CYCLOPEDIA
OF
WORLD
AUTHORS

CYCLOPEDIA
OF
WORLD
AUTHORS

Original title:

MASTERPLOTS CYCLOPEDIA OF WORLD AUTHORS

Edited by

FRANK N. MAGILL

Associate Editor

DAYTON KOHLER

HARPER & ROW, PUBLISHERS

New York, Evanston, and London

190703

CYCLOPEDIA OF WORLD AUTHORS

This work also appears under the title of
Masterplots Cyclopedia of World Authors

Library of Congress catalog card number: 58–12461

PREFACE

THE storyteller has held a unique place in human society since earliest times. His ability to offer entertainment, diversion, or inspiration to his less imaginative fellows has earned for him, or at least for his work, a permanent place in the cultural record of his time. Such a member of the community is usually endowed with an irrepressible impulse which causes his powers of expression to burst their bounds and reveal to all who will listen the story that has taken shape in the recesses of his perceptive being where experience, emotion, and imagination meet and merge.

When these stories spring from an insight and a perception so true and lifelike that they convey abiding human characteristics, they are usually repeated from generation to generation until they blend into the culture they represent.

The *Cyclopedia of World Authors* considers the lives and the works of more than seven hundred fifty creative individuals who have contributed or who are still contributing to the sum total of man's appraisal of himself. These seven hundred fifty authors are the writers represented in the First and Second Series of *Masterpieces of World Literature in Digest Form* and also those who will appear in the Third Series in progress.

A work of this scope and importance could not be accomplished adequately without an enormous amount of aid from scores of scholars who have devoted their lives to research and deduction, and to critical appraisal of the individual writers and their literary achievements. It has been our good fortune to have the assistance of many of the world's foremost experts, scholars who prepared special articles for this book based on intimate acquaintance with the subjects' lives and their creative efforts. More than seventy-five special writers contributed the seven hundred fifty articles included in the Cyclopedia, all the material herein being newly written expressly for this publication. Most of these contributors are listed elsewhere in this volume under "Special Writers and Consultants" and "Additional Contributors and Their Affiliations."

PREFACE

As the work progressed during its almost three years of preparation, a number of scholars, hearing of our project, sent us suggestions and even generously wrote basic material on the subject of their special interest, which is included in various articles. Our appreciation for this voluntary interest is understandable, for in dealing with scholarship—a living, expanding thing—new discoveries and new interpretations can change the entire complexion of an existing opinion.

In presenting this material we have tried to follow a format which gives pertinent information quickly. The author's place and date of birth—and death where applicable—are listed separately. His principal works are then shown in chronological order, separated into various categories such as Novels, Plays, Poems, Essays and the like. Dates shown refer to first publication except in the case of plays, where the date indicates the first presentation, whenever this is known. Foreign titles which have appeared in English are given under the English title as well as the original except when the title is not customarily translated or when the title is self-translating.

The biographical sketches themselves vary in length from one thousand words for some of the more important authors to two hundred words for lesser known writers. Fifty of the more prominent authors are covered by signed articles written by recognized authorities in North America and England. Others were done by the carefully selected and experienced staff upon whom Dayton Kohler and I have come to depend heavily in our work on the several related volumes.

Entries are alphabetical. Articles for authors with common pseudonyms are listed under the pseudonym with a cross reference in the index. Thus, the article on William Sydney Porter appears in the text under Henry, that on Samuel Langhorne Clemens under Twain. But both the pseudonyms and the real names will be found in the Cross-Reference Index with the page references indicated.

Probably the most useful part of this book (certainly the most demanding data to assemble) is that information included under the individual Bibliographical References headings. Librarians and those wishing to study a particular author will often find these sections helpful or time-saving guides to detailed biographical and critical sources on the subject. Here are listed collected editions if they exist, standard or authorized biographies if they exist, books of criticism, and important critical articles in literary publications. Since complete bibliographical references for important authors could easily run to many pages, our entries have often been highly selec-

PREFACE

tive; but we have tried to stress the more up-to-date studies and individual articles whose existence might not be realized without a thorough and time-consuming search through a well-equipped reference library.

We trust that the purpose of this work will be realized. It is obviously not intended to be a group of "biographies"—a project which could fill an entire library—but rather a collection of critical biographical sketches of those authors who appear in *Masterpieces of World Literature in Digest Form,* a work to complement the volumes of digests, adding another dimension to these digests by sketching the author's life, tracing his artistic development, and relating his work to the influences that shaped his career.

I am sure that I speak for all who contributed time and knowledge to the preparation of this book in expressing the hope that its pages will reveal some of the inmost compulsions of the authors under consideration, provide a fundamental rapport with their work, and perchance even momentarily light the mystery that enables one mind to see and speak a truth which will move the generations that follow as long as a human audience exists.

FRANK N. MAGILL

SPECIAL WRITERS AND CONSULTANTS

Gay Wilson Allen
Professor of English
New York University
AUTHOR: _Walt Whitman Handbook;_
The Solitary Singer;
Walt Whitman Abroad
WALT WHITMAN

Walter Allen
AUTHOR: _The English Novel;_
Six Great Novelists
CHARLES DICKENS

Eric J. Batson
Honorary Secretary, The Shaw Society
(London), and
Librarian, City Literary Institute (London)
GEORGE BERNARD SHAW

James F. Beard, Jr.
Associate Professor of English
Clark University
JAMES FENIMORE COOPER

Joseph L. Blotner
Assistant Professor of English
University of Virginia
AUTHOR: _The Political Novel_
JAMES JOYCE
VIRGINIA WOOLF

Roberto Bravo Villarroel
Professor of Spanish Literature
Instituto Tecnológico de Monterrey,
Mexico
CERVANTES

Kenneth W. Cameron
Associate Professor of English
Trinity College
AUTHOR: _Emerson the Essayist;_

The Transcendentalists and Minerva
RALPH WALDO EMERSON

Richard Chase
Associate Professor of English
Columbia University
AUTHOR: _Herman Melville;_
Emily Dickinson;
Walt Whitman Reconsidered;
The American Novel and Its Tradition
HERMAN MELVILLE

Gordon W. Clarke
Associate Professor of English
Eastern Oregon College
SIR JAMES MATTHEW BARRIE

James L. Clifford
Professor of English
Columbia University
AUTHOR: _Young Sam Johnson_
EDITOR: _Johnsonian Studies, 1887–1950_
SAMUEL JOHNSON

Russell Cosper
Professor of English
Purdue University
MOLIÈRE
VICTOR HUGO
MARCEL PROUST

Charles W. Dunn
Professor of English
New York University
EDITOR: _A Chaucer Reader_
GEOFFREY CHAUCER

F. W. Dupee
Associate Professor of English
Columbia University
AUTHOR: _Henry James_

ix

SPECIAL WRITERS AND CONSULTANTS

EDITOR: *The Question of Henry James;*
Henry James: Autobiography
HENRY JAMES

Frederick W. Gwynn
Editor, *College English,* and
Associate Professor of English
University of Virginia
AUTHOR: *Sturge Moore and the Life of Art*
WILLIAM FAULKNER

Moses Hadas
Jay Professor of Greek
Columbia University
AUTHOR: *A History of Greek Literature;*
A History of Latin Literature;
Ancilla to Classical Reading
TRANSLATOR: *Three Greek Romances*
EURIPIDES

M. Clifford Harrison
Chairman, Department of English
Virginia Polytechnic Institute
AUTHOR: *Home to the Cockade City*
JOHN MILTON

Lodwick Hartley
Chairman, Department of English
North Carolina State College
AUTHOR: *This Is Lorence*
LAURENCE STERNE

Thomas H. Johnson
Chairman, Department of English
Lawrenceville School
AUTHOR: *Emily Dickinson: An Interpretive*
Biography
EDITOR: *The Poems of Emily Dickinson;*
The Letters of Emily Dickinson
EMILY DICKINSON

George Burke Johnston
Dean of Applied Science and Business
Administration
Virginia Polytechnic Institute
AUTHOR: *Ben Jonson, Poet*
EDITOR: *Poems of Ben Jonson*
BEN JONSON
SIR WALTER SCOTT

Willis Knapp Jones
Professor of Romanic Languages
Miami University

AUTHOR: *Breve Historia del Teatro*
Latinoamericano
CALDERÓN
LOPE DE VEGA

Abraham C. Keller
Associate Professor of French
University of Washington
GUSTAVE FLAUBERT

Frank Kermode
Professor of English Literature
University of Manchester, England
AUTHOR: *Romantic Image;*
John Donne
EDITOR: *English Pastoral Poetry;*
The Tempest (Arden Edition)
BEAUMONT and FLETCHER
JOHN DONNE

Dayton Kohler
Professor of English
Virginia Polytechnic Institute
WILLA CATHER

Joseph Wood Krutch
Professor Emeritus of Dramatic Literature
Columbia University
AUTHOR: *The Modern Temper;*
Five Masters;
The American Drama Since 1918
EDITOR: *Nine Plays by Eugene O'Neill*
EUGENE O'NEILL

Janko Lavrin
Professor Emeritus of Slavonic Languages
University of Nottingham, England
Member of Slovene Academy of Sciences
and Arts (Jugoslavia)
AUTHOR: *Tolstoy;*
Nikolai Gogol;
Russian Writers—Their Lives and
Literature
LEO TOLSTOY

Ian McGreal
Assistant Professor of Philosophy
Sacramento State College
AUTHOR: *The Art of Making Choices*
DANTE

Francis Claiborne Mason
Professor of English
Gettysburg College
AUTHOR: *This Unchanging Mask*
ROBERT BROWNING

SPECIAL WRITERS AND CONSULTANTS

J. M. Nosworthy
Lecturer in English
University College of Wales
EDITOR: *Cymbeline* (Arden Edition)
SHAKESPEARE
CHRISTOPHER MARLOWE

Fannie Ratchford
Director, Rare Book Collections
University of Texas
AUTHOR: *The Brontës' Web of Childhood;*
Two Poems by Emily Brontë with the
Gondal Background of Her Poems
and Novel
THE BRONTËS

Edgar F. Shannon, Jr.
Associate Professor of English
University of Virginia
AUTHOR: *Tennyson and the Reviewers,*
1827–1851
JANE AUSTEN

Archibald B. Shepperson
Professor of English
University of Virginia
AUTHOR: *The Novel in Motley*
HENRY FIELDING

Marc Slonim
Professor of Comparative Literature
Sarah Lawrence College
AUTHOR: *The Epic of Russian Literature;*
Modern Russian Literature;
Three Loves of Dostoevsky
FYODOR DOSTOEVSKI

Randall Stewart
Chairman, Department of English
Vanderbilt University
AUTHOR: *Nathaniel Hawthorne;*
American Literature and the Christian
Tradition
EDITOR: *The Notebooks of Nathaniel*
Hawthorne
NATHANIEL HAWTHORNE

Lawrance Thompson
Professor of English
Princeton University
AUTHOR: *Fire and Ice:*
The Art and Thought of Robert Frost
ROBERT FROST

Tench Francis Tilghman
Professor of English
Virginia Polytechnic Institute
T. S. ELIOT

Edward Wagenknecht
Professor of English
Boston University
AUTHOR: *Calvalcade of the English Novel;*
Cavalcade of the American Novel;
Longfellow: A Full-Length Portrait;
The Man Charles Dickens: A Victorian
Portrait
EDITOR: *An Introduction to Dickens;*
The Collected Tales of Walter de la Mare
WILLIAM MAKEPEACE THACKERAY
WALTER DE LA MARE

Harry R. Warfel
Professor of English
University of Florida
AUTHOR: *Noah Webster: Schoolmaster*
to America;
Charles Brockden Brown: American
Gothic Novelist;
American Novelist of Today
MARK TWAIN

Carl J. Weber
Roberts Professor of English Literature
Colby College
AUTHOR: *Hardy of Wessex;*
Hardy in America;
Hardy and the Lady from Madison Square
EDITOR: *Letters of Thomas Hardy*
THOMAS HARDY

James Southall Wilson
Edgar Allan Poe Professor of English and
Dean of Graduate Studies, retired
University of Virginia
AUTHOR: *Alexander Wilson: Poet Naturalist*
EDITOR: *The Tales of Edgar Allan Poe*
EDGAR ALLAN POE

Morton Dauwen Zabel
Professor of English
University of Chicago
AUTHOR: *Craft and Character in Modern*
Fiction;
The Make of Man
EDITOR: *Literary Opinion in America;*
The Portable Conrad
JOSEPH CONRAD

ADDITIONAL CONTRIBUTORS AND
THEIR AFFILIATIONS

Matthew J. Bruccoli	*University of Virginia*
Norman T. Burns	*University of Michigan*
Richard A. Condon	*University of Southern California*
John Frederick Frank	*University of Pennsylvania*
O. W. Frost	*Willamette University*
James Gindin	*University of Michigan*
David J. Gordon	*Boston University*
William A. Grant	*Virginia Polytechnic Institute*
John V. Hagopian	*University of Michigan*
Bruce Harkness	*University of Illinois*
John S. Kiefer	*St. John's College, Annapolis*
Robert C. Laing, Jr.	*University of Pittsburgh*
Fred B. McEwen	*University of Pittsburgh*
Preston Newman	*Virginia Polytechnic Institute*
William L. Sandidge	*Virginia Polytechnic Institute*
George Green Shackelford	*Virginia Polytechnic Institute*
Osamu Shimizu	*Columbia University*
E. M. Smith	*Pensacola Junior College*
Grover Smith, Jr.	*Duke University*
M. W. Tillson	*Purdue University*
Richard B. Vowles	*University of Florida*
Chi-Chen Wang	*Columbia University*
Harold H. Watts	*Purdue University*
Irving J. Weiss	*Pennsylvania State University*
William White	*Wayne State University*
William M. White	*Virginia Polytechnic Institute*
Robert F. Whitman	*Princeton University*
Eugene N. Yarrington, Jr.	*University of Illinois*

Jay Hall, Julia Lowry Hall, and Delroy M. Root

CYCLOPEDIA
OF
WORLD
AUTHORS

PIERRE ABÉLARD

Born: Pallet, France
Date: 1079

Died: Chalons-sur-Saône, France
Date: April 21, 1142

PRINCIPAL WORKS

TREATISES: *Sic et Non, Glossulae super Porphyrium.*
AUTOBIOGRAPHY: *Historia Calamitatum,* c. 1132 (*History of My Calamity*).
LETTERS: *Letters of Héloise and Abélard,* 1616.

Born in 1079 at Pallet, Pierre Abélard, although the oldest son of a minor vassal of the dukes of Brittany, gave up his inheritance in order to become a student of philosophy under the celebrated Guillaume de Champeaux (d. 1121). Eventually he broke with Guillaume and set himself up in his own school at Melun from 1101 to 1113. In Paris he studied logic and taught. One of his pupils was Héloise, niece of Canon Fulbert of Notre Dame, a brilliant young girl whom he seduced. Though he married her secretly, ruffians hired by her uncle emasculated Abélard, and he retired to the monastery of St. Denis.

In 1121 the Synod of Soissons cited him for his theological teachings and forced him to burn his *Introductio ad Theologiam.* Still students flocked to him and built for him the Oratory of the Paraclete (The Comforter; i.e., The Holy Spirit), where he taught a moderate realism which anticipated the conceptualism of St. Thomas

Aquinas (1225–1274). Celebrated churchmen of the twelfth century, including John of Salisbury and Arnold of Brescia, studied his influential *Sic et Non,* in which he discussed the contradictory opinions of the church fathers.

Appointed abbot of St. Gildas-en-Rhuys, he established Héloise in the Paraclete as head of a sisterhood. Their correspondence, especially three letters by Héloise, are among the world's greatest love letters.

Condemned for heresy in 1141 by the Council of Sens for teaching that faith could be explained logically, rather than accepted mystically, Abélard died at Chalons-sur-Saône on April 21, 1142, during a journey to defend himself before the Pope in Rome. He was buried in Paraclete, as was Héloise, when she died in 1164. Abélard's writings and letters, though circulated widely in manuscript during the Middle Ages, were not printed in their entirety until the nineteenth century.

BIBLIOGRAPHICAL REFERENCES: There are two editions of the *Letters,* that translated and edited by C. K. S. Moncrieff, 1926, and one by L. K. Short, 1951. See also Charles F. M. de Rémusat, *Abélard,* 1845; Joseph McCabe, *Peter Abelard,* 1901; and Jeffrey G. Sikes, *Peter Abailard,* 1932. The romantic story of the two lovers provided the plot for *Héloise and Abélard,* a novel by George Moore, 1921.

EDMOND FRANÇOIS ABOUT

Born: Dieuze, France
Date: February 14, 1828

Died: Paris, France
Date: January 16, 1885

PRINCIPAL WORKS

NOVELS: *Les mariages de Paris*, 1856 (*The Marriages of Paris*); *Le Roi des montagnes*, 1856 (*The King of the Mountains*); *L'homme à l'oreille cassée*, 1861 (*The Man with the Broken Ear*); *Le nez d'un notaire*, 1862 (*The Notary's Nose*); *Le Roman d'un brave homme*, 1880 (*The Story of an Honest Man*).

Edmond François (Valentin) About was born at Dieuze, France, on February 14, 1828. His studies included several years in a French archeological school in Athens, an experience which he used as the basis for his first book. *La Grèce contemporaine* (*Contemporary Greece*), published in 1854, was a collection of travel sketches and observations on the life and social conditions of the Greeks. He returned to Paris, tried unsuccessfully to become an actor, and began writing for various French newspapers and periodicals. While a journalist, About began writing witty, comic novels, the most famous of which are *The King of the Mountains* and *The Notary's Nose*.

About was well known as a man of wit and charm around Paris in the period of the Second Empire. After the war of 1870, About became more liberal and was soon the powerful and energetic editor of a literary and political periodical called *Le XIX Siècle*. As an editor he exercised a consistent liberal and anti-clerical influence on his generation, and later works such as *The Story of an Honest Man* became more serious forms of social commentary. Widely popular and influential, he was elected to the French Academy in 1884, but before taking his seat he died in Paris on January 16, 1885.

Although his own age respected About most as an editor, a commentator on the current scene, and a serious novelist with an anti-clerical theme, today About is primarily remembered for his comic novels. His wit, his charm, and his ability to mock any form of pretense make his novels still popular.

BIBLIOGRAPHICAL REFERENCES: See Marcel Thiébaut, *Edmond About*, 1936. His work is also discussed briefly in the standard histories of French literature.

HENRY ADAMS

Born: Boston, Massachusetts
Date: February 16, 1838

Died: Washington, D. C.
Date: March 27, 1918

PRINCIPAL WORKS

HISTORY: *The History of the United States during the Administration of Thomas Jefferson*, 1884–1885; *The History of the United States during the Administration of James Madison*, 1888–1889; *Historical Essays*, 1891.
BIOGRAPHY: *The Life of Albert Gallatin*, 1879; *John Randolph*, 1882.

AUTOBIOGRAPHY: *The Education of Henry Adams,* privately printed, 1907; republished, 1918.

PHILOSOPHY OF HISTORY: *Mont-Saint-Michel and Chartres,* privately printed, 1904, and republished, 1913; *The Degradation of the Democratic Dogma,* 1919.

NOVELS: *Democracy: An American Novel,* 1880; *Esther,* 1884.

LETTERS: *A Cycle of Adams Letters, 1861–1865,* edited by W. C. Ford, 1920; *Letters of Henry Adams, 1892–1918,* edited by W. C. Ford, 1938; *Henry Adams and His Friends: A Collection of Unpublished Letters,* edited by H. D. Cater, 1947.

For a man whose father was Charles Francis Adams (1807–1886), American statesman and minister to Great Britain; whose grandfather was John Quincy Adams (1767–1848), the sixth President of the United States, and whose great-grandfather was John Adams (1735–1826), the second President of the United States, Henry Brooks Adams did very well. Despite the burden of family fame, he established himself in literature as a historian and philosopher of history. By branding himself a failure and by writing an autobiography that was an attempt to show the force common to the Virgin and the dynamo, he became an enigmatic success. Consequently, he was more than a mere recorder of events and relic of a great political past; he was a maker of literature and of ideas. Because of his outstanding performances as a historian and philosopher of history he is now as eminent in his own way as his forebears are eminent in political history.

Henry Adams was born in Boston on February 16, 1838. As a boy he profited from a close and friendly relationship with his grandfather, John Quincy Adams. It was primarily through him that Adams developed a moral consciousness of the seriousness and importance of education and of the use of books in the process of becoming educated. The inquisitive mind and the dissatisfied one developed together in him as they had in his grandfather, so that he became no passive scholar but an active critic of events and ideas. When his grandfather died, Henry Adams was only ten years old, but he was to show the effect of John Quincy Adams' influence for the rest of his life.

He attended Harvard University (1854–1858) after a preparatory education at the Boston Latin School and the Epes Dixwell school in Boston. He then went to Europe in order to study civil law at the University of Berlin, but he concentrated on touring about Europe and studying the languages and cultures of various countries. He spent a short time in law study in Quincy, Massachusetts, and then became private secretary to his father, serving him both in Washington and in London. In 1868 he returned to the United States and became a free-lance journalist for two years, writing for the *North American Review, Nation,* and the *New York Post.*

He was married in 1872 to Marian Hooper, two years after his reluctant acceptance of an instructorship in medieval history at Harvard. During this time he was also editor of the *North American Review.* He taught at Harvard until 1877, when he and his wife went to live in Washington, D.C. There he settled down to an intensive writing career. Part of the time he spent abroad, gathering documents

3

in London, Paris, and Madrid, and adding to his knowledge and impressions of Europe.

On December 6, 1885, his wife, ill and depressed since the death of her father over a year before, committed suicide. Adams, although deeply shocked by his wife's death, mentioned it only indirectly in *The Education of Henry Adams.*

Following her death he visited Japan with John La Farge, the American artist and writer. By that time he had produced a distinguished historical biography, *The Life of Albert Gallatin;* a satirical novel of political life, *Democracy;* a less important biography, *John Randolph,* and another novel, *Esther.* Upon his return from his travels with La Farge, Adams worked steadily on his nine-volume history of the administrations of Jefferson and Madison. After another journey with La Farge, this time to the South Seas, he produced his distinctive philosophy of history in the two books, *Mont-Saint-Michel and Chartres* and *The Education of Henry Adams.* The first of these books represents a time when society had achieved unity, the twelfth century; the second, a time when multiplicity had divided men and societies, his own era. Beautifully written, original in conception, these works are generally regarded as his masterpieces. He died in Washington, D.C., on March 27, 1918, shortly after *The Education of Henry Adams,* privately printed in 1906, had been republished in a trade edition.

BIBLIOGRAPHICAL REFERENCES: The only recent biography which offers insight into Adams' esthetic and historical philosophy is Robert A. Hume's *Runaway Star: An Appreciation of Henry Adams,* 1951. A more general biography is James Truslow Adams, *Henry Adams,* 1933; Ernest Samuels, *The Young Henry Adams,* 1948, deals fully with the early years. More specialized studies are found in M. I. Baym, *The French Education of Henry Adams,* 1951; and W. H. Jordy, *Henry Adams: Scientific Historian,* 1952.

See also "Henry Adams," in *Literary History of the United States,* edited by Robert E. Spiller, Willard Thorp, Thomas H. Johnson, and Henry S. Canby, 1948; Louis Zukofsky, "Henry Adams: A Criticism in Autobiography," *Hound and Horn,* III (1930), 333–357, 518–530; IV (1930), 46–72; R. P. Blackmur, "Henry and Brooks Adams: Parallels to Two Generations," *Southern Review,* V (1939), 308–334; *idem,* "Henry Adams: Three Late Moments," *Kenyon Review,* II (1940), 7–29; Herbert Edwards, "The Prophetic Mind of Henry Adams," *College English,* III (1942), 708–721; Nathalia Wright, "Henry Adams's Theory of History: A Puritan Defense," *New England Quarterly,* XVII (1945), 204–210; and M. I. Baym, "Henry Adams and the Critics," *American Scholar,* XV (1945), 79–89.

JOHN ADAMS

Born: Braintree, Massachusetts
Date: October 19, 1735

Died: Quincy, Massachusetts
Date: July 4, 1826

PRINCIPAL WORKS

POLITICAL DOCUMENTS, ESSAYS, AND TREATISES: "Essay on Canon and Feudal Law," in *The True Sentiments of America* . . . (ed. by Thomas Holles), 1768 (published anonymously in Boston, 1765); *Instruction of the Town of Braintree, Massachusetts,* on the Stamp Act, October 14, 1765; Thoughts on Government, 1776; Massachusetts Constitution and Bill of Rights, 1780; A Collection of the State-Papers . . . of the United States of America, 1782; Novanglus and Massachusettensis, 1819 (This work presents most fully in book form the arguments of John Adams and Daniel Leonard concerning the imperial controversy, but they had appeared in abridged fashion in the Boston Gazette in 1774 and at The Hague in 1782 and at London in 1784 as History of the Dispute with America; from its origin in 1754.); A Defense of the Constitutions of the United States of America, 3 vols. 1787–1788 (Volumes 2 and 3 are frequently entitled The Political History of the Italian Republics.); Twenty-six Letters, upon Interesting Subjects, respecting the Revolution of America. Written in Holland in 1780, 1789; A Selection of . . . Patriotic Addresses, 1798; Four Letters . . . between . . . John Adams . . . and Samuel Adams . . . On the important subject of Government, 1802; Discourses on Davila, 1805 (Printed in part in the Gazette of the United States, Philadelphia, 1790); . . . Concerning the British Doctrine of Impressment, 1809; Correspondence between the Hon. John Adams . . . and the late Wm. Cunningham, Esq., 1803–1812, 1823.

John Adams, second President, and the first Vice-President of the United States, was born in the settlement of Braintree in the colony of Massachusetts on October 19, 1735. He was educated at Harvard, graduating in 1755 with the original intention of entering the ministry; but, deciding that he could not subscribe wholeheartedly to Calvinist doctrine, he turned instead to the law and studied in Boston after a brief period of schoolteaching in Worcester. He passed his bar examinations in November of 1758 and set up practice in Braintree. In 1764, following his marriage to Abigail Smith, he established himself in Boston.

Adams' place in American history is assured primarily by the high public offices he held; but even if he had never won a political election, his importance as an active member of the revolutionary party, his eloquence as a spokesman for the revolutionary cause, and his clarity as a definer of constitutional democracy would place him alongside Washington, Jefferson, and Franklin in the foremost rank of our founding fathers. He was both a public figure and a writer on matters of law and government. His writing began in 1765 with his Dissertation on Canon and Feudal Law, and his career as a public figure began with his removal to Boston, for it was then that he first gained wide recognition by successfully defending John Hancock against a charge of smuggling. His association with the patriotic cause came at this same time, and by 1774 he was so thoroughly identified with the movement through his activities and his writings that he was elected along with his more radical cousin, Samuel Adams, to serve as a delegate to the First Continental Congress. He returned to Massachusetts in 1775 but was back in Philadelphia the next year as a member of the committee for framing a Declaration of Independence. When that document was finally drawn up he stood, according to Jefferson, as the strongest "pillar of its support" on the congressional floor.

Committed fully to hostilities with England, he served two years on the Colonies' Board of War and then sailed to France, where he joined Franklin as a commissioner seeking aid for the

5

Colonies. His efforts in France were somewhat ineffectual, owing to his many disagreements with Franklin and to the fact that his uncompromising personality and outspoken attitude ill-fitted him for the role of diplomat. In spite of his disagreements and antagonisms he continued to serve abroad until 1788, treating with the Dutch and serving on the commission for final peace negotiations with Britian.

Upon his return to the new United States, this same straightforwardness and independence of thought brought him into the center of the political controversies over the founding of the new government. A conservative by nature, he has generally been identified with the Federalist point of view, and it was as a Federalist that he held office. But his temperament would not allow him to be a good party man, and his conflict with Alexander Hamilton, his fellow Federalist, was much deeper than his disagreements with Republican Thomas Jefferson. It has been suggested that his election to the vice-presidency was actually engineered by Hamilton in order to put him in a position where he would have as little power as possible—a position, according to Adams' own complaint, in "the most insignificant office the invention of man contrived or his imagination conceived."

The breach with Hamilton closed temporarily, Adams was elected President in his own right in 1796. Conflicts soon broke out again to plague his administration. Hamilton seized complete control of the party on one hand, while the rift with Jefferson widened over Adams' establishment of the National Judiciary System on the other. Thus he stood alone during the election of 1800, and Jefferson was easily victorious.

Through with national politics, Adams retired to his home in Quincy and devoted the rest of his life to his writings and to the observation of the national career of his son, John Quincy Adams. His discourses on government ran to ten volumes when collected by Charles Francis Adams in 1850–1856, and their soundness and vision has prompted one historian to claim that he was "the greatest political thinker that America has yet produced." He died in Quincy, Massachusetts, in 1826, aptly enough, on the Fourth of July, the same day that marked the death of his great friend and political adversary, Thomas Jefferson.

BIBLIOGRAPHICAL REFERENCES: The standard biography of the second President is Gilbert Chinard, *Honest John Adams*, 1933. Grandson Charles F. Adams, *Life of John Adams* (published as Vol. I of *The Life and Works*, Boston, 1850; reprinted in two separate vols., Philadelphia, 1871) serves as basis for most of the older biographies such as John T. Morse, *John Adams*, American Statesmen series, 1885; and Mellen Chamberlain, *John Adams, the Statesman of the American Revolution*, 1898. James T. Adams, *The Adams Family*, 1930, is helpful and has only incidental genealogical orientation. Catherine D. Bowen, *John Adams and the [Coming of the] American Revolution*, 1950, is a fictionalized biography. The best sketch is by Worthington C. Ford in the *Dictionary of American Biography*, in which there is an independent sketch of his wife, Abigail Adams, by Martha Tucker Stephenson.

Mid-twentieth century renewal of interest in John Adams is largely due to two stimulating works: Zoltán Haraszti's *John Adams & the Prophets of Progress*, 1952, and Russell Kirk's *The Conservative Mind*, 1953. The former elaborates upon Adams marginalia in books of his library, in connection with which see *Catalogue of the John Adams Library in the Public Library of the City of Boston*, 1917.

Valuable studies throwing light on varied aspects of his career are: W. L. Smith and Oliver Wolcott, *The Pretensions of Thomas Jefferson to the Presidency Examined; and the Charges against John Adams Refuted*, 1796; Alexander Hamilton, *Letter concerning the Public Conduct and Character of John Adams*, 1800 (2nd ed.), and James Cheetham's *An Answer to Alexander Hamilton's Letter*, 1800; John Wood, *History of the Administration of John Adams*, 1802; Timothy Pickering, *A Review of the Correspondence between . . . John Adams . . . and the late William Cunningham*, 1824 (2nd ed.); Oliver Wolcott, *Memoirs of the Administrations of Washington and Adams*, 2 vols., edited by George Gibbs, 1846; Fisher Ames, *Works of Fisher Ames*, 2 vols., edited by Seth Ames, 1854; Frederick Kidder, *History of the Boston Massacre*, 1870; Henry Adams, *Documents Relating to New England Federalism*, 1877, and *History of the United States during the Administrations of Thomas Jefferson and James Madison*, 9 vols., 1890–1898; Rufus King, *The Life and Correspondence of Rufus King*, 6 vols., edited by Charles R. King, 1894–1900; Gardiner W. Allen, *Our Naval War with France*, 1909; Anson E. Morse, *The Federalist Party in Massachusetts to the Year 1800*, 1909; Correa M. Walsh, *The Political Science of John Adams*, 1915; William A. Robinson, *Jeffersonian Democracy in New England*, 1916; Edmund C. Burnett, *The Continental Congress*, 1941; Leonard D. White, *The Federalists: A Study in Administrative History*, 1948; and Howard C. Rice, *The Adams Family in Auteuil, 1784–1785*, 1956.

The Works of John Adams, 10 vols., edited by Charles F. Adams, 1850–1856, is still standard, but it may be supplemented by the following: *Letters of John Adams, Addressed to His Wife*, 2 vols., edited by Charles F. Adams as vols. III and IV to supplement *Letters of Abigail Adams*, 1841; *Familiar Letters of John Adams and His Wife Abigail Adams, during the Revolution*, edited by Charles F. Adams, 1875; *Correspondence between John Adams and Mercy Warren*, *Correspondence between John Adams and Professor John Winthrop*, and *Warren-Adams Letters, 1743–1814*, in Massachusetts Historical Society, *Collections*, 5th series, IV (1878) and LXXII–LXXIII, 1917–1925; *Correspondence of John Adams and Thomas Jefferson, 1812–1826*, edited by Paul Wilstach, 1925; and *Statesman and Friend: Correspondence of John Adams with Benjamin Waterhouse, 1784–1822*, edited by Worthington C. Ford, 1927. One-volume selections are *The Selected Writings of John and John Quincy Adams*, edited by Adrienne Koch and William Peden, 1946; and *The Political Writings of John Adams: Representative Selections*, edited by George A. Peek, Jr., 1954. A definitive, multi-volume edition of the *Papers* of John Adams is now in progress under the editorship of Lyman H. Butterfield and the auspices of the Massachusetts Historical Society.

JOSEPH ADDISON

Born: Milston, Wiltshire, England   *Died:* London, England
Date: May 1, 1672   *Date:* June 17, 1719

PRINCIPAL WORKS

PERIODICAL ESSAYS: *The Tatler* (about 46 numbers alone, 36 numbers with Richard Steele), 1709–1710; *The Whig Examiner*, 1710; *The Spectator* (with Richard Steele; 298 numbers by Addison alone), 1711–1712, 1714; *The Guardian* (with Richard Steele; 51 numbers by Addison alone), 1713; *The Lover* (as Marmaduke

Myrtle, Gent., with Richard Steele; 2 numbers by Addison alone), 1714; *The Reader* (with Richard Steele; 2 numbers by Addison alone), 1714; *The Free-Holder, or Political Essays,* 1715–1716; *The Old Whig,* 1719.

PLAYS: *Rosamond,* 1707; *Cato,* 1713; *The Drummer, or The Haunted House,* 1716.

Joseph Addison is perhaps best remembered today as the journalistic partner of Richard Steele and as the creator of the quaint and fascinating country gentleman, Sir Roger de Coverley. But to his contemporaries— his friends, his fellow members of the Kit-Cat Club, and even his political and literary enemies, among whom, eventually, were both Swift and Pope —and to those of the later period of "The Age of Enlightenment," he was considerably more. In the opinion of the eighteenth century he was an outstanding poet, a penetrating critic, a major playwright, and a consummate master of style. He was, in short, one of the brilliant literary figures of his time, quite in keeping with the spirit of an age that produced a greater wealth of brilliant literary figures than of lasting literary work.

In addition to all this, he was more than just a literary figure. From the time of his return to England, after the completion of a Continental tour in 1703, until his death in London following a severe attack of asthma and dropsy some sixteen years later, on June 17, 1719, he was an active and articulate member of the Whig Party. He was a Whig member of Parliament from 1708 until his death, and, at other times, according to the vicissitudes of political fortune, he held still higher positions, including those of Commissioner of Appeals (1704– 1708), Undersecretary of State (1706– 1708), and secretary to the Lord Lieutenant of Ireland (1709–1710); moreover, from his first arrival on the Lon- don scene as an erudite young scholar fresh from Oxford until his marriage late in life to the dowager Countess of Warwick (1716), he made it his business to ingratiate himself with the rich and the powerful. Because his career was advanced through preferment, and a politic caution governed all his personal relationships, he was immortalized by Pope as "a tim'rous foe, and a suspicious friend."

Yet for all his desire to rise to the notice of the noble and the great, his own beginnings were not particularly humble. His father, the rector of Milston at the time of Joseph's birth on May 1, 1672, became shortly afterward the dean of Lichfield Cathedral, and he was also a theological writer of some contemporary reputation. Addison's education began in the town that later was to produce, in Samuel Johnson, the greatest figure of the age; it continued there until he was sent to Charterhouse School (1686), where he began his friendship with Richard Steele, a friendship that was to last until the final year of his life.

From Charterhouse he went directly to Queen's College, Oxford in 1687. There he began his literary activities with the composition of scholarly Latin verse, winning enough acclaim to be awarded a probationary fellowship after he had received his Master of Arts degree in 1693. He remained at Oxford five years more, writing classical translations along with his poetry, and was awarded a permanent fellowship at Magdalen College in 1698.

By this time his reputation as a poet

8

and as a rising man of letters had spread to London. Acting with his usual genteel opportunism, he discreetly began to take advantage of his fame, soon winning the patronage of Charles Montagu (later the Earl of Halifax) and with it a pension of three hundred pounds a year—enough to allow him to spend the next four years making a leisurely tour of France and Italy.

The pension ceased with the fall of the Whig government in 1703, and Addison was forced to return to London and to find new sources of preferment. He did not have to wait long. He joined the Whigs' famed Kit-Cat Club, published in 1705 a poem, *The Campaign,* in honor of Marlborough's victory at Blenheim, and was rewarded, upon the Whigs' return to power, with his first government appointment. A book of travel sketches and impressions, *Remarks on Italy,* also appeared in 1705.

His literary career developed along with his political career, and before long the two were joined in his periodical writings. First came an abortive attempt to write for the stage, but after the failure of his opera *Rosamond,* he joined Steele in the production of *The Tatler* in 1709–1710. When *The Tatler* was dropped after 271 numbers, he turned out five numbers of his own periodical, *The Whig Examiner,* but soon rejoined Steele, this time to begin work on their most successful extended publication, the famous *Spectator* papers.

The Spectator, which was, according to Johnson, the best, the most "humorous, urbane and decorous" of all their writings, continued an interrupted existence from 1711 until 1714, running, finally, to 635 numbers, 298 of which (including those on Sir Roger de Coverley) were contributed by Addison. The collaboration with Steele was to continue through *The Guardian, The Lover,* and *The Reader,* but their close relationship, begun in boyhood, was to end in a quarrel over Steele's indebtedness just before Addison's death in 1719. It was then that the name of Steele was added to those of Swift and Pope on the list of Addison's one-time friends who became enemies.

But in spite of his being "willing to wound, and yet afraid to strike," Addison's literary stature continued to grow, reaching its greatest proportions with the success of his tragedy *Cato* in 1713. The play stands now merely as an interesting landmark of literary history, but at the time it secured Addison a reputation as the greatest poet and tragedian of his age, a reputation which lasted for over a century but which has not survived into our own time.

BIBLIOGRAPHICAL REFERENCES: The standard edition of *The Tatler* is that edited by George A. Aitken, 4 vols., 1898–1899. The same editor prepared a collected edition of *The Spectator,* 8 vols., 1898. Another edition of the *Spectator* papers is that of G. Gregory Smith, 8 vols., 1897–1898, reissued in Everyman's Library, 1907. Addison's *Complete Works* have been reprinted in numerous editions, the most recent being edited by A. C. Guthkelch, 2 vols., 1914. A separate edition of the *Letters* was edited by Walter Graham, 1941.

The most recent biography is Peter Smithers, *The Life of Joseph Addison,* 1954 Other biographies include Lucy Aiken, *Life of Joseph Addison,* 2 vols., 1843; W. J. Courthope, *Addison,* 1903; Samuel Johnson, *Lives of the Poets,* edited by G. B.

Hill, 1905; and T. B. Macaulay, *The Life and Writings of Addison,* edited by C. F. Lavell, 1908. See also Bonamy Dobrée, *Essays in Biography,* 1925.

There are three valuable studies of the development of the periodical and the periodical essay: Nathan Drake, *Essays, Biographical, Critical, and Historical, Illustrative of "The Tatler," "Spectator," and "Guardian,"* 1805; G. S. Marr, *Periodical Essayists of the 18th Century,* 1924; and Walter Graham, *English Literary Periodicals,* 1930. See also C. N. Greenough, "The Development of *The Tatler,*" *Publications of the Modern Language Association,* XXXI (1916), 633–667.

An interesting general estimate is by C. S. Lewis in *Essays on the 18th Century Presented to David Nichol Smith,* 1945. Three special articles are Leicester Bradner, "The Composition and Publication of Addison's Latin Poems," *Modern Philology,* XXXV (1938), 359–367; Phyllis Freeman, "Who Was Sir Roger de Coverley"? *Quarterly Review,* CCLXXXV (1947), 592–604; and Silas E. Summers, "Addison's Conception of Tragedy," *College English,* VIII (1947), 245–248.

AESCHYLUS

Born: Eleusis in Attica   Died: Gela, Sicily
Date: c. 525–524 B.C.   Date: 456–455 B.C.

EXTANT PLAYS

The Suppliants, c. 491; *The Persians,* 472; *Seven Against Thebes,* 467; *Prometheus Bound* (?); *Oresteia: Agamemnon, Choëphoroe (Libation Bearers), Eumenides (Furies),* 458.

Aeschylus, writer of tragedy at Athens, was the first dramatist whose tragedies (seven out of about eighty) have been preserved. He was the son of Euphorion, a well-born landowner of Eleusis, the city of the mysteries of Demeter. He fought in the battle of Marathon, 490 B.C., and possibly at Salamis. He won fame at Athens by his tragedies and more than once visited Hiero, King of Syracuse, to produce tragedies there. One tragedy, *Women of Aetna,* he produced to celebrate Hiero's refoundation of Aetna, which had been destroyed in the volcanic eruption of Mt. Aetna in 475 B.C. His death occurred at Gela about 455, during his last visit to Sicily.

Aeschylus' predecessors had developed out of choral songs in honor of gods, a primitive drama with one actor taking the part of all characters in the myth narrated in the song, speaking to the chorus to carry on the story. This form became popular and was established as a regular part of the festival of Dionysus at Athens. Prizes were competed for by poets who submitted three poems each, as well as a farcical afterpiece called a satyr play.

Aeschylus entered this competition first in 499 B.C. (?) with an unknown trilogy. His first prize was won in 484, again with unknown works. The entrance of Aeschylus into competition is a great event in literary history. He transformed tragedy completely. Aristotle tells us of two technical innovations he made that had a profound effect. He reduced the number of the chorus from fifty to twelve and he began using a second actor. This latter change made possible a more flexible drama; two persons of the play could now appear together and converse. The former change signalized the shift to a real emphasis on dramatic interplay.

More important, however, than technical improvements was Aeschylus' change of the tone of tragedy. Partly because of the greater dramatic possibilities that his improvements allowed, Aeschylus fashioned a means of using the old myths to express fundamental questions of human life. He had the imagination to present these themes through characters of grandeur and power, and the poetic gifts to dress them in language of dignity and grace. His powers needed greater scope than a single play provided. Therefore he usually presented real trilogies, three plays based on the same myth.

Although the titles of about eighty of his plays are known, seven only are preserved. However, these seven give us a good view of his development as a dramatist and the variety of his imagination.

The Suppliants tells the story of the fifty daughters of Danaüs who fled with their father from the land of the Nile to Argos, home of their ancestor, Io, to escape unwanted marriage with their fifty cousins, the sons of Danaüs' brother, Aegyptus. With hesitation, and after consulting the citizens, the King of Argos agrees to take the suppliants under his protection. The herald of Aegyptus arrives, makes melodramatic threats to get the girls to return with him, tries to use force, and is finally driven away by the King of Argos. The story is an old and naïve folktale, and the dramatic action is slight. Except for a few scenes there is but a single actor on the stage at any one time, yet the power of the poet to convey pathos and the lovely verse of the choral odes, with their rich tapestry of mythological allusion, show the work of a major poet.

Patriotism dominates *The Persians*. This play is unique among extant tragedies in having a plot drawn not from myth but from recent history, the glorious victory of the Persian war. It is also unusual among Aeschylus' works in not being part of a trilogy, but complete in itself. Aeschylus achieves the detachment necessary for tragedy by setting the scene in Persia and having the chorus and all the characters be Persians—Atossa, the mother of Xerxes; the ghost of Darius, her husband; the unfortunate Xerxes himself; and the chorus of Persian elders. Beginning with their forebodings, the play moves on to reveal in verse of grandeur the catastrophes that befall the invincible army. Through the lamentations of their enemies the Athenian audience relives their god-favored victory. For once in tragedy the spectacle of hybris bringing the downfall of the mighty is seen without fear, though Aeschylus achieves the tremendous feat of infusing a sense of pity for the fallen, enemies though they are.

Seven Against Thebes tells the story of the battle for the throne of Thebes between the two sons of Oedipus, Polynices and Eteocles, who perish in single combat, while the six other Theban champions defeat and kill the Argive leaders who joined Polynices in his attempt to regain the throne. The great stories of Oedipus and Antigone are recalled and foreshadowed, but the play concentrates on the pageantry of the battle. The play is archaic, static; we see groupings rather than movement. But the hold of the Theban story on the imagination of Greeks shines upon it, and we sense the patriotic feelings that made the Greek polis so vital a culture.

Aeschylus' imagination grew more

powerful as he progressed in his art. In the *Prometheus Bound* he raised tragedy to a cosmic level. The old legend of the god who stole fire from Olympus to give to man and thus save man from extinction becomes in Aeschylus' treatment a complex drama of guilt and punishment in which, because the persons of the play are immortal, the mitigating power of death is absent. It portrays the Greek analogue to the Christian doctrine of original sin and atonement. The latter theme is the subject of the lost *Prometheus Unbound*, which followed the extant play in the trilogy. The setting, the chorus, the action, all emphasize the stark aloneness of Prometheus, defying the ineluctable power of Zeus. The one human character, Io, portrays the misery of the condition of man, with just a hint of the relief to follow in the fullness of time. In this play the essence of tragedy, abstracted from all human complexities, is most clearly revealed.

The latest work of Aeschylus, produced in 458 B.C., two years before his death, is the trilogy, *Oresteia*, consisting of *Agamemnon*, the *Libation-Bearers*, and the *Furies*. It is the only trilogy preserved and shows the master's ability to develop a theme through three separate dramas, each complete in itself. In bare outline, the *Agamemnon* enacts the murder of the conqueror of Troy by his faithless wife, Clytemnestra, and her paramour, Aegisthus; the *Libation-Bearers*, the murder of the two by Orestes, the son of Agamemnon and Clytemnestra, impelled by the old law of vengeance; the *Furies*, the justification of Orestes' deed against the claims of vengeance for matricide. The *Agamemnon* is poetically the richest, with its brooding odes dwelling on the cycles of guilt of the house of Atreus, giving a magnificent portrait of the man-hearted queen and the prophetic Cassandra. The second play portrays the agony of Orestes, caught in the contradictory rules of ancient blood-feud. The third play raises the action to the level of the gods, who must find a solution that will reëstablish justice for mankind on the basis of a rational order that finds its expression in the polis, and brings men from barbarism to civilization.

Those final plays show Aeschylus influenced by Sophocles in the greater variety of characters and hence complexity of scenes. On the other hand they remain true to Aeschylus' bold simplicity of imagination. His characters are larger and simpler than life. They are moved to what they do by external forces and yet act of their own wills. They are not suffering puppets any more than they are strong defiers of fate. The tragedies of Aeschylus deal with enigmas rather than recognitions.

BIBLIOGRAPHICAL REFERENCES: The standard prose translation is H. Weir Smyth, *Aeschylus, with an English Translation*, in the Loeb Classical Library, 2 vols., 1922–1926. See also Whitney J. Oates and Eugene O'Neill, Jr., *The Complete Greek Drama*, 2 vols., 1938. For general studies and criticism see also A. E. Haigh, *The Tragic Drama of the Greeks*, 1896; T. D. Goodell, *Athenian Tragedy*, 1920; H. Weir Smyth, *Aeschylean Tragedy*, 1924; J. T. Sheppard, *Aeschylus and Sophocles*, 1927; Gilbert Norwood, *Greek Tragedy*, 1928; Edith Hamilton, *The Greek Way*, 1930; R. C. Flickinger, *The Greek Theater and Its Drama*, 1936 (3rd edition); Gilbert Murray, *Aeschylus: The Creator of Tragedy*, 1940; George D. Thomson, *Aeschylus and Athens*, 1941; P. W. Harsh, *A Handbook of Classical Drama*, 1944; and Moses Hadas, *A History of Greek Literature*, 1950.

AESOP

Born: Unknown
Date: Fl. sixth century B.C. (?)

Died: Unknown
Date: Unknown

PRINCIPAL WORKS

FABLES: *Aesopea* (*Aesop's Fables*).

Though many Greek cities claim to be the birthplace of Aesop, some scholars believe he never existed. He is shown as a dwarf, deformed and ugly, in a marble figure on the Villa Albani, Paris, perhaps to symbolize his "near approach to the lower animals and his peculiar sympathy for their habits." Yet history contains a reference to a "noble statue" of him by Lysippus, in Athens. Velasquez's painting presents him as a sturdy figure in a brown cloak.

Many fables, supposedly by Aesop, have been traced to earlier Indian or fourteenth century B.C. Egyptian versions; somebody, however, wrote them down, perhaps this sixth century B.C. legendary slave of Iadmon of Samos. Tradition tells of his travels to Lydia,

to meet Solon at the court of Croesus, and Periander in Corinth. While visiting Athens, in order to keep its citizens from deposing Pisistratus, legend has him recounting to them the fable of the frogs who asked for a king.

Phaedrus, a Macedonian freedman of Augustus, translated the fables in five volumes of Latin verse. Babrius, in his Mythiambics, versified them two centuries later, and Planudes Maximus, a learned thirteenth century Byzantine monk, compiled a collection in prose, prefaced by his account of Aesop's life. Children and sophisticates have enjoyed the fables ever since. Jean de La Fontaine gave them their most polished and sophisticated form in his *Fables* (1668–1694).

BIBLIOGRAPHICAL REFERENCES: There are numerous editions of the *Fables* in English. See, in particular, Francis Barlow, *The Fables of Aesop,* in English, French, and Latin, 1687; John Gilchrist, *Fables in Six Oriental Languages,* 1803 (Calcutta); Joseph Jacobs, *The Fables of Aesop,* 1889; and Manuel Komroff, *The Great Fables,* 1928.

WILLIAM HARRISON AINSWORTH

Born: Manchester, England
Date: February 4, 1805

Died: Reigate, England
Date: January 3, 1882

PRINCIPAL WORKS

NOVELS: *Rookwood,* 1834; *Crichton,* 1837; *Jack Sheppard,* 1839; *The Tower of London,* 1840; *Old Saint Paul's,* 1841; *Guy Fawkes,* 1841; *Windsor Castle,* 1843; *St. James, or The Court of Queen Anne,* 1844; *The Lancashire Witches,* 1849.

In his own lifetime, William Harrison Ainsworth was well known as an editor and publisher, as well as a

novelist. His activities in editing and publishing were at least as important in his life as were his writing. He was

13

born, Feburary 4, 1805, into the family of a respected Manchester lawyer and, after attending grammar school in Manchester, was himself apprenticed to a lawyer with the intent that he should follow his father's profession. At the death of his father in 1824, however, he left Manchester and continued his studies in London at the Inner Temple. But fate did not intend him for the legal profession. In 1826 he married Anne Francis Ebers, daughter of John Ebers, a prominent London publisher, an occasion that swerved him into activities other than law. At the time of his marriage Ainsworth had already done considerable writing, had published in several periodicals, and had tried to start a magazine of his own, *The Boeotian*. Following his marriage he entered the publishing business, but seems to have been too poor a businessman to succeed. He turned then to writing. *Sir John Chiverton* (1826), a mediocre novel written by Ainsworth and J. P. Aston, had received some praise from Sir Walter Scott. At any rate, sometime in 1830, while traveling on the Continent, Ainsworth seems to have made up his mind to turn seriously to a career of novel-writing. His first success was *Rookwood*, which gave him some economic security, made him temporarily a literary lion, and gave him an entry into the literary and political life which centered about Holland House, the London residence of Lord Holland, who was the social leader of the Whigs. Following that successful novel, Ainsworth continued as a novelist, publishing about forty titles during his life.

But writing was still only one of the activities of Ainsworth's busy life. In 1839 he became editor of *Bentley's Miscellany*, a famous British magazine of the time, to which he had been a contributor. He bought the magazine in 1854 and owned it for fourteen years. He eventually sold the magazine back to its previous owner for a fraction of what he had paid, the value of the magazine having fallen while under his ownership. Before he bought *Bentley's Miscellany*, Ainsworth had edited other periodicals, *Ainsworth's Magazine* and the *New Monthly Magazine*. Although an unsuccessful businessman, Ainsworth made a memorable reputation as an editor of periodicals. He was extremely courteous to contributors and was willing to help them to a greater extent than most of the editors of the time, even to helping them place in other periodicals pieces of writing which he could not use himself. He was also unlike many editors of his time in that he was prompt and fair in paying for work he used.

Ainsworth's novels are historical romances, and his name and work have often been bracketed with those of such authors as Sir Walter Scott, G. P. R. James, Captain Marryat, James Fenimore Cooper, and Charles Lever. Like other writers in this genre, Ainsworth often took liberties with historical facts and utilized peculiarities of language to enliven his fiction. The slang of thieves and highwaymen was a realm of language which he particularly exploited. In *Rookwood*, which made him famous, Ainsworth also utilized the bag of tricks common to the Gothic novelists, bringing in old manor houses, corpses, coffins, and supernatural paraphernalia. A highlight of the novel was Dick Turpin's famous ride on his mare, Black Bess. *Crichton* is reminiscent of Sir Walter

Scott's *Quentin Durward*, with its plot involving a Scottish adventurer and a foundling who turns out to be a noble and beautiful French heiress, along with such historical figures as Henry of Navarre and Catherine de Médicis. More typical of Ainsworth's fiction is *Jack Sheppard*, which is the story of the famous highwayman. Characterization is slight in this novel, taking second place behind robust action and a plentiful supply of realistic, even brutal details. Typical of Ainsworth's excellent narrative ability in passages devoted to portraying action is a hair-raising escape by water through the arches of London Bridge on the flood tide. In addition to Jack Sheppard himself, the reader meets Jonathan Wild, an equally famous British criminal, who is portrayed by Ainsworth as loathsome, cynical, and horribly brutal.

A very popular Ainsworth novel was *Guy Fawkes*, part of which used the setting of Manchester and gave the author an opportunity to exploit his knowledge of the city in which he had been reared. A whole group of Ainsworth's novels are laid against the background of London and the people and events of that city's history. In the group belong *The Tower of London*, *Old St. Paul's*, *Windsor Castle*, and *St. James, or The Court of Queen Anne*. Also of interest is *The Lancashire Witches*, which describes the famous trial at Lancaster in 1612, with long accounts of the outlandish charges made against the persons accused of witchcraft. Like many another voluminous writer, Ainsworth wrote better fiction earlier in his career than he did later. Books continued to flow from his pen until his death at Reigate on January 3, 1882, but most of the later volumes do not measure up to his earlier productions.

Ainsworth's life was never an easy one during adulthood. He tried to carry out two and three careers at one time; along with his output of fiction goes an important lifetime of editing and publishing. Had he been able to forego writing, editing, or business, he might have been more successful than he was. He died still trying to recoup great financial losses incurred in publishing ventures, having to make up by writing popular novels the money he lost as an unsuccessful businessman.

BIBLIOGRAPHICAL REFERENCES: The most recent edition is *The Collected Works of William Harrison Ainsworth*, 12 vols., 1923. There is a bibliography by Harold Locke, *A Bibliographical Catalogue of the Published Novels and Ballads of William Harrison Ainsworth*, 1925. The standard biography is S. M. Ellis, *William Harrison Ainsworth and his Friends*, 1911. See also John Evans, *The Early Life of William Harrison Ainsworth*, 1882; and W. E. A. Axon, *William Harrison Ainsworth, A Memoir*, 1902.

ALAIN-FOURNIER
(Henri Alain Fournier)

Born: Chapelle-d'Angillon, France
Date: October 3, 1886

Died: Bois Saint-Remy, France
Date: September 22, 1914

PRINCIPAL WORKS

NOVEL: *Le Grand Méaulnes*, 1913 (*The Wanderer*).
MISCELLANY: *Miracles*, 1924.

Alain-Fournier, born Henri Alain Fournier at Chapelle-d'Angillon, October 3, 1886, spent a pleasant childhood and went to school at Brest and at Bourges. It was the school at Brest and his experiences there that served as part of the setting for his famous novel, *The Wanderer*. This minor masterpiece, partly based on Alain-Fournier's own life, partly on a loose reconstruction of the life of John Keats, tells of the attempt of a young schoolboy to discover through the haze of experience what is philosophically and psychologically real. Alain-Fournier himself was a symbolist, strongly influenced by the poetry of Rimbaud and Baudelaire; in his novel he was, in part, all of his characters, splitting himself into different types in order to discover some identity and meaning in experience through a symbolic and poetic prose. Philosophically, he was also strongly influenced by the work of Henri Bergson.

After he left school, Alain-Fournier wrote for various contemporary journals in Paris before World War I. During this period of his life *The Wanderer* was well received, and his early death, in the war, was widely mourned. After the war his novel was to have a profound influence on young French writers who found in Alain-Fournier's style a fierce and delicate instrument with which to trace the wanderings of the spirit toward reality. *Miracles*, a collection of Alain-Fournier's poems and eleven of his short stories dealing with his life in Paris, all written between 1905 and 1911, was published posthumously by his friend Jacques Rivière in 1924. Alain-Fournier died at Bois Saint-Remy on September 22, 1914.

BIBLIOGRAPHICAL REFERENCES: The standard translation of *Le Grand Méaulnes* (titled *The Wanderer*, formerly *The Big Méaulnes*), 1946, contains an important introduction by Havelock Ellis. The most recent study is Robert Champigny, *Portrait of a Symbolist Hero: An Existential Study Based on the Work of Alain-Fournier*, 1954, with an extensive bibliography. Robert D. D. Gibson, *The Quest of Alain-Fournier*, 1953, is a very thorough biography. Other studies are in Havelock Ellis, *From Rousseau to Proust*, 1935; Harold March, "The 'Other Landscape' of Fournier," *Publications of the Modern Language Association* LVI (1941), 266–279; David Paul, "The Mysterious Landscape, A Study of Alain-Fournier," *Cornhill*, CLXII (1947), 440–449; and Martin Turnell, "The Legend of Alain-Fournier," *Commonweal*, LIX (1954), 580–582.

PEDRO ANTONIO DE ALARCÓN

Born: Guadix, Spain
Date: March 10, 1833

Died: Madrid, Spain
Date: July 20, 1891

PRINCIPAL WORKS

NOVELS: *El sombrero de tres picos,* 1874 (*The Three-Cornered Hat*); *El Capitán Veneno,* 1881 (*Captain Poison*).

REMINISCENCES AND STUDIES: *Historia de mis libros,* 1884 (*History of My Books*).

Pedro Antonio de Alarcón is an example of a nineteenth century Spanish romanticist almost literally slain by the rise of French realism, which turned him into a conservative in his old age. Born March 10, 1833, in Guadix, a small town in Granada, and unable because of family poverty to study law at the University of Granada, he was urged toward priesthood. At heart, however, he wanted to write, and Sir Walter Scott, Hugo, and Dumas claimed more of his time than his law books. While still at college, he determined on a series of four novels to be set in the four compass points. He started with a tale of the north, *El final de Norma* (*The Final Aria of Norma*), with local color gleaned from guidebooks of Spitzberg. This work, published in 1855, was termed by one critic "fantastic trash still enjoyed by the very young."

With a friend, Alarcón founded a periodical devoted to literature, science, and art. He attempted a play, pleasing to the audience, but lampooned by the critics. With the outbreak of war in Africa in 1859, he enlisted to serve as a soldier-reporter; he returned with a manuscript of his experiences that earned him enough money to finance a trip to Naples to write another travel book.

The years 1872–1884 marked Alarcón's greatest literary activity. Several long novels, *El escándalo* (*Scandal*) in 1875 and *El niño de la bola* (*The Religious Statue of the Globe*) in 1880, were published during this period, as well as some of the novelettes in which he excelled. One of the best is *The Three-Cornered Hat*, based on a somewhat bawdy ballad, "The Miller of Arcos," which Alarcón turned into one of the world's masterpieces of humor. In the archaic town of his childhood, among family treasures, were a scarlet cape and a three-cornered hat which had belonged to his grandfather, a councilman of the town. The story they suggested was written originally to order for a Cuban humorous magazine. It has had several adaptations, including a ballet version by Manuel de Falla in 1919. Another of Alarcón's better works is *Captain Poison*, the story of a misogynist, wounded in Madrid street fighting in 1848 and then hospitalized among three women.

In 1875 Alarcón was elected to the Spanish Academy but the critical attacks on his work, especially on those with religious implication, discouraged him from further fiction writing. He did, however, publish a pathetic *History of My Books* in 1884. Ill following several strokes, he died in Madrid on July 20 (or July 10), 1891.

BIBLIOGRAPHICAL REFERENCES: Alarcón's own account of his literary career is given in *Historia de mis libros*, Vol. XXXII of his *Obras completas*. See also E. Pardo Bazán, "Alarcón, estudio biografico," in *Obras completas*, XXXII; José A. Balseiro, *Novelistas españoles modernos*, 1917; Julio Romano, *Pedro Antonio de Alarcón, el novelista romántico*, 1933; and W. C. Atkinson, "Pedro Antonio de Alarcón," *Bulletin of Spanish Studies*, 1933.

LOUISA MAY ALCOTT

Born: Germantown, Pennsylvania
Date: November 29, 1832

Died: Boston, Massachusetts
Date: March 6, 1888

NOVELS: *Little Women,* 1868; *An Old-Fashioned Girl,* 1870; *Little Men,* 1871; *Eight Cousins,* 1875; *Rose in Bloom,* 1876; *Under the Lilacs,* 1878; *Jack and Jill,* 1880; *Jo's Boys,* 1886.

MISCELLANEOUS: *Flower Fables,* 1854; *Hospital Sketches,* 1863.

Louisa May Alcott, the famous daughter of a famous father, was born in Germantown, Pennsylvania, on November 29, 1832; but her early life was spent in the vicinity of Concord and Boston, where she grew up under the influence of Ralph Waldo Emerson and Henry David Thoreau. Her father, Bronson Alcott, was a transcendentalist, a non-resident member of Brook Farm. Reformer, scholar, and educator, he founded the well-known Temple School in Boston.

Early in life she realized that her impractical father needed financial assistance to run his household. Accordingly she worked as a domestic, as a seamstress, and as a teacher. Her first attempts at writing were the popular melodramas of the period, in which métier she attracted some attention with such early and now forgotten plays as *The Bandit's Bride,* and *The Moorish Maiden's Vow.* Next she wrote poems and stories, some of which were published in *The Atlantic Monthly.* In 1854 appeared her first book, *Flower Fables,* a series of stories written for Ralph Waldo Emerson's daughter Ellen.

During the Civil War she served as a nurse in the Union Hospital in Georgetown. As a result of this experience her health was impaired. The letters she wrote home to her family were later revised and published as *Hospital Sketches* in 1863.

In 1864 her first novel, *Moods,* was published. In 1867 she became editor of a children's magazine, *Merry's Museum.* In the next year *Little Women* appeared, an immediate success both in English and translation. This perennially popular volume described a normal, pleasant American family life. The March family of the novel is drawn from her own family. Jo March is Louisa herself, and the March sisters represent the girls of the Alcott family. Theodore Lawrence (Laurie) is modeled after a young man whom she met in Poland during a trip abroad.

The popularity of *Little Women* was such that at last the family could live without financial worries. But Louisa continued to write other children's stories which attracted an enthusiastic and adoring audience: *An Old-Fashioned Girl, Little Men, Eight Cousins, Rose in Bloom, Under the Lilacs, Jack and Jill,* and *Jo's Boys.* All had their avid readers.

Her last years were spent in Boston, where she died two days after her father, on March 6, 1888. An ardent abolitionist and advocate of women's suffrage, Louisa May Alcott still has a host of admirers, for her sentimental novels continue to attract readers among each new generation of children all over the world. *Little Women,* called the most popular girls' book ever written, is her chief claim to fame.

BIBLIOGRAPHICAL REFERENCES: Most of the books about Louisa May Alcott are intended primarily for children. The standard biography for source material is Ednah

D. Cheney, *Louisa May Alcott: Her Life, Letters and Journals,* 1889. Katherine Anthony, *Louisa May Alcott,* 1938, is a more recent and perceptive study. See also Maria S. Porter, *Recollections of Louisa May Alcott,* 1893; and Lucile Gulliver, *Louisa May Alcott: A Bibliography,* 1932.

RICHARD ALDINGTON

Born: Portsmouth, England   *Died:* Léré, France
Date: 1892   *Date:* July 28, 1962

PRINCIPAL WORKS

POEMS: *Images,* 1915 [*Images Old and New*]; *The Love Poems of Myrrhine and Konallis,* 1917; *Reverie,* 1917; *Images of War,* 1919; *Images of Desire,* 1919; *War and Love,* 1919; *Exile and Other Poems,* 1923; *A Fool i' the Forest,* 1925; *Collected Poems,* 1928; *Hark the Herald,* 1928; *The Eaten Heart,* 1929; *A Dream in the Luxembourg,* 1930 [*Love and the Luxembourg*]; *Poems,* 1934; *Complete Poems,* 1949.

NOVELS: *Death of a Hero,* 1929; *The Colonel's Daughter,* 1931; *All Men Are Enemies,* 1933; *Women Must Work,* 1934; *Very Heaven,* 1937; *Rejected Guest,* 1939.

SHORT STORIES: *At All Costs,* 1930; *Last Straws,* 1930; *Two Stories: Deserter* and *The Lads of the Village,* 1930; *A War Story,* 1930; *Stepping Heavenward,* 1931; *Soft Answers,* 1932.

LITERARY STUDIES: *Literary Studies and Reviews,* 1924; *Voltaire,* 1925; *French Studies and Reviews,* 1926; *Remy de Gourmont: A Modern Man of Letters,* 1928; *D. H. Lawrence,* 1930 [*D. H. Lawrence: An Indiscretion*]; *Portrait of a Rebel,* 1957.

BIOGRAPHY: *Life of Wellington,* 1943 [*The Duke*]; *The Strange Life of Charles Waterton,* 1949; *D. H. Lawrence: Portrait of a Genius, But* . . . , 1950; *Lawrence of Arabia,* 1955; *Portrait of a Rebel,* 1957.

AUTOBIOGRAPHY: *Life for Life's Sake,* 1941.

An influential poet during the Imagist period and a cosmopolite, Richard Aldington, born at Portsmouth in 1892, was educated at Dover College and the University of London. Following the publication of his *Images* in 1915, he was looked up to as a leader of the Imagist school and for a time was editor of *The Egoist,* the main publication of that group. Perhaps his best work has been in the novel (with such bitter war novels as *Death of a Hero*), but he has also written literary criticism, biography, short stories, and many translations from the Greek, Latin, French, and Italian.

He was married from 1913 to 1937 to "H. D.," the American Imagist poet, Hilda Doolittle. After 1916 he served in World War I; his war experience left him penniless and, for eight years, shell-shocked. No doubt these episodes account for the ironic and savage attack on war and on his society which is shown in the very titles of his novels. His "Hero" is anything but that.

After his divorce and remarriage (to Netta McCulloch) in 1937, Aldington turned his attention to a brilliant series of biographical studies. His book on Wellington earned the James Tait Black Memorial Prize for 1947, and his picture of D. H. Lawrence, written out of close personal knowledge of the man, is especially valuable in showing a human and understandable genius. His study of T. E. Lawrence of Arabia received very mixed and controversial reviews in 1955.

BIBLIOGRAPHICAL REFERENCES: Apart from book reviews, there is almost no recent criticism of Aldington. See Thomas McGreevy, *Richard Aldington: An Englishman,* 1931; Glenn Hughes, *Imagism and the Imagists,* 1931; and May Sinclair, "Richard Aldington's Images," *English Review,* XXXII (1931), 397–404.

THOMAS BAILEY ALDRICH

Born: Portsmouth, New Hampshire *Died:* Boston, Massachusetts
Date: November 11, 1836 *Date:* March 19, 1907

PRINCIPAL WORKS

POEMS: *The Bells: A Collection of Chimes,* 1855; *The Ballad of Babie Bell and Other Poems,* 1859; *Cloth of Gold,* 1874; *Flower and Thorn,* 1877; *Mercedes and Later Lyrics,* 1884; *Wyndham Towers,* 1890; *Judith and Holofernes,* 1896.

NOVELS: *The Story of a Bad Boy,* 1870; *Prudence Palfrey,* 1874; *The Queen of Sheba,* 1877; *The Stillwater Tragedy,* 1880; *The Second Son,* 1888.

SHORT STORIES: *Marjorie Daw and Other People,* 1873; *Two Bites at a Cherry,* 1894.

SKETCHES AND STUDIES: *From Ponkapog to Pesth,* 1883; *An Old Town by the Sea,* 1893; *Ponkapog Papers,* 1903.

Thomas Bailey Aldrich, poet, editor, and story-writer, was born in the harbor town of Portsmouth, New Hampshire, on November 11, 1836. Son of Elias Taft Aldrich and Sarah Abba Bailey Aldrich, his early years were spent in New York City, New Orleans, and other parts of the country; but in 1849 he returned to Portsmouth to prepare for Harvard College and to live in the Nutter House which he describes so vividly in *The Story of a Bad Boy.* Here he was a pupil of Samuel De Merritt, a famous schoolmaster of the time.

However, instead of going to college to study literature with Professor Longfellow at Cambridge, he went to New York as a clerk for his uncle, James Frost. In the metropolis he worked diligently in the counting house, but he also had time to write poetry. Some of these early poems were published under various pseudonyms. In 1855 he gained nation-wide acclaim for his "Ballad of Babie Bell," which he wrote on the backs of bills of lading during his working hours. Meanwhile he had become a member of a Bohemian group of writers, among whom were Walt Whitman and Bayard Taylor.

He started his work with the press with a position on the staff of the *Home Journal.* In 1861, during the Civil War, he went to the front with the Army of the Potomac as a reporter. In 1863 he began his distinguished editorial career with the position of managing editor of the *Illustrated News*. Later he moved to Boston as editor of *Every Saturday*.

Meanwhile he had been writing and publishing poems, stories, and novels, some of which had appeared in the *Atlantic Monthly*. In 1881, when his friend William Dean Howells resigned his position as editor of the *Atlantic Monthly*, Aldrich was named to succeed him. He held this position for nine years. After giving up this position he spent his time in traveling and at his home at Tenant's Harbor on the coast of Maine. He died in Boston on March 19, 1907.

During his lifetime Aldrich was highly regarded as a poet, especially for his delicacy and precision of language. In 1865 his collected poems were published in the Ticknor and Fields Blue and Gold Series. His collections of verse include *Cloth of Gold, Mercedes and Later Lyrics,* and *Wyndham Towers*. Some of his most popular lyrics are "Hesperides," "When the Sultan Goes to Ispahan," "Before the Rain," "Tiger Lilies," "Destiny," and "The Bells at Midnight"—the latter a poem written on the death of President Lincoln. Two of his novels, *Prudence Palfrey* and *The Stillwater Tragedy,* were extremely popular in their day. He also wrote numerous short stories. of which "Marjorie Daw" is probably the best known.

BIBLIOGRAPHICAL REFERENCES: The standard biography is Ferris Greenslet, *The Life of Thomas Bailey Aldrich,* 1908. See also Van Wyck Brooks, *New England: Indian Summer,* 1940; and Alexander Cowrie, "Indian Summer Novelist," *New England Quarterly,* XV (1942), 608–621.

CIRO ALEGRÍA

Born: Sartimbamba, Quilca, Peru
Date: November 4, 1909

Principal Works

NOVELS: *La serpiente de oro,* 1935 (*The Golden Serpent*); *Los perros hambrientos,* 1939 (*Hungry Dogs*); *El mundo es ancho y ajeno,* 1941 (*Broad and Alien Is the World*).

Born in northern Peru, at Sartimbamba, on November 4, 1909, and claiming one Irish grandfather, named Lynch, Ciro Alegría spent his boyhood among the common people, often traveling by horseback from coast to selvas and taking shelter at night with Indians or half-breed peasant families. This experience proved excellent training for a *criollista* writer.

After graduating from the national College of San Juan at Trujillo, he wrote for newspapers and bossed a road-building gang. He entered the university in 1930, but was arrested as an *Aprista* plotter against the government and spent eight months in jail until freed by a revolution. When the government regained power, Alegría fled to the Marañón wilderness, where he acquired material for his romantic adventure story, *The Golden Serpent,* the first great novel to depict life in the Peruvian jungles at the headwaters of the Amazon. This prize-winning novel was translated into English in 1943.

Alegría was again a political exile in Chile when he wrote *Hungry Dogs,* a realistic picture of Indians in the northern Peruvian highlands. The novel won a literary prize in Chile. His next novel, *Broad and Alien Is* *the World,* won first prize in the Latin American novel contest for 1941. Unlike other Indianist novelists, Alegría does not concentrate on the ugly side of the lives of the Indians. Their human qualities appeal to his compassion and he writes about them with lyric intensity.

BIBLIOGRAPHICAL REFERENCES: For brief critical studies see Jefferson R. Spell, *Contemporary Spanish American Fiction,* 1944; *Latin American Studies,* I (1945, University of Texas); and A. Torres Rioseco, *The Epic of Latin American Literature,* 1946.

MATEO ALEMÁN

Born: Seville, Spain
Date: September 26, 1547

Died: Mexico
Date: c. 1615

PRINCIPAL WORK

NOVEL: *La vida y hechos del pícaro Guzmán de Alfarache,* Part I, 1599; Part II, 1604 (*The Rogue*).

The sixteenth century in Spain brought a flood of idealistic novels, with one jarring note, the first picaresque novel, introduced by *Lazarillo de Tormes* in 1554. Although religious censorship under Philip II discouraged imitators for a time, the king's death allowed writers to react against idealistic and didactic fiction and to turn to realistic and satirical novels. The author of one of the best, *Guzmán de Alfarache,* was Mateo Alemán, born in Seville on September 26, 1547, who as the son of a prison doctor of Seville had learned about rogues as a child. Trying to follow in his father's profession, Alemán succumbed to love affairs and debts for which he was three times jailed, on the first occasion in Seville in 1580.

Many scholars believe that during his second imprisonment, in Seville in 1602, Cervantes was a fellow prisoner. The two have many points in common: they were born within a few days of each other; they studied under the same teacher, and they wrote at the same time. Perhaps both were in the army in Italy. It is known that both sought assignments in the New World, Alemán successfully. There he died, perhaps within a year of his great contemporary.

Where they differ is in the tone of their writing. Alemán was lacking in love for his fellow men and in a philosophy to compensate for life's trials. His writing has the cruel, heartless quality of the picaresque tradition.

Guzmán, a rogue of Seville, wanders as widely as his author did, lying and stealing in Madrid, Toledo, and Rome, where he was beggar, page to a cardinal and servant of the French ambassador. More important than the plot, however, are the keen observations of life

22

at all social levels, accompanied by a wealth of folk material, proverbs, customs, and philosophical interpolations. The book's chief flaw is its moralizing, inserted so that it might pass the scrutiny of clerical censorship. The story pattern, a series of incidents strung like beads on the personality of its chief character, became the model followed by many Spanish authors ever since. In Germany, Lessing commented on its greatness, and it has also influenced French writers. For some time its first part far surpassed *Don Quixote* in popularity, going into a score of editions in five years and

provoking a spurious sequel in 1602, two years before Alemán published his own sequel. The character of the protagonist is more thoroughly developed than Lazarillo is, but because of its digressions, its bitterness, its literary rather than popular language, it ranks slightly behind the delightful and gay *Lazarillo de Tormes*.

In 1608 Alemán obtained permission to emigrate to Mexico, where a relative was already established. There he wrote a book on Spanish spelling and some religious tracts, and there he died unrecorded in any official document.

BIBLIOGRAPHICAL REFERENCES: For a study of Alemán in English see F. W. Chandler, *Romances of Roguery*, 1899. Standard references in Spanish include Francisco Rodríguez Marín, *Documentos referentes a Mateo Alemán*, 1933; C. Espinosa, *La novela picaresca y el Guzmán de Alfarache*, 1935 (Havana); and E. Moreno Báez, *Guzmán de Alfarache*, 1948.

HERVEY ALLEN

Born: Pittsburgh, Pennsylvania
Date: December 8, 1889

Died: Miami, Florida
Date: December 28, 1949

PRINCIPAL WORKS

NOVELS: *Anthony Adverse*, 1933; *Action at Aquila*, 1938; *It Was Like This*, 1940; *The Forest and the Fort*, 1943; *Bedford Village*, 1944; *Toward the Morning*, 1948; *The City in the Dawn*, 1950.

POEMS: *Wampum and Old Gold*, 1921; *The Bride of Huitzil*, 1922; *Carolina Chansons: Legends of the Low Country*, 1922 (with DuBose Heyward); *Earth Moods and Other Poems*, 1925; *New Legends*, 1929; *Sarah Simon*, 1929; *Songs for Annette*, 1929.

BIOGRAPHY: *Israfel: The Life and Times of Edgar Allan Poe*, 1926.

AUTOBIOGRAPHY: *Toward the Flame*, 1926.

(William) Hervey Allen began writing poetry in the 1920's, but his work in this form was overshadowed both by the scholarly achievement of his two-volume biography of Poe, *Israfel*, and *Anthony Adverse*, a novel of historical romance unsurpassed in sales by any other before Margaret Mitch-

ell's *Gone with The Wind*. During the author's lifetime, 1,500,000 copies of this 1200-page picaresque tale of adventure were sold.

Born in Pittsburgh, Pennsylvania, on December 8, 1889, Allen was educated at the United States Naval Academy but left before graduating to

23

take a degree in economics at the University of Pittsburgh in 1915. On his return from France, where he was wounded while serving as an officer in the A.E.F., he went to live in Charleston, South Carolina. Friendship with another Charleston writer, Du Bose Heyward, led to their collaboration on *Carolina Chansons,* published in 1922.

Three more collections of poetry soon followed, the most ambitious being *Earth Moods and Other Poems,* an attempt to picture evolution as a legendary conflict ending in the supremacy of man. *New Legends,* however, may be Allen's most successful book of verse, a volume reflecting his poetic absorption with the Bermuda islands where he stayed five years to complete *Anthony Adverse.*

The adventurous exploits of Anthony Adverse, born illegitimate son of a runaway wife and a Spanish father, and adopted by his grandfather, a Scottish merchant, are mingled with philosophical musings in Allen's famous novel to create a story full of vivid scenes; but the serious historical objective of the book is not too convincing.

Europe and the eighteenth century are brought to bear on the hero's wanderings and exploits with something of Melville's gravity but much more of the elder Dumas' magic.

In his next venture into historical fiction, Allen restricted himself to the Civil War in *Action at Aquila,* a rather conventional story of a gallant Union hero and a Southern belle. *The Forest and the Fort, Bedford Village,* and *Toward the Morning* were to have been a series of six related novels tentatively titled *The Disinherited* and spanning American history from colonial times through the twenties, but Allen died while working on this ambitious project. The three novels and part of a fourth were collected under one title, *The City in the Dawn,* in 1950.

Perhaps Hervey Allen's most distinguished work was his biography of Poe, *Israfel,* which attempted to trace Poe's achievements and failures to the conditions of his life. It is a work of excellent research, leaning carefully on Freudian psychology to explain Poe's personality.

BIBLIOGRAPHICAL REFERENCES: Criticism of Hervey Allen is limited. For biographical references see *Hervey Allen: American Author,* 1938 (pamphlet). The writer's own theories of historical fiction are presented in "The Sources of *Anthony Adverse,*" *Saturday Review of Literature,* X (1934), 401+, and "History and the Novel," *Atlantic Monthly,* CLXXXIII (1944), 119–120. For related material see also Ernest E. Leisy, *The American Historical Novel,* 1950.

IGNACIO MANUEL ALTAMIRANO

Born: Tixtla, Mexico
Date: November 13, 1834

Died: San Remo, Italy
Date: February 13, 1893

PRINCIPAL WORKS

NOVELS: *Clemencia,* 1869; *La navidad en las montañas,* 1870 (*Christmas in the Mountains*); *El Zarco,* 1901.

SHORT STORIES: *Cuentas de invierno,* 1880 (*Winter Tales*); *Paisajes y leyendas, tradiciones y costumbres de Mexico,* 1884 (*Landscapes and Legends, Traditions and Customs of Mexico*).

POEMS: *Rimas,* 1880.

Teacher, politician, soldier, journalist, poet, novelist, literary inspirer of the young, restorer of centers of learning, Ignacio Manuel Altamirano fills an epoch in the cultural life of Mexico. The spiritual development of this writer, considered his country's greatest in his age, is an example of determination and genius. Of pure Indian blood, he was born on November 13, 1834, in an obscure village in the southwest of Mexico; and at the age of fourteen he still knew no Spanish. He began his studies at the Scientific and Literary Institute of Toluca, then the capital city of the state that contained his native village. In this city he learned Spanish, Latin, French, and philosophy, and had as a teacher of literature the celebrated reformer, Ignacio Ramírez, better known under his pseudonym, El Nigromante (The Necromancer).

After teaching French in a private school in Toluca, he settled in Mexico City and studied at the College of Letrán. He interrupted his studies in order to ally himself with the Revolution of 1854, and after fighting in it he returned to Mexico City to complete his courses in law. Again he took up arms during the War of Reform, and in 1861 he was elected a delegate to the Union Congress. During the French Intervention and the Second Empire he fought in the Republican ranks. After the fall of Maximilian he devoted the rest of his life to teaching and to letters.

"Without resentment of the past or fear of the future" he founded the weekly literary review, *El Renacimiento* (*Renaissance*), in whose columns was brought about the true reconciliation of the conflicting political and literary factions: the conservative and the liberal; the neoclassic and the romantic. The pages of this publication were open to all genres and all ideas. Here the short story, the novel, poetry, criticism, and history shook hands with one another and brought about a literary rebirth in Mexico that was to culminate in the Modernism which marked the end of the nineteenth and the beginning of the twentieth centuries.

The poetic activity of Altamirano produced thirty-two poems written before 1867 and published in 1880 under the title *Rimas.* These poems are especially descriptive and pictorial with a strong Mexican flavor; their subjects and atmosphere indicate the poet's deep preoccupation with the creation of an eminently national literature.

As a novelist, Altamirano was the first, from a literary point of view, to appear in Mexican letters. He was the first concerned with creating an authentic novel; that is to say, a literary work with an artistic form. The plots of his novels are generally sober, weighty, and proportioned. The atmosphere in which they develop is intensely Mexican, completely localized within the provincial geography of Mexico. His characters, although moved by romantic motives, are nonetheless believable, sympathetic, contrasted one with another. In *Clemencia,* laid in the west of the Republic during the war of the French Intervention,

Altamirano succeeds in creating a romantic novel of powerful native coloring. *El Zarco,* a similar novel confined to the State of Morelos, presents a picture of the guerrillas and bandits of that time and of a woman who sacrifices herself to follow a highwayman. In *Christmas in the Mountains,* a short novel of idyllic atmosphere, Altamirano gives us a simple and pleasing account of a Christmas spent in a village in the south of Mexico during the Civil War.

In 1889 Altamirano was named Consul General in Spain and later in France. During a visit to Italy he became ill and went to San Remo in search of health. There he died on February 13, 1893. His ashes were carried to Mexico City and placed in the Hall of Fame.

BIBLIOGRAPHICAL REFERENCES: For biographical and critical studies of Altamirano in English see Carlos González Peña, *History of Mexican Literature,* translated by G. B. Nance and F. J. Dunstan, 1943, and the introduction to the Folio Society edition of *El Zarco the Bandit,* 1957; in Spanish, José Luis Martínez, Introductions to *Clemencia* and *La literatura nacional,* 1949 (Mexico City); and Ralph E. Warner, "Bibliografia de las obras de Ignacio Manuel Altamirano," *Revista Iberoamericana,* III (1941), 465–512; reprinted, 1955 (Mexico City). A useful collection of essays by various hands is *Homaje a Ignacio Manuel Altamirano,* 1935 (Mexico City).

JORGE AMADO

Born: Ilhéos, Bahia, Brazil
Date: August 12, 1912

PRINCIPAL WORKS

NOVELS: *Cacau,* 1933 (*Cacao*); *Suor,* 1934 (*Sweat*); *Jubiabá,* 1935; *Mar Morto,* 1936 (*Sea of the Dead*); *Capitães da Areia,* 1937 (*Beach Waifs*); *Terras do Sem Fin,* 1943 (*The Violent Land*).

Jorge Amado, ranked beside José Lins do Rego as one of the two greatest contemporary Brazilian novelists, is a mulatto who was born on August 12, 1912, at Ilhéos, a city of Negroes in the State of Bahia, about which he wrote a cycle of six sociological novels. Gilberto Freyre complains that Amado distorts reality to seem more real and more Brazilian, and so becomes a master caricaturist rather than a photographic realist. Yet this poet in prose wrote in his *The Violent Land* one of the best descriptions of the tropical jungles, and their effect on men's minds, to come out of South America.

Because of his sociological interest in the masses, whose revolt he under-stands and chronicles, Amado picks his characters from among the downtrodden: the juvenile gangs of the big city in *Beach Waifs,* fishermen in his prize-winning *Sea of the Dead,* and the plantation worker in *Cacao* and *The Violent Land. Sweat* uses as its protagonist a tenement house. Balduíno, an ex-prizefighter and black Don Juan, is the hero of the powerful *Jubiabá,* a novel taking its title from a distortion of the name of the Baldwin locomotive. This work, showing the novelist's intention of symbolizing Afro-Brazilian vitality, has been published in seven languages.

Amado's social novels carry implications beyond their narrow provincial settings. Many reveal the realist author's romantic tendencies in yearning for an imaginary and better future, but his most recent works have been weakened by political preachment along Marxist lines.

BIBLIOGRAPHICAL REFERENCES: For criticism see Erico Verissimo, *Brazilian Literature: An Outline*, 1945; and Samuel Putnam, *Marvelous Journey*, 1948.

EDMONDO DE AMICIS

Born: Oneglia, Italy
Date: October 21, 1846

Died: Bordighera, Italy
Date: March 12, 1908

PRINCIPAL WORKS

NOVELS: *Sull'oceano*, 1889 (*On Blue Water*); *Il Romanzo d'un maestro*, 1890 (*The Romance of a Schoolmaster*); *La Maestrina degli operai*, 1894 (*Won by a Woman*).

SHORT STORIES AND SKETCHES: *La Vita militare*, 1868 (*Military Life in Italy*); *Novelle*, 1872; *Cuore*, 1886 (*The Heart of a Schoolboy*); *Fra sculoa e casa*, 1892; *La Carrozza di tutti*, 1899.

TRAVEL SKETCHES AND IMPRESSIONS: *Spagna*, 1872 (*Spain*); *L'Olanda*, 1874 (*Holland and Its People*); *Ricordi di Londra*, 1874 (*Jottings about London*); *Marocco*, 1876 (*Morocco*); *Constantinopili*, 1878 (*Constantinople*); *Ricordi di Parigi*, 1879 (*Studies of Paris*).

ESSAYS AND STUDIES: *Ritratti letterarii*, 1881; *L'Idioma gentile*, 1905.

Edmondo de Amicis, born at Oneglia, Italy, on October 21, 1846, was educated at a military school in Modena and was, soon after his graduation, made the director of the military garrison at Florence in 1867. While at Florence, he began to write short stories with a strong patriotic flavor and published his first volume, *Military Life in Italy*, in 1868.

In 1870, Amicis left the army and began to write journals of his travels throughout Europe, North Africa, and the Near East. The travel books were all rambling accounts of his journeys through a foreign city or country, full of descriptive comments, leisurely descriptions of scenery, and appreciative estimates of art. The most famous of his travel books is that on Holland, a sensitive account of Dutch village life, Dutch gardens, and the glories of Dutch painting. He moved easily from discussing painting to discussing the life and scenery of the town that had gone into the painting. His travel books were also appreciated for his ability to portray a large festive scene—a bull fight, a pageant, a tulip festival.

In later life Amicis turned his attention to politics. He became a socialist and infused a good deal of political and social doctrine into his later works. In Italy his most popular book was *The Heart of a Schoolboy*, written in the form of a journal in which a schoolboy recounted his day to day experiences. The experiences, in turn, demonstrated how a system of education might be developed to produce a socialist community. Amicis endowed his social ideas with moral value, for he assumed that the community he advocated would bring equality, happi-

27

ness, and good to all men. Amicis was elected to the Italian Chamber of Deputies from Turin, but he never served because he was unwilling to engage in practical political problems. As a writer, however, his Utopian ideas, especially as worked out in the school-boy community in *The Heart of a Schoolboy*, had a strong influence on Italian youth until about the time of World War I. He died at Bordighera on March 12, 1908.

Today Amicis is not revered as a political thinker, nor do his early stories still stir Italians with patriotic pride. But his travel books are still read and enjoyed as gentle rambles, and his later novels, like *The Romance of the Schoolmaster*, are still appreciated for their grace, charm, and artistry. Amicis was never praised for psychological depth or probing analysis of character; but both style and humanity are still visible in the best of his work, and his talent at evoking a purely descriptive scene is still recognized.

BIBLIOGRAPHICAL REFERENCES: There is no helpful book on Amicis in English. See V. Chialant, *Edmondo de Amicis, educatore e artista*, 1911; J. H. Brovedani, *Edmondo de Amicis, l'homme et l'œuvre*, 1914; Mimi Mosso, *I tempi del "Cuore,"* 1925; Benedetto Croce, *La letteratura della nuova Italia*, I, 1929 (3d ed.); and Guido Mazzoni, "L'opera di Edmondo de Amicis," *Nuova Antologia*, CCCLXII (1932), 32–44.

JOHANNA VAN AMMERS-KÜLLER

Born: Delft, Netherlands
Date: August 13, 1884

PRINCIPAL WORKS

NOVELS: *De verzwegan strijd*, 1916 (*The Silent Struggle*); *Maskerade*, 1919 (*Masquerade*); *Het huis der vreugden*, 1922 (*The House of Joy*); *De opstandigen*, 1925 (*The Rebel Generation*); *Tantalus*, 1928; *Jenny Heysten*, 1930 (*Jenny Heysten's Career*); *Vrouwenkruistocht*, 1930 (*No Surrender*); *Heeren, knechten en vrouwen*, 1934 (*The House of Tavelinck*); *Prins incognito*, 1935 (*Prince Incognito*); *Elzelina*, 1940.

Johanna van Ammers-Küller is, with E. and M. Scharten-Antink and Marie Schmitz, the foremost interpreter of Dutch middle-class life after World War I in the tradition of psychological realism that came mainly from France. Her novels probe the social and spirit-ual problems that beset the younger generation during the postwar period of disillusionment.

Born at Delft on August 13, 1884, into a family of lawyers and doctors, she began writing early, publishing a story of romantic love at the age of fifteen in a weekly paper. She continued to write stories until marriage in 1904 and the birth of two children led her to abandon a literary career. Later, after going to London with her husband, she resumed work in fiction and published several novels that gained a wide audience. Between 1912 and 1921 three of her plays were produced. It was, however, not until she went to Amsterdam and wrote *The Rebel Generation* that she became famous.

This novel, said to have been the

28

most popular in Holland in the last fifty years, has been translated into most modern languages and produced successfully as a play. It reviews three generations of Dutch life and is primarily concerned with the emancipation of women in a world of shifting values. *The House of Joy,* equally a best seller, also drew upon the aspirations of woman in the story of a girl's yearning for a theatrical career and the intricate problems that resulted. The same milieu provided the background for a sequel, *Jenny Heysten's Career,* a searching account of the heroine, an impoverished aristocrat, who becomes so corrupted by her stage role that she attempts to act out her affections for the man she loves.

In *No Surrender* youth is shown struggling against standards it refuses to observe. This novel, utilizing the family background of *The Rebel Generation,* concerns an English suffragette forcefully conscious of her aims in life. Common to most of Ammers-Küller's work of this period is a subtlety of detail in characterizing intimate family life and a texture of incidents that carry the reader into her central theme of struggle for identity.

Her latest novels have been romances based upon French and Dutch history. One of her more recent works, *Elzelina,* is about a Dutch parson's daughter who became the mistress of Marshall Ney and accompanied him into the field of Napoleon's campaigns. The novel marks no new departure in Johanna van Ammers-Küller's work, for *The House of Tavelinck* was a successful chronicle drawn from historical sources.

BIBLIOGRAPHICAL REFERENCE: There is no helpful criticism in English. See Johannes Tielrooy, *Panaroma de la Littérature Hollandaise contemporaine,* 1938.

HANS CHRISTIAN ANDERSEN

Born: Odense, Denmark
Date: April 2, 1805

Died: Copenhagen, Denmark
Date: August 4, 1875

PRINCIPAL WORKS

FAIRY TALES AND FANTASIES: *Eventyr,* 1835–1872 (*Tales*).

NOVELS: *Improvisatoren,* 1835 (*The Improvisatore*); *O. T.,* 1836; *Kun en Spillemand,* 1837 (*Only a Fiddler*); *At være eller ikke være,* 1857 (*To Be or Not To Be*).

TRAVEL SKETCHES AND IMPRESSIONS: *Fodreise fra Holmena Canal til Østpynten af Amager,* 1829 (*A Journey on Foot from Holman's Canal to the East Point of Amager*); *I Sverrig,* 1851 (*Pictures of Sweden*); *I Spanien,* 1863 (*In Spain*).

AUTOBIOGRAPHY: *Mit Livs Eventyr* and *Fortsættelse,* 1855 (*The Story of My Life*).

Born on April 2, 1805, in the little town of Odense, Denmark, Hans Christian Andersen lived a life that followed the pattern of some of his fairy story characters. His father was a poor cobbler; his mother took in laundry to help support the family. The paternal grandfather was mildly insane; the grandmother cherished her grandson, telling him stories and myths and handing down tales of horror, superstition, and romance—the very fabric of Danish folk culture as it had come to her.

The cobbler father implanted in his

29

son the desire to lift himself above his humble cottage life. The father had read beyond his station in life; he questioned religion and abhorred superstition. He made toys and a small theater and gave the child companionship and passionately enjoined him to follow his imaginative interests so that he should not be bound to a menial trade.

At eleven Andersen lost his father, and the sheltered life he had led as a well-loved child came to an end. He attended the city school for poor children. There he learned rapidly what he wanted to learn, but he was jeered at by his schoolmates because of his gentle and artistic nature—a forecast of Andersen's own tale of the Ugly Duckling that finally became a Swan. He made friends with an assortment of adults who were more perceptive of his strange eagerness to achieve a mark in the world.

In 1819 he went to Copenhagen. Fiercely determined to find recognition, he tried ballet, singing, and acting; and he all but starved. He was snubbed by theater managers, but his youth won him the friendship of Weyse and Siboni, two musicians. He also attracted the attention of Jonas Collin, who was to be his life-long friend. He had already written a number of poems and in 1829 his first play, *Love on St. Nicholas Tower*, was performed in the Royal Theatre. He fell in love with Riborg Voigt; she inspired poems and sketches but never became his wife. (Here we can be reminded of the Steadfast Tin Soldier with his gaze fixed on the unattainable Ballerina.)

Andersen traveled throughout Denmark and then through Europe to Italy, a country which impressed him vividly. He wrote *The Improvisatore*, a veiled autobiography which was well received, and a psychological novel, *O.T.*, its scenes laid in Denmark. Thus only slowly did he approach the fairy tales that became his final basis for fame.

By this time, however, his social position was secure, and everywhere he was entertained by people of prestige. Nevertheless he frequently sought the astringent criticism of the Collin family, who saw him almost as a member of their household and felt privileged to remind him, as the child reminded the Emperor in Andersen's tale, that it was unwise to be insatiable in one's quest for recognition.

Despite this defect and an extreme sensitivity, Andersen continued to win favor and became the recipient of gifts and honors from various royal houses; for by this time his fairy tales were winning wide favor. He was acclaimed in Germany, Holland, and England; the Danish press, however, affronted him by its restrained attitude toward his foreign success. He was a friend of Jenny Lind, Charles Dickens, the musicians Liszt, Schumann, and Mendelssohn. He was welcomed as a guest anywhere. Although he was eccentric, he was a genuine poet with the sensitive understanding of the artist who perceives widely and deeply.

Andersen was influenced by the Danish philosopher Ørsted, whose principal idea was that the contrast between spirit and nature or between miracle and reality is illusory; in Andersen, the most ordinary objects can suddenly take on strange and haunting life. At any rate Andersen breathed new life into the folk tale; to him reality was more marvelous than any imagined realm because he had the poet's

30

eye for detail. As he labored at his chosen task, he did his countrymen the incidental service of stabilizing their language.

The first series of his *Eventyr*, or Wonder Tales, appeared in 1835, to be followed by a second series in 1838 and a third in 1845. He continued to write groups of these stories yearly until 1872, and it is upon these that his fame rests. He longed to excel as a novelist or dramatist, but his genius lay in telling the ancient folk tale with fresh perception so that the fairy story took on new proportions because of Andersen's remarkable ability to make the simplest description come alive. These tales have been published in nearly every European language and in some Oriental ones as well. They rank with the classics of world literature.

The much-loved Hans Christian Andersen died quietly at the Copenhagen home of friends on August 4, 1875. But the books of fairy stories that he composed have never been closed. They have a freshness and a self-subsistence that defy the attempts of the student whose tool is sociological or psychological explanation. In these tales, as an artist, Andersen triumphed over his shortcomings as a man.

BIBLIOGRAPHICAL REFERENCES: The *Fairy Tales and Legends by Hans Christian Andersen* were issued in London, 1935, and *Fairy Tales from Hans Christian Andersen* New York and London, 1935. Useful bibliographies are Elias Bredsdorff, *Danish Literature in English Translations*, 1950; and the U. S. Library of Congress bulletin, *Catalogue of the Jean Hersholt Collection of Hans Christian Andersen*, 1954. Andersen's autobiography has been translated into English as *The Story of My Life*, 1871, 1872, 1880, ff., and as *The Mermaid Man*, translated and abridged by Maurice Michael, 1955. Biographies are numerous: Robert Nisbet Bain, *Hans Christian Andersen: A Biography*, 1895; Signe Toksvig, *The Life of Hans Christian Andersen*, 1934; C. B. Burnett, *The Shoemaker's Son*, 1943; S. Larsen, *Hans Christian Andersen*, 1949; E. Meynell, *The Story of Andersen*, 1949; and Rumer Godden, *Hans Christain Andersen: A Great Life in Brief*, 1954, probably the best biography of Andersen in English. Critical books include H. S. Holbeck, *Andersen's Religion*, 1947; Svend Dahl and H. G. Topsoe-Jensen, eds., *A Book on the Danish Writer, Hans Christian Andersen, His Life and Work*, 1955, published on the 150th anniversary of the author's birth; and Elias Bredsdorff, *Hans Christian Andersen and Charles Dickens: A Friendship and Its Dissolution*, 1956, including many letters between the two authors.

MAXWELL ANDERSON

Born: Atlantic, Pennsylvania   Died: Stamford, Connecticut
Date: December 15, 1888   Date: February 28, 1959

PRINCIPAL WORKS

PLAYS: *What Price Glory*, 1924 (with Laurence Stallings); *Saturday's Children*, 1927; *Elizabeth the Queen*, 1930; *Night Over Taos*, 1932; *Both Your Houses*, 1933; *Mary of Scotland*, 1933; *Winterset*, 1935; *High Tor*, 1936; *Key Largo*, 1939; *The Eve of St. Mark*, 1942; *Joan of Lorraine*, 1946; *Anne of the Thousand Days*, 1948; *Lost in the Stars*, 1949 (with Kurt Weill); *The Bad Seed*, 1955.

ESSAYS: *The Essence of Tragedy*, 1939; *The Bases of Artistic Creation*, 1942; *Off Broadway*, 1947.

31

Maxwell Anderson, sometimes called America's leading playwright since the death of Eugene O'Neill, was born in Atlantic, Pennsylvania, on December 15, 1888. His father was a minister, and young Anderson traveled widely as his father moved from charge to charge. He was graduated from the University of North Dakota in 1911 and continued his studies at Stanford, graduating with an M.A. in English in 1914. He served as instructor in both these colleges, but later turned to journalism, on the staff of the *Herald* at Grand Forks, North Dakota. He wrote for the San Francisco *Chronicle* and also for the *Bulletin* in the years 1914–1918. From then until 1924 he wrote editorially for such New York papers as the *Evening Globe* and the *World*, as well as *New Republic*. He helped establish *Measure*, a magazine of verse, in 1920. He has been a member of long standing of the Playwrights Group, a company formed by prominent playwrights to produce their own plays. In 1911 he married Margaret Haskett, who died in 1931; his second wife, Gertrude Maynard, died in 1953. He has three sons and one daughter; one son, Alan, directs his father's plays from time to time.

Anderson is sometimes called America's journeyman playwright. His first success, *What Price Glory*, started the rumor that Anderson had himself seen military service, but it was his collaborator, Laurence Stallings (who was to work again with him on other early plays) who contributed his experiences as a Marine in the Fifth Division. The play is probably the best-known war play of modern times. After this success, Anderson met with some reverses, especially those dealt him by the critics who saw his poetry as pedestrian or pretentious. His verse plays aspired to great heights of emotion and played on great themes, but the results were often less than satisfactory. His greatest criticial success was *Winterset,* which reflected his interest in the Sacco-Vanzetti case. He has attempted to depict three English queens, several American statesmen and soldiers, Indians, and many common folk in his verse dramas. With few exceptions these plays are theatrically effective and extremely popular with theatergoers, even though they have been less than satisfactory to the arm-chair critic. Many of his plays have been made into movies with Anderson himself doing the adaptation.

In his critical essays, *The Essence of Tragedy,* Anderson has attempted to formalize his theories of drama, which are possibly more valid in retrospect than as a *modus operandi*. From his discussions it is apparent that he has always started with an Aristotelian concept of unity, and that he believes in an exalted theme, a larger-than-life protagonist, and the tragic flaw; and he has often managed to translate these elements into near-great drama. Certainly he has run the gamut of mythological, historical, and literary themes. He has dared to experiment within the commercial theater and to win out over great obstacles. However, his best plays are all behind him in the 1930's. Since that time he has written of the topical and the typical, often putting a special flourish to an older theme.

BIBLIOGRAPHICAL REFERENCES: A representative selection is Maxwell Anderson, *Eleven Verse Plays,* 1939. For biography and criticism see Barrett H. Clark, *Max-*

well Anderson: The Man and His Plays, 1932; Carl Carmer, "Maxwell Anderson: Poet and Champion," *Theatre Arts Monthly*, XVII (1933), 437–446; Edith J. Isaacs, "Maxwell Anderson," *English Journal*, XXV (1936), 795–804; Harold Rosenberg, "Poetry and the Theatre," *Poetry*, LVII (1941), 258–263; Vincent Wall, "Maxwell Anderson: The Last Anarchist," *Sewanee Review*, XLIX (1941), 339–369; E. Foster, "Core of Belief: Interpretation of the Plays of Maxwell Anderson," *ibid.*, L (1942), 87–100; Arthur M. Sampley, "Theory and Practice in Maxwell Anderson's Poetic Tragedies," *College English*, V (1944), 412–418; H. E. Woodridge, "Maxwell Anderson," *South Atlantic Quarterly*, XLIV (1945), 55–68; Harold Watts, "The Tragedy of Attrition," in *Hound and Quarry*, 1954; and Robert C. Roby, "Two Worlds: Maxwell Anderson's *Winterset*," *College English*, XVIII (1957), 195–202.

SHERWOOD ANDERSON

Born: Camden, Ohio
Date: September 13, 1876

Died: Colón, Panama
Date: March 8, 1941

PRINCIPAL WORKS

NOVELS: *Windy McPherson's Son*, 1916; *Marching Men*, 1917; *Poor White*, 1920; *Many Marriages*, 1923; *Dark Laughter*, 1925; *Beyond Desire*, 1932; *Kit Brandon*, 1936.

SHORT STORIES: *Winesburg, Ohio*, 1919; *The Triumph of the Egg*, 1921; *Horses and Men*, 1923; *Death in the Woods and Other Stories*, 1933.

ESSAYS AND STUDIES: *Sherwood Anderson's Notebook*, 1926; *Hello Towns!*, 1929; *Perhaps Women*, 1931; *No Swank*, 1934; *Puzzled America*, 1935; *Home Town*, 1940.

POEMS: *Mid-American Chants*, 1918; *A New Testament*, 1927.

AUTOBIOGRAPHY: *A Story Teller's Story*, 1924; *Tar: A Midwest Childhood*, 1926; *Sherwood Anderson's Memoirs*, 1942.

PLAYS: *Plays: Winesburg and Others*, 1937.

LETTERS: *Letters of Sherwood Anderson*, edited by Howard Mumford Jones, 1953.

Sherwood Anderson was born in Camden, Ohio, September 13, 1876. His wanderings began in boyhood as his family moved from town to town in Ohio. The father ran a harness shop, worked in harness shops, and painted signs in a succession of jobs, each bringing in less money for his large family. Sherwood, an active young boy, sold newspapers, picked up odd jobs, and wandered around the Ohio towns that were to become the setting for his later stories and novels. Although he read avidly, he had finished only one year of high school when he went to Chicago, in 1896, to work as a day laborer. After serving in the Spanish-American War and attending a prep school for a short time, he returned to Chicago and worked for an advertising agency. He did well in business and soon moved to Elyria, Ohio, where he managed a factory and sold a roof paint called "Roof Fix." Outwardly, during those years, he led a conventional young businessman's life, but at the same time he was trying in poems, short stories, and novels to record his puzzled impressions of American life.

33

Legend has it that Anderson simply walked out of his factory one afternoon in 1912, after deciding to leave industry for writing. Actually, the decision was neither that conscious nor that simple, for the conflicts between his life and his literary ambition had been growing for years and he seemed to suffer a kind of breakdown. After leaving the factory, he wandered aimlessly for four days until he was discovered in Cleveland. Later, leaving his family, he went to Chicago and began to write more seriously and intensely. In Chicago, as a member of a literary group which included Dreiser, Sandburg, Hecht, and others, and stimulated by Harriet Monroe's *Poetry* (founded 1912) and Margaret Anderson's *Little Review* (begun in 1914), Sherwood Anderson found an artistic climate in which he could write.

His first novel, *Windy McPherson's Son,* the story of a Midwestern boy's revolt against his father and against his small home town, appeared in 1916 but received little attention. Three years and several publications later, however, Anderson became well known and widely acclaimed following the publication of *Winesburg, Ohio.* The book is a loosely-structured series of episodes dealing with life and character in a small Midwestern town. Anderson attempted to show, with enormous sympathy, the grim and quietly desperate lives in the small half-industrial town. The novel is centered around young George Willard as he learns to see and understand the town around him. Anderson concentrated on the weak and the maimed, the characters beaten by life in a competitive and mechanical society. He attempted to give life to the groping, half-inarticulate protests of these people.

Winesburg, Ohio was hailed as the authentic voice of the Midwest. Distinguished eastern literary figures such as Waldo Frank, Van Wyck Brooks, and Paul Rosenfeld admired and befriended Anderson. Other writers, such as Theodore Dreiser and Hart Crane, valued his power and insight. *Poor White,* Anderson's next novel, dealt with American society more comprehensively in presenting the wanderings of a lonely, inarticulate young man. Again the novel was well received, and this success, in combination with the short stories in *The Triumph of the Egg* and *Horses and Men,* made Anderson one of the most frequently honored figures on the American literary scene in the early twenties. He received the first annual award given by *The Dial* in December, 1921. His fame spread to Europe, and, a few years later, Virginia Woolf wrote that "Of all American novelists the most discussed and read in England at the present moment are probably Mr. Sherwood Anderson and Mr. Sinclair Lewis."

About this time Anderson began to feel the influence of D. H. Lawrence strongly. He read Lawrence over and over again and attempted to incorporate some of Lawrence's search for the meaning of life through sexual experience into his own novels. *Many Marriages* expresses the point of view that Americans are crippled by the attitude that sexual discussion and experience should be repressed. *Dark Laughter,* in many ways his best novel, uses sex as one of several means for the hero to scrape away the superficialities of modern cosmopolitan life and to get back to the primitive and basic meanings of human experience. In this novel, as well as in most of his other work, Anderson seemed probing, groping, to get at the really meaningful and essential experience of modern society.

After becoming successful, Anderson wandered around both America and Europe, finally settling in Marion, Virginia, where he edited two newspapers, one Republican, one Democrat. He continued to write, although after 1925 his work never reached the depth or the public of his earlier work. He died at Colón, Panama, while on a State Department mission, March 8, 1941.

Critics during the 1920's talked of the depth of his insight, of his warmth and concern for humanity, of his clumsy efforts toward conveying his simple people through a rugged and effective style, of his genuine quality as a spokesman for the frustrations of the man from the small Midwestern town. In the 1940's and 1950's critics have been less inclined to acclaim Anderson as a homespun American genius or to speak of his depth of insight. He is still regarded as a writer of warmth and sympathy who managed to create a rugged, half-articulate style through which to present his characters doomed by society. Much of the literary world today is inclined to agree with an early estimate made by F. Scott Fitzgerald: "He is the possessor of a brilliant and almost inimitable prose style, and of scarcely any ideas at all." For this reason his short stories and his autobiographical writings seem more likely to survive because they are less thesis-ridden than his novels.

BIBLIOGRAPHICAL REFERENCES: There is no collected edition. Convenient one-volume editions are *The Sherwood Anderson Reader,* edited by Paul Rosenfeld, 1947, and *The Portable Sherwood Anderson,* edited by Horace Gregory, 1949. The two leading biographical studies are Irving Howe, *Sherwood Anderson,* 1951, and James Schevill, *Sherwood Anderson: His Life and Work,* 1951. A selection of the letters was edited by Howard Mumford Jones and Walter B. Rideout in 1953. An early critical study was C. B. Chase, *Sherwood Anderson,* 1927. See also T. K. Whipple, *Spokesmen,* 1928; Harlan Hatcher, *Creating the Modern American Novel,* 1935; and Alfred Kazin, *On Native Grounds,* 1942.

Among the outstanding articles on Anderson are Lionel Trilling, "Sherwood Anderson," *Kenyon Review,* III (1941), 293–302; Robert Morss Lovett, "Sherwood Anderson, American," *Virginia Quarterly Review,* XVII (1941), 379–388; Norman Holmes Pearson, "Anderson and the New Puritanism," *Newberry Library Bulletin,* Series 2, No. 2 (1948), 52–70; Bernard Raymund, "The Grammar of Not-Reason: Sherwood Anderson," *Arizona Quarterly,* XII (1956), 48–60, 137–148; John J. Mahoney, "An Analysis of *Winesburg, Ohio,*" *Journal of Aesthetics and Art Criticism,* XV (1956), 245–252; and Jarvis Thurston, "Anderson and *Winesburg,*" *Accent,* XVI (1956), 107–128.

LEONID ANDREYEV

Born: Orel, Russia   *Died:* Kuokkala, Finland
Date: June 18, 1871   *Date:* September 12, 1919

PRINCIPAL WORKS

PLAYS: *K zvezdam,* 1905 (*To the Stars*); *Savva,* 1906; *Zhizn cheloveka,* 1906 (*The Life of Man*); *Tsar Golod,* 1907 (*King Hunger*); *Anatema,* 1909 (*Anathema*); *Prekrasnyye sabibyanki,* 1912 (*The Sabine Women*); *Tot kto polnchayet poshchechiny*, 1915 (*He Who Gets Slapped*); *Sobachit val's*, 1922 (*The Waltz of the Dogs*); *Samson v okovakh*, 1925 (*Samson in Chains*).

NOVELS AND TALES: *Mysl*, 1902 (*A Dilemma*); *Krasny smekh*, 1905 (*The Red Laugh*); *Raskaz o semi poveshennykh*, 1908 (*The Seven Who Were Hanged*); *Sashka Zhegulyov*, 1911.

SHORT STORIES IN TRANSLATION: *The Little Angel and Other Stories*, 1916; *When the King Loses His Head and Other Stories*, 1920.

Leonid (Nikolayevich) Andreyev, a morbid pessimist and mournful humanist, as one critic put it, was born into turbulent times on June 18, 1871. Born and educated in Orel, he continued his training for law in Moscow, where he was awarded a degree at the university in 1896, and in St. Petersburg. Depressed by his background and penury and so uncertain of his future, he was said to have attempted suicide on three occasions; he was restrained by the law from this course in 1894.

Andreyev's training for the law gave him his first writing job as a court reporter, later on the staff of the Moscow *Courier*. His first story, "They Lived," was published in *Zhizn* (*Life*), a monthly magazine, in 1899, arousing interest and attention of the public and critics alike. Maxim Gorky befriended the young writer and urged publication of a series of short stories which appeared in 1901. Some of these caught the eye of the critic Michailovsky. Andreyev also came to the attention of the Countess Tolstoy with a story called "In the Fog," which she labeled indecent in 1902; because of censure he lived for a time in Finland, a country to which he fled later for quite different reasons. He also served a short prison term with his friend Gorky in 1905 for anti-Tsarist activities—this in spite of the fact that he opposed war, dictatorship, capital punishment, and all manner of social evils. Later he supported Kerensky rather than the Bolsheviks, advocating the cause of democracy during World War I.

In his plays he vacillated between realism and symbolism, achieving a greater degree of success in the latter since he could find a wider range for his expression of the deterioration and bitterness he observed at every hand. His two earliest plays, *To the Stars* and *Savva* are realistic in technique. The former tells of an astronomer who assuages his grief over the execution of his revolutionist son by remarking that his troubles are as nothing in the face of all eternity. In *Savva*, Andreyev's most successful early play, he opposes the hold of the Church over the people. *Katerina Ivanovna* presages a theme of Pirandello, for the title character allows herself to become the symbol of the fallen woman her husband erroneously thinks her to be. *The Waltz of the Dogs*, more expressionistic than realistic, shows the defeat of a man at the hands of a brother who schemes for his life insurance and his fiancée who proves disloyal.

This unrelieved gloom, powerful in its mordant irony, is lightened by a Shavian-like comedy called *The Sabine Woman*, in which the Sabine men attempt to rescue their spouses from the ravaging Romans by moderate means, law books, and careful footing— one step back for two forward. *He Who Gets Slapped*, a seemingly flippant play, tells of a man who leaves his unfaithful wife and best friend to become a clown in a circus; he finally kills himself and his beloved circus rider friend to relieve them both of their restrictions imposed by society. One of Andreyev's early symbolic plays, *The Life of Man*, was thought by many to be a travesty. When *Anathema* was produced, many thought the production so far outran the inherent worth of the play that critically it was difficult to evaluate. Certainly the Faust-Mephistopheles theme is not original, nor is the final resolution of the play noteworthy: Faust dies when he finds he cannot help suffering mankind sufficiently while the devil looks on sympathetically but without power. As in many of his other plays, Andreyev advanced interesting hypotheses without convincing proof.

But on his two greatest stories the critical opinion is undivided. *The Red Laugh* proved prophetic of the Russian terror to come; here Andreyev wrote one of the strongest indictments of war ever made. In a preface to the English translation of *The Seven Who Were Hanged,* he says that the story is intended to castigate capital punishment, and the unrelieved anguish of these seven creates an effect of powerful revulsion.

Surely Andreyev showed good judgment in choosing to reject Gorky's acceptance of the Red lie and leaving his native Russia, for his anguished soul could never have survived even a year of Bolshevism so ruthlessly practiced. Disillusioned, he died in exile at Kuokkala, Finland, on September 12, 1919. At present a forgotten man, no doubt he will find eventually a new audience for his brooding, intuitive genius.

BIBLIOGRAPHICAL REFERENCES: There is no collected edition in English, but three plays are contained in *Plays,* an authorized edition translated by L. Meader and F. N. Scott, 1915. The only full-length study available in English is A. S. Kaun, *Leonid Andreyev,* 1924. Two other useful volumes are H. King, *Dostoevsky and Andreyev,* 1934; and Maxim Gorky, *Reminiscences of Tolstoy, Chekhov, and Andreyev,* translated 1934. There is a useful chapter on Andreyev in Janko Lavrin, *Russian Writers, Their Lives and Literature,* 1954. See also D. S. Mirsky, *A History of Russian Literature,* 1934.

JEAN ANOUILH

Born: Bordeaux, France
Date: June 23, 1910

PRINCIPAL WORKS

PLAYS: *L'Hermine,* 1932; *Mandarine,* 1933; *Le Voyageur sans bagage,* 1937; *Le Bal des Voleurs,* 1938 (*Thieves' Carnival*); *Léocadia,* 1939; *Le Sauvage,* 1940; *Eurydice,* 1941 (*Legend of Lovers*); *Antigone,* 1942; *Médée,* 1946; *L'Invitation au Château,* 1947 (*Ring Round the Moon*); *Ardèle,* 1949 (*Cry of the Peacock*); *La Répétition,* 1950; *Colombe,* 1950; *La Valse des toreadors,* 1952 (*The Waltz of the Toreadors*); *L'Alouette,* 1953 (*The Lark*).

Jean Anouilh, one of the most prolific and perturbing of modern French dramatists, can write a play in a month, and many have survived only an equal period on the stage. Nevertheless, in the past decade he has made a considerable impact on the Paris, London, and Broadway theater.

He was born in Bordeaux, France, on June 23, 1910, of parents who combined qualities as strange as any in his plays. His father was a Basque clothes cutter, his mother a French casino violinist. As a child he was permitted to watch the operettas at the casino, and at ten he was already putting together little verse plays in imitation of Rostand. Before beginning law studies at the Sorbonne, he wrote his first full-length play, which has never been published or produced. After college he spent two years writing advertising copy, adding to his income by selling comedy plots to film producers.

At nineteen he wrote a one-act farce, *Humulous le Muet* (published 1945), which displays the salient features of Anouilh's neo-romantic fantasies. The story deals with a mute who is permitted only one word a day and who saves all his words to make a pretty speech to a girl he loves. For years Anouilh wrote play after play without success. In 1931 he became secretary to Louis Javert's theatrical company and in the following year actor Pierre Fresnay succeeded in getting *L'Hermine* produced; it ran for thirty-seven performances. Meanwhile he was turning out plays which have been published or produced since. A change came in his fortunes with *Y'Avait un prisonnier* (1935), which had only a short run but which was bought by Hollywood. As Europe moved toward war the tone of his plays deepened. Occupied France responded to *Antig-*

one, seeing, mistakenly, the struggle between a pure maiden and a tyrant in twentieth century political terms, and on Broadway, in 1946, the play was diversely interpreted, as has been the case with his work ever since. In *Médée* he touched again upon the classic themes of tragedy and death, but presented them with the overtones of fantasy and melodrama which distinguish practically everything he has written. It is perhaps no coincidence that his chief translator and adapter has been Christopher Fry, English poet and dramatist who shares something of Anouilh's temperament.

In spite of his great success in France, Anouilh has in general not been greeted with full critical favor in London and New York. *Ardèle*, translated as *Cry of the Peacock*, and *Eurydice*, the story of Orpheus and Eurydice in modern dress and presented on Broadway as *Legend of Lovers*, had relatively short runs. Eric Bentley has stated that Anouilh is "something of a charlatan . . . excessively clever . . . transforming Strindbergian harshness into scurrility." But *The Lark*, a retold version of the story of Joan of Arc, and *The Waltz of the Toreadors*, acclaimed as the best foreign play of 1956, have added greatly to Anouilh's stature in this country. Theatergoers have discovered that his is an art which entertains, even when it baffles or disturbs.

Anouilh is a shy, reserved man who lives quietly in a Paris suburb. His wife is Monelle Valentin, French actress.

BIBLIOGRAPHICAL REFERENCES: The best study of Anouilh in English is E. O. Marsh, *Jean Anouilh: Poet of Pierrot and Pantaloon*, 1953. See also Hubert Gignoux, *Jean Anouilh*, 1946; J. Didier, *A la recontre de Jean Anouilh*, 1946; Jacques Poujol, "Tendresse et cruaté dans le théâtre de Jean Anouilh," *French Review*, XXV

(1952), 337–347; John C. Lapp, "Anouilh's *Médée*: A Debt to Seneca," *Modern Language Notes*, LXIX (1954), 41–47; Robert Champigny, "Theater in a Mirror: Anouilh," *Yale French Studies*, XIV (1955), 331–335; and Donald Heiney, "Jean Anouilh: The Revival of Tragedy," *College English*, XVI (1955), 331–335—the latter a discussion of the playwright's debt to Greek drama.

LUCIUS APULEIUS

Born: Madaura, Numidia, Africa	*Died:* Carthage (?)
Date: c. 125	*Date:* c. 175

PRINCIPAL WORKS

NOVEL: *Metamorphoses, or The Golden Ass,* c. 150.

TREATISES: *Apologia; De Deo Socratis (On the God of Socrates); De Mundo (On the World).*

Relatively little is known about the life of Lucius Apuleius, born at Madaura, Africa, about 125, the chief source of information being what he said about himself in his *Apologia sive oratorio de magia.* As a young man, according to his own testimony, he was educated in rhetoric at Carthage and in philosophy at Athens. He early became interested in religion and spent some time traveling over the ancient world, including Asia Minor, investigating the mysteries of the religions of his time, a somewhat unusual occupation for one who had become an ardent rationalist. Apuleius went to Rome and lived in that city for an indefinite time, apparently serving as a legal counselor. While on a journey to Africa, he was taken ill at Oea (modern Tripoli) and convalesced in the home of Sicineus Pontianus, who had been a fellow-student years before. During his convalescence, Apuleius won the affections of his host's widowed mother, Aemilia Pudentilla, and they were married. Her family, outraged by the course of events, accused Apuleius of having won his wife's affections by magical arts. Apuleius,

brought before the Proconsul Claudius Maximus, successfully defended himself against the charges. His defense was summed up in the *Apologia.*

Following his trial, Apuleius seems to have gone to Carthage to spend the remainder of his life, which he devoted to studying and writing in literature, religion, and philosophy. His fame as a writer rests on the *Metamorphoses,* which cannot be accurately dated. This work is often referred to as *The Golden Ass,* a title bestowed upon it by readers and critics in the ensuing centuries, rather than by its author, probably to differentiate between it and other works with the same title. In the *Metamorphoses* he seems to have used a well-known narrative used previously by Lucius of Patrae and by Lucian, but Apuleius turned the materials into a beautifully written prose romance in the picaresque style. The ending of the story, in which the goddess Isis helps the hero return from the status of an ass to that of a man, illustrates Apuleius' own interest in religious matters and the tendency of his time to turn to mystical religion. The work is full of wit, humor, and satire. Even today it remains a highly readable work. In the centuries that have passed since Apuleius' time his book has been an influence on such great writers of fiction as Cervantes, Le Sage, and Boccaccio, who found in the *Metamorphoses* materials and techniques which they made their own.

Only a few of Apuleius' philosophical writings are still extant. *On the God of Socrates* and *On the World* are works on Platonism as it was seen in Apuleius' time. Another work, *Florida*, is a collection or anthology of excerpts from speeches by Apuleius. Although he said he wrote a great deal of poetry and several volumes on natural history, they are no longer extant. The date and place of Apuleius' death are not known, although it is claimed that he died in Carthage about 175.

BIBLIOGRAPHICAL REFERENCES: The classic translation in English is William Adlington, *The XI Bookes of the Golden Asse, conteininge the Metamorphosie of Lucius Apuleius*, 1566; revised and reprinted 1893, 1913, and 1915. A more modern translation is that by Robert Graves, 1950. For critical comment see Elizabeth H. Haight, *Apuleius and His Influence*, 1927, and *Essays on the Greek Romances*, 1943; also Charles Whibley, Introduction to *The Golden Ass of Apuleius*, 1893.

THOMAS AQUINAS

Born: Rocca Secca, Italy
Date: c. 1225

Died: Fossanuova, Italy
Date: March 7, 1274

PRINCIPAL WORKS

THEOLOGICAL TREATISES: *Commentaria en Libros Sententiarum*, c.1254 (*Commentary on the Sentences*); *Summa contra Gentiles*, c. 1259–1264; *Summa Theologica*, c. 1265–1274.

Thomas Aquinas is generally agreed to be the towering figure in medieval theology, and to him goes the principal credit for applying the philosophical doctrines of Aristotle to Christianity. The joining of these seemingly divergent streams of thought has had tremendous influence on subsequent theological and philosophical thinking.

Thomas was well prepared by his background for the work that was to engage far and away the major portion of his efforts. Born at Rocca Secca, near Aquino, Italy, about 1225 or 1227, the son of Count Landolfo of Aquino, he was reared in an atmosphere of ease. Having studied at the Abbey of Monte Cassino, he went from there, in 1239, to Naples to study the liberal arts. He then entered the Order of St. Dominic (c. 1243).

Thomas was also fortunate to be able to study under Albert the Great (Albertus Magnus) in Paris from 1245 to 1248. While with Albert in Cologne, after his studies in Paris, he was ordained in the priesthood. Shortly thereafter he received advanced degrees in theology. He spent the rest of his life teaching and writing his great treatises—such as his commentary on the *Sentences* of Peter Lombard (c. 1100–c. 1160)—in Rome, Paris, and Naples.

Of his works, the two most important are his *Summa contra Gentiles*, which defends Christianity in the area of natural theology, and *Summa Theologica,* a work whose three divisions are related to God, Man, and Christ and in which Thomas attempted to summarize all human knowledge. This treatise was left unfinished when he died of a sudden illness on March 7, 1274, at Fossanuova, Italy, while traveling to the General Council of Lyons.

St. Thomas Aquinas, canonized in 1323, remains a central thinker in all Christian theology because of his synthesization of past knowledge and his application of the principles of scholasticism to religion.

BIELIOGRAPHICAL REFERENCES: The *Summa Theologica* has been translated by the Fathers of the English Dominican Province, 3 vols., 1957. A more general edition is *Selected Writings of St. Thomas Aquinas,* edited by M. C. D'Arcy, 1950. Biographical studies include A. D. Sertillanges, *St. Thomas d'Aquin,* 1910; John P. Conway, *St. Thomas Aquinas,* 1911; Edgar De Bruyne, *St. Thomas d'Aquin,* 1928; G. K. Chesterton, *St. Thomas Aquinas,* 1933; Gerald Van, *Saint Thomas Aquinas,* 1947; Angelus Maria Walz, *Saint Thomas Aquinas: A Biographical Study,* translated 1951; and M. C. D'Arcy, *St. Thomas Aquinas,* 1953.

For an introduction to his thought and a discussion of his philosophy see also A. D. Sertillanges, *La Philosophie morale de St. Thomas d'Aquin,* 1916; M. M. de Wulf, *Mediaeval Philosophy Illustrated from the System of St. Thomas Aquinas,* 1922; Etienne Gilson, *Le Thomisme,* translated 1924, and *St. Thomas d'Aquin,* 1925, the latter a study of his ethics; Francesco Olgiati, *The Key to the Study of St. Thomas,* translated 1925; *St. Thomas Aquinas: Being Papers Read at the Sixth Centenary Celebrations,* 1925; and M. D. Chenu, *Introduction à l'étude de St. Thomas d'Aquin,* 1950.

PIETRO ARETINO

Born: Arezzo, Italy
Date: April 20, 1492

Died: Venice, Italy
Date: October 21, 1556

PRINCIPAL WORKS

DIALOGUES: *Ragionamento della Nanna e della Antonia,* 1534 (*Discourse of Nanna and Antonia,* consisting of *The Life of Nuns, The Life of Married Women, The Life of Courtesans*); *Dialogo di Messer Pietro Aretino,* 1536 (*Dialogue by Master Pietro Aretino,* consisting of *Pippa's Education, The Wiles of Men,* and *The Bawd's Trade*); *Ragionamento de le Corti,* 1538 (*Discourse on Courts*); *Dialogo nel quale si parla del gioco,* 1543 (*Dialogue on Games*).

PLAYS: *Il Marescalco,* 1533; *Il Filosofo,* 1533 (*The Philosopher*); *La Cortegiana,* 1534 (*The Courtesan*); *La Talanta,* 1542; *La Horatia,* 1546.

POEMS: *Sonetti Lussuriosi,* 1523 (*Licentious Sonnets*); *La Marfisa,* 1535.

RELIGIOUS STUDIES: *L'Humanità di' Christo,* 1535 (*The Humanity of Christ*); *La Passione di Gesù,* 1534 (*The Passion of Jesus*); *Gli Sette Salmi di Penitentia,* 1534 (*The Seven Penitential Psalms*); *Il Genesi,* 1538 (*Genesis*); *La Vita di Maria Vergine,* 1539 (*The Life of the Virgin Mary*); *La Vita di Catherina Vergine,* 1539 (*The Life of St. Catherine*); *La Vita di San Tomaso Signor d'Aquino,* 1543 (*The Life of St. Thomas Aquinas*).

LETTERS: *Lettere,* 1538, 1542.

Born April 20, 1492, Pietro Aretino, the "Scourge of Princes," was a native of Arezzo, where, according to some sources, his father worked as a poor shoemaker. He seems to have studied literature and painting at Perugia in 1511 or 1512; there is a tradition that he was forced to leave his birthplace because he had composed a sonnet deriding indulgences, and a more doubtful tradition that he was forced to leave Perugia because he had stealthily added worldly detail to a holy picture. His reputation in later life inspired many such tales. About 1516, he went to Rome and soon entered the service of Agostino Chiga, a banker. When, a few years after, he became attached to the court of Pope Leo X, he already possessed some fame as a poet. After the Pope's death in 1521, he waged an unsuccessful fight, by means of pasquinades (satirical verses imprinted on fly-sheets, which were affixed to a certain mutilated statue called "Pasquino"), to promote the election of his patron, Cardinal de' Medici, to the Papal throne. Although the College of Cardinals chose Adrian VI, Aretino, by his scurrilous squibs, won great celebrity. He wisely fled Rome and did not return until the election of Clement VII. In 1523 he fell into disfavor because of his *Sonetti Lussuriosi*, written to accompany a series of sixteen indecent engravings cut by Marcantonio Raimondi. He was soon forgiven and,

returning from another brief exile, began the writing of his first and possibly finest comedy, *La Cortegiana*, which he appears to have drafted early in 1525. In the same year he almost lost his life when stabbed by a henchman of Marcantonio Giberti: he was wounded in five places and was permanently lamed in the right hand.

He left Rome again, campaigned with Giovanni delle Bande Nere, and eventually reached Venice in 1527. There, in close association with Sansovino and Titian, he began a life which, though subject to vicissitudes, was rich in pleasures and literary achievements. He occupied a house on the Grand Canal, and there not only composed most of his later works but also found leisure to consort with his large household of amiable mistresses, the "Aretines." His favorites were Caterina Sandella and Pierina Riccia. In 1538 he narrowly escaped being expelled from Venice for bestiality, and he made a last visit to Rome to be received by Pope Julius III, who had awarded him a pension. He died on October 21, 1556, of apoplexy, and was buried in the church of San Luca at Venice.

The writings of Aretino reflect his spontaneous vitality. He is regarded as the very embodiment of the sixteenth century Italian spirit: scornful, astute, proudly obscene, and as direct as the stiletto.

BIBLIOGRAPHICAL REFERENCES: The best biographical study of Aretino in English is Edward Hutton, *Pietro Aretino, Scourge of Princes*, 1922. See also Giorgio Petrocchi, *Pietro Aretino*, 1951. A good critical study is U. Fresco, *Le Commedie di Pietro Aretino*, 1901.

ARIHARA NO NARIHIRA

Born: Japan
Date: 825

Died: Japan
Date: 880

STORIES AND POEMS: *Ise Monogatari*, ninth century (*Tales of Ise*).
POEMS: *Narihira Ason Shû*, 1819 (*Collected Verse of Narihira*).

Like those of Beau Brummel or Casanova, the life of Arihara no Narihira has been so legendarized that it is difficult to sift fact from fiction. His mother was the daughter of Emperor Kammu (781–806), and the official government chronicle of his time describes Narihira as "graceful of body, beautiful of face, he did as he pleased, and although not greatly endowed with talent or learning, he composed poetry well."

From the anthologies of thirty-one syllable poems and the *Tales of Ise*, which contain the bulk of his poetry, we find that Narihira was a loyal friend of Imperial Prince Koretaka, eldest son of Emperor Montoku, who because his mother was not a member of the then rising Fujiwara clan, was not made heir to the throne. In 872, when the disappointed Koretaka took religious orders, Narihira visited his friend in his self-imposed exile. Narihira's wife was the niece of Koretaka's mother. Narihira had illicit relations with at least one imperial consort, and perhaps for this reason he traveled to eastern Japan. At this time he com-posed his poems which describe the smoke of volcanic Mt. Asama, the snow on Mt. Fuji in summer, and the oyster-snatchers of the Sumida River. He also made a trip to Ise, where at Japan's holiest of holy places, the Grand Shrine of Ise, he had relations with the Imperial Princess who served there as Vestal Virgin and as Head Priestess. She was Koretaka's sister. Another illicit relationship occurred with his sister-in-law.

Such amorous adventures, often indiscriminate, led to the persistent legend that he was the model Lady Murasaki used in her *Tale of Genji*. In his poetry he was one of Japan's greatest in classical times. Another great poet, Ki no Tsurayuki (died 946) described Narihira's poetry as, "having so much heart that he lacked the words to express himself fully, like a withered blossom, its color spent, but still with a lingering fragrance." Narihira has traditionally been counted as one of Japan's six great poets of classical times. He died on the twenty-eighth day of the fifth lunar month, 880, at the age of fifty-five.

BIBLIOGRAPHICAL REFERENCES: Translations of some of Narihira's poems are contained in Judith Gautier and Kimmochi Saionji, *Poemes de la Libelluer*, Paris, 1884; Aisaburo Akiyama, *The Rokkasen*, Tokyo, 1894; Hans-Bethge, *Japanischer Frühling*, Leipzig, 1911; W. G. Aston, *A History of Japanese Literature*, 1937; and Donald L. Keene, ed., *Anthology of Japanese Literature*, 1955. Translations of the *Ise Monogatari* are those by F. Rumpf, *Das Ise Monogatari*, Berlin, 1918; and J. Konrad, *Ise Monogatari*, Petrograd, 1923. Excerpts are also to be found in the *History* by Aston, and the *Anthology* by Keene mentioned above, as well as in Shinobu Orikuchi, "Ise-monogatari," in *Cultural Nippon*, 7, (1939), 97–118.

LUDOVICO ARIOSTO

Born: Reggio, Italy *Died:* Ferrara, Italy
Date: September 8, 1474 *Date:* June 6, 1533

PRINCIPAL WORKS

POEM: *Orlando Furioso,* 1516–1532.
PLAYS: *I Suppositi,* 1509; *La Cassaria,* c. 1510.

Ludovico Ariosto, born in Reggio, Italy, September 8, 1474, was destined to become one of the greatest of Italian poets. His father intended to have him follow the legal profession, and not until Ariosto had finished five years of legal training did his father relent enough to permit the young man to study his first love, classical literature, under the famous Gregorio da Spoleto. But the father's death placed responsibility for the Ariosto family on the shoulders of young Ludovico, and he was to abandon his studies for several years. Beginning about 1495, however, young Ariosto achieved some fame in his own land as a writer of comedies. About 1512 two of his plays were seen on the stage by Ippolito, Cardinal d'Este, who became the young writer's patron and appointed him his emissary to Pope Julius II.

Ariosto's connection with the powerful cardinal lasted until 1517; it ended when Ariosto refused to accompany the cardinal to Hungary and gave as excuses his own ill health, his mother's advanced age, and his literary work and study. At that time the cardinal's brother, Alfonso, Duke of Ferrara, became Ariosto's patron and benefactor. In the duke's employment, Ariosto was appointed governor of Garfagnana, a remote district high in the Apennines, a post the poet retained for three years. Upon being relieved of this difficult and even dangerous post, Ariosto settled in Ferrara, where he spent his time writing comedies, directing his own plays on the stage of a theater he designed and built, and working on his great narrative poem, *Orlando Furioso,* which was completed to his satisfaction in 1532, only a year before his death.

Orlando Furioso, Ariosto's great masterpiece, was begun in 1503. Forty of the forty-six cantos were first published in 1516. The poem, written in *ottava rima,* has often been considered the greatest literary achievement of the Italian Renaissance, and it is usually regarded as the greatest of the poetic romances. The poem was based by Ariosto on a romance of chivalry written by Matteo Maria Boiardo, *Orlando Innamorato,* which Boiardo had left unfinished at his death. The central episode of Ariosto's poem, the jealous frenzy of Orlando, followed the subject matter and utilized the characters found in Boiardo's poem. The setting of *Orlando Furioso* is Paris besieged by the Saracens, and the poem ends, as all good Christian literature of the time did, with the success of the Christians in repulsing the pagans. Of interest in connection with Ariosto's patronage by Cardinal d'Este and the Duke of Ferrara is the fact that Ariosto, in his poem, emphasizes two characters —Ruggiero and Bradamante—who were said to be the ancestors of his patrons.

Within a half century of his death, Ariosto's poem was translated into a dozen languages. Its popularity and influence are indicated also by the fact that its translation into Spanish was mentioned by Cervantes in *Don Quixote* (1605) and that it was one of the influences on Edmund Spenser's *Faerie Queene* (1590–1595).

By comparison with *Orlando Furioso*, Ariosto's other writings are insignificant. His five comedies, one of which he left unfinished, are obviously modeled after the work of the Roman playwrights Plautus and Terence. The poetry in Latin is not as good as that written by other Italian authors of the time, men like Vida, Flaminio, and Sannazaro. The *Satires*, based on the poetry of Horace, are important because they indicate Ariosto's independence of religion. They also indicate a reluctance for marital ties, although Ariosto did marry late in life, his wife being the widow of Tito Strozzi, an Italian poet of the time. Gabriele Ariosto, Ludovico's brother, characterized the famous poet as pious, kind, sympathetic, and free of ambition. Ariosto characterized himself by the epigram placed over the door of his house, a statement that the owner knew the house was small, but that he was satisfied because he had bought it with his own money. He died in Ferrara on June 6, 1533.

BIBLIOGRAPHICAL REFERENCES: The chief studies of Ariosto are Edmund G. Gardner, *The King of the Court Poets*, 1906; J. S. Nicholson, *Life and Genius of Arioso*, 1914; and Benedetto Croce, *Ariosto, Shakespeare and Corneille*, translated 1920. See also T. E. Casson, "Ariosto and the English Poets," *Manchester Literary Club Papers*, LXII (1937), 119–139.

ARISTOPHANES

Born: Athens, Greece
Date: c. 448 B.C.

Died: Athens
Date: c. 385 B.C.

EXTANT PLAYS

The Acharnians, 425; *The Knights*, 424; *The Clouds*, 423; *The Wasps*, 422; *The Peace*, 421; *The Birds*, 414; *Lysistrata*, 411; *Thesmophoriazusae*, 411; *The Frogs*, 405; *Ecclesiazusae*, 392; *Plutus*, 388.

Very little is known of the life of Aristophanes; as a matter of fact, the birth and death dates vary as much as five to ten years either way. His parents were Philippus and Zenodora, and their son was born into the Athenian deme of Cydathenaeon of the tribe Pandionis. The father was a landowner in Aegina, which gave the young playwright certain status. It was a remarkable fact that the lad may not have been out of his teens when his first play, *The Banqueters* (427), which is no longer extant, was produced to great applause. As to his appearance, he was certainly bald by the time he produced *The Peace* in 421; his vitality must have been great since he produced and acted in several of his earlier plays.

Aristophanes, the world's greatest writer of poetical satirical comedy, inherited the traditions of the Old Comedy—broad political and personal abuse, low-comedy farce of an earthy nature, inappropriate flights of poetic fancy, and theatrical conventions of costume, mask, music, and dance. The Age of Pericles allowed its comedians great license and freedom for political satire, a tradition which Aristophanes followed assiduously. He hated the age of decadence, compromise, departure from the vigorous way of life, the "new" sophistries and systems; in short, he used his plays to influence the political, moral, and religious life of his times, and although his was only a delaying action, it was nevertheless a vigorous campaign. Under the farcical exterior, his plays were serious allegories aimed at the emotions rather than the intellect he so mistrusted. His art passed through three major periods and bridged the gap between the Old Comedy and the New.

In the first of the extant plays, *The Acharnians,* Aristophanes won the first prize at the Lenaea in 425 B.C., a remarkable feat for the young actor-director-playwright. This play is remarkable as well in that he introduces the anti-war theme for the first time in history, and he played the part of the protagonist, a simple country man who thoroughly routs the antagonist, a war-monger. *The Knights,* following the next year, so soundly berated the tyrant and usurper Cleon that litigation was put in motion to prove the playwright of foreign birth and therefore disqualify him from competition. Continuing the play-a-year habit, he presented next *The Clouds,* satirizing the modern sophistries personified, although unfairly, by Socrates. This was one of his most widely read and discussed plays. Athens' love of litigation, which he thought wasteful of time and energy, he attacked in *The Wasps;* in the second part he demonstrates how the populace could have benefited from art, literature, and music were it not

for this unfortunate involvement in demagoguery. *The Peace* returns to his original theme, suggesting strongly that Athens should accept the Spartan peace offer and demonstrating the contrast of rural peace and strident war, the making of farm implements and the tools of war.

In his middle period Aristophanes wrote his best-known and greatest plays, thereby advancing dramatic art to a peak of perfection never topped and seldom equaled. *The Birds,* the play he liked best and one containing some of the greatest lyric poetry of all time, advances the Utopian theory that man should begin to build a simpler kingdom. The plan fails, however, when this heavenly birdland is overrun by the same old Athenian complications: litigation, demagoguery, and warfare. *Lysistrata* takes its name from the feminist protagonist who feels that women can end the sad spectacle of war by resisting men's amorous advances. The risqué wit and humor make this one of the best comedies of manners and the most frequently produced Greek play of the modern theater. The *Thesmophoriazusae,* presented that same year, continues a theme begun earlier, that of dramatic criticism, especially of Euripides, whom Aristophanes criticized as unfairly as he did Socrates and for about the same reasons. But in *The Frogs* he combines many elements of criticism—of state, art, reason—into a masterpiece of theater in which Dionysus goes to the underworld to bring back the greatest poet for troubled times. The chorus of frogs chide, admonish, and exhort while the arguments for and against finally agree on Aeschylus, the tragedian of the great period of Greek drama.

46

The last period bridges the final gap from the old Dionysian revel to the bourgeois comedy of Menander. The *Ecclesiazusae* fails to support the facetious view held in *Lysistrata,* for when women intrude themselves into office they establish a novel form of communism, foreshadowing platonic sophistries and satirizing them in advance. *Plutus,* the last extant play under the old master's name, appeared probably in the year before Aristophanes' death. This work looks backward to the preoccupation of the middle period with mythological themes; blind Plutus is given sight and wisdom to see that wealth belongs to those who can sanely use it while the way of the foolish is poverty. This play, with its simple, not topical allusions, struck a vibrant chord for playgoers and readers from antiquity down through the Renaissance.

Aristophanes' three sons carried on the dramatic tradition with some success, for one play—probably written by the father—won a prize in 387 B.C. The youngest son evidently won honors in the New Comedy. But the master's true progeny include such figures as Menander, Plautus, Molière, Congreve, Maugham, and Coward, dramatists who have been able to provoke thoughtful laughter while scourging the laugher.

BIBLIOGRAPHICAL REFERENCES: The standard edition in English is still Benjamin B. Rogers, *The Comedies of Aristophanes,* containing full introductions, critical commentary, and notes, originally published as separate texts, 1852 ff., now reprinted in the Loeb Classical Library, 3 vols., 1924. See also *The Complete Greek Drama,* edited by Whitney J. Oates and Eugene O'Neill, Jr., 2 vols., 1938. For general studies and criticism see also M. Croiset, *Aristophanes and the Political Parties at Athens,* 1909; F. M. Cornford, *The Origin of Attic Comedy,* 1914; Louis P. Lord, *Aristophanes: His Plays and Influence,* 1925; Edith Hamilton, *The Greek Way,* 1930; Gilbert Norwood, *Greek Comedy,* 1932; Gilbert Murray, *Aristophanes: A Study,* 1933; R. S. Flickinger, *The Greek Theater and Its Drama,* 1936 (3rd edition); V. Ehrenberg, *The People of Aristophanes,* 1943; P. S. Harsh, *A Handbook of Classical Drama,* 1944; and Moses Hadas, *A History of Greek Literature,* 1950.

ARISTOTLE

Born: Stagira, Chalcidice
Date: 384 B.C.

Died: Chalcis, Euboea
Date: 322 B.C.

PRINCIPAL WORKS

PHILOSOPHICAL, SCIENTIFIC, POLITICAL, AND CRITICAL TREATISES: *Organon, Physics, De Caelo, De Generatione et Corruptione, Eudemian Ethics, Metaphysics, Politics, Historia Animalium, Meteorologica, Constitutions, Nicomachean Ethics, Poetics, Rhetoric.*

Aristotle, one of the greatest philosophers of history, was born in Stagira, a little town on the peninsula of Chalcidice, in 384 B.C. He was the son of Nicomachus, a physician, and Phaestis. While Aristotle was yet a child his father became court physician to Amyntas II of Macedon, the grandfather of Alexander the Great. From birth Aristotle, as the son of a physician, was a member of the Asclepiadae guild. His interest in science and par-

47

ticularly in biology was only natural, for his family had a long tradition in medicine. Aristotle found himself in a middle-class family, of moderate means, but he was soon without parents, for they died when he was a boy. He became a ward of a friend and relation of the family, Proxenus.

When he was eighteen he became a student under Plato at the Academy in Athens, not primarily because he was interested in philosophy, but because the Academy offered the best education in Greece in science and other basic studies. He distinguished himself as a student, even though there were some who were irritated by his interest in dress and by his lisping, mocking air. He remained with the Academy, always a central figure, but becoming increasingly critical of some of Plato's ideas, until Plato's death in 347.

When Speusippus became the Academy's leader after the death of Plato, Aristotle, who disagreed with the Platonic views which the new head represented, accepted the invitation of Hermias, the King of Atarneus in Mysia, to join him there and become part of a philosophical circle. While with Hermias, Aristotle spent a considerable part of his time studying marine biology along the Aeolic coast, and he also found time to admire and marry Hermias' niece and adopted daughter, Pythias, by whom he had a daughter of the same name.

After spending three years in Mysia, following the assassination of Hermias by agents of the Persians, Aristotle moved to Mytilene on the island of Lesbos where he continued his independent biological research. He then left to undertake the tutelage of Alexander, the thirteen-year-old son of Philip of Macedon. Philip, who had known Aristotle since boyhood, was aware of Aristotle's reputation as a brilliant scientist and philosopher. Aristotle taught Alexander the usual Greek education, with emphasis upon Homer and the dramatists, and with considerable discussion of the philosophy and art of politics. The work was conducted at Pella and later at Mieza, and was virtually terminated when Alexander was appointed regent for his father in 340, while Philip was engaged in a campaign to complete the subjugation of all Greece. Aristotle settled in Stagira and became friends with Antipater, later regent in Greece.

When Philip was assassinated in 336, Aristotle returned to Athens to continue his scientific work. At about that time Speusippus, Plato's successor at the Academy, died, and Xenocrates of Chalcedon was appointed in his place. Aristotle was not tempted to return to the Academy; instead, he decided to start a new school in the Lyceum, a grove sacred to Apollo Lyceius, located to the northeast of Athens. He rented some buildings there and acquired pupils. Because of Aristotle's custom of walking up and down under a covered court, or *peripatos* with a group of students while lecturing or discussing some philosophical or scientific matter, his group became known as the "Peripatetics." The subjects which needed special study and individual attention were taught in the mornings to small groups, while those that could adequately be taught to larger numbers were reserved for the afternoons or evenings. Emphasis was upon biology, history, and philosophy.

During the twelve years he was at the Lyceum, Aristotle gave hundreds of lectures, of which some notes are extant and constitute the material which has come to be identified as his works. He classified the sciences, added to the scientific data in many fields, particularly in biology, encouraged and developed ideas in ethics and politics, and developed logic as a science of reasoning. The Lyceum, largely due to the creative energy of its founder, soon became the outstanding school in Greece, outranking the Academy; and Aristotle, as the most encompassing mind of the age, achieved a preëminence which two thousand years have not dispelled.

Shortly after his return to Athens from Macedon, Aristotle's wife died. He formed a lasting union out of wedlock with a woman of Stagira, Herpyllis, who bore him a son, Nicomachus,

whose name has been used to distinguish the *Nicomachean Ethics,* that version of Aristotle's ethics recorded by his son, from the *Eudemian Ethics,* the version of a pupil, Eudemus.

Alexander died in 323, and as a result of the ensuing anti-Macedonian feeling, Aristotle was charged with impiety, the same capital charge which led to the death of Socrates. The charge, founded on nothing more than some poetry that Aristotle wrote twenty years before to honor the memory of Hermias, was provoked by Aristotle's continued friendship with Antipater of Macedon. Aristotle retreated to Chalcis, accompanied by several of his followers, and died there the following year. His will provided for the emancipation of some of his slaves and protected the rest from being sold.

BIBLIOGRAPHICAL REFERENCES: The standard edition in English is *The Works of Aristotle,* edited by J. A. Smith and W. D. Ross, 11 vols., 1908–1931. A useful one-volume edition of selected essays is *The Basic Works of Aristotle,* 1941. For commentary on the life and work see A. E. Taylor, *Aristotle,* 1912 (rev. ed., 1943); W. D. Ross, *Aristotle,* 1923; J. L. Stocks, *Aristotelianism,* 1925; and G. R. G. Mure, *Aristotle,* 1932.

MATTHEW ARNOLD

Born: Laleham, England
Date: December 24, 1822

Died: Liverpool, England
Date: April 15, 1888

PRINCIPAL WORKS

POEMS: *The Strayed Reveller and Other Poems,* 1849; *Empedocles on Etna,* 1852; *Poems,* 1853; *Poems: Second Series,* 1855; *Merope: A Tragedy,* 1858; *New Poems,* 1867.

ESSAYS AND STUDIES: *On Translating Homer,* 1861; *Essays in Criticism,* 1865; *On the Study of Celtic Literature,* 1867; *Culture and Anarchy,* 1869; *Literature and Dogma,* 1873; *Last Essays on Church and Religion,* 1877; *Discourses in America,* 1885; *Civilization in the United States,* 1888; *Essays in Criticism: Second Series,* 1888.

Matthew Arnold, born at Laleham, December 24, 1822, was the eldest son of the famous schoolmaster, "Arnold of Rugby." The father, Dr. Thomas Arnold, had, as headmaster of that celebrated public school, brought about important changes in English education, not by spectacular reforms, but rather through the force of his character and example, both of which profoundly affected the son. Matthew attended Rugby during his father's headmastership and then matriculated (1841) at Balliol College, Oxford, where he studied classical literature and won the Newdigate Prize for poetry. While at Oxford, he was an intimate friend of Arthur Hugh Clough, whose death he mourned in the pastoral elegy, "Thyrsis" (1866).

Soon after his graduation from Oxford, Arnold became secretary to Lord Lansdowne, by whom he was appointed, in 1851, inspector of schools, a position he held until nearly the end of his life and one which provided him with an income sufficient to relieve him of financial worries. The position was, however, no sinecure; Arnold was sent to the Continent several times to investigate public secondary education in France and Germany, and the numerous volumes of his official reports testify to his industry and his conscientious discharge of his duties. In 1857 he was elected professor of poetry at Oxford and retained the professorship for ten years.

Arnold's poetry was all written during his early years; he later abandoned verse for prose. Even in his own time his poetry never attained the popularity of his great contemporaries, Tennyson and Browning, nor is it as well known today; indeed, he has been called the "great neglected Victorian." It has been said that his range was very narrow and that the "gray elegiac mood" was too pervasive for him ever to be a popular favorite, in spite of the exquisite technique that he could sometimes achieve. He could never accomplish the bravura effects that other poets used to catch the imagination of their readers; he was always calm and aloof. Therefore, he has generally been classed as a poet of the second rank rather than as one of the great poets of his age. Yet in "Dover Beach" he wrote one of the finest poems of the Victorian era, for in it he faced squarely a major problem of the time: the ebb of faith; and in "The Scholar Gypsy" he foreshadowed much of his later criticism of the modern world, "with its sick hurry, its divided aims."

Arnold's literary criticism, to which he turned in the early 1860's and which sprang from his lectures at Oxford, represents some of the most influential writing of the second half of the century; it can even be said that he raised the art of criticism to a level it had not attained since the days of Hazlitt and DeQuincey. Although he admitted that "the critical power is of lower rank than the creative," he still claimed for criticism an important function: its aim was "to know the best that is known and thought in the world" and to "create a current of true and fresh ideas"—both of which phrases became literary bywords. His masters were Goethe and Sainte-Beuve; indeed, he was always much interested in Continental literature. In evaluating poetry, he distrusted the study of historical developments; instead, he advanced his theory of the "touchstone": the reader should have in his memory certain great passages, from Homer, Dante, Shakespeare, Milton, against which other poems could be measured. Literature, he felt, was fundamentally a "criticism of life" and must possess "high seriousness." Milton he regarded as "the one artist of the highest rank in the great style" in England; of the

50

moderns, he was most impressed by Wordsworth.

Arnold's criticism had an enormous effect on the serious reading public of both England and America; as T. S. Eliot has pointed out, "the valuation of the Romantic poets, in academic circles, is still very largely that which Arnold made." But gradually his writing turned toward social criticism and the consideration of the complex problem created by the "ebb of faith" during his time. He was not one of those who saw Victorian England as "the best of all possible worlds"; he hated its materialism and felt that the upper class was materialized; the middle, vulgarized; and the lower, brutalized. The middle-class "Philistines," whom he felt to be the dominant group, must be turned from what he called "Hebraism," which had led to a narrow Puritanism, to "Hellenism," "an unclouded clearness of the mind." Only through culture could their salvation be accomplished. To this task the critic, with his "current of true and fresh ideas," could contribute much.

In 1883 Arnold made a lecture tour in America which furnished the material for his last important books. In 1886 he gave up his inspectorship of schools, and on April 15, 1888, he died quite suddenly in Liverpool.

BIBLIOGRAPHICAL REFERENCES: The standard edition of the poems is *The Poetical Works of Matthew Arnold*, edited by C. B. Tinker and H. F. Lowry, 1950. Because Arnold requested that no biography of him be written, there is no definitive biography. Collections of letters are *The Letters of Matthew Arnold, 1848–1888*, edited by G. W. E. Russell, 1895, and *The Letters of Matthew Arnold to Arthur Hugh Clough*, edited by H. F. Lowry, 1932. *The Notebooks of Matthew Arnold* were edited by H. F. Lowry, Karl Young, and Waldo Hilary, 1952.

For critical studies and incidental biographical materials see George Saintsbury, *Matthew Arnold*, 1899; H. W. Paul, *Matthew Arnold*, 1902; G. W. E. Russell, *Matthew Arnold*, 1904; Hugh Kingsmill, *Matthew Arnold*, 1928; C. H. Harvey, *Matthew Arnold*, 1931; Sir Edmund Chambers, *Matthew Arnold*, 1932; Lionel Trilling, *Matthew Arnold*, 1939; C. B. Tinker and H. F. Lowry, *The Poetry of Matthew Arnold*, 1940; E. K. Brown, *Matthew Arnold: A Study in Conflict*, 1948; and Kenneth Allott, *Matthew Arnold*, 1955.

MIKHAIL ARTSYBASHEV

Born: Kharkov, Russia
Date: October 18, 1878

Died: Warsaw, Poland
Date: March 3, 1927

PRINCIPAL WORKS

NOVELS: *Sanin*, 1907; *U posledney cherty*, 1912 (*The Breaking Point*).
PLAYS: *Zakon dikarya*, 1912 (*The Law of the Savage*); *Voyna*, 1916 (*War*).

Mikhail (Petrovich) Artsybashev, born at Kharkov, Russia, on October 18, 1878, lived through some of the darkest years which that country has known. Affected by his troubled times and by the literary influence of Dos- toevski, he was one of the most negative of all writers and felt that goodness and light exist almost nowhere, certainly not in people. His partially Tartar parentage may be some explanation of his rebellious, nihilistic spirit.

51

His early education was in art, and he had achieved some fame as a caricaturist when he turned to the writing of fiction and drama. Although Artsybashev is not recognized as a first rank writer, his short stories, particularly *Pasha Tumanov* (1901), were popular. With the publication of his first novel, *Sanin,* in 1907, he became an overnight international sensation. The revolt against social traditions and the excessively vivid pictures of vice he presented appealed to the unsettled Russian nation, especially to the young people, who formed Sanin cults and organized their defiance of tradition and restraint. *Sanin* was written when Artsybashev was under thirty, but his maturing years developed in him no relaxation of the brutality and candor of his vision. His next novel, *The Breaking Point,* is typical; it treats of death, sexual irregularity, and suicide. Plays like *War* and *The Law of the Savage* are identical in tone with the novels, except that they have the advantage of being more direct in structure.

Because of his frankness and unwillingness to conform, Artsybashev was imprisoned by the Tsarist government in 1912. After the revolution of 1917 he was almost equally unpopular with the Bolsheviks, even though he had written scathing stories about imperialistic tyranny. He was often sued and berated because of the "immorality" of his works, and in 1923 he left Russia for good. After his departure his novels were often confiscated and burned, and his popularity declined. Although he has never gained critical favor, his work cannot be dismissed. He had a direct style, a good sense of plot, and an attitude toward life which, if not widely accepted, must be understood for literary and historical reasons; he spoke for and to, as Janko Lavrin has pointed out, a demoralized intellectual and political generation. He died in exile at Warsaw, Poland, March 3, 1927, still advocating his doctrines of individuality and the falseness of love.

BIBLIOGRAPHICAL REFERENCES: For brief studies of Artsybashev in English see D. S. Mirsky, *Contemporary Russian Literature,* 1926; Marc Slonim, *Modern Russian Literature,* 1953; and Janko Lavrin, *Russian Writers—Their Lives and Literature,* 1954.

SHOLEM ASCH

Born: Kutno, Poland
Date: November 1, 1880

Died: London, England
Date: July 10, 1957

PRINCIPAL WORKS

NOVELS: *The Village,* 1903; *Mottke the Thief,* 1916; *Uncle Moses,* 1920; *The Mother,* 1925; *Three Cities,* 1933; *Salvation,* 1934; *In the Beginning,* 1935; *The War Goes On,* 1936; *Song of the Valley,* 1939; *The Nazarene,* 1939; *The Apostle,* 1943; *East River,* 1946; *Mary,* 1949; *Moses,* 1951; *A Passage in the Night,* 1953; *The Prophet,* 1955.

SHORT STORIES: *Children of Abraham,* 1942; *Tales of My People,* 1948.

PLAYS: *The God of Vengeance,* 1907; *Mottke the Thief,* 1917.

MISCELLANEOUS: *To America,* 1911; *What I Believe,* 1941; *One Destiny: An Epistle to the Christians,* 1948.

Sholem (or Shalom) Asch, born in Kutno, Poland, on November 1, 1880, and an American citizen since 1920, is the foremost Yiddish novelist in America. At the age of twenty he began writing short stories in Hebrew but soon changed to Yiddish with his first novel, *The Village,* an epic of Jewish patriarchal life.

Throughout his career Asch's principal subjects have been taken from Jewish life. One major group of his novels, plays, and short stories is concerned with the experience of Jews in Europe. Another, dating from his first visit to America in 1910, deals with the Jews of New York City. The third, his most ambitious subject, is his re-creation of Biblical subjects.

Sholem Asch was educated in Rabbinic theology in his native Poland, a background that proved basic to his five-volume work formed on Testamental literature. *The Nazarene,* first of the series, offered interesting Jewish insight into the life and personality of Jesus. This was followed by *The Apostle,* a portrait of St. Paul, and the tender story of "Miriam" in *Mary,* perhaps too imaginatively distant from any source material to be an acceptable characterization of Mary as the Mother of God. *Moses,* called by one critic merely an expanded Exodus, and *The Prophet,* a study of Deutero-Isaiah, complete the Biblical group. The research for these novels, which occupied Asch for more than thirty years, was begun during his first visit to Palestine and continued on later trips to examine archaeological sites. Asch's lifelong attempt to relate Christianity to Judaism as an inevitable development of it is expressed most fully in this series. Unconvinced by criticism that he betrays his own religion and distorts Christianity ("The Gospel according to St. Shalom"), he claims to see in Christ the Messiah bridging their theological division.

As a historical as well as a folk novelist, Asch brings out in his work with assurance the thought and behavior of individuals against a background of time and custom. In *Three Cities* the main character, who leaves St. Petersburg to hide out in the Warsaw Ghetto and finally leads a machine-gun squad in the Moscow revolution, shows this side of his writing most clearly. *The War Goes On,* a study of Germany during the pre-Hitler period, is a work of similar ability. But the essence of Sholem Asch's most personal theme, revelation as it brings man to consciousness of his moral nature, is best seen in *Salvation,* an account of a Hassidic rabbi whose miraculous powers lead him to sin.

The *Jewish Morning Journal* published Asch's first stories in 1908, and after the appearance in the *Jewish Daily Forward* of *To America,* in which he described his first impressions of the country, that newspaper introduced him to American readers in serial form with such novels as *Mottke the Thief* and *Uncle Moses.* He has also written plays, the most famous of which is *The God of Vengeance,* a work that made him internationally known after performances in St. Petersburg, Berlin, and New York.

Aside from his Biblical series, Asch's most widely read novels may be *Three Cities, The Mother,* and *East River.* A writer of great pictorial evocation and sound scholarship, he is frequently overlooked in critical estimates because of his popular appeal.

53

BIOGRAPHICAL REFERENCES: There is no extended biographical study. For criticism see A. A. Roback, *The Story of Yiddish Literature*, 1940; Herman Lieberman. *The Christianity of Sholem Asch*, 1953; Charles A. Madison, "Sholem Asch," *Poet Lore*, XLVI (1940), 303–337; and Oscar Cargill, "Sholem Asch: Still Immigrant and Alien," *College English*, XII (1950), 67–74.

W. H. AUDEN

Born: York, England
Date: February 21, 1907

PRINCIPAL WORKS

POEMS: *Poems*, 1930; *The Orators*, 1932; *The Dance of Death*, 1933; *Poems*, 1934; *Look, Stranger*, 1936; *Spain*, 1937; *Another Time*, 1940; *The Double Man*, 1941; *For the Time Being*, 1944; *Collected Poetry*, 1945; *The Age of Anxiety*, 1947; *Some Poems*, 1947; *Collected Shorter Poems, 1930–1944*, 1950; *Nones*, 1951; *The Shield of Achilles*, 1955; *The Old Man's Road*, 1956.

PLAYS: *The Dog Beneath the Skin*, 1935 (with Christopher Isherwood); *The Ascent of F6*, 1936; *On the Frontier*, 1939 (with Christopher Isherwood).

ESSAYS AND STUDIES: *The Enchaféd Flood*, 1950.

TRAVEL SKETCHES AND IMPRESSIONS: *Letter from Iceland*, 1937 (with Louis MacNeice); *Journey to a War*, 1939 (with Christopher Isherwood).

W(ystan) H(ugh) Auden was born in York, England, on February 21, 1907, the third son of George Augustus Auden, a distinguished physician. After preparing at Gresham's School, Holt, he took his degree at Christ Church College in Oxford University. He taught for five years in a boys' school in Malvern before he became one of a group of young poets which included Stephen Spender, Louis Mac-Neice, and his childhood friend, Christopher Isherwood. Socially and politically in revolt, dabbling in Marxism and experimenting in poetry, this group seemed the most promising among the younger writers of the time. After spending 1928 and 1929 in Germany with Isherwood, Auden returned to England to publish his first book of verse, *Poems*, in 1930. The prose and verse of *The Orators*, two years later, made it clear that his was a substantial and promising talent.

Combining sharp satire and delight in word play with seeming obscurity and private references, his poetry called for action against the depressed condition of England of the 1930's. Another book of verse, *The Dance of Death*, was followed in 1935 by *The Dog Beneath the Skin*, an experimental play written in collaboration with Isherwood. This was also the year of his marriage to Erika Mann, journalist and eldest daughter of novelist Thomas Mann.

Another collaborative verse drama, *The Ascent of F6*, appeared in 1936. In this work, as in the previous one, Auden and Isherwood combined experimental techniques with a concern over social and political problems. Another volume of poetry, *Look, Stranger*, appeared in the same year. Like so many other writers, Auden found his sympathies lay on the side of the Loyalists in the Spanish Civil War.

He went to Spain, and when he returned in 1937 from service there as an ambulance driver, his increasing reputation was further enlarged by the award of the King's Poetry Medal. *Letters from Iceland,* which he published with MacNeice in 1937, *Spain,* of the same year, and *On the Frontier,* another collaboration with Isherwood, showed the deepening, maturing effect of his experiences upon his work. With Isherwood he traveled to China in 1938 to view another war. Their impressions were recorded in the prose volume, *Journey to a War,* which was issued the next year.

In 1939 Auden and Isherwood came to the United States, where Auden was to live and later gain citizenship. *Selected Poems, Another Time,* and *New Year Letter* further consolidated Auden's reputation as the first poet of the generation that came after that of T. S. Eliot. *For the Time Being* and *The Age of Anxiety* showed how Auden's genius had matured and how he could still be technically a virtuoso,

daring and spectacular, though his view of life had deepened, shifting from Marxist to Anglo-Catholic. His latest volumes, *Nones* in 1951 and *The Shield of Achilles* in 1955, revealed the same mastery of his medium. A Guggenheim Fellow in 1942 and 1945, he successfully combined the artistic and the academic life when he served as associate professor of English at the University of Michigan in 1950 and occupied a professorship at Smith College in 1953. In 1954 he was elected to membership in the American Academy of Arts and Letters, from which he is also the recipient of an award for poetry. His appointment as Professor of Poetry at Oxford University came in 1956. In addition to the libretto of Stravinsky's *The Rake's Progress* (1951), he has published *The Enchaféd Flood,* a work of literary criticism, and two books on Kierkegaard. He has also edited selected works of Tennyson and Henry James as well as one volume of Greek literature and three of English poetry.

BIBLIOGRAPHICAL REFERENCES: There is no extended biographical study of Auden. The basic critical study is Richard Hoggart, *Auden: An Introductory Essay,* 1951. An important earlier study is Francis Scarfe, *Auden and After,* 1942. See also Cecil Day Lewis, *A Hope for Poetry,* 1934; Stephen Spender, *The Destructive Element,* 1935; Louis MacNeice, *A Hope for Poetry,* 1936; and J. G. Southworth, *Sowing the Spring,* 1940.

For articles in periodicals see also Stephen Spender, "The Importance of W. H. Auden," *London Mercury,* XXXIX (1939), 613–619; Delmore Schwartz, "The Two Audens," *Kenyon Review,* I (1939), 34–45; Randall Jarrell, "Freud to Paul: Stages in Auden's Ideology," *Partisan Review* (1945), 437–457; Joseph Warren Beach, "The Poems of Auden and the Prose Diathesis," *Virginia Quarterly Review,* XXV (1949), 365–483; and Monroe K. Spears, "Late Auden: The Satirist as Lunatic Clergyman" and "The Dominant Symbols of Auden's Poetry," *Sewanee Review,* LIX (1951), 50–74 and 392–425.

ST. AUGUSTINE
(Aurelius Augustinus)

Born: Tagaste, Numidia   *Died:* Hippo (now Bône, Algeria)
Date: 354   *Date:* 430

55

THEOLOGICAL TREATISES AND COMMENTARIES: *Enarrationes in Psalmos,* 391–430; *De Doctrina Christiana,* 397; *De Trinitate,* 397–401 (*On the Trinity*); *De Genesi ad Literam,* 401–415; *De Civitate Dei,* 413–426 (*The City of God*); *Retractiones,* 426 (*Retractions*).

PHILOSOPHICAL STUDIES: *De Ordine,* 386; *De Beata Vita,* 386; *Soliloquia,* 387 (*Soliloquies*); *De Musica,* 387–389; *De Magistro,* 389.

AUTOBIOGRAPHY: *Confessiones,* 397–401 (*Confessions*).

Next to St. Paul, St. Augustine has probably exerted the greatest influence on Christianity, both Catholic and Protestant, by his books, letters and sermons. Born at Tagaste (now Souk-Ahras), in North Africa, in 354, he was brought up as a Christian by his devout mother, Monica, but when he attended school in Carthage the fascination of rhetoric transformed him into a youthful skeptic. He professed the teachings of Manichaeanism, a philosophy derived from Zoroaster and Buddha by the Persian Mani of the third century. This doctrine stressed the struggle between good and evil, light and darkness.

After completing his education, about 377, Augustine migrated to Rome as a teacher of rhetoric, and in 384 he went to Milan to teach Manichaean philosophy. It was during this period that his earliest treatises resulted from the idea of recording in shorthand the conversations with his mother and his friends, and circularizing them. Under the influence of Ambrose, Bishop of Milan, he became interested in Platonism and, through it, in the Christianity he had rejected. On Easter Day, 387, following a mystic acceptance of faith, he was baptized by Ambrose. Shortly afterward he returned to Tagaste alone, Monica having died at Ostia during the homeward journey. There he lived a rather monastic life and, continuing his theological studies, became a stanch

defender of the faith, not only against followers of his earlier beliefs, but also against other religious sects like the Pelagians, who denied the doctrine of original sin and the fall of man. St. Augustine held that man was essentially corrupt and helpless without God's grace.

In 391, somewhat against his will because of his preference for the retired, contemplative life, he was urged by the congregation of Hippo Regius to be ordained as a priest. Four years later, in 395, he was consecrated bishop, with the understanding that he would occupy the bishopric when the incumbent died. This event occurred in 396, and for the next thirty-four years St. Augustine was in charge of the see of Hippo. Although he rarely ever left the small coastal city, his influence spread throughout the Christian world through the letters which he dispatched to congregations in many lands. About 250 of these, written to admonish, explain, or encourage, still survive. Couched in a colloquial style, they are none the less powerful and persuasive. In them, as in his dialogues, St. Augustine stands as the champion of orthodoxy against the Manichaean, Pelagian, and Donatist heresies of his time. Of his formal treatises, perhaps his greatest dogmatic work was the systematic analysis of Christian doctrine he presented under the title, *On the Trinity.* His philosophical *Soliloquies* were also popular; five hundred years later King Alfred translated a large part of this work for the instruction of his Saxons.

The *Confessions* of St. Augustine provide most of the information about his life. In common with many men of the period, he had kept concubines. He expresses regret at his original lapse from Christianity and often bears witness to the influence of his mother on his life and thinking. The work is a classic of Christian mysticism. The most famous of St. Augustine's works is *The City of God*, in twenty-two books, completed in 426. Christianity,

blamed for the fall of Rome, here finds its apologist. Although the writer reveals himself as a not very systematic thinker, he does present pertinent views on society and outlines the steps by which a new social order could be created by Christianity. An inspiration to many, Augustine's discussion of the city of this world and the city of God is one of the foundation stones of the Christian faith.

In the last years of his life, St. Augustine wrote his *Retractions*, changing and reëvaluating some of his earlier views. He was killed when the Vandals besieged Hippo in 430.

BIBLIOGRAPHICAL REFERENCES: The writings of St. Augustine have now been collected in an edition of the *Works* translated by A. C. Cutler, 1955. Available single works include *The City of God*, translated by John Healey, 1610 (re. eds., 1903 and 1931); John Gibbs and W. Montgomery, *The Confessions of St. Augustine*, 1909; W. J. Sparrow-Simpson, *On the Spirit and the Letter*, 1925; and R. C. Taliaferro, *On Music*, 1931. An edition of Alfred's translation of the *Soliloquies* was published in 1902. The *Selected Letters*, edited by J. H. Baxter, are in the Loeb Classical Library, 1930. For biography see A. Naville, *St. Augustine*, 1872; Louis Bertrand, *Saint Augustine*, 1914; Heinrich H. Lasser, *St. Augustine*, 1931; and S. J. Grabowski, *The All-Present God*, 1954. A useful volume is R. W. Battenhouse, *A Companion to the Study of St. Augustine*, 1955. For a background study of the early Church and its writers see also C. T. Cruttwell, *A Literary History of Early Christianity*, 2 vols., 1893.

JANE AUSTEN

Born: Steventon, Hampshire, England   *Died:* Winchester, England
Date: December 16, 1775   *Date:* July 18, 1817

PRINCIPAL WORKS

NOVELS: *Sense and Sensibility*, 1811; *Pride and Prejudice*, 1813; *Mansfield Park*, 1814; *Emma*, 1815 (dated 1816); *Persuasion*, together with *Northanger Abbey*, 1818.

The seventh of eight children of a rural clergyman respected for his learning and literary taste, Jane Austen, born at Steventon, Hampshire, on December 16, 1775, was the second daughter in a vigorous, able, and affectionate family. Two of her brothers followed their father to Oxford and into the Church, and two others rose to be admirals in the Navy. Except for brief schooling in Oxford, Southampton, and Reading, which ended at the age of nine, she was educated at home, where she learned French, a smattering of

Italian, some history and, in addition to Shakespeare and Milton, gained a thorough acquaintance with the essayists, novelists, and poets of the eighteenth century.

Always somewhat shy but lively and witty, Jane Austen developed into a young lady of cultivated manners and pleasing appearance, who at balls and assemblies enjoyed her share of masculine attention. A brief but genuine romance with a young man whose identity is uncertain ended suddenly with his death. When she was nearly twenty-seven, she accepted, and the next day rejected, the proposal of Harris Bigg-Wither, a friend of longstanding, whom she realized she did not love.

Aside from writing, Jane Austen devoted her life to domestic duties and household affections, and especially to being the companion and confidante of numerous nieces and nephews, who found her unfailingly kind, sympathetic, and amusing.

Having spent the first twenty-five years of her life in the rectory at Steventon, she removed in 1801, upon her father's retirement, with her parents and sister Cassandra to Bath. After her father's death in 1805 and a sojourn of three years in Southampton, she settled with her mother and sister in a cottage belonging to her brother Edward at Chawton, Hampshire, where she resided until two months before her death. Here, working mainly in the general sitting room, she composed the final drafts of all her major works, hurriedly slipping the small sheets under the blotting paper if a visitor or servant appeared. In 1816 her health began to fail; and in May, 1817, she and Cassandra moved to Winchester for adequate medical attention.

Despite weakness and pain, she remained cheerful to the end. Dying peacefully on July 18, 1817, aged forty-one, she was buried in Winchester Cathedral.

Jane Austen's novels, the first published when she was thirty-five and followed by five others in as many years, were the final fruits of an early and painstaking apprenticeship to literature. Three small volumes of juvenilia, *Volume the First* (1933), *Love and Freindship* (1922), and *Volume the Third* (1951), written by the time she was eighteen years old and bearing witness to her youthful talent for mimicry and burlesque, also contain her first serious piece, "Catharine, or the Bower," probably a literary ancestor of *Northanger Abbey*. Her first completed novel, *First Impressions* (the lost original of *Pride and Prejudice*), begun in October, 1796, and finished in August, 1797, her father offered to a publisher without success. In November, 1797, she started *Sense and Sensibility* and in that year and the next wrote *Northanger Abbey*, a revised version of which, entitled *Susan*, she sold in 1803 for ten pounds to the publisher Crosby, who advertised but failed to publish it; finally retrieved in 1816, an amended text appeared posthumously in 1818. *The Watsons* (1871, 1927), a fragmentary progenitor of *Emma*, and *Lady Susan* (1871, 1925), a biting epistolary satire, probably the germ of *Mansfield Park*, have survived in manuscripts written on paper watermarked 1803 and 1805 respectively. Extensively revised or rewritten in 1809–1811, *Sense and Sensibility* was published on October 31, 1811. Favorably received, the edition sold out in less than two years and brought its author one hundred forty

58

pounds. *Pride and Prejudice* appeared in 1813, *Mansfield Park* in 1814, and *Emma* in 1815 (dated 1816). *Persuasion* was issued with *Northanger Abbey* in 1818, and by that date *Sense and Sensibility* and *Mansfield Park* had reached a second edition, *Pride and Prejudice* a third. She was engaged upon the rough draft of the early chapters of a new novel, *Sanditon* (1925), only a few weeks before she died.

Far ahead of her time in the techniques of narration, especially in the control of point of view, Jane Austen, through her fidelity to life, her delineation of character, and her ironic insight, produced sophisticated comedy unsurpassed in the English novel. Entertainment, however, was not her sole aim. Primarily a moral writer striving to establish criteria of sound judgment and right conduct in human relationships, she inculcates the related virtues of self-awareness and unselfishness.

Northanger Abbey, the earliest of the major novels in chronological order of composition, while revealing its kinship to the juvenilia by depending for much of its humor upon burlesque of the Gothic novel, offers much more than mere parody. The education of its callow heroine, Catherine Morland, by examples of the discrepancy between appearance and reality, typifies Jane Austen's method and illustrates her penchant for proportion and symmetry in both literature and life. Although *Sense and Sensibility* also contains an element of literary satire—upon the current novel of feeling—it is essentially a paradigm of the proper balance between self-control and emotion. *Pride and Prejudice,* the most scintillating of her novels and long the popular favorite among them, provides in Elizabeth Bennet one of the most

delightful heroines of fiction. She and Darcy eventually overcome first impressions (note the original title) distorted on both sides by pride and prejudice. With its high proportion of dialogue and with the ironic commentary shifted from the author to a character within the story (Mr. Bennet), this book represents the apex of her dramatic act. Convinced that *Pride and Prejudice* was too playful, she tended to the opposite extreme with *Mansfield Park,* where her irony is chastened and her censure of worldly values borders on didacticism. *Emma,* Jane Austen's masterpiece and profoundest moral comedy, is a study in the self-delusions of vanity. Unified in time (a cycle of one year) and place (Highbury and its environs), the beautifully concentric action revolves, as the title implies, around a dominant heroine, who, having every advantage in life, is a victim only of herself. *Persuasion,* more patently infused with emotion than is customary with Jane Austen, but saved from sentimentality by the full play of her wit, examines, through the person of Anne Elliot, aged twenty-seven, the author's only mature heroine, the conflicting claims of prudence and true love.

Jane Austen's style—unadorned, concise, flexible, and animated—is the ideal instrument for her art. Her dialogue, without resort to slang or obvious tags, shows a precise ear for individual and revealing rhythms of speech. Her ironic detachment and technical skill have established her reputation with modern critics, but the deftness with which she pleases and instructs has endeared her works to generations of readers.

Edgar F. Shannon, Jr.

BIBLIOGRAPHICAL REFERENCES: The definitive edition is *The Novels of Jane Austen,* edited by R. W. Chapman, 5 vols., 1933 (3rd ed.), with a sixth volume added in 1954. The standard biography is W. and R. A. Austen-Leigh's *Jane Austen: Her Life and Letters,* 1913. This work supplements J. E. Austen-Leigh's *Memoir of Jane Austen,* 1870–1871 (reissued 1926). A companion volume to the biography is M. A. Austen-Leigh, *Personal Aspects of Jane Austen,* 1920. Other biographical and critical studies include Geraldine Mitton, *Jane Austen and Her Times,* 1905; F. W. Cornish, *Jane Austen,* 1913; R. B. Johnson, *Jane Austen: Her Life, Her Work, Her Family, and Her Critics,* 1930; Lord David Cecil, *Jane Austen,* 1935; Mary Lascelles, *Jane Austen and Her Art,* 1939; R. A. Austen-Leigh, *Jane Austen and Southampton,* 1949; Elizabeth Jenkins, *Jane Austen,* 1952; Marvin Mudrick, *Jane Austen: Irony as Defense and Discovery,* 1952; and A. H. Wright, *Jane Austen's Novels,* 1953.

A most useful book of Austen studies is R. W. Chapman's *Jane Austen: Facts and Problems,* 1949. In *Speaking of Jane Austen,* 1944, and *More Talk of Jane Austen,* 1949, Sheila Kaye-Smith and G. B. Stern present lively, appreciative table-talk on Jane Austen and her art.

MARIANO AZUELA

Born: Lagos de Moreno, Mexico
Date: January 1, 1873

Died: Mexico City, Mexico
Date: March 1, 1952

PRINCIPAL WORKS

NOVELS: *Mala yerba,* 1909 (*Marcela*); *Los de abajo,* 1915 (*The Underdogs*); *Los Caciques,* 1917 (*The Bosses*); *Las Moscas,* 1918 (*The Flies*); *La luciérnaga,* 1932; *La nueva burguesía,* 1941.

Mariano Azuela, born January 1, 1873, of a middle-class family in Lagos de Moreno, Jalisco, Mexico, was a novelist by avocation who wrote only under the spur of indignation or to cast light on social conflicts in the hopes of bettering conditions. He was the spokesman of the poor; the middle class and the aristocracy did not concern him. His early sentimental novel, *María Luisa* (1907), is based on a tragic case he knew as a medical student in Guadalajara.

Politics also interested him, and he entered the struggle against Mexico's dictator Porfirio Díaz. His *Los fracasados* (1908), English title *The Failures,* attacks the conservatives and the Church, Díaz' chief supporters. *Mala yerba* was his first important novel,

with good characterization and descriptions of national customs.

The overthrow of Díaz in 1910 started a struggle for his successor. Because Azuela sided with Pancho Villa, he had to flee his home when Carranza's army moved in. While serving as doctor with one of Villa's regiments in 1915, Azuela collected material for his greatest book, *The Underdogs,* which he wrote while a fugitive in El Paso. The novel, now regarded as a Mexican classic, first appeared serially in an obscure Spanish paper.

With the end of the Civil War, Azuela returned to Mexico to practice medicine, especially among the poor, and to write sixteen more novels. He was awarded the National Prize for literature in 1949 and another prize in 1950 for his dramatization of *The Underdogs*. Since his novels cover every phase of Mexican life, from the last days of Díaz to the end of the presidency of Lázaro Cárdenas in 1940, Azuela's books make him the historian in fiction of the Mexican Revolution. He died in Mexico City, March 1, 1952.

BIBLIOGRAPHICAL REFERENCES: In addition to the introductions to Azuela's translated works, see in English Jefferson R. Spell, *Contemporary Latin American Fiction*, 1944; in Spanish, A. Torres Rioseco, *Novelistas contemporáneos de América*, 1939 (Santiago de Chile); *idem*, *Grandes novelistas*, 1941; Ernest R. Moore, "Biografía y bibliografía de don Mariano Azuela," *Ábside*, IV, 2 (1940); and Xavier Villaurrutia, "Sobre la novela, el relato y el novelista Mariano Azuela," *La Voz Nueva*, I, 46 (1931); also in *Rueca*, I, 5 (1942), 12–16.

RICCARDO BACCHELLI

Born: Bologna, Italy
Date: April 11, 1891

PRINCIPAL WORKS

NOVELS: *Il Diavolo al Pontelungo*, 1927 (*The Devil at the Long Bridge*); *La Città degli amanti*, 1929 (*Love town*); *Il Mulino del Po*, 1938–1940 (*The Mill on the Po*).

POEMS: *Poemi lirici*, 1914; *Parole d'amore*, 1935.

HISTORY: *La Congiura di Don Giulio d'Este*, 1931.

Born into a well-established and wealthy family, at Bologna, Italy, on April 11, 1891, Riccardo Bacchelli labored for years before he received the recognition due him, for his writing was outside the main stream of Italian literature of his day. While others of his time were producing works of delicate lyricism, Bacchelli was composing long historical romances rather in the manner of the great nineteenth century Italian novelist, Manzoni.

Bacchelli has written only one light-hearted book, the relatively unsuccessful *Love Town*. This is the story of a paternalistic, Utopian city, which true lovers finally see is impossible for them. Other than this book, Bacchelli's social commentary has either been direct or historical. An example of the

first, *The Devil at the Long Bridge*, has for its subject matter the attempt of Mikhail Bakunin to establish socialism in Italy. *The Mill on the Po* is his recognized masterpiece. A somewhat ponderous trilogy, it was first published in serial form in *Nuova Antologia*. In this country the novel appeared in two parts: *The Mill on the Po* (1950) and *Nothing New Under the Sun* (1955). It presents a panorama of Bacchelli's native district in Italy over the span of three generations, and the realistic treatment piles detail upon detail until the years from the decline of Napoleon to the Battle of Vittorio Veneto in World War I are captured within its covers. The controlling theme of the book is the emergence of Italy as a unified, modern nation. This

61

birth takes place, however, not in the large issues and great men of history, but in the small, obscure lives of Italy's common folk.

Though it cannot be said that Bacchelli ever achieved wide popularity, his scholarly approach to a romantic understanding of history did finally bring him great authority in his homeland. This recognition came to him only after nearly a score of years of lonely writing in his early life. Unfortunately, it is now a question whether the renaissance that came in Italian literature after World War II will not eclipse Bacchelli's reputation. Moravia,

Berto, and other such harsh realists speak more directly to and for today's Italy. Within its field, however, Bacchelli's work is not likely be replaced, even though it remains a monument to a slightly outdated style of writing. As a writer of the older generation, Bacchelli is a member of the Accademia Nazionale dei Lencie, the Accademia della Crusca of Florence, and a Grand Officer of the Italian Republic, 1953. His minor works include *Il Rabdomante* (1936), *Il Male d'Africa* (1937), and *La Cometa,* a lively satire (1951).

BIBLIOGRAPHICAL REFERENCES: A brief but comprehensive introduction to Bacchelli in English is T. G. Bergin, "Riccardo Bacchelli," *Italica,* XVII (1940), 64–68. For biography and critical studies in Italian see Pietro Pancrazi, *Scittari italiani del novecento,* 1939; Luigi Menapace, *Saggio intorno al Mulino del Po,* 1947, with a bibliography; Giuseppe Antonio Brunelli, *Manzoni e Bacchelli,* 1951; and A. Bocelli, "Riccardo Bacchelli," *Nuova Antologia,* CCCLXVI (1933), 145–153.

SIR FRANCIS BACON

Born: London, England
Date: January 22, 1561

Died: Highgate, England
Date: April 9, 1626

PRINCIPAL WORKS

ESSAYS AND STUDIES: *Essays,* 1597, 1612, 1625; *The Advancement of Learning,* 1605; *Cogitata et Visa,* 1607; *De Sapientia Veterum,* 1609; *Novum Organum,* 1620; *History of Henry VII,* 1622; *Historia Naturalis et Experimentalis,* 1622; *De Dignitate et Augmentis Scientiarum,* 1623; *New Atlantis,* 1627.

Francis Bacon, founder of the inductive method of modern science, philosopher, politician, and historian, was the son of Sir Nicholas Bacon, an Anglican, Lord Keeper of the Great Seal under Queen Elizabeth. Bacon's mother, Anne Bacon, a Calvinist, second wife of Sir Nicholas, was a Greek and Latin scholar. The family was prosperous. Bacon's uncle by the marriage of his aunt was Sir William Cecil, Lord Burghley, principal ad-

viser to the queen, Lord High Treasurer, and one of the most important men in England.

Born at York House, his father's London residence on January 22, 1561, young Francis Bacon was often seen at court in the company of his father and was known to Queen Elizabeth, who thought the boy extremely clever. He entered Trinity College, Cambridge, in April, 1573, when he was twelve years old. There he achieved a notable academic record and left traces of his youthful arrogance as a critic of the logic and science of his teachers. It seemed to the young student that the logic and philosophy of Aristotle were not adequate as a practical way to knowledge of the world. This criticism, probably irritating to his teachers, was well-taken and provided the theoretical ground for Bacon's philosophy of science. By the time he was fourteen years old he had made his rejection of Aristotle; he was graduated in 1575.

After leaving Trinity College, Bacon decided to study law, and he became a student at Gray's Inn in 1575. His studies were interrupted by a stay of two and a half years in Paris as a member of the staff of the English ambassador, Sir Amias Paulet. During this time he traveled widely and became aware of the new ideas which were gradually supplanting Scholasticism in Europe. Recalled to England in February, 1579, because of the death of his father, he discovered on his arrival that he had been left practically penniless, largely because his father had not completed the division of his estate among his sons, and Francis was the youngest. He was forced to borrow money to complete his law studies.

Bacon, continuing to reflect on the need for new methods in science, had hopes of achieving a philosophy that would liberate students of nature from the artificial restraints of ancient logic and allow their work to have practical value in the world. At the same time he had political ambitions and prepared to set himself up as a man of power at Court. In pursuit of this objective, he became a member of Parliament in 1584. He gradually ingratiated himself with Robert Devereux, the second Earl of Essex, and attempted to use his influence with Essex, who was six years his junior, to secure for himself a responsible position at court. Although Essex was wealthy enough and friendly enough to rescue Bacon from debt and even from debtor's prison, he could not manage to move the queen to make an appointment of his friend. This lack of preferment was partly Bacon's fault, for he was not always politic in his criticism of the queen's policies, particularly of her tax program. He finally managed to be granted an unofficial position in the Queen's Learned Council.

In 1597, Bacon's first published work appeared, a volume of ten *Essays*, containing some of his basic opinions about the need for observation and science and distinguished by their literary charm. The book remains one of Bacon's most popular works.

In the meantime Essex prospered from Bacon's advice and, becoming too confident of his own power, attempted a march on London which ended with his arrest for treason. Commissioned to prosecute his former friend and patron, Bacon performed his duties diligently throughout the trial. This course of action has been interpreted by some as a sign of Bacon's devotion to duty and to the queen, and by others as a sign of his putting personal advancement above friendship. Essex was executed in 1601.

When James ascended to the throne two years later, Bacon managed, through his uncle's petition, to be knighted at the coronation; thereafter his fortunes improved, personally, economically, and politically. In 1605 he wrote his famous *Advancement of Learning*. In 1607 he married Alice Barnham, an alderman's daughter. He

63

became solicitor general in 1613, and four years later received his father's office as Lord Keeper of the Great Seal. When he became Lord Chancellor in 1621 he was created Baron Verulam and Viscount St. Albans.

His *Novum Organum,* published in 1620, was the first part of a great philosophic work which Bacon then conceived, to be entitled *Instauratio Magna.* Although the work was never completed, the parts that were published were sufficient to make Bacon's reputation as one of the most important thinkers of his times. The *Novum Organum* presented Bacon's conclusions about the proper mode of scientific inquiry. He built his ideas on the principle that the study of nature could not proceed from ideas taken a priori, as true without reference to experience, but only from a study of particular cases. In order to attain knowledge, he argued, one must free oneself from certain pernicious preconceptions or "idols," among them the "Idols of the Tribe," the habits of thought peculiar to human beings; "The Idols of the Cave," the prejudices of one's environment; "The Idols of the Market Place," the fallacies resulting from misunderstanding and misusing language; and the "Idols of the Theatre," the erroneous conceptions derived from authority. Bacon suggested that the study of particular events proceed to a consideration of forms, or general features, and that the generalizations be tested by further observation of particular instances. This work was the first significant formulation of the inductive method in science.

But Bacon's philosophical acumen did not save him from prosecution when in the same year he was charged with accepting bribes as Lord Chancellor. While admitting his guilt, Bacon attempted to excuse himself by ingenious distinctions and references to the immorality of the times. However, he was fined 40,000 pounds and sentenced to a prison term in the Tower. Although the sentence was soon remitted, Bacon was forced to leave Parliament and to give up his positions at court. For the next five years he lived in retirement and continued his philosophical writings about scientific procedures. Among the products of that period are the *Historia Naturalis et Experimentalis* and *The New Atlantis,* his conception of a scientific Utopia.

He died at Highgate, April 9, 1626, of pneumonia contracted as a result of an experiment in preserving meat by freezing it. He had left his carriage to gather snow with which to stuff a chicken and was seized with a sudden chill which caused his fatal illness. On his deathbed he wrote, "The experiment succeeded, excellently well."

BIBLIOGRAPHICAL REFERENCES: The standard edition is *The Works of Francis Bacon,* edited by James Spedding, R. L. Ellis, and D. D. Heath, 14 vols., 1857–1874. This edition contains *The Letters and the Life of Francis Bacon,* by Spedding, of which *The Life and Times of Francis Bacon,* 1878, is an abridgement. Special editions of the essays are *A Harmony of the Essays,* edited by Edward Arber, 1871; *Bacon's Essays,* edited by Geoffrey Grigson, 1937; and the *Essays, Advancement of Learning, and Other Pieces,* edited by R. F. Jones, 1937. For biography and criticism see R. W. Church, *Bacon,* 1884; C. D. Broad, *The Philosophy of Francis Bacon,* 1926; "Byron Steel" (Francis Steegmuller), *Sir Francis Bacon, the First Modern Mind,* 1930—an unpretentious and very readable biography; Mary Sturt, *Francis Bacon,* 1932; and

Charles Williams, *Bacon,* 1933; A. Wigfall Green, *Sir Francis Bacon: His Life and Works,* 1952; Thomas H. Jameson, *Francis Bacon: Criticism and the Modern World,* 1954; R. F. Jones, *Ancients and Moderns,* 1936; G. Bullough, "Bacon and the Defence of Learning," in *Seventeenth Century Studies Presented to Sir Herbert Grierson,* 1938; George V. Tovey, "Toward a New Understanding of Francis Bacon's Reform of Philosophy," *Philosophical Review,* LXI (1952), 568–574; and Moody E. Prior, "Bacon's Man of Science," *Journal of the History of Ideas,* XV (1954), 348–370. Related material on essays and essayists will be found in E. N. S. Thompson, *The Seventeenth Century English Essay,* 1926; and W. G. Crane, *Wit and Rhetoric in the Renaissance,* 1937.

JOHN BALE

Born: Cove, Suffolk, England
Date: November 21, 1495

Died: Canterbury, England
Date: November, 1563

PRINCIPAL WORKS

PLAYS: *A Tragedye,* 1538; *The Temptacyon Of Our Lorde,* 1538; *The Three Laws of Nature,* 1538; *Kynge Johan,* c. 1548.

John Bale, outspoken anti-papist Bishop of Ossory was born at Cove, England, on November 21, 1495, and educated by the Carmelites. He took his divinity degree at Jesus College, Cambridge, in 1529. He joined the reformation movement, married, and obtained a post in Suffolk.

Thomas Cromwell, knowing of his popular anti-Catholic morality plays, became his protector. After Cromwell was beheaded in 1540, the playwright and his family fled to Germany. When the Protestant Edward VI came into power, Bale returned and shortly after becoming Bishop of Ossory antagonized the Irish by refusing to be consecrated by Roman rites. When Mary came to the throne he was again in exile, only to return to England after Elizabeth's accession.

Of the forty plays Bale boasted of writing, very few have survived. His most famous play concerns King John; although it is meant to expose Catholicism, it contains the basis for later historical dramas. In this work Bale utilizes the form of the morality play and allows allegorical figures to speak with the historical ones. John, who acts as the champion of the poor widow England against the Pope, is poisoned for his trouble by Dissimulation disguised as a monk. Verity tells of this treachery and Imperial Majesty (meant to represent Henry VIII) takes over the realm and hangs Sedition.

In spite of his bias Bale lamented the destruction of the monasteries and their libraries, and he prepared a catalogue-history of fourteen centuries of English writers (*Illustrium Majoris Britanniae Scriptorum Summarium,* 1548). Queen Elizabeth gave him a living at Canterbury for his declining years, no doubt in recognition of his effective writing and preaching. He died in Canterbury in November, 1563.

BIBLIOGRAPHICAL REFERENCES: The best edition of Bale's dramatic work is *The Dramatic Writings of John Bale, Bishop of Ossory,* edited by John S. Farmer, 1907. A selection of his non-dramatic writings may be found in *Select Works of John*

Bale, D.D., Bishop of Ossory, edited by the Rev. Henry Christmas, 1849. The most important biographical and critical study is Jesse W. Harris, *John Bale: A Study in the Minor Literature of the Reformation*, 1940. Other useful studies are Honor McCusker, *John Bale: Dramatist and Antiquary*, 1942; E. S. Miller, "The Roman Rite in Bale's *King John*," *Publications of the Modern Language Association*, LXIV (1949), 802–822; and C. H. Wheat, *"A Pore Helpe, Ralph Roister Doister,* and *Three Laws,"* *Philological Quarterly*, XXVIII (1949), 312–319.

HONORÉ DE BALZAC

Born: Tours, France
Date: May 20, 1799

Died: Paris, France
Date: August 18, 1850

PRINCIPAL WORKS

NOVELS: *Les Chouans*, 1829 (*The Chouans*); *La Peau de chagrin*, 1831 (*The Magic Skin*); *Le Curé de Tours*, 1832; *Louis Lambert*, 1832; *Le Médecin de campagne*, 1833 (*The Country Doctor*); *Eugénie Grandet*, 1834; *Le Père Goriot*, 1835 (*Father Goriot*); *Séraphita*, 1835; *Le lys dans la vallée*, 1836 (*The Lily of the Valley*); *César Birotteau*, 1837; *Sur Catherine de Médicis*, 1837; *Illusions perdues*, 1839 (*Lost Illusions*); *Pierette*, 1840; *La Femme de trente ans*, 1841 (*A Woman of Thirty*); *Ursule Mirouët*, 1841; *La Rabouilleuse*, 1841 (*A Bachelor's Establishment*); *Modeste Mignon*, 1844; *Un Début dans la vie*, 1844 (*A Start in Life*); *Béatrix*, 1845; *Un Homme d'affaires*, 1847; *Le Cousin Pons*, 1847; *La Cousine Bette*, 1847; *Le Député d'Arcis*, 1847 (*The Member for Arcis*).

SHORT STORIES: *Contes drolatiques*, 1832 (*Droll Stories*).

PLAYS: *Vautrin*, 1840; *Les Ressources de Quinola*, 1842; *Paméla Giraud*, 1843; *Mercadet*, 1851.

Honoré de Balzac was born Honoré Balzac at Tours, France, on May 20, 1799. His father, originally from the peasant stock of the Albigeois, had by this time risen to become director of commissariat to Napoleon's 22nd Division. In 1799, Napoleon himself was returning from Egypt to rule for fifteen years over half of Europe. Thus the first years of Balzac's life passed in the glorious reign of Napoleon, and the emperor's career had a great effect on the young Balzac's mind.

From 1807 to 1814, Balzac was a student, first at the Collège des Oratoriens at Vendôme, then at L'Institut Lepître and L'Institut Sganzer et Beuzelin, both in Paris. Balzac later spoke of these years as "brutalizing";

he found his school a prison. His schoolmates called him fat and red-faced; his masters thought him dull. Balzac found escape from his humiliations in the library. His appetite for reading was indiscriminate and insatiable: he read everything. There in escape from the rigors of his schooling, he was laying the foundation for the vast store of knowledge that would later become a legend about him. These detested years in school, in contrast with the glory of Napoleon, fed his dreams of power and fame, and filled him with contempt for anything less than complete possession of the world. Herein is the essence of his genius as well as his greatest weakness: Balzac seemed almost unable to distinguish his imaginings from actuality, and since imagination can always transcend reality, the world he knew was too small for him.

Leaving school, Balzac in 1816 entered the University of Paris to study jurisprudence. Napoleon had fallen and France was in a state of calm. There were no worlds then to be conquered with arms. But his grandiose dreams of fame and conquest remained with Balzac as he studied law and worked to supplement his allowance in the office of an advocate. In 1819 came his revolt. Balzac left his law clerk's stool and went home to announce that he would be an author. He wrote under a picture of the former Emperor: "What Napoleon could not do with the sword, I shall accomplish with the pen."

His family was thunderstruck, but Balzac was resolved. He arrived at a compromise with his father: he would go to Paris to write for two years; if in that time he did not succeed, he would enter a more secure profession. Balzac moved to a garret at 9 rue Lesdiguières, Paris, and began to write. However, when the two years were almost up, he had produced no work even hopeful of success except a play, *Cromwell,* which had come to nothing, and his father set a date for him to evacuate his room. Then he met a young man, Auguste Le Poitevin, and writing under various pseudonyms began turning out trash in collaboration with him. He made a little money and was granted a reprieve.

With Poitevin, Balzac had entered into utter literary prostitution. In 1821 he returned home, but he continued writing trash of any kind as long as it paid. His chief desire was to earn enough money to be freed from his family. He wrote at a prodigious rate, living almost without sleep at his writing table, stimulated by countless cups of coffee. At this time he met with perhaps the most profound experience of his life and found his self-reliance, but not through his writing. He met Madame Laure de Berny.

Madame de Berny was already forty-five, a grandmother with a daughter older than Balzac. But, almost twenty-two, Balzac had never known love; he found it in this woman. The extent of her influence on his life can be seen in his saying: "There is nothing that can match the last love of a woman who is giving a man the fulfillment of his first love."

Madame de Berny was the turning point in the development of his literary genius, but even she could not save his business sense. When the pressures of his association with her sent him again to Paris, between 1826 and 1828, Balzac entered into three business speculations which, having failed, saw him in debt for 90,000 francs. Ironically, freed from the necessity of driving himself to write for freedom from his parents, he promptly made it necessary to write for freedom from his creditors. He continued to write at an incredible pace, turning out novels, essays, stories, articles, and pamphlets like a machine.

While his genius matured, his debts increased. He found his first fame in 1830 with *Scenes from Private Life* in two volumes. In 1831, he added the "de" to his name, obtained a larger apartment, a valet, a horse and carriage, and began to have political ambitions. In 1833 he met Madame de Hanska, a Russian lady whom he courted for eighteen years before she became his wife. That was the pattern of his life: his dreams stayed always ahead of his achievement. Although the critic Taine called his work the greatest gallery of human portraits since Shakespeare, Balzac died in Paris on August 18, 1850, blind, broken, alone except for his mother in a house not paid for while the wife he had married only the March before waited indifferently in another room for his death.

In more than 350 titles Balzac created and peopled a world of his own, often with more than one hundred characters in a single novel. In his work Balzac despised detail. He sought to distill from the world its pure essence, its universal qualities. He held as an axiom that everything, singly and in combination, acts and reacts upon everything else: all forces are mobile, none free. Moreover, he believed that every life expends an equal sum of energy. One may dissipate that energy upon inconsequentials and live many years, or one may concentrate that energy upon one ideal and live fewer years; but he who lives quickly does not live a shorter time. Therefore, in a work of fiction, only monomaniacs are important. A man is great insofar as he concentrates on one ideal, and tragedy occurs when such concentration is thwarted. Any motive is worthy of tragedy if followed by a single purpose. It is in terms of these ideas that Balzac once exclaimed to the romanticists: "My bourgeois novels are more tragic than your tragic dramas."

Balzac's world is a distillation of our own. He sheers away great quantities of dross and reveals the basic motives which govern human action. His world is poorer than the real world, but it is more intense. His masterwork, in which his world is most fully depicted, is *The Human Comedy*. This work has a wholeness of conception perhaps un-paralleled in literature. Balzac made the first arrangements for the collected edition in 1842. In that year the first three volumes appeared. From 1843 to 1846, at the rate of two to four volumes per year, the first edition was completed at sixteen volumes. For this edition, Balzac wrote his celebrated Preface in which he outlines his plan:

The *Scenes from Private Life* depict childhood and youth, with the false steps to which they are prone. The *Scenes from Provincial Life* show the age of passion, calculation, self-interest and ambition. The *Scenes from Parisian Life* portray finally the various tastes and vices, with all the unbridled forms of behavior of capital cities—for it is there that good and evil meet and have their strongest repercussions.

. . . After . . . these three sections, I was still confronted with the task of showing the kind of existence led by those who are subject to exceptional conditions, in whom the interests of all or several merge, and who stand, so to speak, outside the law. This led me to write the *Scenes from Political Life.*

Dying at Paris on August 18, 1850, Balzac did not live to complete the *Scenes from Military Life* which depict society "when it steps out of itself for the purpose of either defense or conquest," and he barely began the *Scenes from Rural Life* which were to contain "the purest of my characters and the application of the great principles of order, politics, and morals." In concluding his preface, Balzac wrote: "The immeasurable scope of a plan which embraces not only a history and criticism of society, but also an analysis of its evils and an exposition of its principles, justifies me, so I believe, in giving my work the title . . . *La Comédie Humaine.*"

In 1847, *Cousin Bette* and *Cousin Pons* appeared as the last important work published in Balzac's lifetime. Perhaps his greatest work, they crown his last misery. Balzac was already dying—of fifty thousand cups of coffee.

BIBLIOGRAPHICAL REFERENCES: The foundation for all Balzac studies is Vicomte Charles de Spoelberch de Lovenjoul's *Histoire des œuvres d'Honoré de Balzac,* 1888. For other biographical and critical studies see Anatole Cerfberr and Jules Christophe, *Répertoire de la Comédie Humaine,* 1887; André Le Breton, *Balzac l'homme et l'œuvre,* 1905; Ernst Robert Curtius, *Balzac,* 1923; Ethel Preston, *Recherches sur la technique de Balzac,* 1926; Pierre Abraham, *Balzac,* 1929; André Billy, *Vie de Balzac,* 2 vols., 1944; and Albert Béguin, *Balzac visionnaire,* 1946.

For studies of Balzac in English see Stefan Zweig, *Balzac,* 1930; William H. Royce, *Balzac as He Should Be Read,* 1946; Martin Turnell, *The Novel in France,* 1951; and Herbert J. Hunt, *Honoré de Balzac,* 1957. William H. Royce has also published *A Balzac Bibliography,* 1929.

HENRI BARBUSSE

Born: Asnières, France
Date: May 17, 1873

Died: Moscow, Russia
Date: August 30, 1935

PRINCIPAL WORKS

NOVELS: *Les Suppliants,* 1903 (*The Suppliants*); *L'Enfer,* 1908 (*The Inferno*); *Le Feu,* 1916 (*Under Fire*); *Clarté,* 1919 (*Light*); *Les Enchaînements,* 1925 (*Chains*).

SHORT STORIES: *Nous autres,* 1914 (*We Others*).

POEMS: *Pleureuses,* 1895.

BIOGRAPHY: *Meissonier,* 1912; *Jésus,* 1927; *Zola,* 1932; *Stalin,* 1935.

Henri Barbusse was poet, novelist, biographer, editor, and polemicist, but he is likely to be best remembered for his novels. He was born on May 17, 1873, at Asnières, France, to an English mother and a French father, and though he lived some of his childhood years in England, he retained no knowledge of English in his mature life. In 1895 he published a collection of poems titled *Pleureuses,* and in 1903 he wrote his first novel, *The Suppliants.* He attracted the attention of Catulle Mendès, became his protégé, and then married his youngest daughter. In 1908 he published *The Inferno,* the hero of which serves as a model for Colin Wilson's "Outsider" because he had "awakened to chaos."

Barbusse himself was much of an idealist about art and life, and despite the fact that in 1914 he was over forty years old, frail, and newly recovered from tuberculosis, he joined the French army in the belief of the righteousness of the cause. He requested frontline duty, and the request was granted. The experience was more than he had imagined. Although he won three citations for bravery in battle, far more meaningful to him were his impressions of the filth, the futility, and the horror of war. When in 1916 he was invalided out by his third attack of dysentery, he drew on these memories for his most famous work, *Under Fire,* published in 1916. The moral passion of the book, its daring frankness, and the author's precise attention to detail won it the Prix Goncourt in 1917 and its immediate translation into English. Barbusse's reputation was secured; the American edition alone went through seven printings in that year.

Thereafter Barbusse involved himself more and more with prose tracts intended to benefit man. He became one of the intellectuals who saw hope for peace in communism, and he occupied himself almost wholly with spreading this doctrine. In 1931 he wrote a a laudatory book on Russia, and in 1935 he published a biography of Stalin. Both works seem excessively naïve to present-day readers, particularly the doting portrait of Stalin; however, one can say for Barbusse that he was serving an ideal which many people, disillusioned by war, considered man's hope. Barbusse did not live to lose these beliefs; in 1935 while a delegate at the Seventh Congress of the Third International, he contracted pneumonia and died on August 30 in the Kremlin hospital.

BIBLIOGRAPHICAL REFERENCES: Henri Hertz, *Henri Barbusse*, 1919, is a comprehensive critical study of his work. See also J. N. Cru, *Témoins*, 1929. A rather specialized study is Jacques Duclos and Jean Fréville, *Henri Barbusse*, 1946. Colin Wilson discusses Barbusse at some length in *The Outsider*, 1956.

JOHN BARCLAY

Born: Pont-à-Mousson, France
Date: January 28, 1582

Died: Rome, Italy
Date: August 15, 1621

PRINCIPAL WORKS

POEMS: *Satyricon*, Part I, 1603; Part II, 1607; *Sylvae*, 1606.
PROSE ROMANCE: *Argenis*, 1621.
TREATISES: *Apologia*, 1610; *Icon Animorum*, 1614.

Born at Pont-à-Mousson, France, on January 28, 1582, to a French mother and a Scottish barrister-professor father, John Barclay became a leading Latin poet and satirist of his day. He was probably educated at a French Jesuit college. Although most of his works were published in London, he lived there only about ten years; later he lived in France and in Rome. He married Louise Debonaire, a Latin scholar and poetess, in 1605.

Barclay showed a marked facility in Latin and in 1601 wrote a commentary on Statius' *Thebais*. His early poems, *Sylvae*, were first printed in London and in Latin. He is best remembered, however, for his *Satyricon*, a devastating satire, modeled after Petronius, on the Jesuit order. A well-known work, *Argenis*, is a long romance with political implications—an elaborate key to topical allusions provided by the author. He completed the manuscript in 1621, just a few days before his death, at Rome on August 15, the cause of which is unknown but which was attributed to poisoning.

As a Neo-Latin author, Barclay is ranked with the best; he was especially deft in satire. Most of his work reflects the man in his times, an Anti-Papist but not a Reformist. His poetry gives few clues to his character, although he was said to be grave. He was an opportunist, writing always with an eye to money and the patronage of the wealthy. He adhered to Catholicism, even though he disapproved of much Church doctrine. His only son became an abbé shortly after the father's death.

BIBLIOGRAPHICAL REFERENCES: See Jules Dukas, Preface to his bibligraphy of the *Satyricon*, 1889; and A. Collignon, *Notes historiques, littéraires et bibliographiques sur le Satyricon de John Barclay*, 1902.

PÍO BAROJA Y NESSI

Born: San Sebastián, Spain
Date: December 28, 1872

Died: Madrid, Spain
Date: October 30, 1956

PRINCIPAL WORKS

NOVELS: *Tierra vasco* (*Basque Land*), 1900–1909: *La casa de Aizgorri* (*The House of Aizgorri*), *El mayorazgo de Labraz* (*The Lord of Labraz*), and *Zalacaín el aventurero* (*Zalacaín the Adventurer*); *La lucha por la vida* (*The Struggle for Life*), 1904: *La Busca* (*The Quest*), *Mala hierba* (*Weeds*), and *Aurora roja* (*Red Dawn*); *La vida fantástica* (*The Fantastic Life*, 1901–1906: *Aventuras, inventos y mixtificaciones de Silvestre Paradox* (*The Adventures of Sylvester Paradox*), *Camino de perfección* (*The Way of Perfection*), and *Paradox, rey* (*Paradox, King*); *César o nada*, 1919 (*Caesar or Nothing*); *El árbol de la ciencia*, 1922 (*The Tree of Knowledge*); *Memorias de un hombre de acción*, 1913–1931 (*Recollections of a Man of Action*).

ESSAYS AND STUDIES: *El tablado de Arlequín*, 1904; *Nuevo tablado de Arlequín*, 1917.

AUTOBIOGRAPHICAL SKETCHES: *Juventud egolatria*, 1917 (*Youth and Egolatry*).

The father of Pío Baroja y Nessi may have been responsible for his son's writing career. Though a mining engineer, he was also a poet and author of the lyrics for perhaps the only opera in the Basque language, and he brought up the boy, born in San Sebastián, December 28, 1872, on Spanish and Basque ballads and legends. Disliking discipline and rules, young Pío hated school. In one autobiographical work he describes satirically his uninspired teachers. But he did read widely, including translations of Poe, Dickens, Nietzsche, Balzac, and the Russians, and trained himself in observation and self-analysis.

His antipathy toward textbooks caused him to fail twice in his final examinations in the medical school of Valencia, but he finally earned a degree in Madrid, in 1893. However, after one or two dull years spent practicing medicine in a small Basque town, Baroja gave up that career and joined his brother in Madrid to run a bakery. Lack of customers gave him leisure to wander the streets of the Spanish capital and to get acquainted not only with the laboring classes but also with the derelicts of back streets and gutters who figure in his trilogy, *The Struggle for Life*.

A lucky investment allowed him to

71

give up commerce and concentrate on writing. At first he contributed to newspapers, writing articles that attracted the attention of literary leaders like Azorín, who became his friend. Fiction, however, was his chief love. In 1900 he published a volume of short stories, then started on the first of his trilogies, called *The Basque Land,* three novels written in dramatic form and portraying the once healthy Basque culture as it succumbed to alcohol and industrial progress.

Baroja wrote rapidly, sometimes three or four novels a year, with action more prominent than characterization or style. Life has no plan, he said, so a novel that imitated life need have no plot. After reading Balzac, he was seized by the ambition to fictionalize the Spanish scene in several series of novels with such titles as *The Cities* (1920), which includes *Caesar or Nothing* and *The Race.* In these works he points up the failure of modern civilization. He also began a long series called *Recollections of a Man of Action,* comprising semi-historical novels with one of his ancestors as the chief character.

The novels of Baroja, powerful in their restraint and understatement, won him election to the Spanish Academy in 1936. His chief flaw as a novelist is lack of structural unity. He had a marvelous gift for describing people and scenes, but a sudden idea could lead him into reflections unconnected with the plot, digressions which reveal him as a sincere, open-minded liberal. His typical theme is the life of a physical or spiritual vagabond, maladjusted because of his early life, and seeking to break out of the ironic trap of civilization. To Baroja, action is a cure for all ills. Let a man will, and he can recover whatever he has lost, from health to dignity. He criticizes the degeneracy of Spain and shows pessimism about any possible improvement, and even anarchism comes into his philosophical speculation. For such a man it was easy to revive the picaresque novel of Golden Age Spain, as he did in *Zalacaín the Adventurer.*

He never married. He seemed to know little about love, and few of his novels can be classified as love stories. All but one of his nearly one hundred books were banned when Franco took over Spain. From then on until his death in Madrid, October 30, 1956, too old to seek intellectual freedom outside Spain, Baroja lived under the dictatorship, publishing inoffensive novels and memoirs about what he had been and what people had thought of him or said about him.

BIBLIOGRAPHICAL REFERENCES: For studies of Baroja in English see John Dos Passos, *Rosinante to the Road Again,* 1922; Salvador de Madariaga, *The Genius of Spain,* 1923; A. F. G. Bell, *Contemporary Spanish Literature,* 1925; and John T. Reid, *Modern Spain and Liberalism,* 1937; in Spanish, César Barja, *Libros y autores contemporáneos,* 1935; M. Pérez Ferrero, *Pío Baroja y su rincón,* 1938 (Santiago de Chile); José A. Balseiro, *Blasco Ibáñez . . . y Pío Baroja,* 1949; idem, "Homaje a Baroja," *Indice de artes y letras,* 9, Num. 70–71, 1954 (Madrid).

SIR JAMES MATTHEW BARRIE

Born: Kirriemuir, Scotland   *Died:* London, England
Date: May 9, 1860   *Date:* June 19, 1937

PLAYS: *Walker, London,* 1892; *The Professor's Love Story,* 1895; *The Little Minister,* 1897; *Quality Street,* 1901; *The Admirable Crichton,* 1903; *Peter Pan,* 1904; *Alice Sit-by-the-Fire,* 1905; *What Every Woman Knows,* 1908; *The Twelve-Pound Look,* 1910; *Der Tag,* 1914; *A Kiss for Cinderella,* 1916; *The Old Lady Shows Her Medals,* 1917; *Dear Brutus,* 1917; *Mary Rose,* 1920; *Shall We Join the Ladies?,* 1922.

NOVELS: *Better Dead,* 1887; *When a Man's Single,* 1888; *A Window in Thrums,* 1889; *The Little Minister,* 1891; *Sentimental Tommy,* 1896; *Tommy and Grizel,* 1900.

SHORT STORIES: *Auld Licht Idylls,* 1888; *A Window in Thrums,* 1889; *An Auld Licht Manse,* 1893; *A Tillyloss Scandal,* 1893; *Farewell, Miss Julie Logan,* 1931.

BIOGRAPHY: *Margaret Ogilvy,* 1896.

MEMOIRS: *The Greenwood Hat,* 1937.

James Matthew Barrie was born at Kirriemuir, Scotland, May 9, 1860, into the family of a poor Scottish weaver, and no one could have guessed when he was a child that he would one day make his native village famous as the fictional village of Thrums. Despite their poverty, David Barrie and his wife, born Margaret Ogilvy, gave their children all the education they could. The father worked long hours at his loom for many years, and because he did, the mother was much closer to their children than he, particularly in the case of James Matthew Barrie. It was largely through the feminine influence of his mother that Barrie became the man of culture and letters that he was, but her influence made him also a sentimentalist and something of a snob.

Barrie's schooling was acquired in many places, including several schools operated by his brother, A. O. Barrie, himself famous in the British educational world. By dint of hard work James Matthew Barrie was graduated from Edinburgh University and went ahead to take his M.A. in 1882; his university record was undistinguished. Early in 1883 Barrie applied successfully by mail for a job as a writer on the staff of the Nottingham *Journal.* As a journalist Barrie turned out thousands of words weekly on many subjects, although none of his writing for the newspapers was remotely of literary quality. His first literary effort to be published was an article entitled "An Auld Licht Community," in the London *St. James Gazette,* in 1884. This article was written at his parents' home, shortly after Barrie had lost his job in Nottingham. Several other "Auld Licht" sketches followed and were published, launching Barrie's career as a man of letters. Filled with enthusiasm, Barrie moved to London, despite the fact that Frederick Greenwood, editor of the *St. James Gazette,* discouraged the change.

Once in London, Barrie began to write in earnest, and *Better Dead,* a book based on his experience as a journalist, was published. The following year saw three books which cemented the author's popularity, if not his literary position: *Auld Licht Idylls,* a sentimental collection about life in Kirriemuir; *When A Man's Single,* a novel about life as a journalist; and *In Edinburgh Eleven,* sketches of famous men of that city. *A Window in Thrums* was highly popular, but its very success was a mixed blessing for Barrie: it identified him as the leader of the Kailyard School. The term, a derogatory one, was applied by critics to authors who wrote sentimental, humorous fiction about Scottish life, using dialect and ignoring anything which might be considered harsh or ugly. *The Little Minister,* still a favorite with immature and sentimental readers, is typical of the type.

Although he began to write for the stage in 1894, Barrie's career until about 1900 was that of a novelist, for he continued to publish sentimental idylls like *Sentimental Tommy* and *Tommy and Grizel.* But the 1890's were an important decade in many ways for Barrie. In addition to changing careers from that of novelist to dramatist, he changed his personal life also. In 1894 he married an actress, Mary Ansell. The marriage was unsuccessful, however, and a divorce followed in 1909. Perhaps the fault was Barrie's; he was a man who clung throughout life to attitudes of adolescence. The influence of his mother, too, may have marred the marriage. This is the evidence implied in *Margaret Ogilvy,* the biography Barrie published in 1896.

As early as 1891 Barrie had plays on the stage. In that year three of his one-act plays were produced. Odd things happened early in his career, even to his collaborating with A. Conan Doyle on the libretto of *Jane Annie,* an opera. He dramatized several of his prose works, including *The Little Minister.* The star of that play was Maude Adams, who appeared also in *Quality Street* and *Peter Pan.* When she

opened in *The Little Minister* in New York, Barrie came to the United States, taking the opportunity of his being in this country to deny the authorship of several sentimental and scandalous volumes which had been published here.

By 1903 Barrie's reputation as a dramatist was something of a sensation. In that year he had three plays on the stage—*Quality Street, The Admirable Crichton,* and *Little Mary.* In the following year his outstanding success, *Peter Pan,* appeared; the play has endeared Barrie to millions of children, and to adults, too. It is important to remember that Barrie achieved critical acclaim as a dramatist, as well as popularity, as early as the production of *The Little Minister* in 1897. After that time, Barrie's reputation with critics may have wavered, but it always remained high. Of all his plays, and Barrie wrote many, there are some which stand out today above the rest.

The Admirable Crichton, which is perhaps the most enduring, after *Peter Pan,* of all Barrie's work, was unusual at the time of its production, for no one had dreamed before of a play with a butler as the leading character. Novel as it was, the play was a success. On the other hand, *Quality Street* illustrates the charm that Barrie was able to introduce into his plays, a whimsical grace which has kept that play popular ever since.

Best-known to the general public of all Barrie's works is *Peter Pan; or, The Boy Who Never Grew Up,* a play which grew out of games that Barrie played with his friends' children. Out of the play has emerged a whole group of immortal characters: Peter Pan, Wendy, Captain Hook, Mr. Smee, and

Nana the dog. In America and in England the characters and the play have delighted and charmed their audiences, both on the stage and on television.

Two other plays by Barrie deserve notice: *What Every Woman Knows* and *Dear Brutus.* The first-named play is a well-knit affair telling how a woman makes a success out of a dull husband; the latter is similar to *Peter Pan* in that it moves into a dream world where its characters have a second chance at life. In *Dear Brutus,* as in other later works, Barrie preached his creed that one should prefer a heavenly failure to a too-worldly success, a creed most explicit in his rec-

toral address at St. Andrews University in 1922.

Popularity and critical acclaim came to Barrie before his death. His alma mater, Edinburgh University, and St. Andrews (of which he was rector from 1919 to 1922) conferred the LL.D. upon him. English universities were not to be outdone, for Oxford and Cambridge both awarded him the honorary D.Litt. Barrie was created a baronet in 1913, and he received the Order of Merit in 1922, in recognition of his service to his country during World War I. He died in London on June 19, 1937.

Gordon W. Clarke

BIBLIOGRAPHICAL REFERENCES: The Peter Pan Edition, 18 vols., 1929–1941, is the definitive edition. The authorized biography is Denis Mackail's *Barrie: The Story of J. M. B.,* 1941. For other biographical and critical studies see H. M. Walbrook, *J. M. Barrie and the Theatre,* 1922; Thomas Moult, *Barrie,* 1928; F. J. H. Darton, *J. M. Barrie,* 1929; J. A. Hammerton, *Barrie: The Story of a Genius,* 1929; J. A. Roy, *James Matthew Barrie: An Appreciation,* 1937; and W. A. Darlington, *J. M. Barrie,* 1938.

See also Lionel Stevenson, "A Source for Barrie's *Peter Pan,*" *Philological Quarterly,* VIII (1929), 210–214; J. Bailhache, "Le Sentimentalisme de Barrie," *Études Anglaises,* II (1938), 113–119; and Hugh Kingsmill, "J. M. Barrie," *Horizon,* IV (1941), 43–49.

MATSUO BASHÔ

Born: Iga Province, Japan *Died:* Osaka, Japan
Date: 1644   *Date:* 1694

PRINCIPAL WORKS

Matsuo Bashô wrote about seven travel accounts and diaries and twelve works of criticism. There are also thirteen collections of his hokku, nine of his linked verse, and five collections of his letters. Best known of his travel accounts are *Oku no Hoso-michi,* 1702 (*The Narrow Road of Oku*); *Oi no Obumi,* 1709 (*Scraps from My Letterbox*); of collections of his haiku, the undated *Haikai Shichibu-shû* (*Excerpts from Seven Collections of Bashô's Verse*), is most popular.

Born into a warrior family in Iga Province in the year 1644, as a youth Matsuo Jinshichirô served in the house of Tôdô Yoshikiyo, warden of Ueno

Castle, east of the ancient capital of Nara, as the personal retainer of Yoshikiyo's son Yoshitada. Yoshitada was himself interested in the haikai, was a disciple of the poet Kitamura Kigin, and had the nom de plume of Sengin. Apparently they stirred Jinshichirô's interest, for we find early poems of his which were evaluated and corrected by Kigin. Yoshitada died in 1666 when Bashô, as he was to be known in Japanese history, was twenty-two. This was the turning point in his career, for he abandoned further feudal service, an act which made him a virtual outcast from his social class. He seems to have gone to Kyoto, and in 1672 we find him in Edo (now Tokyo), working at a local water works. By this time he had acquired a number of disciples, and one of them offered him a small residence. From that time on he devoted his life to his art. Two schools of haikai poetry were prevalent in Edo at this time, the old Teitoku School, and the newer, more liberal Danrin School headed by Nishiyama Sôin. Bashô preferred the latter, and associated himself with the school's members, but eventually, tiring of their tendency to run to empty witticisms, he turned back to the primitive but honest spirit expressed in the Man'yô-shû (Anthology of a Myriad Leaves) to adapt it to his times, thereby developing the haikai and

haiku (seventeen-syllable epigrammatic verse) to a new height. His poems and writings show his love of nature. In 1684 he began his wanderings through various parts of Japan, composing haiku as he went, and writing his famous travel accounts and diaries. In the middle of 1694 he set out west on another trip, and after having visited various places on the way, he visited his childhood home in Ueno before going on to Osaka, where he fell ill and died. Although a few modest wild oats were not unknown to him in his youth, his master's death and his later tribulations in Edo and on his wanderings made him an introspective and moral man, not devoid of humor.

Actually, the pen name Bashô was given him later. The nom de plume which he used was Tôsei of the Hut of the Bashô. Bashô, meaning plantain, was the name of his residence because a plantain tree grew there. There are numerous schools of the haikai and haiku in Japan today, but they all stem from Bashô, so great has been his influence on Japanese seventeen-syllable poetry. He is Japan's most highly esteemed poet, and one of the greatest figures in Japanese literature.

BIBLIOGRAPHICAL REFERENCES: Because of his importance in Japanese literature, there are at least twelve collected works of Bashô. Some of his works have appeared in translation in The Master Singers of Japan, 1910; Japanese Hokkus, 1910; A Year of Japanese Epigrams, 1911; Japanese Poetry, 1923; Anthology of Haiku, Ancient and Modern, 1932; The Bamboo Broom, 1934; Le Haiku, 1935; Haïkaï de Bahsô et de ses Disciples, 1936; and Anthology of Japanese Literature, 1955. The number of biographies and critical studies are beyond counting, but mostly in Japanese. In English a pioneer work is Basil Hall Chamberlain, "Bashô (1644–94) and the Japanese Poetical Epigram," in Transactions of the Asiatic Society of Japan, XXX (1902), 243–362.

CHARLES BAUDELAIRE

Born: Paris, France
Date: April 9, 1821

Died: Paris
Date: August 31, 1867

POEMS: *Les Fleurs du Mal*, 1857 (*Flowers of Evil*); *Petits Poèmes en Prose*, 1869 (*Little Poems in Prose*).

ESSAYS AND STUDIES: *Les Paradis artificiels*, 1860 (*The Artificial Paradise*); *Richard Wagner et Tannhaeuser à Paris*, 1861; *L'Art romantique* and *Curiosités esthétiques*, 1868–1869.

REMINISCENCES: *Mon Coeur mis à nu*, 1887 (*My Heart Laid Bare*).

Charles (Pierre) Baudelaire, in his youth, provided the classic example of rebellion against domestic restraint, and this rebellion has been used to explain much of his adult personality. He was born in Paris, April 9, 1821; his father died soon after, and his mother married an army officer named Aupick, with whom young Baudelaire was soon at loggerheads. He was educated at the Collège Louis-le-Grand in Paris, and by 1841 the domestic situation had become so strained that his stepfather sent him on a voyage to India which lasted two years. On his return to France, having inherited a small property, Baudelaire established himself as one of the dandies of the Latin Quarter. Before long his extravagance was such that his family had to have his money put in trust.

Baudelaire was intimate with Delacroix and several other painters. Since he himself was not without artistic talent, his first two books were criticisms of art. As a child, he had learned English; hence, he came under the influence of writers not generally known in France. In addition, he was affected by the international "Byronism" of the period, and he read avidly "Monk" Lewis and other writers of the Gothic school. But his most important discovery was of Poe, whose work he encountered in 1846–1847. Through his translations (1856–1865) Poe became better known in France than in America and had a greater effect upon French poetry than upon American.

In 1857 Baudelaire published his great book of poems, *Flowers of Evil*, a volume that almost immediately became a synonym for everything decadent and unwholesome. He and his publisher were prosecuted for offending against public morals; the poems dealing with lesbianism were removed and republished under another title (*Les Épaves*) in Brussels in 1866.

In Baudelaire's poetry there was developed an aspect of Romanticism that was to be much more prominent in France than in England—a preoccupation on the one hand with the morbid and the perverse, and on the other with a deep religious mysticism. He was not above attempting merely to shock the bourgeoisie; yet much of his poetry was a genuine awareness, both psychologically and morally, of the problem of Evil—a problem generally ignored in a century largely devoted to sweetness and light. He pushed the Romantic craving for sensation to its limit, so that Hugo congratulated him on having "created a new shudder"; but the shudder was the genuine one of a man both attracted and repelled by the idea of Sin. His is a literature of inclusion; whereas nineteenth century literature, particularly in Anglo-Saxon countries, was one of exclusion.

Baudelaire was a meticulous craftsman, and French criticism commonly speaks of the "lapidary perfection" of his language. From Poe he had learned the art of brevity, and in this respect he ran counter to the usual Romantic diffuseness. He represented the breakdown of Romanticism and the beginning of modernism. He may be truly considered one of the greatest poets of the century, for he looked far beneath its surface and expressed what he saw.

Baudelaire had only a limited influence in England, where he was responsible for some of the feeble eroticism of Swinburne and was much esteemed by the minor writers of the 1890's. It was the fashion then to admire his spectacular and often specious Satanism; our generation is more inclined to see in him yet another aspect of the struggle for faith—the great problem of his century.

In addition to his poems, Baudelaire published many critical pieces in magazines. In 1864, his finances caused him to move to Brussels. Worn out by alcohol and opium, he spent most of his last years in asylums and died in Paris, August 31, 1867.

BIBLIOGRAPHICAL REFERENCES: Baudelaire's Œuvres complètes were published in 1868–1870. The standard modern edition is that edited by Jacques Crépet, 1922–1950. For studies of Baudelaire in English see James Huneker, Essays, 1929; T. S. Eliot, Selected Essays, 1932; Joseph D. Bennett, Baudelaire: A Criticism, 1946; Percy M. Jones, Baudelaire, 1952; and Louis Untermeyer, Makers of the Modern World, 1955; in French, Charles Asselineau, Charles Baudelaire: sa vie, sa œuvre, 1869; Féli Gautier, Charles Baudelaire, 1904; E. and J. Crépet, Charles Baudelaire, 1906; and F. Porché, La vie douloureuse de Charles Baudelaire, 1926. A recent addition to Baudelaire studies was Baudelaire: A Self-Portrait, a selection of his letters edited by L. B. and F. E. Hyslop, 1957.

VICKI BAUM

Born: Vienna, Austria
Date: January 24, 1888

Died: Hollywood, California
Date: August 29, 1960

PRINCIPAL WORKS

NOVELS: *Grand Hotel*, 1931; *And Life Goes On*, 1932; *A Tale from Bali*, 1937; *The Ship and the Shore*, 1941; *Hotel Berlin '43*, 1944; *Danger from Deer*, 1951.

Vicki Baum has marked her career as novelist since 1914, playwright since 1930, and scenarist since 1932 by almost yearly production. Born in Vienna, she wrote in German until 1937, a year before she became an American citizen; she had come to the United States in 1931 to see the dramatization of *Grand Hotel*, her most famous novel, and stayed.

Grand Hotel, her best-known work, is a good example of Miss Baum's special storytelling gift, grouping as it does sketches of the thoughts and ac-tions of guests in a post-World War I German hotel as their lives interconnect. Her characters, representing diversified national, class, and professional types, appeal to the reader's interest in romantic adventure, the whole interwoven into a complex structure of plot. Fast-moving, skillful in construction, and uncomplicated by more than superficial development of the thematic ideas, Miss Baum's cosmopolitan novels rely on their author's ability to sentimentalize exotic material.

BIBLIOGRAPHICAL REFERENCES: There is no extended biographical or critical study. For a comprehensive brief sketch see Harry R. Warfel, *American Novelists of Today*, 1951. For references to the novels, consult *Book Review Digest*, 1931 ff.

REX BEACH

Born: Atwood, Michigan   Died: Sebring, Florida
Date: September 1, 1877   Date: December 7, 1949

PRINCIPAL WORKS

NOVELS: *Pardners*, 1905; *The Spoilers*, 1906; *The Barrier*, 1907; *The Silver Horde*, 1909; *Big Brother*, 1923; *Son of the Gods*, 1929; *Woman in Ambush*, 1951.

PLAY: *The World in His Arms*, 1946.

AUTOBIOGRAPHY: *Personal Exposures*, 1941.

Rex (Ellingwood) Beach, equally famous for his two-fisted novels of adventure and the movies made from them, died a year before his last, unfinished novel, *Woman in Ambush*, was published. The movie rights had already been sold for one hundred thousand dollars at the end of a long successful career that began with *Pardners* in 1905. *The Spoilers*, his most famous book, was produced in 1912 as the first of the six-reel movies. Beach was the first author to insist upon movie rights in his publishing contracts.

Most of Rex Beach's novels and plays reflected his knowledge and experience of he-man pioneering business ventures in Panama, the oil fields of the Southwest, and the mines and salmon canning factories of Alaska. Strong on action and intrigue, melodramatic in plot, and written in fast-moving style, his fiction is filled with brawls, riots, shootings in the street, and similar manly encounters. He wrote little in later years, having invested his fortune with remarkable success in vegetable-growing and ranching. Incurably ill, he shot himself at his lakeside home in Sebring, Florida, on December 7, 1949. Beach was born in Atwood, Michigan, on September 1, 1877.

BIBLIOGRAPHICAL REFERENCES: There is no authorized biography and almost no criticism. See Robert Van Gelder, *Writers and Writing*, 1946; Cyril Clemens, "My Friend Rex Beach," *Hobbies*, LIV (1950), 138; and L. Nizer, "The Most Unforgettable Character I've Met," *Reader's Digest*, LVIII (1951), 33–37.

PIERRE AUGUSTIN CARON DE BEAUMARCHAIS

Born: Paris, France   Died: Paris
Date: January 24, 1732   Date: May 18, 1799

PRINCIPAL WORKS

PLAYS: *Eugénie*, 1767; *Les Deux Amis, ou le négociant de Lyon*, 1770; *Le Barbier de Séville*, 1775 (*The Barber of Seville*); *Le Mariage de Figaro*, 1784 (*The Marriage of Figaro*).

AUTOBIOGRAPHY: *Mémoires*, 1773–1774.

Pierre Augustin Caron de Beaumarchais, one of the few outstanding French writers of prose comedy during the eighteenth century, is best known for his two great plays, *The Barber of Seville* and *The Marriage of Figaro,* made into operas by Rossini and Mozart, and for his action-filled career as watch-maker, businessman, secret agent, and financier of revolutions. Born in Paris on January 24, 1732, and son of a bourgeois jeweler, Charles Caron, Beaumarchais learned first his father's trade, then became music teacher to one of the daughters of Louis XV. Married advantageously, he became wealthy through careful speculations; these investments enabled him to buy, in 1761, the title of Royal Secretary to Louis, who conferred noble rank upon him. After traveling throughout most of Europe on various official and private missions, he became embroiled in a series of lawsuits in Paris. His accounts of his trials, notably that involving Goëzman, as told in his *Mémoires,* made his reputation as a caustic, effective, and popular writer.

Beaumarchais' literary career was as stormy as his personal life. *The Barber of Seville,* which was based on an unfortunate alliance between his sister and the Spanish writer, José Clavijo, was at first prohibited (1773), then received with great success two years later. This play, which seems to borrow situation and plot from the older Italian comedy and from Molière's *The School for Wives,* ridicules the figure of the jealous guardian. The latter, in love with his young ward, finds himself at the mercy of the girl, her true lover, and several sly servants and persons of lower caste, including Figaro himself. Despite the conventionality of plot and characters—the play abounds in conspiracies and disguises, *quiproquos,* and the usual stock comic situations and types—*The Barber of Seville* is made alive through the dexterity and wit of Beaumarchais, who matches his characters cleverly and puts originality into his scenes through his style, unique in its boldness and diversification.

The Marriage of Figaro continues this same tradition. Here, however, the brilliant sallies of the "barber" take on political significance: Figaro emerges as a strong individual and an even stronger symbol. Henceforth, he will epitomize the spirit of the Revolution —in a sense, then, the spirit of France. Forbidden to be played for several years, the 1784 première of *The Marriage of Figaro* met with total success. In this play Beaumarchais turns comedy into what has been called "universal satire," into diatribes and insinuations against the lawyers, the courtiers, and the privileged classes in general, who, says Figaro, are often inferior to their servants. Like *The Barber of Seville, The Marriage of Figaro* is an elaborate construction of intrigue and incident. The main plot (there are several sub-plots) concerns the outwitting of the Count Almaviva, the romantic lead of *The Barber of Seville* now turned libertine, by Figaro and the women of the play. One of the latter is Figaro's own financée, whom the count is pursuing. The high point of the play is Figaro's famous monologue of the last act, in which he sums up his protests against the prevailing social and political order in France. On the whole, *The Marriage of Figaro* is the most remarkable dramatic production of the century: a mixture of all comic genres, it is a veritable portrait of the period in which it appeared.

Although Beaumarchais wrote several other plays (*Eugénie*, and *Les Deux Amis, ou le négociant de Lyon*), these fall far short of his two masterpieces.

The playwright's last years were marked, typically, by unusual events. He published the first complete edition of the works of Voltaire (1785–1790), furnished arms to the American revolutionists, became a Revolutionary official in France (he had been a secret agent for Louis XVI), and later fled his country as an *émigré*. He died in Paris, May 18, 1799, three years after his return from exile.

BIBLIOGRAPHICAL REFERENCES: There is no standard collected edition in English, although numerous single translations are available. The most recent collected edition in French is the *Théâtre complet*, edited by Pascal Pia, 1956.

Biographies are numerous. Outstanding is John Rivers, *Figaro: The Life of Beaumarchais*, 1922, with a selected bibliography. See also René Dalsème, *Beaumarchais*, *1732–1799*, 1929, with bibliography; Georges Édouard Lemaître, *Beaumarchais*, 1949, a first edition in English with selected bibliography; and Elizabeth S. Kite, *Beaumarchais and the War of American Independence*, 1908. French readers should consult the recent critical work of Jacques Scherer, *La Dramaturgie de Beaumarchais*, 1954. Other studies can be found in Frederick Charles Green, *Minuet: A Critical Survey of French and English Literary Ideas in the Eighteenth Century*, 1935; Clarence D. Brenner and Nolan A. Goodyear, *Eighteenth Century French Plays*, 1927; and C. H. C. Wright, *A History of French Literature*, 1912.

FRANCIS BEAUMONT and JOHN FLETCHER

Beaumont

Born: Grace-Dieu, England   *Died:* Kent (?), England
Date: 1585(?)   *Date:* March 6, 1616

PRINCIPAL WORKS

POEMS: *Salmacis and Hermaphroditus*, 1602; *Poems*, 1640.

PLAYS (BEAUMONT ALONE): *The Woman Hater*, c. 1606 (sometimes attributed); *The Knight of the Burning Pestle*, 1607.

COLLABORATIONS WITH FLETCHER: *The Coxcomb*, 1608–1610; *The Maid's Tragedy*, 1610–1611; *Philaster, or Love Lies a-Bleeding*, c. 1609; *A King and No King*, 1611; *The Scornful Lady*, 1613–1617.

Fletcher

Born: Rye, Sussex, England   *Died:* London, England
Date: December, 1579   *Date:* August, 1625

PRINCIPAL WORKS

PLAYS (FLETCHER ALONE): *The Woman's Prize, or The Tamer Tamed*, c. 1604; *The Faithful Shepherdess*, c. 1609; *Bonduca*, 1609–1614; *Valentinian*, 1610–1614, *Wit*

Without Money, c. 1614; *Monsieur Thomas,* 1610–1616; *The Mad Lover,* c. 1616; *The Loyal Subject,* 1618; *The Humourous Lieutenant,* 1619; *The Wild-Goose Chase.* 1621; *Rule a Wife and Have a Wife,* 1624.

COLLABORATIONS WITH MASSINGER: *Sir John van Olden Barnavelt,* 1619; *The Custom of the Country,* c. 1609; *The False One,* c. 1620; *The Beggars' Bush,* c. 1622; *The Spanish Curate,* 1622; *The Elder Brother,* printed 1637.

COLLABORATIONS WITH SHAKESPEARE: *King Henry VIII,* 1612–1613; *The Two Noble Kinsmen,* 1613.

Francis Beaumont was well-connected, his father being a distinguished lawyer of noble family at Grace-Dieu priory in Leicestershire. Born in 1584 or 1585, Beaumont went up to Oxford in 1597, and in 1600 enrolled at the Inns of Court in London. Like many of his fellow students, he was probably preparing himself not so much for the law as for life as a man of property, and his time would be spent not only in reading but in all manner of fashionable pleasures, including the theater. In 1613 he married Ursula Isley of Sundridge Hall, Kent, and retired to the country; but he died three years after, in the same year as Shakespeare. He was buried in Westminster Abbey.

John Fletcher was also well-connected, the son of Richard Fletcher, an eminent cleric who became Bishop of Bristol and later of London; and he had considerable influence at Court until he fell into disfavor shortly before his death in 1596. John, born at Rye, Sussex, in 1579, was sent to Cambridge at the age of twelve, and may have been intended for the Church; but any such idea was given up at his father's death, which left him dependent upon relatives. Of the years between 1596 and his emergence as a dramatist little is known. He died in the London plague in August, 1625, and was buried in St. Saviours, Southwark.

Beaumont and Fletcher must have met in the early years of the century,

probably while the former was still at the Inner Temple. According to Aubrey they set up house together. They had much in common, in particular a background of wealth and culture; but there was one important difference between them. Fletcher had to make a living, Beaumont had not. Fletcher made a career of the theater, but his friend was an amateur playwright who could and did give up the theater when he pleased. And out of the fifty-odd plays associated with his name, Beaumont had a hand in something between eight and twelve only, though out of that number a high proportion rank with the very best of the fifty, among them *The Knight of the Burning Pestle* (perhaps by him alone), *The Scornful Lady, Philaster, The Maid's Tragedy, A King and No King.* After Beaumont's withdrawal Fletcher continued in full production until his death during the plague of 1625, but he found many other collaborators among the writers of the day. In fact one of these, Philip Massinger, contributed far more to the "Beaumont and Fletcher" plays than Beaumont, and had a hand in such distinguished works as *Sir John van Olden Barnavelt, The False One, The Beggars' Bush, The Elder Brother, The Custom of the Country,* and *The Spanish Curate* before he parted company with Fletcher in 1623.

Beaumont and Fletcher began their

careers as writers for child-actors. Each had failure to start with, though the plays concerned later became famous: *The Knight of the Burning Pestle* and *The Faithful Shepherdess*. Perhaps they over-estimated their audience; if so, they learned their lesson and never did so again. *The Faithful Shepherdess* in particular is an ambitious and subtly experimental play which taught Fletcher much about tragi-comedy, a form which became very popular in his hands a little later. The luck changed when, in 1608, the King's Men, Shakespeare's company and the most powerful of all, leased the play-house at Blackfriars. Formerly this had been used only by children, the adult players confining themselves to large open-air theaters like the Globe. But a change was coming over the audience. It was splitting into classes with different interests, and it was good business to take this more refined indoor theater and cater to a more fashionable audience in dearer seats.

For this theater a new kind of play was needed. It was smaller, had artificial lighting, fairly elaborate scenery, and scope for more music. It could offer its patrons some of the refinements of courtly entertainment. Probably Shakespeare was assigned the task of writing for it: hence the change in his manner about 1608. But also his colleagues secured the services of Beaumont and Fletcher; after 1616 Fletcher worked for nobody else. Their qualifications were obvious: they had written plays for this theater before; they were new men, not trained for, perhaps not interested in, the older type of play that had to appeal to gentleman and workman alike. Above all they were in sympathy with this new audience of gentlemen. The task of reflecting or

appealing to its aesthetic tastes and political prejudices was one they relished. As Dryden says, "They understood the conversation of gentlemen better than Shakespeare." Soon came the first of those successes that kept their reputation higher than Shakespeare's through most of the century. It was *Philaster*, presented c. 1609.

Here, as elsewhere, it is impossible to say just how the collaborators worked, but like all the Fletcher plays *Philaster* is tailor-made for an audience which liked sophisticated emotional appeal, variety of incident, and smooth, easy verse which is not without power, but which seems a little soft beside the great things of the same epoch by Shakespeare and Chapman and Jonson. *Philaster* is a new type of tragi-comedy, combining the poignancy of tragic situations with a happy ending. Out of its highly artificial plot and situations it develops a rich romantic pathos. The same is true of the famous *Maid's Tragedy*, perhaps the best Beaumont and Fletcher play. Here the central situation is the powerlessness of a man to avenge the impurity of his bride because her seducer is the King, hedged by divinity. It combines two themes with strong audience-appeal: the political theme of divine right, much in everyone's mind during the reign of James I (the Blackfriars audience would be on the whole supporters of it) and the sexual theme of female lust and fickleness, a topic treated in endless detail in Beaumont and Fletcher. We may complain about the element of pose in the characterization—everybody seems to be holding an unnatural attitude—or about the crowd-pleasing bawdiness, but we have to admit that this is an expertly made play; and some of the verse, though it is also posed and artificial as if, like one of the characters, it has found "fine new tricks to grieve," is memorable.

It is an old complaint against these writers that they "degraded woman to an object of voluptuous pursuit," and were sycophantically royalist. As for the first charge, it is true that they have no Cordelia or Miranda, and that there are some pretty indecent situations in such plays as *Valentinian, A King and No King,* and *A Wife for a Month.* And it is true that more serious writers like Middleton handled equally suggestive situations in a less provocative way. The charge has some truth in it, but we should remember the wider range of sexual reference permitted to Jacobean writers. As for the second charge, these authors were in sympathy with their class-audience, and working for a company under the official protection of King James himself. Even had they wished to they could hardly have set up as republicans. And they did not wish to.

However we feel about that, the fact remains that Fletcher's considerable poetic gifts and constructional skill, combined with that of many talented collaborators, continued for years to delight an educated public. And if it is true, as most scholars now believe, that he had a large hand in *Henry VIII,* and that Shakespeare contributed to *The Two Noble Kinsmen,* we have presumably to count among his many admirers the greatest dramatist of all.

Frank Kermode

BIBLIOGRAPHICAL REFERENCES: The standard critical edition for Beaumont and Fletcher studies is still Alexander Dyce, ed., *The Works of Francis Beaumont and John Fletcher,* 1843–1846, although this has been superseded in part by the variorum edition of the *Works* (1904 ff.), under the general editorship of A. H. Bullen. For biography and criticism see also G. C. Macaulay, *Francis Beaumont: A Critical Study,* 1883; C. N. Gayley, *Francis Beaumont, Dramatist,* 1914; *Dictionary of National Biography,* Vols. II and VII, 1921; E. K. Chambers, *The Elizabethan Stage,* Vols. III and IV, 1923; Baldwin Maxwell, *Studies in Fletcher and Beaumont, Massinger,* 1939; L. B. Wallis, *Fletcher, Beaumont and Company,* 1947; and W. W. Appleton, *Beaumont and Fletcher,* 1956.

SAMUEL BECKETT

Born: Dublin, Ireland
Date: 1906

PRINCIPAL WORKS

NOVELS: *Murphy,* 1938; *Molloy,* 1951; *Malone Meurt,* 1951 (*Malone Dies*) *L'innommable,* 1953; *Watt,* 1953.

SHORT STORIES: *More Pricks Than Kicks,* 1934.

PLAYS: *En Attendant Godot,* 1952 (*Waiting for Godot*); *All That Fall,* 1957; *Endgame,* 1958.

POEMS: *Whoroscope,* 1930; *Echo's Bones and Other Precipitates,* 1936.

Samuel Beckett, one of the most controversial and difficult writers of the twentieth century, was born in Dublin in 1906. He was educated at the Portora Royal School at Enniskillen, better remembered as Oscar Wilde's school, and received a B.A. in French and Italian from Trinity College, Dublin, in 1927. He spent the next three years as lecturer in English at the École Normale Supérieur in Paris. During this period his first book, a long poem characteristically entitled *Whoroscope*, was published. He returned to Trinity as lecturer in French in 1930 and took his M.A. there. The years 1932–1936 were spent in England or traveling extensively on the Continent. He began writing more intensively, and a long essay on Proust was followed by a collection of short stories entitled *More Pricks Than Kicks* in 1934 and one of poems called *Echo's Bones* in 1936. During these years Beckett was secretary to and a close literary associate of the man who probably influenced him most, James Joyce. In 1929 he assisted Eugene Jolas in editing a collection of critical essays on Joyce, somewhat pompously and puzzlingly entitled *Our Examination Round His Factification for Incamination of Work in Progress*, and later, in Paris, he worked with Joyce on a French translation of the "Anna Livia Plurabelle" section of *Finnegans Wake* (1939).

In 1937 Beckett settled in his adopted land, France, for good. His first two novels, *Murphy*, written in Paris before the war, and *Watt*, written in unoccupied Vaucluse during the hostilities, were the last two works he was to write in English. During 1945–1946 he worked as an interpreter and storekeeper at the Irish Red Cross Hospital at St. Lô, and was decorated for his services there. He returned to Paris in 1947 to write a trilogy in French, *Molloy, Malone Dies*, and *L'innom-*

mable. In 1952 he published his dramatic masterpiece, the baffling *Waiting for Godot*, which was enthusiastically received by Paris critics and audiences, and ran for over three hundred performances. Beckett's own translation has met with a mixed but chiefly enthusiastic response on the American and English stages

Waiting for Godot, a "tragicomedy" with only five characters and almost literally no action, has been called the crystallization of all Beckett's work. The two tramps standing by the roadside, waiting for the unknown, mysterious Godot who never comes, share the spiritual misery and hopelessness, if not the physical deformity, of most of the characters in his novels. Although the dramatic structure of this work prevents it from seeming quite as formless as the novels, which are largely composed of incidents without any logical connection, it shares their taut, poetic language, stream-of-consciousness technique, static quality, and highly personal and therefore extremely difficult symbolism. And, like them, this "bible of pessimism" is often surprisingly, indeed inexplicably, funny. It is no mere coincidence that Beckett's writings, which by the postwar period had been purged of their Irishness and rather conceited wit, are best known and appreciated in France. He shares with Sartre and Camus an intense sense of the pervasiveness of misery, solitude, paralysis of will, and, above all, the horror of nothingness. His obscure and difficult style is peculiarly suited to the portrayal of a world where, amidst obscenity and occasional blasphemy, the characters create their personal hells in the prisons of their own dark minds. If Beckett deserves to be ranked, as he sometimes is, in importance and originality with Kafka and Joyce, it is because, like them, he works to perfect a literary style suited to the probing of the innermost recesses of the human mind. His lastest play, *Endgame*, continues in this vein.

BIBLIOGRAPHICAL REFERENCES: An early introductory study is M. Nadeau, "Samuel Beckett, L'humour et le neant," *Mercure de France*, CCCXII (1951), 693–697. The underlying meanings of his work are discussed with considerable insight by Niall Montgomery in *New World Writing*, V (1954), 324–337; this article includes a bibliography. See also Edith Kern, "Drama Stripped for Inaction: Beckett's *Godot*," *Yale French Studies*, XIV (1954), 41–47; Vivian Mercier, "Beckett and the Search for Self," *New Republic*, CXXXIII (September 19, 1955), 20–21, and "Savage Humor," *Commonweal*, LXVI (1957), 88+; Anon., "Puzzling About Godot," *London Times Literary Supplement*, LV (February 10, 1956), 84; Kenneth Rexroth, "The Point Is Irrelevance," *Nation*, CLXXXII (1956), 325–328; Horace Gregory, "Beckett's Dying Gladiators," *Commonweal*, LXV (1956), 88–92; Herbert Gold, "Beckett: Style and Desire," *Nation*, CLXXXIII (1956), 397–399; Ray Briggs and William Barrett, "Samuel Beckett's World in Waiting," *Saturday Review*, XL (June 8, 1957), 14–16; and Warren Lee, "The Bitter Pill of Samuel Beckett," *Chicago Review*, X (1957), 77–87.

WILLIAM BECKFORD

Born: Fonthill-Gifford, England
Date: September 29, 1759

Died: Bath, England
Date: May 2, 1844

PRINCIPAL WORKS

NOVEL: *Vathek*, 1786.
BURLESQUES: *The Elegant Enthusiast*, 1796; *Amezia*, 1797.
MISCELLANEOUS: *Biographical Memoirs of Extraordinary Painters*, 1780; *Recollections of an Excursion to the Monasteries of Alcobaça and Batalha*, 1835.

William Beckford's father, Lord Mayor of London in 1762 and 1769, was famous for his great wealth and for the fact that he led the opposition to George III's reprehensible and arbitrary conduct toward the city and its government. Born at Fonthill-Gifford, Wiltshire, on September 29, 1759, young William Beckford had an unusual boyhood. His education was received from tutors, including the composer Mozart. At the age of eleven Beckford inherited his father's wealth. When he was twenty Beckford published *Biographical Memoirs of Extraordinary Paint*-ers, a largely humorous volume with its satirical barbs at Dutch and Flemish painters. A short-lived marriage, begun in 1783, ended with the death of Beckford's wife, Lady Margaret Gordon, in 1786. Before her death they had two children, both daughters.

Beckford's best-known book is *Vathek*, almost unique in the history of English literature, having been written originally in French. It is the story of an Arabian caliph who suffers the tortures of the damned and has a wondrous series of supernatural adventures. Beckford intended for the book to be published first in the original French, but its English translator, the Reverend Samuel Henly, published an English version prior to the appearance of the original. *Vathek* was revised twice during the author's lifetime, and some episodes did not appear until posthumous editions. Other books by Beckford are *Modern Novel Writing* (1796), published under the pseudonym of the Right Honorable Harriet Marlow; *Azemia,* published under the pseudonym of Jacquetta Agneta Mariana Jenks; *Al Raoui* (1799), and *Recollections of an Excursion to the Monasteries of Alcobaça and Batalha.*

In his lifetime Beckford was famous for his houses. The first he built, Fonthill Abbey, was eighteen years in the construction and was reputed to have cost more than a quarter of a million pounds. His second, near Bath, England, where he died May 2, 1844, was also magnificent. Beckford's later years were marred by his repeated attempts to obtain a title to add luster to his fortune. Some biographers have felt that the search for a title was the principal motivation of his life.

BIBLIOGRAPHICAL REFERENCES: J. W. Oliver, *The Life of William Beckford,* 1932; Guy Chapman, *Beckford,* 1937; Sacheverell Sitwell, *Beckford and Beckfordism,* 1930; and H. A. N. Brockman, *The Caliph of Fonthill,* 1957. As a background study see Martha P. Conant, *The Oriental Tale in England in the Eighteenth Century,* 1908.

SIR MAX BEERBOHM

Born: London, England
Date: August 24, 1872

Died: Rapallo, Italy
Date: May 20, 1956

PRINCIPAL WORKS

ESSAYS AND SKETCHES: *The Works of Max Beerbohm,* 1896; *More,* 1899; *Yet Again,* 1909; *And Even Now,* 1920; *A Variety of Things,* 1928.

FANTASIES AND SATIRES: *The Happy Hypocrite: A Fairy Tale for Tired Men,* 1897; *Zuleika Dobson,* 1911; *A Christmas Garland,* 1912; *Seven Men,* 1919; *The Dreadful Dragon of Hay Hill,* 1928.

CARICATURES: *Caricatures of Twenty-five Gentlemen,* 1896; *The Poets' Corner,* 1904; *A Book of Caricatures,* 1907; *The Second Childhood of John Bull,* 1911; *Fifty Caricatures,* 1913; *A Survey,* 1921; *Rossetti and His Circle,* 1922; *Things New and Old,* 1923; *Observations,* 1925.

MISCELLANEOUS: *Around Theatres,* 1924; *Mainly on the Air,* 1946.

One of the most "civilized" men of the twentieth century, Sir (Henry) Max(imilian) Beerbohm was born in Kensington, London, on August 24, 1872. He was the youngest child of his father's second marriage. Julius E. E. Beerbohm married sisters, the first bearing three sons and a daughter, of whom the celebrated actor Sir Herbert Beerbohm Tree was most widely known; the second bearing four daughters and a son, Max. He attended Charterhouse School, 1885–1890, and enrolled at Merton College, Oxford, in 1890, remaining there until he was graduated in 1895.

During his undergraduate days at Oxford Beerbohm seems to have

87

avoided most lectures, all athletics, and to have interested himself mainly in his position as "young man about campus," for he made his initial appearances as writer and caricaturist during his college days. He contributed to the first volume of *The Yellow Book,* in 1894, his first published caricatures having previously appeared in three issues of the *Strand Magazine* in 1892. In 1895 he accompanied Beerbohm Tree to America as secretary. Returning to London, he saw his first published book appear in 1896 under the title, *The Works of Max Beerbohm,* complete with a bibliography of his writings supplied by his publisher, John Lane. The same year also saw publication of his first book of drawings, *Caricatures of Twenty-Five Gentlemen.* In 1898, George Bernard Shaw retired as drama critic of the *Saturday Review* and appointed Beerbohm to succeed him, introducing him in phrases often quoted: "The younger generation is knocking at the door; and as I open it there steps spritely in the incomparable Max . . ." Beerbohm conducted the drama criticisms until his own retirement in 1910.

Beerbohm's time was busily filled by drawings, shown at the Leicester Galleries and later issued in book form, essays, stories, criticisms: *The Happy Hypocrite* appeared in 1897 and a second volume of essays, *More,* in 1899; *Yet Again* in 1909; *The Christmas Garland,* a perfect critical caricature-parody of literary figures, in 1912; *And Even Now* in 1920; and the Collected Edition of his writings in 1922–1928.

Various books of caricatures were also appearing, his reputation as a writer and caricaturist developing simultaneously as the obverse and reverse sides of a highly individualized personality. In 1910, Beerbohm married the talented actress, Miss Florence Kahn, who had been born in Memphis, Tennessee, and who had scored great success in Ibsen's plays. After the marriage the Beerbohms retired to the Villino Chiaro near Rapallo, Italy, where they made their home until their deaths. In 1939, Beerbohm was knighted in George VI's Birthday Honours List. Lady Florence died in Italy in 1951. In a secret ceremony only a month before Sir Max's own death on May 20, 1956, he married the British-naturalized German, Miss Elizabeth Jungman, who had been his secretary-companion and a family friend.

When Beerbohm was making his first appearances in the early 1890's, Oscar Wilde announced that he had "mastered the secret of perpetual old age." A courtly wit and satirist, Beerbohm, who seemed old when he was young, aged gracefully and carried his years as a living classic with cavalier ease. His one novel, *Zuleika Dobson,* which appeared in 1911, is a classic fantasy subtitled "An Oxford Love Story." Almost equally well-known are the short stories included in *Seven Men,* in which the "seventh man" of the stories is the author himself. Beerbohm is perhaps next in line to Charles Lamb among England's personal essayists and the master of an individualized and exquisitely disciplined prose style.

BIBLIOGRAPHICAL REFERENCES: The definitive biography is J. G. Riewald's *Sir Max Beerbohm: Man and Writer,* 1953. See also Bohun Lynch, *Max Beerbohm in Perspective,* 1921; Dixon Scott, "Max Beerbohm" in *Men of Letters,* 1916; and A. K. Tuell, "The Prose of Mr. Beerbohm," *South Atlantic Quarterly,* XXX (1931), 190–199.

APHRA BEHN

Born: Wye, England
Date: July (?), 1640

Died: London, England
Date: April 16, 1689

PRINCIPAL WORKS

PLAYS: *The Forced Marriage,* 1670; *The Amorous Prince,* 1671; *The Dutch Lover,* 1673; *The Rover,* 1677; *The Lucky Chance,* 1686; *The Emperor of the Moon,* 1687.
NOVELS: *Oroonoko, or The Royal Slave,* 1688; *Agnes de Castro,* 1688; *The Fair Jilt,* 1688; *The History of a Nun, or The Fair Vow-Breaker,* 1689.

The origins of Aphra Behn, long heralded as the first Englishwoman to become a professional writer and support herself by her pen, are controversial and obscure, and scholars still dispute over the facts available. The sketch in the *Dictionary of National Biography* states that she was the daughter of John Johnson, a barber, and his wife Amy. Another account says that she was born Aphra, or Aphara, Amis. In her childhood a relative, or possibly her foster-father, related to Lord Willoughby, was nominated to the post of Lieutenant-Governor of Surinam. He is believed to have died at sea. There is some evidence, however, that his family went to Surinam and lived there for several years. In Surinam the girl may have been the mistress of William Scot, son of regicide Thomas Scot. She is thought to have returned to England about 1658, and she married a prosperous Dutch merchant named Behn in 1665. The husband died soon afterward, possibly of the plague that swept London in 1666. In the same year Mrs. Behn became a secret agent sent by the British government to Antwerp to gather information for the English in their war against the Dutch. For her work she apparently received little credit or pay. Returning to England to straighten out her affairs, she was un-

successful and was put into a debtor's prison for an indeterminate time.

In 1670 Mrs. Behn's fortunes changed. In that year, which saw publication of *Paradise Lost* and the laureateship given to John Dryden, Mrs. Behn's first play was staged successfully at the Duke's Theater. The play was *The Forced Marriage, or The Jealous Bridegroom.* A second successful play, *The Amorous Prince,* soon followed. But Mrs. Behn's greatest triumph as a dramatist came with the production of her fourth comedy, *The Rover,* which was apparently the most popular play of the year in London, although it has not been so highly regarded since by readers as others she wrote. As the author of *The Rover,* Mrs. Behn was famous, and she became friends with Edmund Waller, John Dryden, and even the notorious Duke of Rochester, the most scandalous rake of the time. John Dryden did her the honor of publishing some of her translations from Ovid, and Sir Peter Lely, the famous painter, did her portrait. Even a second-rate take off on Molière's play *La Malade imaginaire,* was successful under the title of *Sir Patient Fancy* (1678).

During the years after 1677 Mrs. Behn wrote a great deal. After 1682 she did not write for the stage for a time, however, apparently because the Whigs had become angry at her satire of them in *The City Heiress* (1682) and in a prologue she wrote for an anonymous play entitled *Romulus and Hersilia* (1682). While abstaining from writing drama, Mrs. Behn wrote prose and verse. She returned to writing drama in 1686 and soon another comedy, *The Lucky Chance,* was on the boards. Her last play, a three-act farce entitled *The Emperor of the Moon,* was one of the earliest English plays in something other than the traditional five-act structure.

Despite the contemporary success of her drama, Mrs. Behn is better known today as the author of *Oroonoko, or The Royal Slave,* a romantic prose tale, one of several that Mrs. Behn apparently wrote. The tale is an idealized story about a Negro slave in Surinam,

but Mrs. Behn, despite the romanticization in the story, manages to keep the reader's admiration of the hero until the end. Her feat was unusual at the time, for the characters in romantic fiction of the seventeenth century tended, almost without exception, to become artificial and brittle pictures, rather than real flesh-and-blood people. Many of Mrs. Behn's tales, like her own and other typical comedies of the time, exploited sex. In her time, on the stage and in fiction, sex was a commonplace, just as it was in the life of Charles II. But the exploitation was objectionable in the eyes of people in the two centuries and more which followed her death, and it is only recently that readers and scholars, kinder to the whole Restoration period, have taken to an understanding review of her work. She died in London on April 16, 1689.

BIBLIOGRAPHICAL REFERENCES: Montague Summers edited *The Works of Aphra Behn,* 6 vols., 1915. The *Novels* were edited by Ernest A. Baker, 1913. Robert Phelps edited her *Selected Writings* in 1950. There are two recent biographies: V. Sackville-West, *Aphra Behn, The Incomparable Astrea,* 1927; and George Woodcock, *The Incomparable Aphra,* 1948. See also Harrison Gray Platt, Jr., "Astrea and Celadon: An Untouched Portrait of Aphra Behn," *Publications of the Modern Language Association,* XLIX (1934), 544–559; Edward Wagenknecht, "In Praise of Mrs. Behn," *Colophon,* Part XVIII (1934); Wylie Sypher, "A Note on the Realism of Mrs. Behn's Oroonoko," *Modern Language Quarterly,* III (1942), 401–405; and R. M. Hill, "Aphra Behn's Use of Setting," *ibid.,* VII (1946), 189–203.

HENRY BELLAMANN

Born: Fulton, Missouri
Date: April 28, 1882

Died: New York, N.Y.
Date: June 16, 1945

PRINCIPAL WORKS

NOVELS: *King's Row,* 1940; *The Floods of Spring,* 1942; *Victoria Grandolet,* 1944. POEMS: *Cups of Illusion,* 1923.

The son of George Heinrich and Caroline Bellamann, Heinrich Hauer (so christened) Bellamann at first trained as a musician, a career he

magnificently achieved before and during his success as a writer. After having studied under Isidor Philipp and Charles-Marie Widor, Bellamann held posts of importance at Chicora College for Women (1907–1924), the Juilliard Music Foundation (1924–1926), and the Curtis Institute of Music (1931–1932). He was also editor of *Overtones,* a music magazine. Probably it was his interest in music that led him to poetry, for his verse shows the influence of his long study of Debussy.

In 1907 he married the woman who was to encourage his career as a novelist and to become a novelist in her own right. Katherine Jones Bellamann also completed her husband's last, unfinished novel, *Parris Mitchell* of *King's Row* (1948). This is a sequel to *King's Row,* the book that made Henry Bellamann famous. This novel, with its large cast of characters, shows Bellamann's own peculiar and successful blend of horror story, historical sociology, and Freudian psychology. The book also made a sensational success as a motion picture.

Bellamann died suddenly of a heart attack in New York City, June 16, 1945. He was born at Fulton, Missouri, on April 28, 1882.

BIBLIOGRAPHICAL REFERENCES: There is no general criticism of Bellamann. For discussion of his books see *Book Review Digest,* 1940, 1942.

EDWARD BELLAMY

Born: Chicopee Falls, Massachusetts
Date: March 26, 1850

Died: Chicopee Falls
Date: May 22, 1898

PRINCIPAL WORKS

NOVELS: *Six to One: A Nantucket Idyl,* 1878; *Dr. Heidenhoff's Process,* 1880; *Miss Ludington's Sister: A Romance of Immortality,* 1884; *Looking Backward: 2000–1887,* 1888; *Equality,* 1897; *The Duke of Stockbridge: A Romance of Shays' Rebellion,* 1900.

SHORT STORIES: *The Blindman's World and Other Stories,* 1898.

Edward Bellamy, the son of a New England Baptist minister, was born at Chicopee Falls, Massachusetts, March 26, 1850. He was largely self-educated. Although he attended Union College for only a year as a special student, he read widely in history, politics, economics, and literature. As a young man, he wrote editorials for the *Springfield Union* and later helped establish the *Daily News.* For a year or so he wrote book reviews for the New York *Evening Post.*

While working as a newspaperman in Springfield, Bellamy began to write novels. His first work, *Six to One,* was light and romantic, but his second novel, *Dr. Heidenhoff's Process,* a work dealing with sin and a sense of guilt, was impressive enough to have William Dean Howells hail Bellamy as the literary successor to Hawthorne. But Bellamy did not find a wide public or general acclaim until the publication of *Looking Backward* in January, 1888.

Begun simply as a literary fantasy, *Looking Backward* presented a picture of a humane, scientific, and socialistic Utopia in the year 2000. The book sold fewer than 10,000 copies its first year, but then became enormously popular. Others, such as Cyrus Field Willard,

91

a Boston newspaperman, formed clubs to promote Bellamy's social ideas, clubs that soon joined in the "Nationalist Movement." Before long Bellamy became a leader in this movement, editing first the *Nationalist,* then the *New Nation,* and crusading for economic equality, human brotherhood, and the progressive nationalization of industry. Bellamy spoke and wrote frequently for his cause, at the same time working on *Equality,* a sequel to *Looking Backward* which developed more fully the socialistic institutions of the Utopia. In the meantime the movement was enormously popular, its ideas forming a large portion of the platform of the People's Party in the 1892 election.

By the time of Bellamy's death, at Chicopee Falls on May 22, 1898, the "Nationalist Movement" as a political organization had disappeared, and the People's Party had been absorbed by William Jennings Bryan and "Free Silver" in 1896. Yet Bellamy's Utopian concepts, always tinged with fantasy and human values, maintained a romantic influence on thinking young men in both America and Europe. Numerous critics complained about his lack of originality, but his ideas formed the basis of "The League for the Organization of Progress" in Europe (a group which claimed Eduard Beneš, Ramsay MacDonald, Aristide Briand, and Karl Renner as members), and Americans as diverse as Thorstein Veblen, John Dewey, and A. A. Berle, Jr. have acknowledged his influence. It is as the humane and romantic Utopian, campaigning for equality and social justice, rather than as a novelist or profound political thinker, that Bellamy is remembered and read today.

BIBLIOGRAPHICAL REFERENCES: The chief source is Arthur E. Morgan, *Edward Bellamy,* 1944, which includes a bibliography. Morgan is the editor of *The Philosophy of Edward Bellamy,* 1945, a collection of selections from Bellamy's writings together with commentary. Two useful studies appear in Vernon L. Parrington, *Main Currents in American Thought,* Vol. III, 1930; and W. F. Taylor, *The Economic Novel in America,* 1942. See also Robert L. Shurter, "The Literary Work of Edward Bellamy," *American Literature,* V (1933), 229–234.

HILAIRE BELLOC

Born: St. Cloud, France
Date: July 27, 1870

Died: Guildford, Surrey, England
Date: July 16, 1953

PRINCIPAL WORKS

ESSAYS: *On Nothing,* 1908; *On Everything,* 1909; *This and That and the Other,* 1909; *On Anything,* 1910; *On Something,* 1910; *First and Last,* 1911; *At the Sign of the Lion,* 1916; *The Free Press,* 1918; *The Contrast,* 1923; *On,* 1923; *The Road,* 1923; *Conversations with an Angel,* 1928; *Survivals and New Arrivals,* 1929; *Wandering,* 1929; *A Conversation with a Cat and Others,* 1931; *Essays of a Catholic Layman in England,* 1931 [*Essays of a Catholic*]; *The Silence of the Sea,* 1941.

NOVELS: *Emmanuel Burden,* 1904; *Mr. Clutterbuck's Election,* 1908; *A Change in the Cabinet,* 1909; *The Green Overcoat,* 1912; *The Mercy of Allah,* 1922; *Mr. Petre,* 1925; *Belinda,* 1928; *The Missing Masterpiece,* 1929; *The Postmaster-General,* 1932; *The Hedge and the Horse,* 1936.

BIOGRAPHY: *Danton*, 1899; *Robespierre*, 1901; *Marie Antoinette*, 1909; *Oliver Cromwell*, 1927; *James the Second*, 1928; *Joan of Arc*, 1929; *Richelieu*, 1929; *Wolsey*, 1930; *Cranmer*, 1931; *Napoleon*, 1932; *Charles the First, King of England*, 1933; *William the Conqueror*, 1933; *Cromwell*, 1934; *Milton*, 1935; *The Last Rally: A Study of Charles II*, 1940 [*Charles II: The Last Rally*]; *Elizabethan Commentary*, 1942 [*Elizabeth: Creature of Circumstance*].

TRAVEL SKETCHES AND IMPRESSIONS: *The Path to Rome*, 1902; *The Old Road*, 1904; *Algerian Studies and Impressions*, 1906; *Hills and the Sea*, 1906; *The Pyrenees,* 1909; *The Four Men*, 1912; *The Cruise of the "Nona,"* 1925; *Many Cities*, 1928.

HISTORY: *The Historic Thames*, 1907; *The Eyewitness*, 1908; *The French Revolution*, 1911; *The Last Days of the French Monarchy*, 1916; *The House of Commons and the Monarchy*, 1920; *The Campaign of 1812 and the Retreat from Moscow*, 1924; *Miniatures of French History*, 1925; *A History of England*, 1925–1941; *Six British Battles*, 1931; *The Tactics and Strategy of the Great Duke of Marlborough*, 1933; *Characters of the Reformation*, 1936; *The Crusade*, 1937; *Monarchy: A Study of Louis XIV*, 1938 [*Louis XIV*]; *The Great Heresies*, 1938.

POEMS: *Verses and Sonnets*, 1896; *Verses*, 1910; *More Peers*, 1911; *Sonnets and Verse*, 1923; *Ladies and Gentlemen*, 1932.

MISCELLANEOUS: *The Servile State*, 1912; *Europe and the Faith*, 1920; *The Jews*, 1922; *The Catholic Church and History*, 1926; *The Question and the Answer*, 1932.

One of the most prolific writers of the century (Joseph) Hilaire (Pierre) Belloc was the son of a French father and an English mother. Born at St. Cloud, France, on July 27, 1870, he was sent to school in England and remained in England most of his life, becoming a British subject in 1903.

Belloc began writing poems and essays at an early age. Always interested in politics, he was elected to Parliament as a Liberal from South Salford in 1906 and again in 1910. He abandoned active politics to begin, with two life-long friends, G. K. Chesterton and Cecil Chesterton, a new political review called *New Witness*, which first appeared in 1911. In the review Belloc and Cecil Chesterton attacked the current English governmental system and promoted ideas for a unified Europe. (Belloc always revered Napoleon for the latter's effort to create a unified Europe.)

Besides his ties to France and to the Continent, Belloc was an ardent Roman Catholic. For thirty years or more, he and G. K. Chesterton propounded arguments for Roman Catholicism to the intellectuals of England. Belloc began his intellectual crusade with *The Path to Rome*, an account of a walking trip he took from Toul, in northern France, down through Switzerland and northern Italy to Rome. In this book he tried to demonstrate the importance and relevance of the Catholic faith along the way. His view of history, in his many biographies and historical works, was strongly and directly infused with a Roman Catholic point of view. Belloc treated the Reformation as an unfortunate accident and the Enlightenment as a serious mistake, whereas he venerated the Middle Ages. In spite of his proselytizing, Belloc pleaded his case with a vast store of knowledge, charm, and humor; he once claimed that the fact that most British public lavatories were built underground could be attributed to the ultimate effects of the Reformation.

Belloc's lighter side was usually expressed in his verse, especially in his humorous poems for children. His prose style was distinguished by enormous clarity and lucidity; despite a total output of 153 books, he took pains with every sentence and word. He was interested in the derivations of words and in the many connections between French and English.

Belloc was also one of the most provocative essayists of the first half of the twentieth century. While he lived, his home in the English countryside was often full of young intellectual visitors. His writing and his conversation covered the full range of political, social, and religious experience, and he stood out as one of the most vigorous, energetic, and lucid minds of his age, even though many of his particular doctrines and ideas have not been followed by the young intellectuals he was anxious to reach. He died in Guildford, Surrey, on July 16, 1953.

BIBLIOGRAPHICAL REFERENCES: The authorized biography is Robert Speiaght, *The Life of Hilaire Belloc,* 1957. Eleanor and Reginald Jebb, *Testimony of Hilaire Belloc,* 1956, is useful for its domestic picture and the presentation of Belloc's attitudes, points of view, and conversation. See also C. C. Mandell and Edward Shanks, *Hilaire Belloc: The Man and His Work,* 1916; Patrick Braybrook, *Some Thoughts on Hilaire Belloc,* 1924; Robert Hamilton, *Hilaire Belloc,* 1948; Sister M. Madeleva, "Belloc as a Biographer," *Bookman,* LXII (1931), 607–612; Raymond Las Vergnas, "Une personalité anglo-française: Hilaire Belloc," *Revue des Deux Mondes,* VIII Per. 28 (1935), 401–422; Osbert Burdett, "Hilaire Belloc," *London Mercury,* XXX (1935), 133–142; and Anon., "Hilaire Belloc," *London Times Literary Supplement,* LVI (February 8, 1957), 73–74.

JACINTO BENAVENTE Y MARTÍNEZ

Born: Madrid, Spain
Date: August 12, 1866

Died: Madrid
Date: July 14, 1954

PRINCIPAL WORKS

PLAYS: *El nido ajeno,* 1894 (*The Strange Nest*); *Los malhechores de bien,* 1905 (*Perverters of Good*); *Los intereses creados,* 1907 (*The Bonds of Interest*); *Señora Ama,* 1908; *La malquerida,* 1913 (*The Passion Flower*).

Jacinto Benavente y Martínez, who was born in Madrid on August 12, 1866, began writing plays in 1894 for Spanish theatergoers who were accustomed to the artificiality and melodrama of Echegaray. After some experience with youthful puppet plays, brief appearances before the public as an actor, and a season as a circus

clown on European tour, this son of a Madrid physician offered a manuscript to a theatrical manager who had been one of his father's patients. *The Strange Nest,* produced in 1894, had no thesis, no action, and no emotion. It merely satirized upper and middle-class Madrid society. The author concentrated on the rich because, as he ex-

94

plained, the poor had troubles enough, and he did not admire a dramatist who could find humor in poverty. The comedy had a chilly reception. A second attempt at social satire, *Gente conocida (People You Know)*, was better received in 1896. From then until 1902, the end of his first period, Benavente wrote twenty-two plays that held a magnifying glass over the vices of society, but without ever offering a solution. Though he translated Ibsen, as well as Shakespeare and Molière, the more recent dramatists of France were his chief models, especially Henri Lavedan.

In 1903 Benavente adopted a new technique in *La noche de sábado (Saturday Night)*. Less realism, more idealism, and a feminine slant characterized this work. Most of the plays that followed it were set outside Spain, sometimes in imaginary countries. The well-intentioned women who try to make over the morals and lives of others were his target in one of his greatest plays, *Los malhechores de bien*, in 1905. Tradition had it that the first night audience considered it antireligious and walked out of the Lara Theater, but one of those present recently denied that legend.

Two years later, along with ten other plays, long and short, and all produced, came *The Bonds of Interest* in the tradition of the Italian *commedia dell'arte*. It synthesizes the dramatist's genius, his poetry, his idealism, and his irony and skepticism. Crispín, the chief character, is Benavente's greatest male creation. A later play about him, *La ciudad alegre y confiada (The Happy, Confident City)*, was, like most sequels, less successful in 1916, though its patriotic theme evoked some enthusiasm.

Benavente turned to the rural regions of Castile for two of his masterpieces, written in the dialect of the country. The psychological drama *Señora Ama,* the dramatist's favorite, presents his greatest feminine character, a country woman who does not protest her husband's infidelity while she thinks she can give him no children, but who is quick to defend family and inheritance after she has a child. Its picture of ignorance, vice, and corruption existing even outside big cities caused one critic to observe that virtue in Benavente's plays is usually embodied in the women. His men are vain, selfish, and interested in amusement, the sort of reputation Benavente himself acquired when he came to Hollywood, a little man with heavy make-up to conceal his age. But as a realist, he never made any of his characters entirely evil, and he himself had many redeeming features.

In 1913, the year of his election to the Spanish Academy, he wrote another play with the same rural setting, the outstanding *The Passion Flower*. While the first two acts are melodrama, the final action is transferred to the soul of the father. This most moving of his tragedies is the favorite of theatergoers. In English translation, it has had over five hundred performances and was made into a motion picture.

Unfortunately, it represents the high point of Benavente's career. Though two or three plays a year followed, for a total of nearly two hundred, the tendency of the dramatist to moralize or become symbolic proved his downfall. Certainly none of his later plays contributed greatly to his winning of the Nobel Prize for literature in 1922. In 1928 one of the weakest, *Para el cielo y los altares (For Heaven and the Church)*, was forbidden by Dictator

Rivera, who saw in it a criticism of Alfonso XIII, though the author insisted he had Russia in mind.

Benavente was also successful in writing comedies for children. In 1909 he founded a Children's Theater in Madrid. Among the charming plays he wrote for it was *El príncipe que todo lo aprendió en los libros* (*The Prince who Learned Everything from Books*), presented in 1919. For such plays, and for his three great plays in which he showed himself a faithful recorder of contemporary society, Benavente deserves a place in the history of the Spanish stage, whose outstanding figure he was for a period of ten years. He died in Madrid on July 14, 1954.

BIBLIOGRAPHICAL REFERENCES: For critical studies of Benavente in English see Isaac Goldberg, *The Drama of Transition*, 1922; Walter Starkie, *Jacinto Benavente*, 1924; A. F. G. Bell, *Contemporary Spanish Literature*, 1925; and Ernest Boyd, *Studies from Ten Literatures*, 1925. Spanish studies include Federico de Onís, *Jacinto Benavente: estudio literario*, 1923; Angel Lázaro, *Jacinto Benavente: de su vida y de su obras*, 1925, 1935; S. Córdoba, *Benavente desde le conocí*, 1954; and I. S. Estevan, *Jacinto Benavente y su teatro*, 1954.

STEPHEN VINCENT BENÉT

Born: Bethlehem, Pennsylvania
Date: July 22, 1898

Died: New York, N.Y.
Date: March 13, 1943

PRINCIPAL WORKS

POEMS: *Five Men and Pompey*, 1915; *Young Adventure*, 1918; *Heavens and Earth*, 1920; *Tiger Joy*, 1925; *John Brown's Body*, 1928; *Ballads and Poems, 1915–1930*, 1931; *A Book of Americans*, 1933 (with Rosemary Carr Benét); *Burning City*, 1936; *Western Star*, 1943.

SHORT STORIES: *The Barefoot Saint*, 1929; *The Devil and Daniel Webster*, 1937; *Thirteen O'Clock*, 1937; *Johnny Pye and the Fool Killer*, 1938; *Tales Before Midnight*, 1939; *Twenty-five Short Stories*, 1943.

NOVELS: *The Beginning of Wisdom*, 1921; *Young People's Pride*, 1922; *Jean Huguenot*, 1923; *Spanish Bayonet*, 1926; *James Shore's Daughter*, 1934.

Stephen Vincent Benét was born in Bethlehem, Pennsylvania, on July 22, 1898. His father, Colonel J. Walker Benét, was the third generation of the family to make a career of the army. Himself interested in literature, he left his mark on his children—William Rose Benét, Stephen Vincent Benét, and Laura Benét. The young Stephen started his career as a writer by winning prizes from *St. Nicholas Magazine*. He spent his youth mostly on army posts and went to school in Georgia and California. From Yale University he won his B.A. degree in 1919 and his M.A. in 1920. While at Yale he numbered among his friends Thornton Wilder, Archibald MacLeish, and Philip Barry. During his senior year he served as editor of the *Yale Literary Magazine*. He also studied at the Sorbonne in France where he met his wife, Rosemary Carr, also a poet. In 1926 he went again to France, this time to study on a Guggenheim Fellowship for two years and to produce his famous American epic poem of the Civil War, *John Brown's Body*, which was awarded the Pulitzer Prize for poetry in 1929. Outstanding for its historical exactness and sense of patriotism, this book-length narrative poem has become an American classic.

Stephen Vincent Benét was the recipient of many honors besides the Pulitzer Prize. In 1923 his "King David" won the poetry prize in the *Nation* magazine. In 1932 he won the Shelley Memorial award and in 1933 the Roosevelt Medal of the Roosevelt Memorial Association for his contribution to American letters.

Shortly before entering Yale, Benét published in 1915 a volume entitled *Five Men and Pompey*, a series of six dramatic monologues in verse. In 1918 he published *Young Adventure*, a book of poems. His first novel, *The Beginning of Wisdom*, was published in 1921 after his return from Paris. "King David," "The Ballad of William Sycamore, 1790–1880," and *Jean Huguenot*, a novel, appeared in 1923. In 1925 he published a collection of poems entitled *Tiger Joy*. In 1933, with his wife

Rosemary Carr Benét, he published *A Book of Americans*, a collection of poems for children. This was followed in 1936 by *Burning City*, poems reflecting national themes and the decade of crisis in which they were written.

He was the author of such excellent short stories as "Johnny Pye and the Fool Killer" and "The Devil and Daniel Webster." This last story, which first appeared in a collection entitled *Thirteen O'Clock*, has had an interesting subsequent history: it was rewritten as a play, then as a musical (with music by Douglas Moore), and finally as a motion picture entitled *All That Money Can Buy*. Benét is the author of another musical play *The Headless Horseman*, for which Douglas Moore also wrote the music. After his death in New York City in 1943 his collected radio scripts were published under the title of *We Stand Alone* (1945). *Western Star*, the first part of an unfinished narrative on American history, is complete in itself. Published posthumously in 1943, it won the Pulitzer Prize the following year.

BIBLIOGRAPHICAL REFERENCES: There is no full-length biographical or critical study. For briefer articles see Robert M. Lovett, "The American Conflict," *New Republic*, LIV (1928), 51–52; Harriet Monroe, "A Cinema Epic," *Poetry*, XXXIII (1928), 91–96; S. R. Daniels, "A Saga of the American Civil War," *Contemporary Review*, CXLVI (1934), 466–471; Christopher La Farge, "The Narrative Poetry of Stephen Vincent Benét," *Saturday Review of Literature*, XXVII (1944), 106–108; and Paul L. Wiley, "The Phaeton Symbol in *John Brown's Body*," *American Literature*, XVII (1945), 231–242.

ARNOLD BENNETT

Born: Hanley, Staffordshire, England
Date: May 27, 1867

Died: London, England
Date: March 27, 1931

PRINCIPAL WORKS

NOVELS: *A Man from the North*, 1898; *The Grand Babylon Hotel*, 1902; *Anna of the Five Towns*, 1902; *Leonora*, 1903; *The Gates of Wrath*, 1903; *A Great Man*

97

1904; *Teresa of Watling Street*, 1904; *Sacred and Profane Love*, 1905; *Whom God Hath Joined*, 1906; *The Old Wives' Tale*, 1908; *Buried Alive*, 1908; *Clayhanger*, 1910; *Helen with the High Hand*, 1910; *The Card*, 1911 [*Denry the Audacious*]; *Hilda Lessways*, 1911; *The Regent*, 1913 [*The Old Adam*]; *The Price of Love*, 1914; *These Twain*, 1915; *The Lion's Share*, 1916; *The Pretty Lady*, 1918; *The Roll Call*, 1918; *Mr. Prohack*, 1922; *Lilian*, 1922; *Riceyman Steps*, 1923; *Elsie and the Child*, 1924; *Lord Raingo*, 1926; *The Strange Vanguard*, 1928 [*The Vanguard*]; *Accident*, 1929; *Imperial Palace*, 1930.

SHORT STORIES: *Tales of the Five Towns*, 1905; *The Grim Smile of the Five Towns*, 1907; *The Matador of the Five Towns*, 1912; *The Woman Who Stole Everything*, 1927; *The Night Visitor*, 1931.

REMINISCENCES AND JOURNALS: *The Truth About an Author*, 1903; *Things That Have Interested Me*, 1921; *Second Series*, 1923; *Third Series*, 1925; *The Journals of Arnold Bennett*, 1932–1933.

To be an artist, dedicated unselfishly to his art, was hardly the goal which Arnold Bennett established for himself. He was a merchant of words, frankly writing for money, but writing with extraordinary facility and keen observation. That he should have become a writer at all was almost a freak of destiny; that he should be remembered as a notable one is almost as strange. Yet out of a welter of pot-boilers and hack-work his writing rose now and again to a peak which supported him on an equal eminence with the best of his Edwardian contemporaries—Conrad, Galsworthy, and Wells. *The Old Wives' Tale* alone supplies reason enough for gratitude that Arnold Bennett lived and wrote.

(Enoch) Arnold Bennett was born on May 27, 1867, near Hanley, North Staffordshire, one of his immortal Five Towns. His father was a solicitor who had arrived at that station in life after the odd preliminaries of pottery manufacture and pawnbroking. Neither his family nor his early schooling was of the type to provide much impetus towards an interest in letters. It was intended that he, too, should become a solicitor; and, after attending Newcastle Middle School, he settled down in his father's office to study law and serve as a clerk.

This state of affairs did not last long. A family disagreement occurred—Bennett's father had a reputation as a martinet—and young Arnold, at the age of twenty-one, left the Five Towns behind for life in London. At first a solicitor's clerk, vaguely intent on reading law, he soon found other interests. Previously, in the Five Towns, he had dabbled in journalism, contributing to a local newspaper; once in London, he found the time to read voraciously and was influenced by the remark of a friend to think of writing as a means of livelihood. The die was finally cast when, about 1893, the *Yellow Book* accepted a story and *Tit Bits* gave him a twenty-guinea prize. His days as a solicitor's clerk came abruptly to an end, and an aspiring writer was born.

His first journalistic job was on the staff of *Woman*, where he did such unexpected stints as writing beauty tips and advising the lovelorn. A period of freelancing followed, during which he wrote anything and everything which seemed salable. A move to Bedfordshire was followed by another, in 1900, to France, where he lived for eight years. By 1903 he was writing a half million words a year, eclipsing in industry even the indefatigable Trollope, and had won acceptance as a popular novelist. Though sharp in money matters, he was far from being a miser; on the contrary, he enjoyed spending money freely, and he acquired something of a reputation as a ladies' man. In 1907 he married a French actress, Marguerite Hebrard, with whom he lived until their separation in 1921; two years later he became interested in another actress, Dorothy Cheston, who later mothered his only child, Virginia Bennett. Later on, each of the women felt inspired to provide the public with an account of her domestic alliance with the author.

Despite its vitality, Bennett always hated the ugly industrial Midlands from which he had sprung and which provided him with his best literary themes. He is the best historian of the Five Towns; and characters like Constance and Sophia Baines in *The Old Wives' Tales* are unforgettable, both as individual characters and as representatives of the lower middle class, preoccupied with industry, patriotism, and thrift. Of this book, Bennett shrewdly observed that it was the very best that he could do. Though such others novels as *Clayhanger* and *Riceyman Steps* have genuine appeal, none equals Bennett's masterpiece in objective realism, re-creation of place, and skillful evocation of the passage of time.

More colorful than most of his own characters, Arnold Bennett lived life to the hilt, enjoying the clothes, the yacht, and the fine hotels which he earned for himself with his success. Yet he could set these things calmly aside, as during World War I, when called upon to do propaganda work for the government. He toured the United States in 1911, and he found ease and satisfaction during his life in Paris; but at home or abroad, the Five Towns never completely relaxed their hold upon him, either as a man or as a writer. He died in London on March 27, 1931, of typhoid fever.

BIBLIOGRAPHICAL REFERENCES: The most complete and authoritative biography is *Arnold Bennett*, by Reginald Pound, 1952. Earlier studies include L. G. Johnson, *Arnold Bennett of the Five Towns*, 1924; Marguerite Bennett, *Arnold Bennett*, 1925; *idem*, *My Arnold Bennett*, 1931; Rebecca West, *Arnold Bennett Himself*, 1931; and Dorothy C. Bennett, *Arnold Bennett*, 1935. See also Virginia Woolf, *Mr. Bennett and Mrs. Brown*, 1924; Geoffrey West, *The Problem of Arnold Bennett*, 1932; J. B. Simons, *Arnold Bennett and His Novels*, 1936; George Lafourcade, *Arnold Bennett: A Study*, 1939; Wilbur L. Cross, "Arnold Bennett" in *Four Contemporary Novelists*, 1930; Walter Allen, *Arnold Bennett*, 1949; and Louis Tellier, "Arnold Bennett, ou de la mutilation voluntaire," *Revue Anglo-Americaine*, XI (1933–1934), 303–321.

GEORGES BERNANOS

Born: Paris, France   *Died:* Neuilly, Paris
Date: May 5, 1888   *Date:* July 5, 1948

PRINCIPAL WORKS

NOVELS: *Sous le soleil de Satan*, 1926 (*The Star of Satan*); *Journal d'un curé de campagne*, 1936 (*The Diary of a Country Priest*).

POLITICAL ESSAYS: *Les Grands Cimetières sous la lune,* 1938 (*A Diary of My Times*); *Lettre aux Anglais,* 1942 (*Plea for Liberty*).

(Paul Louis) Georges Bernanos, born in Paris on May 5, 1888, spent his childhood in the tiny village of Fressin in Pas de Calais and later attended Vaugerard College, where under Jesuit tutelage he was grounded in a militant Catholicism. This was later deepened and intensified by his studies in law and letters at the University of Paris and L'Institut Catholique. Before beginning his career as writer he fought in World War I and worked for an insurance company. His earliest political publications were savage anti-democratic articles in *Action française, Revue universelle,* and other royalist periodicals. Bernanos believed that democracy was based on materialism leading to political and economic tyranny; therefore he advocated restoration of the French monarchy. Following a serious illness, during which he was preoccupied with sin, mysticism, and mortality, he published *The Star of Satan,* a novel based partly on experiences of the Curé d'Ars, a deeply troubled priest who experienced hallucinations. Most of the novels which followed dealt also with priests—sick and dying, losing their faith, flagellating themselves, or otherwise symboliz-

ing Bernanos' conviction that the Church needed a spiritual cleansing before it could save Western civilization. He won the Grand Prix du Roman of the French Academy for *The Diary of a Country Priest,* the agonized tale of a priest who dies for and from the sins of his village.

In 1936, while in the Balearic Islands, he grew indignant over the atrocities committed by Franco in the Spanish Civil War, and in 1938 he exiled himself to Brazil in bitter protest against the Munich Pact. He supported the Free French led by his old classmate de Gaulle, and returned to France only in 1946. *A Diary of My Times* is a polemic against Franco, which gained Bernanos a great deal of credit among non-Catholics. He died at Neuilly, near Paris, July 5, 1948, of cirrhosis of the liver and was survived by his wife, three sons and three daughters. Despite the fact that a very bitter sense of sin mars his spiritual message, his chief works will no doubt survive because of their intensely dramatic style and keen psychological analyses of religious faith and mysticism.

BIBLIOGRAPHICAL REFERENCES: As yet no full study of Bernanos has appeared in English. For French readers there is Gaëtan Picon, *Georges Bernanos,* 1948. Three useful brief articles are Ben Ray Redman, "Indignant Royalist," *Saturday Review of Literature,* XIX (November 26, 1938), 11; C. P. Bruehl, "Censor of his Age," *Commonweal,* XXIX (1939), 515–518; and Donat O'Donnell, "The Faust of Georges Bernanos," *Orpheus,* II (1949), 73–89.

AMBROSE BIERCE

Born: Horse Cave Creek, Ohio
Date: June 24, 1842

Died: Mexico
Date: 1914(?)

SHORT STORIES: *Nuggets and Dust,* 1872; *Tales of Soldiers and Civilians,* 1891 (reissued as *In the Midst of Life,* 1898); *Can Such Things Be?* 1893; *Battle Sketches,* 1930.

SATIRES: *The Fiend's Delight,* 1872; *Cobwebs from an Empty Skull,* 1873; *Fantastic Fables,* 1899.

POEMS: *Black Beetles in Amber,* 1895; *Shapes of Clay,* 1903.

ESSAYS AND CRITICISM: *The Cynic's Word Book,* 1906 (reprinted as *The Devil's Dictionary,* 1911); *Write It Right,* 1909; *The Shadow on the Dial,* 1909.

TRANSLATION: *The Monk and the Hangman's Daughter,* 1892 (with G. A. Danziger).

Ambrose (Gwinett) Bierce, journalist, short-story writer, and cynical wit, was born in Meigs County near Chester, Ohio, June 24, 1842, on the site of a campmeeting of parents he labeled, characteristically, "unwashed savages." He disappeared into even greater obscurity at the age of seventy-two, having crossed into Mexico during the revolution; one legend is that he was attached for a time to Pancho Villa's staff.

He was educated in a country school with no later university training, although much of his literary fame rests upon a severely impeccable style that depends upon grammatical succinctness for effect. In 1861 he entered the Union army as a volunteer private but rose to the rank of lieutenant and was finally brevetted major. He was twice wounded, once severely in the head at Kennesaw Mountain. A lifelong interest in strategy developed from his experience as a mapmaker while touring the West under General Hazen. Bierce's exacting and unromantic accounts of the Civil War in *Tales of Soldiers and Civilians* (a collection also called *In the Midst of Life*) imaginatively record this period. These tales, in which his feeling for unusual descriptions of nature heightens the intellectual precision of his plots, gave a more inexorable twist to "life's ironies" than did Thomas Hardy's novels and verse during the same period.

After the Civil War Bierce lived in California and wrote for several San Francisco journals and papers. He deserted his wife and three children in 1871 to go to England for four years. There he was associated with the magazine *Fun* and wrote *The Fiend's Delight* and *Cobwebs from an Empty Skull,* a collection of satirical fables. He resumed his journalistic career in California in 1876, acting for the next twenty-one years as the arbiter of literary taste—the unchallenged Dr. Johnson—of the West Coast while writing columns for Hearst's *Sunday Examiner.* Sent to Washington to oppose the railroad lobby of Collis P. Huntington, Bierce wrote for the New York *American* and *Cosmopolitan* until 1909; he produced little between that year and his departure for the Mexican border in 1913.

Bierce's first short story, "The Haunted Valley" (1871), was published in *Overland Monthly.* His earliest sketches, humorous accounts of the mining camps, were published in *Nuggets and Dust.* In these tales there is marked resemblance to Bret Harte; but gradually Poe, whom Bierce greatly admired, became the greater influence on his work, even to the extent of his disavowing the novel as a fictional mode. In 1881 he began printing in periodical form much of the material later published as *The Cynic's Word Book* (now known as *The Devil's Dictionary*). His mordant brevity in this book ("Politeness: The most acceptable hypocrisy.") is the most philosophical form of the columnist's quip that later became a mainstay of American journalism.

Bierce's first volume of satiric verse, *Black Beetles in Amber*, followed his translation, with G. A. Danziger, of *The Monk and the Hangman's Daughter*, from the German of Richard Voss. His second verse collection was *Shapes of Clay*. These did not carry the literary force and conviction of his *Write it Right*, a critical listing of stylistic faults, or of his frank essays in *The Shadow on the Dial*.

Some of the finest short stories in English have been judged Bierce's main contribution to American literature. In "An Occurrence at Owl Creek Bridge" and "The Death of Halpin Fraser" he rivaled Poe, Bierce being less macabre but more forthright in his mockery of circumstance. Above all he had the power to surprise the reader by a deft ending that hung on the edge of impossibility as in "A Tough Tussle" and "The Night Doings at Deadman's". The very title of *Can Such Things Be?* best expresses Bierce's attitude towards the critical events of life that inspire the writer of fiction. The *Collected Works* in twelve volumes (1909–1912) was his legacy to a world he felt incapable of discrimination; in it he published completely everything he had ever written in what may have been a last gesture of defiance.

BIBLIOGRAPHICAL REFERENCES: The standard edition is *The Collected Works of Ambrose Bierce*, 12 vols., 1909–1912. A more recent edition is *The Collected Writings of Ambrose Bierce*, edited by Clifton Fadiman, 1946.

The standard biography is Carey McWilliams, *Ambrose Bierce: A Biography*, 1929. See also Walter Neale, *The Life of Ambrose Bierce*, 1929; C. Hartley Grattan, *Bitter Bierce: A Mystery of American Letters;* and Joseph Noel, *Footloose in Arcadia: A Personal Record of Jack London, George Sterling, Ambrose Bierce*, 1940. Also useful are *The Letters of Ambrose Bierce*, edited by Bertha C. Pope, 1921. For criticism see Van Wyck Brooks, *Emerson and Others*, 1927; Percy H. Boynton, *More Contemporary Americans*, 1927; Arthur M. Miller, "The Influence of Edgar Allan Poe on Ambrose Bierce," *American Literature*, IV (1932), 130–150; George Snell, "Poe Redivivus," *Arizona Quarterly*, I (1945), 49–57; Clifton Fadiman, "Portrait of a Misanthrope," *Saturday Review of Literature*, XXIX (1946), 11–13, 61–62; and Marcus Klein, "San Francisco and Her Hateful Ambrose Bierce," *Hudson Review*, VII (1954), 392–407.

ROBERT MONTGOMERY BIRD

Born: Newcastle, Delaware
Date: February 5, 1806

Died: Philadelphia, Pennsylvania
Date: January 23, 1854

PRINCIPAL WORKS

NOVELS: *Calavar*, 1834; *The Infidel*, 1835; *The Hawks of Hawk-Hollow*, 1835; *Nick of the Woods, or The Jibbenainosay*, 1837; *Peter Pilgrim*, 1838; *The Adventures of Robin Day*, 1839.

PLAYS: *The Gladiator*, 1831; *The Broker of Bogota*, 1834.

Robert Montgomery Bird was born in Newcastle, Delaware, February 5, 1806. He took his M.D. degree from the University of Pennsylvania Medical School in 1827 and practiced briefly before being drawn to the theater. His first great stage success was *The Gladiator*, a play written for the celebrated actor, Edwin Forrest. The story of a Thracian captive in Rome, its themes are family love and personal honor. Bird's soundest play, and the most successful, was *The Broker of Bogota*, first performed in New York in 1834. This is a domestic tragedy about a money-lender whose heart is broken by a faithless son. Like other early plays, it reflects Bird's sustained interest in Latin America.

Throughout his career as a playwright Bird had a working arrangement with Forrest which did not sufficiently protect his own interests; while the actor made a fortune from the plays, Bird earned very little. Consequently, he broke with Forrest and turned to the novel. Two early books dealt with the adventures of Cortez in Mexico. Then Bird began to use frontier materials. His outstanding literary achievement was *Nick of the Woods*, the story of a revenge-mad Quaker who slinks through the Kentucky woods slaughtering Indians. In this novel Bird portrayed the Indian as a barbarian and rejected the noble savage conception of the Red Man.

In 1841 Bird became a professor at the new Pennsylvania Medical College, but he continued to engage in journalism until his health broke under the strain of his labors. He died in Philadelphia, January 23, 1854.

BIBLIOGRAPHICAL REFERENCES: The basic study of Bird is Clement E. Foust, *The Life and Dramatic Works of Robert Montgomery Bird*, 1919. An interesting companion volume is Mary Mayer Bird, *Life of Robert Montgomery Bird, Written by his Wife*, edited by C. Seymour Thompson, 1945. See also A. H. Quinn, "Dramatic Works of Robert Montgomery Bird," *Nation*, CVII (1916), 136–137.

BJØRNSTJERNE BJØRNSON

Born: Kvikne, Norway
Date: December 8, 1832

Died: Paris, France
Date: April 26, 1910

PRINCIPAL WORKS

PLAYS: *Mallem Slagene*, 1857 (*Between the Battles*); *Halte Hulda*, 1858 (*Lame Hulda*); *Kong Sverre*, 1861 (*King Sverre*); *Sigurd Slembe*, 1862 (*Sigurd the Bas-*

tard); *Maria Stuart i Skotland*, 1864 (*Mary Stuart in Scotland*); *De Nygifte*, 1865 (*The Newly Wedded Pair*); *Sigurd Jorsalfar*, 1872 (*Sigurd the Crusader*); *Redaktören*, 1874 (*The Editor*); *En Fallit*, 1874 (*A Bankruptcy*); *Kongen*, 1877 (*The King*); *Leonarda*, 1879; *Det nye System*, 1879 (*The New System*); *En Hanske*, 1883 (*A Glove*); *Over Ævne, Part I*, 1883 (*Beyond Human Power*); *Geografi og Kaerlighed*, 1885 (*Geography and Love*); *Over Ævne, Part II*, 1895; *Paul Lange og Tora Parsberg*, 1898 (*Paul Lang and Tora Parsburg*); *Naar den ny Vinblomstrer*, 1909 (*When the Vineyards are in Bloom*).

NOVELS: *Synnöve Solbakken*, 1857; *Arne*, 1858; *En glad Gut*, 1860 (*A Happy Boy*); *Fiskerjenten*, 1868 (*The Fisher Maiden*); *Magnhild*, 1877; *Det Flager i Byen og paa Havnen*, 1884 (literally, *Flags are Flying in Town and Port*; English translation, *The Heritage of the Kurts*); *Paa Guds Veje*, 1889 (*In God's Way*).

POEMS: *Digte og Sange*, 1870 (*Poems and Songs*); *Arnljot Gelline*, 1870.

Bjørnstjerne Bjørnson was a journalist, a critic, a playwright, a novelist, and a poet—one of the most prolific writers that Norway has produced. His works of fiction were widely read and widely translated; his revolutionary drama paved the way for the triumph of the Norwegian stage under his talented friend and compatriot, Henrik Ibsen. Yet Bjørnson was not, for all these accomplishments, essentially the literary man, the artist. His vocation was Norway. All his work, of which this literary activity was only a part, was singlemindedly dedicated to the attainment of Norwegian cultural and political independence. His early tales and novels were written to present to the urban reading public of greater Christiania (now Oslo) a sympathetic portrayal of the *Bonde*, Norway's sturdy yeoman-agricultural class all in the interests of national unity. His early plays, based on the legends of Norway's Viking greatness, were heroic dramas, attempts to stimulate national pride. His more mature dramatic efforts, the social drama which he left for Ibsen to develop, were written to provide a repertory of native Norwegian plays for a newly formed national theater. His poems were songs in celebration of the beauties of Norway, hymns of national devotion, one of which, "Ja vi elsker dette landet (Yes We Love This Land)" has become the Norwegian national anthem.

This land he loved was a land he knew well. He was born on December 8, 1832, in the small northeastern parish of Kvikne, where his father was pastor. Following his father's transfer, he grew up in Nesset in Romsdal, a district noted for the beauty of its mountains and fjords. In his twelfth year he was sent to school at Molde, the seaport and capital of Romsdal. At this time Norway, though it had been free from the control of Denmark for thirty years, was united with Sweden and under allegiance to the Swedish king, a political union resented by the more nationally conscious of the Norwegians. At Molde, Bjørnson, reading the sagas of Norway's heroic age and studying the works of the patriot-poet Henric Wergeland (1808–1845), developed his determination to do his part to end the alliance and to create a Norway that was wholly free.

He came to Christiania in 1850 to attend the University of Norway, but his interest in poetry and the stage was stronger than his interest in scholarship. He entered the field of journalism and struck his first blow in the cause for cultural independence with a series of articles insisting that incumbent Danish actors be replaced by native Norwegians on the Christiania stage.

This demand was eventually to be carried out. In the meantime, Bjørnson, having written a play of his own, *Between the Battles,* was gaining enough stature in drama circles to be selected as the director of the theater at Bergen, where, for two years (1857–1859), he was successful in putting his nationalistic concepts into action. There a second play of his was produced; during this period his first three works of fiction, *Synnöve Solbakken, Arne,* and *A Happy Boy* were published as well.

In 1860 he received a government stipend to travel to Rome. This was the first of six extended trips he was to take abroad (he visited the United States on a lecture tour in 1880–1881), and with each foreign visit his nationalistic ideas were to be tempered and broadened, though never shaken. The immediate result of this maturing influence was that he left off the writing of his heroic plays and began his drama of social commentary. *The Newly Wedded Pair* was presented in 1865, and nine years later *The Editor* and *A Bankruptcy* were finally produced.

These were followed by *The King* in 1877. They were all controversial, but they were all finally accepted, and with them the theater of Ibsen was launched.

His first trip marked, also, a change in his career. He continued to write for the stage—his finest play, the Second Part of *Beyond Human Power* coming as late as 1895—and he continued to produce novels and poems. But gradually his literary interests decreased as he became more and more involved in public life. Tall, erect, with a mane of blond hair and a tremendous voice, the archetype Viking warrior, he was made the living symbol of his nationalist creed. He was in demand everywhere as an orator, and he went gladly wherever he was invited.

In 1903 his achievements as a writer were honored when he received the Nobel Prize for literature; his greatest award, however, an award for the achievements of his entire life, came two years later when Norway became a completely independent nation for the first time in five centuries. Five years later, his mission accomplished, the foremost of Norwegian nationalists died quietly in Paris, on April 26, 1910.

BIBLIOGRAPHICAL REFERENCES: The novels were edited by Edmund Gosse in 1894, and the *Poems and Songs* were translated by A. Hubbell Palmer in 1915. A recent study is Harold Larson, *Björnstjerne Björnson: A Study in Norwegian Nationalism,* 1944. Brief sketches and appraisals appear in Georg Brandes, *Critical Studies,* 1899; Ashley Dukes, *Modern Dramatists,* 1911; Edwin Björkman, *Voices of Tomorrow: Critical Studies of the New Spirit in Literature,* 1913; Georg Brandes, *Creative Spirits of the Nineteenth Century,* 1923; and A. R. Marble, *The Nobel Prize Winners in Literature, 1901–1931,* 1932.

R. D. BLACKMORE

Born: Longworth, Berkshire, England
Date: June 7, 1825

Died: Teddington, England
Date: January 20, 1900

NOVELS: *Clara Vaughan*, 1864; *Cradock Nowell*, 1866; *Lorna Doone: A Romance of Exmoor*, 1869; *The Maid of Sker*, 1872; *Alice Loraine*, 1875; *Springhaven*, 1887; *Perlycross*, 1894.

POEMS: *Poems by Melanter*, 1853; *The Bugle of the Black Sea*, 1855; *The Fate of Franklin*, 1860; *Fringilla*, 1895.

TRANSLATIONS: The *Georgics* of Vergil, 1862.

R(ichard) D(oddridge) Blackmore's father was an Anglican curate. When Blackmore's mother died shortly after his birth at Longworth, Berkshire, England, on June 7, 1825, the father sent him to live with a grandmother. Blackmore was an unusually shy person and was reticent about his life, so that relatively little is known about him. The reason for his shyness may have been a tendency toward apoplexy that became evident even during his childhood and plagued him throughout life. After attending Blundell School, Blackmore attended Exeter College, Oxford. Following graduation from Oxford, he studied law and was admitted to the bar in 1852. While he was studying law he married. Although his wife was an invalid during most of their married life, her death was a severe blow to Blackmore when she died thirty-six years later.

Dissatisfied with the practice of law soon after he had been admitted to the bar, Blackmore turned to teaching. Teaching, too, proved unsatisfactory. Fortunately for him, an inheritance and poor health gave him the excuse to retire to a life of writing and gardening. As early as his student days at Oxford, Blackmore had begun writing poetry, publishing under the pseudonym of Melanter. Two volumes of poems "by Melanter" appeared in 1854 and 1855. They received little attention from either critics or readers. In 1862 Blackmore published a translation of Vergil's *Georgics*, an event which seems to have settled him on a career as a writer. His first novel, *Clara Vaughan*, was followed by a second, *Cradock Nowell*. His acknowledged masterpiece, *Lorna Doone*, attracted little attention for more than a year after publication. A rumor began, however, that the novel was about the family of the Marquis of Lorne, who had recently married into the family of Queen Victoria. Suddenly sales began to soar; as the novel became known, critics and the reading public became enthusiastic over it. The novel, in the romantic tradition, exploited the regional background of the country Blackmore had known as a boy. The book became, over the years, a minor classic of Victorian fiction, typical of the romantic novelists' attention to action, setting, and the use of the imagination. Other novels by Blackmore are *The Maid of Sker* and *Springhaven*, the latter a tale of England at the time of Napoleon.

Like other minor historical novelists of the nineteenth century, Blackmore has been compared to Sir Walter Scott. The comparison, as is true in most such cases, is unfair to both authors. Blackmore had his own style, and so did Scott. The outstanding characteristic of Blackmore's fiction is the humor and detail which he lavished on many of his minor characters. A noticeable defect is his tendency toward the melodramatic.

People who knew Blackmore declared that gardening, not writing, was his first love. He had a garden full of rare plants, even growing peaches, which then, as now, are a rarity in Britain outside a hothouse. Although he worked alone, Blackmore had many admirers among literary figures of Victorian England and commanded a faithful reading public. He died at Teddington, Middlesex, England, January 20, 1900, and four years later a group of admirers, including James M. Barrie, Thomas Hardy, and Rudyard Kipling, placed a memorial window to him in Exeter Cathedral.

BIBLIOGRAPHICAL REFERENCES: For biography and criticism see Quincy G. Burris, *Richard Doddridge Blackmore: His Life and Novels*, Illinois Studies in Language and Literature, XV (1930); also F. J. Snell, *The Blackmore Country*, 1906.

WILLIAM BLAKE

Born: London, England
Date: November 28, 1757

Died: London
Date: August 12, 1827

PRINCIPAL WORKS

POEMS (Lyric, Symbolic, Didactic): *Poetical Sketches*, 1783; *There Is No Natural Religion*, c. 1788–1794; *All Religions Are One*, c. 1788–1794; *Songs of Innocence*, 1789; *The Book of Thel*, 1789; *The Marriage of Heaven and Hell*, c. 1790; *The French Revolution*, 1791; *For the Sexes: The Gates of Paradise*, 1793; *Visions of the Daughters of Albion*, 1793; *America, A Prophecy*, 1793; *Songs of Experience*, 1794; *Europe, A Prophecy*, 1794; *The First Book of Urizen*, 1794; *The Song of Los*, 1795; *The Book of Ahania*, 1795; *The Book of Los*, 1795; *Milton*, 1804–1808; *Jerusalem, The Emanation of the Giant Albion*, 1804–1820; *Laocoön*, c. 1820; *The Ghost of Abel*, 1822.

ILLUSTRATIONS AND ENGRAVINGS: *The Complaint and the Consolation, or Night Thoughts*, by Edward Young, 1797; *Blair's Grave*, 1808; *The Prologue and Characters of Chaucer's Pilgrims*, 1812; *The Pastorals of Virgil*, 1821; *Illustrations of the Book of Job*, 1825; *Illustrations of Dante*, 1827.

ESSAY: *A Descriptive Catalogue*, 1809.

William Blake, the greatest visionary poet in English, was born on November 28, 1757, the second son of James Blake, a London native of obscure origin who was a hosier by occupation. A few remarkable incidents of Blake's childhood have been recorded, among them the manifestation of his first known vision, when, at the age of four, he beheld God's head at a window and was seized with a fit of screaming. On other occasions he informed his parents that during his walks about the fields he had seen angels; and once he returned to say that the prophet Ezekiel had appeared to him under a tree. He was so fiery-tempered that his father preferred not to send him to school, where he might be whipped, but chose to give him elementary instruction at home. At the age of ten he was enrolled in Henry Pars' drawing school, from which, at fourteen, he advanced to a formal apprenticeship in the engraver's trade under James Basire. He was already writing verse, and several

107

of the pieces collected in *Poetical Sketches* were composed when he was only twelve. Although he passed his early youth in studious application to his technical work, he found time also to increase his familiarity with literature. He read modern philosophers and the poets, far outdistancing his Swedenborgian father. In 1778, having qualified as an engraver, he began to accept commissions from booksellers and was quickly able to assert his professional competence.

In 1781, jilted by a certain Polly Wood, he fell in love with Catherine Boucher; reaching an understanding almost at once, he married her the following year. At their first meeting she had been suddenly overwhelmed with the intuitive knowledge that she had met her destined husband, and she had been forced to leave the room to keep from fainting. The match so easily made was in all respects ideal: Blake taught her to read, write, sketch, and paint, and she became skillful enough to assist his labors. In his transports of artistic and visionary rapture, which often roused him from sleep and sent him irresistibly to his worktable, she would sustain him by sitting immobile for hours at his side. He found that her presence helped him subdue his wilder emotions, thus bringing order to his mind. Perhaps no artist ever had a more affectionately docile wife.

In the closing decade of the century, Blake, working almost frenziedly under the pressure of visionary experience while perfecting his mastery of artistic media, published his lyric *Songs of Innocence* and *Songs of Experience* in such a way as to co-ordinate his different talents. Using a writing substance impervious to acid, he prepared for each page a copper plate inscribed in reverse with the text of a poem and with a decorative frame, and having etched the plate he made impressions in color, afterward in some cases adding other tints by hand. This method he called illuminated printing. He employed it further in issuing his didactic and prophetic works, from *There Is No Natural Religion,* to *The Ghost of Abel.* His final masterpieces, however, the illustrations for the Book of Job and his illustrations of Dante, were engraved from watercolor drawings, as were the illustrations for Young's *Night Thoughts,* Virgil's *Pastorals,* and for numerous other books.

In 1800, Blake formed an association with William Hayley, who engaged him to illustrate a *Life of Cowper,* and he moved from London to Felpham, Sussex, in order to work there with Hayley. The scheme proved unsatisfactory; after three years he went back to London to set up as a publisher of his own writings, for which the commercial arrangement with Hayley had made no provision. Since his works were not in demand, his new venture failed; and as a result he and his wife lived in straitened circumstances, subsisting on commissions from Thomas Butts, already for some years Blake's patron. Butts was the first Blake collector and enthusiast. For an exhibition of his works in 1809, Blake issued a *Descriptive Catalogue* in which, analyzing his painting of the Canterbury Pilgrims, he expounded his artistic theories.

Few traces exist of Blake's activities between 1809 and 1818; but between the latter year and his death in London on August 12, 1827, he emerged as one of the most respected artists in London, where he had many friends, including the well-known painter John Linnell. In this period he attained his zenith as a designer and engraver. Since his lifetime, his work has become more and more a topic of specialized study, and the mystical symbolism of his prophetic books in particular has been subjected to much exegesis.

BIBLIOGRAPHICAL REFERENCES: The standard text is *The Complete Writings of William Blake, with All the Variant Readings*, edited by Geoffrey Keynes, 1957. This edition supersedes the same editor's *The Writings of William Blake*, 3 vols., 1925, and *The Poetry and Prose of William Blake*, 3 vols., 1927. *The Letters of William Blake* were edited by Geoffrey Keynes, 1956. An earlier edition of the *Works* was edited by E. J. Ellis and William Butler Yeats, 3 vols., 1893. *The Prophetic Writings of William Blake* have been edited by D. J. Sloss and J. P. R. Wallis, 2 vols., 1926.

Biographical studies include Alexander Gilchrist, *Pictor Ignotus: The Life of William Blake*, 1863, now available in Everyman's Library; Arthur Symons, *William Blake*, 1907; E. J. Ellis, *The Real Blake*, 1907; Basil de Selincourt, *William Blake*, 1909; H. L. Bruce, *William Blake in This World*, 1926; Osbert Burdett, *William Blake*, English Men of Letters Series, 1926; Mona Wilson, *The Life of William Blake*, 1927; Thomas Wright, *The Life of William Blake*, 2 vols., 1929; Kathleen Raine, *William Blake*, 1951; H. M. Margoliouth, *William Blake*, 1951; and Jacob Bronowski, *William Blake, 1757–1827: A Man without a Mask*, 1954.

Critical studies of Blake as artist and man of letters include J. B. Wicksteed, *Blake's Vision of the Book of Job*, 1910; Darrell Figgis, *The Paintings of William Blake*, 1925; Laurence Binyon, *The Engraved Designs of William Blake*, 1926; Denis Saurat, *Blake and Milton*, 1920, and *Blake and Modern Thought*, 1929; S. Foster Damon, *William Blake: His Philosophy and Symbols*, 1922; Max Plowman, *An Introduction to the Study of Blake*, 1927; Helen C. White, *The Mysticism of William Blake*, 1927; Emily S. Hamblen, *On the Minor Prophecies of William Blake*, 1930; M. O. Percival, *William Blake's Circle of Destiny*, 1938; Mark Shorer, *William Blake: The Politics of Vision*, 1946, a work important for its study of Blake's relationship to the political and social thought of his time; Adrian Van Sindren, *Blake, the Mystic Genius*, 1949; Hal Saunders White, *A Primer of Blake*, 1951; Stanley Gardner, *Infinity on the Anvil: A Critical Study of Blake's Poetry*, 1954; J. B. Wicksteed, *William Blake's Jerusalem*, 1954; G. M. Pedersen, *The Religion of William Blake*, 1954; Hazard Adams, *Blake and Yeats: The Contrary Vision*, 1955; H. C. Goddard, *Blake's Fourfold Vision*, 1956; Laura DeWitt James, *William Blake: The Finger on the Furnace*, 1956; and William Gaunt, *Arrows of Desire: A Study of William Blake and His Romantic World*, 1956.

VICENTE BLASCO IBÁÑEZ

Born: Valencia, Spain
Date: January 29, 1867

Died: Mentone, France
Date: January 28, 1928

PRINCIPAL WORKS

NOVELS: *Arroz y tartana*, 1894 (*Rice and Canoe*); *Flor de Mayo*, 1895 (*The Mayflower*); *La barraca*, 1898 (*The Cabin*); *Cañas y barro*, 1902 (*Reeds and Mud*); *La catedral,* 1903 (*The Shadow of the Cathedral*); *Sangre y arena,* 1908 (*Blood and Sand*); *Los cuatro jinetes del apocalipsis,* 1916 (*The Four Horsemen of the Apocalypse*); *Mare Nostrum,* 1917.

Vicente Blasco Ibáñez is an example of a writer better known and more greatly admired outside his country than in it. Except in his earliest works, where he was truly regional in writing about Valencia, his work is classified by his countrymen as journalistic, based upon any contemporary fad or interest.

He was born January 29, 1867, in Valencia. Perhaps his Aragonese blood gave him a tenacious and rebellious temperament which characterizes his writing as much as does the dreamy idealism of his Valencian environment, for the pen that reinforced his idealism earned him several imprisonments while he was still in school. He was a political exile in France in 1889 for anti-royalist propaganda, and in Italy in 1898 for upholding Cuba's right to revolt. On January 28, 1928, he died in Mentone, France, exiled for attacking Dictator Primo de Rivera. Not until Spain became a republic was his body brought home.

Running away from home at the age of sixteen, Blasco Ibáñez entered the literary world as secretary in the fiction factory of the Spanish writer of thrilling adventure yarns, Manuel Fernández y González. Later he resigned, thinking he might as well sign what he wrote, but his earliest efforts found no publisher. Much later, after he became famous, a number of his earlier pseudo-historical novels appeared in Spain and in translation in American magazines to reveal him as a belated romanticist. His best works are *The Cabin* and the naturalistic *Reeds and Mud,* realistic tragedies of Valencian life.

To escape the tag of regionalist, he began a series of controversial novels attacking social evils, and set in different Spanish cities. The anti-clerical *The Shadows of the Cathedral* contains wonderful descriptions of Toledo. *La bodega* (*Fruit of the Vine*), set in Jerez and published in 1905, attacks the evils of drinking. The very popular *Blood and Sand* attacks Seville's bull fighting. Its motion picture version, with Rudolph Valentino, gave Blasco Ibáñez world renown.

Enlarging his ambition, to devote a novel to each Latin American nation, he was interrupted by World War I, but two novels about the war, *The Four Horsemen of the Apocalypse* and *Mare Nostrum,* made him a best-seller in the United States. Seven of his novels have been dramatized and seven have motion picture versions. He composed too fast, but he was a good observer and he wrote colorfully and with suspense. Most of his novels show vigorous forcefulness in spite of occasional grammatical inaccuracy and crudeness.

BIBLIOGRAPHICAL REFERENCES: Except for John Dos Passos, *Rosinante to the Road Again,* 1922, very little has been written on Blasco Ibáñez in English. See E. Zamacois, *Vicente Blasco Ibáñez,* 1910; C. Pitollet, *Blasco Ibáñez: ses romans et le roman de sa vie,* 1921; R. Martínez de la Riva, *Vicente Blasco Ibáñez,* 1929; and José A. Balseiro, *Vicente Blasco Ibáñez, hombre de acción y de letras,* 1935 (San Juan, P.R.); *idem, Blasco Ibáñez, Unamuno, Valle Inclán y Baroja,* 1949.

GIOVANNI BOCCACCIO

Born: Paris (?), France
Date: 1313

Died: Certaldo, Italy
Date: December 21, 1375

PRINCIPAL WORKS

NOVELS AND TALES: *Il Filocolo, Ameto,* c. 1335–1340; *L'Amorosa Fiammetta,* 1340–1345; *Il Decamerone,* 1348–1353; *Il Corbaccio,* c. 1355.

POEMS: *Il Filostrato,* c. 1335–1340; *La Teseida, L'Amorosa Visione, Il Ninfale Fiesolano,* 1340–1345.

Giovanni Boccaccio was born in 1313, possibly in Paris and probably the illegitimate son of a respectable Florentine merchant then living in France. Boccaccio called himself a citizen of Florence. His father reared him well, giving him a sound education. He studied with Giovanni da Strada, a celebrated grammarian in Florence, and by his own account was from his earliest years devoted to poetry. He tells us he was writing verses at the age of seven years. Very early, however, he was apprenticed to an eminent merchant with whom he remained for six years, and with whom he seems to have traveled about Italy and France. Since the boy was deeply interested in studies, his father next apprenticed him to a professor of canon law, again for six years. Baccaccio was still dissatisfied, still desired to study literature, and felt that the entire twelve years were ill spent.

About 1333 he went to Naples, apparently to resume preparation for a mercantile career, for by that time he had given up the study of law. In Naples he lived in an atmosphere of gaiety emanating from the court of King Robert of Anjou. King Robert had an interest in the arts and kept about him many men of letters, Petrarch among them, though Boccaccio did not meet the great poet until a later time.

He did, however, meet Maria d'Aquino, the natural daughter of King Robert. He saw her first on Easter Eve, 1341, in the Church of San Lorenzo, and they immediately fell in love. Already married, Maria only after much delay gave in to Boccaccio's amorous demands. Though Maria died long before Boccaccio, he cherished her memory until his death and he immortalized her in his works as Fiammetta. He is supposed to have written at her request his first long novel, *Il Filocolo.*

About 1341 Boccaccio reluctantly returned to Florence, apparently to be with his aged father. Between 1340 and 1344, when he was able through the intercession of a friend to go back to Naples, Boccaccio wrote three works treating of Maria: *L'Amorosa Visione* in verse, *Ameto* in prose and verse, and *L'Amorosa Fiammetta* in prose. The last work appears to be the semi-fictional account of his association with Maria.

In 1344 Boccaccio returned to Naples, then ruled by Giovanna, granddaughter of King Robert, and was warmly received because of his literary reputation. It is doubtful if he was in Florence during the plague of 1348, but about that time the death of his father called him back to Florence and he entered the diplomatic service of the republic. Boccaccio's acquaintance with

Petrarch dated from 1350, when as a diplomat he entertained the great scholar-poet during the latter's visit to Florence. The two became good friends, and until Petrarch's death Boccaccio considered the elder man his mentor as well as his friend.

By 1353 the *Decamerone*, begun in 1348, was completed, and this work earned for Boccaccio the title of father of Italian prose. The work consists of one hundred stories supposed to have been told at the rate of ten a day over a period of ten days by seven young ladies and three young men driven from Florence by a plague to take refuge in an abandoned villa near the city. The young people pass the time in their exile by playing games, taking walks, reading, and, in the evenings, telling stories. Each day a ruler is chosen to govern the group that day and to pass judgment on the tales told that evening.

The one hundred stories range from highest pathos to coarsest licentiousness. Many of them were borrowed from other literatures, especially the French, but they have become Boccaccio's own. A description of the plague precedes the stories; a masterpiece of epic grandeur and vividness, it ranks with the writings of Thucydides, Defoe, and Manzoni. The prose of the *Decamerone* is flexible, tender, supple, precise. It renders all the shades of feeling of the Italian nation from the coarse laugh of cynicism to the pathetic sigh of hopeless love. This prose has had great influence on later Italian writers, notably Machiavelli, Aretino, and Bandello. The stories themselves have permeated Western literature. In English literature, Chaucer, Lydgate, Dryden, Keats, and Tennyson are among those who have used the *Decamerone* as a source.

After 1360 Boccaccio's writings were in Latin, and his reputation grew to rank him second only to Petrarch by the time of his death on December 21, 1375, at Certaldo. He was buried there in the Church of Saints Jacopo and Filippo.

BIBLIOGRAPHICAL REFERENCES: There are several reliable biographical-critical studies of Boccaccio: J. A. Symonds, *Giovanni Boccaccio as Man and Author*, 1895; Edward Hutton, *Giovanni Boccaccio,* 1910; T. C. Chubb, *The Life of Giovanni Boccaccio*, 1930; and Catherine Carswell, *The Tranquil Heart: Portrait of Giovanni Boccaccio*, 1937. See also Joseph Wood Krutch, *Five Masters: A Study in the Mutations of the Novel*, 1930; and H. D. Sedgwick, "Boccaccio, An Apology," *Yale Review*, II (1913), 327–342.

ANICIUS MANLIUS SEVERINUS BOETHIUS

Born: Rome, Italy
Date: c. 480

Died: Pavia, Italy
Date: 524

PRINCIPAL WORK

PHILOSOPHY: *De Consolatione Philosophiae*, 523 (*The Consolations of Philosophy*).

Born in Rome about A.D. 480, the philosopher Boethius, who was also called Boetius and Boece, was the last of the Romans and the first of the Scholastics. The family must have been patrician for his father was a consul in 487. At his father's death, Boethius became the ward of the senator Memmius Symmachus and later married his guardian's daughter Rusticiana. Theodoric, Ostrogoth ruler of Rome from 500 on, made Boethius consul in 510. Later, either because of his Christian beliefs or because he was conspiring with Emperor Justin the Elder of the Eastern Roman Empire, Boethius was arrested, imprisoned in Pavia, and executed there without trial in 524. Before his death his sons had been appointed consuls.

While still in favor, Boethius had translated and commented on some of Aristotle's writings, introducing him to the Western World in a work on which a great part of the educational practices of the Middle Ages was based. He had also written treatises on many subjects: Arithmetic, Logic, and especially Music (*De musica*). Other works, perhaps falsely attributed to him, dealt with Christian theology and immortalized him upon his death as the martyred Saint Severinus.

While imprisoned in Pavia, Boethius wrote five books in prose and verse entitled *The Consolations of Philosophy*, a work derived from Plato and Aristotle. In one dialogue, an attempt to find why evil exists in a world where God is the highest good and the truest happiness, Lady Philosophy tells him that the absence of self-knowledge is the source of his weakness. She also comments on the practices of the Goddess Fortuna. This work has influenced thinking ever since. King Alfred translated it into Anglo-Saxon (published at Oxford in 1698). Chaucer made an English version of part of this dialogue, and Queen Elizabeth tried her hand at translating it. Before the invention of printing, translations of Boethius existed in a dozen languages. The earliest English versions in print are by George Colville (London, 1556) and by Viscount Preston (London, 1695).

BIBLIOGRAPHICAL REFERENCES: For translation and critical commentary see H. R. James's translation of the *Consolation*, 1897; H. F. Stewart, *Boethius*, 1891, 1918; E. K. Rand, *Founders of the Middle Ages*, 1928; and H. R. Path, *The Traditions of Boethius*, 1935.

MATTEO MARIA BOIARDO

Born: Scandiano, Italy   *Died:* Scandiano
Date: c. 1440   *Date:* 1494

PRINCIPAL WORK

POEM: *Orlando Innamorato*, 1486–1495.

Matteo Maria Boiardo was the essence of Italian nobility, a successful courtier, soldier, and scholar. Born at Scandiano, near Reggio nell' Emilia, in 1440 or 1441, he found a patron in a wealthy family and was educated at the University of Ferrara. In 1478 he was appointed governor of Reggio. He held several high military posts and took part in the wars against the Venetians. Boiardo did most of his writing to amuse the court of Duke Hercules d'Este, at Ferrara.

The primary influence on Boiardo's

113

Italian sonnets and lyrics was the writing of the ancients, chiefly Herodotus and Apuleius. A skilled scholar in Latin and Greek, he wrote several eclogues in Latin. His major work was the *Orlando Innamorato*, of which he wrote only the first two books, the rest being written by Niccolo degli Agostini after Boiardo's death, which occurred at Scandiano in 1494. Boiardo's verse romance, outstanding in early Italian literature, has a richness of characterization and a variety of scene that provided a basis for the more famous *Orlando Furioso* of Ariosto.

Ariosto's work, written in puristic Tuscan tradition, became the more popular after its appearance in 1515. In 1541, Francesco Berni's revised edition of *Orlando Innamorato* was better received. Some modern critics have claimed that Boiardo's poem is superior to Ariosto's, a judgment made possible by the discovery of Boiardo's manuscripts in the nineteenth century. In any event, the poem, along with Boiardo's many sonnets and shorter poems, is part of the grand tradition of fifteenth century poetry, as was his gentle and courtly life a model of the existence of the fifteenth century Italian nobleman.

BIBLIOGRAPHICAL REFERENCES: Boiardo's complete *Opere* were edited by Angelandrea Zottoli, 2 vols., 1936–1937. *Studi su Matteo Boiardo* contains material published in commemoration of the 400th anniversary of his death, 1894. For biographical and critical studies see Anthony Panizzi, *Boiardo*, 1830–1831; E. W. Edwards, *The Orlando Furioso and Its Predecessor*, 1924; Virgilio Procacci, *La vita e l'opera di Matteo Maria Boiardo*, 1931; and A. Zottoli, *Di Matteo Maria Boiardo*, 1937.

NICOLAS BOILEAU-DESPRÉAUX

Born: Paris, France
Date: November 1, 1636

Died: Paris
Date: March 13, 1711

PRINCIPAL WORKS

POEMS: *Satires*, 1666–1716; *Épîtres*, 1669–1701 (Epistles); *L'Art poétique*, 1674; *Le Lutrin*, 1674.

CRITICISM: *Réflexions critiques sur Longin*, 1693; *Dialogue des héros de roman*, 1713.

Born in Paris on November 1, 1636, Nicolas Boileau-Despréaux, the fifteenth child of a Parliament clerk, was left motherless at two years, a circumstance contributing to the critical and satirical attitude toward life revealed in his work. Educated at the Collège de Beauvais and at the Sorbonne, he abandoned the law for the Church and then left the Church for literature. Thus he followed his brother Gilles, translator of Epictetus, rather than his brother Jacques, canon of Ste. Chapelle.

At twenty-four he published his first satire in imitation of Juvenal; there were eleven others, all more or less didactic verses on the sad state of French letters, together with precepts for their improvement. He strongly preferred the satires of Molière, with whom he, Racine, Chapelle, and Fure-

114

tière joined in an informal literary society. In 1664 he wrote *Dialogue des héros de roman*, first published in 1713, a scathing attack on the outlandish heroic romances of La Calprenède, Mlle. de Scudéry, and others. These early polemical works were followed by his more serious and carefully polished *Epistles;* these brought him to the attention of Louis XIV, who summoned him to court and pensioned him.

These experiences emboldened him to become the leading neo-classicist of his day, the "legislateur du Parnasse" with his verse masterpiece, *L'Art Poétique.* This work, in the tradition of Aristotle, Horace, and Vida, has often been misunderstood as establishing absolute and universal laws for literature. Actually, it is advice for an age based on a prejudiced survey of French literature, an imitation of classical writers, and the sifting out of the best characteristics of each genre: ". . .

zealous for the right, a strict observer of each noble flight, from the fine gold I separate the alloy." *L'Art Poétique* was quickly followed by *Le Lutrin,* a mock epic later imitated by Pope, and a translation of Longinus' *On the Sublime.* The *Œuvres du Monsieur D . . .* (1674) led three years later to his appointment as historiographer by Louis XIV and to his membership in the Académie Française in 1684.

Boileau's satires involved him in bitter controversies during his lifetime. The Jesuits, particularly, found satire to be immoral and un-Christian, and prevented publication of the definitive edition of the collected works which Boileau prepared just before his death in Paris on March 13, 1711. However, he was the greatest literary influence of his age, and when Berriat Saint-Prix came to edit the definitive modern edition in 1830 he found that, in little more than a century, Boileau had been republished some 350 times.

BIBLIOGRAPHICAL REFERENCES: Many editions of Boileau's works have been published. There is no extended or satisfactory study of Boileau in English. For biography and criticism see P. Morillot, *Boileau,* 1891; G. Lanson, *Boileau,* 1891; M. T. Noss, *La Sensibilité de Boileau,* 1932; J. R. Miller, *Boileau en France au dix-huitième siècle,* 1942; and Daniel Mornet, *Nicholas Boileau,* 1942.

JOHAN BOJER

Born: Orkdalsøra, Norway
Date: March 6, 1872

Died: Oslo, Norway
Date: July 3, 1959

PRINCIPAL WORKS

NOVELS: *Et folketog,* 1896 (*A Procession*); *Den evige krig,* 1899 (*The Eternal Strife*); *Moder Lea,* 1900 (*Mother Lea*); *Troens magt,* 1903 (*The Power of a Lie*); *Fangen som sang,* 1913 (*The Prisoner Who Sang*); *Den store hunger,* 1916 (*The Great Hunger*); *Den siste viking,* 1921 (*The Last of the Vikings*); *Vor egen stamme,* 1925 (*The Emigrants*); *Folk ved sjøen,* 1929 (*The Everlasting Struggle*).

Though he has had no work translated into English since 1940, Johan Bojer enjoyed great popularity in America during the 1920's. Galsworthy, Tagore, Hergesheimer, and Cabell all praised his fiction, and after his reputation in America began with the translation of *The Great Hunger* in 1919, four more of his novels were translated by 1920. The change in public taste brought about by the depression made his optimistic realism seem anachronistic amidst the disillusion of Farrell, Dos Passos, and Steinbeck; but his hopefulness was not superficially grounded. Bojer himself had passed through economic and intellectual difficulties in a Norway dominated by the skeptical thought of Ibsen and Strindberg.

The son of a servant girl who was unable to care for him, Bojer was born at Orkdalsøra, March 6, 1872, and was brought up in the country by foster parents. He had little schooling, but at eighteen he went to a free military school for non-commissioned officers at Trondheim. After three years there he scraped out a living at such various occupations as fisherman, salesman, and advertising copywriter. He had his first great success at twenty-four, when he published his first novel, *A Procession*. Able at last to devote all his energies to writing, he married in 1899, traveled about Europe, and sent occasional articles back to Norwegian newspapers until he settled permanently in Norway in 1907.

Always a novelist of ideas, Bojer read widely and constantly. His central theme generally concerns an individual, usually an idealist, in conflict with a hostile environment. His first two novels, *A Procession* and *The Eternal Strife*, describe how idealists are corrupted when they try to be effectual in the democratic political system. Bojer suggests that moral idealism and party politics are natural enemies and, like the Ibsen of *An Enemy of the People*, leaves little hope for the good man in an evil world.

In his third novel, however, Bojer found the values that were, particularly in his later work, to lead him away from moral skepticism. *Mother Lea* presents a peasant woman and her healthy family as normative humanity and ironically contrasts them with a politician who, unable to choose between dreams and action, ruins his family.

His much-admired *The Great Hunger* reconsiders the character of the romantic idealist. The hero, Peer Holm, tries with tremendous energy to win a victory over the hostile natural world. Dissatisfied with all his scientific achievements, reduced to poverty by his enemies, he saves himself from bitter defeat by secretly sowing his corn in his enemy's field, not out of Christian love, but simply to assert man's superiority to the forces which destroy him. Peer's acceptance of man's necessarily unsatisfactory relationship with an imperfect world contrasts sharply with the earlier portrait of a romantic idealist in *The Prisoner Who Sang*. The hero of that novel, in trying to encompass all possible human experience, assumes so many disguises that he eventually finds that he has lost his identity; he ends in prison, singing to himself as he madly imagines himself emperor of the universe.

Bojer's spirit of compromise with life, the sanity of accepting the harshness of one's environment with dignity and courage, is best exemplified by Mother Lea and the peasantry in *The Last of the Vikings* and *The Emigrants*. Knowing nothing of politics and science, knowing only the dangers of daily living, they cannot envision grandiose, delusive schemes for con-

116

quering a universe that will always be more powerful than man, and which will never pay much attention to his aspirations.

BIBLIOGRAPHICAL REFERENCES: The main work on Bojer in English is Carl Gad, *Johan Bojer*, 1920. See also Allen W. Porterfield, "Bojer's Conquest of America," *Bookman*, LVIII, 287–294.

GEORGE HENRY BORROW

Born: East Dereham, England
Date: July 5, 1803

Died: Oulton Broad, England
Date: July 26, 1881

PRINCIPAL WORKS

AUTOBIOGRAPHY: *Lavengro; the Scholar, the Gipsy, and the Priest,* 1851; *The Romany Rye,* 1857.

TRAVEL SKETCHES AND IMPRESSIONS: *The Zincali, or an Account of the Gipsies in Spain,* 1841; *The Bible in Spain,* 1843; *Wild Wales,* 1862.

TRANSLATIONS: *Targum, or Metrical Translations from Thirty Languages,* 1835.

PHILOLOGY: *Romano Lavo-Lil, or Word-Book of the Romany,* 1874.

George Henry Borrow, born at East Dereham, Norfolk, on July 5, 1803, was a *rara avis* of English letters, a man whose life was even more incredibly romantic and picaresque than any of his works. The son of an itinerant recruiting officer, he picked up a catch-as-catch-can education, mainly in Edinburgh. William Taylor, Southey's friend, interested the boy in learning languages, in which he developed a marvelous facility. His curious career as a traveler, autobiographer-novelist, and philologist began when, after a brief period as a solicitor's apprentice in Norwich and a frustrating career as a publisher's hack in the late 1830's, he was sent to Spain as a distributing agent of the British and Foreign Bible Society. He recorded his adventures with colorful embellishments in *The Zincali* and *The Bible in Spain.* In St. Petersburg, he published *Targum,* a curious sort of anthology and literary *tour-de-force* including translations from some thirty languages. Widely hailed as a genius, Borrow became a literary lion and developed a vanity bordering on megalomania. With his royalties and money from Mary Clarke, whom he married in 1840, he bought an estate at Oulton Broad where he permitted gipsy encampments. After a passionate attachment to the British gipsies, he published the first dictionary of their language, followed by two strange and fascinating narratives of gipsy life, *Lavrengo* and its sequel, *The Romany Rye,* which were reprinted in scholarly editions in the early years of the twentieth century. These accounts —actually autobiography written in the form of a picaresque novel—are now his chief claim to an odd niche in English literary history, but they were not very popular in his day, a fact which led him to fulminate bitterly against the British reading public. Borrow protested the genteel novels of the Victorians, especially the "humbug and Philistinism" of Bulwer-Lytton and Disraeli. He became even more a rebellious bohemian, lived a riotous life among the Welsh gipsies, and wrote *Wild Wales* and *Romano Lavo-Lil*. The immense range of his learning can be seen in his translations of the New Testament into Manchu, the Gospel of Luke into Gitanos, "Bluebeard" into Turkish, and into English the Danish *Death of Balder,* a German *Faustus,* the Cambrian *Sleeping Bard,* Russian folk tales, and other works.

He was a powerfully built, striking figure, given to dramatic stances and highly-colored rhetoric, except for gradually increasing periods of gloomy depression. Though by no means a great artist, he ranks with such figures as Occleve, Skelton, Dekker, and others among the vigorous, eccentric, and vastly entertaining men of letters on the second or third shelf of English literature. In his old age he settled in Suffolk, where he died on July 26, 1881, at Oulton Broad. His five main works constitute a highly readable but very untrustworthy and loosely connected autobiography.

BIBLIOGRAPHICAL REFERENCES: The standard edition is *The Works of George Borrow,* edited by Clement K. Shorter, 16 vols., 1923–1924. There is a bibliography compiled by T. J. Wise, *A Bibliography of the Writings in Prose and Verse of George Henry Borrow,* 1912. There are several worth-while studies of Borrow: W. I. Knapp, *Life, Writings, and Correspondence of George Borrow,* 2 vols., 1899; H. Jenkins, *The Life of George Borrow,* 1912; Edward Thomas, *George Borrow,* 1912; C. K. Shorter, *George Borrow and his Circle,* 1913; Samuel M. Elam, *George Borrow,* 1929; and Martin D. Armstrong, *George Borrow,* 1950. See also Shane Leslie, "George Borrow in Spain," *Dublin Review,* CLV (1914), 42–59.

JAMES BOSWELL

Born: Edinburgh, Scotland
Date: October 29, 1740

Died: London, England
Date: May 19, 1795

PRINCIPAL WORKS

BIOGRAPHY: *The Life of Samuel Johnson, LL.D.,* 1791.

JOURNALS: *An Account of Corsica: The Journal of a Tour to That Island; and Memoirs of Pascal Paoli,* 1768; *The Journal of a Tour to the Hebrides with Samuel Johnson, LL.D.,* 1785; *Boswell's London Journal, 1762–1763,* 1950; *Boswell in Holland, 1763–1764,* 1952; *Boswell on the Grand Tour: Germany and Switzerland, 1764,* 1953; *Boswell on the Grand Tour: Italy, Corsica, and France, 1765–1766,* 1955; *Boswell in Search of a Wife, 1766–1769,* 1956.

James Boswell, born in Edinburgh, Scotland, on October 29, 1740, was the oldest son and heir of a distinguished Scottish judge, the proprietor of an ancient estate in Ayrshire who, when raised to the bench, took the title of Lord Auchinleck. Young Boswell was privately tutored as a child.

Following his studies at the Edinburgh High School, he entered the University of Edinburgh. He also studied at the University of Glasgow and, later, at the University of Utrecht, in preparation for a career in law.

As early as 1758 Boswell began keeping a journal and publishing articles in various periodicals. In 1759–1760 he became interested in Roman Catholicism and voiced his determination to become a priest. When Lord Auchinleck, a dour and ardent Scottish Presbyterian, opposed the idea, father and son compromised on the plan of a military career for the young man. Although he did not enter the army when his father took him to London, Boswell remained in the English city, enjoying its society and becoming a friend of many of the great and near-great of that time. On his return to Edinburgh in the following spring of 1761, he entered the university, but he much preferred the social life of the capital, becoming acquainted with young actors, young military officers, and even such a solid man of learning as David Hume. On the pretext of trying for a commission in the guards, Boswell returned to London in 1762; there he met Samuel Johnson, the famous lexicographer and literary dictator, in 1763. Also, in 1763, Boswell crossed the channel to the Continent, partly to study at the University of Utrecht and partly to satisfy his appetite for famous people, good times, and new sights. During his stay on the Continent, Boswell contrived to visit both Voltaire and Rousseau. In 1764 he journeyed to Corsica, which, under the famous patriot, Pasquale Paoli, was then fighting for independence from Genoa. The energetic Boswell became an enthusiast for the Corsican cause, and in 1768 published his *Account of Corsica: The Journal of a Tour of that Island; and Memories of Pascal Paoli* in an effort to secure help for the Corsican patriots. Upon his return to England Boswell also tried to enlist the aid of such men as Lord Chatham and Lord Holland in getting British aid to the Corsicans, but he was unsuccessful in his attempts.

In 1766 Boswell was admitted to the bar in Scotland and practiced law during 1766–1767. His work on the Douglas case, involving the inheritance of a large estate in Scotland, caught Boswell's fancy and he twice wrote about it: *Dorando, a Spanish Tale* (1767) discussed the case under the thin disguise of fiction, and the *Essence of the Douglas Cause* (1767) was an ambitious treatise on the subject. During these years Boswell, always enthusiastic for women, was falling in and out of love many times, and finally he married Margaret Montgomerie, a distant cousin, in November, 1769. Boswell's father, a widower remarried the same day. The younger Boswells had seven children, of whom five survived to maturity.

Although Boswell's chief claim to fame has been his friendship with Samuel Johnson and the biography which grew from it, for many months after his marriage Boswell did not see or correspond with Johnson. The two men did not meet again after the marriage until 1772, when Boswell journeyed to London. Neither Boswell's father nor his wife liked Johnson, and Mrs. Boswell did not share her husband's enthusiasm for travel. During the vacations of the Scottish courts, in the spring of the year, Boswell went to London almost every year between 1772 and 1784. In 1773 Johnson and Boswell made their famous tour of Scotland and the Hebrides, which Boswell recorded in his *Journal of a Tour to the Hebrides with Samuel Johnson, LL.D.* In the same year Boswell was elected to Johnson's famous Literary Club, although some of the members were not enthusiastic about adding his name to the list. The club was made up of such men of fame as Johnson, Burke, Garrick, Goldsmith, and Reynolds. During the 1770's Boswell had financial and domestic problems. His law practice was a slim one, and he could not learn to overlook other women. In addition, his relations with his father were strained, as they had been for years. Despite an allowance from his father, Boswell often barely skirted the abyss of bankruptcy and debtors' prison, and a love of strong drink tended to push him to the verge of alcoholism all his life.

Troubled as he was, Boswell continued to write. A series of seventy-odd papers was published in the *London Magazine* under the title of *The Hypochondriack* (1777–1783). In a better financial condition after his father's death in 1782, Boswell nourished political ambitions and attacked Fox's India Bill in a pamphlet, *A Letter to the People of Scotland* (1783), by which he hoped to gain political support from Lord Lowther; the attempt was unsuccessful. On June 30, 1784, Boswell, visiting in London, saw Samuel Johnson for the last time, for Johnson died the following December. In the years immediately after, Boswell tried to break into politics, but his attempts were unsuccessful. His only government appointment was that of recorder of Carlisle. He was admitted to the English bar, but the number of cases he handled was negligible; and he was unable to shake off his love of liquor. In 1783, while Boswell was in London, his wife died. Following her death he sent his children off to various schools while he himself remained in London, writing on his biography of Johnson and occasionally doing a little legal work. On its appearance in 1791, *The Life of Samuel Johnson, LL.D.* was an immediate success, and two months after its appearance Boswell was elected Secretary of Foreign Correspondence of the Royal Society. The world found in Boswell's *Life of Johnson* something new and wonderful in biographical writing. Boswell did not merely describe a wealth of detail; he made his subject come alive for the reader by means of his sharp, retentive memory, his inveterate habit of making notes on any and all events and conversations, and his complete candor in presenting character and scene. The result is at all times dramatically effective and psychologically revealing. But even the success of his book did not cheer Boswell a great deal. His last years were marked by melancholy and loneliness which he tried to ease with drink and dissipation. He fell ill in the spring of 1795 and died a few weeks later, on May 19, 1795, at his home in London.

During the twentieth century a great mass of Boswell papers, including many of his journals and the complete manuscript of his *Life of Johnson*, was discovered at Malahide Castle, in Ireland. After considerable legal entanglements were cleared away, scholars began to work on them, and the successive volumes of the *Yale Editions of the Private Papers of James Boswell*, beginning with *Boswell's London Journal* in 1950, are now in preparation under the editorship of Frederick A. Pottle and Frank Brady.

BIBLIOGRAPHICAL REFERENCES: The Boswell papers recovered from Malahide Castle were first made available in the privately printed edition of *The Private Papers of James Boswell*, edited by Geoffrey Scott and Frederick A. Pottle. 18 vols., 1928–

1934. The definitive *Yale Editions of the Private Papers of James Boswell,* edited by Frederick A. Pottle and Frank Brady, is now in preparation, 1950 ff. There are separate editions of *Dorando: A Spanish Tale, The Essence of the Douglas Cause,* and *An Account of Corsica,* edited by Sydney C. Roberts, 1923; the *Letters,* edited by Chauncey Brewster Tinker, 2 vols., 1924; *The Hypochondriack,* edited by Margery Bailey, 2 vols., 1928; and *The Journal of a Tour to the Hebrides,* edited from the original ms. by Frederick A. Pottle and Charles H. Bennett, 1936.

To date there is no standard biography incorporating the findings of recent Boswell scholarship. See Percy H. Fitzgerald, *Life of Boswell,* 2 vols., 1891; Chauncey B. Tinker, *Young Boswell,* 1922; Frederick A. Pottle, *The Literary Career of James Boswell, Esq.,* 1929; C. E. Vulliamy, *James Boswell,* 1932; and D. B. Wyndham Lewis, *The Hooded Hawk,* 1947. A useful volume is John L. Smith-Dampier, *Who's Who in Boswell,* 1935.

PAUL BOURGET

Born: Amiens, France
Date: September 2, 1852

Died: Paris, France
Date: December 25, 1935

Principal Works

NOVELS: *Cruelle énigme,* 1885; *André Cornélis,* 1886; *Mensonges,* 1887; *Le Disciple,* 1889; *Cosmopolis,* 1893; *Une Idylle Tragique,* 1896; *L'Étape,* 1902; *Un divorce,* 1904; *L'Émigré,* 1907; *Le Démon de Midi,* 1914; *Nos actes nous suivent,* 1927.

SHORT STORIES: *Pastels,* 1889; *Complications sentimentales,* 1898; *Drames de famille,* 1900; *Anomalies,* 1920.

POEMS: *La Vie inquiète,* 1875; *Edel,* 1877; *Les Aveux,* 1882.

PLAYS: *La Barricade,* 1910; *Le Tribun,* 1911.

ESSAYS: *Essais de psychologie contemporaine,* 1883; *Nouveaux essais,* 1885.

Paul Bourget, born at Amiens, France, on September 2, 1852, is perhaps the outstanding French novelist of a period of French literature not distinguished in this genre, the interval between Zola and Proust. Bookish and precise by nature, Bourget received an education which tended to accentuate rather than diminish these qualities. When viewed against a materialistic age, his life represents a struggle to find a personal religion—one which he will advocate for France as a whole—consisting, for him, of a return to the Catholic Church and to the political point of view of the extreme Right. This struggle is reflected in most of Bourget's

novels, most of which have dated badly but all of which have the merit of their author's sincerity, expressed in an admirably clear style.

Bourget's first works were poetry and criticism, and he continued to write in the latter field throughout his life. His *Essais de psychologie contemporaine* and *Nouveaux essais,* in which the works of ten great French writers of the modern period are studied, represent a successful attempt to "disengage life from the mass of books and sketch a moral portrait of my generation." Bourget's thesis is that his generation is imbued with pessimism deriving from its faith in materialistic

121

science which, he says, is no faith at all. Strongly influenced by Taine, who would not have approved his conclusions, Bourget sees the writers he studies, together with their works, only as symbols of their environment; his criticism of their philosophy is by no means personal and it is not allowed to cloud his opinion of their craftsmanship as artists. In all, Bourget's critical essays fill eleven volumes, and he is at present becoming more and more highly esteemed as a critic while his reputation as a novelist declines.

Yet it was as a novelist that Bourget made his greatest contribution to French literature *per se.* His early works (*Cruelle énigme, André Cornélis,* and *Mensonges*) represent a period of philosophical searching on Bourget's part. As in all of his later novels, his first works are primarily psychological studies of his characters, who are invariably drawn from the upper strata of society. These works, however, while valuable as pictures of the period, show more sensibility than true psychological insight. Also, Bourget's moral and political ideas had not yet crystallized and no "lesson" is to be found here. Bourget the dilettante and cosmopolite appears in two later novels, which, because of their general tone, might be placed with this group: *Cosmopolis* and *Une Idylle tragique.*

The appearance of *Le Disciple* in 1889 marks Bourget's entry into French literature as a truly serious novelist. *Le Disciple* also coincides with a decided change in Bourget's own ideas concerning religion and politics. Bourget, when younger, had been an admirer of Taine, the great determinist. In *Le Disciple,* he tells the story of a youth who is similarly influenced by a deterministic psychologist, whose principles he tries to apply to his own life. The work is a thesis-novel which marks the first of many writings by Bourget in which the bankruptcy of science and materialism is foretold. A return to the Catholic faith and to the virtues of patriotism (equated with adherence to royalist, not republican ideals) is strongly implied.

The "lessons" of *Le Disciple,* which created a critical storm and deeply affected French youth of the day, are carried over to *L'Étape,* in which the principle of social and political equality is attacked. In all of his later novels (*Un divorce, L'Émigré,* and *Le démon de Midi*) Bourget leans more and more heavily on these "lessons." Yet his construction is always excellent, and he examines his fictional subjects with the same discerning eye with which he examines literary ones.

In addition to critical works and novels, Bourget produced two travel-books, *Sensations d'Italie* (1891) and *Outre-mer* (1895) and many short stories such as "Un Saint," "Le Luxe des autres," "Conflits intimes." He died in Paris on Christmas Day, 1935.

BIBLIOGRAPHICAL REFERENCES: There is no collected edition in English translation. A useful volume of selections for French readers is the *Extraits choisis,* edited by Alphonse N. Van Daell, 1894, which includes an autobiographical letter by Bourget, a bibliography, and an introduction.

There is a need for biographies in English. The standard study of Bourget's life and works for French readers is Victor Giraud, *Paul Bourget,* 1934. Recent single volumes of criticism are Walter Todd Secor, *Paul Bourget and the Nouvelle,* 1948, a published thesis containing biography and extensive bibliography; and Norval P.

Barksdale, *Paul Bourget, Literary Ideas as Expressed in his Critical Writings,* 1946. Further studies can be found in Edmund W. Gosse, *French Profiles,* 1905; René Lalou, *Contemporary French Literature,* 1924; and Pierre de Bacourt and J. W. Cunliffe, *French Literature during the Last Half Century,* 1923.

See also E. A. Jones, "Paul Bourget, Apologist for Traditionalism in France," *South Atlantic Quarterly,* XLV (1946), 504–510; and Hugh M. Davidson, "The 'Essais de psychologie contemporaine' and the character of Adrien Sixte," *Modern Philology,* XLVI (August, 1948), 34–48.

ELIZABETH BOWEN

Born: Dublin, Ireland
Date: June 7, 1899

Principal Works

NOVELS: *The Hotel,* 1927; *The Last September,* 1929; *Friends and Relations,* 1931; *To the North,* 1932; *The House in Paris,* 1936; *The Death of the Heart,* 1938; *The Heat of the Day,* 1949; *A World of Love,* 1955.

SHORT STORIES: *Encounters,* 1923; *Ann Lee's and Other Stories,* 1928; *Joining Charles,* 1929; *Look at All Those Roses,* 1941; *The Demon Lover,* 1945; *Ivy Gripped the Steps,* 1946.

MISCELLANEOUS: *Bowen's Court,* 1941; *Seven Winters,* 1942; *The English Novelists,* 1942; *Anthony Trollope,* 1946; *The Shelbourne Hotel,* 1951.

Elizabeth Bowen is, along with Virginia Woolf, usually top-ranked among England's contemporary woman novelists. Of Anglo-Irish descent on both sides of her family, she was born in Dublin on June 7, 1899. At the age of seven, however, she was taken to live in the south of England where, five years later, her mother died. After a period of boarding school in Kent, she went back to Ireland to live; and the last year of World War I found her at work in a shell-shock hospital near Dublin.

Soon thereafter Miss Bowen's desire for a career resulted in her leaving home at the age of nineteen. Her father, who had remarried, coöperated generously with her wish for freedom and travel. During such times, Miss Bowen began to write, producing her first short stories at the age of twenty. Her principal residence became London, with winters in Italy. One of the latter, spent partly in tutoring her aunt's children at Bordighera, later produced *The Hotel,* published in 1927.

In 1923 Miss Bowen was married to Alan Cameron. Following her husband's appointment, in 1926, to a teaching position at Oxford, the Camerons occupied, at nearby Old Headington, a cottage that was once the stable of the village manor house. In 1931 Miss Bowen inherited Bowen's Court, her ancestral home in County Cork, Ireland, and began the practice of spending part of every summer there. A large, square house with Renaissance doors and cornices, the mansion acquired its name from a Captain Bowen of Wales who received the property in reward for services to Cromwell in the Irish campaign. Miss Bowen has interestingly revived this and other memories of the place with *Bowen's Court.*

Aside from distinguished short story

writing, Miss Bowen's reputation largely rests on these novels: *The Hotel, The House in Paris, The Death of the Heart,* and *The Heat of the Day.* In all four the theme revolves around the upper middle class, the social level which she understands best and interprets with clarity and penetration. The author's method is not to emphasize the physical action in her stories; it is, rather, to unfold complex relationships of people, evolving slowly into a conclusion that is logical but necessarily incomplete. In this approach her novels recall those of Henry James, to whose style of writing her own bears very strong resemblances.

This complexity of situation is well illustrated by *The House in Paris,* the situation being one which a child creates by merely existing. In this case, the child is an illegitimate boy, and his ancient problem has rarely been traced with more keenness and sympathy. The same qualities mark *The Death of the Heart,* which explores the trials of adolescence, that No Man's Land between the borders of childhood and maturity. Despite the excellence of these books, however, it was *The Heat of the Day* which gained widespread recognition for Miss Bowen. This novel, a tale of espionage during World War II, embodies an absorbing conflict between love and patriotism. The authenticity of its atmosphere is no accident: the locale is blitz-torn London; and Miss Bowen's London home, though it survived the war, suffered heavily from bombing raids. Also, Miss Bowen, not unlike her heroine, Stella Rodney, was engaged in important wartime activity. Yet the setting and period of this book are no more than incidental, for the story treats of contrasting faiths and loyalties which are altogether timeless.

Since 1941 Miss Bowen has broadened her literary activities to include literary criticism and book reviews for such journals as the *Tatler,* as well as scripts for the B.B.C. During the 1950's she has spent much time in the United States, writing and lecturing. Her own country honored her in 1948, when she was created a Companion of the British Empire.

BIBLIOGRAPHICAL REFERENCES: There is no extended biographical treatment. For criticism see Seán O'Faoláin, *The Vanishing Hero: Studies in Novelists of the 20's,* 1956; Edward Sackville-West, "Ivy Compton-Burnett and Elizabeth Bowen," *Horizon,* XIII (1946), 367–385; David Daiches, "The Novels of Elizabeth Bowen," *English Journal,* XXXVIII (1949), 305–313; and Barbara Seward, "Elizabeth Bowen's World of Impoverished Love," *College English,* XVIII (1956), 30–37.

JAMES BOYD

Born: Dauphin County, Pennsylvania
Date: July 2, 1888

Died: Princeton, New Jersey
Date: February 25, 1944

PRINCIPAL WORKS

NOVELS: *Drums,* 1925; *Marching On,* 1927; *The Long Hunt,* 1930; *Roll River,* 1935; *Bitter Creek,* 1939.

POEMS: *Eighteen Poems,* 1944.

James Boyd, American historical novelist, was born in Dauphin County, Pennsylvania, July 2, 1888, the son of James Yeomans Boyd and Eleanor Gilmore Boyd. He was graduated from Princeton University in 1910. He also attended Trinity College, Cambridge University, for two years. During the First World War he served as a first lieutenant in the American Expeditionary Forces in France. During World War II he set up The Free Company, a group of American writers whose plays, written without charge, were designed as broadcasts to forestall enemy propaganda. In 1917 he married Katherine Lamont and they became the parents of one son and two daughters. After his experiences in the First World War he moved south on the advice of his doctor and took up his residence at Southern Pines, North Carolina, where he devoted his time to writing. When John Galsworthy was traveling in the United States he met Boyd and was favorably impressed with his writing. He encouraged the young author and advised American publishers to watch his works.

James Boyd's novels are natural and realistic. His first volume was *Drums* which has been called the finest novel of the American Revolution. It shows, through the eyes of the central character, Johnny Fraser, the conflicting loyalties of the period. Some scenes of the novel are laid in England and others at sea. In the novel the reader meets John Paul Jones and participates in the historic battle between the *Serapis* and the *Bonhomme Richard*. Later the reader follows the hero to America where Fraser fights under Daniel Morgan. *Marching On* is a novel of the Cape Fear country of North Carolina before the Civil War. The characters involved are the descendants of those in *Drums*. Written from the viewpoint of a sophisticated Southerner, it shows the wastefulness and needless suffering caused by war. It had a considerable influence on the historical novel of the time. *Roll River* has its setting in Harrisburg, Pennsylvania. *The Long Hunt* is a novel of the frontier, *Bitter Creek* a story of the West in the cowpuncher era. Boyd died at Princeton, New Jersey, February 25, 1944. *Eighteen Poems* was published posthumously.

BIBLIOGRAPHICAL REFERENCES: There is no body of criticism on James Boyd. See *Book Review Digest*, 1925 ff.

HUGH HENRY BRACKENRIDGE

Born: Near Campbeltown, Scotland   *Died:* Carlisle, Pennsylvania
Date: 1748   *Date:* June 25, 1816

PRINCIPAL WORKS

NOVEL: *Modern Chivalry*, 1792–1815.

PLAYS: *The Battle of Bunker's Hill*, 1776; *The Death of General Montgomery*, 1777.

MISCELLANEOUS: *A Poem on the Rising Glory of America*, 1772 (with Philip Freneau); *Law Miscellanies*, 1814.

Hugh Henry Brackenridge, born in 1748, at Campbeltown, Scotland, was brought to this country at the age of five. The family settled in western Pennsylvania where Brackenridge grew up on the frontier. He entered Princeton in 1768. At his graduation in 1771 he recited a poem, "The Rising Glory of America," which he had written with Philip Freneau. Epic in intention, the poem is an important contribution to early nationalism. For a brief period he was the head of an academy in Maryland. During the Revolution, in addition to serving as a chaplain, he published two plays, designed for private performance, which praised the heroism of American troops, and also a group of sermons exhorting the troops to carry on bravely.

After studying law in Annapolis, he moved to Pittsburgh in 1781. He made many contributions to the cultural life of that frontier community, and there he wrote *Modern Chivalry,* the book by which he is best remembered. It is a picaresque novel, fashioned after *Don Quixote,* which satirizes incompetence and corruption in the workings of democratic government. By ridiculing the weaknesses of democracy, Brackenridge hoped eventually to strengthen it.

Despite the fact that he satisfied neither side during the Whiskey Rebellion, he was sufficiently well thought of politically to win an appointment to the Supreme Court of Pennsylvania in 1799. He moved to Carlisle in 1801. There he wrote *Law Miscellanies,* his principal contribution to legal literature, and there he died, June 25, 1816.

BIBLIOGRAPHICAL REFERENCES: The biography of Brackenridge is Claude M. Newlin, *The Life and Writings of Hugh Henry Brackenridge,* 1932. There is a bibliography by Charles F. Heartman, *A Bibliography of the Writings of Hugh Henry Brackenridge,* 1932. See also C. M. Newlin, "Hugh Henry Brackenridge: Writer," *Western Pennsylvania Historical Magazine,* X (1928), 224–256; and William W. Edel, "Hugh Brackenridge's Ride," *Boyd Lee Spahr Lectures in Americana,* I (1950), 115–145.

BERTOLT BRECHT

Born: Augsburg, Germany
Date: February 10, 1898

Died: East Berlin, Germany
Date: August 17, 1956

PRINCIPAL WORKS

PLAYS: *Trommeln in der Nacht,* 1922 (*Drums in the Night*); *Baal,* 1922; *Im Dickicht der Stadt,* 1922 (*In the City's Thickets*); *Mann ist Mann,* 1927 (*One Is Another*); *Dreigroschenoper,* 1928 (*The Three-penny Opera,* with Kurt Weill); *Die Rundköpfe und die Spitzköpfe,* 1936 (*Round Heads, Peak Heads*); *The Private Life of the Master Race,* 1944 (in English only); *Furcht und Elend des Dritten Reiches,* 1945 (*The Fears and Miseries of the Third Reich*).

NOVEL: *Dreigroschenroman,* 1934 (*A Penny for the Poor*).

POEMS: *Hauspostille,* 1927; *Lieder, Gedichte und Chöre,* 1934; *Svendbarger Gedichte,* 1939.

Any account of twentieth century German drama will have to take Bertolt Brecht into consideration, and yet he began life in such a way as to make a career as a playwright highly improbable. Born in Augsburg, Germany, February 10, 1898, he began his advanced studies in medicine and science at the universities in Munich and Berlin before finding his career in the theater. Brecht's writings and activity in political affairs, including activity in the Augsburg Revolution, won him a high place on the Nazi list of political criminals after the failure of Adolf Hitler's notorious beer-hall *putsch* in 1923. When the Nazis came to power in 1933, Brecht became an exile from his native land and sought asylum in a series of countries—Russia, France, Norway, and finally the United States, to which he came in 1941. During his exile and until the end of World War II in Europe in 1945, he poured forth a steady stream of plays, radio scripts, and poetry on anti-Nazi themes.

Brecht left the United States in 1947 and in 1949 took up residence in East Berlin, in Russian-controlled Germany where he died on August 17, 1956. He built up a drama company, the Berliner Ensemble, which produced a number of outstanding plays for the East Berlin Deutsches Theater. But Brecht's relationship with the Russian masters of East Germany was not entirely a happy one. His presentation of *The Trial of Lucullus* (written in 1943) at the Deutsches Theater was criticized severely by the Communist press as being too "formalistic." Rumors flew that Brecht had been censured by the authorities and that his play had been banned, but Brecht announced in 1951 that the play had

been withdrawn at his own request, whatever that meant.

Brecht was a peculiar person with many idiosyncrasies. He had a habit of appearing at first-night performances, where formal dress is conventional, in old clothes and with an unshaven beard. Purportedly the character of Brecht is mirrored in Feuchtwanger's novel, *Success*, although the fictional character is an engineer by profession.

As a playwright Brecht first achieved prominence with *Drums in the Night*, a play about a soldier of World War I believed to be dead by his sweetheart, but who returns to find the girl in the act of marrying another man. The returned soldier retrieves his girl and then proceeds to free himself from a revolutionary background. *In the City's Thickets* and *One Is Another*, are the typical Brecht plays in that they, like *Drums in the Night*, use expressionism to the point of grotesque exaggeration and depict the incongruities of human existence. In 1928 Brecht, in collaboration with Kurt Weill, turned to opera with *The Three-penny Opera*, based on John Gay's famous comic opera of the eighteenth century, *The Beggar's Opera* (1728). Translated into English, the work had great popularity in the United States in the 1930's, thanks largely to Brecht's mordant irony and the lively songs. The best-known of Brecht's works is a collection of short plays translated into English during World War II as *The Private Life of the Master Race*, an anti-Nazi work.

Although he was famous and important as a playwright and theatrical director, Brecht was also a novelist and poet. His one novel, *A Penny for the*

Poor, was published in 1934. Three volumes of poetry were published in German during the 1920's and 1930's, with a volume of collected poetry being published in 1947. He also did some translations of Japanese plays into English-language drama in *Der Jasager und der Neinsager* (1930).

At least part of Bertolt Brecht's importance to contemporary theater rests on his theories of the theater arts. His drama, which he directed as well as wrote, became more and more instructive, for he felt that art was a branch of education. He termed his experiments "epic theater," in contrast to the traditional theatrical theory based upon Aristotle. Brecht's notion was that the theater should teach and should appeal to its audience by means of the intellect, rather than the emotions. Brecht tried to replace the suggestive qualities and effects of the traditional theater with what he thought was evidence of a sober, intellectual, and concrete sort. He hoped, not for any catharsis of the spectators' emotions during the play, but rather for a lasting effect similar to that created in a classroom. Nevertheless, when he wished to reach and sway a wide audience, Brecht turned to traditional theatrical means, as he did in *The Private Life of the Master Race.* Apparently in his effort to create a better world, Brecht was willing to try any and all means.

BIBLIOGRAPHICAL REFERENCES: As yet no full study of Brecht has appeared in English. Short evaluations appear in Arthur Eloesser, *Modern German Literature,* 1933, and Jethro Bithell, *Modern German Literature,* 1939. See also Clement Greenberg, "Bertolt Brecht's Poetry," *Partisan Review,* VIII (1941), 114–127; Berthold Viertel, "Bertolt Brecht, Dramatist," *Kenyon Review,* VII (1945), 467–475; and John Gassner, "A Modern Style of Theatre," *Quarterly Journal of Speech,* (February, 1952), 63–75.

HERMANN BROCH

Born: Vienna, Austria
Date: November 1, 1886

Died: New Haven, Connecticut
Date: May 30, 1951

PRINCIPAL WORKS

NOVELS: *Die Schlafwandler,* 1931–1932 (*The Sleepwalkers*); *Die unbekannte Grösse,* 1933 (*The Unknown Quantity*); *Der Tod des Vergil,* 1945 (*The Death of Vergil*); *Die Schuldlosen,* 1950 (*The Guiltless*).

Hermann Broch, born in Vienna on November 1, 1886, was the son of a manufacturer, and it seemed for a while that young Broch would follow the same career. He studied philosophy and mathematics at the French city of Mulhouse and at Vienna, completing his higher education at the University of Vienna. Then Broch went into the textile industry and became director of a textile firm. He married Frances de Rothermann in 1909, and in 1916 he became general manager of the Austrian Textile Concern.

From 1920 to 1928 Broch served also in various governmental positions. But in 1928 he retired from business and went back to his university studies. From that time on he engaged in those activities for which he has be-

128

come famous, as a mathematician, a poet, a novelist, and a philosopher. The piece of writing that made him internationally famous, and the one by which he first became known in the United States, is *The Sleepwalkers*. This 300,000-word trilogy, which was completed in 1932, is an almost prophetic picture of the breaking down of German life as it had been before World War I. *The Sleepwalkers* is quite modern in its method of presenting reality. Broch shows the world as the people in the novel perceive it, using a variety of points of view in a way that is reminiscent of James Joyce. The novel achieved immediate critical acclaim in this country.

His next novel, *The Unknown Quantity*, is a less ambitious work, but is equal to his larger effort in sensitivity, delicacy, and careful probing of the human spirit. In this novel Broch knew his subject well; it is a character study of a doctor of mathematics.

As Hitler's power in Germany grew in the early 1930's, Broch became less popular officially, and he spent some time in prison. He then came to the United States and became an American citizen. Here Broch continued his writing in the fields of philosophy, mathematics, and literature. His work won him a Guggenheim Fellowship in 1941. For several years Broch worked as a researcher at Princeton University; he also was a member of the Office of Public Opinion Research, this work reflecting his increasing interest in politics.

In 1945 Broch's *The Death of Vergil* was published. This poetic treatment of death he had begun as a private endeavor while in a Nazi prison. It added considerably to his stature as a philosophical thinker.

In his last years, prior to his death in New Haven on May 30, 1951, Broch was a lecturer in Germanic Literature at Yale University, where he was known as a strict and exacting teacher, but one who always applied his most severe critical tests to his own work. Although Broch considered the ethical as important as the aesthetic, he himself was highly original in both technique and style. Perhaps the most consistent theme in his writing is the loneliness of men; but he almost always held out hope for humanity, finding it in the principle of brotherhood.

BIBLIOGRAPHICAL REFERENCES: For biographical-critical articles see Edwin Muir, "Hermann Broch," *Bookman*, LXXV, (1932), 664–668; and Fritz Lehner, "Hermann Broch," *Life and Letters To-Day*, XVI, 6 (1936), 64–71.

RICHARD BROME

Born: Uncertain
Date: Uncertain

Died: Probably London, England
Date: 1652 or 1653.

PRINCIPAL WORKS

PLAYS: *The Northern Lass*, 1632; *The Sparagus Garden*, 1635; *The Antipodes*, 1638; *A Jovial Crew, or the Merry Beggars*, 1641.

Richard Brome remains a shadowy figure. The last of the Elizabethan writers of comedy, he has no biographers, left few legal traces of existence, and yet was a friend of the great and near great. Ben Jonson's servant originally, whether menial or secretarial, Brome came from humble beginnings to a place of some prominence. He called himself a playmaker rather than a poet, and he was a writer of popular comedies, satires, masques, and romantic plays which may have totaled fifteen or more. Only four of his plays were published during his lifetime.

Brome wrote for the prominent companies and his plays were acted again and again at the most popular theaters. He collaborated on several occasions with other working dramatists (he disdained the courtly amateurs). Even after the Restoration, his plays were being revised and played. Like his mentor, Ben Jonson, his comedies contained much deft writing and satiric but accurate portrayals of the rollicking age. More important, his art looked toward the comedy of manners and thus served as a bridge between the two great periods of comedy in the theater.

Only from tributes from Jonson and others, his own prologues and play content, and his occasional verse do we know anything about Richard Brome. Modern scholarship indicates that his work deserves more attention than it has thus far received.

BIBLIOGRAPHICAL REFERENCES: Brome's plays have been collected in *The Dramatic Works of Richard Brome*, edited by R. H. Shepherd, 3 vols., 1873. The standard biography is C. E. Andrews, *Richard Brome: A Study of His Life and Works*, 1913. An important critical study is H. F. Allen's *A Study of the Comedies of Richard Brome, Especially as Representative of Dramatic Decadence*, 1912. Other useful studies are T. Miles, "Place-Realism in a Group of Caroline Plays," *Review of English Studies*, XVIII (1942), 428–440; and J. L. Davis, "Brome's Neglected Contribution to Comic Theory," *Studies in Philology*, XL (1943), 520–528.

LOUIS BROMFIELD

Born: Mansfield, Ohio
Date: December 27, 1896

Died: Columbus, Ohio
Date: March 18, 1956

PRINCIPAL WORKS

NOVELS: *The Green Bay Tree*, 1924; *Possession*, 1925; *Early Autumn*, 1926; *A Good Woman*, 1927; *The Strange Case of Miss Annie Spragg*, 1928; *Twenty-Four Hours*, 1930; *The Farm*, 1933; *The Rains Came*, 1937; *Mrs. Parkington*, 1943; *The Wild Country*, 1948.

SHORT STORIES: *Awake and Rehearse*, 1929; *Here Today and Gone Tomorrow*, 1934.

AUTOBIOGRAPHY: *Pleasant Valley*, 1945; *Malabar Farm*, 1948; *From My Experience*, 1955.

Louis Bromfield was born December 27, 1896, in Mansfield, Ohio, received public school education there, and enrolled at Cornell University in 1912 to study agriculture. At Cornell, remembering his early experiences around newspapers, Bromfield decided to write and travel; but he did not completely forget his agricultural interests, and eventually he returned to Ohio to buy and make his Malabar Farm a great showplace and the subject of several of his books. He entered World War I, served in many parts of Europe, and came back to the United States an established newspaper man. From newspaper work he moved to magazine work, to the theater, and to publication as an author.

In 1924 his first published novel appeared. It was *The Green Bay Tree*, which established the author immediately as one of the most popular writers of his day. The book introduced his most memorable character, Lily Shane, and told the story of life in a Midwestern city in which industry was crowding out an old estate. This novel was followed in rapid succession by *Possession, Early Autumn*—which won the Pulitzer Prize for the year—and *A Good Woman*. The first three titles, separate but interrelated novels, were published as a trilogy in 1937 under the inclusive title *Escape*. They are the books which support Bromfield's critical reputation, and they represent him at his fictional best.

Traveling widely, Bromfield began in 1928 to extend and vary his fictional scene, publishing *The Strange Case of Miss Annie Spragg*, his own favorite among his novels; *The Farm*, a novel drawn from family history; *The Rains Came*, in which the scene is India (and from which a highly successful motion picture was made); *Mrs. Parkington; The Wild Country*; and a series of books, partly autobiographical and partly general commentary, dealing with his Malabar Farm in Ohio: *Pleasant Valley, Out of the Earth* (1950), and *From My Experience*.

A prolific writer with vast energies and wide interests, Louis Bromfield spent much of his time in promoting soil conservation and the scientific approach to agriculture generally. He died suddenly at Columbus, Ohio, on March 18, 1956.

BIBLIOGRAPHICAL REFERENCES: The first full-length biographical and critical study is Morrison Brown, *Louis Bromfield and His Books*, 1957. See also Robert Van Gelder, *Writers and Writing*, 1946; Harry R. Warfel, *American Novelists of Today*, 1951; Louise M. Field, "Louis Bromfield, Novelist," *Bookman*, LXXV (1932), 43–48; and Ben R. Redman, *Louis Bromfield and His Books*, 1928 (pamphlet).

THE BRONTËS

Charlotte Brontë

Born: Thornton, Yorkshire, England
Date: April 21, 1816

Died: Haworth, Yorkshire, England
Date: March 31, 1855

PRINCIPAL WORKS

NOVELS: *Jane Eyre*, 1847; *Shirley*, 1849; *Villette*, 1853; *The Professor*, 1857.

Emily (Jane) Brontë

Born: Thornton, Yorkshire, England
Date: July 30, 1818

Died: Haworth, Yorkshire, England
Date: December 19, 1848

NOVEL: *Wuthering Heights,* 1847.
POEMS: *The Complete Poems of Emily Jane Brontë,* 1941.

Anne Brontë

Born: Thornton, Yorkshire, England   *Died:* Scarborough, England
Date: January 17, 1820   *Date:* May 28, 1849

PRINCIPAL WORKS

NOVELS: *Agnes Grey,* 1847; *The Tenant of Wildfell Hall,* 1848.
POEMS (in collaboration): *Poems,* by Currer, Ellis, and Acton Bell, 1846.

On December 29, 1812, the Reverend Patrick Brontë, incumbent of Hartshead, Yorkshire (originally of County Down, in Ireland), was married in Guiseley Church to Maria Branwell, a Cornish lady then visiting in the home of her uncle, the Reverend John Fennell.

Little more than seven years later, having in the meantime served a ministry in Thornton, he was appointed perpetual curate of Haworth. There he removed his family in April, 1820. Eighteen months later Mrs. Brontë died of cancer, leaving six small children: Maria, Elizabeth, Charlotte, Branwell, Emily, and Anne, ranging in age from seven years to twenty months. The emergency was solved when Elizabeth Branwell, Mrs. Brontë's eldest sister, came from Penzance to order the house and bring up the children.

In late summer of 1824, the four older girls were entered as pupils in the Clergy Daughters' School at Cowan Bridge. Precocious in mind but shy in spirit and frail in body, they fell victims to the severity of its routine. Maria and Elizabeth, ill of tuberculosis, were taken home to die, Maria on May 6, and Elizabeth on June 15, 1825. Charlotte and Emily were immediately re-called, and thereafter the Parsonage children knew no formal school room until Charlotte, near the end of her fourteenth year, entered Miss Margaret Wooler's school near Roe Head. Branwell was taught by his father, while the girls received training in household arts from their aunt. Left much to their own devices, the children found endless entertainment in creative plays continued from day to day. Shortly after Charlotte's tenth birthday, they launched a new play centering around twelve wooden soldiers, which absorbed all other household plays, and, having taken permanent form as an imaginary world of escape, nourished and shaped the genius of the family. Not only did the heroes of this play perform great deeds, but, turning authors, artists, and publishers, they recorded them in tiny volumes in proportion to their size—histories, biographies, novels, poems, and dramas.

In January, 1831, the Young Men's Play was interrupted by Charlotte's departure for Roe Head, when Emily and Anne took advantage of the break to withdraw from the family group and set up a play of their own called Gondal. Despite Charlotte's revival of the old creation on her return eighteen months later, and its expansion into a farflung empire called Angria, the younger girls stood aloof, and, from that time on the Brontë children played and wrote in pairs: Charlotte and Branwell, of Angria; Emily and Anne, of Gondal.

Through the years, 1832–1835, the game grew and matured with its creators through an astonishing number of "books." Branwell's productions, closely paralleling Charlotte's in characters and plot, betray his corrupting association with "rough lads of the Village" and the society of the Black Bull Inn. It was time for him to prepare for his chosen work of portrait painting. To help with family expenses, Charlotte, in late summer of 1835, returned to Miss Wooler's school as teacher, taking Emily with her as pupil.

The plan worked out badly. Branwell went to London but did not enter the Royal Academy, as had been planned. Charlotte and Emily, torn from their all-absorbing dream world, inseparable from home surroundings, were miserably homesick. Emily fell so ill that Charlotte sent her home and brought Anne to school in her place. Charlotte herself endured for two years until she collapsed nervously. Back home again, and lost in their writing, both regained health and courage to try again earning a living away from home, Emily in a school near Halifax, Charlotte as a nursery governess. Convinced that health and happiness were not for them away from home, the girls laid plans for a school in the Parsonage. To acquire the needed French, they borrowed from Aunt Elizabeth the money for a term of study in Mme. Héger's school in Brussels. Charlotte and Emily entered this school in February, 1842, leaving Anne in a position as governess in the Robinson family at Thorp Green, where Branwell was tutor. They were making satisfactory progress when they were called home by the death of Aunt Elizabeth in October.

The small legacies which they received from her enabled the older girls to finish out the year quietly at home. But in January, 1843, Charlotte returned to the Pensionnat Héger as teacher-pupil. Without Emily she was lonely. Worst of all, increasing weakness of overstrained eyes raised the spectre of blindness and reinforced M. Héger's frowning advice to give up Angria, the only medium she knew of creative dreaming and writing. Life stretched before her in years of unrelieved teaching, which her soul loathed.

Broken for a time in health and spirit, she returned to Haworth on New Year's Day, 1844. In the summer of 1845, Branwell, having conceived an infatuation for his employer's wife, was dismissed from his post. Already a habitué of drink and drugs, he never again rose above the piteous existence of an addict. Anne returned to the Parsonage with him.

At home the girls found alleviation of their distress in their old creative plays of Angria and Gondal. There is evidence that Charlotte tried by this means to bring her brother back to his rightful place in the group, but his manuscripts of the period show how grievously she failed.

The order was broken in the fall of 1845, when Charlotte accidentally came upon a manuscript volume of Emily's poetry, headed "Gondal Poems," which she read with astonishment at their grandeur and power, and the beauty of their "wild, wailing music." Out of this discovery, a joint volume of verse by the three girls was carefully worked out. For it, each drew from her store of verse (chiefly Angrian and Gondalan) twenty-one pieces, and chose a pseudonym to fit her own initials. The small volume was printed at the authors' expense with £31.10s. from Aunt Elizabeth's legacy: *Poems by Currer, Ellis, and Acton Bell*, London, Aylott and Jones, 8 Paternoster Row, 1846. Charlotte records that only two copies were sold. Disappointment turned the girls more determinedly to their novels already in progress, not the usual run of the Angrian and Gondal mills, but novels of realistic setting designed to please a publisher. Charlotte's, *The Professor*, was a skillful and artistic adaptation of portions of the Angrian creation to a Yorkshire-Brussels setting. Emily's, *Wuthering Heights*, showed many recognizable Gondalan features, traceable through her poems. Anne's, *Agnes Grey*, based on her own experience as a governess, had no kinship to her earlier writing. All three retained their previous pseudonyms.

After months of repeated rejection, *Wuthering Heights* and *Agnes Grey* were accepted by Thomas Cautley Newby of London. *The Professor* continued its rounds until it reached the house of Smith, Elder and Company, who returned it, but with such encouraging advice that Charlotte, on August 24, 1847, dispatched for their consideration a second novel, *Jane Eyre*, in characters and plot incidents derived directly from Angria.

Accepted, and published in October following, *Jane Eyre* was an immediate success. Newby now hastened the publication of *Wuthering Heights* and *Agnes Grey*, encouraging the surmise that they, too, were by the author of *Jane Eyre*, the three Bells being actually one person.

In the meanwhile Branwell had sunken so far out of family life that he knew nothing of his sisters' publishing ventures. Through late summer he grew rapidly worse, dying on September 24. Emily, having taken cold at his funeral, passed rapidly into tuberculosis, and followed him on December 19. Anne, already ill of the family scourge, succumbed on May 28, 1849.

Alone in the Parsonage with her father, Charlotte returned to an interrupted novel (*Shirley*) of Yorkshire local color which had been developed through fifteen years of Angrian writing. In November, 1852, she began the refining and naturalizing of yet another group of her beloved Angrians against a Belgian background. The result, *Villette*, was published in January, 1853.

On June 29 of the next year, she married her father's curate, Arthur Bell Nicholls. Her happiness was of short duration; she died on Easter Eve, March 31, 1855.

Fannie Elizabeth Ratchford

BIBLIOGRAPHICAL REFERENCES: *The Life of Charlotte Brontë*, by Mrs. E. C. Gaskell, 1857, is the pioneer biography, but this work should be supplemented by more recent studies, which include Clement K. Shorter, *Charlotte Brontë and Her Circle*, 1896; F. Macdonald, *The Secret of Charlotte Brontë*, 1914; Rosamond Langbridge, *Charlotte Brontë: A Psychological Study*, 1929; E. F. Benson, *Charlotte Brontë*, 1932; Laura Hinkley, *The Brontës, Charlotte and Emily*, 1947; and Margaret Crompton, *Passionate Search: A Life of Charlotte Brontë*, 1955. The best book on Emily Brontë is Charles Simpson, *Emily Brontë*, 1929; but see also A. M. F. Robinson, *Emily Brontë*, 1883. and Lord David Cecil, *Early Victorian Novelists*, 1934.

For Anne Brontë see Will T. Hale, *Anne Brontë: Her Life and Writings, Indiana University Studies*, XVI, No. 83, 1929.

More general studies of the Brontë family include Clement K. Shorter, *The Brontës: Life and Letters*, 2 vols., 1908; May Sinclair, *The Three Brontës*, 1912; K. A. R. Sugden, *A Short History of the Brontës*, 1929; Lawrence C. Willis, *The Brontës*, 1933; Phyllis Bentley, *The Brontës*, 1947; Ernest Raymond, *In the Steps of the Brontës*, 1948; Lawrence and E. M. Hanson, *The Four Brontës*, 1949; and Margaret Lane, *The Brontë Story*, 1953.

All recent Brontë studies owe a tremendous debt to Fannie E. Ratchford, whose definitive work is *The Brontës' Web of Childhood*, 1941, supplemented by her *Two Poems by Emily Brontë, with the Gondal Background of Her Poems and Novel*, 1934; Introduction to Emily Brontë's *Gondal's Queen*, 1955, with notes; and *Legends of Angria*, edited with W. C. DeVane, 1933. Other specialized studies are C. P. Sanger, *The Structure of Wuthering Heights*, 1926; Leicester Bradner, "The Growth of *Wuthering Heights*," *Publications of the Modern Language Association*, XLVIII (1933), 129–146; Martin Turnell, "*Wuthering Heights*," *Dublin Review*, CCVI (1940), 134–149; and Richard Chase, "The Brontës; or, Myth Domesticated," in *Forms of Modern Fiction*, edited by W. V. O'Connor, 1948. See also the *Transactions and Publications of the Brontë Society*, various dates; in particular, Hilda Marsden, "The Scenic Background of *Wuthering Heights*," Part 67, XIII, No. 2, 1957.

HENRY BROOKE

Born: Rantavan, Ireland
Date: c. 1703

Died: Dublin, Ireland
Date: October 10, 1783

PRINCIPAL WORKS

NOVEL: *The Fool of Quality, or the History of Henry, Earl of Moreland*, 1765–1770.

PLAY: *Gustavus Vasa*, 1739.

POEM: *Universal Beauty*, 1735.

Henry Brooke was born into the family of a Protestant clergyman in County Cavan, Ireland, about 1703. Little is known of his early life until he entered Trinity College, Dublin, at the age of seventeen. He left Dublin for London, where he studied law. For many years he divided his time between London and Dublin, marrying a cousin, Catherine Meares, who had been his ward. His first publication of note was a long philosophical poem, *Universal Beauty*, which helped to gain for him friendship of many English men of letters, including Jonathan Swift and Alexander Pope. Indeed,

Pope may have helped Brooke revise *Universal Beauty*, which some critics have declared to be a forerunner of Darwin's *Botanic Garden*. Brooke also became involved in English politics, as well as literature, becoming an adherent of Frederick, Prince of Wales, in his opposition to the policies of George II. *Gustavus Vasa*, a play based on Swedish history, was barred from the London stage by the censor because of political overtones, although it was successful in printed form. Because of his political activities and the difficulties in which they embroiled him, Brooke returned to Ireland early in the 1740's.

During his years of residence there he wrote several plays, an opera libretto, and numerous political pamphlets, but his literary fame rests almost entirely on *The Fool of Quality*. This novel, picaresque in construction, was a five-volume work influenced by the author's interest in Methodism. (A decade and a half after its publication a revised and abridged edition was produced especially for Methodists by John Wesley.) Late in life Brooke suffered from mental illness. In his old age he was cared for by his daughter Catherine, sole survivor of a family of twenty-two children. Brooke died in Dublin on October 10, 1783.

BIBLIOGRAPHICAL REFERENCES: There is no authorized biography and, aside from the standard histories of the English novel, relatively little critical discussion of his work. See E. A. Baker, Introduction to *The Fool of Quality*, 1906; and Eric Gellert, "The Fool of Quality," *London Mercury*, XXX (1934), 420–428. For general background material see also J. M. S. Tompkins, *The Popular Novel in England, 1770–1800*, 1932.

CHARLES BROCKDEN BROWN

Born: Philadelphia, Pennsylvania
Date: January 17, 1771

Died: Philadelphia
Date: February 22, 1810

PRINCIPAL WORKS

NOVELS: *Wieland*, 1798; *Ormond*, 1799; *Edgar Huntly*, 1799; *Arthur Mervyn*, 1799–1800; *Clara Howard*, 1801; *Jane Talbot*, 1801.

SOCIAL TRACT: *Alcuin: A Dialogue*, 1798.

Charles Brockden Brown is given credit for being the first American to earn a living as a professional author, although he did so for only a few years of his life. He was born on January 17, 1771, into a Philadelphia Quaker family and even as a youngster was addicted to reading voluminously. Because of his constant reading, he earned for himself a reputation as a scholar and genius in Philadelphia. Early in life, too, he began to write, planning three epic poems on Columbus, Pizarro, and Cortez—all notably American rather than European themes. His first published work, entitled "The Rhapsodist" (1789), a glorification of the romantic rebel, appeared in *The Columbian Magazine*, a Philadelphia publication.

Despite his literary bent, Brown's family set him to studying law in 1787, but in 1793 he gave up law and announced that he was henceforth to be a professional writer. After several visits to New York, Brown took up residence in that city, apparently finding, especially in the Friendly Society, the stimulation he needed as a writer. Brown was an ardent admirer of William Godwin, the British radical, who was also a novelist, and Brown's fiction reflects that enthusiasm. *Alcuin: A Dialogue* is really a treatise on the rights of women, using fiction as the bearer of a message. Following that work, Brown turned to writing fiction that more nearly can be called novels, but in which he hoped to teach as well as entertain. Writing at a furious rate, within a few years he wrote and published a number of novels. His best work, *Wieland,* was based on an actual murder case in Pennsylvania. The book is a study in religious psychosis, with the novelty of ventriloquism added. The story is melodramatic and uses many of the devices of the English Gothic fiction of the time, but it is original in that it uses American materials and presents a serious study of a human mind under pressures it does not understand.

In a later novel, *Arthur Mervyn,* Brown made further use of native materials. In 1793 he and his family had fled from Philadelphia, along with hundreds of others, to escape an epidemic of yellow fever. In New York, in 1798, another epidemic of the same disease had killed his close friend, Dr. Elihu Hubbard Smith. In *Arthur Mervyn,* Brown wrote a highly realistic account of the horrors of such an epidemic, describing the effects of the Philadelphia epidemic in 1793 in a manner comparable to Daniel Defoe's description of the London plague of 1665 in his *Journal of the Plague Year.* Other of Brown's novels also made use of American subject matter. Indians and the frontier were introduced into the American novel in *Edgar Huntly,* a work which is also usually considered the first American detective story. Unfortunately, Brown knew little about Indians or the frontier and was unable to present them very realistically. The outstanding characteristic of the novel is the presentation, as in *Wieland,* of a human mind under torment.

There is no doubt that Brown's novels were influenced by European fiction. They had to be, for there were almost no American novels at the time. Scholars usually consider William Hill Brown's *The Power of Sympathy* the first American novel, and it appeared less than a decade before *Wieland.* Brown's greatness comes from the fact that he was willing to use native materials and themes in his work. Too often critics have overemphasized the similarity of Brown's work to that of William Godwin, without giving credit to the American for his own originality.

Despite his output of fiction from 1798 to 1801, Brown made very little money, too little to continue indefinitely as a professional author. To support himself he also edited the *Monthly Magazine and North American Review* in 1799–1800. When the magazine failed, he returned to Philadelphia in 1801 and became a partner in his brothers' mercantile firm. He was married in 1804 to a New York girl, Elizabeth Linn, and they had four children. Following the failure of the family firm in 1806, Brown became an independent merchant. During the last three years of his life he continued to write, but mostly hack work for various periodicals. He died in Philadelphia on February 22, 1810.

BIBLIOGRAPHICAL REFERENCES: Of the biographical studies, William Dunlap, *The Life of Charles Brockden Brown,* 1815, remains an important source book, though often inaccurate. See also Harry R. Warfel, *Charles Brockden Brown, American Gothic Novelist,* 1949; John Erskine, *Leading American Novelists,* 1910; Alexander Cowrie, *The Rise of the American Novel,* 1948; George Snell, *The Shapers of American Fiction, 1798–1947,* 1947; and Warren B. Blake, "Brockden Brown and the Novel," *Sewanee Review,* XVIII (1910), 431–443.

ELIZABETH BARRETT BROWNING

Born: Coxhoe Hall, Durham, England
Date: March 6, 1806

Died: Florence, Italy
Date: June 29, 1861

Principal Works

POEMS: *The Seraphim and Other Poems,* 1838; *Poems, by Elizabeth Barrett Barrett,* 1844; *Poems* (including *Sonnets from the Portuguese*), 1850; *Casa Guidi Windows,* 1851; *Aurora Leigh,* 1857; *Poems before Congress,* 1860; *Last Poems,* 1862.

TRANSLATION: *Prometheus Bound,* 1833.

LETTERS: *Letters of Elizabeth Barrett Browning,* 1897; *Letters of Robert Browning and E. B. Barrett,* 1899.

The most famous feminine poet in English, Elizabeth Barrett Browning achieved her popularity perhaps as much through her romantic courtship and marriage as through her poetic talents, though it is, of course, on her poetry that her reputation finally rests. Hers was a minor talent, well-endowed with a lyric gift, but often lacking the technical control that could have polished her natural lyricism. In her *Sonnets from the Portuguese,* however, the strict limitations of the form gave shape to her lyric expression, and the poems have become the most popular love cycle in the language.

Elizabeth Barrett Moulton was the eldest child of Edward Barrett Moulton, a rich landowner who later changed his surname to Barrett. Born at Coxhoe Hall, Durham, England, on March 6, 1806, she was brought up in the Malvern Hills, a landscape that appears in a number of her poems. A precocious child, she was a good student of the Greek and Roman classics. In 1820, her father had fifty copies of her youthful epic, *The Battle of Marathon,* privately printed. She published anonymously *An Essay on Mind, and Other Poems* (1826), a stiff and sterile performance dominated by the influence of Pope and the classics.

In 1832 the Barretts moved to Sidmouth, Devonshire, where Elizabeth translated Aeschylus' *Prometheus Bound.* The family then made the important move to London in 1835 and soon took up permanent residence at 50 Wimpole Street. There Elizabeth made the literary friendships she needed, and her new friends encouraged her to publish her poetry more frequently. *The Seraphim and Other Poems* received good notices when it appeared in 1838, but it was not popular. But her increased literary activities proved too much for her, a riding accident as a girl and weak lungs having left her a semi-invalid, and in 1838 she was forced to go to the sea resort at Torquay for her health. Edward, her favorite brother, stayed with her and when, after a misunderstanding between them, Edward was drowned, Elizabeth was plunged into an extreme grief from which she was slow to recover.

She returned to Wimpole Street in 1841 and tried to forget her sorrow by working on a modernization of Chaucer with Wordsworth and Leigh Hunt. *Poems, by Elizabeth Barrett Barrett* was praised by the reviewers and she received flattering letters from Carlyle, Poe, and Lowell. In 1845 she received her most important letter, a note of praise from Robert Browning, a little-known poet whose work she admired. They continued the correspondence and met that summer. Browning became a frequent visitor at Wimpole Street. Because Mr. Barrett had forbidden any of his daughters to marry, the pair had a secret courtship which was climaxed on September 12, 1846, when the lovers were secretly married. A week later they left for the Continent. Her father never allowed Elizabeth to see him again, and he returned all her letters unopened. He died unreconciled in 1857.

Settling, for health and economic reasons, in Florence, the Brownings stayed at Casa Guidi, near the Pitti Palace, until Elizabeth's death. Their only child, a son, was born there in 1849. One day Mrs. Browning shyly showed her *Sonnets from the Portu-guese* to her husband; he persuaded her to include them in her 1850 volume. A thorough republican, Mrs. Browning next wrote *Casa Guidi Windows* in an attempt to gain English sympathy for the cause of Italian liberty. The Brownings traveled frequently and visited England in 1851, 1855 and 1856. During her last visit Mrs. Browning wrote *Aurora Leigh,* a narrative poem that has been compared to a psychological novel. Despite its slow-moving plot, the poem had a success equal almost to that of the *Sonnets from the Portuguese.* She had put out new editions of her poems in 1853 and 1856, and by now her reputation was firmly established. Her *Poems before Congress* received mixed reviews, but they did no damage to her popular fame. When she died in Florence on June 29, 1861, she was one of the best-known of Victorian poets.

BIBLIOGRAPHICAL REFERENCES: *The Complete Poetical Works* has been edited by H. W. Preston, 1900. There are four collections of letters: *Letters of Elizabeth Barrett Browning,* edited by F. G. Kenyon, 1897; *The Letters of Robert Browning and Elizabeth Barrett Browning, 1845–1846,* edited by F. G. Kenyon, 2 vols., 1899 (rev. ed., 1930); the *Letters to Her Sister,* edited by Leonard Huxley, 1929; and *Elizabeth Barrett to Miss Mitford,* edited by Betty Miller, 1943.

The definitive biography is Gardner B. Taplin, *The Life of Elizabeth Barrett Browning,* 1957. Other biographical studies include J. H. Ingram, *Elizabeth Barrett Browning, 1888;* I. C. Willis, *Elizabeth Barrett Browning,* 1928; Dorothy Hewlett, *Elizabeth Barrett Browning: A Life,* 1952; and Frances Winwar, *Elizabeth: The Romantic Story of Elizabeth Barrett Browning,* 1957. The story of Robert and Elizabeth Barrett Browning has been told in Osbert Burdett, *The Brownings,* 1929; Virginia Woolf, *Flush,* 1933; Frances Winwar, *The Immortal Lovers,* 1950; Constance Burnett, *The Silver Answer,* 1955; and Dallas Kenmare, *The Browning Love-Story,* 1957. For family background see Jeanette Marks, *The Family of the Barretts,* 1938.

ROBERT BROWNING

Born: Camberwell, London, England
Date: May 7, 1812

Died: Venice, Italy
Date: December 12, 1889

PRINCIPAL WORKS

POEMS: *Pauline,* 1833; *Paracelsus,* 1835; *Sordello,* 1840; *Dramatic Lyrics,* 1842 (*Bells and Pomegranates III*); *Dramatic Romances and Lyrics,* 1845 (*Bells and*

Pomegranates VII); *Christmas Eve and Easter Day,* 1850; *Men and Women,* 1855 (2 vols.); *Dramatis Personae,* 1864; *The Ring and the Book,* 1868–1869 (4 vols.); *Balaustion's Adventure,* 1871; *Prince Hohenstiel-Schwangau,* 1871; *Fifine at the Fair,* 1872; *Red Cotton Night-Cap Country,* 1873; *Aristophanes' Apology,* 1875; *The Inn Album,* 1875; *Pacchiarotto,* 1876; *La Saisiaz* and *The Two Poets of Croisac,* 1878; *Dramatic Idylls: First Series,* 1879; *Dramatic Idylls: Second Series,* 1880; *Jocoseria,* 1883; *Ferishtah's Fancies,* 1884; *Parleyings with Certain People of Importance,* 1887; *Asolando,* 1889.

PLAYS: *Strafford,* 1837; *Pippa Passes,* 1841 (*Bells and Pomegranates* I); *King Victor and King Charles,* 1842 (*Bells and Pomegranates* II); *The Return of the Druses,* 1843 (*Bells and Pomegranates* IV); *A Blot in the 'Scutcheon,* 1843 (*Bells and Pomegranates* V); *Colombe's Birthday,* 1844 (*Bells and Pomegranates* VI); *Luria* and *A Soul's Tragedy,* 1846 (*Bells and Pomegranates* VIII).

TRANSLATION: *The Agamemnon of Aeschylus,* 1877.

The poet Robert Browning was born May 7, 1812, in Camberwell, near London, the son of a learned and genial Bank of England clerk. His father's substantial library, notable for curious history, biography, and anecdote, became an important influence upon the future poet, as were his father's instruction in languages and his mother's Evangelical piety and love of music. Private schooling and a term at the University of London had comparatively little influence on a young man who felt himself destined to be a poet and was admirably prepared for it at home.

He came early under the influence of Shelley, whose techniques and political ideas remained with him somewhat longer than the religious radicalism which Browning repudiated in his earliest significant poem, *Pauline.* After this poem of personal confession, he turned to the "chronicling" of objective characters and the use of the dramatic techniques which were to remain his characteristic concerns.

The first poem of this dramatic kind was *Paracelsus,* published in 1835. The character here examined was that of a historical person, the Renaissance scientist, who, as Browning represented

him, came to know almost too late the nature of true love, without which knowledge is empty.

Turned to stage drama through his friendship with the actor Macready, Browning produced a historical play, *Strafford,* in 1837, which ran for only four nights. He was to make two more attempts at the stage without success: *A Blot in the 'Scutcheon* and *Colombe's Birthday.* But the earlier of these was to lead him toward his destined medium of the short dramatic poem, and his studies in seventeenth-century history for *Strafford* confirmed him in his characteristic political liberalism and sympathy for the common man.

The promising reputation which had begun with *Paracelsus* was spoiled in 1840 by the publication of *Sordello.* Browning's changing conceptions of the central character and an excessive concern with medieval Italian history resulted in a poem which has been called "a bewildering potpourri of poetry, psychology, love, romance, humanitarianism, philosophy, fiction, and history." It continues to be regarded, in spite of modern criticism, as distinguished chiefly by its obscurity.

From 1841 to 1846 he published the inexpensive little series titled *Bells and*

140

Pomegranates, beginning with *Pippa Passes* and including, among other titles, *Dramatic Lyrics, A Blot in the 'Scutcheon, Colombe's Birthday,* and *Dramatic Romances and Lyrics. Pippa Passes* and a number of the shorter poems show him at his best in the dramatic monologue and lyric: "My Last Duchess," "Soliloquy of the Spanish Cloister," "Porphyria's Lover," "The Bishop Orders His Tomb at St. Praxed's Church." The last of these especially is a triumph in one of Browning's special interests, the interpretation of the Italian Renaissance; and in many of the dramatic poems of the series he illustrates the characteristic purpose of his best work: the chronicling, in concrete settings, of individualized human souls in moments of crucial and revelatory experience.

In 1844 Browning noticed a compliment to himself in a poem by the invalid poetess, Elizabeth Barrett. A correspondence and visits followed, Miss Barrett's health improved, and in 1846 they were secretly married and set out for a long and happy residence in Italy, residing first in Pisa and then moving to the now famous Casa Guidi villa in Florence. They followed the revolutionary movements of 1848 with sympathetic liberalism, though Mrs. Browning was more interested in social institutions and her husband in liberty as serving individual growth. They differed more notably in Mrs. Browning's faith in spiritualism and Browning's contempt for it.

Summer visits to London brought them the friendship of Carlyle, Ruskin, Kingsley, and Rossetti. Their son was born in Florence in 1849, and Mrs. Browning died there in 1861.

In 1850 Browning published *Christmas Eve and Easter Day,* in the first of these emphasizing love rather than ecclesiastical forms as essential to Christianity and in the second dealing with religion in its individual aspects. The poems have been called Puritan in spirit.

In 1855 he issued his "fifty men and women" under the title *Men and Women,* highly individualized characters in concrete settings, expressing in their experiences various ideas about love, art, and religion. "Fra Lippo Lippi" affirms the goodness of physical beauty, "Saul" makes human love a prophecy of the revelation of divine love, "Cleon" asserts the ethical pessimism of Greece as against the upstart Christian hope, and in "An Epistle of Karshish" an Arab physician is converted by a study of the case of Lazarus.

After his wife's death Browning returned to England to edit her unpublished poems, to supervise his son's education, and to become a highly popular figure in London society. In 1864 he published *Dramatis Personae,* similar to *Men and Women* as a collection of dramatic sketches, but with even greater emphasis upon ideas and religion. He was honored by Oxford with a fellowship and by Cambridge with an honorary degree. In 1868 he published his *Poetical Works* in six volumes.

In Florence, Browning had picked up an "old yellow book" containing, in print and manuscript, the story of a seventeenth century murder trial. This became the long poem, *The Ring and the Book,* in which the poignant story, rich in Italian background, was interpreted through monologues by nine persons involved in the trial. It is his masterpiece in his most characteristic form, the dramatic monologue.

Although his best work had been done, many volumes were to follow before his death in Venice, December 12, 1889, and burial in Westminster Abbey. Italy, religion, and the world of art had provided him with his best settings; the dramatic monologue was his triumphant art form; the chronicling of souls in growth or crisis was his central substance; optimism was his philosophical bent; and his central doctrine was the "glory of the incomplete"—the supremacy of high and unfulfilled aspiration over low-level, finite achievement. He ranks with Tennyson as one of the two greatest poets of the Victorian era.

Francis Claiborne Mason

BIBLIOGRAPHICAL REFERENCES: The standard edition is *The Complete Poetical Works of Robert Browning*, edited by Augustine Birrell, 1915. The standard biography is W. H. Griffin and H. C. Minchin, *The Life of Robert Browning*, 1938. Other biographical studies include Arthur Waugh, *Robert Browning*, 1900; Edward Dowden, *The Life of Robert Browning*, 1917; Lilian Whiting, *The Brownings: Their Life and Art*, 1917; Fannie Barrett Browning, *Some Memories of Robert Browning*, 1928; and Betty Miller, *Robert Browning: A Portrait*, 1952.

For criticism see E. H. Griggs, *The Poetry and Philosophy of Robert Browning*, 1905; A. K. Cook, *A Commentary upon Browning's "The Ring and the Book,"* 1920; C. W. Hodell, ed., *The Old Yellow Book*, 1927; Frances T. Russell, *One Word More on Browning*, 1927; W. L. Phelps, *Robert Browning: How to Know Him*, 1931; W. C. DeVane, *A Browning Handbook*, 1935; and W. O. Raymond, *The Infinite Moment*, 1950.

A useful volume of general reference is Edward Berdoe, *The Browning Cyclopedia*, 1916.

WILLIAM CULLEN BRYANT

Born: Cummington, Massachusetts
Date: November 3, 1794

Died: New York, N. Y.
Date: June 12, 1878

PRINCIPAL WORKS

POEMS: *The Embargo, or Sketches of the Times: A Satire*, 1808; *Poems*, 1821, 1832, 1834, 1836, 1839; *The Fountain and Other Poems*, 1842; *The White-Footed Deer*, 1844; *Poems*, 1854; *Thirty Poems*, 1864; *Hymns*, 1864, 1869; *The Poetical Works of William Cullen Bryant*, 1876; *The Flood of Years*, 1878.

TRAVEL SKETCHES AND IMPRESSIONS: *Letters of a Traveller*, 1850; *Letters of a Traveller: Second Series*, 1859; *Letters from the East*, 1869.

TRANSLATIONS: *The Iliad of Homer*, 1870; *The Odyssey of Homer*, 1871–1872.

MISCELLANEOUS: *Orations and Addresses*, 1873; *Lectures on Poetry*, 1884.

William Cullen Bryant, born at Cummington, Massachusetts, on November 3, 1794, spent his childhood under the opposing influences of his father, a liberal-minded physician who later became a Unitarian and a member of the state legislature, and his maternal grandfather, a sternly Calvinist farmer who was a deacon in the local church. Bryant, a precocious boy, showed an early interest in politics, religion, and literature, and his first volume of poetry, *The Embargo, or Sketches of the Times: A Satire* was

142

published before his fourteenth birthday in 1808. The principal poem in this volume, "The Embargo," was an attack on President Jefferson in heroic couplets, a work in which young Bryant repeated all the slanders against Jefferson current in New England at the time, adding numerous pious clichés in a childish imitation of the technique of Alexander Pope.

Bryant was also interested in nature and spent many hours roaming through the fields and woods near his home in western Massachusetts. His poetry began to change from measured heroic couplets to a style and diction more like those of Wordsworth. He wrote several versions of the famous "Thanatopsis" while still in his teens, but, since the poem expressed many Unitarian ideas, it had to be hidden from his Calvinist grandfather. Bryant wanted to go to Harvard, and his father agreed; but when his grandfather insisted it was a needless extravagance, the boy was sent to Williams. He spent only one year at Williams before returning to Cummington to study law.

"Thanatopsis," a poem showing how any man might go to his death confident that any faith would save him, appeared in the *North American Review* in 1817. Although the poem— acknowledged as one of the first and best American romantic poems demonstrating an already developed technique—has become accepted as one of the poetic classics in America, it appeared anonymously and evoked little comment for several years. His editors, however, hailed Bryant as a new poetic genius. Bryant wrote industriously, published another volume, *Poems* (containing, among others, "The Yellow Violet" and "To A Water-fowl"), and was invited to deliver the Phi Beta Kappa poem at Harvard in 1821. His Harvard offering, "The Ages," a long exposition of the progress and perfectibility of man, apparently did not impress his academic audience. Bryant also began to contribute to the *North American Review* articles in which he called for a uniquely American poetry uninhibited by eighteenth century English classicism.

In 1825, Bryant left the law and Massachusetts for literary life in New York, where he founded a periodical called the *New York Review and Atheneum Magazine*. Within a year he became an editor of the *Evening Post*. He was connected with the *Evening Post* for the rest of his life, and, as editor, was a constant champion of free speech, civil rights, the abolition of slavery, the rights of labor. His strongly liberal political opinions never worked their way into his poetry, however; most of his poetry remained devoted to nature and romantic religious ideas.

After 1830, Bryant wrote little poetry; "To A Fringed Gentian" is one of the primary exceptions. Bryant spent his later years writing editorials, traveling in Europe and sending essays on his trips back to the *Evening Post*, giving a great many commencement and patriotic addresses, and writing critical articles. He wrote many prose pieces for the paper on Indians or on old legends, but his prose lacked the distinction and originality of his poetry. Although he could become heated in political controversy (especially in his defense of the Abolitionist position before the Civil War), his contemporaries could find little if any strongly felt emotion in his later poetry, his non-political prose, or his conversation. He was regarded as an efficient editor, a writer and judge with high moral principles, but as a somewhat cold, aloof, unapproachable personality. In fact, he seemed to become more and more like the Calvinist grandfather he had originally rebelled against.

Bryant's poetic criticism was regarded as anachronistic even in his later life. As might be expected of the author of a number of fine nature poems, he advocated originality, simplicity, and the treatment of emotion in all poetry. He concentrated on the importance of reaching the reader and stirring his imagination to see the beauty and truth in nature. He was opposed to the strict formalism, measured couplets, and rational satire of eighteenth century verse, and he was forceful in claiming the need for a distinctively American group of poets. These views he set forth in his famous introduction to *A Library of Poetry and Song* (1871), the first true critical anthology in America. Bryant insisted also on the primary importance of morality in poetry, his doctrine being that the good poet has an obligation to make his readers more moral citizens. By the 1870's, however, American poets and intellectuals had become suspicious of direct connections between poetry and morality; to them Bryant sounded like the remnant of an earlier age.

In the last year of his life, Bryant published a long poem, *The Flood of Years*. Like "Thanatopsis," this poem dealt with how a man should face death, how man could rest secure in the knowledge of ultimate good and hope for the future of mankind. The poem was widely praised, not so much for itself, but as a reminder that its author was the first American romantic poet, one of the first in America to glorify both external nature and the spirit of man. Bryant also never lost his belief in political liberty. He collapsed while giving an oration at a dedication of a statue of Mazzini in New York's Central Park, and died two weeks later, on June 12, 1878.

BIBLIOGRAPHICAL REFERENCES: The standard edition, though not definitive, is *The Life and Works of William Cullen Bryant,* edited by Parke Godwin, 6 vols., 1883–1884. All later collections are based on *The Poetical Works of William Cullen Bryant,* 1876, for which Bryant provided the final text. The best one-volume edition is the Roslyn Edition of *The Poetical Works of William Cullen Bryant,* edited by H. C. Sturges and R. H. Stoddard, 1903. A useful book of selections is *Bryant: Representative Selections,* edited by Tremaine McDowell, American Writers Series, 1935.

The basic biography is still Parke Godwin, *A Biography of William Cullen Bryant, with Extracts from His Private Correspondence,* 2 vols., 1883. More recent studies include W. A. Bradley, *William Cullen Bryant,* 1905, and H. H. Peckham, *Gotham Yankee,* 1950. Related material will be found in Allan Nevins, *The Evening Post: A Century of Journalism,* 1922. See also Norman Foerster, *Nature in American Literature,* 1923, and Vernon L. Parrington, *Main Currents in American Thought,* Vol. II, 1927.

JOHN BUCHAN

Born: Perth, Scotland
Date: August 26, 1875

Died: Montreal, Canada
Date: February 11, 1940

PRINCIPAL WORKS

NOVELS: *John Burnet of Barns*, 1898; *Grey Weather*, 1899; *The Half Hearted*, 1900; *The Watcher by the Threshold*, 1902; *Prester John*, 1910 [*The Great Diamond Pipe*]; *The Moon Endureth*, 1912; *The Thirty-Nine Steps*, 1915; *Greenmantle*, 1916; *Mr. Standfast*, 1919; *Huntingtower*, 1922; *Midwinter*, 1923; *The Three Hostages*, 1924; *John McNab*, 1925; *The Dancing Floor*, 1926; *Witch Wood*, 1927; *The Blanket of the Dark*, 1931; *The Free Fishers*, 1934; *The House of the Four Winds*, 1935; *The Island of Sheep*, 1936 [*The Man from the Norlands*]; *Sick Heart River*, 1941 [*Mountain Meadow*].

BIOGRAPHY: *Sir Walter Raleigh*, 1897; *The Marquis of Montrose*, 1913; *Sir Walter Scott*, 1932; *Oliver Cromwell*, 1934.

AUTOBIOGRAPHY: *Memory Hold-the-Door*, 1940 [*Pilgrim's Way*].

John Buchan, later 1st Baron Tweedsmuir, was one of those remarkable men of many talents whom the British Isles are regularly able to produce. He was a prolific writer of history and fiction, a distinguished member of Parliament, a lawyer, editor, director of information for the British government, a churchman, and Governor General of Canada.

He was born in Perth, Scotland, August 26, 1875, to a Free Church minister, John Buchan, and a farmer's daughter, Helen Masterson Buchan. Surviving an early skull injury which kept him in bed for a year, he entered Glasgow University when he was seventeen, and then, having been awarded a scholarship, went to Brasenose College at Oxford, where he won a number of literary prizes and wrote three books.

In 1900 he went to London to study law and was admitted to the Middle Temple bar the following year. During that time he also served as a member of the editorial board of the *Spectator*. He began his career in public service by going with Lord Milner to South

Africa, where he acquired a broadness of outlook that made him a successful administrator. Two years later he returned to England, having by that time completed five novels.

He entered into partnership with the publishers Thomas A. Nelson and Sons in 1907. He married Susan Charlotte Grosvenor, and had three sons and one daughter; his wife provided him with the opportunity for writing and served as his hostess during various government assignments.

After leaving Nelson and Sons, Buchan worked for a time as director of the Reuter Press Agency and then during the First World War, as correspondent for the London *Times*. His most famous novel, *The Thirty-Nine Steps*, was published at that time. While serving next as director of information for the British government, he not only edited Nelson's twenty-four-volume popular history of the war, but also wrote his own four-volume history.

Buchan entered Parliament in 1927 as a conservative member for the Scottish universities, and he held his seat until his appointment in 1935 as Governor General of Canada brought with it the title of Baron Tweedsmuir. He had previously been honored by being made Lord High Commissioner of the Elder Church of Scotland in 1933. He was an agreeable and efficient Governor General, friend to President Roosevelt, and host to King George VI and Queen Elizabeth when the royal pair visited Canada in 1939. Buchan's death at Montreal, February 11, 1940, was the result of a skull injury.

Buchan was a capable, exciting, and prolific writer, even though he led a busy political life and was often able to write only on weekends and during the summers. His historical works, particularly his *Oliver Cromwell,* were well received; but he was most popular for his adventure stories, many of them featuring Richard Hannay, who figures in *The Thirty-Nine Steps, Greenmantle, Mr. Standfast,* and *The Three Hostages.*

BIBLIOGRAPHICAL REFERENCES: Archibald Hanna, *John Buchan, A Bibliography,* 1953, is a comprehensive work. There are four major references: Anna Buchan, *Unforgettable, Unforgotten,* by O. Douglas [pseud.], 1945; Susan Buchan, *John Buchan, by his Wife and Friends,* 1947; Arthur C. Turner, *Mr. Buchan, Writer: A Life of the First Lord Tweedsmuir,* The Torch Biographies, 1949; and Susan Buchan, *The Lilac and the Rose,* 1952. See also John MacFinnan, "John Buchan, Historian and Statesman," *British Annual of Literature,* 1939, 21–23; John W. Wheeler-Bennet, "America's John Buchan," *Virginia Quarterly Review,* XVII (1941), 151–153; and Ferris Greenslet, "John Buchan," *Atlantic Monthly,* CLXXII (September, 1943), 60–64.

GEORG BÜCHNER

Born: Goddelau, Germany
Date: October 17, 1813

Died: Zurich, Switzerland
Date: February 19, 1837

PRINCIPAL WORKS

PLAYS: *Dantons Tod,* printed 1835 (*Danton's Death*); *Leonce und Lena,* printed 1838; *Woyzeck,* printed 1879.

(Karl) Georg Büchner, who died in his twenty-fourth year at the beginning of a promising career in both science and letters, was to achieve posthumous fame almost a century later as a brilliant dramatist and a significant literary figure inspired by the revolutionary "Young Germany" movement of the 1830's. The oldest of six children, he was born on October 17, 1813, at Goddelau, near Darmstadt, Germany, where his father, a former medical officer in Napoleon's army, had taken

service with the Duke of Hesse-Darmstadt. From all accounts the mother was of mild and pleasant disposition, but the father was a severe, freethinking martinet. Although there was little accord between father and son, it is believed that the father's sternness and unorthodox views influenced Büchner toward the naturalistic drama that he wrote.

Having shown an early interest in science, young Büchner prepared himself for a career in medicine at the

146

University of Strasbourg and later at Giessen. During his two years at Strasbourg he became engaged to the parson's daughter who later destroyed some of his manuscripts. At Giessen he became a member of a secret revolutionary society and in 1834 wrote his famous political pamphlet, *Der hessiche Landbote* (*The Hessian Courier*). This document, widely circulated at the time, fell into the hands of the authorities and Büchner was forced to leave Giessen to avoid imprisonment. He returned to his father's house and there, under police surveillance and in constant danger of arrest, wrote his first play, *Danton's Death*, a powerful drama based on the personalities and events of the French Revolution.

Büchner escaped to Strasbourg. There he wrote *Leonce and Lena*, a short satirical comedy which ridicules conventions and praises the self-realization of the individual, and his fragmentary but impressive *Woyzeck*, a psychological tragedy which has for its theme the exploitation of the common man, in this case a conscript driven by jealousy to commit a murder. He wrote a fourth play, *Pietro Aretino*, but of this drama little more is known than the title, for its frankness shocked the parson's daughter and she destroyed it after her fiancé's death. Büchner also translated two of Victor Hugo's plays and began a novel, *Lenz*, never completed because the newspaper for which it was intended was suppressed. In addition, while engaged in these activities, he completed his dissertation for his doctoral degree in medicine and wrote several scientific papers.

By 1836 he was ready to abandon his revolutionary activities and political propaganda for a career in science. Appointed lecturer in comparative anatomy at the University of Zurich, he served there only a few months, dying of typhus after a brief illness on February 19, 1837. His literary remains were not published until 1879. *Woyzeck* was first presented in 1913, *Danton's Death* in 1916. Alban Berg's modern opera, *Wozzeck* (1925), is based on Büchner's tragic play.

BIBLIOGRAPHICAL REFERENCES: The standard collection of Büchner's works is the German-text edition published in 1922. For biography and criticism see H. Lippmann, *Georg Büchner und die Romantik*, 1923; Hans Mayer, *Georg Büchner und seine Zeit*, 1948; Karl Viëtor, *Georg Büchner*, 1950; A. H. J. Knight, *Georg Büchner*, 1951; and Eva Friedrich, *Georg Büchner und die französische Revolution*, 1956.

PEARL S. BUCK

Born: Hillsboro, West Virginia
Date: June 26, 1892

PRINCIPAL WORKS

NOVELS: *The Good Earth*, 1931; *Sons*, 1932; *A House Divided*, 1935; *This Proud Heart*, 1938; *Dragon Seed*, 1942; *The Promise*, 1943; *Pavilion of Women*, 1946; *Peony*, 1948; *Kinfolk*, 1949; *The Hidden Flower*, 1952; *Imperial Woman*, 1956.

BIOGRAPHY AND AUTOBIOGRAPHY: *The Exile*, 1936; *Fighting Angel: Portrait of a Soul*, 1936; *My Several Worlds*, 1954.

TRANSLATIONS: *All Men Are Brothers*, 1933 (*Shui hu chuan*, 2 vols.).

Pearl S(ydenstricker) Buck was born in West Virginia on June 26, 1892, into a missionary family. Her parents, Absalom and Caroline Sydenstricker, took her to China when she was still an infant, and China was her home, except during her college undergraduate days, until 1932. When she was ready to go to college, Pearl Buck's parents sent her back to the United States, where she attended Randolph-Macon Woman's College, in Lynchburg, Virginia, graduating in 1914. While she was an undergraduate Pearl Buck distinguished herself by becoming president of her class and by some amateur literary accomplishments. In 1917 she married John Lossing Buck, also an American missionary to China. Their first five years of marriage were spent in the highly unsettled regions of North China. When her husband became head of the farm-management departments at Nanking University, Pearl Buck began to teach English at the same institution, serving until 1924. She later taught at National Southeastern University, from 1925 to 1927, and at Chung-Yang University, from 1928 to 1930. She lived in Nanking until publication of *The Good Earth* in 1931 made her world-famous as a popular novelist. With that book she achieved fame, not only as a novelist, but as the foremost interpreter of China to Westerners. She and her first husband had two daughters, who returned to America with her. Following her return to the United States she divorced her first husband, later marrying Richard J. Walsh, president of the John Day Company, her publishers. Since

their marriage they have adopted four children; they live on a farm in Pennsylvania.

In addition to her undergraduate degree, Pearl Buck has a master's degree from Cornell University. Honorary degrees have been awarded her by several institutions, including Harvard and Yale. She was also one of the first women to be elected to the American Academy of Arts and Letters. *The Good Earth*, which was highly successful in many ways, won many awards for its author, including the Pulitzer Prize in 1932 and the Howells Medal of the American Academy of Arts and Letters. She was made a member of the National Institute of Arts and Letters in 1936. Her crowning award was the Nobel Prize for Literature, which she received in 1938.

The Good Earth was the first novel of a trilogy *The House of Earth*, which includes *Sons* and *A House Divided*. The trilogy presents the history of a Chinese family through several generations, and it has been compared to the Rougon-Macquart series of novels by Zola. Similarities are especially strong between Pearl Buck's *The Good Earth* and Zola's *La Terre*, the similarities running much deeper than the titles. *The Good Earth* was an exceptionally popular novel. With its American sales alone approximating a million copies, and translations made into twenty or more other languages, the novel stood at the top of the best-seller lists in the United States for more than two years. Despite its vast popularity, or perhaps partly because of it, critics and scholars have been slow to grant Pearl Buck's work a place in literary history, and not only because her books have been concerned with a culture alien to America. Critical appraisals of *The Good Earth* and the later novels have said that the books have their greatest merit in the truthfulness with which China and its people are portrayed, a statement which can scarcely be interpreted as aesthetic acclaim.

Following *The Good Earth*, which is a point of departure in any discussion of Pearl Buck, came other novels which had a more modest success, such books as *The Young Revolutionist* (1932), portraying the Chinese Communist movement, and *The Mother* (1934), which relates the tribulations of a Chinese peasant woman. During the 1930's Pearl Buck also turned to writing books other than novels. *The First Wife and Other Stories* (1932) was her first volume of published short fiction. Like a later volume, *Today and Forever* (1941), it had relatively little appeal to the public, which seemed to have quickly categorized Pearl Buck as a novelist. In addition to her other work, there appeared two volumes of biography, *The Exile* in 1936 and *Fighting Angel* in 1936, portraits of the author's missionary parents. These two books offer a suggestion as to why Pearl Buck broke away from missionary work, inasmuch as they show that she believed that the Christianity of the missions failed to arouse Chinese sympathy for Christianity or the people who represented it. Perhaps that belief has also played a large part in Pearl Buck's continued efforts to help improve understanding between the Chinese and Western peoples. In 1941 she founded the East and West Association, serving as its president for many years. In books her work to improve understanding has continued through such volumes as *Dragon Seed*, *The Promise*, *Pavilion of Women*, *Peony*, *Kinfolk*, *The Hidden Flower*, and *Imperial Woman*. An autobiographical volume, *My Several Worlds*, relates the author's experiences as a person, a writer, and a humanitarian. Also worthy of mention in Pearl Buck's amazing volume of writings is *All Men Are Brothers*, a translation of a Chinese classic, *Shui hu chuan*. She has also written and published a number of books for children.

Pearl Buck considers herself a writer in the Chinese tradition of fiction, a tradition which stresses as its primary purpose the entertainment of the people. Such was her declaration in her Nobel lecture, *The Chinese Novel* (1939). She has also said that she must write, especially novels, and that she cannot be truly happy unless she is writing, either to entertain or to further her humanitarian and liberal beliefs in religion and politics.

BIBLIOGRAPHICAL REFERENCES: There is no full-length biographical or critical study. See Robert Van Gelder, *Writers and Writing*, 1946; Harry R. Warfel, *American Novelists of Today*, 1951; and Phyllis Bentley, "The Art of Pearl S. Buck," *English Journal*, XXIV (1935), 791–800.

FRANK THOMAS BULLEN

Born: London, England
Date: April 5, 1857

Died: Madeira Island
Date: March 1, 1915

ADVENTURE NARRATIVES AND REPORTAGE: *The Cruise of the "Cachalot,"* 1898; *Idylls of the Sea,* 1899; *The Log of a Sea-Waif,* 1899; *The Men of the Merchant Service,* 1900; *With Christ at Sea,* 1900; *Deep Sea Plunderings,* 1901; *The Apostles of the South East,* 1901; *Sea Wrack,* 1903; *Our Heritage—the Sea,* 1906; *Frank Brown, Sea Apprentice,* 1906; *The Call of the Deep,* 1907; *Young Nemesis,* 1909; *Fighting the Icebergs,* 1910; *A Bounty Boy,* 1912; *From Wheel and Outlook,* 1913.

Frank Thomas Bullen, born in Paddington, London, April 5, 1857, was a minor but respected member of the great fraternity of literary seafaring men. He began his independent career at the age of nine as a street urchin and errand boy about the docks of London. At twelve he was rescued from this unpromising existence by his uncle, the master of the *Arabella,* who started him on those nautical adventures which, later, were to furnish him with the material for some fifteen books and a countless number of lectures. First as cabin boy, then as able-bodied seaman, he shipped aboard vessels from various ports of the world until, at the age of eighteen, he found himself in New Bedford, Massachusetts, where he signed for a cruise on the whaler *Cachalot.*

This was a significant sailing for him. When the expedition was over, he returned to London. There he was hired as a clerk in the British government's Meteorological Office, and there he started work on his first and most important book, *The Cruise of the "Cachalot,"* a vivid and detailed account of life on a Yankee whaler.

The book was highly praised—Kipling termed it the finest report on the techniques of whaling that he had ever read—and with its success Bullen left the Meteorological Office to devote all of his energies to professional authorship. From this first achievement until his death on March 1, 1915, while on a trip to the Island of Madeira, he averaged approximately one publication a year, gaining enough prestige as a master of nautical lore to be in demand as a lecturer throughout the British Isles.

BIBLIOGRAPHICAL REFERENCES: There is no full study of Bullen, but his two volumes of memoirs are useful: *The Log of a Sea-Waif,* 1899, and *Recollections,* 1915.

EDWARD GEORGE EARLE BULWER-LYTTON

Born: London, England
Date: May 25, 1803

Died: Torquay, England
Date: January 18, 1873

NOVELS: *Falkland,* 1827; *Pelham, or the Adventures of a Gentleman,* 1828; *The Disowned,* 1829; *Devereux,* 1829; *Paul Clifford,* 1830; *Eugene Aram,* 1832; *Godolphin,* 1833; *The Last Days of Pompeii,* 1834; *Rienzi,* 1835; *Ernest Maltravers,* 1837; *Alice,* 1838; *Night and Morning,* 1841; *Zanoni,* 1842; *The Last of the Barons,* 1843; *Lucretia,* 1846; *Harold,* 1848; *The Caxtons,* 1849; *My Novel, or Varieties of English Life,* 1853; *What Will He Do With It?,* 1859; *A Strange Story,* 1861; *The Coming Race,* 1871; *Kenelm Chillingly,* 1873.

PLAYS: *The Lady of Lyons*, 1838; *Richelieu*, 1839; *Money*, 1840; *Cromwell*, 1842; *The Rightful Heir*, 1869.
POEMS: *The New Timon*, 1847; *King Arthur*, 1849; *St. Stephens*, 1860.
TRANSLATIONS: *The Poems and Ballads of Schiller*, 1844; *Horace's Odes*, 1869.

Edward George Earle Bulwer-Lytton was born in London on May 25, 1803. He was of distinguished ancestry, his father being General William Earle Bulwer and his mother, nee Elizabeth Barbara Lytton, a great heiress. (He added his mother's maiden name to his own when he inherited Knebworth from her in 1843.) The father died in 1807, while young Edward was still a small child, and Mrs. Bulwer moved the family from their estate in Norfolk to London. When he grew old enough, Bulwer's family wished to send him to Eton, but he preferred and was permitted to have his education under tutors who prepared him for Trinity College, Cambridge, where he took a bachelor's and master's degree, graduating in 1826. His scholarly honors were not to end there, however, for both his own university and Oxford granted him honorary degrees after he became famous. Long before he left the university, Bulwer had established himself as a dandy in Victorian London and had published some poetry written in a flamboyant, Byronic fashion. Prior to his marriage in 1827, however, he apparently had no intention of becoming a serious writer, much less of earning a living by his pen.

His marriage to a beautiful but poor Irish girl, Rosina Doyle Wheeler, was opposed bitterly by his mother, who stopped her son's £1000 allowance shortly after the wedding. Finding himself without an income, Bulwer turned to writing, and within the year his first novel, *Falkland*, was published. His first great success came with *Pelham* in 1828, a novel which many persons read with the hope of identifying the originals of the characters drawn from fashionable life in Britain at the time. After the publication of *Pelham*, Bulwer had a great popular reputation; his novels sold readily, and his poetry, if not great, at least found readers. After *Pelham* he wrote one, sometimes two novels a year. Individually his novels did not sell as widely as those of his prominent competitors, Thackeray and Dickens, but his total output was as popular, possibly more so. Bulwer had no choice but to write, for he and his wife lived extravagantly, but he often wrote under great pressure. In addition he found time to enter politics, successfully standing for Parliament on a reform ticket in 1831. Once in Parliament, he remained for a decade. In his private life Bulwer was not so fortunate. His wife, from whom he separated in 1836, came to hate him bitterly, even to caricaturing him in a novel of her own entitled *Cheveley* (1839). She was finally declared in-sane, and the two children of the marriage spent most of their years in the custody and household of their father.

In 1838 Bulwer was made a baronet. In 1843 he inherited his maternal grandfather's estate, Knebworth, and at that time changed his name to the hyphenated Bulwer-Lytton. Changing his politics, Bulwer-Lytton stood for Parliament again in 1852, this time as a Conservative candidate, but once again successfully. He served briefly, too, in 1858–1859 as Colonial Secretary, and in 1866 he was elevated to the peerage, becoming Baron Lytton of Knebworth. Shortly afterward he retired from public life.

During his years of unhappy marriage and happy activity in politics, Bulwer-Lytton continued his prolific writing career. As a novelist he turned to writing novels of crime and violence, with themes as well as social justice. His first such novel was *Paul Clifford*, published in 1830. One of his most famous novels, *Eugene Aram,* falls into this same category. This novel involves both a murder and a motivation for the crime which the author tried to make so understandable and logical that the reader's sympathies would be aroused for the criminal. Then, beginning with *The Last Days of Pompeii,* Bulwer-Lytton wrote a series of exotic historical romances. After *The Last Days of Pompeii,* which presents both paganism and early Christianity, he published novels based on Continental and British history. *Rienzi* gives a picture of Rome. *Leila* presents Spain during Moorish days. *The Last of the Barons* is laid in the time of the War of the Roses. *Harold* deals with the period of the Norman Conquest. These historical romances were written after a careful preparation by the author, and they emphasize characterization, background, and style, rather than action. Unlike most other writers of historical novels,

Bulwer-Lytton actually used great historical figures as his chief characters.

In addition to his historical novels he also wrote fiction concerned with the fantastic, the supernatural, and the terrifying. *Zanoni* is the story of a weird set of adventures occurring over five thousand years to a human being temporarily granted immortality. In *The Caxtons* Bulwer-Lytton turned to the depiction once again of contemporary British life, but in *The Coming Race,* one of his last productions, he created a Utopian fantasy.

Although he is no longer remembered as such, in his own lifetime Bulwer-Lytton was a successful dramatist, as well as a novelist. Three of his plays, extremely popular in their time, were *The Lady of Lyons, Richelieu,* and *Money.*

As a writer Bulwer-Lytton once enjoyed a great popularity, but other writers were often critical, even satirical, of his work; perhaps they resented his successes in literature and politics. While he resented the adverse criticism of his work, he managed to stay on friendly terms with critics and fellow writers, and he knew almost all of the literary men of Victorian England. He died, still active as a writer, at Torquay, January 18, 1873. Most of his novels, once so popular, are now seldom read.

BIBLIOGRAPHICAL REFERENCES: The collected edition is The New Knebworth Edition of the novels, 29 volumes, 1895–1898. The basic biography is Victor A. G. R. Bulwer-Lytton, *The Life of Edward Bulwer, First Lord Lytton,* 2 volumes, 1913 (reissued in 1948). Of interest to specialists are Michael Sadleir, *Bulwer: A Panorama,* 1931 (retitled *Bulwer and his Wife,* 1933), and *The Strange Life of Lady Blessington,* 1935. Of general use to students are E. G. Bell, *Introductions to the Prose Romances, Plays and Comedies of Edward Bulwer, Lord Lytton,* 1914; and Edwin Berry Burgum, *The Literary Career of Edward Bulwer, Lord Lytton,* 1924. See also Lewis S. Benjamin, *Victorian Novelists* by Lewis Melville (pseud.), 1906; and Holbrook Jackson, *Great English Novelists,* 1908.

IVAN ALEXEYEVICH BUNIN

Born: Voronezh, Russia
Date: October 10, 1870

Died: Paris, France
Date: November 8, 1953

PRINCIPAL WORKS

NOVELS: *Derevnya,* 1910 (*The Village*); *Mitina lyubov,* 1924–1925 (*Mitya's Love*); *Zhizn Arseneva; istoki dnei,* 1930 (*The Well of Days*).

SHORT STORIES AND NOVELLAS: *Sukhodol,* 1911–1912 (in *The Elaghin Affair and Other Stories*); *Gospodin iz San Frantsisko,* 1916 (*The Gentleman from San Francisco*); *Bozhie drevo,* 1931 (*God's Tree*).

POEMS: *Listopod,* 1901.

Ivan Alexeyevich Bunin, the only Russian to have won the Nobel Prize for literature (1933), led a hard life despite his international acclaim as one of the very finest modern writers of the novella. Born to a noble but poor family at Voronezh, Russia, on October 10, 1870, Bunin was privately tutored in his native Yelets district before continuing his studies briefly at the University of Moscow. As a man of letters he first attracted attention with his translations of Longfellow and Byron. For this work he was awarded the Pushkin Prize, top honor of the Russian Academy. He seemed, with these translations and his own poems, to be continuing the classical tradition of Russian literature, but in the next few years his verse took a shift toward the symbolical.

He first won popular fame in Russia with the publication of his long, pessimistic novel, *The Village.* Six years later his reputation became international with the publication of *The Gentleman from San Francisco.* This tale was not only specially cited by the Nobel Committee; it was long a model for aspiring modernists among the literati. Its surface, so apparently realistic and detailed, is actually a brilliant method of sustaining the symbolism of

Bunin's theme of the hollowness of vanity. His rich American, after many years devoted solely to business, retires to Capri, planning a gala life. There he immediately dies and is carried back across the Atlantic, having missed out on life entirely. The ship itself, the weather, and the ocean become in the end symbolic. It is no exaggeration to say that the story's blending of realism and symbolism has become the essence of the modern period of writing.

In 1898 Bunin had married the daughter of a Greek refugee and had settled down to a quiet life of travel and writing. With the outbreak of the Russian Revolution, Bunin, who leaned toward the conservative despite his lack of complete acceptance of the Tsarist regime, became an expatriate. Leaving Moscow in 1918, he lived abroad, mainly in Paris. During World War II, he resided in the south of France, in ill health and poverty, his days additionally clouded by his wife's illness. In spite of these difficulties, he is reported to have helped many refugees fleeing from the Nazis during the occupation.

Bunin's attitude toward life was never bitter; though full of the knowledge of the sadness the world can bring, he yet maintained a sense of the nobility and beauty of human endeavor. His last work was *Memories and Portraits,* published in 1951. He died of a heart attack, in relative obscurity, in his Paris home on November 8, 1953.

BIBLIOGRAPHICAL REFERENCES: There is no full-length study of Bunin in English. See G. Struve, "The Art of Ivan Bunin," *Slavonic Review,* XI (1934), 423–436; R. Poggioli, "Ivan Bunin, premio Nobel 1933," *Nuova Antologia,* CCCLXXI (1934), 134–144; Alexander Bakshy, "Nobel Prize for Literature," *American Mercury,* XXXI (1934), 219–223; Nikander Strelsky, "Bunin: Eclectic of the Future," *South Atlantic Quarterly,* XXXV (1936), 273–283; and J. Croisé, "Ivan Bunin, 1870–1953," *Russian Review,* XIII (1954), 146–151.

JOHN BUNYAN

Born: Elstow, England
Date: November, 1628

Died: London, England
Date: August 31, 1688

PRINCIPAL WORKS

NOVELS: *The Pilgrim's Progress,* Part I, 1678; Part II, 1684; *The Life and Death of Mr. Badman,* 1680; *The Holy War,* 1682.

AUTOBIOGRAPHY: *Grace Abounding to the Chief of Sinners,* 1666.

TRACTS: *Some Gospel Truths Opened,* 1656; *The Holy City, or the New Jerusalem,* 1666; *A Confession of My Faith and a Reason for My Practice,* 1671.

Both the career and the writings of John Bunyan are full of interest for the student of the seventeenth century, for his career illustrates the difficulties faced by a convinced Baptist in a society that, after the restoration of Charles II, took a poor view of Puritan views in general. His writings speak clearly of the convictions that enabled Bunyan and others to endure social intolerance and oppression, and at least one of his works—*The Pilgrim's Progress*—is more than a personal and sociological record; it is a work that many generations of readers have regarded as a wonderfully allegorized account of each man's spiritual experience.

Bunyan was one of the least learned and socially humblest of men to attain enduring literary fame. He was born in Elstow, in rural Bedfordshire, of a father who was a tinker, a hereditary trade to which, in due time, Bunyan himself was apprenticed. Baptized on November 30, 1628, he was brought up in an atmosphere of strict Puritanism which imposed checks on his normal youthful behavior and brought on violent mental disturbances. Bunyan could believe, in later years, that his youthful high spirits were displays of vice.

At seventeen he joined the Parliamentary army in the Civil War and took part in the victorious campaigns of 1645. In 1646 he married a poor, pious woman whose only dowry was two religious books. His wife's piety and study of the two books added to his habit of searching his soul for sin. Happily, in 1653, he joined a Baptist society and regained his equilibrium. He soon became a preacher and drew large crowds of laboring people, causing the Royalists to look on him with such suspicion that after the Restoration in

154

1660 and the passage of laws that forbade meetings hostile to the Established Church Bunyan was brought to trial for refusing to give up his preaching. Since, during his confinement, Bunyan's family was penniless and often starving, Bunyan suffered further pangs of guilt. Yet he declined opportunities to renounce his religious belief and remained in prison for twelve years, enjoying only short intervals of freedom. This confinement was at least to the advantage of posterity, for in prison he had ample leisure to read the Bible and Fox's *Book of Martyrs*—his only source of historical knowledge—to write attacks on various religious groups, and to give religious instruction to fellow prisoners. Indeed, much of the first part of *The Pilgrim's Progress* was written in the Bedford gaol. After its publication in 1678, Bunyan's life ran more smoothly. His book and his sufferings made him "the hero of the Baptists," and he preached to vast groups in London and throughout the country. He was even, in the last year of his life, chaplain to the Lord Mayor of London. Bunyan died in London, August 31, 1688.

Bunyan's literary production was abundant and dominated by the preoccupations of faith and religious controversy. Titles of his minor writings read like evangelistic tracts. Even the titles give one a sense of preoccupations different from present ones: "Some Gospel Truths Opened," "A Few Sighs from Hell" (1658), "Light for Them that Sit in the Darkness" (1675), and "A Caution to Stir up to Watch against Sin" (1684).

Better known are Bunyan's longer works, such as *The Holy War*, the principal character of which is Mansoul and the action of which is, as in Bunyan's greatest book, allegorical and shows man beset by the powers of evil and victorious only by the strength of godly resistance and divine grace. On a less exalted level is *The Life and Death of Mr. Badman,* which is an interesting record of contemporary manners and lower middle-class life. The most famous of his works is *The Pilgrim's Progress,* an allegorical account of two journeys taken to the Celestial City, first the journey of the solitary hero, Christian, and then the journey of his family—a journey less grim than Christian's and one genially supervised by Mr. Greatheart. Bunyan's allegory, both in the events and the abstractly named characters, is a dramatic projection of his central religious conviction: that man is saved by God's mercy and not by mortal deeds and mortal obedience to the ancient laws of Moses and current civil law. Symbolic narrow gates and overhanging mountains and dusty rooms all quickly reveal themselves as some aspect of Bunyan's brooding upon the meaning of the Holy Scriptures; and there is no character, from Mr. Worldly Wiseman to the Interpreter, who does not also suggest some aspect of the eternal drama of sin, repentance, grace, and —sometimes—backsliding and eternal damnation.

Criticism of Bunyan naturally points to his highly representative qualities; many aspects of seventeenth century life are opened up by a reading of his works. His books show, further, that he is a man of one book, the Bible; and particularly in *The Pilgrim's Progress* does he fuse into a successful unity the language and landscape of the Scriptures and the scenes, the landscapes, and the humble diction of his own native English countryside. If the book is less fascinating now than it once was, modern readers should remember that they have lost the habit of allegorical thinking; it is a habit that Bunyan found in the Scriptures and one, moreover, which had been normal in the Middle Ages. With Bunyan, it is not the surface reality that counts; it is Truth, both spiritual and eternal.

BIBLIOGRAPHICAL REFERENCES: The standard biography is John Brown, *John Bunyan: His Life, Times, and Work*, in the *Tercentenary Edition* revised by F. M. Harrison, 1928. Important also are W. Y. Tindall, *John Bunyan, Mechanic Preacher*, 1934, and Jack Lindsay, *John Bunyan, Maker of Myths*, 1937. See, further, J. A. Froude, *John Bunyan*, in the English Men of Letters Series, 1880; G. B. Harrison, *John Bunyan: A Study in Personality*, 1928; Mary P. Willcocks, *Bunyan Calling*, 1943; Vera Brittain, *In the Steps of John Bunyan*, 1950; Henri Talon, *John Bunyan: The Man and His Works*, 1951; and Roger Sharrock, *John Bunyan*, 1954. Briefer studies will be found in Edward Dowden, *Puritan and Anglican*, 1900; John Livingston Lowes, *Essays in Appreciation*, 1936; J. W. Mackail, *Studies in Humanism*, 1938; and R. E. Fitch, "A Tale of Two Pilgrims: A Comparison of Bunyan's *Pilgrim's Progress* and Voltaire's *Candide*," *Hibbert Journal*, XLVIII (1950). 388–393.

EDMUND BURKE

Born: Dublin, Ireland
Date: January 12, 1729

Died: Beaconsfield, England
Date: July 9, 1797

PRINCIPAL WORKS

POLITICAL AND PHILOSOPHICAL ESSAYS AND SPEECHES: *A Vindication of Natural Society*, 1756; *A Philosophical Inquiry into the Origin of Our Ideas of the Sublime and Beautiful*, 1757; *An Account of the European Settlements in America*, 1757 (with William Burke); *Thoughts on the Cause of the Present Discontents*, 1770; *Speech on American Taxation*, 1774; *Speech on Moving His Resolutions for Conciliation with the Colonies*, 1775; *Two Letters on Ireland*, 1778; *Speech on Presenting a Plan for the Better Security of the Independence of Parliament*, 1780; *Speech on Reform in the House of Commons*, 1782; *Speech upon Mr. Fox's East India Bill*, 1784; *Speech Relative to the Nabob of Arcot's Debts*, 1785; *Article of Charge against Warren Hastings*, 1788; *Reflections on the Revolution in France*, 1790; *A Letter to a Member of the National Assembly*, 1791; *An Appeal from the New to the Old Whigs*, 1791; *A Letter . . . on the Subject of the Roman Catholics of Ireland*, 1792; *Two Letters on the Proposals for Peace with the Regicide Directory of France*, 1796; *Two Letters on the Conduct of Our Domestic Parties*, 1797.

Edmund Burke, born in Dublin on January 12, 1729, and son of a Protestant father and a Catholic mother, was schooled by Abraham Shackleton, a Quaker who became his lifelong friend. Burke spent five years as a mediocre student at Trinity College, Dublin, before going to London in 1750 to study law. Various unfounded rumors have it that he led a dissipated bohemian life for the next ten years. It is certain only that he never passed the bar and that after his allowance was cut off he did hack writing for a living; his *Vindication of Natural Society*, a satire on Bolingbroke, shows the cast of his political

156

thought in an early mood. In 1756 he married a daughter of Dr. Nugent of Bath; his father-in-law settled with Burke in London and introduced him to "Single-Speech" W. G. Hamilton, a member of Parliament who became Irish Secretary and took Burke with him to Dublin, thus beginning the young man's public career.

In 1759 Burke founded the *Annual Register* (on political and economic matters) with which he was associated until 1788. In 1765 he entered the House of Commons where he remained for twenty-nine years, never becoming a minister and always opposing the ministries of George III. He fought for such causes as the abolition of the slave trade, the Catholic emancipation in Ireland, and the prosecution of the corrupt exploiters of India, especially Warren Hastings. He was particularly embittered when the fourteen-year-long trial of the latter ended in acquittal.

His *Speech on Moving His Resolutions for Conciliation with the Colonies* is, perhaps, the most widely admired of his works. It is full of simple ethical maxims, not in praise of Jeffersonian liberalism, but in favor of British prudence: "The question with me is not whether you have the right to make your people miserable, but whether it is not your interest to make them happy."

When political upheaval broke out in France in 1789, Burke wrote his now famous *Reflections on the Revolution in France,* partly in reaction against the Rev. Richard Price, a non-conformist minister who had dared to compare the political events in France with the Glorious Revolution of 1688. Burke, incensed because the leaders of the French Revolution were mercurial and undependable, was such a profound believer in firm, stable, and responsible government that he could not fathom the depth and the inevitability of the French reaction against the thoroughly corrupt *ancien régime.*

Burke's convictions were always passionate; he distrusted *a priori* theorists of the political left and right, and he believed that government was an organic evolution of centuries-long traditions and institutions, not to be tampered with or repaired like a machine. Though he was a poor orator (it is said that whenever he rose, the members of the House went out to dinner), his speeches were widely read, admired, and discussed for their vigorous prose and political philosophy. When he died at Beaconsfield on July 9, 1797, three years after his son succeeded him in Parliament, his most implacable foe, Fox, urged a public funeral in Westminster Abbey, but Burke's wish was to be buried privately on his estate at Beaconsfield. His life and work have become inextricably woven into the major strands of British political theory and history.

BIBLIOGRAPHICAL REFERENCES: The basic edition of Burke's writings is the *Works,* edited by F. Laurence and W. King, 8 vols., 1792–1827. Of modern editions, the edition of the *Works* edited by W. Willis and F. W. Raffety, 6 vols., 1906–1907, is available in the World's Classics series. The *Correspondence, 1744–1797,* was edited by Earl Fitzwilliam and Sir R. Bourke, 4 vols., 1844; a new and definitive edition is now in preparation. There are various editions of his selected writings.

For biography and criticism see Robert Bisset, *The Life of Burke,* 1798; Sir James Prior, *Memoir of the Life and Character of Burke,* 1824; Thomas Macknight. *History of the Life and Times of Burke,* 3 vols., 1858–1860; John Morley, *Edmund*

Burke: A Historical Study, 1879; E. A. Parkhurst, Edmund Burke: A Study of His Life and Character, 1886; T. S. Pillans, Edmund Burke: Apostle of Justice and Liberty, 1905; John McCunn, The Political Philosophy of Burke, 1913; A. P. I. Samuels, The Early Life, Correspondence and Writings of Burke, 1923; P. Magnus, Burke, 1939; A. M. Osborn, Burke and Rousseau, 1940; Harold J. Laski, Edmund Burke, 1947; T. W. Copeland, Edmund Burke: Six Essays, 1950; and Liam Barry, Our Legacy from Burke, 1952. See also Dixon Wecter, "The Missing Years in Edmund Burke's Biography," Publications of the Modern Language Association, LIII (1938), 1102–1125.

FANNY BURNEY

Born: King's Lynn, England
Date: June 13, 1752

Died: Bath, England
Date: January 6, 1840

Principal Works

NOVELS: *Evelina*, 1778; *Cecilia*, 1782; *Camilla*, 1796; *The Wanderer*, 1814.
JOURNAL AND LETTERS: *Letters and Diaries*, 1842–1846.

Fanny (Frances) Burney, the daughter of Charles Burney, musician and musicologist, was born in King's Lynn, Norfolk, on June 13, 1752. She began to write at the age of ten, and thereafter scribbled incessantly. She was persuaded to burn these youthful effusions, but she published (anonymously) her first novel in 1778: *Evelina, or, A Young Lady's Entrance into the World*. This picture of contemporary society was an immediate success. The narrative of the advancement of a charming heroine of obscure birth and humble surroundings to a position of social prominence obtained for the author the friendship and admiration of Dr. Samuel Johnson and a place in the intellectual life of London. Her second novel, *Cecilia, or, Memoirs of an Heiress* was salvaged from the material of a rejected drama, *The Witlings*; it enjoyed less success. In 1786 Miss Burney accepted the position of lady-in-waiting to the Queen; but the honor proved distasteful to her, and she retired from the court in 1791. In 1793 she married Alexandre D'Ar-

blay, a refugee from France; a son, Alexandre, was born in the following year. D'Arblay reawakened his wife's interest in writing, and soon appeared *Brief Reflections Relative to the Emigrant French Clergy* (1793), a politico-social pamphlet; *Edwy and Elgiva* (1795), a blank verse tragedy which died after one night; *Camilla, or, a Picture of Youth*, a dull but profitable novel; and a comedy, *Love and Fashion* (1800). From 1802 to 1812 Mme. D'Arblay lived in Paris. She published *The Wanderer: or, Female Difficulties* in 1814, duller than *Camilla* but more profitable. She followed her husband to Waterloo in 1815 and in Brussels tended the wounded of that battle; of this experience she left a vivid account in her diary. D'Arblay, wounded in the engagement, was permitted to retire to England, where he died in 1818. Mme. D'Arblay occupied herself thereafter with a life of her father, *Memoirs of Dr. Burney* (1832). She was made a countess by King Louis XVIII. She died at Bath on January 6, 1840, and was buried there.

Charlotte Frances Barrett, Mme. D'Arblay's niece, collected the letters and diaries of her aunt and published them in seven volumes (1842–1846). The diaries were severely edited in the process. *The Early Diary of Fanny Burney* was edited by Mrs. Anne Raine Ellis and published in 1889.

The publication of *Evelina* and the discovery that the author was a woman created a sensation; Mme. D'Arblay was not the first female writer, but she was the first woman to write successfully on a serious level. *Evelina* constituted "an extraordinary proof of woman's increasing importance in literature." Dr. Johnson praised the novel highly and reported that he could not put it down. He had whole scenes of it by heart and considered that one of the characters had never been "better drawn anywhere—in any book by any author."

BIBLIOGRAPHICAL REFERENCES: The most recent collected edition of Fanny Burney was edited in 1930 by F. D. Mackinnon. A recent edition of the diaries is the *Diary and Letters,* edited by Muriel Masefield, 1931. For biographical and critical studies see R. B. Johnson, *Fanny Burney and the Burneys,* 1926; Muriel Masefield, *The Story of Fanny Burney,* 1927; A. A. Overman, *An Investigation into the Character of Fanny Burney,* 1933; Averyl Staples, *Fanny Burney,* 1948; and Emily Hahn, *A Degree of Prudery,* 1950; also "Fanny Burney and the Courtesy Books," *Publications of the Modern Language Association,* LXV (1950), 732–761.

An important contribution to Burney studies is Joyce Hemlow, *The History of Fanny Burney,* 1958, a scholarly work of definitive proportions based on previously unpublished letters, journals, and miscellaneous papers.

ROBERT BURNS

Born: Alloway, Ayrshire, Scotland
Date: January 25, 1759

Died: Dumfries, Scotland
Date: July 21, 1796

PRINCIPAL WORKS

POEMS: *Poems, Chiefly in the Scottish Dialect,* 1786 (Kilmarnock Edition); 1787 (Edinburgh Edition); 1793, 2 volumes.

Although Robert Burns lived only to the age of thirty-seven, he lived with more intensity and produced more memorable writing than most authors who have lived twice as long. He became acquainted with hard work early, on his father's farm in Ayrshire where he was born, January 25, 1759. William Burnes, as he chose to spell it, was a poor tenant farmer who was kept in constant poverty by high rents and poor soil. Robert was put to work in the fields by the age of twelve, and he was doing a man's work at fifteen.

Even while laboring strenuously, however, Burns was an avid reader, stealing moments whenever possible to read Pope, Shakespeare, Milton, Dryden, and any other author whose works he could get.

The two major influences on Burns's early years, aside from his reading, were his father, whom Burns immortalized in *The Cotter's Saturday Night* (1786), and the local folk songs and legends. His earliest schooling he received from John Murdoch, a scholar hired by the farmers of the district, and at the parish school in Dalrymple. In 1773 he was sent to Murdoch's school at Ayr for a brief period. The old notion that Burns was an uneducated clod is quite inaccurate. He learned French well enough to read in that language and he was well grounded in English grammar. During the summer of 1777, while living with an uncle at Ballochneil, he studied mathematics and surveying under Hugh Rodger, schoolmaster at nearby Kirkoswald.

Throughout Burns's early life the history of his family was the story of moving from one poor farm to another. Thus they moved from Mount Oliphant to Lochlie in 1777, and from Lochlie to Mossgiel in 1784, at the death of Burns's father. As a possible source of income, Robert had tried to learn to dress flax in Irvine, but the work was uncongenial; when the flax shop burned down, he returned home immediately. He then spent four years, with his younger brothers, trying to make the farm at Mossgiel pay. By this time Burns had already started those romantic activities for which he is perhaps needlessly famous. He had had affairs with Jean Armour and Mary Campbell by this period in his life, but far more important, he had also started writing verse. He began "The Jolly Beggars" (1799) as early as 1785, and he had done some short songs and poems before that date.

By the time he was twenty-five many of Burns's most strongly expressed ideas were beginning to take shape in his mind. One of the most important of these was his mocking attitude toward Calvinism. Burns devoted much of his verse to exposing what he considered the hypocrisies and pomposities of Calvinism, and he was ever an enemy of the false, seemingly devout ministers, one of whom he pictures mercilessly in "Holy Willie's Prayer" (1799). Of equal importance, and of superior fame, was Burns's love of the countryside and its people. He was always primarily interested in the human significances of things; so, while he was not a nature poet in the Wordsworthian cause, he tried to show the effects of the rural environment on his countrymen.

After several years of fruitless and back-breaking work at the Mossgiel farm, Burns suddenly achieved success. The first edition of his poems came out in the nearby town of Kilmarnock in 1786, and overnight Burns became famous. That he should achieve fame with this group of poems is only fitting, since it contained some of his best work: "The Holy Fair," "The Cotter's Saturday Night," and "Address to the Deil." In this volume, *Poems, Chiefly in the Scottish Dialect,* Burns expressed his love of simple folk and his hate of specious religion.

Owing to the success of this first edition, Burns went to Edinburgh, where he comported himself well and was applauded by the critics. He also had there another love affair, with a Mrs. M'Lehose; this was not a hearty country romance, but an artificial, rather conventional one. Burns had received only twenty pounds for the first edition of the Kilmarnock poems, but he got four hundred for the second edition in 1787. With this money he traveled, had the leisure in which to write, and was able to marry and buy property of his own. In 1788 he made Jean Armour, mother of his four children, his wife and settled down on a farm at Ellisland, near Dumfries. In the next year he was given a post as an excise officer, and in 1791 he moved to Dumfries, where he remained for the rest of his life.

The last years of Burns's life were spent in further writing, including the three hundred songs which he contributed to two collections of Scottish songs, Johnson's *Musical Museum* (1737–1797) and Thomson's *Select Collection of Original Scottish Airs* (1793–1805), and in a fevered defense of the French Revolution and its principles. This latter enthusiasm is evidence of another of his traits, for Burns was a social rebel, never accepting blindly the traditional order of things. In the matter of the revolution, however, his outspoken advocacy earned him only contempt from his fellow citizens. There is considerable doubt about the last five years of Burns's life. Some biographers picture it as a time of dissipation and increasing ill temper, while others paint Burns as a tired but respected member of society. Probably parts of both stories are true. But it is certain that he suffered from melancholy and fits of extreme depression during his last years. His health never having been completely restored after the rigors of his youth and having declined rapidly in his mature years, he died in Dumfries on July 21, 1796.

Burns led a far from happy life. He was always under the burden of poverty, and, although he was socially minded and always a social success, he saw too realistically the faults and weaknesses of his fellow man ever to enjoy complete happiness. His love affairs, too, often gave him pain, and in his poems about the women involved the reader can detect a note of sadness and regret. But his warm and often tender poetry has earned for him a high place among writers of his own time and has made him the national poet of Scotland. Burns was not a great original thinker; he owes much to Robert Fergusson and Allan Ramsay, both for content and style. But his absolute sincerity, his moral honesty and rough ethical code, and his power to supply telling and vivid poetic details place him high in the first ranks of romantic poets. Perhaps the one quality of Burns's verse that appeals most strongly to the reader is the prominent personal note. Burns was a poet for everyone. His little songs or longer poems all speak directly to the reader directly from Burns. In poetry, a type of writing which tends to be most exclusive, Burns was probably the most un-exclusive writer of all. For this reason he has been widely read and admired by people of all ages and from all parts of the world.

BIBLIOGRAPHICAL REFERENCES: The basic edition for all Burns studies is the Library Edition of *The Life and Works of Robert Burns*, edited by Robert Chambers, 4 vols., 1856–1857, and revised by William Wallace, 1896. The standard edition of the *Poems* is that edited by William E. Henley and T. F. Henderson, 4 vols., 1896–1897. See also the *Works*, edited by W. S. Douglas, 6 vols., 1877–1879; the *Poetical Works*, edited by J. L. Robertson, Oxford Standard Authors Series, 1904; *Selected Poems of Robert Burns*, edited by John De Lancey Ferguson, 1926; *Robert Burns: The Poems*, edited by Charles S. Dougall, 1927; and *Poems of Robert Burns*, edited by Lawrence Brander, World's Classics series, 1950. Burns's letters are included in many of the editions of his works. The most reliable modern editions are the *Letters*, edited from original mss. by John De Lancey Ferguson, 2 vols., 1931, and *idem*, *Selected Letters*, World's Classics Series, 1953.

Many of the early biographies of Burns are inaccurate and biased. The standard biography is Franklyn B. Snyder, *The Life of Robert Burns*, 1932. See also Hans Hecht, *Robert Burns*, 1919 (trans., 1936); Catherine Carswell, *The Life of Robert Burns*, 1930; John De Lancey Ferguson, *Pride and Passion: Robert Burns*, 1939; and David Daiches, *Robert Burns*, 1952. A useful brief critical study is David Daiches, *Robert Burns*, 1957.

ROBERT BURTON

Born: Lindley, England   *Died:* Oxford, England
Date: February 8, 1577   *Date:* January 25, 1640

Principal Work

ESSAYS: *The Anatomy of Melancholy,* 1621.

Robert Burton was one of those remarkable men who by some major effort have established places for themselves in literary history. Burton's contribution was *The Anatomy of Melancholy,* a pseudo-scientific investigation into and philosophical discussion of the possibilities of human happiness. This was his only published work of a lifetime spent in scholarly and literary pursuits. However, if one counts the various revised editions (1624, 1628, 1632, 1638, 1651) of the work in which Burton's continuing labors showed themselves, and if one takes into account the extraordinary length and depth of his book, he may be credited with having written much more than many writers of seemingly greater productivity.

Burton was born in Lindley, Leicestershire, on February 8, 1577, the son of Ralph and Dorothy Burton. His preparatory education was at Sutton Coldfield, Warwickshire, and Nuneaton grammar schools. He entered Brasenose College, Oxford, as a commoner in 1593. Six years later he entered Christ Church College of Oxford University. He received his B.D. degree from Christ Church College in 1614. Although he subsequently held various

assignments as a clergyman, he remained at the college until his death. In 1616 he was appointed vicar of St. Thomas in Oxford, and in 1630 he was made rector of Segrave, Leicestershire, by his patron, Lord George Berkeley.

The Anatomy of Melancholy is a study of men which pretends, although the satirical intent is obvious, to be a study of moods from the medical point of view. Burton used the medical treatise form as a device for cramming literary, philosophical, and historical allusions, together with information from the somewhat confused medical sciences, into one vast commentary on the changing modes of human character and human emotion. From a discussion of the kinds and causes of melancholy Burton proceeds to a "Second Partition" on the cure of melancholy, and then enlivens the book with fascinating and (to him) sometimes shocking material on "love melancholy."

Although the title page gave the name "Democritus, Jr." as the author, Burton revealed his identity in a note to the reader which was included in the first edition.

Like a later "anatomist of melan-

162

choly," Sigmund Freud, whose studies of the human spirit have had more attention from psychologists than Burton's more fanciful literary analysis, Burton tried to predict the year of his death. Unlike Freud, who found his fearful calculations incorrect, Burton died early in the year he had chosen, on January 25, 1640.

He also wrote a play, *Philosophaster*, a comedy in Latin which entertained audiences at Christ Church when it was first presented in 1617. The work was not published until 1862.

BIBLIOGRAPHICAL REFERENCES: Modern editions of *The Anatomy of Melancholy* include those of Floyd Dell and Paul Jordan-Smith, 1927, and H. Jackson, Everyman's Library, 3 vols., 1932. For criticism see Paul Jordan-Smith, *Bibliographia Burtoniana: A Study of Robert Burton's "The Anatomy of Melancholy,"* 1931; Bergen Evans and G. J. Mohr, *The Psychiatry of Robert Burton,* 1944; W. R. Mueller, "The Anatomy of Robert Burton's England," *University of California English Studies,* No. 2, 1952; Robert M. Browne, "Robert Burton and the New Cosmology," *Modern Language Quarterly,* XIII (1952), 131–148; and Kimberley S. Roberts and Norman P. Sacks, "Dom Duarte and Robert Burton: Two Men of Melancholy," *Journal of the History of Medicine and Allied Sciences,* IX (1954), 21–37.

SAMUEL BUTLER

Born: Strensham, England
Date: February 8, 1612

Died: London, England
Date: September 25, 1680

PRINCIPAL WORKS

POEM: *Hudibras,* 1663, 1664, 1678.

MISCELLANEOUS: *The Genuine Remains in Verse and Prose of Samuel Butler,* 1759; *Characters, Observations, and Reflexions from the Notebooks,* 1908 (edited by A. R. Waller).

Samuel Butler is remembered chiefly as the author of one of the outstanding satires of the seventeenth century. *Hudibras,* a rollicking burlesque on the followers of Oliver Cromwell, was written as a mock-heroic poem in the tradition of Cervantes' *Don Quixote* (1605), in order to ridicule the Puritans who had controlled England for two decades. The central figure is Hudibras, a "presbyterian true blue" knight, and the theme of the poem is the attempt of this knight and his odd squire Ralpho to put an end to amusements in England. The topical reference is to the closing of the theaters in 1642.

Butler, royalist son of a prosperous Worcestershire yeoman, was born at Strensham on February 8, 1612. He was educated at King's School, Worcester. Later he served as secretary of the Countess of Kent and was also associated with the household of Sir Samuel Luke, a fanatical officer of Cromwell's army and possibly the original of the knight Hudibras.

His poem, part of which had circulated in manuscript before the Restoration in 1660, was published in three parts between 1663 and 1678, and King Charles II was so pleased with the work that he awarded Butler an annual pension of one hundred

163

pounds. Butler also wrote a series of character sketches between 1667 and 1669, but these were not published until 1759. Between 1671 and 1674 he was secretary to George Villiers, Duke of Buckingham. He died in London on September 25, 1680.

BIBLIOGRAPHICAL REFERENCES: The standard edition is the *Collected Works,* Vols. I and II edited by A. R. Waller, 1905, 1908; and Vol. III edited by René Lamar, 1928. Reginald B. Johnson edited the *Poetical Works,* 2 vols., 1893. For biography and criticism see Samuel Johnson, *Lives of the Poets,* 1779; William Hazlitt, *Lectures on the English Comic Writers,* 1819; Jan Veldkamp, *Samuel Butler,* 1923; Dan Gibson, "Samuel Butler," in *Seventeenth Century Studies by Members of the Graduate School, University of Cincinnati,* 1933; and E. A. Richards, *Hudibras in the Burlesque Tradition,* 1937.

SAMUEL BUTLER

Born: Langar, England
Date: December 4, 1835

Died: London, England
Date: June 18, 1902

PRINCIPAL WORKS

NOVELS: *Erewhon,* 1872; *Erewhon Revisited,* 1901; *The Way of All Flesh,* 1903.
ESSAYS AND STUDIES: *Evolution, Old and New,* 1879; *Unconscious Memory,* 1880; *The Humor of Homer,* 1892; *The Authoress of Homer,* 1897; *Shakespeare's Sonnets Reconsidered,* 1899.
TRANSLATIONS: The *Iliad,* 1898; the *Odyssey,* 1900.

Samuel Butler, English novelist and essayist, was born at Langar, Nottinghamshire, December 4, 1835, the son of the Reverend Thomas Butler and the grandson of a Bishop of Lichfield. This clerical ancestry was to have its influence on his writings. He was educated at St. John's College, Cambridge, and was intended for the Church; but, because of religious doubts he declined to take orders, preferring to study painting. The resulting estrangement between his father and himself led him to emigrate to New Zealand in 1859, where he spent five years in sheep farming. He became interested in Darwin and wrote *Darwin Among the Machines* (1863), the germ of *Erewhon.* Returning to England in 1864, he continued his painting, exhibiting regularly, and also composed

music. He became a friend of Darwin, but disagreed with the latter's theory of evolution and wrote several books to advance a theory of his own, which was not taken very seriously by scientists.

Butler's next phase was classical. He became interested in the Homeric question, maintaining that the *Iliad* and the *Odyssey* were by different authors and that the latter was written by a woman. Like his books on evolution, these writings now belong to the curiosities of literature.

Butler's importance lies in his contribution to the reaction against Victorianism. *Erewhon* ("nowhere") is a satire on the machine age and the forerunner of several modern novels. By depicting a society in which the possession of any mechanical device

164

is illegal, he made fun of nineteenth century industrialism, and then proceeded to satirize much of Victorian morality. In *Erewhon* sickness is a crime, whereas crime is a sickness and is treated as such. Thus, society's attitude towards morals is the product of convention; it is as illogical to condemn a man for stealing as to condemn him for contracting influenza.

Butler's really important novel is *The Way of All Flesh*, written between 1873 and 1885 but not published until a year after his death. This book, which Shaw claimed had influenced him greatly, is a satiric portrait of Butler's own childhood. Theobald and Christina Pontifex are his parents, while Butler appears twice: as Overton, the narrator, and as Ernest, the repressed son. It is a terrible picture of the worst side of Victorian family life, with its excessive strictness, exaggerated piety, and hypocrisy. The book is hardly a novel; it is a series of essays in which Butler attacked the shams of the world of his childhood in a clergyman's family and at the same time expressed his philosophy of common sense. His hero is the prototype of the modern youth who revolts against his parents' *mores* and eventually builds a life of his own. It is the story of Butler's own struggle for freedom.

Butler died in London, June 18, 1902.

BIBLIOGRAPHICAL REFERENCES: The collected writings of Samuel Butler have been published in The Shrewsbury Edition, edited by H. F. Jones and A. T. Bartholomew, 20 vols., 1923–1926. The standard biography is H. F. Jones, *Samuel Butler: A Memoir*, 2 vols., 1919. See also Clara G. Stillman, *Samuel Butler: A Mid-Victorian Modern*, 1932; Malcolm Muggeridge, *The Earnest Atheist*, 1937; George Bernard Shaw, Introduction to *The Way of All Flesh*, 1936 (Oxford University Press); Edmund Wilson, *The Triple Thinkers*, 1938; and L. E. Holt, "Samuel Butler's Rise to Fame," *Publications of the Modern Language Society*, LVII (1942), 867–878.

DONN BYRNE
(Brian Oswald Donn-Byrne)

Born: New York, N. Y.
Date: November 20, 1889

Died: County Cork, Ireland
Date: June 18, 1928

PRINCIPAL WORKS

NOVELS: *The Stranger's Banquet*, 1919; *The Foolish Matrons*, 1920; *Messer Marco Polo*, 1921; *The Wind Bloweth*, 1922; *Blind Raftery*, 1924; *O'Malley of Shanganagh*, 1925; *Hangman's House*, 1926; *Brother Saul*, 1927; *Crusade*, 1928; *Field of Honor*, 1929.

SHORT STORIES: *Stories without Women*, 1915; *Changeling and Other Stories*, 1923; *Destiny Bay*, 1928.

MISCELLANEOUS: *Ireland: The Rock Whence I Was Hewn*, 1929.

Donn Byrne (christened Brian Oswald Donn-Byrne) was born on November 20, 1889, in New York City, where his parents were staying while his father, an Irish engineer, was inspecting an American bridge-building project. Within a few months the Donn-Byrnes returned to their home in Armagh. The father died several years later, leaving the family in somewhat straitened circumstances. As a boy Donn Byrne, as he eventually signed himself in his writing, became interested in the Irish national movement. Known in those days as Brian O'Beirne, he appeared frequently at the Glens Feiseanna—Irish festivals—and in spite of his youth formed friendships with a number of organizers of the Sinn Fein. The influences of his boyhood account for the deep interest in Irish life and folkways displayed in his books.

Educated at University College, Dublin, where he studied under Dr. Douglas Hyde, famous Gaelic scholar and later the first president of Eire, he also did work at the Sorbonne and at Leipzig. The story is that he suddenly gave up plans for a diplomatic career and went off to Central or South America to become a cowboy poet. He next turned up in New York. There he worked at a variety of jobs, wrote and published a few romantic poems, and in 1911 married Dorothea Cadogan, soon to be known in her own right as the co-author of the successful play, *Enter Madame*. For a time Donn Byrne supported his family by work on the staffs of the New Standard and the Century dictionaries. His first short stories appeared in *The Smart Set* and *Century*.

Although his first two novels had fair sales and received some critical recognition, his first real success came with *Messer Marco Polo* in 1921. This short novel, a retelling of Marco Polo's adventures in the spirit of an Irish folk tale, captured the attention of critics and readers alike with its imaginative sweep and romantic Gaelic phrasing. *The Wind Bloweth* achieved an equally great success when it appeared in 1922. On the proceeds of these two books Donn Byrne, generous and extravagant by nature, was soon living beyond his means; unable to meet the demands of his creditors, he and his wife decided to retrench and to return to Ireland. There, after a brief stay in England, he wrote *Blind Raftery*, *O'Malley of Shanganagh*, and *Hangman's House*. A visit to Palestine and Syria in 1926 gave him the themes and backgrounds for two novels, *Brother Saul* and *Crusade*. *Field of Honor*, his last novel (published in England as *The Power of the Dog*), showed his growing interest in history, particularly that of the Napoleonic period.

With $10,000 won in a single night at the baccarat tables in Cannes, he bought Coolmain Castle, a country estate in County Cork which he had rented in two previous summers. Several days after his arrival at Coolmain he was killed when the defective steering gear caused his car to swerve off the road and plunge into Courtmacsherry Bay, on June 18, 1928.

The writing of Donn Byrne belongs to the tradition of Synge and other romanticists of the Irish Renaissance. Unfriendly critics have charged that he was a professional Irishman. It is true that his fiction was often self-consciously poetic and lush in Gaelic atmosphere, but only a very real love for a land and an understanding of its people could have produced the novels and short stories which define so clearly his limited but authentic talent.

BIBLIOGRAPHICAL REFERENCES: The full-length biographical study is Thurston Macauley, *Donn Byrne: Bard of Armagh*, 1929. See also A. St. John Adcock, *Gods* of *Modern Grub Street*, 1923; and T. P. O'Connor, *The Genius of Donn Byrne*, 1927 (pamphlet).

GEORGE GORDON, LORD BYRON

Born: London, England   *Died:* Missolonghi, Greece
Date: January 22, 1788   *Date:* April 19, 1824

PRINCIPAL WORKS

POEMS: *English Bards and Scotch Reviewers*, 1809; *Childe Harold's Pilgrimage*, 1812 (Cantos I and II); *The Giaour*, 1813; *The Bride of Abydos*, 1813; *The Corsair*, 1814; *Lara*, 1814; *Hebrew Melodies*, 1815; *The Siege of Corinth*, 1816; *Parisina*, 1816; *Childe Harold's Pilgrimage*, 1816 (Canto III); *The Prisoner of Chillon*, 1816; *Beppo*, 1818; *Childe Harold's Pilgrimage*, 1818 (Canto IV); *Don Juan*, 1819–1824; *The Vision of Judgment*, 1822; *The Island*, 1823.

PLAYS: *Manfred*, 1817; *Cain*, 1821; *Marino Faliero*, 1821; *Sardanapalus*, 1821; *The Two Foscari*, 1821; *Werner*, 1823; *Heaven and Earth*, 1824.

More than 130 years after his death the name of George Gordon, Lord Byron, can still evoke all that was poetic, dramatic, and scandalous about the Romantic Period. But instead of just one Byron, there seem to have been three (and perhaps more): Byron the Adventurer, Byron the Lover, Byron the Poet.

Adventurer he was, with exploits not confined to the drawing-room, and a revolutionist who fought not only with words but with a physical bravery that led to his death.

Born in London on January 22, 1788, Byron was the son of a spendthrift father and a mother whose alternating moods of affection and wild anger left him bewildered. His life was tempestuous from the beginning. Lame, handsome, and with a personality magnetic to both men and women, he embarked in 1809 on a trip to the Near East. His adventures included a shipwreck, a bout with fever, the swimming of the Hellespont, and the rescue of a girl who was about to be drowned. When he returned to England his first speech in the House of Lords was in defense of the working man—a radical start for a young lord. Later, when the scandal of his personal life broke over his head, he was advised not to appear in public, for fear the very sight of him might cause a riot. When he left England for his exile in Europe, friends had to protect his life with firearms.

In Italy, at Ravenna, Byron became again the adventurer. Probably joining the revolutionary Carbonari, he bought guns and ammunition for a revolt against Austrian tyranny. His death at Missolonghi, in Greece, on April 19, 1824, was the result of a fever caught while fighting against the Turks for Greek independence.

There was also Byron the Lover. "Mad, bad, and dangerous to know"—thus Lady Caroline Lamb summed up her first impression of him. Byron's love affairs started early, while he was a student at Harrow, and they continued through Cambridge and the period when he was a darling of London society. In 1814 he married Anne Isabella Milbanke, and his friends thought the match might calm the wild lord; it failed to do so. After the birth of his daughter Ada, he and Lady Byron separated; rumors spread over England, rumors of an incestuous relationship between Byron and his half-sister, Augusta Leigh. No public explanation of their separation was ever advanced by either Byron or his wife, and so the society that had idolized him now turned him, on the basis of rumor alone, into a monstrous villain. He virtually went into exile when he left England in 1816. In Venice, in 1818, Byron the Lover became Byron the Debauchee. Then he met the Countess Teresa Guiccioli, the beautiful young wife of an old man. His love for the Countess was no idle affair of a confirmed libertine. Byron followed her from Venice to Ravenna, from Pisa to Genoa. The arrangements for such a love-life were complicated but in part regularized by Teresa's separation, by Papal decree, from her husband, but it seems characteristically Byronic that his one real love could never be completely his own. Yet he remained her faithful paramour until his death.

Out of these conflicting personalities there was enough left over for Byron the Poet, who remains, after the drama and the swashbuckling are stripped away, a truly major figure among the English Romantics. Certainly the early Byron who awoke to find himself famous was not then a great poet but a versifier who shocked and insulted. His first volume, *Hours of Idleness* (1807), came out while Byron was at Cambridge and the *Edinburgh Review* criticized it scathingly; Byron retaliated with *English Bards and Scotch Reviewers,* equally as scathing. From his trip to the Near East he brought back the first two cantos of *Childe Harold's Pilgrimage.* They made him famous and ex- tremely popular. Volume followed volume until he reached, in 1814, a peak of popularity with *The Corsair,* which sold 10,000 copies on the day of publication. To the second edition Byron added "Lines to a Lady Weeping," which disparaged the Prince Regent. This insult provoked a revolt against him. Next came the scandal in his personal life, and Byron went into the exile that turned him from a weak sensationalist into a great lyric and narrative poet.

On the site of the Battle of Waterloo he composed the famous stanza for a new canto of *Childe Harold.* In Venice (sandwiched between his notorious affairs) he wrote more cantos, and *Manfred,* and the beginning of *Don Juan,* the greatest of his narrative poems. Starting out like a slapstick bedroom farce, *Don Juan* slowly emerges as a beautiful romance between its protagonist and Haidée, a native girl. Along with his new-found poetic strength Byron kept his talent for invective: the dedication of *Don Juan* insults Robert Southey (then Poet Laureate), Coleridge, and Wordsworth, among others.

The charge has been brought that Byron is too topical, too stale for our time. Yet his *The Vision of Judgment,* one of his last works, makes history sound as fresh as a clipping from this morning's newspaper.

The poetry of Byron is as many-sided as the man himself. It ranges from gentle love lyrics like "She Walks in Beauty" and "When We Two Parted" to the pure narrative of "The Prisoner of Chillon" and the biting satire of *The Vision of Judgment.* Byron might well be a product of our own times, so twentieth century in spirit are his love

168

of athletics, his disillusionment, his laughing satire, his genuine spirit of revolt.

England refused this stormy Poet, Adventurer, and Lover a burial in Westminster Abbey; he lies in the fam- ily vault at Hucknall-Torkard Church, near Newstead. But time, which may wash away the muck of sensationalism from his life, will thereby more fully reveal the sparkling facets of his best verse.

BIBLIOGRAPHICAL REFERENCES: The collected works of Byron comprise the *Poems*, edited by E. H. Coleridge, and the *Letters and Journals*, edited by R. E. Prothero, 13 vols., 1898–1904. Important among the volumes of selections are the *Poetical Works*, edited by Paul Elmer More, 1905, and *Don Juan and Other Satirical Poems*, edited by L. I. Bredvold, 1935.

The standard biography is Ethel C. Mayne, *Byron*, 2 vols., 1912, but this work must now be supplemented by Leslie A. Marchand, *Byron: A Biography*, 3 vols., 1957, a monumental and authoritative study incorporating the results of recent Byron scholarship. For biographical studies of Byron as presented by his contemporaries see Thomas Medwin, *Journal of the Conversations of Lord Byron*, 1824; Leigh Hunt, *Lord Byron and Some of His Contemporaries*, 1828; John Galt, *The Life of Lord Byron*, 1830; Thomas Moore, *The Life of Lord Byron with His Letters and Journals*, 1830; and Teresa Guiccioli, *My Recollections of Lord Byron*, 1869. Other studies include Richard Edgecombe, *Byron: The Last Phase*, 1909; Harold Nicolson, *Byron: The Last Journey, April 1823–April 1824*, 1924; Sir John C. Fox, *The Byron Mystery*, 1925; André Maurois, *Byron*, 1930; Peter Quennell, *The Years of Fame*, 1935; *idem*, *Byron in Italy*, 1941; and Iris Origo, *The Last Attachment: The Story of Byron and Teresa Guiccioli*, 1949. See also E. W. Marjarum, *Byron as Skeptic and Believer*, 1938; Elizabeth Boyd, *Byron's Don Juan*, 1945; and Paul Trueblood, *The Flowering of Byron's Genius*, 1945.

JAMES BRANCH CABELL

Born: Richmond, Virginia
Date: April 14, 1879

Died: Richmond, Virginia
Date: May 5, 1958

PRINCIPAL WORKS

NOVELS: *The Eagle's Shadow*, 1904; *The Cords of Vanity*, 1909; *The Rivet in Grandfather's Neck*, 1915; *The Cream of the Jest*, 1917; *Jurgen*, 1919; *Domnei*, 1920; *Figures of Earth*, 1921; *The High Place*, 1923; *The Silver Stallion*, 1926; *Something about Eve*, 1927; *The Way of Ecben*, 1929; *Smirt*, 1934; *Smith*, 1935; *Smire*, 1937; *The King Was in His Counting-House*, 1938; *Hamlet Had an Uncle*, 1940; *The First Gentleman of America*, 1942; *There Were Two Pirates*, 1946; *The Devil's Own Dear Son*, 1949.

SHORT STORIES: *The Line of Love*, 1905; *Gallantry*, 1907; *Chivalry*, 1909; *The Certain Hour*, 1916; *The Music from behind the Moon*, 1926; *The White Robe*, 1928.

ESSAYS AND CRITICISM: *Beyond Life*, 1919; *Straws and Prayer-Books*, 1924; *Some of Us*, 1930; *These Restless Heads*, 1932; *Special Delivery*, 1933; *Ladies and Gentlemen*, 1934; *Let Me Lie*, 1947; *Quiet, Please*, 1952.

AUTOBIOGRAPHY: *As I Remember It*, 1955.

James Branch Cabell was born in Richmond, Virginia, on April 14, 1879. He attended the College of William and Mary, graduating with high honors in 1898, and entered journalism in Richmond. After two years (1899-1901) with the New York *Herald*, he returned and, while working on the Richmond *News*, began the publication of his fictional writings in short stories and novels. Cabell's first major popular success was delayed until the publication of *Jurgen* in 1919; then, ironically, popular attention came largely because the book was banned in several cities through censorship. The publicity attracted both critical and popular attention, and James Branch Cabell enjoyed a huge success throughout the 1920's. By 1929 Cabell believed that a distinct phase of his writing had been completed, and he prepared the Storisende Edition of his collected works under the title *The Biography of the Life of Manuel*. The whole series of eighteen volumes is an interrelated saga of Dom Manuel of Poictesme and tells of characteristic traits passed by him to his descendants. The *Biography* covers centuries in time and has settings in both Europe and America. After 1929 further books by the author were to appear over the signature of Branch Cabell, until in 1942 he resumed his full name.

Cabell is a romanticist with a difference; he is romantic in his subject matter but ironical in his conclusions. His style is polished to brilliancy, frequently teeming with archaisms selected for piquant flavor. He is witty and erudite in his literary background.

Rearranged in time sequence, the books that make up *The Biography of the Life of Manuel* integrate the richly involved story of a swineherd, Manuel, who during the medieval period becomes ruler of the mythical kingdom of Poictesme in what is now the south of France. Progenitor of numerous descendants and characteristics, Manuel after death is legendized into a cultural faith and eventually reappears on earth. Making up the *Biography* are novels, short stories, poems, plays, essays. Among the most significant novels are these: *Figures of Earth* presents the story of Manuel's origin in mythic Poictesme, his rule, and his death; *The Silver Stallion* traces the legendary growth of Manuel as a "Redeemer" who is worshiped by later generations; *Jurgen*, most famous individual novel by Cabell, tells the story of a middle-aged pawnbroker who, seeking his wife Lisa, dons a magic shirt which allows him to return to his youth and enjoy associations with famous beauties of fiction and myth, but who returns to his commonplace life as he knows it and to his wife as he knows her. *The High Place* tells the story of Florian de Puysange, who grasps the ideal romantic goal only to renounce it. *The Rivet in Grandfather's Neck* and *The Cream of the Jest* both tell satirically of Poictesme-like romantic ideals in the American South. Cabell's reiterated theme seems to be that ideals to strive for are more stimulating and satisfying than an ideal actually achieved.

Since 1934 Cabell has published three fictional trilogies, none of them adding greatly to his fame as a novelist. They include *The Nightmare has Triplets*, made up of *Smirt, Smith*, and *Smire; Heirs and Assigns*, made up of *The King Was in His Counting-House, Hamlet Had an Uncle*, and *The First Gentleman of America; It Happened in Florida*, made up of *The*

St. Johns, There Were Two Pirates, and The Devil's Own Dear Son. In 1913 Cabell married Miss Priscilla Bradley, who bore him one son and who died in 1948; in 1950 Mr. Cabell married Miss Margaret Waller Freeman. In his later years he and his wife spent much of their time in Florida. During the late 1930's and the 1940's Cabell's popular and critical position was in eclipse, but Edmund Wilson, a perceptive critic, writing in 1956, has begun among many readers a revival of interest in Cabell's writings.

BIBLIOGRAPHICAL REFERENCES: Books written before 1930 have been collected in the Storisende Edition of *The Works of James Branch Cabell*, 1927–1930. There is no extensive biographical study. For general information on the man and his work see Carl Van Doren, *James Branch Cabell*, 1925, (rev. ed., 1932); H. L. Mencken, *James Branch Cabell*, 1927 (pamphlet); more specialized studies are found in Don M. Bregenzer and Amy Loveman, eds., *A Round Table in Poictesme*, 1924; Warren A. McNeill, *Cabellian Harmonics*, 1928; James P. Cover, *Notes on "Jurgen,"* 1928; and John P. Cranwell and James P. Cover, *Notes on "Figures of Earth,"* 1929.

See also Percy Boynton, *Some Contemporary Americans*, 1924; Stuart P. Sherman, *The Main Stream*, 1927; Henry S. Canby, *American Estimates*, 1930; Russell Blankenship, *American Literature as an Expression of the American Mind*, 1931; Edward Wagenknecht, *Cavalcade of the American Novel*, 1951; Hugh Walpole, "The Art of James Branch Cabell," *Yale Review*, IX (1920), 684–698; Clara F. McIntyre, "Mr. Cabell's Cosmos," *Sewanee Review*, XXXVIII (1930), 278–285; Gay Wilson Allen, "Jurgen and Faust," *Sewanee Review*, XXXIX (1931), 485–492; W. R. Parker, "A Key to Cabell," *English Journal*, XXI (1932), 431–440; Edmund Wilson, "The James Branch Cabell Case Reopened," *New Yorker*, XXXII (1956), 140–168; Edd W. Parks, "Cabell's *Cream of the Jest*," *Modern Fiction Studies*, II (1956), 68–70; and Raymond Himelick, "Figures of Cabell," *Modern Fiction Studies*, II (1956–1957), 214–220.

GEORGE WASHINGTON CABLE

Born: New Orleans, Louisiana   *Died:* St. Petersburg, Florida
Date: October 12, 1844   *Date:* January 31, 1925

PRINCIPAL WORKS

NOVELS: *The Grandissimes*, 1880; *Dr. Sevier*, 1884; *Bonaventure*, 1888; *John March, Southerner*, 1894; *The Cavalier*, 1901; *Bylow Hill*, 1902; *Kincaid's Battery*, 1908; *Gideon's Band*, 1914; *The Flower of the Chapdelaines*, 1918; *Lovers of Louisiana*, 1918.

SHORT STORIES: *Old Creole Days*, 1879; *Madame Delphine*, 1881; *Strange True Stories of Louisiana*, 1889; *Strong Hearts*, 1899.

HISTORICAL AND SOCIAL STUDIES: *History and Present Condition of New Orleans*, 1881; *The Creoles of Louisiana*, 1884; *The Silent South*, 1885; *The Negro Question*, 1890.

George Washington Cable, a man of diverse and lively talents, was born in New Orleans on October 12, 1844. His father was from an old slaveholding family in Virginia, while his mother came of strait-laced Puritan stock; from

171

this contrast may have stemmed some of the contradictions which later marked Cable's adult personality and literary career.

In 1859, on the eve of the Civil War, Cable's father died after a series of business reverses which had brought the family circumstances to the brink of poverty. During the next few years the boy, only fourteen at the time of his father's death, became the mainstay of the family. In 1863 he enlisted in the Confederate cavalry. Twice wounded, he nevertheless served until the end of the war, interspersing his activities as a trooper with self-imposed studies in mathematics, Latin, and the Bible.

For two years after the war Cable was almost completely incapacitated by malarial fever. Recovering slowly, he began to write for the New Orleans *Picayune,* doing a regular column called "Drop Shot." His journalistic career proved short-lived, however, when the paper dropped him for refusing to report theatrical performances. Next, as an accountant and correspondence clerk, he found congenial work with a firm of cotton factors. His marriage, in 1869, to Louise S. Bartlett seemed to complete the pattern by which his life would be ordered.

Suddenly, however—and almost by accident—this course was changed. His passion for self-education had led him to develop mastery of French and to dig into the city archives. Among the latter he found numerous fascinating events which he could not resist using as the basis for narratives of his own. When a literary scout, Edward King, examined his papers for *Scribner's*

Monthly, the result was publication of " 'Sieur George" in the October, 1873, issue of that magazine. *Old Creole Days,* a collection of seven tales, followed six years later. This volume gained for its author instant recognition as a new and interesting interpreter of the South. When the firm for which he worked was eventually dissolved, he seized the opportunity to turn to writing as a full-time occupation. In steady succession appeared *The Grandissimes, The Creoles of Louisiana, Dr. Sevier,* and *The Silent South.* Criticism of his views on the South led him, in 1885, to establish a home for his family in Northampton, Massachusetts. During his later years in New England he became a close friend of Mark Twain, and he continued to write and publish as late as 1918. He died in St. Petersburg, Florida, on January 31, 1925.

A large part of Cable's remarkable energy went into his varied activities as an advocate of social reform. His Puritan inheritance found its outlet in untiring work as a philanthropist, a religious leader, and a Bible-class teacher; and his outspoken views, especially those regarding justice for the Negro, often earned him the resentment of his native South. Nevertheless, it is as a romanticist that the twentieth century most easily identifies George Washington Cable. His early work, for which he is by now best remembered, has established him as a leading exponent of the "local color" school, and his Louisiana tales have preserved an exotic segment of American life which is fast losing its identity.

BIBLIOGRAPHICAL REFERENCES: There is no collected edition. The official biography is Lucy L. C. Biklé, *George W. Cable: His Life and Letters,* 1928, now superseded in many important details by Arlin Turner, *George W. Cable: A Biography,*

1957. The biographical sketch in the *Dictionary of American Biography* is by Fred L. Pattee. See also Harry A. Toulmin, *Social Historians,* 1911; Fred L. Pattee, *A History of American Literature since 1870,* 1915; Arthur Hobson Quinn, *American Fiction,* 1936; Van Wyck Brooks, *The Times of Melville and Whitman,* 1947; Lafcadio Hearn, "The Scenes of Cable's Romances," *Century,* New Series V (1883), 40–47; Edward L. Tinker, "Cable and the Creoles," *American Literature,* V (1934), 313–326; Richard Chase, "Cable and His *Grandissimes,*" *Kenyon Review,* XVIII (1956), 194–204; and Edmund Wilson, "The Ordeal of George Washington Cable," *New Yorker,* XXXIII (Nov. 9, 1957), 172–216.

GAIUS JULIUS CAESAR

Born: Rome, Italy
Date: July 12, 102 (or 100) B.C.

Died: Rome
Date: March 15, 44 B.C.

PRINCIPAL WORKS

HISTORY: *Comentarii,* c. 51 B.C. (*Commentaries*).

Gaius Julius Caesar is better known as a leader than as a writer. However, his histories were models of the simple expository style of composition. Born of a Roman patrician family in either 102 or 100 B.C., he was required to prepare himself for political or military service to the state. He determined upon the military life because a relative, Marius, was the leader of the *populārēs,* the more democratic of the two groups who struggled for control of the state at the time. He was tutored in Greek and Latin literature and rhetoric. When his father died, Caesar at sixteen assumed the *toga virilis.* He was made a priest of Jupiter during the temporary triumph of the *populārēs* led by Marius and Cinna after the civil war which followed the social war of 90–89 B.C. He married Cinna's daughter Cornelia, but when the *optimātēs* party led by Sulla assumed power, he was ordered to divorce her. Refusing, he fled to Asia Minor to join the Roman army under Thermus and there received the highest military award for valor. When he learned of Sulla's death in 78 B.C., he returned to Rome. To further his political career he studied rhetoric at Rhodes under Molon, and then slowly advanced himself in Roman politics by supporting the common people to increase his popularity and by revising the popular assembly. He was made quaestor in 68 B.C. and, through bribery, pontifex maximus following the Catiline conspiracy in 63 B.C. When the Senate welcomed Pompey, whom he had opposed, Caesar went to Spain as its governor. On his return from Spain he formed a ruling coalition with Pompey and Crassus in 60 B.C. He became consul in 59 B.C. and the next year secured his military power by becoming governor of Gaul. His *Commentaries,* the only literary works of his extant, cover his successful activities as a military leader during the subsequent ten years spent in subduing Gaul and Pompey. In the latter years of his governorship the triumvirate gradually disintgerated. Crassus was killed in battle and Julia, Caesar's daughter whom Pompey had married, died. Pompey and Caesar became distrustful

173

of one another. The senate, under the influence of Cicero, sought to reinstate Pompey. Civil war ensued, but with Caesar's victory at Pharsala he became master of the entire Roman world. In 44 B.C., after being made dictator for life, he was murdered in the Senate building.

As dictator, Caesar undertook a complete reorganization of the Roman state. His later writings, such as political pamphlets, grammatical treatises, and even poems, no longer exist. Much of his writing was suppressed by Augustus; only the *Commentaries*, of his longer works, survive. As history and memoirs, and as models of clear expository writing, they give their soldier-author a unique place in literary history.

BIBLIOGRAPHICAL REFERENCES: Editions of the *Commentaries* are numerous. See H. J. Edwards, *The Gallic War*, 1917. For biographical and historical studies see also John Buchan, *Julius Caesar*, 1936; T. Rice Holmes, *The Roman Republic and the Founder of the Empire*, 3 vols., 1923; L. R. Taylor, *Party Politics in the Age of Caesar*; and Gérard Walter, *Caesar: A Biography*, 1947 (trans., 1952).

PEDRO CALDERÓN DE LA BARCA

Born: Madrid, Spain
Date: January 17, 1600

Died: Madrid
Date: May 25, 1681

PRINCIPAL WORKS

PLAYS: *El astrólogo fingido*, c. 1624 (*The Mock Astrologer*); *El príncipe constante*, 1629 (*The Constant Prince*); *La dama duende*, 1629 (*The Fairy Lady*); *Peor está que estaba*, 1630 (*It Is Worse than It Was*); *Mejor está que estaba*, 1631 (*It Is Better than It Was*); *La devoción de la cruz*, c. 1633 (*The Devotion of the Cross*); *El médico de su honra*, 1635 (*The Physician of His Own Honor*); *El mayor encanto amor*, 1635 (*No Magic like Love*); *La vida es sueño*, c. 1635 (*Life Is a Dream*); *El mágico prodigioso*, 1637 (*The Mighty Magician*); *El alcalde de Zalamea*, c. 1642 (*The Mayor of Zalamea*); *El gran teatro del mundo*, c. 1645 (*The Great Theater of the World*).

Born in Madrid on January 17, 1600, Pedro Calderón de la Barca, the national dramatist of Spain who was to dominate his age as thoroughly as Lope de Vega did his, came from a good family of the lower nobility. His father was a secretary of the treasury under two kings and could afford to give his son the best education available. Calderón entered the Royal Jesuit School of Madrid when he was nine, and continued his studies in Alcalá. By the age of fifteen he was ready for the University of Salamanca, where he began writing and producing plays. Upon graduation he returned to Madrid, determined on a literary career and early marked as the greatest lyric poet of his time. He started studying the theater, especially Lope de Vega's plays, but his apprentice period was interrupted by military service in Italy and Flanders.

Back in Madrid, after Lope de Vega's death he wrote plays to be presented in the palace of Philip IV, including the *zarzuela*, or comedy with music, that inaugurated the king's

174

Retiro Theater in 1635. In his bid for popularity, Calderón could not simply imitate Lope de Vega. He had to offer something new. At that time Spanish literature was characterized by Gongorism, a striving for the subtle, involving strained metaphors and an uncommon vocabulary. The new dramatist seized upon this fad to attract attention. But he was too great a craftsman to forget that he had also to produce drama.

The art of the theater had improved in the course of the thirty-five years during which Lope de Vega and his contemporaries had been experimenting. To this new technique Calderón added a skill in versification and a philosophical training, so that, at his best, he reached heights beyond his predecessor's powers. Since plagiarism was not a black and ugly word at that time, provided the new user improved upon his borrowed material, for some of his greatest plays Calderón employed some of Lope de Vega's material and themes. His tragedy, *The Mayor of Zalamea*, the most perfect rural drama of the Golden Age, is a rewriting of Lope de Vega's dashing improvisation of the same title. Half a dozen sources gave him material for his greatest philosophical drama *Life Is a Dream*. There are other instances of his borrowing, but his genius lay in transmuting what he took from others.

Calderón's Jesuitical training and his offices in the Church may explain his preference for his religious plays, rather than his secular output, which ceased after 1650. He never even attempted to collect and publish what he had written. Only because the Duke of Veragua, a descendant of Columbus, requested it, ten months before the dramatist's death, did Calderón draw up a list of his secular plays. It included 111 three-act plays, aside from his sacramental dramas.

The *auto sacramental,* an allegory putting into concrete form the abstract idea of the Holy Communion and performed as part of the Corpus Christi observances, was the dramatic form on which Calderón lavished his poetic ability. He wrote seventy-three of them during his lifetime. It is a pity that the vogue of these religious plays has passed and that his creations, so full of poetic wealth, have been practically forgotten. In one, *The Great Theater of the World,* God is the director, and the actors include people from many walks of life. To the Poor Man, the King, and Discretion, the director gives roles of glory. The Rich Man and Beauty are condemned. In another, Helen of Troy is a lost soul stolen from her husband Menelaus (Christ) by Paris (the Devil). Priam is God; Hecuba, God's idea. In *Los encantos de la culpa* (*The Sorceries of Sin*), a masterpiece of this type of drama, Man, represented by Ulysses, sails in a ship with the Five Senses as crew. As he stops at an island, Sin the Enchantress turns the Senses into beasts. Understanding awakens Man and tells him of the fate of his guides. When he repents, Penance appears to give him flowers stained with the Blood of the Lamb.

In 1681 Calderón's strength failed after he had completed one of two *autos sacramentales* intended for presentation during the Corpus Christi feast, plays similar to those he had written on the same occasion for the past thirty years. He took to his bed and died on May 25, 1681, leaving the second play to be finished by another author.

175

Religion also provided themes for Calderón's longer plays. The Bible and an earlier play by Lope de Vega inspired *Los cabellos de Absolom* (*The Hair of Absolom*). His masterpiece of this type is *The Mighty Magician,* a Faust-like play of a man who gives up his pagan deities in his search for God.

For a totally different type, dramas of jealousy, the strict Spanish honor code provided motivation. Shocking to Anglo-Saxon minds and criticized by many Spaniards, including the *graciosos* or practical-minded comic characters of the plays themselves, the honor code was still carefully observed. Examples are *El pintor de su deshonra* (*The Painter of her Dishonor*) and *The Physician of His Own Honor,* in which even the vague possibility of a wife's unfaithfulness that might stain the family honor is enough to justify the husband in arranging for her death. In stressing theme, Calderón was the great tragic dramatist of Spain as Lope de Vega surpassed in comedy.

Calderón was skilled also in handling the complications of the *comedias de capa y espada,* or cape-and-sword plays. The presentation of local customs and the dramatist's ability to interweave the many threads of the complicated plot are seen at their best in a comedy like *The Fairy Lady.* But the dramatic production of Calderón's that caused German critics to rank him as one of the world's best three, a play still much read and frequently produced even after three hundred years, is *Life Is a Dream,* produced about 1635. It has been translated into many foreign languages; Russia, Sweden, France, Germany, and America have witnessed performances, and to Spanish school children the poetic soliloquy defining Life is as familiar as those of Hamlet. Combining the awakened sleeper theme of the King of the Assassins, the Arabian Nights story of Abou Hassan, and the oriental legend of Barlaam and Josephat with its links to Buddha, Calderón has added elements of his own to make it a symbolic drama of deep philosophy and poetic sentiment.

His scholarly training made Calderón one of the most mathematical, logical, and architectural of dramatists, but his imagination and poetic skill were the magic qualities that brought his plays to life. He is the national dramatist, the best interpreter of the Spanish spirit. He gave his audiences the splendid pageantry that combines Spanish charm and the pride of a cabellero with the religious fervor of the Mystics, and yet he gave his work its strong appeal to the intellect. He crystallized the Spanish thought of the seventeenth century, making it dramatic on the stage, not something to be read only in the study.

Willis Knapp Jones

BIBLIOGRAPHICAL REFERENCES: For studies on Calderón in English see James Fitzmaurice Kelly, *Chapters on Spanish Literature,* 1908; Salvador de Madariaga, *Shelley and Calderón,* 1920; A. Parker, *The Allegorical Dramas of Calderón,* 1920; in Spanish, E. Cotarelo y Mori, *Esayo sobre la vida y obras de don Pedro Calderón,* 1924; and A. Valbuena Prat, *Calderón, su personalidad, su arte dramática, su estilo y sus obras,* 1941.

ERSKINE CALDWELL

Born: White Oak, Georgia
Date: December 17, 1903

PRINCIPAL WORKS

NOVELS: *The Bastard*, 1930; *Tobacco Road*, 1932; *God's Little Acre*, 1933; *Journeyman*, 1935; *Georgia Boy*, 1943; *Tragic Ground*, 1944; *A House in the Uplands*, 1946; *The Sure Hand of God*, 1947; *The Courting of Susie Brown*, 1952.

SHORT STORIES: *American Earth*, 1931; *We Are the Living*, 1933; *Kneel to the Rising Sun*, 1935; *Southways*, 1938; *Jackpot*, 1940; *The Complete Stories of Erskine Caldwell*, 1953.

AUTOBIOGRAPHY: *Moscow Under Fire: A Wartime Diary*, 1941; *Call It Experience*, 1951.

MISCELLANEOUS: *You Have Seen Their Faces*, 1937 (with Margaret Bourke-White); *Say, Is This the U.S.A.*, 1941.

His novels having sold millions of copies, particularly in paperback reprints, Erskine (Preston) Caldwell has become the most popular novelist in America. Born into a ministerial household in White Oak, Georgia, on December 17, 1903, he moved widely about the United States in his early years. Although he has ranged as far away as Maine and Russia, his representative fiction has always been associated with the South. His topic is usually the life of the dispossessed, the down-trodden, the sharecropper, the underdog, white or black. Before he became successful as a writer, he held a wide variety of jobs—football player, pool hall worker, real estate salesman—and attended briefly Erskine College, the University of Pennsylvania, and the University of Virginia.

Although he has published an astounding quantity of fiction, Caldwell has also found time to be foreign correspondent for *Life*, *P.M.*, and the Columbia Broadcasting System. During the 1930's he collaborated with his second wife, the photographer Margaret Bourke-White, in the production of pictorial, sociological books. His *Tobacco Road* was not only a best seller as a book (and a successful movie), but as dramatized by Joseph Kirkland broke all records for the New York stage, including that of the amazing *Abie's Irish Rose*.

A tall, good-humored man, Caldwell has not let either success or the charge of sensationalism turn his head. Consciously leftist in his attitude, he looks upon his books as more than mere entertainment; they are social documents of protest.

BIBLIOGRAPHICAL REFERENCES: There is no authorized biographical study of Caldwell and, in recent years, very little criticism. See Joseph Warren Beach, *American Fiction, 1920–1940*, 1941; W. M. Frohock, *The Novel of Violence in America, 1920–1950*, 1950; Kenneth Burke, "Caldwell: Maker of Grotesques," *New Republic*, LXXXII (1935), 232–235; John Donald Wade, "Sweet Are the Uses of Degeneracy," *Southern Review*, I (1936), 449–466; Peter A. Carmichael, "Jeeter Lester, Agrarian Par Excellence," *Sewanee Review*, XLVIII (1940), 21–29; and John M. Maclachlan, "Folk and Culture in the Novels of Erskine Caldwell," *Southern Folklore Quarterly*, IX (1945), 93–101.

LUIS DE CAMOËNS

Born: Lisbon (?), Portugal   *Died:* Lisbon
Date: 1524   *Date:* June 10, 1580 (?)

PRINCIPAL WORK

POEM: *Os Lusíadas,* 1572 (*The Lusiad*).

Born in 1524, Luis Vaz de Camões (to give his name as he wrote it in Portuguese) has the distinction of having two cities, Lisbon and Coimbra, claim him as a native son. Modern scholarship has been unable to determine which city is correct in its claim, but Lisbon presents a somewhat better case. Camoëns apparently was educated at the University of Coimbra, a flourishing university in the sixteenth century, thanks to the patronage of King João III of Portugal. In the middle 1540's Camoëns left the university for Lisbon. A tradition no longer believed correct held that he went to Lisbon as a tutor; another tradition no longer believed was that he followed a beautiful woman of the court.

By 1547, however, Camoëns had made a name for himself as the author of three successful comedies: *El-Rei Seleuco, Filodemo,* and *Os Amphitryões.* In 1547 he enlisted in the Portuguese army and served in northern Africa for two years; during the campaign he lost the sight of his right eye. Upon his return to Portugal he apparently led a loose life on the edge of court circles, earning himself the sobriquet of "Swashbuckler." In June, 1552, he had the misfortune to wound a court official in a street brawl. Imprisoned, he was released about a year later, apparently with the proviso that he leave the county, for he set sail within a month on a troopship for the Far East, to be gone for seventeen years.

As a soldier in the Orient, Comoëns was stationed at Goa, a city of wealth and luxury. He took part in several expeditions to the coast of Malabar, the shores of the Red sea, and the Persian Gulf. Continuing as a writer, he won local fame as a satirist, and his *Filodemo* was staged successfully at Goa. In 1555 he received an appointment as trustee of property of deceased and absent Portuguese at Macao. He set out for his new post in 1556, arriving there in 1558. Two years later he was accused of misappropriation of funds and was returned to Goa as a prisoner. The trip back was almost fatal. The ship sank, and Camoëns was one of the few survivors, tradition saying that he swam ashore holding his manuscript of *The Lusiad* over his head and out of the water. When he finally arrived in Goa in 1561, he was imprisoned; upon his release he was again arrested for indebtedness. For several years he lived in the severest poverty, almost a beggar. In 1567 he managed to get to Mozambique in the company of Pedro Barreto, ex-governor of Goa. What Camoëns did to keep himself alive in the African colony is unknown; probably he served in some minor government post. In 1569 he left Mozambique, thanks to help from friends, and arrived home in Lisbon the following year.

Camoëns immediately set about seeing to the publication of his great epic poem, and in the following September he received the royal permission to publish *The Lusiad,* which was in print early in 1572. In the spring of that year the poet was awarded a royal pension. During the years that followed Camoëns wrote almost nothing. His poetic genius was apparently worn out by the tribulations he had weathered earlier in life. He died of the plague in Lisbon in 1579 or 1580, the latter year being accepted by most modern scholars, and was hurried into an unmarked grave with other plague victims. Although he is remembered by readers in English for *The Lusiad* alone, he also wrote some very fine but almost untranslatable lyrics in his native language.

BIBLIOGRAPHICAL REFERENCES: *Os Lusíadas,* edited, with an introduction and notes, by J. D. M. Ford, 1946, incorporates recent scholarly research on the Portuguese epic and its author. Recent translations of *The Lusiads* are those by Leonard Bacon, 1950; and W. C. Atkinson, 1952. For biographical and critical studies see Sir Richard Burton, *Camoëns, His Life and His Lusiads: A Commentary,* 1881; Aubrey F. G. Bell, *Luís de Camões,* 1923; and Hernani Cidade, *Luís de Camões,* 1936. For briefer studies see A. F. G. Bell, *Studies in Portuguese Literature,* 1914, and *Portuguese Literature,* 1922; and C. M. Bowra, *From Vergil to Milton,* 1945.

ALBERT CAMUS

Born: Mondovi, Algeria
Date: November 7, 1913

Died: Near Sens, France
Date: January 4, 1960

PRINCIPAL WORKS

NOVELS: *L'Étranger,* 1942 (*The Stranger*); *La Peste,* 1947 (*The Plague*); *La Chute,* 1956 (*The Fall*).

PLAYS: *Caligula,* 1944; *Le Malentendu,* 1944 (*Cross Purposes*); *Les Justes,* 1950.

ESSAYS AND PHILOSOPHICAL STUDIES: *Le Mythe de Sisyphe,* 1942 (*The Myth of Sisyphus*); *L'Homme révolté,* 1951 (*The Rebel*).

SHORT STORIES IN TRANSLATION: *Exile and the Kingdom,* 1958.

Albert Camus, a leading writer of the contemporary French renaissance in literature, was born on November 7, 1913 in Mondovi, Algeria, of a Spanish mother and Alsatian father whose family, to avoid remaining under German domination, had moved to Algeria after the Franco-Prussian War. The family was poor, and the boy's education was possible only because to a considerable extent he earned his own way. He was educated in public schools in Algiers and then at the University of Algiers. While attending the University he worked at various jobs: for an automobile accessory firm, for the weather bureau, and for a shipping company.

In 1936, Camus received a degree in philosophy after writing a thesis on Plotinus and St. Augustine. After graduation he began a career in journalism and also played an active part as manager and actor with a theatrical company in Algiers.

He traveled through Europe and for a time was a member of the staff of *Paris-Soir.* When France fell in 1940

179

he returned to Algeria and taught in a private school in Oran, the setting of his best-known novel, *The Plague.* While in Oran he produced the manuscripts of *The Stranger* and *The Myth of Sisyphus,* works that established him as a significant new writer on the French scene when he returned to France in 1942. In 1940 he was married, and he has a son and daughter.

During World War II Camus became part of the French Resistance and distinguished himself as the editor of *Combat,* an important underground paper. His lucid and provocative editorials and particularly his famous *Lettres à un ami Allemand* (*Letters to a German Friend*)—published separately in France in 1945—brought him considerable critical attention.

For a time Camus and Jean-Paul Sartre, leading figure in the French Existentialist movement, were closely associated, but Camus' criticism of Sartre's continuing support of the Communists brought a complete break between the writers when Sartre published a strong attack on Camus in Sartre's journal, *Les Temps Modernes.*

After the Liberation Camus resigned from *Combat* and became director of the publishing house Librairie Gallimard.

Camus is no longer to be identified with the Existentialists, although his philosophy of the absurd has features in common with atheistic Existentialism. Defining the idea of the absurd in his significant essay, *The Myth of Sisyphus,* he argued that man is confronted by a meaningless universe and that the only value in life comes from maintaining a clear awareness of the opposition (the absurdity) between man and what is not man. His first novel, *The Stranger,* presented an inner portrait of an absurd man driven by accidental events to an act of murder. His later novels, *The Plague* and *The Fall,* and his book of social and political philosophy, *The Rebel,* exhibit a sense of responsibility for the freedom of all men.

Still a relatively young man, Camus was awarded the Nobel Prize in Literature for 1957 and with this recognition it is likely that his stature and influence will continue to grow.

BIBLIOGRAPHICAL REFERENCES: The pioneer full-length study of the man and his work is Albert Maquet, *Albert Camus: The Invincible Summer,* translated from the French, 1957. Another balanced and objective study is Philip Thody, *Albert Camus,* 1957. The discussion in Germaine Brée and Margaret Guiton, *An Age of Fiction: The French Novel from Gide to Camus,* 1957, is mostly descriptive of his subject matter. Camus' personality and work are also discussed in most of the books dealing with Existentialism. For brief critical studies see Philip Hallie, "Camus and the Literature of Revolt," *College English,* XVI (1954), 25–32, 83; Harold A. Dufee, "Camus' Challenge to Modern Art," *Journal of Aesthetics and Art Criticism,* I (1955), 201–205; Herbert S. Gershman, "On *L'Étranger,*" *The French Review,* XXIX (1956), 299–305; and P. Thody, "Albert Camus," *Contemporary Review,* LXXXXII (1956), 349–352.

KAREL ČAPEK

Born: Malé Svatoňovice, Bohemia
Date: 1890

Died: Prague, Czechoslovakia
Date: December 25, 1938

PLAYS: *R.U.R.*, 1921; *Že života hmyzu* (with Josef Čapek), 1921 (*The Insect Play;* also *The World We Live In*); *Věc Makropulos*, 1922 (*The Makropulos Secret*); *Adam Stvoritel* (with Josef Čapek), 1927 (*Adam the Creator*); *Bílá Nemoc*, 1937 (*Power and Glory*); *Matka*, 1938 (*The Mother*).

NOVELS: *Továrna na absolutno*, 1922 (*The Absolute at Large*); *Krakatit*, 1924; *Hordubal*, 1933; *Povětrōn*, 1934 (*Meteor*); *Obyčejný život*, 1935 (*An Ordinary Life*); *Válka s mloky*, 1936 (*War with the Newts*); *První parta*, 1937 (*The Rescue Party*).

SHORT STORIES: *Trapné povídky*, 1921 (*Money and Other Stories*); *Devatero pohádek*, 1931 (*Fairy Tales*).

MISCELLANEOUS: *Anglické listy*, 1923 (*Letters from England*); *Hovory s T. G. Masarykem*, 1928–1935 (*Conversations with Masaryk*).

Although born in Malé Svatoňovice in Yugoslav Bohemia, Karel Čapek and his brother Josef are considered Czech, since their chief works were produced in Prague. In a sense Karel, born in 1890, rose and fell with his country, for his death at Prague on December 25, 1938, signalized the collapse of the young country and his last play, *The Mother*, was anti-dictator though pro-pacifist.

As the sons of a doctor, both Karel and Josef Čapek followed their own inclinations, the latter known primarily as a painter but also as an able collaborator. Karel amazed the world and gave his country its most famous play with *R.U.R.*—and left a lasting neologism, *robot*, in the world's vocabulary. Expressionistic in technique, this brilliant play suggests that Rossun's Universal Robots will replace mankind unless humanity rather than mechanization prevails. His other plays, and those in collaboration with his brother, all attacked modern trends and evils, but none measured up to the success of *R.U.R.*

Among Čapek's other writings are novels and several very good collections of short stories as well as some witty and interesting journalism, *Letters from Italy* (1926). He will be remembered chiefly, however, for his experimental plays which tried to convey the feeling of impending doom. Even though disguised, as in *The Insect Play* (or *The World We Live In*), Čapek's view was that man's greed and rapaciousness will bring on the annihilation of the species.

BIBLIOGRAPHICAL REFERENCES: For brief studies of Čapek in English see Oliver Elton, *Essays and Addresses*, 1939; and René Wellek, "Karel Čapek," *Slavonic Review*, XV (1936–1937), 191–206. See also C. Černý, *Karel Čapek*, 1936; and Aimé van Santen, *Over Karek Čapek*, 1949.

GIOSUÈ CARDUCCI

Born: Val di Castello, Italy
Date: July 27, 1835

Died: Bologna, Italy
Date: February 16, 1907

POEMS: *Rime,* 1857; *Inno a Satana,* 1865 (*Hymn to Satan*); *Levia Gravia,* 1868; *Odi barbare,* 1877–1889 (*Pagan Odes*); *Rime e ritmi,* 1899.

Giosuè Carducci, who in his early writing career sometimes used the pseudonym of Enotrio Romano, was born in Val di Castello, Tuscany, on July 27, 1835; the son of an ardent Italian revolutionist, Michele Carducci, a physician. The father had been imprisoned for taking part in the Italian revolution of 1831. In 1849, because of political activity, the father was forced to flee from his native province of Tuscany to Florence. Carducci was educated in Florence as a boy and began writing poetry while still a child. His poetry won him a scholarship to the normal school connected with the University of Pisa. Following his training there he became a teacher. He applied for a post on the faculty of the municipal college at Arezzo, but his political opinions and his father's political record as a revolutionary caused the college authorities to deny him the appointment. Carducci returned to Florence to become a private tutor. He also turned to literature, becoming one of a group of young men, the "Amici Pedanti," who hoped to reform Italian poetry, to turn it from romanticism to the classical temper. During these years Carducci wrote the poems which were later gathered together in the volume entitled *Rime.* These poems, like Carducci's later poetry, reproduced classical meters. During his years in Florence, Carducci also edited a series of books, mainly pieces of Italian literature. In 1860 he became professor of Italian literature at the University of Bologna, where he lectured for more than forty years, until 1904.

Carducci was a rebel in literary mat-ters, as his father had been in politics. Some of his earlier poems were printed in the journal of the Florentine "Amici Pedanti," which was entitled *Il Poliziano.* In addition to turning to classical meters in *Rime,* Carducci used his poetry as criticism, seeing for the Italy of his day very harmful factors in romantic art and in Christianity. His remedy for what he thought was weakness in Italian culture was a return to the classical in art and to the pagan spirit in religion. Temporarily Carducci seemed to become a conservative with the publication of poems like his "Canzone a Vittorio Emanuele" (1859), but his monarchism was short-lived. He soon returned to his role of gadfly, trying to rouse his countrymen out of spiritual, cultural, and political complacency, as in his notorious *Hymn to Satan.* Satan, in this poem, is a symbol for many things, including free thought and the whole notion of progress. The poem, although written in 1863, was not printed until two years later.

Later volumes of Carducci's poetry included poems on contemporary political events. *Levia Gravia* was a collected edition, including some of the poetry Carducci had written before 1857. In *Decennali* (1871) Carducci published a volume of poems dealing with the contemporary Italian scene and with historical events in Italy. The *Pagan Odes* comprised in all three collections based on Latin models. These poems were an attempt to adapt the prosody of Latin to Italian poetry, an effort earlier Italian poets had tried and in which they had largely failed. Car-

182

ducci's attempts were much more successful than those of his predecessors. As a crowning honor to his life's work, Carducci was awarded the Nobel Prize for literature in 1906, a year before his death at Bologna on February 16, 1907.

BIBLIOGRAPHICAL REFERENCES: The standard biographical and critical study is Benedetto Croce, *Giosuè Carducci*, 1937. See also A. Jeanroy, *Giosuè Carducci, l'homme et le poete*, 1911; and A. M. De Luca, "An Evaluation of Carducci's Polemical Writings," *Italica*, XXVIII (1951), 233–240.

WILLIAM CARLETON

Born: Prillisk, Ireland
Date: March 4, 1794

Died: Dublin, Ireland
Date: January 30, 1869

PRINCIPAL WORKS

NOVELS: *Fardorougha the Miser*, 1839; *Parra Sastha, or the History of Paddy-Go-Easy and His Wife Nancy*, 1845; *Valentine McClutchy*, 1845; *Roddy the Rover*, 1845; *Art Maguire, or the Broken Pledge*, 1847; *The Black Prophet*, 1847; *The Emigrants of Ahadarra*, 1848; *The Tithe-Proctor*, 1849.

SHORT STORIES AND SKETCHES: *Traits and Stories of the Irish Peasantry*, 1830–1833.

William Carleton, born in Prillisk, County Tyrone, Ireland, on March 4, 1794, was educated in Irish hedge schools and later at the classical school at Donagh. As a young man he tried stonecutting, taxidermy, and other means of earning a livelihood, for his family was poor and he was the fourteenth child. Although his family had hoped he would become a priest, Carleton was so changed by a religious pilgrimage in 1813 that he gave up the idea of taking holy orders and became a Protestant. After his marriage to Jane Anderson, in 1822, Carleton worked as a teacher and as a journalist, contributing to many Irish periodicals. He became famous as a writer when a collection of his stories was published as *Traits and Stories of the Irish Peasantry* in 1830. Several editions were sold, and in 1833 a second series was published. *Fardorougha the Miser*, his first novel, was adapted for the stage by a woman named Magrath, but the play was disliked by Carleton and almost proved a failure on the Dublin stage. During his lifetime, Carleton wrote a number of novels, of which *Fardorougha the Miser*, *The Black Prophet*, and *The Emigrants of Ahadarra* are the best. *The Black Prophet* was based on the Irish famine and typhus plague of the 1840's and is typical of the novelist's realism in writing about life in Ireland, especially among the peasants. *The Emigrants of Ahadarra* is an unsparing study of the landlord system. Most of the realistic detail in Carleton's work was based on his own intimate knowledge of Irish life. Although he was a voluminous writer, he had constant financial difficulty until he was awarded a pension of two hundred pounds by Lord John Russell in 1848. Carleton died in Dublin on January 30, 1869.

BIBLIOGRAPHICAL REFERENCES: There has never been a collected edition of Carleton's once popular novels, and only one of his books, *Stories of Irish Life*, has been reprinted in a modern edition (1936). The most recent biographical study is Benedict Kiely, *Poor Scholar*, 1947. See also David J. O'Donoghue, *The Life of William Carleton*, 1896; and Rose Shaw, *Carleton Country*, 1930. The best short criticism is G. Barnett Smith, "A Brilliant Irish Novelist," *Fortnightly Review*, LXVII (1897), 104–116.

THOMAS CARLYLE

Born: Ecclefechan, Scotland   *Died:* London, England
Date: December 4, 1795   *Date:* February 4, 1881

PRINCIPAL WORKS

SOCIAL, PHILOSOPHICAL, AND POLITICAL ESSAYS: *Characteristics*, 1831; *Sartor Resartus*, 1835; *Chartism*, 1839; *On Heroes, Hero-Worship, and the Heroic in History*, 1841; *Past and Present*, 1843; *Original Discourses on the Negro Question*, 1849; *Latter-Day Pamphlets*, 1850; *Shooting Niagara: and After*, 1867; *Last Words of Thomas Carlyle*, 1882.

HISTORY AND BIOGRAPHY: *The French Revolution*, 1837; *Oliver Cromwell's Letters and Speeches, with Elucidations*, 1845; *Life of John Sterling*, 1851; *History of Frederick II of Prussia*, 1858–1865; *The Early Kings of Norway; also an Essay on the Portraits of John Knox*, 1875.

CRITICAL ESSAYS AND STUDIES: *Essay on Goethe's Faust*, 1822; *Life of Schiller*, 1823–1824; *Essay on Richter*, 1827; *The Present State of German Literature*, 1827; *Life and Writings of Werner*, 1828; *Essay on Burns*, 1828; *Voltaire*, 1829; *Sir Walter Scott*, 1838; *Critical and Miscellaneous Essays*, 1839, 1840, 1847.

TRAVEL SKETCHES AND IMPRESSIONS: *Reminiscences of My Irish Journey*, 1849.

AUTOBIOGRAPHY: *Reminiscences*, 1881.

TRANSLATIONS: *Wilhelm Meister's Apprenticeship*, 1824; *German Romance*, 1827.

The childhood of Thomas Carlyle was spent in the village of Ecclefechan, in Dumfriesshire, Scotland, where he was born on December 4, 1795. His father, James Carlyle, was a stonemason. From the age of ten Carlyle attended the grammar school at Annan, and at fourteen he was sent, on foot, to enroll in the University of Edinburgh. Here he remained until 1814, when he left without a degree and became a teacher of mathematics at his old school. Subsequently he held the mastership of a school at Kirkcaldy. His parents, who were devout Calvinists, had wanted him to study divinity and become a minister; but in 1817 he definitely rejected this course of life. For a time he lived in Edinburgh and desultorily read law, but was unable to interest himself in any profession. Weakened by dyspepsia and much troubled in mind by his inability to achieve philosophical or religious certitude, he underwent a period of acute strain which culminated, during the summer of 1822, in his well-known spiritual crisis, recorded in *Sartor Resartus*. By now greatly under the influence of the German philosophers, especially Richter and Fichte, he was beginning to devise a set of beliefs acceptable to himself and was coming to realize that his vocation was to be literary and philosophic. He became absorbed in the poetry of Goethe, with whom he corresponded after the publication of his English translation of *Wilhelm Meister's Apprenticeship.*

In 1826 he married Jane Welsh, an exceptionally brilliant girl who had been a pupil of his friend Edward Irving. Their life together seems to have been tempestuous in the extreme. They lived in Edinburgh two years and then moved to Craigenputtock, an isolated farm in Dumfriesshire. There Carlyle worked painstakingly on the "clothes philosophy" of *Sartor Resartus* and consolidated his whole system of thought; his six years at Craigenputtock were his time of intellectual self-discovery. A few journeys to London sufficed to win him a number of literary friends, including John Stuart Mill. In 1834, after another brief sojourn in Edinburgh, the Carlyles moved to Chelsea, London, so that he might have access to the London libraries to assemble material for his great historical study, *The French Revolution.* This he finally completed early in 1837, after the terrible experience of having to rewrite the whole first volume; he had

lent the manuscript to Mill, and Mill had left it with his friend Mrs. Taylor, whose servant-girl heedlessly used it to light fires. Carlyle had no other copy and had preserved no notes. *The French Revolution,* as soon as it appeared, established his reputation once and for all. The most important of his later works were *Chartism, On Heroes, Hero-worship, and the Heroic in History, Past and Present,* and a six-volume history of Frederick the Great. Surviving his wife by almost fifteen years, Carlyle died in London on February 4, 1881. His highly indiscreet *Reminiscences,* edited by his official biographer, James Anthony Froude, aroused much indignation when they appeared shortly after his death.

Carlyle was a bitter enemy of conformity. He extolled government by an aristocracy of talent, despised democracy and popular political institutions, and damned the French Revolution. He admired the interdependence of classes under feudalism, preached the sacredness of work in opposition to the cult of riches, and scorned mass-production as the bane of fine craftsmanship. He expressed his ideas in an intense, and often somewhat raucous, literary style.

BIOGRAPHICAL REFERENCES: The standard edition is the Centenary Edition, edited by H. D. Trail, 30 vols., 1897–1901. The library of Carlyle correspondence is extensive: *Correspondence of Carlyle and Emerson,* edited by Charles Eliot Norton, 1886; *Correspondence between Goethe and Carlyle,* ed. by Norton, 1887; *Early Letters,* ed. by Norton, 1887; *Letters, 1826–1836,* ed. by Norton, 2 vols., 1888; *Letters to His Youngest Sister,* edited by C. T. Copeland, 1899; *New Letters,* edited by Alexander Carlyle, 2 vols., 1905; *Love Letters of Thomas Carlyle and Jane Welsh,* ed. by A. Carlyle, 2 vols., 1909; *Letters to John Stuart Mill, John Sterling, and Robert Browning,* ed. by A. Carlyle, 1923; *Letters and Memorials of Jane Welsh Carlyle, Prepared for Publication by Thomas Carlyle,* edited by James Anthony Froude, 3 vols., 1883; and *Jane Welsh Carlyle: Letters to Her Family, 1839–1863,* edited by Leonard Huxley, 1924.

The authorized biography is James Anthony Froude, *Thomas Carlyle: History of the First Forty Years of His Life,* 2 vols., 1882, and *Thomas Carlyle: History of His*

Life in London, 2 vols., 1884. For the history of this controversial work see D. A. Wilson, *Froude and Carlyle,* 1898; J. A. Froude, *My Relations with Carlyle,* 1903; J. Crichton-Browne, *Froude and Carlyle,* 1903; J. Crichton-Browne and Alexander Carlyle, *The Nemesis of Froude,* 1903; and Waldo Dunn, *Froude and Carlyle,* 1930. For additional biographical and critical studies see D. A. Wilson, *Life of Carlyle,* 6 vols., 1923–1934, a monumental and well-documented work; also, R. S. Craig, *The Making of Carlyle,* 1908; W. S. Johnson, *Thomas Carlyle: A Study of His Literary Apprenticeship, 1814–1831,* 1911; Louis Cazinmam, *Carlyle,* 1913 (trans., 1932); Osbert Burdett, *The Two Carlyles,* 1931; F. A. Lea, *Carlyle: Prophet of Today,* 1943; Julian Symons, *Thomas Carlyle: The Life and Ideas of a Prophet,* 1952; David Gascoyne, *Thomas Carlyle,* 1952; and John Holloway, *The Victorian Sage: Studies in Argument,* 1953.

LEWIS CARROLL
(Charles Lutwidge Dodgson)

Born: Daresbury, Cheshire, England   *Died:* Guildford, Surrey, England
Date: January 27, 1832   *Date:* January 14, 1898

PRINCIPAL WORKS

FANTASIES AND CHILDREN'S STORIES: *Alice's Adventures in Wonderland,* 1865; *Through the Looking-Glass and What Alice Found There,* 1871; *A Tangled Tale,* 1885; *Sylvie and Bruno,* 1889; *Sylvie and Bruno Concluded,* 1893.

POEM: *The Hunting of the Snark,* 1876.

MATHEMATICAL STUDIES: *Euclid and His Modern Rivals,* 1879; *Curiosa Mathematica,* Part I, 1888; Part II, 1893; *Symbolic Logic, Specimens,* 1894.

Charles Lutwidge Dodgson, who under his pseudonym of Lewis Carroll came to be known to millions as the author of *Alice in Wonderland,* was born at Daresbury, England, January 27, 1832, the son of the rector of Daresbury, the Reverend Charles Dodgson and Frances Jane Lutwidge. He was the eldest of a family of eleven children, with seven sisters and three brothers. After a pleasant and for the most part solitary childhood he attended Richmond School and then Rugby for three extremely unhappy years. In 1851, the year he formally went into residence as a student at Christ Church College, Oxford, his mother died. He was probably deeply affected by her death; his later verses show the affection he felt for his gentle mother, and in his nonsense stories some critics have claimed to find signs of a childhood love for his mother that never matured.

Dodgson spent the rest of his life at Oxford. In 1856, two years after receiving the Bachelor of Arts degree, and after serving as a tutor in mathematics, he was made a regular member of the teaching faculty at Christ Church. Although the significance of the event was unrealized at the time, it was in the previous year, 1855, that he wrote the first lines of his famous "Jabberwocky" poem: "Twas bryllyg, and the slythy toves/Did gyre and gymble in the wabe . . ." This was a scholar's jest, an attempt to parody Anglo-Saxon poetry. He was twenty-three years old at the time.

As a teacher and mathematician, Charles Lutwidge Dodgson was conscientious, precise, sometimes inspired, but usually dull. His students reported finding his lectures very tiresome, even during the period when he was writing *Alice's Adventures in Wonderland*. Dodgson wrote many articles and several books in mathematics and logic, but he would not have been famous if he had relied on them or on his reputation as a teacher.

The pseudonym, Lewis Carroll, was devised in 1856 to accompany a poem which appeared in the magazine *The Train*. It appears to have been derived from the names Lutwidge and Charles by some fanciful logic of his own.

Dodgson had considerable skill as a humorous artist, but his drawings—which some have regarded as comparable to the nonsense drawings by Edward Lear—were rejected when he submitted them to the *Comic Times*. Discouraged, he turned to photography and became an excellent photographer of children and one of the notable amateurs in nineteenth century photography.

In 1856 he met the children of Dean Liddell of Christ Church, and was particularly interested in Alice Liddell, then four years old. A year after his ordination (for taking Holy Orders was a condition of his staying at Christ Church as a mathematics lecturer), on a picnic with another young clergyman and three of the Liddell girls—Alice, then ten years old, among them—Dodgson began in an extemporaneous way the story of *Alice's Adventures Underground*. He wrote the story, after expanding it considerably, and presented the manuscript to Alice. An even longer version was prepared for publication and was illustrated by

John Tenniel, whose drawings have become as famous as the story. The book was published by Macmillan in 1865 with the title *Alice's Adventures in Wonderland*. This extremely popular story full of nonsense and logical fancy was followed by *Through the Looking-Glass and What Alice Found There*. *The Hunting of the Snark*, perhaps the most fascinating of his nonsense poems, became a great favorite with adults and, like the Alice books, continues to be popular. But the author's own favorite work was his long and involved *Sylvie and Bruno* which appeared in two parts, the first in 1889 and the second in 1893. Unfortunately, the public never fully shared the author's love, and compared to the other books it was a failure.

Dodgson's playful temperament, seldom in evidence in the classroom and often made wicked when he turned to criticism of his colleagues at the college, found an outlet in games of logic and mathematics, many of which he invented. He was always fascinated with girls; he liked to read to them, to make up stories for them, to draw them, and to photograph them—sometimes in the nude. But somehow he managed to stay out of trouble, if not free from all criticism. In all probability, his innocence was evident. He never married, but he probably had an unhappy love affair when he was young; the evidence is inconclusive. In any case, analysts have been amusing themselves by studying him; the maker of puzzles was something of a puzzle himself.

This solitary deacon, dull teacher, clever logician, and inspired teller of nonsense tales died of influenza and bronchial complications at Guildford on January 14, 1898. He was still ambitious, with several projects under way, but since he was more and more out of touch with "real life," living, although quite sanely, in the world of his imagination, it was not entirely inappropriate that after a long creative life he finally stopped dreaming.

BIBLIOGRAPHICAL REFERENCES: The collected edition is *The Complete Works of Lewis Carroll*, edited by Alexander Woollcott, 1939 (reprinted 1947), with a critical introduction and illustrations by John Tenniel. The standard bibliography is *A Handbook of the Literature of the Rev. C. L. Dodgson*, 1931, by S. H. Williams and Falconer Madan. Roger L. Green has edited *The Diaries of Lewis Carroll*, 2 vols., 1953, the most complete edition to date. Standard biographies are Langford Reed, *The Life of Lewis Carroll*, 1932; Florence B. Lennon, *Victoria Through the Looking Glass: The Life of Lewis Carroll*, 1945; and Derek Hudson, *Lewis Carroll*, 1954, the first critical biography to make use of the diaries. Other critical works are Walter de la Mare, *Lewis Carroll*, 1932; R. L. Green, *The Story of Lewis Carroll*, 1949; and Phyllis Greenacre, *Swift and Carroll*, 1955. An important short essay is Virginia Woolf, "Lewis Carroll," in *The Moment and Other Essays*, 1948.

JOYCE CARY

Born: Londonderry, Ireland
Date: December 7, 1888

Died: Oxford, England
Date: March 29, 1957

PRINCIPAL WORKS

NOVELS: *Aissa Saved*, 1932; *The American Visitor*, 1933; *The African Witch*, 1936; *Castle Corner*, 1938; *Mister Johnson*, 1939; *Charley Is My Darling*, 1940; *The House of Children*, 1941; *Herself Surprised*, 1941; *To Be a Pilgrim*, 1942; *The Horse's Mouth*, 1944; *The Moonlight*, 1946; *A Fearful Joy*, 1949; *Prisoner of Grace*, 1952; *Except the Lord*, 1953; *Not Honour More*, 1955.

There was nothing precocious about the talent of Joyce Cary. He started writing late and learned his craft slowly and carefully. *Aissa Saved*, his first novel, was rewritten a great many times and he did not publish it until the age of forty-four. In 1936 *The African Witch* was a considerable success, but his reputation was not securely founded before World War II. Despite his late start and slow development, Cary managed to establish himself as one of the leading novelists writing in English before his death in 1957.

Born in Londonderry, Ireland, on December 7, 1888, Cary was descended from a Devonshire family that had settled in Ireland in the seventeenth century. Educated in England and of independent means, he was able to study painting in Edinburgh and Paris. Deciding that he lacked the talent to be a professional painter (though he later illustrated some of his own books), he took his degree at Oxford in 1912.

Still unsettled about a career, Cary joined a Montenegrin battalion to fight in the Balkan War of 1912–1913. He later transferred to Red Cross work and was decorated by the King of Montenegro. In 1913 he joined the Nigerian Political Service as a colonial administrator and served with the West African Frontier Force. Wounds suffered during the Cameroons campaign forced him to retire from the colonial service in 1920. He returned to England and

188

settled in Oxford, where he remained the rest of his life.

At this point, without a profession at thirty-two, Gary decided to become a writer. Feeling that he was inadequately educated to be a serious writer, he began a systematic and broad study of the latest developments in philosophy, history, and economics. It was not a superficial or rapid effort, for it was not until twelve years after his return to England that he published *Aissa Saved,* a novel about a primitive African girl's conversion to Christianity. He continued to make use of his African experience in his more successful novel *The African Witch.* His knowledge of the political and social problems of Africa enabled him powerfully to represent the clash of an advanced and a primitive culture in a story of how an Oxford-educated native prince is opposed by his priestess sister because he wants to bring Christianity and progress to his people.

With the publication of *Herself Surprised,* Cary made a final departure from African materials and established himself as a witty portrayer of English society. In this and the two other books of the trilogy, *To Be a Pilgrim* and *The Horse's Mouth,* Cary achieved his characteristic tone, irony blended with sympathy. He always respects his characters, despite their obvious moral defects; they are full of life and make a forcible impression on the reader. Each novel tells the same story from the point of view of a different principal character. First, Sara Monday, the amorous, light-fingered cook, tells of her downfall; next, the cunning, half-senile old lawyer, Tom Wilcher, reports the events from his perspective; and finally, Jimson, the lusty painter, gives his version. Plot, therefore, is clearly subordinated to character, for Cary was primarily interested in how events modify human character.

Cary employed the same technique in his trilogy about an English politician: *Prisoner of Grace, Except the Lord,* and *Not Honour More.* This was his last major work; but despite lifelong illness and a creeping paralysis in his last years, Cary remained an indefatigable worker, and he left several novels unfinished when he died at his home in Oxford on March 29, 1957.

BIBLIOGRAPHICAL REFERENCES: There is surprisingly little criticism available. See Walter Allen, *Joyce Cary,* 1953; Andrew Wright, *Joyce Cary,* 1957; and George Steinbrecher, Jr., "Joyce Cary: Master Novelist," *College English,* XVIII (1957), 387–395. A biographical sketch appeared in *Time,* LX, Pt. 2 (October 20, 1952), 118–130.

GIOVANNI JACOPO CASANOVA DE SEINGALT

Born: Venice, Italy
Date: April 2, 1725

Died: Dux, Bohemia
Date: June 4, 1798

PRINCIPAL WORKS

AUTOBIOGRAPHY: *Mémoires écrits par lui-même,* 1826–1838.
NOVEL: *Icosameron,* 1788.

Giovanni Jacopo (or Giacomo) Casanova de Seingalt has not suffered an injustice because the world makes his name synonymous with "libertine." In fact, it is largely because of his own efforts that he has acquired this reputation: his *Mémoires* present him as the flamboyant "natural man," bound by no laws but the law of his own nature. While his autobiography is somewhat colored, even the most cursory survey of the facts of his career show him to be the amoral adventurer *par excellence*.

Born in Venice, Italy, on April 2, 1725, he was expelled in his youth from a Venetian seminary for immoral conduct, but his mother saved him from jail by securing for him the protection of the influential Cardinal Acquaviva. Casanova soon began his adventures: he traveled about Europe and the Near East for years, living variously as preacher, businessman, alchemist, musician, diplomat, and journalist. Imprisoned in Venice in 1755 for spying, he made a marvelous escape, which he reports in his *Mémoires,* a section translated by Arthur Machen as *Casanova's Escape from the Leads* (1925). He went to Paris, where he was made head of the national lotteries. He gained a reputation as a financial wizard, and he moved in the best society.

Never the man to stay contented in a secure position, he resumed his travels in 1759. He visited the Netherlands, Germany, Savoy, Switzerland (where he met Voltaire) and Florence (from which he was expelled). At Rome he received the Order of the Golden Spur from the Pope. After a short time at Paris he toured Russia, where he was involved in a scandal and a duel. Fearing arrest in Paris, he fled to Spain, where he stayed until he was expelled from Madrid in 1769. By 1774 he was again employed as a spy, this time for the Venetian state police, but in 1782 he was exiled for libeling one of his patrons.

With few places in Europe where he could safely go, Casanova decided to retire from public life and write down his adventures. With Count Waldstein as his patron, he took a post as librarian at the château of Dux in Bohemia. In 1788 he published *Icosameron,* a strange novel-fantasy which anticipates many modern inventions. In the quiet of the library he also relived his past adventures, fictionalizing them for greater effect, and wrote them in French. These *Mémoires* create an absorbing portrait of a shallow, amoral man whose vitality makes his story rival Cellini's *Autobiography*. The *Mémoires* have been translated into every European language. Casanova died at Dux on June 4, 1798.

BIBLIOGRAPHICAL REFERENCES: The standard edition of the *Memoirs,* though not definitive, is *Mémoires ecrits par lui-même,* collected in 12 vols., 1826–1838. There is a later edition, edited by Raoul Vèze, 7 vols., 1924–1928. For translations into English see those by Arthur Machen, 1894; and by James Stern and Robert Pick, 1955; also *Casanova's Escape from the Leads,* translated and with an introduction by Arthur Machen, 1925. See, further, J. Pollis and Raoul Vèze, *Pages Casanoviennes,* 8 vols., 1925–1926, and *Bibliographie anecdotique et critique des œuvres de Jacques Casanova,* 1926.

For biographical and critical studies in English see Joseph Le Gras, *Casanova, Ad-*

venturer and Lover, translated 1923; Stephan Zweig, Adepts in Self-Portraiture: Casanova, Stendhal, Tolstoy, translated 1928; Guy Endore, Casanova: His Known and Unknown Life, 1929; and James Stuart Montgomery, Incredible Casanova, 1950; in French, Édouard Maynial, Casanova et son temps, 1911; and Joseph Le Gras and Raoul Vèze, Casanova, 1930. A specialized study of particular interest is Paul Nettle, The Other Casanova, a Contribution to Eighteenth Century Music and Manners, 1950.

WILLA CATHER

Born: Gore, Virginia
Date: December 7, 1873

Died: New York, N. Y.
Date: April 24, 1947

PRINCIPAL WORKS

NOVELS: Alexander's Bridge, 1912; O Pioneers! 1913; The Songs of the Lark, 1915; My Ántonia, 1918; One of Ours, 1922; A Lost Lady, 1923; The Professor's House, 1925; My Mortal Enemy, 1926; Death Comes for the Archbishop, 1927; Shadows on the Rock, 1931; Lucy Gayheart, 1935; Sapphira and the Slave Girl, 1940.

SHORT STORIES: The Troll Garden, 1905; Youth and the Bright Medusa, 1920; Obscure Destinies, 1932; The Old Beauty and Others, 1948.

POEMS: April Twilights, 1903 (enlarged edition, 1923).

ESSAYS: Not Under Forty, 1936; Willa Cather on Writing, 1949.

Willa Cather was the last of a generation of writers who lived through the passing of the old frontier, who saw at first hand the region of the homesteader transformed into a countryside of tidy farms and small towns; and she found in the primitive virtues of the pioneer experience her own values as an artist. When the prairie roads "no longer ran about like wild things, but followed the surveyed section lines," they led inevitably to Main Street. This fact colored all her perceptions of a place and its people, gave her writing its center and its roots. The West, the past—one was the physical background of her best work, the other its spiritual climate. The very nature of her materials determined her course as a writer: to record the decline of the prairie frontier and later to find in more traditional societies of the Spanish Southwest and French-Colonial Quebec those resources of the

human spirit which have been almost overwhelmed in the complexities and confusion of the present.

For a talent as special as hers, Willa Cather was fortunate in her time and place. She was born on December 7, 1873, in the Back Creek Valley of northern Virginia, not far from Winchester, where her ancestors had settled late in the eighteenth century. In 1883 her father moved his family to a ranch near Red Cloud, Nebraska, and there she grew up in a region still marked by trails of the Indian and the buffalo. This change from the stability and ordered pattern of life in rural Virginia made a lasting impression on the nine-year-old girl, so that for the rest of her life she was to be concerned with the effects of continuance and change on human character.

During the year the Cathers lived on the Nebraska Divide they had few American neighbors, but Bohemian,

191

Scandinavian, French, and German farmers lived nearby. Free to come and go as she pleased, Willa Cather found a new set of experiences among these people struggling to master a new language and a stubborn soil and to hold their lands through periods of drought and failing credit. Friendships with immigrant neighbors and the classics she read aloud to her grandmothers at night—there was at the time no school she could attend—gave her a deeper knowledge of old cultures than the prairie towns of that day could provide. The lasting impressions of those early years are reflected in that passage in *My Ántonia* in which Jim Burden ponders the lines of the classic poet, *Primus ego in patriam mecum . . . deducam Musas,* and realizes that Vergil had in mind not the Roman state or even a province, but a rural neighborhood, a landscape of fields "sloping down to the river and to the old beech trees with broken tops." Here is the narrow gap that Miss Cather eventually crossed between the frontier of the prairie and the frontier of art.

In 1885 the Cathers moved into Red Cloud, where Willa attended the high school for two years. A great influence on her life at that time was an English storekeeper who taught her to read Latin and Greek; after she matriculated at the University of Nebraska in 1891 she continued her unofficial studies under his guidance during vacations. Graduated in 1895, she went to Pittsburgh a year later to do editorial work for a small magazine before joining the staff of the Pittsburgh *Daily Leader* in 1897. About the same time her poems and short stories began to appear in *McClure's Magazine* and *Cosmopolitan.* Finding newspaper work too exacting for creative writing, she taught in the Pittsburgh high schools from 1901 to 1906. *April Twilights,* a book of poems, was published in 1903, followed two years later by a collection of short stories, *The Troll Garden.* In 1906 she joined the staff of *McClure's Magazine,* where she remained until she published her first novel in 1912.

The first novel is likely to be an unguarded one, and *Alexander's Bridge* was no exception. Bringing together a young Westerner's impressions of charming Boston teas and London drawing rooms, a moral problem out of Edith Wharton, and moral symbolism out of Henry James, the book failed because it did not come out of Miss Cather's own experience but out of her respect for literary tradition. In the meantime, however, she had met Sarah Orne Jewett, who advised her to write of her own region in her own way. Willa Cather profited by this advice; her next three novels enclose vast spaces of prairie, hills, and sky in a world rich and sustaining with homely realism. In *O Pioneers!* the immigrant heroine, Alexandra Bergson, develops the brooding wisdom and deep strength we find in the women of racial myths as she struggles to tame the wild land and bring it to fruition. *The Song of the Lark* tells the story of Thea Kronborg, rising from the crudeness and vulgarity of a Colorado mountain town to have a great career as a singer. In *My Ántonia* the simplicity and generous good nature of Ántonia Shimerda leave her untouched by years of farm drudgery and village spite; her serenity and happiness have their source in her passion for order and motherhood.

But the land which ennobled some natures could also corrupt the weak and breed the mean. As the pioneering impulses dwindled to a second genera-

192

tion's desire for soft jobs and easy money, Miss Cather's disillusionment deepened and found expression in the books of her middle period. The short stories in *Youth and the Bright Medusa* contain pictures of the barrenness and waste imposed by the frontier effort and a career in art. *One of Ours* is a novel of defeat which fails to convince because Claude Wheeler is little more than an abstraction in a conventional novel of art, a fable of the creative spirit blighted by a crass, stupid world. *A Lost Lady* is another story of frustration, but in it Miss Cather had her vision of a dying age and her own disillusionment in its passing under firm control. This was the first example of what she called the novel *démeublé*, fiction stripped of all furnishings to leave the scene bare for the play of emotions. From this time on she was to abandon the full-bodied realistic method in her novels; in her later works her plots take shape naturally from the development of character or the interplay and clash of personalities, and her deeper meanings are conveyed indirectly by images and symbols. In *The Professor's House*, for example, the Blue Mesa looms behind the story of Godfrey St. Peter, an enduring symbol overshadowing the four stories of corruption and betrayal which give the novel its underlying strength and critical force. Beneath its quiet and autumnal mood *The Professor's House* is Miss Cather's most intimate and bitter work, touching American life at so many weak points in our national self-esteem.

This novel also marks a crisis in Miss Cather's career and in her personal reaction against modern materialism. Either she could ease her disillusionment with satire, as many of her contemporaries were doing, or she could preserve in another time and place the mood of serenity and acceptance with which her book ends. The artist who had written "The Sculptor's Funeral" and "A Wagner Matinee" more than twenty years before could not turn back to repeat herself. Her Godfrey St. Peter was a spiritual brother who had written of the conquistadores and the Franciscan friars; she chose to follow him into his region of imagination and history. In her earlier novels she had celebrated, as all America has done, the industry and courage of the pioneer, but she had also showed what no one before her had seen, the essential humanism of his legend. Now she was to trace the fundamental likenesses, presented in the same images of heroism and endurance, between the frontier in its best phase and the influence of historical civilizations. The result was *Death Comes for the Archbishop*, an American masterpiece re-creating a region, a society, and a culture in its account of two dedicated missionary priests and their experiences in the Southwest shortly after the Mexican War. *Shadows on the Rock*, a somewhat similar chronicle of Quebec in the days of Frontenac, is less effective, possibly because the novel lacks, in the French tradition for order and reason, the grander passions of place and human nature that light up *Death Comes for the Archbishop* like desert sunlight.

Willa Cather was to publish three more books before her death in New York City on April 24, 1947. Of the stories in *Obscure Destinies*, "Neighbor Rosicky" is among her best. *Lucy Gayheart* is a minor work bringing together two of Miss Cather's favorite themes, the West and music. In *Sapphira and the Slave Girl* she drew for the first time on memories of her Virginia childhood in a novel of pre-Civil War days, a work suggesting allegorical intentions and filled with disturbing subtleties that criticism has not yet attempted to resolve. *The Old Beauty and Others,* containing her last three stories, was published posthumously in 1948.

Willa Cather thought of the novel as an instrument of culture, not a vehicle for social reportage or character-mongering, and art worth a lifetime's effort and devotion. Her literary masters were the European craftsmen whom she so greatly admired, but her own writing was American in subject and mood. Coming at the end of an era, she tried to recapture a past that existed largely in memory, a past which was once innocent and romantic and heroic. That was her aim and her achievement, and what she had to say she said with honesty and simplicity, with moral subtlety and stylistic evocation. Her fidelity to this vision of experience testifies to her integrity as a person and an artist.

Dayton Kohler

BIBLIOGRAPHICAL REFERENCES: Willa Cather's books have been collected in the Library Edition, 13 vols., 1937–1941. In addition to *The Old Beauty and Others,* 1948, and *Willa Cather on Writing,* 1941, posthumous publications have included *Willa Cather in Europe,* a collection of travel sketches and impressions edited by George N. Kates, who also appended to *Five Stories by Willa Cather,* 1956, a discussion of her unfinished Avignon story which was destroyed at her request after her death. James R. Shively in *Writings from Willa Cather's Campus Years,* 1950, reprints six stories written as an undergraduate at the University of Nebraska. Mildred R. Bennett has also edited a collection of previously uncollected short stories, 1957.

The authorized biography is E. K. Brown, *Willa Cather: A Critical Biography,* 1953, completed by Leon Edel. Much of the material in the official biography derives from Edith Lewis, *Willa Cather Living: A Personal Record,* 1953. Mildred R. Bennett, *The World of Willa Cather,* is useful for the Red Cloud background of Miss Cather's writing. Elizabeth Shepley Sergeant, *Willa Cather: A Memoir,* 1953, is both an informal biography and the record of a friendship. James R. Shively's *Writings from Willa Cather's Campus Years* brings together interesting material from her university days, including reminiscences of classmates.

The most extensive critical study is David Daiches, *Willa Cather: A Critical Introduction,* 1950. For briefer studies in books and periodicals see Stuart P. Sherman, *Critical Woodcuts,* 1926; Elizabeth Shepley Sergeant, *Fire Under the Andes,* 1927; Rebecca West, *The Strange Necessity,* 1931; Arthur H. Quinn, *American Fiction,* 1936; Alfred Kazin, *On Native Grounds,* 1942; Maxwell Geismar, *The Last of the Provincials,* 1947; Francis X. Connolly, "Willa Cather: Memory as Muse," in *Fifty Years of the American Novel,* edited by Harold C. Gardiner, S.J., 1951; Frederick J. Hoffman, *The Modern Novel in America, 1900–1950,* 1951; Edward Wagenknecht, *Cavalcade of the American Novel,* 1952; Robert McNamara, "Phases of American Religion in Thornton Wilder and Willa Cather," *Catholic World,* CXXXV (1932), 641–649; E. K. Brown, "Willa Cather and the West," *University of Toronto Quarterly,* V (1936), 544–566, and "Homage to Willa Cather," *Yale Review,* XXXVI (1946), 77–92; Robert H. Footman, "The Genius of Willa Cather," *American Literature,* X (1938), 123–141; Dayton Kohler, "Willa Cather," *College English,* IX (1947), 8–18; Edward A. and Lillian D. Bloom, "Willa Cather's Novels of the Frontier: A Study in Thematic Symbolism," *American Literature,* XXI

(1949), 71–93, and *"Shadows on the Rock*: Notes on the Composition of a Novel," *Twentieth Century Literature*, II (1956), 70–85; Bernard Baum, "Willa Cather's Waste Land," *South Atlantic Quarterly*, XLVIII (1949), 589–601; and John P. Hinz, "Willa Cather: Prairie Spring," *Prairie Schooner*, XXIII (1949), 82–89, and "*A Lost Lady* and *The Professor's House*," *Virginia Quarterly Review*, XXIX (1953), 70–85. For a complete bibliographical listing see Phyllis Martin Hutchinson, "The Writings of Willa Cather: A List of Works by and about Her," *Bulletin of the New York Public Library*, LX (1956), 267–288, 338–356, 378–400.

GAIUS VALERIUS CATULLUS

Born: Verona, Italy   *Died:* Rome, Italy
Date: c. 84 B.C.   *Date:* c. 54 B.C.

PRINCIPAL WORK

POEMS: *Carmina.*

Catullus ranks with Sappho and Shelley among the world's great lyric poets, yet this son of a wealthy family of Transpadane Gaul, delights more in the flesh than either of the others and is more concerned with the struggle between flesh and spirit. Where he studied is not known, but in 62 B.C. he went to Rome, where he became a leader in the literary and fashionable circles of Roman society. Cicero was his friend. Though he was originally an enemy of Julius Caesar, the two became reconciled. To him and other important Romans Catullus wrote many of his verses.

While there is no record of his marriage, the account of his love affair with "Lesbia," a name suggested by the birthplace of Sappho, comes down in 116 poems, of which three may be spurious. They run the gamut from dawning love to flaming hate when the lady proves faithless. Apuleius, author of *The Golden Ass,* identifies the object of the poems as the notorious Clodia, sister of Clodius and wife (63–59 B.C.) of the noble praetor, Quintus Caecilius Metellus.

Influenced by Greek form and meter, as well as by the early poets of Alexandria, Catullus evolved his own simple style, displayed in "On the Death of Lesbia's Sparrow," and the brief lament at his brother's death. His most ambitious poem is a 408-line epithalamium on the marriage of Peleus and Thetis. Catullus also wrote epigrams, some obscene, some amiable, lampooning the Romans of his day; but his lyric poetry, written with wit, grace, and sensual imagination, is what endures.

BIBLIOGRAPHICAL REFERENCES: Among the available translations of Catullus are Robinson Ellis, *Works, with Commentary,* 1889; Richard Burton, *The Carmina of Catullus,* 1894; F. W. Cornish, *Poems of Catullus,* 1904; and Horace Gregory, *Poems of Catullus,* 1931. See also H. A. J. Monro, *Criticisms and Elucidations of Catullus,* 1905; K. P. Harrington, *Catullus and His Influence,* 1923; Tenney Frank, *Catullus and Horace,* 1928; A. L. Wheeler, *Catullus and the Traditions of Ancient Poetry,* 1934; F. A. Wright, *Three Roman Poets,* 1938; Eric A. Havelock, *The Lyric Genius of Catullus,* 1939; Gilbert Highet, *Poets in a Landscape,* 1957; and Frank O. Copley, *Catullus, the Complete Poetry,* 1957.

LOUIS-FERDINAND CÉLINE
(Louis Fuch Destouches)

Born: Paris, France   *Died:* Paris (?), France
Date: May 27, 1894   *Date:* July 4, 1961

PRINCIPAL WORKS

NOVELS: *Voyage au bout de la nuit,* 1932 (*Journey to the End of the Night*); *Mort à credit,* 1936 (*Death on the Installment Plan*).

POLITICAL STUDIES: *Mea Culpa,* 1937; *Bagatelles pour un massacre,* 1938; *École des cadavres,* 1938.

Louis-Ferdinand Céline, whose real name is Louis Fuch Destouches, was born in Paris on May 27, 1894 to relatively humble Breton parents. While fighting in World War I, he was wounded in the head, shell-shocked, and decorated for bravery. After the war he studied medicine and subsequently practiced in the United States, Africa, and finally back in France, where he worked among the poor at a state clinic in Clichy. During this time he started writing novels which shocked sensitive readers but nevertheless sold well. His *Journey to the End of the Night* and *Death on the Installment Plan* quickly established his reputation; both were subsequently translated into English. After a trip to Russia in 1935, Céline wrote *Mea Culpa,* a report in which he set forth his bitterness against the Soviet. In the next year he published *Bagatelles pour un massacre,* a violently anti-Semitic work, and *École des cadavres,* in which he lashed out at the degeneracy of the French. Naturally, because of the views presented Céline was suspected of having fascist tendencies, although he constantly denied having any such affiliations. After the fall of France in 1940, however, he remained in Paris, where he continued to practice medicine. Accused of collaboration with the Nazis, he fled to Denmark after the defeat of Germany. When the French authorities discovered his whereabouts, they started (but never completed) extradition proceedings against him. He was, nevertheless, imprisoned for a short time in Denmark. Granted amnesty in 1951, he continued to live in exile. His most recent novel is *Guignol's Band,* a disordered study of slum life published in 1954. Before his death the author became partly paralyzed and, according to some, was close to insanity.

The main characters of his novels, Bardamu and Ferdinand, are largely extensions of Céline himself. Much that happens to them is autobiographical, and their ideas are those of their creator. Céline's sentences seem ungrammatical; his style is condensed; and his language is largely the slang of criminals. Some dismiss his novels as mere cheap pornography, but others point out a morbid yet almost noble misanthropy and a certain fierce sincerity in his writing.

BIBLIOGRAPHICAL REFERENCES: The best study in English is Milton Hindus, *The Crippled Giant: A Bizarre Adventure in Contemporary Letters,* 1950. See also Leon

Trotsky, "Novelist and Politician," *Atlantic Monthly,* CLVI (1935), 413–420; G. Truc, "L'Art et la passion de M. Ferdinand Céline," *Revue Hebdomadaire,* VII (1938), 550–565; and J. H. Matthews, "Céline's Journey to the End of Night," *Contemporary Review,* MXCV (1957), 158–161.

BENVENUTO CELLINI

Born: Florence, Italy   *Died:* Florence
Date: November 1, 1500   *Date:* February 13, 1571

PRINCIPAL WORK

MEMOIRS: *The Autobiography of Benvenuto Cellini,* c. 1558–1560; printed 1730.

The son of Giovanni Cellini, a Florentine musician and maker of musical instruments, Benvenuto, born November 1, 1500, was so named (Welcome) as a result of his being the first son born to his parents, who had been married eighteen years.

At fifteen he was apprenticed to a Florentine goldsmith, Marcone, although his father long clung to the hope of making the boy a musician; in fact, largely in deference to the elder's wishes, Benvenuto did become a skillful flutist but resented the interference of "that accursed music" with his own preference for metal working and sculpture.

Always quarrelsome, he was banished from Florence for six months because of a fight, went to Siena and Bologna, where he engaged in more metal work, and at nineteen made his first trip to Rome. There some of his work for the Bishop of Salamanca attracted the notice of Pope Clement VII, to whose court he became attached as a musician. By his own account he took part in the defense of Rome against the army of the Constable de Bourbon, performing, as he puts it, "incredible" feats of valor, including the shooting of the Bourbon himself.

After an interval spent in Florence and at the court of the Duke of Mantua, he returned to Rome, where he was employed in setting jewelry and in executing dies for private medallions, as well as for the papal mint. Still given to violence, by 1529 he seems to have committed at least two homicides and been engaged in some lesser brawls. Having fallen from papal favor, he was reinstated under Paul III. Later he again had to flee to Florence and Venice, only to be pardoned once more.

In 1537 he made his first trip to the court of Francis I of France, this visit a brief one. On his return to Italy he was imprisoned on a charge of having embezzled the gems of a pontifical tiara during the attack upon Rome. His memoirs give a graphic, at times lurid, account of his unsuccessful attempt to escape, the hardships of his imprisonment, his foiling of a poison plot against his life, and his religious visions.

Released at the intercession of the Cardinal of Ferrara, he returned to Francis I, spending about five years in arduous work for the French ruler. In 1545 he returned to his native city of Florence to spend the balance of his

197

life, though not much more serenely than before. He tells, for example, of a violent quarrel with the sculptor Baccio Bandinelli, who had accused Cellini of sexual perversions; of his participation in the defense of Florence in the war with Siena, and of his shabby treatment at the hands of his ducal patrons there. He continued to receive widespread acclaim for his work, however. It is commonly believed that at his death in Florence on February 13, 1571, he was still unmarried and without issue, although some sources say that he married Piera de Salvadore Parigi about 1565.

His works, many of which have been lost, include gold medallions of *Leda and the Swan, Hercules and the Nemean Lion, Atlas Supporting the Sphere,* and the famous salt cellar done for Francis I. Of a more ambitious scope are his bronze group, *Perseus Holding the Head of Medusa,* and silver statues of Jupiter, Mars, Vulcan, and a bust of Julius Caesar.

His *Autobiography,* begun in 1558, is the source for most of the information about him. Racy, direct, and energetic, it is almost as candid as Boswell's journals written two centuries later. With apparently no sense of incongruity Cellini blends sensuous love of beauty, religious fervor, brash self-congratulation, eroticism, haggling, and homicide, so that the work is a crystallization of much that is characteristic of the Italian Renaissance.

BIBLIOGRAPHICAL REFERENCES: The standard study is T. Longueville, *Cellini: His Times and Contemporaries,* 1899. Brief sketches appear in L. Forrer, *Biographical Dictionary of Medalists,* 1904; Sidney Dark, *Twelve Bad Men,* 1928; and Herbert M. Vaughan, *Studies in the Italian Renaissance,* 1930.

MIGUEL DE CERVANTES SAAVEDRA

Born: Alcalá de Henares, Spain
Date: September 29(?), 1547

Died: Madrid, Spain
Date: April 23, 1616

PRINCIPAL WORKS

NOVEL: *El Ingenioso Hidalgo Don Quixote de la Mancha,* First Part, 1605 (*The Ingenious Gentleman, Don Quixote de la Mancha*); Second Part, 1615.

NOVELLAS AND PROSE ROMANCES: *La Galatea,* 1585; *Novelas Exemplares,* 1613 (*Exemplary Novels*); *Los Trabajos de Persiles y Sigismunda,* 1617 (*The Tasks of Persiles and Sigismunda*).

POEM: *Viaje del Parnaso,* 1614 (*Journey to Parnassus*).

PLAYS: *Ocho Comedias y Ocho Entremeses,* 1615 (*Eight Comedies and Eight Interludes*).

In the gallery of universal and eternal symbols there are two figures thrust into fame by the pen of the great writer of the Golden Age of Spain, Miguel de Cervantes Saavedra. These two figures, one sad and gaunt, the other chubby and jovial, are the gentleman Don Quixote de la Mancha and his squire, Sancho Panza. "Thin, shriveled fanciful, and full of various thoughts," the first, and "a man of a good nature but with very little salt in the crown of his head," the second—both constitute an inseparable duality typifying

198

all the aspects of humanity through all the ages.

Miguel de Cervantes Saavedra, author of *El Ingenioso Hidalgo Don Quixote de la Mancha,* was "more versed in misfortunes than in verses." Born in Alcalá de Henares in 1547, probably on September 29, he was baptized on October 9 of the same year. Fourth son of a poor and deaf surgeon, Rodrigo de Cervantes, and Leonor de Cortinas, his wife, the boy tasted at his earliest age the salty bread of poverty. The father followed his profession in Valladolid, and there Cervantes spent some years of his boyhood. Some biographers conjecture that he also lived in Seville and Salamanca for a time, but the only known fact is that by 1567 he was studying in Madrid at the School of General Studies, later the University, under the instruction of Juan López de Hoyos, a professor of humanities who called Cervantes "our dear and beloved pupil." In 1569, as chamberlain in the household of Cardinal Giulio Acquaviva, Cervantes journeyed to Italy, where he had the opportunity to visit Rome, Florence, Milan, Venice, and Naples. These cities, especially the first two, were at the time centers of Renaissance culture, and this experience undoubtedly gave Cervantes the thirst for fame which remained with him for the rest of his life.

In 1570 he enlisted as a soldier in the forces of Diego de Urbina. On October 7, 1571, a date of glory for all Christendom, Cervantes fought in the naval battle of Lepanto, fighting aboard the galley *La Marquesa.* In spite of a high fever and the advice of friends to stay in the cabin of the vessel, he fought as valiantly as any of the others and received three arquebus shots, two in the chest and one in the left hand which left him permanently maimed. Years later the "maimed hero of Lepanto" was to recall gloriously his heroism "in the loftiest occasion that past and present ages saw, nor one which the future shall ever hope to see."

After recovering from his wounds, Cervantes fought in engagements at Navarino, Tunis, and Goletta. When he was on his way back to Spain, the galley *Sol* on which he was traveling was captured by Turkish pirates. Cervantes was taken to Algiers, where he remained a prisoner for the next five years. At least twice he planned his escape, but on each occasion he was betrayed by renegade Christians. Finally, on October 24, 1580, he was ransomed by Juan Gil, a Trinitarian friar.

His return to Spain ended the heroic period of Cervantes' life and began a grimmer period of daily struggles, hardships, and smothering bureaucracy. In 1584 he married Doña Catalina de Palacios. The complete failure of his domestic life echoes through his pastoral romance, *La Galatea,* a work "as vapid and languid as his marriage," says the critic Valbuena Prat. In the discharge of his duties as a commissary deputy procuring wheat for the Invincible Armada he suffered unjustly excommunication and two terms in prison because of the misconduct of one of his subordinates and the defalcation of his insurers. Probably in Seville, and in prison, "where every discomfort has its seat and every dismal sound its abode," he conceived or even traced out the framework of his masterpiece, *Don Quixote.*

In 1605 he was living in Valladolid with his two sisters, his illegitimate daughter, Isabel de Saavedra, and his niece, Constanza de Ovando. The fatal wounding of a gentleman, Don Gaspar de Ezpeleta, outside the house in which Cervantes lived caused the mayor, Don Cristóbal de Villarreal, to suspect that the writer's household was in some way connected with the brawl, and Cervantes and his whole family were arrested. A few days later they were released because nothing could be proved against them, but the investigation revealed certain evidence of very low morality on the part of one of Cervantes' sisters and his daughter, as well as the sordid, poverty-stricken surroundings in which the great novelist lived.

When the court moved to Madrid, Cervantes returned to that city. His life, which had been one of varied experience and uncertain fortune, he now devoted to literary work. The great Cervantine books were published over a period of little more than ten years: in 1605, the First Part of *Don Quixote*, which went into its sixth printing in the same year; in 1613, *Novelas Exemplares*, of which the best are, for their realistic and satirical flavor, "Rinconete," "El Licenciado Vidriera," and "El Coloquio de los perros"; in 1614, *Viaje del Parnaso*, a poem both laudable and ironical on the poets of his time; in 1615, *Ocho Comedias y Ocho Entremeses*. Of the comedies, the best are *El Cerco de Numancia*, a play of great dramatic sweep, and *Los Baños de Argel*, in which he drew upon his memories of his life as a captive in Africa; among the second, or brief comic pieces, *El Retablo de las Maravillas*, in which Cervantes ridiculed the credulity and hypocrisy of the society of his time, and *La Cueva de Salamanca*, a work of great roguishness and graciousness. In the

same year he published the Second Part of *Don Quixote*. *Los Trabajos de Persiles y Sigismunda*, a posthumous work called by Arturo Farinelli "the last romantic dream of Cervantes," appeared in 1617.

In this last work Cervantes foresees his approaching end. The dedication is dated April 19, 1616, four days before his death, and the prologue is a melancholy departure: "Farewell graces, farewell elegances, farewell beloved friends; that I depart dying and wishing to see you soon, happy in the other life." On April 23, 1616, after having joined the Order of Franciscan Tertiaries, Miguel de Cervantes died and was buried in the convent of the Trinitarian nuns in Madrid. His grave is unknown.

Cervantes began to write his immortal masterpiece as a satire on the romances of chivalry which at that time had become a rather foolish fashion in Spain. "Keep your aim set," he wrote in the prologue to the First Part of *Don Quixote*, "on demolishing the ill-founded fabric of these books of chivalry." But step by step, as the story unfolded in his imagination, the initial purpose of his book was giving way to a far greater design; as the work progressed, that primary conception continued to shape itself into a more lofty goal, one complex and universal in its attempt to depict the realistic and the idealistic in mankind. In the prologue to the Second Part Cervantes advised the reader that "in it I give you a Don Quixote of far greater outline"; that is to say, not only the Knight of the Sad Countenance, but beyond this figure a symbol of nobility, love, and justice. Don Quixote is no longer the poor gentleman gone mad, an unfortunate who inspires pity, but the wise and prudent hero who teaches with his life and his word a love for the highest ideals of humanity. Cervantes developed his valiant hero from a simple, middle-aged gentleman upon Rocinante, horse of mockery, to a national and universal personage upon Clavileño, the steed of the ideal and the visionary.

The change in Don Quixote is paralleled by that in Sancho Panza, his squire. Introduced at the beginning as a good-natured rustic, rich in proverbs and shrewd in common sense, he is transformed by the novelist's pen into a spirit purified by the teachings of his master. Sancho becomes a dedicated squire ruling wisely the island of Barataria, a wonderful quixotic utopia. Nor does the novel end here. There comes a moment, sharply indicated by Salvador de Madariaga, in which Don Quixote and Sancho merge in such a manner that Don Quixote becomes Sancho-like and Sancho becomes quixotic, the first moving gradually toward reason, which he fully reaches with his death, and the second making a nobility of aim triumphant in his life.

It is well said that like other great works, Don Quixote has been the subject of much study and many interpretations. It is a book that every reader can read many times, always with fresh joy because of its inexhaustible treasure of humanity, teachings, and ideas of enduring value. It is with reason enough that Marcelino Menéndez y Pelayo, supreme master of Spanish criticism, has called Cervantes the "creator of the realistic modern novel" and Don Quixote the "comic epic of human value, eternal breviary of laughter and prudence."

Roberto Bravo Villarroel

BIBLIOGRAPHICAL REFERENCES: The definitive edition is the *Obras Completas de Miguel de Cervantes Saavedra*, edited by Adolf Bonilla and Rudolph Schevill, 19 vols., Madrid, 1914–1941. Cervantes studies are so extensive in every language that space will not permit more than a selective listing.

For biography and criticism in English see Smollett's *Life* in his translation of *Don Quixote*, Vol. I, 1775; Thomas Roscoe, *The Life and Writings of Miguel de Cervantes Saavedra*, 1839; A. J. Duffield, *Don Quixote, His Critics and Commentators*, 1881; James Fitzmaurice-Kelly, *The Life of Miguel de Cervantes Saavedra*, 1892; idem, *Miguel de Cervantes Saavedra: A Memoir*, 1913; idem, *Cervantes and Shakespeare*, 1916; Rudolph Schevill, *Cervantes*, 1919; W. J. Entwistle, *Cervantes*, 1940; Angel Flores and M. J. Benardete, eds., *Cervantes Across the Centuries*, 1947; Aubrey F. G. Bell, *Cervantes*, 1947; and Gary MacEoin, *Cervantes*, 1950; also Rudolph Schevill, "Persiles y Sigismunda," *Modern Philology*, IV (1906–1907), 1–24, and "Three Centuries of *Don Quixote*," University of California *Chronicle*, XV (1913), 181–206.

For studies in Spanish see Martín Fernández de Navarrete, *Vida de Miguel de Cervantes Saavedra*, 1819; Jerónimo Morán, *Vida de Miguel de Cervantes Saavedra*, 1863; Cristóbal Pérez Pastor, *Documentos Cervantinos*, 1897–1902; Francisco A. de Icaza, *Las "Novelas Ejemplares" de Cervantes*, 1901; José María Asensio y Toledo, *Cervantes y sus obras*, 1902; Miguel de Unamuno, *Vida de Don Quijote y Sancho*, 1905; Marcelino Menéndez y Pelayo, *Discurso acerca de Cervantes y el "Quijote,"* 1905; José Ortega y Gasset, *Meditaciones del Quijote*, 1914; Adolfo Bonilla y San Martín, *De Crítica Cervantina*, 1916; Emilio Cotarelo y Mori, *Últimos estudios cervantinos*, 1920; Arturo Farinelli, *El último sueño romántico de Cervantes*, 1922;

Ramiro de Maeztú, *Don Quixote, Don Juan y la Celestina,* 1926; **and Salvador de** Madariaga, *Don Quixote,* 1935.

See also Raymond L. Grismer, *Cervantes: A Bibliography,* 1950.

GEORGE CHAPMAN

Born: Near Hitchin, England
Date: c. 1559

Died: London, England
Date: May 12, 1634

PRINCIPAL WORKS

PLAYS: *The Blind Beggar of Alexandria,* 1596; *An Humourous Day's Mirth,* 1597; *The Gentleman Usher,* c. 1602; *All Fools,* c. 1604; *Monsieur d'Olive,* 1604; *Bussy d'Ambois,* 1604; *Eastward Ho!,* 1605 (with Jonson and Marston); *Charles, Duke of Byron,* 1608; *May Day,* 1609; *The Revenge of Bussy d'Ambois,* c. 1610; *The Widow's Tears,* printed 1612; *Chabot, Admiral of France,* c. 1613 (with Shirley); *Caesar and Pompey,* c. 1613.

POEMS: *The Shadow of Night,* 1594; *Hero and Leander,* 1598 (a completion of the last four books of Marlowe's poem).

TRANSLATIONS: The *Iliad,* 1598, 1611; the *Odyssey,* 1614; the *Georgics* of Hesiod, 1618; *The Works of Homer,* 1624.

George Chapman is best remembered as the translator of *The Works of Homer.* His massive accomplishment in the field of drama is respected by scholars, but it has not displaced the idea of him as primarily a translator.

Although the date of his birth, near Hitchin, Hertfordshire, is not certain, he was probably a little older than Shakespeare and more than a dozen years older than Ben Jonson, his long-time friend and sometime enemy. According to Anthony à Wood, Chapman attended one of the universities. Possibly, after leaving the university, he served in the Netherlands with the forces of Sir Francis Vere; if so, he shared another experience with Jonson, for the latter trailed a pike in the Netherlands.

Chapman's literary career began no later than 1594, for in that year was published his poem *The Shadow of Night.* Two years later he launched his dramatic career with the performance of his *Blind Beggar of Alexandria* by

the Admiral's Men. After this, Philip Henslowe recorded dramatic activity by Chapman, sometimes alone, sometimes with collaborators. Francis Meres in *Palladis Tamia* (1598) referred to him as one of England's best for comedy and tragedy. His experiments with "humour" comedy precede or coincide with Jonson's earliest efforts.

As it was fitting for such substantial scholars and authors to be, Chapman and Jonson were apparently good friends for many years. Chapman contributed a major commendatory poem to the 1605 Quarto of *Sejanus;* and Jonson reciprocated with a highly complimentary poem for the *Georgics* of Hesiod, translated by Chapman. In 1605 Chapman and Jonson were imprisoned together, apparently because of offense taken at certain satirical passages in *Eastward Ho!.* An old commonplace book now in The Folger Library contains copies of ten letters by the two authors pleading for noble patrons to come to their rescue. Both of the

202

dramatists served Henry, Prince of Wales, and both suffered a serious loss in patronage in his untimely death. Both were co-workers with Inigo Jones, the King's architect and scenic designer, and Inigo seems to have been the rock on which they split. Jonson and Jones both had their share of arrogance and certainty of preëminent merit, and they quarreled violently for many years. Chapman took sides with the architect rather than with his fellow-poet: an unfinished poetic invective against Jonson survives in manuscript. Almost two hundred lines, some obviously in need of revision, pour a stream of able abuse on Jonson, who almost certainly had no knowledge of the piece. Jonson made no known written attack on Chapman, but he dealt numerous and heavy verbal blows at Jones both in printed and manuscript works. When Chapman died, May 12, 1634, Inigo Jones designed his monument. He is buried at St. Giles-in-the-Fields, London.

Chapman is not easy to read, and his plays are seldom if ever performed; but there is a solid and intellectual quality to his writings more satisfactory to cultivated tastes than the glib and the commonplace.

BIBLIOGRAPHICAL REFERENCES: The most recent critical edition is *The Plays and Poems of George Chapman*, ed. by T. M. Parrott, 1910–1914. Phyllis Bartlett edited *The Poems of George Chapman*, 1941. See also J. M. Robertson, *Shakespeare and Chapman*, 1917; *Dictionary of National Biography*, Vol. IV, 1921; E. K. Chambers, *The Elizabethan Stage*, Vol. III, 1923; and C. H. Herford, Percy and Evelyn Simpson, eds., *Ben Jonson*, 1925–1952. (See especially Vols. I, X, and XI).

FRANÇOIS RENÉ DE CHATEAUBRIAND

Born: St. Malo, France
Date: September 4, 1768

Died: Paris, France
Date: July 4, 1848

PRINCIPAL WORKS

NOVELS: *Atala*, 1801; *René*, 1802; *Les Martyrs*, 1809; *Les Natchez*, 1826–1831; *Les Aventures du dernier des Abencérages*, 1826–1831.

POLITICAL AND RELIGIOUS STUDIES: *Essai historique, politique, et moral sur les révolutions anciennes et modernes*, 1797; *La génie du christianisme*, 1802; *De Buonaparte et des Bourbons*, 1814; *Études ou discours historiques*, 1831; *Congrès de Vérone*, 1838.

BIOGRAPHY AND AUTOBIOGRAPHY: *Vie de Rancé*, 1844; *Mémoires d'outre-tombe*, 1849–1850.

François René de Chateaubriand was born September 4, 1768, at St. Malo in the Breton section of France. After studying for the priesthood, Chateaubriand gave up the Church as a career and in 1786 received a commission in the army. In 1787 in Paris he was presented at court. Early in 1791 he joined an expedition in search of the Northwest Passage. Although it was unsuccessful, Chateaubriand developed an interest in primitivism in man and in nature; at this time he also developed a faculty for literary expression.

Back in France only a short time, he

203

became an emigrant after the arrest of Louis XVI. After being wounded on a street in Brussels and abandoned on a beach on Guernsey Island, he made his way to London. Here he lived in poverty, but he was able to accomplish much writing. In his *Essai historique, politique et moral sur les révolutions,* published in England in 1797, he took a stand as a mediator between the extremes of royalist and revolutionary ideas and as a Rousseauistic freethinker in religion. He turned against the revolutionists, however, when he learned how his family had been ill-treated. Shortly after returning to Paris in 1800, he published *Atala, ou les amours de deux sauvages dans le désert.* The book contains many brilliant passages, especially descriptions of nature; yet critics have complained of its rather offensive combination of prudery and sensuousness. His next work was *La génie du christianisme, ou beautés de la religion chrétienne.* This book, although it does not contain very convincing theological arguments, is praised for its sensitive descriptions of Catholic liturgy and symbolism. As part of this work appeared the narrative *René.* Because of its portrayal of a dissatisfied soul, this book is believed to be largely autobiographical.

For the next thirty years Chateaubriand was in and out of favor with the French monarchs—Napoleon, Louis XVIII, and Louis Philippe. During this time he held numerous governmental positions and was attended by a series of mistresses. His complete works were published between 1826 and 1831. After retiring from public life, Chateaubriand died in Paris, July 4, 1848. His autobiographical *Mémoires d'outre-tombe,* posthumously published, exhibit in many ways the man's egotism and shallowness. Chateaubriand is held by literary historians as representing a bridge between the classicism of the eighteenth century and the romanticism of the early nineteenth.

BIBLIOGRAPHICAL REFERENCES: For studies of Chateaubriand in English see Francis H. Gribble, *Chateaubriand and His Court of Women,* 1909, and the more comprehensive biography, André Maurois, *Chateaubriand: Poet, Statesman, Lover,* 1938. Biographical and critical studies in French include Comte de Marcellus, *Chateaubriand et son temps,* 1859; C. A. Sainte-Beuve, *Chateaubriand et son groupe littéraire sous l'empire,* 1872; and Victor Giraud, *La vie romanesque de Chateaubriand,* 1932.

GEOFFREY CHAUCER

Born: London (?), England
Date: c. 1343

Died: London
Date: October 25 (?), 1400

PRINCIPAL WORKS

ABC, The Book of the Duchess, courtly love lyrics, *The Romance of the Rose* (a translation, surviving fragments of which may not be Chaucer's), 1360?–1372; *The House of Fame, The Legend of St. Cecelia* (later used as *Second Nun's Tale*), *Tragedies of Fortune* (later used as *Monk's Tale*), *Anelida and Arcite,* 1372–1380; *The Parliament of Fowls, Palamon and Arcite* (later used as *Knight's Tale*), *Boece* (translation of Boethius' *Consolation of Philosophy*), *Troilus and Criseyde,* philosophical lyrics, *The Legend of Good Women*, 1380–1386; *The Canterbury Tales*, (General Prologue and Groups A and B), *The Treatise of the Astrolabe*, 1387–1392; *The Canterbury Tales* (Groups D, E, F, C, G, H), *retraction*, personal lyrics, 1393–1400.

Geoffrey Chaucer, one of the greatest of English writers, made his living as a civil servant and composed poetry as an avocation. His career, however, was such as to contribute to his literary growth. He was born about 1343 of a prosperous family and reared in London. His father, a wine-importer, was able to find him a position (in 1357 or earlier) as a page boy in the household of King Edward III's daughter-in-law, Elizabeth of Ulster; and from this period on, despite the political uncertainties of the age, Chaucer enjoyed the uninterrupted favor of the members of the court of, successively, Edward, Richard II, and Henry IV, both as a man of affairs and as a poet.

He served as a soldier in France in the campaigns of the Hundred Years' War in 1359–1360 and was sent abroad on at least seven occasions between 1368 and 1387, either to France or Italy, on diplomatic missions. He acquired the training necessary for business, probably at the law school known as the Inner Temple. He acted in London as a Controller of Customs from 1374 to 1385, became a Justice of the Peace in Kent in 1385 and a member of Parliament for the county in 1386, served in London again from 1389 to 1391 as a Clerk of the Works, and was thereafter awarded a less active royal appointment as subforester.

He was married (c. 1366) to Philippa Roet of Flanders, who was lady-in-waiting to Queen Philippa and later to John of Gaunt's second wife Constance. (Chaucer's wife's sister became Gaunt's third wife.) Records suggest that he had two sons and a daughter

and that his wife died in 1387. He died in 1400 in a house which he had rented in the grounds of Westminster Abbey, and he was buried in that section of the Abbey later to become famous as the Poets' Corner.

The maturation of Chaucer's genius can be illustrated by four works. In the *Book of the Duchess* the poet dreams that he shares the grief of a lonely young knight, who proves to be John of Gaunt mourning his newly lost first wife. The conception is original and the expression of sympathy is gracefully tender, but the framework of the dream-vision and the knight's description of his love are strongly influenced by French models.

In the uncompleted *House of Fame*, another dream-vision, the poet is carried off by an eagle to learn whether those who are in the service of Love are happy or not. The self-confident and domineering eagle was suggested to Chaucer by his reading of Dante's *Paradiso* but here plays a novel comic role in a work which tends to parody the artificiality of medieval courtly love conventions.

In *Troilus and Criseyde*, Chaucer's first major achievement, he amplifies Boccaccio's pseudo-classical romance, *Il Filostrato*, giving depth to the sorrowful Troilus, elusiveness to the timid Criseyde, robust comicality to the officious Pandarus, immediacy to the setting, and a new significance to the tragedy of the two lovers separated by the Trojan War.

In *The Canterbury Tales*, a masterpiece even greater than *Troilus* though uncompleted, Chaucer turned to the

205

English scene, as had his contemporaries Langland and Gower, and excelled all the writers of his era in his delineation of the men, women, children, and animals familiar to him in real life. A richly assorted group of pilgrims entertain themselves by telling stories on the way from London to Canterbury. Through his descriptions in the General Prologue and dramatizations in the links connecting the tales he portrays in detail seven members of the feudal order, thirteen people associated with religious life, and fourteen townspeople —the chivalrous Knight, the aristocratic Prioress, the fraudulent Pardoner, the impoverished Canon's Yeoman, the amorous Wife of Bath, the reticent civil servant who is Chaucer himself, and the rest who have gained an independent identity as real as that of Falstaff, Tom Jones, or Becky Sharp. And the tales which Chaucer has supplied match the tellers in their rich variety— the Knight's courtly romance, the Miller's racy fabliau, the Second Nun's pious saint's life, the Nun's Priest's mock-heroic fable, the Pardoner's hypocritical sermon, and the Parson's sincere one.

Like most medieval craftsmen, Chaucer, whether as young apprentice or as mature master, followed the pattern of established models; and his success can therefore be partially explained by the vast extent of his reading of "old, approvèd stories." Sources or analogues have been found for almost all of his works and even for his style. His comic tone, for instance, often seems reminiscent of his favorite Latin poet, Ovid; and his philosophical ideas are usually those of Boethius. He appears to have culled materials in turn from the French —from Machaut, Deschamps, Froissart —then from the Italians—from Dante, Petrarch, and Boccaccio—and finally, perhaps, from his fellow countryman Langland. But the ultimate achievements of the medieval master craftsman were profoundly original. Chaucer's skill as a raconteur; his deftness of characterization and description; his perfection in metrical technique; his understanding of man's religious, moral, and philosophical instincts; his knowledge of life and acceptance of its mingled tragedy and comedy; and his transcendent sense of humor are, in combination, unique.

Charles W. Dunn

BIBLIOGRAPHICAL REFERENCES: The most recent definitive edition of Chaucer is *The Works of Geoffrey Chaucer*, 2nd ed., edited by F. N. Robinson, 1957. For biography and criticism see the following: G. L. Kittredge, *Chaucer and His Poetry*, 1915; R. K. Root, *The Poetry of Chaucer*, 1922 (rev. ed.); G. K. Chesterton, *Chaucer*, 1932; J. L. Lowes, *Chaucer and the Development of his Genius*, 1934; Marchette Chute, *Geoffrey Chaucer of England*, 1946; Muriel A. Bowden, *Commentary of the General Prologue to the Canterbury Tales*, 1948; Nevil Coghill, *The Poet Chaucer*, 1949; W. W. Lawrence, *Chaucer and the Canterbury Tales*, 1950; and Raymond Preston, *Chaucer*, 1952.

Five Hundred Years of Chaucer Criticism, by Caroline F. E. Spurgeon, 3 vols., 1925, is a scholarly work that is both valuable for the student and interesting to the general reader.

ANTON CHEKHOV

Born: Taganrog, Russia
Date: January 17, 1860

Died: Badenweiler, Germany
Date: July 2, 1904

PRINCIPAL WORKS

PLAYS: *Ivanov*, 1889; *Chaika*, 1896 (*The Sea Gull*); *Dyadya Vanya*, 1899 (*Uncle Vanya*); *Tri sestry*, 1901 (*The Three Sisters*); *Vishnyovy sad*, 1904 (*The Cherry Orchard*).

SHORT STORIES IN TRANSLATION: *The Tales of Tchekhov*, 1916–1922 (13 vols.).

REPORTAGE: *Sakhalin*, 1891.

Anton (Pavlovich) Chekhov [also Chekov, Tchehov, and Tchekhov], Russia's foremost playwright and one of the great masters of the short story, was the third child of Pavel Yegorovitch Chekhov, "merchant in the third guild"—that is, the proprietor of a small grocery shop in Taganrog, where the future writer was born on January 17, 1860. When, after an unhappy childhood, he entered Moscow University to study medicine, he assumed the burden and responsibility of supporting the family, which he undertook to do by writing humorous sketches and stories for periodicals. The first of these tales was published in 1880, and in the next seven years he wrote as many as six hundred stories. On graduation in 1884, with health already impaired by hard work and tuberculosis, he took up the practice of medicine, which he was to pursue somewhat desultorily in later years, as inclination and poor health permitted. There would be no lack of patients, but money was always scarce.

His literary aspirations received strong encouragement in 1885 when he made his first visit to the nation's literary capital, St. Petersburg. There he met A. S. Suvorin, wealthy and influential editor of the *New Times*, who invited contributions. His first three stories published in this paper found enthusiastic readers. Actually he was already well known and admired in the city on the strength of earlier stories, most of which he confessed were carelessly written. In the next five years he gave critical attention to his writing and formulated sound theories of art. In a letter in 1887 he pointed out that "a man of letters is not a pastry cook, nor an expert on cosmetics, nor an entertainer; he is a responsible person, under contract to his conscience and the consciousness of his duty . . . [and] he is in duty bound to battle with his fastidiousness and soil his imagination with the grime of life." During this period he came under the influence of Tolstoy. A few of the tales show the impact of Tolstoyan ideas on morality and non-resistance to evil.

In 1890 Chekhov decided to make the arduous journey to Sakhalin Island, penal colony of the tsarist government, to study conditions there. His motives are not clear, for he gave conflicting explanations. However personal the real reasons were, his humanitarian sympathies were genuine enough, and he may have felt an impulse to make practical use of his keen powers of observation and his scientific training. He reported to Suvorin that he spoke with every man, woman, and child on the island. His book based on the survey

—in which, as he said, "I have paid my debt to learning"—helped to bring about changes of policy in the colony, but soon both the investigation and the book were forgotten.

One significant consequence was that Tolstoy's ideas no longer seemed adequate to reach the deep-rooted ills of men. Chekhov's carefully wrought "Ward No. 6" (1892) pointed to the weakness of the "non-resistance" principle, and in 1894, in a letter to Suvorin, he said, "There is more love of humanity in electricity and steam than in chastity and abstention from meat."

Chekhov had already written several plays, but his high reputation as a playwright dates from 1898, when *The Seagull,* a failure at its first performance on October 17, 1896, was presented by Stanislavski and the Moscow Art Theatre. The same group presented *Uncle Vanya* in the autumn of 1899, and the whole troupe went to the author's home in Yalta to petition him for further works from his pen. He obliged with *The Three Sisters,* which brought his subtle methods close to perfection in a deftly articulated story. In the last year of his life *The Cherry Orchard* made his high rank secure. External action in this haunting masterpiece is almost non-existent, for the writer's intention, as in many of his tales, is to project a mood, an elusive state of mind. The central figures are a set of futile but charming gentlefolk, far better able to feel than to act, who having outlived their own day are powerless to adapt themselves to the new.

Chekhov's rise to fame as a playwright coincided with the culmination of his long battle against tuberculosis. In 1897 he suffered a severe attack, and from that day his activities and travels were dictated by his illness. During his stay at Nice, seeking as usual for a tolerable climate, he became a partisan of Zola in connection with the Dreyfus affair. This stand brought him into open conflict with the conservative principles of the St. Petersburg *New Times,* and his close friendship with Suvorin ended. He found a new friend, however, in Maxim Gorky, and in 1901 he married Olga Knipper, a young actress of the Moscow Art Theatre. Much of their wedded life was spent apart, Chekhov in Yalta and his wife in Moscow pursuing her theatrical career, the two of them anxiously querying and reassuring each other by letter as to the quality and durability of their devotion. They were together in Badenweiler, Germany, however, at the time of Chekhov's death on July 2, 1904. His body arrived in Moscow in a coach bearing the legend "Fresh Oysters."

Although Chekhov was occasionally charged with being a writer without a philosophy or a point of view, his stories and plays clearly illustrate his artistic principles and his conception of human truths. The drabness and tedium of life, the ugliness of hardship and poverty, and the silent loneliness of the individual are of course set forth without compromise or palliation, but there are many glimpses of beauty in nature and humanity. The author's very real personal woes never defeated his innate kindliness, his keen sense of humor, his love for his fellowmen, and his faith in the future.

BIBLIOGRAPHICAL REFERENCES: *The Letters of Anton Tchekhov,* translated by Constance Garnett, 1920, provide valuable source material on Chekhov's life. For biographical and critical studies in English see also William Gerhardi, *Chekhov: A*

Critical Study, 1923; Walter H. Bruford, Chekhov and His Russia, 1948; L. Avilova, Chekhov in My Life, 1950; Ronald Hingsley, Chekhov: A Biographical and Critical Study, 1950; and David Magarshack, Chekhov the Dramatist, 1952, and Chekhov: A Life, 1952.

The Tales of Chekhov were translated by Constance Garnett, 13 vols., 1916–1922.

CHARLES WADDELL CHESNUTT

Born: Cleveland, Ohio
Date: June 20, 1858

Died: Cleveland
Date: November 15, 1932

PRINCIPAL WORKS

SHORT STORIES: The Conjure Woman, 1899; The Wife of His Youth, 1899.
NOVELS: The House Behind the Cedars, 1900; The Marrow of Tradition, 1901; The Colonel's Dream, 1905.
BIOGRAPHY: Life of Frederick Douglass, 1899.

Charles Waddell Chesnutt was born in Cleveland, Ohio, on June 20, 1858, but spent his boyhood in North Carolina. There he began teaching at the age of sixteen, becoming principal of the State Normal School at Fayetteville when he was only twenty-three. He left the South in 1883 and settled in Cleveland, where he studied law and was admitted to the bar.

Chesnutt's two main interests were the customs, folklore, and superstitions of Negroes, and the sociological and legal problems with which American civilization confronted his race. For the former he drew upon his early Southern experience, and for the latter, his legal training in the North.

Frederick Douglass, whom Chesnutt made the subject of a book, was one of the first to see the value of Negro folklore; Chesnutt expanded upon Douglass' insight and made such material the focus of many of his stories. His treatment of the Negro in the context of his folklore is quite similar to that of the Uncle Remus stories.

Chesnutt's sociological interests, though civically commendable, proved less fruitful for his art. This is especially true of his novels, in which character and plot are often subordinated to propagandistic and didactic interests. He died at Cleveland on November 15, 1932.

BIBLIOGRAPHICAL REFERENCES: The fullest account of Chesnutt and his fiction is found in Benjamin G. Brawley, The Negro Genius, 1937. See also Jay S. Redding, To Make a Poet Black, 1939; William Dean Howells, "Mr. Charles W. Chesnutt's Stories," Atlantic Monthly, LXXXV (1900), 699–701; John Chamberlain, "The Negro as Writer," Bookman, LXX (1930), 603–611; and "Post-Bellum—Pre-Harlem," Colophon, Part V (1931).

PHILIP DORMER STANHOPE, LORD CHESTERFIELD

Born: London, England
Date: September 22, 1694

Died: London
Date: March 24, 1773

LETTERS: *Letters to His Son,* 1774, 1776, 1778; *Letters to His Godson,* 1776, 1790.

Lord Chesterfield's name has become so synonymous with courtly manners that we are likely to forget that he had a distinguished career in public affairs. Born in London, September 22, 1694, he succeeded to the earldom in 1726. During his public life he was twice ambassador to The Hague, Secretary of State, negotiator of the second Treaty of Vienna (1731), and a very successful lord-lieutenant of Ireland (1746). In 1755 occurred his famous quarrel with Dr. Johnson on the publication of the latter's Dictionary, the story of which can be found in Boswell's *Life of Samuel Johnson.*

The famous letters, for which his name is chiefly remembered, were written to his illegitimate son Philip. They were begun when the boy was quite young and were continued for years.

The purpose was to teach the boy the easy elegance of manner that distinguished his father and to serve as a guide to the fashionable world. To some readers, they have seemed cold, artificial and heartless; to others, they have much of traditional eighteenth century charm. It was the supreme irony that the son never profited from the lessons; he married a woman of low birth and never assumed the position in the world for which his father had tried to prepare him. The son preceded the father in death by five years.

Lord Chesterfield married Melusina von Schulemberg, illegitimate daughter of George I. They had no children, and he was succeeded in the earldom by a distant cousin when he died in London, March 24, 1773.

BIBLIOGRAPHICAL REFERENCES: For biographical and related information see W. H. Craig's *Life,* 1907; R. Coxon, *Chesterfield and His Critics,* 1925; and Samuel Shellabarger, *Lord Chesterfield and His World,* 1951.

G. K. CHESTERTON

Born: London, England
Date: May 29, 1874

Died: Beaconsfield, England
Date: June 14, 1936

Principal Works

ESSAYS AND STUDIES: *The Defendant,* 1901; *Heretics,* 1905; *All Things Considered,* 1908; *Orthodoxy,* 1908; *Tremendous Trifles,* 1909; *What's Wrong With the World,* 1910; *Utopia of Usurers,* 1917; *The Uses of Diversity,* 1920; *Fancies vs. Fads,* 1923; *The Everlasting Man,* 1925; *The Superstitions of the Skeptic,* 1925; *The Outline of Sanity,* 1926; *Generally Speaking,* 1928; *The Thing,* 1929; *Come To Think of It,* 1930; *Avowals and Denials,* 1934; *As I Was Saying,* 1936.

NOVELS: *The Napoleon of Notting Hill,* 1904; *The Man Who Was Thursday,* 1908; *Manalive,* 1912; *The Flying Inn,* 1914.

FATHER BROWN STORIES: *The Innocence of Father Brown,* 1911; *The Wisdom of Father Brown,* 1914; *The Incredulity of Father Brown,* 1926; *The Secret of Father Brown,* 1927; *The Scandal of Father Brown,* 1935.

BIOGRAPHY AND CRITICISM: *Robert Browning*, 1903; *Charles Dickens*, 1906; *George Bernard Shaw*, 1909; *William Blake*, 1910; *Saint Francis of Assisi*, 1923; *Robert Louis Stevenson*, 1927; *Chaucer*, 1932; *St. Thomas Aquinas*, 1933.

POEMS: *The Wild Knight*, 1900; *The Ballad of the White Horse*, 1911; *The Ballad of St. Barbara*, 1923; *The Queen of Seven Swords*, 1926.

Gilbert Keith Chesterton, English essayist, novelist, and poet, was born May 29, 1874, in London. Educated at St. Paul's School, he left in 1891 to study art, but followed his natural literary bent by producing his first book of poems, *The Wild Knight*, in 1900. In 1901 he married Frances Blogg and became a regular contributor to two leading newspapers. Chesterton regarded himself as a journalist, and nothing that was in the news of the day failed to get into his writing. From 1918 on, he edited *G. K.'s Weekly*.

Chesterton the writer, lecturer, and champion of the Catholic faith, remained Chesterton the controversialist; not, however, as an Anglican as opposed to his writings as a Catholic after his conversion in 1922. The general Christian truths he preached in *Orthodoxy* in 1908 he echoed also in *St. Thomas Aquinas* in 1933. He was a controversial thinker whose "chief idea of life" was the awakening of wonder, or of an awareness of a thing as being seen for the first time. He became a master of paradox. Unless a reader's mind is prepared to work along with Chesterton, nothing will come of the reading. He said, for example, that "nothing succeeds like failure," but he was referring to the "failure" of Calvary.

A prolific writer, Chesterton will be remembered longest, in all probability, for his literary criticisms: *Robert Browning*, *Charles Dickens*, *George Bernard Shaw*, *Robert Louis Stevenson*, and *Chaucer*; and for his penetrating religious analyses such as *St. Francis of Assisi*, *The Everlasting Man*, and *The Thing*. A delightful light verse writer and illustrator, he was also a fine rhetorical poet. ("Lepanto," "A Song of the Wheels," and "The Ballad of the White Horse" were all written in 1911.) As a writer of fiction he was most successful in his Father Brown detective stories. But in all his works, including three plays and innumerable essays, he hammers home Christian truths. Through his sociological books, *What's Wrong with the World* and *The Outline of Sanity*, he became with Hilaire Belloc a leading exponent of the policy of economic and political decentralization known as "Distributism."

Possessing a brilliant mind and a huge hulk of a body, this Christian humorist endeared himself to thousands through his writings and extensive lecture tours in Europe, America, and Palestine. His much-touted absent-mindedness and shaggy appearance made him the subject of cartoons and anecdotes. He died June 14, 1936, at Beaconsfield, Buckinghamshire.

BIBLIOGRAPHICAL REFERENCES: Chesterton's *Autobiography*, 1936, is the foundation of source material on his life. For biography and criticism see also Julius West, *G. K. Chesterton: A Critical Study*, 1916; Patrick Braybrooke, *Gilbert Keith Chesterton*, 1922; W. R. Titterton, *G. K. Chesterton: A Portrait*, 1936; Maurice Evans, *G. K. Chesterton*, 1939; Hilaire Belloc, *On the Place of G. K. Chesterton in English*

Letters, 1940; Ada E. Chesterton, *The Chestertons*, 1941; Maisie Ward, *Gilbert Keith Chesterton*, 1943; and Hugh Kenner, *Paradox in Chesterton*, 1947.

CHIKAMATSU MONZAEMON

Born: Probably Kyoto, Japan   *Died:* Japan
Date: 1653   *Date:* January 5 or 6, 1725

Principal Works

PLAYS: *Sonezaki Shinjû*, 1703 (*The Love Suicides at Sonezaki*); *Meido no Hikyaku*, 1711 (*The Courier for Hades*); *Kaoyo Uta-garuta*, 1714 (*Fair Ladies at a Game of Poem Cards*); *Kokusen'ya Kassen*, 1715 (*The Battles of Conxinga*); *Ikutama Shinjû*, 1715 (*Love Suicide at Ikutama*); *Nihon Furisode-hajime*, 1718 (*The Beginning of Love Sleeves in Japan*); *Hakata Kojorô Nami-makura*, 1719 (*The Adventures of the Hakata Damsel*); *Shinjû Ten no Amijima*, 1721 (*The Love Suicide at Amijima*); *Kwan-hasshû Tsunagi-uma*, 1724 (*The Tethered Steed*), *Koi Hakke Hashira-go-yomi*, 1740 (*The Almanac of Love*).

As in the case of Shakespeare, very few details of Chikamatsu Monzaemon's personal life are known. He was probably born in 1653 at Kyoto, to a warrior family. It is disputed whether he died on January 5 or 6, 1725. Although he is credited with more than one hundred puppet plays as well as plays for the Kabuki stage estimated between twenty-six and forty, his authorship of a number of them is disputed.

Chikamatsu Monzaemon's dramas fall into two general types: the historical (the majority) and the domestic. In time, they range from Japan's legendary Age of the Gods to current events of his day. The theme of all his plays is the conflict between love and duty. Virtue is generally triumphant. If the plot does not permit a happy ending, the moral or social code is vindicated by the suicide of the offenders. This is particularly the case with the domestic plays, the tragedies ending in "love suicide," in which the lovers decide that their present plight results from past sins and thus seek the next life where they hope they may become husband and wife. Chikamatsu, with his wide range of knowledge, both in the Japanese classics and in quotations from Chinese writings, ranged widely through Confucian ethics, Buddhist ideas of the after life, and the predicaments of human life. In whatever historical time his play is cast, it is written in the language and the manner of his contemporaries. His puppet plays were mostly written for the famous reciter, Takemoto Gidayû (1651–1714), and his Kabuki plays for the celebrated actor, Sakata Tôjûrô (1647–1709). About 1705 he became staff playwright for the Takemoto Theater; it was after this date that he reached his greatest heights. He is celebrated today as Japan's greatest playwright.

BIBLIOGRAPHICAL REFERENCES: There are three complete works of Chikamatsu, and nine collected works. Critical studies of his plays in Japanese are too many to enumerate. A few of his plays have been translated into English: Asataro Miyamori trans lated *Masterpieces of Chikamatsu,* 1926; Donald L. Keene, *The Battles of Conxinga,* 1951; and Donald H. Shiveley, *The Love Suicide at Amijima,* 1953. His life and works are also dealt with in Sir George B. Sansom, *Japan, a Short Cultural History,* 1943; Faubion Bowers, *Japanese Theater,* 1952; Donald L. Keene, *Japanese Literature,* 1953; Earle Ernst, *The Kabuki Theater,* 1956; and *The Kabuki Handbook,* 1956.

CHRÉTIEN DE TROYES

Born: France   *Died:* France (?)
Date: c. 1150   *Date:* c. 1190

Principal Works

METRICAL ROMANCES: *Erec et Enide,* before 1164; *Cligés,* before 1164; *Lancelot, ou le Chevalier de la Charrette,* after 1164; *Yvain, ou le Chevalier au Lion,* after 1164; *Perceval, ou le Conte du Graal,* c. 1180.

Born in France about 1150, Chrétien de Troyes, author of the earliest extant Arthurian romances, is one of those important medieval writers of whom little is known. Not even his poems can be dated more certainly than the second half of the twelfth century, though they can be listed in chronological order: *Erec et Enid, Cligés, Lancelot, Yvain,* and *Perceval.* The latter, the first use of the Holy Grail motif in Arthurian legend, was left incomplete at Chrétien's death. Other works, including a *Tristan,* have been lost or are of doubtful authorship. *Guillaume d'Angleterre,* a romanticized saint's legend, is also attributed to him.

Chrétien enjoyed the patronage of Marie de Champagne, daughter of Eleanor of Aquitaine, and of Philip of Flanders, and his enormously popular works were translated into Old Norse, German, and English. Even though there is some controversy among scholars concerning his originality of style and subject matter, he cannot be denied an attractive power of characterization. In general, but especially in *Lancelot,* he wrote in the tradition of the code of courtly love and followed the rules of Andreas Cappellanus, except that he seemed to believe love in marriage was possible. *Perceval* (the ultimate source of Wagner's Parsifal) is especially valuable for showing us the medieval ideal of a perfect knight embodying all the Christian virtues. Chrétien died about 1190, probably in Paris.

BIBLIOGRAPHICAL REFERENCES: For translations of the romances into English see W. W. Comfort, *Arthurian Romances,* 1913. See also J. D. Bruce, *The Evolution of Arthurian Romance,* 1928 (2nd ed.); J. R. Reinhard, *Chrétien de Troyes: A Bibliographical Essay,* 1932; and R. S. Loomis, *The Arthurian Tradition and Chrétien de Troyes,* 1949.

WINSTON CHURCHILL

Born: St. Louis, Missouri   *Died:* Winter Park, Florida
Date: November 10, 1871   *Date:* March 12, 1947

NOVELS: *The Celebrity*, 1898; *Richard Carvel*, 1899; *The Crisis*, 1901; *The Crossing*, 1904; *Coniston*, 1906; *Mr. Crewe's Career*, 1908; *A Modern Chronicle*, 1910; *The Inside of the Cup*, 1913; *A Far Country*, 1915; *The Dwelling-Place of Light*, 1917.

SHORT STORIES: *Mr. Keegan's Elopement*, 1903; *The Faith of Frances Craniford*, 1917.

PLAYS: *The Title Mart*, 1905; *Dr. Jonathan*, 1919.

Winston Churchill was regarded, in many of his novels, as an earnest critic of American society in the first two decades of the twentieth century; on these grounds alone he remains permanently interesting, though newer and more penetrating social insights have superseded his.

Churchill was born in St. Louis, Missouri, on November 10, 1871. His education was completed at the U.S. Naval Academy, although he never served in the Navy. Private means, instead, made it possible for him to devote his life to writing. Inspired by the American past, he began as a writer of historical novels; *The Crisis* and *Richard Carvel* were immediate successes. Churchill was read by virtually everyone until the 1920's, when new literary fashions made him seem cumbrous and old-fashioned.

In 1895, Churchill moved to New Hampshire and married. Active in the political life of his state, he was a member of the legislature from 1903 to 1905, and he ran unsuccessfully on the Progressive ticket as a candidate for governor. Perhaps his political activity is indicative of the subject matter he chose to present in his later novels. Even in 1924, his rank was fourth in a list of the ten "greatest" writers since 1900. He had, in his later novels, a tone of moral earnestness which gave real substance to the questions he chose to present. Yet when he tried to resolve the dilemmas he set himself, he fell back upon the genteel and the romantic. His attitude toward the American democratic tradition was dualistic; the wealthy in his novels were usually superior in taste and even in morals. Actually, Churchill was too much a man of his own era to separate his novels from rather full approval of it. His novels became a reflection of the intoxicating growth and wealth which indicated a solution for the old dilemmas. Man had the "new science"; man could control his environment and foresee new ethics. Thus, though in his own time Churchill was regarded as a reformer, his books now gather dust on the shelf. His is a voice from long ago. He concerned himself, with the exception of his early and interesting historical novels, with current problems of divorce, religion, and class relationships; but to these problems he, as a product and endorser of the status quo, had no very compelling answer. In the opinion of Carl Van Doren, Churchill was a romancer first and a critic afterwards, a kind of politician among novelists, morally eager but intellectually naïve. Yet he was both honest and factual in his research and served the truth as he saw it. He died at Winter Park, Florida, on March 12, 1947.

BIBLIOGRAPHICAL REFERENCES: There is no authorized biography. See C. C. Walcutt, *Romantic Compromise in the Novels of Winston Churchill*, 1951; Morris E.
Speare, *The Political Novel*, 1924; Arthur H. Quinn, *American Fiction*, 1936; and
Cyril Clemens, "Visit with the American Winston Churchill," *Hobbies*, LII (1947),
144–145. See also Upton Sinclair, "American Churchill," *Saturday Review of Literature*, XXXIV (June 9, 1951), 24, and the reply by H. O. Lokensgard, *ibid.*, XXXIV
(August 25, 1951), 21.

SIR WINSTON CHURCHILL

Born: Blenheim Palace, England
Date: November 30, 1874

PRINCIPAL WORKS

HISTORY: *Life of Lord Randolph Churchill*, 1906; *The World Crisis*, 1923–1929;
Marlborough: His Life and Times, 1933–1938; *The Second World War*, 1948–1954
(*The Gathering Storm*, 1948; *Their Finest Hour*, 1949; *The Grand Alliance*, 1950;
The Hinge of Fate, 1951; *Closing the Ring*, 1952; *Triumph and Tragedy*, 1954);
A History of the English-Speaking Peoples, 1956–1958 (*The Birth of Britain*, 1956;
The New World, 1956; *The Age of Revolution*, 1957; *The Great Democracies*,
1958).

SPEECHES: *Arms and the Covenant*, 1938; *Step by Step*, 1939; *Into Battle*, 1941;
The Unrelenting Struggle, 1942; *The End of the Beginning*, 1943; *Onwards to
Victory*, 1944; *The Dawn of Liberation*, 1945; *Victory*, 1946; *Secret Session
Speeches*, 1946; *The Sinews of Peace*, 1948.

NOVEL: *Savrola*, 1900.

MISCELLANEOUS: *My African Journey*, 1908; *Liberalism and the Social Problem*,
1909; *My Early Life*, 1930; *Painting as a Pastime*, 1949.

Sir Winston (Leonard Spencer)
Churchill, former Prime Minister of
Great Britain, statesman, historian,
biographer, soldier, and painter, holds
a secure place in the history of nations
and the history of literature. As a personality he is the nineteenth century
hero in a twentieth century world,
bringing to the crises of a totalitarian
and atomic age the urbanity, the moral
sense, and the stubborn courage of an
era in which his father was preëminent
in much the same manner, although
without such challenging opportunities.

He was born at Blenheim Palace,
Oxfordshire, on November 30, 1874.
His father, Lord Randolph Churchill,
was at one time Chancellor of the Ex-

chequer and Leader of the House, and
would have risen to the premiership
had he not resigned over some minor
issue. His mother was the American-
born Jennie Jerome, daughter of a
wealthy American financier. Because
of his parents' involvement in the social
and political life of the times, the boy
would have had a lonely childhood except for the loving attention of his
nurse, Mrs. Everest. He had an unhappy time at various preparatory
schools, did better at Harrow, and at
last began to demonstrate his future
qualities of leadership while a cadet at
the Royal Military College at Sand-
hurst.

His military career began with serv-

215

ice as a sub-lieutenant in the Fourth Hussars, a cavalry regiment. It continued, after a journalistic tour to report on the revolution in Cuba, with the Bengal Lancers in India; he based his first book, *The Malakand Field Force* (1898) on his experiences there. In the Sudan, while attached to the 21st Lancers (1898), he engaged in hand to hand fighting with the dervishes at the battle of Omdurman. A year later he returned to Africa as a correspondent for the *Morning Post*. Captured by the Boers during the South African War, he was sent to prison in Pretoria. His escape became an international sensation which catapulted him into public life.

In 1900 he published his novel, *Savrola*, and in the same year was elected a Conservative member to Parliament. He took an active part in debates and made news again when he "crossed the aisle" to the Liberal party in 1904. His marriage in September, 1908, to Clementine Hozier, daughter of Lloyd's secretary-general, Colonel H. M. Hozier, was a great social event of the London season. In the meantime he had published *Lord Randolph Churchill*, a biography of his statesman-father.

Churchill was First Lord of the Admiralty when World War I began, but he lost his cabinet post after the Dardanelles disaster in which the battleship *Irresistable* was sunk. After six months with the army in France he returned to become Minister of Munitions (1917), Secretary of State for War and Air (1918–1921, and Colonial Secretary (1921). He returned to the Conservatives in 1924 and as Chancellor of the Exchequer achieved fame when he took over the nation's press during the great general strike of May, 1926. The four volumes of his monumental history of the war, *The World Crisis,* appeared between 1923 and 1929. In 1936 he advised King Edward VIII during the abdication crisis and composed the moving speech which Edward delivered in relinquishing the throne.

When World War II began, Churchill was appointed First Lord of the Admiralty and soon afterward became Prime Minister, succeeding Neville Chamberlain, whom he had severely criticized in the months before the war. His stirring speeches (". . . blood, toil, tears, and sweat" and ". . . We shall fight on the beaches . . .") made him a natural symbol of the democratic determination to be victorious and free. During the war he played a determining role in a series of international conferences with President Roosevelt and Stalin, the three national leaders becoming the "big three" of world politics. After the war the Conservatives were defeated by the Labour party in a general election in July, 1945, and Churchill was succeeded by Clement Atlee as Prime Minister. One of his most famous speeches was made at Fulton, Missouri, in March, 1946, when he warned of the "iron curtain" which had come between the U.S.S.R. and countries dominated by it, and the rest of the world. Out of office, Churchill turned to the writing of his six-volume history, *The Second World War.* As the result of the 1951 election he was returned as Prime Minister. He served until his retirement in 1955, when he turned over the ministry to Anthony Eden. Since then he has been engaged in completing *A History of the English-Speaking Peoples,* a project abandoned when he was called to the Admiralty in 1939.

Winston Churchill has been both a maker and recorder of history. If the writer has been for the most part subordinated to the statesman, the reason is that through successive decades of crisis he has stood at the center of the events about which he was later to write, as *The Second World War* makes eloquently clear. Because of the nature of his experience, his view of history is personal rather than academic. Master of a rhetorical style and a coiner of striking images and compelling epithets, he has an ability to dramatize personalities and events rare among professional historians. The distinction of his literary position is this: he is the only national leader who has ever written history on a scale commensurate with that presented in his histories of two world wars and *A History of the English-Speaking Peoples,* works vast in design and yet illuminated at many points by his own knowledge and experience. In recognition of his lasting contributions to historical knowledge he was awarded the Nobel Prize for literature in 1953.

BIBLIOGRAPHICAL REFERENCES: The Churchill bibliography is extensive and varied. For biographical and historical studies see Emrys Hughes, *Winston Churchill in War and Peace,* 1950; John Gilbert Lockhart, *Winston Churchill,* 1951; Lewis Broad, *Winston Churchill, 1874–1952,* 1952; Robert Lewis Taylor, *Winston Churchill, An Informal Study of Greatness,* 1952; Virginia Spencer Cowles, *Winston Churchill: The Era and the Man,* 1953; Francis Neilson, *The Churchill Legend,* 1954; John Marsh, *The Young Winston Churchill,* 1955; Leonard Wibberley, *The Life of Winston Churchill,* 1956; and Alida Sims Malkus, *The Story of Winston Churchill,* 1957.

An informing book dealing with the literary side of Churchill's career is Herbert Leslie Stewart, *Sir Winston Churchill as Writer and Speaker,* 1954. Another specialized study is Geoffrey Williams, *The Wit of Winston Churchill,* 1955. For family background see also Alfred Leslie Rowse, *The Early Churchills: An English Family,* 1956.

COLLEY CIBBER

Born: London, England
Date: November 6, 1671

Died: London
Date: December 12, 1757

PRINCIPAL WORKS

PLAYS: *Love's Last Shift, or the Fool in Fashion,* 1696; *Richard III,* 1700; *She Would and She Would Not,* 1703; *The Careless Husband,* 1704; *The Rival Queens,* 1710; *The Nonjuror,* 1711.

AUTOBIOGRAPHY: *An Apology for the Life of Colley Cibber, Comedian,* 1740.

Colley Cibber is in the unfortunate position of being remembered mainly as the chief target of ridicule in Pope's *Dunciad,* for to be immortalized as the King of Dullness is a poor sort of fame. Although it is certain that Cibber's name would not have been immortal but for Pope, it is also certain that he

217

was far from being dull. He was, in fact, a remarkable actor, a playhouse manager, and a competent, though unoriginal, playwright. He had the misfortune to make the best writers of England his enemies: Cibber suffered not only from the verbal assaults of Pope, but from the wit of Fielding and Johnson. His Whig politics helped him in his career, but also made him a ready butt for the Tory satirists.

Colley Cibber was the eldest son of Caius Gabriel Cibber, a popular and wealthy Danish sculptor. Born in London on November 6, 1671, he left school at sixteen and in 1688 enlisted with his father in the Devonshire volunteers to support the cause of William of Orange. In 1690 he joined Thomas Betterton as an actor at the Drury Lane Theatre. While an actor he wrote the successful *Love's Last Shift*, a play about a rakish husband who reforms when he finds out how much his wife loves him. This play broke the Restoration tradition of libertine comedy and initiated the new taste for sentimental comedy that was to dominate the English stage for almost a century. John Vanbrugh, however, satirized Cibber's sentimental ending by writing *The Relapse* (1696), a play that recounts the further affairs

of the "reformed" husband. Cibber established his reputation as an actor by playing the role of the fop in *both* plays.

The rest of his playwriting was mainly imitative. He adapted Beaumont and Fletcher, Dryden, Molière, Shakespeare, and Corneille to suit the taste of his audience. *The Nonjuror,* for example, was a Whig version of Molière's *Tartuffe,* with the hypocrite now a Roman Catholic priest who incites rebellion; for this political stroke George I awarded him two hundred guineas. Cibber's paraphrase of Shakespeare in *Richard III* was extremely popular and kept the stage until 1821. He became one of the managers of the Drury Lane Theatre in 1711 and for political reasons he was made poet laureate in 1730. Even Cibber knew that he was unsuited to be a poet by nature, and his official odes were commonly ridiculed. His famous *Apology* is a valuable and absorbing account of contemporary English stage history. In 1742 he attained permanent fame when Pope published *The New Dunciad* and in the fourth book made Cibber the "hero." Nevertheless, Colley Cibber outlived many of his enemies and detractors and died a wealthy man in London on December 12, 1757.

BIBLIOGRAPHICAL REFERENCES: There is no modern edition of Cibber's writings, but the *Plays of Cibber* were collected in 5 vols., 1777, with an introductory *Life* by D. E. Parker. Cibber wrote his autobiography in the *Apology,* which is not entirely reliable. Modern biographies are F. D. P. Senior, *The Life and Times of Colley Cibber,* 1928, and the more important *Mr. Cibber of Drury Lane,* 1939, by Richard H. Barker, also containing critical accounts of Cibber's writings and a bibliography. F. S. Tupper, "Colley and Caius Cibber," *Modern Language Notes,* LV (1940), 393–96, adds a supplement to Barker's study. Critical works include William Hazlitt's essay on Cibber in *Lectures on the English Comic Writers,* 1819; Ernest Bernbaum's essay in *The Dramas of Sensibility,* 1914; E. K. Broadus, *The Laureateship,* 1921; and F. W. Bateson, *English Comic Drama, 1700–1750,* 1929. An important article is De Witt Clinton Croissant, "Studies in the Work of Colley Cibber," *Bulletin of the University of Kansas,* I (1912), 1–69, including a bibliography.

MARCUS TULLIUS CICERO

Born: Arpinum (Arpino), Italy
Date: January 3, 106 B.C.

Died: Formiae (Formia), Italy
Date: December 7, 43 B.C.

PRINCIPAL WORKS

ORATIONS: *In Verrem,* 70 B.C. (*Against Verres*); *In Catilinam,* 63 B.C. (*Against Catiline*); *Pro Archia,* 62 B.C. (*For Archias*); *In Pisonem,* 55 B.C. (*Against Piso*); *Pro Milone,* 52 B.C. (*For Milo*); *Pro Marcello,* 46 B.C. (*For Marcellus*); *Philippicae,* 44–43 B.C. (*Philippics*).

TREATISES: *De republica,* 51 B.C. (*On the Republic*); *De legibus,* c. 51–46 (*On Law*); *De finibus bonorum et malorum,* c. 45 (*On the Ends of Good and Evil*); *De natura deorum,* c. 45 (*On the Nature of the Gods*); *De senectute,* c. 44 (*On Old Age*); *De amicitia,* c. 44 (*On Friendship*); *De officiis,* c. 43 (*On Duty*).

What was said of Dryden might also be said of Cicero, that he converted into marble the brick of his native tongue. But Cicero's main interest in language was in how to use it most effectively to persuade people; in the process he shaped it so well that Latin, which had been one of many local ancient dialects, became a universal language. In a letter to Atticus, Cicero said: "Make yourself perfectly easy about the language I employ, I have plenty at my command; but my matter is not original"; but in reality he constantly increased his erudition so that he might meet his own standard of an orator: a good man skilled in speaking. Cicero served a position the newspaper, the church, and the university serve today, and his writings abundantly reveal his genius in all three functions.

Marcus Tullius Cicero, born in Arpinum on January 3, 106 B.C. (four years before Caesar), was not of patrician origin, although his mother's family contained some politicians of high rank. Reared in a country town, he was imbued with the order and stability of the knightly or mercantile class to which his father belonged. Years later, when Cicero became consul, he relied mainly on the support of this class in his attempt to maintain the stability of the Roman republic with conservative policies.

Cicero began his career as a lawyer, for which he prepared long and exactingly. It was ten years between the time he assumed the toga of manhood in 91 B.C. and the day he took a brief and appeared before the public. During the intervening years he studied philosophy and rhetoric under such great teachers as Philo and Molon. His tutor was Diodotus the Stoic. His military experience under Pompey's father was brief; he was underweight and pale, and carrying arms was not his forte. Cicero was always against the use of force to resolve conflict.

Cicero first established his reputation as a defense lawyer (in all of his career he acted as prosecutor not more than a half dozen times). Plutarch refers to his love for praise and glory. Certainly he was ambitious; he once said the side of the defense was more honorable. But he never allowed his ambition to force him to transgress his moral code, part of which was never to use his gifts to further injustice. It was as a successful defender of victims of political injustice that he rose in public esteem. It was his passion for manip-

219

ulating others that made him success-ful later in the Senate. During his consulship he suppressed the Catiline conspiracy (63 B.C.). Banished for the execution of some members of the Catiline group, he was exiled until recalled by Pompey in 57 B.C. He served as proconsul in Cilicia (51–50 B.C.) but returned to join Pompey at the outbreak of the civil war. Although pardoned and allowed by Caesar to re-turn to Rome in 47, he lived in political retirement until his delivery of the Philippics against Antony (44–43 B.C.). Proscribed by the triumvirate, he was put to death at Formiae on December 7, 43 B.C.

Cicero's writings fall into three cate-gories: his philosophic works, his let-ters, and his speeches. His theory of oratory is best revealed in *De Oratore* (55 B.C.). Success in oratory is based on the general culture and philosophic depth of the orator, but the orator must suit the style to the occasion. The orations against Catiline and the *Phi-lippics* best reveal his force. His de-fense of the poet Archias is outstand-ing as an example of his fusing culture with rhetoric. The important period of Cicero's literary production in philos-ophy was 46–44 B.C. He created a philosophical vocabulary for Latin and opened up the wealth of Greek thought to his countrymen. *De Officiis*, a manual of ethics, is the most popular of the works of this period, and reveals his basic identity with Christianity. The letters, first published about A.D. 60, were edited by his secretary Tiro. They reveal a brilliant writing style, as well as the essential nature of Cic-ero, a man of great learning, tact, and charm.

BIBLIOGRAPHICAL REFERENCES: There are many editions of Cicero; see in particular those in the Loeb Classical Library and the translations of *Brutus, On the Nature of the Gods, On Divination,* and *On Duties* by H. M. Poteat, 1950. For biographical and critical studies see E. G. Sihler, *Cicero of Arpinum,* 1914; Torsten Petersson, *Cicero: A Biography,* 1920; and G. C. Richards, *Cicero,* 1935. A useful one-volume edition of selections is Moses Hadas, *Basic Writings of Cicero,* Modern Library, 1951.

WALTER VAN TILBURG CLARK

Born: East Orland, Maine
Date: August 3, 1909

PRINCIPAL WORKS

NOVELS: *The Ox-Bow Incident,* 1940; *The City of Trembling Leaves,* 1945; *The Track of the Cat,* 1949.
SHORT STORIES: *The Watchful Gods and Other Stories,* 1950.

Walter Van Tilburg Clark was born in East Orland, Maine, August 3, 1909, but spent his early childhood in West Nyack, New York. In 1917 the family moved to Reno, Nevada, where the elder Clark assumed the presi-dency of the University of Nevada. Educated in the Reno public schools, he took his B.A. degree at the Univer-sity of Nevada in 1931 and an M.A. the following year. He then returned to New England to attend the Uni-versity of Vermont for two years, tak-ing a second M.A. there in 1934. By this time he had married. For the next ten years he taught English and dramatics and coached athletics in the public schools in Cazenovia, New York.

During this period of school teaching he wrote and published his first two novels and several short stories. *The Ox-Bow Incident* reveals Clark at once as a western novelist. The novel, laid in the Nevada of 1885, deals with a lynching. But Clark's story of cowboys and cattle rustling is not the ordinary local color tale. It is, in the first place, a carefully and tightly constructed narrative. In the second place, it is a perceptive and imaginative examination of the nature and meaning of justice and man's moral responsibility in administering it; it is an investigation into the implications of mob violence. Clark skillfully explores varying reactions to the lynching, from the lawless expression of man's hunting instincts to the delicate subtleties in moral cowardice.

The City of the Trembling Leaves is by comparison a sprawling book. What it has in common with *The Ox-Bow Incident*, however, is its western setting—Reno—and its sensitivity to the landscape of the West, which Clark sees always with a clear and knowledgeable eye. It is a story of maturation, of how a young artist grows to adulthood, finally finding a satisfactory relationship with the girl he loves and composing the symphony he had to write. The book has a certain value as a portrait of the artist as a young man in an indifferent society. The novel is too long because Clark masses detail indiscriminately in the description of places and persons and gives serious attention to almost every adolescent itch felt by his protagonist.

With these two novels behind him, Clark decided in 1945 to give up teaching and devote all his time to writing. He moved with his wife and two children first to Taos, New Mexico, and later to Nevada and California, and Montana.

The Track of the Cat, published in 1949, is the story of how the three sons of a ranching family hunt down and kill a marauding panther, but only after it has caused the death of two of them. This novel represents Clark's most ambitious effort to explore the myth of the West and the place of the white man there. The panther is a symbol of many meanings: of the pristine West before the white man despoiled it, of the Indians' revenge because the white man took the land from them, simply of the power of myth. Through these levels of interpretation the book presents a searching and provocative view of man and nature in the American West.

The Watchful Gods and Other Stories is a selection of Clark's short stories, ten in number, including "The Wind and the Snow of Winter," which won the O. Henry prize in 1945.

BIBLIOGRAPHICAL REFERENCES: There is no full study of Clark. John R. Kuehl, "Walter Van Tilburg Clark: A Bibliography," *Bulletin of Bibliography,* XXII, 1 (1956), 18–20, includes a list of articles about Clark. See Otis W. Coan, *America in Fiction,* 1949. Two useful articles are Vernon Young, "Gods Without Heroes: The Tentative Myth of Walter Van Tilburg Clark," *Arizona Quarterly,* VII, 2 (1951), 110; and Frederic I. Carpenter, "The West of Walter Van Tilburg Clark," *College English,* XIII (1952), 243–248.

JEAN COCTEAU

Born: Maisons-Lafitte, France
Date: July 5, 1891

Died: Milly-la-Forêt, France
Date: October 11, 1963

PRINCIPAL WORKS

PLAYS AND BALLETS: *Parade,* 1917; *Le Bœuf sur le Toit,* 1920; *Orphée,* 1927; *La Voix humaine,* 1930 (*The Human Voice*); *La Machine infernale,* 1934; *Les Parents terribles,* 1938 (*Intimate Relations*); *L'Aigle à deux têtes,* 1946 (*The Eagle Has Two Heads*).

NOVELS: *Le Potomak,* 1919; *Le Grand Écart,* 1923; *Thomas l'imposteur,* 1923; *Les Enfants terribles,* 1929.

POEMS: *Le Cap de Bonne Esperance,* 1919; *Plain-Chant,* 1923; *Poésie, 1916–1923,* 1924; *L'Ange heurtebise,* 1927; *Opéra, 1925–1927,* 1927; *Enigme,* 1931; *Mythologie,* 1934; *Allégories,* 1941; *Poésies,* 1948; *Poèmes, 1916–1955,* 1956.

ESSAYS AND STUDIES: *Le Coq et l'Arlequin,* 1918 (*Cock and Harlequin*); *Lettre à Jacques Maritain,* 1926; *Le Rappel à l'ordre,* 1926 (*A Call to Order*); *Opium,* 1930; *Mon Premier Voyage,* 1936 (*Round the World Again in Eighty Days*); *Poésie Critique,* 1945.

Americans know Jean Cocteau best by gossip, by his drawings, and by such bizarre motion pictures as *Blood of a Poet* (1932) and *Beauty and the Beast* (1945). Readers of art criticism have been interested in his *Cock and Harlequin,* and many novel readers have been impressed by his study of adolescence in *Les Enfants terribles,* which appeared as a novel in 1929 and as a film in 1950.

Cocteau was born into a prosperous and distinguished family at Maisons-Lafitte, France, on July 5, 1891. His father was a lawyer with an active interest in the arts, and Jean, a poet at seventeen and a lover of the theater, knew intimately such persons as Proust, Gide, Nijinsky, Diaghilev, and Stravinsky. Three volumes of poetry were followed by an experimental but successful novel, *Le Potomak,* in 1919.

After the first World War, during which Cocteau served in an ambulance unit, he worked with Picasso and the composer Erik Satie, and later with Stravinsky, in the production of several ballets. An interest in Greek art which developed at that time has continued to show itself in his various works.

He was a very close friend to Raymond Radiguet, the young author of *Devil in the Flesh* (1923), and he was grief-stricken when Radiguet died of typhoid in 1923. He took to opium, and then to religion, and was involved in a lengthy and public correspondence with Jacques Maritain on the subject of Catholicism.

In 1934 he traveled around the world in eighty days in order to win a bet with a Paris newspaper. His report of his journey is given in *Round the World Again in Eighty Days.* Much of his writing has expressed his dissatisfaction with the modern world. His *Lettre aux Américains* (1949) expressed his dissatisfaction with machine-crowded America. In 1955, he was elected to the Académie Française to fill the chair of Jérôme Tharaud. Since 1950 he has lived in semi-retirement at the Villa Santo Sospir, Cap Ferrat, in order to escape "the conspiracy of noise."

222

BIBLIOGRAPHICAL REFERENCES: Cocteau's *Journals*, edited and translated by Wallace Fowlie, 1956, contain an important critical introduction. The standard biography in English is Margaret Crosland, *Jean Cocteau*, 1955. For studies in French see Roger Lannes, *Jean Cocteau*, 1945; Claude Mauriac, *Jean Cocteau ou la vérité du mensonge*, 1945; and Pierre Dubourg, *Dramaturgie de Jean Cocteau*, 1954. For briefer studies see also Edith Sitwell, *A Poet's Notebook*, 1943; and Wallace Fowlie, "Note on Jean Cocteau," *Poetry* LXXXIV (1954), 85–88.

SAMUEL TAYLOR COLERIDGE

Born: Ottery St. Mary, England   Died: Highgate, London, England
Date: October 21, 1772   Date: July 25, 1834

PRINCIPAL WORKS

POEMS: *Poems on Various Subjects*, 1796; *Poems: Second Edition*, 1797; *Lyrical Ballads*, 1798 (with Wordsworth); *Christabel*, 1816; *Sibylline Leaves*, 1817; *Poetical Works*, 1828 (3 vols.).

ESSAYS AND STUDIES: *Addresses to the People*, 1795; *The Friend*, 1809–1810; *The Statesman's Manual*, 1816; *Biographia Literaria*, 1817; *Aids to Reflection*, 1825; *On the Constitution of Church and State*, 1830; *Confessions of an Inquiring Spirit*, 1840.

PLAYS: *The Fall of Robespierre*, 1794 (with Southey); *Remorse*, 1813; *Zapolya*, 1817.

TRANSLATIONS: Schiller's *Wallenstein*, 1800 (*The Piccolomini* and *The Death of Wallenstein*).

Samuel Taylor Coleridge, English poet, critic, and amateur philosopher, was born in Ottery Saint Mary, in Devonshire, on October 21, 1772. In 1782, at the death of his father, a Church of England clergyman, he was sent to the Christ's Hospital school in London. After eight years there he went to Jesus College, Cambridge. Charles Lamb, who wrote an essay about Coleridge as a boy, said that he had a tendency to monopolize conversation, and was interested in metaphysical discussions. His school fellows considered him impractical and eccentric.

In the fall of 1793 Coleridge left Cambridge and enlisted in the Light Dragoons. Discharged the following spring, he traveled in England and Wales. On a visit to Oxford he met Robert Southey, another young radical of the day. Both were sympathetic to the principles of the French Revolution and together they devised the idea of starting a new social settlement free from the prejudices and influences of the English political system. This settlement, to be called a "Pantisocracy," was to be on the banks of the Susquehanna River in America; but lack of funds doomed the plan. Coleridge left Cambridge without a degree in 1794. His marriage in 1795 to Sarah Fricker came about because the pantisocratic plan called for married emigrants.

In 1796 he published *Poems on Various Subjects* and for a few weeks edited the periodical, *The Watchman*, in which he voiced the principles of the French Revolution and of Godwinism. In the next year he settled in Nether Stowey, Somerset, and formed

223

an intimate friendship with Words-worth. Together they conceived the idea of publishing the *Lyrical Ballads,* which, appearing in 1798, is considered a landmark in English literature and the beginning of nineteenth century Romanticism.

The original plan of *Lyrical Ballads* was to upset and defy the old literary standards of the didactic school of Pope. Wanting poetic diction synony-mous with ordinary speech, Words-worth and Coleridge dropped the couplet form and adapted the ballad form from folk songs of the country-side. A new type of character, the peas-ant, was introduced. *Lyrical Ballads* is simple in language and verse forms, and presents simple characters. Cole-ridge's contribution, *The Rime of the Ancient Mariner,* is its best ballad. He took preternatural events with the in-tention of making them seem natural, just as Wordsworth took natural events and put over them a screen of imagi-native wonder.

During a trip with the Wordsworths to Germany, Coleridge attended lec-tures at the universities and became a student of German literature and phi-losophy. This interest led to his intro-duction of German philosophy into England. After his return to England in 1799 he produced a translation of Schiller's *Wallenstein.*

Coleridge acquired the habit of tak-ing opium, which took firm hold on him in 1801. In 1802 he wrote "Dejection, an Ode," in which he seems to make up his mind he never can be a great poet, and at the time he lived in a state of great depression. His attempt to re-cover his health at Malta, where he was secretary to Governor Sir Alexan-der Ball, failed. At home he became es-tranged from his friends and separated from his wife and children. He lived with friends until his death.

In 1808 he delivered a series of lec-tures at the Royal Institution of Lon-don, a course on Shakespeare and Mil-ton, and one on the history of litera-ture. Most of these exist today in frag-mentary form only (Vols. I and II of the *Literary Remains,* 1836–1838).

The Friend, a periodical he began after five months of procrastination, is characteristic of the sick and destitute Coleridge. Advertised as a "weekly" essay on philosophical questions, poli-tics, and allied subjects, it rarely came out on time and folded with the twenty-seventh issue. Coleridge pub-lished a revised edition of *The Friend* in 1818.

He had his first definite quarrel with Wordsworth in 1810 and left the Lake Country for good. Some of the most acute criticism of Wordsworth comes from Coleridge. He attacks Words-worth's extreme primitivism in *Bio-graphia Literaria,* but praises his high degree of imagination. Considered one of the foremost literary critics of the time, in his later years Coleridge set himself up as a kind of London sage, and with partial control over opium he began republishing in 1816, when his two most famous unfinished poems, *Christabel* and "Kubla Khan," along with "Pains of Sleep," appeared. *Chris-tabel* is an example of pseudo-medieval-ism popular with Romantic poets. In descriptive detail and ballad meter Coleridge creates an atmosphere of superstition and pleasing horror. He tried to develop poetry in which the intellect is consciously left out, poetry of imagination and sensibility produc-ing sheer mood.

During his last years he published

224

Sibylline Leaves, Aids to Reflection, and On the Constitution of the Church and State. Today he is recognized as one of the most important Church of England thinkers before the Oxford Movement.

He died in poverty at Highgate, London, on July 25, 1834.

BIBLIOGRAPHICAL REFERENCES: The standard edition of the poems is the *Complete Poetical Works*, 2 vols., edited by E. H. Coleridge, 1912. The best edition of the *Biographia Literaria* is that edited by J. Shawcross, 1907. The standard biographies are J. D. Campbell, *Samuel Taylor Coleridge: A Narrative of Events in His Life*, 1894; E. K. Chambers, *Samuel Taylor Coleridge*, 1938; and Lawrence Hanson, *The Life of Samuel Taylor Coleridge: The Early Years*, 1939. All critical studies have been overshadowed by John Livingston Lowes, *The Road to Xanadu: A Study in the Ways of the Imagination*, 1927. See also J. H. Muirhead, *Coleridge as Philosopher*, 1930; I. A. Richards, *Coleridge on Imagination*, 1934; and Robert Penn Warren, "A Poem of Pure Imagination: An Experiment in Reading," in *The Rime of the Ancient Mariner*, 1946.

COLETTE

Born: St.-Sauveur-en-Puisaye, France
Date: January 28, 1873

Died: Paris, France
Date: August 3, 1954

PRINCIPAL WORKS

NOVELS: (as "Willy" with Henri Gauthier-Villars): *Claudine à l'école*, 1900 (*Claudine at School*); *Claudine à Paris*, 1901 (*Claudine in Paris*); *Claudine en ménage*, 1902 (*Claudine Domesticated*); *Claudine s'en va*, 1903 (*Claudine Takes Off*); (as "Colette Willy"): *La retraite sentimentale*, 1907 (*The Sentimental Retreat*); *Les Vrilles de la vigne*, 1907 (*The Tendrils of the Vine*); *L'Ingénue Libertine*, 1909 (*The Wicked Innocent*); *La Vagabonde*, 1910 (*The Vagabond*); *L'Entrave*, 1913 (*The Shackle*); (as "Colette"): *Chéri*, 1920; *La Maison de Claudine*, 1923 (*Claudine's House*); *La Fin de Chéri*, 1926 (*The End of Chéri*); *Sido*, 1929; *La Seconde*, 1929 (*The Other One*); *Duo*, 1934 (*Duet*); *Bella Vista*, 1937; *Chambre d'Hôtel*, 1940 (*Hotel Room*); *Julie de Carneilhan*, 1941; *Le Képi*, 1943 (*The Kepi*); *Gigi*, 1945.

Sidonie Gabrielle Claudine Colette was born on January 28, 1873, in the Burgundian village of St.-Sauveur-en-Puisaye, where her father, Jules-Joseph Colette, a retired army officer, was the local tax collector. Her interest in literature began early. Besides being a precocious student, she became—inspired by her mother's example—an insatiable reader who soon exhausted the available supply of children's stories and turned, by the age of ten, to such writers as Labiche, Daudet, and Mérimée.

When she was sixteen years old the family moved from St.-Sauveur to Châtillon-Coliquy where she met the rising and ambitious young novelist and music critic, Henri Gauthier-Villars, whom she subsequently married. It was a poor match for Colette, personally, but it was a fortunate one from the literary point of view. The couple settled in Paris, where Colette's high spirited interest in the artistic and theatrical life of the city was hardly consistent with Gauthier-Villars' somewhat pretentious social ambitions. But even though he was displeased by her headstrong actions, he was intrigued by the stories she told him of her escapades as a young girl in Burgundy. The result of these stories was their collaboration, under the pseudonym of "Willy"—a collaboration which produced the financially successful series of *Claudine* novels between 1900 and 1904.

With the end of the collaboration came the end of the marriage. Divorcing her writing partner in 1906, Colette exchanged domesticity for the life that had fascinated her ever since she had come to Paris—the life of the music hall, which she describes so vividly in her novel *The Vagabond*. She was, it turned out, every bit as talented as a dancer and mime as she was as a writer, and she supported herself adequately in the music halls of Paris until her marriage to the statesman-writer, Henri de Jouvenel, in 1910.

As the wife of Henri de Jouvenel she resumed her activities as a novelist, but was interrupted in these pursuits by the outbreak of the first World War. And here a third talent, a capacity for action, displayed itself. Turning her husband's country estate into a hospital, she worked tirelessly as an army nurse, and was made, at the end of the war, a Chevalier of the Legion of Honor.

This was but the first of many public honors that were to be bestowed upon her, for as she grew older she broadened her abilities as a writer. Not only did she continue as a novelist, but she also worked through the twenties and thirties as a practicing journalist as well, contributing everything from critical essays to fashion notes to such periodicals as *Figaro, Le Matin, Femina,* and *Vogue.*

More important than this versatility was the symmetrical development of her skill as a literary artist, her increasing success in (as she herself describes it) taking up her pen and attempting "the perilous and elusive task of seizing and pinning down, under its flexible double-pointed nib, the many-hued, fugitive, thrilling adjective . . . ," and in her ability to find, in her contrasts of intellect and sensuality, the truly human qualities of her characters.

It was this development as a novelist that brought her all later honors. Not only did she rise to be a Grand Officer of the Legion of Honor, but in 1945 she became the only woman ever elected to the Goncourt Academy. In spite of the fact that she was stricken with arthritis toward the end of her life, she still managed to attend the meetings of this august body, the highest tribunal of literary merit in all France.

She died August 3, 1954, and it was then the final honor was bestowed. Although denied Catholic burial for having married twice outside the church (her marriage to Henri de Jouvenel had ended in divorce in 1924 and she had married Maurice Goudeket in 1935), she was given a formal state funeral by the French government, lying in state as a military hero, her literary victories given full acclaim.

BIBLIOGRAPHICAL REFERENCES: Representative selected novels have been reprinted in *Short Novels of Colette,* with an introduction by Glenway Wescott, 1951. The collected edition in French is the *Œuvres complètes,* 15 vols., 1948–1950. A recent and very complete biography is Margaret Crosland, *Colette, A Provincial in Paris* (alternate title, *Madame Colette*), 1954. A reminiscence by her husband, Maurice Goudeket, is *Close to Colette*, 1957.

See also René Lalou, *Contemporary French Literature*, 1924; Milton Stansbury, *French Novelists of Today*, 1935; Richard Hayes, "The Wisdom of Colette," *Commonweal*, LVI, (1952), 536–538; and Sonya Rudikoff, "Colette at Eighty," *Partisan Review*, XX, (1953), 332–338.

WILKIE COLLINS

Born: London, England   *Died:* London
Date: January 8, 1824   *Date:* September 23, 1889

Principal Works

NOVELS: *Antonina*, 1850; *Basil*, 1852; *Hide and Seek*, 1854; *The Woman in White*, 1860; *No Name*, 1862; *Armadale*, 1866; *The Moonstone*, 1868; *Man and Wife*, 1870; *Poor Miss Finch*, 1872; *The New Magdalen*, 1873; *The Two Destinies*, 1875; *The Law and the Lady*, 1876; *The Fallen Leaves*, 1879; *Heart and Science*, 1883.

SHORT STORIES: *After Dark*, 1856; *"Miss or Mrs.?" and Other Stories*, 1873; *The Frozen Deep*, 1874; *Little Novels*, 1887; *The Lazy Tour of Two Idle Apprentices*, 1890 (with Charles Dickens).

PLAYS: *No Thoroughfare*, 1867 (with Charles Dickens); *The New Magdalen*, 1873; *Man and Wife*, 1873; *The Moonstone*, 1877.

ESSAYS AND SKETCHES: *My Miscellanies*, 1863.

TRAVEL SKETCHES AND IMPRESSIONS: *Rambles Beyond Railways*, 1851.

BIOGRAPHY: *Memoirs of the Life of William Collins, R.A.*, 1848.

In his own time (William) Wilkie Collins was regarded by many persons as the equal of Dickens and Thackeray and, in at least two novels, *The Woman in White* and *The Moonstone*, their superior in sheer popularity. In retrospect, his best work can be admired for the very elements that Collins himself esteemed: his emphasis on "the Actual" (his own term) and the element of suspense. Modern readers may qualify their admiration by finding "the Actual" strangely mixed with the melodramatic and the sentimental; and they may find that the suspenseful in Collins has suffered from the widespread imitation of his devices by generations of writers of mystery stories. But in justice to Collins it must be realized that precious gems that bear a curse, unjust confinement in lunatic asylums, and false marriages were more novel in his day than in ours. In his service to "the Actual" he gave expression to his own contempt for many of the Victorian taboos that Dickens and Thackeray submitted to. Collins was a pioneer in anticlericalism and other attacks on British complacency and insularity. He also took up, as in *Fallen Leaves*, such forbidden themes as prostitution and marital infidelity. At both these points he displays a boldness that is today thought to have its origin in Samuel Butler and George Bernard Shaw. It is not, however, strange that these historically important elements in Collins are overlooked; they cannot be detached from his coldly calculated sensationalism that kept his immediate public breathless.

227

The circumstances of his early life contributed to the coexistence in Collins of two opposing drives: a desire for material success and a desire to tell unpalatable truths about the society from which he wished to win this success. Collins' father was William Collins, R.A., who rose in the British art world by careful cultivation of important persons. (These included the well-known artist David Wilkie, the godfather of Wilkie Collins.) The elder Collins united with his search for success Tory political beliefs and a repressive kind of piety. Collins, born in London on January 8, 1824, was a small, weak child who soon learned to detect hypocrisy in his father and his other elders; he had, however, enough taste of comfort and foreign travel to determine to win his share of worldly goods.

Collins was, in his late teens, placed by his father in the office of a tea merchant in London, but he used his evenings and much of his employer's time in literary self-cultivation; he was particularly inspired by the financial success of Charles Dickens. His own first novel, *Antonina, or the Fall of Rome,* was inspired by the grandiose view of the past to be found in such works as Bulwer-Lytton's *The Last Days of Pompeii* (1834). His turn toward "the Actual," which he studied by riding in the London omnibuses, was encouraged by the beginning of his close association with Charles Dickens in 1851 in an amateur theatrical production. Dickens, as editor of *Household Words,* had need of talented assistance; he also found in a man much his junior a stimulating and admiring traveling companion. Throughout their lives the two men abetted each other's tastes in amuse-ment and also left their marks on each other's novels. The growth of closely knit plot-structure in Dickens, e.g., the clues and false clues of *Great Expectations* (1861) shows Collins' influence on Dickens. Collins' increase in humor and the power of lively portraiture was due to Dickens' criticism of Collins' self-conscious and pompous gloom in his early novels.

Collins, like most writers who have a reputation for being "inventive," was always an industrious seeker for material; French police files, newspaper items, and encyclopedia articles aided him. He also exploited to the full, and quite explicitly, incidents in his own life. In 1854 he met his life-long companion, Caroline Graves, whom he never married. The meeting was a romantic night encounter along a suburban road; with this incident *The Woman in White* begins. Caroline Graves had a child; the fate of such a child—its uncertain social position, the cruelty of the secure and righteous toward her—is the subject of *No Name.* Collins' own peculiar position and Caroline's suggested several themes of women suffering at the hands of society.

Collins' correspondence displays a keen concern over his literary profits; with a desire to extend these profits, he turned many of his novels into plays (usually with limited success), and he took a keen interest in the transatlantic publication of his novels and also in their translation into many languages. He displayed kindness toward Hall Caine and was, in his last years, on friendly terms with Oscar Wilde. He was concerned, after Dickens' death, with demonstrating the closeness of his relation to Dickens, especially after the appearance of

228

Forster's *Life of Dickens* (1872–1874). But his last years were a time of acute suffering from the pain of the gout, which Collins could relieve only by draughts of laudanum and unremitting novel-writing (he had not only Mrs. Graves to support but another "morganatic household"). He died in London, his health wrecked by drugs and overwork, on September 23, 1889.

Much contemporary criticism regarded Collins as a wonderful entertainer but an unhealthy one. Actually Collins, unlike Samuel Butler and Shaw, did not give consistent and sustained expression of his views. The chief public battle he fought came early in his career and was in support of the Pre-Raphaelite Brotherhood, of which his brother Charles was a member. Perhaps his greatest legacy to oncoming generations of novelists, in contrast to most writers of sensational fiction, was his emphasis on careful planning and revision. In this respect he goes beyond Dickens and Trollope and looks toward James and many modern novelists.

BIBLIOGRAPHICAL REFERENCES: There are two recent biographies of Collins: Kenneth Robinson, *Wilkie Collins: A Biography*, 1952, and Nuel Pharr Davis, *The Life of Wilkie Collins*, 1956. See also Samuel L. Ellis, *Wilkie Collins, Le Fanu, and Others*, 1931; Malcolm Elwin, *Victorian Wallflowers*, 1934; Michael Sadleir, *Nineteenth Century Fiction*, 1951; and Robert P. Ashley, *Wilkie Collins*, 1952. The most important foreign study is Ernst von Wolzogen, *Wilkie Collins, ein biographisch-kritischer*, 1885.

Reminiscences of Collins or related background material appear also in John Forster, *Life of Dickens*, 1872–1874; Harriet Martineau, *Autobiography*, 1877; William P. Frith, *John Leech: His Life and Work*, 1891; John G. Millais, *The Life and Letters of Sir Everett Millais*, 1899; R. C. Lehmann, *Memories of Half a Century*, 1908; Squire Bancroft, *Recollections of Sixty Years*, 1909; and Frank Archer, *An Actor's Notebooks*, 1912.

For criticism see Walter de la Mare, "The Early Novels of Wilkie Collins," in *The Eighteen-Sixties*, edited by John Drinkwater, 1932; T. S. Eliot, "Wilkie Collins and Charles Dickens," in *Selected Essays*, 1932; Clyde K. Hyder, "Wilkie Collins and *The Woman in White*," *Publications of the Modern Language Association*, LIV (1939), 297–303; and T. W. Hill, "The Enigma of Wilkie Collins," *Dickensian*, XLVIII (1952), 54–57.

WILLIAM CONGREVE

Born: Bardsey Grange, England
Date: February, 1670

Died: London, England
Date: January 19, 1729

PRINCIPAL WORKS

PLAYS: *The Old Bachelor*, 1693; *The Double Dealer*, 1693; *Love for Love*, 1695; *The Mourning Bride*, 1697; *The Way of the World*, 1700.

NOVELLA: *Incognita*, 1692.

William Congreve, English dramatist, was born at Bardsey Grange, Yorkshire, and was baptized on February 10, 1670. His family was an ancient one of high repute. His father being an officer in the army, Congreve was taken when he was about two years old to Youghal, Ireland, where his father took command of the garrison. About 1681, Congreve entered school in Kilkenny. There he met Jonathan Swift, who was three years his senior, and there he "received the first tinctures of letters." He was known to his masters as a boy of talent, most particularly for poetry.

In 1685 Congreve proceeded to Trinity College, Dublin, where Swift had gone three years before. It is probably here that they established the friendship which was to last until Congreve's death. The two youths sat together under the eminent St. George Ashe, and Congreve was apparently a better scholar than Swift; according to Southerne, he enjoyed that reputation. At the close of 1688 Congreve, possibly in the company of Swift, returned to England, Ireland being after the Revolution no place for a gentleman whose family had served the Stuarts to hope for comfort or advancement. For the next two years, Congreve probably remained in Staffordshire with relations. It is probable too that Congreve's first play, not acted until 1693, was composed in Staffordshire about 1690.

In March, 1691, Congreve was admitted to the Middle Temple to study law. As one contemporary reference states, "The severe study of the law had so little relation to the active disposition of the young gentleman, that though he continued for three or four years to live in chambers and pass for a Templar, yet it does not appear that he ever applied himself with diligence to conquer his dislike to a course of life, which had been chosen for him with so little respect either to the turn of his natural parts or the preceding course of his education." He began almost immediately to turn toward litera-ture, becoming by August, 1692, an accepted poet and the friend of Dryden, and consequently the associate of the literati of Dryden's acquaintance. In 1693, he made his debut as a playwright with *The Old Bachelor*. It is as a playwright that we must consider him.

Congreve belonged to a literary tradition of which he was perhaps the climax. It had been almost a blessing to literature that the theaters were closed by Puritan edict in 1642. The stream of English drama which bore on its crest the masterpieces of Shakespeare and Jonson had after them dispersed into muddy shallows. With the reopening of the theaters in 1660, Davenant and Dryden set about to start the stream of tradition anew. Both the critics and playwrights of the day agreed that the purpose of literature was moral instruction, but this credo was mere lip-service. Especially in court circles, a revulsion against all Puritan virtue—natural enough under the circumstances, and enhanced by the influence of French elegance on the returned noble exiles—made the people gluttonous of entertainment. The manners of the court were highly corrupt, and the comedy played for the court was unblushing, hard, cynical, and immoral. Sir George Etherege was the "inventor" of this comedy, but Congreve gave it its apotheosis.

In Restoration comedy true "wit" was the desideratum, and true wit was the other side of true elegance. The truly fine gentleman was a rake, but an elegant, easy, and aloof one. The truly fine lady was often the mistress of a rake, but was an elegant, aloof, and secret one. Pretense and hypocrisy of any kind were by these standards comic. Stock characters, modeled in

230

part on the humours of Jonson, consequently emerged. The True-Wit, male and female, the Wit-would, the Fop, the Superannuated Buck, and his counterpart, the Antiquated Coquette —these were the chief types of dramatic convention. Another convention was the ridicule of the Puritans. Meanwhile, and not unnaturally, the Puritans were clamoring for reform; and they, being on the side of respectability, ultimately won. Congreve was among the unregenerate, and so at last was driven from the boards.

His first play, *The Old Bachelor,* was enormously successful. It is a play involving a series of intrigues. Sir Joseph Wittol, a fool, is gulled into marrying a common woman after Heartwell, the bachelor misogynist, barely escapes her charms. Bellmour, in love with Belinda, takes time out to disguise himself as the fanatic preacher, Tribulation Spintext, in order to cuckold the Puritan banker, Fondlewife. With this play Congreve's reputation seemed assured.

Later in the same year his second play, *The Double Dealer,* failed. This failure is hard to account for, since the plot of this play is more unified than that of its predecessor, being merely the struggle of Mellefont against the jealous Lady Touchwood and against the Iago-like Maskwell to win his charming Cynthia. Maskwell's villainy, however, makes the play almost tragi-comic, and this fact may explain its failure.

Love for Love appeared in 1695, and was long the most popular of Congreve's plays. Valentine, at odds with his father, is threatened with the loss of his estate and with the consequent loss of his beloved heiress, Angelica. The intrigue is deft and filled with suspense, ending at last with a masked marriage which matches the fop Tattle

with the blemished Mrs. Frail instead of with Angelica, as he had supposed.

Congreve's best play, *The Way of the World,* was produced in 1700. This play has an excellent plot, though perhaps Congreve wastes too much time in topical conversation. The play shows the gentleman Mirabell evading the malicious Lady Wishfort, Mrs. Marwood, and her lover Fainall, and persuading the aloof but charming Millamant to marry him. All this is of course conventional: this is not a comedy of love, but of a love-chase. It is highly artificial comedy—all Restoration comedy is—but it is the best of its kind. Mirabell never loses his convincing ease and wit as he faces all the obstacles to his success. Most notable in the comedy are the brilliant dialogues of Mirabell and Millamant. The two characters are perfectly matched; in their conversations the conventions of theatrical love in Restoration comedy are at their height. There is no real emotional involvement felt by the audience, since there is obviously none felt by the characters. It is the most primitive kind of storytelling overlaid with the most sophisticated and shallow kind of intellectual gymnastics; but if one accepts the conventions, it is superb.

Two years before, the Puritans had found their most notable spokesman in the Reverend Jeremy Collier, who could not endure the likes of Tribulation Spintext or bear to see licentiousness presented so entertainingly. His *Short View of the Immorality and Profaneness of the English Stage* (1698) became the voice from the housetops, and it was heard. Congreve replied to Collier's attacks, but after *The Way of the World* was ill-received, he virtually

231

retired from the stage. He held various government sinecures and politely lived out his life with many friends and almost no enemies. He spent much time during his later years with the Duchess of Marlborough to whom he left the most of his estate when he died in London on January 19, 1729.

BIBLIOGRAPHICAL REFERENCES: The standard edition is *The Complete Works of William Congreve*, edited by Montague Summers, 4 vols., 1923. For biography see Edmund Gosse, *The Life of William Congreve*, 1924 (rev. ed.); D. C. Taylor, *William Congreve*, 1931; and J. C. Hodges, *William Congreve, The Man*, 1941. See also, H. T. E. Perry, *The Comic Spirit in Restoration Drama*, 1925; Allardyce Nicoll, *A History of English Drama, 1660–1900*, Vol. I, 1952 (rev. ed.); *The Age of Dryden*, Vol. VIII, in the *Cambridge History of English Literature*; and *Dictionary of National Biography*, Vol. VI.

JOSEPH CONRAD
(Jozef Teodor Konrad Nalecz Korzeniowski)

Born: Berdyczew, Poland
Date: December 3 or 6, 1857

Died: Bishopsbourne, England
Date: August 3, 1924

PRINCIPAL WORKS

NOVELS: *Almayer's Folly*, 1895; *An Outcast of the Islands*, 1896; *The Nigger of the "Narcissus,"* 1897; *Lord Jim*, 1900; *The Inheritors*, 1901 (with Ford Madox Hueffer [Ford]); *Romance*, 1903 (with F. M. Hueffer [Ford]); *Nostromo*, 1904; *The Secret Agent*, 1907; *Under Western Eyes*, 1911; *Chance*, 1914; *Victory*, 1915; *The Shadow-Line*, 1917; *The Arrow of Gold*, 1919; *The Rescue*, 1920; *The Rover*, 1923; *The Nature of a Crime*, 1924 (with F. M. Hueffer [Ford]); *Suspense*, 1925 (unfinished).

SHORT STORIES AND TALES: *Tales of Unrest*, 1898 ("Karain: A Memory," "The Idiots," "An Outpost of Progress," "The Return," "The Lagoon"); *Typhoon*, 1902; *Youth: A Narrative, and Two Other Stories*, 1902 ("Heart of Darkness" and "The End of the Tether"); *Typhoon and Other Stories*, 1903 ("Amy Foster," "Falk," "Tomorrow"); *A Set of Six*, 1908 ("The Informer," "Gaspar Ruiz," "The Brute," "An Anarchist," "The Duel," "Il Conde"); *'Twixt Land and Sea*, 1912 ("A Smile of Fortune," "The Secret Sharer," "Freya of the Seven Isles"); *Within the Tides*, 1915 ("The Planter of Malata," "The Partner," "The Inn of the Two Witches," "Because of the Dollars"); *Tales of Hearsay*, 1925 ("The Warrior's Soul," "Prince Roman," "The Tale," "The Black Mate"); *The Sisters*, 1928; *The Complete Short Stories of Joseph Conrad*, 1933.

PLAYS: *One Day More*, 1917; *The Secret Agent*, 1921; *Laughing Anne*, 1923.

AUTOBIOGRAPHY: *The Mirror of the Sea*, 1906; *Some Reminiscences*, 1912 [*A Personal Record*].

ESSAYS AND STUDIES: *Notes on Life and Letters*, 1921; *Notes on My Books*, 1921; *Last Essays*, 1926.

LETTERS: *Joseph Conrad: Life and Letters*, edited by Gérard Jean-Aubry, 1927; *Joseph Conrad's Letters to His Wife*, 1927; *Conrad to a Friend*, edited by Richard Curle, 1928; *Letters from Joseph Conrad, 1895–1924*, edited by Edward Garnett, 1928; *Lettres françaises de Joseph Conrad*, edited by Gérard Jean-Aubry, 1929;

Letters of Joseph Conrad to Marguerite Poradowska, edited by John A. Gee and Paul J. Sturm, 1940.

Joseph Conrad, one of the finest novelists and stylists of modern English literature, was born as Jozef Teodor Konrad Nalecz Korzeniowski at Berdyczew, in the Ukraine region of Poland, then under Russian rule, on December 3 or 6, 1857. The tradition of both families of Conrad's parentage —of his father, Apollo Nalecz Korzeniowski, a Polish writer, translator, patriot, and nationalist, and of his mother, Ewelina Bobrowska—both of them deriving from the "land-tilling gentry" of the old Poland with connections in the Almanach de Gotha, had for many years been ardently nationalistic, dedicated to the liberation of their country from the occupation of the three powers, Russia, Prussia, and Austria, who had overrun and divided her by the "crime of partition" in the late eighteenth century. In this cause three of Conrad's uncles had died or been exiled to Siberia, and his own father was in 1862 arrested for his activities in the secret Polish National Committee and sentenced to deportation in Russia. Apollo Korzeniowski took his wife and six-year-old son with him into that exile; and when both his parents died as a result of their hardship, Conrad was left an orphan in 1869. Under the guardianship of his uncle Tadeusz Bobrowski, he lived in Kiev and Cracow, attended the St. Anne High School in Cracow, then studied under a tutor, Mr. Pulman, of the University of Cracow, was given the freedom of that city in honor of his father, went on a vacation trip in 1873 with his tutor to Germany, Switzerland, and Italy, saw the sea for the first time from the Lido at Venice, and at the age of seventeen determined to leave his tragic homeland and seek his fortunes in western Europe.

From 1874 to 1878 he lived in southern France, at Marseilles, where he had gone by way of the Vienna Express "as a man might get into a dream." At Marseilles the adventurous and romantic inclinations of his nature found their first outlet. He frequented the *légitimiste* circles of the banker Delestang and his wife, to whom he had carried letters of introduction; and it was as an employee of the banking and shipping firm of Delestang that he entered the French marine service and had his apprenticeship at sea, first on the *Mont-Blanc* to the West Indies late in 1874, again on the *Mont-Blanc* to Martinique in 1875, then on the schooner *St.-Antoine* to the West Indies in 1876–1877. With several young Marseilles friends he also bought a small *tartane,* the *Tremolino,* in which he seems to have engaged in smuggling activities of some kind, possibly on behalf of the Carlists who were attempting to restore Don Carlos to the throne of Spain. He may also have become involved in a romantic relation with a lady of the Carlist circles in Marseilles, as the novel *The Arrow of Gold* suggests, but this matter remains unverified. What appears certain, from a recently discovered letter written by his uncle Tadeusz Bobrowski on March 24, 1879, is that the young Conrad became involved in serious debts in Marseilles and Monte Carlo, that his affairs in France ended in fiasco and serious personal difficulties, and that in these straits he made an attempt on his life. Bobrowski, and later Conrad himself, attempted to disguise this situation with the long-familiar story of a duel with the expatriate American, J. M. K. Blunt, a rival for the favors of "Rita de Lastaola." When he found himself wounded, deserted by his embarrassed Marseilles friends, and faced with the reproof of his guardian uncle who had hastened from Poland to Marseilles to see his disgraced nephew, Conrad determined to redeem himself by taking to the sea in earnest. He found a berth as a common seaman on a British freighter, the *Mavis,* carrying cargoes to the Eastern Mediterranean; and on June 18, 1878, he stepped for the first time on English soil at Lowestoft, "alone in the world," knowing little English, but now at last committed to a seaman's career.

From 1878 to 1894 Conrad spent sixteen years in the British Merchant Service or under various Eastern flags. His voyages took him to the Mediterranean, to Australia, to the Indian Ocean, to India, to Malaya, Sumatra, Java, Borneo, the Philippines, the coasts of China and Indo-China, and around the world. He gained third mate status in 1880, first mate papers in 1883, and his master's papers in 1886, and he achieved his "first command" on the ship *Otago* in 1888–1889. In 1890 he made a harrowing and fateful journey up the Congo in the employ of the Société Anonyme Belge pour le Commerce du Haut-Congo, experiencing there illnesses and mental distress from which he suffered the rest of his life. His last berth was on the *Adowa* early in 1894, and when he returned to London on January 14, 1894, his career as a seaman was over, though he did not yet know it and tried for another six years to return to the stabler life of ships and sea-voyages.

It was at this point that he took up once more the manuscript of a tale he had been writing in the ships and ports of his journeys for five years, the story of a defeated Dutchman he had once known in a remote jungle country of Borneo. By agonized and persistent labor he finished the manuscript, sent it to a London publisher (T. Fisher Unwin), and in 1895 found, to his "perpetual surprise," his first book, *Almayer's Folly,* printed and bound in his hands and a career in literature opening to him. In 1896 he married an Englishwoman, Jessie George. In 1898 his first son, Borys, was born; a second, John Alexander, followed in 1906. He had been naturalized as a British subject in 1886; and now he found himself wholly identified with English life as citizen, author, family man, and professional writer.

Though the art and stylistic mastery of Conrad's books was early recognized by some of his most distinguished contemporaries, Henry James, George Gissing, H. G. Wells, Stephen Crane, and Cunninghame Graham among them, success in any practical or popular sense was many years in coming to him. But his working life now became wholly dedicated to authorship, and his last twenty-nine years saw his books appear in continuous succession. His first novels, *Almayer's Folly* and *An Outcast of the Islands,* were tales of Eastern kingdoms and of European exiles who had met their fate in them; but with *The Nigger of the "Narcissus"* in 1897 he turned to his own memories of the sea and wrote his first masterpiece of style and dramatic narration. "Youth," his first notable short story, told of his first discovery of the East; "Heart of Darkness," a sovereign masterwork of moral and symbolic drama, dealt with his Congo journey of 1890; *Typhoon* shcwed his descriptive powers at their highest; and with *Lord Jim,* in 1900, he achieved his first long novel of classic dimensions in the tale of a dishonored English seaman seeking the recovery of his honor and self-respect in the East.

After collaborating on two minor novels with Ford Madox Hueffer [Ford], Conrad now turned to his most prodigious feat of imaginative creation in the long novel *Nostromo,* a complex drama of civil strife and rival moralities in the South American republic of Costaguana; and the subject of political intrigue or tragedy was to be carried further in *The Secret Agent* and in *Under Western Eyes,* two novels of the "international evil" and Russian danger which he saw as a threat to the stability of Europe and her traditional institutions. *Chance* was his attempt at a modern drama of social persecution and alienation. *Victory* brought his central subject of disillusioned skepticism and the test it imposes on character to its most concise symbolic terms. *The Shadow-Line* treated the experience of his "first command" on the *Otago* in 1888–1889. The minor novel, *The Arrow of Gold,* revived the memory of his Marseilles years and Carlist adventures of 1874–1878. Two works of autobiography had punctuated these fictions: *The Mirror of the Sea* in 1906, and *Some Reminiscences* (later retitled *A Personal Record*) in 1912. Conrad had also written continuously in the shorter forms, and while many of these stories are distinctly minor, some of them achieve his keenest powers of atmospheric and symbolic narrative—"Amy Foster," "Falk," "The Brute," "Il Conde," "Freya of the Seven Isles," and notably the brilliant tale which is a key-story among his works, "The Secret Sharer." His last two completed novels, *The Rescue* and *The Rover,* though personally and thematically significant, show a marked decline in his qualities; and *Suspense* (posthumously published in 1925), which followed *The Rover* as a tale of Napoleonic France, was left half finished when Conrad died suddenly of a heart attack at Oswalds, his last English home, at Bishopsbourne, near Canterbury, on August 3, 1924. He was buried at Canterbury.

Conrad's widest fame perhaps attaches to his tales of the sea and of the East, and he is likewise celebrated as a writer of romantic and heroic subjects. To both these designations he came to object, and his finest work in fact corrects them. For Conrad is at basis a tragic novelist, as he is also essentially a moral and psychological realist whose profounder themes are concerned with problems of guilt and honor, with the tests of conscience and moral justice, and with the secret recriminatory and retributive processes of the human personality. Inclined to the moral and historical pessimism of a constitutional skepticism, he was at the same time impelled toward the principles of that "human solidarity" he insistently invoked as a standard of action and moral commitment; and his characteristic tales show a drama of character forced out of the illusions, isolation, self-deception, or nihilism of the private or uncommitted temperament into the larger moral coherence of society and of humanity. And while some of his richest writing comes in his descriptive and atmospheric art, his greater powers appear when he makes the form and structure of his tales, as well as their stylistic detail and analysis, convey the processes of character, of conscience, and of moral justice. It was for this purpose that he advanced out of impressionism into dramatic and moral realism, out of a richly sensuous art into an art of structural intricacy and analytical capacities. His finest novels and tales show him to be an artist scarcely surpassed in his English generation for the probity of his moral vision, the originality of his plotting and construction, and the searching accuracy of his style. When he wrote his artistic credo in the "Preface" to The Nigger of the "Narcissus" in 1897, he not only defined the moral idea to which he addressed himself— "the solidarity in mysterious origin, in toil, in joy, in hope in uncertain fate, which binds men to each other and all mankind to the visible world"—but also specified the "task" to which he dedicated his talent: "My task which I am trying to achieve is, by the power of the written word, to make you hear, to make you feel—it is, before all, to make you see. That—and no more, and it is everything." By his loyalty to those two principles Conrad made himself a master not only of moral vision but of an art which at its best defines one of the most austere aesthetic purposes in modern fiction, and sets a standard in the novel of the twentieth century.

Morton Dauwen Zabel

BIBLIOGRAPHICAL REFERENCES: Joseph Conrad's work has been collected in various editions and collections. Those published in New York include the Sun Dial Edition, 1920–1921; the Concord, 1923; the Canterbury, 1924; the Memorial, 1925, and the Malay, 1927. The Uniform Edition, 22 vols., London, 1923–1928, is complete except for The Nature of a Crime and the plays. The Collected Edition, 1946 ff., is a reprint. One-volume selections include A Conrad Argosy, edited by William McFee, 1942; The Conrad Reader, edited by A. J. Hoppé, 1946 (reprinted as The Conrad Companion, 1948); and The Portable Conrad, edited by Morton Dauwen Zabel, 1947, 1957.

The authorized biography is Gérard Jean-Aubry's Vie de Conrad, 1947, translated by Helen Sebba as The Sea Dreamer: A Definitive Biography of Joseph Conrad, 1957. Important source material is contained also in G. Jean-Aubry, Joseph Conrad: Life and Letters, 1927, and in other collections of letters previously cited. For biographical information see also (Mrs.) Jessie Conrad, Joseph Conrad as I Knew Him, 1926, and Joseph Conrad and His Circle, 1935; Richard Curle, The Last Twelve Years of Joseph Conrad, 1928; Gustav Morf, The Polish Heritage of Joseph Conrad, 1930; John Dozier Gordan, Joseph Conrad: The Making of a Novelist, 1940; J. H. Retinger, Conrad and His Contemporaries, 1941; and an important new critical biography, Joseph Conrad, by Jocelyn Baines, scheduled for publication in 1958. (See also Jocelyn Baines, "The Affair in Marseilles," London Magazine, IV (November, 1957), 41–46, and "The Young Conrad in Marseilles," London Times Literary Supplement, LVI (December 6, 1957), 748.)

Among the critical studies, Gordan's Joseph Conrad is also important for its account of Conrad's sources. The field of Conrad criticism is extensive. Among the earlier studies are the following: Richard Curle, Joseph Conrad: A Study, 1914; Wilson Follett, Joseph Conrad: A Short Study, 1915; Hugh Walpole, Joseph Conrad, 1916; Ruth M. Stauffer, Joseph Conrad: His Romantic Realism, 1922; Ernst Bendz, Joseph Conrad: An Appreciation, 1923; and Ford Madox Ford, Joseph Conrad: A Personal Remembrance, 1924. Later studies, written after Conrad's death, include Arthur Symons, Notes on Joseph Conrad, 1925; R. L. Mégroz, Joseph Conrad's Mind and

Method, 1931; William W. Bancroft, *Joseph Conrad: His Philosophy of Life*, 1933; Edward Crankshaw, *Joseph Conrad: Some Aspects of the Art of the Novel*, 1936; Josef Ujejski, *Joseph Conrad*, 1939; M. C. Bradbrook, *Joseph Conrad: Poland's English Genius*, 1941; Albert Guerard, Jr., *Joseph Conrad*, 1947; Walter F. Wright, *Romance and Tragedy in Joseph Conrad*, 1949; Oliver Warner, *Joseph Conrad*, 1951; Douglas Hewitt, *Conrad: A Reassessment*, 1952; Paul L. Wiley, *Conrad's Measure of Man*, 1954; E. H. Visiak, *The Mirror of Conrad*, 1955; Thomas Moser, *Joseph Conrad: Achievement and Decline*, 1957; and Richard Curle, *Joseph Conrad and His Characters*, 1957.

Some notably important short essays or studies include Henry James, "The New Novel," in *Notes on Novelists*, 1914; H. L. Mencken, "Joseph Conrad," in *A Book of Prefaces*, 1917; "Hommage à Joseph Conrad," with essays by André Gide, Paul Valéry, H. R. Lenormand, G. Jean-Aubry, André Maurois, André Chevrillon, Edmond Jaloux, Ramon Fernandez, and others, *Nouvelle Revue Française*, Nouvelle Série, CXXXV (December 1, 1924), 649–806; Joseph Warren Beach, "Conrad: Impressionism," in *The Twentieth Century Novel*, 1932; Thomas Mann, "Joseph Conrad's *The Secret Angent*," in *Past Masters and Other Papers*, 1933; E. M. Forster, "Joseph Conrad: A Note," in *Abinger Harvest*, 1936; V. S. Pritchett, "A Pole in the Far East," in *The Living Novel*, 1947; Morton Dauwen Zabel, Introduction to *The Portable Conrad*, 1947, 1957; *idem*, "Conrad: Chance and Recognition," "The East and the Sea," "The Threat to the West," "Conrad in His Age," in *Craft and Character*, 1957; F. R. Leavis, "Joseph Conrad," in *The Great Tradition*, 1949; and Dorothy van Ghent, "On *Lord Jim*," in *The English Novel: Form and Function*, 1953. Introductions written for the following novels are also of critical importance: Morton Dauwen Zabel, *The Nigger of the "Narcissus,"* Harper Modern Classics, 1950, *Under Western Eyes*, New Directions edition, 1951, and *Lord Jim*, Houghton Mifflin Riverside Editions, 1958; Robert Penn Warren, *Nostromo*, Modern Library edition, 1951; and Robert B. Heilman, *Lord Jim*, Rinehart Editions, 1957.

The Joseph Conrad Number of *Modern Fiction Studies*, I (February, 1955), contains a selected checklist of Conrad criticism with an index to studies of the separate works, 30–45. A more complete study of this kind is *Joseph Conrad at Mid-Century: Editions and Studies, 1895–1955*, by Kenneth A. Lohf and Eugene P. Sheehy, 1957.

HENDRIK CONSCIENCE

Born: Antwerp, Belgium   *Died:* Brussels, Belgium
Date: December 3, 1812   *Date:* September 10, 1883

PRINCIPAL WORKS

NOVELS: *In't Wonderjaar 1566*, 1837 (*In the Year of Marvels, 1566*); *De leeuw van Vlaanderen*, 1838 (*The Lion of Flanders*); *Jacob van Artevelde*, 1849; *De Loteling*, 1850 (*The Conscript*); *De arme edelman*, 1851 (*The Poor Nobleman*); *Het geluk van ryk te zyn*, 1855 (*The Happiness of Being Rich*); *Benjamin van Vlaanderen*, 1880 (*Benjamin of Flanders*).

SHORT STORIES: *Phantazy*, 1837 (*Fantasy*).

Leader in the revival of the Flemish vernacular as a vehicle of the literary art, Hendrik Conscience, son of a French father and a Flemish mother, was born in Antwerp on December 3, 1812. During his childhood the family lived for a time in Antwerp and then moved to a flat, desolate stretch of land

237

between Antwerp and Venloo, the setting for much of his later fiction. When he was seventeen, Conscience was sent to Antwerp to study; he supported himself in part by tutoring. In 1830, at the time of the Belgian revolution, he volunteered for the army and served in the ranks until 1837.

Conscience had written some poetry in French while in the army, but when he turned to writing fiction he decided to write in Flemish, a dialect considered by all educated Belgians as too vulgar for literary use. His first book, *In the Year of Marvels, 1566,* was well received in 1837; King Leopold I of Belgium gave the book his personal praise. But Conscience's father was so angry that his son should write a book in Flemish that he turned the young man out of the family home. A collec-

tion of stories and tales, *Fantasy,* appeared in the same year, under royal patronage. Later novels of Belgian life include *The Poor Nobleman, The Miser, The Burgomaster of Liege,* and *Benjamin of Flanders.*

A congress meeting at Ghent in 1841 mentioned Conscience's work as the beginnings of a true national literature, but for many years his novels about homely life, written originally in Flemish, did not achieve popularity. In the 1850's, however, his popularity rose, and his novels were translated into German, French, and English. In later life Conscience held the title of Keeper of the Royal Belgian Museum. When he died in Brussels on September 10, 1883, he was given the state funeral of an important government official.

BIBLIOGRAPHICAL REFERENCES: For biography and criticism see Emmanuel de Bom, *Hendrik Conscience,* 1912; and R. Zellweger, *Les débuts du roman rustique, 1836–1850,* 1941.

BENJAMIN CONSTANT

Born: Lausanne, Switzerland   *Died:* Paris, France
Date: October 25, 1767   *Date:* December 8, 1830

PRINCIPAL WORKS

NOVELS: *Adolphe,* 1815; *Le Cahier rouge,* 1907 (*The Red Notebook*); *Cécile,* 1951.
ESSAYS AND STUDIES: *De la religion considérée dans sa source, ses formes, et ses développements,* 1825–1831.

(Henri) Benjamin Constant de Rebecque, son of a Dutch army colonel, was born at Lausanne, Switzerland, on October 25, 1767. His education was varied; he was tutored in turn by a sadistic German, a Frenchman who boarded him in a brothel, and an unfrocked German priest. His mother having died in giving him birth, he was pampered by his grandmother, aunts, and stepmother. A precocious boy, he

was sent to Oxford (where he was not formally admitted), Erlangen (where he was expelled for relations with a prostitute), and Edinburgh (where he acquired powerful Whig political convictions). Finally, in 1787, he returned to Paris to begin the tumultuous social and political life which he embodied in his writings.

Constant was a Jekyll-Hyde personality, a serious intellectual on the one hand and an unrestrained sensualist on the other. At twenty he formed an alliance with forty-seven-year-old Mme. de Charrière, who for seven years gave him an education in eighteenth century manners. He abandoned her for Mme. de Staël, who maintained one of the most brilliant liberal salons of the age. His two marriages and frequent affairs failed to interfere with his social, literary, and political life. Constant's autobiography is presented under thin disguise in his fiction: *Cécile*, written 1811, *Le Cahier rouge*, written 1812; and *Adolphe*. The last fifteen years of his life were spent in steady writing, mostly political but including his important religious study *De la religion considérée dans sa source, ses formes, et ses développements*. He was regularly elected to the Chamber of Deputies, becoming president four months before he died, December 8, 1830.

BIBLIOGRAPHICAL REFERENCES: The best and most recent study is Harold Nicolson, *Benjamin Constant*, 1949, with a bibliography. This supersedes Elizabeth Schemerhorn, *Benjamin Constant*, 1924. An excellent essay is included in Lord David Cecil, *Poets and Story-tellers*, 1949. A postscript on Constant is included in Geoffrey Scott, *The Portrait of Zélide*, 1927.

JOHN ESTEN COOKE

Born: Winchester, Virginia
Date: November 3, 1830

Died: Clarke County, Virginia
Date: September 27, 1886

PRINCIPAL WORKS

NOVELS: *Leather Stocking and Silk*, 1854; *The Virginia Comedians*, 1854; *Henry St. John, Gentleman*, 1859; *Surry of Eagle's Nest*, 1866; *Fairfax*, 1868; *Mohun*, 1869; *The Heir of Greymount*, 1870; *Her Majesty the Queen*, 1873; *My Lady Pokahontas*, 1885.

BIOGRAPHY: *A Life of Stonewall Jackson*, 1863; *A Life of General Robert E. Lee*, 1871.

ESSAYS: *Hammer and Rapier*, 1870.

HISTORY: *Virginia: A History of the People*, 1883.

John Esten Cooke, born in Winchester, Virginia, November 3, 1830, is an almost-forgotten American novelist whose books have deserved better reputation and greater popularity. His older brother was Philip Pendleton Cooke, noted as a poet and story writer of the ante-bellum South. John Esten Cooke spent his early boyhood on a farm near Winchester, Virginia, but his family moved to Richmond when he was nine years old. In 1846, although he had wanted to attend the University of Virginia, he began to read law in his father's office. By 1848 he had published some poetry and prose, including pieces in *Harper's Monthly* and *The Southern Literary Messenger*. His first real success came with the publication of *The Virginia Comedians*, which was the first of a total of thirty-one books to be published before his death.

During the 1850's, Cooke was an ardent proponent of secession, and he served in the Confederate Army

239

throughout the Civil War, rising from the rank of private to that of captain. During the war years he found time to write *A Life of Stonewall Jackson*, the pioneer study of the great Confederate tactician and general. After the war ended he continued to write, turning again to fiction. His war experience was woven into *Surry of Eagle's Nest* and *Mohun*, among the earliest novels about the Civil War.

Following Lee's surrender at Appomattox, Cooke returned to civilian life in Virginia. In 1867 he married Mary Francis Page and settled at "The Briers," in Clarke County, Virginia, where he divided his time between writing and farming. Work of this later period in his career is varied. *The Heir of Greymount* carries the theme that the best answer to the South's postwar problems is agriculture. *My Lady Pokahontas* is a novel about the early days of Virginia as a British colony. *Virginia* is a history of colonial times. During the 1870's Cooke also wrote *A Life of General Robert E. Lee* and a volume of essays on the Civil War and related military topics, *Hammer and Rapier*. Cooke's untimely death at his home on September 27, 1886, was caused by typhoid fever.

BIBLIOGRAPHICAL REFERENCES: There is only one biography, John O. Beaty, *John Esten Cooke, Virginian*, 1922. Oscar Wegelin, "A Bibliography of the Separate Writings of John Esten Cooke," *American Collector*, I (1925), 96–99 (separately republished, 1925, 1941), does not provide a full listing of periodical publications. Two useful brief evaluations appear in A. H. Quinn, *American Fiction*, 1936; and Jay B. Hubbell, *The South in American Literature*, 1954. For an interesting article, see Carvel Collins, "John Esten Cooke and Local Color," *Southern Literary Messenger*, NS VI (1944), 82–84.

JAMES FENIMORE COOPER

Born: Burlington, New Jersey   *Died:* Cooperstown, New York
Date: September 15, 1789   *Date:* September 14, 1851

PRINCIPAL WORKS

NOVELS: *The Spy*, 1821; *The Pioneers*, 1823; *The Pilot*, 1824; *Lionel Lincoln*, 1825; *The Last of the Mohicans*, 1826; *The Prairie*, 1827; *The Red Rover*, 1827; *The Wept of Wish-ton-Wish*, 1829; *The Water-Witch*, 1830; *The Bravo*, 1831; *The Heidenmauer*, 1832; *The Headsman*, 1833; *The Monikins*, 1835; *Homeward Bound*, 1838; *Home as Found*, 1838; *Mercedes of Castile*, 1840; *The Pathfinder*, 1840; *The Deerslayer*, 1841; *The Wing-and-Wing*, 1842; *The Two Admirals*, 1842; *Wyandotté*, 1843; *Ned Myers*, 1843; *Afloat and Ashore*, 1844; *Satanstoe*, 1845; *The Chainbearer*, 1845; *The Redskins*, 1846; *The Crater*, 1847; *Jack Tier*, 1848; *The Oak Openings*, 1848; *The Sea Lions*, 1849; *The Ways of the Hour*, 1850.

SOCIAL CRITICISM: *Notions of the Americans*, 1828; *Letter of J. Fenimore Cooper to General Lafayette*, 1831; *A Letter to His Countrymen*, 1834; *The American Democrat*, 1838.

TRAVEL SKETCHES: *Sketches of Switzerland*, Parts I and II, 1836; *Gleanings in Europe*, 1837–1838.

HISTORY: *The History of the Navy of the United States of America*, 1839.

Novelist, social critic, and historian, James Fenimore Cooper was perhaps the most productive and versatile American writer of his generation. In his comparatively short literary career (1820–1851), he published thirty-three substantial fictional works, three books of explicit social and political commentary, five travel works, a monumental history of the United States Navy, a book of naval biographies, and an impressive quantity of miscellaneous writing, much of it anonymous and some of it still unknown to scholars. His purpose as man and author, as he declared it, was the intellectual independence of his country, whose thought and art were, he believed, too much dominated by foreign models; and his bold experimentation with indigenous literary materials exerted a powerful formative effect on the literature of the young Republic. His interest for readers today lies mainly in his artistic triumphs in the form of the romance, at present too little understood, and in his pungent and pertinent insights into the development of American and European civilization.

Born at Burlington, New Jersey, on September 15, 1789, Cooper was reared by his wealthy, land-holding father, the Federalist leader of western New York State, in the bustling frontier community of Cooperstown at the foot of Lake Otsego. As a lad, he explored the hills, forests, and lake near his home, devoured fiction, and spun yarns of his own. From his father and his father's associates, he derived a life-long reverence for the Constitution ("on the framing of which all the experience of the past was early brought to bear") and for the exalted ideals of the Federalist founding fathers. Expelled from Yale for a high-spirited prank before he was fifteen, he made an apprentice voyage before the mast and became a midshipman in the then infant Navy, only to have his dream of glorious service afloat shattered by relatively inactive assignments at Oswego and New York City. In 1811, determining to resign his commission and enjoy his considerable patrimony as a gentleman farmer, he married Susan Augusta De Lancey of the well-known Tory family and for the next several years devoted himself to various domestic, agricultural, military, political, religious, and cultural activities in Westchester and Otsego Counties.

When the depression of 1817–1819 swept away his inheritance, Cooper had to seek means of paying his debts and supporting his increasing family. His first novel *Precaution* (1820), a deliberate attempt to produce a best-seller, failed like his other speculations; but the writing so intrigued him that he continued with *The Spy*, a historical romance based on an anecdote of John Jay and on intimate knowledge of the legends and terrain of Westchester County. Its unexpected success at home and abroad turned Cooper decisively to authorship. Moving to New York City in 1822, he soon became a dominant literary figure, founding the Bread and Cheese Club and rallying writers and painters to the cause of distinctively American art. In *The Pioneers,* earliest of the Leatherstocking series, he drew heavily on nostalgic memories of his frontier boyhood; in *The Pilot,* he initiated the vogue of nautical romance; in *Lionel Lincoln,* he attempted in fiction an almost unprecedented exactitude of historical detail; and in *The Last of the Mohicans,* second of the Leatherstocking Tales, he gave his first extended treatment of Indians in a wild forest

241

setting. Though uneven artistically, these experimental romances proved the value of American literary materials and the serious thematic potentialities of the form.

In 1826, Cooper took his family to Europe, where he wrote such favorite romances as *The Prairie,* in which Leatherstocking reappears as an aged trapper-philosopher on the western plains, and *The Red Rover,* a second sea-tale. Friendship with Lafayette and close observation of European aristocracy led to such strenuous efforts to expound and defend American democratic ideas as *Notions of the Americans,* an idealized description of the United States, and *The Bravo, The Heidenmauer,* and *The Headsman,* fictional interpretations of European history. These efforts were misunderstood at home, however; and Cooper returned to New York in 1833 depressed and discouraged, convinced that his countrymen did not understand their own principles. In *The Monikins,* an allegorical satire, in a series of travel books (1836–1837), and in *The American Democrat,* he sought to bring Americans to self-knowledge and to correct the excesses of the Jacksonian era; but, despite the cogency of their observation, these works were almost totally disregarded.

Cooper's return to fiction with *Homeward Bound* and *Home As Found* and publication of his long-deferred *The History of the Navy of the United States of America* precipitated many bitter battles with Whig editors in the press and in libel courts. Despite his numerous controversies, Cooper's final years, spent pleasantly enough in the refurbished family mansion in Cooperstown, were astonishingly productive. Concluding the Leatherstocking Tales with *The Pathfinder* and *The Deerslayer,* he reasserted and afterwards maintained his reputation as a master of romance; but, to the end, he experimented with means of fusing his imaginative materials and his specifically critical interests. These efforts, including *Afloat and Ashore,* its sequel *Miles Wallingford* (1844), the Anti-Rent trilogy—*Satanstoe, The Chainbearer, The Redskins*—and *The Crater* were not notably successful, though *Satanstoe,* the first novel of the Anti-Rent series, has been widely appreciated for its evocation of early Dutch life in New York and Albany. Cooper died at Cooperstown on September 14, 1851, after a prolonged illness.

While Cooper's stature as a social critic has been sufficiently acknowledged by twentieth-century critics, his artistic stature is still disputed. The imaginative appeal of his swift-moving narrative, graphic description, and picturesque characterization is usually conceded; but the complex symbolic structures of his better fiction have been overlooked or misrepresented, so that its intricacy and universality of meaning have been inadequately comprehended. Cooper's weaknesses (occasional turgidity of style, excessive dependence on outworn fictional convention, love of overelaboration, and careless composition) do not disappear when his works are given the strenuous reading they require; but the flaws do not essentially damage the unobtrusive brilliance of the total conceptions.

James F. Beard, Jr.

BIBLIOGRAPHICAL REFERENCES: No complete edition of Cooper's works, no full edition of his letters, and no definitive biography have been published. The Mohawk

Edition of the fiction, 33 vols., 1895–1900, is available and perhaps as satisfactory as any other. Miscellaneous selections from the family papers were published by Cooper's grandson and namesake as *The Correspondence of James Fenimore-Cooper*, 1922. The most informative biographies are those by T. R. Lounsbury, 1883; H. W. Boynton, 1931; Marcel Clavel, 1938; and James Grossman, 1949. Robert E. Spiller in *Fenimore Cooper: Critic of His Times*, 1931, and in numerous articles, editions, and introductions has made the most substantial contributions to modern Cooper scholarship. Useful bibliographies are contained in Robert E. Spiller and Philip C. Blackburn, *A Descriptive Bibliography of the Writings of James Fenimore Cooper*, 1934, and in Robert E. Spiller, *James Fenimore Cooper: Representative Selections*, American Writers Series, 1936. More recent books and articles are listed in the various bibliographies of the American Literature Group of the Modern Language Association.

PIERRE CORNEILLE

Born: Rouen, France   *Died:* Paris, France
Date: June 6, 1606   *Date:* October 1, 1684

PRINCIPAL WORKS

PLAYS: *Mélite*, 1629; *Clitandre*, c. 1631; *La Veuve*, c. 1632; *La Galerie du Palais*, 1632; *La Suivante*, c. 1633; *La Place Royale*, 1633; *Médée*, 1635; *L'Illusion comique*, 1635; *Le Cid*, 1636; *Horace*, 1640; *Cinna*, c. 1640; *Pompée*, c. 1642; *Polyeucte*, c. 1643; *Le Menteur*, 1643; *La Suite du Menteur*, 1644; *Rodogune*, c. 1645; *Héraclius*, 1646; *Don Sanche d'Aragon*, 1649; *Andromède*, 1650; *Nicomède*, c. 1650; *Œdipe*, 1659; *La Toison d'or*, 1660; *Sertorious*, 1662; *Othon*, 1664; *Attila*, 1667; *Tite et Bérénice*, 1670.

Pierre Corneille, born June 6, 1606, was the son of a barrister and king's advocate of great prominence in the thriving city of Rouen. His mother was Marthe le Pesant. He was educated in the Jesuit school in his home town and took his oath as a lawyer four years ahead of the usual time by special dispensation. The brilliant young man followed in his father's footsteps, almost literally, by becoming for a time the king's advocate "over waters and forests," as the title read.

His love of the theater and of literature were early manifest, and he wrote a play for a traveling troupe in 1629; later *Mélite* was popular in Paris. While this comedy would seem crude by modern standards, it broke away from the stultifying conventions of the

times. This and later comedies caused Cardinal Richelieu to include the young Corneille in his group of hack writers who developed the great patron's sketchy ideas into plays for the tennis court theater he had earlier established. But the talented young man soon incurred the displeasure of his patron by doctoring up the ideas. Later he was to become more deeply involved through his failure to observe the "unities" (of time, place, and action) so highly regarded by the new classicists.

In *Médée* he began to show promise as a tragedian, and *L'Illusion comique* of the same year indicated that he had great versatility. By this time he was at work translating and arranging the life of Spain's national hero, the Cid Campeador, into a play which would become more famous than its hero and which would introduce a new play type to theater, the tragi-comedy. The play, produced in 1636, aroused critics, playwrights, and patrons of the arts into a pamphlet war of recurring interest to scholars. The author of the play had little to say, but he was universally scored for bad taste and the failure to observe rules of dramaturgy. The public put its seal of approval on the play, however, and it has inspired a healthy progeny of heroic drama to the present day.

For three years Corneille was in virtual retirement, and then he brought out in *Horace,* dedicated to Richelieu, a tragedy more nearly in keeping with critical edicts. The cardinal then bestowed on the poet a grant of five hundred crowns a year, a sum which allowed the playwright to marry his mistress, Marie de Lampérière. In the following year his father died and he himself suffered an illness, but plays continued to come from his facile pen until his peak year of 1643 when both a great tragedy and comedy were on the boards, *Polyeucte* and *Le Menteur.* About the same time the French Academy finally invited him into their exclusive group after twice rejecting him over a period of disquieting years.

While the master dramatist continued to write plays, finally removing to Paris in order to be more nearly in the center of productions, he never again reached his former level. The influence of Molière and Racine was more and more noticeable on theater patrons, and the old plays of bombast and oratorical display were becoming passé. Corneille turned to a translation of *The Imitation of Christ* (1656) and to essays on dramaturgy, but continued all the while to write plays.

The last ten years of his life were spent in uncertainty of his pension and in doubt as to his following, though there is a record of some verses thanking Louis XIV for ordering the revival of his better works. He was survived by four of his six children, to whom he had been devoted. His love of family seems to have been offset by his indifference to society. His manner was melancholy and reserved; he seems to have suffered fits of depression. While he was agreeably pleased in seeing other works of talent, he felt slighted if he did not receive praise in return. No one can now tell whether his reputed parsimony was based on miserliness or on lack of funds; certainly he never sought out the high and mighty or begged help. He made little enough from his plays, and his pensions came later in life and erratically. He died in Paris, October 1, 1684.

While Corneille has suffered greatly at the hands of influential critics like Boileau and Voltaire, he has been nobly defended by the greatest of playwrights and other writers, such as Molière, Racine, and Balzac. Although modern readers are often wearied by the theatrics and contrivance as well as the rhetorical language of his plays, it must be remembered that what we regard as his weaknesses were strengths in the lackluster theater of his day, and even his weakest plays were better than anything seen previously. In a sense he was the Aeschylus to Racine's Sophocles and Molière's Aristophanes, if one would wish to carry out a neo-classic comparison. Nowhere before or since has so much excitement been contained in so few hours as in his greatest work, *Le Cid.* It is of interest to note that the last heroic play of note took its cue from this renaissance of drama and brought a contemporary of Corneille's to larger-than-life, Cyrano de Bergerac —and that re-creation for us must have had the same theatrical effect as the recalling of the Cid to the French stage.

BIBLIOGRAPHICAL REFERENCES: The most recent edition of the plays is *Chief Plays of Corneille,* translated into blank verse by Lacy Lockert, 1952. An old, but still useful study is François P. G. Guizot, *Corneille and his Times,* 1852. Two valuable briefer studies appear in Benedetto Croce, *Ariosto, Shakespeare, and Corneille,* 1920; and Martin Turnell, *The Classical Moment: Studies of Corneille, Molière, and Racine,* 1947. See also Martin Turnell, "The Great and Good Corneille," *Scrutiny,* VII (1938), 277–301.

CHARLES DE COSTER

Born: Munich, Germany
Date: August 20, 1827

Died: Brussels, Belgium
Date: May 17, 1879

Principal Works

NOVEL: *La Légende et les Aventures héroiques, joyeuses et glorieuses d'Ulenspiegel,* 1867 (*The Legend of Tyl Ulenspiegel*).

FOLK TALES: *Légendes flamandes,* 1858 (*Flemish Legends*); *Les Contes Brabançons,* 1861.

In all Belgian literature the best-known names to English-speaking readers are Maurice Maeterlinck and Émile Verhaeren, and our neglect is nowhere more our loss than with Charles (Theodore Henri) De Coster, the man whom Verhaeren himself called "the father of Belgian literature." Coster, born in Munich, Germany, August 20, 1827, was educated to the law at the University of Brussels. Later he filled a responsible position with the Société Générale, but he found this work too constricting. He wrote, instead, political articles and novels, first as a freelance writer and later as instructor of French literature at the Military School of Brussels. It was here, after a quiet life, that he died, relatively unmourned when one considers what he had done for Belgian letters.

The task Coster set for himself was, as with James Joyce in Ireland, to create the conscience of his race. He believed, however, that the people of the middle class were all "tarred with the same monotony," so he went to the folk and collected their tales, and he went to the Flemish past and studied its history and its painters. These interests gave direction to his talent and shape to his art.

In his collection of folk tales, *Flemish Legends,* we see sketched all the vigor and wit of peasant life turned to a purpose beyond folk learning, beyond art for its own sake. One tale, for example, contains the familiar pact with the devil and three wishes motifs, but the story points to a political moral. Smetse Smee, a Flemish peasant, outwits the devil each time, and the three guises of the devil correspond to three enemies of Flanders, culminating in the one most hated, Philip II of Spain.

That monarch also appears in Coster's greatest book, *Tyl Ulenspiegel.*

245

Here he is villainously opposed to Tyl, the popular, quick-witted, open-hearted prankster of German and Flemish folklore. The subject is ostensibly the sixteenth century revolt of some Low Country provinces against Philip and his hangman in Flanders, the Duke of Alba. But the novel outgrows its historical setting; it is the epic of the race, and Ulenspiegel is the soul of Flan-

ders. Reading Tyl's episodic adventures, we often laugh, but at the same time we are aware of a somber strain that Coster never lets us forget. This is a history chronicle of a people who have suffered and have endured. At Coster's death in Brussels on May 17, 1879 he was unheralded, but succeeding generations have come to know his worth.

BIBLIOGRAPHICAL REFERENCES: There is no satisfactory study of Coster in English. See Joseph Hanse, *Charles De Coster et son œuvre*, 1928; and L. L. Sosset, *Introduction à l'œuvre de Charles De Coster*, 1937.

LOUIS COUPERUS

Born: The Hague, Netherlands
Date: June 10, 1863

Died: De Steeg, Netherlands
Date: July 16, 1923

PRINCIPAL WORKS

NOVELS: *Eline Vere*, 1889; *Noodlot*, 1890 (*Footsteps of Fate*); *Extaze*, 1892 (*Ecstasy*); *De Stille Kracht*, 1900 (*The Hidden Force*); *Langs lijnen van geleidelijk-heid*, 1900 (*The Law Inevitable*); *De Boeken der kleine zielen*, 1901–1903 (*The Book of the Small Souls: Small Souls, The Later Life, The Twilight of Souls, Dr. Adriaan*); *Dionyzos*, 1904; *De Berg Van Licht*, 1905 (*The Mountain of Light*); *Van oude menschen, de dingen, die voorbijgaan*, 1906 (*Old People and the Things That Pass*); *Antiek tourisme*, 1911 (*The Tour*); *Herakles*, 1913; *De Komedianten*, 1917 (*The Comedians*); *Xerxes*, 1919; *Iskander*, 1920; *Het zwevende schaakbord*, 1923 (*The Flitting Chess Board*).

AUTOBIOGRAPHY: *Van en over Mijzelf en Anderen*, 1910–1917 (*Of and Concerning Myself and Others*).

Louis Couperus, born at The Hague, June 10, 1863, brought the modern Dutch novel into the mainstream of European literature by carrying the tradition of Zola's social realism to an extreme. From his first published work, *Eline Vere*, in 1889—the story of a woman without character who feels damned by her heredity—to one of his best novels, *Old People and the Things That Pass*—in which a forgotten crime determines the lives of those who were unborn when it was committed—he developed his own method of situating

personal life in a context of fate. Although Dutch critics accused him of having a perverse and morbid philosophical outlook, his novels were highly successful in his own country and abroad. When he returned to Holland in 1923, after a residence of many years in Italy, his sixtieth birthday was the occasion for a national celebration.

Couperus spent his early years until the age of fifteen in Java, where his father served as a government official, and visited the Dutch East Indies again after 1921 as correspondent for the

Haagsche Post. Much of his work reflects this colonial background.

The Book of the Small Souls, a four volume novel resembling Galsworthy's family saga in its depressing accumulation of detail, is Couperus' most ambitious work, apart from his historical group of novels, *The Mountain of Light, Xerxes,* and *Iskander,* in which he analyzes the downfall of Heliogabalus, Xerxes, and Alexander the Great, respectively, as caused by forces beyond their control. His writings were often relieved by a delicate play of irony that distinguishes *Of and Concerning Myself and Others,* an autobiography interesting for its portrait sketches. Couperus died at De Steeg, near Arnhem, The Netherlands, on July 16, 1923.

BIBLIOGRAPHICAL REFERENCES: There is almost no criticism of Couperus in English. See the essay by Sir Edmund Gosse in *Silhouettes,* 1925; also J. L. Walch, *Louis Couperus,* 1921; J. de Graaf, *Le Réveil litteraire en Hollande,* 1938; and Johannes B. Tielrooy, *Panorama de la littérature hollandais contemporaine,* 1938. *Over Louis Couperus,* 1952, is a collection of studies by various hands.

NOEL COWARD

Born: Teddington-on-Thames, England
Date: December 16, 1899

PRINCIPAL WORKS

PLAYS: *The Vortex,* 1923; *Hay Fever,* 1925; *Fallen Angels,* 1925; *Bitter Sweet,* 1929; *Private Lives,* 1930; *Post Mortem,* 1931; *Cavalcade,* 1931; *Design for Living,* 1933; *Tonight at 8:30,* 1936; *Blithe Spirit,* 1942; *This Happy Breed,* 1943; *Nude with Violin,* 1957.

AUTOBIOGRAPHY: *Present Indicative,* 1937; *Future Indefinite,* 1954.

Noel (Pierce) Coward, who was to become a playwright, actor, composer, stage manager, producer, and sophisticate extraordinary, had unprepossessing beginnings in an atmosphere of genteel poverty in the suburb of London in which he was born on December 16, 1899. His father worked first for a music publisher and later for a piano manufacturer, neither of which occupations appears to have been particularly lucrative. Noel received his formal education at the Chapel Royal School in Clapham, but it ended before he entered his teens. The boy had been acting ever since he could talk, and at the age of ten a part in a children's play called *The Gold Fish* took him from the schoolroom forever, except for a brief and unwelcome return during a three-week engagement in Manchester. His career as an actor continued more or less unbroken until 1918, when he was called for military service. Declared unfit for active duty, he was sent to drill with the Artists' Rifles near London. An accident (he tripped over a board and fell on his head) was followed by lingering illness, and his army career of a few months' duration was ended with an honorable discharge and six months' pension.

His military career behind him, Coward returned to acting and at the same time tried his wings as a playwright. His first few plays were never produced. Although *I'll Leave It To You* (1920) met with rousing success on the London stage before its author had reached his majority, *Vortex* stands as the first of Coward's important plays. In this serious account of a willful, selfish woman's effect on the lives of her son and others around her, we are given a vivid picture of the futile, empty lives of a dying class. *Hay Fever* is the first of a long line of what the world has come to consider typically "Coward" plays, witty, brittle pieces characterized by sophisticated dialogue and perfect timing, portraying the empty, pleasure-seeking lives of the smart "Mayfair set" with a sympathy touched by cynicism. In these deft descriptions of the people of the smart new disillusioned twenties Coward aims many a verbal dagger at Victorian prudery and hypocrisy, yet the world-dreary unhappiness of most of his characters indicates that their way of life is also the object of the author's satire. *Fallen Angels, Private Lives,* and *Design for Living* continue the tradition of the comedy of manners. The nine short plays of *Tonight at 8:30* are presented in a similar vein, although their scope has been broadened to include more than one social class. By the 1930's, however, the brittle wit had sharpened edges of bitterness, and it was obvious that Coward's own disenchantment was increasing. In *Post Mortem,* the story of a dead soldier's return to the world of 1930, the bitterness is uncoated by wit and contemporary audiences found the powerful castigation of their own age hard to take. *Cavalcade* is an interesting and at times moving social chronicle of English life from 1899 to 1930; it presents a world falling apart and in ruins.

Coward's skills also include the composition of delightful music and lyrics, as *The Noel Coward Songbook* (1953) shows. By far the most successful of his revues was *Bitter Sweet.* In this highly romantic, faintly nostalgic piece all his facility in rhyme and scansion, his highly-developed sense of form, and his skillful versification of ordinary speech, are brought into play.

Noel Coward traveled widely during World War II, raising funds and entertaining troops. Many of his experiences are recorded in his *Middle East Diary* (1944), whose flippancy has often been criticized as misplaced and in bad taste. Since the war Coward has lived much as before, unmarried, rich, dapper, well-traveled, and hardworking. Of his later plays, only *Blithe Spirit* measures up to earlier ones in entertainment value; indeed, some regard it as his funniest work, devoid of the usual bitterness. His postwar excursions into movie-making not only show his abilities as actor and director as well as writer but, in such pieces as *Brief Encounter,* indicate that the mature Coward has a hitherto undisplayed knack for telling a sensitive, quietly poignant story. Although Coward's recent comedies indicate that his wit is dated by the era in which it first flourished, his versatility and his ability to catch the spirit of an age seem to guarantee that, in one way or another, his best plays will survive as a minor but permanent chapter in the history of the modern theater.

BIBLIOGRAPHICAL REFERENCES: Coward's plays have been collected in his *Play Parade,* 4 vols., 1949–1953. The best account of his life, although strongly colored by his own personality, is found in the two volumes of his autobiography. See also Patrick Braybrook, *The Amazing Mr. Noel Coward,* 1933; Robert Graecen, *The Art of Noel Coward,* 1953; Frederick Lumley, *Trends in Twentieth Century Drama,* 1956; A. G. Macdonnell, "The Plays of Noel Coward," *Living Age,* CCCXLI (1932), 439–446; J. C. Furnas, "The Art of Noel Coward," *Fortnightly Review,* CXXXIX (1933), 709–716; and Homer E. Woodbridge, "Noel Coward," *South Atlantic Quarterly,* XXXVIII (1938), 239–251.

ABRAHAM COWLEY

Born: London, England
Date: 1618

Died: Chertsey, England
Date: July 28, 1667

PRINCIPAL WORKS

POEMS: *The Mistress,* 1647; *Miscellanies* (containing the "Pindarique Odes" and "Davideis"), 1656.

Abraham Cowley, born in London in 1618, was the seventh child of a London stationer who died before his child's birth. The mother obtained her son's admittance to Westminster School as a king's scholar, and very early the boy demonstrated his ability as a poet; at the age of fifteen he published a collection of poems, *Poetical Blossoms* (1633). In 1637 he entered Cambridge University, where he continued his literary efforts with a pastoral drama, *Love's Riddle* (1638), and *Naufragium Joculare* (1638), a Latin comedy. Cowley received his bachelor's degree from Cambridge in 1639 and his master's degree in 1642. During the English Civil War he sided with the Royalists against the Puritans and was forced to flee to France in 1646.

In exile, he was sent by the Stuarts on diplomatic missions throughout western Europe. One of his chief tasks at court was to code and decode the voluminous correspondence between Charles I and Queen Henrietta Maria, until Charles' death at the hands of the regicides in 1649. A volume of love poetry, *The Mistress, or Several Copies*

of *Love-Verses,* was published in 1647 while the poet was in France. The book was popular throughout the seventeenth century. After Cowley's return to England, his *Miscellanies,* a collection of his poetical works appeared in 1656. This volume included his love poems, the "Pindarique Odes," and his unfinished epic, "Davideis." The odes were highly serious poems; the "Davideis" was a Biblical epic in rhymed verse which had been written in part while Cowley was at Cambridge.

While in England, Cowley was arrested and imprisoned as a spy, but was released on bail. He studied medicine and was given an M.D. degree by Oxford in 1657. He then returned to France to remain there until the Restoration in 1660. Shortly after Charles II ascended the throne, Cowley, awarded a lease of land by the crown, settled in the Surrey countryside until his death at Chertsey on July 28, 1667. During his last years, living in quiet retirement, he wrote eleven essays in the style of Montaigne and composed a series of poems in Latin on flowers and plants.

BIBLIOGRAPHICAL REFERENCES: The writings of Cowley in English have been collected in an edition edited by A. R. Waller, 2 vols., 1905–1906. A good selection of his poetry is *"The Mistress,"* with *Other Select Poems of Abraham Cowley*, edited by John Sparrow, 1926. Of the various critical studies, that by Samuel Johnson in his *Lives of the Most Eminent English Poets*, 1779–1781, is still among the best. See also A. H. Nethercot, *Abraham Cowley: The Muse's Hannibal*, 1926, and J. Loiseau, *Abraham Cowley, sa vie, son œuvre*, 1931.

WILLIAM COWPER

Born: Great Berkhamsted, England
Date: November 26, 1731

Died: East Dereham, England
Date: April 25, 1800

PRINCIPAL WORKS

POEMS: *Olney Hymns*, 1779 (with John Newton); *Poems*, 1782; *The Task*, 1785.

One of the forerunners of English Romanticism, William Cowper was criticized by his contemporaries who, bred to the formal metrics and diction of Pope and Dryden, and to the strong rhythmic patterns of *Paradise Lost*, complained that his verse was too like prose. Some of Cowper's verse justifies this charge, but in *The Task* he developed a new style of blank verse, a relaxed, easy, almost conversational style that was well suited to the rustic, personal content of the poem. The ability to write blank verse that was not dominated by Miltonic rhythms was no small feat, and Cowper's ease led to the fluent blank verse of Wordsworth.

Cowper's life stands in ironic counterpoint to the good-humored, placid subject matter of so much of his poetry. Born at Great Berkhamsted, England, on November 26, 1731, he was from an early age afflicted with a profound melancholy that was deepened by his Calvinistic sense of sin. After a good education, he became a law clerk at eighteen. He fell in love with his cousin, Theodora Cowper, the "Delia" of his poems; her father forbade the match on the basis of consanguinity, but perhaps the young man's melan-

choly had as much to do with the refusal. He was then nominated for a clerkship in the House of Lords, but the formality of an examination before the House terrified him. Rather than face it, he attempted suicide and was committed to an asylum for eighteen months.

In 1765 he went to the country and took up residence with the Unwin family. When the Rev. Morley Unwin died a few years later, Cowper and the Unwins moved to Olney. There he came under the influence of the Rev. John Newton, an evangelical preacher of Methodist principles. Newton's sermons about man's personal relationship to God intensified Cowper's latent melancholy and in 1773, when he was on the verge of marrying Mrs. Unwin, he had a terrible dream in which God ordered him to destroy himself and accept his inevitable damnation. Cowper tried to hang himself, and it was three years before he fully recovered from that seizure of madness. He had other attacks of melancholy in 1787 and 1794. He collaborated with the Rev. John Newton in the writing of *Olney Hymns*, thereby establishing himself

250

with Charles Wesley as one of the great hymnodists of the language.

Cowper's secular fame rests mainly on his *Poems* and *The Task*, the latter a discursive poem ostensibly written about a sofa. His direct expression of personal emotion and his interest in the personal response to natural objects make him a transition figure between the Neo-Classic and Romantic ages. He died at East Dereham, England, on April 25, 1800.

BIBLIOGRAPHICAL REFERENCES: The edition of the *Works*, edited with a *Life* by Robert Southey, 15 vols., 1835–1837, is still of interest to scholars. Standard editions of the *Poems* are those edited by John Bruce for the Aldine Series, 3 vols., 1865; Sir Humphrey S. Milford, 1905 ff.; and Hugh l'A. Fausset, Everyman's Library, 1931. For biographical and critical studies see the *Life* by William Hayley, 3 vols., 1803–1804; Hugh l'A. Fausset, *William Cowper*, 1928; and Lord David Cecil, *The Stricken Deer; or, The Life of William Cowper*, 1929. Also useful is Gilbert Thomas, *William Cowper and the Eighteenth Century*, 1935.

JAMES GOULD COZZENS

Born: Chicago, Illinois
Date: August 19, 1903

PRINCIPAL WORKS

NOVELS: *S.S. San Pedro*, 1931; *The Last Adam*, 1933; *Castaway*, 1934; *Men and Brethren*, 1936; *Ask Me Tomorrow*, 1940; *The Just and the Unjust*, 1942; *Guard of Honor*, 1948; *By Love Possessed*, 1957.

A singular literary event of the 1950's was the sudden, somewhat paradoxical critical and popular recognition accorded to James Gould Cozzens upon the publication of his twelfth novel, *By Love Possessed*. Although he had previously enjoyed a certain measure of respect, Cozzens had never won any marked popularity or even many partisan critics, possibly because he remained aloof from all literary trends and political movements while unspectacularly mastering his craft.

Born in Chicago on August 19, 1903, into a family of New England background, Cozzens was reared in Staten Island, New York, and educated at Kent School and Harvard University. While an undergraduate he published his first novel, *Confusion* (1924), which deals with the career of a jazz-age girl. He took a leave of absence from college but never returned. His next work, *Michael Scarlett* (1925), is a historical novel set in Elizabethan England. A post as tutor in Cuba provided material for two novels, *Cock Pit* (1928) and *Son of Perdition* (1929).

Cozzens' first major work was *S.S. San Pedro*, a short novel based on the sinking of the *Vestris*; this book clearly established his remarkable ability to assimilate the facts of an occupation and to apply them knowledgably. *The Last Adam* examines the character of a forceful doctor in a New England town. A short, rather experimental novel, *Castaway*, deals with the idea of a man alone in a department store after a world-wrecking catastrophe. Cozzens achieved an unusually objec-

251

tive treatment of a clergyman in *Men and Brethren,* a novel about an Episcopal clergyman and his New York parish. *Ask Me Tomorrow* presents an at least partially autobiographical portrait of an American writer-tutor in Europe. A study of a murder trial in a small town, *The Just and the Unjust* was received with what, for Cozzens, was considerable interest. His next novel, *Guard of Honor,* which is possibly his best work, is set at an Air Force training base in Florida during World War II. This book won the Pulitzer Prize. *By Love Possessed,* published thirty-three years after Cozzens' first novel, achieved wide acceptance and high praise; the author was rediscovered, and there was a revival of interest in his earlier writing. This last novel details forty-nine hours in the life of a lawyer in an eastern community; it is a dispassionate chronicle of the varieties of love, ranging from altruism to carnality.

Despite the tardiness and the spectacular quality of James Gould Cozzens' success, his may ultimately prove to be among the firmest reputations in modern American fiction. He writes with a regard for clear English and a disdain for sentimentality; his style is purposely unliterary; and he manages complex structures with ease. All his novels are characterized by restraint and detachment, so that in the past critics have complained of his coldness and general readers have been repelled by his refusal to express sympathy. Nevertheless, Cozzens has created a group of superb male characters, reasonable men who, though necessarily imperfect, fulfill their duties and serve life.

BIBLIOGRAPHICAL REFERENCES: There is relatively little criticism of Cozzens' fiction. See Granville Hicks, "The Reputation of James Gould Cozzens," *College English,* XI (1950), 177–183; also Bernard DeVoto, "The Editor's Easy Chair," *Harper's* CXCVIII (1949), 70–73; John Fischer, "The Editor's Easy Chair," *ibid.,* CCXV (1957), 14–20; and *Time,* LXX (September 2, 1957), 72–78.

GEORGE CRABBE

Born: Aldeburgh, England
Date: December 24, 1754

Died: Trowbridge, England
Date: February 3, 1832

PRINCIPAL WORKS

POEMS: *Inebriety,* 1775; *The Candidate,* 1780; *The Library,* 1781; *The Village,* 1783; *The News-Paper,* 1785; *Poems,* 1807; *The Borough,* 1810; *Tales in Verse,* 1812; *Tales of the Hall,* 1819.

George Crabbe, born at Aldeburgh, Suffolk, on December 24, 1754, was the eldest son of a schoolmaster and revenue officer. In his youth, while apprenticed to a surgeon at Woodbridge, he met his future wife, Sarah Elmy, whom he addressed in his poems as "Mira." After practicing surgery for a time he began to despair of his aptitude for the profession, and in 1780, bearing with him his accumulated poems in manuscript, he went to London in the hope of subsisting by literature. (His didactic poem *Inebriety* had appeared in 1775.) Failing to sell anything but *The Candidate,* he applied to Edmund Burke, who became his patron and arranged for him to take holy orders. Crabbe, ordained in 1781, was given the curacy of his birthplace. In 1783, the year of his marriage, *The Village* was published, and in 1785, *The News-Paper.*

His financial circumstances improved little by little, but he brought out no more poems until 1807, when a collected edition was issued. He achieved some popularity with *The Borough* and *Tales in Verse,* and he gained the friendship of Sir Walter Scott. His wife's mind failed in her last years; she died in 1813. He himself lived until February 3, 1832, dying at Trowbridge, Wiltshire, where he had become rector in 1814.

Crabbe's poems have had many admirers, not the least of whom was Jane Austen. But having lagged behind the romantic poetical fashion in its own day, his work has seldom been judged on its substantial intrinsic merits.

BIBLIOGRAPHICAL REFERENCES: The earliest collection was the *Works*, 8 vols., 1834. The *Poetical Works* was edited by A. W. Ward, 3 vols, 1905–1906. More recent editions include *The Poetical Works of George Crabbe*, edited by A. J. and R. M. Carlyle, 1932 (rev. ed.), and *The Life and Poems of the Reverend George Crabbe by His Son*, edited by E. M. Forster, 1933. The standard biography is George Crabbe, *The Life of the Reverend George Crabbe*, 1834. Other studies include A. C. Ainger, *Crabbe*, 1903; René Huchon, *George Crabbe and His Times*, 1907; and *The Poems of George Crabbe: A Literary and Historical Study*, 1933.

HART CRANE

Born: Garrettsville, Ohio
Date: July 21, 1899

Died: Gulf of Mexico
Date: April 27, 1932

PRINCIPAL WORKS

POEMS: *White Buildings*, 1926; *The Bridge*, 1930; *Collected Poems*, 1933.
LETTERS: *The Letters of Hart Crane*, edited by Brom Weber, 1952.

(Harold) Hart Crane was a potentially great poet who was unable to channelize into his art sufficient energy of unifying order to balance the disorder of his personal life. Handicapped from childhood by the "curse of sundered parentage," he engaged in sexual and occupational perversities that further split him until he returned figuratively to the womb, actually to the sea, as a suicide at the age of thirty-three. Born in Garrettsville, Ohio, July 21, 1899, the only child of a prosperous family of New England background, Crane suffered a pattern of father-jealousy of the first male child which produced in him a panic over the obvious rejection that resulted eventually in *The Bridge*, an attempt on a highly abstract verbal plane to bring those "things together again which should never have been divided." However, before creating this culminating work he drifted from city to city from his sixteenth year on, writing poetry as he moved. Following publication of one of his poems in *The Little Review* when he was eighteen, he rejected an opportunity to go to college; instead, pursuing his interest in books, he found a job in

253

a bookstore in New York. He soon left this for work in a munitions plant, followed by employment in a Lake Erie shipyard, serving the while as associate editor of a little magazine, *The Pagan*. He finally went into advertising in New York after World War I.

More poems were published in *avant-garde* magazines like *The Dial*. Encouraged by such writers as Allen Tate and Laura Riding, he secured funds from philanthropist Otto Kahn in 1925 and quit advertising to devote his full time to poetry. *White Buildings,* his first volume, was published with a foreword by Allen Tate. Crane was a poet of the city; the loneliness in material standards was aggravated in him by his feeling of inadequacy. (His father, a successful businessman, was at him until his own death a year before his son's to give up the "poetry nonsense.") The objective purpose of these poems was to fuse the artifacts of the city with romantic idealizations of the past to create a modern romanticism for city life. It was an attempt in the tradition of Walt Whitman, the poet Crane most admired. His poetry fell short of his goal; unlike Whitman, he was not willing to reveal himself frankly—although he expressed himself fully. The result was a confused combination of clear, brilliant imagery and incoherent private symbolization. What he needed most, some critics felt, was a theme to embody his uncoördinated imagery.

After three years of further travel, including Europe, Crane finished and published *The Bridge*. A theme had been found, and the result won him the Levinson Prize from *Poetry* in 1930 and a Guggenheim Fellowship the following year. The poem is a triumph of the use of the principle of "objective correlative" in which the images are arranged on the basis of emotional rather than logical effect, with the meaning emerging in the reader's mind at the end—depending, of course, upon the quality of the mind. The language is still occasionally poorly arranged grammatically, however, and the element of confusion, heightened by certain completely private passages, still exists to a degree sufficient to mark the work as a whole imperfect, though impressive in many of its parts.

Crane was not able to achieve necessary order in his art, and for a man of his sensitivity it was the only way for survival—other than self-discipline, which he was even less capable of achieving. Returning from Mexico, where he had gone during the year of his fellowship, he jumped into the Gulf of Mexico on April 27, 1932. His body was not recovered.

BIBLIOGRAPHICAL REFERENCES: *The Collected Poems of Hart Crane,* edited by Waldo Frank, 1933 (reissued 1946), includes an introduction and previously uncollected poems. The correspondence has been published in *Letters, 1916–1932,* edited by Brom Weber, 1952. Philip Horton's biography, *Hart Crane,* 1937, is excellent and is in no way superseded by Brom Weber, *Hart Crane,* 1948, which includes an appendix of uncollected prose and poetry. *Hart Crane, A Bibliography,* 1955, is by Hershel D. Rowe.

Commentary by an associate appears in Gorham B. Munson, *Destinations,* 1928. Crane has been the subject of a flood of magazine articles, and it is possible here only to list what seem to be the leading ones: Yvor Winters, "The Progress of Hart Crane," *Poetry,* XXXVI (1930), 153–165—an essentially unfriendly view; Morton

Dauwen Zabel, "The Book of Hart Crane," *ibid.*, XLII (1933), 33–39; Waldo Frank, "An Introduction to Hart Crane," *New Republic*, LXXIV (1933), 11–16; R. P. Blackmur, "New Thresholds, New Anatomies: Notes on a Text by Hart Crane," *The Double Agent*, 1935; Allen Tate, *Reactionary Essays on Poetry and Ideas*, 1936; F. R. Leavis, "Hart Crane from this Side," *Scrutiny*, VII (1939), 443–446; Malcolm Cowley, "Remembering Hart Crane," *New Republic*, CIV (1941), 504–506; Howard Moss, "Disorder as Myth: Hart Crane's *The Bridge*," *Poetry*, LXII (1943), 32–45; and Joseph Frank, "Hart Crane: American Poet," *Sewanee Review*, LVII (1949), 156–158.

STEPHEN CRANE

Born: Newark, New Jersey
Date: November 1, 1871

Died: Badenweiler, Germany
Date: June 5, 1900

PRINCIPAL WORKS

NOVELS: *Maggie: A Girl of the Streets*, 1893; *The Red Badge of Courage: An Episode of the American Civil War*, 1895; *George's Mother*, 1896; *The Third Violet*, 1897; *Active Service*, 1899; *The O'Ruddy*, 1903 (completed by Robert Barr).

SHORT STORIES: *The Little Regiment and Other Episodes of the American Civil War*, 1896; *The Open Boat and Other Tales of Adventure*, 1898; *The Monster and Other Stories*, 1899; *Whilomville Stories*, 1900; *Wounds in the Rain: War Stories*, 1900.

POEMS: *The Black Riders*, 1895; *War Is Kind*, 1899.

HISTORY: *Great Battles of the World*, 1901.

Stephen Crane was the fourteenth child born into the ministerial household of the Reverend Jonathan Crane and his wife Mary, at Newark, New Jersey, on November 1, 1871. The father's frequent moves to pastorates in New Jersey and New York gave the youngest Crane an opportunity to grow up under changing environments and stimuli. As a boy he shocked his family by announcing his disbelief in hell, a protest against the apparent futility of his father's devoted service to Methodism. Ideals with which the Reverend Jonathan Crane sternly allied himself did not correspond to life as his son came to know it. Stephen later wrote, "He was so simple and good that I often think he didn't know much of anything about humanity." Although physically frail, Stephen was essentially an outdoorsman. At Lafayette College (1889–1890) and at Syracuse University (1890–1891) he distinguished himself at boxing and as a shortstop on the varsity team. Years later, Joseph Conrad paid tribute to him as a good shot and a fine horseman. Mary Crane's death ended her son's college career, and he was never to be formally well educated. His real education sprang from a keen ability to observe and learn from the life around him.

Crane moved to New York City where he lived a precarious five years as a free lance writer for the newspapers. While working for *The Herald*, the fledgling reporter studied the intimate nature of the Bowery. He slept in Bowery shelters, for he wanted the truth of the life he witnessed. None escaped his keen observation: the beggar, the vagrant, the harlot—the life of the East Side world. During the two

255

days before Christmas of 1891, the twenty-year-old reporter wrote his first novel. The characters were nameless and the book untitled. A brother, William Crane, suggested a title, *Maggie: A Girl of the Streets*. Meanwhile *The Herald* had either fired Crane or he had dismissed himself. Actually, Crane was not a successful reporter. Copy which he submitted was rich in impressions but often lacked the basic facts of the event.

Maggie was not a respectable book. Its author, having borrowed a thousand dollars from his brother William, published it early in 1893 under a pseudonym, Johnston Smith. Impressed by *Maggie*, Hamlin Garland became the first established writer to show faith in Crane's talent, but the book did not sell; only a hundred copies of the seven hundred printed were sold. It was not until 1896 that the book was reissued under its author's name. In it Crane had discovered the slum as literary material; thus naturalism entered American letters, and from that obscure beginning his feeling for dialect and his knowledge of American life fastened his fiction in reality. In contrast to the light romances of its period, *Maggie* proclaimed a world without virtue. Since Crane's outlook was cynical, he was not disposed to cry the cause of his heroine, Maggie Johnson, nor to expect a reform of the environment which spawned her. Then, too, Maggie is never lifelike enough to evoke pity. She resembles a figure in a Greek drama whose fate is sealed before the play begins.

Through his reading and endless conversations with Civil War veterans, young Stephen had grown up intrigued by war. In ten days and nights of intense labor he wrote the first American novel to describe not only what a soldier did but how he felt. Written in Edmund Crane's home at Lakeview, New Jersey, *The Red Badge of Courage* first appeared in installment form in *The Philadelphia Press*, the manuscript having been sold to Irving Bacheller's newspaper syndicate in February, 1894, for less than a hundred dollars. Publication in book form was delayed until October 3, 1895, for the author, commissioned by the Bacheller syndicate, was away traveling in the West, the Southwest, and Mexico. With his second novel Crane was established as a major novelist, but success and fame were never to bring him much money.

The Red Badge of Courage depicted a youth confused and battered about by war as Crane had been by life. Written about the little man, the book appealed to the American mind. Henry Fleming, the farmer's boy, seemed real enough. Even the officers were human. Crane, always eager for new sensations and with a seeming personal delight in danger, wrote of war as he imagined it. In the tense and telegraphic manner peculiar to him, he flashed a series of individual pictures of war, each heightened by color images reflecting the psychological horror of the event. Henry Fleming's fear was one which Crane himself felt, and Henry's victory over fear was not a true victory. It stands for that effort which man manages somehow to make. Man sees; despite his seeing, he goes onward.

Crane's characters do not fashion their worlds. Things happen to them, and under stress they react as the event dictates. The author feels no sentimental concern for Maggie or Henry; they mirror the brutal forces of their environments and are not distinct personalities. Maggie's mind is not entered by the novelist, but it seems certain that she will be battered to death by an environment which she is powerless to escape. Henry's mind is entered, and in entering it the author unlocks the thoughts and emotions of mankind at war.

Shipwrecked off the coast of Florida while serving with a Cuban filibustering expedition in 1896, Crane experienced hardships which may have contributed to his early death. In Jacksonville he met Cora Taylor, a woman older than himself, who was to follow him as he covered the Greco-Turkish War for *The New York Journal*. Stephen and Cora were married in Greece.

Notoriety arising from false reports that he was addicted to liquor and morphine may have influenced Crane's decision to establish residence in England. Having developed strong friendships with Joseph Conrad and Henry James, he remained in England except for a brief return to cover the Spanish-American War for *The World*. Crane was brave if not foolhardy under fire, and the fatigue of battle further broke his health. Conrad, perhaps Crane's most intimate friend, was displeased to witness at Brede Place, Sussex, shortly before Crane's death, an unhappy talent lost in a maze of hack work.

On assignment as a special writer for the *London Morning Post*, he collapsed, ill from the tuberculosis which caused his death in Badenweiler, Germany, on June 5, 1900, after a futile trip to the Black Forest in search of a cure. His body was returned to the family plot in Elizabeth, New Jersey.

A trail-blazer of unquestioned sincerity, Crane felt and knew that what he wrote was of the essence of truth. Portraying a universe without meaning or order, he sensed only that his task was to point out the cutting irony of circumstances and to probe the fate of his experimental men and women as they reacted to the intensely cruel pressures of a meaningless yet always victorious circumstance. Within these limits he perfected an art; beyond them, during the short time allotted him, he did not care to explore. It may be that he saw no reason to explore, for it may be that he saw nothing there.

BIBLIOGRAPHICAL REFERENCES: The standard edition is *The Works of Stephen Crane*, edited by Wilson Follett, 12 vols., 1925–1927; and by the same editor, *The Collected Poems of Stephen Crane*, 1930. For biography and criticism see Thomas Beer, *Stephen Crane: A Study in American Letters*, with an Introduction by Joseph Conrad, 1923; John Berryman, *Stephen Crane*, in the American Men of Letters Series, 1950; Edward Garnett, "Stephen Crane and His Work," in *Friday Nights*, 1922; Matthew Josephson, *Portrait of the Artist as American*, 1930; Alfred Kazin, *On Native Grounds*, 1942; V. S. Pritchett, *The Living Novel*, 1946; Alexander Cowie, *The Rise of the American Novel*, 1948; R. W. Stallman, Introduction to *The Red Badge of Courage*, Modern Library edition, 1951; Daniel G. Hoffman, Introduction to *The Red Badge of Courage*, Harper's Modern Classics edition, 1957; also H. T. Webster, "Wilbur F. Hinman's *Corporal Si Klegg* and Stephen Crane's *Red Badge of Courage*," *American Literature*, II (1939), 285–293; John Schroeder, "Stephen Crane Embattled," in *University of Kansas City Review*, XVII (1950), 119–129; and Scott C. Osborn, "Stephen Crane's Imagery: 'Pasted Like a Wafer,'" *American Literature*, XXIII (1951), 362.

PROSPER JOLYOT DE CRÉBILLON

Born: Dijon, France   Died: Paris, France
Date: January 13, 1674   Date: June 17, 1762

PRINCIPAL WORKS

PLAYS: *Idoménée*, 1705; *Atrée et Thyeste*, 1707; *Électre*, 1709; *Rhadamiste et Zénobie*, 1711; *Pyrrhus*, 1726; *Catilina*, 1748; *Le Triumvirat*, 1754.

The famous father of a notorious son, Prosper Jolyot de Crébillon was born in Dijon on January 13, 1674. Like his father before him, he studied for the law. His early education completed in a Jesuit school, he attended the Collège Mazarin, and became an advocate in Paris. When a series of tragedies, the death of his young wife and his father, left him with two small sons and many enemies jealous of his early dramatic successes, he went into retirement for a number of years. Success returned with *Pyrrhus*, one of his many plays in the heroic, neo-classic tradition; and in 1731 he was elected to the French Academy. A post as royal censor in 1735 was followed by a pension from Madame de Pompadour and a sinecure in the royal library.

Voltaire, said to have written a depreciation of Crébillon out of jealousy of the only other ranking tragic poet of the age, was also quick to duplicate his work. Though their plays are not often read now—and never produced—Crébillon's are more stageworthy, even though marked with bombast, inaccurate history, false tears, and horrific scenes. He died in Paris at an advanced age on June 17, 1762, survived by his novelist son, Claude Prosper Jolyot de Crébillon the controversial writer of the lascivious *The Sofa* (1745).

BIBLIOGRAPHICAL REFERENCES: Jean G. Palache, *Four Novelists of the Old Regime*, 1926, includes a study of Crébillon. See also M. Dutrait, *Crébillon*, 1895.

MICHEL-GUILLAUME JEAN DE CRÈVECŒUR

Born: Lesches, near Caen, France   Died: Sarcelles, France
Date: January 31, 1735   Date: November 12, 1813

PRINCIPAL WORKS

LETTERS AND ESSAYS: *Letters from an American Farmer*, 1782; *Voyage dans la haute Pensylvanie et dans l'État de New York*, 1801 (*Travels in Pennsylvania and New York*); *Sketches of Eighteenth Century America*, 1925.

One of the first and certainly one of the most artistic depicters of colonial America was a man who did not learn English until he was sixteen, Michel-Guillaume Jean de Crèvecœur, who published his first book in London under the pseudonym of J. Hector St. John. Descended from an old Norman family, he was born at Lesches, France, on January 31, 1735, and educated by Jesuits. He came to America in 1754, married, and in 1769 settled on a farm in Orange County, New York. After three months in prison on suspicion of espionage during the American Revolution, he returned to France. There Rochefoucauld befriended him, arranged for the publication of his letters, and got him a consulship in New York. On his return to America in 1783, Crèvecœur found his farm burned, his wife dead, his family scattered. He then threw himself zealously into developing French-American relationships.

His great work, *Letters from an American Farmer,* contains political philosophy, economics, agronomy, and colonial history, but it is chiefly marked by a visionary idealism, certitude that America could be the brave new world. The descriptions of Nantucket and Martha's Vineyard are particularly idyllic. However, he strikes a dark note in describing the terrible institution of Negro slavery in "Descriptions of Charles-Town."

The picturesque *Voyage dans la haute Pensylvanie et dans l'État de New York* pretends to be a translation from an early Oneida Indian manuscript, but the work is actually based on his own early travels with his friend, Benjamin Franklin.

Ill health constantly interrupted his diplomatic work and finally in 1790 he returned to France, where he lived with his daughter and son-in-law until his death at Sarcelles on November 12, 1813.

BIBLIOGRAPHICAL REFERENCES: There is no collected edition. A reprint of the 1792 *Letters,* edited with a preface by William P. Trent and an introduction by Ludwig Lewisohn, was published in 1904 (reissued, 1925). The story of the recovered *Sketches,* edited by Henri L. Bourdin, Ralph H. Gabriel, and Stanley T. Williams, 1925, is told in Bourdin and Williams, "The Unpublished Manuscripts of Crève-cœur," *Studies in Philology,* XXII (1925), 425–432.

Biographical studies include Julia P. Mitchell, *St. Jean de Crèvecœur,* 1916, and Howard C. Rice, *Le Cultivateur Americaine; Étude sur l'Œuvre de Saint John de Crèvecœur,* 1933. For briefer studies see the article by Stanley T. Williams in the *Dictionary of National Biography* and Vernon L. Parrington, *Main Currents in American Thought,* Vol. I, 1927.

DAVID CROCKETT

Born: Limestone, Tennessee
Date: August 17, 1786

Died: The Alamo, San Antonio, Texas
Date: March 6, 1836

PRINCIPAL WORKS

AUTOBIOGRAPHY: *A Narrative of the Life of David Crockett,* 1834.

TRAVEL SKETCHES: *An Account of Col. Crockett's Tour to the North and Down East,* 1835.

The "real" Davy Crockett who was born at Limestone on the Tennessee frontier on August 17, 1786, has all but yielded his place on the stage to the more striking images of him created by political manipulators and hero worshipers. While he was yet living he was fast becoming a legend as the bear hunter of the Shakes, the deadly marksman with his lethal grin, the droll yarn-spinner, the coonskin hero of Whiggism. His death at the Alamo on

March 6, 1836, made him a demigod. His motto "Go ahead" expressed the national sentiment of his America, as he himself was the embodiment of the romantic daring and energy of the frontier.

It was not until he became a magistrate that Crockett learned to read and write. After two terms in the Tennessee legislature he was sent to Congress in 1827 as a partisan of Jackson, under whose command he had served as scout in the campaign against the Creeks. During his first two terms he broke with the administration, and in his third he vigorously opposed Jackson's policy concerning the United States Bank. Defeated for reëlection in 1835 he went to Texas, where he was killed the following year, with Travis and Bowie, in the defense of the Alamo.

Aside from a few letters, very little of the works sometimes attributed to Crockett can be ascribed with confidence to his sole authorship. Even his speeches in Congress were probably touched up by a friend before being recorded, and the *Life* of Van Buren (1835) was largely the work of another. Both *Sketches and Eccentricities of Col. David Crockett* (1833) and *Col. Crockett's Exploits and Adventures in Texas* (1836), whoever wrote or compiled them, make use of Crockett's stories and belong to the vast body of legend concerning him. The *Narrative* itself, though bearing signs of another helping hand, is substantially Crockett's work. Valuable as a general picture of the times it achieves distinction as a realistic account of frontier life, and its language often attains a classic directness and simplicity.

BIBLIOGRAPHICAL REFERENCES: The chief biographical study of Crockett is Constance Rourke, *Davy Crockett*, 1934. The Crockett tales have been collected in Richard M. Dorson, *Davy Crockett: American Comic Legend*, 1939. The general subject of the American folk hero is covered in Frank Shay, *Here's Audacity! American Legendary Heroes*, 1930. Interested readers should also consult *A Narrative of the Life of David Crockett*, 1834, which purports to be an autobiography.

E. E. CUMMINGS

Born: Cambridge, Massachusetts
Date: October 14, 1894

Died: North Conway, New Hampshire
Date: September 3, 1962

PRINCIPAL WORKS

POEMS: *Tulips and Chimneys*, 1923; &, 1925; *XLI Poems*, 1925; *Is 5*, 1926; *Christmas Tree*, 1928; *W: Seventy New Poems*, 1931; *No Thanks*, 1935; *1/20 Poems*, 1936; *50 Poems*, 1940, *1 × 1*, 1944; *Poems: 1923–1954*, 1954.

PLAYS: *Him*, 1927; *Tom: A Ballet*, 1935; *Santa Claus: A Morality*, 1946.

NOVEL: *The Enormous Room*, 1922.

MISCELLANEOUS: *Eimi*, 1933; *i: six nonlectures*, 1953.

E(dward) E(stlin) Cummings (whom his critics sometimes disparagingly refer to as "lower case cummings" because of the trick typography of his poems) was born in Cambridge, Massachusetts, on October 14, 1894. His father was the Rev. Edward Cummings, who taught English at Harvard and Radcliffe and was a well-known preacher and lecturer. E. E. Cummings also attended Harvard, receiving his A.B. in 1915 and his M.A. in 1916. A year later he and Slater Brown, a Harvard friend, enlisted in the ambulance service and served as drivers for six months in France. Because of an error of the military censor, Cummings spent three months in a French prison. Out of this experience came *The Enormous Room*, a prose account of life in a military prison that contains none of the usual bitterness and self-pity found in such works. Instead Cummings looks at the daily life and the strange characters in the enormous room with the saucy eye and original wit so evident in his poems. Incidentally, Cummings refers to a friend of his in the novel as B; in the last few pages he is revealed as Brown. *The Enormous Room* may not be the most powerful book to come out of World War I, but it is certainly one of the most original and interesting.

After his release from the French prison, Cummings served as a private in the American infantry until the Armistice. He then returned to New York for two years. After this he spent some time in Paris, where he won recognition both as a poet and a painter. Cummings shuttled between these two cities for many years and finally settled in New York.

Between Cummings' first book, *Tulips and Chimneys*, and his *Poems, 1923–1954*, there is a sort of consistent inconsistency. His recurring themes are conventional: nature, which he treats with charming lyricism; love, which for Cummings can be idyllic or brutally sensual; the underdogs, both men and women, whom he tenderly champions; and the blatant materialism of our times, which he excoriates in witty satire. In the presentation of these themes Cummings turns into a fearless experimenter. Apparently believing that poems nowadays are read rather than recited, he uses every trick of typography to heighten his meaning; at his best he can picture his scene with the arrangement of words (as in "Sunset") or intensify his colloquial style (as in "Poem, or Beauty Hurts Mr. Vinal").

In 1952 Cummings was invited to deliver the Charles Eliot Norton lectures in poetry at Harvard. Characteristically, he refused to become a lecturer. His witty (and frequently wise) series of comments on poetry are entitled and published as *i: six nonlectures*.

In 1955 he received a special citation from the National Book Awards Committee for his collected poems.

About the middle of his career Cummings appeared headed for the oblivion of an *avant-garde* poet who fails to bound ahead of his competitors; but his complete work, although it shows no greater breadth now than in its beginning, reveals a poet who cannot be dismissed as an upstart innovator: his voice is an authentic one of our times and one that contains an element so frequently lacking in his dour contemporaries: a sense of humor.

BIBLIOGRAPHICAL REFERENCES: There is no extensive biographical study of Cummings, but the Cummings Number of *The Harvard Wake*, No. 5, (Spring, 1946) contains brief biographical and critical sketches by various hands. For further criticism see R. P. Blackmur, *The Double Agent*, 1935; Allen Tate, *Reactionary Essays in*

Poetry and Ideas, 1936; Babette Deutsch, *Poetry in Our Time,* 1956 (2nd ed.); also John Peale Bishop, "The Poems and Prose of E. E. Cummings," *Southern Review,* IV (1938), 173–186; Samuel I. Hayakawa, "Is Indeed 5," *Poetry,* LII (1938), 284–292; John Finch, "New England Prodigal," *New England Quarterly,* XII (1939), 643–653; and John Arthos, "The Poetry of E. E. Cummings," *American Literature,* XIV (1943), 372–383.

RICHARD HENRY DANA

Born: Cambridge, Massachusetts
Date: August 1, 1815

Died: Rome, Italy
Date: January 6, 1882

PRINCIPAL WORKS

TRAVEL AND ADVENTURE: *Two Years Before the Mast,* 1840; *To Cuba and Back,* 1859.

Richard Henry Dana, Jr., was born in Cambridge, Massachusetts, August 1, 1815, the son of Richard Henry Dana, critic and editor. He enrolled at Harvard University in 1831, but bad health and failing eyesight caused him to resign. Instead of taking a pleasure trip to Europe he sailed before the mast as a common sailor on the brig *Pilgrim.* This voyage around Cape Horn to California and Oregon furnished the material for his celebrated work, *Two Years Before the Mast.* Published in 1840, this book had a wide influence on other writers about the sea, and its realistic approach was much imitated. In this volume Dana was successful in bringing to public attention the hardships of a sailor's life. Today the book is also valuable as a picture of life in California in the nineteenth century.

After returning home from his trip Dana finished Harvard in 1837 and entered the law school there. After graduation he opened his law offices, specializing in maritime law. He also published *The Seaman's Friend* (1841) dealing with the responsibilities, duties, and legal rights of the sailor, a manual which was widely recognized and used both in the United States and in England. In 1859 he published *To Cuba and Back.*

Interested in politics, he early joined the Free Soil Movement. He was also an early member of the Republican Party. In 1860 he was interested in the presidential campaign and was appointed to the office of United States District Attorney for Massachusetts by President Lincoln. Meanwhile he won the *Amy Warwick* case, which was concerned with blockading Southern ports. In 1866 he published his extensive compendium on International Law entitled *Wheaton's International Law.* Thirteen years of litigation followed. In 1866 he ran for Congress unsuccessfully. In 1876 he was nominated by President Grant as Minister to England, but the Congress did not confirm the appointment. He also achieved distinction when he was asked to prosecute Jefferson Davis. In 1877 he was a member of a commission which met in Nova Scotia concerning problems of fisheries which arose between Britain and the United States. In 1879 he retired from his distinguished duties as a lawyer to spend the rest of his life writing and traveling. His death occurred in Rome on January 6, 1882.

Though he achieved his greatest fame
as a lawyer, he is chiefly remembered
for his famous story of life at sea, *Two
Years Before the Mast.*

BIBLIOGRAPHICAL REFERENCES: The definitive biography of Dana is Charles Francis
Adams' *Richard Henry Dana,* 1890. There is also an excellent essay on this writer
in Bliss Perry's *The Praise of Folly and Other Papers,* 1923.

GABRIELE D'ANNUNZIO

Born: Near Pescara, Italy
Date: March 12, 1863

Died: Gardone Riviera, Italy
Date: March 1, 1938

PRINCIPAL WORKS

POEMS: *Primo Vere,* 1879 (*First Verses*); *Canto Nuovo,* 1882 (*New Cantos*); *Terra
Vergine,* 1883 (*Virgin Ground*); *San Pantaleone,* 1886; *Il Poema Paradisiaco,* 1893
(*The Poem of Paradise*); *Le Laudi,* 1903–1912.

NOVELS: *Il Piacere,* 1889 (*The Child of Pleasure*); *L'Innocente,* 1892 (*The Intruder*); *Giovanni Episcopo,* 1892 (*Episcopo and Company*); *Il Trionfo della Morte,*
1894 (*The Triumph of Death*); *Le Vergini delle Rocca,* 1896 (*The Maidens of
the Rocks*); *Il Fuoco,* 1900 (*The Flame of Life*).

PLAYS: *Il Sogno d'un mattino di primavera,* 1897 (*The Dream of a Spring Morn-
ing*); *Il Sogno d'un tramonto d'autumno,* 1898 (*The Dream of an Autumn Sunset*);
La Città morta, 1898 (*The City of Death*); *La Gioconda,* 1899; *Francesca,* 1902
(*Francesca da Rimini*); *La Figlia di Jorio,* 1904 (*The Daughter of Jorio*).

Gabriele D'Annunzio, born near Pescara, Italy, on March 12, 1863, dedicated himself to literature as a fifteen-
year-old schoolboy when he wrote a
prize story that was published by an
Italian magazine. His first book of
verses, *First Verses,* was published
when he was sixteen, and he followed
this success with several other books of
poems. He was widely acclaimed as a
native genius, as a spirited and genuine
romantic poet. His first novel, *The
Child of Pleasure,* brought him many
new readers and increased his reputation as the romantic hero fighting
against mechanism and conventionality
in the modern world. D'Annunzio did
his best to live up to his reputation,
surrounding himself with luxury in his
elaborate homes (his career was always
financially successful) and a parade of
many wealthy or artistic mistresses. He

had an affair with Eleonora Duse that
lasted for several years in the 1890's.
In the meantime D'Annunzio's fame
spread all over Europe, where he was
alternately praised as the modern romantic hero and damned as a licentious
devil.

As a member of the Chamber of
Deputies he moved from the extreme
right to the extreme left to political indifference in the course of his three-
year term. After 1900 he spent a good
deal of time in France, always writing
very conscientiously, until he returned
to Italy to serve his native land in
World War I. During the war, D'Annunzio was one of the first Italian pilots;
he lost the sight of one eye while on a
reconnaissance mission for the Italian
Air Force. His war service is best
known, however, for his dramatic seizure of the disputed city of Fiume in

the name of the Italian government. D'Annunzio marched in with his troops and took over the city in September, 1919. Although he was opposed by the British, French, and American governments, even by the responsible Italian government (at one point, he even declared war on the Italian government), he managed to rule Fiume for nearly sixteen months before Italian troops came to relieve him and under the treaty of Rapallo restored the city to independence. One of the few Italians who approved D'Annunzio's gesture in Fiume was Benito Mussolini. D'Annunzio, in recognition of his service at Fiume, became Prince of Monte Nevoso in 1924.

D'Annunzio published a great deal during his life. Often, his work was criticized as derivative or as a pastiche of current literary styles. His novels, in particular, seemed to reflect other trends, for *The Child of Pleasure* parroted the sensitive and sensuous French novel of the day; *The Intruder* echoed the gloomy introversion of many Russian novels, and *The Triumph of Death*, with its suicide pact, seemed to parrot the German romantic novel with its *weltschmerz*. But to analyze D'Annunzio's lack of originality or lasting value is to forget the extraordinary range and popularity of the legend of the man and his life. As the popular romantic figure with the restless soul and dramatic gesture, he seems, more than most writers, to belong to a particular and irrevocable age. D'Annunzio died March 1, 1938, at Gardone Riviera, Italy.

BIBLIOGRAPHICAL REFERENCES: The colorful career of D'Annunzio provides rich material for biographers. Tommaso Antongini, *D'Annunzio*, 1936, is translated from the Italian. Berlita Harding, *Age Cannot Wither*, 1947, tells the story of Duse and D'Annunzio; this work includes a bibliography. One of the best books on the material is Frances Winwar, *Wingless Victory*, 1956, a biography of Duse and D'Annunzio, which includes an excellent bibliography. See also Charles Herford, "Gabrielle d'Annunzio," *Bulletin of the John Rylands Library*, V (1918–1920), 418–444.

DANTE ALIGHIERI

Born: Florence, Italy
Date: May, 1265

Died: Ravenna, Italy
Date: September 13 or 14, 1321

PRINCIPAL WORKS

POEMS: *Vita Nuova*, c. 1292 (*The Young Life*); *Commedia*, c. 1320 (later *La Divina Commedia, The Divine Comedy*).

TREATISES: *De Vulgari Eloquentia*, c. 1305 (*On the Illustrious Vernacular*); *Convivio*, c. 1307 (*The Banquet*); *De Monarchia*, 1310–1312 (*On Monarchy*).

Dante Alighieri, author of *The Divine Comedy*, was born in May, 1265, into a Florentine family of noble lineage but humble circumstances. His father was Alighiero di Bellincione d'Alighiero, of a family which can be traced back to the second crusade. His mother's name was Bella; she may have been the daughter of Durante di Scolaio degli Abati, a name that would

264

account for the "Dante," a contraction of "Durante." Dante's family was connected with the Guelphs, the papal party antagonistic to the imperial Ghibellines. He was baptized in the San Giovanni Baptistery.

Despite the family's financial status, Dante was somehow able to be educated as a gentleman, and he probably studied rhetoric in Bologna. He formed a close friendship with the poet Guido Cavalcanti and also a less worthy relationship with the abusive poet Forese Donati. Part of Dante's youth was spent in military service; he was a mounted soldier fighting with the Florentine Guelphs when they defeated the Aretines at Campaldino in 1289.

Not much else of Dante's early life is known, but perhaps the most significant events from the perspective of literary history were those involving a Florentine girl, Beatrice, or Bice, Portinari, later the wife of Simone de' Bardi. Dante first met her when he was nine and she was eight, and from the first moment he was fascinated by her. Although he saw her several times during the next nine years, she never spoke to him until one May morning in 1285. The depth of his emotional response and the increasing role she played in his life as an image of everything good and divine is known because of Dante's love poems in his *Vita Nuova*, composed over a period of years and finally gathered together about the year 1292. This same Beatrice came to play a significant role as his sponsor in his trip through Paradise, as told in his *The Divine Comedy*.

Upon returning to his chambers, after having been greeted by Beatrice, young Dante composed his first known sonnet. When he sent the poem to several famous poets, a reply from Guido Cavalcanti began his strongest friendship.

Since Dante was a romantic poet, aware of the customs of his day and influenced by them, he thought it proper to be seen with other young ladies so as to hide his love of Beatrice. Consequently, when he saw her again she failed to greet him, and the effect of this rebuff was devastating—at least, at first, before the experience became one from which he drew strength as a poet. Each experience involving Beatrice gave him new lyrical images and prompted new ideas concerning her spiritual significance. The poems which were to become the *Vita Nuova* continued to grow.

Dante may have been a distraught witness at Beatrice's wedding party when she married Simone de' Bardi, sometime about 1285, although he may have been solaced by the realization that the marriage was a family arrangement, not a matter of the heart. When Beatrice's father died, probably sometime in the latter part of 1289, Dante began to reflect on death and to fear that it might come to Beatrice. In fact, it soon did; his romanticism had not in this case exceeded itself; Beatrice died on June 8, 1290, about six months after her father.

Dante's sorrow was followed by reflection, his reflection by imagination; soon he was poetically imagining Beatrice as one of the glories of paradise. He enjoyed a romantic interlude with a consoling woman, but he soon regarded his behavior as faithless to the memory of Beatrice. Gathering his scattered poems together, reworking and ordering them, he formed them into a complete volume, *Vita Nuova*, a work celebrating the new life which his love of Beatrice made possible.

His interest in lyrical expression was tempered from the beginning by the desire to discipline his poetry both by reference to the poetic conventions and by self-imposed intellectual constraints. The philosophies of Aristotle and Aquinas were preëminent in those days, and like other young poets and intellectuals of his time Dante believed that it was his duty to know as much as possible of their ideas. About 1290, when Dante was twenty-five, he began an intensive two or three year study of philosophy, some of it, in all probability, with the Franciscans of Santa Croce.

A year or two later he married Gemma di Manetto Donati, in accordance with an arrangement made by his father about fourteen years earlier. Boccaccio, who wrote of Dante's meetings with Beatrice, also told of this marriage, giving the impression that Gemma left Dante little time for writing and reflection, and that she made him take part in small talk with her friends. However, Boccaccio cannot be trusted as a historian. In any case, there were children of this marriage: Jacopo, Pietro, Antonia (who may have been the "Beatrice" who became a nun at Ravenna), and perhaps Johannes.

After his marriage Dante became active in the political life of Florence. In order to be eligible for election to the councils, in 1295 he joined the guild of physicians and apothecaries, probably because a young man of philosophic and artistic interests was acceptable there. He was consequently elected and summoned to several councils, and then, as a result of his service as an ambassador to San Gimignano,

was elected in 1300 as one of the six priors of Florence—the highest office in the city—and served for two months, from June 15 to August 15, leaving office just in time to escape being excommunicated by Pope Boniface VIII. By that time the Guelphs had split into two factions. The Blacks, led by Corso Donati, were sympathetic to the Pope; the Whites, headed by Vieri de' Cerchi, refused an invitation from the Pope to make peace with the Blacks and restore unity to the Guelphs. Consequently, Dante and other municipal leaders recommended the banishment from Florence of the leaders of both factions—including his best friend, Guido Cavalcanti of the Whites, who died in exile. Then, in the effort to forestall the plans of Pope Boniface to use Charles of Valois, the French prince, for the recovery of Sicily and the conquest of the Tuscany rebels, Dante—who was by that time a White—was sent with two others in 1301 as envoys to the Pope. While Dante was in Rome, Charles entered Florence and took control of the city in support of the Blacks. On January 27, 1302, Dante and four other Whites were charged with barratry and as punishment were fined and exiled. On March 10, since Dante failed to appear, it was declared that he would be burned alive if he reëntered Florence. Later the same sentence was passed on his sons, to take effect when they reached the age of fourteen.

For the next twenty years, until his death, Dante lived in exile, staying in various cities: San Godenzo, Forli, Verona, and Ravenna. He made several attempts to be readmitted to Florence —including the writing of The Divine Comedy—and would perhaps have succeeded had he been willing to do public penance and had he not written an angry letter to the Florentines accusing them of crimes against honest men. When the Holy Roman Emperor Henry VII descended into Italy to restore peace, Dante hoped that the emperor's victory would pave the way for his readmission to Florence. He wished the emperor success and paid him homage, but he would not join him in the fight against Florence. Dante's hopes were ended, however, when the death of Henry in 1313 put an end to the Italian campaign.

Dante's positive efforts to express his ideas of right action and civic duty and to say something about the kind of language appropriate to poetry resulted in two treatises, *On the Illustrious Vernacular* and *The Banquet*, composed in the period 1304–07. But these works were never completed because he interrupted them to begin a master poem,

one in which Beatrice would function as the spirit of everything good and divine, the spirit of love, guiding Dante through Paradise: the *Commedia* (known to later generations, who added a word, as *The Divine Comedy*).

According to Dante, the poem has four levels of meaning: the literal, the allegorical, the moral, and the anagogical—that is, it tells of Dante's trip through Hell, Purgatory, and Paradise; it shows how the soul progresses; it suggests the right way of life; and it relates man's state to the Divine.

Shortly after completing his greatest poem, the outstanding work of the medieval period, Dante died on September 13 or 14 in 1321 in Ravenna, after having contracted some disease, perhaps malaria, on his return from a mission to Venice.

Ian McGreal

BIBLIOGRAPHICAL REFERENCES: Of the many editions of *The Divine Comedy* in English, two of the most recent and in many ways the best are the translations of the *Inferno* and the *Purgatorio* by Dorothy L. Sayers, Penguin Classics series, 1949 and 1955. There are two important contemporary accounts of his life, Giovanni Boccaccio's *Vita di Dante* and Leonardo Bruni's *Vita,* both appearing in English translation by J. R. Smith, 1901. The standard modern biography is Michele Barbi, *Dante: Vita, opere e fortuna,* 1933 (English translation, 1954). Important recent contributions to Dante studies are Dorothy L. Sayers, *Introductory Papers on Dante,* 1954, and *Further Papers on Dante,* 1957.

See also Giovanni Scartazzini, *Enciclopedia dantesca,* 3 vols., 1896–1905; Paget Toynbee, *Dante Alighiere,* 1910; Francesco Torraca, *Studi danteschi,* 1912; *idem, Nuovi Studi danteschi,* 1921; Charles H. Grandgent, *Dante,* 1916; Benedetto Croce, *La Poesia di Dante,* 1921 (English translation, 1922); Corrado Ricci, *L'ultimo refugio di Dante Alighieri,* 1921 (2nd ed.); Karl Vossler, *Medieval Culture: An Introduction to Dante and His Times,* 2 vols., 1929; T. S. Eliot, *Dante,* 1929 (reprinted in *Selected Essays,* 1932); Charles Williams, *The Figure of Beatrice: A Study in Dante,* 1943; Umberto Cosmo, *A Handbook to Dante Studies,* 1947; and Aldo Vallone, *La critica dantesca contemporeana,* 1953.

CHARLES DARWIN

Born: Shrewsbury, England
Date: February 12, 1809

Died: Down, England
Date: April 19, 1882

SCIENTIFIC ESSAYS AND STUDIES: *On the Origin of Species by Means of Natural Selection*, 1859; *The Variation of Animals and Plants under Domestication*, 1868; *The Descent of Man, and Selection in Relation to Sex*, 1871.

JOURNAL: *Diary of the Voyage of H.M.S. "Beagle,"* 1839.

The work of Charles (Robert) Darwin is of inestimable importance in the history of man and the history of science, and the publication of his *Origin of Species* in 1859 marks a turning point in the thinking of the Western world. Somewhat ironically, Darwin studied for two different professions before he turned to biology and science.

Darwin, grandson of Erasmus Darwin, was born at Shrewsbury, England, on February 12, 1809; his father was a physician and his mother a daughter of the noted English potter, Josiah Wedgwood. Darwin's mother died when he was eight years old, and his rearing was largely at the hands of older sisters. As a boy he attended Shrewsbury School, then under the direction of Dr. Samuel Butler, an educator who, devoted to a classical regimen of learning, deplored young Darwin's attention to chemistry in a home laboratory. Darwin's father intended his son for the medical profession, and so young Charles Darwin entered Edinburgh University in 1825. The study of medicine proved distasteful, however, and in 1828 Darwin entered Cambridge University to prepare himself for a career as an Anglican clergyman. While at Cambridge he became friendly with John Stevens Henslow, the famous professor of botany, through whom Darwin received his opportunity to sail as a naturalist on the official British exploration ship, H.M.S. *Beagle*.

At first Darwin's father refused to consent to this change of careers, but at the urging of Josiah Wedgwood he finally withdrew his objections and young Darwin, as the unpaid naturalist, sailed on the *Beagle* for South America and the Pacific Ocean on December 27, 1831. When he left England, Darwin was practically uneducated in science, certainly untried as a specialist in science. When he returned to England in 1836, almost five years later, he had had an unequaled practical education and experience in science, having acquired first-hand experience in methodical scientific observation over a large portion of the earth's surface. His experience, by giving him a tremendous knowledge of living creatures, had already turned his thinking to the possibility of evolution. In his travels he had seen many living creatures and organisms of his own age and from earlier geological eras. In the years immediately after his return to England, Darwin spent his time disposing of his collections of specimens and writing and editing the voluminous reports that came from the five-year exploratory trip, including the *Zoölogy of the Voyage of H.M.S. "Beagle"* (1840–1846). The voyage had taken its toll of Darwin's constitution, however, and he never again experienced good health. Two years after his marriage to Emma Wedgwood, a cousin, he was forced to leave London to take up residence in the countryside near Down, where excitement and nervous tension were at a minimum. Years later, when his books created a storm of protest and controversy, ill-health required Darwin to leave the defense of his work to Thomas Henry Huxley and others. In fact, for more than forty years weakness and illness prevented Darwin's working for more than a few hours at a time.

Although it was not published until 1859, *The Origin of Species* began to take form in Darwin's writings as early as 1842; a manuscript of 1844 clearly defines the theory. At the urging of Lyell, Darwin began to compile the results of years of research and study, but before he was finished, in June, 1858, Darwin received a manuscript from A. R. Wallace, then in Malaya, in which an identical theory of mutation was set forth. Upon the advice of fellow scientists, Wallace's paper and one by Darwin were presented to the Linnean Society in July, 1858. The full book, *On the Origin of Species,* was published the following year. In 1868 certain aspects of his theory were more fully developed in *The Variation of Animals and Plants under Domestication. The Descent of Man* grew in its turn out of the 1868 volume and included man as one of the animals which had evolved through the epochs of geological history. During the rest of his life Darwin gave his time to publishing papers and books on botany, works of very little interest to a general reader. He died at his home near Down, Kent, on April 19, 1882.

Darwin's most important books are remembered as landmarks in history because they gave weight to what had previously been merely hypotheses. Linnaeus had already classified man as an anthropoid, but it was left for Darwin to present evidence of an overwhelming kind for the hypothesis. Today evolution is an accepted fact; although not every biologist is a Darwinian, there is not one of stature and reputation who does not believe in some form of evolution.

BIBLIOGRAPHICAL REFERENCES: The principal writings of Charles Darwin have now been collected in *The Darwin Reader,* edited by Marston Bates and Philip S. Humphrey, 1957. There is also a definitive edition of *Charles Darwin's Diary of the Voyage of H.M.S. "Beagle,"* edited by Nora Barlow, 1934. A collection of Darwinian excerpts, *What Darwin Really Said,* was edited by Julian Huxley, 1929.

The standard biography is Francis Darwin, *The Life and Letters of Charles Darwin,* 3 vols., 1887 (rev. ed., 1911). For other biographical and critical studies see also Leonard Huxley, *Darwin,* 1921; Gamaliel Bradford, *Darwin,* 1926; G. A. Dorsey, *The Evolution of Charles Darwin,* 1927; Geoffrey West, *Charles Darwin: The Fragmentary Man,* 1937; H. G. Wells, *Charles Darwin: A Portrait,* 1938; and Sir Arthur Keith, *Darwin Revalued,* 1955.

ALPHONSE DAUDET

Born: Nîmes, France
Date: May 13, 1840

Died: Paris, France
Date: December 16, 1897

PRINCIPAL WORKS

NOVELS: *Le Petit Chose,* 1868 (*The Little Good-for-Nothing*); *Les Aventures prodigieuses de Tartarin de Tarascon,* 1872 (*Tartarin of Tarascon*); *Robert Helmont,* 1874; *Fromont jeune et Risler aîné,* 1874 (*Fromont and Risler*); *Jack,* 1876; *Le*

Nabab, 1877 (*The Nabob*); *Les Rois en exil,* 1879 (*Kings in Exile*); *Numa Roumestan,* 1881; *L'Evangéliste,* 1883; *Sapho,* 1884; *Tartarin sur les Alpes,* 1885 (*Tartarin on the Alps*); *L'Immortel,* 1888; *Port Tarascon,* 1890.

SHORT STORIES AND SKETCHES: *Lettres de mon moulin,* 1869 (*Letters from My Mill*); *Contes du lundi,* 1873 (*Monday Tales*); *Contes choisis, la fantaisie et l'histoire,* 1879.

POEMS: *Les Amoureuses,* 1858.

BIOGRAPHY AND MEMOIRS: *Lettres à un absent,* 1871 (*Letters to an Absent One*); *Les Femmes d'artistes,* 1874 (*Artists' Wives*); *Trente ans de Paris,* 1887 (*Thirty Years in Paris*); *Souvenirs d'un homme de lettres,* 1888 (*Memories of a Man of Letters*).

PLAYS: *La Dernière Idole,* 1862; *Les Absents,* 1863; *L'Œillet blanc,* 1864; *Le Frère âiné,* 1868; *L'Arlésienne,* 1872.

Alphonse Daudet is among the most durable of the literary figures of France in the last half of the nineteenth century. His poetic approach to realism has made him universally popular, for, unlike his contemporaries, he wrote with a sympathy and a cautious optimism that produced an appealing tenderness without recourse to mawkish sentimentality. Critics, who find his prose difficult to define, have termed him variously a realist, a naturalist, an impressionist, and an independent. Daudet himself professed to follow no school, maintaining all such inflexibility to be absurd.

A native of Nîmes, in Provence, where he was born on May 13, 1840, and where his family struggled to preserve a rapidly failing silk weaving business, Daudet grew up in a period of financial crises which taught him sympathy for all human failings. At sixteen he was forced to take a position as a novice instructor in a small provincial school at Alais where he suffered innumerable humiliations and hardships, most of which he later incorporated into his first novel, *The Little Good-for-Nothing.* Two years later he joined his brother in Paris to seek his fortune as an author. Believ-

ing himself destined to be a poet, Daudet made his debut with a small volume of poetry patterned after the romantic verses of Alfred de Musset. Entitled *Les Amoureuses,* the collection had a vogue in the salons of the period and brought him to the attention of the Duc de Morny, who hired him as a secretary. It was at this time that Daudet was stricken with a nervous disease which was to plague him until his death.

Once settled in Paris, Daudet began a succession of novels and collections of short stories which were to establish him firmly as an important author. *Letters from My Mill* is a volume of short stories whose setting is Daudet's beloved Provence; the work contains some of Daudet's most delightful sketches. The Franco-Prussian war produced *Letters to an Absent One,* a collection of semi-historical reminiscences of the war. In 1872 he published the first of the amusing Tartarin trilogy, *Tartarin of Tarascon,* the story of a Provençal who sets out for Algeria to make good his boasts that he is a first-rate killer of lions. *Tartarin on the Alps* and *Port Tarascon* complete the trilogy. Crowned by the French Academy, *Fromont and Risler*, wherein a jealous, scheming wife ruins a prosperous business partnership, is considered by many to be Daudet's finest novel, marking the point at which Daudet turned from his native Provence to write of the manners and mores of the Second Empire. *Jack* is a two-volume treatise of the struggles of a young boy to come to terms with life in the face of an indifferent mother and her pseudo-intellectual lover. *The Nabob* depicts the attempts of a wealthy Tunisian expatriate to buy respectability in Parisian society. *Kings in Exile* gives a vivid picture of the plight of exiled royalty struggling to maintain a life it can no longer afford.

Other novels exploring various segments of Parisian society include *Numa Roumestan*, a novel of manners; *Sapho*, concerning the vicissitudes of a young provincial who finds a mistress in Paris only to become ensnared by her demanding love, and *L'Immortel*.

In addition to his novels and poems Daudet wrote several dramas, the best known of which is *L'Arlésienne*, based on one of his short stories. He frequently contributed art and theater criticism to journals and newspapers, along with his short stories and articles.

Although he was never elected to the French Academy, Daudet remains one of the most beloved and respected authors of France. His novels enjoyed an enormous vogue in their day, and their exceptional sensitivity has never lost its attraction for admirers of the man who saw himself as a "marchand de bonheur." He died in Paris on December 16, 1897.

BIBLIOGRAPHICAL REFERENCES: The works of Daudet have been issued in 24 vols., 1898–1900. A recent full study is G. Vera Dobie, *Alphonse Daudet*, 1949. Brief studies appear in Henry James, *Partial Portraits*, 1894; Brander Matthews, *The Historical Novel, and Other Essays*, 1901; and Arthur Symons, *Studies in Prose and Verse*, 1904.

SIR WILLIAM DAVENANT

Born: Crown Inn, Oxford, England
Date: February, 1606

Died: London, England
Date: April 7, 1668

PRINCIPAL WORKS

PLAYS: *The Cruel Brother*, 1627; *The Wits*, 1634; *Love and Honour*, 1634; *The Platonic Lovers*, 1636; *The Unfortunate Lovers*, 1638; *The Siege of Rhodes*, 1656; *The Playhouse to be Let*, 1659.
POEM: *Gondibert*, 1651 (unfinished).

William Davenant (or D'Avenant), born at Oxford in February, 1606, himself encouraged the legend that William Shakespeare was his father. It was said that the elder Davenant's Crown Inn was a favorite stopover of the great poet, although there exists no evidence to prove any intimacy between Mistress Davenant and Shakespeare. The innkeeper later became mayor of Oxford, where his son was educated in Lincoln College. Before taking a degree, however, William quit school to go into the service of royalty.

Davenant was associated in London with the theater of Inigo Jones and

Ben Jonson, and when these two quarreled, Davenant wrote for Jones *The Temple of Love* (1635), a masque which was played before the queen to much applause. After Jonson's death, Davenant became poet laureate in 1638. Although an ardent loyalist, he must have had the protection of Cromwell during the time the theaters were closed, for there are records to show that he at one time had "entertainments" in four separate theaters. After his political activities had led to several sentences, accusations, imprisonments, and general difficulties in England, France, and at sea, he was apparently saved by Milton's intercession.

After the Restoration, Davenant was given a license to open a new theater, The Duke, in Lincoln's Inn Fields, where he produced masques, spectacles, adaptations, operas, and bombastic love-and-honor tragedies. His own best plays are *The Wits, Love and Honour,* and *The Platonic Lovers.* He was said to have been influential enough under Charles II to return a favor and save Milton's life in 1660. He died in London on April 7, 1668, and was buried in the Poet's Corner of Westminster Abbey. On his tomb is an inscription reminiscent of Ben Jonson's, "O rare Sir William Davenant!"

BIBLIOGRAPHICAL REFERENCES: Davenant's *Dramatic Works* were collected by James Maidment and W. H. Logan in 1872–1874 in 5 vols., and the *Selected Poems* were edited by Douglas Bush in 1943. The standard biography is Arthur H. Nethercot, *Sir William D'Avenant, Poet Laureate and Playwright-Manager,* 1938. Important critical works are Cornell Marsh Dowlin, *Sir William Davenant's Gondibert, Its Preface, and Hobbes' Answer: A Study in English Neo-Classicism,* 1934; Alfred Harbage, *Sir William Davenant, Poet Venturer,* 1935 (includes a bibliography); and E. C. Marchant, *Sir William Davenant,* 1936. See also the essay on Davenant's art in Leah Jonas, *The Divine Science,* 1940; and Leslie Hotson's remarks in *The Commonwealth and Restoration Stage,* 1928.

H. L. DAVIS

Born: Roane's Mill, Oregon
Date: October 18, 1896

Died: San Antonio, Texas
Date: October 31, 1960

PRINCIPAL WORKS

NOVELS: *Honey in the Horn,* 1935; *Harp of a Thousand Strings,* 1947; *Beulah Land,* 1949; *Winds of Morning,* 1952; *The Distant Music,* 1957.
SHORT STORIES: *Team Bells Woke Me,* 1953.
POEMS: *Proud Riders,* 1942.

Although some of H(arold) L(enoir) Davis' writing presents locales such as North Carolina, Paris, or Natchez, the scenes of most of his fiction are laid in that region of the United States in which he was born and grew up, the Columbia River Valley of Oregon. The son of a country

schoolteacher, Davis was born in the now-vanished community of Roane's Mill, Oregon, on October 18, 1896, at a time when the American frontier and all it represented in the political, economic, and sociological patterns of American life was fast disappearing. The fact is important, for the passing

272

of frontier life—its values, personal justice, and colorful people—forms the subject matter characteristically associated with his work.

One of the features of frontier life which distinguishes it from our own was the early maturation of the child, a pattern necessitated by the rugged physical conditions of the environment, and the immediate economic needs of the family to which the child belonged. Davis' own childhood exemplifies this experience. At the age of nine he was working as a devil for the printer of a frontier newspaper; at twelve he was punching cattle and herding sheep; at seventeen he was a deputy sheriff responsible for maintaining law and order among the rough-and-tumble migratory workers who frequented the area. By the time he finished high school he had traveled extensively throughout the state and worked at a great variety of jobs.

Davis attended Stanford University briefly, and then, during the years of World War I, served with the American cavalry along the Mexican border. In the meantime he had become interested in literature, and he began to publish his poems in the well-known periodical *Poetry*. His work was talented enough to win him the Levinson Prize in 1919. Davis' concern with technique, his ability to convey the mood and tone of a location and the stylistic precision which characterizes his novels were probably formed under this early poetic discipline. *Proud Riders*, a book of his poems, was published in 1942.

During his apprentice years Davis helped to support himself by singing Western songs on a Seattle radio station. At the suggestion of H. L. Mencken, Davis turned from poetry to prose, concentrating at first on the short story. A number of his early efforts were published by the *American Mercury* and other magazines. Some of these early stories were collected in *Team Bells Woke Me*. Davis was awarded a Guggenheim fellowship in 1932. He went to Mexico with the intention of writing more poetry while he was there. Instead, he began work on his first novel, *Honey in the Horn*, the novel that won him the Harper Prize in the year of its publication and the Pulitzer Prize in 1936.

Almost twelve years elapsed before the appearance of Davis' second book *Harp of a Thousand Strings*, a historical novel which abandoned the Oregon locale for Tripoli and Napoleonic France. His later novels, *Beulah Land*, *Winds of Morning*, and *The Distant Music*, returned to the transitional frontier society of the Pacific Northwest.

Davis is perhaps best associated with two other distinguished writers whose works have grown out of the American West—Walter Van Tilburg Clark and A. B. Guthrie, Jr. Like them, he is not content to write "Westerns" in which melodrama is a substitute for character analysis, or to make sentimental re-creations of defunct societies a valid excuse for bad writing. He is first and foremost a careful craftsman who has brought into the province of art material which had previously been treated by many critics as a sub-literary genre. Davis has accomplished his objective largely because of his moral insight and his concern with style. As a result of this concern he has created a sensitive vehicle which is capable of communicating both the poetic immediacy of nature and the moral depth of the characters who people it.

BIBLIOGRAPHICAL REFERENCES: There is very little biographical or critical material available on Davis. For a detailed autobiographical sketch see *Rocky Mountain Herald*, XCI (December 29, 1951), 1–2. See also Carl Sandburg, "Something About H. L. Davis," *Rocky Mountain Herald*, XC (April 1, 1950), 1–2; and Dayton Kohler, "H. L. Davis: Writer in the West," *College English*, XIV (1952), 133–140.

CLARENCE DAY

Born: New York, N. Y.
Date: November 18, 1874

Died: New York
Date: December 28, 1935

PRINCIPAL WORKS

BIOGRAPHY AND REMINISCENCE: *God and My Father*, 1932; *Life with Father*, 1935; *Life with Mother*, 1937.

ESSAYS AND SKETCHES: *This Simian World*, 1920; *The Crow's Nest*, 1921 (revised and enlarged as *After All*, 1936); *In the Green Mountain Country*, 1934.

DRAWINGS AND VERSES: *Thoughts without Words*, 1928; *Scenes from the Mesozoic*, 1935.

Clarence (Shepherd) Day, "a thoroughbred New Yorker," was born on Murray Hill, on November 18, 1874, the son of the owner of the Gwynne and Day stock brokerage firm, and the grandson of the founder of the New York *Sun*. He attended St. Paul's School in Concord, New Hampshire, and then Yale, where he was elected secretary of his class (1896) and editor of the class year book. After graduation he entered his father's firm and a year later was made a partner. Later he purchased a seat on the Exchange. Day enlisted in the Navy in April of 1892 and served as a pay yeoman on the *Nahant*, the old Civil War monitor still in use at the time.

A crippling arthritic disease struck Day in 1899; after several futile trips to Arizona and Colorodo for his health he was forced to settle down in New York City, a bed-ridden invalid for life. His career parallels in some ways those of Parkman and Bradford, two other men who refused to resign from life because of severe physical handi-

caps. Day was able to hold a pencil between his thumb and third finger and manipulate it by flexing a muscle in his shoulder. Despite these difficulties he wrote several books, drew Thurberian cartoons, and carried on a large correspondence with Yale classmates and friends.

For a while he edited *Metropolitan Magazine* and was a regular contributor to the *New Republic*. He kept up a mild interest in Wall Street during these years, but concentrated most of his efforts on writing. In 1928 he married Katherine Briggs.

Day had always been known and admired by a small, devoted group of readers; but when his *Life with Father* appeared in 1935 his fame and reputation spread quickly. More than 110,000 copies of the work were sold during its first year of publication. Always modest, Day said, "I'm not what they call a real writer. I write chiefly to pay the bills, not because of Higher Reasons." His irony and wit, while always trenchant, were essentially humane and sympathetic and his satire was always tempered by the personal suffering that he daily experienced. He died from pneumonia on December 28, 1935, the very year in which large groups of readers were beginning to appreciate for the first time his unusual gifts.

BIBLIOGRAPHICAL REFERENCES· There is no authorized biography and almost no criticism. See Henry S. Canby, "Clarence Day, Jr.," *Saturday Review of Literature*, XII (August 24, 1935), 18, and *ibid.*, XXI (November 18, 1939), 8–9.

THOMAS DAY

Born: London, England
Date: June 22, 1748

Died: Wargrave, Berkshire, England
Date: September 28, 1789

PRINCIPAL WORKS

NOVEL: *The History of Sandford and Merton*, 1783, 1787, 1789.
POEM: *The Dying Negro*, 1773
POLITICAL AND SOCIAL TRACTS: *The Desolation of America*, 1777; *Reflections on the Present State of England and the Independence of America*, 1782; *Letters of Marius*, 1784; *Dialogue between a Justice of the Peace and a Farmer*, 1785.

Thomas Day is one of the minor English authors who is remembered for a single work, although in his case the situation is not so strange, for he turned to writing only in order to propagandize. Born in London, June 22, 1748, into the family of a customs collector, he was educated at Charterhouse School and at Corpus Christi College, Oxford. While at the university he read Rousseau and became an enthusiastic supporter of that author's doctrines, even to the point of trying to put them into practice. After leaving the university, Thomas Day went back to London, read law, and was admitted to the bar in 1775. He did not practice law, however, but devoted his energy and time to carrying out his ideas of social and educational reform. Early evidence of his interest in reform is found in *The Dying Negro*, a narrative poem taking to task the American patriots who were at the time seeking independence from Great Britain while supporting Negro slavery in the colonies.

Having both money and inclination, Day took on the education of two orphan girls, one of whom he thought he would marry, making his choice on philosophical principles. Both young women proved unsuitable as prospective spouses, however, and after considerable search Day finally found what seemed to him to be the ideal woman for him to marry, an heiress and reformer named Esther Milnes. Both were interested in many kinds of reforms, and, among other things, they experimented in agriculture and politics. Although he wrote several volumes, both fiction and non-fiction, Thomas Day is seldom remembered for anything but *Sandford and Merton*, a novel which compares, through the experiences of two boys, the effects of a conventional education with those of an education close to nature. Sandford is the child of convention, and

275

Merton is the child of nature. The doctrine of the novel is too palpable for most readers nowadays, but the book is a good example of the novel of propaganda of the times. The novel is almost completely lacking in humor, and its simplicity of educational reform seems now at least to be absurd. But the author, who lived by his principles, died by them; in an effort to prove that gentle handling could control any animal, he was thrown from a horse and killed at Wargrave, September 28, 1789.

BIBLIOGRAPHICAL REFERENCES: Biographical studies include Michael Sadleir, *Thomas Day, An English Disciple of Rousseau*, 1928; G. W. Gignilliat, *The Author of Sandford and Merton: A Life of Thomas Day, Esq.*, 1932; and S. H. Scott, *The Exemplary Mr. Day*, 1935. See also Allene Gregory, *The French Revolution and the English Novel*, 1915.

DANIEL DEFOE

Born: St. Giles, London, England
Date: 1660

Died: Moorfields, London
Date: April 26, 1731

PRINCIPAL WORKS

NOVELS: *The Life and Strange Surprizing Adventures of Robinson Crusoe, of York, Mariner*, 1719; *The Memoirs of a Cavalier*, 1720; *The Life, Adventures and Piracies of the Famous Captain Singleton*, 1720; *The Fortunes and Misfortunes of the Famous Moll Flanders*, 1722; *A Journal of the Plague Year*, 1722; *The History and Remarkable Life of Colonel Jacque*, 1722; *Roxana, or The Fortunate Mistress*, 1724; *The Memoirs of Captain Carleton*, 1728.

SHORT STORY: *A True Relation of the Apparition of One Mrs. Veal*, 1706.

POEM: *The True-Born Englishman*, 1701.

TRACTS: *An Essay Upon Projects*, 1697; *The Shortest Way with the Dissenters*, 1702.

MISCELLANEOUS: *A Tour Thro' the Whole Island of Great Britain*, 1724–1727; *A General History of the Pirates*, 1724–1728; *The Complete English Tradesman*, 1725–1727.

Daniel Defoe, best known as the author of *Robinson Crusoe*, is a writer whose journalistic writing still has an appeal because of its assertion of common sense principles and whose works of fiction are also convincing because of the same accent of common sense and esteem for fact.

Few writers have written more voluminously and continuously than Defoe. Though there is uncertainty about the authorship of some works attributed to him, three nineteenth century students compiled separately lists of Defoe's work; the number varies from 183 works of genuine authorship to 254. It was in the midst of such abundant and ceaseless journalism that Defoe produced his works that are remembered; but like the works that are now forgotten, his novels were designed to be in our phrase "newsworthy," to stimulate or satisfy public curiosity and, in some cases, to purify it.

His most famous work, *The Life and Strange Surprizing Adventures of*

276

Robinson Crusoe, was founded on Dampier's *Voyage Round the World* (1697) and on Alexander Selkirk's adventures as actually told by Selkirk to Defoe. Thus, a work that commenced as "news" nevertheless took form as the classic story of civilized man alone with nature. Crusoe's shipwreck, his solitude, and his man Friday open wide vistas of adventure to every reader. Further, Defoe had amazing capacities for creating imaginative detail. His *Journal of the Plague Year* strikes the reader as an eye-witness account of hideous disaster; yet actually Defoe was writing at a distance of several decades. Similar perceptions about his talent can be supported by *Moll Flanders* and other works; whatever sort of adventure Defoe treats has the accent of truth. The events may be startling, but the tone in which they are told is sober, moralistic, even plodding. Such narrative one cannot doubt.

Defoe's life is like much of his work, a mixture of the utterly commonplace and the exciting. He was born in 1660 in the parish of St. Giles, London, to a Nonconformist family and was educated at Morton's Academy at Stoke Newington. He participated in Monmouth's rebellion (1685) but escaped punishment. He took up the business of hosier factor and married Mary Tuffley, by whom he had seven children. Later he became a merchant, dealing in Spanish and Portuguese goods; he even visited Spain. In 1692 his business failed, but he honorably paid off his creditors, a fact attested to by witnesses; he then became secretary and finally owner of a tile works at Tilbury. From this wealth of practical experience came, in 1698, an early and remarkable publication of Defoe's, *An Essay Upon Projects,* which contained far-sighted practical suggestions on road systems, insane asylums, schools for women, military colleges, and other subjects. Benjamin Franklin acknowledged his indebtedness to this study. But it was the vital question of religious conformity which produced the first of a long series of pamphlets in which Defoe argued the position of the nonconformists; the most famous of these was *The Shortest Way with the Dissenters,* published anonymously in 1702. When the authorship was discovered, a price was put on his head in an advertisement describing Defoe as "a middle-sized spare man about forty years old, of a brown complexion and dark brown-colored hair, but wears a wig; a hooked nose, a sharp chin, grey eyes, and a large mole near his mouth"—a description, it may be remarked, in Defoe's own sober and factual vein. Finally apprehended, fined, put in the pillory three times, he was forced to find sureties for his behavior. Defoe spent only one year in prison, thanks to the aid of the influential Robert Harley.

After his release from prison Defoe began *The Review* (February, 1704). Published three times a week, this work extends to more than eight volumes. The publication contained news as well as essays on subjects of trade and national policy. There were also discussions of minor problems of morals and manners in the Scandal Club columns; these probably influenced the form soon taken by the *Tatler* and *Spectator* papers.

Defoe, like some of his heroes, united adventure and business. Involved in secret political missions for Robert Harley, Defoe wrote a *History of the Union* which appeared in 1709. In 1715 he was indicted for libel of

Lord Annesley, whom he accused of using the army in Ireland to join a Jacobite rebellion. Before his trial he published *An Appeal to Honor and Justice,* an apologia that gives one some insight into Defoe's busy life. He was imprisoned and gained his freedom only by consenting to become a government agent. He was also a subeditor of *Mist's Journal,* a Jacobite publication which he agreed to chasten and tame.

In 1719 *Robinson Crusoe* had instant success. In 1724 came *A Tour Thro' the Whole Island of Great Britain,* followed soon after by *A New Voyage round the World,* apparently drawn only from the author's wide reading and colored by his creative imagination, but apparently verified by his amazing zest for accurate detail.

All this journalistic activity must have built up a substantial income. However, Defoe did not die in his own home at Stoke Newington but in Moorfields, on April 26, 1731. It is known that at this time Defoe's journalistic employment came to an end, perhaps because Mist discovered he was a government agent and let it be known to other editors. Mist himself was imprisoned for attacking Defoe physically; perhaps he even planned further revenge. At any rate, in his last years Defoe wrote anonymously or under the name "Andrew Moreton"; in the summer previous to his death he was in hiding. For these reasons there is uncertainty about his final years, but all available facts show him to be like his Captain Singleton, a man of vigor, willing to shoulder the burden of his courageous convictions. His life casts a confirming light over his most famous books; the materials may be startling, but, written as they were by a man of affairs and simple moral perceptions, there is no nonsense in them.

BIBLIOGRAPHICAL REFERENCES: There is no complete edition of Defoe. The best known of his works have been reprinted in *Novels and Selected Writings,* 14 vols., 1927. The standard biography in English is James R. Sutherland, *Defoe,* 1954. An important study in French is Paul Dottin, *Daniel Defoe et ses Romans,* 3 vols., 1924, rather poorly translated in part as *The Life and Surprising Adventures of Daniel Defoe,* 1929. See also William Minton, *Daniel Defoe,* 1879; John F. Ross, *Swift and Defoe: A Study in Relationship,* 1941; William Freeman, *The Incredible Defoe,* 1950; and Brian Fitzgerald, *Daniel Defoe: A Study in Conflict,* 1954. A delightful book of non-scholarly pretensions is Walter de la Mare, *Desert Islands and Robinson Crusoe,* 1930.

JOHN WILLIAM DE FOREST

Born: Seymour, Connecticut
Date: March 31, 1826

Died: New Haven, Connecticut
Date: July 17, 1906

PRINCIPAL WORKS

NOVELS: *Seacliff,* 1859; *Miss Ravenel's Conversion from Secession to Loyalty,* 1867; *Overland,* 1871; *Kate Beaumont,* 1872; *The Wetherel Affair,* 1873; *Honest John Vane,* 1875; *Playing the Mischief,* 1875; *Irene the Missionary,* 1879; *The Bloody Chasm,* 1881; *A Lover's Revolt,* 1898.

TRAVEL SKETCHES AND IMPRESSIONS: *Oriental Acquaintance,* 1856; *European Acquaintance,* 1858.

AUTOBIOGRAPHY AND REMINISCENCE: *A Volunteer's Adventures,* 1946; *A Union Officer in the Reconstruction,* 1948.

HISTORY AND ETHNOLOGY: *History of the Indians of Connecticut,* 1851.

John William De Forest, born at Seymour, Connecticut, on March 31, 1826, was a member of a wealthy and cultured New England family. Poor health, however, prevented him from following family tradition in his education and instead of attending Yale he took a two-year trip to the Near East. On his return he assembled the *History of the Indians of Connecticut,* the first book of its kind and one which is still consulted by ethnologists for its accuracy and detail.

De Forest then spent several years abroad, traveling, collecting material for books and studying foreign languages. He returned to America, married, and was living in Charleston, South Carolina, when the Civil War broke out. With his wife and child he escaped on the last boat to leave that port before the attack on Fort Sumter. Back in Connecticut he organized a group of volunteers and led them through a series of Civil War battles. De Forest recorded his experiences in a journal, later published as *A Volunteer's Adventures.* It remains one of the best accounts of life in the Union Army. The journal also served as an important source of material for his excellent but neglected novel, *Miss Ravenel's Conversion.*

Factual, accurate, and realistic, De Forest failed to achieve the recognition he deserved from a generation which preferred sentimentalized versions of "the irrepressible conflict." Only recently has his realism been appreciated by critics who, like William Dean Howells, admire the way in which De Forest worked, "with a sort of disdainful honesty to the effects of art."

He died at New Haven on July 17, 1906.

BIBLIOGRAPHICAL REFERENCES: For biographical details and critical comment see Gordon S. Haight, Introduction to *Miss Ravenel's Conversion,* 1939; Stanley T. Williams, Introduction to *A Volunteer's Adventures,* 1946; Clara F. McIntyre, *John William De Forest: Pioneer Realist, University of Wyoming Publications,* IX (1942), No. I; and Thomas O'Donnell, "De Forest, Jan Petten, and Stephen Crane," *American Literature,* XXVII (1956), 578–580. A good contemporary estimate is Clarence Gordon, "Mr. De Forest's Novels," *Atlantic Monthly,* XXXII (1873), 611–621. The sketch in the *Dictionary of American Biography* is brief but helpful.

THOMAS DEKKER

Born: London, England
Date: c. 1572

Died: Clerkenwell(?), London
Date: 1632?

PRINCIPAL WORKS

PLAYS: *Old Fortunatus,* 1599; *The Shoemaker's Holiday,* 1599; *Patient Grissell,* 1600 (with Chettle and Haughton); *Satiromastix,* 1601; *Sir Thomas Wyatt,* 1602; *The Honest Whore,* Part I, 1604 (with Middleton); Part II, c. 1605; *Westward*

Ho!, 1604 (with Webster); *Northward Ho!*, 1605 (with Webster); *The Whore of Babylon*, c. 1606; *The Roaring Girl*, c. 1610 (with Middleton); *If It Be Not Good, the Devil Is In It*, c. 1611; *Match Me in London*, c. 1613; *The Virgin Martyr*, c. 1620 (with Massinger); *The Witch of Edmonton*, 1621 (with Ford and W. Rowley); *The Wonder of a Kingdom*, 1623 (with Day); *The Sun's Darling*, 1624 (with Ford); *The Noble Soldier*, 1631 (with Day and S. Rowley).

MISCELLANEOUS: *The Magnificent Entertainment*, 1603 (with Jonson and Middleton); *The Wonderful Year*, 1603; *The Seven Deadly Sins of London*, 1606; *The Bellman of London*, 1608; *Lanthorn and Candlelight*, 1608; *The Gull's Hornbook*, 1609.

Through the mist of the centuries Thomas Dekker appears a somewhat threadbare and shabby figure, but he arouses more affection and stimulates more delight than some of his greater contemporaries. Biographical facts about him are relatively rare, even for an Elizabethan dramatist. Much of his dramatic writing was hackwork, frequently done with collaborators. He is chiefly remembered as author of the delightful *Shoemaker's Holiday* and the satirical *Gull's Hornbook*, and as Ben Jonson's literary enemy.

In his *English Villainies* (1632) Dekker claims threescore years, and in his *Seven Deadly Sins of London* and *Rod for Run-aways* he speaks of London as his birthplace. J. H. Penniman accepts the identification of the playwright with the Thomas Dekker who had two daughters baptized in St. Giles, Cripplegate (1594 and 1602). Church registers also record the burial of a Dekker son and daughter in 1598. E. K. Chambers simply states that neither Dekker's parentage nor his marriage can be traced with certainty.

As a writer Dekker first appears in 1598 in Philip Henslowe's records, but he may have written for Henslowe before that year. In 1598 Henslowe had to obtain his release from prison, and in 1599 his release from arrest. During the next few years Dekker had a prolific career as playwright, writing for the Admiral's Men (Henslowe's company), for Worcester's company, for the Chamberlain's Men, and for Paul's Boys.

In 1601 he became involved in the War of the Theaters on the side of Marston. Jonson attacked them both in *Poetaster*, and Dekker retaliated with an uproarious caricature of Jonson in *Satiromastix*. Jonson worked out a Roman setting for both plots of *Poetaster*, but Dekker bundled Horace and the other Romans into the subplot of a play dealing with William Rufus of England. Enemies or not, Jonson and Dekker shared in the writing of the *Entertainment* performed for James I at the time of his Coronation in 1603.

In addition to his copious dramatic output, Dekker wrote a number of prose pamphlets on contemporary subjects, the best known of which is *The Gull's Hornbook*, a valuable document in that it gives a first-hand, if biased, picture of the behavior of Jacobean gallants in various places, including the theater. In 1613 Dekker was imprisoned for debt, apparently for some six years. After his release he resumed his dramatic career, collaborating chiefly with Ford. Sir Edmund Chambers believes that he was probably the Thomas Dekker buried on August 25,

1632, at St. James's Church, Clerkenwell.

Including doubtful and lost works, Chambers lists about fifty plays in which Dekker had a hand; he ascribes eighteen surviving plays to him. Although this dramatic work is uneven, as might be expected from the author's evident haste and collaboration with others, Dekker is one of the more popular minor dramatists of his day. *The Shoemaker's Holiday* is an almost inevitable choice for any anthology of the period, and it has been a popular theatrical success in the twentieth century, both on the professional and the collegiate stage. At least one of the author's songs, "Sweet Content" from *Patient Grissell,* has won its place in the anthologies of English literature.

BIBLIOGRAPHICAL REFERENCES: The earlier edition of *Thomas Dekker's Dramatic Works,* edited by R. H. Shepherd, 1873, is being superseded by *The Dramatic Works of Thomas Dekker,* edited by Fredson Bowers, now in progress, 1953, 1955, ff. Selected plays have been reprinted in *Thomas Dekker,* edited by Ernest Rhys, in the Mermaid Series, n. d. J. H. Penniman edited *Jonson's "Poetaster" and Dekker's "Satiromastix,"* 1913.

See also *Ben Jonson,* edited by C. H. Herford, Percy Simpson, and Evelyn Simpson, 1925–1952; E. K. Chambers, *The Elizabethan Stage,* Vol. III, 1923; Henry W. Wells, *Elizabethan and Jacobean Playwrights,* 1939; G. B. Harrison, *Elizabethan Plays and Players,* 1940; and T. M. Parrott and R. H. Ball, *A Short View of Elizabethan Drama,* 1943.

WALTER DE LA MARE

Born: Charlton, Kent, England
Date: April 25, 1873

Died: Twickenham, England
Date: June 22, 1956

PRINCIPAL WORKS

POEMS: *Songs of Childhood,* 1902; *Poems,* 1906; *The Listeners,* 1912; *A Child's Day,* 1912; *Peacock Pie,* 1913; *The Sunken Garden,* 1917; *Motley and Other Poems,* 1918; *The Veil and Other Poems,* 1922; *Down-adown-Derry,* 1922; *The Captive and Other Poems,* 1928; *Poems for Children,* 1930; *Old Rhymes and New,* 1932; *The Fleeting and Other Poems,* 1933; *Memory and Other Poems,* 1938; *Collected Poems,* 1941; *Collected Rhymes and Verses,* 1944; *The Burning Glass,* 1945; *The Traveller,* 1946; *Inward Companion,* 1950; *Winged Chariot,* 1951; *O Lovely England,* 1953.

NOVELS AND FANTASIES: *Henry Brocken,* 1904; *The Three Mulla-Mulgars,* 1910; *The Return,* 1910; *Memoirs of a Midget,* 1921; *At First Sight,* 1928.

SHORT STORIES: *The Riddle,* 1923; *Broomsticks and Other Tales,* 1925; *The Connoisseur,* 1926; *On the Edge,* 1930; *The Wind Blows Over,* 1936; *The Picnic,* 1941; *Collected Stories for Children,* 1947; *A Beginning and Other Stories,* 1955.

MISCELLANEOUS: *Crossings: A Fairy Play,* 1921; *Come Hither,* 1923; *Ding Dong Bell,* 1924; *Stories from the Bible,* 1929; *Desert Islands and Robinson Crusoe,* 1930; *Early One Morning in the Spring,* 1935; *Behold, This Dreamer!,* 1939; *Pleasures and Speculations,* 1940; *Love,* 1943; *Private View,* 1953.

Of French Huguenot and Scottish ancestry, Walter (John) de la Mare was born at Charlton, Kent, April 25, 1873, and died at Twickenham, Middlesex, June 22, 1956. He was educated at St. Paul's Cathedral Choir School, where he founded *The Choristers' Journal*. Though he never went to college, Oxford, Cambridge, and St. Andrews all gave him honorary doctorates. Declining knighthood, he accepted both the C.H. (1948) and the O.M. (1953).

In his early days de la Mare used the pseudonym "Walter Ramal." In the 1890's he wrote for such periodicals as *The Cornhill Magazine*, *The Sketch*, *The Pall Mall Gazette*. For many years he reviewed widely, especially for the *London Times Literary Supplement*. In 1902, Andrew Lang persuaded Longmans to publish his first book, *Songs of Childhood*.

From 1890 to 1908 de la Mare worked as a statistician for the Anglo-American Oil Company; in later years he devoted all his time to literature. He was married to Constance Ingpen and became the father of four children.

Though one of the friendliest and most accessible of men, de la Mare was one of the most independent of writers. He followed his own inspiration and stood apart from all literary movements. He was one of the great masters of the supernatural story; as a poet of childhood he was without a peer. His genius was as highly individualized as Blake's, though without Blake's eccentricity. No writer of our time has been more deeply loved.

De la Mare is best known as a poet; even his prose is essentially the product of a poet's mind. For all that, more than one critic has called *Memoirs of a Midget* the greatest British novel of the twentieth century. A very prolific writer, he also produced many learned and highly-individualized anthologies, quite unlike any others in literature, and critical and ruminative works, often difficult of classification. His voice may still be heard on a long-playing record, "Walter de la Mare Reading" (Caedmon TC 1046), in which he converses and reads the story, "The Princess," plus twelve of his poems.

Memoirs of a Midget has its kinship to the work of Dickens and Emily Bronte, but it is both a highly original and a distinctively modern novel. Like de la Mare's poems, it shows great sensitiveness to nature; like many of his tales, it hovers at times on the edge of the supernatural. Essentially, however, it is a serious study of human relationships, centering around the conflict between society and the individual. The reader is absorbed in the life history of Miss M., who longed passionately to share the world upon equal terms with other human beings. He sympathizes intensely with her passionate response to beauty, her consuming desire to know the meaning of life, and he shudders for her when she degrades herself. Though the novel is not didactic, its values are sound and sure, and the world in which its action is staged is a world of unimaginable terrors where the final word is love's.

Edward Wagenknecht

BIBLIOGRAPHICAL REFERENCES: There is no full-length biographical study of Walter de la Mare. For biographical data and criticism see R. L. Mégroz, *Walter de la Mare: A Biographical and Critical Study*, 1924; Forrest Reid, *Walter de la Mare: A Critical Study*, 1929; Henry C. Duffin, *Walter de la Mare: A Study of His Poetry*, 1949; Storm Jameson, "Mr. de la Mare and the Grotesque," *English Review*, XXXIV (1922), 424–430; John Freeman, 'The Work of Walter de la Mare," *Quarterly Re-*

view, CCXXXVII (1922), 32–47; Edward Wagenknecht, "Walter de la Mare's 'The Riddle,' A Note on the Teaching of Literature with Allegorical Tendencies," *College English*, XI (1949), 72–80 and *Cavalcade of the English Novel*, 1954 (rev. ed).

Tributes to Walter de la Mare on his Seventy-fifth Birthday, 1948, is a symposium containing essays by Lord David Cecil, Edmund Blunden, Graham Greene, and others.

MAZO DE LA ROCHE

Born: Toronto, Canada
Date: 1885

Died: Toronto, Canada
Date: July 12, 1961

PRINCIPAL WORKS

NOVELS: *Jalna*, 1927; *Whiteoaks of Jalna*, 1929; *Finch's Fortune*, 1931; *The Master of Jalna*, 1933; *Young Renny*, 1935; *Whiteoak Harvest*, 1936; *Growth of a Man*, 1938; *Whiteoak Heritage*, 1940; *Wakefield's Course*, 1941; *The Building of Jalna*, 1944; *Return to Jalna*, 1946; *Mary Wakefield*, 1949; *Renny's Daughter*, 1951; *The Whiteoak Brothers: Jalna—1923*, 1953; *Variable Winds at Jalna*, 1954.

SHORT STORIES: *The Sacred Bullock*, 1939; *A Boy in the House*, 1952.

PLAY: *Whiteoaks*, 1936.

Most of the novels of Mazo de la Roche have been set at Jalna, her fictional estate in Canada where all life revolves around an isolated and self-contained family living in an old tradition with old values. Her novels have a steady and loyal public for whom her self-contained world comes to represent a valuable and important—almost Trollopian—island in the midst of the modern world.

Miss de la Roche, having published several earlier novels, first reached a wide public in 1927 when *Jalna* won a $10,000 prize given by the *Atlantic Monthly*. With accuracy, grace, and introspective insight, she first depicted the family and the world which was to serve as the basis for much of her future work. Other typical novels dealing with Jalna are *Whiteoaks*, *Finch's Fortune*, *Young Renny*, *Whiteoak Harvest*, *Growth of a Man*, *The Building*

of Jalna, and *Mary Wakefield*—the last showing the impingement of the outside world, in the form of a governess, on people and events at Jalna. The popularity of Miss de la Roche's work can be demonstrated by the fact that a dramatized version of *Whiteoaks* was highly successful in New York and ran for two years in London.

Born in Toronto in 1885, Miss de la Roche has, for the most part, preferred the same quiet isolation that characterizes Jalna. She has lived in rural Canada, caring for her family, her land, her dogs and horses. At various times she has lived in England and in Sicily, but she has managed to maintain the same kind of isolation and self-sufficiency there. Although, in her novels, her family may have its turbulent and dramatic moments, the values of family, propriety, and independence remain supreme.

BIBLIOGRAPHICAL REFERENCES: The primary source of biographical information is Mazo de la Roche, *Ringing the Changes: An Autobiography*, 1957. See also J. Moore,

283

"Canadian Writers of Today," *Canadian Forum,* XII (1932), 380–381; and H. Eayrs, "Bookman Profiles," *Canadian Bookman,* XX (1938), 17–22.

GRAZIA DELEDDA

Born: Nuoro, Sardina
Date: September 27, 1875

Died: Rome, Italy
Date: August 16, 1936

PRINCIPAL WORKS

NOVELS: *Il Vecchio della montagna,* 1900; *Elias Portolu,* 1903; *Cenere,* 1904 (*Ashes*); *Nostalgie,* 1905; *L'Ombra del passato,* 1907; *L'Edera,* 1908 (*The Ivy*); *Canne al Vento,* 1913; *L'Incendio nell' oliveto,* 1918; *La Madre,* 1920 (*The Mother*); *Annalena Bilsini,* 1928.

SHORT STORIES: *I Giochi della Vita,* 1905; *Chiaroscuro,* 1912; *Il Fanciulla nascosto,* 1915.

Grazia Deledda was born on September 27, 1875 in the primitive Sardinian village of Nuoro which she has utilized as the background for most of her fiction. In that backward community she was forced largely to educate herself, and she found her amusement, even as a child, in reading and writing. Her first published article was in a fashion magazine; before long she was contributing successfully to Sardinian literary and political papers and journals. Knowing no other environment than her island, she began to write stories about its people and their setting. Her first major publication of fiction appeared in *La Tribuna,* published in Rome. Before she was twenty-one she had published three novels, all dealing with Sardinian life.

Very few of Grazia Deledda's many novels have been translated into English, most translators saying they are difficult to convert into English idiom. As a result, she is relatively unknown in the United States and Great Britain, although she is widely read on the Continent. During her lifetime she was a shy and retiring, even timid woman, but fame came to her unsolicited when in 1926 she was elected to the Italian

Academy, and in the same year was awarded the Nobel Prize in Literature. She was the second woman to receive that award, Selma Lagerlöf, Swedish novelist, having preceded her in 1909.

In 1897, at the age of twenty-two, Grazia Deledda married an Italian named Madesani, a civil employee of the Italian war ministry, and after her marriage left Sardinia. She and her husband took up residence in Rome, and there they resided, except for short intervals, until the novelist's death on August 16, 1936. Although famous, Grazia Deledda devoted herself to her home and her family. In addition to her very considerable output of fiction, she also wrote two plays and collaborated on a third, all successfully produced in Rome.

In her earlier writings Grazia Deledda tended toward a sentimental picture of Sardinian life, but in her later novels she turned to moving tragedies of human experience. In *Elias Portoliu* she presented a convict who, though in love with his sister-in-law, refused to marry the woman even after she had become a widow. *Ashes* tells the story of a tragic relationship between a woman and her illegitimate child, with the son eventually driving his mother to suicide. *The Ivy* presented an equally tragic theme in the relationship between a man and a woman servant who murdered for his sake and then found expiation in marriage to her master. In her greatest novel, *The Mother*, Grazia Deledda portrayed the shame of a mother who first realized the dream of seeing her son become a priest and then had to watch him fail by falling victim to sin and lust. *Cosima* (1937), a posthumous book, is partly autobiographical.

BIBLIOGRAPHICAL REFERENCES: A basic discussion of Grazia Deledda in English is the essay in Domenico Vittorini, *The Modern Italian Novel*, 1930. See also Mercede Mundula, *Grazia Deledda*, 1929; Lacy Collison-Morby, *Modern Italian Literature*, 1911; and Allesandro de Bosdari, *Studies in Foreign Literature*, 1928.

THOMAS DELONEY

Born: London (?), England
Date: c. 1543

Died: Unknown
Date: 1600 (?)

Principal Works

PROSE ROMANCES: *The Pleasant History of John Winchcomb in His Younger Years Called Jack of Newberry*, c. 1597; *The Gentle Craft*, c. 1587–1598; *Thomas of Reading, or the Six Worthy Yeomen of the West*, c. 1600.

Thomas Deloney was a hack writer of Elizabethan London (where he was probably born in 1543), the author of innumerable occasional ballads and broadside sheets as well as a pioneer in English prose fiction. He had learned the trade of a weaver as a boy and he began writing ballads on contemporary events while working at his trade in Norwich. About 1585 he moved to London, where he seems to have devoted all his time to writing. He was the author of many ballads, which at the time were printed on single sheets of paper and hawked about the streets. Deloney, according to tradition, was the successor to William Elderton, the chief balladeer of the early 1580's. Although many of his ballads have long since been lost, there are two collections of his work: *The Garland of Goodwill* (c. 1604) and *Strange Histories* (c. 1607). These collections were apparently made after the author's death.

It is for his work as a writer of prose narratives that Deloney is usually remembered by students of literature. His best-known work is *The Pleasant History of John Winchcomb in His Younger Years Called Jack of Newberry*, usually referred to nowadays as *Jack of Newberry*. The earliest extant edition is one of 1619, which is labeled the eighth edition. The volume is a realistic prose narrative extolling the virtues of weavers, the author's fellow tradesmen. Another prose narrative by Deloney is *The Gentle Craft*, in two parts, in which he glorified shoemakers. This work probably influenced Thomas Dekker's *The Shoemaker's Holiday* (1599), a popular play. A third prose narrative by Deloney is *Thomas of Reading* (earliest extant edition, 1612), praising the clothiers of England. All three narratives combine romantic and realistic techniques in dealing with phases of the life of Elizabethan trades and crafts against semi-historic backgrounds.

The ultimate fate of Thomas Deloney is unknown. He simply disappeared from literary history about 1600.

BIBLIOGRAPHICAL REFERENCES: The standard edition is *The Works of Thomas Deloney*, edited by F. O. Mann, 1912. See also A. Chevalley, *Thomas Deloney*, 1926; and Llewellyn Powys, "Thomas Deloney," *Virginia Quarterly Review*, IX (1933), 578–594.

WILLIAM DE MORGAN

Born: London, England
Date: November 16, 1839

Died: London
Date: January 15, 1917

PRINCIPAL WORKS

NOVELS: *Joseph Vance: An Ill-Written Autobiography*, 1906; *Alice-for-Short*, 1907; *Somehow Good*, 1908; *It Never Can Happen Again*, 1909; *When Ghost Meets Ghost*, 1914.

William (Frend) De Morgan is an unusual figure in the history of English literature, for he wrote and published his first novel at the age of sixty-seven, following his retirement from a long career in art and industry. Son of Augustus De Morgan, the famous nineteenth century mathematician and logician, he was born in London on November 16, 1839, and educated at University College, where his father was a member of the faculty. In 1859 he entered the Royal Academy School to take a course in art; there he became one of a student group that included Dante Gabriel Rossetti, Edward Burne-Jones, and William Morris, who became lifelong friends.

As an artist, De Morgan spent most of his early career working and experimenting in pottery and tile. Particularly interested in pottery glazes and techniques lost to modern craftsmen, he rediscovered through research some of the methods used to produce the brilliant blue and green glazes of ancient pottery. His first published writings were scientific papers in the field of ceramics. Later he founded a company for the manufacture of artistic tile and pottery, even inventing some of the tools and machinery needed for his factory, and his products became famous for their artistic and utilitarian qualities. He married Evelyn Pickering, an artist, in 1887; they had no children. From 1890 on, they spent part of every year in Italy for the sake of De Morgan's health.

Retired from active business in 1905, De Morgan turned to fiction, at his wife's suggestion, while convalescing from a serious illness. His first novel was *Joseph Vance*, a leisurely tale told in the form of an autobiography, somewhat in the manner of Dickens' *David Copperfield*. The book was well received, and its modest success encouraged De Morgan to continue writing.

286

Six novels followed, none as successful as the first; but only two, *An Affair of Dishonor* (1910) and *A Likely Story* (1911), can be considered truly inferior. The two novels published after his death owe more to his wife than to De Morgan. Because his models in fiction were the novelists popular when he was young, notably Dickens, De Morgan has been called a late Victorian. *Alice-for-Short,* according to its author, contains a portrayal of the writer in the character of Charles Heath.

During World War I, De Morgan resumed his scientific studies. He was working on methods and devices for defense against submarines and aircraft when he contracted influenza and died in London on January 15, 1917.

BIBLIOGRAPHICAL REFERENCES: The best biographical study is A. M. W. Stirling, *William De Morgan and His Wife,* 1922. For criticism see Will T. Hale, "William De Morgan and the Early Victorians," *Indiana University Studies,* VIII, No. 50, 1921.

DEMOSTHENES

Born: Attica, Greece
Date: 384 B.C.

Died: Calauria, Greece
Date: October, 322 B.C.

PRINCIPAL WORKS

ORATIONS: *Against Androtion,* 355; *Against the Law of the Leptines,* 354; *Symmories,* 354 (*On the Navy Boards*); *Against Timocrates,* 352; *Against Aristocrates,* 352; *First Philippic,* 351; *For the Rhodians,* 351; *First and Second Olynthiacs,* 349; *Third Olynthiac,* 348; *On the Peace,* 346; *Second Philippic,* 344; *On the Embassy,* 343; *Third Philippic,* 341; *On the Affairs of the Chersonese,* 341; *On the Crown,* 330.

Born at Paeania in 384 B.C., Demosthenes was the greatest of the Greek orators, an Athenian patriot who used his skill at declamation to arouse the citizens of Athens to regain their civic pride and to resist the efforts of Philip II of Macedon to conquer Greece.

When Demosthenes was seven his father, who bore the same name, died; and his mother, Cleobule, was left with very little money to care for him and his sister, since the executors of the estate embezzled most of it. Demosthenes was an awkward child, with little strength, and he was handicapped by a speech defect which he later overcame—although probably not by putting pebbles in his mouth. He received a good education of the standard sort, and special instruction in rhetoric. He then went on to the study of law with a famous probate lawyer of the time, Isaeus.

In 360 Demosthenes was commander of a ship in the Athenian fleet, but his first ventures into public life were as a lawyer, and one of his important early cases was one initiated by himself in which he unsuccessfully attempted to win back some of the money that had been embezzled from his father's estate. Then, as one trained both in law and rhetoric, Demosthenes went on to the profession of writing cases to be delivered orally in court. The experience which he acquired

287

stood him in good stead when he began in 355 to attempt to influence the political life of Athens by his speeches in the general assembly.

His most famous orations were the three *Philippics,* and the most famous of the three was the third, delivered in 341. In his speeches he warned the people of Athens that civic reform and a revival of civic spirit were needed if Athens was to hold its place in the world. He cited cases of corruption in public administration and demanded action. When Philip of Macedon seemed to have the subjugation of Athens as one of his objectives, Demosthenes warned the people of Athens that democracy could not survive if Philip were to conquer them. He urged the necessity of taxes, of military service, of a strong fleet, and of continued attention to political and military affairs.

He traveled throughout Greece, attempting to form an alliance of the various cities against Macedon.

In 338 Philip scored a final victory against the allied city-states at the battle of Chaeronea. Demosthenes then worked to secure funds from Persia, Philip's next target, in order to build up anti-Macedonian forces. When Philip died in 336 and Alexander became king of Macedon, the Athenian cause was recognized as hopeless for the time being. Demosthenes restricted his campaign against Macedon. In order to restore confidence in Demosthenes as a public leader, his friend Ctesiphon proposed that Demosthenes be given a gold wreath or crown. This act was denounced as illegal by Aeschines, whom Demosthenes had accused in 343 of accepting bribes; and Aeschines brought suit. In one of his most famous orations, *On the Crown,* Demosthenes defended his record and won the case.

Demosthenes then concentrated on developing the internal strength of Athens, but his work was halted when he was found guilty of appropriating to himself some gold that had been in possession of a deserter from Alexander's forces who had been captured by the Athenians. (Demosthenes' guilt was never actually established.) He was imprisoned because he could not pay the fine, but he escaped and went into exile. When Alexander died in 323 Demosthenes was recalled to Athens and acclaimed. At the battle of Crannon in 322 Athens was defeated by the Macedonians, and Demosthenes fled to the island of Calauria, where he took poison to avoid being captured by the soldiers of Antipater, the Macedonian leader.

BIBLIOGRAPHICAL REFERENCES: There are various editions of Demosthenes' orations in English translation, the most complete being those of Charles R. Kennedy, *The Orations of Demosthenes,* 6 vols., in Bohn's Classical Library, 1852–1870, and A. W. Pickard-Cambridge, *The Public Orations of Demosthenes,* 2 vols., 1912. Among the available biographical and historical studies of Demosthenes and his period are R. C. Jebb, *The Attic Orators,* 2 vols., 1876; S. H. Butcher, *Demosthenes,* in the Classical Writers series, 1893; A. W. Pickard-Cambridge, *Demosthenes and the Last Days of Greek Freedom,* 1914; Charles D. Adams, *Demosthenes and His Influence,* 1927; and W. D. Jaeger, *Demosthenes: The Origin and Growth of His Policy,* 1938.

THOMAS DE QUINCEY

Born: Manchester, England
Date: August 15, 1785

Died: Edinburgh, Scotland
Date: December 8, 1859

PRINCIPAL WORKS

ESSAYS AND STUDIES: *Confessions of an English Opium Eater,* 1822; *The Logic of Political Economy,* 1844; *Collected Writings,* edited by David Masson, 1889–1890 (14 vols.).

NOVEL: *Klosterheim,* 1832.

Thomas De Quincey, a close associate of Coleridge and Wordsworth, deserved to be near the center of the great Romantic Movement in England. Like the other Romantics, he placed great emphasis on feeling; like some of them, he was a master of the curious and obscure in literature; and he was a creator of a poetic prose that, in its range of diction and display of surprising fancy, is the equal of any writing of his time. It is prose written by an isolated man, a man in whom dream and vigor are not antithetical.

De Quincey was born in Manchester, August 15, 1785, the fifth child in a family of eight children. His busy and stern parents soon alienated De Quincey, who was a sensitive and quiet child much in need of understanding. The boy's only comfort within his own family was an unusually close devotion to one of his sisters, whose untimely death left him alone, disturbed, and morose.

Since both of De Quincey's parents were well-educated and interested in scholarship, he at least did not lack for opportunity of study. A brilliant if somewhat unbalanced boy, he could read, write, and speak Greek "as though it were his native tongue" by the age of fifteen. Dissatisfied with the restrictions of his home and also by his own shortcomings, De Quincey ran off at the age of seventeen. For almost a

year he hid in London, where he led a frugal and difficult life of study and introspection. Here he performed his deep reading of English poets, a reading characteristic of all the Romantics. This period he later called an "impassioned parenthesis of my life." Reunited with his family, he was allowed to enter Oxford in 1803. There he quickly won the reputation of brilliant scholar and conversationalist, but left without taking a degree in 1808.

When De Quincey was about twenty he became subject to severe pain. Some say it was a stomach disorder; others, that it was a combination of eyestrain and astigmatism. Upon a friend's suggestion, he started to use laudanum for relief from his discomfort. Apparently as a child he had been subject to deep dreams or visions; and since he was not adjusted either to himself or the people around him, it is natural to suppose that he welcomed the artificial, remote dream world that the continued use of opium led him into. It was a habit he submitted to for over twenty years; then, for no explainable reason, he disciplined himself and ceased its use. This was a period of immeasurable physical and emotional torture for De Quincey; but world literature is the richer for it.

After college he made the acquaintance of the Lake poets and, in 1816, married; both relations were happy ones, in part because of the charm of De Quincey's own nature, which was courteous, playful, and firm. His life was one of much literary toil, he supported himself and his large family by contributions to *Blackwood's, Hogg's Weekly Instructor,* and other magazines, whose editors gave him—as must seem to readers of modern periodicals—very free rein. He touched a wide variety of topics and—as in the celebrated "Flight of a Tartar Tribe"—in a way quite imaginative and fanciful.

De Quincey moved to Edinburgh, leaving behind such London friends as Lamb and Hazlitt, like him masters of a colored and personal style. (It was these friends who encouraged him to write *the Confessions of an English Opium Eater,* the work that brought him fame and assured him the attention of editors and publishers.) De Quincey continued his periodical writing until his death in Edinburgh, December 8, 1859. It is said that when the quantity of his writing became too voluminous for his lodgings, he would simply move away from the mass and start fresh elsewhere.

Representative samples of his ability to take an assigned topic and effect a personal transmutation of it appear in "Joan of Arc" (1847) and "On Murder Considered as One of the Fine Arts" (1827). De Quincey's reminiscences of the Lake poets reveal a unique view of the great men of his day. In all his writing De Quincey well illustrates a famous literary distinction of his own creation between the literature of knowledge and the literature of power. He may begin on a theme which suggests that the writer will convey knowledge (information or instruction); but few essays conclude without creating in the reader a sense of unexpected and, indeed, ungovernable fantasy at work.

BIBLIOGRAPHICAL REFERENCES. For many years the standard biographical and critical study was David Masson, *De Quincey,* 1887; but this work has now been superseded by Horace Ainsworth Eaton, *Thomas De Quincey,* 1936, and Edward Sackville-West, *Thomas De Quincey: His Life and Work,* 1936. See also Malcolm Elwin, *De Quincey,* 1935; John C. Metcalf, *De Quincey: A Portrait,* 1940; Sigmund K. Proctor, *Thomas De Quincey's Theory of Literature,* 1943; and John E. Jordan, *Thomas De Quincey: Literary Critic,* 1952.

CHARLES DICKENS

Born: Landport, England
Date: February 7, 1812

Died: Gadshill, England
Date: June 9, 1870

PRINCIPAL WORKS

NOVELS: *The Pickwick Papers,* 1836–1837; *Oliver Twist,* 1837–1839; *Nicholas Nickleby,* 1838–1839; *The Old Curiosity Shop,* 1840–1841; *Barnaby Rudge,* 1841; *Martin Chuzzlewit,* 1843–1844; *Dombey and Son,* 1846–1848; *David Copperfield,* 1849–1850; *Bleak House,* 1852–1853; *Hard Times,* 1854; *Little Dorrit,* 1855–1857; *A Tale of Two Cities,* 1859; *Great Expectations,* 1860–1861; *Our Mutual Friend,* 1864–1866; *The Mystery of Edwin Drood,* 1870.

CHRISTMAS BOOKS: *A Christmas Carol,* 1843; *The Chimes,* 1844; *The Cricket on the Hearth,* 1845; *The Battle of Life,* 1846; *The Haunted Man,* 1848.

SKETCHES AND TALES: *Sketches by Boz*, 1836; *Sketches of Young Gentlemen*, 1838; *Sketches of Young Couples*, 1840; *The Uncommercial Traveller*, 1860; *George Silverman's Explanation*, 1868.

PLAYS: *The Strange Gentleman*, 1836; *The Village Coquettes*, 1836; *Mr. Nightingale's Diary*, 1851 (with Mark Lemon); *No Thoroughfare*, 1867 (with Wilkie Collins).

TRAVEL SKETCHES AND IMPRESSIONS: *American Notes*, 1842; *Pictures from Italy*, 1846.

MISCELLANEOUS: *A Child's History of England*, 1853; *The Life of Our Lord*, 1934.

Charles Dickens, British novelist, was born at Landport, near Portsmouth, England, February 7, 1812, the son of a minor government clerk. Owing to his parents' incompetence in money matters, at the age of ten, when the family moved to London, occurred the episode that many critics have found traumatic in its effect on the emotional and creative life of the novelist: that "deep sense of abandonment," symbolized for him by his parents' complacent relegation of him to the sordid drudgery of work in Warren's blacking warehouse. One side of its effect on him is almost certainly the way in which we find, at or near the center of so many of his novels, a suffering, neglected child; another, the almost hallucinatory intensity of his rendering of the externals of human beings. The episode was brief, and he returned to school, to leave at fifteen, his real education having been gained from the novels of Cervantes, Le Sage, Fielding, and Smollett, and his exposure to the London scene during his "abandonment." He became first a lawyer's clerk and then a shorthand reporter in the courts and the House of Commons.

His first book, *Sketches by Boz*, stemmed from his work as a journalist; it led to his being commissioned to write the text accompanying a collection of comic drawings about Cockney sportsmen which was to be published in monthly parts. "I thought," he wrote later, "of Mr. Pickwick"; and with the appearance of Sam Weller in Chapter X the success of *The Pickwick Papers* was not merely assured but unprecedentedly sensational. From then on, Dickens was the most popular of all English novelists in his lifetime and probably for posterity too.

Even while *The Pickwick Papers* was appearing, however, *Oliver Twist* was being published as a continued story in a magazine. The two novels show the two sides of Dickens' genius. *Pickwick* is a work of pure humor, in which the crudities and miseries of the real world are sterilized by laughter and the vicious are objects of comedy, good things in themselves, without reference to moral judgment, because they are seen as comic. The world of *Pickwick* is almost fairyland: in *Oliver Twist* fairyland has become the country of nightmare; the bad fairies have become ogres. There is still laughter, but it has become savage, satirical; the appeal is to derision. On the surface, *Oliver Twist* is an exposure novel, an attack on the working of the poor law of the day, but its real theme is the fate of innocence and weakness. The savage comedy, seen in a character like Bumble, is accompanied by equally savage melodrama, the melodrama of the Jew Fagin and the robber Bill Sikes.

From then on, fairyland and nightmare exist side by side in Dickens' novels. During the first part of his career,

291

these novels are naïve in form, based on eighteenth century picaresque, in which we follow the fortunes of the hero who gives his name to the book, as in *Nicholas Nickleby* and *Martin Chuzzlewit*. The weaknesses of structure inherent in picaresque fiction were accentuated by Dickens' practice of writing for serialization and by his lack of what today would be called the artistic conscience: Martin Chuzzlewit was sent to America not because the pattern of the novel demanded it but because sales were falling off and an element of novelty seemed called for to revive interest. Today we read the earlier novels for their incidentals, not for their plots; for the scenes at Dotheboys Hall and the character of Mrs. Nickleby in *Nicholas Nickleby;* for the wonderful Pecksniff and the sublime Mrs. Gamp —as a comic creation second only to Falstaff in English literature—in *Martin Chuzzlewit.*

The masterpiece of this first part of Dickens' career is the semi-autobiographical *David Copperfield,* the most varied of the earlier works and the best proportioned, containing, too, some of his most delightful characters, among them Mr. Micawber, modeled on his father. The darkening of his genius is already apparent, however, in *Dombey and Son;* and henceforth his criticism of the age, which up to then had largely dealt with specific abuses, becomes general, focusing on the theme of money. The humor is no longer that of delighted appreciation of the absurd, but bitterly sardonic, as in the rendering of Mr. Podsnap in *Our Mutual Friend.* Plot becomes much more highly organized; and at the same time a rich symbolism enters his fiction, sometimes

as an extraordinary intensification of atmosphere, as in the description of Dombey's house in *Dombey and Son,* sometimes as a feature of the London scene, like the dust-piles which dominate *Our Mutual Friend,* sometimes even as an atmospheric condition, as in the fog that enshrouds the beginning of *Bleak House.* Symbolism of this kind was something almost entirely new in English fiction; and while his contemporaries preferred the earlier books, where he is "the unique portrayer of comical eccentrics" and the stress is on high spirits and the gospel of kindliness, critics in our time have tended more to admire the later novels, with their dark poetic sweep, the passionate intensity of their symbolism, and their affinity, in mood engendered, both with the later Elizabethan tragedy and with Dostoevski. Outstanding also among the later works are *Little Dorrit,* which is partly autobiographical in inspiration, and *Great Expectations.* His mystery story, *Edwin Drood,* was unfinished. He wrote two historical novels, *Barnaby Rudge,* based on the Gordon Riots of eighteenth-century London, and *A Tale of Two Cities,* on the French Revolution. *A Christmas Carol in Prose* is the most famous of his shorter pieces.

Dickens married in 1836 and separated from his wife in 1858. His first visit to the United States, in 1841, resulted in *American Notes,* a work which, together with the American chapters in *Martin Chuzzlewit,* was extremely resented in America. A second visit, in 1867, was a triumphant success. He died at his home at Gadshill on June 9, 1870.

Walter Allen

BIBLIOGRAPHICAL REFERENCES: The most recent collected edition of Dickens appeared in 1937–1938; it includes three volumes of letters. The authorized biography is John Forster's *The Life of Charles Dickens,* 1872–1874, but this has been supplemented and superseded in part by Edgar Johnson, *Charles Dickens: His Tragedy and Triumph,* 2 vols., 1953. For other biographical studies see Ralph Straus, *Charles Dickens: A Biography from New Sources,* 1928; Una Pope-Hennessy, *Charles Dickens,* 1946; Hesketh Pearson, *Charles Dickens: His Character, Comedy, and Career,* 1949; and Jack Lindsay, *Charles Dickens: A Biographical and Critical Study,* 1950. Edward Wagenknecht, *The Man Charles Dickens,* 1929, is a sympathetic study of Dickens' personality.

For criticism see George Gissing, *Charles Dickens,* 1898; G. K. Chesterton, *Charles Dickens,* 1906; George Santayana, *Soliloquies in England,* 1922; Stefan Zweig, *Three Masters,* 1930; George Orwell, *Dickens, Dali, and Others,* 1946; and Walter Allen, *Six Great Novelists,* 1955. For briefer studies consult the available bibliographies and *The Dickensian,* a periodical published quarterly by the Dickens Fellowship.

EMILY DICKINSON

Born: Amherst, Massachusetts
Date: December 10, 1830

Died: Amherst
Date: May 15, 1886

Principal Works

POEMS: *Poems,* 1890; *Poems: Second Series,* 1891; *Poems: Third Series,* 1896; *The Single Hound,* 1914; *Further Poems,* 1929; *Unpublished Poems,* 1936; *Bolts of Melody: New Poems,* 1945; *The Poems of Emily Dickinson,* edited by Thomas H. Johnson, 3 vols., 1955.

LETTERS: *Letters of Emily Dickinson,* edited by Mabel Loomis Todd, 2 vols., 1894 (enlarged, 1931); *The Letters of Emily Dickinson,* edited by Thomas H. Johnson, 3 vols., 1958.

Emily Dickinson, born in Amherst, Massachusetts, December 10, 1830, was a daughter of Edward and Emily (Norcross) Dickinson. Her father, a graduate of Yale College, practiced law in Amherst, engaged in politics, and was treasurer of Amherst College for thirty-seven years. Her brother, William Austin Dickinson, eldest of the three children, after graduation from Amherst College and Harvard Law School, took up the practice of law in Amherst and succeeded his father in 1872 as college treasurer. At the time of his marriage in 1856 to Susan Gilbert, his father built the couple a house on land adjoining the homestead. Lavinia, the youngest child, like her sister Emily, never married and lived at home. A year after Edward Dickinson's death in 1874, Mrs. Dickinson became paralyzed, and the sisters shared the task of caring for their invalid mother until her death in 1882. Thus Emily Dickinson throughout her life was intimately a part of the daily routines of all members of her family. The closeness of ties was a distinguishing mark of the Dickinsons, and regulated Emily's domestic existence.

Small in stature, with chestnut hair and brown eyes, Emily Dickinson was remembered for her plain features and vivacity. Even as a girl her droll wit gave her singularity. She was natural, with an eager interest in people and books. During her youth on one or two occasions she visited relatives in Boston, and her letters home report events with sprightly detail. Having completed her preparatory training in Amherst Academy, at sixteen she was admitted to the second-year class at Mount Holyoke Female Seminary, in September, 1847. Though she was enthusiastic about her new life there, at least during the first months, and completed the year creditably, she did not return to graduate. Her home thenceforth became her physical world. Early in 1855 she and Lavinia spent a month in Washington with their father, then a member of Congress. During the years 1864 and 1865 she was compelled to sojourn for several months in Cambridge and Boston to undergo treatment for an eye affliction, the nature of which is unknown. The trouble was corrected and she returned, quite literally never to leave her home again.

Though none of her early poetry survives, the supposition is that she began writing verse in her early twenties, encouraged by a young law student in her father's office, Benjamin Newton. He removed to Worcester in 1850, married soon after, and died in 1853; but his importance is reflected in her continued references to him as her earliest guide. She seems to have experienced seven or eight years of great poetic creativity, commencing in 1858. In that year she began collecting into "volumes" the brief, neatly transcribed lyrics which for the most part were known only to a few people during her lifetime. These packets, some eighty in number, consist each of a few sheets of folded stationery, loosely threaded at the spine. By 1862 she felt enough assurance in the quality of her verse so that she responded to an *Atlantic Monthly* article by Thomas Wentworth Higginson, written as advice to young contributors. She enclosed in her letter four of her best poems, asking his criticism. The originalities of her nervous style, her innovations in metric and rhyme patterns led him to reply that he felt her writing was uncontrolled. His opinion she accepted as a verdict that the public would not care for her poetry, and she never willingly allowed publication of her verses in her lifetime. But the correspondence thus initiated with Higginson was continued steadily, and he became, as she later called him, her "safest friend."

Emily Dickinson gradually withdrew from all physical encounters except those which did not exhaust her, for the emotional intensity of her nature became so acute as to be an embarassment to her. After 1870 letters became almost her sole way of maintaining association with the large group of friends, nearby or at a distance, whose existence was deeply important to her. She communicated her poems by enclosing them in her letters, and over the years many thus came to the attention of her sister-in-law, Susan Dickinson; Colonel Higginson; Samuel Bowles, publisher of the *Springfield Republican*; Dr. Josiah Holland, Bowles's associate, and later founder of *Scribner's Monthly*; and the poet and novelist, Helen Hunt Jackson. Only seven poems were published in her lifetime, all anonymously, and most of them surreptitiously by friends who wished to see them in print. Among her contemporaries only Mrs. Jackson seems genuinely to have believed that Emily Dickinson was a poet of true distinction.

During her late twenties Emily Dickinson came to feel a deep attachment for the Reverend Dr. Charles Wadsworth of Philadelphia, to whom she referred after his death in 1882 as her dearest earthly friend. In the last decade of her life she was evidently in love with Otis P. Lord, associate justice of the Supreme Court of Massachusetts. A contemporary and lifelong friend of her father's, Lord and his wife (who died in 1877) had been frequent guests of the Dickinsons. The surviving drafts of Emily's letters to him suggest that he may have offered marriage to her. But though her emotional response was deep, clearly she could not alter the pattern of her restricted life. His death in 1884 followed closely upon others in the circle of her close friendships. Her own health deteriorated rapidly soon thereafter, and she succumbed to nephritis on May 15, 1886, aged fifty-five.

After Emily Dickinson's death, her sister Lavinia discovered the many hundred manuscript poems, and persuaded Higginson, who was assisted by Mabel Loomis Todd, to edit a slender volume: *Poems by Emily Dickinson* (1890). Though the reviews for the most part were discouraging, the demand for the volume was heartening, and in the following year the two editors brought out *Poems: Second Series*. Mrs. Todd edited two volumes of *Letters* in 1894, and two years later a further selection of verses: *Poems: Third Series*. No more appeared until Emily Dickinson's niece, Martha Dickinson Bianchi issued *The Single Hound* in 1914, followed by *Further Poems* in 1929 and *Unpublished Poems* in 1936. In 1945 Mrs. Todd and her daughter Millicent Todd Bingham brought out *Bolts of Melody*; with its appearance, virtually all the Dickinson poems were finally in print.

The distinguishing nature of the Dickinson poetry is its conciseness and intensity. The lyrics are brief and usually concerned with such "flood subjects" as the phenomena of nature, the themes of love, death, and immortality. Her prosodic patterns all stem from meters familiar to her in hymn books, but her skill at introducing new rhymes, metric forms, and varying poetic feet—often within a single poem—are originalities which have given added richness to versification. Never commonplace, her language draws upon the homely phrases native to her speech. Her diction is laconic, stripped to the fewest words in order to gain fleetness. She delighted, like the seventeenth century metaphysical poets with whom she is affined, in the paradox: in balancing side by side the concrete and abstract, the minute and the transcendent, the serious and the comic, the usual and the least expected. The awkwardness of her style no longer offends, as it appears to have done before the public was awakened to her true inventiveness, for it is now recognized as the manner by which her startling paradoxes are quickened and given their immediacy.

Thomas H. Johnson

BIBLIOGRAPHICAL REFERENCES: Autograph copies of most of the Dickinson poems are extant, as well as a great many letters. The two great collections are at Amherst College and Harvard University. *The Poems of Emily Dickinson*, 3 vols., 1955, ed. by T. H. Johnson, is a variorum edition. The same editor prepared *The Letters of Emily Dickinson*, 3 vols., 1958, fully annotated. Three biographies are George F. Whicher, *This Was a Poet*, 1939; Richard Chase, *Emily Dickinson*, 1951; and T. H. Johnson, *Emily Dickinson: An Interpretive Biography*, 1955. Two books by Millicent Todd Bingham are useful as source material: *Ancestors' Brocades*, 1945, and account of the early publishing of poems and letters; and *Emily Dickinson's Home: Letters of Edward Dickinson and His Family*, 1955.

DENIS DIDEROT

Born: Langres, France
Date: October 5, 1713

Died: Paris, France
Date: July 30, 1784

PRINCIPAL WORKS

ESSAYS AND STUDIES: *Pensées philosophiques*, 1746 (*Thoughts on Philosophy*); *Lettre sur les aveugles*, 1749 (*Letter on the Blind*); *Lettre sur les sourds et muets*, 1751 (*Letter on the Deaf and Dumb*); *L'Encyclopédie*, 1751–1772; *Supplement au voyage de Bougainville*, 1796 (*Supplement to the Voyage of Bougainville*); *Paradoxe sur le comédien*, 1830 (*The Paradox of the Comedian*); *Le Rêve de d'Alembert*, 1830 (*D'Alembert's Dream*).

NOVEL: *Le Neveu de Rameau*, 1823 (*Rameau's Nephew*).

SHORT STORIES AND SKETCHES: *Bijoux indiscrets*, 1748.

PLAYS: *Le Fils naturel*, 1757; *Le Père de famille*, 1758.

Like so many of his famous contemporaries, Denis Diderot was of respectable, even humble origin, and lived the life of a public controversialist. Born in Langres, France, on October 5, 1713, he early rebelled against his Jesuit background, refusing to go into the solid professions of law or medicine. Instead, he became a bookseller's hack, married a woman with whom he could not live, and led a bohemian existence.

His conversation, always his great talent, attracted the notice of Rousseau, Grimm, and even Catherine the Great, who once saved the great encyclopedist from penury by buying his library and then making him her librarian. His aesthetic, philosophic, and literary judgments made such an impression that he was commissioned to translate Chambers's famous *Cyclopedia*, but in the process he so enlarged the original plan that the monumental *Encyclopedia* resulted. For twenty years he fought to keep the volumes coming off the press but everywhere met with objections, accusations, and all manner of persecution. Diderot's enlightened views on science and religion drew Philistine scorn. Finally, worn out and destitute, he himself wrote and read proofs on the last parts, only to have the printer mutilate the copy by self-imposed censorship. Voltaire observed that such ingenuity paid Diderot only a fourth of what an army contractor makes in a day. He died in Paris on July 30, 1784.

Diderot's collected works total twenty volumes, ranging from a delightful farce-comedy, to tragedy, poetry, philosophy, aesthetics, criticism, politics, and religion. He made numerous translations. Yet he was not a great writer at all. His works, however, inspired all his French contemporaries, as well as Lessing and Goethe in Germany. He was not the atheist his detractors said, but believed only in religious tolerance and speculative freedom. His philosophy was a simple sort of casuistry, somewhat didactic though sympathetic. But as a critic of art, literature, and drama he is sometimes read today, for none of his contemporaries presents such balanced judgment. Unfortunately, he founded no school nor was he widely emulated, but many have praised his faithfulness to the subjects he discussed.

BIBLIOGRAPHICAL REFERENCES: Diderot's *Œuvres* were published in 1821–1834 in 26 vols. Good selections of the works, in English, are *French Thought in the Eighteenth Century*, edited by Romain Rolland, André Maurois, and Edouard Herriot, 1953; and *Rameau's Nephew and Other Works*, edited in the Anchor Books by Jacques Barzun and Ralph H. Bowen, 1956. The *Correspondence* was edited by Georges Roth, 1955, with an important preface and notes. A good bibliography is Herbert Dieckmann, *Inventaire du Fonds Vandeul, et Inédits de Diderot*, 1951. Probably the best biographies are André Billy, *Diderot*, 1932, in French; and Lester G. Crocker, *The Embattled Philosopher: A Biography of Denis Diderot*, 1954, in English. Important critical books are John M. Morley, *Diderot and the Encyclopaedists*, 2 vols., 1886; Joseph E. Barker, *Diderot's Treatment of the Christian Religion in the Encyclopédie*, 1941, with bibliography; Eric M. Steel, *Diderot's Imagery: A Study of a Literary Personality*, 1941; Otis Edward Fellows and Norman L. Torrey, eds., *Diderot Studies*, 2 vols., 1950–53, containing essays in French and English, with a bibliography; Aram Vartanian, *Diderot and Descartes: A Study of Scientific Naturalism in the Enlightenment*, 1953; and Arthur M. Wilson, *Diderot: The Testing Years, 1713–1759*, 1957. Havelock Ellis's essay on Diderot in *The New Spirit*, 1890, is also interesting.

ISAK DINESEN
(Baroness Karen Blixen-Finecke)

Born: Rungsted, Denmark
Date: October 17, 1885

Died: Rungsted, Denmark
Date: September 7, 1962

PRINCIPAL WORKS

SHORT STORIES: *Seven Gothic Tales*, 1934; *Winter Tales*, 1942; *Last Tales*, 1957.
NOVEL: *Gengaeldelsens veje*, 1944 (*The Angelic Avenger*, as Pierre Andrézel).
TRAVEL SKETCHES AND IMPRESSIONS: *Out of Africa*, 1937.
ESSAYS: *Daguerreotypes*, 1951.

Karen Dinesen, born at Rungsted, Denmark, on October 17, 1885, was the daughter of a Danish officer and popular writer on hunting subjects. Educated in Copenhagen, she later studied painting in Paris and Berlin. Upon her marriage to Baron Bror Blixen-Finecke in 1914, she and her husband were given by their families a coffee plantation in British East Africa. Divorced in 1921, she continued to manage the plantation alone until the economic world situation forced her to abandon the project in 1931, when she returned to her family home near Elsinore. Since that time she has won a wide audience of readers with her Gothic fiction. She writes with equal facility in either Danish or English, and most of her books have appeared almost simultaneously in both languages.

The publication of *Seven Gothic Tales* in this country created a mild sensation in 1934. Into a literary world then dominated by the proletarian novel, "Isak Dinesen" wandered rather like a reveler strayed from a *bal masqué* who had forgotten to take off his fancy dress. Written in an artificial, highly mannered style and with early nineteenth century settings, the stories contained a good deal of "Gothic" strangeness and some horror; but they were overlaid with a strictly modern psychology and philosophizing. Though somewhat operatic, they pleased because they were so different from the current fiction of the depression decade.

Out of Africa, the result of her African experience, was praised by many for its sensitive evocation of the native scene. During the German occupation of Denmark during World War II, she wrote (in Danish and under a different pseudonym) a novel which under the same Gothic disguise attacked the Germans so subtly that the true intent of the book was never grasped by the Nazis. It appeared in this country in 1947 as *The Angelic Avenger. Last Tales* is a collection of stories written over the past decade.

In her short fiction Baroness Blixen belongs to the nineteenth century tradition of E. T. A. Hoffmann, Edgar Allan Poe, and Villiers de l'Isle Adam. Although some readers may feel that, in arranging the fantastic staging for her stories, the author's cleverness sometimes overreaches itself, her work is interesting to those who, tired of realism, do not object to an artificial style and an elaborate machinery of ghosts, duels, and floods, or a reliance upon "trick" plots.

BIBLIOGRAPHICAL REFERENCES: The most carefully considered study in English is John Davenport, "A Noble Pride: The Art of Karen Blixen," *Twentieth Century,* CLIX (1956), 264–274. See also Hans Brix, *Blixens Eventyr,* 1949; Aage Hendrikson, *Karen Blixen og marionetterne,* 1952; and Claidi Jorgen, *Contemporary Danish Authors,* 1952.

BENJAMIN DISRAELI

Born: London, England
Date: December 21, 1804

Died: London
Date: April 19, 1881

PRINCIPAL WORKS

NOVELS: *Vivian Grey,* 1826–1827; *The Young Duke,* 1831; *Contarini Fleming,* 1832; *The Wondrous Tale of Alroy,* 1833; *Henrietta Temple, A Love Story,* 1836; *Venetia,* 1837; *Coningsby,* 1844; *Sybil,* 1845; *Tancred,* 1847; *Lothair,* 1870; *Endymion,* 1880.

BURLESQUES: *The Voyage of Captain Popanilla,* 1828; *Ixion in Heaven,* 1833; *The Infernal Marriage,* 1833.

BIOGRAPHY: *The Political Biography of Lord George Bentinck,* 1852.

HISTORICAL STUDIES: *England and France,* 1832; *Vindication of the English Constitution,* 1835; *The Spirit of Whiggism,* 1836.

Benjamin Disraeli, born in London, December 21, 1804, was the son of Isaac D'Israeli, a well-known literary commentator and biographer. Like the title character of his sensational first novel, *Vivian Grey,* he was privately educated—chiefly in his father's library—and took the "grand tour." He chafed at his law studies and with a powerful self-assurance wrote a quick succession of shallowly brilliant novels: *The Young Duke, Contarini Fleming,* and *The Wondrous Tale of Alroy,* as well as a group of political pamphlets and a trio of burlesque extravaganzas, *The Voyage of Captain Popanilla, Ixion in Heaven,* and *The Infernal Marriage.* Then, despite the handicaps of his Jewish heritage and his foppish manners, he brazenly experimented with politics. Failing as a radical, he was elected to Parliament as a Tory. Out of this experience he wrote his three best-known novels, *Coningsby,* sometimes referred to as "the best novel of politics ever written"; *Sybil,* and *Tancred.* He gave up his writing temporarily, married in 1839 the widow of

his colleague Wyndham Lewis, then gradually rose to be three times Chancellor of the Exchequer, and, finally, Prime Minister from 1867–68 and again from 1874–80.

During his second term of office, when he was knighted, he took a name from his first novel and became the first Earl of Beaconsfield. In his later years he resumed his writing and became an intimate friend of Queen Victoria. He died in London, April 19, 1881.

In *The Political Biography of Lord George Bentinck,* Disraeli summed up the basic message of all his social novels in the principle: "the few for the many; not the many for the few." Despite his many detractors, political and literary, he bluffed, schemed, fought, and insisted on his way to success—and achieved it.

BIBLIOGRAPHICAL REFERENCES: The best edition is the Bradenham Edition of *The Novels and Tales of Benjamin Disraeli,* with an introduction by Philip Guedalla, 12 vols., 1926–1927. The fullest biography is William F. Monypenny and G. E. Buckle, *The Life of Benjamin Disraeli,* 1929. There are several other useful biographies: E. T. Raymond, *Disraeli: Alien Patriot,* 1925; Edward G. Clark, *Benjamin Disraeli,* 1926; D. L. Murray, *Disraeli,* 1927; and André Maurois, *Disraeli,* 1928. See also M. E. Speare, *The Political Novel,* 1924.

JOHN DONNE

Born: London, England   *Died:* London
Date: 1572   *Date:* March 31, 1631

PRINCIPAL WORKS

POEMS: *An Anatomy of the World: The First Anniversary,* 1611; *Of the Progress of the Soule: The Second Anniversary,* 1612; *Poems by J. D.,* 1633.

THEOLOGICAL ESSAYS AND STUDIES: *Pseudo-Martyr,* 1610; *Ignatius His Conclave,* 1611; *Devotions Upon Emergent Occasions,* 1624; *Juvenalia: or Certain Paradoxes and Problems,* 1633; *Biathanatos,* 1646; *Essays in Divinity,* 1651.

SERMONS: *Six Sermons on Several Occasions,* 1634; *LXXX Sermons,* with *The Life and Death of Dr. Donne,* by Izaak Walton, 1640; *Fifty Sermons,* 1649; *XXVI Sermons,* 1660.

LETTERS: *Letters to Several Persons of Honour,* 1651; *A Collection of Letters,* made by Sir Tobie Mathews, Kt., 1660.

John Donne, born in London, probably early in 1572, was the son of a prosperous London tradesman. His mother, who came of more distinguished family, was a Roman Catholic, and the poet was educated in that faith. His claim that his family had suffered for the faith is borne out by the fact that his brother died in prison after being charged with concealing a priest; and his own career was long hindered by his recusancy. Jesuit training left permanent traces on his mind. In a book on suicide (*Biathanatos*) he said that his interest in the subject stemmed from first-hand knowledge of the persecuted Jesuits; and this also gave him the right in another book (*Pseudo-Martyr*) to analyze and condemn their desire to achieve martyrdom at the hands of the civil authorities. Compelled by his religion to leave Oxford without a degree, Donne studied law at the Inns of Court in the 1590's; but at this time he also read widely in theology. He was trying to decide which of the two Churches that claimed to be truly Catholic—the Roman and the Anglican—was the right one. The date of his decision in favor of the Church of England is uncertain, but we know it was taken many years later, after intense study and not merely to clear the way to worldly advancement.

This was not his whole life at the Inns of Court. He took his place in the world of wit and fashion, made friends with the gifted youth of his time, became "a great visitor of ladies." Despite his reputation for hard study, in many languages and many subjects, he also began at this time a series of highly original, occasionally improper, love-poems. These circulated widely in manuscript and grew famous, in spite of his later distaste for them; eventually they were published in 1633, after his death. In our own time these *Songs and Sonets* have achieved a remarkable celebrity. They are often very difficult—even Ben Jonson, Donne's friend, found them so—and some of the most difficult are also the most profound, like the "Nocturnall upon S. Lucies Day." Many of them, however —and this applies also to the *Elegies* —are merely learned jokes about love, like "The Flea," or paradoxes ridiculing conventional morality, like "Elegy xvii." Others again are apparently serious love-poems, like "The Feaver"; but even these are, as Dryden complained, calculated to "perplex the minds of the fair sex with the nice speculations of philosophy." One or two poems seem to be addressed to his wife. In fact there is a variety of occasions and moods; but nearly all the poems are alike in abjuring the usual smoothness of Elizabethan love-poetry. They are "harsh," to use Donne's word, with a harshness usually thought of as more proper to satire, which he was also writing at this time. This quality will disturb modern readers less than the obscurity of the thought; most need help from a learned edition to read these poems.

When he left the Inns of Court, Donne traveled in Italy and Spain, and took part in two naval expeditions (1596 and 1597). He was trying to make his way in the world. In 1598 he became secretary to the powerful Sir Thomas Egerton, but ruined his chances by secretly marrying Lady Egerton's niece, Ann More, in December 1601. He went to prison and lost his job. Forgiven but not reinstated, he lived for some years in relative poverty and discomfort at Mitcham, then a village outside London, with his rapidly growing family. Being poor, he sought patronage, writing complimentary and elegiac verse, some of it excellent, for the great Countess of Bedford, Sir Robert Drury, and others. He "ghosted" for the Bishop of Durham in anti-Romanist controversy, but refused to enter the Church. When the belated payment of his wife's dowry gave him a spell of leisure, he wrote *Pseudo-Martyr* and the witty *Ignatius his Conclave* against the Jesuits; and a work of theology, *Essayes in Divinity,* written about 1614 but not published until 1651. *Biathanatos* was also written at this time.

Eventually the King himself made it clear that Donne would not achieve advancement outside the Church; and in 1615, at the age of nearly forty-three, he was ordained. Thenceforth he wrote little verse, and that of relatively small importance; his religious poetry belongs mostly to 1607–1615. Instead, he wrote and preached sermons which established him as one of the greatest of preachers in an age of great pulpit oratory. His wife died in 1617, and he celebrated her memory in a magnificent sermon and a fine sonnet. In 1621 he became Dean of St. Paul's, a somber priest much given to thoughts of death, but happy in the rejection of "the mistress of my youth, Poetry" for "the wife of mine age, Divinity." In 1623, seriously ill, he wrote *Devotions upon Emergent Occasions,* a set of religious meditations on his disease which, for all their solemnity, show that he remained in his strange way the wittiest of writers. In Lent, 1631, he preached the famous and terrible sermon called "Deaths Duell" before Charles I, and then ordered the grim monument of himself in his shroud,

which survived the great fires of 1666 and 1940, and may still be seen in St. Paul's. Donne died in London on March 31, 1631, and Izaak Walton, his first biographer, has made notorious the histrionic composure of his deathbed.

Donne's reputation as a poet faded rapidly, and was not fully revived until the present century. His influence on modern poetry has been considerable, because poets admire the intellectual vigor of his work, his range of learned reference, and his wit. It has also been thought, not quite correctly, that his attitude to the new science of his time, for example to the discovery of Copernicus, was that of a man who saw an older and more stable world breaking up, so that his mood resembled that of some modern intellectuals. This is a distorted view; but distortion is probably inevitable, because there is a great deal of Donne, and not much of it is read. What is well known is the love-poetry and the religious poetry. Of the love-poetry it is true to say that the modern reader, with an effort, can recover some of the delight and surprise it must have given to Donne's friends. The religious poetry, much of it based on Catholic techniques of meditation still in use by Anglo-Catholics at that time, has an equal appeal. It is characterized by the same agility of intellect, here associated with religious passion; and although it sometimes declines into clever trifling that offends modern taste, it remains a remarkable record of spiritual turbulence. As a prose writer Donne achieved almost unrivaled greatness in the sermon; it was the form that suited him best, and it is unlucky that it hardly suits us at all, so that his sermons are not much read nowadays, and the picture we have of Donne is consequently incomplete. Nevertheless, his rediscovery as a poet has added to our tradition a fine example of mascu- line strength and intellectual power in English verse.

Frank Kermode

BIBLIOGRAPHICAL REFERENCES: The standard edition of the poems, complete with introductory essay and notes, is *The Poems of John Donne*, edited by Sir H. J. C. Grierson, 2 vols., 1912. Other editions are the *Complete Poems*, edited by A. B. Grosart, 2 vols., 1872; *Poems*, edited by E. K. Chambers, 2 vols., 1896; *Poems*, edited by Hugh l'Anson Fausset, Everyman's Library, 1931; *Complete Poems*, edited by R. E. Bennett, 1942; and *Donne: The Divine Poems*, edited by Helen Gardner, 1952. The *Works*, edited by Henry Alford, 6 vols., 1839, contains sermons, letters, and the *Devotions*. A definitive edition of the *Sermons* is now in preparation under the editorship of H. H. Umbach and Evelyn M. Simpson, with 6 vols. in print to 1957. For the general reader the best edition is probably *The Complete Poetry and Selected Prose*, edited by John Hayward, Nonesuch Library, 1929. Another edition of selections is *John Donne: Poetry and Prose*, edited by H. W. Garrod, 1946.

Sir Edmund Gosse's *The Life and Letters of John Donne*, 2 vols., 1899, remains the standard biography in spite of incompleteness and inaccuracies. Izaak Walton, *The Life and Death of Dr. Donne*, originally prefixed to LXXX Sermons, 1640, and separately published in an enlarged edition in 1658, though not always accurate, shows the viewpoint of a contemporary and friend. For criticism see Evelyn M. Simpson, *A Study of the Prose Works of John Donne*, 1924 (rev. ed., 1948); Hugh l'Anson Fausset, *John Donne: A Study in Discord*, 1924; George Williamson, *The Donne Tradition*, 1930; R. C. Bald, *Donne's Influence in English Literature*, 1932; M. A. Rugoff, *Donne's Imagery*, 1939; M. F. Maloney, *John Donne: His Flight from Mediaevalism*, 1944; J. B. Leishman, *The Monarch of Wit*, 1951; K. W. Gransden, *John Donne*, 1954; James Clay Hunt, *Donne's Poetry: Essays in Literary Analysis*, 1954; and Frank Kermode, *John Donne*, 1957.

Some notably important essay studies include Mario Praz, *Secentismo e Marinismo in Inghilterra: John Donne—Richard Crashaw*, 1925; Theodore Spencer, ed., *A Garland for John Donne*, 1931, containing essays by T. S. Eliot, Mario Praz, John Sparrow, George Williamson, Evelyn M. Simpson, John Hayward, Mary P. Ramsay, and Theodore Spencer; Joan Bennett, *Four Metaphysical Poets*, 1934 (rev. ed., 1953); J. B. Leishman, *The Metaphysical Poets*, 1934; and Rosemond Tuve, *Elizabethan and Metaphysical Imagery*, 1947.

JOHN DOS PASSOS

Born: Chicago, Illinois
Date: January 14, 1896

PRINCIPAL WORKS

NOVELS: *One Man's Initiation: 1917*, 1920; *Three Soldiers*, 1921; *Streets of Night*, 1923; *Manhattan Transfer*, 1925; *The 42nd Parallel*, 1930; *1919*, 1932; *The Big Money*, 1936; *U. S. A.*, 1937 (*The 42nd Parallel*, *1919*, and *The Big Money*); *Adventures of a Young Man*, 1939; *Number One*, 1943; *The Grand Design*, 1948; *District of Columbia*, 1953 (*Adventures of a Young Man*, *Number One*, and *The Grand Design*); *Chosen Country*, 1951; *Most Likely to Succeed*, 1954.

POEMS: *A Pushcart at the Curb*, 1922.

PLAYS: *The Garbage Man,* 1926; *Airways, Inc.,* 1928; *Three Plays,* 1934.

TRAVEL AND REPORTING: *Rosinante to the Road Again,* 1922; *Orient Express,* 1927; *In All Countries,* 1934; *Journeys Between Wars,* 1938; *State of the Nation,* 1944; *Tour of Duty,* 1946.

HISTORICAL ESSAYS AND STUDIES: *The Ground We Stand On,* 1941; *The Head and Heart of Thomas Jefferson,* 1953; *The Men Who Made Our Nation,* 1956.

Of Portuguese-American ancestry, John (Roderigo) Dos Passos was born in Chicago on January 14, 1896, and educated at Harvard, from which he was graduated in 1916. During the First World War he served in the ambulance corps, and from his experiences grew his first novel to attract attention, *Three Soldiers,* a contribution to a large body of fiction, both European and American, which aimed to strip war of any shreds of glamour or romance that might still cling to it. Disillusioned like so many of the now famous "lost generation," Dos Passos next turned his attention to an exhaustive study of the American scene, trying to pack into *Manhattan Transfer* and the trilogies that followed it a picture, as nearly complete as possible, of American society during a significant and crucial period of our national history.

During his early career as a novelist Dos Passos displayed distinctly leftist and unorthodox sympathies that he carried into practice to the extent of being jailed for joining a picket line during the furor that attended the Sacco-Vanzetti case. This was the period of the so-called "proletarian" novel, a type that he did much to form, not only by his technical devices but especially by his sympathies with the underdog, those whom he considered to be exploited and abused by the American system. During the depression years, when so much in our national life was under sharp criticism, the point of view maintained by Dos

Passos and his imitators had great popularity and influence.

In massive novels crowded with characters, like *U.S.A.* and *District of Columbia,* the real protagonist is, as has often been remarked, society itself. That is to say, the author exerts as much effort to describe and make real the social scene of a given period as a traditional novelist would expend upon the development of a human hero. The "characters," in the conventional sense of the word, are subordinate to society; the important point is the effect that the social and particularly the economic milieu has upon the individual. Thus it is vital for the success of the book that the reader be given as vivid a picture of the era as is possible. To accomplish this purpose, Dos Passos employed a variety of technical devices: the "Camera Eye," which focused on atmospheric details subjectively and impressionistically rendered; the "Newsreel," made up of snatches of popular songs, quotations from speeches, reproductions of newspaper headlines and related reportage of the time, and interpolated biographical sketches of real personages whose activities coincided with those of his fictional creations. It was a kind of literary *découpage* which at times was very successful. The accuracy of detail, adding up to a portrait of modern America, won the highest praise of Sinclair Lewis, himself a master of realistic reporting.

The Spanish civil war was a disillusioning experience to Dos Passos, as it

303

was to many writers; it was to turn his sympathies toward the political Right and to deepen his interest in American history and the democratic tradition. It was a shift, however, which lost him the support of some of his earlier admirers. Further, critics were not so kind to his more recent novels; the documentary style, they felt, had been overworked. Nevertheless, Dos Passos' novels are important in that they reveal varied aspects of American life from a sociological viewpoint hitherto largely ignored.

BIBLIOGRAPHICAL REFERENCES: There is no full-length biographical or critical study. For evaluations of Dos Passos' work see Granville Hicks, *The Great Tradition*, 1933; Joseph Warren Beach, *American Fiction, 1920–1940*, 1941; Maxwell Geismar, *Writers in Crisis*, 1942; Alfred Kazin, *On Native Grounds*, 1942; George Snell, *The Shapers of American Fiction*, 1947; W. M. Frohock, *The Novel of Violence in America*, 1950; and J. W. Aldridge, *After the Lost Generation*, 1951.

See also Alan Calmer, "John Dos Passos," *Sewanee Review*, XL (1932), 341–349; Michael Gold, "The Education of John Dos Passos," *English Journal*, XXII (1933), 87–97; Bernard DeVoto, "John Dos Passos: Anatomist of Our Time," *Saturday Review of Literature*, XIV (1936), 3–4, 12–13; Delmore Schwartz, "John Dos Passos and the Whole Truth," *Southern Review*, IV (1938), 351–367; Lionel Trilling, "The America of John Dos Passos," *Partisan Review*, IV (1938), 26–32; Granville Hicks, "Politics and John Dos Passos," *Antioch Review*, X (1950), 85–98; and Milton Rugoff, "Dos Passos, Novelist of Our Time," *Sewanee Review*, XLIX (1941), 453–494.

FYODOR MIKHAILOVICH DOSTOEVSKI

Born: Moscow, Russia
Date: November 11, 1821

Died: St. Petersburg, Russia
Date: February 9, 1881

PRINCIPAL WORKS

NOVELS: *Bednyie lyudi*, 1846 (*Poor Folk*); *Selo Stepanchikovo i evo obitateli*, 1859 (*The Hamlet of Stepanchikovo*); *Unizhonnyie i oskorblyonnie*, 1861 (*The Humiliated and the Wronged*); *Zapiski iz Mertvovo Doma*, 1861–1862 (*Notes from the House of the Dead*); *Zapiski iz podpolya*, 1864 (*Notes from the Underground*); *Igrok*, 1866 (*The Gambler*); *Prestupleniye i nakazaniye*, 1866 (*Crime and Punishment*); *Idiot*, 1868 (*The Idiot*); *Besy*, 1871–1872 (*The Possessed*); *Podrostok*, 1875 (*A Raw Youth*); *Bratya Karamazov*, 1879–1880 (*The Brothers Karamazov*).

JOURNAL AND ESSAYS: *Dnevnik pisatelya*, 1873, 1876–1878 (*The Diary of a Writer*).

Fyodor Mikhailovich Dostoevski (also Fëdor or Fiodor Dostoevsky), the great Russian novelist, was born on November 11, 1821, in Moscow, where his father, an impoverished nobleman, was a resident physician at Mariinsky Hospital for the poor. Fyodor, with his four brothers and two sisters, lived on the hospital grounds and at an early age became familiar with suffering, misfortune and death. He was brought up by his morose and hot-tempered father in an atmosphere of strict discipline and religious piety. His mother who came from a family of well-to-do Moscow merchants, was kind and

304

sickly; she died when her son was not yet sixteen. Sent in 1837 to St. Petersburg School for Military Engineering, Fyodor spent there four depressing years. In 1839 his father was murdered by his mishandled serfs, and Fyodor remained alone, without money or friends. Freud believes that this tragic event, in conjunction with an Oedipus complex, caused the beginning of Dostoevski's epilepsy: he suffered from it all his life.

In 1844 he resigned his position as military draughtsman to devote himself completely to writing. After years of poverty and privations he attained considerable success with his first novel *Poor Folk,* published in 1846; in it he followed Gogol's humanitarian tradition and depicted a humble governmental clerk who loves an orphan girl but, despite all his sacrifices, is unable to secure her happiness. *The Double,* published the same year and dealing with the problem of split personality in E. T. A. Hoffmann manner, and other stories (among them the romantic *The Landlady,* the autobiographical *White Nights,* and the unfinished but highly revelatory *Netochka Nezvanova*) failed to find favor with the critics.

In 1849 Dostoevski was arrested as a member of the clandestine Petrashevsky Society—a group of young radicals who dreamt of freedom, criticized Russian autocracy, and discussed Utopian socialism; later he was, together with nineteen friends, sentenced to death, brought to the execution place, and put in front of a firing squad. At the last moment, however, it was announced that the tsar had commuted the capital punishment into one of penal servitude. After this horrible experience Dostoevski spent four years as a convict in Siberia and had to submit to treatment so inhuman that only glimpses of it can be caught in his *Notes from the House of the Dead.* In 1854 he was sent for another four years as a private in an infantry regiment to Semipalatinsk, an Asiatic hellhole. In 1857 he married Maria Isayeva, a young consumptive widow, and in 1858, after nine years of ordeals and forced silence, he was allowed to return to St. Petersburg and to resume his literary activities. By this time, a man of thirty-eight, he had lost most of his youthful illusions and he underwent a religious conversion. In the next few years, which form the second period of his development as a novelist, he edited monthly magazines and published *The Hamlet of Stepanchikovo,* a satirical novelette containing ironic character sketches; *The Humiliated and Wronged,* a novel of frustrated love and suffering, which, despite its melodramatic devices, revealed the same morbid sensitivity and compassion for the poor and disinherited as in *Poor Folk;* and *Notes from the Underground,* one of his most significant works: its despicable hero builds challenging philosophical and social theories in order to rationalize his own sadistic and masochistic drives.

Dostoevski worked always under pressure, and the constant lack of money forced him to write hastily and to deliver unpolished copy to publishers and magazine editors in a steady and speedy flow. After the death of his hysterical wife in 1864 and a tempestuous love affair with the twenty-year-old Apollinaria Suslova, who served as the prototype for several of his feminine portrayals (particularly in the highly autobiographical *The Gambler*), Dostoevski married in 1867 his stenog

305

rapher, the young Anna Snitkina. The following year, in order to escape his creditors, he went abroad with his wife and spent four years in Germany, Italy, and Switzerland. This sojourn strengthened his negative attitude toward the Western way of life. His second wife became his faithful companion, gave him children and the peace of a family, put order into his involved financial affairs, and succeeded in curing him of his gambling passion which, until 1871, made him lose money at each roulette table in Europe. They returned to Russia in 1871, and settled in St. Petersburg. By that time Dostoevski was recognized at home as a great writer, and his fame began to spread abroad. *Crime and Punishment* opened the third and most important period of his career, in which he wrote his greatest works. Most of them were novels of murder and passion or stories of morbid introspection, such as *The Eternal Husband* (1870). In *Crime and Punishment,* Raskolnikov, a poor student, kills an old woman moneylender on the assumption that extraordinary individuals have the right to disregard the accepted moral code, but falls victim of his own doubts and of his unbearable isolation. Prince Myshkin, the simple-hearted and Christ-like figure of *The Idiot,* is the embodiment of kindliness and brotherhood but he is unable to cope with hatred and destruction raging around him and is finally crushed by them. In *The Possessed,* a long novel with strong political overtones and a sarcastic portrayal of Turgenev, a group of atheistic rebels, fools, and demonic egotists unleash the forces of evil in an attempt to stir up a revolutionary movement which would lead to an egalitarian, soulless, antheap-like

society, and cause only suicide, murder, arson, and utter confusion. In *A Raw Youth* an adolescent driven by will to power and vague idealism dreams of becoming a millionaire, but is confronted with blackmail and vice. And in *The Brothers Karamazov,* Dostoevski's masterpiece, a multi-level tragedy of parricide, he alternates metaphysical discussions and prophetic tales (such as his "Legend of Grand Inquisitor," a weird forecast of authoritarian theory and practice) with psychological analysis of human nature and superb portrayals of intellectual rebel, emotional wastrel, trivial knave, and Christian knight. The author's faith in the ultimate triumph of spiritual values and of religion of Christ finds in this novel its highest expression. In his *Speech on Pushkin* (1880) Dostoevski gave a new meaning to his Slavophile creed, preached the union of Russia and the West through the Orthodox concept of love and the national striving for universality which he claimed to be a typically Russian trait. In his *Diary of a Writer* (1873–1880, with interruptions), however, Dostoevski the journalist criticized Russian intellectuals from the position of national conservatism, and defended the autocratic government and the Greek Orthodox Church. These writings were labeled as reactionary by liberal and later by communist critics. Dostoevski died at St. Petersburg on February 9, 1881.

The impact of Dostoevski's work can be explained by its tremendous representational power, by its psychological intensity, and by its moral and philosophical wealth. In his fiction he hardly ever offered definite solutions but he never ceased raising most disturbing questions. One of his main themes was the problem of freedom and of suspension of morality; therefore he was attracted by crime and the various forms of transgression by which man challenges the accepted code of behaviour and the existing social and moral order. While deeply concerned with the justification of evil and suffering on earth, Dostoevski tried to define man's condition and limitations, and in his constant religious quest, which often assumed a tormented manic character, strove for a reconciliation of human and divine. As a psychological writer, he explored man's nature in depth, and discovered the hidden roots of its duality: by showing man in crisis situations he revealed his most intimate subconscious drives and pathological complexes. This gave his heroes a peculiar dimension of morbidity and exaggeration. Dostoevski insisted that one and the same man was equally capable of highest virtue and lowest sin, of coarse carnal fury and of pure idealistic flight. The purification and redemption of man through suffering and sacrifice is connected in Dostoevski with the affirmation of Christian faith, and his positive hero in *The Brothers Karamazov*, Alesha, reaches some kind of religious epiphany through deeds of love and compassion. Dostoevski's psychological novel, often disguised as a mystery story, is actually a novel of ideas presented in a dramatic form. All his main themes are lived through in a highly personal and intense manner by passionate men and women who move around in despair, pain, lust, and madness. A wonderful builder of plots, Dostoevski often recurs to theatrical devices. The structure of his novels is often loose and the accumulation of horrors is sometimes on the border of bad taste. Yet all these shortcomings are redeemed by intensity, suspense, and psychological illuminations. Today he is hailed as the precursor of modern psychology of the unconscious and the pathological, as one of the masters of Nietzsche and of the existentialists, and as a source of literary influence to be traced in such different writers as Gide, Mann, Faulkner, and many others.

Marc Slonim

BIBLIOGRAPHICAL REFERENCES: Among numerous works on Dostoevski, for the biographical data see Avrahm Yarmolinsky, *Dostoyevsky: A Life*, 1934; Henri Troyat, *The Firebrand: The Life of Dostoevsky*, 1946; and Marc Slonim, *Three Loves of Dostoevsky*, 1955. For critical comment see André Gide, *Dostoievski*, 1923; Stefan Zweig, *Three Masters*, 1930; N. A. Berdyaev, *Dostoevsky*, 1934; Janko Lavrin, *Dostoevsky*, 1947; also A. Meier-Graefe, *Dostoevsky: The Man and His Work*, 1928; and E. J. Simmons, *Dostoevski: The Making of a Novelist*, 1940.

CHARLES M. DOUGHTY

Born: Suffolk, England
Date: August 19, 1843

Died: Sissinghurst, England
Date: January 20, 1926

PRINCIPAL WORKS

TRAVEL SKETCHES AND IMPRESSIONS: *Travels in Arabia Deserta*, 1888.

POEMS: *Under Arms*, 1900; *The Dawn in Britain*, 1906; *Adam Cast Forth*, 1908; *The Cliffs*, 1909; *The Clouds*, 1912; *The Titans*, 1916; *Mansoul*, 1920.

Of a landed county family, Charles M(ontagu) Doughty was born at Theberton Hall, Suffolk, on August 19, 1843. At various times he studied at King's College, London, and the universities of Oxford, Cambridge, Leyden, and Louvain. While still an undergraduate at Cambridge, he spent a year (1863–1864) studying the Norwegian glaciers and returned to England to publish his findings in *On the Jöstedal Brae Glaciers in Norway.* After his graduation he continued to study— archeology, geology, geography, and early English literature—without any apparent pattern or purpose. In 1870 he left England, going through Holland, Italy, Spain, and Athens, before he reached Egypt in 1874.

Doughty also made several expeditions into the Sinai Peninsula, charting the geological formations and making maps of the terrain. He then returned to Europe and wrote to the Royal Geographical Society in London, offering his information and requesting funds for further exploration. He was refused, for the Society felt it had all the information on the Sinai Peninsula it needed.

Returning to the Near East, Doughty traveled throughout northwestern Arabia for two years (1876–1878) with a group of Bedouins, living in their tents, making many notations on the land, the geology, and the customs of the tribes. On his return to England in 1879 he gave numerous reports to the Society concerning the geology and geography of Arabia. The Arabian expedition formed the basis of Doughty's major work, *Travels in Arabia Deserta,* an account not only of his scientific

findings, but also of the customs and behavior of the tribe of Bedouins among whom he lived. The book became enormously popular both because of its scientific interest and because of the curiosity aroused by adventures in an unknown land.

Apart from three years spent writing in Italy, Doughty did not leave England again. Having always considered himself a poet, he began to work very earnestly at a long epic poem dealing with the founding of Britain. The six-volume work was finally published, when he was sixty years old, as *The Dawn in Britain.* Despite his patriotic glorification of the English race, Doughty did not, with this poem, reach the wide and appreciative audience he anticipated. Nevertheless, he continued writing long poems: *Adam Cast Forth,* dealing with the origin of the first human family in Arabia; *The Cliffs,* a long satire on contemporary British complacency in the face of a threatened and imaginary invasion; *The Titans,* a long hymn praising the origin of man and his development of scientific knowledge, and the allegorical *Mansoul,* a poem dealing, as the subtitle indicates, with "the Riddle of the World." In his later years *Travels in Arabia Deserta* brought him fame, and he was awarded the Royal Geographical Society's Founder's Medal in 1912. He died at Sissinghurst on January 20, 1926.

Doughty's admirers have unqualified praise for his style. When writing of his travels in Arabia, he employed an archaic and ironic quality that seemed a splendid instrument for presenting Arabic manners and speech. In his

308

poetry the same style, without the irony, led some to praise his purity of language and others to ignore his work as boring and archaic. His admirers compared his poetry to Spenser's rich, full, lavish verse (and Doughty honestly felt he was glorifying his own age as Spenser had his); other critics felt Doughty was only elaborating on conventional patriotism and notions of progress. Today he is admired solely for his fascinating accounts of life and geography in Arabia, and *Travels in Arabia Deserta* is secure in its place as a classic narrative of travel and adventure.

BIBLIOGRAPHICAL REFERENCES: David G. Hogarth, *The Life of Charles M. Doughty*, 1928, is a well-documented biographical study. See also Barker Fairley, *Charles M. Doughty: A Critical Study*, 1927; idem, "The Dawn in Britain after Fifty Years," *University of Toronto Quarterly*, XXVI (1957), 149–164.

GEORGE DOUGLAS
(George Douglas Brown)

Born: Ochiltree, Ayrshire, Scotland
Date: January 26, 1869

Died: London, England
Date: August 28, 1902

PRINCIPAL WORK

NOVEL: *The House with the Green Shutters*, 1901.

George Douglas, born George Douglas Brown, at Ochiltree, Scotland, on January 26, 1869, was educated at the University of Glasgow and at Oxford. He then went to London where he contributed articles to periodicals and worked as a reader for the publisher John Macqueen. Douglas's first literary effort was a boy's book, *Love and a Sword* (1899), written under the pseudonym of Kennedy King.

Douglas drew on his Scottish background for his only major novel, *The House with the Green Shutters*, a story of the grim and somber aspects of Scottish life. The novel was widely acclaimed as a realistic portrait of the hard life of the Scot, and Douglas's sense of the grim rustic defeated by a world he never made caused critics to praise and describe him as a Scottish Thomas Hardy. Douglas also injected some Scottish dialect into the book, attempting to give his readers as complete a picture of the different qualities of life in Scotland as he possibly could. His work has had some influence on more recent Scottish writers, although they have carried the use of Scottish dialect and the notion of Scotland as a separate culture and a separate country much further than Douglas did. But the grim tone, the feeling that life is primarily a losing battle in a hard, northern land, is still frequent in Scottish writing.

Douglas made elaborate plans to write a vast historical romance, based in the period of Cromwell, but he died in London, August 28, 1902, before any significant amount of work was done on the project.

BIBLIOGRAPHICAL REFERENCES: The mainstream of English literature has swept past Brown. There is no collected edition. The only full study is C. Lennox, *George*

Douglas Brown, A Memoir, and Reminiscences of Brown by Andrew Melrose, 1903.
Other material appears in Edwin Muir, *Latitudes*, 1924.

LLOYD C. DOUGLAS

Born: Columbia City, Indiana   *Died*: Los Angeles, California
Date: August 27, 1877   *Date*: February 13, 1951

PRINCIPAL WORKS

NOVELS: *Magnificent Obsession*, 1929; *Green Light*, 1935; *Disputed Passage*, 1939;
The Robe, 1942; *The Big Fisherman*, 1948.

Lloyd C(assel) Douglas, one of the most popular novelists of his period, was able to present certain aspects of the Christian truth in a narrative form that had for many of his readers effects of inspiration and truth. As his career suggests, he spent many years in religious work, unconsciously preparing for the work that filled out his career.

Son of a clergyman, Douglas was born in Columbia City, Indiana, on August 27, 1877. His education included attendance at Wittenberg College and Hamma Divinity School, from which he received his B.D. degree in 1903. For the next twenty-five years he held six pastorates in the United States and Canada. He served also as chaplain of the First Infantry, District of Columbia (1908–1911) and as director of religious work at the University of Illinois (1911–1915).

At fifty-two Douglas left the pulpit to devote his time exclusively to writing. In his first two novels, *Magnificent Obsession* and *Forgive Us Our Trespasses* (1932), he had found what he had "advertised" for in the title of his first book of essays, *Wanted—a Congregation* (1920), and he kept his large "congregation" of readers through eleven novels and two volumes of inspirational essays. *The Robe*, for example, based on speculation about the fate of the garment worn by Christ at the Crucifixion, sold over two million copies. This, like all of Douglas' fiction, is a story concerned with the self-enrichment that results from the serving of others.

Critics deplored his clichés, announced that his characters were puppets, and found the conduct of action in the novels melodramatic; and Douglas at least agreed that his characters were "tiresomely decent . . . and everything turns out happily in the end." He added that he came into writing too late "to take on any airs about it." Deluges of letters thanking Douglas for the comfort to be found in his novels were more important to the clergyman-turned-novelist than the objections of literary critics. He died, at the height of his popularity, in Los Angeles, California, on February 13, 1951.

BIBLIOGRAPHICAL REFERENCES: There is no full-length biographical or critical study. See Edmund Wilson, *Classics and Commercials*, 1951; and *Book Review Digest*, 1929 ff.

NORMAN DOUGLAS

Born: The Vorarlberg, Austria   *Died:* Capri, Italy
Date: December 8, 1868   *Date:* February 9, 1952

PRINCIPAL WORKS

NOVELS: *South Wind*, 1917; *They Went*, 1920; *In the Beginning*, 1927.

TRAVEL: *Siren Land*, 1911; *Fountains in the Sand*, 1912; *Old Calabria*, 1915; *Alone* 1921; *Together*, 1923; *One Day*, 1929; *Summer Islands, Ischia and Ponzo*, 1931.

AUTOBIOGRAPHY: *Looking Back*, 1933.

MISCELLANEOUS: *London Street Games*, 1916; *D. H. Lawrence and Maurice Magnus*, 1924; *Experiments*, 1925; *Some Footnotes on East and West*, 1929 [*Good-Bye to Western Culture*]; *Capri: Materials for a Description of the Island*, 1931; *Late Harvest*, 1946.

Seldom has a writer, on the strength of one novel, been made the object of such a cult as that centered around Norman Douglas after *South Wind* had become well known. It was his only book to achieve any wide degree of popularity, yet because of it he overshadowed for a time writers of much more solid accomplishment.

Douglas, the descendant of a very ancient Scottish family, was born in Austria, December 8, 1868. Because he disliked the English public schools he was sent to the gymnasium at Karlsruhe in 1883, where he became a fluent linguist. While a student, he contributed articles on zoölogy to scientific publications. He joined the British Foreign Office in 1893 and in 1894 was sent to St. Petersburg; however, he soon withdrew from government service to become a writer, eventually settling on the island of Capri.

His first book, *Unprofessional Tales*, (1901) had almost no sale; ten years later his second, *Siren Land*, got published only through the help of Joseph Conrad and Edward Garnett. It was during the blackest period of the First World War that he attained celebrity with *South Wind*.

It would seem that, during every literary period, there must be what might be called a "coterie novel," familiarity with which becomes the hallmark of the cognoscenti. Such a role was played by *South Wind* as its fame gradually spread to the United States and it was taken up by the literary sophisticates. Not to have read the novel was the sign of a kind of intellectual barbarism. Its special tone fitted in with the prevailing enthusiasm for the work of James Branch Cabell and Ronald Firbank in that these three writers provided escape literature of a highly sophisticated kind which could be enjoyed by readers who would not be attracted by the ordinary examples of such. Polish, urbanity, and a gentle cynicism were important, and the artificial atmosphere thus created satirized bourgeois society and its standards.

Like many Englishmen, Douglas seems to have been fascinated by Southern Europe, where he spent most of his adult life. The setting of *South Wind* is the Mediterranan island of "Nepenthe," inhabited by an extraordinary group of eccentrics who have, in various ways, succumbed to the local atmosphere. By viewing most of the story through the eyes of an English Bishop, Douglas emphasized his theme: the eternal contrast between Northern and Southern Europe. Nepenthe is, in miniature, the Mediterranean world, unchanged throughout the centuries, whose ripe, immemorial charm Douglas described appreciatively and with exquisite humor.

Unfortunately, *In the Beginning,* so eagerly awaited by the admirers of *South Wind,* fell far short of its predecessor. In this novel and in *The Angel of Manfredonia* (1929) it was clear that the master of sophisticated irony had lost his touch. Douglas died at Capri, February 9, 1952.

BIBLIOGRAPHICAL REFERENCES: There is no authorized biography. See E. D. MacDonald, *Bibliography of the Writings of Norman Douglas, with Notes by Norman Douglas* (1927); H. M. Tomlinson, *Norman Douglas* (1931); Richard McGillivray, *Norman Douglas* (1933); also Elizabeth D. Wheatley, "Norman Douglas," *Sewanee Review,* XL (1932), 55–67.

SIR ARTHUR CONAN DOYLE

Born: Edinburgh, Scotland
Date: May 22, 1859

Died: Crowborough, England
Date: July 7, 1930

PRINCIPAL WORKS

SHERLOCK HOLMES STORIES: *A Study in Scarlet,* 1887; *The Sign of Four,* 1890; *The Adventures of Sherlock Holmes,* 1892; *The Memoirs of Sherlock Holmes,* 1894; *The Hound of the Baskervilles,* 1902; *The Return of Sherlock Holmes,* 1905; *The Valley of Fear,* 1915; *His Last Bow,* 1917; *The Case-Book of Sherlock Holmes,* 1927.

NOVELS OF HISTORY AND ADVENTURE: *Micah Clarke,* 1888; *The White Company,* 1891; *The Exploits of Brigadier Gerard,* 1896; *The Lost World,* 1912.

To Sir Arthur Conan Doyle goes the honor of having created one of the best known and most popular characters in English literature. Sherlock Holmes, the gaunt and brillant detective of 221B Baker Street, London, was brought to life by Doyle in fifty-six short stories and four novelettes published between 1887 and 1927. Doyle's tales of crime and detection have so enthralled readers that Sherlock Holmes (aided by stage, screen, radio, and television imitations) has become a permanent part of our language. Despite his obligation to such detective writers of the past as Edgar Allan Poe, Doyle created the first truly great detective of fiction, and he popularized and vitalized the detective story as a fictional form.

Doyle was born in Edinburgh, Scotland, of Irish parents, May 22, 1859. He was graduated from Edinburgh University's school of medicine in 1884 and began to practice medicine in England. To supplement his income he wrote a tale of murder and revenge called *A Study in Scarlet,* featuring Sherlock Holmes as its central character. Doyle based Holmes' keen powers of observation and deduction upon Dr. Joseph Bell, a former teacher, who had long impressed his students with his ability to diagnose patients with a quick glance.

Although *A Study in Scarlet,* the first of the Holmes novelettes, was published in 1887, it deservedly gained little success. Doyle, however, was urged by an American editor to continue the exploits of his detective, and he wrote *The Sign of Four,* the best of the novelettes, and produced a series of twenty-four short stories. These first twenty-four stories were published in book form in *The Adventures of Sherlock Holmes* and *The Memoirs of Sherlock Holmes.*

The success of these works enabled Doyle to give up his medical career. But he had become bored with his creation, and in "The Final Problem," the last story in *The Memoirs,* he described Holmes' death at the hands of his arch enemy, Professor Moriarty. Doyle's readers were shocked and outraged: they were not to be denied their hero. In the face of great public clamor Doyle at last relented and resurrected Holmes. The series continued with *The Hound of the Baskervilles* in 1902; the last of the novelettes, *The Valley of Fear,* was published in 1915. The later short stories were published in book form in *The Return of Sherlock Holmes, His Last Bow* and *The Case-Book of Sherlock Holmes.* Almost all of the stories were told in the first person by Holmes' close companion,

Dr. John Watson, whose vague intellect offered the perfect reflector for Holmes' genius.

Arthur Conan Doyle was an active, public spirited man, and an extremely prolific writer. In his own time he was known for many works other than the Holmes stories, and today some of them deserve attention. *The White Company* remains a classic novel of chivalric adventure; and *Micah Clarke,* a story of Monmouth's rebellion, *The Exploits of Brigadier Gerard,* and *Sir Nigel* (1906) are all spirited historical romances. In *The Lost World* Doyle originated the idea of an isolated land of prehistoric life existing in the twentieth century, and in *Danger!* (1914) he predicted the German submarine blockade of the British Isles. He was knighted in 1902 for his defense of the conduct of the British army in *The Great Boer War* (1900).

Arthur Conan Doyle was primarily a superb romancer; he possessed virtually no capacity for dullness. His vigor and sense of adventure infused almost everything he wrote with an uncomplicated air of excitement. Today the best of the Sherlock Holmes stories are puzzling and original mystery stories, but they also absorb us in an atmosphere of sinister doings in London at the turn of the century which is at once nostalgic and exciting. Doyle died in Crowborough on July 7, 1930.

BIBLIOGRAPHICAL REFERENCES: A convenient one-volume edition is *The Works of A. Conan Doyle,* 1928. There is a bibliography by Harold Locke, *A Bibliographical Catalogue of the Writings of Sir Arthur Conan Doyle,* 1928. Of primary interest is Doyle's autobiography, *My Memories and Adventures,* 1924. There are several reliable biographies: John Lamond, *Arthur Conan Doyle: A Memoir,* 1931; Hesketh Pearson, *Conan Doyle, His Life and Art,* 1943; and John D. Carr, *The Life of Sir Arthur Conan Doyle,* 1949.

Sherlock Holmes has been the subject of separate studies: H. W. Bell, *Sherlock Holmes and Dr. Watson,* 1932; and Vincent Starrett, *The Private Life of Sherlock*

Holmes, 1933. See also *The Baker Street Journal*, 1946 ff. and *The Sherlock Holmes Journal*, 1952 ff.

There are three reliable sources of information about the history of the literature of crime: F. W. Chandler, *The Literature of Roguery*, 2 vols., 1907; H. D. Thomson, *Masters of Mystery: A Study of the Detective Story*, 1931; and Howard Haycraft, *Murder for Pleasure: The Life and Times of the Detective Story*, 1942.

MICHAEL DRAYTON

Born: Hartshill, England
Date: 1563

Died: London, England
Date: December 23, 1631

PRINCIPAL WORKS

POEMS: *The Harmonie of the Church*, 1591; *Idea, the Shepherd's Garland*, 1593 (republished, c. 1605 in *Poems Lyric and Pastoral* and again as *Pastorals*, 1619); *Piers Gaveston*, 1593; *Idea's Mirror*, 1594; *Matilda*, 1594; *Endimion and Phoebe*, 1595; *The Tragical Legend of Robert, Duke of Normandy*, 1596; *Mortimeriados*, 1596 (republished as *The Barons' Wars*, 1603); *England's Heroical Epistles*, 1597; *Legend of the Great Cromwell*, 1607; *Poly-Olbion*, 1612–22; *Nimphidia*, 1627; *Shepherd's Sirena*, 1627; *The Muses' Elizium*, 1630.

Michael Drayton, born at Hartshill, Warwickshire, in 1563, may have been the most voluminous as well as the most dedicated poet of his period. His *Poly-Olbion*, ten years in the writing, is one of the longest poems in English, a varied topographical and historical celebration of England's glories, but it represents only one type of his poetic works, which included his earliest volume, the biblical paraphrases, *The Harmonie of the Church*; the sonnet series, *Idea's Mirror*, and the mock-heroic *Nimphidia*.

Drayton's finest work is *The Muses' Elizium*, finished the year before his death, in which the combination of his talents for realistic expression and dignified artifice were enhanced by a firm idealism. His vigorous sonnets, among them the famous "Since there's no help, come let us kiss and part" (from *Idea's Mirror*), showed him leading toward this fluent style.

He collaborated on more than twenty plays of which only one has survived, and his historical poems are of only passing interest; but his continued fascination with England's past found successful expression in *England's Heroical Epistles*, modeled on Ovid, imaginary letters exchanged between such famous personages as Henry II and Fair Rosamond and Edward IV and Jane Shore. *Nimphidia* contains two of his most charming pastoral poems and a critical verse letter to Henry Reynolds.

Drayton died in London on December 23, 1631, and was buried in Westminster Abbey.

BIBLIOGRAPHICAL REFERENCES: J. W. Hebel has edited *The Complete Works of Michael Drayton*, 5 vols., 1931–1941. For biographical and critical studies see Olivier Elton, *Michael Drayton: A Critical Study*, 1905; and Bernard H. Newdigate, *Michael Drayton and His Circle*, 1941.

THEODORE DREISER

Born: Terre Haute, Indiana
Date: August 27, 1871

Died: Hollywood, California
Date: December 28, 1945

PRINCIPAL WORKS

NOVELS: *Sister Carrie*, 1900; *Jennie Gerhardt*, 1911; *The Financier*, 1912; *The Titan*, 1914; *The "Genius,"* 1915; *An American Tragedy*, 1925; *The Bulwark*, 1946; *The Stoic*, 1947.

SHORT STORIES: *Free and Other Stories*, 1918; *Twelve Men*, 1919; *Chains: Lesser Novels and Stories*, 1927; *A Gallery of Women*, 1929.

PLAYS: *Plays of the Natural and Supernatural*, 1916 (*The Girl in the Coffin*, *The Blue Sphere, Laughing Gas, In the Dark, The Spring Recital, The Light in the Window, "Old Ragpicker"*); *The Hand of the Potter: A Tragedy in Four Acts*, 1918.

AUTOBIOGRAPHY: *A Book about Myself*, 1922 (republished as *Newspaper Days*, 1931); *Dawn*, 1931.

ESSAYS: *Hey Rub-a-Dub-Dub*, 1920.

TRAVEL SKETCHES: *A Traveler at Forty*, 1913; *A Hoosier Holiday*, 1916; *The Color of a Great City*, 1923.

POLITICAL AND SOCIAL STUDIES: *Dreiser Looks at Russia*, 1928; *Tragic America*, 1931.

POEMS: *Moods, Cadenced and Declaimed*, 1926, 1928.

Theodore Dreiser, born in Terre Haute, Indiana, on August 27, 1871, is probably the most puzzling figure in twentieth century American literature. No other major author has survived so much hostile criticism. Nor has any other author of his stature displayed so much paradoxical thinking. Yet despite his inconsistencies and blunders, Dreiser's position is unshakable. His influence on the naturalistic American novel has been enormous; moreover, there is in his writing a peculiar power and honesty that is not to be found anywhere else.

The son of a desperately poor and narrowly religious family, Dreiser developed intense feelings about poverty and social restraint that are manifest in all his work. After a spotty schooling in various Indiana towns, he became a journalist and worked for newspapers and magazines in several cities. This work and his searching reading formed the education for his literary career. The greatest influence on Dreiser's thinking was his study of the evolutionary writers—especially Spencer, Huxley, and Darwin—who taught him to view life as a massive struggle for survival. Starting from these ideas he worked out his own theories about human behavior in terms of compulsions or "chemisms."

Sister Carrie, his first novel, was suppressed by its publisher, thus initiating Dreiser's long series of battles with censorship. This novel tells the story of a beautiful, materialistic girl who accepts a liaison in preference to the conditions of sweatshop labor. Especially impressive is the documentation of George Hurstwood's gradual collapse and suicide. What the Grundy clan found objectionable in *Sister Carrie* was not the use of a "fallen woman," but rather Dreiser's unconventional view of her; instead of punishing

315

Carrie, he seems to say that she was justified in seeking her welfare as best she could. *Sister Carrie* exhibits all of Dreiser's merits and defects: the clumsy writing, the overpowering earnestness, the loose construction, the massing of realistic detail.

Dreiser's next novel, *Jennie Gerhardt*, is another study of a kept woman; but Jennie is a nobler character, a lower-class girl who leaves her wealthy lover when she realizes that she stands in the way of his career. After this work came the first volume of the Frank Cowperwood "trilogy of desire": *The Financier* (published 1912, revised 1927), followed by *The Titan* in 1914, and *The Stoic* in 1947. These novels comprise a wide examination of American finance from the time of Lincoln and deal with the life of a ruthless tycoon. As a boy Cowperwood sees a lobster devour a squid and realizes, "Things lived on each other—that was it." *The "Genius"* again brought Dreiser into conflict with the censors, but this time he was championed by H. L. Mencken. Eugene Witla, the hero of the novel, is a gifted realistic painter whose sexuality conflicts with his artistic career.

An American Tragedy, Dreiser's highest achievement, was also the victim of censorship. The protagonist, Clyde Griffiths, attempts to drown his pregnant mistress because marriage to her would ruin his hopes of a rich marriage. He proves too indecisive; but the boat overturns, and he is convicted of murder. While awaiting execution, Clyde comes to understand the extent of his guilt. In contrast to this angry book, *The Bulwark*, Dreiser's mellow-est novel, tells the story of a Quaker banker whose faith is deepened by the failure of his family life.

Dreiser's stories have been collected in *Free, Twelve Men, Chains,* and *A Gallery of Women. Plays of the Natural and Supernatural,* published in 1916, was followed by a tragedy, *The Hand of the Potter. Hey Rub-a-Dub-Dub* is a collection of essays. His other writings include political studies and poems, as well as books of travel sketches and reminiscence. Dreiser's autobiography, written with characteristic frankness, is contained in *A Book About Myself*—republished in 1931 as *Newspaper Days*—and *Dawn.*

Theodore Dreiser was neither a clear nor original thinker. Though he assimilated many of the ideas of the evolutionists, he remained enough of a skeptic to show marked ambiguities in his work. He is both a determinist and a sentimentalist, evoking considerable pity for his defeated characters. Although he appears to believe that it is proper for a man to grab as much as possible from an indifferent or malevolent society, he came to accept many of the ideas of communism. The main theme in Dreiser's work is that of the conflict between the individual and society. In keeping with this theme, his characters are, typically, either weaklings or strong figures who seize what they want.

Dreiser died in Hollywood, California, on December 28, 1945. Although it now seems certain that his reputation will endure, it is difficult to forecast what final judgment the critics and literary historians will pass on him. It is hard to measure a giant.

BIBLIOGRAPHICAL REFERENCES: Biographical and critical studies include Burton Rascoe, *Theodore Dreiser*, 1925; Dorothy Dudley, *Dreiser and the Land of the Free,*

1946; Robert H. Elias, *Theodore Dreiser: Apostle of Nature*, 1949; Helen Dreiser, *My Life with Dreiser*, 1951; and F. O. Matthiessen, *Theodore Dreiser*, 1951.

See also H. L. Mencken, "Theodore Dreiser," in *A Book of Prefaces*, 1917; Vernon L. Parrington, *Main Currents of American Thought*, III, 1930; Joseph Warren Beach, *The Twentieth Century Novel*, 1932; Granville Hicks, *The Great Tradition*, 1933; E. B. Burgum, *The Novel and the World's Dilemma*, 1947; George Snell, "Theodore Dreiser: Philosopher," in *Shapers of American Fiction*, 1947; F. J. Hoffman, *The Modern Novel in America, 1900–1950*, 1951; Edward Wagenknecht, *Cavalcade of the American Novel*, 1952; and Maxwell Geismar, *Rebels and Ancestors*, 1953.

JOHN DRYDEN

Born: Northamptonshire, England *Died:* London, England
Date: August 9 (?), 1631 *Date:* May 1, 1700

Principal Works

POEMS: *Heroic Stanzas*, 1659; *Astraea Redux*, 1660; *Annus Mirabilis*, 1667; *Alexander's Feast, or The Power of Music*, 1697; *Fables Ancient and Modern*, 1700.

SATIRES IN VERSE: *Absalom and Achitophel*, 1681; *The Medall*, 1682; *MacFlecknoe, or a Satyr upon the True-Blew-Protestant Poet, T. S.*, 1682; *Religio Laici*, 1682; *The Hind and the Panther*, 1687.

PLAYS: *The Indian Emperor*, 1665; *Secret Love, or The Maiden Queen*, 1667; *Tyrannic Love, or The Royal Martyr*, 1669; *Almanzor and Almahide*, 1670–1672; *Marriage à la Mode*, 1673; *Aurengzebe*, 1675; *All for Love*, 1678; *The Spanish Friar*, 1681; *Don Sebastian*, 1690; *Cleomenes, The Spartan Hero*, 1692; *Love Triumphant*, 1694.

ESSAYS AND CRITICISM: *An Essay of Dramatic Poesy*, 1668; *A Defence of an Essay of Dramatic Poesy*, 1668; *Of Heroic Plays*, 1672; *Preface to the Fables*, 1700.

TRANSLATIONS: Ovid's *Epistles*, 1680; *The Works of Vergil*, 1697.

John Dryden, English poet, dramatist, and critic, was born at Aldwinkle All Saints, in Northamptonshire, probably on August 9, 1631. He was educated at Westminster School and Trinity College, Cambridge, where he received his B.A. degree in 1654.

After honoring Cromwell in *Heroic Stanzas*, he welcomed the restoration of Charles II in 1660 in *Astraea Redux*. Thereafter he remained a royalist and a Tory. Dryden in 1663 married Lady Elizabeth Howard and proved an affectionate father for their three sons. His poem on the Dutch war and the Great Fire of London was *Annus Mirabilis*. From this time until 1681 he produced plays.

As a man of letters his life may be divided into three periods: 1657–1681, primarily a dramatist; 1681–1688, a satirist; and 1688–1700, a translator. It was in 1688 that he became poet laureate with the title of Historiographer-Royal being conferred two years later.

Dryden's most important prose work, *An Essay of Dramatic Poesy*, appeared in 1668. Here, as master of his "other harmony" of prose, he upholds the reputation of English dramatists and defends his principles of composition. This work takes the form of a dialogue between Neander (Dryden) and others in which Neander defends the English drama of preceding generations. At the same time he argues that English

317

drama has much to gain by the observance of exact methods of construction without abandoning entirely the freedom which English writers had always claimed. Rhyme in serious drama he also upholds, elaborated upon in *A Defence of an Essay of Dramatic Poesy*, a statement of his views of rhymed couplets in tragedy. Dryden was the first to employ the rhymed couplet in the dialogue of an ordinary stage play.

Notable also in this first period are *Almanzor and Almahide, or the Conquest of Granada*, a rhymed heroic play, and *All for Love*, a seventeenth century version of Shakespeare's *Antony and Cleopatra*.

It was during this period that the Royal Society was chartered in 1662. It became the popularizing body for the idea of universal correctness of language, with Dryden its great exponent. His idea was to establish a highly selective language for poetry. Moreover, the use of this language would improve the writings of any poet. Thus *All for Love* is Dryden's formal, correct modernization in blank verse of Shakespeare's materials. In transforming Milton's *Paradise Lost* into rhymed drama, Dryden makes his language fit his own thoughts, but it is the inexact thought of Milton. He is considered a genius at finding the exact words that express exactly his mind. Clarity and balance are keynotes of his style. His critical essays (prefaces to his works) are standards of clear writing. As a critic he is excellent in his praise of Shakespeare, Jonson, and Chaucer.

Political events in London in the years 1678 to 1680 revolved around the Popish Plot, followed by the attempt of the Whigs, led by the Earl of Shaftesbury, to force Charles to exclude his brother, the Duke of York (Catholic) from the succession. It was the Whigs' purpose to substitute the King's illegitimate son, the Duke of Monmouth. Shaftesbury was waiting his trial for high treason when Dryden began his satires with *Absalom and Achitophel*, in which he supports the King and the Tories and presents brilliant portraits of the chief Whig politicians. In 1682 the polemical warfare in which he became involved called forth *MacFlecknoe or a Satyr upon the True-Blew-Protestant Poet, T. S.* "T. S." stood for Thomas Shadwell, a supporter of Shaftesbury. This work served as a model for Pope's *Dunciad*. In March, 1682, Dryden published *The Medall: a Satyre against Sedition*, which ridicules the medal struck to commemorate Shaftesbury's acquittal.

His most personal poem, *Religio Laici*, attacked the Papists. In 1686, however, he was converted to the Catholic Church and *The Hind and the Panther* is an allegorical argument for his new faith. The hind of spotless white is the Roman Church while the panther ready to spring is the English Church established by Henry VIII. The Independent or Puritan church is a bear; the Quaker, a quaking hare, and the Baptist, a bristling boar.

The revolution of 1688 brought ruin to Dryden's worldly prosperity. He now lacked official assistance and the position as poet laureate. He had begun as a translator in 1680 with Ovid's *Epistles;* now he finished a complete version of Juvenal and Persius and a translation of Vergil. Noteworthy at this time is the famous ode, *Alexander's Feast*, of 1697. Following was a volume of translations and adaptations from Chaucer, Boccaccio, Ovid, and Homer titled *Fables, Ancient and Modern*.

Dryden died in London on May 1, 1700. While his family was preparing to bury him as well as their poverty could afford, a large subscription was raised. His body was borne in state to Westminster Abbey, where he is buried in the Poets' Corner near Chaucer and Spenser.

BIBLIOGRAPHICAL REFERENCES: The definitive edition, replacing that of Sir Walter Scott, 1808 (revised by George Saintsbury, 1882–1893), will be *The Works of John Dryden*, edited by E. N. Hooker, H. T. Swedenberg, and others, 1956 ff. For biography and criticism see Samuel Johnson, *Lives of the Poets*, 1779–1781; George Saintsbury, *Dryden*, in the English Men of Letters Series, 1881; L. N. Chase, *The English Heroic Play*, 1909; and Mark Van Doren, *The Poetry of John Dryden*, 1920. See also Allardyce Nicoll, *A History of English Drama, 1660–1900*, 1952 (rev. ed.); *The Age of Dryden* in the *Cambridge History of English Literature*, Vol. VIII; and *Dictionary of National Biography*, Vol. VI.

ALEXANDRE DUMAS *père*

Born: Villers-Cotterets, France
Date: July 24, 1802

Died: Puys, France
Date: December 5, 1870

PRINCIPAL WORKS

NOVELS: *Les Trois Mousquetaires*, 1844 (*The Three Musketeers*); *Le Comte de Monte-Cristo*, 1844; *Vingt ans après*, 1845 (*Twenty Years After*); *Les Frères corses*, 1845 (*The Corsican Brothers*); *Marguerite de Valois*, 1845; *Le Chevalier de Maison Rouge*, 1846; *Agénor de Mauleon*, 1846; *La Dame de Monsoreau*, 1846 (*Chicot the Jester*); *Mémoirs d'un Médecin*, 1846–1848 (*Memoirs of a Physician*); *Les Quarante-cinq*, 1848 (*The Forty-Five Guardsmen*); *Dix ans plus tard, ou le Vicomte de Brage-lonne*, 1848–1850 (*The Vicomte de Bragelonne*); *Le Collier de la reine*, 1849–1850 (*The Queen's Necklace*); *Le Tulipe noire*, 1850 (*The Black Tulip*); *Ange Pitou*, 1852 (*The Taking of the Bastille*); *La Comtesse de Charny*, 1853–1855.

PLAYS: *Henri III*, 1829; *Christine*, 1830; *Napoleon Bonaparte*, 1831; *Antony*, 1831; *Mademoiselle de Belle-Isle*, 1839.

Alexandre Dumas, the most famous of the French romantic novelists, was born at Villers-Cotterets, July 24, 1802. His father, General Dumas, had been born in San Domingo, the illegitimate son of the Marquis de la Pailleterie and a Negress. Taking his mother's name, he came to France early in the Revolution and entered the army, where he had a brilliant career, rising under Napoleon to the rank of major general of cavalry. But he offended Napoleon by his outspoken criticism, and retired to Villers-Cotterets, where he died, leaving his widow and their four-year-old son in straitened circumstances.

Young Dumas, with only a scanty education, began life in the office of a local solicitor. While still quite young, he was writing plays in collaboration with a Swedish friend. In 1823 he went to Paris and obtained a position in the household of the Duc d'Orleans. He continued to write vaudeville sketches and melodramas, and entered into a liaison with a dressmaker, Marie Catherine Labay, by whom he had a son, the younger Alexandre Dumas.

319

As a dramatist, Dumas was much influenced by seeing some of Shakespeare's plays which were being produced in Paris at this time. His *Henri III* has been called the first great triumph of the romantic drama in France, and through it he won the friendship of Hugo and Vigny. It was at the end of this period that he married an actress, Ida Ferrier.

It was during the 1840's that Dumas, working with several collaborators, particularly Auguste Maquet, produced the novels on which his fame rests. The question of how much he owed to his collaborators is a vexed one; suffice it to say that none of these men was ever able to do any original work, and their function seems to have been to find plot-material and to sketch the broad outlines of the story. The element that gave life to the books was Dumas' genius.

The first of these novels, and probably the greatest "cloak and sword" story ever written, was *The Three Musketeers*. Using some seventeenth century memoirs as a source, Dumas created the immortal figures of D'Artagnan, Athos, Porthos, and Aramis, who have won the affection of generations of readers. The novel won wide acclaim throughout Europe, being a particular favorite of Thackeray and later of Lang and Stevenson. Realizing his success, Dumas continued the adventures of his heroes, carrying them, in four more stories, from the time of Louis XIII and Richelieu to their old age in the early reign of Louis XIV with the great mystery of the Man in the Iron Mask. By skillfully introducing such actual figures as Anne of Austria, Buckingham, Mazarin, and Fouquet, he succeeded in giving an air of verisimilitude to the novels; the reader feels genuinely that he is living in the period and sharing the adventures of the swashbuckling guardsmen. Unlike most historical novelists, he was able to achieve growth in his characters, so that the four friends are quite different men at the ends of their lives from the young men first encountered. Dumas possessed a real sense of history; the reader can understand the changing times as the young Louis XIV begins to eclipse all those about him, and the musketeers become anachronisms from another age.

Though not nearly so well known, the series of novels dealing with the France of the last Valois Kings is almost the equal of the Musketeer series. Dumas was especially fascinated by the court of Henri III and gave a strangely sympathetic portrait of this last degenerate member of a once virile House. In these novels, the two great antagonists are Henry of Navarre and Catherine de Médicis, and the popular conception of the latter as the embodiment of subtle and relentless cruelty probably stems from these books, as the portrait of Richard III has been indelibly fixed by Shakespeare. Here Dumas again created one of his greatest characters in Chicot, gentleman-jester to Henri III and an incomparable swordsman. The secondary figure of Dom Gorenflot has been considered second only to Falstaff among comic creations.

In the midst of these historical novels appeared *The Count of Monte Cristo*, equally famous in its fashion. While the story does not contain any character as great as D'Artagnan or Chicot, the clever plot has made it a perennial favorite, first as a novel and later as a play.

The later life of Dumas was remarkably like that of Scott. He, too, built a huge country house, "Monte Cristo," and toiled equally hard to keep up with his expenses. He founded a theater for the production of his own plays, and its failure added to his financial woes. In spite of his preoccupation, as a writer, with the French Monarchy, he remained a Republican in politics and hailed the Revolution of 1848. The coup d'état of 1851 caused him to flee to Brussels, but his sojourn there enabled him to straighten out his financial affairs.

Dumas' prodigious literary productivity can be gauged from the fact that the French edition of his works fills 277 volumes. But it is as a novelist that he has survived. The inevitable comparison is between him and Scott, and from this comparison Dumas emerges as the greater writer in their particular genre. His novels have much more life and movement; the action is not slowed by the interminable descriptions and digressions that make tedious so much of Scott's work. He had a better sense of plot construction; above all, an irrepressible gaiety pervades his books. Nothing in Scott can equal the picnic of the Musketeers in the trenches before La Rochelle, nor could Scott give to his historical figures the reality that Dumas gave to Richelieu or Catherine de Médicis. Truly, "they order these matters better in France."

Having lived a life more romantic than any of his novels, Dumas spent his last years at the mercy of his creditors. He died at the home of his son at Puys, near Dieppe, on December 5, 1870.

BIBLIOGRAPHICAL REFERENCES: The best books on Dumas in English are Arthur F. Davidson, *Alexandre Dumas Père: His Life and Works,* 1902; H. A. Spurr, *The Life and Writings of Alexandre Dumas,* 2 vols., 1929 (rev. ed.); Herbert Gorman, *The Incredible Marquis, Alexandre Dumas,* 1929; and A. C. Bell, *Alexandre Dumas,* 1950. See also L. H. Lecomte, *Alexandre Dumas,* 1904. An important background study is André Maurois, *Les trois Dumas,* 1957, translated as *The Titans,* 1958.

ALEXANDRE DUMAS, *fils*

Born: Paris, France
Date: July 27, 1824

Died: Paris
Date: November 27, 1895

PRINCIPAL WORKS

NOVEL: *La Dame aux camélias,* 1848 (*The Lady of the Camelias*).

PLAYS: *La Dame aux camélias,* 1852 (*Camille*); *La Question d'argent,* 1857 (*The Question of Money*); *Le Fils naturel,* 1858 (*The Natural Son*); *Le Père prodigue,* 1859 (*The Prodigal Father*); *L'Étrangère,* 1876 (*The Stranger*).

POEMS: *La Chronique,* 1842; *Péchés de jeunesse,* 1847.

ESSAYS: *Nouvelle lettre de Junius,* 1870; *Tue-la, Monsieur Alphonse,* 1874; *La Recherché de la paternité,* 1883.

Illegitimate son of the famous novelist and a dressmaker named Marie Labay, the younger Dumas was born in Paris July 27, 1824, at a time when his father was merely a little-known writer of melodramas and vaudeville sketches. The stigma of his illegitimate birth embittered his childhood and later furnished the material for several of his plays. Forced by his father's bankruptcy to fend for himself, the young man began his literary career in 1847 with a book of poems, which was followed by a novel, *The Lady of the Camelias*, in 1848. This novel he dramatized the following year, but because of censorship restrictions it could not be produced until 1852, when the author's influence with the new government of Napoleon III finally got the play on the boards.

By the end of the 1850's Dumas had become a rich man; he continued, however, to write plays for many more years. In his later dramas appeared such famous figures as Bernhardt and Coquelin. These plays were much admired for their skillful construction, witty dialogue, and mastery of theatrical technique. The elder Dumas, however, criticized his son for preaching too much and for trying to turn the stage into a debating platform for moral issues, generally those arising from problems of adultery and illegitimacy.

Of the sixteen plays that Dumas wrote, only *Camille* has survived, mainly because it offers a good acting part. It is much better known, however, in Verdi's operatic version, *La Traviata* (1853).

Dumas died in Paris on November 27, 1895.

BIBLIOGRAPHICAL REFERENCES: For biographical and critical studies see H. S. Schwartz, *Dumas fils, Dramatist*, 1927; Frank A. Taylor, *The Theatre of Dumas fils*, 1937; and N. C. Arvin, *Alexandre Dumas, fils*, 1939. An excellent study of the Dumas family is André Maurois, *The Titans*, 1957 (American ed., 1958).

DAPHNE DU MAURIER

Born: London, England
Date: May 13, 1907

PRINCIPAL WORKS

NOVELS: *Jamaica Inn*, 1936; *Rebecca*, 1938; *Frenchman's Creek*, 1941; *Hungry Hill*, 1943; *My Cousin Rachel*, 1951; *The Scapegoat*, 1957.

SHORT STORIES: *Come Wind, Come Weather*, 1941: *Kiss Me Again, Stranger*, 1952.

PLAYS: *The Years Between*, 1945; *September Tide*, 1948.

BIOGRAPHY: *Gerald: A Portrait*, 1934; *The du Mauriers*, 1937.

Daphne du Maurier, born in London on May 13, 1907, comes from a family much concerned with the arts, and it is little wonder that she writes well and fluently. Her grandfather was the novelist and artist, George du Maurier, writer of the famous *Trilby*. Her parents were both of the theater —her father, Sir Gerald, being a notable actor and manager.

The Loving Spirit, Miss du Maurier's first novel was published in 1931. It was followed by *I'll Never Be Young Again* (1932) and *The Progress of Julius* (1933). Miss du Maurier's initial success in the United States was achieved with a series of historical cloak-and-dagger romances, many of which were related from the viewpoint of the belabored heroine. The best remembered of these novels is *The King's General* (1946). A prolific and com-

322

pelling storyteller, Miss du Maurier's other works in this genre are: *Jamaica Inn, Frenchman's Creek, Hungry Hill,* and *Mary Anne* (1954). She is also the author of two plays, *The Years Between* and *September Tide;* a biography of her father, *Gerald: A Portrait,* and *The du Mauriers,* a semi-fictional story of her ancestors. Her other works include *Happy Christmas* (1940) and *The Parasites* (1949).

Rebecca is Miss du Maurier's best-known work, and it has been widely imitated since its publication in 1938. Its success may be credited to the studied blending of a Gothic atmosphere of mystery with the more subtle psychological suspense of a modern thriller. Miss du Maurier has returned to this formula in many of her more recent works such as *Kiss Me Again Stranger, My Cousin Rachel,* and *The Scapegoat.*

BIBLIOGRAPHICAL REFERENCES: There is very little criticism on Daphne du Maurier. See LaTourette Stockwell, "Best Sellers and the Critics," *College English,* XVI (1955), 214–221; also *Book Review Digest,* 1931 ff.

GEORGE DU MAURIER

Born: Paris, France
Date: March 6, 1834

Died: London, England
Date: October 8, 1896

PRINCIPAL WORKS

NOVELS: *Peter Ibbetson,* 1891; *Trilby,* 1894; *The Martian,* 1897.

The grandson of a Frenchman of noble family who had fled to England during the Revolution, George (Louis Palmella Busson) du Maurier was born in Paris, March 6, 1834, the son of a French father and an English mother. In his youth he oscillated between Paris and London; his early education was conducted in Paris between 1847 and 1851. In 1851 he returned to London to study chemistry at the wish of his father, who wanted to make a scientist of him. He had, however, little interest in science, and, in 1856, he went back to Paris to study art and removed soon afterward to Antwerp to continue his work. It was during his student days in Paris that he had many of the experiences that he was later to use as literary material. Early in life he lost the sight of one eye, but the loss did not handicap him in his career.

In 1860 he returned to England to begin his work as an illustrator, first for *Once A Week* and then for *Punch,* whose staff he joined in 1864 on the death of John Leech. Gradually he brought about a change in the subject matter of *Punch's* drawings. Previously the satire had been directed at the foibles of the middle class; now the object was the fashionable world, particularly the *nouveaux riches* and those of literary pretensions. It has often been noted that, in addition to their artistic merits, du Maurier's drawings, because of his close attention to the details of clothes and furnishings, have genuine importance for the social historian. After working successfully for *Punch,* du Maurier became illustrator for the *Cornhill Magazine.* This connection

323

gave him the opportunity to illustrate some of the foremost literary productions of the time.

Early in his career, du Maurier discovered that he had a talent for light verse in either English or French—he was bilingual—and began to develop this gift in case his eyesight should fail and his work as an artist end. From *vers de société* he progressed to more ambitious efforts, and at the suggestion of Henry James he submitted *Peter Ibbetson* to *Harper's Magazine*, in which it appeared serially. Many of the scenes of the novel, made into an opera by Deems Taylor in 1931, were drawn from memories of his own childhood. For the same magazine he wrote the enormously popular *Trilby*, which was later dramatized and produced in London by Beerbohm Tree. For the background of this story he used the details of his student days in Paris, many of the characters being drawn, in whole or in part, from actual people. Young ladies were discouraged from reading it, as the heroine was an artists' model who posed in the nude; yet the book had great success in England, since poor Trilby's better nature is developed through contact with the English characters. The novel gives a sentimentalized picture of Bohemian life, and the plot is pure melodrama; yet in this novel, in the character of the strange, sinister Svengali, du Maurier created a character whose name has become part of the language, no mean achievement.

Du Maurier died at his home in London, October 8, 1896.

BIBLIOGRAPHICAL REFERENCES: There is no official biography, but for family reminiscences see Daphne du Maurier, *Gerald: A Portrait*, 1934, and *The du Mauriers*, 1937. See also *The Young George du Maurier: A Selection of His Letters, 1860–1867*, edited by Daphne du Maurier, 1951; Henry James, *Partial Portraits*, 1888; and Felix Moscheles, *In Bohemia with du Maurier*, 1896.

OLAV DUUN

Born: Namdalen, Norway
Date: November 21, 1876

Died: Oslo, Norway
Date: September 13, 1939

PRINCIPAL WORKS

NOVELS: *Juvikfolke*, 1918–1923 (*The People of Juvik: The Trough of the Wave, The Blind Man, The Big Wedding, Odin in Fairyland, Odin Grows Up, The Storm*); *Medmenneske*, 1929 (*Fellow Beings*); *Ragnhild*, 1931; *Siste leveåre*, 1933 (*The Last Year of Life*).

Olav Duun, a schoolteacher in northern Norway in the vicinity of Trondheim, did not begin to write until after he was thirty years old. He then began to draw on the traditions of the Namdalen region where he had been born on November 21, 1876. In his novels he presents a vivid picture of peasant freeholders fiercely battling against nature for survival.

Duun's first notable achievement was his long saga, *The People of Juvik*, published between 1918 and 1923. This work consists of six volumes dealing with one family from the end of the eighteenth century to the beginning of the twentieth, and it traces the gradual rise of the family from grim brutality to an altruistic sense of ideals. Duun glorified the independent peasant, the man of the land who represented purpose and importance. *The People of Juvik* became well known, and Duun followed it with other novels depicting the solid people and traditions of northern Norway, until his death in Oslo on September 13, 1939.

Duun was also distinguished as one of the first and most able Norwegian writers to write in *landsmål*, the language of the people, particularly those in rural areas in the north. Until his time, most Norwegians felt *landsmål* crude and undignified, and most literature was written in *riksmal*, the language of government, officialdom, and the cities (*riksmål* is very close to Danish). By his example Duun, with an enormous talent for conveying the speech of his people, accomplished a great deal for the growing cause of *landsmål* as both a national and a literary language. The qualities of *landsmål*, its tradition, its simplicity, its closeness to the people and the land, served as the perfect instrument for Duun's work.

BIBLIOGRAPHICAL REFERENCES: Duun's best-known work, *The People of Juvik*, is available in a six-volume translation, 1930–1935. A good but brief introduction in English is P. D. Carleton's essay, "Olav Duun, a Spokesman of Peasants," *American-Scandinavian Review*, XVI (1928), 741–742. Rolv Thesen is the author of three studies: *Menneske og maktene*, 1941; *Olav Duun*, 1946; and *Seks unge om Olav Duun*, 1950. See also A. Øverland, *Olav Duun*, 1926; and Alv Grimseth Schjelderup, *Dikteren Olav Duun*, 1945.

JOSÉ ECHEGARAY Y EIZAGUIRRE

Born: Madrid, Spain
Date: March 10, 1833

Died: Madrid
Date: September 27, 1916

PRINCIPAL WORKS

PLAYS: *El libro talonario*, 1874 (*The Checkbook*); *La Esposa del vengador*, 1874 (*The Avenger's Wife*); *O locura o santidad*, 1877 (*Madman or Saint*); *El gran Galeoto*, 1881 (*The Great Galeoto, The World and His Wife*); *El hijo de don Juan*, 1892 (*The Son of Don Juan*); *El loco Dios*, 1900 (*The Mad God*).

In an autobiographical sonnet about his method of writing, José Echegaray y Eizaguirre once declared:

I choose a passion, an idea indite,
A problem, situation, or a trait,
And deep within someone whom I create
I plant it like a charge of dynamite.

And the explosion engineered by this master of melodrama, by which the hero reveals his many changes, brought new life to the dull Spanish stage that preceded him. Galdós wrote of the "brilliant apparition of the genius of Echegaray upon the Spanish scene."

From then on until the arrival of Benavente, this dramatist with a Basque name, this many-sided man, engineer, physicist, economist, and Academician of Natural Sciences, was monarch of the Spanish theater. Though he once declared his earliest memory as a child of three was of sitting on his mother's lap in a theater, he had no further connection with the stage until after he was forty. Then, during a quarter century of dramatic activity, he composed a total of sixty-four plays of all types, half in prose and half in verse, combining romanticism with the positivist spirit of his times.

Those who see in the profession of the architect Thomas Hardy the explanation of his well-built novels will also give credit to one of Spain's greatest mathematicians for his well-figured plots. Echegaray's times were responsible for the excessive passion of his characters, but only the dramatist can be criticized for the forced conflicts and the abuse of contrived theatrical effects. Yet the powerful and impressive scenes and the intense emotions of the characters gave his audiences no opportunity for cool reflection that would have revealed the falseness of some of his basic situations. Nevertheless, two of his tragedies are undoubted masterpieces.

Influenced by the time-spirit, Echegaray's first plays are romantic in tone. *The Checkbook*, showing that crime is always punished, was performed under a pseudonym in 1874, since its author was Minister of the Treasury at the time. His *The Avenger's Wife*, later that year, was a success when performed under his own name. Like other plays of this period, it is a morality in verse blending romanticism with the classicism of the Golden Age. The honor code of Calderón, for instance, is the basis of Echegaray's first outstanding play, *Madman or Saint*, whose theme is that man's chief end is moral perfection. Lorenzo, the protagonist, is impelled by a quixotic sense

of honor to put right his false social position even though it brings misfortune to everyone. The play is written in prose.

After a number of lesser successes, Echegaray went back to verse for his second masterpiece, the one preferred by most critics, *The Great Galeoto*, which attacks the vice of slander. Its universality has been proved by performances in many countries and in seven languages. It was the play chosen to honor the dramatist in 1904 when he won the Nobel Prize in Literature.

As Echegaray became acquainted with the European theater of his time, Ibsen, Strindberg, and Sudermann increasingly directed his attention to character analysis and realism. In 1885 he abandoned verse in *Vida alegre y muerte triste* (*Gay Life and Sad Death*), which brought complaints from the public about his morbidity and surrender to naturalism. Protests grew louder after the performance of *The Son of Don Juan*, the tragedy of a man who inherits disease from his dissolute father. But crowds still thronged the theater for his last triumph, *The Mad God*, written when he was almost 70.

Echegaray specialized in tragedy and declared: "The height of art is tears, sorrow, and death." But he cannot be accused of lack of humor. *Un crítico incipiente* (*A Fledgling Critic*), performed in 1891, and *El poder de la impotencia*, (*The Power of the Weak*), which followed it the next year, have their amusing moments of satire against those who can do no good themselves, but keep others from doing it.

Although the day of Echegaray is over, he must be given credit for having guided the Spanish theater to the modern thesis play. If his plays are rarely staged today, the reason is that his pupils have surpassed their teacher. He died in Madrid, September 27, 1916, the city of his birth on March 10, 1833.

BIBLIOGRAPHICAL REFERENCES: For biographical and critical material see Isaac Goldberg, *The Drama of Transition*, 1922; A. F. G. Bell, *Contemporary Spanish Literature*, 1925; Annie Marble, *Nobel Prize Winners in Literature*, 1925; in Spanish, L. Anton del Olmet and A. García Garraffa, *Los grandes españoles: Echegaray*, 1912; A. González Blanco, *Los dramaturgos españoles*, 1917; M. Bueno, *Teatro español contemporáneo*, 1919; A. Quintero, "Echegaray, dramaturgo," *Boletín de la Real Academia Española*, XIX (1932); and in French, H. Courzon, *Le théâtre de José Echegaray*, 1912.

MARIA EDGEWORTH

Born: Black Bourton, England   *Died:* Edgeworthstown, Ireland
Date: January 1, 1767   *Date:* May 22, 1849

PRINCIPAL WORKS

NOVELS: *Castle Rackrent*, 1800; *Belinda*, 1801; *The Modern Griselda*, 1804; *Leonora*, 1806; *The Absentee*, 1812; *Vivian*, 1812; *Patronage*, 1814; *Harrington*, 1817; *Ormond*, 1817; *Helen*, 1834.

SHORT STORIES AND MORAL TALES: *The Parents' Assistant*, 1796–1800; *Moral Tales for Young People*, 1801; *Popular Tales*, 1804; *Tales of Fashionable Life*, 1809–1812.

MISCELLANEOUS: *Letters to Literary Ladies*, 1795; *Essays on Practical Education*, 1798 (with Richard Lovell Edgeworth); *Essay on Irish Bulls*, 1802 (with R. L. Edgeworth).

Maria Edgeworth, born at Black Bourton, Oxfordshire, England, on January 1, 1767, continued in the tradition of Fanny Burney to write the type of novel that culminated in the masterpieces of Jane Austen: the novel of manners. Of a generation that believed fiction could influence conduct, her stated purpose in writing was to diminish the frivolity of the times. One of a family of twenty-one children whose father was Richard Lovell Edgeworth, an Irish educator, her first stories were didactic and addressed to children. They included the six-volume series, *The Parents' Assistant*, *Moral Tales for Young People*, and *Popular Tales*, books inspired by her father who "helped" her in their construction. Naturally simple in manner, the characters in these tales were either good or evil with no allowance made for extenuating circumstances. (The part her father played in her career was both positive and negative; while he encouraged her authorship, his taste was poor, and he enthusiastically not only criticized but actually changed portions of a work before it went to the publishers. For example, the ending of *Belinda* is his.)

Maria Edgeworth's local color novel for adults was a permanent contribution to literature; her example influenced Scott to write his own stories with Scottish backgrounds and to some degree inspired Cooper and Thackeray as well. Using Ireland as her locale,

Miss Edgeworth portrayed the Irish realistically in her adult novels, and without apparent moral teaching. Acting as her father's agent on his Irish estate, she said what she knew of the tenant system at first hand. Thus she became one of the first to introduce the lower classes into fiction; but, since her general attitude was one based on reason rather than emotion, many of the characterizations were comic rather than realistic. Schooled by her father in empiricism, she admired the philosophy of utilitarianism with its emphasis on common sense and conservatism. Not only primitivism but sensibility generally was against her persuasion. As the Irish of this time were nearly the opposite in philosophy and habits of these principles, it is all the more surprising to find Miss Edgeworth presenting good-humored and sympathetic portraits of her servants and rustics.

Castle Rackrent is usually considered her best novel. The story, told as seen by an old servant, traces the degeneration of a contemporary Irish estate under the mismanagement of several squires and the emotionalism and lack of common sense of the tenants. Without principles, these people blindly follow money until there is none. Though written in the tone of the manners novel, the plot is actually a tragedy. *The Absentee* is similar in theme and plot, except that the mismanagement of the Irish estate in this case becomes nonmanagement while the hero is away in London trying to maintain a social status in society.

Ormond offers as its theme, implicit rather than stated, the idea that passion without reason is nothing more than sentimentality. *Vivian* presents the theme that reason without action is only procrastination, in one respect the reverse of the theme presented in *Ormond*. Whether or not any human being would ever be capable of all the virtues hinted at in these novels, they pleased a wide public both professional and general. Maria Edgeworth died at Edgeworthstown, County Longford, Ireland, on May 22, 1849.

BIBLIOGRAPHICAL REFERENCES: The basic biographical study is F. A. Edgeworth, *A Memoir of Maria Edgeworth, with a Selection from Her Letters*, 3 vols., 1867. See also A. J. C. Hare, *The Life and Letters of Maria Edgeworth*, 2 vols., 1894; Emily Lawless, *Maria Edgeworth*, 1904; Theodore Goodman, *Maria Edgeworth, Novelist of Reason*, 1936; Isabel C. Clarke, *Maria Edgeworth: Her Family and Friends*, 1950; and P. N. Newby, *Maria Edgeworth*, 1950. Related materials are found in Harriet and Edgeworth Butler, *The Black Book of Edgeworthstown and Other Edgeworth Memoirs, 1585–1817*, 1927. Also useful is *Maria Edgeworth: Chosen Letters*, edited by F. V. Barry, 1931.

WALTER D. EDMONDS

Born: Boonville, New York
Date: July 15, 1903

PRINCIPAL WORKS

NOVELS: *Rome Haul*, 1929; *The Big Barn*, 1930; *Erie Water*, 1933; *Drums Along the Mohawk*, 1936; *Chad Hanna*, 1940; *The Wedding Journey*, 1947.

SHORT STORIES: *Mostly Canallers*, 1934; *Young Ames*, 1941; *In the Hands of the Senecas*, 1947; *The Boyds of Black River*, 1953.

HISTORY: *The First Hundred Years*, 1948; *They Fought with What They Had*, 1951.

Walter D(umaux) Edmonds was born on July 15, 1903, in Boonville, a small town in the heart of the upstate New York area which serves as the locale for his historical novels. His father, who operated a New York City law practice from his country farm, was a lineal descendant of the Reverend Peter Bulkeley of Concord, and his mother, Sarah Mays Edmonds, came from a family which had been involved in the witchcraft episodes around Salem. Edmonds grew up in the Erie Canal territory, and spent many hours of his boyhood listening to the colorful stories of the old canallers in the region around Boonville.

His parents sent him to St. Paul's School in Concord, New Hampshire, and then to Choate School in Wallingford, Connecticut. He later said that these years were "miserable" for him, and that it was not until he attended Harvard University that he discovered learning could be enjoyable. At Harvard, Edmonds studied with Professor Copeland and became editor of the *Harvard Advocate*. When Professor Copeland, impressed by Edmonds' work, sent one of his stories, "The End of the Towpath," to *Scribner's Magazine*, it was accepted for publication. In 1926, the year of his graduation from Harvard, he won second prize in an intercollegiate contest conducted by *Harper's*. Following his graduation, Ellery Sedgwick, then the editor of the *Atlantic Monthly*, suggested to Edmonds that he write a novel about the canal area he knew so well. The novel which he wrote during the winter of 1927–1928 was *Rome Haul*, published in 1929. It proved an immediate success, and from that time on Edmonds has concentrated his full effort on writing.

Most of his novels have been historical in character, re-creating in place and period the history of the upstate New York region. The action of *Drums Along the Mohawk* covers the years between 1776 and 1784; one of the best examples of the regional chronicle ever written in America, it tells how events on the frontier during the Revolutionary War affected the lives of settlers in the Mohawk Valley. *Erie Water* is the story of the building of the Erie Canal between 1817 and 1825. *Rome Haul* shows the canal in the 1850's, before the railroads stripped it of romance and glory. *The Big Barn* deals with the efforts of upstate landowners, in the period of the Civil War, to preserve the large estates which united the culture of the Eastern seaboard with the crude, bluff vigor of the frontier. *Chad Hanna* is a story of circus life along the canal in its heyday. *The Boyds of Black River* presents a picture of Mohawk Valley farm life shortly after the turn of the century. *The Wedding Journey* is another story of the Erie Canal when it was a gateway to the West. Edmonds once summed up his work by saying that its purpose was "to tell, through the lives of everyday people, the story of New York State and its key periods in history."

He has also written a number of

shorter books for young readers: *The Matchlock Gun* (1941), *Tom Whipple* (1942), *Wilderness Clearing* (1944), *Cadmus Henry* (1949), *Mr. Benedict's Lion* (1950), and others. In these there is the same documentary accuracy combined with atmospheric feeling that we find in his historical novels.

Edmonds has received a number of honors for the imaginative fullness and vigor of his re-creation of a segment of the American past, and the importance of his contribution has also been recognized by honorary degrees from Union College, Rutgers University, Colgate, and Harvard. He has served as a member of the Board of Overseers of Harvard University and has, in recent years, divided his time between his farm in Boonville and the academic environs of Cambridge, Massachusetts.

BIBLIOGRAPHICAL REFERENCES: There is no full-length biography and very little criticism. Walter D. Edmonds, "How You Begin a Novel," *Atlantic Monthly*, CLVIII (1936), 189–192, is useful for information on the writer's methods of research. See also Dayton Kohler, "Walter D. Edmonds: Regional Historian," *English Journal*, XXVII (1938), 1–11; and R. M. Gay, "The Historical Novel: Walter D. Edmonds," *Atlantic Monthly*, CLXV (1940), 656–658.

JONATHAN EDWARDS

Born: East Windsor, Connecticut
Date: October 5, 1703

Died: Princeton, New Jersey
Date: March 22, 1758

PRINCIPAL WORKS

RELIGIOUS TREATISES: *God Glorified in the Work of Redemption*, 1731; *A Faithful Narrative*, 1731; *Some Thoughts Concerning the Present Revival of Religion in New England*, 1742; *True Grace*, 1753; *The Freedom of the Will*, 1754; *The Great Christian Doctrine of Original Sin Defended*, 1758.
AUTOBIOGRAPHY: *Personal Narrative*, 1765.

Jonathan Edwards, born in East Windsor, Connecticut, October 5, 1703, was converted to the Calvinistic doctrine of absolute divine sovereignty at twenty, after tutoring by a family chosen for the purpose and subsequent study at Yale, from which he was graduated in 1720. Happily married at twenty-four to Sarah Pierrepont, whom he memorialized in a charming brief essay, he continued the family tradition of preaching and sparked a religious revival in the 1740's with one of his most famous sermons, "Sinners in the Hands of an Angry God." In Edwards the Puritan spirit in America reached its epitome of expression. Because of increasing material prosperity, the leaders of New England life had allowed their strict Calvinistic zeal to relax; Edwards tautened the straps until, in a gesture of frustration, his own congregation, led by defecting relatives, forced him to resign in 1750. Sermons like "Sinners in the Hands of an Angry God" had been too much for them; one could not serve God only—so the man of God had to go. He spent the rest of his life, except for his last year as president of the College of New Jersey, now Princeton University, as a missionary among Indians.

330

Edwards believed the world existed for the glory of God. A combination of logician and mystic, his views reappear in Emerson and the New England transcendental movement of the first half of the nineteenth century. Edwards died of smallpox at Princeton, March 22, 1758.

BIBLIOGRAPHICAL REFERENCES: There have been several collected editions of Edwards' work of which the first American edition, edited by Samuel Austin, 8 vols., 1808–1809, is the most complete. An early *Life* is that of Samuel Hopkins, 1765, which contains the *Personal Narrative* and other essays not separately published in Edwards' lifetime. The standard modern biography is Ola E. Winslow, *Jonathan Edwards, 1703–1758: A Biography,* 1940. For biographical and critical studies see also H. B. Parkes, *Jonathan Edwards, the Fiery Puritan,* 1930; A. C. McGiffert, *Jonathan Edwards,* 1932; and the excellent brief study, Perry Miller's *Jonathan Edwards,* in the American Men of Letters Series, 1949. The best introduction to Edwards' work is *Jonathan Edwards: Representative Selections,* edited by Clarence H. Faust and Thomas H. Johnson, American Writers Series, 1935.

See also C. L. Parrington, *Main Currents in American Thought,* Vol. I, 1927; Henry S. Canby, *Classic Americans,* 1931; and for background information Joseph Tracy, *The Great Awakening: A History of the Revival of Religion in the Time of Edwards and Whitfield,* 1841.

PIERCE EGAN

Born: London, England
Date: 1772

Died: London
Date: August 3, 1849

PRINCIPAL WORKS

NOVELS: *Life in London,* 1821–1828; *The Life of an Actor,* 1824; *Finish to the Adventures of Tom, Jerry, and Logic,* 1828.
SPORTING SKETCHES: *Boxiana, or, Sketches of Modern Pugilism,* 1818–1824.

There are, in the history of the English novel, many relatively minor figures who, because of some quality of their writing or some type of subject material they used, have a strong influence on the subsequent course of that history. Such a man was Pierce Egan. He was a journalist and sportswriter who affected the writing of a giant in the novel, Charles Dickens.

Egan was born in London in 1772. Although he made that city his home for the rest of his life, he traveled as much as any man of his time; it has been said that he knew every city in England, and knew it well. For the early part of his life Egan wrote sporting articles and news stories for London newspapers on a free-lance basis. He was continually traveling throughout Great Britain to cover prize fights, horse races, and any other kind of sporting event. By 1812 his reputation for this sort of reporting was made, and in that year he secured a permanent position and married. Two years later his son, Pierce Egan the younger, was born. Young Egan became almost equally famous as a writer and as an illustrator, often working in conjunction with his father.

The older Egan, famous for his

331

knowledge of high and low life in London, and for his witticisms, decided to write the adventures of a group of young rakes in London. This serialized piece of fiction is far and away his most important work, and its full title is an indication of its nature: *Life in London; or the Day and Night Scenes of Jerry Hawthorn, Esq., and his Elegant Friend, Corinthian Tom, accompanied by Bob Logic, the Oxonian, in their Rambles and Sprees through the Metropolis.* The immediate and tremendous popularity of this series can be attributed to the vivid style and the lively, contrasting pictures of waste and poverty existing side by side. There were many imitations of *Life in London;* it was later dramatized and performed in both England and the United States.

The sequel, *Finish to the Adventures,* creates tragic ends for most of the characters and has an oddly moral tone, but it still has an abundance of adventure and shows an advance in literary style.

Egan also attempted a more ambitious piece of fiction, *The Life of an Actor,* which he dedicated to one of the greatest of all British actors, Edmund Kean. In addition, Egan edited a sporting weekly and turned out several non-fictional works about sports and the life of the sporting class. He also covered famous trials of the day and wrote journalistic histories of several notorious criminals.

In his last years Pierce Egan enjoyed a quiet retirement and the friendship and admiration of many in the social, sporting, and literary worlds. In a literary way he was admired by one of the most important English people, Charles Dickens, for many literary historians believe that the latter's *Pickwick Papers* was based in part on Egan's colorful portrayals of English sporting life. Egan died in London on August 3, 1849.

BIBLIOGRAPHICAL REFERENCES: There is no full-length biography and almost no criticism. For a brief criticism see Ernest A. Baker, *The History of the English Novel,* Vol. VII, 1936. See also William Makepeace Thackeray, *Roundabout Papers,* 1863; and J. C. Hotton, Introduction to *Life in London,* 1870.

EDWARD EGGLESTON

Born: Vevay, Indiana
Date: December 10, 1837

Died: Lake George, New York
Date: September 2, 1902

PRINCIPAL WORKS

NOVELS: *The Hoosier Schoolmaster,* 1871; *The End of the World,* 1872; *The Mystery of Metropolisville,* 1873; *The Circuit Rider,* 1874; *Roxy,* 1878; *The Hoosier Schoolboy,* 1883; *The Graysons,* 1887; *The Faith Doctor,* 1891.

SHORT STORIES: *Book of Queer Stories and Stories Told on a Cellar Door,* 1871; *The Schoolmaster's Stories,* 1874; *Queer Stories for Boys and Girls,* 1884.

HISTORY: *Brant and Red Jacket,* 1879; *A History of the United States,* 1888; *The Beginners of a Nation,* 1896; *The Transit of Civilization from England to America in the Seventeenth Century,* 1901.

Edward Eggleston was born in Vevay, Indiana, on December 10, 1837. His childhood was a sequence of serious illnesses interrupted occasionally by brief periods of precarious health. Despite concerted efforts to give him the life of a normal child, he was able to attend only two years of public school, and the rest of his early education came from the reading he was able to do as his health allowed.

Eggleston studied for a time at the Amelia Academy in Virginia and then, in another effort to regain his health, went to the rural regions of Minnesota. Here he became a circuit rider for the Methodists. By the time he was twenty-four he was regarded as the leading minister of his faith in Minnesota.

After a period in which he wrote children's stories and achieved a reputation through his contributions to literary periodicals, Eggleston went to New York to become editor of *Hearth and Home,* a magazine which came to national prominence under his editorship. *The Hoosier Schoolmaster,* first published in the magazine, was largely responsible for the sudden fame of both the periodical and its editor. The book sold over 20,000 copies in its first year of publication, and was translated into several languages for distribution abroad.

Eggleston's later career alternated between editorial duties, religious work, creative writing and, once again, the sickbed. He retired to Lake George, New York, and built "Owl's Nest," the home of his remaining days, where he died on September 2, 1902.

Throughout his life Eggleston turned to literature only when health forced him to give up his ministerial duties. His creative output frequently reflected this fact, for moral and didactic purposes often governed the structure and tone of his fiction. In the latter part of his career he turned to historical exposition. It was his belief that he had been writing history in novels and that the new field was no radical departure from the old.

Eggleston's character, which pervades all of his writing, was best summed up by his brother: "In all his life . . . Edward Eggleston never permitted himself to do any act that his conscience forbade, or to leave undone any duty that his conscience enjoined. But while in childhood the dogmas in which he had been trained gave law to his thought, his intellect, as he grew older, asserted its right to question the authority of those dogmas, and he did so with utter fearlessness, and with the same conscientious courage that had in childhood led him to obey at whatever cost."

BIBLIOGRAPHICAL REFERENCES: The most authoritative study is William Pierce Randel, *Edward Eggleston,* 1946, which contains an extensive bibliography. This may be supplemented by the biography written by his brother, George C. Eggleston, *The First of the Hoosiers,* 1903. The best brief biographical sketch is by Ralph L. Rusk, *Dictionary of American Biography.* See also Meredith Nicholson, *The Hoosiers,* 1900. Briefer studies include John T. Flannagan, "The Hoosier Schoolmaster in Minnesota," *Minnesota History,* XVIII (1937), 347–370, and "The Novels of Edward Eggleston," *College English,* V (1944), 250–258; Charles Hirschfield, "Edward Eggleston: Pioneer in Social History," in *Historiography and Urbanization: Essays in American History in Honor of W. Stull Holt,* edited by Eric F. Goldman,

1941; Spencer T. Benjamin, "The New Realism and a National Literature," *Publications of the Modern Language Association*, LVI (1941), 1116–1132; and James A. Rawley, "Edward Eggleston, Historian," *Indiana Magazine of History*, XL (1944), 341–352.

GEORGE ELIOT
(Marian or Mary Ann Evans)

Born: Near Nuneaton, England   *Died:* Chelsea, London, England
Date: November 22, 1819   *Date:* December 22, 1880

PRINCIPAL WORKS

NOVELS: *Scenes from Clerical Life*, 1858 (*The Sad Fortunes of the Reverend Amos Barton, Mr. Gilfil's Love Story,* and *Janet's Repentance*); *Adam Bede,* 1859; *The Mill on the Floss,* 1860; *Silas Marner,* 1861; *Romola,* 1863; *Felix Holt, Radical,* 1866; *Middlemarch,* 1871–1872; *Daniel Deronda,* 1876.

NOVELLA: *The Lifted Veil,* 1859.

POEMS: *How Lisa Loved the King,* 1867; *The Spanish Gypsy,* 1868; *The Legend of Jubal,* 1870.

ESSAYS: *The Impressions of Theophrastus Such,* 1879.

TRANSLATION: Strauss's *Life of Jesus,* 1846.

George Eliot was a pen name used by Marian or Mary Ann Evans. She was born on November 22, 1819, at Arbury Farm, Warwickshire, in the parish of Chivers Coton, and was baptized at what has since become the famous Shepperton Church. Her mother was Christina Pearson. Her father was Robert Evans, a carpenter, builder, and agent. Part of her early life was spent at Griff, an ancient red brick house of considerable charm. She attended numerous schools, at one of which she became an intimate friend of Miss Lewis, with whom she exchanged letters for years and who did much to deepen her strong sense of religion. Thus at the age of seventeen she already had an excellent background of education when her mother's death in 1836 and her sister's marriage made it necessary that she return home to look after the house for her father. Meanwhile, however, she continued her study with lessons in Greek, Latin, Italian, and German. She was also an accomplished musician, though shy of appearing in public. When her father gave up his duties on the estate, he removed in 1841 to Coventry. Here at twenty-two she came under a new and liberal influence. Among her new circle of friends were Mr. and Mrs. Charles Bray and Charles Hennell. Both men were writers, Bray having already published *The Philosophy of Necessity* in 1841. Hennell was the author of *An Inquiry Concerning the Origin of Christianity* (1838). Such influences caused the girl to question the evangelical beliefs which had always been such a strong and wholesome influence on her life. In fact, her liberal attitude and her refusal to attend church caused a temporary rift with her stern father. However, a reconciliation was effected and she returned to church, continuing to live with him until his death in 1849, upon which she inherited a small income for life.

334

Thus far she had spent two years translating David Friedrich Strauss's *Life of Jesus*, which was published in 1846 with the author's preface. Printed anonymously, the volume is said to have brought its author only twenty pounds. After her father's death she traveled for a time on the Continent, spending about a year in Geneva. Upon her return to England she accepted a position as assistant editor of the *Westminster Review* (1850–1853). During this period her distinguished circle of friends included James A. Froude, John Stuart Mill, Thomas Carlyle, Harriet Martineau, Herbert Spencer, and George Henry Lewes. The last of this group was serving then as the editor of *The Leader*. Miss Evans was strongly attracted to Lewes, who was not living with his mentally ill wife at the time. Flying in the face of public opinion, these two formed a union which they regarded as the same as a marriage, despite the lack of legal sanction—an arrangement which lasted until Lewes' death in 1878.

Meanwhile she continued her scholastic pursuits, working mostly on translations and on articles for *The Leader*, the *Westminster Review*, and the *Saturday Review*. Her first attempt at fiction was *The Sad Fortunes of The Reverend Amos Barton*, the first story in her *Scenes from Clerical Life*. First published in *Blackwood's Magazine* upon the insistence of Lewes, who recognized their merit, these short novels later appeared in two volumes in 1858. Once started on fiction, Marian Evans had at last found her proper métier. In 1859 she published *Adam Bede* under the pen name of George Eliot, which she continued to use in all her later writings. The next year marked the publication of the three-volume edition of *The Mill on the Floss*, which she had first named *Sister Maggie*. By this time George Eliot had joined the ranks of the successful and popular novelists: *Silas Marner, Romola,* and *Felix Holt, Radical* were avidly read by a large and eager public. Her works were admired by Dickens, Bulwer-Lytton, Trollope, Mrs. Gaskell, Reade, and Thackeray.

The Mill on the Floss, Adam Bede, and *Silas Marner* were skillfully written pictures of provincial life, in some instances drawn from the author's own observations, background, and family. During a trip to Italy she had collected the material for *Romola*, a historical novel of the period of Savonarola. Remarkable for its pictures of Florentine life, its outstanding character is Tito Melema. *Felix Holt*, her only novel concerned with politics, hardly ranks with the other famous titles. Published in 1868, *The Spanish Gypsy*, a blank-verse poem containing drama and narrative, was intended (said its author) to show doctrines of duty and heredity. Her next novel was *Middlemarch: A Study of Provincial Life*, which marked a return to her earlier locale. Probably based on her early life in Coventry, it draws a remarkable picture of middle-class life in an English town. Her last novel, *Daniel Deronda*, was published in 1876.

Having attained notable success as a writer, she and Lewes could now enjoy scholastic pursuits as they wished. They traveled on the Continent and visited the English universities; they even purchased a home in the country. But this life came to an end with the death of Lewes in 1878. Deeply grieved, she finally finished *The Impressions of Theophrastus Such*, a collection of essays which came out in

1879. She also edited Lewes' unpublished works.

Before Lewes' death, the couple had known J. W. Cross, a New York banker. He had also been of considerable service to the widow in settling her affairs. Mutual ties of sympathy brought the pair together, and they were married in the spring of 1880 at St. George's, Hanover Square. After returning to London from a trip to the Continent, Mrs. Cross caught a cold at a concert. She died in London on December 22, 1880.

George Eliot, for under this famous name she is known the world over, has been called the most distinguished English woman novelist. Certainly her novels, and particularly those dealing intimately with English life, reach a high point of wisdom, wit, and human understanding.

BIBLIOGRAPHICAL REFERENCES: The standard edition is The Warwickshire Edition, 25 vols., 1908; included is the authorized *Life, Letters, and Journals*, by J. W. Cross. Earlier biographical and critical studies include Oscar Browning, *The Life of George Eliot*, 1890; William Mottram, *The True Story of George Eliot*, 1906; Charles Gardner, *The Inner Life of George Eliot*, 1912; and Mary H. Deakin, *The Early Life of George Eliot*, 1913. For recent additions to the biographical-critical canon see A. T. Kitchel, *George Lewes and George Eliot: A Review of the Records*, 1933; Anne Freemantle, *George Eliot*, 1933; Joan Bennett, *George Eliot: Her Mind and Art*, 1948; Gerald Bullett, *George Eliot: Her Life and Books*, 1948; F. R. Leavis, *The Great Tradition*, 1948; L. and E. M. Hanson, *Marian Evans and George Eliot*, 1952; *The Letters of George Eliot*, edited by Gordon S. Haight, Vols. I and II, 1952, 1954; and Robert Speaight, *George Eliot*, 1954.

Shorter studies of George Eliot in books and journals are so numerous that a critical bibliography is badly needed.

T. S. ELIOT

Born: St. Louis, Missouri
Date: September 26, 1888

PRINCIPAL WORKS

POEMS: *Prufrock and Other Observations*, 1917; *Poems*, 1919; *Ara Vos Prec*, 1920; *The Waste Land*, 1922; *Poems, 1909–1925*, 1925; *The Journey of the Magi*, 1927; *A Song for Simeon*, 1928; *Animula*, 1929; *Ash Wednesday*, 1930; *Marina*, 1930; *Triumphal March*, 1931; *Sweeney Agonistes*, 1932; *Collected Poems, 1909–1935*, 1936; *Old Possum's Book of Practical Cats*, 1939; *Four Quartets*, 1943 ("Burnt Norton," "East Coker," "The Dry Salvages," and "Little Gidding").

PLAYS: *The Rock: A Pageant Play*, 1934; *Murder in the Cathedral*, 1935; *The Family Reunion*, 1939; *The Cocktail Party*, 1949; *The Confidential Clerk*, 1953.

ESSAYS: *Ezra Pound: His Metric and Poetry*, 1917; *The Sacred Wood*, 1920; *Homage to John Dryden*, 1924; *For Lancelot Andrewes*, 1928; *Dante*, 1929; *Thoughts After Lambeth*, 1931; *John Dryden: The Poet, The Dramatist, The Critic*, 1932; *The Use of Poetry and the Use of Criticism*, 1933; *After Strange Gods*, 1934; *Elizabethan Essays*, 1934; *The Idea of a Christian Society*, 1939; *The Music of Poetry*, 1942; *The Classics and the Man of Letters*, 1942; *Notes Toward the Definition of Culture*, 1948;

Poetry and Drama, 1951; *The Three Voices of Poetry,* 1954; *On Poetry and Poets,* 1957.

BIOGRAPHY: *Charles Whibley: A Memoir,* 1931.

The most controversial and influential poet of our time, Nobel Prize winner T(homas) S(tearns) Eliot was born in St. Louis, September 26, 1888, the descendant of a New England family, a branch of which established itself in St. Louis in the 1830's. The poet was educated at Harvard, where he studied under Babbitt and Santayana; later he continued his education in the Harvard Graduate School, the Sorbonne, and Merton College, Oxford. He taught for a time in a school near London, worked in Lloyd's Bank, edited *The Criterion* (a quarterly review), and became a director of the publishing firm of Faber and Faber. In 1927 he became a British subject. From 1932 on he became a familiar figure to American college audiences through several series of lectures.

Although Eliot's first volume of poems appeared in 1917, it was not until 1922 that he achieved celebrity with *The Waste Land.* Seldom has a poem created such a furor. By some it was acclaimed as America's most important modern poem; by others it was denounced as a deliberate hoax. His unusual technique: the elliptical style studded with phrases in foreign tongues, quotations and echoes used for evocative effect, his erudition, were too difficult for most readers. Yet it was soon realized that he had treated an important subject—the aridity of modern life, the horror of a civilization dying of spiritual drought—in a significant way and with a fresh poetic technique. The poem became the Bible of the "lost generation."

Ash Wednesday created equally great consternation, this time among the admirers of the earlier poem. For here Eliot dealt with the most important of all modern questions, that of belief: the dilemma of the modern man who wants to believe and yet who cannot, because of his spiritual dryness, his over-intellectuality. By approaching the problem in the penitential spirit of Lent, by accepting the religious solution ("suffer me not to be separated/ And let my cry come unto Thee"), Eliot antagonized many of his admirers among the secular-minded generation of 1930, who could not believe in his sincerity (*vide* Edmund Wilson in *Axel's Castle*) or who felt that he had betrayed his earlier position. But all had to admit that the poem attained heights of verbal beauty unequaled in any other contemporary verse.

In the twenty years between *The Waste Land* and *Four Quartets,* Eliot had achieved the rank of a major poet. It was no longer possible to consider him as merely a willful obscurantist or to attribute to him, as an early critic did, only "perverse brilliance." Through familiarity, his poetic technique had become better understood. Yet the *Quartets,* in spite of the careful exegesis to which they have been subjected, remain hard reading—more because of the philosophic difficulty of the theme (time and history) than because of the language. Though they are great poetry, their appeal is to a very limited audience, and they well illustrate the extreme demands that the best modern verse makes upon the reader. Much of the difficulty of modern poetry is the result of Eliot's influence; yet until the technique for reading this poetry has become part of the average reader's literary experience, it is probable that Eliot will remain the poet of the few who are willing to make the intellectual effort necessary for the understanding of his work.

Eliot's criticism appeared concurrently with his poetry, and with equally important effect. It has become a commonplace to say that he, quite literally, brought about a revolution in taste. He called attention to long-neglected writers: the metaphysicals, especially Donne; seventeenth century divines; the less familiar Elizabethans; Dryden. Through his influence, Dante, who had become the province of academic specialists, regained popularity. The reputations of the Romantic poets declined. But most important of all, Eliot's criticism has been written from the Christian point of view; he, more than anyone else, overturned the secular, humanistic attitude of the 1920's and 1930's. So unfamiliar to most readers was the Anglo-Catholic approach that many of the most acute of them could not believe that he meant what he said. Just as the sincerity of *Ash Wednesday* was doubted, so were the ideas of many of his essays considered as merely a pose. Yet to Eliot, more than any other modern writer, is due the credit for the swing from the intellectual Left to the Right, so that now it is the traditionalists who have the offensive. Even his strongest opponents could not deny his genuine scholarship, his enormous reading, and his careful judgments.

Eliot's most recent work has been in the drama. As far back as 1930 he wrote, apropos of the future of poetry: "The ideal medium for poetry, to my mind, and the most direct means of social 'usefulness' for poetry, is the theatre." Beginning with *The Rock*— which was a pageant rather than a drama, and for which he wrote the choruses—Eliot has been experimenting in various ways in an effort to find some effective modern equivalent of the blank verse of the Elizabethans, by means of which the poetic drama might be revitalized. It is perhaps too early to attempt an estimate of the effect that he may have had on the modern theater. Certainly several of his plays —even *Murder in the Cathedral*, in spite of what would hardly seem a popular subject—have had excellent runs on the professional stage, though some of this success may have been due to the author's reputation. It is true that a great poet does not always make a dramatist, and to many readers the plays have seemed the least successful of Eliot's works. Perhaps the plays lack a real sense of the theater; perhaps the poetic drama cannot now be revived. But by breaking with nineteenth century dramatic realism, and yet attempting something more than a mere imitation of Elizabethan tragedy, Eliot continues to demonstrate his importance in contemporary literature.

Tench Francis Tilghman

BIBLIOGRAPHICAL REFERENCES: There is no authorized biography. With the exception of *The Confidential Clerk*, all of Eliot's major work in poetry and the drama appears in *The Complete Poems and Plays of T. S. Eliot*, 1952. Essay collections are *Selected Essays*, 1932, and *Essays, Ancient and Modern*, 1936.

The foundation of all Eliot studies is still F. O. Matthiessen's *The Achievement of T. S. Eliot: An Essay on the Nature of Poetry*, 1935. Other major studies include George Williamson, *The Talent of T. S. Eliot*, 1929; Thomas McGreevy, *Thomas*

Stearns Eliot: A Study, 1931; Elizabeth Drew, T. S. Eliot: The Design of His Poetry, 1949; Leonard Unger, The Art of T. S. Eliot, 1949; H. L. Gardner, The Art of T. S. Eliot, 1950; and George Williamson, A Reader's Guide to T. S. Eliot, 1953. There are two collections of critical essays from various sources: T. S. Eliot: A Selected Critique, edited by Leonard Unger, 1948, and T. S. Eliot: A Symposium, edited by Richard March and Tambimuttu, 1948.

See also Bonamy Dobree, The Lamp and the Lute, 1929; Babette Deutsch, Poetry in Our Time, 1956; Morton D. Zabel, "T. S. Eliot in Mid-Career," Poetry, XXXVI (1930), 330–337; G. M. Turnell, "Tradition and T. S. Eliot," Colosseum, I (1934), 44–54; Theodore Morrison, "Ash Wednesday: A Religious History," New England Quarterly, XI (1938), 266–286; Philip Wheelwright, "The Burnt Norton Trilogy," Chimera, I (1942), 7–18; Genevieve M. Foster, "The Archetypal Imagery in T. S. Eliot," Publications of the Modern Language Association, LX (1945), 567–587; William Blisset, "The Argument of T. S. Eliot's Four Quartets," University of Toronto Quarterly, XV (1946), 115–126; T. Weiss, "T. S. Eliot and the Courtyard Revolution," Sewanee Review, LIV (1946), 289–307; David Daiches, "Some Aspects of T. S. Eliot," College English, IX (1947), 115-122; and John Lawlar, "The Formal Achievement of The Cocktail Party," Virginia Quarterly Review, XXX (1954), 431–451.

RALPH WALDO EMERSON

Born: Boston, Massachusetts   *Died:* Concord, Massachusetts
Date: May 25, 1803   *Date:* April 27, 1882

PRINCIPAL WORKS

ESSAYS AND LECTURES: *Nature,* 1836; *The American Scholar,* 1837; *An Address Delivered Before the Senior Class in Divinity College, Cambridge . . . ,* 1838; *Essays,* 1841; *Orations, Lectures and Addresses,* 1844; *Essays: Second Series,* 1844; *Representative Men: Seven Lectures,* 1850; *English Traits,* 1856; *The Conduct of Life,* 1860; *Society and Solitude,* 1870; *Letters and Social Aims,* 1876; *Lectures and Biographical Sketches,* 1884; *Miscellanies,* 1884; *Natural History of the Intellect,* 1893.

POEMS: *Poems,* 1847; *May-Day and Other Pieces,* 1867; *Selected Poems,* 1876.

JOURNALS: *The Journals of Ralph Waldo Emerson,* edited by E. W. Emerson and W. E. Forbes, 1909–1914 (10 vols.).

LETTERS: *The Letters of Ralph Waldo Emerson,* edited by Ralph L. Rusk, 1939 (6 vols.).

Ralph Waldo Emerson was born in Boston, Massachusetts, on May 25, 1803, and died in nearby Concord on April 27, 1882. Essayist, poet, and lecturer, he might be called the "Coleridge" of the American Renaissance because of his seminal influence on creative minds as various as Melville, Whitman, Dickinson, Hawthorne, Alcott, Thoreau, Very, and Margaret Fuller. He was the leader of "Transcendentalism," a warm, intuitional, religious, aesthetic, philosophical, and ethical movement, which, as a tributary of European Romanticism, proclaimed a theoretical and practical way of life and a new humanism based upon ancient classical and oriental supernaturalism. He maintained the "infinitude" or spiritual expansiveness of the individual person when divinely awakened. His earliest philosophic roots were Plato, Plotinus, Berkeley and the Scottish philosophers; later, Wordsworth, Coleridge, Goethe, Carlyle, Herder, Gérando, Swedenborg, the Methodists, Quakers, and certain Anglican divines; still later, the writers of China, Persia, and India.

Emerson was graduated from Harvard University in 1821, taught school for a while, and then studied theology in Cambridge. Licensed as a Unitarian clergyman in 1826, he was pastor (1829–1832) of the Second Church, Boston, preaching memorable sermons that foreshadowed his future career as essayist. He resigned his pastorate in 1832, partly because of his desire to reach a larger audience and partly in protest against certain rites which seemed to him anachronistic in progressive "Liberal Christianity." (His arguments against the Lord's Supper were drawn from a Quaker source.) Without prospects, in 1832–1833 he visited Europe to see Landor, Wordsworth, Coleridge and Carlyle; and upon his return began a long career as public lecturer and moral philosopher in the recently launched lyceum movement.

By 1834, he was settled in Concord, which has since become a kind of Mecca. Then he launched the first of three memorable challenges in *Nature*, published in 1836—a repudiation of both lukewarm Christianity and American materialism. It is a well-organized statement of his earliest idealism, showing the natural world to be a present messiah or viceregent of God, capable of developing the soul of man, and a mute teacher on the various levels of commodity, aesthetics, language, discipline, and spiritual illumination or mysticism. The final chapter contains a dream or prophecy of man's future or potential greatness on an earth transformed into a new Eden, sung by his alias, the "Orphic Poet." (Coleridge's distinction between the Reason and the Understanding and Swedenborg's doctrine of the divine Influx were basic categories during this period.) The second challenge, his Phi Beta Kappa address, *The American Scholar*, in 1837, urged the abandonment of imitative pedantry and declared America's literary independence from England. The training of the man of letters should be primarily Nature (the mediatrix between God and man) and secondarily an active participation in life. Books, the preservers of tradition, he relegated to the scholar's "idle times." In the third challenge, his *Address at Divinity College* in 1838, he proclaimed a God that *is* in distinction to a God that *has been*—a God that *speaks* rather than one who *has spoken* in ancient times, openly renouncing traditional Christianity and its deification of Jesus. Herein he summarized his Transcendental or spiritual philosophy, already outlined in *Nature*, stressed the *impersoneity* of deity, and elevated the Categorical Imperative of Kantian morality. This decade of his life (1833–1843) was characterized largely by a militant subjectivity and by a lofty optimism regarding the possibilities of the individual, but the middle years brought doubts and conflicts which necessitated a tempering of his idealism and a shift from the inner world of Self to the objective world—to an increasing awareness of man's animal inheritance and limitations.

Though still only a *leitmotiv*, these viewpoints make their appearance in

Essays: First Series and Essays: Second Series, which are condensations and revisions of earlier platform addresses —still, probably, his most popular works at home and abroad. Of these essays, "History" celebrates no chronology but rather an existential awareness in the individual soul of the ever-present Deity. "Self-Reliance" proclaims the God-in-man or Coleridgian Reason as the true Self in opposition to the brutish or animal Understanding which most men commonly exercise. (This doctrine of the true Self became the basis of Emerson's lofty individualism and theory of democracy.) "Compensation" reveals an instantaneous spiritual judgment upon thoughts, acts and conditions, illustrating the corresponding alterations or retributions taking place within the inner man. "The Over-Soul" and "Spiritual Laws" develop the doctrine of Transcendent Ultimate Reality and that of man's being a microcosm between it and the natural world. In them Emerson explores the subtle manifestations or laws of spiritual phenomena. "Friendship" owes much to the Swedenborgian doctrines of Influx and the "hells" and to the doctrine of *Quantum sumus, scimus* ("Like only can know like"), proclaimed by Coleridge, who echoed the Neo-Platonists of all ages. "The Poet" predicts Walt Whitman, who either read it in print or heard it as a lecture before the appearance of *Leaves of Grass*. (He addressed Emerson as "dear Master.") "It is not metres, but a metre-making argument that makes a poem." For Platonic Emerson, the poet is the only "complete man," whereas most people are only half-men. The poet receives a greater flow of divine energy or power than others; and he alone is articulate enough to express in words his intuitions of eternal beauty. Expression, indeed, is the principal evidence of his completeness. (Emerson's theory of art, in this essay, is Romantic receptionism.) "Politics," a practical application to the State of his doctrine of the individual, shows a keen awareness of American affairs in the midst of which the immortal soul or Self must be developed. "To educate the wise man the State exists, and with the appearance of the wise man the State expires."

Emerson's late works show an increasing acquiescence to the state of things, less reliance on the Self, and greater trust in the Over-soul conceived of as outside and beyond the Self. His *Poems* appeared in 1846, supplemented by *May-Day* in 1867; their importance is beginning to be appreciated. *Representative Men,* showing a philosophical indebtedness to Victor Cousin, may be interestingly contrasted with Carlyle's *On Heroes, Hero-Worship, and the Heroic in History* (1841). Emerson's visits to England in 1834 and 1847 provided rich observations for *English Traits,* published in 1856. His ripest work, *Conduct of Life,* ending in the sublime prose of "Illusions," reveals a developed humanism and a modest view of man's melioration under the limitations imposed by freedom and fate. *Society and Solitude* marks a falling off. He had the assistance of an editor or literary executor for *Letters and Social Aims.* James Elliot Cabot also supervised the posthumous *Lectures and Biographical Sketches, Miscellanies,* and *Natural History of the Intellect.* In his late years, Emerson issued *Parnassus* (1874), an anthology of favorite English and American poems. When they

341

are fully published, his remarkable journals will probably provide the best portrayal of the American mind and genius during the changing ethos of the vital nineteenth century.

Kenneth Walter Cameron

BIBLIOGRAPHICAL REFERENCES: The standard edition, though not definitive, is the Centenary Edition, *The Complete Works of Ralph Waldo Emerson*, edited and annotated by his son, Edward Waldo Emerson, 12 vols., 1903–1904. The Concord Edition, 1904, is a reprint. There are also volumes of supplementary material, including *The Uncollected Writings: Essays, Addresses, Poems, Reviews, and Letters by Ralph Waldo Emerson*, edited by Charles C. Bigelow, 1912; *Uncollected Lectures by Ralph Waldo Emerson*, edited by Clarence F. Gohdes, 1933; *Young Emerson Speaks: Unpublished Discourses on Many Subjects*, edited by Arthur C. McGiffert, 1938; and Jeanne Kronman, "Three Unpublished Lectures by Ralph Waldo Emerson," *New England Quarterly*, XIX (1946), 98–110. The most complete edition of the journals at the present time is *The Journals of Ralph Waldo Emerson*, edited by E. W. Emerson and W. E. Forbes, 10 vols., 1909–1914. *The Letters of Ralph Waldo Emerson*, edited by Ralph L. Rusk and containing more than 2,000 previously unpublished letters, correlates previous editions of Emerson's correspondence.

Among the one-volume editions available the most important is the recent *Selections from Ralph Waldo Emerson*, edited by Stephen E. Whicher, 1957. Earlier one-volume selections and their editors include Bliss Perry, *The Heart of Emerson's Journals*, 1926, and *The Heart of Emerson's Essays*, 1933; Frederic I. Carpenter, *Ralph Waldo Emerson: Representative Selections*, in the American Writers Series, 1934; and for the general reader, Mark Van Doren, *The Portable Emerson*, 1946.

The definitive biography is Ralph L. Rusk, *The Life of Ralph Waldo Emerson*, 1949, but two earlier works are still of great value: Edward Waldo Emerson, *Emerson in Concord: A Memoir Written for the "Social Circle" in Concord, Massachusetts*, 1888; and Oliver Wendell Holmes, *Ralph Waldo Emerson*, American Men of Letters Series, 1885. In the field of general criticism, F. O. Matthiessen's *American Renaissance*, 1941, has not been surpassed. For studies in Emerson's sources and philosophy, see Kenneth Walter Cameron, *Emerson the Essayist*, 2 vols., 1945, a work extending and growing out of this author's earlier *Ralph Waldo Emerson's Reading*, 1941. Emerson's Orientalism is dealt with in Frederic I. Carpenter, *Emerson and Asia*, 1930; Arthur Christy, *The Orient in American Transcendentalism*, 1932; and Kenneth W. Cameron, "A Dissertation on Emerson's Orientalism at Harvard," prefixed to his edition of Emerson's prize poem, *Indian Superstition*, 1954. Important attempts to integrate the many sides of Emerson and evaluate the transitions in his speculative outlook include Vivian C. Hopkins, *Spires of Form: A Study of Emerson's Aesthetic Theory*, 1951; Sherman Paul, *Emerson's Angle of Vision*, 1952; and Stephen E. Whicher, *Freedom and Fate: An Inner Life of Ralph Waldo Emerson*, 1953.

The serious student must not ignore the valuable monographs on Emerson's poems by Carl Ferdinand Strauch, who, for some years, has been at work on a definitive edition of the poetry. The best survey of research prior to 1950 is Frederic I. Carpenter's *Emerson Handbook*, 1953. New resources appear in Kenneth Walter Cameron, *The Transcendentalists and Minerva: Cultural Backgrounds of the American Renaissance with Fresh Discoveries in the Intellectual Climate of Emerson, Alcott and Thoreau*, 3 vols., 1958; in his *Emerson, Thoreau and Concord in Early Newspapers*, 1958; and in his announced *Transcendental Climate*, 3 vols.

Annual bibliographies, scholarly articles, interpretations, and facsimiles of Emerson's manuscripts appear in the *Emerson Society Quarterly*, established in 1955.

DESIDERIUS ERASMUS

Born: Rotterdam, Netherlands
Date: October 27, 1466(?)

Died: Basel, Switzerland
Date: July 12, 1536

PRINCIPAL WORKS

THEOLOGICAL AND PHILOSOPHICAL TREATISES: *Adagia,* 1500 (*Adages or Proverbs*); *Enchiridion militis christiani,* 1503 (*Manual of the Christian Knight*); *Moriae encomium,* 1509 (*The Praise of Folly*); *Institutio principis christiani,* 1515 (*The Education of a Christian Prince*); *Colloquia,* 1516 (*Colloquies*).

Erasmus, Christian humanist of the northern Renaissance, known primarily for his satirical *The Praise of Folly,* was an illegitimate child born in Rotterdam probably on October 27, 1466, the son of a priest whose name may have been Roger Gerard. Erasmus later called himself "Desiderius Erasmus Roterodamus." "Erasmus" was his given Christian name, "Rotterdammensis," as it originally was, indicated the city of his origin, and "Desiderius" was his own idea; it means "beloved" and is taken as the Latin equivalent of the Dutch name "Gerard."

When Erasmus was four years old he went to school at Gouda, where his father's family lived, and five years later went to Deventer with his mother to study there. In 1484 his mother died of the plague, and Erasmus returned with his brother Peter to Gouda. Their father died, and the boys passed into the care of three guardians, the principal one being Peter Winckel, a schoolmaster. Erasmus was finally sent to a monastery at Steyn in 1488 and Peter to one at Sion, after a brief period at school in Bois-le-Duc.

Erasmus was ordained in 1492, and in the next year he left the monastery to become secretary to the Bishop of Cambrai. He then managed to receive permission to attend the University of Paris, and was there from 1495 to 1499.

But he disliked the scholastic atmosphere of the university, and he was discouraged when his early poems and essays aroused little interest. He managed to find a patroness, the Lady of Veere at Tournehem, and then a traveling companion in young Lord Mountjoy, who went with him to England. In England he was very much impressed by John Colet, the Dean of St. Paul's, and was encouraged to do serious work in theology. Ironically, a work of the Paris years then appeared, *Adagia,* a highly successful collection of Latin proverbs which made humanism popular in Europe. Through a chance request, Erasmus prepared a Christian manual to give practical advice for guiding disillusioned and simple-minded soldiers back to the true faith. The book, *Manual of the Christian Knight,* expressed Emasmus' contempt for mere ceremony and form in religion, and urged a return to the meaning and spirit of the Scriptures.

From 1506 to 1509 Erasmus worked in Italy, where he received his doctorate in theology from Turin in 1506. In 1509 he completed *The Praise of Folly,* a book he conceived while crossing the Alps from Italy on his way to England. He dedicated the book to Sir Thomas More, his friend, partly because it was the sort of book More

343

would enjoy and partly because the Greek word for "fool" is "moros." The book is a kind of sermon, delivered by Folly, in which the claim is made that everything worth while in life has been done by fools. Erasmus used his satire to praise the simple kind of self-denial which is the heart of Christian love, and at the same time he damned as fools those who would glorify themselves by ecclesiastical abuses.

Erasmus traveled widely and knew many important scholars and churchmen. *The Praise of Folly* has remained his most famous book, although he distinguished himself with a controversial Latin edition of the New Testament and scored another satiric triumph with his *Colloquies* in 1516.

During the controversy over Luther, Erasmus attempted to stay uncommitted, sympathizing with Luther's attack on empty forms and indefensible dogma but disapproving of open conflict in religion. He finally attacked Luther on the free-will issue and thereby allied himself with the conservative elements within the church. Erasmus died at Basel, Switzerland, July 12, 1536.

BIBLIOGRAPHICAL REFERENCES: There is no recent edition of the complete *Works* of Erasmus. P. S. and H. M. Allen and H. W. Garrod have edited the *Opus Epistolarum,* 11 vols., 1906–1947. The standard biographical study is Johan Huizinga, *Erasmus of Rotterdam,* translated 1952, a work containing a selection of the letters. Also useful is *Erasmus and His Times: A Selection from the Letters of Erasmus and His Circle,* edited by G. S. Facer, 1951. See also P. S. Allen, *The Age of Erasmus,* 1914; Preserved Smith, *The Age of Erasmus,* 1920, and *Erasmus: A Study of His Life, Ideals, and Place in History,* 1923; J. B. Pineau, *Erasmus, sa pensée religieuse,* 1924; A. Hyma, *The Youth of Erasmus,* 1930; Margaret M. Phillips, *Erasmus and the Northern Renaissance,* 1949; José Chapiro, *Erasmus and Our Struggle for Peace,* 1950; Stefan Zweig, *Erasmus: The Right to Heresy,* translated 1951; and Jesse K. Sowards, *Thomas More and the Friendship of Erasmus, 1499–1517: A Study in Northern Humanism,* 1952.

SIR GEORGE ETHEREGE

Born: Maidenhead (?), England
Date: 1635 (?)

Died: Paris (?), France
Date: 1691

PRINCIPAL WORKS

PLAYS: *The Comical Revenge, or Love in a Tub,* 1664; *She Would if She Could,* 1667; *The Man of Mode, or Sir Fopling Flutter,* 1676.

LETTERS: *The Letterbook of Sir George Etherege,* edited by Sybil Rosenfield, 1928.

Sir George Etherege is one of those intriguing figures in history about whom biographers, literary historians, and other scholars wish they knew more. Only a few facts covering a relatively short number of years in his life are known. Even the spelling of his name is somewhat in doubt, there being evidence that his family spelled it "Etheredge." His family apparently lived in Oxfordshire, although there are papers which indicate that a grandfather (who spelled his name "Etherege") lived at Maidenhead, Berkshire, where George was reputedly born in 1635. George Etherege may have spent some time at Cambridge University. He may have studied law at the Inns of Court. He may have spent many years living abroad. But all this is merely conjecture, and no concrete evidence is available. He first came to notice when his play *Love in a Tub*, produced in London in 1664, made him famous.

Love in a Tub is actually the subtitle of the play; its real title was *The Comical Revenge.* The play has been considered by scholars to be the first comedy distinctly in the tradition of the Restoration period, when Charles II was on the British throne. The accent of the play is on wittiness, and the theme is a "war" between the sexes. In the years that followed *Love in a Tub*, Etherege became a figure of some notoriety in Restoration London. A compatriot of Sedley and the infamous Duke of Rochester, both notorious rakes and scoundrels, Etherege cut a wide swath as a beau and wit, almost like one of the characters in a comedy of the times. He apparently had a love affair with Mrs. Barry, a famous actress, and she allegedly bore him a daughter. In 1667 *She Would if She Could* was produced, a satirical comedy with two pairs of lovers for the comedy of manners and some low characters for comedy that was and is reminiscent of Ben Jonson's comedy of humours early in the same century.

Between 1667 and 1671 Etherege seems to have been in Charles II's diplomatic service, probably at Constantinople for a time, and perhaps also in Sweden. He was sent on one occasion to The Hague as a representative of Charles II. For a five-year period from 1671 to 1676 he seems to have done nothing except follow a dissolute existence. Then appeared his last comedy, *The Man of Mode,* in which he may have portrayed himself as the hero. Following the success of this play he apparently married a rich but little-known widow, Mary Arnold. Rumor at the time said that he had bought the title he received in order to win her or that he was given the title as a reward by the king for having done so.

In 1685 he was appointed British ambassador at Ratisbon, and from his letters written while in that official capacity comes the best knowledge of him. They indicate that he was tolerant and well-mannered—too tolerant and well-mannered to become a great diplomat or a great playwright; he adopted the pose at least of a man who shunned enthusiasms. His dissoluteness offended the people of Ratisbon, and he left under a cloud. Just how or when or where he died is still a mystery, although he is thought to have been killed by a fall while in Paris in 1691. The faults he had were not his alone; they were typical of the man-about-town, the loyal courtier of Charles II. He invented the comedy of intrigue, but others developed it. Perhaps money, fame, and women came too easily for him. At least his contemporaries all admitted that he was an affable and good-natured companion, and they nicknamed him "Gentle George" and "Easy Etherege."

BIBLIOGRAPHICAL REFERENCES: The plays appear with Introduction and notes in *The Dramatic Works of Sir George Etherege,* edited by H. F. B. Brett-Smith, 1927. See also Edmund Gosse, *Seventeenth Century Studies,* 1883; Allardyce Nicoll, *His-*

tory of *Restoration Comedy, 1600–1700,* 1923; Bonamy Dobrée, *Restoration Comedy, 1600–1720,* 1924; *Dictionary of National Biography,* Vol. VI; Dorothy Foster, "Notes on Sir George Etherege," *Review of English Studies,* VIII (1932); and Dale Underwood, *Etherege and the Sevententh Century Comedy of Manners,* 1957.

EURIPIDES

Born: Salamis
Date: c. 485 B.C.

Died: Macedonia
Date: c. 406 B.C.

EXTANT PLAYS

Alcestis, 438 B.C.; *Cyclops* (?); *Medea,* 431; *Children of Herakles,* c. 430; *Hippolytus,* 428; *Andromache,* c. 426; *Hecuba,* c. 425; *The Suppliants,* c. 424; *Herakles Mad,* c. 420; *Ion* (?); *Iphigenia in Tauris,* c. 420; *Trojan Women,* 415; *Electra,* 413; *Helen,* 412; *The Phoenician Women,* c. 410; *Orestes,* 408; *The Bacchae,* 405; *Iphigenia in Aulis,* c. 405.

Euripides, latest of the three great Attic tragedians, was born on Salamis c. 485 and died in Macedonia c. 406 B.C. Conservatives, represented mainly by the comic poets, complained of his debasing tragedy by introducing ragged heroes, immoral women, and the subversive casuistry of the sophists. He was not, as they allege, of low birth and unhappy in his marriages, though he may well have been a bookish recluse. He is more obviously concerned than are his predecessors with current political and social problems—we can trace his growing disillusionment with the Peloponnesian War from the *Andromache* to the *Trojan Women*—but he never held public office, won only four prizes, and was ready to leave Athens for Macedonia (c. 408) at the end of his life. After his death his plays far outstripped his rivals' in popularity. Of the ninety-two he wrote nineteen (as against seven each for Aeschylus and Sophocles) are extant; these include the *Cyclops,* of uncertain date, our only complete satyr drama, and the *Rhesus,* whose genuineness is question-

able. It is worth noting that the surviving plays were written in Euripides' middle and later years.

The formalism of Greek tragedy, because of its religious origin and associations, made marked deviations from the accepted subject matter and structure impossible, but within the traditional pattern Euripides effected startling changes in manner and substance. Instead of the traditional palace or temple façade his setting may be a peasant's hut or a remote barbaric shrine. The persons, whatever grand names they bear, are recognizable contemporary types; Sophocles remarked that whereas he represented people as they should be Euripides represented them as they are. Vocabulary, syntax, and meter (in the spoken parts) are far removed from the formal grandeur of his predecessors and virtually colloquial. The plots are richer in intrigue, and a detached character, frequently a deity, often introduces the play with an explanatory prologue. Most characteristic is Euripides' use of the "god out of the machine" to impose a traditional or happy ending where the course of the action would point to a different conclusion.

The availability of this device to effect a prescribed consummation allows the playwright greater freedom within the play, but almost always Euripides purposely makes the contrived ending difficult to accept and seems to hope that the intelligent part of the audience will supply the tragic ending the action implies. The choral odes are often little more than detachable interludes of song and dance to punctuate the episodes; as independent lyric utterance the odes have a new immediacy and suppleness and poignancy. The psychologic background and clarification which Aeschylus and Sophocles put into their choruses Euripides often presents in set speeches of his characters. Sometimes he will interrupt the unity of a play with a preachment, like Medea's attack on marriage, or even a joke, like the parody of the Aeschylean recognition scene in the *Electra*.

These innovations in manner are all functions of a more significant innovation in spirit. In Euripides' hands tragedy moved from the heroic to the bourgeois, from the abstract and timeless to the concrete and immediate, from theological speculation to social reform. His strategy is to transpose the traditional legends to a contemporary key, and to weigh the character of the actors and the morality of their actions by a realistic rather than an idealistic gauge. A decent man like Jason uses Medea badly because he shares the common view, which the result shows us was mistaken, that women and non-Greeks are inferior. A decent man like Admetus is willing to let his wife die for him because he too, wrongly as we see, thought women inferior. Hippoly-

tus was abnormally afraid of sex because he himself suffered from the stigma of bastardy. Electra turned psychopath and brutally murdered her quite conventional mother and stepfather because of false notions of *noblesse oblige*. Basic to Euripides' criticism is the sophists' distinction between *physis* and *nomos,* nature and convention.

Does a belief or institution—the superiority of Greek over barbarian, man over woman, king over commoner, the legitimate over the base-born—rest on nature or convention? If on nature we can only yield, as we yield to the law of gravity or to the gods. (It is a mistake to say Euripides was a rationalist; he may not have liked the gods, but plays like the *Hippolytus* or the *Bacchae* show that he believed in them.) Euripides is not concerned, as Aeschylus is, to justify apparent flaws in the universe. But so much of human misery derives from outworn conventions, which having been made by men should be reformed by men. By contrast with Sophocles' tragic doom, which is only illuminated, not mitigated, by heroism, Euripides is optimistic in envisaging the possibility of improvement and humanitarian in his sympathy for the individual victims of the flaws in society's conventions. He is at once philosophic, in his general reflections, and sensitive to the private suffering of his appealingly human characters. It is because of his concern for human rather than heroic characters (and that is why women figure so largely in his plays) that his treatment tends to be pathetic rather than tragic.

Euripides is above all a poet, not merely a pamphleteer or even merely an inspired teacher. His intellectuality and his impatience with illusion did

347

not blunt his sensitivity to the beauty and worth of all life. There are no villains in his plays (unless it be Apollo, and especially in the *Ion*), only sick sufferers. And it is because his apprehension of the world and its people is so encompassing and so essentially lyrical that his plays are sometimes badly constructed and sometimes crowded but always directly appealing. Audiences found him warm and relevant long after his starker predecessors had grown cold and remote. It is Euripides, not Aristophanes, who is the direct antecedent of Menander's comedy of manners, and so the progenitor of the main stream of European drama.

Moses Hadas

BIBLIOGRAPHICAL REFERENCES: The best book on Euripides in English is G. M. A. Grube, *The Drama of Euripides,* 1941. Gilbert Norwood, *Essays on Euripidean Drama,* 1955, is penetrating and suggestive. There are excellent chapters on Euripides in G. Norwood, *Greek Tragedy,* 1920, and H. D. F. Kitto, *Greek Tragedy,* 1950 (rev. ed.). See also Moses Hadas, *A History of Greek Literature,* 1950; *idem, Ancilla to Classical Reading,* 1954.

See also *The Complete Greek Drama,* edited by Whitney J. Oates and Eugene O'Neill, Jr., 2 vols., 1938.

JOHN EVELYN

Born: Wotton, Surrey, England
Date: October 31, 1620

Died: Wotton
Date: February 27, 1706

PRINCIPAL WORKS

MEMOIRS: *Diary,* 1818–1819.

POLITICAL TREATISES: *Of Liberty and Servitude,* 1649 (translated from the French of La Mothe Le Vayer); *The State of France,* 1652; *A Character of England,* 1659; *Apology for the Royal Party,* 1659.

SCIENTIFIC TREATISES: *Sylva, or a Discourse on Forest Trees,* 1664; *Terra; the Compleat Gardener,* 1693 (translated from the French of Quintinie).

John Evelyn, who recorded faithfully in his famous *Diary* the times of Charles I, Cromwell, and Charles II, was born into wealth at Wotton, the family estate in Surrey, on October 31, 1620. Reared by his maternal grandmother, he preferred to go to free schools rather than to Eton. Although he attended Balliol College, Oxford, he took no degree. After a brief period as a soldier he returned to Wotton.

Unable to remain neutral in the civil strife of the 1640's, he received permission to go abroad, where he was befriended by Sir Richard Browne.

Evelyn married Browne's daughter, Mary, when she was about twelve, although she did not live with him for some years after. Their union resulted in six sons and three daughters; one of his great sorrows was that only one son and two daughters lived to adulthood.

During the period of the Commonwealth John Evelyn lived mostly in France. In 1652, believing the Royalist cause lost, he settled at Sir Richard Browne's estate at Deptford. During this time he occupied himself with gardening and conservation, meanwhile carrying on a clandestine correspondence with Charles Stuart. He was always in royal favor during the Restoration, but he was never able to procure lucrative posts. He acted faithfully, though in minor and strenuous roles, as commissioner for improving streets, inspector of charitable institutions, and commissioner of the mint. He must have held twenty petty offices during his lifetime. His greatest honor was that as one of the promoters and early director of the Royal Society. He was secretary of the organization in 1672 and was twice offered the presidency.

While his diary, covering his life and times from 1620 to 1706, is chiefly remembered, his writings included political and economic tracts, and translations from French of scientific writings. It is inevitable, however, that his diary should be compared with that of Pepys, his good friend. Evelyn had not the wit, sense of malice, or inquisitiveness of Pepys, but he was a better reporter of events and possessed a more sane and conservative mind. While Pepys covered only a few years of Charles II's reign, Evelyn provides a document of over fifty years. Evelyn indicated at every turn his deep devotion to his family, a love of tradition, of established religion, of the natural world. Nor was he lacking in appreciation of art, music, or architecture, although he disapproved of the scandalous doings in the court of Charles II and in the theaters.

All in all, John Evelyn is the exemplar of the Age of Reason, which he ushered in. Compared to the later sages of that period, he is the nature's gentleman from whom this age could learn much about civilized living. On the death of his older brother he inherited Wotton in 1699. He died there on February 27, 1706.

BIBLIOGRAPHICAL REFERENCES: The first complete edition of Evelyn's *Diary* is that of E. S. de Beer, 6 vols., 1955. The *Miscellaneous Works* were edited in 1825 by William Upcott. There is a bibliography, Geoffrey L. Keynes, *John Evelyn*, 1937. There are two excellent studies of Evelyn's life and of his technique as a diarist: Arthur Ponsonby, *John Evelyn*, 1933; and Clara Marburg, *Mr. Pepys and Mr. Evelyn*, 1935. Also valuable is Walter G. Hisock, *John Evelyn and Mrs. Godolphin*, 1951. See also Ponsonby's *English Diaries*, 1923.

GEORGE FARQUHAR

Born: Londonderry, Ireland
Date: 1678

Died: London, England
Date: April, 1707

PRINCIPAL WORKS

PLAYS: *Love and a Bottle*, 1699; *The Constant Couple*, 1700; *Sir Harry Wildair*, 1701; *The Inconstant, or The Way to Win Him*, 1702; *The Twin Rivals*, 1702; *The Stage Coach*, 1704; *The Recruiting Officer*, 1706; *The Beaux' Stratagem*, 1707.

George Farquhar was born the son of William Farquhar, a clergyman, in Londonderry, Ireland, 1678. When seventeen years old, he entered Trinity College, Dublin, under the patronage of the Bishop of Dromore, but was soon expelled. Whether his expulsion resulted from a profane joke or from the death of his patron is not known, but the latter cause is the more likely. After leaving the college, he became for a while a corrector for the press of a bookseller, and then became an actor in Dublin. In a fencing scene in Dryden's *Indian Emperor,* however, Farquhar forgot to change his sword for a foil and almost killed a fellow actor. He never acted again.

He arrived in London about 1697 and devoted himself to writing comedies. He had met the famous comedian, Robert Wilkes, in Dublin, and it was perhaps Wilkes' influence that got Farquhar's first play, *Love and a Bottle,* on the boards at Drury Lane in 1699. In 1703, Farquhar married in the expectation of a fortune, only to find himself deceived. In spite of this trick which left him penniless, Farquhar harbored no resentment; but the remainder of his short life was spent in a constant struggle against poverty. While writing the second act of *The Beaux' Stratagem,* Farquhar realized he had a mortal illness. He completed the play and lived through its third night at the Haymarket Theatre before his death in April, 1707.

Farquhar has been called the last notable figure in the Restoration tradition, but he belongs perhaps more properly to the eighteenth century. In the year preceding his first play the steady clamor of the Puritans for reform found its most notable voice in the pamphlet, *A Short View of the Immorality and Profaneness of the English Stage,* penned by the Reverend Jeremy Collier. Collier was not the first to object to the cynical irreligiousness of the stage, nor was he the last, but he gained the most attentive audience. One doubts whether Farquhar was actually much moved by the clergyman's protestations, but he knew that many playgoers were, and he made a virtue of necessity; in his seven comedies and a farce, there is a definite transitional trend toward what was to culminate during the first half of the eighteenth century in the sentimental comedies of Cibber and Steele.

In Farquhar's plays, elegance as the social desideratum is replaced by naturalness. He has one of his ladies, Aurelia, say, "I take good manners to be nothing but a natural desire to be easy and agreeable to whatever conversation we fall into," and this principle is as fitting for a cook as for a courtier. His stage gentlemen are not merely drawing-room dandies; they are more real, more human, more capable of genuine emotion than their predecessors. Virtue is no longer a subject for mockery. Servants, bawds, and constables step forth from the wings into notable and organic roles, and sentiment begins to reappear on the stage in considerable force. For instance, in *The Twin Rivals,* Richmore, a wealthy fine gentleman, is prevented from raping Aurelia by the last-minute intervention of Trueman. Trueman thereupon reproaches Richmore for the wrongs done to another lady, Clelia. Richmore immediately says, "Your youthful virtue warms my breast, and melts it into tenderness," and forthwith agrees to marry the wronged Clelia. Etherege and Congreve must have smiled elegant and cynical smiles, but Cibber and Steele must have been filled with melting joy.

By the time of Farquhar's death Restoration comedy was almost dead as well, and with it real dramatic comedy, which was not to live again until resurrected by Goldsmith and Sheridan; and even then it was not the same.

But in Farquhar's career that moribund comedy breathes a few last healthy breaths. Farquhar replaced with human interest and a somewhat vulgar "character" the depraved witty elegance of the earlier Restoration. He emphasized story above the scintillant, empty brilliance of his predecessors. He is always natural, never strained, and the advances he made over his contemporaries in construction and general moral tone are striking in view of his age.

BIBLIOGRAPHICAL REFERENCES: The standard edition is *The Dramatic Works of George Farquhar*, edited by A. C. Ewald, 2 vols., 1892. A recent biography is Willard Connely, *Young George Farquhar*, 1949. See also Bonamy Dobrée, *Restoration Comedy, 1600–1720*, 1924; H. T. E. Perry, *The Comic Spirit in Restoration Drama*, 1925; Allardyce Nicoll, *A History of English Drama, 1600–1900*, Vol. I, 1952 (rev. ed.); and *Dictionary of National Biography*, Vol. VI.

JAMES T. FARRELL

Born: Chicago, Illinois
Date: February 27, 1904

PRINCIPAL WORKS

NOVELS: *Young Lonigan*, 1932; *Gas-House Maginty*, 1933; *The Young Manhood of Studs Lonigan*, 1934; *Judgment Day*, 1935; *Studs Lonigan: A Trilogy*, 1935 (*Young Lonigan, The Young Manhood of Studs Lonigan, Judgment Day*); *A World I Never Made*, 1936; *No Star Is Lost*, 1939; *Father and Son*, 1940; *My Days of Anger*, 1943; *Bernard Clare*, 1946; *The Road Between*, 1949; *This Man and This Woman*, 1951; *Yet Other Waters*, 1952; *The Face of Time*, 1953.

SHORT STORIES: *Calico Shoes*, 1934; *Guillotine Party*, 1935; *Can All This Grandeur Perish?* 1937; *$1000 a Week*, 1942; *To Whom It May Concern*, 1944; *When Boyhood Dreams Come True*, 1946; *The Life Adventurous*, 1947; *An American Dream Girl*, 1950; *French Girls Are Vicious*, 1956.

ESSAYS AND STUDIES: *A Note on Literary Criticism*, 1936; *The League of Frightened Philistines*, 1945; *Literature and Morality*, 1947; *Reflections at Fifty*, 1954.

James T(homas) Farrell remained a naturalistic writer during the 1930's at a time when the trend was toward symbolism or a highly selective realism. If he did not see life as a whole he saw it steadily, through gray-tinted glasses. He tells the same story of the life of the Irish in a Chicago slum over and over again, but he has retained a purely reportorial attitude on this phase of life which he knows so intimately, having been a part of it. In his fiction there is nothing that had to be invented. During the time Farrell was growing up in the Chicago South Side it was one of the harshest slums in America, and his *Studs Lonigan* trilogy (*Young Lonigan, The Young Manhood of Studs Lonigan,* and *Judgment Day*) is the story of the life of a childhood friend hardened by the environment until death saves him.

Farrell, born on the South Side on February 27, 1904, had the usual Catholic parochial education in Chicago; however, unlike most of his friends he went on to college, first to De Paul and then to the University of Chicago. Here he determined to be a writer, although his interests up to that time,

351

except for a brief experience as reporter for a Hearst paper, were chiefly in sports; other part-time jobs had included clerking and selling. First publishing in periodicals, he gained critical attention with his early novels and achieved popular notice in 1937 when *A World I Never Made* was examined by a New York court on the grounds of obscenity. The year before he had received a fellowship from the Book-of-the-Month Club for *Studs Lonigan*. Throughout his career Farrell has maintained his purpose of "exposing conditions," but his later novels, including the Danny O'Neill series which in many ways parallels his own life, have not sustained the tension of the Lonigan trilogy. He has matured, however, as a socio-literary critic, and his self-assumed role of the outsider, aligned with no particular group, gives his latest statements on the culture generally, and the publishing business specifically, a valuable objectivity.

BIBLIOGRAPHICAL REFERENCES: The best brief criticism of Farrell is Joseph Warren Beach, *American Fiction: 1920–1940*, 1941. See also Oscar Cargill, *Intellectual America*, 1941; Alfred Kazin, *On Native Grounds*, 1942; George Snell, *The Shapers of American Fiction, 1798–1947*, 1947; W. M. Frohock, *The Novel of Violence in America, 1920–1950*, 1950; Robert M. Lovett, "James T. Farrell," *English Journal*, XXVI (1937), 347–354; and Calder Willingham, "A Note on James T. Farrell," *Quarterly Review of Literature*, II (1944), 120–124.

WILLIAM FAULKNER

Born: New Albany, Mississippi
Date: September 25, 1897

Died: Oxford, Mississippi
Date: July 6, 1962

PRINCIPAL WORKS

NOVELS: *Soldier's Pay*, 1926; *Mosquitoes*, 1927; *Sartoris*, 1929; *The Sound and the Fury*, 1929; *As I Lay Dying*, 1930; *Sanctuary*, 1931; *Light in August*, 1932; *Pylon*, 1935; *Absalom, Absalom!*, 1936; *The Wild Palms*, 1939; *The Hamlet*, 1940; *Go Down, Moses*, 1942; *Intruder in the Dust*, 1948; *Requiem for a Nun*, 1951; *A Fable*, 1954; *The Town*, 1957.

SHORT STORIES: *These Thirteen*, 1931; *Doctor Martino and Other Stories*, 1934; *The Unvanquished: Sartoris Stories*, 1938; *Knight's Gambit*, 1949; *Collected Short Stories of William Faulkner*, 1950.

POEMS: *The Marble Faun*, 1924; *A Green Bough*, 1933.

William Faulkner is associated inevitably with a small area of land in northern Mississippi, where he was born (in New Albany) September 25, 1897, and where he has long lived (Oxford)—having abandoned it only for piecework in Hollywood in the 1930's and 1940's and for cultural missions to foreign countries (via the State Department) and to American college students (at the University of Virginia) in the 1950's. Against the background of a versatile and violent great-grandfather, Colonel William C. Falkner— who wrote the popular *The White Rose of Memphis*, published in 1880, before being murdered by a business rival—a mother who still paints, and a younger brother who has published three novels, Faulkner showed an early gift for sketching, storytelling, and verse-writing, but he was nearing thirty when his first book was published (*The Marble Faun*, 1924, poems). By that time he had read widely in Western classics under the guidance of a local lawyer named Phil Stone, had been trained as a pilot by the R.F.C. in Canada during World War I too late for combat, and had stayed around home doing odd jobs, studying briefly at the nearby University of Mississippi, and writing short stories which editors returned.

It was in bohemian New Orleans that Faulkner was encouraged by Sherwood Anderson, who got the younger writer's first novel published in 1926 while Faulkner was traveling around Europe. *Soldier's Pay*, like Hemingway's *The Sun Also Rises* of the same year, concerns the problems of the post-war "lost generation"; Faulkner's maimed Donald Mahon returns to Georgia to be rejected by his flapper fiancée but appreciated by a war widow before his early death. *Mosquitoes*, which followed a novel the writer destroyed, is a disjointed satirical tale of New Orleans artists and aesthetes, whose company the individualistic Faulkner apparently found enervating. In his third novel, *Sartoris*, he discovered his proper milieu—family life in his own Mississippi county (which he later christened Yoknapatawpha) as affected by the vicissitudes of Southern history. True, Bayard Sartoris is the romantic veteran of World War I who loses himself in alcohol, cruelty, and suicide, but Aunt Jenny, Old Bayard, the Benbows, the McCallums, and the Snopeses are original characters to be developed or counterparted in later, more successful Yoknapatawpha stories that reach back in setting to 1820.

In six months during 1928, Faulkner took a big creative leap and wrote the first of a half-dozen major novels, all of which were experimental in technique, shocking in violence and sexuality, and overwhelming in their embodiment of the dignity and indignity of man. *The Sound and the Fury* may be a tale of the Compson family's decline partly told by the idiot son Benjy, by the neurotic son Quentin, and the heartless son Jason, about an alcoholic father, a self-centered mother, and a promiscuous sister and her promiscuous daughter, but its disorder becomes a powerful parable when set against the order of the astute but faithful Negro servant Dilsey ("They endured," Faulkner wrote later). Having rewritten that novel five times before publication, Faulkner then dashed off a horrendous first draft of *Sanctuary* in order to make money, and (during six weeks on the night shift in a power plant) the back-country family tale of *As I Lay Dying*. The latter consists of fifty-nine short interior monologues mostly concerning the varying relationships of husband, lover, sons, daughter, and neighbors to the dying and dead Addie Bundren. When Faulkner got the galley proofs of *Sanctuary*, he rewrote the book—not with the result of making its sexual, moral, and social degenerates less shocking, but apparently of investing the wild tale of rape, murder, and nymphomania with a significant indictment of the evil of both hypocrisy and amorality. *Sanctuary* made Faulkner famous, but neither the critics nor the public understood it until much later, nor did they solve the riddle of *Light in August*, whose Joe Christmas is caught in a vortex of sexual, racial, religious, and community pressures. *Py-lon* was a second-rank story of a *femme fatale* involved with an air circus, two lovers, and a quixotic newspaperman at Mardi Gras, but *Absalom, Absalom!* rose again to the heights. In a suspended and suspenseful sequence reconstructed by Quentin Compson (of *The Sound and the Fury*), the novel concentrates on Faulkner's most tragic protagonist, Thomas Sutpen (1807–1869), who achieves his magnificent "design" of creating a great house out of nothing, but fails to sustain his line because he rejects the human beings who compose it.

The Civil War was the romantic subject of most of the connected stories in *The Unvanquished*, and the ravages of love in the twentieth century was the unromantic subject of *The Wild Palms*, which consists of two separate tales (the other called *Old Man*) whose chapters alternate. *The Hamlet* and *Go Down, Moses* returned to the fertile earth of Yoknapatawpha. The former, the first in an uncompleted trilogy centering on the aggressive, amoral Flem Snopes and his odious, if comic, clan, is made up of linked tales, the most famous of which is the tall-story masterpiece, "Spotted Horses." *Go Down, Moses* looks like a collection of stories, but Faulkner sees it as a novel, and it does embody his most complex family saga, that of the McCaslin-Edmonds-Beauchamp group, which begins with ante-bellum miscegenation and incest, proceeds through social comedy, romantic primitivism, and Christian renunciation—especially in the great short novel, *The Bear*—and ends with fifth-generation disintegration. After World War II) when his books were out of print) Faulkner filled a gap in this saga with *Intruder in the Dust*,

not so much a story of the proud Negro Lucas Beauchamp as of the teen-age white boy who learns painfully how to treat him as a human being. *Requiem for a Nun* revived the ugly characters of *Sanctuary* to seek their salvation in the frame of a play with long stage directions.

In 1954 Faulkner published a totally new long novel conceived a dozen years before and set in the France of 1918. *A Fable*, which consciously allegorizes the events of the false Armistice into the events of Christ's last days, caused some confusion for the reader but gained the National Book Award and the Pulitzer Prize for the writer. The latest novel, *The Town*, takes up Flem Snopes after *The Hamlet* and sets him down in "Jefferson" (Oxford, Miss.) to take over.

During this thirty-year period of publication, Faulkner's magazine stories were issued in collections—*These Thirteen*, *Dr. Martino*, and *Knight's Gambit*—the last being the adventures of the highly articulate small-town lawyer Gavin Stevens, who appears in other works. After Faulkner received the Nobel Prize for 1949, these and other items were reprinted in various collections, but it was Malcolm Cowley's superb anthology *The Portable Faulkner* (1946) that first demonstrated a unity as well as a variety that appealed to more than a coterie of readers. In his extensive body of work, Faulkner displays styles as various as Picasso's, but the most typical expression is a syntactically demanding, ornate but precise, diffuse but flowing series of long sentences, easy to parody but impossible to match—the very signal of the most original and substantial American writer of the century.

Frederick L. Gwynn

BIBLIOGRAPHICAL REFERENCES: There is no authorized biography of William Faulkner. For some information, see Robert Cantwell, "The Faulkner's: Recollections of a Gifted Family," *New World Writing* II (1952), 300–315; and Robert Coughlan, *The Private World of William Faulkner*, 1954. For extended critical studies consult Irving Howe, *William Faulkner: A Critical Study*, 1952; W. L. Miner, *The World of William Faulkner*, 1952; and W. V. O'Connor, *The Tangled Fire of William Faulkner*, 1954. See also Alfred Kazin, *On Native Grounds*, 1942; Joseph Warren Beach, *American Fiction 1920–1940*, 1942; Maxwell Geismar, *Writers in Crisis*, 1942; F. J. Hoffman, *The Modern Novel in America, 1900–1950*, 1951; F. J. Hoffman and Olga W. Vickery, eds., *William Faulkner: Two Decades of Criticism*, 1951; L. D. Rubin, Jr., and R. D. Jacobs, eds., *Southern Renascence: The Literature of the Modern South*, 1953; and Richard Chase, "Faulkner—The Great Years," in *The American Novel and Its Tradition*, 1957. See, further, Warren Beck, "William Faulkner and the South," *Antioch Review*, I (1941), 82–94, and "Faulkner's Point of View," *College English*, II (1941), 736–749; also Dayton Kohler, "William Faulkner and the Social Conscience," *College English*, XI (1949), 119–127. Some interesting comments by Faulkner on his own work are given in "Faulkner at the University: A Classroom Conference," edited by Frederick L. Gwynn and Joseph L. Blotner, *College English*, XIX (1957), 1–6.

The best introduction to the Yoknapatawpha sequence is *The Portable Faulkner*, edited by Malcolm Cowley, 1946. The William Faulkner Number of *Modern Fiction Studies*, II (1956), contains a selected checklist of criticism of Faulkner with an index to studies of his separate books, 150–164.

JOSÉ JOAQUÍN FERNÁNDEZ DE LIZARDI

Born: Mexico City, Mexico   *Died:* Mexico City
Date: November 15, 1776   *Date:* June 21, 1827

PRINCIPAL WORKS

NOVEL: *El periquillo sarniento*, 1816 (*The Itching Parrot*).

AUTOBIOGRAPHY: *Noches tristes y día alegre*, 1818 (*Sad Nights and Happy Day*).

José Joaquín Fernández de Lizardi had no college education, but he taught himself French, and so came under the influence of French philosophy. He commented on Rousseau's ideas of education in *La Quixotita y su prima* (*Little Miss Quixote and Her Cousin*), in 1819. At heart he was a journalist, however, and he took advantage of relaxed censorship in Mexico to found a liberal journal, *El Pensador mexicano* (The Mexican Thinker). This paper, established in 1812, gave him his nickname and pseudonym. He also wrote poetry and drama, and in the autobiographical dialogues of his sufferings during the revolution, *Sad Nights and Happy Day*, he introduced romantic prose to the New World in 1818.

He will be best remembered as the author of the first Latin American novel, *The Itching Parrot*, a title deriving from a pun on the name of the chief character, Pedro Sarmiento, whose schoolboy costume of green coat and yellow trousers earned him the nickname of "Parrot." This picaresque novel, springing up in Mexico two centuries after its counterpart in Spain had disappeared, criticized social customs at the end of Mexico's viceregal period. The publication of the first sixteen

355

chapters got their author into political difficulties, so that its complete publication was delayed until after his death. Censorship did not prevent him, however, from writing several other novels and many political pamphlets for which he was both excommunicated and imprisoned. He was born in Mexico City, November 15, 1776, and died there on June 21, 1827.

BIBLIOGRAPHICAL REFERENCES: For studies of Fernández de Lizardi in English see Jefferson R. Spell, *The Life and Works of José Fernández de Lizardi*, 1931; *idem*, "The Genesis of the First Mexican Novel," *Hispania*, XIV (1931), 53–58; G. González Peña, *History of Mexican Literature*, 1943; and Katherine Anne Porter, Preface to *The Itching Parrot*, 1942 (reprinted in K. A. Porter, *The Days Before*, 1952); in Spanish, González Obregón, *Novelistas mexicanos: Don José Fernández de Lizardi*, 1938 (Mexico); and Mariano Azuela, *Cien años de novela mexicana*, 1947 (Mexico).

ANTÓNIO FERREIRA

Born: Lisbon, Portugal
Date: 1528(?)

Died: Lisbon
Date: November, 1569

PRINCIPAL WORKS

PLAYS: *Bristo*, c. 1553; *Inês de Castro*, c. 1558.
POEMS: *Poemas Lusitanos*, 1598 (*Portuguese Poems*).

Born in Lisbon, Portugal, about 1528, António Ferreira, one of the founders of Portuguese classicism and a follower of the poet and playwright Sá de Miranda (1485–1558), was the son of a member of the household of the Duke of Coimbra. Educated in Canon Law at the University of Coimbra, he later became a professor there. Though Ferreira was inspired by Horace and employed Italian verse forms, he wrote in the Portuguese language because of national pride, and his collected verse was called *Lusitanian* (*Portuguese*) *Poems*.

In 1552 he completed a volume of sonnets in praise of some unidentified lady. With more success he compiled a second volume of sonnets, this time to D. Maria Pimentel, whom he won as his wife. His complete poetic output of Latinized odes, epigrams, sonnets, and epithalamiums, was published posthumously by his son in 1598.

While serving as the king's privy councilor and magistrate, he wrote the earliest completely Portuguese tragedy, *Inês de Castro*, Sá de Miranda's *Cleopatra* (1550) having been set in Egypt. Ferreira's play is considered the best of its kind of the sixteenth century. Inspired by Terence, Ferreira wrote a plotted comedy, *Bristo*, dedicated in the name of the University to Prince John, and he was also the author of a comedy of character, *O Cioso* (*The Jealous Husband*). Both plays were published in 1622.

Sent in 1567 to Lisbon on a government mission, Ferreira remained there, until his death during a plague in November, 1569.

BIBLIOGRAPHICAL REFERENCES: The *Complete Works* of Ferreira in Portuguese were published, with notes by António Castilho, in Rio de Janeiro, 2 vols., 1865.

356

There is an English translation by T. M. Musgrave, *Inez de Castro*, 1825. See also J. de Castilho, *António Ferreira, poeta quinhentista*, 3 vols., 1875.

LION FEUCHTWANGER

Born: Munich, Germany
Date: July 7, 1884

Died: Los Angeles, California
Date: December 21, 1958

PRINCIPAL WORKS

NOVELS: *Die hässliche Herzogin*, 1923 (*The Ugly Duchess*); *Jud Süss*, 1925 (*Power*); *Erfolg*, 1930 (*Success*); *Der Jüdische Krieg*, 1932 (*Josephus*); *Die Geschwister Oppenheim*, 1934 (*The Oppermanns*); *Die Söhne*, 1935 (*The Jew of Rome*); *Der falsche Nero*, 1936 (*The Pretender*); *Exil*, 1940 (*Paris Gazette*); *Josephus and the Emperor*, 1942 (*Der Tag wird kommen*); *Simone*, 1944; *Goya oder der arge Weg der Erkenntnis*, 1951 (*This is the Hour*).

POEMS: *Pep: J. L. Wetcheek's American Song Book*, 1929.

PLAYS: *Warren Hastings*, 1927; *Die Petroleuminseln*, 1927 (*The Petroleum Islands*); *Wird Hill amnestiert?* 1927.

AUTOBIOGRAPHY: *Moskav*, 1937 (*Moscow*); *Unholdes Frankreich*, 1942 (*The Devil in France*).

The son of a rich Jewish businessman, Lion Feuchtwanger, born at Munich, July 7, 1884, was well educated in pre-World War I Germany (his Ph.D. thesis was on Heine). In Germany he is probably best known to this day as a dramatist and as an adaptor of Greek plays, but in the English-speaking world he is justly famed for his long, somewhat ponderous historical novels. These books of his middle period seemed to breathe fresh life into the genre; they flash with modern psychology and with relevance to the turmoil of today's world. In fact, the English translations of his novels have always been more successful than the originals, and several of the latest books, beginning with *Josephus and the Emperor*, have appeared only in English.

Married in 1912 to Marthe Löffler, Feuchtwanger left Germany only to be caught in Italy by the outbreak of war in 1914. After his escape to his homeland, he was conscripted into the army. Permitted to return to civilian life, he began the modernist period of his writing, and he became active in the *avant-garde* movement, not only as a writer but as a publicist and a producer of the new drama. In this stage of his development he was bitterly anti-war, especially in his adaptation of the *Peace* of Aristophanes. World fame came to him a short time later with his historical novel, *The Ugly Duchess*, a story having a fourteenth century background.

Probably his best work is the Josephus trilogy, which is more historically accurate than his latest books. In Josephus, learned and Jewish like himself, Feuchtwanger apparently found just the right kind of hero to inspire his best writing. His novels written after World War II are marred by inaccuracies. *'Tis Folly to be Wise*, based on

357

the life of Rousseau, shows the oddities of Feuchtwanger's interpretation of the past and a rearrangement of historical fact.

Though begun in Germany, the Josephus sequence was completed in the United States. Partly because he was Jewish, partly because he was a liberal, Feuchtwanger was persecuted by Nazi Germany. He emigrated to Russia, London, Paris, and after the fall of France in World War II he fled to Spain. Finally, having adopted various disguises, he escaped from Europe. He finally settled in California.

His poetry, though often lighter than his fiction, is not well known in this country. Except for *Pep* (published under the name "Wetcheek," a literal translation of "Feuchtwanger"), little is available. His own regret about his writing concerns his drama. He feels that his finest plays have had little success, while the mediocre ones have won wide acclaim and have been often produced in his homeland.

BIBLIOGRAPHICAL REFERENCES: Robert Van Gelder, *Writers and Writing*, 1946, contains a section on Feuchtwanger. See also John Werner, *Die Geschichtsauffasung Lion Feuchtwangers in seiner Josephus-Trilogie*, 1954.

HENRY FIELDING

Born: Near Glastonbury, England
Date: April 22, 1707

Died: Lisbon, Portugal
Date: October 8, 1754

PRINCIPAL WORKS

NOVELS: *The History of the Adventures of Joseph Andrews, and his Friend Mr. Abraham Adams*, 1742; *The History of the Life of the Late Mr. Jonathan Wild the Great*, 1743; *Tom Jones, the History of a Foundling*, 1749; *Amelia*, 1751.

PLAYS: *Love in Several Masques*, 1728; *The Temple Beau*, 1730; *The Life and Death of Tom Thumb the Great*, 1730; *The Covent Garden Tragedy*, 1731; *Pasquin*, 1736; *The Historical Register*, 1737.

JOURNAL OF TRAVEL: *The Journal of a Voyage to Lisbon*, 1755.

Henry Fielding was born in Somersetshire on April 22, 1707, probably at Sharpham Park near Glastonbury, the home of his grandfather, Sir Henry Gould. When he was two and a half years of age his parents moved to a home of their own at the village of East Stour in the adjoining county of Dorset. The remarriage of his father, after his mother's death in 1718, brought on a bitter family quarrel, partly concerned with money, and a lawsuit which resulted in Fielding and his sisters and brother being made wards of Chancery, with their grandmother, Lady Gould, as their principal guardian. The old lady allowed her grandson far more freedom than was advisable for so boisterous and high-spirited a boy. He was sent to school at Eton between the ages of thirteen and eighteen and there received a thorough and valuable education, especially in the Greek and Latin classics. There followed three more years of complete freedom in the country, spent mainly in hunting, fishing, visiting various country estates, and courting half a dozen or more young girls. Early in 1728 he was in London, where his first play was produced at Drury Lane just before his twenty-first birthday. It was based in part on his unsuccessful attempt, at the age of eighteen, to abduct a beautiful young heiress, aged sixteen. Although the play was moderately successful, it was decided that he should go to Holland for further study at the University of Leyden, where he remained for most of the next two years.

On his return to England in 1730, he found himself without any regular means of support, even though his improvident father had promised him an income of £200. He began writing plays for a living and was launched on his career with the assistance of his cousin, Lady Mary Wortley Montagu, and the American, James Ralph, a friend of Benjamin Franklin then living in London. At the end of seven years he was the author of twenty-one plays, the majority of which had been successfully produced. Although he was then unquestionably England's most popular living dramatist, his career was brought to an end by the Licensing Act of 1737. This provided for government censorship of all plays before they could be produced and was aimed directly at Fielding, who had offended the powerful Prime Minister, Sir Robert Walpole, by his sharp political satires.

He then turned to the study of law and was called to the bar in less than three years, although the average time required was six or seven. He never developed a lucrative practice, however, and was obliged to supplement his income with his pen. During the next fourteen years he edited and chiefly wrote four periodicals, wrote and published four novels and a very large number of tracts and pamphlets, mostly political. As a reward for his political services, he was in 1748 appointed Justice of the Peace for Westminster and a few months later for Middlesex as well. Although the position had brought his predecessor an income of about £1000, Fielding received only about a third of that amount because, unlike the other corrupt "trading justices" of the time, he declined to accept bribes. He labored so ardently and so successfully that he practically cleared of crime one of the worst districts of London and in so doing established England's first efficient detective force, which has since developed into the famous Criminal Investigation Department of Scotland Yard. Largely through his influence, Parliament passed Acts greatly improving criminal laws and through his efforts the scandalous practice of holding public executions was abolished for a time. However, his attempts to abolish debtors' prisons and to establish institutions for the proper care of minor criminals and the poor failed and his suggestions were not put into effect until a century after his death.

In the summer of 1754 the ill health which had plagued his existence for more than a decade caused him to journey to Lisbon for the benefit of the warm climate. He died there the following October at the age of forty-seven and was buried in the Protestant Cemetery on a hill outside the city.

Fielding's outspoken honesty and his gift for witty, biting satire made him many enemies, who abused him roundly in print without much regard for the truth. Until recently, much of the mud that was slung at him has stuck to his reputation. Careful investigation by modern scholars, especially Wilbur L. Cross, has shown that he was by no means the dissipated rake his earlier biograhers were led to believe him. A principal cause of criticism and merciless abuse was that after the death of his first wife—the beautiful Charlotte Cradock whom he adored and made the model for Sophia Western in *Tom Jones*—he married her maid. His motive for this action was that she was about to bear his child and he wanted to save her from disgrace. Few if any other men of his generation would have behaved as decently.

In physique he was tall, handsome, and well made. His high spirits, convivial nature, and great wit as a conversationalist made him one of the most sought-after of companions. Those who knew him well knew him to be scrupulously honest, generous to a fault, and wise in the ways of the world. The most democratic of men, he chose his friends for what they were rather than for who they were.

Although Fielding was immensely popular as a dramatist in his own day and although several of his plays held the boards until the end of the eighteenth century, there is only one, *Tom Thumb the Great*, which is at all widely read today. Nearly all of them are topical and require a knowledge of contemporary events to be fully understood. He edited and largely wrote four periodicals of which two *The Champion* and *The Covent-garden Journal* are among the best of their time. All four of his novels, *Jonathan Wild, Amelia, Joseph Andrews,* and *Tom Jones,* are rewarding reading today, especially the latter two, which are read and studied in most American schools and colleges.

To his masterpiece *Tom Jones,* Fielding devoted all the art of which he was master and all the wisdom he had gained from a life lived to the hilt. Its greatness lies not so much in its wealth of characters and incidents, abundant and splendid as they are, nor in its plot, which Coleridge overenthusiastically declared to be one of the three most perfect ever divised. It is rather in the open-minded acceptance of human nature as it is and in the enlightened view of life, at the same time panoramic and profound. In this book we see life as clearly as the light of comedy can show it. We breathe and move in the sparkling, invigorating air which pervades also the *Odyssey* and *Don Quixote* and the comedies of Shakespeare and Molière.

Archibald B. Shepperson

BIBLIOGRAPHICAL REFERENCES: The most recent edition of the complete works is that edited by W. E. Henley and others, 16 vols., 1903. The novels are available in the Shakespeare Head Press Edition, 10 vols., 1926. The standard biography is Wilbur L. Cross, *The History of Henry Fielding,* 3 vols., 1918, a basic work which has not been superseded by the more recent scholarship and detailed study presented in Frederick H. Dudden, *Henry Fielding: His Life, Works, and Times,* 2 vols., 1952. There are a number of shorter but reliable biographical and critical studies: Austin Dobson, *Fielding,* 1883; Frederick T. Blanchard, *Fielding the Novelist,* 1926; H. K. Benerji, *Henry Fielding: His Life and Works,* 1929; Ethel M. Thornbury, *Henry Fielding's Theory of the Comic Prose Epic,* University of Wisconsin Studies in Language and Literature, No. 30, 1931; F. O. Bissell, Jr., *Fielding's Theory of the Novel,* 1933; B. M. Jones, *Henry Fielding, Novelist and Magistrate,* 1933; W. R. Irwin, *The Making of Jonathan Wild,* 1941; and Elizabeth Jenkins, *Henry Fielding,* 1947.

For general studies of the novel and Fielding's influence on its development see Ernest A. Baker, *The History of the English Novel*, Vol. IV, 1930, 1950; Robert M. Lovett and H. S. Hughes, *The History of the Novel in England*, 1932; and Edward Wagenknecht, *Cavalcade of the English Novel*, 1943. See also Kenneth Chester Slagle, *The English Country Squire as Depicted in English Prose Fiction from 1740 to 1800*, 1938.

Additional references will be found in F. Cordasco, *Henry Fielding: A List of Critical Studies from 1895 to 1946*, 1946.

VARDIS FISHER

Born: Annis, Idaho
Date: March 31, 1895

PRINCIPAL WORKS

NOVELS: *Toilers of the Hills*, 1928; *Dark Bridwell*, 1931; *In Tragic Life*, 1932; *Passions Spin the Plot*, 1934; *We Are Betrayed*, 1935; *No Villain Need Be*, 1936; *Children of God: An American Epic*, 1939; *City of Illusion*, 1941; *The Mothers*, 1943; *Darkness and the Deep*, 1943; *The Golden Rooms*, 1944; *Intimations of Eve*, 1946; *Adam and the Serpent*, 1947; *The Divine Passion*, 1948; *The Valley of Vision*, 1951; *The Island of the Innocent*, 1952; *God or Caesar*, 1953; *Pemmican*, 1956; *A Goat for Azazel*, 1957.

POEMS: *Sonnets to an Imaginary Madonna*, 1927.

Vardis (Alvero) Fisher was born on March 31, 1895, in Annis, Idaho, the son of Joseph and Temperance Thornton, Mormon converts. He spent his early life in a log cabin on the frontier. He received his A.B. degree at the University of Idaho and his M.A. and his Ph.D. degrees from the University of Chicago. After graduation he taught at both universities; he also served in the First World War as a corporal.

In 1918 he married Leona McMurtrey. In 1928 he married Margaret Trusler and, in 1940, Laurel Holmes. During the years of the depression he was the director of the Federal Writers' Project in Idaho. Almost without help he wrote *The Idaho Guide* and *The Idaho Encyclopedia*. *Toilers of the Hills* and *Dark Bridwell* present Laurentian themes in a Western setting. His first work to attract attention was a thinly disguised biographical at-tempt, a tetralogy consisting of the following titles: *In Tragic Life, Passions Spin the Plot, We Are Betrayed,* and *No Villain Need Be.*

His best known work is his long historical novel *Children of God* which tells the fascinating story of the Mormon movement under Joseph Smith and Brigham Young. In 1939 it won the Harper Novel Prize. *City of Illusion* is a story of the Comstock Lode and *The Mothers* is a fictionalized account of the Donner Party tragedy. In a planned twelve-volume series called *The Testament of Man*, he traces the development of mankind from prehistoric days. Some of the titles are *Darkness and the Deep, The Golden Rooms, Intimations of Eve, Adam and the Serpent,* and *The Island of the Innocent. Pemmican* is a novel of the early fur trade in the Northwest.

361

BIBLIOGRAPHICAL REFERENCES: There is no comprehensive critical study. See George Snell, *The Shapers of American Fiction: 1798–1947*, 1947; Harry R. Warfel, *American Novelists of Today*, 1951; and John Peale Bishop, "The Strange Case of Vardis Fisher," *Southern Review*, III (1937), 348–359.

EDWARD FITZGERALD

Born: Near Woodbridge, England   *Died:* Merton, Norfolk, England
Date: March 31, 1809   *Date:* June 14, 1883

PRINCIPAL WORKS

BELLES-LETTRES: *Euphranor: A Dialogue on Youth*, 1851.
TRANSLATIONS: *Six Dramas of Calderón*, 1853; *Rubáiyát of Omar Khayyám*, 1859 (revised 1868, 1872, 1879); Aeschylus' *Agamemnon*, 1865; Sophocles' *Oedipus Rex* and *Oedipus at Colonus*, 1880–1881.

Born in Suffolk on March 31, 1809, into a prosperous family originally named Purcell, Edward FitzGerald was able, after his graduation from Trinity College, Cambridge, to devote his life to study, literary dabbling, and the pursuits of a country gentleman. In his Suffolk home he took up the study of Greek, Spanish, and Persian. He became the friend of Tennyson, Thackeray, and Carlyle; but was the object of a bitter poem by Browning occasioned by a slurring reference on Fitz-Gerald's part to Mrs. Browning's death and her novel in verse, *Aurora Leigh*.

FitzGerald's translations—or rather, free adaptations—from the Greek and Spanish are of no literary interest. It was his version of the eleventh-century Persian philosopher, scientist, and poet Omar that made him famous. Following his usual method, he adapted rather than translated, until the result was almost an original poem. At first the book had no sale; but in 1860 it was accidentally discovered by Rossetti, who showed it to Swinburne and others. Its reputation rapidly spread; revised versions were published; and by the end of the century it was the most quoted poem in English. Its haunting music and its facile Epicureanism made it popular among a generation that had wearied of Victorian moralizing. It has become trite through excessive quotation, yet some of its lines have become part of every man's literary heritage. FitzGerald died at Merton, England, on June 14, 1883.

BIBLIOGRAPHICAL REFERENCES: *The Letters and Literary Remains of Edward Fitz-Gerald* were edited by William A. Wright, 7 vols., 1902–1903. The standard biography is Thomas Wright, *The Life of Edward FitzGerald*, 2 vols., 1904. See also Arthur C. Benson, *Edward FitzGerald*, 1905; Morley Adams, *Omar's Interpreter: A New Life of Edward FitzGerald*, 1909; Alfred M. Terhune, *The Life of Edward FitzGerald*, 1947; and Peter DePolmay, *The Paradox of Edward FitzGerald*, 1950.

F. SCOTT FITZGERALD

Born: St. Paul, Minnesota   *Died:* Hollywood, California
Date: September 24, 1896   *Date:* December 21, 1940

NOVELS: *This Side of Paradise*, 1920; *The Beautiful and Damned*, 1922; *The Great Gatsby*, 1925; *Tender Is the Night*, 1934; *The Last Tycoon*, 1941.

SHORT STORIES: *Flappers and Philosophers*, 1920; *Tales of the Jazz Age*, 1922; *All the Sad Young Men*, 1926; *Taps at Reveille*, 1935; *The Stories of F. Scott Fitzgerald*, 1951.

F. Scott Fitzgerald achieved early success with the publication of his first novel when he was twenty-four. He was acclaimed as the laureate of the jazz age; but when that era became unfashionable, the epithet was converted to stigmatize Fitzgerald as the playboy of American literature. Then, after his death, his reputation was gradually re-established on the basis of a fair assessment of his achievements. His writing was intensely autobiographical: not so much in the sense that he actually reported events in his life, but rather that he applied his work to interpret his career and evaluate the hectic time in which he lived.

Francis Scott Key Fitzgerald was born in St. Paul, Minnesota, on September 24, 1896. During his boyhood in that city he developed strong feelings about youth, romantic love, wealth, and success. These glamorous ideas were carried east to prep school and then to Princeton University. At Princeton he neglected his studies for literary activities, and dropped out of college to join the army in World War I. While stationed in Alabama he fell desperately in love with Zelda Sayre but lacked the means to marry her. When he became convinced after demobilization that the conventional road to success was too long, Fitzgerald quit his job to rewrite the novel he had been working on since college.

This Side of Paradise won immediate success with its blend of *weltschmertz* and wild college life. The author-celebrity married his southern belle and plunged into expensive living. For the rest of his life Fitzgerald was to be involved in a cycle of extravagant expenditure and writing himself out of debt. The novel was followed by *Flappers and Philosophers*, a collection of short stories. Fitzgerald's story output was very high—it eventually amounted to 160—for stories supplied him with money to meet his expenses while working on novels. Although he wrote stories primarily to earn money quickly, Fitzgerald's body of truly fine stories places him as one of the chief American short story writers.

The Beautiful and Damned, a novel dealing with the emotional and spiritual collapse of a wealthy young man during an unstable marriage, was less successful than Fitzgerald's first novel. The second novel was followed by *Tales of the Jazz Age*, a collection which included "May Day." An attempt to repair his finances with a play, *The Vegetable, or From President to Postman* (1923), proved unsuccessful.

The rich promise of Fitzgerald's earlier work was abundantly fulfilled by *The Great Gatsby*. In this novel treating a romantic racketeer's deep love for a rich and selfish married woman, the writing is perhaps unequalled for its lucidity and euphony. *All the Sad Young Men*, Fitzgerald's next collection, included "The Rich Boy" and "Absolution."

363

Following the critical success of *The Great Gatsby*, Fitzgerald's personal difficulties began to close in on him. In addition to the ever-present financial problems, his heavy drinking and his wife's mental breakdown forestalled work on the next novel. After several false starts, *Tender Is the Night* was completed at an inauspicious time. Although many critics now judge this study of a brilliant young doctor's disintegration to be Fitzgerald's finest work, the depression-ridden 1930's were unenthusiastic about a novel dealing with rich expatriates. *Taps at Reveille*, Fitzgerald's last story collection, included the Basil stories and "Babylon Revisited."

Fitzgerald then turned to screen-writing, and was engaged in a novel about a Hollywood producer when he died in that town on December 21, 1940. This unfinished novel, *The Last Tycoon*, was well-received; some critics felt that the prose style showed an even greater power and grace than that of *The Great Gatsby*. A final Fitzgerald volume, *The Crack-Up* (1945), edited by Edmund Wilson, gathered together autobiographical pieces, letters, notebook selections, and critical tributes.

After a period of neglect, F. Scott Fitzgerald was the subject of a remarkable literary revival in the 1950's. He now appears to be firmly established in the very first rank of American writers.

BIBLIOGRAPHICAL REFERENCES: The best biographical and critical study of Fitzgerald is Arthur Mizener, *The Far Side of Paradise*, 1951. Representative critical studies have been reprinted in a volume edited by Alfred Kazin, *F. Scott Fitzgerald: The Man and His Work*, 1951. See also Paul Rosenfeld, "F. Scott Fitzgerald" in *Men Seen*, 1925; Maxwell Geismar, *The Last of the Provincials*, 1947; J. W. Aldridge, *After the Lost Generation*, 1951; John Berryman, "F. Scott Fitzgerald," *Kenyon Review*, VIII (1946), 103–112; Anon., "Power Without Glory," *London Times Literary Supplement*, XLIX (1950), p. 40; Henry D. Piper, "Fitzgerald's Cult of Disillusion," *American Quarterly*, III (1951), 69–80; Edwin Fussell, "The Stature of Scott Fitzgerald," *Kenyon Review*, XIII (1951), 530–534; William Barrett, "Fitzgerald and America," *Partisan Review*, XVIII (1951), 345–353; Tom Burnam, "The Eyes of Dr. Eckleburg: A Re-examination of *The Great Gatsby*," *College English*, XIV (1952), 7–12; Marius Bewley, "Scott Fitzgerald's Criticism of America," *Sewanee Review*, LXII (1954), 223–246; and R. W. Stallman, "Gatsby and the Hole in Time," *Modern Fiction Studies*, I (November, 1955), 2–16.

The Crack-Up, edited by Edmund Wilson, 1945, contains autobiographical sketches, letters, and selections from Fitzgerald's notebooks. *The Disenchanted*, by Budd Schulberg, 1951, is a novel based on Fitzgerald's career and personality.

GUSTAVE FLAUBERT

Born: Rouen, France
Date: December 12, 1821

Died: Croisset, near Rouen
Date: May 8, 1880

PRINCIPAL WORKS

NOVELS: *Madame Bovary*, 1857; *Salammbô*, 1862; *L'Éducation sentimentale*, 1869 (*A Sentimental Education*); *La Tentation de Saint-Antoine*, 1874 (*The Temptation of Saint Anthony*); *Bouvard et Pécuchet*, 1881.

SHORT STORIES: *Trois Contes:* "La Légende de Saint-Julien-l'Hospitalier," "Un Cœur simple," "Hérodias," 1877 (*Three Tales*).

TRAVEL SKETCHES: *Par les champs et par les grèves.* 1885.

LETTERS: *Lettres à George Sand*, 1884; *Letters*, edited by Richard Rumbold, 1951.

Gustave Flaubert, French novelist, was born in Rouen on December 12, 1821. His father was a doctor and director of the Rouen city hospital, his mother a retiring woman of bourgeois background. High-strung and imaginative, Gustave eagerly consumed all the fanciful stories that he could induce his nurse or his neighbors to tell him. As a student he joined in the anti-classical revolt which was sweeping France. Solitary by nature and not of a happy temperament, Flaubert became absorbed with literature and history and early became aware of his vocation as a writer.

During a summer vacation in 1836 he became emotionally attached to Mme. Élisa Schlésinger—an attachment which he recorded shortly afterwards in *Les Mémoires d'un fou.* He found a companion and confidant in Alfred Le Poittevin, with whom he was to have a deep and lasting intellectual friendship. Flaubert's mood throughout his youth was in keeping with the fashionable romantic temper, one of ennui and lassitude, partly genuine, partly affected. He suffered, throughout his life, from fits of depression.

In 1839 Flaubert traveled to Corsica, stopping in southern France for sightseeing and amorous adventures. After his return he wrote *Novembre*, a romantic tale of love and longing. In the autumn of 1842 he became a law student in Paris, where he renewed acquaintance with Mme. Schlésinger (who refused to become his mistress). In January, 1844, he suffered a serious nervous attack and spent a year recuperating. He then abandoned the idea of a law career and became committed to literature, his romantic ideas having meanwhile become profoundly altered, especially in the direction of a de-emphasis on subjectivism.

Upon the death of his father in 1846 Flaubert inherited a comfortable annuity and pursued his literary career with fervor. In July he met the poetess Louise Colet, with whom he was to have a stormy liaison. In the spring of the following year he took an extended trip through Brittany, which he described in *Par les champs et par les grèves*, a work which first shows Flaubert's almost paralyzing capacity for self-criticism and his determination to avoid self-revelation.

Glad to see the July monarchy overthrown, Flaubert participated in a minor way in the revolution of February, 1848. He then completed *The Temptation of Saint Anthony*, which he had begun in 1846, but his friends Louis Bouilhet and Maxime du Camp urged him to discard the manuscript in favor of subjects where his rhetorical bent would have less scope. In the opinion of many critics, the *Temptation*, though not a superior book, more purely reflects Flaubert's temperament than his later, more successful works.

With du Camp, Flaubert set out in October, 1849, on a journey of more than eighteen months to Egypt, Syria, Palestine, Greece, and Italy, a journey during which he partook of much sightseeing and some love-making. In the course of his travels he deepened

365

his understanding of humanity, which he detested no less than before. In autumn, 1851, he began work on *Madame Bovary,* which was to absorb him until its completion in April, 1856. His extreme pains with the style of *Madame Bovary* were rewarded when, upon publication, the book was acclaimed by the discriminating public. (The broader success of the novel was due to a widely publicized morals suit against the author.) *Madame Bovary,* a study of the effects of romantic notions on a sensitive girl, ranks as one of the great novels of European literature. In it the author was undoubtedly effecting a self-cure, for Emma Bovary primarily embodies character traits and yearnings of the author. The book has usually been considered a masterpiece of realism, but stylistically Flaubert had little in common with his realist contemporaries, who had no time for his type of quest for beauty. He was, in this sense, much closer to Chateaubriand and Gautier. As for realism in the sense of a dispassionate examination of reality, Flaubert carried the doctrine to its farthest limits, avoiding judgments and stoutly maintaining that the artist's function is to understand humanity, not to explain or reform it. His approach has been characterized as objective, scientific, deterministic. His observation and his efforts to express reality through the perfect word and phrase were tireless and uncompromising; he was never hurried or harried by ambition for fame or success.

In 1857 Flaubert began his research for *Salammbô,* traveling to the site of ancient Carthage in order to develop a feel for his material. Published in November, 1862, *Salammbô* was totally unappreciated by the critics. After some unsuccessful attempts at theater, Flaubert decided upon *A Sentimental Education,* a novel about Paris in the 1840's. In this work the most scrupulous historical documentation is fused with personal reminiscences so numerous as to make the book a gold mine for Flaubert's biographers. This novel, published in November, 1869, Flaubert considered his masterpiece, but it met with hostility from the critics and indifference from the public. Flaubert next reworked his manuscript of *The Temptation of Saint Anthony,* which he published in 1874, without success.

In his last years Flaubert's best friend was the Russian novelist Turgenev, but for the most part he lived in relative solitude, whether in Paris or in Croisset, near Rouen. His scorn for humanity had become more intense and more generalized with each novel, and in the comic *Bouvard et Pécuchet,* unfinished at his death, he presented a devastating picture of the emptiness of modern man's most fundamental aspirations. In 1875–1877 Flaubert wrote *Three Tales* ("La Légende de Saint-Julien-l'Hospitalier," "Un Cœur simple," and "Hérodias"). Of the three stories "Un Cœur simple" is the most remarkable, showing none of Flaubert's irony and misanthropy but only the tenderness and compassion which often characterize the last works of the greatest artists. The *Three Tales* were immediately and almost universally hailed as masterpieces.

In spite of his scorn for fame, Flaubert's fierce artistic integrity and cult of perfection made him, in his late years, France's most eminent and respected literary artist. He gave counsel generously to many young writers, especially Guy de Maupassant, whom he

subjected to a long and rigid appren- Croisset, apparently of apoplexy, on
ticeship. Despite his fame, Flaubert May 8, 1880, and was buried in
suffered in his last years from financial Rouen.
insecurity. He died at his home in

Abraham C. Keller

BIBLIOGRAPHICAL REFERENCES: There are few books in English on Flaubert. A good
introduction is Francis Steegmuller, *Flaubert and Madame Bovary*, 1939. See also
J. M. Murry, *Countries of the Mind*, 1921; L. O. Shanks, *Flaubert's Youth: 1821–
1841*, 1927; Edmund Wilson, *The Triple Thinkers*, 1938; and Philip Spencer,
Flaubert, 1952. Also see Caroline Gordon, "Notes on Faulkner and Flaubert," *Hudson Review* (1948), 222–232; and R. W. Stallman, "Flaubert's *Madame Bovary*,"
College English, X (1949), 195–203.

The chief studies in French are by René Dumesnil, especially *G. Flaubert,
l'homme et l'œuvre*, 1932 (and later editions).

ANTONIO FOGAZZARO

Born: Vicenza, Italy   Died: Vicenza
Date: March 25, 1842   Date: March 7, 1911

PRINCIPAL WORKS

NOVELS: *Malombra*, 1881 (*The Woman*); *Daniele Cortis*, 1885; *Il Mistero del
poeta*, 1888 (*The Mystery of the Poet*); *Piccolo mondo antico*, 1896 (*The Patriot*);
Piccolo mondo moderno, 1900 (*The Man of the World*); *Il Santo*, 1905 (*The Saint*);
Leila, 1910.

SHORT STORIES: *Fedele*, 1887; *Racconti brevi*, 1894.

POEMS: *Miranda*, 1874; *Valsolda*, 1876 (expanded 1886).

PLAYS: *Scene*, 1903.

ESSAYS AND STUDIES: *Discorsi*, 1898; *Ascensioni umane*, 1899.

Antonio Fogazzaro was born in Vicenza, Italy, on March 25, 1842, of
devout Catholic parents. This moral
climate of his childhood influenced the
author to varying degrees throughout
his life. He was first educated to the
law at Turin and Milan; however, he
made a poor clerk and later declared
that he would have preferred death to
the legal profession. Instead, he turned
to literature. His poetic romance *Miranda*, published at his father's expense in 1874, justly received little
favorable notice. *Valsolda*, a collection of lyrics, showed even less promise.
Fogazzaro's religious faith had earlier
left him; now he saw his literary hopes

dying. Then one November day in the
Euganean hills, while reading *La
Philosophie du Credo*, by Gratry, his
belief flooded back, giving him a new
sense of confidence and of dedication.

Shortly after, at thirty-nine, Fogazzaro published his first novel, *Malombra*, a work in which he sounded
his major theme: the attempt of a man
with a passionate nature to lead the
religious life. The novel was a success,
and from this time Fogazzaro's career
was determined.

Next came *Daniele Cortis*, which
caused Verga to call him "one of the
very finest [novelists] in European literature." Daniele and Elena are in love,

367

but she is married to a worthless husband. When their moment comes for a decision, they mutually agree, on moral grounds, no longer to see each other or even to correspond. The renunciation, judging by Fogazzaro's letters, parallels one in his own life at that time. Further, both renunciations reveal very clearly Fogazzaro's lifelong concern with the effects of belief on conduct.

In the following years Fogazzaro published *Fedele,* a collection of tales, *The Mystery of the Poet,* and some lectures on Darwinian evolution. These last reflect his interest as a follower of Rosmini, a liberal churchman, in a vital regard for ideas from the position of intellectual Catholicism. These studies occasioned a good deal of comment, and in some quarters Fogazzaro began to be examined for heresy.

In 1895, Fogazzaro finished *The Patriot.* This novel, dealing with the *Risorgimento,* was meant, according to Fogazzaro, to "show the different effects of suffering on people whose mental attitudes differ." It was the first of three novels (with *The Man of the World* and *The Saint*) in a family chronicle. Particularly notable in *The Patriot* is the idealized portrait of Franco Maironi (based on Fogazzaro's memory of his father), who through faith in Catholicism finds strength to endure suffering. *The Man of the World* takes for its hero Piero, the son of Franco. Again the autobiographical implications are clear, as once more the hero is made to accept the moral responsibilities of marriage and to deny himself an adulterous love. The trilogy is completed in *The Saint,* Fogazzaro's best single work, in which Piero becomes a monk and takes the name Benedetto. The novel is characterized by its cry for reform within the Church and its emphasis on good deeds, precisely the positions which caused it to be placed on the Index.

Fogazzaro submitted to this decree and with *Leila* he made peace with his religion. Soon after a serious operation on his liver became necessary. On March 7, 1911, three days after his operation, he was given extreme unction, and that same day he died at his villa near Vicenza. He left behind him a reputation which placed him only second to Manzoni among nineteenth century Italian novelists.

BIBLIOGRAPHICAL REFERENCES: For biography and criticism see Sebastiano Rumor, *Antonio Fogazzaro,* 1920 (2nd ed.); Tommaso Gallarati-Scotti, *La Vita di Antonio Fogazzaro,* 1920 (English trans., 1922); Lucienne Portier, *Antonio Fogazzaro,* 1937; Piero Nardi, *Antonio Fogazzaro,* 1938; Ernesto Balducci, *Antonio Fogazzaro,* 1952; and Antonio Piromalli, *Fogazzaro e la critica,* 1952.

THEODOR FONTANE

Born: Neuruppin, Germany
Date: December 30, 1819

Died: Berlin, Germany
Date: September 20, 1898

PRINCIPAL WORKS

NOVELS: *Vor dem Sturm,* 1878 *(Before the Storm); Grete Minde,* 1880; *Ellernklipp,* 1881; *L'Adultera,* 1882; *Schach von Wutherow,* 1883; *Graf Petöfy,* 1884

(Count Petofy); *Cécile*, 1887; *Irrungen, Wirrungen*, 1888 *(Trials and Tribulations)*; *Frau Jenny Treibel*, 1892; *Effi Briest*, 1895; *Der Stechlin*, 1898.

POEMS: *Gedichte*, 1851; *Balladen*, 1861.

AUTOBIOGRAPHY: *Meine Kinderjahre*, 1894 *(My Childhood Years)*; *Von Zwanzig bis Dreissig*, 1898 *(From Twenty to Thirty)*.

TRAVEL SKETCHES AND IMPRESSIONS: *Ein Sommer in London*, 1854; *(A Summer in London)*; *Jenseit des Tweed*, 1860 *(Beyond the Tweed)*; *Wanderungen durch die Mark Brandenburg*, 1862–1882.

CRITICISM: *Causerien über das Theater*, 1905.

The work of Theodor Fontane, born at Neuruppin, December 30, 1819, is usually divided into three periods. The first is the period of his historical novels, when he was under the influence of Sir Walter Scott. *Before the Storm* and *Schach von Wutherow*, both novels of the Napoleonic Wars, are characteristic of this period. The second, introduced by *Trials and Tribulations* in 1888, is characterized by fiction in the vein of Zola's naturalism. In his third period he wrote psychological novels of Berlin life, of which the outstanding examples are *Frau Jenny Treibel* and *Effi Briest*, his masterpiece. During his first period he also wrote ballads on Scottish subjects; one of the best known, "Archibald Douglas," has continued to be popular.

Fontane had been trained as an apothecary but later branched out into literary activities as a member of several Berlin literary societies, particularly *Der Tunnel über der Spree*, during its most vigorous years. He traveled to England as a foreign observer for the Prussian ministerial press and later collected his travel experiences in two volumes, *A Summer in London* and *Beyond the Tweed*. Numerous trips through his native province resulted in *Wanderings Through the Mark Brandenburg*. During his later years he reviewed the productions at the Royal Theater for the *Vossiche Zeitung*. He died in Berlin, September 20, 1898.

BIBLIOGRAPHICAL REFERENCES: The best study of Fontane in English is Conrad Wandrey, *Theodor Fontane: A Critical Study*, 1920. See also Franz Servaes, *Theodor Fontane*, 1900; L. A. Shears, *The Influence of Walter Scott on the Novels of Theodor Fontane*, 1922; Heinrich Spiero, *Fontane*, 1928; Felix Bertaux, *A Panorama of German Literature, 1871–1931*, 1935; and Gilbert Waterhouse, *A Short History of German Literature*, 1946.

ESTHER FORBES

Born: Westboro, Massachusetts
Date: 1894 (?)

PRINCIPAL WORKS

NOVELS: *O Genteel Lady*, 1926; *A Mirror for Witches*, 1928; *Miss Marvel*, 1935; *Paradise*, 1937; *The General's Lady*, 1938; *The Running of the Tide*, 1948; *Rainbow on the Road*, 1954.

HISTORY: *Paul Revere and the World He Lived In*, 1942.

Born at Westboro, Massachusetts, in 1894(?) into a literary environment and surrounded from her earliest childhood by the traditions and the lore of New England history, Esther Forbes began the practice of her calling as a novelist at the age of thirteen—a practice which, according to her own report, has been going on ever since. Publication, however, did not follow until 1926, when she had been graduated from Bradford Academy (1912), had attended the University of Wisconsin for two years (1916–1918), had worked six years on the editorial staff of a publishing company, and had married (1926) Albert J. Hoskins, whom she later divorced.

O Genteel Lady, though historical, is concerned chiefly with a woman's revolt against the stifling conventions of Victorian times and is not in keeping with the spirit or the subject matter of her later works. In her second novel, A Mirror for Witches, the writer attained her greatest critical success by exploiting for the first time her long-collected store of knowledge concerning early New England. This period of history continued to serve her well: for example, in her romance, Paradise, she went back to the time of King Philip's War (1675–1676); in The General's Lady she created a setting in Revolutionary times; and in Rainbow on the Road she vividly depicted rural life in New England during the 1830's. In fact, though primarily a novelist, Miss Forbes won her highest public acclaim as a historian when, in 1943, her best-selling Paul Revere and the World He Lived In brought her the Pulitzer Prize for history.

BIBLIOGRAPHICAL REFERENCES: For critical comment see Esther Forbes, "Why the Past?" in What Is a Book? edited by Dale Warren, 1935; and Dale Warren, "Esther Forbes and the World She Lives In," Publishers' Weekly, CXLV (1944), 1844–1845. For discussion of individual books see, further, Book Review Digest, 1926, 1928 ff.

FORD MADOX FORD

Born: Merton, England
Date: 1873

Died: Deauville, France
Date: June 26, 1939

PRINCIPAL WORKS

NOVELS: The Shifting of the Fire, 1892; The Inheritors, 1901 (with Joseph Conrad); Romance, 1903 (with Joseph Conrad); Benefactor, 1905; The Fifth Queen, 1906; An English Girl, 1907; Privy Seal, 1907; The Fifth Queen Crowned, 1908; Mr. Apollo, 1908; The "Half Moon," 1909; A Call, 1910; The Portrait, 1910; Ladies Whose Bright Eyes, 1911; The Panel, 1912; Mr. Fleight, 1913; The Young Lovell, 1913 [Ring for Nancy]; The Good Soldier, 1915; The Marsden Case, 1923; The Nature of a Crime, 1924 (with Joseph Conrad); Some Do Not, 1924; No More Parades, 1925; A Man Could Stand Up, 1926; The Last Post, 1928; A Little Less Than Gods, 1928; When the Wicked Man, 1931; The Rash Act, 1933; Henry for Hugh, 1934; Vive le Roi, 1936.

POEMS: Poems for Pictures, 1900; The Face of the Night, 1904; From Inland and Other Poems, 1907; Songs from London, 1910; High Germany, 1911; Collected

Poems, 1913; Antwerp, 1915; On Heaven, 1918; Poems Written on Active Service, 1918; New Poems, 1927; Collected Poems, 1936.

REMINISCENCES: Thus to Revisit, 1921; Joseph Conrad, A Personal Remembrance, 1924; No Enemy, 1929; Return to Yesterday, 1931; It Was the Nightingale, 1933; Mightier than the Sword, 1938.

CRITICISM AND STUDIES: Ford Madox Brown, 1896; The Cinque Ports, 1900; Rossetti, 1902; Hans Holbein, the Younger, 1905; The Pre-Raphaelite Brotherhood, 1907; Henry James, 1913; Between St. Dennis and St. George, 1915; A Mirror to France, 1926; The English Novel, 1929.

Ford Madox [Hueffer] Ford was born at Merton, England, in 1873. His father was a music critic of German origin, Franz Xaver Hüffer; his mother was Catherine Ernely Madox Brown, daughter of a pre-Raphaelite artist. As a privileged child in an environment of eminent Victorians, his formal schooling at Praetoria House and University College School, London, could not match the artistic and literary influences that surrounded him at home. At eighteen he traveled on the Continent and became a Roman Catholic in order to please his rich German relatives.

The Brown Owl, a fairy story, marked Ford's debut in print in 1892. After his early marriage, Ford settled in Kent where he devoted himself to writing. Here he met Joseph Conrad with whom he shared a fundamental agreement upon the role of technique in the novel. The two fledgling authors collaborated over a period of five years in a partnership which produced two novels, The Inheritors and Romance.

From 1892 to 1902, Ford turned out nine published volumes, including biography, fiction, poetry and travel. Just before his thirtieth birthday the strain of so much activity took its toll in a nervous breakdown. Despite his illness he worked on a fictional treatment of the ill-starred Catherine Howard which eventually became a clever trilogy: The Fifth Queen, Privy Seal, and The Fifth Queen Crowned. In 1905 the reception of his The Soul of London gave his recovery a physical and financial boost. This success was followed by the high point of his public career in England, the editorship of The English Review (1908–1909).

The financial failure of this brilliant journal and an unfortunate liaison brought his short glory to an end. His unsuccessful attempt to arrange a divorce from his wife served only to further alienate his former friends. Two novels of this period, however, fared well. Ladies Whose Bright Eyes exhibited Ford's satirical analysis of medieval England combined with a facile grasp of le mot juste. The Good Soldier, a story of psychological, religious, and moral violence between the sexes, reflected his own painful marital situation.

World War I provided an escape from his personal difficulties. By the time he emerged from it in 1919, a victim of shell-shock and gassing, the Imagist movement had felt the impact of his vers libre, On Heaven. For a few years he lived in modest agrarian style in Sussex with a young woman artist. Here he changed his name to Ford, ostensibly to avoid the anti-Prussian reaction that pervaded England.

His semi-absence from the literary scene ended in 1922 when he went to Paris and became editor of the trans-

atlantic review, a short-lived periodical whose contributors included Pound and Joyce. In France, where his reputation was high as a result of his perceptive book on the French nation, *Between St. Dennis and St. George,* Ford was a patriarch to the Bohemian, expatriate circle. Across the Channel, however, antagonism to him was increased by *Joseph Conrad, A Personal Remembrance,* a book he wrote after Conrad's death in 1924.

Issued in the same year was *Some Do Not,* the first of four novels dealing with Christopher Tietjens, a unique character creation in twentieth century fiction personifying the Tory, Christian gentleman of immense intellect and humanity living in a hostile, crumbling world. In the three succeeding books, *No More Parades, A Man Could Stand Up,* and *The Last Post,* Ford combined his finest technique, including most intricate use of the timeshift, with some far-sighted ideas about the individual, society, war, politics, and religion.

During the course of sixty-five years Ford displayed a legendary personality, further exaggerated by his own sensational autobiographies, *Return to Yesterday* and *It was the Nightingale,* which could only be shadowed by the factual legacy of his literary output of seventy-five books. He died in Deauville, France, on June 26, 1939.

BIBLIOGRAPHICAL REFERENCES: Interesting but often factually incorrect are Ford's volumes of autobiography: *Memories and Impressions,* 1911; *Thus to Revisit,* 1921; *It Was the Nightingale,* 1933; and *Mightier than the Sword: Memories and Criticisms,* 1938. Three reliable books are Richard Aldington, *Life for Life's Sake,* 1941; Douglas Goldring, *South Lodge,* 1943; and *Trained for Genius,* 1949 (published in England as *The Last Pre-Raphaelite,* 1948). See also Granville Hicks, "Ford Madox Ford—A Neglected Contemporary," *Bookman,* LXXII (1930), 364–370; and Mark Schorer's introduction to *The Good Soldier,* 1951.

JOHN FORD

Born: Ilsington, England
Date: 1586 (Baptized April 17, 1586)

Died: Unknown
Date: c. 1640?

PRINCIPAL WORKS

PLAYS: *The Witch of Edmonton,* 1621 (with Dekker); *The Sun's Darling,* 1624 (with Dekker); *The Lover's Melancholy,* 1628; *'Tis Pity She's a Whore,* c. 1628; *The Broken Heart,* c. 1629; *Love's Sacrifice,* 1630; *The Chronicle History of Perkin Warbeck,* c. 1633; *The Fancies Chaste and Noble,* c. 1635; *The Lady's Trial,* 1638.

MISCELLANEOUS: *Fame's Memorial,* 1606; *Honor Triumphant,* 1606; *A Line of Life,* 1620.

John Ford was born in Ilsington, Devonshire, in 1586. He probably entered Exeter College, Oxford, in 1601; he entered the Middle Temple in 1602, but there is no evidence that he ever practiced law. His earliest known literary composition is *Fame's Memorial,* an elegy on the death of the Earl of Devonshire which contains a tribute to that nobleman's widow, the former Penelope Devereux, the supposed Stella of Sir Philip Sidney's sonnets.

At least four of Ford's plays, perhaps including his earliest, are lost. Four are included in the list of plays destroyed by John Warburton's cook. The unfortunate fame of this woman, one Betsy Baker, rests on her destruction of a large number of play manuscripts, some unique, which she used as "pie-bottoms" or as fire-starters. The first two of Ford's surviving plays were written in collaboration with Dekker. Of the seven surviving plays by Ford alone, three carry his reputation: *'Tis Pity She's a Whore, The Broken Heart*, and *The Chronicle History of Perkin Warbeck*. The first of these has been a favorite illustration of the "decadence" of Stuart drama because of its sensationalism and moral horror; the second is interesting for its connections with Sidney's *Arcadia* and its use of the theme of Sidney's *Astrophel and Stella* for its tragic plot; the third is a worthy, if slightly anemic, descendant of Shakespeare's history plays. After the production of Ford's latest play in 1638, he vanishes from the records except for a late tradition of retirement.

BIBLIOGRAPHICAL REFERENCES: The standard edition is *John Ford's Dramatic Works*, edited by Henri de Vocht, 1927. Representative dramas are in *John Ford*, edited by H. Ellis, Mermaid Series, n. d. See also H. W. Wells, *Elizabethan and Jacobean Playwrights*, 1939; T. M. Parrott and R. H. Ball, *A Short View of Elizabethan Drama*, 1943; and C. Leech, *John Ford and the Drama of His Time*, 1957.

C. S. FORESTER

Born: Cairo, Egypt
Date: August 27, 1899

PRINCIPAL WORKS

NOVELS: *Beat to Quarters*, 1927; *The Gun*, 1933; *The African Queen*, 1935; *The General*, 1936; *Ship of the Line*, 1938; *Flying Colours*, 1939; *To the Indies*, 1940; *The Captain from Connecticut*, 1941; *The Ship*, 1943; *Commodore Hornblower*, 1945; *Lord Hornblower*, 1946; *Lieutenant Hornblower*, 1952; *The Good Shepherd*, 1955.

BIOGRAPHY: *Napoleon*, 1924; *Josephine*, 1925; *Louis XIV*, 1928; *Nelson*, 1929.

HISTORY: *The Age of Fighting Sail*, 1956.

C(ecil) S(cott) Forester is best known for his series of novels depicting the fictional saga of Horatio Hornblower of the English Navy during the Napoleonic era. However, he has also written other lively stories, and an early one, *The African Queen*, though purposed as a spoof on adventure tales, was accepted by critics and public alike as a uniquely exciting work.

Forester was born in Cairo on August 27, 1899. Well-traveled and a lover of the sea, he was educated in England and studied medicine at Guy's College in London. With the publication of his first novel he abandoned medicine for writing, and the popularity of *Payment Deferred* (1924) on the stage and screen assured him a sufficient income to continue his literary career.

As a successful writer of sea tales, Forester invites comparison with Frederick Marryat, a popular novelist of the early Victorian period. However, where Marryat is farcical Forester is realistic, and where Marryat's story and style are meandering Forester's are racy. The Forester hero is essentially a man's man (even the timid Cockney who carries a missionary maiden safely down a treacherous African river in his asthmatic steam launch, *The African Queen*); his most famous character, Horatio Hornblower, is always admirable though at times guilty of errors in judgment. Although the plotting of the Hornblower series is conventional, the novels nevertheless carry the reader along by their simple yet evocative language and realistic characterizations. An English reviewer once said, commenting on a book on marionettes by Forester, "Whilst novelists may often be accused of making puppets of their characters, Forester succeeds in making characters of his puppets."

BIBLIOGRAPHICAL REFERENCES: A good introduction to the fiction of C. S. Forester is L. R. Muirhead, "Novelist of Action," *Fortnightly Review*, CLVII (1945), 414–419. For single titles see also *Book Review Digest*, 1927 ff.

E. M. FORSTER

Born: London, England
Date: January 1, 1879

Principal Works

NOVELS: *Where Angels Fear to Tread*, 1905; *The Longest Journey*, 1907; *A Room with a View*, 1908; *Howards End*, 1910; *A Passage to India*, 1924.

SHORT STORIES: *The Celestial Omnibus and Other Stories*, 1911; *The Eternal Moment and Other Stories*, 1928; *Collected Short Stories*, 1948.

ESSAYS: *Abinger Harvest—A Miscellany*, 1936; *Two Cheers for Democracy*, 1951.

BIOGRAPHY: *Goldsworthy Lowes Dickinson*, 1934; *Marianne Thornton: A Domestic Biography*, 1797–1887, 1956.

CRITICISM: *Aspects of the Novel*, 1927; *Virginia Woolf*, 1942.

HISTORY AND TRAVEL: *Alexandria: A History and a Guide*, 1922; *Pharos and Pharillon*, 1923; *The Hill of Devi*, 1953.

E[dward] M[organ] Forster, the dean of contemporary English novelists, was born in London on January 1, 1879, and educated at Tonbridge School and King's College, Cambridge, where he became friendly with G. Lowes Dickinson. By the time he was twenty he had worked on a novel, although he never finished it. After graduation, he published short stories, some of them appearing in the *Independent Review*. In 1905 he published his first novel, *Where Angels Fear to Tread*, written during his residence in Italy. The novel is laid in that country, and its theme is the impact of a foreign culture on provincial personalities. The next year Forster prepared a school edition of the *Aeneid* (1906). Tonbridge School and Cambridge are the settings for Forster's second novel, *The Longest Journey*, a book dealing with the problem of illusion and reality and the conflict between people who are

374

whole and honest and those who are false and hypocritical. *A Room With a View*, published in 1908, may very well have been conceived five years before. It is a comedy, and like the first novel is laid in Italy.

Forster had returned to England in 1907 and it was there that he finished *A Room With a View*. He also began at this time to lecture at the Working Men's College. In 1910 *Howards End* appeared, felt by many to be Forster's masterpiece. The essential conflict in this novel is embodied in the Schlegel and Wilcox families, the former representing the inner life, the life of art and thought and generous impulses toward man, and the latter representing the outer life, the life of affairs, of telegrams and hurry and anger. Forster here raises the question whether we can reclaim the roots of tradition in the modern world where there is flux even in the hearts of men. His answer is a qualified yes, if men and women are truly perceptive and they are moved by love.

In 1911 Forster made his first trip to India, accompanying G. Lowes Dickinson. During the first World War he did civilian war work in Alexandria and contributed a series of essays to the *Egyptian Mail* which later appeared under the title *Pharos and Pharillon*. He also wrote at this time

Alexandria: A History and Guide. Back in London after the war, he engaged in literary journalism briefly and in 1921 returned to India, where he served as secretary to the Maharajah of Dewas. His Indian experience provided the background for *Passage to India,* his most celebrated novel and the winner in 1925 of the Femina Vie Heureuse and the James Tait Black Memorial prizes. The novel is a sensitive rendering of the clash of English and Indian temperaments and cultures. Misunderstanding, prejudice, and suspicion poison decent human relationships and work to keep even men of good will apart. Only the elderly Mrs. Moore, a mystic, seems able to penetrate the barriers.

In 1927 Forster was invited to deliver the Clark Lectures at King's College, Cambridge. These were published in the same year as *Aspects of the Novel,* his most substantial and influential volume of criticism. In 1934 he published a life of his friend Dickinson and in 1936 *Abinger Harvest* appeared, a collection of reviews. *The Hill of Devi* deals with his Indian experiences. *Marianne Thornton* is a biography of his great-aunt. Forster has been much honored, most recently by Queen Elizabeth II, who conferred upon him the Order of Companions of Honour in 1953.

BIBLIOGRAPHICAL REFERENCES: The most detailed and comprehensive study of E. M. Forster is Lionel Trilling, *E. M. Forster: A Study,* 1943. For discussion of his earlier writings Rose Macaulay, *The Writings of E. M. Forster,* 1938, is still valuable.

Briefer studies in books include Bonamy Dobrée, *The Lamp and the Lute: Studies in Six Modern Authors,* 1929; Katherine Mansfield, *Novels and Novelists,* 1930; E. B. C. Jones, "E. M. Forster and Virginia Woolf," in *The English Novelists,* edited by Derek Verschoyle, 1936; D. M. Hoare, *Some Studies in the Modern Novel,* 1938; Virginia Woolf, *The Death of the Moth and Other Essays,* 1942; Austin Warren, *Rage for Order: Essays in Criticism,* 1948; Lord David Cecil, *Poets and Story-Tellers,* 1949; and D. S. Savage, *The Withered Branch,* 1950. See also Peter Burra, "The Novels of E. M. Forster," *New Century,* CXVI (1934), 581–

594; E. K. Brown, "E. M. Forster and the Contemplative Novel," *University of Toronto Quarterly*, III (1934), 349–361; Montgomery Belgion, "The Diabolism of E. M. Forster," *Criterion*, XIV (1934), 57–73; F. R. Leavis, "E. M. Forster," *Scrutiny*, VII (1938), 185–202; and H. M. McLuhan, "Kipling and Forster," *Sewanee Review*, LII (1944), 332–343.

ANATOLE FRANCE
(Jacques Anatole Thibault)

Born: Paris, France
Date: April 16, 1844

Died: Near Tours, France
Date: October 12, 1924

Principal Works

NOVELS: *Le Crime de Sylvestre Bonnard*, 1881 (*The Crime of Sylvestre Bonnard*); *Les Désirs de Jean Servien*, 1882 (*The Aspirations of Jean Servien*); *Thaïs*, 1890; *La Rôtisserie de la Reine Pédauque*, 1893 (*At the Sign of the Reine Pédauque*); *Les Opinions de Jérôme Coignard*, 1893 (*The Opinions of Jerome Coignard*); *Le Lys Rouge*, 1894 (*The Red Lily*); *L'Orme du Mail*, 1897 (*The Elm Tree on the Mall*); *Le Mannequin d'Osier*, 1897 (*The Wicker-Work Woman*); *L'Anneau d'Améthyste*, 1899 (*The Amethyst Ring*); *Monsieur Bergeret à Paris*, 1901 (*Monsieur Bergeret in Paris*); *L'Île des Pingouins*, 1908 (*Penguin Island*); *La Vie de Jeanne d'Arc*, 1908 (*The Life of Joan of Arc*); *Les Dieux ont Soif*, 1912 (*The Gods are Athirst*); *Le Révolte des Anges*, 1914 (*The Revolt of the Angels*).

ESSAYS: *La Vie Littéraire*, 1888–92 (*On Life and Letters*); *Le Jardin d'Epicure*, 1894 (*The Garden of Epicurus*).

Anatole France was born Jacques Anatole Thibault on April 16, 1844, the son of a Parisian bookseller with one of the stalls along the Seine. The father, François Thibault, was nicknamed France, and Anatole began to use the pseudonym for the poems he wrote as a boy. Educated at a religious school, the Collège Stanislas, he received a thorough and disciplined education in both religion and the classics. The classical side of his education, however, had the greater impact, for he quickly became skeptical about religion and began writing precise, neo-classic poems.

After writing several unsuccessful novels, France found both his private style and public success in *The Crime of Sylvestre Bonnard* in 1881. France portrayed Bonnard, an old classical scholar, with charm, humor, a great

deal of erudition, and an edge of irony. Gently skeptical about religion, about science (although France had acknowledged Darwin, Taine, and Renan as his masters during his schooldays), about scholarship, France began to develop a graceful, discursive style. At about this time, France was taken up by a wealthy literary patron, Madame Arman de Caillavet. While Madame de Caillavet introduced France to the world of the literary salon in Paris, she also made sure he worked and she helped change his attitude gradually from that of the skeptical dilettante to that of an energetic champion of Dreyfus and other social causes. After France and his wife were divorced in 1892, he began to work at the home of Madame de Caillavet, an association that lasted until her death in 1910.

In 1886, France began to contribute weekly essays on literary life to *Le Temps*. At first the essays were mild and pleasant excursions into literary topics, but they soon began to assume a more biting and skeptical manner toward the Church and the established institutions of the day. His attacks against Christianity became more explicit in his novel *Thaïs,* in which he saved the licentious courtesan and damned the religious hermit while maintaining a constant ironic attitude toward conventional Christianity. In this novel, as in one written a few years later, *At the Sign of the Reine Pédauque,* France also demonstrated a kind of robust and Rabelaisian sensuality not apparent in his earlier work. The latter novel particularly, with the jovial and voluptuous Abbé Coignard as its hero, indicated new range, power, and emphasis in France's writing. By this time France, famous as the creator of the memorable and spirited Abbé Coignard and as the ironic opponent of conventional Christianity, was called by some of his contemporaries a nineteenth century version of the great eighteenth century rationalists, Voltaire and Diderot.

In 1897, like many of his countrymen, France was suddenly caught up in the Dreyfus case. Influenced in part by Madame de Caillavet, a woman of Jewish ancestry, France signed Zola's famous petition, *I Accuse,* and wrote frequent articles attacking the prejudices of the Army and the Church. His next three novels were violently partisan; *The Elm Tree on the Mall, The Wicker-Work Woman,* and *The Amethyst Ring* were all dissections of the narrowness and prejudice of all classes of French society. These novels villified the Church and the Army as the

bastions of ignorant and provincial French life. Reference to the Dreyfus case became even more explicit in *Monsieur Bergeret in Paris.*

France's connection with the Dreyfus case and his attacks on the Church brought him into closer contact with the Left in French politics. He began to speak at radical meetings, and after 1900 he at various times embraced socialist and anarchist causes. He could not long remain a violent partisan, however, for his sense of irony and his genuine skepticism soon led him to treat the parties and institutions of the Left with the same ironic attitude he had once applied to the Church and to scholarship. In fact, his best known work, *Penguin Island,* poked fun at all of French society, at the socialists, the Dreyfusards, at those who would establish a perfect human society, as well as at the familiar targets of the Church and the Army. Similarly, his other well-known works of later years, *The Gods are Athirst* and *The Revolt of the Angels,* berate all organizations in society and lift the satire to a universal plane.

France is still noted for his style, a sense of language touched with irony at all the foibles of mankind. This style was not at its best as an instrument for partisan causes, and, unlike Zola, France is not remembered primarily as a Dreyfusard or a social reformer. France was at his best in those works where he exercised his gift for satire, for rationally probing at all the pretense and foolishness of man and his institutions: *The Crime of Sylvestre Bonnard, Penguin Island,* and *The Revolt of the Angels.*

France was widely honored in his later years. Although his books were placed on the Index by Papal decree in 1922, he was venerated throughout France and most of the Western world. He was regarded as a patriotic hero throughout the First World War when he wrote articles championing the Allied cause and looking forward to world peace. He was awarded the Nobel Prize for literature in 1921 for "the most remarkable literary work of idealistic stamp." His death occurred on October 12, 1924, at La Béchellerie, near Tours.

BIBLIOGRAPHICAL REFERENCES: The standard edition is the *Œuvres Complètes Illustrées*, 25 vols., 1925–1935. Selected editions include *Writings of Anatole France*, 4 vols., 1931; and *Six Great Novels of Anatole France*, 1936. The most adequate bibliography is found on pp. 206–54 of Marjorie R. McEwen's critical work, *Anatole France in the United States*, 1945. Biographical works include Jean Jacques Brousson, *Anatole France Himself: A Boswellian Record by His Secretary*, 1925; and I. M. J. de Bölöni, *Rambles With Anatole France*, 1926. Full-length critical biographies are numerous. See Lewis P. Shanks, *Anatole France*, 1919; J. L. May, *Anatole France: The Man and His Work*, 1924; H. M. Chevalier, *The Ironic Temper: Anatole France and His Time*, 1932; E. P. Dargan, *Anatole France: 1844–1896*, 1937; and, most important, Jacob Axelrad, *Anatole France: A Life Without Illusion*, 1944. Other critical works are Barry Cerf, *Anatole France: The Degeneration of a Great Artist*, 1926; and L. B. Walker, *Anatole France and the Greek World*, 1950. Essays in books include Bradford Torrey, *Friends on the Shelf*, 1906; and Algar L. Thorold, *Six Masters in Disillusion*, 1909.

BENJAMIN FRANKLIN

Born: Boston, Massachusetts
Date: January 17, 1706

Died: Philadelphia, Pennsylvania
Date: April 17, 1790

PRINCIPAL WORKS

AUTOBIOGRAPHY: The *Autobiography*, first printed as *Mémoires*, Paris, 1791; William Temple Franklin edition from imperfect text, 1816; John Bigelow edition, 1868.

ESSAYS: *The Dogood Papers*, 1722; *A Dissertation on Liberty and Necessity, Pleasure and Pain*, 1725; *Articles of Belief and Acts of Religion*, 1728; *Busybody Papers*, 1728–1729; *A Dialogue Between Philocles and Horatio*, 1730; *Poor Richard's Almanack*, 1732–1757 (the proverbs were compiled in *The Way to Wealth*, 1757, and *Father Abraham's Speech*, 1760); *Essays on Human Vanity*, 1735; *Reflections on Courtship and Marriage*, 1746; *Plain Truth*, 1747; *The Interest of Great Britain Considered*, 1760; *A Parable Against Persecution*, 1764; *Cool Thoughts on the Present Situation of Our Public Affairs*, 1764; *An Edict of the King of Prussia*, 1773; *Rules by Which a Great Empire May Be Reduced to a Small One*, 1773; *The Ephemera*, 1778; *Political, Miscellaneous and Philosophical Pieces*, 1779; *The Whistle*, 1779; *Dialogue Between Franklin and the Gout*, 1780; *The Handsome and the Deformed Leg*, 1780; *Remarks Concerning the Savages of North America*, 1784; *Art of Procuring Pleasant Dreams*, 1786; *On the Slave Trade*, 1790.

STATE PAPERS: "Albany Plan of Union, 1754," in Franklin's *Works* and *Documents of American History* (2 vols., ed., Henry S. Commager, 5th ed., hereafter cited as Commager's *Documents*), I, 43–45; "Examination of Dr. Franklin [by the House of Commons concerning the Stamp Act, 1766]," *A Collection of Scarce and Interesting Tracts* . . . , 1787, reprinted in *Shaping the American Tradition* (ed., Louis

M. Hacker, 1947), 196–202; "Treaty Plan of 1776," *Policy of the United States Toward Maritime Commerce in War* (2 vols., ed., Carlton Savage, 1934), I, 132–134, and *The Record of Diplomacy* (ed., Ruhl J. Bartlett, 1947; hereafter cited as Bartlett's *Records*), 17–19; "Treaty of Amity and Commerce Between the United States and France, 1778," *Treaties and Other International Acts of the United States of America* (8 vols., ed., Hunter Miller, 1931–1948; hereafter cited as Miller's *Treaties*), II, 3–27, and Bartlett's *Records*, 24–26; "Treaty of Alliance Between the United States and France, 1778," Miller's *Treaties*, II, 35–47, and Commager's *Documents*, I, 105–107; "Treaty of Peace Between the United States and Great Britain, 1783," Miller's *Treaties*, II, 151–157, and Commager's *Documents*, I, 117–119.

SCIENTIFIC PAPERS: *Observations on the Increase of Mankind, Peopling of Countries, etc.,* 1751–1755; *Experiments and Observations on Electricity,* 1751–1754; *On Smoky Chimneys,* 1785; *Observations Relative to . . . the Academy in Philadelphia,* 1789.

Benjamin Franklin was born at Boston on January 17, 1706, the son of Abiah Folger and Josiah Franklin, a poor soap boiler and tallow chandler. His formal education between 1714 and 1716 consisted of tutoring and a year's study at the Boston Grammar School. He eventually acquired prodigious learning from his own experience, which included vast readings in American, British, and West European books and newspapers.

After working almost two years for his father, Benjamin was apprenticed to his half-brother, James Franklin, editor of the *New England Courant* (1721–1723). James encouraged his brother's first known literary efforts, the "Silence Dogood Papers," satirical imitations of Cotton Mather's *Essays to Do Good.* Theocratic officialdom was outraged by these and other articles, and they warned the editor to desist in them. Shortly before the *Courant* was suppressed, Franklin broke the terms of his indenture in 1723 to emigrate to Philadelphia with little besides the clothes on his back. He worked for a year in a printing house there. Encouraged by and with a letter of recommendation from Pennslyvania's eccentric Governor Keith,

Franklin then sought his fortune in England. After saving enough from London printing jobs to return to Philadelphia in 1726, he clerked for a merchant before establishing himself as a printer.

In 1727 Franklin founded the Junto discussion group, the first American adult education class. In 1730 he became sole owner of the *Pennsylvania Gazette.* In 1731 he started the Philadelphia Library, the first American circulating library. He promoted Philadelphia's advanced street paving, cleaning, and lighting. In 1751 he helped found the City Hospital and the present University of Pennsylvania. He soon gravitated into Colonial politics and patronage: postmaster of Philadelphia (1737), state printer, clerk (1736–1750) and member (1744–1754) of the Pennsylvania Assembly, member of several Indian commissions, delegate to the intercolonial Albany Congress (1754), deputy (1737–1753) and joint (1753–1775) postmaster-general for British North America, and Pennsylvania's agent at London (1757–1762, 1764–1775).

The most sustained of Franklin's literary productions was *Poor Richard's Almanack,* whose proverbs illustrate his understanding that Puritan virtues had immense utilitarian value. A Deist and Natural Rights philosopher believing in the perfectibility of Man, Franklin felt obligated to show others how they, too, could rise from rags to riches by consciously leading a frugal, industrious life. He considered experiential tests superior to a system's logical consistency in evaluating the worth of concepts, but he carefully distinguished between the end and means. Franklin's *Almanack* sold about 10,000 copies per issue and enabled him to retire in 1748 from active conduct of his printing and newspaper business, from which he thereafter derived an income of £1,000 yearly.

To devote himself to moral and natural philosophy and to further their study by others, Franklin established the American Philosophical Society at Philadelphia in 1743. The popular conception of him as merely the inventor of practical gadgets, like his stove and lightning rod, does great injustice to Franklin the abstract scientist. He discovered the first law of electricity, conservation of charge, gave to electrical charges their positive and negative designations, and deduced that electrical properties of bodies depend on their shape, a fact which controls condenser design. His compendious *Experiments and Observations on Electricity* won for him at home and abroad memberships in the major cultural and scientific societies and many honorary degrees. In a different field, Franklin's discovery that Atlantic nor'easters move against the wind is a fundamental in the science of weather. In *Observations on the Increase of Mankind,* he anticipated theories later elaborated by the Rev. Thomas Malthus.

At the Albany Congress of 1754, Franklin advanced his prophetic plan of union which embodied the federal principle. He always asserted that adoption of his plan, rejected by the colonies and by Parliament, would have averted the American Revolution. Representing Pennsylvania at London in disputes with the Penn proprietors, in 1766 he helped persuade Parliament to repeal the Stamp Act as an impractical measure. His humility and reasonableness won new friends for America and increased his prestige so that other colonies designated him their agent. Although he feared that the disputes between Parliament and the Colonies were irreconcilable, he labored for conciliation until the Coercive Acts of 1775.

Returning home, Franklin represented Pennsylvania in the Second Continental Congress. On the committee to draw up a declaration of independence, he made a few changes in Jefferson's draft. Chairman of the foreign affairs committee, he drafted the Treaty Plan of 1776. Although he was not on the constitutional committee, his was the strongest single influence on the Articles of Confederation because he submitted a revised plan of union and because his 1776 Constitution for Pennsylvania afforded practical examples of the operation of the unicameral legislature, an executive of weak powers, and a denial of compulsive force by central authority—all soon to be salient features of the new federal government.

Appointed by Congress in 1776 as one of three Treaty Commissioners, Franklin went to France, where his *Œuvres* had been published in translation in 1773 and where his prestige was so great that he completely overshadowed his co-commissioners. The canny Franklin's intimacy with Foreign Minister Vergennes helped win in 1778 recognition of the United States' independence and a treaty of alliance with France. A few months later he became sole plenipotentiary to France. After Franklin had already begun in 1781 separate negotiations with Great Britain, he, John Adams, and John Jay formed a Peace Commission which effected a separate armistice, to the ostensible surprise and indignation of Vergennes. This preliminary, however, made possible the signature of a general peace treaty at Paris in 1783. Upon Franklin's longstanding request, he was recalled to America in 1785.

Pennsylvania honored the ailing Franklin with the presidency of its Executive Council (1785–1787). As one of its delegates to the Federal Convention in 1787, Franklin made few specific proposals, but his affable spirit, shunning the doctrinaire, promoted compromises based on practical experience. His federal principle was greatly strengthened, but his other notions of governmental machinery found little or no place in the new constitution.

Franklin married in 1730 Deborah Read (d. 1774). Devoted, illiterate, and a good housewife, she bore him two daughters, one of whom survived infancy and married Richard Bache. Tolerant of her husband's infidelities, Deborah even reared his illegitimate son William Franklin, later Royal Governor of New Jersey and a Loyalist.

It was to guide William that Franklin began his *Autobiography* in 1771 at Twyford, England. Written in the manner of *The Spectator,* it is his best work stylistically, but its judgments are harsh on himself. Franklin completed his memoirs up to the year 1757. He died at Philadelphia on April 17, 1790, and European countries joined America in mourning the passing of a man whom David Hume had hailed as the first philosopher and great man of letters in the New World.

BIBLIOGRAPHICAL REFERENCES: Preparation of a scholarly, multi-volume edition of *The Papers of Benjamin Franklin* is now in progress under the editorship of Leonard W. Larabee and Whitfield J. Bell, Jr., under the auspices of the American Philosophical Society and Yale University. Of the older editions, *The Writings of Benjamin Franklin,* edited by Albert H. Smyth, 10 vols., 1905–1907, is still standard, though it omits many selections found in *The Complete Works of Benjamin Franklin,* edited by John Bigelow, 10 vols., 1887–1889. The first great edition of Franklin's *Works,* edited by Jared Sparks, 10 vols., 1836–1840, is still useful for its notes. Of the one-volume selections, the following are particularly valuable: Carl Van Doren, *Benjamin Franklin and Jonathan Edwards: Selections from their Writings,* 1920, and *Benjamin Franklin's Autobiographical Writings,* 1945; Frank L. Mott and Chester E. Jorgenson, *Benjamin Franklin: Representative Selections, American Writers* series, 1936; Nathan G. Goodman, *A Benjamin Franklin Reader,* 1945; and I. Bernard Cohen, *Benjamin Franklin: His Contribution to the American Tradition, Makers of the American Tradition* series, 1953.

The best sketch is Carl Becker's in the *Dictionary of American Biography,* separately reprinted in 1946. The best of the older biographies is George S. Fisher, *The True Benjamin Franklin,* 1889, reprinted in 1926. The best recent biography (which is also the best-documented one-volume biography) is Carl Van Doren, *Benjamin Franklin*, 1938.

Other biographies and special works which are especially helpful are Bernard Fayë, *Franklin, Apostle of Modern Times*, 1929; Verner W. Crane, *Benjamin Franklin: Englishman and American*, 1936, and *Benjamin Franklin and a Rising People*, 1954; Gerald Stourzh, *Benjamin Franklin and American Foreign Policy*, 1954; James Parton, *Life and Times of Benjamin Franklin*, 3 vols., 1874; Evarts S. Scudder, *Benjamin Franklin: A Biography*, 1939; John B. McMaster, *Benjamin Franklin as a Man of Letters*, 1887; John C. Oswald, *Benjamin Franklin, Printer*, 1917; Ruth L. Butler, *Doctor Franklin: Postmaster General*, 1928; and James B. Nolan, *General Benjamin Franklin: The Military Career of a Philosopher*, 1936.

Charles L. Sanford, *Benjamin Franklin and the American Character*, Amherst *Problems in American Civilization* Series, 1955, is a superb collection of selections on Franklin from (besides those cited above) the writings of George Washington, John Adams, Frank Davidson, A. Whitney Griswold, Gladys Meyer, Charles Angoff, D. H. Lawrence, Stuart P. Sherman, and Herbert W. Schneider.

For a full account of the *Autobiography* and its various editions see Max Farrand, *The Autobiography of Benjamin Franklin: A Restoration of a "Fair Copy,"* 1949; and *Benjamin Franklin's Memoirs, Parallel Text Edition*, 1949.

HAROLD FREDERIC

Born: Utica, New York   *Died:* Henley-on-Thames, England
Date: August 19, 1856   *Date:* October 19, 1898

Principal Works

NOVELS: *Seth's Brother's Wife*, 1887; *The Lawton Girl*, 1890; *In the Valley*, 1890; *The Copperhead*, 1893; *The Damnation of Theron Ware*, 1896; *March Hares*, 1896; *Gloria Mundi*, 1898; *The Market Place*, 1899.

Harold Frederic was born in Utica, New York, August 19, 1856, the son of Henry deMotte Frederic, who died when the child was only eighteen months old. Young Frederic experienced a poverty-stricken boyhood; however, starting as an office boy for the Utica *Observer*, he progressed rapidly in the newspaper world, becoming editor-in-chief of the Albany *Evening Journal* in 1882. Two years later he joined the staff of the *New York Times* as London correspondent and never returned to America. Although Frederic remained typically American, not caring greatly for European culture and never bothering to learn a foreign language, he became an extremely effi-

cient European reporter. He made a trip through the cholera-stricken areas of southern France and Italy, writing extensively on what he saw, and in 1891 he went to Russia to investigate the persecution of the Jews in that country. The result of that trip was *The New Exodus: A Study of Israel in Russia* (1892). The bitterness of his articles caused his virtual exclusion from Russia. Like other journalists of the period, he became interested in the personality of William II and wrote a study of that controversial monarch. Frederic died October 19, 1898, at Henley-on-Thames.

Frederic produced ten volumes of fiction, writing carelessly and hurriedly

382

—sometimes 4,000 words a day. His early books were local color novels of the Mohawk Valley region; he then turned to historical novels of the Revolution and the Civil War (*The Copperhead*), treating his materials with more realism than was common at the time.

His one important novel, and the only one to survive, is *The Damnation of Theron Ware*, published in England as *Illumination*. This story has had considerable influence on modern American fiction, particularly upon the work of Sinclair Lewis, who refers to it in *Main Street* as a favorite of his heroine. Into this novel Frederic incorporated two themes that have been further developed by later writers: the cultural barrenness of the American small town and the hypocrisy of much of American Protestantism. The novel

is thus an ancestor of both *Main Street* and *Elmer Gantry*. By making his pathetic hero a Methodist minister, Frederic shocked many readers; however, he shrewdly grasped the greatest weakness of a large segment of the American Protestantism of his time: its appalling narrow-mindedness and its lip-service to moral platitudes. Theron Ware, a product of this starved environment, catches, through the Roman Catholic members of his community, a glimpse of a world beyond that of the American small town, yet his heritage debars him from entering this world and brings him to ruin when he tries to do so. In this study of the last stages of Puritanism, Frederic took an important step away from the popular romantic fiction of his day towards the modern realistic treatment of American life.

BIBLIOGRAPHICAL REFERENCES: As yet no full study of Frederic has appeared. A good introduction to the study of Frederic is contained in A. H. Quinn, *American Fiction*, 1936. Two useful articles are Carey McWilliams, "Harold Frederic: 'A Country Boy of Genius,'" *University of California Chronicle*, XXXV (1933), 21–34; and Charles C. Walcutt, "Harold Frederic and American Naturalism," *American Literature*, X (1939), 11–22.

DOUGLAS SOUTHALL FREEMAN

Born: Lynchburg, Virginia   Died: Richmond, Virginia
Date: May 16, 1886   Date: June 13, 1953

PRINCIPAL WORKS

BIOGRAPHY: *R. E. Lee*, 1934–1935; *Lee's Lieutenants*, 1942–1944; *George Washington*, 1948–1957 (completed by John Alexander Carroll and Mary Wells Ashworth).
MISCELLANEOUS: *Virginia—A Gentle Dominion*, 1924; *The Last Parade*, 1932; *The South to Posterity*, 1939.
EDITOR: *A Calendar of Confederate Papers*, 1908; *Lee's Dispatches*, 1914.

Douglas Southall Freeman, born in Lynchburg, Virginia, on May 16, 1886, was the son of a former Confederate soldier prominent in the United Confederate Veterans. His parents took him

to Richmond when he was six years old. He attended Richmond College and upon being graduated in 1904 he enrolled at the Johns Hopkins University, which had awarded him a fellowship

383

in history. At the early age of twenty-two he received his doctorate. He then accepted an assignment to write articles on taxation for the Richmond *Times Dispatch*. For two years he was secretary to the Virginia Tax Commission. His period of intense activity began in 1915, when he became the editor of the Richmond *News Leader*. He was later made Rector and President of the Board of the University of Richmond, gave commutation lectures in journalism at Columbia University, and was appointed to numerous committees and foundations. By maintaining an inflexible time schedule, he was able to work at many tasks concurrently.

Freeman ranks as one of the most learned biographers and historians of the Civil War. His *R. E. Lee*, in four volumes, the first two being honored with a Pulitzer Prize, was followed by the equally impressive *Lee's Lieutenants*, in three volumes. His *George Washington*, projected as an eight-volume work, of which he completed six before he died in Richmond on June 13, 1953, has been widely acknowledged to be a definitive study. The seventh and final volume of this monumental work, published in 1957, was written by John Alexander Carroll and Mary Wells Ashworth, who had worked as research associates on the earlier books of the series.

BIBLIOGRAPHICAL REFERENCES: There is no authorized biography or extended critical study. See Dumas Malone, "The Pen of Douglas Southall Freeman," an introduction to Freeman's *George Washington*, VI, 1954. See also *Book Review Digest*, 1948 ff.

PHILIP FRENEAU

Born: New York, N. Y.
Date: January 2, 1752

Died: Near Freehold, New Jersey
Date: December 18, 1832

PRINCIPAL WORKS

POEMS: *A Poem on the Rising Glory of America*, 1772 (with H. H. Brackenridge); *The American Village*, 1772; *General Gage's Confession*, 1775; *The British Prison Ship*, 1781; *The Poems of Philip Freneau*, 1786; *Poems Written Between the Years 1786 and 1794*, 1795; *Poems Written and Published during the Revolutionary War*, 1809; *A Collection of Poems . . . Written Between the Year 1797 and the Present Time*, 1815.

MISCELLANEOUS: *A Journey from Philadelphia to New York, by Robert Slender, Stockingweaver*, 1787; *The Miscellaneous Works of Mr. Philip Freneau*, 1788; *Letters on Various Interesting and Important Subjects*, 1799.

Philip (Morin) Freneau, born in New York City on January 2, 1752, was the first noteworthy American poet both as the partisan versifier of colonial independence and as a romantic poet of the American scene. His political poems during the American Revolution, notably *The British Prison* Ship, established him as a powerful satirist, while his greatest work, "The House of Night" (1779) with its atmospheric descriptions, its whippor-wills and Jack o'Lanterns, proved his originality as the first poet to use themes from American nature. Freneau's poems, first printed in the

United States Magazine and the *Freeman's Journal*, of which he was editor (1781–1784), came out in several collected editions, the most important of which were those of 1786, 1795 and 1815.

Freneau left Princeton University in 1771 after writing his first patriotic poem, "The Rising Glory of America," with H. Henry Brackenridge. He began his career as political pamphleteer in 1775, attacking English generals and Tories with revolutionary fervor. In 1775 he sailed for the West Indies and spent two years at Santa Cruz. From then until 1790 he spent much of his time at sea, sometimes as master of a freight sloop; some of his best lyrics were written during these years, among them "The Jamaica Funeral" and "Santa Cruz."

In 1789 he became editor of the *New York Daily Advertiser*. In 1792, influenced by Jefferson and Madison, he established the *National Gazette* in Philadelphia (October 31, 1791–October 23, 1793) and campaigned vigorously against the Federalists. In the pages of this paper Freneau became notorious as a critic of Hamilton, Washington, and Adams and as a fervent exponent of Republicanism. His reputation smirched by his political opponents, he retired to Mount Pleasant, his home near Freehold, New Jersey, in 1794. Poverty forced him to return to the sea as captain of coastwise trading vessels. After his house burned down in 1815 he earned his living as an itinerant tinker and clock mender. Caught in a blizzard, he froze to death near Freehold, New Jersey, on December 18, 1832. Recent research has absolved Freneau of much of the political calumny heaped upon him by his enemies during his lifetime.

BIBLIOGRAPHICAL REFERENCES: The standard edition of the poems, though not definitive, is *The Poems of Philip Freneau, Poet of the American Revolution*, edited by Fred L. Pattee, 3 vols., 1902–1907. A supplementary volume is *The Last Poems of Philip Freneau*, edited by Lewis Leary, 1946. A useful one-volume edition of selections is *Poems of Freneau*, edited by H. H. Clark, 1929. There is no complete edition of the prose.

The most recent biography is Lewis Leary, *That Rascal Freneau: A Study in Literary Failure*, 1941. See also Mary S. Austin, *Philip Freneau, the Poet of the Revolution*, 1901; Moses C. Tyler, *The Literary History of the American Revolution*, Vol. I, 1897; Annie R. Marble, *Heralds of the American Revolution*, 1907; Paul E. More, *Shelburne Essays, Fifth Series*, 1908; and Vernon L. Parrington, *Main Currents in American Thought*, Vol. I, 1927.

SIGMUND FREUD

Born: Freiberg, Moravia
Date: May 6, 1856

Died: London, England
Date: September 23, 1939

PRINCIPAL WORKS

SCIENTIFIC ESSAYS AND STUDIES: *Zur Auffassung der Aphasien*, 1891 (*Aphasia*); *Studien über Hysterie*, 1895 (*Studies of Hysteria*, with J. Breuer); *Die Traumdeutung*, 1900 (*The Interpretation of Dreams*); *Über den Traum*, 1901 (*On Dreams*); *Zur Psychopathologie des Alltagslebens*, 1904 (*The Psychopathology of Everyday Life*); *Der Witz und seine Beziehung zum Unbewussten*, 1905 (*Wit and its Rela-*

tion to the Unconscious); *Drei Abhandlungen zur Sexualtheorie*, 1905 (*Three Contributions to the Theory of Sex*); *Über Psychoanalyze; Fünf Vorlesungen gehalten zur 20jährigen gründungsfeier der Clark University in Worcester, Mass.*, 1909 (*Five Lectures on Psychoanalysis*); *Totem und Tabu*, 1913 (*Totem and Taboo*); *Vorlesungen zur Einführung in die Psychoanalyse*, 1917 (*Introductory Lectures on Psychoanalysis*); *Jenseits des Lustprinzips*, 1919 (*Beyond the Pleasure Principle*); *Das Ich und das Es*, 1923 (*The Ego and the Id*); *Neue Folge der Vorlesungen zur Einführung*, 1932 (*New Introductory Lectures in Psychoanalysis*); *Der Mann Moses und die Monotheistische Religion*, 1939 (*Moses and Monotheism*); *An Outline of Psychoanalysis*, 1949.

Sigmund Freud, Austrian psychiatrist and originator of theories and methods of psychoanalysis, was born on May 6, 1856, in Freiberg, Moravia, the son of Jakob Freud, a merchant in wool, and Amalie Nathansohn Freud. When inflation in the early 1850's severely damaged the economy of Freiberg, and anti-Semitism became common, the Freud family moved to Leipzig, and then to Vienna. The years in Vienna were at first unpleasant ones for Freud, who preferred the country to the city. When he was nine years old, he entered high school a year earlier than normal and had a brilliant record there, graduating *summa cum laude* and rewarded with a trip to England two years later.

Without much enthusiasm for medicine itself, but compelled by an interest in learning more about man in the universe, he entered the University of Vienna in 1873 and received his M.D. on March 31, 1881, after doing considerable important research work in histology. His first publications date from his university days.

E. W. von Brücke of the Physiological Institute at which Freud studied and worked advised the young doctor to abandon a theoretical career because he was too poor to afford it. Freud resigned his position in 1882 and entered the General Hospital in Vienna, where he acquired experience in surgery, psychiatry, and dermatology. In 1885 he was appointed Lecturer in Neuropathology, a position of considerable importance at that stage in his career, and one that was awarded only after extensive survey of his published papers and other qualifications. Freud's experimental work with cocaine prepared the way for Carl Koller's discovery of cocaine as an anesthetic.

In December, 1883, he became engaged to be married to Martha Bernays, whom he married in 1886 after some feuding with her mother and brother. The Freuds were happily married for fifty-three years and had three sons and three daughters.

Freud's career began slowly, and at first the couple existed in a state of near poverty. While in Paris, shortly before his marriage, Freud had met and studied with J. M. Charcot, the neurologist, and had gained permission to translate some of Charcot's lectures for publication in book form. Charcot's studies of hysteria interested Freud and provided impetus for his own work. His first book was *Aphasia*, a significant contribution to neurology, but one that was ignored by most of the journals and critics.

Freud's reputation got its first real impetus with the presentation in 1893 of a paper "On the Psychical Mechanism of Hysterical Phenomena," which he presented in collaboration with Josef Breuer. From December, 1880, to June, 1882, Breuer had treated a woman with a complicated case of hysteria ("Anna O." i.e., Bertha Pappenheim), and in the course of the treatment discovered that when she recounted the circumstances surrounding her hallucinations and other symtoms, her symptoms disappeared. Breuer continued to treat her by this "cathartic" method, combined with hypnotism. The cathartic method interested Freud, for it showed that the symptoms of hysteria could be treated even though the neurological basis of hysteria was not known. When Freud added to the analytic technique of catharsis a method he called "free association," developed in the period between 1892 and 1895, he made his most significant contribution to the field. The free association technique involved allowing the patient to speak freely of past experiences without being interrupted or controlled by the analyst. In his *Studies of Hysteria,* which he wrote with Breur, Freud began to approximate the method that in 1896 he named "psychoanalysis." By this method the analyst overcomes the patient's resistance to recounting unpleasant memories and affecting transference, an emotional re-creation of traumatic experiences. The role of the unconscious began to play a leading part in Freud's discussions.

Through a self-analysis conducted in 1897 Freud began to appreciate the importance of dreams and the role of infant sexuality in understanding the genesis of neuroses, and *The Interpretation of Dreams,* his most important book, appeared in 1900. His challenging place in psychiatry was fixed with his *Three Contributions to the Theory of Sex,* which aroused a great deal of antagonism and criticism because of Freud's theories about infant sexuality, and particularly his ideas concerning incest wishes in children.

In 1909, with the assistance of Bleuler and Jung, he founded the *Jahrbuch für Psychoanalytische und psychopathologische Forschungen.* That same year he lectured at Clark University in Worcester, Massachusetts, and received an honorary LL.D. The Internationl Psychoanalytical Association was founded in 1910.

Freud's relations with his colleagues Jung and Adler were broken off in 1913, partly for personal reasons stemming from professional conflicts and partly because of Adler and Jung's conviction that Freud was over-emphasizing sexual factors. During the 1920's Freudianism became an important phase of the development of modern thought.

Near the end of his life Freud concentrated on applied psychoanalysis, of which such works as *New Introductory Lectures in Psychoanalysis* and *Moses and Monotheism* were the result. In 1938 he moved to England when the Nazis occupied Austria. Suffering from cancer of the jaw, he labored to complete his final work, *An Outline of Psychoanalysis.* He died in London on September 23, 1939.

BIBLIOGRAPHICAL REFERENCES: The literature on Freud is so extensive that any bibliographical listing must be tentative and highly selective. His most important books are available in translation and a definitive edition of his *Gesammelte Werke* is now appearing under the editorship of his daughter, Anna Freud, and others, 1942 ff. The authorized biography, written by a friend and associate for many years, is Ernest Jones, M.D., *The Life and Work of Sigmund Freud*, 3 vols., 1953–1957, a study based partly on private papers and material previously unpublished. Part of Freud's own story is told in *Selbsdarstellung* (*An Autobiographical Study*, 1946). Other biographies include Fritz Wittels, *Sigmund Freud: His Personality, His Teaching, and His School*, 1924; Hanns Sachs, *Freud: Master and Friend*, 1944; Maurice Natenberg, *The Case History of Sigmund Freud*, 1955; and R. L. Schoenwald, *Freud: The Man and His Mind, 1856–1956*, 1956.

For more specialized studies of his theories and work see A. L. Beeley, *Freud and Psychoanalysis*, 1931; F. H. Bartlett, *Sigmund Freud: A Marxian Study*, 1938; A. A. Brill, *Freud's Contribution to Psychiatry*, 1944; Frederick J. Hoffman, *Freudianism and the Literary Mind*, 1945; Edward Glover, *Freud or Jung*, 1950; Gregory Zilboorg, *Sigmund Freud: His Exploration of the Mind of Man*, 1951; Calvin S. Hall, *A Primer of Freudian Psychology*, 1954; W. G. Cole, *Sex in Christ and Psychoanalysis*, 1955; Lionel Trilling, *Freud and the Crisis of Our Culture*, 1955; and H. L. Philip, *Freud and Religious Belief*, 1956.

GUSTAV FREYTAG

Born: Kreuzburg, Silesia　　　　　　*Died:* Wiesbaden, Germany
Date: July 13, 1816　　　　　　　　*Date:* April 30, 1895

Principal Works

NOVELS: *Soll und Haben*, 1855 (*Debit and Credit*); *Die verlorene Handschrift*, 1864 (*The Lost Manuscript*); *Die Ahnen*, 1872–1880 (*The Ancestors*).

PLAYS: *Die Valentine*, 1847; *Graf Waldemar*, 1850; *Die Journalisten*, 1854; *Die Fabier*, 1859.

HISTORIOGRAPHY: *Bilder aus der deutschen Vergangenheit*, 1859–1867 (*Pictures of German Life*).

Gustav Freytag, born in Kreuzburg, Silesia, on July 13, 1816, was trained as a philologist under Hoffmann von Fallersleben and Karl Lachmann. As a writer, he represents the supreme application of German historical idealism to the novel in his most ambitious undertaking, *The Ancestors,* an epical series in seven parts which carry the reader from the migrations of the fourth century through the development of folk and national consciousness to the revolution of 1848. This work evolved out of his scholarly *Pictures of German Life,* a historical study of the German spirit that stresses the hereditary contributions of the lower and middle classes to national history and culture.

Freytag was editor of the Leipzig periodical *Die Grenzboten* from 1848 to 1860, out of which experience came *Die Journalisten,* his most famous play, an exaggerated satire of the newspaper office. His finest novel was *Debit and Credit,* a tightly knit account of commercial life which reveals his strong faith in the working class.

The greater part of Freytag's work has been described as connecting realism with romanticism just as his method of writing seems to have channeled scholarship toward popular appreciation. The principal characters in his fiction and drama were of the same type; his elegant style and clearness of expression were distinctive. Some of Freytag's other works in-

388

clude the critical volume, *Die Technik des Dramas* (1863) and *The Lost Manuscript,* a novel of university life. His works were often reissued and were first collected in 1888. He died on April 30, 1895, at Wiesbaden, Germany.

BIBLIOGRAPHICAL REFERENCES: The most important source for biographical material is Freytag's autobiography, *Erinnungen aus meinen Leben,* 1887. The standard biography is Conrad Alberti, *Gustav Freytag,* 1885. See also L. M. Price, *The Attitude of Freytag and Julian Schmidt towards English Literature, 1848–1862,* 1915; A. Kohut, *Gustav Freytag als Patriot und Politiker,* 1916; and Christa Barth, *Gustav Freytags "Journalisten,"* 1949.

JEAN FROISSART

Born: Valenciennes, France
Date: c. 1338

Died: Chimay, Belgium
Date: c. 1410

PRINCIPAL WORKS

HISTORY: *Chronique de France, d'Angleterre, d'Écosse et d'Espagne,* 1373–1410 (*Chronicle of France, England, Scotland, and Spain*).
POEMS: *Paradis d'Amour,* c. 1378; *Méliador,* c. 1384.

Jean Froissart, one of the liveliest and most prolific writers of the Middle Ages, descended from Flemish stock. He was born about 1338 at Valenciennes, France. His father probably served the nobility with his brush, being a painter of armorial bearings; Froissart himself served the nobility with his pen, producing all manners of chronicles, romances, occasional poems, and lyrics. At eighteen he presented himself with glowing credentials to Queen Philippa of England and was appointed secretary and royal historiographer. He traveled throughout England and Scotland collecting everybody's views on battles and wars, all of which he faithfully recorded. Then, in 1366, he began a long series of travels throughout Europe, visiting almost every court and collecting various prizes, benefices, and pensions for his chivalric accounts of men and events. As a cleric, Froissart from time to time was assigned as priest to various parishes, but he never had the patience to carry out the unexciting duties of masses, marriages, and funerals. He was too much a man of the world, a world which he was determined to see at first-hand and to record—not always with realistic fidelity to historical truth, but with the fascinating vividness of his imagination.

His famous *Chronicles* depict the major events of Western Europe from 1325 through the Hundred Years' War and crusades to the murder of Richard II. It is one of the most graphic accounts ever produced of any age and is spiced throughout with delightful autobiographical tidbits. His other works include the *Paradis d'Amour,* imitated by Chaucer, and the Arthurian romance, *Méliador.*

Despite the fact that throughout his life he was the intimate of royalty and nobility and the friend and colleague of the greatest poets and historians of the fourteenth century (Deschamps, Machaut, Cuvelier, and Chaucer), he died an obscure death, about 1410, at Chimay, Belgium, and was buried unsung in an unmarked grave.

BIBLIOGRAPHICAL REFERENCES: The standard edition of Froissart is the *Chroniques*, edited by K. de Lettenhove, 25 vols., 1867–1877. There is an English translation by Lord Berners, edited by W. P. Ker, 6 vols., 1901–1903. The most authoritative study is F. C. Shears, *Froissart, Chronicler and Poet*, 1930. See also Mme. Darmesteter, *Froissart*, 1894; G. L. Kittredge, "Chaucer and Froissart," *English Studies*, XXVI (1899); M. Wilmotte, *Jean Froissart*, 1942; and B. J. Whiting, "Froissart as Poet," in *Medieval Studies*, VIII, 1946.

EUGÈNE FROMENTIN

Born: La Rochelle, France
Date: October 24, 1820

Died: La Rochelle
Date: August 27, 1876

PRINCIPAL WORKS

NOVEL: *Dominique*, 1862.

TRAVEL SKETCHES AND IMPRESSIONS: *Un été dans le Sahara*, 1857 (*A Summer in the Sahara*); *Une Année dans le Sahel*, 1858 (*A Summer in the Sahel*); *Voyage en Égypte*, 1935.

CRITICISM: *Les Maîtres d'autrefois*, 1876 (*The Masters of Past Time*).

Eugène Fromentin is remembered in literary history for his only novel *Dominique*, published in 1862, but his amateur's success in this form was perhaps indebted to his originality as a painter and art critic. *Dominique* is a sentimental novel of love and renunciation, so vivid and analytical that it has been compared to *Adolphe* (1816) and *The Princess of Clèves* (1678). In this work the author succeded in exploring the depths of feeling in his autobiographical hero with the same romantic intensity he devoted to his researches in painting.

Fromentin, born in La Rochelle on October 24, 1820, studied art in Paris between 1839 and 1843 and later traveled widely in North Africa where he painted scenes of desert and Arab life that distinctly foreshadowed Impressionism. He wrote of his travels in three books: *A Summer in the Sahara, A Summer in the Sahel,* and *Voyage en Égypte,* which records his trip with Gautier and Louise Colet to attend the opening of the Suez Canal in 1869. *The Masters of Past Time,* published two years after he was elected to the Goncourt Academy, is his one contribution to art criticism, a work in which he dealt with the Dutch and Flemish schools of painting more acutely than any other critic of his time.

Dominique, however, remains his most remarkable accomplishment. Only the marriage of his childhood friend, Madeleine, causes Dominque, the young hero, to realize that he loves her. Although she divines his feeling, she chooses her duty and he returns to his native town. The clarity of descriptive detail in the handling of this situation reflects his painter's sensibility but does not overshadow his psychological perceptiveness.

Fromentin died in La Rochelle on August 27, 1876.

BIBLIOGRAPHICAL REFERENCES: For biographical and critical studies see E. Champion, *Essai de bibliographie critique,* 1924; Albert Thibaudet, *Intérieurs: Baudelaire, Fromentin, Amiel,* 1924; C. Raynaud, *La genèse de Dominique,* 1937; V. Giraud, *Fromentin,* 1945; and André Lagrange, *L'art de Fromentin,* 1952.

ROBERT FROST

Born: San Francisco, California
Date: March 26, 1874

Died: Boston, Massachusetts
Date: January 29, 1963

PRINCIPAL WORKS

POEMS: *A Boy's Will,* 1913; *North of Boston,* 1914; *Mountain Interval,* 1916; *New Hampshire: A Poem with Notes and Grace Notes,* 1923; *West-Running Brook,* 1928; *A Further Range,* 1936; *A Witness Tree,* 1942; *A Masque of Reason,* 1945; *Steeple Bush,* 1947; *A Masque of Mercy,* 1947; *How Not to Be King,* 1951; *And All We Call American,* 1958.
PLAY: *A Way Out,* 1929.

There is more than passing significance in the anomaly that this decidedly New England poet happened to be born on March 26, 1874, in San Francisco. Robert (Lee) Frost has frequently admitted that when he settled in New England, at the age of eleven, he so prided himself on being a California city-boy that he felt a decided hostility toward the "north of Boston" region and toward Yankee taciturnity. Perhaps it was the shock of newness which sharpened his response to so much that he later came to admire and to capture with such accurate precision in his poems.

Robert Frost's father, William Prescott Frost, had been a native of New Hampshire; but he had bitterly rejected New England because of his Copperhead political sympathies, following the Civil War. After he had been graduated, with honors from Harvard College in the Class of 1872; after he had served for one year (1872–1873) as Headmaster of Lewistown

(Pa.) Academy, where he had met, courted, married (1873) an immigrant Scottish schoolteacher named Isabelle Moody, William Prescott Frost had taken his bride to San Francisco, where he worked as newspaper reporter and editor, from 1873 until his untimely death at the age of thirty-five, from tuberculosis, in 1885. His strongly democratic political sympathies were reflected in his decision to name his first-born child after the distinguished Confederate general, Robert E. Lee. But in spite of all his cumulative hatreds of New England, William Prescott Frost had requested, shortly before his death, that he be buried in his native New England. Thus it happened that his widow took their two children (the younger child, Jeanie Florence Frost, had been born in 1876) across the continent with the casket, for the interment, in Lawrence, Massachusetts, where the dead man's parents then lived. Because Mrs. Frost could not afford the cost of the return trip to

California, she settled with her children in the land strange to them all, and for several years earned a living by teaching in various schools, starting in Salem, New Hampshire. Certainly the strong influence of Robert Frost's widowed mother had a profound effect on his development. Her Scottish loyalties, particularly her intense religious preoccupations (which caused her to relinquish her inherited Calvinistic Presbyterianism in favor of an ardent Swedenborgian belief) may account in part for the tantalizing blend of practicality and mysticism in Robert Frost's poetry.

In 1892, Robert Frost was graduated from Lawrence High School, as class poet and as co-valedictorian. He shared this latter honor with a sensitive, brilliant, attractive girl named Elinor Miriam White, whom he married three years later, in 1895. Before his graduation from high school, he had so completely dedicated himself to a poet's career that he found no comparable attraction in any other possible profession. His paternal grandfather, however, was so anxious to make a lawyer of the gifted young man that he persuaded him to enter Dartmouth College in the fall of 1892, with all expenses paid. Characteristically, Robert Frost asserted his independence by leaving Dartmouth, unceremoniously, before he had completed his first semester there. During the next few years his quietly dedicated aim was concealed beneath apparent aimlessness: he earned his living in miscellaneous ways. Intermittently, he taught school, worked as bobbin boy in a Lawrence woolen mill, tried newspaper reporting, and did odd jobs. Throughout these years he continued to write poems which he kept sending to news-

paper and magazine editors, without success. Finally, when the *New York Independent* sent him his first check, for a poem entitled "My Butterfly," in November, 1894, he celebrated the event by having six of his poems printed in book form, under the title, *Twilight,* and in a limited edition of only two copies, one for his fiancée, Elinor White, and one for himself.

After his marriage, at the age of twenty-one, Robert Frost spent two years helping his mother run a small private school in Lawrence. Then, deciding to prepare himself for more advanced teaching, he entered Harvard University as a special student, with the plan to concentrate on Latin literature. After two years of study at Harvard (1897–1899), he again grew impatient with formal study, and abandoned it with no prospect save that of his continuing desire to become distinguished as a poet.

In a sense, an important turning point occurred at this time, when a doctor warned him that his chronically precarious physical condition suggested the threat of tuberculosis, and that country life might be beneficial. So it happened that he turned farmer. His paternal grandfather, somewhat baffled but solicitous, bought him a small farm in Derry, New Hampshire, where Robert Frost raised poultry, and came to be known as "the egg man," from 1900 to 1905. Still more a poet than a farmer, during this period, he found in the New Hampshire countryside and its people an appealing kind of raw material for lyrics and dramatic narratives. By 1905 he had written the majority of the poems which later constituted his first two published volumes. Neither farming nor poetry provided adequate support for his growing family of three daughters and one son, and from 1905 to 1911 he taught various subjects in the Pinkerton Academy at Derry. His success as a provocative teacher brought him the invitation to join the faculty of the New Hampshire Normal School at Plymouth, and in 1911 he moved his family there, from Derry.

Never wavering from his secret goal, and increasingly impatient with various diversions and hindrances, Robert Frost taught at the New Hampshire Normal School only one year before he decided to make a desperate gamble in favor of an out-and-out literary life. In the autumn of 1912 he sailed for England with his family, a venture made possible by the cash sale of his Derry farm and by a small annual income which came from the estate of his deceased paternal grandfather. The Frosts rented an inexpensive cottage on the edge of fields and woods in Beaconsfield, Buckinghamshire, and more or less "camped it," as the poet went seriously to work. Within three months after his arrival in England he had sorted out his previously written poems into an arrangement for two volumes of poems, had submitted to a London publisher the manuscript of *A Boy's Will,* and had signed a contract. The British reviews of his first book were little more than lukewarm; but the critical response to his dramatic narratives, published a year later in *North of Boston,* enthusiastically hailed a new poetic voice. Thus, at the age of forty, after twenty years of patient devotion to his art, Robert Frost had won recognition in England which attracted the attention of critics and editors in his native land.

Both volumes brought with them literary acquaintances and friendships in England, including such familiar names as Ezra Pound, Edward Thomas, F. S. Flint, T. E. Hulme, and Lascelles Abercrombie. With the encouragement of Abercrombie, the Frost family moved from Beaconsfield to the idyllic Gloucestershire countryside, near the Malvern Hills, in the spring of 1914. Only the outbreak of war caused the Frosts to make plans for returning to the United States, and with some difficulty arrangements were completed. By the time they reached New York, in February of 1915, both *A Boy's Will* and *North of Boston* had been published in American editions, and the latter quickly became a best seller.

Robert Frost returned to New Hampshire and bought a small farm in the White Mountain region, near Franconia; but his growing literary reputation brought almost immediate demands for public readings and lectures, with much-needed remunerations. In less than a year after his return from England, he had given readings in most of the New England states, in Illinois, Texas, Pennsylvania, and New York. He became one of the first American poets to make arrangements with various universities to join a faculty as a creative writer, without submitting too often to the treadmill of regular teaching. From 1916 to 1920 he was a professor of English at Amherst College. From 1921 to 1923 he was Poet in Residence at the University of Michigan. After returning to Amherst for two years, he went back to spend one more year at the University of Michigan as a Fellow in Letters. From 1926 to 1938 he was again a professor of English at Amherst, on a part-time teaching basis. From 1939 to 1943 he was Ralph Waldo Emerson Fellow of Poetry at

Harvard; from 1943 to 1949 he was Ticknor Fellow in the Humanities at Dartmouth; in 1949 he was appointed Simpson Lecturer at Amherst, on a permanent basis.

Among the many honors and awards which Robert Frost has received, the following are outstanding: He was awarded the Pulitzer Prize for Poetry, in 1924, 1931, 1937, 1943. He was elected to membership in the National Institute of Arts and Letters in 1916; to membership in the American Academy of Arts and Letters in 1930. On the occasion of his seventy-fifth birthday, the United States Senate adopted a resolution extending him felicitations. In 1955, the State of Vermont named a mountain after him, in the town of his legal residence, Ripton. More than thirty colleges and universities have given him honorary degrees, and in the spring of 1957 he returned to the British Isles to receive honorary degrees from Oxford, Cambridge, and the National University of Ireland.

The qualities of Robert Frost's seemingly simple poetic idiom are actually complicated, subtle, elusive. At first glance, many of his lyric, descriptive, and narrative poems may seem to deserve particular merit solely because they precisely observe little-noticed details of natural objects and rural characters. Some readers may be content to settle for these qualities. But the poet's obvious pleasure in faithfully recording cherished images provides the solid foundation on which a subtly poetic superstructure is wrought. Even in his least lyrics, Robert Frost manages to achieve a strongly dramatic element, primarily through a sensitive capturing of voice tones, so that the so-called "sound of sense" adds a significant dimension of meaningfulness to all his poems. More than that, his imagery is developed in such a way as to endow even the most prosaically represented object with implied symbolic extensions of meaning. Finally, through the blend of matter and manner, Robert Frost's poems frequently transcend the immediate relationships of the individual to self, to others, to nature, to the universe, as they probe the mysteries around which religious faith is built. While the totality of his separate poetic moods may explore many possible attitudes toward human experience, his poems repeatedly return to an implied attitude of devout reverence and belief, which constitute the infallible core of his understatements.

Lawrance Thompson

BIBLIOGRAPHICAL REFERENCES: Robert Frost's relatively small output of poetic work has been selected and collected in various editions, none definitive; but the selections are of particular interest because they so largely represent the poet's own winnowings and arrangements. The first *Selected Poems* appeared in 1923 and contained forty-three poems; it was revised in 1928, with the addition of fourteen poems; it was again revised in 1934, with a total of seventy-three poems. An English edition of the *Selected Poems* appeared in 1936: sixty-two poems "chosen by the author," and significantly rearranged by him. This edition also contained introductory essays by W. H. Auden, C. Day Lewis, Paul Engle, and Edwin Muir. Another kind of selection appeared in 1943, with a biographical introduction and notes by Louis Untermeyer, under the title, *Come In;* reprinted in 1946 under the title, *The Pocket Book of Robert Frost's Poems.* In 1955, a *Selected Poems* appeared in the London "Penguin

Poets" series, with a new arrangement by Robert Frost and with a preface by C. Day Lewis.

The first *Collected Poems* appeared in 1930; it was reissued and enlarged in 1939, containing a preface ("The Figure a Poem Makes") by Robert Frost; it was reissued and enlarged in 1949, with the title changed to *Complete Poems*.

Robert Frost's prose, which has its own distinct flavor and quality, deserves to be better known. Much of it is scattered through ephemeral publications, as for example his "Education by Poetry—a Meditative Monologue," which appeared in the *Amherst Graduates' Quarterly* for February, 1931. A collected volume of his prose, now in preparation, will include the best of his essays, addresses, informal talks, and radio and television interviews.

No adequate biography of Robert Frost has yet been published, although several are now in preparation. Among fragmentary biographical studies, already published, are the following: Gorham B. Munson, *Robert Frost: A Study in Sensibility and Good Sense*, 1927; Lawrance Thompson, "Robert Frost's California Boyhood," in *Princeton Alumni Weekly* for November 9, 1956; and Sidney Cox, *A Swinger of Birches: A Portrait of Robert Frost*, 1957.

Among the many critical studies and appreciations of Robert Frost's poetry, the most extended is *Fire and Ice: The Art and Thought of Robert Frost*, by Lawrance Thompson, 1942. Outstanding essays or discussions, in books of varied scope, include the following, chronologically arranged. "Robert Frost," in Amy Lowell, *Tendencies in Modern American Poetry*, 1917; "Robert Frost," in Percy H. Boynton, *Some Contemporary Americans*, 1924; "The Soil of the Puritans," in Carl Van Doren, *Many Minds*, 1924; "Robert Frost, Good Greek Out of New England," in Elizabeth Shepley Sergeant, *Fire Under the Andes*, 1927; "The Neighbourly Humour of Robert Frost," in G. R. Elliott, *The Cycle of Modern Poetry*, 1929; "The Instincts of a Bard," by R. P. Blackmur, in *The Nation*, CXLII 1936, 817–819; "The Horatian Serenity of Robert Frost," in Horace Gregory and Marya Zaturenska, *A History of American Poetry: 1900–1940*, 1942; various references in Louise Bogan, *Achievement in American Poetry: 1900 to 1950*, 1951; and two essays in Randall Jarrell, *Poetry and the Age*, 1953.

A comprehensive bibliography, now in process of revision is W. B. S. Clymer and Charles R. Green, *Robert Frost: A Bibliography*, 1937. For purposes of research, the most valuable collection of books and manuscripts, newspaper and magazine files, may be found in the Jones (public) library at Amherst, Massachusetts.

CHRISTOPHER FRY

Born: Bristol, England
Date: December 18, 1907

PRINCIPAL WORKS

PLAYS: *The Boy with a Cart*, 1937; *A Phoenix Too Frequent*, 1946; *The Firstborn*, 1946; *Thor, with Angels* 1948; *The Lady's Not for Burning*, 1948; *Venus Observed*, 1949; *A Sleep of Prisoners*, 1951; *The Dark Is Light Enough*, 1954.

TRANSLATIONS: *Ring Round the Moon*, 1950 (after Jean Anouilh); *The Lark*, 1955 (after Jean Anouilh); *Tiger at the Gates*, 1955 (after Jean Giraudoux).

Christopher Fry (originally Harris) was born December 18, 1907, the son of an Anglican lay-preacher in the city of Bristol; in 1925 he adopted his

395

maternal grandmother's surname, Fry, on becoming a Quaker, the faith of his mother's family. He was educated at the Bedford Modern School. After finishing his studies he became an actor and then a schoolmaster, teaching at the Hazelwood Preparatory School from 1928 to 1931. Returning to the theater, he acted in repertory; in 1935 he wrote a musical comedy, *She Shall Have Music*. The same year he composed his first drama, *Siege*, which has been neither staged nor published. He next wrote on commission a play, *Open Door*, about the life of John Barnardo, the founder of the Barnardo orphanages; a religious festival play, *The Boy with a Cart*; and two pageants, *The Tower* and *Thursday's Child*, both staged in 1939. For a brief period, before he was called up for national service in 1940, he directed the Tunbridge Wells Repertory Players. At this date he was working on *The Firstborn*, which he completed in his limited free time while assigned to noncombat duty.

Since World War II Fry's stature as a poet-dramatist has become unmistakable. Besides *The Boy with a Cart* and *The Firstborn*, the latter a tragedy, he has written the festival plays *Thor, with Angels* and *A Sleep of Prisoners*; translations of Anouilh and Giraudoux;

and four brilliant comedies, *A Phoenix Too Frequent*, *The Lady's Not for Burning*, *Venus Observed*, and *The Dark Is Light Enough*. All have been produced; and in America no less than in England the virtuosity of Fry has been widely praised. There seems to be a general consensus that, in the present state of the theater, the future of poetic drama lies with dramatists who, like Fry, are also poets rather than with poets who, like Eliot, are also dramatists.

Fry's dramatic verse seems to have bewildered many of his critics; and undeniably, in both *The Lady's Not for Burning* and *Venus Observed*, his buoyant flights of imagery and his sometimes baroque rhetoric are surprising at first encounter. But such effects are not interruptive. The most imaginative passages, instead of standing isolated as poems to be recited by the actors, reinforce characterization. That is, they are expressions of the characters rather than meditations by the author. Fry's symbolism is primarily dramatic, not poetic, and to this fact is attributable his success in communicating, through the medium of the theater, a sacramental view of life usually associated with the devotional lyric.

BIBLIOGRAPHICAL REFERENCES: There is no collected edition of Fry's plays. A good full-length critical study is Derek Stanford, *Christopher Fry: An Appreciation*, 1952. A shorter study by Stanford is *Christopher Fry*, in the *Writers and their Work* series, 1954. A cover article which included a review of *The Lady's Not for Burning* was published in *Time*, LVI (Nov. 20, 1950), 58–64. Also helpful is Ben Ray Redman's "Christopher Fry: Poet-Dramatist," *College English*, XIV (1953), 191–197. Fry states some of his own aims and theories in "Poetry in the Theatre," *The Saturday Review of Literature*, XXXVI (March 21, 1953), 18–19, 33–34.

ÉMILE GABORIAU

Born: Saujon, France   *Died:* Paris, France
Date: November 9, 1835   *Date:* September 28, 1873

NOVELS: *L'Affaire Lerouge*, 1866 (*The Widow Lerouge*); *Le Dossier 113*, 1867 (*File No. 113*); *Le Crime d'Orcival*, 1867 (*The Mystery of Orcival*); *Monsieur Lecoq*, 1869; *L'Argent des autres*, 1874 (*Other People's Money*).

Émile Gaboriau was born at Saujon, France, November 9, 1835. After an uneventful childhood and a brief period of service in the cavalry, he arrived in Paris, where he eventually began to write sensational serial stories for the daily newspapers. Since he specialized in romances of crime, he spent much time in police courts and morgues searching for material. Turning to the novel, Gaboriau soon produced the popular *The Widow Lerouge*, in which the detection of crime is an important theme; this work has the distinction of being called the world's first true detective novel. There followed in quick succession fourteen novels, of which four can be classified as detective fiction. His life was brief; he died in Paris on September 28, 1873, at the age of thirty-seven.

Many of Gaboriau's novels were soon translated into English, first in America and then in England. Devotees of detective fiction point out the influence of Gaboriau's novels on the subsequent development of the form. His *Monsieur Lecoq* in many ways is the prototype of many a latter-day ingenious detective. In his novels, although the solution of the mystery is often skillfully worked out, such a solution is often not the climax of the story. Melodramatic family scandal is basic to most of his works. Gaboriau's novels are sensational, discursive, and verbose; yet, without a doubt, they are significant contributions to a popular literary type.

BIBLIOGRAPHICAL REFERENCES: There is no authorized biography. For criticism and comment see Marius Topin, *Romanciers contemporains*, 1876; Régis Messac, *Le "detective novel" et la pensée scientifique*, 1929; and François Fosca, *Histoire technique du roman policier*, 1937.

RÓMULO GALLEGOS

Born: Caracas, Venezuela
Date: August 2, 1884

PRINCIPAL WORKS

NOVELS: *Reinaldo Solar*, 1920; *Doña Bárbara*, 1929; *Cantaclaro*, 1931; *Canaima*, 1935.
PLAY: *El milagro del año*, 1911 (*The Miracle of the Year*).

Graduated from the Law School in Caracas, Venezuela, where he was born on August 2, 1884, Rómulo Gallegos became a teacher in 1912 to finance his marriage. He founded a magazine and wrote unsuccessful dramas and short stories until Dictator Juan Gómez suspended the magazine. His first novel, *Reinaldo Solar*, attacked crooked politics. Not until the publication in Spain of *Doña Bárbara* in 1929 did Gallegos achieve an international reputation. In this story of jungle violence, the symbolism of calling the chief woman Bárbara (barbarous) and the hero Santos (saintly) is obvious. The novel has gone through many editions and a filming.

While a voluntary political exile in Spain, Gallegos wrote *Cantaclaro,* the story of a wandering minstrel. Some critics consider it his greatest novel; others call it complicated and undigested. He returned to political satire in *Canaima,* banned by Gómez.

Following the dictator's death in 1935, Gallegos returned to Venezuela and wrote *Pobre negro (Poor Negro).* This novel, published in 1937, deals with a nineteenth century Venezuelan slave. An Indian girl, educated in New York to work for the advancement of her race, is the heroine of *Sobre la misma tierra (On the Same Earth),* published in 1949.

Gallegos not only wrote about politics, but he also campaigned twice for the presidency of Venezuela. In 1947 he was elected to serve until 1952, but he was overthrown by a military junta in 1949. An exile in Cuba, he wrote and published there in 1952 a work titled *La brizna de paja en el viento, (Straws in the Wind),* a study of political unrest. In all his writing this novelist, who ranks close to the top among authors of his continent, shows himself an ardent moralist with deep faith in nonviolence and in the true ethics of Christianity.

BIBLIOGRAPHICAL REFERENCES: Studies of Gallegos are found in D. F. Ratcliff, *Venezuelan Prose Fiction,* 1933; A. Torres Rioseco, *Novelistas contemporáneos de América,* 1939 (Santiago de Chile); *idem, Grandes novelistas,* 1941; Jefferson R. Spell, *Contemporary Spanish American Fiction,* 1944; G. Arciniegas, "Novela y verdad en Gallegos," *Cuadernos Americanos,* July-August, 1954; and J. A. Crow, "Essays of Rómulo Gallegos," *Hispania,* XXXVII (1955), 35–40.

JOHN GALSWORTHY

Born: Kingston, Surrey, England   *Died:* London, England
Date: August 14, 1867   *Date:* January 31, 1933

PRINCIPAL WORKS

NOVELS: *Jocelyn,* 1898 (as John Sinjohn); *Villa Rubein,* 1900 (as John Sinjohn); *The Island Pharisees,* 1904; *The Man of Property,* 1906; *The Country House,* 1907; *Fraternity,* 1909; *The Patrician,* 1911; *The Dark Flower,* 1913; *The Freelands,* 1915; *Beyond,* 1917; *Saint's Progress,* 1919; *In Chancery,* 1920; *To Let,* 1921; *The Forsyte Saga,* 1922 (containing *The Man of Property, In Chancery, To Let,* and the connecting interludes, "The Indian Summer of a Forsyte" and "Awakening"); *The White Monkey,* 1924; *The Silver Spoon,* 1926; *Swan Song,* 1928; *A Modern Comedy,* 1929 (containing *The White Monkey, The Silver Spoon, Swan Song,* and the two interludes, "A Silent Wooing" and "Passers By"); *Maid in Waiting,* 1931; *Flowering Wilderness,* 1932; *Over the River,* 1933 [*One More River*]; *End of the Chapter,* 1934 (containing the three foregoing).

SHORT STORIES: *From the Four Winds,* 1897 (as John Sinjohn); *A Man of Devon,* 1901 (as John Sinjohn); *Five Tales,* 1918; *Tatterdemalion,* 1920; *Captures,* 1923;

Caravan: The Assembled Tales of John Galsworthy, 1925; *On Forsyte 'Change,* 1930; *Soames and the Flag,* 1930.

PLAYS: *The Silver Box,* 1906; *Strife,* 1909; *Justice,* 1910; *The Pigeon,* 1912; *The Fugitive,* 1913; *The Skin Game,* 1920; *Loyalties,* 1922; *Old English,* 1924; *Escape,* 1926.

ESSAYS: *A Commentary,* 1908; *A Motley,* 1910; *The Inn of Tranquility,* 1912; *The Little Man,* 1916; *A Sheaf,* 1916; *Another Sheaf,* 1919; *The Burning Spear,* 1919; *Castles in Spain,* 1927; *Candelabra,* 1932.

LETTERS: *Letters from John Galsworthy, 1900–1932,* edited by Edward Garnett, 1934.

Literary recognition came slowly but surely to John Galsworthy, English novelist, dramatist, poet, and man of letters. By the time of his death in 1933, general opinion had accorded him first place among British novelists; and his most memorable creations, the Forsytes, were as warmly considered and discussed as if they had been real people of flesh and blood.

Not unlike the members of his famous fictional family, Galsworthy began life with a silver spoon in his mouth. He was born at Kingston, Surrey, on August 14, 1867, the son of John and Blanche Bailey Galsworthy. The boy's father was of Devonshire yeoman stock; his mother belonged to an old Worcestershire family, its annals studded with provincial squires and men of commerce. The elder Galsworthy, after migrating to London, had achieved solid prosperity as a lawyer and director of many companies. His position in life assured, he—a man in his middle forties—proceeded with calmness and confidence to found the family in which young John was to be the second child of four. To the senior John Galsworthy the elder Forsytes probably owe many of their distinguishing traits, for he is said to have had a strong measure of "tenacity" and "the possessive instinct." Nevertheless, the son's fondness for his father was always strong; and the latter's saving love of the arts and his feeling for nature made him a natural progenitor of the sturdy and lovable Old Jolyon.

His schoolboy days, however, revealed little indication of what the younger John was to become. At Harrow, where he went in 1881, he excelled in running and football rather more than as a scholar. Neither there nor at Oxford did he show any great tendency toward a literary career. In fact, real ambition in any direction lay dormant, though he did graduate with honors in law and was called to the bar in 1890. But he showed little interest in practicing his profession; instead, being under no financial stress, he set out on a series of extensive journeys which carried him to such distant spots as Canada, the Fijis, Australia, and Russia. His first long voyage was marked by a chance meeting with Joseph Conrad, then chief officer of *The Torrens,* with whom he sailed from Australia to South Africa. This was the beginning of a strong friendship, which was terminated only by Conrad's death in 1924.

Neither his early education nor his fleeting contact with Conrad had provided the spark which would ignite Galsworthy's literary aspirations. Fate set that privilege aside for Ada Galsworthy, the girl who had married his

399

cousin Arthur. Charming and intelligent, Ada was trapped by a tragic Victorian marriage which enlisted the sympathetic concern not only of her friends but also of her husband's own family. Her plight aroused John's pity; love was soon to follow. Out of consideration for the feelings of John's father, their love affair was concealed until after his death; in 1904, however, they went together to Dartmoor. Subsequently they were served with divorce papers and eventually were married on September 23, 1905.

It was at Ada's suggestion, early in their acquaintance, that Galsworthy began to write. Throughout the rest of his career, her encouragement and understanding made a strong contribution to his success. His acknowledgment of this debt is most clearly expressed in the dedication of The Forsyte Saga, the best of his work, as the fittest to be dedicated to "the dearest and most lovely companion, the most faithful helpmate, and the best natural critic a man ever had."

Success did not come all at once. Between 1897 and 1901 appeared his first four volumes: From the Four Winds, Jocelyn, Villa Rubein, and A Man of Devon. Issued under the pseudonym of John Sinjohn, the books, though immature, disclosed interesting potentialities. Here and there they also revealed such of the author's personal concerns as the strife between social classes and the mistreatment of animals. Introduced into these tales were even a few characters who—more completely developed and rounded out— were to reappear in The Forsyte Saga.

The year 1906 really marked Galsworthy's literary coming of age. His arrival as a dramatist of stature was heralded by the initial performance, in that year, of The Silver Box. In this play, as in many to follow, Galsworthy adopted the course taken by Pinero and Shaw in dramatizing social problems: Strife pinpointed industrial troubles; Justice turned a devastating spotlight on the wretched condition of prisons. But 1906 is even more important for the introduction of a book which is the cornerstone of the author's success. It was The Man of Property, which, though a separate book in itself, would later become the first part of The Forsyte Saga. Galsworthy did not at first see The Man of Property as one of a series. Not for many years did In Chancery and To Let complete the saga proper. This fascinating trilogy, with its appealing interludes, is a penetrating treatment of that new and prosperous middle class which had come in with industrialism. Prominent in the novels of Dickens and Thackeray, where they were hated by the one and scorned by the other, the most searching and sustained analysis of their class was the one which flowed from Galsworthy's pen. In it he recorded, half sympathetically and always with interest, their worship of wealth, their clinging to family, and their arch conservatism. Soames Forsyte, perhaps the most completely realized of all Galsworthy's characters, is still only one of the many Forsytes who reveal different facets of English middle-class society. The Saga is, by general agreement, the high-water mark of Galsworthy's achievement; though he chose to extend the Forsyte story into two later trilogies, A Modern Comedy and End of the Chapter, they add little to his reputation as a writer.

After the First World War, Galsworthy was offered a knighthood, which he refused. In 1929 he did, however, accept the Order of Merit, and in 1932 he was awarded the Nobel Prize. Honorary degrees from Oxford, Cambridge, and several other universities attest to the high esteem which his later years brought to him. While the flood tide of his popularity has now receded, there seems no reason to doubt that *The Forsyte Saga* will hold securely to its place in the front rank of English novels. Galsworthy died in London on January 31, 1933. By his direction his ashes were scattered to the winds.

BIBLIOGRAPHICAL REFERENCES: The authorized biography is by H. V. Marrot, *The Life and Letters of John Galsworthy*, 1936; see also M. E. Reynolds, *Memories of John Galsworthy*, 1937, and Ada Galsworthy, *Over the Hills and Far Away*, 1938. Among the critical studies are the following: Sheila Kaye-Smith, *John Galsworthy*, 1916; André Chevrillon, *Three Studies in English Literature*, 1923; Natalie Croman, *John Galsworthy*, 1933; Wilbur L. Cross, "John Galsworthy" in *Four Contemporary Novelists*, 1930; and Edouard Guyot, "Diagnostique du Forsytisme," *Revue Anglo-Americaine*, X (1933), 290–300.

JOHN GALT

Born: Irvine, Ayrshire, Scotland   *Died:* Greenock, Scotland
Date: May 2, 1779   *Date:* April 11, 1839

PRINCIPAL WORKS

NOVELS: *The Ayrshire Legatees*, 1820–1821; *Annals of the Parish*, 1821; *Sir Andrew Wylie*, 1822; *The Provost*, 1822; *The Entail*, 1823; *Lawrie Todd*, 1830.
AUTOBIOGRAPHY: *Autobiography*, 1833.

John Galt, born in Irvine, Scotland, May 2, 1779, was the son of a Scottish sea-captain. His education was received through private tutors and irregular attendance at various schools, and upon finishing school he entered the British customs service at Greenock, Scotland. A few years later he left the customs service to become a clerical employee of a private business house. In 1804 he left Scotland and journeyed to London where, shortly after his arrival he published and then immediately suppressed an epic poem entitled *The Battle of Largs* (1804). He found employment in business, but when his firm failed he began to study law at Lincoln's Inn. That study ended within a few months, however, and Galt began a three-year tour which took him as far from England as Greece and Turkey.

Upon his return to London in 1811 he became editor of the *Political Review*. He began writing and published two books in 1812, a *Life of Wolsey* and a volume relating his adventures abroad. He married Elizabeth Tilloch, daughter of a fellow editor, in 1813. The Galts had three sons, all born between 1814 and 1817. This family Galt supported by his editorship, by writing articles for *Lives of the British Admirals*, and by some writing of fiction. His fame as an author began in 1820, when *Blackwood's Magazine* began publishing his novel, *The Ayrshire Legatees*. *Annals of the Parish* gave that fame a secure foundation. After *Annals of the Parish* was published,

401

Galt continued as a professional writer, but none of his later work reached the popularity or the critical acclaim awarded that book. Most of his stories and novels are set, like *Annals of the Parish,* in a Scottish background. Galt was a prolific, if little-remembered author. In his lifetime he saw published sixty books, twelve plays, and an uncounted number of articles.

In the history of the novel he is regarded as something of a pioneer realist, but the passing years have not granted him, as he claimed for himself, a rating equal to that of Sir Walter Scott. In addition to his career as a writer, Galt served his government as secretary to a commission sent to Canada to investigate land claims. After 1828 he wrote furiously in an effort to keep out of debtor's prison. He died, after having suffered a series of strokes, at Greenock, Scotland, April 11, 1839.

BIBLIOGRAPHICAL REFERENCES: The standard collected edition is *The Works of John Galt,* edited by D. S. Meldrum and William Roughead, 10 vols., 1936. The best bibliography is B. A. Booth, "A Bibliography of John Galt," *Bulletin of Bibliography,* XVI (1936), 7–9. Biographies are by Robert Kay Gordon, *John Galt,* 1920, with bibliography; and J. W. Aberdein, *John Galt,* 1936. Critical works are H. W. Thompson, *A Scottish Man of Feeling,* 1931; and Frank Hallam Lyell, *A Study of the Novels of John Galt,* 1942, with an important bibliography. Essays in books are by William Maginn, "John Galt," in *A Gallery of Illustrious Characters,* edited by W. Bates, 1873; Hugh Walker, *Three Centuries of Scottish Literature,* 2 vols., 1893; J. H. Millar, *Scottish Prose of the Seventeenth and Eighteenth Centuries,* 1912; and George Kitchen, "John Galt," *Edinburgh Essays on Scots Literature,* 1934. An important magazine article is Francis Jeffrey's "Secondary Scottish Novelists," *Edinburgh Review,* XXXIX (1823), 159–196.

FEDERICO GARCÍA LORCA

Born: Fuentevaquero, Spain
Date: June 5, 1899

Died: Near Granada, Spain
Date: August, 1936

PRINCIPAL WORKS

POEMS: *Libro de poemas,* 1921 (*Book of Poems*); *Canciones,* 1927 (*Songs*); *Romancero gitano,* 1928 (*Gypsy Ballads*); *Llanto por Sánchez Mejías,* 1935 (*Lament for the Death of a Bullfighter*); *Poeta en Nueva York,* 1940 (*Poet in New York*).

PLAYS: *Bodas de sangre,* 1933 (*Blood Wedding*); *Yerma,* 1934; *La Casa de Bernarda Alba,* 1936.

Partly, at least, because of his death at the hands of the Falangists in the early days of the Spanish Civil War, but in a greater part because of his literary achievements, Federico García Lorca has come to be regarded as the outstanding modern Spanish poet. He was born in the village of Fuentevaquero, in the province of Andalusia, June 5, 1899, and educated at the University of Granada, where he studied law and literature. By 1919 he had settled in Madrid and by 1927 had become well known as a poet through his *Book of Poems* and *Songs.* In 1929 he spent a year in New York, being especially fascinated by Harlem and the life of the Negroes there, an experience that greatly affected some of his later work. Upon returning to Spain, he turned his attention to the drama, writing plays and directing a traveling theater. From all accounts, he was a man of great personal charm and celebrated for his reading of his own poems. In August, 1936, near the village of his birth, he was shot by the adherents of Franco, apparently at the order of the authorities in Granada. So great was the esteem in which García Lorca was held outside his native country, that it has been claimed that his murder, more than any other act of Franco's government, lost it much of the sympathy of the Spanish-speaking world.

The admirers of García Lorca's poetry have laid particular stress upon the beauty and the originality of the metaphorical language in which he expressed himself. The poet himself told of his delight in the spontaneous metaphors of the peasants of his province —metaphors drawn from nature as experienced by the peasant. His writing also expressed his love for Spanish folk songs. The two influences of folk speech and folk poetry are obviously behind his own verse. It is primitive art, yet modern in the poet's deliberate effort to revivify language by seeking new and startling images. The similes are derived through the physical senses; they are "realistic" and yet often strained, as though the poet were pushing language to its limits. This technique is characteristic of much modern verse. García Lorca's work differs, however, by the degree to which his images spring from the violence and tragedy in the lives of the Spanish peasants and gipsies. There is peasant naïveté (the Archangel Gabriel is described as wearing an embroidered jacket and patent-leather shoes) and yet there is an astonishing preoccupation with blood and horror. Thus his verse represents a reaction against the highly intellectual poetry of the last thirty years.

The plays he wrote contain this same deliberate primitivism. The obvious comparison here is with Synge, since both sought to break away from nineteenth century realism and to restore poetic tragedy by returning to the life of the peasant. However interesting it may be, *Blood Wedding* nevertheless falls short of great tragedy because the characters are types not sufficiently individualized. The drama contains, however, the same strange yet weirdly beautiful language as do the poems.

BIBLIOGRAPHICAL REFERENCES: The full-length study in English is Edwin Honig, *García Lorca*, 1944. See also Angel del Rio, *Revista hispanica moderna*, VI (1940), 193–260; Herschel Brickell, "A Spanish Poet in New York," *Virginia Quarterly Review*, XXI (1945), 386–398; and Helen E. Sackett, "García Lorca and the Doctrinal Issue," *South Atlantic Quarterly*, XLVII (1948), 480–490.

HAMLIN GARLAND

Born: West Salem, Wisconsin
Date: September 14, 1860

Died: Hollywood, California
Date: March 4, 1940

PRINCIPAL WORKS

NOVELS: *Jason Edwards, An Average Man,* 1892; *A Little Norsk,* 1892; *A Spoil of Office,* 1892; *Rose of Dutcher's Coolly,* 1895; *The Spirit of Sweetwater,* 1898 (reissued as *Witch's Gold*, 1906); *Boy Life on the Prairie*, 1899; *The Eagle's Heart*, 1900; *Her Mountain Lover*, 1901; *The Captain of the Gray Horse Troop*, 1902; *Hesper*, 1903; *The Light of the Star*, 1904; *The Tyranny of the Dark*, 1905; *The Long Trail*, 1907; *Money Magic*, 1907 (reissued as *Mart Haney's Mate*, 1922); *The Moccasin Ranch*, 1909; *Cavanagh, Forest Ranger*, 1910; *Victor Ollnee's Discipline*, 1911; *The Forester's Daughter*, 1914.

SHORT STORIES: *Main-Travelled Roads*, 1891; *Prairie Folks*, 1893; *Wayside Courtships*, 1897; *Other Main-Travelled Roads*, 1910; *They of the High Trails*, 1916; *The Book of the American Indian*, 1923.

AUTOBIOGRAPHY AND REMINISCENCE: *A Son of the Middle Border*, 1917; *A Daughter of the Middle Border*, 1921; *Trail-Makers of the Middle Border*, 1926; *Back-Trailers from the Middle Border*, 1928; *Roadside Meetings*, 1930; *Companions on the Trail: A Literary Chronicle*, 1931; *My Friendly Contemporaries: A Literary Log*, 1932; *Afternoon Neighbors*, 1934.

POEMS: *Prairie Songs*, 1893.

ESSAYS: *Crumbling Idols*, 1894; *Out-of-Door Americans*, 1901; *The Westward March of American Settlement*, 1927; *Joys of the Trail*, 1935.

PLAY: *Under the Wheel*, 1890.

BIOGRAPHY: *Ulysses S. Grant: His Life and Character*, 1898.

(Hannibal) Hamlin Garland was born on a farm near West Salem, in Wisconsin, on September 14, 1860, and moved with his family to the Iowa prairie at the age of eight. There he remained during early youth, accustomed to the hard rural life he described in his books. In 1881, after graduating from Cedar Valley Seminary in Osage, Iowa, he taught school for a year in Illinois, but was soon attracted by the cultural prestige of Boston, where he spent a winter reading in the public library, penniless and unknown. Here he first became influenced by the writings of Henry George and Herbert Spencer, who gave him the ethical and social inspiration to orient clearly his exposure of Western agricultural life.

A trip back to his father's Dakota farm in 1887 confirmed Garland in his desire to write about the life of the plains, and upon Joseph Kirkland's suggestion he began his first stories, printed in *Century, Harper's Weekly*, and *Arena*. Garland became famous and moved to Chicago in 1893, remaining there until 1916. He then moved to New York and in 1930 to Los Angeles, where he died on March 4, 1940.

Main-Travelled Roads, Garland's first collection of stories, is one of the most important books in American literary history, a conscious record of the Midwestern farmer's plight during the rapid growth of industrialization. The stories are harsh and objective, aware of a vanishing pioneer dream and hopeless in view of the future. *Prairie Folks*, published in 1893, continued this theme of the "blight as well as the bloom of the frontier." In the essays of *Crumbling Idols*, Garland went from social to cultural awareness of the changes in Western life, regretting its backwardness and suggesting the possibilities of drama in the development of towns and cities. He followed Whitman in advising the artist to tell the truth of the life he saw about him. *Rose of Dutcher's Cooley*, his best novel, puts this idea into practice in the story of a talented girl who found poetry in savage Chicago. *A Son of the Middle Border,* the last of Garland's notable writings, is his autobiographical summation of the agrarian illusion he had seen dispelled. The sequels to this book, among them *A Daughter of the Middle Border* and *Trail-Makers of the Middle Border,* could not recapture the vision of his earlier book. Much of Garland's other work was romantic fiction of little importance.

BIBLIOGRAPHICAL REFERENCES: Garland's best books were collected in the Border Edition, 11 vols., 1895–1910. There is no authorized biography, but his autobiographical writings provide excellent source materials for the story of his life. For critical studies in books and periodicals see Lucy L. Hazard, *The Frontier in American Literature,* 1927; Vernon L. Parrington, *Main Currents in American Thought,* III, 1930; Arthur H. Quinn, *American Fiction,* 1936; Ferner Nuhn, *The Wind Blew from the East,* 1942; Walter F. Taylor, *The Economic Novel in America,* 1942; Lars Åhnebrink, *Beginnings of Naturalism in American Fiction,* 1950; Edward Wagenknecht, *Cavalcade of the American Novel,* 1952; B. P. McElderry, "Hamlin Garland and Henry James," *American Literature,* XXIII (1952), 433–446; and Bernard L. Duffy, "Hamlin Garland's 'Decline' from Realism," *ibid.,* XXV (1953), 69–74.

DAVID GARNETT

Born: Brighton, England
Date: March 9, 1892

PRINCIPAL WORKS

NOVELS: *Lady into Fox,* 1922; *A Man in the Zoo,* 1924; *The Sailor's Return,* 1925; *Go She Must!,* 1927; *No Love,* 1929; *The Grasshoppers Come,* 1931; *Pocahontas, or, The Nonpareil of Virginia,* 1933; *Beany-Eye,* 1935; *Aspects of Love,* 1955.

SHORT STORIES: *The Old Dovecote and Other Stories,* 1928.

AUTOBIOGRAPHY: *The Golden Echo,* 1953; *Flowers of the Forest,* 1956; *The Familiar Faces,* 1957.

REPORTAGE: *War in the Air,* 1941.

David Garnett was born into a highly gifted literary family on easy terms with the greatest men of letters of the last century. His grandfather was Richard Garnett, superintendent of the British Museum reading room, and his father was Edward Garnett (1868–1937), essayist and playwright, who as a publisher's reader discovered Conrad and Doughty. His mother was Constance Garnett, famed translator of Tolstoy, Dostoevski, and Turgenev. In the first volume of his autobiography,

The Golden Echo, Garnett, born at Brighton on March 9, 1892, has described a marvelous boyhood. When he was five, Conrad taught him seamanship in a laundry basket rigged with sails made of sheets. W. H. Hudson took him bird-watching; Hilaire Belloc made adult jokes with him; G. B. Shaw watched him at play, dubbed him "a born actor"; Ford Madox Ford took him to tea with Henry James at Rye, and H. G. Wells argued socialism with him. His mother, deeply sympathetic with the Russian revolutionary movement, constantly had as house guests political exiles from Russia.

At the age of twelve David accompanied his mother (who was serving as a secret courier) to wartime Russia, where he rode horses across the steppes, played the balalaika, and in general had a magnificently adventurous time. Such experiences contributed to his being a restless and undisciplined student. To prepare for college entrance exams he crammed at London Tutorial College, where he became involved in a futile cloak-and-dagger plot to free an Indian friend, Vinayak Savarkar, from British imprisonment for treason. Then for five years he studied botany at the Royal College of Science and made frequent vacation trips and love trysts in France, Germany, Russia —the most delightful excursion being a walking trip through the Tyrol with D. H. and Frieda Lawrence in 1912. During those years he also became an intimate of the famed Bloomsbury Group: Geoffrey and Maynard Keynes, Adrian and Virginia Stephen (later Virginia Woolf), Leonard Woolf, Clive Bell, Roger Fry, and others.

In the second volume of his autobiography, *Flowers of the Forest,* Garnett has described how he refused to fight in World War I. He served instead with the Quakers rebuilding villages in France and later as an agricultural laborer in Surrey, but as a pacifist he suffered a great struggle of conscience. After the war he became interested in writing and published a novel, *Dope Darling* (1919), under the pseudonym of Leda Burke. Then with *Lady into Fox,* in 1922, he "officially" joined the Bloomsbury Group with which in every other way he had identified himself. That novel, a fantasy about the strange married life of a man whose wife turns into a fox, won both the Hawthornden and the James Tait Black prizes, and was the first of a series of pleasant, witty books: *A Man in the Zoo,* about a man who offered himself as an exhibit in the London Zoo; *The Sailor's Return,* about a sailor who brings an exotic, dark-skinned woman to live in a drab little English village; *The Grasshoppers Come,* about a grounded plane caught in a plague of locusts, and other novels and short stories equally fascinating and entertaining.

During the 1920's Garnett also tried his hand at bookselling; his failure is recounted in *Never Be a Bookseller* (1929). He was more successful as a publisher after founding the Nonesuch Press with Francis Birrell and Francis Meynell. Later he became a director of Rupert Hart-Davis, Ltd.

After many years as a discreet bohemian and intellectual radical, Garnett served as an intelligence officer in World War II and wrote the stirring account, *War in the Air.* In 1942 he married Angelica Bell, daughter of Clive Bell, but as his recent writing shows, the responsibilities of military, marital, and business life have not seriously modified his Bloomsbury vision of the world.

BIBLIOGRAPHICAL REFERENCES: Of primary importance is Garnett's autobiography, *The Golden Echo,* 1953; *Flowers of the Forest,* 1955; and *The Familiar Faces,* 1957. See also Gerald Gould, *The English Novel of Today,* 1924; Desmond MacCarthy, *Criticism,* 1932; and Frank A. Swinnerton, *The Georgian Scene,* 1935 (published in England as *The Georgian Literary Scene,* 1935).

MRS. ELIZABETH GASKELL

Born: Chelsea, London, England
Date: September 29, 1810

Died: Holybourne, England
Date: November 12, 1865

PRINCIPAL WORKS

NOVELS: *Mary Barton*, 1848; *Cranford*, 1853; *Ruth*, 1853; *North and South*, 1855; *My Lady Ludlow*, 1858; *Sylvia's Lovers*, 1863; *Cousin Phyllis*, 1864; *Wives and Daughters*, 1866.

BIOGRAPHY: *Life of Charlotte Brontë*, 1857.

Elizabeth Cleghorn (Stevenson) Gaskell, born in Chelsea, London, on September 29, 1810, was the eighth child of a Unitarian minister. Her father, although a clergyman, became a farmer and, eventually, keeper of the records at the National Treasury in London. Her mother died while Elizabeth Gaskell was still an infant, and the baby was put in the care of an aunt. According to her own account, Elizabeth Gaskell's childhood was a happy one, spent mostly at Knutsford (the Cranford of her later fiction) in rural Cheshire. In 1825, at the age of fifteen, she began her first formal schooling at Stratford-upon-Avon. She left boarding school in 1827 when her father became ill. In the same year a brother was lost at sea, and her father died two years later.

After her father's death, Elizabeth, a pretty and personable young woman, stayed with various relatives. On a visit to Manchester she met a young Unitarian minister, William Gaskell, whom she married in August, 1832. The young couple settled in Manchester. William Gaskell served as a minister in that city until his death and also taught English history and literature at the New College and the Workingman's College in Manchester. During the first decade of her marriage Elizabeth Gaskell showed little inclination to a literary career, except for a descriptive piece published in William Howitt's *Visits to Remarkable Places* (1840). During the early years of her marriage, Mrs. Gaskell had five children, the fifth a son. The death of her son from scarlet fever in 1844 spurred her to write as a means of alleviating her grief. Her first work was the novel *Mary Barton*, published anonymously. An immediate success, it brought her the friendship of Dickens and and a congratulatory letter from Thomas Carlyle. The novel, subtitled *A Tale of Manchester Life*, realistically portrayed the lives of the poor and showed the factory owners as callous and indifferent to their employees' welfare. The success of *Mary Barton* encouraged Mrs. Gaskell to write for the magazines.

Cranford, a volume of sketches rather loosely called a novel, appeared serially (1851–1852) in Dickens' *Household Words* before publication as a book in 1853. *Ruth* was Mrs. Gaskell's second novel; it was a plea for a single standard of sexual morality for both men and women. *North and South* found Mrs. Gaskell applying herself once again to a study of the relations between capital and labor. In 1855 she proposed to write a biography of Charlotte Brontë, which appeared in 1857. Some difficulties over statements which Miss Brontë had made and which were printed in the biography caused Mrs. Gaskell temporarily to suspend writing. Social life in literary circles took the place of writing.

Although she returned to writing again in the early 1860's, Mrs. Gaskell had ceased to write her best work. On November 12, 1865, she died suddenly of a heart attack at Alton, a country house near Holybourne, Hampshire, which she had bought a short time before.

BIBLIOGRAPHICAL REFERENCES: Mrs. Gaskell's writings have been collected in the Knutsford Edition, edited by A. W. Ward, 8 vols., 1906. The standard biography is Annette B. Hopkins, *Elizabeth Gaskell: Her Life and Work*, 1952. For biography and criticism see also J. J. Van Dulleman, *Mrs. Gaskell, Novelist and Biographer*, 1924; A. S. Whitfield, *Mrs. Gaskell: Her Life and Work*, 1929; Elizabeth Haldane, *Mrs. Gaskell and Her Friends*, 1930; and Yvonne ffrench, *Mrs. Gaskell*, 1949. Supplementing these is the *Letters of Mrs. Gaskell and Charles Eliot Norton, 1855–1865*, edited by Jane Whitehill, 1932. An interesting brief study is H. P. Collins, "The Naked Sensibility: Elizabeth Gaskell," *Essays in Criticism*, III (1952), 60–72.

THÉOPHILE GAUTIER

Born: Tarbes, France
Date: August 31, 1811

Died: Neuilly, France
Date: October 23, 1872

PRINCIPAL WORKS

NOVELS: *Mademoiselle de Maupin*, 1835; *Le Roman de la momie*, 1856; *Le Capitaine Fracasse*, 1861–1863.

POEMS: *Poésies*, 1830; *Albertus*, 1833; *La Comédie de la mort*, 1838; *Émaux et camées*, 1852.

PLAYS: *Le Tricorne enchanté*, 1845; *Pierrot posthume*, 1845; *La Juive de Constantine*, 1846.

TRAVEL SKETCHES AND IMPRESSIONS: *Voyage en Espagne*, 1843; *Italia*, 1852; *Constantinople*, 1854; *Voyage en Russie*, 1866.

CRITICISM: *Exhumations littéraires*, 1834–1835; *Les Grotesques*, 1844.

Théophile Gautier was born at Tarbes in the south of France on August 31, 1811, but shortly afterward moved with his family to Paris, where he received his education. He avidly studied art and the literature of the sixteenth and early seventeenth centuries. Coming early under the influence of the Romantics, Gautier formed a group of young writers who were noted for their excesses in actively denouncing the Classicists and in vigorously defending such Romantics as Victor Hugo. Some of Gautier's early literary essays soon impressed the critic, Sainte-Beuve. Gautier's second poetic work, *Albertus*, impressed the critics with its felicitous language and excellent description. Switching to a new medium, he then brought out a novel, the popular *Mademoiselle de Maupin*.

From 1836 until his old age, in order to augment his income, Gautier wrote theater and art criticism for Paris newspapers. He was a good-tempered critic, pointing out the good points of a work of art rather than its faults. Gautier was able to travel from time to time, and in works like *Voyage en*

Espagne, Italia, Constantinople, and Voyage en Russie the writer caught the individual color and atmosphere of these interesting places. During this period he continued writing fiction, such as the successful Le Roman de la momie and Le Capitaine Fracasse. The latter illustrates elements of the picaresque and contains more humor than his other works. Gautier's most significant work, however, is probably the volume of poems entitled Émaux et camées. The emphasis in these short poems is on form, language, and imagery.

In spite of Gautier's early adulation of the Romantics, both his verse and prose demonstrate that in many ways he was far from adhering to their principles. In his poetry, for example, he was more interested in form than in the expression of emotions. In Émaux et camées especially, critics have hailed the plastic quality of his verse; "carved gems" these poems were called. Through exact language and appropriate descriptive details Gautier kept his imagery under control at all times. Because of the lack of emotion and ideas in his verse some unfriendly critics have labeled his poetry "mere prettiness." But in his verse Gautier was clearly a forerunner of the Parnassians. His prose also reflects this dominant interest in form. In his novels he seems more interested in the backgrounds of his stories than in the stories themselves, in the physical characteristics of his characters than in the characters themselves. Both in practice and in precept Gautier was an early advocate of the "art for art's sake" school of aesthetic philosophy. He died in Neuilly on October 23, 1872.

BIBLIOGRAPHICAL REFERENCES: An edition of Gautier's Complete Works was translated and edited by F. C. de Sumichrast, 12 vols., 1900–1903, and in 24 vols., 1907. There is no adequate biography in English, although Sainte-Beuve's essay may be consulted in his Famous French Authors: Biographical Portraits of Distinguished French Writers, 1879. For French readers Maxime du Camp, Théophile Gautier, 1890, is a good biography; and biographical-critical information is furnished by Emile Bergerat, Théophile Gautier, Entretiens, Souvenirs, et Correspondance, 1911. Critical works are Helen Patch, The Dramatic Criticism of Théophile Gautier, 1922; and Louise Bulkley Dillingham, The Creative Imagination of Théophile Gautier: A Study in Literary Psychology, 1927, containing probably the best bibliography in English. Leon Henry Vincent's essay on Gautier in The Bibliotaph, and Other People, 1898, is worth consulting. Short critical articles include Horatio E. Smith, "The Brief-Narrative Art of Théophile Gautier," Modern Philology, XIV (1916–1917), 647–664; F. B. Barton, "Laurence Sterne and Théophile Gautier," ibid., XVI (1918–1919), 205–212; A. E. Carter, "Théophile Gautier on the Conception of Decadence," University of Toronto Quarterly, XXI (1951), 53–63; and A. E. Carter, "The Cult of Artificiality," ibid., XXV (1956), 452–466.

JOHN GAY

Born: Barnstaple, England
Date: September, 1685

Died: London, England
Date: December 4, 1732

PRINCIPAL WORKS

POEMS: Wine, 1708; Rural Sports, 1713; The Fan, 1714; The Shepherd's Week, 1714; Trivia, 1716; Poems on Several Occasions, 1720; Fables in Verse, 1727, 1738.

PLAYS: *The Wife of Bath,* 1713; *The What-D'-Ye-Call-It,* 1715; *The Captives,* 1724; *The Beggar's Opera,* 1728; *Polly,* printed 1729; *Acis and Galatea,* 1732.
PAMPHLET: *The Present State of Wit,* 1711.

John Gay, English poet and playwright, was born at Barnstaple, Devonshire, in September, 1685. He attended a free grammar school and served an apprenticeship to a cloth merchant in London. Next he worked in 1712 as secretary to the Duchess of Monmouth. Before this time he had written "Wine," a poem in blank verse which argued that water-drinkers could not be successful writers. Also in 1711 he wrote a pamphlet entitled *The Present State of Wit,* praising periodical authors. In 1713 appeared his poem *Rural Sports,* modeled after Alexander Pope's *Windsor Forest* and dedicated to Pope. His next two poems were the result of Pope's friendship: *The Fan,* a mock epic, and *The Shepherd's Week,* a group of pastorals. In the summer of 1714 he went to Europe with Lord Clarendon as his secretary.

The What-D'-Ye-Call-It is a light farce making fun of the tragedies of the time and contains his popular lyric " 'Twas When the Seas Were Roaring." *Trivia, or the Art of Walking the Streets of London* describes minutely and interestingly street scenes and happenings of the time and is a valuable source of information on eighteenth century manners. Another play, *Three Hours After Marriage* (1717), written with Pope and Arbuthnot, was not successful. In 1720 a collection of his poems was made by Tonson and Lintot in two volumes. This anthology contained the attractive lyric "Sweet Williams's Farewell to Black-Ey'd Susan." The first edition of his well-known *Fables* in verse was published in 1723. In 1724 his tragedy, *The Captives,* was acted at the Drury Lane Theatre, one night's performance being at the express command of the Prince and Princess of Wales.

On January 28, 1728, *The Beggar's Opera* was performed at Lincoln Inn's Fields with marked success. A musical play, it was written at the suggestion of Swift that a Newgate pastoral would make a good topic for a play. This popular drama had a long run, a revival, and a tour of the provinces. According to a popular epigram *The Beggar's Opera* made Gay rich and Rich (the producer) gay. The success of this play, in which he satirized Sir Robert Walpole, led Gay to write a sequel in which he used some of the same characters, and he named the play *Polly* after the heroine of the first play. For obvious reasons the production was forbidden on the stage, but this fact made its sale greater at the book stores. He also wrote most of the libretto for *Acis and Galatea,* performed in 1732, for which Handel composed the music. *Achilles* (1733), another opera, and two more plays were presented after his death.

John Gay is best remembered for *The Beggar's Opera,* the *Fables,* and some of his well-known lyrics. He died in London, December 4, 1732. On his tomb in Westminster Abbey the epitaph which he composed reads:

Life is a jest, and all things show it;
I thought so once, and now I know it.

BIBLIOGRAPHICAL REFERENCES: The most recent edition of Gay's *Works* was edited by J. C. Faber, 1926. For biography and criticism see Samuel Johnson, *Lives of the*

Poets, 1754; William Makepeace Thackeray, *The English Humorists*, 1853; L. Melville, *The Life and Letters of John Gay*, 1921; and W. E. Schultz, *Gay's Beggar's Opera*, 1923.

STEFAN GEORGE

Born: Büdesheim, Germany
Date: July 12, 1868

Died: Near Locarno, Switzerland
Date: December 4, 1933

PRINCIPAL WORKS

POEMS: *Hymnen*, 1890 (*Hymns*); *Pilgerfahrten*, 1891 (*Pilgrimages*); *Algabal*, 1892 (*Heliogabalus*); *Die Bücher der Hirten und Preisgedichte; der Sagen und Sänge; und der hängenden Gärten*, 1895 (*The Book of Eclogues and Eulogies; Legends and Lays; and The Hanging Gardens*); *Das Jahr der Seele*, 1897 (*The Year of the Soul*); *Der Teppich des Lebens und die Lieder von Traum und Tod*, 1899 (*The Tapestry of Life and Songs of Dream and of Death*); *Maximin*, 1906; *Der siebente Ring*, 1907 (*The Seventh Ring*); *Der Stern des Bundes*, 1914 (*Star of the Covenant*); *Das Neue Reich*, 1928 (*Kingdom Come*).

Stefan (Anton) George, born in Büdesheim, Germany, on July 12, 1868, invented at the age of nine a secret language to express emotions he felt German was inadequate to render; later he developed a Romance polyglot in which he wrote several poems. This concern with linguistic research he brought to scholarly fruition, becoming adept in Greek and Latin as well as all the modern languages of importance. After 1888 he visited London and Paris, perfecting his studies, and then went on to Spain. Denmark and Italy were his goals after 1890. Refusing to consider himself bound to Germany, he moved freely through Europe in quest not only of experience—Mallarmé introduced him to Verlaine as a "second Werther"—but also of a highly personal vision in art. He left his native land in 1933 for Switzerland and died near Locarno, December 4, 1933.

In *Hymns*, George's first important book of poems influenced by the Symbolists, he clearly expressed his preoccupation with man as an emergent being in the cycles of nature, and he continued in *Pilgrimages* to develop a conception of the poet as a sacred wanderer who must strive to be understood. At this time he began publishing the irregular periodical *Die Blätter für die Kunst* (1892–1919) with Hofmannsthal and Paul Gérardy, a series now rare, in which some of the finest artistic and critical contributions of a new German spirit were printed anonymously. In his translations from Mallarmé, Baudelaire, Rimbaud, and other French poets of this period, George was the first to bring to German readers their innovations of language and reorientation of art in modern society.

In *The Year of the Soul*, George's suggestive technique of description expressed his deepest belief in nature as controlled and changed by man. The quest of the lonely artist for companionship was reinforced in these pages which, with the other two volumes of his middle period, *The Tapestry of Life* and *The Seventh Ring*, are often considered his greatest achievement. In the later of these volumes his

411

sense of prophetic mission, of the poet as solitary hero in a new community, is confirmed. With his last book, *Kingdom Come*, George's poetic grasp of the foreboding present is tempered by his image of civilization triumphant. Like Hölderlin, George saw the poet as filling the emptiness in man's life caused by estrangement from God. Toward this fulfillment he dedicated his life along severe ascetic and moral principles, demanding similar behavior on the part of his disciples of *"der George Kreis"* (The George Circle), as they were known.

The finest of George's poems, such as "Die Spange" ("The Clasp") and "Das Licht" ("Light") are incisive and almost sculptured in style, their greatest effects achieved by nuances of image within the strict mold of form. His most elusive ideas were usually restrained by a Hellenic sense of order in verse.

BIBLIOGRAPHICAL REFERENCES: *Poems by Stefan George*, translated by Carol N. Valhope and Ernst Morwitz, 1943, contains both the German and English texts. See also E. L. Duthie, *L'Influence du symbolisme français dans le renouveau poétique de l'Allemagne*, 1933; Ernst Morwitz, *Die Dichtung Stefan George*, 1934; E. G. Winkler, *Stefan George, Gestalten und Probleme*, 1937; and E. K. Bennett, *Stefan George*, 1954. A useful background study is C. M. Bowra, *The Heritage of Symbolism*, 1943.

EDWARD GIBBON

Born: Putney, England
Date: April 27, 1737

Died: London, England
Date: January 16, 1794

PRINCIPAL WORKS

HISTORY: *The History of the Decline and Fall of the Roman Empire*, 1776–1788.
CRITICISM: *Essai sur l'Étude de la Littérature*, 1761; *Critical Observations on the Sixth Book of the Aeneid*, 1770.
AUTOBIOGRAPHY: *Memoirs of My Life and Writings*, 1796 [*Miscellaneous Works*].

Edward Gibbon, born at Putney, Surrey, England, on April 27, 1737, stemmed from an old and wealthy Kentish family. His father, also named Edward, was a member of Parliament from 1734 to 1747 and was also a colonel in the Hampshire militia. The future historian was the only one of his seven children who survived infancy, and for a long time it was doubtful whether or not he would live through childhood. Puny and weak and tortured by undiagnosed leg-aches in his youth, he grew, through physical inaction, to a repellent obesity, enduring, throughout his latter years, the severe pains of gout. As a result, his life was for the most part sedentary, devoted almost completely to intellectual pursuits. He never married, though his studies were broken by one short love affair. His services as a somewhat disinterested member of Parliament in 1774 and again in 1782, and as a commissioner of the Board of Trade from 1779 to 1782, plus a tour of duty in his father's militia regiment (whereby he was forced to become temporarily "a soldier and an Englishman") were the only interruptions to his constant and self-indulgent studiousness. Thus his life is mainly a summary of his studies, his thoughts, and his writings.

Gibbon's formal education began in a day-school at Putney, was continued at the school of one Dr. Wooddeson at Kingston-on-Thames, and was brought to the university level at Westminster. He entered Magdalen College, Oxford, in 1752, after a two-year retirement at Bath, and there spent what he termed "the most idle and unprofitable months" of his life. At Oxford he developed an interest in Catholicism. When his father discovered his intention of becoming a convert, he was summarily removed and put under the tutelage of a Calvinist minister in Lausanne, Switzerland. There he gave up Catholicism, learned French (which became his "second native language"), and turned to the serious study of Latin.

His father, having sent him to Lausanne to remove him from a religious infatuation, found it necessary to demand his return in order to separate him from an amatory one. In Switzerland, Gibbon had met Susanne Curchod, later the mother of Mme. de Staël, and had requested permission to marry her. Paternal disapproval kept them apart for a time; finally relations were severed completely when Gibbon failed to keep an appointment with Rousseau that Mlle. Curchod had arranged for him.

Freed now from all emotional entanglements, Gibbon was able to devote himself to the building of a library and to the writings that were to precede his final and major work. He also began his service in the militia and turned his experience into profit by pursuing at the same time a course of study in military literature. There followed an extended visit to Italy (1764–65), the founding of the Roman Club in London, and the writing of a few minor historical essays.

Work on his masterpiece was not to begin until after his father's death in 1770. Gibbon then sold his country estate, moved to London, and began to take part in the stimulating intellectual life of the town. If Boswell's authority is to be trusted, he was no welcome addition to Dr. Johnson's literary circle.

Though he contributed little, he himself profited greatly; the stimulation he received from others proved what he needed to concentrate on his projected work.

The first volume of the *Decline and Fall* was published in 1776, with immediate success. Not only was Gibbon suddenly famous; he was also the subject of bitter controversy touched off by his chapters on the growth of Christianity. Except for rather desultory activities in public office, the rest of his days were spent either in finishing or in defending his one great work. His erudite and effective *Vindication* appeared in 1779, followed by Volumes II and III in 1781. Gibbon then moved to his beloved Lausanne and settled there, library and all, to finish the last three volumes. These appeared, finally, in 1788. Gibbon remained in Lausanne, fat, feeble, and gout-ridden, until his death during a visit to London on January 16, 1794.

BIBLIOGRAPHICAL REFERENCES: For a complete listing see Jane E. Norton, *A Bibliography of the Works of Edward Gibbon*, 1940. His shorter writings were first collected in his *Miscellaneous Works*, edited by the Earl of Sheffield, 2 vols., 1796, and increased to 5 vols., 1814; re-edited by J. B. Bury, 1907. The standard edition of Gibbon's autobiography is *The Memoirs of the Life of Edward Gibbon*, edited by G. B. Hill, 1900. R. E. Prothero edited the *Letters* in 2 vols., 1896, and D. M. Low the *Journal* in 1929.

There is no standard biography. See G. M. Young, *Edward Gibbon*, 1932; Edmund Blunden, *Edward Gibbon and His Age*, 1935; R. B. Mowat, *Gibbon*, 1936; and D. M. Low, *Edward Gibbon*, 1937. See also J. B. Black, *The Art of History*, 1926.

ANDRÉ GIDE

Born: Paris, France   *Died:* Paris
Date: November 22, 1869   *Date:* February 19, 1951

PRINCIPAL WORKS

NOVELS AND NOVELLAS: *L'Immoraliste*, 1902 (*The Immoralist*); *La Porte étroite*, 1909 (*Strait Is the Gate*); *Les Caves du Vatican*, 1914 (*The Vatican Swindle*); *La Symphonie pastorale*, 1919 (*The Pastoral Symphony*); *Les Faux-Monnayeurs*, 1926 (*The Counterfeiters*); *L'École des femmes*, 1929 (*The School for Wives*); *Thésée*, 1946 (*Theseus*).

PLAYS: *Philoctète*, 1899 (*Philoctetes*); *Le Roi Candaule*, 1901 (*King Candaules*); *Œdipe*, 1931 (*Œdipus*); *Le Retour*, 1946 (*The Return*).

POEMS: *Les Cahiers d'André Walter*, 1891 (*The Notebooks of André Walter*); *Les Poesies d'André Walter*, 1892 (*The Poems of André Walter*); *Les Nourritures terrestres*, 1897 (*Fruits of the Earth*); *Les Nouvelles Nourritures*, 1935 (*New Fruits of the Earth*).

CRITICAL STUDIES: *Prétextes*, 1903 (*Pretexts*); *Nouveaux Prétextes*, 1911 (*Further Pretexts*); *Dostoïevsky*, 1923; *Journal des Faux-Monnayeurs*, 1926 (*Journal of "The Counterfeiters"*); *Essai sur Montaigne*, 1929 (*Montaigne*); *Interviews imaginaires*, 1943 (*Imaginary Interviews*); *Poétique*, 1947 (*A Definition of Poetry*).

TRAVEL SKETCHES AND IMPRESSIONS: *Voyage au Congo*, 1927 (*Travels in the Congo*); *Retour de l'U.R.S.S.*, 1936 (*Return from the U.S.S.R.*).

JOURNALS: *Journal, 1889–1939*, 1939 (*The Journals of André Gide*); *Pages de Journal, 1939–1942*, 1944 (*Extracts from the Journals, 1939–1942*); *Journal, 1942–1949*, 1950; *Deux Interviews imaginaires suivies de Feuillets*, 1946 (*Dialogues on God*).

LETTERS: *Lettres*, 1930; *Correspondence Francis Jammes et André Gide, 1899–1938*, 1948; *Correspondence Paul Claudel et André Gide, 1899–1926*, 1949.

André Gide was a distinguished French writer, the significance of whose work was finally recognized by the award of the Nobel Prize in 1947. This award was the termination of a long debate that had for many decades been carried on in France: the question was whether Gide, a writer of great talent and diversity, should be given official sanction and recognition such as membership in the French Academy indicates. During much of his career Gide was suspect because of his explicit revelation in *Corydon* (1924) of his own sexual tastes. Also, from 1937 on, his *Return from the U.S.S.R.* stood—in the minds of left-wing critics—as the record of Gide's retreat from a whole-hearted admiration of post-revolutionary Russia. Indeed, Gide's whole career, in a way that is more typical of France than of other countries, was a constant theme for debate and speculation. Did aesthetic excellence allow one to overlook a writer's challenge to conventional social patterns? Did this excellence permit one to overlook the damage Gide may have done to young and impressionable readers? These questions were asked by distinguished contemporaries like Paul Claudel and François Mauriac.

The circumstances of Gide's origins underlined these questions. He was born of respectable parents in Paris on November 22, 1869, and he was reared in a household where Protestant piety and artistic responsiveness were closely aligned. His education was thorough, and he had the financial security to make early literary experiments such as *The Notebooks of André Walter*, experiments that soon placed him within the confines of literary coteries that included Stephen Mallarmé and Pierre Louÿs.

Against this cultivated background of privilege and taste, Gide's personal history unfolded: a history which is explicitly avowed in memoirs (*Journals*, 1939, 1950; *Et Nunc Manet in Te*, 1951) and which is displayed slightly altered in works of fiction like *The Immoralist* and *The Counterfeiters*. As Gide reveals this history, we see in the foreground a struggle to choose between inherited patterns of behavior—norms that were Protestant and devout—and faithfulness to the impulses which the writer found in his own nature. Gide married his cousin, Madeleine Rondeaux, in 1895 and thereafter regarded her as a principle

of stability in his life. But his deep regard for her did not seriously interrupt his own moral experiments which, when they came to her knowledge, led Madame Gide to destroy all the correspondence that she had had, over the years, with her husband. Gide's remarks show us that he did not regard with indifference the agonies of his wife; he too experienced pain because part of his nature drew him away from her and the sober piety of French Protestantism (Gide's work is full of phrases that remind us that he was a constant reader of the Gospels). But Gide felt just as strongly the need to be faithful to his own emotional nature, whatever the cost in personal tragedy and social scandal. He lived his life and wrote his books in terms of his own tastes. It is on this ground that Gide made a great appeal in a century that was already critical of the old certainties typified by religion and traditional morality.

The events of Gide's life are a record of the publication of many books and of wide-ranging travels in Europe and Africa that were in accord with his restless spirit. In his early years he found the cultures of North Africa particularly attractive. Toward the end of the 1920's he was strongly attracted by the social experiments of Soviet Russia and finally traveled in that country. His report, in 1936, on what he found there—the triumph of an unimaginative dictatorship over the social aspirations of the 1917 revolution—aroused almost as much controversy as the personal avowals of *Corydon*. Because of his censures on Russia, Gide was the center of a storm that did not abate until the beginning of World War II. This experience convinced Gide that an artist underwent an unwise risk when he involved himself in current problems, and during World War II he would not allow his private loyalties to become involved in the great conflict as they had been by the Russian experiment and, still earlier, by the abuses of French colonial policy in the Congo.

Gide's own writing is, with the exceptions noted, a monument to his convictions that a writer's first and final duty is to his work and not to special moral and social problems that exist in the society to which he belongs. Faithfulness to an artistic task, Gide decided, lay at the center of an artist's morality; he must avoid bowing to the protests of the society he addresses. Even more painful, he must ignore the protests of his own conscience which speaks for the partial truths of his childhood. Gide's works frequently express this emphasis on aesthetic faithfulness by presenting us a character who is a writer and who writes a book in the book which Gide

himself is writing. Such a character appears in *The Counterfeiters;* we also possess a *Journal of "The Counterfeiters"* which Gide composed while he was writing the novel itself. This emphasis on art and the self as it is involved in the creation of art suggests the myth of Narcissus.

Gide was strongly drawn, as Justin O'Brien points out in his *Portrait of André Gide* (1953), by many of the ancient myths and also by scriptural narratives. Gide was convinced that the old tales were naïve only on the surface; actually, they offered the modern writer inexhaustible suggestions for creation. Indeed, the tales are richer than the codes men have associated with them; Gide's defenders consider that he was successful, in part, because he detached himself from the codes and sought the reality, whether in ancient myth or in the sorrow and delight of his own life and art.

Gide died in Paris on February 19, 1951.

BIBLIOGRAPHICAL REFERENCES: The best and most extensive study of André Gide in English is Justin O'Brien, *Portrait of André Gide*, 1953. For other biographical and critical studies, both European and American, see also René Lalou, *André Gide*, 1928; Klaus Mann, *André Gide and the Crisis of Modern Thought*, 1943; Van Meter Ames, *André Gide*, 1947; Henri Massis, *D'André Gide à Marcel Proust*, 1948; L. Thomas, *André Gide: The Ethic of the Artist*, 1950; Roger Martin du Gard, *Recollections of André Gide*, 1953; J. C. McLaren, *The Theatre of André Gide*, 1953; and Marsalet Delmas, *André Gide, L'enchaîné*, 1955.

SIR WILLIAM SCHWENCK GILBERT

Born: London, England
Date: November 18, 1836

Died: Harrow Weald, England
Date: May 29, 1911

PRINCIPAL WORKS

LIBRETTOS: *Trial by Jury*, 1875; *The Sorcerer*, 1877; *H.M.S. Pinafore*, 1878; *The Pirates of Penzance*, 1880; *Patience*, 1881; *Iolanthe*, 1882; *The Mikado*, 1885; *Ruddigore*, 1887; *The Yeoman of the Guard*, 1888; *The Gondoliers*, 1889.
POEMS: *Bab Ballads*, 1869.

Sir William Schwenck Gilbert has a name indissolubly linked with that of the British composer, Sir Arthur Sullivan. Both men produced work individually—and Gilbert might be remembered for his *Bab Ballads* and Sullivan for his famous composition, "The Lost Chord"—but the individual works of each man are eclipsed by what the two did working together. They gave all who share in Anglo-Saxon culture a new set of phrases, characters, and melodies. This is in itself a considerable achievement; and the very existence of works like *H.M.S. Pinafore* and *The Mikado* gives the lie to a twentieth century stereotype for the Victorian Age: that it was a time in which hypocrisy and prudery were rife. As all the operettas suggest, the Victorian period was able to generate in Gilbert and Sullivan deadly critics of pomposity and emotional and intellectual dishonesty. Moreover, as the record of the popularity of the Savoy operettas shows, there was a large public eager to respond to satire and to ridicule which was far from gentle.

Gilbert, born in London on November 18, 1836, was the son of William Gilbert, a retired naval surgeon. At the age of two, while traveling with his parents, he was kidnapped by brigands in Naples and returned for a ransom price of twenty-five pounds; the incident is not without parallel in the Savoy operettas, which are full of the confusions of identity that may overtake a child in his early years.

Gilbert's first schooling was in France; his later education, interrupted by the Crimean War, was completed at King's College, University of London, in 1857. He served for four years in the Education Department of the Privy Council until a small inheritance enabled him to resign and begin the practice of law, a profession he had been studying in his spare time. Thus the young man had, in a comparatively short time, actual experience of the army, the civil service, and the law. These were the three respected institutions which bore the brunt of his witty and satirical writing.

In 1867, Gilbert, now an established literary personage, married Lucy Turner, a daughter of a captain of engineers. He was a regular contributor of copy and drawings to *Fun*, the rival of *Punch*; here appeared his delightful *Bab Ballads*. His deftness of rhyme and trenchancy of insight were already apparent in these light verses, which point toward his successes in his operettas. Gilbert's famous collaboration with Sullivan came about after the two men met and worked as amateur producers of sketches and music at the Gallery of Illustration. Their first joint production, a burlesque, *Thespis, or the Gods Grown Old*, was presented in 1871. It is worth noting that already Gilbert was finding Greek mythology and fairy tales in general a fertile mine of subjects. Before the two men achieved their destiny of close coöperation, Gilbert produced a few witty comedies in which, it must be confessed, wit comes out a second best to Victorian sentiment, the same sentiment that he was later to parody with great skill.

Gilbert and Sullivan's first serious collaboration was *Trial by Jury*. Produced by D'Oyly Carte in 1875, it met with such immediate approval that the producer formed the Comedy Opera Company. There followed in quick succession *The Sorcerer, H.M.S. Pinafore, The Pirates of Penzance,* and

Patience. During its run, *Patience* was transferred from the Opera Comique to the Savoy, which Carte had built especially for the Gilbert and Sullivan works. Included in the "Savoy operas" were *Iolanthe, The Mikado, Ruddigore, The Yeomen of the Guard,* and *The Gondoliers.* Almost without exception, the works took their themes from a perception of bureaucratic bungling, grotesque aspects of current modes of sentiment (romance is always taken with a smile), or topical sensations, such as the aestheticism of Oscar Wilde which suggested features of *Patience.* Whatever their inspiration, certain of the works, notably *The Mikado* and *H.M.S. Pinafore,* seem to hit off officialdom decisively; and the popularity of these works does not falter.

During the production of *The Gondoliers,* Gilbert, a temperamental and sensitive person, quarreled with Carte over financial arrangements. Sullivan was drawn into the disagreement, and the partnership was virtually dissolved. There was later collaboration, but without memorable results. In later years Gilbert built a theater of his own in London, bought an estate in Middlesex, and lived the life of a country gentleman. He was knighted in 1907. Four years later, on May 29, 1911, he was drowned at Harrow Weald, Middlesex.

It is the opinion of some critics that the two men created a new form of theatrical representation. Although songs had been used as incidental effects by other nineteenth century writers, Gilbert was the first to see the music as part and parcel of the characterizations and the plot. Even the rhythms of many of his lines seem to have the power to suggest the sort of music that Sullivan actually provided for them.

BIBLIOGRAPHICAL REFERENCES: The Gilbert and Sullivan operettas are available in various editions. See François Cellier and Cunningham Bridgeman, *Gilbert and Sullivan and Their Operas,* 1914; Hesketh Pearson, *Gilbert and Sullivan,* 1935; and William A. Darlington, *The World of Gilbert and Sullivan,* 1950; also Edith A. Browne, *W. S. Gilbert,* 1907. For all true Savoyards, George F. Dunn, *A Gilbert and Sullivan Dictionary,* 1936, is indispensable.

JEAN GIONO

Born: Manosque, France
Date: March 30, 1895

PRINCIPAL WORKS

NOVELS: *Colline,* 1929 (*Hill of Destiny*); *Un de Baumugnes,* 1929 (*Lovers Are Never Losers*); *Regain,* 1930 (*Harvest*); *Jean le bleu,* 1932 (*The Blue Boy*); *Le Chant du monde,* 1934 (*Song of the World*); *Que ma joie demeure,* 1935 (*Joy of Man's Desiring*); *Batailles dans la montagne,* 1937 (*Battles in the Mountain*); *Le Hussard sur le toit,* 1951 (*The Horseman on the Roof*); *La Moulin de Pologne,* 1952 (*The Malediction*).

PLAY: *Lanceurs de graines,* 1937 (*Sowers of Seed*).

Refus d'obéissance, 1937 *(Refusal to Obey)*; *Pour saluer Mel-ville,* 1940 *(Salute to Melville).*

Jean Giono was born at Manosque, in the Alpine section of France on March 30, 1895. His father was a cobbler and his mother a laundress from Paris. When he was sixteen Giono left school in order to help support his family; he became a bank messenger and eventually a clerk in the bank. During his youth he read the Bible and the works of Homer, about the only books available to him. From Homer especially he absorbed pantheistic notions which impregnated most of his subsequent writings. Serving at Verdun during World War I, he was horrified by much of what he saw. This aversion to war has influenced some aspects of his later writing.

A volume of verse, *Accompagnés de la flute* (1924), and a short story, "Champs," in the *Nouvelle Revue Française* brought recognition to Giono. An extensive publication of novels during the late twenties and thirties established Giono as a serious practitioner of *avant-garde* literature. Two of his earliest and best works were *Hill of Destiny* and *Harvest,* characterized as novels of the soil. A new note was struck in *Le Grand Troupeau* (1931) which portrayed the horrors of war. *The Blue Boy,* set in the author's native Provence, is largely autobiographical. Two more excellent novels of the soil were *Song of the World* and *Joy of Man's Desiring. Refusal to Obey* and *Précisions* (1939), written in the shadow of World War II, brought out Giono's strong pacifism. During these productive years Giono also wrote some excellent short stories.

In 1939 Giono was imprisoned briefly for inciting the peasants of his native region to oppose war. During World War II he retained a tolerant attitude toward the Vichy government. Because of this attitude the National Book Committee blacklisted him after the War. During the forties Giono translated *Moby Dick* into French, wrote a critical work on Melville, *Salute to Melville,* and produced more novels. *The Horseman on the Roof* is set in Paris during the cholera epidemic of 1838. *The Malediction* is the story of a family doomed by strange fate.

In most of his work Giono celebrates the soil and those who till it. He sees these simple peasants as a separate race rather than as another class. Critics have praised the bold metaphors by which he joins man with nature. His novels, however, contain more of a naturalistic than a pastoral quality. Giono's prose style is vigorous, almost epic, yet poetic.

BIBLIOGRAPHICAL REFERENCES: For biography and criticism see Christian Michel-felder, *Jean Giono et les religions de la terre,* 1938; Jacques Pugnet, *Jean Giono,* 1955; and Romée de Villeneuve, *Jean Giono, ce solitaire,* 1955. A good introduction is *Giono par lui-même,* edited by Claudine Chonez, 1956.

JEAN GIRAUDOUX

Born: Bellac, France
Date: October 29, 1882

Died: Paris, France
Date: January 31, 1944

PLAYS: *Siegfried*, 1928; *Amphitryon 38*, 1929; *La Guerre de Troie n'aura pas lieu*, 1935 (*Tiger at the Gates*); *Electre*, 1937; *La Folle de Chaillot*, 1945 (*The Madwoman of Chaillot*).

NOVELS: *Suzanne et le Pacifique*, 1921; *Juliette au pays des hommes*, 1924; *Bella*, 1926; *Églantine*, 1927.

REPORTAGE AND TRAVEL: *Lectures pour une ombre*, 1918; *Amica America*, 1919.

POLITICAL ESSAYS: *Pleines Pouvoirs*, 1939.

Born in Bellac, France, on October 29, 1882, (Hippolyte) Jean Giraudoux grew up in the Haute Vienne and remained a "provincial" throughout his cosmopolitan life. Educated at the École Normale Supérieure in Paris, he spent a year at Harvard University as instructor in French and representative for *La Figaro*, was horrified by American materialism and the frenzy over Harvard-Yale football games, and returned to Paris. There he failed German in the *agregation* exams and turned to journalism for *Le Matin* and the *Paris-Journal*. In 1910 he was attached to the press bureau of the Foreign Affairs Ministry, thus beginning a career of diplomatic activity at the Quai d'Orsay.

In World War I, Giraudoux served as a sergeant, later sub-lieutenant, was badly wounded, and received the Legion of Honor. In 1916 he went to Portugal as a military instructor and later went to America in the same capacity. After the war he served for eight years in Turkey with a commission appointed to inspect allied war damage.

Influenced strongly by Gide and Proust, Giraudoux nevertheless developed a unique literary style which handles languages as Monet and Pissarro handle paint. His impressionism appears with his very first book *Provinciales* (1909), followed by an account of his American experience, *L'École des Indifférents* (1911), and a report of his adventures in World War I, *Lectures pour une ombre*. His most important novels are *Simon le Pathétique* (1918), partly autobiographical; *L'Adorable Clio* (1920), a piquant farewell to arms; *Suzanne et la Pacifique; Siegfried et le Limousin* (1922), concerning an amnesic French prisoner of war who becomes a political power in Germany; and *Bella*, a *roman à clef* dealing with Parisian political life. *Pleins Pouvoirs*, published in 1939, was a critique of French foreign affairs and internal politics. Giraudoux also achieved considerable success as a dramatist with Louis Jouvet starring in the major plays: *Amphitryon 38, Intermezzo* (1933), and *La Guerre de Troie n'aura pas lieu*. Americans know him best from Broadway productions of *Tiger at the Gates*, and *The Madwoman of Chaillot*.

Giraudoux continued his political activities to the very end, serving as Daladier's propaganda director and emissary between Paris and Vichy; however, he refused a ministry to Athens in order to continue his writing. He died in occupied Paris on January 31, 1944.

BIBLIOGRAPHICAL REFERENCES: There is no collected edition in English, but numerous individual translations are available, the best of which are by Christopher Fry. The standard edition in French is *Le Théâtre complet*, 16 vols., 1945–1951.

English biographies and critical studies are lacking. For French readers there is Paul Morand, *Giraudoux, Souvenirs de notre jeunesse suivi de Adieu à Giraudoux,* 1948, which includes previously unpublished letters, documents, and photographs. See also C. E. Magny, *Précieux Giraudoux,* 1945; and Marianne M. Campiche, *Le théâtre de Giraudoux et la condition humaine,* 1954. In English, see articles in Frederick Lumley, *Trends in Twentieth Century Drama,* 1956, with a selected bibliography; also Milton Stansbury, *French Novelists of Today,* 1935; and G. E. Lamaître, *Four French Novelists,* 1938.

Recent articles in periodicals include Georges May, "Marriage vs. Love in the World of Giraudoux," *Yale French Studies,* XI (1953), 106–115; and Walter A. Strauss, "Giraudoux. The Tragedy of Disharmony," *Emory University Quarterly,* XI (1955), 18–29.

GEORGE GISSING

Born: Wakefield, England   *Died:* St. Jean-Pied-de-Port, France
Date: November 22, 1857   *Date:* December 28, 1903

PRINCIPAL WORKS

NOVELS: *Workers in the Dawn,* 1880; *The Unclassed,* 1884; *Isabel Clarendon,* 1886; *Demos,* 1886; *Thyrza,* 1887; *A Life's Morning,* 1888; *The Nether World,* 1889; *The Emancipated,* 1890; *New Grub Street,* 1891; *Born in Exile,* 1892; *The Odd Women,* 1893; *In the Year of Jubilee,* 1894; *The Paying Guest,* 1894; *Sleeping Fires,* 1895; *The Whirlpool,* 1897; *The Town Traveller,* 1898; *Our Friend the Charlatan,* 1901; *The Private Papers of Henry Ryecroft,* 1903; *Veranilda,* 1904.
CRITICISM: *Charles Dickens: A Study,* 1898.

George (Robert) Gissing was surely one of the most unfortunate and miserable men ever to achieve a place in the world of letters, and his novels constitute a broad panorama of dismal lives, meticulously recorded without the slightest trace of warmth, humor, or hope.

Born in Wakefield, England, on November 22, 1857, he was educated at a Quaker academy and later won a scholarship at Owens College, Manchester. But his career as a classical scholar was cut off by an unhappy relationship with a prostitute whom he desperately hoped to reform, and he was imprisoned for theft. Upon his release he fled to the United States, where he sold some short stories to the Chicago *Tribune.* He returned to England and endured a brief marriage to the same prostitute who had earlier embroiled him in crime. Determined to become an author, he wrote a novel which never found a publisher and has since been lost. His second novel, *Workers in the Dawn,* was published in 1880 at his own expense. Failing to find a public, Gissing retreated further into the slums. Before he could become utterly corrupted he was rescued by Frederick Harrison, who made him tutor to his sons. Once again Gissing took up his pen and wrote a rapid succession of novels which were Victorian in form but certainly not in subject matter. These included *The Unclassed,* one of the first environmental studies of prostitution; *Demos,* a bitter account of social agitation among the working classes; *Thyrza,* the sordid story of a London working girl; *The Nether*

World, a realistic tale of slum life and the underworld; *New Grub Street,* an assault on unscrupulous publishers and the stupid reading public; *The Odd Women,* a view of old age among poor, uncultured, and unmarried women, and almost a dozen similar portraits of despair among the underprivileged segments of Victorian society.

Gradual improvement of his affairs brought about a perceptible but only slightly increased cheerfulness reflected in his autobiographical *The Private Papers of Henry Ryecroft,* published in the year before his death, which occurred at St. Jean-Pied-de-Port, France, on December 28, 1903. The work shows his relief at escaping to the country after a dismal life of grinding poverty, illness, and a second unfortunate marriage to a woman who refused to grant him a divorce. Earlier (in *The Unclassed*) he had written: "Art nowadays must be the mouthpiece of misery, for misery is the keynote of modern life"; at the end he wrote: "The artist is moved and inspired by the supreme enjoyment of some aspect of the world about him . . . an emotion of rare vitality." Gissing spent his last years living in the Pyrenees with

a highly cultured, sensitive, and intelligent Frenchwoman. Apart from his twenty-three realistic novels, Gissing wrote two small collections of short stories, a series of introductions to the Rochester edition of Dickens, an unfinished historical novel of Rome, *Veranilda,* and an account of holiday travels, *By the Ionian Sea* (1901).

Had Gissing's circumstances been more secure, he might well have become more than a second-rate social chronicler, for he read and loved the classics deeply and managed to make several pilgrimages to Italy and Greece. He was the first person to write an intelligent and discerning study of Charles Dickens, in which he skillfully analyzed Dickens' realistic characters, particularly his women, and traced Dickens' stylistic debt to the masters of eighteenth century fiction. Gissing's own style is frankly related to that of the French naturalists of the late nineteenth century. Even though he lacked sufficient vitality, both personally and in his art, to achieve a front rank in English literary history, he has won the esteem of such discriminating critics as Henry James, H. G. Wells, and Virginia Woolf.

BIBLIOGRAPHICAL REFERENCES: There are several reliable biographical-critical studies of Gissing: M. Yates, *George Gissing,* 1922; Frank A. Swinnerton, *George Gissing, A Critical Study,* 1923; R. C. McKay, *George Gissing,* 1933; and S. V. Gapp, *George Gissing, Classicist,* 1936. See also Jackson I. Cope, "Definition as Structure in Gissing's Ryecroft Papers," *Modern Fiction Studies,* III (1957), 127–140.

ELLEN GLASGOW

Born: Richmond, Virginia   *Died:* Richmond
Date: April 22, 1874   *Date:* November 20, 1945

PRINCIPAL WORKS

NOVELS: *The Voice of the People,* 1900; *The Battle-Ground,* 1902; *The Deliverance,* 1904; *The Wheel of Life,* 1906; *The Ancient Law,* 1908; *The Romance of a Plain Man,* 1909; *The Miller of Old Church,* 1911; *Virginia,* 1913; *Life and*

Gabriella, 1916; *The Builders,* 1919; *One Man in His Time,* 1922; *Barren Ground,* 1925; *The Romantic Comedians,* 1926; *They Stooped to Folly,* 1929; *The Sheltered Life,* 1932; *Vein of Iron,* 1935; *In This Our Life,* 1941.

SHORT STORIES: *The Shadowy Third and Other Stories,* 1923.

POEMS: *The Freeman and Other Poems,* 1902.

ESSAYS: *A Certain Measure,* 1943.

AUTOBIOGRAPHY: *The Woman Within,* 1954.

By birth and tradition Ellen Glasgow was as deeply involved as John Esten Cooke or Thomas Nelson Page in the historical situation and society of her region, but from the beginning her path cut straight across the elegiac romanticism of the plantation school of fiction. That literature, which came into being partly to redeem the pride of a defeated people, served its purpose for the age in which it was written, and its nostalgic recapture of the past held a certain dignity and grace. Too often, however, it was true to ideals which were in turn false to practice in human conduct. As an apprentice novelist, Ellen Glasgow was forced to look elsewhere for the lessons of experience.

Born in Richmond, Virginia, on April 22, 1874, Ellen (Anderson Gholson) Glasgow grew up in a society which had emerged from the Civil War with its principles, if not its property, almost intact. Her mother came from an aristocratic family of the Tidewater; her father, descended from Scotch-Irish pioneers who had settled west of the Blue Ridge, was the manager of an ironworks which had manufactured cannon for the Confederacy. Perhaps it was her good fortune that as a child she was too delicate for formal education. Her real teachers—John Stuart Mill, Hume, Voltaire, Plato, Darwin, Huxley, Adam Smith—she found in the books in her father's library; no university in the South could have provided a more liberal education at the time. Although the University of Virginia did not admit women, she read for, and passed, the honors examination in political economy. These studies prepared her for lifelong revolt against an apathy of war memories and a code of evasive idealism whose only meaning lay in a backward look toward glory. Although writers of an earlier generation spoke eloquently for the tradition uprooted at Appomattox, their sentiments were too cloying for a girl who had read literary masterpieces as well as the great scientists and philosophers.

More personally, as she told in her posthumous autobiography, *The Woman Within,* domestic tensions and the experience of a love doomed to unfulfillment helped to shape a philosophy of life that was essentially tragic and gave her deeper insight into the gap between appearance and reality. Skepticism became the natural habit of her mind, flowering eventually in the novel of manners and reflecting with indulgent irony the final disenchantment of a society caught in the entanglement of its social and moral code.

Few writers have revealed more candidly the influences contributing to the development of a point of view and a literary method. Fielding gave her the model of his comic epic in prose. Tolstoy showed that a writer may remain provincial and yet fasten on universals. Jane Austen provided a depth of critical penetration and an illuminating irony which sets everything in its proper place within a small conservative society. The novels of Balzac and Zola demonstrated a method for tracing patterns of change through whole social groups. Her apprenticeship began early. By the time she was eighteen she had secretly written and destroyed her first novel. She then began to write *The Descendant,* but because of grief and shock at the time of her mother's death it was not published until 1897. This novel was followed a year later by *Phases of an Inferior Planet.* These are minor works on a minor theme, the escape of the Virginian to New York; in them Miss Glasgow had not yet found the proper subject for her method and style. That moment came with *The Voice of the People* in 1900, the story of Nick Burr and his climb from the poverty and misery of a poor dirt-farmer's family to become governor of Virginia. This was the first of her novels written, as she said later, out of her determination to write of the South not sentimentally, as a stricken province or a lost, romantic legend, but as part of the larger human world.

In the Virginia Edition of her works, for which she wrote the series of critical prefaces later reprinted in *A Certain Measure,* Miss Glasgow divided her best novels into three groups. The first of these is a cycle designed as a social history of the Commonwealth, beginning with a picture of plantation society and the war years in *The Battle-Ground* and ending, in *Virginia* and *Life and Gabriella,* with ironic studies of woman's place in the traditional code of gentility. In her novels of the Reconstruction period—*The Deliverance, The Voice of the People,* and *The Romance of a Plain Man*—Miss Glas-

gow tells of the rise of the new middle class, the sturdy, honest, hard-working Scotch-Irish families who have given the South its real backbone running like a "vein of iron" beneath surface pleasantries of custom and tradition. Closely associated with these "Novels of the Commonwealth" are her three "Novels of the Country." *The Miller of Old Church,* rich in its atmosphere of the Virginia countryside, sustains much of its action in a pastoral mood, but without sentimentality or the limitations of local color quaintness. Always at her best in her portrayal of women, Miss Glasgow created her best character in Dorinda Oakley of *Barren Ground,* in which the plot, characterization, and mood combine to make this story of rural change one of the wisest and most compelling of modern American novels. *Vein of Iron* presents another notable heroine, Ada Fincastle, in a novel which spans the course of Virginia history from a grandmother's memories of the mountain frontier to the depression years of the 1930's.

The "Novels of the City," are three brilliant comedies of manners which relate Miss Glasgow's fiction not only to the history of her state but also to the history of literature. Her skepticism and wit have full play in *The Romantic Comedians,* a novel dissecting the heart and mind of the traditionally gallant Southern gentleman, and in *They Stooped to Folly,* slyly malicious in its picture of a "perfect" marriage set against a background of changing moral standards. *The Sheltered Life* presents the last act in a long drama of sentimentality and sham. *In This Our Life,* her last novel, closer to the social histories than the comedies of manners, brings Miss Glasgow's study of Virginia society down to the summer of 1939. In the story of the Timberlake family she shows on a domestic level and against an urban background a world falling apart in loneliness and cruelty and fear. This is the most pessimistic of her novels; its mood of deep despair is scarcely leavened by the bright quality of her wit.

Ellen Glasgow's fiction is of one piece, a prescription of the "blood and irony" that she recommended for the South in 1925. After years of "benev-

olent neglect" many honors came to her toward the end of her career. Elected to the American Academy of Arts and Letters in 1938, she was awarded the Howells Medal in 1940 and in the same year the *Saturday Review of Literature* plaque for distinguished service to American letters. She received the Southern Authors' Prize in 1941 and *In This Our Life* was named for the Pulitzer Prize in 1942. She died at her home in Richmond on November 20, 1945.

BIBLIOGRAPHICAL REFERENCES: Ellen Glasgow's representative novels have been collected in two editions, neither definitive: the Old Dominion Edition, 8 vols., 1929–1933, and the limited Virginia Edition, 12 vols., 1938. Both contain the prefaces republished in *A Certain Measure*, 1943, to which the author added a thirteenth essay on *In This Our Life*. There is no full-length biography, although at least two were reported in preparation in 1957. For biographical material the best source is *The Woman Within*, 1954, and for discussion of her theories of the art of fiction the essays in *A Certain Measure*.

For brief studies in books or pamphlets see Louise Maunsell Field, *Ellen Glasgow: Novelist of the Old and the New South*, 1923; Stuart P. Sherman, *Critical Woodcuts*, 1926; Dorothea L. Mann, *Ellen Glasgow*, 1927, with additional sketches by James Branch Cabell, Joseph Collins, and Carl Van Vechten; James Branch Cabell, *Some of Us*, 1930; Emily Clark, *Innocence Abroad*, 1931; Friedrich Brie, *Ellen Glasgow*, 1931; Arthur H. Quinn, *American Fiction*, 1936; N. Elizabeth Monroe, *The Novel and Society*, 1941, and "Ellen Glasgow: Ironist of Manners," in *Fifty Years of the American Novel*, edited by Harold C. Gardiner, S.J., 1951; Alfred Kazin, *On Native Grounds*, 1942; Frederick J. Hoffman, *The Modern Novel in America, 1900–1950*, 1951; Edward Wagenknecht, *Cavalcade of the American Novel*, 1952; Maxwell Geismar, *Rebels and Ancestors: The American Novel, 1890–1915*, 1953; and John Edward Hardy, "Ellen Glasgow," in *Southern Renascence*, edited by Louis D. Rubin, Jr., and Robert D. Jacobs, 1953.

Critical studies in periodicals include Isaac F. Marcosson, "The Personal Ellen Glasgow," *Bookman*, XXIX (1909), 619–621; Edward Mims, "The Social Philosophy of Ellen Glasgow," *Journal of Social Forces*, IV (1926), 495–503; Sara Haardt, "Ellen Glasgow and the South," *Bookman*, LXIX (1929), 133–139; Kenneth Murdock, "Folly and the Ironist," *Virginia Quarterly Review*, V (1929), 596–600. William A. Parker, "Ellen Glasgow: A Gentle Rebel," *English Journal*, XX (1931) 187–194; James Southall Wilson, "Ellen Glasgow's Novels," *Virginia Quarterly Review*, IX (1933), 595–600; Léonie Villard, "L'Œuvre d'Ellen Glasgow, romancière américaine," *Revue Anglo-Américaine*, XI (1933), 97–111; Marjorie Kinnan Rawlings, "Regional Literature of the South," *College English*, I (1940), 381–389; Herschel Brickell, "Miss Glasgow and Mr. Marquand," *Virginia Quarterly Review*, XVII (1941), 405–417; Dayton Kohler, "Recognition of Ellen Glasgow," *English Journal*, XXXI (1942), 523–529; Grace Stone, "Ellen Glasgow's Novels," *Sewanee Review*, L (1942), 289–301; H. Blair Rouse, "Ellen Glasgow in Retrospect," *Emory University Quarterly*, VI (1950), 30–40; Frederick P. McDowell, "Ellen Glasgow and the Art of the Novel," *Philological Quarterly*, XXX (1951), 328–347; and Barbara Giles, "Character and Fate: The Novels of Ellen Glasgow," *Mainstream*, IX (1956), 20–31.

WILLIAM GODWIN

Born: Wisbeach, England
Date: March 3, 1756

Died: London, England
Date: April 7, 1836

PRINCIPAL WORKS

NOVELS: *The Adventures of Caleb Williams, or Things as They Are*, 1794; *St. Leon: A Tale of the Sixteenth Century*, 1799.
POLITICAL PHILOSOPHY: *The Inquiry concerning Political Justice and its Influence on General Virtue and Happiness*, 1793; *Of Population*, 1820.
HISTORY: *History of the Commonwealth*, 1820–1824.

William Godwin, born at Wisbeach, England, on March 3, 1756, made dissent the theme of his life. In a sense he was born to this theme, being the seventh of thirteen children in the family of a dissenting minister. Because of the father's religious views, the children were reared in a strict, Puritanic tradition. As a boy Godwin was educated at various academies run by and for nonconformists. Trained for the ministry, he entered church work in 1771. But he continued to study philosophy and by 1782 so completely disagreed with his sect that he left the ministry to earn a living by writing. Taking up residence in London, he became a hack writer, an atheist, and a radical.

Godwin's first book, the key to his thinking, was *Political Justice*, published in 1793. The volume received wide attention, and according to report the author narrowly escaped being prosecuted for his unorthodox views. In the book Godwin announced his principle of dispassionate advocation of extremes; the work is a compendium criticizing society, advocating a new ethics, and prophesying a Utopian fu-

ture. People, thought Godwin, could exercise reason in all activities and through education could learn to apply the basic motivation of pleasure and pain to all their activities, thus producing a new ethics and a better society.

In 1792 Godwin met Mary Wollstonecraft, notorious at the time for her *Vindication of the Rights of Women*. In 1796 they began to live together without marriage, such conduct being basic to their principles, but they bowed to convention and married when Mary became pregnant. In 1797 Mary Godwin died a few days after giving birth to a daughter, leaving Godwin with two small children. One was their infant daughter, who became the wife of the poet Shelley, and the other was Mary Godwin's illegitimate child by Gilbert Imlay, an American novelist. Soon after becoming a widower, needing help in his household, Godwin married Mary Jane Clairmont, a widow with two children, one of whom, Clara ("Claire"), was to obtain notoriety as Lord Byron's mistress. To this marriage was born Godwin's own son William, who had a brief literary career of his own.

426

During the 1790's Godwin published two novels. His first, *Caleb Williams*, published in 1794, is his best known. It portrays what Godwin saw as the power of the privileged few opposed to the helplessness of the many poor people, and it was intended as an indictment of society, a fictional presentation of the same principles Godwin had presented in *Political Justice* just a year before. In addition to being a novel with a social purpose, *Caleb Williams* is an interesting study in suspense and fear, even terror. In his second novel, *St. Leon*, Godwin wrote a historical romance, heavy with Gothicism, about sixteenth century England. His later novels are less important simply because they are less interesting and tend to be dull. In this category are *Fleetwood* (1805), *Mandeville* (1817), *Cloudsley* (1830), and *Deloraine* (1833). He also wrote several biographies, including one of Geoffrey Chaucer, several volumes of history, two plays, and volumes in philosophy. Only *Political Justice* and *Caleb Williams* have received long-term popular or scholarly attention.

Godwin's life after his second marriage was dismal. His wife operated a publishing house and embittered her own and her husband's life by a combination of shrewishness and bankruptcy. Money troubles dogged Godwin constantly; Percy Bysshe Shelley, his son-in-law, contributed for a time to his support. Godwin suffered a stroke in 1818, but he continued writing to earn a living. Only in 1833, just three years prior to his death, did he have any financial relief. At that time the British government gave him a sinecure as a yeoman usher of the exchequer, a post which gave him financial security. He died in London on April 7, 1836. But even then he was not left in peace, for when a railroad was put through St. Pancras' cemetery in London his body had to be disinterred and moved to another grave.

BIBLIOGRAPHICAL REFERENCES: There is no collected edition of Godwin, but his two chief works are available in good editions: *Political Justice*, edited by R. A. Preston, 1926, and *Caleb Williams*, edited by Van Wyck Brooks, 1926. There are several reliable studies of Godwin's career and influence: C. K. Paul, *William Godwin, his Friends and Contemporaries*, 2 vols., 1876; H. N. Brailsford, *Shelley, Godwin and Their Circle*, 1913; F. K. Brown, *William Godwin*, 1926; and George Woodcock, *William Godwin*, 1946. See also Sir Leslie Stephen, *English Thought in the Eighteenth Century*, Vol. II, 1902; and Ernest A. Baker, *The History of the English Novel*, Vol. V, 1929.

JOHANN WOLFGANG VON GOETHE

Born: Frankfort-on-Main, Germany
Date: August 28, 1749

Died: Weimar, Germany
Date: March 22, 1832

PRINCIPAL WORKS

PLAYS: *Götz von Berlichingen*, 1774; *Clavigo*, 1774; *Egmont*, 1778; *Iphigenie auf Tauris*, 1779, 1787 (*Iphigenia in Tauris*); *Torquato Tasso*, 1781, 1790; *Faust, ein Fragment*, 1790; *Faust I*, 1808; *Faust II*, 1832.

NOVELS: *Die Leiden des jungen Werther*, 1774 (*The Sorrows of Young Werther*); *Wilhelm Meisters Lehrjahre*, 1795–1796 (*William Meister's Apprenticeship*); *Die*

Wahlverwandtschaften, 1808 (*Elective Affinities*); *Wilhelm Meisters Wanderjahre*, 1821–1829 (*Wilhelm Meister's Travels*).

POEMS: *Reineke Fuchs*, 1794 (*Reynard the Fox*); *Römische Elegien*, 1795 (*Roman Elegies*); *Hermann und Dorothea*, 1798; *Westöstlicher Diwan*, 1819 (*The West-Eastern Divan*).

Satire: *Götter, Helden und Wieland*, 1774 (*Gods, Heroes, and Wieland*); *Die Xenien*, 1796 (with Friedrich Schiller).

SCIENTIFIC ESSAYS: *Beiträge zur Optik*, 1791–1792; *Morphologie*, 1817–1829.

TRAVEL SKETCHES: *Italienische Reise*, 1816–1817 (*Italian Journeys*).

AUTOBIOGRAPHY: *Aus meinem Leben; Dichtung, und Wahrheit*, 1811–1833 (*Poetry and Truth from My Own Life*).

Johann Wolfgang Goethe, poet, dramatist, philosopher, scientist, and leader of the German intellectual renaissance of the late eighteenth century, was born to a wealthy Frankfort lawyer and his wife on August 28, 1749. Goethe's poetic gift may well have come from his gay and witty mother, whose love of storytelling was early transmitted to her son. Educated at home in an atmosphere of learning and refinement, the boy displayed an unusual facility for languages and versification. An unwilling law student at the University of Leipzig at the age of sixteen, his adolescent disgust with all book learning set the mood for the germination of his masterpiece, *Faust* (1831), which was not to be completed for fifty years. Goethe occupied his time less with studying than with writing verse and two plays, and with what was to become another lifelong habit, falling in love. With these early, relatively insignificant compositions, the author established his practice of highly subjective writing. Later he would learn to universalize the particular, but few of his great works are without a hard core of personal experience.

Recuperating at home from a serious illness during the winter of 1768 and all of 1769, Goethe fell deeply under the influence of a pietist friend of his mother and developed a mystic, deeply personal religious feeling. This preoccupation, along with an intense interest in "natural magic" and all things occult, was soon left behind, but its mark is strongly imprinted on *Faust*. In 1770 Goethe went to Strasbourg to study, this time more medicine than law. Here he made the acquaintance of the German poet, philosopher, and radical patriot, Johann Gottfried von Herder, who taught the young man to admire Homer and Shakespeare and all folk poetry alike as representing the true spirit of their epoch and peoples. He imbued the youth with pride in Germany's cultural heritage and, above all, taught him to regard genuiness of feeling and fullness of life rather than correctness and good taste as the true criteria of good literature.

Under Herder's influence Goethe became a leader of the important *Sturm und Drang* (Storm and Stress) movement, a romantic reaction against the restrictiveness of classical and French influences on literature. Its followers sought to break free of all authority, to put off all that was artificial and contrived and to return to "nature" and "reality," to the intuitive and emotional side of man's nature. The influence of this movement dominates *The Sorrows of Young Werther,* a sentimental novel inspired by another of Goethe's love affairs, this one at Wetzlar in 1772. Written as a series of letters, following the style of Samuel Richardson and Jean Jacques Rousseau, this tale of the effects of love on a sensitive, impressionable youth caused an immediate sensation when it was published and has remained a classic of its type ever since. For all its power and emotional appeal, however, this rather mawkish and morbid book plunged much of the literary world into an orgy of *Weltschmerz* and brooding pessimism from which it was long in recovering.

In 1775 Goethe left his native Frankfort at the invitation of young Karl August, Duke of Weimar, and went to visit the court. The prince and the poet soon became fast friends and a few weeks' visit became a lifetime stay. During his years at Weimar Goethe held various important governmental posts and eventually received a diploma of nobility which allowed him to use the *von* before his surname. Here he pursued studies in mathematics, optics, geology, botany, and anatomy, laying the foundations for scientific papers in which he disagreed with Newton's theory of optics, announced his discovery of a new bone in the skull, and prepared the way for Darwin and Huxley by his investigations into plant and animal life. In 1786 he went to spend a year and a half in Italy, mostly in Rome and Naples. Goethe's Italian sojourn marks an important turning point in his literary development. Abandoning the romantic outpourings of his *Sturm und Drang* period, he strove toward the classical ideals of tranquility of mind and harmony of form. He recast his

play, *Iphigenia in Tauris,* from rhythmic prose into mellifluous blank verse, and when the final version was published in 1787, his treatment of this ancient theme showed his return to the rules of classical forms he had earlier cast off. His *Roman Elegies,* superb elegaic couplets published after his return to Weimar, reflect this new spirit, as well as the inspiration of his latest love, Christiane Vulpius, who was to become his wife in 1806, after she had borne him several children. *Torquato Tasso,* a dramatic consideration of the conflict the author felt in his own mind between the claims of art and of practical affairs, is another of the poetic dramas which are the culmination of the second phase of Goethe's artistic development. Reflective and lyrical rather than dramatic in a stage sense, they show a sensitive understanding of human nature and a newly positive outlook on life and the joys of love.

In 1794 began a friendship between Goethe and the playwright Friedrich Schiller which was to last until the latter's death in 1805. The men had a salutary influence on each other, Schiller continually inspiring the enthusiasm of Goethe, who in turn steadied the thinking of his friend. The two collaborated on the publication of a magazine, *Die Horen,* and together wrote *Die Xenien,* a collection of biting epigrams. Under his friend's influence Goethe finally completed and published *Wilhelm Meister's Apprenticeship* in 1796. This novel, which he had begun some ten years before as the tale of a youth's discovery of his theatrical vocation, had by now grown into a leisurely, discursive novel of eight books in which the author used the framework of young Wilhelm's apprenticeship for life to develop his own philosophy of the necessity of self-discipline in the conduct of living, and to give a minute description of contemporary German life. Another product of this period is the patriotic poem in stately Homeric hexameters, *Hermann and Dorothea*. Written against a background of the upheavals following the French Revolution, for which Goethe felt little sympathy, this idyllic and gently humorous poem displays the warm and human side of the poet's nature at its best.

In the turbulent years of the Napoleonic era Goethe isolated himself from world politics, occupying himself with his literary pursuits, his scientific studies, and work on his autobiography, *Poetry and Truth from My Own Life*. This autobiography is essentially an old man's romantic recollection of his youth, filled with inaccuracies but displaying the beauty of his mature prose style. It was not until 1831, a year before the author's death, that *Faust* was finally published. This dramatic poem, which reflects Goethe's mental and literary development from youth to old age, is the eternal saga of man's struggle for perfection. Lifting many of his own experiences to the level of universal truths, Goethe recounts Faust's bargain with the devil, who will claim his soul at the very moment when he gives him "something worth living for." Disenchanted in turn by knowledge, power, and sensual pleasure, Faust is truly happy only when he becomes engaged in useful, humanitarian labor; and thus God takes his soul at the moment the devil is about to claim it. The great difference between the two parts of this philosophical drama reflects the fact that the first part was written in youth, the second in maturity and old age. From the subjective romantic realism of the first part, which is dominated by the tragic figure of its heroine, Margaret, he turns to a depersonalized symbolic depiction of the climax of Faust's struggle in the second. The complicated symbolism of the "classical" second part makes it far more difficult to understand than the "romantic" first. Taken together, they represent the two most important phases of their author's genius as well as the masterly summation of his philosophy and the culmination of his poetic art. The poet died on March 22, 1832, shortly after the completion of his life work, and was buried by the side of his patron, Duke Karl August, and his friend, Schiller, in the ducal mausoleum at Weimar.

BIBLIOGRAPHICAL REFERENCES: The bibliography of Goethe's own writings is tremendous, his *Gesamtausgabe*, 1887–1918, running to 133 volumes. Most of his important books are available in translation, and there are more than fifty versions of *Faust*, Part I, in English. Perhaps the best known is the translation into rhymed couplets by Alice Raphael, 1930. Other translations in verse include those by J. Anster, 1835, now in the World's Classics series; by Anna Swanwick, in Bohn's Classics, 1849; by Bayard Taylor, 1870, reissued in the Modern Library; and by Philip Wayne, 1949, in the Penguin Classics series. Bayard Quincy Morgan has a translation in prose, 1954. Parts I and II of *Faust* have been translated by Louis MacNeice, 1951. Goethe's autobiography, long unprocurable, was translated by R. O. Moon, 1949. Ludwig Lewisohn, *Goethe: The Story of a Man*, 2 vols., 1949, is a biographical anthology compiled from writings by Goethe and his contemporaries. An excellent background study is Berthold Biermann, *Goethe's World as Seen in Letters and Memoirs*, 1949.

Two useful volumes of selections are *The Permanent Goethe,* edited by Thomas Mann, 1948; and *Goethe: Wisdom and Experience,* edited by Ludwig Curtius and Hermann J. Weigand, 1949.

For most readers the best introduction to Goethe is still George Henry Lewes, *Life of Goethe,* 1855, reissued in Everyman's Library. The most carefully documented biography is W. Bode, *Goethe,* 9 vols., 1920–1927. For biography and criticism see also Rudolf Magnus, *Goethe as a Scientist,* 1906 (tr. 1949); P. H. Brown, *Goethe,* 1920; Benedetto Croce, *Goethe,* 1923; J. G. Robertson, *Goethe,* 1927; Barker Fairley, *Goethe as Revealed in His Poetry,* 1932, and *A Study of Goethe,* 1946; Ernst Cassirer, *Rousseau, Kant, Goethe,* 1945; C. R. Buxton, *Prophets of Heaven and Hell,* 1949; Albert Schweitzer, *Goethe,* 1949; Karl Viëtor, *Goethe the Poet,* 1949; Arnold Bergstraesser, *Goethe's Image of Man and Society,* 1949; Thomas Mann, *Essays of Three Decades,* 1949; and R. D. Gray, *Goethe the Alchemist,* 1952.

NIKOLAI VASILYEVICH GOGOL

Born: Sorochintzy, Russia
Date: March 31, 1809

Died: Moscow, Russia
Date: March 4, 1852

PRINCIPAL WORKS

NOVELS: *Mertvye dushi,* 1842 (*Dead Souls*); *Taras Bulba,* 1842 (expanded version).

SHORT STORIES AND TALES: *Vechera na khutore bliz Dikanki,* 1831–1832 (*Evenings on a Farm near Dikanka*); *Mirgorod,* 1835 ("Taras Bulba," "Viy," "The Old-World Landowners," "How the Two Ivans Quarreled"); *Arabeski,* 1835 (*Arabesques*).

PLAYS: *Revizor,* 1836 (*The Inspector General*); *Zhenit'ba,* 1842 (*The Marriage*).

Nikolai Vasilyevich Gogol was born on March 31, 1809, at Sorochintzy, in the Ukraine, the son of a Cossack landowner. In 1821 he went to the provincial grammar school in Nyezhin, which he attended until 1828. Being of a secretive disposition, Gogol made few friends, even as a child, and he turned to writing at an early age, actually finishing a boyish tragedy entitled *The Brigands.* After leaving school he went to St. Petersburg. Shortly after his arrival there he published, under the pseudonym of V. Alov, an idyllic poem, *Hans Kuchelgarten* (1829), but this work was so harshly ridiculed by the critics that Gogol destroyed as many copies as he could. Deciding to go to America, he traveled as far as Lübeck. There, his funds exhausted, he changed his mind

about migration to the New World and returned to St. Petersburg. He found a post in a government office, settled down to writing, and made the acquaintance of Pushkin and other writers and editors of the capital. As a minor figure in St. Petersburg literary circles, he found it relatively easy to have his writings published in periodicals. *Evenings on a Farm near Dikanka,* a two-volume collection of Cossack stories in which he drew upon memories of his childhood, was well received by readers and critics; Borodin used one of the stories as the basis for an opera. *Mirgorod* was a collection of longer tales, among them "Taras Bulba," his historical romance of fifteenth century Cossack life which he republished in a considerably expanded version in 1842. *Arabesques,* published

431

in 1835, contained a miscellany of stories and essays.

In the meantime Gogol had left the Russian civil service and had become a teacher of history at a school for young women. He became enthusiastic for a career as a historian and planned a history of the medieval period in Little Russia, a work to extend through eight or nine volumes. The work was never written, but on the strength of his plans and through the influence of friends Gogol was appointed professor of history at the University of St. Petersburg. As a lecturer Gogol was a failure, being unprepared to teach his subject, and he resigned after less than a year, in 1835.

Although he had published several volumes of fiction and had worked hard at his literary efforts between 1829 and 1835, Gogol does not seem to have thought of a career as a literary man during that time. Only after the appearance of his satirical play, *The Inspector General*, did he think seriously of literature as a life work. The play, a mordant satire on the Russian bureaucracy of the times, was produced only because of the friendly aid of Tsar Nicholas I in getting it past the censors. The people of officialdom hated the play, but the intellectuals praised Gogol's drama immensely. Shortly after the comedy was produced Gogol went abroad, staying away from Russia, except for brief visits, from 1836 to 1848. During those years he continued to write, and his earlier writings were given adulatory praise by Russians. Following the death of Pushkin, in 1837, Gogol considered himself the leader of Russian literature. In 1840 the first part of *Dead Souls* was finished, and Gogol took it to Moscow for publication. At the same time it

appeared, in 1842, he published the first collected edition of his earlier works, which included his most famous tale, *The Overcoat*.

The publication of *Dead Souls* marks the apex of Gogol's career. Like his great comedy, *The Inspector General*, Gogol's novel is satirical in its account of an unscrupulous rogue who tries through a loophole in Russian taxation and registration at the time, to buy the names of dead serfs to mortgage their labor to the government. For a time the book was taken to be an ordinary realistic satire, but in more recent years critics have seen it as a kind of prophetic work which caricatures what was in Gogol's mind. The book is no longer considered the Russian equivalent of the Spanish *Don Quixote*, which it at least superficially resembles.

Gogol seems to have been the victim of people who wished to reform Russia, and perhaps more than a little of his reputation is the result of their lionizing him. They saw in him a willing spokesman, and he was only too ready to be a leader toward the regeneration of Russia. In a sense Gogol's ability as a creative writer fell victim to his sense of a moral mission. He thought of *Dead Souls* as an epic and planned a second part that would show the regeneration of rogues, but after a great deal of work he destroyed his manuscripts. In 1847 he produced a highly didactic work, *Uybrannye mesta iz perepiski s drazyami* (*Selected Passages from Correspondence with Friends*), in which he preached a doctrine of conformity. The work aroused resentment, and some of Gogol's admirers, expressing disgust that he should write such a book, accused him of excessive pride and of falsifying

Christianity. For an introspective mind like Gogol's such accusations were dangerous. In an effort to redeem himself, for he believed himself damned, he undertook a pilgrimage to the Holy Land. The trip was a religious failure for him, and Gogol considered himself hopelessly lost, giving up to the idea that all of his earlier work was sinful. In another attempt to redeem himself he set to work to write the second part of *Dead Souls*. All the time he worked his health, both physical and mental, became worse. His physical health was especially damaged by ascetic practices he inflicted upon himself. In an excess of mortification, or perhaps a bout with madness, he destroyed his manuscripts, including the unfinished second part of his novel. Afterward he claimed that Satan had played a joke on him and made him do it. Within a few months, obviously suffering from mental illness, Gogol died in Moscow on March 4, 1852.

In some respects Gogol seems never to have reached maturity. He was never married and seemingly never in love. His attitude toward women was mostly that of a boy, impersonal and asexual, in his personal life and in his writings. Although Gogol has received high praise in Russian literature, his contribution was largely inspirational. (It was Dostoevski who said, "We all came out of *The Overcoat*".) Later generations, however, may come to feel that his work has been overrated.

BIBLIOGRAPHICAL REFERENCES: The standard edition is the *Works of Gogol*, translated by Constance Garnett, 6 vols., 1922–1928. *Nikolai Gogol*, 1947, by V. V. Nabokov is probably the most sensitive biography; nevertheless, two other recent studies are wholly reliable—Janko Lavrin, *Nikolai Gogol*, 1952, and David Magarshack, *Gogol: A Life*, 1957. Janko Lavrin's *Russian Writers—Their Lives and Literature*, 1954, includes an excellent chapter on Gogol. D. S. Mirsky, *A History of Russian Literature*, 1934, is still valuable. For recent articles see Nina Brodiansky, "Gogol and His Characters," *Slavonic and East European Review*, XXXI (1953), 36–57; L. I. Strakhovsky, "The Historianism of Gogol," *ibid.*, XII (1953), 360–370; Winston Weathers, "Gogol's *Dead Souls*: The Degrees of Reality," *College English*, XVII (1955), 159–164; and A. Michael, "Gogol and Dickens," *Slavonic and East European Review*, XXXIV (1956), 443–459.

CARLO GOLDONI

Born: Venice, Italy	Died: Paris, France
Date: February 25, 1707	Date: January 6, 1793

PRINCIPAL WORKS

PLAYS: *Belisario*, 1734; *Momolo cortesan*, 1738 (*Momolo the Courtier*); *La Donna di garbo*, 1743; *Il Cavaliere e la dama*, 1749 (*The Gentleman and the Lady*); *La Bottega di caffè*, 1750 (*The Coffee House*); *Il Bugiardo*, 1750 (*The Liar*); *La Locandiera*, 1753 (*The Mistress of the Inn*); *Gl'innamorati*, 1759; *I Rusteghi*, 1760; *Le Baruffe chiozzotte*, 1761; *Le Bourru bienfaisant*, 1771 (*The Beneficent Bear*).

AUTOBIOGRAPHY: *Mémoires de Carlo Goldoni*, 1787.

Born near St. Thomas' Church in Venice, on February 25, 1707, Carlo Goldoni was the son of Giulio of Modena, a physician. After removing to

Rome and then Perugia, the doctor abandoned his son in Rimini, after putting him in charge of a professor whom the boy disliked and deserted in order to follow a troupe of strolling players. Goldoni showed an early interest in puppets and wrote a play for them at the age of eight. His favorite reading consisted of plays, and he was influenced by the comedies of Cicognini as well as Machiavelli's *Mandragola*.

For a time he prepared himself for the law, studying in Venice and Pavia but taking his degree in Modena. Even in his student days he devoted much time to the theater and was driven from Pavia because of a satire directed at the leading citizens. He was devoted to Molière's belief that drama must break from the superficial and mirror man's essential nature. Attempting tragedy for his first professionally produced play, *Amalasunta* (1732), he was unsuccessful. He broke from the *commedia dell'arte* theater of rigid improvisation, then on the decline, and gave the Italian theater new life with sparkling satires on war, male supremacy, foppish manners, and other matters of social satire. He wrote as many as fifteen plays a year and became so well known that he was called to France and the court of Louis XVI, who bestowed on him a pension for life. The Revolution, however, forced him to live out his last years in poverty. He died in Paris on January 6, 1793.

BIBLIOGRAPHICAL REFERENCES: Apart from the *Memoirs*, edited, with an introduction by W. A. Drake, 1926, the chief source for biographical information is Joseph S. Kennard, *Goldoni and the Venice of his Time*, 1920. Of use in studying Goldoni's critical principles and literary aims is *Goldoni on Playwriting*, by F. C. L. van Steenderen, with an introduction by H. C. Chatfield-Taylor, 1919. This volume is a collection of passages from Goldoni's writings. For an extensive bibliography on Goldoni see H. C. Chatfield-Taylor, *Goldoni: A Biography*, 1913.

OLIVER GOLDSMITH

Born: Ballymahon, Ireland
Date: November 10, 1728

Died: London, England
Date: April 4, 1774

PRINCIPAL WORKS

NOVEL: *The Vicar of Wakefield*, 1766.

PLAYS: *The Good-Natured Man*, 1768; *She Stoops to Conquer*, 1773.

POEMS: *The Traveler*, 1764; *The Deserted Village*, 1770.

ESSAYS AND STUDIES: *Enquiry into the Present State of Polite Learning in Europe*, 1759; *The Citizen of the World*, 1762.

Oliver Goldsmith was born on November 10, 1728, son of a Protestant clergyman in Ballymahon, a small and poor village in County Longford, Ireland. When Oliver was two years old his father succeeded to a more lucrative parish and moved his family to Lissoy, Westmeath. There was little in Goldsmith's early life to point him toward literature—not education, not any early manifested talent. He was first taught at home by a maid-servant;

then at the Lissoy village school; still later in first one and then another of various boarding schools as the occasion demanded. Small in stature, pitted with smallpox, awkward in manner, he was the butt of his schoolmates' jokes, and was to his schoolmasters "a stupid, heavy blockhead." Curiously, and in spite of the tradition our psychological novelists have established in situations of this kind, Goldsmith was not soured on life; nor was he filled with great ambitions for proving his worth to the world. His characteristic good nature was not altered, and his characteristic indolence held fast.

About the time he was to enter college, his sister married a well-to-do young man and his father felt obliged to send her forth with a suitable dowry. Perhaps this gallant and prideful care left the girl in comfortable circumstances, but the resultant depletion of the family treasury made it necessary for young Oliver to attend the university as a sizar instead of as a pensioner. This was a blow to the boy's pride, but with characteristic good humor, he let himself be won over to the idea. He passed the college entrance examination—last on the list—and entered Trinity College in 1745.

His academic standing and economic status at Trinity College are largely matters of conjecture, but we know that he was baited and occasionally beaten by his tutor and that he was perpetually without funds. His father died about this time and Oliver was made dependent on the kindness of his uncle, Mr. Contarine, who apparently had a fund of that fine virtue: Goldsmith continued to petition him for money which was promptly lost at the gaming tables or spent in roisterous frolics. One such frolic in Oliver's rooms was interrupted by a surprise visit from Oliver's tutor, who, in righteous indignation at such unrestraint, struck the boy before his friends. Goldsmith's sanguinity was for once overcome, and he retaliated in a noble fashion: he packed his bags in the night and left school. He was persuaded to return, however; the departure was condoned somehow, and he was graduated in 1749—last on the list.

The next years were chiefly devoted to idleness and a penniless Grand Tour through Europe, ostensibly in search of a medical degree. In his petitions to his uncle for money he cited the names of more than one famous scholar from whose fount he was drinking deeply of learning. Modern investigation has found not one of those men to have been existent, at that time or any other. Nevertheless, Oliver got his medical degree somehow, somewhere, though it was not founded on enough knowledge for him to practice in England.

Oliver arrived in London about 1756, penniless, without work, and without ideas for any. He worked intermittently at proof-reading for Samuel Richardson's press, at ushering for a school, and finally gravitated almost as a last resort to hack-writing, living the while in first one and then another of London's slum garrets. His first hack-writings (1757) were book reviews for the bookseller Griffiths, a hard taskmaster. Goldsmith and Griffiths quarreled often, and soon their association was all but broken off. Ever thereafter, Goldsmith continued to inveigh against critics, of whose number he himself had been an unwilling member. His first public criticism of professional criticism appeared in *An Enquiry into the Present State of Polite Learning in*

435

Europe, in which little volume he kicked enough notable critical shins to attract attention. It is for this notoriety chiefly that the book is noteworthy, though the graceful, supple, antithetical style so characteristic of the mature Goldsmith was already beginning to be apparent in his writing.

The reputation—or notoriety—that this book got for him also secured for him the editorship of *The Bee,* a weekly periodical which shortly failed, but not before Goldsmith was sought out by Smollett, who wished him to write for the *British Magazine,* and by the great Samuel Johnson, who made him a protégé.

This latter recognition marked the turn in his literary career, but not in his financial circumstances. For though Goldsmith made considerable money in his later years, became and has remained one of the most popular English writers, he died in London on April 4, 1774, in debt for £2000.

Goldsmith's most notable literary works are now but two: *The Vicar of Wakefield,* a novel, and *She Stoops to Conquer,* a play. Two others, *The Deserted Village,* a poem, and *The Good-Natured Man,* a play, should perhaps also be mentioned, the first because of its lasting popularity; the second because of its pertinence to his last and best comedy.

The Vicar of Wakefield structurally follows the Book of Job: "You take a good man, overwhelm him with successive misfortunes, show the pure flame of his soul burning in the midst of the darkness, and then, as the reward of his patience and fortitude and submission, restore him gradually to happiness, with even more flocks and herds than before." The plot of the novel, as was usual with Goldsmith, is

the weak part of the story, being full of wild improbabilities. The strong part of the story, that which has made the book so popular, is its simple but perfect description of domestic life, set forth even in the midst of incremental distresses in a style idyllically tender, pathetic, slyly humorous, and full of grace and charm. This graceful style, reminiscent of Pope, and this warm sly humor, distinctive of Goldsmith, permeate the best of his work and guarantee him an audience so long as these traits appeal to men.

The Deserted Village shows these traits of Goldsmith in verse. The piece is anachronistic in that it looks back past the verse forms of Collins and Thomson and Gray to the heroic couplets of Pope. But the couplet in Goldsmith's hands is not the tool for flagellant satire that it was for Pope: it is as precise, but more warm and human. The poem presents the economic difficulties of rural life, the dangers of luxury and "trade's unfeeling train" in "Auburn, loveliest village of the plain." The story the poem tells is, according to Macaulay, "something that never was, and never will be, seen in any part of the world." That may well be; but the nostalgia and the easy presentation of the poem make it very gratifying to read, and one of the most popular poems in English literature.

It is in the drama, however, with two comedies, that Goldsmith's influence on his successors has been most felt. With Steele and Cibber in the first quarter of the eighteenth century, the not unnatural reaction against the immorality of Restoration plays culminated in a type of comedy hardly worthy of the name. The popular plays had by Goldsmith's time all become the weeping, sentimental kind; everything vulgar

436

and vigorous was left out. Drama had perhaps not been in a worse state since the theaters were closed upon Shirley in 1642. Goldsmith was moved to animosity, a rare feeling for him. In his *Enquiry into . . . Learning* in 1759, he had attacked the managers of the theaters for their abject pandering to the public taste, and had offended David Garrick. In 1768, when the *Good-Natured Man* appeared at Covent Garden, Garrick had not forgotten. He produced Hugh Kelley's latest weeping comedy at Drury Lane in competition with Goldsmith's play to hurt its success. Perhaps he needed not have bothered. Goldsmith had been restrained and apprehensive even in the play's composition. He wept after its production. The play has touches of the easy dialogue that would later make *She Stoops to Conquer,* and some excellent scenes—notably that one which most offended the taste of the audience, in which two bailiffs masquerade as fine gentlemen—but in the whole there is a lack of focus and structure and overall comic effect. The play was a gesture, however, that bade well for the future.

When *She Stoops to Conquer* appeared five years later, it was a rousing success, and has remained one of the half dozen most popular comedies in English drama. It was early recognized as almost farce, and while it was ill-bred in Goldsmith's time to laugh loudly, the play made Horace Walpole "laugh very much." Like *The Vicar of Wakefield,* the play is defective in plot and in plausibility. The continued mistaking of the Hardcastle mansion for an inn, and the inability of bashful young Marlow to tell a barmaid from a young lady—these things do not stand analysis. But while one is seeing the play, these things do not matter. The natural and homey action, not artificially sensitive as in sentimental comedy nor artificially brittle as in Restoration comedy, and the nice compromise between the old Anglo-Saxon slapstick and intellectual wit combine to make the play a comic masterpiece.

The play is not overtly anti-sentimental; Goldsmith had learned his lesson. But it restored true humor to English comedy and it taught playgoers to laugh again. They went away from the playhouse with wet eyes as usual, but for a different reason from the usual one. They felt less pious perhaps, but they were in better spirits. Goldsmith wrote once: "Innocently to amuse the imagination in this dream of life is wisdom." If that be accepted as true, then Oliver Goldsmith, with all his many faults, was very wise.

BIBLIOGRAPHICAL REFERENCES: The latest edition is *The Works of Oliver Goldsmith,* edited by J. W. M. Gibbs, 5 vols., 1884–1886. Also available are, *The Plays of Oliver Goldsmith,* 1901, and *Complete Poetical Works of Oliver Goldsmith,* 1906, both edited by Austin Dobson; *New Essays by Oliver Goldsmith,* edited by R. S. Crane, 1927; and *The Collected Letters of Oliver Goldsmith,* edited by K. C. Balderston, 1928. The most thorough biography is Sir James Prior, *The Life of Oliver Goldsmith,* 2 vols., 1837. There are a number of other reliable studies: John Forster, *The Life and Times of Oliver Goldsmith,* 2 vols., 1854; Austin Dobson, *The Life of Oliver Goldsmith,* 1899; H. J. Smith, *The Citizen of the World,* 1926; and Temple Scott, *Oliver Goldsmith Bibliographically and Biographically Considered,* 1928. See also James Boswell, *Life of Samuel Johnson,* edited by C. B. Tinker, new edition, 1953.

IVAN ALEXANDROVICH GONCHAROV

Born: Simbirsk, Russia
Date: July 18, 1812

Died: St. Petersburg, Russia
Date: September 28, 1891

PRINCIPAL WORKS

NOVELS: *Obyknovennaya Istoria,* 1847 (*A Common Story*); *Oblomov,* 1858; *Obryv,* 1869 (*The Precipice*).

TRAVEL AND DESCRIPTION: *Fregat Pallada,* 1856 (*The Frigate Pallas*).

Ivan Alexandrovich Goncharov was born at Simbirsk on July 18 (July 6 O.S.), 1812, into a well-to-do merchant family living the manorial life of idle Russian gentry, the class for which the future novelist was to establish an enduring symbol in the character of Oblomov. His uneventful adult life was spent in St. Petersburg as a civil servant and later as a literary censor. Although he was, according to Tolstoy, a thorough townsman, Goncharov demonstrated in his novels a profound concern for the disintegration of gentry traditions. *A Common Story,* published when its author was already thirty-five, traces the disillusioning sentimental education of an idealist who makes the transition from an idyllic country estate to St. Petersburg at the cost of becoming a smug opportunist.

In 1849 Goncharov published *The Dream of Oblomov,* a lyrical evocation of the lost paradise of childhood and manorial life, which was later incorporated into his masterpiece, *Oblomov.* The hero, who gives the novel its title, is a cultured, intelligent man of generous impulses who is hopelessly slothful and ineffectual—indeed for a number of pages he cannot even get out of bed—and who sinks slowly and undramatically into the depths of what he himself calls "Oblomovism." This char-acterization was immediately recognized as representing a significant type in Russian society, and the name Oblomov became proverbial. In his autobiographical essay, *Better Late than Never* (1870), Goncharov himself remarked that he intended to present the lethargy of Russia in contrast to the ferment of foreign influences; the author's unconscious sympathy, however, is obviously for Oblomov.

Goncharov worked slowly on another novel, *The Precipice,* which shows again a talented, intelligent man doomed to remain a dilettante and a young man torn between the old values and the new. The book contains, besides, a sympathetic portrait of an old-style grandmother, and an unsympathetic portrait of a modern nihilist.

In addition to novels, Goncharov wrote during this time a handful of stories and a long account of a trip to Japan, *The Frigate Pallas.* After retirement in 1867 he wrote reminiscence, criticism, a few stories, and in the 1870's a curious book, *An Uncommon Story* (not published until 1924), which shows Goncharov in a pathological light, suffering from the delusion that Turgenev and others had stolen his ideas. He lived quietly until his death in St. Petersburg on September 28 (September 15 O.S.), 1891.

BIBLIOGRAPHICAL REFERENCES: The prime source for biographical, critical, and bibliographical information is Janko Lavrin, *Goncharov,* 1954. See also Lavrin,

Russian Writers—Their Lives and Literature, 1954. Reliable critical estimates of Goncharov are included in Richard Hare, *Russian Literature,* 1947; and Marc Slonim, *The Epic of Russian Literature,* 1950.

THE GONCOURTS
Edmond Louis Antoine Huot de Goncourt

Born: Nancy, France   *Died:* Champrosay, France
Date: May 26, 1822   *Date:* July 16, 1896

Jules Alfred Huot de Goncourt

Born: Paris, France   *Died:* Paris
Date: December 17, 1830   *Date:* June 20, 1870

Principal Works

NOVELS: *Charles Demailly,* 1860; *Sœur Philomène,* 1861; *Renée Mauperin,* 1864; *Germinie Lacerteux,* 1865; *Manette Salomon,* 1867; *Madame Gervaisais,* 1869.

HISTORY: *Histoire de la société française pendant la Révolution,* 1854; *Portraits intimes du dix-huitieme siècle,* 1857–1858; *La Femme au dix-huitieme siècle,* 1862; *L'art dix-huitieme siècle,* 1859–1875.

AUTOBIOGRAPHY: *Le Journal des Goncourt,* 1887–1896.

Edmond and Jules de Goncourt were for the most part brought up and educated by their mother, their father having died when the brothers were quite young. Although Edmond was early sent away to school, Jules, a more delicate boy, received much of his education at home. After their mother's death in 1848 the young men, being in comfortable financial circumstances, established themselves in Paris quarters and embarked upon a long career of writing, historical research, art collecting, and travel.

In their younger days many of their vacations were spent traveling on the Continent. Much of their early writing appeared in two newspapers started by their cousin. As a climax to their journalistic career, they were on one instance hauled into court for having written what was felt to be an immoral piece. From journalism they turned their attention to historical subjects. Having acquired an avid interest in the eighteenth century, they published a small group of remarkable works picturing aspects of French society during that period. These books were grounded in careful research among the minor documents of the age, playbills, popular ballads, engravings. Not only did the Goncourts have an interest in the past, but they also had a fine curiosity about what they saw of the people and places around them in the present. Accordingly, they began to write novels in which they described, rather thinly disguised, people who had interested them and places which they had known. *Renée Mauperin* for example, was suggested by a high-spirited and intelligent young girl who had attracted the brothers years before. *Germinie Lacerteux* is largely a portrait of their housekeeper who, as the brothers learned after her death, had

439

been leading a double life and had thereby incurred many debts and a fatal disease. Although these and a few other novels produced some stir in literary circles, they did not all receive complete approbation by either critics or public.

By this time the Goncourt brothers had become well-known figures in Paris. They took an interest in struggling young writers and artists, and they numbered among their literary friends figures like Sainte-Beuve, Gautier, Flaubert, George Sand, and Zola. In *The Goncourt Journals* they present a lively and intimate picture of life in Paris during these years. In these pages one finds recorded much of the brilliant conversation at the literary Magny dinners, choice gossip about the great and near-great of Parisian society, and minute observations of two perceptive men on everything from a young girl in an omnibus to a Japanese vase. Exquisite taste and keen intellect illuminate many of the pages.

In his late thirties Jules de Goncourt began to grow sickly and eventually lost many of his faculties of both body and mind. Some of the most moving pages in the *Journal* are those of Edmond in which he describes this pitiful final illness of his brother, who died in Paris on June 20, 1870. Edmond lived on for twenty-six years, writing a few novels (*La fille Elisa*, 1878; *La Faustin*, 1882; *Chérie*, 1884) and working on plans which he and his brother had conceived for an Academy to help struggling writers. This is the Académie des Goncourt, founded in 1900.

The novels of the Goncourts have a secure place in the history of fiction because of their insistence on stark realism. In this respect they influenced several later writers, notably Zola and Daudet. In an almost clinical manner they record the most minute details, many of them sordid, of a human life or a human institution. In doing so, however, they seem to sacrifice a certain amount of unity of theme and tightness of plot construction; consequently, their influence has been in the field of subject matter and style.

BIBLIOGRAPHICAL REFERENCES: For biography and criticism see M. A. Belloc and M. Shedlock, *Edmund and Jules de Goncourt*, 1895; Laura Martin Jarman, *The Goncourt Brothers: Modernists in Abnormal Psychology*, 1939; and George Saintsbury, *A History of the French Novel*, 1917–1919.

CAROLINE GORDON

Born: Todd County, Kentucky
Date: October 6, 1895

PRINCIPAL WORKS

NOVELS: *Penhally*, 1931; *Aleck Maury, Sportsman*, 1934; *None Shall Look Back*, 1937; *The Garden of Adonis*, 1937; *Green Centuries*, 1941; *The Women on the Porch*, 1944; *The Strange Children*, 1951; *The Malefactors*, 1956.
SHORT STORIES: *The Forest of the South*, 1945.

Caroline Gordon, wife of the poet and critic, Allen Tate, has written novels and short stories since the publication of her first book, *Penhally* in

1931, and she has taught writing at Columbia and other universities. The region around Clarksville, Tennessee, near which she was born on October 6, 1895, is the scene of her first four novels, and, indeed, the locale as well as the refined and complex sense of ante-bellum Southern culture in her work relates it to that of William Faulkner, Katherine Anne Porter, and Eudora Welty. Miss Gordon, named a Guggenheim Fellow in 1932 and awarded the second O. Henry prize in the same year, won early recognition of her "unsalable" fiction.

Her writing is sensuous and sugges-tive rather than explicit, impressively tragic without being spectacular. In *None Shall Look Back* the Civil War slowly breaks the spirit of almost all her characters; in *The Women on the Porch* love in New York becomes worthless without a sense of attach-ment to tradition; and in many of her short stories evil is shown gradually encroaching on a world of innocence. The historical poignancy of a vanished Southern tradition has perhaps become theologically defined in later novels such as *The Strange Children* and *The Malefactors*, works implying that alienation is part of man's destiny.

BIBLIOGRAPHICAL REFERENCES: There is no extensive criticism of Caroline Gordon. See Andrew Lytle, "Caroline Gordon and the Historic Image," *Sewanee Review*, LVII (1949), 560–586; Vivienne Koch, "The Conservatism of Caroline Gordon," in *Southern Renascence: The Literature of the Modern South*, edited by Louis D. Rubin, Jr., and Robert D. Jacobs, 1953; and Willard Thorp, "The Way Back and The Way Up: The Novels of Caroline Gordon," *Bucknell Review*, VI (1956), 1–15. *Critique*, I (1956), 3–78, contained articles on Caroline Gordon by various hands.

MAXIM GORKY
Aleksei Maksimovich Peshkov

Born: Nizhni-Novgorod, Russia
Date: March 28, 1868

Died: Moscow, Russia
Date: June 18, 1936

PRINCIPAL WORKS

NOVELS: *Foma Gordeyev*, 1899; *Troye*, 1901 (*Three Men*); *Byvshie lyudi*, 1905 (*Creatures That Once Were Men*); *Mat*, 1907–1908 (*Mother*); *Ispoved*, 1908 (*The Confession*); *Delo Artamonovykh*, 1925 (*The Artamonov Business*); *Klim Samgin— Sorok let*, 1927–1936 (*The Life of Klim Samgin: The Bystander*, 1930; *The Magnet*, 1931; *Other Fires*, 1933; *The Specter*, 1938).

PLAYS: *Meschane*, 1902 (*The Smug Citizens*); *Na dne*, 1902 (*The Lower Depths*); *Dachniki*, 1905 (*Summer Folk*); *Starik*, 1915 (*The Judge*); *Yegor Bulichov*, 1932; *Dostigayev i drugiye*, 1934 (*Dostigayev and the Others*).

AUTOBIOGRAPHY: *Detstvo*, 1913 (*My Childhood*); *Vlyudyakh*, 1915–1916 (*In the World*); *Moi Universitety*, 1923 (*My Universities*).

In the work of Aleksei Maksimovich Peshkov, who renamed himself Maxim Gorky (or Gorki, Bitter), can be dis-covered the recent history of the Rus-sian people, their politics, and their literature. More than any other author he succeeded in mirroring the hectic times which gave him birth, set his style, and supported his efforts. Born into pain and degradation at Nizhni-Novgorod, March 28, 1868, he made everything he wrote a biography of Russia in upheaval. Early orphaned from his upholsterer father and peasant mother, he was brought up by his tyrannical grandfather and a sympathetic grandmother. At the age of nine he was apprenticed to a shoemaker, only to run away as cabin boy on a Volga River steamer. A genial cook taught him to read, the most important single event in his life. He had only two years of formal schooling, attended by so much hardship that he later attempted suicide by shooting himself through the lung. The succession of jobs, wanderings, and hardships makes up a bitter anthology of misery which he was forever describing, not only in his reminiscences but in his novels and plays as well.

His first real opportunity came when a lawyer from his home town (later renamed Gorky) hired the young drifter and helped to educate and civilize him. But Gorky's innate love of wandering and observing forced him to travel to other parts of Russia, and it was from this trip that he gained confidence in his ability to portray his people and their ways. He turned to journalism and wrote his first story for a Tiflis paper in 1892; from that time on he made his way by his pen. He attracted the interest of two great literary men, Korolenko and Chekhov, both of whom proved influential in developing his talents in fiction and drama respectively. He married in 1896 while a writer for the *Samarskaya Gazete,* and in 1898 he published his first collection of short stories. These established his fame in Europe and America as well as Russia.

Chekhov's introduction of Gorky to the Moscow Art Players led to a memorable event in world theater: by persuasion Gorky wrote an anti-middle-class play *The Smug Citizens,* which aroused controversy when produced but which convinced him that the theater could be a mouthpiece for his revolutionary beliefs. *Na dne,* known in English as *The Lower Depths,* became the proletarian drama of the century; anthologized everywhere though not often staged these days, it produced a great furor which has only recently died down. In this work Luka, the wandering pilgrim, brings peace and hope to the downtrodden Russian poor but may well have caused uprising everywhere. The play with its romantic and mystic overtones is almost certainly not the great play it was once thought to be, but it served its author's purpose. His revolutionist activities thereafter made him the spokesman for the masses, and in 1905 he was involved in the uprising which caused him to flee the country. A brief visit to America to raise funds for the revolutionary cause left him embittered at his lack of success; he then returned to Russia where he worked on a literary magazine from 1913 to the Revolution. He sided with the Bolsheviks at that time but broke with them immediately after, and in 1922 he left the country in disagreement over censorship. In 1928 he returned for a visit and fell once more under the sway of communism, this time as Russia's favorite son and one of the heroes of the Revolution. His conformity and party working seem amazing in this man who had never sided long with any faction, but apparently the effort was a genuine one. As Stalin's voice, he published a work known in English as *On*

Guard for the Soviet Union (1933), a sharp criticism of his country's critics and an official statement on political behavior.

It is extremely difficult to say what work of Gorky's will live: most certainly he will find no posterity in his political, social, or historical-critical works. His brief sketches of Russian life found scattered throughout his stories and novels and his sympathetic evocations of pity and compassion for the peasants will no doubt be long read and admired. He is a kind of amalgam of the three great Russians whom he knew, admired, and wrote about: Tolstoy, Chekhov, and Andreyev. No doubt his concessions to political expediency will hurt his reputation for some time to come, and indeed his drive to propagandize puts him well below those three greats, at least in artistry. On the other hand, the genius of the man shows through most strikingly in the frankly autobiographical works; in fact, his observations of Russian life are so highly colored by his own emotional and intuitive responses that the soul of the man is seen everywhere. Many critics, since they see everywhere the compassionate and sympathetic individualist, feel certain that he did not really approve of the New Russia, except as a means to an end—and a very different end indeed. This viewpoint gives some credence to the belief that he was actually murdered, and not by the anti-Stalinists who suffered the death penalty for alleged complicity in the plot, but by order of the Party. His death occurred at Moscow on June 18, 1936.

BIBLIOGRAPHICAL REFERENCES: Of primary interest are Gorky's volumes of autobiography: My Childhood, 1913; In the World, 1915–1916; My University Days, 1923 (also published as My Universities), and Fragments From My Diary, 1924. The first three are in a convenient one-volume edition, The Autobiography of Maxim Gorky, translated by Isidor Schneider, 1949. Three biographical studies may be singled out: M. J. Olgin, Maxim Gorky: Writer and Revolutionist, 1933; A. I. Roskin, From the Banks of the Volga, translated 1946; and Filia Holtzman, Young Maxim Gorky, 1868–1902, 1948. Interesting studies appear in J. G. Huneker, Iconoclasts, 1905; and Ashley Dukes, Modern Dramatists, 1911. See also Stefan Zweig, "Maxim Gorki," Virginia Quarterly Review, V (1929), 492–501.

GOTTFRIED VON STRASSBURG

Born: Germany (?)
Date: Late twelfth century (?)

Died: Unknown
Date: Unknown

PRINCIPAL WORK

EPIC POEM: Tristan und Isolde, c. 1210.

So little is known of the life of Gottfried von Strassburg, the German court poet, that it seems remarkable any of his work would yet remain. He most certainly lived during the thirteenth century in the city that formed his name, and he wrote the finest extant version of the Tristan and Isolde story. He seems not to have come from a noble family since he is addressed as *meister* rather than *herr*.

There is little doubt of his erudition,

443

for his allusions to learned things, his knowledge of earlier versions of the central legend, his sophisticated poetic forms all show wide education. In his version Tristan goes to Ireland in order to bring back Isolde, bride of his uncle, the King of Cornwall. By mistake the two drink a love potion and so are bound irrevocably to one another. For a time they deceive the cuckold king. When their guilty love is revealed, Tristan flees to Normandy, where he marries a different Isolde and where he is wounded by a poisoned spear. Only the Irish Isolde can cure him, but the jealous wife makes him believe she cannot come. His death moves the king to pity, and he has the lovers buried side by side. This latter part is taken from fragments written in continuation by two followers of Gottfried, Ulrich von Türheim and Heinrich von Freiberg.

It is now fairly certain that Gottfried alone succeeded in the task so many other French and German poets had tried: Chrétien de Troyes, the *trouvère* Thomas, and Eilhart von Oberge among others who attempted the Tristan and Isolde theme. Many translations have been made of the epic, but none improves upon the original. The psychological overtones, the deft poetic insights, and the lack of didacticism make this one of the unique and original masterpieces of world literature. Richard Wagner did well to use this version in his famous music drama.

BIBLIOGRAPHICAL REFERENCES: The prime sources of information about the work of Gottfried von Strassburg are the various editions of his work. *The Story of Tristan and Iseult*, rendered into English by Jessie L. Weston, 1907, is in condensed form. *Tristan und Isolt: A Poem*, edited by August Closs, 1947, includes an introduction, notes, glossary, and facsimiles. *The "Tristan and Isolde" of Gottfried von Strassburg*, translated and edited by Edwin H. Zeydel, 1948, includes an introduction, notes, and connecting summaries.

REMY DE GOURMONT

Born: Bazoches-en-Houlme, France
Date: April 4, 1858

Died: Paris, France
Date: September 27, 1915

PRINCIPAL WORKS

NOVELLAS AND TALES: *Histoires magiques*, 1895; *Les Chevaux de Diomède*, 1897 (*The Horses of Diomede*); *Le Pèlerin du silence*, 1906; *Un Nuit au Luxembourg*, 1906 (*A Night in the Luxembourg*); *Un Cœur virginal*, 1907 (*A Virgin Heart*).

PLAYS: *Lilith*, 1892; *Théodat*, 1894; *Le Vieux Roi*, 1897; *L'Ombre d'une femme*, 1925.

POEMS: *Hiéroglpyhes*, 1894; *Les Saintes du Paradis*, 1898; *Les Divertissements*, 1912.

ESSAYS AND STUDIES: *Le Livre des Masques*, 1896 (*The Book of Masques*); *Esthétique de la langue française*, 1899; *Le Problème du style*, 1902; *Epilogues*, 1903–1913; *Promenades littéraires*, 1904–1927; *Promenades philosophiques*, 1905–1909.

Remy de Gourmont was an example of a literary type not uncommon in the nineteenth century, the detached observer of life. Never an active participant in everyday affairs, he seems nevertheless to have observed and understood almost everything that went on around him.

Born on April 4, 1858 in Bazoches-en-Houlme, an obscure village in Normandy, he went to Paris in 1883, after having been educated in Caen, a northern seaport near the English Channel. In this year he took the only regular job he ever held, as an assistant librarian at the Bibliothèque Nationale, a position from which he was subsequently discharged in 1891 for writing an article displeasing to the authorities. In that same year, he helped to found the *Mercure de France,* a publication to which he contributed for the next twenty years.

The book which first displayed Gourmont's critical abilities at their fullest was his *The Book of Masques,* critical studies dealing with the authors of the Symbolist School, a group that profoundly affected Gourmont's art and thought. This series was followed by his *Epilogues,* a set of sketches on contemporary life published in the *Mercure.* One of the most valuable achievements of Gourmont's early critical work was his calling attention to the writings of then little known men such as Huysmans, Mallarmé, and Nietzsche. Later studies, *Promenades littéraires* and *Promenades philosophiques,* covered a wide range of intellectual topics. But Gourmont's interest lay chiefly in matters of style and

in literature as a pure art form, as he demonstrated in his *Le Problème du style.* One of the salient features of his artistic approach to literature was his practice of breaking up traditional images and ideas into parts so that these divisions could be individually analyzed and reassembled into new patterns and associations.

After 1891, Gourmont lived the life of a semi-recluse, observing and noting, but not engaging in life actively. The most intense part of his life was lived in his own mind, as reflected in his novelettes, *The Horses of Diomede, A Night in the Luxembourg,* and *A Virgin Heart.* Although few of his characters really come alive, these novels are illuminated by a lucid and individual intelligence. In *A Night in the Luxembourg* he reveals also his defiance of religious convention.

Remy de Gourmont died of a cerebral hemorrhage in Paris on September 27, 1915, while writing a condemnation of the German bombing of Rheims Cathedral after the invasion of 1914. At last the detached, coolly logical critic and philosopher had been moved to patriotic passion. Never popular with the general public, Gourmont has always had a small but enthusiastic following among those who could appreciate his profound and subtle literary theorizing.

BIBLIOGRAPHICAL REFERENCES: Some of Gourmont's fiction, including *A Night in the Luxembourg* and *A Virgin Heart,* is available in translation. Richard Aldington has edited *Selections from the Writings of Remy de Gourmont,* 1928. For biography and criticism see Richard Aldington, *Remy de Gourmont, Modern Man of Letters,* 1928; P. E. Jacob, *Remy de Gourmont,* 1932; and G. Rees, *Remy de Gourmont: Essai de bibliographie intellectuelle,* 1939.

KENNETH GRAHAME

Born: Edinburgh, Scotland　　　　　　　Died: Pangbourne, England
Date: March 8, 1859　　　　　　　　　　Date: July 6, 1932

PRINCIPAL WORKS

FANTASY: *The Wind in the Willows,* 1908.
BELLES-LETTRES: *Pagan Papers,* 1893; *The Golden Age,* 1895; *Dream Days,* 1898.
MISCELLANEOUS: *The Headswoman,* 1898; *The Kenneth Grahame Book,* 1933; *First Whisper of "The Wind in the Willows,"* 1944.

Kenneth Grahame, author of *The Wind in the Willows,* one of the most beloved books of the twentieth century, was born in Edinburgh on March 8, 1859. Orphaned at an early age, he was brought up by relatives in Berkshire and was educated at St. Edward's School, Oxford, and Summertown. He became a clerk in the Bank of England in 1879, and after nineteen years' service he was appointed Secretary of the Bank, in which capacity he retired, in 1908, after two serious illnesses. (The second of these was caused by a wound he suffered when a lunatic fired off a revolver in the bank.) Withdrawing to his boyhood home at Blewbury, Grahame and his wife spent almost a quarter of a century in enjoyment of the tranquil Berkshire countryside; their life was marred, in 1920, by the death of their only child, Alastair, who was killed by a train while an undergraduate at Oxford. After his retirement Grahame wrote only spasmodically. His later writings include introductions to a few books, among them his anthologies, *The Cambridge Book of Poetry for Children* (1916) and *The Cambridge Book of Poetry for Young People* (1916). For the most part he devoted his leisure to reading and to observations of nature.

Grahame's literary career began in the 1880's with occasional poetry and with prose essays, the latter encouraged by W. E. Henley, who published some of them in the *National Observer.* When Grahame prepared a collection of these under the title *Pagan Papers,* in 1893, the book met with immediate success. In the next three or four years he contributed other prose sketches to *The Yellow Book,* and in 1895 he issued his second volume, *The Golden Age,* combining material from the first with pieces he had written in the interim since its publication. A sequel, *Dream Days,* appeared in 1898. *The Golden Age* and *Dream Days,* drawn from Grahame's own childhood, give some of the most charming and nostalgic glimpses of child life in all of English *belles-lettres.*

The Wind in the Willows was started informally as a series of stories told by Grahame to his six-year-old son, nicknamed "Mouse." In 1907 the child was sent away for a seaside holiday, and during his absence the father wrote frequent letters expanding the chronicle of Mole, Ratty, Toad, and Badger, the heroes of his narrative. These letters, published as *First Whisper of "The Wind in the Willows,"* under the editorship of Grahame's widow, Elspeth Grahame, show the impeccable sensitivity of his style even in his first drafts. *The Wind in the Willows,* though slow to establish itself in the public admiration, eventually surpassed his earlier books in popularity. Its jollity and coziness appear certain to remain attractive, despite a vein of sentimentality; this, moreover, is not unwholesome. The book has been sympathetically illustrated by E. H. Shepard, Arthur Rackham, and others. Parts of it were dramatized in 1929 by the late A. A. Milne as *Toad of Toad Hall*. Several of Grahame's stories, among them "The Reluctant Dragon," have been adapted for motion pictures. He died in Pangbourne, England, on July 6, 1932.

BIBLIOGRAPHICAL REFERENCES: *The Kenneth Grahame Book*, 1933, contains a posthumous collection of his unpublished work. See also P. R. Chalmers, *Kenneth Grahame: Life, Letters and Unpublished Work*, 1933; A. Pryce-Jones, "Kenneth Grahame," *London Mercury*, XXVI (1932), 446–449; and E. Holt, "Kenneth Grahame: An Appreciation," *Bookman* (London), LXXXII (1932), 234. See also D. M. Fyrth, *Étude littéraire Kenneth Grahame*, 1937.

HARLEY GRANVILLE-BARKER

Born: London, England
Date: November 25, 1877

Died: Paris, France
Date: August 31, 1946

PRINCIPAL WORKS

PLAYS: *Three Plays*, 1909 (*The Marrying of Ann Leete, The Voysey Inheritance, Waste*); *The Madras House*, 1910; *Three Short Plays*, 1917 (*Rococo, Vote by Ballot, Farewell to the Theatre*); *The Secret Life*, 1923; *His Majesty*, 1928.

ESSAYS AND STUDIES: *A National Theatre*, 1907 (with William Archer); *The Exemplary Theatre*, 1922; *Prefaces to Shakespeare*, 1927–1929; *Associating with Shakespeare*, 1932; *The Study of Drama*, 1934; *On Poetry in Drama*, 1937; *The Perennial Shakespeare*, 1937.

Though not born to the theater, Harley (Granville) Granville-Barker—a judicious combining of his parents' names—received most of his education in a dramatic school stock company at Margate. He made his debut as an actor at the age of fourteen, and he wrote his first play at sixteen. At twenty-eight he became a theater manager, producing plays by Ibsen, Shaw, and other writers of the new and realistic school of drama. His acting career ended in 1910, though he continued managing until 1914. One of the last plays he produced was Hardy's *The Dynasts* in 1914. From this time to his death, however, he achieved fame and greatness through his critical writings. He also translated plays by Arthur Schnitzler, Sacha Guitry, Martínez Sierra, Álvarez Quintero, and Jules Romains.

No one has written more searchingly than Granville-Barker on the production of Shakespeare, for here he combines his knowledge of acting, producing, writing, and criticism. As a result of his intellectual pursuits, he received honorary degrees from Oxford, Edinburgh, and Reading; he was a Fellow of the Royal Society of Literature and was also a visiting professor at Yale and Harvard. In the years preceding World War II, he held the post of Director of the British Institute of the University of Paris. Born in London, November 25, 1877, he died in Paris on August 31, 1946.

BIBLIOGRAPHICAL REFERENCES: The most extensive biographical and critical study is Charles B. Purdom, *Harley Granville Granville-Barker: Man of the Theatre, Dramatist, and Scholar*, 1955. See also Dixon Scott, *Men of Letters*, 1916; Archibald Henderson, *European Dramatists*, 1918; Hesketh Pearson, *The Last Actor-Managers*, 1950; George Bernard Shaw, "Barker's Wild Oats," *Harper's*, CLXXXXIV (1947), 49–53; and Alan S. Downer, "Harley Granville-Barker," *Sewanee Review*, LV (1947), 627–645.

ROBERT GRAVES

Born: Wimbledon, England
Date: July 26, 1895

PRINCIPAL WORKS

POEMS: *Over the Brazier*, 1916; *Fairies and Fusiliers*, 1917; *Country Sentiment*, 1920; *The Pier Glass*, 1921; *Whipperginny*, 1923; *Mock Beggar Hall*, 1924; *Welchman's Hose*, 1925; *The Marmosite's Miscellany*, 1925; *Poems: 1914–1926*, 1927; *Poems: 1929*, 1929; *Poems: 1926–1930*, 1931; *Collected Poems*, 1938; *No More Ghosts*, 1940; *Poems: 1938–1945*, 1946; *Collected Poems: 1914–1947*, 1948; *Poems and Satires*, 1951; *Collected Poems*, 1955.

NOVELS: *My Head! My Head! Being the History of Elisha*, 1925; *I, Claudius*, 1934; *Claudius the God*, 1934; *Count Belisarius*, 1938; *Sergeant Lamb of the Ninth*, 1940 [*Sergeant Lamb's America*]; *Proceed, Sergeant Lamb*, 1941; *Wife to Mr. Milton*, 1943; *The Golden Fleece*, 1944 [*Hercules, My Shipmate*]; *King Jesus*, 1946; *The Islands of Unwisdom*, 1949; *Seven Days in New Crete*, 1949 [*Watch the Northwind Rise*], 1949; *Homer's Daughter*, 1955; *They Hanged My Saintly Billy*, 1957.

ESSAYS AND STUDIES: *The English Ballad*, 1921; *On English Poetry*, 1922; *The Meaning of Dreams*, 1924; *Poetic Unreason*, 1925; *Contemporary Techniques of Poetry*, 1925; *Another Future of Poetry*, 1926; *Lawrence and the Arabs*, 1927; *John Skelton*, 1927; *Impenetrability, or the Proper Habit of English*, 1926; *Lars Porsena, or the Future of Swearing*, 1927; *A Survey of Modernist Poetry*, 1927 (with Laura Riding); *Mrs. Fisher, or the Future of Humour*, 1928; *The Real David Copperfield*, 1933; *The White Goddess*, 1947; *The Common Asphodel*, 1949; *Occupation: Writer*, 1950; *The Crowning Privilege*, 1955; *Adam's Rib*, 1955.

AUTOBIOGRAPHY: *Goodbye to All That*, 1929.

BELLES-LETTRES: *But It Still Goes On*, 1930; *The Greek Myths*, 1955.

TRANSLATIONS: *The Golden Ass*, 1950; *Lives of the Twelve Caesars*, 1957.

Robert (Ranke) Graves came by his literary heritage in part through family tradition; his father, Alfred Perceval Graves (1846–1931), was a gifted Irish poet. Born in Wimbledon, July 26, 1895, the younger Graves was reared in London. He was schooled at Charterhouse and, like most of his generation, fought in World War I. He suffered a head wound which gave him one of his several scars; his broken nose resulted from a mishap at football. (Graves was always athletic and once received an Olympic Games award.) During the war, like Siegfried Sassoon, a fellow officer in the Royal Welch Fusiliers, Graves wrote verse while at the front. His poems, if inferior to those of Sassoon and Wilfred Owen, share with their work a vivid sense of the absolutely unromantic truth of battle. In his autobiography, *Goodbye to All That,* Graves describes with verve and frankness his wartime experiences. *Fairies and Fusiliers,* though rarely voicing the horror characteristic of Owen's verse, exhibits some of its same bitterness; it perhaps differs most in being often ironic. A mild flippancy is detectable throughout Graves's early period.

Discharged after the war, Graves moved with his wife to Wales. Here he wrote two more volumes of poetry. He then decided to take a degree at Oxford and enrolled as an undergraduate of St. John's College. The effect of Oxford life was to subdue some of Graves's high spirits, and in this period he published several books on critical theory and poetic analysis. As he increased in learning, he introduced into his own poetry fascinating subtleties drawn from his readings in philosophy and psychoanalysis.

In 1926 he was appointed professor of English in the University of Cairo, where he remained but one year. When he and his wife were separated in 1927, Graves went to live in the Balearic Islands. A literary association with the American poet Laura Riding, with whom he was to operate at Minorca a small publishing enterprise for the better part of a decade, produced the acute but querulous critical study *A Survey of Modernist Poetry.* By this time he had published nine more books of verse and had started his practice of frequently reprinting his collected editions. He had already written his biography of Lawrence of Arabia, his monograph on John Skelton (whom at an early stage he had imitated), and his unconventional *Lars Porsena, or the Future of Swearing.*

Graves's first novel, *My Head! My Head! Being the History of Elisha,* is remarkable chiefly for its title. This and his next novel showed him chiefly as a facile stylist; but *I, Claudius* and *Claudius the God,* the former a winner of both the Hawthornden Prize and the James Tait Black Memorial Prize, suggest also that besides being one of the most interesting poets of contemporary England, Graves is very nearly the most arresting storyteller. Although he seldom depicts the modern scene, and has no great talent at psychological manipulation of character, he has few masters at the art of romantic narration. *Wife to Mr. Milton* makes a shrewd guess, infuriating to votaries of the author of *Paradise Lost,* about the causes of Milton's marital discord. *King Jesus,* which has infuriated others for reasons of faith, is in many ways both enlightened and enlightening. *Seven Days in New Crete* is a fantasy based on Graves's speculations concerning Cybele, the Great Mother, whose supposedly universal cult in primitive Europe constitutes the subject of his remarkable treatise, *The White Goddess. Homer's Daughter* pays the tribute of fiction to Samuel Butler's hypothesis that the *Odyssey* was composed by a woman.

Graves now resides at Minorca with his second wife. He writes incessantly, always witty, imaginative, and iconoclastic.

BIBLIOGRAPHICAL REFERENCES: There is no full-length biography or critical study. For articles in books or periodicals see Frank Swinnerton, *The Georgian Literary Scene,* 1951 (6th ed.); Nelson Algren, "Sentiment with Terror," *Poetry,* LV (1939),

157–159; Richard Church, "Robert Graves, A Traveller in the Desert," *Fortnightly Review,* CLV (1941), 384–391; Horace Gregory, "Robert Graves: A Parable for Writers," *Partisan Review,* XX (1953), 44–54; and C. M. Bowra, "Greek Myths," *Sewanee Review,* LXIV (1956), 498–507.

THOMAS GRAY

Born: London, England   *Died:* Cambridge, England
Date: December 26, 1716   *Date:* July 30, 1771

PRINCIPAL WORKS

POEMS: *Elegy in a Country Churchyard,* 1751; *Six Poems by Mr. T. Gray,* 1753; *Odes by Mr. Gray,* 1757; *Pindaric Odes,* 1758; *Poems by Mr. Gray,* 1768.

In judging the poetic output of Thomas Gray, two schools of thought have gradually developed. One holds that he is the most distinguished of the minor poets; the other, that he is assuredly the least prolific of the major ones. Whichever view finally prevails, it is certainly true that Gray was concerned with the quality rather than the quantity of his verse. Essentially a scholar, with scholarly instincts, he shaped and reshaped his lines with a patience and discipline almost unmatched in the annals of English poetry. To call his best work the ultimate expression of neo-classical art would be only half accurate; it also contains, sometimes half-hidden, the seeds of a momentous change in English poetry.

Born at Cornhill in London on December 26, 1716, Gray was the only one of a family of twelve children to survive infancy. His father, like Milton's, was a money scrivener; unfortunately, he had the additional characteristics of being a brutal, neglectful parent and something of a ne'er-do-well. As a result, the father and mother separated; and Gray's mother joined her sister in a millinery establishment which prospered sufficiently to allow Gray to attend Eton. Here he became intimate with Richard West, son of the Lord Chancellor of Ireland, and Horace Walpole, the Prime Minister's son. A career at Cambridge followed, a career which, with minor interruptions, was to stretch on to the end of his life.

Studies at Cambridge were broken by a tour of Italy and France (1739–1741), taken in the company of young Walpole; but the trip ended in a quarrel which disrupted, though only temporarily, the friendship of the travelers. After reaching home again, Gray postponed his return to Cambridge for two years, though he had not yet taken his degree; this interval he spent with his mother at the village of Stoke Poges. Here, in 1742, he wrote his first important poems: "Ode to the Spring," "Ode on a Distant Prospect of Eton College," and "Hymn to Adversity." About the same time he started the famous "Elegy in a Country Churchyard," which was published in 1751. Returning to Cambridge, he took up residence first at Peterhouse and then at Pembroke, becoming a bachelor of civil law. Thereafter his life followed the placid course of a scholar interested in literature, history, science, and music.

Though Gray's modern reputation rests largely on the admirable "Elegy," his significance as a poet far outreaches the slenderness of his literary output. Discernible in his work was that interest in nature and in the past which was curiously at variance with the rigid tenets of neo-classicism. This type of interest places him with the forerunners of that full-blown Romanticism which Coleridge and Wordsworth would usher in a generation after his death. His role as a transitional poet is especially well illustrated by "The Bard" (1757) and by his later odes, "The Fatal Sisters" (1761) and "The Descent of Odin" (1761).

Gray never married. In 1757 he was offered the poet laureateship of England, which he refused—probably because of the low repute which it had acquired under recent holders of the office. In 1768 he accepted the post of Professor of History and Modern Languages at Cambridge. His health, always fragile, suffered from painful attacks of gout in his later years. At his death in Cambridge, on July 30, 1771, he was buried beside his mother in the churchyard of Stoke Poges.

BIBLIOGRAPHICAL REFERENCES: *The Works of Thomas Gray, in Prose and Verse* were collected by Sir Edmund Gosse, 4 vols., 1885. The standard bibliographies are C. S. Northup, *A Bibliography of Thomas Gray*, 1917, supplemented by H. W. Starr, *A Bibliography of Gray, 1917–51*, 1953. Robert W. Ketton-Cremer's biography, *Thomas Gray*, 1955, is authoritative, but should be supplemented by William Powell Jones, *Thomas Gray, Scholar: The True Tragedy of an Eighteenth Century Gentleman*, 1937 (containing two previously unpublished notebooks); and Lord David Cecil, *Two Quiet Lives: Dorothy Osborne, Thomas Gray*, 1948. Critical works include Sir Edmund Gosse, *Gray*, English Men of Letters Series, 1882; William Henry Hudson, *Gray and His Poetry*, 1927; and H. W. Starr, *Gray as a Literary Critic*, 1941. Important chapters in books are Lytton Strachey, "Gray and Cowper," in *Characters and Commentaries*, 1933; B. I. Evans, "Gray and Blake," in *Tradition and Romanticism*, 1940; Geoffrey Tillotson, "On Gray's Letters: Gray the Scholar Poet," in *Essays in Criticism and Research*, 1942; and Lord David Cecil, "The Poetry of Gray," in *Poets and Storytellers*, 1949. Critical articles include C. F. Gray, "Thomas Gray and the Fine Arts," *Essays and Studies*, XXX (1945), 50–81, and H. W. Starr, "Gray's Craftmanship," *Journal of English and Germanic Philology*, XLV (1946), 415–429.

HENRY GREEN
Henry Vincent Yorke

Born: Near Tewkesbury, England
Date: 1905

PRINCIPAL WORKS

NOVELS: *Blindness*, 1926; *Living*, 1929; *Party Going*, 1939; *Caught*, 1943; *Loving*, 1945; *Back*, 1946; *Concluding*, 1948; *Nothing*, 1950; *Doting*, 1952.

Henry Green, born near Tewkesbury, England, in 1905, has hidden behind the mask of pseudonymity very successfully, and little is known of his personal life beyond the few scattered facts he has divulged. His real name is

451

Henry Vincent Yorke; his family owned the factory where he worked as a laborer and which he now manages. Beginning at the age of six, he was educated away from home until he took his degree from Oxford at twenty-two. At twelve he was sent to Eton, where he wrote *Blindness,* a novel about a schoolboy who is forced to come to terms with his gradual loss of sight.

After leaving Oxford he began work at the lowest rank in the family foundry at Birmingham. He was greatly impressed by the vitality of the laboring class and wrote *Living,* a study of working-class life. It was quite successful, though it gained much of its reputation because it could be classed as a proletarian novel, a form that had a considerable vogue at the time. Actually, *Living* is not concerned, like the proletarian novel, with extolling the virtues of the working class in order to prescribe a plan for class action; rather, the author sees the workers as a breed able to preserve its vitality in spite of the deadening forces of a machine civilization. Green stands apart from the workers and gives an eloquent gasp of wonder.

The circumstances of Green's life have enabled him to range freely among the social classes of Britain. A nephew of Lord Leconfield, he knows the upper classes as well as the lower. *Party Going* is an ironic jibe at a group of young rich people who are delayed by fog on their trip to a party in France. They spend the night in a railroad station where commoners press near them and show their superior resources for meeting difficulties. His work in the National Fire Service during the war supplied him with the material for *Caught,* a novel of distrust and misunderstanding among the social classes. *Loving* examines the servant class closely, with respect but without sentimentality.

Green's style is sharply individual, belonging to the tradition of the remakers of language, the tradition of James Joyce. Unlike Joyce, Greene's liberties with syntax are small ones; but they are nevertheless prominent. He frequently omits the article and generally tries for a bare, sometimes harsh style that often succeeds in bringing out the power latent in commonplace, familiar words.

BIBLIOGRAPHICAL REFERENCES: There is no extensive biographical or critical study of Green. See Walter Allen, "Henry Green," in *Modern British Writing,* edited by D. Val Baker, 1947; and Philip Toynbee, "The Novels of Henry Green," *Partisan Review,* V (1949), 487–498.

JULIAN GREEN

Born: Paris, France
Date: September 6, 1900

PRINCIPAL WORKS

NOVELS: *Mont Cinère,* 1926 (*Avarice House*); *Adrienne Mésurat,* 1927 (*The Closed Garden*); *Léviathan,* 1929 (*The Dark Journey*); *Épaves,* 1931 (*The Strange River*); *Le Visionnaire,* 1934 (*The Dreamer*); *Minuit,* 1936 (*Midnight*); *Varouna,* 1941 (*Then Shall the Dust Return*); *Moira,* 1950; *Le malfaiteur,* 1956 (*The Transgressor*).

SHORT STORIES: *Le Voyageur sur la Terre,* 1927 (*The Pilgrim on the Earth*); *Christine and Other Stories,* 1930 (in English).

PLAYS: *Sud,* 1953 (*South*); *L'Ennemi,* 1954 (*The Enemy*).

AUTOBIOGRAPHY AND REMINISCENCES: *Journals, 1928–1954,* Vols. I–VI, 1938–1955 (*Personal Record,* 1928–1939); *Memories of Happy Days,* 1942 (in English).

CRITICISM: *Suite Anglais,* 1927.

Julian (or Julien) Green was born of American parents in Paris on September 6, 1900. His father was from Virginia, his mother originally from Georgia; at the time the father's business had taken the family to Paris. Although Julian attended French schools and, therefore, learned to speak French fluently, he was required at home to learn English thoroughly. At home also his mother, who was an Episcopalian, held daily Bible readings with her family. Thus Green was early affected by the awe and mystery of religion, as well as by its significance to him. After his mother's death, he became converted to Roman Catholicism in 1915, only to enter a period of apostasy later on. His journals, however, record with deep feeling and humility the account of his return to faith in 1939.

During World War I, since he was at first too young to join the army, he served in the American Field Service, in which he saw service at the front in both France and Italy. In 1918 he was able to join the French artillery. After the war an uncle in the United States persuaded Green to pursue his studies at the University of Virginia. While he was there, the university literary magazine published a short piece of his called "The Apprentice Psychiatrist," an early work holding promise of his later novels. After three years, however, Green became homesick for France and returned without having completed his course of study.

After a brief period of art studies Green determined on writing for his career. His first novel, *Avarice House,* was favorably received in France and the United States. The setting is Virginia, which he had known during his university days and where some of his American relatives lived. The story is a rather unpleasant one about a niggardly and cruel mother and her neurotic daughter. His second novel, *Adrienne Mésurat,* written shortly after, was more mature. Here the setting is a French provincial town, the particular atmosphere of which he has caught well. The main character is a persecuted, embittered, and bored young girl who, when her one *grande passion* is rejected, loses her reason completely. This work was awarded a prize for the best French work suitable for English translation, and the translation, *The Closed Garden,* was chosen as a selection by one of the national book clubs. His next novel was *Léviathan,* a rather sordid story of a man's unrequited passion for a rather shabby village girl. This work, translated into English as *The Dark Journey,* was the Harper Prize novel for 1929. Perhaps his most bizarre novel is *The Dreamer,* which concerns a sickly young man who imagines himself inhabiting a chateau peopled with a small group of quite weird inhabitants.

Since these early successes Green has interspersed novel writing with short stories, plays, and books of personal recollections. His *Journals*, published in separate volumes between 1938 and 1955, contain reflections on such subjects as death and God as well as glimpses into his literary friendships with such writers as André Gide and Gertrude Stein. During World War II, after the fall of France, Green resided in the United States, where he lectured at various colleges and wrote one of his few English works, *Memories of Happy Days*, in which he poignantly described his boyhood life in France. During the war he also served with the United States Army.

In *Moira* he returned to an American setting to present a psychological study of a country boy at an American university in the South during the 1920's. More recently he has written two plays, *South* and *The Enemy*. The setting of the former is again the South in the United States; the action takes place shortly before the Civil War. *The Transgressor* presents an intensely psychological theme against a French provincial background.

Critics have commented on Green's impeccable French style. His backgrounds are usually well conceived. The tone of most of his work is excessively somber. Most of his characters are highly neurotic. These qualities give his novels their distinctive blend of external melodrama and inward psychological intensity. His later work is marked also by a spirit of devout mysticism.

BIBLIOGRAPHICAL REFERENCES: For critical studies of Julian Green in English see Samuel Stokes, *Julian Green and the Thorn of Puritanism*, 1955; Milton H. Stansbury, *French Novelists of Today*, 1935; Edmond Jaloux, "Julien Green," *American Bookman*, LXVII (1928), 34–35; Dayton Kohler, "Julian Green: Modern Gothic," *Sewanee Review*, XL (1932), 139–148; Anon., "Paris and Savannah," *London Times Literary Supplement*, L (June 22, 1951), 381–383; in French, Marc Eigeldinger, *Julien Green et la tentation de l'irréel*, 1947; and Charles E. Koëlla, "La Puissance du rêve chez Julien Green," *Publications of the Modern Language Association*, LIV (1939), 597–607.

GRAHAM GREENE

Born: Berkhamstead, England
Date: October 2, 1904

PRINCIPAL WORKS

NOVELS: *The Man Within*, 1929; *It's a Battlefield*, 1934; *England Made Me*, 1935 [*The Shipwrecked*]; *Brighton Rock*, 1938; *The Power and the Glory*, 1940 [*The Labyrinthine Ways*]; *The Heart of the Matter*, 1948; *The End of the Affair*, 1951; *The Quiet American*, 1955.

ENTERTAINMENTS: *Stamboul Train*, 1932 [*Orient Express*]; *A Gun for Sale*, 1936 [*This Gun for Hire*]; *The Confidential Agent*, 1939; *The Ministry of Fear*, 1943; *The Third Man* and *The Fallen Idol*, 1950; *Loser Take All*, 1955.

SHORT STORIES: *The Basement Room*, 1935; *Nineteen Stories*, 1947; *Twenty-one Stories*, 1954.

PLAYS: *The Living Room*, 1953; *The Potting Shed*, 1957.

ESSAYS: *The Lost Childhood and Other Essays*, 1951.

TRAVEL SKETCHES AND IMPRESSIONS: *Journey Without Maps*, 1936; *The Lawless Roads*, 1939 [*Another Mexico*].
POEMS: *Babbling April*, 1925.

Graham Greene, one of the few modern writers to win wide acceptance from both the critics and the book-buying public, was born at Berkhamstead, Hertfordshire, England, on October 2, 1904. After attending Berkhamstead School, of which his father was headmaster, he went to Balliol College, Oxford, and from there to a staff position on the London *Times* (1926–1930). While an undergraduate at Oxford, he published his only book of verse, *Babbling April*. His first novel, *The Man Within*, appeared in 1929. He married Vivien Dayrell-Browning in 1927; they have a son and a daughter.

An intellectual convert to Roman Catholicism (1929), Green divides his fiction into two groups: the entertainments, which are crime stories of great fascination, and the novels, which often deal with much the same subject matter but which are presented on a higher level of moral seriousness, with deep probing into such matters as sin, the nature of faith, and the possibility of redemption. Nearly all his fiction has been successful, and nearly all the books have been excitingly filmed. So cinematic is Greene's imagination that some of his books (*The Third Man*, for example) have been written for the motion pictures before being adapted to book form.

If criticism sets aside the entertainments, though they are fine enough to have satisfied many authors, Greene's fiction may be classified in three groups. His first three novels are socio-psychological books presenting life and crime from a rather specialized political point of view. *England Made Me* is a rather confusing *roman à clef* centering on the "Swedish Match King," the late Ivar Kreuger.

Greene's second period began with *Brighton Rock*, when he deliberately started to write novels on religious themes. It has been noted that in these religious novels Greene frequently uses the same manhunt or chase pattern that forms the framework of his entertainments. But he has refined the adventure story to force it into an ethical treatment of evil, pity, sin, and possible damnation. In *Brighton Rock* the young gangster, Pinkie, is pursued by the police, by a rival gang, by a woman ignorant of evil; but most importantly, Pinkie is pursued by God, Who wants him to repent. Freudian psychology enters the book in that, because of his ugly boyhood, Pinkie is unable to love. Hence he is, no doubt, damned for his evil. In *The Heart of the Matter*, set in Africa where Greene for a time resided, the adulterous Scobie may not be damned. Scobie falls through excess of pity for the sufferings of people around him. It is also fairly clear that the whiskey priest of *The Power and the Glory* is a better man than the cold policeman who hunts him down. The last religious book, *The End of the Affair*, is weaker: Greene's portrait of a saint is not nearly so convincing as are his pictures of the sinful.

With *The Quiet American*, Greene seems to feel that he has turned from religious or Roman Catholic issues; but the same dwelling on evil and the damage produced by moral ignorance

455

is apparent to most readers. Many believe that in this book Greene for the first time fails to give sufficient credit to that which he attacks—the secular, innocent attitude toward life.

Greene's travel books, excellent in themselves, have given him the subject matter for some of his best novels. *The Lawless Roads* is a record of travel in Mexico during the religious disturbances of the 1930's; on the factual level it parallels *The Power and the Glory*. It was as a newspaper correspondent in Indo-China that Greene collected much of the material in *The Quiet American*.

Less successful as a playwright, Greene has written two problem plays, both of which show the same rather pessimistic attitude toward life that he presents in his novels. The not well-known children's stories, such as *The Little Train* (1947) and *The Little Horse Bus* (1952), are thoroughly delightful. His essays are most valuable for an understanding of the novelist's mind. For example, they tell us that Greene's determined belief in the evil of this world came to him before his religious conversion.

In addition to his great output of fiction, Greene is also active in the London publishing world and in various important causes concerning authorship, public opinion, and censorship.

BIBLIOGRAPHICAL REFERENCES: Graham Greene's books are published in the Uniform Edition, London, 1947 ff. For biographical and critical studies see Paul Rostenne, *Graham Greene: Témoin des temps tragiques*, 1949; Kenneth Allott and Miriam Farris, *The Art of Graham Greene*, 1951; Marie-Béatrice Mesnet, *Graham Greene and the Heart of the Matter*, 1954; Francis Wyndham, *Graham Greene*, 1955; and John Atkins, *Graham Greene: A Biographical and Critical Study*, 1957.

For briefer critical studies in books and magazines see also Walter Allen, "Graham Greene," in *Writers of Today*, edited by D. Val Baker, 1946; Henry Reed, *The Novel Since 1939*, 1947; P. H. Newby, *The Novel, 1945–1950*, 1951; Donat O'Donnell, *Maria Cross*, 1952; Seán O'Faoláin, *The Vanishing Hero*, 1956; Anthony West, *Principles and Persuasions*, 1957; Morton Dauwen Zabel, *Craft and Character in Modern Fiction*, 1957; Allen W. Gore, "Evelyn Waugh and Graham Greene," *Irish Monthly*, LXXVII (1949), 16–22; Henry A. Grubbs, "Albert Camus and Graham Greene," *Modern Language Quarterly*, X (1949), 33–42; Neville Braybrook, "Graham Greene: Pioneer Novelist," *College English*, XII (1950), 1–9; Bruce Marshall, "Graham Greene and Evelyn Waugh," *Commonweal*, LI (1950), 551–553; Jean-H. Roy, "L'œuvre de Graham Greene ou un christianisme de la damnation," *Les Temps Modernes*, LII (1950), 1513–1519; Richard J. Voorhees, "The World of Graham Greene," *South Atlantic Quarterly*, L (1951), 389–398; Kenneth A. Lohf, "Graham Greene and the Problem of Evil," *Catholic World*, CLXXIII (1951), 196–199; William D. Ellis, Jr., "The Grand Theme of Graham Greene," *Southwest Review*, XLI (1956), 239–250; R. W. B. Lewis, "The Fiction of Graham Greene: Between the Horror and the Glory," *Kenyon Review*, XIX (1957), 56–75; R. B. W. Lewis, "The 'Trilogy' of Graham Greene," *Modern Fiction Studies*, III (1957), 195–215; Karl Patten, "The Structure of The Power and the Glory," *ibid.*, 225–234; Beekman W. Cottrell, "Second Time Charm: The Theatre of Graham Greene," *ibid.*, 249–255; and Herbert R. Haber, "The Two Worlds of Graham Greene," *ibid.*, 256–268.

The Graham Greene Number of *Modern Fiction Studies*, III (1957), contains a selected bibliography by Phylis Hargreaves, with an index to studies of his separate works, 269–288.

ROBERT GREENE

Born: Norwich, England
Date: c. July, 1558

Died: London, England
Date: September 3, 1592

Principal Works

PLAYS: *Alphonsus, King of Aragon*, c. 1587; *A Looking-glass for London and England*, c. 1588 (with Lodge); *Orlando Furioso*, c. 1588; *Friar Bacon and Friar Bungay*, c. 1589; *James IV*, c. 1590.

NOVELLAS: *Mamilia*, 1580; *Perimedes the Blacksmith*, 1588; *Pandosto*, 1588; *Pandosto and Menaphon*, 1589.

TRACTS AND PAMPHLETS: *Greene's Mourning Garment*, 1590; *Greene's Never Too Late*, 1590; *Greene's Farewell to Folly*, 1591; *A Notable Discovery of Coosnage*, 1591; *The Second and Last Part of Conny-catching*, 1592; *The Third and Last Part of Conny-catching*, 1592; *The Black Book's Messenger*, 1592; *Greene's Groatsworth of Wit Bought with a Million of Repentance*, 1592.

Robert Greene was born at Norwich in 1558. He studied at Cambridge, where his life appears to have been dissipated, and the dissipation persisted during his subsequent travels in Italy and Spain. His life in general, as described in his various autobiographical pamphlets, is not edifying, and he died, appropriately, after an orgy of pickled herrings and Rhenish wine, on September 3, 1592, in London.

Greene was a prolific and versatile writer. His Euphuistic prose romances, though popular in their day, hold little interest now, but the pamphlets, some of which relate to the Marprelate controversy, still make lively reading and are biographically indispensable. It is claimed, possibly by Greene himself in a famous passage in *The Groatsworth of Wit*, and certainly by one "R. B.," that his plumes were purloined by other writers. If, as seems probable, this implies that Greene was a dramatic innovator whose ideas were stolen by other dramatists, including Shakespeare, the allegation is manifestly ab-

surd, for Greene was not, on the face of it, a conspicuously original writer. Just as his prose tales owe much to Lyly, so do his earlier plays run heavily into debt to Marlowe and Kyd. *Alphonsus, King of Aragon* closely follows the style of *Tamburlaine*, while *Orlando Furioso* follows the same model but adds a good deal of Senecan matter directly inspired by *The Spanish Tragedy*. There is little that is memorable in these or in *A Looking-glass for London and England*, which Greene wrote in collaboration with Lodge. His sole claim to dramatic distinction rests on *Friar Bacon and Friar Bungay* and *James the Fourth*, two romantic comedies in which individual qualities are at last apparent. *Friar Bacon* is an extraordinary compound of comedy, tragedy, pastoral, romance, magic, and buffoonery. It has no recognizable structure and could in fact end at any point after the beginning of the third act. Yet Friar Bacon himself serves to unify the curious jumble by

457

virtue of his magic. The results of his necromancy, as Greene depicts them, must have made this the most spectacular Elizabethan play since *Tamburlaine*. *James the Fourth*, a more orthodox romance based on a novella by Cinthio, bears what was perhaps an intentionally misleading title, for it was written at a time when other dramatists were making capital out of the post-Armada vogue for chronicle histories. These, it would seem, were the vested interest of Shakespeare, Marlowe, and Peele; and Greene's title may have been retaliation for his exclusion, which accounts also for his bitter attacks in *The Groatsworth of Wit*.

Greene refers to a comedy which he wrote in collaboration with a 'young Juvenal, that biting satirist,' presumably Nash, but this has not survived. Various anonymous plays have been attributed to him, including *George-a-Greene*, *Selimus*, and the pseudo-Shakespearian *Locrine*. The evidence is interesting but far from conclusive, and the fact that Francis Meres, who is usually precise, does not mention Greene among the writers of tragedy, seems to rule out his claims to *Selimus* and *Locrine*.

BIBLIOGRAPHICAL REFERENCES: The most recent edition is *The Plays and Poems of Robert Greene*, edited by J. C. Collins, 2 vols., 1905. See also J. J. Jusserand, *The English Novel in the Time of Shakespeare*, 1890; E. J. Castle, *Shakespeare, Bacon, Jonson, and Greene*, 1897; C. R. Gayley, "Robert Greene: His Life and the Order of His Plays," in *Representative English Comedies*, edited by Gayley, 1903; G. E. Woodberry, "Greene's Place in Comedy," *ibid.*; E. K. Chambers, *The Elizabethan Stage*, Vol. III, 1923; and *Dictionary of National Biography*, Vol. VIII.

LADY AUGUSTA GREGORY

Born: Roxborough, Ireland
Date: March 5, 1852

Died: Coole Park, Gort, Ireland
Date: May 22, 1932

PRINCIPAL WORKS

PLAYS: *Spreading the News*, 1904; *Kincora*, 1905; *The White Cockade*, 1905; *Hyacinth Halvey*, 1906; *The Rising of the Moon*, 1906; *The Unicorn from the Stars and Other Plays*, 1908 (with William Butler Yeats); *Seven Short Plays*, 1909; *The Image*, 1910; *The Full Moon*, 1911; *Irish Folk-history Plays*, 1912; *New Comedies*, 1913; *Three Wonder Plays*, 1922; *The Story Brought by Brigit*, 1924; *On the Racecourse*, 1926; *Three Last Plays*, 1928.

FOLKLORE AND HISTORY: *A Book of Saints and Wonders*, 1906; *The Kiltartan History Book*, 1909; *The Kiltartan Wonder Book*, 1910.

ESSAYS: *Coole*, 1931.

AUTOBIOGRAPHY: *Our Irish Theatre*, 1913.

TRANSLATIONS: *Poets and Dreamers*, 1903; *Gods and Fighting Men*, 1904; *The Kiltartan Molière*, 1910; *The Kiltartan Poetry Book*, 1918; *Mirandolina*, adapted from Goldoni's *La Locandiera*, 1924.

Not to be confused with an actress who died in 1895, Lady Gregory was born Isabella Augusta Persse at Roxborough, County Galway, on March 5,

1852. Daughter of a wealthy landowner, she was educated privately. In 1881 she married Sir William Henry Gregory, well-known Orientalist and Irish M.P. who died in 1892. They had one son.

The turning point in her life came about through a meeting with William Butler Yeats, who urged Lady Gregory, Edward Martyn, and George Moore, among others, to write folk plays of the Irish people. One result of this literary movement was the Irish literary revival and the founding of the Irish National Theatre Society, later the Abbey Theatre in 1903. (Yeats's *The Countess Kathleen,* produced at Lady Gregory's insistence, culminated in the famous Abbey group, to which she gave her interest, ability, enthusiasm, and financial support.) Though overshadowed as an author by Yeats and Synge, her *Rising of the Moon, The Work-* *house Ward,* and *Hyacinth Halvey,* are excellent in their kind. Many of her plays are masterpieces of suspense, folk humor, and incisiveness. She translated plays from Molière's French and Goldoni's Italian into Irish country speech, no mean achievement in itself. As business manager, director, and "the godmother" of the Abbey Theatre she gained her fame, for the group would never have been able to perform without her steady guiding hand.

Her later years were saddened by the death of her son, an aviator killed in World War I, and of her good friends of the group. Though the Abbey Theatre has burned since her death, which occurred at Coole Park, Ireland, May 22, 1932, her influence is still felt in the modern theater, for without her pioneering work such an original genius as Sean O'Casey would possibly not be writing plays today.

BIBLIOGRAPHICAL REFERENCES: There is no extended biographical or critical study. Many details of Lady Gregory's life are given in her *Journals, 1916–1930,* edited by Lennox Robinson, 1947. The best brief study is that by Lennox Robinson in the *Dictionary of National Biography.* See also William Butler Yeats, *The Cutting of an Agate,* 1912; Cornelius Weygandt, *Irish Plays and Playwrights,* 1913; and Dawson Byrne, *The Story of Ireland's Great Theatre,* 1930.

GERALD GRIFFIN

Born: Limerick, Ireland
Date: December 12, 1803

Died: Cork, Ireland
Date: June 12, 1840

PRINCIPAL WORKS

NOVELS: *The Collegians,* 1828; *The Invasion,* 1832; *The Duke of Monmouth,* 1836.

SHORT STORIES: *Tales of the Munster Festivals,* 1827–1832.

PLAY: *Gisippus,* 1842.

Gerald Griffin, born in Limerick, Ireland, December 12, 1803, and son of a well-to-do brewer in Limerick, received a rather irregular education. As a boy he studied with a tutor part of the time and attended schools in Limerick and Longhill. He later went to England and studied for a time at the University of London, intending to become a lawyer. He turned to writing and became the author of nine novels, although only three were published during his lifetime. The most famous of his novels is *The Collegians.* He also wrote several volumes of short stories, as well as an opera, *The Noyades* (1826), and a play, *Gisippus,* which was written sometime before he was twenty.

In his works Griffin dealt generally with the people and countryside of his native Ireland, being especially fond of materials dealing with the lives of fishermen and smugglers on the Irish coast, with peasant life, and with the differences between the lives of the peasants and the landed gentry. As a poet he achieved popularity in Ireland because his lyrics were concerned with Ireland and Irish life. In his maturity Griffin came to doubt life and entered the Society of the Christian Brothers

under the name of Brother Joseph in 1838. At the time he feared the moral influence of his writings and destroyed many of his manuscripts. Before he finished his novitiate, however, he contracted typhus and died on June 12, 1840, at Cork. His tragedy, *Gisippus,* which had escaped destruction at his hands, was produced in London by Macready in 1842, two years after the author's death, and was regarded as a stage success at the time. Some years later Dion Boucicault created a famous melodrama, *The Colleen Bawn,* from *The Collegians.* Later critics have been in agreement that Griffin, although known as a novelist, was a better artist with the short story than he was with the novel, for the longer pieces of his prose tend to lose unity; the simplicity of the tales, which in them is a virtue, becomes a fault in his longer fiction.

BIBLIOGRAPHICAL REFERENCES: The standard edition is *The Works of Gerald Griffin,* 8 vols., 1842–1843. There are two biographies separated by a century: *The Life of Gerald Griffin,* by his brother, Daniel Griffin, 1843; and W. S. Gill, *Gerald Griffin, Poet, Novelist, Christian Brother,* 1941. See also H. S. Krans, *Irish Life in Irish Fiction,* 1903.

FRANZ GRILLPARZER

Born: Vienna, Austria
Date: January 15, 1791

Died: Vienna
Date: January 21, 1872

PRINCIPAL WORKS

PLAYS: *Die Ahnfrau,* 1817 (*The Ancestress*); *Sappho,* 1818; *Das Goldene Vlies,* 1821 (*The Golden Fleece*); *König Ottokars Glück und Ende,* 1823 (*King Ottokar: His Rise and Fall*); *Des Meeres und der Liebe Wellen,* 1831 (*The Waves of the Sea and of Love*); *Der Traum, ein Leben,* 1834 (*The Dream, a Life*); *Die Jüdin von Toledo,* 1872 (*The Jewess of Toledo*).
POEMS: *Tristia ex Ponto,* 1835.

Born in Vienna on January 15, 1791, Franz Grillparzer lived there almost his entire life. Although he often felt that the city had a stultifying atmosphere for artists, he knew that he

could not live anywhere else. His father was a lawyer, a man of cold and unsocial nature; but Grillparzer's mother was emotional and warm. The young man entered the University of

460

Vienna as a law student in 1807, but his father's death and the resulting shortage of funds forced him to leave and engage in private tutoring. He soon became a government clerk, later a librarian. Grillparzer held various civil service posts until his retirement in 1856.

He was an unstable man, given to fits of depression and melancholy. His family history (both his mother and a brother committed suicide) may be an explanation of this gloomy tendency, or his dark moods may have been caused by his dissatisfaction with the political situation in Vienna. Metternich was then in power, and the strict censorship of Grillparzer's plays was a constant harassment for the sensitive playwright.

The first of his plays, *The Ancestress,* was a dark and bloody verse tragedy that made him famous. Even this early work revealed Grillparzer's unerring dramatic sense and his ability to write fine poetry. His next play, *Sappho,* is based on classical material and contains the essense of classical directness and simplicity. Grillparzer's historical tragedies, the trilogy *The Golden Fleece,* which tells two sides to the story of Jason's search for the Golden Fleece, and *King Ottokar: His Rise and Fall,* caused him further trouble with the censor; and Grillparzer suffered untold torments of spirit. These tragedies enforce a fairly con-

stant theme of his work, the vanity of human desires and the pettiness of worldly glory. He thought that people should remain in the stations in life which destiny had chosen for them and not try to rise by fierce ambition. He favored the simple life.

In 1826 Grillparzer suffered a particularly deep fit of depression which fortunately did not impair his dramatic abilities, and his later work. *The Waves of the Sea and of Love* and *The Dream, a Life,* show him at his height as a poetic dramatist. In these plays he united a deep understanding of human psychology, sound dramatic technique, and excellent verse. His only comedy, *Weh' dem, der lügt* (1838, *Thou Shalt Not Lie*), was unsuccessful.

Grillparzer's failure to find appreciation during his lifetime was one cause of his despondency. On his eightieth birthday, however, a national festival was declared. Even this celebration did not cheer him; it came too late and his gloom was too deep. This gloom and the tension between his life and his art can be read in Grillparzer's plays. He wrote, really, about the emotional disturbances of his own life. He died in Vienna on January 21, 1872, still an unhappy man but a writer who had a tremendous influence on later dramatists and who has been compared in his tragic stature to Shakespeare.

BIBLIOGRAPHICAL REFERENCES: Studies of Grillparzer in English include G. Pollack, *Franz Grillparzer and the Austrian Drama,* 1907; Douglas Yates, *Franz Grillparzer,* 1946; Frederic E. Coenen, *Franz Grillparzer's Portraiture of Men,* 1951; and Gisela Stein, *The Inspiration Motif in the Works of Franz Grillparzer,* 1955. For briefer studies consult also Patricia Drake, "Grillparzer and the Dream," *Modern Language Quarterly,* XII (1951), 72–85; and Myra R. Jessen, "Conflicting Views in the Evaluation of Grillparzer," *ibid.,* XV (1954), 67–73.

J. J. C. VON GRIMMELSHAUSEN

Born: Gelnhausen, Germany　　　　　*Died:* Renchen, Germany
Date: c. 1622　　　　　　　　　　　*Date:* August 17, 1676

PRINCIPAL WORKS

NOVELS: *Der abenteuerliche Simplicissimus, Teutsch, d.h., die Beschreibung des Lebens eines seltsamen Vaganten, genannt Melchior Sternfels von Fuchsheim,* 1669 (*Simplicissimus the Vagabond*); *Die Erzbetrügerin und Landstörtzerin Courasche,* 1670 (*The Female Vagrant*).

Johann (Hans) Jakob Christoffel von Grimmelshausen, born c. 1622, was the son of an innkeeper in Gelnhausen. His parents, who were Protestants, were probably killed in the sack of Gelnhausen in 1631, after that city was captured by the Hessians during the Thirty Years' War. As a child, Grimmelshausen was taken prisoner by the Hessian and Croat soldiers. Later he was in the Hessian ranks, serving until 1648. During this time he apparently began writing down what he saw, perhaps even organizing what he wrote.

Upon leaving military service in 1648, Grimmelshausen became a bailiff or administrator for the estates of a noble family near Gaisbach, Germany. After twelve years of service there he was dismissed as bailiff, but he found a similar position with another family, which he retained for five years. Early in the 1660's Grimmelshausen became a convert to Roman Catholicism. Whether his conversion was prompted by spiritual reasons has been questioned by some scholars of German literature, but some worldy benefit accrued from his conversion. In 1667 the Bishop of Strassbourg made Grimmelshausen an administrator of lands at Renchen, in the Schwarzwald or Black Forest, in Bavaria.

Whatever writings he may have done prior to 1665 must be conjectured, but after that date Grimmelshausen seems to have written regularly to augment a rather slender income. His best work, and his most widely known, is *Simplicissimus the Vagabond,* a picaresque novel published in several parts in 1669. The book is semi-autobiographical, beginning with the childhood of the hero and realistically describing his adventures during the Thirty Years' War. The realism, which makes the book a valuable social document, proved too much for the nineteenth century, whose critics condemned both the novel and its author for bad taste. In the latter part of the book the mood changes when Simplicissimus seeks a spiritual peace by renunciation of the world for life on a desert island. *Die Erzbetrügerin und Landstörtzerin Courasche* is a somewhat similar novel about the career of a female rogue. While most of Grimmelshausen's work deals with the common people, he also wrote three novels about courtly life: *The Innocent Joseph* (1667), *Dietwald and Amelinde* (1670), and *Proximus and Lympida* (1672). He died in Renchen, Germany, on August 17, 1676.

BIBLIOGRAPHICAL REFERENCES: The only available biographical and critical study in English is K. C. Hayens, *Grimmelshausen,* 1932. There is also a brief survey in

William Rose, *Men, Myths and Movements in German Literature*, 1931. See also Artur Bechtold, *Grimmelshausen und seine Zeit*, 1919; Johannes Alt, *Grimmelshausen und der Simplicissimus*, 1936; Jan Hendrik Scholte, *Der Simplicissimus und sein Dichter*, 1950; and Walter Roch, *Richter ihrer Zeit: Grimmelshausen, Swift, Gogol*, 1956.

GUILLAUME DE LORRIS

Born: Lorris, Loiret, France
Date: 1215 (?)

Died: Unknown
Date: c. 1240

AND

JEAN DE MEUNG

Born: Meung-sur-Loire, France
Date: c. 1250

Died: Paris, France
Date: c. 1305

Principal Work

poem: *Le Roman de la Rose*, Part I, c. 1237 (*Romance of the Rose*); Part II, 1275–1280.

In the first half of the thirteenth century, a French court poet, Guillaume de Lorris (also written Loury, Lory, and Lorrys), completed some 4,000 lines of the *Romance of the Rose*, an allegory on the psychology of Love, but left the work unfinished at his death. Forty years later it was completed by another poet of the court, named Jehan Clopinel (or Chopinel), known also as Jean de Meung, who added about 18,000 lines. There is a vast difference in the two authors and in their contributions to this allegory, a difference partly due to changes in civilization. The early thirteenth century troubadour, Guillaume, was full of courtly ideals, and his contribution is charming and frequently subtle. The Lover visits a park to which he is admitted by Idleness. Sharing the woods and lawns with him are Cupid, Pleasure, and Delight. Finally he comes upon the Rose and is given permission to kiss her. Their mutual pleasure irritates Jealousy, her guard, who

forthwith drives the Lover from the park.

With the passing of a half century, Jean de Meung who had previously translated Boethius' *Consolations of Philosophy* and the *Letters of Abélard and Héloïse*, was moved to complete the story in verse. He had come under bourgeois influences and was temperamentally incapable of delicate satire; his contribution is marked by brutal satire of the clergy and the nobility, the same spirit that fills his satirical *Testament*, written against the mendicant friars, between 1291 and 1296. He also shows his bitterness toward women and their wiles. In Jean's sequel there is more digression than story. Abuse of power is satirized, and though eventually there is a happy ending with the Lover winning the Rose, after an extended courtship, the reader must first read through much speech-making by Nature, Reason, Genius, and A Friend.

The high regard in which the *Ro-*

mance *of the Rose* was held in its time is proved by the existence of several hundred manuscript copies of its 22,000 lines. A translation of half of the first part is attributed to Geoffrey Chaucer.

BIBLIOGRAPHICAL REFERENCES: The best text in French, with commentary, is that of the Sociéte des Anciens Textes Français, 3 vols., 1893. For a translation in English see Frederick S. Ellis, *Romance of the Rose*, 1900 (rev. ed., 1932).

RICARDO GÜIRALDES

Born: Buenos Aires, Argentina
Date: February 13, 1886

Died: Paris, France
Date: October 6, 1927

PRINCIPAL WORKS

NOVELS: *Raucho*, 1917; *Rosaura*, 1922; *Don Segundo Sombra*, 1926.
SHORT STORIES: *Cuentos de muerte y de sangre*, 1915 (*Tales of Death and Blood*).
TRAVEL SKETCHES: *Xaimaca*, 1923 (*Jamaica*).

Ricardo Güiraldes, the son of a rich Argentine rancher, was born on his father's estate near Buenos Aires on February 13, 1886. France attracted him at an early age, and he was reading French when he entered high school. This influence is revealed in the volume of poetry he published at the age of twenty-nine. He spent much of his life in Paris and died there, October 6, 1927.

His boyhood on the ranch threw him into the company of the gauchos, one of whom, Segundo, was his teacher in the lore of the pampas. This cowboy was the inspiration for at least one of his short stories of violence, published in 1915, and for the novel about his childhood, written while homesick in Paris, that was to establish his fame. Previously Güiraldes had been influenced by the Vanguardist movement to compose the stories *Raucho, Rosaura,* and the travel book *Jamaica,* but nostalgia in France cured him of fads and his poetic sensitivity transmuted the crude material of early gaucho literature into a story as popular with children as with adults. This novel, *Don Segundo Sombra,* is a South American classic dealing with the ordinary life of a gaucho, but the author's originality colors it and his modern technique gives newness to the old tradition.

Güiraldes had other activities. He was a Congressman and at one time the mayor of Buenos Aires. His poetry is frivolous and mystic. His stories are romantic and realistic. But his love for his native country and his ability as a writer find their ideal combination in one novel, *Don Segundo Sombra.*

BIBLIOGRAPHICAL REFERENCES: Available biographical-critical studies include Angel Flores, "Latin American Writers: Ricardo Güiraldes," *Panorama* (Pan American Union), December, 1940; A. Torres Rioseco, *Novelistas contemporáneos de América,* 1939 (Santiago de Chile); *idem, Grandes Novelistas,* 1941; and Jefferson R. Spell, *Contemporary Spanish American Fiction,* 1944.

GUNNAR GUNNARSSON

Born: Valthjófsstadir, Iceland
Date: May 18, 1889

PRINCIPAL WORKS

NOVELS: *Af Borgslaegtens Historie,* 1912–1914 (*The History of the Family at Borg*); *Livets Strand,* 1915 (*The Shore of Life*); *Varg i Veum,* 1916 (*The Outcast*); *Edbrødre,* 1918 (*The Sworn Brothers*); *Salige er de Enføldige,* 1920 (*Seven Days' Darkness*); *Kirken paa Bjerget,* 1924–1928 (*The Church on the Mountain*); *Jon Arason,* 1930; *Hvide-Krist,* 1934 (*The White Christ*); *Graamand,* 1936 (*Gray Man*); *Advert,* 1937 (*The Good Shepherd*); *Heiðaharmur,* 1940 (*The Heath Laments*); *Salumessa,* 1952; *Brimhenda,* 1954.

SHORT STORIES: *Smaa Historier,* 1916; *Trylle og andet smaakram,* 1939 (*Trylla and Other Small Fry*).

PLAYS: *Drengen,* 1917; *Smaa Skuespil,* 1917; *Dyret med Glorien,* 1922; *Rævepelsena eller Ærlighed varer lengst,* 1930.

POEMS: *Digte,* 1911.

Gunnar Gunnarsson, who has written in both Icelandic and Danish, settled in Copenhagen after a high school education in his native Iceland, where he was born on May 18, 1889, at Valthjófsstadir. At first he joined a number of his countrymen who hoped to reach a large audience by writing in Danish, but he soon reacted against their cosmopolitan views to describe the lives of his ancestors and the fixed ways of his homeland in two notable series of novels. The four-volume "Borg" novels, about three generations of Icelandic farmers, first brought him fame in his adopted language. The most popular of these has been translated as *Guest the One-Eyed* (trans. 1920). In the autobiographical five-volume series titled *The Church on the Mountain* his gloomy concentration on the rocky terrain of Iceland and his portrayal of rugged heroes living close to the soil were forcefully expressed.

These novels were translated as *Ships in the Sky* and *Night and the Dream,* both published in 1938.

The Shore of Life, a story about the failure of a country priest and the enervating weakness of the people around him, may be Gunnarsson's finest work. He has always been concerned with intense moral struggles; especially powerful is his account of the destruction of a mind through villainy in *Seven Days' Darkness.* As an interpreter of Northern life he has been compared to Knut Hamsun and Johannes V. Jensen. Primarily a novelist, he has written several plays and a volume of poetry.

Gunnarsson returned to Iceland in 1938 to write *The Heath Laments,* in his own language. Master of an elegant style, he is now at work on a series of novels designed to dramatize the history of Iceland from the age of the Vikings to the present.

BIBLIOGRAPHICAL REFERENCES: For brief studies of Gunnarsson in English see Stefán Einarsson, *History of Icelandic Prose Writers, 1800–1940,* 1948; and W. W. Worster, "Four Icelandic Writers," *Edinburgh Review,* CCXXXVIII (1923), 302–

319. See also Kjeld Elfelt, *Gunnar Gunnarsson*, 1927; S. Einarsson, "Gunnar Gunnarsson," *Skírnir*, CXII (1938), 138–160; and H. de Boor, "Gunnar Gunnarsson," *Nordische Stimen*, IX (1939), 180–183.

A. B. GUTHRIE, JR.

Born: Bedford, Indiana
Date: January 13, 1901

Principal Works

NOVELS: *The Big Sky*, 1947; *The Way West*, 1949; *These Thousand Hills*, 1956.

A(lfred) B(ertram) Guthrie, Jr., American journalist, teacher, and novelist, was born in Bedford, Indiana, on January 13, 1901. His family soon moved to Choteau, Montana, a rough settlement not far from the Blackfoot Reservation. Here Mr. Guthrie, Sr., served as teacher and principal of the local high school. He began early to instill an interest in historical subjects in his sons. Later he gave up his school work to become a publisher of newspapers and tried to interest his sons in journalism. Accordingly, Guthrie enrolled at the University of Washington. He took his degree from the University of Montana in 1913. In college he worked for a regional paper, *The Frontier,* and he was graduated with honors.

After trying his hand at numerous jobs in all parts of the United States, he was hired as a reporter for the *Lexington Leader* in Lexington, Kentucky. He held this position for twenty years, during which time he worked up to the editorship of the paper. His first book, a mystery story entitled *Murders at Moon Dance,* was published in 1943. In 1944, on a fellowship at Harvard University, he was influenced by Professor Theodore Morrison to start work on *The Big Sky,* an exciting story of the opening of the Far Western frontier. Realistically written, it covers the period from 1830 to 1843. In 1947 he gave up his editorial duties in Lexington and published, in 1949, *The Way West,* a novel which continues the story of the opening of the West, telling the story of a group of people who traveled over the Oregon Trail from Missouri to Oregon in the 1840's. This book was chosen as a Book-of-the-Month-Club selection in 1949 and in 1950 was awarded the Pulitzer Prize for fiction. In the fall of 1956 Guthrie published *These Thousand Hills,* a story of Montana in the 1880's which describes the cattlemen as they begin to fence off the land and settle down.

At present Mr. Guthrie teaches creative writing at the University of Kentucky and spends his summers in Montana, where he is the owner of a ranch. His wife is the former Harriet Helen Larson of Choteau, Montana.

BIBLIOGRAPHICAL REFERENCES: For biographical data and criticism see Harry R. Warfel, *American Novelists of Today,* 1951; and Dayton Kohler, "A. B. Guthrie, Jr., and the West," *College English,* XII (1951), 249–256.

HĀFIZ
Shams ud-din Mohammed

Born: Shiraz, Persia
Date: c. 1320

Died: Shiraz
Date: c. 1388

PRINCIPAL WORK

POEMS: The *Divan*, c. 1350.

Hāfiz was the pen name of Shams ud-din Mohammed, the most celebrated of the Persian lyric poets. As a youth he studied poetry, theology, and philosophy under Shaik Mahmūd 'Aṭṭār, a famous dervish of the time in the Moslem world. Hāfiz's first literary patron was the Shah of Fars, Abu Ishaqi Inju. Twelve years of serene life ended for Hāfiz when the shah was ousted in 1353 by the ascetic Mubariz ud-din Muhammad Mozaffari. Judging from Hāfiz's poetry, in which he chafes at even the thought of asceticism, the five-year reign of Mubariz ud-din must have been a most unhappy time for the poet. But in 1358 Shah Shuja, overthrew his father, returned Fars to a more genial rule, and became the patron of Hāfiz.

By this time Hāfiz had established his reputation in the Moslem world.

Although he remained in Fars, he seems to have had several offers of patronage from neighboring rulers who wanted the poet to grace their courts with his presence and poetry. According to references in his poetry, Hāfiz was married and had a son who was lost while still a youth; little else is known of his personal life. His most important work is the *Divan* (or *Dīwān*), composed of more than five hundred poems, most of them short pieces in the form called *ghazals*. Students of Persian poetry claim for the *ghazals* of Hāfiz the height of subtlety and lyric expression. Although much of his poetry is about natural beauty, drinking, and love, Hāfiz was a truly religious man, and he satirized hypocrisy in both laymen and religious leaders. He was born in Shiraz about 1320 and died there about 1388.

BIBLIOGRAPHICAL REFERENCES: Translations in verse include Gertrude L. Bell, *Poems from the Divan of Hāfiz*, 1928 (2nd ed.); C. K. Street, *Hāfiz in Quatrains*, 1946; and A. J. Arberry, *Fifty Poems of Hāfiz*, 1947. A prose translation was made by H. Wilberforce Clarke, 2 vols., 1891 (Calcutta). See also Sir Gore Ouseley, *Biographical Notices of Persian Poets*, 1846; Claud Field, *Persian Literature*, 1912; and C. K. Street, *Hāfiz, the Tongue of the Hidden*, 1928.

H. RIDER HAGGARD

Born: Norfolk, England
Date: June 22, 1856

Died: London, England
Date: May 14, 1925

PRINCIPAL WORKS

NOVELS: *King Solomon's Mines*, 1885; *She*, 1887; *Allan Quatermain*, 1887; *Jess*, 1887; *Colonel Quarich, V. C.*, 1888; *Cleopatra*, 1889; *The World's Desire*, 1890 (with Andrew Lang); *Beatrice,* 1890; *Eric Brighteyes,* 1891; *Nada the Lily,* 1892; *Ayesha* 1905.

AUTOBIOGRAPHY: *The Days of My Life,* 1926.

Past generations have esteemed H(enry) Rider Haggard as an ingenious teller of tales in the tradition of Robert Louis Stevenson; he was a master of effects of exotic suspense, and in this he has been equaled by the motion picture but hardly surpassed. He added to these qualities heroes who were manly and self-reliant, men immersed in either danger from native populations or awesome encounters with the occult.

Born at Bradenham Hall in Norfolk, on June 22, 1856, Haggard possessed a first-hand knowledge of Africa. At nineteen he went to South Africa as secretary to Sir Henry Bulwer, governor of Natal. Later, holding a position on the staff of the special commissioner, Sir Theophilus Shepstone, he finally became a master of the High Court of the Transvaal.

In 1879 he married and read for the bar, to which he was called in 1884. He felt drawn to literary work, however, and in 1882 he published his first book, *Cetywayo and His White Neighbours,* written in defense of Shepstone's policy, which had been overthrown when the Boers took over the Transvaal. Though the book was received favorably at the Cape, it did not draw the general attention that Haggard later won. Two novels—*Dawn* (1884) and *The Witch's Head* (1885), the latter treating a British defeat at Isandhlwana—appeared without stirring notice. But in 1885, *King Solomon's Mines,* inspired by the Zimbabwe ruins, achieved an immediate and spectacular success. Then followed a veritable flood of tales, their scenes chiefly laid in Africa, in which descriptions of exotic landscapes lead easily to apparitions of the goddesses of strange, lost religions; *She* and *Allan Quatermain* are good examples.

Haggard displayed in his own life the union of the practical and the romantic which marks his heroes. He displayed an intense interest in rural and agricultural problems. He himself was not only a practical farmer on his Norfolk estate but also a member of several commissions which studied agricultural and social conditions. Some of these reports evolved into *The Poor and the Land* (1905). Haggard was knighted in 1912.

At the time of his death in London on May 14, 1925, it was suggested that he was the superior of Kipling; but, though Haggard shared some of the greater writer's characteristics, he may at best be regarded only as a gifted and typical man of his time.

BIBLIOGRAPHICAL REFERENCES: A good source of biographical material is Haggard's autobiography, *The Days of My Life,* 2 vols., 1926. For biography and criticism in books and periodicals see also Katherine Mansfield, *Novels and Novelists,* 1930; E. C. Rashleigh, "Romances of Rider Haggard," *Living Age,* CCCIV (1920), 598–604; Edward Shanks, "Sir Rider Haggard and the Novel of Adventure," *London Mercury,* XI (1924), 71–79; H. G. Hutchinson, "Sir Rider Haggard's Autobiography," *Edinburgh Review,* CCXLIV (1926), 343–355; and Stella Gibbons, "Voyage of Rediscovery," *Fortnightly Review,* CLVIII (1945), 401–406.

RICHARD HAKLUYT

Born: Unknown
Date: c. 1552

Died: London, England
Date: November 23, 1616

PRINCIPAL WORKS

HISTORIES: *Divers Voyages touching the Discoverie of America*, 1582; *The Notable History, containing four Voyages made by certain French Captains into Florida; The Principal Navigations, Voyages, and Discoveries of the English Nation*, 1589, 1598–1600 (3 vols.); *A Particular Discourse concerning Westerne discoveries written in the year 1584*, 1877.

Although Richard Hakluyt, born c. 1552, enjoyed a successful career in the Church, he was, from his youth, driven by a boundless enthusiasm for the literature of the sea. In 1582 he published *Divers Voyages touching the Discoverie of America* and, five years later, *The Notable History, containing four Voyages made by certain French Captains into Florida*. In 1589 appeared the first edition of the great collection for which he is chiefly known, *The Principal Navigations, Voyages, and Discoveries of the English Nation*.

The book ranges from Geoffrey of Monmouth's story of the fabulous conquest of Iceland by King Arthur to a Dutch chronicler's account of the defeat of the Spanish Armada, from the mythical discovery of America by the Welsh prince Madoc to the voyages of Cabot, Drake, Cavendish, Frobisher, and Gilbert. In it one senses not only the immense courage of men facing the unknown dangers of uncharted seas, but also the amazingly business-like attitude they took toward their formidable tasks. By bringing to light a number of important accounts of events that had been obscure, Hakluyt helped to focus the public imagination on the all-important affairs of discovery and colonization.

Later he published several other translations and books of explorations, but none as important as *The Principal Navigations*. He rose to the arch-deaconry of Westminster and, appropriately, in 1605 was given the living of James Town, the prospective capital of Virginia. He died in London, November 23, 1616, and was buried in Westminster Abbey.

BIBLIOGRAPHICAL REFERENCES: The best edition of *The Principal Navigations* is the edition edited by Edmund Goldsmid, 16 vols., 1885–1890. The Hakluyt Society edition in 12 vols., 1903–1905, is a reliable reprint of the second edition. Editions of Hakluyt's other major works are *Divers Voyages Touching the Discoverie of America and the Islands Adjacent*, edited by John Winter Jones 1850; *A Discourse Concerning Western Planting*, edited by Charles Deane and with an introduction by Leonard Woods, 1877; *The Original Writings and Correspondence of the Two Richard Hakluyts*, edited by E. G. R. Taylor, 1935—all published by the Hakluyt Society. Important critical studies are G. B. Parks, *Richard Hakluyt and the English Voyages*, 1928, and *Richard Hakluyt and his Successors*, edited by Edward Lynam for the Hakluyt Society, 1946. Important articles are K. R. Andrews, "New Light on Hakluyt," *Mariner's Mirror*, XXXVII (1951), 299–307; and Paul Whittek, "The Turkish Documents in Hakluyt's 'Voyages,'" *Bulletin of the Institute of Historical Research*, XIX (1942), 121–39.

EDWARD EVERETT HALE

Born: Boston, Massachusetts   *Died:* Roxbury, Massachusetts
Date: April 3, 1822   *Date:* June 10, 1909

PRINCIPAL WORKS

NOVELS: *G. T. T.*, 1877; *Our Christmas in a Palace*, 1883; *East and West*, 1892.
SHORT STORIES: *If, Yes, and Perhaps*, 1868; *Back to Back*, 1878; *Crusoe in New York*, 1880; *For Christmas and New Year*, 1906.
MICELLANEOUS: *The Ingham Papers*, 1869; *Ten Times One Is Ten*, 1871; *The Sermon on the Mount*, 1886; *Studies in American Colonial Life*, 1895; *James Russell Lowell and His Friends*, 1899; *A New England Boyhood*, 1893; *Memories of a Hundred Years*, 1902; *"We, the People,"* 1903.

Edward Everett Hale's father was editor of the Boston *Daily Advertiser,* his uncle the distinguished orator, Edward Everett, and his great-uncle the legendary Nathan Hale. His own career reflected the patriotic zeal, religious devotion, and humanitarian interests with which his family name had long been associated. Born in Boston on April 3, 1822, he was graduated from Harvard University in 1839, taught at the Boston Latin School, studied theology, and then entered the ministry as a Unitarian clergyman.

Hale was a moralist and reformer. He worked indefatigably as a preacher, a contributor to and editor of periodicals, and as a founder and organizer of charitable societies. Through his writing and organizations he sought to correct what he felt to be injustices in the American scene. Hale began his literary career with a series of short stories which apeared in the *Atlantic Monthly.* The moral import of Hale's stories and their pedagogical approach to social and moral problems is perhaps best indicated by the fact that several of them led to the formation of religious and charitable organizations. His best remembered short story, "The Man Without a Country," included in *If, Yes, and Perhaps,* was written to arouse patriotic sentiments and thus rally people to the wavering Union cause. Another of his best-known stories, "My Double; and How He Undid Me," was published in the same volume. A prolific writer, he published several books under the pseudonym Col. Frederic Ingham. He died at Roxbury, Massachusetts, June 10, 1909.

BIBLIOGRAPHICAL REFERENCES: There is no collected edition of Hale's writings. His autobiographical volumes (*A New England Boyhood and Other Bits of Autobiography*, 1900; *Memories of a Hundred Years*, 2 vols., 1902) are supplemented by the official biography by Edward Everett Hale, Jr., *The Life and Letters of Edward Everett Hale*, 2 vols., 1917. A briefer and more readable work is Jean Holloway, *Edward Everett Hale: A Biography*, 1956. See also E. E. Hale, Jr., "Edward Everett Hale," *Outlook*, LXXXV (1907), 801–805; and T. W. Higginson, "Edward Everett Hale," *ibid.*, LXXXXII (1909), 403–406.

LUDOVIC HALÉVY

Born: Paris, France
Date: January 1, 1834

Died: Paris
Date: May 8, 1908

Principal Works

NOVELS: *Un Scandale,* 1860 (*A Scandal*); *L'Abbé Constantin,* 1882 (*The Abbé Constantin*); *Deux Mariages,* 1885 (*Two Marriages*); *Mon camarade Moussard,* 1886 (*My Friend Moussard*).

SHORT STORIES: *Kari-kari,* 1892.

PLAYS (with Henri Meilhac): *Frou-frou,* 1869; *Le Réveillon,* 1872; *La Boule,* 1875; *La Cigale,* 1877; *La Petit Mère,* 1880.

LIBRETTOS: *La Belle Hélène,* 1864; *Barbe bleue,* 1866; *La Grande Duchesse de Gérolstein,* 1867; *La Périchole,* 1868; *Carmen,* 1875; *Le Petit Duc,* 1878; *La Petite Mademoiselle,* 1879.

Ludovic Halévy was fortunate in his artistic background. His father, Léon Halévy, was a poet and versatile man of letters; his uncle was a successful opera librettist, and his grandfather was a noted architect. Born in Paris, January 1, 1834, he attended the lycée Louis-le-Grand and at eighteen, entered the civil service and held various minor governmental posts until 1865, when he retired to devote his entire time to writing.

He had met Offenbach in 1855, and the latter's *Orpheus in the Underworld,* for which Halévy did a prologue, made the young writer famous. In 1860 Halévy met Henri Meilhac, with whom he wrote a total of seventy-nine theatrical works. The influence of Halévy's uncle may have had much to do with his early interest in the stage. Perhaps the most famous comic opera

for which the two collaborators wrote a libretto was *La Périchole.* Both writers did their best work in depicting gay scenes of Paris life, scenes which displayed their wit and penetrating observation. Halévy's best-known libretto was written on Bizet's *Carmen.*

After 1881 Halévy turned his powers of observation to more serious creation in his novels. The most famous of these, and the one work for which he will always be remembered, is *The Abbé Constantin,* a heart-warming tale of human benevolence which won him entrance into the French Academy. Halévy did almost no writing in his last years, but he encouraged and aided younger writers. He died in Paris, May 8, 1908, beloved for his kindness and admired for the graceful play of his penetrating wit.

BIBLIOGRAPHICAL REFERENCES: The representative plays have been collected in *Théâtre de Meilhac et Halévy,* 8 vols., 1900–1902. See also Félix Gaiffe, *La Rire et la scène française,* 1932.

ALEXANDER HAMILTON

Born: Nevis, British West Indies
Date: January 11, 1755

Died: New York, N. Y.
Date: July 12, 1804

POLITICAL ESSAYS, LETTERS, AND DOCUMENTS: *A Full Vindication of the Measures of Congress*, 1774 (reprinted in *The Works of Alexander Hamilton*, edited by Henry Cabot Lodge, 2nd ed., 12 vols., 1904, hereafter cited as *Works*, I, 1–52); *The Farmer Refuted*, 1775 (*Works*, I, 53–177); *Propositions [Offered in the Philadelphia Convention] for a Constitution of Government* (*Works*, I, 347–378); *Letters from Phocion [on Tory Enfranchisement]*, 1784 (*Works*, IV, 230–240); *The Federalist*, 1788 (*Works*, Vols., XI and XII, with index); *[First Report on the] Public Credit*, 1790 (*Works*, II, 227–327); *[Report on the] National Bank*, 1790 (*Works*, III, 388–495); *[Report on] Manufactures*, 1791 (*Works*, IV, 70–198); *[Second Report on the] Public Credit*, 1795 (*Works*, III, 199–301); *[Letters by] No Jacobin*, 1793 (*Works*, V, 17–49); *Americanus [Condemns Discrimination against British Goods]*, 1794 (*Works*, V, 74–96); *Horatius* and *Camillus: Defence of Mr. Jay's Treaty*, 1795 (*Works*, V, 189–491; VI, 3–197); *Letters of Pacificus*, 1796 (*Works*, IV, 432–489); "The Jefferson Controversy" (*Works*, VII, 299–306); *Observations on Certain Documents contained in . . . The History of the United States for the Year 1796, in which the Charge of Speculation against Alexander Hamilton . . . is fully Refuted [but his Affair with Mrs. Reynolds Admitted]*, 1797 (*Works*, VII, 369–479); *Letter . . . Concerning the Public Conduct and Character of John Adams*, 1800 (*Works*, VII, 309–365).

Alexander Hamilton was born on Nevis, British West Indies, on January 11, 1755, the illegitimate son of one James Hamilton and Mrs. Rachel Fawcett Levein. A penniless orphan at thirteen, he was apprenticed to a merchant. His 1772 newspaper account of a hurricane influenced charitable islanders to finance his education at Elizabethtown, New Jersey, and at King's (Columbia) College, 1772–1776. A premedical student, he became interested in debate and wrote newspaper essays culminating in *A Full Vindication of the Measures of Congress*, published in 1774. In purple passages, he appealed to racial, religious, and economic prejudice against Parliament's pretensions, while professing moderation.

A Revolutionary militia captain in 1776, Hamilton became a lieutenant-colonel as aide-de-camp to Washington. Although a good secretary and confidential adviser, he coveted personal glory in combat. After disputing with Washington and resigning in 1781, he was given a colonelcy and command of an assault at Yorktown. Hamilton supplied secret war news to New Yorkers like Philip Schuyler, whose daughter Elizabeth he married in 1780.

Retiring from active service in 1782, he successfully prepared himself for the bar and served briefly as Continental tax collector in New York, whose legislature gave him little cash, Delphic agreement to his proposal that the states enlarge Congress' power, and his own election to Congress, 1782–1783 and 1788–1789. In pamphlets and in Congress, Hamilton advocated a peacetime standing army, restitution of Loyalist franchise and property, and congressional control over trade, tariffs, and its own bureaucracy. His prospect of a "great Federal Republic" instead of disunited "petty" states appealed more to merchants than the "laboring poor." As early as 1779, Hamilton proposed a national bank with high profits for wealthy investors and tax schedules weighing heaviest upon farmers and artisans. In the army mutinies of 1783, he first encouraged unpaid soldiers to frighten Congressmen into closer unity and then urged their forcible suppression.

A member of the 1786 Annapolis Convention to consider interstate problems and foreign trade, Hamilton and James Madison were largely responsible for its adjournment to Philadelphia in 1787 to revise the Articles of Confederation. Brief service in the New York legislature in 1786 secured liberalization of divorce laws, enfranchisement of Tories, enlargement of Columbia University (of which he was long a Trustee), and participation in the convention. At Philadelphia he despaired of republican government and unsuccessfully advocated British-style government of "the rich and well born," a lifetime executive and Senate chosen by indirect and restricted election, a triennial assembly elected by universal suffrage, an executive veto over federal and state laws and the elimination of states. Contributing little to the Constitution, Hamilton urged all delegates to sign it "as better than nothing." The kindest light in which Hamilton's proposals may be viewed is that he consciously overstated his reactionary case to create a position from which to bargain with advocates of decentralized liberty. He recognized that popular opinion would countenance only a republic, and he was determined to make it as supremely powerful and strong as he could.

Although ever considering the Constitution a "frail and worthless fabric," Hamilton fought for its ratification in the New York convention and in newspaper essays. His fifty-three contributions to *The Federalist,* together with those of Madison and John Jay, form the Constitution's greatest commentary and America's greatest contribution to political philosophy. Hamilton argued the indispensability of a strong nation to avoid foreign aggression, fragmentation, and commercial disadvantages. He postponed New York's decision until so many states ratified it that she did likewise, in fear of unprofitable exclusion.

Hamilton's chief fame rests upon his career as Secretary of the Treasury, 1789–1795. Reform of national finances, upon which the Confederation foundered, was accomplished by his bold, comprehensive program, attuned to demands for solvency, despite questionable details, and delivered in written reports to Congress on public credit in 1790 and 1795, the national bank in 1790 and manufactures in 1791. Continental currency had already been repudiated, but staggering foreign and domestic debts since 1776 remained owing by the state and central governments. Hamilton guaranteed full repayment of both, despite demands by Madison's followers to prefer original domestic creditors above subsequent speculators, many of whom were Hamiltonians who, unlike Hamilton, profited by advance knowledge of his financing. By a close decision, the federal government assumed state debts, more because Jefferson and Madison disliked obstructing the new government at the outset than because they bargained with Hamilton to establish the national capital on the Potomac. Hamilton's Report on manufactures, propounding protective tariffs for infant industries, and his establishment of the bank, justified by his

473

theory of implied powers, were anathema to the Republicans. His meddling in foreign affairs antagonized Jefferson further and started a newspaper war. Hamilton's indiscreet confidences to the British minister would today be held treasonable. Congressional censure of Hamilton for violating instructions in the disposition of new foreign loans, although admitted subsequently, was avoided by Washington's reluctant sharing of responsibility. Backwoods objections to whiskey excises were stifled by him with more force than necessary. During the French Revolutionary wars, Hamilton's desire for a neutrality stricter than consistent with the Franco-American Alliance and his opposition to Madison's proposals to discriminate against British trade until she dealt fairly with America on their frontiers and at sea were almost thwarted, but negotiation and ratification of Jay's Treaty effected both his foreign and domestic policies.

Following his retirement to New York legal practice in 1795, Hamilton's governmental influence remained great. He shared with Madison the background for Washington's Farewell Address. He so intrigued against John Adams in the election of 1796 and so dominated his cabinet that they became enemies. In 1797 Republican investigation of Hamilton's secretaryship caused his admission of an illicit liaison with a certain Mrs. Reynolds to save his official integrity. Threat of war with France in 1798 made him Washington's second-in-command of a provisional army, but Adams' diplomacy averted war. Adams' assertion that Hamilton was under British influence evoked Hamilton's publication of a diatribe against Adams which contributed to Federalist defeat in 1800. Hamilton's influence in the electoral college to break the tie in favor of Jefferson over Burr was more motivated by vindictiveness against his New York rival than by statesmanship. His libelous participation in the New York gubernatorial election of 1804 defeated Burr. When Burr justifiably challenged him, Hamilton refused to apologize. They dueled at Weehawken, New Jersey, on July 11, 1804, and Hamilton was wounded. He died the next day at New York, survived by his wife and children.

BIBLIOGRAPHICAL REFERENCES: Allan Nevins, "Alexander Hamilton," in the *Dictionary of American Biography* is the best sketch. There are two "best" biographies, one pro and the other anti: Broadus Mitchell's *Alexander Hamilton: From Youth to Maturity, 1755–1788*, 1957, the first of a projected two-volume work, whose fault is that it seeks to explain away Hamilton's anti-republicanism; and Nathan Schachner's *Alexander Hamilton*, 1946, which is weak in research and detail and whose waspish picking at Hamilton's flaws seriously impairs its objectivity. Louis M. Hacker, *Alexander Hamilton in the American Tradition*, 1957, paints the subject in unbelievably democratic colors. Of the older biographies, John T. Morse, *Life of Alexander Hamilton*, 2 vols., 1876, and William G. Sumner's *Alexander Hamilton*, 1890, are superior to Henry J. Ford's *Alexander Hamilton*, 1920. Allan McL. Hamilton, *The Intimate Life of Alexander Hamilton*, 1910, contains valuable materials and attempts to correct the filiopietistic John C. Hamilton's *The Life of Alexander Hamilton*, 1840, and *History of the United States of America as Traced in the Writings of Alexander Hamilton and his Contemporaries*, 9 vols., 1857–1865. Henry C. Lodge, *Alexander Hamilton*, 1882, is biased and uncritical. At the opposite extreme of partisanship is Claude G. Bowers, *Jefferson and Hamilton: The Struggle for Democracy in America*,

1925. Gertrude Atherton made scholarly researches which she embodied in her excellent novel about Hamilton, *The Conqueror*, 1902. Important Hamiltonian materials have been published in the *William and Mary Quarterly*, Series III, especially Douglass Adair, "The Authorship of the Disputed Federalist Papers," *op. cit.*, I, (April and July, 1944), 97–122, 235–264; Harold Larson, "Alexander Hamilton: the Fact and Fiction of His Early Years," *op. cit.*, IX (April, 1952), 139–151; and *Alexander Hamilton, 1755–1804, Bicentennial Number, op. cit.*, XII (April, 1955), No. 2.

There is currently afoot preparation of a multi-volume edition of *The Papers of Alexander Hamilton* sponsored by Columbia University under the executive editorship of Harold C. Syrett. Until its publication *The Works of Alexander Hamilton*, edited by Henry C. Lodge, 12 vols., 1904 (2nd ed.), remains standard, except where it omits selections found in John C. Hamilton, *The Works of Alexander Hamilton*, 7 vols., 1850–1851. Extremely useful compilations, usually from Lodge's text, are *Alexander Hamilton and the Founding of the Nation*, edited by Richard B. Morris, 1957; and *Alexander Hamilton's Papers on Public Credit, Commerce and Finance*, edited by Samuel McKee, Jr., 1934.

Exclusive of biographies of Hamilton's contemporaries, specialized and general works which are useful are Thomas P. Abernethy, *The Burr Conspiracy*, 1954; Henry Adams, *Documents Relating to New England Federalism*, 1877, *The Life of Albert Gallatin*, 1879, and *History of the United States during the Administrations of Thomas Jefferson and James Madison*, 9 vols., 1889–1891; Leland D. Baldwin, *The Whiskey Rebels: The Story of a Frontier Uprising*, 1939; John S. Bassett, *The Federalist System, 1789–1801*, 1906; Charles A. Beard, *An Economic Interpretation of the Constitution of the United States*, 1913, and *Economic Origins of Jeffersonian Democracy*, 1915; Samuel F. Bemis, *Jay's Treaty: A Study in Commerce and Diplomacy*, 1923; Albert S. Bolles, *The Financial History of the United States from 1789 to 1860*, 1883; James Bryce, *The Predictions of Hamilton and De Tocqueville*, 1887; Edmund C. Burnet, *The Continental Congress*, 1941; Joseph Charles, *The Origins of the American Party System*, 1956; Rudolph Cronau, *The Army of the American Revolution and Its Organization*, 1923; Davis R. Dewey, *The Financial System of the United States*, 1928 (10th ed.); William A. Ganoe, *The History of the United States Army*, 1942 (rev. ed.); John T. Holdsworth, *The First Bank of the United States*, 1910; Merrill Jensen, *The New Nation: A History of the United States During the Confederation, 1781–1789*, 1950; Benson J. Lossing, *Pictorial Field Book of the American Revolution*, 2 vols., 1850–1851; John C. Miller, *Crisis in Freedom: The Alien and Sedition Acts*, 1951; Allan Nevins, *History of Bank of New York and Trust Company, 1784 to 1934*, 1934; Victor H. Palsits, ed., *Washington's Farewell Address with transliterations of all of the drafts of Washington, Madison & Hamilton*, 1953; William J. Schultz and M. R. Caine, *Financial Development of the United States*, 1937; William G. Sumner, *A History of Banking in the United States*, 1896; Raymond Walters, Jr., *Albert Gallatin, Jeffersonian Financier and Diplomat*, 1957; Leonard D. White, *The Federalists*, 1948; Charles Warren, *The Making of the Constitution*, 1929; Emily S. Whiteley, *Washington and His Aides-de-Camp*, 1936; Woodrow Wilson, *Congressional Government*, 1885; Carl C. Van Doren, *Secret History of the American Revolution*, 1941; Charles H. Van Tyne, *The American Revolution*, 1905, and *The War of Independence*, 1929.

DASHIELL HAMMETT

Born: St. Mary's County, Maryland   *Died:* New York, N. Y.
Date: May 27, 1894   *Date:* January 10, 1961

PRINCIPAL WORKS

NOVELS: *The Maltese Falcon,* 1930; *The Glass Key,* 1931; *The Thin Man,* 1932.

(Samuel) Dashiell Hammett is the successful innovator of a form of detective fiction that dominates the genre today, the mystery novel in which the detective is as tough as the quarry he pursues and sometimes as immoral. Hammett's list of works is shorter than that of many writers of detective fiction, but his two most famous detectives, Sam Spade and Nick Charles, are the ancestors of the hard-drinking, hard-knuckled, and saturnine heroes of the novels of Raymond Chandler, Mickey Spillane, and others.

Born on the Maryland Eastern Shore on May 27, 1894, Hammett was educated at the Baltimore Polytechnic Institute. Shortly after he left school he went through a variety of occupations as newsboy, messenger boy, clerk, stevedore, and private detective, occupations that have since been very use-ful to him as a writer. He developed his method of horror and shock in *Red Harvest* (1929) and *The Dain Curse* (1929) but failed to win popular favor until he published *The Maltese Falcon* in 1930. In 1946–1947 he was an instructor in the Jefferson School of Social Science in New York. Hammett was active in both wars, and in recent years he has been touched by several investigations into Communist front organizations.

Hammett's success as a writer was for some years overshadowed by the almost independent life which two of his characters, Nick and Nora Charles, achieved in a series of motion pictures and radio and television programs. Additional Hammett titles are *Adventures of Sam Spade* (1944) and *Continental Operator* (1945).

BIBLIOGRAPHICAL REFERENCES: There is no extended biographical study or criticism. For a brief sketch see Elizabeth Sanderson, "Ex-detective Hammett," *Bookman,* LXXIV (1932), 516–518.

KNUT HAMSUN

Born: Lom, Norway   *Died:* Grimstad, Norway
Date: August 4, 1859   *Date:* February 19, 1952

PRINCIPAL WORKS

NOVELS: *Sult,* 1890 (*Hunger*); *Mysterier,* 1892 (*Mysteries*); *Ny jord,* 1893 (*Shallow Soil*); *Redaktør Lynge,* 1893 (*Editor Lynge*); *Pan,* 1894; *Svœrmere,* 1904 (*Dreamers*); *Under høstsjernen,* 1907 (*Under the Autumn Star*); *Benoni,* 1908; *Rosa,* 1908; *En vandrer spiller met sordin,* 1909 (*A Wanderer Plays on Muted Strings*); *Børn av tilden,* 1913 (*Children of the Age*); *Segelfoss by,* 1915 (*Segelfoss Town*); *Markens grøde,* 1917 (*Growth of the Soil*); *Konerne ved vandposten,* 1920

(The Women at the Pump); Landstrykere, 1927 *(Vagabonds); August,* 1930; *Men livet lever,* 1933 *(The Road Leads On); Ringen slutet,* 1936 *(The Ring Is Closed).*
PLAY: *Livet ivold: skuespil i fire akter,* 1910 *(In the Grip of Life).*

Although essentially a Norwegian author, Knut Hamsun may be claimed in part by America because he spent some of his formative years in the United States. He was born at Lom, Norway, into what the Scandinavians refer to as the "peasant aristocracy" on August 4, 1859, that momentous year which saw the appearance of Darwin's *Origin of Species* and the birth of John Dewey, both of whom became landmarks in the course of Western thought and civilization. By the age of nineteen Hamsun had composed a few poems and had attempted a novel. As a young man he hoped to enter the University of Christiania, and he worked at all kinds of jobs in order to save up enough money. Finding himself unable to save the necessary funds for a university education in his native land, he, like tens of thousands of his generation in Europe, emigrated to the United States. Also, like so many of his fellow Scandinavian immigrants, he made his way to the Middle West. Roaming about Wisconsin and Minnesota, he worked at many short-time jobs on farms and in the towns. Disappointed at finding so little opportunity in America, he returned to his native Norway in 1884 and there lectured about the United States and his experiences in this country. Two years later he returned to America to spend the years 1886–1888 in the Middle West. His activities during the second American period included lectures on literature in Minneapolis, hard work as a harvest hand in the wheat fields of North Dakota, and an unhappy period as a horse-car con-

ductor in Chicago. He is reputed to have been dismissed from the last-named job because he insisted upon reading while he should have been working at collecting fares from the passengers.

Upon his return to Norway in 1889 Hamsun wrote an essay entitled "Cultural Life of Modern America," a highly critical work about American life and a reflection of what the author had seen as an emigrant to the United States. The essay was followed by *Hunger* in 1890, the first of Hamsun's great novels. This book was so successful that Hamsun acquired enough money and prestige to continue as a professional writer. He settled in a little fishing village near Grimstad, in his native Norway. He married and reared five children.

Growth of the Soil, which was published in 1917, is Hamsun's best and most popular novel, a work rich in both form and content. Translated into English in 1920, it also won for Hamsun the Nobel Prize for literature in the same year. In this book the author reveals his great power as a regionalist and as a rural naturalist, in the literary sense of that term. As a regionalist he presents beautifully the setting of a rural community in northern Norway, making extensive use of both local language and customs. As a literary naturalist he portrays life in the hard countryside of northern Norway as it is, refusing to glamorize rural life, although he sees some mystical elements in it. Hamsun, who knew well both city and rural life, saw urban existence as a corrosive influence on humanity.

Isak, Inger, and their sons, in *Growth of the Soil*, are not idealized, nor is their life, but it is compared favorably with life in a more complex civilization. Indeed, urban civilization is the real villain of the novel. Only those characters, like Isak, who cling to the soil and wrest a livelihood from it find a successful existence. As a literary naturalist Hamsun is a little difficult to analyze. There are times when the characters seem more like Rousseau's noble savage than, for example, the peasants in Zola's naturalistic *Earth* (1887). This is true not only of *Growth of the Soil*; it is true also of *Pan, Vagabonds, August,* and *The Road Leads On*. The central character in each of these books is close to nature and stays as far as possible from the culture of the city. In a sense, too, each of these characters is like his creator, Knut Hamsun, who after being an urban city-dweller chose to live the simple life in a Norwegian fishing village. There is, too, at least a suspicion that Hamsun was comparing in abstract fashion his own relatively agricultural Norway to the urban and industrialized United States, a land which had been none too kind to him during the years he spent in America. Certainly Hamsun always felt that urban life, with its cities and factories and their attendant prohibitions and conventions, was an unnatural, if not vicious, environment for mankind.

Upon first reading Hamsun's novels, the reader may wonder how the author could ever have been awarded the Nobel Prize for literature. In the original Norwegian, or in translation, his style seems primitive, even childlike. The apparent characteristics are misleading, for Hamsun's style is a careful one and well suited to his subject matter and his themes. Much of his writing is a carefully constructed prose poetry which owes something, at least, to the style of the Old Testament, especially the King James version. Poetic repetition and complicated parallelism abound, although the diction is simplicity itself, and Hamsun's style is noticeably independent of the adjectives so common in American writing.

Unlike his countrymen, Knut Hamsun felt a strong kinship with the Germans. During both the great world wars he sympathized with the activities of Germany. Even the German occupation of Norway under the Nazis during World War II failed to arouse his resentment. As a result, many of Hamsun's fellow Norwegians, who actively resented the German occupation, nursed ill-feeling for him after 1945. Beyond a fine, no official action was taken against him by the Norwegian government, however, because of his advanced age. Hamsun died at Grimstad on February 19, 1952, in his ninety-third year.

BIBLIOGRAPHICAL REFERENCES: The pioneer study of Knut Hamsun in English is Hanna Astrup Larsen's *Knut Hamsun*, 1922. Other studies include *Knut Hamsun: His Personality and His Outlook upon Life*, 1922; Walter A. Berendsohn, *Knut Hamsun*, 1929; and Einar Skavlan, *Knut Hamsun*, 1929. See also W. W. Worster, *Growth of the Soil*, Vol. II, 1921; Edwin Bjorkman, Introduction to *Hunger*, 1922; Alrik Gustafson, *Six Scandinavian Novelists*, 1940; and W. G. Allen, *Renaissance in the North*, 1946.

478

THOMAS HARDY

Born: Higher Bockhampton, England *Died:* Dorchester, England
Date: June 2, 1840   *Date:* January 11, 1928

PRINCIPAL WORKS

NOVELS: *Desperate Remedies,* 1871; *Under the Greenwood Tree,* 1872; *A Pair of Blue Eyes,* 1873; *Far from the Madding Crowd,* 1874; *The Hand of Ethelberta,* 1876; *The Return of the Native,* 1878; *The Trumpet-Major,* 1880; *A Laodicean,* 1881; *Two on a Tower,* 1882; *The Mayor of Casterbridge,* 1886; *The Woodlanders,* 1887; *Tess of the D'Urbervilles,* 1891; *Jude the Obscure,* 1895; *The Well-Beloved,* 1897.

SHORT STORIES: *Wessex Tales,* 1888; *A Group of Noble Dames,* 1891; *Life's Little Ironies,* 1894; *A Changed Man,* 1913.

POEMS: *Wessex Poems,* 1898; *Poems of the Past and the Present,* 1901; *Time's Laughingstocks,* 1909; *Satires of Circumstance,* 1914; *Moments of Vision,* 1917; *Late Lyrics and Earlier,* 1922; *Human Shows, Far Phantasies, Songs and Trifles,* 1925; *Winter Words,* 1928; *Collected Poems,* 1931.

PLAYS: *The Dynasts: A Drama in Three Parts,* 1903, 1906, 1908; *The Famous Tragedy of the Queen of Cornwall,* 1923.

MISCELLANEOUS: *Life and Art,* 1925; *Letters: Transcribed from the Original Autographs in the Colby College Library,* 1954.

About three miles east of Dorchester, in Dorset, England, there is a hamlet known as Higher Bockhampton. In a thatched-roof cottage which still stands at one end of this hamlet, Thomas Hardy was born on June 2, 1840. The place of his birth is important, for it is the center of a region he learned to know and love—a region he called "Wessex" and wrote about in all his books.

The first of these books was published in 1871 when Hardy was nearly thirty-one years old and was still lacking in literary training and experience. His entire schooling had been confined to eight years between the ages of eight and sixteen. For five years he had worked as an apprentice in the drafting office of a Dorchester architect, John Hicks. When Hardy was twenty-one he went to London and found employment with Arthur Blomfield, a successful metropolitan architect, and remained with him for five years. But Gothic churches and old manor houses never succeeded in crowding books out of the central place in Hardy's affections. During his years in London, he tried his hand at composing verses, and when he discovered that editors showed no readiness to publish his poems, he turned at the age of twenty-seven to novel-writing.

Hardy called his first attempt at fiction *The Poor Man and the Lady.* He sent his manuscript to Alexander Macmillan, the London publisher, who replied encouragingly but found too many faults in the work to be willing to print it. Hardy thereupon tried a second publisher, Chapman & Hall, and was fortunate enough to have his manuscript placed in the hands of their reader, George Meredith, the novelist. Meredith had an interview with Hardy and advised him to suppress *The Poor Man* (because of the vehemence of its social satire) and to write another novel "with more plot." Hardy took Meredith's advice and wrote *Desperate Remedies,* which was published anonymously and at his own expense in 1871. This was the beginning of a quarter-century's activity as one of the most successful and influential novelists that England has produced.

Like *Desperate Remedies,* Hardy's next novel, *Under the Greenwood Tree,* was published anonymously. In 1872 he was invited to contribute a story for serialization in *Tinsleys' Magazine* and this novel, *A Pair of Blue Eyes* (1873), was the first to carry his name. When *Far from the Madding Crowd* was serialized in the *Cornhill Magazine* in 1874, the acclaim from critics as well as from the general public was cordial enough to encourage Hardy to do three things: he discarded further use of anonymity, he gave up all further practice as an architect, and in September, 1874, he married.

In the twenty years that followed, Hardy turned out ten more full-length novels, besides numerous short-stories and articles. His fourteenth and last novel, *Jude the Obscure,* resulted in such an outcry that Hardy, always over-sensitive to criticism, shrank from further attempt to find expression in fiction and returned to his first love, poetry. In 1898 he surprised the world by publishing *Wessex Poems,* and throughout the next thirty years he produced volume after volume of verse until, by the time of his death, he had composed nearly a thousand poems. In addition to this achievement in metrical composition, Hardy wrote a gigantic dramatic epic on the Napoleonic wars which he called *The Dynasts* (published in three parts, 1904, 1906, 1908).

As stated above, Hardy's success with *Far from the Madding Crowd* enabled him to marry. He had met Emma L. Gifford, the young lady who became his wife, when he had gone to Cornwall in 1870 to supervise the restoration of a dilapidated church. Ten years after this marriage, he built a house near Dorchester, and from 1885 on, his address remained "Max Gate." He had no children. Mrs. Hardy died in 1912 and was buried in the country churchyard beside the Stinsford parish church which Hardy had attended as a boy. He had these words carved on her tombstone: "This for remembrance." The reader interested in the significance of this inscription should examine Hardy's poignant "Poems of 1912–1913" in his volume, *Satires of Circumstance, Lyrics and Reveries.*

In 1914 Hardy married again. Miss Florence Emily Dugdale, who had helped him with research on *The Dynasts,* became the second Mrs. Hardy. When Hardy died, on January 11, 1928, burial in the Poets' Corner in Westminster Abbey was offered, but there were many people who felt that an author whose heart had always been with Wessex folk among Wessex scenes ought not to have that heart carried off to alien soil. Hardy's heart was accordingly buried in the grave of his first wife at Stinsford, while his ashes were deposited next to those of Charles Dickens in Westminster Abbey.

In the course of the three decades that followed Hardy's death, there came to be general critical agreement that his literary output was of very uneven quality. Some of his novels are excellent, others are mediocre, or worse; and many of his poems have seemed harsh and unmusical, even to modern ears attuned to the discordant. But a reading of Hardy's best novels and a study of his best poems will show the same gifted author at work in both. There is the same attentive eye for nature in all seasons and in all her moods, the same tender, sympathetic heart, and the same sorrowing mind. In studying this record of Hardy's earlier years, the reader should avoid making the all-too-common mistake of thinking that his novels were all written from a single, unchanging point of view. Hardy grew and developed, his philosophy of life matured, and the novels show this development. *Far from the Madding Crowd*, and *The Return of the Native* are the most "fatalistic" (to use an overworked word that needs strict definition); *The Mayor of Casterbridge*, in which Hardy quotes "Character is Fate," marks a distinct shift in his viewpoint; and *The Woodlanders, Tess of the D'Urbervilles,* and *Jude the Obscure* are all three written by an older author with a riper social outlook and a clearer understanding of the causes of human unhappiness. The reader who grasps this immense advance on Hardy's part over the fragile charm of *Under the Greenwood Tree* will have no difficulty in understanding why, when John Dewey was asked to name, among books published in the last fifty years, the twenty-five which he regarded as the most influential, he put *Tess of the D'Urbervilles* first among English novels, or why Henry C. Duffin, when appraising the entire literary career of the Wessex author, called *Jude the Obscure* "the greatest of Hardy's novels."

Carl J. Weber

BIBLIOGRAPHICAL REFERENCES: For scholarly accuracy and balanced appraisal Carl J. Weber's *Hardy of Wessex: His Life and Literary Career,* 1940, is the outstanding critical biography among the masses of Hardy studies. Other important biographies include Florence Hardy, *The Early Life of Thomas Hardy, 1840–1891,* 1928; idem, *The Later Years of Thomas Hardy, 1892–1928,* 1930; Evelyn Hardy, *Thomas Hardy: A Critical Biography,* 1954. For critical studies see Lascelles Abercrombie, *Thomas Hardy: A Critical Study,* 1912; Arthur Symons, *A Study of Thomas Hardy,* 1927; Mary Ellen Chase, *Thomas Hardy: From Serial to Novel,* 1927; Samuel C. Chew, *Thomas Hardy: Poet and Novelist,* 1928; A. S. McDowell, *Thomas Hardy: A Critical Study,* 1931; Lord David Cecil, *Hardy the Novelist,* 1946; H. C. Webster, *On a Darkling Plain,* 1947; Albert J. Guerard, *Thomas Hardy: The Novels and Stories,* 1949; and Carl J. Weber, *Hardy in America,* 1952.

The Thomas Hardy Centennial Issue of *The Southern Review,* V (1940), contains articles on Hardy as viewed by Allen Tate, Jacques Barzun, and other contemporary critics. Carl J. Weber has also published *The First Hundred Years of Thomas Hardy, 1840–1940: A Centenary Bibliography of Hardiana,* 1942, and has edited *Hardy Letters,* 1954.

JOEL CHANDLER HARRIS

Born: Eatonton, Georgia
Date: December 9, 1848

Died: Atlanta, Georgia
Date: July 3, 1908

PRINCIPAL WORKS

UNCLE REMUS TALES: *Uncle Remus: His Songs and His Sayings,* 1880; *Nights with Uncle Remus,* 1883; *Daddy Jake the Runaway,* 1889; *On the Plantation,*

1892; *Uncle Remus and His Friends*, 1892; *Told by Uncle Remus*, 1905; *Uncle Remus and Br'er Rabbit*, 1907; *Uncle Remus and the Little Boy*, 1910.

SHORT STORIES AND SKETCHES: *Mingo and Other Sketches in Black and White*, 1884; *Free Joe and Other Georgian Sketches*, 1887; *Balaam and His Friends*, 1892; *Stories of Georgia*, 1896; *Tales of the Home Folks in Peace and War*, 1898; *Chronicles of Aunt Minervy Ann*, 1899; *On the Wing of Occasions*, 1900.

NOVEL: *Gabriel Tolliver*, 1902.

Joel Chandler Harris was the first writer to create out of diverse Negro oral dialect stories in the South in the nineteenth century a local color literature of lasting form. Though he wrote numerous children's stories, newspaper articles, and novels of the Negro and the mountaineer, he is remembered today chiefly for his Uncle Remus stories, ten volumes of which have been published. Born December 9, 1848, to a deserted mother near Eatonton in Putnam County, Georgia, he was educated in a local private school and encouraged to write by his mother. At the age of fourteen he became a printer's devil on *The Countryman*, but in 1864 he was forced by the approach of Union troops to leave the area. After working as a reporter on newspapers in Macon, Georgia, and New Orleans, he returned to Eatonton and wrote humor pieces for the Savannah *Morning News*. In 1876 he became a staff writer for the Atlanta *Constitution*, with which he remained twenty-four years.

At the age of twenty-nine Harris began a study of Negro folklore and dialect and attempted to reproduce the material realistically in sketches. The pieces appeared in newspapers in both the North and the South, and were so successful a volume of them was published as *Uncle Remus: His Songs and Saying* in 1880. The character of Uncle Remus was not dissimilar to that of Harris, kindly, even of temperament, yet shrewd and devoted to the side of the underdog. It was Remus's delight in the methods used by the underdog members—especially Br'er Rabbit—of his bestiary that so infected the readers of these tales. By reader demand Harris produced hundreds of these pieces and, from 1907 until his death, at Atlanta, Georgia, on July 3, 1908, even edited the *Uncle Remus's Magazine*. Actually a fable, each piece is particularly connected to the other by the dialect of the narrator, Uncle Remus. While the homely philosophy revealed is not unattractive, it is this unique verbal form, especially the syntax, which makes the piece as a whole delightful reading.

BIBLIOGRAPHICAL REFERENCES: There is no collected edition, but a useful volume is *Joel Chandler Harris: Editor and Essayist: Miscellaneous Literary, Political, and Social Writings*, edited by Julia C. Harris, 1931. Mrs. Harris is also the author of the most authoritative biography, *The Life and Letters of Joel Chandler Harris*, 1918, which includes a bibliography. Robert L. Wiggins, *The Life of Joel Chandler Harris From Obscurity in Boyhood to Fame in Early Manhood*, 1918, includes a bibliography and important early writings of Harris.

Shorter studies may be found in W. M. Baskervill, *Southern Writers*, Vol. I, 1902; C. Alphonso Smith, *Southern Literary Studies*, 1927; A. H. Quinn, *American Fiction*, 1936; Robert E. Spiller, Willard Thorp, Thomas H. Johnson, and Henry S. Canby, eds., *The Literary History of the United States*, Vol. II, 1948; and Jay B.

Hubbell, *The South in American Literature*, 1954, the best single work on the subject.

See also John Stafford, "Patterns of Meaning in *Nights with Uncle Remus*," *American Literature*, XVIII (1946), 89–108, and Louise Dauner, "Myth and Humor in the Uncle Remus Tales," *American Literature*, XX (1948), 129–143.

BRET HARTE

Born: Albany, New York   *Died:* Camberley, Surrey, England
Date: August 25, 1836   *Date:* May 5, 1902

PRINCIPAL WORKS

SHORT STORIES: *The Luck of Roaring Camp*, 1870; *Stories of the Sierras*, 1872; *Mrs. Skagg's Husbands*, 1873; *Tales of the Argonauts*, 1875; *The Twins of Table Mountain*, 1879; *Flip and Other Stories*, 1882; *In the Carquinez Woods*, 1883; *The Argonauts of North Liberty*, 1888; *A Sappho of Green Springs*, 1891; *Colonel Starbottle's Client*, 1892; *A Protégée of Jack Hamlin's*, 1894; *The Bell-Ringer of Angel's*, 1894; *Barker's Luck and Other Stories*, 1896; *Mr. Jack Hamlin's Meditation*, 1899.

NOVELS: *M'liss: An Idyll of Red Mountain*, 1873; *Gabriel Conroy*, 1876.

PARODIES: *Condensed Novels*, 1867; *Condensed Novels: Second Series*, 1902.

POEMS: *Poems*, 1871; *East and West Poems*, 1871; *Poetical Works of Bret Harte*, 1896.

(Francis) Bret(t) Harte, who found fame with two short stories and a humorous poem, is better known in literary history for his short stories of the West. Of Hebrew, Dutch, and English descent, he was born in Albany, New York, on August 25, 1836. His indigent parents moved from city to city in the East until, after the death of the father, his mother went to California to marry a new husband, and Harte and his sister moved after them. During the next few years he was engaged in school teaching, typesetting, mining, politics, and finally journalism. In 1857 he became a typesetter on the *Golden Era* in San Francisco. Though serving in a nonliterary capacity, he wrote poems and local-color sketches on the side, and in 1865 edited a book of western verse, *Outcroppings*. In 1868 he was made editor of the newly founded *Overland Monthly* in San Francisco. The second issue contained his "The Luck of Roaring Camp," and in January, 1869, "The Outcasts of Poker Flat" appeared in the same magazine. Though both caught the approving attention of readers in the East, the accidental publication of his poem, "Plain Language from Truthful James" (familiarly known as "The Heathen Chinee") produced his greatest popularity. It resulted in an offer, which he accepted, of $10,000 to write for the *Atlantic Monthly* for a year, and in 1871 he left for the East. The volume *East and West Poems* appeared that same year. However, his work soon declined in popularity and, running into debt after the failure of a magazine venture, he entered the United States consular service. After posts in Germany and Scotland he lost his political appointment in 1885 and he moved to

London where he remained, isolating himself from his past, until he died at Camberley, Surrey, on May 5, 1902.

The prose work of Harte has many of the same faults of his verse: it is melodramatic and poorly constructed. ("Plain Language from Truthful James" had actually been printed only because a form of an issue of the *Overland Monthly* was discovered to be one page short and the poem, one among many considered too poor for publication, was used.) However, as with the verse, the prose also contained a sentimental point of view of the West which suited at the time preconceptions of the West among Eastern and British readers who never had been there. Except for the verse and two or three short stories (the novels are bad), none of Harte's writing is widely read today.

BIBLIOGRAPHICAL REFERENCES: The latest collection is The Argonaut Edition, *The Works of Bret Harte*, 25 vols., 1914. Other useful collections are *Stories and Poems and Other Uncollected Writings by Bret Harte*, edited by Charles M. Kozlay, 1914; *The Complete Poetical Works of Bret Harte*, 1899; and *The Letters of Bret Harte*, edited by Geoffrey Bret Harte, 1926. A valuable book is the American Writers Series volume, *Bret Harte: Representative Selections, with Introduction, Bibliography, and Notes*, 1941, edited by Joseph B. Harrison. There are two volumes of biography by Harte's friend Thomas E. Pemberton, *Bret Harte: A Treatise and a Tribute*, 1900, and *The Life of Bret Harte*, 1903. Three other biographies are Henry W. Boynton, *Bret Harte*, 1903; Henry C. Merwin, *The Life of Bret Harte, with Some Account of the California Pioneers*, 1911; and George R. Stewart, Jr., *Bret Harte: Argonaut and Exile*, 1931—the most reliable single work. For a brief estimate, see Arthur H. Quinn, *American Fiction*, 1936.

HARTMANN VON AUE

Born: Probably in Swabia
Date: c. 1170

Died: Unknown
Date: Between 1210 and 1220

PRINCIPAL WORKS

EPIC POEMS: *Erec der Wunderaere*, c. 1192 (*Erec the Wonder-Worker*); *Gregorius oder der guote Sündaere*, c. 1195 (*Gregory, or the Good Sinner*); *Der arme Heinrich*, between 1192 and 1202 (*Poor Henry*); *Iwein*, finished before 1204.

With Gottfried von Strassburg and Wolfram von Eschenbach, Hartmann von Aue (or Ouwe) was one of the foremost writers of the Middle High German court epic. Little is known of his life, but it is believed that he spent his youth in a monastery and later served a noble at Aue, somewhere in Swabia. At some time during the last two decades of the twelfth century, he went with a band of crusaders to Palestine.

His first work, *Erec the Wonder-Worker*, is one of the earliest known poems in German on the Arthurian cycle, the tale of an uxorious knight who neglects his chivalric duties. *Iwein* tells of a knight who, mindful of Erec's example, errs at the other extreme and overstays his time at King Arthur's court, although he had promised his wife to return in a year. Both these somewhat didactic tales were patterned after those of Chrétien de Troyes.

Poor Henry, of uncertain date, is Hartmann's most famous narrative poem, later retold by Longfellow and Rossetti. It tells of a knight who, stricken with leprosy, is miraculously cured by the faith of a poor virgin willing to sacrifice herself for him. In it Hartmann brings German to an early point of full literary expression. He is also recognized for shorter lyrics, poems of the crusades, and *Gregory, or the*

Good Sinner, a medieval version of the Oedipus myth, about a militant knight who, after unknowingly committing incest with his mother, returns sanctified from a long period of penance and becomes pope. This legendary tale provided the plot of Thomas Mann's novel, *The Holy Sinner* (1951). Hartmann is believed to have been born in Swabia about 1170 and to have died between 1210 and 1220.

BIBLIOGRAPHICAL REFERENCES: See J. K. Bostock, *Der Arme Heinrich,* 1941; and Edwin Hermann Zeydel and Bayard Quincy Morgan, *The Gregorius of Hartmann von Aue,* 1955. For background studies see also Lewis Spence, *A Dictionary of Medieval Romance and Romance Writers,* 1913; Thomas Calvin, *A History of German Literature,* 1928; and Gilbert Waterhouse, *A Short History of German Literature,* 1952.

GERHART HAUPTMANN

Born: Obersalzbrunn, Germany
Date: November 15, 1862

Died: Agneterdorf, Silesia
Date: June 8, 1946

PRINCIPAL WORKS

PLAYS: *Vor Sonnenaufgang,* 1889 (*Before Dawn*); *Das Friedensfest,* 1890 (*The Reconciliation*); *Einsame Menschen,* 1891 (*Lonely Lives*); *Die Weber,* 1892 (*The Weavers*); *Der Biberpelz,* 1893 (*The Beaver Coat*); *Hanneles Himmelfahrt,* 1893 (*Hannele*); *Die versunkene Glocke,* 1897 (*The Sunken Bell*); *Fuhrmann Henschel,* 1899 (*Drayman Henschel*); *Der arme Heinrich,* 1902 (*Henry of Auë*); *Rose Bernd,* 1903; *Und Pippa tanzt,* 1906 (*And Pippa Dances*); *Der Bogen des Odysseus,* 1914 (*The Bow of Odysseus*); *Der weisse Heiland,* 1920 (*The White Savior*).

NOVELS: *Der Narr in Christo, Emmanuel Quint,* 1910 (*The Fool in Christ, Emanuel Quint*); *Atlantis,* 1912; *Der Ketzer von Soana,* 1918 (*The Heretic of Soana*).

MEMOIRS: *Das Abenteuer meiner Jugend,* 1937 (*The Adventure of My Youth*).

Gerhart Hauptmann, probably Germany's greatest modern playwright, was born November 15, 1862, the son of an innkeeper in the Silesian village of Obersalzbrunn. As a child he grew up under the influence of his parents' Moravian religion in a home that was remarkable for its air of piety and mysticism. As a young man Hauptmann failed to prepare himself adequately for a career at one of the German universities and as a result studied agriculture for a time. He left the soil, however, to study art at the Royal College of Art at Breslau in 1880–1881. He went to Rome to study sculpture in 1883. Between these two periods of study he traveled throughout western Europe. Leisure for him to begin a career of writing was afforded by a marriage to a wealthy German girl in 1885. He and his wife were divorced ten years later. That period of marriage left its scars upon Hauptmann, who later referred to the time as one of torture.

As early as 1885 Hauptmann became interested in politics, especially in the liberal Social-Democrat movement. He joined a liberal literary society called "Through," and soon became associated with Otto Brahm's Freie Bühne (Free Stage) in Berlin. His *Before Dawn* was produced in the theater's first season. The play, a study of degeneracy among newly-rich Silesian peasants, was a sensation at the time because of its naturalism. Hauptmann described the degeneracy with frankness, and he used the appropriate German dialects for each character. The play indicates the influence of Zola's naturalistic fiction on Hauptmann's dramatic theory and practice. During the next three years Hauptmann wrote plays such as *The Reconciliation* and *Lonely Lives,* stories of middle-class and domestic misery which remind the modern reader of Ibsen's drama. *The Weavers,* produced in 1892, brought him world fame. In this drama about starving workmen in eighteenth century Germany, Hauptmann made use of a collective hero, a device often utilized by later collectivist authors in every genre. As might be expected, liberal groups throughout Europe hailed *The Weavers* as a rallying point for socialists and labor. Before imparting to the play purely political motives, however, one should recall that a grandfather of the dramatist had been one of the weavers whose abortive revolt was stifled in Silesia.

Hauptmann wrote continuously after his success with *The Weavers,* which was followed by such varied works as *The Beaver Coat, Hannele,* *The Sunken Bell, Henry of Auë* and others. Many honors were bestowed upon him. During his lifetime he received honorary degrees from the universities at Prague, Oxford, Leipzig, and from Columbia University in New York. In 1912 he was awarded the Nobel Prize for literature. His reputation suffered, however, from a fault which revealed itself in his personal life and his work. Hauptmann was a changeable man, seldom constant in anything. From his Social-Democrat position in the 1890's he moved so far as to become a functionary of the Nazi regime after Adolf Hitler came to power in 1933. In his work he moved from one kind of drama to another, with the result that many critics have come to feel that he was once overrated and that his work from 1920 to his death in 1946 is unimportant. Today he seems to have been one of those unfortunate literary persons who points the way but never travels very far on the road himself.

Some idea of the different kinds of plays written by Hauptmann can be seen in the following examples. *And Pippa Dances* is a poetic romance about the search for beauty in a world of force and brutality. *The White Savior* is a play about the conquest of the Aztec civilization in Mexico by Cortez. A journey to Greece in 1907 prompted Hauptmann to reinterpret part of the Homeric epics in *The Bow of Odysseus.* In *Veland* (1925) he wrote a play involving terror and the supernatural, somewhat reminiscent of *Medea,* for the main character flies away on manmade wings after deeds of violent revenge. *Iphigenia in Delphi* (1941) and *Iphigenia in Aulis* (1944) indicate Hauptmann's interest in Greek culture and history, especially its drama. In

Till Eulenspiegel (1928) he tried to give epic proportions to his picture of life in postwar Germany. Despite these varied efforts, *The Weavers* and *The Beaver Coat* remain his best-remembered plays.

Hauptmann was also outstanding in the field of fiction. *The Fool in Christ, Emanuel Quint,* published in 1910, has been called one of the great religious novels of the century. Other well-known novels are *Atlantis* and *The Heretic of Soana.* He died at Agneterdorf, Silesia, June 8, 1946.

BIBLIOGRAPHICAL REFERENCES: The plays are available in English in *The Dramatic Works of Gerhart Hauptmann,* 9 vols., edited by Ludwig Lewisohn, 1912–1929. A basic biographical study is Karl Holl, *Gerhart Hauptmann; His Life and Work,* 1913. The most recent biography is Hugh F. Garten, *Gerhart Hauptmann,* 1954. See also Otto Heller, *Studies in Modern German Literature,* 1905; J. G. Huneker, *Iconoclasts,* 1905; Barrett H. Clark, ed., *A History of Modern Drama,* 1947; and Allardyce Nicoll, *World Drama,* 1949.

NATHANIEL HAWTHORNE

Born: Salem, Massachusetts
Date: July 4, 1804

Died: Plymouth, New Hampshire
Date: May 19, 1864

PRINCIPAL WORKS

NOVELS: *Fanshawe,* 1828; *The Scarlet Letter,* 1850; *The House of the Seven Gables,* 1851; *The Blithedale Romance,* 1852; *The Marble Faun,* 1860; *Septimius Felton,* 1872; *Doctor Grimshawe's Secret,* 1882.

SHORT STORIES: *Twice-Told Tales,* 1837 (2nd ed., 1842; 3rd ed., 1851); *Grandfather's Chair,* 1841; *Famous Old People,* 1841; *Mosses from an Old Manse,* 1846 (2nd ed., 1854); *The Snow Image and Other Twice-Told Tales,* 1851; *A Wonder Book for Girls and Boys,* 1851; *Tanglewood Tales,* 1853.

ESSAYS: *Our Old Home,* 1863.

JOURNALS: *The American Notebooks,* 1932; *The English Notebooks,* 1941.

Nathaniel Hawthorne, one of the greatest of all American fiction writers, was born in Salem, Massachusetts, July 4, 1804, and died in Plymouth, New Hampshire, May 19, 1864.

His first American ancestor William Hathorne (the *w* was added by Nathaniel himself while he was in college) came to Massachusetts Bay from England with John Winthrop in 1630, and as a magistrate ordered the whipping of a Quakeress in Salem; William's son John was one of the three judges who presided over the Salem witch trials in 1692. Nathaniel was sensitively aware of this inheritance. These men were important figures in the early history of the Massachusetts Bay Colony; they were also guilty of great crimes. The family fortunes had declined since those early days (Nathaniel's father was a ship captain who died in a distant port when the boy was only four years old), and Nathaniel often wondered whether the decline was a punishment for the sins of his (as he called them) "sable-cloaked, steeple-crowned progenitors."

After his graduation from Bowdoin College (where Longfellow, a life-long friend, was a classmate) in the class of 1825, Hawthorne returned to his mother's house in Salem, where, after the publication of an immature "college novel," *Fanshawe,* in 1828, he settled down to hard application to the craft of fiction. He read much, wrote much, and destroyed much of what he wrote. The result was the appearance in the periodical press of many remarkable stories (or "tales," as he preferred to call them), published anonymously, and the collection in book form of many of these in 1837 under the title *Twice-Told Tales* (the first work to bear the author's name on the title page). Hawthorne was employed in the Boston Custom House in 1839–1840 (his publications having brought him very little money), and in 1841 he joined the socialist community at Brook Farm, where he stayed about six months. Meanwhile, he had met and fallen in love with Sophia Peabody, and she with him, and after their marriage on July 9, 1842, they went to the "Old Manse" in Concord, Massachusetts, to live. The story of the three years there, as recorded in Hawthorne's *American Notebooks* and his essay *The Old Manse,* is one of the most charming of marital idyls.

Writing more and still more "tales," he brought out in 1846 a second collection entitled *Mosses from an Old Manse;* and, his success still consisting more of esteem than of money, he took a post in the Salem Custom House in 1846, a post which (being a good Democrat) he received from the Democratic administration of James K. Polk, and from which (being not without political enemies in his local precinct) he was ousted in 1849 by the Whig administration of Zachary Taylor. Though greatly angered at the

time, Hawthorne later saw the loss of his job as a blessing in disguise: for in the gloom of this seeming misfortune, he sat down to write *The Scarlet Letter.* This novel (or "romance," as he preferred to call this, and his other longer fictions) proved to be his greatest book, and made him famous.

For a year and a half following the publication of *The Scarlet Letter* Hawthorne lived in the Berkshires, near Lenox, where he wrote *The House of the Seven Gables,* published in 1851, and enjoyed the stimulating friendship of Herman Melville, whose *Moby Dick,* published in the same year, was dedicated to Hawthorne. Returning to Eastern Massachusetts (he always preferred the ocean to the mountains), he wrote at West Newton *The Blithedale Romance,* based upon his Brook Farm experience and published in 1852. In 1853, he went with his wife and three children (Una, Julian, and Rose) to Liverpool, England, where he served four years as United States Consul, a comparatively lucrative post to which he had been appointed by President Franklin Pierce, whose devoted friendship went back to their college days together at Bowdoin. The Hawthornes were in Italy in 1858–1859, and in 1860, shortly after the publication of *The Marble Faun* (which was based upon Italian experiences, and appeared first in England as *Transformation*), they returned to "The Wayside," in Concord, where Hawthorne spent the remaining four years of his life. These were years of sadness, frustration, and failing health. He managed to bring out a fine collection of essays about England, *Our Old Home,* but the old skill at fiction-writing seemed to have deserted him. His death occurred while he, accompanied by the faithful Pierce, was on a recuperative journey to the White Mountains. Mrs. Hawthorne, who lived seven years longer, religiously devoted her widowhood to the publication of her husband's journals.

Hawthorne is a symbolic writer whose greatness seems to grow with the passing years. Discerning critics and readers of the mid-twentieth century and later seem tireless in discovering "layers" of meanings in his fiction. Hawthorne's work is seen more and more clearly as a criticism of life, a weighing of conflicting forces, a dramatization of the dilemmas and ambiguities which beset the human condition. His attitude toward life can be called "Puritan," but more properly it is broadly Christian in that he is concerned always with the conflict between good and evil, and the consequences to mankind which flow from "Original Sin."

In his greatest book, Arthur Dimmesdale, the Puritan minister, has committed adultery with Hester Prynne. Arthur is conscience-stricken, while Hester, a symbol of "emancipation," feels that she has not sinned. "What we did," she said, "had a consecration of its own." The tension is tautly drawn between the Puritan (or Christian) respect for law and conscience and the "Romantic" insistence upon the supremacy of the private impulse. Hester is sympathetically treated, and the Romantic position is allowed its full weight—so much so that many modern readers have believed that the Romantic position, that is, the glorification of individual desire, contains the theme of the story. But Arthur, not Hester, is the protagonist, and the resolution of the tension is brought about, not by Hester's plan of elopement, but by Arthur's confession of guilt before his assembled parishioners. The resolution (where one looks especially for "meaning") is Christian in the sense that the protagonist, after a long, agonizing conflict within himself, surrenders his own will to the Divine Will, and becomes able to say, "Father, not my will but Thine be done."

Hawthorne everywhere is concerned with moral problems which are also personality problems. The blemish on Georgiana's cheek in *The Birthmark* is a fascinating symbol of human imperfection. In *The House of the Seven Gables,* the author deals with the problem of heredity; in *The Blithedale Romance,* with the problem of reform; in *The Marble Faun,* with the problem of good and evil. "Is sin, then, like sorrow," Kenyon asks in the last named work, "an element of human education, through which we struggle to a higher and purer state than we could otherwise have attained? Did Adam fall, that we might ultimately rise to a loftier paradise than his?" The answers in Hawthorne to questions like these are never pat and categorical. Rather is he content to describe both sides of the human coin: the heroic and the ignoble, the unselfish and the selfish, the angelic and the diabolic. It is beside the point, critically, to apply to Hawthorne such adjectives as "morbid" or "pessimistic." He is rather a "realist" in the only worth-while sense of that word: in the sense, that is, that he holds a true mirror to our common fallible humanity. It is for this reason, as well as his meticulous craftsmanship, that he has been attracting a growing audience of thoughtful readers in modern times.

Randall Stewart

489

BIBLIOGRAPHICAL REFERENCES: The standard edition is still *The Complete Works of Nathaniel Hawthorne*, ed. by George P. Lathrop, 12 vols., 1883. Important early biographies are Julian Hawthorne, *Nathaniel Hawthorne and His Wife*, 2 vols., 1884, and George E. Woodberry, *Nathaniel Hawthorne*, 1902. A reliable factual biography is Randall Stewart, *Nathaniel Hawthorne*, 1948. See also Newton Arvin, *Nathaniel Hawthorne*, 1929; F. O. Matthiessen, *American Renaissance*, 1941; Mark Van Doren, *Nathaniel Hawthorne*, 1949; R. H. Fogle, *Hawthorne's Fiction: The Light and the Dark*, 1952; Hyatt Waggoner, *Hawthorne: A New Evaluation*, 1955; Floyd Stovall, ed., *Eight American Authors: A Review of Research and Criticism*, 1956; and Roy R. Male, *Hawthorne*, 1957. More specialized studies are found in the following: Julian Green, *Un puritan homme de lettres, Nathaniel Hawthorne*, 1928; L.-E. Chrétien, *La Pensée morale de Nathaniel Hawthorne*, 1932; Jane Lundblad, *Nathaniel Hawthorne and European Literary Tradition*, 1947; Q. D. Leavis, "Hawthorne as Poet," *Sewanee Review*, LIX (1951), 179–205, 426–458; and Randall Stewart, "Hawthorne and Faulkner," *College English*, XVII (1956), 258–262. Randall Stewart edited and annotated *The American Notebooks of Nathaniel Hawthorne*, 1932, and *The English Notebooks*, 1941.

WILLIAM HAZLITT

Born: Maidstone, England
Date: April 10, 1778

Died: London, England
Date: September 18, 1830

PRINCIPAL WORKS

INFORMAL AND LITERARY ESSAYS: *The Round Table*, 1817; *Table Talk*, 1821–1822; *The Spirit of the Age, or Contemporary Portraits*, 1825; *The Plain Speaker*, 1826; *Winterslow*, 1839; *Sketches and Essays*, 1839.

CRITICAL STUDIES: *Characters of Shakespeare's Plays*, 1817; *Lectures on the English Poets*, 1818; *Views of the English Stage*, 1818; *Lectures on the English Comic Writers*, 1819; *Dramatic Literature of the Age of Elizabeth*, 1821.

AUTOBIOGRAPHY: *Liber Amoris, or the New Pygmalion*, 1823.

BIOGRAPHY: *Life of Napoleon*, 1828.

One of the great English Romantic critics, William Hazlitt, born in Maidstone, England, on April 10, 1778, was also one of the first great journalistic essayists. He was a political liberal, writing eloquent defenses of the principles of the French Revolution, and he replied savagely to the attacks of the Scottish Tory reviewers, though he himself was not free from politically prejudiced literary criticism. He attacked the later work of the Lake Poets, mainly because they had turned politically conservative. All his work is marked by a complete independence of spirit. He cannot be classed with any particular "school" of criticism; he is simply a courageous, honest, and sensitive man who brought his serious mind to bear upon literature.

Hazlitt inherited his liberalism from his father, a Unitarian minister who sympathized with the American fight for independence. In 1783 the Rev. William Hazlitt emigrated with his family to America, but after an unsuccessful struggle he returned to England in the winter of 1786. He took a small parish in Wem, Shropshire, where young William Hazlitt attended school. In 1793 Hazlitt was sent to the Hackney Theological College to become a dissenting minister. He soon decided against that profession and returned to Wem. He heard Coleridge preach at Shrewsbury in 1798, and the poet's influence and example after their meeting encouraged him in his study of metaphysics. The next year he visited Coleridge and met Wordsworth.

In 1802 Hazlitt decided to become a portrait painter like his brother John, and he went to Paris to copy pictures at the Louvre. Four months later he returned to London; he had decided that he could never be a very good painter. He lectured for a time on modern philosophy but later turned to journalism. He was a Parliamentary reporter and then the drama critic for the *Morning Chronicle;* he also contributed articles to Leigh Hunt's *Examiner.*

His *Characters of Shakespeare's Plays* is a basic work in Shakespearean criticism, and his *Dramatic Literature of the Age of Elizabeth* directed attention toward some of the more neglected playwrights of that period.

Hazlitt's marriage to Sarah Stoddart in 1808 was a miserable match of two opposed temperaments. He had a passionate affair with the ignorant daughter of his landlord; *Liber Amoris* records the history of the attachment. He finally freed himself from the girl, divorced his wife, and married a Mrs. Bridgewater. Toward the end of his life his publisher suffered financial difficulties, and Hazlitt died in poverty, on September 18, 1830, in London. Modern criticism regards him as an important critic, a master of the familiar essay, and a distinguished prose stylist.

BIBLIOGRAPHICAL REFERENCES: The *Complete Works* of Hazlitt have been edited by P. P. Howe, 21 vols., 1933. A useful volume is *The Essays: A Selection,* edited by C. M. Maclean, 1949. There is a *Bibliography of Hazlitt* by Geoffrey Keynes, 1931. At least three good biographies have been published: Augustine Birrell, *Hazlitt,* English Men of Letters Series, 1902; P. P. Howe, *Life of William Hazlitt,* 1922; and C. M. Maclean, *Born Under Saturn: A Biography of William Hazlitt,* 1944. Good material on Hazlitt appears in M. H. Law, *The English Familiar Essay in the Early Nineteenth Century,* 1934. Worth-while critical judgments appear in the essays included in George Saintsbury, *Collected Essays and Papers,* 1924; H. W. Garrad, *The Profession of Poetry, and Other Lectures,* 1929; and Virginia Woolf, *The Second Common Reader,* 1935. See also C. I. Patterson, "William Hazlitt as a Critic of Prose Fiction," *Publications of the Modern Language Association,* LXVIII (1953), 1001–1016.

LAFCADIO HEARN

Born: Leucadia, Ionian Islands
Date: June 27, 1850

Died: Tokyo, Japan
Date: September 26, 1904

PRINCIPAL WORKS

NOVELS: *Chita: A Memory of Last Island,* 1889; *Youma,* 1890.

TALES AND SKETCHES: *Stray Leaves from Strange Literature,* 1884; *Some Chinese Ghosts,* 1887; *Kotto,* 1902; *Kwaidan,* 1904; *The Romance of the Milky Way,* 1905.
TRAVEL SKETCHES AND IMPRESSIONS: *Two Years in the French West Indies,* 1890; *Glimpses of Unfamiliar Japan,* 1894; *In Ghostly Japan,* 1899.

MISCELLANEOUS: *Gleanings in Buddha-Fields,* 1897; *Exotics and Retrospectives,* 1898; *Japan: An Attempt at Interpretation,* 1904.

Lafcadio Hearn is an excellent example of a writer who is remembered for a delicate, continuously responsive sensitivity and a carefully wrought style.

Born in the Ionian Islands on June 27, 1850, he was the son of a British army surgeon and a young Greek woman of a respected family. Her elopement with a member of the unpopular British occupational forces broke ties with her own family; thus, when she could not follow her husband to the West Indies, she and the infant Lafcadio went to Ireland to live with Surgeon Hearn's family. There, religious differences, the language barrier, and her keen sensitivity to the criticism of her in-laws and—later—of her returned husband led to a mental collapse from which she never completely recovered. She eventually returned to the Ionian Islands, married a compatriot, and died in a mental hospital on Corfu.

Hearn was left in Ireland to live an unsettled life as the ward of a very devout great-aunt, becoming prey to all sorts of fears, especially of the supernatural. He was educated at home by tutors and at a church school in Normandy before being sent to Saint Cuthbert's College near Durham, England. Here his imaginative pranks and winning nature won him many friends among the students.

Hearn left college without a degree because of three personal tragedies. Extremely myopic, he lost the sight of one of his eyes when it was accidentally struck by a classmate during a game. About this same time, his great-aunt lost her wealth through the business speculations of a relative she wished to help, and Hearn's own father, who might have contributed financially to his schooling, died on a return voyage from service in India. His father's money was left to three daughters by a second marriage.

The great-aunt, now senile, resorted to the desperate expedient of sending Hearn to Cincinnati, Ohio, where a distant relative had settled. She died soon after without ever knowing what terrible hardships her ward suffered before he received help from an English printer who gave him paternal affection and training for the superlative work he was to do for Cincinnati and New Orleans newspapers. In Cincinnati, he made his reputation locally by reporting the minute details of a sensational tan-yard murder and by writing sympathetically and perceptively about the levee life of Negro roustabouts. In New Orleans, he attacked corruption in city government, praised George Washington Cable's writing about Louisiana Creoles, reconstructed tales from Arabian and Chinese literatures, and, above all, through his translations in newspapers, introduced Zola, Maupassant, and Loti to an American reading public.

Twice he visited the West Indies, where the color and charm of native life made an immediate appeal to his senses. Exotic travel sketches and two novelettes about Creole life gained him an international audience before he departed for Japan in 1890 on an assignment from Harper and Brothers.

Hearn planned to stay in Japan for only a short time, but he was so thrilled with the veritable fairyland he discovered in Japan that he spent the rest of his life there, identifying himself with the Japanese by marrying into a Japanese family and by becoming a naturalized Japanese citizen. His penetrating studies of customs and legends and his acute interpretations of the Japanese were translated into many languages. In 1895, after teaching in several secondary schools, he was made professor of English literature in the Imperial University of Tokyo.

When he died in Tokyo on September 26, 1904, he was buried with Buddhist rites in a Buddhist cemetery. This was his wish—to die and be cremated and buried like the Japanese, though he himself was not a Buddhist. Today Hearn is nowhere so highly regarded as in Japan. Certainly, in Japan, as in so many other places, Hearn had re-created in exquisitely stylized prose whatever was wonderful and weird and beautiful.

BIBLIOGRAPHICAL REFERENCES: The authorized biography is Elizabeth Bisland, *The Life and Letters of Lafcadio Hearn*, 2 vols., 1906. Since it glosses over certain aspects of Hearn's life and work, it should be supplemented by such later studies as Nina H. Kennard, *Lafcadio Hearn*, 1912; Edward Larocque Tinker, *Lafcadio Hearn's American Days*, 1924; Vera McWilliams, *Lafcadio Hearn*, 1946; Marcel Robert, *Lafcadio Hearn*, 3 vols., 1950–1954 (Tokyo); and O. W. Frost, *Young Hearn*, 1957 (Tokyo). Also useful are the collections of letters: *Letters from the Raven*, edited by Milton Bronner, 1907, and *The Japanese Letters of Lafcadio Hearn*, edited by Elizabeth Bisland, 1910.

For briefer studies see Percy H. Boynton, *More Contemporary Americans*, 1927; Oscar Lewis, *Hearn and His Biographers: The Record of a Literary Controversy*, 1930; Matthew Josephson, *Portrait of the Artist as American*, 1930; Elizabeth Bisland, "Some Martinique Letters of Lafcadio Hearn," *Harper's*, CXLII (1921), 516–525; Henry Tracy Kneeland, "Lafcadio Hearn's Brother," *Atlantic Monthly*, CXXXI (1923), 20–27; E. C. Beck, "Letters of Lafcadio Hearn to His Brother," *American Literature*, IV (1932), 167–173; Ray M. Lawless, "A Note on Lafcadio Hearn's Brother," *ibid.*, X (1938), 80–83; and H. E. Rudkin, "Lafcadio Hearn," *Notes & Queries*, CLXXVII (1939), 419–422.

FRIEDRICH HEBBEL

Born: Wesselburen, Germany
Date: March 18, 1813

Died: Vienna, Austria
Date: December 13, 1863

PRINCIPAL WORKS

PLAYS: *Judith*, 1840; *Genoveva*, 1841; *Maria Magdalena*, 1843; *Herodes und Mariamne*, 1848; *Agnes Bernauer*, 1851; *Gyges und sein Ring*, 1854 (*Gyges and His Ring*); *Die Nibelungen*, 1855–1860.

NOVELLAS: *Ezrälungen und Novellen*, 1855.

POEMS: *Mutter und Kind*, 1859.

JOURNAL: *Tagebücher*, 1885–1887 (*Diary*).

Friedrich Hebbel was born in Schleswig-Holstein on March 18, 1813, the son of a poor mason who was hostile to his young son's ambitions. "Poverty," Hebbel wrote of him years later in his interesting *Diary*, "had taken the place

493

of his soul." When Hebbel was fourteen his father died, and the future dramatist was recommended by a teacher to a local magistrate whom he served as secretary for eight years, in the meantime reading widely, writing verse and drama under the influence of Uhland and Schiller, and participating in amateur theatricals.

A few plays were published in a Hamburg magazine whose editor offered Hebbel money toward a university education if he would come to Hamburg. Spending the next few years there, at the University of Heidelberg, and in Munich, lecturing, studying law, and writing, he suffered from bitter poverty which was partially relieved by his liaison with a seamstress whom he met in Heidelberg in 1836. Meanwhile he was developing his philosophical position; when he returned to Hamburg in 1839, he was ready to embark upon his career as a playwright. *Judith* was completed in 1840, *Genoveva* (in verse) in 1841, and *Maria Magdalena* in 1843, the last completed in Paris where he had gone upon receiving some money from the King of Denmark.

He went to Rome in 1844 and to Vienna in 1845. There, moved by the warm reception he received, he settled for good. Despite the claims of the woman who had borne him children, Hebbel married an actress he met in Vienna in 1846 and entered upon another important period of playwriting. *Herodes und Mariamne, Agnes Bernauer, Gyges and His Ring,* and his *Die Nibelungen* trilogy, like his earlier plays, were not staged at once in puritanical Vienna. When they were finally performed, with Hebbel's wife playing leading roles, widespread recognition secured for him the Order of Maximilian in Bavaria and the Schiller Prize in Berlin. He died in Vienna on December 13, 1863.

Although Hebbel wrote several volumes of verse and some stories, his reputation rests on his dramas. Applying Hegel's dialectical method to the analysis of character, he showed how the act of self-assertion, which was necessary and not in itself evil, often led to destruction. Several of his plays describe relationships between male and female heroes of history and legend in which the assertive male brings about his own destruction through his blindness to the nature of woman as person rather than as object. His plays dealing with contemporary life, notably *Maria Magdalena,* often considered his masterpiece, make clear the characteristic sociological basis of his work by showing the strong influence of social conventions and values on the actions of men and women. It is not surprising that Ibsen acknowledged Hebbel as one of his teachers.

BIBLIOGRAPHICAL REFERENCES: There are many accounts of Hebbel in the history of the European theater. More extended studies in English include T. M. Campbell. *The Life and Works of Friedrich Hebbel,* 1919; G. Brychan Rees, *Hebbel as a Dramatic Artist,* 1930; Edna Purdie, *Friedrich Hebbel,* 1932; and Sten Gunnar Flygt, *Friedrich Hebbel's Conception of Movement in the Absolute and in History,* 1952. For recent brief studies see Walter Naumann, "Hebbel's *Gyges und sein Ring," Monatshefte,* XLIII (1951), 253–270; Wolfgang Liepe, "Ideology Underlying the Writings of Freidrich Hebbel," *Yearbook of the American Philosophical Society* (1953), 221–225; *idem,* "Hebbels philosophisches Jugendmärchen 'Die einsamen Kinder,'" *Hebbeljarbüch* (1954), 9–39. A good comparative study is K. H. Becker, *Kleist and Hebbel,* 1904.

THOMAS O. HEGGEN

Born: Fort Dodge, Iowa
Date: December 23, 1919

Died: New York, N.Y.
Date: May 19, 1949

PRINCIPAL WORK

NOVEL: *Mister Roberts,* 1946.

Thomas O. Heggen began a literary career, which was as promisingly brilliant as it was disappointingly brief, at the University of Minnesota in 1937. There Heggen, born in Fort Dodge, Iowa, on December 23, 1919, but reared in Oklahoma and Minnesota, served his writing apprenticeship as a reporter for the *Minnesota Daily* and for *Ski-U-Mah,* the campus humor magazine, devoting himself, according to a classmate's report, much more to his journalistic activities than to the demands of the classroom. In spite of this alleged neglect of scholarship, he received his B.A. degree from Minnesota in 1941, and with it he traveled east to secure a job on the editorial staff of the *Reader's Digest.*

His initial tenure with the *Reader's Digest* was short-lived, for soon after Pearl Harbor he enlisted in the United States Navy, serving until October of 1945, and spending the greater part of his tour of duty in the Pacific, where the actions and reactions portrayed in his novel were experienced and observed at first hand.

The war over, he returned to the *Reader's Digest.* But again his stay was short, and the events of his three and a half remaining years tempestuous. There was the publication of *Mister Roberts* in 1946; the novel brought immediate fame and monetary success. There was a marriage that survived only a few months. There was the collaboration with Joshua Logan from which emerged the successful and popular stage version of *Mister Roberts* (1948). Then there was a new play which was started but never finished. And finally there was the death by drowning in the bathtub of his New York apartment on May 19, 1949, seven months before his thirtieth birthday.

BIBLIOGRAPHICAL REFERENCES: There is no full study of Heggen. See Victor Cohn, "Mister Heggen," *Saturday Review of Literature,* XXXII (June 11, 1949), 19. The text of *Mister Roberts* together with an introduction by Joshua Logan appeared in *Theatre Arts Monthly,* XXXIV (1950), 57–104.

VERNER VON HEIDENSTAM

Born: Olshammar, Sweden
Date: July 6, 1859

Died: Övralid, Sweden
Date: May 20, 1940

PRINCIPAL WORKS

POEMS: *Vallfart och vandring år,* 1888 (*Pilgrimage and Years of Wandering*); *Dikter* 1895 (*Poems*); *Ett folk,* 1902 (*A Nation*); *Nya Dikter,* 1915 (*New Poems*).

NOVELS AND TALES: *Hans Alienus,* 1892; *Karolinerna,* 1897–1898 (*The Charles Men*); *Helige Birgittas pilgrimsfärd,* 1901 (*St. Bridget's Pilgrimage*); *Folkungaträdet,* 1905–1907 (*The Tree of the Folkungs*).

One of the great Swedish writers of the modern era, Verner von Heidenstam was born on July 6, 1859, at Olshammar, Närke, Sweden. After several years of travel through the Mediterranean and the East, Heidenstam returned to Sweden in 1887 to become a vigorous participant in the literary struggles against a rising Scandinavian realism. His first publication was a book of poems based on Eastern themes, *Pilgrimage and Years of Wandering,* which appeared in 1888. With this work the Swedish literary renaissance began, and Heidenstam contributed to its romanticist development with more Oriental themes in *Endymion* (1889) and *Hans Alienus.* The latter is an epic dealing with a journey in search of beauty, a metamorphosed autobiography.

Then, like Fröding and Strindberg, he turned to literary theory and criticism. He attacked the sordid realism of the time and espoused a vigorous nationalism and historicism. Heidenstam's creative work expressing these values began with *Poems* in 1895 and attained powerful expression in *The Charles Men,* a cycle of tales which glorified Sweden in the time of Charles XII. A note of stoic moralism is sounded in *St. Bridget's Pilgrimage* and the historical theme is further developed in *The Tree of the Folkungs,* a novel of medieval Sweden and the rise of the powerful Folkung dynasty which flourished in the thirteenth century. A year after the publication of his *New Poems* he received the Nobel Prize for literature and the Henrik Steffens Prize two years before his death at Övralid on May 20, 1940. He ranks with Selma Lagerlöf among the leading romanticists of his day.

BIBLIOGRAPHICAL REFERENCES: The best brief critical study in English is the essay in Alrik Gustafson, *Six Scandinavian Novelists,* 1930. For biography and criticism see John Landquist, *Verner von Heidenstam,* 1909; also F. Böök, *Sveriges moderna litteratur,* 1921, and *Verner von Heidenstam,* 2 vols., 1945–1946; and Victor Svanberg, *Poesi och politik,* 1931. For a specialized study see, further, Harold H. Borland, *Nietzsche's Influence on Swedish Literature,* 1956, a work containing special reference to Strindberg, Ola Hansson, Heidenstam, and Fröding.

HEINRICH HEINE

Born: Düsseldorf, Germany
Date: Probably December 13, 1797

Died: Paris, France
Date: February 17, 1856

PRINCIPAL WORKS

POEMS: *Gedichte,* 1822 (*Poems*); *William Ratcliff,* 1823; *Almansor,* 1823; *Buch der Lieder,* 1827 (*Book of Songs*); *Deutschland, Ein Wintermärchen,* 1844 (*Germany: A Winter's Tale*); *Neue Gedichte,* 1844 (*New Poems*); *Atta Troll,* 1847; *Romanzero,* 1851; *Der Doktor Faust,* 1851 (*Doctor Faust*); *Letzte Gedichte,* 1869 (*Last Poems*).

496

ESSAYS AND STUDIES: *Zur Geschichte der Religion und Philosophie in Deutschland,* 1834–1835 (*On the History of Religion and Philosophy in Germany*); *Die Romantische Schule,* 1836 (*The Romantic School*); *Shakespeares Mädchen und Frauen,* 1838 (*Shakespeare's Maidens and Matrons*); *Die Götter im Exil,* 1853 (*Gods in Exile*); *Geständnisse,* 1853–1854 (*Confessions*).

TRAVEL SKETCHES AND IMPRESSIONS: *Reisebilder,* 1826–1831 (*Pictures of Travel*).

Heinrich Heine was born of Jewish parents in Düsseldorf, Germany, on or about December 13, 1797. At the age of seventeen he tried, unwillingly, to engage in a business career, first in Frankfort-am-Main and later in Hamburg under a rich uncle, Salomon Heine, a Hamburg banker. During these years he fell in love with his uncle's daughter, Amalie, who inspired his earliest lyrics "Youthful Sorrows." In 1819, although his interests were already decidedly literary, Heine went to the University at Bonn as a law student. A year later he attended the University of Göttingen, from which he eventually received his degree in 1825, after interrupting his law studies for a time to pursue his more literary and artistic interests in Berlin. The year of his graduation he was received into the Lutheran Church, a practical measure he viewed with misgivings.

Heine had already published his first book of poems in 1822, followed by two romantic verse plays of little dramatic importance. After leaving Göttingen he began to travel, visiting the North Sea and England as well as various German cities in a fruitless attempt to find a university position. No longer in love with Amalie, he was next attracted to her younger sister, Therese, the inspiration for his poems in the "Home-Coming Cycle" (1826). In 1826, *Die Harzreise* appeared, a mixture of impressionistic travel sketches and verses that forms the first volume of *Pictures of Travel.* Three other installments were published, the last one in 1831, and in that year, weary of his failure to find a congenial post and restless in contemporary Germany, he went to Paris, a voluntary exile in the new constitutional monarchy.

His *Book of Songs,* Heine's most important collection of poetry during his period of residence in Germany, comprised all his work to that time; it contained some of his finest poems— "Belshazzar," "The Two Grenadiers," and the "Pilgrimage to Kevlaar." His characteristic notes of romantic longing for liberty as well as nervous irony are first fully revealed in this volume.

Heine himself said that before emigrating to France he had been a poet, afterwards a journalist, critic, and historian. This statement is largely true, although poetic inspiration never left him completely in spite of his absorption in philology, philosophy, and religion. The short *lieder* in *New Poems* are lyrical in intensity and his satirical love poems as biting as ever.

From about 1836 to 1848, although it is doubtful that he ever became a French citizen, Heine received a pension from the French government, and he returned to his native land only twice. He had met his "Mathilde," an uneducated Frenchwoman, in 1834 and married her in 1841. Soon the nervous disorders he had been accustomed to for many years became more severe and from the middle of the 1840's he suffered from spinal paralysis. During the last eight years of his life he was an invalid, confined to his bed, his days softened only by his wife's devoted care and visits from distinguished writers who recognized his genius.

As early as 1833 Heine had begun sending to *Europe Littéraire* and *Revue des Deux Mondes* the essays later collected in *Religion and Philosophy in Germany* and *The Romantic School*, works which treat respectively of German thought from Luther to Hegel and of the German Romantic poets. These are the witty and shrewd reflections of a comprehensive mind; rather than systematic studies, the preoccupations of an imaginative scholar.

Atta Troll, its hero an escaped bear whose advice to his cubs makes up the major part of the poem, is a long polemic in trochaics that served to express Heine's condemnation of the political and artistic shams of his day. It released the poet's feelings about topical affairs but is limited in its appeal now. With *Romanzero* Heine reinvigorated his dispersed poetic energies in a series of poems that reach the heights of tenderness, delicacy, and somber wit of which he was so variously capable. These comprise ballads, lyrical cycles, and shorter songs, including the famous "Hebrew Melodies." At this time Heine also wrote a ballet libretto called *Doctor Faust* and a prose fantasy, *The Gods in Exile.* His last important works were the *Last Poems,* in which the poems are more savage, mocking, ribald, and his *Confessions,* a defense of his connection with the Romantic school. "Die Passion Blume" was the last of Heine's poems, written a week or two before his death; with characteristic irony it describes a dead man lying in a tomb sculptured in Hellenic and Biblical bas-reliefs which quarrel noisily while he communes with Death itself. Heine died in Paris on February 17, 1856.

BIBLIOGRAPHICAL REFERENCES: *The Complete Works of Heinrich Heine* were translated into English by C. G. Leland and others, 13 vols., 1892–1905. There are numerous biographical studies, in German and English, by M. J. Wolff, 1923; H. G. Atkins, 1929; H. Walter, 1930; Max Brod, 1934; and F. E. Hirth, 1950. Of special interest is P. Beyer, *Der junge Heine,* 1911. Critical studies in English will be found in Matthew Arnold, *Essays in Criticism: First Series,* 1865, and George Eliot, *Essays,* 1884. More recent studies are Barker Fairley, *Heinrich Heine: An Interpretation,* 1954; and Max Brod, *Heinrich Heine: The Artist in Revolt,* 1956. See also Georg Brandes, *Det unge Tyskland,* 1890, and *Main Currents in Nineteenth Century Literature,* 1906; and Ilse Weidekampf, *Traum und Wirklichkeit in der Romantik und bei Heine,* 1932.

LILLIAN HELLMAN

Born: New Orleans, Louisiana
Date: June 20, 1905

PRINCIPAL WORKS

PLAYS: *The Children's Hour,* 1934; *Days to Come,* 1936; *The Little Foxes,* 1939; *Watch on the Rhine,* 1941; *The Searching Wind,* 1944; *Another Part of the Forest,* 1946; *The Autumn Garden,* 1951.

Lillian Hellman, born in New Orleans on June 20, 1905, spent most of her childhood in New York City. Except for visits to relatives in the Deep South during school vacations, her background was entirely urban, and she was educated at New York and Columbia universities. After leaving college she worked for a publisher, wrote book reviews, and read plays for theatrical producers. Out of these activities came her interest in the theater. The report of a famous nineteenth century Scottish trial gave her the theme for her first produced play, *The Children's Hour*. This drama contains the tone of all her work: two teachers are accused of sexual perversion in a girls' boarding school, but while the question of guilt serves to give suspense to the play the true theme is the imbalance of evil over good in the personalities of the people involved. After the rather unsuccessful handling of a proletarian theme in *Days to Come*, Miss Hellman traveled in Russia and Spain, where she saw at first hand the havoc of the civil war. The threat of fascism gave eloquent motivation to *Watch on the Rhine*, presented in 1941.

Between *Days to Come* and *Watch on the Rhine*, Miss Hellman had written *The Little Foxes*, which is for most audiences and readers her best-known play. The drama is impressive in its spectacle of moral ruin and decay as the South of 1900 is invaded by the competitive, acquisitive tactics of modern capitalism. *The Searching Wind*, dealing with the social and moral roots of war, was followed by *Another Part of the Forest*, in which the playwright revived the people of *The Little Foxes* in an earlier chapter of their chronicle of defeat. *The Autumn Garden* is a comedy-drama about a group of people at a summer resort, all of whom feel that they have failed in life.

Active in many leftist political organizations, Lillian Hellman was called before the House Un-American Activities Committee in 1952, but she refused to testify whether she had ever been a Communist. She has stated that she believes more in the rights of working men than in other rights. Her recent activities in the theater have included the adaptation of *The Lark* (1955) from the French of Jean Anouilh and the libretto for the musical show, *Candide* (1956).

BIBLIOGRAPHICAL REFERENCES: There is no full-length biography and very little criticism. See Lillian Hellman, Introduction to *Four Plays*, 1942; also Joseph Wood Krutch, *The American Drama Since 1918*, 1939; John Mason Brown, *Broadway in Review*, 1940; Brooks Atkinson, *Broadway Scrapbook*, 1947; Margaret Case Harriman, "Miss Lily of New Orleans," *New Yorker*, XVII (1941), 22–35; and J. R. Isaacs, "Lillian Hellman: A Playwright on the March," *Theatre Arts Monthly*, XXVIII (1944), 19–24.

ERNEST HEMINGWAY

Born: Oak Park, Illinois   *Died:* Ketchum, Idaho
Date: July 21, 1899   *Date:* July 2, 1961

PRINCIPAL WORKS

NOVELS: *The Torrents of Spring*, 1926; *The Sun Also Rises*, 1926; *A Farewell to Arms*, 1929; *To Have and Have Not*, 1937; *For Whom the Bell Tolls*, 1940; *Across the River and into the Trees*, 1950; *The Old Man and the Sea*, 1952.

SHORT STORIES: *Three Stories & Ten Poems,* 1923; *In Our Time,* 1924 (enlarged edition, New York, 1925); *Men Without Women,* 1927; *Winner Take Nothing,* 1933; *The Fifth Column and the First Forty-nine Stories,* 1938.

SPORT AND TRAVEL SKETCHES: *Death in the Afternoon,* 1932; *Green Hills of Africa,* 1935.

Oak Park, Illinois, seems as unlikely a birthplace for Ernest Hemingway as does Hailey, Idaho, for Ezra Pound; but it was in Oak Park—a quiet, middle-class, somewhat puritanical suburb of Chicago—that the boy who was to become the champion, in his bare-bones prose, of the hard-drinking, hard-loving, hard-fighting life was born on July 21, 1899. His father, a doctor, took him on hunting and fishing trips to Horton Bay, Michigan, and his experiences there, rather than in Oak Park, gave him the material for short stories (such as "Big Two-Hearted River" and "Indian Camp") that appeared in *In Our Time.* In Oak Park young Hemingway contributed to *Trapeze,* his high school newspaper, and wrote the class prophecy for the 1917 yearbook, but not until he worked for the *Kansas City Star* as a reporter did he begin to develop (aided by the *Star's* fine editorial staff) the style which eventually became as distinctive as Shakespeare's and which has influenced scores of contemporary writers.

Hemingway wanted to get into the First World War. When he was turned down by the army because of poor eyesight, he joined an American ambulance unit, later transferred to the Italian Arditi; after only seven days on the front lines he was seriously wounded. But war's fascination had taken hold of him: he covered the Greco-Turkish War in 1920, the civil war in Spain in 1937, and the Allied invasion of Europe in 1944. War and death comprise a major part of his subject matter, from the vignettes of *In Our Time* to *Across the River and into the Trees.*

After the Armistice, Hemingway came back to the United States and married Hadley Richardson, a childhood Michigan friend. She was the first of four wives. (The others, with the dates of his marriages, were Pauline Pfeiffer, a Paris fashion writer for *Vogue,* 1927; Martha Gellhorn, a writer, 1940; and Mary Welsh, a correspondent for *Time,* 1944.) Hemingway tried newspaper work again, this time in Toronto, but a restless postwar disillusionment came upon him, his editor proved grimly unsympathetic, and so Hemingway left for Europe to become, after the Greco-Turkish War interlude, a part of Paris and "the lost generation." That name was created by Gertrude Stein; and she, Ezra Pound, and Sherwood Anderson had the greatest "literary" influence on his early writing. In 1923 he published *Three Stories & Ten Poems* in Dijon. One of these stories, "My Old Man" is very Andersonian, but the books that followed this modest volume—*In Our Time; The Torrents of Spring,* a burlesque of Anderson's style; *The Sun Also Rises,* a novel that is really a long, sparkling short story; and *Men Without Women,* another collection of brilliant short stories—show that Hemingway had absorbed his influences and become a craftsman whose ear for dialogue was flawless and a taster of life who savored emotions by rolling them, as it were, on his tongue.

Financial success came in 1929 with *A Farewell to Arms.* Although this novel lacks the sparkle of *The Sun Also*

500

Rises, its emotional impact is greater and its war scenes are raw, vivid, and true.

Between wars and books, Hemingway occupied himself with many virile sports, and sport has provided him with some of his best material. An accomplished amateur boxer in his youth, he has used the prize-ring background in the stories "Fifty Grand" and "The Battler." His absorption with bullfighting appears in *The Sun Also Rises*, in short stories like "The Undefeated," and, of course, in that clever compendium of bullfighting and literary philosophy, *Death in the Afternoon*. In 1934 he went on an African safari; the following year he published *The Green Hills of Africa*, chiefly concerned with big-game hunting. Another trophy of this trip was the much-anthologized story, "The Snows of Kilimanjaro." Hemingway also likes to fish, and though the size of the catch has increased from the trout of "Big Two-Hearted River" to the giant marlin of *The Old Man and the Sea*, the thrill of the strike is the same.

War came again in the late 1930's. With the outbreak of the fighting in Spain, Hemingway raised money to buy ambulances for the Madrid Loyalists; in February, 1937, he sailed for Spain to cover the war for the North American Newspaper Alliance and to collect the material that was to become, in 1940, *For Whom the Bell Tolls*, his own favorite of his novels, and a book that is certainly more mature, because of its concern with moral values, than anything he had previously published. From Spain he returned to Key West, Florida, but he continued his interest in the fight against fascism. When the United States entered World War II, Hemingway for a while helped the Navy spot submarines in the Caribbean, then covered the land fighting in Europe, where he was nicknamed "Papa" by the new generation of fighting men. After the war he wrote a novel about an aging soldier, *Across the River and into the Trees*, a disappointing effort in which many critics have detected two flaws rarely found in Hemingway—the banal and the phoney. But with *The Old Man and the Sea* he quickly bounded back into favor, and the warmth and humanity of this story (though it seems strangely repetitious) probably did more than anything else to win for him the 1953 Nobel Prize as well as the Pulitzer Prize in the same year.

Following another African hunting trip on which he was once reported dead after a series of airplane crashes, Hemingway settled down with his wife Mary on a sprawling ranch in Cuba. As he mellowed there, many acclaimed him as the greatest living writer. This judgment can be disputed: he is an unquestioned master of the short story, but his novels lend themselves to fragmentation so well that the reader wonders if these too might not have been better as a series of stories. In spite of his obvious drumbeats (on the chest) for an over-glamorized masculinity, Hemingway stands as a stylist whose words ring clean and true and whose touch with love and hate and courage is as gentle-firm as that of a doctor's fingers, probing, trying to find the strength and the sickness in our times.

BIBLIOGRAPHICAL REFERENCES: There is no full-length biographical study of Hemingway, but biographical and critical materials are contained in the following: Carlos Baker, *Hemingway: The Writer as Artist*, 1952; Philip Young, *Ernest Hemingway*,

1952; Charles A. Fenton, *The Apprenticeship of Ernest Hemingway*, 1954. For briefer studies see H. J. Muller, *Modern Fiction: A Study in Values*, 1937; Maxwell Geismar, *Writers in Crisis*, 1942; Alfred Kazin, *On Native Grounds*, 1942; E. B. Burgum, *The Novel and the World's Dilemma*, 1947; W. M. Frohock, *The Novel of Violence in America, 1920–1950*, 1950; F. J. Hoffman, *The Modern Novel in America, 1900–1950*, 1951; R. B. West, Jr., *The Short Story in America, 1900–1950*, 1951.

John K. M. McCaffery, Jr., has edited an important collection of critical studies, *Ernest Hemingway: The Man and His Work*, 1950. See also David Daiches, "Ernest Hemingway," *College English*, II (1941), 725–736; Malcolm Cowley, "Hemingway at Midnight," *New Republic*, CXI (1944), 190–195; *idem*, "Hemingway and the Hero," *New Republic*, CXI (1944), 754–758; Robert Penn Warren, "Ernest Hemingway," *Kenyon Review*, IX (1947), 1–28 (reprinted in enlarged version as introduction to Modern Standard Authors edition of *A Farewell to Arms*, 1949); Melvin Backman, "The Matador and the Crucified," *Modern Fiction Studies*, I (August, 1955), 2–11; B. S. Oldsey, "Hemingway's Old Men," *Modern Fiction Studies*, I (August, 1955), 31–35; Warren Beck, "The Shorter Happy Life of Mrs. Macomber," *Modern Fiction Studies*, I (November, 1955), 28–37; Robert C. Hart, "Hemingway on Writing," *College English*, XVIII (1957), 314–320.

The Ernest Hemingway Number of *Modern Fiction Studies*, I (August, 1955), contains a selected checklist of criticism of Hemingway with an index to studies of his separate works, 36–45.

LOUIS HÉMON

Born: Brest, France   Died: Chapleau, Ontario, Canada
Date: October 12, 1880   Date: July 8, 1913

Principal Works

NOVELS: *Maria Chapdelaine*, 1916; *La Belle que voilà*, 1923; *Colin Maillard*, 1924.

The fame of Louis Hémon is based almost entirely on one novel, *Maria Chapdelaine*, although some of his earlier work was published as a result of the fame he achieved after the reprinting of the novel in 1921. In France he is valued chiefly as a stylist, but in Canada he is regarded as the first great voice of a national literature. The Canadian government has even renamed localities in his honor: there is now a Lake Hémon and a Lake Chapdelaine.

It is odd that the man who captured the spirit of pioneering Canada actually lived less than two years in that country. Born in France on October 12,

1880, son of the inspector-general of the University of Brest, Hémon was educated at the University of Paris, where he studied Oriental languages to prepare himself for colonial service. In 1903, however, he went to England; he worked as a clerk in London and married there. While in England he wrote numerous articles and stories on sports for French newspapers and magazines. In 1911, after his wife died, he emigrated to Canada, where he took a job as translator in Montreal.

In 1912 he became a farm laborer for eight dollars a month in the village of Péribonka, near Lake St. John, in northern Quebec. He admired his employer, Samuel Bédard, and his family and later made M. Bédard the model for Samuel Chapdelaine and his sister-in-law, Eva Bouchard, the model for Maria. After six months' labor in clearing the land, Hémon left the Bédards and wrote *Maria Chapdelaine* during the first part of 1913. He mailed his manuscript to *Le Temps,* a Parisian newspaper, and immediately set out on a walking tour of the west in search of new material. He was walking on the railroad tracks near the little town of Chapleau, Ontario, when he was struck and killed by a train on July 8, 1913.

The novel attracted little attention when it appeared serially in *Le Temps* in January and February of 1914. In 1916 it was published in Montreal in book form, but only in a limited edition. The Paris edition of 1921 sold over four hundred thousand copies; a number of American editions were very popular, and there was great interest in this polished chronicler of modern pioneer life. Hémon is admired for his fresh perception of pioneer character and a severity of style that prevented his love for the land and simple characters from degenerating into sentimentality.

BIBLIOGRAPHICAL REFERENCES: For biographical and critical studies see Allan McAndrew, *Louis Hémon, sa vie et son œuvre,* 1936; Louvigny de Montigny, *La Révanche de Maria Chapdelaine,* 1937; Damase Potvin, *Le Roman d'un roman: Louis Hémon à Peribonka,* 1950; also René Bazin, *"L'Auteur de Maria Chapdelaine: Louis Hémon,"* *Revue des Deux Mondes,* LXII (1921), 528–554.

O. HENRY
William Sydney Porter

Born: Greensboro, North Carolina
Date: September 11, 1862

Died: New York, N. Y.
Date: June 5, 1910

PRINCIPAL WORKS

SHORT STORIES: *Cabbages and Kings,* 1904; *The Four Million,* 1906; *The Trimmed Lamp,* 1907; *Heart of the West,* 1907; *The Gentle Grafter,* 1908; *The Voice of the City,* 1908; *Roads of Destiny,* 1909; *Options,* 1909; *Whirligigs,* 1910; *The Two Women,* 1910; *Strictly Business,* 1910; *Sixes and Sevens,* 1911; *Rolling Stones,* 1912; *Waifs and Strays,* 1917.

William Sydney Porter, universally known by his pen name, "O. Henry," was born on September 11, 1862, in Greensboro, North Carolina, where his father was a physician. His schooling was meager; at fifteen, he was given a job in a store kept by his uncle, a pharmacist. In 1882, threatened by pulmonary weakness, he went to stay on a large ranch in La Salle County,

Texas. Two years later he moved to Austin and found employment as a bookkeeper. For four years he worked as a draftsman in the Land Office there. He was clandestinely married in 1887 to Athol Estes, a seventeen-year-old girl whom he had met while both were members of a Presbyterian church choir. Early in 1891 he was appointed teller in the First National

Bank of Austin. At the end of 1894, having bought the proprietorship of a humorous weekly paper, Brann's *Iconoclast* (afterwards *The Rolling Stone*), he resigned his position to try his hand at cartooning, writing, and editing. He had previously contributed literary sketches to the *Detroit Free Press* and other newspapers. In the spring of the next year, confronted with the failure of his publishing venture, he went to Houston and became a columnist for the Houston *Daily Post*. His collected "Postscripts" show the wit and agility of mind he was to display in his short stories. His wife, who was discovered to be tubercular, remained at first in Austin but later joined him.

In 1896 Porter was indicted for having misappropriated funds, totaling $1153.68, while an employee of the First National Bank of Austin. He started for Austin to stand trial, but on the way reversed his direction and on reaching New Orleans took ship for Honduras. On arriving there, he fell in with Al Jennings, an outlaw train-robber. For the greater part of a year, Porter and the two Jennings brothers made common cause as fugitives, traveling all the way around the South American continent and at last stopping in Mexico. At the beginning of 1897, having got word that his wife was dangerously ill, Porter went back to Austin. Mrs. Porter died the following summer. Tried for embezzlement, Porter was convicted and sentenced to a five-year term, beginning March, 1898, in the Federal division of the Ohio State Penitentiary. Although he was technically guilty, he may only have been extremely careless in keeping the bank's records; he always insisted that he had not profited. In prison, he renewed his friendship with

Al Jennings, now a fellow inmate; wrote fiction, which he readily sold, and worked in the prison pharmacy. After serving three years and three months of his sentence he was discharged for good behavior.

On his release he joined his daughter in Pittsburgh and in the spring of 1902 moved to New York. This final change both made and broke him. Up to this time he had drawn the subject-matter of his stories from experiences in the Southwest and in Latin America; plunging into the turmoil of "Bagdad on the Subway," as he called it, he perceived that the city held, in its masses of people and its infinite scenes, the multiplicity of events that he required to stimulate his imagination. In New York he frequented not only the parlors of his respectable friends but also sweat-shops, low theaters, wharves, warrens, and dives, the breeders of disease and violence. Seeing in all this only the human perplexity and delusion, he put into his work a humorous pathos; he was kindly ironic where other writers might have been satirical. His first collection, *Cabbages and Kings,* was followed by fourteen more, several being posthumous. He wrote prolifically, averaging more than a story a week for some years, and was never without a market. At this rate he might have become rich; but he squandered his income by drinking heavily, leaving munificent tips in restaurants, and giving gold pieces to beggars. His attempts to write successful plays came to nothing; it was obvious that the scope of his gift did not extend beyond the short story. His health deteriorated; he became actively tuberculous; and in the final years before he died, in New York on June 5, 1910, he made several trips to Asheville for rest. He was survived by his second wife, Sara Lindsay Coleman.

The claim made by some of his contemporaries that O. Henry was an American Dickens, Maupassant, or Kipling will, of course, not bear examination. His characters were blurry, his expository style was marred by nonfunctional slang, his plots were factitious and over-dependent on the trick surprise ending that became his hallmark. But it is no exaggeration to say that he bequeathed to the American short story an awareness of formal economy that has had a distinct effect. Perhaps for every writer whose work has suffered from his influence there are a hundred who could benefit from a study of his craftsmanship.

BIBLIOGRAPHICAL REFERENCES: There are numerous collections and reprints of O. Henry's short stories. The basic collected edition is *The Complete Writings of O. Henry*, 14 vols., 1917. Other collected editions include *The Complete Works of O. Henry*, 1927, reissued in 1937, with a preface by William Lyon Phelps, and again in 1953, in 2 vols., with a foreword by Harry Hansen. Among the editions of selections are *Selected Stories from O. Henry*, edited by C. Alphonso Smith, 1922; *The Voice of the City and Other Stories by O. Henry*, with an introduction by Clifton Fadiman, 1935; and *Best Short Stories of O. Henry*, edited by Bennett Cerf and Van H. Cartmell, 1945.

The authorized life is C. Alphonso Smith, *O. Henry Biography*, 1916. More recent studies are Robert H. Davis and Arthur B. Maurice, *The Caliph of Bagdad*, 1931; E. Hudson Long, *O. Henry: The Man and His Work*, 1949; and Gerald Langford, *Alias O. Henry*, 1957. See also Fred L. Pattee, *The New American Literature*, 1930; Arthur H. Quinn, *American Fiction*, 1936; Van Wyck Brooks, *The Confident Years, 1885–1915*, 1952; L. W. Payne, Jr., "The Humor of O. Henry," *Texas Review*, IV (1918), 18–37; and Luther W. Courtney, "O. Henry's Case Reconsidered," *American Literature*, XIV (1943), 361–371.

GEORGE HERBERT

Born: Montgomery Castle, Wales
Date: April 3, 1593

Died: Bemerton, Wiltshire, England
Date: March 2 (?), 1633

PRINCIPAL WORKS

POEMS: *Parentalia*, 1627; *The Temple: Sacred Poems and Private Ejaculations*, 1633.

DEVOTIONAL COMMENTARY: *A Priest to the Temple, or The Country Parson, His Character and Rule of Holy Life*, 1652.

The fifth son of an aristocratic family, George Herbert was born at Montgomery Castle, Wales, on April 3, 1593. He was educated by his mother, whom he characterizes so touchingly in his famous *Parentalia*, the only volume published within the poet's lifetime. From the age of twelve and until he was seventeen he studied at Westminster School. Winner of a scholarship to Trinity College, Cambridge, he received his B.A. in 1613 and stayed on as minor fellow and later as major fellow until he received his M.A. in

1616. He distinguished himself as a Latin and Greek scholar and wrote Latin verses for publication while at Cambridge.

When he was twenty-three he became prelector in rhetoric and in 1619 through his and others' earnest solicitations he became public orator. He distinguished himself, one might say almost outdid himself, in the service of James I, and he received many royal favors for his diligence.

The death of the king and the reversal of policies set Herbert on the road which was to immortalize him— that of clergyman and Christian poet. On being ordained deacon in 1626, he resigned his post as orator of Cambridge and became prebendary of Layton Ecclesia.

In 1629 he married Jane Danvers, who was, according to Izaak Walton, Herbert's first biographer, a most pious and pleasant person. In 1630 King Charles I presented him with the living of Bemerton, near Salisbury. There he not only rebuilt the church and parsonage but also became a most sought after and impassioned preacher. Walton called him "holy Herbert." Three years later he died of consumption and was buried under the altar of Bemerton Church on March 3, 1633. The poems contained in The Temple were collected and published in the same year by his friend Nicholas Ferrar.

BIBLIOGRAPHICAL REFERENCES: The most satisfactory edition of Herbert is The Works of George Herbert, edited by F. E. Hutchinson, 1941. The best biographical study is Joseph H. Summers, George Herbert, 1954; and the most useful critical study is Rosemond Tuve, A Reading of George Herbert, 1952. Other important studies are Rosemary Freeman, "Herbert and the Emblem Books," Review of English Studies, XVII (1941), 150–165; L. C. Knights, "George Herbert," Scrutiny, XII (1944), 171–186; and Joseph H. Summers, "Herbert's Form," Publications of the Modern Language Association, LXVI (1951), 1055–1072. See also Lewis L. Martz, The Poetry of Meditation, 1955.

JOSEPH HERGESHEIMER

Born: Philadelphia, Pennsylvania
Date: February 15, 1880

Died: Sea Isle City, New Jersey
Date: April 25, 1954

PRINCIPAL WORKS

NOVELS: The Lay Anthony, 1914; Mountain Blood, 1915; The Three Black Pennys, 1917; Gold and Iron, 1918 (Wild Oranges, Tubal Cain, The Dark Fleece); Java Head, 1919; Linda Condon, 1919; Cytherea, 1922; The Bright Shawl, 1922; Balisand, 1924; Tampico, 1926; The Party Dress, 1929; The Limestone Tree, 1931; The Foolscap Rose, 1934.

SHORT STORIES: The Happy End, 1919; Quiet Cities, 1928.

BIOGRAPHY AND HISTORY: Swords and Roses, 1929; Sheridan, 1931.

AUTOBIOGRAPHY: The Presbyterian Child, 1923; From an Old House, 1925.

TRAVEL SKETCHES: San Cristóbal de la Habana, 1920.

Joseph Hergesheimer was born of Pennsylvania Dutch stock in Philadelphia, Pennsylvania, on February 15, 1880. Shy, and frequently ill as a child, he attended Quaker School and, planning a career as a painter, enrolled at the Philadelphia Academy of Fine Arts in 1897. At twenty-one, he inherited enough money to allow him to live and paint in Italy for a few years, but he suffered a nervous breakdown and returned to the United States, abandoning painting for a career as a writer.

Progress as a writer was slow; there were lean years of trial-and-error apprenticeship. In 1907 he married Miss Dorothy Hemphill, settled in West Chester, Pennsylvania, and made that city his home for the rest of his writing career. His first novel, *The Lay Anthony*, appeared in 1914. His success followed rapidly, and became established with the novel *The Three Black Pennys* in 1917. This is a realistic but exotically styled novel set against the Pennsylvania iron industry and deals with three generations of a single family of iron-masters. His best fiction combines realism and romance, usually against historical settings, and includes such books as *Java Head, Linda Condon, The Bright Shawl, Balisand,* and *The Limestone Tree.* He also wrote short stories, the historical-biographical sketches in *Swords and Roses,* a biography of Sheridan, an account of the restored Pennsylvania farmhouse where he made his home, *From an Old House,* and some critical articles. For nearly twenty years before his death, on April 25, 1954, at Sea Isle City, New Jersey, Hergesheimer wrote very little for publication.

BIBLIOGRAPHICAL REFERENCES: An authorized biography is in preparation. Autobiographical material will be found in *The Presbyterian Child,* 1923, and *From an Old House,* 1925. See also James Branch Cabell, *Joseph Hergesheimer, An Essay in Interpretation,* 1921; idem, *Some of Us,* 1930; Geoffrey West, "Joseph Hergesheimer," *Virginia Quarterly Review,* VIII (1932), 95–108; and Leon Kelly, "America and Mr. Hergesheimer," *Sewanee Review,* XL (1932), 171–193.

JOSÉ HERNÁNDEZ

Born: Near Buenos Aires, Argentina
Date: November 10, 1834

Died: Belgrano, near Buenos Aires
Date: October 21, 1886

PRINCIPAL WORKS

POEMS: *Martín Fierro,* 1872; *La vuelta de Martín Fierro,* 1879 (*The Return of Martín Fierro*).

José Hernández, Argentine poet, soldier, political office holder, champion of minorities, was born at the Estancia Pucyrredón, Province of Buenos Aires, November 10, 1834, and died in Belgrano, October 21, 1886. He lacked the education of other Argentine writers about the gauchos—Hidalgo, del Campo, and Ascasubi—because illness halted his formal education after the primary division, yet he was the poet read by the gauchos about whom he wrote. However, sixty thousand copies of the first part of his epic poem, *Martín Fierro,* were sold before he could persuade himself to go on with its sequel. Country pulperías stocked copies, along with other essentials like tobacco and food, for the cattle herders to purchase and read around their campfires. Hernández was so closely identified with his work that as the robust, bearded man strode along Buenos Aires streets, people addressed him as "Don Martín." There the popular dessert of quince jelly and cheese is still called a "Martín Fierro."

The first part of this epic of the pampas has more interest and more beauty, but the second part, in which the author pleads for fair treatment of the gaucho by the corrupt government, is admirable because of old Vizcacha and his gaucho philosophy.

In one of the many places that the footloose poet and his Buenos Aires wife, Carolina González del Solar (married in 1863) settled, he founded the newspaper *Río de la Plata* and ran it for a year before his enemy, President Sarmiento, closed it. He also wrote a handbook on farming and animal husbandry in 1881, but nothing else from his pen will have the permanence of his crudely rhymed yarn of a typical gaucho, told in the authentic folk language that Hernández learned on the estancia of his mother's family. For seventy-five years it has been an integral part of Argentine culture.

BIBLIOGRAPHICAL REFERENCES: Among the studies of Hernández and his gaucho epic are J. M. Salaverría, *El poema de la Pampa*, 1917; Calixto Oyuela, *Antología poética hispanoamericana*, II, 1919 (Buenos Aires); Henry A. Holmes, *Martín Fierro: An Epic of the Argentine*, 1923; Ricardo Rojas, *Los gauchescos*, 1924 (Buenos Aires), and Preface to Martín Fierro, 1937 (Buenos Aires), and Elutario F. Tiscornia, *Martín Fierro, comentado y anotado*, 1925 (Buenos Aires).

HERODOTUS

Born: Halicarnassus, Asia Minor
Date: 484 B.C.

Died: Thurii, Italy
Date: c. 425 B.C.

PRINCIPAL WORK

HISTORY: *Herodoti Historiae*, c. 430 B.C. (*The History of the Persian Wars*).

Only from references in his own works and occasional mention by Encyclopedists like the tenth century Suidas can details of Herodotus' life be obtained. He relates that his parents were Lyxes and Dryo, wealthy people of the upper class, and that his birthplace, Halicarnassus, was part of the Persian Empire until he was thirty years old. His many quotations and references to dozens of authors show the scope and quantity of his reading, and his apparent familiarity with foreign scenes indicates how widely he traveled in Egypt, Scythia, Asia Minor, and various Greek states. Although he tried to test the validity of his sources, the interest rather than the veracity of many of the related incidents appealed to him most. Herodotus must be read with caution. For that reason, some scholars prefer Thucydides (q.v.).

Herodotus earned the name of "Father of History" for his detailed account of the wars of the Greeks and the Persians between 500 and 479 B.C. This work is the earliest example of secular narrative of events. Interested in causation, he tried to establish strict chronology and in doing so became the first historian in the West. True, he includes all he had been able to

508

learn about earlier culture and history, without much effort to see deep meaning or discuss movements or trends, but the result is a colorful yet neat and serious story, presented by a master of prose style, who does suggest the lessons inherent in the events. The work is eminently readable.

Part of it was written in Samos and in Athens during a period when Herodotus was in exile, probably for taking part in a revolution. His uncle Panyasis is known to have been executed as a conspirator, and later Herodotus returned to Halicarnassus to help overthrow the tyrant Lygdamis and labor to get his city to join the Athenian Confederacy. When he left home permanently about 447 B.C., perhaps because he felt he was not appreciated, Herodotus settled in Athens where, in 445, the city voted him ten talents, a sum estimated at $10,000. Because it did not give him what he wanted most, citizenship, he left Athens to help found a colony of Greeks in Thurii, Italy, where he lived for the rest of his life, his death occurring about 425 B.C. His history was not printed in its original Greek until Aldus Manutius made an edition in 1502, divided into nine books, each named after one of the Muses. Previously, in 1474, the work had been published in Latin.

BIBLIOGRAPHICAL REFERENCES: A classic translation is B. R., *The Famous Historie*, 1584 (reissued, with an introduction by Leonard Whibley, 1924). See also George Rawlinson, *The History of Herodotus*, 1858–1860 (rev. ed., 1928); G. C. Macaulay, *The History of Herodotus*, 2 vols., 1890; and A. D. Godley, *Herodotus, with an English Translation*, 4 vols., 1921–1924. See also C. V. Langlois and Charles Seignobos, *An Introduction to the Study of History*, 1898, and T. R. Glover, *Herodotus*, 1924.

ROBERT HERRICK

Born: London, England
Date: August 24, 1591

Died: Dean Prior, England
Date: October, 1674

PRINCIPAL WORK

POEMS: *Hesperides, or the Works both Human and Divine of Robert Herrick, Esq.*, 1648.

A poet who found his poetic inspiration in the pagan poets, especially Anacreon, Horace, Catullus, and Martial, Robert Herrick seems hardly suited for a career in the Church. Least of all was he suited for a rural parish. Herrick had earlier associated with Ben Jonson and his witty followers, so he was understandably dissatisfied with his ignorant country congregation and looked upon his Devonshire residence as an imprisonment among the barbarians. It is said that he once threw his sermon at his inattentive parishioners. But he found some consolation, nevertheless, in the pagan qualities of the local songs and dances; and he loved his pet menagerie, particularly the pig he taught to drink.

He was born in London on August 24, 1591, about the time Shakespeare began to write for the stage, and he died in the same year as John Milton. His father, a prosperous goldsmith, died when Herrick was an infant, but he was aided by his rich uncle, Sir William Herrick, jeweler to the king. He was apprenticed to his uncle, but his academic talents made it advisable to send him to St. John's, Cambridge, at the age of twenty-two. He took his degree in 1617 and his M.A. in 1620. Little is known of the next nine years of his life, but he probably spent them associating with Jonson and his circle. In 1629 Herrick became vicar at Dean Prior, Devonshire. Despite his dislike for his new surroundings, he began to write poetry that exalted the charms of rusticity. He stayed in this rural setting until 1647, when he was removed from his position because he refused to subscribe to Parliamentary reforms. He then went to London and collected his twelve hundred short poems into his single volume, *Hesperides*, published in 1648. Many of his lyrics were anthologized and set to music. In 1662 he was restored to his parish and lived there until his death in October, 1674.

Though some of his poems are devotional, Herrick's most representative lyrics are full of pagan delights. His style is not Petrarchan but classic; among the English poets he followed Marlowe and Jonson rather than the metaphysical wit of Donne. He revised diligently and as a result his metrics and stanzaic patterns are pleasingly varied. Herrick's talents were little appreciated during most of the eighteenth century, but his idyllic charms captured the attention of the Romantic audience and his reputation has increased steadily ever since.

BIBLIOGRAPHICAL REFERENCES: The most recent annotated edition is *The Poetical Works of Robert Herrick*, 1956, edited by L. C. Martin. There is a bibliography, S. A. and D. R. Tannenbaum, *Robert Herrick, A Concise Bibliography*, 1949. The best life and the outstanding scholarly work is F. W. Moorman, *Robert Herrick, A Biographical and Critical Study*, 1910. A less solid biography is E. I. M. Easton, *Youth Immortal*, 1934.

JOHN HERSEY

Born: Tientsin, China
Date: June 17, 1914

PRINCIPAL WORKS

NOVELS: *A Bell for Adano*, 1944; *The Wall*, 1950; *The Marmot Drive*, 1953; *A Single Pebble*, 1956.

WAR REPORTAGE: *Men on Bataan*, 1942; *Into the Valley*, 1943; *Hiroshima*, 1946.

John (Richard) Hersey is a writer whose tremendous success is an interesting phenomenon of the years that followed upon World War II. In a time when prose fiction ran a very poor second to informational and historical works, Hersey's books continued to have a great success. To understand the attention his books have received, one should bear in mind that Hersey is primarily the novelist-as-reporter. When he writes a creative novel, as in *The Wall* or *A Single Pebble*, he convinces many readers that his novel

510

is primarily fact fictionized. When he writes a direct report, as in *Hiroshima*, his report is more than fact; it has the sharp detail and psychological insight that give life to a work of fiction.

Hersey, born into a missionary family at Tientsin, China, on June 17, 1914, could speak Chinese before he spoke English. As a child, he was taken on a two-year trip around the world. He received his education in the United States at Hotchkiss and Yale, and he moved from his first job, that of secretary to Sinclair Lewis, to positions on *Time* and *Life* magazines. He was a vigorous and intrepid reporter of World War II and often underwent the sort of danger described in *Into the Valley*, which reports the adventures of an ambushed group of men in the Pacific theater of war. In *A Bell for Adano*, which won the Pulitzer Prize in 1945, Hersey drew upon his knowledge of the invasion of Sicily and gave us not a literal report but a smoothly fictionized account of the first contacts between the American troops and the Italians. Hersey returned to vivid reporting in his most impressive book, *Hiroshima*; his reproduction of the recollections of a few Japanese who experienced the first atomic explosion

stirred the world. Hersey's visits to Hitler's ghettos in Poland inspired *The Wall*. A little to one side of Hersey's usual techniques are two works: *The Marmot Drive,* in which an ordinary rural pleasure is given political overtones by allegory, and *A Single Pebble,* a work in which Hersey tries to recapture, in fictitious form, recollections of his early years in China.

Whatever Hersey's change of pace, his works are animated by a quick responsiveness to the results of misery and oppression in all quarters of the globe, and he re-creates, either in reporting or in fiction, whatever has come into his field of vision. That vision, driven by his liberal sympathies, has covered some of the chief disaster spots of the twentieth century. In the work of Hersey many readers find a supplement to what the news magazines present them.

Critical opinion of Hersey generally recognizes these merits, but a minority report on Hersey suggests that he travels too far and too fast to be taken as a serious creative novelist and that his careful documentation covers a lack of perception of the inner workings of personality which is the mark of a first-rate novelist.

BIBLIOGRAPHICAL REFERENCES: There is no extended biographical or critical study. See Norman Cousins, "John Hersey," *Saturday Review of Literature,* XXXIII (March 4, 1950), 15; Milton Rugoff, "John Hersey: From Documentary Journalism to the Novelist's Art," *New York Herald-Tribune Book Review,* XXVII (August 20, 1950), 3+; and Kelsey Guilfoil, "John Hersey: Fact and Fiction," *English Journal,* XXXIX (1950), 355–360. For a discussion of Hersey's literary position as he sees it, consult also his article, "The Novel of Contemporary History," *Atlantic Monthly,* CLXXXIV (1949), 80+.

HESIOD

Born: Ascra, Boeotia
Date: Unknown; fl. c. 735 B.C.

Died: Oeneon, Locris
Date: Unknown

PRINCIPAL WORKS

POEMS: *Works and Days; Theogony.*

One of the chief sources about the mythology of the early Greeks is the poem *Theogony,* ascribed to a man so nebulous that some scholars claim Hesiod was only the personification of the Boeotian school of poetry as that other vague poet, Homer, typified the Ionic school. Still, *Works and Days,* while marking a high point in Greek didactic poetry, with its precepts, fables, and allegories, provides a portrait of its author, whatever his name, as a placid but hard-working Boeotian farmer whose father came from the Aeolic Cyme in Asia Minor at a time when the writer was just old enough to look after the flocks. The poet further reveals himself as a bachelor and a misogynist because of the marital troubles of his older brother.

Apparently, after his father's death, that brother bribed a corrupt judge to give him all of Hesiod's inheritance, too, so the poet went to Orchomenus and Naupactus and was finally, by tradition, murdered in the sacred enclosure of the Nemean Zeus at Oeneon. By command of the Delphic Oracle, his remains were removed to Orchomenus.

Works and Days describes daily life on a farm, with maxims for farmers, and a list of lucky and unlucky days for farm chores, interspersed with caustic council for his grasping brother. The *Theogony* traces the genealogy of the gods of ancient Greece.

BIBLIOGRAPHICAL REFERENCES: Translations of Hesiod available in English include those by A. W. Mair, in *Oxford Library of Translations,* 1908; H. G. Evelyn-White, *Hesiod,* 1914; J. A. Sinclair, *Hesiod, Works and Days,* 1932; and A. S. Way, *Hesiod in English Verse,* 1934. See also A. R. Burn, *The World of Hesiod,* 1937, and F. Solmsen, *Hesiod and Aeschylus,* 1949.

HERMANN HESSE

Born: Calw, Germany
Date: July 2, 1877

Died: Montagnola, Switzerland
Date: August 9, 1962

PRINCIPAL WORKS

NOVELS: *Peter Camenzind,* 1904; *Gertrud,* 1910 (*Gertrude and I*); *Rosshalde,* 1914; *Demian,* 1919; *Siddhartha,* 1922; *Der Steppenwolf,* 1927 (*Steppenwolf*); *Narziss und Goldmund,* 1930 (*Death and the Lover*); *Das Glasperlenspiel,* 1943 (*Magister Ludi*).

SHORT STORIES: *Knulp,* 1915.

POEMS: *Gedichte,* 1922; *Trost der Nacht,* 1929.

Hermann Hesse is still thought of as a German writer, although he has lived in Switzerland for fifty years and has acquired Swiss citizenship. He was born in Germany on July 2, 1877, at Calw, a small town in the Black Forest; his father, Johannes Hesse, was a religious journalist and a missionary. The influence of his father's religiosity is apparent in much of Hesse's work, particularly in the earlier fiction. Hesse's education included both classical schooling and study in the theological preparatory school at Maulbroun. During his youth he was a mechanic for a time, and also a bookseller in Basel. His advanced studies included literature and the history of art. He has also traveled extensively, touring Italy and going as far as India, where his father had done missionary work.

One of his earliest novels, *Peter Camenzind*, displays Hesse's ability to recall with understanding and acute observation the scenes of his childhood in a provincial atmosphere. This book, along with another early romantic novel, *Unterm Rad* (1905), deals with the conflicts of youth. Both are written in a direct and engaging style. In another early novel, *Gertrude and I*, his choice of intimate, lowly subject matter pertaining to small-town life again gives evidence of his interest in recollections of the past. In these early books Hesse writes with much warmth and delicacy.

The coming of World War I was a disillusioning experience for Hermann Hesse and his postwar novels, beginning with *Demian* and continuing in *Steppenwolf*, became more expression-istic and indicative of their writer's deep interest in modern psychology. Harry Haller, the hero of *Steppenwolf*, is a mixture of civilized moderation and barbarity. Whereas Hesse's earlier novels avoided strong conflict, his later work has dealt with the dominance of the "masses" over the individual and his creative force. After *Steppenwolf*, Hesse's fiction stressed classical tradition at the expense of his previous romanticism. This stress is seen in such later works as *Death and the Lover* and *Magister Ludi*. Hesse has lived in Switzerland since early in this century, and from this neutral ground he has watched with dismay the crumbling of social and intellectual values in the modern age. His social and political attitudes are also reflected in a large body of essays on contemporary topics. Several collections of his poetry have been published. One of the most personal of his books is *Siddhartha*, based on his travels in India, which brings together the themes of father and son relationships and self-discovery through Indian mysticism. In 1946 he was awarded the Nobel Prize for literature. He is now in the main current of the modern German novel, and in his latest work can be found interior monologue and abstract symbols.

BIBLIOGRAPHICAL REFERENCES: For biography and criticism see Hugo Ball, *Hermann Hesse*, 1927—a work continued by Anni Carlsson, 1947; H. R. Schmid, *Hermann Hesse*, 1928; Gotthilf Hafner, *Hermann Hesse, Werk und Leben*, 1954; Weibel Kurt, *Hermann Hesse und die deutsche Romantik*, 1954; and Käte Nadler, *Hermann Hesse*, 1956. For brief studies in English see also M. Benn, "An Interpretation of the Work of Hermann Hesse," *German Life and Letters*, 1950 (3); Seymour L. Flaxman, "Der Steppenwolf: Hesse's Portrait of the Intellectual," *Modern Language Quarterly*, XV (1954), 349–358); Joseph Mileck, "The Prose of Hermann Hesse: Life, Substance and Form," *German Quarterly*, XXVII (1954), 163–174; Murray B. Peppard, "Hermann Hesse's Ladder of Learning," *University of Kentucky Foreign Language Quarterly*, III (1956), 13–20; and Ruth Domino, "The Hunchback and Wings," *Approach*, II (1957), 20–28.

DUBOSE HEYWARD

Born: Charleston, South Carolina
Date: August 31, 1885

Died: Tryon, North Carolina
Date: June 16, 1940

PRINCIPAL WORKS

NOVELS: *Porgy,* 1925; *Angel,* 1926; *Mamba's Daughters,* 1929; *Peter Ashley,* 1932; *Lost Morning,* 1936; *Star Spangled Virgin,* 1939.

SHORT STORY: *The Half-Pint Flask,* 1929.

POEMS: *Carolina Chansons: Legends of the Low Country,* 1922 (with Hervey Allen); *Skylines and Horizons,* 1924; *Jasbo Brown and Selected Poems,* 1931.

PLAYS: *Porgy,* 1927 (with Dorothy Heyward); *Brass Ankle,* 1931; *Mamba's Daughters,* 1939 (with Dorothy Heyward).

DuBose Heyward was born in Charleston, South Carolina, on August 31, 1885. His formal schooling ended when he left high school to work. After an attack of poliomyelitis at eighteen, he worked as a cotton checker on the Charleston waterfront. At twenty-one he established with a boyhood friend a fairly prosperous insurance firm in Charleston. About this time Heyward began to write short stories and poetry, and in 1920, with John Bennett and Hervey Allen, he organized the Poetry Society of South Carolina. Heyward edited the *Year Book* (1921–1924) of the society and was elected its president in 1924. Allen and Heyward collaborated in the verse collection, *Carolina Chansons* and the latter published a second volume of poetry, *Skylines and Horizons,* in 1924. Heyward had begun to attend the MacDowell Colony in 1921 and there he met and married Dorothy Hartzell Kuhns, herself a playwright, in 1923. Their only child, Jenifer, was born in 1930.

In 1924 Heyward relinquished his insurance business in Charleston and undertook a series of lecture tours. His first novel, *Porgy,* was based on Negro life in Charleston and published in 1925. The hero is a crippled beggar who defends Bess, his woman, from her former lover, Crown, and eventually kills him, only to lose her to a drunken sport who abducts her to Savannah. A second novel, *Angel,* had a background of the North Carolina mountains. A long short story, "The Half-Pint Flask," was published in the *Bookman* (1927) and reprinted in book form two years later. *Mamba's Daughters* was a more ambitious novel of white and colored people in Charleston. Next came *Peter Ashley,* a historical novel of South Carolina before the Civil War. In these works Heyward became the first white author to treat Negroes honestly, sincerely, and sympathetically, and to represent the Gullah dialect of the sea islands authentically.

With the assistance of Dorothy Heyward, *Porgy* was considerably tightened, dramatized, and produced in 1927 in New York and later in London. *Mamba's Daughters* was similarly produced in 1939. An original play, *Brass Ankle,* appeared in 1931. He also wrote two less successful novels, *Lost Morning,* and *Star Spangled Virgin.*

The story of Porgy first caught the attention of George Gershwin in 1926, but it was not until 1935 that the opera *Porgy and Bess,* based on the play,

514

reached the stage. Gershwin wrote the music, the Heywards the libretto, and the Heywards and Ira Gershwin the lyrics. This was the first and has been the most successful serious American folk opera.

DuBose Heyward died at Tryon, North Carolina, June 16, 1940.

BIBLIOGRAPHICAL REFERENCES: The chief study of Heyward is Frank Durham, *DuBose Heyward*, 1954. See also Emily Clark, *Innocence Abroad*, 1931.

THOMAS HEYWOOD

Born: Lincolnshire, England
Date: c. 1573

Died: Clerkenwell, London, England
Date: August, 1641

PRINCIPAL WORKS

PLAYS: *The Four Prentices of London*, c. 1592; *King Edward IV*, Parts I and II, 1599; *How a Man May Choose a Good Wife from a Bad*, 1602; *The Royal King and the Loyal Subject*, c. 1602; *A Woman Killed with Kindness*, 1603; *The Wise-Woman of Hogsdon*, c. 1604; *If You Know Not Me, You Know Nobody*, Parts I and II, 1605; *The Rape of Lucrece*, c. 1605; *Fortune by Land and Sea*, c. 1609 (with W. Rowley); *The Golden Age*, 1610; *The Silver Age*, 1610; *The Brazen Age*, 1610; *The Iron Age*, Parts I and II, c. 1613?; *The Captives*, 1624; *The English Traveler*, c. 1624; *The Fair Maid of the West*, Parts I and II, 1631; *A Maidenhead Well Lost*, 1632; *A Challenge for Beauty*, c. 1634; *The Late Lancashire Witches*, 1634 (with Brome); *Love's Mistress*, 1634.

MISCELLANEOUS: *Troia Britannica*, 1609; *An Apology for Actors*, 1612; *Gunakeion* 1624; *England's Elizabeth*, 1631; *The Hierarchy of Blessed Angels*, 1635; *The Exemplary Lives and Memorable Acts of Nine [of] the most Worthy Women of the World*, 1640; *The Life of Merlin, Surnamed Ambrosius*, 1641.

Although the most commonly quoted statement about Thomas Heywood is Charles Lamb's characterization of him as "a sort of prose Shakespeare," the most striking thing about him is his almost incredible productivity. In the Epistle to *The English Traveler*, printed in 1633, Heywood calls the play "one reserved amongst two hundred and twenty, in which I have had either an entire hand, or at least a main finger." He also wrote numerous non-dramatic works in verse and prose and was a prolific translator. Considering his career as a professional actor, one finds this gigantic literary output phenomenal.

Heywood claimed himself a Lincolnshire man. Recently discovered testimony in a lawsuit of 1623 gives his age in one place as "50 yeares or neare upon" and in another as "49 or thereabouts." These statements would place his birth in late 1573 or 1574. A seventeenth century tradition states that he was "a fellow of Peter House," but official records to prove this have not been found. In *An Apology for Actors* he tells of being in residence at Cambridge University, but does not give the college.

The first reference to Heywood in Philip Henslowe's *Diary* records payment for a play in 1596. In 1598 he bound himself to Henslowe's company as an actor, and continued to write

515

plays. Some idea of the importance of the dramatists' position in this age of great drama is shown by the fact that Heywood received less for writing *A Woman Killed with Kindness* than Henslowe spent on the dress for the actor playing Mrs. Frankford.

Perhaps because of the effect of the plague on theatrical activity, Heywood turned more to writing and publishing in 1608 and following years. During this period he began *The Lives of All the Poets,* which apparently perished in manuscript. If this book contained lives of Heywood's contemporaries, its loss deserves deep mourning.

Although E. K. Chambers was unable to find any trace of Heywood as actor after 1619, C. J. Sisson has recently discovered records of a lawsuit involving the Red Bull Company which indicate that he was still active as a shareholder in 1623. Heywood wrote plays as late as 1634 and other works until the year of his death, 1641. In 1631 he became City Poet and wrote a series of Lord Mayor's Shows.

The texts of seven of these annual pageants were published. The register of St. James's Church, Clerkenwell, records his burial on August 16, 1641.

Heywood's writings often show haste and carelessness, and not always inspiration; they often show bad taste. Nevertheless, they have many poetic and dramatic merits. *A Woman Killed with Kindness* is not the work of a prose Shakespeare but of a lesser poet; its Biblical imagery is extremely appropriate to the Christian theology of the play, which stresses forgiveness rather than revenge; especially appropriate is such a passage as "I thank thee, maid; thou, like an angel's hand,/Hast stayed me from a bloody sacrifice." This speech is undergirded by the story of Abraham and Isaac, but the application is very different from that of the old story. In spite of Heywood's condescending attitude toward his plays, they (especially *A Woman Killed with Kindness*) hold up his literary reputation.

BIBLIOGRAPHICAL REFERENCES: The collected edition is *Heywood's Dramatic Works,* edited by John Pearson, 1874. Other editions are *The Best Plays of Thomas Heywood,* edited by A. W. Verity for the Mermaid Series, 1888, and *A Woman Killed With Kindness and The Fair Maid of the West, by Thomas Heywood,* edited by Katharine Lee Bates, 1917. See also A. M. Clark, *Thomas Heywood, Playwright and Miscellanist,* 1931; C. J. Sisson, "The Red Bull Company and the Importunate Widow," *Shakespeare Survey* 7, 1954; E. K. Chambers, *The Elizabethan Stage,* Vols. II and III, 1923; Henry W. Wells, *Elizabethan and Jacobean Playwrights,* 1939; and T. M. Parrott and R. H. Ball, *A Short View of Elizabethan Drama,* 1943.

JAMES HILTON

Born: Leigh, Lancashire, England
Date: September 9, 1900

Died: Long Beach, California
Date: December 20, 1954

PRINCIPAL WORKS

NOVELS: *Catherine Herself,* 1920; *And Now Goodbye,* 1931; *Goodbye Mr. Chips,* 1933; *Lost Horizon,* 1933; *We Are Not Alone,* 1937; *Random Harvest,* 1941; *So Well Remembered,* 1945; *Time and Time Again,* 1953.

As the famous biographer of a fictional professor, James Hilton was himself the son of a schoolmaster. Born at Leigh, England, on September 9, 1900, he was educated in the succession of schools where his father taught. Later he attended Leys School and Christ's College, Cambridge, where he received his baccalaureate in history and English in 1921. He not only distinguished himself in scholarship but he also proved an able soldier-officer in the university R.O.T.C.

A professional writer at seventeen, when he published an article in the *Manchester Guardian*, he published his first novel at the age of twenty. The royalties from *Catherine Herself* were so meager that he continued in journalism, writing from England two articles a week for the Dublin *Irish Independent*. Although recognized as a young writer of ability, his first financial success came from *And Now Goodbye*, which enabled him to give all his time and energy to fiction. Commissioned to write a short story of some length to be published in a supplement of the *British Weekly*, a short month before the story was due he wrote *Goodbye Mr. Chips* while bicycling on the Continent—and made his deadline. Successful as it was in England, its success in America was even greater. In 1934 Hilton submitted the manuscript to the *Atlantic Monthly*, where

it was published to great popular acclaim. It then went into many printings as a short novel, and finally was dramatized by the author for both stage and screen. While many think of the book, its author, and also the hero as jejune and sentimental, millions of readers and viewers remember the lovable old schoolmaster with great affection. From this time on, James Hilton was one of the best-paid writers of all time.

If he portrayed the stock image of a professor, he extended the metaphor of Utopia to its farthest reaches in *Lost Horizon*, first published in England in 1933 where it was awarded the Hawthornden Prize in 1934; but it was not widely acclaimed until the American publication several years later. This too received even greater attention after dramatization, as did nearly all Hilton's later works. Unfortunately, James Hilton did not live up to his early promise, and his final novels are disappointing.

He turned to his American admirers altogether in his last years, making California his home and Hollywood his headquarters. He continued to write and lecture and was much in demand everywhere, especially for articles in high-grade magazines and scenarios for motion pictures. He died of a lingering illness in Long Beach, California, on December 20, 1954.

BIBLIOGRAPHICAL REFERENCES: An early study of Hilton is in Carroll Sibley, *Barrie and His Contemporaries*, 28–47. An interview was printed in the *Bookman*, LXXXVI (1934), 192. See also George Stevens, *Lincoln's Doctor's Dog and Other Famous Best Sellers*, 1939; Frank Luther Mott, *Golden Multitudes*, 1947; and Cyril Clemens, "My Friend, James Hilton," *Hobbies*, LXI (1956), 106–107.

THOMAS HOBBES

Born: Westport, England
Date: April 5, 1588

Died: Hardwick Hall, England
Date: December 4, 1679

ESSAYS AND STUDIES: *De Cive*, 1642 (*The Citizen*); *Human Nature*, 1650; *Leviathan*, 1651; *Questions concerning Liberty, Necessity, and Chance*, 1656; *Behemoth*, 1679.

The first great materialistic philosopher in England to challenge theological orthodoxy, Thomas Hobbes was an alien in his own country. Neither the Church of England nor the Puritan party could tolerate the materialistic foundation of his philosophy, and as a result he became a great controversialist whose very life was sometimes in danger. Despite his fears of physical harm, he managed to produce a tremendous volume of work during his long life, his political theory and his doctrine of psychological determinism being his most important contributions to moral philosophy.

Until he was past the age of forty, however, Hobbes did little philosophical work. Born at Westport on April 5, 1588, he entered Oxford at fifteen; at the university he studied Greek and Roman authors almost exclusively. Following his graduation he made a living as a tutor to the second and third Earls of Devonshire. During these years he traveled in Europe, published a translation of Thucydides, and became acquainted with the thought of Montaigne and Galileo. He left England in 1640 in fear of the Parliament and took up residence among the philosophers of Paris. *Leviathan*, his great defense of the authoritarian state, turned even the exiled Royalists against him because of its irreligion. Hobbes fled for his life back to London, where Parliament chose to let him alone. He carried on many public disputes, his most famous being his defense of psychological determinism against Bishop Bramhall. At his death at Hardwick Hall, December 4, 1679, Hobbes was both revered as a sage and hated as the enemy of virtue and religion.

BIBLIOGRAPHICAL REFERENCES: Hobbes' *Complete Works* were collected by Sir William Molesworth, 11 vols., 1839–45. More recently, the *Leviathan* was edited by M. Oakeshott, 1946. Hugh Macdonald and Mary Hargreaves, *Hobbes: A Bibliography*, 1952, is standard. A good biography is Sir Leslie Stevens, *Hobbes*, English Men of Letters Series, 1904. Important critical works include John Laird, *Hobbes*, 1934; R. P. Russell, *The Natural Law in the Philosophy of Hobbes*, 1939; and R. M. MacIver, *Leviathan and the People*, 1939. More recent works are D. G. James, *The Life of Reason: Hobbes, Locke, Bolingbroke*, 1949; John Bowle, *Hobbes and His Critics: A Study in Seventeenth-Century Constitutionalism*, 1951; F. L. Windolph, *Leviathan and Natural Law*, 1951; and Leo Strauss, *Political Philosophy of Hobbes*, translated by E. M. Sinclair, 1952. An important critical article is D. M. Wolfe's "Milton and Hobbes: A Contrast in Social Temper," *Studies in Philology*, XLI (1944), 410–426.

ERNST THEODOR AMADEUS HOFFMANN

Born: Königsberg, East Prussia
Date: January 24, 1776

Died: Berlin, Germany
Date: June 25, 1822

SHORT STORIES AND TALES: *Phantasiestücke*, 1814–1815 (*Weird Tales*); *Nacht-stücke*, 1817 (*Night Pieces*); *Seltsame Leiden eines Theaterdirektors*, 1818 (*Strange Sufferings of a Theater Director*); *Die Serapions-Brüder*, 1819–1821 (*The Serapion Brethren*).

NOVELS: *Die Elixiere des Teufels*, 1815–1816 (*The Devil's Elixir*); *Lebensansichten des Katers Murr*, 1821–1822 (*Murr the Tomcat*).

Ernst Theodor Amadeus Hoffmann, born in Königsberg on January 24, 1776, was at one time perhaps the most influential German author both in his own country and elsewhere; Heine, Keller, Storm, Gautier, Balzac, Musset, and Poe were all indebted to him, and Offenbach wrote an opera based on his tales. At the beginning of the Romantic Movement he showed the way towards the representation of fantasy as an ingredient of everyday life, by using not only supernatural devices but also abnormal states of mind to accent and account for the horror of commonplace events.

Hoffmann, a diligent government official most of his life, first turned his artistic attention to music as a theater director and composer; the opera *Undine* (1816) survives as his most important work in this field. Also a suc-

cessful illustrator and caricaturist, he did not fully embark on a literary career until the appearance of his first collection of *Weird Tales* in 1814. These stories were followed by a story of temptation and sin, *The Devil's Elixir*, in 1815–1816. In *The Serapion Brethren*, he wrote of a literary club whose competitive tales make up the book itself. *Murr the Tomcat* was a satire against sham art and culture in the supposed memoirs of Hoffmann's pet tomcat. In his most effective stories Hoffman wrote of the region between fact and belief, using ghosts, clairvoyants, hypnotism, and psychological abnormality to turn the plot. He was a careless stylist, relying more upon invention and idea than artistic expression. An acknowledged master of Gothic effects, he died in Berlin on June 25, 1822.

BIBLIOGRAPHICAL REFERENCES: There are numerous books on Hoffmann in various languages. A good introductory study in English is Harvey Hewett-Thayer, *Hoffmann: Author of the Tales*, 1948. See, in German, Arthur Sakheim, *E. T. A. Hoffmann: Studien zu seiner Persönlichkeit und seinen Werken*, 1908; Hans von Wolzogen, *E. T. A. Hoffmann, der deutsche Geisterseher*, 1922; E. von Shenck, *E. T. A. Hoffmann: ein Kampf um das Bild des Menschen*, 1939; and Arthur Gloor, *E. T. A. Hoffmann*, 1947; in French, Raymond Lyon, *Les contes d'Hoffmann: étude et analyse*, 1948; and Jean Mistler, *Hoffmann le fantastique*, 1951.

OLIVER WENDELL HOLMES

Born: Cambridge, Massachusetts   *Died:* Boston, Massachusetts
Date: August 29, 1809   *Date:* October 7, 1894

PRINCIPAL WORKS

POEMS: *Poems*, 1836; *Urania: A Rhymed Lesson*, 1846; *Poems*, 1846; *Poems*, 1849; *The Poetical Works of Oliver Wendell Holmes*, 1852; *Songs of the Class of*

MDCCCXXIX, 1854; *Songs and Poems of the Class of 1829,* 1859; *Songs in Many Keys,* 1862; *The Poems of Oliver Wendell Holmes,* 1862; *Humorous Poems,* 1865; *Songs and Poems of the Class of Eighteen Hundred and Twenty-nine,* 1868; *Songs of Many Seasons, 1862–1874,* 1875; *The Iron Gate and Other Poems,* 1880; *Before the Curfew and Other Poems,* 1888.

NOVELS: *Elsie Venner,* 1861; *The Guardian Angel,* 1867; *A Mortal Antipathy,* 1885.

ESSAYS: *The Autocrat of the Breakfast-Table,* 1858; *The Professor at the Breakfast-Table,* 1860; *The Poet at the Breakfast-Table,* 1872; *Over the Teacups,* 1891.

BIOGRAPHY: *John Lathrop Motley,* 1879; *Ralph Waldo Emerson,* 1885; *Memoir of Henry Jacob Bigelow,* 1891.

TRAVEL: *Our Hundred Days in Europe,* 1887.

MEDICAL STUDIES: *Medical Essays, 1842–1882,* 1883.

Oliver Wendell Holmes, last of the great literary "Brahmins" of the nineteenth century, was in every way a true member of that class which he described in his novel *Elsie Venner* as "this . . . harmless, inoffensive untitled aristocracy" whose qualities of intellectual leadership "are congenital and hereditary." He could list among his ancestors on his mother's side the Phillipses, the Wendells, the Quincys, the Hancocks, and even Anne Bradstreet; and his father, the Reverend Abiel Holmes was descended from a long line of Calvinistic Connecticut divines. Moreover, he further demonstrated the hereditary qualities of his tradition by passing the genes of greatness on to his son, Oliver Wendell Holmes, Jr., for thirty years Associate Justice of the United States Supreme Court.

If versatility can be considered a Brahmin trait, Holmes possessed that, too. He is remembered today as a writer, particularly as a humorous essayist who wrote *The Autocrat of the Breakfast-Table* and as the author of such light verse as "The Deacon's Masterpiece, or, The Wonderful One-Hoss Shay" and of philosophical lyrics like "The Chambered Nautilus." When his three novels are added to

his humorous works, his versatility as a writer can be seen. But his versatility was not limited to his writing. He displays it in his life. He was also, at various times, a practicing physician, a professor of anatomy at Dartmouth, a professor of anatomy at Harvard, Dean of the Harvard Medical School, and a lecturer of note both on subjects of science and of literature.

He was born on August 29, 1809, in Cambridge, Massachusetts, where his father was minister of the First Congregational Church. In the Brahmin tradition, he was educated at Harvard, being graduated in the class of 1829. He next attended law school, the only result of which was some twenty poems including the much-quoted "Old Ironsides." Medicine seemed more congenial than law, and he changed his curriculum accordingly. He completed his domestic studies in 1833 and, after a grand tour and a year's medical training in Paris, began his professional practice in Boston.

Since he was more the theorist than the practitioner, and because the personality that was to make him the great humorist was not one that would inspire the confidence of patients, it

520

was natural that he should turn to the academic side of his profession. He accepted the professorship of anatomy and physiology at Dartmouth, returning to Boston in 1840 to marry Amelia Lee Jackson and to take over a similar post at the Harvard Medical School.

Settled in Boston, he began, with his lectures and his contributions to the famous Saturday Club, to establish a reputation as a poet and a wit. The reputation was purely local at first, but by 1857, when James Russell Lowell became editor of the *Atlantic Monthly,* Holmes won national fame as the author of that immortal series of essays, *The Autocrat of the Breakfast-Table,* which ran in the *Atlantic* for two years. These were followed in 1859–1860 by *The Professor at the Breakfast Table,* and by *The Poet at the Breakfast Table* in 1872. Finally, as an octogenarian, Holmes contributed still another series, *Over the Teacups,* which appeared in the *Atlantic* in 1891, just three years before his death.

It was in these pieces that he demonstrated his greatest literary talent: his ability to write prose in a sprightly, conversational style which set the pattern for the modern magazine and newspaper humorist–columnist. The sharp and penetrating form of Holmes's essays lacks the sentimentality of his own period and seems to hark back to the satire of Augustan England. It was in these pieces, too, that much of his liveliest verse appears. "The Wonderful One-Hoss Shay" is from Number Twelve of *The Autocrat,* his cleverly altered "Come! fill a fresh bumper" from the first.

His writings were not confined to the *Atlantic,* nor his wit to his writings. Besides his work as a humorist, he wrote novels—though these were comparatively unsuccessful—clever but ephemeral occasional verse, biographies, and a number of respected scientific discourses. Besides the humor of his printed works is the legendary humor of his many lectures, in public and in the university classroom.

Except for a trip abroad in 1886 (from which came his book, *One Hundred Days in Europe*), he remained in Boston until he died there on October 7, 1894, a true Brahmin of the time when Boston was still the literary capital of the country.

BIBLIOGRAPHICAL REFERENCES: The standard edition is the Riverside Edition of *The Writings of Oliver Wendell Holmes,* 13 vols., 1891–1892, reissued in 1892 as the Standard Library Edition of *The Works of Oliver Wendell Holmes,* increased to 15 vols. in 1896 with the addition of John T. Morse's *Life and Letters of Oliver Wendell Holmes.* The best one-volume edition of the poems is *The Complete Poetical Works of Oliver Wendell Holmes,* edited by Horace E. Scudder, 1895. A useful book of selections is *Oliver Wendell Holmes: Representative Selections,* edited by S. I. Hayakawa and Howard Mumford Jones, American Writers series, 1939.

The standard biography is the Morse *Life and Letters,* 2 vols., 1896. See also Mark A. De Wolfe Howe, *Holmes of the Breakfast-Table,* 1939, and Eleanor M. Tilton, *Amiable Autocrat,* 1947. The best short study is by Mark A. De Wolfe Howe, *Dictionary of American Biography.*

HOMER

Born: Ionia (?), Greece
Date: c. 9th Century, B.C.

Died: Greece
Date: c. 9th Century, B.C.

The *Iliad,* c. 800 B.C.; the *Odyssey,* c. 800 B.C.

Any biography of Homer as the modern reader thinks of a biography is an impossibility. All that can be done is to theorize tentatively on the basis of conflicting traditions, evidence within the *Iliad* and the *Odyssey,* and some slight relevant archaeological evidence. The two great Homeric epics are facts, and "Homer" is an author, fact or fiction, to account for them. Some classical scholars have argued for single authorship of the great poems, while other scholars have argued for a community of authorship. Contemporary scholarship leans heavily in favor of the theory that Homer, the author of the *Iliad* and the *Odyssey,* was a single person.

The great difficulty with which the student of Homer is faced is the great antiquity of the Homeric poems, which were written long before any extant literary records were kept. And yet the poetry of Homer was famous, even revered, in ancient Greece. Both the *Iliad* and the *Odyssey* were recited by rhapsodies, in public, at the Panathenaea in Athens every four years in classical times. It would appear that there were attempts to create some biography as early as the times of Plato and Aristotle. Eight different "Lives" of Homer from classical times are known, the fullest being credited to Herodotus, in Ionic Greek. Herodotus' and the other accounts seem to be made up of conjecture and tradition, fortified by possible deductions from passages within the *Iliad,* the *Odyssey,* and other poems sometimes attributed to Homer. Most of the early accounts agree that Homer was blind, elderly,

and poverty-stricken, a poet who wandered from city to city in ancient Greece. Although tradition has it that seven cities claimed to be his birthplace, tradition cannot even agree on which seven made the claim. There is agreement, however, that Homer came originally from somewhere in Ionia. But just when the poet flourished is not and probably never will be known. The biographical record attributed to Herodotus put Homer's death in 1102 B.C., but other accounts give dates varying from 685 to 1159 B.C. Recent archaeological discoveries lending indirect help with dates cause modern scholars to place Homer's life somewhere in the ninth century before Christ, or a little later.

In many cases, the text of a piece of literature furnishes evidence of the author's origin and dates, but the *Iliad* and the *Odyssey* do not give much help. The language of the two poems is unique, being a combination of Ionic and Attic Greek. In addition, the very nature of the epic conventions, as well as some very ancient Greek terms, baffle modern scholars and apparently puzzled also people of classical times. The nature of the epic conventions hides the author and causes him to use stylized language, and the very ancient terms can be given only tentative meanings. What we have in the way of texts of the Homeric poems were set some generations after Homer, perhaps as late as the sixth century before Christ, and are the probable results of a collation of texts which have long since disappeared.

Whether in the future we shall ever

522

know more about Homer or his poetry is doubtful. The available knowledge of the Greek world before 600 B.C. is altogether too dim. Almost nothing is known even of Greek political life before the time of the Athenian tyrant, Pisistratus. Even the very existence of Troy and the Trojan War was doubted prior to the archaeological discoveries by Schliemann in the nineteenth century. Schliemann's discovery of a series of cities on what is believed to have been the site of Troy indicates that there is at least some historical basis for the events recited in the Homeric poems. Indeed, evidence has been found that indicates which of the layers of ruins is that of the city about which Homer wrote.

The most logical conjecture is that soon after the end of the Trojan War, which occurred about 1200 B.C., stories sung to some musical accompaniment sprang up in Greece. These songs were well-known and spread widely through Greek culture, the action and characterization becoming common knowledge. As the centuries passed, these short pieces were probably joined together in many ways. Then at some time near 800 B.C. an unknown poet, whom we call Homer, brought together parts of the traditions and made the artistic creations which were very similar to the epics we now know as the *Iliad* and the *Odyssey*. The poet's sources were many, and the varied sources account for differences in customs, dialect, and action found in the poems. This theory does not detract from Homer, for he was the poet who organized these materials into artistic masterpieces, giving unity, point, and purpose to the materials he presented. Unfortunately, his poems had to be passed on by oral transmission for a time, and the oral transmission allowed for changes and additions which have affected some details, so that what we have is no longer quite what Homer wrote. Such changes seem to have affected only minor details, however, rather than the overall unity and tone of these poems from the dawn of Western civilization.

One should not linger too long over the biographical problems presented by Homer. Nor should one lament that we know so little about him or the history of his poems. The fact is that we have the poems. They still retain the beauty and grace which he gave them almost 2500 years ago. As works of art and as inspiration for later art they have been—and still are—magnificent.

BIBLIOGRAPHICAL REFERENCES: There are many translations of the Homeric epics in varying degrees of literary merit and scholarly accuracy. For general reading the translations by E. V. Rieu in the Penguin Classics library are recommended. See also S. E. Bassett, *The Poetry of Homer*, 1938; Rhys Carpenter, *Folk Tale, Fiction, and Saga in the Homeric Epics*, 1946; and Mark Van Doren, *The Noble Voice*, 1946.

ANTHONY HOPE
Sir Anthony Hope Hawkins

Born: London, England
Date: February 9, 1863

Died: Tadworth, England (?)
Date: July 8, 1933

NOVELS: *The Prisoner of Zenda*, 1894; *Rupert of Hentzau*, 1898; *Double Harness*, 1904.

SKETCHES: *The Dolly Dialogues*, 1894.

Anthony Hope Hawkins was born at London, February 9, 1863, the younger son of the Rev. Edward Connerford Hawkins. He attended Balliol College, Oxford, where he had a distinguished record as an athlete and scholar. After settling in London, he read law, and was called to the bar in 1887. By 1893 he had published five novels, become a successful barrister, and taken some part in politics; hence, three possible careers stood open to him. The choice was made in the autumn of 1893, when the plot of *The Prisoner of Zenda* came into his mind. By writing two chapters a day, he finished the novel in a month. It at once became enormously popular, being hailed by Andrew Lang and Robert Louis Stevenson. The novel was soon dramatized, and was produced by Sir George Alexander. In the same year appeared *The Dolly Dialogues*, an equally popular volume of sketches.

Although he wrote eighteen novels and three plays and considered *Double Harness* his best work, Hawkins will always be remembered as the author of *The Prisoner of Zenda*. In this novel he established a type that was to be copied repeatedly both in England and America: the stock setting of a mythical Balkan kingdom where a handsome, debonair, well-born, and self-sacrificing English—and later American—hero rescues from various entanglements a beautiful princess. For a generation the map of Europe was constantly being remade to include replicas of his Ruritania, and his naïve and melodramatic plot went through endless variations. It was the kind of novel that perfectly suited the taste of the period, which, in popular fiction, strongly inclined toward a dashing and romantic story and was willing to accept such in a contemporary setting. It was a pleasant and sunlit world, untroubled by international problems and unshadowed by the horrors of two world wars. The Balkans were merely a group of quaint and remote principalities, not to be taken too seriously, where almost any romantic adventure might take place. Realism in the English novel was still in the formative stage and was heartily disliked by the general reader.

Hawkins turned to another field in *The Dolly Dialogues*, the social world of London during the period when that world was at its height. These sketches, which consist of half-humorous, half-sentimental conversations, displayed a great gift for catching the tone of fashionable talk of that time. If for no one else, they have value for the social historian.

Although Hawkins has little to offer to the modern reader, he possessed the ability to tell a good story, an ability lacking in some much greater novelists.

Hawkins was knighted for war services in 1918. He died on July 8, 1933, probably at Tadworth, England.

BIBLIOGRAPHICAL REFERENCES: See Sir Charles Mallet, *Anthony Hope and His Books* (1935); also A. St. J. Adcock, *Gods of Modern Grub Street* (1923).

GERARD MANLEY HOPKINS

Born: Stratford, Essex, England   *Died:* Dublin, Ireland
Date: June 11, 1844   *Date:* June 8, 1889

PRINCIPAL WORKS

POEMS: *Poems of Gerard Manley Hopkins, Now First Published, with Notes by Robert Bridges,* 1918; *Complete Poems,* 1947.

LETTERS: *The Letters of Gerard Manley Hopkins to Robert Bridges,* 1935; *The Correspondence of Gerard Manley Hopkins and Richard Watson Dixon,* 1935; *Further Letters,* 1937.

MISCELLANEOUS: *Notebooks and Papers of Gerard Manley Hopkins,* 1936.

In his lifetime few others than his teacher and confessor, R. W. Dixon, and Coventry Patmore, friend and correspondent, knew of the genius Gerard Manley Hopkins. Neither the *Dictionary of National Biography* nor the eleventh edition of the *Encyclopedia Britannica* makes space for one of the most highly praised of modern poets. A quick glance at his life, however, makes one wonder how he or his poems ever became known.

A precocious child, Hopkins, born at Stratford on June 11, 1844, was reared and educated in Highgate where Dixon may have first recognized the talents of this sensitive soul, although the famous correspondence did not begin until nearly twenty years later. Always inward, and an eager reader, Hopkins won a prize for a poem in 1859. He later won a prize for a poem "A Vision of Mermaids" (1862) which was reprinted in *Poems* accompanied by a Blake-like sketch. His interest and ability in music, especially composition, were early manifest.

From 1863 to 1867, Hopkins attended Oxford, where he met Robert Bridges, later Poet Laureate and collector of Hopkins' poems. Here he was converted to Catholicism, at which time he reputedly burned all his poems, most of which must have been repro-

duced later if content is any guide. He is said to have studied also under John Henry Newman, later Cardinal, in a Jesuit school in Birmingham.

After his novitiate he taught classics at Stonyhurst, Lancashire Catholic College, and later he was Professor of Greek, Royal University of Ireland. He seems to have started writing again in 1875 with the poem "The Wreck of the Deutschland," a lament for the death of five nuns who were going into exile. Certainly his voluminous letter writing began at this time and continued until his death in Dublin on June 8, 1889, of typhoid.

Modern critics have given Hopkins credit for introducing the offbeat "sprung" rhythm into poetry, although there is evidence to show that such innovation began with the Elizabethan and metaphysical poets. Even so, Hopkins possessed the finest ear for extremely sensitive alliteration, assonance, and dissonance of any recent poet. His concept of poetry as "inscape," internal landscape, is most revealing and useful; this is a principle the New Critics have used to support the view that a poem is an entity, capable of arousing within each reader a complete emotional response. In a sense even Dadaism arose from such an idea, a kind of surrealistic, highly personal response. Hopkins' themes, mystical and exalted, show the man's great genius and intensity, and his religious leanings indicate that he was ecstatic in the spirit of the great Spanish poets of the Renaissance.

As a theorist he is often thought of as a poet's poet, and his explanations sometimes surpass his verse in sheer imaginative power. Like Melville, Hopkins wrote for another generation than his own; like Thoreau, he marched to the rhythm of a different and distant drum.

BIBLIOGRAPHICAL REFERENCES: For biography and criticism see G. F. Lahey, *Gerard Manley Hopkins,* 1930; E. E. Phare, *The Poetry of Gerard Manley Hopkins: A Survey and Commentary,* 1933; John Pick, *Gerard Manley Hopkins: Priest and Poet,* 1942; W. H. Gardner, *Gerard Manley Hopkins,* 1944; and Geoffrey Grigson, *Gerard Manley Hopkins,* 1955. See also Herbert Read, *In Defence of Shelley and Other Essays,* 1936; F. R. Leavis, *New Bearings in English Poetry,* 1938; David Daiches, *Poetry and the Modern World,* 1940; and J. G. Southworth, *Sowing the Spring: Studies in English Poets from Hopkins to MacNeice,* 1940. There are two excellent collections of critical studies by various hands: *Immortal Diamonds: Studies in Gerard Manley Hopkins,* edited by Norman Weyand, 1949, and *Gerard Manley Hopkins [by] the Kenyon Critics,* 1949. Also see *A Hopkins Reader,* edited and with an introduction by John Pick, 1953.

HORACE
Quintus Horatius Flaccus

Born: Venusia (Venosa), Italy
Date: December 8, 65 B.C.

Died: Rome, Italy
Date: November 27, 8 B.C.

PRINCIPAL WORKS

POEMS: *Satires,* 35, 30 B.C.; *Epodes,* 30 B.C.; *Odes,* 23–13 B.C.; *Carmen Seculare,* 17 B.C.

TREATISE: *Ars Poetica,* 13–8 B.C. (*The Art of Poetry*).

LETTERS IN VERSE: *Epistles,* 20–13 B.C.

No other Latin poet has so greatly influenced modern poetry, English or the Latin tongues, as Horace. The son of an Apulian tax collector, freed by one of the patrician Horatii family from which he took his name, young Horace was taken to Rome by his father for the education he could not get in his home town of Venusia, where he was born December 8, 65 B.C. Later he went to Athens to continue his studies. There he met Brutus, a fugitive after the assassination of Julius Caesar, and enrolled in the republican army of Brutus and Cassius. He commanded part of a legion at the Battle of Philippi (42 B.C.) where Octavius and Antony were victorious. His father dead and his small estate confiscated, Horace secured a minor post in the treasury. About the same time his poems brought him to the attention of Vergil, through whose offices Horace became the clerk and protégé of Maecenas, wealthy patron of the arts. When Augustus offered Horace a post as private secretary, the poet chose to remain with his benefactor, who gave him the famous villa in the Sabine Hills, still visited by tourists. Horace admired Augustus' efforts to secure peace, however, and wrote many admiring poems to him.

In his earliest poetry Horace reveals Greek influence. His writing was cruel and heartless and his satires were bitter attacks on individuals, but as he grew older he mellowed. He became more Roman, and after the death of his friend Vergil in 19 B.C., Horace became the chief representative of the Augustan Age of Roman literature. Always a master of poetic form, his satires became generalized, though never as popular as his odes. He also became interested in literary criticism and wrote *The Art of Poetry* as precepts for a young dramatist. As an urban Epicurean, he presented in his odes (gems of light verse translated by some of the world's great poets) charming pictures of contemporary society. Those describing his Sabine farm show his love for nature, though never to the exclusion of the city.

Horace never married, since marriage was considered unfashionable by literary people, but his amorous poetry reveals him as anything but a celibate. He died at Rome on November 27, in the year 8 B.C.

BIBLIOGRAPHICAL REFERENCES: There are translations of Horace by many hands. These include *The Complete Works of Horace*, edited with an introduction by Casper J. Kraemer, Jr., 1936, and various selections: Charles E. Bennett, *Horace, Odes and Epodes*, 1901; W. H. Mills, *Fifty Odes of Horace*, 1920; H. Rushton Fairclough, *Satires, Epistles and Ars Poetica*, 1926; and John C. Rolfe, *Horace, Satires and Epistles*, 1935. See also A. W. Verall, *Studies in Horace*, 1884; J. D. D'Alton, *Horace and His Age*, 1917; A. Y. Campbell, *Horace: A New Interpretation*, 1924; Tenney Frank, *Catullus and Horace*, 1928; H. D. Sedgwick, *Horace, A Biography*, 1947; Gilbert Highet, *Poets in a Landscape*, 1957; and Eduard Fraenkel, *Horace*, 1957. Useful also is W. Y. Sellar, *Roman Poets of the Augustan Age*, 1892.

A. E. HOUSMAN

Born: Fockbury, England
Date: March 26, 1859

Died: Cambridge, England
Date: April 30, 1936

PRINCIPAL WORKS

POEMS: *A Shropshire Lad*, 1896; *Last Poems*, 1922; *More Poems*, 1936; *Collected Poems*, 1939.

CRITICISM: *The Name and Nature of Poetry*, 1933.

CLASSICAL STUDIES: *Editions of Manilius*, 1903–1931; *Juvenal*, 1905; *Lucan*, 1926.

Despite the title of his most famous volume, A(lfred) E(dward) Housman was born, not in Shropshire, but at Fockbury, in the neighboring county of Worcestershire, March 26, 1859, the son of Edward Housman, a solicitor, and the elder brother of Laurence Housman, author and artist. He was educated at St. John's College, Oxford (1877–81), but failed to take honors in *literae humaniores*. This failure apparently embittered his spirits and temporarily turned him away from an academic career. When he left Oxford, he obtained in 1882 a position in the Patent Office in London and devoted his evenings to classical studies. In 1892 he was offered the Latin professorship at University College, London, which he held until 1911. In that year, against strong competition, he was elected to the Latin professorship at Cambridge, where he became a Fellow of Trinity College and spent the rest of his life.

Although Housman is known to the general public only as a poet, his poetry represented but a small part of his life's work. His main efforts were in classical scholarship, particularly Latin, and in this special world he obtained a formidable reputation. He was especially famous for his biting sarcasm when dealing with the productions of less competent scholars, usually Germans. He denied harboring an animus against that nation; but since, in his highly specialized field, most of the work was done by Germans, they inevitably became the victims of his satire. It was characteristic that he could spend thirty years on a second-rate poet such as Manilius, but one whose work afforded interesting problems in Latin usage and textual criticism.

Of all the poets of modern times, none has won so great a reputation from such a small body of work. The volumes are slender and most of the poems consist of but a few quatrains. That twenty-five years should have elapsed between his first and second books is indicative of his careful workmanship. It has been suggested that the discipline of classical scholarship, as well as the terseness of the Latin language, had an important influence on his own highly compressed style.

Housman himself said that the three great influences on his poetry were Shakespeare's songs, the Scottish border ballads, and the poems of Heine—all three of which achieve their effects with the greatest economy of means. *A Shropshire Lad* represented a reaction against the luxuriance of Victorian poets like Tennyson, Browning, and Swinburne.

Housman always kept his themes and their consequent emotions within a very narrow range. Repeatedly he returned to the same ideas: the passing of spring and of youth, the brevity and tragedy of life. The wind will strip the petals from the flowering trees; the boys and girls, now so brave and young, will all too soon be lying in their narrow beds of clay. It is a bitter, uncompromising, tragic view of life, devoid of hope. To contend against the inexorable tragedy of life is vain, yet a man must make the struggle against hopeless odds—"As I strap on for fighting/My sword that will not save."

The criticism brought against Housman's poetry was twofold: first, that he over-indulged in certain mannerisms of language, and that he artificially cultivated a tragic attitude. There is some validity in the first charge; to the second, we have his own answer:

They say my verse is sad: no wonder;
  Its narrow measure spans
Tears of eternity, and sorrow,
  Not mine, but man's.

Housman was apparently the perfect university don, reserved, withdrawn, immensely erudite. He never married, and he died in Cambridge April 30, 1936.

BIBLIOGRAPHICAL REFERENCES: There is no definitive biography. Memoirs of A. E. Housman appear in two books by his brother, Laurence Housman, *A. E. Housman*:

Some Poems, Some Letters, and a Personal Memoir, 1937, and The Unexpected Years, 1937. See also Katherine Symons and others, Alfred Edward Housman: Recollections, 1936; A. S. F. Gow, A. E. Housman: A Sketch, 1936; Percy Withers, A Buried Life: Personal Recollections of A. E. Housman, 1940; F. T. Grant Richards, A. E. Housman, 1897–1936, 1942; and O. Robinson, Angry Dust: The Poetry of A. E. Housman, 1950; also Stephen Spender, "The Essential Housman," Horizon, I (1940), 295–301; and A. F. Allison, "The Poetry of A. E. Housman," Review of English Studies, XIX (1943), 276–284.

Theodore G. Ehrsam published A Bibliography of A. E. Housman, 1941. This was supplemented by Robert Stallman, "An Annotated Bibliography of A. E. Housman: A Critical Study," Publications of the Modern Language Association, LX (1945), 463–502.

E. W. HOWE

Born: Treaty, Indiana
Date: May 3, 1853

Died: Atchison, Kansas
Date: October 3, 1937

PRINCIPAL WORK

NOVEL: The Story of a Country Town, 1883.

E(dgar) W(atson) Howe, journalist and novelist, born May 3, 1853, at Treaty, Indiana, belongs to that class of prolific writers whose energy and direction come out most clearly in a book only once during a long career. His first and best novel, The Story of a Country Town, set in Middle Western Twin Mounds, is noteworthy in American literature for its small-town realism and its stark exposure of nastiness and loneliness. He was among the first to denigrate frontier life and portray the Midwest less in the tradition of the American Dream than in the grimness of its daily order. For these qualities he belongs in the same category as Hamlin Garland and Edgar

Lee Masters, and he was noticed with appreciation by Mark Twain and William Dean Howells. The story itself, revealing conjugal betrayal in three families, is still overpowering, although in a period after Freud its undercurrent of male sexual repression reads more like a document of social psychology.

Howe published several other novels and two books of essays, but he was successful chiefly in the biting paragraphs of his journalism. He published the Golden Globe in Colorado and later the Atchison, Kansas, Daily Globe, the best-known American single sheet. He also established E. W. Howe's Monthly in 1911. He died at Atchison on October 3, 1937.

BIBLIOGRAPHICAL REFERENCES: Howe told much of the story of his own life in his autobiography, Plain Folks, 1929. For a discussion of his novel see Carl Van Doren, Introduction to The Story of a Country Town, 1927; and Vernon L. Parrington, Main Currents in American Thought, III, 1930.

WILLIAM DEAN HOWELLS

Born: Martins Ferry, Ohio
Date: March 1, 1837

Died: New York, N.Y.
Date: May 11, 1920

NOVELS: *Their Wedding Journey,* 1872; *A Chance Acquaintance,* 1873; *A Foregone Conclusion,* 1875; *The Lady of the Aroostook,* 1879; *The Undiscovered Country,* 1880; *A Modern Instance,* 1882; *A Woman's Reason,* 1883; *The Rise of Silas Lapham,* 1885; *Indian Summer,* 1886; *The Minister's Charge,* 1887; *April Hopes,* 1888; *Annie Kilburn,* 1889; *A Hazard of New Fortunes,* 1890; *The Quality of Mercy,* 1892; *An Imperative Duty,* 1892; *The World of Chance,* 1893; *The Coast of Bohemia,* 1893; *A Traveler from Altruria,* 1894; *The Day of Their Wedding,* 1896; *A Parting and a Meeting,* 1896; *An Open-Eyed Conspiracy,* 1897; *The Landlord at Lion's Head,* 1897; *Their Silver Wedding Journey,* 1899; *Ragged Lady,* 1899; *The Kentons,* 1902; *The Son of Royal Langbrith,* 1904; *Through the Eye of the Needle,* 1907; *New Leaf Mills,* 1913; *The Leatherwood God,* 1916.

SHORT STORIES: *A Fearful Responsibility and Other Stories,* 1881; *Christmas Every Day,* 1893.

PLAYS: *The Parlor Car,* 1876; *Out of the Question,* 1877; *A Counterfeit Presentment,* 1877; *The Register,* 1884; *A Sea-Change,* 1888; *The Albany Depot,* 1892; *A Letter of Introduction,* 1892; *The Unexpected Guests,* 1893; *A Previous Engagement,* 1897; *Room Forty-five,* 1900; *The Smoking Car,* 1900; *An Indian Giver,* 1900; *Parting Friends,* 1911.

TRAVEL SKETCHES: *Venetian Life,* 1866; *Italian Journeys,* 1867; *Tuscan Cities,* 1886; *London Films,* 1905; *Certain Delightful English Towns,* 1906; *Roman Holidays,* 1908; *Seven English Cities,* 1909; *Familiar Spanish Travels,* 1913.

AUTOBIOGRAPHY AND REMINISCENCE: *A Boy's Town,* 1890; *My Year in a Log Cabin,* 1893; *Impressions and Experiences,* 1896; *Stories of Ohio,* 1897; *Letters Home,* 1903; *My Mark Twain,* 1910; *Years of My Youth,* 1916; *Eighty Years and After,* 1921; *The Life in Letters of William Dean Howells,* 1928.

ESSAYS AND CRITICISM: *Criticism and Fiction,* 1891; *My Literary Passions,* 1895; *Literary Friends and Acquaintances,* 1900; *Heroines of Fiction,* 1901; *Literature and Life,* 1902; *Imaginary Interviews,* 1910.

Concerning the literary greatness of William Dean Howells, some dissent is now being heard on the grounds that he is too quiet and unhurried for our own frenetic generation, but it is hard to exaggerate the influence which he once exerted upon American writing. A prolific and versatile author of novels, plays, essays, poems, reviews, travel pieces—the author of too much, it must be said—he achieved a remarkable degree of success in consistently expressing himself with ease, exactness, and felicity. Furthermore, his long connection with the *Atlantic Monthly* and other important publications enabled him to encourage some potentially able writers to whom an editor's approval could make a great difference. The list of struggling authors thus benefited would be a long one; and it would show such notables-to-be as Mark Twain and Henry James, both of whom received Howells' endorsement at times when it was needed most.

Howells was born March 1, 1837, at Martins Ferry, Ohio. His father, William Cooper Howells, was of Welsh descent, a former Quaker who had drifted into the "New Church" of Emanuel Swedenborg; his mother, Mary Dean Howells, was of Irish and Pennsylvania Dutch stock. The elder Howells was a man of ability and character whose craftsman's skill as a printer was offset by a distressing lack of business acumen. With, eventually, ten mouths to feed, he led a wandering and straitened life as editor and printer in various sections of Ohio; and his second son, William Dean, got much of his education in a printing office. Fortunately, there have been worse places, as Bret Harte and Mark Twain could have joined Howells in testifying. The latter's formal schooling occupied as little as sixteen or eighteen months; and these were in random doses, mainly at Hamilton, Ohio. Nevertheless, the boy's keen appetite for learning was soon discernible to and encouraged by his understanding father. William eagerly read and wrote; he developed a passion for languages, at one period studying five simultaneously, and he acquired such a devotion to Heinrich Heine that Lowell was later to write: "You must sweat the Heine out of you as men do mercury."

At fourteen Howells became a compositor on the *Ohio State Journal* at Columbus. Other newspaper jobs followed, but the young man found time to write and send off poetry to the *Atlantic Monthly,* some of it finding acceptance. Energy and ambition began to pay off, though all was not clear sailing. One of his biggest handicaps was a sort of psychic malaise, featuring a fear of hydrophobia, which haunted his childhood and adolescence, once driving him into a complete breakdown. Nevertheless, Howells' will was indomitable. At twenty-one he was dining with the governor of the state; at twenty-four—largely as the result of a campaign life of Lincoln—he was appointed American Consul at Venice. His four years in Venice were the

equivalent of a university education for Howells; they gave him not only an acquaintance with the riches of Europe but enough time to read, write, and improve his knowledge of languages. During his consulship, in 1862, he married Elinor Meade of Brattleboro, Vermont, whom he had previously met in Columbus. Their stay abroad inspired the writing of *Venetian Life* and *Italian Journeys,* which were published in 1866 and 1867.

Returning to America in 1865, Howells intensified his pursuit of a literary career. After a few months of free-lancing in New York, a break came when he was offered the post of editorial assistant on *The Nation.* Even this, however, was merely the prelude to one of the most important steps of his life. Early in 1866 he attracted the attention of James T. Fields, editor of the *Atlantic Monthly;* and a few weeks later, on his twenty-ninth birthday, he became assistant editor of that influential literary organ. For fifteen years Howells' fate and fortunes were to be connected with those of the *Atlantic;* in 1872 he became chief editor, remaining in that capacity until 1881, when he resigned to devote himself more exclusively to writing. During his years with the *Atlantic* he exercised a wide and wholesome influence, mediating busily between the old and the new, compromising differences between East and West, and sponsoring such new and diverse talents as those of Mark Twain and Henry James. Not even these activities, however, could shut off the flow of his own writing; and his contributions to the *Atlantic* began to display, more and more strongly, the type of realistic writing which stamps his major pieces of fiction.

531

The quality of Howells' realism finds effective illustration in what are generally considered his best novels: *A Modern Instance, The Rise of Silas Lapham*, and *A Hazard of New Fortunes*. In these, he largely concerns himself with everyday people and the realistic translation of their experiences. However, his picture of humanity omitted the rougher aspects of life, and his standards of good taste did not permit the revelations of sex and violence which punctuate the writing of the twentieth century. Because of these omissions, the characters of his novels have been accused of being commonplace, but it is certain that modern realism owes a debt to Howells' pioneering which it has not always been very prompt to acknowledge.

After leaving the *Atlantic* in 1881, Howells moved to New York, which had become the publishing center of the nation. There he wrote novels for the *Century Magazine* and became literary adviser to Harper and Brothers; in 1900 he took over editorship of The

Easy Chair, that notable department of *Harper's Monthly*. Novels and shorter fiction continued to pour from his pen, with side excursions into poetry and drama. In literary criticism, also, he achieved what some literary historians consider his finest work, reaching its peak with *Criticism and Fiction* in 1891.

Howells' later years were rich in honors. His last two decades brought satisfying recognition to a man who, despite varying estimates of his literary significance, had always refused to compromise on matters involving principle. Harvard, Yale, and Columbia conferred degrees upon him; Oxford bestowed a doctorate of literature in 1904; leading institutions sought his services as lecturer and teacher. For many years he was president of the American Academy of Arts and Letters. Before his wife's death in 1909 he frequently traveled abroad with her; afterwards his companion became his daughter Mildred. Howells died May 11, 1920, at his home in New York.

BIBLIOGRAPHICAL REFERENCES: Aside from the epistolary autobiography, *The Life in Letters of William Dean Howells*, edited by Mildred Howells, 2 vols., 1928, there is no standard biography. Edwin H. Cady in *The Road to Realism: The Early Years of William Dean Howells, 1837–1885*, 1956, traces the story of his life through the publication of *The Rise of Silas Lapham*. The best critical studies are Delmar G. Cooke, *William Dean Howells: A Critical Study*, 1922; Oscar W. Firkins, *William Dean Howells: A Study*, 1924; and Everett Carter, *Howells and the Age of Realism*, 1954. See also Clara and Rudolph Kirk, Introduction to *William Dean Howells: Representative Selections*, American Writers Series, 1950; Arthur H. Quinn, *American Fiction*, 1936; Alexander Cowie, *The Rise of the American Novel*, 1948; and Gordon S. Haight, "Realism Defined: William Dean Howells," in *Literary History of the United States*, Vol. II, edited by Robert E. Spiller, Willard Thorp, Thomas H. Johnson, and Henry S. Canby, 1948.

W. H. HUDSON

Born: Quilmes, Argentina
Date: August 4, 1841

Died: London, England
Date: August 18, 1922

NATURE STUDIES AND ESSAYS: *The Naturalist in La Plata*, 1892; *Birds in a Village*, 1893; *Idle Days in Patagonia*, 1893; *Nature in Downland*, 1900; *Birds and Man*, 1901; *Hampshire Days*, 1903; *The Land's End*, 1908; *Afoot in England*, 1909; *A Shepherd's Life*, 1910; *Adventures among Birds*, 1913; *The Book of a Naturalist*, 1919; *A Traveller in Little Things*, 1921; *A Hind in Richmond Park*, 1922; *Men, Books, and Birds*, 1925.

NOVELS: *The Purple Land That England Lost*, 1885; *A Crystal Age*, 1887; *Fan*, 1892 (as Henry Harford); *Green Mansions*, 1904; *Ralph Herne*, 1923.

SHORT STORIES: *El Ombú*, 1902 (reissued as *South American Sketches*, 1909; American edition, *Tales of the Pampas*, 1916); *A Little Boy Lost*, 1905; *Dead Man's Plack* and *An Old Thorn*, 1920.

AUTOBIOGRAPHY: *Far Away and Long Ago*, 1918.

LETTERS: *153 Letters from W. H. Hudson*, edited by Edward Garnett, 1923 (American edition, *Letters from W. H. Hudson*, 1901–1922).

W(illiam) H(enry) Hudson, naturalist and author, was born at Quilmes, a short distance west of Buenos Aires, on August 4, 1841. His father, Daniel Hudson, was of English descent; born in Marblehead, Massachusetts, Daniel had left New England under threat of tuberculosis to seek a softer climate in Argentina. There six children were born to him and his wife, who had been Katherine Kimball of Maine. William Henry, the fourth of their five sons, was a strong, alert child who rode his pony about the pampas and developed an absorbing interest in the bird life of the great plains. From these contacts with nature he learned much that was later to be of benefit, quite possibly more than he learned from the ill-equipped tutors who were available to conduct his formal training.

At the age of twenty-eight, Hudson left South America to take up permanent residence in England. The death of his father the year before had severed the last strong tie with his boyhood home. Furthermore, during his teens an attack of rheumatic fever had weakened Hudson's heart; and the Argentine was no place for a man who could not lead an active outdoor life.

Hudson's earliest years in England were marked by poverty and loneliness. For a time he became secretary to an eccentric archaeologist, who often lacked money to pay him. In 1876 he married Emily Wingreave, a gentle soul fifteen years older than Hudson, who admired her husband unreservedly, though never completely understanding his peculiar gifts and qualities. Two experiments in running a boarding house failed, and finally the Hudsons settled in a dreary house, near Westbourne Park, which had been left to Mrs. Hudson by her sister.

Though he had been writing steadily since arrival in England, literary recognition came to Hudson with extreme slowness. One of his best books, now known as *The Purple Land*, was published in 1885; and in 1887 came his Utopian romance, *A Crystal Age*. Neither book created much stir, but in 1892 *The Naturalist in La Plata* received favorable attention; thereafter Hudson's books won increasing, though still modest, circulation. In 1918 came the history of his childhood,

Far Away and Long Ago; though highly regarded, it is probably less read than *Green Mansions,* brightly-colored romance of the bird-girl Rima, set against the background of Venezuelan forests. Especially popular in America, it effectively combines Hudson's gifts as a storyteller with his deep feeling for nature.

Hudson died in London on August 18, 1922. His literary following has, if anything, grown larger since his death. This development is possibly due to the fact that an increasingly urban civilization has learned to value nature more than in the author's own time. Hudson's style is simple and direct; at its best, it gracefully embodies the author's almost mystical sense of natural beauty. Very appropriately, Hudson's London memorial is a bird sanctuary, established in Hyde Park in 1925.

BIBLIOGRAPHICAL REFERENCES: Useful biographical studies are Morley Roberts, *W. H. Hudson: A Portrait,* 1925, and H. C. Goddard, *W. H. Hudson, Bird Man,* 1928. See also F. M. Ford, *Portraits from Life,* 1937; Richard Curle, "W. H. Hudson," *Fortnightly Review,* CXII (1922), 612–619; Robert H. Charles, "The Writings of W. H. Hudson," *Essays and Studies by Members of the English Association,* XX (1935); and James V. Fletcher, "The Creator of Rima, W. H. Hudson," *Sewanee Review,* XLVIII (1933), 908–918.

RICHARD HUGHES

Born: Weybridge, Surrey, England
Date: April 19, 1900

PRINCIPAL WORKS

NOVELS: *A High Wind in Jamaica,* 1929 [*The Innocent Voyage*]; *In Hazard,* 1938.

SHORT STORIES: *A Moment of Time,* 1926; *The Spider's Palace,* 1931; *Don't Blame Me,* 1940.

PLAYS: *The Sisters' Tragedy and Three Other Plays,* 1926 [*A Rabbit and a Leg*].

POEMS: *Gypsy-Night and Other Poems,* 1922; *Confessio Juvenis,* 1926.

Though his reputation is limited to a small public, Richard (Arthur Warren) Hughes has had a considerable critical success with his small output of books. A writer of plays, short stories, poems, and novels, his distinction is based mainly on his two novels. Critics have almost unanimously acclaimed his stylistic skills and his portrayal of the springs of character.

Born of Welsh parentage in Weybridge, England, April 19, 1900, Hughes was educated at Charterhouse School and Oriel College, Oxford.

While still at Oxford, he traveled widely on the Continent. When "The Sisters' Tragedy" was produced, George Bernard Shaw called it "the finest one-act play ever written." Published in England as *A High Wind in Jamaica,* *The Innocent Voyage* drew praise from the critics for its adroit handling of melodrama, its imaginative power, and its grasp of the child's mentality. In 1943 a dramatic version was produced on Broadway, but with little success.

After *The Innocent Voyage* Hughes concentrated on fiction. *In Hazard* was compared favorably with another story of a storm at sea, Conrad's *Typhoon* (1903); some critics even thought the style better in some respects. Hughes still publishes an occasional short story in American magazines. Two volumes of his short stories for children have been well received: *The Spider's Palace* and *Don't Blame Me*.

BIBLIOGRAPHICAL REFERENCES: There is almost no criticism available on Hughes. *Richard Hughes: An Omnibus*, 1931, includes an autobiographical introduction. His collected plays were published in *The Sisters' Tragedy and Three Other Plays*, 1924; American edition, *A Rabbit and a Leg. High Wind in Jamaica* is in the Modern Library. Hughes' work as a playwright is covered in James E. Agate, *The Contemporary Theatre, 1924*, 1925. For reviews see *New Republic*, LVIII (1929), 312; *Saturday Review of Literature*, VII (1932), 673; and *Saturday Review* CXXXXVIII (1929), 355.

THOMAS HUGHES

Born: Uffington, England
Date: October 20, 1822

Died: Brighton, England
Date: March 22, 1896

PRINCIPAL WORKS

NOVELS: *Tom Brown's School Days*, 1857; *Tom Brown at Oxford*, 1861.
HISTORY: *Alfred the Great*, 1869.

Thomas Hughes, author, lawyer, and active socialist, was born at Uffington, Berkshire, England, October 20, 1822, the son of an editor and writer. Thomas and his fellow siblings were reared by a grandmother, their mother dying while they were still young. After attending a school at Twyford for a time, Thomas Hughes and his older brother entered Rugby, which was then under the guidance of Dr. Thomas Arnold, famous as an educator and as the father of Matthew Arnold, the Victorian writer. After finishing Rugby, Thomas Hughes entered Oxford University, where he took his degree in 1845. He went down to London after receiving his degree and began to study law, being admitted to the bar in 1848. In the same year he married Frances Ford, who bore him several children. Under the influence of Frederick Denison Maurice, Hughes became a Christian Socialist. He helped found Working Men's College in London and served as its principal from 1872 to 1883.

Hughes' first literary effort, and his most famous, is *Tom Brown's School Days*, written under the pseudonym of "An Old Boy." In this book Hughes painted an idealized picture of life in the British public school which has influenced the world's notions of that kind of school and childhood in Victorian England. Those who knew Hughes claimed that the hero of his book, a high-minded and unselfish lad, bore a great resemblance to the author. Other books by Hughes are *Religio Laici* (1861), *Tom Brown at Oxford* (an inferior sequel to his first success), *Alfred the Great*, and *Memoir of a Brother* (1873). During the 1850's and 1860's Hughes continued his work in the profession of law, becoming a

535

Queen's Counselor in 1869. He also served in Parliament as a Liberal Unionist from 1865 to 1874. On the third of his three visits to the United States, in 1879, he helped found a cooperative colony in Rugby, Tennessee. The colony, like many another in nineteenth century America, was unsuccessful, and it cost Hughes a great deal of money. In his later years Hughes continued to serve society by working for reforms in both his church and in society. He died at Brighton on March 22, 1896.

BIBLIOGRAPHICAL REFERENCES: See Thomas Hughes, *Memoir of a Brother*, 1873; also *Dictionary of National Biography Supplement*, 1912; and M. L. Parrish and B. K. Mann, *Charles Kingsley and Thomas Hughes*, 1936.

VICTOR HUGO

Born: Besançon, France
Date: February 26, 1802

Died: Paris, France
Date: May 22, 1885

PRINCIPAL WORKS

NOVELS: *Han d'Island*, 1823; *Bug Jargal*, 1826; *Le Dernier jour d'un condamné*, 1829; *Notre Dame de Paris*, 1831 (*The Hunchback of Notre Dame*); *Les Misérables*, 1862; *Les Travailleurs de la mer*, 1866 (*The Toilers of the Sea*); *L'Homme qui rit*, 1869 (*The Man Who Laughs*); *Quatre-vingt-treize*, 1874 (*Ninety-Three*).

POEMS: *Odes et poésies diverses*, 1822; *Odes et ballades*, 1826; *Les Orientales*, 1829; *Les Feuilles d'automne*, 1831; *Les Chants du crépuscule*, 1835; *Les Voix intérieures*, 1837; *Les Rayons et les ombres*, 1840; *Les Châtiments*, 1853; *Les Contemplations*, 1856–1857; *La Légende des siècles*, 1859, 1877, 1883 (three series); *Les Chansons des rues et des bois*, 1865; *L'Année terrible*, 1872; *L'Art d'être grand-père*, 1877; *Le Pape*, 1878; *La Pitié suprême*, 1879; *L'Ane*, 1880; *Les Quatre Vents de l'esprit*, 1881; *La Fin de Satan*, 1886; *Toute la lyre*, 1889–1893; *Dieu*, 1891.

PLAYS: *Cromwell*, 1827; *Hernani*, 1830; *Marion De Lorme*, 1831; *Le Roi s'amuse*, 1832; *Lucrèce Borgia*, 1833; *Marie Tudor*, 1833; *Angelo*, 1835; *Esmeralda*, 1836; *Ruy Blas*, 1838.

MISCELLANEOUS: *Littérature et philosophie mêlées*, 1834; *William Shakespeare*, 1864; *Choses vues*, 1887; *En voyage: Alpes et Pyrénées*, 1890.

In France, Victor Hugo's fame rests chiefly on his enormous output of romantic poetry; in America he is known best for two novels. Although he was a successful playwright in his time, only *Hernani* is now remembered outside scholarly circles.

Victor (Marie) Hugo was born at Besançon, to Joseph Hugo and Sophie Trébuchet, on February 26, 1802. His father was a crude and lusty officer in Napoleon's army. His mother, of more reserved disposition, rather quickly tired of her amorous husband. As a relief from his attentions, she entered into a liaison with LaHorie, a general opposed to Napoleon, while her husband was stationed in Germany, Italy, and Spain. Victor and his two older brothers spent some time with their father in Elba, and later, when Joseph was made a governor in Spain, Sophie took the children there to see that they shared in his wealth and influence. Most of Victor's childhood was spent, however, in a quiet house with a big garden in the rue des Feuillantines, Paris. The children frequently saw the gentle LaHorie, in hiding from the wrath of Napoleon.

Hugo began to write poetry early. When he was fifteen, his work was honorably mentioned by the French Academy; in 1819 he received first prize from the Academy of Floral Games at Toulouse. Two years later Louis XVIII gave him a royal prize, and by the time he was twenty-five, Hugo was the acknowledged leader of the "Young Poets," a coterie that included Alfred de Musset and the critic Sainte-Beuve. His first published work was a volume of poems in 1822. An early meeting with Chateaubriand, when he was only seventeen, had been important in forming his artistic bent.

After Hugo fell in love with a neighbor girl, Adèle Foucher, he carried on a long, idealistic courtship. His parents opposed the match, however, because Hugo had no means to support a wife. His mother's death and a state pension smoothed out the difficulties enough so that Adèle and Victor were married on October 14, 1822. The wedding breakfast was saddened when Eugène, Victor's older brother, suddenly went insane, supposedly because he was also in love with Adèle. To the young couple were born by 1829 five children, of whom two boys and two girls survived.

Hugo's first play, *Cromwell*, was a stage failure but gained him critical esteem. *Marion De Lorme*, his second drama in time of composition, was censored and barred from presentation; it was printed in 1931, following the great financial and critical success of *Hernani*, performed in 1830.

Adèle Hugo, a pretty, commonplace woman, became weary of trying to keep up with her restless, creative husband and tired of frequent childbirth. In defense she undertook a mild flirtation with Sainte-Beuve, by this time a family friend. More curiously Hugo, who had been a devoted husband and father and a fiery advocate of chastity for men, took a mistress, Juliette Drouet. It was a strange coupling. Juliette had had several other lovers, had borne a daughter, and was accustomed to a bohemian life. Hugo kept her in seclusion on a strict budget, but to the end of her life Juliette never thought of another man.

This sudden change in Hugo's character is hard to account for. During the rest of his life he was a questing satyr, continuously involved with women. On one occasion he was caught *in flagrante* by a jealous husband and the woman was imprisoned. At another time he and his own son were rivals for the charms of the beautiful Alice Ozy; the father won. At the age of seventy-six he made a conquest of comely Blanche, a servant girl who desperately wanted to bear his child. Yet none of these amorous excursions interfered with his work, his marriage, or his permanent liaison with Juliette.

With publication of *The Hunchback of Notre Dame* in 1831, election to the French Academy, and elevation to the peerage, Hugo became a prominent figure in French life. He had in his youth been a royalist, but he gradually changed sides. Taking an increasingly active part in politics, he became an ardent champion of the left, bitterly opposed to Napoleon III, and in 1848 he founded a newspaper, *L'Événement*.

Because of his fame he was allowed his liberty, but his son Charles was imprisoned. When Napoleon came to absolute power in 1851, Hugo was forced into exile. After a short stay in Brussels, he settled in the Channel Islands, first on Jersey and then on Guernsey. At each remove Juliette was installed in suitable quarters discreetly apart from the family dwelling. Adèle spent a good deal of time in Paris, and Juliette was quietly accepted as part of the family.

Hugo's resentment of the authoritarian regime meant nineteen years of exile. These were productive years. In addition to the vast *La Légende des Siècles,* as well as other collections of poetry, he published three novels during this period. *Les Misérables,* the best known of his fiction, sold over seven million copies by the end of the century. His fame made him a world figure. Keenly interested in the American Civil War, he wrote several times to Lincoln. He also defended John Brown and wrote in support of Garibaldi, the Italian patriot.

After Adèle died in 1868, many expected him to marry Juliette, but she remained his open and respected mistress. With the outbreak of the Franco-Prussian War in 1870 the Empire fell, and Hugo returned to his beloved Paris. His welcome was tumultuous. He was still active in politics and writing, and even made a balloon ascension in 1878. Juliette died in 1883, and Victor Hugo followed her two years later, on May 22, 1885.

Hugo began writing in the heyday of romanticism and continued well into the naturalistic period. His poetry is a landmark of the romantic movement in France, and his novels, though full of digression and extravagance, are widely read. Interest in Hugo the man continues unabated. His long, rich life, his prolific writing, and his incredible vigor—all offer a fascinating subject to biographers.

Russell Cosper

BIBLIOGRAPHICAL REFERENCES: The *Œuvres Complètes* appeared in 48 vols., 1880–1889; the complete *Novels* were published in English in 28 vols., 1892–1894; and the *Works* appeared in English in 18 vols., 19— (the Royal de Luxe edition). Autobiographical information is furnished by *The Memoirs of Victor Hugo,* translated by John W. Harding, preface by Paul Meurice, 1899; and an early biography was published by Mme. Victor Hugo in 1887, *Victor Hugo, by a Witness of His Life.* Recent biographies, all of which include bibliographies, are Matthew Josephson, *Victor Hugo: A Realistic Biography of the Great Romantic,* 1942; E. M. Grant, *The Career of Victor Hugo,* Harvard Studies in Romance Languages, XXI, 1945; and André Maurois, *Olympio: ou La Vie de Victor Hugo,* 1954, translated by Gerard Hopkins, 1956. Critical works include A. C. Swinburne, *A Study of Victor Hugo,* 1886; Kenneth Ward Hooker, *The Fortunes of Victor Hugo in England,* 1938; William D. Pendell, *Victor Hugo's Acted Dramas and the Contemporary Press,* 1947; and Maurice Gay, *Victor Hugo, Spiritualiste,* 1955.

DAVID HUME

Born: Edinburgh, Scotland
Date: April 26 (O.S.), 1711

Died: Edinburgh
Date: August 25, 1776

ESSAYS AND STUDIES: *A Treatise of Human Nature*, 1739–1740; *Essays, Moral and Political*, 1741–1742; *An Enquiry Concerning Human Understanding*, 1748; *Political Discourses*, 1751; *An Enquiry Concerning the Principles of Morals*, 1751; *Four Dissertations*, 1757; *Two Essays*, 1777; *Dialogues Concerning Natural Religion*, 1779.

HISTORY: *History of England*, 1754–1761; *Natural History of Religion*, 1757.

No doubt the most thoroughgoing British skeptic of the eighteenth century was David Hume, Scottish philosopher and historian. Born in Edinburgh on April 26, (O.S.), 1711, he received his early schooling there and later began the study of law at the University of Edinburgh. Disliking the legal profession, however, and also the commercial career he began at a counting-house in Bristol, he was finally permitted to study literature in France (1734–1737). There he wrote the germinal *Treatise of Human Nature*. Published anonymously in 1739 and practically unread, it was later (1777) repudiated by Hume; but it contains the key ideas which he polished and enlarged in his subsequent writings. On his return to Scotland he wrote his *Essays, Moral and Political*, but failed to secure an appointment to the Chair of Moral Philosophy at Edinburgh. In the next few years he served as tutor to the near-mad Marquis of Annandale, then as Judge-Advocate-General to General James Sinclair, with whom he served on a diplomatic mission to France. In 1748 he issued his *Philosophical Essays Concerning Human Understanding*, later called *An Enquiry Concerning Human Understanding*, which included the highly controversial *Essay on Miracles*. Clerical opposition to this book and the subsequent *Enquiry concerning the Principles of Morals* prevented his appoint-

ment as successor to his friend Adam Smith at the University of Glasgow.

He then became keeper of the library of the Faculty of Advocates Library and a prominent member of intellectual circles in Edinburgh. Access to innumerable reference works encouraged his historical bent, and he began a comprehensive history of England from Julius Caesar to his own day, a popular work continued into the nineteenth century with additions by Smollett and others. Meanwhile he published *Four Dissertations* (on Religion, the Passions, Tragedy, and Taste, with two others, Suicide, and the Immortality of the Soul, added posthumously). From 1763–1766 he served as secretary and sometime *Chargé-d'affaires* with the British Embassy in Paris. There he befriended Rousseau, brought him back to England, and secured a pension for him; but the friendship was abruptly terminated under mysterious circumstances. Hume himself received a pension and served briefly as General Conway's undersecretary of state (1767–1768) before retiring to spend his life in writing and presiding over the intellectual life of Edinburgh, where he died on August 25, 1776.

Hume's dazzlingly brilliant logic has always offended the deeply religious and the incurably romantic. As an enemy of metaphysics he cleared the ground for nineteenth century positivism and utilitarianism with his opposi-

539

tion to all *a priori* thought and his rigorous insistence on induction from psychological data. However, in his life and writings he amply demonstrated his own favorite principle that virtue could exist apart from religion.

BIBLIOGRAPHICAL REFERENCES: There is no complete edition of Hume's works, although the *Philosophical Works*, including all the essays, was published in 1826, 1836, and 1854 in 4 vols. J. Y. T. Greig collected *The Letters of David Hume*, 1932, supplemented by *New Letters*, edited by Raymond Klibansky and E. C. Mossner, 1954. T. E. Jessop, *A Bibliography of Hume and of Scottish Philosophy from Hutcheson to Lord Balfour*, 1938, is helpful. The standard biography for many years was J. H. Burton, *David Hume*, 2 vols., 1846, but it has been largely replaced by the following: Thomas Henry Huxley, *Hume*, English Men of Letters Series, 1879; J. Y. T. Greig, *David Hume*, 1931; E. C. Mossner, *The Forgotten Hume, Le Bon David*, 1943; and *The Life of David Hume*, 1954. Critical books include C. W. Hendel, *Studies in the Philosophy of David Hume*, 1925; R. W. Church, *Hume's Theory of the Understanding*, 1935; L. F. V. Kruse, *Hume's Philosophy in His Principal Work, A Treatise of Human Nature, and in His Essays*, translated by P. T. Federspiel, 1939; N. K. Smith, *The Philosophy of David Hume: A Critical Study of Its Origins and Central Doctrines*, 1941; H. H. Price, *Hume's Theory of the External World*, 1948; C. R. Morris, *Locke, Berkeley, Hume*, 1949; and D. G. C. MacNabb, *David Hume: His Theory of Knowledge and Morality*, 1951. Also important is John Bennett Black's essay on Hume in *The Art of History*, 1926.

A. S. M. HUTCHINSON

Born: India
Date: June 2, 1879

PRINCIPAL WORKS

NOVELS: *Once Aboard the Lugger*, 1908; *The Happy Warrior*, 1912; *The Clean Heart*, 1914; *If Winter Comes*, 1920; *This Freedom*, 1922; *One Increasing Purpose*, 1925; *The Uncertain Trumpet*, 1929; *Big Business*, 1932; *The Soft Spot*, 1933; *As Once We Were*, 1938; *He Looked for a City*, 1940; *It Happened Like This*, 1942.
SHORT STORIES: *The Eighth Wonder*, 1923.
AUTOBIOGRAPHY: *A Year That the Locust . . .* , 1935.

A(rthur) S(tuart) M(enteth), Hutchinson, son of General H. D. Hutchinson, distinguished soldier and well known as the author of several military textbooks, was born June 2, 1879, during his father's tour of duty in India; and he grew up in an environment of garrison life. It was expected that he was to follow his father's profession, but when his poor health forced him to choose otherwise he was

sent back to England to study medicine.

His tenure at medical school lasted but three years, his determination to become a writer being stronger than his desire to work for a medical degree, and in 1908 his career as an author was launched with the publication of his first novel, *Once Aboard the Lugger*. In 1912 he became editor of the *Daily Graphic*, a position which he held for four years, during which time two more of his novels saw print. His progress as editor and writer was suspended temporarily in 1916 when he finally realized his ambition to be a soldier; he served first with the Royal Engineers and later with the British Army of Occupation. Returning to his literary tasks after the war, he produced his most successful and most widely read work, *If Winter Comes,* in 1920. A slow and meticulous writer, he averaged a book about every two and a half years from that time until 1942.

Following the success of *If Winter Comes* he enjoyed a fair amount of popularity, his works being published regularly in the United States as well as in England. Because of his romanticism and a tendency toward an excess of sentimentality, however, what critical recognition he has received has been slight.

BIBLIOGRAPHICAL REFERENCES: The best source on Hutchinson's life is his autobiography, *A Year That the Locust* . . . , 1935. See also *Book Review Digest,* 1920 ff.

ALDOUS HUXLEY

Born: Godalming, Surrey, England
Date: July 26, 1894

PRINCIPAL WORKS

NOVELS: *Crome Yellow,* 1921; *Antic Hay,* 1923; *Those Barren Leaves,* 1925; *Point Counter Point,* 1928; *Brave New World,* 1932; *Eyeless in Gaza,* 1936; *After Many a Summer Dies the Swan,* 1940; *Time Must Have a Stop,* 1944; *Ape and Essence,* 1948; *The Genius and the Goddess,* 1955.

SHORT STORIES: *Limbo,* 1920; *Mortal Coils,* 1922; *The Little Mexican and Other Stories,* 1924 [*Young Archimedes*]; *Two or Three Graces,* 1926; *Brief Candles,* 1930.

ESSAYS AND STUDIES: *On the Margin,* 1923; *Along the Road,* 1925; *Jesting Pilate,* 1926; *Essays New and Old,* 1926; *Proper Studies,* 1927; *Do What You Will,* 1929; *Holy Face and Other Essays,* 1929; *Music at Night,* 1931; *Texts and Pretexts,* 1932; *Beyond the Mexique Bay,* 1934; *The Olive Tree,* 1936; *Ends and Means,* 1937; *The Art of Seeing,* 1942; *The Perennial Philosophy,* 1945; *Themes and Variations,* 1950; *The Devils of Loudun,* 1952; *The Doors of Perception,* 1954.

POEMS: *The Burning Wheel,* 1916; *Jonah,* 1917; *The Defeat of Youth,* 1918; *Leda,* 1920; *Arabia Infelix,* 1929; *The Cicadas and Other Poems,* 1931.

PLAYS: *The World of Light,* 1931; *The Gioconda Smile,* 1950.

Aldous (Leonard) Huxley is the son of Leonard Huxley, English author and editor, himself the son of T. H. Huxley, the famous English biologist and essayist. Aldous Huxley's mother was Julia Arnold, daughter of Thomas Arnold, Matthew Arnold's brother. It is not surprising, then, that Aldous Huxley has made an eminent name for himself as a writer and philosophical essayist, although one could not have predicted from his family background his peculiar passage from novelist of manners and caustic critic of contempo-

541

rary society to defender and disciple of mystical philosophies and religions. Few critics of Huxley's work have had the range of intellectual experience and conviction which he has passed through; consequently, there has been a tendency for those who admire his earlier satirical novels to regard the later mystical emphasis as a sign of a "loss of nerve"; while those who sympathize with his effort to find new ways to an understanding of the perplexing modern world are inclined to regard the earlier work as the superficial product of a mind too soon disillusioned. Perhaps, as one might expect, the truth is somewhere in between: there is an underlying sense of value and respect for honor in even the most brittle of his books; on the other hand, his advocacy of mysticism has been tolerant and responsible from the outset, hardly what one might expect from a frightened man.

Huxley's education fitted his family background. Born at Godalming, England, on July 26, 1894, he went to preparatory school and then to Eton (1908–1911). But an eye disease interrupted his education and for two years he was almost blind, compelled to learn Braille and touch typewriting. Although his eyes improved somewhat and he was able to go on to Balliol College, Oxford, it was not until about 1935, when he began training his eyes according to a method devised by an American doctor, W. H. Bates, that he made any significant improvement. Huxley reported his experience and endorsed the Bates system in his book, *The Art of Seeing*.

After graduating from Oxford in 1915 he worked at various jobs during the war, teaching and doing administrative work for the government. In 1919 he married Maria Nys, a Belgian, and by her had one son, Matthew. He joined the staff of the *Athenaeum* that same year, and then moved on to a job as dramatic critic for the *Westminster Gazette*.

He was financially able to move to Italy with his wife and son in 1923, and the family lived there intermittently until 1930, when Huxley bought a house in Southern France. In the meantime the Huxleys enjoyed frequent visits with D. H. Lawrence and his wife Frieda in France and Italy. Lawrence died in 1930, and in 1933 Huxley edited Lawrence's letters for publication.

In 1934 the Huxleys traveled in Central America and the United States and finally settled in Southern California in a suburb of Los Angeles. For a time Huxley worked in Hollywood, writing screen treatments of the story of Madame Curie, of the novel *Pride and Prejudice*, and of some of his own short stories.

In his novels from *Crome Yellow*, published in 1921, through *Point Counter Point*, seven years later, he had written brilliantly and cynically about the empty lives and pretenses of modern men. Then, in *Brave New World*, a depressing portrait of a regimented scientific future, he predicted that with scientific control and conditioning human beings would become either infantile or mad. By the time he settled in California he had, partly through the influence of Lawrence, begun to take an interest in the possibility of mystical modes of knowing, and he was receiving instruction in the arts of mystical contemplation. Thus, by the time he came to write a new foreword for *Brave New World* in 1946, he was able to refer to himself as having been, in 1932, an "amused, Pyrrhonic aesthete," and to indicate an interest in the kind of sanity attainable by pursuing man's "Final End, the unitive knowledge of the immanent Tao or Logos, the transcendent Godhead or Brahman." *The Perennial Philosophy* is an anthology of the utterances of various mystics, with commentaries supplied by Huxley.

Huxley's wife died on February 12, 1955. Since her death he continues to live and work in California.

BIBLIOGRAPHICAL REFERENCES: A representative selection of Huxley's works is *The World of Aldous Huxley: An Omnibus of His Fiction and Non-Fiction Over Three Decades*, edited, with an introduction, by Charles J. Rolo, 1947. There is no standard biography, but John Atkins, *Aldous Huxley: A Literary Study*, 1956, is an adequate critical biography. See also Alexander J. Henderson, *Aldous Huxley*, 1936, and Jocelyn Brooke, *Aldous Huxley*, 1954; these works include bibliographies. For briefer studies in books and critical essays see also André Maurois, *Poets and Prophets*, 1935; C. E. M. Joad, *Return to Philosophy*, 1936; David Daiches, *The Novel and the Modern World*, 1939; Harry Slochower, *No Voice Is Wholly Lost*, 1946; D. S. Savage, *The Withered Branch*, 1950; J. H. Roberts, "Huxley and Lawrence," *Virginia Quarterly Review*, XIII (1937), 546–557; Helen Estrich, "Jesting Pilate Tells the Answer: Aldous Huxley," *Sewanee Review*, XLVII (1939), 63–81; William Y. Tindall, "The Trouble with Aldous Huxley," *American Scholar*, XI (1942), 452–464; R. C. Bald, "Aldous Huxley as a Borrower," *College English*, II (1942), 183–187; Frederick T. Hoffman, "Aldous Huxley and the Novel of Ideas," *ibid.*, VIII (1946), 129–137; H. T. Webster, "Aldous Huxley: Notes on a Moral Evolution," *South Atlantic Quarterly*, XLV (1946), 372–383; Carlyle King, "Aldous Huxley's Way to God," *Queen's Quarterly*, LXI (1954), 80–100; and Margaret Church, "Aldous Huxley's Attitude Toward Duration," *College English*, XVII (1956), 388–391.

THOMAS HENRY HUXLEY

Born: Ealing, England
Date: May 4, 1825

Died: Eastbourne, England
Date: June 29, 1895

PRINCIPAL WORKS

SCIENTIFIC ESSAYS AND STUDIES: *Evidence as to Man's Place in Nature*, 1863; *The Physical Basis of Life*, 1868; *Lay Sermons*, 1870; *Critiques and Addresses*, 1873; *Science and Morals*, 1886; *Essays Upon Some Controverted Questions*, 1892; *Evolution and Ethics*, 1893.

AUTOBIOGRAPHY: *Autobiography*, 1889.

Thomas Henry Huxley, born at Ealing, England, on May 4, 1825, was the son of an assistant master in a public school, but he had only two years in the "pandemonium of a school" before he began, at seventeen, a course of medical studies at Charing Cross Hospital. But in his boyhood he had read widely and indulged his curiosity in all sorts of ways, even to observing an autopsy when he was thirteen. Following his graduation in 1845 he published his first scientific paper and joined the Royal College of

Surgeons. The Arctic explorer, Sir John Richardson, secured for him a billet as assistant surgeon aboard H.M.S. *Rattlesnake,* a post which Huxley used primarily to study the surface life of the tropical seas. His papers, based on data collected during the four-year voyage, and published by the Royal Society, helped to establish the concepts of *ectoderm* and *endoderm* in evolution. He was elected to the Royal Society in 1852. In the following year he was awarded the Royal Medal for his contributions to science.

Dedicated to a rigorous inductive method, he attacked the idealistic evolutionists, Richard Owen and Lorenz Oken, and insisted that "there is no progression from a lower to a higher type, but a more or less complete evolution of one type." Darwin's *Origin of Species* (1859) was a turning point in Huxley's life; from then on he devoted himself largely to research, publication, and public debate relating to the theory of evolution. In *Zoölogical Evidences as to Man's Place in Nature,* Huxley demonstrated that anatomically man is in body and brain one with the animal world. Having been appointed lecturer to the School of Mines in 1854 and to the Geological Survey in 1855, he turned his attention to the role of fossils in evolutionary studies and concluded that if the hypothesis of evolution had not existed, the paleontologist would have had to invent it.

His dedicated public life included service on ten Royal Commissions, the posts of secretary (1871–1880) and president (1881–1885) of the Royal Society, and membership of the London School Board (1870–1872). In the latter position he strongly influenced the British concept of elementary education, with his demands that in addition to the three R's, courses be added in physical education, home economics, the various aesthetic arts, and natural science in school laboratories.

During his lifetime his scientific fame and his notoriety derived from his vigorous public controversies over the doctrine of evolution, controversies that led him to be erroneously identified simply as a "materialistic atheist." He enjoyed debating with such men as Gladstone and Bishop Wilberforce, and attacking fundamentalist Christian concepts upon premises such as "There is no evidence of the existence of such a being as the God of the Theologians," or "The cosmic process has no sort of relation to moral ends." But he also asserted that "the substance of matter is a metaphysical unknown—as is the substance of mind," and that "atheism is on purely philosophical grounds untenable." In the tradition of Hobbes and Descartes, he believed that man must learn to subdue through social organization the qualities of ape and tiger that originally made for his survival.

Though sentimentalists and anti-intellectualists have always despised him, none can deny his own dedicated, moral life and the power of his compelling, pellucid prose. His grandsons, Julian and Aldous, have each developed a single facet of his rich personality, the former as one of Britain's leading scientists, the latter as a novelist and twentieth century metaphysical speculator.

In his last years Huxley, suffering from a painful illness, was unable to fulfill the duties of the Privy Councillorship which he accepted in 1892, and he died at Eastbourne on June 29, 1895. Standing for all that was best in the Victorian agnostic tradition, his influence was, and still is, enormous.

BIBLIOGRAPHICAL REFERENCES: Huxley's most important work appears in *Collected Essays of Thomas Henry Huxley*, 9 vols., 1898. There are various editions of selected writings, including *Essays by Thomas Henry Huxley*, edited by F. Barry, 1929. See also *The Scientific Memoirs of Thomas Henry Huxley*, edited by M. Foster and E. R. Lankester, 5 vols., 1898–1902.

The standard biography is *The Life and Letters of Thomas Henry Huxley*, by his son Leonard Huxley, 2 vols., 1900 (rev. ed., 3 vols., 1913). See also P. C. Mitchell, *Thomas Henry Huxley*, 1900; H. F. Osborn, *Huxley and Education*, 1910; Clarence E. Ayres, *Huxley*, 1932; and Houston Peterson, *Huxley: Prophet of Science*, 1932. A lively and stimulating study of the period is William Irvine, *Apes, Angels, and Victorians: The Story of Darwin, Huxley, and Evolution*, 1955. For a study of the scientific and religious controversies which agitated the nineteenth century see the essays reprinted in *The Order of Creation: The Conflict between Genesis and Geology*, n.d., and *Christianity and Agnosticism: A Controversy*, 1889.

J(ORIS)-K(ARL) HUYSMANS
Charles Marie Georges Huysmans

Born: Paris, France
Date: February 5, 1848

Died: Paris
Date: May 13, 1907

PRINCIPAL WORKS

NOVELS: *Marthe*, 1876; *Les Sœurs Vatard*, 1879; *À rebours*, 1884 (*Against the Grain*); *Là-bas*, 1891 (*Down There*); *En route*, 1895; *La Cathédrale*, 1898; *L'Oblat*, 1903 (*The Oblate*); *Les Foules de Lourdes*, 1905 (*The Crowds of Lourdes*).

Descendant of a Dutch family of painters, Charles Marie Georges Huysmans, who wrote under the pseudonym of J.-K. Huysmans, was born in Paris on Febrary 5, 1848. For thirty years he worked in the Ministry of the Interior, thus providing himself with a small income so that he could devote his free time to literature. His first volume of stories showed the influence of Baudelaire; he next came under the influence of Zola, whom he knew well, and he wrote a series of novels of everyday life in which he tried to outdo his master in the field of naturalism.

The influence of Zola was short-lived, however, and Huysmans turned to another field. With the publication of *Against the Grain* he produced his most important novel and the first volume of a loosely-connected series. This story of the decadent aristocrat, the Duc des Esseintes, had a great influence on French and English writers of the 1890's and, thinly-disguised, is described in Wilde's *The Picture of Dorian Gray*. The jaded duc, seeking in bizarre fashions for new and unattainable sensations, was the prototype for the *fin de siècle* hero.

With *Down There* Huysmans continued the work begun in *Against the Grain,* changing his hero's name to Durtal and giving him a different social background. These novels are a spiritual autobiography, overlaid with much esoteric learning, of Huysmans' own struggle towards faith. Durtal is a man shorn of all religious belief, thoroughly mired in the sins of the flesh, yet a product of the Christian tradition and thus aware of the void in his life caused by his loss of faith. The novel deals with modern diabolism—the details being drawn from actual happenings in contemporary Paris—and with the history of the medieval sadist, Gilles de Rais. In the subsequent volumes, Durtal goes first to a Trappist monastery and finally to the city of Chartres, where he becomes a Benedictine oblate. The last volumes are hardly novels at all; the plots are reduced to a minimum, and the author concerns himself with elaborate discussions of medieval religious symbolism and the lives of saints and mystics. Thus Huysmans was able to display his considerable erudition.

Aside from his influence on the artificial literature of the 1890's, Huysmans has a genuine importance in that he so well depicted a characteristic problem of the late nineteenth century: the struggle to regain the religious faith which, particularly in Roman Catholic countries, had been lost by so many. Neither sensual indulgence nor the enjoyment of art could fill the vacuum; there remained for the individual only the long, uphill road that might lead to faith and peace.

Having become a devout Roman Catholic, Huysmans died in Paris, after a painful illness, May 13, 1907.

BIBLIOGRAPHICAL REFERENCES: The most extensive and interpretive study of Huysmans in English is James Laver, *The First Decadent, Being the Strange Life of J.-K. Huysmans*, 1954. See also James Huneker, "The Pessimist's Progress: J.-K. Huysmans," *North American Review*, CLXXXVI (1907), 41–51; and Fr. Lefèvre, *Entretiens sur J.-K. Huysmans*, 1931.

IBARA SAIKAKU

Born: Osaka, Japan
Date: c. 1642

Died: Osaka(?)
Date: 1693

PRINCIPAL WORKS

NOVELS: *Koshoku Gonin Onna*, c. 1685 (*Five Women Who Loved Love*); *Nihon Eitai-gura*, 1688 (*Japanese Treasury for the Ages*); *Seken Mune-sanyô*, 1692 (*Mental Calculations of the World*); *Saikaku Ori-dome*, 1694 (*Saikaku's Last Weavings*).

POEMS: Innumerable haikai.

Details of the personal lives of artists in feudal Japan are seldom known except through their works, for most of them rose from obscure origins, and Saikaku was no exception. Even the year of his birth must be calculated back from his age at time of death. He was born into the low social class of merchants, but his family seems to have had means. His wife died early, leaving him a blind daughter who also died young. He left his family business in the hands of a manager to free himself, and traveled, frequently not returning for half a year at a time.

From his works we know that he began his literary life as a writer of haikai (seventeen-syllable epigrams linked into long poems) and a disciple of Nishiyama Sôin (1605–1682), head of the Danrin School of poetry. His earliest known poem is dated 1666, probably prior to his study under Sôin, and signed "Kaku'ei." As a poet, Saikaku is best known for his mass production of seventeen-syllable verse. In 1677 he composed 1,600 such verses at one sitting. Two years later, in a single sitting, he composed 3,000, followed by 4,000 in 1680 and a reputed 23,500 in 1684, more than one every four seconds.

After Sôin's death Saikaku turned his productive talents to fiction as well as poetry. His prose tales fall into three general types: those dealing with warriors and their code of loyalty; those dealing with merchants and their business of making money; and those dealing with the carnal pleasures. So well known did the last type become that frequently Saikaku is remembered only for his erotic tales. The first of these was also the first fiction he wrote, the *Koshoku Ichidai Otoko*, 1682 (*The Love Life of One Man*), in which the hero, Yonosuke, the son of a well-to-do merchant family, roams around the country, making love to men and women alike until, exhausting his money, he is forced to work. Finally, having recovered his fortune, he sails to the Island of Women on a fabulous ship outfitted with every manner of riches. It has frequently been said that Saikaku used Lady Murasaki's *Tale of Genji* as a model for his work, but the style differs radically; Saikaku was describing the Japan of his day through the eyes of a member of the merchant class among other people in similar circumstances. His talents as a poet undeniably influenced his style which is a mixture of classical and colloquial language, and his narrative runs mostly in meter, weaving quotations from poem after poem into the text, so that an extensive knowledge of seventeen-syllable verse is necessary in order to read his fiction with understanding. These qualities make it almost impossible to translate his works into any other language without losing much of the original flavor.

Until about 1687 his principal works were of the erotic variety: the best known of which are the *Kôshoku Ichidai Onna*, 1686 (*The Love Life of One Woman*); the *Kôshoku Gonin Onna; Honchô Nijû Fukô*, 1686 (*The Twenty Unfilials of Japan*), a lampoon on the Chinese tales of twenty-four filial sons and daughters, and the *Nanshoku Ô-kagami*, 1687 (*The Great Mirror of Love of Males*). During this period he also wrote a few puppet plays.

From then on he devoted his production to descriptions of the life of loyalty and obligation of feudal warriors, and the greed of merchants. The most famous of these are the *Buke Giri Monogatari*, 1688 (*Tales of Warrior Obligations*), and *Japanese Treasury for the Ages*. In 1692 he published *Mental Calculations of the World*, and the *Naniwa Miyage* (*Gift from Naniwa*). The latter was his last publication during his lifetime. His *Eitai-gura, Mune-sanyô*, and his posthumously published *Saikaku's Last Weavings* are considered his masterpieces describing the ideals and lives of the merchant class. As a poet his voluminous production won him acclaim, and he had a number of disciples who later distinguished themselves. He wrote about twenty-one novels in which he developed a type of fiction known as "Books of the Floating World," and his influence can be seen in the works of many writers who followed him. Unsurpassed in earlier periods, he was also the greatest novelist of common origin on the Japanese literary scene in his own time.

BIBLIOGRAPHICAL REFERENCES: There are at least six *Complete Works of Saikaku*, and more than that number of his *Collected Works*. There are seventeen collections of his verse. Among the translations in English, the most readily available is that of *Koshoku Gonin Onna*, published as *Five Women Who Loved Love*, 1956. His life and works are also described in Ken Sato, translator, *Ebara, Saïkakou (Ibara Saikaku), Contes d'Amour des Samouraïs*, Paris, 1927; Georges Bonmarchand, translator, "Koshoku-Ichidai-Onna. Vie d'une Amie de la Volupté," in *Deutsche Gesellschaft für Natur- und Völkerkunde Ostasiens (Tokyo), Jubiläumsband*, II (1933), 270–304; Walter Donat, "Aus Saikaku: Fünf Geschichten von liebenden Frauen," in *Deutsche Gesellschaft für Natur- und Völkerkunde Ostasiens (Tokyo), Jubiläumsband*, I (1933), 263–280; and Jan Rahder, "Saikaku's *Life of a Voluptuous Woman*, Book II (*Koshokuichidai onna*)," in *Acta Orientalia*, XIII (1934), 292–318. See also W. G. Aston, *A History of Japanese Literature*, 1933, and Donald L. Keene, *Anthology of Japanese Literature*, 1955. Biographies and critical studies in Japanese are innumerable.

HENRIK IBSEN

Born: Skien, Norway   Died: Christiania (Oslo), Norway
Date: March 20, 1828   Date: May 23, 1906

PRINCIPAL WORKS

PLAYS: *Gildet paa Solhaug*, 1852 (*The Banquet of Solhaug*); *Fru Inger til Østraat*, 1857 (*Mistress Inger at Østraat*); *Hæmændene paa Helgeland*, 1858 (*The Warriors at Helgeland*); *Kjærlighedens Komedie*, 1862 (*Love's Comedy*); *Kongs Emnerne*, 1863 (*The Pretenders*); *Brand*, 1866; *Peer Gynt*, 1867; *De Unges Forbund*, 1867 (*The Young Men's Union*); *Kejser og Galilæer*, 1871 (*Emperor and Galilean*); *Samfundets Støtter*, 1877 (*The Pillars of Society*); *Et Dukkehjem*, 1879 (*A Doll's House*); *Gjengangere*, 1881 (*Ghosts*); *En Folkefiende*, 1882 (*An Enemy of the People*); *Vildanden*, 1884 (*The Wild Duck*); *Rosmersholm*, 1886; *Fruen fra Havet*, 1888 (*The Lady from the Sea*); *Hedda Gabler*, 1890; *Bygmester Solness*, 1892 (*The Master Builder*); *Lille Eyolf*, 1894 (*Little Eyolf*); *John Gabriel Borkman*, 1896; *Nar vi Döde vågner*, 1899 (*When We Dead Awaken*).

No amount of criticism, biased or sound, can dislodge Henrik (Johan) Ibsen from his place as the father of modern drama. Despite the marked provincial quality which permeates his plays, he, as no one else, wrecked outmoded conventions of life and theater. In short, he brought life to the stage and set the tone for the modern era.

Born to upper middle-class parents in Skien, Norway, on March 20, 1828,

Ibsen lived an early life of poverty after his father suffered bankruptcy in 1836. His lot did not change even after he was apprenticed to an apothecary in Grimstad when he was sixteen. There loneliness drove him into the arms of a servant girl, who bore him an unwanted child who added to his financial burden for fourteen years.

Vowing he would succeed, and still seeking escape from hopelessness, he turned to literary creation. From early childhood, the theater had fascinated him. His early attempt at drama, *Katilina* (1850, *Catiline*), brought him two good friends who in turn helped him to escape Grimstad for Oslo where *Catiline* was published. The driving force felt in Ibsen's subsequent work is exhibited in this early play.

Ostensibly in Oslo to attend the University, Ibsen busied himself at many jobs. Most important, he met Ole Bull, the violin virtuoso. Bull, founder of the Bergen National Theater, was seeking a dramatist-apprentice; in Ibsen he found his man. During the next six years in Bergen, Ibsen, a serious student of dramaturgy, wrote an annual play to fulfill his agreement with Bull while he soaked up theater-craft. There, too, he met Susanna Thoresen, who shortly afterward became his wife.

Called to the directorship of The Norwegian Theater in Oslo in 1857, he accepted a position which demanded strenuous efforts and boundless energy. Denied the opportunity to write, and close to a physical breakdown, Ibsen resigned in 1862.

To write, he needed freedom from financial worry. It came in the form of grants and fellowships which permitted him to travel and study. From this point on he steadily matured as a dramatist. Up to 1862 he had written nine plays, all interesting as milestones in his development but none theatrically important. The first fruit of his new leisure was *The Pretenders*, a lengthy but moving historical tragedy set in the period of the Norwegian civil wars. Consistently underrated, it is a powerfully constructed and psychologically motivated drama, marking at once both the peak and the termination of Ibsen's historical-romantic period.

A more mature mind and dramatic technique can be seen in *Brand*, now seldom produced. This play is an attack on the complacency and spiritual poverty of the average citizen of the time, and, lashing the sanctimonious fraud, admonishes us to be true to ourselves, whatever that self may be.

Brand, a great success, won acclaim and royalties for its author, who equaled or surpassed it with *Peer Gynt* in 1867. Peer, the antithesis of Brand, is the incarnation of man's vacillation, instability, and opportunism. His story, told as a poetic fantasy, is long and diffuse, but it has magnificent characters in Peer and Ase and some highly memorable scenes. It stands as a distinguished and unique *tour de force*.

While living mostly in Dresden during the next decade, Ibsen developed a new style which resulted in his famous realistic dramas. A minor work, *The Young Men's Union*, an attack on the liberal politicians of the day, is an embryo example of his new genre and, along with *The Pillars of Society*, is important largely because Ibsen's developing prose style and dramatic technique are visible.

Between these two attempts at realism, Ibsen spent too much time on the cumbersome *Emperor and Galilean*. Unintegrated and unevenly characterized, it was consciously conceived and written to be a masterpiece. Critical judgment must deny the claim.

But his new realism made its full impact felt in *A Doll's House* and *Ghosts*. Taken together they are an unprecedented indictment of conventions which had long denied individual freedom. In the former play, Ibsen made his contribution to the feminist movement. When Ibsen emancipated Nora from her toy house, outraged outcries were heard round the civilized world. *Ghosts* treats of heredity and venereal disease. As drama the play created a new standard of excellence. It is tautly human and natural yet permeated with the conviction that man is controlled by the "dead hand of the past." Its suggestion of fate and retribution remind one of Greek tragedy.

These plays were received by the public with unveiled abuse. Vilified and scorned, Ibsen hastily wrote a rebuttal, the ironic comedy *An Enemy of the People*. The story concerns the embattled Dr. Stockmann, striving to clean up the infected municipal baths of a small Norwegian town. Thwarted at every turn, Stockmann, attacks the "compact majority" who are always wrong. Stockmann is Ibsen in disguise.

By 1882, Henrik Ibsen, now fifty-four years old, had been residing in Munich and Rome for some years. He was poised, confident, and successful. At this point two new elements enter his work: compassion and symbolism. The lovely work, *The Wild Duck*, is a contemplative, poetic play which analyzes illusions and ideals and concludes, with Hedvig's death, that truth-telling idealism is destructive to the thin thread of human happiness. The analysis of idealism is carried even further in *Rosmersholm*. When idealism results in human destruction, idealism is no match for awakened conscience which in the end drives the Reverend Rosmer and Rebecca West to their deaths. *Rosmersholm*, remarkable for its dramatic projection of the complexities of the unconscious, is static and seldom produced.

Two years later came a minor play, *The Lady from the Sea*. Confusing and elusive, its potential is unrealized. But Ibsen's delvings into the complexities of human motivation found integration in *Hedda Gabler*, generally held to be the finest character study Ibsen created. Hedda is an aristocratic relic who cannot adjust to a new, democratic world—she can only die, which she does with style.

After *Hedda Gabler* was published, Henrik Ibsen went home to Norway. He had spent most of his mature life abroad and perhaps this self-imposed rustication plus a natural poetic nature turned his thoughts inward. Henceforth his plays were concerned with weariness, failure, and wasted lives.

The best product of Ibsen's declining years, *The Master Builder*, is a powerful study in pessimism. Solness, the architect, cannot live down his sick conscience. Fearing the younger generation, he tries to outdo youth and dies in the attempt.

After the failure of *Little Eyolf*, a confused play of remorse lacking dramatic action, came *John Gabriel Borkman*, which, provocative but static, is more successful. A study of the betrayal of love for material gain, it is the story of a financial tycoon, who, bankrupted, was imprisoned. Now, years later, he finds freedom and courage only when it is too late.

The dramatist's final work, *When We Dead Awaken*, is a protest against everything that deprives men of happiness. "When we dead awaken, what do we really see then?" Ibsen asks, only to answer, "We see that we have never lived."

A year later Ibsen suffered a paralytic stroke and never wrote again. Rich in honor and reward, but with paralysis almost total and his mind unsettled, Ibsen died at Christiania (Oslo), on May 25, 1906.

All his life Ibsen opposed every convention or tendency that denied the fulfillment of the individual. Not only was he the friend and counselor to modern man and woman, but his pioneering of psychological motivation in drama has had incalculable effect on all subsequent dramatic writing. Every modern playwright has gone to school to Henrik Ibsen.

BIBLIOGRAPHICAL REFERENCES: The standard collected edition in English is *The Collected Works of Henrik Ibsen,* edited by William Archer, 1906–1912. The Viking Edition, 1917, includes a volume of biographical studies by Edmund Gosse, Edward Dowdin, and James Huneker. Archer's introductions to the plays form an important body of Ibsen criticism.

An authoritative biography is Halvdan Koht, *The Life of Ibsen,* 2 vols., 1931. Older standard biographies are Henrik Bernhard Jaeger, *Henrik Ibsen, 1828–1888: A Critical Biography,* 1890; Montrose J. Moses, *Henrik Ibsen: The Man and his Plays,* 1908, with a selected bibliography.

Standard critical works are A. E. Zucker, *Ibsen the Master Builder,* 1929, and George Bernard Shaw, *The Quintessence of Ibsenism,* 1913 (rev. ed.). See also Otto Heller, *Henrik Ibsen—Plays and Problems,* 1912, with a selected bibliography; Janko Lavrin, *Ibsen: an Approach,* 1913, with a selected bibliography; and Hermann J. Weigand, *The Modern Ibsen: A Reconsideration,* 1925. Excellent recent studies are Brian Westerdale Downs, *Ibsen, the Intellectual Background,* 1946, and *A Study of Six Plays by Ibsen,* 1950; Muriel Clara Bradbrook, *Ibsen the Norwegian: A Revaluation,* 1948; and Peter Tennant, *Ibsen's Dramatic Technique,* 1948, with a selected bibliography. Bergliot Ibsen's *The Three Ibsens,* 1952, contains new and previously unknown material; and Francis Bull's short study, *Ibsen, the Man and the Dramatist,* 1954, is an excellent introduction to Ibsen studies.

For briefer studies see also James Huneker, *Iconoclasts,* 1905; John Gassner, *Masters of the Drama,* 1945; Eric Bentley, *The Playwright as Thinker,* 1946; Barrett H. Clark and George Freedley, *A History of Modern Drama,* 1947; C. F. Engelstad, "Henrik Ibsen and the Modern Theatre," *World Theatre,* VI, No. I (1957), 5–26; and F. W. Kaufmann, "Ibsen's Conception of Truth," *Germanic Review,* XXXII (1957), 83–92.

JORGE ICAZA

Born: Quito, Ecuador
Date: April 10, 1906

PRINCIPAL WORKS

NOVELS: *Huasipungo,* 1934 (*Peonage*); *En las calles,* 1935 (*In the Streets*); *Cholos,* 1938 (*Half Breeds*); *Huaira pamushcas,* 1948 (*Children of the Wind*).

SHORT STORIES: *Seis relatos,* 1948 (*Six Tales*).

PLAYS: *El intruso,* 1929 (*The Intruder*); *Flagelo,* 1936 (*The Scourge*).

Of the many novelists of Ecuador, the best known internationally is a realist of Quito whose works denounce the shameless exploitation of the Indians. Jorge Icaza born in Quito, April 10, 1906, began as a dramatist while still a student at the University. He and some classmates, with his wife Marina Moncayo as leading lady, barnstormed the nearby villages with a repertory of old Spanish farces and some of Icaza's own comedies. His popularity diminished in 1931 when he began writing serious plays, and when he announced a dramatization of *Le Dictateur*, by Jules Romains, in 1933, the performance was forbidden by the government. Icaza then turned to the novel.

The great success of his first attempt, *Huasipungo*, confirmed him in his choice of a career. Its six translations include Russian and Chinese, and an English version which was published in *International Literature* in Moscow in 1936. Since then, though he has done such dramatic sketches as *The Scourge*,

his chief work has been novel writing and running a bookstore in Quito.

His first novel was followed by *In the Streets*, which won a national prize, though it is not so good as the first novel. *Half Breeds* has stark realism, and *Children of the Wind* also depicts the Indians as scarcely above the level of animals, debased by their white overlords. His most recent work, *Six Tales*, told naturalistically, shows incidents building up to a savage climax. There are such Indians in Ecuador, it is true, but in his concentration on their repulsive side Icaza gives a distorted picture of the inhabitants of his country.

BIBLIOGRAPHICAL REFERENCES: For information on Icaza see E. Suárez Calimano, "Dos novelas de Jorge Icaza," in *Nosotros*, I: Second Series, 1936, 315–319; A. Torres Rioseco, *La novela en la América hispana*, 1939; *idem*, "Nuevas tendencias en la novela," *Revista Iberoamericana*, I (1939); A. B. Franklin, "Ecuador's Novelists at Work," *Inter-American Quarterly*, II (1940), 37–38; and Jefferson R. Spell, *Contemporary Spanish American Fiction*, 1944.

WASHINGTON IRVING

Born: New York, N.Y.   *Died:* Irvington, New York
Date: April 3, 1783   *Date:* November 28, 1859

PRINCIPAL WORKS

TALES AND SKETCHES: *The Sketch Book of Geoffrey Crayon, Gent.*, 1819–1820; *Bracebridge Hall; or, The Humorists*, 1822; *Tales of a Traveller*, 1824; *The Alhambra*, 1832; *Legends of the Conquest of Spain*, 1835 (printed in *The Crayon Miscellany*).

SATIRES: *Letters of Jonathan Oldstyle, Gent.*, 1802–1803; *Salmagundi; or, The Whim-Whams and Opinions of Launcelot Longstaff, Esq., and Others*, 1807–1808 (with J. K. Paulding and William Irving); *A History of New York from the Beginning of the World to the End of the Dutch Dynasty*, 1809.

HISTORY AND ROMANCE: *A History of the Life and Voyages of Christopher Columbus*, 1828; *A Chronicle of the Conquest of Granada*, 1829; *Voyages and Discoveries of the Companions of Columbus*, 1831.

NOVEL: *Astoria*, 1836.

BIOGRAPHY: *The Life of Oliver Goldsmith*, 1849; *The Lives of Mahomet and His Successors*, 1850; *The Life of George Washington*, 1855–1859.

ESSAYS: *Wolfert's Roost and Other Papers*, 1855; *Spanish Papers and Other Miscellanies*, 1866.

Born in New York City on April 3, 1783, son of a prosperous merchant of Scottish descent, Washington Irving was the youngest child in a family of eleven children. A frail child, he grew up in a household that catered to him whenever it could. He spent eleven years in school and then began to read law in 1798. For more than four years he studied law and engaged in the busy social life of the city, despite a weak constitution that sent him on several excursions up the Hudson River in search of more healthful surroundings. During those years of study he also began to write; some of his contributions were published in the New York *Morning Chronicle,* edited by his brother Peter, under the pseudonym of Jonathan Oldstyle, Gent.

Because of his continuing tendency toward tuberculosis, Washington Irving's family sent him off to southern Europe in 1804. During his two years away from America he visited most of the cities of France, traveled into the lands on the Mediterranean, and enjoyed himself immensely. His health improved steadily, despite the fact that he endured hardships and some danger, including pirate attacks, desert travel, and all the inconveniences of the horse-drawn conveyances of the time. Although he was bent on having an enjoyable time while he was in Europe, he took the time to fill notebooks and diaries with data on his observations and impressions. The journals he kept indicate that he was more interested in people than in institutions. Notes on the theater, for which he maintained a lifelong enthusiasm, like the notes about operas, dances, and flirtations, show he often had greater interest in those subjects than he did in cathedrals, classical ruins, and art galleries.

Upon his return to the United States from Europe, Irving passed the examinations and was admitted to the New York bar, setting up as a lawyer in an office he shared with his brother John, on Wall Street. In the long run, however, law was to be less important in the following years than his associations with literary young men such as James K. Paulding. The young men, including Irving's brother William, embarked upon a project that became the twenty numbers of *Salmagundi,* published between January, 1807, and January, 1808. These papers are strongly reminiscent of the style and purpose of the style-conscious and didactic *Spectator* written by Addison and Steele almost a century before. During the same months Irving began a project that eventually became *Knickerbocker's History of New York,* a work which first showed Irving as having antiquarian interests and which is still a source of enjoyment to any reader who can recognize the burlesquing of various kinds of prose style which Irving put into the work. In 1809 tragedy hit Irving's life; his fiancée, Matilda Hoffman, daughter of a prominent New York barrister, died. After her death, he seemed to lose interest in women, and he never married.

In 1810, following his father's death, Irving went into his family's cutlery business as a partner with his two brothers, William and Peter. The firm did an extensive business, both in the

United States and in England. In 1811 Irving traveled to Washington, D.C., as the agent of his firm during the session of Congress; however, his exact business in the city has always remained vague. Letters he wrote at the time indicate that his duties did not keep him from enjoying to the full the social activity of the nation's capital. As a result of the business depression of 1812, he was back in Washington as a member of a committee of merchants from New York who sought help from the federal government. Upon his return he busied himself in two capacities, as the editor of the *Analectic Magazine* in Philadelphia and as a colonel on the staff of Governor Tompkins of New York during the War of 1812.

Leaving New York in 1815, Washington Irving crossed the Atlantic a second time, not realizing that seventeen years would pass before he returned to America. Shortly after his arrival in England the combination of his brother Peter's death and another business depression put Washington Irving in charge of the Liverpool branch of the family business. When affairs of the firm went from bad to worse, bankruptcy was declared in 1817. At that point in his life Irving, then past thirty, decided to live by his pen in spite of the fact that he had been away from any writing activity for almost a decade. In February of 1818 he had the first number of his *Sketch Book* ready for publication, and the others soon followed. *The Sketch Book*, published serially in England and in the United States, made Irving a popular author, although readers knew him only by the pseudonym of Geoffrey Crayon. Another volume of short pieces, *Bracebridge Hall*, followed soon after and assured his future success. These two volumes, *The Sketch Book* and *Bracebridge Hall*, contain some of Irving's best-known and best-loved work: "Rip Van Winkle," "The Legend of Sleepy Hollow," such essays as "John Bull" and "Traits of Indian Character," humorous sketches like "The Stout Gentleman."

After finishing *Bracebridge Hall*, Irving crossed the English Channel to visit the Continent and settled in Dresden for several months before returning to Paris to collaborate with John Howard Payne on some plays, the best of which was *Charles the Second; or, The Merry Monarch*. Shortly after his return to London, *Tales of a Traveler* appeared in 1824. This volume, like the earlier *Sketch Book* and *Bracebridge Hall*, shows Irving as a writer in the romantic temper, writing tales of the unusual, the exotic, and the supernatural, a far cry from the obvious neo-classicism of the *Salmagundi* papers. Irving was soon to turn to a somewhat different subject matter that confirmed fully his romantic tendencies. In 1826 he went to Madrid to become a member of the American Legation. While in Spain he began the study and writing which were to bear fruit in his *Life and Voyages of Christopher Columbus*. In 1828–1829 Irving toured Spain, remaining for some time in the Alhambra and gathering material for his *Conquest of Granada*, which was history in a far different vein from the light-hearted burlesque of *Knickerbocker's History of New York*.

The year 1832 found new changes for Irving. He returned to America to be met with great enthusiasm. *The Alhambra*, a volume in the "gothic"

554

tradition was published, and Irving, as a member of a government commission, made a long trip into the West. Between 1832 and 1841 little work of literary importance came from Irving; his western tour resulted in journalistic and historical writings: *A Tour of the Prairies, Astoria,* and *The Adventures of Captain Bonneville* (1837), which he digested from B. L. E. Bonneville's famous *Journal.* From 1842 to 1846 Irving was back in Spain as the United States minister to that country; he left Spain to journey to England in the capacity of envoy in the negotiations over the Oregon controversy and returned home to the United States in 1846.

Upon his return to America he remodeled his famous home at Sunnyside and settled down to a quieter life. His final years were spent in arranging a revised edition of his writings, doing research in the National Archives, and producing his biographies of Mahomet and George Washington, the latter a ponderous five-volume work. Irving died at Irvington, New York, November 28, 1859, shortly after the publication of the final volume of his biography of Washington.

Today Washington Irving's continued popularity rests on parts of three volumes—*Knickerbocker's History of New York, The Sketch Book,* and *Bracebridge Hall.* To the student of literature he is probably much more important than he is to the general reader: he brought to world literature much that is romantic and picturesque in American life and legend; he was the first native writer to receive critical and popular approval in this country and in Europe; and he was a prose stylist whose influence is still apparent in our national literature.

BIBLIOGRAPHICAL REFERENCES: The standard text is the Author's Uniform Revised Edition of *The Works of Washington Irving,* 21 vols., 1860–1861, reissued in the Spuyten Duyvel Edition, 12 vols., 1881. There are various editions of the separate works aside from *The Sketch Book:* including *Washington Irving Diary, Spain, 1828–1829,* edited by C. L. Penney, 1926; *Knickerbocker's History of New York,* edited by Stanley T. Williams and Tremaine McDowell, 1927; *The Poems of Washington Irving,* edited by W. R. Langfield, 1931; *Washington Irving on the Prairies, or, A Narrative of a Tour in the Southwest,* edited by Stanley T. Williams and Barbara D. Simison, 1937; and *The Western Journals of Washington Irving,* edited by John F. McDermott, 1944. There are two editions of letters edited by G. S. Hellman, *Letters of Washington Irving to Henry Brevoort,* 1915, and *Letters of Henry Brevoort to Washington Irving,* 1916. *The Journals of Washington Irving* were edited by W. P. Trent and G. S. Hellman, 3 vols., 1919. Stanley T. Williams has also edited five volumes of the *Journals,* 1927–1937. Useful one-volume editions are *Washington Irving: Representative Selections,* edited by Henry A. Porchman, American Writers series, 1934, with a critical introduction and a bibliography, and *Selected Writings of Washington Irving,* edited by Saxe Commins, Modern Library, 1945.

The definitive critical biography is Stanley T. Williams, *The Life of Washington Irving,* 2 vols., 1935. The basis biographical study, however, is Pierre M. Irving, *The Life and Letters of Washington Irving, by His Nephew,* 4 vols., 1862–1864. Other biographical studies include Charles Dudley Warner, *Washington Irving,* American Men of Letters Series, 1881; H. W. Boynton, *Washington Irving,* 1901; and G. S. Hellman, *Washington Irving, Esquire,* 1925. There are two bibliographies: W. R.

Langfield and P. C. Blackburn, *Washington Irving: A Bibliography*, 1933; and Stanley T. Williams and Mary A. Edge, *A Bibliography of the Writings of Washington Irving: A Check List*, 1936. For a complete critical bibliography, including articles in books and periodicals, see *Literary History of the United States*, edited by Robert E. Spiller, Willard Thorp, Thomas H. Johnson, and Henry S. Canby, Vol. III, 1948.

CHARLES JACKSON

Born: Summit, New Jersey
Date: April 6, 1903

PRINCIPAL WORKS

NOVELS: *The Lost Weekend*, 1944; *The Fall of Valor*, 1946; *The Outer Edges*, 1948.
SHORT STORIES: *The Sunnier Side*, 1950; *Earthly Creatures*, 1953.

Charles (Reginald) Jackson has achieved a considerable reputation as a writer of psychological fiction. Though he has had no formal training in psychology, his intuition and personal observation provide material for his popular stories of the abnormal and perverse.

He was born in Summit, New Jersey, on April 6, 1903, studied at Syracuse University, and later became a staff writer for the Columbia Broadcasting System. In 1939 he became a free-lance script writer and taught radio writing while working on *The Lost Weekend*, which reviewers and doctors praised for the accuracy of its presentation of a dipsomaniac's psychology. Jackson also adapted the novel for the popular film. His years as a script writer had taught him realistic dialogue and the dramatic presentation of character, his chief artistic virtues; in his later work he continued to concentrate on prose fiction and the lives of abnormal humanity. In 1946 he published *The Fall of Valor*, a novel about the disintegration of a college professor who develops a strange affection for a Marine war hero. His latest novel, *The Outer Edges*, studies the social effects of the brutal murder of two little girls by a mentally defective youth. He has also written two volumes of short stories: *The Sunnier Side* and *Earthly Creatures*.

BIBLIOGRAPHICAL REFERENCES: A good biographical sketch is Lincoln Barnett's pamphlet "Lost Novelist," 1948. An interview may be found in Harvey Breit, *The Writer Observed*, 1956. See also Harry R. Warfel, *American Novelists of Today*. 1951; *Saturday Review of Literature*, XXXIII (April 15, 1950), 25; and *Time*, LI (June 21, 1948), 108.

JENS PETER JACOBSEN

Born: Thisted, Jutland, Denmark
Date: April 7, 1847

Died: Thisted
Date: April 30, 1885

NOVELS: *Fru Marie Grubbe,* 1876; *Niels Lyhne,* 1880.
SHORT STORIES: *Mogens og andre Novellen,* 1882 (*Mogens and Other Stories*).
POEMS: *Digte og Udkast,* 1886.

The life of Jens Peter Jacobsen began in the fishing village of Thisted, Denmark, on April 7, 1847, and ended there on April 30, 1885. Within that brief span of time Jacobsen traveled very little; his one trip to France was made in an attempt to arrest the consumption that eventually killed him. The body of his creative work is small, with two novels, a book of poems, and a few short stories composing the total. However, of his two novels, *Niels Lyhne* is important enough to cause his name to be placed beside that of his friend and mentor, Georg Brandes, on the list of the foremost Danish writers of the nineteenth century.

Although it was brief, Jacobsen's career was a full one when his scientific accomplishments are added to his literary works. He went from his small fishing village to the University of Copenhagen where, besides reading widely in the works of such writers as Goethe, Schiller, Shakespeare, Kierkegaard, Heine, Byron, and Tennyson, he studied tirelessly in the natural sciences, winning, upon his graduation in 1868, a gold medal for his thesis on a microscopic marsh plant.

His education completed, he devoted himself to writing in both fields, the literary and the scientific, and artfully joined his two interests in a successful short story, "Mogens," title story of a volume of short fiction published in 1882. Jacobsen's greatest contribution to the Danish scientific world, however, was his translation into his native language of Darwin's *Origin of Species,* completed the next year, and his greatest contribution to literature was his scientifically discerning study of human decay presented in his novel *Niels Lyhne.*

BIBLIOGRAPHICAL REFERENCES: The best study of Jacobsen in English is the essay in Alrik Gustafson, *Six Scandinavian Novelists,* 1940. See also Georg Christensen, *Jens Peter Jacobsen,* 1910; and Anna Linck, *Jens Peter Jacobsen,* 1911. Georg Brandes, *Det Moderne Gennembruds Mænd,* 1883, presents a study of Jacobsen by a friend and contemporary.

HENRY JAMES

Born: New York, N. Y.   Died: London, England
Date: April 15, 1843   Date: February 28, 1916

Principal Works

NOVELS: *Roderick Hudson,* 1876; *The American,* 1877; *The Europeans,* 1878; *Daisy Miller,* 1879; *An International Episode,* 1879; *Confidence,* 1880; *Washington Square,* 1881; *The Portrait of a Lady,* 1881; *The Bostonians,* 1886; *The Princess Casamassima,* 1886; *The Reverberator,* 1888; *The Tragic Muse,* 1890; *The Other House,* 1896; *The Spoils of Poynton,* 1897; *What Maisie Knew,* 1897; *In the Cage,*

1898; *The Awkward Age*, 1899; *The Sacred Fount*, 1901; *The Wings of the Dove*, 1902; *The Ambassadors*, 1903; *The Golden Bowl*, 1904; *Julia Bride*, 1909; *The Outcry*, 1911; *The Ivory Tower*, 1917; *The Sense of the Past*, 1917.

SHORT STORIES: *A Passionate Pilgrim*, 1875; *The Madonna of the Future*, 1879; *The Siege of London*, 1883; *Tales of Three Cities*, 1884; *The Author of Beltraffio*, 1885; *The Aspern Papers*, 1888; *The Lesson of the Master*, 1892; *The Real Thing*, 1898; *Terminations*, 1895; *Embarrassments*, 1896; *The Two Magics: The Turn of the Screw* and *Covering End*, 1898; *The Soft Side*, 1900; *The Better Sort*, 1903; *The Finer Grain*, 1910; *A Landscape Painter*, 1919; *Travelling Companions*, 1919; *Master Eustace*, 1920.

AUTOBIOGRAPHY: *A Small Boy and Others*, 1913; *Notes of a Son and Brother*, 1914; *The Middle Years*, 1917.

PLAYS: *Theatricals: Tenants and Disengaged*, 1894; *Theatricals, Second Series: The Album* and *The Reprobate*, 1895; *The Complete Plays of Henry James*, 1949.

TRAVEL SKETCHES AND IMPRESSIONS: *Transatlantic Sketches*, 1875; *Portraits of Places*, 1883; *A Little Tour in France*, 1884; *English Hours*, 1905; *The American Scene*, 1907; *Italian Hours*, 1909.

CRITICISM: *French Poets and Novelists*, 1878; *Hawthorne*, 1879; *Partial Portraits*, 1888; *Essays in London*, 1893; *Views and Reviews*, 1908; *Notes on Novelists*, 1914; *Within the Rim*, 1918.

The world of Henry James's novels, with its international outlook, its very intimate human relationships, and its ideal abundance of money, distinction, intelligence, and good will, was derived in part from the circumstances of his own childhood and youth. He was born in New York City on April 15, 1843, the second son of Henry James and Mary Walsh James, both of whom belonged to wealthy New York State families of Irish Protestant descent. Henry James, Senior, was a dissident religious philosopher, a man of many ideas, an affectionate father, and a charming if highly independent social figure. His personal vitality and speculative mind descended to the eldest son, William James, the future scientist and philosopher, and in some degree to the younger brothers, Wilkinson and Robertson, and the younger sister, Alice. The Jameses were a gifted and vivacious circle; and their frequent changes of residence in the United States (Albany, New York, Newport,

Cambridge); the lengthy stay they made in Europe during Henry's boyhood; the perpetual experiments in schooling to which the young Jameses were subjected—all this promoted the self-sufficiency of the family as a whole and the close interdependence of its members on one another. Henry and William were, and remained, especially intimate.

Illness and mental tension also haunted the James family. Passive and withdrawn in childhood, Henry suffered a back injury in his nineteenth year which made him a semi-invalid throughout his youth. He never married. His experience was notably inward and his mind highly contemplative from the start. He felt unsure of his talents and of his place in the family, the United States, and the world. But these uncertainties determined him in his search for a vocation and a mind of his own. From his early love of paintings and stage plays arose a passion for artistic form and for

558

the representation of life in what he called "images." In the Europe, especially the Paris, of his boyhood he found the image of a high culture and a complex social history as distinguished from the more meager culture and history of his own country at the time. He profited by the James family culture in the degree that he gently dissociated himself from some of its ideals, retaining the family faith in self-culture and moral disinterestedness but pursuing these aims from a point of view which was more international, aristocratic and conservative. Despite his family's wealth and his own preference for good society, he largely supported himself by his writings and was a tireless critic of the manners and morals of good society.

These and other considerations made him finally take up residence in Europe. Meanwhile he had served his literary apprenticeship in the United States. At Cambridge, where he was briefly enrolled in the Harvard Law School in 1862, he applied himself seriously to writing and formed enduring literary friendships with William Dean Howells, Charles Eliot Norton and others. His first publication seems to have been an unsigned tale, "A Tragedy of Error," which appeared in the *Continental Monthly* in February, 1864. He was soon a steady contributor of stories, critical articles, and travel essays to American periodicals. Between 1868 and 1874 he made two long stays in Europe; and in 1872, after a prolonged debate with himself and others, he decided to settle in Europe. Paris, where he first resided and where he came to know Turgenev, Flaubert and other writers, proved uncongenial for his purposes, and in 1876 he removed to England. London was

for many years his home; but in 1898 he acquired a small estate in Rye, Sussex, which was his main residence for the rest of his life. He continued to travel in Europe and paid three lengthy visits to America. He had a genius for friendship and its amenities, including letter writing. For many years his social life in Europe was very active; he frequented fashionable society as well as that of other writers and artists, English, American, and French. Essentially he remained a rather solitary bachelor, preoccupied with his own art and point of view as a kindly but austere moralist. His literary reputation, which was high in his early London years, declined during the later 1880's; and in the next decade he turned to writing for the theater in the hope of recouping his losses. The experiment failed; and gradually he ceased to expect a wide popularity. His novels became increasingly intricate and original in language and form; and while they antagonized the large public, they attracted readers of advanced taste. His remarkable powers of conversation were also widely appreciated. He left, said one listener, "a deep impression of majesty, beauty and greatness." Beginning in 1907, there appeared The New York Edition of the Novels and Tales of Henry James, for which he selected, revised, and prefaced his writings. In 1911, following the death of William James, he issued two autobiographical volumes, *A Small Boy and Others* and *Notes of a Son and Brother*; the fragment of a third, *The Middle Years*, was published posthumously. With the outbreak of the war of 1914, he devoted himself to England's cause and in 1915 he made the sympathetic gesture of becoming a British subject. But his health was failing, and following a heart attack he died in London on February 28, 1916, aged 72.

James's work is massive and complex and, in its themes and techniques, extremely various. The twenty-six volumes of the New York Edition include only about two-thirds of his published fiction, which ranges in scope and subject from great international panoramas like *The Wings of the Dove* to unpretentious comedies of manners, fables of the artist life, ghost stories, and anecdotal tales. He was most famous in his lifetime for novels and stories showing the impact of Europeans and Americans on one another. His best early writings (e.g. *Daisy Miller, The American, The Europeans,* and *The Portrait of a Lady*) deal with this subject; and he returned to it in the three long novels of his later maturity (*The Ambassadors, The Wings of the Dove,* and *The Golden Bowl*). In the later 1880's and the 1890's, he wrote much on the subject of English life proper or American life proper (e.g. *The Bostonians, The Princess Casamassima, The Spoils of Poynton, What Maisie Knew, The Awkward Age*). These books, which had little success in their day, have since been recognized as among his greatest. Besides his fiction, he also wrote biographies (of Hawthorne and William Wetmore Story), literary essays, and cultural studies (*The American Scene*), and was one of the major Anglo-American critics between the age of Matthew Arnold and that of T. S. Eliot.

His fiction and his criticism rest on the same general interests and assumptions. Like Matthew Arnold he was greatly concerned with the state of culture, and he believed that culture included art, ideas, and manners, but consisted essentially in "the perfection of the self." In all his major novels, his men and women seek self-knowledge and self-mastery along with knowledge of the world and pleasure in the world's appearances. He was, Joseph Conrad said, "the historian of fine consciences." Men and women become true heroes for James in the degree that they reach a state of consciousness concerning their own natures and aims, cast off their illusions and their emotional dependency on other persons, act decisively on the data of consciousness, and are willing to renounce some immediate material advantage in the expectation of some ultimate and higher good. This is success in life for Henry James; while failure and evil, which also abound in his fictional world, consist in the substitution of material aims and of personal power for the practice of intelligence, good will, and love. His high evaluation of human consciousness gives rise to the peculiar methods of the James novel. The events of the story are transmitted to us through the minds of the chief protagonists. The minds of his observers frequently develop in clarity and power of sympathy as the story progresses, though sometimes they remain closed to reality and record experience falsely. From these methods arises the profound irony of many of James's performances; and some few of his tales (*The Sacred Fount, The Turn of the Screw*) seem to be deliberate exercises in ambiguity. Other similar tales ("The Aspern Papers," "The Beast in Jungle"), in which the observer is denied real vision altogether or until the last moment, may be James's most original and perfect writings. In recent years, some

English critics claim him for the great tradition of novel writing in that country, while some American critics describe him as among the greatest of our own writers, the disciple of Haw-thorne and the forerunner of T. S. Eliot. Both claims are justified by the range of his sympathy, knowledge, and art.

F. W. Dupee

BIBLIOGRAPHICAL REFERENCES: The standard but incomplete edition is the New York Edition of *The Novels and Tales of Henry James,* 26 vols., 1907–1917, containing the author's final revisions and valuable prefaces. A London edition, *The Novels and Stories of Henry James,* 36 vols., was published 1921–1923. Percy Lubbock edited *The Letters of Henry James,* 2 vols., 1920. Varied selections include *The Art of Henry James: Critical Prefaces,* edited by R. P. Blackmur, 1934; *The Great Short Novels of Henry James,* edited by Philip Rahv, 1944; *Stories of Writers and Artists,* edited by F. O. Matthiessen, 1944; *The Short Stories of Henry James,* edited by Clifton Fadiman, 1945; *The American Novels and Stories of Henry James,* edited by F. O. Matthiessen, 1947; *The Notebooks of Henry James,* edited by F. O. Matthiessen and K. B. Murdock, 1947; *The Ghostly Tales of Henry James,* edited by Leon Edel, 1948; *The Portable Henry James,* edited by Morton Dauwen Zabel, 1951; and *Henry James: Autobiography,* edited by F. W. Dupee, 1956.

An important addition to the biographical and critical canon was Leon Edel's *Henry James: The Untried Years, 1843–1870,* 1953, the first of three projected volumes which promise to become the definitive biography. An early comprehensive study is Pelham Edgar, *Henry James: Man and Author,* 1927. A recent valuable study is F. W. Dupee, *Henry James,* in the American Men of Letters Series, 1951 (rev. ed., 1956). See also E. L. Cary, *The Novels of Henry James: A Study,* 1905; Joseph Warren Beach, *The Method of Henry James,* 1918; Theodora Bosanquet, *Henry James at Work,* 1924; Van Wyck Brooks, *The Pilgrimage of Henry James,* 1925; Cornelia P. Kelly, *The Early Development of Henry James,* University of Illinois Studies in Language and Literature, XV (1930), Nos. 1–2; Stephen Spender, *The Destructive Element,* 1935; F. O. Matthiessen, *Henry James: The Major Phase,* 1944; idem. *The James Family,* 1947; F. W. Dupee, ed., *The Question of Henry James,* 1945; Elizabeth Stevenson, *The Crooked Corridor,* 1949; and Henry S. Canby, *Turn West, Turn East: Mark Twain and Henry James,* 1951.

The Henry James Special Number of *Modern Fiction Studies,* III (1957) contains an extensive and valuable selected checklist of James criticism with an index to studies of separate works, 73–96.

WILLIAM JAMES

Born: New York, N. Y.
Date: January 11, 1842

Died: Chocorua, New Hampshire
Date: August 26, 1910

PRINCIPAL WORKS

PHILOSOPHY AND PSYCHOLOGY: *The Principles of Psychology,* 1890; *The Will to Believe and Other Essays,* 1897; *Human Immortality,* 1898; *Talks to Teachers on Psychology,* 1899; *The Varieties of Religious Experience,* 1902; *Pragmatism,* 1907; *A Pluralistic Universe,* 1909; *The Meaning of Truth: A Sequel to "Pragmatism,"* 1909; *Some Problems of Philosophy,* 1911; *Memories and Studies,* 1911; *Essays in Radical Empiricism,* 1912; *Collected Essays and Reviews,* 1920.

561

William James, oldest son of the anti-ecclesiastical Swedenborgian mystic Henry James, Sr., and elder brother of novelist Henry James, was born in New York City on January 11, 1842. In keeping with their father's theories of education and life, the brothers had a similar upbringing: irregular schooling in America and Europe, extensive travel, parental encouragement to follow their own interests in art and science.

In 1865, after a brief study of art under William M. Hunt and an interrupted period of training at the Harvard Medical School, William James accompanied the great Louis Agassiz on the Thayer zoölogical expedition to explore the reaches of the Amazon River. Poor health caused him to return to Boston, where he resumed his medical studies before he went to Germany in 1867. There he worked with Helmholtz, Bernard, and Virchow. In 1869 he took his medical degree at Harvard, but continuing illness prevented his beginning a practice. As a semi-invalid in his father's house James experienced a terrific mental turmoil which ended with his decision, influenced by reading Renouvier, that his "first act of free will shall be to believe in free will." From his abandonment of all determinisms and his embracing of an "open" rather than a "blocked" universe stem all his later discoveries in psychology and philosophy.

From 1872 to 1876 he taught physiology at Harvard University. Then he began a series of transitions of interest to physiological psychology and psychological philosophy which were to occupy him throughout the rest of his career at Harvard. In the first phase he developed, independently of C. G.

Lange, the James-Lange theory that emotions are simply the feelings that accompany bodily changes stimulated by the perception of exciting objects. This and other psychophysical theories are embodied in his *Principles of Psychology,* published in 1890. Having established the first psychological laboratory in America, James turned next to a decade-long interest in religion and ethics which found expression in a variety of essays and books and culminated in the Gifford lectures at the University of Edinburgh, *The Varieties of Religious Experience.* These studies, empirical rather than dialectical, represent a search into the actual nature of the religious experience for evidence of supernatural forces.

The next phase of James's career was concerned with Pragmatism, the theory of which he inherited from Charles S. Peirce and modified. In his hands it became a method for judging the truth and value of any idea strictly in terms of the practical consequences of that idea; i.e., the difference to human behavior and experience that the idea makes. His lectures at the Lowell Institute in 1906 and Columbia University in 1907 were embodied in *Pragmatism: A New Name for Old Ways of Thinking,* a work in which he applied the pragmatic test to a wide variety of issues. The resulting new relativism became the controversial and revitalizing philosophy of the early twentieth century. He was elected president of the American Philosophical Association in 1906.

In 1907 James taught his last class at Harvard, where he was lionized by students and faculty alike. In his last three years he pushed his practical approach further and further into metaphysical realms, producing *A Pluralistic Universe, The Meaning of Truth,* and his two posthumous publications, *Some Problems of Philosophy* and *Essays in Radical Empiricism*. Despite his growing ill health, he remained active as a lecturer and consultant to students. A trip to Bad-Nauheim, Germany, failed to improve his weekened physical condition and he returned to the United States with his brother Henry in the summer of 1910. Survived by his wife and four children, he died at Chocorua, New Hampshire, on August 26, of the same year.

BIBLIOGRAPHICAL REFERENCES: There is no collected edition of James's treatises and essays, but a number of his works are available in separate editions. A good volume of selections is *The Philosophy of William James, Drawn from His Own Works,* edited by Horace M. Kallen, 1925. The basic biographical study is Ralph Barton Perry, *The Thought and Character of William James,* 2 vols., 1935. See also Henry James, *A Small Boy and Others,* 1913, and *Notes of a Son and Brother,* 1914; C. Hartley Grattan, *The Three Jameses,* 1932; and Lloyd Morris, *William James: The Message of a Modern Mind,* 1951.

JOHN JAY

Born: New York, N. Y.
Date: December 12, 1745

Died: Bedford, New York
Date: May 17, 1829

PRINCIPAL WORKS

POLITICAL DOCUMENTS AND TREATISES: *The Definitive Treaty of Peace between Great Britain and the United States of America, 1783; An Address to the People of the State of New-York on the Subject of the Constitution Agreed Upon at Philadelphia, 1788; The Federalist, 1788; Treaty of Amity, Commerce, and Navigation between His Britannic Majesty and the United States of America, 1795.*

John Jay was born at New York City on December 12, 1745, the son of Mary Van Cortlandt and Peter Jay, who was a rich merchant of French Huguenot descent. Jay was graduated from King's College (now Columbia University) in 1764 and admitted to the bar in 1768. He married in 1774 Sarah Livingston, daughter of the Revolutionary governor of New Jersey and cousin of Jay's law partner.

Jay was a member of the 1773 mixed commission to establish the boundary between New York and New Jersey. Between 1775 and 1777, he was successively on New York's Committee of Correspondence, in the first two Continental Congresses and in the New York legislature. Having helped frame New York's constitution, Jay became chief justice of the state supreme court, 1777–1779. He resigned to return to Congress, of which he was president, 1778–1779. Sent as special envoy to Spain, he secured $170,000 in secret aid, but no recognition of independence.

As joint Treaty Commissioner with Franklin and Adams at Paris, 1782–1783, he participated in the negotiation of the peace preliminaries between the United States and Great Britain. His insistence that Britain expressly recognize the commissioners as agents of the Republic of the United States delayed negotiation and may have unwittingly barred cession of Canada to the new republic. He joined Adams in urging Franklin to ignore the French in concluding these preliminaries, although this flouted their Congressional instructions. After the general peace of 1783, Jay declined offers to become minister to Great Britain or France, but he was drafted by Congress as Secretary of Foreign Affairs, 1784–1790. His otherwise capable administration was perplexed by difficulties with Spain, and Congress overrode his proposal to waive Mississippi navigation to get Spanish trading rights.

Ever an advocate of stronger government, Jay joined with Hamilton and Madison in writing five of *The Federalist* essays, all on constitutional or foreign affairs. His *Address to the People of the State of New-York* is believed by many to have been more influential in securing ratification than *The Federalist,* if only because it was briefer and earlier on the scene. Appointed the first Chief Justice of the United States Supreme Court, 1790–1795, Jay handed down the famous Chisholm *v.* Georgia decision in a manner so vigorously nationalistic that Georgia and her sister states secured adoption of the eleventh amendment to protect themselves.

Jay was defeated for the governorship of New York in 1792 on the Federalist ticket. He was sent by Washington in 1794 to negotiate a settlement with Great Britain which sought British evacuation of frontier areas and trade and maritime concessions. Hamiltonian finance required no interruption of trade, inasmuch as nine-tenths of America's revenue depended on tariffs. Jay was, therefore, not really in a position to bargain, and the treaty which bears his name is described as the price paid for peace and stability when the federal union was being established. The treaty provided for settlement by mixed commissions of spoliation claims, debts, and boundaries, but did not specify any enlargement of neutral rights or trading concessions with the British Isles or the West Indies in return for a guarantee for twenty-five years of freedom from tariff discrimination. Britain did promise to evacuate the frontier areas which she had illegally retained since 1783.

Upon Jay's return from England, he was elected Governor of New York, serving two terms, 1795–1801. His administration was upright and conservative. Declining further renomination as Governor or Chief Justice of the U.S. Supreme Court, he retired to Bedford in Westchester County, New York, where he died on his 800-acre farm on May 17, 1829, survived by two sons and five daughters.

A measure of Jay's moral rectitude which sets him apart from Hamilton as a truly great Federalist at all times occurred in the election of 1800. Hamilton urged a special session of the outgoing Federalist legislature to select presidential electors untainted by Republicanism. Jay conceived that to do so would serve "party purposes which I think it would not become me to adopt."

BIBLIOGRAPHICAL REFERENCES: The standard edition of Jay's works is *The Correspondence and Public Papers of John Jay,* edited by Henry P. Johnston, 4 vols., 1890–1893. The best biography is Frank Monaghan, *John Jay: Defender of Liberty,*

1935, which is also one of the best-balanced biographies of the Federalists. Best of the older biographies is George Pellew, *John Jay*, 1890. William Jay, *The Life of John Jay with Selections from his Correspondence and Miscellaneous Papers*, 2 vols., 1833, is kindly described as a filial biography. The best brief sketch is Samuel F. Bemis, "John Jay," in the *Dictionary of American Biography*.

Special works bearing upon some aspects of Jay's career are Samuel F. Bemis, *Jay's Treaty: A Study in Commerce and Diplomacy*, 1923; *idem*, "John Jay," *American Secretaries of State and Their Diplomacy*, 1927–1929 (Vol. I, 193–285); Charles Warren, *The Supreme Court in United States History*, 1926 (rev. ed., Vol. I, 31–124); Frank Monaghan, ed., *The Diary of John Jay during the Peace Negotiations of 1782*, 1934 (rev. ed.); and, *idem*, *Some Conversations of Dr. Franklin and Mr. Jay*, 1783–1784, 1936.

ROBINSON JEFFERS

Born: Pittsburgh, Pennsylvania
Date: January 10, 1887

Died: Carmel, California
Date: January 21, 1962

Principal Works

poems: *Californians*, 1916; *Tamar and Other Poems*, 1924; *Roan Stallion, Tamar, and Other Poems*, 1925; *The Women at Point Sur*, 1927; *Cawdor and Other Poems*, 1928; *Dear Judas and Other Poems*, 1929; *Descent to the Dead*, 1931; *Thurso's Landing and Other Poems*, 1932; *Give Your Heart to the Hawks*, 1933; *Solstice and Other Poems*, 1935; *The Beaks of Eagles*, 1936; *Such Counsels You Gave to Me*, 1937; *Be Angry at the Sun*, 1941; *The Double Axe*, 1948; *Hungerfield and Other Poems*, 1953.

plays: *Medea*, 1946; *The Cretan Woman*, 1954.

The lines are sometimes as rough and jagged as rocks, the human characters often seem as twisted as a wind-battered cypress, the flashes of beauty are as cleanly cruel as the sweeping dive of a hawk—yet the poetry of Robinson Jeffers speaks out like an elemental prophecy and stands aloof from the poetic cults that eddy and swirl in contemporary literature.

Born in Pittsburgh on January 10, 1887, (John) Robinson Jeffers spent a great deal of his childhood traveling about Europe with his parents. Some of their stops included Zurich, where he went to kindergarten, London, and Edinburgh. At the age of fifteen he came back to America and the next year his family moved to California, the region Jeffers has chosen as the

background of his poetry. At eighteen he graduated from Occidental College in Los Angeles. After that, according to Jeffers' own account, came desultory years at the University of Southern California, the University of Zurich, the Medical School in Los Angeles, the University of Washington, all with faint interest. As he states, "I wasn't deeply interested in anything but poetry."

In 1912 he published *Flagons and Apples*, a volume that contained little hint of his later distinctive and powerful style. The next year he married Una Call Custer and the following summer they planned a trip to England. But the First World War broke out and they turned back to the village of Carmel, on the California coast. The country around Carmel Bay, wild and rugged, possessed a beauty that appealed to Jeffers; it was there that he built a house and, with his own hands, an observation tower. And there he has lived in virtual seclusion ever since.

After *Californians*, Jeffers brought out in 1924 the book, *Tamar and Other Poems*, that brought him fame. The volumes came swiftly after that: *Roan Stallion, Tamar, and Other Poems, The Women at Point Sur, Cawdor, Dear Judas, Thurso's Landing, Give Your Heart to the Hawks*, and others. At first the philosophy that emerges from Jeffers' violent and tragic narrative poems and from his lyrics seems unrewardingly bleak: mankind is introverted, cruel, and at best only a blundering step toward some higher form of life. But he reveals for us the beauty of permanence in rocks, sea, and sky. In 1938 appeared *The Selected Poetry of Robinson Jeffers*, in which the poet displays his rugged power and his inconsistencies of outlook. Many critics feel that Jeffers' contribution to poetry may lie in the cut-from-stone beauty of his lyrics and not in the narratives that heap the horror and violence too high.

Dramatic success has come to Jeffers late in his career with the Broadway production of his *Medea* in 1947. Judith Anderson gave a sensational performance in this play, a free adaptation from the Greek. He followed *Medea* with a revival in 1950 of his earlier play, *The Tower beyond Tragedy*, first printed in *Roan Stallion, Tamar, and Other Poems*.

In *The Double Axe* and *Hungerfield*, readers have detected a declining power in Jeffers' work, but he has never been accorded the prominence he deserves. This age of literary movements and splinter groups has been baffled by this lonely figure of despair. The horrors of future atomic warfare may prove him a major prophet.

BIBLIOGRAPHICAL REFERENCES: George Sterling's *Robinson Jeffers: The Man and the Artist*, 1926, is the pioneer study of Jeffers; the most recent is Radcliffe Squires, *The Loyalties of Robinson Jeffers*, 1956. The most extensive general study is Lawrence C. Powell, *Robinson Jeffers: The Man and His Work*, 1934 (rev. ed., 1940). See also Louis Adamic, *Robinson Jeffers: A Portrait*, 1929; Rudolph Gilbert, *Shine, Perishing Republic: Robinson Jeffers and the Tragic Sense in Modern Poetry*, 1936; and Melba B. Bennett, *Robinson Jeffers and the Sea*, 1936.

Shorter estimates and critical studies include Morton D. Zabel, "The Problem of Tragedy," *Poetry*, XXXIII (1929), 336–340; John Gould Fletcher, "The Dilemma of Robinson Jeffers," *Poetry*, XLIII (1934), 338–342; Hyatt H. Waggoner, "Science and the Poetry of Robinson Jeffers," *American Literature*, X (1938), 275–288; Frederick I. Carpenter, "The Values of Robinson Jeffers," *American Literature*, X (1940), 353–366; and R. W. Short, "The Tower Beyond Tragedy," *Southern Review*, VII (1941), 132–144.

THOMAS JEFFERSON

Born: Albemarle County, Virginia
Date: April 13, 1743

Died: Monticello, Virginia
Date: July 4, 1826

PRINCIPAL WORKS

POLITICAL ESSAYS, LETTERS, AND DOCUMENTS: *A Summary View of the Rights of British America*, 1774; *The Declaration of Independence*, 1776; *Notes on the Estab-*

lishment of a Money Unit, 1784; Notes on the State of Virginia, 1784–1785; A Manual of Parliamentary Practice, 1801; The Address of Thomas Jefferson to the Senate, 1801; The Life of Captain Lewis, 1817.

Thomas Jefferson was born on April 13, 1743, at Shadwell in Albemarle County, Virginia, the son of Jane Randolph and Peter Jefferson. He liked to emphasize his father's frontier experiences as surveyor and cartographer instead of his family's prominent antecedents. Educated in private schools and at William and Mary, he was admitted to the bar in 1767 by his teacher, George Wythe. Throughout life, he persevered in the study of agronomy, anthropology, archaeology, architecture, astronomy, biblical and legal history, botany, music, philology, and the latest scientific discoveries of his age. Between 1770 and 1810, he built Monticello, a Palladian mansion on the mountaintop of his estate. He married in 1772 Mrs. Martha Wayles Skelton, and they had two daughters who attained maturity.

As an organizer of political parties, Jefferson was not an orator. His forte lay more in committee work than in personal correspondence or persuasion. In "his country" of Virginia, he served as Burgess (1768–1775), Delegate (1776–1779), and Governor (1779–1781). His written address to the Virginia Convention of 1774 is famous: *A Summary View of the Rights of British America.* This natural-rights document denied Parliament's colonial authority and any bonds other than voluntary submission to the king. It demanded free trade in products not essential to the mother country and an end of British colonial taxation. He was a principal author of the 1776 Virginia constitution, whose preamble foreshadowed the Declaration of Inde-

pendence. His bills for the abolition of entails, primogeniture and the *lex talionis* were accompanied by those establishing religious freedom and educational reform. All were enacted, although the last was limited to deistic substitution of foreign languages, law and medicine for religious curricula at William and Mary. His wartime governorship was unhappy because of his reluctance to exceed constitutional authority. After British capture of Richmond and pursuit of Governor and Legislature into the Shenandoah Valley, Jefferson welcomed the election of a successor with dictatorial powers. He had helped transfer the capital from Williamsburg to Richmond, and he subsequently designed the capitol after the Maison Carrée of Nîmes. To answer Buffon's and Raynal's thesis that humans and animals degenerated in the New World, he wrote his *Notes on Virginia,* valuable for its statistical description of that commonwealth's economy, fauna, flora, polity and society.

Among Jefferson's accomplishments in congressional committees (1775–1776, 1783–1784) were the adoption of the present units of currency, plans for foreign trade agreements, and organization of the Northwest Territory. His Declaration of Independence listed grievances against the King instead of Parliament. Inspired by John Locke, it emphasized inalienable rights of humans, the social compact theory, but no absolute equality.

In 1784 he joined Franklin and Adams in Europe and helped negotiate a commercial treaty with Prussia. As Minister to France (1785–1789), he gained concessions for American cereals, fish products, naval stores, and rice and tobacco in French domestic and colonial markets. He more influenced the early leaders of the French Revolution than *vice versa* and was optimistic of its result, despite excesses wrought in the name of liberty. Favoring stronger union, Jefferson endorsed the Federal Constitution after the addition of the first ten amendments. Home from France, he was persuaded by Washington to become Secretary of State (1789–1793). His reports on foreign commerce, the mint, neutrality, and weights and measures belong to this period. At first not hostile to Hamilton's schemes for assumption of state debts and funding them with those of the central government, Jefferson increasingly suspected that Hamilton favored private, monarchical privilege at public expense in incorporating the Bank of the United States and ratifying Jay's Treaty with Great Britain. In this, Jefferson established common ground with proto-Republicans led by his friend and neighbor, James Madison. Defeated for the Presidency by John Adams in 1796, Jefferson served as Vice President, 1797–1801. With Madison, he was the author of the four Kentucky and Virginia Resolutions (1798–1800) which protested the Alien and Sedition Acts as violations of the Bill of Rights and as extreme centralization of authority inconsistent with the tenth amendment. Although subsequently claimed as precedents by advocates of nullification and secession, these resolves avoided charges of disunion even though asserting that a substantial minority of the states could interpose their authority through constitutional conventions. They formed admirable

campaign documents in the "Revolution of 1800," in which moderate Federalists deserted the ultras to join with the Republicans in electing Jefferson President (1801–1809).

In his first inaugural he spoke for abatement of partisanship, avoidance of the intrigues of Europe, limitations of both executive and central government by strict interpretation of the constitution, in favor of balanced power within the federal government and between the federal government and the states. Acquisition of the Louisiana Territory violated strict construction, but was shortly thereafter authorized by Congress. Jefferson dispatched the Lewis and Clark expedition to gather varied information about this virtually unknown empire. Preferring militia to standing armies or navies, his administration both crushed the Tripolitanian pirates and reduced the national debt. Removal of old Federalists from office was criticized, but it pales in comparison with spoils-seeking patronage since 1828. Increasing difficulties with France and Great Britain over neutral, maritime trading rights during the Napoleonic wars plagued his second term, and Jefferson's embargo on trade with both belligerents caused much protest.

In retirement, Jefferson advised his successors Madison and Monroe, agreeing with the former in declaring war on Great Britain in 1812 and with the latter in warning the monarchs of Europe not to molest the newly freed Latin American republics. Acquisition of Florida by 1821 was the culmination of Jefferson's Spanish policy of the 1790's. Largely responsible for assembling the first Library of Congress, which was destroyed by the

British in 1814, he sold his own library to the federal government for a nominal sum as a replacement. His contributions to the American Philosophical and Colonization Societies were important aspects of his later years, but he considered the greatest achievement of this period of his life to be the founding of the University of Virginia (1819), of which he was a benefactor and architect. These benefactions, added to a lifetime of public service in which his own finances suffered, he could ill afford in the depression following the panic of 1819. On the verge of bankruptcy, this most versatile of America's presidents died at Monticello on July 4, 1826, the fiftieth anniversary of the Declaration of Independence.

BIBLIOGRAPHICAL REFERENCES: *A Summary View of the Rights of British America* is elaborately annotated in *The Papers of Thomas Jefferson* (13 vols. to date, ed. by Julian P. Boyd and others, Princeton, 1950ff.) I, 121–137; as are the following: "The Virginia Constitution [of 1776]," *ibid.*, I, 329–386. "The Revisal of the Laws [of Virginia]," 1776–1786, *ibid.*, I, 560–564, II, 305–664; "Plan for Government of the Western Territory," *ibid.*, VI, 581–617; and "Draft of a Model Treaty," *ibid.*, VII, 479–490. "Jefferson's Opinion on the Constitutionality of the Bank" is conveniently available in *Documents of American History* (edited by Henry S. Commager, 5th ed., New York, 1948), I, 158–160; "The Kentucky and Virginia Resolutions," *ibid.*, I, 178–184; "Jefferson's First Inaugural Address," *ibid.*, I, 186–189. Jefferson's *Notes On Virginia* are available in many editions. Interesting posthumous publications are Jefferson's *An Essay towards Facilitating Instruction in the Anglo-Saxon and Modern Dialects of the English Language* (New York, 1851); and *The Life and Morals of Jesus of Nazareth* available in several editions.

In addition to works cited above, *The Writings of Thomas Jefferson*, 20 vols., edited by Andrew A. Lipscomb and Albert E. Bergh, 1903–1904, is the most complete of the older collections, but it does not have the accuracy of *The Writings of Thomas Jefferson*, 10 vols., edited by Paul L. Ford, New York, 1892–1899. *Jefferson Himself*, edited by Bernard Mayo, 1942, portrays the life and beliefs of the subject in his own words, all adequately footnoted. Two of the five volumes which will comprise Dumas Malone's definitive biography, *Jefferson and His Time*, have appeared: *Jefferson the Virginian*, 1948, and *Jefferson and the Rights of Man*, 1951. Henry S. Randall, *The Life of Thomas Jefferson*, 3 vols., 1858, remains the best complete biography. Gilbert Chinard, *Thomas Jefferson: The Apostle of Americanism*, 1929, is the best treatment of French influences on Jefferson. Marie Kimball, *Jefferson: The Road to Glory*, 1943, *Jefferson: War and Peace*, 1947, and *Jefferson: The Scene of Europe*, 1950, are good from the *beaux-arts* point of view. Sarah N. Randolph, *The Domestic Life of Thomas Jefferson*, 1871, is still useful. The best short sketch is Dumas Malone's "Thomas Jefferson," in *Dictionary of American Biography*, Vol. X.

JOHANNES V. JENSEN

Born: Farsø, Denmark
Date: January 20, 1873

Died: Copenhagen, Denmark
Date: November 25, 1950

PRINCIPAL WORKS

NOVELS: *Danskere*, 1896 (*Danes*); *Einar Elkjaer*, 1898; *Intermezzo*, 1899; *Kongens Fald*, 1900–1901 (*The Fall of the King*); *Skovene*, 1904 (*The Forests*); *Madame d'Ora*, 1904; *Hjulet*, 1905 (*The Wheel*); *Den lange Rejse*, 1908–1922 (*The Long Journey*).

SHORT STORIES: *Himmerlandshistorier*, 1898–1910 (*Himmerland Stories*); *Eksotiske Noveller*, 1907–1909 (*Exotic Stories*).

POEMS: *Digte*, 1906 (*Poems*).

ESSAYS: *Dyrenes Forvandling*, 1927 (*The Transformation of Animals*); *Aandens Studier*, 1928 (*Stages in the Development of the Mind*).

Johannes V(ilhelm) Jensen, Nobel Prize-winning novelist of Denmark, left behind him, when he died in 1950, over sixty volumes of published works which included poetry, short stories, and essays along with his many novels, and which extended even to the drama with a number of his own plays and a translation into the Danish of Shakespeare's *Hamlet*. In spite of this amazingly large output, his international reputation rests mainly on a single work, *The Long Journey*, an epic six-volume novel on the beginnings and history of the Teutonic race.

The publication of *The Long Journey* marks the high point in an extensive career which began in the 1890's at the University of Copenhagen. Born at Farsø, North Jutland, January 20, 1873, Jensen, an aspiring young student of hardy Himmerland peasant stock, had gone to Copenhagen with the intention of studying medicine, but there a fortunate indoctrination in the world of letters compelled him to change plans. He abruptly left the university without his degree and determined to devote himself to travel and to writing. In 1897 he came to the United States, remaining for a time in Chicago where, fascinated, he made those observations of Midwest urban culture that were to serve as background for two of his early novels. Before these were written he turned to his own native background, bringing

out in 1898 his first collection of short stories, *Himmerland Stories*, based on the memories of his Jutland childhood.

His writing and traveling continued throughout the first quarter of the century, during which time he developed some definite theories about the purpose and meaning of literature. Attacking the traditionalist attitudes of Georg Brandes and his followers, he demanded a new Danish novel based on the naturalistic concepts of the contemporary French and Americans. To further his cause, he did all he could to spread the fame of Hemingway in Denmark; also, going back in time both for scientific cause and stylistic example, he preached the virtues of Darwin and Walt Whitman as well. Before his death he became perhaps the most influential writer in Denmark, the leader of a growing school of young novelists.

Nor were his interests, as the influence of Darwin indicates, confined to literature alone. Science and history were both well within the scope of his broad intellectual concerns, and it was his interest in history as well as his abilities in the novel that brought him to his greatest literary triumph. *The Long Journey* is history as well as art, and it deals, not with individual characters, but with an entire people, the Cimbrians, who, according to Jensen, had their origins in his own native Himmerland and from there surged out to make their way, as the great Teutonic race, over all of Europe and even into Asia.

Vast as it is, *The Long Journey* is only one of Jensen's experiments in many different literary fields. He was to continue his writings for over a decade more and to extend his interests into philosophy and journalism as well. Awarded the Nobel Prize for literature in 1944, he died in Copenhagen on November 25, 1950.

BIBLIOGRAPHICAL REFERENCES: There is almost no helpful criticism of Jensen in English. For brief studies see Signe Toksvig, "Johannes V. Jensen," *American-Scandinavian Review*, XXXI (1943), 343–346; and J. Nyholm. "The Nobel Prize Goes Nordic," *Books Abroad*, XIX (1945), 131–135. See also Otto Gelsted, *Johannes V. Jensen*, 1913; H. P. E. Hansen, *Johannes Vilhelm Jensen og hans Tid*, 1930; Alf Henriques, *Johannes V. Jensen*, 1938; and Aage Schiøttz-Christensen, *Om sammerhaengen i Johanss V. Jensens forfatterskab*, 1956.

JEROME K. JEROME

Born: Walsall, England
Date: May 2, 1859

Died: Northampton, England
Date: June 14, 1927

PRINCIPAL WORKS

NOVELS: *Three Men in a Boat*, 1889; *Paul Kelver*, 1902.

PLAYS: *When Greek Meets Greek*, 1888; *Susan in Search of a Husband*, 1906; *The Passing of the Third Floor Back*, 1908.

Jerome K(lapka) Jerome, born in Walsall, England, May 2, 1859, began to earn his own living at an early age, and from the age of fourteen on was a railway clerk, a teacher, an actor, and a newspaperman. From his career as an actor came his first book, *On the Stage and Off* (1885). His first play, *Barbara*, was produced in 1886. Fame came to him with the publication of *Three Men in a Boat*, a comic novel which made Jerome a popular author in England and abroad. During the 1890's Jerome edited and published several periodicals, including *The Idler*, which he founded with Robert Barr in 1892, and *To-day*, a weekly newspaper. He himself considered *Paul Kelver* his best novel.

Following the production of *Barbara*, Jerome had no real name as a dramatist until long after he was established in his reputation as a humorist and a novelist. His reputation as a playwright began with *The Passing of the Third Floor Back* in 1908. While he wrote many plays afterward, this play is the only one that is remembered.

During World War I, Jerome broke off writing; despite his age he served as an ambulance driver for the French. After the war he returned to writing and produced, among other things, a memoir, *My Life and Times* (1926). He died while making an automobile tour of England in 1927. His work has gone largely unnoticed since his death.

BIBLIOGRAPHICAL REFERENCES: Although Jerome K. Jerome has received very little critical attention, items worth consulting include his own *Miscellany of Sense and Nonsense from the Writings of Jerome K. Jerome*, 1923, and his autobiography, *M,*

Life and Times, 1926. A good biography is Arnold Moss, *Jerome K. Jerome: His Life and Works*, 1929. For background material see also A. B. Walkley, *Playhouse Impressions*, 1892.

SARAH ORNE JEWETT

Born: South Berwick, Maine   *Died:* South Berwick
Date: September 3, 1849   *Date:* June 24, 1909

PRINCIPAL WORKS

SHORT STORIES: *Deephaven*, 1877; *Old Friends and New*, 1879; *A White Heron and Other Stories*, 1886; *The King of Folly Island*, 1888; *Strangers and Wayfarers*, 1890; *A Native of Winby*, 1893; *The Life of Nancy*, 1895; *The Country of the Pointed Firs*, 1896; *The Queen's Twin*, 1899.
NOVELS: *A Country Doctor*, 1884; *A Marsh Island*, 1885; *The Tory Lover*, 1901.

Born in South Berwick, Maine, on September 3, 1849, Sarah Orne Jewett lived a quiet and happy childhood distinguished only by the fact that she developed a keen interest in people and an insight into culture through traveling about the countryside with her father, who was a country doctor. Her interest in the people of Maine never diminished, even though she later traveled widely in Europe. She seems to have been much more interested in the people of the coastal villages and upland farms of Maine than she was in such friends as William Dean Howells, Annie Fields, and Thomas Bailey Aldrich, famous literary personages of the time. Miss Jewett's private life was always undistinguished; she never married, nor did she go to college, although Bowdoin College awarded her an honorary Litt.D. degree in 1901, making her the first woman to receive such a degree from that institution.

What education Miss Jewett had she acquired by herself or at the local academy in Berwick. As a young woman she began to serve a writer's apprenticeship by writing for children's magazines. Her first published attempt at adult fiction appeared in the *Atlantic Monthly* for December, 1869, when she was but twenty years old. By 1877 she had published many stories in periodicals and collected thirteen of them into a volume published as *Deephaven* in 1877. During the following two decades Miss Jewett continued to write many stories for magazines and collected them at intervals in volumes. Of the several collections, two are outstanding: *Tales of New England* (1890), selected from earlier volumes, and *The Country of the Pointed Firs*, published in 1896. Critics, scholars, and fellow authors have termed the latter volume one of the great examples of American regional fiction during the period 1865–1900. Willa Cather, famous American woman writer, enthusiastically, if extravagantly, compared *The Country of the Pointed Firs* in greatness to Mark Twain's *Huckleberry Finn* and Hawthorne's *The Scarlet Letter*.

The Country of the Pointed Firs, as well as other volumes by Miss Jewett, has sometimes been called a novel. The book is divided into chapters, but each "chapter" is really a separate local color character sketch, with the series held together by the simple device of having a summer visitor to the fictional town of Dunnet Landing, Maine, narrate the fiction through her impressions. The device is a common one in Miss Jewett's writings, and she used it as early as her first collection, *Deephaven*, in 1877.

All of Miss Jewett's important writings deal with the country she knew so well, the coastal towns and upland farms of Maine. Her method of approach to her material is realistic, and her brand of realism is very similar to the realism of the commonplace familiar to readers of William Dean Howells. Some readers have been dismayed because the subject matter—background, characters, and action—is often so simple and commonplace as to seem to border on the trivial. Twentieth century readers, reared on a lustier diet of fiction—like that of Hemingway and Faulkner—may find Miss Jewett's work boring, despite a poetic air which pervades it. Perhaps Miss Jewett's fiction, like that of other women authors of the nineteenth century, is to become fare for the passionate few, rather than for a wide but less enthusiastic group of readers.

Technically, the fiction written by Miss Jewett is outstanding, despite the shortcomings some readers may find in it. She studied the craft of writing more seriously than most writers, being an avid student of fiction-writing and especially the work of Zola, Tolstoy, Flaubert, and Henry James. She appreciated their work because they, like her, gave weight in their writings to the commonplace, even the trivial, lending an importance to elements in everyday life which ordinarily are not seen thoroughly enough to be regarded as important. Like Henry James, Miss Jewett sought to see beneath the surface of existence. The result is that her stories attain artistry, although they may seem brittle. Certainly she has given American literature a better picture of New England than such writers as Harriet Beecher Stowe and Rose Terry Cooke.

Perhaps the only serious weakness in Miss Jewett's work is that she saw everything and wrote about everything from the standpoint of a woman. Her female characters are splendidly portrayed, as is their life, but the world of men seems to have been outside her abilities, or at least she regarded it as of little consequence for her art.

Rather than whole volumes, present-day readers tend to read individual stories from her work. Some which seem particularly attractive for readers now are "A White Heron," "Marsh Rosemary," "A Lost Lover," "Miss Tempy's Watchers," and "The Courting of Sister Wisby."

In addition to her stories and some juvenile fiction, Miss Jewett made brief excursions into other areas of writing. She wrote a non-fictional *Story of the Normans* (1887) and three novels. Her first novel, *A Country Doctor*, described in fiction the character and life of her father. In *The Tory Lover* she attempted a historical novel dealing with John Paul Jones and a company of men he recruited from her native Berwick, Maine. She died in the town of her birth on June 24, 1909.

BIBLIOGRAPHICAL REFERENCES: The best study is F. O. Matthiessen, *Sarah Orne Jewett*, 1929. See also Jean Sougnac, *Sarah Orne Jewett*, 1937; Willa Cather, Introduction to *The Best Stories of Sarah Orne Jewett,* 2 vols., 1925; Arthur H. Quinn, *American Fiction,* 1936; C. M. Thompson, "The Art of Miss Jewett," *Atlantic Monthly,* XCIV (1904), 485–497; E. M. Chapman, "The New England of Sarah Orne Jewett," *Yale Review,* III (1913), 157–172; Martha H. Shackleford, "Sarah Orne Jewett," *Sewanee Review,* XXX (1922), 20–26; Edward Garnett, *Friday Nights,* 1922; and Anon, "The New England Spirit," *London Times Literary Supplement,* XLVI (1947), p. 602.

See also Carl J. Weber, *A Bibliography of the Published Writings of Sarah Orne Jewett,* 1949, and *Letters of Sarah Orne Jewett Now in the Colby College Library,* 1948; also "New England Through French Eyes Fifty Years Ago," *New England Quarterly,* XX (1947), 385–396.

JUAN RAMÓN JIMÉNEZ

Born: Moguer, Spain   *Died:* San Juan, Puerto Rico
Date: December 24, 1881   *Date:* May 29, 1958

PRINCIPAL WORKS

POEMS: *Almas de violeta,* 1900 (*Violet Souls*); *Diario de un poeta recién casado,* 1916 (*Diary of a Recently Married Poet*); *Estío,* 1917 (*Summer*); *Sonetos espirituales,* 1917 (*Spiritual Sonnets*); *Poesía escogida,* 1917 (*Selected Poems*); *Segunda antología poética,* 1919 (*Second Anthology of Poetry*); *Poesía en prosa y verso,* 1923 (*Poetry in Prose and Verse*); *Animal de fondo,* 1949 (*Brute*).
SKETCHES: *Platero y yo,* 1914–1917 (*Platero and I*).

Juan Ramón Jiménez, who shared with Antonio Machado Ruiz (1875–1939) the highest pinnacle among twentieth century Spanish lyric poets, was born in the village of Moguer, Andalusia, on December 24, 1881. He received his early education at the Jesuit school in Santa María, near where Columbus outfitted his expedition for the New World. After completing his formal study at the University of Seville, he continued to educate himself by reading the old Spanish ballads in the *Romanceros* and the poems of the seventeenth century perfectionist Góngora y Argote and those of Bécquer, whom Jiménez regarded as the initiator of modern Spanish poetry. The poetry of the Romantic Movement in England and Germany also inspired him, as did the French Symbolist poets. In addition, he stud- ied painting and music, both of which left an imprint on his literary work.

His literary career began during the period of transition that marked the closing years of the nineteenth century, and Jiménez's first publication at the age of seventeen indicated his choice between continuing his study of law in Seville or devoting himself to literature. These verses, sent to *Vida nueva,* of Madrid, though over-decorated and florid, nevertheless attracted the attention of the magazine's more famous contributors, resulting in an invitation to come to the capital to have a share in the reform of Spanish poetry. Signed to the invitation were two of the greatest names in Madrid literary circles, the Spanish poet, Francisco Villaespesa, and Rubén Darío, the meteoric New World writer.

In April, 1900, eighteen-year-old

Jiménez went to Madrid, taking with him a portfolio of verses that were to make up the volume *Nubes* (*Clouds*). His new friends encouraged him to add enough poems to make two volumes. Darío suggested the name for one, *Violet Souls*, and Villaespesa wrote the preface. But the excitement of Madrid was too much for Jiménez, and he returned to quiet Moguer to await the appearance of his books. About that time a business failure plunged the family into poverty and his father died. The appearance of his two volumes of poems that flaunted literary conventions brought violent attacks from the critics and sent the sensitive writer to a sanatorium. His general reticence and withdrawal from active life date from this period.

Jiménez's next two volumes, *Rimas* (1902, *Rhymes*), whose title proves his kinship to Bécquer, and *Arias tristes* (1903, *Sad Airs*), turned criticism into admiration. Darío's enthusiasm was boundless, and the friendship of these completely different poets, whose only resemblance was their dedication to their art, was formed to last until Darío's death in 1916. Jiménez called the Nicaraguan "My dear Master," and was addressed in turn as "My dear Poet."

Jiménez lived in Madrid from 1912 until 1916, when he sailed to America to marry poetess Zenobia Camprubí Aymar in New York. His account of this trip is *Diary of a Recently Married Poet*, a volume of great importance in the development of modern Spanish poetry. It marks also the beginning of his new phase in writing, as does the publication of his most famous work, *Platero and I*, a series of prose poems about a donkey of Moguer. The French *Figaro* called it "One of two or three books capable of giving back to the people their childhood soul," and critics generally rate it as one of the great classics of modern Spanish literature.

Following his marriage, Jiménez returned to Madrid, where his wife opened a handicraft shop so he could go on writing. Here he lived until the outbreak of civil war drove him from Spain. At first he lived and taught in Baltimore, but in 1951, for the sake of the climate, he went to Puerto Rico, where he has lived ever since and where his wife died shortly after he was awarded the Nobel Prize for literature in 1956.

The poetry of Jiménez has shown a continual development from his florid early style, against which he rebelled in the ballads of his *Pastorales* (1905). His life has been spent revising all his previous poetry in an attempt to purify it. In his present style of free verse that he calls "la poesía desnuda" (naked poetry), he has cleared away all the decoration of rhyme and meter. The result is work more subtle and difficult to understand. As the Nobel Committee declared, his poems are "modernistic sculptures made out of a few metal pieces with emptiness between them wherein their artistic meaning is expressed."

BIBLIOGRAPHICAL REFERENCES: Before he was named for the Nobel Prize in 1956, Jiménez was almost unknown in English translation. Two editions of *Platero and I* are now available, a distinguished rendering of the complete text by Eloïse Roach, 1957, and a scholarly but incomplete translation by William and Mary Roberts, 1957. J. B. Trend published *Fifty Spanish Poems of Jiménez* in 1956, and D. F. Fogelquist has translated and edited *The Literary Collaboration and Personal Corro-*

spondence of Darío and Jiménez, 1956. There is no authorized biography, but Juan Ramón Jiménez, "Recuerdos al primer Villaespesa," *El Sol* (Madrid), May 10, 1936, is helpful for its autobiographical account of the writer's first journey to Madrid. See also Andrés González Blanco, "Juan Ramón Jiménez," in *Los contemporáneos*, 1907–1909; Rafael Cansinos-Asséns, *La nueva literatura*, 1917; Pedro Henríquez Ureña, "La obra de Jiménez," in *Cursos y conferencias*, XIX (1919, Buenos Aires); Aubrey F. G. Bell, *Contemporary Spanish Literature*, 1925; E. Nedderman, *Die Symbolistichen Stilemente im Werke von Juan Ramon Jimenez*, 1935; Carmen Gómez Tejera and Juan Asencio Alvarez-Torre, Introduction to Jiménez, *Poesía puertorriqueña*, 1936 (Havana); Gastón Figueira, *J. R. Jiménez, poeta de la inefable*, 1944 (Montevideo); and Graciela Palau de Nemes, *Vida y obra de Juan Ramón Jiménez*, 1957.

JIPPENSHA IKKU

Born: Fuchû, Suruga Province, Japan   *Died:* Edo, Japan
Date: 1765   *Date:* 1831

PRINCIPAL WORKS

Jippensha Ikku wrote a total of fifty-four works, most famous of which is his *Dochû Hiza-kurige* and its sequel, *Zoku Dochû Hiza-kurige*, 43 volumes, 1802–1822, part of which is available in English translation under the title *Hizakurige* (Kobe, 1929; reprinted in Tokyo, 1952).

In youth Jippensha Ikku, born in Fuchû, Suruga Province, in 1765, served in the household of the feudal Lord Odagiri. Sometime in his middle twenties he resigned and set out on his wanderings. At one time he lived in the house of a story chanter. He married into the family of a lumber merchant, but the marriage soon ended in divorce. His first literary work, a puppet play which he co-authored under the pseudonym Chikamatsu Yoshichi (Yoshichi being his real personal name) was published in 1789 when he was twenty-four. In the fall of 1794 he went to Edo (later Tokyo) and stayed in the house of a paper merchant, where he is said to have worked at the trade of making paper. In 1795 he published a novel which he illustrated himself. The work, called the *Shingaku Tokei-gusa* (*Around the Clock with Heart Studies*) dealt with a prostitute of the

Nightless City of Edo (the Yoshiwara) who became a devotee of the then prevalent Shingaku ("Heart Study") movement, an attempt to combine Buddhism and Shintô in the interest of Chinese philosophy and ethics, and who served twelve customers, one for every hour of the night. The work was an overnight success. From this time a flood of works flowed from his brush, and in 1802, when the *Hiza-kurige* (Shank's Mare) series appeared, he hit the height of his popularity. So popular was this series that it was reputed to have increased the price of paper in Edo. In order to get material for this series he made a number of journeys along the roads which he described. About 1802, or a few years previously, he married into another family, and was again divorced. He married a third time, this time maintaining his own identity, and had a son and daughter.

576

He read widely, was a comic poet of some fame, and a calligrapher as well as a painter. Toward the end of his life he suffered a stroke from overdrinking and lost the use of his hands and legs. He never amassed a fortune; before he died in straitened circumstances in Edo he was supported by his daughter, who had become a dancing instructress.

Because of the humorous nature of the Shank's Mare series, he has given the impression that he himself was a gay, humorous person, but such does not seem to have been the case. He was a reticent man. During his travels he was busy taking notes at the various tea shops he visited, and he seldom volunteered conversation with his fellow travelers. When his daughter had become a dancing instructress and was desired by a certain feudal lord as a concubine, Ikku refused the nobleman's request. When it was written of him that at one time he had worked as a gate keeper at a certain Buddhist temple during his youth, he took it as an affront to his character. Evidently it was his observation of the frailties and inconsistencies of human nature which led to his dealing with humor.

As a writer of humor, which gives him an important position in the history of Japanese literature, he is often ranked with Kyokutei Samba (1776–1822), but their natures were entirely different. Samba was reasoning and logical, whereas Ikku was passionate and emotional. Samba's humor was one of irony and cynicism, while Ikku's was robust and earthy.

Ikku died in Edo in 1831.

BIBLIOGRAPHICAL REFERENCES: The works of Jippensha Ikku are collected in the Teikoku Bunko Series I, Vol. 9, and in Series II, Vols. 21 and 23. All the biographies and critical studies concerning him are to be found as articles in various literary periodicals. In non-Japanese languages, other than the translation of his Hiza-kurige mentioned above, there is Serge Elisséev, "Jippensha Ikku et le Hizakurige," in *Japon et Extrême-Orient*, 5 (1924), 439–448. He is mentioned in such general histories of Japanese literature as that by W. G. Aston, *A History of Japanese Literature*, 1937.

SAMUEL JOHNSON

Born: Lichfield, England
Date: September 18, 1709

Died: London, England
Date: December 13, 1784

PRINCIPAL WORKS

ESSAYS: *The Rambler*, 1750–1752; *The Idler*, 1758–1760.

LEXICOGRAPHY: *Dictionary of the English Language*, 1755.

BIOGRAPHY: *Life of Richard Savage*, 1744; *Lives of the Poets*, 1779–1781.

POEMS: *London*, 1738; *The Vanity of Human Wishes*, 1749.

NOVEL: *The History of Rasselas, Prince of Abyssinia*, 1759.

PLAY: *Irene*, 1749.

MISCELLANEOUS: *Marmor Norfolciense*, 1739; *A Compleat Vindication of the Licensers of the Stage*, 1739; *Miscellaneous Observations on the Tragedy of Macbeth*, 1745; *The Plays of William Shakespeare*, 1765; *The False Alarm*, 1770; *Thoughts on Falkland's Islands*, 1771; *The Patriot*, 1774; *Journey to the Western Islands of Scotland*, 1775; *Taxation No Tyranny*, 1775.

TRANSLATIONS: *Voyage to Abyssinia,* by Father Lobo, 1735; *Commentary* on Pope's *Essay on Man,* by Jean Pierre de Crousaz, 1738–1739.

Samuel Johnson was born at Lichfield, Staffordshire, on September 18, 1709 (new style dating). His father was a provincial bookseller, and it was through browsing in his shop that the boy acquired much of his remarkable knowledge. Physically handicapped, with bad eyesight and facial disfigurements, he later developed a pronounced neurotic "tic." Showing early emotional instability, he was ever afterwards subject to long fits of lassitude and depression.

In the grammar schools of Lichfield and Stourbridge, and for some thirteen months at Oxford, he was well grounded in the classics, but because of financial difficulties left the university in 1729 without a degree. During the next few years all attempts to find a permanent post as a teacher failed; then in 1735 he married a widow over twenty years his senior, with whose small fortune he set up his own school. When this, too, proved unsuccessful, he and his wife late in 1737 moved to London. There followed a decade of poverty and distress in the city, as Johnson eked out a meager livelihood as translator and hack writer. He aided Edward Cave in editing the *Gentleman's Magazine,* providing fictionalized accounts of the proceedings in parliament, and short biographies, essays and poems. Independently he was involved in other large projects, and *con amore* wrote a revealing life of his erratic friend in misery, Richard Savage. *The Life of Richard Savage* is now recognized as an important milestone in the development of the art of biography.

In 1746 he signed a contract with a group of booksellers to produce a dictionary of the English language, but it was not until 1755 that the work, in two large folio volumes, finally appeared. Meanwhile, he had written two imitations of Juvenal in sonorous couplets, *London* in 1738 and *The Vanity of Human Wishes* in 1749, called by T. S. Eliot "among the greatest verse Satires of the English or any other language." His blank verse tragedy *Irene* was produced at Drury Lane in February, 1749, with meager success. Early in the 1750's he wrote some two hundred periodical essays entitled *The Rambler.*

With the publication of the *Dictionary* his reputation was established, but fame brought little immediate financial return. So in June, 1756, he issued proposals for a new edition of Shakespeare, and in the same year was largely responsible for a new periodical *The Literary Magazine or Universal Review.* For two years, from April, 1758, to April, 1760, he contributed a weekly essay under the title of *The Idler* to a newspaper, the *Universal Chronicle.* Depressed by the fatal illness of his mother, whom he had not seen for almost twenty years, and needing money for her expenses, he dashed off in the evenings of a single week what is perhaps his most characteristic work, the philosophical tale now known as *Rasselas.*

After the death in 1752 of his beloved wife, Johnson more and more sought diversion and companionship in the coffee houses and taverns, gradually drawing around him a brilliant circle including some of the most eminent men of his age, among them Edmund Burke, Sir Joshua Reynolds, Oliver Goldsmith, and David Garrick. As the years passed, his fame as a talker and sage equaled that as a writer.

In 1762 his financial difficulties were alleviated by a royal pension of £300 a year, and for the rest of his life he wrote only what he wished. There now began the period so brilliantly chronicled by the young Scot, James Boswell, whom he met in May, 1763. In January, 1765, he met the brewer Henry Thrale and his talkative wife, in whose comfortable homes he spent much time during the next eighteen years. Of his late published works the most notable were a series of political pamphlets hurriedly written in the early 1770's; an account of his journey with Boswell to the western islands of Scotland; and a series of biographical and critical prefaces to an extensive edition of the English poets of the seventeenth and early eighteenth centuries. At last, a prey to asthma, dropsy, and other ailments, he died in pious resignation on December 13, 1784, at London.

In his own day Johnson was best known as a lexicographer, essayist, and critic. Yet because of Boswell's genius and a general shift of sensibility, the next century regarded him chiefly as an eccentric character in a great book. He was loved and admired as the epitome of British bullheadedness and as the patron saint of clubbability, but only rarely were his works taken down from the shelves. The twentieth century is again taking Johnson seriously as a creative artist and critic.

The basic quality of his mind was skeptical. Except in religion, which he would never allow himself to question,

he was always searching for truth but, despite dogmatic remarks made in the heat of argument, never certain of finding it. It was this fundamental pyrrhonism which made him politically conservative, for he could never be convinced of the perfectibility of human institutions. Good men, he felt, were more to be desired than changes of government. For him abstract moral principles carried more weight than political or economic considerations. Even his notorious prejudices were largely grounded in ethical judgments: the Scots were too commercially minded; the American colonists were slave-owners who had stolen land from its rightful owners and were interested only in financial independence.

As a literary critic, he was neither a rigid theorist nor a bigoted follower of neo-classic rules, for he tended to rely instead on common sense and empirical knowledge. While his aesthetic appreciation was limited by an insistence, as he was reading, on understanding clearly how each rhetorical figure worked, within his own frame of reference he was a perceptive and acute judge. Always ready to shift ground if necessary, he had one criterion in mind: the power of a work to please and instruct. Nothing produced by man, he was convinced, could be perfect. Thus it was the duty of a critic to point out defects as well as merits in every work of art. But because of his forceful style the listing of defects is often more memorable than extensive general praise.

At its worst Johnson's prose is overly formal and ponderous; at its best, forceful, direct, and pungent. Its difficulty for some modern readers stems not from any excessive use of hard words or long sentences, for many of his most characteristic utterances are monosyllabic, but from a constant stress on abstract ideas. Yet such a style is eminently suited to one who is remembered as a powerful thinker and moralist.

James L. Clifford

BIBLIOGRAPHICAL REFERENCES: There is no recent or critical edition of the works of Samuel Johnson. There are definitive editions of *Samuel Johnson's Prefaces and Dedications,* by A. T. Hazen, 1937; *The Poems of Samuel Johnson,* by D. N. Smith and E. L. McAdam, 1941; and *The Letters of Samuel Johnson,* by R. W. Chapman, 3 vols., 1952. The standard biography is still James Boswell's *The Life of Samuel Johnson, LL.D.,* ed., G. B. Hill; revised and enlarged by L. F. Powell, 6 vols., 1934, 1950. Other important biographical studies are Sir John Hawkins, *The Life of Samuel Johnson,* 1787; G. B. Hill, ed., *Johnsonian Miscellanies,* 2 vols., 1897; Joseph Wood Krutch, *Samuel Johnson,* 1944; and James L. Clifford, *Young Sam Johnson,* 1955.

For criticism see Walter Raleigh, *Six Essays on Johnson,* 1910; J. E. Brown, *The Critical Opinions of Samuel Johnson,* 1926; W. B. C. Watkins, *Johnson and English Poetry before 1660,* 1936, and *Perilous Balance,* 1939; W. K. Wimsatt, Jr., *The Prose Style of Samuel Johnson,* 1941, and *Philosophic Words: A Study of Style and Meaning in the "Rambler" and "Dictionary" of Samuel Johnson,* 1948; B. H. Bronson, *Johnson Agonistes and Other Essays,* 1946; W. T. Cairns, *The Religion of Dr. Johnson and Other Essays,* 1946; E. L. McAdam, Jr., *Dr. Johnson and the English Law,* 1951; Jean H. Hagstrum, *Samuel Johnson's Literary Criticism,* 1952; B. B. Hoover, *Johnson's Parliamentary Reporting,* 1953; W. J. Bate, *The Achievement of Samuel Johnson,* 1955; J. H. Sledd and G. J. Kolb, *Dr. Johnson's Dictionary: Essays in the Biography of a Book,* 1955; and Arthur Sherbo, *Samuel Johnson: Editor of Shakespeare,* 1956. James L. Clifford's *Johnsonian Studies, 1887–1950: A Survey and Bibliography,* 1951, provides a comprehensive bibliographical guide.

MARY JOHNSTON

Born: Buchanan, Virginia
Date: November 21, 1870

Died: Warm Springs, Virginia
Date: May 9, 1936

PRINCIPAL WORKS

NOVELS: *Prisoners of Hope,* 1898; *To Have and to Hold,* 1900; *Audrey,* 1902; *Sir Mortimer,* 1904; *Lewis Rand,* 1908; *The Long Roll,* 1911; *Cease Firing,* 1912; *Hagar,* 1913; *The Witch,* 1914; *The Fortunes of Garin,* 1915; *The Wanderers,* 1917; *Foes,* 1918; *Michael Forth,* 1919; *Sweet Rocket,* 1920; *Silver Cross,* 1922; *1492,* 1922; *Croatan,* 1923; *The Slave Ship,* 1924; *The Great Valley,* 1926; *The Exile,* 1927; *Hunting Shirt,* 1931; *Miss Delicia Allen,* 1933; *Drury Randall,* 1934.

PLAY: *The Goddess of Reason,* 1907.

HISTORY: *Pioneers of the Old South,* 1918.

Mary Johnston was born on November 21, 1870, at Buchanan, Virginia, one of several children of Major John W. Johnston, a Confederate veteran whose family was connected with that of General Joseph E. Johnston. A delicate child, educated by governesses and tutors, she lived at home until she was nineteen; browsing in her father's library, she became an avid reader, particularly of history. With her father, who was a widower, she traveled in Europe and in 1893 moved to New York. During her four-year residence there, she was bedridden, and in default of an active life she began to write. Her first novel, *Prisoners of Hope*, was little noticed; her second, *To Have and to Hold*, a romantic story of the Virginia Colony, became a best seller. Her third novel, *Audrey*, repeated this success. Although her subsequent work was less enthusiastically received, she was henceforth provided with an independent career. She was never married. Upon her father's death, she moved to Richmond and afterward to Three Hills, the house she built at Warm Springs, Virginia. Here, after an operation, she died on May 9, 1936.

In the United States, even more than is true in England, the historical novel, through its influence on major realistic writers, has earned a place of high repute in the literary scene. For this reason, the work of minor historical novelists is here regarded as less incidental than in England. In its own right, furthermore, the genre has been dignified by the approval of a large reading public. Dozens of American historical novelists have attained a success that, measured in commercial terms, might have aroused envy in Sir Walter Scott. If the achievements of Mary Johnston do not now seem remarkable, the cause is that a new generation has surpassed them; half a century ago they were extraordinary.

Miss Johnston will be remembered as a creator of historical verisimilitude and as a skillful narrator. She did not confine herself to American locales and events, but was perhaps at her best when depicting these. *The Long Roll* and its sequel, *Cease Firing*, are romances of the Civil War period. Her zeal in the cause of women's rights prompted her two feminist novels, *Hagar* and *The Wanderers;* her socialist pacifism produced *Foes.* The last named was the first of a series of novels having mystical bearings, indebted in some measure to her interest in Buddhism; of these, the most noteworthy are *Michael Forth* and *Sweet Rocket.* *The Exile* is a tale of spiritual trial in a setting of the future.

BIBLIOGRAPHICAL REFERENCES: There is no extended biographical study of Mary Johnston and very little criticism. A good introduction to her fiction, especially in relation to its spiritual significance, is Edward Wagenknecht, "The World and Mary Johnston," *Sewanee Review*, XLIV (1936), 188–206. This material is presented in somewhat different fashion in the same author's *Cavalcade of the American Novel*, 1952. See also Grant Overton, *Cargoes for Crusoes*, 1924, and Arthur Hobson Quinn, *American Fiction: An Historical and Critical Survey*, 1936.

MAURUS JÓKAI

Born: Komárno, Hungary
Date: February 19, 1825

Died: Budapest, Hungary
Date: May 5, 1904

PRINCIPAL WORKS

NOVELS: *Erdély aranykora*, 1852 (*Midst the Wild Carpathians*); *Egy Magyar nábob*, 1853–1854 (*A Hungarian Nabob*); *Szomorú napok*, 1856 (*The Day of Wrath*); *A köszivü ember fiai,* 1869 (*The Baron's Sons*); *A fekete gyémantok,* 1870 (*Black Diamonds*); *Az arany ember,* 1872 (*A Modern Midas*); *A tengerszemü hölgy,* 1890 (*Eyes Like the Sea*); *Nincsen ördög,* 1891 (*There Is No Devil*).

Maurus (also Móricz or Mór) Jókai was born at Komárno, Hungary, on February 19, 1825. By the time he was twenty he had written his first play, *Zsidó fiu* (1845, *The Jew Boy*). The partial success of this work decided him on his career as a writer, and he abandoned the law to apply himself vigorously to this end. Before he was fifty he had finished twenty-nine long novels, some poetry, humorous articles, dramas, and sixty-eight volumes of tales. He had also made a good marriage with Róza Laborfalvi and had established himself as the great living figure in Magyar literature. He had fought in the unsuccessful revolt against Austria in 1848 and was deeply involved in political journalism. He founded *Hon,* a Magyar patriotic newspaper, and in 1860 was sentenced to a month of solitary confinement for printing his views. His novels continued to express nationalistic sentiments and were widely published abroad, serving in this way both his literary hopes and the aspirations of his people.

Jókai's work has often been compared to that of Dickens, Dumas, and Scott. Like them he was not above melodrama, and also like them he was loved by his readers. When he died in Budapest on May 5, 1904, he was accorded a public funeral by unanimous vote of the legislature.

BIBLIOGRAPHICAL REFERENCES: John Bell Henneman, *Shakespearean and Other Papers,* 1911, includes an essay on Jókai. See also Kálmán Mikszáth, *Jókai élete es kora,* 1907; and F. Zsigmond, *Jókai,* 1924.

HENRY ARTHUR JONES

Born: Grandborough, England
Date: September 28, 1851

Died: London, England
Date: January 7, 1929

PRINCIPAL WORKS

PLAYS: *The Silver King,* 1882 (with Henry Herman); *Saints and Sinners,* 1884; *The Middleman,* 1889; *Judah,* 1890; *The Dancing Girl,* 1891; *The Case of Rebellious Susan,* 1894; *Michael and His Lost Angel,* 1896; *The Liars,* 1897; *Mrs. Dane's Defence,* 1900; *Joseph Entangled,* 1904; *The Evangelist,* 1907; *Mary Goes First,* 1913; *The Lie,* 1914; *The Pacifists,* 1917.

ESSAYS: *The Renascence of the English Drama,* 1895.

Henry Arthur Jones, born at Grandborough on September 28, 1851, was the son of a Buckinghamshire farmer. Leaving school at the age of twelve, he became an apprentice in a draper's shop, then a clerk in London, and later a commercial traveler. He educated himself through wide reading. After he saw his first play, at the age of eighteen, he started writing plays at once, and considering his backgrounds and experience he achieved phenomenal success in the theater. Although none of his hundred plays would please a modern audience because of his artistic limitations—easy submission to the mores of his day and tedious moralizing—he was an important pioneer in the beginnings of modern drama.

Along with Oscar Wilde and Sir Arthur Wing Pinero he fought for honesty and literacy in drama, and thus paved the way for Shaw, Galsworthy, and Barrie as well as the emancipated age of drama in our time. He did his best work in melodrama, including such works as *The Silver King* and *Mrs. Dane's Defence*; and in sparkling high comedy: *The Case of Rebellious Susan, The Liars,* and *Mary Goes First. The Liars* has been called the best English comedy of manners of the nineteenth century. Bernard Shaw regarded Jones as a better playwright than his noted contemporary, Sir Arthur Wing Pinero. He died in London on January 7, 1929.

BIBLIOGRAPHICAL REFERENCES: A selection of Jones' plays, *Representative Plays,* 4 vols., 1926, edited by Clayton Hamilton, includes a historical, biographical, and critical introduction. A full-length biography is Jenny Doris Arthur Jones, *The Life and Letters of Henry Arthur Jones,* 1930 (American edition, *Taking the Curtain Call),* which includes a bibliography. F. K. Walter's bibliography, "Reading List on Henry Arthur Jones," *Bulletin of Bibliography,* VI (1911), 273–275, is helpful but badly outdated.

Another full-length study is Richard A. Cordell, *Henry Arthur Jones and the Modern Drama,* 1932. Books which include studies of Jones are William Archer, *The Old Drama and the New,* 1923; Ashley Dukes, *The Youngest Drama,* 1923; Max Beerbohm, *Around Theatres,* 2 vols., 1924; and Allardyce Nicoll, *British Drama,* 1932. Also helpful is Marjorie Northend's "Henry Arthur Jones and the Development of the Modern English Drama," *Review of English Studies,* XVIII (1942), 448–463.

BEN JONSON

Born: Westminster (?), England
Date: June 11, 1573 (?)

Died: Westminster
Date: August 6, 1637

PRINCIPAL WORKS

PLAYS: *The Case Is Altered,* 1597?; *Every Man in his Humour,* 1598; *Every Man out of his Humour,* 1599; *Cynthia's Revels,* 1600; *Poetaster,* 1601; *Sejanus,* 1603; *Volpone,* 1605; *Epicœne, or The Silent Woman,* 1609; *The Alchemist,* 1610; *Catiline,* 1611; *Bartholomew Fair,* 1614; *The Devil Is an Ass,* 1616; *The Staple of News,* 1626; *The New Inn,* 1629; *The Magnetic Lady,* 1632; *A Tale of a Tub,* 1633; *The Sad Shepherd* (fragment).

MISCELLANEOUS: *The King's Entertainment in Passing to his Coronation,* 1603; *The Masque of Blackness,* 1605; *The Masque of Beauty,* 1608; *The Masque of Queens,* 1609; *Oberon, the Fairy Prince,* 1611; *Pleasure Reconciled to Virtue,* 1618; *The Gypsies Metamorphosed,* 1621; *Chloridia,* 1630; *Epigrams,* 1616; *The Forest,* 1616; *The Under-wood,* 1640; "To the Memory of my Beloved, the Author, Mr. William Shakespeare," 1623; *The English Grammar,* 1640; *Discoveries,* 1641.

One of the most colorful personalities and able writers of the age of Shakespeare, Ben Jonson left so vigorous an impression on his time that even today he is viewed with intense partisanship, hostile or friendly. However, there are many doubtful dates and gaps in his biography. He was, according to some late traditions, born at Westminster in 1572 or 1573. Some contemporary accounts place the death of his father, "a reverend preacher," when Ben was seventeen or when he was in the sixth form at Westminster School. The *Conversations* by Drummond of Hawthornden (1619?) state that the father died a month before his son's birth. Since this account is supposedly Jonson's own, it has been generally accepted. All accounts agree that after the father's death, the widowed mother married a bricklayer, and that for a while young Ben practiced his stepfather's trade.

In the sixteenth century the burst of poetic energy and the accompanying public demand for poetry owed much to England's grammar schools. Edmund Spenser studied under Richard Mulcaster, a renowned educator, at the Merchant Tailors School in London; Shakespeare was almost certainly trained in the excellent grammar school at Stratford; and Jonson sat at the feet of William Camden, one of the finest scholars of his day, at Westminster School. From Camden, Jonson drew his delight and his competence in classical languages and literatures, and learned much of his own country's history and literature.

After leaving Westminster School, probably in 1588, Jonson was a bricklayer, a soldier, and a traveling actor. According to Mark Eccles, he was probably the Benjamine Johnson who married Anne Lewis on November 14, 1594. A six-month-old daughter and a seven-year-old son of the Jonsons met untimely deaths. The brief poems written by the grieving father show a tenderness not common to the rugged, often rough-tongued, dramatist. During his acting career he performed as Hieronimo in Thomas Kyd's *The Spanish Tragedy,* and later sold additions to *Jeronymo* (obviously the *Spanish Tragedy*) to Philip Henslowe, the manager of the Admiral's Men. The surviving additions to the play are not unanimously accepted as Jonson's. Other plots and parts of plays sold to Henslowe have been lost. Little is known about the career as a soldier; the *Conversations* carry an account of a spectacular single combat, and one of the epigrams recalls with pride the fact that the author is a combat veteran.

In 1597 Jonson and two other actors were imprisoned for their part in *The Isle of Dogs,* chiefly written by Thomas Nash. One of these actors was Gabriel Spencer, who in the following year was killed by Jonson in a duel. Spencer's death led to Jonson's second recorded brush with the law, which nearly ended his life; however, he was able to plead benefit of clergy, which any Latinist could do, and he saved himself by reading his "neck verse."

This fortunate escape helped make 1598 a memorable year for Jonson. In that year Francis Meres recorded him as one of "our best for Tragedie," and the theatrical company of Burbage and Shakespeare produced his *Every Man in his Humour*—his first resounding success—the realistic comedy that marked his future path. This

584

company (the Lord Chamberlain's, later the King's Men) produced nine of Jonson's plays; but unlike Shakespeare, Jonson did not write almost exclusively for one company.

Between 1599 and 1603 he took part in the War of the Theatres. Jonson's *Poetaster* and Dekker's *Satiromastix* were the main battles in this bloodless conflict. Except for the disgruntled Jonson, who temporarily turned his back on comedy as a result of the War, the participants apparently did not take it too seriously. As a stimulant to theatrical attendance the feud may have been more commercial than emotional.

In 1603 *Sejanus,* one of Jonson's two surviving tragedies, was performed with Shakespeare and Burbage among the principal tragedians. In the same year began Jonson's long career as writer of court masques which led to his position as Poet Laureate in fact if not in name. Except for his third imprisonment (probably in 1605 for his part in *Eastward Ho*), Jonson enjoyed a decade of triumphs as his prestige grew in the theater, at court, and in literary circles. His collaboration with the famous architect Inigo Jones led to his acquaintance with notable musicians and graphic artists. This triumphant period was rounded out by the publication of the first folio edition of his *Works* in 1616, the year of the death of Shakespeare. Until the publication of Jonson's Folio, plays had little literary standing; hence the idea of considering plays "works" aroused much ridicule. But the literary world owes Jonson an incalculable debt: his Folio begot the much more famous, but less satisfactory, First Folio of Shakespeare in 1623. Had Shakespeare edited his own Folio as Jonson did his, many a ream of paper and much printer's ink would have been saved in the ensuing years. Still, the Shakespeare Folio has been justly adored "almost t'idolatrie," for without it a substantial body of the work of England's favorite poet would be lost.

After 1616, though less happy and less triumphant, Jonson's life was not devoid of incident or accomplishment. In 1618 he journeyed to Scotland on foot and paid a much-discussed visit to Drummond of Hawthornden. Their recorded conversations have been heavily used as biographical source material. According to the *Conversations* both Oxford and Cambridge conferred Master of Arts degrees on Jonson for his literary merits, not for residence study. The Register of the University of Oxford records the granting of the degree on July 17, 1619. Official evidence for the Cambridge degree is missing. In 1623 he contributed to the Shakespeare Folio the excellent poem "To the Memory of my Beloved, the Author, Mr. William Shakespeare." In the same year he suffered a disastrous fire which destroyed many manuscripts, including some of his own unpublished works. C. J. Sisson recently discovered that in 1623 he was in residence at Gresham College, and may possibly have been a teacher of rhetoric at the College.

In his last years he was stricken with palsy, then paralysis. He was neglected by King Charles. Inigo Jones triumphed over him in their long quarrel. His late plays were largely failures on the stage, but he continued to write plays, masques, and poems almost to the end of his life. Although in comparison with the masterpieces of his prime they indi-

585

cate a considerable decline in power, they are far from being contemptible literature. Several of his noble patrons, notably the Digbys and the Earl of Newcastle, stood by him in his adver-

sity. When he died—at Westminster, on August 6, 1637—his followers published a memorial volume of verse filled with extravagant praise.

George Burke Johnston

BIBLIOGRAPHICAL REFERENCES: *Ben Jonson's Conversations with William Drummond of Hawthornden,* c. 1619; summarized in the 1711 Folio of Drummond's *Works;* printed in 1842; completely edited in Vol. I of the Oxford *Ben Jonson)* remains a primary source book in the study of Jonson's life and personality. The most recent biography is Marchette Chute, *Ben Jonson of Westminster,* 1953. Important editions of the works are *Ben Jonson,* edited by C. H. Herford, Percy Simpson, and Evelyn Simpson, 1925–1952; *The Poems of Ben Jonson,* edited by B. H. Newdigate, 1936; and *Poems of Ben Jonson,* edited by George Burke Johnston, 1954.

See also Maurice Castelain, *Ben Jonson: l'homme et l'œuvre,* 1907; G. G. Smith, *Ben Jonson,* 1919; E. K. Chambers, *The Elizabethan Stage,* Vols. III and IV, 1923; J. A. Gotch, *Inigo Jones,* 1928; John Palmer, *Ben Jonson,* 1934; K. A. McEuen, *Classical Influence on the Tribe of Ben,* 1939; and George Burke Johnston, *Ben Jonson: Poet,* 1945.

JAMES JOYCE

Born: Dublin, Ireland
Date: February 2, 1882

Died: Zurich, Switzerland
Date: January 13, 1941

PRINCIPAL WORKS

NOVELS: *A Portrait of the Artist as a Young Man,* 1916; *Ulysses,* 1922; *Finnegans Wake,* 1939.

SHORT STORIES: *Dubliners,* 1914.

POEMS: *Chamber Music,* 1907; *Pomes Penyeach,* 1927.

PLAY: *Exiles,* 1918.

LETTERS: *Letters of James Joyce,* edited by Stuart Gilbert, 1957.

There was little in James Augustine Aloysius Joyce's family background to indicate that he was to become the most influential novelist of the first half of the twentieth century. His birth in Dublin on February 2, 1882, was the first of the fifteen that marked the union of mild Mary Jane Murray and witty, volatile, improvident John Stanislaus Joyce. Sometime medical student, petty politician, and office-holder, John Joyce managed to send his eldest son to Clongowes Wood College, County Kildare, in September

of 1888. Declining family fortunes caused the father to withdraw him in 1891. As a day student, James Joyce continued his classical Jesuit education at Belvedere College in Dublin until 1898. At University College he contributed essays to the college magazine. He was scarcely eighteen when the prominent English *Fortnightly Review* published "Ibsen's New Drama," his perceptive appraisal of the art of the great Henrik Ibsen, in order to read whose plays Joyce had learned Norwegian. On October 31, 1902, he received his degree and a month later left Ireland for the Continent, visiting William Butler Yeats briefly in London on his way.

In Paris, as in Dublin, he found himself unable to attend medical school —he planned to combine medicine with writing. Half a year's poverty there ended when he was summoned home to his dying mother. In the year following her death in August, 1903, he taught school, consorted with lively companions, and wrote. He sent off a manuscript of thirty-six poems entitled *Chamber Music* to be offered to a London publisher, jotted notes for the short story volume *Dubliners,* and began *Stephen Hero,* an autobiographical novel. In this year he had also fallen in love, and on October 8, 1904, he and Nora Barnacle, a straightforward young girl from Galway, left Ireland together for Paris. In Pola and Trieste Joyce worked as a language teacher in the Berlitz school system, barely making enough for themselves and their son Giorgio, born July 27, 1905. In November Joyce sent *Dubliners* to an English publisher, beginning the nine years of rejections and disputes over alleged impropriety and irreligiousness that were to pass before the stories would appear. The year 1907 was marked by the birth of a daughter, Lucia, and the appearance of *Chamber Music.* The form of these finely wrought, musical love lyrics suggested the discipline and simplicity of Ben Jonson; their content recalled the romantic melancholy of the early Yeats.

Brief trips to Dublin in 1909 and 1910 were followed by a third in 1912, to fight for *Dubliners,* which was Joyce's last visit to his native land. *Stephen Hero,* most of it burned in despair in 1907, had been rewritten in a compressed, highly disciplined form as *A Portrait of the Artist as a Young Man.* Through Ezra Pound, American poet and *avant-garde* leader, the novel was accepted early in 1914 for serial publication in the new magazine, *The Egoist.* This success was crowned by the June publication of *Dubliners.* Some reviewers praised the author of the fifteen short stories for realism. Few realized that these polished portrayals of people afflicted with moral paralysis were also freighted with symbolic meanings and religio-mythic references. Having earlier resisted the temptation to call this book *Ulysses at Dublin,* Joyce had in the spring begun a big novel to be called *Ulysses.* In this same year he wrote *Exiles,* a rather static play, strongly influenced by Ibsen, which dealt with the problem of the possibility of complete spiritual freedom between two lovers. The Joyces moved to Zurich in June, 1915. There he continued his teaching, their poverty only a little relieved by funds from friends and relatives. But Joyce's reputation began to grow as both *Dubliners* and *A Portrait of the Artist as a Young Man* were published in New York in 1916. Several critics saw the semi-autobiographical novel as a work of genius, a realistic portrayal, through protagonist Stephen Dedalus, of a young artist's growth, revolt, and dedication against a background of family and religious conflict in politically strife-ridden Ireland. But as with *Dubliners,* fewer critics perceived the pervasive symbolism or the highly allusive, strictly disciplined, and densely textured character of the prose which was an integral part of the novel's meaning. A favorable review upon publication in England was counterbalanced by Joyce's sufferings from glaucoma and Nora's nervous breakdown. In 1917 portions of *Ulysses* appeared in *The Egoist*. A year later it began in serial form in *The Little Review*, only to be halted by court order in 1920 on the grounds of indecency.

In that same year the family moved to Paris, where a year and a half later Shakespeare and Company published *Ulysses* on February 2, 1922, Joyce's birthday. It received one of the most diverse and violent receptions ever accorded a great book. To some, this story of a single day in the lives of Stephen Dedalus and Leopold and Molly Bloom was an obscene picture of base people in a shabby Dublin. To others, these modern events, with their detailed correspondences to those of the *Odyssey*, symbolically elaborated fundamental themes in human experience. Displaying a mastery of a dazzling variety of prose styles, the difficult and erudite novel was on one level the most realistic treatment of a city in literature and on another level an intense exploration in depth of human nature through unforgettable characters whom the reader knew through their very thoughts, sometimes presented only half articulated in their streams of consciousness. By the time a celebrated legal opinion admitted the novel into the United States in 1933, Joyce had become a *bête noire* to conservatives, a prophet

to the *avant-garde,* and an internationally known modern master.

Handicapped by failing sight despite ten serious operations on his eyes, Joyce worked on. Excerpts from *Work in Progress,* later to be titled *Finnegans Wake,* revealed that he had virtually invented a new language. Spiced with borrowings from more than a dozen languages, the words were combined and spelled in such a way as to offer several denotations and connotations in a series of puns and word plays which loaded each individual verbal unit with literal and symbolic meaning. After its appearance in 1939, commentaries gradually explicated the novel for an almost wholly baffled public. They showed that Joyce was trying to compress the history and experience of the race into one night's time through the sleeping, dreaming, and waking experiences of Humphrey Chimpden Earwicker (Everyman), his wife Anna Livia Plurabelle (the great feminine force in life and nature), their twin sons, Shem and Shaun, and their daughter, Issy. More allusive, densely wrought, and demanding than all his previous works together, this novel is still a source of literary debate. Meditating a sequel, *The Reawakening,* Joyce was interrupted in his work by World War II and escaped with his family to Zurich, only to die there as a result of a perforated ulcer on January 13, 1941.

Joseph L. Blotner

BIBLIOGRAPHICAL REFERENCES: The authorized biography is *James Joyce,* by Herbert Gorman, 1939. An important newer study is Stanislaus Joyce, *My Brother's Keeper: James Joyce's Early Years,* 1958. Other books in the critical canon are Stuart Gilbert, *James Joyce's "Ulysses,"* 1930; Louis Golding, *James Joyce,* 1933; Frank Budgen, *James Joyce and the Making of "Ulysses,"* 1934; Harry Levin, *James Joyce: A Critical Introduction,* 1941; Joseph Campbell and H. M. Robinson, *A Skeleton*

Key to Finnegans Wake, 1944; Leon Edel, *James Joyce: The Last Journey,* 1947; R. M. Kain: *Fabulous Voyager: James Joyce's Ulysses,* 1947; Alan Parker, *James Joyce,* 1948; W. Y. Tindall, *James Joyce: His Way of Interpreting the Modern World,* 1950; L. A. G. Strong, *The Sacred River,* 1951; John J. Slocum and Herbert Cahoon, *A Bibliography of James Joyce,* 1953; Adaline Glasheen, *A Census of Finnegans Wake,* 1956; Hugh Kenner, *Dublin's Joyce,* 1956; and Marvin Magalaner and R. M. Kain, *Joyce: The Man, The Work, The Reputation,* 1956.

For articles in books see David Daiches, *The Novel and the Modern World,* 1939; *idem,* "James Joyce: The Artist as Exile" in *Forms of Modern Fiction,* edited by W. V. O'Connor, 1948; Edmund Wilson, *Axel's Castle,* 1931; *idem,* "The Dream of H. C. Earwicker" in *The Wound and the Bow,* 1947; D. S. Savage, *The Withered Branch,* 1950; and Arland Ussher, *Three Great Irishmen,* 1953.

See also Edwin Muir, "James Joyce: The Meaning of *Ulysses,*" *Calendar of Modern Letters,* I (1925), 347–355; Cyril Connolly, "The Position of Joyce," *Life and Letters,* II (1929), 273–290; Joseph Prescott, "James Joyce: A Study in Words," *Publications of the Modern Language Association,* LIV (1939), 304–315; *idem,* "Homer's *Odyssey* and Joyce's *Ulysses,*" *Modern Language Quarterly,* III (1942), 427–444; Ernest Bernbaum, "The Crucial Question Regarding Finnegans Wake," *College English,* VII (1945), 151–154; R. P. Blackmur, "The Jew in Search of a Son," *Virginia Quarterly Review,* XXIV (1948), 96–116; M. Magalaner, "James Joyce and the Myth of Man," *Arizona Quarterly,* IV (1948), 300–309; Hugh Kenner, "Baker Street to Eccles Street: The Odyssey of a Myth," *Hudson Review,* I (1949), 481–500; R. G. Kelly, "James Joyce: A Partical Explanation," *Publications of the Modern Language Association,* LXV (1949), 26–39; Edward Duncan, "Unsubstantial Father: A Study of the 'Hamlet' Symbolism in Joyce's *Ulysses,*" *University of Toronto Quarterly,* XIX (1950), 126–140; Stanislaus Joyce, "James Joyce: A Memoir," *Hudson Review,* II (1950), 485–515; A. M. Klein, "The Black Panther—A Study of Joyce," *Accent,* X (1950), 139–154; F. J. Thompson, "A Portrait of the Artist Asleep," *Western Review,* XIV (1950), 245–253; Hugh Kenner, "Joyce and Ibsen's Naturalism," *Sewanee Review,* LIX (1951), 75–96; Joseph Prescott, "Notes on Joyce's *Ulysses,*" *Modern Language Quarterly,* XIII (1952), 149–162; Richard Ellman, "The Backgrounds of *Ulysses,*" *Kenyon Review,* XVI (1954), 337–386, and "The Limits of Joyce's Naturalism," *Sewanee Review,* LXIII (1955), 567–575; and William Empson, "The Theme of *Ulysses,*" *Kenyon Review,* XVIII (1956), 26–52.

Additional critical studies have been reprinted in *James Joyce: Two Decades of Criticism,* edited by Seon Givens, 1948.

JUVENAL
Decimus Junius Juvenalis

Born: Aquinum, Italy   *Died:* Egypt?
Date: c. 55   *Date:* c. 135

PRINCIPAL WORKS

POEMS: *Satires,* 112–128.

Born at Aquinum, Italy, about A.D. 55, Juvenal was the poet of the Age of Trajan. Of his cruelly biting satires written between 100 and 128, sixteen, in five volumes, are still preserved. From them, a reader deduces that

589

Juvenal disliked almost everything in the life of his time. There is a brief characterization of him in a poem written by Martial. A conservative Roman who scorned the soft life of the fashionable and wealthy, he lashed in quotable epigrams against their follies and vices. Fools as well as philosophers are subject to his savage denunciation. His humor is grim, but his pictures are unforgettable, especially of the affectations and immorality of women of high society.

Several editions of his work contain prefatory biographies, but these show little agreement in details. Apparently Juvenal was the son of a freedman.

Tradition says also that he practiced declamation, like Demosthenes, with a pebble in his mouth. Wisely, not until after Domitian's death did he publish his tragic satires. They show considerable development over the disunited productions of Petronius and Horace. An actor, taking personally the satire probably aimed at Domitian's favorite actor, Paris, is believed to have persuaded Trajan to banish Juvenal under the guise of a military appointment, to Egypt, though some claim that he was sent to Britain. According to a fourth century biographer, the poet died in exile at the age of eighty, "of vexation and disgust."

BIBLIOGRAPHICAL REFERENCES: Translations in English include *The Satires of Decimus Junius Juvenalis*, by John Dryden and others, 1697, reissued many times; Alexander Leeper, *Thirteen Satires of Juvenal*, 1902; A. F. Cole, *The Satires of Juvenal*, useful for its introduction and notes, 1906; and George Gilbert Ramsay, *Juvenal and Persius*, 1918. See also Inez B. Scott, *The Grand Style in the Satires of Juvenal*, 1927; and Gilbert Highet, *Juvenal the Satirist*, 1954, and *Poets in a Landscape*, 1957.

FRANZ KAFKA

Born: Prague, Czechoslovakia
Date: July 3, 1883

Died: Klosterneuburg, Austria
Date: June 3, 1924

PRINCIPAL WORKS

NOVELS: *Der Process*, 1925 (*The Trial*); *Das Schloss*, 1926 (*The Castle*); *Amerika*, 1927.

SHORT STORIES: *Die Verwandlung*, 1915 (*Metamorphosis*); *Das Urteil*, 1916 (*The Judgment*); *In der Strafkolonie*, 1919 (*In the Penal Colony*); *Ein Landarzt*, 1919 (*The Country Doctor*); *Beim Bau der chinesischen Mauer*, 1931 (*The Great Wall of China*).

MISCELLANEOUS: *A Franz Kafka Miscellany* (1940); *Parables* (1947); *The Diaries of Franz Kafka*, ed. by Max Brod (1948–1949); *Briefe an Milena*, 1952 (*Letters to Milena*); *Dearest Father* (1954).

A member of a Czech Jewish family, Franz Kafka was born in Prague July 3, 1883, the son of a prosperous dealer in wholesale fancy goods whose dominant personality may have contributed to his son's sense of inadequacy. Kafka took his law degree in 1906 at the German University of Prague and later secured a minor position with the Austrian Government. He was dogged by ill health, twice being prevented from marrying, and spent much time in various sanatoriums. The privations of the war, from which he was exempt because of his government post, increased his illness. In 1923 he formed a liaison with a very young Jewish girl, Dora Dymant, and experienced a brief period of happiness, but died of tuberculosis at Klosterneuburg, June 3, 1924.

Kafka's diaries reveal a sensitive, introspective personality haunted by a conviction of failure. Characteristically, his three novels were never finished, and he told his friend, Max Brod, to destroy all of his unpublished manuscripts. This request Brod refused to carry out; instead, he put Kafka's manuscripts and papers together as best he could. The novels were translated into English during the 1930's and have been widely acclaimed.

Kafka is an extremely difficult writer, lacking the surface charm that might attract some readers to attempt the task of untangling the obscure allegories in which he elected to clothe his plots set amid dream-like, surrealist landscapes. Max Brod has called the novels a trilogy of loneliness, while Edwin Muir has pointed out the similarity between *The Castle* and *Pilgrim's Progress*. Each story depicts the struggle of the individual towards salvation; the difference is that the seventeenth century Christian knew exactly what road he must take and what obstacles he would meet, whereas Kafka's hero must contend against unseen forces that he can never understand. This circumstance points to what has been considered the central theme of Kafka's work: that man must strive to find his right place and his true vocation in a universe whose pattern he can never fully comprehend. "There is a right way of life, and the discovery of it depends on one's attitude to powers which are almost unknown," wrote Edwin Muir, translator of *The Castle*. Thus the hero of Kafka's novel can never reach the Castle, and yet he cannot understand why he has failed.

In Kafka, we have a profoundly moral writer who was endeavoring to express, by a difficult technique, the problem of modern man who, product of an age of skepticism, struggles vainly to act in accordance with divine wishes. Kafka may be compared with Huysmans, who dealt with the same problem in nineteenth-century terms. In spite of his obscure and at times unsatisfactory technique, Kafka has been viewed by many critics as one of the greatest writers of our age.

BIBLIOGRAPHICAL REFERENCES: The chief source of biographical information on Kafka is found in Max Brod, *Franz Kafka: A Biography*, 1937. A more recent study is M. Carrouges, *Franz Kafka*, 1948. See also Charles Neider, *The Frozen Sea: A Study of Franz Kafka*, 1948; W. Hubben, *Four Prophets of Our Destiny*, 1952; N. A. Scott, *Rehearsals of Discomposure*, 1952; Philip Rahv, "Franz Kafka: The Hero as Lonely Man," *Kenyon Review*, I (1939), 60–74; and Austin Warren, "Kosmos Kafka," *Southern Review*, VII (1941), 350–365.

KALIDASA

Born: Ujjain (?), India　　　　　*Died*: India
Date: Probably fifth century　　　*Date*: Unknown

PLAYS: *Sakuntalā* (*The Lost Ring*); *Mālavikāgnimitra* (*Mālavikā and Agnimitra*); *Vikramorvasī* (*Urvashī Won by Valor*).

POEMS: *Raghuvansa* (*The Dynasty of Raghu*); *Kumārasambhava* (*The Birth of Kumāra*); *Meghadūta* (*The Cloud Messenger*); *Ritusamhāra* (*The Seasons*). All dates of original composition or presentation are unknown.

Legends concerning the life of the Indian poet and dramatist Kalidasa (or Kālidāsa) abound, but almost no facts are known about him. Scholars have placed the date of his birth as early as the third or as late as the sixth century of the Christian era; current theories seem to favor the fifth. Even less is known about his place of birth. A long-popular legend which made Kalidasa one of the "nine gems," or wise men, at the brilliant court of King Vikramaditya I at Ujjain during the so-called "Sanskrit Renaissance" has been discredited by some modern authorities. What little is actually known of the poet's life, that he must have been well-educated and widely traveled in his own land, has been gleaned from a careful study of his own writings.

Kalidasa, the most famous writer of the post-Vedic period of Sanskrit literature, produced seven works still extant: three plays, two epic and two lyric poems. All his works are characterized by their delicate, lyrical quality, and by a sensitivity both to human feelings and to the beauties of nature. His poetry, all unrhymed, is closer to Greek and Latin forms than to English blank verse in that the rhythm depends upon the quantity of syllables rather than upon accent.

The plays of Kalidasa, of which *Sakuntala* (or *Shakuntala*) is the most famous, are in prose, richly intermingled with lyric and descriptive verse-stanzas. They all tell the story of the love between a king and a nymph-maiden who, after being separated by a series of violent and supernatural misfortunes, are happily reunited. The dramas, whose heroines are among the most appealing in all literature, follow closely the elaborate conventions of Indian dramaturgy.

BIBLIOGRAPHICAL REFERENCES: *Shakuntalā and Other Writings of Kālidāsa* is a collection translated by A. W. Ryder, 1912. See also A. Bernedale Keith, *The Sanskrit Drama in Its Origin, Development, Theory and Practice*, 1924. An earlier study is H. H. Wilson, *The Hindu Theatre*, 1871.

IMMANUEL KANT

Born: Königsberg, Germany
Date: April 22, 1724

Died: Königsberg
Date: February 12, 1804

PHILOSOPHICAL ESSAYS AND STUDIES: *Allgemeine Naturgeschichte und Theorie des Himmels*, 1755 (*General History of Nature and Theory of the Heavens*); *Beobachtungen über das Gefühl des Schönen und Erhabenen*, 1764 (*Observations on the*

Sense of the Beautiful and the Sublime); Kritik der reinen Vernunft, 1781 (Critique of Pure Reason); Kritik der praktischen Vernunft, 1788 (Critique of Practical Reason); Kritik der Urteilskraft, 1790 (Critique of Judgment); Religion innerhalb der Grenzen der blossen Vernunft, 1793 (Religion Within the Limits of Mere Reason).

Immanuel Kant, perhaps the most influential philosopher in the Western world since Aristotle, was born on April 22, 1724, in the East Prussian city of Königsberg, his lifelong home. After graduating from the university in 1746, he was for some nine years a tutor. In 1755 he became *Privatdozent* at the university and in 1770 a professor. He never traveled far from the city, nor, from 1755 on, did his interest extend beyond the precincts of his academic retreat, so that the external events of his life were few and limited in their physical scope. The course of his existence was inward, the action that he was involved in taking place in the abstract fields of logic and illuminated by the non-diurnal light of purest reason. Thus an examination of his life, however cursory, must deal with these immanent actions, for without them there would be no life worth mentioning.

Kant's first rational activities were scientific and mathematical, resulting in a theory of the nebular origin of the solar system which anticipated the hypothesis later developed by the astronomer Laplace. His natural bent, however, inclined him toward work in pure philosophy, and it was in that realm that his greatest accomplishments were made. He began as an adherent of the rationalist school of Leibniz and Wolff, but by 1763 he had reversed his position, coming under the influence of Hume when the Scotsman's writings became known in Germany. Unable to synthesize from the works of his pred-

ecessors a metaphysics suitable to him, Kant set out to construct a system of his own; it was his hope to develop a metaphysics that would establish a basis of truth for the discoveries of science and at the same time would allow for a belief in God and immortality. In order to do this, Kant discovered that he would first have to make an examination of the cognitive faculties of mankind.

He began his *Critique of Pure Reason* in 1770 as an examination of the cognitive faculties in preparation for the development of a system of metaphysics. When the book was completed eleven years later, there was no need for the metaphysical discussion; the *Critique* was a metaphysics in itself, and in it Kant had, at least to his own satisfaction, achieved his two ends: he had demonstrated a system that asserts man's *a priori* knowledge in matters pertaining to science, but which, at the same time, removes all matters of God and immortality from the sphere of scientific reasoning and places them in the realm of faith.

Kant went on to extend these principles in two of his later works. But although he had demonstrated his theories to his own satisfaction, he had not done so to the satisfaction of those who came after him. His *Critique*, since its first appearance, has been subjected to the severest criticism; it has been called "The merest patchwork or mosaic of scraps, specimens of which have been collected by the hundreds," and it has been claimed that in it Kant "flatly

593

contradicts himself in almost every chapter." Still, the influence of his work, particularly on the writers and poets of the Romantic Era, has been tremendous, and any modern approach to the study of philosophy must deal with his assertions in one way or another.

During his later years Kant received, and rejected, invitations to lecture and teach in other universities. He died in Königsberg on February 12, 1804.

BIBLIOGRAPHICAL REFERENCES: The most important of Kant's writings are easily available in translation. A good introduction is Norman Kemp Smith, *Commentary on Kant's Critique of Pure Reason,* 1929 (rev. ed.). Another useful volume is *The Philosophy of Kant as Contained in Extracts from His Own Writings,* translated and edited by John Watson, 1908. See also H. S. Chamberlain, *Kant,* 1905; H. A. Pritchard, *Kant's Theory of Knowledge,* 1909; R. M. Winley, *Kant and His Philosophical Revolution,* 1911; A. D. Lindsay, *Kant,* 1934; Ernst Cassirer, *Rousseau, Kant, Goethe,* 1945; H. J. Paton, *Categorical Imperative: A Study of Kant's Moral Philosophy,* 1948; and A. Teale, *Kantian Ethics,* 1951. For an existentialist view see also Martin Heidegger, *Kant und das Problem der Metaphysik,* 1929. Two interesting comparative studies are G. W. Ardley, *Aquinas and Kant,* 1950; and Ludwig Muth, *Kleist und Kant,* 1954.

KAO TSE-CH'ENG

(Kao Ming)

Born: China
Date: c. 1305

Died: China
Date: c. 1368

PRINCIPAL WORK

DRAMA: The *P'i P'a Chi* (*Story of the Guitar,* sometimes *Lute Song*).

Tse-ch'eng is the *tzu* or derived name of Kao Ming, generally accepted as the author of *Story of the Guitar,* though one source gives the credit to a certain Kao Shih, who had the same *tzu.* Kao was a native of Wenchow in Chekiang. He passed his *chin-shih* examinations in 1345 and held minor government posts, first in his native province and later in Fukien.

When the uprisings which were to overthrow the Yuan dynasty broke out, he refused to become involved in such precarious political maneuvers. Holding himself aloof, he retired to the greater security of private life and took up residence in what is modern Ningpo.

It is said, as it is of many other writers who lived into the Ming dynasty, that he received an invitation to serve in the new government but declined the honor.

BIBLIOGRAPHICAL REFERENCES: See, in English, H. A. Giles, *History of Chinese Literature,* 1901. Studies in Chinese include Wang Kuo-wei, *Sung-yuan Hsi-ch'u Shih* (*History of Sung-Yuan Drama*), 1915; and Cheng Chen-to, *Chung-kuo Wen-hsueh Shih* (*History of Chinese Literature*), 1932.

SHEILA KAYE-SMITH

Born: St.-Leonard's-on-Sea, England
Date: February 4, 1887

Died: Northiam, Sussex, England
Date: January 14, 1956

PRINCIPAL WORKS

NOVELS: *The Tramping Methodist*, 1908; *Starbrace*, 1909; *Three Against the World*, 1914 [*The Three Furlongers*]; *Sussex Gorse*, 1916; *Tamarisk Town*, 1919; *Green Apple Harvest*, 1920; *Joanna Godden*, 1921; *The End of the House of Alard*, 1923; *The George and the Crown*, 1925; *Shepherds in Sackcloth*, 1930; *The History of Susan Spray*, 1931 [*Susan Spray*]; *Gallybird*, 1934; *Superstition Corner*, 1934; *Rose Deeprose*, 1936; *The Lardners and the Laurelwoods*, 1948.

SHORT STORIES: *Joanna Godden Married and Other Stories*, 1926; *A Wedding Morn*, 1928; *Faithful Stranger*, 1938.

POEMS: *Willow's Forge*, 1914; *Saints in Sussex*, 1923.

BELLES LETTRES: *John Galsworthy*, 1916; *Anglo-Catholicism*, 1925; *Mirror of the Months*, 1931; *Speaking of Jane Austen*, 1943 (with G. B. Stern); *More Talk of Jane Austen*, 1949 (with G. B. Stern); *The Weald of Kent and Sussex*, 1953.

AUTOBIOGRAPHY: *Three Ways Home*, 1937; *All the Books in My Life*, 1956.

Sheila Kaye-Smith was born on February 4, 1887 at St.-Leonard's-on-Sea, Sussex, the shire whose atmosphere she was to recapture in many of her novels. In her girlhood, as she relates in her autobiography, *Three Ways Home,* she had three ambitions: to live alone in the country, to become a famous novelist of rural life, and to be "extremely High Church." All three were realized, in a different form: she lived many years in Sussex, not alone but happily married to Theodore Penrose Fry; by her Sussex novels she achieved distinction, if not superlative fame; and, like her husband, who at the time of their marriage was a Church of England clergyman, she became in 1929 a Roman Catholic. Her father, a physician with a practice at Hastings, and her mother, the daughter of a French Huguenot who had emigrated from the Channel Islands to Scotland, were both Protestants. Although she describes herself as having been a nervous child, it seems unlikely that her early, abortive impulse toward Catholicism was prompted by any hostility

to her gentle and affectionate parents.

Miss Kaye-Smith has revealed her imaginative tendencies in childhood. Like the Brontë sisters at a comparable age, she created fictional characters and plots. By the time she was fifteen she had composed (but not written) between forty and fifty romances. In her last two years at school she wrote thirteen novelettes in exercise books. After the publication of two novels she underwent a spiritual crisis, becoming in turn an agnostic and a Swedenborgian. *Sussex Gorse*, her first major novel, appeared in 1916; in this period Miss Kaye-Smith was living in London, employed in government wartime service. She became interested in the Oxford Tractarian movement, and in *The Challenge to Sirius* (1917) she used its history, not with much sympathy, as background.

At the end of 1918, feeling a positive call to religious conversion, she became an Anglo-Catholic. The novels *Tamarisk Town, Green Apple Harvest,* and *Joanna Godden* followed this event but had no marked Anglo-Catholic

595

orientation. *The End of the House of Alard,* on the other hand, let her religious position be known. All these novels were well received; *Joanna Godden,* her first novel centering on the life of a woman, inaugurated her real success. All, moreover, were Sussex narratives, concerned with rural people and written with rich appreciation of their dialect. During these years Miss Kaye-Smith acquired the designation "Sussex novelist"; critics suggested a comparison of her work with that of the "Wessex novelist," Thomas Hardy.

After her marriage in 1924, Miss Kaye-Smith assisted her husband in his London parish. They moved to a Sussex farm, Little Doucegrove, some months before leaving the Church of England. There, until shortly before her death on January 14, 1956, she continued her writing. Her later work includes two studies of Jane Austen, written with the novelist G. B. Stern.

BIBLIOGRAPHICAL REFERENCES: Most of the essential details on Miss Kaye-Smith's life and personality have been presented in her two volumes of autobiography. For criticism see Robert T. Hopkins, *Sheila Kaye-Smith and the Weald Country,* 1925; Andrew E. Malone, "The Novelist of Sussex: Sheila Kaye-Smith," *Fortnightly Review,* CXX (1926), 199–209; and Karl Arns, "Sheila Kaye-Smith," *Zeitschrift für Englischen Unterricht,* XXVI (1927), 268–279.

JOHN KEATS

Born: Moorfields, London, England
Date: October 29 (or 31), 1795

Died: Rome, Italy
Date: February 23, 1821

PRINCIPAL WORKS

POEMS: *Poems,* 1817; *Endymion,* 1818; *Lamia, Isabella, The Eve of St. Agnes, and Other Poems,* 1820.

John Keats, English poet, was born October 29 or 31, 1795, in Moorfields, London, where his father managed a livery stable. John, the eldest child, had two brothers, George and Tom, and a sister Fanny. After the death of their father in 1804, and of their mother in 1810, the children were under the care of guardians. The boys attended school at Enfield where John became a close friend of Charles Cowden Clarke, the headmaster's son. Clarke introduced Keats to Spenser's *Faerie Queene,* which became the inspiration for his own first poetry.

In 1811 Keats was apprenticed to a surgeon in Edmonton. About this time he finished his first translation of the *Aeneid.* As a young medical student he worked steadily and passed his examinations before the Court of Apothecaries in 1816. Although he continued his studies in Guy's and St. Thomas's hospitals briefly, he was more interested in writing poetry.

In London Clarke showed Keats' verses to Leigh Hunt, who published in his newspaper Keats' first important poem, "On First Looking into Chapman's Homer" (1815). Hunt was a worthy man and kind to Keats, but from him Keats acquired many words and turns of phrase not considered "good" in the best English tradition. "Cockney," it was termed by the reviewers of Keats' first volume, *Poems,* published in 1817. He eventually overcame a great many of these faults, but the fact was that he was an urban Londoner associated in the minds of his contemporaries with the "cockney" world of Hunt. His consequent struggle was with his own natural virtues and talents and his opposing environmental factors.

His first work showed promise, though it was immature. He delighted in the world of eye, ear, and touch, and he made a constant effort to make the senses talk. Seeming to have hated abstractions of all sorts, his tendency was toward the concrete, individual object, rather than to use an image abstracted from many things and presented as a generality. In his imaginative projection of sensation into various other forms, Keats would ask, for example, how it might feel to be a ripple of water—and then proceeded to record his impression with intense poetical feeling.

In 1817 he went alone to the Isle of Wight and began work on *Endymion*, published the following year. Endowed with common sense and a decided critical ability, Keats tells us in the preface that *Endymion* is a splendid failure. But it is an excellent example of Keats' Hellenism at a time when Greek art was on exhibition in England. Hunt had earlier introduced him to Benjamin Robert Haydon, a painter who took Keats to see the Elgin marbles. Keats himself had some knowledge of Latin but none of Greek. He took from translations certain emotional elements of Greek civilization; the more unrestricted side intoxicated with beauty and color. The first line of *Endymion* is one of his most famous: "A thing of beauty is a joy forever."

After a walking tour of Scotland with Charles Armitage Brown in the summer of 1818, Keats developed tuberculosis. Prior to this his brother Tom had developed tuberculosis and brother George and his wife were starting to America to live. After Tom's death Keats lived with Brown at Hampstead and began work on *Hyperion*. There he fell completely in love with Fanny Brawne, an attractive seventeen-year-old girl who lived close by. Even though his health was failing rapidly, Keats, consumed with passionate love, began the most creative period of his life. Within the period of a year he completed "The Eve of St. Agnes," "La Belle Dame sans Merci," and the odes "To a Nightingale," "On a Grecian Urn," "To Psyche," and "On Melancholy." At Winchester he finished "Lamia" and wrote the ode "To Autumn." In February, 1820, Keats realized his illness was fatal. His last volume, *Lamia, Isabella, The Eve of St. Agnes, and Other Poems,* appeared in July, 1820.

An advance in technique can be seen in all these poems, especially in the narrative ones. "Isabella," started six months before the first draft of "The Eve of St. Agnes," shows the romantic tendency to dwell on detail rather than the telling of the story. Also, with Keats as an impassioned advocator of Isabella's cause, the story loses the classical aloofness of Boccaccio, from whom Keats took the tale. Ottava rima is its measure, suggestive of Chaucer, one of Keats' models along with Spenser (especially in his first works), Shakespeare, Milton, Dryden, and others. "The Eve of St. Agnes" uses medieval motifs, makes little attempt at narration, but is successful pictorially. "Lamia" is generally considered the most successful of these three narratives. The story is told in a classical, forthright manner and with vigor. "To Autumn" is viewed by most critics as a classic of pure description. It is his most impersonal poem, an example of how, as his art developed, he became less emotionally involved. Keats began with sensuousness, but throughout the short career of this extraordinarily talented young man, he tried to arrive at the best poetry he was capable of writing, not simply to force his art to serve any particular personal whimsies.

During the earlier part of his career he had arranged a sort of program of what he hoped to do in "Sleep and Poetry." For a time he would content himself with poetry of beautiful things that the senses can perceive. Afterward he would write noble poetry of agonies and strife. Never did he write didactic or moralistic poetry. Also, he had what may be called an anti-intellectual attitude toward poetry; he attempted to feel his way into the matter of the poem. The end result was that his later works were poetry of the highest order. He was the most promising of the Romantic poets.

Keats sailed in September, 1820, for Rome with his friend, Joseph Severn, an artist. He had a final relapse in Rome on December 10, and on February 23, 1821, he died. He was buried in the Roman Protestant Cemetery. At his wish his non-prophetic epitaph was, "Here lies one whose name was writ in water."

BIBLIOGRAPHICAL REFERENCES: The standard edition of the poems is H. W. Garrod, *The Poetical Works of John Keats*, 1939. H. B. Forman, *The Poetical Works and Other Writings of John Keats*, was revised by M. B. Forman, 8 vols., 1938–1939. M. B. Forman has also edited *The Letters of John Keats*, 1931 (rev. ed., 1947). Sidney Colvin, *John Keats: His Life and Poetry, His Friends, Critics, and After-Fame*, 1917, is the standard critical biography. Robert Gittings, *John Keats: The Living Year*, 1954, is a valuable work of criticism.

See also Amy Lowell, *John Keats*, 2 vols., 1925; J. Middleton Murry, *Keats and Shakespeare: A Study of Keats's Poetic Life from 1816 to 1820*, 1925; idem, *Studies in Keats, New and Old*, 1930; H. W. Garrod, *Keats*, 1926; C. D. Thorpe, *The Mind of John Keats*, 1926; M. R. Ridley, *Keats' Craftsmanship: A Study in Poetic Development*, 1933; C. L. Finney, *The Evolution of Keats' Poetry*, 2 vols., 1936; Douglas Bush, *Mythology and the Romantic Tradition in English Poetry*, 1937; W. J. Bate, *Negative Capability: The Intuitive Approach to Keats*, 1939; idem, *The Stylistic Development of John Keats*, 1945; and R. H. Fogle, *The Imagery of Keats and Shelley: A Comparative Study*, 1949.

GOTTFRIED KELLER

Born: Zurich, Switzerland
Date: July 19, 1819

Died: Zurich
Date: July 15, 1890

PRINCIPAL WORKS

NOVEL: *Der grüne Heinrich*, 1854–1855.

SHORT STORIES: *Die Leute von Seldwyla*, 1856–1874 (*The People of Seldwyla*); *Sieber Legenden*, 1872 (*Seven Legends*); *Der Züricher Novellen*, 1878 (*Short Novels of Zurich*); *Das Sinngedicht*, 1881.

POEMS: *Gesammelte Gedichte*, 1883.

Gottfried Keller, born at Zurich on July 19, 1819, is the outstanding Swiss writer of poetic realism. His father died when he was young and he was first apprenticed to a landscape painter. But as the result of his interest in politics he published some verses in 1846 which made possible a brief interim of formal study at Heidelberg.

An abortive attempt at writing drama resulted in his turning to the novel and short story. Written in German, his short stories still are considered the best in that language. *The People of Seldwyla*, for example, is a collection of tales presenting an imaginary town in Switzerland but describing accurately the people, customs, emotions, and tragedies which are typical of Swiss life. His first novel is an autobiographical work resembling *Wilhelm Meister* (1795) in its philosophical overtones. In his later novellas dealing with Zurich life he turned to patriotic motifs with religious overtones.

In all his writing Keller was a spokesman of democracy, a man with an easy tolerance, a belief in the good in human nature, and a kindly humor. Although tolerant, he was not without strong convictions. In *Martin Salander* (1886), an unfinished novel, Keller struck out at shallowness and political intrigue while affirming his faith in the stability and soundness of Swiss democracy. His style, in fiction and poetry, is simple, colorful, sincere, and heartwarming in its humanitarianism. He is considered the most beloved writer of Switzerland. He died in Zurich on July 15, 1890.

BIBLIOGRAPHICAL REFERENCES: An edition of Keller's *Gesammelte Werke* was published in Berlin, 8 vols., 1908–1912. For biography and criticism see Albert Köster, *Gottfried Keller*, 1907; Edward F. Hauch, *Gottfried Keller as a Democratic Idealist*, 1916; August Krehbiel, *Gottfried Keller's Attitude toward Literary Criticism and Theory*, 1918; Thomas Roeffler, *Gottfried Keller: ein Bildnis*, 1931; E. Ackerknecht, *Gottfried Keller*, 1939; and William I. Schreiber, "Gottfried Keller's Use of Proverbs and Proverbial Expressions," *Journal of English and Germanic Philology*," LIII (1951), 514–523.

JOHN PENDLETON KENNEDY

Born: Baltimore, Maryland
Date: October 25, 1795

Died: Newport, Rhode Island
Date: August 18, 1870

PRINCIPAL WORKS

NOVELS: *Swallow Barn*, 1832; *Horse-Shoe Robinson*, 1835; *Rob of the Bowl*, 1838.
HISTORY AND BIOGRAPHY: *Defense of the Whigs*, 1843; *Memoirs of the Life of William Wirt*, 1849; *The Border States*, 1861; *Mr. Ambrose's Letters on the Rebellion*, 1865.

John Pendleton Kennedy, son of a distinguished and well-to-do Baltimore family, was born on October 25, 1795. He spent his early years studying the classics, attending the theater, participating in debating societies and, later, preparing himself for a career in the law. Shortly after his graduation from Baltimore College, Kennedy interrupted his plans to volunteer in the

War of 1812. After his return from active duty he practiced law, found its details boring, and took every free moment to read and write "the humanizing generalities of literature. . . ."

By 1820, elected to the Maryland legislature, he had taken a firm stand in opposition to slavery. In the years that preceded the Civil War he did his utmost to placate the extremists of both North and South, and carried on a voluminous correspondence with men of influence in both sections in an effort to solve some of the problems and hostilities. A member of Congress from Maryland, 1838–1839 and 1841–1845, he fought for a Congressional appropriation to test Morse's telegraph; it was largely as a result of Kennedy's persistence that the appropriation was made. He also served as Secretary of the Navy, 1852–1853.

Politically, Kennedy was a Unionist. He believed that the South had no right to secede because the states "did not exist before the union of the Revolution but [were] derived from that union." When the conflict broke out he did everything he could of a humanitarian nature to ease the miseries of those affected by it.

Kennedy had married Elizabeth Gary, the daughter of a wealthy cotton mill owner, in 1829. His own resources and those into which he had married enabled him to lead an untroubled and aristocratic life. Kennedy used some of his money to support struggling artists, because he felt that "his own prosperous circumstances gave them a claim upon his kindness." For a time he was the patron of Edgar Allan Poe, who regarded Kennedy's *Horse-Shoe Robinson* as a book that would place its author "in the very first rank of American novelists." This novel, a tale of the American Revolution, was preceded by *Swallow Barn,* a story of plantation life in Virginia, the first of many such works to be set in that state.

Some critics hold that Kennedy's marriage into wealth was a turning point in his career, and that he became conservative and undemocratic as a result of it. But the support he gave to literary figures, his political humanitarianism, and the tone of genial gentility which characterizes his novels and personal correspondence seem to indicate that Kennedy's wealth did little more than to permit him to broaden his sympathies and to give them the material support his money could provide. He died at Newport, Rhode Island, August 18, 1870.

BIBLIOGRAPHICAL REFERENCES: *The Collected Works of John Pendleton Kennedy,* 10 vols., 1871, includes the authorized biography by Henry T. Tuckerman, *The Life of John Pendleton Kennedy.* The only other full-length biography is Edward M. Gwathmey, *John Pendleton Kennedy,* 1931. Valuable introductions appear in Jay B. Hubbell's edition of *Swallow Barn,* 1929, and in Ernest E. Leisy's edition of *Horse-Shoe Robinson,* including a useful bibliography, 1937. Of primary interest is Hubbell, *The South in American Literature,* 1954. See also John E. Uhler, "Kennedy's Novels and his Posthumous Works," *American Literature,* III (1932), 471–479.

SØREN KIERKEGAARD

Born: Copenhagen, Denmark
Date: May 5, 1813

Died: Copenhagen
Date: November 11, 1855

RELIGIOUS PHILOSOPHY: *Enten-Eller*, 1843 (*Either/Or*); *Gjentagelsen*, 1843 (*Repetition*); *Frygt og Baeven*, 1843 (*Fear and Trembling*); *Philosophiske Smuler*, 1844 (*Philosophical Fragments*); *Begrebet Angst*, 1844 (*The Concept of Dread*); *Stadier paa Livets Vej*, 1845 (*Stages on Life's Way*); *Afsluttende uvidenskabelig Efterskrift*, 1846 (*Concluding Unscientific Postscript to the Philosophical Fragments*); *Opbyggelige Taler i forskjellig Aand*, 1847 (*Edifying Discourses in Various Spirits*); *Christelige Taler*, 1848 (*Christian Discourses*); *Sygdommen til Doden*, 1849 (*The Sickness Unto Death*); *Synspunkter for min Forfattervirksomhed*, 1849 (*The Point of View for My Work as an Author*); *Indøvelse i Christendom*, 1850 (*Training in Christianity*).

Søren Aabye Kierkegaard was born on May 5, 1813, in a great house facing the New Market Square in Copenhagen, and he spent his life in that city while devoting most of his efforts to the development and communication of a philosophy and way of life that was his personal response to the Christian religion and to the world about him. Although his early work expressed more of a faith in philosophy than in religion, he is the founder of Christian existentialism, and his work has influenced in a profound way such thinkers as Ibsen, Heidegger, Jaspers, and Barth. Many of his ideas have been incorporated also into the works of atheistic existentialists like Sartre and Camus.

Kierkegaard's father, Michael Pedersen Kierkegaard, was driven by a compelling sense of anxiety and guilt because as a child, while tending sheep in the cold, he had cursed God for allowing him to suffer. Søren was the seventh child of Michael Kierkegaard's second wife; the first wife died childless after two years of married life. The family was prosperous since Michael Kierkegaard had been brought to Copenhagen by his uncle and had built a small business into a flourishing concern; when his first wife died, he retired (at the age of forty) and lived on his securities. The father was a strict patriarch, profoundly religious and melancholy. His dominance was a continuous and depressing influence on his children, and it probably played an important part in affecting Søren's attitudes toward Christianity. Nevertheless, it appears that his childhood was on the whole a happy one, possibly because of the careful attention and good humor of his mother, Ane Sørensdatter Lund.

As a result of the various influences upon him, Søren Kierkegaard developed the conviction that he was somehow intended to be a sacrifice, and that it was his mission in life to rebel against the God who made suffering. Only gradually, as the years passed, did these beliefs disappear.

A fall from a tree injured his back and probably led to a series of ailments that plagued him during his lifetime; the injury may have been connected also with the final illness that resulted in his death.

Kierkegaard entered the University of Copenhagen in 1830. A series of deaths, including the death of his mother, had reduced the Kierkegaard family to the father, Søren, and one brother by 1834. In that year or the following a moral revelation, never made entirely explicit, from the father to the son so affected Søren Kierkegaard that he referred to it as "the great earthquake." It seems probable that the father had engaged in sensual crimes, and had perhaps violated the woman who later became his second wife. The presentiment or knowledge of his father's crimes and guilt aroused a sense of anguish and dread in Søren Kierkegaard, and he became estranged from his father and from God. Before his father's death in 1838, however, father and son were reconciled.

He returned to the practice of Christian communion and began to explore the possibility that the subjective is the sign of truth, and that religion is more of a revelation of reality than philosophy. In 1840 he received his theology degree from Copenhagen, and in the same year became engaged to Regina Olsen. He finally broke the engagement because he thought that the necessity for keeping secret his father's guilt made marriage impossible.

Kierkegaard's major philosophical works, published under pseudonyms, appeared in the period 1843 to 1846. His "Edifying Discourses," published at various times, were under his own name and were intended to make clear the religious intention of his other works. He was persecuted after an attack on the *Corsair,* a comic journal, by having his works ridiculed in the paper, and he was often involved in controversy. Shortly before his death, on November 11, 1855, at Copenhagen, he made his criticism of "official Christianity" clear in a series of pamphlets entitled *The Instant.* His work was a reflection of a progression in action from the aesthetic to the ethical and finally to the religious. He died believing in God but not in communion from the hands of a parson, a "royal functionary."

BIBLIOGRAPHICAL REFERENCES: Recent biographical and critical studies of Kierkegaard are so extensive that only a selective listing will be possible. The standard biography is Johannes Hohlenberg, *Søren Kierkegaard,* 1948 (trans. 1954). Representative selections from his works, most of which are available in translation, have been collected by Robert Bretall in *A Kierkegaard Anthology,* 1951. See also E. L. Allen, *Kierkegaard: His Life and Thought,* 1935; J. A. Bain, *Søren Kierkegaard: His Life and Religious Teaching,* 1935; Walter Lowrie, *Kierkegaard,* 1938, and *A Short Life of Kierkegaard,* 1942; T. H. Coxall, *Kierkegaard Studies,* 1948, and *Kierkegaard Commentary,* 1956; M. C. Pearce, *Søren Kierkegaard: A Study,* 1948; Rudolph Friedmann, *Kierkegaard,* 1949; William Hubben "Kierkegaard," in *Four Prophets of Our Destiny,* 1952; James Daniel Collins, *The Mind of Kierkegaard,* 1953; and Arland Ussher, *Journey Through Dread: A Study of Kierkegaard, Heidegger, and Sartre,* 1955.

CHARLES KINGSLEY

Born: Holne, England
Date: June 12, 1819

Died: Eversley, England
Date: January 23, 1875

PRINCIPAL WORKS

NOVELS: *Alton Locke,* 1850; *Yeast,* 1851; *Hypatia,* 1853; *Westward Ho!* 1855; *Two Years Ago,* 1857; *Hereward the Wake, "Last of the English,"* 1866.
FAIRY TALE: *The Water Babies,* 1863.

Charles Kingsley, born in Holne, Devonshire, England, on June 12, 1819, was the son of an Anglican clergyman. Although three sons of the family, Charles, George Henry, and Henry, became famous as authors in Victorian England, Charles was the most famous. After an unimpressive record at school, he entered King's College in London when he was seventeen. Matriculation at King's College was probably for the convenience of the family, for Charles' father had become rector of a church in London. After two years, however, Charles Kingsley left to finish his education at Cambridge University. While still at Cambridge he met Fanny Grenfell and fell in love with her, but her family was opposed to the match because Kingsley had already made for himself a reputation as a rather wild and radical young man who followed Samuel Taylor Coleridge, Thomas Carlyle, and Frederick Denison Maurice in his thinking.

After graduation from Cambridge, Kingsley was ordained as an Anglican clergyman and sent as a curate to Eversley, on the edge of Windsor Forest, in Hampshire. In 1844 he succeeded to the living at Eversley as rector and married Fanny Grenfell. In addition to his work as a clergyman he had begun to write, having started a biography of St. Elizabeth of Hungary in 1842. The biography turned out eventually to be a poetic drama, *The Saint's Tragedy* (1848). During the early years of his marriage, Kingsley augmented his slender income by teaching and lecturing. But in 1848, a year of revolution in Europe as well as the

year of the publication of Kingsley's first book, the young clergyman began to take an active interest in Christian Socialism, and wrote a number of papers and pamphlets in support of the movement. Thus his first two novels, *Alton Locke* and *Yeast,* reflect his interest and enthusiasm for reform. The latter novel appeared in part in *Fraser's Magazine* in 1848, but it was discontinued because of its so-called radicalism. Kingsley's idea of reform, then misunderstood, was not one of revolution; rather it was the awakening of the higher classes to their real responsibilities for the masses. The period 1848 to 1851 was a difficult one in many ways for Kingsley. He suffered from health so poor that he had to give up within a few months an appointment in 1848 as professor of English literature at Queen's College, London.

By 1851, Kingsley's health had improved and he had also solved many of his problems and misunderstandings about reform. *Hypatia,* his next novel, presented a vivid picture of a past social state. His wife became ill in 1853 and had to leave Eversley. With her on an enforced vacation, Kingsley wrote his novel of romantic adventure entitled *Westward Ho!*

As the years passed, the feelings which had run against him as a young man disappeared in conservative circles. In 1859 he was appointed one of the chaplains in ordinary to Queen Victoria, an honorary post. In 1860 he was appointed professor of modern history at Cambridge. A popular juvenile book, *Water Babies,* was written to entertain his younger children. Kingsley's controversy with John Henry Newman in 1864 led to the latter's famous *Apologia pro vita sua* (1864).

During the early 1870's Kingsley was honored with several church appointments, but ill health kept him from arduous duties. He and his wife toured Canada and the United States in 1874, after visiting their son in the United States. Kingsley's health declined until his death at Eversley, Hampshire, on January 23, 1875.

BIBLIOGRAPHICAL REFERENCES: The standard biography is Margaret F. Thorp, *Charles Kingsley, 1819–1875*, 1937. Still of interest for its domestic pictures is Mrs. Kingsley's *Charles Kingsley: His Letters and Memories of His Life*, 1877. See also Guy Kendall, *Charles Kingsley and His Ideas*, 1947; Una Pope-Hennessy, *Canon Charles Kingsley*, 1949; and Stanley T. Williams, "*Yeast*: A Victorian Heresy," *North American Review*, CCXII (1920), 697–704.

HENRY KINGSLEY

Born: Barnack, England
Date: January 2, 1830

Died: Cuckfield, England
Date: May 24, 1876

PRINCIPAL WORKS

NOVELS: *The Recollections of Geoffrey Hamlyn*, 1859; *Ravenshoe*, 1862; *Austin Elliott*, 1863; *The Hillyars and the Burtons*, 1865; *Leighton Court*, 1866; *Silcote of Silcotes*, 1867; *Stretton*, 1869; *Mademoiselle Mathilde*, 1868; *Old Margaret*, 1871; *Hetty*, 1871; *Oakshott Castle*, 1873.

FANTASY: *The Boy in Grey*, 1871.

Henry Kingsley, born at Barnack, Northamptonshire, England, on January 2, 1830, was the son of an Anglican clergyman and a younger brother of Charles Kingsley, the well-known Victorian novelist. Henry Kingsley, never so successful as his older brother during his lifetime, is today given higher rank by many English critics. After some time at the King's College School, in London, Henry Kingsley went to Oxford University in 1850, to stay for three years. As a student at Oxford he was neither successful nor very conscientious, preferring to spend his time in social and athletic pursuits. He not only wasted his three academic years at the university, but he also ran himself seriously into debt. A timely inheritance paid off his indebtedness, and in 1853 he migrated to Australia to seek his fortune in the Australian goldfields. Unsuccessful in his search for gold, he worked at all kinds of minor jobs to make a living. While in Australia he began to write his first novel, *The Recollections of Geoffrey Hamlyn*.

Kingsley returned to England in 1858, and his novel about the Australian goldfields appeared the following year. Following its success, Kingsley, then living with his parents, began to contribute to various periodicals and wrote a second successful novel, *Ravenshoe*.

In 1864, Kingsley married Sarah Maria Kingsley Haselwood, a cousin, and they settled in a cottage at Wargrave, in Berkshire. Among Kingsley's friends by that time were such notables as Matthew Arnold, George Meredith, and Algernon Charles Swinburne. Since the author's income was insufficient to take care of his hospitality and the costs of his wife's illnesses, and his later novels failed to meet with public approval as expressed in sales, financial pressure finally caused him to become editor of the Edinburgh *Daily Review* in 1869. He was unsuited to newspaper editorship however, and in 1870, when the outbreak of the Franco-Prussian War provided an excuse, he seized it to go to the Continent as a war correspondent. He returned to England in the following year, left the newspaper shortly afterward, and resumed, in London, the writing of fiction. A fantasy, *The Boy in Grey*, and two novels, *Old Margaret* and *Hetty*, all published in 1871, proved failures upon publication. At her husband's insistence, Kingsley's wife sought financial aid from Charles Kingsley, her husband's brother. Assistance was forthcoming at first, but continued requests were more than the Charles Kingsleys were able or willing to meet.

Henry Kingsley wrote and published several other novels, but none was successful with critics or the reading public. Kingsley himself considered *Oakshott Castle* his best book. The Kingsley fortunes continued downward, although a small inheritance in 1873 kept him and his wife from outright poverty. Shortly after his brother's death in 1875, Henry Kingsley was found to have cancer of the throat and mouth. He resolved to leave London to spend his last months in the English countryside. He took a cottage in Cuckfield, in Sussex, where he died a few months later, on May 24, 1876.

BIBLIOGRAPHICAL REFERENCES: There is no extensive body of biographical or critical material available on Kingsley, aside from that in the standard histories of the English novel. See S. M. Ellis, *Henry Kingsley, 1830–1876*, 1931.

RUDYARD KIPLING

Born: Bombay, India
Date: December 30, 1865

Died: London, England
Date: January 18, 1936

PRINCIPAL WORKS

POEMS: *Departmental Ditties*, 1886; *Barrack Room Ballads*, 1892; *The Seven Seas*, 1896; *Recessional and Other Poems*, 1899; *The Five Nations*, 1903; *The Years Between*, 1919; *Rudyard Kipling's Verse*, 1940.

SHORT STORIES: *In Black and White*, 1888; *Plain Tales from the Hills*, 1888; *Soldiers Three*, 1888; *Under the Deodars*, 1888; *Life's Handicap*, 1891; *Many Inventions*, 1893; *The Day's Work*, 1898; *Traffics and Discoveries*, 1904; *A Diversity of Creatures*, 1917; *Debits and Credits*, 1926; *Limits and Renewals*, 1932.

CHILDREN'S STORIES: *The Jungle Book*, 1894; *The Second Jungle Book*, 1895; *Captains Courageous*, 1897; *Stalky & Co.*, 1899; *Just-So Stories*, 1902; *Puck of Pook's Hill*, 1906; *Rewards and Fairies*, 1910.

NOVELS: *The Light That Failed*, 1890; *The Naulahka: A Story of West and East*, 1892 (with Wolcott Balestier); *Kim*, 1901.

TRAVEL SKETCHES: *Letters of Marque*, 1891; *From Sea to Sea*, 1899; *Letters of Travel*, 1920.

Joseph Rudyard Kipling was born in Bombay on December 30, 1865; born at some distance from the center of empire, he was to become one of the chief expressers of the ideas that allowed the English to regard their great power with complacency or optimism. To many contemporary eyes, he justified the "white man's burden"; he also showed how it could be carried with efficiency and dignity.

Kipling was the first child of John Lockwood Kipling, architectural sculptor at the Bombay School of Arts, and Alice Macdonald Kipling. Both parents were children of Methodist ministers and contributed to the Biblical accent in many of Kipling's works. Like many other Anglo-Indian children, Kipling was sent to England for his education. Since he was nearsighted, Kipling could take little part in athletics; instead he spent his spare time writing for and editing the school paper at the United Services College at Westward Ho!, North Devon, the school that is portrayed in *Stalky & Co.* His school journalism led to professional journalism when Kipling returned at seventeen to India to work on the staff of the Lahore *Civil and Military Gazette.* Various assignments for this paper and the Allahabad *Pioneer* gave Kipling the opportunity to travel and provided abundant material for his books, which were then beginning to appear. From the publication of *Departmental Ditties* in 1886, the young writer found a wide—some would say a predestined—public for his poetic and narrative impressions of the Indian subcontinent as viewed from a certain distance. It was a dis-

tance, later critics have suggested, in which full knowledge and considerable condescension are mingled, in which sympathy and impatience are paradoxically mingled. This, certainly, is the note that is struck in *Plain Tales from the Hills* and it is a note that sounds, with some variations, throughout his work.

Kipling's own life, as a summary indicates, was full of the motion and change that many of his contemporaries regarded as the mark of a notable man. Kipling left India and spent three years of travel that took him to every continent. In the United States he married in 1892 Miss Caroline Starr Balestier of Vermont; there he lived until 1896, when, because of a disagreement with his brother-in-law, the Kiplings went to England to live. Kipling continued to win both great financial rewards and fame by work as a writer, literary and journalistic. He did not, and here he differed from many writers who are taken more seriously by contemporary criticism, turn aside from the chance to cover newsworthy events. Thus, he went as a newspaper correspondent on English naval cruises, made a second visit to America, and went to South Africa to report on the English forces in the Boer War. So great was the popular veneration for Kipling that his checks were preserved rather than cashed, his signature being worth more than the amount of the check. Kipling in his later years continued to mingle writing and action and covered events in World War I.

Kipling's greatest honor lay in the indefatigable public that responded to his vivid, decided insights into the role of beneficent imperialism and, more sensitively, into the differences between cultures brought into startling contact by conquest (e.g., *Kim*, 1901). But he was also the recipient of many specific honors, such as the Doctor of Laws degree from McGill University (1899), the Doctorate of Letters, Oxford (1907), and Cambridge (1908). Further, when in 1907 he became the first Englishman to win the Nobel Prize for Literature, it became apparent that his special sort of greatness was recognized beyond the confines of the English-speaking world. That he failed to become poet laureate on three possible occasions was—twice at least—the result of temporary difficulties rather than a reflection on his eminence; in 1892 he was in disfavor with Victoria, to whom he had referred as "the widow of Windsor," and in 1930 there was concern over Russia's reaction to honors accorded a poet who had once referred to Russia as "the bear that walks as a man."

Kipling died in London, January 18, 1936. He was buried in the Poet's Corner of Westminster Abbey, between Dickens and Hardy, between a writer who had been both popular and great and one who had been chiefly great. As a survey of criticism suggests, it is still an open question whether Kipling was great as well as popular, whether Kipling is—like both Dickens and Hardy—for the ages or interestingly symptomatic of his own times. On the day after Kipling's death, General Sir Ian Hamilton wrote in the London *Observer*: "His death seems to me to place a full stop to the period when war was a romance and the expansion of our Empire a duty." Kipling's whole literary output

was a brilliant expression of an attitude later out of favor. He urged action at the expense of refinement of perception and rigorous analysis of the presuppositions on which action rests. He prolonged Carlyle's gospel of work and the hero; he seemed unsympathetic to democracy and many liberal causes, such as the emancipation of women; and his veneration for the signs and tools of material progress has seemed to some persons uncritical. In Kipling's eyes, neither the resolute man nor the steam engine could do wrong.

That the judgment of Kipling is not closed is indicated by the fact that T. S. Eliot could, in 1942, write seriously of Kipling. Eliot points out that Kipling writes transparently, "so that our attention is directed to the object and not to the medium." Kipling had great economy of words, had an "unsurpassed" ability with ballads, and was in "Recessional" a great hymn writer. One might add to this praise the observation that Kipling's energy was poured out in a variety of forms in a way that few more recent writers can imitate. Though *The Light That Failed* was Kipling's only attempt at the conventional novel, he poured out tales for adult readers, tales for children (e.g., *The Jungle Books, Just-So Stories*, and *Captains Courageous*), and poetry stirring to persons of differing ages. It is this manly variety that is his distinguishing mark. It is possible to accuse him, as did Richard Le Gallienne, of honoring "everywhere the brute and the bully." But such a judgment overlooks the perceptiveness and even the tenderness that, paradoxically, are interwoven with that which is strikingly typical and topical.

607

BIBLIOGRAPHICAL REFERENCES: Of the various collected editions of Kipling's work the Burwash Edition, 28 vols., 1941, is definitive. The authorized biography is Charles Edmund Carrington's *The Life of Rudyard Kipling*, 1956. See also W. M. Hart, *Kipling the Story-Writer*, 1918; R. T. Hopkins, *Rudyard Kipling: A Character Study*, 1921; Patrick Braybrooke, *Kipling and His Soldiers*, 1926; G. C. Beresford, *Schooldays with Kipling*, 1936; F. F. Van de Water, *Rudyard Kipling's Vermont Feud*, 1937; Edward Shanks, *Rudyard Kipling: A Study in Literature and Political Ideas*, 1940; Hilton Brown, *Rudyard Kipling: A New Appreciation*, 1945; Rupert Croft-Cooke, *Rudyard Kipling*, 1948; and Bonamy Dobree, *Rudyard Kipling*, 1951; also André Maurois, *Prophets and Poets*, 1935; Edmund Wilson, *The Wound and the Bow*, 1941; Lionel Stevenson, "The Ideas in Kipling's Poetry," *University of Toronto Quarterly*, I (1932), Edith Merielees, "Time and Mr. Kipling," *Virginia Quarterly Review*, XI (1935), 37–46; and 467–489; Basil Williams, "Rudyard Kipling," *Nineteenth Century*, CXIX (1937), 291–302.

Two recent books of selections with critical introductions are *A Choice of Kipling's Verse*, edited by T. S. Eliot, 1942; and *A Choice of Kipling's Prose*, edited by W. Somerset Maugham, 1952.

HEINRICH VON KLEIST

Born: Frankfort-on-Oder, Germany   *Died:* Near Potsdam, Germany
Date: October 18, 1777   *Date:* November 21, 1811

PRINCIPAL WORKS

PLAYS: *Die Familie Schroffenstein*, 1803 (*The Feud of the Schroffensteins*); *Penthesilea*, 1808; *Der Zerbrochene Krug*, 1808 (*The Broken Jug*); *Das Käthchen von Heilbronn*, 1810; *Der Prinz von Homburg*, 1821 (*The Prince of Homburg*).
NOVELLA: *Erzählungen*, 1810.

Heinrich (Wilhelm) von Kleist was a man of many moods, all of which show up in his plays and novelettes and occasional poetry. A native of Frankfort, he was born on October 18, 1777, and had a slight education before he joined the Prussian Army in 1792. He soon tired of military life and, desiring to study philosophy and law in Frankfort, retired as a lieutenant in 1799. His studies were brief, and in 1800 he secured a post in the Ministry of Finance in Berlin. Abandoning this position before long, Kleist then traveled in Europe before he went to Switzerland and settled down to write. He soon became dissatisfied with his work here, however, and returned to Berlin in 1802. He visited

Goethe and Schiller at Weimar, but remained discouraged about his own writing. After further travels he returned to Frankfurt and in 1804 secured another government job.

Kleist's short life seemed destined for mishap. In 1807, on the way to Dresden, he was arrested by the French authorities as a spy and spent six months in prison. In the same year he settled in Dresden and with Adam Müller published the journal *Phöbus*, in which many of his poems appeared. When this project failed, Kleist went to Prague but stayed there only briefly before returning to Berlin to write editorials for the *Berliner Abendblätter*, a political journal.

Many times during his itinerant and

608

unsettled life, Kleist had offered one or another of his friends a suicide pact in which he offered to shoot the friend and then himself. In Henriette Vogel, for whom he is thought to have had a form of warped passion, he apparently found a friend of similar temperament. On November 21, 1811, she was found shot to death next to the body of Kleist, who had evidently carried out the pact he had so morbidly offered.

Although his work often received a cool reception during his lifetime, a fact which kept him on the borderline of poverty much of the time and in a state of depression for a large part of his life, Kleist achieved posthumous eminence as a dramatist and storyteller. He seemed to alternate between gloomy tragedy, as in *The Feud of the Schroffensteins* and *Penthesilea,* and realistic comedy, like *The Broken Jug.* His tragedy was stark and often gory, as in *The Prince of Homburg.* His outstanding novelette, *Michael Kohlhaas* (1810), is set in the Middle Ages and exemplifies a strong trait, perhaps the trait of Kleist's that explains his unsettled and turbulent life; he was a Romantic, possessing the gloom and world-weariness that so often characterized the Romantic of the late eighteenth and early nineteenth centuries. Most of his best work was not published until after his death, and thus he did not live to see the acceptance of his work as being in the best tradition of the Romantic period.

BIBLIOGRAPHICAL REFERENCES: A good introduction to Kleist in English is Richard March, *Heinrich von Kleist,* 1954. See also A. Conrad, *Heinrich von Kleist als Mensch und Dichter,* 1896; K. H. Becker, *Kleist and Hebbel,* 1904; F. Braig, *Heinrich von Kleist,* 1925; H. M. Woolf, *Kleist als politischer Dichter,* 1947; and Marthe Robert, *Heinrich von Kleist, dramaturge,* 1955. There is also an essay on Kleist in Stefan Zweig, *Baumeister der Welt,* 1951. For a discussion of the plays in their relation to the history of European drama see also Georg Brandes, *Main Currents in Nineteenth Century Literature,* II, 1906; and R. M. Smith, *Types of Historical Drama,* 1928. For an interesting recent comparative study see Ludwig Muth, *Kleist und Kant,* 1954.

ERIC KNIGHT

Born: Menston, Yorkshire, England   *Died:* Surinam
Date: April 10, 1897   *Date:* January 15, 1943

PRINCIPAL WORKS

NOVELS: *Song on Your Bugles,* 1936; *The Flying Yorkshireman,* 1938; *You Play the Black and the Red Comes Up,* 1938; *Now Pray We for Our Country,* 1940; *Lassie Come Home,* 1940; *This Above All,* 1941; *Sam Small Flies Again,* 1942.

The title of Eric (Mowbray) Knight's best-known story, *The Flying Yorkshireman,* might well be taken as figuratively descriptive of himself. He was born on April 10, 1897, in Yorkshire, where, at the age of twelve, he went to work in a textile factory. After various industrial jobs he joined members of his family who had emigrated to the United States. Intending an artistic career, he studied at the Boston Museum of Fine Arts and elsewhere.

He served in the Canadian Army during World War I and afterwards wrote for newspapers in Philadelphia, eventually specializing in dramatic criticism. In the early 1930's a film-writing assignment took him to Hollywood; later with his wife he settled in Pleasant Valley, Pennsylvania, to do free-lance writing. He revisited Yorkshire in 1938.

Knight will be remembered longest for his tales of the artful, irrepressible Sam Small, the Yorkshireman who mastered levitation, and for the novels *You Play the Black and the Red Comes Up* (published in 1938 under the pseudonym "Richard Hallas") and *This Above All*. The last was turned into a screenplay by Robert C. Sherriff.

In 1942, Knight was commissioned a major in the film unit of the Special Services section, United States Army. On January 15, the following year, he was among those killed when a United States military transport plane, bound for Africa, crashed in the Surinam jungle.

BIBLIOGRAPHICAL REFERENCES: Knight's letters to Paul Rotha have been edited by Rotha in *Portrait of a Flying Yorkshireman*, 1952. A biographical sketch is in *National Cyclopedia of American Biography*, 1942. Knight is interviewed in Robert Van Gelder, *Writers and Writing*, 1946. See also Elizabeth Montgomery, *The Story Behind Modern Books*, 1949.

ARTHUR KOESTLER

Born: Budapest, Hungary
Date: September 5, 1905

PRINCIPAL WORKS

NOVELS: *The Gladiators*, 1939; *Darkness at Noon*, 1940; *Arrival and Departure*, 1943; *Thieves in the Night*, 1946; *The Age of Longing*, 1951.

AUTOBIOGRAPHY: *Dialogue with Death*, 1938; *Scum of the Earth*, 1941; *Arrow in the Blue*, 1952; *The Invisible Writing*, 1954 (Second volume of *Arrow in the Blue*).

ESSAYS: *The Yogi and the Commissar*, 1945; *Insight and Outlook*, 1949; *Promise and Fulfillment*, 1949.

Arthur Koestler writes in his autobiographical *Arrow in the Blue* that his story is a "typical case-history of a central-European member of the educated middle classes, born in the first years of this century." It is true that Koestler's life is typical, not in the sense that he is an average European, but in the sense that on a personal plane he has lived through Europe's contemporary and continuing crisis brought about by the political presence of communism. He was an active Communist intellectual; he was imprisoned in Spain by the Fascists and sentenced to be executed; he was imprisoned by the French and English. When he broke with the Communist Party, he wrote one of the most effective novels of protest against it: *Darkness at Noon*. He has explained the attraction and repulsion of communism in his contribution to the collection of essays by former Communists, *The God That Failed* (1950), but for the whole story of his shifting back and forth between an ethics of conscience and an ethics of action one must go to his autobiographical works, to his novels, and to his essays—particularly to *The Yogi and the Commissar*.

Arthur Koestler's grandfather escaped from Russia during the Crimean War, when, for unknown reasons, the name Köstler, with variants of it, was adopted to hide his identity. Koestler's father, Henrik Köstler, was an energetic, would-be inventor, a maker of radioactive products, including soap, brass polish, and cleaning powder; his mother came from an old Jewish family of Prague. Arthur Koestler was born in Budapest, September 5, 1905. After the outbreak of World War I ruined the father's business, the family moved to Vienna and was never to have a permanent home again.

Koestler's interest in Zionism led him in 1926 to destroy the record of his studies at the University of Vienna. He went to Palestine to work for the Zionist movement, but after a probationary period, during which he worked in the fields, he was rejected. He suffered from poverty, failed as an architect, worked as a lemonade vender in Haifa, for a tourist agency, as a land surveyor's assistant, and as an editor (for three issues) of a German-language paper in Cairo. He finally secured a job as correspondent for the Ullstein chain of newspapers and was sent to Jerusalem in September, 1927. During the next four years he worked for Ullstein in the Middle East, Paris, and Berlin. One of his assignments was as correspondent on the Graf Zeppelin when it made an expeditionary flight to the North Pole region.

Koestler was a member of the Communist Party from 1931 to the spring of 1938. He traveled in the U.S.S.R. and in 1936 went to Spain ostensibly as correspondent for the London *News Chronicle*. In February, 1937, he was captured by the Fascists and for over three months expected execution. He was released after protests from England.

After being imprisoned as an alien by the French in the infamous camp Le Vernet, Koestler spent several months after his release in January, 1940, trying to get to England. He spent six weeks in Pentonville Prison in England and then joined the British Army. He worked for the Ministry of Information in London during the war. His *Darkness at Noon* and the two parts of *Arrow in the Blue* rank among the most revealing and influential anticommunist documents of our time.

BIBLIOGRAPHICAL REFERENCES: Koestler has told much of his own story in his autobiographical volumes: *Spanish Testament*, 1937; *Scum of the Earth*, 1941; *Arrow in the Blue*, 1952; and *The Invisible Writing*, 1954. A *New Yorker* sketch by Koestler, "The Koestler Saga," XXVIII (July 26, 1952), 21–22, supplies only family history. A good full-length study is John Alfred Atkins, *Arthur Koestler*, 1956. V. S. Pritchett, *Books in General*, 1953, includes a study of Koestler. Also of interest are Ben Ray Redman, "Arthur Koestler: Radical's Progress," *College English*, XIII (1951), 131–136; and Spencer Brown, "Arthur Koestler, the Mellow Machine Gun," *American Mercury*, LXXV (1952), 99–103.

THOMAS KYD

Born: London, England

Date: November, 1558

Died: London (?)

Date: 1594

PRINCIPAL WORKS

PLAYS: *The Spanish Tragedy,* c. 1585; sometimes attributed, *Arden of Feversham,* 1592 (in collaboration).

TRANSLATIONS: *The Householder's Philosophie,* 1588; *Cornelia,* 1593.

Thomas Kyd was born in London in November, 1558. Son of a London scrivener, he was educated at Merchant Taylors School, where he was probably contemporary with Spenser. It is unlikely that he proceeded to a university, and little is known about the rest of his life save that, in 1593, he was arrested and charged with some libel which concerned the state. His rooms were searched and certain allegedly atheistical papers were found. He disclosed, under torture, that these were Marlowe's. He died in 1594, a year after his release, apparently in penury and disowned by his parents.

The Kyd canon is hopelessly indeterminate. Certainty attaches to his two translations, *The Householder's Philosophie* and *Cornelia,* and it is highly probable that *The Spanish Tragedy,* dated c. 1585, is wholly his. A sensational pamphlet, *The Murder of John Brewen,* has been ascribed to Kyd on ambiguous evidence, and his claim to the lurid tragedy of *Soliman and Perseda* (1592) is by no means established. A fair case exists for regarding him as, at least, part author of the powerful domestic tragedy, *Arden of Feversham.* The trouble is that *The Spanish Tragedy,* like Marlowe's *Tamburlaine,* was widely imitated, so that much of the internal evidence cited by critics is suspect. A punning allusion by Nash in 1589 suggests, though it does not prove, that Kyd wrote the play of *Hamlet* on which Shakespeare's masterpiece was based.

The Spanish Tragedy, on which Kyd's reputation and importance alike depend, is perhaps the most influential play ever written. The story of the revenge of Hieronimo and Belimperia is transformed into roaring melodrama which has little formal structure and is tragedy only in the sense that it piles up deaths and atrocities. Elizabethan tragedy in the hands of Marlowe and Shakespeare soon rendered this kind of play obsolete, but the type of revenge pattern developed by Kyd proved more enduring. Many of his devices—the Stoic hero, the Machiavellian villain, the ghost, madness, procrastination, the play within a play, and others—remained part of the stock-in-trade, and Shakespeare turned all of them to account in *Hamlet.* It can, in fact, be argued that Shakespeare alone apprehended the broader implications of *The Spanish Tragedy:* its presentation of revenge as a fine art and its extension of tragedy from the individual to the state. Kyd's rhetoric and bombast, though long popular with the groundlings, were much ridiculed by later dramatists. There is much in *The Spanish Tragedy* that is linguistically preposterous, but the verse in its tenderer elegiac moments contains some exquisite cadences.

The 1602 edition of *The Spanish Tragedy* contains certain additional passages which were evidently intended to replace the dated scenes depicting Hieronimo's madness. Henslowe's diary reveals that Ben Jonson was paid for supplying certain additions in 1601 and 1602, but those printed in the quarto are quite un-Jonsonian. They are of extraordinary power and intensity and have been claimed for Webster by Lamb and FitzGerald, and for Shakespeare by Coleridge.

BIBLIOGRAPHICAL REFERENCES: The only complete edition is *The Works of Thomas Kyd*, edited by F. S. Boas, 1901. See also A. W. Ward, *History of English Dramatic Literature*, Vol. II, 1899; E. K. Chambers, *The Elizabethan Stage*, Vol. III, 1923; and *Dictionary of National Biography*, Vol. XI.

PIERRE CHODERLOS DE LACLOS

Born: Amiens, France
Date: October 19, 1741

Died: Taranto, Italy
Date: September 5, 1803

PRINCIPAL WORK

NOVEL: *Les Liaisons dangereuses*, 1782.

Pierre (Ambroise François) Choderlos de Laclos, born in Amiens, France, on October 19, 1741, was the type of Renaissance writer-fighter-politician, born too late. His family, Spanish in background, was less conspicuous than the name would imply, having gained it from an ancestor who was a valet to King Louis XIV.

Laclos' early life was that of a soldier, although he himself added a dimension to the usual military education by reading widely, especially in the early English novelists. While on duty as an artillery captain in Grenoble, he wrote verses and a libretto based on a novel, both insignificant. He wrote his celebrated novel, *Les Liaisons dangereuses*, while on a six-month leave from his post. This incendiary work caused the military great concern, but it won fame for its author and fifteen hundred francs. A number of articles, some critical of the army, finally forced Laclos to seek a discharge after twenty-eight years of service, but not before he had been made a Knight of St. Louis.

Laclos became secretary to the Duke of Orléans, at that time reported the richest man in France, and he soon became a court favorite in the dissolute years before the French Revolution. Although he went with the duke to England before the Revolution began, he himself was favorable to the common cause, having written many political articles on the subject. Later he returned to France and turned to pamphlet writing for the proletariat. A change of events brought Laclos back to the army, into prison, and finally to a position in which he was free to write, conduct experiments, and carry on political activities. He praised Napoleon and was rewarded by a command in the Army of Naples. But the rigors of life in the field and the organization of his group overtaxed his strength; he died at Taranto, Italy, on September 5, 1803. A collection of his letters was published in 1904 and a volume of his poems in 1908.

BIBLIOGRAPHICAL REFERENCES: For a study of Laclos in English see John G. Palache, *Four Novelists of the Old Regime: Crébillon, Laclos, Diderot, Bretonne*, 1926.

MADAME MARIE DE LA FAYETTE

Born: Paris, France   *Died:* Paris
Date: March 16, 1634   *Date:* May 25, 1693

PRINCIPAL WORKS

NOVELS: *La Princesse de Montpensier,* 1662; *Zaïde,* 1670; *La Princesse de Clèves,* 1678; *La Comtesse de Tende,* 1927.
MISCELLANEOUS: *Histoire de Madame Henriette d'Angleterre,* 1720; *Memoirs de la cours de France,* 1731.

Marie-Madeleine Pioche de la Vergne, later the Comtesse de La Fayette, was the daughter of Marc Pioche de la Vergne, a gentleman of Paris who was important enough to have the Marshal of France and a niece of Cardinal Richelieu as his daughter's godparents. Marie, born in Paris on March 16, 1634, was educated privately, but evidently was educated well; later, as lady-in-waiting to the queen, and as a member of the most intellectual circles of the capital, she was known for her wit and for her ability to converse freely in Latin. She was married to François, Comte de La Fayette, when she was twenty-two years old. The couple lived for a time at the count's country estate in Auvergne, but after she had borne her husband two children Mme. de La Fayette returned to Paris, to remain there for the rest of her life.

Her literary interests soon brought her to the attention of her most talented contemporaries; she became acquainted with Molière, and knew Scarron, Boileau, and Mme. de Scudéry as well. In her own court circles she was one of an intimate group that included Mme. de Sévigné and the Duc de La Rochefoucauld, with whom she shared a house until he died in 1680. Her best books were written during this period of literary and personal association.

It has been established beyond doubt that Mme. de La Fayette wrote the novels ascribed her, even though she denied them explicitly. Her second book, *Zaïde,* could possibly have been the work of Segrais, a scholar who served in her household until 1676 and who put his signature to the work, but modern scholarship doubts even that. Certainly *La Princesse de Montpensier, La Princesse de Clèves,* and *La Comtesse de Tende,* which, unpublished in her lifetime, was discovered in an eighteenth century magazine and printed in book form in 1927, show too great an understanding of court life and too great a restraint to have been written by anyone but this keenly intelligent and marvelously talented Frenchwoman who was literally a hundred years ahead of her time. Mme. de La Fayette died in Paris on May 25, 1693.

BIBLIOGRAPHICAL REFERENCES: An edition of Mme. de La Fayette's *Œuvres* appeared in 1928. Two volumes of her *Correspondence* were published in 1942. The standard life is Harry Ashton, *Madame de La Fayette, sa vie et ses œuvres,* 1922. See also C. A. Sainte-Beuve, *Portraits de femmes*, 1884; Émile Magne, *Madame de Lafayette en ménage*, 1926, and *Le Cœur et l'esprit de Madame de Lafayette*; and Martin Turnell, *The Novel in France*, 1950.

JEAN DE LA FONTAINE

Born: Château Thierry, France   *Died:* Paris, France
Date: July 8, 1621   *Date:* April 13, 1695

PRINCIPAL WORKS

FABLES IN VERSE: *Fables*, Books I–VI, 1668; *Fables*, Books VII–XI, 1673–1679; *Fables*, Book XII, 1694.

NOVELS: *Amours de Psyché et de Cupidon*, 1669; *Adonis*, 1669.

SHORT STORIES: *Contes*, 1665; *Nouveaux contes*, 1671.

POEMS: *Poème de la captivité de Saint Malo*, 1673; *Poème du Quinquina*, 1682.

PLAYS: *Ragotin*, 1684; *Le Florentin*, 1685; *La Coupe enchantée*, 1688.

One of the world's greatest writers of fables was an easy-going, absent-minded Frenchman, who was content to let others arrange his life. Jean de La Fontaine's parents were of the middle class. His father earned his living as forest ranger in the Duchy of Château Thierry, where La Fontaine was born on July 8, 1621, and where he was brought up. He studied at Rheims and at the age of twenty entered the seminary to prepare for a churchly career; however, his interest in law led to a change of vocation. In 1647, through family pressure, he married the well-to-do Marie Héricart, ten years younger than he, "a beautiful and chaste woman," according to one biographer, "who drove him to despair." They lived together for eleven years and had one son before their separation in 1658.

La Fontaine was thirty when he began his literary career. A friend of the dramatists Racine and Molière, he was encouraged in 1651 to adapt Terence's *Eunuchus* for the Paris stage. La Fontaine's version, *L'Eunuque*, was performed with fair success. Soon afterward he began versifying fables, some

suggested by Aesop, some original, and their popularity increased his literary reputation. In 1656 Nicholas Fouquet, Superintendent of Finances and the confidential agent of Cardinal Mazarin, bestowed an annual pension of 1,000 livres on La Fontaine in return for four poems a year. Fouquet's arrest for embezzlement in 1661 ended that pension, but the Duchess of Château Thierry then granted La Fontaine a living. The fondness of the Duke for Ariosto probably prompted La Fontaine to write his *Contes*, spicy retellings of Boccaccio as well as local scandals, published in 1665. In that same year he received an appointment as gentleman to the dowager Duchess of Orléans, who provided him with a home in the Luxembourg. When she died, Madame de la Sablière became a combination of mother and mistress to La Fontaine, and he lived at her house for the next twenty years. At her death, another admirer, Hervart, looked after this childlike person whose disregard of business matters and absent-mindedness became legendary.

615

In Paris, with his needs provided for, La Fontaine thought only of his writing. Friendship with Champmeslé (Charles de Chevillet, 1645–1701) interested him in writing operetta librettos and plays to be performed by the actress wife of his friend. But poetry always held his greatest interest. By 1668 he had collected enough of his *Fables* to publish them in six books, dedicated to the Dauphin of France. Ten years later five more volumes appeared with a prefatory eulogy to Mme. de Montespan, but this indirect appeal for royal favor failed because she was already being supplanted as the king's favorite. The final book of *Fables*, the twelfth, published in 1694, was dedicated to the young Duke of Burgundy.

La Fontaine was first proposed for membership in the Royal Academy in 1682, but Louis XIV and his Minister of Finance Colbert remembered the poet's friendship with Mazarin and other of their enemies and his election failed. The next year, after Colbert's death, La Fontaine and his friend Boileau were nominated at the same time. The Academicians, to the king's disgust, voted for La Fontaine. Louis neglected to sanction his admission until there was another vacancy, when La Fontaine and Boileau were both seated.

After a severe illness that made him repent of his frivolous writing, La Fontaine adapted some Psalms, engaged in moral meditation, and died at Hervart's house in Paris on April 13, 1695. He was buried in the Cemetery of the Holy Innocents.

BIBLIOGRAPHICAL REFERENCES: There are numerous modern translations of the Fables. See Edward Marsh, *Forty-two Fables*, 1924; *More Fables*, 1925; and *Collected Fables*, 1930; Joseph Auslander and Jacques Le Clercq, *The Fables of La Fontaine*, 1930; and Marianne Moore, *The Fables of La Fontaine*, 1954. For biography and criticism see Emile Faguet, *Jean de La Fontaine*, 1900; André Hallays, *Jean de La Fontaine*, 1922; Jean Giraudoux, *Les cinq tentations de La Fontaine*, 1938; Pierre Clarac, *La Fontaine*, 1947; and P. A. Wadsworth, *Young La Fontaine*, 1952.

PÄR LAGERKVIST

Born: Växjö, Sweden
Date: May 23, 1891

PRINCIPAL WORKS

NOVELS: *Det eviga leendet*, 1920 (*The Eternal Smile*); *Gäst hos verkligheten*, 1925 (*Guest of Reality*); *Bödeln*, 1933 (*The Hangman*); *Dvärgen*, 1944 (*The Dwarf*); *Barabbas*, 1949; *Sibyllan*, 1956 (*The Sibyl*).

SHORT STORIES: *Järn och människor*, 1915 (*Iron and Men*); *Onda sagor*, 1924 (*Evil Tales*); *I den tiden*, 1925 (*In That Time*); *Kämpande ande*, 1930 (*Struggling Spirit*); 1930; *The Eternal Smile and Other Stories*, 1954.

PLAYS: *Den osynlige*, 1923 (*The Invisible One*); *Han som fick leva om sitt liv*, 1928 (*He Who Lived His Life Over Again*); *Konungen*, 1932 (*The King*); *Bödeln*, 1934 (*The Hangman*); *Mannen utan själ*, 1936 (*The Man Without a Soul*), 1936; *Seger i mörker*, 1939 (*Victory in the Dark*); *Midsommardröm i fattighuset*, 1941

(*Midsummer Dream in the Poor House*); *Dramatik*, 1946 (*Collected Plays*); *Den vises sten*, 1947 (*The Philosopher's Stone*); *Låt människan leva*, 1949 (*Let Man Live*); *Barabbas*, 1953.

POEMS: *Ångest*, 1916 (*Anguish*); *Den lyckliges väg*, 1921 (*Path of the Happy*); *Hjärtats sånger*, 1926 (*Songs of the Heart*); *Vid lägereld*, 1932 (*By the Campfire*); *Genius*, 1937; *Sång och strid*, 1940 (*Song and Battle*); *Dikter*, 1941 (*Collected Poems*); *Hemmet och stjärnan*, 1942 (*The Home and the Star*); *Aftonland*, 1953 (*Evening Land*).

When Pär (Fabian) Lagerkvist received the Nobel Prize in 1951, the world was suddenly made aware of a new oracular voice, a teller of moral tales of severely classical pattern. But in his native Sweden, Lagerkvist had been a member of the Royal Academy of Eighteen since 1940 and had, as early as 1913, largely instigated the modern literary revolution in that country. Born of middle-class Lutheran parentage at Växjö, in the southern province of Småland, on May 23, 1891, Lagerkvist exposed himself only summarily to the academic education of Upsala (1911–1912); instead he plunged into a literary life that embraced all forms. In *Word Art and Picture Art* (1913) he applied the principles of cubistic painting to liberate lyric poetry from nineteenth century constraints; in *Theatre* (1918) he issued a powerful manifesto that perpetuated the expressionism of Strindberg and paved the way for his own dramas of fantasy. Equally important, in his first volume of poems, *Anguish*, he established the dark, lyrical tone that has characterized his work in every genre.

The Eternal Smile gathers folk elements into Lagerkvist's first important moral tale, one which becomes, as the title suggests, a kind of *divina commedia; Guest of Reality*, transparently autobiographical, reveals an almost pathological awareness of death in its luminous insights into childhood experience. The Nazification of Germany deepened Lagerkvist's political awareness to the point of his writing a series of Swiftian satires and that trenchant portrayal of brutality *The Hangman*, first successful as a novel and later as a play.

Lagerkvist's reputation began to be noised abroad with *The Dwarf*, in which a court retainer of the Florentine Renaissance becomes a symbol of that which is eternally twisted and malevolent in man. Ultimately Lagerkvist's focus came to bear on the meaning of a deity that could play so many searing cosmic jokes on mankind. In *Barabbas*, the novel which brought him the Nobel Prize, Lagerkvist examines the significance of Calvary through the guilt-ridden and very modern eyes of Barabbas, the thief whose reprieve released a cross to Christ.

"It is the measure of Lagerkvist's success," wrote André Gide, "that he managed so admirably to maintain his balance on a tightrope which stretches across the dark abyss that lies between the world of reality and the world of faith." But little faith reveals itself in *The Sibyl*, a taut and magnificent tale, unless it is a reaffirmed faith in human love. For in this fusion of Christian and classical myth, the divine is "neither noble nor sublime . . . but malignant and dangerous and fatal."

617

BIBLIOGRAPHICAL REFERENCES: For biographical and critical studies in the Scandinavian languages see G. M. Bergman, *Pär Lagerkvists Dramatik,* 1928; G. Fredén, *Pär Lagerkvist,* 1934; R. Fearnley, *Pär Lagerkvist,* 1950; Jöran Mjöberg, *Livsproblemet hos Lagerkvist,* 1951; *Pär Lagerkvist: Från Gudstanken till Barabbas,* 1952; and H. Schück et al., *Illustrerad Svensk Litteratur Historia,* Volume VIII, Stockholm, 1952.

Studies in English include Richard B. Vowles, "Pär Lagerkvist: Dramatist of the Soul," *Saturday Review of Literature,* XXXIV (December 1, 1951), 15, 54, 56; Lars Åhnebrink, "Pär Lagerkvist: a Seeker and a Humanist," *Pacific Spectator,* VI (1952), 400–412; N. Braybrooke, "Lagerkvist and his *Barabbas,*" *Queen's Quarterly,* LIX (1952), 367–372; W. Gustafson, "Pär Lagerkvist and his Symbols," *Books Abroad,* XXVI (1952), 20–23; Jöran Mjöberg, "Pär Lagerkvist and the Ancient Greek Drama," *Scandinavian Studies,* XXV (1953), 46–51; R. D. Spector, "The Limbo World of Pär Lagerkvist," *The American-Scandinavian Review,* XLIII (1955), 271–274; Richard B. Vowles, Introduction to *The Eternal Smile and Other Stories,* 1954, xi–xix; and, in somewhat revised form, "The Fiction of Pär Lagerkvist," *Western Humanities Review,* VIII (1954), 111–117.

SELMA LAGERLÖF

Born: Mårbacka, Värmland, Sweden
Date: November 20, 1858

Died: Mårbacka
Date: March 16, 1940

PRINCIPAL WORKS

NOVELS: *Gösta Berlings saga,* 1891 (*The Story of Gösta Berling*); *Jerusalem,* 1901–1902; *Liljecronas hern,* 1911 (*Lilliecrona's Home*); *Kejseren af Portugalien,* 1914 (*The Emperor of Portugallia*); *Bannlyst,* 1918 (*The Outcast*); *Löwensköldska ringen,* 1925 (*The Ring of the Löwenskölds: The General's Ring, Charlotte Löwensköld, Anna Svärd*).

TALES AND LEGENDS: *Osynliga länkar,* 1894 (*Invisible Links*); *En Herrgårdssägen* 1899 (*From a Sweidsh Homestead*); *Kristuslegender,* 1904 (*Christ Legends*); *Nils Holgerssons underbara resa genom Sverige,* 1906–1907 (*The Wonderful Adventures of Nils*).

AUTOBIOGRAPHY AND MEMOIRS: *Mårbacka,* 1922–1932 (*Mårbacka, Memories of My Childhood, The Diary of Selma Lagerlöf*).

MISCELLANEOUS: *Höst,* 1933 (*Harvest*).

Sweden, like the rest of Scandinavia, is one of the most energetically progressive and forward-looking nations of modern Europe. In the midst of its modernism, however, it still honors Selma (Ottiliana Lovisa) Lagerlöf, who was the romantic voice of a Sweden that is fast fading. By the last decade of the nineteeth century, Swedish literature was following the lead of the great realistic movement.

The style and subject matter had been set by Balzac, Flaubert and Zola, and serious artists were seeking ways to express the latest scientific discoveries in literary form. Into this cultural situation came a woman whose sensibility had been shaped by the folk legends of agrarian Sweden and who was not concerned with demonstrating scientific truths in literature. Selma Lagerlöf wrote *The Story of Gösta Berling* and

618

with this work began a long career as Sweden's leading romantic novelist.

One of a large family, Selma, born at Mårbacka on November 20, 1858, was a sickly child. At the age of three she was stricken with a disease, possibly poliomyelitis, that left her lame for the rest of her life. Unable to play with the other children, she read all the books on her father's large estate and absorbed the folk legends of Värmland from her grandmother and the servants. At fifteen she began to write poetry; at twenty-two she went to Stockholm to study for a teaching career. In 1882 she entered the Royal Women's Superior Training Academy and in 1885 she began teaching at a girl's school at Landskrŏiva in Skåne. She thought about the legends of her Värmland home and in 1890 began writing *The Story of Gösta Berling* in her spare time. She reworked the material many times, even experimenting with a poetic version, but she finally modeled her style on the romantic rhetoric of Thomas Carlyle, whose work she admired. When she learned that the literary magazine *Idun* was holding a competition, she entered her five completed chapters and won first prize. Soon after, the novel was published and had a resounding success; it broke all the rules of realistic writing, but it tapped the interest of the Swedish people in their immediate past.

Her next book, *Invisible Links*, was successful enough to allow her to support herself by writing. She left teaching in 1895 and began to travel on a grant arranged for her by King Oscar and Prince Eugene. Miss Lagerlöf toured the Near East in 1900 and in Jerusalem met a group of Dalecarlian peasants who had gone there in order to live like the first Christians. Attracted by their idealism, she wrote *Jerusalem*, a two-volume novel about the conflict of religious conviction with the peasant love for inherited farmland. The story sweeps from Sweden to Jerusalem and this scope, together with the fine characterizations, made Selfa Lagerlöf world famous.

When the National Teachers' Association commissioned her to write a group of stories telling of the folklore and geography of the various areas of Sweden, she produced the folk-fantasy known in translation as *The Wonderful Adventures of Nils*, a textbook that has become an enduring children's classic. Her trilogy, *The Ring of the Löwenskölds*, also had a great international success. It is a study of inherited character traits which are destroying a family until the curse is removed by a peasant girl.

Miss Lagerlöf's own values were firmly rooted in the Värmland earth. She lived most of her life at Mårbacka, the family manor, and cared for the tenant farmers until her death. In 1909 she became the first woman to win the Nobel Prize for literature and in 1914 the first woman to become a member of the Swedish Academy. The two great wars affected her deeply; she gave her Nobel gold medal to the Finnish defense fund shortly before her death at Mårbacka on March 16, 1940.

BIBLIOGRAPHICAL REFERENCES: Biographical and critical studies in English include Hanna Astrup Larsen, *Selma Lagerlöf*, 1932; and Alrik Gustafson, *Six Scandinavian Novelists*, 1940. There is also W. A. Berendsohn's *Selma Lagerlöf*, 1931, an abridged translation of the German edition of 1927. See also Johan Mortensen, *Selma Lagerlöf*, 1908; Stella Arvidson, *Selma Lagerlöf*, 1932; Elin Wägner, *Vie de Selma Lagerlof*, 1950; and Lars Ulvenstam, *Den åldrade Selma Lagerlöf*, 1955.

CHARLES LAMB

Born: London, England   Died: Edmonton, England
Date: February 10, 1775   Date: December 27, 1834

PRINCIPAL WORKS

ESSAYS: *Essays of Elia*, 1823; *Last Essays of Elia*, 1833.

CRITICISM: *Specimens of English Dramatic Poets, Who Lived about the Time of Shakespeare, with Notes*, 1808.

POEMS: *Blank Verse*, 1798 (with Charles Lloyd); *Poetry for Children*, 1809 (with Mary Lamb); *Album Verses*, 1830; *The Poetical Works of Charles Lamb*, 1836.

TALES AND STORIES: *A Tale of Rosamund Gray and Old Blind Margaret*, 1798; *Tales from Shakespeare*, 1807 (with Mary Lamb); *Adventures of Ulysses*, 1808; *Mrs. Leicester's School*, 1809 (with Mary Lamb).

PLAYS: *John Woodvil, A Tragedy*, 1802; *Mr. H.*, 1806.

Charles Lamb was born in Crown Office Row, Inner Temple, London, on February 10, 1775. His father, described under the name Lovel in Lamb's essay "The Old Benchers of the Inner Temple," was an assistant and servant to Samuel Salt, a member of Parliament. Through the generosity of Salt, Lamb in 1782 was allowed to enroll in the celebrated charity school, Christ's Hospital, where he continued for seven years; among his fellows was Samuel Taylor Coleridge. In 1789 he left school and became a clerk in the South Sea House. In 1792 he went to work for the East India Company, first in the accountant's office and later, on the recommendation of Salt, in the examiner's office. Here, except for a six-week period of derangement (1795–1796), when he was confined in a madhouse, he was employed for thirty-three years, the span of time coinciding with his principal literary activities. In 1796 his sister Mary, ten years his senior, who shared with him a heredi-

tary mental disorder marked by recurrent mania, stabbed their mother to death. The responsibility of caring for Mary devolved upon Charles and proved a source of anxiety for the rest of his life; she survived him, dying in 1847.

To Lamb's close friendship with Coleridge is to be credited his emergence as a poet, and in Coleridge's *Poems on Various Subjects* (1796) were included four sonnets by Lamb. Through Coleridge, Lamb established friendships with Dorothy and William Wordsworth, with Robert Southey, and with Charles Lloyd. In 1798, under the joint authorship of himself and Lloyd, appeared a volume entitled *Blank Verse*, assembling some of his best lyrics, among them "The Old Familiar Faces." The same year saw the publication of his prose romance *A Tale of Rosamund Gray*, a melodramatic and sentimental story with sources in Lamb's family misfortunes. The income from his clerkship at the

East India House, though assured, was small, and Lamb augmented his means by writing humorous sketches for newspapers. Aspiring to less transitory fame, he composed and offered to the actor John Kemble a tragedy, *John Woodvil*, which drew heavily on his favorites, the Elizabethans. Undeterred by indifference to this effort, he wrote a farce, *Mr. H.*, and enjoyed enthusiastic hopes when it was scheduled to be staged at Drury Lane. Produced in December, 1806, it was greeted with derision; Lamb added his own hisses to those of the audience.

Mary Lamb had been approached by the wife of William Godwin (later Shelley's father-in-law) with the request that she prepare for Godwin, who was publishing books for children, a collection of prose versions of Shakespeare's plays. Accordingly, with her brother's help, she wrote *Tales from Shakespeare*. The work achieved instant success, and Godwin got out a complete two-volume edition of the twenty tales, as well as several illustrated sixpenny pamphlets each containing one. Charles Lamb wrote paraphrases of six tragedies; Mary, the remainder. He had already conceived one slight juvenile story for Godwin's list, and afterwards he furnished others, including *Adventures of Ulysses*, based on the *Odyssey*, and *Mrs. Leicester's School*, the latter being chiefly the work of Mary Lamb.

Leigh Hunt, in 1810, began to edit a quarterly magazine, *The Reflector*. To this Lamb contributed some of his finest critical pieces, notably the essays on Hogarth and on Shakespeare's tragedies. His steady absorption in the works of the old dramatists had resulted in his *Specimens of English Dramatic Poets*, appreciatively annotated; the essays published through Hunt brought out even more distinctly his genius as an interpreter of the English literary past. Unfortunately, *The Reflector* was short-lived, and this fact, with the improvement in Lamb's salary from the East India Company, diminished his incentive to write. Until 1820 he wrote little else, though the publication of his *Works* (1818), in two volumes, attracted favorable notice. Upon the inauguration of the *London Magazine*, he found a new outlet for his ideas, and in the next four or five years he wrote industriously. His pseudonym "Elia" he took, without asking leave, from an Italian fellow clerk. In the popular mind, Lamb is best known for the essays published under this name. In 1825, he was pensioned by the Company and almost at once redoubled his studies in the drama. But his writing days were near their end. As Mary Lamb's mental instability grew, his worries multiplied. In 1834 Coleridge died. Two months later Lamb fell while walking in the London road near his house at Edmonton, Middlesex, and a few days later, December 27, 1834, he died of an infection, diagnosed as erysipelas, spreading from a facial scratch. He was in his sixtieth year.

The friends of Charles Lamb knew him as a convivial man of placid temper. Coleridge, with a hint of a pun on Lamb's surname, characterized him as "gentle-hearted Charles." Such indeed is the impression conveyed by the Elia essays, which are blended of graciousness and humor. No reader ever forgets "The Praise of Chimney-Sweepers," "Witches and Other Night Fears," "Christ's Hospital Five and Thirty Years Ago," "The Two Races of Men," "Sanity of True Genius," "Dream Children: A Reverie," or

"Confessions of a Drunkard." These desultory familiar essays, numbering several of his best, reveal Lamb's sentiment. They also exemplify the scope of his fancy, and so does his style, with its histrionic mannerisms and its quaint archaic terms learned from Sir Thomas Browne, Robert Burton, and other seventeenth century originals. But Lamb was no mere amiable eccentric: his intelligence, as manifested in his voluminous letters and in his formal criticism, was of extremely high quality. He far surpassed Coleridge in orderliness of mind and may possibly have equaled him in sensibility. The proof of Lamb's powers lies in his remarkable insight into the minor Elizabethan and Jacobean drama, which, by his critical evaluations, he revived from its two centuries of neglect as literature.

BIBLIOGRAPHICAL REFERENCES: The standard edition is *The Works of Charles and Mary Lamb,* edited by E. V. Lucas, 7 vols., 1903, reissued in 6 vols., 1912. Another edition is the *Works in Prose and Verse,* edited by Thomas Hutchinson, 2 vols., 1909. Useful one-volume editions of selections include *Twenty Essays of Elia,* edited by Daniel Varney, 1932; *Essays and Letters,* edited by J. M. French, 1937; and *The Portable Charles Lamb,* edited by J. M. Brown, 1949. Of particular interest for its combination of selections and biographical text is *Charles Lamb and Elia,* edited by J. E. Morpurgo, 1948.

The standard biography is E. V. Lucas, *The Life of Charles Lamb,* 2 vols., 1905 (rev. ed., 1921), supplemented by the same writer's edition of the *Letters,* 3 vols., 1935. Other biographical studies include F. V. Morley, *Lamb Before Elia,* 1932; Edmund Blunden, *Charles Lamb and His Contemporaries,* 1933; A. C. Ward, *The Frolic and the Gentle: A Centenary Study of Charles Lamb,* 1934; J. May Lewis, *Charles Lamb,* 1934; E. C. Ross, *The Ordeal of Bridget Elia: A Chronicle of the Lambs,* 1940; Katharine Anthony, *The Lambs,* 1945; and Edmund Blunden, *Charles Lamb,* 1954. For criticism see M. H. Law, *The English Familiar Essay in the Nineteenth Century,* 1934; G. L. Barnett, *The Evolution of Elia,* 1952; and William K. Seymour, *Charles Lamb as a Poet,* 1953.

FRIEDRICH DE LA MOTTE-FOUQUÉ

Born: Brandenburg, Germany
Date: February 12, 1777

Died: Berlin, Germany
Date: January 23, 1843

PRINCIPAL WORK

NOVEL: *Undine,* 1811.

Baron Friedrich (Heinrich Karl) de la Motte-Fouqué, born in Brandenburg, Germany, February 12, 1777, followed his grandfather, General de la Motte-Fouqué, distinguished under Frederick the Great, in serving in the Prussian Guards. He fought in the Campaign of 1794 as well as in the War of Liberation, 1813. But the pen attracted him more than the sword.

The critic August von Schlegel encouraged Fouqué by publishing his first book in 1804; from then on this fertile writer turned out a variety of products, including criticisms and discussions of Romanticism, then coming into vogue.

As a poet, he wrote deft lyrics, ringing epics, and poetic modernizations of well-known medieval poems. In 1808 he published *Sigurd der Schlangentödter*, the first German dramatization of the *Nibelungen* saga.

Turning to the short tale, Fouqué wrote *Undine*, based on a fourteenth century legend; the work inaugurated a never-ending series of mermaid stories. Heine said of it: "The fragrance of poetry and the songs of the nightingale were put into words by Fouqué, and he called it *Undine*." The author made an opera libretto of it for music by Ernst Hoffmann, performed in 1816.

Undine has the virtues of Romanticism, with its vividness and sentiment; but critics note the author's exaggerations and inaccuracies, as he drew on his imagination, rather than on research, for the details of feudal and chivalric life. While he continued writing until his death, at Berlin on January 23, 1843, he never again equaled this work for popularity.

BIBLIOGRAPHICAL REFERENCES: The story of Fouqué's life to 1813 is told in his autobiography, *Lebensgeschichte des Baron Friedrich de la Motte-Fouqué*, 1840. For biography and criticism see also E. Hagemeister, *Fouqué als Dramatiker*, 1905; Lother Jentne, *Fouqué als Erzähler*, 1910; T. Krämer, *Das romantische Ritterepos bei Fouqué*, 1913; G. Mehlis, *Die deutsche Romantik*, 1922; and J. Haupt, *Elementargeister bei Fouqué, Immermann und Hoffmann*, 1923.

WALTER SAVAGE LANDOR

Born: Warwick, England
Date: January 30, 1775

Died: Florence, Italy
Date: September 17, 1864

PRINCIPAL WORKS

DIALOGUES: *Imaginary Conversations*, 1824–1848; *The Citation and Examination of William Shakespeare . . . Touching Deer-Stealing*, 1834; *Pentameron and Pentalogia*, 1837.

LETTERS: *Pericles and Aspasia*, 1836.

POEMS: *Poems*, 1795; *Gebir*, 1798; *Hellenics*, 1847; *Italics*, 1848; *Heroic Idylls*, 1863.

PLAY: *Count Julian*, 1812.

Seldom does a man of wealth, without a degree or a profession, become an outstanding poet, but this in brief is the life of Walter Savage Landor, born at Warwick, England, on January 30, 1775. His education was irregular at best; he was early removed from Rugby in favor of a private tutor, and in 1794 he was rusticated from Trinity College, Cambridge, for firing a shot in a political dispute. At the age of twenty, after his father had given him an independent allowance, he brought out his first poems. In these he immediately established his reputation as satirist and epigrammatist. Shortly afterward he inherited a fortune from his father and removed to fashionable Bath. Much of his inheritance he squandered by outfitting a regiment and fighting with the Spaniards against the French at La Coruña. From this experience came the lofty and heroic closet-drama, *Count Julian.*

His domestic life was stormy at best. Having married Julia Thuillier in 1811, he removed to the Continent after domestic and legal strife in 1818, and was finally separated from his wife in 1835. In the meantime, he was writing his best work. The *Imaginary Conversations,* written over a period of some twenty years, range widely in theme and time and present such figures as Diogenes and Plato, Lucullus and Caesar, Henry VIII and Anne Boleyn, Rousseau and Malesherbes. The *Pentameron* records conversations between Boccaccio and Petrarch. *Pericles and Aspasia* purports to be an exchange of letters which mirror the life of Athens in its golden age.

Landor's career continued stormy, and in his old age he became embroiled in litigation over libelous writings as well as his contested estate. During these latter years he did many of his Latin poems and epigrams as well as dramatic dialogues. He was friendly with such writers as Robert Southey, Charles Lamb, and Robert Browning, and for a time he carried on a literary feud with Lord Byron. Always the hot-head and incendiary, he was in turn gentle to children and animals, a nature lover, and generous to a fault. He died in Florence, Italy, September 17, 1864.

His literary life, from the time he was twenty until he was nearly ninety, is hard to assess. He was a stylist in the Latin tradition, coming midway between Milton and Shelley. His drama, like that of the later Victorians, was interesting as poetry but unplayable, and his poetry sometimes degenerated into banal verse, though at its best it was heightened to sublimity. As an essayist he was irreproachable, Swiftian, satiric, incisive in his praise or condemnation. He paid tribute to the younger literary figures of his day before they were generally recognized.

Within recent years a revival of interest in Landor has become increasingly evident. This, certainly, is only poetic justice, for he remains one of the great eccentrics in English literature and a fascinating personality once the truth is separated from prejudiced opinions against him.

BIBLIOGRAPHICAL REFERENCES: The standard edition, although not definitive, is *The Complete Works of Walter Savage Landor,* edited by T. E. Welby and Stephen Wheeler, 16 vols., 1927–1936. The *Poems* have been edited by Stephen Wheeler, 3 vols., 1937, and *Imaginary Conversations* by Ernest de Selincourt, 1915. A representative selection from his poetry and prose was included in *Selections from Landor,* edited by Sidney Colvin, 1904 (rev. ed.).

There is no standard biography, but for biographical and critical studies see John Forster, *Walter Savage Landor,* 1869, reprinted in an edition of the *Works,* 8 vols., 1876; Sidney Colvin, *Landor,* English Men of Letters Series, 1881; H. C. Minchin, *Last Days, Letters and Conversations with Walter Savage Landor,* 1934; Michael Elwin, *Savage Landor,* 1942; and Robert H. Super, *Walter Savage Landor: A Biography,* 1954. Briefer studies include Stephen Leslie, *Hours in a Library, Third Series,* 1879; George Saintsbury, *Essays in English Literature, 1780–1860,* 1895; and Helene Richter, "Walter Savage Landor," *Anglia,* L (1926), 123–152, 317–344, and LI (1927), 1–30.

WILLIAM LANGLAND

Born: Shropshire (?), England
Date: c. 1332

Died: London (?), England
Date: c. 1400

PRINCIPAL WORKS

POEMS: *The Vision of William, concerning Piers the Plowman,* c. 1395; *Richard the Redeless,* c. 1395 (attributed).

Like most medieval authors, the poet who wrote *The Vision of William, concerning Piers the Plowman* is almost anonymous. His name is often thought to have been William Langland, but his biography is mostly hypothetical, being drawn almost entirely from what seem to be autobiographical references in the poem. He was probably educated at a Benedictine monastery in the Malvern hills and became a clerk with minor orders in the Church. He eked out a slender living in London by singing in churches and by copying legal documents. He wrote the first version of his poem about 1362, revised and greatly expanded it about 1377, and revised it again about 1395.

The poem is digressive and rather formless; it consists of a series of visions with few necessary connections. The verse is alliterative and without rhyme, in the older pre-Norman style. The use of allegory for satiric purposes, however, comes from the French tradition begun by Jean de Meung's work in *Le Roman de la rose.* Its realistic satire and simple moral power constitute its prime virtues. Langland considers simplicity in religion and social relations and the recognition of the value of honest labor as the foundations of a healthy society. The poem was extremely popular in the fourteenth and fifteenth centuries, and its values inspired the religious reformers of the sixteenth century.

Langland is thought to have been born at Cleobury Mortimer, Shropshire, England, about 1332 and to have died in London about 1400, though such claims are in dispute.

BIBLIOGRAPHICAL REFERENCES: Good editions of *Piers Plowman* are those of W. W. Skeat, 10th edition, 1928, and the critical edition by Thomas A. Knott and David C. Fowler, 1952. Biographical and critical works include A. H. Bright, "William Langland's Early Life," *London Times Literary Supplement,* XXIV (Nov. 5, 1925), 739, and XXV (Sept. 9, 1926), 596. Other important critical works are G. A. Thomas, *A Study of the Influence of Piers Plowman,* 1927; Greta Hart, *Piers Plowman and Contemporary Religious Thought,* 1938; D. W. Robertson and Bernard Huppé, *Piers Plowman and Scriptural Tradition,* 1951; and Nevill Coghill, "The Pardon of Piers Plowman," *Proceedings of the British Academy,* XXX (1947), 303–357. See also J. J. Jusserand's account of the authorship controversy, *The Piers Plowman Controversy,* 1910.

SIDNEY LANIER

Born: Macon, Georgia
Date: February 3, 1842

Died: Lynn, North Carolina
Date: September 7, 1881

PRINCIPAL WORKS

POEMS: *Poems,* 1877; *Poems of Sidney Lanier,* 1884.

NOVEL: *Tiger-Lilies,* 1867.

CRITICISM AND BELLES-LETTRES: *The Science of English Verse,* 1880; *The English Novel and the Principle of Its Development,* 1883; *Music and Poetry,* 1898; *Retrospects and Prospects,* 1899; *Shakespeare and His Forerunners,* 1902.

TRAVEL: *Florida: Its Scenery, Climate, and History,* 1875.

Among nineteenth century American poets, Sidney Lanier may be ranked in order behind Whitman, Poe, and Emily Dickinson. He was a master of the craft of versification without possessing, as has been charged against Poe, a vulgar ear. Lanier was born in Macon, Georgia, on February 3, 1842. He was taught music in childhood, a fact of great moment to his growth as a poet. At fourteen he entered Oglethorpe College and was graduated in 1860. He spent one year as a tutor in English there. Intending an academic career, he hoped to proceed to Heidelberg, but the outbreak of the Civil War precluded such a design. Lanier enlisted as a Confederate private and was in service four years. When he was released from the Federal military prison at Point Lookout, Maryland, in 1865, his health was shattered. The tuberculosis that would eventually kill him was already latent. His one novel, *Tiger-Lilies,* a weak but informative anti-war story, he had begun while in the Confederate signal service.

He worked as a hotel clerk, as a schoolmaster, and as an assistant in his father's law office. After his marriage to Mary Day in 1867, he underwent financial hardship: there was little demand for poets or musicians in central Georgia. At the same time his malady grew worse. Looking for a tolerable climate, he went to San Antonio, Texas, in 1872; but the following year he felt the need to accept an appointment as first flutist in the Peabody Orchestra in Baltimore. There his work was appreciated, and he had the good fortune to become friends with Bayard Taylor. Through Taylor, he had poems published in *Lippincott's Magazine* and obtained the commission to write a cantata for the Centennial Exposition at Philadelphia in 1876. He eked out his other resources by preparing a guidebook to Florida and by other writings. In 1879 he was named to the faculty of the Johns Hopkins University and gave two series of lectures, one on the English novel, another on the science of prosody. On September 7, 1881, he died at Lynn, North Carolina, where he had gone in a last effort to recruit his broken strength.

Lanier is distinguished for his profound knowledge of the analogies between poetry and music and for his application of musical theory to his own verse. Among his finest poems are "The Marshes of Glynn," suggested by a visit to the Georgia coast near the town of Brunswick, and "The Symphony," a quasi-orchestral composition on the theme of the enmity between commercialism and man's vital nature.

BIBLIOGRAPHICAL REFERENCES: The standard edition is *The Centennial Edition of Sidney Lanier,* 10 vols., under the general editorship of Charles R. Anderson, 1945.

Useful volumes of Lanier's selected writings include *Select Poems of Sidney Lanier*, edited by Morgan Callaway, Jr., 1895; *Selections from Sidney Lanier: Prose and Verse*, edited by Henry W. Lanier, 1916; and *Selected Poems of Sidney Lanier*, edited by Stark Young, 1947.

An excellent early biography of Lanier is Edwin Mims, *Sidney Lanier*, 1905. See also Aubrey H. Starke, *Sidney Lanier: A Biographical and Critical Study*, 1933; and Lincoln Lorenz, *The Life of Sidney Lanier*, 1935. For studies of Lanier's prosody see George Saintsbury, *History of English Prosody*, 1910; and Gay Wilson Allen, *American Prosody*, 1935. Lanier in the light of modern criticism is presented in Robert Penn Warren, "The Blind Poet: Sidney Lanier," *American Review*, II (1933), 27–45; and John Crowe Ransom, "Hearts and Heads," *ibid.*, II (1934), 554–571.

RING LARDNER

Born: Niles, Michigan   *Died:* East Hampton, New York
Date: March 6, 1885   *Date:* September 25, 1933

Principal Works

short stories: *Gullible's Travels*, 1917; *How to Write Short Stories*, 1924; *The Love Nest and Other Stories*, 1926; *Round Up*, 1929.

novels: *You Know Me Al*, 1916; *The Big Town*, 1921.

humorous and satirical sketches: *Treat 'Em Rough*, 1918; *Own Your Own Home*, 1919; *The Real Dope*, 1919; *Symptoms of Being 35*, 1921; *What of It?*, 1925; *The Story of a Wonder Man*, 1927; *Lose with a Smile*, 1933; *First and Last*, 1934.

rhymes: *Bib Ballads*, 1915; *Regular Fellows I Have Met*, 1919.

play: *June Moon*, 1930 (with George S. Kaufman).

Ring(gold Wilmer) Lardner represents the culmination of a long line of American colloquial humorists; but he applied his mastery of slang to satire. His pessimism assumed Swiftian dimensions, and his oblique commentaries on the human race are full of acid.

Ring Lardner, born on March 6, 1885, grew up in prosperous surroundings in Niles, Michigan. After abandoning the study of engineering, he stumbled into journalism in 1905. Through 1919 he worked as a sportswriter on several papers, mainly in Chicago. His marriage in 1911, which produced four sons, was very happy. In 1913 Lardner took over "In the Wake of the News," a column in the *Chicago Tribune*. The Jack Keefe stories, written as a series of semi-lit-

erate letters by an oafish baseball player, began appearing in 1914; they were collected into an epistolary novel, *You Know Me Al*, in which Keefe, a selfish and cruel braggart, exposes all his obnoxious qualities in his own letters chronicling his athletic career. This was followed by *Treat 'Em Rough*—which deals with Keefe's adventures in World War I—*Own Your Own Home*, and *The Real Dope*. *The Big Town* is a brash Midwesterner's account of his experiences in New York City.

How to Write Short Stories, published in 1924, is the central work in Ring Lardner's career. The title is typical of his refusal to believe that he was a significant writer, but the collection included "Alibi Ike," "Some Like

Them Cold," "The Golden Honeymoon," and "Champion," which was one of the earliest debunking sports stories. *What of It?*, a collection of magazine pieces came next, and in 1926 his second major book of short stories, *The Love Nest and Other Stories*, which included "Haircut." A mock autobiography, *The Story of a Wonder Man*, and two more collections of stories and sketches, *Round Up* and *Lose with a Smile*, followed.

Despite his high output of fiction, Lardner never abandoned his newspaper column and syndicate writing. To this he added theater and movie work. Although he was anxious for a stage success, the closest he came was in *June Moon*, on which George S. Kaufman collaborated. This great burden of work and the strain of physical excesses caught up with him early, and he suffered years of illness before he died. While sick he wrote a series of brilliant radio articles for the *New Yorker* in 1932 and 1933. He died at his home in East Hampton, Long Island, on September 25, 1933.

In his own time there was a firm group of critics who claimed Ring Lardner as one of the chief American satirists. Since then this estimate has slowly been gaining currency, so that his enormous wit is sometimes in danger of being forgotten by the people who praise him as a critic of humanity.

BIBLIOGRAPHICAL REFERENCES: A convenient one-volume edition is *The Portable Ring Lardner*, edited with an introduction by Gilbert Seldes, 1946. The only full study is Donald Elder, *Ring Lardner*, 1956. See also Carl Van Doren, *Many Minds*, 1924; Maxwell Geismar, *Writers in Crisis*, 1942; F. Scott Fitzgerald, *The Crack-Up*, 1946; and Edmund Wilson, *The Shores of Light*, 1952.

FRANÇOIS LA ROCHEFOUCAULD

Born: Paris, France
Date: September 15, 1613

Died: Paris
Date: March 17, 1680

PRINCIPAL WORKS

MAXIMS: *Réflexions ou sentences et maximes morales*, 1665–1678.

MISCELLANEOUS: *Portrait*, 1658; *Mémoires sur la régence d'Anne d'Autriche*, 1662.

François, Duc de La Rochefoucauld, the cynical French aphorist of the seventeenth century, was born into the nobility and educated primarily as a soldier and a courtier. He never considered himself a man of letters, but he did admit in his *Portrait* that "I write good prose, I compose good verse; and, if I desired the glory that comes with such things, I believe that with little work I could acquire for myself a sufficient reputation." The irony of his life, and perhaps the basis for much of the cynicism that his maxims display, stemmed from the fact that in the affairs of government, the one area in which his ambitions lay, he acquired for himself no reputation at all, while what fame he actually achieved in his lifetime, and his entire reputation as far as posterity is concerned, came entirely from those writings which were not originally intended for publication.

As has been suggested by F. G.

628

Stevens, his editor and translator, the times were not right, either for the employment of La Rochefoucauld's great intellectual gifts in affairs of state or for the full development of his talents as a writer. In the first place, as a nobleman and as a member of the military caste, he received a minimum of education. Born in Paris on September 15, 1613, he was married for family purposes at the age of fifteen and began his active service as an officer of the king a year later. In the second, his was not a period during which any nobleman in France could aspire to a high position in the government. Louis XIII was an absolute monarch, and the only delegation of power in the realm was into the hands of two successive Cardinal ministers, first Richelieu, and then, after his death in 1642, the Italian, Mazarin.

The situation was, certainly, one to embitter a young man of La Rochefoucauld's temperament; and in the end he was completely disillusioned— but not until he had twice tried to do something about it. The first attempt was by means of a conspiracy with Louis's queen, Anne of Austria, who, suspected justifiably by Richelieu of plotting with Spain, suggested to La Rochefoucauld that he abduct her and carry her to the Netherlands. La Rochefoucauld readily agreed, but the plot was discovered and he was promptly thrown into the Bastille, but later banished to his country estates. When Louis XIII died shortly after Richelieu, and Anne became regent for the five-year-old Louis XIV, La Rochefoucauld returned to court in expectation of favor to repay his former devotion. He found, instead, that the queen mother was completely under the domination of Mazarin and that he was no closer to an important position than he had been under the late king. This fresh source of disillusionment prompted him to join forces with the Prince de Condé in the Frondist rebellion that began in 1648 and ended without victory for the rebels in 1653. La Rochefoucauld had fought for the entire duration of the uprising and had been wounded severely, but again nothing had come of his efforts.

He returned once more to the capital, resigned finally to live out his days as an ineffectual courtier. There he became attached to the literary circle that contained such brilliant figures as Mme. de Sablé, Mme. de Sévigné, and, particularly his writing companion and reputed mistress, Mme. de Lafayette, author of *The Princess of Clèves*. Within this group he found a worthy subject for his brilliant and penetrating mind, his famous *Maxims* that tear the protecting film from human vanity and expose it to the harsh glare of his studied cynicism. He died in Paris on March 17, 1680.

BIBLIOGRAPHICAL REFERENCES: La Rochefoucauld's *Œuvres complètes* were edited by L. Martin-Chauffier in 1935. The standard translation in English is *The Maxims of François, Duc de La Rochefoucauld*, translated and edited by F. G. Stevens, 1935. For biographical studies see Jean Bourdeau, *La Rochefoucauld*, 1895, and Morris Bishop, *The Life and Adventures of La Rochefoucauld*, 1951. An excellent critical study is Sister Mary F. Zeller, *New Aspects of Style in the Maxims of La Rochefoucauld*, 1954.

D. H. LAWRENCE

Born: Eastwood, England
Date: September 11, 1885

Died: Vence, France
Date: March 2, 1930

Principal Works

NOVELS: *The White Peacock,* 1911; *The Trespasser,* 1912; *Sons and Lovers,* 1913; *The Rainbow,* 1915; *Women in Love,* 1920; *The Lost Girl,* 1920; *Aaron's Rod,* 1922; *Kangaroo,* 1923; *The Boy in the Bush,* 1924; *The Plumed Serpent,* 1926; *Lady Chatterley's Lover,* 1928; *The Virgin and the Gipsy,* 1930.

POEMS: *Love Poems and Others,* 1913; *Amores,* 1916; *Look! We Have Come Through,* 1917; *New Poems,* 1918; *Bay,* 1919; *Tortoises,* 1921; *Birds, Beasts, and Flowers,* 1923; *Pansies,* 1929; *Nettles,* 1930; *Last Poems,* 1932; *Fire and Other Poems,* 1940.

SHORT STORIES: *The Prussian Officer and Other Stories,* 1914; *England, My England,* 1922; *The Ladybird,* 1923; *St. Mawr,* together with *The Princess,* 1925; *The Woman Who Rode Away,* 1928; *Love Among the Haystacks,* 1930; *The Lovely Lady and Other Stories,* 1933; *A Modern Lover,* 1934.

ESSAYS: *Psychoanalysis and the Unconscious,* 1921; *Fantasia of the Unconscious,* 1922; *Studies in Classic American Literature,* 1923; *Reflections on the Death of a Porcupine,* 1925; *Phoenix,* 1936.

PLAYS: *The Widowing of Mrs. Holroyd,* 1914; *Touch and Go,* 1920; *David,* 1926; *A Collier's Friday Night,* 1934.

TRAVEL SKETCHES: *Twilight in Italy,* 1916; *Sea and Sardinia,* 1921; *Mornings in Mexico,* 1927; *Etruscan Places,* 1932.

LETTERS: *The Letters of D. H. Lawrence,* edited by Aldous Huxley, 1932.

The passion, conflict, turmoil, and striving that were to mark the brief life and fiery art of D(avid) H(erbert) Lawrence were there before him, clustering about his cradle in the grimy mining town of Eastwood in Nottinghamshire, England. Ten years before his birth on September 11, 1885, a genteel, ambitious schoolmistress, Lydia Beardsall, had married an untamed, intensely physical coal miner, John Arthur Lawrence, only to learn in bitterness thereafter that they inhabited different worlds even while they lived in the same house and raised five children. Physically delicate, their sensitive fourth child cleaved to his mother and with her encouragement excelled at school and went on to win a scholarship to Nottingham High School in his twelfth year. After graduation he worked briefly and unhappily as a manufacturer's clerk in 1899 until he suffered a serious attack of pneumonia. After a long convalescence he took a position as a pupil-teacher in the Eastwood British School in 1902. He taught there and then at Ilkeston, Derbyshire, until September, 1906, when he entered Nottingham University (having two years earlier placed in the First Division of the First Class in the nationwide King's Scholarship Examination) for a two years' academic program leading to an Arts degree. Qualified as a teacher two years later, he became junior assistant-master at Davidson Road School, in Croydon, a suburb of London. He was to teach there until November, 1911, when he was struck down again by pneumonia.

As early as 1905, however, his literary interests had begun to burgeon. Sharing the joys of voracious reading with Jessie Chambers, the daughter of a family at whose home he had spent part of his convalescence five years earlier, he had begun to experiment with verse and fiction. At the same time he was being torn by the conflicting emotional demands of Jessie and his mother, which he was to record so vividly in *Sons and Lovers*. His mother's death, in January, 1911, was followed in a few weeks by the publication of the novel he had begun with Jessie's encouragement: *The White Peacock*. The story of a girl and two suitors, narrated by a character strongly resembling Lawrence, it enunciated many of the themes he was to treat throughout his career: competition between the over-cerebral, over-civilized man and the earthy, vital one, as well as the need for truth and naturalness in the relation between men and men, and men and women. *The Trespasser*, based on the work of a London friend, Helen Corke, was a very uneven novel of frustrated love which followed a year later. In 1913 Lawrence's reputation began to grow, for he published not only a book of poems, but the powerful *Sons and Lovers*, to many his finest novel. Strongly autobiographical, it relates the growth of a sensitive young man in a coal-mining environment through emotional turmoil in his relations with a spiritual sweetheart, an earthy one, and his possessive mother, from whose influence he liberates himself only after her death.

A year earlier Lawrence's personal life had undergone as great a change as his professional one. A month after they had met in April, 1912, Lawrence had eloped with Frieda von Richthofen Weekley, mother of three small children and wife of a professor of philology at Nottingham University. This was the first move of the many which were to continue for the rest of Lawrence's life and to take him around the world. While Frieda and Lawrence lived in poverty on the continent he continued at work on poems, short stories, a novel, and a play. They returned to England in 1914, when they were married, to find themselves the objects of hostility and absurd charges of pro-German sympathies with the outbreak of World War I. An added blow was the reaction to *The Rainbow*, published in 1915. This novel of three generations of people like Lawrence's own, with its forthright treatment of sexual passion and conflicting values and philosophies, was denounced as obscene by many reviewers, and the entire edition was destroyed by court order. Poverty stricken, compelled to leave Cornwall by the military, and badgered by the conscription authorities despite incipient tuberculosis, the Lawrences briefly lived in borrowed apartments in London and cottages in Berkshire before departing for Italy for three years in 1919. The books of poems which had followed *The Rainbow* were themselves followed by *Women in Love*, which used some of the same characters as the earlier novel and introduced clearly recognizable fictional portraits of J. M. Murry, Katherine Mansfield, Bertrand Russell, and Ottoline Morrell as well as Frieda and Lawrence himself. The novel, which showed the influence of the new psychological concepts of Sigmund Freud, seemed to contain a rejection of European culture and to plead for allegiance to a vital and primitive one which would reinfuse

631

life and awareness of fundamental human drives. Besides his preoccupation with what he felt to be healthy and spiritual sexuality, there was throughout the book his vivid intuition about people, his preternatural sensitivity to nature, and his ability to infuse life into whatever he described. Clear too was his belief in the necessity for following instinctual feelings, for blood consciousness, as he called it, rather than sterile cerebral consciousness. This book far overshadowed *The Lost Girl* of the same year, an attempt, after the manner of Arnold Bennett's naturalism, to write a novel that would sell well. His ideas about psychology were elaborated in essay form in *Psychoanalysis and the Unconscious* and *Fantasia of the Unconscious.*

Invited in 1921 to come and live at Taos, New Mexico, by Mabel Dodge Luhan, who was building an artists' colony there, Frieda and Lawrence set out for the American southwest by way of Ceylon, New Zealand, and Australia. Before they reached America, in September 1922, Lawrence was to have absorbed enough material for two novels of Australia. They were preceded by *Aaron's Rod,* which dealt with the attempt of an established man, in the familiar mining environment, to start all over in middle life. In addition to his earlier themes, Lawrence had introduced two new ones: the drive to power and to domination over one's fellows. These studies were amplified by *Kangaroo* in 1923, a novel in which a man much like Lawrence is torn between the claims of Kangaroo, political leader of the Australian miners, and those of his own wife. This idea of the prophet, the leader of an almost-Utopia, was to loom larger with time in Lawrence's own thought

and personality. *The Boy in the Bush* of the same year is a rewritten version of a novel by Martin Skinner, an adventure novel of early nineteenth century West Australia.

When the Lawrences arrived in Taos in September, 1922, he found himself as much at harmony as he was ever to be with any place. In Old and New Mexico the plains and mountains, the Indians with their tribal brotherhood and primitivism, all seemed to Lawrence a part of the answer to the problem of European decadence and personal fulfillment. Building, gardening, riding, baking, painting, Lawrence found time too to write verse and begin a novel presenting a modern incarnation of the Aztec god Quetzalcoatl. *The Plumed Serpent* was a violent novel in which both Christianity and sophisticated Europeans bowed before the strength of the blood consciousness of Indian primitivism and the primal instinctive behavior of its representatives. But now a near-fatal tuberculous hemorrhage complicated by malaria showed Lawrence how ill he was. His visa thus unrenewable, Lawrence returned to England and thence to Italy. Here in 1928 he privately printed *Lady Chatterley's Lover,* whose reception, with charges of obscenity and with seizures and threats of prosecution, dwarfed those of his earlier works. With unprecedented frankness of language and accuracy of detail, Lawrence presented the fulfillment of the unsatisfied wife of a maimed aristocrat by an ex-officer, now a game-keeper and a vital Lawrentian hero. *The Virgin and the Gipsy* was also set in England and bore many similarities in tone and character to *Lady Chatterley's Lover.* Lawrence's health steadily worsened, and

632

after a month in a sanatorium, on his insistence he was moved to a villa at Vence, above Cannes. There on March 2, 1930, with Frieda at his side, he died. He left behind him an extraor- dinarily large body of work for so short a career, nearly all of it strongly marked by his unmistakable literary and philosophical imprint. His body was later reinterred at Taos.

BIBLIOGRAPHICAL REFERENCES: No other writer of modern times has provoked so many slanted biographies or such a mass of controversial criticism. The fullest and most balanced biography is Harry Thornton Moore, *The Intelligent Heart: The Story of D. H. Lawrence*, 1955. Other biographical and personal studies include J. Middleton Murry, *The Son of Woman*, 1931; *idem, Reminiscences of D. H. Lawrence*, 1933; Catherine Carswell, *Savage Pilgrimage*, 1932; Mabel Dodge Luhan, *Lorenzo in Taos*, 1932; Horace Gregory, *Pilgrim of the Apocalypse*, 1933; Frieda Lawrence, *Not I But the Wind*, 1934; E. T., *D. H. Lawrence: A Personal Record*, 1935; Hugh Kingsmill, *The Life of D. H. Lawrence*, 1938; Knud Merrild, *A Poet and Two Painters*, 1939; Richard Aldington, *D. H. Lawrence: Portrait of a Genius But—*, 1950; Harry T. Moore, *The Life and Work of D. H. Lawrence*, 1951; Witter Bynner, *Journey with Genius*, 1951; and E. G. Fay, *Lorenzo in Search of the Sun*, 1953.

For criticism see W. Y. Tindall, *D. H. Lawrence and Susan His Cow*, 1939; Anthony West, *D. H. Lawrence*, 1950; William Tiverton, *D. H. Lawrence and Human Existence*, 1951; Dallas Kenmare, *Firebird: A Study of D. H. Lawrence*, 1951; Mark Spilka, *The Love Ethic of D. H. Lawrence*, 1955; Mary Freeman, *D. H. Lawrence: A Basic Study of His Ideas*, 1955; F. R. Leavis, *D. H. Lawrence, Novelist*, 1955; and Graham Hough, *The Dark Sun: A Study of D. H. Lawrence*, 1957.

The Achievement of D. H. Lawrence, edited by Frederick J. Hoffman and Harry T. Moore, 1953, is a collection of selected critiques from the great body of Lawrence criticism. See also William White, *D. H. Lawrence: A Check-List, Writings about D. H. Lawrence, 1931–1950*, 1950.

T. E. LAWRENCE

Born: Tremadoc, North Wales
Date: August 15, 1888

Died: Moreton, England
Date: May 19, 1935

PRINCIPAL WORKS

TRAVEL AND ADVENTURE: *Seven Pillars of Wisdom*, 1926; *Revolt in the Desert*, 1927 (an abridgment).

SOCIAL CRITICISM: *The Mint*, 1926.

LETTERS AND JOURNAL: *The Diary of T. E. Lawrence, MCMXI*, 1937; *The Letters of T. E. Lawrence*, 1938.

TRANSLATION: *The Odyssey of Homer*, 1932.

MISCELLANEOUS: *Crusader Castles*, 1936; *Oriental Assembly*, 1940.

The biographical details of T(homas) E(dward) Lawrence, adventurer, soldier, archeologist, and writer, are common knowledge, though it is now difficult to separate fact from fancy. Born at Tremadoc, North

Wales, on August 15, 1888, he lived an unsettled childhood as his family moved about between England and France. In 1896 they settled in Oxford. There Lawrence attended the Oxford High School, where he won a first in English.

Interested in local archeology as a boy, he continued in that field of study during his undergraduate years at Jesus College, Oxford, from 1907 to 1910. During the winter of 1909–1910 he wrote his first book, *Crusader Castles*. From this time until 1914 he served in many capacities on explorations of Syria, Northern Mesopotamia, and Egypt. There he developed the knowledge and abilities which led to his now legendary exploits in Arabia.

With the outbreak of war in 1914, the British Intelligence Department in Egypt appointed Lawrence staff captain, and he served in this capacity through 1916. At his own request he was then granted a leave of absence in Arabia, where he immediately began the unification of the Arab chieftains and principalities—no small task when one considers the central strength of Turkey, at that time trying to disunify and conquer all Arabs. Lawrence successfully organized border raids, attacks on caravans, destruction of transportation and communication lines, and he himself led many victorious missions if the account given in *Seven Pillars of Wisdom* can be taken as documentary evidence. This book, compiled in several sections and printed in various forms, many consider the best adventure book of our time, perhaps of all time. The book has had a curious history. From extensive notes Lawrence completed the first draft, only to lose almost the entire manuscript. He then rewrote from memory the second text, his notes having been destroyed after the completion of each section. The book, printed first in a limited edition in 1926, did not reach a general audience until 1935, the popular edition before that date being an abridgment of the original titled *Revolt in the Desert*.

Along with his successful resistance to the Turks, Lawrence brought his army into collaboration with the British in Syria and again aided in opening the way to Damascus. These exploits won him top military honors, most of which he refused, and a chance to represent the Arabs at the Peace Conference. He retired from the army with the rank of colonel. He continued writing and rewriting his great work until 1921 when he became a political adviser to the Colonial office on near Eastern affairs.

The remainder of his story calls for psychoanalysis rather than biography. Evidently Lawrence's abhorrence of publicity, distrust of politics, and general antipathy toward society made him attempt a number of disguises. In 1922 he enlisted in the air force as Aircraftman Ross, only to receive a discharge after his identity was discovered. As Private T. E. Shaw he served in the Royal Tank Corps and later rejoined the Royal Air Force under the same name. After honorable service in England and India, he received a discharge a few months before his death at Moreton, England, the result of a motorcycle accident, on May 19, 1935.

In the years since his death Lawrence has attracted more attention, if that is possible, than he did in his lifetime. Of his boyhood and young manhood the record is now nearly complete, a fascinating revelation of a mercurial and universal mind which could grasp language, science, literature, history, and still allow its owner to travel, fight, converse, write in a veritable whirl-pool of energy and activity. A small man with no vices, he maintained his youthful vigor and appearance so well that the world was shocked to learn he was almost fifty when he died.

BIBLIOGRAPHICAL REFERENCES: There is no authorized biography and many of the details of fact and interpretation in Lawrence's career are still matters of dispute. There are two bibliographies: E. W. Duval, T. E. *Lawrence: A Bibliography*, 1928, and an earlier study by T. German-Reed, *Bibliographical Notes on T. E. Lawrence's "Seven Pillars of Wisdom" and "Revolt in the Desert,"* 1928. For biography see Lowell Thomas, *With Lawrence in Arabia*, 1924; Robert Graves, *Lawrence and the Arabs*, 1927 [*Lawrence and the Arabian Adventure*]; Basil H. Liddell-Hart, *T. E. Lawrence in Arabia and After*, 1934; and A. W. Lawrence, ed., *T. E. Lawrence by His Friends*, 1937. For briefer studies see R. P. Blackmur, "T. E. Lawrence," in *The Expense of Greatness*, 1940; and Herbert Read, "Lawrence of Arabia" and "The Seven Pillars of Wisdom," in *A Coat of Many Colors*, 1945. For an adverse opinion on Lawrence see also Richard Aldington, *Lawrence of Arabia: A Biographical Inquiry*, 1955. David Garnett has edited *The Essential T. E. Lawrence*, 1951.

HALLDÓR KILJAN LAXNESS

Born: Reykjavík, Iceland
Date: April 23, 1902

PRINCIPAL WORKS

NOVELS: *Undir Helgahnúk*, 1924 (*Under the Holy Mountain*); *Vefarinn mikli frá Kasmír*, 1927 (*The Great Weaver from Kashmir*); *Thú vínvidur hreini*, 1931; *Fuglinn í fjörunni*, 1932 (the two foregoing combined as *Salka-Valka*, 1934); *Sjálfstætt fólk I–II*, 1934–1935 (*Independent People*); *Ljós heimsins*, 1937; *Höll sumarlandsins*, 1938; *Hús skáldsins*, 1939; *Fegurd himinsins*, 1940; *Íslandsklukkan*, 1943 (*The Bell of Iceland*); *Hid ljósa man*, 1944 (*The Slender Fairy*); *Eldur í Kaupinhafn*, 1945 (*Fire in Copenhagen*); *Atómstödin*, 1948 (*The Atomic Base*); *Gerpla*, 1952 (*The Heroes*).

SHORT STORIES: *Nokkrar sögur*, 1923; *Fótatak manna*, 1933.

PLAYS: *Straumrof*, 1934; *Íslandsklukkan*, 1950; *Silvurtunglid*, 1954 (*The Silver Moon*).

POEMS: *Kvædakver*, 1930.

ESSAYS: *Althýdubókin*, 1929 (*The Book of the People*); *Dagleid á fjöllum*, 1937 (*A Day's Journey to the Mountains*).

TRAVEL SKETCHES AND IMPRESSIONS: *Gerska æfintýrid*, 1939 (*The Russian Adventure*).

The foremost literary figure of modern Iceland, Halldór (Gudjonsson) Kiljan Laxness has broken with the older cultural tradition of the island, both in philosophy and style. Although his novels imitate the old Norse epics in scope, his method and manner are quite different. He blends lyricism with realism and often takes a satirical attitude toward the society he depicts. His political radicalism makes him critical of existing institutions and of the people who allow them to exist; his search is directed toward

635

urban values that can replace the old agrarian ways of life.

He was born in Reykjavík on April 23, 1902, but spent his boyhood at Laxness, a farm to which his family moved when he was three years old. Prosperous farmers, his parents sent him to the gymnasium in Reykjavík for his education, but he remained there only one year; the chief event of his schooldays was his introduction to a group of student poets and the literary circles of the capital. In 1919, following his father's death, he began the series of wanderings which have marked his life ever since. Most of the tales in his first book of short stories were written as he moved from one Scandinavian country to another. In 1921–1922 he was in Germany. Denied entry to the United States in 1922, he returned to Europe and spent a year in a monastery in Luxembourg. There he became a convert in 1923 and wrote *Under the Holy Mountain*, a novel reflecting his religious experience. After a pilgrimage to Lourdes and a short stay in an English monastery he returned to Iceland in 1924. In Italy, in 1925, he wrote *The Great Weaver from Kashmir*, which caused something of a sensation when it appeared in Iceland in 1927. Laxness spent the years 1927–1930 in Canada and the United States; criticized for his activities in the leftist press, he returned to Iceland under threat of deportation in 1930.

Laxness achieved international fame when Gunnar Gunnarsson translated the two parts of *Salka-Valka* into Danish in 1934. This novel, an overnight success in Copenhagen, was also translated for publication in England and the United States. Equally well received was *Independent People,* which dealt with the life of the Icelandic farmer very much as *Salka-Valka* had presented life in an Icelandic fishing village. This work was followed, 1937–1940, by the long tetrology translated into the Dutch as *The Light of the World.* A later trilogy—*The Bell of Iceland, The Slender Fairy,* and *Fire in Copenhagen*—deals with Icelandic life in the eighteenth century. *The Atomic Base* is a political satire, *The Heroes* a literary satire on the themes and style of the old sagas; both have been subjects of controversy in the writer's homeland. In his most recent work Laxness has introduced a strong strain of autobiography into his fiction. A writer of varied talents, he has also written essays, travel books, and poetry, and he has had considerable success as a dramatist.

Laxness' later travels have included trips to Russia and the United States. He was awarded the Stalin Prize in 1943 and the Nobel Prize for literature in 1955.

BIBLIOGRAPHICAL REFERENCES: For brief critical studies of Laxness in English see Stefán Einarsson, *History of Icelandic Prose Writers, 1800–1940,* 1948; and S. A. Magnússon, "Halldór Kiljan Laxness, Iceland's First Nobel Prize Winner," *American-Scandinavian Review,* XLIV (1956), 13–18. Peter Hallberg is the author of three studies: *Halldór Kiljan Laxness,* 1952; *Den store vävaren,* 1954; and *Skaldens hus,* 1956. See also Ivar Eskeland, *Halldór Kiljan Laxness,* 1955; and Laurence S. Thompson, "Halldór Kiljan Laxness," *Books Abroad,* XXVIII (1954), 298–299.

LAYAMON

Born: Unknown
Date: Twelfth century

Died: Unknown
Date: Early thirteenth century(?)

PRINCIPAL WORK

VERSE CHRONICLE: *Brut,* c. 1205 *(Brutus).*

Layamon (properly Laȝamon; frequently modernized Lawman), the son of Leovenath, cannot be precisely dated, though it is known that he lived during the second half of the twelfth century. Allusions in his *Brut* indicate that his great medieval version of the story of Arthur was written sometime after 1189, when King Henry II died, but before May, 1206, when King John forbade the payment of Peter's pence. All that is known about Layamon is drawn from autobiographical asides in his one surviving work. He was a humble priest at Ernley (Areley Regis) on the banks of the Severn River in Worcestershire. "One day it came into his mind" to narrate the great deeds of the English and he sought out books on the subject. With Bede's *Ecclesiastical History* in Old English and in Latin, and Wace's *Roman de Brut* (1155) in Old French, he proceeded to fashion a highly imaginative rewriting of the latter into alliterative Middle English verse. Wace's 15,000 lines were expanded into 32,000, constituting the first and only account of King Arthur in English until the fourteenth century. Layamon, in a rich poetic idiom crowded with vivid images drawn from nature, not only reproduced the entire Arthurian legend known to his day, but also invented many of the now immortal features of that legend. It is he who introduced the Round Table, a massive wooden oval that could seat 1600 knights without a quarrel over precedence at table. Other innovations include gifts from elves at Arthur's birth, magic armor made by spirit smithies, and the dream which warned Arthur of Mordred's treachery.

BIBLIOGRAPHICAL REFERENCES: The standard edition of Layamon's *Brut* was edited by Sir Frederic Madden, 3 vols., 1847. A good recent text is the *Arthurian Chronicles,* also containing Wace's *Romance,* in Everyman's Library, 1912. Critical works include S. J. McNary, *Studies in Layamon's Verse,* 1904; G. J. Visser, *Layamon: An Attempt at Versification,* 1935; and Niels Bøgholm, *The Layamon Texts: A Linguistical Investigation,* 1944. An important essay is D. Everett, "Layamon and the Earliest Middle English Alliterative Verse," in *Essays on Middle English Literature,* edited by P. Kean, 1955. Other brief criticisms are R. H. Fletcher, "Layamon and Geoffrey of Monmouth," *Publications of the Modern Language Association,* XVIII (19C3), 91–94; Frances Lytel Gillespy, "Layamon's Brut: A Comparative Study in Narrative Art," *University of California Publications in Modern Philology,* III (1916), 361–510, with bibliographical footnotes; J. S. P. Tatlock, "Epic Formulas," *Publications of the Modern Language Association,* XXXVIII (1923), 494–529, and his "Laȝamon's Poetic Style," in *Manly Anniversary Studies,* 1923; H. C. Wyld, "Layamon as an English Poet," *Review of English Studies,* VI (1930), 1–30; Rudolph Willard, "Layamon in the Seventeenth and Eighteenth Centuries," *Texas University Studies in English,* XXVII (1948), 239–278, with bibliographical footnotes; and Roland Blenner-Hassett, "A Study of the Place Names in Lawman's *Brut*," *Stanford University Publications in Language and Literature*, IX (1950), 1–77, with bibliography.

JOSEPH SHERIDAN LE FANU

Born: Dublin, Ireland   *Died:* Dublin
Date: August 28, 1814   *Date:* February 7, 1873

PRINCIPAL WORKS

NOVELS: *The House by the Churchyard*, 1863; *Wylder's Hand*, 1864; *Uncle Silas*, 1864; *Guy Deverell*, 1865; *Haunted Lives*, 1868; *The Wyvern Mystery*, 1869.
SHORT STORIES: *In a Glass Darkly*, 1872; *The Watcher and Other Weird Stories*, 1894.

Joseph Sheridan Le Fanu, born in Dublin on August 28, 1814, was the son of the Dean of the Irish Episcopal Church and an off-shoot of the famous Sheridans of Ireland. His grandmother was Alice Sheridan Le Fanu, a witty poet and playwright and sister of Richard Brinsley Sheridan, author of *The Rivals* and *The School for Scandal*. As a student at Trinity College, Dublin, Le Fanu contributed stories to the *Dublin University Magazine*, which he ultimately edited and used as an outlet for most of his twelve novels. Though he passed his bar examination in 1839, he eschewed the practice of law in order to follow a literary career. Le Fanu became famous overnight with two stirring ballads, "Shamus O'Brien" and "Phaudhrig Crohoore." Drawn to the occult, the uncanny, and the ominous, he undertook a series of horror stories, some of which are considered to rank with those of Wilkie Collins. The early historical novels, such as *The Cock and Anchor* (1845) and *Torlogh O'Brien* (1847), seem to modern taste

too exaggerated to be effective. But *The House by the Churchyard*, his masterpiece, and *Uncle Silas*, his best-known work, are distinguished by their ingenious plots and tightly-knit construction.

A play, *Beatrice*, his one attempt to emulate his granduncle, was a failure and has not survived, but his stories of terror and suspense were enormously popular and still pack a punch. One of his early works, "A Chapter in the History of the Tyrone Family" (1839), reprinted in *The Watcher and Other Weird Stories*, has powerfully lurid and violent scenes that have been suggested as a source for Emily Brontë's *Wuthering Heights*. Le Fanu is frequently dismissed by literary historians as a "mere incident of the mid-century," but if the genre of the mystery story is considered a significant branch of literature, Le Fanu must be ranked as one of the important novelists of nineteenth century Ireland. Le Fanu died at Dublin on February 7, 1873.

BIBLIOGRAPHICAL REFERENCES: Le Fanu has not received the critical attention that the best of his writing merits. For a study of his genre novels see S. M. Ellis, *Wilkie Collins, Le Fanu, and Others*, 1931.

MIKHAIL YURIEVICH LERMONTOV

Born: Moscow, Russia   Died: Pyatigorsk, Russia
Date: October 15, 1814   Date: July 27, 1841

PRINCIPAL WORKS

POEMS: *Ismail-Bey,* 1832; *Hadji Abrek,* 1835; *Peshya o Kuptze Kalashnikove,* 1837 (*A Song about Tsar Ivan Vasilyevich, His Body-Guard and the Valiant Merchant Kalashnikov*); *Borodino,* 1837; *Na smert' Pushkina,* 1837 (*On the Death of a Poet*); *Mtsyri,* 1840 (*The Novice*); *Demon,* 1841 (*The Demon*).

NOVEL: *Heroï Nasheva vremeni,* 1839 (*A Hero of Our Time*).

PLAYS: *Menschen und Leidenschaften,* 1830 (*Men and Passions*); *Strannyŭ chelovek,* 1831 (*A Queer Fellow*); *Maskarad,* 1835 (*The Masquerade*).

Mikhail Yurievich Lermontov, who carried Pushkin's lyricism further into the European Romantic current, is in many ways the Russian counterpart of Leopardi, Musset, and Byron. Educated at the University of Moscow, from which he withdrew in 1832 to enroll in a military school in St. Petersburg, and commissioned in the Guards, he saw military service in Georgia and Novgorod and lived a hard and active life, frequently being engaged in duels. He was killed July 27, 1841, at the age of twenty-six at Pyatigorsk, in the Caucasus, his death the result of a duel he had forced upon a friend over an unimportant matter.

Lermontov began writing as a precocious child of twelve, but he first achieved fame with his ode on the death of Pushkin. This poem, containing accusations against the Court, could not be printed but was circulated in written copies; it brought Lermontov a sentence of banishment to a regiment stationed in the Caucasus. His earliest work was Byronic in style, gloomy and proud and strongly lyrical in its sense of independence. His strange poem, *The Demon,* planned at fifteen, contains the essence of his visionary loneliness in the story of a lost Angel who hopes to find paradise in the love of a woman but who is cheated by her death. In this work, as in *Ismail-Bey* and *Hadji Abrek,* he draws largely upon the Caucasian setting of his army life.

Many of Lermontov's shorter poems, such as "The Angel" and "The Sail" have attained lasting popularity in Russia. *The Novice,* the story of a Circassian orphan, and *A Song about Tsar Ivan Vasilyevich, his Body-Guard and the Valiant Merchant Kalashnikov,* written as a folk tale in concrete and extremely realistic phrasing, are two of his best long poems, but he also mastered the form of the novel in *A Hero of Our Time.* This, the first psychological novel in Russian, is mostly autobiographical, full of Lermontov's own passion for love and violence in the person of an officer in the Caucasus.

Lermontov was born in Moscow on October 15, 1814.

BIBLIOGRAPHICAL REFERENCES: The best brief critical study available in English is the chapter-essay in Janko Lavrin, *Russian Writers,* 1954. For other biographical and critical studies see Henri Troyat, *L'étrange destin de Lermontov; biographie,* 1952;

Georg Brandes, *Impressions of Russia*, 1899; A. Brueckner, *A Literary History of Russia*, 1908; Maurice Baring, *An Outline of Russian Literature*, 1915; G. A. Aleksinski, *Russia and Europe*, 1917; C. P. L. Dennis, "Mikhayl Yurevich Lermontov: A Brief Account of His Life and Poetry," *Poetry Review*, XVI (1925), 304–312, 392–403; and Samuel H. Cross, "Mikhail Yurevich Lermontov," *American Review on the Soviet Union*," IV (1941), 25–51.

ALAIN RENÉ LE SAGE

Born: Sarzeau, Morbihan, France
Date: May 8, 1668

Died: Boulogne, France
Date: November 17, 1747

PRINCIPAL WORKS

NOVELS: *Le Diable boiteux,* 1707; *L'Histoire de Gil Blas de Santillane,* Parts I and II, 1715; Part III, 1724; Part IV, 1735.

PLAYS: *Crispin rival de son maître,* 1707; *Turcaret,* 1709.

Alain René Le Sage, author of a hundred farces and parodies and of novels as Spanish as those of Spain, was born on a tiny peninsula of Brittany on May 8, 1668, in the town of Sarzeau. The death of his notary father left him an orphan at fourteen. He studied law, but by the time he was twenty-five a literary career in Paris seemed more attractive. There, his friend, the Abbé de Lyonne, brought to his attention the literature of Spain, and he began translating the plays of its Golden Age. He also made a French translation of the pseudo-continuation of *Don Quixote,* of which even most Spaniards have never heard.

He was forty when he scored two triumphs, one with a one act play, *Crispin rival de son maître,* accepted and performed at the Comédie Française, and the other with the novel *Le Diable Boiteux,* suggested by the Spaniard Guevara's story of the devil who removed the rooftops in Madrid so that their inhabitants could be satirized.

Continuing with the theater, Le Sage was Molière's nearest rival in real comedy, especially with the realistic *Turcaret,* an attack on those who farmed out government taxes. His quarrel with actors at the Comédie Française set him writing for the Opéra-Comique and the Théâtre de la Foire. By himself, or with collaborators, he provided dozens of plays ridiculing the vices of society during the last years of the reign of Louis XIV; these plays were performed and then lost.

In the field of the novel, with his masterpiece *Gil Blas de Santillane,* he created the first French example of material realism and by it made himself the father of the French picaresque novel. Some details were borrowed from earlier Spanish authors, but much of his own invention was so close in spirit to Spain that for years Spanish scholars sought his Spanish sources.

Unable to find a rich patron, he struggled for money and recognition. His marriage to the daughter of a cabinet maker brought him only a small dowry and three sons and a daughter. To provide them with food, he turned out potboilers. One was his *Vie et aventures de M. de Beauchêne* (1732), a story about a pirate based partly on a diary obtained from Beauchêne's widow in Tours and partly on his imagination, especially when piecing out the volume by the inclusion of adventures among the Iroquois of Canada and the Indians of Mexico and South America. Le Sage also transcribed the memoirs of the adventuress Marie Petit and other works. From the Spanish he adapted novels of roguery, like *Guzman d'Alfarache* (1732), *Estévanille Gonzalès* (1734), and *Le Bachelier de Salamanque* (1736).

He was a good father who gave his children all possible advantages. One son entered the priesthood and provided for his father in his declining years. Another became a famous star of the Comédie Française. In his later years, Le Sage was afflicted by deafness, which he satirized. He died at Boulogne, France, on November 17, 1747.

BIBLIOGRAPHICAL REFERENCES: The best study of Le Sage in English is C. O. Pierson, *The Dramatic Works of Alain-René Lesage: An Analysis and Comparison*, 1930. See also Léo Claretie, *Le Roman en France au début du XVIIIᵉ siècle*, 1890; Emile Faguet, *Dixhuitième siècle*, 1890; George Saintsbury, *Essays on French Novelists*, 1891; and Eugene F. Linthilhac, *Le Sage*, 1893.

GOTTHOLD EPHRAIM LESSING

Born: Kamenz, Germany
Date: January 22, 1729

Died: Brunswick, Germany
Date: February 15, 1781

PRINCIPAL WORKS

PLAYS: *Miss Sara Sampson*, 1755; *Minna von Barnhelm*, 1767; *Emilia Galotti*, 1771; *Nathan der Weise*, 1779 (*Nathan the Wise*).

ESSAYS AND STUDIES: *Laokoön*, 1766; *Hamburgische Dramaturgie*, 1769; *Wie die Alten den Tod gebildet*, 1769; *Die Erziehung des Menschengeschlechts*, 1780.

Born January 22, 1729, in Kamenz, a small city of northeastern Saxony, of a family originally Slavic but citizens of Germany for centuries, Gotthold Ephraim Lessing mingled in his character the energetic ruggedness of the frontier with the discipline of civilization that turned it into intellectual and aesthetic channels. As the oldest son of the city's chief pastor, the boy attended the Latin School and the famous St. Afra in Meissen, where students were up at 4:30 A.M. for a long day at their books. Introduced by his mathematics teacher to the writers of Europe, Lessing studied longer and harder than his schoolmates.

He attended the University of Leipzig in 1746, sent by his father to study theology; but Karoline Neuber, who was striving to develop a serious German theater, encouraged Lessing to use his knowledge of the classics to write an original play. His *Der junge Gelehrte* (*The Young Scholar*) was performed in 1748; at the news, his disapproving father summoned him home and would not let him return until he promised to concentrate on medicine, if he lacked aptitudes for the Church. Unfortunately, money difficulties because of his friendship for the actors sent him fleeing to Wittenberg. In Berlin, a friendly journalist

641

found him employment translating ancient history, writing plays, and editing a magazine devoted to the drama. He eventually returned to Wittenberg to work for a master's degree (1751). Here he met the philosopher Moses Mendelssohn, grandfather of the composer, and the "German Socrates" who inspired Lessing's *Nathan the Wise*.

Back in Berlin he wrote his first important play, *Miss Sara Sampson,* a "tragedy of common life" growing out of his acquaintance with the character-revealing novels of Fielding and from a play, *The London Merchant,* by George Lillo. Lessing's critical sense showed him the weakness of German drama with its dependence on a frivolous French theater. He championed the imitation of Shakespeare and Sophocles.

The Seven Years' War found him employed in Breslau as secretary to its governor, General von Tauentzien, and for five years Lessing had respite from his continual state of poverty. The death of a friend in the war suggested the idea of a series of letters on contemporary literature, supposedly written by a wounded soldier. Lessing also clarified his ideas on poetry as a dynamic form and the plastic arts as a plastic form, in the volume *Laokoön,* a landmark in aesthetic criticism. While superseded now, this pioneer work had an immense influence over several generations. At Breslau he wrote also his greatest drama, *Minna von Barnhelm,* not published until 1767. The patriotic background and the soldier protagonist with his ideas of honor attracted local interest, while the blend of pathos and humor contributed to its universal appeal.

In 1767 the port city of Hamburg, wishing to become also a center of cuture, invited the dramatist and critic to establish there a national theater. After two vain years spent fighting petty intrigue and pressures to present only French box office successes, Lessing resigned his post. But his critical articles discussing the work of the theater, published as *Hamburgische Dramaturgie,* became the basis upon which a real German national art was eventually constructed.

In debt and discouraged, Lessing took a library job at Wolfenbüttel. He experienced a brief happiness when he fell in love with and married a widow, but she died in childbirth in 1778. He found comfort in getting ready his only great tragedy, *Emilia Galotti,* which forecasts the coming social revolution, and in writing his dramatic poem in blank verse, *Nathan the Wise,* a plea for toleration from the representatives of three religions, the Jew Nathan, a Christian Knight Templar, and the Mohammedan Saladin. The carping of Christian zealots about this work made Lessing's declining years unhappy. He died alone and in debt at Brunswick on February 15, 1781, but his life and writings had prepared the way for the great poets and philosophers who were to give Germany her literary reputation.

BIBLIOGRAPHICAL REFERENCES: Two important studies of Lessing in English are H. B. Garland, *Lessing: The Founder of Modern German Literature,* 1937; and J. G. Robertson, *Lessing's Dramatic Theory,* 1939. For studies in German see Erich Schmidt, *Lessing,* 1899; G. Kettner, *Lessings Dramen,* 1904; A. M. Wagner, *Lessing,*

1931; Otto Mann, *Lessing, Sein und Leistung,* 1949; Heinrich Schneider, *Lessing, zwölf biographische Studien,* 1951; and Franz Mehring, *Die Lessing-Legende,* 1953.

CHARLES JAMES LEVER

Born: Dublin, Ireland

Date: August 31, 1806

Died: Trieste, Italy

Date: June 1, 1872

PRINCIPAL WORKS

NOVELS: *The Confessions of Harry Lorrequer,* 1839; *Charles O'Malley, The Irish Dragoon,* 1841; *Jack Hinton, Guardsman,* 1843; *Arthur O'Leary,* 1844; *Tom Burke of "Ours,"* 1844; *The O'Donoghue,* 1845; *St. Patrick's Eve,* 1845; *The Knight of Gwynne,* 1847; *The Martins of Cro' Martin,* 1847; *Confessions of Con Cregan,* 1849; *Roland Cashel,* 1850; *The Daltons,* 1852; *Sir Jasper Carewe,* 1855; *The Fortunes of Glencore,* 1857; *Davenport Dunn,* 1859; *One of Them,* 1861; *A Day's Ride,* 1863; *Barrington,* 1863; *The Bramleighs of Bishop's Folly,* 1868; *Lord Kilgobbin,* 1872.

Though classified as an Irish novelist, Charles James Lever, born in Dublin on August 31, 1806, was the son of English parents. He studied at Trinity College, Dublin, 1822–1827; there his escapades and some of his classmates provided later fictional material. He studied medicine at Göttingen, with interruptions to go as a ship's doctor to Canada, where he lived for a time with backwoods Indians. Finally he became a physician in 1831. Although the Licensing Board had doubts about his serious intentions, a cholera epidemic required doctors, and they licensed him. The death of his parents, who had opposed his marriage, allowed him to marry in 1833.

To eke out his income, Lever drew on his experiences for a string of anecdotes published serially in the newly founded *Dublin University Magazine* as the *Confessions of Harry Lorrequer,* (1837–1840). The work appeared in book form in 1839. From 1840–1842 he was semi-officially connected with the British Embassy in Brussels, where retired British officers supplied him with details for the vivid battle scenes that characterize his novels.

Charles O'Malley, a good example of military romance, appeared first in the *Dublin University Magazine,* followed by *Jack Hinton, Guardsman,* and *Tom Burke of "Ours."* Though critics scorned them, the public was so enthusiastic over Lever's work that in April, 1842, he was invited to edit the magazine to whose success he had contributed. The circle of Irish contributors he assembled increased its circulation. But his living expenses, including gambling losses, were so great, and squabbles in the editorial office so annoying, that Lever returned to Brussels, where his writings brought high prices. He went to Florence in 1847.

As he grew older, youthful zest gave way to a more reflective style, first evident in *Roland Cashel.* In 1857 he was appointed British consul at La Spezia, Italy, where he continued to write novels and articles. In 1867 he was transferred to Trieste. But he disliked the climate and hated the society. The death of his wife was the culminating blow. However, his last novel, *Lord Kilgobbin*, shows some of his old spirit. He died of a heart condition at Trieste on June 1, 1872.

To read Lever's best work is like listening to a born storyteller relating one anecdote after another about an interesting protagonist. Lever had no idea about plot or dramatic unity, but his characters, vigorous though never subtle, are unforgettable. One critic nominated Major Monsoon as a nineteenth century Falstaff, and Mickey Free as the Irish Sam Weller. Some Irishmen, however, maintain he defamed the Irish people and that his figures are not typical. In his preface to *Major Barbara*, George Bernard Shaw acknowledged his own debt to Lever, particularly to the anti-romantic *A Day's Ride*.

BIBLIOGRAPHICAL REFERENCES: There is an edition of the *Novels of Charles Lever,* 37 vols., 1897–1899. *The Confessions of Harry Lorrequer* is available in the Nelson Classics. W. J. Fitzpatrick, *The Life of Charles Lever,* 1884, and Edmund Downey, *Charles Lever: His Life in his Letters,* 2 vols., 1906 have been superseded by Lionel Stevenson's *Dr. Quicksilver: The Life of Charles Lever,* 1939. See also J. H. Friswell, *Modern Men of Letters,* 1870.

CECIL DAY LEWIS

Born: Ballintubber, Ireland
Date: April 27, 1904

PRINCIPAL WORKS

POEMS: *Beechen Vigil and Other Poems,* 1925; *Country Comet,* 1928; *Transitional Poem,* 1929; *From Feathers to Iron,* 1931; *The Magnetic Mountain,* 1933; *A Time to Dance and Other Poems,* 1935; *Overtures to Death,* 1938; *Poems in Wartime,* 1940; *Word Over All,* 1943; *Short is the Time: Poems, 1936–1943,* 1943; *Poems, 1943–1947,* 1948; *Italian Visit,* 1953; *Pegasus and Other Poems,* 1957.

NOVEL: *The Starting Point,* 1937.

TRANSLATIONS: Vergil's *Georgics,* 1940; *The Aeneid,* 1952.

ESSAYS: *A Hope for Poetry,* 1934; *The Poetic Image,* 1947; *Notable Images of Virtue,* 1954.

PLAY: *Noah and the Waters,* 1945.

Cecil Day Lewis (original name Day-Lewis) was a leading figure among the young British poets who in the 1930's were concerned chiefly with themes of social protest, and his reputation both in that unsettled decade and since seems solid and secure. He was born on April 27, 1904, in Ballintubber, Ireland; his father was an English clergyman, his mother a descendant of Oliver Goldsmith. During his childhood the family returned to England. He began to write verses when he was six and at the Sherbourne School he was several times awarded the Poetry Prize. At Wadham College, Oxford, he first became affiliated with the literary group which included W. H. Auden, Stephen Spender, Louis MacNeice, and others, and with Auden he edited the 1927 volume of Oxford Poetry.

Leftist in politics, the group with which Lewis was associated made violent and often obscure protest against conditions of the 1930's, primarily in the areas of sociology and politics. But their verse was often characterized by esoteric imagery and private allusion, so that many readers found themselves bewildered by verse that ranged in style from the gravely satirical to the frivolously diffuse. Among some readers and critics this poetry came to be known as "coterie verse"; nevertheless it was a significant reflection of the uncertainty of the decade.

Lewis has made perhaps the most successful adjustment of any of the group to popular taste and needs. More concerned with the individual in his later work and less with ideological causes, he has softened his attacks on what he once thought of as the weakening culture of the modern world and on religion, although there is still no evidence of revealed religion in his writing. This change is apparent in the verse written during the years when he was teaching at various colleges before he turned to poetry as his essential occupation in 1935. The war deepened in him a sense of responsibility; his verse about the dangers of fascism is sharp and severe, and in the poems of his middle period he showed awareness of the social weaknesses that open the way for aggression.

He is also distinguished as a writer of prose. He has written several books on the nature of poetry and its function which have given him considerable stature as a critic. His first novel, *The Starting Point*, has been followed by a series of entertaining mystery stories published under the pen name of Nicholas Blake. But poetry remains his first interest. Never an exclusive poet, he has done much to bring poetry to the common man. He has lectured successfully on the subject and, with his wife, Jill Balcon, has given extremely popular readings from his own work. In recent years he has become interested in poetry for children and has tried in a number of ways to help them develop an appreciation of verse. Although his own poetry sometimes lacks flexibility and is written in a deliberately casual manner, critics agree that his work has an economy of words and often a biting tone that makes it exceptionally suitable for the treatment of modern themes.

Lewis was made Professor of Poetry at Oxford in 1951. Recently his name has been mentioned for the office of the next poet laureate of England.

BIBLIOGRAPHICAL REFERENCES: The most comprehensive study is Clifford Dyment, *C. Day Lewis*, 1955. See also Dilys Powell, *Descent from Parnassus*, 1934; Francis Scarfe, *Auden and After*, 1942; James G. Southworth, "Cecil Day Lewis," *Sewanee Review*, XLV (1937), 469–484; Campbell Nairne, "The New Professor of Poetry," *John O'London's Weekly*, LX (1951), 1–2.

MATTHEW GREGORY LEWIS

Born: London, England
Date: July 9, 1775

Died: At Sea
Date: May 14, 1818

NOVEL: *Ambrosio, or, The Monk*, 1796.

PLAYS: *The Castle Spectre*, 1796; *The East Indian*, 1799; *Alphonso, King of Castile*, 1801; *Adelgitha*, 1807.

POEMS: *The Love of Cain*, 1799; *Poems*, 1812.

MEMOIRS: *The Journal of a West India Proprietor*, 1834.

Matthew Gregory ("Monk") Lewis was a gifted child handicapped by divided parents. Born in London on July 9, 1775, son of a prominent, forbidding father and a beautiful, artistic mother, from his public school days until his death he was kept in a constant state of anxiety over his unsuccessful efforts to love and be loved by both while trying to avoid acting as a buffer between them. The result was that he remained emotionally an adolescent until his death, although in many ways he was attentive and kind and properly ambitious. His psychological immaturity and possibly sexual abnormality combined with a strong imagination, a natural sensitivity, and a facility of language channelized into the romance of horrors for which Horace Walpole (1717–1797) and Mrs. Ann Radcliffe (1764–1823) had prepared the reading public. While at Oxford he wrote plays and poetry based on works long popular. At Weimar he became immersed in German Romanticism through the works of Tieck, Spiess, and Kotzebue. Appointed an attaché to the British legation at The Hague in 1794, he spent most of his time while in the foreign service writing his notorious novel, *Ambrosio, or, The Monk*. Published in 1796, the book created a sensation because of its blend of nightmare evil, sexual frankness, and fantastic supernaturalism. When he was elected to the House of Commons in the same year, discussion of Lewis as the author of *The Monk* required that a second edition be issued, and after he and his publisher were indicted for using literature for sensational purposes, a third, but expurgated, edition was needed to satisfy the curious public. Several of the plays he wrote later were successful on the stage, but none achieved the notoriety of his novel.

Lewis served in Parliament until 1802. In 1815 he went to Jamaica on business in connection with a plantation he had inherited. He returned there in 1817 and died at sea while on his way back to England, May 14, 1818.

BIBLIOGRAPHICAL REFERENCES: There is no adequate critical study of Lewis. The Grove Press edition of *The Monk*, 1951, contains interesting commentary by Louis F. Peck and John Berryman. See also L. F. Peck, "The Monk and Le Diable Amoureux," *Modern Language Notes*, LXVIII (1953), 406–408. For studies of Lewis's novel and the writer's relation to his period see, further, Edith Birkhead, *The Tale of Terror*, 1921; Eino Railo, *The Haunted Castle*, 1927; and the Rev. Montague Summers, *The Gothic Quest*, 1938.

SINCLAIR LEWIS

Born: Sauk Center, Minnesota
Date: February 7, 1885

Died: Rome, Italy
Date: January 10, 1951

PRINCIPAL WORKS

NOVELS: *Our Mr. Wren,* 1914; *The Trail of the Hawk,* 1915; *The Innocents,* 1917; *The Job,* 1917; *Free Air,* 1919; *Main Street,* 1920; *Babbitt,* 1922; *Arrowsmith,* 1925; *Mantrap,* 1926; *Elmer Gantry,* 1927; *The Man Who Knew Coolidge,* 1928; *Dodsworth,* 1929; *Ann Vickers,* 1933; *Work of Art,* 1934; *It Can't Happen Here,* 1935; *The Prodigal Parents,* 1938; *Bethel Merriday,* 1940; *Gideon Planish,* 1943; *Cass Timberlane,* 1945; *Kingsblood Royal,* 1947; *The God-Seeker,* 1949; *World So Wide,* 1951.

SHORT STORIES: *Selected Short Stories of Sinclair Lewis,* 1935.

PLAY: *Jayhawker,* 1935 (with Lloyd Lewis).

The literary decade of the 1920's was dominated by two figures: H. L. Mencken and (Harry) Sinclair Lewis, who, more than any other writers, gave to that era of "debunking" its special tone. Quite appropriately, Lewis was born in Sauk Center, Minnesota ("Gopher Prairie"), on February 7, 1885, the son of Dr. Emmet J. Lewis, who furnished him with part of the character of Arrowsmith. After graduating from Yale in 1908, Lewis spent many years at all sorts of work, mainly journalism, wandering from California to the East Coast. His first marriage, to Grace Hegger in 1914, ended in divorce in 1925; in 1928 he married the famous newspaper correspondent, Dorothy Thompson, from whom he was divorced in 1942.

Lewis presents the rather unusual phenomenon of a writer who, after a period of purely conventional apprenticeship, suddenly found his true expression and for a decade produced a series of extremely important novels, only to relapse for the rest of his career into hack work of no lasting significance. Thus, his earlier and later novels can be disregarded. It was in five books written during the 1920's

that he said what he had to say, and even during these years he wrote the undoubtedly second-rate *Mantrap.*

Before 1920, Lewis had published five novels, all insignificant; then, according to legend, he announced that he was at last going to write a book to please himself. The result was *Main Street,* which had an immediate and enormous success following its unheralded publication in 1920. Using the knowledge gained as a youth spent in a typical small town, Lewis shattered forever the sentimental tradition clinging around American village life. Though he located Gopher Prairie in the part of the country that he knew best, Lewis made it clear that his story would have been much the same in any small town in the United States: they are all alike, he implied, in their pettiness, dreariness, and dullness, victims of the "village virus" which destroys initiative and makes the complacent inhabitants intolerant of values other than their own. For them, Gopher Prairie is the ultimate triumph of civilization.

In *Babbitt,* his most successfully executed novel, Lewis undertook a more representative theme: the character of the typical businessman, the "go-getter" with his materialistic standards, hypnotized by his own slogans of success, yet gnawingly aware that his life is somehow empty. His tragi-comic revolt is short-lived, but it symbolizes the failure of American middle-class life to bring any real satisfaction to these people who are materially so successful and comfortable.

Arrowsmith did not infuriate so many readers, since its satire of commercialized science did not touch as many individuals and it contained the sympathetic character of Leora, the hero's first wife. It is a competent novel, with some memorable figures, but it is more limited than the other books Lewis wrote during this period. Yet it was probably his most popular novel and the one for which he was offered the Pulitzer Prize in 1926. This prize he refused.

The next novel, *Elmer Gantry,* was Lewis' most slashing attack on any segment of American life and the book that angered the greatest number of people. In it Lewis satirized with intense bitterness the more fundamentalist sects of American Protestantism. The main character, a clergyman, is a monster of hypocrisy equal to any of the villains of Dickens, yet at the end of the novel, after a temporary reversal, he is poised for further triumphs—a biting comment on America. Also included was a caricature of a famous evangelist of that period. The novel is naïve, for Lewis knew very little about religion, but the attack was badly needed at a time when many churchmen had put the weight of their churches behind Prohibition and similar hypocrisies. Yet its very timeliness for 1927 makes it more "dated" than the other novels Lewis wrote during this period.

In *Dodsworth* Lewis returned to the scenes of *Babbitt,* dealing now with the very rich members of that world. His aim was to point out that American life, even at this high financial level of ease and security, is an empty thing, that the very success, so much striven for, does not bring happiness, that the typical American, preoccupied with making money, does not know what to do with himself once the money is made. Added to this picture was that of Dodsworth's wife, seeking in a series of affairs, each more hectic than the last, for some romantic thrill that she feels she has missed.

Although Lewis wrote ten more novels and, in 1930, became the first American to be awarded the Nobel Prize for literature, his important work had been completed by the end of the 1920's. He was a typical product of the decade which, with Mencken, he had dominated, and they together accomplished a much-needed task. Though both were devoid of taste and imagination, their pungent satire, appealing to the younger generation, successfully punctured the great national complacency; never again, as has often been pointed out, could Americans regard themselves with the same placid self-satisfaction. The cult of "boosterism" had received a mortal wound.

Even in his best novels, Lewis was an extremely uneven writer and apparently totally lacked the power of self-criticism. His often naïve view of social problems was probably the result of his early socialist sympathies; he resembled Dickens in his over-simplification of human situations. Yet he had something of Dickens' power of creating caricatures, which he used in place of characters: we have never known a man exactly like Babbitt, but he is a composite of all the businessmen of our acquaintance. In addition, Lewis possessed an eye for characteristic detail and an ear for actual American speech which, added to his careful preparation, give to his novels a solid reality. He was the perfect photographer; each scene, each speech is authentic and recognizable.

Lewis died in Rome on January 10, 1951. His last novel, *World So Wide*, appeared after his death.

BIBLIOGRAPHICAL REFERENCES: The authorized biography of Sinclair Lewis is now in preparation. Grace Hegger Lewis has presented a highly personal portrait in *With Love from Gracie: Sinclair Lewis, 1912–1925*, 1956. Earlier biographical studies include Oliver Harrison, *Sinclair Lewis*, 1925; and Carl Van Doren, *Sinclair Lewis: A Biographical Sketch*, 1933. Biographical details may also be found in *From Main Street to Stockholm: Letters of Sinclair Lewis, 1919–1930*, edited by Harrison Smith, 1952, and *The Man from Main Street: A Sinclair Lewis Reader*, 1953.

For critical commentary see Carl Van Doren, *The American Novel*, 1921 (rev. ed., 1940); Vernon L. Parrington, *Sinclair Lewis: Our Own Diogenes*, 1927; Régis Michaud, *The American Novel To-day*, 1928; Vernon L. Parrington, *Main Currents in American Thought*, Vol. III, 1930; Alfred Kazin, *On Native Grounds*, 1942; C. Carroll Hollis, "Sinclair Lewis: Reviver of Character," in *50 Years of the American Novel, 1900–1950*, edited by Harold C. Gardiner, S.J., 1952; Edward Wagenknecht, *Cavalcade of the American Novel*, 1952; and Frederick J. Hoffman, *The Twenties: American Writing in the Postwar Decade*, 1955.

See also Howard Mumford Jones, "Mr. Lewis's America," *Virginia Quarterly Review*, VII (1931), 427–432; Lewis Mumford, "The America of Sinclair Lewis," *Current History*, XXXIII (1931), 529–533; Granville Hicks, "Sinclair Lewis and the Good Life," *English Journal*, XXV (1936), 265–273; Lloyd Morris, "Sinclair Lewis, His Critics and Public," *North American Review*, CCXLV (1938), 381–390; Joseph E. Baker, "Sinclair Lewis, Plato, and the Regional Escape," *English Journal*, XXVIII (1939), 460–468; Leo and Miriam Gurko, "The Two Main Streets of Sinclair Lewis," *College English*, IV (1943), 288–293; and Frederick I. Carpenter, "Sinclair Lewis and the Fortress of Reality," *ibid.*, XVI (1955), 416–423.

WYNDHAM LEWIS

Born: Maine
Date: 1886

Died: London, England
Date: March 7, 1957

PRINCIPAL WORKS

NOVELS: *Tarr*, 1918; *The Childermass*, 1928; *The Apes of God*, 1930; *Snooty Baronet*, 1932; *The Revenge for Love*, 1937; *Self-Condemned*, 1954; *The Human Age: Monstre Gai* and *Malign Fiesta*, 1955; *The Red Priest*, 1956.

SHORT STORIES: *The Wild Body*, 1927; *Rotting Hill*, 1951.

ESSAYS AND STUDIES: *The Art of Being Ruled*, 1926; *The Lion and the Fox: The Role of the Hero in Shakespeare's Plays*, 1927; *Time and Western Man*, 1927; *Paleface*, 1929; *The Diabolical Principle and the Dithyrambic Spectator*, 1931; *The Doom of Youth*, 1931; *The Old Gang and the New Gang*, 1933; *Men without Art*, 1934; *America and Cosmic Man*, 1948.

AUTOBIOGRAPHY: *Blasting and Bombardiering,* 1937; *Wyndham Lewis: The Artist from "Blast" to Burlington House,* 1939; *Rude Assignment: A Narrative of My Career Up-to-Date,* 1950.

(Percy) Wyndham Lewis, born in Maine in 1886, was taken to England by his English parents while he was still an infant. After two years at Rugby, where he revealed little enthusiasm for anything except painting, he was entered in the Slade School of Art in London with the approval of his mother who was herself a painter. From there he went to Paris on an allowance that was to continue during all of his creative years. Here began his initial expression of enmity for the effects of the "cashnexus" on morality and art and government, an attitude that was to continue throughout his career. He was first recognized as an artist for his abstract paintings. It was not until he had returned to England that he did his first writing for *Blast* (1914–1915), which he edited with Ezra Pound.

After an interlude in the army during World War I, Lewis continued with his painting and began to write professionally, referring to himself as that kind of an artist who excites people to retributory action. (His self-analysis was accurate: what he said has brought rejection and ostracization from almost all established institutions.) His first novel, *Tarr,* was naturalistic, revealing a strong influence of nihilism derived from the nineteenth century Russian novelists. His rejection of majority taste and curbs on individual freedom continued in his important work, *The Art of Being Ruled,* and reached its strongest expression in *Rude Assignment,* his informal and aggressive autobiography. The work is a brilliant exposition of the position of the man of good will and intelligence today. It also shows a waste of energy and time in its detailed concern over the problems of a writer that no reader who is not a writer would find meaningful. However, handled as a work of art, the book could have been an expression of the average individual caught in the center of amoral competitive organizational life.

While Lewis cannot be labeled "fascist," "communist," or "anti-social" without contradicting his own explicit defense in various publications, the tone of almost all of his work is that of the satirist whose object of satire is the ways of democracy. Unlike Shaw, he did not have the sense of humor which the man of sensitivity needs to survive in a democracy. As a word artist he wrote as a painter, of the outside. "Art is the science of the outside of things; natural science is the science of the inside of things." The order that is art was to him the symbolization of life dead. (Thus the seeming disorder of Joyce and Woolf was not art to him, whereas that of Eliot was.) His language was always fresh and vivid, his point of view that of the protesting individualist of sensitivity, his attitude satiric.

During World War II and after Wyndham Lewis spent much of his time in various parts of the United States and Canada. He died in London on March 7, 1957. The most important published work of his last years was *The Human Age,* a continuation of *The Childermass.* A final section, *The Trial of Man,* is to be published posthumously.

650

BIBLIOGRAPHICAL REFERENCES: For biographical and critical studies see Geoffrey Grigson, *A Master of Our Time*, 1951; Hugh Kenner, *Wyndham Lewis*, 1954; and Geoffrey Wagner, *Wyndham Lewis: A Portrait of the Artist as the Enemy*, 1957. An excellent study of *The Human Age* is Hugh Kenner, "The Devil and Mr. Lewis," *Shenandoah*, VII (1955), 15–30. See also Michael Ayrton, "Tarr and Flying Feathers," *ibid.*, 31–43; and Anon., "Classic Inhumanism," *London Times Literary Supplement*, LVI (August 2, 1957), 465–467.

JONAS LIE

Born: Drammen, Norway   *Died:* Near Oslo, Norway
Date: November 6, 1833   *Date:* July 5, 1908

PRINCIPAL WORKS

NOVELS: *Den Fremsynte*, 1870 (*The Visionary*); *Tremasteren "Fremtiden" eller Liv Nordpaa*, 1872 (*The Barque "Future," or Life Up North*); *Lodsen og hans Hustru*, 1874 (*The Pilot and His Wife*); *Thomas Ross*, 1878; *Adam Schrader*, 1879; *Rutland*, 1880; *Familjen paa Gilje*, 1883 (*The Family at Gilje*); *Kommandørens Døtre*, 1886 (*The Commodore's Daughters*); *Niobe*, 1893.

SHORT STORIES: *Fortaellinger og Skildringer fra Norge*, 1872 (*Tales and Descriptions of Norway*); *Trold*, 1891–1892.

POEMS: *Digte*, 1866–1867; *Faustina Strozzi*, 1875.

PLAYS: *Grabows Kat*, 1880; *Lystige Koner*, 1894; *Lindelin*, 1897.

Jonas (Lauritz Edemil) Lie one of Norway's most prolific nineteenth century novelists, was born at Drammen on November 6, 1833. The son of a town sheriff, he grew up in the city of Tromsö, where his youthful impressions of the wild sea-going life provided material for many of his later novels. He studied for a time at the naval academy but was forced to resign because of poor eyesight. At the University of Christiana, preparing for a career in law, he was the fellow student of Bjørnson and Ibsen. He practiced law with varying success for many years until financial pressures following a bankruptcy forced him to turn to journalism. He had little success until he and his wife (a cousin, Thomasine Lie, whom he married in 1860) collaborated on a brief romantic novel, *The Visionary*, published in 1870. With royalties from that book he traveled to Rome, where he continued to write.

In quick succession he published a volume of short stories in 1871 and two novels, *The Barque "Future"* and *The Pilot and His Wife*. These works established him as one of Norway's leading novelists and brought him a government pension. He then traveled through Germany and returned home, where he devoted his efforts to realistic novels of nineteenth century Norwegian life; among the best is *The Family at Gilje*, published in 1883. After a brief sojourn in Germany, Lie settled at Paris, where he wrote *The Commodore's Daughters* and *Niobe*. He finally ended his voluntary exile to spend the last six years of his life on native soil, writing a two-volume collection of romantic folk tales, *Trold*,

651

and preparing a 14-volume edition of his *Collected Works* (1902–1904). He died at his home near Christiania (Oslo) on July 5, 1908. In spite of his popularity in Norway, Lie has been generally ignored outside his native country. Nevertheless, anyone who seeks a detailed picture of Norwegian domestic life of a hundred years ago will find the best representation in the novels of Jonas Lie, a writer almost unexcelled as a painter of milieu.

BIBLIOGRAPHICAL REFERENCES: The best introduction to Lie in English is Alrik Gustafson, *Six Scandinavian Novelists,* 1940. See also H. H. Boyesen, *Essays on Scandinavian Literature,* 1895; J. Wiehr, "Women Characters of Jonas Lie," *Journal of English and Germanic Philology,* XXVIII (1929), 41–71+; and Hanna Astrup Larsen, "Jonas Lie," *American-Scandinavian Review,* XXI (1933), 461–471. Among the critical studies published abroad are Arne Garborg, *Jonas Lie,* 1893; Erik Lie, *Jonas Lie En livsskildring,* 1933; and Frederik Paasche, *Jonas Lie,* 1933.

ABRAHAM LINCOLN

Born: Hardin County, Kentucky   Died: Washington, D. C.
Date: February 12, 1809   Date: April 15, 1865

Principal Works

Editions of Lincoln's writings are so varied that a comparative listing of separate items is impossible within brief space. The most recent and comprehensive of the complete works is *The Collected Works of Abraham Lincoln,* edited by Roy P. Basler, Marion Dolores Pratt, and Lloyd A. Dunlap, 9 vols., 1953.

Abraham Lincoln has long been a fascinating subject for biographers and critics; in fact, the sixteenth President of the United States has probably inspired more published comment and analysis than any other American. Yet, this unceasing and unsparing scrutiny, though it has uncovered many details of his life and character, has not removed that ultimate veil which shrouds the secret of genius. Despite all that research can do—and perhaps fortunately so—the investigation of Lincoln's heritage and training fails to account for his facility in statesmanship or his eloquence as spokesman of a troubled time.

As the world knows, the birthplace of Abraham Lincoln was a log cabin in what is now Larue County, Kentucky; as it knows equally well, the date of his birth was February 12, 1809. His early surroundings were typical of the pioneer country, crude and primitive by modern standards. The parents of Lincoln were unlettered and undistinguished; it is ironic that their illiteracy should produce one of the most expressive voices of our history. Little is known of Nancy Hanks Lincoln, although a large measure of that mental and spiritual vigor discernible in her son is popularly supposed to have been derived from her. The father, Thomas Lincoln, was an unsuccessful carpenter and farmer; he acquired a reputation for instability and indecision, possibly because of his wandering ways and his tendency to work only hard enough to get by. In Abraham Lincoln's own words, he was born "in the most humble walks of life."

In 1816 the Lincolns moved to Indiana, where life was even barer and more uncomfortable than it had been in Kentucky. There, when young Abe was only nine, his mother died. A year later Thomas Lincoln found another wife in good-natured Sarah Bush Johnston, a sensible, energetic widow who managed to bring some order out of the chaos in the Lincoln household and to inspire in young Abe Lincoln a warm and lasting affection. Fortunate in at least this respect, the boy passed into adolescence and young manhood, acquiring, during a brief, one-year brush with formal schooling, an elementary knowledge of reading, writing, and ciphering. Yet this hard-working farm boy attained, somehow, a passion for knowledge and a definite interest in words and ideas.

Nor was this interest to prove a temporary one, despite the lack of intellectual stimuli in his youthful experience. During the years that followed—removal to Illinois, storekeeping, practicing law, marrying a Kentucky belle, becoming an indefatigable candidate for one political office or another—Lincoln was steadily blending that mixture of experience and reflection which would find its full flavor in the Gettysburg Address. His later accomplishments as a speaker and as a writer, overshadowed by the political and military crises which dominated his career, were never given their due by his contemporaries. Only by later generations of Americans was proper recognition accorded to such uniquely eloquent utterances as the speech at Gettysburg, the Second Inaugural Address, and the Letter to Mrs. Bixby.

Understandably, it was hard for the American public—Lincoln's friends and enemies alike—to associate the Rail Splitter from Illinois with literary polish and excellence. They sneered at his lack of education and background, choosing to ignore the amazing zest for reading and study which filled great gaps in his formal training. A vast body of general information was at the command of the frontier lawyer who was to become President of his country, and his favorite authors covered a wide range from Shakespeare to Artemus Ward. Though lacking the mannered style of popular contemporary orators like Edward Everett, Lincoln's presidential addresses and papers showed his ability to think clearly and express himself clearly, to organize his material logically, and to adapt his style to widely varying types of audiences. This style had terseness, emotional appeal, and strength. Scorning conventional artifice, he relied on directness and vigor, and his language was capable of achieving dignity and even poetry of expression. But Lincoln himself did not fully realize his gifts. He considered his Gettysburg effort a failure, with audience reaction and subsequent press comment serving only to strengthen this opinion.

This speech, which stands on an eminence all its own, was delivered on November 19, 1863. From the beginning, it was considered merely an incidental feature of ceremonies connected with the dedication of the National Cemetery at Gettysburg. Lincoln was invited, almost as an afterthought, to make a few appropriate remarks after the featured speaker, Edward Everett, had finished his address. He received only about two weeks' notice, and no one, not even Lincoln, expected his remarks to require especial preparation. Nor did they. As the story goes, they were scribbled on a slip of paper as his train approached Gettysburg. Nevertheless, they achieved the important object of lifting the nation's thoughts above the immediate stresses and hatreds of the Civil War. Lincoln's great humanity overflowed into his few simple words of dedication, and the prevailing note emphasized the broad significance of the Civil War as a vindication of popular rule.

The same note of humanity dominates Lincoln's letters, notable among these being the beautiful consolation of Mrs. Bixby for the loss of her sons in battle. Nevertheless, Lincoln's shrewdness sometimes dictated a different and more practical use of correspondence. Lacking the present-day techniques and devices of presidential publicity, he sometimes answered criticism or appealed to the people by preparing a careful letter; this, though addressed to an individual or a delegation, would really be intended for the ear of the nation as a whole. Such an epistle was the elaborate letter written to E. Corning and others, June 12, 1863, explaining his policy of arbitrary arrests and pointing out the inability of the courts to deal with rebellion. Another important letter of this type, to J. C. Conkling, defended the Emancipation Proclamation as a means of saving the Union.

Because of the pressure of public events, Lincoln made comparatively few public addresses after becoming President. Nevertheless, his death from the assassin's bullet in Washington, D.C., on April 15, 1865, cost the nation not only a statesman but a man whose singularly effective use of words allows him a respected position in our literary history. Though not technically a man of letters, what he wrote and spoke came from such depths of experience and feeling that it takes a well deserved place among American literary models. In spite of the fact that he wrote nothing with an exclusively artistic intent, the literary remains of Abraham Lincoln can be logically included among our proudest possessions.

BIBLIOGRAPHICAL REFERENCES: The edition of Lincoln's writings incorporating the results of recent historical scholarship is *The Collected Works of Abraham Lincoln,* edited by Roy P. Basler, Marion Dolores Pratt, and Lloyd A. Dunlap, 9 vols., 1953—a monumental work sponsored by the Abraham Lincoln Association. Still of importance, though not definitive, is the *Complete Works* edited by John G. Nicolay and John Hay, 12 vols., 1905. Two convenient samplings are The Modern Library edition of *The Life and Writings of Abraham Lincoln,* edited by Philip Van Doren Stern, 1942, and *Abraham Lincoln: His Speeches and Writings,* edited by Roy P. Basler, 1946. A thorough listing of Lincoln material will be found in Jay Monaghan, *Lincoln Bibliography, 1839–1939,* 2 vols., 1945. Leading studies have been evaluated in Paul M. Angle, *A Shelf of Lincoln Books,* 1946.

The authorized biography is by John G. Nicolay and John Hay, *Abraham Lincoln: A History,* 10 vols., 1890. A fine account of the pre-Presidential Lincoln is W. H. Herndon and J. W. Weik, *Herndon's Lincoln: The True Story of a Great Life,* 3 vols., 1889 (edited, 1930, by Paul M. Angle). Carl Sandburg's six-volume biography is of basic importance—*Abraham Lincoln: The Prairie Years,* 2 vols., 1926, and *Abraham Lincoln: The War Years,* 4 vols., 1939—issued in a condensed one-volume edition, 1954. Beside this classic work by a poet-historian may be set the biography by scholar-historian James G. Randall: *Lincoln the President: From Springfield to Gettysburg,* 2 vols., 1945; *Lincoln the President: Midstream,* 1952; and *Lincoln the*

President: *Last Full Measure*, 1955, completed by Richard N. Current after Randall's death in 1953. Earlier studies by Randall are *Lincoln and the South*, 1945, and *Lincoln the Liberal Statesman*, 1947. An interesting experiment in Lincoln biography, sponsored by the Abraham Lincoln Association, is the work titled *Lincoln Day by Day*, a carefully documented account of his life from 1809 to 1861, issued in four volumes by various editors between 1933 and 1941. See also Lord G. R. B. Charnwood, *Abraham Lincoln*, 1916; Ida M. Tarbell, *The Life of Abraham Lincoln*, 2 vols., 1917; Albert J. Beveridge, *Abraham Lincoln, 1809–1858*, 2 vols., 1928; Roy P. Basler, *The Lincoln Legend*, 1935; and Benjamin P. Thomas, *Abraham Lincoln*, 1952. A recent popular biography is Stephen Lorant, *The Life of Abraham Lincoln*, 1955.

More specialized studies include Harry Pratt, *Concerning Mr. Lincoln*, 1944, a study of Lincoln as he appeared to his contemporaries; Reinhard H. Luthin, *The First Lincoln Campaign*, 1944; William B. Hesseltine, *Lincoln and the War Governors*, 1948; Donald W. Riddle, *Lincoln Runs for Congress*, 1948; Robert S. Harper, *Lincoln and the Press*, 1951; and T. Harry Williams, *Lincoln and His Generals*, 1952. For background studies see also Margaret Leech, *Reveille in Washington*, 1941; Allan Nevins, *The Ordeal of the Union*, 2 vols., 1947, and *The Emergence of Lincoln*, 2 vols., 1950; Kenneth P. Williams, *Lincoln Finds a General*, 1950; Henry Steele Commager, *The Blue and the Gray: The Story of the Civil War as Told by Participants*, 2 vols., 1950; and Bruce Catton, *Mr. Lincoln's Army*, 1951.

Two periodicals are important for Lincolniana: *The Abraham Lincoln Bulletin*, 1923–1939, and *The Abraham Lincoln Quarterly*, 1940 ff.

VACHEL LINDSAY

Born: Springfield, Illinois   *Died*: Springfield
Date: November 10, 1879   *Date*: December 5, 1931

Principal Works

poems: *The Tramp's Excuse and Other Poems*, 1909; *Rhymes to Be Traded for Bread*, 1912; *General William Booth Enters into Heaven*, 1913; *The Congo and Other Poems*, 1914; *The Chinese Nightingale and Other Poems*, 1917; *The Golden Whales of California and Other Rhymes in the American Language*, 1920; *Going-to-the-Sun*, 1923; *Going-to-the-Stars*, 1926; *The Candle in the Cabin*, 1926; *Johnny Appleseed and Other Poems*, 1928; *Every Soul Is a Circus*, 1929.

autobiography and travel: *Adventures While Preaching the Gospel of Beauty*, 1914; *A Handy Guide for Beggars*, 1916.

miscellaneous: *The Golden Book of Springfield*, 1920; *The Litany of Washington Street*, 1929.

(Nicholas) Vachel Lindsay, perhaps America's most publicity-conscious poet, was a native of Illinois. He was born in Springfield, November 10, 1879, in a house which Lincoln had often visited and in which his wife's sister had lived. Lindsay's parents were both of Scottish ancestry; his father had been a Kentucky doctor, and his mother came of Virginia and Maryland stock. The parents were devout members of the Christian (Campbellite) Church, and Lindsay's mother, particularly, possessed strong artistic leanings. His family background contributed naturally to the author's interest in Southern themes, including the Negro; it also helps to account for his successful interlocking of such interests as religion, poetry, and art, as well as the evangelistic fervor of his verse.

After graduating from the Springfield High School in 1897, young Lindsay attended Hiram College in Ohio for three years. Here he came under the influence of a strong academic tradition in oratory, an influnce permanent enough to affect his later literary work. After abandoning the idea of entering the ministry, he studied art at the Art Institute of Chicago (1900–1903) and at the New York School of Art (1904–1905). His early efforts in art and poetry attracted some critical approval, but little financial return. Unperturbed, he found ways of earning a livelihood which made a strange pattern. For a while, he lectured for the Y.M.C.A. in New York, then for the Illinois Anti-Saloon League; he issued the *Village Magazine* in 1910; and he indulged in long walking tours through the South, the Southwest, and the Industrial East. On these tours he traveled alone and carried no baggage, using as his only currency his poems, which he traded for bed and board. In 1913 he published *General William Booth Enters into Heaven,* his first significant volume of poetry. It attracted little notice, but his next volume, *The Congo and Other Poems,* caught the popular fancy with what has been described as "an infectious blend of rhyme, religion, and ragtime."

Lindsay fully merited Hamlin Garland's description of him as "highly individualized." As he grew older this individuality sometimes wandered into eccentricity, both personal and literary. For example, he often attracted startled attention by his habit of dining publicly with a number of huge dolls set up at his table. In poetry, however, his innovations were usually more easy to justify. The insistent rhythms of his verse were strikingly appropriate to a subject matter generally noisy, colorful, and exciting—stampeding buffalo, a tribal dance, or the commotion of autos or trains. Lindsay became a popular reciter of his own poems; and his audiences found unforgettably impressive the manner in which, throwing back back his head and closing his eyes, he chanted and sometimes sang such poems as "The Congo." In 1920 he became the first American poet to be honored with an invitation to recite his poems at Oxford University. In the shadow of his more sensational achievements, however, are conventional poems like "The Eagle That Is Forgotten" and "Abraham Lincoln Walks at Midnight," which are marked by high seriousness and calm dignity.

Lindsay's flair for publicity and his real originality served as a decided spur to poetic interest in the early twentieth century, although the quality of his own work began a noticeable decline as early as 1917, with *The Chinese Nightingale and Other Poems.* He was married in 1925 to Elizabeth Conner. After living for a time in her home state of Washington, he returned to Springfield. Given to periods of despondency, he committed suicide on December 5, 1931.

BIBLIOGRAPHICAL REFERENCES: There is no definitive edition of Lindsay's works, for *Collected Poems of Vachel Lindsay,* 1923, revised and reissued in 1925, contains none of his later books. *Selected Poems of Vachel Lindsay,* edited by Hazleton Spencer, 1931, is representative of the poet's work.

For biography and comment see Albert E. Trombly, *Vachel Lindsay, Adventurer,* 1929; Edgar Lee Masters, *Vachel Lindsay: A Poet in America,* 1935; Mark Harris, *City of Discontent: An Interpretive Biography,* 1952; Thomas K. Whipple, *Spokesmen,* 1928; Henry M. Robinson, "The Ordeal of Vachel Lindsay: A Critical Reconstruction," *Bookman,* LXXV (1932), 6–9; William R. Moses, "Vachel Lindsay: Ferment of the Poet's Mind," *Southern Review,* I (1936), 828–836; and Austin Warren, "The Case of Vachel Lindsay," *Accent,* VI (1946), 230–239.

JOSÉ LINS DO RÊGO

Born: Pilar, Paraíba, Brazil   *Died:* Rio de Janeiro(?), Brazil
Date: June 2, 1901   *Date:* September 12(?), 1957

PRINCIPAL WORKS

NOVELS: *Menino de engenho,* 1932 (*Plantation Lad*); *Doidinho,* 1933 (*Daffy Lad*); *Banguê,* 1934 (*The Old Plantation*); *Moleque Ricardo,* 1935 (*Black Richard*); *Usina,* 1936 (*Sugar Refinery*); *Fogo morto,* 1943 (*Dead Fires*); *Eurídice,* 3rd ed., 1948.

Northeast Brazil, like the Deep South of the United States, depended on slaves to work its plantations. Born at Pilar, Paraíba, on June 2, 1901, José Lins do Rêgo (Cavalcanti) was brought up in this region at a time when the plantation system was declining before the disrupting forces of modern society. When his mother died shortly after his birth, his father left him in the care of aunts and an old grandfather who owned a string of sugar plantations extending from the ocean to the *sertão,* that region plagued by alternate drought and floods.

Educated for the legal profession in Paraíba and Pernambuco, Lins do Rêgo became professor of law, prosecuting attorney in a small town of Minas Gerais (1925), and bank inspector. In 1932 he undertook to portray in his *Sugar Cane Cycle* the economic and social conflicts of his native region, in five novels built around Carlos de Mello, who embodied autobiographical details drawn from Lins do Rêgo's prodigious memory as Carlos

grew up, went to school, circulated among his colored friends in the city, and witnessed the decline of the aristocratic plantation owners.

Lins do Rêgo was already well known when he moved to Rio de Janeiro to enter the newspaper world. He married Filomena Massa; they have three daughters. He is an uneven writer. He stands out among the increasing number of excellent Brazilian novelists for his character drawing and his simple, direct language, but his writing is flawed by the speed with which he produces a novel a year and by his lack of dialogue. His defenders see in his preference for narrative soliloquy the influence of professional oral storytellers he heard as a boy.

Among his later works, *Pedra Bonita* (1938, *Wondrous Rock*) with its picture of fanaticism in the *sertão,* is founded on actual happenings. *Agua Mãe* (1941, *Mother-Water*) is a ghost story of eerie moods that won the Felipe d'Oliveira award as the best

657

novel of the year in 1941. *Dead Fires,* a novel with excellent dialogue and characters like the Quixote-like Captain Vitorino Carneiro da Cunha (differing from the morbid Carlos de Mello) goes back to the sugar plantations to follow the rise and fall of the epileptic Lula de Hollanda, aristocratic master of Santa-Fe. Another departure from Lins do Rêgo's earlier style is *Eurídice,* a psychological novel about sex, in which he is seen experimenting with new themes.

In 1956, elected to the Academia Brasileira de Letras, he was supposed to eulogize his predecessor in his acceptance speech, but shocked the members by declaring that the man never wrote anything remotely resembling literature. It is doubtful if the same statement will ever be made about José Lins do Rêgo.

BIBLIOGRAPHICAL REFERENCES: There is almost no criticism on Lins do Rêgo in English. See Fred P. Ellison, *Brazil's New Novel,* 1954. A more specialized study is Henry H. Carter, *Lins do Rêgo's "Banguê" and Freyre's "Sobrados e Mucambos,"* 1952.

TITUS LIVIUS

Born: Patavium (Padua), Italy
Date: 59 B.C.

Died: Padua
Date: A.D. 17

PRINCIPAL WORK

HISTORY: *Ab Urbe Condita Libri* c. 26 B.C.–A.D. 14, (*Annals of the Roman People*).

Livy, greatest prose writer of the Augustan Age, was born of a noble family and spent most of his life in Rome. He left a son and a daughter. A student of rhetoric, he admired Demosthenes and Cicero and adapted the oratorical style to his narration, with an added touch of poetry.

His purpose being "To do my duty to the memory of the deeds of the most important people on earth," he wrote the *Annals of the Roman People* in 142 books, covering eight centuries from the time of Romulus and Remus (753 B.C.) to the death of young Drusus, brother of Emperor Tiberius, in 9 B.C. Apparently the history was intended to be issued in installments, since there are prefaces at four intervals in the work. Though only Books I–X and XXI–XLV still exist, fragments of the other volumes and their summaries in epitome give a good idea of the general scope and content of the whole work.

Livy gathered material from many ancient Greek and Roman sources, but confessed: "I neither affirm nor deny the traditions engendered by poets." Certainly the accuracy of the details is often dubious; the variety of his sources resulted in many inconsistencies. But Livy wrote with the enthusiasm of a patriotic Roman, and though Macaulay complained that no other historian had ever showed "so complete an indifference to truth," his vivid descriptions and swift narrative still provide good reading. He was born at Padua, Italy, in 59 B.C. and died there A.D. 17.

BIBLIOGRAPHICAL REFERENCES: The first complete translation in English was Philemon Holland, *The Roman Historie*, 1600, several times re-edited and still interesting. The acceptable modern editions are the translation by Canon Roberts in Everyman's Library, 6 vols., 1912, and those by various hands in the Loeb Classical Library, 13 vols., 1919–1930. See also R. S. Conway, *Harvard Lectures on the Virgilian Age*, 1928; Tenney Frank, *Life and Literature of the Roman Republic*, 1930; and M. L. W. Lainster, *The Greater Roman Historians*, 1947.

RICHARD LLEWELLYN
(Richard David Vivian Llewellyn Lloyd)

Born: St. David's, Wales
Date: 1907

PRINCIPAL WORKS

NOVELS: *How Green Was My Valley*, 1939; *None But the Lonely Heart*, 1943; *A Few Flowers for Shiner*, 1947; *Mr. Hamish Gleave*, 1955.

Richard (David Vivian) Llewellyn (Lloyd) was born in 1907 in that section of Wales which he described so well in his most important novel, *How Green Was My Valley*. His education, by his own admission, was chaotic, gathered piecemeal in St. David's, Cardiff, and London. Sent to Italy at the age of sixteen to study the hotel business, he began his apprenticeship in the kitchen. Meanwhile he studied art and sculpture in Venice. While working with an Italian movie unit, he began to feel the need for a more solid existence; he was not yet out of his teens when he joined H.M. Regular Army in which he served five years. During this time he got a taste of world travel, which has since become his avocation.

Returning to civilian life in 1931, he took a job as a movie extra and then became a writer for a penny film magazine. From these beginnings he rose successively in the motion picture industry to become assistant director, scenarist, production manager, and finally director.

Between periods of making films he wrote *Poison Pen*, a melodrama produced in London in 1938, and the success of this effort started him on his career as a professional writer. His first novel was *How Green Was My Valley*, the manuscript of which was begun at St. David's, added to in India, revised in Cardiff, and put into final shape in London. Immensely popular, the novel sold fifty thousand copies in England and twice that number when it was published in the United States the following year.

In the meantime Llewellyn had returned to military life, first as transportation officer in the Entertainment Battalion Services Association, later as a lieutenant in the Welsh Guards. His next novel also showed a change of course; *None But the Lonely Heart* is the story of a Cockney tough whose mother's blind devotion is most touching. Since the war Llewellyn has divided his time between traveling and writing. In addition to *Mr. Hamish Gleave*, based on the disappearance of

659

Guy Burgess and Donald Maclean behind the Iron Curtain in 1951, he has written several romantic novels for younger readers.

BIBLIOGRAPHICAL REFERENCES: For criticism of Llewellyn's novels see the *Book Review Digest*, 1940 ff.

LO KUAN-CHUNG

Born: Shantung(?), China
Date: c. 1320

Died: Unknown
Date: c. 1380

PRINCIPAL WORKS

NOVEL: The *San-kuo chih yen-i* (*Romance of the Three Kingdoms*).

In his list of contemporary libretto writers (*Hsu Lu-kuei Pu*), Chia Chung-ming speaks of Lo Kuan-chung as "a friend of disparate years" (*i.e.,* an older friend) and of a reunion in 1364 after what must have been a long separation. This would place Lo's birth around 1320. His native home is given as T'ai-yuan in Shansi, but there is good reason to believe that he was a native of Shantung and worked in Hangchow in Chekiang, which was from the twelfth to fourteenth centuries an important center of the theater and of the storytellers' guilds. Most sources are agreed that his real name was Pen, Kuan-chung being his *tzu* or derived name.

Chia lists three plays by him and speaks of him as a lyricist of great originality. One of these, dealing with the life of the founder of the Sung dynasty, has come down to our time.

He is chiefly remembered as the author of *Romance of the Three Kingdoms,* but it must be remembered that the version which has been translated into English and which has been generally read in China was extensively revised and enlarged by Mao Tsung-kang in the latter part of the seventeenth century and that even the earliest known version (1494) probably bears little resemblance to Lo's work, if he did write such a romance at all. All available evidence indicates that works of fiction published in the fourteenth century were more in the nature of prompt-books than well developed compositions intended for the reading public (Cf. note on Shih Nai-an). Lo is also credited with the authorship of three or four other historical romances in addition to the *Shui Hu Chuan* (*All Men Are Brothers*), more often attributed to Shih Nai-an.

BIBLIOGRAPHICAL REFERENCES: See, in English, Richard G. Irwin, *The Evolution of a Chinese Novel: Shui Hu Chuan;* 1953; in Chinese, Ho Hsin, *Shui-hu Yen-chiu,* 1954 (Shanghai).

VASCO DE LOBEIRA

Born: Oporto (?), Portugal
Date: c. 1360 (?)

Died: Elvas (?), Portugal
Date: c. 1403

CHIVALRIC ROMANCE: *Amadís de Gaul*, 1508.

The name of Lobeira is extremely vexing to scholars of Spanish and Portuguese literature, for it is not certain (and perhaps never will be) whether João de Lobeira (fl. 1258–1285) or Vasco de Lobeira (fl. 1385–1403) is principally responsible for *Amadís de Gaul*, the romance which Cervantes invokes as the cause of Don Quixote's madness. The great scholar of Iberian literature, A. F. G. Bell, believes that the prose romance is by Vasco, based upon an earlier poetic version by his ancestor João in the reign of King Dinis. The work was first published in four books by Garci Ordóñez (or Rodríquez) de Montalvo in 1508.

Fifteenth and sixteenth century sources refer to a Vasco de Lobeira who was knighted by King João I on the field of Aljubarrota about 1385. Since *Amadís de Gaul* was first referred to some thirty-five years earlier, this would mean either that Vasco was older than sixty when knighted or very young when he wrote his romance—unless we assume that the reference in 1350 was to a poetic version by João de Lobeira. Vasco's father left a will, dated 1386, in which he stipulated that if his widow were to remarry, the estate should go to Vasco. The fact that Vasco's mother later married a Castilian knight may mean that Vasco was influenced to compose or translate his novel into Spanish. In any event, no original Portuguese manuscript is extant, and the question remains one of academic dispute. One thing is certain: the tale exerted a powerful influence on French, Spanish, English, and Italian literature through the sixteenth and seventeenth centuries, with subsequent romancers adding tales and adventures to swell the original three books to fourteen. The places and dates of Vasco's birth and death are not known.

BIBLIOGRAPHICAL REFERENCES: The accepted version of *Amadís de Gaul* in English is an abridged translation made by Robert Southey, 1803. For discussion of the problem of authorship and sources see A. F. G. Bell, *Portuguese Literature*, 1922; W. J. Entwistle, *The Arthurian Legend in the Literatures of the Spanish Peninsula*, 1925; and G. S. Williams, "The Amadís Question," *Review Hispanique*, XXI (1909).

JOHN LOCKE

Born: Wrington, England
Date: August 29, 1632

Died: Oates, High Laver, England
Date: October 28, 1704

PRINCIPAL WORKS

ESSAYS AND STUDIES: *Epistola de Tolerantia*, 1689 (*Letters on Toleration*); *Two Treatises of Government*, 1690; *An Essay concerning Human Understanding*, 1690; *Some Thoughts concerning Education*, 1693; *The Reasonableness of Christianity as Delivered in the Scriptures*, 1695.

John Locke, English rationalist philosopher of the seventeenth century, is best known for his monumental *Essay Concerning Human Understanding*, which was to furnish basic premises, not only for the coming eigtheenth century Age of Reason and the deistic theology upon which many of its ideas were based, but also for the incipient Industrial Revolution with its rising entrepreneur class, and for political revolution in America.

Born in Wrington, Somersetshire, on August 29, 1632, he was the son of a Puritan attorney of Somerset, also named John Locke, who had served as a captain in the Parliamentary army under Cromwell and who lost a considerable part of his fortune at the time of the Restoration in 1660. This financial setback was an important factor in the life of young John Locke, for it meant that he was unable to lead the life of quiet contemplation he desired. Instead, he was forced to make a career of public office and to tie himself unwillingly to the changing circumstances of a patron. Because of this forced dependence on political patronage his important works were not written until the final quarter of his life.

His first opportunity for a life of contemplation was denied because of his religious convictions. Although he had received his master's degree from Oxford in 1658 and held minor positions at the university for a period of six years, permanent tenure was denied him because of his refusal to take holy orders; he had by then abandoned Puritanism and taken a stand against state religion, as he shows in his *Letters on Toleration*. True to his principles, he left Oxford rather than submit to governmental policies of required conformity.

Having received an appointment as secretary to Sir Walter Vane, Locke traveled with him on a mission to Brandenburg in 1665. Finding public activity inimical to philosophical thought, he refused to accompany Vane on a second mission. Instead, he took his small patrimony (what was left of his father's estate in 1660 had been divided among himself and three brothers) and pursued the study of chemistry and medicine. Although political influence kept him from receiving a medical degree, his scientific genius soon won him both the respect of his colleagues and a fellowship in the Royal Society in 1668. He also gained the patronage of Anthony Ashley Cooper, soon to become the first Earl of Shaftesbury, whose household physican he became. He also served as tutor and personal secretary and was, following Shaftesbury's rise to the chancellorship in 1672, appointed government secretary of presentations at a salary of five hundred pounds. In 1673 he became president of the Board of Trade.

These lucrative posts were lost with Shaftesbury's first fall from power, but a pension of a hundred pounds a year left him free to take up his scholarly activities in Holland. Still he was to be harassed by politics. Shaftesbury was now branded a traitor and Locke became a fugitive from extradition proceedings, unable to return to England until after the revolution of 1688 and the accession of William of Orange. Then he was restored to office with the position of Commissioner of Appeals. His famous *Essay* appeared two years later. During the remaining fourteen years of his life, spent mostly in the household of Sir Francis Masham, he was free to continue the work that was to influence so strongly the whole course of Western thought. He died at High Laver on October 28, 1704.

BIBLIOGRAPHICAL REFERENCES: John Locke's works have been reprinted in various editions. For biography and analysis see A. C. Fraser, *Locke*, 1890; Samuel Alexander, *Locke*, 1908; R. I. Aaron, *John Locke*, 1937; and J. G. Gwilym, *Life of Reason*, 1949. A more specialized study is Kenneth Maclean, *John Locke and the English Literature of the Eighteenth Century*, 1936. See also *British Empirical Philosophers*, edited by A. J. Ayer and Raymond Winch, 1952.

ROSS LOCKRIDGE, JR.

Born: Bloomington, Indiana
Date: April 25, 1914

Died: Bloomington
Date: March 6, 1948

PRINCIPAL WORK

NOVEL: *Raintree County*, 1948.

Ross (Franklin) Lockridge, Jr., wrote only one book, committing suicide in his thirty-fourth year shortly after it was published in 1948. Born April 25, 1914, in Bloomington, Indiana, where his father taught at Indiana University, Lockridge taught on the same English faculty and at Simmons College while working on his novel.

Raintree County reflects the novelist's personal concern with place and time. Set in Indiana, it attempts to encompass the popular democratic vigor of mid-nineteenth century American social history by means of flashbacks. The novel follows the experiences of one man, John Shawnessy, through the events of one day, July 4, 1892, which symbolically represents the author's theme of "encyclopedia Americana" with its school picnics, local post office gatherings, and political speeches. But the actual time covered is from 1844 to 1892; what Lockridge attempted was a re-creation, on a tremendous scale, of American society and history in the decades before and after the Civil War.

Lockridge, who spent seven years writing his work, considered it a major effort. Because of its loose realism and experimental devices of style and language, suggesting a combination of Thomas Wolfe and Joyce, the novel gained wide attention when it was first published. Full-bodied in its teeming sense of life, *Raintree County* is more than historical panorama. It is also poetic insight and myth, and in spite of certain obvious crudities it remains an interesting and ambitious effort to create a living legend of the national experience. Lockridge's death occurred in Bloomington on March 6, 1948.

BIBLIOGRAPHICAL REFERENCES: There is almost no criticism of Lockridge. See William York Tindall, "Many-leveled Fiction: Virginia Woolf to Ross Lockridge," *College English*, X (1948), 65–71; and *Book Review Digest*, 1948.

JACK LONDON

Born: San Francisco, California
Date: January 12, 1876

Died: Santa Rosa, California
Date: November 22, 1916

PRINCIPAL WORKS

NOVELS: *A Daughter of the Snows*, 1902; *The Call of the Wild*, 1903; *The Sea Wolf*, 1904; *The Game*, 1905; *White Fang*, 1906; *Before Adam*, 1906; *The Iron*

Heel, 1907; *Martin Eden*, 1909; *Burning Daylight*, 1910; *Adventure*, 1911; *Smoke Bellew*, 1912; *John Barleycorn*, 1913; *The Valley of the Moon*, 1913; *The Mutiny of the Elsinore*, 1914; *The Star Rover*, 1915; *The Scarlet Plague*, 1915; *Jerry of the Islands*, 1917; *Michael, Brother of Jerry*, 1917; *Hearts of Three*, 1920.

SHORT STORIES: *The Son of the Wolf*, 1900; *The God of His Fathers*, 1901; *The Faith of Men*, 1904; *Tales of the Fish Patrol*, 1905; *Moon-Face*, 1906; *Love of Life*, 1906; *When God Laughs*, 1911; *The House of Pride*, 1912; *The Strength of the Strong*, 1914; *Dutch Courage*, 1922.

PLAY: *Theft*, 1910.

ESSAYS: *Revolution and Other Essays*, 1910.

Jack (John Griffith) London, the ardent Socialist whose individualistic tales of adventure have long made him the idol of American boys, was born in the squalor of a San Francisco slum on January 12, 1876. His mother was a girl called Flora Wellman, his father an Irish adventurer and roving astrologer, W. H. Chaney. A few months after the child's birth Flora married John London, whose name was to be adopted and made famous by a child not his own.

Increasing poverty forced London to leave school after the eighth grade; thenceforth his literary education was dependent upon the books he borrowed from the Oakland Public Library. The fictional productions of his maturity reflect the influence of his early favorites, Rudyard Kipling, Karl Marx and, later, Herbert Spencer and Friedrich Nietzsche. Not that young London had much leisure for reading; during the five years after he left school he was an oyster pirate, a seaman, an unsuccessful Yukon prospector, and a tramp throughout the entire North American continent. In 1893, shortly after he had won a newspaper prize for his account of a typhoon off Japan, he spent a month in a Niagara Falls jail as a vagrant. Upon his release he returned to Oakland and, intending to mend his ways, entered high school there. After only a year he passed the entrance ex-

aminations of the University of California with high honors. After only one semester he left college for financial reasons, to devote himself to the writing which was to be his principal occupation for the rest of his life.

In 1898 the *Overland Monthly* published London's tale of the Yukon, *To The Man on the Trail*, the first of a steady stream of stories which were to pour from his prolific pen. By 1903 he had published more than one hundred pieces in periodicals as well as eight full-length volumes. During that year *The Call of the Wild* appeared, the story of the magnificent lone dog Buck, king of the Alaskan wilderness, which has become something of an American classic. But London's socialistic class-consciousness was already warring with his love of adventurous individualism; during the same year the American public was shocked to read his first-hand account, in *The People of the Abyss*, of life among the derelicts of London, who grubbed for garbage in the mud as food.

During the next ten years London's novels followed upon each other with amazing rapidity. Whether dealing with high adventure and the thrills of the individual torn loose from the encumbrances of civilization, battling nature as in *The Sea Wolf*, or with the growing consciousness of the downtrodden masses under a powerful leader, as in *The Iron Heel,* his books are alike in their exaltation of violence and essential solitude. This love of violence is reflected in the very titles of some of the later books, as in *The Strength of the Strong* or *The Abysmal Brute.* Only two of the novels, *Martin Eden* and *John Barleycorn,* are frankly autobiographical, but most of them reflect some aspects of the author's own character and ideals. The fortune his writing quickly brought him London spent with reckless abandon, seeking to "show the world" and satisfy his own ego with his enormous ranch, his fantastic yacht, his many loves. But neither writing nor his pursuit of pleasure could ward off the despair which came increasingly to supplant the glorious illusions in his mind. On November 22, 1916, at the age of forty, Jack London took his own life at Santa Rosa, California.

At its best, Jack London's style is characterized by color, vigor, and brutal directness rather than by literary refinement or excellence; at its worst it is that of any cheap, pot-boiling hack. But it is for the tales of violence conceived by his fertile imagination, not for beauty of prose style, that London is remembered. Socialist though he may have been by intellectual choice, he was at heart an unadulterated individualist and romantic, and his personal dream was not the Socialist paradise of mass security but the primordial wilderness, untouched by civilization, where every man and beast is king in his own domain. Egotism and vitality were the keys to London's personality, just as they are the central qualities of all his books. It was as "king of the adventure story" that Jack London was hailed in his own era and is read and remembered today.

BIBLIOGRAPHICAL REFERENCES: The best-documented story of London's life is Charmian London, *The Book of Jack London,* 2 vols., 1921. See also Irving Stone, *Sailor on Horseback,* 1938; and Joan London, *Jack London and His Times: An Unconventional Biography,* 1939. Reminiscences of London and related background studies will also be found in Stephen Graham, *The Death of Yesterday,* 1930; Georgia L. Bamford, *The Mystery of Jack London,* 1931; and Joseph Noel, *Footloose in Arcadia,* 1940.

For criticism see Thomas K. Whipple, *Study Out the Land,* 1943; H. L. Mencken, *Prejudices, First Series,* 1919; Lewis Mumford, "Jack London," *New Republic,* XXX (1922), 145–147; Stephen Graham, "Jack London," *English Review,* XXXVIII (1924), 732–737; C. Hartley Grattan, "Jack London," *Bookman,* LXVIII (1929), 667–671; and Charles C. Walcutt, "Naturalism and the Superman in the Novels of Jack London," *Papers of the Michigan Academy of Science, Arts and Letters,* XXIV (1938), 89–107.

HENRY WADSWORTH LONGFELLOW

Born: Portland, Maine
Date: February 27, 1807

Died: Cambridge, Massachusetts
Date: March 24, 1882

PRINCIPAL WORKS

POEMS: *Voices of the Night,* 1839; *Ballads and Other Poems,* 1842; *The Belfry of Bruges and Other Poems,* 1846; *Evangeline: A Tale of Acadie,* 1847; *The Seaside and the Fireside,* 1850; *The Song of Hiawatha,* 1855; *The Courtship of Miles*

Standish, 1858; *Tales of a Wayside Inn,* 1863; *Flower-de-Luce,* 1867; *Christus: A Mystery,* 1872; *The Hanging of the Crane,* 1874; *The Masque of Pandora and Other Poems,* 1875; *Kéramos and Other Poems,* 1878; *Ultima Thule,* 1880; *In the Harbor: Ultima Thule,* Part II, 1882.

PROSE ROMANCES: *Hyperion,* 1839; *Kavanagh: A Tale,* 1849.

PLAY: *The Spanish Student,* 1843.

ESSAYS: *Outre-Mer: A Pilgrimage Beyond the Sea,* 1833–1834; *Drift Wood,* 1857; *From My Armchair,* 1879.

TRANSLATION: *The Divine Comedy of Dante Alighieri,* 1867–1869.

The best loved American poet of his day, Longfellow has since suffered a literary eclipse from which he is only now slowly emerging. In popularity, at home and abroad, he once surpassed such fellow New Englanders as Emerson, Thoreau, Hawthorne, Lowell, and Holmes; and, despite continuing modern assault on his points of vulnerability, his position as our leading household poet seems likely to remain unshaken.

Henry Wadsworth Longfellow was born in Portland, Maine, on February 27, 1807. His father was an influential lawyer, and his mother's family went back to that Priscilla and John Alden whose romance was told in *The Courtship of Miles Standish.* A talented, bookish lad, Longfellow entered Bowdoin College at fifteen; at his graduation, he was offered Bowdoin's newly established professorship of modern languages. European study was a preliminary requirement, and so in 1826 the young man began that long and loving dalliance with the treasures of the Old World which was to color his experience and give flavor to his writing. From this, the first of four excursions abroad, he returned in 1829 to begin five years of teaching at his alma mater.

In 1834 Harvard called Longfellow to its Smith professorship of modern languages. Another European tour was to precede his new duties; and Long-

fellow was accompanied abroad by his wife, the fragile Mary Potter of Portland, whom he had married in 1831. Her death at Rotterdam was Longfellow's first great sorrow. Eight years later he proposed to Frances Appleton; and eighteen years of domestic happiness followed, only to end in a second disaster when Mrs. Longfellow was fatally burned in an accident at home.

Aside from these personal tragedies, Longfellow's adult years constitute a remarkable story of uninterrupted success and growing prestige. In 1839 his first book of verse, *Voices of the Night,* gained for him wide and prompt recognition with such poems as "The Psalm of Life" and "Excelsior." In 1854 he resigned the Harvard professorship to devote himself exclusively to writing. Such longer works as *Evangeline, The Song of Hiawatha,* and the first part of *Tales of a Wayside Inn* swept the poet forward on a flood-tide of acclaim and affluence. At sixty-one, during his last trip to Europe, he received honorary degrees from Oxford and Cambridge. At seventy-five he published a volume of poems entitled *In the Harbor;* a few weeks later, stricken by sudden illness, he died, on March 24, 1882, at Cambridge, Massachusetts.

Modern criticism has made much of Longfellow's frequent didacticism and lack of profundity, with less attention being given to his compensating merits as a poet. Among these is a craftsmanship and versatility which give grace and fluency to his work. Never a slavish imitator of his European literary models, he served, rather, as a link between the Old World and the New; and he contributed to American culture such distinguished translations as that of the *Divine Comedy*. Even more important was the degree of attention which was given to narrative poems based on American themes and historical incidents, most of them hitherto ignored as poetic material. If not the greatest, Longfellow is still his country's most representative poet, the writer venerated by the masses because he understood the aspirations and sorrows of everyday life and was able to express them in tones of unmistakable simplicity and sincerity.

BIBLIOGRAPHICAL REFERENCES: The standard edition for Longfellow is *The Complete Poetical and Prose Works* in the Riverside Edition, edited by H. E. Scudder, 11 vols., 1896. The standard biography is still Samuel Longfellow, *The Life of Henry Wadsworth Longfellow*, 2 vols., 1886, to which a third volume, *Final Memorials*, was added in 1887. Other biographical studies include G. R. Carpenter, *Henry Wadwsorth Longfellow*, 1901; C. E. Norton, *Henry Wadsworth Longfellow A Sketch of His Life*, 1907; H. S. Gorman, *A Victorian American: Henry Wadsworth Longfellow*, 1926; Lawrance Thompson, *Young Longfellow, 1807–1843*, 1938.

For criticism see G. R. Elliott, "The Gentle Shades of Longfellow," in *The Cycle of Modern Poetry*, 1929; Howard M. Jones, "Longfellow," in *American Writers on American Literature*, edited by John Macy, 1931; Odell Shepherd, *Longfellow*, in the American Writers Series, 1934; and Gay Wilson Allen, *American Prosody*, 1935.

AUGUSTUS BALDWIN LONGSTREET

Born: Augusta, Georgia
Date: September 22, 1790

Died: Oxford, Mississippi
Date: July 9, 1870

PRINCIPAL WORKS

TALES AND SKETCHES: *Georgia Scenes, Characters, Incidents, Etc. in the First Half Century of the Republic*, 1835.

POLEMICS: *Letters on the Epistle of Paul to Philemon, or the Connection of Apostolic Christianity with Slavery*, 1845; *A Voice from the South*, 1847; *Letters from President Longstreet to the Know-Nothing Preachers of the Methodist Church South*, 1855.

The author of *Georgia Scenes*, Augustus Baldwin Longstreet, belonged to a New Jersey family which, late in the eighteenth century, had migrated to Augusta, Georgia, where he was born, September 22, 1790. Like his friend John C. Calhoun, he attended Yale and the Litchfield Law School in Connecticut. He practiced law and entered politics after his marriage in 1817 to Frances Eliza Parkes, of Greensboro. His *Georgia Scenes* appeared, under the pseudonym "Timothy Crabshaw," in the Milledgeville *Southern Recorder* and in his newspaper, the Augusta *State Rights Sentinel*, which he edited from 1834 to 1836. He endorsed Calhoun's nullification doctrines and wrote fiercely in defense of slavery, appealing to scriptural warrant. He was a devout Methodist. After his ordination, he served as the president of Emory College, Oxford, Georgia (1839–1848), of Centenary College (1849), of the University of Mississippi (1849–1856), and of South Carolina College, later the University of South Carolina (1857). Although he welcomed secession, he was unprepared for the Civil War when it came; he appears to have been much chastened by the time it ended. He died at Oxford, Mississippi, July 9, 1870.

Edgar Allan Poe, reviewing *Georgia Scenes* in the *Southern Literary Messenger*, praised its vigor and realism. Certainly the work, with its photographic portrayal of the coarseness and starkness of "Cracker" life, heralded a new era in American letters. The influence of this work is apparent in the romances of Mark Twain and in the strain of frontier humor that runs through the writing of William Faulkner.

BIBLIOGRAPHICAL REFERENCES: The standard biographical and critical work is John Donald Wade, *Augustus Baldwin Longstreet: A Study of the Development of Culture in the South*, 1924. There is also an excellent brief sketch in Jay B. Hubbell, *The South in American Literature*, 1954. Although Longstreet is mentioned only incidentally, an important background study of frontier humor is found in Constance Rourke, *American Humor*, 1931.

LONGUS

Born: Lesbos(?), Greece
Date: Between second and fifth centuries A.D.

Died: Unknown
Date: Unknown

PRINCIPAL WORK

PASTORAL ROMANCE: *Daphnis and Chloë*, date unknown.

As is the case with another masterpiece of Greek literature, the *Iliad*, not even the name of the author of *Daphnis and Chloë* is certain. All that is actually known about the writer whose name has come down through the centuries as Longus, is that he was a native of one of the islands in the eastern Aegean Sea, possibly the island of Lesbos. He probably wrote during the second or third century A.D., although some experts place him as late as the fifth. No other works by the same author are known to exist.

Daphnis and Chloë, the romantic tale of two children, reared by shepherds, who fall in love and after many trials discover their true identities and marry happily, is said to be among the first novels ever written. It shares with other early "novels" a romantic plot full of violent mishaps, supernatural occurrences, and a final happy reunion, a measured style of the type later termed euphuistic, and a reliance on such stock characters (taken from Menander) as the parasite and the nurse. Longus is unique, however, in the grace of his prose style, his sense of humor, his use of a pastoral setting, and the fact that he puts psychological as well as physical barriers between his lovers.

Longus' fanciful tale, full of literary allusions to Homer and other Greek poets, is characterized above all by its magnificent descriptions of scenes of natural beauty. As the writer says in his prologue, his aim was to put into words a painting which told a love story.

The first translation of *Daphnis and Chloë* into English was by Angell Daye, in 1587, and the tale had a great influence on Elizabethan literature, as the plots of Greene's *Pandosto* (1588) and Shakespeare's *The Winter's Tale* (1611) testify. It is highly probable that John Lyly, whose hero Euphues gave his name to a rhetorical style of writing, was himself greatly influenced by the style of Longus.

BIBLIOGRAPHICAL REFERENCES: Available modern translations are thos by George Moore, 1924, and Moses Hadas, in *Three Greek Romances,* 1953. The Thornley translation of 1657 was edited by J. M. Edmonds, 1924. For criticism and commentary see John C. Dunlop, *History of Prose Fiction,* 1888; E. Rohde, *Der griesche Roman,* 1900; F. A. Todd, *Some Ancient Novels,* 1940; and Elizabeth H. Haight, *Essays on Greek Romances,* 1943.

ELIAS LÖNNROT

Born: Sammatti, Nyland, Finland
Date: April 9, 1802

Died: Nyland
Date: March 19, 1884

PRINCIPAL WORKS

POEMS AND COMPILATIONS: *Kantele,* 1829–1831 (*Folk Songs*); *Kalevala,* 1835; *Kanteletar,* 1840 (*Lyric Poems*).

MISCELLANEOUS: *Sananlaskuja,* 1842 (*The Proverbs of Finland*); *Finske-Svenskt lexikon,* 1866–1880 (*Finnish-Swedish Dictionary*).

Elias Lönnrot was one of those little known men who, through their extreme diligence and unusual ability, help to re-create the past glory and artistic history of a nation. Born at Sammatti, Finland, on April 9, 1802, he labored throughout most of his career to preserve the old folk legends and poetry of Finland in readable form. His formal education, however, was directed toward medicine. Educated at the University of Åbo and later at Helsinki, he was qualified as a physician.

Lönnrot's real interest was not in medicine but in philology. By 1827 he was writing articles on the nature of the early Finnish language, and he soon began to collect old legends and folk tales. In 1833 he settled in the rural district of Kajana, presumably as a doctor, but most of his time was spent in touring the countryside of Finland, nearby parts of Russia, and even Lapland, searching out fragments of old stories and verse. He was thus engaged in building collections of the national literature of Finland. His most important work was the *Kalevala,* a collection of folk literature which became the national epic of Finland. Lönnrot's work went far beyond simply collecting, which in itself was laborious, often done on foot for days at a time; he also had to edit and connect the fragmental items of the epic, often supplying connective material. Most of the source material was preserved only in oral tradition, and his work involved careful research combined with truly creative imagination. He was rewarded for his labors by an appointment to the Chair of Finnish Literature at the University of Helsinki. He died in Nyland on March 19, 1884.

BIBLIOGRAPHICAL REFERENCES: The best study of Lönnrot in English is O. A. Kallio, *Elias Lönnrot*, 1921. See also B. F. Godenhjelm, *Handbook of Finnish Literature*, trans. by E. D. Butler, 1896. A recent study is A. Anttila, *Elias Lönnrot*, 1945.

PIERRE LOTI
(Louis Marie Julien Viaud)

Born: Rochefort, France
Date: January 14, 1850

Died: Hendaye, France
Date: June 10, 1923

PRINCIPAL WORKS

NOVELS: *Aziyadé*, 1879; *Rarahu*, 1880 (reprinted as *Le Mariage de Loti*); *Le Roman d'un Spahi*, 1881; *Mon frère Yves*, 1883 (*My Brother Yves*); *Pêcheur d'islande*, 1886 (*An Iceland Fisherman*); *Madame Chrysanthème*, 1887; *Le Roman d'un enfant*, 1890 (*A Child's Romance*); *Fantôme d'Orient*, 1892; *Ramuntcho*, 1897; *Judith Renaudin*, 1898; *Les Désanchantées*, 1906.

JOURNAL: *Journal intime, 1878–1881,* 1925.

Pierre Loti was the pseudonym of Louis Marie Julien Viaud, who was born at Rochefort, France, on January 14, 1850, and who served for many years in the French Navy. During the years in which he sailed throughout the world and got to know many strange lands, he wrote a number of semi-autobiographical novels which proved immensely popular in all languages. He was elected to the French Academy in 1891. In 1910 Loti retired from active duty with the navy, but rejoined the service during World War I. He died in retirement at Hendaye on June 10, 1923.

Many of Loti's novels are set in the lands he visited. *Le Mariage de Loti*, for example, is set in Tahiti, *Madame Chrysanthème* in Japan. Such novels usually center about a primitive, but rather melancholy, love affair between a native girl and a French sailor, and they contain much vivid description in which the author caught well the sights, sounds, and smells of exotic scenes and places. Other novels are set nearer home. *An Iceland Fisherman* pictures life among the Breton fishermen, and *Ramuntcho* is a story of the Basque country. A mood of pessimism pervades these works. In his novels Loti is emotional rather than thoughtful and more interested in a poetic, romantic style than in plot construction.

BIBLIOGRAPHICAL REFERENCES: Loti's romances have been collected in his *Œuvres complètes*, 11 vols., 1894–1911. For biographical and critical studies in English see Edmund B. d'Auvergne, *Pierre Loti: The Romance of a Great Writer*, 1926; Albert

Guérard, *Five Masters of French Romance,* 1916; and Stuart P. Sherman, *Critical Woodcuts,* 1927; in French, Nicolas Serban, *Pierre Loti, sa vie et son œuvre,* 1924; and Robert de Traz, *Pierre Loti,* 1948.

RICHARD LOVELACE

Born: Kent, England *Died:* London, England
Date: 1618 *Date:* 1658

PRINCIPAL WORKS

POEMS: *Lucasta,* 1649; *Posthume Poems,* 1659.

In both his art and life Richard Lovelace played the role of the perfect courtier grandly. During the Parliamentary Wars both he and his family served King Charles I. A favorite of Queen Henrietta, Lovelace learned all the courtly graces, and in his poetry, as much as in his dress, he followed the elegant fashions of the time.

Of a noble family, Lovelace was born in Kent in 1618. He took his degree from Oxford before he went to the court of London. Having petitioned in Commons for the king, he was imprisoned in 1642. While in prison he wrote his famous lyric, "To Althea, from prison." He was soon released on bail but was required to remain in London for the duration of the Parliamentary Wars. After the defeat of the king he went to France, was wounded at the siege of Dunkerque in 1646, and returned to England in 1648. Imprisoned again, he collected and published a volume of his poems, *Lucasta,* in 1649. Having spent his fortune in the king's cause, he lived the rest of his life dependent on the generosity of his friends. After his death in London in 1658, his brother Dudley collected his literary remains and published them in *Posthume Poems.* Apart from a few excellent lyrics, Lovelace's poetry has the extravagance of Donne without his wit or synthesizing powers. It is rhetorical and artificial in the best Cavalier manner, but there is little of permanent interest in it.

BIBLIOGRAPHICAL REFERENCES: The standard edition is *The Poems of Richard Lovelace,* edited by C. H. Wilkinson, 1930. For biography and criticism see C. H. Hartmann, *The Cavalier Spirit and Its Influence on the Life and Work of Richard Lovelace,* 1925.

SAMUEL LOVER

Born: Dublin, Ireland *Died:* St. Helier, Jersey
Date: February 24, 1797 *Date:* July 6, 1868

PRINCIPAL WORKS

NOVELS: *Rory O'More,* 1837; *Handy Andy,* 1842.
SHORT STORIES: *Legends and Stories of Ireland,* 1831–1834.
POEMS: *Songs and Ballads,* 1839.

671

Although remembered today chiefly as a minor novelist, Samuel Lover in his own day had a reputation as a painter, musician, song writer, and novelist. Born on February 24, 1797, he was the son of a Dublin stockbroker who hoped that his son would follow the family profession. At the age of twelve, the boy was sent out of Dublin into the countryside to improve his health, and it was then that Lover became acquainted with the rural Irish who played such a prominent part in his fiction years later. At the age of fifteen he was taken from school to start an apprenticeship in his father's business, which proved to be uncongenial to a person with Lover's artistic interests and talent. At the age of seventeen, Samuel Lover struck out on his own and began to support himself as a painter, author, and song writer. By his thirtieth year he had established himself as a portraitist and married Lucy Berrel, daughter of a Dutch architect.

Samuel Lover's first published book was a collection of tales and Irish legends which had previously appeared in various periodicals. A greater success, although in another realm of art, came in 1835, when Lover's portrait of Paganini was chosen by the Royal Academy for an exhibit in London. That success caused Lover to take up residence in London. His first novel, *Rory O'More*, was an immediate success, both as a novel and as a play. Trouble with his eyes caused Lover to leave painting for a career as a writer of fiction, and his best-known novel, *Handy Andy*, appeared in 1842. During the 1840's Lover added to his income by giving public performances of readings from his writings and renditions of his own songs. Those entertainments and his novels gave Samuel Lover importance as a spokesman for the Irish. He is often credited with changing for the better the popular conception of the Irish in England and in America. His first wife having died, Lover was remarried in 1852 to Mary Jane Wandby. He died at St. Helier, on the isle of Jersey, Channel Islands, on July 6, 1868.

BIBLIOGRAPHICAL REFERENCES: The collected edition is *The Works of Samuel Lover*, New Library Edition, 6 vols., 1902, with a biographical and critical introduction by James J. Roche. *Handy Andy* is available in Everyman's Library, and there is an edition of the *Poetical Works*, 1880. There are two biographies: William Bayle Bernard, *The Life of Samuel Lover*, 1874, with selections from the correspondence and unpublished papers; and Andrew J. Symington, *Samuel Lover*, 1880, with selections from the writings and correspondence. See also Lewis Melville, *Victorian Novelists*, 1906.

JAMES RUSSELL LOWELL

Born: Cambridge, Massachusetts
Date: February 22, 1819

Died: Cambridge
Date: August 12, 1891

PRINCIPAL WORKS

POEMS: *Class Poem*, 1838; *A Year's Life*, 1841; *Poems*, 1844; *Poems, Second Series*, 1848; *The Vision of Sir Launfal*, 1848; *The Biglow Papers*, 1848; *A Fable for Critics*, 1848; *Poems*, 1849; *Ode: Recited at the Commemoration of the Living and Dead Soldiers of Harvard University*, 1865; *The Biglow Papers, Second Series,*

1867; *Under the Willows and Other Poems,* 1869; *The Cathedral,* 1870; *Three Memorial Poems,* 1877; *Heartsease and Rue,* 1888; *Last Poems,* 1895; *Four Poems,* 1906.

ESSAYS AND STUDIES: *Conversations on Some of the Old Poets,* 1845; *Fireside Travels,* 1864; *Among My Books,* 1870; *My Study Windows,* 1871; *Democracy and Other Addresses,* 1887; *Political Essays,* 1888; *Latest Literary Essays and Addresses,* 1891; *The Old English Dramatists,* 1892; *Lectures on English Poets,* 1897.

James Russell Lowell, born in Cambridge, Massachusetts, on February 22, 1819, and a life-long leader of the Cambridge group of nineteenth century literary New Englanders, managed to crowd a number of careers into his seventy-two years of life. He was at various times, and sometimes concurrently, a poet, a radical political writer, a conservative political writer, a satirist, an editor, a critic, a diplomat, and a teacher; and in all of these efforts he won the praise of his contemporaries. Today his reputation as poet and as critic has considerably diminished, indicating perhaps that much of the greatness attributed to him during his lifetime was due to the force of his personal qualities as a speaker and public figure, and to his urbanity and wit. But even though modern re-evaluation has diminished his stature as an artist, it must still be admitted that if he is not, as has been claimed, the "largest, best rounded personality in our literature," he is still one of the most active and most versatile we have had.

This versatility was demonstrated as early as his college days. As a New England Brahmin, he naturally attended Harvard, and there he read widely but studied indifferently. He began his career as a poet with contributions to the college magazine, *Harvardiana,* which he edited during his final year. He was also elected class poet, an honor which he was unable to enjoy completely because of the fact that he was rusticated to Concord during the graduation exercises and was thus unable to deliver the class poem.

His graduation from Harvard was in 1838. The next two years were devoted to the study of law. Although he received his law degree (1840), and set up practice for a time, his primary interest was in literature, and to that he soon completely turned, publishing his first volume of poetry, *A Year's Life,* in 1841 and making his first professional venture as an editor with the founding of the short-lived *Pioneer* in 1843.

It was in this period following his graduation from law school that his political and social radicalism came to the fore. In 1844 he had married Maria White of Watertown, and it has been suggested that his stands as an extreme abolitionist with transcendental leanings—in an attitude more natural to Concord than to Cambridge—were influenced more by her strong beliefs than by his own natural inclinations. The fact that, after her death in 1853, Lowell retreated to more and more conservative positions certainly lends weight to the validity of the suggestion. But however much Mrs. Lowell influenced her husband in these matters, it cannot be denied that the first few years of their marriage were by far the most poetically productive of his life. And of these years, 1848 was undoubtedly the greatest, for in that year he published the three works on which his diminished reputation now rests—

673

The Vision of Sir Launfal, The Biglow Papers, and *A Fable for Critics.*

This period marked the height of his career as a poet, for his production decreased as his critical and academic interests grew. He wielded his satirical pen once again during the Civil War with a second series of *Biglow Papers,* but these did not have the wit nor the spontaneity of their originals.

The decline of his work as a poet did not mean inactivity, however, but, rather, an increase of his other work. In 1855 he gave the Lowell lectures at Harvard and then succeeded Longfellow there as Smith Professor of Modern Languages, becoming head of the department of French, Spanish, and Belles-Lettres in 1856. He became the first editor of the *Atlantic Monthly* in 1857, held that post for two years, and then resigned to become editor of the *North American Review.* During this period he also found time to travel extensively in Europe and to marry Miss Frances Dunlap, his daughter's governess, three years after the death of his first wife.

Following the war and his brief resurgence as a poet, he resigned as editor of the *North American Review* (1872) and turned his attention to problems of government and politics. A thorough conservative by that time, he espoused the Republican cause and was rewarded for his party services with the ambassadorship to England in 1880, remaining at the Court of St. James until 1885 when he was recalled by Cleveland. His final years were spent in lecturing and in the writing of literary and social criticism, though one last volume of poetry, *Heartsease and Rue,* appeared in 1888, the same year as the publication of his *Political Essays.* Three years later, on August 12, 1891, he died at Elmwood, the house of his birth, but for over a quarter of a century his reputation as one of the greatest writers of the century lived on.

BIBLIOGRAPHICAL REFERENCES: The most comprehensive collection of Lowell's writings is the Elmwood Edition of *The Complete Writings of James Russell Lowell,* edited by Charles Eliot Norton, 16 vols., 1904. Useful also is *The Complete Poetical Works of James Russell Lowell,* edited by Horace E. Scudder, 1897, 1917. Material not printed in the Elmwood Edition is available in *New Letters of James Russell Lowell,* edited by M. A. DeWolfe Howe, 1932; and *The Uncollected Poetry of James Russell Lowell,* edited by Thelma M. Smith, 1950. Another useful one-volume edition is *James Russell Lowell: Representative Selections, with Introduction, Bibliography, and Notes,* edited by Harry H. Clark and Norman Foerster, 1947.

The standard life is Horace E. Scudder, *James Russell Lowell: A Biography,* 2 vols., 1901. See also E. E. Hale, Jr., *James Russell Lowell and His Friends,* 1899; Ferris Greenslet, *James Russell Lowell: His Life and Work,* 1905; and Richmond C. Beatty, *James Russell Lowell,* 1942.

LUCIAN

Born: Samosata, Syria   *Died:* Egypt (?)
Date: c. 120   *Date:* c. 200

PRINCIPAL WORKS

RHETORICAL SKETCHES: *Tyrannicide; Praise of a Fly; Phalaris I and II; Dipsas.*
SATIRES OF PHILOSOPHY: *Hermotimus; Cock; Demonax; Icaromenippus; Sale of Lives; Zeus Cross-examined; Voyage to the Lower World; Fisher.*

Outstanding among second century Greek satirists under the Roman Empire was the wit and Sophist Lucian (or Lucianus). Among his eighty writings, mostly in masterly Attic prose, are rhetorical, critical, and biographical works. Two mock tragedies about bad government and fifty-three epigrams are also attributed to him.

Lucian, born at Samosata, Syria, about A.D. 120, began as an apprentice to his uncle, a sculptor, then turned to the study of Rhetoric. He practiced law unsuccessfully in Antioch before finding his forte in writing discourses. He also traveled widely in Macedonia, Asia Minor, Italy, and Gaul, where he lectured and wrote a satirical two-volume *True History* that influenced Rabelais and Swift, as he told of space ships and battles between moon men and sun dwellers. But his fame rests on attacks on fraud in vigorous satirical dialogues, often imitated, that formed his most mature writing. He was an intellectual mocker.

In 165 Lucian settled in Athens to remain for twenty years; then, in spite of his expressed scorn for people who sell their opinions to the government, he accepted an official appointment to Egypt. Suidas, who calls him "The Blasphemer," since "he alleged the stories told of the gods are absurd," hands out poetic justice by declaring that Lucian died in Egypt about 200, torn to pieces by dogs.

BIBLIOGRAPHICAL REFERENCES: There are various translations of Lucian in English: John Dryden, *The Works of Lucian*, 4 vols., 1710; S. T. Irwin, *Six Dialogues of Lucian*, 1894; Francis Hickes, *The True History*, 1894; H. W. and F. G. Fowler, *The Works of Lucian of Samosata*, 4 vols., 1905; and A. M. Herman, *Lucian with English Translation*, 8 vols., 1913.

For background material and critical comment see F. G. Allison, Introduction to *Lucian: Selected Writings*, 1905; *idem, Lucian: Satirist and Artist*, 1926; J. J. Chapman, *Lucian and Greek Morals*, 1931; and Elizabeth H. Haight, *Essays on the Greek Romances*, 1943.

TITUS LUCRETIUS CARUS

Born: Rome, Italy   *Died:* Rome
Date: c. 98 B.C.   *Date:* 55 B.C.

PRINCIPAL WORK

PHILOSOPHY: *De rerum natura*, c. 60 B.C. (*On the Nature of Things*).

The Roman philosophical poet Lucretius was a disciple of Epicurus (c. 342–270 B.C.), who taught that pleasure is the only good and aim of all morality, but insisted a life of pleasure must be founded on honor, prudence, and justice. All that is known about Lucretius as a man are some forty words in Jerome's *Chronica Eusebii*, which, under the year 94 B.C. declares: "Titus Lucretius the poet is born. Rendered insane by a love potion, he wrote some books which Cicero afterward emended and he later killed himself by his own hand in his forty-fourth year." The exact day can be determined by a history of Vergil that declares the poet assumed his *toga virilis* on the day Lucretius died. However, all the details do not fit, and the story of his insanity after his wife gave him a love philter may be the invention of some anti-Epicurean to discredit his great work.

On the Nature of Things, in six books of hexameter verse, is a didactic work based on the fourth century B.C. "Laughing Philosopher" Democritus as well as on the doctrines of Epicurus. Lucretius declares that man is lord of himself and need not fear either death or the gods; that man's soul is made up of atoms and therefore controlled by natural laws, and that the soul and the body are mutually interdependent and cease to exist at the same time. Lucretius preached that man should see clearly, think seriously, and, believing in his own independence, face life bravely.

BIBLIOGRAPHICAL REFERENCES: Available translations in prose are those by H. A. J. Munro, 1864 (4th ed., revised 1920–1928); W. H. D. Rouse, 1924; in verse by William Ellery and Leonard, 1916; and R. C. Trevelyn, 1937. See also George Santayana, *Three Philosophical Poets*, 1910; J. Veitch, *Lucretius and the Atomic Theory*, 1875; John Masson, *The Atomic Theory of Lucretius*, 1884; G. D. Hadzsits, *Lucretius and His Influence*, 1935; and Edward E. Sikes, *Lucretius, Poet and Philosopher*, 1936.

JOHN LYLY

Born: Canterbury (?), England
Date: c. 1554

Died: London, England
Date: November, 1606

PRINCIPAL WORKS

PLAYS: *Campaspe*, 1584; *Sapho and Phao*, 1584; *Galathea*, c. 1585; *Endymion*, 1588; *Midas*, 1589; *Mother Bombie*, c. 1589; *Love's Metamorphosis*, c. 1589; *The Woman in the Moon*, c. 1593.

NOVELS: *Euphues, the Anatomy of Wit*, 1579; *Euphues and his England*, 1580.

John Lyly appeared on England's literary horizon at the same time as Sir Philip Sidney and Edmund Spenser, and each man made important contributions to the splendid literature which followed. In the twentieth century both Lyly and Spenser have fallen on evil days, Lyly with more justification, perhaps, than Spenser. However, Lyly influenced such later writers as Shake- speare and Ben Jonson; he showed the importance of prose as an art form, and he made literature of plays.

Like most of the literary Elizabethans he left no information about his childhood. He was the grandson of the famous Latin grammarian William Lyly, whose popular fame lasted long enough for Ben Jonson to use his name in a joke in *The Magnetic Lady*

(1634). John's father was Peter Lyly, who held a diocesan office at Canterbury. Reckoning backward from the year 1569, when he entered Oxford at age sixteen or thereabouts, according to Anthony à Wood, Lyly's biographers have assigned his birth to 1553 or 1554. He received his B.A. from Magdalen College, Oxford, in 1573, and his M.A. in 1575. In 1579 he was incorporated M.A. of Cambridge University. Accounts of his college life indicate that he was more addicted to the creative than the scholarly arts, but these assumptions may have been due to knowledge of his later life.

Lyly's interest in literature, like Spenser's, was apparently secondary to his interest in political advancement. Again like Spenser, he suffered much disappointment. It is ironical that in both instances the literary activities which failed to gain the desired courtly preferment for the authors gained lasting fame for them.

Lyly's literary reputation was made in 1579 with *Euphues, the Anatomy of Wit*, a bit of courtly prose fiction. The number of editions and the flood of imitations indicate its impressive popularity, which led to a sequel, *Euphues and his England*, a year later. Both books contain much philosophizing; and both are written in the ornate and distinctive style since known as Euphuism, with much alliteration, balanced phrases, artificial images, and frequent references to "unnatural natural history," such as the Fish Scolopidus, which changes color with the phases of the moon. After these two books Lyly abandoned the field of the prose novel to his imitators and turned to drama.

Euphues and His England was dedicated to Edward de Vere, Earl of Oxford, son-in-law of the powerful Lord Burghley. Under Oxford's patronage, perhaps under his influence, Lyly began to write for the theater, and also set up a company of boy actors. Not one of Lyly's eight surviving comedies appears to have been written for one of the adult companies. Since they were of the family of *Euphues*, they were probably more effective and appealing when acted by children.

In 1583 Lyly married Beatrice Browne of Yorkshire. In 1584 his theatrical ventures must have failed, for he was imprisoned for debt. Presumably Oxford had him released. His one-time friend, later enemy, Gabriel Harvey, attacked him in one of the pamphlets in the Marprelate controversy, saying: "Would God, Lyly had always been Euphues, and never Paphatchet." On this information Lyly has been accepted as the author of *Pap with an Hatchet* (1589), one of the pamphlets defending the bishops.

Although Lyly held a court position as "Esquire of the Body" and served in Parliament four times, he never became Master of the Revels, which was the height of his ambition. Several of his surviving letters are devoted to complaints at his courtly disappointments.

According to the register of the Church of St. Bartholomew the Less, Lyly had two sons and a daughter. The first son, born in 1596, lived only a year; the second was born in 1600; the daughter in 1603. The Church register records Lyly's burial on November 30, 1606.

BIBLIOGRAPHICAL REFERENCES: The standard edition is *The Complete Works of John Lyly*, edited by R. Warwick Bond, 1902. Edward Arber edited *Euphues, The*

Anatomy of Wit and *Euphues and his England,* 1868. For biographical and critical studies see J. Dover Wilson, *John Lyly,* 1905; A. Feuillerat, *John Lyly,* 1910; V. M. Jeffrey, *John Lyly and the Italian Renaissance,* 1921; F. E. Schelling and M. W. Black, *Typical Elizabethan Plays,* 1949; E. K. Chambers, *The Elizabethan Stage,* Volume III, 1923; Henry W. Wells, *Elizabethan and Jacobean Playwrights,* 1939; and T. M. Parrott and R. H. Ball, *A Short View of Elizabethan Drama,* 1943.

ANDREW LYTLE

Born: Murfreesboro, Tenn.
Date: December 26, 1902

Principal Works

NOVELS: *The Long Night,* 1936; *At the Moon's Inn,* 1941; *A Name for Evil,* 1947; *The Velvet Horn,* 1957.
BIOGRAPHY: *Bedford Forrest and His Critter Company,* 1931.

Andew Lytle, born in Murfreesboro, Tennessee, on December 26, 1902, has been one of the least productive of the group of Vanderbilt University students who as "The Fugitives" formed in the 1920's the nucleus of what was to become a dominant force in contemporary American literature. He was one of twelve Southern writers, including John Crowe Ransom, Allen Tate, Robert Penn Warren, Donald Davidson, and others, who published *I'll Take My Stand* (1930). This was the manifesto of that small group of intellectuals who, fearing that finance capitalism was leading the nation to a totalitarian state, urged a return to economic agrarianism and social patricianism. (The same group published *Who Owns America* in 1936.) Lytle was later a member of the "47 Workshop" in playwriting at Yale, an amateur actor in the new little theater movement of the 1920's, and eventually a teacher of English, including creative writing, at colleges in the East and South.

None of the four novels of Lytle has had serious critical attention. *The Long Night,* a powerful study of personal passions and deep regional feeling, has as its theme the change of character the Civil War forced on many men. The hero recovers his former humaneness but loses all purpose. *At the Moon's Inn* is a naturalistic portrayal of the actions of men searching for gold with De Soto. *A Name for Evil* symbolizes the plight of Western civilization in a ghost story dealing with a couple who restore a Southern mansion. *The Velvet Horn,* set against a background of rural Tennessee shortly after the Civil War, is rich in regional feeling and mythic implications in its account of man's perennial search for identity and wholeness.

BIBLIOGRAPHICAL REFERENCES: There is no extended biographical study, almost no criticism. See Harry R. Warfel, *American Novelists of Today,* 1951; Walter Sullivan, "Southern Novelists and the Civil War," in *Southern Renascence,* edited by Louis D. Rubin, Jr., and Robert D. Jacobs, 1953; John Crowe Ransom, "Fiction Harvest,"

Southern Review, II (1936), 403–405; and Brewster Ghiselin, "Trial of Light," *Sewanee Review,* LXV (1957), 657–665. For further discussion of individual books see also *Book Review Digest,* 1931 ff.

THOMAS BABINGTON MACAULAY

Born: Rothley Temple, England   *Died:* Campden Hill, London, England

Date: October 25, 1800   *Date:* December 28, 1859

Principal Works

HISTORY: *The History of England from the Accession of James the Second,* Vols. I and II, 1848; Vols. III and IV, 1855; Vol. V, 1861.

LITERARY ESSAYS: *Essay on Milton,* 1825; *Essay on John Dryden,* 1828; *John Bunyan,* 1830; *Samuel Johnson,* 1831; *Lord Bacon,* 1837; *Leigh Hunt,* 1841; *The Life and Writings of Addison,* 1843.

HISTORICAL AND POLITICAL ESSAYS: *Hallam,* 1828; *Mill on Government,* 1829; *Saddler's Law of Population,* 1830; *John Hampden,* 1831; *Burleigh and His Times,* 1832; *Horace Walpole,* 1833; *William Pitt, Earl of Chatham,* 1834; *Gladstone on Church and State,* 1839; *Lord Clive,* 1840; *Warren Hastings,* 1841; *Frederick the Great,* 1842.

POEMS: *Lays of Ancient Rome,* 1842.

Thomas Babington Macaulay was born at Rothley Temple, Leicestershire, October 25, 1800, the son of Zachary Macaulay, a prominent philanthropist and abolitionist. The boy was abnormally precocious; before he was eight he had written a history of the world and a three-canto romance in the manner of Scott. In 1818 he matriculated at Trinity College, Cambridge, where he wrote the prize poems in 1819 and 1821. He was called to the bar in 1826, and in 1830 he entered Parliament from the "pocket borough" of Calne, which was given to him by Lord Lansdowne. His maiden speech, on the Reform Bill, made a tremendous sensation. Representing various constituencies, he remained in Parliament off and on until 1847. He became a specialist on Indian affairs, and from 1834 to 1838 was in India as a member of the Supreme Council.

Macaulay established his literary reputation in 1825 with an essay on Milton, published in the *Edinburgh Review,* at that time the most influential journal in England. The essay attracted wide attention, far in excess of its merits. He had already become a famous conversationalist in an age when conversation was an art, and was a familiar figure at Holland House, entree to which signified social success. Some found his conversation, loaded with recondite references, overwhelming, for he read books almost as fast as he could turn the pages and never forgot a detail. He was "a book in breeches."

In spite of his duties in the House of Commons, which he discharged most conscientiously, Macaulay continued to write for the *Edinburgh Review,* contributing essays generally on literary subjects. But his great work and the one that brought him the most fame and money was his *History of England.* Within a generation after its

679

publication it had sold 140,000 copies in Great Britain alone and had been translated into every European language. For many readers, indeed, it long remained *the* history of England, for it was written from the liberal Whig point of view, which was the dominant one in Victorian England.

Macaulay, more than any other great writer of his time except perhaps Dickens, seems to us to embody all the qualities associated with the word "Victorian": the hard common-sense, the optimism, the complacency, the satisfaction with material progress. He said what the average reader wanted to hear, and he said it in effective, if artificial, style. His prejudices were obvious, but they were the prejudices of his readers; he saw everything in black or white, a characteristic which appealed to the great middle-class reading public, which was impatient of subtle theorizing.

Macaulay's mind was unquestionably powerful but limited. He knew nothing about science, art, or philosophy, but this blindness did him no harm with his readers. And his prodigious memory enabled him to produce endlessly the illustrations and references with which his work abounds.

But even in his own day there were some discerning critics who saw his weaknesses: his too-sweeping judgments, his cocksureness, his oracular certainty on all questions. Today, with the reaction against Victorianism, his reputation has dwindled. His once-famous style no longer appeals. Our historical values have changed; we no longer see history through the eyes of a nineteenth century Whig, and we can even find something good to say of James II. The *Lays of Ancient Rome* are read, if at all, only by children.

Macaulay was raised to the peerage in 1857, but ill-health limited his activities, and he never spoke in the House of Lords. He died at Campden Hill, December 28, 1859; and since he had never married, his barony became extinct.

BIBLIOGRAPHICAL REFERENCES: Macaulay's *Collected Works* were first published in eight volumes in 1866. The standard biography, one of the greatest in the language, is Sir George Otto Trevelyan's *The Life and Letters of Lord Macaulay*, 2 vols., 1875. Other studies include, J. Cotter Morison, *Macaulay*, in the English Men of Letters Series, 1882; Arthur W. M. Bryant, *Macaulay*, 1932; and Richard Croom Beatty, *Lord Macaulay: Victorian Liberal*, 1938.

CARSON MCCULLERS

Born: Columbus, Georgia
Date: February, 19, 1917

PRINCIPAL WORKS

NOVELS: *The Heart Is a Lonely Hunter*, 1940; *Reflections in a Golden Eye*, 1941; *The Member of the Wedding*, 1946.
NOVELLA: *The Ballad of the Sad Café*, 1951.
PLAYS: *The Member of the Wedding*, 1950; *The Square Root of Wonderful*, 1957.

Like William Faulkner, Carson McCullers has her literary kinship with those older, midnight-haunted writers —Poe and Hawthorne and Melville among them—who projected in fable and with symbol the story of America's unquiet mind. Her writing is also deeply rooted in the Southern scene, in her case, however, not a charted province of the imagination but a more generalized landscape that includes Georgia mill towns, a dusty crossroads hamlet, an army post in peacetime. Against this regional background she has created a world of symbolic violence and tragic reality indirectly lighted by the cool Flaubertian purity of her style. Of the writers of her generation, none has been more consistent or thoroughgoing in achieving a sustained body of work. The underlying unity of her novels, short stories, and plays is partly the result of her pervasive theme of loneliness and desire, partly the working of a special sensibility by which she gives to everyday reality an aspect of the fantastic and the fabulous. This quality of dualism in her writing allows her imagination to function simultaneously on two levels, one real and dramatic, the other poetic and symbolic.

Carson (Smith) McCullers was born in Columbus, Georgia, on February 19, 1917. The situation of her family was such that her parents could give her few advantages. (The character of Mick Kelly in The Heart Is a Lonely Hunter, a girl struggling against the confusion of her adolescence and living most intensely in her daydreams and her passion for music, suggests autobiographical overtones.) Shy, precocious, bitter, she began to write shortly after her graduation from high school. At the same time she con-

sidered making her career in music. In 1935 she went to New York with the intention of studying at Columbia University and the Juilliard School of Music, but on her arrival she lost her tuition money on the subway and was forced to take a series of part-time jobs while going to school at night. When Story bought two of her short stories she was encouraged to go ahead with her writing. In 1937 she married J. Reeves McCullers, who died in Paris in 1953. She was a Guggenheim fellow in 1942 and 1946. In 1943 she received an award from the American Academy of Arts and Letters.

All of Carson McCullers' writing turns on the plight of the loving and the lonely, and it is this view of moral and spiritual isolation as the inescapable condition of man that made The Heart Is a Lonely Hunter so impressive as a first novel when it appeared in 1940. Although the book shows certain limitations which may be accounted for by the author's youth and inexperience, it nevertheless remains a remarkable work for a twenty-two-year-old to write. It is the story of John Singer, a deaf-mute who by his speechlessness holds a strange attraction for a group of frustrated people drawn to him because his gentleness and silence seem in themselves a form of wisdom: an adolescent girl with a deep, unfulfilled love of music, a restaurant owner made lonely by his wife's death, a footloose, drunken workman who has read Marx and formulated a vague philosophy of world brotherhood, and a colored doctor dedicated to curing the physical and social ills of his race. But Singer is the most vulnerable of all. When his only friend, a Greek mute, dies in an insane asylum, he commits suicide.

The complications and ironies of this

novel make it the broadest social picture Carson McCullers has attempted. In contrast, the world of *Reflections in a Golden Eye* is restricted and intense. Here the swift unfolding of physical violence and psychological horror is designed to reveal man's capacity for error, cruelty, self-deception, and destruction. In a sense the army post of the setting is the world in miniature and the characters are the weak, the skeptical, the predatory, the lonely, the primitive, and the lost of its society. Louis Untermeyer called this novel "one of the most uncanny stories ever written in America." *The Member of the Wedding* shows adolescence as a period of loneliness and groping shot through with private fantasy and furious outbreak against a complacent adult society. Twelve-year-old Frankie Addams seizes upon her soldier brother's approaching wedding as a chance to will herself into the social community, only to discover that the bride and groom must of necessity reject her and that she must fend for herself. This novel, reducing the total idea of moral isolation to a fable of simple outlines and a few eloquently dramatic scenes, was dramatized by the writer; it was named for both the Donaldson Award and the New York Drama Critics Circle Award in 1950.

In 1951, in recognition of Carson McCullers' growing critical importance, her publishers brought out an omnibus volume containing her three novels, six short stories, and the long title story, *The Ballad of the Sad Café*. This account of gruff, squint-eyed Amelia Evans, her ex-convict husband, and a miserable hunchback named Cousin Lymon brings together the thematic implications of Carson McCullers' work in one concentration of violence, horror, and anguish. *The Square Root of Wonderful* was produced in 1957. Although the play was not all that the critics had hoped for after the freshness and simple eloquence of *The Member of the Wedding*, it nevertheless contained its moments of revelation to make plain the writer's conviction that the square root of wonderful is the understanding of love.

BIBLIOGRAPHICAL REFERENCES: There is no extended biographical or critical study. See Dayton Kohler, "Carson McCullers: Variations on a Theme," *College English*, XIII (1951), 1–8; Oliver Evans, "The Theme of Spiritual Isolation in Carson McCullers," in *New World Writing*, First Selection, 1952, 297–310; Anon., "Human Isolation," *London Times Literary Supplement*, LII (July 17, 1953), 460; Jane Hart, "Carson McCullers, Pilgrim of Loneliness," *Georgia Review*, XI (1957), 53–58; and Frank Durham, "God and No God in *The Heart Is a Lonely Hunter*," *South Atlantic Quarterly*, LVI (1957), 494–499. The view of European criticism is reflected in Erling Christie, "Carson McCullers og Hjertenes Fangenskap," *Vinduet* (Oslo), IX (1955), 55–62.

WILLIAM MCFEE

Born: At sea
Date: June 15, 1881

PRINCIPAL WORKS

NOVELS: *Aliens*, 1914; *Casuals of the Sea*, 1916; *Captain Macedoine's Daughter*, 1920; *Command*, 1922; *Race*, 1924; *Pilgrims of Adversity*, 1928; *North of Suez*,

1930; *The Harbourmaster*, 1931; *No Castle in Spain*, 1933; *The Beachcomber*, 1935; *Derelicts*, 1938; *The Watch Below*, 1940; *Spenlove in Arcady*, 1941; *Ship to Shore*, 1944; *Family Trouble*, 1949; *The Adopted*, 1952.

SHORT STORIES: *A Port Said Miscellany*, 1918; *Sailors of Fortune*, 1929; *Sailor's Bane*, 1936.

ESSAYS AND SKETCHES: *Letters from an Ocean Tramp*, 1908; *An Ocean Tramp: An Engineer's Notebook*, 1921; *Harbours of Memory*, 1921; *Swallowing the Anchor*, 1925; *Born to Be Hanged*, 1930; *More Harbours of Memory*, 1934; *Sailor's Wisdom*, 1935.

TRAVEL SKETCHES AND IMPRESSIONS: *Sunlight in New Granada*, 1925.

BIOGRAPHY: *The Life of Sir Martin Frobisher*, 1928.

AUTOBIOGRAPHY: *In the First Watch*, 1946.

William McFee writes with authority when he writes his stories of the sea, for not only was he a sailor, rising to the rank of a chief engineer before settling down in Connecticut in 1922, but he was literally born on the ocean, the son of a British sea captain who took his young Canadian wife with him for company on his transoceanic voyages.

Shortly after William McFee's birth on June 15, 1881, his father retired, taking up residence near London. There the boy attended school and then served for three years as a mechanical apprentice. Once his apprenticeship was over, he worked as an engineer and also as a salesman for a laundry machine manufacturing company. Meanwhile he read widely, lectured, and met literary men, an association that stimulated his own desire to write. In 1906 he resigned his sales job to begin a five-year tour as a seaman. His background in mechanics led him naturally to the engine-room and to a position as engineer's mate. Eventually, he became chief engineer on the S.S. *Fernfield*, establishing his own real-life counterpart of his Chief Engineer Spenlove, central figure of many of the novels he was later to write.

His first book, *Letters from an Ocean Tramp*, appeared in 1908. Four years later McFee came to the United States with the intention of devoting his full time to literature, but after a short period of time ashore he secured a chief's license in the American Merchant Marine and entered the employ of the United Fruit Company. In 1914, following the outbreak of World War I, he returned to England. During the war he served as an engineering officer on a British transport, later as a sub-lieutenant in the navy. In the meantime he had turned to fiction in his writing. *Aliens*, his first novel, was published in 1914, followed by *Casuals of the Sea* two years later.

After the war McFee returned to the United States. For several years he again served as an engineer in the United Fruit Company fleet until the demands of his writing led to a more settled life ashore. Throughout his years as a professional writer the sea, its adventures, and the wealth of shipboard lore gathered by McFee during his years at sea have remained alive in his books. Over twenty novels plus an amount of non-fictional material on the ways of ships and life afloat have followed his initial success with *Aliens* and *Casuals of the Sea*. His Chief Engineer Spenlove has become a well-known character in fiction. In recognition of his contributions to the literature of the sea, Yale University conferred on him an honorary degree in 1936.

Although McFee has had commercial success and relatively wide recognition, he has met with very little critical attention. The inevitable comparison with Conrad leaves him wanting, and he has been accused of using Spenlove as a mere mouthpiece for announcing the social or moral ideas that have interested him. In his own defense he claims that he is only interested in writing straightforward and simple adventure stories, in spinning yarns of the sea. Certainly his life, from its very beginning, gives him the authority to do just that.

BIBLIOGRAPHICAL REFERENCES: For biographical material the best source, though not complete, is the autobiographical account, *In the First Watch*, 1946. See also Harry E. Maule, *William McFee*, 1928; Christopher Morley, Introduction to *Casuals of the Sea*, 1931; and Harry R. Warfel, *American Novelists of Today*, 1951. James T. Babb, *A Bibliography of the Writings of William McFee*, 1931, contains an introduction and notes by McFee.

JOAQUIM MARIA MACHADO DE ASSÍS

Born: Rio de Janeiro, Brazil
Date: June 21, 1839

Died: Rio de Janeiro
Date: September 29, 1908

PRINCIPAL WORKS

NOVELS: *Memórias pósthumas de Braz Cubas*, 1881 (*Posthumous Memoirs of Braz Cubas*); *Quincas Borba*, 1891 (*Philosopher or Dog?*); *Dom Casmurro*, 1900 (*Mr. Grumpy*).
POEMS: *Crisálidas*, 1864; *Falenas*, 1870; *Americanas*, 1875.

Though in Brazil the color line is not drawn, the fact that Machado de Assís had a Negro father may be the explanation of much that is incomprehensible in his life and writing. During most of his life he wore a beard that concealed his negroid features. His novels reveal what some call "smiling, bitter pessimism," and others, "sad, bitter irony." Samuel Putnam declared that white Brazilian authors defend the Negro and his culture; those with mixed blood are the doubters and the pessimists.

Joaquim Maria Machado de Assís, born in Rio de Janeiro, June 21, 1839, began his literary career as a poet in the transition period between Romanticism and Brazilian Parnassianism, which was less objective and impersonal than the French prototype. He also wrote excellent short stories. His first three novels, beginning with *Resurreicão* (*Resurrection*) in 1872, though in the Romantic vein, betray a realistic author intent on suppressing emotion. His first great success was *Posthumous Memoires of Braz Cubas*, whose supposed author beyond the grave wrote "with the pen of jesting and the ink of melancholy" to prove that nothing leads to nothing. *Philosopher or Dog?* introduces Machado de Assís' only really virtuous character, and he a madman. In this work the administrator of the estate of a wealthy Rio philosopher learns that nothing is permanent except the affection of the dog that was the rich man's heir.

Best as a starting point for those who wish to know the works of this outstanding author of Brazil, whose complete works fill thirty-one volumes, is *Mr. Grumpy*, a work which helps to explain why its author is classified as Brazil's first true psychological novelist. In it, life is portrayed as it is, looking neither to its evil nor to its goodness, but delving into the soul of the unhappy and weak character who ponders the reasons for his wife's unfaithfulness and then decides that he is happy because they have no children to inherit "the legacy of his misery."

In Machado de Assís' novels, the journey rather than the goal is his pleasure, with pauses for reflection and contemplation. Action is unimportant. The novelist deals with ideas, turned by his magic into characters with human form. He makes no attempt to solve the problems of society.

Though short and far from good-looking, near-sighted and suffering continuous fears that an attack of epilepsy in the street might cause him to make a spectacle of himself, Machado de Assís has been called by Verissimo "the highest expression of our literary genius, the most eminent figure of our literature." Perhaps he was a "man of half-tints, of half words, of half ideas, of half systems"; but when the Brazilian Academy of Letters was founded in 1897, Machado de Assís was elected president and re-elected every year until his death, September 29, 1908. A flawless choice of words, force and originality of thought, and masterly control of form characterize him. Perhaps he was disillusioned, but he looked on life with a brave smile and with his dying breath he whispered: "Life is good."

BIBLIOGRAPHICAL REFERENCES: There is very little writing on Machado de Assís in English. See Isaac Goldberg, *Brazilian Literature*, 1922, with bibliography; Erico Verissimo, *Brazilian Literature: An Outline*, 1945; and Samuel Putnam, *Marvelous Journey*, 1948.

ARTHUR MACHEN

Born: Caerleon, England
Date: March 3, 1863

Died: Beaconsfield, England
Date: December 15, 1947

PRINCIPAL WORKS

NOVELS: *The Great God Pan*, 1894; *The Inmost Light*, 1894; *The Three Impostors*, 1895; *The House of Souls*, 1906; *The Hill of Dreams*, 1907; *The Great Return*, 1915; *The Terror*, 1917; *The Shining Pyramid*, 1923; *A Fragment of Life*, 1928; *The Green Round*, 1933.

SHORT STORIES AND TALES: *The Chronicle of Clemendy, or, The History of the IX Joyous Journeys*, 1888; *The Angels of Mons, The Bowmen, and Other Legends of the War*, 1915.

ESSAYS AND STUDIES: *The Anatomy of Tobacco*, 1884; *Hieroglyphics*, 1902; *Strange Roads*, 1923; *The London Adventure*, 1924; *The Canning Wonder*, 1925; *Dreads and Drolls*, 1926; *Notes and Queries*, 1926.

AUTOBIOGRAPHY: *Far Off Things*, 1922; *Things Near and Far*, 1923.

TRANSLATIONS: *The Heptameron, or, Tales and Novels of Marguerite, Queen of Navarre,* 1886; *The Memoirs of Jacques Casanova,* 1894.

Arthur Machen, Welsh writer of the bizarre and supernatural, was born at Caerleon, Monmouthshire, the sole child of a High Church clergyman in Wales, on March 3, 1863. He was an introspective, imaginative, almost mystical child, forced to spend most of his time by himself. He was educated in private schools, but the family's poverty kept him from achieving a first-class education. In his early reading he came under the influence of De Quincey and various medieval writers, and traces of that interest show in his later work.

His childhood experiences are probably reflected in his most famous novel, *The Hill of Dreams,* which is obviously autobiographical to a considerable extent.

He worked as a clerk in a publishing house in Paddington, then as a teacher, and finally as a free-lance writer. None of these vocations satisfied him, and even writing was a great labor which he never relished.

His best-known works, after *The Anatomy of Tobacco,* which appeared under the pseudonym Leolinus Siluriensis, were *The Three Imposters* and *The Hill of Dreams.* The latter novel was rejected by the publishers when it was first submitted, and it was ten years after its completion before it finally appeared. Ironically, it was his masterpiece.

In 1902 Machen joined the Benson Shakespearian Repertoire and toured with them. While with the company he met an actress who became his wife and the mother of his two children, Hilary and Janet. He joined the staff of the London *Evening News* when he was fifty years old, still restless, still poor, and still dedicated to an exquisite and other-worldly style of literature which never brought financial reward. He worked for the *News* for ten years.

Machen finally gave up writing entirely. He could not be popular even when he tried. Nevertheless, he had many appreciative friends among critics and other writers, and he entertained them as often as his budget would allow. He was a congenial man with a liking for children, and with a quick wit and a sense of humor.

His most popular story was "The Bowmen," published in the volume *The Angels of Mons, The Bowmen, and Other Legends of the War.* Machen had been profoundly disturbed by the death of five thousand soldiers at the Battle of Mons in 1914, and in his mystical short story he wrote of St. George and his archers joining forces with the English soldiers to strike down the Germans. Many readers, including men who had fought at Mons, took the story as true.

In 1943 a committee, including George Bernard Shaw, Max Beerbohm, and T. S. Eliot, was formed to help Machen financially. He died in a nursing home in Beaconsfield, England, on December 15, 1947.

BIBLIOGRAPHICAL REFERENCES: There is a collected edition, *The Works of Arthur Machen,* 9 vols., 1923. Henry Danielson, *Arthur Machen, A Bibliography,* 1923, includes an introduction and notes by Machen. Two good biographies are available, Vincent Starrett, *Arthur Machen: A Novelist of Ecstasy and Sin,* 1918; and William F. Gekle, *Arthur Machen, Weaver of Fantasy,* 1949. These are supplemented by his autobiographical books: *Far Off Things,* 1922; *Things Near and Far,* 1923; and *A Few Letters from Arthur Machen,* 1932. An interesting volume is Machen's *Precious Balms,* 1924, a collection of criticisms of his works. A range of opinion may be found in pieces dealing with Machen in several volumes: Starrett, *Buried Caesars,* 1923; Stuart P. Mais, *Some Modern Authors,* 1923; Carl Van Vechten, *Excavations: A Book of Advocacies,* 1926; and Arthur St. J. Adcock, *The Glory That Was Grub Street,* 1928.

NICCOLÒ MACHIAVELLI

Born: Florence, Italy   *Died:* Florence
Date: May 3, 1469   *Date:* June 22, 1527

PRINCIPAL WORKS

POLITICAL PHILOSOPHY: *Dell' arte della guerra,* 1521 (*The Art of War*); *Discorsi sopra la prima deca di Tito Livio,* 1531 (*Commentary on the First Ten Books of Livy*); *Istorie fiorentine,* 1532 (*History of Florence*); *Il principe,* 1532 (*The Prince*).
PLAY: *Mandragola,* 1524.

Niccolò Machiavelli, whose *Prince* set forth in realistic and cynical fashion the principles of action a ruler must use to gain and hold power, was born on May 3, 1469, into a family with a long tradition in Florentine politics. His father, Bernardo Machiavelli, was a lawyer who was forced into an ignoble position as a treasury official in Florence because his dwindling inheritance was no longer adequate to support him and his family. Niccolò, growing up during the period of Savonarola's greatest activity, was twenty-eight years old when the reformer-monk, after having been the most powerful spiritual leader in Florence, was arrested, tortured, and hanged as a heretic in March, 1498.

Machiavelli began his political life a few months after Savonarola's death. Having served briefly as a minor clerk, he was then appointed as a secretary to the Second Chancery, largely through the influence of his friend Marcello Virgilio Adriani, head of the First Chancery. He was sent on a number of minor diplomatic missions, the first important one being a mission to Forli in 1499, where he attempted unsuccessfully to discover the sentiments toward Florence of Caterina Sforza. He traveled twice to the court of King Louis XII, marched with Pope Julius II in 1506, and visited the Emperor Maximilian in 1508, but the most impressive political figure he met was Cesare Borgia, whose political tricks and murders he knew at first hand. Borgia later became the prototype for the model of statecraft in *The Prince.* He was married in 1502 to Marietta Corsini, by whom he had several children.

In 1512, following the fall of the Republic and the return of the Medici to power in Florence, Machiavelli, in spite of attempts on his part to win over the Medici by unasked-for advice, was dismissed from his office in the Chancery. He was forty-three and not wealthy; his pay had never been enough to enable him to put money aside. In 1513 he was arrested because his name was on a list prepared by conspirators who planned to murder Giuliano Medici. While under torture he strongly declared his loyalty to the Medici, but he was not readily believed. After four weeks in prison he was released.

He dedicated most of his remaining days to writing. *The Prince*, written in 1513, first appeared in 1532. This guide to power politics, with Cesare Borgia as the ideal prince, was both the natural product of his experiences with raw politics and an attempt on his part to win the favor of Lorenzo the Magnificent. His comic drama, *Mandragola*, was also written about this time, and it soon became popular because of its swift plot and clever dialogue. His *History of Florence* has often been praised for its historical and literary value. The *Commentary on Livy*, a more liberal and republican political study than *The Prince*, is regarded by many critics as a more important product of Machiavelli's experience than his more famous work.

He died in Florence on June 22, 1527, shortly after an unsuccessful attempt was made to find a place for him in the newly restored republican government. Ironically, the man who dissected the essence of Renaissance power was never able to use it to his own political advantage.

BIBLIOGRAPHICAL REFERENCES: The standard modern translation of *The Prince* is that by L. A. Bard, with an introduction by Lord Acton, 1891. Two important studies in English are A. H. Gilbert, *Machiavelli's "The Prince" and Its Forerunners*, 1939; and J. H. Whitfield, *Machiavelli*, 1947. Recent studies in Italian include Achille Norsa, *Niccolò Machiavelli*, 1948; and Federico Bruno, *Romanità e modernità del pensiero de Machiavelli*, 1952. See also Ralph Roeder, *The Man of the Renaissance*, 1933; Valeriu Marcu, *Accent on Power*, 1939; and L. Collison-Morley, "Machiavelli and the World Today," *Contemporary Review*, CLXX (1946), 289–293.

HENRY MACKENZIE

Born: Edinburgh, Scotland
Date: August, 1745

Died: Edinburgh
Date: January 14, 1831

PRINCIPAL WORKS

NOVELS: *The Man of Feeling*, 1771; *The Man of the World*, 1773; *Julia de Roubigné*, 1777.
PLAY: *The Prince of Tunis*, 1773.

Henry Mackenzie, who was called by many the "Scottish Addison," was born in Edinburgh in August, 1745. Following education at the high school and at the university of that city, he studied law, and in 1765, at the age of twenty, he went to London for a time to study English exchequer practice. Upon his return to Edinburgh, be became the law partner of George Inglis, who was attorney for the Crown. Mackenzie later succeeded Inglis in that position. About the time he returned to Scotland from England, Mackenzie began to write his famous sentimental novel, *The Man of Feeling*. For several years after its completion the novel went from publisher to publisher without arousing sufficient interest to assure its publication. When it did appear in

1771, it was published anonymously, and an English clergyman at Bath, one Eccles, claimed to have written it. Henry Mackenzie came forward to acknowledge his authorship of the book, but even then the false claim was maintained even to Eccles' having his claim commemorated upon his tombstone.

The Man of Feeling, like other novels of its genre in eighteenth century England, was vastly over-sentimental; even for the times it was a rather poorly written work. Despite these faults, as seen by modern criticism and scholarship, the novel was a very popular one when it was first published. Mackenzie wrote two other novels, *The Man of the World* and *Julia de Roubigné.* He also attempted a career as a playwright, but his *Prince of Tunis* had only a limited success; his later plays can be described only as failures.

Mackenzie married Penuel Grant in 1776, and the couple had eleven children. Mackenzie was an important figure in Edinburgh life and society in his time, being a friend to such great and famous Scottish authors as Robert Burns and Sir Walter Scott, who dedicated *Waverly* to Mackenzie and later edited an edition of his collected novels. Mackenzie was for many years a literary dictator in Edinburgh, active in literary societies and editing such journals as *The Mirror* (1779–1780) and *The Lounger* (1785–1787). He was also an enthusiastic hunter and lover of the outdoors. He died at Edinburgh on January 14, 1831.

BIBLIOGRAPHICAL REFERENCES: The best early account of Mackenzie and his fiction is Sir Walter Scott's prefatory memoir to the *Collected Novels of Henry Mackenzie,* 1831. The most recent full-length study is H. W. Thompson, *A Scottish Man of Feeling,* 1931.

ARCHIBALD MACLEISH

Born: Glencoe, Illinois
Date: May 7, 1892

PRINCIPAL WORKS

POEMS: *Tower of Ivory,* 1917; *The Happy Marriage,* 1924; *The Pot of Earth,* 1925; *Streets in the Moon,* 1926; *The Hamlet of A. MacLeish,* 1928; *New Found Land,* 1930; *Conquistador,* 1932; *Frescoes for Mr. Rockefeller's City,* 1933; *Public Speech,* 1936; *Land of the Free,* 1938; *America Was Promises,* 1939; *Actfive and Other Poems,* 1948; *Collected Poems, 1917–1952,* 1952; *Songs for Eve,* 1954.

PLAYS: *Nobodaddy,* 1925; *Panic,* 1935; *The Fall of the City: A Verse Play for Radio,* 1937; *Air Raid: A Verse Play for Radio,* 1938; *The American Story,* 1944; *This Music Crept by Me upon the Waters,* 1953; *J.B.,* 1958.

ESSAYS AND STUDIES: *The Irresponsibles,* 1940; *The American Cause,* 1941; *A Time to Speak,* 1941; *A Time to Act,* 1942; *American Opinion and the War,* 1942; *Poetry and Opinion: the "Pisan Cantos" of Ezra Pound,* 1950; *Freedom Is the Right to Choose: an Inquiry into the Battle for the American Future,* 1951.

The career of Archibald MacLeish has completed a cycle beginning in the academic world and returning to it. Born in Glencoe, Illinois, on May 7, 1892, he attended Yale University, where he was elected to Phi Beta Kappa, and Harvard University, from which he was graduated LL.B. in

1919. During the American participation in World War I, he saw twelve months' active duty in France, having enlisted in 1917 and having been advanced to the rank of captain. Accompanied by his wife and family, he went to Harvard as an instructor in government after taking his law degree. In 1920, he began the practice of law in Boston, but three years later he turned entirely to the writing of poetry. To his first volume, *Tower of Ivory,* he now added a succession of books of verse, written for the most part in Paris, where he spent several winters until 1928, the year he took up residence in Connecticut. He traveled informally in Mexico; the resultant poem, *Conquistador,* received the Pulitzer Prize for poetry in 1933. In the 1930's he became affiliated with the staff of *Fortune.* Like his poetry of the same period, his contributions to this magazine reveal his growing social-consciousness, aroused by the economic and political crises of the era.

MacLeish's public services began in 1939, when President Franklin D. Roosevelt appointed him Librarian of Congress. He held the office until 1944. In 1941–1942 he was the director of the Office of Facts and Figures; the following year he became the assistant director of the Office of War Information. As Assistant Secretary of State in 1944–1945, he maintained his interest in postwar international coöperation and gained experience which he put to use in helping to organize UNESCO. He rejoined the Harvard faculty as Boylston Professor of Rhetoric and Oratory in 1949.

As a poet, MacLeish has developed through several stages. His early poems were traditionalistic; an allegorical mystery-play, *Nobodaddy,* held no great promise of his later achievements as a poetic dramatist. *Streets in the Moon,* a maturer work which owed much to contemporary models, including Conrad Aiken, Ezra Pound, and T. S. Eliot, showed more delicate craftsmanship. This volume contains the often-quoted "Ars Poetica," with its imagistic tribute to the integrity of poetry. *The Hamlet of A. MacLeish* was as much influenced by Jules Laforgue as by Elizabethan models. *New Found Land* marked a new transition to American themes. *Conquistador,* a narrative in modified *terza rima,* was based on the *True History of the Conquest of New Spain,* by Bernal Díaz del Castillo. MacLeish's dissatisfaction with the expatriates was fully apparent in *Frescoes for Mr. Rockefeller's City;* this group of poems satirized "decadence" and acclaimed the vitality of America. His politically conservative tone in this volume gave way, in turn, to a liberal note in his verse-play *Panic,* in *Public Speech,* in the radio drama *The Fall of the City,* and in *Land of the Free.* *America Was Promises* presaged the optimism of MacLeish's prose writings during World War II, when he was concerned to fortify the American cause of liberal democracy. That he had kept his faith in the independent dignity of art was illustrated when, in 1950, he defended the award of the Bollingen Prize to Ezra Pound for *The Pisan Cantos,* to whose political overtones he was naturally hostile. The issuance of *Collected Poems, 1917–1952* was recognized with a second Pulitzer Prize and with the Bollingen Prize and the National Book Award in 1953. His most recent poems and plays show signs of a return to certain poetic mannerisms of his expatriate period.

BIBLIOGRAPHICAL REFERENCES: The early collection of MacLeish's poems was *Poems, 1924–1933*, followed by *Collected Poems, 1917–1952*. The most recent bibliography is the checklist by Frances Cheney in Allen Tate, *Sixty American Poets, 1896–1944*, 1945.

MacLeish has been the subject of considerable critical examination in the periodicals; only a partial listing can be given here. Early articles include Morton Dauwen Zabel, "The Compromise of Archibald MacLeish," *Poetry*, XXXVI (1930), 270–275, and "Cinema of Hamlet," *ibid.*, XLIV (1934), 150–159; Harriet Monroe, "Archibald MacLeish," *ibid.*, XXXVIII (1931), 150–155; and George Dangerfield, "Archibald MacLeish: An Appreciation," *Bookman*, LXXII (1931), 493–496. Later estimates include Dayton Kohler, "MacLeish and the Modern Temper," *South Atlantic Quarterly*, XXXVIII (1939), 416–426; Edmund Wilson, "Archibald MacLeish and 'The Word,'" *New Republic*, CIII (1940), 30–32; M. D. Zabel, "The Poet on Capitol Hill," *Partisan Review*, VIII (1941), 2–19; Eleanor M. Sickels, "Archibald MacLeish and American Democracy," *American Literature*, XV (1943), 223–227; and Hyatt H. Waggoner, "Archibald MacLeish and the Aspect of Eternity," *College English*, IV (1943), 402–412, the latter an examination of his thought.

JAMES MADISON

Born: Port Conway, Virginia　　　　　　*Died:* Orange County, Virginia
Date: March 16, 1751　　　　　　　　*Date:* June 28, 1836

PRINCIPAL WORKS

POLITICAL ESSAYS, LETTERS, AND DOCUMENTS: Nos. 10, 14, and 37–58, *The Federalist*, 1788; *Letters of Helvidius*, 1796; *Examination of the British Doctrine which subjects to Capture a Neutral Trade not open in time of Peace*, 1806; "Virginia Statute of Religious Liberty of 1786," in *Documents of American History*, edited by Henry S. Commager, 1949 (5th edition), I, 125–126; "The Virginia and Kentucky Resolutions of 1798–1799," *ibid.*, I, 178–184; "Madison's War Message [of 1812]," *ibid.*, 207–209; "Madison's Veto of Bonus Bill of 1817," *ibid.*, I, 211–212; "Journal of Debates in the Federal Convention of 1787," in *The Writings of James Madison*, edited by Gaillard Hunt, 1900–1910, Vols. III and IV; Speeches in Congress on "Imports," *ibid.*, V, 346–361; "Amendments," *ibid.*, V, 370–389, 414–417; "Location of the Capital," *ibid.*, V, 418–425, and VI, 6–18; "Assumption," *ibid.*, V, 438–461; "Discriminiating Duties," *ibid.*, VI, 1–5, 203–208; "The Jay Treaty," *ibid.*, VI, 263–301; "Special [Peace] Message to Congress, 1815," *ibid.*, VIII, 324–326; "Veto Message [on the National Bank], 1815," *ibid.*, VIII, 327–330.

James Madison was born on March 16, 1751, at Port Conway, King George County, Virginia, the son of Nelly Conway and Colonel James Madison. His antecedents had pioneered lands in Orange County, where he inherited the 5,000-acre estate "Montpelier," whose mansion he commissioned William Thornton to rebuild. Tutors prepared him in the classics, French, and Spanish. He received his B.A. from Princeton in 1771 after two years of study, principally in history, government, and debate. Illness compelled his return to "Montpelier," self-study of law, and civilian service during the Revolutionary War.

A member of the Virginia Committee of Safety in 1775, the Constitutional Convention in 1776, the Executive Council in 1778–1780, and the House of Delegates in 1776, 1783–1786, and 1799, this free-thinking Anglican advocated religious freedom and disestablishment of his Church. Refusal to treat voters to liquor at the polls caused his only political defeat, reëlection to the House of Delegates in 1777. In Virginia, Madison established his reputation for meticulous detail, linguistic ability, and grasp of principles of government.

A delegate to the Continental Congress (1780–1783 and 1786–1789), Madison kept valuable notes of its proceedings, consistently advocated that the confederation raise revenue by a uniform tariff, and voiced the ambitions of the Trans-Allegheny. He helped persuade Congress to honor Virginia's ownership and gift of the Northwest Territory, and he blocked northern mercantile proposals to exchange Mississippi navigation for Spanish trading concessions.

Madison's fame rests primarily upon his contributions to the Federal Convention at Philadelphia in 1787. In hopes of broader interstate compromises he had participated in the compromise of Virginia's and Maryland's maritime differences which led to the convention. Although not the convention's official secretary, he kept daily notes of its proceedings. He became the leading advocate of national government with coercive power as the alternative to monarchy or fragmentation. Although Edmund Randolph presented the Virginia Plan to the convention, Madison's influence upon it was immense, minimizing small-state fears, advocating a two-house legislature with different terms of office based upon population alone, and favoring strong executive and judicial departments as

protection against omnipotent central government. Although asserting in 1787 federal power to incorporate a national bank, he vetoed as President in 1812 the recharter of such a bank, denying that the "general welfare" clause enlarged federal power. He opposed restriction of the slave trade and reiterated his federal ratio of congressional representation. Insisting that experience, not theory, guide constitution-making, Madison is justly called "Father of the Constitution."

While at New York to persuade the old Congress to submit the new Constitution to the states without amendments, he collaborated with Alexander Hamilton and John Jay to promote ratification by essays, collected as *The Federalist* (2 vols., New York, 1788). Only Washington's endorsement did more to foster ratification. *The Federalist* is America's most important constitutional commentary and contribution to political science. In his essays Madison argued that only the central government could reconcile economic rivalries, that property deserved protection from ephemeral popular majorities, and that states would not lose their identity under the federal system.

In Virginia's 1788 ratifying convention, Madison led Federalists against such opponents as George Mason and Patrick Henry. His support for Kentucky's approaching separation from Virginia possibly contributed to the narrow Federalist victory.

In the House of Representatives, 1789–1797, Madison not only helped frame the first ten amendments and revenue laws, but he became the focus of the new Republican Party. Initially reluctant to embarrass the untried government by opposing the Federalists' early measures, he came to protest

Hamilton's fiscal schemes as enrichment of speculators at popular expense. Sharing his friend Jefferson's enthusiasm for early French revolutionary reforms and bitter at Great Britain's illegal retention of border forts and interference with American trade, Madison condemned Hamiltonian measures he considered subservient to the British. He advocated commercial discrimination against the British, unless they dealt more fairly with America, and opposed Jay's Treaty, saying that the United States gained nothing by promising freedom from such discrimination.

Madison's collaboration with Jefferson in the Kentucky and Virginia Resolutions of 1798–1800 protested impingement of the ultra-Hamiltonian Alien and Sedition Acts upon fundamental freedom guaranteed by the Bill of Rights. His theory that a state could interpose its authority against that of the federal government required concurrent action by other states and avoided the stigma of disunion. The Resolutions made powerful campaign documents in the Republican victory of 1800.

As Jefferson's Secretary of State, 1801–1809, and as President, 1809–1817, Madison by commercial discrimination against the warring British and French tried to secure recognition of America's neutral maritime rights, complete control of her territory, and pacification of the western Indians. Ever a nationalist and superb politician, he restrained "War Hawks" like Henry Clay and John C. Calhoun from precipitate war with Great Britain. Ignorant that she was about to desist violation of American sovereignty because of his and Jefferson's policies of peaceful coercion, Madison led the nation into what he declared a just and unavoidable war against Great Britain.

Madison the politician was better than Madison the commander-in-chief. American defeats in Canada and the humiliation of the British burning of Washington must be balanced against disunionist sentiment in New England inimical to more centralized military measures than the inefficient militia system. The inclusion of War Hawk Clay and New Englander John Quincy Adams as American peace negotiators is indicative of Madison's political mastery in making palatable a peace *in statu quo ante bellum*.

As an elder statesman, Madison continued important services to his commonwealth and nation as Jefferson's successor as Rector of the University of Virginia, President of the American Colonization Society, and President of the Virginia Constitutional Convention of 1829–1830. He married Mrs. Dolly Payne Todd in 1794 and died without issue at "Montpelier," Orange County, Virginia, on June 28, 1836.

BIBLIOGRAPHICAL REFERENCES: The standard edition of Madison's works is *The Writings of James Madison,* edited by Gaillard Hunt, 9 vols., 1900–1910. Two earlier editions do not duplicate each other: *The Madison Papers,* edited by Henry D. Gilpin, 3 vols., 1840, and the Congressional Edition of *The Letters and Other Writings of James Madison,* 4 vols., 1865. Gilpin's edition contains the first but slightly inaccurate publication of Madison's *Journal* of the Federal Convention. For Madison papers see also *Documents in American History,* edited by Henry S. Commager, Vol. I, 1949 (5th edition). Also, there is currently in progress a twenty-two volume edition of *The Papers of James Madison,* under the editorship of Leonard D. White,

William T. Hutchinson, and William M. E. Rachal, which will be published beginning in 1960.

Julius W. Pratt's "James Madison," in the *Dictionary of American Biography*, XII, 184–193, is the best brief biographical sketch, even though it did not have the benefit of such recent scholarship as Irving Brant's definitive biography in progress *James Madison*, 5 vols., 1941 ff., which carries the subject up to 1812. Sometimes, however, Brant seems too preoccupied with attacking Henry Adams' unfair treatment of Madison in his *History of the United States of America during the Administrations of Thomas Jefferson and James Madison*, 9 vols., 1889–1891. William C. Rives' oldfashioned *History of the Life and Times of James Madison*, 3 vols., 1859–1868, does not go beyond 1797, but it is an important source since Rives was a family friend who had access to both Madison's and Jefferson's papers before their dispersal. The best one-volume biography is Gaillard Hunt, *The Life of James Madison*, 1902.

Important supplements to the above, with the exception of the memoirs and biographies of Madison's contemporaries, are: *James Madison, 1751–1836, Bicentennial Number, William and Mary Quarterly*, 3rd series, VIII, (Jan., 1951), No. 1; Douglass Adair, "The Authorship of the Disputed Federalist Papers," *William and Mary Quarterly*, 3rd ser., I (April and July, 1944), 97–122, 235–264; Henry Adams, ed., *Documents Relating to New-England Federalism, 1800–1815*, 1877; John S. Bassett, *The Federalist System, 1789–1801*, 1906; Kendrick C. Babcock, *The Rise of American Nationality, 1809–1819*, 1906; Charles A. Beard, *An Economic Interpretation of the Constitution of the United States*, 1913, and *Economic Origins of Jeffersonian Democracy*, 1915; Francis F. Beirne, *The War of 1812*, 1949; Edmund C. Burnet, *The Continental Congress*, 1941; Alfred L. Burt, *The United States, Great Britain and British North America from the Revolution to the Peace after the War of 1812*, 1940; Edward Channing, *The Jeffersonian System, 1801–1811*; Joseph Charles, *The Origins of the American Party System*, 1956; Isaac J. Cox, *The West Florida Controversy, 1798–1813*, 1918; Theodore Dwight, *The Hartford Convention*, 1933; Max Farrand, *Framing the Constitution*, 1918, and *The Fathers of the Constitution*, 1921; Hugh B. Grigsby, *The Virginia Convention of 1829–1830*, 1854, *The Virginia Convention of 1776*, 1855, and (ed. by R. A. Brock) *The History of the Virginia Federal Convention of 1788*, 2 vols., 1890; James K. Hosmer, *The History of the Louisiana Purchase*, 1902; Merrill Jensen, *The New Nation: A History of the United States During the Confederation, 1781–1789*, 1950; Adrienne Koch, *Jefferson and Madison: The Great Collaboration*, 1950; Alfred T. Mahan, *Sea Power in its Relation to the War of 1812*, 2 vols., 1919; John C. Miller, *Crisis in Freedom: The Alien and Sedition Acts*, 1951; Victor H. Palsits, ed., *Washington's Farewell Address in facsimile with transliterations of all of the drafts of Washington, Madison & Hamilton*, 1935; Julius W. Pratt, *Expansionists of 1812*, 1925; Fred Roadell, *Fifty-five Men: The Story of the Constitution*, 1936; Louis C. Schaedler, "James Madison, Literary Craftsman," *William and Mary Quarterly*, 3rd ser., III, 515–533 (Oct., 1946); Louis M. Sears, *Jefferson and the Embargo*, 1927; James M. Smith, *Freedom's Fetters: The Alien and Sedition Laws and American Civil Liberties*, 1956; Carl Van Doren, *The Great Rehearsal*, 1948; Charles Warren, *The Making of the Constitution*, 1928; Leonard D. White, *The Federalists*, 1948, and *The Jeffersonians*, 1951; and Charles M. Wiltse, *The Jeffersonian Tradition in American Politics*, 1935.

MAURICE MAETERLINCK

Born: Ghent, Belgium   *Died:* Nice, France
Date: August 29, 1862   *Date:* May 6, 1949

Principal Works

PLAYS: *La Princesse Maleine,* 1889; *L'Intruse,* 1890 (*The Intruder*); *Les Aveugles,* 1890 (*The Blind*); *Pélléas et Mélisande,* 1892; *Intérieur,* 1894; *Aglavaine et Sélysette,* 1896; *Monna Vanna,* 1902 *L'Oiseau bleu,* 1909 (*The Blue Bird*).

POEMS: *Serres chaudes,* 1889 (*Hot Houses*).

ESSAYS: *Le Trésor des humbles,* 1896 (*The Treasure of the Humble*); *La Sagesse et la destinée,* 1898 (*Wisdom and Destiny*); *Le Temple enseveli,* 1902 (*The Buried Temple*).

NATURAL HISTORY: *La Vie des abeilles,* 1901 (*The Life of the Bee*); *L'Intelligence des fleurs,* 1907; *La Vie des termites,* 1927; *La Vie des fourmis,* 1930 (*The Life of the Ant*).

Maurice Maeterlinck was famous both as a dramatist and as an essayist. The two activities, however, were but aspects of his persistent attempt to discover, on a purely personal basis, a mysticism that should be both satisfactory and sustaining. Since he addressed a world that was in part distressed by the apparent disappearance of religious meaning, he had the good fortune to win an attentive, respectful public, but he was never without critics who questioned the profundity of his mysticism and the merit of his dramas.

Maeterlinck was born at Ghent on August 29, 1862, and was educated in that Belgian city. He lived, as a young man, for some time in Paris, where he came into contact with the Symbolist school of French poetry, a school that was in partial accord with his own mystical aspirations. After the death of his father, Maeterlinck returned to Ghent, where, until World War II, he spent much of his time. His private means allowed him to devote his life to literature. He published his first work, a book of poems, *Hot Houses,* and a play, *The Princess Maleine,* in 1889. That poetic drama moved a critic in *Figaro* to call him "the Belgian Shakespeare," a title that remained with him, for better or worse, the rest of his life. Maeterlinck had widest attention during the first decade and a half of the twentieth century, when his *Pélléas and Mélisande* was turned into a famous opera by the French composer Debussy, and his fantasy, *The Blue Bird,* was played throughout the world. Other plays won less attention; critics judged they perceived thinness and pomposity.

Maeterlinck's essays, on occasion, won hardly less attention than his plays. He early published a study of the German poet, Novalis (1772–1801), whose mixture of mysticism and sensory awareness Maeterlinck found most congenial. *The Life of the Bee,* the product of direct observations carried out at Maeterlinck's estate at Oostacker, was received as a fascinating study of the bee, a classic of its kind because of its interesting blending of natural history, fancy, and philosophy.

Maeterlinck's characteristics make his work unique; his dramatic charac-

695

ters live intense lives concerned with the mystery of the soul, and his prose studies take up, more discursively, the same topic. Critics have found this work marked by high purpose and also, many suggest, by "nebulous mysticism." The ring which Mélisande drops into the well, the bird which the children pursue in his most famous play—these can be regarded as short cuts to profound truths or as substitutes for exact thought. Surprisingly enough, his plays have been produced successfully for audiences which have no apparent interest in mysticism.

Maeterlinck's honors included the award of the Nobel Prize for literature in 1911, the title of Count of the Kingdom of Belgium in 1932, and his election to the French Academy in 1937. He was resident in the United States during the Second World War; afterwards, he returned to France and resided on the Riviera until his death at Nice on May 6, 1949.

Maeterlinck, who dealt extensively in symbols, had the fortune to become a symbol himself; the entity that is his life and work speaks for the confusions of the *fin de siècle* thought and the pursuit of possible reconciliations and syntheses.

BIBLIOGRAPHICAL REFERENCES: For biographical and critical studies of Maeterlinck in English see Clark Macdonald, *Maurice Maeterlinck, Poet and Philosopher,* 1915; and Patrick Mahoney, *The Magic of Maeterlinck,* 1951; in French, Maurice Lecat, *Maurice Maeterlinck en pantoufles,* 1939; *idem, Maurice Maeterlinck et son œuvre,* 1950; and Antonio Rapisarda, *La Double vie de Maeterlinck,* 1949. Brief critical analyses of his plays also appear in E. E. Hall, *Dramatists of Today,* 1911; and Archibald Henderson, *European Dramatists,* 1918.

STÉPHANE MALLARMÉ

Born: Paris, France
Date: March 18, 1842

Died: Valvins, France
Date: September 9, 1898

PRINCIPAL WORKS

POEMS: *L'Après-midi d'un Faune,* 1876 (*The Afternoon of a Faun*); *Poésies,* 1887; *Vers et Prose,* 1893; *Poésies complètes,* 1899.

ESSAYS AND STUDIES: *Les Dieux antiques,* 1880; *La Musique et les lettres,* 1894 (*Music and Letters*); *Divagations,* 1897.

Stéphane Mallarmé led two lives: the calm, quiet life of a schoolteacher and the disturbed inner life of a startling innovator in French poetry. That his life attracted less attention, perhaps notoriety, than the careers of Verlaine and Rimbaud is due largely to the seemingly serene routine he followed.

His beginnings gave no hint of the turbulence that was to follow. Born in Paris on March 18, 1842, he received good but not unusual schooling at Auteuil and Sens; the only unusual event of his early life was a trip to England during which he studied the English language, which he taught when he returned to France. Another event, striking in its effect, however, was his early discovery of the poetry of Baudelaire, the rebellious but skillful French poet

696

whose *Flowers of Evil* (1857) created a sensation in the nineteenth century.

On his return from England, Mallarmé taught English in southern France, from 1862 to 1873. When he moved to Paris, where he spent the rest of his life, his real work as the virtual leader of the Symbolists began. He became professor of English in the Lycée Fontanes, and held that post until 1892. His outward professional career and his domestic life with his wife and daughter seemed regular and uneventful until, in 1874, he began to write poetry and criticism. In these early works he became a pioneer in the principles of Symbolist verse, but he was not "discovered" until 1884, when Verlaine and Joris Karl Huysmans recognized him as the leader of the new movement toward a more mystical type of poetry. Only one piece of writing from this early period is generally remembered, and *The Afternoon of a Faun* is primarily known because it inspired the musical prelude of Debussy.

Mallarmé produced only a small volume of actual writing, and his work was counted generally unsuccessful. Perhaps his most effective influence was achieved in the small Tuesday meetings which he held in his home. At these intimate affairs he read his poetry to his guests and lectured to them on the principles of Symbolism, a movement whose first members were called "decadents." One of the most important of these principles was Mallarmé's belief that poetry should suggest, or connote, the interior life of the poet, not express it in concrete terms. His purpose was an attempt at communication which transcends customary language.

In later publications like *Poésies complètes, Vers et Prose,* and *Divagations,* he intensified his ideas and exemplified them in his verse. As he grew older his writing became more obscure and incomprehensible; it often seemed as though this vagueness of meaning was what he was striving for. Indeed, one of his great achievements was his realization of "nothingness," and his appreciation of the beauty that lies within it. He was always searching for new standards and new ways of achieving deep poetic expression, but when he began eliminating all punctuation in poetry and devising a new punctuation and syntax for prose, many people thought that he had gone too far. Although some of his poetry is jewel-like in its brilliance, most of his work is limited in its effects. He was exceedingly self-critical, a quality which kept him from creating abundantly by drawing rigorous aesthetic limits around what he did produce. However, for those who can follow Mallarmé through the tortuous paths of his mystical suggestions the reward is great; and his influence on younger French poets of his period was almost equal to the immense influence that he has had on twentieth century poetry by both English-speaking and French poets. Mallarmé died quietly at Valvins, near Fontainebleau, on September 9, 1898, after a career as a revivifying, if not universally accepted, force in French poetry. Among the influences on Mallarmé himself was Edgar Allan Poe, whose poems he translated into French in 1888.

BIBLIOGRAPHICAL REFERENCES: Mallarmé's *Œuvres complètes* were edited by Henri Mondor and G. Jean-Aubry in 1945. An edition of the *Poems,* in English translation, was published by Roger Fry in 1936. Two contemporary tributes to the poet are to be found in J. K. Huysmans, À rebours, 1884, and in Paul Verlaine, Les Poètes maudits, 1884. The standard biography is Henri Mondor, Vie de Mallarmé, 2 vols., 1941. Other biographical and critical studies include Paul Valery, Varieté II, 1929; Pierre Beausire, Essai sur la poésie et la poétique de Mallarmé, 1942; Grange Wooley, Stéphane Mallarmé, 1942; Francis de Miomandre, Mallarmé, 1948; and Robert Goffin, Mallarmé vivant, 1956. For a perceptive background study see also Arthur Symons, The Symbolist Movement in Literature, 1900.

EDUARDO MALLEA

Born: Bahía Blanca, Argentina
Date: August 14, 1903

Principal Works

NOVELS AND TALES: Cuentos para una inglesa desesperada, 1926 (Stories for a Desperate Englishwoman); La ciudad junto al río inmóvil, 1936 (The City beside the Motionless River); Fiesta en noviembre, 1936 (Fiesta in November); La Bahía de silencio, 1940 (The Bay of Silence); Todo verdor perecerá, 1941 (All Verdure Shall Perish); Las águilas, 1943 (The Eagles); Rodeada está de sueño, 1944 (She is Surrounded by Dreams); El retorno, 1946 (The Return); El vínculo, 1946 (The Bond); Los Rembrandts, 1946; La rosa de Cernobbio, 1946; La torre, 1951 (The Tower).

ESSAYS: Historia de una pasión argentina, 1937 (History of an Argentine Passion).

Descendant of the diplomat-author-educator Sarmiento, Eduardo Mallea was born on August 14, 1903, in desolate, wind-swept Bahía Blanca, Argentina, the setting for much of his writing. After his primary instruction by an Australian woman, his physician father took him to Buenos Aires, where he studied law until the sale of some children's stories turned him to literature as a career. In 1926 his first collection of fantastic but frantic Stories for a Desperate Englishwoman opened the way for a voyage to Europe and brought him the literary editorship of La Nación, of Buenos Aires. A lecture trip to Italy later resulted in Nocturno europeo (1935), an example of his technique of using a slim fictional plot to tie together his ideas. It won him the first of many literary prizes.

His History of an Argentine Passion, with its hero Adrian seeking relief for his tormented soul in the Confessions of Saint Augustine and in Spanish mysticism, contains many autobiographical elements. His confessed admiration in it for Proust, James Joyce, and Franz Kafka explains Mallea's The Bay of Silence, the work which firmly established him as a modern novelist who expresses philosophical implications in a pungently lyric style and who excels in descriptions of the city. It describes Martin Tregua as a student in Buenos Aires and in his relationship in Europe with the disillusioned, frustrated, married Gloria, with whom he finds solace at the Bay of Silence. In Fiesta in November, Mallea presents three complicated and temperamental women in a literary feat inspired by the November execution of the poet García Lorca. Between chapters about the useless rich of Buenos Aires, fearing supression of

698

liberty and thought, are sections of another short story about soldiers murdering a liberal poet for having ideas.

Mallea later began a cycle about the fortunes of the Ricarte family, built by the pioneering efforts of the immigrant Don Leon, almost destroyed by his bookish son and his wasteful wife, but again on the rise in the person of vague, liberal Roberto of the third generation. The initial volume, *The Eagles,* named from the family estate, was followed in eight years by *The Tower;* a third volume, *Tempestad (The Storm),* was in preparation in 1957.

Stefan Zweig insisted that Mallea's *All Verdure Shall Perish* should be published in Europe, and José Lins do Rêgo made a Portuguese version of it for Brazil. Hemingway and others recognized Mallea's skill with words and ideas by voting one of his representative works into an anthology, *The Best of the World* (1950). Mallea has tried to create a style typically Argentine; his vivid word pictures as he portrays his characters, solitary souls in pain seeking freedom and self-expression, reveal his patriotic belief that his native land is a paradise even if the inhabitants possess many weaknesses.

BIBLIOGRAPHICAL REFERENCES: Some of Mallea's fiction appeared in English, including *The Bay of Silence,* translated by S. E. Grummon, 1940, and *Fiesta in November,* translated by Alis De Sola for the anthology of the same title published in 1942. For biography and criticism see Emilio Suárez Calímaco, *Directrices de la novela y del cuento argentino,* 1933 (Buenos Aires); Roberto F. Giusti, "Panorama de la literatura argentina contemporánea," in *Nosotros,* II, No. 68 (Buenos Aires, 1941); Juan Pinto, *Literatura argentina,* 1941 (Buenos Aires); Roque Esteban Scarpa, "Lecturas americanas," Zig-Zag (Santiago de Chile, 1943), 187–195; Arturo Torres Rioseco, *Epic of Latin American Literature,* 1946; Arnold Chapman, "Manuel Gálvez y Eduardo Mallea," *Revista Iberoamericana,* XIX (1953), 71–78; José Manuel Topete, "Eduardo Mallea y el laberinto de la agonía," *ibid.,* XX (1955), 117–151; Agustín del Saz, *Resumen de la historia de la novela hispanoamericana,* 19 (Barcelona, n.d.), 190–192; and Guillermo Díaz Plaja, *El novelista argentino Eduardo Mallea,* Instituto de Problemas Hispanoamericanos (Madrid, n.d.).

SIR THOMAS MALORY

Born: Warwickshire (?), England   *Died:* London (?)
Date: Early fifteenth century   *Date:* March 14, 1471

PRINCIPAL WORK

PROSE ROMANCE: *Le Morte d'Arthur,* c. 1469; printed 1485.

On July 31, 1485, from the press of William Caxton, the first English printer, issued the great collection of Arthurian romances known as *Le Morte d'Arthur.* Caxton's preface names the author as Sir Thomas Malory but gives no further information about him. At the end of the volume stands a farewell to the reader (an *explicit*) in which the author begs prayer for his "good delyveraunce," states that the book was finished in the ninth year of the reign of King Edward the Fourth (that is, after March 4, 1469), and names himself as "Syr Thomas Maleore, knyght."

The only historical figure now known with whom this Sir Thomas Malory could be identified was a member of an old Warwickshire family. He came into his father's estates about 1433 and with "one lance and two archers" was in the train of Richard Beauchamp at the siege of Calais in 1436. In 1455 he was a member of Parliament for Warwickshire. But at this point his career underwent a drastic change; within the next five or six years he was accused of and tried for a number of crimes: cattle raiding, extortion, breaking and entering, theft, rape, sedition, and attempted murder. He was imprisoned eight times and twice made dramatic escapes. After this interlude of lawlessness, he is known to have followed the Earl of Warwick on his expedition into Northumberland in 1462, probably was present at the siege of Alnwick, which lasted until January 30, 1463, and very likely went over with Warwick to the Lancastrians. When the king granted general pardons to the rebels in 1468, Malory was excluded from the amnesty by name. He died on March 14, 1471, possibly as a prisoner, and was buried near Newgate.

The identification of Malory, the author of the Le Morte d'Arthur, with Malory, the traitor, burglar, and rapist, was supported by the information found in a manuscript version of the work discovered in 1934 in the library of Winchester College. This manuscript contains several explicits which were suppressed in the printed version; one of them says specifically that the book was "drawyn by a knyght presoner Sir Thomas Maleorre." Perhaps more important, the manuscript shows that Caxton treated Malory's work with considerable freedom and that many of the inconsistencies and garbles in the text are traceable to the printing house rather than to the author. The most reliable modern edition, therefore, is one like that of Eugène Vinaver, which is based on the Winchester manuscript rather than Caxton's version of the text.

The book consists of the legends of Sir Launcelot, Sir Gareth, Sir Tristram, and the Holy Grail, as well as the stories of Arthur's coming to the throne, his wars with the Emperor Lucius, and his death. Malory's sources were principally French romances, which he translated into vigorous and resonant English prose. The earliest written tales clung closely to the sources, the departures being chiefly to extol the virtues of the high order of knighthood. Later, however, Malory seems to have gained more confidence, and his changes in the source material took the form of reordering and altering to increase the aesthetic value of the story. The last-written work, *The Most Piteous Tale of the Morte Arthur,* which is based partly on a French romance and partly on an English stanzaic poem, is thought to be the greatest; in it Malory's genius reached its highest pitch in describing the wonderful deeds of heroes in the service of a great national leader.

BIBLIOGRAPHICAL REFERENCES: The most recent scholarly edition is *The Works of Sir Thomas Malory,* edited by Eugène Vinaver, 3 vols., 1947. A convenient modernized text is in Everyman's Library, 2 vols., 1906. There are several useful full-length studies: Vita D. Scudder, *Le Morte d'Arthur of Sir Thomas Malory and its Sources,* 1917; Edward Hicks, *Sir Thomas Malory, His Turbulent Career,* 1928; and Eugène

Vinaver, *Malory*, 1929. See also Nellie S. Aurner, *Caxton, Mirrour of Fifteenth-Century Letters*, 1926. For two articles pioneering the identification of Malory, see George Lyman Kittredge, "Who Was Sir Thomas Malory?" *Harvard Studies and Notes in Philology and Literature*, V (1896), 85–106; and E. K. Chambers, *Sir Thomas Malory, English Association Pamphlet*, No. 51, 1922.

ANDRÉ MALRAUX

Born: Paris, France
Date: November 3, 1901

PRINCIPAL WORKS

NOVELS: *Les Conquérants*, 1928 (*The Conquerors*); *La Voie royale*, 1930 (*The Royal Way*); *La Condition humaine*, 1933 (*Man's Fate*); *Le Temps du Mépris*, 1935 (*Days of Wrath*); *L'Espoir*, 1937 (*Man's Hope*).
CRITICISM: *Essais de psychologie de l'art*, 1947–1950 (*The Psychology of Art*).

André Malraux was born of well-to-do parents in Paris on November 3, 1901. After obtaining a traditional classical education at his lycée, he studied Sanskrit, Chinese, and archeology at the School of Oriental Languages. In 1923 he went to Indo-China, where he father was a civil servant. There Malraux entered upon a series of adventures which have provided rich material for his novels. In Indo-China he first dug for ancient statues in the ruins of fallen temples, but he soon became an active member of the Young Annam League which was seeking dominion status for the country of Cambodia. From here he moved on to China, where he became active in the Kuomintang, the revolutionary and nationalist party which was gaining control of most of China during the late 1920's. His first important novel, *The Conquerors*, concerns an insurrection against the British in Hong Kong. The hero, Garine, is a professional revolutionist who fights for ideals but who, when the Chinese achieve their immediate ends, is no longer interested in their problems. Malraux's next novel, *The Royal Way*,

is the story of three rebels against society as they face the jungles of Indo-China, the savage Cambodian natives, and French soldiers. Three years later appeared one of his most celebrated novels, *Man's Fate*. The book depicts the turbulent Chinese Revolution of 1927. The main characters are of all types, both revolutionists and counter-revolutionists; there are, for example, a young Chinese intellectual idealist, a Russian nihilist, a French capitalist, a German chief of police, and Chiang Kai-shek. But along with these main characters there is the important part that China itself plays, with its motley populace and the dirty, noisy, smelly streets of its crowded cities. The book was awarded the Goncourt Prize.

When the revolution collapsed following a series of betrayals, Malraux returned to Paris after collecting Graeco-Buddhist art in Persia and Afghanistan. In 1934 he flew into the Arabian desert, where he claimed to have discovered the legendary capital of the Queen of Sheba. Shortly thereafter *Days of Wrath* was published. This novel, tighter in structure than his previous ones, concerns the imprisonment of a Communist propagandist in a Nazi prison; it was a book club selection in the United States. During the early and mid-thirties Malraux was in Paris writing on aesthetic theories and attending mass metings at which he defended imprisoned German Communists or protested the invasion of Ethiopia. By 1936, however, he was in Spain in the thick of the Civil War. He organized an air corps for the Loyalists and made several flights into Fascist territory. During part of this time he also toured the United States in an effort to raise funds for the Loyalists. His *Man's Hope* is a monumental novel recounting the first months of this conflict. Critics have hailed its imaginative power and have praised the supple prose of its style.

During World War II Malraux served in the French tank corps, was captured by the Germans, escaped, became a leader of guerrillas in the Resistance, was wounded, and finally was decorated with the British Distinguished Service Order. Since the war he has been a loyal and vociferous supporter of General Charles de Gaulle.

Malraux's monumental critical work entitled *The Psychology of Art* was translated in three volumes, and a condensed one-volume English version of it also appeared as *The Voices of Silence* in 1953. Called one of the most valuable works on the aesthetics of art, the book stresses the fact that the essences of past civilizations survive in the great art they have produced.

BIBLIOGRAPHICAL REFERENCES: There is no complete edition of Malraux's works, but his most important books are available in translation. The most adequate bibliography is found in W. M. Frohock's excellent critical study, *André Malraux and the Tragic Imagination*, 1952, supplemented by his "Note for a Malraux Bibliography," *Modern Language Notes*, LXV (1950), 392–95. This book may also be used for the chief biographical facts, or, for French readers, Claude Mauriac, *Malraux*, 1946, will serve. Other critical books in French are Gaëtan Picon, *André Malraux*, 1945, and Jeanne Delhomme, *Temps et Destin: Essai Sur André Malraux*, 1955. Essays in books include Janet Flanner, *Men and Monuments*, 1957. Short critical articles are Nicola Chiaromonte, "Malraux and the Demons of Action," *Partisan Review*, XV (1948), 776–789 and 912–923; W. M. Frohock, "Notes on Malraux' Symbols," *Romanic Review*, XLII (1951), 274–281; Joseph Frank, "Malraux and the Image of Man," *New Republic*, (August 30, 1954), 18–19; Michael Harrington, "André Malraux: Metamorphosis of the Hero," *Partisan Review*, XXI (1954), 655–663; and "Man's Quest," *Time Magazine* cover story on Malraux, LXVI (July 18, 1955), 24–30.

THOMAS MANN

Born: Lübeck, Germany
Date: June 6, 1875

Died: Zurich, Switzerland
Date: August 12, 1955

PRINCIPAL WORKS

NOVELS: *Buddenbrooks*, 1901; *Königliche Hoheit*, 1909 (*Royal Highness*); *Der Zauberberg*, 1924 (*The Magic Mountain*); *Joseph und seine Brüder*, 1933–1943 (*Joseph and His Brothers*): I. *Die Geschichten Jaakobs*, 1933 (*Joseph and His Brothers: Tales of Jacob*); II. *Der junge Joseph*, 1934 (*Young Joseph*); III. *Joseph*

702

in Ägypten, 1936 (*Joseph in Egypt*); IV. *Joseph, der Ernährer,* 1943 (*Joseph the Provider*); *Lotte in Weimar,* 1939 (*The Beloved Returns*); *Die vertauschten Köpfe,* 1940 (*The Transposed Heads*); *Doktor Faustus,* 1947 (*Doctor Faustus: The Life of the German Composer Adrian Leverkuhn as Told by a Friend*); *Der Erwählte,* 1951 (*The Holy Sinner*); *Bekenntnisse des Hochstaplers Felix Krull,* 1954 (*Confessions of Felix Krull, Confidence Man*).

NOVELLAS: *Tristan,* 1903; *Tonio Kröger,* 1903; *Der Tod in Venedig,* 1913 (*Death in Venice*); *Unordnung und frühes Leid,* 1926 (*Disorder and Early Sorrow*); *Mario und der Zauberer,* 1930 (*Mario and the Magician*); *Das Gesetz,* 1944 (*The Tables of the Law*); *Die Betrogene,* 1953 (*The Black Swan*).

SHORT STORIES: *Der kleine Herr Friedemann,* 1898 (*Little Herr Friedemann*); *Das Wunderkind,* 1914 (*The Infant Prodigy*); *Herr und Hund,* 1919 (*A Man and His Dog*); *Wälsungenblut,* 1921 (*The Blood of the Walsungs*); *Stories of Three Decades,* 1936.

ESSAYS AND STUDIES: *Betrachtungen eines Unpolitischen,* 1918; *Bemühungen,* 1922; *Rede und Antwort,* 1922; *Die Forderung des Tages,* 1930; *Leiden und Grösse der Meister,* 1935; *Freud und die Zukunft,* 1936; *Order of the Day: Political Essays and Speeches of Two Decades,* 1942; *Essays of Three Decades,* 1947.

Thomas Mann, regarded by many critics as one of the outstanding novelists of the twentieth century, was born in Lübeck, Germany, to Johann Heinrich Mann, a grain merchant and senator of Lübeck, and Julia da Silva-Bruhns Mann, the daughter of a German planter in Brazil and his Portuguese-Creole wife. Thomas Mann had two brothers and two sisters; the sisters committed suicide—Carla, in 1910 and Julia in 1927. The eldest child of the family, Heinrich Mann, became a distinguished novelist himself. As a child, before his school days, Thomas Mann enjoyed a prosperous and relaxing family life; he loved the holidays at Travemünde and knew the comfortable security of German bourgeois life.

His father wanted Thomas to become a grain merchant like himself, and the boy was sent to a military school where he was thoroughly unhappy—a young verse writer among bullying students and schoolmasters. When he was fifteen, his father suddenly died from blood poisoning. The business failed, and Thomas' mother took his brothers and sisters to Munich where he rejoined them after completing his studies. In Munich he was a fire insurance clerk. He sold his first story, *Gefallen,* the story of a fallen woman, in 1894.

When he tired of business life—after a year—he attended lectures at the University of Munich, auditing courses without officially matriculating. When his brother Heinrich suggested that Thomas join him in Rome, he welcomed the suggestion. The brothers lived in Palestrina, where Thomas began his first novel, *Buddenbrooks,* the book that was to make him famous and contribute to his winning, in 1929, the Nobel Prize in Literature. The novel portrays a merchant family, and the society of which it is a part, with all its pretenses and weaknesses. Nevertheless, the young writer, faithful to his own experience, was not entirely scornful of that society and regarded the members of it as fundamentally worth while.

While Mann was still in Rome, his first volume of short stories, *Little Herr*

Friedemann, was published. He returned to Munich and joined the staff of the journal *Simplicissimus,* but resigned before completing *Buddenbrooks* on which he continued to work. The book was completed after two and a half years of work and was published at the end of 1900 (with the date 1901). Although the novel did not receive immediate critical attention or popular success, it soon gained momentum and by a year after its publication its young author was famous. The short work, *Tonio Kröger,* helped to secure his reputation. Success in literature was then enhanced by success in love: in 1905 he married Katja Pringsheim, the daughter of a mathematics professor. By that marriage he had six children, and of them Erika Mann achieved attention as a war correspondent and actress, while the eldest son, Klaus, distinguished himself as a writer.

Mann's second novel, *Royal Highness,* the result of an attempt to write a comic novel, was not as well received as *Buddenbrooks,* but Mann's status as a novelist was not diminished. From his experiences in Venice with his wife in 1911 he gained the emotional impressions which he used with haunting effect in his famous novella, *Death in Venice.* This work is characteristic of the decadent, morbid, poetic, and ironic stories and novels which came from Mann, intermittently, until the new constructive phase marked by the Joseph novels. In a lesser writer the combination of the decadent and the creative would have been not only impossible, but, if attained, perhaps objectionable; but in Mann the author's control gave the material a distinctive dark charm which made it fascinating, as if he were presenting evil—evil sanctified by art.

The outstanding work of that period derives from visits he made to his wife while she was a tuberculosis patient in Switzerland; it is *The Magic Mountain,* a novel which is both the story of a young man attempting to resist the morbid atmosphere of a tuberculosis sanitarium and, on another level, an evaluation of the morbid character of Western civilization prior to the first World War.

Although Mann was not directly involved in World War I and tended to accept the view that the artist must keep free of political matters, as time went on he became more and more involved in the political life of his times, not as a politician, but as a critic and as an apologist for the free, creative life. In 1933 his daughters in Germany warned him by telegram that he had better stay in Switzerland where he was vacationing with his wife; they wired that the housecleaning would be too much for him. The Nazis burned his books and in 1936 deprived him of his German citizenship. In 1938 he moved to Princeton, N. J., and continued his work, much of it a criticism of contemporary Europe's new dark age. In 1941 he moved to Pacific Palisades, California, and in 1944 he became a United States citizen. The cultural ties and charms of Europe continued to work on him, however, and he returned to Europe to settle in Switzerland. Before he died he had the satisfaction of finding that he had won new popularity in Germany, and he paid visits and lectured in both zones. He died of phlebitis in Zurich on August 12, 1955.

BIBLIOGRAPHICAL REFERENCES: There is no extensive biographical study of Mann. See Arthur Eloesser, *Thomas Mann: Sein Leben und seine Werke,* 1925 (Berlin);

Käte Hamburger, *Thomas Mann's Roman "Joseph und seine Brüder*, 1945 (Stockholm); James Cleugh, *Thomas Mann: A Study*, 1933; H. J. Weigand, *Thomas Mann's Novel "Der Zauberberg*," 1933; Harry Slochower, *Three Ways of Modern Man*, 1937; J. M. Lindsay, *Thomas Mann*, 1954; also William Troy, "Thomas Mann: Myth and Reason," *Partisan Review*, V (1938), 24–32 and 51–64; P. B. Rice, "Thomas Mann and the Religious Revival," *Kenyon Review*, VII (1945), 361–377; D. J. Enright, "The Forgotten Novelist: A Survey of Thomas Mann," *Focus II* (1946), 104–116; and R. P. Blackmur, "Hans Castorp, Small Lord of Counterpositions," *Hudson Review*, I (1948), 318–339. See also Charles Neider, ed., *The Stature of Thomas Mann*, 1947; and Klaus W. Jonas, *Fifty Years of Mann Studies, A Bibliography of Criticism*, 1955.

KATHERINE MANSFIELD
(Kathleen Mansfield Beauchamp)

Born: Wellington, New Zealand   *Died:* Fontainebleau, France
Date: October 14, 1888   *Date:* January 9, 1923

PRINCIPAL WORKS

SHORT STORIES: *In a German Pension*, 1911; *Prelude*, 1918; *Je ne parle pas français*, 1920; *Bliss and Other Stories*, 1920; *The Garden Party and Other Stories*, 1922; *The Doves' Nest and Other Stories*, 1923; *Something Childish and Other Stories*, 1924; *The Aloe*, 1930.

POEMS: *Poems*, 1923.

AUTOBIOGRAPHY: *The Journal of Katherine Mansfield*, 1927; *The Scrapbook of Katherine Mansfield*, 1939.

ESSAYS AND STUDIES: *Novels and Novelists*, 1930.

LETTERS: *The Letters of Katherine Mansfield*, 1929; *Katherine Mansfield's Letters to John Middleton Murry, 1913–1922*, 1951.

One of the great shapers of the modern short story, Katherine Mansfield was a colonial who had escaped to the cosmopolitanism of London and the Continent, only to find some of the richest sources of her art in the New Zealand from which she had fled. Born Kathleen Beauchamp in Wellington on October 14, 1888, she was the third daughter of Harold Beauchamp, a banker later to be knighted. At the age of five Kathleen went to school outside Wellington at Karori. Imaginative and withdrawn, she did not respond well to formal education and discipline, but by the time the Beauchamps were entered in the Wellington College for Girls in 1897, she had already won a composition prize with an entry prophetically called "A Sea Voyage." By 1900, in still another school, Kathleen had developed an interest in the cello and in a boy prodigy, Arnold Trowell, from whose father she took lessons. Kathleen first saw London in 1903, where her father had taken her and her sisters to be educated at Queen's College, Harley Street. She studied desultorily there, taking lessons at the Royal Academy of Music, and developing her art, watching and observing while, concomitantly, her hypersensitivity and incipient neuroticism increased. Immersed in *fin de siècle* at-

705

mosphere and the writings of Wilde, Pater, Verlaine, and others, she became secretly engaged to Arnold Trowell, who was giving increasingly successful concerts. Her distraction at the knowledge of his waning ardor was made desperate by her father's summons home in 1906.

Back in New Zealand, but in rebellion against being there, she had decided by the spring of 1907 that writing, not music, was her forte, and she began to work earnestly at short stories and verse. But neither the publication of three of her stories in *The Native Companion,* a Melbourne monthly, nor a six-week trip into the bush could make her forget her aim. She gained it in July of 1908 when she secured her father's reluctant consent and, with a £100 yearly allowance, returned to England. At first she lived at an unmarried ladies' hostel and then at the Trowells'. But she was soon in despair, for Arnold no longer loved her, and besides she found herself in financial straits, unable to live comfortably even when she supplemented her allowance by touring with an opera company and working as a movie extra. In March, 1909, funereally dressed, she contracted a hasty marriage with George Bowden, a young musician, only to leave him a few days later. Mrs. Beauchamp joined her and, finding her pregnant but not by her husband, took her to Woerishofen, Bavaria. There her child was stillborn and the decline in her health began.

When she returned to England in 1910, A. R. Orage published some of her work, signed "Katherine Mansfield," in *The New Age.* Collected with other stories, it was published as *In A German Pension* in 1911. The next year saw her fateful meeting with John Middleton Murry, already a rising literary journalist. Soon they began to live together, impecunious and unable to marry until 1918, when Bowden divorced her. Despite illness, insecurity, and depression, she continued to write, temporarily exhilarated by the visit of her young brother Leslie, on his way to the front in the summer of 1915. His death in action shortly thereafter brought heartbreak which no amount of work and travel in France and England could assuage. Her thoughts turned to her homeland. Embodied in "Prelude," among other stories, they appeared under the imprint of the Hogarth Press, founded by her friends, Leonard and Virginia Woolf. Other work of hers had previously appeared in *Signature,* which she had begun with Murry and D. H. Lawrence.

Her sufferings in France during the winter of 1917–1918, where she had sought a milder climate than that of England, made it clear that she, like her great predecessor and master, Chekhov, was the victim of what was to be incurable tuberculosis. Virtually an invalid by the end of the war, she was in lonely separation from Murry, who was in London earning a living as editor of *The Athenaeum,* to which she contributed. *Bliss And Other Stories,* published in 1920, helped her growing reputation, but her personal exigencies were becoming desperate. Like her friend, D. H. Lawrence, Katherine Mansfield found her last years filled with continuous unsuccessful trips from one place to another in search of health. But she did not possess Lawrence's inner certitude, so that there was the corollary travail of a fruitless spiritual pilgrimage as well.

By 1922, when she published *The Garden Party And Other Stories,* her work was appearing in America as well as England. X-Ray treatments in Paris seemed for a time to help her wasted lungs, but finally, in the last phase of her desperate search, she entered the Gurdjieff Institute for the Harmonic Development of Man at Fontainebleau. As her wasted body grew even more debilitated under an unfavorable physical environment, her questing spirit grew calmer. There her last and fatal hemorrhage occurred on January 9, 1923, the year in which *The Doves' Nest And Other Stories* confirmed her place as one of the most accomplished experimentalists and shapers of the modern short story.

Katherine Mansfield's work was intensely autobiographical, and throughout her career her protagonists often approximated her own age, interests, and temperament. Her favorite themes were family relationships, parental and marital, most often somberly treated. Excelling at the portrayal of children, she was able at her best to enter into the souls of her characters and turn them outward for her reader to see and understand. Her technique, much of it revolutionary in her own time, was marked by the use of the stream-of-consciousness method, skillful shifts in point of view from one character to another, and evocation of mood through poetically appropriate gesture and detail. Almost lyrical, her art bypassed conventional narration, ellipsizing naturalistic detail and de-emphasizing the traditional plot structure to produce, like James Joyce and Virginia Woolf, works of art which conveyed the greater truth found in the portrayal of the essence of character and experience itself.

BIBLIOGRAPHICAL REFERENCES: Katherine Mansfield's short stories have been collected in chronological sequence in *The Short Stories of Katherine Mansfield,* 1945. The standard biography is Anthony Alpers, *Katherine Mansfield: A Biography,* 1953, a work containing much new material not found in Ruth E. Mantz and John Middleton Murry, *The Life of Katherine Mansfield,* 1933. Francis Carco, *Souvenirs sur Katherine Mansfield,* 1934, contains reminiscences by a French writer upon whom Katherine Mansfield modeled several of her characters.

The basic critical study is Sylvia Berkman, *Katherine Mansfield: A Critical Study,* 1951. For briefer criticism see André Maurois, *Prophets and Poets,* 1935; A. Sewell, *Katherine Mansfield: A Critical Essay,* 1936; David Daiches, *The Novel in the Modern World,* 1939; L. E. Rillo, *Katherine Mansfield and Virginia Woolf,* 1944; John Middleton Murry, *Katherine Munsfield and Other Literary Portraits,* 1949; Katherine Anne Porter, *The Days Before,* 1952; Louis Gillet, "Katherine Mansfield," *Revue des Deux Mondes,* VIIe Période, XXIV (1924), 929–942; Edward Wagenknecht, "Katherine Mansfield," *English Journal,* XVII (1928), 272–284; Sidney Cox, "The Fastidiousness of Katherine Mansfield," *Sewanee Review,* XXXIX (1931), 158–169; Gerard Jean-Aubry, "Katherine Mansfield, *Revue de Paris,* XXXVIIIe An, V (1931), 57–72; and Arnold Whitridge, "Katherine Mansfield," *Sewanee Review,* XLVIII (1940), 256–272.

ALESSANDRO MANZONI

Born: Milan, Italy
Date: March 7, 1785

Died: Milan
Date: May 22, 1873

NOVEL: *I Promessi Sposi*, 1825–1827 (*The Betrothed*).

PLAYS: *Il Conte di Carmagnola*, 1820; *Adelchi*, 1822.

POEMS: *Carme in Morte di Carlo Imbonati*, 1806; *Urania*, 1809; *Inni Sacri*, 1812–1817.

HISTORICAL TREATISE: *Storia della Colonna infame*, 1842.

Alessandro (Francesco Tommaso Antonio) Manzoni, one of Italy's outstanding novelists on the basis of a single book, *The Betrothed*, was born in Milan, March 7, 1785, presumably the son of Pietro Manzoni and his wife Giulia Beccaria, although there is some evidence to show that he was in fact the son of Giovanni Verri, one of his mother's lovers. Manzoni's grandfather was Cesare Beccaria, the famous Italian criminologist. Manzoni's mother, legally separated from Pietro Manzoni, went to Paris with a wealthy Milanese banker, Count Carlo Imbonati, in 1796. Her son was sent to various religious schools in Merate, Lugano, and Milan. His grandfather had died of an apoplectic stroke on November 28, 1794, and his father took little interest in him; consequently, Alessandro was miserable and lonely at school. When his education was completed in 1801 he lived for four years with his father in Milan, where he attended lectures and enjoyed the freedom of city life. About this time he began writing poems and making the acquaintance of other young writers in Milan.

In 1804 he received an invitation from Carlo Imbonati to stay with him and Alessandro's mother in Paris, but before he reached Paris Imbonati was dead. Although he had never met Imbonati, Manzoni's elegy, *Carme in Morte di Carlo Imbonati*, was written in an effort to console his mother. The count's will made Alessandro and his mother financially independent; in addition to his fortune they inherited his villa at Brusuglio, near Milan. During his stay in Paris young Manzoni met Claude Fauriel, Madame Condorcet, and others who introduced him to the new Romantic movement in French literature. He returned to Italy in 1807.

In 1808 Manzoni married Henriette Blondel, daughter of a Swiss Calvinist banker. His wife became increasingly interested in Jansenism and in 1810, after she had joined the Catholic Church, they were remarried in a Catholic ceremony in Paris. At the time Manzoni, a rationalist, was but nominally Catholic; however, an intense emotional experience soon after his remarriage brought about a genuine conversion. His poems, the *Inni Sacri* published during the period between 1812 and 1817, reflect his concern with religious matters.

The Manzonis moved to the villa at Brusuglio, where in spite of revolution, Austrian occupation, and business difficulties the author spent his remaining years. In 1820 his first tragedy, *Il Conte di Carmagnola* appeared and was received with adverse criticism, although Goethe came to Manzoni's defense. When Napoleon died Manzoni wrote his most famous ode, "Il Cinque Maggio" (1821), and followed that with another tragedy, *Adelchi*. His most famous work, the historical novel *The Betrothed*, brought him literary fame, and he spent most of his remaining creative effort on revisions and additions to this work and in writing minor essays.

In 1833 Henriette died. Four years later he married Countess Teresa Borri-Stampa, a widow, who died in 1861. Of his six daughters, five died young; his three sons were spendthrifts, drunkards, and trouble-makers, and the eldest died one month before his father. Manzoni died on May 22, 1873, two weeks after he had been injured in a fall on the steps of the church of San Fedele in Milan.

BIBLIOGRAPHICAL REFERENCES: Manzoni's *The Betrothed* is now available in a distinguished translation by Archibald Colquhoun, 1951. There are two important critical biographies in English: Archibald Colquhoun, *Manzoni and His Times*, 1954; and Bernard Wall, *Alessandro Manzoni*, 1954. See also Luigi Tonelli, *Manzoni*, 1928; Attilio Momigliani, *Alessandro Manzoni*, 1929; Benedetto Croce, *Alessandro Manzoni*, 1930; Domenico Budini, *Alessandro Manzoni*, 1940; Giorgio Bonfiglioli, *Manzoni, la vita e le opere*, 1949; Giuseppe A. Brunelli, *Introduzione allo studio del Manzoni*, 1949; Barbara Reynolds, *The Linguistic Writings of Alessandro Manzoni*, 1950; and Lucienne Portier, *Alessandro Manzoni*, 1955. An excellent brief introduction to *The Betrothed* is the unsigned review, "The Greatest Italian Novel," *London Times Literary Supplement*, L (August 3, 1951), 484.

RENÉ MARAN

Born: Fort-de-France, Martinique
Date: November 15, 1887

PRINCIPAL WORK

NOVEL: *Batouala*, 1921.

For a person who has written nearly a book a year since 1918, René Maran is given little attention by the English-speaking world. His chief claim to fame is his Goncourt Prize novel, *Batouala*, the first book by a Negro author to be so honored. Maran was born on November 15, 1887. There is disagreement on his birthplace, but it is fairly certain he did not leave Martinique until he was four years old, never to return. He attended the lycée in Bordeaux, which he always claimed as home.

From 1909 until 1925 he was in the Civil Service, the only Negro of the group which carried on diplomatic affairs in French Equatorial Africa. His first book of poems as well as his novels, short stories, and essays reflect this experience. He states that he spent six years, off and on, writing his best work by observing the ways of the tribal groups and learning their languages. Some critics felt that he included too much dialect for the average reader; certainly he caught the exotic flavor of the continent better than anyone has done since Pierre Loti, as one reviewer put it. In his own introduction, Maran sharply questions how much the white man puts the burden on his colored colonials. Since winning the Goncourt Prize in 1921, he has described the flora and fauna of Africa, its native peoples and their problems, and other such matters for a variety of periodicals ranging from *Le Monde Illustré* to *Candide*.

Maran's latest books include one on

709

the legends and customs of the Ubangi, the explorations of Livingstone, and the lives of a number of pioneers in Africa in addition to novels and adventure books describing wild animal life. To date *Batouala* is the only one of his books translated into English, but with the mounting tensions on the Dark Continent, it might be well to hear from a Negro who knows and loves that continent and who is a lucid spokesman for its people.

BIBLIOGRAPHICAL REFERENCES: There is almost no criticism of Maran in English. See *Dictionaire National des Contemporains,* Vol. III, 1939, and the author's preface to *Batouala,* translated by H. Seltzer, 1922.

MARCUS AURELIUS

Born: Rome, Italy
Date: April, 121

Died: Vienna (?)
Date: March 17, 180

PRINCIPAL WORK

PHILOSOPHICAL ESSAYS: *Meditations.*

Born in Rome sometime in April, 121, Marcus Annius Verus, later named Marcus (Aelius) Aurelius (Antoninus), was one of two writers who are identified forever with the philosophy of Stoicism. The other, Epictetus, was originally a slave; Marcus Aurelius was an emperor of Rome who, educated by private tutors, studied poetry and rhetoric. About the age of twelve he became interested in Stoicism, and at twenty-five he began the study of this philosophy and the law. In 161, when he was forty, Marcus Aurelius became the emperor of Rome, devoting most of his reign to defending the empire from marauders from Europe and Asia.

Extremely popular with his subjects, Marcus Aurelius was on of the most benevolent of emperors, and his treatment of slaves and orphans was generous beyond his times. His only cruelty was to the members of the new Christian religion, but his objection was not to the religion as such, but to the fact that it was not a state religion and therefore harmed the solidarity of Rome. After his death, March 17, 180, in Vienna or Sirmium, he was deified.

His reign marked an unsettled period in Roman history. Besides the foes outside the empire, Rome was plagued by earthquakes and pestilence. It is perhaps fortunate for history that Marcus Aurelius was one of the world's greatest Stoics, feeling always that one should seek not happiness but serenity. His great work, the *Meditations,* is the record of a life led on Stoic principles. It has been praised highly for its practical morality and the absence of abstract statements with little basis in everyday experience. Written originally in Greek, the *Meditations* were first published in 1558.

BIBLIOGRAPHICAL REFERENCES: Recent biographical and historical studies of Marcus Aurelius include H. D. Sedgwick, *Marcus Aurelius,* 1944; Aristide Calderini, *Marco Aurelio, Antonio imperatore,* 1950; and A. S. L. Farquharson, *Marcus Aurelius: His Life and His World,* 1951. A good background study is E. V. Arnold, *Roman*

Stoicism, 1911. See also Will Durant, *The Story of Philosophy*, 1926 (rev. ed., 1954).

PIERRE DE MARIVAUX

Born: Paris, France
Date: February 4, 1688

Died: Paris
Date: February 12, 1763

Principal Works

NOVELS: *La Vie de Marianne*, 1731–1741 (*Marianne*); *Le Paysan parvenu*, 1735 (*The Upstart Peasant*); *Pharamond*, 1737.

PLAYS: *Les Effets surprenants de la sympathie*, 1713 (*The Surprising Effects of Sympathy*); *La Surprise de l'amour*, 1722 (*The Surprises of Love*); *Le Jeu de l'amour et du hasard*, 1730 (*The Game of Love and Chance*); *L'École des mères*, 1732 (*The School for Mothers*); *Le Legs*, 1736 (*The Legacy*); *Les Fausses confidences*, 1737 (*False Secrets*); *L'Épreuve*, 1740 (*The Test*).

Pierre Carlet de Chamblain de Marivaux is chiefly remembered through coinage of the word *Marivaudage*, alluding to his use of a highly meticulous though sentimental style copied by the eighteenth and nineteenth century novelists. Born in Paris on February 4, 1688, he himself was the son of a financier who created the family name implying nobility and who was the director of the mint at Riom.

Writing for journals and periodicals having helped to shape his peculiar style, he wrote Addison-like essays for the Paris *Mercure* from 1717. He began writing plays for the Comédie Italienne (although the Comédie Française occasionally produced one of his thirty-odd plays) in 1720. He married and lost his wife and his fortune within a very few years of his initial successes; thereafter he lived by his pen.

Marivaux started several journals which might have enjoyed success had his habits of publication been more regular. In 1731 he began writing his great work, the novel *Marianne*, one of the landmarks in the development of the novel. He began two other novels, *The Upstart Peasant*, which had promises of even greater distinction, and *Pharamond*.

His last years were not remarkable. Elected to the French Academy in 1742, he was the friend of the great Fontenelle, Helvétius, and Madame de Pompadour, but he incurred the wrath of Voltaire through his unsparing criticism of the rising *Philosophes*. He died in Paris on February 12, 1763.

BIBLIOGRAPHICAL REFERENCES: A recent work on Marivaux in English is R. K. Jamison, *Marivaux: A Study in Sensibility*, 1941. See also Gustave Larroumet, *Marivaux, sa vie et ses œuvres*, 1882; Gaston Deschamps, *Marivaux*, 1897; Arthur Tilley, *Three French Dramatists: Racine, Marivaux, Musset*, 1933; Claude Roy, *Lire Marivaux*, 1947; and Marcel Arland, *Marivaux*, 1950.

CHRISTOPHER MARLOWE

Born: Canterbury, England
Date: February 6, 1564

Died: Deptford, England
Date: May 30, 1593

PRINCIPAL WORKS

PLAYS: *Dido, Queen of Carthage,* c. 1585 (with Nash); *Tamburlaine,* Parts I and II, c. 1586–1587; *The Jew of Malta,* 1589; *The Massacre at Paris,* c. 1590; *Edward the Second,* 1591; *The Tragedy of Doctor Faustus,* 1592.

POEMS: *Hero and Leander,* 1598 (completed by Chapman); "The Passionate Shepherd to His Love," 1599.

Christopher Marlowe, English playwright, was born at Canterbury, February 6, 1564, and was murdered at Deptford, May 30, 1593. Marlowe was educated at King's School, Canterbury, and at Corpus Christi College, Cambridge (B.A. 1584: M.A. 1587). His original intention of taking orders was abandoned in favor of play writing, state service, and, apparently, political intrigue. His first plays and poems belong to his Cambridge days, but the lure of the public theaters took him to London, where he spent the rest of his life. In 1589 he and his fellow-dramatist, Thomas Watson, were involved in a fatal assault on one William Bradley in Norton Folgate, but their plea of self-defense was accepted. It seems that Marlowe was known by this time as an exponent of unorthodox religious and political opinions. He was arrested on a charge of atheism in May, 1593 (see under Kyd, Thomas), but was fatally wounded in a brawl at Deptford before he could be brought to trial. His assailants, Ingram Frizer, Robert Poley and Nicholas Skeres, are known to have been connected with various shady political intrigues, and it it probable that the murder of Marlowe was intended to safeguard the interests of the Walsingham family. The whole episode is perplexing, but no importance attaches to the absurd theory that

Marlowe survived into the seventeenth century and wrote the plays which responsible opinion assigns to Shakespeare.

Marlowe's literary beginnings were as a translator of Lucan and Ovid, but when he turned to Vergil's *Aeneid,* he did so as a dramatist. *Dido, Queen of Carthage* was printed after Marlowe's death as a play written jointly with Thomas Nash, though Nash's share cannot have been very extensive. The source material for the first part of *Tamburlaine* was doubtless gathered at Cambridge, where Marlowe had access to books outside the general run. In matter and manner it is an astounding product of the uninhibited Renaissance imagination and, as such, took London by storm, even though it was evidently performed under primitive conditions. The sequel, written and presented c. 1587, is a more professional affair and shows some measure of dramatic advance. *The Jew of Malta* was perhaps influenced by Kyd's *Spanish Tragedy.* It is, despite recent critical dicta, a characteristic revenge tragedy, fraught with horrors and sensationalism. *The Massacre at Paris* has survived only in a deplorably corrupt text, but even this reveals something of the vigor and powerful dramatic conflict of the original. Many critics have unwisely condemned this play out of hand, but the probability is that it was a masterpiece in its kind. *Edward the Second,* the first real historical play and the first great English tragedy, shows a remarkable maturing of Marlowe's tragic genius, and this is fully maintained in the last play, *Doctor Faustus,* presented in 1592. *Doctor Faustus* was evidently planned by Marlowe and much of it was certainly executed by him, but many scenes, especially in the middle acts, are the work of another hand. Whether this implies original collaboration, or the completion of a play left unfinished at the time of Marlowe's sudden death cannot be determined. One lyric, "The Passionate Shepherd to his Love," and the narrative fragment, *Hero and Leander,* survive as evidence of Marlowe's compelling excellence in non-dramatic forms.

Marlowe's plays up to 1590 are tragedies which show no real tragic sense and little skill in dramatic contrivance. Formally the two *Tamburlaine* plays are chronicle drama, and *The Jew of Malta* a revenge tragedy, but interest centers on a single character who is a mouthpiece for rhetorical declamation and a perpetrator of monstrous violence. How far these so-called "supermen" are projections of Marlowe's own personality or ideals remains a moot point. It is likely that he was fascinated by the spectacle of man in pursuit of the infinite and by crude exemplars of Machiavellian doctrine, but the final tragedies prove conclusively that he outgrew the impulse to traffic in horrors and moved to a compassionate, though still perplexed, view of human affairs. Character types such as Tamburlaine, Barabas, and Guise may well have been determined by the particular talents and preferences of Edward Alleyne, the leading actor of

the Lord Admiral's Company, and it is surely significant that *Edward the Second,* written for Pembroke's men, abandons the superman in favor of an even distribution of parts, a feature which it shares with the earlier *Dido,* written for a boys' company.

Such clues to Marlowe's personality as the plays seem to offer may be illusory, and often run counter to the received biographical evidence, which, in its turn, is misleading. It has always to be borne in mind that Marlowe's death was almost certainly a political expedient, and that his assailants and accusers were desperate and perjured men. On the other hand, Nash, Drayton, and especially Edward Blount, the publisher, wrote of him with affection, and Shakespeare's allusion to him as "dead shepherd" strongly suggests that he was a person of gentle parts. Most of the gibes at religion, the crown, and so forth collected by Richard Baines are undoubtedly authentic and are corroborated by Kyd's letters to Sir John Puckering, but it is hard to know how much reliance can be placed on seemingly outrageous statements which have been wrenched from their contexts. Marlowe's "Atheism," actually a form of unitarianism, may have been a passing phase, a very riband in the cap of youth, and *Doctor Faustus* in all its parts suggests that by 1592 Marlowe had moved to a more orthodox position. The importance of Baines's note lies in the fact that, in its own slipshod and malicious way, it confirms the impression left by the plays as a whole—that Marlowe was an earnest seeker after truth who was not prepared to submit complacently to acceptance of the existing order. Mr. T. S. Eliot claims that he is the most thoughtful of the Elizabethan dramatists. This is perhaps a half rather than a whole truth, but it is evident that Marlowe's mind reached out beyond the Ptolemaic and neo-Platonic orthodoxy of his time, and that the basic Elizabethan notion of order and degree was something which he and all his tragic heroes set out to challenge. It can scarcely be pretended that he supplies the full answer to any of the questions that he raises, but the important thing is that they were raised at all, both in respect of the existing outlook and of the imaginative synthesis which grew out of Marlowe's virtual anarchy. Marlowe's tragic irony lies in the opposition between man's illusion that his progress is an infinite, vertical ascent and the reality that he moves on Fortune's wheel. His heroes rise from base beginnings to sovereign power and to a self-assurance from which they are flung headlong to destruction. Such an outlook on human affairs can obviously degenerate into cynicism, and it is true that the splendors of *Tamburlaine* were succeeded by the murky nihilism of *The Jew of Malta* and the sardonic complexities of *The Massacre at Paris*, but Marlowe's essential humanity emerges in the final plays, and here, within his relatively simple and uniform tragic pattern, he contrives fascinating variety of action invested with moral and emotional tones of infinite subtlety and suggestion.

J. M. Nosworthy

BIBLIOGRAPHICAL REFERENCES: The standard edition is *The Works and Life of Christopher Marlowe*, general editor, R. H. Case, 6 vols., 1930–1933. Also valuable is the one-volume, old-spelling edition, *The Works of Christopher Marlowe*, edited by C. F. Tucker Brooke, 1910. W. W. Greg's edition of *Doctor Faustus, 1604–1616*, 1950, is an important contribution to Marlowe scholarship. For biography and criticism see also A. W. Ward, *A History of Dramatic Literature*, Vol. I, 1887; J. G. Lewis, *Marlowe: Outlines of His Life and Works*, 1891; J. H. Ingram, *Christopher Marlowe and His Associates*, 1904; E. K. Chambers, *The Elizabethan Stage*, Vol. III, 1923; Leslie Hotson, *The Death of Christopher Marlowe*, 1925; Una Ellis-Fermor, *Christopher Marlowe*, 1926; J. E. Bakeless, *Christopher Marlowe: The Man in His Time*, 1937; idem, *The Tragicall History of Christopher Marlowe*, 1942; P. H. Kocher, *Christopher Marlowe*, 1946; and Harry Levin, *The Overreacher: A Study of Christopher Marlowe*, 1952.

JOHN PHILLIPS MARQUAND

Born: Wilmington, Delaware
Date: November 10, 1893

Died: Newbury, Massachusetts
Date: July 16, 1960

PRINCIPAL WORKS

NOVELS: *The Unspeakable Gentleman*, 1922; *The Black Cargo*, 1925; *Warning Hill*, 1930; *Haven's End*, 1933; *The Late George Apley*, 1937; *Wickford Point*, 1939; *H. M. Pulham, Esq.*, 1941; *So Little Time*, 1943; *B. F.'s Daughter*, 1946; *Point of No Return*, 1949; *Melville Goodwin, U.S.A.*, 1951; *Sincerely, Willis Wayde*, 1955.

MISCELLANEOUS: *Thirty Years*, 1954.

John P(hillips) Marquand is, in the opinion of many readers, the inheritor of the mantle of Sinclair Lewis as an attentive reporter of social customs, personal ambitions, and class structures in modern American society, but unlike Lewis, whose social satire is laid on with a heavy hand, Marquand presents his pictures of upper-class New England life with a clarity and simplicity that keep the reader from immediately sensing the real bitterness of the novelist's observations. Indeed, Marquand works a vein of good-mannered but tart social comment that can be found also in the novels of William Dean Howells and Ellen Glasgow.

Marquand is admirably equipped for the task to which he has set himself in his fiction. He was born in Wilmington, Delaware, on November 10, 1893, into a well-to-do family with New England connections; his great-aunt was the celebrated Margaret Fuller of Trascendentalist fame, and his ancestral town of Newburyport, Massachusetts, is a town whose aura of tradition he has reflected in *Wickford Point* and other novels. But Marquand's youth was not a financially secure one; his family lost money in the crash of 1907, and when Marquand went to Harvard (Class of '15), he was forced to depend on scholarships and the help of friends. Marquand had a keen sense of being ostracized and consequently is able to look at his chosen subject-matter from both sides of the tracks; his recognition from the Harvard *Lampoon* did not close the wound which social exclusion from the university clubs had given him.

After college Marquand accumulated war experience on the Mexican border and in France, but he did not find this experience of danger and fear especially suggestive in a literary way. More stimulating were several years spent in an advertising agency in New York; he could not take seriously an office full of Phi Beta Kappas involved in merchandising. After two years with the New York *Tribune* he returned to New England to write his first novel, a cloak-and-dagger narrative titled *The Unspeakable Gentleman*. For almost a decade and a half afterwards, until the appearance of *The Late George Apley* in 1937, Marquand was a productive writer of stories that appeared regularly in the *Saturday Evening Post* and *Collier's,* work that, in Marquand's own later judgment, naïvely accepts the morality of the success story and the superficial social observation of a fashionable photographer. Toward the end of this period he had great success with a series of detective stories about a Japanese detective, Mr. Moto, who, understandably, had to be withdrawn from circulation about 1941 but who was revived in *Stopover, Tokyo* (1957).

Against the advice of friends, Marquand wrote his first serious novel, *The Late George Apley,* and had the satisfaction of winning the Pulitzer Prize. The novel, an attack on the Brahmin class of Boston, is, like Marquand's later social dissections, doubly chilling because of the simplicity and quietness with which the attack goes forward. The failure of his central character to achieve his own early hopes and to respond to the real chances for life and experience furnishes a pattern for many of the later Marquand novels. The hero of many a subsequent tale is shrewd enough to see what he really is or could be; he is not adventurous enough to realize this vision and instead accepts the "diminished thing" (the phrase is that of Robert Frost, another New Englander) that is life according to the wishes of one's wife and the pressures of one's "social role."

Marquand has been married twice, each time, as one of his characters would put it, "very well." Marquand's first wife, from whom he was divorced in 1935, warned him of his projected novel about Apley: "That's a good book to write if you want to leave Boston, that's all."

Marquand's own career since 1937 has been one of unwavering success measured by the books he has written: *Wickford Point, H. M. Pulham, Esq., So Little Time, Point of No Return, Sincerely, Willis Wayde,* and others. Meanwhile membership on the board of a book club, involvement in the productions of stage versions of several of his novels, and continuous writing are activities protracting his early success as a writer for the "slicks" into his second career as a writer whose social comment and criticism are taken with real seriousness. For example, Gran-

ville Hicks has pointed out that Marquand is a better observer of class structure in Newburyport than are W. Lloyd Warner and his staff of sociologists in their scientific study of the Massachusetts town in *The Social Life of a Modern Community.* But negative criticism points to the continued deftness of Marquand's style; apparently such criticism would be pleased if Marquand wrote with less skill. Other critics are not pleased that Marquand in the long run accepts and tolerates a society whose shortcomings he identifies brilliantly. As to this latter point, it may be doubted that a person who rejected the social structure that tolerates Willis Wayde and other Marquand characters could write of the perplexed heroes with the understanding which Marquand can always summon. Marquand himself is a Unitarian, but his novels present man involved in the problems of the twentieth century only insofar as those problems are *not* religious.

BIBLIOGRAPHICAL REFERENCES: The writer is the subject of a literary study done in the Marquand manner, Philip Hamburger's *J. P. Marquand, Esq.,* 1952. For briefer criticism and commentary see also the essay on Marquand in Joseph Warren Beach, *American Fiction, 1920–1940,* 1941; and Charles A. Brady "John Phillips Marquand: Martini-Age Victorian," in *Fifty Years of the American Novel, 1900–1950,* edited by Harold C. Gardiner, S.J., 1952; Harlan Hatcher, "John Phillips Marquand," *College English,* I (1939), 107–118; Herschel Brickell, "Miss Glasgow and Mr. Marquand," *Virginia Quarterly Review,* XVII (1941), 405–417; Nathan Glick, "Marquand's Vanishing American Aristocracy: Good Manners and the Good Life," *Commentary,* IX (1950), 435–441; and Granville Hicks, "Marquand of Newburyport," *Harper's,* CC (1950), 101–108.

FREDERICK MARRYAT

Born: London, England
Date: July 10, 1792

Died: Langham, England
Date: August 9, 1848

PRINCIPAL WORKS

NOVELS: *The Naval Officer, of Scenes and Adventures in the Life of Frank Mildmay,* 1829; *The King's Own,* 1830; *Peter Simple,* 1834; *Jacob Faithful,* 1834; *The*

Pirate and Three Cutters, 1836; *Mr. Midshipman Easy*, 1836; *Japhet in Search of a Father*, 1836; *Snarleyyow, or The Dog Fiend*, 1837; *The Phantom Ship*, 1839.

Frederick Marryat, born in Westminster, London, July 10, 1792, was the second son of Joseph Marryat, a member of Parliament. He was not well educated, and his home and school life made him miserable. After repeated attempts to run away, each attempt ending in capture and caning, he was allowed to join the English Navy in 1806. Strong in body and favored by social status, he saw active service in the Napoleonic and Burmese wars and soon became a commander. But the writing of an article against impressment ended prospects of advancement in his naval career. However, as his private log shows, he already took much pleasure in writing. After his first novel, *Frank Mildmay*, was published in 1829, he resigned to enjoy his enthusiasm for the sea vicariously as well as to tell in his novels of the essential cruelty of the service.

Marryat tried to be both man of fashion and man of letters. Always in debt, he worked rapidly. From 1832 to 1835 he edited the *Metropolitan Magazine*, and during that period five of his best novels appeared in its pages. Influenced by Smollett, only one of his tales, *The King's Own*, was a tragedy.

The rest were comedies that often went into farce. The major theme was the corruption of a young man by an immoral institution—the English Navy—whose success was the result of bloodthirsty cruelty to both its own members and the enemy. However, Marryat believed in the myth that it was the destiny of the English to rule the world.

A writer of good descriptive power, his characters were sharp portraits of men who had responsibility but little ability and of youths who were loyal. His stories for children fit the mode of the time of Victoria: one should follow one's religious teachings and consider the home the center of life. Though he became an individualist because his father could not see him as an individual, he always wrote with an eye for the market. And it was his catering to the mass market that caused Poe to claim his very success proved his mediocrity as a writer. However, his style is pleasingly simple, his humor often delightful, his pathos genuine; and he is still read today. *Mr. Midshipman Easy* is considered his best work. He died at Langham, England, August 9, 1848.

BIBLIOGRAPHICAL REFERENCES: The standard edition is *The Novels of Captain Marryat*, edited by R. B. Johnson, 26 vols., 1929–1930. The official biography is Florence Marryat, *Life and Letters of Captain Marryat*, 2 vols., 1872. Two modern studies of value are Christopher Lloyd, *Captain Marryat and the Old Navy*, 1939; and Oliver Warner, *Captain Marryat: A Rediscovery*, 1953. Of great interest is "The Captain's Death Bed" in Virginia Woolf, *The Captain's Death Bed and Other Essays*, 1950. See also, Michael Sadleir, "Captain Marryat," *London Mercury*, X (1924), 495–510.

JOHN MARSTON

Born: Coventry (?), England   *Died:* London, England
Date: 1576 (Baptized October 7, 1576)   *Date:* June 24, 1634

PLAYS: *Antonio and Mellida*, 1599; *Antonio's Revenge*, 1599; *Jack Drum's Entertainment*, c. 1600; *What You Will*, 1601; *The Dutch Courtesan*, 1603; *The Malcontent*, 1604; *Parasitaster, or The Fawn*, c. 1605; *Eastward Ho!*, 1605 (with Chapman and Jonson); *Sophonisba*, 1606; *The Insatiate Countess*, c. 1610 (with William Barksteed).

POEMS: *The Metamorphosis of Pygmalion's Image and Certain Satires*, 1598; *The Scourge of Villainy*, 1598.

John Marston, probably born in Coventry and baptized there on October 7, 1576, was the son of an English lawyer and his Italian wife. He attended Brasenose College, Oxford, from February 4, 1592, to February 6, 1594, when he received his B.A. degree. He entered the Middle Temple, but his father's statement of disappointment indicates that the young man did not complete his legal training.

Marston's first known works were books of poetic satire: *The Metamorphosis of Pygmalion's Image* and *The Scourge of Villainy*. In them the young poet lashes himself into somewhat conventional anger against the abuses of the times. In September, 1599, Philip Henslowe recorded payment to "Mr. Maxton the new poete." Making allowance for Henslowe's customary spelling difficulties, one may assume the new poet is Marston. Very soon Marston turned from Henslowe's company to Paul's Boys, revising for them *Histriomastix* (c. 1599) and writing the two Antonio plays and *Jack Drum's Entertainment*. Because of the uncertainty of dating the plays it is not clear whether *Antonio's Revenge* influenced *Hamlet* or was influenced by it; both plays owed much to Thomas Kyd's *Spanish Tragedy*.

Perhaps Marston is best remembered for his part in the so-called War of the Theaters, in which Ben Jonson was on one side, and Marston and Thomas Dekker were on the other. E. K. Chambers suggests that Marston helped Dekker with the anti-Jonsonian *Satiromastix* (1601); but Fredson Bowers, Dekker's latest and most excellent editor, does not credit Marston with a share in the play. At any rate, *What You Will* contains an apparent attack on Jonson. Jonson's *Poetaster* (also 1601) lacerated both Marston and Dekker. However, by 1604 any breach between Jonson and Marston must have been healed, for Marston dedicated his *Malcontent* to Jonson in that year. In 1605 commendatory verses by Marston appeared in Jonson's *Sejanus*; and Marston, Chapman, and Jonson collaborated in the writing of *Eastward Ho!* Satirical passages in the last play led to the imprisonment of Chapman and Jonson; but Marston escaped recorded punishment at this time, though the other writers claimed that they did not write the offensive passages.

According to E. K. Chambers, Marston was married to "Mary, probably the daughter of one of James's chaplains." He was imprisoned in 1608, and his career as a practicing dramatist ended with his *Insatiate Countess* apparently unfinished. The assumption is that William Barksteed, or Barksted, finished the play, as a quarto version of it was printed under his name. Barksteed was a minor actor, poet, and dramatist.

Marston took holy orders and obtained a parish church in Hampshire in 1616. He resigned his pastorate in 1631 and died three years later, on June 24, 1634, in Aldermanbury Parish, London.

Though guilty of verbal excesses, for which Jonson chastised him in *Poetaster*, Marston is a worthy minor poet and dramatist. He is still readable, though hardly alive on the modern stage.

BIBLIOGRAPHICAL REFERENCES: There are two editions of Marston's writings: *The Works of John Marston*, edited by A. H. Bullen, 1887; and *The Plays of John Marston*, edited by H. H. Wood, 1934–1938. See also E. K. Chambers, *The Elizabethan Stage*, Vols. II and III, 1923; Henry W. Wells, *Elizabethan and Jacobean Playwrights*, 1939; G. B. Harrison, *Elizabethan Plays and Players*, 1940; and T. M. Parrott and R. H. Ball, *A Short View of Elizabethan Drama*, 1943.

MARTIAL
(Marcus Valerius Martialis)

Born: Bilbilis, Spain　　　　　*Died:* Bilbilis
Date: c. A.D. 40　　　　　　　*Date:* c. 104

PRINCIPAL WORKS

EPIGRAMS IN VERSE: *Liber Spectaculorum*, 80; *Xenia*, 84; *Apophoreta*, 84.

Although Martial (Marcus Valerius Martialis) was born in Bilbilis, Spain, about A.D. 40 and did not go to Rome until 64, he was completely a Roman, and he has given posterity one of the best pictures of Roman life in his time that exists. His arrival in Rome was not ostentatious, and he remained poor for a few years; but he soon became acquainted with the famous literary men of the time—Pliny, Lucan, Juvenal—and acquired rich patrons. He received benefits from the Roman Emperors Titus and Domitian.

Martial was often accused of being a toady to his wealthy patrons; certainly it is known that he was often unhappy over the necessity to be witty and entertaining for them, but he was a loyal friend and was generally well liked. He was given an estate in Spain to which he returned in 94 to spend there the last few years of his life, dying at Bilbilis about 104.

The epigram was Martial's poetic specialty, and he wrote a total of fourteen books of satiric verse. About 575 of his epigrams have been preserved, and from these it can be seen that he wrote about almost every phase of Roman life, sharply pinpointing the gentle and gracious as well as the false and disgusting. His epigrams, running from two lines to over thirty in length, are written in a variety of meters, but they have in common a sharp twist of phrase and meaning at the end, a kind of punch line.

Martial's epigrams are often bitter, but at times, especially when he was writing of country life or his Spanish homeland, he was capable of deep warmth of feeling. The epigram in English literature owes much to his clear insight and skillful versatility.

BIBLIOGRAPHICAL REFERENCES: Martial's epigrammatic poems, translated by W. C. A. Ker, are in the Loeb Classical Library, 2 vols., 1930. Another collection, *Martial: The Twelve Books of Epigrams*, was translated by J. A. Pott and F. A. Wright, 1926. For biography and criticism see G. Boissier, *Tacitus and Other Studies*, translated by W. G. Hutchison, 1906; T. K. Whipple, *Martial and the English Epigram*, 1925; and Luigi Illuminati, *Marziala nella vita e nell' arte*, 1951. For a background study of the satirists of the Silver Age see J. W. Duff, *Roman Satire*, 1936.

ROGER MARTIN DU GARD

Born: Neuilly-sur-Seine, France   *Died:* Bellême, France
Date: March 23, 1881   *Date:* August 22, 1958

PRINCIPAL WORKS

NOVELS: *Devenir*, 1908; *Jean Barois*, 1913; *Les Thibaults*, 1922–1940 (*The World of the Thibaults*); *La Confidence africaine*, 1932; *Vieille France*, 1933 (*The Postman*).

PLAYS: *Le Testament de Père Leleu*, 1920; *La Gonfle*, 1928; *Un Taciturne*, 1931 (*A Man of Few Words*).

Roger Martin du Gard achieved his reputation as a novelist with the publication of *Jean Barois* in 1913. After the war, during which he served in the motor transport division, he undertook his magnum opus, an eight-volume work called *Les Thibaults*, the first volumes of which came out in the early 1920's and the last, called simply *Epilogue*, in 1940. In recognition of his performance in this cyclical work, he was awarded the Nobel Prize for literature in 1937.

Martin du Gard was born at Neuilly, March 23, 1881, into an established, well-to-do Catholic family of lawyers and magistrates. He has made this same bourgeois class the subject of his novels, and even though his theme is revolt and disintegration he seems to have inherited from his background the qualities for which he is most often praised: integrity, solidity, sense. He was educated at the best lycées in Paris and in 1906 he received from the École de Chartres the advanced degree of archivist-paleog-

rapher. His scholarly temperament is evident in his fiction; André Gide in his *Journals* remarked that Martin du Gard was interested in general laws of behavior rather than in exceptional cases and that he envied him his obstinate patience in pursuing his goal. In his Nobel Prize speech Martin du Gard referred to himself as an "investigator as objective as is humanly possible." In his fiction he strives for and achieves an almost photographic fidelity, especially notable in his dialogue, and the virtual elimination of a personal style.

His work in many ways invites comparison with the scientific naturalistic novel of the late nineteenth century, except that Martin du Gard is less committed to a thesis than Zola, for example, and interested more in the family situation and the ideological and psychological conflicts in the minds of his characters than in the broad economic organization of society. His work would perhaps be more comparable to the Edwardian family saga except for

720

its rigidly analytic and unsentimental tone. *Jean Barois* describes a young man torn between the religious view of life which was implanted in him and the scientific view to which he is drawn. The problem is carried further in *The World of the Thibaults*, which gives us a full portrait of a French family (and a large segment of French society besides) between the years 1903 and 1914: the father, successful, autocratic, moralistic, insensitive, and his two sons who try but ultimately fail to come to terms with their powerful bourgeois indoctrination. Antoine, the elder, compromises, tries to save what he can of the old values and becomes a doctor; the younger, Jacques, sets himself in complete revolt as a writer and a socialist. Gide commented that Martin du Gard put most of himself into Antoine and implied that his interest in Jacques was part of the author's "extraordinary and anxious desire to acquire certain qualities that are quite opposed to his nature, mystery,

shadow and strangeness." In this novel it is Antoine who debates his position with an old Abbé because he cannot rationalize the contradictions in his nature to his satisfaction. The author himself withholds judgment in this struggle.

Martin du Gard has also been a successful playwright. Two farces, *Le Testament du Père Leleu* and *La Gonfle,* which are excellent descriptions of peasant mentality and language, were produced for Jacques Copeau at the Vieux Colombier. A third play, *A Man of Few Words,* deals impartially, as does *The Postman* and several other lesser works, with the problem of sexual abnormalities.

During the Second World War, as he had done during most of his life, Martin du Gard lived quietly, for the most part in the country, indifferent to personal interviews, public appearances, or polemics. In 1953 he published some brief recollections of his friend André Gide.

BIBLIOGRAPHICAL REFERENCES: The most comprehensive study in English is H. C. Rice, *Roger Martin du Gard and the World of the Thibaults,* 1941. See also René Lalou, *Roger Martin du Gard,* 1937; Pierre Brodin, *Les écrivains français l'entre deux guerres,* 1942; and David Tylden-Wright, *The Image of France,* 1957.

GREGORIO MARTÍNEZ SIERRA

Born: Madrid, Spain
Date: May 6, 1881

Died: Madrid
Date: October 1, 1947

PRINCIPAL WORKS

PLAYS: *El ama de la casa,* 1910 (*The Housekeeper*); *Canción de cuna,* 1911 (*Cradle Song*); *El Reino de Dios,* 1915 (*The Kingdom of God*); *Sueño de una noche de agosto,* 1918 (*The Romantic Young Lady*); *Don Juan de España,* 1921; *Triángulo,* 1930.

NOVEL: *Tú eres la paz,* 1906 (*Ana María*).

Gregorio Martínez Sierra was born in Madrid on May 6, 1881, and died there October 1, 1947. The story of his

life is virtually the story of the dramas, novels, poetry, and essays he wrote. The program for a New York per-

721

formance of *Cradle Song* first explained the feminine charm long felt in the work of Martínez Sierra, when it listed as his previously unknown collaborator, his wife María de la O Lajárraga, a feminist, lecturer, and writer in her own right. Their *Vida y dulzura* (*Life and Sweetness*) was well received in 1908, then several fanciful plays preceded the realistic *La sombra del padre* (*Shadow of the Father*), a study of family life produced in 1909. Their first real success, however, was *The Housekeeper,* followed the next year by their most popular play, the delightful *Cradle Song,* the story of a foundling left in an orphan asylum. Recently it was revealed that the father of Martínez Sierra's wife was the medical consultant for a convent, like the only male character in the comedy, and her sister, a Mother Superior, was the inspiration for the Prioress in this play.

Several plays a year preceded *The Kingdom of God,* another great success in several languages, including English. The drama covers more than a half century in the life of its feminine protagonist.

Besides writing plays, Martínez Sierra translated some of the best of European plays for presentation in the experimental Eslava Theater of Madrid, off the main thoroughfare but in the main currents of contemporary drama. For this theater which he directed, he made the best translation into Spanish of Ibsen's *The Doll's House.* However, Madrid audiences preferred his adaptation under the title *Mamá* (1912), truer to the Spanish character since, instead of giving up and abandoning home and family, as Nora did, the Spanish mother in this play fights to hold her family together. Its happy ending is explained by Martínez Sierra when he asserts his belief that human nature is essentially good and can be counted on to choose the way that will come out right.

Though this author wrote verse in the modernist manner, as well as several novels, his comedies of manners have done most to enhance his reputation. While uncomplicated, his characters are human and real. The action and the emotions are simple. In practically all of his forty plays, women have the principal roles, handled with insight and psychology, and the style is poetic. There is nothing base or low in the plays, but rather a spirit of optimism, and because of the dramatist's humor, they avoid over-sentimentality. Martínez Sierra is a good representative of Spain's theater at its best.

BIBLIOGRAPHICAL REFERENCES: Many of Martínez Sierra's plays have been translated into English. See the forewords to *Plays of G. Martínez Sierra,* 1915–1923; A. F. G. Bell, *Contemporary Spanish Literature,* 1925; and A. González Blanco, *Los Dramaturgos españoles contemporáneos,* 1917.

ANDREW MARVELL

Born: Winestead, England
Date: March 31, 1621

Died: London, England
Date: August 16, 1678

PRINCIPAL WORKS

POEMS: *Miscellaneous Poems,* 1681; *Poems on Affairs of State,* 1689; *Horatian Ode to Cromwell,* 1776.

SATIRE: *The Rehearsal Transposed,* 1672–1673.

Andrew Marvell, born at Winestead, Yorkshire, England, on March 31, 1621, was the son of an Anglican clergyman who became master of the Hull Grammar School. Having received his early education under his father at Hull, he entered Cambridge University in 1633 and received his bachelor's degree in 1638. As many men did at the time, he remained at Cambridge. In 1640 his father died, and two years later, apparently with his inheritance, Marvell began a four-year tour of the Continent. Although he began writing poetry while still at the university, few of Marvell's love lyrics or bucolic poems were published during his lifetime, his contemporary fame resting largely upon his satire.

During the English civil war Marvell, although not a Puritan himself, sided with the Cromwellians. From 1650 to 1652 he was tutor in the household of Lord Fairfax, a general in Cromwell's forces, and not long afterward tutor to Cromwell's ward, William Dutton; most of his best-known poems were written at this time. Although John Milton tried to get Marvell a post with the Puritan government in 1653, he did not actually receive an appointment until 1657. In 1659, a year before the Restoration of the Stuarts, he was elected to Parliament for Hull, a post he held until his death.

When Charles II became king, Marvell thought monarchy would be good for England, but he soon found himself in disagreement with the crown and began a long series of satires against the king and his government. The satires were so outspoken that they passed from hand to hand or were printed in secret, always anonymously. Only in the case of religious oppression did Marvell feel safe in admitting his authorship of satire, as he did for the two parts of *The Rehearsal Transprosed*. Just before his death Marvell published an anonymous pamphlet, *An Account of the Growth of Popery and Arbitrary Government in England* (1677). For some years it was thought that opponents, enraged by the satire, had poisoned its author, but his death in London on August 16, 1678, was caused by an overdose of opiates administered by his physician in ignorance.

BIBLIOGRAPHICAL REFERENCES: The standard edition is *The Poems and Letters of Andrew Marvell*, edited by H. M. Margoliouth, 2 vols., 1927. Biographical and critical studies include Augustine Birrell, *Andrew Marvell*, English Men of Letters series, 1905; V. Sackville-West, *Andrew Marvell*, 1929; and M. C. Bradbrook and M. G. L. Thomas, *Andrew Marvell*, 1940. An important study in French is Pierre Legouis, *André Marvell, Poète, puritain, patriote*, 1928. For briefer studies see M. C. Bradbrook, "Marvell and the Poetry of Rural Solitude," *Review of English Studies*, XVII (1941), 37–46; Douglas Bush, "Marvell's 'Horatian Ode,'" *Sewanee Review*, LX (1952), 361–376; and Joseph H. Summers, "Marvell's 'Nature'," *Journal of English Literary History*, XX (1953), 121–135.

KARL MARX

Born: Trier, Germany
Date: May 5, 1818

Died: London, England
Date: March 14, 1883

POLITICAL PHILOSOPHY: *Das Kapital*, 1867.

Karl (Heinrich) Marx, famous theorist who laid the foundation of modern communism, was born in Trier, Germany, on May 5, 1818, the son of a Jewish lawyer who had his practice in Treves. The father became a convert to Christianity while Karl Marx was a small child, and the entire family was baptized and received into Christianity in 1824, when Karl was but six years old. As a boy Karl attended the schools in Trier. Beginning his university career in 1835, he attended the German universities at Bonn and Berlin, where he studied law, history, and philosophy. In 1842 he received the degree of doctor of philosophy from the University of Jena. Because Marx's radical views and temperament prevented his being accepted into the academic world of a university as a faculty member, he began a career in journalism and became one of the editors of the *Rheinische Zeitung* in Cologne; his socialistic articles contributed to the suppression of this periodical by the government the following year. A few months later Marx married Jenny von Westphalen, daughter of a prominent government official, who remained loyal all her life to her husband. Although German on her father's side, she was of British descent on her mother's side of the family. Forced to leave Prussia within a few months of their marriage, the couple went to Paris.

In Paris Marx became associated with Arnold Ruge, and together they planned a socialist periodical, the *Deutsch-französische Jahrbücher*, a project that died quickly. The one issue of the periodical contained two articles by Marx on the Jewish question and Hegel's criticism of law; in the latter Marx declared that political freedom could come only by the proletariat's dissolution of government as it was then known, dissolution to be achieved by violence. Unlike most of the other socialists of his time, Marx already believed in political warfare as the key to success. An important side aspect of the short-lived *Jahrbücher* was that it brought together Marx and Friedrich Engels. The two men, working together, produced a volume, *Die heilige Familie oder Kritik der kritischen Kritic*, excoriating the intellectual Hegelian articles and their authors so prevalent at the time, including Bruno and Edgar Bauer, with whom Marx as a member of the "Freien," had once been on the friendliest of terms in Berlin. Once again, in this new book, Marx proposed that socialism be a working-class movement. After its publication he continued to contribute to periodicals and became a friend of Heinrich Heine, the poet. A relatively calm period in life ended, however, when the Prussian government requested the French to oust Marx. From France he went to Brussels, where he wrote and in 1847 published *La Misère de la philosophie* (*The Misery of Philosophy*), an attack on Proudhon's economic philosophy. Joined in Brussels by Engels, Marx became a part of the proletarian socialist movement, joining a league of German workers, the League of the Just, which had secret chapters in many European cities. This organization's philosophy of action coincided largely with that of Marx. The organization soon became the League of Communists, and for it Marx and Engels wrote the now famous *Manifest der Kommunisten* (*The Communist Manifesto*), published in 1848. A few weeks later revolution broke out in France. Believing this revolt the forerunner of a similar revolution in his native Prussia, Marx and Engels went immediately to Cologne to found a journal, *Neue rheinische Zeitung*, whose subtitle was "An Organ of Democracy." The paper openly advocated nonpayment of taxes, armed resistance, and revolution. The paper was quickly suppressed, and Marx was tried for high treason. Although acquitted, he was expelled by the Prussian authorities. He went to Paris for a time but, forced to leave France, he and his wife crossed the Channel to England and settled in London, where they spent the rest of their lives.

In London, Marx and his family lived precariously. He tried to reorganize the Communist League, but the results were hopeless. He also tried to revive the *Neue rheinische Zeitung*, but without success. Three children born during the years of poverty died while quite young. At last Marx received an appointment as a correspondent for the New York *Tribune* and his financial condition began to improve. His letters to the *Tribune*, later reprinted, were anti-Russian, in reaction to what Marx viewed as the tyranny of the tsarist regime.

In 1859 Marx published one of his most important pieces of writing, *Zur Kritik der politischen Ökonomie* (*A Critique of Political Economy*), which was planned as the first volume in a series of volumes to discuss all aspects of political economy. This long and ambitious project was never completed, but the published volume, rewritten and published as *Das Kapital*, was translated into English in the same year.

When in 1864 the International Working Men's Association was formed in London, Marx was an important figure in the organization. He soon became its unofficial leader, formulating its policy, explaining the organization's purposes to the members, and writing its pronouncements. This organization flourished for several years until historical events doomed it to eventual failure and finally, in July, 1876, it was formally dissolved at a congress of workers held in Philadelphia. Marx had practically left the organization by 1872, turning from it to spend his time working on the second and third volumes of *Das Kapital*, which he left in manuscript at his death. Illness frequently interrupted Marx's work during his later years, and the death of his wife in December, 1881, was a severe blow from which he himself never recovered. Karl Marx, proponent of revolution and proletarian violence, died quietly at his home in London on March 14, 1883, leaving three daughters and a set of doctrines destined to shake civilization to its roots. The posthumous volumes of *Das Kapital* were published by Engels, 1885–1894.

BIBLIOGRAPHICAL REFERENCES: A good introduction to Marx's life and philosophy is Max Beer, *Life and Teaching of Karl Marx*, 1921. For biography and political and economic commentary see also Wilhelm Liebknecht, *Karl Marx: Biographical Memoirs*, translated 1901; L. B. Boudin, *The Theoretical System of Karl Marx*,

1907; Benedetto Croce, *Historical Materialism and the Economics of Karl Marx*, 1914; Achille Loria, *Karl Marx*, 1920; Karl Kantsky, *The Economic Doctrines of Karl Marx*, 1925; A. D. Lindsay, *Karl Marx's "Capital,"* 1925; Max Eastman, *Marx, Lenin and the Science of Revolution*, 1926; Harold J. Laski, *Communism*, 1927; E. H. Carr, *Karl Marx*, 1934; Isaiah Berlin, *Karl Marx: His Life and Environment*, 1948; Edmund Wilson, *The Triple Thinkers*, 1948; and P. M. Sweezy, *Theory of Capitalist Development*, 1956.

PHILIP MASSINGER

Born: Salisbury, England
Date: c. November 24, 1583

Died: London, England
Date: c. March 18, 1640

PRINCIPAL WORKS

PLAYS (MASSINGER ALONE): *The Duke of Milan*, c. 1621; *The Bondman*, c. 1623; *The Maid of Honor*, c. 1623; *A New Way to Pay Old Debts*, c. 1625–1626; *The Roman Actor*, 1626; *The City Madam*, c. 1632; *The Bashful Lover*, 1636.

COLLABORATIONS WITH FLETCHER: *The Custom of the Country*, c. 1609; *Sir John Van Olden Barnavelt*, 1619; *The False One*, c. 1620; *The Beggar's Bush*, c. 1622; *The Spanish Curate*, 1622; *The Elder Brother*, printed 1637.

Philip Massinger was the son of Arthur Massinger, "gentlemen," of an old Salisbury family. The father had two degrees from Oxford and served Henry Herbert, second Earl of Pembroke, in confidential matters. His son Philip was baptized at St. Thomas's, Salisbury, on November 24, 1583, and may have served as a page in Wilton, the home of the Herberts. On May 14, 1602, Philip was entered in St. Alban's Hall, Oxford. Anthony à Wood surmises that Henry Herbert supported Philip at Oxford until he offended his patron by adopting the Roman Catholic faith, and Wood implies that Philip left Oxford without a degree because he "applied his mind more to poetry and romance . . . than to logic and philosophy." The withdrawal from Oxford was probably due to his father's death in 1606.

Several years later, Philip Massinger was in London, writing in collaboration with Nat Field, Daborne, and Fletcher. Henslowe, the great theatrical proprietor, in 1613 records money paid in advance to these associates. Though Field, Fletcher, and Massinger joined the King's Men in 1616, yet Massinger wrote three plays for the Queen's Men in 1623. After Fletcher's death in 1625, Massinger remained as chief playwright for the most important King's Men until his death. He died in London and was buried March 18, 1640, in the churchyard of St. Saviour's, reputedly in the same grave as Fletcher. Massinger's widow inherited the pension that the fourth Earl of Pembroke had bestowed upon the dramatist.

Tragedies, comedies, and tragicomedies that show Massinger's hand in their composition number about fifty-four plays. At least fifteen were written unaided; some two dozen show collaboration with other dramatists, the majority being with Fletcher; still others are probably revisions of older plays with an occasional scene or passage interpolated. About eleven plays are now lost.

Undoubtedly the most popular of

726

his plays is *A New Way to Pay Old Debts* a realistic comedy of intrigue with an English atmosphere. Though the plot was suggested by Middleton's *A Trick to Catch the Old One,* Ben Jonson furnished the true model for such humor characters as Greedy, Marrall, and Furnace. Sir Giles Overreach and his foil, Wellborn, are admirably conceived. This play, as well as *The City Madam* shows Massinger's ability to mingle the realistic comedy of intrigue with the comedy of humours that Ben Jonson had taught him.

Massinger's greatest claim to distinction probably rests upon his stage-craft and his skill in dramatic construction. Likewise, Massinger's ability to write moral and rhetorical declamations is superior to that of most of his contemporaries. Probably for these reasons, Massinger judged *The Roman Actor,* a tragedy, as "the most perfect birth of my Minerva." A play within the play motivates the main action; a second marks the climax; a third presents the death of Paris, the actor-hero, at the hands of the Emperor Domitian. With great fervor the dramatist defends the stage for all times.

Massinger had learned the art of writing tragicomedies in his collaboration with Fletcher. Seven unaided tragicomedies are attributed to Massinger. Characterizations in *The Bondman, The Maid of Honor,* and the others are thoroughly adequate; the new Senecan Stoicism gives a sense of moral earnestness; the speeches are rhetorical and didactic; and finally, with his usual mastery of plot, Massinger brings about a happy ending that "wants death."

After the Restoration, the actor Betterton especially liked *The Bondman* and was attracted by Paris to *The Roman Actor. A New Way to Pay Old Debts* continues to hold the stage.

BIBLIOGRAPHICAL REFERENCES: The most extensive study is A. H. Cruickshank, *Philip Massinger,* 1928. See also Sir Leslie Stephen, *Hours in a Library,* Series III, 1879; *Dictionary of National Biography,* Vol. XIII (1921); T. S. Eliot, *Selected Essays, 1917–1932,* 1932; and Baldwin Maxwell, *Studies in Beaumont, Fletcher and Massinger,* 1939.

EDGAR LEE MASTERS

Born: Garnett, Kansas
Date: August 23, 1869

Died: Melrose Park, Pennsylvania
Date: March 5, 1950

PRINCIPAL WORKS

POEMS: *A Book of Verses,* 1898; *The Blood of the Prophets,* 1905; *Songs and Sonnets,* 1910; *Spoon River Anthology,* 1915; *Songs and Satires,* 1916; *The Great Valley,* 1916; *Toward the Gulf,* 1918; *Starved Rock,* 1919; *Domesday Book,* 1920; *The Open Sea,* 1921; *The New Spoon River,* 1924; *Selected Poems,* 1925; *The Fate of the Jury: An Epilogue to Domesday Book,* 1929; *Lichee Nuts,* 1930; *The Serpent in the Wilderness,* 1933; *Invisible Landscapes,* 1935; *The Golden Fleece of California,* 1936; *Poems of People,* 1936; *The New World,* 1937; *More People,* 1939; *Illinois Poems,* 1941.

PLAYS IN VERSE: *Richmond,* 1902; *Lee: A Dramatic Poem,* 1926; *Jack Kelso,* 1928; *Gettysburg, Manila, Acoma,* 1930; *Godbey,* 1931; *Dramatic Duologues,* 1934; *Richmond,* 1934.

PLAYS: *Althea,* 1907; *The Trifler,* 1908; *The Leaves of the Tree,* 1909; *Eileen,* 1910; *The Locket,* 1910; *The Bread of Idleness,* 1911.

NOVELS: *Mitch Miller,* 1920; *Children of the Market Place,* 1922; *The Nuptial Flight,* 1923; *Skeeters Kirby,* 1923; *Mirage,* 1924; *Kit O'Brien,* 1927; *The Tide of Time,* 1937.

BIOGRAPHY: *Levy Mayer and the New Industrial Era,* 1927; *Lincoln, the Man,* 1931; *Vachel Lindsay: A Poet in America,* 1935; *Whitman,* 1937; *Mark Twain: A Portrait,* 1938.

AUTOBIOGRAPHY: *Across Spoon River,* 1936.

HISTORY: *The Tale of Chicago,* 1933; *The Sangamon,* 1942.

Edgar Lee Masters was the first major twentieth century writer to emphasize the psychological rather than the sociological in delineating the American character. After years of writing traditional poems on traditional themes inspired particularly by his reading of English romantic writers, he turned in his early forties to the inhabitants of his home town for subject matter. Using *The Greek Anthology* as his model, and with the encouragement of William Marion Reedy, he produced a landmark in American poetry when his *Spoon River Anthology* was published in 1915. His attitude was that of the naturalists immediately preceding him; but unlike them he showed no interest in the economic condition of men nor a desire for its reform. Rather he centered his focus on the minds of his characters, emphasizing the sterility in village thought in a society where tradition had broken down.

Masters, born in Garnett, Kansas, on August 23, 1869, lived his childhood in Petersburg and his early youth in Lewistown, near Spoon River, all small Illinois towns. Though his natural interest was literature, his father had him study law and work in his law office, refusing to send him through college because there was "no money in it." He started to write,

however, and by his middle twenties he had had verses printed in Chicago papers and had done general newspaper work. After he was admitted to the bar he moved to Chicago where, within twenty years, he had achieved financial affluence and social position as a lawyer. During this time he wrote and published undistinguished verse and verse plays. In addition, he was active in politics, supporting Bryan and Altgeld, and served as the president of the Jefferson Club of Chicago. He came to know writers such as Theodore Dreiser, and with the sudden emergence of new literary interest in Chicago in the second decade of the twentieth century he joined the group supporting *Poetry* and received encouragement from such poets as Masefield, Amy Lowell, Lindsay, and Sandburg. The first group of poems to become a part of the *Spoon River Anthology* appeared on May 29, 1914, in *Reedy's Mirror;* epitaphs written by dead townspeople who were presumably telling the truth at last, the poems were a sardonic comment upon the mental aberrations and spiritual poverties in a town. When the book itself appeared it met with violent attacks but sold well. In 1916 Masters received *Poetry's* Levinson Prize.

Masters became ill at this time, emo-

728

tionally exhausted from the creation and defense of over two hundred poems of the same type. The war had replaced other interests as the center of everyone's world, and he went back to his earlier rhetorical style, in many instances reworking former pieces. During the next two decades he produced a series of novels, none financially or critically successful, biographies, plays, histories, and poetry, but he was never able to produce another equal to his masterwork, though he revealed in everything he wrote a searching for deep inner truth. That he also wrote of the beauty in life few people noticed, *Spoon River* having bracketed him in their minds. Disillusioned and broken in health, he died at Melrose Park, Pennsylvania, on March 5, 1950.

BIBLIOGRAPHICAL REFERENCES: There is no collected edition, authorized biography, or extensive critical study of Edgar Lee Masters. Details of his life will be found in *Across Spoon River*, 1936, which deals also with other literary figures of the Chicago Renascence. For briefer critical estimates see Amy Lowell, *Tendencies in Modern American Poetry*, 1917; Conrad Aiken, *Scepticisms*, 1919; Harry Hansen, *Midwest Portraits*, 1923; Alfred Kreymborg, *Our Singing Strength*, 1929; Babette Deutsch, *Poetry in Our Time*, 1952 (rev. ed., 1956); Julius W. Pratt, "Whitman and Masters: A Contrast," *South Atlantic Quarterly*, XVI (1917), 155–158; John Cowper Powys, "Edgar Lee Masters," *Bookman*, LXIX (1929), 650–656; and Herbert E. Childs, "Agrarianism and Sex: Edgar Lee Masters and the Modern Spirit," *Sewanee Review*, XLI (1933), 331–343.

COTTON MATHER

Born: Boston, Massachusetts
Date: February 12, 1663

Died: Boston
Date: February 13, 1728

PRINCIPAL WORKS

SERMONS, TRACTS, CHURCH HISTORY, BIOGRAPHY: *The Declaration of the Gentlemen, Merchants, and Inhabitants of Boston*, 1689; *Memorable Providences: Relating to Witchcraft and Possessions*, 1689; *The Present State of New England*, 1690; *Wonders in the Invisible World*, 1693; *Pietas in Patriam*, 1697; *Eleutheria: or an Idea of the Reformation in England*, 1698; *Pastoral Letter to the English Captives in Africa*, 1698; *A Family Well-Ordered*, 1699; *Reasonable Religion*, 1700; *Magnalia Christi Americana, or The Ecclesiastical History of New England from its First Planting*, 1702; *A Faithful Man, Michael Wigglesworth*, 1705; *The Negro Christianized*, 1706; *Corderius Americanus: or the Good Education of Children*, 1708; *Bonifacius*, 1710 (*Essays to Do Good*); *Brethren Dwelling together in Unity*, 1718; *The Christian Philosopher*, 1721; *The Angel of Bethsada*, 1722; *Parentator*, 1724; *Ratio Disciplinae*, 1726; *Manuductio ad Ministerium*, 1726.

Cotton Mather, born in Boston, Massachusetts, on February 12, 1663, was one of the outstanding leaders of the early New England Puritan theocracy, and also one of the last. He came to power at a time when the control of the church was nearing its end —one hastened in no small part by his unpopularity and poor judgment.

Cotton was the son of Increase Mather and eventually succeeded him as minister of the Second, or Old North Church in Boston, but only after having served as his father's assistant from 1680 until 1723, the year of Increase Mather's death. During much of his tenure as assistant minister he was actually in full charge, however, his father being either absent on political missions (as in the Andros affair, which took him to England) or engaged in other activities, such as those connected with his duties as president of Harvard University.

As the son of a leading minister, and as a child destined to become one of the theocratical rulers of the colony, Cotton Mather naturally attended Harvard. A nervous, over-sensitive, precocious child, he was a college student at the age of twelve. His first intentions were to study medicine because of a nervous stutter which he felt would keep him from the ministry, but he mastered this defect through sheer determination, and began his duties at Old North Church upon his graduation in 1680, becoming ordained with the receipt of his master's degree in 1685.

Refusing a call from New Haven, he remained at the Old North Church for the rest of his life, growing more pedantic and more dictatorial each year. His nervousness grew to neurosis and his religious convictions to fanaticism. He attempted to rule as a tyrant, but the times for such religious tyranny were drawing to a close. Thus his career ended in a series of frustrations. Governor Dudley, whom he could not control as he had Phips and whom he could not get rid of (as he and his father had Andros), was in charge of the colony; Harvard had refused to select him as his father's successor to the president's chair; his name was besmirched by the Salem witch trials (he has been cleared by historians of any direct part in these, but is still held guilty of sins of omission in regard to them), and one of his sons was a thankless ne'er-do-well.

These late frustrations would indicate that as politician, as educator, as judge, and as father, he had failed. But as a writer, if sheer bulk rather than quality is important, and if pedantry rather than discerning scholarship is an admirable trait, he was a distinguished success. His various duties as shepherd of his flock caused him all too frequently to take pen in hand, and the total wordage of his writing is enormous. Its importance today, however, is slight though some works, such as the *Magnalia Christi Americana*, which traces the development of the colony from its earliest times, are of interest and value to the historian.

There was, on the other hand, one field in which Mather did not experience frustration, and one writing which retains its value. The field is that of science, and for his *Sentiment of the Smallpox Inoculated* (1721) he became the first American ever elected to the Royal Society (1713). He died at Boston on February 13, 1728.

BIBLIOGRAPHICAL REFERENCES: There is no collected edition of Cotton Mather's diverse writings. Reprints of separate works are listed in Thomas J. Holmes, *Cotton Mather: A Bibliography of His Works*, 3 vols., 1940. A useful book of selections is *Selections from Cotton Mather*, edited by Kenneth B. Murdock, 1926.

The basic biography is Barrett Wendell, *Cotton Mather: The Puritan Priest*, 1891 (reissued, 1926). See also Abijah P. Marvin, *The Life and Times of Cotton Mather*, 1892; and Ralph P. and Louise Boas, *Cotton Mather*, 1928. The best brief account of his life and work is Kenneth B. Murdock, "Cotton Mather," *Dictionary of National Biography*.

CHARLES ROBERT MATURIN

Born: Dublin, Ireland   *Died:* Dublin
Date: 1780   *Date:* October 30, 1824

PRINCIPAL WORKS

NOVELS: *The Fatal Revenge, or The Family of Montorio,* 1807; *The Wild Irish Boy,* 1808; *The Milesian Chief,* 1812; *Women, or Pour et Contre,* 1818; *Melmoth, the Wanderer,* 1820; *The Albigenses,* 1824.
PLAYS: *Bertram,* 1816; *Manuel,* 1817; *Fredolfo,* 1817.

Charles Robert Maturin, who was born in the city of Dublin in the year 1780, was the son of an official in the Irish postoffice and the grandson of Gabriel Maturin, who had been Jonathan Swift's successor as Dean of St. Patrick's, Dublin. Maturin was educated at Trinity College, Dublin, and afterward became curate of Loughrea and then of St. Peter's, Dublin. In 1803 he married Henrietta Kingsbury.

His early novels, *The Fatal Revenge, The Wild Irish Boy,* and *The Milesian Chief* were published under the pseudonym Dennis Jasper Murphy. Extreme in their Gothic style and dramatic character, the novels met with small success and much criticism—". . . the false creation of a heat-oppressed brain," as one critic described them—but the young author was fortunate in winning the interest of Sir Walter Scott, who found in the novels something of the quality he sought in his own work. At the time Scott was not established in his writing career; his famous novels and poems were yet to be written. Consequently, Scott referred Maturin to Byron, at that time the target of severe criticism from the Edinburgh reviewers but beginning to be prominent in literary circles. Through his influence, Maturin's tragedy, *Bertram,* was produced at the Drury Lane Theatre in 1816, with Edmund Kean playing the lead. A French version of the play was produced in Paris. The moderate success of *Bertram* was followed by the failure of two other tragedies, *Manuel* and *Fredolfo.*

Of his novels, *Melmoth the Wanderer* is his masterpiece, and one of the most famous of the Gothic romances popular in the early nineteenth century. It so impressed Honoré de Balzac that he wrote a sequel, *Melmoth réconcilié* (1835). Maturin died in Dublin, October 30, 1824.

BIBLIOGRAPHICAL REFERENCES: There is no collected edition of Maturin; but there is a good edition of his chief novel, *Melmoth the Wanderer,* 3 vols., 1892, which includes a memoir and a bibliography. There are two full studies, Nielo Idman, *Charles Robert Maturin: His Life and Works,* 1923, and William Scholten, *Charles Robert Maturin, the Terror Novelist,* 1933. Of primary importance is a standard study of the literature of terror, Edith Birkhead, *The Tale of Terror,* 1921. See also Oliver Elton, *A Survey of English Literature, 1780–1830,* I, 1912.

W. SOMERSET MAUGHAM

Born: Paris, France
Date: January 25, 1874

PRINCIPAL WORKS

NOVELS: *Liza of Lambeth,* 1897; *The Making of a Saint,* 1898; *The Hero,* 1901; *Mrs. Craddock,* 1902; *The Merry-go-round,* 1904; *The Bishop's Apron,* 1906; *The Explorer,* 1907; *The Magician,* 1908; *Of Human Bondage,* 1915; *The Moon and Sixpence,* 1919; *The Painted Veil,* 1925; *Cakes and Ale,* 1930; *The Narrow Corner,* 1932; *Theatre,* 1937; *Christmas Holiday,* 1939; *The Razor's Edge,* 1944.

SHORT STORIES: *Orientations,* 1899; *The Trembling of a Leaf,* 1921; *The Casuarina Tree,* 1926; *Ashenden, or The British Agent,* 1928; *Six Stories Written in the First Person Singular,* 1931; *Ah King,* 1933; *Cosmopolitans,* 1936; *Creatures of Circumstance,* 1937; *The Mixture as Before,* 1940; *Collected Short Stories,* 1952 (3 vols.).

PLAYS: *A Man of Honour,* 1903; *Lady Frederick,* 1907; *Penelope,* 1909; *Mrs. Dot,* 1912; *The Tenth Man,* 1913; *Landed Gentry,* 1913; *The Land of Promise,* 1913; *The Unknown,* 1920; *The Circle,* 1921; *East of Suez,* 1922; *Caesar's Wife,* 1922; *Our Betters,* 1923; *The Unattainable,* 1923; *Loaves and Fishes,* 1924; *The Letter,* 1925; *The Constant Wife,* 1926; *The Sacred Flame,* 1928; *The Bread Winner,* 1930; *For Services Rendered,* 1932; *Sheppey,* 1933; *Collected Plays,* 1951 (3 vols.).

TRAVEL SKETCHES: *The Land of the Blessed Virgin,* 1905 (rev. ed., *Andalusia,* 1920); *On a Chinese Screen,* 1922; *The Gentleman in the Parlour,* 1930.

ESSAYS AND STUDIES: *Don Fernando,* 1935; *The Summing Up,* 1938; *A Writer's Notebook,* 1949; *Ten Novels and Their Authors,* 1954 [*The Art of Fiction*].

The long life of W(illiam) Somerset Maugham offers one a view of the fashions and current ideas during more than half a century. Maugham exploited shrewdly and brilliantly the public taste of his time; a deft and facile workman in both the novel and the drama, for many decades he managed to be faithful both to his international public and to himself. His basic idea rests on a perception of the relativity of human morals; his works illustrate this perception entertainingly and sometimes penetratingly.

An outline of Maugham's own life suggests that he has always been situated where different codes are offering their ironic contrasts. Of Celtic extraction, Maugham was born January 25, 1874, in Paris, where his father was attached to the British Embassy. Maugham's mother, an extraordinary

beauty, died of tuberculosis of the lungs when Maugham was eight; the author has said that fifty years of active living—he is as widely traveled as any modern writer—have failed to heal the wound caused by his mother's death. His father died two years later of cancer, and Maugham went to live with his father's brother, a vicar in Whitstable near the mouth of the Thames. Life in this small town offered a sharp contrast to Paris. At thirteen Maugham entered preparatory school at Canterbury, where his first year was "a veritable purgatory," his masters bullying him because of his speech difficulty and frail health. Because of this ill treatment, Maugham refused to go on to Oxford to study for the clergy; instead, he spent a year at Heidelberg in "intellectual stimulation." During this time, he defined his agnosticism and decided on writing as a profession. But before he succeeded at this, he was, briefly, a public accountant and a student at St. Thomas's Medical School in Lambeth, across the Thames from the House of Parliament. Work at this charity hospital made a lasting impression on Maugham and his writing. He obtained a sound knowledge of science and developed a respect for the scientific method, a perception that strengthened his proclivity to realism in writing. He also acquired a knowledge of mankind, especially regarding the "unaccountability of human nature." Moreover, the hospital gave him his material for his first novel, *Liza of Lambeth,* published in 1897. The success of this book diverted Maugham from a medical career. He never practiced medicine but, in the drama, the novel, and the essay, became one of the most successful authors in English literary history. His personal history has included marriage (1915 to 1927) and extensive wanderings, which have allowed him to savor to the full the contrasts of codes and customs he had already, as a child of ten, come to note.

To learn of Maugham's youth and young manhood, one has but to know Philip Carey in *Of Human Bondage.* Philip's bondage because of his clubfoot, patterned after Maugham's stammering, makes reader identification easy for young people, who are likely to find in the novel the effect of catharsis of Maugham and escape from "certain tormenting memories of the past."

Maugham, as he records in *The Summing Up,* trained himself as a writer of a prose singularly clear and unobtrusive by reading such masters of lucidity and simplicity as Dryden, Swift, Arnold, Voltaire, and Hume;

his prose protracts the irony and disillusionment of some of these masters. This accent appears in both his plays and his fiction.

His comedies are studies of manners, usually among the well-to-do; *Our Betters, The Circle,* and *The Constant Wife* are highly entertaining studies of persons who arrive at moral crossroads and find no signposts. Maugham can strike grimmer notes in his dramas, but a play like *The Letter* only shows us the characters of the comedies exploring the grimmer implications of their pursuit of distraction as they fly from uncertainty. Maugham, who sometimes underplays his real skill, explains his success as a dramatist by saying that he has followed two maxims: "Stick to the point and, whenever you can, cut."

Maugham's fiction offers him more freedom and allows him to display to the full an urbane, curious, and—some readers judge—unprejudiced mind. The merit of *Of Human Bondage* has already been suggested; the hero "frees" himself from the tyranny of existence by deciding that the meaning of existence is but the pattern each man wills to create. In many of Maugham's other novels, we see men less fully studied than the hero of his best novel who also try to trace out (Maugham's phrase echoes Henry James) "the pattern in the carpet." *The Moon and Sixpence* traces the revolt of a Gauguin-type artist against conventional duty; *Cakes and Ale* contains an ironical analysis of the submission to convention made by a great writer (popularly supposed to be Thomas Hardy). *The Razor's Edge* even gives us a pursuit of meaning in life which skirts the edge of Hindu mysticism; some supporters of the

733

earlier Maugham supposed that the writer was merely trying to draw profits from a current public interest in the religious novel. But other and earlier writing suggested that Maugham's urbane interest had already extended to Loyola as well as the inhabitants of Lambeth. Readers who find that it is the temper of the man rather than his power as a creative artist that most draws them should not overlook *Don Fernando,* which blends philosophy, criticism, and travel, and other non-fiction books in which he reveals that part of his nature which he judges the public has a right to observe.

BIBLIOGRAPHICAL REFERENCES: J. W. Jonas published *A Bibliography of the Writings of W. Somerset Maugham,* 1950. The best study of Maugham is Richard A. Cordell's *W. Somerest Maugham,* 1937. For biography and criticism see also C. S. McIver, *William Somerset Maugham,* 1936; R. H. Ward, *William Somerset Maugham,* 1937; Cyril Connolly, *The Condemned Playground,* 1946; and John Brophy, *Somerset Maugham,* 1952. For shorter studies see Theodore Spencer, "Somerset Maugham," *College English,* II (1940), 1–10; and W. O. Ross, "W. Somerset Maugham: Theme and Variations," *ibid.,* VIII (1946), 113–122.

GUY DE MAUPASSANT

Born: Château de Miromesnil, France
Date: August 5, 1850

Died: Paris, France
Date: July 6, 1893

PRINCIPAL WORKS

SHORT STORIES: *La Maison Tellier,* 1881; *Mademoiselle Fifi,* 1882; *Contes de la bécasse,* 1883; *Clair de lune,* 1884; *Miss Harriet,* 1884; *Les Sœurs Rondoli,* 1884; *Toine,* 1885; *Yvette,* 1885; *Contes et nouvelles,* 1885; *Contes du jour et de la nuit,* 1885; *Monsieur Parent,* 1886; *La Petite Roque,* 1886; *La Horla,* 1887; *Le Rosier de Mme. Husson,* 1888; *La Main gauche,* 1889; *L'Inutile beauté,* 1890.

NOVELS: *Une Vie,* 1883 (*A Woman's Life*); *Bel-Ami,* 1885; *Mont-Oriol,* 1887; *Pierre et Jean,* 1888; *Fort comme la mort,* 1889; *Notre cœur,* 1890.

PLAYS: *Histoire du vieux temps,* 1879; *Musotte,* 1891.

(Henri René Albert) Guy de Maupassant, born on August 5, 1850, at Château de Miromesnil, was descended from an old French family; his grandfather was a wealthy landowner in Lorraine, and the writer's father was a stockbroker in Paris. As a boy, Maupassant went to school at Yvetot, in Normandy, and later attended the lycée at Rouen. During his childhood and youth in Normandy he observed and absorbed a great deal of the life he was later to use so effectively in his fiction. Significant in the author's life was the separation of his parents when he was eleven years old, the mother retaining custody of the child. His mother, a sister of a close friend of Flaubert, turned to Flaubert for advice after her husband had left her. That association brought Maupassant into French literary circles. Although he was often a member of gatherings which included such famous writers of the nineteenth century as Flaubert, Turgenev, Zola, and Daudet, he seems to have had little interest at the time in a career of writing for himself; as an

adolescent he was much more interested in sports, especially rowing.

Maupassant's education was interrupted by the Franco-Prussian War, in
which he served as a member of the
French Army. After the war he entered
the French civil service, first with the
Ministry of the Navy and later with
the Ministry of Public Instruction.
During the years between 1873 and
1880 he also served a literary apprenticeship under the tutelage of Flaubert.
A volume of poetry, *Des Vers* (1880),
attracted little attention, except to involve its young author in a lawsuit.
Maupassant, realizing his weakness as
a poet, concentrated on developing
his powers as a writer of prose fiction.
Within a short time "Boule de suif,"
a short story or *conte*, appeared in
Soirées de Médan (1880), a collection
of tales which included work by such
famous and recognized authors as Zola
and Huysmans. Maupassant's story
about the Franco-Prussian War out-
shone all the others, and the author's
reputation was made. The lessons he
had learned from Flaubert—precision,
conciseness, characteristic and accurate
detail—had proved their value. Following up his success with vigor, Maupassant within the ensuing decade published more than thirty volumes of
short stories, plays, novels, and travel
sketches. The first collection of short
stories published under his own name
was *La Maison Tellier*, which appeared in 1881.

Mademoiselle Fifi, a particularly fine
collection of short stories, added weight
to Maupassant's growing reputation
and popularity in 1883. Like most of
his volumes of stories, it contained a
relatively long title story and a group
of shorter pieces. *Une Vie*, published

in the same year as *Mademoiselle Fifi*,
was Maupassant's first novel. As an example of naturalism in literature, it is
a masterpiece. In it is portrayed the
life of a Norman woman of the nineteenth century, the disillusionment
and heartbreak of the theme presented
with the naturalistic writer's objectivity
and frankness. Censorship of this book
only increased its popularity, thus contributing to Maupassant's financial
success with the novel and a second
collection of stories, *Contes de la
bécasse*, published in the same year.
The material success he enjoyed as a
writer enabled Maupassant to leave
the French civil service.

The years 1884–1885 were those in
which Maupassant produced a great
deal of fiction of very high caliber. To
those years belong the short story
collections, *Clair de lune, Miss Harriet,
Les Sœurs Rondoli, Toine, Yvette,
Contes et nouvelles*, and *Contes du
jour et la nuit*. The best of these deal
with the author's favorite and familiar
subjects: the Franco-Prussian War, the
peasants of Normandy, and petty bu-
reaucrats of the French civil service.
Because of the craftsmanship Maupassant displayed, he became a model
for writers in both English and French,
and some authorities have seen in his
work the origin of the well-made but
stereotyped story so common to the
magazines, a type more notable for its
facile style than anything else. More
thoughtfully presented was *Bel-Ami*, a
novel about a vicious rascal whose ugliness of spirit was hidden by his handsome face. A statement of Maupassant's
theory of fiction appeared in his preface
to *Pierre et Jean*, in which he declared
himself a complete literary naturalist,
approaching his material with objec-

tivity and detachment, describing life with utter frankness, and reflecting a personal conception of a deterministic universe. In presenting his theories in practice, Maupassant, like other writers of naturalistic fiction, often became biased in the direction of pessimism in his choice of characters and detail, with the result that readers of his work, especially his novels, found themselves in a depressing fictional world.

During 1886–1887 Maupassant began to show signs of mental illness, probably the result of venereal disease.

A sea voyage to improve his health enabled him to make some gains toward recovery. From that experience he extracted a travel book, *Sur l'eau* (1888). His difficulties recurred, however, and after 1890 he practically ceased to write. A general paralysis began to assail him, as well as severe hallucinations. Maupassant went to Cannes, on the Mediterranean, to spend the winter of 1891–1892, but he was taken back to Paris after an attempt at suicide in January, 1892. He died in Paris on July 6, 1893.

BIBLIOGRAPHICAL REFERENCES: The standard edition is the *Œuvres complètes*, edited by A. Gillon and E. Choreau, 15 vols., 1934–1938. The collected edition in English is *The Works of Guy de Maupassant*, translated by Marjorie Laurie, 19 vols., 1923–1929. A good introduction to Maupassant will be found in Henry James, *Partial Portraits*, 1888. Other biographical and critical studies in English include Ernest Boyd, *Guy de Maupassant*, 1926; Francis Steegmuller, *Maupassant*, 1950; and Edward Daniel Sullivan, *Maupassant the Novelist*, 1954. See also Edouard Maynial, *La Vie et l'œuvre de Maupassant*, 1906; René Dumesnil, *Guy de Maupassant*, 1933; Victor Harold Hoving, *Guy de Maupassant*, 1946; Ernst Leo Sander, *Maupassant*, 1951; Pierre Borel, *Le Vrai Maupassant*, 1951; and André Vial, *Guy de Maupassant et l'art du roman*, 1954.

FRANÇOIS MAURIAC

Born: Bordeaux, France
Date: October 11, 1885

PRINCIPAL WORKS

NOVELS: *Le Baiser au lépreux*, 1922 (*A Kiss for the Leper*); *Genitrix*, 1923 (translated with *Le Baiser au lépreux* as *The Family*); *Le Désert de l'amour*, 1925 (*The Desert of Love*); *Orages*, 1925; *Thérèse Desqueyroux*, 1927 (*Thérèse*); *Destins*, 1928 (*Lines of Life*); *Ce qui était perdu*, 1930 (*That Which Was Lost*); *Le nœud de vipères*, 1932 (*Vipers' Tangle*); *Le mystère Frontenac*, 1933; *La fin de la nuit*, 1935; *Le Mal*, 1935 (*The Enemy*); *Les anges noirs*, 1936 (*The Black Angels*); *Les Chemins de la mer*, 1939 (*The Unknown Sea*); *La Pharisienne*, 1941 (*A Woman of the Pharisees*); *Le Sagouin*, 1951 (*The Little Misery*); *L'Agneau*, 1954 (*The Lamb*).

PLAYS: *Asmodée*, 1938 (*The Intruder*); *Les Mal Aimés*, 1945; *Passage du malin*, 1948; *Le feu sur la terre*, 1951.

BIOGRAPHY: *Vie de Racine*, 1928; *Vie de Jésus*, 1936.

ESSAYS: *Petits essais de psychologie religieuse*, 1920; *Proust*, 1926; *Le Roman*, 1928; *Dieu et Mammon*, 1929; *Le jeu di-saint*, 1931 (*The Eucharist*); *Le Romancier et ses personnages,* 1933; *Journal, 1932–1939,* 1947; *Mes grands hommes,* 1949 (*Men I Hold Great*).

POEM: *Le Sang d'Atys,* 1940.

Since the death of André Gide, François Mauriac has been called the grand old man of French literature; he is more the conscience of France. One of the great Roman Catholic writers of our time, born into the strictest orthodoxy, at Bordeaux, France, on October 11, 1885, he received his early education in parochial schools. His mother reared the family of four boys and a girl, all of whom turned to such professions as medicine, literature, religion, and law, and in a sense, the youngest son turned to all of these through his one hundred or more literary works.

Mauriac's childhood, aside from the rigors of a Jesuit education, was idyllic since he lived in turn on the many beautiful estates controlled by his family. He early developed a sense of solitude and reflection, and he became a voracious reader. At the lycée in Bordeaux he studied under André Gide's brother-in-law, winning a first prize in French. In Paris he was admitted to the École de Chartes, but more important he gained the friendship of Barrès and Bourget, who helped launch his career. Through them he published, in typical French fashion, a collection of verse, *Les Maints Jointes* (1909).

A short retreat with Dominican monks was followed by the establishment of a journal of Catholic arts and letters, *Les Cahiers* (1912). The next year was noteworthy in that he published his first novel and married Jeanne Lafont. However, their honeymoon was interrupted by war; Mauriac enlisted as a hospital assistant and served until incapacitated by malaria.

His first popular success was *A Kiss for the Leper;* it was largely for this work the French Academy awarded him the Grand Prix du Roman. By the early 1930's he had written literary criticism, biography, and plays in addition to a miscellany of articles on divergent subjects. In 1932 he was elected president of the Societe des Gens de Lettres. In 1933 he occupied Brieux's chair in the French Academy.

Mauriac's novels echo man's persistence in striking out against the world's sins, but it is noteworthy that he himself actually fought for these beliefs as a part of the French Resistance movement, for which he wrote anti-German articles at the risk of death. In 1952 he achieved international recognition with the Nobel Prize in Literature. In an important interview he has discussed the compulsion which forces him to go on writing in the hope that each novel will be the one which will allow him to rest; the perfect work. He himself prefers his poetry; all his novels have poetic overtones. Consistently Mauriac has maintained that man's struggle for perfection, from which he fell and to which he must ever strive, is the mission of life. He has represented the Church as hypocritical and man as malignant, but always with a belief that eventually good must triumph over evil. His writings reveal sensual imagination, the psychology of sin, and true faith in a kind of uneasy balance. His novels reveal the power and the glory and many things besides, and his style is as subtle as the themes he presents.

737

The writer lives quietly on his wife's country estate in Vémars, twenty miles from Paris, in surroundings suited to a writer whose message is the need of truth in the modern world and salvation to be gained only through Christian austerity.

BIBLIOGRAPHICAL REFERENCES: For studies of Mauriac in English see Martin Jarrett-Kerr, *François Mauriac*, 1954; and Wallace Fowlie, "Mauriac's Dark Hero," *Sewanee Review*, LVI (1948), 39–57; in French, Charles du Bos, *Mauriac et le problème du romancier catholique*, 1933; Amélie Fillon, *François Mauriac*, 1936; Georges Hourdin, *Mauriac, Romancier chrétien*, 1945 (2nd ed.); R. Laffont, *Mauriac et l'art du roman*, 1946; and Nelly Cormeau, *L'Art de François Mauriac*, 1951. See, further, Gérard de Catalogne, *Une Genération*, 1930; and C. E. Magny, *Histoire du roman français depuis 1918*, 1950.

HERMAN MELVILLE

Born: New York, N. Y. *Died:* New York
Date: August 1, 1819 *Date:* September 28, 1891

PRINCIPAL WORKS

NOVELS: *Typee*, 1846; *Omoo*, 1847; *Mardi*, 1849; *Redburn*, 1849; *White Jacket*, 1850; *Moby Dick*, 1851; *Pierre*, 1852; *Israel Potter*, 1855; *The Confidence Man*, 1857; *Billy Budd, Foretopman*, 1924.

SHORT STORIES: *Piazza Tales*, 1856.

POEMS: *Battle Pieces and Aspects of the War*, 1866; *Clarel*, 1876; *John Marr and Other Sailors*, 1888; *Timoleon*, 1891.

MISCELLANEOUS: *Journal Up the Straits*, 1935; *Journal of a Visit to London and the Continent*, 1948.

Herman Melville's first five books were based in part on the varied experiences of his youth. It is therefore necessary to have the main facts of the author's early life before us.

Melville was born in New York City on August 1, 1819. His family was of English, Scotch, and Dutch ancestry and had some claims to eminence on both sides. Both the Presbyterianism of his father and the Dutch Reformed views of his mother gave Melville that partly Calvinistic concern with good and evil which we find in his writings, most notably *Moby Dick*. Melville's father, a prosperous merchant until 1826, failed financially in that year of depression and died in 1832, leaving the family close to poverty.

After a number of years in Albany as a student and a clerk, Melville embarked in 1837 on his first voyage, as a cabin boy on a merchant ship bound for Liverpool. In 1841 he sailed from New Bedford on the whaleship *Acushnet*, beginning a series of adventures in the Pacific which lasted until 1844. Returning to New York, he began to write of his experiences.

His first book, *Typee*, was a popular success, and this exciting narrative, part memoir, part romance, which described the hero's sojourn among the cannibals of the Marquesas Islands, remained for

738

many decades the author's most widely known work. *Omoo*, a sequel to *Typee*, was followed by *Mardi*. This book, which readers found baffling, begins as a travel narrative but quickly becomes a fanciful mixture of allegory, satire, and extravaganza somewhat in the tradition of the imaginary voyage, such as *Gulliver's Travels*. A new note of stark and somber realism is struck in *Redburn*, based on Melville's voyage to Liverpool. The note of realism is maintained in *White Jacket,* a book which benefits from Melville's memories of his days as a common sailor aboard the U.S.S. *United States,* on which he had returned from the Pacific in 1844. The best of these early books is *Typee*, although parts of *Redburn* are moving and authentic and certain scenes in *White Jacket* rival Smollett's in their vivid impression of sea-going life.

But *Typee* turned out to be something of an evil fate for its author, since it had conditioned Melville's available audience to pleasurable travel romance. Unwilling and unable to continue in the *Typee* vein, Melville lost his audience and suffered more and more, as he grew older, from his increasing sense of alienation from the conventional life of his time. Even *Moby Dick,* which seems to us now one of the great books of world literature, had no more than a scattered reputation until about 1920. And only in recent years has Melville been generally accepted as one of the greatest of American writers.

Moby Dick was written mostly in Pittsfield, Massachusetts, where Melville, now married and beginning to raise a family, had settled in 1850. Like the early novels, *Moby Dick* mirrors actual experience, being an account of the author's voyage on the *Acushnet.*

The accepted view of *Moby Dick* is that as Melville first conceived it, it was to be merely a realistic narrative. As he wrote, however, the pursuit of the whale, which was to constitute the main plot, took on ever new meanings. This imaginative proliferation was the result of the natural unfolding of Melville's genius, but also of his reading, at the time, of Shakespeare and Hawthorne. Besides being a magnificent account of the whaling enterprise, the book became, as Melville reconceived it, an epic romance.

Moby Dick has manifold meaning, but its complexity is often exaggerated. Much confusion can be avoided by noting that the white whale is not allegorical, and therefore cannot be explained as "standing for" this or that. The whale is a poetic symbol deliberately intended to reflect the ambiguity of nature, at once terrible and beautiful, threatening and beneficent. It is a part of Captain Ahab's madness that he understands the whale allegorically, thinking of it (and thus thinking of nature itself) as representing Evil. In Ahab we see a man alienated from mankind by a fanatical will and intellect which have distorted all the genial emotions into a vindictive hatred of life itself. All the rich poetry of life, so memorably expressed by Melville, is unavailable to him. Whether or not Ahab is intended in a sinister way as the representative American individualist, it is certain that, in the manner of epics, *Moby Dick* copiously reflects the folkways of the culture that gave it birth.

The later writings of Melville may be dealt with briefly, although he wrote several interesting works at Pittsfield and later in New York, where he was a District Inspector of Customs from 1866 until 1885. *Pierre* is a powerful but incoherent melodrama of incest and struggling genius, murkily reflecting Melville's own inner struggles. *The Confidence Man* is a dark comedy or masque, having for its central figure an elusive character representing the huckstering tendencies of American life as Melville saw them—from ordinary salesmanship to Emersonian transcendentalism. Sometimes extremely effective, the book never quite finds a way of clearly expressing the author's intense satire. Certain prose pieces of the 1850's, like *Bartleby the Scrivener, Benito Cereno,* and *The Encantadas,* are next to perfect in their way, and *Israel Potter* is, though not a great, a neglected piece of picaresque narrative. After the Civil War Melville wrote poetry. But his poems, with certain notable exceptions, such as

"The Portent," "Shiloh," and "The Maldive Shark," are the work of a thoughtful amateur rather than a skillful poet.

There remains *Billy Budd,* the product of Melville's last years. In its concern with the inhumanity of martial law, it reminds us of *White Jacket.* But in the hanging of the the innocent Billy by Captain Vere, a good and honorable man, Melville found one of his most effective symbols for the inscrutable ambiguity of the universe and of the moral ideas man derives from the universe. As befits the author's last work, the tone is one of elegy and recompense. *Billy Budd* stands near the top of Melville's achievement, a fitting last word of the all but unknown author who died on September 28, 1891, and was obscurely buried in a New York cemetery.

Richard Chase

BIBLIOGRAPHICAL REFERENCES: The collected edition is *The Works of Herman Melville,* 16 vols., London, 1922–1924. An American edition, still without definitive proportions, is in preparation under the general editorship of Howard P. Vincent. For biographical and critical studies see the following: Raymond Weaver, *Herman Melville: Mariner and Mystic,* 1921; John Freeman, *Herman Melville,* 1926; Lewis Mumford, *Herman Melville,* 1929; Charles R. Anderson, *Melville in the South Seas,* 1939; William Braswell, *Melville's Religious Thought,* 1943; W. E. Sedgwick, *Herman Melville: The Tragedy of Mind,* 1944; Howard P. Vincent, *The Trying Out of Moby Dick,* 1949; Richard Chase, *Herman Melville: A Critical Study,* 1949; Geoffrey Stone, *Melville,* 1949; Newton Arvin, *Herman Melville,* 1950; Leon Howard, *Herman Melville: A Biography,* 1951; Jay Leyda, *The Melville Log: A Documentary Life of Herman Melville,* 1951; Eleanor Melville Metcalf, *Herman Melville: Cycle and Epicycle,* 1953; and E. H. Rosenberry, *Melville and the Comic Spirit,* 1955.

See also Willard Thorp, Introduction to *Melville* in the American Writers series, 1931, and Introduction to *Moby Dick,* Oxford University Press, 1947; R. P. Blackmur, *The Expense of Greatness,* 1940; F. O. Matthiessen, *American Renaissance,* 1941; and W. H. Auden, *The Enchafèd Flood,* 1950.

MENANDER

Born: Athens, Greece
Date: 342 B.C.

Died: Athens
Date: 291 B.C.

PLAYS: *Epitrepontes (Arbitration)*; *Perikeiromene (The Girl with the Shorn Locks)*; *Samia (The Girl from Samos)*.

With Menander, born at Athens in 342 B.C., the Greek New Comedy came into being, plays in which such devices as the chorus and intervention by the gods were replaced by themes of commonplace Athenian life, treated with subtle humor. Through his influence on such Romans as Plautus and Terence, who was called "Half-Menander," he determined the form of later comedies of manners. From Homer he took his "call of the blood" theme, the recognition of lost relatives, but his thematic treatments of a good woman sinned against, and a man reformed by woman's love were of his own devising.

A bust in the Vatican, supposed to represent Menander, gives a squint to this son of wealthy Athenians, Diopeithes and Hegesistrate. The tyrant Demetrius of Phalerum was his classmate while studying with Theophrastus (died 287 B.C.), the successor to Aristotle in the Peripatetic School and author of thirty vivid character sketches: *The Flatterer, The Grumbler, The Newsmaker, The Miser,* and

others. Because of his wealth, Menander could choose his own career. He decided to follow his playwright uncle Alexis. His first play *Orge (The Self-Tormenter)* was written in 324, but he failed in the annual drama contests until 316. During his lifetime he wrote more than a hundred dramas, with the titles of eighty recorded, but he won the wreath only eight times. It has been charged that his most successful competitor Philemon, though greatly inferior, had influence with the judges.

Though invited by Ptolemy Soter to Alexandria, and urged to visit Macedonia, Menander remained in Athens until his death by drowning in the Bay of Phalerum in 291. He was buried beside Euripides. After his death Menander was considered not only the best representative of the New Comedy, but of Greek Comedy as a whole. For a long time, his work was considered wholly lost, but recent discoveries of papyrus in Alexandria and Cairo have allowed Gilbert Murray to reconstruct two of his plays of intrigue.

BIBLIOGRAPHICAL REFERENCES: An excellent historical and literary study is P. E. Le-Grand, *The New Greek Comedy,* 1917. See also L. A. Post, *Three Plays of Menander,* 1929; and Gilbert Murray, *Two Plays by Menander,* 1945. For critical comment see also A. W. Gomme, *Essays in Greek History and Literature,* 1937.

H. L. MENCKEN

Born: Baltimore, Maryland
Date: September 12, 1880

Died: Baltimore
Date: January 29, 1956

PRINCIPAL WORKS

ESSAYS AND STUDIES: *George Bernard Shaw—His Plays,* 1905; *The Philosophy of Friedrich Nietzsche,* 1908; *A Book of Prefaces,* 1917; *In Defense of Women,* 1918; *Prejudices* (in six series), 1919–1927; *Notes on Democracy,* 1926; *Treatise on the*

Gods, 1930; *Treatise on Right and Wrong*, 1934; *Generally Political*, 1944; *A Mencken Christomathy*, 1949.

PHILOLOGY: *The American Language*, 1919; *First Supplement*, 1945; *Second Supplement*, 1948.

AUTOBIOGRAPHY: *Happy Days*, 1940; *Newspaper Days*, 1941; *Heathen Days*, 1943.

SATIRE: *A Book of Burlesques*, 1916.

PLAYS: *The Artist*, 1912; *Heliogabalus: A Buffoonery in Three Acts*, 1920 (with George Jean Nathan).

"The Gaseous Vertebrata who own, operate and afflict the universe have treated me with excessive politeness," H(enry) L(ouis) Mencken wrote in his autobiography, as he recalled how satisfactory his life had been, so that he would not wish one detail of it changed. He was born in Baltimore, September 12, 1880, in a family of the "comfortable and complacent bourgeoisie," largely of German descent, and was educated in his native city where he lived all of his life. For many years he was on the staff of the Baltimore *Sun;* in 1914 he became editor of *The Smart Set,* and from 1924 to 1933 he edited *The American Mercury,* the liveliest magazine of that decade. In 1930 he married Sarah Powell Haardt, who died in 1935.

Despite the recent interest in Fitzgerald and the early Hemingway and Faulkner, it was not these writers who dominated the 1920's. Rather, the two important figures at the time, those who really attracted attention, were Mencken and Sinclair Lewis; and perhaps only someone who can recall that decade can understand how great their influence was. Just as the novels of Lewis, satirizing so much in American life, were hailed or damned according to the point of view of the reader, so the pungent essays of Mencken, slaughtering so many sacred cows, evoked cries of delight or anguish. The objects of their satire were much the same—the provincialism, narrowness, hypocrisy, and self-satisfaction of America—and while their methods were often crude, the two writers accomplished salutary results.

Mencken's writing can be divided into two parts: literary criticism and criticism of the national political and social scene. As a literary critic, he appealed to the then younger generation because of the freshness of his point of view, the vivid phrases by which he expressed himself, and his scorn of the venerable academic critics such as More, Babbitt, and Sherman. To the irreverent college students of those days, his slashing attacks on some hitherto-revered "Dr. Professor" were highly stimulating, for it was an iconoclastic era. The chief target of his satire was the Puritan tradition in American letters, with all that it meant of literary taboos. Viewed in retrospect, however, his literary criticism has not stood up well. Though he championed some writers of merit, such as Conrad, his range was narrow and his taste often deplorable. His obvious preference was for purely naturalistic fiction such as that of Dreiser. His limited imagination was evidenced by his inability to appreciate or even understand poetry. Nor was his criticism based on any reasoned aesthetic; it was purely subjective, a matter of likes and dislikes. Yet he was fearless in defending unpopular causes, and he succeeded in

742

admitting some much-needed light and air.

His comments on national affairs were of a piece with his literary criticism and directed against similar targets: America's ingrown Puritanism, displayed at that time in the grotesque farce of Prohibition; the national cult of "boosterism"; public idols such as Woodrow Wilson—all were attacked, while the author was either hailed or vilified. The satire was not subtle; it was said that Mencken's weapon was not the rapier but the bludgeon. It may have been, however, that the latter was the more suitable weapon at the moment. In the course of his bitter reflections on the national *mores* he displayed genuine wit and coined some phrases that have become a part of the language: "the Bible belt" and "the booboisie," for example. So great was his prestige at that time, that to write "Menckenese" was the ambition of most university literati. These essays often still provide amusing reading, yet they were so topical, so tied in with situations and events peculiar to the 1920's, that they are already dated.

Mencken was always the individualist, the foe of the mass-mind and of mass-culture. Toward religion, he was, as he freely admitted, a complete skeptic; and the ascendency during the 1920's of the more fanatical aspects of fundamentalism gave him some excellent subjects for satire. Politically, he was a tory, with little faith in democracy and a detestation of all radical movements, reforms, and paternalism. Actually much of this attitude, which disturbed so many readers, was merely a restatement of traditional American individualism. Above all, he was the enemy of humbug wherever found in our national life.

A very different aspect of Mencken's work were the volumes of *The American Language,* on which he spent years of research. These books have been acclaimed by scholars as important contributions to philology, and yet his characteristic wit makes fascinating reading of an otherwise dry subject. It is probable that *The American Language* will outlive all his other books.

In 1948 Mencken suffered a stroke which incapacitated him for further writing. He died in Baltimore, January 29, 1956.

BIBLIOGRAPHICAL REFERENCES: The authorized biography is William R. Manchester's *Disturber of the Peace: The Life of H. L. Mencken,* 1951. For other biographical and critical studies see Isaac Goldberg, *The Man Mencken: A Biographical and Critical Survey,* 1925; Ernest Boyd, *H. L. Mencken,* 1927; Edgar Kemler, *The Irreverent Mr. Mencken,* 1950; and Charles Angoff, *H. L. Mencken,* 1956.

For articles and essays in books see also Stuart P. Sherman, *Americans,* 1922; *idem,* "H. L. Mencken as Liberator," in *Critical Woodcuts,* 1927; Joseph W. Beach, *The Outlook for American Prose,* 1926; Walter Lippman, *Men of Destiny,* 1927; Elizabeth S. Sergent, *Fire Under the Andes,* 1927; James Branch Cabell, *Some of Us,* 1930; Van Wyck Brooks, *Sketches in Criticism,* 1932; Louis Kronenberger, "H. L. Mencken," in *After the Genteel Tradition,* edited by Malcolm Cowley, 1936; and Bernard Smith, *Forces in American Criticism,* 1939.

GEORGE MEREDITH

Born: Portsmouth, England   *Died:* Box Hill, Surrey, England
Date: February 12, 1828   *Date:* May 18, 1909

NOVELS: *The Shaving of Shagpat,* 1856; *Farina,* 1857; *The Ordeal of Richard Feverel,* 1859; *Evan Harrington,* 1861; *Sandra Belloni, or Emilia in England,* 1864; *Rhoda Fleming,* 1865; *Vittoria,* 1867; *The Adventures of Harry Richmond,* 1871; *Beauchamp's Career,* 1876; *The Egoist,* 1879; *The Tragic Comedians,* 1880; *Diana of the Crossways,* 1885; *Lord Ormont and His Aminta,* 1894; *One of Our Conquerors,* 1891; *The Amazing Marriage,* 1895; *Celt and Saxon,* 1910 (unfinished).

SHORT STORIES: *The Tale of Chloe,* 1879; *The Case of General Ople and Lady Camper,* 1890.

POEMS: *Poems,* 1851; *Modern Love,* 1862; *Poems and Lyrics of the Joy of Earth,* 1883; *Ballads and Poems of Tragic Life,* 1887; *A Reading of Earth,* 1888; *A Reading of Life,* 1901; *Last Poems,* 1909.

ESSAY: *On the Idea of Comedy and the Uses of the Comic Spirit,* 1897 (first separate publication).

A highly original writer, perhaps too original and idiosyncratic ever to be very popular, George Meredith has always been one of those unfortunate writers whose work is more praised than read. He did not receive much popular attention until he was past fifty, and after that, though he received most of the honors his fellow writers could award, he never attracted the general reader as Dickens, Thackeray, or Trollope did. An age in which the ability to invent a lively plot was highly valued was not likely to be much pleased by a novelist who, like his equally neglected contemporary Henry James, was almost exclusively interested in the subtle depiction of human motivation. Meredith's style also gave the common reader trouble: it was epigrammatic and involved, totally unlike the swift narrative flow of the prose of Dickens or Thackeray. In his poetry Meredith again refused to conform to popular taste; his diction was often rough, his syntax obscure, in contrast to the melodic sweetness of the popular Tennysonian tradition.

His style, however, is admirably suited to his purposes. He considered it the purpose of art to correct the excesses of men in society and to bring them closer to the ideal of the golden mean. His novels usually expose the flaws in human beings so that the reader may eliminate them in himself. His celebrated lecture, *On the Idea of Comedy and the Uses of the Comic Spirit,* delivered in 1877 but not published separately until 1897, is one of the great expressions of the moral value of literature. To this end he developed a style that is leisurely yet challenging, designed to penetrate to the hidden motivations of character by pithy thrusts and subtle implications. His poetry, too, is highly metaphoric; Meredith's nimble mind is too impatient always to make the transitions from image to image clear, and the result is a colorful, affecting style that sometimes cannot fully bear the thought of the poem. His observations of nature are fresh and vivid, and his poetry generally tries to reconcile the forces of passion and intellect.

The son of a naval outfitter, Meredith was born at Portsmouth, England, on February 12, 1828. He received a good early education but was forced to support himself rather than go to college, and he took to journalism in order to secure a reasonably steady income. In 1849 he married Mrs. Mary Ellen Nicholls, a widow almost seven years his senior. The daughter of Thomas Love Peacock, she was a talented and witty woman who was quite unsuited to the even more talented and witty Meredith. The marriage was unhappy; after 1858, when Mrs. Meredith went to Capri with another man, unreconcilable. After her death in 1861 Meredith told the psychological history of their estrangement in the brilliant lyric sequence, *Modern Love*. In 1864 he married Marie Vulliamy and two years later he served as a war correspondent in the Austro-Italian War of 1866. On his return to England he edited the *Fortnightly Review* and worked as a publisher's reader. A careful and sensitive critic, he gave needed encouragement to Thomas Hardy and George Gissing.

Meanwhile Meredith was slowly gaining a reputation as a novelist. His first important novel, *The Ordeal of Richard Feverel*, had little success, though it is a fine study of the emotional growth of a young man. The complex characterization and the delicately shaded style of *Evan Harrington* and *Beauchamp's Career* attracted a small but growing group of readers, but it was not until his comic masterpiece,

The Egoist, appeared in 1879 that he received much popular attention. *Diana of the Crossways,* published in 1885, was his first novel to have a great popular success.

In the same year his second wife died. Meredith's own health was poor. Although a spinal ailment confined him to a wheelchair, he became in his last years the intellectual leader of his time. To his home at Box Hill, just outside of London, came aspiring young men, and Meredith, grown dogmatic and certain, was free with his literary advice. Following the death of Tennyson in 1892, Meredith was made president of the Society of Authors, thereby becoming the titular head of English letters. In 1905 he was awarded the Order of Merit and the medal of the Royal Society of Literature. At his death, on May 18, 1909, at Box Hill, he was England's most honored author and the last of the great Victorians.

Meredith's technique as a novelist is to use the point of view not of an onlooker, but of a particular character. In this way he can describe the peculiar emotion of the character and, with his powerfully figurative style, catch the interest of the reader. As a result, his characters are extremely complex and varied. His heroines are particularly well drawn and are perhaps the finest since Shakespeare.

BIBLIOGRAPHICAL REFERENCES: The fiction, poetry, and letters of George Meredith have been collected in the Memorial Edition, edited by G. M. Trevelyan, 29 vols., 1909–1912. There are several separate collections of letters: *Letters,* edited by W. M. Meredith, 2 vols., 1912; *Letters to Edward Clodd and C. K. Shorter,* edited by T. J. Wise, 1913; and *Letters to Alice Meynell,* 1923.

Biographical and critical studies are numerous. See G. M. Trevelyan, *The Poetry and Philosophy of George Meredith,* 1906; E. J. Bailey, *The Novels of George Meredith,* 1907; Richard Curle, *Aspects of George Meredith,* 1908; James Moffatt, *George Meredith: A Primer to the Novels,* 1909; Joseph Warren Beach, *The Comic Spirit in George Meredith,* 1911; Constantin Photiadès, *George Meredith: sa vie, son imagination, son art, sa doctrine,* 1911 (translated 1913); J. H. E. Crees, *George Mere-*

dith: A Study of His Works and Personality, 1918; S. M. Ellis, *George Meredith: His Life and Friends in Relation to His Work,* 1920; René Galland, *George Meredith: les cinquante premières années,* 1923; J. B. Priestley, *George Meredith,* 1926; Mary Sturge Gretton, *The Writings and Life of George Meredith,* 1926; R. E. Sencourt, *The Life of George Meredith,* 1929; Sir Osbert Sitwell, *The Novels of George Meredith and Some Notes on the English Novel,* 1947; Siegfried Sassoon, *Meredith,* 1948; W. F. Wright, *Art and Substance in George Meredith,* 1953; and Lionel Stevenson, *The Ordeal of George Meredith,* 1953.

DMITRI MEREJKOWSKI

Born: St. Petersburg, Russia   *Died:* Paris, France
Date: August 14, 1865   *Date:* December 9, 1941

Principal Works

NOVELS: *Smert Bogov,* 1895 (*The Death of the Gods*); *Voskresenie Bogi,* 1902 (*The Romance of Leonardo da Vinci*); *Antikhrist: Pëtr i Aleksei,* 1905 (*Peter and Alexis*).
ESSAY: *Tolstoi i Dostoyevski,* 1902 (*Tolstoy as Man and Artist, with an Essay on Dostoevski*).

Though Dmitri Merejkowski [also Dmitry Sergeyevich Merezhkovsky] wrote many poems and essays, he is known in the Western world chiefly for his historical romances. One of the last Russian novelists to write out of the philosophical backgrounds of "Old Russia," his philosophical difficulties represent the intellectual and moral struggles of the aristocracy as it lost political power to the lower classes. His trilogy of novels, called by the general title *Christ and the Antichrist* (1895–1905), were intended to set forth a solution to modern man's religious doubts and to present an alternative to both ascetic Christianity and hedonism by fusing the flesh and the spirit into a new religious philosophy.

His early years prepared him especially well for his career as a writer. Born in St. Petersburg on August 14, 1865, he was brought up as a member of the aristocracy by his noble father. He had a good classical education and, on entering the University of St.

Petersburg in 1884, he studied the Greek and Roman civilizations intensively. A brilliant student, he completed in two years the studies that supplied him with the backgrounds for his best novels. He also read widely in scientific philosophy, but these studies left his religious nature unsatisfied. He began to try to synthesize materialism and spirituality into a new whole.

He traveled to the Caucasus because of a lung condition and there met and married Zinaida Hippius, the leading poetess of Russia. They traveled for many years in Greece, Italy, and Asia Minor, and spent very little time in their native country. About 1900 he formulated the religion of "The New Road." For a time he and his wife conducted a salon devoted to the discussion of this new religion that tried to reconcile the egoism of Nietzsche and the altruism of Tolstoy, but the repressive Tsarist regime soon dissolved this unorthodox little society. Because he had sympathized with the 1905

746

revolutionists, Merejkowski was compelled to flee to Paris. He returned to Russia in 1910 and opposed World War I. He opposed the Bolsheviks even more vigorously and was sent to Siberia in 1918. He escaped to Paris in 1920. There he and his wife spent their remaining years writing polemical tracts against Soviet materialism and books explaining 'The New Way." Merejkowski died December 9, 1941, during the occupation of Paris, perhaps of malnutrition.

His novels, though clumsily constructed, show a raw power in the presentation of impressive historical scenes. *The Death of the Gods* (sometimes titled *Julian the Apostate*) makes full use of his knowledge of ancient Mediterranean culture. The sweep of historical events is absorbing and the philosophical theme, though it tends to make characters mere embodiments of ideas, provides a unifying perspective as the trilogy ranges freely over European history. Merejkowski sees the complete rout of the paganism represented by Julian as an unfortunate event, but his spirits rise as he tells of the resurrection of the dead gods during the Renaissance; *The Romance of Leonardo da Vinci* celebrates the restoration of fleshly values to the ascetic European world. Leonardo represents the fusion of flesh and spirit that Merejkowski sought. But Antichrist rises again in Peter the Great, and Merejkowski is aware, in *Peter and Alexis,* that the struggle to achieve a balance between the demands of the flesh and the spirit is a constant one.

In his book *Tolstoy as Man and Artist, with an Essay on Dostoevski,* Merejkowski attacked Tolstoy because he was not interested in the supernatural and praised Dostoevski because he was concerned with both the natural and supernatural worlds. It was for similar reasons that he attacked Soviet communism: this new Antichrist, with its materialistic foundations, was a danger to the synthesis Merejkowski hoped would become a final and enduring belief for all men.

BIBLIOGRAPHICAL REFERENCES: *The Romance of Leonardo da Vinci,* in the Guerney translation, is available in the Modern Library, 1928. For a biography see J. Chuzeville, *Dmitri Merezhkovsky,* 1922. Biographical information may be found in Valentine Snow, *Russian Writers,* 1946. Reliable critical appraisals are included in Richard Hare, *Russian Literature,* 1947; and Marc Slonim, *Modern Russian Literature,* 1953.

PROSPER MÉRIMÉE

Born: Paris, France
Date: September 28, 1803

Died: Cannes, France
Date: September 23, 1870

PRINCIPAL WORKS

NOVELS: *La Chronique du regne de Charles IX,* 1829 (*The Chronicle of the Reign of Charles IX*); *La Double Meprise,* 1833 (*The Double Mistake*); *Les Âmes du Purgatoire,* 1837 (*Souls in Purgatory*); *Colomba,* 1840; *Carmen,* 1847.

SHORT STORIES: *Mosaique,* 1833 (*Mosaics*).

PLAYS: *Théâtre de Clara Gazul,* 1825 (*The Theater of Clara Gazul*).

POEMS: *La Guzla,* 1827.

747

HISTORY: *Essai sur la guerre sociale,* 1841; *Histoire de Don Pèdre,* 1843; *La Conjuration de Catalina,* 1844; *Le faux Démétrius,* 1852.

ESSAYS AND STUDIES: *Mélanges historiques et littéraires,* 1855; *Portraits historiques et littéraires,* 1874; *Études sur les arts au moyen âge,* 1874.

Prosper Mérimée, born in Paris, September 28, 1803, was not the greatest French writer of the nineteenth century. To claim that he was the greatest of an era that produced Victor Hugo and Dumas fils, Stendhal and Balzac, Baudelaire, Zola, and Flaubert would be foolhardy, if not absurd. Yet, if he was not the greatest, he was certainly one of the most versatile; and though he certainly was not the most productive, he was, perhaps, the least dedicated. And it is this lack of dedication that gives him his charm and his importance. At a time when writers tended to take themselves (and to be taken) very seriously, and when the murky seas of Germanic Romanticism threatened to inundate completely the level plain of Gallic thought, Mérimée stood indifferently on his own personal promontory, observant, uncommitted, and completely dry, beginning his literary career with two of the most thorough hoaxes ever perpetrated on a reading public, and ending it with a tale of bestiality designed to shock the ladies of the Empress Eugénie's court.

For Mérimée could afford to be indifferent. Despite his claim that *Carmen* was written because its author was in need of a new pair of pants, Mérimée never had to rely on his pen either for financial support or for individual prestige. His success in the novel and the short story was but one of his many accomplishments: he was also a lawyer, a career public official important enough in his position as Inspector General of Public Monuments to be retained through two great changes in

power (the end of the Bourbon Restoration in 1830 and the abdication of Louis-Philippe in the Revolution of 1848) and to be made a senator under Louis-Napoléon, a painter of some small talent, a lover of some great notoriety, an authority on Russian literature, a member of the French Academy (elected in 1844), and a mentor and friend (though not, as has been held, the father) of the empress of the French. Moreover, he was born into an artistic environment and was accustomed to association with people of talent from his earliest days.

His father was Léonor Mérimée, a highly regarded academic painter of the period who, shortly before Prosper's birth in 1803, was made secretary of the École des Beaux Arts. Prosper, his only child, and a sickly one at that, was spoiled and pampered by a mother who was also a talented artist.

His early interest in painting was natural, but it was subordinated early to his one greatest desire—the acquisition of knowledge. To further this end he enrolled in the École de Droit and received his degree in law at the age of twenty. Some two years before, however, he had met Stendhal, who was to become a lifelong friend and who was immediately to stimulate his interest in authorship. Mérimée began a play, but here his comic indifference intervened. Instead of the serious *Cromwell* (never published), there emerged a whole series of plays, mock romances by a fictitious Spanish actress, complete with a spurious autobiography.

This hoax, *The Theater of Clara Gazul*, had hardly been discovered when Mérimée audaciously succeeded with a second, *La Guzla*, a collection of ballads reputedly from the unwritten works of one Hyacinthe Maglanovich, a Dalmatian bard who performed on a miraculous one-stringed instrument.

Content with his hoaxes (written, he claimed, to demonstrate the simplicity and basic absurdity of the use of local color), he turned next to the novel, producing his ironic *Charles IX* in 1829.

His career as a public official began the next year, and with it came journeys, not only throughout France, but to all parts of Europe. His work as an archeologist developed his powers of observation, and his travels gave him much to observe. His tales and novels were the result: *Carmen* grew out of a number of incidents observed during trips to Spain—one as early as 1830—and *Colomba* was inspired by an official tour of Corsica in 1839. In these stories and novels Mérimée's indifference crystallized into an aesthetic detachment that allowed him to shape his fictional materials into his most enduring triumph, that of form.

Ironically, for all his indifference, his public triumphs did not endure through his lifetime. After having survived two political upheavals, he was forced from office with the fall of the Second Empire in 1870, and died a few months later at Cannes, on September 23, 1870.

BIBLIOGRAPHICAL REFERENCES: *The Writings of Prosper Mérimée*, edited with a preface by George Saintsbury, appeared in 8 vols. in 1906. The *Letters*, edited by Maurice Perturier in French, have appeared in several installments, the sixth volume being published in 1948; and the *Correspondance Générale* in 1956. The most adequate biography in English is G. H. Johnstone, *Prosper Mérimée: A Mask and a Face*, 1927, also containing a good bibliography. For French readers Pierre Marie Augustin Filon, *Mérimée*, 1898, is standard. Elizabeth Balch, *An Author's Love: Being the Unpublished Letters of Prosper Mérimée's "Inconnue,"* 1889, is an interesting fictitious document. Essays in books include Adolphe Jullien, *Paris Dilettante au Commencement du Siècle*, 1884; Walter Pater, *Miscellaneous Studies*, 1895; Arthur Symons, *Studies in Prose and Verse*, 1904; and Algar L. Thorold, *Six Masters in Disillusion*, 1909. A good critical article is Albert J. George's "Prosper Mérimée and the Short Prose Narrative," *Symposium*, X (1956), 25–33.

THOMAS MIDDLETON

Born: London, England
Date: April, 1580 (Baptized April 18)

Died: Newington Butts, London
Date: 1627 (Buried July 4)

PRINCIPAL WORKS

PLAYS: *The Old Law*, c. 1599 (revised by Massinger); *Blurt, Master Constable*, 1601 (authorship doubtful); *The Family of Love*, c. 1602; *The Phoenix*, c. 1604; *A Trick to Catch the Old One*, c. 1605; *A Mad World, My Masters*, c. 1606; *Michaelmas Term*, c. 1606; *Your Five Gallants*, c. 1607; *The Roaring Girl*, c. 1610 (with Dekker); *A Chaste Maid in Cheapside*, 1611; *No Wit, No Help like a Woman's*, c. 1613; *The Witch*, c. 1615; *More Dissemblers besides Women*, c. 1615; *A Fair Quarrel*, 1616 (with William Rowley); *The Widow*, c. 1616 (with Fletcher);

Hengist, King of Kent, or The Mayor of Quinborough, c. 1618; *Anything for a Quiet Life,* c. 1621 (with Webster?); *Women Beware Women,* c. 1621; *The Changeling,* 1622 (with Rowley); *The Spanish Gipsy,* 1623 (with Ford and Rowley); *A Game at Chess,* 1624.

MISCELLANEOUS: *The Wisdom of Solomon Paraphrased,* 1597; *Micro-Cynicon, Six Snarling Satires,* 1599; *Running Stream Entertainment,* 1613; *The Triumphs of Truth,* 1613; *Civitatis Amor,* 1616.

For about three centuries little definite information was available about the life of Thomas Middleton. Even now a full-scale biography could hardly be compiled. E. K. Chambers believed him to be one of two Thomas Middletons who entered Gray's Inn in the 1590's. Mark Eccles, in 1931, established the currently accepted identification and furnished biographical facts. Thomas Middleton was the son of William Middleton, a London bricklayer with a coat of arms, able to write himself "gentleman." Thomas entered Queen's College, Oxford, in 1598. His first published work, a versified *Wisdom of Solomon Paraphrased,* was followed by other pamphlets in prose and verse.

He began his career as a playwright with Philip Henslowe's company, the record of his employment being in 1602. Later he composed for other companies, including Paul's Boys and the King's Men. The canon and chronology of his dramatic work are very uncertain: some of his works were written in collaboration; some were revised by other playwrights years after the original writing. Several of his plays are lost. He took part in writing entertainments for official occasions. In the 1604 edition of *The Magnificent Entertainment: Given to King James . . . the 15. of March. 1603,* Thomas Dekker, ignoring the contribution of his enemy Ben Jonson to the work, gave generous credit to Middleton for a much less significant share. Middleton's writing of city pageants and masques was the apparent reason for his being appointed City Chronologer of London in 1620. His last play was a satirical political allegory, *A Game at Chess,* 1624. This dealt too boldly with international politics; after a brief run it was banned and the Globe Theater itself closed. The play is most unusual in that the author's manuscript survives. The author's final work was a Lord Mayor's Pageant in 1626.

Although Middleton's reputation is primarily that of a comical realist and satirist, he left at least two very effective tragedies of evil: *Women Beware Women* and *The Changeling,* the latter written with William Rowley. His bawdy farce, *A Chaste Maid in Cheapside,* is a worthy and amusing forerunner of Restoration comedy. Middleton was born in London in April, 1580, and died there in 1627.

BIBLIOGRAPHICAL REFERENCES: The standard edition is *The Works of Thomas Middleton,* edited by A. H. Bullen, 1885–1886. Representative dramas are included in *The Best Plays of Thomas Middleton,* with an Introduction by A. C. Swinburne, Mermaid Series, 1887. See also *A Game at Chesse,* by Thomas Middleton, edited by R. C. Bald, 1929; *English Drama, 1580–1642,* edited by C. F. Tucker Brooke and N. B. Paradise, 1933; *Elizabethan and Stuart Plays,* edited by C. H. Baskervill, V. B. Heltzel, and A. H. Nethercot, 1934; *Typical Elizabethan Plays,* edited by F. E.

Schelling and M. W. Black, 1949; *The Dramatic Works of Thomas Dekker,* edited by Fredson Bowers, Vol. II, 1955; Pauline C. Wiggin, *An Inquiry into the Authorship of the Middleton-Rowley Plays,* 1897; E. K. Chambers, *The Elizabethan Stage,* Vol. III, 1923; W. D. Dunkelm, *The Dramatic Technique of Thomas Middleton in the Comedies of London Life,* 1925; Mark Eccles, "Middleton's Birth and Education," *Review of English Studies,* VII (1931), 431–441; Henry W. Wells, *Elizabethan and Jacobean Playwrights,* 1939; and T. M. Parrott and R. H. Ball, *A Short View of Elizabethan Drama,* 1943.

KÁLMÁN MIKSZÁTH

Born: Szklabonya, Hungary *Died:* Budapest, Hungary
Date: January 16, 1847 *Date:* May 28, 1910

PRINCIPAL WORKS

NOVELS: *Szent Péter esernyöje,* 1895 (*St. Peter's Umbrella*); *Besztercze ostroma,* 1895 (*The Siege of Besztercze*); *A fekete város,* 1910 (*The Black City*).

SHORT STORIES: *A tót atyafiak,* 1881 (*The Slovak Folk*); *A jó Palóczok,* 1882 (*The Good People of Palóc*).

Kálmán Mikszáth was born in Szklabonya, Hungary, on January 16, 1847, the son of an innkeeper and butcher descended from a family of Lutheran gentry. Despite family hardships, he received a law degree from the University of Budapest and for a time eked out a living as a county clerk and journalist. Many of his later short stories which treat debt and poverty with comic irony stem from this period. His journalistic fortunes improved as he moved from one newspaper to another until, in 1871, he began to publish fiction. His fame rapidly increased; he was elected to the national literary societies, awarded the grand prize of the Hungarian Academy, granted an honorary degree from the University of Budapest, and elected President of the Hungarian Society of Journalists.

Despite a turbulent personal life (he divorced and remarried his wife, and saw his young son die), Mikszáth's writings generally show a detached, humorous attitude toward human foibles and frailities with only occasional touches of bitterness. Even his most explicitly "problem" novels are filled with wit and fantasy as characters from different centuries and classes confront each other with a comic hostility and bewilderment. He was, however, not a rebel, but a conservative country gentleman who loved the common people.

Mikszáth received national honors in 1908, when an estate was purchased and presented to him; his birthplace was named after him, and essays, monographs, and books devoted to his work were published. His stories and novels constitute a collected edition of fifty volumes (1931). He died in Budapest on May 28, 1910.

BIBLIOGRAPHICAL REFERENCES: There is no useful criticism of Mikszáth in English. A. Schöpflin is the author of two studies, *Magyar irók,* 1919, and *Mikszáth Kálmán,* 1941. See also M. Rubinyi, *Mikszáth Kálmán élete és müvei,* 1917.

JOHN STUART MILL

Born: London, England
Date: May 20, 1806

Died: Avignon, France
Date: May 8, 1873

PRINCIPAL WORKS

PHILOSOPHICAL, POLITICAL, AND SCIENTIFIC ESSAYS: *A System of Logic,* 1843; *Principles of Political Economy,* 1848; *On Liberty,* 1859; *Thoughts on Parliamentary Reform,* 1859; *Considerations on Representative Government,* 1861; *Utilitarianism,* 1863; *Auguste Comte and Positivism,* 1865; *England and Ireland,* 1868; *The Subjection of Women,* 1869; *On the Irish Land Question,* 1870; *Three Essays on Religion,* 1874.

AUTOBIOGRAPHY: *Autobiography,* 1873.

The intellectual leader of a liberal movement that profoundly influenced Western political thought, John Stuart Mill was also a fine literary stylist. His prose style is clear and balanced, admirably suited to bear the weight of his political and social thinking. He developed the Utilitarian movement, started by his father, James Mill, into a political force for humanitarian social developments. His *The Subjection of Women* was an early blow in the fight for women's rights, and his *On Liberty* remains, with Milton's *Areopagitica* (1644), a classic defense of individuality against authoritarianism in all its forms.

Mill, born in London on May 20, 1806, is also a classic example of the precocious child; he himself always insisted that he had no more than average ability, but merely profited from an earlier start than most children. Under the tutelage of his father, Mill acquired an immense background of knowledge. At his earliest recollection he knew Greek; Latin came harder because it was started later. At eleven he began to write a history of Rome; at twelve he began the serious study of logic. By the age of fourteen he was solidly grounded in mathematics, political theory, economics, and history, as well as logic and the classical languages. In 1823 he started as clerk in the India House, a firm in which he eventually succeeded his father as director. But the education his father had given him had excluded emotional development, and in 1826 Mill had a great spiritual crisis. He became aware of his own emotional needs and eventually, particularly through the study of Wordsworth, he was able to resolve his difficulties. After this crisis he saw the need for humanizing the *laissez-faire* doctrines of the Utilitarians until they met emotional as well as economic human needs.

In 1830 he met Mrs. Taylor, an invalid for whom he developed, with the full knowledge of her intellectually inferior husband, what was apparently a platonic attachment. He married her, after the death of her husband, twenty-one years later. He edited the *London Review,* the organ of Utilitarian thought, from 1835 to 1840 and gave early recognition to Tennyson. *A System of Logic* was a great work in the development of scientific, empirical thinking. He was elected to the House of Commons for a term lasting from 1865 to 1868; he worked for a way to have minority opinions heard more, for he always feared that democracies could become tyrannous. His *Autobiography*, a sensitive record of his emotional and intellectual development, appeared in the year of his death at Avignon, France, on May 8, 1873.

BIBLIOGRAPHICAL REFERENCES: Most of the essential details of Mills's life are presented in his *Autobiography*, re-edited by Harold J. Laski in 1944. There is also a collection of *Letters*, edited by H. S. R. Elliot, 2 vols., 1910. For biographical and critical studies see W. L. Courtney, *The Life of John Stuart Mill*, 1889; H. K. Garner, *John Stuart Mill and the Philosophy of Mediation*, 1919; Emery Neff, *Carlyle and Mill*, 1924; and C. L. Street, *Individualism and Individuality in the Social Philosophy of John Stuart Mill*, 1940. For an earlier study see A. Bain, *John Stuart Mill: A Personal Criticism*, 1882. For background studies of his life and work see also Leslie Stephen, *The English Utilitarians*, Vol. III, 1900; James Seth, *English Philosophers and Schools of Philosophy*, 1912; and Rudolf Metz, *A Hundred Years of British Philosophy*, 1938.

EDNA ST. VINCENT MILLAY

Born: Rockland, Maine
Date: February 22, 1892

Died: Austerlitz, New York
Date: October 19, 1950

PRINCIPAL WORKS

POEMS: *Renascence and Other Poems*, 1917; *A Few Figs from Thistles*, 1920; *Second April*, 1921; *The Ballad of the Harp-Weaver*, 1922; *Poems*, 1923; *The Buck in the Snow and Other Poems*, 1928; *Fatal Interview*, 1931; *Wine from These Grapes*, 1934; *Conversation at Midnight*, 1937; *Huntsman, What Quarry?*, 1939; *Make Bright the Arrows*, 1940; *There Are No Islands Any More*, 1940; *Collected Sonnets*, 1941; *The Murder of Lidice*, 1942; *Collected Lyrics*, 1943; *Mine the Harvest*, 1954.

PLAYS: *Aria da Capo*, 1919; *The Lamp and the Bell*, 1921; *Two Slatterns and a King*, 1921; *The Princess Marries the Page*, 1932.

OPERATIC LIBRETTO: *The King's Henchman*, 1926 (with a score by Deems Taylor).

MISCELLANEOUS: *Distressing Dialogues*, 1924; *Reflections on the Sacco-Vanzetti Tragedy*, 1927 (with William G. Thompson, John Dewey, and C. I. Claflin); *Letters*, 1952.

TRANSLATION: *Flowers of Evil*, 1936 (with George Dillon).

Of twentieth century American poets, no other perhaps has excited so much popular interest as Edna St. Vincent Millay, for her verse, despite the intricacies of its rhetoric, spoke directly and intensely of the emotions and both inspired and shocked the generation to whom she first became a symbol of female freedom. Born in Rockland, Maine, on February 22, 1892, Vincent Millay (as she was known to her family) began writing verse in adolescence, won several poetry prizes from St. *Nicholas* magazine, and at nineteen composed her first adult poem, "Renascence," published in *The Lyric Year* in 1912. "Renascence" was warmly admired by the poet Arthur Davison Ficke, for whom Miss Millay conceived a romantic attachment that gave rise to some of her best and most tender love sonnets. In 1917, following her graduation from Vassar, she went to New York to look for roles as an actress. Her one-act play, *Aria da Capo*, was produced at the Provincetown Playhouse in 1919. In 1923 she was married to Eugen Jan Boissevain. That same year she received a Pulitzer Prize for *The Ballad of the Harp-Weaver*. Under a pseudonym, "Nancy Boyd," she issued a collection of essays with the title *Distressing Dialogues;* these had appeared in *Vanity Fair*. In 1925, after a voyage to the Orient, she and her husband moved into Steepletop, a house they had acquired in the Berkshires near Austerlitz, New York. Always an eager traveler, Miss Millay considered this her permanent home; here, surviving her husband by fourteen months, she died in solitude on October 19, 1950.

Miss Millay's work up to *Conversation at Midnight* may be regarded as a continuous personal testament. The same vivacity evident in her letters emerges in her poetry, but in the concentrated form of a passionate devotion to life. Her creed was hedonistic; high among her themes was resentment that death would pitilessly smother joy, and it was not accidental that she was a close student of the Roman elegiac poets, especially Catullus. Her later poems are more impersonal. Although an active social consciousness had led her, in 1927, to plead with zeal and anger for the lives of Sacco and Vanzetti, she hardly displayed before the 1940's a generalized concern with the problems of humanity. During World War II, however, the character of her work changed. The results were not altogether favorable: her true *métier* was the poetry of love and grief by which, in the beginning, her fame had been crystallized.

BIBLIOGRAPHICAL REFERENCES: The standard text is *The Collected Poems of Edna St. Vincent Millay*, 1956. There is no authorized life, although several are reported in preparation. Vincent Sheehan presents an interesting but rather sentimentalized personality portrait in *Indigo Bunting: A Memoir of Edna St. Vincent Millay*, 1951. The *Letters of Edna St. Vincent Millay* were edited by Allan Ross Macdougall, 1952. A pioneer critical study is Elizabeth Atkins, *Edna St. Vincent Millay and Her Times*, 1936.

For briefer studies see Rica Brenner, *Ten Modern Poets*, 1930; Harriet Monroe, "Edna St. Vincent Millay," *Poetry*, XXIV (1924), 260–266; John H. Preston, "Edna St. Vincent Millay," *Virginia Quarterly Review*, III (1927), 342–355; Edward Davison, "Edna St. Vincent Millay," *English Journal*, XVI (1927), 671–682; Edd W. Parks, "Edna St. Vincent Millay," *Sewanee Review*, XXXVIII (1930), 42–49; Arthur E. Du Bois, "Edna St. Vincent Millay," *ibid.*, XLIII (1935), 80–104; John Crowe Ransom, "The Poet as Woman," *Southern Review*, II (1937), 783–806; and James S. Dabbs, "Edna St. Vincent Millay: Not Resigned," *South Atlantic Quarterly*, XXXVII (1938), 54–66. The latest checklist is by Frances Cheney in Allen Tate, *Sixty American Poets*, 1945.

ARTHUR MILLER

Born: New York, N. Y.
Date: October 17, 1915

Principal Works

PLAYS: *The Man Who Had All the Luck*, 1944; *All My Sons*, 1947; *Death of a Salesman*, 1949; *The Crucible*, 1953; *A View from the Bridge*, 1955.

NOVEL: *Focus*, 1945.

REPORTAGE: *Situation Normal*, 1944.

As he himself tells it, Arthur Miller was born in Harlem, October 17, 1915, to a well-to-do Austrian-American father and an American mother. He was such a poor student in high school that only his special plea that he wanted to be a writer allowed him to enter the University of Michigan; evidently the letter exhibited his ability. This turn toward the academic occurred only after several years' work in miscellaneous jobs, one of which was in a warehouse on Tenth Avenue. *The Brothers Karamazov* was the first great book he can remember reading, a work which determined his desire to write.

Under the tutelage of Kenneth Rowe, Miller wrote several prize one-acters while at Michigan. He was in the School of Journalism at the time and previously had seen only one play and read a few of Shakespeare's works. He wrote several plays a year while at Michigan, some of which have been produced.

He returned to New York as a hack writer, for radio and television mainly, and as an aspiring novelist. His one novel, *Focus*, received some acclaim in the early forties, but his first full-length, professionally-produced play quickly overshadowed it. *All My Sons* proved to be timely since its theme was corruption in important places: here the small-parts manufacturer father indirectly causes the plane crash death of his own son. As a movie, Miller's dramatized version became well known everywhere, and he attracted the attention of Elia Kazan.

Death of a Salesman, produced in 1949, was awarded the Pulitzer Prize for drama and Miller himself won recognition as a strong rival to Tennessee Williams as the best young American playwright. The Kazan production was carried almost without rewriting into a movie; through both successes the play itself became a best seller for the armchair theater critics.

At least in part for criticism of his political activities, Arthur Miller wrote a stinging condemnation of twentieth century witch-hunting in *The Crucible*, purportedly about the Salem witch trials. *A View from the Bridge* was made up of two one-act plays, "A Memory of Two Mondays" and the title piece. The printed version contained a long preface, "On Social Plays," in which Miller defined and defended his position as a playwright.

BIBLIOGRAPHICAL REFERENCES: *Collected Plays*, 1957, is a very convenient volume for students of Arthur Miller; it includes a provocative introduction by the author. Articles by two drama critics who covered the plays may be found in Brooks Atkinson, *Along Broadway*, 1947; and John Mason Brown, *Still Seeing Things*, 1950. A valuable study of the development of Miller's basic themes is William Wiegand, "Arthur Miller and the Man Who Knows," *Western Review*, XXI (1957), 85–103. See also *Time*, LIII (February 21, 1949), 74–76; D. E. Schneider, "Play of Dreams," *Theatre Arts Monthly*, XXXIII (1949), 18–21; and Paul N. Siegel, "Willy Loman and King Lear," *College English*, XVII (1956), 341–345.

JOHN MILTON

Born: London, England
Date: December 9, 1608

Died: London
Date: November 8, 1674

PRINCIPAL WORKS

POEMS: *Poems,* 1645 (containing "On the Morning of Christ's Nativity," "L'Allegro," "Il Penseroso," "Lycidas," and other lyrics); *Paradise Lost,* 1667; *Paradise Regained,* 1671; *Samson Agonistes,* 1671.

MASQUE: *Comus,* 1634 (printed 1637).

PAMPHLETS AND TRACTS: *Of Reformation Touching Church Discipline,* 1641; *The Doctrine and Discipline of Divorce,* 1643; *Of Education,* 1644; *Areopagitica,* 1644; *Of the Tenure of Kings and Magistrates,* 1649; *Eikonoklastes,* 1649; *Pro Populo Anglicano Defensio,* 1651.

John Milton was born when the summer of Elizabethan joy was yielding to the autumn of Jacobean folly and the winter of Puritan discontent. The day was December 9, 1608; the place, above his father's scrivener's shop, Bread Street, Cheapside, London.

The future poet's grandfather, Richard Milton, a yeoman and underranger, lived near Oxford. Unswervingly Roman Catholic, he disinherited his son John for joining the Church of England. The latter, however, fared to London, where he earned a satisfactory fortune to provide comforts for himself, his wife, and their three children, John, Christopher, and Anne. The home above the Bread Street shop must have possessed a cultural, artistic air, for John senior was a musician and composer; and when the firstborn child showed eagerness for reading and study there was ample parental encouragement. The boy John enrolled as a day student at St. Paul's School and was also tutored privately by a Scottish curate, Thomas Young. At St. Paul's the lad formed an abiding friendship with Charles Diodati—"perhaps the warmest human relationship which Milton ever experienced."

In 1625, when sixteen, Milton entered Christ's College, Cambridge. Fellow students dubbed him the "Lady of Christ's"—referring derisively to his meticulous conduct or more complimentarily to his benignly handsome face. The one visible rift in his Cambridge career occurred in 1627, when because of a disagreement with his tutor, William Chappell, he was briefly suspended. His period of rustication proved enjoyable, however, for he went up to London, attended theaters, visited parks, and eyed city girls. Returning to Cambridge, he was allowed a new tutor. Besides studying consistently, he wrote Latin verse and several English poems, the best being "On the Morning of Christ's Nativity." On schedule he took the B.A. and M.A. degrees and departed from the university in 1632.

John Milton's father had wanted his son to take holy orders in the Established Church, but, when the young man was averse to the ministry and to the Church of England itself, the parent attempted no coercion. Undoubtedly he remembered the bitterness of his own father's attitude.

The young university graduate showed no interest in a business or profession. Fortunately his father, with means sufficient, had retired to Horton, a village in Buckinghamshire, seventeen miles west of London. From 1632 to 1638 John lived quietly and pleasantly under the parental roof, where, according to his own statement, he "spent a long holiday turning over the Latin and Greek authors." At Horton his poetic genius flowered in "L'Allegro," a glorification of the mirthful man; "Il Penseroso," an extolling of the pensive soul; *Comus,* a masque; and "Lycidas," a combination elegy and satire, which berated corrupt members of the clergy—"blind mouths," whom he was finding increasingly offensive.

Visiting Italy in 1638, Milton met the scientist Galileo. He returned to England in August, 1639, as threats of civil conflict grew constantly darker. In the ensuing war between Charles I and Parliament, Milton espoused the latter cause as the people's fight for freedom. He was no soldier, but he battled with his pen. In 1649 he was appointed Latin Secretary to Oliver Cromwell, with the duty of translating foreign diplomatic correspondence. Moreover, he voluntarily composed propaganda pamphlets. So strong was his sense of consecration that, though his doctor warned continued writing would cost his eyesight, he completed his *Defence of the English People*—an attempted justification of the execution of King Charles. He paid the predicted price: at forty-three he became totally blind. With Andrew Marvell as his assistant, he retained the Latin secretaryship until dismissed by General Monk in 1659.

Milton's religion typified the man and the time. A Christian trinitarian in a broadly orthodox sense, he found short contentment with any sect. After Episcopal rearing, he turned Presby-terian, only later, dissatisfied, to aver, "New *Presbyter* is but old *Priest* writ large." Independent best characterizes him. Prelatic authoritarianism of any flavor offended him. "True religion is the true worship and service of God, learned and believed from the word of God only," he wrote. And further: "Heresy . . . is a religion taken up and believed from the traditions of men, and additions to the word of God."

With the restoration of Charles II in 1660 Milton went into uneasy retirement in London and in the village of Chalfont St. Giles near Horton. The Royalist government, reinstated by a Puritan-sickened, Cromwell-sated citizenry, did him no harm.

Milton married three times. His first wife, Mary Powell, the seventeen-year-old daughter of a Cavalier squire, left him shortly after their wedding in 1643. Their separation might have been permanent had the king's troops been victorious; but when in 1645 Cromwell's triumph became too apparent, Mary, spurred by relatives who needed an alliance on the winning side, sought her husband, fell on her knees, and effected a reconciliation. She bore Milton three daughters—Anne, Mary, and Deborah—and a son who died in infancy. The wife herself died in 1652. The second marriage was in 1656 to Katharine Woodcock, who survived only fifteen months. The third wife, Elizabeth Minshull, wedding the blind poet in 1663, outlived him.

As early as 1639 Milton had wanted to write a master poem. Whether it should be epic or dramatic, national or religious, he long pondered. By 1642 he had a list of subjects, but the Civil War and his prosaic tasks for the Commonwealth delayed his start. He accom-

757

plished his literary ambition only when physical blindness permitted spiritual visions and when political defeat provided leisure necessary for contemplation. About 1658 he began *Paradise Lost* and in 1663 completed it. This blank verse religious epic in twelve books is unique in the English language. Its purpose, to "justify the ways of God to men," transcends sectarianism. Its allegory of Satan, Sin, and Death at the gates of Hell; its graphic scenes of Heaven's war; its unintentional humor in the embellished account of Adam's fall; its softly cadenced final lines—all enthrall one's soul like the majestic music of a cathedral organ. The sequel epic, *Paradise Regained*—a paraphrase of Christ's temptations—is inferior in quantity and poetic quality.

Milton's final long poem, *Samson Agonistes,* is religious drama. Its blind protagonist, duped by Dalila, imprisoned by Philistines, dying in victory, is an autobiographical figure.

The poet's strength, like Samson's, ebbed. Happily in his last years his wife Elizabeth was diligent to comfort him. He in turn was vocally appreciative. His custom was to rise at four or five, hear a chapter of the Bible, eat and drink temperately, get someone to lead him about the streets for exercise, listen to music, smoke a pipe of tobacco, and dictate to any available amanuensis. In "his house, near Bunhill Fields, without Moorgate" a visitor saw him in "black clothes, and neat enough, pale but not cadaverous, his hands and fingers gouty and with chalk-stones." Death came on Sunday, November 8, 1674. His remains were buried near his father's in the chancel of St. Giles' Church, Cripplegate, while in the glory of world-wide epic creation

". . . his clear Sprite
Yet reigns o'er earth; the third among the sons of light."

M. Clifford Harrison

BIBLIOGRAPHICAL REFERENCES: The standard modern edition is that edited by F. A. Patterson and others, 18 vols., 1931–1938. The standard biography is David Masson, *The Life of John Milton,* 7 vols., 1881–1896 (rev. ed.). The best biography of recent years is J. H. Hanford, *John Milton, Englishman,* 1949. For biography and criticism see also Walter Raleigh, *Milton,* 1900; N. G. Tarrant, *John Milton,* 1908; Alden Sampson, *Studies in Milton,* 1913; Robert Bridges, *Milton's Prosody,* 1921 (rev. ed.); E. M. W. Tillyard, *The Miltonic Setting, Past and Present,* 1938; C. S. Lewis, *A Preface to Paradise Lost,* 1942; Douglas Bush, *Paradise Lost in Our Time,* 1945; C. M. Bowra, *From Vergil to Milton,* 1945; J. S. Diekhoff, *Milton's Paradise Lost: A Commentary,* 1946; B. Rajan, *Paradise Lost and the Seventeenth Century Reader,* 1947; F. M. Krouse, *Milton's Samson and the Christian Tradition,* 1949; James Thorpe, ed., *Milton Criticism: Selections from Four Centuries,* 1950; Cleanth Brooks and J. E. Hardy, eds., *Poems of Mr. John Milton with Essays in Analysis,* 1951; E. M. W. Tillyard, *Studies in Milton,* 1951; also T. S. Eliot, "Milton," *Sewanee Review,* LVI (1948), 185–209; and A. S. P. Woodhouse, "Pattern in *Paradise Lost," University of Toronto Quarterly,* XXII (1953), 109–127.

MARGARET MITCHELL

Born: Atlanta, Georgia   *Died:* Atlanta
Date: November 8, 1900   *Date:* August 16, 1949

NOVEL: *Gone with the Wind,* 1936.

Margaret (Munnerlyn) Mitchell, born in Atlanta, Georgia, on November 8, 1900, was the daughter of Eugene Muse Mitchell, an attorney and president of the Atlanta Historical Society. Atlanta's history meant Civil War history and the perceptive young daughter of the Mitchell household developed a keen interest in this event and its lingering impact even as a child. What she later did with this lore caused the biggest splash in American publishing history. To describe her one novel requires superlatives: biggest seller in a single day (50,000 copies) and in a single year (2,000,000 copies); most widely translated (22 languages); longest fiction translated into Braille (30 volumes); greatest motion picture hit (seen by 91,000,000 people in 17,000 theaters, earned a profit of $30,000,000 for producers). Margaret Mitchell attended Smith College for one year and later received an honorary M.A. degree from that institution. Required to return home when her mother died, she started a career in journalism on the Atlanta *Journal* as "Peggy Mitchell" in 1922.

Three years later she married John R. Marsh, a power company executive, to whom she dedicated her book. A year later a slow-healing sprained ankle caused her to resign her position with the newspaper and the ten-year writing job which resulted in *Gone with the Wind* got under way, the last part first.

The title taken from Ernest Dowson's poem "Cynara," *Gone with the Wind* was published on June 30, 1936, and among the many awards which followed were the Pulitzer Prize in 1937 and the American Booksellers' Association award in the same year. The book owes its immense popular appeal to its sustained narrative and the finely drawn characters. Scarlett O'Hara and Rhett Butler become vivid personalities whose all-too-human emotions absorb the reader and keep him racing along through 1,037 pages.

Margaret Mitchell wrote no other book. On a summer evening in 1949 she was struck down by a taxicab on an Atlanta street and died shortly thereafter, on August 16.

BIBLIOGRAPHICAL REFERENCES: Biographical and critical material on Margaret Mitchell is scarce. For brief discussions see Frank Ernest Mott, *Golden Multitudes,* 1947, 255–258; and Ernest E. Leisy, *The American Historical Novel,* 1950, 171–173. See also "Backdrop for Atlanta," *Time,* XXVIII (July 6, 1936), 62; and Editorial, *Saturday Review of Literature,* XVII (January 8, 1938), 8.

S. WEIR MITCHELL

Born: Philadelphia, Pennsylvania   *Died:* Philadelphia
Date: February 15, 1829   *Date:* January 4, 1914

PRINCIPAL WORKS

NOVELS: *In War Time,* 1885; *Roland Blake,* 1886; *Far in the Forest,* 1889; *Characteristics,* 1892; *When All the Woods Are Green,* 1894; *Hugh Wynne, Free*

Quaker, 1897; *The Adventures of François*, 1899; *Dr. North and His Friends*, 1900; *Circumstance*, 1901; *Constance Trescott*, 1905; *The Red City*, 1907; *John Sherwood, Iron Master*, 1911; *Westways*, 1913.

NOVELETTES AND SHORT STORIES: *Thee and You*, 1880; *Hephzibah Guinness*, 1880; *Little Stories*, 1903; *A Diplomatic Adventure*, 1906; *The Guillotine Club and Other Stories*, 1910.

POEMS: *Collected Poems*, 1896; *The Wager*, 1900.

S(ilas) Weir Mitchell, life-long Philadelphian, earned an immortal niche in the history of American medicine before achieving a somewhat more modest place in American letters. Born February 15, 1829, the son of a doctor and academician, Mitchell received his medical degree at twenty-one and went to Paris to study under Claude Bernard, the famous physiologist. He returned to do pioneer research in a variety of fields (such as the discovery of the double-poison in snake venom), but he is most famous for his "rest cure" therapy of neurotics. A specialist in neurology and toxicology, he published a total of 171 scientific papers, mostly in the field of neurology. From this experience he learned to make the careful psychological analyses which pervade his fiction. Powerfully drawn to literature, he postponed, on the advice of physician-author Oliver Wendell Holmes, serious commitment to a literary career until he was well established as a neurologist; but after 1880 he published on the average of a book of poems or fiction every year until his death.

Mitchell's brother, first wife, and daughter, all died of diphtheria, and his second wife outlived him only a few days, but his son succeeded to his practice just as Mitchell had succeeded his father. In his later years he enjoyed considerable prestige as trustee of his alma mater, the University of Pennsylvania, as president of the Franklin Inn, and as recipient of honorary de-grees from the leading European and American universities. Despite his professional experimentation, he was basically a conservative and highly moralistic personality, dramatic evidence of which was displayed when he flung the Philadelphia Public Library copy of Freud into the fire.

His poems except for "Ode on a Lycian Tomb," an elegy to his daughter, have not outlived him, but his novels are still read by the general public as curiosa and by students of literature as forerunners of the modern psychological novel. "The Case of George Dedlow," his first story, concerned a Civil War basket case; it was published anonymously in the *Atlantic Monthly* in 1886. His first novel, *In War Time*, has for its setting a Philadelphia army hospital and portrays the moral weakness of a Dr. Ezra Wendell; *Roland Blake* has as its central character Octopia Darnell, a neurotic woman whose bold characterization caused a minor revolution in American fiction in 1886; she was the first of a series of possessive feminine neurotics he depicted in his fiction. *Hugh Wynne, Free Quaker*, written in six weeks and considered his masterpiece, is a historical novel, based on his own eighteenth century ancestors. This is the most popular novel of the American Revolution ever written. Although a romance, the novel contains realistic character studies of such actual person-

760

ages as Washington, Hamilton, Benedict Arnold, Dr. Benjamin Rush, and other figures of the time. *The Adventures of François,* a novel of Paris in the days of the French Revolution, was his own favorite. In *Characteristics* and its sequel, *Dr. North and His Friends,*

Mitchell experimented with a new type of fiction, a combination of narrative, essay, and dialogue. In his later works he returned to the historical themes which had established his reputation. He died in Philadelphia on January 4, 1914.

BIBLIOGRAPHICAL REFERENCES: Mitchell's writings were collected in the Author's Definitive Edition, 16 vols., 1913–1914. The standard biography is Anna Robeson Burr, *Weir Mitchell, His Life and Letters,* 1929, but this work has been superseded in large part by Ernest Earnest, *S. Weir Mitchell, Novelist and Physician,* 1950. See also Charles W. Burr, *S. Weir Mitchell, Physician, Man of Science, Man of Letters, Man of Affairs,* 1920; Charles R. Brown, *They Were Giants,* 1934; Arthur Hobson Quinn, *American Fiction,* 1936; Felix E. Schelling, "S. Weir Mitchell, Poet and Novelist," in *Shakespeare Biography and Other Papers,* 1937; and Max Farrand, "Hugh Wynne, A Historical Novel," *Washington Historical Quarterly,* I (1907), 101–108.

MARY RUSSELL MITFORD

Born: Alresford, England
Date: December 16, 1787

Died: Swallowfield, England
Date: January 10, 1855

PRINCIPAL WORKS

TALES AND SKETCHES: *Our Village; Sketches of Rural Character and Scenery,* 1824–1832; *Belford Regis; or Sketches of a Country Town,* 1835; *Country Stories,* 1847; *Atherton and Other Tales,* 1854.

PLAYS: *Julian,* 1823; *The Foscari,* 1826; *Rienzi,* 1828; *Charles the First,* 1834.

POEMS: *Miscellaneous Verses,* 1806; *Christina, The Maid of the South Seas,* 1806; *Blanche,* 1806; *Miscellaneous Poems,* 1810; *Watling Hill,* 1812.

Mary Russell Mitford, born at Alresford, Hampshire, on December 16, 1787, was the only child of Dr. George Mitford, a country physician who was better known as a gambler and spendthrift than as a practitioner of medicine, but who had, apparently, the charm to inspire an attitude of unquestioning adoration in his frail but talented daughter. In any case, a single-minded devotion to her father stands out as the main theme of Miss Mitford's personal life and as the direct practical motivation of her writing, for in an attempt to recoup the second fortune squandered by her father she

turned from the unprofitable composition of poems to the writing of those discerning sketches of rural life that remain her most important contribution to literature.

The first squandered fortune had been her mother's; the second had been her own, the winnings from the lottery ticket her father had given her on her tenth birthday. This prize of twenty thousand pounds provided both for her father's ostentatious living and for her own education at a French school in London (1798–1802), where she distinguished herself in the study of Romance literature.

With the dissipation of the lottery winnings by 1822, she turned from the long sentimental poems she had been writing and began a professional literary campaign on two fronts. Her first play, *Julian*, was produced in 1823, and in 1819 the first series of *Our Village* sketches appeared in the *Ladies' Magazine*. Three more plays saw production in the next twelve years. The *Our Village* sketches were published in book form in 1824, with four more volumes added to the series by 1832. The success of her fiction allowed her to continue writing in this congenial vein. She edited a collection of American sketches in 1832, published *Belford Regis,* another series of sketches based on the pattern of *Our Village,* in 1835, and ended her career with *Atherton and Other Tales* in 1854.

During this time she remained unmarried and in poor health: her father, who lived until she was fifty-six, claimed all her affection as well as all her money; she survived him only by eleven years, dying at Swallowfield on January 10, 1855.

BIBLIOGRAPHICAL REFERENCES: Biographical studies include William J. Roberts, *Mary Russell Mitford: Her Life and Friendship,* 1913; Marjorie Astin, *Mary Russell Mitford: Her Circle and Her Books,* 1930; Vera Watson, *Mary Russell Mitford,* 1949; and Caroline Mary Duncan-Jones, *Miss Mitford and Mr. Harness: Records of a Friendship,* 1955. There are numerous collections of her letters: *The Life of Mary Russell Mitford in a Selection of Her Letters,* edited by A. G. K. L'Estrange, 3 vols., 1870; *Letters of Mary Russell Mitford,* edited by Henry Chorley, 1872; *The Friendship of Mary Russell Mitford in Letters,* edited by A. G. K. L'Estrange, 2 vols., 1882; and her *Correspondence with Charles Boner and John Ruskin,* edited by Elizabeth Lee, 1915.

MOLIÈRE
(Jean Baptiste Poquelin)

Baptized: Paris, France　　　　　　*Died:* Paris
Date: January 15, 1622　　　　　　*Date:* February 17, 1673

PRINCIPAL WORKS

PLAYS: *Les Précieuses ridicules,* 1659 (*The Romantic Ladies*); *L'École des maris,* 1661 (*The School for Husbands*); *Les Fâcheux,* 1661 (*The Bores*); *L'École des femmes,* 1662 (*The School for Wives*); *Tartuffe,* 1664; *Don Juan,* 1665; *L'Amour médecin,* 1665 (*Love as a Doctor*); *Le Médecin malgré lui,* 1666 (*The Doctor in Spite of Himself*); *Le Misanthrope,* 1666; *Amphitryon,* 1668; *Georges Dandin,* 1668; *L'Avare,* 1668 (*The Miser*); *Le Bourgeois gentilhomme,* 1670 (*The Bourgeois Gentleman*); *Les Femmes savantes,* 1672 (*The Learned Ladies*); *Le Malade imaginaire,* 1673 (*The Hypochondriac*).

Not much of the detail of Molière's life is known, but of his reputation as France's comic genius there is no doubt. He was a popular and appreciated playwright in his lifetime; since his death his fame has spread and his plays continue to delight audiences.

Jean Baptiste Poquelin was baptized on January 15, 1622, in the Parisian church of Saint Eustache. In all probability he was born on the same day. His father Jean was a prosperous upholsterer who held a royal commission. His mother was Marie Cressé.

At the age of ten Jean Baptiste was sent to the Collège de Clermont, a school conducted by the Jesuits. Afterward he studied law and perhaps in 1641 took a law degree at Orléans. It is thought that in 1642 he accompanied Louis XIII to Narbonne and Lyons as a substitute for his father. Somehow during these formative years he fell in love with the theater, a love he never lost. According to legend his maternal grandfather took him often to performances at the Hôtel de Bourgogne. In any event, in 1643 he formed with three members of the Béjart family a theatrical company called L'Illustre Théâtre.

The leading spirit of the Béjarts was Madeleine, a woman five years older than Jean Baptiste, experienced in acting and in love-making. It must have been a scandal, for the Poquelin family was solid bourgeois and acting as a profession was held in low esteem. Jean Baptiste's infatuation for Madeleine lasted for years until it cooled to friendship. Until her death Madeleine was his guide, business helper, and leading actress.

The young company tried out briefly in Rouen, and then returned to Paris under the patronage of Gaston, Duc d'Orléans. By 1644 the company had failed; Jean Baptiste had begun signing his name Molière; and as the director of the troupe he had been in prison three times for debt. To escape their troubles, Molière and the Béjarts joined another company under Dufresne and spent the years from 1645 to 1658 in the provinces, chiefly at Lyons. Tradition has it that this provincial apprenticeship was difficult and filled with hardship; in fact, the life of strolling players was anything but easy. Molière, however, soon advanced to the position of director, and the patronage of the Duc d'Épernon stood him in good stead even during the civil wars of the Fronde. At Lyons, probably in 1655, he produced his first play, *L'Étourdi* (*The Blunderer*). He added a number of actors to his troupe, among them Mlles. duParc and deBrie. Again according to legend he enjoyed the favors of both.

In October of 1658 Molière returned to Paris under the sponsorship of the king's brother. The production of *The Romantic Ladies* on November 18, 1659, made him the most discussed dramatist of the day. This satire exposed mercilessly the affectations of high society, particularly the fashionable preciosity in speech. In spite of the controversy raised in the elegant world by the play, Molière continued to please most playgoers. He was astute enough also to court the young Louis XIV, and royal patronage helped him maintain his preëminence.

The School for Husbands and *The School for Wives* were both concerned with the theme of an aging husband married to a young wife. This theme was a reflection of his own life; for on February 20, 1662, he married Armande Béjart, the nineteen-year-old sister of his mistress Madeleine. The marriage was not happy for a number of reasons; in all probability Armande was guilty of indiscretions with her gallant admirers.

The next few years were difficult ones. Both *Tartuffe* and *Don Juan* were censured by secular and ecclesiastical authorities. In spite of the friendship of Louis XIV, Molière had difficulty in presenting these dramas. (*Tartuffe*, although written five years before, could not be presented in its entirety until 1669.) In 1665 occurred the famous break with Racine, who took his *Alexandre* away from Molière's company and gave it to a rival troupe. The following year Molière suffered an attack of pleurisy which left both lungs affected. Although *The Doctor in Spite of Himself* was a great success, he lost heavily on his production of Corneille's *Attila*. About this time Molière was estranged from Armande. The couple were not reunited until 1671, just before the death of Madeleine. In 1672 their son and third child was born.

In 1673 Molière was playing in *The Hypochondriac*. He gave his usual fine performance at the fourth showing of the new play, but afterward he complained of his health. He died that same night. His widow had to appeal to both the Archbishop of Paris and the king for permission to have Molière buried in sanctified ground. Ironically, the Archbishop de Champvallon, who so grudgingly allowed space in a cemetery but forbade church services and required burial at night, was himself a libertine of scandalous repute.

Molière's entire adult life was intimately allied with the theater. In addition to writing plays, he directed and acted; and for many years he was manager of his own company. As a person, he seems to have been attractive to women but much less so to men. His well-publicized connections with La Fontaine and Racine were literary rather than personal. He was unexcelled as a comic actor in spite of his halting speech. Unlike many in his profession, he became wealthy. He was shrewd in cultivating royal favor and hard-headed in business. More important is the fact that Molière left a canon of comedy unique in Western literature.

All his plays are marked by humor and good sense. Many of his scenes are broadly farcical, but underneath the buffoonery is a steady and searching criticism of society. He is never bitter or pompous, and his continued appeal to readers and playgoers is testimony of his understanding of man.

Russell Cosper

BIBLIOGRAPHICAL REFERENCES: The standard collected edition in French is the *Œuvres de Molière*, edited by Eugene Despois and Pierre Mesnard, 1873–1927. It includes the best biography of Molière, and a bibliography complete up to 1893. There are several collected editions in translation; among these is *The Plays of Molière in French and English*, edited by A. R. Waller, 1907, which includes an introduction by George Saintsbury. A single volume of selected plays is *Plays by Molière*, Modern Library edition, 1924, with an introduction by Waldo Frank.

The standard critical study in English is Brander Matthews, *Molière, His Life and His Works*, 1916. Other excellent studies are John Leslie Palmer, *Molière*, 1930, with a selected bibliography; and Henry C. Lancaster, *A History of French Dramatic Literature in the Seventeenth Century*, Part III, *The Period of Molière*, 1652–1672, 2 vols., 1936. Other studies can be found in Ferdinand Brunetière, *Essays in French Literature*, 1898; Charles A. Sainte-Beuve, *Portraits of the Seventeenth Century*, translated 1904; Martin Turnell, *The Classical Moment; Studies of Corneille, Molière, and Racine*, 1948; Elbert B.O.E. Borgerhoff, *The Freedom of French Classicism*, 1950; François Mauriac, *Men I Hold Great*, 1951; H. Carrington Lancaster, *Literary Masterpieces of the Western World*, 1953; and Georges Poulet,

Studies in Human Times, 1956. For French readers, see the excellent articles in Jules Lemaître, Impressions de Théâtre, 1920, (Vols. 1, 3, 4, 6, 8, and 11).

See also W. G. Moore, "Tartuffe and the Comic Principle in Molière," Modern Language Review, XLIII (1948), 47–53; and Theophil Spoerri, "The Smile of Molière," Yale French Studies, V (1950), 51–65.

FERENC MOLNAR

Born: Budapest, Hungary   Died: New York, N. Y.
Date: January 12, 1878   Date: April 1, 1952

Principal Works

PLAYS: Az ördög, 1907 (The Devil); Liliom, 1909; A testör, 1910 (The Guardsman); A hattyú, 1920 (The Swan); Játék a kastélyban, 1925 (The Play's the Thing); Olympia, 1928.

NOVELS: Egy gazdátlan csónak története, 1901 (The Derelict Boat); Éva, 1903; Rabok, 1907 (Prisoners); A Pál-uccai fiuk, 1907 (The Paul Street Boys); Zenélö angyal, 1933 (Angel Making Music).

REPORTAGE: Haditudósitó naplója, 1916 (The Diary of a War Correspondent).

Born in Budapest, into a wealthy Jewish merchant family, on January 12, 1878, Ferenc Molnar lived the life that he so often characterized in his plays: the witty, sophisticated, leisured life of the cultured bohemian. He was educated as a lawyer, at the universities in Budapest and Geneva, and his first literary work was a brilliant discussion of the psychology of crime. By the time he was eighteen he was writing for a Budapest paper whose circulation he increased greatly by his scintillatingly witty essays and character sketches; he also married the editor's daughter, Margaret Vaszi. He was soon divorced, only to marry and then remarry—his third wife was the celebrated Hungarian beauty and actress, notable for her successes with Max Reinhardt, Lili Darvas. During World War I he served as a war correspondent for the Central Powers, but he remained neutral politically between the two wars.

While he wrote much fiction—little has been translated into English—his dramas were his forte with the exception of the novel, The Paul Street Boys, a story of a Hungarian adolescence. The Devil, his first important play, came out that same year. This work shows the Devil as an engaging fellow who is a master of means to marital infidelity. Liliom first appeared two years later, unsuccessfully, only to become one of the most produced plays of the century ten years later. This roughneck barker hero, who became Billy Bigelow in the American musical version, Carousel, epitomizes the modern misfit who can do no good no matter how good his intentions. The Guardsman is a witty play on the triangle theme in which the husband disguises himself in order to find out if his wife will carry on a flirtation; she ends by informing him that she was aware of the disguise all along. In The Swan the young princess who falls in love below her station is advised to give up her tutor friend rather than go out into a world where her regal qualities will only be grotesque like a swan out of water. His final important work, *The Play's the Thing*, contains a most delightful play-within-a-play, contrived by a group of theatrical folk to prevent a young actress from straying from her composer fiancé. In all these plays, except perhaps *Liliom*, the romantic, effervescent touch of the charming and elegant playwright makes for exceptionally good theater. But Molnar's brilliance of writing faded fast, and his latter years were spent in reliving his former successes.

In the early years of the last war, Molnar settled in the United States where he continued to write plays which proved to be only potboilers. Recent productions of his best works may have encouraged him in his latter years; however, he could never re-create the charm and gaiety his writing possessed in his long-lost youth. He died in New York City, April 1, 1952.

BIBLIOGRAPHICAL REFERENCES: A convenient volume is *The Plays of Ferenc Molnar*, 1929. The only biography seems to be George Halasz, *Ferenc Molnar, the Man Behind the Monocle*, 1929. Of primary importance is Emro J. Gergely, *Hungarian Drama in New York, American Adaptations, 1908–1940*, 1947, with a bibliography. See also Frank W. Chandler, *Modern Continental Playwrights*, 1931.

MICHEL EYQUEM DE MONTAIGNE

Born: Near Bordeaux, France
Date: February 28, 1533

Died: Near Bordeaux
Date: September 13, 1592

PRINCIPAL WORKS

ESSAYS: *Essais*, Books I–II, 1580; Books I–II, revised, 1582; Books I–II, revised, with Book III, 1588; Books I–III, further revised and augmented, 1595.

The father of Michel de Montaigne, Pierre Eyquem, was a wealthy trader whose grandfather, Ramon Eyquem, had acquired the Château de Montaigne, near the town of Castellan, in Périgord, in the last quarter of the fifteenth century. In his youth, Pierre Eyquem had served in the armies of Francis I, but had returned to became a prominent citizen of Bordeaux and at length its mayor. His wife, Antoinette de Lopez (or Louppes), member of a Jewish family of Spanish derivation, had embraced the Protestant faith. Michel Eyquem, their third child and eldest son, was born at the Château de Montaigne on February 28, 1533; in maturity he chose to discard his patronymic in favor of the estate name. The future essayist was baptized a Catholic and was reared without his mother's direct supervision; at his father's insistence he had nurses and godparents selected from the peasantry. Montaigne reports that in childhood, by a pleasant conceit of his father's, he was always awakened by the playing of music. Pierre Eyquem had further resolved that his son should learn no French before becoming proficient in Latin; the tutor set over him was a German who was directed to use Latin to make himself understood. The servants being required to follow the tutor's example, the boy spoke no other language before the age of six. He was then sent to the College of Guienne, at Bordeaux, where he improved his acquaintance with Latin literature. It is recorded that he distinguished himself in the performance of Latin plays written by his masters, including the poet George Buchanan.

At thirteen he was withdrawn from the college and went, it is believed, to Toulouse, to read law in preparation for an official career. In these circumstances he formed a friendship with a fellow lawyer a few years his senior, Étienne de la Boétie, who exerted a strong influence on his character and opinions. After a journey with his father to Paris, he undertook, in 1557, a legal practice at the Parlement of Bordeaux, but he seems to have stayed there only a year. He was in royal service at the siege of Thionville in 1558, and on occasions in 1559 and 1560 he attended court functions. In the next seventeen years he was intermittently employed in advisory and diplomatic capacities. Charles IX, Henry III, and Henry of Navarre all gave him commissions of trust; at length, in 1577, Henry of Navarre, duplicating the honor accorded to Montaigne by Henry III, appointed him Gentleman Ordinary of the King's Chamber. But the bestowal of the Order of St. Michael, in 1571, really marked the end of his active career in the service of the court. He had been married in 1565 to Françoise de la Chassaigne, and the responsibilities of his estate, which he had inherited at his father's death three years thereafter, as well as his own distaste for the violence of political life urged him into retirement. On his thirty-eighth birthday (a few weeks before the close of the year 1571, according to the reckoning then in use), he formally carried out his determination to go into seclusion and devote himself to learning, and he caused a

Latin memorial of this action to be inscribed on the walls of his study.

The first memoranda for the famous *Essais* may be dated from 1572. Montaigne was horrified by the massacre of St. Bartholomew's Day, and his early essays took on a philosophic complexion in response to the turbulence of the age. Already he was expressing the dispassionate view of life, the humane tolerance for which he was to become celebrated. Stimulated by the reading of Seneca and the Stoics and of Plutarch, whose *Moralia* and *Lives* had newly appeared in Jacques Amyot's French translation, and fortified in mind by an undogmatic skepticism proceeding necessarily from his reverence for truth, he set forth his personal reflections with a frankness compatible with his announced purpose of writing for himself and not for the world. But his actual intention was otherwise; he wished both to teach and to influence, and in his aspiration he has been amply justified. After the first edition of the *Essais* in 1580, he enlarged his work to three books in the third edition of 1588. The essence of his thought is to be found in the long essay "Apology for Raimond Sebond," in the second book. This composition, ostensibly a vindication of Sebond's tractate *Theologia naturalis* (*Natural Theology*), which Montaigne at his father's behest had translated into French and had later published (1569), seems in fact to constitute a reasoned assault on the dogmas of Christianity.

In 1579, having suffered an attack of the stone and believing his life to be threatened, he came out of retirement and braved a tour lasting almost a year and a half through Germany and Switzerland to Italy. While abroad, he learned that arrangements had been made to elect him mayor of Bordeaux. Yielding to the king's desire, he accepted the office and in 1583 allowed himself to be re-elected for a second term of two years. In 1588 he traveled to Paris to see the third edition of the *Essais* through the press. Through the machinations of the Catholic League, he was briefly imprisoned, but was released at the instance of Catherine de Médicis. In Paris he became friends with Marie de Jars de Gournay, a young woman of great learning, whom he honored with the title of "daughter by adoption." She, after his death, obtained from his widow a copy of the 1588 edition profusely annotated by him, and with it she established a revised text; this, when corrected by means of another annotated copy that Mme. Montaigne had presented to a convent at Bordeaux, formed the basis of the practically definitive fourth edition of 1595.

After receiving the last rites of the Church, Montaigne died of quinsy on September 13, 1592, at the Château de Montaigne.

BIBLIOGRAPHICAL REFERENCES: The definitive edition in English is *The Complete Works of Montaigne,* translated by Donald M. Frame, 1957—a monumental work containing the essays, travel journal, and letters. The standard edition of the *Essais* was edited by F. Strowski and others, 5 vols., 1906–1933. The *Essays* have also been translated into English by E. J. Trechmann, 1946; this edition contains an important critical introduction by J. M. Robertson.

For studies of Montaigne in English see Mary E. Lowndes, *Michel de Montaigne,* 1898, still valuable for its account of Montaigne's life and character; Grace Norton, *Studies in Montaigne,* 1904; Edward Dowden, *Michel de Montaigne,* 1905, containing an excellent bibliography; Alan M. Boase, *The Fortune of Montaigne in France, 1580–1669,* 1935; and Donald M. Frame, *Montaigne's Discovery of Man: The Humanization of a Humanist,* 1955; in French, Paul Bonnefon, *Montaigne, l'homme et l'œuvre,* 1893, and *Montaigne et ses amis,* 1898; Paul Stapfer, *Montaigne,* in the *Grands écrivains,* 1895; Pierre Villey, *Les Sources et l'évolution des Essais,* 1908; André Gide, *Essai sur Montaigne,* 1929; Pierre Moreau, *Montaigne, l'homme et l'œuvre,* 1939; Charles Dédéyan, *Montaigne chez ses amis anglo-saxons,* 1946; and Pierre Barrière, *Montaigne, gentilhomme français,* 1948.

CHARLES DE MONTESQUIEU

Born: Near Bordeaux, France
Date: January 18, 1689

Died: Paris, France
Date: February 10, 1755

PRINCIPAL WORKS

SATIRE: *Lettres persanes,* 1721 (*Persian Letters*).

POLITICAL PHILOSOPHY: *Considérations sur les causes de la grandeur et de la décadence des Romains,* 1734 (*Considerations of the Sources of the Grandeur and Decadence of the Romans*); *L'Esprit des lois,* 1748 (*The Spirit of the Laws*).

Charles Louis de Secondat, Baron de la Brède et de Montesquieu, was born on January 18, 1689, at Château La Brède, the French country seat of his wealthy and noble family. The title of Montesquieu came to him from a paternal uncle, while the title of La Brède came from his mother's family.

His mother died when Montesquieu was but seven years old, and soon afterward he began his education at the Oratorian School at Juilly, France. In 1716, while still a young man, Montesquieu succeeded to his uncle's title and position as president of the Bordeaux parlement. The previous year he had married a plain but wealthy heiress, Jeanne Lartigue, with whom he led a happy, if uneventful, married life.

During the period between 1716 and 1728, Montesquieu held his position as president of the Bordeaux parlement and began a career as scholar and author by contributing articles to the Bordeaux Academy on philosophical, scientific, and political subjects. His earliest work of note was his *Persian Letters,* supposedly written by two Persian gentlemen traveling in Europe, in which he satirized European society, literature, politics, and religious institutions. Proposed as a candidate for the French Academy in 1725, he was elected but not seated because of a rule that members must be residents of Paris. He finally became a member in 1728, after he had given up his presidency of the Bordeaux parlement and moved to the capital. Shortly after his election to the Academy he began a four-year tour of Europe.

Upon his return to France, Montesquieu took up residence at La Brède, rather than at Paris, and resumed his literary career. *Considerations of the Sources of the Grandeur and Decadence of the Romans* was published anonymously in 1734, but there was little secrecy about the author's identity. The work ascribed the decadence and eventual fall of Rome to the loss of political virtue and liberty. Because of his love of Parisian life, as well as the quiet of his estate at La Brède, Montesquieu took almost twenty years to produce his next and greatest book, *The Spirit of the Laws.* This thirty-one volume work, which friends advised the author not to publish, was put on the Index of the Roman Church and almost received a public censure from the Sorbonne. Both moves indicated the liberal quality of the book and the fact that it foreshadowed many later clerical and political reforms. The book soon found favor in other countries, and eventually it became the authoritative source for moderate reforms in France. This work is probably the best-written and most important early work on comparative government; aristocratic Montesquieu certainly did not realize how he was pointing the way to the French Revolution three decades after his death in Paris on February 10, 1755.

BIBLIOGRAPHICAL REFERENCES: A good introduction to Montesquieu is the essay in George Saintsbury, *French Literature and Its Masters*, 1946. For biography and criticism see H. A. Barckhausen, *Montesquieu, ses idées et ses œuvres*, 1907; Joseph Didieu, *Montesquieu, l'homme et l'œuvre*, 1943; and Pierre Barrière, *Montesquieu*, 1946. A more specialized study is F. T. H. Fletcher, *Montesquieu and English Politics*, 1939.

GEORGE MOORE

Born: County Mayo, Ireland
Date: February 24, 1852

Died: London, England
Date: January 21, 1933

NOVELS: *A Modern Lover*, 1883; *A Mummer's Wife*, 1885; *A Drama in Muslin*, 1886; *A Mere Accident*, 1887; *Spring Days*, 1888; *Mike Fletcher*, 1889; *Vain Fortune*, 1890; *Esther Waters*, 1894; *Evelyn Innes*, 1898; *Sister Teresa*, 1901; *The Lake*, 1905; *The Brook Kerith*, 1916; *Héloise and Abélard*, 1921; *Ulick and Soracha*, 1926; *Aphrodite in Aulis*, 1930.

SHORT STORIES: *Celibates*, 1895; *The Untilled Field*, 1903; *In Single Strictness*, 1922; *Peronnik the Fool*, 1926; *A Flood*, 1930.

PLAYS: *The Strike at Arlingford*, 1893; *The Bending of the Bough*, 1900; *The Apostle*, 1911; *Elizabeth Cooper*, 1913; *Esther Waters*, 1913; *The Coming of Gabrielle*, 1920; *The Making of an Immortal*, 1927; *The Passing of the Essenes*, 1930.

AUTOBIOGRAPHY: *Confessions of a Young Man*, 1888; *Memoirs of My Dead Life*, 1906; *Hail and Farewell!* 1911–1914 (*Ave*, 1911; *Salve*, 1912; *Vale*, 1914); *Avowals*, 1919; *Conversations in Ebury Street*, 1924.

ESSAYS AND SKETCHES: *Reminiscences of the Impressionist Painters*, 1906; *A Storyteller's Holiday*, 1918; *The Talking Pine*, 1932.

POEMS: *Flowers of Passion*, 1878; *Pagan Poems*, 1881.

The prolonged, chameleonic career of George Moore is unified only by a constant dedication to the aesthetics of literature, to the perfection of his style. Born at Moore Hall, in County Mayo, on February 24, 1852, the eldest son of a wealthy Irish landowner, horse-breeder, and M.P., Moore led a rowdy boyhood in west Ireland before his family moved to London in 1869. There Moore showed his first interest in literature and art. In 1873, on a small inherited income, he went to Paris (where Manet painted his famous portrait) to continue his studies in art. Discovering that his bent was toward the literary rather than the plastic arts, he wrote two books of Baudelairian verse, *Flowers of Passion* and *Pagan Poems*, before financial reverses forced his return to slum quarters in London. There he began the Zola-esque phase of his career and wrote a series of eight realistic novels beginning with *A Modern Lover*, an unusually frank story of a painter's sexual life in London and Paris, and *A Mummer's Wife*, a portrayal of a shopkeeper's wife who elopes with the manager of a traveling troupe of actors. In 1894 this phase of his career culminated in a major work, *Esther Waters*, the carefully disciplined, objective story of a young servant girl's seduction and struggle to rear her son to fine young manhood.

Celibates, *Evelyn Innes*, and *Sister Teresa* make up an intermediate period of fiction concerning neurotic heroes, Wagnerites, and religious sensualists, all of whom reveal Moore's responsiveness to current ideas and his readiness to experiment; eventually he expunged these works from the canon. In 1901, outraged by Kitchener's brutalities in the Boer War, Moore left England and for ten years was an active figure in the Irish Literary Renaissance. His enthusiastic experiences with the Abbey Theater and with such co-workers as Yeats, Synge, Lady Gregory, Æ, and others, are freely and maliciously recounted in his autobiographical trilogy *Hail and Farewell!* Moore's slim fictional output during this phase, definitely representing a break with

770

naturalism and an affinity for the style of Turgenev and Walter Pater, consisted of a beautiful volume of Irish stories, *The Untilled Field*; a novel, *The Lake,* about a young priest's escape from "the prison of Catholicism"; and the semi-autobiographical and ingenious *Memoirs of My Dead Life.*

After his return to England in 1911, Moore undertook a new and final phase, considered by many critics his most beautiful and polished, giving the impression he had at last achieved a goal toward which he had been moving all his life. In a powerful reaction against the religious *kitsch* art of the late Victorian and Edwardian era, he wrote *The Brook Kerith* and *Héloise and Abélard.* The former is a fantasy based on the idea that Christ did not die on the cross; rather, he was revived by Joseph and led the life of a Palestinian shepherd. In a strange yet effective climax, he encounters Paul, who has been preaching Christ's resurrection and divinity. For background material Moore traveled to Palestine and studied details of landscape and setting, but despite his careful artistry in this work there was a considerable outcry against his irreverence. *Héloise and Abélard* is a richly detailed historical novel about the famous lovers up to the moment when they are separated and about to begin their celebrated letters.

In his last years, Moore heavily revised much of his earlier work and published still glossier novels of which few have sufficient life embodied in the lacquered prose to warrant critical attention. Apart from his poems and novels, he wrote nine plays, seven volumes of reminiscence, and nine books of essays and belles-lettres. He died in London on January 21, 1933.

BIBLIOGRAPHICAL REFERENCES: Moore's writings have been collected in the Carra Edition, 21 vols., 1922–1924, and the Ebury Edition, 20 vols., 1936–1938. There are several collections of letters: *Moore versus Harris,* 1925; *Letters from George Moore to E. Dujardin, 1886–1922,* 1929; and *George Moore in Quest of Locale,* 1931. Supplementing the autobiographical books is Geraint Goodwin, *Conversations with George Moore,* 1929. The authorized biography is Joseph Hone, *The Life of George Moore,* 1936. See also John Freeman, *A Portrait of George Moore in a Study of His Work,* 1922; Humbert Wolfe, *George Moore,* 1931; and Charles Morgan, *Epitaph on George Moore,* 1935.

THOMAS MOORE

Born: Dublin, Ireland
Date: May 28, 1779

Died: Bromham, England
Date: February 25, 1852

PRINCIPAL WORKS

POEMS: *Epistles, Odes and Other Poems,* 1806; *Irish Melodies,* 1807–1834; *Lalla Rookh,* 1817; *The Loves of the Angels,* 1823.

SATIRES: *The Two-Penny Post Bag,* 1813; *The Fudge Family in Paris,* 1818; *Fables for the Holy Alliance,* 1823.

BIOGRAPHY: *Life of Sheridan,* 1825; *Life of Byron,* 1830; *Life and Death of Lord Edward Fitzgerald,* 1831.

Thomas Moore was born on May 28, 1779, the son of a prosperous Dublin merchant. After study in grammar school, he entered Trinity College, Dublin, in 1794, one of the first Roman Catholic students to be admitted to that institution. In the same year two poems by Moore appeared in the periodical *Anthologia Hibernica*. During his college years, Moore made a translation of Anacreon in verse which he took with him to London in 1799, when he entered the Middle Temple to study law; *Odes of Anacreon* was published in 1800, with an accepted dedication to the Prince of Wales. In 1803 Moore set out for Bermuda as a government appointee, but he decided en route to tour the United States and Canada and then return to England, leaving his post in charge of a deputy. *Epistles, Odes and Other Poems*, published in 1806, contains references to his travels. In 1807 he began to publish a series of volumes entitled *Irish Melodies*, with music by Sir John Stevenson. These volumes, highly popular, provided Moore with about £500 a year. During the next few years, at odds with the Regent, Moore wrote a series of satires which were collected in *The Two-Penny Post Bag* in 1813. In 1811 Moore married Bessie Dyke, a young actress, by whom he had several children, all of whom were a disappointment to their father and failed to outlive him. Real fame as a writer came to Moore with *Lalla Rookh,* a long narrative poem with Oriental flavor. Other works followed, but none was so popular or so well-remembered. A biography of Lord Byron appeared in 1830. Moore also wrote a biography of Sheridan, the famous eighteenth century playwright. A novel, *The Epicurean* (1827), was not very successful. Moore's later years, made comfortable by a government pension, were spent at Slopeton Cottage, in Wiltshire. For many non-literary people Moore remains the author of the ever-popular, romantic "Believe Me, if All Those Endearing Young Charms" and a collection of patriotic Irish airs. He also edited an edition of Byron's *Works* and *Letters and Journals* (1832–1833). He died at Bromham, England, on February 25, 1852.

BIBLIOGRAPHICAL REFERENCES: The standard edition is *The Poetical Works of Moore,* edited by A. D. Godley, 1910. An edition of the *Memoirs, Journal and Correspondence of Thomas Moore* was edited by Lord John Russell, 8 vols., 1853–1856. A more recent but abridged edition of the journal is *Tom Moore's Diary: A Selection* edited by J. B. Priestley, 1925. For biography and criticism see Stephen Gwynn, *Thomas Moore,* English Men of Letters series, 1904; W. F. Trench, *Tom Moore,* 1934; H. M. Jones, *The Harp That Once—A Chronicle of the Life of Thomas Moore,* 1937; and L. A. G. Strong, *The Minstrel Boy: A Portrait of Tom Moore,* 1937.

ALBERTO MORAVIA
(Alberto Pincherle)

Born: Rome, Italy
Date: November 28, 1907

PRINCIPAL WORKS

NOVELS: *Gli Indifferenti,* 1929 (*The Time of Indifference*); *Le Ambizioni Sbagliate,* 1935 (*Wheel of Fortune*); *La Mascherata,* 1941 (*The Fancy Dress Party*); *Agostino,*

1944; *La Romana,* 1947 (*The Woman of Rome*); *La Disubbidienza* (*Disobedience;* printed, as *Luca,* with *Agostino* in *Two Adolescents*); *L'Amore Conjiugale,* 1949 (*Conjugal Love*); *Il Conformista,* 1951 (*The Conformist*); *Il Disprezzo,* 1954 (*A Ghost at Noon*); *La Ciociara,* 1957 (*Two Women*).

SHORT STORIES IN TRANSLATION: *Bitter Honeymoon and Other Stories,* 1956; *Roman Tales,* 1957.

Alberto Moravia, whose real name is Alberto Pincherle, usually sets the scene of his fiction in his native Rome, although what he has to say about the lives of the lower and middle classes is not limited to his locale. On the contrary, his insights into modern life are so universal that he has won widespread recognition throughout Europe and in America. His popularity in the United States has grown steadily since 1949, and in 1952 France awarded him the Legion of Honor.

The son of a successful architect of Venetian ancestry, Moravia was born in Rome on November 28, 1907. When he was nine, he contracted tuberculosis of the bone, with the result that he was forced to spend long periods of time in bed. Unable to attend school, he was privately educated. At a sanatorium where he spent two years he began work on his first novel, *The Time of Indifference,* which was completed before he was twenty. This novel, which describes in vivid detail the moral rootlessness of modern youth, was published at the writer's expense. A tremendous success in Italy, it did not long survive its translation into English as *The Indifferent Ones* in 1932. A second translation, *The Time of Indifference,* fared much better after the appearance of *The Woman of Rome* in 1949.

During the 1930's Moravia traveled widely in Europe and America, meanwhile supporting himself by writing non-political articles for Italian papers.

His second novel attracted the unfavorable attention of the censorship that prevailed during Mussolini's regime; by official order, the book was not reviewed in the Italian press. In 1941 he published *The Fancy Dress Party,* a story of politics and love in an imaginary country and a thinly veiled satire on a Fascist dictator. This novel, apparently published with Mussolini's knowledge and approval, was nevertheless withdrawn within a month under circumstances which made it impossible for Moravia to write under his own name. A second pseudonym which he adopted was also suppressed. Active in anti-Fascist journalism after the fall of Mussolini, and marked for arrest when the Germans occupied Rome, Moravia and his wife fled in an effort to reach the Allied lines in the Cassino area. After hiding in a mountain hut for several months they finally found safety with the American Fifth Army in the spring of 1943.

In the postwar work which has made him internationally famous, Moravia searches for the human values that can give coherence to life in the disordered modern world. His central ethical theme is that love, a free and complete commitment to another human being, is the value which alone sustains man in a grasping, fragmented society. In *The Woman of Rome,* Moravia sympathizes with Adriana because she never sells her capacity for love; his contempt is reserved for those who enslave themselves spiritually. In *Conjugal Love,* a dilettante novelist almost loses his wife before he learns to love unselfishly. The hero of *The Conformist* readily barters his individuality for a cheap success. *A Ghost at Noon* is another unsparing analysis of the tensions underlying married life and of the moral nihilism resulting from self-deception and conflict between the mores of a social group and the primitive instincts of the individual.

Moravia is as frank in his sexuality as the late D. H. Lawrence. As in Lawrence also, the sensuality which often passes for love among people of disordered lives becomes a symptom of the social and spiritual malaise of our time. The astringent technique and psychological intensity of Moravia's writing has made him a leading figure in the neo-realistic movement which has revitalized postwar Italian literature.

BIBLIOGRAPHICAL REFERENCES: Moravia's principal works are now available in translation. For criticism see Carlo L. Golino, "Alberto Moravia," *Modern Language Journal*, XXXVI (1952), 15–20; Thomas G. Bergin, "The Moravian Muse," *Virginia Quarterly Review*, XXIX (1953), 215–225; Giovanni Cecchetti, "Alberto Moravia," *Italica*, XXX (1953), 153–167; Charles J. Rolo, "Alberto Moravia," *Atlantic Monthly*, CXCV (February, 1955), 69–74; Giovanni Fincato, "Ambiguità di Moravia," *Humanitas* (Brescia), XI (1956), 669–673; and Frank Baldanza, "The Classicism of Alberto Moravia," *Modern Fiction Studies*, III (1958), 309–320. For a background study of contemporary trends see, further, Nicola Chiaromonte, "Realism and Neorealism in Contemporary Italian Literature," *College English*, XIV (1953), 431–439.

SIR THOMAS MORE

Born: London, England
Date: February 7, 1478

Died: London
Date: July 7, 1535

PRINCIPAL WORKS

POLITICAL ROMANCE: *De Optimo Reipublicae Statu, deque Nova Insula Utopia*, 1516 (*Utopia*).

MISCELLANEOUS: *The Life of John Picus, Earl of Myrandula*, c. 1510; *A Dialogue of Sir Thomas More*, 1529; *An Apology of Sir Thomas More, Knight*, 1533; *History of King Richard III*, 1543; *A Dialogue of Comfort against Tribulation*, 1553.

Thomas More, son of a British lawyer and judge, was born in London on February 7, 1478 (some scholars say 1477). At the age of thirteen he became a page to the Archbishop of Canterbury, a post he held until he was sent to Oxford University in 1492. His father, intending his son for a legal career and suspicious of the teachings at the university, withdrew his son and sent him to London in 1494 to begin the study of law at the Inns of Court and at Lincoln's Inn (1496). Some-

time later, probably in 1497, More became interested in the religious life, taking upon himself the discipline of the Carthusian order during the period 1499–1503. Although he was in Parliament in 1504, More aroused the anger of Henry VII and was forced to retire temporarily from public life. For a time he devoted himself to the study of music, French, mathematics, and astronomy, but, his mind turning again to religion, he considered becoming a priest. Marriage to Jane Cult (or Colt) in 1505 ended his dilemma. The young couple settled in Bucklesbury, where they were twice visited by Erasmus, who dedicated his *Praise of Folly* (1511) to More. Domestic life was broken by his wife's death in 1511, but he remarried within a short time, taking as his wife a widow named Alice Middleton.

After the death of Henry VII in 1509, More resumed his public career and soon attracted the favorable attention of both Henry VIII and Wolsey. In 1518 he was appointed to the Privy Council. He attended the king at the Field of the Cloth of Gold in 1520 and a year later was made under-treasurer and knighted. In 1529 he succeeded Wolsey as chancellor, the first layman to hold that office in England; apparently Henry thought that the new chancellor would favor the royal divorce from Queen Catherine. More had signed the impeachment of Wolsey and remained silent when Parliament passed acts limiting the power of the clergy in 1531, but he refused to lend approval to the divorce. When Henry proclaimed himself head of the Church in 1532, More asked permission to resign his chancellorship, a request quickly granted. His resignation cost him much in financial and personal security. When he refused to attend the coronation of Anne Boleyn, he created as much resentment in the king as he had hitherto incurred favor. Charged with receiving bribes, he was proved innocent; he was also acquitted on a charge of treason. The crisis in his affairs came in 1534, when Parliament passed a bill giving Anne Boleyn's children the right of succession and forcing an oath of allegiance to the king as the supreme authority of the Church. More, refusing to make such an acknowledgment, was imprisoned in the Tower of London. Tried on a charge of treason, he was found guilty and executed on July 7, 1535, and his severed head was hung on London Bridge. For his loyalty to the Pope and his martyrdom on behalf of the Church, he was beatified in 1886 and canonized in 1935.

Important as he is in British history and in the crisis of antagonism between Catholicism and Protestantism in the sixteenth century, More also has a place in the history of literature as the author of *Utopia*, published originally in Latin but translated into English in 1551. Utopia is an island described by a fictitious mariner who supposedly sailed with Amerigo Vespucci. The book suggests such reforms as community of goods, universal education, and the establishment of an academy of learning. It also retains such institutions of More's time as slavery and monarchy. The work is usually considered a companion piece to Erasmus' *Praise of Folly*. More's *History of King Richard III* is also important as the source of Shakespeare's *Richard III*.

BIBLIOGRAPHICAL REFERENCES: The basic biography is William Roper, *The Life and Death of Sir Thomas More*, 1625 (rev. ed., 1935). Other biographical studies include E. M. G. Routh, *Sir Thomas More and His Friends*, 1934; R. W. Chambers, *Sir Thomas More*, 1935; L. A. Paul, *Sir Thomas More*, 1953; E. E. Reynolds, *Saint Thomas More*, 1953; and John Farrow, *The Story of Thomas More*, 1954. More specialized studies are W. E. Campbell, *More's Utopia and His Social Teaching*, 1930, and *Erasmus, Tyndale, and More*, 1949; and R. W. Chambers, *The Place of Sir Thomas More in English Literature*, 1937.

JAMES JUSTINIAN MORIER

Born: Smyrna, Turkey
Date: January 8, 1784

Died: Brighton, England
Date: March 19, 1849

PRINCIPAL WORKS

NOVELS: *The Adventures of Hajji Baba of Ispahan*, 1824; *The Adventures of Hajji Baba of Ispahan in England*, 1828; *Zohrab the Hostage*, 1832; *Ayesha: the Maid of Kars*, 1834.

TRAVEL AND DESCRIPTION: *A Journey Through Persia, Armenia, and Asia Minor to Constantinople in the Years 1808 and 1809*, 1812; *A Second Journey Through Persia*, 1818.

A characteristic of the Romantic period in English literature was the use of exotic material, particularly in the "Oriental." All of the little that James Justinian Morier wrote contained this characteristic. It was superior work because, educational as well as entertaining, it was about foreign people of the author's own experiences. Morier was born on January 8, 1784, at Smyrna, Turkey, son of a British consul of Huguenot extraction. After education at Harrow in England, Morier himself served in the consular service in Persia. Retiring in England on a pension in 1817, he wrote tales until 1824, when he was sent as a special commissioner to Mexico. He is best known for *The Adventures of Hajji Baba of Ispahan*. Although foreign in locale and picaresque in action, the material, based on fact, was treated realistically. In the sequel, *The Adventures of Hajji Baba of Ispahan in England*, the purpose of social criticism was no longer veiled. The later novels are sentimental and unreal, and at best are but typical of the lighter reading of the day. Morier died at Brighton, England, March 19, 1849.

BIBLIOGRAPHICAL REFERENCES: *Hajji Baba* is in the Everyman's Library and the World's Classics. Sir Walter Scott's review of *Hajji Baba* appeared in the *Quarterly Review*, XXXIX (1829), 73–96. See also "The Sun and the Pen," *London Times Literary Supplement*, XLVIII (July 22, 1949), 473.

DINAH MARIA MULOCK

Born: Stoke-upon-Kent, England
Date: April 20, 1826

Died: Shortlands, Kent, England
Date: October 12, 1887

PRINCIPAL WORKS

NOVELS: *The Ogilvies*, 1849; *Olive*, 1850; *The Head of the Family*, 1851; *John Halifax, Gentleman*, 1857; *A Life for a Life*, 1859; *Mistress and Maid*, 1863; *Christian's Mistake*, 1865; *A Noble Life*, 1866; *Two Marriages*, 1867; *A Brave Lady*, 1870; *Hannah*, 1872; *The Little Lame Prince*, 1874 (juvenile); *The Laurel Bush*, 1876; *Young Mrs. Jardine*, 1879.

SHORT STORIES AND SKETCHES: *Avillion and Other Tales*, 1853; *Nothing New*, 1857; *Romantic Tales*, 1859; *Domestic Stories*, 1860; *Lord Erlestoun and Other Stories*, 1864; *The Unkind World and Other Stories*, 1870.

POEMS: *Poems*, 1859; *Songs of Our Youth*, 1875; *Thirty Years*, 1880.
BIOGRAPHY: *Fifty Golden Years: Incidents in the Queen's Reign*, 1887.

Dinah Maria Mulock (Craik) was one of the many minor female novelists produced by nineteenth century England. Her father, Thomas Mulock, was something of ne'er-do-well. At the time of his daughter's birth, April 20, 1826, he was operating in the capacity of a Non-conformist preacher at Stoke-upon-Trent, but he soon left this calling for some nebulous business scheme, transferring the support of his family to his wife.

Mrs. Mulock, consequently, was forced to open a school in her home. She was assisted in this venture by her eldest daughter, Dinah, a precocious girl who had begun writing poetry at the age of ten. Mother and daughter continued to run the school until 1840, at which time Mrs. Mulock inherited a sizable fortune. Here pedagogy was exchanged for travel. The entire family (Mr. Mulock had returned along with the inheritance) toured Europe for the next four years, and Dinah had the opportunity to study French, Italian, Greek, Latin, and even Erse.

In 1844 the unpredictable Thomas Mulock left home for good and the remainder of the family settled in Staffordshire. The next year Mrs. Mulock died, leaving Dinah in charge of the younger children and the fortune.

Dinah, now nineteen, employed her talents in the writing of poems and stories for children. Four years later she turned to adult fiction with the production of *The Ogilvies* in 1849, a novel which she dedicated to her mother. After this maiden effort, she produced some twenty more novels, not to mention sundry volumes of poems, tales, and children's stories in the course of a career that reached its greatest height with the publication of *John Halifax, Gentleman* in 1857.

Miss Mulock was married in 1864 to George Lillie Craik, a publisher eleven years her junior. She lived with him and, later, an adopted daughter at Corner House, Shortlands, Kent, until her death on October 12, 1887.

Mrs. Craik's reputation as a novelist is no greater than that of the general run of the often dull, always sentimental, and frequently over-didactic lady fiction writers of Victoria's day. Yet in *John Halifax, Gentleman* she produced one work which makes demands upon the attention of the modern reader. She is remembered also as a woman of great tenderness and charity, one whose moral emphasis was, if somewhat unsound artistically, at least always sincere.

BIBLIOGRAPHICAL REFERENCES: There is no collected edition of Dinah Mulock. The only biography is Louisa Parr, *The Author of "John Halifax, Gentleman," A Memoir*, 1898; *idem, Women Novelists of Queen Victoria's Reign*, 1897. See also R. B. Johnson, *The Women Novelists*, 1918.

MULTATULI
(Eduard Douwes Dekker)

Born: Amsterdam, Netherlands
Date: March 2, 1820

Died: Nieder-Ingelheim, Netherlands
Date: February 19, 1887

Principal Works

NOVEL: *Max Havelaar,* 1860.
PLAY: *Vorstenschool,* 1875 (*The School for Princes*).
SATIRE: *Minnebrieven,* 1862.

Eduard Douwes Dekker, who used the pseudonym Multatuli, was for many years a colonial administrator in the Dutch East Indies, principally in Java. Born in Amsterdam on March 2, 1820, he went to Java in 1838, and by 1857 he was the official resident at Bantam. In 1846 he married Everdine van Wijnbergen. After her death he married a second time, in 1875, to Mimi Hamminck Schepel, who as his widow and literary executor published her husband's collected works in 1892.

During his years as a colonial administrator in the Dutch East Indies, Dekker observed many incidents and situations he regarded as scandalous. Becoming outspoken against the abuses, he alienated by his frankness and candor many of his fellow administrators. Either dismissed or forced to resign from his post, he returned to Holland determined to expose in detail the situation which had aroused him. A series of articles in periodicals and a number of pamphlets were the result of his determination. He also wrote a novel to present the abuses of the Dutch colonial system, especially the abuse of free labor by the administrators. The novel, *Max Havelaar,* was published under his pseudonym of Multatuli in 1860. *Minnebrieven,* ostensibly a collection of love letters, was a satire on the abuses of the colonial system. *The School for Princes,* a drama based on the same need for reforms, had limited contemporary success on the stage. During the years from 1862 to 1877 Dekker assembled his miscellaneous works and published them as a series of volumes entitled *Ideën,* translated into English in 1904. *Max Havelaar,* best known of his works was first published in English in 1868; other translations have followed. Dekker died at Nieder-Ingelheim on February 19, 1887.

BIBLIOGRAPHICAL REFERENCES: The introduction written by D. H. Lawrence for *Max Havelaar,* 1927, is also a good introduction to the work and personality of Dekker. See also J. de Gruyter, *Het leven en de werken van Eduard Douwes Dekker,* 2 vols., 1920; C. E. du Perron, *De Man van Lebak,* 1937; and A. J. Barnouw, *The Dutch,* 1940.

LADY MURASAKI SHIKIBU

Born: Japan
Date: c. 978

Died: Japan
Date: c. 1030

Principal Work

NOVEL: *Genji Monogatari,* c. 1004 (*The Tale of Genji*).

Lady Murasaki Shikibu, foremost writer of the Heian period in Japanese literature, had every advantage of birth and education. A member of a family

778

that had produced mikados and statesmen, she was the granddaughter of Fujiwara no Kanesuki, celebrated Japanese poet. As a girl she was considered something of a prodigy of learning, even in an age when Japanese women of noble birth were generally much better educated than their European contemporaries. While still in her teens Lady Murasaki was well read in Chinese and Japanese literature, and had already written both prose and verse. Widowed early, after a brief marriage to an officer in the Imperial Guard, she was called to court by the Empress-consort Akiko as chief maid of honor.

Lady Murasaki's long association with the imperial court provided her with the leisure to continue her writing, which included many short poems and a diary, still extant. It also gave her a personal familiarity with the customs and character types so important in her best-known work, *The Tale of Genji*. *The Tale*, a prose narrative in fifty-four books dealing with the loves and adventures of a fictional character, Genji, and his son Kaoru, represents a higher achievement in Japanese literature than that of any earlier period, and the work is considered by many the finest novel Japan has produced. With a keen eye for character and manners, Lady Murasaki describes realistically, but in a formal style, the upper-class world of the age just preceding her own. Although it is filled with charm and humor, the dominant tone of *The Tale of Genji* is one of sadness at the declining splendor of a sophisticated and aristocratic society.

Lady Murasaki was born about 978 and died about 1030.

BIBLIOGRAPHICAL REFERENCES: *The Tale of Genji* is available to English-speaking readers in the translation by Arthur Waley, 1925. The *Diary* has been reprinted in *Diaries of Court Ladies of Old Japan,* translated by Annie Shepley Omori and Kochi Doi, 1925. Brief accounts of Lady Murasaki Shikibu's life and work are given in J. Ingram Bryan, *The Literature of Japan,* 1930; and Donald L. Keene, *Japanese Literature,* 1953.

HENRI MURGER

Born: Paris, France
Date: March 24, 1822

Died: Paris
Date: January 28, 1861

PRINCIPAL WORK

NOVEL: *Scènes de la vie de Bohème,* 1848 (*The Bohemians of the Latin Quarter*).

Henri Murger once said that "Bohemia is the preface to the hospital, the Academy, or the morgue." The honor of membership in the French Academy never came to him, but he did spend a long time in hospitals until severe arthritis, aggravated by the malnutrition he suffered during his many years in "Bohemia," caused his premature death at the age of thirty-eight.

Murger never knew anything but the poverty that was the enduring fact of typical bohemian life. Born at Paris into the family of a poor tailor on March 24, 1822, he existed on his small salary as secretary to Count Alexei Tolstoy. *The Bohemians of the Latin Quarter* was first published serially, accounting, perhaps, for its structural looseness. A dramatic version, written in collaboration with Théodore Barrière (1849), had an even greater success. But Murger, like Baudelaire, his fellow bohemian, had little success in taking care of money when he had it. Despite his considerable fame and the recognition he received when Napoleon III gave him the Legion of Honor, he died penniless on January 28, 1861.

Though he wrote a number of other novels and plays (*Le Pays Latin*, 1852; *Les Buveurs d'eau*, 1855; *Le Sabot rouge*, 1858), and a volume of poetry, Murger is remembered almost exclusively for his novel depicting the lives of the impoverished artists in the Latin Quarter of nineteenth century Paris, the story on which Puccini's opera *La Bohème* is based.

BIBLIOGRAPHICAL REFERENCES: For the story of Murger and the artistic life of his time see in English Arthur Moss and Evalyn Marvel, *The Legend of the Latin Quarter*, 1946; in French, Georges Montorgueil, *Henri Murger, romancier de la Bohème*, 1929.

ALFRED DE MUSSET

Born: Paris, France
Date: December 11, 1810

Died: Paris
Date: May 1, 1857

PRINCIPAL WORKS

PLAYS: *Nuit vénitienne*, 1830 (*Venetian Night*); *Les Caprices de Marianne*, 1833 (*The Caprices of Marianne*); *On ne badine pas avec l'amour*, 1834 (*No Trifling with Love*); *Lorenzaccio*, 1834; *Nuit de décembre*, 1835 (*December Night*); *Il ne faut jurer de rien*, 1836 (*One Never Can Tell*); *Il faut qu'une porte soit ouverte ou fermée*, 1847 (*A Door Should Either Be Open or Closed*).

POEMS: *Contes d'Espagne et d'Italie*, 1829 (*Romances of Spain and Italy*); *Poésies diverses*, 1831; *Le Spectacle dans un fauteuil*, 1833 (*A Show from an Easy Chair*); *Poésies nouvelles*, 1840.

AUTOBIOGRAPHY: *Confession d'un enfant du siècle*, 1836 (*Confessions of a Child of the Century*).

(Louis Charles) Alfred de Musset was born into an aristocratic family in Paris on December 11, 1810. Both his parents were literary; his father wrote biography and criticism and his mother created charades and playlets for such notables as Scribe and Duveyrier. Both Alfred and Paul, later his famous biographer, delighted in literary exercises and talk. Before he was eighteen, Alfred showed unmistakable signs of genius that were fostered by Hugo, Mérimée, and Sainte-Beuve, the latter exerting great influence on the young

writer and his career. Musset's first popular success, achieved at nineteen, was *Romances of Spain and Italy*.

A failure on stage, *Venetian Night* was an interesting play; unfortunately, it temporarily turned the young poet from the theater, where his genius finally manifested itself. In 1833 the two most important events in his life occurred: the writing of *The Caprices of Marianne*, which is still a classic part of the repertory of the Théâtre Français, and his ill-fated liaison with George Sand (described by both Sand in *Elle et lui* 1859, and Paul de Musset in *Lui et elle*, 1860) which affected the rest of the poet's life adversely. The much publicized Italian journey of the lovers ended in violent quarrels and an abrupt break-off.

Musset gained stature as an artist even after such a debilitating experience. *Lorenzaccio*, a favorite of Sarah Bernhardt for many years, may have been written in Venice in 1834. His *Confessions of a Child of the Century* contains some interesting political ideas and some very good writing. In 1834, in another justifiably famous work, *No Trifling With Love*, he defended romance in a play thought to be an expression of his own love affair. Another comedy, *One Never Can Tell*, reveals

Musset's musings and fatalism under the guise of brilliant dialogue and clever situation. In his last years he turned more and more to poetry and journalism, although great lapses cropped up between periods of diligent writing. By 1848, however, his reputation increased as his plays won larger audiences. His curtain raisers were standard fare not only in the Théâtre Français but also in the Théâtre Historique.

Elected to the French Academy in 1852, he died in Paris on May 1, 1857. For the past century his work has been kept alive by his excellence of language,, his keen wit, and his sophisticated satire.

BIBLIOGRAPHICAL REFERENCES: The basic biographical study is Paul de Musset, *Biographie d'Alfred de Musset*, 1877. A good recent study is P. van Tieghem, *Musset, l'homme et l'œuvre*, 1945. The best brief study in English is in Henry James, *French Poets and Novelists*, 1876. The story of Musset's liaison with George Sand has been told in two books: *Elle et lui*, by George Sand, 1859, and Paul de Musset, *Lui et elle*, 1860.

THOMAS NASH

Born: Lowestoft, Surrey, England
Date: 1567

Died: Yarmouth (?), England
Date: 1601

PRINCIPAL WORKS

NOVEL: *The Unfortunate Traveller*, 1594.

PLAY: *Summer's Last Will and Testament*, 1592.

PAMPHLETS: *Strange News of the Intercepting of Certain Letters*, 1592; *Christ's Tears over Jerusalem*, 1593; *Have with You to Saffron Walden, or Gabriel Harvey's Hunt Is Up*, 1596.

Thomas Nash (or Nashe), dramatist, novelist, and pamphleteer, was born in 1567 in Lowestoft, England, the son of William Nash, a minister, and his second wife Margaret. He spent several years at St. John's College, Cambridge, and received his B.A. degree in 1585. By 1588 he was

living in London, trying to make a living with his pen as one of the University Wits. *A Countercuff to Martin Junior, Martin's Month's Mind*, and *Pasquil's Apology* are sometimes attributed to him. Among his friends were Greene, Daniel, Lodge, and Marlowe. At this time the Puritan writers, under

781

the pseudonym of Martin Marprelate, were attacking the bishops and the government of the Church. Using the name Pasquil, Nash joined the controversy against the Puritans, especially against Gabriel Harvey. His contributions to the "paper war" include *Strange News of the Intercepting of Certain Letters*, *Christ's Tears over Jerusalem*, and *Have with You to Saffron Walden, or Gabriel Harvey's Hunt Is Up*.

The most notable of his works was a picaresque novel of romantic adventure entitled *The Unfortunate Traveller, or The Life of Jack Wilton*, the story of a page who attended the Earl of Surrey on his Grand Tour and who married a Venetian lady. The realistic use of detail in this work set the pattern for the novels of Defoe. Nash also wrote several plays, and the title page of Marlowe's *Dido, Queen of Carthage* credits him with the joint authorship, or possibly the completion, of that work. *Summer's Last Will and Testament*, originally a masque presented at the house of Sir George Carey, was produced in 1592. A lost play, *The Isle of Dogs* (1597), a slanderous work of which he wrote at least a part, led to his being sentenced to the Fleet prison, a sentence he seems to have avoided somehow. He died in 1601, probably at Yarmouth.

BIBLIOGRAPHICAL REFERENCES: The standard edition of Nash's *Works* was edited by R. B. McKerrow, 1904–1910. See also J. J. Jusserand, *The English Novel in the Time of Shakespeare*, 1890; F. G. Harman, *Gabriel Harvey and Thomas Nashe*, 1923; Fredson T. Bowers, "Thomas Nashe and the Picaresque Novel," in *Studies in Honor of John Calvin Metcalf*, 1941; and *Dictionary of National Biography*, Vol. XIV.

JOHN HENRY NEWMAN

Born: London, England
Date: February 21, 1801

Died: Birmingham, England
Date: August 11, 1890

PRINCIPAL WORKS

THEOLOGICAL TRACTS AND STUDIES: *Tract XXXVIII*, 1834; *Tract XLI*, 1834; *Tract XC*, 1841; *Lectures on the Prophetical Office of the Church*, 1837; *Lectures on Justification*, 1838; *An Essay on the Development of Christian Doctrine*, 1845; *An Essay in Aid of a Grammar of Assent*, 1870; *Causes of the Rise of Arianism*, 1872; *Stray Essays on Controversial Points*, 1890.

AUTOBIOGRAPHY: *Apologia pro Vita Sua*, 1864 (*History of My Religious Opinions*).

NOVELS: *Loss and Gain*, 1848; *Callista: A Sketch of the Third Century*, 1856.

POEMS: *Verses on Religious Subjects*, 1853; *The Dream of Gerontius*, 1866; *Verses on Various Occasions*, 1868.

ESSAYS ON EDUCATION: *Discourses on the Scope and Nature of University Education*, 1852; *Lectures and Essays on University Subjects*, 1859; *The Idea of a University Defined*, 1873.

John Henry Newman, who was to be the outstanding figure in nineteenth century English theology, was born in London on February 21, 1801, the oldest son of John Newman, a banker. After private schooling at Ealing, young Newman entered Trinity College, Oxford, in 1817. Before this time, however, he had felt, at age fifteen, a strong call to religion, almost a conversion to deeply religious ways. This force was so great that he changed from a course in law to the study of divinity in 1820.

Graduated in 1820, he was made a fellow of Oriel College the next year. By 1831 Newman was made select preacher before the college, having been ordained an Anglican deacon in 1824. While returning from a visit to Italy in 1832, he wrote his most famous hymn, "Lead, Kindly Light." In July, 1833, he heard John Keble preach his famous sermon on the weaknesses of English government in matters of religion. Profoundly moved by this strong appeal, he and several others prepared and published a series of theological tracts called *Tracts for the Times,* (1833–1841). These publications marked the real beginning of the Oxford Movement, later called Tractarianism from the name of the series. Newman and his friends wanted a more secure and severe basis of doctrine for the Church of England; they felt that the Church had fallen from the high ideals and disciplines of the past, and they advocated a return to the more authoritative faith of previous eras.

In 1836 Newman became editor of the *British Critic* and was able to exert considerable influence in his praise of the "middle life" of the Anglican faith as opposed to the extremes of other religions. About the same time he began to see the firmness of the Catholic position, and learned to admire its principle of authority. In his last tract, *Tract XC,* published in 1841, Newman displayed his weakening opposition to Catholicism, and after retiring as editor he wrote *An Essay on the Development of Christian Doctrine,* a work defending the Catholic Church from a historical standpoint. In September of 1843 he resigned his living at St. Mary's Anglican Church at Oxford, and two years later he was admitted into the Catholic Church.

He was ordained a priest, in Rome, in 1847, and in the next year he returned to England, finally settling at Edgbaston Oratory in Birmingham, where he remained for most of the last forty years of his life. In 1851 he was appointed rector of the newly created Catholic University of Ireland, in Dublin, where he wrote his justly famous series of lectures, *Discourses on the Scope and Nature of University Education,* later revised as *The Idea of a University Defined.* He resigned his rectorship and returned to Edgbaston in 1858.

The great work of Newman's life resulted from an attack made on his sincerity by Charles Kingsley, who had slanderously attacked Newman's integrity. In his *Apologia pro Vita Sua,* published in 1864, Newman answered all attacks and by his obvious sincerity and brilliant writing in this religious autobiography turned the tide of public opinion in his favor. With the general approbation of the English people he continued setting up religious schools. In 1870 he produced *An Essay in Aid of a Grammar of Assent,* a delicately reasoned defense of religious belief which greatly increased his reputation. This reputation was so favorable that when Pope Leo XIII offered Newman a cardinal's hat in February of 1879, most Englishmen were pleased by the honor conferred. He became Cardinal Newman on May 12, 1879. After his return from Rome he resided at Edgbaston until his death on August 11, 1890.

Since his time Newman has stood for sincerity and devotion in religious matters. The extent to which his works are still published is sure evidence of his influence, and there are many Newman Societies established in his honor. The depth of his religious conviction may also be found in his one great poem, *The Dream of Gerontius*, written while his ever-failing health was in a precarious state. This deep and moving poem shows that had Newman chosen, he could have been one of the leading poets of the nineteenth century as well as an outstanding theologian.

BIBLIOGRAPHICAL REFERENCES: John Henry Newman edited the Uniform Edition of his writings, 1869–1881. There are numerous editions of single and selected works. One useful and representative volume is *Newman, Prose and Poetry*, selected by Geoffrey Tillotson, Reynard Library series, 1957. The standard biographies are Anne Mozley, *The Life and Correspondence of John Henry Newman*, 1892; and Wilfrid Ward, *The Life of John Henry Cardinal Newman*, 2 vols., 1912. See also William Barry, *Newman*, 1904; J. C. May, *Cardinal Newman*, 1930; and C. F. Harrold, *John Henry Newman*, 1945. A more specialized study is J. J. Reilly, *Newman as a Man of Letters*, 1927. For an introduction to the story of the Oxford Movement see also W. G. Hutchinson, ed., *The Oxford Movement: Being a Selection from Tracts of the Times*, 1906—an edition containing eighteen of the tracts, including Nos. XXXVIII and XC, by Newman; T. B. Kittredge, *The Influence of Newman on the Oxford Movement*, 1914; H. L. Stewart, *A Century of Anglo-Catholicism*, 1929; A. H. T. Clarke, "The Passing of the Oxford Movement," *Nineteenth Century and After*, LXXI (1912), 133–147, 341–346; and E. G. Selwyn, "The Future of the Oxford Movement," *ibid.*, 532–546.

SIR ISAAC NEWTON

Born: Woolsthorpe, England
Date: December 25, 1642

Died: Kensington, England
Date: March 20, 1727

PRINCIPAL WORKS

SCIENTIFIC ESSAYS AND TREATISES: *Philosophiae Naturalis Principia Mathematica*, 1687 (*The Mathematical Principles of Natural Philosophy*); *Treatise on Optics*, 1704; *Arithmetica Universalis*, 1707 (*Universal Arithmetic*); *Analysis per Equationes Numero Terminorum Infinitas*, 1711 (*Analysis by Equations of an Infinite Number of Terms*); *The Method of Fluxions and Infinite Series*, 1736.

Isaac Newton, posthumous son of a Lincolnshire farmer, was born at Woolsthorpe on December 25, 1642. His scientific interests became apparent at an early age; as a child he made drawings of new types of windmills and of a self-propelled carriage. In 1661 he entered Trinity College, Cambridge, where he came under the influence of Dr. Isaac Barrow, a famous professor of both Greek and mathematics. At the university he studied Kepler's work on optics and Descartes' principles of geometry. During most of 1665 and 1666, Newton was absent from Cambridge because of the plague. During this time he studied at his family home

784

in Lincolnshire, where he developed the binomial theorem, invented differential and integral calculus (although some authorities claim that most of the credit for the invention of the calculus should go to Dr. Barrow), computed the area of hyperbola, and began his speculations about the nature of gravity. He later developed most of these speculations and published them in his first and most famous work, *The Mathematical Principles of Natural Philosophy*, in 1687. When Newton returned to Cambridge in 1667, he was appointed a fellow of Trinity. He began lecturing on optics in 1669 and made experiments that enabled him to correct existing telescopes. He also, at this time, developed his theory on the transmission of light, and later published his lectures and theories in his *Treatise on Optics* in 1704.

Appointed Lucasian professor in 1669, Newton spent most of his life at Cambridge, lecturing, working on his experiments, formulating his laws and theories, writing. He became a fellow of the Royal Society in 1672; thereafter all his work was presented first in the form of papers read to the Society before publishing. His scientific life was enlivened by several long controversies. Dr. Robert Hooke, a fellow English scientist, disputed Newton's theory of light in a long argument which made light one of the principal topics for discussion in the scientific world of the time. Newton carried on a long correspondence with Leibniz, the German philosopher, and John Bernoulli, the latter two claiming that Leibniz had discovered the calculus. Newton also differed strongly with Flamsteed, the British Astronomer-Royal, on astronomy and lunar theory.

Despite these long controversies, Newton was recognized as the foremost scientist of his time throughout the Western world. His eminence brought him other honors and responsibilities, some of which, he felt, merely took time needed for scientific studies. He was named a delegate to resist the encroachment of the Crown on Cambridge by James II in 1687. As a result of his work in limiting royal interference in university affairs, Newton was elected to Parliament in 1689, after the abdication of James II, as the representative from Cambridge. He soon resigned, but was elected again in 1701. He was Warden of the Royal Mint in 1699. In 1703 he became President of the Royal Society and in 1705 he was knighted by Queen Anne. He died at Kensington on March 20, 1727.

Although his principal fame rests on his scientific work, Newton's theological ideas also strongly influenced men for a hundred years after his death. He felt that God had set the universe in motion, which then operated by natural law with God standing by to provide the remedy should the functioning of natural law break down or wear out. This notion of God as only first cause was widely held among scientists and intellectuals throughout the eighteenth century.

BIBLIOGRAPHICAL REFERENCES: The basic biography is Sir David Brewster, *Memoirs of the Life, Writings, and Discoveries of Sir Isaac Newton*, 2 vols., 1855. Recent biographical and analytical studies include L. T. More, *Isaac Newton*, 1934; and E. N. da Costa Andrade, *Isaac Newton*, 1950. For more specialized studies on the scientific and philosophic aspects of his work see W. W. R. Ball, *Essay on Newton's Principia*, 1893; P. G. Tait, *Newton's Laws of Motion*, 1899; Helene Metzger,

Attraction universelle et religion naturelle chez quelques commentateurs anglais de Newton, 1938; H. W. Turnbull, *Mathematical Discoveries of Newton*, 1945; and M. H. Nicolson, *Newton Demands the Muse*, 1946.

MARTIN ANDERSEN NEXÖ

Born: Copenhagen, Denmark   Died: Dresden, East Germany
Date: June 26, 1869   Date: June 1, 1954

PRINCIPAL WORKS

NOVELS: *Pelle Erobreren*, 1906–1910 (*Pelle the Conqueror*); *Ditte Menneskebarn*, 1917–1921 (*Ditte, Girl Alive!*, 1920; *Ditte, Daughter of Man*, 1921; *Ditte, Toward the Stars*, 1922); *Midt i en Jerntid*, 1929 (*In God's Land*); *Morten hin Röde*, 1945 (*Morten the Red*).

AUTOBIOGRAPHY: *Scoldag*, 1903 (*Days in the Sun*); *Et Ille Krae*, 1932 (*A Little Mite*); *Under aaben Himmel*, 1935 (*Under the Open Sky*); *For Lud og koldt Vand*, 1937 (*Roughing It*); *Vejs Ende*, 1939 (*The End of the Road*).

Martin Andersen Nexö was born into poverty, and though he was to emerge from it in later years, poverty was to leave its mark on him and to lend its color to his life and his writing. Born on June 26, 1869, he was the fourth child of eleven sired by a drunken peasant who had moved from Neksö to the slums of Copenhagen and had married there the daughter of a German immigrant. With the father constantly drunk and the mother frequently indisposed, the sickly Martin and an older brother were faced with the task of supporting the family, a task which they accomplished by peddling cherries from a pushcart.

Their impoverished situation was lightened somewhat when, with the outbreak of the Prussian War, the family moved back to Neksö. There Martin was hired out as a herd boy. Living in the open air, he improved temporarily in health.

At twelve he was sent to work on a farm belonging to the widow of the Danish poet Mollack; this experience proved to be the turning point of his life. The poet's widow, impressed by his intelligence, took an interest in him and had him sent to Peder Moller's school in Odense. Within two years he was an instructor at the school and was composing poems and sketches.

His poor health returned at this point, however; but again his patroness came to his aid, providing him with funds for a walking trip into Southern Europe. The trip lasted until 1896. Much of it was spent in Spain and Italy, where he lived in the countryside among the peasants or among the masses in the slums of large cities. It was at this time, he said, that he learned that "poverty is international." It was at this time, also, that the memory of his own early poverty combined with these current observations to begin what was eventually a complete conversion to Marxism.

These Marxist tendencies were to appear ten years later in his first important work. He had begun his writing career with newspaper articles about his trip, but had suspended his efforts while attending the Danish Normal School upon his return. Appointed an instructor at Frederiksberg, he resumed his writing but received little attention until the publication of the first volume of *Pelle the Conqueror* in 1906.

Pelle the Conqueror was his first proletarian novel, a lengthy undertaking running to four volumes over a span of four years. Proclaiming the triumph of Danish social-democracy, it was highly successful in gaining readers, so that Nexö was encouraged to attempt another work in the same vein. This time he changed from a proletarian hero to a proletarian heroine, creating his *Ditte* novel which ran to five volumes.

With the success of these two ambitious works, Nexö was established as a spokesman of the masses, a crusader against the poverty he knew so well. The rest of his life was spent in producing what was frankly propaganda for the Marxist cause. After World War I, he went to Germany to study the Communist movement there; he remained until Hitler's rise to power.

Back in Denmark he continued his contributions to leftist periodicals and wrote a series of autobiographical works on the theme of his first-hand knowledge of poverty. He was captured by the Nazis when they invaded Denmark during World War II but escaped into Sweden in 1943. After the war he settled in East Germany and continued his propagandistic writing until his death at Dresden on June 1, 1954.

BIBLIOGRAPHICAL REFERENCES: The best introduction to Nexø in English is the essay in Harry Slochower, *Three Ways of Modern Man*, 1937. See also K. K. Nicolaisen, *Martin Andersen Nexø*, 1919; and W. A. Berendsohn, *Martin Andersen Nexø*, 1948.

FRIEDRICH WILHELM NIETZSCHE

Born: Röcken, Saxony
Date: October 15, 1844

Died: Weimar, Germany
Date: August 25, 1900

PRINCIPAL WORKS

PHILOSOPHICAL DISCOURSES: *Die Geburt der Tragödie*, 1872 (*The Birth of Tragedy*); *Unzeitgemässe Betrachtungen*, 1873–1876 (*Thoughts out of Season*); *Menschliches, Allzumenschliches*, 1878 (*Human, All Too Human*); *Morgenröte*, 1881 (*The Dawn of Day*); *Die fröhliche Wissenschaft*, 1882 (*The Joyful Wisdom*); *Also sprach Zarathustra*, 1883–1885 (*Thus Spake Zarathustra*); *Jenseits von Gut und Böse*, 1886 (*Beyond Good and Evil*); *Zur Genealogie der Moral*, 1887 (*The Genealogy of Morals*); *Der Fall Wagner*, 1888 (*The Case of Wagner*); *Götzendämmerung*, 1889 (*Twilight of the Idols*); *Der Antichrist*, 1902 (*The Antichrist*); *Nietzsche contra Wagner*, 1901; *Ecce Homo*, 1908.

Friedrich Nietzsche, who proclaimed in his philosophy that men could become supermen, rising beyond good and evil, leaving behind them the slave morality of Christianity, was the son of a Lutheran pastor in the village of Röcken, Saxony. He was christened

Friedrich Wilhelm Nietzsche, to honor the King of Prussia, Frederick William IV, on whose birthday, October 15, he was born in 1844.

When Nietzsche was four years old, his father injured himself falling on some stone steps and died after a year's mental and physical illness. For years Friedrich was disturbed by the idea that he might inherit insanity from his father; but although he did go insane in 1889, it seems more likely that his madness was the result of a syphilitic infection.

After the pastor's death Nietzsche was taken with his sister Elizabeth to Naumburg where his mother's family, the Oehlers, lived. He was brought up in the midst of five women: his mother, his grandmother, two aunts, and his sister. Naturally, he was overprotected, overcaressed, and overruled. It is not surprising that in later life some of his most bitter language is directed against women: in *Thus Spake Zarathustra* he advised: "Thou goest to woman? Do not forget thy whip."

As a young boy Nietzsche was well-behaved and conscientious. When he was fourteen he attended a school in Pforta, five miles from Naumburg. Until he was eighteen he was a bright, regular student; but then he began to miss classes, to get drunk in beer halls, and to spend more time listening to music than studying. However, he managed to graduate from Pforta. He entered the University of Bonn in October, 1864, to study theology and philosophy. Apparently he spent a considerable amount of time drinking beer, singing with the student corps, and talking about or actually venturing out with women; and the result was that he came to regard his year there as a "lost year" and the student life as coarse and expensive.

He then undertook the study of philology at the University of Leipzig under Professor Ritschl. He applied himself diligently to the study of languages but amused himself with walks, music, and reading. He found in Schopenhauer a philosopher worthy of serious study, and he avidly went through *The World as Will and Idea* (1818) after finding a copy in a Leipzig book shop. The notion that everything is a manifestation of the will to live appealed to Nietzsche, and he was emotionally in accord with Schopenhauer's pessimism; but as he reflected on Schopenhauer's philosophy and attempted to reconcile it with his own opinions, he began to believe that the will to power is the basic force in the universe, that man's duty is not to extinguish the will to life, as Schopenhauer had urged, but to accept existence and to become strong.

In 1867 he was compelled to serve in the Prussian cavalry despite his claim that his health was poor and he had a widowed mother to support. He was released after a fall from a horse tore his chest muscles and fractured his ribs. The following year he enjoyed two triumphs: an article of his was published in a philological journal and won critical acceptance from professional scholars; and he accepted a chair in philology at the University of Basel. His doctorate in philosophy was awarded without his writing a thesis. But his academic career was interrupted by the Franco-Prussian War. He served in the German ambulance corps for a short time until he was discharged after an attack of dysentery and diphtheria.

Having met the composer Wagner in Leipzig, Nietzsche reintroduced himself when Wagner, with his mistress Cosima von Bülow, settled in Triebschen, Switzerland. A strong friendship developed, and Nietzsche's first book, *The Birth of Tragedy from the Spirit of Music*, was a defense of the thesis that Wagner represented the triumph of the Dionysian spirit over the Apollonian. The book was dismissed by philologists, and Nietzsche's reputation as a scholar was fatally damaged. In ill health and with few students he continued at Basel until 1879 when he was pensioned at the age of thirty-four. His friendship with Wagner declined as Wagner's popular fame increased, and Nietzsche later charged Wagner with having succumbed to the destructive influence of Christianity.

He traveled to France, to Italy, to Germany, and then back to Switzerland. During the next ten years he produced his greatest works, the most famous being *Thus Spake Zarathustra*, in which he urged that men assert their natural power against the slave morality of Christianity. His ideas were more carefully developed in *Beyond Good and Evil* and *The Genealogy of Morals*.

In 1882 he had a disillusioning experience with a young Finnish girl, Lou Salomé, who was willing to join him in the search for truth, but not in marriage. His friendships were never of long duration; although he was generally regarded as a genius, he was also considered impossible to live with. He was often in poor health, suffering headaches, nausea, nervous disturbances, and eye trouble. In December 1888 or January 1889 he became insane, and he was taken to a mental hospital in Basel. Later his mother moved him to Jena, and in 1897 his sister Elizabeth took him to Weimar, where he died on August 25, 1900. His last ten years were spent in a state of complete, although not violent, insanity.

His work has had a considerable influence on Nazi and totalitarian type political thinkers. Some critics have maintained, however, that a proper reading of Nietzsche will show his basic antipathy to movements in which physical and economic power is the basic force to be utilized.

BIBLIOGRAPHICAL REFERENCES: All of Nietzsche's works are available in English translation. For biography and critical comment see C. A. Bernoulli, *Franz Overbeck und Friedrich Nietzsche: Eine Freundschaft*, 1908; E. Forster-Nietzsche, *The Life of Nietzsche*, translated by A. M. Ludovici, 1912–1915; Charles Andler, *Nietzsche, sa vie et sa pensée*, 1920–1931; and Crane Brinton, *Nietzsche*, 1948.

IPPOLITO NIEVO

Born: Padua, Italy
Date: November 30, 1831

Died: At sea
Date: March 4 (?), 1861

PRINCIPAL WORKS

NOVELS: *Angelo di Bontà*, 1855 (*Angel of Goodness*); *Il Conte pecoraio*, 1857 (*The Shepherd Count*); *Le Confessioni di un ottuagenario*, 1867 (*Confessions of an Octogenarian*).

POEMS: *Versi*, 1854; *Le Lucciole*, 1858; *Amori Garibaldini*, 1860.

The one truly great novel of mid-nineteenth century Italy is Ippolito Nievo's *Confessions of an Octogenarian*, written between December, 1857, and August, 1858, and published six years after the writer's death. This masterpiece was preceded by two collections of poems, several plays, and

789

two novellas which may be described as the beginning of modern Italian realism. *Angel of Goodness* re-creates eighteenth century Venice with minute fidelity to detail in manners and dialect, while *The Shepherd Count* sets a similar story in Nievo's own day and region. Both are poetically conceived, yet realistic in the depiction of Italian peasant life.

Nievo, born in Padua on November 30, 1831, was descended from a patrician family of Venetian background. During his student days at Mantua and Pisa he became interested in the cause of Italian freedom. Graduated from the University of Padua in 1855, he wrote poems and plays that on at least one occasion involved him in difficulties with the Austrian authorities. In May, 1859, following the outbreak of hostilities between Austria and the Italian patriots, he joined the rebels under the leadership of Garibaldi and fought at Varese, San Fermo, and Calatafimi. One of Garibaldi's "Thousand," he was at Naples in charge of administrative duties in 1861. Ordered to return to Palermo, he sailed, March 4, 1861, aboard a ship believed to have foundered during the voyage; there were no survivors to tell what had happened to the ship or its company.

The *Confessions* is written as the autobiography of one Carlo Altoviti, who tells of the rambling castle in which he grew up, of his turbulent love for the daughter of a countess, and of his final peace in maturity. The chapters dealing with Altoviti's boyhood experience are particularly impressive. But the manuscript was never revised by the author and is thus somewhat loose and rambling in structure. Nievo had intended, possibly for patriotic reasons, to call his novel *The Confessions of an Italian*. However, its publisher in 1867 thought the title too political and renamed it *The Confessions of an Octogenarian*, by which the book is still generally known. Competent criticism has declared that this is the only Italian novel which can be compared with Manzoni's *The Betrothed*.

BIBLIOGRAPHICAL REFERENCES: There is no complete translation of the *Confessions* in English. The section telling of Altoviti's boyhood, translated by Lovett F. Edwards, was published as *The Castle of Fratta* in 1954 and under the same title was enlarged in 1957 to include the later sections dealing with Italy in the Napoleonic era. An excellent brief introduction to Nievo is the translator's prefaces to these editions. The complete text of the *Confessions* was edited by B. Chiurlo, 1941. Riccardo Bacchelli has also edited a book of selecitons titled *Le piu belle pagine di Ippolito Nievo*, 1929. For more extended biography and criticism see also D. Montovani, *Ippolito Nievo, il poeta soldato*, 1932; Ugo Gallo, *Nievo*, 1932; and G. Galati, *Nievo*, 1940.

CHARLES NORDHOFF and JAMES NORMAN HALL
Charles Nordhoff

Born: London, England   *Died:* Santa Barbara, California
Date: February 1, 1887   *Date:* April 11, 1947

PRINCIPAL WORKS

NOVELS: *The Fledgling*, 1919; *Picaro*, 1921; *The Pearl Lagoon*, 1924; *The Derelict*, 1928.

James Norman Hall

Born: Colfax, Iowa
Date: April 22, 1887

Died: Papeete, Tahiti
Date: July 5, 1951

PRINCIPAL WORKS

NOVELS: *Dr. Dogbody's Leg,* 1940; *Lost Island,* 1944; *Far Lands,* 1950.

POETRY: *The Friends,* 1939; *Word for His Sponsor,* 1949.

MISCELLANEOUS: *Kitchener's Mob,* 1916; *High Adventure,* 1918; *Flying with Chaucer,* 1930; *The Tale of a Shipwreck,* 1935; *Under a Thatched Roof,* 1942; *"Forgotten Ones" and Other True Tales of the South Seas,* 1952; *My Island Home,* 1952.

Nordhoff and Hall in Collaboration

PRINCIPAL WORKS

NOVELS: *Mutiny on the Bounty,* 1932; *Men Against the Sea,* 1933; *Pitcairn's Island,* 1934; *The Hurricane,* 1936; *The Dark River,* 1938; *No More Gas,* 1940; *Botany Bay,* 1941; *Men Without Country,* 1942; *High Barbaree,* 1945.

MISCELLANEOUS: *The Lafayette Flying Corps,* 1921; *Faery Lands of the South Seas,* 1921; *Falcons of France,* 1929.

Charles (Bernard) Nordhoff, the senior member of the writing team of Nordhoff and Hall, was born in London of American parents on February 1, 1887. Brought back to Philadelphia at the age of three, he grew up in California and Mexico, worked for two years on a Mexican sugar plantation, and attended Stanford University for one year before finally settling down in Cambridge, Massachusetts, long enough to receive a degree from Harvard in 1909. And these peripatetic early years were to set the restless pattern of his entire life. Not waiting for the United States to enter the war, he enlisted in the French Ambulance Corps in 1916, becoming, later, a pilot in the French Air Service, and serving, finally, in the Lafayette Flying Corps after this country's participation had begun.

James Norman Hall began life in a quieter fashion. Born in Colfax, Iowa, on April 22, 1887, and educated in the public schools there, he did not leave the Middle West until after his graduation from Grinnell College in 1910. From Grinnell he went to Boston, where he worked as an agent for the Society for the Prevention of Cruelty to Children and where he first met Ellery Sedgwick, editor of the *Atlantic Monthly,* who was later to encourage his literary efforts. With the outbreak of war his life became every bit as turbulent as Nordhoff's. In August of 1914 he enlisted in Lord Kitchener's "The First Hundred Thousand." He next joined the French Flying Service, but later transferred, as Nordhoff had done, to the Lafayette Flying Corps. He distinguished himself as an ace before being shot down behind the German lines and spending the last six months of hostilities as a prisoner of war.

The two first met while serving as members of the Lafayette Flying Corps, and their amazingly productive collaboration began when they were commissioned to write the Corps' history. This task completed, they went together to Tahiti. There they wrote independently at first. But becoming interested in the tales they had heard concerning Pitcairn Island, they revived their partnership and under the sponsorship of Sedgwick, who helped them in securing necessary documents from England, they set to work on the island's fascinating history, producing in 1932 their first novel together, the first book of the *Bounty* trilogy, *Mutiny on the Bounty*. The success of this work, both as a novel and as a motion picture, cemented their partnership. The trilogy was completed with *Men Against the Sea* and *Pitcairn's Island*.

Six other novels resulted from their collaboration, which lasted through the writing of *High Barbaree*. No other approached the brilliance of their initial effort, but the smoothness of their teamwork continued to amaze critics. They augmented and balanced each other; the result of their rapport is, according to an understandingly partial Sedgwick, unique in the history of fiction.

Their partnership was ended by the death of Nordhoff, who died at Santa Barbara, California, April 11, 1947. Hall, who had settled in Tahiti and had married the half-Tahitian daughter of a British sea captain, survived until 1951, dying at Papeete on July 5.

BIBLIOGRAPHICAL REFERENCES: Hall's *My Island Home*, 1952, is an unfinished autobiography which tells little of his adult personal life but does discuss his collaboration with Nordhoff. This collaboration is also dealt with in Ellery Sedgwick, "James Norman Hall, 1877–1951," *Atlantic Monthly*, CLXXXVIII (1951), 19–21; and James McConnaughey, "By Nordhoff and Hall," *Saturday Evening Post*, CCX (1938), 12–13+. A somewhat unsatisfactory critical article is Murray D. Welch, "James Norman Hall: Poet and Philosopher," *South Atlantic Quarterly*, XXXIX (1940), 140–150. See also Horace Sutton, "A Day on Bounty Bay," *Saturday Review*, XXXIV (July 14, 1956), 25–26; Walter G. Smith, "James Norman Hall, 1887–1951," *Atlantic Monthly*, CLXXXVIII (October, 1951), 22+; Robert Van Gelder, *Writers and Writing*, 1946; and Harvey Breit, *The Writers Observed*, 1956.

FRANK NORRIS

Born: Chicago, Illinois
Date: March 5, 1870

Died: San Francisco, California
Date: October 25, 1902

PRINCIPAL WORKS

NOVELS: *Moran of the Lady Letty*, 1898; *Blix*, 1899; *McTeague*, 1899; *A Man's Woman*, 1900; *The Octopus*, 1901; *The Pit*, 1903; *Vandover and the Brute*, 1914.
SHORT STORIES: *A Deal in Wheat and Other Stories*, 1903; *The Third Circle*, 1909.
ESSAYS: *The Responsibilities of the Novelist*, 1903.

Frank Norris wrote in 1899: "Tell your yarn and let your style go to the devil. We don't want literature, we want life." Yet the life he portrayed in his novels was more naturalistic—emphasizing the brutality in man, the sordid in experience—than realistic; and his works are more the dramatiza-

792

tion of his obsession with power and bigness than the "truth" of either the times or the characters of his fiction.

The oldest son of a wealthy jewelry manufacturer and a doting mother, he was born in Chicago on March 5, 1870, and christened Benjamin Franklin Norris, Jr. When he was fourteen, his family moved to San Francisco; the bustling and varied life of that city as well as his wide reading stimulated his boyish imagination and turned him away from all thoughts of a business career. Encouraged by his mother, he began the study of art and spent a year at the Atelier Julien in Paris. In 1890 he entered the University of California, read Darwin and Zola, and began *McTeague*. After four years at the university, without taking a degree, he transferred to Harvard. There, encouraged by Professor Lewis E. Gates, he worked at *McTeague* and completed *Vandover and the Brute*.

During the Boer War he was in South Africa as a correspondent for the San Francisco *Chronicle*. After editorial experience on *The Wave*, a magazine published in San Francisco, he went to New York to work for the S. S. McClure syndicate. In 1898 he went to Cuba to report on the Spanish-American War. Following his return to New York, he married and became a reader for the firm of Doubleday, Page and Company. As a publisher's reader, he was the discoverer of Theodore Dreiser's *Sister Carrie* (1900).

Physically frail as a boy, Norris had greatly admired his powerful, aggressive father, but was rejected by him because of the boy's obedience to his artistic, possessive mother. When his parents were divorced, Norris apparently suffered a form of psychological split; his brief career as a writer has been explained as an attempt at refusion by attempting big things to please his father while traveling along the path of art which his mother has laid out for him. He never completed either of the two great trilogies he planned, yet his books gave promise of what he might have achieved as a writer of the naturalistic school. In his projected Epic of the Wheat, for example, he wished to express his indignation over as well as his admiration for the men who through organization and exploitation had taken over the economic and social control of America. The expansion of the railroads alone had produced vast outer conflicts and inner tensions, the latter principally because there was no frontier left for the less aggressive and the ethical to flee to. Norris wrote of both the aggressors and those in conflict with them, but in his emphasis on the business of social conflict rather than on character, in his preoccupation with the sordid, shocking, and depressing, and in his obsession with size and violence, he was frequently the traditional romantic in reverse. In addition, he mixed his literary styles, sometimes writing realistically and sometimes weaving into his work an almost mystic poetical quality. This fusion of the naturalistic and the poetic makes him a distinctive writer, as well as an artistic failure in all his novels except *McTeague*.

Vandover and the Brute, although published last, was the first written of his novels. (The loss of the manuscript during the San Francisco fire accounts for the long-delayed publication). It is a thinly disguised tale of Norris' own attempt to find release from his unhappy relationship with his incompatible parents, a work in which he relived his own defeats in dilettante debauchery and prophesied his doom as a broken cleaner of closets. Of little interest for the average reader today, it curiously fits a prejudice of the time in its philosophy that anyone born to wealth deserved a miserable and impoverished end.

Superior in every way to the Nietzschean primitivism of *Moran of the Lady Letty* and the semi-autobiographical *Blix*, *McTeague* also presents the theme of indulgence and punishment, but within a milieu quite different from that of Norris himself. More objective in treatment, it is also more a work of the creative imagination in the manner of Zola; melodramatic situations and exaggeration of the degree of brutality and avarice in American life mar but do not destroy the sheer driving power of narrative in this story of a crude, brutal dentist corrupted by his passion for gold.

Norris was not to find another subject suited to his talents until he conceived his Epic of the Wheat. In *The Octopus*, the first novel of his proposed trilogy, he tells of the planting and harvesting of the wheat; the fertile land is presented as a symbol of force in a plot centering on conflict between the farmers of the San Joaquin Valley in California and the Southern Pacific Railroad, an industrial octopus with tentacles of steel. In this novel the human antagonists are doomed to defeat, but the prevailing mood of pessimism is in part redeemed by a conclusion which suggests the tradition of the sentimental novel in its assurance that everything has occurred for the best, that no matter how many lives are destroyed in the production of wheat more lives are sustained by it as food. *The Pit* continues the story of wheat through the speculation and exploitation of the Chicago grain market. This novel is less an artistic melange, but the work suffers from the writer's reversion to memories of his own family for some of his situations and scenes. In it the main protagonists are drawn after his father and mother, with the mother choosing the wrong lover (a businessman rather than an artist) for her husband. As in the case of *The Octopus*, the characters are overdrawn and the naturalistic tone is blurred by the note of personal mysticism at the end.

Norris had sketchily outlined a third novel, *The Wolf*, which would deal with the need for and the consumption of wheat abroad. But this book, like the trilogy he had planned on the Battle of Gettysburg, was never written. He died in San Francisco on October 25, 1902, from the post-operative effects of appendicitis.

BIBLIOGRAPHICAL REFERENCES: The writings of Frank Norris were collected in the limited Argonaut Manuscript Edition and a trade edition, 10 vols., 1928. A later collection of previously unpublished stories and sketches is *Frank Norris of "The Wave,"* edited by Oscar Lewis, 1931. The standard biography is Franklin Walker, *Frank Norris: A Biography*, 1932. The best critical work is Ernest Marchand, *Frank Norris: A Study*, 1942, which contains a bibliography. See also Kenneth S. Lynn, *The Dream of Success*, 1955; and Richard Chase, *The American Novel and Its Tradition*, 1957.

THOMAS NORTON and THOMAS SACKVILLE

Norton

Born: London, England
Date: 1532

Died: Sharpenhoe, England
Date: March 10, 1584

PRINCIPAL WORK

TRANSLATIONS: *Calvin's Institutes*, 1561.

Sackville

Born: Buckhurst, Sussex, England
Date: 1536

Died: London, England
Date: April 19, 1608

PRINCIPAL WORKS

POEMS: "Induction" and "The Complaint of Henry, Duke of Buckingham" from *A Mirror for Magistrates*, (2nd ed.), 1563.

Norton and Sackville in Collaboration

PRINCIPAL WORK

PLAY: *Gorboduc, or Ferrex and Porrex*, 1562.

Norton and Sackville are literary twins bound together in their humble sphere as surely as Beaumont and Fletcher or Gilbert and Sullivan. Both lived full lives with active careers in government, and both wrote independently; but their surest hold on fame is their joint effort, *Gorboduc*, the first blank-verse tragedy in English. When *Gorboduc* was written, *King Lear* loomed in the mists of the future.

According to the early text of *Gorboduc*, Thomas Norton wrote the first three acts, and Thomas Sackville the last two. Norton was born in London in 1532 and was probably educated at Cambridge University. He was admitted to the Inner Temple in 1555. At about the same time he married the daughter of Archbishop Cranmer, whose Protestantism he followed with increasing intensity. In 1557 he contributed to *Tottel's Miscellany*; of

course his work there was overshadowed by the poems of the more famous Sir Thomas Wyatt and Henry Howard, the Earl of Surrey. *Gorboduc* was produced before Queen Elizabeth I on January 18, 1562 (new style). It was published first in 1565 and in an improved text in 1570.

In 1558 he was elected to Parliament, and in 1562 he represented Berwick in Parliament. He held other important positions in the Queen's government. After the death of his first wife he married a niece of his Archbishop father-in-law. His second wife lost her mind as a result of violent religious fanaticism. The latter part of Norton's own career was spent in fanatical activities as a militant Calvinist. He wrote numerous controversial tracts against the Catholics, and his violence as a persecutor led to his imprisonment in the Tower in 1583. He

795

was, however, released before his death at Sharpenhoe, Bedfordshire, on March 10, 1584.

Born at Buckhurst, Sussex, in 1536, Thomas Sackville was the son of Sir Richard and Lady Winifrede Sackville, and grandson of Sir John Bridges, Lord Mayor of London. Presumably, like Norton, he went to Cambridge; he was admitted to the Inner Temple and called to the bar. In 1554 he married the daughter of Sir John Baker; they had four sons and three daughters. In 1557 he was elected to Parliament.

After beginning his political career he began a very successful and promising literary one. Norton's small niche in literary history would probably be vacated if Gorboduc were taken away; but Sackville would have a secure, though minor, place even without the famous tragedy. His "Induction" from A Mirror for Magistrates is an important transitional piece in a relatively barren poetic period between Chaucer and Spenser. It is written in respectable verse and still holds an occasional place in anthologies; it is by no means unreadable even to modern tastes. Spenser prefixed to The Faerie Queene a sonnet addressed to Sackville.

However, Sackville turned from his promising literary career to devote himself to an impressive political life. He became Lord Buckhurst in 1567, Chancellor of the University of Oxford in 1591, member of the Privy Council and Lord Treasurer in 1603, and Earl of Dorset in 1604. His death at the council table in Whitehall on April 19, 1608, in his eighth decade, was a fitting and dramatic one.

Nevertheless, the impressive political careers of the two men would not have kept their names as much alive as their single tragedy has. Gorboduc is honored and studied as a noble progenitor and prototype of perhaps the greatest glory of English literature: Elizabethan tragedy. Although it gains much from the classical learning of its authors, it draws much of its life from native sources: it is part classical tragedy, part medieval morality, and part political propaganda. Its main purpose was to convince Queen Elizabeth of the necessity of establishing a definite succession to the Crown, in order to avoid civil war of the sort depicted in the play. Its solid structural and stylistic virtues and its thoughtfulness outweigh the currently accepted notion that it is dull.

BIBLIOGRAPHICAL REFERENCES: For biographical and critical studies see *Dictionary of National Biography*, Vols. XIV and XVII, 1921; E. K. Chambers, *The Elizabethan Stage*, Vol. III, 1923; and C. R. Baskervill, V. B. Heltzel, and A. H. Nethercot, *Elizabethan and Stuart Plays*, 1934.

KATE O'BRIEN

Born: Limerick, Ireland
Date: December 3, 1897

PRINCIPAL WORKS

NOVELS: *Without My Cloak*, 1931; *Mary Lavelle*, 1936; *Pray for the Wanderer*, 1938; *The Last of Summer*, 1943; *That Lady*, 1946 [*For One Sweet Grape*]; *The Flower of May*, 1953.

PLAYS: *Distinguished Villa*, 1926; *The Bridge*, 1927; *The Schoolroom Window*, 1937; *That Lady*, 1949.

MISCELLANEOUS: *Farewell, Spain*, 1937; *English Diaries and Journals*, 1943; *Teresa of Avila*, 1951.

Kate O'Brien was born on December 3, 1897, at Limerick, the "Mellick" of her novels. Going to London as a young woman, she wrote for newspapers and from journalism turned to drama. Her first play, *Distinguished Villa*, the only one of her six plays thus far published, was staged successfully in London in 1926; it was followed the next year by *The Bridge*. After moving to Spain, where she lived until the Falangist Civil War, Miss O'Brien achieved her more substantial reputation as a novelist. She has continued, however, to write for the theater and has adapted to that medium three narratives of her own, including her historical novel, *That Lady*.

A psychological novelist, Miss O'Brien is expert in her handling of modern techniques. Thematically, *The Last of Summer* is characteristic: The heroine, an actress reared in France, visits for the first time her father's childhood home in Ireland, where she is forced to cope with the family of her domineering aunt. The tension between the girl's warm, equable temperament and the neuroses of the cousin with whom she falls in love causes an inevitable exposure of divided emotional loyalties. Also, Miss O'Brien has frequently been concerned with failures of the artistic spirit to quicken sympathy in the conservative, Catholic Irish middle class.

BIBLIOGRAPHICAL REFERENCES: See Matthew Hoehn, ed., *Catholic Authors*, 1948; and Harvey Breit, "Talk with Kate O'Brien," *New York Times Book Review*, December 4, 1949, 22.

SEAN O'CASEY

Born: Dublin, Ireland
Date: March 31, 1884

PRINCIPAL WORKS

PLAYS: *The Shadow of a Gunman*, 1923; *Juno and the Paycock*, 1924; *The Plough and the Stars*, 1926; *The Silver Tassie*, 1929; *Within the Gates*, 1933; *The Star Turns Red*, 1940; *Purple Dust*, 1940; *Red Roses for Me*, 1942; *Oak Leaves and Lavender*, 1946; *Cockadoodle Dandy*, 1949; *The Bishop's Bonfire*, 1955.

AUTOBIOGRAPHY: *I Knock at the Door*, 1939; *Pictures in the Hallway*, 1942; *Drums Under the Windows*, 1945; *Inishfallen, Fare Thee Well*, 1949; *Rose and Crown*, 1952; *Sunset and Evening Star*, 1954.

MISCELLANEOUS: *The Story of the Irish Citizen Army*, 1919; *Windfalls*, 1934; *The Flying Wasp*, 1936; *The Green Crow*, 1956.

Sean O'Casey, Irish playwright who was one of the chief adornments of the Irish theater during its time of glory, is to be mentioned along with Yeats, Synge, and Lennox Robinson. He differs from these and other Irish playwrights in that he does not go to the time of Irish legend, as does Yeats, or to the chiefly picturesque village life, as do Robinson and Lady Gregory. Instead, his plays are a reflection of the troubled political and economic currents of his own time. He has the color of his own day; he eschews "local color." His plays are permanently interesting because his final concern is human nature, but human nature under the pressures which the history and the economic structure of the twentieth century have created. Consequently, his audiences are asked to give their attention to the inefficacy of certain decaying institutions; they are asked to weigh seriously certain hopes which have stirred men in this century.

That this should be O'Casey's accent is suggested by the course of his life. O'Casey, born in the Dublin slums on March 31, 1884, was the son of a Wicklow mother and a Limerick father, and one member of a numerous family that had to exist on limited means after the father's early death. In childhood Sean O'Casey, suffering from a severe eye disease which kept him from formal schooling except for about three years, taught himself and became interested in literature, especially the works of Shakespeare, Milton, and later poets. At eighteen he began work as a laborer and, becoming interested in the Irish Nationalist Movement, he was active in the Sinn Fein activities and the Easter Rebellion of 1916. At that time he also learned Gaelic.

He wrote his first play for the dramatic class of the National Club, but the group could not perform it, nor could that famous institution, the Abbey Theatre, where it was also sent. Two more plays followed unsuccess-fully; but the fourth, *The Shadow of a Gunman,* was produced successfully. Other plays followed: *June and the Paycock, The Plough and the Stars,* and *The Silver Tassie.* O'Casey went to England in 1926; he married and has two sons and a daughter.

Like their author, O'Casey's dramas are deeply engaged in the events of his time. His characters know the sharp bite of poverty; they are stirred into action, now heroic, now comic, by the misery which they endure and by hopes for social improvement which they only partly understand. But unlike many dramas which also have for their point of departure the temporary but very real difficulties of a country (e.g., the plays sponsored by the Federal Theatre in the United States during the 1930's), O'Casey's plays continue to interest audiences that have little or no grasp of the Irish-British tensions of the second decade of our century and have no intrinsic stake in the Catholic-Protestant tensions of Ireland itself. Instead, O'Casey creates, at least in his early plays, a haunting, tragicomic spectacle of misery and revolution thriving in the decayed mansions which, with their spacious rooms and beautiful stairways, offer an ironic counterpoint to the inelegant speech and the abortive hopes of the modern proletariat who rent out the rooms. Moments of violence, moments of grotesque indignity, and moments of awkward and sincere poetry follow each other in O'Casey's plays of the 1920's. Some of O'Casey's later plays abandon the realistic texture of his early work and offer symbolic presentation of O'Casey's insights into modern society. But even these plays of a symbolic nature, like *Within the Gates* and *Red Roses for Me,* display the gift of biting language that was from the start O'Casey's particular gift. O'Casey has called himself a Communist, but he makes clear that this political attitude is a purely personal one since he scorns the political Communists. Certainly this is the attitude that informs many of his plays; the social criticism bitingly conveyed is the result of O'Casey's direct reaction to the paradoxes of modern life; he follows no line laid out by a party committee.

O'Casey's later life, much of it devoted to the composition of his interesting recollections of his early days, is a kind of exile from Ireland and, more extensively, from all lands and creeds and literary groups. His later plays record his loyalty to the powers of direct perception and his impatience with what he regards as social, religious, and political shibboleths.

BIBLIOGRAPHICAL REFERENCES: Although highly subjective and frequently colored by prejudice, *Mirror in My House,* the collected edition of the autobiographies of Sean O'Casey, 1939–1954, provides the best source of biographical material. For a more objective picture see Jules Koslow, *The Green and the Red: Sean O'Casey, the Man and His Plays,* 1950. For briefer studies see also John Gassner, *Masters of the Drama,* 1940, 1945; Brooks Atkinson, *Broadway Scrapbook,* 1947; Peter Kavanagh, *The Story of the Abbey Theatre from Its Origins in 1899 to the Present,* 1950; John Gassner, "The Prodigality of Sean O'Casey," *Theatre Arts Monthly,* XXXV (1951), 52–53+ (June), 54–55+ (July), 48–49+ (August); and J. C. Trewin, "Lord of Language," *Drama,* No. 35 (Winter, 1954), 34–38.

CLIFFORD ODETS

Born: Philadelphia, Pennsylvania
Date: July 18, 1906

Died: Los Angeles, California
Date: August 14, 1963

PRINCIPAL WORKS

PLAYS: *Waiting for Lefty,* 1935; *Awake and Sing,* 1935; *Till the Day I Die,* 1935; *Paradise Lost,* 1935; *Golden Boy,* 1937; *Rocket to the Moon,* 1938; *Night Music,* 1940; *Clash by Night,* 1941; *The Big Knife,* 1949; *The Country Girl,* 1950.

Clifford Odets, born in Philadelphia, Pennsylvania, on July 18, 1906, was reared in middle-class surroundings but grew up to write some of the most controversial proletarian dramas of our time. Educated in the Bronx, New York City, he left high school after his second year to seek a career in the entertainment field. From 1925 to 1927 he directed a drama group on the radio, and read poetry there and in vaudeville. Other jobs included announcing, script writing, creating sound effects arranging, and acting with a stock company on a summer theater circuit. These activities led him to work with the Theatre Guild in 1928 and to membership in the Group Theatre at the beginning of the depression in 1930. It was while acting with this latter organization that he wrote and had produced by it three plays in 1935, *Awake and Sing!, Waiting for Lefty,* and *Till the Day I Die.* In tune with the prevailing mood of pessimism, the plays were not only financially successful: they won Odets the Yale Drama Prize for that year and an invitation from Hollywood to write motion picture scripts. Though failing to produce a memorable film, he wrote *Golden Boy* in 1937, his best play and perhaps the only one (with the possible exception of *The Country Girl*) likely to survive on the basis of good theater.

All of Odets's plays of the 1930's were basically social criticism or propaganda for proletarian collectivism. All the characters are Americans dispossessed not only of economic opportunity but also of their very dignity. The Berger family in *Awake and Sing!* could find suicide of the old to collect insurance the only method of survival for the young. During World War II Odets frankly espoused the Russian way of life with his adaptation of *The Russian People*. He was not incuriously silent after the war, in the light of the revelations of Russian manners. The beginning of the 1950's saw him turning toward the world of American entertainment, out of which has come so far *The Big Knife* and *The Country Girl*, the latter made into a prize-winning motion picture in 1954.

BIBLIOGRAPHICAL REFERENCES: A useful volume is *Six Plays of Clifford Odets*, Modern Library, 1939. There is as yet no full-length study of Odets, but reliable estimates of the early portion of his career may be found in Burns Mantle, *Contemporary American Playwrights*, 1938; and Joseph Wood Krutch, *The American Drama Since 1918: An Informal History*, 1939. An interesting profile is John McCarten's "Revolution's Number One Boy," *New Yorker*, Jan. 22, 1938, 21–27. See also E. J. Isaacs, "Clifford Odets," *Theatre Arts Monthly*, XXIII (1939), 257–264; John Gassner, "The Long Journey of Talent," *ibid.*, XXXIII (1949), 25–30; and R. S. Warshow, "Poet of the Jewish Middle Class," *Commentary*, I (1946), 17–22.

SEÁN O'FAOLÁIN

Born: Cork, Ireland
Date: February 22, 1900

PRINCIPAL WORKS

NOVELS: *A Nest of Simple Folk*, 1933; *Bird Alone*, 1936; *Come Back to Erin*, 1940.

SHORT STORIES: *Midsummer Night Madness and Other Stories*, 1932; *There's a Birdie in the Cage*, 1935; *A Purse of Coppers*, 1937; *Teresa*, 1946; *The Man Who Invented Sin*, 1948; *The Finest Stories of Seán O'Faoláin*, 1957.

BIOGRAPHY: *The Life Story of Eamon De Valera*, 1933; *Constance Markievicz*, 1934; *King of the Beggars: A Life of Daniel O'Connell*, 1938; *The Great O'Neill*, 1942.

PLAY: *She Had to Do Something*, 1938.

TRAVEL AND MISCELLANEOUS: *The Silver Branch*, 1938; *An Irish Journey*, 1940; *The Irish*, 1948; *Summer in Italy*, 1950; *South to Sicily*, 1953.

Seán O'Faoláin was born in Cork, Ireland, February 22, 1900, the son of Denis Whelan and his wife Bridget Whelan. An Irish nationalist, he adopted the Gaelic variant of his name as part of a personal campaign to reassert the values of the Irish past.

O'Faoláin's education began at the Presentation Brothers' School in Cork and continued with advanced study at the National University of Ireland, which awarded him an M.A., and as a Comonwealth Fellow at Harvard University from 1926–1928, where he received a second master's degree. He fought in the Irish Revolution (1918–1921) and then, when the Sinn Fein party split into a right and left wing because of differing policies concerning the treaty with England, O'Faoláin took the Republican side during the civil war and became director of publicity for the Republican Army.

O'Faoláin spent the academic year 1928–1929 at Harvard as a John Harvard Fellow. During the following year he taught Gaelic at Harvard and Anglo-Irish literature at Boston College. During the next three years he was lecturer in English at St. Mary's Training College, Strawberry Hill. He did not enjoy teaching and consequently welcomed the freedom which soon came through his fiction and biographies.

His first volume of short stories, *Midsummer Night Madness and Other Stories*, was published in 1932 and immediately brought him to the attention of those who were looking for the distinctive Irish combination of compassion for the "simple folk" of Ireland and a sense of the close relationship between heroism and a spirit of independence. The stories are concerned with Irish life from the period of the Easter Rebellion of 1916, a consequence of the Sinn Fein movement for complete independence of Ireland, through the days following the establishment in 1921 of the Irish Free State. The book was nominated for the Femina Prize and brought an invitation to him to become a charter member of the Irish Academy of Letters.

With his first novel, *A Nest of Simple Folk,* he achieved the kind of critical and popular response which made financial independence as a writer possible. He returned to Ireland where he continued his writing, becoming more and more interested as time went on in the writing of biographies and travel books.

Since World War II he has traveled in Europe and the United States, spending some time as a lecturer in 1954 at the Graduate School of Princeton University. Perhaps his most controversial and widely read piece in the United States has been his article, "Love Among the Irish" which appeared in *Life Magazine* on March 16, 1953. In that article he developed many of his familiar themes: the restrictive effects of Irish family traditions, the dangers of church censorship, the marriage problem for the Irish young people whose lives are conditioned and inhibited by provincial traditions of church, state, and family. His attitude has made him a controversial writer, a critic as well as a realist; but in his work there is a stubborn devotion to Ireland which belies his advice to the young to get out of Ireland.

His reputation as a biographer and travel writer has gradually supplanted his earlier fame as a short story writer and novelist. Although there has been a change of literary medium O'Faoláin continues to be concerned with realistic portrayals of the people and the country of Ireland, and consequently there is a continuity to his work.

BIBLIOGRAPHICAL REFERENCES: There is no extended biographical or critical study. For criticism and comment see Seán O'Faoláin, Introduction to *The Finest Stories of Seán O'Faoláin,* 1957; Malcolm Cowley, "Yeats and O'Faoláin," *New Republic,* XCVIII (February 15, 1939), 49–50; and J. V. Kelleher, "Seán O'Faoláin," *Atlantic Monthly,* CXCIX (May, 1957), 67–69.

LIAM O'FLAHERTY

Born: Aran Islands, Ireland
Date: 1896

PRINCIPAL WORKS

NOVELS: *Thy Neighbor's Wife*, 1923; *The Black Soul*, 1924; *The Informer*, 1925; *Mr. Gilhooley*, 1926; *The Assassin*, 1928; *The House of Gold*, 1929; *The Puritan*, 1931; *Skerrett*, 1932; *The Martyr*, 1933; *Famine*, 1937; *Land*, 1946; *Insurrection*, 1950.

SHORT STORIES: *Spring Sowing*, 1926; *The Tent and Other Stories*, 1926; *The Fairy-Goose and Two Other Stories*, 1927; *The Mountain Tavern and Other Stories*, 1929; *The Wild Swan and Other Stories*, 1932; *Two Lovely Beasts and Other Stories*, 1948; *The Stories of Liam O'Flaherty*, 1956.

AUTOBIOGRAPHY: *Two Years*, 1930; *Shame the Devil*, 1934.

BIOGRAPHY: *The Life of Tim Healy*, 1927.

Liam O'Flaherty is an Irish novelist who has always had a direct knowledge of the land and a genuine compassion for the people of Ireland. He has concerned himself in his work almost exclusively with the poor and the laboring, and his efforts as a writer have been to communicate a sense of their dignity and their worth. Born in the Aran Islands in 1896, O'Flaherty began life in a struggling community where primitive conditions were imposed by a barren land. As Robert Flaherty's motion picture, *Man of Aran*, shows, no setting would be more likely to give a youth the full appreciation of the problems of bare survival and of the courage it takes to resolve those problems. O'Flaherty's novels express his acute awareness of the stubborn courage and perseverance demanded of those who would live in the Aran Islands and in other barren parts of Ireland.

He was educated by Catholic priests as a postulant for the priesthood, and then at Rockwell College, Blackrock College, and University College in Dublin. He left the college to join the Irish Guards and served on the Western Front, in France, for six months during the First World War. He was wounded in 1917 and discharged with a disability pension.

As O'Flaherty relates in his autobiographical *Two Years*, the two years after his discharge from the army were a period of extensive travel and experience in various temporary jobs. His travels ranged from Ireland to South America, through the United States and Canada, and to Turkey. During the course of his travels he undertook menial employment of various kinds. According to his report—not always trustworthy, say the critics—he was a lumberjack in Canada, a brewer's fireman, a night porter in a hotel, a miner, a printer's devil in Boston, a worker in a canned milk factory, a waiter, a dish washer, a bank clerk, a stoker, and a deckhand. While working in a tire factory in Hartford, Connecticut, he began writing short stories.

Whatever the actual facts of his wanderings—facts which may never be determined because of what one reviewer called O'Flaherty's "magnificent lies"—there is no question but that he did travel extensively, probably over four continents, and that he was usually associated with the poor and

802

the laboring class wherever he happened to be.

After working at a number of jobs on the eastern coast of the United States, he returned to Ireland and promptly achieved notoriety and expulsion from Ireland for joining unemployed workers in seizing a public building in Dublin. This was but one instance of his active left-wing political activity, motivated apparently not by intellectual idealism but by a spontaneous and intimate sympathy for the underprivileged.

After being forced to leave Ireland, he traveled to England and established residence there. In 1923 his first novel, *Thy Neighbor's Wife*, appeared, followed the next year by *The Black Soul*. With his third novel, *The Informer*, O'Flaherty won a mass audience. His vivid treatment of the psychological and political aspects of common Irish life in a time of civil war made this novel a particularly effective work of naturalistic realism. The force of the novel was retained in translations and O'Flaherty achieved world recognition. He was married to Margaret Barrington in 1926. His travels have resulted in *A Tourist's Guide to Ireland* (1929) and *I Went to Russia* (1931).

O'Flaherty's earlier novels tended to focus upon some one troubled individual, while his later works, such as *Famine* and *Land* are novels of nineteenth century Ireland, depicting the general character of Irish life and conveying its distinctive mood. With *Insurrection* in 1950 O'Flaherty once again won the wholehearted endorsement of most critics, many of whom acknowledged the book as equal to or better than *The Informer*. The action takes place during the 1916 Easter uprising in Ireland and concerns a young Irishman who is killed helping the cowardly son of a woman he meets in a pub. The book has been praised for its poetry and its pathos; it was regarded as "taut, humorous, tragic," and the *Saturday Review of Literature* critic declared that it may be the best O'Flaherty has done. Although some reviewers thought that the novel needed greater scope and that O'Flaherty should have given his characters more individuality, the consensus seemed to be that O'Flaherty's skill as a writer and his knowledge of common life in Ireland keep him very much in the forefront of contemporary Irish writers.

BIBLIOGRAPHICAL REFERENCES: For biographical material see O'Flaherty's two autobiographical studies, *Two Years*, 1930, and *Shame the Devil*, 1934. For brief criticism see also William Troy, "The Position of Liam O'Flaherty," *Bookman*, LXIX (1929), 7–11; and C. H. Warren, "Liam O'Flaherty," *Bookman* (London), LXXVII (1930), 235–236. O'Flaherty is also discussed in J. von Sternemann, "Irische geschichten," *Die Neue Rundschau*, XLII (1931), 521–539.

JOHN O'HARA

Born: Pottsville, Pennsylvania
Date: January 31, 1905

PRINCIPAL WORKS

NOVELS: *Appointment in Samarra*, 1934; *Butterfield 8*, 1935; *Hope of Heaven*, 1938; *A Rage to Live*, 1949; *The Farmer's Hotel*, 1951; *Ten North Frederick*, 1955.

John O'Hara, novelist and short story writer, is one of the chief practitioners in the so-called hard-boiled school of American fiction. His writing is marked by a callous tone and a blunt attitude toward sexual matters; his characters typically belong to the moneyed Ivy League country club set or are members of the demimonde of Broadway and Hollywood. O'Hara gilds his realism, however, with an encyclopedic knowledge of group customs and manners combined with an accurate reproduction of characteristic speech. In a way, he is a special sort of social historian, a tough Horace Walpole. There is, nonetheless, a peculiar ambivalence in O'Hara's attitude toward his material: although he detests the snobbery of his rich characters, the author himself is somehow fascinated by their way of life. Readers who strongly object to O'Hara's brutality perhaps fail to realize that his presentation of frustration and cruelty is in fact an indictment of lives that have abandoned their potentiality for understanding and generosity.

Born on January 31, 1905, in Pottsville, Pennsylvania—which is probably the Gibbsville of his fiction—O'Hara attended preparatory schools but not college. After serving an apprenticeship at an assortment of jobs, he succeeded at screen writing and journalism. In 1934 *Appointment in Samarra* launched him as a promising literary figure. This work, which may be his best, is set in Gibbsville during the prohibition era and describes the circumstances leading to the suicide of a member of the young married set.

Butterfield 8 deals with the death of a party-girl, and is probably based on the Starr Faithful case. *Hope of Heaven* treats the unsuccessful love affair of a screen-writer. *A Rage to Live* is a large work dealing with a married woman who is unable to stay her amatory urges. *The Farmer's Hotel*, a novelette, describes a violent crime among a group of snow-bound travelers. *Ten North Frederick*, also set in Gibbsville, is a strongly-written story of the dissolution of a successful lawyer who secretly longs to be president. This novel received the National Book Award.

O'Hara is also a prolific worker in the short story field. He is especially expert at what has become known as the *New Yorker* type of story, a tight sketch in which a character exposes some lack in his nature or in which a dramatic situation is undramatically stated. His stories have been collected in *The Doctor's Son, Files on Parade, Pipe Night,* and *Hell Box. Pal Joey,* a series of loosely connected letters by a shallow night-club entertainer, was used by O'Hara for the book of a Rodgers and Hart musical in 1940. One of the first well-plotted musical dramas, it had a highly successful revival in 1952. *A Family Party* is a short story issued as a book. *Sweet and Sour* (1954) is a collection of newspaper columns.

Although it is likely that John O'Hara learned some lessons from Hemingway and Fitzgerald, his work is sufficiently individualized to place him as one of the most distinctive American writers now active.

BIBLIOGRAPHICAL REFERENCES: There is no extensive body of criticism on O'Hara. For a good summing up of his present literary position see John Portz, "John O'Hara Up to Now," *College English*, XVI (1955), 493–499, 516. See also *Book Review Digest*, 1934 ff.

EUGENE O'NEILL

Born: New York, N. Y. *Died:* Boston, Massachusetts
Date: October 16, 1888 *Date:* November 27, 1953

Principal Works

PLAYS: *Thirst and Other One-Act Plays*, 1914; *Bound East for Cardiff*, 1916; *Before Breakfast*, 1916; *The Moon of the Caribbees and Six Other Plays of the Sea*, 1919; *Beyond the Horizon*, 1920; *Gold*, 1920; *The Emperor Jones, Diff'rent*, and *The Straw*, 1921; *The Hairy Ape, Anna Christie*, and *The First Man*, 1922; *The Dreamy Kid*, 1922; *All God's Chillun Got Wings*, 1924; *Welded*, 1924; *Desire Under the Elms*, 1925; *The Great God Brown, The Fountain*, and *The Moon of the Caribbees*, 1926; *Marco Millions*, 1927; *Lazarus Laughed*, 1927; *Strange Interlude*, 1928; *Dynamo*, 1929; *Mourning Becomes Electra*, 1931 (*Homecoming, The Hunted*, and *The Haunted*); *Ah! Wilderness*, 1933; *Days Without End*, 1934; *The Iceman Cometh*, 1946; *A Moon for the Misbegotten*, 1952; *Long Day's Journey into Night*, 1956; *A Touch of the Poet*, 1957.

Eugene (Gladstone) O'Neill, American playwright, is often regarded as the most important writer for the theater this country has produced. He was born in New York City, October 16, 1888, the son of the popular melodramatic actor James O'Neill and of the latter's wife, Ella Quinlan. In O'Neill's posthumous and frankly autobiographical play *Long Day's Journey into Night* (completed by 1941 but neither published nor produced until 1956) the father appears as an improvident bohemian, lavish in speculation and with boon companions but parsimonious and unsatisfactory as the head of a family; the mother as a loving, somewhat conventional woman wrecked by the habit of drug-taking contracted during an illness and encouraged by the disorderliness of the domestic establishment. The future playwright attended various private schools, sometimes accompanied his father on tour, and grew into an unhappy, rebellious young man. He was dismissed at the end of his first year at Princeton University and spent five years as a drifter, going as a common sailor on voyages to South America and Europe, later working briefly as a reporter on the New London (Conn.) *Telegraph*.

Some months spent during 1912 in a tuberculosis sanitarium marked the turning point of his life. In the hospital he read widely in the modern drama and, profoundly impressed by Ibsen, even more by August Strindberg, he determined to become a playwright. He spent some time as a student in Professor George Pierce Baker's course at Harvard and saw the first production of one of his plays in 1916, when an amateur group calling itself The Provincetown Players acted his short romantic melodrama, *Bound East for Cardiff*, first at Provincetown, Massachusetts, then at its tiny theater in New York's Greenwich Village. Other one-act melodramas, based like the first

805

on his experience as a sailor, followed, and in 1920 his first full-length, professionally produced play, *Beyond the Horizon*, won the Pulitzer Prize. Passionally committed to his task and extremely prolific, he was soon turning out a rapid succession of plays, all somber in tone but otherwise exhibiting a great variety of themes and styles. Some were commercially produced, others by amateur and semi-amateur groups; but all helped make him before long the most discussed American playwright.

Among the more notable plays of this period were *The Emperor Jones*, *The Hairy Ape*, and *The Great God Brown*, together with his earlier, first great popular success, *Anna Christie*, which differed from these other plays in being realistic rather than "experimental" and "expressionistic" in method. The success of *Desire Under the Elms* in 1924 led to his association with the Theater Guild, the leading "art theater," which produced his two most widely discussed plays, the enormously long *Strange Interlude* in 1928 and the trilogy, *Mourning Becomes Electra*, a modernization of the Greek legend as told by Aeschylus, in 1931. Less notable plays appeared between these outstanding successes, which were not again approached until *The Iceman Cometh* was produced in 1946. In 1936 he became the first American playwright to receive the Nobel Prize, but ill health resulting from Parkinson's disease made composition increasingly difficult for him during the next decade. Two late plays failed to achieve Broadway production during his lifetime, and O'Neill was physically almost incapacitated for several years before his death in Boston on November 27, 1953. He was survived by his third wife, the actress Carlotta Monterey, who became his literary executor.

O'Neill was the author of one comedy, *Ah! Wilderness*, but this play is by no means a completely merry work. The most persistent characteristic of his total writing is its tragic view of life, presented in various ways and seeming to range from prosaic, pessimistic naturalism, through the classic version of man redeemed and ennobled by suffering, to the mystical exultation of *Lazarus Laughed*.

In all of O'Neill's plays, in one way or another, the phrase used by his master Strindberg, "Men are pitiable creatures," is always implicit. The great and even bewildering variety of styles and subject matter is, like the presence of different sociological and psychological theories, less the result of changes in thought than simply of repeated attempts, none found quite satisfactory, to objectify and express his tragic sense of life. Men are seen as pitiable creatures for many reasons, but most significantly they want something which the universe does not seem to provide. O'Neill explicitly stated that it was this seeming "maladjustment" to the universe rather than any political or social maladjustment which interested him most. What does seem to change from play to play is the conclusion to be drawn from man's situation in an alien universe. Sometimes, as in *The Iceman Cometh* (the most nihilistically pessimistic of the plays), O'Neill seems to say that only the deluded are either happy or wise; in other plays he seems to be saying, instead, either that man's aspiration toward the unattainable is his justification and his glory or even, as in *Lazarus Laughed* and perhaps also in

Days Without End, that the universe does hide a saving secret which an occasional individual can penetrate.

O'Neill's greatness has not been universally recognized, and during the decade before his death some insisted that he had been greatly over-estimated. The surprise occasioned by *Long Day's Journey into Night*—one of the most impressive of his plays—stimulated a debate which seems likely to swing definitely in his favor. His unfriendly critics have brought many charges, accusing him especially of over-ambition in his attempt to rival the great tragic writers of the past, of relying too heavily upon Freudian psychology, and of a lack of either precision or beauty in the writing of dialogue. To the first of these charges it is sometimes replied that high ambition was precisely what the modern drama, too content with small subjects and small themes, most conspicuously

lacked and that the Freudianism evident enough in some of his best-known work is not a doctrine being preached but simply a proper use of what is, after all, one of the most important ways in which modern man is accustomed to look at himself and his problems. The third charge was more serious. O'Neill wrote rapidly, sometimes clumsily and repetitiously. There is little wit and in the words little of that poetry upon which Tragedy is sometimes said to depend. Yet the effectiveness of his plays was demonstrated at the time when they were new and continues to be demonstrated today by both the posthumous plays and several revivals. Whatever absolute value may ultimately be put upon O'Neill's work, it seems likely that he will continue to be regarded as the most impressive playwright so far to appear in the United States.

Joseph Wood Krutch

BIBLIOGRAPHICAL REFERENCES: There is no biographical or critical study dealing with the whole of O'Neill's life and career, and there is no complete edition of his plays, the latest being *The Plays of Eugene O'Neill,* 12 vols., 1934–1935. The best book on O'Neill is Barrett H. Clark, *Eugene O'Neill: The Man and His Plays,* 1947 (rev. ed.). Other studies include S. K. Winther, *Eugene O'Neill: A Critical Study,* 1934; R. D. Skinner, *Eugene O'Neill: A Poet's Quest,* 1935; and Edwin A. Engel, *The Haunted Heroes of Eugene O'Neill,* 1953.

See also "The Playwright Unbound: Eugene O'Neill," in T. H. Dickinson, *Playwrights of The New American Theater,* 1925; "Eugene O'Neill, Poet and Mystic," in Arthur H. Quinn, *A History of the American Drama from the Civil War to the Present Day,* Vol. II, 1936 (rev. ed.); "Tragedy: Eugene O'Neill," in Joseph Wood Krutch, *The American Drama Since 1918,* 1939 (rev. ed.); *idem,* Introduction to *Nine Plays,* 1941; Barrett H. Clark, "Aeschylus and O'Neill," *English Journal,* XXI (1932), 699–710; Homer E. Woodbridge, "Eugene O'Neill," *South Atlantic Quarterly,* XXXVII (1938), 22–35; Clara Blackburn, "Continental Influences on Eugene O'Neill's Expressionistic Drama," *American Literature,* XIII (1941), 109–133; F. I. Carpenter, "The Romantic Tragedy of Eugene O'Neill," *College English,* VI (1945), 250–258; and George Jean Nathan, "O'Neill: A Critical Summation," *American Mercury,* LXIII (1946), 713–719.

JOSÉ ORTEGA Y GASSET

Born: Madrid, Spain
Date: May 9, 1883

Died: Madrid
Date: October 18, 1955

PRINCIPAL WORKS

ESSAYS AND STUDIES: *España invertebrada,* 1922 (*Invertebrate Spain*); *El tema de nuestro tiempo,* 1923 (*The Modern Theme*); *La deshumanización del arte,* 1925 (*The Dehumanization of Art*); *La rebelión de las masas,* 1930 (*The Revolt of the Masses*); *Misión de la universidad,* 1930 (*The Mission of the University*); *Del Imperio romano,* 1941 (*Concord and Liberty*); *Historica como sistema,* 1941 (*Towards a Philosophy of History*).

One of the most eminent Spanish philosophers of modern times, a figure whose influence was felt beyond his native country, José Ortega y Gasset, was born in Madrid on May 9, 1883. He was educated at a Jesuit school at Málaga and at the University of Madrid, where he later held the professorship of metaphysics. From 1906 to 1910 he studied in Germany. Returning to Spain, he obtained his professorship in 1911. He published widely in newspapers and reviews, and in 1923 founded the *Revista de Occidente,* which became an important and influential periodical. His announced mission at the time was to "Europeanize Spain" and to combat its traditional cultural isolation.

Ortega y Gasset, long a foe of the monarchy, naturally favored the revolution that overthrew Alfonso XIII in 1931. Indeed, he has been called one of the "Fathers of the Republic," and was elected a deputy from León. But the victory of Franco drove him from Spain, and he spent many years in exile in France, Portugal, and South America. For a time he held a professorship at the University of San Marcos in Peru. In 1945 he returned to Spain.

The first of his books to be translated into English, and the work on which his reputation in the English-speaking world chiefly rests, is *The Revolt of the Masses,* which attained considerable popularity in this country during the 1930's. The title is, to some degree, deceptive, for the author was not dealing with proletarian revolution, as the word "masses" might suggest. Rather, he was concerned with what he regarded as the significant phenomenon of the twentieth century: the emergence of the "mass man" into a position of power. The author recognizes, among human beings, two types: the superior man, intellectually disciplined, cultivated, always demanding more of himself and striving to raise himself still higher; and the "common" man, self-satisfied, lacking in standards, making no demands upon himself, content to be like everyone else. These two classes, the author takes pains to emphasize, have nothing to do with the traditional social divisions; indeed, Ortega y Gasset rather scorns the old European nobility. It is a question of a moral and intellectual elite, the members of which may come from any social milieu.

The fantastic increase in the population of Europe—according to the author, it never rose above 180 millions from the sixth century to 1800, but by 1914 it had reached 460 millions—has produced a continent swarming with people; and the "mass man," thrust upward by sheer force of numbers, has taken over all the functions previously exercised by the superior minority. Through him, all traditional values of European civilization are threatened: "the vulgar proclaims and imposes the right of vulgarity, or vulgarity as a right." Since the masses "neither should nor can direct their own personal existence, and still less rule society in general," Europe is in danger of being destroyed by a kind of internal barbarian invasion.

Ortega y Gasset was not, as his words might seem to imply, an admirer of the dictatorships emerging into European politics at that time; on the contrary, he detested them. He was merely re-emphasizing the traditional European reliance on a small group of genuinely superior men to direct its affairs. This attitude, so different from the American enthusiasm for the "age of the common man," may account for much of the popularity of the book in this country. Ortega y Gasset died in Madrid on October 18, 1955.

BIBLIOGRAPHICAL REFERENCES: Ortega y Gasset's principal works are available in translation. For biography and criticism see Joaquín Iriarte, *Ortega y Gasset*, 1942; José Ferrater Mora, *Ortega y Gasset*, 1957; R. Alonso, *En torno de pensamiento de Ortega y Gasset*, 1946; Julian Marias, *Ortega y Gasset y la idea de la razón vital*, 1948, and *Ortega y tres antípodes*, 1950; E. R. Curtius, "Spanische Perspektiven," in *Die Neue Rundschau*, XXXV (1924); L. Araquistain, "Ortega y Gasset: profeto del fracas de las masas," in *Leviatán*, VII (1934) and VIII (1935); and D. White, "One of the Twelve: The Life and Thought of Ortega y Gasset," *Religion in Life*, XXV (1956), 247–258. A more specialized study is José Sanchez Villaseñor, *Ortega y Gasset: Existentialist*, 1949, an examination of Ortega y Gasset's philosophical attitudes in the light of modern existentialist doctrine.

GEORGE ORWELL
(Eric Hugh Blair)

Born: Motihari, India
Date: 1903

Died: London, England
Date: January 23, 1950

PRINCIPAL WORKS

NOVELS: *Burmese Days*, 1934; *A Clergyman's Daughter*, 1935; *Keep the Aspidistra Flying*, 1936; *Coming Up for Air*, 1939; *Nineteen Eighty-Four*, 1949.

SATIRE: *Animal Farm: A Fairy Story*, 1945.

ESSAYS: *Inside the Whale*, 1940; *Critical Essays*, 1946; *Shooting an Elephant*, 1950.

AUTOBIOGRAPHY: *Down and Out in Paris and London*, 1933; *Such, Such Were the Joys*, 1953.

MISCELLANEOUS: *The Road to Wigan Pier*, 1937; *Homage to Catalonia*, 1938.

Eric Hugh Blair was born in 1903 at Motihari in Bengal, India, the son of a Customs and Excise official of Scottish descent. Although his father soon retired on a small pension, the modest family resources were strained to send the boy in 1911 to a fashionable English preparatory school. Accepted at a reduced rate because of the likelihood of his winning a scholarship, he crammed successfully and won one to Eton in 1917. Lonely, imaginative, and insecure among the children of the well-to-do, he studied at Eton until 1921, reading Shaw, Wells, and other advanced writers and doing some writing of his own. Deciding not to try for a scholarship to Cambridge, he took a job in the Indian Imperial Police, intending to choose his own way of life when he would be pensioned off at forty. The five years between 1922 and 1927 which he spent in this service in Burma were unhappy ones. He was torn between opposed feelings: shame, guilt, and outrage at the often brutal workings of colonialism, and inability to feel more than contemptuous sympathy for its native victims.

Returning home on leave in 1927, he quit the service, took his terminal leave pay, and went to Paris to live on it for a year and a half while he wrote short stories and novels which no one published. With his money spent and the depression on, he plummeted down into the depths of poverty, at times seeming to make his plunge an act of expiation for feelings of guilt attaching to his Burma days. By a combination of public charity, a dishwashing job (in Paris), and a few loans, he managed to survive, tasting the bitterness of extreme penury in both Paris and London. The years between 1929 and 1935 saw him supporting himself as a private tutor, a teacher in cheap private schools, and (for a year and a half between 1932 and 1934) a part-time assistant in a Hampstead Heath bookshop. By this time, however, he had been published, as George Orwell, in various magazines such as The Adelphi, and in January,

1933, his first book, the autobiographical Down and Out in Paris and London, had appeared to receive high praise from the critics. His portraits of the people of this nether world and his etchings of the miseries of their surroundings were lit up by the flame of his social consciousness.

In his first novel, Burmese Days, he presented a decaying empire, his writing—not illusioned like Kipling's or sympathetic like Forster's—serving him as a purgative for some of his feelings of guilt at having been part of a system he loathed. In A Clergyman's Daughter, Orwell drew upon his experience as a schoolteacher, hop-picker, and down-and-outer. This novel, with its amnesic protagonist, shows the inadequacy of the Church and its philosophy in an acquisitive society. There was now a slight income from his writing (an average of $15 a week from 1930 to 1940) to permit him to escape to Essex, where he kept a pub, a village store, and a flock of hens. In 1936 he married Eileen O'Shaughnessy. In the same year Keep the Aspidistra Flying was published. A novel about a young man who escapes from, but finally capitulates to, the advertising industry in order to permit rather unromantic matrimony, it presents a gray, shabby middle-class life dominated by money. Increasingly active as a Socialist by this time, Orwell recorded the experiences of his stay in a depressed area of Britain in The Road to Wigan Pier. A choice of the Left Book Club, this documentary study displayed Orwell's strong sympathy for the laboring classes.

By Christmas of 1936 Orwell had decided to go to Spain to do a series of newspaper articles about the Spanish Civil War. When he arrived there, he felt compelled instead to join the military force of the anarchist-affiliated P.O.U.M. organization, fighting on the side of the Loyalists. A bullet through the throat put an end to his service in May, and when the Communists crushed the P.O.U.M. in Barcelona, Orwell barely escaped the country. All this was recorded graphically in clear, vivid prose in *Homage to Catalonia*.

Despite the tuberculosis aggravated by his hardships in Spain, Orwell continued to work, publishing in 1939 *Coming Up for Air*. This novel of a man returning to find the old home town destroyed by gray suburban developments was dominated by the conviction of impending war. When the war came, Orwell served as a sergeant in the Home Guard and as a member of the Indian Service of the B.B.C. In the last year of the war, as his own health further declined, his wife died suddenly from the combined effects of a minor operation and poor nutrition.

Animal Farm, published in 1945, was his most successful single work, a classically-written Swiftian animal story which was on one level a satiric allegory of Stalinism and on another of totalitarianism in general. Now a prominent, successful author and journalist, the ill, tired man went in 1947 to live with his sister and adopted son on the island of Jura, off the west coast of Scotland. He had hoped there to complete a new novel about the totalitarian future he saw, but in 1949 he found it necessary to enter a sanatorium in Gloucestershire. *Nineteen Eighty-Four*, completed in University College Hospital, London, was a horrifying vision of a world in which all the old values were systematically eradicated, language was deliberately made rudimentary to prevent unorthodox thought, and three superstates dominated an enslaved planet. The author's avowed faith in the proletarians was but a feeble flicker against the overpowering gloom of this fictional relation of personal and national horror. By late 1949, when he had married Sonia Brownwell, George Orwell had envisioned another novel. Planned as a new departure into a study of human relationships, it died with him when he succumbed after a tuberculous hemorrhage on January 23, 1950.

BIBLIOGRAPHICAL REFERENCES: There are three interesting and significant biographical and critical studies of Orwell by Laurence Brander, 1954, John Atkins, 1954, and Christopher Hollis, 1956. See also Tom Hopkinson, *George Orwell*, 1955 (pamphlet); Kenneth M. Hamilton, "G. K. Chesterton and George Orwell: A Contrast in Prophecy," *Dalhousie Review*, XXXI (1951), 198–205; Charles I. Glicksberg, "The Literary Contribution of George Orwell," *Arizona Quarterly*, X (1954), 234–245; Philip Rieff, "George Orwell and the Post-Liberal Imagination," *Kenyon Review*, XVI (1954), 49–70; Richard J. Vorhees, "George Orwell: Rebellion and Responsibility," *South Atlantic Quarterly*, LIII (1954), 556–565; R. H. Rovere, "George Orwell," *New Republic*, CXXXV (1956), 11–15; Robert F. Gleckner, "1984 or 1948?" *College English*, XVIII (1956), 95–99; and Richard J. Vorhees, "*Nineteen Eighty-Four*: No Failure of Nerve," *ibid.*, 101–102.

THOMAS OTWAY

Born: Trotton, Sussex, England
Date: March 3, 1652

Died: Tower Hill (?), London, England
Date: April 14 (?), 1685

PLAYS: *Alcibiades,* 1675; *Don Carlos,* 1676; *The Cheats of Scapin,* 1677 (adapted from Molière); *Friendship in Fashion,* 1678; *The Orphan,* 1680; *The Soldier's Fortune,* 1681; *Venice Preserved, or a Plot Discovered,* 1682; *The Atheist,* 1684 (the second part of *The Soldier's Fortune*).

Although the son of a poor Anglican curate, Thomas Otway, born at Trotton, March 3, 1652, was educated at Winchester School and Oxford University. He left the university in 1672, however, before receiving a degree. Just what he did between leaving the university and the production of his first play, the bombastic *Alcibiades,* is unknown. The following year a second play, a tragedy in heroic couplets entitled *Don Carlos,* was produced, an adaptation of St. Real's French tragedy with the same title. *Don Carlos* proved successful on the stage and made Otway's reputation as a leading playwright of the time. His success gave Otway acquaintance and friendship with the famous people of the stage and court. Otway wrote mainly for the famous actor Betterton, including a number of tragedies and comedies adapted from the French drama of Molière and Racine.

Rejected by a self-seeking actress, Mrs. Barry, for whom he bore a lifelong love, Otway joined the English army in 1678 and received a commission as ensign within a short time. He re-turned to London the next year and began writing again, turning to blank verse in his domestic tragedy, *The Orphan, or The Unhappy Marriage.* *The Soldier's Fortune* was a successful original comedy which utilized Otway's military experience. His greatest play, *Venice Preserved,* followed in 1682. One more play, *The Atheist,* a continuation of *The Soldier's Fortune,* was produced in 1684. Although successful on the stage and in print, Otway's works were insufficient to produce an income for him, and his life was full of financial difficulty. He was an impetuous man and reputedly fought several duels successfully. He died in questionable circumstances. Several accounts, none verified, have been offered as to the manner of his death in his thirty-fourth year, but the most common is that he died in a shop near the sponging house in which he was then living. In his plays Otway illustrated the tendency of the drama of the Restoration period to move away from heroic bombast to sentimentality and pathos.

BIBLIOGRAPHICAL REFERENCES: The outstanding edition of Otway is J. C. Ghosh's, *Works,* 2 vols., 1932. The sole biography is R. G. Ham, *Otway and Lee,* 1931. Aline M. Taylor, *Next to Shakespeare: Otway's "Venice Preserv'd" and "The Orphan,"* and *their History on the London Stage,* 1950, is the most recent full study devoted to Otway; it includes a bibliography. Still valuable for a survey of the subject is Bonamy Dobrée, *Restoration Tragedy,* 1929. See also Aline Mackenzie, "*Venice Preserv'd* Reconsidered," *Tulane Studies in English,* I (1949), 81–118.

OUIDA
(Marie Louise de la Ramée)

Born: Bury St. Edmunds, England   *Died:* Viareggio, Italy
Date: January 7, 1839   *Date:* January 25, 1908

PRINCIPAL WORKS

NOVELS: *Held in Bondage*, 1863; *Strathmore*, 1865; *Chandos*, 1866; *Idalia*, 1867; *Under Two Flags*, 1867; *Tricotrin*, 1868; *A Dog of Flanders*, 1872; *Pascarel*, 1873; *Signa*, 1875; *Ariadne*, 1877; *Moths*, 1880; *A Village Commune*, 1881; *In Maremma*, 1882; *Othmar*, 1885; *The Tower of Taddeo*, 1890; *The Massarenes*, 1897; *La Stregha*, 1899; *The Waters of Edera*, 1900.
ESSAYS: *Critical Studies*, 1900.

Ouida, born at Bury St. Edmunds, England, January 7, 1839, was the pseudonym of Marie Louise Ramé, daughter of a French language teacher and an Englishwoman. As a young woman Ouida changed her surname to what seemed to her the more romantic and dignified "de la Ramée." The family background and childhood of Ouida are vague. Her father disappeared while she was still a child, and she and her mother, then in France, returned to England to take up residence in London. In 1860, just in her twenties, Ouida began to contribute fiction to *Bentley's Miscellany*. Her stories were about glamorous, unreal, and romantic life, but they found an enthusiastic, even fascinated, body of readers, so that for a time Ouida was a very popular author. Sir Arthur Quiller-Couch was among the critics who praised her. Her first novel was *Held in Bondage*, her first real success *Strathmore*, and her best-known, and probably best, *Under Two Flags*.

Even as a child, Ouida, as she preferred to be called even in private life, was egocentric. She displayed an unusual propensity for falling in love, a trait which caused her unhappiness, for her love was often unrequited, and probably led to the misanthropy which she made so obvious in later life. Once a success, Ouida tried to make herself into a great lady. She moved to Florence, Italy, and purchased a large house. She became an irritating, even despicable, personality, insulting her friends, her acquaintances, and her publishers. In 1894 she removed to Lucca, Italy, to live on a more lavish scale than ever, with no attention to the expense of her way of life. But declining popularity as an author cost her the large income she once had, and the last decade of her life she spent almost in poverty. Her only real income in that time was a small pension from the British government. In old age she suffered from blindness in one eye and painful illness. She died in Viareggio, Italy, on January 25, 1908, and was buried in that country. Although adults have almost forgotten her work, children still find such stories as *Two Little Wooden Shoes* and *A Dog of Flanders* interesting.

BIBLIOGRAPHICAL REFERENCES: The New York edition of Ouida's *Complete Works* was published in 12 volumes. Elizabeth Lee, *Ouida: A Memoir*, 1914, is a good biography, but it is inferior to Eileen Bigland, *Ouida, the Passionate Victorian*, 1950, probably the best single work on Ouida's life and art. The only full-length critical work is Yvonne ffrench's *Ouida: A Study in Ostentation,* 1938, containing a good bibliography. Critical essays in books include G. S. Street, "An Appreciation of Ouida," in *Quales Ego,* 1896; Max Beerbohm, *More,* 1899; Carl Van Vechten, *Excavations,* 1926; and Malcolm Elwin, *Victorian Wallflowers,* 1934. A brief magazine article is Rose Macaulay, "Eccentric Englishwomen, IV: Ouida," *Spectator,* CLVIII (1937), 855–856.

PUBLIUS OVIDIUS NASO

Born: Sulmo, Italy   *Died:* Tomi (Now Constanta, Rumania)
Date: March 20, 43 B.C.   *Date:* A.D. 18

PRINCIPAL WORKS

POEMS: *Amores; Heroides (Letters from Heroines); Ars amatoria (Art of Love); Remedium amoris (Love's Remedy); Medicina faniei (Face Lotions); Metamorphoses,* all written before A.D. 8; *Tristia (Sorrows); Ex Ponto (Letters from Pontus),* A.D. 8–18.

Publius Ovidius Naso (Ovid) was born in the Italian Apennines, northeast of Rome, at Sulmo on March 20 of the last year of the Republic. He was brought up under the absolute rule of Augustus. His works depict the life of rich and fashionable Romans during the second half of Augustus' reign, and with his death the Golden Age of Roman literature came to an end.

Ovid's father, of an equestrian family whose estates were never confiscated, sent the boy and his brother from Abruzzi to Rome, where they were educated by two famous rhetoricians, Arellius Fuscus and the Spanish-born friend of Seneca, Marcus Porcius Latro, who formed Ovid's literary style. Horace read his poems to Ovid, and Aemilius Macer, who traveled with him to Athens, Troy, and Sicily, made him acquainted with the writings of Vergil.

On their return to Rome, Ovid was offered a political career in the Senate, but he chose literature. He married three times. Personal experience undoubtedly inspired the creation of his imaginary Corinna whom he celebrated in forty-four short poems and the five-volume *Amores* which he later prudently reduced to three. His fourth marriage, to a girl of the Fabian family, brought him favor with the Empress Livia. Women were influential in Roman life, and women figure largely in Ovid's poetry, with a balance between romance and realism and a tongue-in-cheek humor. His *Letters from Heroines* were imaginary epistles from the old heroines of antiquity to their absent husbands and lovers.

His *Art of Love* caused the greatest furor. This guide book for lovemaking, with two volumes for men and one for women, has been called the most immoral book ever written by a man of genius. Because it ran counter to Augustus' attempts at moral reforms, Ovid tried to repair the damage by writing *Love's Remedies,* telling how to end love affairs, but he was banished in 8 A.D. to the half-barbaric town of Tomi at the mouth of the Danube, more probably for what he knew of scandals at court than for what he had disclosed.

814

Though he wrote scores of letters to influential Romans and five volumes of *Sorrows* to describe the wretchedness of his exile and to present pleas for forgiveness, even Tiberius upon his succession to the throne refused to pardon him, thus suggesting that the reason for Ovid's banishment was something more than licentious writing or even meddling in the love intrigues of Augustus' granddaughter Julia. He remained in Tomi until his death in A.D. 18.

Ovid's greatest work was the fifteen books of *Metamorphoses,* written in hexameters to recount miraculous transformations that range through classical mythology from the change of chaos to cosmos in the world down to the tale of Julius Caesar's metamorphosis into a star. The Alexandrian poets as well as old legends provided material for this cyclic work. At the time of his banishment, he burned his own manuscript, but other copies had been made and so the work has survived.

BIBLIOGRAPHICAL REFERENCES: There are a number of modern translations: Robinson Ellis, *The Amores of Ovid,* 1912; F. A. Wright, *Ovid's The Lover's Handbook,* 1923; F. J. Miller, *Metamorphoses,* 2 vols., 1916; A. L. Wheeler, *Tristia and Ex Ponto,* 1924; J. H. Mozley, *The Art of Love and Other Poems,* 1929; and Rolphe Humphries, *Ovid: The Art of Love,* 1957. See also Edward K. Rand, *Ovid and His Influence,* 1925; Herman Frankel, *Ovid, a Poet Between Two Worlds,* 1945; and Gilbert Highet, *Poets in a Landscape,* 1957.

THOMAS NELSON PAGE

Born: Hanover County, Virginia
Date: April 23, 1853

Died: Hanover County
Date: November 1, 1922

PRINCIPAL WORKS

NOVELS: *On Newfound River,* 1891; *Red Rock,* 1898; *Gordon Keith,* 1903; *John Marvel, Assistant,* 1909; *The Red Riders,* 1924.

SHORT STORIES: *Marse Chan,* 1884; *In Ole Virginia,* 1887; *The Burial of the Guns,* 1894.

JUVENILES: *Two Little Confederates,* 1888; *The Old Gentleman of the Black Stock,* 1897.

ESSAYS AND STUDIES: *The Old South,* 1892; *Social Life in Old Virginia,* 1897.

BIOGRAPHY: *Robert E. Lee, Man and Soldier,* 1911.

Thomas Nelson Page was a product of the ante-bellum South, and the romance of the pre-Civil War period influenced all his thinking and his writing, as did the Civil War itself. He was born on a plantation in Hanover County, Virginia, on April 23, 1853, and lived there until he entered college. He attended Washington College (later Washington and Lee University) from 1869 to 1872, but was forced to leave before graduation by lack of sufficient money for his expenses. An important influence upon him during those undergraduate years was Robert E. Lee, president of the institution, who took a personal interest in young Page. After leaving college, Thomas Nelson Page found employment as a tutor and studied law with his father.

In 1873 he entered the University of Virginia and received the LL.B. degree in 1874. During the following decade he practiced law, married, and continued the writing he had begun while at Washington College.

Page's first fame came with the publication of a story in Negro dialect, "Marse Chan," in the *Century Magazine*. In 1893 he left the practice of law altogether and moved to Washington, D.C., for by that time he had acquired sufficient reputation as a man of letters and a lecturer to assure himself of an income. In the next twenty years he lectured and wrote, his stories, novels, and social studies being almost completely about the South before, during, and immediately after the Civil War. His works reflected his own romantic and idealized notions about the South. He believed that the antebellum South had been a happy place for both slaves and masters, and he attempted in his writings to present such a sympathetic picture that the North would change its views and the breach between the two sections be healed.

From being a man of letters, Page became a diplomat in 1913, when President Wilson appointed him ambassador to Italy, a post Page held until 1919. He was sympathetic toward the Italians and tried to support Italy's position in the peace negotiations at Paris after World War I. Failing to be helpful that way, he wrote a highly sympathetic volume, *Italy and the World War* (1920). Ill health prevented any further serious writing during the remainder of his life, and his last novel, *The Red Riders*, was left unfinished when he died at his Hanover County home on November 1, 1922.

BIBLIOGRAPHICAL REFERENCES: The collected edition is *The Novels, Stories, Sketches and Poems of Thomas Nelson Page*, 18 vols., 1906–1918. The official biography by Rosewell Page is not altogether satisfactory, *Thomas Nelson Page: A Memoir of a Virginia Gentlemen*, 1923. Of importance is the major study of Southern literature, Jay B. Hubbell, *The South in American Literature, 1607–1900*, 1954. See also Edwin Mims, "Thomas Nelson Page," *Atlantic Monthly*, C (1907), 109–115; and Charles W. Kent, "Thomas Nelson Page," *South Atlantic Quarterly*, VI (1907), 263–271.

THOMAS PAINE

Born: Thetford, England
Date: January 29, 1737

Died: New Rochelle, New York
Date: June 8, 1809

PRINCIPAL WORKS

POLITICAL PAMPHLETS AND ESSAYS: *The Case of the Officers of the Excise*, 1772; *Common Sense*, 1776; *The Crisis*, 1776–1783; *Public Good*, 1780; *Dissertations on Government, . . . Bank and Paper-Money*, 1786; *The Rights of Man*, 1791–1792; *Opinion de Thomas Paine . . . concernant le judgement de Louis XVI*, 1792; *Letter to George Washington*, 1796.

DEISTIC PHILOSOPHHY: *The Age of Reason*, 1795–1797.

Thomas Paine was born at Thetford, England, on January 29, 1737, the son of Frances Cocke and Joseph Paine. After grammar school he was apprenticed at thirteen in his Quaker father's trade as a corsetmaker until he left home at nineteen. Briefly a privateer, a schoolmaster, a grocer, and a tobacconist, he was twice discharged as an exciseman. His second discharge resulted from lobbying at Parliament for higher salaries for excisemen. He met Benjamin Franklin at Westminster and received letters of introduction from him when Paine left for America in 1774.

After his arrival at Philadelphia, Paine edited *The Pennsylvania Magazine,* contributed articles to the *Pennsylvania Journal* on recent inventions, in which he was widely read, and wrote miscellaneous papers. Publication of *Common Sense* in 1776 established his fame and probably sold 500,000 copies at a loss. He urged America's moral obligation to the world to seek independence for its own sake and to free the almost-uncontaminated continent from monarchy by establishing a strong federal republic. Enlisting in the Continental army in the same year, he began *The Crisis* essays with the phrase "These are the times that try men's souls." The influence of the sixteen *Crisis* pamphlets did much to preserve morale during the winter at Valley Forge.

Secretary of the Continental Congress, 1777–1779, Paine became needlessly embroiled in disputes concerning the administration of secret French aid and was dismissed from his post at French request. Clerk of the Pennsylvania Assembly, 1779–1781, he resigned to undertake a brief mission to France. After the Revolutionary War, New York gave him a farm at New Rochelle and Pennsylvania gave him £500 for his services.

While living at New Rochelle and at Bordentown, New Jersey, 1782–1787, he continued his writings for efficient taxation, against paper money, and for federal supervision of western lands occupied by Virginia. He also experimented in iron bridge construction, which led him to England in 1787. His bridge was successful in all ways except financially. Paine was welcomed in England by Charles James Fox and Edmund Burke and in France by Condorcet. In reply to Burke's condemnation of revolutionary France, Paine published in 1791–1792 his *Rights of Man,* in which he urged an English revolution to establish a republic as the only way to guarantee equal, individual rights of liberty, porperty, security, and resistance to oppression. This book sold about 200,000 copies and caused Paine's banishment from Great Britain.

Although ignorant of French, Paine took advantage of honorary French citizenship to gain election to the French Convention. Associated with the Girondists, he played a minor role, except for speaking against the execution of Louis XVI. Arrested and deprived of citizenship, 1793–1794, he was freed upon James Monroe's instance. Living at Paris until 1802 with the Bonneville family, he published there the epitome of deism, *The Age of Reason* in which he discounted the Trinity, claims for Biblical consistency, and the paternity of Christ, while stoutly asserting the existence of a God. He also wrote the unjust *Letter to Washington,* accusing the president of conniving at his arrest in France.

These two last publications made Paine anathema to the Federalists and an embarrassment to the Republicans, whose states-rights cause he embraced upon his return to America in 1802.

His last years were spent as an ill, bohemian resident of New York and New Rochelle with inconsequent literary production. Cared for by Madame de Bonneville, he died at New Rochelle on June 8, 1809, and was buried on his farm because consecrated ground was denied him. In 1819, William Cobbett transferred his remains to England. He was twice married without issue: first, to Mary Lambert, who died within a year of their marriage in 1759, and lastly to Elizabeth Ollive in 1771, from whom he was legally separated in 1774.

Paine's talents as a revolutionary propagandist were not excelled in the last quarter of the eighteenth century. Although subsequently damned as an atheist, his religious views were not exceptionable in his own day; however, they still cloud his name.

BIBLIOGRAPHICAL REFERENCES: The critical edition of Paine's works is *The Writings of Thomas Paine*, edited by Moncure D. Conway, 4 vols., 1894–1896. W. M. Van der Weyde's *The Life and Works of Thomas Paine*, 10 vols., 1925, does not add substantially to the Conway edition. The standard biography is Moncure D. Conway, *The Life of Thomas Paine*, 2 vols., 1892, a study which exaggerates the importance of its subject but is generous in citation of sources. Also authoritative is W. E. Woodward, *Tom Paine: America's Godfather*, 1945. Howard Fast, *Citizen Tom Paine*, 1943, exaggerates his leftist proclivities. The best brief sketch is Crane Brinton, "Thomas Paine," *Dictionary of American Biography*, XIV, 159–166. A convenient one-volume edition is *Thomas Paine: Representative Selections*, edited, with an introduction, by H. H. Clark, American Writers series, 1944.

FRANCIS PARKMAN

Born: Boston, Massachusetts
Date: September 16, 1823

Died: Jamaica Plain, Massachusetts
Date: November 8, 1893

PRINCIPAL WORKS

TRAVEL SKETCHES AND IMPRESSIONS: *The California and Oregon Trail*, 1849.
HISTORY: *History of the Conspiracy of Pontiac*, 1851; *Pioneers of France in the New World*, 1865; *The Jesuits in North America in the Seventeenth Century*, 1867; *The Discovery of the Great West*, 1869 (*La Salle and the Discovery of the Great West*, 1879); *The Old Regime in Canada*, 1874; *Count Frontenac and New France Under Louis XIV*, 1877; *Montcalm and Wolfe*, 1884; *A Half Century of Conflict*, 1892.
NOVEL: *Vassall Morton*, 1856.

Francis Parkman's background was a fortunate one for a person who was to become a writer. He was born, September 16, 1823, into a wealthy and cultured Boston family; his father was a clergyman, and his mother came from a socially prominent New England family. Even when Parkman later became an invalid, he always had enough of his grandfather's fortune on which to live comfortably. Few men have so carefully and sensibly prepared themselves for their life's work. Although he showed moderate aptitude in his studies and some skill at writing, his most pleasurable hours were spent tramping through wooded country. In 1840 he entered Harvard, where he joined several clubs and was popular with his fellow students. He always did well in courses he liked—he was quite fond of poetry—and he was elected to the Phi Beta Kappa fraternity. Even then he was intensely interested in Indians and frontier life. Here, too, he often went on extended expeditions into wild country on foot or by canoe. He was a sportsman and a good shot.

In 1843, while still a student at Harvard, Parkman went to Europe and toured the Continent. On his return he was graduated and entered the law school. His first publication, in 1845, was a series of five sketches on his rambles during vacations, published in *The Knickerbocker, or New York Magazine.* His most important trip took him west as far as Wyoming, and from there he returned by way of the Southwest. On this trip he gathered much material about Indians and the Oregon Trail, about which he was to write so knowingly.

On his return Parkman was struck by the extreme nervous disorder that was to plague him for the rest of his life. In 1846 he retired to Boston to regain his health. There he had a major breakdown and went to Brattleboro, Vermont, to cure himself. He then started to write *The California and Oregon Trail,* published in 1849. In 1848 he started his *History of the Conspiracy of Pontiac,* the first of a series of volumes on his main historical topic, the struggle between France and England for the possession of the North American continent. He wrote this, and his other histories, under severe strain from his ailment, the sufferings of which are hinted in his one novel, *Vassall Morton.*

The book that definitely established his reputation as a great American historian was *Pioneers of France in the New World.* In this work, as well as in all his others, Parkman was scrupulous in using primary sources to document his statements. His last two books, *Montcalm and Wolfe* and *A Half Century of Conflict,* completed his historical survey of the titanic conflict of the two great European powers for control of North America.

Beset by ill health and its depressing mental effects, Parkman was never morbid; and although he could have lived comfortably without working, he always felt that he must have an occupation. His careful preparation for this occupation and his diligence in trying to capture the spirit of a past time, along with a rich and colorful narrative style, have made him, in the opinion of many readers, the greatest of American historians. His interests were varied, and he was professor of horticulture in the Harvard agricultural school, 1871–1872. He died at Jamaica Plain, near Boston, on November 8, 1893.

BIBLIOGRAPHICAL REFERENCES: Parkman's *Works* are collected in the New Library Edition, 12 vols., 1902. An important *Representative Selections* was edited by W. L. Schramm, 1938, with critical introduction, notes, and bibliography. There are three authoritative biographies: Henry Dwight Sedgwick, *Francis Parkman,* American Men of Letters Series, 1904; C. H. Farnham, *A Life of Francis Parkman,* 1910; and Mason Wade, *Francis Parkman, Heroic Historian,* 1942. Critical works include Otis A. Pease, *Parkman's History: The Historian As Literary Artist,* 1953; John Fiske's essay on Parkman in *A Century of Science and Other Essays,* 1900; and E. F. Wyatt, "Francis Parkman: 1823–1893," *North American Review,* CCXVIII (1923), 484–496.

BLAISE PASCAL

Born: Clermont-Ferrand, France
Date: June 19, 1623

Died: Port Royal, France
Date: August 19, 1662

PRINCIPAL WORKS

ESSAYS: *Provinciales*, 1656–1657; *Pensées*, 1670.

Blaise Pascal, born on June 19, 1623, was a precocious child tutored at home in Clermont-Ferrand and, later, in Paris by his father. During Pascal's boyhood his father displeased Cardinal Richelieu by objecting to the Cardinal's handling of some financial matters and went into temporary exile. The Cardinal later relented and appointed Pascal's father intendant of Rouen in 1639, a post he held for nine years. During the years in Rouen, Pascal became acquainted with Corneille, the famous dramatist. In 1646 the Pascal family became interested in Jansenism, although Blaise Pascal himself seems to have been at the time more interested in science than in religion. He had written a geometric treatise at the age of seventeen, and his first complete demonstration of the barometer in 1647 was only one of his many achievements in mathematics and physics.

In 1650 the Pascal family returned to Paris, where Pascal's father died in the following year. Jacqueline Pascal, a sister, joined a convent at Port Royal. During this period, in which Pascal seems to have written his essays on the passions of love, the author is supposed to have led a dissolute life. In 1654 he underwent a mystic experience at the convent at Port Royal and a few months later retired from the world. During 1656 he came out of retirement briefly to defend Antoine Arnauld from an attack by the Jesuits, publishing a series of letters entitled *Provinciales*.

Pascal continued to live a quiet, religious life within the walls of Port Royal until his death on August 19, 1662. Eight years later a committee of Jansenists, headed by the Duc de Roannez, Pascal's friend, edited and published the *Pensées*, fragments salvaged from a projected but unfinished work to be called *Apologie de la religion catholique*. Because of religious biases, however, this and other early editions failed to do justice to Pascal. Only nineteenth century and later editions, made from the original manuscripts, are trustworthy. It is rather as a pioneer in science and mathematics than as an author that Pascal is an important person in world history.

BIBLIOGRAPHICAL REFERENCES: The Pascal bibliography is extensive. Among recent studies in English are Morris Bishop, *Pascal: The Life of a Genius*, 1936; H. F. Stewart, *Pascal's Apology for Religion*, 1942; and F. T. H. Fletcher, *Pascal and the Mystical Tradition*, 1954. See also Jacques Chevalier, *Pascal*, 1922; Ehrhard Bucholz, *Blaise Pascal*, 1942; Henri Lefebre, *Pascal*, 1949; Jean Mesnard, *Pascal, l'homme et l'œuvre*, 1951 (tr. 1952); and Jean Steinmann, *Pascal*, 1954. An interesting comparative study is D. G. M. Patrick, *Pascal and Kierkegaard*, 1948. See also R. H. Soltau, *Pascal: The Man and the Message*, 1927.

WALTER PATER

Born: London, England
Date: August 4, 1839

Died: Oxford, England
Date: July 30, 1894

PRINCIPAL WORKS

ESSAYS AND STUDIES: *Studies in the History of the Renaissance*, 1873; *Appreciations, with an Essay on Style*, 1889; *Plato and Platonism*, 1893; *Miscellaneous Studies*, 1895.

NOVELS: *Marius the Epicurean*, 1885; *The Child in the House*, 1894.

TALES AND SKETCHES: *Imaginary Portraits*, 1887.

Walter (Horatio) Pater was born in London on August 4, 1839. Having attended King's School in Canterbury and graduated B.A. from Queen's College, Oxford, he was made Fellow of Brasenose College, Oxford, from which he received his M.A. degree in 1865. With this college he was connected in some capacity during most of the rest of his life. During vacations, however, he often traveled on the Continent. He died at Oxford after a brief illness, on July 30, 1894.

Much of Pater's literary output consisted of critical essays on aesthetic subjects, most of which were collected in such works as *Studies in the History of the Renaissance* and *Apprecia-* tions, with an Essay on Style. Critics have spoken of his sensual approach to art, and some are bothered by a certain subjective impressionism in his criticism. Pater also wrote a few romances, the most famous of which is *Marius the Epicurean*. There is a relation between these romances and his critical works because in the romances he seems to advocate that life itself be approached as an art. Through elaborate sentences with delicate shadings he worked continually for perfection of expression in his prose style. Although Pater spent most of his life in academic seclusion, he had a profound influence on a group of perceptive younger artists and critics.

BIBLIOGRAPHICAL REFERENCES: Pater's works are collected in the New Library Edition of the Works of Walter Pater, 10 vols., 1910. The standard bibliography is C. A. and H. W. Stonehill, *Bibliographies of Modern Authors*, Series 2, 1925. The best biographies are Thomas Wright, *The Life of Walter Pater*, 2 vols., 1907; and A. C. Benson's *Walter Pater*, English Men of Letters Series, 1906, which includes a critical bibliography. Other critical works include Helen H. Young, *The Writings of Walter Pater: A Reflection of British Philosophical Opinion From 1860 to 1890*, 1933; and R. C. Child, *The Aesthetic of Walter Pater*, 1940. Short critical articles are G. G. Hough, "Walter Pater" in *The Last Romantics*, 1949; Geoffrey Tillotson, "Arnold and Pater: Critics Historical, Aesthetic, and Otherwise," in *Criticism and the Nineteenth Century*, 1951; R. V. Johnson, "Pater and the Victorian Anti-Romantics," *Essays in Criticism*, IV (1954), 42–57; and Lord David Cecil's published lecture, *Walter Pater: The Scholar-Artist*, 1955.

ALAN PATON

Born: Natal, South Africa
Date: January 11, 1903

NOVELS: *Cry, the Beloved Country,* 1948; *Too Late the Phalarope,* 1953.
SOCIAL STUDIES: *The Land and People of South Africa,* 1955; *South Africa in Transition,* 1956 (with Dan Weiner).

Perhaps more a great humanitarian than a novelist, sensitive Alan Paton has nevertheless written two very fine novels about racial problems in Africa. Born in Pietermaritzburg, Natal, on January 11, 1903, he writes out of lifelong familiarity with the land and its people, white and black.

Though always interested in literature, Paton first chose a career in science and became a science teacher in the school at the African village of Ixopo, which was later to figure in *Cry, the Beloved Country.* Later he was for a number of years the principal of a reformatory for African boys. There he brought many badly needed improvements to the institution. Today he is considered one of South Africa's leading experts on prison reform.

In 1928 he married Doris Olive Francis; their work is among tuberculosis patients in Natal. They have two children, David and Jonathan. By religion, Paton is an Anglican.

After abandoning two novels, Paton began *Cry, the Beloved Country* in 1946 while on a tour studying prison systems. The book, published in 1948, enjoyed an overnight success. *Too Late the Phalarope,* probably because of its heavy style, has not been as well received. Both novels have been dramatized.

In addition to his hospital work, Paton is also active in a Non-European Boys' Club movement, and in the Liberal Association of South Africa, which, challenging white supremacy in Africa, favors all and any civilized men.

BIBLIOGRAPHICAL REFERENCES: Aside from book reviews, there is almost no criticism on Paton. Sheridan Barker, "Paton's Beloved Country and the Morality of Geography," *College English,* XIX (1957), 56–61, presents an interesting explication of *Cry, the Beloved Country.*

THOMAS LOVE PEACOCK

Born: Weymouth, England
Date: October 18, 1785

Died: Lower Halliford, England
Date: January 23, 1866

PRINCIPAL WORKS

NOVELS: *Headlong Hall,* 1816; *Melincourt,* 1817; *Nightmare Abbey,* 1818; *Maid Marian,* 1822; *The Misfortunes of Elphin,* 1829; *Crotchet Castle,* 1831; *Gryll Grange,* 1860.
POEMS: *The Monks of St. Mark,* 1804; *Palmyra and Other Poems,* 1806; *The Genius of the Thames,* 1810; *The Philosophy of Melancholy,* 1812; *Sir Proteus: a Satirical Ballad,* 1814; *Rhododaphne,* 1818.

Thomas Love Peacock, born at Weymouth, Dorsetshire, England, on October 18, 1785, was a literary barnacle, following the ship of English Romanticism for the ride though not a part of it. Until his early thirties he wrote poetry that was intended to inspire readers as that of the Romantics did. However, it was only the shell of poetry; it contained rhyme and meter and exotic material, but the meat—emotion—was absent. This passage from *Rhododaphne* is typical:

All other fires are of the earth,
And transient: but of heavenly
  birth
Is Love's first flame, which howso-
  ever
Fraud, power, woe, chance, or fate
  may sever
From its congenial source, must
  burn
Unquenched, but in the funeral
  urn. (Canto VII)

Actually Peacock was in spirit and temperament a classicist. He was precocious as a child and although he did not attend college, he was well-read in Latin and Greek (having taught himself the two languages for pleasure's sake). Among his favorite classical authors were Sallust, Tacitus, and Lucian. Of an even disposition, he walked along country roads and stopped by graveyards and mountain streams as was the prevailing practice of the Lake poets. But he collected ideas, not emotional experiences. (One idea was that a Welsh girl whom he had met on a walking tour through Wales would be a good wife to marry; when he had advanced in the East India Company to a salary sufficient to support a family ten years later he wrote to her to be his bride. She remembered and accepted.) However, he was not ignorant of the Romantic movement; many of the poets, like Shelley, were his good friends. And it was the combination of his practical brain, his enjoyment of literature, and his sense of humor that produced his real contribution to literature, a series of seven novels satirizing the whole intellectual and artistic movement of the day.

In reality a conservative, successful businessman, Peacock was unsympathetic to the new ideas of the time primarily because they went beyond reason, which is to say they were to him unreasonably romantic. Using the method of irony, he satirized radicalism, medievalism, and transcendentalism as well as individual romanticists like Wordsworth, Coleridge, Byron, and Shelley. Five of the seven novels —all but *Maid Marian* and *The Misfortunes of Elphin*—follow the same plan: a group of eccentric guests at a house party reveal the folly of their romantic persuasions in witty talk and inane action. Each guest, of course, is a caricature of a contemporary figure. The other two novels are burlesques of legends, the first of Robin Hood and the second of the Welsh (supra). The critic Saintsbury felt that this last novel was the best, although *Crotchet Castle* has remained the most popular. The main purpose of all the works was "to make a joke of things." Peacock died at Lower Halliford, Chertsey, on January 23, 1866.

BIBLIOGRAPHICAL REFERENCES: The standard edition of Peacock's works is the Halliford Edition, edited by H. F. B. Brett-Smith and C. E. Jones, 10 vols., 1923–1924; it includes a biographical introduction and full bibliographical and textual notes. J. B. Priestly, *Thomas Love Peacock* in the English Men of Letters Series, 1927, is the most adequate biography, although Carl Van Doren, *The Life of Thomas Love Peacock*, 1911, is still important. Critical works include A. Martin

Freeman, *Thomas Love Peacock, a Critical Study,* 1911; A. B. Young, *The Life and Novels of Thomas Love Peacock,* 1904; H. R. Fedden, "Peacock," in *The English Novelists,* edited by D. Vershoyle, 1936; and Olwen W. Campbell, *Peacock,* in the English Novelists Series, 1953. An important article is O. Burdett, "Thomas Love Peacock," *London Mercury,* VIII (1923), 21–32.

GEORGE PEELE

Born: London, England   *Died:* London (?)
Date: 1558   *Date:* 1596

PRINCIPAL WORKS

PLAYS: *The Arraignment of Paris,* 1584; *Edward the First,* 1593; *David and Bethsabe,* 1594; *The Old Wives' Tale,* 1595.
POEMS: *Polyhymnia,* 1590; *The Honour of the Garter,* 1593; *Anglorum Feriae,* 1595.

George Peele was born in London in 1558 and died in 1596. He studied at Oxford and after leaving the university wrote for the stage and produced various patriotic occasional poems, of which the best known are *Polyhymnia, The Honour of the Garter,* and *Anglorum Feriae.* These poems suggest that he moved in court circles, and such is certainly the impression left by his first play, *The Arraignment of Paris,* which was performed before Elizabeth by the Children of the Chapel Royal. The Peele canon offers many difficulties, and only the publication dates of his plays are known. In addition to *The Arraignment of Paris,* these comprise *Edward the First, David and Bethsabe, The Old Wives' Tale.* The two last named are pirated and corrupt texts.

Very little is known about Peele's life, except that his latter days were spent in poverty and sickness. He was evidently very much a public figure in his own day. Many tales and pranks were attributed to him, and his reputation as a jester survived long after his death. The character George Pieboard (i.e. a peel or baker's shovel) in the pseudo-Shakespearian comedy, *The Puritan Widow* (1607), doubtless presents him as his contemporaries saw him.

Peele does not rank high as a dramatist, but it is not unreasonable to regard him as a lyric poet who, for pecuniary advantage, turned to a medium for which he was not naturally suited. Of his lyrical gifts there can be no doubt and the songs in his plays have a verbal felicity that is almost Tennysonian. *The Arraignment of Paris* and *The Old Wives' Tale* are successful within their limits precisely because they exist at a gentle and unconstrained pastoral level which allows full scope for lyricism. *David and Bethsabe,* which draws freely on *Samuel* and *The Song of Solomon,* is a notable attempt to present Hebrew pastoral but the general effect is marred by Peele's attempts to bring off the more heroic parts of his material in the grand Marlovian manner. There is probably a measure of topical satire in *The Old Wives' Tale,* but the merit of the play lies in its deft and impalpable presentation of a tale of magic and spells. It has affinities with *Comus* (1634), and it is likely that Peele's work influenced Milton far more than is generally recognized.

BIBLIOGRAPHICAL REFERENCES: The only complete edition of the plays is *The Works of George Peele*, edited by A. H. Bullen, 2 vols., 1888. See also F. B. Gummere in *Representative English Comedies*, edited by C. R. Gayley, 1903; E. K. Chambers, *The Elizabethan Stage*, Vol. III, 1923; and *Dictionary of National Biography*, Vol. XV.

SAMUEL PEPYS

Born: London (?), England
Date: February 23, 1633

Died: Clapham, England
Date: May 26, 1703

PRINCIPAL WORKS

MEMOIRS: *Diary, 1660–1669,* 1825; first complete publication, 1848–1849. *Memoirs Relating to the State of the Royal Navy of England,* 1690.

Samuel Pepys, born on February 23, 1633, probably in London, was a man of wide interests and varied affairs: an inveterate playgoer and a minor patron of the arts, a conscientious husband and householder, a responsible public official, and a friend (sometimes a self-acknowledged flatterer) of the great and the powerful. All this we know from his *Diary,* his own candid and unaffected portrayal of himself. Yet it must be remembered that the *Diary,* as detailed and as thorough as it is for its own specified time, deals with only nine years in a life that lasted a full seventy.

Although not much of importance had happened to Samuel Pepys before he began his famous project in 1660, his many affairs continued long after poor eyesight forced him to give up his record in 1669; and twice, in the period between the ending of the *Diary* and the quiet ending of his life in 1703, his fortunes fell and rose again. Although the full publication of the *Diary* in 1849 transformed him suddenly into a literary figure, it should also be re-

membered that he was not, neither to himself nor to his contemporaries, primarily a man of letters. He was what would be called in modern terminology a "career" admiralty official. He served twenty-eight years in the Admiralty Department, was twice Secretary of the Admiralty, and was acknowledged, after the "Bloodless Revolution" ended his career in 1688, as the foremost authority on naval matters in all England.

His admiralty career began significantly enough with the restoration of the Stuarts in 1660. His life up to that time had been a genteel struggle with poverty, for his family, though well connected, was, by his own admission, "never very considerable." He had gone through Magdelene College, Cambridge, as a scholarship student (receiving a B.A. in 1653 and an M.A. in 1660), had married in 1655 the fifteen-year-old daughter of a penniless French expatriate, and had lived for some time under the patronage of a wealthy cousin, Sir Edward Montagu. This nobleman, later the first Earl of

825

Sandwich, was a stanch supporter of Charles II and played no small part in the triumph of the royal cause. As his good fortune swelled with the resurgence of the Stuarts, so the good fortune of Samuel Pepys increased as well. Pepys' first official appointment was to a minor position in the Exchequer, but on July 13, 1660, he moved to the Navy Office, becoming, later that same year, Clerk of the Privy Seal and a Justice of the Peace.

This triumphal year is covered by the *Diary*. During the remaining eight years of that chronicled account, the triumphs continue. Pepys' finances improve. Able to afford books, he begins the collection of his famous library (now preserved at Cambridge); he can dress his wife in cautious finery; and he can, when his basically puritan conscience allows, indulge in his favorite delights, the theater and wine. His prestige increases, too; he is known to the king. The Duke of York becomes his friend and his pupil in naval matters. By 1689 the lowly government clerk has become a prominent official; the unknown Cambridge scholar has become a respected practical authority; the former Roundhead sympathizer has become a friend of royalty.

But, as Pepys well learned, one who attaches himself to the politically great and who enjoys their triumphs must also endure their defeats. Once the national relief at the removal of the Puritans had died away, the reaction against the policies of the two royal brothers—a reaction accelerated greatly by popular disapproval of their personal conduct and, particularly, of James's avowed Catholicism—set in. The reaction had immediate repercussions; since there was much dis-

approval over the temporary Dutch naval supremacy, and the Duke of York was closely associated with the Navy, the Admiralty received much of the reactionary force. The first of a number of setbacks came even before the end of the *Diary*, but the honor of the Admiralty was saved by Pepys himself. In 1688, in an eloquent speech before the House of Commons, he defended his colleagues of the Navy Department against a charge of financial mismanagement and temporarily, at least, kept the anti-Stuart forces at bay.

The reaction being too strong to be held back indefinitely, Pepys was to be injured by it personally before it was finally ended. Following an excursion to France and Holland in 1669, he returned to England to stand for Parliament. He was supported in this venture by the Duke of York, but he lost the election when his interests were turned from politics to bereavement over his wife's death. He stood again, after having been appointed Secretary of the Admiralty for the first time, in 1673; and here his connections with the future James II worked against him. He won the election but was not, for some months, allowed to take his seat because of a trumped up charge that he, like his royal friend and patron, was a Roman Catholic.

This was not the only time that he was to be the victim of conspiracy and guilt by association. On May 22, 1679, he was imprisoned in the Tower of London on a charge of collaborating with the French, an accusation as spurious as the earlier one. When his accusers could not muster enough evidence to have him brought to trial, he was eventually released. Although no action was taken against him, he was forced to remain in the Tower from May to the following February, even though it was widely admitted that he was guiltless.

In June of 1684, after a visit to Tangier, he was reappointed to his Admiralty Secretaryship and was once again elected to Parliament. He continued in office during the brief reign of the fourth Stuart and retired, peacefully enough, when William of Orange arrived to become the constitutional co-monarch of England. Even in retirement Pepys was harassed for his long friendship with the now-deposed king. Once again (June, 1689) he was imprisoned. Once more he went untried. Finally, in deference to his age and his ill health, he was released, uncharged, and was allowed to live out his remaining four years in the quiet retreat of Clapham.

From this last retirement came the only written work published under his name during his lifetime, his *Memoirs of the Royal Navy*. These papers were accepted as his final vindication. He died on May 26, 1703, with full honors restored, secure in his reputation as a naval authority, as a valuable man of public office, and as a respected former President of the Royal Society. Thus his reputation remained, fading slowly in the pages of Restoration history, until the first deciphering of his *Diary* over a century later.

BIBLIOGRAPHICAL REFERENCES: The standard edition of the *Diary* is that edited by Henry B. Wheatley, 10 vols., 1893–1899; but eventually this work will be superseded by the unabridged transcription in preparation by F. M. C. Turner, the Pepysian Librarian. Another edition of the *Diary*, edited from Mynors Bright and with an introduction by John Warrington, 1953, is available in the Everyman Library. Other published writings by Pepys include *Memoirs Relating to the State of the Royal Navy*, edited by Joseph R. Tanner, 1906; *Private Correspondence and Miscellaneous Papers*, edited by Joseph R. Tanner, 2 vols., 1926; *Further Correspondence*, edited by Joseph R. Tanner, 1929; *Letters and Second Diary*, edited by R. G. Howarth, 1932; *Shorthand Letters*, edited by Edwin Chappell, 1933; *The Tangier Papers*, edited by Edwin Chappell, 1935; and *The Letters of Samuel Pepys and His Family Circle*, edited by Helen Truesdell Heath, 1955.

The standard biography is Sir Arthur Bryant, *Samuel Pepys*, 3 vols., 1933–1938. See also Henry B. Wheatley, *Samuel Pepys and the World He Lived In*, 1880 (2nd ed.); Joseph R. Tanner, *Samuel Pepys and the Royal Navy*, 1920, and *Mr. Pepys: An Introduction to the Diary*, 1925; Lord Arthur Ponsonby, *Samuel Pepys*, 1928; John Drinkwater, *Pepys: His Life and Character*, 1930; and Clara Marburg, *Mr. Pepys and Mr. Evelyn*, 1935. For briefer studies see, further, *Occasional Papers Read at Meetings of the Samuel Pepys Club*, 2 vols., 1917–1925.

JOSÉ MARÍA DE PEREDA

Born: Polanco, Spain
Date: February 6, 1833

Died: Polanco
Date: March 1, 1906

PRINCIPAL WORKS

NOVELS: *El buey suelto*, 1877 (*Footloose*); *Pedro Sánchez*, 1883; *Sotileza*, 1884; *Nubes de estío*, 1891 (*Summer Clouds*); *Peñas arriba*, 1895 (*Ascent to the Heights*).

Spanish literature is full of regional novelists who describe in their fiction the people and customs of the corner of Spain in which they live. Of them all, the greatest was José María de Pereda, the youngest of twenty-two children of a wealthy family of Polanco, near Santander, Spain, where José was born February 6, 1833. Having grown up full of the conservative ideas of his social class, he journeyed, at the age of nineteen, to Madrid, to enter artillery school. There his dislike of mathematics and his disgust with mob rule as he saw it during the revolution of 1854 turned him against the capital. Although he returned later to serve in Congress, political corruption made even more attractive the quiet of his country home in the north, and he spent the rest of his life in Santander.

For something to do, Pereda founded a newspaper, *La abeja montañesa* (*The Mountain Bee*), and for it he wrote a series of descriptive sketches. Later he collected eighteen of them into his first volume, *Escenas montañesas* (*Mountain Scenes*), published in 1864. This book revealed Pereda as the Spanish writer with the truest feeling for nature. Mountains and sea play as important a part in his stories as people do. Civilization, he believed, destroys men's souls.

The traditions of his mountainous homeland, never overrun by the Moors who conquered most of the rest of Spain, are more truly Spanish than those of southern Spain, occupied by foreigners through the fifteenth century. For his portrayal of the patriarchal life of his region, the conservative Pereda was accepted during his lifetime as more truly Spanish than any of his contemporaries. Some of his books can still serve as guidebooks for tourists to the city and countryside of Santander. Also, it is hard to imagine that this novelist who believed that liberal thinkers are the incarnation of all that is evil could have had as his greatest friend the liberal Benito Pérez Galdós, with whom he took a walking trip through Galicia and Portugal and who sponsored his election to the Spanish Academy in 1897.

Pereda was against anything new. His fervent Catholicism turned him against the naturalism of Zola which colored the work of other writers of Spain. But in spite of the idealization of some of his characters, Pereda was not a true romanticist. Menéndez y Pelayo classifies Pereda's style as "idealized realism." Especially realistic is his reproduction of the speech of the common people. Though he was an aristocrat, his sympathetic short story, "La leva" ("The Draft"), telling of the conscription of lowly Santander fishermen, is one of the greatest ever written in Spain.

Uncertain at first of his capabilities as a writer, Pereda was very sensitive to critical opinion. Following the publication of *De tal palo, tal astilla* (*Chip of the Old Block*) in 1879—his uncompromising answer to Pérez Galdós' anti-clerical novels—critics declared that his painting of love was cold. In 1882 he replied with *El sabor de la tierruca* (*Redolent of the Soil*), an idyl describing village life and the charms of the Santander region. When this work provoked the comment that his novels had a limited horizon, he changed his scene to Madrid in the unsettled times he had known there as a student, and wrote Spain's best modern picaresque novel, *Pedro Sánchez,* the story of a political adventurer.

His most popular novel, *Sotileza,* one of the two best sea tales in Spanish literature, was written to portray the noble virtues and incorruptible faith of Santander fishermen, as well as their miserable living conditions. Ten years later, when the critics declared he was "written out," Pereda replied with *Ascent to the Heights,* considered by many his best novel. This work describes the healing effects of nature on a Madrid idler who takes over his uncle's mountain estate. With its sale of 5,000 copies during the first week equaled in its time only by Pérez Galdós, the book brought about Pereda's election to the Spanish Academy in 1897.

Pereda's flaws lie in the weakness of his plots and his inability to portray women, especially those of the upper class, who appear in his pages chiefly as snobs or caricatures. Only the lower class women get sympathetic treatment in his pages, as in his handling of the orphan heroine of *Sotileza.*

Pereda showed little understanding of modernism. For this reason, during his lifetime, some critics were blinded to his talents by their dislike for his social and religious beliefs. A later revaluation of his writing, however, won for him a high place among Spanish novelists for his vivid style, his delicacy of observation, his forceful and enormous vocabulary, and his realistic creation of living people. He died in Polanco on March 1, 1906.

BIBLIOGRAPHICAL REFERENCES: For biographical and critical material see Boris de Tennenberg, *L'Espagne littéraire,* 1903; J. Montera, *Pereda: Biografía crítica,* 1919; E. Gómez de Baquero, *El renacimiento de la novela española en el siglo XIX,* 1924; J. Camp, *José María de Pereda, sa vie, son œuvre, et son temps,* 1937; R. Gullon, *Vida de Pereda,* 1944; and José A. Balseiro, *Novelistas españoles contemporáneos,* 1947.

BENITO PÉREZ GALDÓS

Born: Las Palmas, Canary Islands
Date: May 10, 1843

Died: Madrid, Spain
Date: January 4, 1920

PRINCIPAL WORKS

NOVELS: *Saragossa,* 1874; *Doña Perfecta,* 1876; *Gloria,* 1876–1877; *Marianela,* 1878; *Fortunata y Jacinta,* 1886–1887; *Angel Guerra,* 1890–1891; *Episodios nacionales,* 1872–1912 (*National Episodes*).

PLAYS: *La loca de la casa,* 1893 (*The Madwoman in the House*); *La de San Quintín,* 1894; *Electra,* 1900; *Mariucha,* 1903; *El abuelo,* 1904 (*The Grandfather*).

Regionalism in the Spanish novel developed because of Spain's circumscribed provinces and the difficulty of traveling from one to another. So each novelist wrote best about his "patria chica" or restricted region. Benito Pérez Galdós, born at Las Palmas, the

Canary Islands, May 10, 1843, had an eye for the whole of the nation. His English school environment in the Canary Islands may also explain why he differed on so many social questions from the views of most Spaniards.

At the age of twenty Pérez Galdós

829

was sent to Madrid to study law, but books bored him. He liked people. When he found that his pen could earn him a living, he tried his hand at plays and short novels. His first long book, begun in 1867, was finally published in 1870. Between then and 1918, he wrote seventy-seven novels and twenty-one plays. His greatest success lay in the novel. Because he believed that fictional people should behave and talk like real people, he became the father of the modern Spanish novel and its greatest practitioner, with only his friend Pereda to contest that claim. But he was realistic only as one who cannot forget that beauty is also essential.

A trip to Paris, where he became acquainted with the novels of Balzac, determined Pérez Galdós to re-create in fiction the history of nineteenth century Spain. In 1873, the first volume of *National Episodes* appeared, called *Trafálgar*, dealing with the naval battle of 1805. In two years he completed the first series of ten volumes, ending with the battle of Arapilis in 1812 and including in Volume VI an account of the heroic defense by the citizens of Saragossa against the French. The next series of ten volumes, covering events through 1834, was started at once and completed in four years. Then Pérez Galdós abandoned the project for twenty years. He started again in 1898 and wrote feverishly until his blindness in 1912 prevented the careful research on which he based his historical novels. By this time he had completed forty-six of the series, covering seventy years of Spain's history and weaving in a vast panorama of 1,243 people, according to a dictionary compiled by Professor Glenn Barr.

Of his other novels, those called by the author "novels of the first epoch," three are among his best. He deals with the clerical problem in *Doña Perfecta* and with religious bigotry in *Gloria,* a theme also handled in his *La Familia de León Roch (The Family of Leon Roch)* in 1879. To this period also belongs *Marianela,* considered Spain's best sentimental novel, the tragedy of an ugly orphan after the blind boy who has idealized her regains his sight.

The rest of Pérez Galdós' fictional output, his "contemporary novels" about social and ethical themes, includes the great but lengthy *Fortunata y Jacinta,* which presents the idea that the hope of Spain is in its lower class; *Angel Guerra,* which deals with the mysticism of a political idealist, and *Misericordia* (1897), another novel about the lower class, its central figure a Christlike priest.

While turning out novels, Pérez Galdós realized that more money could be earned by successful plays than by books, and so he dramatized some of his novels and wrote original plays. His aim was to correct the exaggerated situations and unnatural dialogue then in vogue. Because he lacked a basic sense of the dramatic as well as a feeling for the stage, however, only a few of his plays were successful. *The Grandfather* is probably the best.

In 1897 he accepted an invitation to become a member of the Royal Spanish Academy, an honor he had previously refused. He also took up politics and entered Congress as a reform delegate against a corrupt monarchy and its supporters. As president of the Coalition, he wrote and campaigned until blindness ended his political activities. For a time he kept on writing, dictating a few plays and a novel, but by that time other writers had captured the public fancy. Political enmities, financial troubles, and the fact that he had never married, brought him loneliness at the end of his life. He died in Madrid, January 4, 1920.

In his many novels, even those produced because of financial necessity, Pérez Galdós reveals a vigorous creative power and a knowledge of people, especially of Madrid, through whose streets he roamed all his life. He is the interpreter of the national spirit; and while his preaching sometimes flaws his writing, he was the outstanding novelist of Spain in the nineteenth century.

BIBLIOGRAPHICAL REFERENCES: For studies of Pérez Galdós in English see Isaac Goldberg, *The Drama of Transition*, 1922; Salvador de Madariaga, *The Genius of Spain*, 1923; L. B. Walton, *Pérez Galdós and the Spanish Novel of the Nineteenth Century*, 1927; H. C. Berkowitz, *Pérez Galdós: Spanish Liberal Crusader*, 1948; and W. T. Pattison, *Benito Galdós and the Creative Process*, 1954; in Spanish, Clarín, *Galdós*, 1912; Salvadaor de Madariaga, "Benito Pérez Galdós," in *Semblanzas literarias contemporáneos*, 1924; J. Casalduero, *Vida y obra de Galdós*, 1943 (Buenos Aires); José A. Balseiro, *Novelistas españoles contemporáneos*, 1947; and A. del Río, *Estudios galdósianos*, 1953.

ST.-JOHN PERSE

Born: An island near Guadeloupe
Date: May 31, 1887

Principal Works

POEMS: *Éloges*, 1910; *Anabase*, 1924 (*Anabasis*); *Amitié du Prince*, 1924 (*The Friendship of the Prince*); *Exil*, 1942; *Vents*, 1953.

Alexis St.-Léger Léger, the French poet who writes under the pseudonym of St.-John Perse, was born May 31, 1887, on a small, family-owned island, the Island of St. Léger les Feuilles, off Guadaloupe. His early education explains in part the symbolic and esoteric nature of his poetry; his first intellectual influences came from a Roman Catholic bishop and from a nurse who was a Hindu priestess of Shiva. His formal education, begun in France when he was eleven years old, was liberal in the fullest sense of the word. The studies of medicine, letters, and law all combined to fashion the background that was to make him not only a poet but also a distinguished statesman.

It was as a diplomat that he became known to his countrymen, and it was in the French diplomatic corps that he made his public career. He entered the foreign service in 1914, served in Peiping from 1917 to 1921, and acted as consultant on Asiatic affairs during the Washington conference on disarmament in 1922. He served in the foreign office under Aristide Briand and on Briand's death became Permanent Secretary of Foreign Affairs, holding that position until the Nazi invasion of France. Refusing to become a collaborationist, he fled to England, traveled from there to Canada, and finally, at the behest of Archibald MacLeish, came to the United States to act as Consultant of French Poetry to the Library of Congress.

Léger's career as a poet ran concurrently with his career as a diplomat, but he had managed, at least as far as reputation was concerned, to keep the two separated. He published little, and always under the pseudonym St.-John Perse, concealing his artistic identity so well that few, if any, of his colleagues in the diplomatic service knew of his literary career. Among fellow poets, however, he became known, despite the infrequency of his publications, as a writer of great accomplishment and considerable scope.

His first collection of poems, Èloges, came out in 1910, and though a few individual lyrics had been pirated earlier, this was his first acknowledged appearance in print. Fourteen years

later Anabasis, the work now considered his masterpiece, was published. This work established him as a worthy successor to Arthur Rimbaud in the school of French Symbolism; the poem was compared favorably with Rimbaud's A Season in Hell, and its author praised for his ability to portray the "subconscious mastered by reason." Anabasis also brought him to the attention of poets in this country and in England, and T. S. Eliot published an English translation in 1930. Whatever work Léger produced between 1924 and 1940 will never be seen, much less praised. His manuscripts were left behind when he fled the Nazis. Since the war Léger has published two additional volumes, both equal in merit to those done earlier in France, Exil in 1942 and Vents in 1953. In 1960, he was awarded the Nobel Prize in Literature.

BIBLIOGRAPHICAL REFERENCES: For brief studies of Saint-John Perse in English see T. S. Eliot, Preface to Anabasis, 1930, reissued with additional notes by Hugo von Hofmannsthal, Valery Larbaud, and Giuseppe Ungaretti, 1949; Archibald MacLeish, "A Note on Alexis Saint-Léger Léger," Poetry, LIX (1942), 330–337, and "The Personality of Saint-John Perse," in Exile and Other Poems, 1949; John Gould Fletcher, "Like a Sky Above Orchards," New Republic, CXI (1944), 282; Roger Caillois, "The Art of Saint-John Perse," translated by H. M. Chevalier, Sewanee Review, LIII (1945), 198–206; Wallace Fowlie, "Saint-John Perse," Poetry, LXXIX (1951), 31–35; and K. G. Chapin, "Saint-John Perse: Notes on Some Poetic Contrasts," Sewanee Review, LX (1951), 65–81.

For more extended biographical and critical studies see also Maurice Saillet, Saint-John Perse, 1952; Alain Bosquet, Saint-John Perse, 1953; Roger Caillois, Poétique de Saint-John Perse, 1954; and Pierre Guerre, Saint-John Perse et l'homme, 1954.

FRANCESCO PETRARCH

Born: Arezzo, Italy
Date: July 20, 1304

Died: Arquà, Italy
Date: July 19, 1374

PRINCIPAL WORKS

POEMS: Epistles, 1326–1374; Le Rime, after 1327; Africa, 1338–1342; I Trionfi, c. 1352–1374 (The Triumphs).

BIOGRAPHY: De viribus illustribus, c. 1338 (Concerning Famous Men).

Francesco Petrarch (Petracco), the most famous literary man of Italy next to Dante, was born in Arezzo on July 20, 1304, while his father, the notary Ser Petracco, was a political exile under the edict of 1302. His mother took him to the Tuscan town of Incisa, but when he was nine they joined his father in Avignon. At fifteen Petrarch was studying law, first in Montpellier from 1316 to 1320 and later, until 1323, at Bologna in Italy. The death of his father removed the pressure that he become a lawyer, but it also deprived him and his brother of their inheritance. Under the encouragement of Giacomo (or Jacopo) Colonna, he took minor church orders and turned to the classics. Late in 1326 or early in the next year he returned to Avignon, home of the Pope.

That was a fateful move. There, on April 6, 1327, he saw a lovely lady in the church of Santa Clara. He never revealed her identity, but always referred to her as Laura, and to her he wrote a total of 366 poems making up a collection of odes, sonnets, and lyrics that ranks as one of the world's greatest volumes of love poems. Others have identified her as a French lady, Laura de Noves, who had married a rich burgher two years earlier and who had eleven children by him before her death, during the plague, on April 6, 1348. (Petrarch's patron, Bishop Colonna, died about the same time.) In the traditions of chivalry, Laura welcomed the tribute of the poet, but held him at a distance for twenty years. Petrarch's poems to Laura run the gamut from passion to anger at love unrequited, and even express struggles with his conscience over his religious obligations. But his feelings for her did not prevent his having affairs with other women, by whom he had children, a son Giovanni in 1337, and a daughter Francesca in 1343. They were later legitimatized by a papal decree.

In 1335, Colonna secured for Petrarch a canonry at Lombez, in the region of the Pyrenees. Two years later Petrarch bought himself a small house at Vaucluse, near Avignon, with the intention of becoming a recluse and devoting himself to writing. An eager student of history, he produced a series of biographies, *Concerning Famous Men,* and began an epic in classical Latin about Scipio Africanus and the Punic Wars. He called it *Africa.*

Always eager for acclaim, Petrarch arranged for a public ovation for himself at the court of King Robert of Naples early in 1341, and another one, in Rome, in April of the same year, when he was crowned poet laureate. He tried to return to his writings, but, well-known by this time, he had many calls for his services. Although he had boasted of his republican theories, rulers and even Pope Clemente VI sent him on diplomatic missions. Rarely had he leisure to write more sonnets of delicacy and technical excellence that later set the form for the Elizabethan sonnet of England, through translations by Henry Howard, Earl of Surrey, and Sir Thomas Wyatt.

In 1350, Petrarch, on his way to Rome, stopped in Florence to see his great friend Boccaccio (1313–1375). For a time, beginning in 1362, he lived in Padua, where he was a canon of the Church, and then in Venice, where he and Boccaccio met for the last time. In 1369 he moved to a villa in nearby Arquà, where he died quietly five years later, on July 19, 1374.

Petrarch has been called the "First Modern Man of Letters." With his interest in ancient cultures, his collection of books, coins, and medals of antiquity, he was a forerunner of Humanism. Through him, the medieval period made its transition to the Italian Renaissance.

BIBLIOGRAPHICAL REFERENCES: Petrarch's sonnets are available in several translations, the latest being that by Joseph Auslander, 1931. For biography and commentary see J. H. Robinson, *Petrarch, the First Modern Scholar*, 1898; H. Holloway-Calthorp, *Petrarch: His Life and Times*, 1907; Henry Reeve, *Biography of Petrarch*, 1912; E. H. R. Tatham, *Petrarca, the First Modern Man of Letters: His Life and Correspondence*, 1925–1926; and J. H. Whitfield, *Petrarch and the Renascence*, 1943; also Umberto Bosco, *Francesco Petrarca*, 1946; and Rosario Verde, *Studio sulla Rima del Petrarca*, 1950. Central to all modern Petrarchan scholarship is *Studi petrarcheschi*, edited by C. Calcaterra, 3 vols., 1948–1950. Briefer studies in English include Murray Potter, *Four Essays*, 1917; and E. H. Wilkins, *Studies in the Life and Works of Petrarch*, 1955.

GAIUS PETRONIUS ARBITER

Born: Unknown
Date: Unknown

Died: Cumae, Italy
Date: c. 66

PRINCIPAL WORK

PICARESQUE SATIRE: *Satyrica*, c. 60 (*Satyricon*).

A certain Gaius Petronius did exist. Plutarch, probably by a slip, referred to him as Titus Petronius, but Tacitus, in his annals for A.D. 66, tells of the death of Gaius Petronius, a brilliant, cynical man of pleasure who was as famous for his idleness as most men are for their industry. This Petronius was a man of culture, noted for his frankness. Tacitus also cites his political experiences, first as a proconsul of Bithynia, and later as a consul and administrator. When Petronius abandoned diplomacy and returned to the licentiousness of Nero's court, he became the emperor's *Arbiter Elegantiae*, the arbiter of elegance and master of the court revels.

Envy brought about his death. The emperor's previous favorite, Tigellinus, forced a slave to testify to Petronius' plots with the traitor Scaevinus and soldiers were sent to place Petronius under house arrest at Cumae. Disgraced and politically suspect, Petronius knew how to die elegantly. He cut his veins in such a way that his death would seem natural, and during his last hours he bandied conversation and songs with his companions. In his will, instead of lauding the emperor, as was customary, he attacked Nero's unnatural vices, describing them so accurately that the emperor searched among his courtiers for an informer. His suspicions finally fell on a companion of his revels, Silia, the wife of a senator, and she was executed.

There is no positive proof that Petronius wrote the *Satyricon*, usually attributed to him. However, the medley of ribaldry, anecdotes, and cynical philosophy and moralizing is just what Nero's favorite might have written, a supposition strengthened by the fact that a first century grammarian referred to the author as "arbiter."

Whether he or some other Roman of the same name wrote all that has been lost and the 146 chapters of Books 15 and 16 that are still preserved, the author of the *Satyricon* was forced to invent the narrative formula for adventures involving his mouthpiece Encolpius and two friends. It was necessary to forget courtly speech and put into the mouths of his characters the plebian Latin of the market place, with its wealth of slang, puns, and obscenities difficult for the ordinary student of Latin. The result is such a remarkable picture of the ordinary Roman citizen that one regrets the lost portion of the work but is grateful that its popularity among ancient anthology compilers preserved as many episodes as we still have of a work which offers entertainment on every level, from the outrageously scabrous in human conduct to delicate and refined judgment in literature and art.

BIBLIOGRAPHICAL REFERENCES: The *Satyricon* is available in a number of translations of varying quality and completeness. See in particular those by J. M. Mitchell, 1922, and M. Heseltine, Loeb Classical Library, 1913. *Trimalchio's Dinner* was translated by H. T. Peck, 1898. See also E. H. Haight, *Essays on Ancient Fiction*, 1936; and H. W. Hawley, "Quaestiones petronianae," in *Harvard Studies in Classical Philology*, II (1891), 1–40. The standard background study is J. W. Duff, *Roman Satire*, 1936.

BORIS PILNYAK
(Boris Andreyevich Vogau)

Born: Mozhaysk, Russia   *Died:* ?
Date: September 29, 1894   *Date:* 1937 (?)

PRINCIPAL WORKS

NOVELS: *Goly god*, 1922 (*The Naked Year*); *Ivan da Marya*, 1923 (*Ivan and Maria*); *Tretya stolitsa*, 1923 (*The Third Capital*); *Mashiny i volki*, 1925 (*Machines and Wolves*); *Mat' syra zemlya*, 1926 (*Mother Damp Earth*); *Mahogany*, 1929; *Volga vpadayet v Kaspiyskoye more*, 1930 (*The Volga Falls to the Caspian Sea*); *Rozhdeniye cheloveka*, 1935 (*The Birth of a Man*); *Sozrevaniye plodov*, 1936 (*The Ripening Fruit*).

SHORT STORIES: *Bylyo*, 1920; *Tales of the Wilderness*, 1925.

Perhaps Boris Pilnyak, famous for *The Naked Year*, a portrait of Russia in chaos, can be regarded as a symbol of the distinctive confusion and tragedy that is characteristic of the U.S.S.R. under Communist domination. As a revolutionary intellectual, he tended to accept the Communist revolution as a genuine people's revolt; as a student of nature and a sympathizer with the common man, he tended to discover and to report the degenerating effects

835

of communism on the people of Russia. Because of the adverse criticism implicit in his writings, he was criticized by government leaders, although in other times he has been honored by them. The result is that since 1938 there has been no news of Pilnyak from the U.S.S.R., and there is a rumor that he has been executed.

The son of educated, middle class parents of German, Slavic, and Tartar extraction, he was born Boris Andreyevich Vogau in a small town near Moscow on September 29, 1894. Graduated from the Nizhni-Novgorod school in 1913, he also attended the University of Kolomna and the Moscow Institute of Commerce, where he studied business finance and administration. As one exempt from military service because of poor eyesight, he was able to devote a considerable amount of time to writing, much of it unpublished; his pseudonym is derived from the title of an unpublished novel. He achieved fame with *The Naked Year,* published seven years after Pilnyak had begun to

sell some of his work. The book is an electrifying portrait of the revolution, reflecting in a realistic and fresh way its enthusiasm, its horror, and its human spirit.

Pilnyak's concern for the people of Russia and the elementary forces at work within the great land led him to be critical in his later works of the brutalized Bolsheviks and of the careless waste of human lives, as set forth in his account of the building of the dam at Kolomna in *The Volga Falls to the Caspian Sea.* His short novel *Mahogany,* published in Berlin in 1927, was denounced as anti-revolutionary and banned in the U.S.S.R. Pilnyak traveled extensively in Russia, Germany, England, the Near East, and the Far East. In 1931 he toured the United States and wrote a bitter commentary on his experiences in *O.K.* (1933).

Pilnyak's fate remains a mystery. He was last heard of in 1937, and it is believed that he was liquidated in the Stalinist purge of that year.

BIBLIOGRAPHICAL REFERENCES: For a brief study of Pilnyak in English see Gleb Struve, *Twenty-five Years of Soviet Russian Literature,* 1944. See also A. Voronsky, "Boris Pilnyak," in *Literaturnye tipy,* 1927; A. Paley, *Literaturnye portrety,* 1928; and B. P. Kozmin, "Boris Pilnyak," in *Pisateli sovremyonnoi epokhi,* Vol. II, 1937.

PINDAR

Born: Cynoscephalae, Greece
Date: c. 522 B.C.

Died: Argos, Greece
Date: c. 443 B.C.

Principal Works

POEMS: *Epinicia,* 502–452 B.C.

Pindar was born at Cynoscephalae, near Thebes, about 522 B.C. Through his parents, Daiphantus and Cleodice, of a family claiming descent from Cadmus, founder of Thebes, Pindar could regard ancient Greek gods and heroes

as part of his family. As training for his poetic career, Pindar began to study the flute, first in Thebes under his uncle Scopelinus, later in Athens. He began writing odes at the age of twenty, losing in his first competition to a poetess named Corinna, because he neglected to use mythology. His lesson learned, for the next fifty years he was highly regarded for his paeans to Apollo and Zeus and his hymns to Persephone and others.

The home of this Boeotian was chiefly Thebes, but he frequently visited Athens, then coming into literary supremacy, and spent several years at the court of Hieron of Syracuse. There he wrote what was to be called the Pindaric Ode, the epinician, a poem to welcome home the victors in the national games—the Pythian, the Isthmian, the Nêmean, and the Olympic. Pindar's formula was to select a myth and then in some way re-

late it to the victor and provide words for the chorus to use in the parade. From internal evidence, many of the forty-five odes that survive intact can be dated by the games whose victors he celebrates.

High moral tone, patriotism, and religious fervor characterize the works of this outstanding Greek lyric poet. Though he wrote them to order, and was paid for them, the odes show no signs of cheapening art for cash. Not until they were imitated in England in the seventeenth and eighteenth centuries did the form become debased. Only fragments of Pindar's other poems survive. He died in Argos about 443.

BIBLIOGRAPHICAL REFERENCES: The fullest translation of Pindar in English is L. F. Farnell, *The Works of Pindar*, 3 vols., 1930–1932, a work valuable for critical commentary. Earlier translations are those in prose by Ernest Myers, 1874, and in verse by T. C. Baring, 1875. An excellent recent translation is Richard Lattimore, *The Odes of Pindar*, 1947. For critical comment see also D. M. Robinson, *Pindar, Poet of Eternal Ideas*, 1936; Gilbert Norwood, *Pindar*, 1945; and J. H. Finley, *Pindar and Aeschylus*, 1955.

SIR ARTHUR WING PINERO

Born: London, England
Date: May 24, 1855

Died: London
Date: November 23, 1934

PRINCIPAL WORKS

PLAYS: *Mayfair*, 1885; *The Profligate*, 1889; *Lady Bountiful*, 1890; *The Hobby Horse*, 1892; *The Second Mrs. Tanqueray*, 1893; *The Weaker Sex*, 1894; *The Notorious Mrs. Ebbsmith*, 1895; *Trelawney of the Wells*, 1898; *The Gay Lord Quex*, 1899; *Iris*, 1901; *His House in Order*, 1905; *The Thunderbolt*, 1909; *Mid-Channel*, 1909; *The Big Drum*, 1915; *The Enchanted Cottage*, 1922.

Arthur Wing Pinero had a career and a theater deeply interesting to the historian of the English drama; in his work one sees the partial impact of Continental themes and ideas, from Sardou, the master of the well-made play, to Ibsen, the creator of the theater of ideas. In Pinero, for two decades, the

English found their leading practicer of these imported skills.

Pinero, born on May 24, 1855, was the son of a Jewish solicitor in London. With a private school education as a foundation, he read for the law in his father's office, but with no serious intentions of becoming a solicitor. At the age of nineteen he joined the Theatre Royal in Edinburgh, soon supplementing his bit-role acting by writing short dramatic pieces as supplements to longer plays. After the success of *The Money Spinner* (1880) he was able to forego the pretense of being an actor and to devote his time to playwriting. Between 1885 and 1887 he wrote three successful farces for the Court Theatre in London. In these he presented "possible people doing improbable things"; that is, he shifted the emphasis from farcical situations to character. This was a foreshadowing of his greater successes during the 1890's, beginning with *The Second Mrs. Tanqueray* in 1893. In this play, and those that followed, he added to his technically deft work the themes and social insights which his public regarded as daring and thought-provoking. For two decades the English press and public regarded each new Pinero play as a likely source of controversy, for his plays usually amounted to a criticism of the current sexual patterns based, Pinero would have his audiences believe, on appearances rather than on sincere attraction and devotion. As a matter of fact, Pinero's homegrown versions of

the Continental "problem plays" always contained incidents quite as shocking to current taste as the slamming of the door at the end of Ibsen's *A Doll's House;* for example, in *The Notorious Mrs. Ebbsmith* the rebellious heroine momentarily throws the Holy Scriptures into the fire. Dramatic strokes like these won Pinero his temporary reputation as an iconoclast.

It was a reputation that waned. During the last twenty years of his life Pinero had the bitterness of seeing his fame and public dwindle. To audiences that began to respond to Eugene O'Neill and Sean O'Casey, Pinero's representations of upper-class infidelity came to seem mannered and unreal. Of his more than fifty pieces, many found neither a producer nor a publisher; it was no comfort for him to recall that he had been knighted in 1909. His last successful play, *The Enchanted Cottage,* is a strange blend of the delicate sentimentalism of J. M. Barrie and cynical realism. Although his is no longer a great name in the theater, it cannot be denied that he measured shrewdly the taste of a generation. Pinero died in London on November 23, 1934.

BIBLIOGRAPHICAL REFERENCES: There is no collected edition, but Clayton Hamilton edited *The Social Plays of Arthur Wing Pinero,* 1917–1919, with a general introduction and critical prefaces to each play. For biography and criticism see Wilbur D. Dunkel, *Sir Arthur Wing Pinero: A Critical Biography with Letters,* 1941; also H. H. Fyfe, *Sir Arthur Wing Pinero's Plays and Players,* 1930; and Edward Everett Hale, *Dramatists of Today,* 1911. A good foreign estimate is Wilibald Stöcker, *Pineros Dramen: Studien über Motive, Charaktere und Technik,* 1911.

LUIGI PIRANDELLO

Born: Girgenti, Sicily   *Died:* Rome, Italy
Date: June 28, 1867   *Date:* December 10, 1936

PRINCIPAL WORKS

PLAYS: *Così è—se vi pare,* 1917 (*Right You Are—If You Think So*); *Il Piacere dell' onesta,* 1917 (*The Pleasure of Honesty*); *L'uomo, la bestia e virtù,* 1918 (*Man,*

Beast, and Virtue); Sei Personaggi in cerca d'autore, 1921 (Six Characters in Search of an Author); Vestire gli ignudi, 1922 (Naked); Enrico IV, 1922 (Henry IV); Ciascuno a suo modo, 1924 (Each in His Own Way); Lazzaro, 1929; Come tu mi vuoi, 1930 (As You Desire Me); Questa sera si recita a soggetto, 1930 (Tonight We Improvise).

NOVELS: L'esclusa, 1901 (The Outcast); Il fu Mattia Pascal, 1904 (The Late Mattia Pascal); Si gira, 1916 (Shoot); I Vecchi e i giovani, 1913 (The Old and the Young).

SHORT STORIES: Amori senza amore, 1894; Beffe della morte e della vita, 1902; Bianche e nere, 1904; Erma bifronte, 1906; Il Carneval dei morti, 1921.

ESSAYS AND STUDIES: Umorismo, 1908; Arte e scienza, 1935.

Luigi Pirandello, winner of the Nobel Prize for literature in 1934, became a force in twentieth century drama by calling attention to the limitations of the school of the "well-made" play, the poetic drama, and the naturalistic drama of the nineteenth century. He offered in their place a "theater" that the Italians called "grottesco" and that elsewhere has been called expressionistic. However named, Pirandello's theater directs our attention to the psychological reality that lies beneath social appearances and overt social action. He found inadequate the "well-made" plays of Scribe and Sardou which, like later Hollywood products, are cleverly contrived to excite and divert. He rejected the overwrought and often insincere language of the poetic drama of Gabriele D'Annunzio and Sem Benelli, for he aimed at language closer to that of normal impassioned speech. Finally, he rejected not so much the subject matter of the naturalistic theater of Brieux as its assumptions: that drama is a branch of sociology. Drama, if a branch of anything, was to Pirandello a branch of psychology; and it is superior to psychology in that the dramatist who investigates mental states is not bound by a theory or dogma as are Freud and Jung. The dramatist's only obligation is to be faithful to his insights into the particular situation he treats. (With Pirandello, it is usually an abnormal situation upon which the dramatist broods imaginatively.)

But it was not only opposition to literary fashions in the Italian world that was productive in Pirandello. The conditions of his own life made contributions to his literary production; these conditions created problems that, in his many plays and almost countless stories, he tried to study and resolve.

Pirandello was born on June 28, 1867, of a well-to-do family in Girgenti, Sicily, which at that time was a backward and violent section of Italy, a region in which each man had to protect his own rights and live in expectation of violence. Pirandello was also early impressed by the special civil and religious privileges accorded the upper classes to which he as a boy belonged. In short, he did not need wider experience to reveal to him the elements of hypocrisy and cruelty implicit in human life.

Later experiences helped to underline this lesson. When he attended the University of Rome, he encountered academic pedantry and was saved from total disgust only by a kindly professor. After further training in Germany, Pirandello returned to Sicily and discovered that he and his fiancée of long standing had lost interest in each other.

839

Instead, in 1894, he married a girl of his father's choosing, Antonietta Portulano. For some years the young couple lived easily in Rome, but Signora Pirandello's allowance from her father ceased; the Sicilian sulphur mines of the father had been ruined by floods. When Signora Pirandello became insane, Pirandello did not confine her to an asylum but, until her death in 1918, lived with her and watched over her. During these years his life and the lives of his three children were distorted by the jealous frenzies of Signora Pirandello, who unceasingly accused her husband of infidelity. The family was also poor; Pirandello taught in a teachers' college. During these years he also continued to write and publish; he tried to give expression to the insights that his life, early and late, had stimulated in him. Until after World War I, Pirandello was ignored in his own country. It was the international popularity of *Six Characters in Search of an Author* that finally won him recognition, a recognition that was still grudging on the part of the Italian Fascist government, which regarded Pirandello as decadent.

Decadent or not, Pirandello's themes are now generally regarded as important. As early as 1904, in his novel, *The Late Mattia Pascal*, Pirandello had called attention to the gap between what a man is and what he must seem to be if he is to live in conformity with his social role. *Six Characters in Search of an Author* makes a similar contrast between the conventional bonds that hold persons together and the real bonds of passion and injury that connect one person with another. *As You Desire Me* presents an amnesia victim whose sense of identity depends not on her self-knowledge but on whether a man—possibly her former husband—believes that she is the person she claims to be. *Henry IV* poses another difficult problem, typical of Pirandello and, we now know, closely related to his personal tragedy: what does the word "sanity" mean? And is "sanity" the possession of the "normal" majority or of the persons endowed with a peculiar and distorting insight?

As this inspection suggests, Pirandello was an asker of questions. He questioned the wisdom of taking sense impressions, surface appearances, and sanity for granted. In this respect he resembles many other twentieth century writers. Pirandello's influence has been considerable, especially in his own country, where more recent Italian writers like Ugo Betti and Diego Fabbri have imitated his technique and have continued his merciless and exhaustive scrutiny of human motives and actions. He died at Rome on December 10, 1936.

BIBLIOGRAPHICAL REFERENCES: For criticism of Pirandello in English see Domenico Vittorini, *The Drama of Luigi Pirandello*, 1935; Lander MacClintock, *The Age of Pirandello*, 1951; and Alba Fazia, *Luigi Pirandello and Jean Anouilh*, 1954. See also J. L. Palmer, *Studies of the Contemporary Theatre*, 1927; William A. Drake, *Contemporary European Writers*, 1928; and Eric Bentley, Introduction to *Naked Masks: Five Plays by Luigi Pirandello*, 1952.

PLATO

Born: Athens, Greece
Date: 427 B.C.

Died: Athens
Date: 347 B.C.

PRINCIPAL WORKS

PHILOSOPHIC DIALOGUES: The order of the *Dialogues* is not known, but the following sequence has been suggested by Campbell and Lutoslawski: *Apology, Euthyphro, Crito, Charmides, Laches, Protagoras, Meno, Euthydemus, Gorgias, Lysis, Cratylus, Symposium, Phaedo, Republic, Phaedrus, Theaetetus, Parmenides, Sophist, Politicus, Philebus, Timaeus, Critias, Laws.*

Born at Athens in 427 B.C. and named at birth Aristocles, Plato, the most famous and probably the most important of the Greek philosophers, was the son of Ariston and Perictione, Athenian aristocrats. The family of Ariston traced its descent to Codrus, presumably the last king of Athens, and Perictione was a descendant of Solon, the Athenian lawgiver. Plato probably enjoyed a comfortable boyhood as the youngest member of a wealthy family. He had two brothers, Glaucon and Adeimantus, and a sister, Potone.

When Plato was still a child his father died, and his mother then married Pyrilampes, an active supporter of the policies of Pericles. His uncle, Charmides, and another relation, Critias, were also involved in the political life of the time and were prominent in the oligarchy that came into power at the end of the Pelopennesian War in 404 B.C. Under these circumstances it was natural for Plato to regard political life as one of the duties of the conscientious citizen, and the philosophy of politics as one of the scholar's noblest pursuits.

From his boyhood Plato was acquainted with Socrates, and his friendship with the elderly philosopher convinced him that the search for truth, philosophy, was essential to any effec-

tive political life. Plato's early ambition to be a statesman was encouraged by Charmides and his friends, but when Plato observed that the thirty rulers of Athens, among them his relatives and associates, were even more vicious in their governmental practices than their predecessors, and, furthermore, that they were attempting to involve Socrates in the illegal arrest of a fellow citizen, he began to have qualms as to a career in politics. His misgivings were confirmed when the leaders of the democracy that followed the oligarchy charged Socrates with impiety and with corrupting the youth of Athens; Socrates was brought to trial, condemned, and executed. Plato decided that until philosophers became kings, or kings became philosophers, there was no practical value to be gained if an honest man entered political life.

In all probability, Plato was more than once engaged in active military service. He possibly entered service when he was eighteen and may have served for five years with the cavalry during the last years of the Pelopennesian War. He may also have been involved in 395, when Athens was once more at war.

After the death of Socrates in 399 Plato went to Megara with some other friends of Socrates and visited Euclides, a distinguished philosopher who had been present at the death of Socrates. He may have traveled, but he soon returned to Athens and began his own writing.

When Plato was about forty years old, he made a trip to Italy and Sicily, where he was dismayed by the luxurious, sensual life customary among the wealthy. On the positive side, he made friends with Archytas, the virtual ruler of Tarentum, in Italy. Archytas was not only a strong and respected leader, but also an eminent mathematician, and he and Plato discussed many of the interesting features of Pythagoreanism, with which Plato had first become fascinated in Athens. In Sicily, Plato visited Syracuse, where he became acquainted with Dionysius, the tyrant of the city, and with Dion, the brother-in-law of Dionysius. Dion, then about twenty years old, was inspired by Plato's ideas about the proper kind of state and resolved to become the kind of noble political leader that Plato sketched out for him. While inspiring Dion, however, Plato was irritating Dionysius, who had little interest in philosophy. According to some sources, Plato was seized by a Spartan envoy who shipped him off to Aegina, where he was offered for sale as a slave but was saved by Anniceris, a friend from Cyrene, who ransomed him.

When he returned to Athens about 387 Plato founded a school in which scientific and political studies would be undertaken by young men actually engaged in the task of acquiring knowledge. The school was located outside the city gates where Plato owned a house and garden. Since the place was known as the "Academy," the school acquired that name, and for forty years Plato devoted most of his time to the school. The *Dialogues* for which he is

famous were composed, in great part, at the Academy and in connection with its activities. Among the young men who became his pupils were Dion, who followed Plato to Athens; Aristotle, who joined the school when he was eighteen, and others who were either princes or destined to become important political figures.

In 367, Dionysius of Syracuse died and his power, which by that time extended over Hellenic Sicily and Italy, passed to his son, Dionysius II. Through the influence of Dion, who was the new ruler's uncle, Plato was invited to Syracuse to teach philosophy to the young Dionysius; and he reluctantly accepted. Instruction was practically impossible because of suspicion and intrigue at court, and four months after Plato's arrival Dion was banished on the ground that he was plotting against the ruler. When the war with Carthage broke out, Plato left Sicily, promising to return when peace was established if Dion should be allowed to return to Syracuse.

In 361, Plato returned to Sicily at the urging of Dion, still under banishment. When Dionysius continued to refuse to allow Dion's return and made matters worse by confiscating his property, Plato protested. He was made a virtual prisoner and was in danger from Dionysius' bodyguards, but finally he was released through the intervention of his friend Archytas of Tarentum. He returned to Athens in the summer of 360.

For the next thirteen years Plato taught and wrote at the Academy, composing the later dialogues, among them the *Laws*. He died in 347 and was buried on the grounds of the Academy.

Plato is famous for the intellectually

lively portrait of Socrates which he presented in his earlier dialogues, and for his theory of Ideas, eternal, changeless forms of things by reference to which knowledge is possible. In his *Republic* he set forth his ideas of the ideal state, one founded on conceptions of law and justice.

BIBLIOGRAPHICAL REFERENCES: The standard translation is Benjamin Jowett, *The Dialogues of Plato*, 5 vols., 1892, reprinted in various modern editions. An excellent book of selections is John Burnet's translation of *Euthyphro, Apology, Crito, and Phaedo*, 1924. Perhaps the best introduction to the man and the writings is A. E. Taylor, *Plato: The Man and His Work*, 1927. For analysis and criticism see also J. A. Stewart, *The Myths of Plato*, 1905, and *Plato's Doctrine of Ideas*, 1909; A. E. Taylor, *Platonism*, 1924; John Burnet, *Platonism*, 1928; Paul Shorey, *What Plato Said*, 1933, and *Platonism, Ancient and Modern*, 1938; G. M. A. Grube, *Plato's Thought*, 1935; A. D. Winspear, *The Genesis of Plato's Thought*, 1938; Raymond Sinneterre, *Introduction à l'étude de Platon*, 1948; Guy C. Field, *The Philosophy of Plato*, 1949; Victor Goldschmidt, *La religion de Platon*, 1949; David Grene, *Man in His Pride: A Study in the Political Philosophy of Thucydides and Plato*, 1950; Catherine Rau, *Art and Society: A Reinterpretation of Plato*, 1951; William D. Ross, *Plato's Theory of Ideas*, 1951; and R. B. Levinson, *In Defense of Plato*, 1953. An excellent background study is G. C. Field, *Plato and His Contemporaries*, 1930.

TITUS MACCIUS PLAUTUS

Born: Sarsina, Italy
Date: c. 255 B.C.

Died: Rome (?), Italy
Date: 184 B.C.

Principal Works

PLAYS: *Miles Gloriosus*, c. 206 B.C. (*The Braggart Soldier*); *Stichus*, 200; *Aulularia*, c. 195 (*The Pot of Gold*); *Pseudolus*, 191 (*The Trickster*); *Bacchides*, c. 189; undated: *Amphitruo*; *Asinaria* (*The Ass Comedy*); *Captivi* (*The Captives*); *Casina*; *Cistellaria* (*The Casket*); *Curculio*; *Menaechmi*; *Mercator* (*The Merchant*); *Mostellaria* (*The Haunted House*); *Rudens* (*The Slipknot*); *Trinummus*; *Vidularia* (*The Chest*).

Titus, son of Titus, was born about 255 B.C. in Sarsina, the capital of the Umbrian people of central Italy, only a dozen years after they came under the sway of Rome. Being a freeman, the ambitious Titus could leave home and go south along the Flaminian Way to Rome, which was still a city of thatch and timber. Because some of the Roman generals had become lovers of the theater in Syracuse, where they saw adaptations by a Greek slave, Andronicus, a Greek tragedy and a comedy had featured the Ludi Romani of 240 B.C. Temporary wooden platforms made the theater, and the audience brought their own chairs. (Rome's first permanent theater was built by Pompey, in 55 B.C.) This rude drama attracted young Titus. History records he worked "in operis artificium scenicorum," which might mean he was a stage carpenter, a minor actor, or even a flute player who entertained the spectators between the acts. It has been said that he was nicknamed Maccus after a dissolute character of the farces and that he himself, with characteristic humor, assumed the name Plautus (Flatfoot).

Somehow he made money, and quickly lost it. Scholars speculate that he hired a ship to carry merchandise for sale in Greece; this circumstance would explain his knowledge of Greek and the poverty that drove him to grinding corn for a baker. About 206 B.C. he wrote two plays based on Greek originals. One, *The Braggart Soldier,* was especially successful. With actors clamoring for more of his productions, Titus soon became an established playwright.

At this time, besides Greek plays in translation, Roman audiences had three kinds of dramatic entertainment: satirical medleys of songs and stories, dialogues attacking political and military leaders, and broad farces, performed by masked actors, imitating the coarsest sort of Greek pantomime. Plautus, who knew the "New Comedy" of Athens that had replaced the genre of Aristophanes after the loss of Athenian independence made it dangerous to lampoon citizens, borrowed some light social drama of Menander and his imitators, incorporated some of the technique of the farces, and, while retaining the Greek setting, added Roman local color and topics to give them greater appeal, often so timely that it is possible to date the year of composition.

Apparently the audience did not find it incongruous to have supposedly Greek characters mentioning Roman praetors and aediles, or using the verb *pergraecari* (to act like a Greek) when they meant "lead a dissolute life."

When his popularity with comedies about deceitful servants and parasitical followers earned Roman citizenship for the Umbrian, he changed his nickname Maccus, with its connotation of "clown," into the patrician name Maccius, and became Titus Maccius Plautus. In his day he had detractors; Quintilian criticized him, and Horace commented that if Plautus got his cash he never cared whether his comedies stumbled or stood. Modern critics attack his immorality and the use he made of comedy's early privilege, because of its religious connections, to gloss over its licentiousness. It is true that he was not an originator; the plays whose plots he invented show him at his worst. But when he stays close to his Greek sources, embellishing his work with the salty flavor of common Latin speech, he merits his reputation as the master of Roman comedy.

Originally 130 plays were attributed to him. Later Varro (116–27 B.C.) reduced to twenty and a fragment the number definitely accredited, with nineteen more possibly his work. As he himself borrowed from Greek predecessors, so later playwrights made use of his work. The *Menaechmi* inspired Shakespeare's *Comedy of Errors.* His *Aulularia* was rewritten by Ben Jonson, Molière, Thomas Shadwell, and Hooft, and it probably influenced Fielding in the composition of *The Miser.* Dryden, too, adapted his work. Plautus' humor, combined with pictures of the homely life of the common people and lively satire of the wealthy, makes him one of the greatest of Roman dramatists. He died, probably in Rome, in 184 B.C.

BIBLIOGRAPHICAL REFERENCES: For translations of the extant plays of Plautus, see G. E. Duckworth, *The Complete Roman Drama,* 2 vols., 1942; and Paul Nixon, *Plautus with English Translation,* 5 vols., 1916–1938. For critical and background studies see also A. Y. Sellar, *The Roman Poets of the Republic,* 1889; W. W. Blancké, *The*

Dramatic Values in Plautus, 1918; J. T. Allen, *Stage Antiquities of the Greeks and Romans,* 1927; Gilbert Norwood, *Plautus and Terence,* 1932; F. A. Wright, *Three Roman Poets,* 1932; and William Beare, *The Roman Stage,* 1950.

PLUTARCH

Born: Chaeronea, Boeotia, Greece   *Died:* Chaeronea
Date: c. 45   *Date:* c. 125

PRINCIPAL WORKS

BIOGRAPHY: *Parallel Lives,* 105–115.

ESSAYS AND TREATISES: *Opera moralia (Moral Works).*

Plutarch the biographer was born about A.D. 45 at Chaeronea, in Boeotia, a district that had always had the unlucky reputation of producing stupid men. Plutarch himself shared the belief, though he could have professed that in his own person he belied it. He came of a wealthy magisterial family. In youth he studied philosophy under Ammonius of Delphi, who is thought to have been of the Academic school, or possibly of the Stoic. Plutarch's works show traces of Stoic teaching, especially as regards steadfastness under pain, but they reject the Stoic idea of rewards and punishments for the dead. They embrace the Pythagorean doctrine of metempsychosis. Plutarch is said to have visited Egypt; in view of the knowledge of Egyptian mythology and religion exhibited in his *On Isis and Osiris,* the probability is high. He is known to have been initiated into the Dionysiac mysteries. He journeyed to Rome, and there, it is assumed, wrote his moral treatises. There, certainly, he became renowned as a teacher of philosophy, and he is declared by some authorities to have been appointed Trajan's tutor. He gained the friendship of the consul Sosius Senecio, and was himself elevated by Trajan to the consular rank. On his retirement, he returned to

Greece, where he held the procuratorship under Hadrian. He passed his later years at Chaeronea, where he died about A.D. 125, as archon and as priest of Apollo. Although his Roman literary contemporaries are silent concerning him, he was revered by Eusebius and Aulus Gellius.

In medieval and modern times, Plutarch has been one of the most widely read Greek authors, chief attention being accorded to his *Parallel Lives.* The collection, first printed at Florence in 1517, enjoyed the particular distinction of providing Shakespeare, through Sir Thomas North's English translation (1579) of the Amyot French version, with the plots of *Julius Caesar, Antony and Cleopatra, Coriolanus,* and (in part) *Timon of Athens.* The plan of the *Lives,* which seem to belong to Plutarch's later period, was to set beside each other, in pairs, illustrious Greek and Roman commanders or statesmen and then, in a separate esssay, to compare their traits of character for the purpose of moral instruction. Thus, with Theseus he compared Romulus; with Alcibiades, Coriolanus; with Aristides, Cato; with Demosthenes, Cicero. In all, forty-six lives are extant; to these are appended four others unconnected with one another. Furthermore several of the comparative essays have been lost. The greatest virtue of the *Lives* consists in Plutarch's richness of anecdotal detail, for his circumstantial disclosures of homely incident are often illuminating as well as startling. The *Lives* are deeply learned and must have required an enormous amount of research. Their greatest flaw results from Plutarch's tendency to distort facts when dealing with personages concerning whom, for moral reasons, he was biased.

His other works, far more voluminous, have a good deal of philosophic and antiquarian interest. They fall into various classifications in accordance with their emphasis upon political, scientific, historical, moral, or religious matters. Among them should be mentioned *The Malignity of Herodotus,* reflecting Plutarch's dislike for that historian's preference of Athens to Sparta; the essay *On the Face Appearing on the Disk of the Moon;* the treatise *Whether an Old Man Ought to Engage in Politics;* and the disquisition *On Isis and Osiris,* a source of much material to early students of Egyptian culture. In the esssay *On the Cessation of Oracles* occurs the memorable story of the voice that cried, from the island of Paxi, "Great Pan is dead!"—a tale often stimulating, in later times, to the romantic fancy. Plutarch wrote a *Consolation to Apollonius,* much imitated in the Renaissance, and a *Consolation to His Wife,* by which he hoped to mitigate her grief over the death of their little daughter Timoxena.

BIBLIOGRAPHICAL REFERENCES: The *Lives,* translated by Bernadotte Perrin, 11 vols., 1914–1926, are in the Loeb Classical Library. Another edition, translated by John Dryden, 1683, and revised by Arthur Hugh Clough, 1864, has been reprinted as a Modern Library Giant. The basic translation of the *Moralia* is that by Philemon Holland, 1603. The translation by F. C. Babbitt and others, 14 vols., is also in the Loeb Classical Library. T. G. Tucker and A. O. Prickard have also translated selections from the *Moralia,* 2 vols., 1913–1918. For commentary see R. C. Trench, *A Popular Introduction to Plutarch,* 1873; John Oakesmith, *The Religion of Plutarch,* 1903; K. M. Westaway, *Educational Theory of Plutarch,* 1931; and Moses Hadas, *A History of Greek Literature,* 1950.

EDGAR ALLAN POE

Born: Boston, Massachusetts
Date: January 19, 1809

Died: Baltimore, Maryland
Date: October 7, 1849

PRINCIPAL WORKS

POEMS: *Tamerlane and Other Poems,* 1827; *Al Aaraaf, Tamerlane and Minor Poems,* 1829; *Poems,* 1831; *The Raven and Other Poems,* 1845; *Eureka: A Prose Poem,* 1848.

SHORT STORIES: *Tales of the Grotesque and Arabesque,* 1840 (2 vols.); *Tales,* 1845.

NOVELLA: *The Narrative of Arthur Gordon Pym,* 1838.

CRITICISM: *The Literati,* 1850.

The parents of Edgar Allan Poe were David Poe and Elizabeth Arnold Poe. They had three children: William Henry Leonard, Edgar, and

846

Rosalie. Edgar was born on January 19, 1809, in Boston. His mother died in Richmond, Virginia, on December 8, 1811, and the circumstances of David Poe's death are unknown. It is believed that he died not long before or after the death of his wife. The pretty little boy, Edgar, though not legally adopted, became a member of the childless family of John Allan, a Scottish tobacco merchant of the Richmond firm of Ellis and Allan. He was given the name of Edgar Allan and treated as the son of the family. When Mr. Allan sailed for England to establish a branch of the firm, Edgar went with him and his wife. He was kept in an English school most of the time until the Allans returned home in 1820. After further school days in Richmond, Poe was taken to Charlottesville where on February 14, 1826, he was entered as a student in the University of Virginia. He continued as a student for the more than ten months' session until it closed in December. He excelled in his classes, but he accumulated some debts over which he and Mr. Allan quarreled; and as a result Poe left Richmond a penniless youth.

Why Poe chose to go to Boston is unknown but he arranged there for the publication of a little volume of poems, *Tamerlane and Other Poems*, and on May 26, 1827, he enlisted under the name of Edgar A. Perry in the United States Army. In 1829 he secured a discharge from the army and entered West Point in 1830 as a cadet. After the death of his first wife, John Allan married again. Soon afterward there was a final break with Poe and Poe himself was dismissed from the Academy. He had published *Al Aaraaf, Tamerlane and Minor Poems*

in 1829 and upon leaving West Point he published *Poems, Second Edition*, 1831. There followed an obscure period in Baltimore before he went to Richmond in 1835 to work on the *Southern Literary Messenger* until the end of 1836. He had married his cousin, Virginia Clemm, in 1836, and he now took her and his aunt, Mrs. Clemm, to New York, but soon he removed to Philadelphia where he became first an associate editor of *Burton's Gentleman's Magazine* and later editor of its successor, *Graham's Magazine*. In April, 1844, he returned to New York and in 1846 rented the little cottage in Fordham, just out of the city, where Virginia died on January 30, 1847, and where Poe and Mrs. Clemm continued to live until Poe's death. He had published stories and articles in various magazines and had worked on the New York *Mirror* and edited the *Broadway Journal*.

Of his books, *The Narrative of Arthur Gordon Pym* was published in 1838, *Tales of the Grotesque and Arabesque*, in two volumes, in 1840, *Tales* and *The Raven and Other Poems* in 1845, and *Eureka* in 1848. The publication of his prize-winning story, "The Gold Bug" in the Philadelphia *Dollar Newspaper* in 1843 brought him some recognition, but he became famous in 1845 with the printing of "The Raven" in the *Evening Mirror* and the *Whig Review*. In 1849, the year in which appeared "Annabel Lee," "The Bells," and others of his best-known poems, Poe visited Norfolk and Richmond on a lecture tour. He had broken his engagement to marry the poetess, Mrs. Helen Whitman, and in Richmond he had become engaged to his former sweetheart, Sarah Elmira Royster, now the widow Shelton. From the time of his leaving Richmond his movements are unknown until he was found in an unconscious condition in Baltimore. He died in a hospital on October 7, 1849. In the churchyard of the Westminster Presbyterian Church he was interred the next day. His wife, Virginia, was later removed from the vault of the Valentines, owners of the Fordham cottage, to a place beside his grave.

Edgar Allan Poe is as important for his influence upon the literature of the world as he is for the works in themselves. He is known as poet, critic, short story writer, and mystic theorist. The quality of about twenty of his poems is unique. He was an innovator in the field of pure poetry and of symbolism. Of lesser importance was his mastery of certain technical devices, such as assonance, rhythm and rhyme, as evidenced in his "The Raven," "The Bells," and "Ulalume." His influence was especially great in France through Baudelaire, Mallarmé, and the Symbolists. Certainly, "To Helen," "Annabel Lee," "The Haunted Palace," "The Raven," "Israfel," "The City in the Sea," and "Ulalume" are among the most universally admired short poems in the language.

Poe, at the time of his death, was best known in America as a critic. He defined the short story and developed the theory of what has come to be known as "pure poetry."

His prose tales were unique for his day. He invented the detective story, as illustrated by such tales as "The Murders in the Rue Morgue" and "The Purloined Letter." His most characteristic tales were stories of impressionistic effect, often containing a psychological theme or built on a study of conscience, as seen in "Ligeia" or "William Wilson"; or tales of terror, such as "The Black Cat," "The Telltale Heart," or "The Cask of Amontillado."

The magic of Poe, his power to arouse our terror, and to make us partake of the sensations that he evokes by his stories as though we had lived them, are the effects of his conscious art. His poems are remarkable for their beauty and melody, his tales for the intensity with which the artist brings us under his spell. He is associated especially with his dark and terror-filled stories with which all readers are familiar and he is, perhaps, the world's master of the macabre. He was the product of the Gothic influence infused with the curiosity as to all things psychological that came from Germany. When all the stories that he wrote, however, are considered, he is seen to have a wider range as a prose writer than is generally recognized.

James Southall Wilson

BIBLIOGRAPHICAL REFERENCES: The standard editions are *The Complete Works of Edgar Allan Poe*, edited by James A. Harrison, 17 vols., 1902, now out of print, and the less complete but reliable *Works of Edgar Allan Poe*, edited by George E. Woodberry and Edmund C. Stedman, 10 vols., 1894–1895 (reprinted 1914); but a new edition is needed to incorporate the letters and other findings of recent scholarship. One such contribution is John W. Ostrom, *The Letters of Edgar Allan Poe*, 2 vols., 1948. The best editions of the short stories are James Southall Wilson, *Tales of Edgar Allan Poe*, 1927; and Killis Campbell, *Poe's Short Stories*, 1927. The latter also edited *The Poems of Edgar Allan Poe*, 1917.

The standard biography is Arthur H. Quinn, *Edgar Allan Poe: A Critical Biogra-*

phy, 1941. See also J. H. Ingram, *Edgar Allan Poe: His Life, Letters, and Opinions,* 2 vols., 1880; George E. Woodberry, *The Life of Edgar Allan Poe, Personal and Literary,* 2 vols., 1885 (rev. ed., 1909); Hervey Allen, *Israfel: The Life and Times of Edgar Allan Poe,* 2 vols., 1926; and N. B. Fagin, *The Histrionic Mr. Poe,* 1949.

See also Margaret Alterton, *Origins of Poe's Critical Theory,* 1925; Norman Foerster, *American Criticism,* 1928; S. F. Damon, *Thomas Holley Chivers, Friend of Poe,* 1930; Killis Campbell, *The Mind of Poe and Other Studies,* 1933; Gay Wilson Allen, *American Prosody,* 1935; Van Wyck Brooks, *The World of Washington Irving,* 1944; and "Edgar Allan Poe," in *The Literary History of the United States,* Vol. II, edited by Robert E. Spiller, Willard Thorp, Thomas H. Johnston, and Henry S. Canby, 1948.

For briefer criticism and special studies consult the extensive bibliography in *The Literary History of the United States,* Vol. III, 689–696.

POLITIAN
(Angelo Ambrogini)

Born: Montepulciano, Italy
Date: July 14, 1454

Died: Florence, Italy
Date: September 24, 1494

PRINCIPAL WORKS

PLAY: *Orfeo,* 1480 (*Orpheus*).
POEMS: *Sylvae,* 1512; *Le Stanze,* 1518.
ESSAYS: *Miscellanea,* 1489.

Angelo Ambrogini, who called himself Poliziano and Politian, from his birthplace, was a humanist who studied the philosophy of Plato under Marsilio Ficino and Aristotle under Argyropulos. A true man of the Renaissance, he displayed a modern spirit in his ability to express his classical learning in understandable, popular forms.

At the age of nineteen he attracted the attention of Lorenzo de' Medici (1449–1492) by his Latin version of a part of the *Iliad,* and he was asked to tutor Lorenzo's son Piero. Besides being canon of the cathedral of Florence, he developed the scientific method of textual criticism in his lectures on Greek and Roman literature at the University of Florence, where he had among his students Johann Reuchlin and William Grocyn. His pastoral play, *Orpheus,* was produced in Mantua in 1480, during a brief period of estrangement from the Medicis. After his death his original verses in Latin, including *Manto, Rusticus, Nutricia,* and *Ambra,* were published in twelve books in Paris in 1512. He also wrote poems in Italian, of which the most famous is *Le Stanze,* written to celebrate the skill and courage of Giuliano de' Medici in a tournament. His translations from the Greek include works by Plato, Epictetus, and Plutarch.

As one of the earliest poets of the Italian Renaissance, he revealed the lyrical qualities of the Italian language in *Le Stanze.* His idyllic *Orpheus* is one of the first plays in that language, and since it was also set to music, it can be classified as an early Italian opera. Born in Montepulciano, Italy, on July 14, 1454, he died at Florence, September 24, 1494.

849

BIBLIOGRAPHICAL REFERENCES: There is a translation of *Orpheus* by Louis E. Lord, 1931. For biographical studies see W. P. Gresswell, *Memoirs of Angelus Politianus,* 1805; Pietro Serrasi, *Vita de Angelo Poliziano,* 1808; and M. A. Boccalaro, *Angelo Poliziano: it poeta del bel canto,* 1951. For background and related materials see also William Roscoe, *Life of Lorenzo de' Medici,* 1803 (10th ed., 1889); H. O. Taylor, *Thought and Expression in the Fifteenth Century,* 1920; and John Addington Symonds, *The Renaissance in Italy,* 1875–1886, Modern Library, 1935.

MARCO POLO

Born: Venice (?), Italy	*Died:* Venice
Date: c. 1254	*Date:* January 9, 1324

PRINCIPAL WORK

DESCRIPTION AND TRAVEL: *The Travels of Marco Polo,* c. 1299.

Much of Marco Polo's early life is still in question, including the place and date of his birth. Marco's father was one of three Venetian brothers who had formed a business partnership as merchants. Nicolo Polo, Marco's father, and Maffeo Polo are known to have been at the court of Kublai Khan in the 1260's. The Khan apparently became interested enough in religion to send the two men back to Italy to request that the Pope send Christian missionaries to his land. When the Polos arrived home in 1269, they found that Pope Clement IV had died the year before. They waited for the election of a new Pope before setting off once again for China, taking with them young Marco Polo and letters explaining the cause for their delay. They were followed some months later by two Dominican monks, but these missionaries never reached their destination.

According to Marco Polo's own account, his father and uncle hoped to journey to China by sea, taking ship on the Persian Gulf. Finding that plan impossible to follow, they traveled overland to the court of Kublai Khan, passing on their way through lands explored by no other white man until the nineteenth century and arriving at their destination in 1275, when Marco Polo was about twenty or twenty-one years old. Kublai Khan, pleased to see the Venetians, made them welcome at his court. Young Marco studied the languages of Kublai Khan's dominions and entered the service of that great ruler. Traveling for the Khan took Marco Polo over much of Asia: into the Chinese provinces of Shansi, Shensi, Szechuen, and Yunnan, and into the areas now known as Burma and Tibet. Marco Polo, finding that the Khan took great interest in all phases of life, took many notes on his travels and reported in great detail to Kublai Khan, who seems to have listened personally to the young Venetian. Apparently Kublai Khan esteemed Marco Polo, for the latter even served for a time as the governor of the province of Yangchow. Apparently the two elder Polos served Kublai Khan in the capacity of military advisers.

So important and rich did the three Europeans become that they grew fearful of what jealous courtiers or a new ruler might do to them in the event of Kublai Khan's death. Fearing the worst, they petitioned the Khan to permit them to return to their homeland; their wish was not at first granted, however. An opportunity presented itself finally in 1286. The Khan of Persia, a relative of Kublai Khan, sent a delegation to request a Mongol bride for their ruler, and the envoys who presented the request asked that the three Venetians might accompany them back to Persia. In 1292 the party set out by sea for Persia. Two years later they arrived at the court of Arghan Khan and were given permission to continue on to Venice. They arrived in their home city in 1295, twenty-four years—almost a quarter of a century—after their departure. Having left Venice a stripling, Marco Polo returned a mature and experienced man of about forty.

During 1298 a war broke out between Venice and Genoa. The Genoese assembled a fleet to attack Venice, and the latter city prepared to defend itself. A Venetian naval force under Andrea Dandolo set out to meet and destroy the attacking Genoese vessels; aboard one of the Venetian galleys, as its commander, was Marco Polo. The Venetians were defeated, and among those who found themselves prisoners of war was Marco Polo, who remained a captive in Genoa for almost a year, not being freed until the summer of 1299. During his imprisonment at Genoa, Marco Polo wrote his famous narrative of travels and adventures, or rather he dictated them to a fellow prisoner, one Rusticiano of Pisa, who acted as amanuensis, taking down the *Travels* in French.

Little is known of Marco Polo's life after his release from Genoese imprisonment. By his will, made on January 9, 1324, the day he died in Venice, it is known that he left a wife and three daughters, but other information is scanty. Indeed, aside from his own account, little is known of any of Marco Polo's life. Scholars have searched diligently in the Venetian archives, but they have found little information of consequence. And yet Marco Polo was influential for more than two centuries, through the detailed account of his adventures that he left behind. Many of the maps of the fourteenth and fifteenth centuries were based on his information; even Christopher Columbus owned a Latin translation of the *Travels,* into which he wrote notes.

The Travels of Marco Polo is in two parts. The first part is the actual narrative, while the second part consists of passages describing various places and parts of Asia, particularly portions of the empire of Kublai Khan. The earliest manuscript, perhaps the original, is believed to be one in the National Library at Paris. Altogether there are some eighty manuscripts in existence, and as is usually the case the various manuscripts differ considerably. While the *Travels* have importance as a historical document, the book is of negligible literary value. It is a plainly written account of experiences fascinating in themselves.

BIBLIOGRAPHICAL REFERENCES: Convenient editions of *The Travels of Marco Polo, the Venetian* are the Everyman's Library, 1921, and the Modern Library, 1931. The most generally useful volume on Polo is Henry H. Hart, *Venetian Adventurer,* 1947, with a full bibliography. Other studies are R. Alluli, *Marco Polo,* 1923; and Luigi F. Benedetto, *Marco Polo,* translated 1931. The stories of several great travelers are included in Merriam Sherwood and Elmer Mantz, *The Road to Cathay,* 1928. A valuable general study is J. N. L. Baker, *The History of Geographical Discovery and*

Exploration, 1931. See also Sir Edward D. Ross, "Marco Polo and his Book," *Proceedings of the British Academy,* XX (1934), 181–205. For fictionalized accounts of Marco Polo's adventure see Donn Byrne, *Messer Marco Polo,* 1921; and Eugene O'Neill, *Marco Millions,* 1928.

HENRIK PONTOPPIDAN

Born: Fredericia, Denmark   *Died:* Ordrup, Denmark
Date: July 24, 1857   *Date:* August 21, 1943

Principal Works

NOVELS: *Det forjættede Land,* 1891–1895 (*The Promised Land*); *Lykke-Per,* 1898–1904 (*Lucky Peter*); *Dødes Rige,* 1912–1916 (*The Kingdom of the Dead*); *Mands Himmerig,* 1927 (*Man's Heaven*).
SHORT STORIES: *Stækkede Vinger,* 1881; *Landsbybilleder,* 1883; *Krøniker,* 1890.
PLAY: *De vilde Fugle,* 1902.

Much of the major writing done in Scandinavia for the last seventy-five years has been in some degree pessimistic, for writers there have been very much aware of the intellectual currents flowing through Europe, chiefly of scientific materialism which conflicted with the traditional values of a Christian society. Most of the intellectuals accepted the methods of scientific inquiry and were disillusioned with democracy because of the people's reluctance to accept social change that would bring the social organization into harmony with scientific principles. Ibsen, Strindberg, and Hamsun are all, to some extent, tragic artists. Henrik Pontoppidan also protested against the complacency of his society because it refused to be honest in facing the new knowledge.

Born in Fredericia, Denmark, on July 24, 1857, Henrik Pontoppidan, son of a provincial clergyman, went to Copenhagen to study engineering. At the age of twenty, while engaged in scientific studies, he suddenly realized that he wished only to be a writer. He left college and supported himself by teaching high school. He hated the facile religious sentimentality prevalent in the school, and he disliked the easygoing way of life of the Danish people because it lacked the emotional and intellectual intensity that he respected.

Pontoppidan's early work, of which *The Promised Land* is representative, protests against the injustices of peasant life; his hopes for reform rest with liberal politics, though he is aware that the hardness of human hearts cannot easily be overcome. A little later, in the eight volumes of *Lucky Peter,* he used autobiographical material to portray the life of a representative Dane in modern Denmark. In *The Kingdom of the Dead,* Pontoppidan reached the nadir of his pessimism: in five volumes he shows his disappointment with the results of liberalism and despairs of social progress. He never fully emerged from this pessimism. Though he had entered politics and had served a short time in the Danish legislature, he withdrew from public life entirely during his last years. He wrote little after his retirement; his last important novel, *Man's Heaven,* is a bitter attack upon those who failed Denmark during

World War I: the politicians, the journalists, the isolationists, and the war profiteers.

Pontoppidan, under the influence of Georg Brandes, took up the techniques of realism and wrote with great accuracy of various social groups. His style is smooth and apparently effortless. He represents the most modern elements in Danish thought; it was for this that he was awarded the Nobel Prize for literature in 1917. He died at his home at Ordrup, Charlottenlund, Denmark, on August 21, 1943.

BIBLIOGRAPHICAL REFERENCES: A good introduction to Pontoppidan in English is Hanna Astrup Larsen, "Pontoppidan of Denmark," *American-Scandinavian Review*, XXXI (1943), 231–239. The most carefully documented study of his life and work is C. M. Woel, *Henrik Pontoppidan*, 2 vols., 1945. A brief sketch also appears in Annie Russell Marble, *The Nobel Prize Winners in Literature, 1901–1931*, 1932.

ALEXANDER POPE

Born: London, England
Date: May 21, 1688

Died: Twickenham, England
Date: May 30, 1744

PRINCIPAL WORKS

PASTORAL POEMS: *Pastorals*, 1709; *Windsor Forest*, 1713.

DIDACTIC POEMS: *Essay on Criticism*, 1711; *Moral Essays*, 1731–1735; *Essay on Man*, 1733–1734.

SATIRES: *The Rape of the Lock*, 1712–1714; *The Dunciad*, 1728–1743; *Imitations of Horace*, 1733–1737; *The Epistle to Dr. Arbuthnot*, 1735.

TRANSLATIONS: Homer's *Iliad*, 1715–1718; the *Odyssey*, 1725–1726.

Alexander Pope, English poet, was born in London, May 21, 1688, son of a prosperous linen merchant and his second wife. The fact that Pope's parents were Roman Catholics had a bearing on the amount of education he received and his economic and social status. Schools and universities were closed to him; he could not buy or inherit land; he paid double taxes, and he could not legally live within ten miles of London. He was educated at irregular times by private tutors, mostly priests, but for the most part he, on his own, "dipped into a great number of English, French, Italian, Latin and Greek poets." This was no meager education in itself, for poets of the early 1700's copied many forms and ideas from the classical writers of ancient Rome and the period was called the Augustan Age. Pope himself became known as the "prose and reason" poet.

At the age of twelve a serious illness left him a hunch-backed cripple, four feet, six inches tall. Yet before he was seventeen he was admitted into the society of London wits, and men of fashion encouraged this young prodigy. By the time he was thirty he was acclaimed the chief poet of his times.

Pope's first important publication was his *Pastorals* in 1709. Two years later at the age of twenty-three his more famous *Essay on Criticism* was published. As very polite conversation, it is typical of the eighteenth century "salon"-type verse. Here Pope gives some of his popular sayings: "A little learning is a dangerous thing"; "To

853

err is human, to forgive divine," and "Fools rush in where angels fear to tread." In the first section of the poem he tells of the chaotic state of criticism of his time; in the second he expounds his main rule of following nature, and in the final part he explains that the rules to be observed in writing must be studied in the works of great classical writers—Horace and Vergil, for example. They should not be slavishly imitated but should serve as guides. Pope himself was greatly influenced by Milton and Dryden. *The Rape of the Lock,* printed as a short poem in 1712 and in an elaborate form in 1714, is one of the finest early eighteenth century products. In a satirical way it catches, sums up, and presents in artistic form the spirit of the age. His use of myth makes it unusual for the period.

In his translation of *Homer,* his chief employment for twelve years, Pope consciously dressed Homer in the language of his century. In so doing he accustomed the English ear to the regular rhythms and beats of Homer. He also undertook a translation of the *Odyssey,* done partly by directing collaborators. The two translations were so successful in sales that Pope is reportedly the first English poet to make a fortune by his writing.

"Eloisa to Abelard," which appeared in a volume of poems in 1717, has medieval color and a melancholy tone. Pope left this romantic type, however, and returned to neo-classical forms.

In 1718 he moved to Twickenham on the Thames, where he lived with the widowed mother to whom he was devoted. Pope never married. His love for Lady Mary Wortley Montagu came to a bitter end. Later he fell in love with Martha Blount, and during the last ten years of his life he spent some part of every day with her.

Toward the end of his life Pope's fame as a moralist and satirist increased. Most of the distinguished men of his day were among his friends or enemies. The latter he ridiculed in the mock-heroic *Dunciad,* published in 1728 and republished in 1729.

The *Essay on Man* was also connected with controversies of the time. Designed as one of a series of philosophic poems, it gives proof that by training and temperament Pope was not a philosophical poet, at the same time presenting excellent examples of Pope's technique in building from abstract observation or a general idea to particular illustrations. Also noteworthy of his later years was his *Epistle to Dr. Arbuthnot,* which shows artistic progress in his ability to handle the couplet. Here he gives it ease and a conversational quality in contrast to the stiff and more formal use in *Essay on Criticism.*

The "school of Pope," with its great attention to matters of style and its concern for poems technically "perfect," was considered dull and lifeless and was detested by nineteenth century artists. Pope and his contemporaries are more kindly received today. In them we see elegant, correct, useful, and reasonable literature, although this writing is not necessarily profound.

Pope died at his Twickenham, Middlesex, villa on May 30, 1744.

BIBLIOGRAPHICAL REFERENCES: Earlier standard editions of Alexander Pope are being superseded by the continuing volumes of the Twickenham Edition, edited by Geoffrey Tillotson and others, 1938 ff. The best general biography is W. J. Courthope, *Life of Pope,* in Vol. V of Pope's *Works,* edited by Whitwell Elwin and W. J.

Courthope, 10 vols., 1871–1889. See also Samuel Johnson, *Lives of the Poets,* 1781; Edith Sitwell, *Alexander Pope,* 1930; George Sherburn, *The Early Career of Alexander Pope,* 1934; and R. K. Root, *The Poetical Career of Alexander Pope,* 1938.

For criticism see also Geoffrey Tillotson, *On the Poetry of Pope,* 1938; J. E. Tobin, *Alexander Pope, 1744–1944,* 1945; Austin Warren, "The Mask of Pope," in *Rage for Order,* 1948; Cleanth Brooks, "The Case of Miss Arabella Fermor," in *The Well-Wrought Urn,* 1949; W. K. Wimsatt, "Rhetoric and Poems: The Example of Pope," in *English Institute Essays,* 1949; and Maynard Mack, " 'Wit and Poetry and Pope': Some Observations on His Imagery," in *Pope and His Contemporaries: Essays Presented to George Sherburn,* edited by James L. Clifford and Louis A. Landa, 1949.

JANE PORTER

Born: Durham, England   *Died:* Bristol, England
Date: 1776   *Date:* May 24, 1850

PRINCIPAL WORKS

NOVELS: *Thaddeus of Warsaw,* 1803; *The Scottish Chiefs,* 1810.

Born in Durham, England, in 1776, Jane Porter was the daughter of an army officer who died when she was three years old. Soon afterward the widowed mother took the family to Edinburgh to live, but shortly before 1803 the entire family moved to London, where Jane Porter began to write. Her first book was the story of a Polish exile entitled *Thaddeus of Warsaw.* The book had an amazing success with critics and the public; among the people who sent a congratulatory message to the author was Kosciusko, world-renowned Polish patriot. With the publication of her novel, Jane Porter became as well known as her brother, Sir Robert Ker Porter, a painter, and her sister, Anna Maria Porter, also a popular novelist of the period.

The best novel to come from her pen was *The Scottish Chiefs,* a historical romance of the kind later made famous by Sir Walter Scott, who was a childhood friend of Jane Porter. Indeed, *The Scottish Chiefs* is one of the few historical novels prior to Scott's Waverley series which still commands a body of readers. After her initial success as a novelist, Jane Porter turned to the writing of plays. Her first effort was never staged, and her second was a failure so complete that it ended her career as a dramatist. A number of later novels were written and published, but none caught the public or critical fancy as did her first two. Jane Porter, who never married, spent much of her life in literary and artistic society and lived a happy and serene life, although somewhat financially embarrased in her later years. She died in Bristol on May 24, 1850.

BIBLIOGRAPHICAL REFERENCES: For a study of Jane Porter and her times see Mona Wilson, *These Were Muses,* 1924.

KATHERINE ANNE PORTER

Born: Indian Creek, Texas
Date: May 15, 1894

PRINCIPAL WORKS

NOVELETTES AND SHORT STORIES: *Flowering Judas,* 1930 (enlarged 1935); *Hacienda,* 1934; *Noon Wine,* 1937; *Pale Horse, Pale Rider,* 1939; *The Leaning Tower and Other Stories,* 1944.

ESSAYS: *The Days Before,* 1952.

TRANSLATIONS: *Katherine Anne Porter's French Song-Book,* 1933; *The Itching Parrot,* by José Joaquín Fernández de Lizárdi, 1942.

The critical reputation of Katherine Anne Porter is in inverse ratio to the volume of her published work. Never one to rush into print, she has eyed her writing with such sharp scrutiny that only a comparatively small amount of it has appeared in book form, yet on the basis of five novelettes and three collections of short stories she has been acclaimed as one of the outstanding literary figures of her generation, an important influence on younger writers, and a stylist comparable to Hawthorne and Flaubert.

A descendant of Daniel Boone, Miss Porter was born on May 15, 1894, in a small community near San Antonio, Texas. She spent her girlhood in Texas and Louisiana and received most of her formal education in small convent schools in the South. More important to her development was the fact that she spent her childhood in a home in which there existed both incentive and opportunity to read. By the time she was fifteen she had absorbed a wide variety of literature; she once said that it would be possible for her to write an autobiography based on her reading alone. She spent her youth writing and destroying manuscripts "quite literally by the trunkful," and she was thirty before her first story was published. In

the meantime she had eked out a living by doing book reviews, political articles, editing, rewriting, and what she terms "hack writing of every sort." Twice married and divorced and the recipient of a number of literary honors and awards, she has lived in New Orleans, Chicago, Bermuda, Mexico, New York, Berlin, Paris, and Hollywood.

If the surface aspects of her life appear unfixed and variable, they are in sharp contrast to her inner self, which has remained constant in her efforts to resolve life's complexities in art. In her own words, "This has been the basic and absorbing occupation, the intact line of my life which directs my actions, determines my point of view, and profoundly affects my character and personality, my social beliefs and economic status and the kinds of friendships I form." The first fruits of her apprenticeship appeared in 1930 with the publication of *Flowering Judas,* which was reissued in 1935 with four stories added. *Pale Horse, Pale Rider,* containing three novelettes, followed in 1939. Although Miss Porter liked the title story best, most readers have preferred *Noon Wine,* a psychological tale involving events of unexpected violence on a small farm in Texas. Her most recent book of fiction is *The Leaning Tower and Other Stories.* In 1952 she published *The Days Before,* a collection of her critical writings and essays. For some time now she has committed herself to two long-term projects, a biography of Cotton Mather and a full-length novel. The latter, at which her publishers have darted hopeful glances from year to year, has thus far inspired two titles, *No Safe Harbor* having been discarded in favor of *The Ship of Fools.*

Perhaps the most obvious reason for Miss Porter's importance, in spite of so small an output, is that she is an incomparable stylist. Precise, subtle, poetic, strong yet delicate, her prose has above all a rare quality of stylistic verisimilitude. Unlike many modern authors, whose language always sounds characteristically like themselves, she has a genius for adapting her prose to the specific situation and character under discussion, and for reflecting the personality, background, and quality of thought and vocabulary of each of the widely varied characters she depicts. Rhythm, tone, imagery, and choice of words contribute to the organic unification of her prose and its subject matter. Only the purity, sharpness, and concentration of the writing provide the clues that the thoughts and words of the poor dairy farmer in *Noon Wine* and of the harassed, bullying movie producer in *Hacienda* are creations of the same mind. Writing always in the third person, Miss Porter is nonetheless extraordinarily successful in making what she writes seem to flow from within the brain of the character she is portraying.

Closely related to style is the skill with which she handles her subject matter. Modern Americans of all sorts, their relationships, and the extreme difficulty of self-fulfillment and self-understanding in the world of today are her concern. Two of the "Miranda" novelettes, *Old Mortality* and *Pale Horse, Pale Rider,* deal respectively with the rather conventional themes of self-understanding and the will-to-death. But the last words of the first story indicate the precarious and temporary nature of Miranda's climactic realization of herself, while the ending of the second portrays the quiet awfulness of being doomed to live. Avoiding the extremes of romantic optimism and nihilistic pessimism, the author presents her quiet negativism, her recognition of the wasteland that is modern life, with a subtlety that stops just short of inconclusiveness. With quiet but dramatic irony as her chief tool, whether it is the irony of reflection in the "Miranda" stories or the horrifying irony of action in *Noon Wine,* Miss Porter brilliantly portrays the difficulties involved in ordinary, decent everyday living in our time. Carefully treading the narrow way between objective realism and aesthetic sensibility, she presents a vision of the world which is completely her own, familiar to our view and yet capable of suggesting the deeper realities of symbol and myth.

BIBLIOGRAPHICAL REFERENCES: There is no full-length biography. A pioneer critical study aiming at a comprehensive survey of her work is Harry John Mooney, Jr., *The Fiction and Criticism of Katherine Anne Porter,* 1957. Of particular importance in an understanding of Miss Porter's background of subject matter and method of composition is her essay, " 'Noon Wine': The Sources," in *The Yale Review,* XLVI (1956), 23–39. For additional critical studies see also Ray B. West, Jr., "Katherine Anne Porter: Symbol and Theme in 'Flowering Judas,'" in *The Art of Modern Fic-*

tion, by R. B. West, Jr., and R. W. Stallman, 1949; and "Katherine Anne Porter and 'Historic Memory,'" in *Southern Renascence,* edited by Louis D. Rubin, Jr., and Robert D. Jacobs, 1953; Edmund Wilson, *Classics and Commercials,* 1950; Lodwick Hartley, "Katherine Anne Porter," *Sewanee Review,* XLVIII (1940), 206–216, and "The Lady of the Temple: The Critical Theories of Katherine Anne Porter," *College English,* XIV (1953), 386–391; Margaret Marshall, "Writers in the Wilderness: Katherine Anne Porter," *Nation,* CL (1940), 473–475; Robert Penn Warren, "Katherine Anne Porter: Irony with a Center," *Kenyon Review,* IV (1942), 29–42; Vernon A. Young, "The Art of Katherine Anne Porter," *New Mexico Quarterly,* XV (1945), 326–341; Robert B. Heilman, "The Southern Temper," *Hopkins Review,* VI (1952), 5–15; and Charles A. Allen, "Katherine Anne Porter: Psychology as Art," *Southwest Review,* XLI (1956), 223–230. For bibliography see Edward Schwartz, "Katherine Anne Porter: A Critical Bibliography," with an introduction by Robert Penn Warren," *Bulletin of the New York Public Library,* LVII (1953), 211–247.

EZRA POUND

Born: Hailey, Idaho
Date: October 30, 1885

Principal Works

POEMS: *A Lume Spento,* 1908; *A Quinzaine for This Yule,* 1908; *Personae,* 1909; *Exultations,* 1909; *Provença,* 1910; *Canzoni,* 1911; *Ripostes,* 1912; *Lustra,* 1916; *Quia Pauper Amavi,* 1919; *Hugh Selwyn Mauberley,* 1920; *Umbra,* 1920; *Poems, 1918–1921,* 1921; *A Draft of XVI Cantos,* 1925; *Personae: The Collected Poems of Ezra Pound,* 1926; *A Draft of Cantos 17–27,* 1928; *A Draft of XXX Cantos,* 1930; *Eleven New Cantos, XXXI-XLI,* 1934; *Homage to Sextus Propertius,* 1934; *The Fifth Decad of Cantos,* 1937; *Cantos LII-LXXI,* 1940; *The Pisan Cantos, LXXI-LXXXV,* 1948; *The Cantos of Ezra Pound,* 1948; *Section: Rock-Drill, 85–95 de los cantares,* 1956.

ESSAYS AND STUDIES: *Pavannes and Divisions,* 1918; *ABC of Economics,* 1933; *Jefferson and/or Mussolini,* 1935; *Social Credit: An Impact,* 1935; *Polite Essays,* 1937; *Culture,* 1938 [*Guide to Kulchur*]; *What Is Money For?,* 1939.

LITERARY CRITICISM: *The Spirit of Romance,* 1910; *Instigations,* 1920; *How to Read,* 1931; *The ABC of Reading,* 1934; *Make It New,* 1934.

BIOGRAPHY AND AUTOBIOGRAPHY: *Gaudier-Brzeska,* 1916; *Indiscretions, or Une revue de deux mondes,* 1923.

TRANSLATIONS: *The Sonnets and Ballate of Guido Cavalcanti,* 1912; *Cathay,* 1915 (Translated for the most part from the Chinese of Rihaki, from the notes of Ernest Fenollosa); *Certain Noble Plays of Japan, from the Manuscripts of Ernest Fenollosa,* 1916; *Dialogues of Fontenelle,* 1917; *The Natural Philosophy of Love,* by Remy de Gourmont, 1922; *Confucius: The Great Digest and The Unwobbling Pivot,* 1947; *The Classic Anthology Defined by Confucius,* 1954; Sophocles' *Women of Trachis,* 1957.

LETTERS: *The Letters of Ezra Pound, 1907–1941,* 1950.

Ezra Pound's is a special case in the literary history of our time. One of the most controversial figures in a confused and stormy period, an imitator on the

858

one hand and a brilliant innovator on the other, he has been highly praised and savagely attacked. Certainly no one can doubt his influence on the technique of contemporary verse; there are few poets who have written since the 1920's who have done so without knowledge of the *Cantos*, Pound's tremendous but obscure work in progress. Time alone can tell whether he will survive as a major poet in his own right or as an influential poetry propagandist. However, since his poetry as well as his promotion of literature is discussed widely and freely at the present time, both the man and his work demand, and receive, considerable critical attention.

Ezra (Loomis) Pound was born in Hailey, Idaho, on October 30, 1885, but when he was two he was taken to Pennsylvania by his parents. His mother was a distant relative of Henry Wadsworth Longfellow. A precocious youth, he attended the University of Pennsylvania when he was fifteen but later transferred to Hamilton College, where he received the degree of Ph.B. in 1905. For the next two years he taught Romance languages at the University of Pennsylvania. However, the disciplines of teaching bored him, and after a short time at Wabash College in Indiana he went to Europe in 1908. There he remained, proclaiming that American civilization in general was unbearable, shifting his residence whenever the possibility of a new poetry group appeared, inspiring or attacking other writers while creating on his own. *A Lume Spento*, his first book of poems, was printed in Venice in 1908. *Personae*, his first characteristic book of poems, was published in London in 1909.

Pound was in and out of London until 1920, positively helping such varied writers as T. S. Eliot (who once called him "il miglior fabbro"), William Butler Yeats, and Wyndham Lewis to shape their styles, and for two years serving as London editor of the *Little Review* (1917–1919). During this time successive volumes of his own poetry appeared, all employing Imagist or experimental techniques. Between 1920 and 1924 he lived in Paris, one of the leaders of the expatriate "lost generation" group of writers who congregated there after World War I. In 1924 he went to Italy to live, his long residence at Rapallo broken only by a visit to the United States in 1939. Refusing to leave Italy at the beginning of World War II, he became a radio propagandist for the fascist Italian government. After the war he was imprisoned to stand trial for treason; however, when he was declared insane, he was committed to St. Elizabeth's Hospital in Washington, D. C.

Early in his career Pound demonstrated the intensity and extrasensory foresight of a prophet. He anticipated the fad for things Oriental with his publication of *Cathay*, a free translation into English of verse by the Chinese poet Rihaku. In addition, continuing his scholarly research, begun years before, into medieval literature, especially the Italian and the Provençal, he made free translations of such buried writers as Cavalcanti in *The Sonnets and Ballate of Guido Cavalcanti*, Arnaut Daniel, Sextus Propertius, and others. R. P. Blackmur in his *Language As Gesture* states that Pound is a better poet as a translator than as an originator, for "lacking sufficient substance of his own to maintain an intellectual discipline, he is always

859

better where the discipline of craftsmanship is enough." Certainly this is true of Pound's major opus, a series of original cantos with sources grounded in medieval and modern history, Greek mythology, Chinese culture, and minor classics, which will number about one hundred when finished. In the ninety-five cantos now published there is a juxtaposition of past worlds and the present that reminds one of Eliot's *The Waste Land* (1922). However, here the parallel ends, for the allusions to the past are all to the special past Pound found in his special readings, rather than to a heritage in great works familiar to readers. In addition, in the *Cantos* Pound uses language ideographically, as if the English words could serve the same function as Chinese characters. The result is often unintelligible, but at the same time there are individual lines of great beauty. It was for this work that Pound received the Bollingen Prize in Poetry in 1949, an award which provoked one of the most heated critical battles of the decade.

Pound is probably the best teacher of language of his generation. His encouragement of the early works of others who later became rightfully famous was always just, and what he has written of writing generally, as in his *The ABC of Reading*, is clear and true. (Curiously, outside the field of literature his judgments were twisted to the point of monomania.) It is as a teacher and propagandist that he best has served: an odd, wild, gifted man.

Today, living quietly with his wife at St. Elizabeth's, Pound is free to continue his writing and to receive visitors who come to see him daily.

BIBLIOGRAPHICAL REFERENCES: There is no collected edition of Pound's poetry or prose. All the verse he wishes to preserve, exclusive of the *Cantos,* was printed in *Personae,* 1926; reissued with additional poems, 1949. His major critical writings have been collected in *Literary Essays of Pound,* edited and with an introduction by T. S. Eliot, 1952.

There is no authorized or extended biographical study. The most detailed critical study of his poetry is Hugh Kenner, *The Poetry of Ezra Pound,* 1951. Earlier estimates of his work include T. S. Eliot, *Ezra Pound: His Metric and Poetry,* 1917 (unsigned), and the introduction to *Selected Poems,* 1928; Carl Sandburg, "The Work of Ezra Pound," *Poetry,* VII (1916), 249–257; Conrad Aiken, *Scepticisms,* 1919; and Louis Untermeyer, *American Poetry Since 1900,* 1923. The basic essay for all recent Pound studies is Richard P. Blackmur, "The Masks of Ezra Pound," in *The Double Agent,* 1935. See also F. R. Leavis, *New Bearings in English Poetry,* 1932; Edith Sitwell, *Aspects of Modern Poetry,* 1934; Allen Tate, *Reactionary Essays on Poetry and Ideas,* 1936; Alice S. Admur, *The Poetry of Ezra Pound,* 1936; Babette Deutsch, *Poetry in Our Time,* 1952 (rev. ed., 1956); and H. H. Watts, *Ezra Pound and the Cantos,* 1952. *Examination of Ezra Pound,* edited by Peter Russell, 1950, contains a collection of essays by various hands.

The controversy over the Bollingen Prize in Poetry is aired in two volumes of specialized critical studies: *The Case of Ezra Pound,* edited by Charles Norman, 1948, and *The Case Against the Saturday Review,* edited by the editors of *Poetry,* 1949.

JOHN COWPER POWYS

Born: Shirley, Derbyshire, England

Date: October 8, 1872

Died: Wales

Date: June 17, 1963

PRINCIPAL WORKS

NOVELS: *Wood and Stone,* 1915; *Rodmoor,* 1916; *Ducdame,* 1925; *Wolf Solent,* 1929; *A Glastonbury Romance,* 1932; *Weymouth Sands,* 1934; *Jobber Skald,* 1935; *Maiden Castle,* 1936; *Morwyn,* 1937; *Owen Glendower,* 1940; *Porius,* 1951; *The Inmates,* 1952.

SHORT STORIES: *The Owl, the Duck, and—Miss Rowe! Miss Rowe!* 1930.

POEMS: *Odes and Other Poems,* 1896; *Poems,* 1899; *Wolf's-bane,* 1916; *Mandragora,* 1917; *Samphire,* 1922.

ESSAYS AND STUDIES: *Visions and Revisions,* 1915; *Confessions of Two Brothers,* 1916 (with Llewelyn Powys); *Suspended Judgments,* 1916; *The Complex Vision,* 1920; *Psychoanalysis and Morality,* 1923; *The Religion of a Sceptic,* 1925; *The Meaning of Culture,* 1929; *In Defence of Sensuality,* 1930; *Dorothy M. Richardson,* 1931; *A Philosophy of Solitude,* 1933; *The Pleasures of Literature [The Enjoyment of Literature],* 1938; *The Art of Growing Old,* 1944; *Dostoievsky,* 1947; *Rabelais,* 1948; *In Spite Of: A Philosophy for Everyman,* 1953; *Atlantis,* 1954.

AUTOBIOGRAPHY: *John Cowper Powys: Autobiography,* 1934.

John Cowper Powys, born in Derbyshire, England, on October 8, 1872, is a member of an extraordinarily artistic family. His father was a minister of the Church of England, his mother was a descendant of the poets William Cowper and John Donne. Although John Cowper Powys is an exceptionally prolific writer, his two brothers, Llewelyn and Theodore Francis, turned out before they died a volume of work almost equal to his own. Of the other eight Powys children, one sister became a novelist and poet, another sister a painter, another brother an architect. All of them shared an inheritance of Celtic imagination.

Powys, graduated from Corpus Christi College, Cambridge, began his career as a lecturer in the United States and Britain. His approach to figures like Carlyle, Ruskin, and Tennyson was peculiarly romantic; he would try to intuit the essential nature of the man about whom he was speaking and would often identify himself with that person. As a result, his literary criticism is emotionally based and his comments frequently reveal more about Powys than they do about the subject of the lecture. Despite this subjective quality, or perhaps because of it, he was a very successful lecturer.

His father having granted him an annuity of sixty pounds, Powys began the risky career of writing. He had been influenced by the pantheism of Wordsworth and the Celtic romanticism of the early Yeats. Soon after his graduation from Cambridge he met Thomas Hardy, who advised him to study the bizarre techniques of Edgar Allan Poe. Consequently, Powys' novels frequently deal with subject matter from the Welsh past that lends itself to a presentation of grotesque and fantastic scenes. *Porius,* for example, exploits fifth century Wales for its Arthurian romance and for the exotic religious rituals of the Druids. His historical novels allow his imagination free rein; as a result they are frequently overloaded and lacking in artistic control. His novels of the present are likely (as in *The Inmates,* the story of a love affair in an insane asylum) to deal with bizarre subjects and characters.

After 1910 a case of ulcers caused Powys frequently to spend his winters in America. In 1928 he settled in the United States, living mostly in New York and Hollywood until he returned to England in 1934.

He lived out his life in Wales, the land in which his imagination almost continually dwelt.

BIBLIOGRAPHICAL REFERENCES: There is as yet no full-length biographical or critical study devoted to John Cowper Powys alone. The best source for information about his life and work is his *Autobiography,* supplemented by *Confessions of Two Brothers,* written with Llewelyn Powys, 1916. For studies of his family background and related material see also Richard H. Ward, *The Powys Brothers,* 1935; Louis N. Wilkinson, *Welsh Ambassadors,* 1936, and *The Brothers Powys,* 1947; John Cowper Powys, "Four Brothers," *Century,* CX (1925), 553–560; and Gilbert E. Govan, "The Powys Family," *Sewanee Review,* XLVI (1938), 74–90.

LLEWELYN POWYS

Born: Dorchester, England　　　　　*Died:* Davos Platz, Switzerland
Date: August 13, 1884　　　　　　*Date:* December 2, 1939

PRINCIPAL WORKS

ESSAYS AND STUDIES: *Ebony and Ivory,* 1923; *Thirteen Worthies,* 1923; *Black Laughter,* 1924; *The Cradle of God,* 1929; *The Pathetic Fallacy: A Study of Christianity,* 1930; *Impassioned Clay,* 1931; *Now That the Gods Are Dead,* 1932; *Earth Memories,* 1934; *Glory of Life,* 1934; *Damnable Opinions,* 1935; *Dorset Essays,* 1935; *The Twelve Months,* 1936; *Somerset Essays,* 1937; *Rats in the Sacristy,* 1937; *A Baker's Dozen,* 1939; *Swiss Essays,* 1947.

NOVELS: *Apples Be Ripe,* 1930; *Love and Death,* 1939.

TRAVEL SKETCHES AND IMPRESSIONS: *A Pagan's Pilgrimage,* 1931.

AUTOBIOGRAPHY: *Confessions of Two Brothers,* 1916 (with John Cowper Powys); *Skin for Skin,* 1925; *The Verdict of Bridlegoose,* 1926.

BIOGRAPHY: *Henry Hudson,* 1927.

Llewelyn Powys, born in Dorchester, England, August 13, 1884, was the eighth of eleven children of Charles Francis Powys, an Anglican clergyman. Two of his elder brothers, John Cowper and Theodore Francis, became well-known writers.

In spite of his close relationship with his oldest brother, John Cowper, Llewelyn went through Sherborne School and Cambridge, and began to teach school with little thought of becoming a writer. In 1909 he contracted tuberculosis and spent several years in Switzerland. After he had recovered to some extent, he went to Africa to become a stock farmer in Kenya. During his five-year stay in Africa (1914–1919) he began to write. He published two series of essays and sketches about his life in Africa as *Ebony and Ivory* and *Black Laughter.* In 1920 he came to

New York, writing stories, articles, and personal essays for various periodicals. While in America, he married Alyse Gregory, managing editor of *The Dial*. His autobiographical observations of America, sparked with a sharp wit, appeared in *The Verdict of Bridlegoose*. Powys' essays covered a great range, any subject from a sensory description of a street to herbalism in the sixteenth century. Despite his wide range of concern, knowledge, and literary allusion, his work has been criticized as too much concerned with trivia about well-known people, too journalistic, or too gossipy.

In 1928 Powys traveled to Palestine; his work thereafter demonstrated considerably more substance. The account of the trip to Palestine, *A Pagan's Pilgrimage*, shows an interest in an appreciation of theology and biblical tradition from the point of view of a non-believer. Powys followed this book with *Impassioned Clay*, which attempts to survey man's history and constant search for comfort in the supernatural.

Powys, calling upon youth to be strong and free from the need for spiritual comfort and religious systems, referred to this book as the "Devil's handbook."

In his last years, Powys' tuberculosis forced him to live in Switzerland. He kept writing, ever more seriously calling for independence from religion and opposition to Nazism. His most comprehensive work, published posthumously as *Love and Death,* is an "imaginary autobiography" in which he attempted to get at the meaning of all his experience. After a long illness he died at Davos Platz, Switzerland, on December 2, 1939.

Powys' work found a devoted audience, especially in America. For many readers, his elaborate and allusive style enriched the value of his observations. For others, his style seemed too elaborate, pretentious, and falsely poetic. Between these extremes, however, it is generally agreed that he always maintained a great range of observations and a genuinely independent sense of judgment.

BIBLIOGRAPHICAL REFERENCES: The fullest biographical study is Malcolm Elwin, *Life of Llewelyn Powys*, 1946. Other books and articles dealing with the Powys' family are listed in the bibliography of John Cowper Powys.

T. F. POWYS

Born: Shirley, Derbyshire, England
Date: December 20, 1875

Died: Sturminster Newton, England
Date: November 27, 1953

PRINCIPAL WORKS

NOVELS: *Black Bryony,* 1923; *Mark Only,* 1924; *Mr. Tasker's Gods,* 1925; *Mockery Gap,* 1925; *Innocent Birds,* 1926; *Mr. Weston's Good Wine,* 1927; *Kindness in a Corner,* 1930; *Unclay,* 1931; *Make Thyself Many,* 1935; *Goat Green,* 1937.

SHORT STORIES: *The Left Leg,* 1923; *Feed My Swine,* 1926; *A Strong Girl,* 1926; *A Stubborn Tree,* 1926; *What Lack I Yet?,* 1927; *The Rival Pastors,* 1927; *The Dewpond,* 1928; *The House with the Echo,* 1928; *Fables,* 1929 (reissued as *No Painted Plumage*); *Christ in the Cupboard,* 1930; *The Key of the Field,* 1930; *Uriah on the Hill,* 1930; *The White Paternoster,* 1930; *The Only Penitant,* 1931; *Uncle Dottery,* 1931; *When Thou Wast Naked,* 1931; *The Two Thieves,* 1932; *The Tithe Barn,*

1932; *Captain Patch,* 1935; *Bottle's Path and Other Stories,* 1946; *God's Eyes A-Twinkle,* 1947.

ESSAYS AND STUDIES: *An Interpretation of Genesis,* 1908; *The Soliloquy of a Hermit,* 1916.

Of the three Powys brothers distinguished in literature—John Cowper, Theodore Francis, and Llewelyn—the second, though not the most famous, was without doubt the one with the most original genius. T. F. Powys, whether owing to some occult Cymric strain or to some chance of breeding, may be numbered among those writers to whose narrative talent is added a mystical insight. Born in Derbyshire on December 20, 1875, and educated at private schools, he had reached the age of forty-seven before his first volume of fiction appeared; but he had practiced his craft in silence for many years. In general he may be grouped with such writers as Violet Paget, Lord Dunsany, Algernon Blackwood, Kenneth Grahame, and Arthur Machen, all of whom drew inspiration from the hypothesis that nature is tenanted by animistic forces. The Edwardian decade and after was a great period of haunted literature, as much an age of tales about fauns, banshees, and goblins as it was of social-protest novels and comic-opera romances. This was the period when Powys began to write.

Unlike those of his contemporaries who, in the tradition of Celtic folklore, contrasted the normal human world with a realm of supernatural creatures, Powys depicted an inward haunting, the presence of the cosmic powers of good and evil in man himself. His hu-man characters are almost incarnations, and hence they often have an allegorical quality: in *Unclay* the central figure, John Death, is Death; in *Mr. Weston's Good Wine* Mr. Weston is God. But Powys always emphasized human traits; his personages seem as homely and local as the rustic Dorset villages through which they move.

Powys' technique arose from his acute perception of nature's unseen powers. It would be misleading to speak of "possession," or of "immanent spirits," or to regard him as an ordinary pantheist. Such terms imply a dualism in which the material and the spiritual, however intermingled, remain distinguishable. Powys conceived rather a complete, monistic identification of all nature, human and external, with the passionate intelligence of a Creator responsible alike for beauty and for pain. Powys' insistence on the truth of matter explains the occasional elements of horror, and even of foulness, in his stories.

His philosophical essays, *An Interpretation of Genesis* and *The Soliloquy of a Hermit,* set forth the ideas that later became visible in his fiction. Powys, after his marriage in 1905, went to reside in the small Dorset community of Sturminster Newton, staying in comparative seclusion there until his death on November 27, 1953.

BIBLIOGRAPHICAL REFERENCES: The best critical article on T. F. Powys is Donald MacCampbell, "The Art of T. F. Powys," *Sewanee Review,* XLII (1934), 460–473. For background studies of the Powys family and related materials see the bibliography of John Cowper Powys.

WILLIAM HICKLING PRESCOTT

Born: Salem, Massachusetts　　　　　　*Died:* Salem
Date: May 4, 1796　　　　　　　　　　*Date:* January 28, 1859

PRINCIPAL WORKS

HISTORY: *History of Ferdinand and Isabella,* 1837; *History of the Conquest of Mexico,* 1843; *History of the Conquest of Peru,* 1847.

When Washington Irving decided to write the history of Columbus and the Spaniards in the New World, he found the field already occupied by William Hickling Prescott, son of an eminent lawyer and a graduate of Harvard University, class of 1814. After considerable travel in Europe, Prescott had abandoned the idea of following in his father's footsteps and decided to become a writer specializing in historical narratives.

Despite an accident of his college days that had blinded him in one eye and left him only limited vision in the other, he devoted himself assiduously to research in preparation for his chosen career. Foreign works were read to him and he wrote on a frame for the blind, producing in 1837, after ten years of toil, his monumental *History of Fer-* dinand and Isabella. At regular intervals thereafter he issued multiple-volume works that described in colorful and dramatic detail, reminiscent of Sir Walter Scott, the Spanish struggle for the dominance of Latin America. He considered his greatest accomplishment to be *History of the Conquest of Mexico.* Its companion work is *History of the Conquest of Peru.* To Prescott, history was primarily the vivid account of heroic figures, such as Cortez and Montezuma; in spite of his scholarly mastery of his sources he was not a writer of philosophic depth or scientific thoroughness. In 1858, while at work on the third volume of his *History of Philip II,* he suffered an apoplectic stroke. He died in Salem on January 28, 1859, the town in which he had been born on May 4, 1796.

BIBLIOGRAPHICAL REFERENCES: The standard edition is the Montezuma Edition of *The Works of William H. Prescott,* edited by Wilfred H. Munro, 22 vols., 1904. Prescott's great-grandson, Roger Wolcott, edited *The Correspondence of William Hickling Prescott, 1833–1847,* 1925—a work supplemented by Clara L. Penny, ed., *Prescott: Unpublished Letters to Gayangos in the Library of the Hispanic Society of America,* 1927. Useful one-volume editions are the *Conquest of Mexico* and the *Conquest of Peru,* issued together in the Modern Library, 1936, and *William Hickling Prescott: Representative Selections,* edited by William Charvat and Michael Kraus, American Writers Series, 1943.

The standard biography is George Ticknor, *Life of William Hickling Prescott,* 1864. The best brief biographical sketch is that by Roger B. Merriman in the *Dictionary of American Biography;* the best critical sketch is the introduction to Charvat and Kraus, *Prescott: Representative Selections,* 1943. See also Rollo Ogden, *William Hickling Prescott,* American Men of Letters Series, 1904; Harry T. Peck, *William Hickling Prescott,* English Men of Letters Series, 1905; and Van Wyck Brooks, *The Flowering of New England,* 1936.

THE ABBÉ PRÉVOST

Born: Hesdin, Artois, Flanders   *Died:* Chantilly, France
Date: April 1, 1697   *Date:* November 23, 1763

PRINCIPAL WORKS

NOVELS: *Mémoires et aventures d'un homme de qualité,* 1728–1731 (*Memoirs and Adventures of a Man of Quality*); *L'Histoire du Chevalier des Grieux et de Manon Lescaut,* 1731 (*The History of the Chevalier des Grieux and Manon Lescaut*); *Le Philosophe anglais, ou Histoire de Monsieur Cleveland, fils naturel de Cromwell,* 1731–1739 (*The English Philosopher, or the History of Mr. Cleveland, Natural Son of Cromwell*); *Le Doyen de Killerine,* 1735–1740 (*The Dean of Coleraine*); *Histoire d'une Grecque moderne,* 1740 (*The History of a Modern Greek Lady*).

MISCELLANEOUS: *Histoire de Marguerite d'Anjou, Reine d'Angleterre,* 1740; *Histoire de Guillaume le Conquérant,* 1742; *Histoire générale des voyages,* 1745–1770; *Lettres de Mentor à un jeune seigneur,* 1764 (*Letters of Mentor to a Young Nobleman*).

Antoine François Prévost, who called himself "Prévost d'Exiles," and who is generally referred to as the Abbé Prévost, was born on April 1, 1697, at the village of Hesdin, in Artois, Flanders. Influenced by his masters at the Jesuit school there, he entered upon a novitiate in Paris in 1713, at the age of sixteen. After two years he proceeded to the Collège de La Flèche, but for reasons now unknown he stayed only one year. Enlisting as a soldier, he completed a term of service, following which he applied, without success, for readmission to his novitiate. It is said that he was tricked by the military into re-enlisting, and that he deserted and escaped to Holland. At length he made his way home. Conjecturally, he soon thereafter met the girl who was to become the heroine of his most famous prose romance, *The History of the Chevalier des Grieux and Manon Lescaut,* but the factual basis of the tale is obscure. Whatever may have occurred, the issue was tragic, and in 1720 Prévost revived his earlier intention of becoming a churchman. He first went to the monastic community of St. Maur

at the Abbey of Jumièges, and, being taken into the priesthood six years later at St. Germer de Flaix, he continued with the Benedictines until 1728. In that year, while at the abbey of St.-Germain-des-Prés, he abandoned the order, very much as he had abandoned the army, and took ship for London.

He remained in England some months, working on *Memoirs and Adventures of a Man of Quality,* of which *Manon Lescaut* was the seventh volume, and on *Cleveland,* another long, episodic romance full of swashbuckling. He spent the years between 1729 and 1733 in Holland, where he wrote a few translations. Various improbable legends became attached to his name in these years. After another sojourn in London, he obtained forgiveness of the Benedictines and was reinstated. Having no great fondness for the conventual life, he secured office outside the monasteries and devoted much time to literature and gallantry. In 1754 he received preferment as Abbé of St. Georges de Gesnes. He died near Chantilly on November 23, 1763.

Prévost was on friendly terms with both Voltaire and Rousseau. He translated John Dryden's *All for Love*, Frances Sheridan's *Memoirs of Miss Sidney Bidulph*, and Samuel Richardson's novels (though doubt has been raised as to his responsibility for the version of *Pamela*) and converted them into shallow narratives of rapid action. His fame rests on his contribution to French romantic prose.

BIBLIOGRAPHICAL REFERENCES: The standard biography is V. Schroeder, *L'Abbé Prévost, sa vie, ses romans*, 1898. See also Henry Harrisse, *L'Abbé Prévost, histoire de sa vie et de ses œuvres*, 1896; and Henri Roddier, *L'Abbé Prévost, l'homme et l'œuvre*, 1955. A more specialized study is Paul Hazard, *Études critiques sur Manon Lescaut*, 1929. See also Berenice Cooper, *The Abbé Prévost and the Modern Reader*, Transactions of the Wisconsin Academy of Sciences, Arts and Letters, XLII, 1953, and *The Abbé Prévost and the Jesuits*, ibid., XLIII, 1954.

J. B. PRIESTLEY

Born: Bradford, Yorkshire, England
Date: 1894

PRINCIPAL WORKS

NOVELS: *Adam in Moonshine*, 1927; *The Good Companions*, 1929; *Farthing Hall*, 1929 (with Hugh Walpole); *Angel Pavement*, 1930; *Faraway*, 1932; *Wonder Hero*, 1933; *The Doomsday Men*, 1938; *Blackout in Gretley*, 1942; *Bright Day*, 1946; *Jenny Villiers*, 1947; *Festival at Farbridge*, 1951 [*Festival*].

PLAYS: *Dangerous Corner*, 1932; *The Roundabout*, 1933; *Eden End*, 1934; *Laburnum Grove*, 1934; *Time and the Conways*, 1937; *Music at Night*, 1938.

ESSAYS AND STUDIES: *George Meredith*, 1926; *Thomas Love Peacock*, 1927; *Apes and Angels*, 1928; *English Humour*, 1929; *English Journey*, 1934; *Midnight on the Desert*, 1937; *Rain Upon Gadshill*, 1939.

J(ohn) B(oynton) Priestley was born in Bradford, England, in 1894. After secondary schooling at Bradford, he enlisted in the army at the beginning of World War I, served with the army in France, and was invalided out as an officer. Convalescing, he entered journalism by writing for the *Yorkshire Observer*. He entered Cambridge in 1919, and established a reputation for himself as essayist and critic before receiving his degree from Cambridge. His literary criticisms and reviews had made Priestley a well-known figure before he started his career as a novelist with *Adam in Moonshine* in 1927.

Priestley's first major success in fiction was *The Good Companions*, which appeared in 1929. It enjoyed a very large success in both Britain and America. During 1929 he collaborated with his friend Hugh Walpole to write a humorous romance, *Farthing Hall*, which was published in the same year. Similar in appeal to *The Good Companions, Angel Pavement*, a long romantic novel, English in tradition, appeared in 1930. Other representative novels include *Wonder Hero; The Doomsday Men*, an adventure; *Blackout in Gretley*, a story of and for wartime; *Bright Day*, another war novel;

Jenny Villiers, a story of the theater; and *Festival at Farbridge,* published in America as *Festival.*

Mr. Priestley has been three times married: to Miss Patricia Tempest, who died in 1925, to Miss Mary Wyndham Lewis, and to Miss Jacquetta Hawkes, with whom he has collaborated on the travel sketches appearing in *Journey Down a Rainbow* (1955).

BIBLIOGRAPHICAL REFERENCES: There is no extended biographical or critical study. See Edward Shanks, "Mr. Priestley's Novels," *London Mercury,* XXVI (1932), 240–247; T. Frederick, "J. B. Priestley," *English Journal,* XXVII (1938), 371–380; and R. W. Whidden, "Priestley and His Novels," *Queen's Quarterly,* XLVIII (1941), 57–62.

FREDERIC PROKOSCH

Born: Madison, Wisconsin
Date: May 17, 1909

PRINCIPAL WORKS

NOVELS: *The Asiatics,* 1935; *The Seven Who Fled,* 1937; *Night of the Poor,* 1939; *The Skies of Europe,* 1941; *The Conspirators,* 1943; *Age of Thunder,* 1945; *The Idols of the Cave,* 1946; *Storm and Echo,* 1948; *Nine Days to Mukalla,* 1953; *A Tale for Midnight,* 1955.

POEMS: *The Assassins,* 1936; *The Carnival,* 1938; *Death at Sea,* 1940; *Chosen Poems,* 1944.

Frederic Prokosch was born at Madison, Wisconsin, May 17, 1909. His father, Edouard P. Prokosch, was a distinguished philologist and Sterling Professor of Linguistics at Yale. His mother, Mathilde Dapprich Prokosch, was a concert pianist. Both parents were Austrian. Since the family traveled considerably, the boy was educated at schools in Wisconsin, Pennsylvania, New York, Texas, Connecticut, England, Austria, France, and Germany. He attended Haverford College and was graduated at the top of his class in 1926. He received his M.A. degree from Haverford in 1928.

Prokosch began his graduate work for the Ph.D. in English Literature at the University of Pennsylvania and was awarded the degree in 1932 after further work at Yale University. His thesis subject, based upon a study of pseudo-Chaucerian manuscripts, was entitled "Chaucerian Apocrypha." From 1931–33 he taught at Yale, and continued there as a research fellow for two more years.

In 1935 Prokosch's first novel, *The Asiatics,* met an encouraging critical reception. His extensive academic background, together with experience in travel and a poetic and philosophic temperament, yielded a rare kind of book for a writer of that period, a book which differed from realistic novels with American settings in concerning itself with Asiatic scenes and philosophic attitudes. This peculiar and effective combination became characteristic of most of his work. His book of poems, *The Assassins,* published the following year, showed that he was a capable writer in more than one dimension.

During the academic year 1936–37 Prokosch taught at New York University and then, as a Guggenheim Fellow, he continued his work at Cambridge University. His best-known book, *The Seven Who Fled*, appeared in 1937 as the winner of the Harper Novel Award. The story of seven European refugees traveling from Central Asia to Shanghai and critically surveying their lives on the way provided the author with ample apportunity to express his pessimistic, anti-materialistic point of view. Once again he followed a prose work with a volume of poetry, *The Carnival*, in 1938. A third volume of poems, *Death at Sea*, appeared two years later, and the following year, 1941, he received the Harriet Monroe Lyric Prize from *Poetry* magazine.

During World War II Prokosch worked abroad for the Office of War Information, spending two years (1943–1944) as an attaché in the American Legation in Stockholm. After the war he went to Rome on a Fulbright Scholarship.

During his college days and afterward Prokosch developed championship skill in tennis and squash; he was squash champion of Connecticut in 1933, and he won the squash rackets championship of France in 1939, the championship of Sweden in 1944.

Although some critics have charged Prokosch with being decadently romantic, arguing that by his preoccupation with Oriental and African settings he has neglected the realities of life in favor of travel fantasies, others have found in his novels and poems a careful craftmanship and a poetic sense which give them literary stature. In addition, his poetry and fiction represent an attempt to portray and probe into the intellectual and spiritual malaise characteristic of this century. His poems particularly reflect a sincere preoccupation with the dark state of the world. Most of his novels follow the experiences of a small group of perplexed Westerners traveling through new countries and thereby acquiring new perspectives and insights. An underlying serious intent saves his novels from the merely exotic class and helps Prokosch to maintain his position as a contemporary writer of vividness and force.

BIBLIOGRAPHICAL REFERENCES: There is no full-length study available. For brief critical studies see Dayton Kohler, "Frederic Prokosch," *English Journal*, XXXII (1943), 413–419; and Richard C. Carpenter, "The Novels of Frederic Prokosch," *College English*, XVIII (1957), 261–267.

MARCEL PROUST

Born: Paris, France
Date: July 10, 1871

Died: Paris
Date: November 18, 1922

Principal Works

NOVELS: *À la recherche du temps perdu*, 1913–1927 (*Remembrance of Things Past*), in seven parts: *Du Côté de chez Swann*, 1913 (*Swann's Way*); *A l'ombre des jeunes filles en fleurs*, 1918 (*Within a Budding Grove*); *Le Côté de Guermantes*, 1921 (*The Guermantes Way*); *Sodome et Gomorrhe*, 1921 (*Cities of the Plain*); *La Prisonnière*,

1923 (*The Captive*); *Albertine disparu,* 1925 (*The Sweet Cheat Gone*); *Le Temps retrouvé,* 1927 (*The Past Recaptured*); *Jean Santeuil,* 1951.

ESSAYS AND STUDIES: *Les Plaisirs et les jours,* 1896 (*Pleasures and Days*); *Pastiches et mélanges,* 1919; *Contre Sainte-Beuve,* 1954 (*Against Sainte-Beuve*).

Marcel Proust was born in Paris on July 10, 1871. His father was a successful physician, wealthy enough to provide abundantly for his family. He married a Jewess who was a devoted mother to her sons, but since the younger Robert was robust and quite normal, she gave special attention to the weaker Marcel. Until the age of nine, Marcel lived a normal if sheltered life. Then a violent attack of asthma increased his dependence on his mother. A very strong attachment between them grew up and colored the rest of Marcel's life.

In spite of his physical weakness Marcel went to school fairly regularly, and in the Lycée Condorcet excelled in philosophy and composition. His schoolmates recognized his ability. The chief contributor to a precocious periodical put out by the most intellectual members of his class, he made enduring friendships among them. At the age of seventeen his formal schooling ended, but even before this time Proust had been visiting the literary salons. He was handsome and witty and became a favorite of the famous. Among the men of letters he met were the younger Dumas, Renan, Halévy, and Anatole France. He wrote short pieces which won him a kind of reputation as a precious dilettante, and his gift for mimicry assured him a place in the most brilliant salons. This phase of his life was interrupted in 1889 when he was called up for military service. He ranked seventy-third in a company of seventy-four. At the end of his year of service he returned

to Paris, quite content to live on a generous allowance from his parents. To please his father, he made some attempt to prepare for a profession, even reading law for a while. Then by means of an examination, he was appointed honorary attaché at the Mazarine library. He served several years, but his work was only nominal; he frequently took long leaves on the plea that he was engaged in urgent writing. His first book, a slender volume of diverse pieces called *Pleasures and Days* appeared in 1896.

Toward the end of the 1890's the Dreyfus affair, with its sinister overtones of anti-Semitism, rocked France. To his credit, Proust took an active role in the agitation to clear Captain Dreyfus, to some extent because he himself was part Jewish. In 1903 his father died, and the family was further disrupted by Robert's marriage. Proust's health became worse; his bouts with asthma were appallingly severe, and he went out only infrequently. By 1905 he had recovered sufficiently to accompany his mother on a trip to Evian, but their holiday was cut short by Mme. Proust's illness. He brought her home to die.

From 1905 until his own death in 1922 Proust lived as an invalid, leaving his bed only at intervals, morbidly conscious of his wasted youth, unable to surmount the melancholy of the loss of his mother. True, he had written one book, translated several of Ruskin's works into French, contributed to periodicals, and worked secretly on a novel, but he felt himself capable of more serious work. And indeed he was. Between 1906 and 1913 he finished the plan of what has been called the greatest novel of the century, *Remembrance of Things Past,* and completed the first part, *Swann's Way,* published in 1913; the succeeding six parts (three published posthumously) were written between debilitating asthmatic spells and bronchial attacks.

In view of Proust's personality and health, his achievement is remarkable. Most of his productive years after 1905 were spent propped up in bed, the air thick with vapors to ease his breathing, the windows closed and shuttered. He always had his linen warmed before putting it on, and he habitually wore numerous woolen waistcoats. He left the house only after sundown on the occasions when he was well enough to get up, muffled in a heavy overcoat even in summer, and carrying an umbrella. From time to time he invited in a few friends who dined sumptuously around his bed on chicken and beer. On rarer occasions he dined alone late at night at the Ritz, swathed in fur coat and scarf, his hands covered with dirty white gloves, surrounded by obsequious waiters whom he tipped extravagantly.

Although he retained the friendship of many women, and although he several times made attempts at love affairs, he felt himself incapable of love for women; the theme of homosexuality clouded his life and found expression in parts of his novel. Balancing this inversion is the fact that all sorts of people were attracted to him, and he was lavishly generous to anyone in distress.

The publication of *Swann's Way* was little noticed; in fact, Proust had to bring it out at his own expense. Even so perceptive a critic as Gide could see little merit in it. The second volume, delayed by the war, was almost equally unnoticed for a time by the public, but a number of critics saw the great merit of the work. Léon Daudet especially was convinced of its greatness, and thanks largely to his efforts, Proust was awarded the Prix Goncourt at the age of forty-seven.

At last Proust was famous. He enjoyed briefly the letters that poured in and the homage of friends and admirers, but he kept on working. Proofs were revised and rewritten until the margins were covered and the edges tattered. Before his death in Paris on November 18, 1922, he completed the vast work, a monument to his genius.

Remembrance of Things Past is a search for lost days, an evocation of mood and emotion. It is also a resigned acknowledgement that time is a destroyer, that the past is dead. In form the novel is an innovation—it is built on recurring themes of people, loves, ambitions, frustrations. It is in large part autobiographical, and Proust's circle furnished models for many of the characters. In spite of unconventional sentences and long sections without paragraph breaks, Proust was a meticulous craftsman, detailed and realistic in his descriptions. In addition to its intensely personal dissection, the work is a canvas of social history.

As artist and innovator, Proust is unique. As a person he was weak, abnormal, handicapped. In comparison his novel becomes a more astonishing feat. Since it continues increasingly to attract critical attention, its place in world literature seems assured.

Shortly after World War II Bernard de Fallois, French scholar, discovered among Proust's notebooks and un-classified manuscripts two previously unknown early works, the apprentice and unfinished novel, *Jean Santeuil*, and an important critical study, *Contre Sainte-Beuve*. These works throw considerable new light on Proust's literary activities and his development as a writer.

Russell Cosper

BIBLIOGRAPHICAL REFERENCES: The Proust bibliography is one of the most extensive in modern letters. A useful general study in André Maurois, *À la recherche de Marcel Proust*, 1949 (English translation, *Proust: Portrait of a Genius*). For biographical and critical studies in French see Robert de Billy, *Marcel Proust: Lettres et conversations*, 1930; Ramon Fernandez, *Proust*, 1930; Jacques Bret, *Marcel Proust: Étude critique*, 1946; Edmond Kinds, *Marcel Proust*, 1947; François Mauriac, *Du côté de chez Proust*, 1947 (*Proust's Way*); in English, Clive Bell, *Proust*, 1929; Derrick Leon, *Introduction to Marcel Proust*, 1940; Harold March, *The Two Worlds of Marcel Proust*, 1948; F. C. Green, *The Mind of Proust*, 1949; and Walter A. Strauss, *Proust and Literature: The Novelist as Critic*, 1957.

See also Joseph Wood Krutch, *Five Masters*, 1931; Edmund Wilson, *Axel's Castle*, 1931; Wallace Fowlie, *Clowns and Angels*, 1943; Martin Turnell, *The Novel in France*, 1950; Janko Lavrin, "Dostoievsky and Proust," *Slavonic Review*, V (1927), 609–627; and A. J. Roche, "Proust as a Translator of Ruskin," *Publications of the Modern Language Association*, XLV (1930), 1214–1218.

P'U SUNG-LING

Born: Tzu-ch'uan, Shantung, China
Date: June 5, 1640

Died: Shantung, China
Date: February 5, 1715

PRINCIPAL WORKS

NOVELS AND TALES: *Liao-chai chih-i*, 1766 (*Strange Stories from a Chinese Studio*); *Hsing-shih yin-yuan chuan*, 1870 (*Marriage as Retribution*); *Liao-chai Ch'üan-chi*, 1936 (*Collected Works*, excluding the two above).

P'u Sung-ling's ancestors were probably of Turkic origin and came to China with the Mongol armies around the middle of the thirteenth century. Two of them were governors of Shantung in the last two or three decades of the Yuan dynasty (1279–1368), but nothing was heard of the family again until 1592, when a granduncle of the author became a *chin-shih* and later served a term as magistrate. P'an, the author's father, also studied for the examinations, but after failing several times to pass the first hurdle, he turned to trade. He was apparently the most distinguished member of the clan in his day, for it was recorded that in 1647 he led a successful defense of his village against a band of marauders who had sacked several neighboring cities.

P'u Sung-ling was the third of four sons. He passed his *hsiu-ts'ai* examinations with highest honors in 1658. In 1685 he became a salaried licentiate, and in 1710 a senior licentiate; but the *chü-jen* degree, the next in order, eluded him, though he attended the examinations regularly until he was past sixty. As a result he was thwarted in his ambition, shared by all litero-crats of traditional China, of entering government service, and he was forced to content himself with serving as secretary to more fortunate friends (from 1670 to around 1692) and in teaching in the family schools of the local gentry (until 1710).

The major portion of *Strange Stories from a Chinese Studio* must have been completed by 1679, the date of the preface, but internal evidence suggests many subsequent additions, one as late as 1707. The book was circulated in manuscript during the author's lifetime and was much esteemed by some of his more prominent contemporaries. Upon its publication in 1766, it was an immediate success and became *the* collection of strange tales for literate readers. For the traditional literocrat, his stories are masterpieces of the polished, allusive, classical style; for the modern reader, they represent a radical advance over all previous examples of the same genre because of the richness of invention displayed by the author and the touch of humanity which he gives to all his ghosts, fox fairies, and flower spirits, and which make them seem real, if not probable.

Until 1932, the *Chih-i* was about the only work by which P'u Sung-ling was known. But in that year Hu Shih published his study of the *Hsing-shih Yin-yuan chuan* (*Marriage as Retribution*) and proved conclusively that this epic novel of a hen-pecked husband, which had appeared anonymously in 1870, was also written by P'u. Because of the interest aroused by this discovery and the recognition of this hitherto neglected novel as one of the two or three greatest works of Chinese fiction (the other two being the *Chin P'ing Mei* and the *Hung Lou Meng*), the unpublished works of the author were sought out and published in 1936 under the title of *Liao-chai Ch'üan-chi* (*Collected Works*). The two books of prose and three of verse in the literocratic tradition included in the collection occasioned no surprise, but the rest of the material would have seemed incredible if Hu Shih's study had not prepared us for it, for this comprises seven short satires and eleven longish romances in the *ku-tz'u* or *t'an-tzu* forms (somewhat like the *chante-fable* of medieval French) of the popular tradition. Some of these last, elaborations of stories of wicked mothers-in-law, jealous wives, and hen-pecked husbands, had appeared in briefer forms in the *Chih-i*. In thus dealing with the same set of themes in three different mediums—first in the short tale form, then as romances in prose and verse, and finally in a long epic novel—P'u Sung-ling is unique in the history of Chinese literature.

BIBLIOGRAPHICAL REFERENCES: The best and most comprehensive biographical study of P'u Sung-ling in English is the article by Fang Chao-ying in *Eminent Chinese of the Ch'ing Period*, edited by A. W. Hummel, 1944. Full-length biographies are unknown to traditional Chinese literature; the official biographies as found in histories, in family archives, or on tomb inscriptions are always sketchy and unrevealing. The most detailed biographical information is cast in the form of a chronological record (*nien-p'u*), in which the known facts of the subject's life, in so far as it is possible to determine through his own and other people's writings, are set down in the words of the sources, generally without comment. There is such a record of P'u Sung-ling appended to the *Liao-chai ch'üan-chi*; it was compiled by Lu Ta-huang, editor of the collected works.

ALEXANDER PUSHKIN

Born: Moscow, Russia
Date: June 6, 1799

Died: St. Petersburg, Russia
Date: February 10, 1837

PRINCIPAL WORKS

POEMS: *Ruslan and Ludmila,* 1821; *Kavkarski plennik,* 1820–1821 (*The Prisoner of the Caucasus*); *Eugeny Onegin,* 1823–1831 (*Eugene Onegin*); *Graf Nulin,* 1825 (*Count Nulin*); *Poltava,* 1828; *Medny vsadnik,* 1832 (*The Bronze Horseman*).

NOVELS: *Arap Petra Velikogo,* 1828 (*The Negro of Peter the Great*; unfinished); *Dubrovsky,* 1832–1833; *Kapitanskaya dochka,* 1836 (*The Captain's Daughter*).

SHORT STORIES: *Pikovaya dama,* 1834 (*The Queen of Spades*); *Povesti Belkina,* 1834 (*The Tales of Belkin*).

PLAYS: *Boris Godunov,* 1826; *Rusalka,* 1836.

FOLK TALES: *Skazki,* 1831–1834 (*Fairy Tales*).

Alexander (Sergeyevich) Pushkin, Russia's first important and still greatest poet, was descended on his father's side from a family of impoverished nobility and on his mother's from an Abyssinian officer in the service of Peter the Great. Pushkin was proud of both heritages, and the distinctive character of his verse, a combination of classical form and romantic feeling, may have been influenced by them.

Born in Moscow on June 6, 1799, he studied at home and at the Lyceum (1811–1817), where he absorbed Latin and eighteenth century French literature and began publishing verses: spirited anacreontics, political epigrams, and in 1820 a long narrative poem, *Ruslan and Ludmila.* This work, like much of his later work, was based on folk material. At the age of twenty he was already acknowledged the new leader of Russian poetry. To the tsarist government he was also (and continued to be throughout his life) politically suspect. He was as precocious in love as he was in verse and in St. Petersburg (1818–1820) threw himself with his characteristic love of life into a round of sensual adventures.

In 1820, as the result of his patriotic "Ode to Liberty," he was sent to the Caucasus as a nominal state official but in reality an exile. There, during the next four years, he wrote his first mature poems, *The Prisoner of the Caucasus, The Fountain of Bakhchisaray* (1822), *The Robber Brothers* (1822), and *The Gypsies* (1823–1824), all showing in their exotic settings and romantic characterizations the influence of Byron. He also began in 1823 his masterpiece, *Eugene Onegin,* a novel in verse modeled on Byron's *Don Juan* and not completed until 1831. But Pushkin's poem resembles Byron's only superficially (and less as the work proceeds) in its buoyant tone and theme of love. It has greater unity of form, mellower wisdom, and more profound characterization; the story of Eugene, the callow amorist, simply rejected by the romantic, noble Tatyana who continues to love him even after she is married to another, merits the claim of having launched the great Russian novel.

Dismissed from the service in 1824, for the next two years Pushkin was confined by the government to his mother's estate near Pskov. Here, seeking a less subjective theme, he wrote his play, *Boris Godunov,* an imitation of Shakespearean tragedy rather stilted in tone and lacking in cumulative effect. Although Pushkin's theme is individual rather than political freedom, the play was censored as anti-monarchial. Its reputation today rests chiefly on the Moussorgsky opera based on Pushkin's text.

After 1826 Pushkin was kept under closer government surveillance in Moscow and St. Petersburg. Several notable short verse plays dealing with kinds of evil (*The Covetous Knight, Mozart and Salieri, The Stone Guest*) were written in 1830 just before his marriage to Natalia Goncharova, a beautiful empty-headed girl much younger than he, who, if we can trust one of his letters to a friend, was his one hundred thirteenth conquest. After this date he wrote mostly history, criticism, and fiction. His most important stories, written in terse, bare narrative style, are *The Queen of Spades,* a tale of supernatural evil, and *The Captain's Daughter,* a romantic novel of love and heroism played out against a back-ground of provincial life and the Pugachev Rebellion of 1773.

Forced into a dull round of court affairs by his wife and subject to continuous government censorship and restraint in spite of his patriotic poems, *Poltava* and *The Bronze Horseman,* Pushkin found married life onerous. Involved in domestic intrigue and scandal, he challenged a guardsman named d'Anthès and was fatally wounded in a duel fought to defend his wife's honor. He died two days later on February 10, 1837, at St. Petersburg.

Pushkin's reputation, at its height in the 1820's, fell during the last years of his life but revived rapidly after 1880, when Dostoevski delivered the famous commemorative address in which he stressed Pushkin's role in the formation of a Russian national consciousness. It is still too low in the West because of the special difficulties in translating his work, particularly his large body of lyric poetry beloved by Russian-speaking peoples.

BIBLIOGRAPHICAL REFERENCES: Pushkin's most important works are available in translation. For biographical and critical studies in English see D. S. Mirsky, *Pushkin,* 1926; E. J. Simmons, *Pushkin,* 1937; and Janko Lavrin, *Pushkin and Russian Literature,* 1947, and *Russian Writers,* 1954; in French, Henri Troyat, *À Pouchkine; biographie,* 2 vols., 1953. For bibliography see also Avrahm Yarmolinsky, *Pushkin in English,* 1937.

FRANÇOIS RABELAIS

Born: Chinon, France
Date: c. 1495

Died: Paris (?), France
Date: 1553

PRINCIPAL WORK

SATIRE: *Gargantua and Pantagruel,* 1532-1564.

Concrete facts about the life of François Rabelais are few and far between. The dates and places of his birth and death are at best only guess-work—the best guesses being 1495 at Chinon, France, for his birth and 1553 at Paris for his death—and the gaps in his career are many. As is so often true of men with colorful personalities but uncertain biographies, his life is obscured by a mist of legend and anecdote. There is, for instance, the story that Rabelais, finding himself without money in Lyons, obtained free transportation to Paris by pretending that he was involved in a plot to poison the king. Probably equally apocryphal are the well-known words attributed to him on his deathbed: "Down with the curtain; the farce is done! I am going to seek a great perhaps." Our understanding of Rabelais the man is further confused by his relationship to the bitter religious and political controversies that raged in Europe during his lifetime. As an exponent of rationality and common sense, and enemy of narrow-minded dogmatism of any sort, it was almost inevitable that Rabelais should become the victim of bigotry and cant, and that he and his writing should be denounced by extremists on both sides of moderation. He was characterized by Calvin as a debauched libertine, and by the Catholics as an infamous drunkard; and both epithets, whether justified or not, have stuck.

About all we know for certain about Rabelais is that he was, at various times, a monk, a doctor of medicine, an editor, and, for all time, a writer. The first specific record that we have of him is his signature on the certificate of a purchase made by the Franciscan monastery at Fontenay-le-Comte in 1519, evidence that suggests, because of his apparent importance in the abbey, that he had taken orders several years earlier. We next hear of Rabelais corresponding with Guillaume Budé, secretary to King François I and one of the foremost scholars in Europe. At the same time he was familiar with the group of scholars gathered around André Tiraqueau, one of the most learned judges in France. Moved, it would seem, by a growing interest in intellectual matters, Rabelais received permission from the Pope in 1524 to transfer from the Franciscans at Fontenay to a Benedictine monastery at Maillezais, a change which gave him the advantage of both the protection of his friend, Geoffroi d'Estissac, Bishop of Maillezais, and the relative sophistication and scholarship of the Benedictines. By 1530 he had left the order and taken on secular garb, and in November of that year he was graduated as bachelor of medicine from the University of Montpellier.

In 1532 Rabelais was in Lyons, the intellectual center of France, where he edited and published some medical and scholarly works, was physician at the Hôtel-Dieu, and produced his first original work in *Pantagruel,* or Book II of what was later to become *Gargantua and Pantagruel.* The following year his work was censured by the Faculty of Theology of the University of Paris. In 1534 Rabelais went to Rome in the train of his friend and patron, Cardinal Jean du Bellay, apparently in hopes of regularizing his somewhat anomalous relationship with the Church. His wishes were realized, and in reply to his petition excusing his leaving the order, a papal bull was issued permitting him to rejoin the Benedictines, to assume ecclesiastical office, and to practice medicine. Rabelais, who in the meantime had published *Gargantua,* or Book I of his masterpiece, took advantage of this dispensation almost immediately, becoming canon of St. Maur the next year and, in 1537, taking the degrees of licentiate and doctor of medicine at Montpellier. In 1540 he seems to have been in Italy, and by 1546 he was in Metz, while the recently published *Tiers Livre,* Book III of *Gargantua and Pantagruel,* was being condemned by the Sorbonne. Two years later part of Book IV was published in Lyons—for which a rare copyright was granted by Henry II—and in 1552 the completed Book IV appeared in Paris, to be immediately proscribed by Parliament. In 1553 Rabelais resigned two curacies which he had received several years before from the du Bellay family, and some time before the end of the year he was dead. Nine years later, in 1562, sixteen chapters of what is now Book V appeared under the title, *Ringing Island by Master François Rabelais,* and in 1564 the complete Book V was published in Paris. Its authenticity has often been questioned, and it is probable that some parts of it were edited from unfinished notes left by the author. In 1567 all five books were published together for the first time.

Apart from such inferences as can be gleaned from these meager biographical data, all our knowledge of the philosophy or personality of the man called Rabelais is based on his one extant work and masterpiece, *Gargantua and Pantagruel.* This rollicking and uninhibited tale of the birth, education, and adventures of the "huge giant Gargantua" (Book I) and of his son Pantagruel (Books II–V) leaves the reader with the impression that its author was a man of keen satiric wit, of comprehensive, if not profound, learning, but above all, of a tremendous and all-inclusive enthusiasm for life. Rabelais ends his prefatory address "To My Reader" with the admonition, "Live Happy," and this *joie de vivre* colors every word he wrote. Himself a monk, he was the inveterate enemy of scholasticism, pedantry, superstition, the unnatural rigors of monasticism, and all that was narrow or crabbed or fanatic. An admirer of what was best and noblest in Renaissance humanism, Rabelais had a profound respect for enlightened education and learning (he would make Pantagruel "an abyss of knowledge"). At the same time, reason, for Rabelais, is very close to instinct, and to "follow nature" (where nature is civilized and well-bred) is the true road to the happy life. The one rule of the saturnalian Abbey of Thélème (Book I) is, "Do as thou wilt"; nature is good, and everything that limits and restricts the freedom to "be yourself" is rotten. But Rabelais was not simply a pagan hedonist; instinct for him seems to include faith in God and a future life. "Laughter is the essence of mankind," and joy is the highest form of worship. Consistent with these principles, Rabelais has added immeasurably to the joy of mankind.

BIBLIOGRAPHICAL REFERENCES: The basic and best-known translation in English is *The Works of the Famous Mr. Francis Rabelais,* translated by Sir Thomas Urquhart and Peter Le Motteux, 1653–1694. Recent translations include those by Samuel P. Putnam, 1929; and Jacques Le Clercq, 1936. An abridgement of the Putnam translation was published as *The Portable Rabelais* in 1946. Among the recent biographical and critical studies in English are A. F. Chappell, *The Enigma of Rabelais,* 1924; Samuel P. Putnam, *Rabelais, Man of the Renaissance,* 1929; John Cowper Powys, *Rabelais: His Life,* 1948; and D. B. Wyndham Lewis, *Doctor Rabelais,* 1957; in French, J. Plallard, *La Vie et l'œuvre de Rabelais,* 1939; and J. Charpentier, *Rabelais et la génie de la Renaissance,* 1941.

JEAN BAPTISTE RACINE

Born: La Ferté-Milon, France
Date: December, 1639

Died: Paris, France
Date: April 26, 1699

PRINCIPAL WORKS

PLAYS: *Andromache,* 1667; *Les Plaideurs,* 1668; *Britannicus,* 1669; *Bérénice,* 1670; *Bajazet,* 1672; *Mithridate,* 1673; *Iphigénie,* 1674; *Phèdre,* 1677; *Esther,* 1689; *Athalie,* 1691.

Jean Baptiste Racine is remembered, along with Pierre Corneille, as a leader of the classical revival in the drama of seventeenth century France. His father was a solicitor and local official in the town of La Ferté-Milon, but both parents died soon after Jean's birth in December, 1639, and the boy was brought up by his Jansenist grandparents. He attended school, first at Beauvais, and later at the famous Jansenist monastery of Port-Royal, where he wrote quite passable odes in both Latin and French while still in his teens. By the time he had left the Collège d'Harcourt he had composed an ode in honor of the marriage of Louis XIV which had earned him 600 livres from the monarch, written two unsuccessful dramas, formed a friendship with La Fontaine and liaisons with several of the leading actresses of the day. A few years later he also became a friend of the famous critic and arbiter of French taste, Boileau, who remained his mentor and friendly censor for much of his life.

The years between 1664 and 1673 were marked by the highly favorable reception of two plays, *La Thébaïde* (1664) and *Alexandre Le Grand* (1665), the second of which raised Racine to the rank of Corneille in public opinion, and by an extremely unpleasant exchange of pamphlets with the Jansenists at Port-Royal, who hated the theater and his involvement

in it. It was in *Andromache* that Racine displayed the heights of his particular genius, the ability to combine the strict requirements of the highly formalized Senecan drama which dominated the French stage with a revived interest in human motivation and characterization. Like his other great tragedy, *Phèdre, Andromache* not only employs a classical Greek theme, but also follows the classical rules and unities of Aristotle as they had come to be interpreted on the seventeenth century French stage by the master of the classical renaissance, Corneille. At the same time Racine devotes all his skill to the creation of warm, human characters, and in such figures as Hermione and Phèdre draws a highly sympathetic (some say sentimentalized) picture of the victims of grand and fatal passions. Like Corneille, he regards human passion as a destructive force but, unlike his rival, he feels a genuine sympathy for its victims. This outlook, combined with almost uniformly brilliant versification, has made Racine almost as popular in our century as he was in his own.

Andromache was followed in fairly close succession by a long series of successful plays on classical, biblical, or Oriental themes: *Les Plaideurs* (his charming and only comedy), *Britannicus, Bérénice, Bajazet, Mithridate,* and *Iphigénie.* In 1677 the series was climaxed by *Phèdre,* the story of the Grecian woman whose uncontrollable love for her stepson brings on a series of disasters and her own destruction. Perhaps the greatest of Racine's tragedies, it was also, however, the unluckiest. Influential enemies had commissioned another *Phèdre* to be written for presentation at the same time as his, and Racine's play was nearly driven from the stage in consequence. After this blow the playwright retired almost completely from dramatic writing, abandoned his lifelong libertine habits in favor of a reconciliation with the puritans of Port-Royal, married, and settled down to a comfortable life as a courtier and royal historiographer. He also raised seven children, two sons and five daughters.

Racine wrote only two more plays during the remaining twenty years of his life, both composed especially for the young girls who attended the school at St. Cyr established by Louis XIV's last mistress, Madame de Maintenon, for the education of poor girls from noble families. *Esther* and *Athalie,* while lacking the intense passions of the earlier tragedies, possess a delicacy and perfection of construction, characterization, and versification all their own. The choruses, set to the music of Moreau, the court composer, are particularly lovely.

Except for a short history of Port-Royal and several minor pieces, Racine was silent after 1691. His declining years were marked by a loss of friends and of literary and royal favor. He died in Paris on April 26, 1699. He was buried at Port-Royal.

BIBLIOGRAPHICAL REFERENCES: The standard edition of Racine is that edited by Paul Mesnard in the *Collection des grands écrivains de la France,* 1865–1874. There is also an English edition, *The Dramatic Works of Jean Racine,* translated by R. B. Boswell, 1889–1890. For recent studies of the playwright see Alexander F. B. Clark, *Jean Racine,* 1939; Jean Giraudoux, *Racine,* 1950; and Geoffrey Brereton, *Jean Racine: A Critical Biography,* 1951.

MRS. ANN RADCLIFFE

Born: London, England
Date: July 9, 1764

Died: London
Date: February 7, 1823

PRINCIPAL WORKS

NOVELS: *A Sicilian Romance,* 1790; *The Romance of the Forest,* 1791; *The Mysteries of Udolpho,* 1794; *The Italian, or, The Confessional of the Black Penitents,* 1797; *Gaston de Blondeville,* 1826.

Mrs. Ann (Ward) Radcliffe, although little known today, was considered the greatest romanticist of her age, both for her imaginative plotting and for her poetic prose. Her novels have become a minor landmark in English literary history because their author formulated a Gothic school of writing that owed more to her invention than to the influence of her contemporaries in the same genre, and her tales of terror are unblurred by the awkward supernaturalism of Walpole, the sentimentality of Clara Reeves, or the turgid horrors of Matthew Gregory Lewis.

Born in London on July 9, 1764,

879

Ann Ward included among her ancestors the celebrated classical scholar, Dr. S. Jebb. Stimulated by her wide reading, she delighted as a child in daydreams of things supernatural; however, a shy, asthmatic girl isolated in a society of her elders, she was not encouraged to exercise her abilities or to express herself. At twenty-three, pretty and demure, she married William Radcliffe, the future editor of the *English Chronicle*. Living in London, intimate with literary people, and childless, she began to write. Her first book, *The Castles of Athlin and Dunbayne* (1789), went almost unnoticed, but her second, *A Sicilian Romance*, established her reputation as a master of suspense and description. With *The Romance of the Forest*, published in 1791, she attracted the attention of a wide reading public. For her fourth novel, *The Mysteries of Udolpho*, she received £500 before it was published.

This novel typifies the two strongest elements in Mrs. Radcliffe's fiction: the suggestion of imminent evil and the atmosphere of refinement and beauty. Juxtaposed, each element intensifies the other. Mrs. Radcliffe carries the reader into a beautiful Eden, and by contrasting excellent description with vague references to impending doom an effect of mystery and terror results. That some terrible mystery suggested by a low groan from a distant tomb or an uncertain light on a castle stairs turns out to be wind or moonlight does not alter the effect of the story. Mrs. Radcliffe discriminated carefully between terror and horror, and her ability to evoke the former while avoiding the latter points to her skillful handling of atmosphere and dramatic situation.

Mrs. Radcliffe's novels are built on the same plot: a chaste, helpless young woman achieves a good marriage after a series of attempts on her life by sinister villains in an exotic setting. Although the plots are improbable and the characters are two-dimensional to the modern reader, the novels had great influence on other writers of the time, notably Scott and Byron; early in Scott's career he was hailed as Mrs. Radcliffe's successor, and certainly Schedoni, the villain of *The Italian*, is the forerunner of the Byronic hero.

Although she was in literature a mistress of the strange and picturesque, her own biography is commonplace because of the regularity of her life, and modern scholarship now discounts the contemporary belief that madness, induced by the terrors she created, accounts for the long interval of time between the publication of *The Italian* and her posthumous *Gaston de Blondeville*. A figure deserving more attention in literary history than she has received, Mrs. Radcliffe died in London on February 7, 1823.

BIBLIOGRAPHICAL REFERENCES: There is no collected edition and most of Mrs. Radcliffe's novels are out of print. A modern edition of *The Italian* was issued as *The Confessional of the Black Penitents* by the Folio Society of London in 1956. For biography and criticism see Clara F. McIntyre, *Ann Radcliffe in Relation to Her Time, Yale Studies in English*, LXII, 1920; and A. A. S. Wieten, *Mrs. Radcliffe: Her Relation to Romanticism*, 1926. For more general studies of the Gothic Revival and its writers see also Dorothy Scarborough, *The Supernatural in Modern English Fiction*, 1917; Edith Birkhead, *The Tale of Terror*, 1921; Eino Railo, *The Haunted Castle*, 1927; the Rev. Montague Summers, *The Gothic Quest*, 1938, and *A Gothic Bibliography*, 1941.

CHARLES-FERDINAND RAMUZ

Born: Cully, Switzerland
Date: November 24, 1878

Died: Cully
Date: May 23, 1947

PRINCIPAL WORKS

NOVELS: Le Règne de l'esprit malin, 1917 (The Reign of the Evil One); Présence de la mort, 1922 (The End of All Men); La Grande Peur dans la montagne, 1926; (Great Fear in the Mountain); La Beauté sur la terre, 1927 (Beauty on Earth); Derborence, 1935 (When the Mountain Fell).

Charles-Ferdinand Ramuz was born on November 24, 1878, in Cully, a small town on Lake Geneva in the canton of Vaud. He studied at the University of Lausanne and in 1902 moved to Paris where he intended to develop his capacities as a writer and to achieve independence of style and originality in content. During the next twelve years he wrote diligently, producing several novels and numerous poems and short stories. Becoming increasingly dissatisfied with life in Paris and with his work, he began to believe that isolation in France neither liberated him nor provided him with the kind of material he was best equipped to handle. Consequently, he resolved to return to his birthplace and to write in the midst of the life he remembered and valued. In 1914 he settled down once more in Cully and began a flow of work about the Swiss people he understood so well, writing of fishermen and simple farmers, of craftsmen and peasants.

His decision was soon shown to be wise. A series of novels concerned with Swiss life came from Cully, bringing success and recognition to their author. Writing in a sympathetic way about the people he knew, he won a wide audience; and although there were critics who claimed that he was allowing his metaphysical and mystical interests to cloud his clear vision of the people of Switzerland, there was enough of the beauty and virtue of the land in his books to make them widely acceptable. Ramuz explained in a critical discussion of his work that he intended to communicate the basic emotions of actual life not by philosophic analysis and not by contrived situations, but by selecting those features of actual life which would best exemplify the very qualities he was concerned to share.

He was considered for the Nobel Prize in 1945, a tribute to the enduring quality of his work and to his productivity. Two years later, on May 23, 1947, he died at Cully as the result of an operation.

BIBLIOGRAPHICAL REFERENCES: There is no helpful criticism of Ramuz in English. See Emmanuel Buenzod, C.-F. Ramuz, 1928; P. Kohler, L'Art de C.-F. Ramuz, 1929; C. Guyot, Comment lire C.-F. Ramuz, 1946; André Tissot, C.-F. Ramuz, ou, Le drame de la poésie, 1947, and L'Expérience poétique de C.-F. Ramuz, 1947; Bernard Voyenne, C.-F. Ramuz et la sainteté de la terre, 1948; Lucien Girardet, Notre Ramuz, 1952; and Hélène Cingria, Ramuz, notre parrain, 1956.

JOHN CROWE RANSOM

Born: Pulaski, Tennessee
Date: April 30, 1888

PRINCIPAL WORKS

POEMS: *Poems About God*, 1919; *Chills and Fever*, 1924; *Grace After Meat*, 1924; *Two Gentlemen in Bonds*, 1927; *Selected Poems*, 1945.

CRITICISM: *The World's Body*, 1938; *The New Criticism*, 1941.

ESSAYS AND STUDIES: *I'll Take My Stand: The South and the Agrarian Tradition*, by Twelve Southerners, 1930; *God Without Thunder: An Unorthodox Defense of Orthodoxy*, 1930.

John Crowe Ransom, besides being a fine, though hardly prolific poet in his own right, is perhaps the most influential critic in America of the past quarter century. His influence has stemmed from three sources: the examples he has set in his own poetry; the pronouncements he has made as the leader of two related but distinct literary movements, Southern Agrarianism and the New Criticism; and the power of selection he has exerted in the past twenty years as the editor of the *Kenyon Review*. His influence has been strongly felt, not in literary circles alone, but in the academic world as well (though it must be admitted that today, as far as poetry is concerned, it is difficult to distinguish between the two sectors, so greatly do they overlap). A college teacher himself since 1914 and a professor, first at Vanderbilt and then at Kenyon, since 1924, Ransom's application of the principles of the New Criticism to the teaching of literature has challenged the older historical approach and has been adopted, in part at least, by many of his adherents throughout the country.

Ransom was born in Pulaski, Tennessee, on April 30, 1888, and he began his academic training at Vanderbilt, the original seat of the Southern Agrarians. He was graduated from Vanderbilt in 1909, and then, after studying for four years as a Rhodes Scholar at Oxford, he returned to Vanderbilt as an instructor in English in 1914. There he remained, except for two years spent as a Field Artillery Officer in France during World War I, until he moved to Kenyon in 1937.

His literary activity, which can be divided into two distinct parts (the poetic corresponding to the period at Vanderbilt, the critical to the one at Kenyon), began in 1919 with the publication of *Poems about God*. In 1922 he became one of the founders of the Agrarian magazine, *The Fugitive*, which he edited until its demise in 1925. The previous year had marked the publication of *Chills and Fever*, his second, and, aside from his *Selected Poems*, best volume of verse. In it he realized most fully his own critical conditions for a modern poetry of metaphysical wit, of clarity and restraint, and of a "perfect anonymity"; and at least two of the pieces—the title poem and "Bells for John Whiteside's Daughter"—can readily be cited among the best that have been written in the century. In 1925 he was also one of the "Twelve Southerners" who contributed to the Agrarian manifesto, *I'll Take My Stand*.

Two other slim volumes of verse appeared before his departure from Vanderbilt, but the publication of *Chills and Fever* was the high point of his work as a poet, though the appearance of his *Selected Poems* in 1945 re-established his reputation, and his receiving of the Bollingen Prize in Poetry and the Russell Loines Memorial Award from the American Institute of Arts and Letters in 1951 has kept it deservedly alive.

BIBLIOGRAPHICAL REFERENCES: There is no extended biographical or critical study of John Crowe Ransom. The most comprehensive survey is *Homage to John Ransom: Essays on His Work as Poet and Critic,* a symposium by various of his contemporaries, *Sewanee Review,* LVI (1948), 367–476. See also Vivienne Koch, "The Poetry of John Crowe Ransom," in *Modern American Poetry,* edited by B. Rajan, 1952; Isabel Gamble, "Ceremonies of Bravery: John Crowe Ransom," in *Southern Renascence: The Literature of the Modern South,* edited by Louis D. Rubin, Jr., and Robert D. Jacobs, 1953; and John M. Bradbury, "Ransom as Poet," *Accent,* XI (1951), 45–57.

RUDOLPH ERICH RASPE

Born: Hanover, Germany
Date: 1737

Died: Muckross, Donegal, Ireland
Date: 1794

PRINCIPAL WORK

MOCK-HEROIC CHRONICLE: *Baron Münchausen's Narrative of His Marvellous Travels and Campaigns in Russia,* 1786.

While most people have heard of the mendacious Baron Münchausen, whose *Narrative* competes in foreign translation with classics like *Robinson Crusoe, Gulliver's Travels,* and *Pilgrim's Progress,* the author of the book is practically a forgotten man. Perhaps this is just as well, since Rudolph Erich Raspe, born at Hanover, Germany, in 1737, had little admirable about him except a misused ability to absorb. Little is known about his lower-class family, though they provided him with funds for his study at the universities of Göttingen and Leipzig between 1756 and 1760. After graduation, he spent a year tutoring the son of a noble. Later he became a librarian, first at Hanover, then at Göttingen. Here he translated from the French a philosophic work by Leibniz, pub-lished by the university in 1765, wrote verses in Latin, studied Percy's *Reliques of Ancient English Poetry,* and composed a long allegorical poem on a medieval theme. With Jakob Mauvillon (1743–1794), he founded *The Cassel Spectator,* for which he wrote articles about his many interests and hobbies.

For his study of mammoths during the Ice Age, the Royal Society of England made him an Honorary Fellow, and after the appearance of a volume on ancient gems and medals, the landgrave sent him to Italy to collect specimens. When he was detected stealing and selling the best of them, he was arrested but escaped and fled to England. The warrant for his arrest provides a description of him, as "a long-faced man with small eyes, crooked nose, red hair under his stumpy periwig, and a jerky gait."

In England Horace Walpole and other admirers helped pay his debts until details of his rascality arrived from the Continent; he was then expelled from the Royal Society. Because of his smattering of geology, he became an assayist with a mining company at Dolcoath, in Cornwall. Here he did the only writing that has survived him. In Germany he had known an eccentric old soldier, Hieronymus von Münchausen (1720–1797), who amused his guests and burlesqued his exaggerating gamekeeper by telling highly imaginative yarns as solemn truth. Sure that a book published in England would never reach the eyes of the original Münchausen, Raspe set down some of the yarns he remembered, invented others, and issued the book locally. A great success, the work was republished at Oxford in 1786. Neither brought Raspe much cash, but when a London bookseller bought the rights and sandwiched the original tales between a prefatory chapter and fifteen additional sketches at the end, the volume began a literary trend that still prevails in tall-story fiction. The first German edition of the tales appeared in 1786.

Raspe, having concocted a scheme for amalgamating silver and gold, collected money for his experiments and then fled to a remote section of Ireland, where he died of scarlet fever in 1794.

BIBLIOGRAPHICAL REFERENCES: There are many editions of the tales of Baron Münchausen. A recent biography is John Carswell, *Romantic Rogue, Being the Life and Times of Rudolf Erich Raspe*, 1950. See also Thomas Seccombe, Introduction to *The Surprising Adventures of Baron Münchausen*, 1895. A more specialized study is Carl Muller-Frauruth, *Die deutschen Lügendichtungen auf Münchausen*, 1881.

MARJORIE KINNAN RAWLINGS

Born: Washington, D.C.   *Died:* St. Augustine, Florida
Date: August 8, 1896   *Date:* December 14, 1953

PRINCIPAL WORKS

NOVELS: *South Moon Under*, 1933; *Golden Apples*, 1935; *The Yearling*, 1938; *The Sojourner*, 1953.
SHORT STORIES: *When the Whippoorwill*, 1940.
SKETCHES: *Cross Creek*, 1942.

Marjorie Kinnan Rawlings was born in Washington, D.C., on August 8, 1896. She attended the University of Wisconsin, where she was graduated in 1918. Later she worked with the Young Women's Christian Association at national headquarters as publicity writer and magazine assistant. There followed a period of writing feature articles for various newspapers until her retirement to Florida in 1928 to raise oranges in her grove at Cross Creek and to devote more time to creative writing of her own. Most of her published work has its setting in central Florida in the section around Cross

Creek, where she made her home and was accepted by the natives.

Her first novel, *South Moon Under*, appeared in 1933 and was selected as the choice of one of the national book clubs. Its period is about 1900, its theme the difficulties of a hunter's life in the Florida scrub country. In 1935 came *Golden Apples*, which tells the struggles of a young boy and his sister who take over an abandoned estate, raise oranges, and find satisfactions in their progress; it is set in the 1890's.

Marjorie Kinnan Rawlings' best novel, *The Yearling*, appeared in 1938. It is the story of twelve-year-old Jody Baxter as he grows from boyhood to an early maturity. Jody makes a pet of a fawn, Flag, which grows to maturity, ruins the crops, and has to be killed. Jody's story, set in 1870, is one of the great regional works in American writing, and it has had tributes comparing it with *Huckleberry Finn*. *The Yearling* won the Pulitzer Prize as the outstanding novel of 1938.

Mrs. Rawlings has written short stories in *When the Whippoorwill* (1940), an autobiographical account of the author's life in Florida in *Cross Creek* (1942), and a delightful discussion of food and its preparation in *Cross Creek Cookery* (1942). Her last book, *The Sojourner*, was her first novel with a northern setting. Mrs. Rawlings' death from a cerebral hemorrhage occurred in St. Augustine, Florida, on December 14, 1953.

BIBLIOGRAPHICAL REFERENCES: Very little has been written about Marjorie Kinnan Rawlings. See Harry R. Warfel, *American Novelists of Today*, 1951; also *Book-of-the-Month Club News*, March, 1938.

CHARLES READE

Born: Oxfordshire, England
Date: June 8, 1814

Died: London, England
Date: April 11, 1884

PRINCIPAL WORKS

NOVELS: *Peg Woffington*, 1853; *Christie Johnstone*, 1853; *It Is Never Too Late to Mend*, 1856; *The Cloister and the Hearth*, 1861; *Hard Cash*, 1863; *Griffith Gaunt*, 1866; *Foul Play*, 1868; *Put Yourself in His Place*, 1870; *A Terrible Temptation*, 1871; *A Woman Hater*, 1877.

PLAYS: *The Ladies' Battle*, 1851; *Angelo*, 1851; *A Village Tale*, 1852; *Masks and Faces*, 1852 (with Tom Taylor); *The Lost Husband*, 1852; *Gold*, 1853; *The Courier of Lyons*, 1854 (*The Lyons Mail*); *Peregrine Pickle*, 1854; *Drink*, 1879.

Charles Reade, born at Ipsden House, June 8, 1814, was the youngest in a family of eleven children born to a wealthy family of the landed gentry in Oxfordshire. Unlike his brothers, who were given the usual "public school" education, Charles Reade was educated at home by tutors. As a result of the private education he was faced with difficulties, personal and academic, when he entered Oxford. He had not learned to get along with people, nor had he acquired the academic knowledge he should have had. During his four years at Oxford, from 1832 to 1835, he received honors, apparently more by luck than ability and, in the case of a Vinerian Scholarship, by absolute chicanery. After leaving Oxford he went to London, studied law, and in 1843 was admitted to the bar, although he never actively practiced law. From 1837 to 1848 Reade, who was independently wealthy, spent his time in relative idleness. He traveled a great deal in Europe, adding to his collection of Cremona violins. Returning to London in 1849, he began to write plays. His first successful production was a comedy, *The Ladies' Battle*. Within two years five other plays were produced, and Reade made many friends among theatrical people, among them Laura Seymour, the famous actress, who was his friend and adviser until her death in 1879.

It was at the suggestion of Mrs. Seymour that Reade first turned to fiction. She suggested that he turn a play into a novel, and so *Masks and Faces* became the novel *Peg Woffington*. In 1856 Reade's first long novel was published, *It Is Never Too Late to Mend*. Following the publication of this novel, Reade turned his efforts almost exclusively to writing fiction rather than drama. His *White Lies* appeared in serial form in the *London Journal*, in 1856–57. Serial publication was common at the time. His greatest novel, *The Cloister and the Hearth*, appeared in 1861. Part of that novel had been published earlier under the title "A Good Fight" in a periodical, *Once a Week*. The story had proved so popular that Reade decided to expand it into its eventual four-volume length.

Probably under the influence of Charles Dickens, who was Reade's friend, the author turned from writing historical romances to writing problem novels. Just how much influence Dickens had on this change is impossible to assess, but as the editor of *All the Year Round,* in which much of Reade's fiction appeared, the influence was probably great. After his change to problem novels, Reade wrote such volumes as *Hard Cash, Griffith Gaunt,* and *Foul Play*. During his career as a writer, Reade wrote more than twenty novels, and he wrote, too, almost as many plays. Of all his works, only *The Cloister and the Hearth* draws any wide group of readers today. His problem novels deal with problems that have long since been solved or alleviated, and so are uninteresting to modern-day readers. The plays are deemed by most scholars to be too stagy and melodramatic. None has found any acceptance on the stage for years, although Reade himself thought that his dramatic work was more important than his fiction, even to requesting that the title of dramatist be put first upon his tombstone. He never lost interest in the novel, however, and when he died in London, April 11, 1884, he left a completed novel, *A Perilous Secret* (1884), ready for publication.

BIBLIOGRAPHICAL REFERENCES: The authorized biography is C. L. and Compton Reade, *Charles Reade, A Memoir,* 2 vols., 1887. A more recent study is Malcolm Elwin, *Charles Reade, A Biography,* 1934. See also A. C. Swinburne, *Miscellanies,* 1886; Walter C. Philips, *Dickens, Reade and Collins, Sensation Novelists,* 1919; and A. M. Turner, *The Making of the Cloister and the Hearth,* 1938.

FORREST REID

Born: Belfast, Ireland
Date: June 24, 1876

Died: Warrenpoint, Ireland
Date: January 4, 1947

PRINCIPAL WORKS

NOVELS: *The Kingdom of Twilight,* 1904; *The Garden God,* 1906; *The Bracknels,* 1911; *Following Darkness,* 1912 (reissued as *Peter Waring,* 1937); *The Gentle Lover,* 1913; *At the Door of the Gate,* 1915; *The Spring Song,* 1916; *Pirates of the Spring,* 1920; *Pender among the Residents,* 1922; *Uncle Stephen,* 1931; *Brian Westby,* 1934; *The Retreat,* 1936; *Young Tom,* 1944.

SHORT STORIES: *Retrospective Adventures,* 1941.

ESSAYS AND STUDIES: *W. B. Yeats: A Critical Study,* 1915; *Illustrators of the Sixties,* 1928; *Walter de la Mare: A Critical Study,* 1929; *Milk of Paradise, Some Thoughts on Poetry,* 1946.

AUTOBIOGRAPHY: *Apostate,* 1926; *Private Road,* 1940.

Forrest Reid, Irish author of childhood and the supernatural, was born on June 24, 1876, in Belfast, Ireland, the son of Robert Reid and his wife Frances Matilda Parr Reid. He was the youngest of twelve children. Perhaps when Forrest Reid became a novelist he never demanded commercial success because he had grown accustomed in his childhood to having enough, but never more than enough, of the necessities of life. His father met with business misadventures and lost considerable money investing in ships which tried unsuccessfully to run a Civil War blockade to the United States. As a boy, Reid enjoyed a close family life, but spent a large amount of time by himself, roaming the fields of Ulster and developing his imaginative powers to the point where dream and reality became almost, but not quite, indistinguishable. He became interested in memory, in time, in the spiritual demands of animals, and in a kind of youthful pantheism. He was tutored at home until he was eleven; he hardly ever attended church, perhaps because he found his needs met during his wanderings over the countryside.

He was educated at the Royal Academical Institution in Belfast and then at Christ's Church, Cambridge, where he received his B.A. He was not impressed by Cambridge, nor by intellectual company of the sort he found there, and he was happy to return to Belfast. He lived in a small suburban house, doing most of his own housekeeping and leading a simple life. He took a job as a clerk in a Belfast tea warehouse and enjoyed working there, performing simple duties, receiving an adequate income, and using his mind imaginatively in the creation of ideas and stories.

His first novel was *The Kingdom of Twilight,* a book he later wished he could disown; but the story was good enough to interest Henry James, who wrote to Reid and encouraged him. Reid responded by dedicating his second book, *The Garden God,* to James. In 1911 he made the acquaintance of E. M. Forster, to whom he dedicated *Following Darkness.* This book was later rewritten and appeared as *Peter Waring* in 1937.

Reid continued to write novels and critical studies, building a small but enthusiastic group of readers. He amused

887

himself by playing croquet, at which he was so expert that he became a champion and made periodic trips to England to engage in tournaments. He loved dogs, as his readers know, and made them his close companions. He had a loyal group of literate and appreciative friends. He enjoyed bridge, book hunting, print collecting, dog shows, and stamp collecting. These interests were satisfied by the small income he received from his books, and he was content to be free to write as he pleased.

His trilogy, *Tom Barber* (published in one volume in 1955), will probably endure as his masterpiece, for as the culmination of his work in the novel it has all the virtues of Reid at his best: the radiance of happy childhood, the peculiar aura of supernatural elements, a continuous beauty of setting and character, and a charming and restrained humor. The trilogy is composed of novels written in reverse order to the chronology of the story: *Uncle Stephen*, the last of the series, appeared first in 1931; *The Retreat*, in 1936; and *Young Tom*, with which the trilogy begins, in 1944. Probably no better expression of the spirit of Reid's own childhood can be found than in this evocation of the experiences of Tom Barber.

In his work he sought what in his autobiography, *Apostate*, he called "a sort of moral fragrance." But since his novels present that atmosphere of good and evil as it made itself felt to him in his childhood, his novels are not burdened but enlightened by the depth of his moral involvement. His biographer, Russell Burlingham, characterized his work as "a world full of sunlight and earth's loveliness, yet ever haunted by mystery and fringed with dream."

Reid was a member of the Irish Academy of Letters, and a recipient of an Honorary D.Litt. from Queen's University in Belfast in 1933. Unmarried, he lived most of his life at 13 Ormiston Crescent in Belfast. He died on January 4, 1947, at Warrenpoint, Ireland.

BIBLIOGRAPHICAL REFERENCES: The fullest account of Reid's life is given in his two autobiographical accounts; in addition, *Private Road*, 1940, contains an interesting analysis of his novels in the light of his personal vision of experience. For biography and criticism see also Russell Burlingham, *Forrest Reid: A Portrait and a Study*, 1953, with an introduction by Walter de la Mare; also E. M. Forster, *Abinger Harvest*, 1936.

ERICH MARIA REMARQUE
(Erich Paul Remark)

Born: Osnabrück, Germany
Date: June 22, 1897

PRINCIPAL WORKS

NOVELS: *Im Westen nichts Neues*, 1929 (*All Quiet on the Western Front*); *Der Weg zurück*, 1931 (*The Road Back*); *Drei Kameraden*, 1937 (*Three Comrades*); *Flotsam*, 1941; *Arc de Triomphe*, 1946 (*Arch of Triumph*); *Der Funke Leben*, 1952 (*Spark of Life*); *Zeit zu Leben und Zeit zu Sterben*, 1954 (*A Time to Love and a Time to Die*); *Der schwarze Obelisk*, 1956 (*The Black Obelisk*).

Erich Maria Remarque, author of *All Quiet on the Western Front,* perhaps the outstanding novel of modern war, is from a Roman Catholic family of French descent. His father was a bookbinder and the family name was Remark.

Educated in Osnabrück, where he was born on June 22, 1897, he was drafted into the German Army during World War I when he was eighteen. He was wounded several times. After his discharge he received a government-sponsored education for teaching, but a year's experience convinced him that he was not suited to the academic life. He tried his hand at various occupations: drama critic, a salesman for a tombstone company, test driver for a Berlin tire company, advertising copywriter for an automobile company, part-time organist in an insane asylum, and assistant editor of *Sportbild,* an illustrated sports magazine. Some of his bizarre experiences were later incorporated in his satirical novel, *The Black Obelisk.*

In his spare time and between jobs he worked on a war novel, *All Quiet on the Western Front,* which was an immediate success when it was published in 1929, selling over a million copies during the first year of its sales in Germany and enjoying a similar success in translation. There have been three motion picture versions of the book, and it is likely that the simplicity and directness of the style will enable the book to stand beyond its own time as a memorable portrait of men at war.

In 1932, after a divorce which ended a nine-year marriage, he married for a second time. In order to find the freedom to write and to regain his health, Remarque and his wife built a house at Porto Ronco on Lake Maggiore in Switzerland, where Remarque had been living intermittently since 1929.

His second novel, *The Road Back,* represented an attempt to convey a sense of the overwhelming challenge facing soldiers returning to a defeated country. His third book, *Three Comrades,* continued his narrative exposition of the effects of war on Germany, the subject matter that has most concerned Remarque. His continued protests against uncivilized force made him one of the targets of Nazi vilification, and early in their rise to power the Nazis included his books among those that were publicly burned.

The Switzerland stay ended in 1939, when Remarque moved to the United States. In 1947 he became a naturalized citizen. Since that time he has lived in Los Angeles and New York and has made return visits to his home at Lake Maggiore.

His most recent novel, *The Black Obelisk,* although new in method, since it can be characterized as a tragic farce, seems particularly suited to Remarque, for it allows him to be humane while desperate, satirical while moral, compassionate while censorious, and sane while commenting on lunacy. The novel has aroused considerable attention and has intensified an interest in Remarque's play, *The Last Station,* which has had an enthusiastic reception in Berlin and Vienna.

BIBLIOGRAPHICAL REFERENCES: There is no full-length biographical or critical study. See W. K. Pfeiler, *War and the German Mind,* 1941; James Gray, *On Second Thought,* 1946; and Robert Van Gelder, *Writers and Writing,* 1946.

ALFONSO REYES

Born: Monterrey, Mexico
Date: May 17, 1889

Died: Mexico City, Mexico
Date: December 27, 1959

PRINCIPAL WORKS

ESSAYS AND STUDIES: *Cuestiones estéticas,* 1911 (*Esthetic Questions*); *Visión de Anáhuac,* 1917; *Retratos reales e imaginarios,* 1920 (*Portraits, Real and Imaginary*); *Simpatías y Diferencias,* 1921–1926 (*Sympathies and Differences*); *Cuestiones Gongorinas,* 1927 (*Questions Relating to Góngora*); *Capítulos de Literatura Española,* 1939 (*Chapters concerning Spanish Literature*); *La Crítica en la Edad Ateniense,* 1941 (*Criticism in the Athenian Age*); *La Experiencia literaria,* 1942 (*Literary Experience*); *Ultima Thule,* 1942; *El Deslinde: Prolegómenos a la Teoría literaria,* 1952 (*The Boundary Line: Prolegomenon to Literary Theory*).

SHORT STORIES AND TALES: *El Plano Oblicuo,* 1920 (*The Oblique Plane*); *Quince Presencias,* 1955.

POEMS: *Obra poética,* 1952 (*Poetic Works*).

"The art of expression," wrote Alfonso Reyes, "did not appear to me as a rhetorical function, independent of conduct, but a means of realizing human feeling." Thus this Mexican writer defined and justified his literary vocation, so faithfully and completely fulfilled during the fifty years of his writing that he has justly been called by one of his critics, "the most accomplished example of the man of letters in México."

Born in Monterrey, capital of the State of Nuevo León in Mexico, on May 17, 1889, he was the son of General Bernardo Reyes, at that time governor of the state and a prominent politician in the regime of President Porfirio Díaz.

Having begun his schooling in his native city, Alfonso Reyes moved later to Mexico City where, in 1913, he received the professional title of lawyer. Here in Mexico City, in 1909, there appeared a generation of writers who engaged in a vigorous intellectual revolution which had enormous repercussions in Mexican culture. These writers were united in a movement called "El Ateneo de la Juventud"

(The Athenaeum of Youth). Reyes was the youngest member of this group and was side by side with other writers who, afterwards, were also primary figures in the intellectual life of modern Mexico: José Vasconcelos, Antonio Caso, Martín Luis Guzmán, Enrique González Martínez. The basic aims of this group were the study and understanding of Mexican culture, the assimilation of current philosophies, literary criticism, and, above all, interest in and knowledge of universal ideas.

Immersed in these intellectual currents, Reyes left for Europe in the service of Mexican diplomacy. France, Spain, Argentina and Brazil gave testimony to his great culture and to his diplomatic skill. In Madrid he collaborated with the Center of Historical Studies as a member of the Department of Philosophy under the direction of D. Ramón Menéndez Pidal, and was also invited to contribute to the pages of *El Sol* (*The Sun*), headed by José Ortega y Gasset. In 1939, after twenty-five years—except for a few intermissions—of diplomatic service, he returned to Mexico and pursued his literary activities with the greatest

890

enthusiasm. The universities of California, Tulane, Harvard, Havana, Princeton, and Mexico conferred honorary degrees on him, and in 1957, in recognition of his faithful and constant dedication to letters, he was named president of the Mexican Academy of Language, of which he had been a corresponding member since 1918.

The Alfonso Reyes bibliography is very extensive. During his fifty years as a writer—in 1906, at the age of seventeen, he wrote his first sonnet, "Mercenario"—his indefatigable pen has produced no less than three hundred titles, among them books of poems, criticism, essays, memoirs, plays, novels and short stories, prefaces, newspaper articles, non-literary works and translations. As a constant element of his work one finds, as much in his prose as in his verse, the lyricism that gives to his books a tone that is agreeable and gracious, ingenious and subtle. In his poetry are evident the influences of Góngora and Mallarmé combined with a personal taste for the picturesque and colloquial. In his preferred medium, the essay, he treats of a great variety of subjects. His best literary criticism is to be found in the essays of *Literary Experience,* in which he pours forth his own experiences in the profession of a writer, and in

"Sobre la estética de Góngora," with which he opens the doors to the modern study and understanding of that baroque Spanish poet. Important among his strictly literary works is *Visión de Anáhuac,* a poetic study of Mexican history; among the humanistic studies, *Discurso por Virgilio,* (*Address in Behalf of Virgil,* 1931) containing both profound classical and American flavor; among the works with fantastic and dreamlike themes so much to Reyes' taste are included those in *Arbol de pólvora.*

In 1952, with a profound understanding of the function of a writer, Reyes produced a volume, the greatest of his critical works, on the literary phenomenon: *The Boundary Line: Prolegomenon to Literary Theory.* Here he analyzes the limitations of the artistic work of expression, style, aesthetic problems, semantics, philology, and the philosophy of language.

"American, European, universal," thus Federico de Onís has described Reyes. These epithets are well spoken if one considers that this Mexican writer, through his native sensibility, his classic form, and the universality of his subjects, is, as the same critic avers, "the most successful example of a citizen of the international world of letters, both ancient and modern."

BIBLIOGRAPHICAL REFERENCES: A work that is indispensable to all Reyes studies is the two-volume *Páginas sobre Alfonso Reyes* (I: 1911–1945, II: 1946–1957), a critcial anthology with an extensive bibliography compiled at and published by the University of Nuevo León, Monterrey, Mexico, 1955–1957. See, in particular, Jean Cassou, "Alfonso Reyes"; Azorín, "Azorín habla de la personalidad literaria de Alfonso Reyes"; Gabriela Mistral, "Un hombre de México"; Juan Ramón Jiménez, "Alfonso Reyes"; Karl Vossler, "El Monterrey de Alfonso Reyes"; Waldo Frank, "Note on Alfonso Reyes"; José María González de Mendoza, "Los temas mexicanos en la obra de Alfonso Reyes"; Federico de Onís, "Alfonso Reyes"; J. B. Trend, "Alfonso Reyes"; Luis Leal, "La Generación del Centenario"; Raimundo Lida, "Alfonso Reyes y sus Literaturas"; and José Luis Martínez, "La Obra de Alfonso Reyes." Supplementing this monumental work is the *Catálogo de índices de los libros de Alfonso Reyes,* with a foreword by Alfonso Rangel Guerra, a bulletin of the University of Nuevo León University Library, 1955.

Carlos González Peña, *History of American Literature,* translated 1943 (rev. ed.), contains a section on Reyes. See also Luis Garrido, *Alfonso Reyes,* 1954 (Mexico); Raimundo Lazo, *La personalidad, la creación y el mensaje de Alfonso Reyes,* 1955 (Havana); Manuel Olguín, *Alfonso Reyes, ensayista: vida y pensamiento,* 1956 (Mexico); José Luis Martínez, "La prosa de Alfonso Reyes," in *Literatura mexicana siglo XX, 1910–1949,* I, 1949 (Mexico); José María González de Mendoza, Introduction to *Verdad y Mentira,* 1950; and Manuel Alcalá, "Alfonso Reyes, el mexicano universal," *Filosofía y Letras,* XXVII (1955), Nos. 53–54, 149–164. "Our Alfonso Reyes," essays by Albert Guerard, Muna Lee, Ramón Sender, Antonio Castro Leal, and others, appeared in *Books Abroad,* XXIX (Spring, 1955).

LADISLAS REYMONT

Born: Kobiele Wielkie, Poland   *Died:* Warsaw, Poland
Date: May 7, 1867   *Date:* December 5, 1925

PRINCIPAL WORKS

NOVELS: *Komedjantka,* 1896 (*The Comedienne*); *Fermenty,* 1897; *Ziemia obiecana,* 1899 (*The Promised Land*); *Sprawiedliwie,* 1899 (*Justice*); *Chłopi,* 1902–1909 (*The Peasants*); *Marzyciel,* 1910 (*The Dreamer*); *Wampir,* 1911 (*The Vampire*); *Rok 1794,* 1914–1919 (*The Year 1794*).

SHORT STORIES: *Przed switem,* 1902; *Burza,* 1908; *Przysięga,* 1917; *Za frontem,* 1919 (*Behind the Lines*); *Bunt,* 1924; *Krosnowa i swiat,* 1928.

Ladislas Reymont, Polish novelist and short story writer and 1924 winner of the Nobel Prize in Literature was born Wladyslaw Stanislaw Rejmont, on May 7, 1867, at Kobiele Wielkie, the son of a comparatively poor country church organist. His childhood was unhappy and far from promising; he was not only poor in his studies, but so erratic in his efforts that he never completed school. He was several times apprenticed to various shops and trades but failed to hold any position long. His father, himself concerned about earning enough as organist and farmer to keep his family going, was particularly unsympathetic and stern with the boy; and the mother's piety merely made his failures seem worse. His one saving grace was his enthusiastic interest in the books which his brother brought to him, and in solitude the

family's black sheep began to build the interest in literature which was ultimately to make him one of Poland's notable novelists. He was particularly interested in the book *Lilla Weneda,* (1840) a romantic historical novel by Słowacki. Later on he found the historical novels of Sienkiewicz, and he read them eagerly, vowing to pattern his work after Sienkiewicz.

His first adventures away from home were with a traveling theatrical company with which the penniless boy traveled for a year. His experiences were later reflected in *The Comedienne.*

When he returned from his theatrical venture, his father found employment for him on the Warsaw-Vienna railroad, where he managed to hold a job long enough to get a considerable amount of reading done. When he was

892

about twenty-six years old, even though he had no funds, he decided to take a chance on establishing himself in Warsaw. He lived there in poverty and consoled himself by writing short stories. The stories finally were accepted by the Cracow *Myśl* (*Thought*) and the Warsaw *Prawda* (*Truth*). Having come to the attention of editors, although not yet famous, Reymont managed to win an assignment to write a report on Jasna Góra, a Polish shrine at Częstochowa, with which he was well acquainted, having spent some months there and having at one time considered becoming a lay brother at the shrine. The result was *Pielgrzymka do Jasnej Góry* (1895), *A Pilgrimage to Jasna Góra*).

The following year saw the publication of the novel about his theatrical wanderings, *The Comedienne,* and that moderately successful work was followed by *Fermenty* in 1897. Reymont was beginning to establish himself as a realistic writer who had considerable sympathy for the workers of Poland but very little faith in an industrialized society. His lack of enthusiasm for the then prevalent positivistic faith in science and industry was even more marked in the novel *The Promised Land,* a severe criticism of industry and its leaders, so colorful and bitter in its content that certain passages were deleted by the censor. The novel, like most of his work, reflected his own experience, this time the experience of working in a factory in Łódź, a job he held in 1897.

The positive side of his criticism of industrialized society was given in what turned out to be his most famous novel, *The Peasants,* a long, somewhat disorganized portrait of the severe life of the peasants, written over a seven year period and published from 1902 to 1909. Despite Reymont's pessimistic and fatalistic predilections, he managed to make the point that, at least from his point of view, the hard life of the peasants contributed more to the dignity of man than the city could. Reymont had been injured and had to spend a year and a half in bed; it was while convalescing that he began work on *The Peasants.*

After *The Peasants,* Reymont's work failed to satisfy the expectations which his previous novels had aroused. Becoming interested in spiritualism through Madame Blavatsky in England, he decided to write stories in which he would emphasize the psychological aspects of life. Unfortunately he was not adept at such a level, and he confused the psychological with the phenomena of spiritualism. The result was *The Dreamer* and *The Vampire,* two mediocre novels.

He regained some critical respect with his novel *The Year 1794,* a story of eighteenth century Polish political and social life, but the book was not as effective as the earlier emotional, turbulent books of factory and peasant life.

Reymont visited the United States in 1920 and traveled to various large cities to raise money for Polish relief. He was awarded the Nobel Prize in Literature in 1924 and was honored the following year by a folk congress in which his novels and his social action were reviewed and praised. Four months later he died in Warsaw, on December 5, 1925.

BIBLIOGRAPHICAL REFERENCES: Reymont's best fiction is available in translation. For biographical and critical studies see Ignacy Matuszewski, *Twórczości Twórcy,*

1904; Jan Lorentowicz, *Ladislas Reymont, Essai sur son œuvre*, 1925; Frank L. Schoell, *Les Paysans de Ladislas Reymont*, 1925; Z. Falkowski, *Władysław Reymont, Człowiek i tworca*, 1929; and J. Krzyżanowski, *Władysław Stanisław Reymont, Tworca i dzieło*, 1937. Brief studies of Reymont in English include Ernest Boyd, "Wladyslaw Reymont, *Saturday Review of Literature*, I (November 29, 1924), 317–318; A. Stender-Peterson, "Reymont, Winner of the Nobel Prize," *Living Age*, CCCXXIV (1925), 165–169; and E. M. Almedinger, "Ladislas Reymont, Peasant and Writer," *English Review*, XLII (1926), 119–122.

ELMER RICE

Born: New York, N. Y.
Date: September 28, 1892

PRINCIPAL WORKS

PLAYS: *On Trial*, 1914; *The Adding Machine*, 1923; *Close Harmony*, 1924 (with Dorothy Parker); *Wake Up, Jonathan*, 1928 (with Hatcher Hughes); *Cock Robin*, 1929 (with Philip Barry); *Street Scene*, 1929; *See Naples and Die*, 1930; *Counsellor-at-Law*, 1931; *We, the People*, 1933; *Between Two Worlds*, 1935; *American Landscape*, 1939; *Flight to the West*, 1941; *Dream Girl*, 1945; *The Grand Tour*, 1951; *The Winner*, 1954.

NOVELS: *A Voyage to Purilla*, 1930; *Imperial City*, 1937; *The Show Must Go On*, 1949.

Elmer (L.) Rice, born Elmer Reizenstein in New York City on September 28, 1892, was considered during the 1920's to be as expert as O'Neill in the use of symbolism in drama. However, unlike O'Neill, only one successful play, *Dream Girl*, has come from his hands in the past quarter of a century. Though Rice did not complete high school, he managed to work his way through the New York University Law School and was graduated *cum laude* in 1912; he passed the bar examinations the same year. However, dissatisfied with the lack of quick success the legal profession presented, he wrote *On Trial* evenings, and when it was successfully produced in 1914 he gave up the law for literature. He collaborated with Hatcher Hughes, Dorothy Parker, and Philip Barry on plays and wrote movie scenarios also. Two of his best-known plays are

The Adding Machine and *Street Scene*; each stresses a main thesis of the playwright, that metropolitan life corrodes character and causes unnecessary alienation among people. The first is the most symbolic of any of his plays in technique, with scenery and action distorted in an expressionistic manner as seen through the eyes of the main character, Mr. Zero, a man who has as much emotional life as the adding machine he punches all day. The second play is an example of selective realism at its best, with a slice of a city tenement area as the protagonist. The effect is one of deep pity and terror. Rice had difficulty in finding a producer for *Street Scene*, and the producer who finally presented it was at first considered unwise. However, it won the Pulitzer Prize for drama and later was made into a highly successful movie. After its success Rice produced

894

successfully the next two of his own plays. He was a regional director of the Federal Theatre in 1935 and directed dramatic shows in a housing settlement. After World War II he joined Maxwell Anderson, S. N. Behr-man, Sidney Howard, and Robert Sherwood to form the Playwrights' Producing Company, an organization for the financing and producing of plays by the playwrights themselves.

BIBLIOGRAPHICAL REFERENCES: A convenient volume is *Seven Plays*, 1950. There is still no full-scale study of Elmer Rice, but brief critical estimates may be found in three works: A. H. Quinn, *A History of the American Drama from the Civil War to the Present Day*, 1936; Burns Mantle, *Contemporary American Playwrights*, 1938; and Joseph Wood Krutch, *The American Drama Since 1918: An Informal History*, 1939. Of basic importance is R. L. Collins, "The Playwright and the Press: Elmer Rice and his Critics," *Theatre Annual*, VII (1948–49), 35–58. See also Meyer Levin, "Elmer Rice," *Theatre Arts Monthly*, XVI (1932), 54–62.

DOROTHY M. RICHARDSON

Born: Berkshire, England   *Died:* Beckenham, England
Date: 1873   *Date:* June 17, 1957

PRINCIPAL WORKS

NOVELS: *Pilgrimage: Pointed Roofs*, 1915; *Backwater*, 1916; *Honeycomb*, 1917; *The Tunnel*, 1919; *Interim*, 1919; *Deadlock*, 1921; *Revolving Lights*, 1923; *The Trap*, 1925; *Oberland*, 1927; *Dawn's Left Hand*, 1931; *Clear Horizon*, 1935; *Dimple Hill*, 1938.

MISCELLANEOUS: *The Quakers Past and Present*, 1914; *John Austen and the Inseparables*, 1930.

Like James Joyce, Marcel Proust, Virginia Woolf, and Katherine Mansfield, Dorothy M. Richardson, who was born in Berkshire in 1873, began early in her career to use what were then still experimental techniques in order to portray with fullness and intimacy her own sensitive reactions to experience. Unlike them, however, she has seen her works less and less read with the passage of time, although both critics and fellow novelists have noted and praised her part in enlarging the scope of the novel.

A secluded early childhood was followed by the traumatic experience of the breakup of her home when she was seventeen. Although she continued her work—writing poems, short stories, and essays—her first book was not published until fifteen years later, when *The Quakers Past and Present* appeared in 1914. The twelve-volume autobiographical novel, *Pilgrimage*, began in 1916 with *Pointed Roofs*, the first book in the series. The most recent one, *Dimple Hill* came out in 1938, the same year as the omnibus edition of *Pilgrimage*. The central figure, Miriam Henderson, has been likened to Joyce's Stephen Dedalus. Everything in the novels is filtered through the consciousness of the protagonist and presented by means of the stream-of-consciousness technique. Although the subtlety and sensitivity

895

of the artist's perceptions have been praised, the absence of important action and the lack of sufficient selectivity and condensation have been criticized. The wife of artist Alan Odle, Miss Richardson died at Beckenham, England, on June 17, 1957.

BIBLIOGRAPHICAL REFERENCES: Criticism of Dorothy Richardson's fiction is not extensive. See John Cowper Powys, *Dorothy M. Richardson*, 1931; May Sinclair, Introduction to *Pointed Roofs*, 1919; Lawrence Hyde, "The Work of Dorothy Richardson," *Adelphi*, II (1924), 508–517; and Harvey Eagleson, "Pedestal for a Statue," *Sewanee Review*, XLII (1934), 42–53. Edward Wagenknecht discusses her work in the chapter titled "Stream-of-Consciousness," *Cavalcade of the English Novel*, 1943 (rev. ed., 1954).

HENRY HANDEL RICHARDSON
(Ethel Florence Richardson Robertson)

Born: Melbourne, Australia
Date: January 3, 1870

Died: Hastings, England
Date: March 20, 1946

PRINCIPAL WORKS

NOVELS: *Maurice Guest*, 1908; *The Getting of Wisdom*, 1910; *The Fortunes of Richard Mahony*, 1930 (a trilogy comprising *Australia Felix*, 1917; *The Way Home*, 1925; *Ultima Thule*, 1929); *The End of a Childhood*, 1934; *The Young Cosima*, 1939.

AUTOBIOGRAPHY: *Myself When Young*, 1948.

When Sinclair Lewis said in 1941 that *The Fortunes of Richard Mahony* was "a truly major work of fiction of the twentieth century," he was giving belated recognition to one of the most neglected novelists of modern times. "Henry Handel Richardson" was the pseudonym of Ethel Florence Lindesay Richardson (also known as Henrietta Richardson), born in Melbourne, Australia, on January 3, 1870. After her education in Melbourne she went to Germany about 1890 and studied to become a concert pianist. In 1895 she married J. G. Robertson, who in 1903 became professor of German literature at the University of London. Turning from music to literature, she published at widely separated intervals the novels which have caused her to be hailed since her death as the most distinguished among Australian novelists.

An uncompromising realist, she made the facts of her family the facts of her fiction. Her first novel, *Maurice Guest*, is the story of a musician who suffers ostracism for living like a genius when he was not one; this is probably the most imaginative of her books. *The Getting of Wisdom* partly reflects the writer's schooldays and the experiences that may cause a sensitive young girl to become a writer. Then came the novels that make up *The Fortunes of Richard Mahony: Australia Felix, The Way Home,* and *Ultima Thule.* The trilogy traces the career of a man who went to Australia to find success, failed, and returned home to renew his former position. Rejected in his earlier associations and surroundings, he disintegrated spiritually and died. The work is based on the life of the writer's father. Critical recognition and some measure of popular success came with the last novel of the series. In 1934 Miss Richardson published *The End of a Childhood,* a sequel to her second novel. Her final work of fiction was *The Young Cosima,* a biographical novel dealing with twelve years in the life of the daughter of Franz Liszt. Miss Richardson died at her home in Sussex on March 20, 1946. Her un-finished autobiography, *Myself When Young,* appeared posthumously.

BIBLIOGRAPHICAL REFERENCES: The most comprehensive literary study is Nettie Palmer, *Henry Handel Richardson,* 1950 (Sidney). See also Norman Bartlett, "Pioneers of a New World Literature," *South Atlantic Quarterly,* LXIX (1950), 30–41.

SAMUEL RICHARDSON

Born: Derbyshire, England
Date: 1689

Died: London, England
Date: July 4, 1761

PRINCIPAL WORKS

NOVELS: *Pamela, or Virtue Rewarded,* 1740; *Clarissa, or The History of a Young Lady,* 1747–1748; *Sir Charles Grandison,* 1753–1754.
LETTERS: *The Correspondence of Samuel Richardson,* 1804.

About Samuel Richardson's life and personality there seems to be a great deal of information, most of it uninteresting. He was born in 1689, the son of a Derbyshire joiner and a pious but nowise unusual mother. As a boy, his thoughtful and serious nature would have recommended him for the Church, but his parents could not afford the requisite education. Instead, after moderate schooling, he was apprenticed to a London printer, John Wilde. He proved a conscientious worker for a demanding master, and in due time reaped his reward by marrying his employer's daughter and succeeding to the business. By dint of hard work and honesty his became one of the most prosperous and sought-after publishing concerns in London.

There is no evidence that Richardson had any youthful ambitions to be a writer; he was over fifty, and a successful businessman, when he stum-bled, quite by accident, into his role as "father" of the English novel. From youth to old age, Richardson was unusually fond of what he characteristically called "epistolary correspondence." As a boy in Derbyshire he had been commissioned by various young ladies to compose or embellish their love letters, and in the process he had gained considerable insight into feminine emotional life and had developed an imagination that took pleasure in creating in detail fantasies concerned with the distresses of love. Later, as an apprentice, he carried on a long correspondence, often on moral subjects, with a man he describes as being a "master of the epistolary style." With this background in letter-writing, it was not unusual that two bookseller friends should suggest that he turn his talents to account by publishing a volume of model letters of various sorts. Richardson took up the idea, but characteristically amended it by proposing that the letters should teach not only how to write but also "how to think and act justly and prudently in the common concerns of human life."

The book, entitled *Familiar Letters,* appeared in 1741, but in the meantime Richardson, while writing a connected group of letters "to instruct handsome young girls, who were obliged to go out to service, . . . how to avoid the snares that might be laid against their virtue," remembered an appropriate story told him some twenty-five years before, and *Pamela,* published in 1740, was born. Perhaps the best concise description of this milestone in the development of the novel is given by Richardson himself on the title page: *Pamela: or Virtue Rewarded. In a Series of Familiar Letters from a beautiful Young Damsel, to her Parents. Now first published in order to cultivate the Principles of Virtue and Religion in the Minds of the Youth of both Sexes. A Narrative which has its Foundation in Truth and Nature; and at the same time that it agreeably entertains, by a Variety of curious and affecting Incidents, is entirely divested of all those Images, which, in too many Pieces calculated for Amusement only, tend to inflame the Minds they should instruct.* The book was not only an immediate and unparalleled success—with the average reader for its detailed descriptions of situations and emotions that at times approach the salacious, with the pious for its moral rectitude—but by adding to the realism of Defoe a power of minute mental analysis which Defoe did not possess, it set a new fashion in fiction, the novel of sensibility.

For all its success, and its importance as both one of the first epistolary novels and the prototype of the novel of sentimental analysis, *Pamela* is not without its faults. Although Richardson makes dramatic use of the letter-writing technique, the device demands an annoying degree of almost priggish self-righteousness on the part of the heroine. Further, the morality of the "lesson" taught is not above suspicion. Pamela defends her virtue valiantly, but not without an eye to the main chance, and in the end is rewarded handsomely by an offer of marriage from her master and would-be seducer.

Richardson's next novel, *Clarissa, or The History of a Young Lady,* avoids both these weaknesses. The story, which tells of the "Distresses that may attend the Misconduct both of Parents and Children in Relation to Marriage," is a truly tragic one. Not only is the characterization in this novel superbly handled, and always believable, but the central dilemma is more genuinely a moral one than in *Pamela;* the problem is not whether Clarissa will be seduced, but whether she can forgive her seducer. But the heroine is no pale, self-righteous prude. Indeed, in this novel Richardson rises to the height of his powers as a novelist, both in his ability to present moving and convincing situations and in his power to describe minutely human emotions at times of extreme stress.

Richardson's last novel, *Sir Charles Grandison,* is an attempt to depict a model good man and fine gentleman combined. Like the others, it is in epistolary form; and although the characterization and analysis of emotions are still excellent, it lacks the intense central dilemma that holds the attention in the first two books, and tends to make tedious reading.

898

After *Sir Charles Grandison* Richardson wrote little more of any importance. He continued to prosper in business, grew rich, was elected Master of the Stationers' Company, was employed to print the journals of the House of Commons, and was eventually appointed Law Printer to the king. Full of years and honors, he died in Parson's Green, London, on July 4, 1761.

Colorless as Richardson was personally, and pedestrian and prolix as his style often became, his importance in the history of the novel should not be underestimated. His books have an extraordinary power which at first attracts and in time holds the reader, and his ability to describe and his insight into the workings of the female heart are unusual. Although English fiction which came after him followed slightly different lines, it is impossible to deny Richardson the credit for inaugurating the novel of sensibility, which for a time became the fashion even more on the Continent than in England.

BIBLIOGRAPHICAL REFERENCES: There are two modern editions of Richardson's novels, that edited by Ethel M. M. McKenna, 20 vols., 1902, and the Blackwell Edition, 19 vols., 1930. The basic source for all biographical studies is *The Correspondence of Samuel Richardson*, edited by Anna L. Barbauld, 6 vols., 1804. The standard modern biography is Alan D. McKillop, *Samuel Richardson, Printer and Novelist*, 1936. See also Clara L. Thomson, *Samuel Richardson*, 1900; Austin Dobson, *Samuel Richardson*, 1902; Brian W. Downs, *Richardson*, 1928; Paul Dottin, *Samuel Richardson, imprimeur de Londres*, 1931; and William M. Sale, Jr., *Samuel Richardson, Master Printer*, 1950. Two companion books to Richardson studies are W. M. Sale, *Samuel Richardson: A Bibliographical Record of His Literary Career*, 1936; and Francesco Cordasco, *Samuel Richardson: A List of Critical Studies Published from 1896 to 1946*, 1948.

CONRAD RICHTER

Born: Pine Grove, Pennsylvania
Date: October 13, 1890

PRINCIPAL WORKS

NOVELS: *The Sea of Grass*, 1937; *The Trees*, 1940; *Tacey Cromwell*, 1942; *The Free Man*, 1943; *The Fields*, 1946; *Always Young and Fair*, 1947; *The Town*, 1950; *The Light in the Forest*, 1953; *The Lady*, 1957.

SHORT STORIES: *Early Americana*, 1936.

PHILOSOPHICAL STUDY: *The Mountain on the Desert: A Philosophical Journey*, 1955.

Our leading specialist in early Americana, Conrad (Michael) Richter was born on October 13, 1890, in Pine Grove, Pennsylvania, a town which his great-grandfather, a major in the War of 1812 and a local store and tavern keeper, helped to name. His father was a minister, as were his grandfather, a great-uncle, and an uncle; he feels that his interest in the American past goes back beyond them to earlier ancestors who were soldiers, country squires, traders, farmers. During his boyhood, as his father moved from charge to charge, he became familiar with sections of the state where old habits of living and speech still survived, and these early impressions are reflected in his books. In those days it was expected that he would study for the ministry, but at fifteen he finished high school and went to work driving a wagon over the mountains of central Pennsylvania.

A variety of jobs followed—work in a machine shop, in a coal breaker, on a farm, reporting for Johnstown and Pittsburgh papers. At nineteen he was editor of a country weekly. For two years he worked as a private secretary in Cleveland, Ohio. After a brief mining venture in the Coeur d'Alenes he returned to Pennsylvania to set up a small publishing business of his own. During the next decade his writing was divided between magazine fiction and several nonfiction books of scientific-philosophical theorizing such as *Human Vibration* (1925) and *Principles of Bio-physics* (1927). *Brothers of No Kin*, a collection of short stories, was published in 1924. He married Harvena M. Achenbach in 1915. The Richters have one daughter, Harvena, a poet and short story writer.

In 1928 Conrad Richter sold his business and moved his family to New Mexico. Interested from childhood in stories of pioneer days, he found in the American Southwest a region not long removed from the everyday realities of the frontier experience. Out of the files of old newspapers, diaries, letters, land deeds, account books, and from tales heard at first hand from older settlers in the Southwest, he filled his notebooks with material which eventually became the short stories collected in *Early Americana*. Chronologically and technically, these stories make a good

introduction to the whole body of his fiction because they reveal the working of a specialized point of view. Projected by memory or time into a middle distance where his people act freely, away from the distractions and confusion of the present, the rigors and dangers of the frontier do not enlarge upon life for pictorial or dramatic effect; they are its actual substance. If the present intrudes briefly on the past, as it does in several of the stories, it is only because the lives of his people extend into our own time. In these stories the reader may trace the development of a narrative method. It is not the simple pastness of the past that is important but the effect gained by a useful frame of reference.

In *The Sea of Grass,* his first novel, the story of the passing of the great ranges is told long after the events have taken place by an observer who has reflected on the meaning of deeds of betrayal and violence viewed years before. On a domestic level the account of Colonel Jim Brewton and his cattle empire, of the wife who deserted him for a self-seeking politician, and of their outlaw son parallels a picture of the spacious land ravaged by conflict and greed. The same mold of reminiscence shapes *Tacey Cromwell,* in which the vividly realized atmosphere of an Arizona mining town in its boom days is the background for the story of a dance-hall fancy woman, her gambler lover and his small half-brother, and the miner's orphan whom she adopts. Her attempts at respectability fail when the children are taken from her by the town's prim housewives and her lover deserts her to make a proper marriage. Tacey's story is moving but never sentimentalized, realistically presented by a boy innocent of the social

900

implications but candidly observant of the results. *Always Young and Fair,* also told by an observer, presents a small-town heiress who after the death of her lover in the Spanish-American War renounces the world as represented by the Pennsylvania community in which she lives. In his other, more objective, novels Richter has limited his story to the point of view and the idiom of his period. *The Free Man* tells of Henry Dellicker, a Palatine redemptioner who ran away from his Philadelphia master and as Henry Free made a new life for himself among the freedom-loving Pennsylvania German settlers resisting British authority on the farming frontier beyond the Blue Mountains. *The Light in the Forest* deals with a white boy reclaimed from his Indian captors. His efforts to return to the wild forest life and his friendship with a young Indian uncover deeper meanings, the Emersonian idea that for everything given in human society something fundamental is taken away. *The Lady* marks a return to Richter's earlier method; this story of some events surrounding an unsolved disappearance in the New Mexico Territory is told by a youthful observer and participant.

Conrad Richter's major work is the trilogy made up of *The Trees, The Fields,* and *The Town,* novels tracing the history of a pioneer family in the Ohio Valley from the wilderness years of the eighteenth century to the period of the Civil War. The story, following the life of Sayward Luckett from girlhood in the woods to matriarchal old age in the town of Americus, Ohio, begins with a picture of the hardship and waste which frontier life imposed on those who subdued the savage land and ends with its characters involved in the political, social, and moral problems of modern society. These books are wholly in the American grain; on a deeper level than that of action and character they touch upon matters complex and still obscure in the national consciousness: the restlessness, the violence, the communal guilt and shame, the inner loneliness, the secret fears. That Richter sees in his writing undertones of symbolism and myth is indicated by *The Mountain on the Desert,* a book written to extend the themes of his novels and to define his vitalistic philosophy. This deeper texture makes the past a necessary condition of his work, not to create a painted backdrop for appropriate action, as in most historical novels, but to effect a dimension which gives spatial depth to his perspective of meaning.

BIBLIOGRAPHICAL REFERENCES: Conrad Richter's article, "The Early American Quality," *Atlantic Monthly,* CLXXXVI (September, 1950), 26–30, provides insight into his literary point of view and historical interests. For criticism see Bruce Sutherland, "Conrad Richter's Americana," *New Mexico Quarterly,* XV (1945), 413–422; Dayton Kohler, "Conrad Richter: Early Americana," *College English,* VIII (1947), 221–227; Frederic I. Carpenter, "Conrad Richter's Pioneers: Reality and Myth," *College English,* XII (1950), 77–82; and John T. Flanagan, "Folklore in the Novels of Conrad Richter," *Midwest Folklore,* II (1952), 5–14.

LYNN RIGGS

Born: Claremore, Oklahoma
Date: August 31, 1899

Died: New York, N. Y.
Date: June 30, 1954

PRINCIPAL WORKS

PLAYS: *Big Lake,* 1927; *Sump'n Like Wings,* 1928; *A Lantern to See By,* 1928; *Roadside,* 1930; *Green Grow the Lilacs,* 1931; *Russet Mantle,* 1936; *Cherokee Night,* 1936; *Toward the Western Sky,* 1951.

To the public, Lynn Riggs is only remotely associated with *Oklahoma;* in fact, his *Green Grow the Lilacs* on which the musical is based proved to be the playwright's only popular success. He was, however, a very good poet whose true field was that type of folk play which often lacks widespread appeal.

Riggs was born August 31, 1899, at Claremore, Oklahoma, into the life he portrayed so well in his best work. His father was a rancher, and the family was on good terms with the Rogers family of Claremore. He attended the local schools and the state university, sandwiching his education with a variety of jobs, some associated with writing. His poems were published in national magazines before any of his plays were accepted commercially. *Borned in Texas,* produced as *Roadside* in 1930, was an instant failure on Broadway despite the fact that

Arthur Hopkins, Barrett Clark, and others believed in it.

Green Grow the Lilacs, which followed, received an excellent Theatre Guild production in 1931. This same group insisted that Rodgers and Hammerstein revise the play as a musical; out of this collaboration *Oklahoma* was born. In the meantime, Riggs went right on writing, occasionally appearing as visiting lecturer in universities, and assisting in productions, mostly non-professional, of his later works. He died in New York City on June 30, 1954.

Second only to Paul Green in the provocative use of folklore in drama, Riggs was never a popular playwright, yet he continued to write and produce individually excellent plays. No one else has yet taken his place, and criticism has not yet evaluated his minor but significant contribution to the American drama.

BIBLIOGRAPHICAL REFERENCES: Lynn Riggs received little critical attention. In the absence of full studies, survey volumes must be consulted: Richard D. Skinner, *Our Changing Theatre,* 1931; Montrose J. Moses and John Mason Brown, eds., *The American Theatre as Seen by its Critics, 1752–1934,* 1934; and John Mason Brown, *Two on the Aisle,* 1938. See also, Stanley Vestal, "Lynn Riggs: Poet and Dramatist," *Sewanee Review,* XV (Autumn 1929), 64–71—an important article; R. L. Lowe, "The Lyrics of Lynn Riggs," *Poetry,* XXXVIII (1931), 347–349; and Lee Mitchell, "A Designer at Work," *Theatre Arts Monthly,* XVIII (1934), 874–877.

RAINER MARIA RILKE

Born: Prague, Czechoslovakia
Date: December 4, 1875

Died: Valmont, Switzerland
Date: December 29, 1926

PRINCIPAL WORKS

POEMS: *Leben und Lieder*, 1894 (*Life and Songs*); *Traumgekrönt*, 1897 (*Dream-crowned*); *Mir zur Feier*, 1899 (*For My Rest*); *Das Buch der Bilder*, 1902 (*The Book of Pictures*); *Das Stundenbuch*, 1905 (*Poems from the Book of Hours*); *Die Weise von Liebe und Tod des Cornets Christoph Rilke*, 1906 (*The Tale of the Love and Death of Cornet Christopher Rilke*); *Neue Gedichte*, 1907–1908 (*New Poems*); *Fünf Gesänge*, 1914 (*Five Songs*); *Duineser Elegien*, 1923 (*Duino Elegies*); *Die Sonette an Orpheus*, 1923 (*Sonnets to Orpheus*).

PLAYS: *Ohne Gegenwart*, 1898 (*Without the Present*); *Tägliche Leben*, 1902 (*Everyday Life*).

ESSAYS: *Worpswede*, 1903; *Auguste Rodin*, 1903.

STORIES AND TALES: *Am Leben Hin*, 1899 (*To a Lost Life*); *Zwei Prager Geschichten*, 1899 (*Two Prague Stories*); *Geschichten vom Lieben Gott*, 1900 (*Stories of God*).

NOVEL: *Aufzeichnungen des Malte Laurids Brigge*, 1910 (*The Notebook of Malte Laurids Brigge*).

LETTERS: *Briefe an einen jungen Dichter*, 1929 (*Letters to a Young Poet*); *Briefe an eine junge Frau*, 1930; *Gesammelte Briefe*, 1939–1941; *Selected Letters of Rainer Maria Rilke, 1902–1926*, 1946.

In his poetry, Rainer Maria Rilke, born at Prague on December 4, 1875, transcended the cloying limitations of Romanticism, devoting his creative energies to what has been called an eternal "struggle for clarity and coherence." It is somewhat ironic, in view of his search for a static and depersonalized system of images, that his own life—and, still more ironically, his death—should have conformed so perfectly to the stereotyped romantic image of The Poet. He was, in fact, all of those things that a Romantic Poet should be: a sickly, sensitive, and misunderstood young man, constantly harassed and frequently crushed by the unfeeling demands of a cruel materialistic society; a wanderer searching hopelessly for a land of peace and of truth; and, most aptly, a passionate but faithless lover, a true worshipper of the muse in her earthly as well as in her sublime incarnations.

On this latter point, it has been said that "women always played a decisive part in determining Rilke's life." The course of this life can be plotted by a consideration of the decisive parts that, successively, these women played. First there was the mother and the familiar Byronic rejection theme. At ten the spoiled but unloved Maria was packed off to military school where he remained until, broken in health, he was allowed to exchange the rigors of military discipline for the dreariness of a business education. This phase he endured until the second woman in his life appeared upon the scene. She was a young governess with whom he eloped. When Rilke repented his rash action and returned to Prague, he discovered that his mother had moved to

903

Vienna and that his father had disowned him. Here an uncle, one Jaroslav Rilke, came to his rescue, providing him with tutors and supporting him while he attended the University of Prague.

His attendance there was short-lived, however, because of his uncle's untimely death. But at this point a second mistress, his "bright flame," Valery David-Rhonfeld, exerted her influence. The result was his first collection of poems, *Life and Songs,* published at her expense, and his transfer to the more congenial atmosphere of the University of Munich.

It was at Munich that he began earnestly to pursue his vocation as a poet, and it was from Munich that his long and restless wanderings began. With the publication of his fifth volume of verse, *For My Rest,* his artistic abilities were firmly established, but his desire for a "spiritual homeland" was unsatisfied. He left Munich for Russia, where he visited Tolstoy and met Clara Westoff, a talented young sculptress, a pupil of Rodin, who was then working at the artists' colony at Worpswede. She and Rilke were married in 1901, and for a time the two lived happily in a productive partnership of their respective creative endeavors.

Financial pressure finally destroyed their artistic idyl. Rilke was forced to find work. He had by this time become reconciled with his father, who obligingly offered him a job in a bank. The younger Rilke was horrified. He accepted, instead, a commission to write a critical biography of his wife's great master, Auguste Rodin. In Paris he met the great sculptor, who immediately became his idol. Rilke remained with Rodin for over a year, publishing his monograph, *Auguste Rodin,* and then, after traveling for his failing health first into Italy and next to Denmark, the land of his other great idol, Peter Jacobsen, he returned to France to become Rodin's secretary, an occupation hardly compatible with his poetic temperament. After a year Rilke returned to his literary works.

A productive period which ended with the second volume of *New Poems,* called "his first really mature poetry," was followed by the resumption of his wanderings and the influence of still another woman, the Princess Marie von Thurn und Taxis-Hohenlohe, who allowed him the use of her castle overlooking the Adriatic and who inspired him to renewed creative activity. But soon again he was wandering, not stopping until the war interrupted both his travels and his writing. After the war he settled down in Switzerland, where he produced his final and his greatest poetic triumphs, his *Duino Elegies* and his *Sonnets to Orpheus,* and where he met the last woman who was to influence his life. It is not known who she was, but she was beautiful enough to inspire the ill and aging Rilke to pick a rose for her. The rose pricked his finger. A fatal infection set in. The poet died, symbolically wounded fatally by the eternal poetic symbol of love, at Valmont, Switzerland, on December 29, 1926.

BIBLIOGRAPHICAL REFERENCES: Rilke's major works are now available in translation, the most recent being *Poems, 1906–1926,* translated by J. B. Leishman, 1957. For biographical and critical studies see Lou Andreas-Salomé, *Rainer Maria Rilke,* 1928; Federico Olivero, *Rainer Maria Rilke,* 1929; F. Gundolf, *Rainer Maria Rilke,* 1936; Katharina Kippenberg, *Rainer Maria Rilke,* 1935; E. M. Butler, *Rainer Maria Rilke,*

1941; Nora Wydenbruck, *Rilke, Man and Poet*, 1949; F. W. van Heerikhuizen, *Rainer Maria Rilke: His Life and Work*, translated 1952; and William Laurens Graff, *Rainer Maria Rilke: Creative Anguish of a Modern Poet*, 1956. *Rainer Maria Rilke: Aspects of His Mind and Poetry* was edited by William Rose and G. Craig Houston, 1938. For brief studies see also Frank Wood, "Rainer Maria Rilke: Paradoxes," *Sewanee Review*, XLVII (1939), 586–592, and "Rilke and D. H. Lawrence," *German Review*, XV (1940), 213–223; Barker Fairley, "Rainer Maria Rilke: An Estimate," *University of Toronto Quarterly*, XI (1942), 1–14; and Ernst Rose, "Rainer Maria Rilke and the Heroic," *German Review*, XVIII (1943), 266–276.

ARTHUR RIMBAUD

Born: Charleville, France
Date: October 20, 1854

Died: Marseilles, France
Date: November 10, 1891

Principal Works

poems: *Une Saison en Enfer*, 1873 (*A Season in Hell*); *Les Illuminations*, 1886 (*Illuminations*); *Reliquaire*, 1891 (*Reliquary*); *Poésies complètes*, 1895; *Le Bateau ivre*, 1920 (*The Drunken Boat*); *Les Stupra*, 1923 (*Debaucheries*).

letters: *Lettres de Jean-Arthur Rimbaud, Égypte, Arabie, Éthiopie*, 1899; *Lettres de la vie littéraire*, 1931.

The life of (Jean Nicolas) Arthur Rimbaud was brief, lasting a scant thirty-seven years, and his life as a poet was briefer still, ending with the completion of *A Season in Hell* in 1873, only a little over three years after his first stormy entrance into Paris in 1870. Yet in this brief tenure as a poet he managed to compose enough verse to fill a sizable volume, and, what is much more important than quantity, he managed to write with such power and such vision that he changed the whole course of the French Symbolist movement and exerted an influence that is still being felt in literature today.

His vision was a dual one, angelic and diabolic at the same time. He followed it compulsively and agonizingly, or, rather, he was driven by it from one excess to another, and from one country to another over two continents, until finally his spiritual agony became a physical one and he was consumed by it completely.

The story of his life has been called a saint's legend in reverse. Like the saint, he was seeking complete truth, a perfect communion with God: that was the angelic side of his vision. Like the saint, he knew that he would have to put aside completely the things of this world, but he would do so not through deprivation but through excess. That was the diabolic side of his experience, the descent into hell. That is one way of looking at the facts. Another would be to say simply that he was the victim of a compulsive neurosis and that in one stage of his progressive disease he was compelled to write some brilliant poetry. But whatever it was, vision or neurosis, he was driven, and his life was one of pain.

Born in Charleville, France, on October 20, 1854, he was writing poems by the time he was fifteen, and by sixteen, through the guidance of a rhetoric professor named Georges Izambard, he had already become an anticlerical revolutionary. When he was sixteen he left the college in Charleville and made his first pilgrimage to Paris. This started out by train, but because he did not have enough money for his fare he was thrown in jail upon arrival. Shipped back to Charleville, he refused to return to his studies but set off again for the capital, this time on foot.

On this second trip to Paris he met Verlaine. Some of Rimbaud's early poems had been printed in *La Revue* and *La Charge,* and Verlaine, having read them, was anxious to meet their young author. The two were introduced by Bretagne—who also introduced Rimbaud to occultism—and their tempestuous and abnormal relationship began. Verlaine had only recently been married, but he found the handsome younger poet more attractive than his pregnant wife. Mme. Verlaine objected to the association. Rimbaud returned home for a time, composed a number of poems at Charleville, and then traveled to Brussels, where Verlaine, leaving his wife and newborn child, met him. The two continued to London, remaining there for almost a year while Rimbaud wrote his first *Illuminations.*

He left Verlaine for the second time in April, 1873. His career as a poet was almost over when he returned to France and began *A Season in Hell.* But the relationship with Verlaine was not entirely finished; Rimbaud went once more to Brussels, where Verlaine was staying, reunited with his wife. The three met and an altercation ensued in which Verlaine wounded Rimbaud in the wrist with a bullet from the pistol he had bought to take his own life. Verlaine was sentenced to two years in prison and Rimbaud left Brussels.

Once more in Charleville, he resumed his writing, finishing his *Illuminations* and *A Season in Hell* and finding, with the latter, that there was no more in poetry for him. With the end of his writing career, his wanderings began again. Driven by a form of madness, he traveled throughout Europe, mostly on foot, searching for the true action that would mean life to him. Not finding it, he joined the Dutch colonial army, but soon deserted and traveled home once more. Finally, in April, 1880, he left for Africa, and there, for eleven years, he remained as an exporter, a gun-runner, and even, it has been suggested, a trader in slaves. However deep he went into the back country, he could not travel far enough to fulfill his haunted vision or relieve his compulsion. He died shortly after his thirty-seventh birthday, after a rheumatic infection of the right leg had sent him to Marseilles for treatment. When his condition grew worse, the leg was amputated, but the infection spread. Rimbaud died, feverish and tormented, on November 10, 1891.

BIBLIOGRAPHICAL REFERENCES: Rimbaud's *Œuvres complètes,* with a critical preface by Paul Claudel, appeared in 1929. H. de Bouillane de Lacoste has edited three critical editions of the poet's work: *Poésies complètes,* 1939; *Une Saison en Enfer,* 1941; and *Les Illuminations,* 1949. The best single book on Rimbaud in English is Enid Starkie, *Rimbaud,* 1947 (rev. ed.). For biography and criticism see also D. Berrichon, *Vie de Arthur Rimbaud,* 1897; J. M. Carré, *La Vie aventureuse d'Arthur*

Rimbaud, 1926; Benjamin Fondane, *Rimbaud le voyau*, 1933; C. A. Hackett, *Le Lyrisme de Rimbaud*, 1938; H. de Bouillane de Lacoste, *Rimbaud et le problème des Illuminations*, 1949; and Jacques Gengoux, *La Pensée poétique de Rimbaud*, 1950.

ELIZABETH MADOX ROBERTS

Born: Perryville, Kentucky
Date: October 30, 1881

Died: Orlando, Florida
Date: March 13, 1941

PRINCIPAL WORKS

NOVELS: *The Time of Man*, 1926; *My Heart and My Flesh*, 1927; *Jingling in the Wind*, 1928; *The Great Meadow*, 1930; *A Buried Treasure*, 1931; *He Sent Forth a Raven*, 1935; *Black Is My Truelove's Hair*, 1938.

SHORT STORIES: *The Haunted Mirror*, 1932; *Not by Strange Gods*, 1941.

POEMS: *Under the Tree*, 1922; *Song in the Meadow*, 1940.

Among the writers who have given new perspectives to Southern life and character in fiction, Elizabeth Madox Roberts is notable for her sympathetic portrayal of humanity and the poetic qualities of her style. To the folk materials of her region she added the techniques of the modern novel of sensibility. As a result the final effect of her writing is quite different from anything found in the older local colorists whose stories demonstrate an art based on pictures of the quaint and strange enclosing sentimental or melodramatic plots. Local in her choice of setting but never provincial in outlook, she transformed her Kentucky background into a landscape of the imagination and the spirit, filled it with living figures realistically and regionally true to its manners and its climate but recognizable as part of the greater human world as well.

Elizabeth Madox Roberts was born in Perryville, October 30, 1881, in the Pigeon River country where her family had settled generations before. Among her earliest recollections were a grandmother's stories of ancestors

who came over Boone's Trace in the 1770's; thus the history of Kentucky became for her a personal account of family tradition. Ill during much of her early life, she lived for several years in the Colorado Rockies after her graduation from high school. *In the Great Steep's Garden*, an uneven but promising first book of poems, appeared in 1915. Two years later she entered the University of Chicago, from which she was graduated in 1921. During her undergraduate days, a member of a literary group that included Glenway Wescott and Yvor Winters, she wrote poetry and prose, winning the McLaughlin Prize for essay writing and the Fisk Prize for a group of poems which, expanded, became *Under the Tree*, published in 1922.

Miss Roberts came to the writing of fiction after several false starts during the years of her literary apprenticeship in New York. One novel had been started but abandoned in despair and another was left unfinished when she began *The Time of Man*, which brought her critical recognition and public fame in 1926. Working on her

907

second novel during a stay in California, she wrote day after day in her Santa Monica apartment, watched from her windows the rolling surf of the Pacific, and grew eager to return to Kentucky. Perhaps that is why the limits of the state expand to become a satirical symbol of American civilization in her third novel, *Jingling in the Wind*, rewritten from an unfinished version preceding *The Time of Man*. When these books appeared, however, Miss Roberts had already returned to Kentucky to make her permanent home in Springfield. Having found in the tradition and life of her own region those roots and ties which the writer must possess if his work is to draw any meaning from man's relation to his time and place, in her life as in her books she made a segment of the Kentucky landscape her measure of the larger world.

This was a child's world in *Under the Tree*, a poetic anthology of childhood impressions. But the same world has grown vast and strangely cruel to Ellen Chesser in *The Time of Man* as she scrawls her name with a fingertip upon empty air and ponders the mystery of her identity. Among her people pioneering impulses have dwindled to the restlessness of the tenant farmer; her life is a series of removals through a tragic cycle of love, desertion, marriage, and the beginning of another pilgrimage when her children have begun to repeat in legend fashion the story of her earlier migrations. A work of poetic realism, the novel is as timeless as a pastoral or a folk ballad and seemingly as effortless in design. Darkness of the spirit hangs over *My Heart and My Flesh*, in which the aristocratic, futile world of Theodosia Bell dissolves in hunger, madness, and the

emotional shock of murder. *Jingling in the Wind*, a less successful effort, brings *Candide* and *Alice in Wonderland* into Kentucky, and attempts a travesty on the Babbitts, professional optimists, and brisk salesmen of our industrial civilization. *The Great Meadow*, a re-creation of the historic past, is a prose monument to the pioneer; in the story of Diony Hall, her heroine, Miss Roberts tried to catch the spirit and even the accents of her grandmother's tales of the settlement of Kentucky.

A Buried Treasure is an old morality story retold, presenting the situation which arises when a pot of hidden gold brings unexpected wealth to those who do not know what to do with it. The short stories of *The Haunted Mirror* represent further crystallization of experience, a compression of inarticulate lives into moments of significance and perception: an awakening to life in "The Sacrifice of the Maidens," the terror of love in "The Scarecrow," the candid spectacle of death in "Death at Bearwallow," the tragedy of violence in "Record at Oak Hill." *He Sent Forth a Raven*, set against the first two decades of the present century, dramatizes in mystic and poetic fashion the conflict between the outer realities of man's world and darker passions of the human spirit.

The cloudy mysticism which critics and readers found puzzling in *He Sent Forth a Raven* does not appear in her last novel, *Black Is My Truelove's Hair*. As simple in outline as the folk song from which its title was taken, it is saved from thematic bareness by Miss Roberts' richly colored landscapes and her sensitive perceptions of her people. The novel is a prose ballad of love betrayed, a ballad with a happy ending, however, and it is written in prose that sings.

Elizabeth Madox Roberts never forgot that she was a poet before she became a novelist. From time to time, in the intervals between books, her poems appeared in various magazines. In 1940 the best of these were printed in *Song in the Meadow,* a collection of lyrics in which she spoke in her own person as a poet. *Not by Strange Gods,* a second book of short stories, was her last published work. She died of anemia in Orlando, Florida, on March 13, 1941.

BIBLIOGRAPHICAL REFERENCES: There is no authorized biography. The first extended critical study is Harry M. Campbell and Ruel E. Foster, *Elizabeth Madox Roberts: American Novelist,* 1956. For criticism in books and periodicals see also Harlan Hatcher, *Creating the Modern American Novel,* 1935; Edward Wagenknecht, *Cavalcade of the American Novel,* 1952; Glenway Wescott, "Elizabeth Madox Roberts: A Personal Note," *Bookman,* LXXI (1930), 12–15; Mark Van Doren, "Elizabeth Madox Roberts: Her Mind and Style," *English Journal,* XXI (1932), 521–528; J. Donald Adams, "Elizabeth Madox Roberts," *Virginia Quarterly Review,* XII (1936), 80–90; Francis L. Janney, "Elizabeth Madox Roberts," *Sewanee Review,* XLV (1937), 388–410; Alex M. Buchan, "Elizabeth Madox Roberts," *Southwest Review,* XXV (1940), 463–481; Dayton Kohler, "Elizabeth Madox Roberts: A Regional Example," *Mountain Life and Work,* XXII (Fall, 1946), 5–8; and Earl H. Rovit, "Recurrent Symbolism in the Novels of Elizabeth Madox Roberts," *Boston University Studies in English,* II (Spring, 1956), 35–54.

THOMAS WILLIAM ROBERTSON

Born: Newark, England
Date: January 9, 1829

Died: London, England
Date: February 3, 1871

PRINCIPAL WORKS

PLAYS: *David Garrick,* 1864; *Society,* 1865; *Ours,* 1866; *Caste,* 1867; *School,* 1869; *M.P.,* 1870.

Thomas William Robertson, born at Newark, England, on January 9, 1829, was born also into the theatrical world, for his father and mother were both members of the profession. Because his parents were on the road with a company a great deal, Robertson was cared for much of the time by a distant relative, his great-uncle's widow. Robertson himself made his first appearance on the stage at the age of five. As early as 1843, when but fourteen, he left school to become a stagehand and prompter with his father's players, the Lincoln Company. In 1848, following the dissolution of the Lincoln Company, Robertson went to London, where he found work in the smaller theaters.

His career as a dramatist began with *A Night's Adventure* (1851), but during the 1850's his success as a playwright was slight. During those years he acted with provincial touring companies, wrote, and tried unsuccessfully to enlist in the British Army. In 1856 he married Elizabeth Burton, an actress. Upon the death of their second child in 1858, Robertson returned to London with his family. There he worked as an editor, free-lance writer, and translator. Still his success was so slight that he seriously considered opening a tobacco shop. His fortunes changed, however, when *David Garrick* was produced in 1864. There followed a whole series of successful plays, produced at London's Prince of Wales Theatre: *Society, Caste,* his most famous play, and others. Most of

Robertson's plays combine sentiment and a superficial worldliness in a fashion which caused critics in his time to dub them "cup-and-saucer drama." Robertson's health failed in 1870, and he made a journey to Torquay to recuperate in December of that year. The effort to restore his health failed, however, and he died in London, February 3, 1871.

BIBLIOGRAPHICAL REFERENCES: The best edition of Robertson's plays is *Principal Dramatic Works,* 2 vols., 1889, with a memoir by his son, T. W. S. Robertson. *Caste* and *Society* were edited by T. Edgar Pemberton, 1905. The standard biography is by T. Edgar Pemberton, *Life and Writings of T. W. Robertson,* 1893. Valuable information from his actress-manager appears in Sir Squire and Lady Bancroft, *Recollections of Sixty Years,* 1909. The only full critical study is Maynard Savin, *Thomas William Robertson: His Plays and Stagecraft,* 1950. Of basic importance is Sir Arthur Wing Pinero, "The Theatre of the 'Seventies," in *The Eighteen-Seventies,* edited by H. Granville-Barker, 1929. See also J. H. Friswell, *Modern Men of Letters,* 1870; and C. F. Armstrong, *Shakespeare to Shaw,* 1913.

EDWIN ARLINGTON ROBINSON

Born: Head Tide, Maine
Date: December 22, 1869

Died: New York, N. Y.
Date: April 6, 1935

PRINCIPAL WORKS

POEMS: *The Torrent and the Night Before,* 1896; *The Children of the Night,* 1897; *Captain Craig,* 1902; *The Town Down the River,* 1910; *The Man Against the Sky,* 1916; *Merlin,* 1917; *Lancelot,* 1920; *The Three Taverns,* 1920; *Avon's Harvest,* 1921; *Roman Bartholow,* 1923; *The Man Who Died Twice,* 1924; *Dionysus in Doubt,* 1925; *Tristram,* 1927; *Fortunatus,* 1928; *Three Poems,* 1928; *Sonnets 1889–1927,* 1928; *Cavender's House,* 1929; *Modred, a Fragment,* 1929; *The Glory of the Nightingales,* 1930; *Matthias at the Door,* 1931; *Nicodemus,* 1932; *Talifer,* 1933; *Amaranth,* 1934; *King Jasper,* 1935; *Collected Poems,* 1937.

Edwin Arlington Robinson has been called the last American writer in the nineteenth century tradition of rationalism and psychological understanding, a figure more akin in spirit to the novelists Henry James and Edith Wharton than to any other American poet of his time. Dedicated to his craft of verse and unwilling to disperse his energies in other fields, he became that rarity in literature, a professional poet

who was critically admired (especially after the publication of *The Man Against the Sky* in 1916) and financially successful after the sales of *Tristram* in 1927.

As a boy Robinson showed no distinctive talents. Born in Head Tide, Maine, on December 22, 1869, he went to Harvard for two years without intending to take a degree and then returned to Gardiner, Maine, the Tilbury Town of his early poems, where his father's declining business was located. An apparent failure in life like his own characters Miniver Cheevy and Mr. Flood, Robinson nevertheless wrote steadily and in 1896 privately published his first book, *The Torrent and the Night.* A year later he published *The Children of the Night,* containing "Luke Havergal," later widely known in anthologies, and "The Clerks," two poems marking the appearance of his brief dramas of insight into personality, written in a lucid style of intellectual seriousness.

When his third book, *Captain Craig,* was published in 1902, Robinson was working in New York as a train checker on the subway. During this period Theodore Roosevelt became interested in him and not only offered him a custom house sinecure in 1905 but also wrote a critical commendation of the poet's work for *The Outlook.* Four years later, under the Taft administration, Robinson resigned from the post Roosevelt had found for him in the New York custom house.

The remaining events of Robinson's life were undistinguished except by the fulfillment of his talent in frequent publications of his books. Regularly, after 1911, he divided his time between New York in the winter and the Mac-Dowell Colony in New Hampshire during the summer, supported in part by a legacy and a trust fund established by his friends. Gradually honors came to him: a fiftieth birthday celebration by the New York *Times Book Review* in 1911, three Pulitzer prizes for the 1921 edition of *Collected Poems, The Man Who Died Twice,* and *Tristram;* various poetry prizes, honorary degrees from colleges and universities, the

Gold Medal of the National Institute of Arts and Letters in 1929, and the posthumous award of the Medal of the International Mark Twain Society following his death in New York City on April 6, 1935.

Robinson was a poet of major ambition who seemed to combine New England moral integrity and dryness of manner with something of Browning's psychological curiosity and Hardy's involvement with fate. The fact that his work should suggest a Puritan sensibility dissolved in the mainstream of English narrative verse, combined with a mastery of formal techniques, has resulted in divided critical opinion. At the same time his tendency toward prolixity in blank verse and a sort of romantic realism relying on cleverness made him accessible to a public not usually eager for poetry; indeed, such later long works as *Matthias at the Door, Talifer,* and *Amaranth* were written with a novelist's awareness of his readers.

It is in his short poems and those of medium length that Robinson is most compelling. "For a Dead Lady," from *The Town Down the River;* "Eros Turannos," a perfect match of wit in form with stark understanding of life, from *The Man Against the Sky;* "The Wandering Jew," from *The Three Taverns,* and "The Sheaves," one of his finest sonnets, from *Dionysus in Doubt,* are all among the clearest examples of his literary cultivation and mastery of purpose. In these he demonstrates his ability to make symbolic thought and the play of ideas poetic with little sensuous imagery. Other poems in *The Man Who Died Twice* and *Nicodemus,* his last impressive volume, also develop his concern with failure and defeat, especially the plight of the potential artist, to the point of unflinching awareness.

The Arthurian trilogy (comprising *Merlin,* a study of romantic love; *Lancelot,* a study of the modern doubter, and *Tristram,* a detailed story of defeated passion based largely on Malory) is his most famous group of poems. But it is doubtful if Robinson's attempt at a major achievement here did more than diffuse his narrative power for the sake of full expression. In his work he was always shifting between the long poem in blank verse and the shorter self-contained stanza forms; since his attitude toward man and destiny was not passionate but skeptical and intellectually firm, it is the laconic expression of his mind in a verse form that is most convincing. The long works of his later years, concluding in 1935 with *King Jasper,* a modern allegory of industrial civilization, did not add much to a reputation already firmly grounded in the philosophical qualities which made his poetry a moral criticism of society and the age.

BIBLIOGRAPHICAL REFERENCES: There are various editions of Robinson's *Collected Poems* dating from 1921; the standard text is *The Collected Poems of Edwin Arlington Robinson,* 1937, containing additions from his later work. Collections of his letters are the *Selected Letters,* edited by Ridgely Torrence, 1940; *Letters of Edwin Arlington Robinson to Howard George Schmitt,* edited by Carl J. Weber, 1943; and *Untriangulated Stars: Letters of Edwin Arlington Robinson to Harry de Forest Smith, 1890–1905,* 1947. The biographies which may be regarded as standard are Hermann Hagedorn, *Edwin Arlington Robinson: A Biography,* 1938; and Emery Neff, *Edwin Arlington Robinson,* 1948.

For criticism and analysis see Lloyd Morris, *The Poetry of Edwin Arlington Robinson,* 1923; Ben Ray Redman, *Edwin Arlington Robinson,* 1926; Mark Van Doren, *Edwin Arlington Robinson,* 1927; L. M. Beebe, *Edwin Arlington Robinson and the Arthurian Legend,* 1927; Charles Cestre, *An Introduction to Edwin Arlington Robinson,* 1930; R. W. Brown, *Next Door to a Poet,* 1937; Robert P. T. Coffin, *New Poetry of New England: Frost and Robinson,* 1938; Estelle Kaplan, *Philosophy in the Poetry of Edwin Arlington Robinson,* 1940; Yvor Winters, *Edwin Arlington Robinson,* 1946; and Barnard Ellsworth, *Edwin Arlington Robinson,* 1952. Briefer estimates include Percy H. Boynton, *Some Contemporary Americans,* 1924; Thomas K. Whipple, *Spokesmen,* 1928; Alfred Kreymborg, *Our Singing Strength,* 1929; E. E. Pipkin, "The Arthur of Edwin Arlington Robinson," *English Journal,* XIX (1930), 183–195; Floyd Stovall, "The Optimism behind Robinson's Tragedies," *American Literature,* X (1938), 1–24; C. E. Van Norman, "Captain Craig," *College English,* II (1941), 462–475; Louise Dauner, "Avon and Cavender: Two Children of the Night," *American Literature,* XIV (1942), 55–65; and Richard Crowder, "Men Against the Sky," *College English,* XIV (1953), 269–276.

For other bibliographical listings see also Lillian Lippincott, *A Bibliography of the Writings and Criticisms of Edwin Arlington Robinson,* 1937; supplemented by Charles B. Hogan, "Edwin Arlington Robinson: New Bibliographical Notes," *Papers of the Bibliographical Society of America,* XXXV (1941), 115–144.

FERNANDO DE ROJAS

Born: Puebla de Montalbán (?), Spain
Date: 1475?

Died: Near Talavera (?), Spain
Date: April, 1541

NOVEL: *Comedia de Calisto y Melibea* (*La Celestina*), 1499 (second edition, 1501).

The author of Spain's first realistic novel, *La Celestina*, one of the gems of its national literature, remains a shadowy figure. Even proof that he wrote this novel in dramatic form lies mainly in an acrostic of the 1501 Sevilla edition of twenty-one acts, which gives his home as Montalbán. He may have been born there, about 1475, or in Toledo, if scholars are right in assuming that city as the location of his only known work. A prefatory letter declares that while a student at the University of Salamanca he found the first act and finished the other fifteen acts of the Burgos edition, 1499, at the rate of an act a day during a vacation period.

Modern scholarship has turned up a few more facts and made some deductions. In 1525, Alvaro de Montalbán, accused of relapses into the practice of Jewish faith, claimed that his daughter had married the "converso" Fernando de Rojas, author of *La Celestina*. "Converso" need not mean that Rojas was a new convert; indeed, it is probable that the author of this dialogue-novel was born and brought up in the Christian faith and studied under Nebrija. At all events, when he died in April, 1541, he was a member of the religious order of La Concepción de la Madre, and in his will he directed that his body be buried in the church of the Monastery of Talavera. In 1584 his grandson sought documents to prove he was an *hidalgo*, or man of pure Spanish blood traceable back through his great-grandfather.

Whoever he was, Rojas wrote a novel that critics like Cervantes praised as divine, in spite of its basically human tone, and one that all admire for its realistic character drawing. Not only are those of the lower class true to life, including the go-between Celestina, but even flowery Calisto, the lover, is a typical Petrarch-inspired *galán*. Why Rojas did not boldly claim the book can only be surmised. Perhaps as a lawyer he did not want to be known as a dabbler in fiction. Certainly he did not fear the Inquisition as a Jew, since documents proved he was respected, nor as an author, since the censors never questioned his novel until 1640, long after his death. *La Celestina* went through 120 editions in thirty-five years, with translations into Italian (1506), German (1520), and French (1527). It was the first Spanish volume put into English, in 1530.

BIBLIOGRAPHICAL REFERENCES: See C. L. Penny, *A Book Called Celestina*, 1954; also the Preface to the Clásicos Castellanos Edition, 1913; Foulché-Delbosc, "Observations sur La Célestine," in *Revue Hispanique*, VII, 28–80, IX, 171–199; R. E. House, "Notes on the Authorship of the Celestina," in *Philological Quarterly*, II, 38–47, III, 81–91; and Ruth Davis, "New data on Authorship of Act I of Calisto and Melibea," in *University of Iowa Studies* (1928); and Otis H. Green, "The Judaism of Rojas," in *Hispanic Review*, XV, 3 (1947).

ROMAIN ROLLAND

Born: Clamecy, France
Date: January 29, 1866

Died: Vézelay, France
Date: December 30, 1944

Principal Works

NOVELS: *Jean-Christophe*, 1904–1912; *Colas Breugnon*, 1919; *Clérambault*, 1920; *Pierre et Luce*, 1920; *L'Âme enchantée*, 1922–1933 (*The Soul Enchanted*).

PLAYS: *Aërt*, 1898; *Les Loups*, 1898 (*The Wolves*); *Le Triomphe de la raison*, 1899; *Danton*, 1900; *Le Quatorze Juillet*, 1902 (*The Fourteenth of July*); *Le Jeu de l'amore et de la mort*, 1924 (*The Game of Love and Death*); *Robespierre*, 1939.

BIOGRAPHY: *Vie de Beethoven*, 1903; *Vie de Michel-Ange*, 1906; *Vie de Tolstoi*, 1911; *Handel*, 1901; *Mahatma Gandhi*, 1924; *Beethoven, Les Grandes époqués créatrices*, 1929 (*Beethoven the Creator*); *Goethe et Beethoven*, 1930; *Charles Péguy*, 1944.

AUTOBIOGRAPHY: *Le Voyage intérieur*, 1942 (*The Journey Within*).

POLEMICS: *Au-dessus de la mêlée*, 1915 (*Above the Battle*).

LETTERS: *Les Cahiers des Romain Rolland et Malwida von Meysenbug, 1890–1891*, 1933.

Romain Rolland, Nobel Prize novelist, biographer, and playwright, is known primarily as the author of *Jean-Christophe*, the ten-volume story of a German musician. Rolland was born on January 29, 1866, in Clamecy, France, the son of a notary. His mother was religious and a lover of music. As a boy Rolland experienced poor health, but he amused himself with music and reading, becoming an admirer of Shakespeare.

He attended the collège in Clamecy until he was fourteen, and then continued his education at the schools St. Louis and Louis-le-grand in Paris. In 1886 he entered the École Normale Supérieure, at that time distinguished by its faculty and its scientists in residence, among them Louis Pasteur. He specialized in history with Gabriel Monod. During that period he began to make the acquaintance of distinguished writers and critics, including Ernest Renan, whose influential *Histoire des Origines du Christianisme* (1863–1883) had made him one of the most eminent of French historians, and Leo Tolstoy, author of *War and Peace*. Rolland wrote to Tolstoy because he was depressed by the materialistic life around him and wanted to discuss the matter with Tolstoy. He was also interested in Tolstoy's aesthetic theories.

In 1889 he received his bachelor's degree and went on to the École Française d'Archeologie et d'Histoire in Rome, where he studied history and archaeology. During the next two years he studied, traveled in Italy and Sicily, and formed a close friendship with the aging Malvida von Meysenbug, author of *Memoirs of an Idealist* and friend of Mazzini, Wagner, Nietzsche, and other eminent men of the period.

Rolland then returned to Paris and married Marie Bréal, daughter of Michel Bréal, the philologist. Rolland's doctorate was granted in 1895; his thesis was *The Origins of the Opera in Europe: Before Lully and Scarlatti*. His first published drama, succeeding a considerable number of unpublished dramas on the Italian Renaissance period, was *Saint Louis* (1897). While teaching at the École Normale Supérieure he became a friend of Richard Strauss, Gabriele d'Annunzio, and Eleonora Duse. In 1898 he wrote an important play, *The Wolves*, which had as its subject the Dreyfus affair. Soon afterward his friend Charles Péguy founded a fortnightly publication entitled *Cahiers de la Quinzaine*, in which, from 1900 on, Rolland published most of his important work, including *Jean-Christophe*.

Jean-Christophe established Rolland's reputation in the literary world; in it he used his hero as a device for the criticism of the materialistic emphasis in France, and the dramatic values of the work made poignant the telling analysis of contemporary culture. Upon the completion of the novel, Rolland was awarded the Grand Prize in Literature by the French Academy (1913), and two years later he received the Nobel Prize in Literature, after a recommendation by Anatole France for the French Academy.

In the meantime he suffered extreme criticism from France for the pacifist articles he wrote from Switzerland during the first World War. While in Switzerland he worked for the Red Cross and argued for peace by writing a series of careful apologetic articles. These were published as *Above the Battle* in 1915. His courageous and reasoned defense of his position against war later won him praise from many of France's outstanding intellectuals. After the war he spent two years in Paris. He then returned to Switzerland with his father and sister to live at Villeneuve, where he resided until 1938. While there he commenced an intensive study of India and made the friendship of Gandhi, subject of a biography he published in 1924.

His next important novel was the seven-volume *The Soul Enchanted*. Although this novel enhanced Rolland's reputation, it did not eclipse the standing of *Jean-Christophe* as the novelist's masterpiece.

Over a period of years Rolland advocated a people's theater, and in defense of his humanitarian philosophy wrote a series of plays on themes of revolutionary heroism. From 1900 to 1939 he wrote eight of a projected cycle of twelve plays. Before the turn of the century he had written other series of plays, among them *Les Tragédies de la foi*. He also achieved considerable distinction with his biographies, particularly with his studies of Beethoven, Michelangelo, Tolstoy, and Gandhi.

Rolland made a trip to Moscow in 1935 as the guest of Maxim Gorky, shortly before Gorky's death. While in Russia he met Stalin and other leaders of the government in Moscow. Politically, however, Rolland was bitterly opposed to totalitarian forms of government and regarded himself as a republican with socialist tendencies. During the occupation in World War II he was under house arrest by the Vichy government, but he continued to work and produced his biography of Charles Péguy. He died on December 30, 1944, at his home in Vézelay, France.

BIBLIOGRAPHICAL REFERENCES: For critical studies of Rolland in English see Stefan Zweig, *Romain Rolland, the Man and His Work*, translated 1921; Helen Whitman Machau, *The Popular Theatre Movement in France: Romain Rolland and the Revue d'art dramatique*, 1950 (pamphlet); and William Thomas Starr, *Romain*

Rolland and a World at War, 1956. See also Paul Seippel, *Romain Rolland, l'homme et l'œuvre*, 1913; P. J. Jouve, *Romain Rolland vivant, 1914–1919*, 1920; Christian Sénéchal, *Romain Rolland*, 1933; A. R. Levy, *L'idéalisme de Romain Rolland*, 1946; Maurice Descotes, *Romain Rolland*, 1948; and René Arcos, *Romain Rolland*, 1950.

O. E. RÖLVAAG

Born: Dønna, Helgeland, Norway   Died: Northfield, Minnesota
Date: April 22, 1876   Date: November 5, 1931

Principal Works

NOVELS: *Amerika-breve*, 1912 (*Letters from America*; as Paul Mørck); *Paa glemte veie*, 1914 (*On Forgotten Paths*; as Paul Mørck); *To tullinger*, 1920 (*Two Simpletons*); *Længselens baat*, 1921; *I de dage*, 1924 (*In Those Days*); *Riket grundlægges*, 1925 (*The Kingdom Is Founded*); *Giants in the Earth*, 1927 (translated from *I de dage* and *Riket grundlægges*); *Peder Seier*, 1928 (*Peder Victorious*); *Pure Gold*, 1930 (translation of *To tullinger*); *Their Father's God*, 1931 (translation of *Den signede dag*, 1931); *The Boat of Longing*, 1933 (translation of *Længselens baat*).

ESSAYS: *Omkring fædrearven*, 1925 (*Concerning Our Heritage*).

O(le) E(dvart) Rölvaag was born on April 22, 1876, on the Island of Dønna off the coast of Norway. Although his father was a veterinarian, the family was one of peasant fishermen stock, and for a time young Rölvaag also secured his livelihood from the sea. His formal education was slight, for he had only a few weeks' schooling a year. In 1896, determined to come to America, he refused the command of a fishing boat and emigrated to South Dakota. There he worked for a year on an uncle's farm to earn enough money to attend college.

At home Rölvaag had been regarded as a poor student but an avid reader, particularly the novels of Cooper, Dickens, Haggard, Marryat, Dumas, and Verne, as well as those of such Scandinavian writers as Topelius, Lie, and Bjørnson. In this country he added to his love of reading a strong incentive to learn and during the next six years achieved a brilliant record in scholarship. He first attended Augus-

tana College, a small preparatory school in Canton, South Dakota, and from there went to St. Olaf College at Northfield, Minnesota, graduating with honors in 1905. He then returned to Norway for a year of graduate study at the University of Oslo prior to accepting a position in the Department of Norwegian at St. Olaf.

His relations with St. Olaf continued until a few months before his death a quarter of a century later. He settled in Northfield, married Marie Bergdahl in 1908, and became a citizen of the United States in 1908. In 1910 he received a Master of Arts degree from St. Olaf and eventually was honored with a full professorship. His career as a writer began somewhat obscurely during these years of scholastic activity. Upon his return to St. Olaf he had written his first novel, *Nils og Astri, eller Brudstykker av Norsk-Amerikansk Folkeliv . . . Fragments of Norwegian-American Popular Life*), but this work had gone unpublished. He continued his literary efforts now with *Letters from America* which was printed in Norwegian under a pseudonym in 1912. It was Rölvaag's belief that close relationships between the American immigrants and their fellows in the homeland should be maintained, and his early novels were an attempt to secure this relationship. Written in Norwegian, they depicted the trials and the triumphs of pioneers in the New World.

Rölvaag's interest in the preservation of his homeland culture caused him some difficulty with the rise of strong national feeling during World War I, but criticism and abuse only increased his determination. He continued to write in Norwegian and to advocate the maintenance of Scandinavian folkways in the face of all opinion to the contrary. This was his belief and practice throughout his life, but eventually he was to exchange his native Norwegian for his adopted English in his creative work. This change was brought about through the help of the journalist Lincoln Colcord. Rölvaag had published two novels in Norwegian, *I de dage* and *Riket grundlægges*, both of which dealt with the struggles of the nearly Norwegian settlers in the Dakotas. Colcord, appreciating the power of these two works, persuaded Rölvaag to turn them into English,

working with him to help the novelist capture American idiom in its clearest form. The result was *Giants in the Earth*, Rölvaag's great "Saga of the Prairie," published in 1927.

Three more novels in English, *Peder Victorious, Pure Gold*, and *The Boat of Longing*, followed his first work in his adopted language, but no other could match the strength or scope of his masterpiece, and it is on *Giants in the Earth* that his reputation as a novelist still rests. The book, praised by such critics as Vernon Parrington and such fellow Midwestern writers as Carl Sandburg, has been lauded as "the finest and most powerful novel that has been written about pioneer life in America."

The success of Rölvaag's writings in English failed to diminish his interest in his native language or old-world traditions. He was made a Knight of St. Olaf by King Haakon in 1926 and was a guest of the Norwegian government at the Ibsen centennial celebration in 1927–1928. Although there were many such demands on his time, he continued his teaching in spite of the fact that he suffered from angina pectoris, a disease to which he finally succumbed at Northfield on November 5, 1931, three months after his retirement from St. Olaf.

BIBLIOGRAPHICAL REFERENCES: There is no collected edition of Rölvaag's work. The authorized biography is Theodore Jorgensen and Nora O. Solum, *Ole Edvart Rölvaag: A Biography*, 1939. The best brief account of his career is the essay by Einar Haugen in the *Dictionary of National Biography*. Perhaps the best introduction to the novels is Vernon L. Parrington, *Main Currents of American Thought*, III, 1930.

For criticism see also Julius E. Olson, "Rölvaag's Novels of Norwegian Pioneer Life in the Dakotas," *Scandinavian Studies and Notes*, IX (1926); George L. White, Jr., "Ole Edvart Rölvaag: Prophet of a People," *Scandinavian Themes in American Fiction*, 1937; Percy H. Boynton, *America in Contemporary Fiction*, 1940; Joseph E. Baker, "Western Man Against Nature: *Giants in the Earth*," *College English*, IV (1942), 19–26; and Richard Beck, "Rölvaag, Interpreter of Immigrant Life," *North Dakota Quarterly*, XXIV (1956), 26–30.

PIERRE DE RONSARD

Born: Vendômois, France
Date: September 11, 1524

Died: Touraine, France
Date: December 26 (?), 1585

PRINCIPAL WORKS

POEMS: *Odes*, Books I–IV, 1550; Book V, 1552; *Amours de Cassandre*, 1552; *Hymnes*, 1555; *Elégies, mascarades et bergeries*, 1565; *La Françiade*, 1572.

The most important literary movement in sixteenth-century France centered around the "Pléiade," a group of seven poets. Although the manifesto of the group, *Defénse et Illustration de la Langue Française*, was written by Du Bellay, Pierre de Ronsard remains the most famous of the coterie. He was born September 11, 1524, at his family's Château de la Poissonnière near Vendôme, the son of an official of the household of Francis I. After a short period at the College of Navarre in Paris, he was appointed a royal page. Later he spent three years in Great Britain and was sent on various diplomatic missions. He was a special favorite of Charles IX, who called Ronsard his "master of poetry."

The aim of the Pléiade was to reform French verse by adhering more closely to classic models: "Follow the Ancients" was their motto. This program led to a violent literary quarrel.

During the next two centuries Ronsard's reputation waned. He was revived by the Romanticists; but the standard French criticism is still that the Pléiade "over-classicized" French poetry. However, the charm of Ronsard's nature-verse and the magnificence of his language and metrics are admitted and admired. Ronsard died at the priory of St.-Côme near Tours and was buried December 27, 1585.

BIBLIOGRAPHICAL REFERENCES: The best studies of Ronsard in English are D. B. Wyndham Lewis, *Ronsard*, 1944, and an earlier study by Humbert Wolfe, *Ronsard and French Romantic Poetry*, 1935. For biographical and critical studies in French see P. Champion, *Ronsard et son temps*, 1905; P. de Nolhac, *Ronsard et 'l'humanisme*, 1921; and P. Laumonier, *Ronsard*, 1923.

CHRISTINA ROSSETTI

Born: London, England
Date: December 5, 1830

Died: London
Date: December 29, 1894

PRINCIPAL WORKS

POEMS: *Goblin Market and Other Poems*, 1862; *The Prince's Progress and Other Poems*, 1866; *Sing Song*, 1872; *A Pageant and Other Poems*, 1881; *Verses*, 1893; *New Poems*, 1896.

DEVOTIONAL STUDIES: *Speaking Likenesses*, 1874; *Seek and Find*, 1879; *Called Be the Saints*, 1881; *Letter and Spirit*, 1882; *Time Flies*, 1885; *The Face of the Deep*, 1892.

Christina (Georgina) Rossetti, born in London on December 5, 1830, was the sister of Dante Gabriel Rossetti, and the youngest child of a Neapolitan

918

political refugee who had settled in England and who became, eventually, Professor of Italian at King's College, University of London. She began to write poetry very early in her life, and when she was seventeen a small volume of her work was printed at her grandfather's private press. A year later, in 1848, one of her lyrics was published in *The Athenaeum*. When Dante Gabriel Rossetti founded the Pre-Raphaelite magazine, *The Germ*, in 1850, she became one of its frequent contributors, using the pseudonym Ellen Alleyn. Twelve years later her first volume, *Goblin Market and Other Poems*, appeared publicly. She continued to write until the end of her life, but only four more volumes, including her poems for children, were published during her lifetime.

Although her creative life extended over a long period, her output, in terms of quantity, was not extensive for two reasons. The first had to do with the form of the poetry she wrote and the fact that she was essentially a composer of brief lyrics. Like precious gems, they were small but clear and of exceeding value; but since she wrote only when she felt the possibility of perfection, her work was understandably limited. The other reason for her small poetic output was her extreme religious devotion. As she grew older she turned more and more from her poetry to the writing of her religious prose, expending her creative energy on this less artistic genre. Yet it cannot be said that her religious interests worked against her poetry, for the poetry itself is imbued completely with her religious feelings. Some lyrics, such as "Three Enemies," "Weary in Well-Doing," and "A Better Resurrection" are specifically religious in theme and subject matter. In all she wrote, at the root if not in stalk and branch, is her religious preoccupation.

This preoccupation was dominant in her personality as well. Sickly most of her life, and an actual invalid during her last years, she turned more and more from the world until she became almost a complete recluse. In her youth she had refused two different suitors because they did not conform to her Church of England beliefs and had chosen instead to remain with her equally devout mother. Having channeled all of her emotional energies into her religion, nevertheless in the end she was tormented by doubt, not of her beliefs but of her own worthiness. It was in this spirit that she cried out, "My life is like a faded leaf/My harvest dwindled to a husk," taking no consolation in the fact that the pure freshness of some of her lyrics will remain green for centuries. She died in London on December 29, 1894.

BIBLIOGRAPHICAL REFERENCES: The standard edition of the *Poetical Works* was edited by William Michael Rossetti, 1904 (rev. ed., 1924). For biography and criticism see H. T. M. Bell, *Christina Rosetti: A Biographical and Critical Study*, 1898; Justine de Wilde, *Christina Rossetti, Poet and Woman*, 1923; M. F. Sandars, *The Life of Christina Rossetti*, 1930; Dorothy M. Stuart, *Christina Rossetti*, English Men of Letters Series, 1930; Fredegond Shove, *Christina Rossetti: A Study*, 1931; and Eleanor W. Thomas, *Christina Georgina Rossetti*, 1931. For background studies of the Rossetti family and the period see also R. D. Waller, *The Rossetti Family, 1824–1854*, 1932; and Frances Winwar, *Poor Splendid Wings: The Rossettis and*

DANTE GABRIEL ROSSETTI

Born: London, England
Date: May 12, 1828

Died: Birchington, England
Date: April 9, 1882

PRINCIPAL WORKS

POEMS: *Poems,* 1870; *Ballads and Sonnets,* 1881; *Collected Works,* 1886.
TRANSLATIONS: *Early Italian Poets,* 1861 (retitled *Dante and His Circle,* 1874).

Dante Gabriel Rossetti was born in London, May 12, 1828, the son of Gabriele Rossetti, a political refugee from Naples, and the brother of Christina, the poet, and of William Michael Rossetti, later to be the historian of the Pre-Raphaelites. He attended King's College School in London and then various art schools, finally becoming a pupil of Ford Madox Brown. It was in 1848 that Rossetti, Millais, and Holman Hunt founded the Pre-Raphaelite Brotherhood that was to be a storm center in English art for many years. In 1850 they began their magazine, *The Germ,* in which Rossetti published some of his early poems. The paintings of the group were bitterly attacked by Dickens and by the conventional critics; it was only through the influence of Ruskin, then the aesthetic dictator of art and culture, that the public finally accepted the Pre-Raphaelites and their work.

In 1851 Rossetti became engaged to Elizabeth Siddall, whose peculiar beauty had fascinated him and who had become his model; but they were not married until 1860. She was consumptive; their marriage was unhappy because of Rossetti's increasing indifference, and in 1862 she died of an overdose of laudanum, probably a suicide. Then followed the melodramatic

gesture of Rossetti's burying the only manuscript of his poems in her coffin and the gruesome sequel of their exhumation in 1869.

Very early, Rossetti came under the influence of Percy's *Reliques* (1765), the poems of Scott, and various medieval romances; and these influences, plus the avowed medievalism of the Pre-Raphaelites, gave to his poetry its special tone. He excelled in the imitation or adaption of the border ballads; his "Sister Helen" has been considered one of the best literary ballads of the nineteenth century. To the stark language of the old poems he added the luxuriant coloring and mysticism of the Pre-Raphaelites. His sonnet-sequence, "The House of Life," inspired by his love for Elizabeth Siddall, has also been highly praised. Pre-Raphaelite poetry is out of fashion now, being considered overly-decorated and artificial; yet at the time it was a relief from the didacticism of much Victorian verse.

After 1868 Rossetti became subject to fits of melancholia aggravated by the attack on him in 1871 by Robert Buchanan, in an anonymous essay, "The Fleshly School of Poetry." His failing eyesight eventually made him abandon painting for poetry. His last years were made bearable only through the devoted attention of his brother. He died April 9, 1882, at Birchington, near Margate.

BIBLIOGRAPHICAL REFERENCES: Biographical and critical studies of Rossetti are extensive, and there are numerous collections of his letters. Of particular interest is D. G. Rossetti's Family Letters, edited by William M. Rossetti, 1895, who also edited Pre-Raphaelite Diaries and Letters, 1900, and Rossetti Papers, 1862–1870, 1903. Biographical and critical studies include William M. Rossetti, Ruskin, Rossetti: Pre-Raphaelitism, 1899; F. G. Stephens, D. G. Rossetti, 1894; A. C. Benson, Rossetti, in the English Men of Letters Series, 1904; Evelyn Waugh, Rossetti: His Life and Work, 1928; R. L. Mégroz, Dante Gabriel Rossetti, 1929; Viola Hunt, The Wife of Rossetti, 1932; Frances V. Winwar, Poor Splendid Wings, 1933; idem, The Rossettis and Their Circle, 1934; William Gaunt, The Pre-Raphaelite Tragedy, 1942; O. Doughty, A Victorian Romantic: D. G. Rossetti, 1949; Gordon Hough, The Last Romantics, 1949; and J. Heath-Stubbs, The Darkling Plain, 1950.

EDMOND ROSTAND

Born: Marseilles, France
Date: April 1, 1868

Died: Paris, France
Date: December 2, 1918

PRINCIPAL WORKS

PLAYS: Les Romanesques, 1894 (The Romancers); La Princesse lointaine, 1895 (The Faraway Princess); La Samaritaine, 1897 (The Woman of Samaria); Cyrano de Bergerac, 1897; L'Aiglon, 1900 (The Eaglet); Chantecler, 1910; Le Bois sacré, 1909 (The Sacred Wood); La dernière nuit de Don Juan, 1921 (Don Juan's Last Night).

POEMS: Les Musardises, 1890.

This descendant of Corneille and Hugo, the last great romanticist of the theater, was born in Marseilles, April 1, 1868, the son of a prominent journalist and economist. Like so many other dramatists, his education was in law, although his interest was in poetry. Again, like many other writers, his first publication was a book of verse, Les Musardises, which appeared in 1890. The fact that he lived in comfortable means made it possible for him to write as little as he pleased, though he did put a polish of romance and a luster of history—and histrionics—on all his theater pieces.

In 1890 he married the poetess Rosemonde Gérard and settled in Paris as a professional writer. While he never sought praise or even approval—indeed his inclinations and interests and tastes ran counter to the feeling of the times —he won both in the 1894 Comédie Française production of The Romancers, a slight comedy in which the young lovers take their cues from Romeo and Juliet. For Sarah Bernhardt he wrote several plays; in The Faraway Princess she played the title role, falling in love with a troubadour; in L'Aiglon the Divine Sarah essayed the role of Napoleon's ineffectual son.

Edmond Rostand's penchant for writing starring roles for outstanding actors gave the world its most famous poetic drama, the historical romance, Cyrano de Bergerac, starring the great Coquelin. Before the year of its pro-

921

duction ended, the play had been translated into several languages, and it has been produced everywhere in the civilized world. The swashbuckling hero, a romanticized version of the historical personage bearing that same name, is a household word standing for the idealist who refused to give in to the demands of the world.

So great was the young playwright's reputation that in 1900 he was appointed an Officer of the Legion of Honor, and in 1901 he became a member of the French Academy. His health failing in that same year, he built a villa in southern France where he lived most of the time until his death in Paris, December 2, 1918. His writing was affected by ill health and diminished energy, but he did write one more play which has, especially here in America in the last ten years, received more and more attention. *Chantecler* was also written for Coquelin, who died before it was finished; Lucien Guitry, however, took on the role of the famous rooster who thought that he was the one who brought the sun up in the morning. The slight fable-satire has some of Rostand's best writing in it, and it perfectly expresses its author's disillusioned point of view: Chantecler finds that while he does not control the world he can at least tend valiantly his own henyard.

Few critics consider Rostand much more than a one-play author, but a consideration of his last play, based on the Don Juan theme of self-delusion, would lead one to think that his best plays might have been yet to come. In this and other plays he shows himself a master of language, subtle irony, magnificent spectacle, and ingenious manipulation. In a time when sordid realism seemed to win the day, theatergoers everywhere were grateful for the light touch of fantasy and romance; and while Rostand did not change the temper or the times, he at least managed to make time stand still in the romantic world of his creation.

BIBLIOGRAPHICAL REFERENCES: *The Plays of Edmond Rostand*, translated by Henderson Daingerfield and published in 1921. A good edition of *Cyrano de Bergerac* is that translated by Brian Hooker, with an introduction by Clayton Hamilton, Modern Library, 1951. There is no standard biography in English, but a brief life is found in the first chapter of Hobart Ryland, *The Sources of the Play "Cyrano de Bergerac,"* 1936. This book also contains a brief bibliography in addition to its main critical contents. Biographies in French include Paul Faure, *Vingt Ans d'Intimité avec Edmond Rostand*, 1928; M. J. Premsela, *Edmond Rostand*, 1933; and Rosemonde Gerard, *Edmond Rostand*, 1935. Essays in books include those by Edward Everett Hale, Jr., in *Dramatists of Today*, 1910; G. K. Chesterton, *Twelve Types*, 1910; B. H. Clark, *Contemporary French Dramatists*, 1915; A. Duclaux, *Twentieth Century French Writers*, 1919; Eugène Évrard, *Nos Mandarins*, 1920; F. W. Chandler, *The Contemporary Drama of France*, 1921; W. L. Phelps, *Essays on Modern Dramatists*, 1921; and Hugh Allison Smith, *Main Currents of Modern French Drama*, 1928. Short critical essays are the Count de Soissons "Edmond Rostand," *Contemporary Review*, CXV (1919), 188–195; Stark Young's review of Walter Hampden in *Cyrano de Bergerac*, *New Republic*, XXXVII (1923), 18–19; Philip Lewis, "The Idealism of Rostand," *Contemporary Review*, CLXXIV (1948), 34–37; and C. D. Brenner, "Rostand's *Cyrano de Bergerac*: An Interpretation," *Studies in Philology*, XLVI (1949), 603–611.

JEAN JACQUES ROUSSEAU

Born: Geneva, Switzerland
Date: June 28, 1712

Died: Ermenonville, France
Date: July 2, 1778

PRINCIPAL WORKS

NOVELS: *Julie ou La Nouvelle Héloïse,* 1760 (*The New Héloïse*); *Émile, ou de l'éducation,* 1762 (*Émile*).

MEMOIRS: *Les Confessions,* 1784.

ESSAYS AND STUDIES: *Discours sur les arts et sciences,* 1750; *Discours sur l'inégalité des conditions,* 1754; *Lettre à d'Alembert sur les spectacles,* 1758; *Contrat social,* 1762; *Lettres de la montagne,* 1763; *Rêveries d'un promeneur solitaire,* 1782; *Dialogues,* 1784.

Jean Jacques Rousseau, French philosopher, novelist, and essayist, was born June 28, 1712, in Geneva. The fact that his mother died at his birth he referred to as the first of his misfortunes. When he was twelve years old his father, a watchmaker of restless disposition, abandoned him, and he was placed by an uncle under the tutelage of a pastor of Boissy. Himself a man of many moods and little stability, Rousseau's life was made up of wanderings and positions held for very short periods of time until he settled, more or less, to a life as a writer.

At fourteen he was apprenticed to an engraver; at sixteen he ran away and contacted a Catholic priest who sent him to Madame Louise de Warens at Annecy. She in turn sent him to the seminary of Turin, where it is reported he was converted to Catholicism in nine days. For brief periods he was a lackey in two aristocratic households but returned eventually to Annecy. His study for the priesthood lasted two months. He studied music and gave a very unsuccessful concert, but he did obtain a few pupils. Next he tried to find employment in Paris but failed and returned to Madame de Warens. He also turned down the position she obtained for him as clerk

in the census bureau. This was at the age of nineteen. For the next eleven years he lived as Madame de Warens' protégé, lover, and intendant. At her small farm he began his first serious reading and studying for a musical and literary career.

When he was thirty years old, he met two influential ladies in Paris and through them many writers, musicians, and scientists. Diderot became an intimate friend. Through his associations he became secretary to the Comte de Montaigu, French ambassador in Venice, but he was dismissed from his post following a quarrel after one year. About 1744 he took as his mistress a servant, Thérèse Levasseur. Reportedly they had five children whom he consigned to a foundling home. They were married twenty years later.

Rousseau achieved sudden fame in 1750 with his prize winning *Discours sur les arts et sciences* given before the academy of Dijon. To the academy's contest question, "Have the arts and sciences contributed to improve morals?" Rousseau answered impassionately in the negative. Quite the contrary, wrote Rousseau, in that the arts and sciences, the results of institutions and civilization, tended to corrupt man's natural goodness. Furthermore, only countries (no examples cited) which are strong and virtuous are able to retain primitive simplicity. His third main point was that the rewards of progress are corruption and military defeat.

Three years later he competed for another prize at Dijon, the subject being the origin of inequality among men, and whether it is authorized by natural law. In his *Discours sur l'iné-galité des conditions* he said that in mankind's march from the original state of nature to modern society, the tribal state is the happiest one; in this, the natural, primitive state, there are no inequalities of social position, rank, or inherited wealth. Furthermore, all development beyond this tribal period he condemned for the introduction of private property, an inequality result-ing in a handful of the mighty and the rich as against millions living in squalor and obscurity.

Rousseau preached that the trouble with the world was that selfish laws and customs and spiritual bigotry—ab-solutism in state and church—had changed man's natural bent and cut him off from the heritage of equality, reason, and benevolence.

Although these ideas were not new, nor his alone by any means, their very real significance lay in the fact that Rousseau presented them concretely at one of those culminating points of his-tory. His ideas became the battle cry of a new age and found powerful ex-pression in the French Revolution, and they also permeated nineteenth cen-tury literature. Rousseau has been called the "father of Romanticism" be-cause of the influence he exerted on Wordsworth and Shelley in England and on Herder, Schiller, and Kant in Germany.

He tended to break the hold of all external sanctions in state, church, lit-erature, and society. Individual free-dom he exalted; constituted authority he condemned. By temperament and training he was averse to control and restraint. He believed in natural im-pulse as opposed to discipline, in emo-tion as against reason. He established the predominance of feeling over the patient investigation of fact.

His *The New Héloïse* and *Émile* further exemplify his chief paradox that a barbarian (the natural man) is superior to a modern European. *The New Héloïse* is the story of Julie, a baron's daughter who marries a count after she has had a scandalous affair with a young man of the middle class. The count asks the young man to join them in "a union of hearts." Note-worthy in the rather tedious work is Rousseau's interest in the common people coupled with his glorifications of nature. *Émile* has given him the title of "father of modern education." It would seem that his ideal system of education was the one that least hin-dered the development of the pupil's native or natural bent.

In *Contrat social* ("Man is born free and everywhere he is in chains"), he developed the theories of Hooker and Locke that all government rests upon the consent of the governed. His ideal government was one which least checks the individual and gives to the indi-vidual the maximum of direct control in all state affairs.

The deistic doctrine expressed in *Émile* (Rousseau is termed an "emo-tional" deist) was opposed by the Catholic Church. To avoid arrest Rous-seau went to Berne and to Prussia. His reply to the attack made upon *Émile* by the Archbishop of Paris was his famous *Lettre à M. de Beaumont* (1763).

Expelled from Geneva, his house stoned, Rousseau went to England at the invitation of David Hume, whom he later suspected of conspiring with his enemies. He returned to France and finally settled in Paris in 1770. There he completed his *Confessions* and in 1776 wrote a series of dialogues with himself. *Rêveries d'un promeneur solitaire* also belongs to this period. He died at Ermenonville, near Paris, of apoplexy, on July 2, 1778.

BIBLIOGRAPHICAL REFERENCES: The standard biography is John Morley's *Rousseau*, 1873. Other biographical and critical studies in English include Frederika Macdonald, *Jean Jacques Rousseau*, 2 vols., 1906; Irving Babbitt, *Rousseau and Romanticism*, 1919; and Matthew Josephson, *Jean-Jacques Rousseau*, 1931; in French, E. Ritter, *La Famille et jeunesse de Rousseau*, 1896; Jules Lemaître, *Jean-Jacques Rousseau*, 1907; L. Ducros, *Jean-Jacques Rousseau de Genève à l'Hermitage, 1712–1757*, 1908; and Albert Schinz, *La Pensée de Jean-Jacques Rousseau*, 1929. See also the *Annales de la Société Jean-Jacques Rousseau*, 1905 ff.

JUAN RUIZ DE ALARCÓN

Born: Taxco, Mexico
Date: c. 1581

Died: Córdoba, Spain
Date: August 4, 1639

PRINCIPAL WORKS

PLAYS: *El tejedor de Segovia,* (*The Weaver of Segovia*); *Las paredes oyen,* (*Walls Have Ears*); *La verdad sospechosa,* (*Truth Suspected*).

One of the four great dramatists of Spain's Golden Age, Juan Ruiz de Alarcón y Mendoza, the most modern in spirit, was born at Taxco, Mexico, about 1581, and educated in Mexico before he went to Spain in 1600 for postgraduate study. Back in Mexico in 1608, Ruiz de Alarcón hoped to teach in the University. Rejected because of his hunchback, he left Mexico forever in 1613.

How much of his dramatic technique is due to his Mexican upbringing has been much discussed, for few of his twenty-four recognized comedies mention his homeland. As a dramatist he was more interested in character and less in plot than was Lope de Vega, and his thesis plays, illustrating moral truths through a character personifying a vice, greatly influenced Corneille, Molière, and the Italian Goldoni.

Because playwriting was only an avocation, beyond his regular work on the Council of the Indies, the professional dramatists hated and reviled Ruiz de Alarcón, and performances of his plays were frequently interrupted by unexplained accidents on the stage. Discouraged, he did little writing during the last ten years of his life. Collections of his plays were printed in 1628 and 1634. He died in Córdoba, Spain, on August 4, 1639.

BIBLIOGRAPHICAL REFERENCES: Ruiz de Alarcón's *Comedias escogidas* (*Selected Comedies*) were published in Madrid, 2 vols., 1867, and in *Classicos Castellanos*, 1918. For studies in English see James Fitzmaurice Kelly, *Chapters on Spanish Literature*, 1908, and Dorothy Schons, "The Mexican Background of Alarcón,"

Publications of the Modern Language Association, LVII (1942), 89–104; in Spanish, Rodríguez Marín, Data para la biografía de Ruiz de Alarcón, 1912; Pedro Henríquez Ureña, Don Juan Ruiz de Alarcón, 1915 (Havana); Julio Jiménez Rueda, Ruiz de Alarcón y su tiempo, 1939 (Mexico); Antonio Castro Leal, Ruiz de Alarcón, su vida y su obra, 1943 (Mexico); and Genaro Fernández MacGregor, "La Mexicanidad de Alarcón," in Letras de Mexico, II, 8 (August 15, 1939).

JOHN RUSKIN

Born: London, England
Date: February 8, 1819

Died: Brantwood, Coniston, England
Date: January 20, 1900

PRINCIPAL WORKS

ART CRITICISM: *Modern Painters,* Vols. I–V, 1843–1860; *The Seven Lamps of Architecture,* 1849; *Pre-Raphaelitism,* 1850; *The Stones of Venice,* Vols. I–III, 1851–1853; *Lectures on Art,* 1870; *Aratra Pentelici,* 1871; *The Eagle's Nest,* 1872; *Ariadne Florentina,* 1873–1876; *Val d'Arno,* 1874; *Mornings in Florence,* 1875–1877; *St. Mark's Rest: The History of Venice,* 1877–1884; *The Bible of Amiens,* 1880–1885; *Lectures on Landscape,* 1898.

SOCIAL CRITICISM: *The Construction of Sheepfolds,* 1851; *Unto This Last,* 1860, 1862; *Munera Pulveris,* 1862; *Sesame and Lilies,* 1865; *The Ethics of the Dust,* 1866; *The Crown of Wild Olive,* 1866; *Time and Tide,* 1867; *Fors Clavigera,* 1871–1884.

NATURE STUDIES: *Proserpina,* 1875–1886; *Love's Meinie,* 1873–1878; *Deucalion,* 1875–1883.

NOVELLA: *The King of the Golden River,* 1851.

AUTOBIOGRAPHY: *Praeterita,* 1885–1889.

During his lifetime John Ruskin acted in several capacities as a man of letters, writing as an aesthetician, an art historian, a poet, a writer of a fairy tale, and as the author of works on reform and economics. Born in London, February 8, 1819, he was the only child of parents who could and did lavish upon him a great deal of wealth and affection. In addition to study at King's College, in London, and at Christ Church College, Oxford, he traveled extensively through Europe. As early as 1837–1838 he wrote a series of articles on "The Poetry of Architecture" for *London's Architectural Magazine.* A defense of Turner's painting led him to write the voluminous *Modern Painters,* which appeared

volume by volume from 1843 to 1860. The work became a treatise on art in general, a defense of painting being done at the time, and a formulation of the five categories Ruskin believed conveyed by art: power, imitation, truth, beauty, and relation.

In 1848 Ruskin married Euphemia Chalmers Gray, then nineteen years old, for whom he had written his novel-fairy tale, *The King of the Golden River,* in 1841. The marriage was unsuccessful and was annulled in 1854, with Miss Gray later marrying Millais, the artist, in the following year. Millais and other Pre-Raphaelite artists were friends of Ruskin, who supported their movement, especially in *The Stones of Venice.* After 1857

Ruskin became interested in writing as a social reformer, his most famous works in this vein being *Unto This Last*. As a reformer Ruskin also helped found the Working Men's College in London in 1854, and he gave lessons in drawing and lectured to groups at that institution. During the 1860's Ruskin wrote much and lectured, despite mental illness. One important book of this period was *Sesame and Lilies,* a collection of essays on aesthetic topics addressed primarily to young people. From 1870 to 1890 he wrote and traveled between increasingly severe attacks of mental illness, and the last decade of his life has been described, because of his condition, as a living death. He died at Brantwood, Coniston, England, on January 20, 1900.

BIBLIOGRAPHICAL REFERENCES: The *Works* of Ruskin have been edited by E. T. Cook and Alexander Wedderburn, 39 vols., 1903–1912; this includes an extensive bibliography. A useful selection is P. C. Quennell's edition of *Selected Writings,* 1952. The most thorough biography is E. T. Cook, *The Life of John Ruskin,* 2 vols., 1911. Three briefer biographical studies are Frederick Harrison, *John Ruskin,* English Men of Letters Series, 1902; A. Williams-Ellis, *The Exquisite Tragedy: An Intimate Life of John Ruskin,* 1928; and P. C. Quennell, *Ruskin: The Portrait of a Prophet,* 1949. A valuable handbook is R. H. Wilenski, *John Ruskin: An Introduction to Further Study of his Life and Work,* 1933. Advanced readers may consult H. A. Ladd, *The Victorian Morality of Art: An Analysis of Ruskin's Esthetic,* 1932. A provocative essay on Ruskin appears in Virginia Woolf, *The Captain's Death Bed and Other Essays,* 1950.

W. CLARK RUSSELL

Born: New York, N. Y.
Date: February 24, 1844

Died: Bath, England
Date: November 8, 1911

PRINCIPAL WORKS

NOVELS: *John Holdsworth, Chief Mate,* 1875; *The Wreck of the Grosvenor,* 1877; *My Watch Below,* 1822; *Round the Galley Fire,* 1883; *The Romance of a Midshipman,* 1898.

POEMS: *The Turnpike Sailor,* 1907.

W(illiam) Clark Russell, though of English parentage, was born in New York City, February 24, 1844. His father, Henry Russell, a well-known singer, was playing in America at the time. His mother, Isabella Lloyd Russell, was a distant relative of Wordsworth and herself a writer. W. Clark Russell entered the maritime service at the age of thirteen and remained until 1865. Prior to sea service he had been educated at Winchester School, in England, and abroad. After retiring from the sea he worked for several British newspapers, including the Newcastle *Daily Chronicle* and the London *Daily Telegraph,* staying with the latter until 1889. In 1874 Russell began writing, intending a career as a popular novelist, and during the remainder of his life produced the very remarkable total of fifty-seven volumes. His output included novels of life at sea, lives of Dampier (1889), Nelson (1890), and Collingwood (1891), several collections of short stories, and a volume of light, entertaining poetry

Although his works have never had serious scholarly consideration, they were read and admired by a whole generation of British readers. His best-known work, and the only one with a lasting body of readers, is *The Wreck of the Grosvenor,* one of his earliest novels. During the late nineteenth century many reforms came about in the British merchant marine, and part of the credit has usually been bestowed upon Russell and his books, which brought public attention to the need for improving what were admittedly deplorable conditions. Russell, who was the father of Sir Herbert Russell, a well-known writer on naval subjects, died at Bath, November 8, 1911.

BIBLIOGRAPHICAL REFERENCES: There is no authorized biography, almost no criticism. See W. J. Ward's memoir, "A National Asset," printed as an introduction to *Fathers of the Sea,* 1911. For a study of Russell in relation to his time and literary generation see also R. R. Bowker, "London as a Literary Center," *Harper's,* LXXVII (1888), 3–26.

VIKTOR RYDBERG

Born: Jönköping, Sweden
Date: December 18, 1828

Died: Stockholm, Sweden
Date: September 22, 1895

PRINCIPAL WORKS

NOVELS: *Fribytaren på Ostersjön,* 1857 (*The Freebooter of the Baltic*); *Singoalla,* 1858; *Den siste Athenaren,* 1859 (*The Last Athenian*); *Vapensmeden,* 1891 (*The Armorer*).
ESSAYS: *Romerskadagar,* 1875–1876 (*Roman Days*).
POEMS: *Dikter,* 1882.

(Abraham) Viktor Rydberg, born at Jönköping into a lower class Swedish family on December 18, 1828, had a difficult childhood. It may have been this hard period which turned him toward the later romantic writing for which he became famous. Influenced in his early youth by contemporary liberal pressures, he studied at the University of Lund and in 1854 turned to journalism.

In 1855 he joined the staff of the leading newspaper of the city of Göteborg, and his romantic novels first appeared as serials in the columns of this newspaper. The first of these works, *The Freebooter of the Baltic,* won him some acclaim; it contains evidences of the idealism that was to be more fully developed in his later novels. Of his novels, *The Last Athenian* is the most famous. By the time it appeared in 1859, Rydberg was generally regarded in the first rank of Swedish novelists.

Turning to religion, he produced the first Swedish modern critical study of the Bible, *The Bible's Teaching about Christ* (1862). Besides his work in the novel and in theological criticism he also produced a great deal of material in the fields of aesthetics, philosophy, and psychology. His translation of Goethe's *Faust* in 1876 shows the profound influence that the earlier German writer had upon Rydberg's romanticism.

Rydberg appeared on the Swedish literary scene after a relatively barren period. Historically, he was one of the last of the Romanticists, and certainly one of the few idealists of the period, but his romantic idealism has survived the opposing naturalism that was soon to follow in Scandinavian literature. He died in Stockholm on September 22, 1895.

BIBLIOGRAPHICAL REFERENCES: There is almost no helpful criticism of Rydberg in English. The most comprehensive study is K. Warburg, *Viktor Rydberg, en levnadsteckning*, 2 vols., 1900. See also Ö. Lindberger, *Prometeustanken hos Viktor Rydberg*, 2 vols., 1938. A brief study of his verse is Charles Wharton Stork's essay, "The Poetry of Viktor Rydberg," in *Schelling Anniversary Papers*, edited by A. C Baugh, 1923.

HANS SACHS

Born: Nuremberg, Germany
Date: November 5, 1494

Died: Nuremberg
Date: January 19, 1576

PRINCIPAL WORKS

PLAYS: *Die Wittenbergisch Nachtigall*, 1523 (*The Wittenberg Nightingale*); *Lucretia*, 1527; *Der farendt Schüler im Paradeis*, 1550 (*The Wandering Scholar from Paradise*); *Das heisse Eisen*, 1551 (*The Hot Iron*); *Die ungleichen Kinder Evä*, 1553; *Das Narrenschneiden*, date uncertain.

Lovers of Wagner will recognize the *meistersinger* Hans Sachs, the greatest of his time, as the principal character in *Die Meistersinger*. Surprisingly, his present fame does not rest on his songs and poems but on the 208 dramas which helped keep the German theater alive in the sixteenth century.

Sachs was born and died in Nuremberg, a contemporary and disciple of Martin Luther, having been born November 5, 1494. He forsook his early training as a shoemaker to become a wandering troubador, the highest calling in a day when the arts were revered with more than lip service. His apprenticeship over, he became master of his guild in 1517. After fifty years of composition he was said to have composed, before he died on January 19, 1576, more than four thousand songs, two thousand tales in verse, and 208 plays, thirty-four volumes in all exclusive of the songs which were not collected for publication. His plays were in the folk tradition of the *Fastnachtsspiel*, the humorous plays for Shrovetide, a form paralleling the development of drama in England at the same time. But Germany was torn by strife over the Reformation and consequently had little patience with delightful trifles. Even Sachs, who wrote a poem of tribute to Luther, was forbidden to write for some few years until his own town sided with the reformer.

The avidity with which Hans Sachs wrote, the propitious times in which he lived, and the care with which his works were preserved all contribute to the great knowledge we have of this man and his work. Wagner was justly paying tribute to one of the men on whose shoulders he stood.

BIBLIOGRAPHICAL REFERENCES: There are various editions of the works of Hans Sachs in German. For critical commentary see Francis M. Ellis, *Hans Sachs Studies*, 1941; and John Gassner, *Masters of the Drama*, 1945.

CHARLES AUGUSTIN SAINTE-BEUVE

Born: Boulogne-sur-Mer, France
Date: December 23, 1804

Died: Paris, France
Date: October 13, 1869

PRINCIPAL WORKS

CRITICISM: *Tableau historique et critique de la poésie française au XVIe siecle*, 1827; *Portraits littéraires*, 1832–1839; *Histoire de Port Royal*, 1840–1848; *Portraits littéraires* (Second Series), 1844; *Portraits de femmes*, 1844; *Portraits contemporains*, 1846; *Châteaubriand et son groupe*, 1849; *Causeries de lundi*, 1851–1862 (*Monday Chats*); *Étude sur Virgile*, 1857; *Nouveaux lundis*, 1863–1870; *Premiers lundis*, 1874–1875.

POEMS: *La vie, les poésies et les pensées de J. Delorme*, 1829 (*The Life, Poems, and Thoughts of Joseph Delorme*); *Consolations*, 1830; *Pensées d'août*, 1837 (*Harvest Thoughts*).

NOVEL: *Volupté*, 1832.

Charles Augustin Sainte-Beuve, the greatest literary critic since Aristotle, was born to humble conditions, a posthumous child whose mother could ill-afford the education his brilliance demanded. After beginning his education in Boulogne, where he was born on December 23, 1804, he completed his studies in the Collège Charlemagne and the Collège Bourbon, in Paris. When a former teacher invited his bright student to write reviews for *Le Globe*, Sainte-Beuve abandoned the study of medicine, begun a year before, and devoted his time to writing.

Although he wrote for the influential *Globe*, and so gained the attention of Goethe and Victor Hugo, and for *La Revue de Paris* as well, his early reputation was largely bound in with *La Revue des Deux Mondes*. The columns he wrote for these papers he collected in seven volumes of *Portraits*. During this period of his life he fell in love with Adèle, wife of Victor Hugo, an affair which caused a separa-

tion from his old friend and fellow writer. In 1844 he was elected to the French Academy; he was received there by Hugo, with whom he had become reconciled. Through an error in posting, he was accused of receiving money for intelligence work in the 1848 revolution; consequently, he resigned his post in the Mazarin Library and went to teach French literature at the University of Liége. Another teaching post he held was at the École Normale Superieure from 1858 to 1862; he had previously resigned the chair in Latin poetry at the Collège de France after a few lectures.

Sainte-Beuve, who prided himself on his workaday journalism, produced his greatest series of critical articles in his *Monday Chats*, written for *Le Constitutionnel* and later for *Le Moniteur*. These, when collected, eventually filled fifteen volumes. Thirteen additional volumes were accumulated from his final series, *Nouveaux lundis*. Of all the literary figures of the period, he alone continued to write and prosper under the Empire, and he was made a senator in 1865. In the last year of his life he severed his connection with the official government journal, *Moniteur*, as the result of a political dispute. He died, unable longer to write even for the cause of the new freedom, in Paris on October 13, 1869.

Although he wrote poetry and a novel, Sainte-Beuve's reputation rests on his literary portraits of French authors and his analysis of their works. His classic definition of a literary classic is included in every compilation of criticism; his books are familiar to students everywhere. Attempts to discredit him, begun during his lifetime, have never been successful because his position is virtually unassailable.

BIBLIOGRAPHICAL REFERENCES: The most recent critical biography in English is Sir Harold Nicolson, *Sainte-Beuve*, 1957. An earlier study that is still useful is George McLean Harper, *Sainte-Beuve*, 1909. See also Lewis Freeman Mott, *Sainte-Beuve*, 1925. For biography and criticism in French see Gabriel D'Haussonville, *Sainte-Beauve, sa vie et ses œuvres*, 1875; Gustave Michaut, *Sainte-Beuve*, 1921; L. F. Choisy, *Sainte-Beuve, l'homme et le poète*, 1921; Victor Giraud, *La vie secrète de Sainte-Beuve*, 1935; Maxime Leroy, *La pensée de Sainte-Beuve*, 1940, and *Vie de Sainte-Beuve*, 1947; André Billy, *Sainte-Beuve, sa vie et son temps*, 1952; and Maurice Allemand, *Portrait de Sainte-Beuve*, 1954. For briefer studies see, further, Mary Fisher, *A Group of French Critics*, 1897; and Gustav Pollak, *International Perspective in Criticism*, 1914.

ANTOINE DE SAINT-EXUPÉRY

Born: Lyons, France
Date: June 29, 1900

Died: Southern France
Date: July 31 (?), 1944

PRINCIPAL WORKS

NOVELS: *Courrier sud*, 1928 (*Southern Mail*); *Vol de nuit*, 1931 (*Night Flight*).

ESSAYS: *Terre des hommes*, 1939 (*Wind, Sand, and Stars*); *Pilote de Guerre*, 1942 (*Flight to Arras*); *Lettre à un otage*, 1944 (*Letter to a Hostage*); *Citadelle*, 1948 (*The Wisdom of the Sands*).

JUVENILE: *Le petit prince*, 1943 (*The Little Prince*).

Antoine de Saint-Exupéry, born in Lyons, France, on June 29, 1900, joined the French Army Air Force in 1921. After serving as a pilot, he left the Air Force in 1926 and became a commercial pilot flying the routes from France to West Africa and South America. At the same time he began to write about flying, producing first a novel, *Southern Mail*, in which a young French aristocrat, full of impossibly romantic notions, first faces the realities of life and an unhappy love affair through the discipline of flying. In his next novel, *Night Flight*, Saint-Exupéry further developed the importance of flying by establishing a conflict between the "night flight" representing danger, achievement, and man's purpose on the one hand, and the life of home and domesticity on the other. These novels also showed his mastery of a rich, dense, powerfully poetic style well-suited to convey his ideas about flying and man.

For several years during the mid-

931

thirties, Saint-Exupéry had difficulty getting a job flying. He then became a foreign correspondent, covering the May Day celebration in Moscow in 1935 and the 1937 siege of Madrid for *Paris-Soir,* and the outbreak of the Spanish Civil War, in 1936, for *L'Intransigeant.* These experiences deepened both his political and religious interests so that by the time he was ready to write *Wind, Sand, and Stars* he had switched from the novel to a form of personal essay or autobiography. It was André Gide, always a strong admirer of Saint-Exupéry, who is supposed to have suggested this change in form. *Wind, Sand, and Stars* is more political and religious, more thoughtful and metaphysical, than his earlier work, yet it still reflects his direct experiences, particularly his account of a plane crash in the Sahara Desert, and flying still provides both the form for the book and the necessary function for the author.

When World War II began, Saint-Exupéry returned to the Air Force. Shot down, he managed to escape through Portugal to the United States. He then wrote *Flight to Arras,* an account of his wartime experiences widely read in the United States as evidence that not all Frenchmen had succumbed to complacency and indifference in the face of the Nazi invasion and Vichy collaboration. He remained in the United States, writing, voicing his convictions about his responsibilities for his fellow human beings and his feelings of unity with his flight crew, his country, and all men, until he was able to help organize and rejoin the French forces. In his last days he wrote *The Wisdom of the Sands,* published posthumously in 1948. This book, though not always smooth or coherent, stands as the most complete account of his ideas. It is a long "poem" in prose, full of meditations on God and death and love and man's fate, stressing (in a manner some critics have called Nietzschean) man's need for the discipline and creativity afforded by an activity like flying.

Saint-Exupéry was widely admired for his rich, poetic style and his insight. He received the Prix Femina-Vie Heureuse in 1931 and the Grand Prize of the French Academy in 1939. In the United States and England he was even more famous as a spirited, authentic, and articulate voice of the French resistance, and as a writer who used in creative forms the sense of purpose and discipline wrought by human technology.

His death remains a mystery of the war. It is thought that he was shot down over Southern France on July 31, 1944.

BIBLIOGRAPHICAL REFERENCES: Saint-Exupéry's books are available in translation; there is no collected edition. Two recent studies in English are Richard Rumbold and Lady Margaret Stewart, *The Winged Life,* 1953; and Maxwell Austin Smith, *Knight of the Air: The Life and Works of Antoine de Saint-Exupéry,* 1956. Recent biographies in French include René Delange, *La vie de Saint-Exupéry,* 1948; Armand Bottequin, *Antoine de Saint-Exupéry,* 1949; Jules Roy, *Passion de Saint-Exupéry,* 1951; and Jean Bruce, *Saint-Exupéry, pilote légendaire;* in German, Walter Bauer, *Der Gesang von Sturmvogel,* 1949.

SAKI
(Hector Hugh Munro)

Born: Akyab, Burma   *Died:* Beaumont Hamel, France
Date: December 18, 1870   *Date:* November 14, 1916

PRINCIPAL WORKS

SHORT STORIES: *Reginald,* 1904; *Reginald in Russia,* 1910; *The Chronicles of Clovis,* 1911; *Beasts and Super-Beasts,* 1914; *The Square Egg,* 1924; *The Complete Short Stories of Saki,* 1930.

NOVELS: *The Unbearable Bassington,* 1912; *When William Came,* 1913.

Hector Hugh Munro, an English short story writer and journalist, was born December 18, 1870, in Akyab, Burma, where his father was a colonel in the Bengal Staff Corps and Inspector General of the Police. Because of his mother's death he was reared in England with his elder brother and sister by his grandmother and two aunts in Pilton, near Barnstable, North Devon. He went to grammer school at Exmouth and Bedford, and during his youth was interested in drawing and art. When his father retired from the army he took over the boy's education and accompanied him on a tour of Europe.

In 1893 Munro returned to Burma to join the police force—a position which was the result of his father's influence. But the young man suffered so severely from fever that he returned to England in 1894 to try to make a living from writing. Employed by the *Westminster Gazette,* he wrote the political sketches called *Alice in Westminster,* which were published in book form in 1902. It was during this period that he first used his pen name, Saki. Derived from *The Rubáiyát of Omar Khayyám,* Saki is the name of the cupbearer. In 1902 his *Not So Stories,* written in a satiric vein, were published anonymously. From 1902 to 1908 he traveled as foreign correspondent for

the *Morning Post* to the Balkans, Russia, Poland, and France. His serious volume entitled *The Rise of the Russian Empire,* a history of Russia at the time of Peter the Great, had already been published in 1900.

In 1904 *Reginald,* the first volume of his inimitable short stories, was published. It was followed by *Chronicles of Clovis* and *Beasts and Super-Beasts,* both successful. In 1912 appeared *The Unbearable Bassington,* an excellent short novel of social satire written in the clever epigrammatic style of Oscar Wilde.

Saki's short stories, his chief claim to fame, are still widely read and enjoyed. They are likely to retain their popularity because of their sparkling wit and clever humor. Notable for the unexpected phrase, many of his tales are concerned with unusual animals or witty sophisticated young men. Dealing frequently with unconventional subjects or practical jokes, they are not likely to be true to life. Yet they often have a morbid fascination.

In 1910, when Munro returned to England from the continent, he bought a cottage in Surrey, where he did much of his story-writing. Meanwhile he was writing also for the *Bystander* and the *Daily Express.* In 1913 he published *When William Came,* an imagined pic-

933

ture of what British life would be like under German rule. In 1914 he refused a commission and enlisted in the First World War. He was killed on November 14, 1916, near Beaumont Hamel in France. *The Toys of Peace* (1919) and *The Square Egg* were published after his death.

BIBLIOGRAPHICAL REFERENCES: A biographical sketch by Ethel M. Munro, included in *The Square Egg*, 1924, was reprinted in *The Complete Short Stories of Saki*, 1930. A memoir by Rothay Reynolds was printed in *The Toys of Peace*, 1919.

FELIX SALTEN
(Siegmund Salzmann)

Born: Budapest, Hungary
Date: September 6, 1869

Died: Zurich, Switzerland
Date: October 8, 1945

PRINCIPAL WORKS

NOVELS: *Der Hund von Florenz*, 1921 (*The Hound of Florence*); *Bambi*, 1923; *Florian*, 1933 (*Florian, the Emperor's Stallion*); *Perri*, 1938; *Bambis Kinder*, 1939 (*Bambi's Children*).

Felix Salten (pseudonym of Siegmund Salzmann), who was internationally known in his later years for his animal stories that delighted children and adults alike, was born in Budapest on September 6, 1869. His family was poor and, according to his own account, he was largely self-taught. A journalist at seventeen, he was for many years associated with the Viennese *Neue Freie Presse*, the most influential newspaper in Austro-Hungary before World War I. He began his literary career as a writer of historical, romantic, and satirical novels widely read throughout Central Europe. President of the Austrian P.E.N. Club at the time of the Nazi invasion, he took refuge in Switzerland in 1939 and died at Zurich, after a long illness, on October 8, 1945.

Bambi, translated in 1928, became a popular children's book and brought its author wide fame when it was made into a feature-length cartoon by Walt Disney. This lucidly written and moving story of a red deer growing up in the innocence of the great forest describes also the threat by humans (creatures of the "third arm") to the freedom of life in the wilds. By delicately transferring human ideals to his animals, the writer succeeds in a kind of allegory which preserves a delicate balance between a world of reality and one of fancy. Salten once referred to Gottfried Keller as a primary influence on his work.

The Hound of Florence had been Salten's first children's book. After *Bambi, Florian, the Emperor's Stallion,* and *Perri,* the story of a squirrel, appeared. This is perhaps as haunting a book as his story of the deer; in it he created the character of an inarticulate three-year-old girl who understands animals better than humans. With *Good Comrades* (1942) and *Forest World* (1942), Salten's peculiar talent was confirmed as that of an imaginative observer who could sometimes capture the flow of sympathy between the natural orders of humans

934

and animals. *Jibby the Cat* (1948) and *Little World Apart* (1948), both published after his death, added little to his achievement.

He also wrote travel books about America and Palestine and nearly forty novels, most of them hack work and untranslated, as well as short stories, dramas, and essays. *The Private* (1899), an anti-militaristic play, was his most notable writing for the theater.

BIBLIOGRAPHICAL REFERENCES: There is no comprehensive biographical study and almost no criticism. For discussions of the novels, see the *Book Review Digest*, 1928 ff.

FLORENCIO SÁNCHEZ

Born: Montevideo, Uruguay
Date: January 17, 1875

Died: Milan, Italy
Date: November 7, 1910

PRINCIPAL WORKS

PLAYS: *M'hijo el dotor,* 1903 (*My Son, the Lawyer*); *La gringa,* 1904 (*The Foreign Girl*); *Barranca abajo,* 1905 (*Retrogression*); *Los Muertos,* 1905 (*The Dead*).

The theater of the River Plate region was just beginning to deal with local types when Florencio Sánchez was born, in Montevideo, Uruguay, January 17, 1875, the first of eleven children of a middle class family. His father's political activities kept the family on the move and prevented the children from receiving much of a formal education. Florencio worked as secretary and in various jobs on newspapers. His first play was written for the entertainment of a club of political protesters to which he belonged. His second attempt was censored by city officials of Rosario, where he was a newspaper reporter, but when its performance was prevented, he worked all night setting it in type and had it ready for the public to read the next morning. He rewrote his first play as a musical comedy, *Canillita* (1902), which takes its title from its newsboy hero. The success of the play put that word into the Argentine language as a nickname for all newsboys.

A desire to show his sweetheart that he amounted to something forced Sánchez into the writing of his first important play, *My Son, the Lawyer* in 1903. During its rehearsal, the theater doorkeeper refused admission to the stoop-shouldered, shabbily dressed author with Indian features, because he looked like a tramp. Following the success of this tragedy, came a total of twenty plays, eight long dramas and twelve one-act sketches, products of the six years that comprised Sánchez' activities as a dramatist. He wrote rapidly, often on telegraph blanks, and did his best work in noisy bars and among crowds.

He reported that it took only one day to complete the four-act *The Foreign Girl,* called by one critic "the tragedy of the Argentine race." The play has technical flaws in starting slowly and ending twice, for the third act really answers the question whether the easy-going Argentine can withstand the industrious Italians and the final act merely restates the problem and provides a happy ending, with its

935

preachment that the country's hope lies in work and an amalgamation of native and foreigner. The emotions of the play, however, and the realistic pictures of people and life on the pampas have made it Sánchez' most popular play.

Technically better is *Retrogression* (sometimes called *Down the Ravine*), the tragedy of a good gaucho driven to despair and suicide by the unworthy and nagging women about him. In general, the author has neither interest in nor sympathy with the women of his plays. They are hardly more than puppets to develop his ideas and story.

From 1905 on, Sánchez turned his attention to the city, writing nine plays about the lower classes and five tragedies about the middle and upper classes. These works are characterized by social problems and realistic treatment tending toward naturalism. But Sánchez was no follower of Zola. He saw a "tragic fatality of character and circumstance," but he also had sympathy for his creations as the victims of the society in which they live. In wanting to make them over, he followed Ibsen, thereby gaining his nickname, "El Ibsen criollo."

Having dominated the Argentine and Uruguayan theater, Sánchez longed for a hearing in Europe. Several of his plays had already been translated and played in Italian. In 1909 he persuaded his government to send him to Italy. But after he arrived, his long years of irregular living demanded a reckoning. He contracted tuberculosis, and in 1910 the dramatist who had helped introduce realism into the theater of the River Plate died on November 7, and was buried in Milan. In 1921 the Uruguayan government brought home the ashes of its most distinguished playwright.

Perhaps Florencio Sánchez is not great compared to masters of the theater who have exerted great influence outside their own countries. His writing is uneven, with some of his situations trite and weak. He did inspire writers in his own land, however, and his many good qualities have made his theater a cultural heritage of the River Plate region, where he has had few equals and no superiors.

BIBLIOGRAPHICAL REFERENCES: For critical studies see Isaac Goldberg, *The Drama of Transition*, 1922; Ruth Richardson, *Florencio Sánchez and the Argentine Theatre*, 1933; Julio Imbert, *Florencio Sánchez, vida y creación*, 1954 (Buenos Aires); and Willis K. Jones, "The *Gringa* Theme in River Plate Drama," *Hispania*, XXV (1942), 326–332.

GEORGE SAND
(Amandine Lucile Aurore Dupin Dudevant)

Born: Paris, France   *Died:* Nohant, La Châtre, France
Date: July 1, 1804   *Date:* June 8, 1876

PRINCIPAL WORKS

NOVELS: *Indiana*, 1832; *Valentine*, 1832; *Lélia*, 1833; *Lavinia*, 1833; *Le Secrétaire intime*, 1834 (*The Private Secretary*); *Léone Léoni*, 1834; *Jacques*, 1834; *André*, 1835; *Simon*, 1836; *Mauprat*, 1837; *Les Maîtres mosaïstes*, 1837 (*The Masters of Mosaic*); *La Dernière Aldini*, 1837–1838 (*The Last of the Aldini*); *Les Sept Cordes*

de la Lyre, 1839 (*The Seven Strings of the Lyre*); *Le Compagnon du tour de France,*
1841 (*The Journeyman-Joiner*); *Horace*, 1841–1842; *Consuelo*, 1842–1843; *La
Comtesse de Rudolstadt*, 1843–1844 (*The Countess of Rudolstadt*); *Jeanne*, 1844;
Le Meunier d'Angibault, 1845 (*The Miller of Angibault*); *Le Péché de M. Antoine*,
1845 (*The Sin of Monsieur Antoine*); *La Mare au diable*, 1846 (*The Devil's Pool*);
Lucrezia Floriani, 1846; *François le Champi*, 1847–1848 (*François the Waif*); *La
Petite Fadette*, 1848–1849 (*Little Fadette*); *Mont-Revêche*, 1852; *La Filleule*, 1853
(*The Goddaughter*); *Les Maîtres sonneurs*, 1853 (*The Master Bell-Ringers*); *Adriani*,
1854; *Le Diable aux champs*, 1855–1856 (*The Devil in the Fields*); *La Daniella*,
1857; *Les Beaux Messieurs de Bois-Doré*, 1857–1858 (*The Gentlemen of Bois-Doré*);
L'Homme de neige, 1858 (*The Snow Man*); *Elle et Lui*, 1859 (*She and He*); *Jean
de la Roche*, 1859; *Le Marquis de Villemer*, 1860 (*The Marquis of Villemer*); *La
Famille de Germandre*, 1861 (*The Germandre Family*); *Valvèdre*, 1861; *Tamaris*,
1862; *Antonia*, 1862; *Mademoiselle La Quintinie*, 1863; *Laura*, 1864; *La Confession d'une jeune fille*, 1864 (*The Confession of a Young Girl*); *Monsieur Sylvestre*,
1865; *Le Dernier Amour*, 1866 (*The Last Love*); *Cadio*, 1867; *Pierre qui roule*,
1869 (*Rolling Stone*); *Nanon*, 1872; *Ma Soeur Jeanne*, 1874 (*My Sister Jeanne*);
Flamarande, 1875; *La Tour de Percemont*, 1875–1876 (*The Tower of Percemont*).

PLAYS: *Cosima*, 1840; *François le Champi*, 1849; *Claudie*, 1851; *Le Mariage de
Victorine*, 1851; *Mauprat*, 1853; *Maître Favilla*, 1855; *Le Marquis de Villemer*,
1864; *L'Autre*, 1870 (*The Other One*).

MISCELLANEOUS: *Lettres d'un Voyageur*, 1834–1836 (*Letters of a Traveler*); *Lettres
à Marcie*, 1837 (*Letters to Marcie*); *Un hiver à Majorque*, 1841 (*A Winter at
Majorca*); *Histoire de ma Vie*, 1854–1855 (*Story of My Life*).

In Amandine Lucile Aurore Dudevant, nee Dupin, known to posterity
as George Sand, were united two quite
dissimilar lines of heredity. On the
mother's side her origins were obscure;
Sophie Delaborde, a humble Parisian
modiste, was a bird-trainer's daughter.
On the father's side her pedigree was
brilliant; Maurice Dupin was a dashing officer only a few generations removed from royalty, being the son of
M. Dupin de Francueil (who had
numbered among his friends Jean
Jacques Rousseau) and of Marie Aurore, a granddaughter of Augustus the
Strong of Saxony. Maurice Dupin and
his wife Sophie were married in the
late spring of 1804, and their child
Aurore was born in Paris on July 1.
In 1808 Dupin was killed in a fall
from horseback. Submitting to necessity, Sophie turned the little girl over
to the haughty Mme. Dupin de Fran-

cueil, who undertook the responsibility
of the child's education. Reared at the
family estate of Nohant, Aurore was
privately tutored and, at thirteen, was
sent for schooling to the Convent des
Dames Anglaises at Paris, where she
remained three years. At eighteen, her
grandmother having died, she was
married to Casimir Dudevant, and she
soon bore a son and a daughter. In
1831 she left her husband and took up
residence in Paris.

Fully aware of her literary genius,
she resolved to maintain herself by
writing and to carve out a place of eminence in the world of letters. Her first
intimate association, dating from 1831,
was with a young advocate, Jules Sandeau, with whom she collaborated on
two novels, both signed "J. Sand." The
next novel, *Indiana*, she wrote alone,
but she issued it in 1832 under the
name "Georges Sand"; this, anglicized

soon afterward, became her invariable pseudonym. Having quarreled with Sandeau, she entered upon a liaison with Alfred de Musset and accompanied him to Italy. In Venice she fell ill; while recovering, she had an affair with her physician, Dr. Pietro Pagello. The consequent rift between herself and Musset was never closed. In 1837, Franz Liszt arranged an introduction between George Sand and Frédéric Chopin, whose love she succeeded in winning, though after some difficulty. The next winter she escorted Chopin, who was in fragile health, to the island of Majorca, where for a few months they lodged in a half-ruined monastery. The nine-year period of their alliance was for both a time of splendid artistic productivity. She manifested strong political interests in the 1840's while engaged, paradoxically, in the writing of her pastoral novels. A few years later, she retired to her childhood home at Nohant and passed the remainder of her life there, dying on June 8, 1876.

George Sand's novels may be classified as belonging to four main periods of development. In her first or feminist period, from 1832 to about 1837, they reflected her emotional rebellion against the bonds of marriage. In her second period, ending about 1845, they acquired a larger consciousness of social and philosophical problems; and this awareness gave rise not only to the socialist novels—*The Journeyman-Joiner, Horace, The Miller of Angibault,* and *The Sin of Monsieur Antoine*—but also to *Consuelo* and *The Countess of Rudolstadt.* Some of these works influenced the American poet, Walt Whitman. In her third or pastoral period, ending about 1856, her novels presented chiefly rural scenes and peasant characters; such was the case with *The Devil's Pool, François the Waif, Little Fadette,* and *The Master Bell-Ringers.* In her final period, up to 1876, her fiction explored a large variety of themes in an increasingly vigorous style. Among the best of her later novels are *The Marquis of Villemer* and the anticlerical *Mademoiselle La Quintinie.*

BIBLIOGRAPHICAL REFERENCES: The best work on George Sand in English is the biography by Andre Maurois, *Lélia,* translated from the French in 1953. In French there is the monumental work by Marie Louise Pailleron, *George Sand, histoire de sa vie,* 3 vols., 1938–1953. See also Magdeleine Paz, *La Vie d'un grand homme, George Sand,* 1947; Jeanne Galzy, *George Sand,* 1950; and Pierre Salamon, *George Sand,* 1953.

CARL SANDBURG

Born: Galesburg, Illinois
Date: January 6, 1878

PRINCIPAL WORKS

POEMS: *Chicago Poems,* 1916; *Cornhuskers,* 1918; *Smoke and Steel,* 1920; *Slabs of the Sunburnt West,* 1922; *Good Morning, America,* 1928; *The People, Yes,* 1936; *Complete Poems,* 1950.

BIOGRAPHY: *Abraham Lincoln: The Prairie Years,* 1926; *Steichen the Photographer,* 1929; *Mary Lincoln, Wife and Widow,* 1932 (with Paul M. Angle); *Abraham Lincoln: The War Years,* 1939.

NOVEL: *Remembrance Rock,* 1948.

AUTOBIOGRAPHY: *Always the Young Strangers,* 1952.

CHILDREN'S STORIES: *Rootabaga Stories,* 1922; *Rootabaga Pigeons,* 1923; *Potato Face,* 1930.

MISCELLANEOUS: *The American Songbag,* 1927; *A Lincoln and Whitman Miscellany,* 1938; *Storm over the Land,* 1942; *Home Front Memo,* 1943.

"As American as Carl Sandburg"—this phrase may well become a part of our language, for in spite of his universal appeal Sandburg seems a writer who could only have sprung from America, the land where big men rise from small beginnings, where people are restless, inventive, jacks of all trades. The Sandburg story began in Galesburg, Illinois, on January 6, 1878. Carl (August) was the second child of August and Clara Anderson Sandburg. Legend says that his father, a blacksmith, changed his name from Johnson to Sandburg to avoid confusion with the other August Johnsons in Galesburg, but Carl himself (perhaps to increase confusion) quotes his mother as saying the name was originally Danielson.

The restlessness of America came early. His schooling was fitful and at thirteen he began the first of many jobs that sound almost like a poetic cataloging from one of his own works: newsboy, milkman, bottle washer, scene shifter, potter's helper, hobo, icehouse worker, painter's apprentice. The tour as a hobo (which included the traditional sock on the jaw by a brakeman) took him through Kansas, Nebraska, Colorado. When he came back to Galesburg in 1898, he began wearing out his hands by sandpapering wood for a painter, but the *Maine* went down in Havana harbor and the restless Carl joined Company C, Sixth Infantry Regiment of Illinois Volunteers. The war took him to Puerto Rico and almost, but not quite, into battle.

Returning once more to Galesburg, Carl decided to enter Lombard College there. About the same time he began to write. He was editor-in-chief of the school paper and, to sustain his versatility, captain of the basketball team. Leaving Lombard without graduating (though the college later awarded him one of his many honorary degrees), he again roamed the United States, finally settling in Milwaukee as an organizer for the Wisconsin Socialist Democratic Party. In 1904 he published *In Restless Ecstasy,* a pamphlet of twenty-two poems which reveal the beginnings of his famous style. In 1908 he married Lillian Steichen, sister of the outstanding photographer. After several years as secretary to the mayor of Milwaukee, Sandburg moved to Chicago, his "City of the Big Shoulders," and with this move he became a newspaperman. But the poet was there, too; in 1914 he published in Harriet Monroe's *Poetry: A Magazine of Verse* his poem "Chicago," a rugged, hard-punching tribute. With this success he produced his volumes of verse at regular intervals: *Chicago Poems, Cornhuskers, Smoke and Steel, Slabs of the Sunburnt West, Good Morning, America,* and *The People, Yes.* Although some of the poems are weak and misty, these books contain America, the ugliness and the beauty, all sung by a man who can "tear his shirt" on one page and on the next steal softly in "on little cat feet."

Sandburg continued to make his living as a newspaperman. During World War I he was Stockholm correspondent for the Newspaper Enterprise Associates and later an editorial writer for the Chicago *Daily News*.

In 1920 still another Sandburg emerged, the lecturer and singer of folk songs. Equipped with a voice as powerful and wide-ranging as his poetry, Sandburg gave performances in which he talked philosophy, read his poems, and sang the ballads of our country. With these ballads he filled *The American Songbag* in 1927.

Sandburg is known as a biographer of Lincoln, but this flat statement is a pale inadequacy. Without sacrificing his own individuality, Sandburg has become, by combining admiration and research, almost a latter-day Lincoln, a man who looks at things as Lincoln did. Author and subject seem to blend in the poetic prose of *Abraham Lincoln: The Prairie Years* and *Abraham Lincoln: The War Years*. In 1954 he condensed these six volumes into one. His biography brought him a Pulitzer Prize in 1940, making some of his admirers wonder whether it will be Sandburg the poet or Sandburg the biographer who will be long remembered.

Long remembered he is likely to be, for there are still other sides to this versatile, inventive writer. His *Rootabaga Stories* and *Potato Face*, full of the fanciful repetition that is so much a part of childhood, have become classic stories for childern. Because there seemed to be so few literary forms left to conquer, Sandburg tried a novel and in 1948 produced *Remembrance Rock*, a rambling saga of Americans from Plymouth days to the present. With some readers and critics Sandburg's encounter with the novel came out, at best, as a draw; but his triumph is clearcut when it comes to autobiography, for *Always the Young Strangers* is an account of his early years that is written with the charm, strength, and twinkle only he can blend so persuasively.

Honors have come late to Sandburg, but they are many. Among them are his selection as a Phi Beta Kappa poet at Harvard and the Litt.D. that university later awarded him. One of his most triumphant days came in 1953 on his seventy-fifth birthday. At a dinner in his honor the tributes included one from the homeland of his parents when he received Sweden's Commander Order of the Northern Star. As a part of the general celebration, Sandburg returned to his birthplace, Galesburg, and read the poems and sang the ballads that have made him famous. Radio and television widened his audience even more; his deep voice and his craggy face overhung by hair that looks like a slab of the sunburnt west have penetrated the American living room. This man has done so many things (in 1934 a lecturer at the University of Hawaii and at present a raiser of goats at his home in Flat Rock, North Carolina) and has written so well in so many forms (think of the *Rootabaga Stories* and then of *The People, Yes*, a poetic compendium of our tall tales and our slangy speech) that he has become, if it can be said of one man, the voice of America.

BIBLIOGRAPHICAL REFERENCES: The standard texts of Sandburg's poetry are *The Complete Poems of Carl Sandburg*, 1950, and *Selected Poems of Carl Sandburg*, edited by Rebecca West, 1926, with a valuable critical introduction. There is no fully detailed biographical study, although several have been reported in preparation.

Sandburg has told the story of his early years in *Always the Young Strangers*, 1952. The only other study of significance is Karl W. Detzer, *Carl Sandburg: A Study in Personality and Background*, 1941. The most recent bibliography is the checklist by Frances Cheney in Allen Tate, *Sixty American Poets, 1890–1944*, 1945.

Earlier estimates of Sandburg's writing include Conrad Aiken, "Poetic Realism: Carl Sandburg," in *Scepticisms*, 1919; Stuart P. Sherman, *Americans*, 1922; Harry Hansen, *Midwest Portraits*, 1923; Percy H. Boynton, *Some Contemporary Americans*, 1924; Paul Rosenfeld, "Carl Sandburg," in *Port of New York*, 1924; and Bruce Weirick, *From Whitman to Sandburg in American Poetry: A Critical Survey*, 1924. The commentary on the Lincoln biographies is extensive and important. For criticism of *The Prairie Years* consult the *Book Review Digest*, 1926. A collection of reviews of *The War Years*, by Charles A. Beard, Robert E. Sherwood, and others, was reprinted in the pamphlet, *The Lincoln of Carl Sandburg*, 1940. See also Allan Nevins, "Abraham Lincoln in Washington," *Saturday Review of Literature*, XXI (December 2, 1939), 3–4+; Joseph Auslander, "A Poet Writes Biography," *College English*, I (1940), 649–657; and Oscar Cargill, "Carl Sandburg: Crusader and Mystic," *ibid.*, XI (1950), 367–372. *Carl Sandburg's "Remembrance Rock,"* n.d., contains a selected critical commentary on Sandburg's novel. For later estimates of the poems see also Thomas K. Whipple, *Spokesmen*, 1928; Newton Arvin, "Carl Sandburg," in *After the Genteel Tradition*, edited by Malcolm Cowley, 1936; Babette Deutsch, *Poetry in Our Time*, 1952 (rev. ed., 1956); William Carlos Williams, "Carl Sandburg's Complete Poems," in *Selected Essays*, 1954; Charles H. Compton, "Who Reads Carl Sandburg?" *South Atlantic Quarterly*, XXVIII (1929), 190–200; Morton Dauwen Zabel, "Sandburg's Testament," *Poetry*, XLIX (1936), 33–45; and Babette Deutsch, "Poetry for the People," *English Journal*, XXVI (1937), 265–274.

GEORGE SANTAYANA

Born: Madrid, Spain *Died:* Rome, Italy
Date: December 16, 1863 *Date:* September 26, 1952

PRINCIPAL WORKS

PHILOSOPHY: *The Sense of Beauty*, 1896; *The Life of Reason*, 1905–1906 (*Reason in Common Sense*, 1905; *Reason in Society*, 1905; *Reason in Religion*, 1905; *Reason in Art*, 1905; *Reason in Science*, 1906); *Scepticism and Animal Faith*, 1923; *The Realms of Being*, 1927–1940 (*The Realm of Essence*, 1927; *The Realm of Matter*, 1930; *The Realm of Truth*, 1938; *The Realm of Spirit*, 1940).

ESSAYS AND CRITICAL STUDIES: *Interpretations of Poetry and Religion*, 1900; *Three Philosophical Poets: Lucretius, Dante, and Goethe*, 1910; *Winds of Doctrine*, 1913; *Character and Opinion in the United States*, 1920; *Soliloquies in England and Later Soliloquies*, 1922; *Dominations and Powers*, 1951.

POEMS: *Sonnets and Other Verses*, 1894; *A Hermit of Carmel and Other Poems*, 1901; *Poems*, 1922.

NOVEL: *The Last Puritan: A Memoir in the Form of a Novel*, 1935.

PLAY: *Lucifer: A Theological Tragedy*, 1899.

AUTOBIOGRAPHY: *Persons and Places*, 1944; *The Middle Span*, 1945; *My Host the World*, 1953.

George Santayana, whose fame derives from his role as an urbane and skeptical philosopher endowed with an excellent literary style, was born in

Madrid, December 16, 1863, of nominally Catholic parents, Augustín Ruiz de Santayana and Josefine Borráis. He was christened Jorge Augustín Nicholas Ruiz de Santayana y Borráis.

Until he was nine years of age, he knew no English; his parents, although well-educated in the arts, spoke Spanish in the home. In 1872 Santayana's mother returned to the United States to fulfill an agreement with her former husband, George Sturgis, to educate the three Sturgis children in the United States. In 1872 George Santayana, then nine, joined her and the Sturgis children in Boston. His father, who brought him to the United States, returned to Spain after spending one winter in Boston.

Santayana was educated at the Brimmer School, the Boston Latin School, and Harvard University. In 1883 he returned to Spain to visit his father and there expressed his dissatisfaction with academic life. However, since neither military nor diplomatic service seemed advisable, he decided to continue his work at Harvard. He received his B.A. and a fellowship in 1886 and spent the following two years at the University of Berlin. He then returned to Harvard and in 1889 received the M.A. and Ph.D. in philosophy.

At that time Harvard University was enjoying its greatest philosophical period; on the faculty were William James, Josiah Royce, and George H. Palmer. Although Santayana became a member of that august faculty in 1889 and was to some extent naturally influenced by the ideas about him, he remained for the most part solitary and independent in his work. Santayana ascribed his preference for isolation and his inability to feel at home in America to his Spanish-Catholic background;

he adopted the lifelong attitude of following his particular interests, but wished others happiness in their own individual pursuits.

While he was teaching at Harvard, he had as students a number of persons who later achieved their own kinds of fame, among them T. S. Eliot, Conrad Aiken, Felix Frankfurter, and Walter Lippmann.

In 1912, having received a legacy which made retirement possible, Santayana left the faculty at Harvard and returned to Europe, where he spent the remainder of his life. He stayed for a brief time in Spain and France and spent five years in England. Later he settled in Rome where he felt most at ease as a solitary and contemplative writer of philosophical works and critical essays. During World War II he found sanctuary in the grounds of a convent in Rome. There during the last years of his life his work quietly proceeded, interrupted only occasionally by walks and brief talks with visitors. He died at the convent of the Little Company of Mary on September 26, 1952.

Santayana achieved popular notice with his novel, *The Last Puritan*, and near the end of his life with his autobiography, *Persons and Places*. Perhaps his most controversial work was his *Interpretations of Poetry and Religion*, in which he expressed his conviction that religion is primarily a work of the imagination.

George Santayana is regarded by professional philosophers as a careful and sometimes illuminating thinker whose primary virtue nevertheless consists in the fine literary use he has made of his ideas. Technically, he would be regarded as a naturalist and critical

942

realist, as one who regards knowledge as a construction from the basic elements of experience, the sense data, which show by their essence, their character, the changeless, universal relationships in the realm of essense. His most important philosophical works are *Scepticism and Animal Faith, The Realms of Being,* and *The Life of Reason. The Realms of Being* is composed of four books, separately published: *The Realm of Essence, The Realm of Matter, The Realm of Truth,* and *The Realm of Spirit.*

BIBLIOGRAPHICAL REFERENCES: The standard collected edition is the Triton Edition of *The Works of George Santayana,* 14 vols., 1936–37. *The Letters of George Santayana* were edited with introduction and commentary by Daniel Cory, 1955. George W. Howgate's critical biography, *George Santayana,* 1938, is acceptable if not definitive. Critical books are Van Meter Ames, *Proust and Santayana: The Aesthetic Way of Life,* 1937; Paul Arthur Schilpp, ed., *The Philosophy of George Santayana,* 1940, containing Santayana's autobiography and a bibliography to 1940; Mary C. E. Kinney, *A Critique of the Philosophy of George Santayana in the Light of Thomistic Principles,* 1942; W. E. Arnett, *Santayana and the Sense of Beauty,* 1955; Irving Singer, ed., *Essays in Literary Criticism of George Santayana,* with an introduction, "Santayana as a Literary Critic," 1956; and Irving Singer, *Santayana's Aesthetics,* 1957. See also the essay by A. A. Bowman in *A Sacramental Universe,* 1939. Articles in magazines include Daniel Cory, "A Study of Santayana," *Journal of Philosophic Studies,* II (1927), 349–364; G. W. Howgate, "Santayana and Humanism," *Sewanee Review,* XLIII (1935), 49–57; Q. D. Leavis, "The Critical Writings of George Santayana," *Scrutiny,* III (1935), 278–295; Daniel Cory, "The Later Philosophy of Mr. Santayana," *Criterion,* XV (1936), 379–392; and D. C. Williams, "Of Essence and Existence in Santayana," *Journal of Philosophy,* LI (1954), 31–42.

SANTÔ KYÔDEN

Born: Edo, Japan   Died: Edo
Date: 1761   Date: 1816

PRINCIPAL WORKS

Santô Kyôden has more than ninety-two works of prose fiction to his credit. Some of the best known are *Chûshin Suiko-den,* 1789 (*A Tale of the Forty-seven Loyal Retainers*); *Fukushû Kidan Asaka no Numa,* 1803 (*Murder and Revenge of Swamp of Asaka*); *Udonge Monogatari,* 1804 (*Fortune's Wheel*); *Inazuma-byôshi,* 1806 (*Trouble in the House of Sasaki*), and its sequel, *Honchô Sui-bodai Zenden,* 1809.

Santô Kyôden was born at Edo in 1761, the eldest son of Iwase Nobuaki, who himself was the adopted son of a pawnbroker in Edo (later Tokyo). In 1773 his father left the pawnbroker's family to strike out on his own, and later he became a minor city official. Kyôden was apprenticed to a print artist, Kitao Shigemasa, and also studied chanting and playing the samisen. As an artist's apprentice he learned to paint well, and also became acquainted with writers of his day. By the time he was seventeen he also knew the pleasure quarters of the city, but he seems to have been a modest spender.

and a contemporary system of "Dutch treat" bears his name. As a wood block print artist he became famous in the last twenty years of the eighteenth century. He produced some excellent work, more or less in the manner of his instructor, Shigemasa, but showing flashes of individual technique, power, composition, and use of color. His favorite subjects were the inmates of the Yoshiwara. Some of the most interesting were the illustrations he did for his own writings. After ten years he seems to have become so busy with his writing that he gave up painting before he might have reached further development.

His first published work was *Kaichô Riyaku no Meguri-ai*, 1778 (*The Way the Cards Fall*), which he published at the age of seventeen. But he won popular acclaim with his *Edo-umare Uwaki no Kabayaki*, 1785 (*Vanity and Disillusion*). His first attempt to write a type of short story then current and dealing with the gay quarters was *Musuko-beya*, 1785 (*Guide Book to Behavior in the Gay Quarters*). This was a form in which he excelled, but in 1791 he was sentenced to house confinement in handcuffs for fifty days for this type of writing. From this time Kyôden turned to the production of more legitimate fiction, such as *A Tale of the Forty-seven Loyal Retainers* which he had already published two years previously, but in this field he was not quite the equal of Kyokutei Bakin (1767–1848). Both his wives were former inmates of the Yoshiwara, and much to everyone's surprise, both of them turned out to be excellent wives. After his father's death in 1799, Kyôden succeeded to the family business as handbag merchant and had a modest success with handbags made of cloth or paper, decorated with his own illustrations. He also made and sold patent medicines. He died at Edo in 1816.

BIBLIOGRAPHICAL REFERENCES: Most of the works and all of the biographies of Santô Kyôden are still in Japanese. Of the former, two works have been translated into non-Japanese languages: *Fortune's Wheel (Udenge Monogatari)* in *The Japan Magazine*, XVIII, XIX, and XX (1928–1929); and *Der treue Ritter Uto Yasugata (Utô Yasukata Chûgi-den)* in *Deutsche Gesellschaft für Natur-und Völkerkunde Ostasiens*, 5 (Tokyo, 1891). A brief description of his life and works appears in W. G. Aston, *A History of Japanese Literature*, 1937.

SAPPHO

Born: Eresos, Lesbos
Date: Unknown; fl. c. 600 B.C.

Died: Sicily (?)
Date: Unknown

EXTANT POEMS

Ode to Aphrodite; fragments of 8 (or 9) books of lyric poetry.

Sappho, or "Psappho" as she called herself, was born on the Greek Island of Lesbos, in the Aegean Sea, west of Turkey, and flourished in the sixth century B.C. The tenth century Byzantian lexicographer Suïdas gave her father's name as Scamandronymus, and her mother was Cleis. Hers must have been an aristocratic family because her brother Larichus was a cupbearer in the prytaneum of Mytilene, a duty assigned to only those of noble birth. Another of her brothers, Charaxus, is mentioned in her poetry as being in love with a slave girl whom he bought and freed.

Sappho is supposed to have exchanged love poetry with her fellow countryman Alcaeus, who died about 580 B.C. She married Cercylas of Andros, and had a daughter named Cleis. She lived for some years in Sicily and a statue was erected in her honor at Syracuse. There is no foundation for the legend that she became so enamored of the youthful fisherman Phaon that she threw herself from the Leucadian rock when he ignored her.

Regard for her poetry caused the ancients to rank her with Homer and

Archilochus and moved Plato in *Phaedrus* to call her the "Tenth Muse." All except seven stanzas of an ode to Aphrodite and a few fragments of lesser lyrics were lost for centuries. Recently papyrus rolls turned up in Egypt to provide mutilated but authentic samples. Some appear to have been written for a society of aristocratic girls, others to friends.

Sappho wrote in the Aeolic dialect, pure but simple love poems, full of passion, with vivid phrasing and a variety of meters. The so-called Sapphic stanza comprising three long and one short lines was much used by Catullus and Horace. Ovid and Swinburne, who translated her, also show her influence. It is thought that she died in Sicily.

BIBLIOGRAPHICAL REFERENCES: There are translations by Francis Fawkes in A. Chalmers, *Works of English Poets*, 1810. See also E. M. Cox, *Poems of Sappho*, 1924; and Edgar Lobel, *Sapphous Mele: Fragments of the Lyrical Poems of Sappho*, 1925.

Books about Sappho are largely conjectural. See Mary M. Patrick, *Sappho and the Island of Lesbos*, 1912; David M. Robinson, *Sappho and Her Influence*, 1924; A. E. P. Weigall, *Sappho of Lesbos*, 1932; and Margaret Goldsmith, *Sappho of Lesbos: A Psychological Reconstruction of Her Life*, 1938.

WILLIAM SAROYAN

Born: Fresno, California
Date: August 31, 1908

PRINCIPAL WORKS

SHORT STORIES: *The Daring Young Man on the Flying Trapeze*, 1934; *Inhale and Exhale*, 1936; *Three Times Three*, 1936; *The Gay and Melancholy Flux*, 1937; *Little Children*, 1937; *Love, Here Is My Hat*, 1938; *The Trouble with Tigers*, 1938; *Peace, It's Wonderful*, 1939; *My Name Is Aram*, 1940; *The Assyrian and Other Stories*, 1950; *The Bicycle Rider in Beverly Hills*, 1952.

NOVELS: *The Human Comedy*, 1943; *The Adventures of Wesley Jackson*, 1946; *Rock Wagram*, 1951; *The Laughing Matter*, 1953; *Mama, I Love You*, 1956; *Papa, You're Crazy*, 1957.

PLAYS: *My Heart's in the Highlands*, 1939; *The Time of Your Life*, 1939; *Love's Old Sweet Song*, 1940; *The Beautiful People*, 1941; *Razzle Dazzle*, 1942; *The Human Comedy*, 1943; *Get Away, Old Man*, 1944; *Plays*, 1950; *The Cave Dwellers*, 1957.

MEMOIRS: *The Adventures of William Saroyan*, 1950.

William Saroyan is interesting to students of American literature because he illustrates, in his generation, the same sort of self-conscious simplicity and naïveté that has been the stock-in-trade of American writers ever since Artemus Ward and Mark Twain. Saroyan's simplicity is, to be sure, marked with his awareness of his Armenian ancestry and it is suffused with his own sense of the basic goodness of all persons, particularly those who are obscure and naïve, and the undeniable value of being alive. To Saroyan there is no problem, political or international, that could not be solved by an appeal to the basic good will present in all men.

Saroyan was born on August 31, 1908, in the Armenian section of Fresno, California, one of what he calls the tribe of "proud and angry Saroyans." His elementary school days were marked by truancy and punishment by the principal. Formal education held no attraction for Saroyan; out of sheer boredom he left high school at fifteen after, as he says, he had read every book in the Fresno Public Library. He then went into his uncle's law office, where he read law and learned shorthand and typing.

Although he wrote voluminously during his early years (some four hundred short stories and essays) at the same time that he worked at a dozen different jobs, "The Daring Young Man on the Flying Trapeze," published in Story in 1933, was his first published writing. In it Saroyan revealed his impetuous "love for life" and what he calls his "jump in the river and start to swim immediately" technique. The next few years saw the steady publication of his short stories, all marked by an impressionistic manner and a sentimental exaltation of characters ranging from Armenian-American workers to middle-class businessmen. As might be expected from the fact that he is a self-made writer, most of his characters are optimistically associated with the glory of the American dream.

Saroyan's exuberance is not diminished in his plays, three of which were produced on Broadway within a little over a year. In his dramas he also gives us his special version of the American dream, the idea that worldly success means nothing and that only purity and brilliance of aspiration count. The glory of America is that it is the place where such aspirations are possible and, at least in the America Saroyan knows, are cheerfully accepted. My Heart's in the Highlands deals with an unsuccessful poet and his son; The Time of Your Life shows the essential goodness of man when a wealthy drunkard gives money to a forlorn group of people in a San Francisco bar, people who wish only to pursue their hopes and dreams. For this play Saroyan was awarded the Drama Critics' Circle Award and the Pulitzer Prize for 1940; he refused the Pulitzer award on the grounds that the play was "no more great or good" than anything else he had written. Saroyan's next two plays—Love's Old Sweet Song, a farce-comedy set on a California farm, and The Beautiful People, similar in theme to The Time of Your Life—seemed less attractive, possibly because they marked no advance of ideas or technique. What is true of his plays is true also of his later novels and short stories; from them one gets chiefly a sense of repetition, though even the most banal of his works continue to be enlivened by occasional

946

flashes of poetry and insight. Nowhere is Saroyan's ardent belief in the fundamental goodness of people better illustrated than in his most typical novel, *The Human Comedy*: The "comédie humaine" of Balzac is a parade of greed, lust, and lost illusions, but Saroyan's "human comedy" is, if it be true, a cause for rejoicing because baser motives can always be transformed into noble ones, and human brotherhood is diffused.

BIBLIOGRAPHICAL REFERENCES: There is no full-length biography. For criticism see Harlan Hatcher, "William Saroyan," *English Journal*, XXVIII (1939), 169–177; George Jean Nathan, "Saroyan: Whirling Dervish of Fresno," *American Mercury*, LI (1941), 303–308; Philip Rahv, "William Saroyan: A Minority Report," *ibid.*, LVII (1943), 371–377; Edwin B. Burgum, "The Lonesome Young Man on the Flying Trapeze," *Virginia Quarterly Review*, XX (1944), 392–403; and William J. Fisher, "What Ever Happened to Saroyan?" *College English*, XVI (1955), 336–340, 385. Saroyan is also included in the group of California writers discussed by Edmund Wilson in *The Boys in the Back Room*, 1941.

JEAN-PAUL SARTRE

Born: Paris, France
Date: June 21, 1905

PRINCIPAL WORKS

PHILOSOPHICAL ESSAYS: *L'Imagination*, 1938; *L'Imaginaire*, 1940; *Esquisse d'une théorie des émotions*, 1940 (*Essay on the Emotions*); *L'Être et le Néant*, 1943 (*Being and Nothingness*); *L'Existéntialisme est un humanisme*, 1946 (*Existentialism and Humanism*).

NOVELS: *La Nausée*, 1938 (*Nausea*); *Les Chemins de la Liberté*, 1945–   (*The Roads to Freedom*): *L'Âge de Raison*, 1945 (*The Age of Reason*); *Le Sursis*, 1945 (*The Reprieve*); *La Mort dans l'Âme*, 1949 (*Troubled Sleep*); *La dernière chance*, in preparation.

SHORT STORIES: *Le Mur*, 1939 (*The Wall*).

PLAYS: *Les Mouches*, 1942 (*The Flies*); *Huis-Clos*, 1944 (*No Exit*); *Les Mains sales*, 1948 (*The Red Gloves*; also *Dirty Hands*); *Le Diable et le bon Dieu*, 1951 (*Lucifer and the Lord*).

Jean-Paul Sartre, the leading French existentialist, was born in Paris on June 21, 1905. His father died in Indo-China while Sartre was yet a child. The boy was educated at the Lycée de la Rochelle and then, during the first World War, at the Lycée Henri IV. He entered the École Normale Supérieure in 1925 and took his *Agrégation de Philosophie* with high honors in 1928. He then became a teacher in Laon, and later in Le Havre and Neuilly. During the next five years he made several tours, visiting Egypt, Greece, and Germany. During his stay in Berlin he spent a short time as a *pensionnaire* at the Institut Français, where he studied the philosophies of Edmund Husserl, Martin Heidegger, and Søren Kierkegaard, all important influences in the development of his atheistic existentialism.

As a teacher in Paris in 1935 he began work on his theories of the imagination and the emotions. His first novel, *Nausea,* emphasized the breakdown of meaning and the nausea resulting from a sudden apprehension of the existence of things. This concern with the recognition of existence as a starting point in a man's creative life was shown further in a volume of short stories, *The Wall,* which appeared the following year.

Drafted into the French army as a private, he left his teaching position at the Lycée Pasteur at Neuilly in September, 1939. He was sent to the Maginot Line, and in June, 1940, was taken prisoner by the Germans and held until repatriation nine months later. In the meantime critics were acknowledging Sartre's psychological acumen and ingenuity as shown in his recently published books on the imagination and the emotions.

After returning to France in 1941 Sartre took a writer's role in the resistance. He wrote for *Combat,* the lively intellectual underground paper then edited by Albert Camus. At the same time he continued his teaching at the Lycée Pasteur and then at the Lycée Condorcet.

His first play, *The Flies,* a carefully executed expression of the right of a man to reject old gods and to define himself by independent action, was performed in Paris during the German occupation in 1942. Received as a moving play in support of man's freedom, it naturally had poignant significance to French audiences during the occupa-

tion. Another play, *No Exit,* presented Hell as a rather dull living room where persons who had failed to act in life had to put up eternally with one another's presence and conversation. These plays and the later *The Red Gloves* aroused considerable interest in New York audiences when they were produced in the United States.

Being and Nothingness, a long philosophical work published in 1943, assured Sartre's status as a responsible and creative philosopher, although some critics assumed that the popularity of existentialism could be accounted for only by supposing its leader to be superficial. During the latter half of the 1940's Sartre and other intellectuals made the Café de Flore in Paris the center of the growing existentialist movement. He visited the United States in 1945–1946 and lectured at American colleges and universities. In 1946 he founded the review *Les Temps Modernes* in which his essays and fiction have since been appearing. An attack on Albert Camus in Sartre's journal led to a schism between the two former philosophical friends, primarily because of Sartre's advocacy of Communist programs.

Sartre's most sustained effort in fiction has been his four-volume series *The Roads to Freedom,* of which three novels, *The Age of Reason, The Reprieve,* and *Troubled Sleep* have appeared in this country. He continues to be one of France's most stimulating writers.

BIBLIOGRAPHICAL REFERENCES: The Sartre bibliography is extensive and any listing at this time must be highly selective. The basic study in English is Iris Murdoch, *Sartre, Romantic Rationalist,* 1953. Other books on this controversial figure include Herbert Read, *Existentialism, Marxism, and Anarchism,* 1949; Peter J. Dempsey, *The Psychology of Sartre,* 1950; Maurice Natanson, *A Critique of Jean Paul Sartre's Ontology,* 1951; Alfred Stern, *Sartre: His Philosophy and Psychoanalysis,* 1953; Wilfrid Desan, *The Tragic Finale,* 1954; and Arland Ussher, *Journey Through*

Dread: A Study of Kierkegaard, Heidegger, and Sartre, 1955. See also C. E. Magney, *Les Sandales d'Empédocle,* 1945; R. Campbell, *Jean-Paul Sartre ou une littérature philosophique,* 1945; F. Jeanson, *Le Problème moral et la pensée de Sartre,* 1947; C. Varet, *L'Ontologie de Sartre,* 1948; Nelly Cormeau, *Littérature existéntialiste: le roman et la théâtre de Jean-Paul Sartre,* 1950; Henri Paissac, *Le dieu de Sartre,* 1950; and Hans Heinz Holz, *Jean Paul Sartre,* 1951. See also Hazel E. Barnes, "Jean Paul Sartre and the Haunted Self," *Western Humanities Review,* X (1956), 119–128; and Robert G. Olson, "The Three Theories of Motivation in the Philosophy of Jean-Paul Sartre," *Ethics,* LXVI (1956), 176–187.

SIEGFRIED SASSOON

Born: Brenchley, Kent, England
Date: September 8, 1886

PRINCIPAL WORKS

POEMS: *The Old Huntsman and Other Poems,* 1917; *Counter-Attack and Other Poems,* 1918; *War Poems,* 1919; *Picture Show,* 1920; *Recreations,* 1923; *Selected Poems,* 1925; *Satirical Poems,* 1926; *The Heart's Journey,* 1928; *Poems of Pinchbeck Lyre,* 1931; *Vigils,* 1935; *Rhymed Ruminations,* 1940; *Poems Newly Selected 1916–1935,* 1940; *Collected Poems,* 1947; *Sequences,* 1956.

NOVELS: *The Memoirs of George Sherston,* 1937 (comprising *Memoirs of a Fox-Hunting Man,* 1928; *Memoirs of an Infantry Officer,* 1930; *Sherston's Progress,* 1936).

AUTOBIOGRAPHY: *The Old Century and Seven More Years,* 1938; *The Weald of Youth,* 1942; *Siegfried's Journey 1916–1920,* 1945.

BIOGRAPHY: *Meredith,* 1948.

The literary reputation of Siegfried (Lorraine) Sassoon will rest, to a considerable extent, on his vigorous war poems, written at the front between 1914 and 1918. Like those of Wilfred Owen, whom Sassoon influenced and encouraged, they testify bitterly to the ingloriousness of modern warfare. Such pieces as "The Rear-Guard" and "Counter-Attack" express the aversion and horror which led Sassoon, then an officer in the British Army, to become a pacifist and to refuse further military duty. To a later generation, he is better known for the autobiographical novels which relate what he has called his "mental history," the chronicle of his youth and of the spiritual crisis produced on the battlefield. Of these works the three earliest, *Memoirs of a Fox-Hunting Man, Memoirs of an Infantry Officer,* and *Sherston's Progress* mask their author under the alias "George Sherston"; fictional in form, they nevertheless present a reflective survey of personal events recorded voluminously in Sassoon's diaries. His more formal autobiographies, *The Old Century and Seven More Years, The Weald of Youth,* and *Siegfried's Journey 1916–1920,* re-examine much of the same ground from a later point of view undisguisedly his own. *Memoirs of a Fox-Hunting Man,* awarded both the Hawthornden Prize and the James Tait Black Memorial Prize in 1929, is delightful for its spare, restrained style, conveying in understatement a strong nostalgia for prewar society. Sassoon has used the pseudonyms Pinchbeck Lyre, Sigmund Sashûn, and Saul Kain.

The Sassoons have been eminent chiefly in the realm of English finance. However, Siegfried Sassoon, born at Brenchley, September 8, 1886, and reared by his artist mother in rural Kent (his parents had separated in his childhood), grew up in an atmosphere determined by literature, painting, and summonses to fox meets. He attended Clare College, Cambridge, for two years, until defeated by apathy toward the History Tripos. In the years preceding World War I, he published anonymously several collections of imitative verse, and also tried playwriting. During this period, a narrative poem written in Masefield's manner shows great technical exactitude.

During the war Sassoon received the Military Cross for heroism in action. While recuperating at home from a throat wound, he issued in 1917 a manifesto denouncing the prolongation of the conflict. Although he desired court-martial in order to spread his views, friends had him certified temporarily insane, and subsequently he was placed in a sanatorium in Edinburgh, where he met Wilfred Owen. Later he volunteered to rejoin the forces, served in Palestine and again in France, and suffered a second wound. He was promoted to the rank of captain in the Royal Welsh Fusiliers. He has latterly disowned pacifism, and in the 1951 Honors List was designated a Commander of the British Empire.

BIBLIOGRAPHICAL REFERENCES: The best source for information on Sassoon is his autobiography as told in *The Old Century and Seven More Years*, *The Weald of Youth*, and *Siegfried's Journey*. His fiction is discussed at some length in F. J. H. Darton, *From Surtees to Sassoon*, 1931. For criticism of his poetry see Harold Monro, *Some Contemporary Poets*, 1930; Thomas S. Moore, *Some Soldier Poets*, 1920; Edmund Blunden, "Siegfried Sassoon's Poetry," *London Mercury*, XX (1929), 156–166; and Alexander H. Sackton, "Two Poems on War: A Critical Exercise," *University of Texas Studies in English*, XXXI (1951), 120–124.

FRIEDRICH SCHILLER

Born: Marbach, Germany
Date: November 10, 1759

Died: Weimar, Germany
Date: May 9, 1805

PRINCIPAL WORKS

PLAYS: *Die Raüber*, 1781 (*The Robbers*); *Don Carlos*, 1787; *Wallenstein*, 1798–1799; *Maria Stuart*, 1800; *Die Jungfrau de Orleans*, 1801 (*The Maid of Orleans*); *Die Braut von Messina*, 1803 (*The Bride of Messina*); *Wilhelm Tell*, 1804.

NOVELS: *Der Verbrecher aus verlorener Ehre*, 1786 (*The Criminal, in Consequence of Lost Reputation*); *Der Geisterseher*, 1787–1789 (unfinished).

POEMS: *Xenien*, 1796 (with Goethe); *Gedichte*, 1800–1803.

HISTORY: *Geschichte des dreissigjährigen Krieges*, 1790–1792 (*History of the Thirty Years' War*).

ESSAYS AND STUDIES: *Über den Grund des Vergnügens an tragischen Gegenständen*, 1792; *Über die tragische Kunst*, 1792; *Über das Pathetische*, 1793; *Über Anmut und Würde*, 1793 (*On Grace and Dignity*); *Über naive und sentimentalische Dichtung*, 1795–1796 (*On Naïve and Sentimental Poetry*).

950

(Johann Christoph) Friedrich von Schiller, born on November 10, 1759, at Marbach, Germany, was the son of an officer in the army of the Duke of Württemberg. His parents intended that Johann should enter the ministry of the Lutheran Church, and to this end sent him to the Latin school at Ludwigsburg, then the ducal residence. Duke Karl Eugen of Württemberg, in common with other semi-independent German princelings, had delusions of grandeur, and he tried to imitate the "grand style" of the Bourbons by making his court into a kind of Bavarian Versailles. He lived lavishly, if crudely, ruling largely through sycophants and irresponsible adventurers. At Ludwigsburg young Schiller saw much of the ways of the world and learned early to hate social and political tyranny.

Among the duke's many projects was a military school, established to train the sons of his officers for the public service. When he was fourteen Schiller was offered a scholarship at the academy, a princely favor not to be rejected by his parents, even though it meant giving up their plans for his future. He began as a student of law, but did badly, and when the school was moved to Stuttgart two years later, he transferred to the study of medicine. But in spite of his formal education, young Schiller's true interests did not seem to lie in divinity or law or medicine, but in literature. Although the strict discipline of the academy prevented easy access to contemporary writing, contraband works of the revolutionary "Sturm und Drang" authors found their way into his hands and were avidly read. Under the influence of this reading, and possibly of his own reaction to the world of Ludwigsburg, Schiller began his first play, The Robbers, a wild, romantic melodrama of social injustice and rebellion.

In 1780, Schiller was honorably dismissed from the academy, although without a doctor's degree, and was assigned as army doctor to a regiment of invalid soldiers at Stuttgart. To augment his meager income he decided to borrow money and publish his play. As a book, The Robbers was largely ignored, but it came to the attention of Dalberg, director of a theater at Mannheim, who in 1782 produced a revised version which was a tremendous success. Dissatisfied with an unpleasant job, and flattered by his sudden notoriety into the conviction that he was born to be a writer of tragedy, Schiller deserted the Württemberg army and fled to Mannheim in a neighboring principality. Dalberg was at first reluctant to associate himself with a refugee from another state, but by 1783 it was apparent that the Duke of Württemberg had ignored the desertion, and Schiller received a one-year contract as theater-playwright. In the following year two new plays were produced at Mannheim, neither of which enjoyed anything like the success of The Robbers, but which were, like that play, characterized by a vehement, high-keyed prose and radical sentiments.

Schiller's contract with Dalberg was not renewed, and in 1784 he moved to Leipzig and then to Dresden, where he published his journal, Die rheinische Thalia, and worked in a desultory manner on a new play, Don Carlos. This tragedy, finished in 1787, represents in many ways the midpoint in Schiller's development as a dramatist. As is true of the earlier Mannheim plays, the language is often high-pitched and the action confusing; like them, the plot deals with an idealist, the Marquis Posa, who is destroyed by his own fanaticism, but, as in the later plays, the form is poetic and the thought mature.

After the completion of *Don Carlos* there was a hiatus of ten years in Schiller's dramatic output. In 1787 he went to Weimar, where he made the acquaintance of the poet Herder, and finally settled in Jena. In his reading for *Don Carlos*, Schiller had become interested in the Spanish-Dutch conflict of the sixteenth century, and as a result decided to devote himself to the writing of history. In 1788 he published his *Geschichte des Abfalls der vereinigten Niederlande (History of the Defection of the Netherlands)*, and during the next four years wrote the impressive *History of the Thirty Years' War*. Although Schiller's success as a historian led to his appointment as professor at the University of Jena, his work in that field is more notable for its literary qualities than for its historical accuracy or scientific objectivity. He instinctively sided with the oppressed and rebellious, and his republican sympathies colored his prose as well as his plays.

While at Jena, Schiller divided his time between history and philosophy. His concern was primarily with the study of aesthetics, although that is never, in his thinking, entirely divorced from ethics. His best-known essays in this field are *On Grace and Dignity* and *On Naïve and Sentimental Poetry*.

Schiller first met Goethe in Jena, and from 1794 on they were close friends and literary allies. Partly through Goethe's influence, Schiller's interest in writing poetry revived. Together they made a study of the epic style, and out of this interest grew a number of ballads and romanzas which are still among Schiller's most popular works. During this period Schiller also wrote several reflective lyrics expressing the humane idealism and high ethical aspirations which characterized his thought. Goethe was also at that time the director of the small theater at Weimar, where Schiller moved in 1799, and the two friends often worked together selecting and adapting plays for production there. The renewed contact with the stage quite naturally reawakened Schiller's love for the drama, and the remaining years of his life were spent writing poetic plays for the Weimar theater. With a burst of energy he wrote in rapid succession his five greatest plays: the *Wallenstein* trilogy, made up of *Wallenstein's Camp* (1798), *The Piccolomini* (1799), and *Wallenstein's Death* (1799); *Mary Stuart, The Maid of Orleans, The Bride of Messina,* and *William Tell*. The last, undoubtedly Schiller's most popular play, is an intensely human drama dealing with the rebellion of the Swiss people against their Austrian rulers. In the midst of writing still another historical play, *Demetrius,* Schiller contracted the illness which led to his premature death on May 9, 1805.

Schiller has always been considered among the greatest of German dramatists. Although poetic in form, his last plays are by no means lyrical, their force lying in their sonorous, sometimes rhetorical language, and in the intense sincerity of the playwright's idealism. His characteristic themes are those of persecution and tyranny, for Schiller, writing at the height of German Romanticism, was in both philosophy and politics the representative dramatist of his age.

BIBLIOGRAPHICAL REFERENCES: A comprehensive edition of Schiller's works is the *Säkularausgabe*, edited by E. von der Hellen, 16 vols., 1904–1905. The pioneer study of Schiller in English is Thomas Carlyle, *The Life of Friedrich Schiller*, 1845, still useful in spite of the difficulties of the style. For more recent estimates see J. G. Robertson, *Schiller after a Century*, 1906; H. B. Garland, *Schiller*, 1949; William Witte, *Schiller*, 1949; and E. L. Stahl, *Friedrich Schiller's Drama, Theory, and Practice*, 1954. For biographical and critical studies in German see C. von Wolzogen, *Schillers Leben*, 1830; Reinhard Buchwald, *Schiller*, 2 vols., 1937, and *Schiller und Beethoven*, 1946; Ernst Müller, *Der junge Schiller*, 1943; Kurt May, *Friedrich Schiller: Idee und Wirklichkeit im Drama*, 1948; Bernhard Martin, *Schiller und Goethe*, 1949; and Melitta Gerhard, *Schiller*, 1950.

ARTHUR SCHOPENHAUER

Born: Danzig (free city)
Date: February 22, 1788

Died: Frankfurt-am-Main, Germany
Date: September 21, 1860

PRINCIPAL WORKS

PHILOSOPHICAL TREATISES: *Die Welt als Wille und Vorstellung*, 1818 (*The World as Will and Idea*); *Über den Willen in der Natur*, 1836 (*On the Will in Nature*); *Die beiden Grundprobleme der Ethik*, 1841 (*The Two Fundamental Problems of Ethics*); *Parerga und Paralipomena*, 1851 (*Essays*).

Arthur Schopenhauer, the unacademic, pessimistic, woman-hating, self-glorifying philosopher, was born on February 22, 1788, into a rich merchant family living in the free city of Danzig. His father, Heinrich Schopenhauer, was a liberal thinker, a Voltairian, who admired England and feared that Prussia would annex Danzig. When his fears were realized in 1793, the Schopenhauers hurriedly moved to Hamburg. Arthur lived there with his family for four years, and then at the age of nine was placed with a French family in Le Havre in order that he might learn the French language for its commercial value.

In 1803, when he was fifteen, he was placed with an English cleric's family and attended the boarding school there. He was disturbed by the cant and hypocrisy of his instructors and consequently was irritated by the daily rounds of prayers. After three months he returned and was sent on a European tour, having promised that upon his return he would enter his father's business. True to his word, but against his inclinations, he became a clerk in a commercial house in Hamburg.

In 1805 the death of his father, presumably as a suicide, freed Schopenhauer from the business career he disliked. His mother, a popular novelist, had been handicapped by domestic ties, although there is reason to believe she had not wholly respected them; she moved to Weimar and established a literary salon which attracted many intellectuals, artists, and lovers. The most distinguished member of her circle was the elderly Goethe. Although Arthur was impressed by his mother's friends, he thought them romantic and flighty,

953

and he disapproved of his mother's love affairs. He quarreled with her violently, and they parted; loathing each other, they maintained their hatred until their deaths.

Schopenhauer then studied the classics at the Gymnasium at Gotha, before going on to the University of Göttingen, where he studied Plato, Kant, and other philosophers under Schulze. Two years later he moved to Berlin, where he studied the natural sciences and, with distaste, heard Fichte lecture. At Jena, to which he hurried when Prussia declared war against France, he completed his doctorate, and his thesis, in 1813, became his first book, *Über die vierfache Wurzel des Satzes vom Zureichenden Grunde (On the Fourfold Root of the Principle of Sufficient Reason).*

In 1818, in his most important work, *The World as Will and Idea,* he presented his basic philosophy to the effect that everything is a manifestation of the will, and that since life is misery, man's objective should be to eliminate the will. The work, disregarded at the time, did not become popular or famous until after Schopenhauer had published his later books.

During the 1820's he had a brief and unsuccessful phase as a lecturer at the University of Berlin, withdrawing when he failed to obtain a professorship. From 1831 until his death he lived in solitude at Frankfurt-am-Main, convinced of his own genius and devoting his time to his writing and to his poodle Atma (meaning, the world-soul). He died of a heart attack following pneumonia on September 21, 1860.

BIBLIOGRAPHICAL REFERENCES: The principal works of Schopenhauer are available in English translations by various hands. For the general reader a good introduction to his philosophy is *The Living Thoughts of Schopenhauer,* edited by Thomas Mann, 1940. For biography and analysis see Helen Zimmern, *Arthur Schopenhauer,* 1876; Kuno Fischer, *Schopenhauer,* 1877; Wilhelm Gwinner, *Schopenhauer,* 1878; William Wallace, *Life of Schopenhauer,* 1902—a basic book among the biographical studies; Georg Simmel, *Schopenhauer and Nietzsche,* 1907; André Fauconnet, *L'Esthétique de Schopenhauer,* 1913; V. J. McGill, *Schopenhauer: Pessimist and Pagan,* 1931; Frederic Copleston, *Arthur Schopenhauer, Philosopher of Pessimism,* 1946; Arthur Hübscher, *Arthur Schopenhauer, ein Lebensbild,* 1949; and Hugo Busch, *Das Testament Arthur Schopenhauers,* 1950.

OLIVE SCHREINER

Born: Cape Province, Africa
Date: March 24, 1855

Died: Cape Town, South Africa
Date: December 12, 1920

PRINCIPAL WORKS

NOVELS: *The Story of an African Farm,* 1883; *Trooper Peter Halket of Mashonaland,* 1897; *From Man to Man,* 1926; *Undine,* 1928.

SHORT STORIES: *Dreams,* 1891; *Dream Life and Real Life,* 1893.

LETTERS: *The Letters of Olive Schreiner,* 1924.

Olive (Emilie Albertina) Schreiner, born at the Wittebergen Mission Station in the African Cape Province on March 24, 1855, was the daughter of

954

a Methodist missionary of German descent and English background. She was largely self-educated, for her family lived too far away from any schools for her to attend. At the age of fifteen she became a governess for a Boer family living on the edge of the Karoo Desert, and while still in her teens she began working on what was to be her famous novel, *The Story of an African Farm*. When it was completed, unable to find a publisher, she invested her limited savings in a trip to England to find a publisher. When the book appeared in 1883, under the pseudonym "Ralph Iron," the author's true identity soon became known, and, since the novel was critical of Christianity and feministic, it created a kind of notoriety for its writer. Olive Schreiner remained in England for eight unhappy years before returning to her native Africa;

during this time she became a close friend of Havelock Ellis.

In 1894 she married S. C. Cronwright (who later added Schreiner to his name), a Boer farmer and lawyer, with whom she collaborated in writing *The Political Situation*, 1895. As her literary executor he saw also to the publication of her posthumous books. They had one child, a daughter who died in infancy. During the Boer War, Olive Schreiner was strongly pro-Boer (her second novel, *Trooper Peter Halket of Mashonaland*, had satirized Cecil Rhodes), but a pacifist during World War I. She died at Cape Town on December 12, 1920. Although she wrote much in later life, relatively little was published until after her death. Two novels, a collection of short fiction, and an edition of her letters appeared posthumously.

BIBLIOGRAPHICAL REFERENCES: The fullest biographical account is *The Life of Olive Schreiner*, written by her husband, S. C. Cronwright-Schreiner, 1924. See also Margaret Lawrence, *The School of Femininity*, 1936; and V. Buchanan Gould, *Not Without Honour*, 1948.

MICHAEL SCOTT

Born: Cowlairs, Scotland
Date: October 30, 1789

Died: Glasgow, Scotland
Date: November 7, 1835

PRINCIPAL WORKS

NOVELS: *Tom Cringle's Log*, 1829–1833; *The Cruise of the Midge*, 1834–1835.

Son of a Glasgow merchant, Michael Scott was born at Cowlairs, Scotland, on October 30, 1789, and educated at the high school in Glasgow and at the University of Glasgow. He went to Jamaica in 1806, sent there as an estate manager. In 1810 he founded his own business at Kingston. Many of the incidents recorded in his fiction occurred on trips that he took about the West Indies as a businessman. Scott returned

to Scotland for a time in 1817. While there he married Margaret Bogle, of Glasgow; they had several children in later years. Scott returned to Jamaica, to remain from 1818 to 1822. Although he remained a merchant until his death, he apparently began to write seriously during the early 1820's.

Tom Cringle's Log began appearing as a series of sketches in *Blackwood's Magazine* in 1829 and ran intermittently until its completion in 1833. As the numbers appeared, the story became very popular, although the identity of its author was not known until some time after Scott's death, which occurred at Glasgow on November 7, 1835.

Tom Cringle's Log did not appear in book form under that title until it was printed in France in 1834, as a volume in Baudry's "European Library." The book's effectiveness and popularity undoubtedly stemmed from the exotic setting and the fact that Scott wrote humorously and a first hand of life in the West Indies. Scott's second novel, The Cruise of the Midge, also appeared serially and anonymously. Like the first, it ran in Blackwood's Magazine, 1834–1835. Critics were not as lavish in their praise of the second book as they had been of the first, and readers found its humor forced. The novel first appeared in book form in France in 1836. Scott never loomed large on the literary scene, and his work has gone relatively unnoticed by literary scholars.

BIBLIOGRAPHICAL REFERENCES: There is no full-length biography and almost no criticism available. Apart from brief sketches in the standard biographical dictionaries, the best source of information on Michael Scott will be found in Sir George Douglas, The Blackwood Group, 1897.

SIR WALTER SCOTT

Born: Edinburgh, Scotland
Date: August 15, 1771

Died: Abbotsford, Scotland
Date: September 21, 1832

PRINCIPAL WORKS

NOVELS: Waverley, 1814; Guy Mannering, 1815; The Antiquary, 1816; The Black Dwarf, 1816; Old Mortality, 1816; Rob Roy, 1818; The Heart of Midlothian, 1818; The Bride of Lammermoor, 1819; A Legend of Montrose, 1819; Ivanhoe, 1820; The Monastery, 1820; The Abbot, 1820; Kenilworth, 1821; The Pirate, 1822; The Fortunes of Nigel, 1822; Peveril of the Peak, 1823; Quentin Durward, 1823; St. Ronan's Well, 1824; Redgauntlet, 1824; The Betrothed, 1825; The Talisman, 1825; Woodstock, 1826; Chronicles of the Canongate, 1927 (The Two Drovers, The Highland Widow, The Surgeon's Daughter); The Fair Maid of Perth, 1828; Anne of Geierstein, 1829; Count Robert of Paris, 1831; Castle Dangerous, 1831.

POEMS: The Lay of the Last Minstrel, 1805; Marmion, 1808; The Lady of the Lake, 1810; The Vision of Don Roderick, 1811; The Bridal of Triermain, 1813; The Lord of the Isles, 1815; Rokeby, 1815.

MISCELLANEOUS: The Life and Works of John Dryden, 1808; The Life and Works of Jonathan Swift, 1814; The Life of Napoleon Buonaparte, 1827.

In spite of physical handicaps Walter Scott lived a full, varied life and created an impressive body of writings. Stricken with infantile paralysis before he was two years old, and alternating between periods of physical vigor and serious ailments throughout his life, he loved and practiced outdoor sports for most of his sixty-odd years.

Born in Edinburgh, August 15, 1771, he was a product of the eighteenth century as well as of the romantic nineteenth. As a child he was a voracious reader and avid listener to tales and legends, particularly those of his native Scotland. His copious reading was stored in a retentive memory and used to advantage in his writings; and his interest in folklore led to his collection and publication of Scottish ballads. Although not a brilliant student, he was praised for his ability to enjoy and understand the Latin poets. He entered the University of Edinburgh in 1783, but after a year at college he suffered one of his severe illnesses and had to return home. He spent his convalescence with a sympathetic uncle, Captain Robert Scott, who encouraged his literary interests.

He studied law in his father's office; and in spite of a disinclination for the profession, he was admitted to the bar in 1792. He made use of his legal experiences in his novels, especially *Redgauntlet,* in which his friend William Clerk served as model for Darsie Latimer, and Scott himself for Allan Fairford. When he was twenty he cast his eye on a lovely fifteen-year-old girl, Williamina Belsches. After an unsuccessful courtship of five years he lost her to a rival and indulged his sorrow for a time with melancholy self-dramatization out of keeping with his usual behavior.

In 1797, when the fear of a Napoleonic invasion seized Great Britain, Scott was the moving force in forming a volunteer home-guard unit, in which he held the position of quartermaster. In spite of his crippled leg he was a bold and expert horseman, and apparently was disappointed at not engaging Napoleon's forces. In the same year, on a tour of the Lake Country with his brother John and his friend Adam Ferguson, he met Charlotte Carpenter (Charpentier), daughter of a French royalist and ward of an English nobleman. This time his courtship was both short and successful, and he married his Charlotte on Christmas Eve, 1797. Their first child died in infancy, but four children reached maturity, two sons and two daughters.

In 1799 Scott was appointed Sheriff-depute of Selkirkshire; the position brought him a steady income and not-too-onerous duties. Seven years later he became Clerk of the Session in Edinburgh, adding to his steady income and increasing his routine labors considerably.

Although he translated for publication Gottfried Bürger's *Lenore* (1799) and Goethe's *Goetz von Berlichingen* (1799) and collected and edited—often revised—ballads in his *Minstrelsy of the Scottish Border* (1802–1803), he won his first recognition as a poet in 1805 with *The Lay of the Last Minstrel* and became a major literary figure in England with *Marmion* and *The Lady of the Lake*. His subsequent long poems added little to his reputation. Shortly after the publication of *The Lay of the Last Minstrel* he formed a partnership (Scott to be a silent partner) with the printer James Ballantyne, an old school friend. During his poetic career Scott completed two major works of scholarship, an eighteen-volume edition of Dryden and a nineteen-volume edition of Swift, either of which would have made a reputation for a professional scholar.

In 1814, with the anonymous publication of *Waverley*, Scott began a new literary career and his most illustrious, for he is now considered primarily a historical novelist, more than either poet or scholar. Scott gave reasons for not acknowledging the authorship of his novels; but at least one reason was a childish delight in mystification, a puckish joy in throwing dust into the public eye. Between 1814 and his death in 1832, he completed about thirty novels and novelettes, several long poems, a large mass of miscellaneous writings, and a nine-volume *Life of Napoleon*.

Scott was the first baronet created by George IV (1820). By this time he had bought acres of land and was sinking a fortune in Abbotsford. One friend who helped plan Abbotsford and stock its library was Daniel Terry, the actor-manager who produced dramatic versions of several of Scott's works, making an especial hit as Bailie Jarvie in *Rob Roy*. Scott's publishing ventures were in bad circumstances which grew worse; in 1826 Constable and Ballantyne failed. Instead of taking refuge in bankruptcy, Scott undertook to write himself and his colleagues out of debt. Few men have displayed more fortitude under adversity. To cap the material loss he suffered a severe spiritual one in the death of his beloved wife. His grief was profound, but he continued to write. In 1830, apparently as a result of his Herculean labors under stress, he suffered his first stroke of apoplexy. He recovered and continued work until recurring strokes paralyzed him and practically destroyed his mind. He died September 21, 1832, still in debt; but his son-in-law, John Gibson Lockhart, cleared the debts with the proceeds of his superb biography of the baronet.

Scott's merits as man and writer entitle him to a position much nearer his former reputation than he now holds. One of his admirers called him a combination of Shakespeare and Samuel Johnson. Those who think of him only as a cloak-and-sword romancer overlook his remarkable gift of creating comic characters and his broad view of human nature in all walks of life. He was greatly admired by Balzac and Dumas; and wise critics from Goethe to the present have been impressed with his humane wisdom.

George Burke Johnston

BIBLIOGRAPHICAL REFERENCES: There is no recent scholarly edition of Scott's works. The Border Edition of the *Waverley Novels*, 48 vols., 1892–1894, contains notes by Andrew Lang. John Gibson Lockhart's *Memoirs of the Life of Sir Walter Scott, Bart.*, 1837–1838, is still the standard biography. See also John Buchan (Lord Tweedsmuir), *Sir Walter Scott*, 1932; Sir Herbert Grierson, *Sir Walter Scott, Bart.*, 1938; Hesketh Pearson, *Sir Walter Scott*, 1954; and Paul N. Landis, "The Waverley Novels, or a Hundred Years After," *Publications of the Modern Language Association*, LII (1937), 461–473.

MADELEINE DE SCUDÉRY

Born: Le Havre, France
Date: 1607

Died: Paris, France
Date: June 2, 1701

PRINCIPAL WORKS

NOVELS: *Ibrahim, ou l'illustre bassa*, 1641; *Artamène, ou le grand Cyrus*, 1646–1653; *Clélie*, 1654–1661; *Almahide, ou l'esclave reine*, 1661–1663.
ESSAY: *Le Discours de la gloire*, 1671.

Madeleine de Scudéry was the sister of Georges de Scudéry, a famous dramatist and poet of seventeenth century France. Born in Le Havre in 1607, she went to Paris to live with her brother and soon became well-known in French literary circles as a member of the group known as the Rambouillet coterie. Being a forceful personality, she became a person of consequence in Paris, succeeding Mme. de Rambouillet as the leading hostess of literary Paris in the late 1640's. The salon she established was called the *Société du samedi,* the Saturday Club. As a result of her efforts, Madeleine de Scudéry became the first "bluestocking" of the European literary world. She enjoyed the friendship of Louis XIV and other royalty, as well as that of such famous literary figures as Boileau.

She began to publish prose romances in 1641, when *Ibrahim, ou l'illustre Bassa* appeared. In an age when French romances earned notoriety for their length, hers were longer than most; *Artamène,* was published in ten volumes. It was followed by *Clélie,* and *Almahide.* Though they ostensibly presented an Oriental setting and Oriental heroes and heroines, these romances used the language and action of seventeenth century France, the characters often being recognizable people of the writer's fashionable circle. The romances were published anonymously or under her brother's name, but there is little doubt that she wrote them herself. They were outstandingly popular at the time, at least in aristocratic circles. A writer of essays and other prose studies as well as fiction, Mlle. de Scudéry was the first winner of the prize for French eloquence with her *Discours de la gloire* in 1671. She died in Paris on June 2, 1701.

BIBLIOGRAPHICAL REFERENCES: For biography and criticism see Claude Aragonnés, *Madeleine de Scudéry, reine de tendre,* 1934; and Maurice Magendie, *Le Roman français au XVIIᵉ siècle,* 1932.

LUCIUS ANNAEUS SENECA

Born: Corduba (now Córdoba), Spain   *Died:* Near Rome, Italy
Date: c. 4 B.C.   *Date:* A.D. 65

PRINCIPAL WORKS

PHILOSOPHICAL TREATISES: *De consolatione ad Marciam,* c. 40–41 (*Consolation Addressed to Marcia*); *De ira,* c. 41–44 (*On Anger*); *De brevitate vitae,* c. 49 (*On the Briefness of Life*); *De clementia,* c. 55 (*On Clemency*); *De vita beata,* c. 58 (*On the Happy Life*); *De beneficiis,* c. 62–64 (*On Benefits*); *Naturales quaestiones,* c. 62–64 (*Natural Questions*); *Epistulae morales,* c. 63.

PLAYS: *Hercules furens, Troades, Phoenissae, Medea, Oedipus, Phaedra, Agamemnon, Thyestes, Hercules Oetaeus.*

SATIRE: *Apocolocyntosis,* c. 55 (*Pumpkinification*).

Lucius Annaeus Seneca, born about 4 B.C., was the son of Annaeus Seneca, a famous rhetorician of Córdoba. The family possessed wealth and high rank, and at an early age Seneca was sent to Rome to be educated. As a student of rhetoric and philosophy, the young man came to the notice of the Emperor Caligula, under whose patronage he entered the Roman senate and

959

gained fame as an orator. Accused by the Empress Messalina of a love affair with Caligula's sister, Seneca was banished to Corsica by the Emperor Claudius. Many of Seneca's philosophical writings were written during his exile, but his conduct while in Corsica apparently exhibited little of the stoicism he advocated. Unhappy in his banishment, he begged to be recalled to Rome. In 49 Agrippina, the new wife of Claudius, procured his return and made him a tutor to her eleven-year-old son Domitius, later the Emperor Nero.

Seneca and Sextus Afranius Burrus, prefect of the Praetorian guard, exercised great influence over Nero and were, according to Tacitus, responsible for the mildness which marked the early years of that monarch's reign. Through Nero, Seneca was for a time virtually the ruler of Rome, but after the death of Burrus in 62, his position as an adviser became dangerous because of the restraints he tried to impose on his debauched and brutal master. New advisers to Nero, who cared little for good government or justice, were at the emperor's ear. Nero was constantly in need of money, and Seneca was wealthy, enormously so. Moreover, enemies had pointed out to the emperor that Seneca was Nero's greatest rival at oratory and poetry, that Seneca was very popular with the Romans, and that he had disparaged Nero's poetry and horsemanship. Seneca, learning of the dangerous situation, went to Nero and asked permission to retire from public life. Although Nero refused to grant permission, Seneca appeared less and less at court and spent much of his time in the privacy of his estate near Rome.

In 65 Seneca was accused of plotting against Nero. Ordered by the emperor to commit suicide, Seneca cut the veins of his wrists and while entertaining friends at his villa near Rome allowed himself to bleed to death. Although some authorities in the past have thought Seneca was a Christian, there is no accepted evidence that he was.

It is difficult to associate Seneca's writings with his life, for too little information has been saved which relates the two. In his philosophical writings, Seneca delineated a stoicism that he himself apparently failed to practice. In addition to his philosophical writings, Seneca left nine tragedies, probably designed to be read rather than to be viewed on the stage. During the period between 1580 and 1640, Seneca's plays greatly influenced Elizabethan and Jacobean dramatists; stage devices like ghosts, murders, and long-winded harangues by the chief characters were borrowed directly from Senecan drama. Some authorities have maintained that the Senecan plays are an adjunct to his philosophical writings, each play illustrating a point of Stoic doctrine, *Thyestes*, for example, dealing with retribution. Dating of the plays is next to impossible.

BIBLIOGRAPHICAL REFERENCES: The principal works of Seneca, in translations by various hands, are available in the Loeb Classical Library. The plays, translated by F. J. Miller and by Ella Isabel Harris, are in *The Complete Roman Drama*, edited by George E. Duckworth, 2 vols., 1942. See also W. C. Summers, *The Silver Age of Latin Literature*, 1920; Francis C. Holland, *Seneca*, 1920; F. L. Lucas, *Seneca and Elizabethan Tragedy*, 1922; T. S. Eliot, *Selected Essays*, 1932; and André de Bovis, *La Sagesse de Sénèque*, 1948.

WILLIAM SHAKESPEARE

Born: Stratford-upon-Avon, England   *Died:* Stratford-upon-Avon
Date: April (23?), 1564   *Date:* April 23, 1616

PRINCIPAL WORKS

PLAYS: *Henry VI*, Parts I, II, and III, 1589–1591; *Richard III*, 1592–1593; *The Comedy of Errors*, 1592–1594; *Titus Andronicus*, 1593–1594; *The Taming of the Shrew*, 1593–1594; *Two Gentlemen of Verona*, 1594–1595; *Love's Labour's Lost*, 1595; *Romeo and Juliet*, 1594–1596; *Richard II*, 1595–1596; *A Midsummer Night's Dream*, 1595–1596; *King John*, 1596–1597; *The Merchant of Venice*, 1596–1597; *The Merry Wives of Windsor*, 1597–1601; *Henry IV*, Parts I and II, 1597–1598; *Much Ado About Nothing*, 1598–1599; *Henry V*, 1598–1599; *Julius Caesar*, 1599–1600; *As You Like It*, 1599–1600; *Twelfth Night*, 1599–1600; *Hamlet*, 1600–1601; *Troilus and Cressida*, 1601–1602; *All's Well That Ends Well*, 1602–1604; *Othello*, 1604; *Measure for Measure*, 1604–1605; *King Lear*, 1605; *Macbeth*, 1606; *Antony and Cleopatra*, 1606–1607; *Coriolanus*, 1607–1608; *Timon of Athens*, 1605–1608; *Pericles*, 1608; *Cymbeline*, 1609; *The Winter's Tale*, 1610–1611; *The Tempest*, 1611; *Henry VIII*, 1612–1613 (with Fletcher).

POEMS: *Venus and Adonis*, 1593; *The Rape of Lucrece*, 1594; *The Passionate Pilgrim*, 1599; *The Phoenix and the Turtle*, 1601; *Sonnets*, 1609.

William Shakespeare, greatest of English poets and dramatists, was born at Stratford-upon-Avon in 1564 and died there in 1616. The biographical data, though sufficient to demolish the Baconian and other heresies, are not helpful in other respects. The view that Shakespeare attended Stratford Grammar School, though inherently probable, remains a surmise, and little is known of his activities prior to 1590, save that he married Anne Hathaway in 1582 and had three children by her.

Most of Shakespeare's working life was spent in London, and allusions, friendly and otherwise, show that by 1592 he was a dramatist of recognized achievement. Francis Meres, in *Palladis Tamia* (1598), virtually establishes that his supremacy in comedy, tragedy, and narrative poetry was generally acknowledged, and this view is endorsed by later testimony, notably that of Ben Jonson. From 1594 on Shakespeare was associated exclusively with the Lord Chamberlain's company, which became the King's company in 1603. This was the most stable and prosperous of the Elizabethan dramatic companies. It built the Globe Theatre in 1599, and acquired the Blackfriars private theater in 1608.

So far as can be ascertained, Shakespeare's career as a dramatist covers the period c. 1590 to c. 1612. His early years show him working in all categories. Chronicle histories are a conspicuous feature of the years 1590–1599, and these reflect England's self-awareness at a time when the threat from Spain was still acutely felt. The same period saw the maturing of his comic genius, through such minor masterpieces as *Love's Labour's Lost* and *A Midsummer Night's Dream*, to the three great comedies, *The Merchant of Venice*, *Much Ado about Nothing*, and *As You Like It*. Two early tragedies, *Titus Andronicus* and *Romeo and Juliet*, promise far more than they actually perform, and *Julius Caesar*, though flawless in conception and execution, lacks urgency and depth. By the end of the century Shakepeare's achievement had equalled, but not surpassed, that of Chaucer, the greatest of his predecessors. The foremost lesson so far learnt was that human and poetic truth, as embodied in Falstaff, is greater than the historical truth of Hal and Hotspur.

After 1600, Shakespeare bade farewell to romantic comedy in the incomparable *Twelfth Night,* and appears to have devoted one or two years to earnest contemplation of both life and art. *Hamlet* is the first of the great tragedies and also the first of a group of deeply contemplative dramas, often referred to as "problem plays," comprising *Troilus and Cressida, All's Well that Ends Well,* and *Measure for Measure,* which furnish an ample background to Shakespeare's whole output. When the tragic hero emerges again in *Othello,* his appeal is more directly emotional than Hamlet's, and this impassioned conception prevails in *King Lear* and *Macbeth.* In these titanic masterpieces man's response to the workings of a relentless and malign destiny is explored and exploited to the full, and the terrible logic of the action is communicated in language of ever-increasing urgency and intensity. *Antony and Cleopatra,* despite its superlative poetry, fails to secure a comparable tragic effect, but looks forward to the regenerative pattern of the late romances. *Timon of Athens* is excessive in its pessimism, and was left unfinished, but *Coriolanus* triumphantly affirms Shakespeare's capacity for recovery. Though outwardly uninviting in both matter and manner, its emotional impact proves terrific, and its psychology is penetrating. The plays of Shakespeare's final period are dramatic romances which present improbable persons and incidents and draw freely upon the musical and spectacular elements popular in the Court masques of the period. Here the themes of atonement and reconciliation, earlier treated in *All's Well that Ends Well* and *Measure for Measure,* are co-ordinated in a general pattern of regeneration symbolized by the heroines. *Pericles* and *Cymbeline* are uncertain in their handling of complicated plot material, but *The Winter's Tale* is magnificent and intense and *The Tempest* confers perfection on these endeavors. *Henry VIII,* last of the canonical plays, is thought to have been written in collaboration with Fletcher. *The Two Noble Kinsmen* purports to be the product of the same partnership, but the alleged Shakespearian scenes have been denounced by many competent critics. Attempts to claim other dramatic works of the period for Shakespeare have, in the main, proved abortive, though it has now been established, beyond reasonable doubt, that *The Book of Sir Thomas More* (British Museum MS. Harley 7368) contains three pages of his work in autograph.

Dryden justly claimed that Shakespeare "was the man who of all Modern, and perhaps Ancient Poets, had the largest and most comprehensive soul." He is the supreme interpreter of human relationships, the supreme percipient of human frailties and potentialities. It is often alleged that he is no philosopher, that his mind is neither mystical nor prophetic, that the beatific vision of Dante is beyond his scope. Even so, his thought, governed by the Christian neo-Platonism of his day, is earnest and profound, and his writings as a whole reveal a consistent, coherent, and possibly distinctive philosophical system. The comedies move ultimately to an acute awareness of the mutability of human affairs, and this sense of time's implacability is crystallized in the Sonnets and communicated, with inexpressible poignancy, in *Twelfth Night*. In the historical plays the curse which falls upon the commonwealth through the deposition and murder of an anointed king is pursued through successive manifestations of violence and anarchy, of which Falstaff is made finally the most potent symbol, until expiation is complete in Henry Tudor. Here the manipulation of history is determined by a clearly-ordered conception of political morality no less than by an artistic conscience. The same outlook is more flexibly presented in *Hamlet*, and Ulysses' great exposition of degree in *Troilus and Cressida* summarizes the acquired political wisdom of a decade. But there is no break in continuity, and Ulysses' speech is equally applicable to the great tragedies, in which Shakespeare contemplates the chaos that ensues when "degree is suffocate." Cognate with the doctrine of degree, and informing the histories and tragedies at all stages, is the concept of absolute justice. Portia, in *The Merchant of Venice*, pleads that mercy is above justice, and this is exemplified, in strenuous and practical terms, in *Measure for Measure*. The conflict between justice and mercy is a conspicuous feature of the great tragedies, notably *King Lear*, and is ultimately resolved, in its tragic context, in *Coriolanus*, when the hero spares Rome and gains his greatest victory—that over himself. *Cymbeline* and *The Winter's Tale*, albeit artificially, plunge into chaos comparable to the chaos of the tragedies, but the resolution now is in terms of reconciliation and regeneration instead of sacrifice and waste. Music, the prime function of the Creation, becomes increasingly prominent in these final romances, each of which looks clearly towards the harmony and unity of the Golden Age. The Platonic vision of the Many and the One, which informs these plays and carries them nearly into mysticism, though dramatically new, is something which Shakespeare had earlier achieved in certain of the *Sonnets* and in the concentrated intricacy of *The Phoenix and the Turtle*, published in Robert Chester's *Love's Martyr* in 1601.

Criticism has often erred in emphasizing particular aspects of Shakespeare's art. With him, action, thought, character, and language are not separable elements; and our response, in theater and study alike, must be to a complex unity in which dramatic conceptions are simultaneously natural and poetic, and language, unique and infinitely creative. The greatest Shakespeare critics—Dryden, Johnson, Coleridge and Bradley—can always be read with profit and delight, and the enormous mass of twentieth century criticism contains much that is of value; but if we have ears to hear and a heart to understand we shall always find that Shakespeare is his own best interpreter.

J. M. Nosworthy

BIBLIOGRAPHICAL REFERENCES: Because of the extensive range of Shakespeare studies since 1900, even a tentative bibliography would fill a number of pages and would require separate listings for the individual plays. Only general areas of study and criticism can be indicated here. Standard editions are the *Cambridge Shakespeare*, edited by W. G. Clark and W. A. Wright, 9 vols., 1863–1866; the *New Variorum,* edited by H. H. Furness and others, 1871 ff.; the *Arden Shakespeare,* edited by W. J. Craig and R. J. Case, 39 vols., 1899–1924; the *New Cambridge,* edited by J. Dover Wilson, 1921 ff.; the *Kittredge Shakespeare,* edited by G. L. Kittredge, 1936; and the *New Arden,* under the general editorship of Una Ellis-Fermor, 1951 ff.

For biography see J. Q. Adams, *A Life of William Shakespeare,* 1923; E. K. Chambers, *William Shakespeare: A Study of Facts and Problems,* 2 vols., 1930; Leslie Hotson, *Shakespeare versus Shallow,* 1931; *idem, I, William Shakespeare,* 1937; J. Dover Wilson, *The Essential Shakespeare,* 1932; Hazleton Spencer, *The Art and Life of William Shakespeare,* 1940; Ivor Brown, *Shakespeare,* 1949; and Marchette Chute, *Shakespeare of London,* 1949.

General background studies include *Shakespeare's England,* edited by Walter Raleigh, 2 vols., 1916; E. K. Chambers, *The Elizabethan Stage,* 4 vols., 1923; Muriel St. C. Byrne, *Elizabethan Life in Town and Country,* 1925; Hardin Craig, *The Enchanted Glass,* 1936; G. B. Harrison, *Elizabethan Plays and Players,* 1940; G. E. Bentley, *The Jacobean and Caroline Stage,* 2 vols., 1941; Theodore Spencer, *Shakespeare and the Nature of Man,* 1942. For criticism see A. C. Bradley, *Shakespearean Tragedy,* 1904; *idem, Oxford Lectures on Poetry,* 1909; M. W. MacCallum, *Shakespeare's Roman Plays,* 1910; E. K. Chambers, *Shakespeare: A Survey,* 1925; G. Wilson Knight, *The Wheel of Fire,* 1930; W. W. Lawrence, *Shakespeare's Problem Comedies,* 1931; E. E. Stoll, *Art and Artifice in Shakespeare,* 1933; Caroline F. E. Spurgeon, *Shakespeare's Imagery,* 1936; Mark Van Doren, *Shakespeare,* 1939; Harley Granville-Barker, *Prefaces to Shakespeare,* 2 vols., 1946; Lily B. Campbell, *Shakespeare's "Histories,"* 1947; R. B. Heilman, *This Great Stage,* 1948; T. M. Parrott, *Shakespearean Comedy,* 1949; Donald Stauffer, *Shakespeare's World of Images,* 1949; and Karl J. Holzknecht, *The Backgrounds of Shakespeare's Plays,* 1950.

BERNARD SHAW

Born: Dublin, Ireland   *Died:* Ayot St. Lawrence, England
Date: July 26, 1856   *Date:* November 2, 1950

PRINCIPAL WORKS

PLAYS: *Widowers' Houses,* 1893 [1892]*; *Plays, Pleasant and Unpleasant,* 1898 (*Pleasant: Arms and the Man* [1894], *Candida* [1897], *The Man of Destiny* [1897], *You Never Can Tell* [1899]; *Unpleasant: Widowers' Houses, Mrs. Warren's Profession* [1902], *The Philanderer* [1905]); *Three Plays for Puritans,* 1901 (*The Devil's Disciple* [1897], *Caesar and Cleopatra* [1901], *Captain Brassbound's Conversion* [1900]); *Man and Superman,* 1903 [1905]; *John Bull's Other Island,* 1907 (*John Bull's Other Island* [1904], *How He Lied to Her Husband* [1904], *Major Barbara* [1905]); *Press Cuttings,* 1909; *The Doctor's Dilemma,* 1911 (*The Doctor's Dilemma* [1906], *Getting Married* [1908], *The Shewing-up of Blanco Posnet* [1909]); *Misalliance,* 1914 (*Misalliance* [1910], *The Dark Lady of the Sonnets* [1910], *Fanny's First Play* [1911]); *Androcles and the Lion,* 1916 (*Androcles and the Lion* [1913], *Overruled* [1912], *Pygmalion* [1913]); *Heartbreak House,* 1919 (*Heartbreak House* [1920], *Great Catherine* [1913], *Playlets of the War*); *Back to Methuselah,* 1921 [1922]; *Saint Joan,* 1924 [1923]; *The Apple Cart,* 1929; *Too True to Be Good,* 1934 (*Too True to Be Good* [1932], *A Village Wooing* [1934],

* *Dates of first performances which differ from dates of book publication are set within brackets.*

On the Rocks [1933]); *The Simpleton of the Unexpected Isles*, 1936 (*The Simpleton of the Unexpected Isles* [1935], *The Six of Calais* [1934], *The Millionairess* [1936]); *Geneva*, 1939 [1938]; *In Good King Charles's Golden Days*, 1939; *Buoyant Billions*, 1951 [1949].

NOVELS: *Cashel Byron's Profession*, 1886; *An Unsocial Socialist*, 1887; *Love among the Artists*, 1900; *The Irrational Knot*, 1905; *Immaturity*, 1930.

SHORT STORIES AND TALES: *The Adventures of the Black Girl in Her Search for God*, 1932; *Short Stories, Scraps, and Shavings*, 1934.

ESSAYS AND STUDIES: *The Quintessence of Ibsenism*, 1891; *The Sanity of Art*, 1895; *The Impossibilities of Anarchism*, 1893; *The Perfect Wagnerite*, 1898; *Dramatic Opinions and Essays*, 1906; *Common Sense about the War*, 1914 (reprinted as *What I Really Wrote about the War*, 1931); *The Intelligent Woman's Guide to Socialism and Capitalism*, 1928; *The League of Nations*, 1929; *Major Critical Essays*, 1930; *Our Theatres in the Nineties*, 1932 (3 vols.); *Music in London, 1890–1894*, 1932 (3 vols.); *Essays in Fabian Socialism*, 1932; *Pen Portraits and Reviews*, 1932; *London Music in 1888–1889*, 1937; *Everybody's Political What's What*, 1944.

AUTOBIOGRAPHY: *Shaw Gives Himself Away: An Autobiographical Miscellany*, 1939; *Sixteen Self Sketches*, 1949.

LETTERS: *Letters from George Bernard Shaw to Miss Alma Murray*, 1927; *Ellen Terry and Bernard Shaw: A Correspondence*, 1931 (with Ellen Terry); *Some Unpublished Letters of George Bernard Shaw*, 1939; *Bernard Shaw and Mrs. Patrick Campbell: Their Correspondence*, 1952.

(George) Bernard Shaw, dramatist, essayist, and critic, was born of Irish Protestant parents in Dublin on July 26, 1856. From his unsuccessful father and a "wicked uncle" he inherited his Shavian sense of fun and anticlimax and his "superficial blasphemy," from his mother a deep love and knowledge of music, which, with his keen interest in the spoken and written language, was to prove his most enduring love and one of the greatest influences on his work.

In 1876 Shaw left Ireland for good. Though not susceptible to its "Celtic twilight," he was to its natural beauty, the joy of which, he declared, was to remain with him all his life. His work retains what G. K. Chesterton called "the virginity and violence of Ireland. . . . a strange purity and a strange pugnacity." Before he left, he had made his first excursion into print, in a form that was to remain with him to the end a favorite means of expression: a letter to the press. This first one, written to *Public Opinion* in April 1875 on the advent of the famous "firm of American evangelists," Moody and Sankey, deals maturely enough with the unsavory effect on individuals of sudden conversion. True religion is not to be had on the cheap.

In London, where his mother had preceded him, having left her unloved husband to devote herself to music-teaching, young Shaw soon abandoned clerking and turned to literature by writing five novels between 1879 and 1883. All were commercially rejected or unsuccessful; the best are *Love Among the Artists* and *Cashel Byron's Profession*. Written for the most part in an early Shavian prose bearing traces of strained Victorian elegance, they are insufficiently enlivened by the virile colloquialism he later added to form the supple and athletic prose of his prefaces and plays. The genuine Shavian style was developed the hard way, by "a teeming and tumultuous life spent on many platforms, from the British Association to the triangle at the corner of Salmon's Lane in Limehouse." From this vital public speaking experience (1883–1895), Shaw learnt both how easy it is to lose an audience and yet how very much people are prepared to take in the way of serious thought and provocative ideas if entertainingly and strategically presented in dialectically dramatic form leavened with humor. He also acquired the great virtue of courtesy in debate and respect for his adversary's opinions, and to this his plays owe much—not least the great Trial Scene in *Saint Joan*, in which he is, if anything, "too fair" to the Inquisition.

An encounter (1882) with Henry George and the reading of Karl Marx had turned his thoughts towards socialism, and while any direct propagation of it is absent from his plays, his faith in it is the backbone of all his subsequent work. As he himself said, an understanding of economics was to him what a knowledge of anatomy was to Michelangelo, and it stood him in good stead not only as a local government councilor in St. Pancras (in North London) but on the Executive Committee of the small but influential Fabian Society, to which he devoted himself selflessly (1884–1911) and for which he edited *Fabian Essays* (1889) and wrote many well-known socialist tracts.

Political and public speaking activities did not prevent Shaw's taking proudly to journalism (he welcomed it as another platform), and it was as "Corno di Bassetto," music critic for the new *Star* newspaper (1888–1890),

that he made what was, perhaps, his first indelible mark on the intellectual and artistic consciousness of his times. In this and in his later music criticism for *The World* (1890–1894) and, above all, in his dramatic criticism for the *Saturday Review* (1895–1898), he was in fact attempting, as De Quincey said of Wordsworth, to create the taste by which he was to be appreciated. To this period also belong *The Quintessence of Ibsenism* and *The Perfect Wagnerite*, tributes to fellow "artist-philosophers" and revelatory as much of the author as of their subjects.

The rest of Shaw's life, especially after his marriage (1898) to the wealthy Charlotte Payne-Townshend, is mainly the history of his plays. Those written between 1892 and the end of the century may be said to be the extension of his theater criticism in more directly dramatic form. The first of these, *Widowers' Houses*, was actually begun in 1885 in collaboration with his great friend and fellow-Ibsenite, William Archer, but was finished quite independently in 1892 as the result of the challenge he felt to produce the drama he had been advocating. Into the earliest plays, which include *Mrs. Warren's Profession, Arms and the Man,* and *Candida* (one of the first of Shaw's remarkable gallery of marvelous feminine portraits), creeps already the Shavian theme of conversion—from dead system and outworn morality towards a more creatively vital approach to life—and it is further developed in *Three Plays for Puritans* written between 1897 and 1899: *The Devil's Disciple, Caesar and Cleopatra,* and *Captain Brassbound's Conversion.* These also develop Shaw's scathing attitude to the routineers and slaves of petty bourgeois morality and his fondness for the exponents of original virtue and for those, true to their own faiths, who live in defiance of accepted codes.

His quest for a new religion or purer ethical approach to life reaches its first apotheosis in the Hell Scene of *Man and Superman*, "a Comedy and a Philosophy" in which Don Juan advocates, against the barren worldliness of Everyman and the more eloquent hedonistic desires of the Devil, the ecstasy of philosophical thought and the true joy of man's unceasing creative evolutionary urge for world betterment as well as for his own self-improvement. This theme was further developed, refined, and possibly enfeebled in *Back to Methuselah*, the longest if not the greatest of all Shaw's attempts, in play and preface, to expound the gospel of Creative Evolution and the Life Force, which he had taken over from Butler and Bergson and to which he added his own more Shavianly socialistic and naturalistically mystical yearnings.

With the turn of the century, Shaw found fame at last, first on the Continent and in the United States, and then, with the important advent in his life of the actor-director-playwright, Granville Barker, in England itself during the Court Theater season of 1904–1907. Notable plays of this "second period" include *John Bull's Other Island*, *Major Barbara*, and *The Doctor's Dilemma*, which with the two more purely disquisitory plays, *Getting Married* and *Misalliance*, testify to the growing encyclopedic range of the Shavian drama. In 1909 Shaw was "investigated" by the Joint Select Committee on Stage Censorship and declared all his plays to be "conscientiously immoral." Every advance in

thought and conduct is made by immoralists and heretics, and from now on Shaw's attitude to men and affairs, manners and customs, and to current morality becomes ever more astringent, his religious views ever more "catholic and comprehensive," anti-Fundamentalist and non-anthropomorphic. In a long line of plays, from *The Shewing-up of Blanco Posnet* the same year, through *Androcles and the Lion* (his "religious pantomime"), *Heartbreak House*, *Saint Joan*, and onwards to the very end, he is seeking to distill the pure elixir of religion from the muddy faiths of mortal men, desperately trying not to empty out the baby with the dirty bath-water. The stern Shavian morality of complete individual responsibility, self-discipline, heroic effort without thought of reward or "atonement," and unsentimental and non-sexual regard for one's fellow beings is detectable in even a delightful "potboiler" like *Pygmalion*. In *Saint Joan*, whom Eric Bentley has said Shaw would have had to invent had she never existed, is synthesized the aspiring religious greatness of all Shaw's noblest characters and his impassioned devotion to what Bentley calls his "Both/And" view of life.

In 1925 Shaw was awarded the Nobel Prize for literature, but gave away the money to start the Anglo-Swedish Literary Foundation. In 1931 he visited Russia, and in 1932, with Mrs. Shaw, made a world tour which included the United States and a memorable address on political economy at the Metropolitan Opera House. Greater perhaps than any of the plays written in the last years of his life are the two prose works, *The Intelligent Woman's Guide to Socialism and Capitalism*, and *The Adventures of*

967

the Black Girl in Her Search for God. The later plays, except for *The Apple Cart,* have scarcely received adequate public stage presentation, and those such as *Too True To Be Good* and *The Simpleton of the Unexpected Isles* show signs of striking a newer and even more experimental dramatic note altogether.

Shaw sought to be not only a great radical reformer, like Dickens (by whom he was much influenced, not least in his humor and characterization), but a synthesizer of all that was best in the thought of his times as well. His plays, *sui generis,* are richly endowed with striking characterization, colorful situation, and intellectual but dramatic argument. His importance lies in providing a bridge between the old and the new and in showing a way forward that need not be unduly contemptuous of all that is best in what went before. He is the Socratic gadfly that questions all things, yet steadfastly holds fast to that which is good. His clean astringent style is a healthy example to all who would write of serious matters without solemnity (he is the Mozart of literature), and his personal and professional pride in fine workmanship is an inspiration beyond the merely literary to those who study his life and work. Leaving no school and few, if any, avowed disciples, his influence is wide wherever his plays are performed or his works read. And that, in spite of some not unnatural decline in his personal popularity in the British Isles after his death at the age of ninety-four on November 2, 1950, seems to be everywhere.

Eric J. Batson

BIBLIOGRAPHICAL REFERENCES: There are two collected editions of Shaw's *Works,* the limited Ayot St. Lawrence Edition, 30 vols., 1930, and the Standard Edition, 36 vols., 1931 ff. Excellent one-volume collections are the *Complete Plays,* 1931 (enlarged eds., 1934, 1938), and the *Complete Prefaces,* 1934 (enlarged ed., 1938). The authorized biography is Archibald Henderson's monumental *George Bernard Shaw: Man of the Century,* 1956. The best critical study is Eric Bentley's *Bernard Shaw,* 1947 (rev. ed., 1957).

Shaw studies are so extensive that any listing must be highly selective. For biography and criticism see H. L. Mencken, *George Bernard Shaw: His Plays,* 1905; Holbrook Jackson, *George Bernard Shaw,* 1907; G. K. Chesterton, *George Bernard Shaw,* 1909; Julius Bab, *Bernard Shaw,* 1909; John Palmer, *Bernard Shaw: An Epitaph,* 1915; H. C. Duffin, *The Quintessence of Bernard Shaw,* 1920 (enlarged ed., 1939); Edward Shanks, *Bernard Shaw,* 1924; Archibald Henderson, *Table Talk of G.B.S.,* 1925; *idem, Bernard Shaw, Playboy and Prophet,* 1932; J. S. Collis, *Shaw,* 1925; Frank Harris, *Bernard Shaw,* 1931; André Maurois, *Poets and Prophets,* 1935; Hesketh Pearson, *G.B.S.: A Full-Length Portrait,* 1942; *idem, G.B.S.: A Postscript,* 1951; Stephen Winsten, ed., *G.B.S., 90,* 1946; *idem, Days with Bernard Shaw,* 1948; C. E. M. Joad, *Shaw,* 1949; A. C. Ward, *Bernard Shaw,* 1950; Blanche Patch, *30 Years with G.B.S.,* 1951; Desmond MacCarthy, *Bernard Shaw,* 1951; and Louis Kronenberger, ed., *George Bernard Shaw: A Critical Survey,* 1953, an anthology of Shaw criticism written by various hands, 1901–1951.

See also C. L. and V. M. Broad, *A Dictionary to the Plays and Novels of Bernard Shaw,* 1929; X. Heydet, *Shaw-Kompendium* (in German), 1936; and Raymond Mander and Joe Mitchenson, *Theatrical Companion to Shaw: A Pictorial Record of the First Performances of the Plays of George Bernard Shaw,* 1954. In 1958 Dan H. Laurence had in preparation an authoritative Shaw bibliography.

MARY WOLLSTONECRAFT GODWIN SHELLEY

Born: London, England
Date: August 30, 1797

Died: Bournemouth, England
Date: February 1, 1851

PRINCIPAL WORKS

NOVELS: *Frankenstein,* 1818; *Valperga,* 1823; *The Last Man,* 1826; *Lodore,* 1835; *Falkner,* 1837.

TRAVEL SKETCHES: *The Journal of a Six Weeks' Tour,* 1814; *Rambles in Germany and Italy,* 1844.

Authorship of *Frankenstein* was not the only claim to distinction possessed by Mary Wollstonecraft Shelley. The daughter of a radical philosopher and and an early feminist, the wife of an unconventional boy genius, she early came to know life as something of a roller-coaster; and her masterpiece of fictional horror was only one of the more important incidents in an existence heavily underscored with drama.

The future novelist and mate of Percy Bysshe Shelley was born in London, August 30, 1797, the child of William Godwin and Mary Wollstonecraft. Bereaved of her mother almost immediately, she was reared in a bewildering clutter of family which included a stepmother, a stepbrother, a stepsister, a half-brother, and a half-sister. As Mary grew up she increasingly idolized her dead mother, for whose loss she was inclined to blame herself. The depth of this feeling was one of the important factors in her girlhood, the other being the atmosphere of intellectual discussion and debate which enveloped her father and his many visitors.

One of these visitors was a twenty-one-year-old youth whose mental accomplishments had made quite an impression upon William Godwin. The impression darkened when, a month before her seventeenth birthday, Mary Godwin eloped with Percy Bysshe Shelley, casually disregarding the fact that he was already in possession of a wife. More than two years passed before the suicide of Harriet Shelley allowed Shelley and Mary to legalize their marriage. All evidence available points to a reasonably happy union, though Mary's mind, clear and penetrating as it was, experienced times of bafflement in dealing with the unpredictable Shelley. On the other hand, Mary sometimes succumbed to periods of melancholy, which the death of her first three children did much to deepen.

Frankenstein was written in the Shelleys' first Italian days, during their companionship with Byron. So remarkable an achievement is it, especially for a girl of twenty, that it undoubtedly owes much of its sustained quality to the intellectual stimulation provided by the Shelley circle. The author's only novel to attain permanent reputation, it is an appealing combination of strangeness and reality, skillful in its plot structure and enlivened by sharp character contrasts. Published in 1818, *Frankenstein* was an immediate sensation; and its repeated dramatizations have given its title the familiarity of a household word. Other novels of Mary Shelley were to follow, but the author never regained the touch that would lift her fiction above the level of mediocrity. After Shelley's death, his widow's life became a struggle to secure bread and ensure the proper education of the only surviving Shelley child, Percy Florence. Nevertheless, *The Last Man* is interesting for its expression of Mary Shelley's liberal social and political views, and *Lodore* has the fascination of a veiled autobiography.

After her husband's death, Mary refused various offers of marriage: among her suitors were Shelley's friend Trelawny, John Howard Payne and—reportedly, at least—Washington Irving. After the death of Sir Timothy Shelley in 1844, her financial situation became somewhat easier. One of the disappointments of her later years was the discovery that she lacked the strength to complete a long-planned biography of her husband. She died on February 1, 1851, at the age of fifty-three, and was buried at Bournemouth.

BIBLIOGRAPHICAL REFERENCES: There is no edition of Mary Shelley's works. Frederick L. Jones has edited *The Letters of Mary W. Shelley*, 2 vols., 1944, and *Mary Shelley's Journal*, 1947. The standard biography is Mrs. Julian Marshall, *The Life and Letters of Mary Wollstonecraft Shelley*, 2 vols., 1889. Three more recent and less formal studies are R. G. Grylls, *Mary Shelley, A Biography*, 1938; Muriel Spark, *Child of Delight*, 1951; and Elizabeth Nitchie, *Mary Shelley, Author of "Frankenstein,"* 1953. See also W. E. Peck, "The Biographical Element in the Novels of Mary Wollstonecraft Shelley," *Publications of the Modern Language Association,* XXXVI (1923), 196–219.

PERCY BYSSHE SHELLEY

Born: Field Place, Sussex, England
Date: August 4, 1792

Died: Off Viareggio, Italy
Date: July 8, 1822

PRINCIPAL WORKS

POEMS: *Queen Mab,* 1813; *Alastor, or The Spirit of Solitude,* 1816; *The Revolt of Islam,* 1818; *Rosalind and Helen,* 1819; *Epipsychidion,* 1821; *Adonais,* 1821; *Hellas,* 1822; *Posthumous Poems,* 1824; *Poetical Works,* 1839.

PLAYS: *The Cenci,* 1820; *Prometheus Unbound,* 1820.

TRACTS AND STUDIES: *The Necessity of Atheism,* 1811; *An Address to the Irish People,* 1812; *A Refutation of Deism,* 1814; *A Defence of Poetry,* 1840.

Percy Bysshe Shelley, English poet, was born at Field Place, near Horsham, Sussex, August 4, 1792, the eldest son of a landed country squire. After some tutoring he was sent to Syon House Academy, where his shyness exposed him to brutal bullying. Entering Eton in 1804, he lived as much apart as possible, a moody, sensitive, and precocious boy with the nickname of "mad Shelley." Here he wrote *Zastrozzi* (1810), a wild Gothic romance, *Original Poetry by Victor and Cazire* (1810), and another inferior Gothic romance, *St. Irvyne, or The Rosicrucian,* published in 1811.

Shelley matriculated at University College, Oxford, in 1810. He and Thomas Jefferson Hogg were expelled the following year for publishing and sending to bishops and heads of colleges their pamphlet, *The Necessity of Atheism.* At this time Shelley fell in love with Harriet Westbrook, daughter of a retired hotel-keeper. They eloped, and despite Shelley's open break with the conventions of the Christian religion and particular scorn for the marriage ceremony, they were married in Edinburgh in August, 1811. Both fathers contributed to their support for the next three years, spent wandering in southern England, Ireland, and Wales.

In 1813 their first child was born in London and Shelley's first long poem, *Queen Mab,* was published. Meanwhile, marriage with Harriet was proving a failure. In May, 1814, Shelley met Mary, the daughter of William and Mary Wollstonecraft Godwin. Mary shared his belief that marriage was only a voluntary contract. Harriet left for her father's home, and Shelley and seventeen-year-old Mary eloped to Switzerland, accompanied by Claire Clairmont, Mary's half-sister. When they returned to England in September, Shelley proposed to Harriet that she come live with Mary and him; however, there was no reconciliation.

Mary bore a son in 1816 (the year of *Alastor, or The Spirit of Solitude*). They, with Claire, spent the summer in Switzerland and became close friends of Byron. Soon after they returned to England in the autumn, they heard Harriet had drowned herself. Shelley was now free to marry Mary Godwin (December 30, 1816), but a court order denied him the custody of his two children by Harriet.

After he had completed *The Revolt of Islam,* revised version of his earlier *Laon and Cythna,* the Shelleys and Claire Clairmont, with her child by Byron, went to Italy. There Shelley remained the rest of his life, wandering from Lake Como, Milan, Venice, Este, Rome, Florence, and Pisa to other cities and sections. Much time was spent with Byron. *Julian and Maddalo* (1818) is a poem in the form of a conversation between Shelley (Julian) and Byron (Maddalo). Next followed *The Masque of Anarchy* (1819), a revolutionary propaganda poem; *The Cenci,* a realistic tragedy; and *Prometheus Unbound,* a lyric tragedy completed in 1819 and published in 1820. Earlier in the same year, at Pisa, he wrote some of his most famous lyrics, "The Cloud," "Ode to the West Wind," and "Ode to a Skylark."

The chief productions of 1821 were *Epipsychidion,* a result of his platonic relationship with Countess Emilia Viviani; an uncompleted prose work, *A Defence of Poetry,* published after his death, and *Adonais,* an elegy inspired by the death of John Keats. From his wide reading, he was most greatly influenced by Plato, Lucretius, Spinoza, Rousseau, Hume, and Southey. Godwin's influence lasted until Shelley's death.

His final poem, *The Triumph of Life,* was incomplete at the time he was drowned, July 8, 1822, while sailing off Viareggio. His body was first buried in the sand, then cremated. The ashes were buried in the Protestant cemetery at Rome, January 21, 1823.

The nineteenth century notion of the sensitive poetic soul owes a great deal to the ideal young man (*Alastor*—"the brave, the beautiful—the child of grace and genius") built up largely by Shelley of Shelley. Yet in the history of English literature, Shelley is not as important as Wordsworth or as influential as Byron (more popular as a poet), or Keats. The public was shocked at his defiance of the conventions of life. Today he has many admirers, but for those who dislike Romantic poetry in general, Shelley is a particularly vulnerable target. Unquestionably he could give a song-like character to his verse, for his was the light, lyrical tone. He was a lover of unusual colors, blurred outlines, and large effects. He was also a lover of startling and frank realism and had an obvious passion for the mysterious and far away. In technique he illustrated something more concrete by the less concrete. What Shelley starts to define often results in vague though pretty images. He offers emotion in itself, unattached, in the void.

Because of his sensibility, perhaps, he was at war with the conventions of society from childhood. As a political dreamer he was filled with the hope of transforming the real world into an Arcadia through revolutionary reform. As a disciple of Godwin he directed *Queen Mab* against organized religion. The queen shows the human spirit that evil times, in the past and present, are due to the authority of Church and State. In the future, however, when love reigns supreme, the chains of the human spirit will dissolve; mankind will be boundlessly self-assertive and at the same time temper this self-assertion by a boundless sympathy for others. Then a world will be realized in which there is neither inferior nor superior classes or beings. The end of *Prometheus Unbound* gives this vision of humanity released from all evil artificially imposed from without (one of Rousseau's main tenets), a humanity "where all things flow to all, as rivers to the sea," and "whose nature is its own divine control."

Shelley sets up a humanity glorified through love; he worships in the sanctuary left vacant by "the great absence of God." (His youthful atheism lacked warmth and in the end he turned to a type of pantheism.) Love, as exemplified in his personal life, is a passionate kind of sensuality which becomes his simple moral code with no duty, blame, or obligation attached. The reign of love when no authority was necessary was his millennium.

BIBLIOGRAPHICAL REFERENCES: The best editions of Shelley are the Julian Edition of the *Complete Works,* edited by Roger Ingpen and Walter E. Peck, 10 vols., 1926–1930; and the *Complete Poetical Works,* edited by Thomas Hutchinson, 1933. The standard biography is Newman I. White, *Shelley,* 2 vols., 1940. See also Thomas Medwin, *The Life of Percy Bysshe Shelley,* 1847 (rev. ed., 1913); Edward Dowden, *The Life of Percy Bysshe Shelley,* 2 vols., 1886; André Maurois, *Ariel,* 1923; and Edmund Blunden, *Shelley: A Life Story,* 1946.

For criticism see H. L. Hoffman, *An Odyssey of the Soul: Shelley's Alastor,* 1933; C. H. Grabo, *The Magic Plant,* 1936; Carlos Baker, *Shelley's Major Poetry,* 1948; R. H. Fogle, *The Imagery of Keats and Shelley,* 1949; K. N. Cameron, *The Young Shelley,* 1950; Sylva Norman, *Flight of the Skylark: The Development of Shelley's Reputation,* 1954; and Neville Rogers, *Shelley at Work,* 1957; also David L. Clark, "Shelley and Shakespeare," *Publications of the Modern Language Association,* LIV (1939), 261–287; E. K. Gibson, *"Alastor:* A Reinterpretation," *ibid.,* LXII (1947), 1022–1046; and Bennett Weaver, *"Prometheus Bound* and *Prometheus Unbound,"* *ibid.,* LXIV (1949), 115–133.

RICHARD BRINSLEY SHERIDAN

Born: Dublin, Ireland   *Died:* London, England
Date: October (?), 1751   *Date:* July 7, 1816

PRINCIPAL WORKS

PLAYS: *The Rivals,* 1775; *Saint Patrick's Day,* 1775; *The Duenna,* 1775; *The School for Scandal,* 1777; *The Critic,* 1779.

Richard Brinsley (Butler) Sheridan, the playwright who with Goldsmith effected the revival of English comedy after the coma into which it had lapsed at the hands of Cibber and Steele, led a more romantic life in actuality than most romantic novelists could invent for fiction. He achieved his striking dramatic successes while still in his twenties; then turned his remarkable talents and energies from the theater to politics.

He was born to a heritage of genius. His paternal grandfather had distinguished himself in the classics at Trinity College, Dublin, had taken Holy Orders, and had set up a school in Dublin which for a time produced nearly £1,000 a year. Thomas Sheridan, his father, took his M.A. at Trinity College and at the Theatre Royal in Dublin achieved fame as an actor second only to David Garrick. Sheridan's mother was an accomplished writer of popular novels, and the author of three plays, one of which Garrick pronounced "one of the best comedies he ever read."

Richard Sheridan, the son of this tradition who brought it to its height, was born in 1751 in Dublin. He went at seven years of age under the tutelage of Mr. Samuel Whyte, but after a year moved with his family to England where, in 1762, he was sent to Harrow. There he was under the tutelage of two remarkable scholars, Dr. Robert Sumner and Dr. Parr. He gained a reputation for pranks for which his masters, though they knew he was responsible, could not bring him to account. In spite of these pranks, however, and in spite of his indolence and carelessness, Sheridan at Harrow achieved both the esteem of his schoolfellows and the admiring attention of his masters. Dr. Parr wrote of him: "He would have done little among the mathematicians at Cambridge; he would have been a rake, or an idler, or a trifler at Dublin, but . . . at Oxford he would have become an excellent scholar."

Sheridan was brought home from Harrow to London when he was eighteen. In London for a time he received private tuition from Mr. Lewis Kerr. He had already at Harrow distinguished himself in poetry. In 1771 he published jointly with a friend some translations of "Aristaenetus" which were treated favorably by the critics, but ignored by the public.

About this time one of the most colorful romances in or out of fiction began when Sheridan met, while residing at Bath, the celebrated Maid of Bath, Elizabeth Ann Linley, then eighteen years old. Remarkably blessed with personal beauty and charm and with extraordinary musical talents, all enhanced by the publicity her profession as a singer had gained her, Miss Linley had almost innumerable hearts and fortunes at her feet. Of them all, Sheridan's gained the most attention.

Himself handsome, dashing, somewhat rakish, yet entirely a gentleman, his wit and elegance and devotion presented in his now-famous love verses —these things won her favor. But one Major Mathews, a married man and a friend of the girl's family, had for some time taken advantage of the familiarity his age and position granted him to be indiscreetly attentive to Miss Linley in public and to make shameful proposals to her in private. Repulsed, he is said to have threatened to ruin her reputation if he could not undermine her virtue. She confided in Sheridan, and was persuaded to run away with him to France where they were secretly married.

They were searched out and brought home by the girl's father (the marriage still secret), and Sheridan forthwith dueled with Mathews and forced him to retract publicly some vicious publications he had made about the eloped lovers. Mathews, to regain his reputation, called Sheridan out a second time. In a fierce and bloody duel in which both men broke their swords after wounding each other, Sheridan was this time sorely hurt. Hearing of his wounds, his wife confessed their secret marriage, and they were again married by license in Bath. The year was 1773.

Sheridan, pridefully and delicately rejecting all thoughts of profiting from his wife's already proved talents, set about seeking an independence by his own unproved merits. Under these circumstances he began his dramatic career.

Between 1775 and 1779 Sheridan produced five plays, on two of which his reputation rests. The least important pieces need little comment. *The Duenna* was a comic opera which broke all previous records for full-length plays with seventy-five performances during its first season. Its plot and the music account for its popularity, not the wit of its lines. In 1777 Sheridan made a sterilized adaptation of Vanbrugh's *The Relapse* in *A Trip to Scarborough;* the adaptation was competent and effective. His last original play, *The Critic,* is the least important of the three major works he produced. Appearing in 1779, it follows in the tradition of the Duke of Buckingham's *Rehearsal* and Henry Fielding's *Tom Thumb.* It was successful because it had topical interest, and because it was full of "robust good fun." But it is with *The Rivals* and *The School for Scandal* that Sheridan has made his place in the drama.

The Rivals, the first of Sheridan's plays, represents the short step upward from Goldsmith's *She Stoops to Conquer* to witty and elegant comedy in the maner of Congreve, but purged of his impurities. Because of poor acting and because of the unfortunate offense taken by the Irish gentry to Sir Lucius O'Trigger, the play was soundly damned at its first performance. Withdrawn from the stage, emended, and properly rehearsed, the play returned after eleven days to take the town. The excessively romantic young Lydia Languish is delightfully charming and funny. And Mrs. Malaprop is one of the best comic characters in English literature. From her comes our word "malapropism," and there has been no greater mistress of such than she herself. Her projected schooling for girls is representative of her "nice derangement of epitaphs":

"I would send her, at nine years old, to a boarding school, in order to learn a little ingenuity and artifice. Then,

Sir, she should have a supercilious knowledge of accounts;—and as she grew up, I would have her instructed in geometry that she might know something of the contagious countries;—but above all, she should be mistress of orthodoxy, that she might not misspell, and mis-pronounce words so shamefully as girls usually do."

Two years later, in 1777, *The School for Scandal* appeared. Meanwhile Sheridan had become part owner and manager at Drury Lane. He was thus able to cast his own players, and the result was a tremendous success. For Horace Walpole, "there were more parts performed admirably . . . than I almost ever saw in any play." Sheridan had also learned much about his craft from his close association with the theater, for a comparison of the earlier drafts of the play with its finished form reveals his mastery of the art of revision: "The dialogue . . . was set down with such exquisite Congreve-like precision that it enforced excellence of delivery." The play has poise, dignity, and a "dazzling glitter of wit"; indeed, it has been urged, a surfeit of wit. However, "audiences seldom balk at too much wit; only critics do that."

If Sheridan sought to discredit sentimentalism, this play accomplished his aim, "but sentimentalism is only an ingredient in the rich sauce of his satire. He gives us the quintessence of a scandal-loving society. . . . He can be serious, but not too serious," and he "enlivens the whole with incessant sparkling wit."

Shortly thereafter Sheridan turned from the theater of the drama to the theater of politics, where he played a leading role for more than thirty years. Whether or not that was a loss to letters we shall never know, for he distinguished himself in both occupations. He died in London, July 7, 1816. It must be said, moreover, that he and Goldsmith did not stop sentimental comedy: it lived on; it lives yet. But of all the plays writen from 1660 to our own day, *The Rivals* and *The School for Scandal* are among the half dozen most popular. And as long as men can laugh at themselves they will hold that popularity.

BIBLIOGRAPHICAL REFERENCES: The collected edition is *The Plays and Poems of Richard Brinsley Sheridan*, edited by R. Crompton Rhodes, 3 vols., 1928. This editor is also the author of the standard biography, *Harlequin Sheridan: The Man and the Legends*, 1933. Other biographical and critical studies include Walter Sichel, *Sheridan*, 2 vols., 1909; Lewis Gibbs, *Sheridan: His Life and His Theatre*, 1948; and W. A. Darlington, *Sheridan, 1751–1816*, 1951. For criticism see, further, Ernest Bernbaum, *The Drama of Sensibility*, 1915; and Allardyce Nicoll, *A History of Late Eighteenth Century Drama*, 1927.

ROBERT C. SHERRIFF

Born: Kingston-on-Thames, England
Date: June 6, 1896

PRINCIPAL WORKS

PLAYS: *Journey's End*, 1929; *Badger's Green*, 1930; *Windfall*, 1933; *Home at Seven*, 1950; *The White Carnation*, 1953; *The Long Sunset*, 1955.

975

NOVELS: *The Fortnight in September,* 1931; *Greengates,* 1936; *The Hopkins Manuscript,* 1939; *Chedworth,* 1944; *Another Year,* 1946; *King John's Treasure,* 1954.

The versatility of Robert C(edric) Sherriff goes unrecognized by those who know him only as the author of *Journey's End,* one of the most successful war dramas of modern times, for he has gained fame also as a writer for motion pictures and as a novelist. Born at Kingston-on-Thames, near London, on June 6, 1896, he entered an insurance office at seventeen and, apart from service in World War I, in which he was wounded at Ypres and reached the rank of captain, worked for ten years as an insurance adjuster. His introduction to a literary life was accidental. In 1921 he was asked to contribute a dramatic piece to be presented at Kingston for the benefit of the School Chapel Restoration Fund. After he had written other plays for the Kingston Rowing Club, his heightened interest in drama led to *Journey's End;* this, through the good offices of Bernard Shaw, was produced in 1929. After the London production of a second play, *Badger's Green,* in 1930, Sherriff interrupted his career to read for a bachelor's degree at New College, Oxford.

Sherriff has published six other plays and an equal number of novels. In addition he has been responsible for a number of screenplays, of which perhaps the most distinguished were *The Road Back* (1932) and *Lady Hamilton* (1941).

BIBLIOGRAPHICAL REFERENCES: There is no full-length biographical or critical study. See W. A. Darlington, "Keying Down: The Secret of *Journey's End,*" *Theatre Arts Monthly,* XIII (1929), 493–497; Ernest Short, *Theatrical Cavalcade,* 1942; and Stark Young, *Immortal Shadows,* 1948. "Persons and Personages," *Living Age,* CCCXXXIX (1931), 590–592, contains an interview with Sherriff.

ROBERT E. SHERWOOD

Born: New Rochelle, New York   *Died:* New York, N. Y.
Date: April 4, 1896   *Date:* November 14, 1955

PRINCIPAL WORKS

PLAYS: *The Road to Rome,* 1927; *Waterloo Bridge,* 1930; *Reunion in Vienna,* 1931: *The Petrified Forest,* 1934; *Idiot's Delight,* 1936; *Abe Lincoln in Illinois,* 1938; *There Shall Be No Night,* 1940; *The Rugged Path,* 1945.
NOVEL: *The Virtuous Knight,* 1931.
BIOGRAPHY: *Roosevelt and Hopkins: An Intimate History,* 1948.

Robert E(mmet) Sherwood's association with the Democratic Party during the 1930's and the 1940's can be regarded, like his plays, as an expression of liberal sympathies and hopes; his theater is full of those who resist the imposition of tyranny of persons and superior power and the tyranny that results when outworn ideas continue to be cherished.

The events of Sherwood's life suggest that he moved freely in the world and had reasons for feeling that he knew whereof he spoke. Born in New

Rochelle, New York, on April 4, 1896, he was the son of Arthur Murray Sherwood, an investment broker and devotee of the theater, and Rosina Sherwood, a well-known painter and illustrator. Sherwood was educated at Milton Academy and at Harvard, where his first play, *Barnum Was Right*, was produced by the Hasty Pudding Club. During World War I, after being rejected by the U.S. Army because of his height (he was six feet seven inches tall, he joined the famous Canadian Black Guard, and was gassed and wounded at Vimy Ridge. Discharged from the service in 1919, he became the dramatic editor of *Vanity Fair*, but he left this magazine in protest against the dismissal of Dorothy Parker for an unfavorable review. He moved to the old *Life*, then a humorous magazine, as co-editor and motion picture critic, becoming the first conscientious movie reviewer on the staff of any major American magazine. After 1928 he devoted his time to writing plays and scenarios. With Maxwell Anderson, S. N. Behrman, Sidney Howard, and Elmer Rice, he formed the Playwrights' Company in 1938; this action was a protest against the Theatre Guild's production of too many plays by European dramatists. Later, during World War II, he was an influential adviser to Franklin D. Roosevelt. Out of this experience came a book that is one of Sherwood's claims to fame, *Roosevelt and Hopkins: An Intimate History*, which required some thirty months of writing and culling from the forty filing cases of Harry Hopkins' papers. Critical reaction at once observed that Sherwood had not written for the popular market. The book was labeled Sherwood's "finest drama and the most titanic in scale

that he has so far written" and "the delight of the journalist and the arsenal of the historian." (This book won Sherwood his fourth Pulitzer Prize; the other three had been for his plays, *Idiot's Delight*, *Abe Lincoln in Illinois*, and *There Shall Be No Night*.)

Sherwood's drama, from the farcical *Road to Rome* onward, is concerned with a small set of recurrent problems: What are the impersonal forces that shape history; do these forces interfere unjustly with private happiness; and does the thoughtful man have any chance to dominate the tyranny of impersonal power and outworn rule? Thus, in *Idiot's Delight* the love affair of two vaudeville "artists" is played out against the backdrop of power politics; at the end, even though bombs are dropping, the human spirit has some kind of triumph. Earlier, in *The Petrified Forest*, Sherwood had told much the same story, except that here the lovers had faced not bombs but an inhuman killer. Sherwood again was concerned with the assertion of man's dignity in a world that showed little concern for it. This same regard for human dignity appears in Sherwood's play about Lincoln and in his last significant drama, *There Shall Be No Night*, a play in which the exigencies of altering diplomatic alignments have resulted in transfers of setting from Finland to Greece and finally, in 1957, to Hungary. The setting changes but the story does not; against these national backgrounds enlightened, "decent" people confront the dragon of force and perversion of truth; they go down in material defeat, but the moral victory is theirs. This is a view of human destiny which Sherwood shared with many men of his generation:

977

Man is still the master of his own destiny if he wishes to be, for he can be truly defeated only by his own desire for defeat. Sherwood's theater is a deft and sometimes illuminating expression of this typical twentieth century insight. He died in New York City on November 14, 1955.

BIBLIOGRAPHICAL REFERENCES: There is no extended biographical or critical study. For articles in books and periodicals see Louis Nizer, *Between You and Me,* 1948; John Mason Brown, *Still Seeing Things,* 1950; Edith J. R. Isaacs, "Robert Sherwood: Man of the Hours," *Theatre Arts Monthly,* XXIII (January, 1939), 31–34, 37–40; John Mason Brown, "On a Larger Stage," *Saturday Review of Literature,* XXXI (November 13, 1948), 54–58; John Gassner, "Robert Emmet Sherwood," *Atlantic Monthly,* CLXIX (January, 1942), 26–33; and Maxwell Anderson, "Robert E. Sherwood," *Theatre Arts Monthly,* XL (February, 1956), 26–27.

SHIH NAI-AN

Born: China
Date: Unknown; fl. fourteenth century

Died: China
Date: Unknown

PRINCIPAL WORK

NOVEL: The *Shui Hu Chuan* (*All Men Are Brothers*).

Nothing is definitely known about Shih Nai-an, the man who has been generally accepted as the author of *All Men Are Brothers* ever since Chin Sheng-t'an wrote in 1644 his seventy-chapter version of the novel with a preface of his own composition and forged Shih's name to it, though an equally good claim can be made for Lo Kuan-chung (*q.v.*). Until the early 1930's all that could be said of Shih was that he probably flourished in the middle decades of the fourteenth century and was perhaps an older contemporary of Lo. Then a census taker reported that he had come upon two documents in the archives of a Shih clan in the Tung-t'ai district of Kiangsu. These give the information that Shih Nai-an's real name was Erh or Tzu-an, that he was born in 1226 and died in 1370, that he passed his *chin-shih* examinations in 1331, and that after serving two years as a magistrate of Ch'ien-t'ang in Chekiang, he resigned because of the usual disagreement with superiors and devoted the rest of his life to writing. A list of his writings is given, which include not only the *Shui Hu Chuan* (under a slightly different title) but also several additional historical romances generally attributed to Lo, with the remark that he was helped in his work by his pupil Lo Kuan-chung. At first the report was hailed as a great literary find, but soon doubts began to be voiced. It would seem at this date that either the census taker had been imposed upon by the Shih family or else we have been imposed upon by him.

Actually neither Shih nor Lo could be the author of the extant versions of the novel, of which there are at least five (in 100, 110, 115, 120, and 124 chapters respectively) which antedate Chin's version. Historical and legendary romances such as the *Shui Hu* and *San Kuo* lived first in the oral tradition

978

of professional storytellers. After a time some of them were set down in crude, sketchy form and were used largely as prompt-books. Shih and Lo were probably famous storytellers of their time; it is also possible that they wrote some of these prompt-books, which have since been lost. It is only natural that when literary hacks began to make up more elaborate reading versions of these romances from about the middle of the sixteenth century on, they should appropriate the Shih-Lo names rather than give their own, since it was not to one's credit in those days to be responsible for such "trash."

BIBLIOGRAPHICAL REFERENCES: The most familiar version of the *Shui Hu Chuan* in English is the translation by Pearl Buck, *All Men Are Brothers*, 1933. Critical studies include Richard G. Irwin, *The Evolution of a Chinese Novel: Shui Hu Chuan*, 1953; and Ho Hsin, *Shui-hu Yen-chiu (A Study of the Shui-hu)*, 1954 (Shanghai).

JAMES SHIRLEY

Born: London, England
Date: Baptized September 7, 1596

Died: London
Date: October 29, 1666

PRINCIPAL WORKS

PLAYS: *Love Tricks, or the School of Compliment,* 1625; *The Maid's Revenge,* 1626; *The Wedding,* c. 1627; *The Witty Fair One,* 1628; *The Grateful Servant,* 1629; *The Traitor,* 1631; *Love's Cruelty,* 1631; *Hyde Park,* 1632; *The Young Admiral,* 1633; *The Bird in a Cage,* 1633; *The Gamester,* 1634; *The Example,* 1634; *The Opportunity,* 1634; *The Lady of Pleasure,* 1635; *The Royal Master,* c. 1637; *The Doubtful Heir,* c. 1639; *The Gentleman of Venice,* 1639; *The Humorous Courtier,* 1640; *The Cardinal,* 1641.

MASQUES: *The Triumph of Peace,* 1634; *Cupid and Death,* 1653; *The Contention of Ajax and Ulysses,* 1659.

Another in the long line of preacher-writers, James Shirley, born in London in September, 1596, received his education at the Merchant Taylors' School, St. John's College, Oxford, and St. Catherine's College, Cambridge. After receiving his M.A. he became a parish priest and teacher at St. Albans; he left this post because of scruples which led to his becoming a Roman Catholic.

About 1625 he lodged in Gray's Inn and began to write plays, mostly for the Queen's Company. Until the closing of the theaters in 1642 he wrote over forty plays still extant. He then returned to teaching but continued to write occasional "entertainments" and masques. Severely burned in the Great Fire of London, he and his wife fled to St. Giles' parish. They died there a day later, October 29, 1666, and were buried in the same grave.

Shirley, coming late in the great age, was no innovator, but he wrote excellent tragedy, sprightly comedy, and masques with some surprising twists. *The Cardinal* is often reprinted as one of the best romantic tragedies, the last of the Jacobean Age. His comedy, *The Gamester,* looks forward to the realistic comedy of manners, and the *Lady of Pleasure* is a highly entertaining, fast-paced comedy in the older tradition.

BIBLIOGRAPHICAL REFERENCES: The standard edition is *The Dramatic Works and Poems of James Shirley*, edited by Alexander Dyce, 6 vols., 1833. The best biographical and critical study is A. H. Nason, *James Shirley, Dramatist*, 1915. See also Edmund Gosse, *James Shirley*, 1888; R. S. Forsythe, *The Relation of Shirley's Plays to Elizabethan Drama*, 1914; C. F. Brooke, ed., *English Drama, 1580–1642*, 1933; and Thomas Marc Parrott and Robert Hamilton Ball, *A Short View of Elizabethan Drama*, 1943.

MIKHAIL SHOLOKHOV

Born: Kruzhlino, Russia
Date: May 24, 1905

PRINCIPAL WORKS

NOVELS: *Aloyshkino Serdtse*, 1925 (*The Heart of Aloyshka*; also *Alexander's Heart*); *Dvukhmuznaya*, 1925 (*The Woman with Two Husbands*); *Lazorevaya Steppe*, 1926 (*The Blue Steppes*); *Tikhiy Don*, 1928–1938 (*And Quiet Flows the Don* and *The Don Flows Home to the Sea*; combined as *The Silent Don*, 1942); *Podnyataya Tselina*, 1932–1933 (*Seeds of Tomorrow*; in England, *Virgin Soil Upturned*); *Oni srazhalis za rodinu*, 1944 (*They Fought for Their Country*).

SHORT STORIES: *Donskiye Razkazy*, 1925 (*Tales of the Don*).

Mikhail (Aleksandrovich) Sholokhov, epic novelist of the Cossacks, was born in Kruzhlino, a small village near Veshenskaya on the River Don. When he was born, on May 24, 1905, his parents were unmarried, but in 1912 the marriage ceremony was performed and the child was legitimatized. His father was a farmer, a cattle buyer, a clerk, and later the owner of a power mill. The family was poor, but the parents nevertheless managed to send the boy to school near Moscow. Sholokhov's mother, half-Turkish and half-Cossack, was an illiterate woman of strong determination; she learned to read and write in order to be able to correspond with her son while he was away at school.

Sholokhov, forced to leave his school at Voronezh because of the German invasion, returned to his home when he was fifteen. His plans to teach school upset by the revolution, he was assigned by the Bolsheviks to various jobs, among them an assignment in a statis-tical bureau, as a freight handler, as a food inspector, and as a mason. In 1922, during bandit raids in the region, he participated in some of the fighting.

When he was eighteen he began to write for various newspapers and magazines, and he wrote some short fiction before beginning his long novel and eventual masterpiece, the Don Cossack tetralogy, which was translated into English as *And Quiet Flows the Don* (1934) and *The Don Flows Home to the Sea* (1940) before the whole was combined as *The Silent Don* in 1942. This monumental work, composed over a ten-year period, appeared in Russia in four separate volumes in 1928, 1929, 1933, and 1938. With the first volume of the novel, the author became famous. His analysis in depth into the lives of the Cossacks, showing how history was forcing them into new social roles, became popular because it was an intimate portrait of realistic regional life. Also, the novel expresses something of the power and human dignity

980

of the human beings whose lives it portrays. Ivan Dzerzhinsky, the Soviet composer, used the Don novels as the basis of a highly popular opera, and it was a successful film. Largely on the basis of this work, Sholokhov received the Stalin Prize in 1941. Over a million copies of the book were sold in the U.S.S.R. during its first year of publication, and before Volume IV appeared, the novel had gone through seventy-nine editions, had been translated into thirty-eight languages, and had sold over four and a half million copies.

Sholokhov's work on *The Silent Don* was not continuous. In 1932 he completed the first volume of a two-volume work, *The Seeds of Tomorrow*; the second volume appeared the following year. This novel, dealing with the building of a *kholkoz*, or collective farm, was also a great success in Russia and in other countries. Like the Don novel, it was filmed and made into an opera by Dzerzhinsky. It was also presented as a four-act play by Krasheninikova at the Simonov Studio Theatre.

Until 1941, Sholokhov lived a quiet life in the Veshenskaya region, where he wrote, farmed, hunted, fished, and entertained his friends. When the Nazis invaded Russia in 1941, he became one of Russia's "fighting correspondents," settling in Moscow where he now lives.

In 1937 he was elected Deputy to the Supreme Soviet. He is a member of the Academy of Sciences of the U.S.S.R. and of the Praesidium Union of Soviet Writers. In 1955, during an official state celebration of his fiftieth birthday, he received the Order of Lenin. During World War II he worked on a war novel and on short stories. He is married to Maria Petrovna and has four children.

Sholokhov has been criticized as a Communist apologist, but most readers of his works agree in regarding him as an artist who has managed to triumph over the propagandist; and he is valued as an epical writer who has portrayed a significant aspect of contemporary Russian life.

BIBLIOGRAPHICAL REFERENCES: A brief introductory sketch to Sholokhov is Isidor Schneider, "The Quiet Don Flows Home," *Soviet Russia Today*, IX (1941), 10–11+. More extensive studies are V. Goffenshefer, *Mikhail Sholokhov*, 1940; and I. G. Lezhnёv, *Mikhail Sholokhov*, 1948. See also George Reavey, *Soviet Literature Today*, 1946; and Gleb Struve, *Soviet-Russian Literature*, 1951.

JOSEPH HENRY SHORTHOUSE

Born: Birmingham, England
Date: September 9, 1834

Died: Birmingham
Date: March 4, 1903

PRINCIPAL WORKS

NOVELS: *John Inglesant*, 1880; *The Little Schoolmaster Mark*, 1883–1884; *Sir Percival*, 1886; *The Countess Eve*, 1888; *Blanche, Lady Falaise*, 1891.

SHORT STORIES: *A Teacher of the Violin*, 1888.

ESSAYS: *The Platonism of Wordsworth*, 1882; *The Royal Supremacy*, 1899.

Joseph Henry Shorthouse was born into a Quaker family of Birmingham on September 9, 1834. In his childhood he developed a stammer which embarrassed him all his life, and because of that speech impediment he was, except for a brief stay at Tottenham College at the age of fifteen, educated by tutors at home. At the age of sixteen he entered his father's business, a manufacturing concern in Birmingham. In business, despite his handicap, he proved very successful. Although born a Quaker, he had apparently less sympathy for his parents' religion than for others. Throughout his life he evidenced an interest in spiritualism, however, and after his marriage to Sara Scott, in 1857, he became a convert to the Church of England.

An attack of epilepsy in 1862, while Shorthouse was still in his twenties, forced him to turn to literary study and writing which afforded him the quiet, restful existence he needed. For ten years, from 1866 to 1876, Shorthouse worked on his novel, *John Inglesant.* It lay in manuscript for three years before Shorthouse printed it privately in 1880 for distribution to friends. At the suggestion of Mrs. Humphry Ward, the writer, it was published for the trade in 1881 and became very popular. Other novels, none so successful, by Shorthouse are *The Little Schoolmaster Mark, Sir Percival,* and *The Countess Eve.* He also wrote an essay on *The Platonism of Wordsworth* and a volume of stories, *A Teacher of the Violin and Other Tales.* Shorthouse's *John Inglesant* aroused surprise, and it remains a still amazing work because of its vivid descriptions of Italy, a land the author did not know at first hand, and its quality of mysticism not ordinarily associated with writings by men of business. Shorthouse died at Edgbaston, Birmingham, on March 4, 1903.

BIBLIOGRAPHICAL REFERENCES: The collected edition of *The Novels of Joseph Henry Shorthouse* is in 6 vols., 1891–1894. The official, and only, biography is *The Life, Letters, and Literary Remains,* edited by Sarah Shorthouse, 2 vols., 1905. Two excellent views of Shorthouse appear in P. E. More, *Shelburne Essays, III,* 1906; and Sir Edmund Gosse, *Portraits and Sketches,* 1912.

Special studies of *John Inglesant* are available: H. E. West, *"John Inglesant" and "Sartor Resartus," Two Phases of Religion,* 1884; J. Durham, *"Marius the Epicurean" and "John Inglesant,"* 1905; W. K. Fleming, "Some Truths About John Inglesant," *Quarterly Review,* CCXL (1925), 130–148; and M. Polack, *The Historical, Philosophical, and Religious Aspects of "John Inglesant,"* 1934—the most valuable work on the subject.

SHUDRAKA

Born: India
Date: c. 100 B.C.

Died: India
Date: Unknown

PRINCIPAL WORK

PLAY: *Mrcchakatikā (The Little Clay Cart).*

Shudraka (also spelled "Sūdraka" or "Çudraka") is possibly a legendary prince who never really existed. Tradition has it that he lived in the first or second century before Christ, and *The* *Little Clay Cart,* a Sanskrit drama of political intrigue and romantic comedy has been attributed to him by tradition. The *Sutradhara,* a later Sanskrit manuscript, ascribes the play to him and describes him as a student of the *Vedas*, a mathematician, and an expert on women and elephants. Shudraka's authorship of the play is disputed, however, and some scholars believe that its author was Dandin (fl. 7th century), a Sanskrit author best known for a picaresque narrative entitled *Dasakumāracharita* (*The Adventures of the Ten Princes*). It may well be, however, that neither Shudraka nor Dandin actually wrote the play, for it seems to date from the fifth century of the Christian era, six or seven centuries

after Shudraka's supposed dates and about two centuries before Dandin's lifetime. It seems likely that *The Little Clay Cart* was written at the beginnings of a golden age of Sanskrit drama under the Gupta kings of Kanauj, who ruled over the greater part of India during the fourth and fifth centuries of the Christian era. The play would belong then to that great age of Sanskrit drama which includes the anonymous *Mudrārākṣasa* (*The Prime Minister's Ring*) and Kalidasa's famous *Sakuntala*.

BIBLIOGRAPHICAL REFERENCE: For an excellent background study of Indian drama see A. Bernedale Keith, *The Sanskrit Drama in Its Origin, Development, Theory and Practice*, 1924.

SIR PHILIP SIDNEY

Born: Penshurst, England
Date: November 30, 1554

Died: Arnhem, Netherlands
Date: October 17, 1586

PRINCIPAL WORKS

POEMS: *Astrophel and Stella*, 1591.
PROSE ROMANCE: *Arcadia*, 1590.
CRITICAL ESSAY: *Defence of Poesie*, 1595 (also called *Apologie for Poetry*).

Although Philip Sidney came from a noble family, he received no title until 1583, when he was knighted. His father, Sir Henry Sidney, was a member of a highborn family, and most of Philip Sidney's near relatives were titled; but for most of his life Sidney was poor. A man of steadfast character, he was affected somewhat by the vicissitudes of his life, but his influence on English literature was that of a chivalrous, courtly gentleman.

Born at Penshurst, in Kent, on November 30, 1554, he was entered at Shrewsbury School, near Ludlow Castle, in 1564, and from there he went to Oxford in 1568; he also studied at Cambridge. In 1572 he started an extended tour of Europe. Throughout his life Sidney was intensely interested in learning. He studied the writers of the past but was not bound to them, having an independent spirit. He was generally recognized as a young man of charm, intelligence, and good judgment.

He returned to England in 1575 and remained at court until he was sent to Austria and Germany in 1577. While in England, he labored sedulously to defend his father's policies and position. By 1578 he was becoming known in the world of letters. In that year he wrote *The Lady of the May*, a masque performed before the queen. But his success at court was short-lived; he was disgraced along with the Earl of Leicester, in whose affairs he had become involved. His virtual banishment to the home of his sister, the Countess of Pembroke, at Wilton, may well have been a blessing, for it was there that he began writing the *Arcadia* for his sister's amusement. This work, first begun in 1580, was later revised and added to by Sidney, and the later version is usually considered to be better.

Sidney, permitted to return to court, wrote the great sonnet sequence, *Astrophel and Stella,* which is perhaps best known. The "Stella" in this largely autobiographical and very sincere poetic narrative was Penelope Devereux, daughter of the Earl of Essex, and an early love of Sidney's. The lady had been forced into a marriage of convenience with Lord Rich, and some of Sidney's disappointment may be sensed in these sonnets.

In 1583 Sidney was knighted, and in the same year he married Frances, the daughter of Sir Francis Walsingham. Before and during these events Sidney had been producing what was probably the most truly influential piece of writing he ever did. This was his *Defence of Poesie,* which raised an almost wholly new set of standards for English poetry. By poesie Sidney meant any form of imaginative writing.

Sir Philip Sidney was more than a courtier or literary figure; he was also a man of affairs. A champion of the Protestant cause in Europe, with his primary animosity directed against Spain, in 1585 he was given a command in Holland and made governor of Flushing. He engaged valiantly in several battles during that year. On September 22, 1586, he was severely wounded in a cavalry charge. The famous story is often told, as an example of Sidney's fine sense of humanity and chivalry, of how he refused a cup of water and ordered it to be given to a soldier near him on the battlefield. Sidney died of his wound on October 17, 1586. Following his death he was universally mourned and widely elegized.

Because none of his writing was actually published during his lifetime, most of Sidney's widespread influence was posthumous; nevertheless it was considerable: His *Arcadia,* although essentially a romance, achieves epic qualities and contains some richly developed passages; his *Astrophel and Stella,* perhaps the most fully written sonnet sequence in English, shows a marked improvement in poetic technique over its forerunners; and, with the writing of *Defence of Poesie,* he injected into the rich blood of English literature a necessary impetus toward imaginative but restrained writing. The influence of his genius was felt throughout English writing of the following centuries.

BIBLIOGRAPHICAL REFERENCES: Sidney's writings have been collected in *The Complete Works of Sir Philip Sidney,* edited by A. Feuillerat, 4 vols., 1912–1926, including both versions of the *Arcadia.* The most important studies of his life and works in English are J. A. Symonds, *Sir Philip Sidney,* English Men of Letters Series, 1886; M. W. Wallace, *The Life of Sir Philip Sidney,* 1915; Mona Wilson, *Sir Philip Sidney,* 1932; and A. H. Hill, *Astrophel,* 1937. Of particular importance, in French, is Michael Poirier, *Sir Philip Sidney, le chevalier poète élizabéthain,* 1948. A more specialized study is K. O. Myrick, *Sir Philip Sidney as a Literary Craftsman,* 1940.

For complete references see S. A. Tannenbaum, *Sir Philip Sidney: A Concise Bibliography*, 1941.

Recent studies include A. G. D. Wiles, "Parallel Analyses of the Two Versions of Sidney's *Arcadia*," *Studies in Philology*, XXXIX (1942), 167–206; F. L. Townsend, "Sidney and Ariosto," *Publications of the Modern Language Association*, LXI (1946), 97–108; P. A. Duhamel, "Sidney's *Arcadia* and Elizabethan Rhetoric," *Studies in Philology*, XLV (1948), 119–133; and Michael F. Krouse, "Plato and Sidney's *Defence of Poesie*," *Comparative Literature*, VI (1954), 138–147.

HENRYK SIENKIEWICZ

Born: Wola Okrzejska, Poland
Date: May 5, 1846

Died: Vevey, Switzerland
Date: November 15, 1916

PRINCIPAL WORKS

NOVELS: *Ogniem i mieczem*, 1884 (*With Fire and Sword*); *Potop*, 1886 (*The Deluge*); *Pan Wołodyjowski*, 1887–1888 (*Pan Michael*); *Bez dogmatu*, 1891 (*Without Dogma*); *Rodzina Połanieckich*, 1895 (*Children of the Soil*); *Quo Vadis?* 1896; *Krzyżacy*, 1900 (*The Teutonic Knights*).

Poland's greatest novelist was born on May 5, 1846, near Lukow, in Russian Poland, of a family that belonged to the country gentry. Educated by a tutor who shared his interest in history with his charge, Henryk Sienkiewicz attended the University of Warsaw. There, as one of the Young Positivist admirers of Auguste Comte, he became convinced that all knowledge can be observed through the human senses, including not only colors and sounds, but also their interrelationship. Although he and the other Positivists did not follow their master in scorning the microscope as an attempt to peer beyond human observation, they were interested in the how, rather than the why, of changes. This group largely revolutionized Poland's literary life following the 1863 revolt against Russia; then, and throughout his life, Sienkiewicz was noted for his hatred of Russia.

He began his literary career with his humorous *A Prophet in his Own Country* (1872). Four years later, motivated by his anti-Russian feelings as well as by a spirit of adventure, he emigrated from Poland as a member of a socialistic colony that settled at Anaheim, near Los Angeles. He remained in the United States until 1878, studying the life of Polish immigrants and sending articles back to newspapers in Warsaw. The differences in culture between Poland and the United States, as well as the unwillingness of the colonists to co-operate brought failure to the project. Sienkiewicz returned to Warsaw to make his living as a journalist.

Reading Scott and Dumas inspired him to do something similar for his own land. Discarding his Positivist theories, he began a trilogy dealing with seventeenth century Poland as it tried to establish national unity through wars with the Swedes, Turks, and Cossacks. In *With Fire and Sword, The Deluge,* and *Pan Michael,* the central character, Zagloba, has been likened to Falstaff and to Ulysses because of his combination of heroism and buffoonery.

Interested also in psychology and modern social problems, Sienkiewicz wrote about contemporary Poland in *Without Dogma,* and *Children of the Soil.* After these works he apparently realized that his real talent lay in the romantic field, for he returned to the manner of his earlier successes and in *Quo Vadis?* re-created in colorful detail Roman life under Nero. The best developed character in the novel is the epicure Petronius Arbiter. Since one of the purposes of Sienkiewicz's writing was "to strengthen the heart and to help maintain the Polish national spirit," he included in his Roman picture two Polish countrymen, the heroine Lygia and the giant Ursus. The popularity of the novel was enormous. Translated into thirty languages, it is undoubtedly the best known work of Polish literature, far better known than the same author's four-volume *The*

Teutonic Knights, also known as *The Knights of the Cross.* The narrowness of Sienkiewicz's intellectual sympathies is frequently blamed for some of the flaws in this and his other novels, yet his ability to write with dash and fire has never been questioned; his award of the Nobel Prize for literature in 1905 was universally acclaimed.

Because of his literary status and his anti-Russian sentiments, Sienkiewicz was frequently sought by the patriots to lead them in their movement for the liberation of Poland. During the First World War, he and the pianist Paderewski organized a committee to help Polish war victims. While working for the Polish Red Cross in Switzerland, Sienkiewicz died at Vevey on November 15, 1916. In 1924 his body was taken to Cracow, former capital of Poland, for burial in the ancient cathedral.

BIBLIOGRAPHICAL REFERENCES: Most of Sienkiewicz's novels are available in translation. The most comprehensive biographical study in English is Monica M. Gardner, *The Patriotic Novelist of Poland, Henryk Sienkiewicz,* 1926. See also Waclaw Lednicki, *Henryk Sienkiewicz,* 1946, and *Bits of Table Talk,* 1956; W. L. Phelps, *Essays on Modern Novelists,* 1910; and L. E. Van Norman, "Henryk Sienkiewicz's Poland," *Bookman,* XLIV (1917), 412–426.

FRANS EEMIL SILLANPÄÄ

Born: Hämeenkyrö, Finland
Date: September 16, 1888

PRINCIPAL WORKS

NOVELS: *Hurskas kurjuus,* 1919 (*Meek Heritage*); *Hiltu ja Ragnar,* 1923 (*Hiltu and Ragnar*); *Nuorena nukkunut,* 1931 (*The Maid Silja;* also *Fallen Asleep While Young*); *Miehen tie,* 1932 (*A Man's Road*); *Ihmiset suviyössä,* 1934 (*People in a Summer Night*); *Elokuu,* 1941 (*Harvest Month*).
SHORT STORIES: *Töllinmäki,* 1925.

Frans Eemil Sillanpää, winner of the Nobel Prize for literature in 1939, began life as a peasant's son in the Finnish town of Hämeenkyrö, September 16, 1888. As a child he displayed a great aptitude for science; consequently he was sent to the Imperial Alexander University at Helsingfors. But at the university he found more excitement in the company of writers, artists, and musicians (among whom, at that time, was the composer Sibelius) than he did in the laboratory. As a result of this new interest, he faced a great emotional crisis in his life. Having decided that his vocation was writing, he left the university without taking his examinations for a degree and returned home on Christmas Eve of 1913. Since that time his interests have followed no other course.

He published his first novel in 1916 and in that same year married a servant girl who was to bear him seven children. His second novel, *Meek Heritage*, concerned with the clash of the Reds and the Whites in the Finnish Revolution, won him fame in his own country and a government pension for life. Translated into a number of languages, the novel also helped to establish his international reputation. *The Maid Silja*, published in 1931, was equally popular at home and abroad. In 1936 Sillanpää was made an honorary doctor of philosophy by the Finnish government. Three years later he was awarded the Nobel Prize.

BIBLIOGRAPHICAL REFERENCES: For brief studies of Sillanpää in English see L. Viljanen, "Sillanpää," *American-Scandinavian Review*, XXVIII (1940), 49–53; R. Beck, "Sillanpää—Finland's Winner of the Nobel Prize," *Poet Lore*, XLVI (1940), 358–363; and Agnes Rothery, "Novels from Finland," *Virginia Quarterly Review*, XVI (1940), 296–299. For more extended studies see T. Vaaskivi, *Frans Eemil Sillanpää*, 1937; Edwin J. H. Linkomies, *Sillanpää*, 1948; and Rafael Koskimies, *Sillanpää*, 1948.

IGNAZIO SILONE

Born: Pescina dei Marsi, Italy
Date: May 1, 1900

PRINCIPAL WORKS

NOVELS: *Fontamara*, 1933; *Pane e vino*, 1936 (*Bread and Wine*); *Il Seme sotto la neve*, 1940 (*The Seed Beneath the Snow*); *Una manciata di more*, 1952 (*A Handful of Blackberries*).

PLAY: *Ed egli si nascose*, 1945 (*And He Hid Himself*).

SATIRE: *La scuola dei dittatori*, 1938 (*The School for Dictators*).

Ignazio Silone was born on May 1, 1900, in Pescina dei Marsi in the Abruzzi district of the Italian Apennines. His real name, Secondo Tranquilli, later was dropped to save his family from Fascist persecution. Born the son of a small landowner, he became active in the labor movement as a young boy. In 1917, as secretary for the land workers of the Abruzzi district, he was brought into court on charges of organizing an anti-war demonstration. One of the founders of the Italian Communist Party, by 1921 he was editor of a weekly newspaper in Rome and a daily in Trieste. Even after Mussolini's rise to power, Silone remained in Italy, printing illegal newspapers and carrying out other assignments. He also made trips to Moscow in 1921 and 1927 for the Italian Communist Party. Before he broke with the Party in 1930 and became anti-Communist, he had lost a brother who had died in a Fascist prison and he himself had been imprisoned and then expelled in various European countries.

Taking up residence in Switzerland in 1930, he set to work on his first novel, published in 1933 as *Fontamara*. It describes the systematic destruction by the Black Shirts of a small Italian town which has attempted to resist the Facists. A propagandistic novel which is nonetheless powerful and affecting, it ends with a plea for action against the scourge. Silone's finest book, *Bread and Wine*, tells the story of Pietro Spina, a revolutionist who returns to the Abruzzi district for refuge while he tries to regain his health. Disguised as a priest, he finds the best aspects of his youthful religiousness returning. Carrying out his undercover work, he achieves a kind of regeneration, attempting a fusion of the best of both Christianity and Marxism. *The School for Dictators* was a book of satiric dialogues against Fascism. His third novel, *The Seed Beneath the Snow*, followed the further activities

of Pietro Spina among the peasants and small landowners of Silone's native district. With the Allied invasion of Italy, Silone slipped back into Italy disguised as a priest and spent the remainder of the war as a member of the underground.

In 1945 Silone published a drama, *And He Hid Himself*, which was based on the activities of Pietro Spina. At the war's end he became manager of the newspaper *Avanti!* and, as a member of the Constituent Assembly, the leader of the left wing of the Italian Democratic Socialist Party. In 1952, two years after he had retired from political life to devote himself to literature, Silone published *A Handful of Blackberries*. This novel, set in postwar Italy, was the powerful story of an ex-Communist's attempt to break away from the Party, despite its retributory attempts against him and his sweetheart, and to resume his work for the peasants against the great landowners. Silone is now active in Italian and international writers' associations. His latest novel is a philosophical tale, *The Secret of Luke*.

BIBLIOGRAPHICAL REFERENCES: Aside from reviews of individual books, there is very little helpful criticism of Silone in English. See Edmund Wilson, "Two Survivors: Malraux and Silone," *New Yorker*, XXI (September 8, 1945), 74–78+; James T. Farrell, "Ignazio Silone," *Southern Review*, IV (1939), 771–783; and Julien Steinberg, *Verdict of Three Decades*, 1950.

WILLIAM GILMORE SIMMS

Born: Charleston, South Carolina
Date: April 17, 1806

Died: Charleston
Date: June 11, 1870

PRINCIPAL WORKS

NOVELS: *Guy Rivers*, 1834; *The Partisan*, 1835; *The Yemassee*, 1835; *Mellichampe*, 1836; *Pelayo*, 1838; *Richard Hurdis*, 1838; *The Damsel of Darien*, 1839; *The Border Beagles*, 1840; *The Kinsmen*, 1841 (*The Scout*, 1854); *Beauchampe*, 1842; *Helen Halsey*, 1845; *Count Julian*, 1845; *Katherine Walton*, 1851; *The Golden*

Christmas, 1852; *As Good as A Comedy*, 1852; *Vasconselos*, 1853; *The Sword and Distaff*, 1853 (*Woodcraft*, 1854); *The Forayers*, 1855; *Eutaw*, 1856; *Charlemont*, 1856; *The Cassique of Kiawah*, 1859.

SHORT STORIES: *The Wigwam and the Cabin*, 1845–1846.

HISTORY: *A History of South Carolina*, 1840; *South Carolina in the Revolution*, 1854.

POEM: *Atalantis*, 1832.

William Gilmore Simms, born in Charleston, South Carolina, on April 17, 1806, was known in his lifetime as a novelist, short story writer, poet, historian, and journalist; but his reputation rests today on his novels.

Simms's childhood was an unusual one. His mother died while he was still an infant, and his father left the baby in the care of its maternal grandmother. Under her care he seems to have had but casual schooling, but he read widely and listened intently to his grandmother's stories of the Revolutionary War as it had occurred in the South. In 1816, when the boy was ten years old, his father, a frontiersman who had gone westward toward the Mississippi River, paid a visit to Charleston, and eight years later the boy went to visit his father on his plantation in what is now Mississippi. Upon his return to Charleston after that visit Simms published some poems, most of them with a Byronic flavor. In 1828 he entered upon the editorship of a short-lived magazine entitled *The Tablet*. After its failure he became editor of the Charleston *City Gazette*, which opposed the election of John C. Calhoun. Because of the political animosity he incurred as a result, plus the deaths of his wife, grandmother, and father, Simms left for the North, where he found friends and a future.

Some early work was published shortly after he left Charleston, but his first important success came with the publication of *Guy Rivers* in 1834. A story of gold-mining in northern Georgia, the novel, packed with action, is a romantic piece of writing, but one with a realistic, native theme. His next work was *The Partisan*, which was probably inspired by his grandmother's accounts of the Revolutionary War. In the same year appeared *The Yemassee*, destined to remain his most popular book. It is an exciting tale of early days in South Carolina, especially important because of the realistic portrayal of the Indians. Indeed Simms's portrayal of the Indians has been adjudged by scholars to be essentially better than the more popular, idealized pictures given by James Fenimore Cooper in his novels. Simms's realism was a little too much for his own day. Two of his novels, *Beauchampe* and *Charlemont*, both about a celebrated Kentucky murder case, were considered in his lifetime too realistic for what was then called good taste, although they seem tame enough for today.

Following his second marriage in 1836, Simms's life began to change. Filling the position of a wealthy planter on his wife's plantation and rearing a family of fifteen children made him an outstanding spokesman for the Southern notion of Greek democracy in America, a concept which implied a defense of slavery. Simms's theories on slavery were found in his *History of*

989

South Carolina. His viewpoint and his reputation as an author made him a great man in the South, but they caused unpopularity in the North. While his works were in vogue before the Civil War, they were neglected afterward. All Simms's important writing came before that war, for while the war ruined his reputation in the North, it also destroyed his home and way of life in the South.

Simms's reputation has been slow in returning. For a half century his books were out of print, except for *The Yemassee.* A frequent comparison of Simms to Cooper as a novelist generally is without critical foundation and really unfair to Simms. His novels are vigorous, and the materials he used and the

realism he employed were his own. He wrote about South Carolina during the eighteenth century and about the pre-Civil War frontier, then east of the Mississippi River. He celebrated little-known elements of American history and culture. In three kinds of fiction he excelled: the border romance, of which *Guy Rivers* is his best; the novel of Indian warfare, of which *The Yemassee* is a classic; and the romance about the American Revolution, of which *The Partisan* is a good example. In addition to fiction, poetry and history, Simms also wrote biographies of Francis Marion, Captain John Smith, and Nathaniel Greene.

Simms died in Charleston, June 11, 1870.

BIBLIOGRAPHICAL REFERENCES: *The Works of William Gilmore Simms,* 20 vols., 1853–1866 is not complete. *The Letters of William Gilmore Simms* have been edited by Mary C. Simms Oliphant, Alfred T. Odell, and T. C. D. Eaves, 5 vols., 1952–195–. The standard biography is William P. Trent, *William Gilmore Simms,* 1892. Alexander Cowie's 1937 edition of *The Yemassee* includes an introduction and an excellent bibliography. Outstanding studies of Simms appear in Vernon L. Parrington, *Main Currents in American Thought,* Vol. II, 1927; Van Wyck Brooks, *The World of Washington Irving,* 1944; and Jay B. Hubbell, *The South in American Literature, 1607–1900,* 1954, the latter the leading work on the subject of Southern literature.

MAY SINCLAIR

Born: Rock Ferry, Cheshire, England
Date: 1865 (?)

Died: Aylesbury, England
Date: November 14, 1946

PRINCIPAL WORKS

NOVELS: *Audrey Craven,* 1897; *Two Sides of a Question,* 1901; *The Divine Fire,* 1904; *The Helpmate,* 1907; *The Creators,* 1910; *The Three Sisters,* 1914; *Tasker Jevons,* 1916 [*The Belfry*]; *The Tree of Heaven,* 1917; *Mary Olivier,* 1919; *Mr. Waddington of Wyck,* 1921; *Anne Severn and the Fieldings,* 1922; *The Life and Death of Harriet Frean,* 1922; *A Cure of Souls,* 1924; *The Rector of Wyck,* 1925.

SHORT STORIES: *The Judgment of Eve,* 1908 [*The Return of the Prodigal*]; *Uncanny Stories,* 1923; *The Intercessor,* 1931.

POEM: *The Dark Night,* 1924.

BIOGRAPHY: *The Three Brontës,* 1912.

May Sinclair is an unusual British author in that her work found a wider, more enthusiastic audience in America than it did in her native England. Born in Cheshire, probably in 1865, she was educated at home and at Ladies' College, Cheltenham. As a girl she wrote poetry and philosophical criticism, some of which was published. Her first published short story appeared in 1895, and her first novel, *Audrey Craven*, in 1897. But real fame as a novelist waited for almost a decade, until the publication of *The Divine Fire* in 1904. A biography, *The Three Brontës*, published in 1912, was followed by another successful novel, *The Three Sisters*, which showed the influence of her Brontës studies.

During World War I May Sinclair, who was then and throughout her life unmarried, served with an ambulance unit on the front in Belgium and worked with the Hoover Relief Commission. After World War I she lived a quiet life that was unbroken except for several visits to the United States. Miss Sinclair worked steadily, pro-ducing more than a dozen books, until invalidism made writing impossible. Outstanding among her later books are *Mary Olivier* and *Anne Severn and the Fieldings*. *Uncanny Stories* is a volume of short fiction reflecting her interest in the supernatural and spiritualism. Her lifelong interest in philosophy, especially idealism, resulted in a study, *The New Idealism* (1922). In the 1920's she wrote several light satirical comedies of manners; *Mr. Waddington of Wyck* and *A Cure of Souls* belong to this genre. *The Dark Night* is a long narrative poem.

As early as the writing of *Mary Olivier*, May Sinclair had begun utilizing the subconscious in her fiction, very much in the manner of Dorothy Richardson, and she has been termed one of the pioneers in the stream-of-consciousness technique. As a young woman she was a suffragette, and throughout her life she maintained an interest in feminist movements. She died on November 14, 1946, at Aylesbury, England.

BIBLIOGRAPHICAL REFERENCES: May Sinclair has received very little critical attention. See Frank Swinnerton, *The Georgian Literary Scene*, 1934; W. C. Frierson, *The English Novel in Transition*, 1942; C. A. Dawson Scott, "May Sinclair," *Bookman*, LII (1920), 246–249; and Jean de Bosschere, "Charity in the Work of May Sinclair," *Yale Review*, XIV (1924), 82–94.

UPTON SINCLAIR

Born: Baltimore, Maryland
Date: September 20, 1878

PRINCIPAL WORKS

NOVELS: *The Journal of Arthur Stirling*, 1903; *The Jungle*, 1906; *The Metropolis*, 1908; *King Coal*, 1917; *100%*, 1920; *They Call Me Carpenter*, 1922; *Oil! A Novel*, 1927; *Boston*, 1928; *Mountain City*, 1930; *Roman Holiday*, 1931; *Co-op*, 1936; *Little Steel*, 1938; *World's End*, 1940; *Between Two Worlds*, 1941; *Dragon's Teeth*, 1942; *Wide Is the Gate*, 1943; *Presidential Agent*, 1944; *Dragon Harvest*, 1945; *A World to Win*, 1946; *Presidential Mission*, 1947; *One Clear Call*, 1948; *O Shepherd, Speak!*, 1949; *The Return of Lanny Budd*, 1953.

PLAYS: *Plays of Protest*, 1912; *Singing Jailbirds*, 1924; *Bill Porter*, 1925; *Oil!*, 1925; *Depression Island*, 1935; *Marie Antoinette*, 1939; *The Enemy Had It Too*, 1950.

ESSAYS AND STUDIES: *Our Bourgeois Literature*, 1905; *The Profits of Religion*, 1918; *The Brass Check: A Study in American Journalism*, 1919; *The Goose-Step: A Study of American Education*, 1923; *The Goslings: A Study of the American Schools*, 1924; *Mammonmart*, 1925; *The Cup of Fury*, 1956.

Upton (Beall) Sinclair has been one of the most prolific writers, one of the most widely read, and one of the least recognized writers of our time. The trouble lies probably in the tractarian nature of his writings, for from the beginning of his career Sinclair has been a reformer. He still is, for his most recent book, *The Cup of Fury*, published in 1956, is an analysis of the effect of alcohol, with the conclusion that other writers, had they abstained from liquor like Upton Sinclair, would have been greater writers and would have written much more. The book is, in effect, an old-fashioned temperance tract, an attempt to reform.

Born in Baltimore, Maryland, on September 20, 1878, Sinclair began his career as a prodigy. He finished secondary school when he was twelve and became a student at the City College of New York at the age of fourteen. From the age of fifteen he supported himself in part by writing stories for the pulp magazines. After finishing college, he married in 1900 and, while threatened with poverty, began to write serious novels. His first five books, published between 1901 and 1906, gave him little encouragement, for they produced together less than a thousand dollars. Before leaving college Sinclair had become a Socialist, and his political views influenced his writing. His first fame came with the publication of *The Jungle*, an exposé of the Chicago stockyards which, in its final chapters, becomes a mere Socialist tract. With the proceeds of this book, which was a best seller that still finds readers, Sinclair founded Helicon Hall, a cooperative community at which Sinclair Lewis was temporarily a furnace man. Upton Sinclair continued to write at a furious pace, also becoming a publisher during 1918–1919 with *Upton Sinclair's Magazine*. Beginning with *The Profits of Religion*, in 1918, he wrote a series of non-fictional works on the effects of capitalism in America, from the viewpoint of a Socialist. The series, which has the collective title of *The Dead Hand*, reviewed such phases of American culture as the schools, the colleges, newspapers and publishing, art, and literature.

In private life, as well as in public life, Upton Sinclair had difficulties. He was divorced in 1911 and remarried in 1913. In 1915 he and his second wife, Mary Craig Kimbrough, a poetess, moved to California. In 1923 Sinclair founded the California chapter of the American Civil Liberties Union. Several times he ran for political office, seeking seats in the U.S. House of Representatives and the Senate. He also ran for the governorship of California, twice as a Socialist and once, in 1934, as a Democratic nominee.

In his novels of the period 1917–1940, Upton Sinclair exploited many areas of contemporary life. *King Coal* described conditions in the Colorado coal fields. *Oil!* described life in the oil fields of California, with looks also at the young motion picture industry. *Little Steel* described conditions and strikes in the steel mills during the 1930's.

During the thirteen years between 1940 and 1953, Upton Sinclair labored at a series of novels relating the events of the whole world from 1913 to 1950, including World War I, the peace negotiations after that war, the rise to power of Hitler and Mussolini, the Spanish Civil War, the Munich debacle, Roosevelt's election and re-elections, World War II, and the aftermath of World War II. The whole series is tied together picaresquely and romantically by the character of Lanny Budd, son of a wealthy munitions manufacturer. Lanny Budd, a young man with Socialist leanings, travels far and wide, meets many people, happens usually to be at the right spot at the right time, and even serves as a special agent for Franklin D. Roosevelt.

More recent works by Sinclair include *Another Pamela* (1950), a twentieth-century version of Richardson's novel about virtue rewarded; *The Enemy Had It Too,* a play about the atomic age; and *A Personal Jesus* (1952), Sinclair's own interpretation of the Christ.

Probably no contemporary American writer of fiction has been read by so many people in this country and abroad or been translated into so many languages. Upton Sinclair has been a best seller in other countries when he was not one at home, but that popularity probably rests on social and political bases, rather than on any artistic values. At times Sinclair has employed pseudonyms, among them Clarke Fitch, Frederick Garrison, and Arthur Stirling.

BIBLIOGRAPHICAL REFERENCES: There are two convenient compilations of Sinclair's work, *An Upton Sinclair Anthology,* edited by I. O. Evans, 1934; and *Upton Sinclair Anthology,* edited by Irving Stone and Lewis Browne, 1947. Of primary interest is Sinclair's autobiography, *American Outpost: A Book of Reminiscences,* 1932 (published in England as *Candid Reminiscences: My First Thirty Years*). A significant early evaluation is Floyd Dell, *Upton Sinclair: A Study in Social Protest,* 1927. A range of critical estimates may be found in Van Wyck Brooks, *Emerson and Others,* 1927; Harry Hartwick, *The Foreground of American Fiction,* 1934; Harlan Hatcher, *Creating the Modern American Novel,* 1935; and A. H. Quinn, *American Fiction,* 1936. See also Walter Lippmann, "Upton Sinclair," *Saturday Review of Literature,* IV (1928), 641–643.

ISRAEL JOSHUA SINGER

Born: Bilgoraj, Poland
Date: November 30, 1893

Died: New York, N. Y.
Date: February 10, 1944

PRINCIPAL WORKS

NOVELS: *The Brothers Ashkenazi,* tr., 1936; *East of Eden,* tr., 1939.
SHORT STORIES: *Pearl,* 1922; *The River Breaks Up,* 1938.
PLAY: *Yoshe Kalb,* 1932 (*The Sinners*).

Israel Joshua Singer, Yiddish writer, was born on November 30, 1893, in Bilgoraj, Poland. The son of a rabbi,

he studied the Talmud as a boy, but at seventeen developed more worldly interests which led him finally to newspaper work. In 1922 he became the Warsaw representative of the *Jewish Daily Forward*. The paper sent him to Russia in 1926 and made him an editor when he emigrated to the United States in 1934.

Pearl, his first volume of stories, was highly successful in Europe and it was followed by more stories and a book about Russia, but Singer's reputation rests on two novels: *The Brothers Ashkenazi*, translated in 1936 and sent through eleven editions before 1939, and *East of Eden*, translated in 1939. The first shows the social,

economic, and political forces which affect an industrial town in Poland in the course of the nineteenth century and focuses on the contrasting fortunes of twin brothers. The more somber *East of Eden* traces the desperate careers of a poor, dispossessed family and particularly of the son who turns hopefully to communism, only to be bitterly disillusioned. A dramatic adaptation of a third novel, *The Sinners*, added to Singer's fame when it was produced in New York in 1932.

Singer died in New York on February 10, 1944.

BIBLIOGRAPHICAL REFERENCES: There is no full-length biographical or critical study. See John Cournos, "Three Novelists: Asch, Singer and Schnéour," *Menorah Journal* XXV (1937), 81–91.

ELSIE SINGMASTER

Born: Schuylkill Haven, Pennsylvania
Date: August 29, 1879

Died: Gettysburg, Pennsylvania
Date: September 30, 1958

PRINCIPAL WORKS

NOVELS: *Katy Gaumer*, 1915; *Basil Everman*, 1920; *Ellen Levis*, 1921; *Bennett Malin*, 1922; *The Hidden Road*, 1923; *Keller's Anna Ruth*, 1926; *What Everybody Wanted*, 1928; *Swords of Steel*, 1933; *The Magic Mirror*, 1934; *The Loving Heart*, 1937; *Rifles for Washington*, 1938; *A High Wind Rising*, 1942; *I Speak for Thaddeus Stevens*, 1947; *I Heard of a River*, 1948.

SHORT STORIES: *Gettysburg*, 1913; *Bred in the Bone*, 1925; *Stories to Read at Christmas*, 1940.

JUVENILES: *Emmeline*, 1916; *John Baring's House*, 1920; *A Boy at Gettysburg*, 1924; *"Sewing Susie,"* 1927; *Virginia's Bandit*, 1929; *You Make Your Own Luck*, 1929; *Stories of Pennsylvania* (I-IV), 1937–1940; *The Isle of Que*, 1948.

REGIONAL STUDY: *Pennsylvania's Susquehanna*, 1950.

The fiction of Elsie Singmaster may be clearly charted in geography and time. She is the novelist of Pennsylvania, more particularly of the Pennsylvania German region from the colonial period to the present. First in time are her stories of the early settlements in *A High Wind Rising* and *I Heard of a River*, set against the years

when French and Indian raiders swept over the Warrior Road and Carlisle and Lancaster stood on a disputed frontier between the French lands on the Ohio and English territory along the Schuylkill and the Delaware. Later the history of the state widens into the history of the nation in her Revolutionary War novel, *Rifles for Wash-*

ington, and again in *I Speak for Thaddeus Stevens* and in her stories of the three bloody days at Gettysburg in 1863. For a later time she has written novels and tales of small-town and country life. These are regional rather than historical, for in them she makes vivid and real the Pennsylvania German countryside of red barns and fieldstone houses, the landscape of her sturdy, patriarchal Mennonites, Dunkers, and Amish, with their strange religious dress, their slow unchanging ways of conduct and belief, their simple pieties and old superstitions. This is her own region as well, and she has brought to it her whole vision and understanding as a writer.

Elsie Singmaster was born on August 29, 1879, in the Lutheran parsonage at Schuylkill Haven, Pennsylvania. Her father, the Reverend John Alden Singmaster, had among his ancestors one who studied under Martin Luther and another who was the first Lutheran minister ordained in this country. Part of her childhood was spent at Macungie, the Millerstown of her fiction, where her father had been called to a pastorate of six churches between Allentown and Reading, and she gathered impressions of this locality as she drove about with him when he went to preach to the different congregations in his charge. English was always spoken in the Singmaster home, Mrs. Singmaster being a Quaker of English descent, but from playmates and neighbors the younger Singmasters learned the hybrid mixture of English and German known as Pennsylvania Dutch. This was the only language known to the first teacher who taught her rhetoric.

If her early education was at best rudimentary, there were always good books to read in her father's library. By the time she was eleven she had begun to write stories of her own. Later, at Cornell and Radcliffe, she continued to write sketches of Pennsylvania life and character, partly to set down her observations clearly and partly to explain a foreign-seeming group of people whom she thought misunderstood. She sold her first story in 1905. By the time of her graduation from Radcliffe in 1907 she had already contributed to *Scribner's, Century,* and the *Atlantic Monthly.* In 1912 she married Harold Lewars, a musician, and went to live in Harrisburg. After his death in 1915 she made her permanent home in Gettysburg, where her father was the president of the Lutheran theological seminary.

Elsie Singmaster had already written a number of stories and several books for children when she published *Katy Gaumer,* her first novel, in 1915. Katy is one of Miss Singmaster's typical heroines, a Pennsylvania German girl eager to acquire the learning which will prepare her for life in a larger world. *Basil Everman,* its scene a college town which may be identified as Gettysburg, deals with the influence a young writer of genius has on a group of people of the college and the town many years after his death. *Ellen Levis* and *Keller's Anna Ruth* are stories of gentle, self-sacrificing young women, handicapped by environment, who in the end win for themselves a better future according to their natures and their needs. *Bennett Malin,* darker in mood and implications, tells of a man who builds a false, bright world about himself on a shaky foundation of literary theft. *What Everybody Wanted* shifts its scene to Maryland to present a light and amusing account of human vanity and desire. *The Magic Mirror,* making a return to a more familiar Pennsylvania setting, brings to life a community, a countryside, and a strange but rich way of life through the experiences of Jesse Hummer, whose ambition is to tell the story of his people after he becomes a writer.

Her later novels reveal a renewed interest in historical themes. In *Rifles for Washington* she presents the events and battles of seven years of war from a boy's point of view because she wanted to stress the element of action, the sense of things happening, which would make the deepest impression on a boy's mind. Like many of her stories, this book is juvenile fiction only in the sense that it deals with a youthful hero. *A High Wind Rising* is a regional chronicle dealing with the early settlements and the part played by the Pennsylvania Germans under Conrad Weiser in holding the land for the

English during the French and Indian wars. *I Speak for Thaddeus Stevens* is a biographical novel throwing new light on the powerful political figure of the Civil War period. *I Heard of a River* is another story of the early settlements. Of Miss Singmaster's short stories, the most vivid and moving are the Civil War tales in *Gettysburg,* the most amusing her stories of the Mennonite Shindledecker sisters in *Bred in the Bone.* Much of her magazine fiction has never been collected.

A writer of quiet but satisfying richness and depth within her chosen field, Elsie Singmaster has never attracted a wide reading public or the attention of popular criticism. One reason may be that as examples of work done within a clearly defined regional tradition, her books have owed almost nothing to literary fashion. For much the same reason they will lose little when fashions change.

BIBLIOGRAPHICAL REFERENCES: There is no extended biographical or critical study. See Harry R. Warfel, *American Novelists of Today,* 1951; Edward Wagenknecht, *Cavalcade of the American Novel,* 1952; also Dayton Kohler, "Elsie Singmaster," *Bookman,* LXXII (1931), 621–626, and "Elsie Singmaster and the Regional Tradition," *Commonwealth,* I (September, 1947), 15–18.

ADAM SMITH

Born: Kirkcaldy, Scotland
Date: June 5, 1723

Died: Edinburgh, Scotland
Date: July 17, 1790

PRINCIPAL WORKS

ESSAYS AND TREATISES: *Theory of Moral Sentiments,* 1759; *An Inquiry into the Nature and Causes of the Wealth of Nations,* 1776; *Considerations Concerning the First Formation of Languages,* 1790; *Essays on Philosophical Subjects,* 1795.

Born at Kirkcaldy in Fifeshire, Scotland, on June 5, 1723, Adam Smith studied at the University of Glasgow, where he came under the influence of the famous professor of moral philosophy, Francis Hutcheson. Smith

then studied at Balliol College, Oxford, for six years before returning to Scotland to lecture in rhetoric and polite literature at the University of Edinburgh. His lectures were popular and, unlike those of many of his contemporaries, attracted listeners from the town as well as from the university.

Smith returned to the University of Glasgow in 1751 as professor of logic; in the same year he was appointed to the chair in moral philosophy. At this time Smith was strongly under the influence of his close friend, the historian and philosopher David Hume, and shared in a milder form much of Hume's skepticism. (For example, Smith never took holy orders, an unusual circumstance for a professor of moral philosophy in Scotland at that time.) In 1759, Smith published his *Theory of Moral Sentiments,* in which he claimed that sympathy or feeling was the foundation for all our moral sentiments or judgments. He felt that evil or wrongdoing was punished by remorse in the individual, and that certainly remorse was the most painful of the human sentiments. His position was not very far from that of current philosophers who claim that ethical principles are merely statements of our own emotions.

Even at this early date Smith was highly interested in economics. He often talked of trade and political economy in his lectures, and he urged both students and young businessmen from the growing commercial city and port of Glasgow to attend his lectures. Many criticized him, and one of his colleagues later sneered that "he had converted the chair of moral philosophy into a professorship of trade and finance."

Smith's unconventional lectures attracted a good deal of notice. Late in 1762, the wealthy Duke of Buccleuch became interested in Smith and hired him as his private tutor. Smith left the university and traveled with his patron to France, where he lived for more than two years and met physiocratic economic philosophers like Turgot, Helvétius, and Quesnay. Becoming more and more convinced of the need for coherent study of the principles of political economy, Smith returned from France and spent ten years studying and writing his famous *Wealth of Nations.* Classic statement of the doctrine of laissez faire, this book established the idea that national progress could be best achieved with private initiative and enterprise limited only by the bounds of justice. Although a good deal of Smith's theorizing was borrowed from his French associates, his copious illustrations and his applications of his principles to current problems in England and Scotland insured him a wide and interested audience.

Although he wrote little after the *Wealth of Nations,* the book and its author were both famous. Smith made frequent trips to London where he had a good deal of influence on the Prime Minister, William Pitt, and his opinion was sought on almost all tax legislation passed by Parliament after the disastrous Stamp Act. Widely honored, he was made commissioner of customs for Scotland in 1777 and in 1787 was elected rector of the University of Glasgow. He died in Edinburgh on July 17, 1790.

In later life, Adam Smith came to represent a kind of calm, rational, principled Augustan. He was intimate with many of the great of his age, Hume, Gibbon, and Dr. Johnson (although the last apparently never forgave him for an unkind review of his famous dictionary in the *Edinburgh Review*); and he enjoyed discussing philosophy, semantics, history, politics, and economics in the various London clubs. He was a man apparently without fanaticism or a doctrinaire approach. Despite his advocacy of free trade and unrestricted operation of the law of supply and demand, he did acknowledge the necessity for government control in such matters as education and the public highways. Interested in many phases of the intellect, he was the first to synthesize and articulate many of the economic principles and problems that grew out of the rapid industrial and commercial expansion of his age.

BIBLIOGRAPHICAL REFERENCES: For biography and critical commentary see F. W. Hirst, *Adam Smith*, 1904; A. W. Small, *Adam Smith and Modern Sociology*, 1907; W. R. Scott, *Adam Smith as Student and Professor*, 1937; Charles Ryle Fay, *Adam Smith and the Scotland of His Day*, 1956; and Joseph Cropsey, *Polity and Economy: An Interpretation of the Principles of Adam Smith*, 1957.

BETTY SMITH

Born: Brooklyn, N. Y.
Date: December 15, 1897

PRINCIPAL WORK

NOVEL: *A Tree Grows in Brooklyn*, 1943.

Betty Smith, like Francie Nolan, was born in Brooklyn (December 15, 1897) and went to college in Michigan. Enrolled as a part-time student at the University of Michigan, she studied writing, particularly playwriting, almost exclusively. In 1930 she published two short plays in a volume written by drama students at Michigan, and in 1931 she won the first prize of $1,000 in the Avery Hopwood competition, mainly for her work in fiction. Even then she was developing the material she used later in her popular novel; one of her winning stories was called "Death of a Singing Waiter."

She continued her studies at the Yale School of Drama and was awarded playwriting fellowships by the Rockefeller Foundation and the Dramatists' Guild. Although she has published or produced over seventy one-act plays, it was not until she wrote *A Tree Grows in Brooklyn* that she received widespread public recognition. The novel was praised mainly for its lyrical treatment of naturalistic subject matter and for its realistic dialogue. She collaborated with George Abbott to write a musical version for the stage.

She again turned from her interest in drama to write a second novel, *Tomorrow Will Be Better*, another story of hope in tenement life, but this book was not nearly so well received as her first. Her prime interest remains in the theater.

BIBLIOGRAPHICAL REFERENCES: For critical comment on Miss Smith's novels see the *Book Review Digest*, 1943, 1948.

TOBIAS SMOLLETT

Born: Dalquhurn, Scotland   *Died:* Antignano, Italy
Date: March, 1721   *Date:* September 17, 1771

PRINCIPAL WORKS

NOVELS: *Roderick Random,* 1748; *Peregine Pickle,* 1751; *Ferdinand, Count Fathom,* 1753; *Sir Launcelot Greaves,* 1760–1762; *The Expedition of Humphry Clinker,* 1771.
TRANSLATIONS: *Gil Blas,* 1749; *Don Quixote,* 1755; *The Works of Voltaire,* 1761–1769.
MISCELLANEOUS: *A Complete History of England,* 1757–1758; *The Reprisal,* 1757; *The Modern Part of an Universal History,* 1759–1766; *A Continuation of the Complete History of England,* 1760–1761; 1765; *Travels in France and Italy,* 1766; *The Present State of All Nations,* 1768–1769; *The Adventures of an Atom,* 1769.

Tobias Smollett, born in March, 1721, at Dalquhurn near Bonhill, Scotland, had the ill fortune in his own time and today to be in competition with Henry Fielding. The result is that Smollett's moon has been obscured by Fielding's sun. This is a great pity, for, despite the unattractive behavior of many of his characters and the general brutality of his novels, there is much pleasure to be found in the pages of Smollett.

A poor and hot-tempered Scot, Smollett was a real-life replica of one of his own literary creations. After study at Glasgow University, he went to London to seek his fortune. After a hitch in the navy as surgeon's mate, he remained for a time in the West Indies, where he fell in love with Nancy Lascelles, daughter of a Jamaica planter, whom he later married. In 1744 he was back in London doctoring and writing. His first novel, *Roderick Random,* was a picaresque work which strung together a series of episodes through which the hero ultimately finds love and wealth. Many readers have been repelled by Roderick's selfishness and coarseness; but, as in all of Smollett's novels, there is a plenitude of delight to be found in the minor

characters, who are treated as humor types. Lieutenant Tom Bowling, eccentric sea dog, and Morgan, a Welsh surgeon, are two such figures. Because of his interest in naval life, Smollett has been called the father of the nautical novel. The picture of shipboard life and the account of the disastrous attack on Cartagena in *Roderick Random* are among the earliest literary protests against naval abuses.

Peregrine Pickle, his next novel, mined the vein of *Roderick Random.* Again, a young man with roguish tendencies achieves security after a series of adventures and amours. Commodore Hawser Trunnion, Smollett's finest picture of an old salt, graces this novel. *Ferdinand, Count Fathom,* published in 1753, is a novel remarkable chiefly for the baseness of its hero, a thoroughly villainous ingrate who is made to undergo an unconvincing reformation. This was followed by *Sir Launcelot Greaves,* a lackluster imitation of *Don Quixote.*

Then in the year of his death Smollett published *The Expedition of Humphry Clinker,* at once his masterpiece and his happiest book. This epistolary novel employs a trip through the British Isles as the framework for the exhibition of a brilliant set of humor characters. Chief among them is Matthew Bramble, a kindhearted man who unsuccessfully tries to hide his goodness behind a gruff manner. Bramble is accompanied by his sister Tabitha, a grotesque virago who finally succeeds in marrying Lieutenant Obadiah Lismahago, a terrible-tempered Scot. The novel takes its title from a starveling whom Bramble befriends and who turns out to be Bramble's natural son. The episode of the discovery of Humphry's identity is unsurpassed in the English novel.

In addition to his novels, Smollett labored prodigiously at a number of literary projects in which he was sometimes the coördinator of the work of several hack writers. He translated *Gil Blas, Don Quixote,* and *The Works of Voltaire.* He edited *The Critical Review* (1756–63), *The British Magazine* (1760–67), and *The Briton* (1762–63). He also wrote or edited a group of multiple-volume works: *A Complete History of England, A Continuation of the Complete History of England, A Compendium of Voyages* (1756), *The Modern Part of an Universal History,* and *The Present State of All Nations.* In the field of poetry he wrote "The Tears of Scotland" (1746?, 1753), "Advice, a Satire" (1746), "Reproof, a Satire" (1747), and "Ode to Independence" (1773). Smollett was very ambitious for a stage success; after the failure of his tragedy *The Regicide* (1749) he enjoyed a small hit with a farce, *The Reprisal.*

Ill health sent Smollett abroad, and out of his trips came *Travels in France and Italy,* a curious mixture of laughter and anger. *The Adventures of an Atom* is a scurrilous political satire in which events attributed to Japan stand for occurrences in England.

It is difficult to avoid the conclusion that despite his obvious lapses in taste Tobias Smollett possessed one of the most remarkable talents in all of English literature. He died at Antignano, near Leghorn, Italy, on September 17, 1771.

BIBLIOGRAPHICAL REFERENCES: The most authoritative study of Smollett is Lewis M. Knapp's *Tobias Smollett: Doctor of Men and Manners,* 1949. See also Lewis Melville, *The Life and Letters of Tobias Smollett,* 1927; Lewis M. Kahrl, *Tobias Smollett, Traveler-Novelist,* 1945; F. W. Boege, *Smollett's Reputation as a Novelist,* 1947; also Howard S. Buck, *A Study in Smollett, Chiefly "Peregrine Pickle,"* 1925; Louis L. Martz, *The Later Career of Tobias Smollett,* 1942; and Rufus Putney, "The Plan of *Peregrine Pickle,*" *Publications of the Modern Language Association,* LX (1945), 1051–1065.

SNORRI STURLUSON

Born: Odda (?), Iceland
Date: 1179

Died: Reykjaholt, Iceland
Date: September 23, 1241

PRINCIPAL WORKS

HISTORY: The *Prose Edda,* c. 1220; *Heimskringla,* c. 1230–35 (*Sagas of the Norwegian Kings*).

Snorri Sturluson (or Sturleson), Iceland's best-known writer and historian of the Norse kings, was born at or near Odda in 1179, the scion of a family of powerful Icelandic chiefs. He received an ecclesiastical education at the home of his foster-father at Odda, a cultural center, and read volumes of history and poetry at an early age. Eager for wealth and power, he made a highly advantageous marriage, which brought him several great estates, and became a lawyer, eventually rising to the position of president of the Icelandic legislative assembly and of the highest court of the land. Still seeking power and adventure, Snorri journeyed to Norway and became a favorite of King Haakon, who made him a court chamberlain. Returning to Iceland as Haakon's vassal several years later, he became embroiled in quarrels with other nobles, including some of his own relatives. He was killed at Reykjaholt on September 23, 1241, by agents of the Norwegian king, against whom he had turned traitor in the course of his scheming for self-aggrandizement.

For all his ambition and avarice, Snorri was apparently regarded by his contemporaries as a pious and patriotic man. Certainly the *Heimskringla* indicates his diligent striving after historical accuracy and his desire to immortalize the deeds and characters of the great Norse kings "from the beginning" (i.e. the days of the legendary migrations from Asia) through the reign of Sverri, which ended in 1177. His sources are many: the writings of Ari Torgelson the Wise, the early eleventh century priest-historian; the oral collections of traditions as handed down in ballad form by the scalds or bards, and the legendary biographies

of the two King Olafs. To all this material Snorri added much knowledge gleaned from his own studies and observations in Norway.

Although he takes his chronology and many of his facts from Ari, Snorri's style is completely his own. He sets forth his critical standards in the preface to his work, saying that he trusts most sources which are closest in time to the events described, and that even these things may not be true but are only "believed to be true by old and wise men." Only in his account of the miracles of St. Olaf does he abandon his scientific approach to history.

Snorri's history is set forth in the form of a series of brilliant biographies, from which every irrelevant detail which does not contribute to the characterization has been carefully rejected. He borrows from Thucydides and Plutarch the device of putting into his characters' mouths speeches, not as they were actually spoken, but as they might have been. In "The Life of St. Olaf," the only section of the *Heimskringla* which has survived unabridged, he describes not only the king's great deeds but also details of his everyday life which give the character depth and reality.

Snorri is also credited with the *Prose Edda*, a "primer for young poets" which describes the creation and the rise of paganism, the Norse mythological system and legends attributable to the god of poetry, and lays out the rules and theories of ancient verse forms. Although in prose, the language of the *Edda* is highly poetical.

BIBLIOGRAPHICAL REFERENCES: The translation of the *Heimskringla* by Samuel Laing is available in Everyman's Library. *The Stories of the Kings of Norway,* translated from the Icelandic by William Morris and Eríkr Magnússon, 3 vols., 1893–1905, is supplemented by a fourth volume containing a *Life* by Magnússon. See also

S. Nordal, *Snorri Sturluson,* 1920; and Fredrik Paasche, *Snorre Sturlason og Sturlungerne,* 1922.

SOCRATES

Born: Athens, Greece
Date: c. 470 B.C.

Died: Athens
Date: 399 B.C.

Socrates did not make a written record of his teachings. What is known of his philosophy comes from the *Dialogues* of Plato (q.v.) in which Socrates is the central figure.

What is known of Socrates, the great Greek philosopher, comes primarily from two of his pupils, Xenophon and Plato. The account of Socrates by Plato in the *Dialogues* is generally taken as being, on the whole, the more reliable report, both of the character and the teachings of Socrates.

Socrates, born in Athens about 470 B.C., was the son of Sophroniscus, a sculptor, and Phænarete, a non-professional midwife. The family was neither poor nor wealthy, and Socrates received the usual elementary education in gymnastics and music, to train the body and the mind. He may have planned to follow his father's occupation, and there are some reports that he actually did produce some works of sculpture; but he apparently decided that he was more at ease with ideas than with stone. He had a reflective, almost mystical temperament at times, and throughout his lifetime had the habit of assuming some immobile position, a kind of trancelike state, during which he sometimes believed himself to hear a supernatural voice that warned him against certain acts he was considering. He claimed that when he disregarded the voice, he got into trouble.

He is pictured as a short, snub-nosed person with widely spaced, perhaps protruding eyes, and broad nostrils. The comic dramatists of the time, Aristophanes, Amipsias, and Eupolis, made him the subject of satirical dramas in which his physical traits as well as his dialectical habits were exaggerated. He lived simply, wearing the same garment winter and summer and traveling barefoot in all seasons. He ate and drank moderately, although he could drink more wine than most men without being affected. He was married to Xanthippe, a woman who seemed to suit him, although later critics tried to give her a shrewish reputation; she bore Socrates at least two children.

Socrates began his philosophical studies with the ideas of Pythagoras, Parmenides, Heraclitus, Anaxagoras, Anaximander, Zeno, and others. Because of the conflicting and sometimes fantastic ideas he found in these philosophies concerning the nature of the universe, he came to the conviction that more was to be gained by a study of justice and goodness. He combined his interest in ethics and the philosophy of politics with a faith in the capacity of the mind to clarify itself by working out the inconsistencies in various notions through a conversational technique which has come to be known as the "Socratic method." He claimed that if there were any truth in the report that the Oracle at Delphi had called him the wisest man in Greece, it was only because, unlike others, he recognized his own ignorance. He believed that he had a mission in life to make men aware of the limitations and defects in their beliefs and thus, by knowing themselves, to prepare for knowledge.

He wandered the streets and market places of Athens, and when young men, politicians, or other bystanders became involved in conversation with him about justice, honor, courage, or some other matter with which philosophy could be concerned, Socrates would adroitly question them, leading them to an awareness of the inadequacy or falsity of their ideas. Since his ability was obvious and his insight undeniable, those who knew his method began to regard his profession of ignorance as either ironic or sophistical, and opinion was divided as to whether he was a beneficial genius or a dangerous nuisance.

Before he was forty Socrates had established himself as a remarkable teacher and philosopher; he was known and respected by many of the leading philosophers, politicians, and sophists of his time, including Protagoras, with whom Socrates had one of his most famous debates. Others who at various times came to be companions of Socrates during his conversational tours of Athens were Crito, Charmides (Plato's uncle), Critias (Plato's mother's cousin), Plato, Xenophon, Alcibiades, Adimantus and Glaucon (Plato's brothers), Callias (son of the wealthiest Athenian of the time), and Nicias (an outstanding Athenian democrat).

Socrates' role as "gadfly" (his own term) to the Athenian people irritated the democratic leaders more and more, particularly because he was closely associated with Alcibiades, who in 415

B.C. led the Sicilian expedition that ended in defeat for Athens, and with Critias, leader of the Thirty Tyrants imposed on the city by the Spartans after the defeat of the Athenians ended the Peloponnesian War in 404 B.C. That defeat was blamed in part on the new ideas with which, so it was charged, Socrates had corrupted the youth of the city. In 399 B.C., after the democracy was restored, and despite the commendable military record he had made during the war, Socrates was brought to trial on the charges of impiety and corrupting the young. In an eloquent and dignified defense he argued that he had been fulfilling a mission to goad the Athenians into searching for truth, that he was no man's master, and that he would accept acquittal only if it could be had without a sacrifice of his principles. When he was found guilty and was asked to propose a punishment, he claimed that he deserved to be rewarded for his services to Athens, but that he would agree to pay a fine. Condemned to death, he died after drinking hemlock, having refused the opportunity to escape and go into exile.

Plato's dialogues about Socrates' trial and death, the *Apology*, the *Crito*, and the *Phaedo*, together constitute one of the most moving portraits of all dramatic literature and are probably fairly reliable historically.

Socrates is famous for his questioning method, for his belief that if one knows the good he will seek it, for his theory of knowledge as the recollection of ideas, for his conception of the soul and his attempted proofs of the soul's immortality, and for the theory of Ideas which Plato adopted and expanded. He is also remembered as

1003

much for his courage and his clear idealism as for his philosophy, and he remains one of the greatest figures in Western history.

BIBLIOGRAPHICAL REFERENCES: The primary sources of our knowledge of the life and teachings are the *Dialogues* of Plato and the *Memorabilia* of Xenophon. See in particular the *Euthyphro, Apology, Crito,* and *Phaedo,* translated by John Burnet, 1924. A. E. Taylor is the author of two books on Socrates: *Varia Socratia,* 1911, and *Socrates,* 1951. See also G. C. Field, *Plato and His Contemporaries,* 1930; Constantin Ritter, *Sokrates,* 1931; R. W. Livingston, *Portrait of Socrates,* 1940; Arthur Hübscher, *Sokrates,* 1950; and Cora Mason, *Socrates, the Man Who Dared to Ask,* 1953.

SOPHOCLES

Born: Colonus, near Athens, Greece
Date: c. 496 B.C.

Died: Athens
Date: 406–405 B.C.

EXTANT PLAYS

Antigone, 441; *Ajax* (?); *Women of Trachis* (?); *Oedipus Tyrannus,* c. 429; *Electra,* c. 411; *Philoctetes,* 409; *Oedipus at Colonus,* 401.

Few facts of Sophocles' biography are known. He was born about 496 B.C. at Colonus in Attica, near Athens, and his father's name was Sophillus, said by tradition to have been a carpenter, a blacksmith, or a sword-cutler. Perhaps he owned slaves skilled in these trades. At least Sophocles moved in the best society and was not lampooned by the comic writers for low birth, as was his rival Euripides. He married legitimately a woman named Nicostrate, who bore him a son Iophon. His second wife, a woman of Sicyon, was, according to Athenian law, not legally a wife. She bore him illegitimate children, including a son Ariston, whose son, Sophocles, was legitimized, wrote tragedies, and staged his grandfather's *Oedipus at Colonus* immediately after the latter's death. In his old age the poet kept a mistress, Archippe, whom he named his heiress, but she was cheated of her legacy.

It is reported that as a boy he was handsome and well educated in the conventional music and gymnastics,

that he was chosen to lead the chorus that celebrated the victory of Salamis in 480 B.C. He studied music under Lampros, an outstanding professional musician (the term is broader than today), and he learned the art of writing tragedy from Aeschylus, with whom he was eventually to compete and sometimes defeat. His first production was offered in 468 B.C. but the names of the tragedies then presented are not certainly known. It is generally agreed that the *Antigone* was the first of his surviving plays to be produced. This is dated by the fact that its popularity is credited with getting him elected to the board of ten generals (another of whom was Pericles), whose term of office occurred during the Samian war of 441–439 B.C.

Sophocles was already a public figure. He had been elected to the board of Hellenotamiai, the treasurers of the Athenian League, in 443. This was the year in which the tribute list was revised, and therefore the office was exceptionally responsible. He held the generalship again some years later. Of his qualities as a general we know only that Pericles once said to him, "You may know how to write poetry, but you certainly don't know how to command an army."

An uncertain tradition connects Sophocles with the introduction of the worship of Asclepius, the god of healing, at Athens, makes him a priest of a mysterious healer god Alon (or Alkon), and has the Athenians decree him heroic honors under the name Dexion (Receiver) after his death. This tradition may reflect his interest in Ionian medicine. He certainly knew the historian Herodotus, and from the language of his plays, as well as from other sources, we are fairly certain that he was aware of the growing interest in the technical aspects of language, from which the sciences of grammar, rhetoric, and logic took their start.

Sophocles' personality impressed his contemporaries with its gentleness and even temper. He lived, of course, through the great Periclean Age of Athens—until 406 or 405—and came to symbolize to a later generation the largeness, serenity, and idealism of that time. His dramas reflect these qualities in the idealized aspect of their heroes, the ease and skill of their dramatic construction, and the calm beauty of many of their choral odes. They have, however, something more than these qualities. The hero of a Sophoclean tragedy is at bottom intransigent. He is destroyed by circumstances, only partly, if at all, of his own making, which would crush into nothingness a lesser man. Yet, though destroyed he is not crushed. For us, as spectators, he retains in his ruin the integrity of his nature. Sophocles' dramatic skill consists in his ability to reveal this quality through

speeches of the characters and songs by the chorus. His heroes are intelligent. Though they do not foresee their approaching doom, they recognize it when it is at hand for what it is. The action of most of the tragedies consists in showing by dialogue or monologue the steps by which this awareness is achieved. Sophocles uses the chorus well to heighten this effect. The chorus sympathizes with the hero, but feels terror at his suffering. They would be crushed by it. They often give expression to pessimism about life as a result of being close observers of the tragic fate of the hero. This pessimism is often wrongly attributed to Sophocles himself.

Not all of the extant tragedies—seven out of some one hundred twenty he wrote—exactly fit this pattern. Sophocles had a variety of things to say, but he is most Sophoclean in the plays that do fit it to a greater or less degree. Antigone, the daughter of Oedipus, is the starkest tragic figure in her self-isolation in the cause of her brother's burial. *Oedipus Tyrannus* shows the hero weaving for himself an involuntary net of dire circumstance to discover his own undoing. Even in his last play, *Oedipus at Colonus*, Sophocles shows us the same hero, still maintaining his integrity and ending in the awe-filled isolation of a mysterious death. *Ajax* is a variation on the theme. The hero has in madness disgraced himself. Suicide and its consequences in regard to his burial raise the problem of the place of the hero in a world of politicians and small minded men. Herakles in the *Women of Trachis* literally goes through fire to purge away his human weakness. Only the *Philoctetes* mutes the theme. Though the hero suffers and stands firm, a happy ending is brought about by the intervention of a god. *Electra,* dealing with the old theme of the punishment of the murderers of Agamemnon, is more a melodrama than a tragedy. Orestes and Electra do the bloody deed and rejoice at the end. They, too, preserve their integrity, but at the cost for the spectators of appearing devoid of human feeling. This statement could not be made of any other Sophoclean heroes that we know.

Sophocles is said by Aristotle, in the *Poetics,* to have introduced a third actor. This device made possible more varied scenes, with three viewpoints possible at one time. He also is said to have invented scene-painting.

Sophocles lacks Aeschylus' brooding and dark grandeur, his cosmic back-ground to man's fate, the grim, majestic gods who tread his stage. Perhaps for this reason Sophocles gave up the practice of presenting three plays on a single subject. For him the gods who appear on the stage are dramatic devices. The real motive forces are less tangible; they are gods ultimately, but working through an oracular screen and in man's inner character. Sophocles' language, therefore, is tenser and more ironic than Aeschylus', his poetry is more metaphor and allusion and less verbal ornament. Finally, he was probably more rationally intelligent than Aeschylus, less direct in feeling. He once said to Aeschylus, "Even if you do the right thing, you don't know why." Sophocles certainly knew why.

BIBLIOGRAPHICAL REFERENCES: The standard edition in English is R. C. Jebb, *Sophocles, The Plays and Fragments,* containing critical commentary and full notes, 7 vols., 1885–1896. For translations see also F. Storr, *Sophocles, with an English Translation,* in the Loeb Classical Library, 2 vols., 1919; and Whitney J. Oates and Eugene O'Neill, Jr., *The Complete Greek Drama,* 2 vols., 1938. For general studies and criticism see also A. E. Haigh, *The Tragic Drama of the Greeks,* 1896; J. T. Sheppard, *Aeschylus and Sophocles,* 1927; Gilbert Norwood, *Greek Tragedy,* 1928; Edith Hamilton, *The Greek Way,* 1930; R. C. Flickinger, *The Greek Theater and Its Drama,* 1936 (3rd edition); W. N. Bates, *Sophocles: Poet and Dramatist,* 1940; P. W. Harsh, *A Handbook of Classical Drama,* 1944; C. M. Bowra, *Sophoclean Tragedy,* 1945; and Moses Hadas, *A History of Greek Literature,* 1950.

ROBERT SOUTHEY

Born: Bristol, England
Date: August 12, 1774

Died: Greta Hall, Keswick, England
Date: March 21, 1843

PRINCIPAL WORKS

POEMS: *Ballads,* 1796–1798; *Joan of Arc,* 1796; *Thalaba the Destroyer,* 1801; *Madoc,* 1805; *The Curse of Kehama,* 1810; *Roderick, the Last of the Goths,* 1814; *The Vision of Judgment,* 1821.

BIOGRAPHY: *Life of Nelson,* 1813; *Life of Wesley,* 1820; *Sir Thomas More,* 1829.

HISTORY: *History of Brazil,* 1810; *History of the Expedition of Orsua and Crimes of Aguirre,* 1821; *History of the Peninsular War,* 1823.

TRANSLATIONS: *Amadis de Gaul,* 1805; *Palmerin of England,* 1807; *Chronicle of the Cid,* 1808.

One of the hardiest of English poet laureates, Robert Southey held that post for the last thirty years of his life, from 1813 to 1843. During that time he also held a firm grip on the attention of the English reading public, though the twentieth century has removed him from the pedestal that it still allows Wordsworth and Coleridge. Nevertheless, he was a man of many parts and much energy, and even today it is impossible to dismiss him as a factor in the literary scene of the Romantic era.

Son of a Bristol linen draper, Southey was born in Bristol on August 12, 1774. At the age of three he was surrendered to the care of a maternal aunt, Elizabeth Tyler, of Bath, a lady distinguished by both her personal attractiveness and imperious temper. The latter found employment against her nephew's school, Westminster, when young Robert was expelled for an article about flogging, which he had written for the school paper. Another sympathetic relative, the Reverend Herbert Hill, sent him on to Oxford where, after Christ Church rejected him because of the Westminster incident, he was accepted at Balliol in November, 1792.

At Oxford, according to Southey's own confession, his chief interests turned out to be boating and swimming. He did, however, briefly espouse the cause of the French Revolution; at Oxford, too, he first met Coleridge, who promptly converted him to Unitarianism and Pantisocracy. The two youths jointly sponsored an idealistic scheme to establish a perfect community on the banks of the Susquehanna in Pennsylvania. The venture died stillborn, for lack of funds, but not before Southey and Coleridge had equipped themselves with helpmates in the persons of the Fricker sisters. Another even more dubious byproduct of their scheme was Southey's sudden loss of his aunt's patronage; that strong-minded person, accidentally hearing of the Utopian project, promptly dismissed him from her house and her affections.

After various temporary employments, Southey settled at Keswick in 1803, where his family shared a double house with the Coleridges. Here he devoted himself completely to literature, forming a connection with the *Quarterly Review* and turning out a steady stream of books, poems, and articles. Of these, comparatively few are read today. Modern taste does not respond to the ambitious epic poems which were Southey's chief stock in trade, though *Thalaba the Destroyer, Madoc,* and *The Curse of Kehama* achieved considerable contemporary success. A few shorter poems, such as "The Battle of Blenheim" and "The Inchcape Rock," have survived the blight which has overtaken most of Southey's poetry; but modern criticism prefers the author's prose to his verse, especially as regards such outstanding biographies as his *Life of Nelson* and a *Life of Wesley*.

Though the laureateship, in 1813, brought added recognition to Southey, its effect was offset by a series of family tragedies. The deaths of his much-loved son and a daughter were followed by an additional blow, the loss of his wife's sanity. Mrs. Southey died in 1837, and two years later Southey was married again, to Caroline Bowles; but his health had already broken under the strain. Four years after his second marriage, he succumbed to an attack of brain fever, dying at Keswick on March 21, 1843. Wordsworth attended his funeral, and memorials were placed in Westminster Abbey and Bristol Cathedral.

BIBLIOGRAPHICAL REFERENCES: Southey's letters provide valuable source material. Of the various editions, the first and most complete is *The Life and Correspondence of the Late Robert Southey*, edited by his son, Charles Cuthbert Southey, 6 vols., 1849–1850. See also John Dennis, *Robert Southey: The Story of His Life Written in His Letters*, 1894. The best brief biography is Edward Dowden's *Southey*, in the English Men of Letters Series, 1879. See also W. Haller, *The Early Life of Robert Southey, 1774–1803*, 1917; and Jack Simmons, *Robert Southey*, 1945.

STEPHEN SPENDER

Born: London, England
Date: February 28, 1909

PRINCIPAL WORKS

POEMS: *Nine Entertainments*, 1928; *Twenty Poems*, 1930; *Poems*, 1933; *Poems*, 1934; *Vienna*, 1935; *The Still Centre*, 1939; *Ruins and Visions*, 1942; *Poems of Dedication*, 1947; *Returning to Vienna*, 1947; *The Edge of Being*, 1949; *Collected Poems, 1928–1953*, 1955.

CRITICISM: *The Destructive Element*, 1936; *The Creative Element*, 1954.

PLAYS: *Trial of a Judge*, 1938.

ESSAYS: *Forward from Liberalism*, 1937; *Life and the Poet*, 1942, *Citizens in War and After*, 1945; *Shelley*, 1952; *The Making of a Poem*, 1955.

TRAVEL SKETCHES AND IMPRESSIONS: *European Witness*, 1946; *Learning Laughter*, 1953.

AUTOBIOGRAPHY: *World Within World*, 1951.

SHORT STORIES: *The Burning Cactus*, 1936.

NOVEL: *The Backward Son*, 1940.

Stephen (Harold) Spender was born on February 28, 1909, in London, the son of an English father, journalist Edwin Harold Spender, and a German-Jewish mother, Violet Schuster Spender. After attending University College School and University College, Oxford, which he left in 1931 without taking his degree, he became associated in London with the vocal and promising group of young poets which included Christopher Isherwood, W. H. Auden, Louis MacNeice, and C. Day Lewis. As early as 1928 he had published a book of verse called *Nine Entertainments*, which was followed by *Twenty Poems* two years later. It was not until 1933, however, with the publication of *Poems*, that he began to receive widespread recognition. Critics applauded the lyrical, Shelleyan quality of his poetry which was infused, however, with the Marxist views of the decade. Although he was always an individualist and never a doctrinaire Communist, much of his poetry was based upon a criticism of capitalism and espousal of the cause of the proletariat and revolutionary movements. *Vienna* showed his awareness of the events which were producing the ominous political tensions of Europe, and in 1937, while he was attending the leftist International Writers' Congress in Spain, he found himself in the midst of the Spanish Civil War. A drama, *Trial of a Judge*, was not as successful as his lyric writing had been.

In 1939, the year he published *The Still Centre*, Spender became co-founder with Cyril Connolly of the influential literary magazine, *Horizon*, only to break with Connolly over political policy in 1941. From 1941 through 1944 he served as a member of the London Auxiliary Fire Service, still managing to continue his work, however, and to publish *Ruins and Visions* in 1942. Like many other disillusioned artists and intellectuals, but considerably later than some, he broke with communism after the war, recording his struggle in *The God That Failed*. In postwar years his reputation as a poet has declined somewhat (unlike that of his friend and colleague Auden) while his stature as a critic and prose writer has grown. In 1936 he had published *The Burning Cactus*, a book of short stories, and in 1940 the novel, *A Backward Son*. *World Within World* was a sensitive, reflective, and at times lyrical autobiography which further showed his versatility as a mature man of letters. *Collected Poems, 1928–1953*, which was published in 1955, emphasized the fact that though he might not be a twentieth century Shelley, he is an influential and a major modern poet. In addition to editing three anthologies of English poetry, he has translated two volumes of the work of Rainer Maria Rilke and one of the poetry of Federico García Lorca. Since 1953 co-editor of *Encounter*, he continues as a prolific poet-critic-editor whose career has in many ways been typical of that of the literary artist of his generation.

BIBLIOGRAPHICAL REFERENCES: For biographical detail the most reliable work is the poet's autobiography, *World Within World*, 1951. Most of the books dealing with English literature of the 1930's contain material on Spender; see in particular Francis Scarfe, "Stephen Spender: A Sensitive," in *Auden and After*, 1942. See also James G. Southworth, "Stephen Spender," *Sewanee Review*, XLV (1937), 272–284; C. I. Glicksberg, "Poetry and the Social Revolution," *Dalhousie Review*, XVII (1938), 493–503; and Willis D. Jacobs, "The Moderate Poetical Success of Stephen Spender," *College English*, XVII (1956), 374–378.

EDMUND SPENSER

Born: London, England
Date: c. 1552

Died: Westminster, London
Date: January 13, 1599

PRINCIPAL WORKS

POEMS: *The Shepheardes Calender*, 1579; *The Faerie Queene*, 1590–1596; *Daphnaïda*, 1591; *Complaints*, 1591; *Colin Clout's Come Home Again*, 1595; *Astrophel*, 1595; *Amoretti*, 1595; *Epithalamion*, 1595; *Fowre Hymns*, 1596; *Prothalamion*, 1596.

POLITICAL TRACT: *View of the Present State of Ireland*, 1633 (written in 1596).

Edmund Spenser was one of three children born, probably in 1552, to John and Elizabeth Spenser. He tells us in *Prothalamion* that London was his birthplace. With his brother he attended the Merchant Taylors' School under the famous educator Richard Mulcaster, whose progressive theories

1009

included even education for women, though he was unable to put this practice into effect. Under Mulcaster the principal studies were Hebrew, Greek, Latin, French, English, and music; the students also had experience in acting, which the master thought of considerable educational value.

When Spenser was still in his teens, his first published poetry appeared in *A Theatre wherein be represented . . . the miseries & calamities that follow voluptuous Worldlings* (1569). In the same year he entered Pembroke College, Cambridge. At college he was apparently a wide reader rather than a profound scholar. Among his favorite classical authors were Plato, Aristotle, and Vergil; among his later favorites, Chaucer and Ariosto. At Cambridge began his lasting friendship with Gabriel Harvey, the pedantic target of much Elizabethan wit and barbed satire. Also at Cambridge he imbibed Puritan leanings. As both Mulcaster and Harvey were stanch advocates of English composition rather than Latin specialization, Spenser was a worthy protégé of both men. He received his M.A. degree from Cambridge in 1576, and left to visit some of his family in Lancashire.

His first trip to Ireland, the scene of much of his mature life, was probably made in 1577. In 1578 he was in London as secretary of Dr. John Young, Bishop of Rochester. In 1579 the first major event of his literary career took place, the publication of *The Shepheardes Calender*. Looking back over the great peaks of *Paradise Lost* and the Elizabethan drama, the modern reader can hardly realize the impact the *Calender* must have had on the poetic circle of its day. A good preparation for a modern

reader would be a retirement of several weeks spent with the poetry written and published between 1500 and 1579; after this Spenser would be a revelation. The *Calender,* published anonymously, was dedicated to Sir Philip Sidney, and was furnished with notes by a mysterious E. K.—supposedly a close friend of the author—with great inside knowledge, but with very convenient ignorance about any matter which might have political repercussions. In general it has been assumed that E. K. was Spenser's friend Edward Kirke, but that most of the notes were furnished or inspired by Spenser himself. Obviously the pastoral names of the characters sometimes cloak actual individuals, but some may have been entirely fictitious. For example, much throwing about of brains has gone into the identification of Rosalind, Colin Clout's beloved. Was she an early sweetheart? Was she an aristocratic patroness treated with the conventional love-fiction that Queen Elizabeth received from her courtiers? Or was she a fictional mistress? There are several answers, but no certain one. Colin Clout remained Spenser's poetic nom de plume in the autobiographical *Colin Clout's Come Home Again* and in the sixth book of *The Faerie Queene.*

As the dedication of the *Calender* indicates, by 1579 Spenser was acquainted with Sir Philip Sidney; and he also knew Sidney's uncle, the Earl of Leicester, who had a distinguished career as a patron (see Eleanor Rosenburg, *Leicester, Patron of Letters,* 1955). For some reason the Earl did not take the interest in Spenser that the latter hoped for—or, indeed, that his ability justified. It is ironical that today Leicester is more remembered for his half-hearted patronage of Spenser than for his whole-hearted patronage of many others.

In 1580 Spenser went to Ireland as a secretary of Lord Grey de Wilton, the Lord Deputy of Ireland, whose policies he defended in verse and prose for many years to come. For about eight years he lived in or near Dublin. During this period the friendship between Spenser and Lodowick Bryskett developed. Bryskett's *Discourse of Civil Life* (1606) contains an account of a courtly conversation with Spenser in a literary company. Bryskett also contributed poems to Spenser's *Astrophel*, the memorial volume on the death of Sir Philip Sidney. He was Clerk of the Council of Munster, in which province Spenser lived from 1588 to 1598, serving for part of that time as Bryskett's deputy.

In 1589 Sir Walter Raleigh visited Spenser in Munster. The visit was recorded in *Colin Clout's Come Home Again,* the dedicatory letter of which is dated 1591. Spenser returned Raleigh's visit and brought with him to London three books of *The Faerie Queene,* on which he had been working for about a decade. To his great disappointment the visit did not lead to an eminent position in the Court; but he did gain a pension of fifty pounds, by no means a contemptible amount—if, as J. B. Fletcher stated, the poet ever collected it. The first three books of *The Faerie Queene* were published in 1590. The next six years were productive ones, climaxed by the publication in 1596 of the first six books of the masterpiece, bringing it to the halfway point. Only a scant surviving fragment takes the poem any further toward completion. These productive years of writing and publishing were filled with turmoil and disappointment. For ten years Spenser was harassed by lawsuits instigated by Lord Roche of Fermoy, who earned thereby an unenviable immortality.

The final decade of Spenser's life was not, however, a period of unmitigated gloom: in 1594 he married Elizabeth Boyle and celebrated his love and marriage by publishing his sonnets, *Amoretti,* and his magnificent marriage hymn, *Epithalamion.* Some skeptics believe the sonnets were originally written to another girl; but the general view is that the sequence is unique in the Tudor period in being written and addressed to the poet's wife. The couple had three children (a fourth one believed in formerly has now been attributed to gossip alone).

In 1598, in Tyrone's rebellion, Spenser's Irish home, Kilcolman Castle, was sacked. He and his family escaped first to Cork and then to England; but within a month after his return to his native land he died. He was buried near Chaucer's tomb in what is now known as Poets' Corner in Westminster Abbey.

Probably no poet of comparable merit and former reputation in English literature suffers a comparable neglect today. Perhaps in the future, readers will regain the taste for allegory and the skills for deciphering it with pleasure. If so, they will find that Spenser is far more than a mere painter with words and that he is thoroughly relevant to modern times.

BIBLIOGRAPHICAL REFERENCES: The foundation of all modern Spenser studies is *The Works of Edmund Spenser,* 10 vols., 1932–1945, a variorum edition edited by Edwin Greenlaw, Charles G. Osgood, Frederick M. Padelford, and Roy Heffner. See also J. C. Smith and E. de Sélincourt, *The Poetical Works of Edmund Spenser,* 1912.

Other biographical and critical studies include C. H. Whitman, *A Subject-Index to the Poems of Edmund Spenser*, 1918; W. L. Renwick, *Edmund Spenser*, 1925; H. S. V. Jones, *A Spenser Handbook*, 1930; B. E. C. Davis, *Edmund Spenser*, 1933; Janet Spens, *Spenser's Faerie Queene*, 1934; C. S. Lewis, *The Allegory of Love*, 1938; A. C. Judson, *The Life of Edmund Spenser*, 1945; L. Bradner, *Spenser and the Faerie Queene*, 1948; and Jefferson B. Fletcher, "Edmund Spenser," *Encyclopedia Americana*, Vol. XXV (1955).

BENEDICTUS DE SPINOZA

Born: Amsterdam, Netherlands   *Died:* The Hague, Netherlands
Date: November 24, 1632   *Date:* February 20, 1677

Principal Works

PHILOSOPHICAL TREATISES: *Renati des Cartes principia philosophiae*, 1663 (*Principles of Descartes' Philosophy*), with *Cogitata metaphysica* (*Metaphysical Thoughts*); *Tractatus theologico-politicus*, 1670 (*Theological-Political Treatise*); *Opera posthuma*, 1677 (*Posthumous Works*): *Ethica ordine geometrico demonstrata* (*Ethics*), *Tractatus politicus* (*Politics*), *De intellectus emendatione* (*On the Improvement of the Understanding*), *Epistolae doctorum quorundam virorum ad B.D.S. et auctoris responsiones* (*Letters and Replies*), *Compendium grammatices linguae Hebraeae* (*Hebrew Grammar*); *Tractatus de Deo et homine eiusque felicitate*, 1862 (*A Short Treatise on God, Man, and His Well-being*).

Benedictus de Spinoza, the great Dutch philosopher who tried to demonstrate the existence and nature of God in a geometrically precise fashion, was christened Baruch, the son of Michael and Hannah Deborah de Spinoza, descendants of Jews who, having been forced into the Catholic faith and having practiced their Jewish religion in secret, fled from Spain and Portugal during the Inquisition. Michael Spinoza was a merchant, only moderately prosperous, and Baruch, born in Amsterdam on November 24, 1632, was the third child of his second wife. Baruch's mother died when he was six years old, and Baruch was probably left in the care of Rebecca, the remaining child of Michael Spinoza's first marriage.

He attended a local Hebrew school where his education began with the Hebrew alphabet and proceeded through the Old Testament and the Talmud. When he was eight years old his father married for the third time, and the family soon moved to better quarters as the father's business improved. The boy's studies continued; his work was so promising that he went on to advanced studies at a Hebrew academy, Etz Hayim, and remained there from 1645 to 1652.

Sometime in the course of his studies Spinoza began to doubt the truth of what he was being taught. Although he followed the Hebrew tradition, at the same time he began to study philosophy and gradually to convince himself that he was not interested in being a rabbi. His questioning attitude became apparent to his fellow students, and in 1656, two years after his father's death, he was excommunicated by the Jews. Feeling against him was intense; at one time before the excommunication someone had tried to assassinate him. Spinoza, believing himself to be right in his doubts, quietly settled in Amsterdam and took up the trade of grinding lenses. The work was arduous and painstaking, and the dust irritated his lungs, but he was able to devote his nights to study, particularly to the reading of Descartes. Fascinated with Descartes' method of building up proofs from ideas that could not be doubted, he began to consider constructing an account of reality that would have geometrical exactness.

He changed his name from Baruch to Benedictus, the Latin form of Baruch, which means "blessed," and thereby completed his liberation from the traditions of his fathers. He studied Latin with the Dutch scholar Van den Enden, and there were rumors that he was attracted to his tutor's daughter. If he was, nothing came of it; and Spinoza finally left Amsterdam and moved to the village of Rijnsburg. While he was there he wrote his first philosophical work, *Principles of Descartes' Philosophy*, an attempt to put into geometric form the philosophy of Descartes. At the same time he was working on other projects, the most important being his *Ethics;* and he was spending a considerable amount of time corresponding and helping visiting students who came to him from Amsterdam. He moved to The Hague, and in 1670 his second book appeared, the *Theological-Political Treatise.* It caused a furor, for the philosopher's conception of God and reality was quite different from the orthodox Christian and Jewish views. The Dutch Synod prohibited the work; the Catholics put it on the Index, and its anonymous author was condemned as the devil. When Spinoza became known as the author, the criticism abated to some extent because of his quiet manner and scholarly reputation, but it never wholly died down during his lifetime.

Offered the chair of philosophy at Heidelberg, he refused the post in order to be free both in his opinion and in his time to write. He continued to grind lenses during the day and to write philosophy at night. Pleasant in his personal relationships, he had many good friends. His death came at The Hague on February 20, 1677 from tuberculosis, probably as the result of having breathed glass dust over the years. As he had planned it, his principal works were published after his death; and the quality of them is such that Spinoza has become one of the most famous and respected of philosophers.

BIBLIOGRAPHICAL REFERENCES: The Spinoza *Opera* appeared in 4 vols. in 1926. Abraham Wolf edited the *Correspondence* in 1928. For biographical and analytical studies see H. H. Joachim, *A Study of the Ethics of Spinoza*, 1901; Abraham Wolf's commentary on *A Short Treatise on God, Man, and Well-being*, 1910; J. A. Gunn, *Benedict Spinoza*, 1925, with a bibliography; R. P. Mackeon, *The Philosophy of Spinoza*, 1928; Leon Roth, *Spinoza*, 1929; H. F. Hallett, *Aeternitas: A Spinozistic Study*, 1930; Lewis Browne, *Blesséd Spinoza*, 1932; H. A. Wolfson, *The Philosophy of Spinoza*, 2 vols., 1934; David Bidney, *The Psychology and Ethics of Spinoza*, 1940; Stuart Hampshire, *Spinoza*, 1951; Ruth L. Saw, *The Vindication of Metaphysics: A Study in the Philosophy of Spinoza*, 1951; Paul Siwek, *Au cœur du spinozisme*, 1952; and G. H. R. Parkinson, *Spinoza's Theory of Knowledge*, 1954.

MADAME DE STAËL

Born: Paris, France
Date: April 22, 1766

Died: Paris
Date: July 14, 1817

PRINCIPAL WORKS

NOVELS: *Delphine*, 1802; *Corinne*, 1807.

ESSAYS: *Lettres sur le caractère et les écrits de J. J. Rousseau*, 1788; *De l'Influence des passions*, 1796 (*The Influence of the Passions*); *De la littérature considerée dans ses rapports avec les institutions sociales*, 1800 (*The Influence of Literature on Society*); *De l'Allemagne*, 1810 (*Germany*); *Considérations sur la révolution française*, 1818 (*Considerations on the Principal Events of the French Revolution*).

A leader of the movement to destroy the classical influence on French literature and thought, Anne Louise Germaine de Staël, nee Necker, brought Romantic thought to the forefront of French consciousness. A friend of writers, scientists, and statesmen since childhood, she grew up in an atmosphere of intellectical freedom. Her salon provided a meeting place for literary and political radicals and her literary work introduced the current of German Romanticism into French culture.

Born in Paris on April 22, 1766, the daughter of Jacques Necker, finance minister of Louis XVI, she married the Swedish ambassador to Paris, the Baron de Staël-Holstein, largely because he would be too ineffectual to disturb her love affairs; she divorced him in 1797. To escape the Reign of Terror, she fled to Coppet, Switzerland, where she bore the Comte de Narbonne's son.

She visited England and returned to Paris, where she began her famous love affair with Benjamin Constant. Napoleon exiled her for her political activities in 1803, and she set up her salon at Coppet. During her long exile she traveled widely and wrote her most important book, *Germany*, which became a source book for French Romanticism. In 1811 she married Albert de la Rocca, who survived her by one year.

Apart from her books on literature and society, Madame de Staël wrote two romantic novels, *Delphine* and *Corinne*, and introduced the popular figure of the misunderstood heroine into French literature. A believer in the inevitability of progress, she set the themes for much of the literature of nineteenth century France and England. She died in Paris on July 14, 1817.

BIBLIOGRAPHICAL REFERENCES: The most comprehensive biographical studies are Lady Blennerhasset, *Madame de Staël et son temps*, 1887–1889; and D. G. Larg, *Madame de Staël*, 2 vols., 1926–1928. A more recent study is Olga Taxis-Bordogna, *Madame de Staël*, 1949. See also Paul Gautier, *Madame de Staël et Napoleon*, 1903; also Pierre Kohler, *Madame de Staël et la Suisse*, 1918, and *Au château de Coppet*, 1952.

PUBLIUS PAPINIUS STATIUS

Born: Naples, Italy
Date: c. 45

Died: Naples
Date: c. 96

PRINCIPAL WORKS

POEMS: *Thebais; Achilleid; Silvae.*

Publius Papinius Statius, born in Naples about 45, was a poet of the court of the Emperor Domitian (81–96) and wrote adulatory poetry for that emperor who had no taste for verse. Statius' father had been a poet and the son began early and competed frequently, and usually successfully, in poetic contests in Naples. One clue to his success may be his public acknowledgment that the public never saw his verse until it had been approved by the Divine Emperor.

Victor at Domitian's festival at Alba, where he was awarded the coveted gold wreath from Domitian's hands, he entered the quinquennial Capitoline competition in 94, but failed to win the oakleaf crown. Discouraged, he returned to Naples and died in that city about A.D. 96.

It took Statius twelve years to complete the twelve books of his Vergilian poem, the *Thebais.* Only fragments remain of his epic about the early life of Achilles. In his own time, and through the Middle Ages, Statius was overesteemed as an epic poet. His *Silvae* are pleasant occasional verses about his friends, the emperor, and his wife Claudia. He also wrote a birthday ode to Lucan, valuable because of its comments on earlier writers.

BIBLIOGRAPHICAL REFERENCES: See *Works of Statius,* translated by D. A. Slater, in Oxford Library of Translations, 1908; and J. H. Mozley, *Statius with English Translations,* 2 vols., 1928.

SIR RICHARD STEELE

Born: Dublin, Ireland
Date: March, 1672

Died: Near Carmarthen, Wales
Date: September 1, 1729

PRINCIPAL WORKS

PLAYS: *The Funeral, or Grief-à-la-Mode,* 1701; *The Lying Lover,* 1703; *The Tender Husband,* 1705; *The Conscious Lovers,* 1722.

ESSAYS: *The Tatler,* 1709–1710, and *The Spectator,* 1711–1712 (with Addison); *The Plebeian,* 1718; *The Theatre,* 1720.

ETHICAL TREATISES: *The Christian Hero,* 1701.

Sir Richard Steele was born in Dublin in March, 1672, the son of an attorney. Both his parents died when he was a child, and he became the ward of a prominent uncle, Henry Gascoigne. Through his uncle's influence he entered the Charterhouse School in 1684, where he met and became the lifelong friend of Joseph Addison. In 1689 he followed Addison to Oxford University, but while Addison remained to take his M.A. and to become a fellow, Steele left without a degree in 1694 to enlist as private in a regiment of guards under the command of his uncle's employer, the Duke of Ormond. On the strength of a poem which he published anonymously, he became in the following year an ensign in Lord Cutts' regiment.

1015

By 1700 he was Captain Steele, stationed at the Tower, and the friend of Sir Charles Sedley, Vanbrugh, Congreve, and other wits and writers of the day. In that same year Dryden died, and Congreve published his last important play, these two latter events marking the sunset of Restoration comedy.

His life as a soldier stationed at the Tower led Steele into excesses of which he repented, and which caused him to publish in 1701 a little book, *The Christian Hero,* to prove "that no principles but those of religion are sufficient to make a great man." The sentiments expressed in this little volume lost him his popularity among his fellow soldiers, and to regain that popularity he wrote his first comedy, *The Funeral, or Grief à-la-Mode,* for "Nothing can make the town so fond of a man as a successful play."

This play, which met with "more than expected success," illustrates the tendency of the age to react against libertine elegance and to return to bourgeois respectability. In it Steele attacks the mockery of grief in the person of Sable the undertaker; the mockery of justice in Puzzle the lawyer; and the popular dramatic disregard for women in the persons of Lady Sharlot and Lady Hariot. This stanch stand for morality is readily seen as unusual when compared with that in the plays of Etherege, Congreve, and even Vanbrugh. The "more than expected success" of this play led Steele to write *The Lying Lover* in 1703; this work was, however, "dam'd for its piety," as Steele himself said. Steele tried again in 1705 with *The Tender Husband* which had somewhat more success than its predecessor, but even so,

Steele wrote no more plays for seventeen years.

He entered, instead, into politics (quite actively from 1707 to 1710), and he began to write periodical essays, most significantly in collaboration with his old friend Addison. These two men, with some little help from other writers now forgotten except by scholars, published first *The Tatler,* which appeared three times weekly from 1709–1710, and later *The Spectator,* which appeared daily from 1711–1712. Of both papers Steele was the fathering genius.

In both these forerunners of the modern newspaper, Steele, writing on subjects ranging from descriptions of London and of life in the country to articles on dueling and the question of immortality, preached the gospel of reformed gentility and true gentle manliness to oppose the artificial elegance symbolized by Etherege's Dorimant; and he preached in a style supple and precise, warm and penetrating, a style later used by Benjamin Franklin as a model when he was teaching himself to write. In the dedication to the first collected volume of *The Tatler* (1710), Steele wrote, "The general purpose of this paper, is to expose the false arts of life, to pull off the disguises of cunning, vanity, and affectation, and to recommend a general simplicity in our dress, our discourse, and our behavior."

It is indicative of the trend toward "rational conduct" that these papers were imminently successful in an age when journals, like the lilies of the field, bloomed today and were cast tomorrow in the fire. It is moreover indicative of the influence they had—or the trend they reflected—that when Steele's last play, *The Conscious Lovers,* appeared at Drury Lane in

1722, it ran for eighteen nights and was a great success.

In this play, the contrast with the Restoration is complete. The characters are not fine ladies and gentlemen, but frankly middle class. The lovers do not fence verbally through four acts about their affection before they dare to confess it in the fifth; their mutual love is clear throughout the play, though no amorous words pass between them. Young Bevil, the hero, is not even tainted with rakishness, but is thoroughly upright and worthy; and the solution to the plot which occurs in the last act just in time to show virtue rewarded with wealth, and consequent lifelong happiness, appeared then not at all incongruous, but achieved its purpose of moving the audience to compassion.

Though the play has a well-knit structure—even the startling denouement is handled with sureness and restraint—and though the expression is easy and natural, it celebrates the funeral of Restoration comedy and the coming of age of sentimental comedy. True dramatic comedy is dead, for whatever the faults of Restoration comedy, and they were many, it was dramatic, it was brilliant, and it was funny. Reformation was required, not revolution. But *The Conscious Lovers* banished vice and for a time, at least, theatrical immorality was dead. That dramatic comedy was dead as well seemed at the time unimportant. One imagines Steele would have been pleased, not offended, at Hazlitt's apt remark: "It is almost a misnomer to call them comedies; they are rather homilies in dialogues."

In any case, Sir Richard Steele had temporarily achieved the purpose he set forth in *The Tatler*. In that respect, he must have gone peacefully to his death. He died September 1, 1729. He lies buried in St. Peter's Church, Carmarthen, Wales.

BIBLIOGRAPHICAL REFERENCES: The standard edition of *The Tatler* was edited by George A. Aitken, 4 vols., 1898–1899. There are two modern editions of *The Spectator,* that edited by G. Gregory Smith, 8 vols., 1897–1898, reissued in Everyman's Library, 1907; and the edition by George A. Aitken, 8 vols., 1898. Aitken also edited Steele's *Dramatic Works,* 1894 and 1903. Rae Blanchard has edited several volumes of the miscellaneous works: *The Christian Hero,* 1932; the *Correspondence,* 1941; *Tracts and Pamphlets,* 1944; *Occasional Verses,* 1952; and *The Englishman,* 1955.

The fullest biography is G. A. Aitken, *Life of Richard Steele,* 2 vols., 1889, with a bibliography. The most recent life is Willard Connely, *Sir Richard Steele,* 1934. Still useful is Austin Dobson, *Richard Steele,* 1886. See also the Addison bibliography for studies on the development of the periodical and the periodical essay.

JOHN STEINBECK

Born: Salinas, California
Date: February 27, 1902

PRINCIPAL WORKS

NOVELS: *Cup of Gold,* 1929; *To a God Unknown,* 1933; *Tortilla Flat,* 1935; *In Dubious Battle,* 1936; *Of Mice and Men,* 1937; *The Grapes of Wrath,* 1939; *The Moon Is Down,* 1942; *Cannery Row,* 1945; *The Wayward Bus,* 1947; *Burning*

Bright, 1950; *East of Eden*, 1952; *Sweet Thursday*, 1954; *The Short Reign of Pippin IV: A Fabrication*, 1957.

SHORT STORIES: *The Pastures of Heaven*, 1932; *Saint Katy the Virgin*, 1936; *The Red Pony*, 1937; *The Long Valley*, 1938; *The Pearl*, 1947.

MISCELLANEOUS: *The Forgotten Village*, 1941; *Sea of Cortez*, 1941; *Bombs Away*, 1942; *A Russian Journal*, 1948.

John (Ernst) Steinbeck's career as a novelist allows us to view a man who has enjoyed great popularity and, for long periods of time, serious literary acclaim. This double success is in part due to the fact that his books gave expression to the social and economic tensions that were at work during the period of his greatest success. *The Grapes of Wrath*, in particular, appeared at an opportune moment when the fate of the "Okies" in his novel seemed also to reflect the fate of the nation.

Steinbeck once wrote inquirers for biographical data: "Please feel free to make up your own facts about me as you need them. I can't remember how much of me really happened and how much I invented. . . . Biography by its very nature must be half-fiction." Nevertheless, the records show that he was born in Salinas, California, on February 27, 1902. His father was active in local politics, and his mother was a schoolteacher in the Big Sur country. At nineteen Steinbeck went to Stanford University, where intermittent enrollment and part-time jobs for six years did not lead to a degree. From California he went to New York via the Panama Canal by freighter and continued to live by casual jobs as newspaperman, hod carrier on the construction of New York buildings, chemist, and day laborer. In retrospect, this drifting career seems admirably designed to fit him to be the novelist of the submerged classes and to speak for those who were not able to speak for themselves.

Steinbeck's first three books sold fewer than three thousand copies, but after the popular attention given *Tortilla Flat* in 1935 he moved rapidly into the literary spotlight. *In Dubious Battle* is a study of the confused currents of self-interest and generous emotion involved in a strike of California fruit pickers. In it one sees, as one has seen ever since, Steinbeck's generous social sympathies qualified by his personal skepticism about the possibility of reform and social progress. This same sympathy played over two itinerant farm hands in *Of Mice and Men*. In these novels phases of life that more conventionally trained writers would be powerless to handle took on vivid reality.

Steinbeck's full critical acclaim came in 1939 with *The Grapes of Wrath*, awarded the Pulitzer Prize in 1940 and hailed as the twentieth century *Uncle Tom's Cabin*. Social dislocation, the indifference of large-scale economy to private well-being, the havoc wrought by uninformed prejudice—all these important themes find expression in this work. The chief family in the novel, the Joads, became as famous as Sinclair Lewis' Babbitt of twenty years before; both are almost common nouns in our language. Critics were able to point out that the Joads are the "noble savages" of the twentieth century, endowed with much the same dignity and purity of intent that Rousseau

1018

and his followers once imagined existed in the American Indian. Critics also pointed to literary sophistication in the novel: interchapters of general comment have a Whitmanesque note, and the conclusion that some readers found shocking is a carefully contrived passage of symbolism.

No subsequent book of Steinbeck's has made a similar impact on the national consciousness, but in novels like *Cannery Row* Steinbeck has underlined his claims to a class and a region as his proper subject matter. Certain veins of inverse sentimentality are easy to distinguish in both *Cannery Row* and *The Wayward Bus*; it is a self-evident truth that in Steinbeck's world the virtues of generosity and kindness are found only on the lower rungs of the social ladder, among those very persons whom more fortunate persons call "sinners." It is also apparent that Steinbeck resents the increasing

mechanization of our culture and, in romanticizing the dignity of the poor and the outcast, he is defending the proper dignity of all men.

East of Eden is a story which, in a sense, is about Steinbeck's own people, one that comes into a focus in a study of the reaction two brothers give to past scandal in their family; the ne'er-do-well brother survives the shock of discovering his mother's profession, but the brother who has lived for conscious purity and uprightness disintegrates when confronted by the truth. In this novel Steinbeck appears once more as the advocate of unconscious, spontaneous patterns of behavior.

Steinbeck's career, subsequent to his initial success, has been one which mingles travel, journalism, and public utterance on questions of the day. At his best he touches the conscience of his generation and, incidentally, shows us how that conscience works.

BIBLIOGRAPHICAL REFERENCES: There is no authorized biography. Two critical studies important for general reference on the man and his books are Harry T. Moore, *The Novels of John Steinbeck: A First Critical Study,* 1939; and Peter Lisca, *The Wide World of John Steinbeck,* 1957. See also Lewis Gannett, *John Steinbeck, Personal and Bibliographical Notes: A Pamphlet,* 1939. A useful introduction to the work is *The Portable Steinbeck,* edited by Pascal Covici, with an introduction by Lewis Gannett, 1943 (enlarged, 1946).

For briefer studies see Percy H. Boynton, *America in Contemporary Fiction,* 1940; Edmund Wilson, *The Boys in the Back Room,* 1941; Maxwell Geismar, *Writers in Crisis,* 1942; W. M. Frohock, *The Novel of Violence in America,* 1950; John S. Kennedy, "John Steinbeck: Life Affirmed and Dissolved," in *Fifty Years of the American Novel,* edited by Harold C. Gardiner, S.J., 1952; Charles Child Walcutt, *American Literary Naturalism, A Divided Stream,* 1957; Claude E. Jones, "Proletarian Writing and John Steinbeck," *Sewanee Review,* XLVIII (1940), 445–456; Frederic I. Carpenter, "The Philosophical Joads," *College English,* II (1941), 315–325; Lincoln R. Gibbs, "John Steinbeck, Moralist," *Antioch Review,* II (1942), 172–184; Woodburn Ross, "John Steinbeck: Earth and Stars," *Missouri Studies in Honor of A. H. R. Fairchild,* 1946; and Frederick Bracher, "Steinbeck and the Biological View of Man," *Pacific Spectator,* III (1949), 302–310. The most ambitious treatment of Steinbeck criticism to date is *Steinbeck and His Critics: A Record of Twenty-five Years,* a collection of comprehensive and significant essays edited by E. W. Tedlock, Jr., and C. V. Wicker, 1957.

STENDHAL
(Marie Henri Beyle)

Born: Grenoble, France
Date: January 23, 1783

Died: Paris, France
Date: March 23, 1842

PRINCIPAL WORKS

NOVELS: *Armance,* 1827; *Le Rouge et le noir,* 1830 (*The Red and the Black*); *La Chartreuse de Parme,* 1839 (*The Charterhouse of Parma*); *Lamiel,* 1889; *Lucien Leuwen,* 1894, 1926–1927 (I, *The Green Huntsman*; II, *The Telegraph*).

NOVELLAS: *L'Abbesse de Castro,* 1839; *Romans et nouvelles,* 1854; *Nouvelles inédites,* 1855.

AUTOBIOGRAPHY: *Journal,* 1923–1924.

Stendhal, born Marie Henri Beyle at Grenoble, France, on January 23, 1783, was the most "unromantic" figure of France's Romantic period (1830–1848), yet he ranks with Hugo, Balzac, Flaubert, and Zola as one of the greatest French novelists of the nineteenth century. Always of an independent nature, he left his Grenoble birthplace at an early age to seek his fortune in Paris. There he obtained a position in the Ministry of War and, in 1800, became a dragoon in the army of Napoleon. He accompanied the army in the Italian, Prussian, and Russian campaigns, serving with distinction until the fall of Napoleon in 1814. Still a young man, he spent the next seven years in Milan, scene of *The Charterhouse of Parma,* one of his two masterpieces. The rest of his life was spent as an independent and stubborn consular officer of France, mainly in Trieste and in Civitavecchia. Tempestuous love affairs occupied a considerable amount of his time, and some of the events connected with these are to be found in his writings. He died at Paris on March 23, 1842.

Stendhal's writing career began in 1814 in Milan. There he produced two studies, *Haydn, Mozart and Métastase* (1814) and *Rome, Naples and Flor-*ence (1817). He also contributed several critical essays to British literary journals during this period, and his name was better known in England then than it was in France. Stendhal's first novel, *Armance,* appeared in 1827. Five years earlier, he had written a searching study of one of his own love affairs under the title *De l'Amour.* None of these early writings received significant attention. In 1830 appeared the first of Stendhal's two unquestioned masterpieces, *The Red and the Black.* The title indicates the strife between the Napoleonic spirit of the military and the power of the clergy, whom Stendhal detested. The protagonist of the novel, Julien Sorel, has come to typify the post-Revolutionary *arriviste* in France. Much of Stendhal is in this character. Sorel is a poor tutor who makes love to his student's mother in order to further his own ambitions. When this woman, his first mistress, betrays him to a second, he attempts to kill her and is condemned to die. In addition to giving a profound psychological study of Sorel, *The Red and the Black* also furnishes an excellent representation of the social upheaval which France had undergone during the years since the Revolution. Sorel epitomizes the uprooted peasant, the man of mediocre talent who is intelligent enough to wish above all to avail himself of the limitless opportunities offered those like him under the Republic.

During the years 1831–1838, Stendhal wrote (but did not publish) two autobiographical works (*Souvenirs d'égotisme* and *La Vie d'Henri Buclard*) and one novel, *Lucien Leuwen*. Stendhal's greatest novel, *The Charterhouse of Parma*, was published in 1839. This is the story of Fabrice del Dongo (roughly the equivalent of Julien Sorel) and his relations with a duchess and a highwayman. The story is laid in nineteenth century Italy, although the most famous passage is a realistic description of the Battle of Waterloo as seen through the young hero's eyes. Stendhal, who professed to love Italy better than France, succeeds admirably in painting a true picture of life in a petty Italian principality, and his study of the loves and intrigues of his characters is again brilliant. This work, like *The Red and the Black*, shows Stendhal at his best: careless of form, but willing to put his brilliant energy and his stubborn and egotistical mind to the task of recording, with effective economy of detail, the minutiae and grandeur of life. Stendhal is not above using improbable characters and situations, but his study of both is brutally exact. Thus he is called both romantic and realist.

In his own day Stendhal was not appreciated, and only Balzac saw much worth to his novels. But in the late 1880's, with the appearance of his unpublished works, there occurred a curious literary revival; he was praised by both the naturalists and the psychologists. His reputation grows with each year, and his journals, recently published, have enjoyed a great success. Stendhal, it has been said, went further than any other writer of France in reconciling the two great literary traditions of that country, classical simplicity and romantic imagination.

BIBLIOGRAPHICAL REFERENCES: Stendhal's *Œuvres Complètes* were published in 79 vols., 1927–1937. His most important works are available in English translation; the most recent to appear was Robert Sage's translation of *The Private Diaries of Stendhal*, 1953. The growing literary stature of Stendhal as a novelist has produced a variety of biographical and critical studies. There are three good introductions in English to his personality and work: F. C. Green, *Stendhal*, 1939; Matthew Josephson, *Stendhal, or the Pursuit of Happiness*, 1946; and Howard Clewes, *Stendhal: An Introduction to the Novelist*, 1950. Studies in French include Leon Blum, *Stendhal et le Beylisme*, 1914; Paul Arbelet, *La Jeunesse de Stendhal*, 2 vols., 1919; Armand Caraccio, *Stendhal, l'homme et l'œuvre*, 1951; Henri Martineau, *L'œuvre de Stendhal*, 1951; Jean Prévost, *La Création chez Stendhal*, 1951; Jules Alciatore, *Stendhal et Helvetius*, 1952; and *Stendhal et Maine de Biran*, 1954.

For briefer studies see also Lytton Strachey, *Books and Characters*, 1922; Stefan Zweig, *Adepts in Self-Portraiture*, 1928 (trans., 1929); François Mauriac, *Petits essais de psychologie religieuse*, 1933; Meyer Levin, *Toward Stendhal*, *Pharo III*, 1945; Irving Howe, "Stendhal: The Politics of Survival," in *Politics and the Novel*, 1957; and Victor Brombert, "Stendhal: Creation and Self-Knowledge," *Romantic Review*, XLIII (1952), 190–197.

JAMES STEPHENS

Born: Dublin, Ireland
Date: February 2, 1882

Died: London, England
Date: December 26, 1950

PRINCIPAL WORKS

POEMS: *Insurrections*, 1909; *The Lonely God and Other Poems*, 1909; *The Hill of Vision*, 1912; *The Rocky Road to Dublin*, 1915; *Songs from the Clay*, 1915; *Green Branches*, 1916; *Reincarnations*, 1918; *The Outcast*, 1929; *Theme and Variations*, 1930; *Strict Joy*, 1931; *Collected Poems*, 1954.

NOVELS: *The Charwoman's Daughter*, 1912 [*Mary, Mary*]; *The Crock of Gold*, 1912; *The Demigods*, 1914; *Deirdre*, 1923; *In the Land of Youth*, 1924.

SHORT STORIES: *Here Are Ladies*, 1913; *Etched in Moonlight*, 1928.

PLAY: *Julia Elizabeth*, 1929.

James Stephens, born to a poor Irish family on February 2, 1882, grew up in the slums of Dublin and for the most part educated himself by reading widely. To earn a living he taught himself stenography. While working as a stenographer, he began to write poems and stories, some of which were praised by George W. Russell (Æ), who read them in manuscript. But the praise of an established writer was still insufficient to secure publication, and Stephens found editors and publishers uninterested in his work. His first success did not come until he was thirty, when *The Crock of Gold* was published. *The Crock of Gold*, although never exceptionally popular, has become a minor classic because a respectable number of readers have found it appealing through more than four decades, its splendidly written fantasy appealing to literary appetites tired of realism and naturalism. The book won the Polignac Prize for 1912. A series of novels attempting to create a new mythology for Irish literature followed, the best-known being *Deirdre*, awarded the Tailteann Gold Medal.

Among Stephens' lifelong interests was almost every phase of Gaelic culture, language, art, and literature. As an authority on Gaelic art, he served for some years as an assistant curator of the Dublin National Gallery. Among his amusements was singing Irish folk songs, playing an accompaniment on the concertina.

As an adult Stephens spent much time away from his native city and land. He visited the United States a number of times, for both short and long periods, coming to the United States for the first time in 1925. Just a decade later he spent most of a year on the West Coast, lecturing on literature and Gaelic culture at the University of California. In other ways than lecturing Stephens left an imprint on American higher education. Two anthologies which he edited with E. L. Beck and R. H. Snow have been standard college textbooks for almost a quarter of a century: *English Romantic Poets* (1933) and *Victorian and Later English Poets* (1934). Between the two world wars Stephens also spent a great deal of time in France, especially Paris. In spite of his travels abroad, Stephens remained an ardent Irish nationalist, belonged to the Sinn Fein movement, ardently supported Eamon De Valera, the Irish political leader and president

1022

of Eire. During World War II, however, he felt obliged to go counter to Irish neutrality and he declared himself a supporter of the Allies. The British government granted him a pension in 1942.

In addition to his novels and poetry, none of which has had any truly wide popularity in America, Stephens tried his hand at other literary forms. Here *Are Ladies* and *Etched in Moonlight* are collections of stories. *Irish Fairy Tales* (1920) is a volume for children. *Julia Elizabeth* is an attempt in drama. *On Prose and Verse* (1928) is a critical study of literature.

Stephens was married and had two children. He died on December 26, 1950, in London, where he had resided for a number of years.

BIBLIOGRAPHICAL REFERENCES: There is no authorized biography or extended critical study. See Æ (George W. Russell), *Imaginations and Reveries*, 1916; Iola A. Williams, *John Collings Squire and James Stephens*, 1922; Ernest Boyd, *Portraits: Real and Imaginary*, 1924; Edward Davison, *Some Modern Poets*, 1928; Cornelius Weygandt, "The Riddling of James Stephens," in *Tuesdays at Ten*, 1928; David Morton, *The Renaissance of Irish Poetry*, 1929; Frank Swinnerton, *The Georgian Literary Scene, 1910–1935*, 1935; and Groff Conklin, "James Stephens, Metrist," *English Journal*, XXV (1936), 268–277.

LAURENCE STERNE

Born: Clonmel, Ireland
Date: November 24, 1713

Died: London, England
Date: March 18, 1768

PRINCIPAL WORKS

NOVEL: *The Life and Opinions of Tristram Shandy, Gent.*, 1759–1767.

TRAVEL MISCELLANY: *A Sentimental Journey through France and Italy*, 1768.

SATIRE: *A Political Romance*, 1759.

SERMONS: *The Sermons of Mr. Yorick*, 1760–1769.

LETTERS AND JOURNALS: *Letters from Yorick to Eliza*, 1773; *Sterne's Letters to His Friends on Various Occasions*, 1775; *Letters of the Late Rev. Mr. Sterne to His Most Intimate Friends*, 1775; *Journal to Eliza*, 1904.

Laurence Sterne, the most delightfully eccentric of English novelists, was born in Clonmel, Ireland, on November 24, 1713, the son of an Irish woman and an ensign in the English army whose regiment had just been transferred to Ireland from Dunkirk. Though his parentage was undistinguished, Sterne's father came from an old family in Yorkshire, where a great-grandfather had been an archbishop. A childhood spent in the rigors of camp-following undoubtedly had a harmful effect on the novelist's frail constitution; but the experience provided him with details of barracks life and campaign reminiscences that ultimately enriched his great novel with such authentic creations as Uncle Toby and Corporal Trim.

Between 1723 and 1731, the year of his father's death, Sterne was in school at Halifax, Yorkshire. In 1733, after two years of idleness at Elvington, he was enrolled as a sizar in Jesus College, Cambridge, through the grudging benevolence of relatives. At Cambridge he indulged in the easy, convivial university life of the time. Not surprisingly he discovered an incapacity for mathematics and a contempt for formal logic. Nevertheless, he did considerable reading, developing a deep admiration for John Locke, whose philosophy was to be the most important single influence on his thinking. He also formed a close friendship with John Hall-Stevenson, later the hypochondriac author of *Crazy Tales* (1762). Cambridge granted Sterne a B.A. in 1737 and an M.A. in 1740.

As a matter of expediency rather than religious conviction, he took holy orders. He was ordained deacon in 1737 and inducted into the vicarage of Sutton on the Forest in 1738. Two years later he received a prebendal stall in the York Cathedral. In 1744 he acquired the parish of Stillington, near Sutton.

In 1741, after a "sentimental" courtship he married the homely but well-connected Elizabeth Lumley. A daughter, Lydia, was born in 1747. The Sternes, however, were never really compatible. Not only was Mrs. Sterne ill-tempered but she also suffered aberrations which, according to gossip, were not allayed by her husband's "small, quiet attentions" to various ladies. Actually, there is evidence that Sterne treated his wife with commendable patience. And though he was not averse to paying attention to other women, his philandering was chiefly sentimental—as was, for example, his affair with Catherine ("Kitty") Fourmantelle, a singer from London who came to York in 1759.

In Sutton, Sterne spent twenty years of relative obscurity, serving two parishes with some conscientiousness, unsuccessfully farming his glebe, and making occasional trips to York to preach his turn in the cathedral or to dabble in diocesan politics. He found amusement in hunting, skating, fiddling, and painting, as well as in social gatherings at Newburgh Priory, the seat of Lord Fauconberg, and in the ribald carousals of the "Demoniacks" at Hall-Stevenson's Skelton Castle. He later immortalized his role of "heteroclite parson" in his portrait of Yorick.

In 1759 his participation in local church politics produced a satire called *A Political Romance* (later renamed *The History of a Good Warm Watch-Coat*). Though all but a few copies were burned to prevent embarrassment to the diocese, its success among Sterne's friends gave him the impetus to embark on *Tristram Shandy*, the first two volumes of which came out in York in December of the same year. Introduced to London through the enthusiasm of David Garrick, the novel so impressed the capital with its whimsicality, eccentric humor, and indecorum that it was immediately successful. In fact, when Sterne journeyed down to London in the spring of 1760, he found himself a social lion. Never had the city seen such a witty, hedonistic priest whose lustrous eyes and ebulliently secular conversation so enchantingly belied his black garb, his pale face, thin body, and hollow chest.

But disapprobation soon followed success. Literary men like Walpole, Goldsmith, and Richardson condemned the book for various evils ranging from tediousness to indecency; and a flood of hostile articles, pamphlets, and bad imitations poured from the press. When the author brought out the first two volumes of the *Sermons of Mr. Yorick* (1760), the comminatory chorus grew—chiefly because the title bore the name of "a *Jester. . . . in an obscene romance.*"

Returning to Yorkshire, Sterne received from Lord Fauconberg the living of Coxwold, to which "sweet retirement" he moved his family. Here for the rest of his life his home was a rambling gabled house that he called Shandy Hall. In January, 1761, he was again in London to see two more volumes of *Tristram* published. Though the critical reception was now unfavorable, the books sold well. Sterne returned to Coxwold, completed two more volumes, and was back in November for their publication. This time his reputation soared again. The story of Le Fever, Trim's animadversions on death, and Uncle Toby's campaigns had won universal applause.

Weakened by a serious hemorrhage from chronically weak lungs, Sterne set out for France in 1762 in a "race with death." Recovering in Paris, he was brilliantly lionized by the cream of French intellectual society. He later settled with his family in Toulouse. Back in Coxwold in 1764, he completed volumes seven and eight of Tristram Shandy, including an account of his tour through France and the affair of Uncle Toby and the Widow Wadman. These came out in January, 1765. Two more volumes of sermons followed in January, 1766.

Once again on the Continent in 1766, Sterne had a "joyous" winter in France and Italy. Though hemorrhages were becoming more frequent, he returned during the year to his desk in Coxwold, and by January, 1767, he was on hand in London for the appearance of the ninth volume of *Tristram Shandy.* During this winter he indulged in his famous sentimental affair with Eliza Draper, the young wife of an official of the East India Company, for whom he kept the *Journal to Eliza* after her departure for Bombay.

Late in February, 1768, Sterne brought out *A Sentimental Journey through France and Italy.* Its triumphant reception he was permitted to enjoy only briefly. An attack of influenza that developed into pleurisy proved more than his disease-wracked body could bear. He died in London on March 18, 1768, and was buried at St. George's, Hanover Square.

Sterne's work, like his life, is marked with a refreshing unconventionality. Though the *Sermons* (1760–69) lack religious conviction and orginality of material, they preach a warm benevolence and a comfortable morality in a style that can be at once graceful and dramatic. *A Sentimental Journey*—in which Sterne substituted his traveler's sentimental adventures for the conventional accounts of nations, peoples, and memorable sights in travel books—is a nearly perfect small masterpiece.

The humor of *Tristram Shandy* is plainly in the tradition of Rabelais, Cervantes, and Swift; and its borrowings range from Robert Burton to miscellaneous curiosa. Superficially, the novel may seem merely like an engaging hodge-podge full of tricks, including black, marbled, and blank pages, omitted chapters, unorthodox punctuation and typography, and numerous digressions. But *Tristram Shandy* is far from planless. By insisting on the importance of opinions about action rather than on that of action itself Sterne opened unexplored avenues into the inner lives of his superbly ingratiating characters and achieved a new architectonic principle based on the mind as Locke had illuminated it in the *Essay on Human Understanding*. At the same time he achieved a new concept of time in fiction, a fascinating awareness of the life process itself, and a fresh concept of comedy based on the idea of individual isolation in a world where each person is a product of his own peculiar association of ideas.

Lodwick Hartley

BIBLIOGRAPHICAL REFERENCES: The standard edition is the *Life and Works of Laurence Sterne*, edited by Wilbur L. Cross, 12 vols., 1904. See also *Letters*, edited by L. P. Curtis, 1935; and *Tristram Shandy*, edited by James A. Work, 1940. The standard biography is Wilbur L. Cross, *The Life and Times of Laurence Sterne*, 2 vols., 1929. Other full-length biographical and critical studies include Walter Sichel, *Sterne: A Study*, 1910; Lodwick Hartley, *This is Lorence*, 1943; L. V. Hammond, *Sterne's "Sermons of Mr. Yorick,"* 1946; and E. N. Dilworth, *The Unsentimental Journey of Laurence Sterne*, 1948.

See also Edward Wagenknecht, *Cavalcade of the English Novel*, 1943; Walter Allen, *The English Novel*, 1954; Herbert Read, The Sense of Glory, 1929; Virginia Woolf, "The 'Sentimental Journey'" in *The Second Common Reader*, 1932; W. B. C. Watkins, "Yorick Revisited," in *Perilous Balance*, 1939; Theodore Baird, "The Time-Scheme of Tristram Shandy and a Source," *Publications of the Modern Language Association*, LI (1936), 803–820; Walter L. Myers, "O, the Hobby Horse," *Virginia Quarterly Review*, XIX (1943), 268–277; Lodwick Hartley, "Tristram and the Angels," *College English*, IX (1947), 62–69; Louis D. Rubin, Jr., "Joyce and Sterne: A Study in Affinity," *Hopkins Review*, III (1950), 1–15; and Wayne Booth, "Did Sterne Complete Tristram Shandy?" *Modern Philology*, XLVIII (1951), 172–183.

JAMES STEVENS

Born: Albia, Iowa
Date: November 15, 1892

PRINCIPAL WORKS

TALES AND SKETCHES: *Paul Bunyan*, 1925; *Homer in the Sagebrush*, 1928; *Saginaw Paul Bunyan*, 1932.
NOVELS: *Brawnyman*, 1926; *Mattock*, 1927; *Big Jim Turner*, 1948.

James (Floyd) Stevens, born in Monroe County, Iowa, on November 15, 1892, has always been drawn to the great outdoors, the rivers and forests of America. His novels, short stories, and journalistic writings constitute, on the whole, a partial autobiography and an account of the realistic and mythic heroes of the lumberman, fisherman, and pioneer laborer.

Stevens' strongest claim to a place in literary history is his first book, *Paul Bunyan*, published in 1925. Although one reviewer said that it "converted folklore to farce," most critics were laudatory: "James Stevens merits to be known by this epical work as the prose Homer of American mythology"; "No one but Mark Twain has been able to set down tall tales with such winning conviction." By 1948, the book had sold over 200,000 copies and Stevens issued a new edition, adding a chapter which described a fabulous log run up the Columbia River with tame whales doing the work.

Paul Bunyan was followed by *Brawnyman,* which describes in a ragged, raw style the life of a hobo laborer, Jim Turner, who hops freights from job to job. *Mattock* is based on Stevens' fourteen months in France as an infantryman in World War I. It is Private Parvin Mattock's vernacular account of a farm boy's shocking experiences in the AEF; it closes with the first convention of the American Legion.

Homer in the Sagebrush, a collection of magazine stories of the Northwest frontier was criticized for being too raw, lacking artistic form. His next collection, *Saginaw Paul Bunyan,* seemed, on the other hand, "too prosy and correct . . . a saga in pseudo-literary style." Stevens continued to produce novels and stories, the most significant being *Big Jim Turner,* an autobiographical social chronicle of the early 1900's—railroading and lumber, labor agitation, the IWW, Eugene V. Debs. Although picturesque and often forceful, his later books have never quite fulfilled the expectations aroused by *Paul Bunyan.*

BIBLIOGRAPHICAL REFERENCES: Harry R. Warfel, *American Novelists of Today,* 1951, gives a biographical sketch. Studies are: Stuart Sherman, *The Main Stream,* 1927; Elizabeth Montgomery, *The Story Behind Modern Books,* 1949; and Daniel Hoffman, *Paul Bunyan,* 1952. See also Stevens' "Medicine Men," *American Mercury,* XXVIII (1933), 487–497, and his "Folklore and the Artist," *ibid.,* LXXX (1950), 343–349.

WALLACE STEVENS

Born: Reading, Pennsylvania
Date: October 2, 1879

Died: Hartford, Connecticut
Date: August 2, 1955

PRINCIPAL WORKS

POEMS: *Harmonium,* 1923; *Ideas of Order,* 1935; *Owl's Clover,* 1936; *The Man with the Blue Guitar,* 1937; *Parts of a World,* 1942; *Notes Toward a Supreme Fiction,* 1942; *Esthétique du Mal,* 1945; *Transport to Summer,* 1947; *Three Academic Pieces,* 1947; *A Primitive Like an Orb,* 1948; *The Auroras of Autumn,* 1952; *Collected Poems,* 1954.

ESSAYS: *The Necessary Angel: Essays on Reality and the Imagination,* 1951.

MISCELLANEOUS: *Opus Posthumous,* 1957.

The vice-presidency of a large insurance firm seems an unlikely job to nurture a poet, yet Wallace Stevens throve in both business and literature. No part-time writer, he became one of America's outstanding poets of this century. A juggler with words and a painter of brightly colored pictures of the world, he turned them into poetry that is imaginative, romantic, pictorial, and musical.

Stevens was born in Reading, Pennsylvania, on October 2, 1879. From 1897 to 1900 he attended Harvard University. He then entered the New York Law School, was admitted to the bar in 1904, and began the practice of law in New York City. His first poems appeared in 1913, but he winnowed his work carefully and not until 1923 did he publish his first volume, *Harmonium*. During those early years he also wrote one-act verse plays, but he failed to include them in the books published during his lifetime.

In 1916 he began work for the Hartford Accident and Indemnity Company, becoming vice-president in 1934. He continued to write steadily during the 1920's; however, not until twelve years after *Harmonium* did he bring out *Ideas of Order*, which contains poems whose meanings are often cryptic and elusive, a mixture of chromatic bravura and quiet reflection. But in this book, as in the volumes that followed at fairly regular intervals, the quick wit and the subtly tuned music are always present. In *The Man with the Blue Guitar* he expressed his concern for man's problem in a confused world; in his later work he suffered with our growing despair. Stevens felt that a poet could lead mankind from troubled reality into a serene world of the imagination; for him art became the "supreme fiction," the only reality in a disordered age which had seen the loss of personality, the imperatives of change within a fragmented society, the developing crisis of belief.

For his *Collected Poems* Stevens won a Pulitzer Prize in 1955. He died in Hartford, Connecticut, on August 2 of that year. With the publication of *Opus Posthumous* in 1957 the canon of his delicate and precise yet meaningful art is virtually complete.

BIBLIOGRAPHICAL REFERENCES: The standard edition, although not definitive, is *The Collected Poems of Wallace Stevens*, 1954. *Opus Posthumous*, containing additional poems, aphorisms, essays, and dramatic sketches, was edited by Samuel French Morse, 1957.

There is no authorized biography. The major critical study to date is William Van O'Connor, *The Shaping Spirit: A Study of Wallace Stevens*, 1950. Of bibliographical importance is Samuel French Morse, *Wallace Stevens: A Preliminary Checklist of His Published Writings*, 1954. For critical articles in periodicals see Gorham Munson, "The Dandyism of Wallace Stevens," *Dial*, LXXIX (1925), 413–417; Morton Dauwen Zabel, "The Harmonium of Wallace Stevens," *Poetry*, XXXIX (1931), 148–154; R. P. Blackmur, "Examples of Wallace Stevens," *Hound and Horn*, V (1932), 223–255; Hi Simons, "'The Comedian as the Letter C': Its Sense and Significance," *Southern Review*, V (1940), 453–468, "The Humanism of Wallace Stevens," *Poetry*, LXI (1942), 448–452, and "The Genre of Wallace Stevens," *Sewanee Review*, LIII (1945), 566–579; Wylie Sypher, "Connoisseur in Chaos: Wallace Stevens," *Partisan Review*, XIII (1946), 83–94; Marius Bewley, "The Poetry of Wallace Stevens," *Partisan Review*, XVI (1949), 895–915; Harold H. Watts, "Wallace Stevens and the Rock of Summer," *Kenyon Review*, XIV (1952), 122–140; Donald Davie, "'Essential Gaudiness': The Poems of Wallace Stevens," *Twentieth Century*, CLIII (1953), 455–462; Elder Olson, "The Poetry of Wallace Stevens," *College English*, XVI (1955), 395–402; R. P. Blackmur, "The Substance That Prevails," *Kenyon Review*, XVII (1955), 94–110; Randall Jarrell, "The Collected Poems of Wallace Stevens," *Yale Review*, XLIV (1955), 340–353; William Carlos Williams, "Wallace Stevens," *Poetry*, LXXXVII (1956), 234–239; and Howard Nemerov, "The Poetry of Wallace Stevens," *Sewanee Review*, LXV (1957), 1–14.

The Wallace Stevens Number of the *Harvard Advocate*, CXXVII, No. 3 (December, 1940), contained essays and statements by Marianne Moore, F. O. Matthiessen, Robert Penn Warren, William Carlos Williams, and others.

ROBERT LOUIS STEVENSON

Born: Edinburgh, Scotland   *Died:* Apia, Samoa
Date: November 13, 1850   *Date:* December 3, 1894

PRINCIPAL WORKS

NOVELS: *Treasure Island,* 1883; *Prince Otto,* 1885; *The Strange Case of Dr. Jekyll and Mr. Hyde,* 1886; *Kidnapped,* 1886; *The Merry Men,* 1887; *The Black Arrow,* 1888; *The Master of Ballantrae,* 1888; *The Wrong Box,* 1889 (with Lloyd Osbourne); *The Wrecker,* 1892 (with Lloyd Osbourne); *Catriona,* 1893 [*David Balfour*]; *The Ebb-Tide,* 1894 (with Lloyd Osbourne); *Weir of Hermiston,* 1896 (unfinished); *St. Ives,* 1897 (completed by Arthur Quiller-Couch).

SHORT STORIES AND SKETCHES: *The New Arabian Nights,* 1882; *More New Arabian Nights,* 1885 (with Mrs. Stevenson); *Island Nights' Entertainments,* 1893.

TRAVEL SKETCHES AND IMPRESSIONS: *An Inland Voyage,* 1878; *Travels with a Donkey,* 1879; *The Silverado Squatters,* 1883; *Across the Plains,* 1892; *The Amateur Emigrant,* 1895; *In the South Seas,* 1896.

POEMS: *A Child's Garden of Verses,* 1885; *Underwoods,* 1887; *Ballads,* 1890.

ESSAYS AND STUDIES: *Virginibus Puerisque,* 1881; *Familiar Studies of Men and Books,* 1882; *Memories and Portraits,* 1887; *Father Damien,* 1890.

Robert Louis (Balfour) Stevenson, born in Edinburgh on November 13, 1850, has achieved fame by his romantic life nearly as much as by his romantic fiction, for his life displays the same dualism between romantic adventure and grim reality that the discerning reader finds in much of his writing. Stevenson's brief forty-four year life was a nearly constant journey in search of adventure and relief from the agonies of tuberculosis, with which he was afflicted from early childhood. His father, Thomas Stevenson, a successful Edinburgh lighthouse engineer, hoped for a law career for his only son; but, though Robert did study to be a barrister, he soon commenced a life of traveling that took him to Switzerland, France, the United States, and, finally, the South Seas. In each place Stevenson found adventure; and when he did not find it ready-made, he created it for himself out of his teeming imagination.

Although Stevenson is best known for his fiction, he was a prodigious essayist. The vivid impressions made by the places he visited are found recorded in such brilliant travel sketches and essays as *An Inland Voyage,* which tells of a canoeing trip through Belgium and France, and *Travels with a Donkey in the Cévennes,* which deals with his journeys in southern France. In these books Stevenson shows his fine eye for color and vivid impressions, that sort of sensitivity that was to add so much to the popularity of his fiction.

He had always been ambitious to write and had prepared himself laboriously for a literary career. His famous statements about how he copied the style of great writers such as Lamb, Hazlitt, Defoe, and Hawthorne, and about how he was always writing, polishing, and correcting are evidence of this ambition. So, too, is the delicate, precise, but rich style that his fiction achieves.

Stevenson fell in love with Mrs. Fanny Osbourne in France and went to California in 1879 to marry her after she had secured a divorce from her husband. This trip caused a break with Stevenson's family, who were opposed to the alliance, and he suffered many hardships until he acquired a measure of fame and prosperity with the publication of his first major work, *Treasure Island*, written chiefly for the entertainment of his stepson, Lloyd Osbourne. This most famous and loved of adventure stories demonstrated Stevenson's ability at colorful narration and his technique of using a relatively minor character as observer and narrator. *Kidnapped* was immediately popular, but it never attained the following of *Treasure Island*. A striking contrast to these tales of romantic adventure is *The Strange Case of Dr. Jekyll and Mr. Hyde*, perhaps the most famous of all Stevenson's fiction; this grim story of dual personality is moralistic and filled with Stevenson's concern for ethical problems.

Again in search of improved health, Stevenson left California and traveled in the United States, his longest stay being in Saranac Lake, a health resort in the Adirondacks. He stayed there during 1887–1888. While at Saranac Lake he wrote *The Master of Bal-lantrae*, a tale of the Jacobite struggle, the same subject dealt with in the earlier *Kidnapped*. In *The Black Arrow* he went farther back in time to the Wars of the Roses; this book contains a lively picture of late medieval times.

In a final desperate effort to regain his health, Stevenson moved to the South Seas and settled on the island of Samoa. There he found a serenity that encouraged his literary efforts. He was considered a truly great man by the natives, and he took an active interest in Samoan politics. In his last years he was very productive, turning out *The Wrecker* with Lloyd Osbourne, his stepson, and *David Balfour*, a sequel to *Kidnapped* but a more able literary performance.

Stevenson died suddenly of apoplexy on December 3, 1894, leaving unfinished his *Weir of Hermiston*, the work that is generally regarded as his masterpiece. In this fragment Stevenson manifests the culmination of his constant efforts to improve his style and displays again his conviction that the romance of life is, to the individual, more real than what critics and other materialistic novelists of his period were praising as detached objectivity. Criticism is still sharply divided over the whole body of his work, but he holds a firm place in the favor of all children and of all adults who believe that romance is a valid part of life.

BIBLIOGRAPHICAL REFERENCES: Complete editions of Stevenson's works are the Swanston Edition, 25 vols., 1911–1912, with an introduction by Andrew Lang, and the Tusitala Edition, 35 vols., 1923–1924. Sir Sidney Colvin has edited the *Letters* in 4 vols., 1911. The standard bibliography is by W. F. Prideaux, *A Bibliography of the Works of Robert Louis Stevenson*, 1903, revised by F. V. Livingston, 1917. Good biographies are J. C. Furnas' *Voyage to Windward*, 1951; and Charles Neider's edition of *Our Samoan Adventure*, 1955, which includes a previously unpublished three-year diary and rare photographs. Important critical works are Frank Swinnerton, *Robert Louis Stevenson: A Critical Study*, 1923; J. A. Steuart, *Robert Louis Steven-*

son: *Man and Writer. A Critical Biography*, 2 vols., 1924; David Daiches, *Robert Louis Stevenson*, 1946, and *Stevenson and the Art of Fiction*, 1951. Informative essays include H. W. Garrod's "The Poetry of Robert Louis Stevenson" in his *The Profession of Poetry*, 1929, and "The Poetry of Stevenson" in *Essays Presented to Sir Humphrey Milford*, 1948.

JAMES STILL

Born: Double Creek, Alabama
Date: July 16, 1906

PRINCIPAL WORKS

NOVEL: *River of Earth*, 1940.
SHORT STORIES: *On Troublesome Creek*, 1941.
POEMS: *Hounds on the Mountain*, 1937.

A Kentuckian by adoption, James Still was born on Double Creek, Chambers County, Alabama, on July 16, 1906. His boyhood ambition was to be a veterinarian like his father, and among his earliest recollections are the nights he spent with his father while they nursed a sick animal on some neighbor's farm. When he was seventeen he entered Lincoln Memorial University at Harrogate, Tennessee. There he worked in a rock quarry and in the school library to pay his expenses. After his graduation in 1929 he completed work for his M.A. degree at Vanderbilt University in 1930 and spent a year at the University of Illinois Library School. For the next six years he was librarian at the Hindman Settlement School in Knott County, Kentucky. One of his duties was to carry boxes of books, twenty to the carton, over mountain trails to supply one-room schools without libraries of their own. During those years he tramped over every ridge and hollow mentioned in his books, which have their settings in the region of hill farms and coal camps scattered along the branch waters of Little Carr and Troublesome creeks.

In 1937 he published *Hounds on the Mountain*, a book of poems highly praised for their regional freshness and the lyric beauty of their style. In the meantime, at work on his first novel, he went to live in a log cabin between Deadmare Branch and Wolfpen Creek. *River of Earth* appeared in 1940. Covering two years in the life of a mountain family, it is a simple but moving chronicle of the hill country presented through the eyes of a boy growing into a realization of the strange, bewildering world of human relationships and of man's responsibilities within that world. The story, which falls easily into a pattern of memory, loses nothing in the episodic manner of its telling, and the whole is tuned to a clear colloquial style that holds echoes of old proverbs and hill-born wisdom as well as the occasional incorrectness of folk speech in its idiom. *River of Earth* was selected for the Southern Authors' Award in 1941. *On Troublesome Creek* is a collection of short stories in much the same pattern and mood, set against a landscape where the lives of men and women follow the round of the seasons in an almost timeless cycle of birth, growth, seed-time, and death.

During World War II James Still served with the U. S. Army Air Force in Africa and the Middle East. He was a Guggenheim fellow in 1946, and in 1947, in recognition of "his gift of style and mastery of character and scene," he received a special award from the Academy of Arts and Letters and the National Institute of Arts and Letters. More recently he has been the librarian at the Hindman school and a member of the faculty at the annual writers' conference sponsored by Morehead State College. He remains an unhurried and scrupulous writer whose tales of the Kentucky mountains appear from time to time in magazines and short story anthologies.

BIBLIOGRAPHICAL REFERENCES: There is no extended biographical or critical study. See Dayton Kohler, "Jesse Stuart and James Still: Mountain Regionalists," *College English*, III (1942), 523–533; also the *Book Review Digest*, 1937, 1940, 1941.

BRAM STOKER

Born: Dublin, Ireland
Date: 1847

Died: London, England
Date: April 20, 1912

Principal Work

NOVEL: *Dracula*, 1897.

Born in Dublin, Ireland, in 1847, Bram (Abraham) Stoker, famous for his sensational novel, *Dracula*, was a sickly child, so weak that he was unable to stand up alone until the age of seven. He outgrew his childhood weakness, however, and became a champion athlete while at Dublin University, from which he was graduated in 1867. For the next ten years he drudged away as an Irish civil servant. From 1871 to 1876 Stoker served as an unpaid drama critic for the Dublin *Mail*, work which won for him the friendship of Henry Irving, the actor. As a result of their friendship, Stoker served as Irving's manager for many years.

After touring America with Irving, Stoker wrote a series of lectures about life in the United States to deliver to English audiences. The success of the lectures when printed in pamphlet form caused Stoker to consider other kinds of writing. *Dracula* appeared in 1897. Negligible as literature, the book is really no more than a *tour de force* combining werewolves, vampires, hypnotism, and unhappy spirits. It is horrifying, and yet it is compelling, and it has achieved notoriety, if not fame, as a novel, a stage play, and several motion picture versions. The work represents a late nineteenth century development of the earlier Gothic novel, and its marked success stimulated other authors to imitate the type. Other works by Stoker worth noting are *The Jewel of Seven Stars* (1904), a novel; and *Personal Reminiscences of Henry Irving* (1906), the latter recording Stoker's life with Irving and with the Lyceum Theatre. During his last years Stoker was also on the literary staff of the London *Telegraph*. He died in London on April 20, 1912.

BIBLIOGRAPHICAL REFERENCES: An excellent study of the Gothic novel and its writers is Dorothy Scarborough, *The Supernatural in Modern English Fiction*, 1917.

PHIL STONG

Born: Keosauqua, Iowa   *Died:* Washington, Connecticut
Date: January 27, 1899   *Date:* April 26, 1957

PRINCIPAL WORKS

NOVELS: *State Fair*, 1932; *Stranger's Return*, 1933; *Village Tale*, 1934; *Week-End*, 1935; *Buckskin Breeches*, 1937; *The Long Lane*, 1939; *Return in August*, 1953.

Following graduation from the public schools of Keosauqua, Iowa, where he was born on January 27, 1899, Phil (ip Duffield) Stong went to Drake University, from which he was graduated in 1919. After some graduate study at Columbia University (1920–1921) and at the University of Kansas, (1923–1924) Stong wrote editorials for the Des Moines *Register* and later taught courses in journalism and speech at Drake University. In 1925 he went to New York City, working successively for the Associated Press, the North American Newspaper Alliance, *Liberty*, *Editor and Publisher*, and the New York *World*. In 1931 he began to devote all his time to creative writing.

Stong's first published novel, *State Fair*, was an immediate success, bringing him economic security and a strong reputation. The novel was made into a motion picture, with Will Rogers in one of the lead roles; after World War II the story was again filmed, this time in color. One of the immediate results of the first motion picture version was that the author was able to repurchase the farmstead which had belonged to his maternal grandfather. After 1932 Stong published a number of novels, but none has achieved the popularity of his first. Most of his fiction is about Iowa and the people from the rural areas and small towns of that state.

In his work Stong presented Midwest farm life as a full and pleasant one, not the horror which some other writers, following Hamlin Garland's example, have portrayed. *Stranger's Return* relates the return to happy farm life of a young woman who went East to marry a newspaperman. *Village Tale* presents life and an episode of unusual violence in a small Iowa railroad town. *Week-end* exposes the shams of supposedly sophisticated New Yorkers. *Farmer in the Dell* (1935) drew upon Stong's experience in Hollywood and presents an Iowa farmer's brief experience as a Hollywood actor. In 1937 Stong reached back into history for *Buckskin Breeches*, which tells of one family's migration from Ohio to Iowa early in the nineteenth century.

Later novels draw upon different kinds of materials. *The Iron Mountain* (1942), a study of a Finnish woman's impact on a Scandinavian and Balkan community in the famous Mesabi country of Minnesota makes skillful use of dialects. *Our Destiny* (1942) is a topical novel describing the effect of the Pearl Harbor attack and World War II on an Iowa farm family and their way of life. *Jessamy John* (1947) is a fictional presentation of John Law and the fabulous Mississippi Bubble. None of these later novels, all well-done pieces of fiction, has achieved great popularity or won critical acclaim; Stong remained for most readers the author of a single novel, *State Fair*.

In addition to these novels, Stong turned out a host of other volumes, including a number of books for children. One of them, *The Hired Man's Elephant* (1939), won the New York *Herald Tribune* prize for juvenile fiction in that year. Also in 1939 appeared Stong's study of the horse in America, *Horses and Americans*. Other non-fictional items include *Hawkeyes* (1940), a history of Iowa; *If School Keeps* (1940), an autobiographical volume; and *Marta of Muscovy* (1947), a biography of the wife of Peter the Great. Stong's last novel was *Return in August*, a sequel to *State Fair* which picks up Margy Drake twenty years after the first volume left her and her romance.

BIBLIOGRAPHICAL REFERENCES: For autobiographical material see Stong's *If School Keeps*, 1940. Elizabeth Rider Montgomery, *The Story Behind Modern Books*, 1949, is useful. The pamphlet, "*Buckskin Breeches* by Phil Stong, a Selection of the Discoverers," 1937, was reprinted as prefatory material in the limited edition of his *Buckskin Breeches*. See also Harry R. Warfel, *American Novelists of Today*, 1951.

HARRIET BEECHER STOWE

Born: Litchfield, Connecticut
Date: June 14, 1811

Died: Hartford, Connecticut
Date: July 1, 1896

PRINCIPAL WORKS

NOVELS: *Uncle Tom's Cabin, or Life Among the Lowly*, 1852; *Dred: A Tale of the Great Dismal Swamp*, 1856; *The Minister's Wooing*, 1859; *The Pearl of Orr's Island*, 1862; *Agnes of Sorrento*, 1862; *Oldtown Folks*, 1869; *Pink and White Tyranny*, 1871; *My Wife and I*, 1871; *We and Our Neighbors*, 1875; *Poganuc People*, 1878.

SHORT STORIES AND SKETCHES: *Sam Lawson's Oldtown Fireside Stories*, 1872.

TRAVEL SKETCHES: *Sunny Memories of Foreign Lands*, 1854.

Harriet (Elizabeth) Beecher Stowe presented two regional backgrounds in her fiction: the South before the Civil War and the rural area of New England (Maine). Her novels of the antebellum South, were less authentic as well as more melodramatic in style. They were more popular, however, because of the timeliness of their theme and the antislavery feeling they created.

Born in Litchfield, Connecticut, on June 14, 1811, Harriet Elizabeth Beecher was the daughter of a famous minister, the Reverend Lyman Beecher, and sister of Henry Ward Beecher.

She was educated in the school of her older sister Catherine, who encouraged her inclination to write. The family moved to Cincinnati when Harriet was eighteen. There she married Calvin Ellis Stowe, a professor in the Lane Theological Seminary, and spent eighteen years across the river from a slave state.

Uncle Tom's Cabin, written after the Stowes had moved to Maine, brought its author immediate worldwide fame. The literature of the period generally was influenced by a humanitarian impulse, and Mrs. Stowe had a ready audience for her romantic, even melodramatic history of the relations of a group of southern white families and their slaves. Of her material, she said, "Two nations, the types of two exactly opposite styles of existence, are here struggling; and from the intermingling of these two a third race has arisen, and the three are interlocked in wild and singular relations, that evolve every possible combination of romance." She added, "It is the moral bearings of the subject involved which have had the chief influence in its selection."

The success of her first novel encouraged Mrs. Stowe to write a second on the same theme. The Dred Scott decision, stating that the Negro is not a human being, served as the catalyst for *Dred*, a novel in which her purpose of showing the general corruption of Christian principles brought on by slavery remained the same. Attacked by the critics, like the first novel, for artistic faults, mainly those of artificiality of language, contrived plotting, and sentimental characterizations, the book was less popular than its predecessor.

Turning next to her New England background, Mrs. Stowe wrote four novels in a manner that did not increase her fame but did raise her position on the ground of literary merit. These novels were *The Minister's Wooing, The Pearl of Orr's Island, Oldtown Folks,* and *Poganuc People.* She also wrote society novels and in *Agnes of Sorrento* produced a didactic historical romance. Mrs. Stowe was the first writer to use New England dialect for the sake of realism, becoming a pioneer in the tradition of Mary E. Wilkins Freeman and Sarah Orne Jewett. But her constant interpolation of Christian aphorisms and her use of routine plots kept these novels on the level of conventional nineteenth century romance and local color fiction. A daughter of the transcendental period, she was the most famous sentimental novelist of her time. She died at Hartford, Connecticut, July 1, 1896.

BIBLIOGRAPHICAL REFERENCES: The collected edition is *The Writings of Harriet Beecher Stowe,* 16 vols., 1896. There are several authorized biographies: Annie A. Fields, *Life and Letters of Harriet Beecher Stow,* 1897; Charles E. Stowe, *Life of Harriet Beecher Stowe: Compiled from her Journals and Letters,* 1899; and Charles E. Stowe and Lyman Beecher Stowe, *Harriet Beecher Stowe: The Story of her Life,* 1911. There are two recent biographies: Catherine Gilbertson, *Harriet Beecher Stowe,* 1937; and Forrest Wilson, *Crusader in Crinoline: The Life of Harriet Beecher Stowe,* 1941—the most valuable single work. A useful critical study is Charles H. Foster, *The Rungless Ladder: Harriet Beecher Stowe and New England Puritanism,* 1954. See also Constance Rourke, *Trumpets of Jubilee,* 1927; and Jay B. Hubbell, *The South in American Literature,* 1954.

LYTTON STRACHEY

Born: London, England
Died: March 1, 1880

Died: Wiltshire, England
Date: January 21, 1932

PRINCIPAL WORKS

BIOGRAPHY: *Eminent Victorians,* 1918; *Queen Victoria,* 1921; *Elizabeth and Essex,* 1928; *Portraits in Miniature,* 1931.

ESSAYS AND STUDIES: *Landmarks in French Literature,* 1912; *Books and Characters, French and English,* 1922; *Characters and Commentaries,* 1933.

The new movement in biography as a literary form began in England with (Giles) Lytton Strachey as World War I came to an end. Its chief characteristic was debunking and its main flaw parochialism, but at his best Strachey managed to exude a maximum of the first with a minimum of the second. Born in London on March 1, 1880, Strachey came from a family distinguished in the army, the civil service, and literature. His mother, Lady Jane Strachey, was a respected essayist and an amateur student of French literature; Lionel Strachey, a cousin, had established a literary reputation in the United States; another cousin, John St. Loe Strachey, was the brilliant editor of the *Spectator* from 1898 to 1925, and his children, John Strachey and Mrs. Amabel Williams-Ellis, were both writers.

A delicate child of marked but rather special talents, Lytton Strachey was limited in his choice of profession. At Trinity College, Cambridge, he distinguished himself in his studies, composed verses, and won the Chancellor's Medal with his poem, "Ely." Fearing that he lacked true creative power, however, he dallied with literature in the critical essays which he wrote while living with his mother on an independent income. Almost feminine in outlook, he was sociable but catty. When aroused, usually by some sign of weakness in another, he became feline, verbally dissecting his victim. Eventually this habit was channelized into written sketches of the great and the near-great of the Victorian Age, and some of these were in turn published as *Eminent Victorians* in 1918. As biography, his style

was new to the English public but it caught their fancy and the book sold well. Actually Strachey had been strongly influenced by French biographers, especially Sainte-Beuve—his first publication was *Landmarks in French Literature* in 1912—and their naturalistic approach suited his predilection for accentuating the negative in personal relations. Bothered by his own physique, he laid emphasis on others' weak points, especially among the famous in politics or letters.

Consciously or not, he was effecting in his attitude a new realism to which his readers reacted, not in terms of scorn but rather with greater insight and sympathy. With flaws the sacrosanct Victorian figures became more human and thus more lovable. Especially true was this in the reaction to his *Queen Victoria.* While this biography was just as iconoclastic as the others in its portrait of the queen, the very style of the book, witty and concise, brought her to life as a woman as no similar work or public eulogy had ever done. Emphasizing personality rather than idea, he brought his subject down to the human level. His greatest popular success, *Elizabeth and Essex,* was the most obvious in its revelation that the author was judging the world by what was within himself, a man much different from what his exterior signified.

Never marrying, he moved with his mother to Bloomsbury, London, on a whim. By chance there were other literary people in the neighborhood, and they were welcomed at the Strachey home. Among them were

1036

Virginia Woolf and E. M. Forster. Though known later as the Bloomsbury Group, their only tie besides sociability was a desire to reveal the warm current of fallibility beneath the façade of conventionality in English life. Among the members of the so-called Bloomsbury Group Strachey found his spiritual home and his friends, who shared his interest in the excercise of clarity, restraint, and precision as the basis of literary style. These qualities are all apparent in the portrait gallery of minor, even obscure, figures whom Strachey presents in his *Portraits in Miniature*, the best book of his lifetime. He died on January 21, 1932, at Ham Spray House in Wiltshire, a country residence he had bought with his royalties from *Queen Victoria*.

BIBLIOGRAPHICAL REFERENCES: Lytton Strachey's books have been reprinted in the *Collected Works*, 6 vols., 1948. The standard biography is Charles Richard Sanders, *Lytton Strachey: His Mind and Art*, 1957. For biography and criticism see also Mark Longaker, *Contemporary Biography*, 1934; André Maurois, *Prophets and Poets*, 1935; Edgar Johnson, *One Mighty Torrent*, 1937; Cyril Clemens, *Lytton Strachey*, 1942; Max Beerbohm, *Lytton Strachey: The Rede Lecture*, 1943; George Carver, *Alms for Oblivion*, 1946; George Gordon, *The Lives of Authors*, 1950; also D. S. Mirsky, "Mr. Lytton Strachey," *London Mercury*, VIII (1923), 175–184; Desmond MacCarthy, "Lytton Strachey as a Biographer," *Life and Letters*, VIII (1932), 90–102; Vincent Sheean, "Lytton Strachey: Cambridge and Bloomsbury," *New Republic*, LXX (1932), 19–20; Guy Boas, "Lytton Strachey," *English Association Pamphlets*, No. 93, (1935); Leonard Bacon, "An Eminent Post-Victorian," *Yale Review* XXX (1941), 310–324; and Charles Richard Sanders, "Lytton Strachey's Conception of Biography," *Publications of the Modern Language Association*, LXVI (1951) 295–315.

AUGUST STRINDBERG

Born: Stockholm, Sweden
Date: January 22, 1849

Died: Stockholm
Date: May 14, 1912

PRINCIPAL WORKS

PLAYS: *Mäster Olof*, 1872–1881; *Lycko-Pers resa*, 1882 (*Lucky Peter's Travels*) *Fadren*, 1887 (*The Father*); *Fröken Julie*, 1888 (*Miss Julie*); *Komraterna*, 1888 (*The Comrades*); *Fordringsägare*, 1888 (*Creditors*); *Paria*, 1888–1889 (*Pariah*); *Den Starkare*, 1889 (*The Stronger*); *Bandet*, 1893 (*The Link*); *Till Damaskus*, I and II, 1898 (*To Damascus*); *Advent*, 1898; *Brott och Brott*, 1899 (*Crimes and Crimes*); *Gustavus Vasa*, 1899; *Erik XIV*, 1899; *Gustavus Adolphus*, 1900; *Påsk*, 1900 (*Easter*); *Kronbruden*, 1901 (*The Bridal Crown*); *Carl XII*, 1901; *Dödsdansen*, 1901 (*The Dance of Death*); *Svanevit*, 1901 (*Swanwhite*); *Ett Drömspel*, 1901 (*The Dream Play*); *Kristina*, 1903 (*Queen Christina*); *Till Damaskus*, III, 1904; *Spöksonaten*, 1907 (*The Spook Sonata*).

NOVELS: *Röda rummet*, 1879 (*The Red Room*); *Hemsöborna*, 1887 (*The Dwellers of Hemsö*); *Den romantiske klockaren på Rånö*, 1888 (*The Romantic Sexton of Rånö*); *I Havsbandet*, 1890 (*By the Open Sea*); *Fagervik och Skamsund*, 1902 (*Fairhaven and Foulstrand*); *Swarta Fanor*, 1904 (*Black Banners*).

SHORT STORIES: *Giftas*, I and II, 1886–1888 (*Married*).

August Strindberg, greatest of Swedish writers and one of the few real geniuses among modern dramatists, was born in Stockholm on January 22, 1849. He barely escaped illegitimacy, for his father, a bankrupt shipping agent, married his servant-mistress just before August's birth; three boys had been born before the marriage, and of the numerous children born later, four survived to crowd the tiny flat of the impoverished family. The over-sensitive boy was unhappy at home and unhappier at school, where he felt himself tormented because of his vulgar origins and where he was exasperated by a school system geared to the most stupid children. Upon the death of his mother, whom August idealized, his father married his young housekeeper, much to August's pain and humiliation.

At secondary school he was stimulated by the study of science, and to the end of his life he was a student of geology, astronomy, biology, and chemistry. He attended Uppsala University but was unhappy there, poor, lonely, confused. Leaving the university without taking a degree, he engaged in a bewildering series of activities, becoming at various times a teacher, a tutor, an actor, a journalist, a political radical, a landscape painter, a medical student, a playwright, a librarian, a Sinologist, a poet, a chemist, a novelist, and an autobiographer.

Most of all he was a dramatist who gradually attained fame over all Europe, though at home his genuine distinction was difficult for his compatriots to discern through the clouds of scandal surrounding his melodramatically unsuccessful marriages, the shocking notoriety resulting from his frankly autobiographical books, subjective novels, and short stories, and his bizarre conduct during periods of near-insanity and frightening religious mania. Although none of the many studies of Strindberg has succeeded in making him a completely understandable human being, nearly half a century after his death the "mad genius" strikes us more and more as a great genius, less and less as a madman. In fact, five years preceding his death, on May 14, 1912, Strindberg ended his Continental exile and again lived in Stockholm, where he was associated with an intimate theater for the presentation of his plays and where he became a respected public figure. But he was still frustrated and tormented in his search for certainty, and his literary record of volcanic adventures of mind and spirit made him a violent and controversial figure to the end.

Just how important a figure Strindberg is in modern drama no American or British critic can say with authority, largely because most of his plays have never been translated into English. (The translations are slowly being done, thanks to Bernard Shaw, who gave his Nobel Prize money for this purpose.) The consensus of critics is, however, that he is one of the greatest playwrights of the modern movement. A few, including the late Eugene O'Neill, consider him the greatest dramatic genius of the past century.

The sweep of his dramatic output is breathtaking: historical verse plays, fairy plays, romances, dozens of realistic and naturalistic plays, moralities, religious dramas, plays of complete cynicism and pessimism, and the earliest expressionistic plays. Not only was he far more versatile than any other modern playwright, but he attained distinction in every genre he attempted. The reader is sharply conscious of the dynamic intellect on every page of Strindberg. His plays, except for *The Father* and *Miss Julie,* are infrequently performed in America, although he is receiving increased attention in the more and more significant theaters off Broadway, where at least six of his plays were performed in 1956 and 1957.

Strindberg's historical and religious dramas and his social-reform or crusading plays have little interest for the British and American critics, who feel that Strindberg reached his full stature in his revolutionary naturalistic and expressionistic plays. The former reflect, if not a pathological misogyny, at least the most ferocious anti-feminism ever to appear in drama. *The Father, Comrades, The Dance of Death,* and *Creditors* have as their central theme the duel of the sexes, in each of which the woman is more unscrupulous, selfish, and conscienceless than the man. *The Father* is one of the most terrifying tragedies ever written, partly because Strindberg poured into it experience from his own shattered marriage, partly because there is no alleviation of hope, and partly because of the superb construction and swift tempo which sweep the playgoer or reader along in breathless horror to the tragic and cynical final curtain. Present in this work are echoes of Greek tragedy (the Omphale motif) and of Shakespeare (Iago cleverly planting the seeds of doubt), but *The Father* is modern in its sharp study of a crumbling mind. *The Com-*

rades is not a tragedy but is no less an intense expression of Strinberg's misogyny, his contempt for Ibsen's and Nora Helmer's ideal of marriage as a companionship of equals. To Strindberg, woman has neither the integrity nor the intelligence to succeed as a comrade or partner. *The Dance of Death* exploits the same theme, that the underside of love is hate and only tragedy can result from their inseparableness.

Almost as famous and well known as *The Father* is *Miss Julie,* a powerful story of an aristocratic girl who gives herself to an impudent, attractive servant and who in disgust takes her own life immediately afterward. Here Strindberg makes the man as odious as the woman, although Julie is somewhat more aggressive. *Miss Julie* is a classic naturalistic tragedy in its careful presentation of character as a product of heredity and environment.

Strindberg stands as the father of expressionistic drama, which was carried to its greatest success in Germany after World War I and which went into decline as a dramatic form in the 1930's. But echoes of expressionism are still heard in many modern plays, where its techniques have been utilized to some extent by O'Neill, Rice, Williams, Miller, Millar, Anouilh, Priestley, and others. *To Damascus* is the first real expressionistic drama. In it Strindberg abandoned traditional dramatic techniques in order to dramatize his own inferno of soul in his search for religious certainty. His other two great expressionistic dramas are *The Dream Play* and *The Spook Sonata.* This latter play Eugene O'Neill admired extravagantly, and its influence is to be found in a number of his plays.

BIBLIOGRAPHICAL REFERENCES: The collected works of Strindberg were edited by J. Landquist, 55 vols., 1911–1921. In translation, *Plays by August Strindberg*, 4 vols., 1912–1916, contains valuable introductions by Edwin Bjorkman. For biography and criticism see Nils Erdmann, *August Strindberg*, 1924; C. E. W. L. Dahlström, *Strindberg's Dramatic Expressionism*, 1930; V. J. McGill, *August Strindberg: The Bedeviled Viking*, 1930; A. Jolivet, *Le Théâtre de Strindberg*, 1931; G. A. Campbell, *Strindberg*, 1933; Martin Lamm, *August Strindberg*, 1942; Elizabeth Sprigge, *The Strange Life of August Strindberg*, 1949; Eugen Diem, *August Strindberg: Leben und Werk*, 1949; Maurice Gravier, *Strindberg et le théâtre moderne*, 1949; Karl Jaspers, *Strindberg und van Gogh*, 1949; Brita M. Mortensen and Brian W. Downs, *Strindberg: An Introduction to His Life and Work*, 1949; Nils Norman, *Den unge Strindberg och bäckelserörelsen*, 1953; also see John Gassner, *Masters of the Drama*, 1945; Eric Bentley, *The Playwright as Thinker*, 1946; and Barrett H. Clark and George Freedley, *A History of the Modern Drama*, 1947.

L. A. G. STRONG

Born: Plympton, Devonshire, England Died: Guilford, England
Date: March 8, 1896 Date: August 17, 1958

PRINCIPAL WORKS

NOVELS: *Dewer Rides*, 1929; *The Jealous Ghost*, 1930; *The Garden*, 1931; *The Brothers*, 1932; *Sea Wall*, 1933; *Corporal Tune*, 1934; *The Seven Arms*, 1935; *The Last Enemy*, 1936; *The Swift Shadow*, 1937; *Laughter in the West*, 1937; *The Open Sky*, 1939; *The Bay*, 1941; *Trevannion*, 1948; *The Hill of Howth*, 1953; *Deliverance*, 1955.

SHORT STORIES: *Doyle's Rock and Other Stories*, 1925; *The English Captain*, 1929; *The Big Man*, 1931; *Don Juan and the Wheelbarrow*, 1932; *Tuesday Afternoon*, 1935; *Sun on the Water*, 1940; *Travellers*, 1945; *Darling Tom*, 1952.

POEMS: *Dallington Rhymes*, 1919; *Dublin Days*, 1921; *Twice Four*, 1921; *Says the Muse to Me, Says She*, 1922; *Eight Poems*, 1923; *The Lowery Road*, 1923; *Seven*, 1924; *Difficult Love*, 1927; *At Glenan Cross*, 1928; *Northern Light*, 1930; *Selected Poems*, 1931; *March Evening*, 1932; *Call to the Swan*, 1936; *The Body's Imperfection*, 1957.

BIOGRAPHY: *The Minstrel Boy*, 1937; *John McCormack*, 1941; *Maude Cherrill*, 1950; *Dr. Quicksilver*, 1955.

CRITICISM AND BELLES-LETTRES: *Common Sense About Poetry*, 1932; *A Letter to W. B. Yeats*, 1932; *Life in English Literature*, 1932 (with Monica Redlich); *The Hansom Cab and the Pigeons*, 1935; *The Sacred River*, 1949; *The Writer's Trade*, 1953.

L(eonard) A(lfred) G(eorge) Strong was born, March 8, 1896, in Devonshire. Of three-fourths Irish descent, he spent part of his childhood in the vicinity of Dublin. Retaining stanch ties with his Irish Protestant heritage, he has drawn upon early memories in much of his fiction. He was educated on scholarships at Brighton College and at Wadham College, Oxford. Exempted from military service on account of disability, he began to teach at Summer Fields, a preparatory school near Oxford, in 1917. Here he remained twelve years; in 1930 he moved to London to devote his full time to writing. Interested in speech and its development, he has taught oral interpretation of drama and has broadcast for the B.B.C. In addition, owing apparently to his mixed cultural background, he has maintained an interest in regional dialects, expert knowledge of which he reveals in his poems of rustic life.

Strong became known first for his poems, some of which show affinities with the work of Hardy and the poet of Spoon River. His succinct lyric portrayals of provincial life express satire, pathos, and laughter of delight. Outstanding among his poems are "An Old Woman, Outside the Abbey Theatre," which is epigrammatically ironic in a manner worthy of Yeats, and "The Mad Woman of Punnet's Town," which depicts vitality and joy. After deciding to live by his writing, he concentrated in the main on works of prose; most of his novels, short stories, and essays have been published in rapid succession. As a novelist, he is at his best in treatments of rural domestic scenes. He excels in his realistic handling of conversation; his descriptive style tends to be somewhat dry. Of late years, he has written several crime stories, featuring the character of Ellis McKay, a Scotland Yard detective indifferently successful at solving cases by induction. In these short novels, Strong, like his friend Nicholas Blake (C. Day Lewis), holds to the British tradition of "playing fair" with the reader.

With the English public he has achieved great celebrity as the author of short stories; but, though many of these are available in collected editions, they seem to be little known in America. For the collection entitled *Travellers*, in 1945, Strong was awarded the James Tait Black Memorial Prize. His other works include juveniles and several penetrating critical studies, notably his study of James Joyce in *The Sacred River*.

BIBLIOGRAPHICAL REFERENCES: There is no extensive criticism of Strong and his work. See R. L. Mégroz, *Five Novelist Poets of Today*, 1933; and Dayton Kohler, "L. A. G. Strong," *Bookman*, LXXIII (1931), 570–575.

JESSE STUART

Born: W-Hollow, Riverton, Kentucky
Date: August 8, 1907

PRINCIPAL WORKS

NOVELS: *Trees of Heaven*, 1940; *Taps for Private Tussie*, 1943; *Foretaste of Glory*, 1946; *Hie to the Hunters*, 1950; *The Good Spirit of Laurel Ridge*, 1953.

SHORT STORIES: *Head o' W-Hollow*, 1936; *Men of the Mountains*, 1941; *Tales from the Plum Grove Hills*, 1946; *Clearing in the Sky*, 1950; *Plowshare in Heaven: Tales True and Tall from the Kentucky Hills*, 1958.

POEMS: *Man with a Bull-Tongue Plow*, 1934; *Album of Destiny*, 1944; *Kentucky Is My Land*, 1952.

AUTOBIOGRAPHY: *Beyond Dark Hills*, 1938; *The Thread That Runs So True*, 1949; *The Year of My Rebirth*, 1956.

JUVENILES: *Mongrel Mettle*, 1944; *The Beatinest Boy*, 1953; *A Penny's Worth of Character*, 1954; *Red Mule*, 1955.

"Kentucky is my land," says Jesse Stuart. His life and work make good his claim. Hill-born, he writes about his region with the assurance of one whose familiarity with a place and its people was bred in the bone. All this is as it should be. His forebears had been Kentuckians for generations: the Hiltons, rebels, Democrats, country preachers, lovers of book learning and bright colors, and the Stuarts, hardy fighters, Republicans, heavy drinkers, good workers, tellers of tales. Lustiest of the clan was old Mitch Stuart, the Civil War veteran and mountain feudist celebrated in "Elegy for Mitch Stuart," the first poem his grandson sold to a magazine of national circulation. From stories of these people and their mountain neighbors Jesse Stuart absorbed the background of folk wisdom, family legend, and community experience which gives his writing its local coloring and flavor.

A son of Mitchell and Martha (Hilton) Stuart, the unlettered but earthwise parents to whom he has paid tribute in his autobiographical studies, Jesse (Hilton) Stuart was born on August 8, 1907, in a one-room log cabin overlooking W-Hollow, near Riverton, Kentucky. He had his first schooling at nearby Plum Grove, but he never finished a complete term because he was needed to help with the clearing and cropping on the seven rented farms on which he lived as a boy. At the age of nine be began to hire out to the other farmers of the neighborhood for twenty-five cents a day. When he was eleven he left school, and for the next four years he harvested corn and worked on a paving gang in the summertime and cut timber in the winter. He entered the Greenup County High School when he was fifteen. During vacations throughout his high school years he took charge of the farm so that his father would be free to work for the C&O Railway. About the same time he discovered the poetry of Robert Burns and began to write poems of his own on whatever was at hand—scraps of paper, tobacco sacks, even poplar leaves. Restless after finishing school, he ran away with a carnival. Fired, he got a job as a blacksmith in a steel mill.

This experience convinced him that an education was more important than anything else. In 1926, with $30 he had saved, he went to Lincoln Memorial University at Harrogate, Tennessee. There he worked in the hay fields, in a rock quarry, and in the college kitchen to pay his fees. He ran track, edited the college paper, and wrote about 500 poems. Some of these were later printed in *Harvest of Youth* (1930), a book long out of print and now almost unavailable. Graduated in 1929, he went home and taught in public schools for two years before beginning graduate work at Vanderbilt University in 1931. After a dormitory fire destroyed his clothes, his thesis, some poems, and part of a novel, he managed to get along on one meal a day until the end of the session. He never rewrote his thesis and so failed to qualify for a degree, but he wrote a book-length term paper which his professor called "crudely written and yet beautiful, tremendous, and powerful." He returned to teaching, becoming superintendent of the Greenup County schools and later principal of McKell High School. In the early 1930's his crusade to improve the conditions of secondary education in his county made him a number of enemies, exposed him to physical violence, and involved him in thirty-two lawsuits; but in the end he and his backers won their fight. This is the story he has told in *The Thread That Runs So True.* His book of regional poems, *Man with a Bull-Tongue Plow* appeared in 1934, *Head o' W-Hollow,* a collection of short stories, two years later. In 1937 he went to Europe on a Guggenheim fellowship and in Scotland rewrote his Vanderbilt term paper, published in 1938 as *Beyond Dark Hills.* He married Naomi Deane Norris in 1939; they have one daughter, Jessica Jane. Their W-Hollow home, remodeled from an old house once rented by Mitchell Stuart, is part of a timbered farm covering 785 acres over which Jesse Stuart has tramped, worked, and hunted all his life. His longest period of time away from his homeplace came when, enlisting as an apprentice seaman early in 1944 and commissioned several months later, he served in the Naval Reserve during World War II.

Jesse Stuart's writing is never far away from the poetry with which he began. *Man with a Bull-Tongue Plow,* a collection of 703 sonnets re-creating in lyric language and mood the Kentucky landscape in all lights and seasons and bringing roaringly to life his people of the hills, has been followed by two more books of poems, *Album of Destiny* and *Kentucky Is My Land.* In his prose the same poet's imagination blends with the realist's sharp eye and the gusty, tall story humor of the fabulist. There is a sense in which Stuart's early novels and short stories mark the late flowering of an old tradition in American literature rather than the beginning of a new one. Certainly his talent for anecdote and character drawing goes back through Mark Twain, the Sut Lovingood papers, and

Augustus Longstreet's *Georgia Scenes* to the anonymous frontier storytellers who in comic elaborations of character and drawling reminiscence dramatized the pioneer experience with shrewd appraisal and salty enjoyment. *Trees of Heaven* is filled with tags of frontier realism and rough humor in its account of the grudge fight between settler and squatter as personified by patriarchal Anse Bushman and shiftless Boliver Tussie. *Taps for Private Tussie,* winner of the Thomas Jefferson Southern Award in 1943, tells what happens after the same Tussie clan comes into $10,000 of government insurance money when soldier Kim Tussie is reported killed overseas. *Mongrel Mettle,* which goes back to the manner of the old beast fables, has a dog for its central figure. Although it was written as a book for younger readers, adults continue to read it as folk allegory. *Foretaste of Glory* deals with the agitation caused in a small Kentucky town by a prophecy that the world will end in September, 1941. *Hie to the Hunters* is the story of a city boy who finds a new life among the fox hunters and tobacco growers of the hill country. If this novel and *The Good Spirit of Laurel Ridge* seem more restrained in treatment and style than Stuart's earlier fiction, the reason is that the patterns of mountain life are in a process of change. Paved roads, the automobile, good schools, radio, the movies, and two world wars have brought urban ways into the hills; Jesse Stuart's books are a documentation of this transition. The same shift in emphasis and tone may be traced through his four collections of short stories and his recent tales for younger readers.

Always in demand as a lecturer,

Jesse Stuart had just concluded a talk before a college audience at Murray, Kentucky, in October, 1954, when he was stricken with a coronary occlusion. Part autobiography, part regional chronicle, *The Year of My Rebirth* tells the story of his gradual recovery. Late in his convalescence he received a tribute of affection and respect from his friends and neighbors in Greenup County. October 15, 1955, was proclaimed Jesse Stuart Day by the governor of the state and at Greenup a monument honoring him as poet, novelist, and educator was unveiled in recognition of this writer whose books have given shape and life to the Kentucky hills.

BIBLIOGRAPHICAL REFERENCES: Jesse Stuart's three autobiographical books are valuable for the outline of his life and the light they throw on his background and personality. For brief biographical and critical studies see Harry R. Warfel, *American Novelists of Today*, 1951; Charlotte Salmon, "Jesse Stuart," *Southwest Review*, XXI (1936), 163–168; Dayton Kohler, "Jesse Stuart and James Still: Mountain Regionalists," *College English*, III (1942), 523–533; Marguerite Shelburne, "Jesse Stuart, Young Man of the Mountains," *Holland's*, LXVI (December, 1947), 8–9; and William D. Moore, "Jesse H. Stuart, Teacher," *Educational Forum*, XXI (1956), 75–80.

HERMANN SUDERMANN

Born: Matziken, East Prussia
Date: September 30, 1857

Died: Berlin, Germany
Date: November 21, 1928

PRINCIPAL WORKS

NOVELS: *Frau Sorge*, 1887 (*Dame Care*); *Der Katzensteg*, 1889 (*Regina*); *Das hohe Lied*, 1908 (*The Song of Songs*); *Der tolle Professor*, 1926 (*The Mad Professor*); *Die Frau des Steffen Tromholt*, 1927 (*The Wife of Steffen Tromholt*); *Purzelchen*, 1928 (*The Dance of Youth*).

PLAYS: *Die Ehre*, 1889 (*Honor*); *Sodoms Ende*, 1891 (*The Man and His Picture*); *Heimat*, 1893 (*Magda*); *Die Schmetterlingsschlacht*, 1895 (*The Battle of the Butterflies*); *Das Glück im Winkel*, 1895 (*The Vale of Content*); *Morituri*, 1896; *Die drei Reiherfedern*, 1899 (*The Three Herons' Feathers*); *Johannisfeuer*, 1900 (*The Fires of St. John*); *Sturmgeselle Sokrates*, 1903; *Stein unter Steinen*, 1905.

SHORT STORIES: *Im Zwielicht*, 1886; *Geschwister*, 1888; *Die Reise nach Tilsit*, 1917 (*The Excursion to Tilsit*).

AUTOBIOGRAPHY: *Das Bilderbuch meiner Jugend*, 1922 (*Book of My Youth*).

Hermann Sudermann, German novelist and playwright, regarded during his lifetime as one of Germany's great modern dramatists, was born on September 30, 1857, the son of a brewer who worked in the village of Heydekrug. The Sudermann family was Mennonite and from Holland; an ancestor was Daniel Sudermann (1550–1632), a moralistic writer. Hermann Sudermann's birthplace, Matziken, in East Prussia, was a village where German and Lithuanian elements were mixed, and it was from the rich local strain of folk tales and customs that he was able to draw late in his career in order to put new life into his work.

He received his early education at

1044

the Realschule in Elbing, but as a result of his family's near-poverty he was compelled to go to work at the age of fourteen as apprentice to a chemist. He then entered the Realgymnasium in Tilsit. His advanced education was received at the university in Königsberg, where he studied philology and history, and at the University of Berlin. While in Berlin, to which he came at the age of twenty, he was tutor of the children of Hans von Hopfen (1835–1904), a writer by whom Sudermann was to some extent influenced in his own creative work.

In 1881 and 1882 Sudermann was an editor of *Deutsches Reichsblatt,* a political journal. At the time his political views were fairly liberal, but after leaving the editorship he became increasingly conservative; he was later charged with allowing considerations of royalties to affect his political convictions.

His writing career began with the writing of short stories, and a first collection, *Im Zwielicht,* appeared in 1886. The following year saw the publication of *Dame Care,* a sentimental example of German romanticism, but skillful enough in its portrayal of persons of various classes to make it one of Sudermann's most successful novels. Neither this book nor *Regina* achieved popular recognition until after the overwhelming reception accorded to his play *Honor,* which opened at the Lessing Theatre in Berlin on November 27, 1889. The play had originally been intended as a tragedy, but following the advice of others Sudermann gave it a happy ending which satisfied the audiences that first saw it. *Honor* shows the influence of Nietzsche on Sudermann; the play is in effect a pseudo-intellectual attack on the mo-

rality of the lower classes. With this play Sudermann's highly successful career as a dramatist was launched, and his novels suddenly began to sell in considerable numbers.

Magda, another successful drama, made Sudermann's name known all over Europe, and the play became a favorite vehicle for the leading actresses of the day: Bernhardt, Mrs. Campbell, Duse, and Modjeska. Sudermann wrote his plays at a fortunate time, and he was careful to achieve the kind of technical finish that would make them popular; consequently, although he enjoyed considerable fame for a number of years and was ranked with Gerhart Hauptmann, his plays lost favor when the fashion changed, and neither the audiences nor the critics seemed to care. Sudermann, concentrating on the novel during the last few years of his life, managed to produce enough satisfactory work to establish himself as an important novelist.

The play, *The Man and His Picture,* like *St. John's Fire* provided some critics with evidence to support their claim that Sudermann was a writer with an honest social conscience, that he was freeing German drama from the French influence and replacing romanticism with naturalism. However, Sudermann's portrayals of the vicious social life of fashionable Berlin never quite succeeded in losing the drawing-room comedy touch; perhaps the very features which accounted for his quick success were also accountable for the decline of interest in his plays. Of his novels, *Dame Care* and *The Song of Songs* are now generally regarded as his best, and the short stories in *The Excursion to Tilsit* contain much of his best writing.

Sudermann lived in a villa at Grunewald, a suburb of Berlin, and at his castle at Blankensee, near Trebbin, which he purchased from play royalties. He was married in 1891 to Klara Schultz Lauckner, a widow and a writer. He died in Berlin on November 21, 1928.

BIBLIOGRAPHICAL REFERENCES: For biography and criticism see K. Busse, *Hermann Sudermann, sein Wesen und sein Werke*, 1927; and Irmgard Leux, *Hermann Sudermann*, 1931; also Alfred Kerr, *Das neue Drama*, I, 1917; and E. Feise, "Stilverwirrung in Sudermann's 'Frau Sorge,'" *Germanic Review*, V (1930), 225–237.

EUGÈNE SUE

Born: Paris, France
Date: January 20, 1804

Died: Annecy, France
Date: August 3, 1857

PRINCIPAL WORKS

NOVELS: *Les Mystères de Paris*, 1842–1843 (*The Mysteries of Paris*); *Le Juif errant*, 1844–1845 (*The Wandering Jew*).

Born in Paris on January 20, 1804, Eugène Sue, whose real name was Marie Joseph Sue, was the son of a distinguished surgeon who had served with Napoleon's armies. At his baptism, Sue's sponsors were Prince Eugène Beauharnais and the Empress Joséphine; it was his godfather's name that Sue adopted as part of his pseudonym. Educated at private schools in Paris, he later studied medicine and became a surgeon. From 1823 to 1829 he served aboard ships of the French Navy as a naval surgeon, taking part in the French campaign against Spain in 1823 and in the battle of Navarino in 1828. At his father's death Sue inherited a large fortune and retired from the navy. Returning to Paris, he became a fashionable young man-about-town, but the life bored him and he turned to writing as an outlet for his energies.

Sue is reputed to have become a novelist by accident when an editor outlined a novel of the sea and suggested that Sue was the man to write the book because of his experience in the navy. *Plick et Plock* (1831) was the first of a series of sea novels which brought him critical praise as "the French James Fenimore Cooper." Sainte-Beuve, the eminent French critic, claimed that Sue was the first Frenchman to exploit the sea for French literature and the first author to make use of the Mediterranean Sea for literature. Anxious to become a serious man of letters, Sue turned to writing historical works, including a history of the French Navy (1837) in five volumes. He then wrote historical romances, the two best-known being *Jean Cavalier* (1840) and *Latréaumont* (1837).

His most famous novels, *The Mysteries of Paris* and *The Wandering Jew* resulted from his interest in social problems. The former, taking the reader through episodes of lower-class and underworld Paris, presented the social misery Sue saw in his city; his attempts at reform were comparable to those of Dickens in England at the time. In *The Wandering Jew*, Sue attempted to allegorize in the wretched man doomed to wander for centuries the long, weary journey of humanity in its search for just social structures. Although both novels are long and rambling, they illustrate the writer's ability to combine dramatic episodes with moral earnestness. Extremely popular in France, the books were also circulated widely in translation. A later work of moral earnestness, though never popular, was *Les Sept péchés capitaux* (1847–1849, *The Seven Cardinal Sins*), with stories illustrating each of the sins.

After the revolution of 1848, Sue stood for a seat in the French assembly representing Paris. He served in that chamber until the *coup d'état* of 1851 aroused his opposition and he went to live in exile in Haute-Savoie. He died there on August 3, 1857.

BIBLIOGRAPHICAL REFERENCES: Recent biographical and critical studies are Paul Ginisty, *Eugène Sue*, 1929; and N. Atkinson, *Eugène Sue et le roman-feuilleton*, 1929. A contemporary literary portrait is that by Eugène de Mirecourt, 1855.

GAIUS SUETONIUS TRANQUILLUS

Born: Britain (?)
Date: c. 70

Died: Rome (?), Italy
Date: c. 140

PRINCIPAL WORKS

BIOGRAPHY AND HISTORY: *De viris illustribus*, 106–113 (*Concerning Illustrious Men*); *De vita Caesarum*, c. 120 (*Lives of the Caesars*).

Since his father was military tribune of the XIII Legion, Gaius Suetonius Tranquillus may have been born in Britain or Africa about A.D. 70. He studied in Rome and became a lawyer and teacher of rhetoric. Part of his *De grammaticis* still exists. He also traveled widely. He accompanied Governor Pliny (The Younger) to Bithynia in 112. He also served for a time (119–121) as private secretary to Emperor Hadrian, but lost favor apparently for inattention to the empress while Hadrian was in Britain.

Suetonius' fame rests on his historical biographies of famous men. He collected anecdotes about figures in the public eye and set them down with more attention to their interest than to their accuracy. So he was a chronicler, rather than a historian. He made no attempt at general impression or psychological interpretation, but his stories about Horace and Terence, among other famous men, and his private lives of the twelve Caesars cover ground untouched by any contemporary except Tacitus and Dio Cassius. Many later biographers have taken him as a model. It is believed that he died in Rome about 140.

BIBLIOGRAPHICAL REFERENCES: A translation reissued many times is Philemon Holland, *The History of Twelve Caesars*, 1606 (rev. eds., 1923, 1931). More recent translations include Alexander Thomson, *Lives of the Twelve Caesars*, 1901 (rev. ed., 1914); and J. C. Rolfe, *Suetonius*, 2 vols., 1914. See also D. H. Stuart, *Epochs of Greek and Roman Biography*, 1928.

ROBERT SMITH SURTEES

Born: Northumberland, England
Date: May 17, 1803

Died: Brighton, England
Date: March 16, 1864

PRINCIPAL WORKS

NOVELS: *Jorrocks' Jaunts and Jollities,* 1838; *Handley Cross, or the Spa Hunt,* 1843, 1854; *Hillingdon Hall, or the Cockney Squire,* 1845; *Hawbuck Grange, or the Sporting Adventures of Thomas Scott, Esq.,* 1847; *Mr. Sponge's Sporting Tour,* 1853; *Ask Mamma, or the Richest Commoner in England,* 1858; *Plain or Ringlets?* 1860; *Mr. Facey Romford's Hounds,* 1865.

TECHNICAL AND SPORTING MANUALS: *The Horseman's Manual,* 1831; *The Analysis of the Hunting-Field,* 1846.

Like Anthony Trollope, Robert Smith Surtees re-created in his novels a limited but significant phase of the social milieu of his time. The world of his fiction, although small, is admirably self-contained and complete in every detail within its boundaries of the kennel and the stable, the hunting fields and the drawing rooms of the English squirearchy. Against this background he presented a cross section of Victorian society: the aristocracy entrenched behind barriers of caste and privilege, the new middle class trying to rise above its origins in trade, tuft-hunters and amiable blackguards aping the gentry and living at the expense of their social betters, sturdy yeoman farmers, the laboring tenantry, comic yokels. These people fill a series of sporting novels lively with humor and pungent with that flavor of satire which was Surtees' master bias as a writer.

Descended from an ancient country family that took its name from the River Tees, Robert Smith Surtees was born at The Riding, Northumberland, on May 17, 1803. His boyhood was spent at Hamsterley Hall, near Durham, a seventeenth century manor bought by his father in 1810. A younger son without prospects of in-heritance, he was educated at Ovingham School and at the Durham Grammar School, and in 1822 was articled to a solicitor at Newcastle-on-Tyne in preparation for a career in law. Three years later he transferred to the office of another solicitor in Bow Churchyard, London. Admitted in Chancery in 1828, he abandoned law for journalism a year later and became a hunting correspondent for the *Sporting Magazine.* His first book, combining his knowledge of law with his interest in sport, was *The Horseman's Manual,* published in 1831. In the same year his older brother died and Surtees became the heir to Hamsterley, a change of fortune which probably influenced his decision to join Rudolph Ackermann in founding the *New Sporting Magazine,* which he edited until 1836. For the third issue of the magazine, in July, 1831, he wrote the first of the humorous sketches dealing with John Jorrocks, the sporting Cockney grocer of Great Coram Street. This series, continued until September, 1834, proved so popular that the publishing house of Chapman and Hall planned a similar miscellany which resulted in Dickens' *Pickwick Papers.* Opposed to repeal of the Corn Laws, Surtees stood unsuccessfully for Parliament in 1837.

Following his father's death in 1838, he returned to Hamsterley to lead the life of a country landlord and hunting squire. He married in 1841 and in the following year was appointed a justice of the peace and deputy lieutenant for Durham County. He was also for a time a major in the Durham Militia, an experience he later satirized in his account of the Heavysteed Dragoons. He became high sheriff of Durham County in 1856.

A shy, unsentimental, taciturn man, Surtees, after *The Horseman's Manual,* would not allow his name to be used in connection with his books. Published anonymously, the Jorrocks sketches were collected in 1838 as *Jorrocks' Jaunts and Jollities, or the Hunting, Shooting, Racing, Driving, Sailing, Eating, Eccentric and Extravagant Exploits of that Renowned Sporting Citizen, Mr. John Jorrocks of St. Botolph Lane and Great Coram Street.* On its appearance the book was completely eclipsed by the greater popularity of *Pickwick Papers,* which had been published a year before, so much so that friendly critics were forced to defend the author of *Jorrocks' Jaunts and Jollities* against charges of plagiarism. The third edition of 1843 contained the fifteen colored plates by Henry Alken which have become the familiar illustrations of this humorous classic. The adventures of Jorrocks were continued in *Handley Cross,* also published in 1843 but not expanded to its full proportions until 1854. This book, now considered Surtees' masterpiece, received little attention at the time; the reappearance of Jorrocks as a Master of Fox Hounds gave Surtees every opportunity to ridicule social snobbery and the idea that fox hunting was a fashionable sport to be enjoyed only by the rich, and a snobbish age repaid him with its neglect. Jorrocks made his last appearance in *Hillingdon Hall,* where as a country squire he was allowed to voice Surtees' own views on agriculture and reform. The election of his hero to Parliament at the end of the novel hints that Surtees may have intended to continue the series with an account of the Cockney grocer in politics. If so, the plan was abandoned. Instead, *Hillingdon Hall* was followed in 1846 by *The Analysis of the Hunting-Field,* a collection of sporting sketches of a rather technical nature, and in 1847 by *Hawbuck Grange.*

Surtees' first real success came in 1853 with *Mr. Sponge's Sporting Tour.* Here is the ancient rogue story transformed into a satirical comedy of manners, with a cast that includes aristocratic bores and wastrels, ambitious social climbers, dishonest horse dealers, patronizing masters of hounds, the raggle-taggle of the army and the stage. This was the first of Surtees' books to be illustrated by John Leech, whose drawings for *Mr. Sponge* and later novels are almost as familiar as the author's text. The novel had been serialized in the *New Monthly Magazine,* edited by William Harrison Ainsworth. Ainsworth, anxious to print another work by Surtees, had contracted for the publication of *Young Tom Hall, his Heartbreaks and Horses.* Before many installments had appeared, however, Ainsworth printed an advertisement giving Surtees' name as the author of the new serial. Surtees was angry and Ainsworth tactless; as a result Surtees stopped work on the novel, which promised to be one of his best. Although the book was never completed, it was not a total loss: *Ask*

Mamma and *Plain or Ringlets?* contain a few characters and several episodes he was able to salvage for later use. After *Handley Cross* and *Mr. Sponge's Sporting Tour* these novels are decidedly inferior and reveal too plainly the patchwork of their design. But Surtees was once more at his best in *Mr. Facey Romford's Hounds,* a comic hunting novel and sly satire in which Mr. Sponge and Lucy Glitters, his actress wife, reappear. Surtees did not live to see his last novel in print. At work on an autobiographical work to be called *Sporting and Social Recollections,* he and his wife had gone to Brighton for a short holiday. He died there on March 16, 1864.

Surtees is not one of the eminent Victorians. His field was limited and he had no imagination for anything which lay outside his own experience. But he knew the town as well as the country, and he had seen the agricultural England of his youth transformed by the development of the railway and the growth of factories. Writing of these things, he became what most of the major Victorians, except Thackeray, were not, a social historian and a novelist of manners. His true genius, however, was in creating the comic character; among English novelists he is second only to Dickens in this respect. Jorrocks, in the gallery of great humorous characters, stands only a notch or two below Falstaff, Parson Adams, Mr. Pickwick, and Mr. Micawber. Mr. Sponge and Facey Romford are rogues, but their vulgarity and cunning point to the underlying spirit of an age.

BIBLIOGRAPHICAL REFERENCES: There are several modern editions of Surtees; the most recent, although not definitive, is that issued by the Folio Society, 9 vols., 1949–1956, with reproductions of the original hand-colored illustrations by Leech, Alken, and Hublot K. Browne. *Robert Smith Surtees: Scenes and Characters* is a book of selections edited by Cyril Ray, 1948.

There is no authorized biography. E. D. Cumings, *Robert Smith Surtees, Creator of 'Jorrocks,'* 1924, contains an autobiographical sketch. Later biographical and critical studies include Frederick Watson, *Robert Smith Surtees,* 1933; and Leonard Cooper, *R. S. Surtees,* 1952. See also Hugh S. Gladstone, *Shooting with Surtees,* 1928; F. J. Harvey Darton, *From Surtees to Sassoon,* 1931; Anthony Steel, *Jorrocks' England,* 1932; Una Pope-Hennessy, *Durham Company,* 1941; G. G. French, *John Jorrocks and Other Characters,* 1947; Moira O'Neill, "Some Novels by Surtees," *Blackwood's,* CXCIII (1913), 535–542, and "The Author of 'Jorrocks,'" *Blackwood's,* CCXC (1924), 857–868; W. C. Rivers, "The Place of Robert Smith Surtees," *London Mercury,* X (1924), 605–613; John Shand, "Squire Surtees," *Atlantic Monthly,* CLXXV (January, 1945), 91–96; and Robert L. Collison, "Robert Smith Surtees: Satirist and Sociologist," *Nineteenth Century Fiction,* VII (1952), 202–207.

EMANUEL SWEDENBORG

Born: Stockholm, Sweden
Date: January 29, 1688

Died: London, England
Date: March 29, 1772

PRINCIPAL WORKS

SCIENTIFIC TREATISES: *Opera philosophica et mineralia,* 1734 (*Philosophical and Scientific Works*).

RELIGIOUS TREATISES: *Arcana Coelestia,* 1749–1756 *(Heavenly Secrets); Heaven and Hell,* 1758; *Divine Love and Wisdom,* 1763; *The True Christian Religion,* 1771.

Emanuel Swedenborg was born Emanuel Swedberg—at Stockholm, January 29, 1688—the son of Dr. Jesper Swedberg, professor of theology at the University of Uppsala and Bishop of Skara who, raised to the rank of the nobility for services to the Swedish crown, later changed his name to Swedenborg. By Swedenborg's own account, his childhood was unusual in that he spent much time in spiritual thought and in conversation with clergymen on matters of faith. He attended the University of Uppsala, taking his degree in 1709. He then traveled in England, Holland, France, and Germany before returning to Sweden in 1715. During his travels he studied wherever he went, and upon his return he entered Uppsala once again to study science and engineering. Charles XII of Sweden, who had become a friend and admirer of Swedenborg, appointed him assessor on the Swedish board of mines, a post Swedenborg filled until 1747 and for which he received a salary for the rest of his life. In 1724, Swedenborg was offered a post as professor of mathematics at Uppsala, but he declined, saying he did not wish to be limited to theorizing. Prior to 1720, Swedenborg had published a volume of Latin verse and more than twenty treatises on scientific and mechanical subjects. The scientific works prior to 1721 were largely in Swedish, but the later writings, regardless of subject, were written in Latin. Most of Swedenborg's works were published outside Sweden, the arrangements being made during his many trips abroad. His first major work in philosophy and theology was the

Principia, which was one volume in the three-volume *Philosophical and Scientific Works,* published in 1734. In the same year he published *Prodromus philosophiae ratiocinantis de infinito et causa finali creationis,* a work dealing with the relations of the finite to the infinite and the body to the soul. During the next few years Swedenborg turned his attention to anatomy, hoping to find the seat of the soul. Two works on anatomy resulted from his studies. These works, to which little attention was paid, anticipated many modern physiological theories.

In addition to being a scientist, Swedenborg was a mystic. According to his report, he experienced God on three occasions between 1743 and 1745. During the third of the spiritual experiences Swedenborg, according to his own account, was called upon to reveal what he called the "Doctrine of the New Jerusalem." He then turned his energies to religious inquiry, dividing his time between stays in Sweden, England, and Holland while he wrote works of Biblical interpretation and oversaw their publication. Among the important books of this period was *Heavenly Secrets,* an eight-volume work giving a revealed interpretation of the Bible. *Heaven and Hell* describes the future of mankind after death. *The Last Judgment* (1758) tells of a mystical experience in which God revealed to Swedenborg a vision of doomsday. The last of many theological works from Swedenborg's hand was *The True Christian Religion,* in which he set forth his New Church doctrines. Although he did not found a sect or attempt to do so, later adherents to his doctrines did form a sect of their own, the New Jerusalem Church.

Swedenborg died on March 29, 1772,

while on one of his visits to England. Temporarily buried in London, his body was later removed and interred in a place of honor in the cathedral at Uppsala.

BIBLIOGRAPHICAL REFERENCES: The Swedenborg bibliography is extensive. For biography and commentary see R. L. Tafel, *Documents Concerning the Life and Character of Emanuel Swedenborg*, 3 vols., 1875–1877; M. Lann, *Swedenborg*, 1915, and *Upplysningstidens Romantik*, 1918–1920; E. Kleen, *Swedenborg*, 1917–1919; George Trobridge, *Swedenborg: His Life, Teaching and Influence*, 1918; *Letters and Memorials of Emanuel Swedenborg*, translated and edited by Alfred Acton, 1948; Signe Toksvig, *Emanuel Swedenborg, Scientist and Mystic*, 1948; and C. S. Sigstedt, *The Swedenborg Epic: The Life and Works of Emanuel Swedenborg*, 1952. See also James Hyde, *A Bibliography of the Works of Emanuel Swedenborg*, 1897.

JONATHAN SWIFT

Born: Dublin, Ireland   *Died:* Dublin
Date: November 30, 1667   *Date:* October 19, 1745

PRINCIPAL WORKS

SATIRICAL FICTION: *A Tale of a Tub*, 1704; *Travels into Several Remote Nations of the World . . . by Lemuel Gulliver*, 1726 [*Gulliver's Travels*].

ESSAYS AND TRACTS: *A Discourse on the Dissensions between the Nobles and Commons in Athens and Rome*, 1701; *The Battle of the Books*, 1704; *The Sentiments of a Church of England Man*, 1708; *An Argument against Abolishing Christianity*, 1708; *A Project for the Advancement of Religion*, 1709; *The Conduct of the Allies*, 1711; *The Public Spirit of the Whigs*, 1714; *The Drapier Letters*, 1724; *A Modest Proposal for Preventing the Children of Poor People of Ireland from Being a Burden to Their Parents*, 1729.

POEMS: *Petition to Frances*, 1700; *Miscellanies*, 1708–1711; *Cadenus and Vanessa*, 1713; *On Poetry: A Rhapsody*, 1733; *Verses on the Death of Dr. Swift, Written by Himself*, 1739.

Jonathan Swift, with perhaps the keenest mind and sharpest tongue in an age marked by intellectual brilliance, was a mass of contradictions. Dedicated to the ideals of rationality and common sense, he approached the irrational in his contempt for man's failure to live up to his ideal; profoundly distrustful of all "enthusiasm" or fanaticism, he was himself something of an enthusiast in his glorification of "pure reason"; possessed of one of the clearest and most direct styles in the English language, the subtleties of his irony were misunderstood in his own and later ages.

Although biographical details will never adequately explain either the genius or the contradictions of a man life Swift, the combination of extreme pride and a position of dependence on the favors of the rich or powerful does throw some light on the persistent dissatisfaction with life as it is that colors almost all his work. Born in Dublin on November 30, 1667, the son of an impecunious Englishman who had settled in Ireland, Swift was educated at Trinity College with the aid of a wealthy uncle. In 1688 he left Ireland and became secretary to Sir William Temple at Moor Park, Surrey. Temple was not a congenial master, and Swift chafed to be independent in the more exciting world of London. It was the cultured Sir William, however, who gave polish to the somewhat uncouth young man, and introduced him into his own world of wit and polite learning, and it was in his behalf that Swift entered the controversy over the relative merits of the "ancients" and the "moderns" in his *Battle of the Books*. In this brilliant example of neo-classical mock-heroic prose, Swift pours out his contempt on the self-righteous complacency of modern criticism and poetry. During this same period (1696–1698) Swift, on his own behalf, wrote *A Tale of a Tub*, a burlesque history of the Church in which his genius first revealed itself in its full force. Just as important as his tale of the degradation of the Church through selfishness and fanaticism are the numerous digressions on moral, philosophical, and literary subjects. It was also at Moor Park that Swift first met Esther Johnson, possibly Temple's illegitimate daughter, the "Stella" of his later life.

In 1694, dissatisfied with Moor Park, Swift returned to Ireland, where he was ordained an Anglican priest, but after a dreary year in an Irish parish he was back in England. Between 1708 and 1714 he was in London, and during that period he achieved his greatest triumphs, social, literary, and political. He quickly became familiar with the literary lights of the age, Steele, Addison, Pope, Gay, and Arbuthnot. He wrote pieces for Steele's *Tatler*, and entered Church controversies with such essays as his brilliantly ironic *Argument to prove that the Abolishing of Christianity in England, may . . . be Attended with some inconveniences* In 1710, partly from hopes of personal advancement, and partly through a passionate interest in defending the prerogatives of the Church, Swift switched his allegiance from the Whig to the Tory party. This move won him the enmity of Whigs such as Addison and Steele, but gained him even more powerful friends in Robert Harley and Henry St. John, leaders of the new Tory ministry. Swift's political writing, in the Tory *Examiner* (which he edited briefly, from 1710–1711) and in pamphlets attacking Robert Walpole and the Duke of Marlborough, was a powerful aid to the Tory administration in its attempts to discredit the Whig "war party." For his untiring labors Swift hoped, and expected, to be rewarded with ecclesiastical preferment, perhaps a bishopric. But the memories of men who have risen to high places are notoriously short. Finally, in 1713, Swift was made Dean of St. Patrick's Cathedral, Dublin—virtually exiled from England. When the Tory ministry collapsed in 1714, all hope ended, and Swift returned to Ireland for good, disillusioned and bitter. Probably the best picture of Swift's mind during this period of political writing, as well as of the behind-the-scenes intrigue of London politics, is to be found in the charming and frank letters which make up the *Journal to Stella* (1766–1768), his correspondence with his protégée and friend, Esther Johnson. This was also the period in which Esther Vanhomrigh, whom he had met in London, followed him to Ireland. The "Vanessa" of his poem *Cadenus and Vanessa,* she died in 1723.

Bitter as he was, Swift's energy and wit could not long be stifled, and he turned his talents to defending Irish political and economic interests against the English. In such pamphlets as *The Drapier's Letters,* in which he protests against the circulation of debased coinage in Ireland, or his ironic masterpiece, *A Modest Proposal,* in which he suggests that for the Irish to sell their infants as food is their only defense against economic starvation by England, Swift not only continued his war with the Whig administration, but won the love and respect of all Ireland. During this period (1721–1725), he also worked intermittently on his greatest and best-known work, *Travels into Several Remote Nations of the World,* better known to us today as *Gulliver's Travels.*

Gulliver's Travels, Swift's final word on man and human nature, is a witty and at times vitriolic comment on man's abuse and perversion of his God-given reason. Books I and II, the account of voyages to Lilliput and Brobdingnag, deal with the corruption of practical reason, as it operates in the social and political worlds. Books III and IV are concerned with theoretical reason, either in its misuse, as among the Laputans or in the Academy of Lagado, or in its ideal application among the Houyhnhnms. Swift's brutal characterization of man as a despicable Yahoo (Book IV) has led many readers to feel that the intensity of his misanthropy destroys the validity of his work as satire. But bitter as Swift was at man's failure to live up to his ideal of rationality and common sense, the very fact that he wrote *Gulliver's Travels* suggests his recognition of the existence of such a goal, or at least his hope that man could be stimulated to reach it. For those who can rise above the smug satisfaction of having read *Gulliver's Travels* as a children's classic, Swift's satire and irony can scarcely help producing a serious re-evaluation of the principles by which we live.

Swift's health had never been good, and by 1740 mental decay had seriously weakened his mind. In 1742 guardians were appointed for him since he was on the verge of insanity. He died in Dublin on October 19, 1745.

BIBLIOGRAPHICAL REFERENCES: The basic edition is the Dublin edition of the *Works,* published by George Faulkner, 4 vols., 1735, with later editions edited by John Hawkesworth, 12 vols., 1755; Sir Walter Scott, 19 vols., 1814; and Temple Scott, Bohn Classical Library, 12 vols., 1897–1908. The standard modern edition of the *Prose Works* is in preparation by Herbert Davis, 1939 ff. The *Poems* have been edited by Harold Williams, 3 vols., 1937. There are three important collections of letters: Swift's *Correspondence,* edited by F. Elrington Ball, 6 vols., 1910–1914; *Vanessa and Her Correspondence with Jonathan Swift,* edited by Alexander M. Freeman, 1921; and *The Letters of Swift to Charles Ford,* edited by David Nichol Smith, 1935. A useful one-volume edition of selections is *The Portable Swift,* edited by Carl Van Doren, 1948.

The standard biography is Sir Henry Craik, *The Life of Jonathan Swift,* 2 vols., 1894. The best critical study is Richard Quintana, *The Mind and Art of Jonathan Swift,* 1936. For additional biographical and critical studies see Carl Van Doren, *Swift,* 1930; W. B. C. Watkins, *Perilous Balance,* 1939; G. Wilson Knight, *The*

Burning Oracle, 1939; R. W. Jackson, Swift and His Circle, 1945; R. C. Churchill, He Served Human Liberty, 1946; Herbert Davis, The Satire of Jonathan Swift, 1947; Evelyn Hardy, The Conjured Spirit, 1949; and J. M. Bullit, Jonathan Swift and the Anatomy of Satire, 1953.

The literature on Gulliver's Travels is extensive. See W. A. Eddy, Gulliver's Travels: A Critical Study, 1923; A. E. Case, Four Essays on Gulliver's Travels, 1945; Harold Williams, The Text of Gulliver's Travels, 1952; H. M. Dargan, "The Nature of Allegory as Used by Swift," Studies in Philology, XIII (1916), 159–179; J. B. Moore, "The Role of Gulliver," Modern Philology, XXV (1928), 469–480; Samuel Kliger, "The Unity of Gulliver's Travels," Modern Language Quarterly, VI (1945), 401–415; Edward Stone, "Swift and the Horses: Misanthropy or Comedy," ibid., X (1949), 367–376; Ellen D. Leyburn, "Certain Problems of Allegorical Satire in Gulliver's Travels," Huntington Library Quarterly, XIII (1950), 161–189; H. D. Kelling, "Some Significant Names in Gulliver's Travels," Studies in Philology, XLVIII (1951), 413; K. M. Williams, "Gulliver's Voyage to the Houyhnhnms," English Literary History, XVIII (1951), 275–286; Irvin Ehrenpreis, "Swift and Satire," College English, XIII (1952), 309–312; and H. D. Kelling, "Gulliver's Travels: A Comedy of Humours," University of Toronto Quarterly, XXI (1952), 362–375.

Edith Sitwell's novel, I Live Under a Black Sun, 1938, is based on the life of Swift.

ALGERNON CHARLES SWINBURNE

Born: London, England
Date: April 5, 1837

Died: London
Date: April 10, 1909

PRINCIPAL WORKS

POEMS: Poems and Ballads, 1866 [Laus Veneris]; Songs Before Sunrise, 1871; Poems and Ballads: Second Series, 1878; Songs of the Springtides, 1880; Tristram of Lyonesse, 1882; A Midsummer Holiday, 1884; Poems and Ballads: Third Series, 1889; The Tale of Balen, 1896.

PLAYS: The Queen Mother, 1860; Rosamond, 1860; Atalanta in Calydon, 1865; Chastelard, 1865; Bothwell, 1874; Erechtheus, 1876; Mary Stuart, 1881; Marino Faliero, 1885; Locrine, 1887.

CRITICISM: William Blake, 1868; Essays and Studies, 1875; A Note on Charlotte Brontë, 1877; A Study of Shakespeare, 1880; A Study of Victor Hugo, 1886; A Study of Ben Jonson, 1889; Studies in Prose and Poetry, 1894; The Age of Shakespeare, 1908.

Swinburne's fame as a poet rests on several claims: his dexterity in manipulation of verse; his subject matter, which often glorified the life of the senses or argued for the necessity of social change; and certain oddities in his actual career. In all of these claims, we can see a man at odds with his age and yet drawing strength from his surroundings since they incited him to his protests.

Swinburne was descended from English nobility. The mother of the future revolutionary poet was the daughter of the Earl of Ashburnham, and his father was Admiral Charles Henry Swinburne. Algernon Charles Swinburne enjoyed fully the advantages of his

1055

background. From his mother he acquired a literary taste, a love of the French and Italian languages and literatures, and a thorough knowledge of the Bible. He was also able to read such critical writers as Victor Hugo and W. S. Landor, both advocates of republicanism and both objects of Swinburne's hero worship. From a grandfather in Northumberland, Swinburne learned hatred of monarchy and disapproval of the hereditary privileges of the House of Lords.

Born in London, April 5, 1837, Swinburne early discovered his poetic vocation. Acquaintance in childhood with Wordsworth and Samuel Rogers confirmed his intent by the time he was fifteen. The next decade brought Swinburne the companionship and encouragement of the leading literary figures of the period: Tennyson, Ruskin, and among the Pre-Raphaelites, William Morris, Edward Burne-Jones, and Dante Gabriel Rossetti. Swinburne's youthful claims to attention led Burne-Jones to welcome him thus: "We have hitherto been three, and now there are four of us." Swinburne modeled for some of Rossetti's paintings and had the painter's personal direction in his writings. Further, his affiliation with the Pre-Raphaelite movement drew attention to his work, which early struck his contemporaries as clever, audacious, and erudite. From *Atalanta in Calydon* and *Chastelard,* published in 1865, Swinburne's place in public awareness was important, and remained so for about fifteen years.

Swinburne's themes—glorification of the senses and the assertion of man's dignity—are but two aspects of his central impatience with restraint; the only restraint that Swinburne ever welcomed was that imposed by rather elaborate and even archaic poetical forms. In *Poems and Ballads* he scandalized his times with outspoken endorsement of sensuality; in *Songs Before Sunrise* he stirred them deeply with apostrophes to the insurgent republicans of Italy. In these years he was also a prose propagandist for the Pre-Raphaelites and a defender of his own literary practices. Against a charge made by the *Saturday Review* that with colors intense and violent he effected an "audacious counterfeiting of strong and noble passion by mad, intoxicated sensuality," Swinburne protested against a literary age which "has room only for such as are content to write for children and girls."

The revolt in Swinburne's own life had to be curbed. In 1879 Theodore Watts-Dunton took Swinburne from London to save him from the effects of acute alcoholic dysentery. Although the move to Putney and simplicity probably extended Swinburne's life, it took the essential fire from his writings. He relinquished the idea of political freedom; he turned from poetry to literary criticism more and more; he was capable, as the young Swinburne with his impassioned seriousness would not have been, of composing parodies on the work of prominent Victorian poets like Tennyson, Rossetti, and himself. The prose of his last years is far removed from his Pre-Raphaelite struggles and contemporary politics; he took up his early enthusiasm for the drama of Elizabethan England, of which he wrote brilliantly in criticism which scholarship finds subject to correction.

Upon his death in London, April 10, 1909, Swinburne was buried near his family at Bonchurch, Isle of Wight—

his family from which, at every phase of his career, he had been sharply separated.

Swinburne has been described as a man more "elf-like than human." He was just over five feet tall and thin; he had a massive head thatched with shaggy red hair. His bizarre appearance brought him failure in love and, it can be believed, gave him reason for heightening heretical behavior which led to his removal from Eton and Oxford, behavior that later led him to refuse a degree from the great university that had ejected him. It is not surprising that he welcomed the onslaught of Darwinism; nor did the poet of the senses and political action find admirable Robert Browning's optimism and Tennyson's aspirations toward immortality. Here again, as might be expected, he departed from his era's canons of taste and created his own philosophy and forms.

BIBLIOGRAPHICAL REFERENCES: The definitive edition is *The Complete Works of Algernon Charles Swinburne*, edited by Edmund Gosse and T. J. Wise, 20 vols., 1925–1927. The same editors published a separate edition of the *Letters*, 2 vols., 1919. The standard biography is Edmund Gosse, *The Life of Algernon Charles Swinburne*, 1917, a work supplemented by Sir Herbert Grierson, *Swinburne*, 1953. See also T. E. Welby, *Swinburne: A Critical Study*, 1914; Harold Nicolson, *Swinburne*, 1926; Samuel C. Chew, *Swinburne*, 1929; Georges Lafourcade, *Swinburne: A Literary Biography*, 1932; C. K. Hyder, *Swinburne's Literary Career and Fame*, 1933; and Humphrey Hare, *Swinburne: A Biographical Approach*, 1949.

FRANK SWINNERTON

Born: Wood Green, England
Date: August 12, 1884

PRINCIPAL WORKS

NOVELS: *The Merry Heart*, 1909; *The Casement*, 1911; *The Happy Family*, 1912; *Nocturne*, 1917; *September*, 1919; *Coquette*, 1921; *The Three Lovers*, 1922; *Young Felix*, 1923; *The Elder Sister*, 1925; *Summer Storm*, 1926; *A Brood of Ducklings*, 1928; *Sketch of a Sinner*, 1929; *The Georgian House*, 1932; *Elizabeth*, 1934; *Harvest Comedy*, 1937; *The Two Wives*, 1939; *The Fortunate Lady*, 1941; *Thankless Child*, 1942; *A Woman in Sunshine*, 1945; *A Flower for Catherine*, 1951; *A Month in Gordon Square*, 1953.

ESSAYS AND STUDIES: *George Gissing*, 1912; *R. L. Stevenson*, 1914; *Tokefield Papers*, 1927; *A London Bookman*, 1928; *The Georgian Scene*, 1934 (English edition, *The Georgian Literary Scene*, 1935); *The Bookman's London*, 1951; *Background with Chorus*, 1956.

AUTOBIOGRAPHY: *Swinnerton, An Autobiography*, 1936.

Frank (Arthur) Swinnerton, born in a London suburb on August 12, 1884, was a precocious boy who avowedly taught himself to read at the age of four. A series of illnesses as a child, including diphtheria, paralysis, and scarlet fever, caused poor health through most of his later boyhood.

He decided early to be a journalist and became an office boy for a newspaper company at the age of fourteen. In 1900 having decided to become a man of letters rather than a journalist, he found work with J. M. Dent & Co., British publishers. Six years later he left this firm to join the staff of Chatto & Windus, another British publishing house. Following the publication of a not too successful novel of his own Swinnerton became an editor for the firm, in which position he continued for almost two decades. Before he was thirty Swinnerton had published several books, novels, and critical biographies. His first outstanding success came in 1917 with *Nocturne*, a short but almost perfect Cockney idyl. Since that time he has continued to publish novels and literary essays. *A London Bookman, Tokefield Papers,* and *The Bookman's London* are volumes of essays. *The Georgian Literary Scene* is a work of literary criticism; it is, with *Harvest Comedy,* one of the two books Swinnerton considers his best. From 1937 to 1942 he was chief reviewer of fiction for the London *Observer.* During World War II he served his government as a civil servant in the Ministry of Information. His first wife was Helen Dircks, a poet. His second wife, whom he married in 1924, was Mary Dorothy Bennett; they have one daughter. Critics have never been enthusiastic for Swinnerton's works, though he is considered a competent novelist and a dependable storyteller.

BIBLIOGRAPHICAL REFERENCES: Most of Swinnerton's own story has been told in his autobiography and in collections of essays like *Tokefield Papers, The Bookman's London,* and *Background with Chorus.* There is comparatively little criticism. See *Frank Swinnerton,* a pamphlet containing sketches by Arnold Bennett, H. G. Wells, and Grant M. Overton, 1920; A. Rotter, *Frank Swinnerton und George Gissing, eine kritische studie,* 1930; R. C. McKay, *George Gissing and His Critic Frank Swinnerton,* 1933; and Thomas Beer, "Frank Swinnerton," *Bookman,* LVIII (1923–1924), 404–409.

JOHN MILLINGTON SYNGE

Born: Newton Little, Ireland
Date: April 16, 1871

Died: Dublin, Ireland
Date: March 24, 1909

PRINCIPAL WORKS

PLAYS: *In the Shadow of the Glen,* 1903; *Riders to the Sea,* 1904; *The Well of the Saints,* 1905; *The Tinker's Wedding,* 1907; *The Playboy of the Western World,* 1907; *Deirdre of the Sorrows,* 1910.

POEMS: *Poems and Translations,* 1910.

TALES AND SKETCHES: *The Aran Islands,* 1907.

Although Synge was long considered the greatest Irish dramatist, his eminence is now challenged by Sean O'Casey, who certainly is not the superior of the older playwright in tragic or comic power, or in beauty of language, but who exhibits far greater versatility and productive powers. Synge's five completed plays all deal with the Irish peasant; about 1900 all literary Ireland was fascinated by the peasant and his primitive culture— William Butler Yeats, Æ., Douglas Hyde, Padraic Colum, Lady Gregory, and others were recording his stories and trying to capture the lilting poetry of his speech. Just before Synge died, however, he told Yeats that he was tired of the peasant on the stage and planned a play of Dublin slum life. Had he not died at the early age of thirty-eight, his dramatic work might have had the sweep of O'Casey's.

John Millington Synge was born in Newton Little, near Dublin, on April 16, 1871, the son of a barrister and grandson of the translator of Josephus. He attended private schools until he was fourteen, then studied for three years with a tutor. Later, while a student at Trinity College, Dublin, he also studied music at the Royal Irish Academy and became a more than competent pianist and violinist. After receiving his degree, he went to Germany to study music and German, then to Italy for further language study, and finally to Paris, where he wrote verse and studied French literature. With his small legacy he might have spent the rest of his life as a minor poet and critic, if William Butler Yeats had not met him in Paris and urged him to go to Galway and the Aran Islands to study the peasants, whose rich if primitive life had never been treated in literature. Synge left his Latin Quarter hotel, went to Wicklow, Kerry, and the Aran Islands, and for some years lived among the peasants, carefully studying their life and speech. With his genius for companionship this association bore rich rewards —articles in British weeklies, a book of great beauty, *The Aran Islands,* and finally his classic folk plays.

At the same time the Irish Literary Revival, which had started in the 1890's, was advancing with spectacular success, its happiest manifestation being the famed Abbey Theatre, founded in 1904 for the production of native plays. For over a decade more good plays were written in tiny Ireland than in the entire United States. Synge's devotion to the Abbey and his close friendship with its other literary advisers made the performance of his own plays there inevitable. Because he failed to idealize the Irish national character or concern himself with passionate nationalism, his plays provoked hostile demonstrations at the Abbey when first produced, but they are now accepted, even by the Irish, as the greatest classics of the Abbey Theatre.

In the Shadow of the Glen, derived from an old folk tale, is sharp with satire, and was at first resented as a slur on Irish womanhood. *Riders to the Sea,* considered the greatest short tragedy in modern drama, has as its themes the eternal conflict of man and nature and man's dignified submission to fate; every line in the play has a solemn music, rhythmical and poetic, yet with genuine folk-flavor. *The Well of the Saints* is a sardonic comedy, a tragic-farce of the flavor of Anouilh's *Waltz of the Toreadors* a half century later. *The Playboy of the Western World* is one of the great modern comedies— satirical, boisterous, exquisitely beautiful in language. The crude humors of *The Tinker's Wedding* are in contrast to the legendary, poetic theme of *Deirdre of the Sorrows,* left unfinished at Synge's death. He died in a nursing home in Dublin, March 24, 1909.

BIBLIOGRAPHICAL REFERENCES: Synge's plays, sketches, and poems have been collected in his *Complete Works,* 1935. There is no authorized biography. For biographical and critical studies see P. P. Howe, *John Millington Synge: A Critical Study,* 1912; Maurice Bourgeois, *John Millington Synge and the Irish Theatre,* 1913; John Masefield, *John M. Synge: A Few Personal Recollections,* 1915; Daniel Corkery, *Synge and Anglo-Irish Literature,* 1931; A. D. Estill, *The Sources of Synge,* 1939; and L. A. G. Strong, *John Millington Synge,* 1941. Synge and his work are also treated briefly in the following: Cornelius Weygandt, *Irish Plays and Playwrights,* 1913; Lady Augusta Gregory, *Our Irish Theatre: A Chapter of Autobiography,* 1913; William Butler Yeats, *Dramatis Personae,* 1936; Una Ellis-Fermor, *The Irish Dramatic Movement,* 1939; John Gassner, *Masters of the Drama,* 1940, 1945; and Ronald Peacock, *The Poet in the Theatre,* 1946.

CORNELIUS TACITUS

Born: Comum (Como?), Italy   *Died:* Rome (?), Italy
Date: c. 55   *Date:* c. 120

PRINCIPAL WORKS

BIOGRAPHY: *De vita et moribus Julii Agricolae,* c. 98 (*Life of Agricola*).
HISTORY: *Historiae,* c. 116; *Annales,* c. 119.
TREATISES: *Dialogus de oratoribus,* c. 76–77 (*Dialogue on Orators*); the *Germania,* c. 98.

The life of (Publius or Gaius) Cornelius Tacitus is known only from autobiographical allusions in the remains of his works and from eleven letters written to him by Pliny the Younger. This remarkable republican lived through the reign of nine emperors from Nero to Trajan. As a brilliant lawyer, senator and consul, he was a close observer of public affairs, and his dismay at the degeneration of his age and his fear of tyranny are expressed in pithy language. His *Dialogue on Orators* laments the decay of education and eloquence; the *Life of Agricola* is a fine biography with a sketch of Britain under the Romans; *Concerning the Geography, the Customs and Manners, and the Tribes of Germany,* a valuable classic despite its errors, contrasts the free barbarians with the servile Romans; the *Histories* include a fascinating, prejudical account of the Jews; and the *Annals* provide a philosophy of history.

Despite the "singularly blessed time" of his last years, Tacitus could never shake off the morbid effects of Domitian's reign of terror. Nevertheless, convinced of Rome's corruption, he served loyally and well, receiving in 99 a special vote of thanks from the Roman Senate. He recorded the society more than he cured it, however; and his works collectively give us a vivid panoramic view of the empire in the first century. Many modern historians still subscribe to his dictum that "history's highest function is to rescue merit from oblivion, and to hold up as a terror to base words and actions the reprobation of posterity."

The places and dates of Tacitus' birth and death are not definitely known.

BIBLIOGRAPHICAL REFERENCES: There are numerous editions of Tacitus in modern translation. See in particular *The Complete Works of Tacitus,* edited and with an introduction by Moses Hadas, 1942. Translations of selected works include George Gilbert Ramsay, *The Annals of Tacitus*, 2 vols., 1904–1909; W. Hamilton Fyfe, *Dialogus, Agricola, and Germania*, 1908; *idem, The Histories*, 2 vols., 1912; William Peterson and Maurice Hutton, *Dialogus, Agricola, and Germania*, 1914; and Clifford H. Moore, *The Histories*, 4 vols., 1925–1937. See also M. L. W. Laistner, *Greater Roman Historians*, 1947; and Clarence W. Mendell, *Tacitus: The Man and his Work*, 1957.

HIPPOLYTE TAINE

Born: Vouziers, France   *Died:* Paris, France
Date: April 21, 1828   *Date:* March 9, 1893

Principal Works

essays and studies: *Essai sur Tite-Live*, 1856 (*Essay on Livy*); *Les philosophes classiques du XIXᵉ siècle en France*, 1857 (*The Classic Philosophers of the Nineteenth Century in France*); *Essai sur La Fontaine et ses fables*, 1860; *Histoire de la littérature anglaise*, 1863–1869; *Philosophie de l'art*, 1865; *Nouveaux essais de critique et d'histoire*, 1865; *De l'idéal dans l'art*, 1867; *Théorie de l'intelligence*, 1870.
history: *Les Origines de la France contemporaine*, 1875–1894 (*The Origins of Contemporary France*).

Hippolyte (Adolphe) Taine, born at Vouziers, France, on April 21, 1828, was educated at the Collège Bourbon and the Normal School in Paris. After leaving school, he became a teacher at Toulon, but because of his political views he was appointed to successively poorer posts until he left teaching entirely in 1852 and devoted his time to study and writing. In 1853 he completed his *Essay on La Fontaine and His Fables*, written as the thesis for his doctorate at the Sorbonne. He immediately began his *Essay on Livy* which, entered in competition, won him an award from the French Academy in 1855. Early in 1854, however, Taine had suffered a breakdown in health because of his arduous program of writing. After a period of enforced rest he resumed his literary activities by contributing articles on various subjects to periodicals. One series of articles, published as *The Classic Philosophers of the Nineteenth Century in France*, first suggested Taine's theory

of the application of scientific methods to psychological and metaphysical research. The book attracted considerable interest and helped to spread the author's critical fame. A revised version of his doctoral essay on La Fontaine was published in 1860.

In 1864, Taine received two appointments, both of which gave him security and left him free to study and write. He became examiner at Saint-Cyr and professor of aesthetics and art history at L'École des Beaux Arts. In the same year he published a study of John Stuart Mill, under the title *Le Positivisme anglais*. In the meantime his famous *History of English Literature* had appeared, a work illustrating how determinism could be applied to the study of literature by utilizing the elements of race, milieu, and moment. During the years from 1864 to 1870 Taine fulfilled his tasks at Saint-Cyr and lectured at L'École des Beaux Arts. At the same time he was engaged in

1061

writing his books on aesthetics and art. A general study of the philosophy of art appeared in 1865 and was followed by volumes on various phases of art and the philosophy of art. He married Mlle. Denuelle, the daughter of an architect, in 1868.

The Franco-Prussian War ended that happy period in Taine's life and turned his thinking into new paths. Anxious to ascertain the cause of France's weakness and political instability, and feeling that they were traceable to the French Revolution of 1789, Taine began what was to be his greatest work, his study of the origins of contemporary France. He worked at it constantly, even giving up his professorship in 1884 to avail himself of more time; even so, he left it unfinished when he died in Paris on March 9, 1893. The methods that Taine used in this work were the same quasi-scientific and deterministic methods he had already utilized successfully in his studies of literature and art. The book marked Taine as one of the great intellectual leaders of the nineteenth century, the leader of a generation in France which sought in art, literature, and history to find truth that could be regarded as "objective" and "scientific."

BIBLIOGRAPHICAL REFERENCES: For biography and critical analysis see Gabriel Monod, *Les Maîtres de l'histoire*, 1894; M. E. Boutmy, *Taine, Scherer, Laboulaye*, 1901; F. C. Roe, *Taine et l'Angleterre*, 1924; Victor Giraud, *Hippolyte Taine*, 1928; André Chevrillon, *Taine, formation de sa pensée*, 1932; Maxime Leroy, *Taine*, 1933; Georges Léotard, *L'erreur de Taine*, 1949; and André Cresson, *Hippolyte Taine*, 1951. A recent specialized study is Sholom Jacob Kahn, *Science and Aesthetic Judgment: A Study of Taine's Critical Method*, 1953.

BOOTH TARKINGTON

Born: Indianapolis, Indiana
Date: July 29, 1869

Died: Indianapolis
Date: May 19, 1946

PRINCIPAL WORKS

NOVELS: *The Gentleman from Indiana*, 1899; *Monsieur Beaucaire*, 1900; *The Conquest of Canaan*, 1905; *His Own People*, 1907; *The Flirt*, 1913; *Penrod*, 1914; *The Turmoil*, 1915; *Penrod and Sam*, 1916; *Seventeen*, 1916; *The Magnificent Ambersons*, 1918; *Ramsey Milholland*, 1919; *Alice Adams*, 1921; *Gentle Julia*, 1922; *The Midlander*, 1923; *Growth*, 1927 (*The Turmoil*, *The Magnificent Ambersons*, and *The Midlander*); *Penrod Jashber*, 1929; *Young Mrs. Greeley*, 1929; *Presenting Lily Mars*, 1933; *Little Orvie*, 1934; *The Heritage of Hatcher Ide*, 1941; *The Fighting Littles*, 1941; *Kate Fennigate*, 1943; *Image of Josephine*, 1945.

SHORT STORIES: *In the Arena*, 1905; *The Fascinating Stranger and Other Stories*, 1923.

PLAYS: *The Guardian*, 1907 (with Harry Leon Wilson); *Mister Antonio*, 1916; *The Gibson Upright*, 1919 (with Harry Leon Wilson); *Clarence*, 1919.

REMINISCENCES: *The World Does Move*, 1928.

(Newton) Booth Tarkington was born in Indianapolis, Indiana, on July 29, 1869. He attended Phillips Exeter Academy and Purdue University and was graduated from Princeton. Primarily interested in art, he preferred to make drawing his career, until financial necessity turned him to writing. After an inauspicious beginning he gradually achieved loyal popularity from readers and considerable acclaim from critics. His first popular success in fiction was *Monsieur Beaucaire*, a romantic novelette that helped call attention to his first novel, *The Gentleman from Indiana*, which had appeared in 1899. Today, Tarkington is perhaps most widely known for his stories of youth and teen-agers: *Penrod, Penrod and Sam, Penrod Jashber*, and *Seventeen*. These are "American Boy" stories, comic but very human and appealing. Perhaps his best novel, *Alice Adams*, appeared in 1921 and won the Pulitzer Prize for fiction in 1922. *The Magnificent Ambersons* had earlier won the same prize. In 1933 Tarkington was awarded the Gold Medal of the National Institute of Arts and Letters.

Tarkington was twice married, to Miss Laurel Louisa Fletcher, of Indianapolis, in 1902, and to Miss Susannah Robinson, of Dayton, Ohio, in 1912. He was a prolific writer, with successful ventures in the short story and the drama, but it is chiefly as a novelist that he is remembered. Among his other representative novels are *The Conquest of Canaan, His Own People, The Flirt, The Turmoil, Ramsey Milholland, Gentle Julia, The Midlander*, and *Young Mrs. Greeley*. A trilogy dealing with the industrial development of the Middle West came out in 1927 under the title of *Growth*; it included *The Turmoil, The Magnificent Ambersons*, and *The Midlander*.

Tarkington, who suffered difficulties with his eyesight for years, became totally blind in 1930, but his sight was partially restored by a series of operations. For the last thirty-five years of his life he divided his time between his home in Indianapolis and his house in Kennebunkport, Maine. He died May 19, 1946, in Indianapolis.

BIBLIOGRAPHICAL REFERENCES: The only full-length biography is James Woodress, *Booth Tarkington: Gentleman from Indiana*, 1955, a work based extensively on the Tarkington papers at Princeton University. Two other works indispensable to Tarkington studies are the unfinished autobiography, *As It Seems to Me, Saturday Evening Post*, CCXIV (July 5–August 23, 1941); and Dorothy R. Russo and Thelma L. Sullivan, *A Bibliography of Booth Tarkington, 1869–1946*, 1949. See also Robert C. Holliday, *Booth Tarkington*, 1918; Asa D. Dickinson, *Booth Tarkington: A Sketch*, 1926 (pamphlet); and Kenneth Roberts, *I Wanted to Write*, 1949.

TORQUATO TASSO

Born: Sorrento, Italy
Date: March 11, 1544

Died: Near Rome, Italy
Date: April 25, 1595

PRINCIPAL WORKS

POEMS: *Rinaldo*, 1562; *Gerusalemme Liberata*, 1580–1581 (*Jerusalem Delivered*).
PLAY: *Aminta*, 1573.

Torquato Tasso, born at Sorrento on March 11, 1544, was the son of Bernardo Tasso (1493–1569), a famous Italian poet exiled from Naples during

1063

his son's childhood. Tasso spent his early years in Naples with his mother, a woman of wealth and rank who sent him to school to the Jesuits. When he was ten, he joined his father at Pesaro, where he and the heir to the Duke of Urbino were tutored together. In 1557 his father sent him to study law at the University of Padua. Finding the law uninteresting, he turned before long to the study of philosophy and poetry. A few of his poems appeared as early as 1561, but real fame came with the publication of *Rinaldo,* a romantic epic published while the eighteen-year-old author was still a student at Padua.

After a short period of study at the University of Bologna, Tasso returned to Padua, and by 1565 he had found a wealthy patron in Cardinal Luigi d'Este, a member of the noble house of Ferrara that Tasso was to celebrate in his *Jerusalem Delivered.* This was the later title of the epic poem, *Goffredo,* which he had begun at Bologna. The next five years of his life were happy and busy ones, except for the death of his father in 1569. A year later Tasso traveled with the cardinal to Paris, where he met Ronsard and other French writers of the period. A short time later a difference of opinion on religious matters caused him to exchange the cardinal's patronage for that of Duke Alfonso d'Este of Ferrara. *Aminta,* his charming pastoral drama, added to his literary fame after its initial presentation at Ferrara in 1573.

Jerusalem Delivered, Tasso's great masterpiece, was completed the following year and was read publicly to the Duke of Ferrara and the court in 1575. Having chosen Vergil as his model, Tasso followed the Roman poet's strict adherence to unity, style, and form. The subject matter of the poem is the First Crusade, the theme dealing with the efforts of the forces of evil, personified by the beautiful sorceress Armida, to keep the crusaders under Godfrey of Bouillon from capturing the Holy City. Although classic in form, the poem is closer to medieval romance in its use of allegory and in the romantic interest supplied by love affairs between Christian knights and pagan heroines. Following the reading of *Jerusalem Delivered,* Tasso became ill, probably of malaria, and suffered delusions that attempts were being made on his life. When he asked for permission to leave the court, the duke was patient but firm in his refusal; perhaps he feared that Tasso, if angered or allowed to leave Ferrara, might dedicate his poem to the Medici family of Florence. It is thought that Tasso became temporarily insane about this time, for in 1577 he was placed under the medical care of the Franciscans at Ferrara.

In July of that year he escaped in the disguise of a peasant and went to Sorrento to take refuge with his sister Cornelia. His condition improved and he was in Ferrara again in 1578. After a year spent wandering about Italy he returned to Ferrara and openly accused Duke Alfonso of trying to poison him. He was then confined to an insane asylum for seven years. Although denied liberty of movement, he was permitted to receive visitors and was given spacious apartments in which to live. During this time, in 1580, an inaccurate version of *Goffredo* was printed in Venice. A year later the complete work was published at Ferrara under its present title, *Jerusalem Delivered.* Publication was by order of the duke after Tasso's manuscript had been seized along with his other effects; when the work appeared he received nothing for the poem which made him famous throughout Europe.

Through the effects of friendly Vincenzio Gonzaga, Prince of Mantua, Tasso was released in 1586 and allowed to go to Mantua to live under the protection of the prince. There he wrote *Torrismondo* (1586) before he became a wanderer again. From 1587 to 1594 he traveled aimlessly about Europe, a victim of physical illness, mental weakness, and poverty.

Gerusalemme Conquistata, a sequel to *Jerusalem Delivered* but a much inferior work, was published in 1593. In 1594 arrangements were made to crown him poet laureate at the court of Pope Clement VIII and to grant him a suitable pension. But honors and money came too late. Before the ceremony could be performed, Tasso retired to the monastery of St. Onofrio, near Rome, and announced that he was entering the monastery to die, as he did less than a month later, on April 25, 1595.

BIBLIOGRAPHICAL REFERENCES: Standard translations of *Jerusalem Delivered* are those by Sir Edward Fairfax, 1600, frequently reprinted, and J. K. James, 1884. The standard biography is A. Solerti, *La Vita di Torquato Tasso*, 3 vols., 1895. For biographical and critical studies in English see Robert Milman, *Life of Tasso*, 2 vols., 1850; and William Boulting, *Tasso and His Times*, 1907. Recent European studies include Lafranco Caretti, *Studi sulle rime del Tasso*, 1950; Leo Ulrich, *Torquato Tasso. Studien zur Vorgeschichte des Secentismo*, 1951; Benedetto Croce, *Poeti e scrittori del pieno e del tardo Rinascimento*, 1952; and B. T. Sozzi, *Studi sul Tasso*, 1954.

EDWARD TAYLOR

Born: Leicestershire, England
Date: c. 1645

Died: Westfield, Massachusetts
Date: June 24, 1729

PRINCIPAL WORK

POEMS: *The Poetical Works of Edward Taylor* (including "God's Determinations" and "Sacramental Meditations"), 1939.

The poetry of Edward Taylor, New England mystic, is a fairly recent, but highly important, literary discovery. The manuscripts which contained some three hundred poems had lain untouched for over two centuries before they were resurrected by Thomas H. Johnson in 1937. Johnson edited a selection of the poems and in 1939 published them, along with a biographical sketch and a critical introduction, in *The Poetical Works of Edward Taylor*. And his efforts proved to be well worth the trouble. Taylor, who wrote in a style imitative of the seven-

teenth century metaphysicals, demonstrated a fairly high degree of poetical competency, especially in his long, semi-dramatic "God's Determinations," which has been called "perhaps the finest single poetic achievement in America before the nineteenth century."

As for the author of the poems, little is known about him before his arrival in Boston in 1668. It is believed that he was born about 1645 near Sketchley in Leicestershire, that he attended a Non-Conformist school, and that he came to this country because he could not take the oath of conformity then demanded of all English clergymen; but none of these conjectures is certain.

Following his arrival in Massachusetts, however, his activities were well documented. First, he was admitted to Harvard as a sophomore and was given the post of college butler; he was graduated in 1671. Next, he went to the settlement of Westfield as minister and remained there for the rest of his life, marrying twice, begetting fourteen children, quieting the Indians, acting as a physician, and in general caring for the physical as well as the spiritual well-being of his flock.

All this time he was writing his poetry. The masterpiece, "God's Determination," was probably written around 1690, and the "Sacramental Meditations," which are irregular in quality, over an extended period of time after that. The manuscript of the poems was inherited by his grandson, Ezra Stiles, who respected his ancestor's injunction that "his heirs should never publish it." The poems were deposited in the library of Yale College during Stiles' presidency, and they remained there until their discovery in 1937.

Taylor died at Westfield on June 24, 1729.

BIBLIOGRAPHICAL REFERENCES: The best biographical and critical sketch is Thomas H. Johnson, Introduction to *The Poetical Works of Edward Taylor*, 1939. Some extracts from Edward Taylor's diary were also printed in the *Processes of the Massachusetts Historical Society*, XVIII (1881), 4–18, but the original manuscript has apparently been lost. For critical studies see Thomas H. Johnson, "The Discovery of Edward Taylor's Poetry," *Colophon*, New Graphic Series I, No. 2, (1939), 101–106; Austin Warren, "Edward Taylor's Poetry: Colonial Baroque," *Kenyon Review*, III (1941), 355–371; Wallace C. Brown, "Edward Taylor, An American Metaphysical," *American Literature*, XVI (1944), 186–197; and Willie T. Weathers, "Edward Taylor: Hellenistic Puritan," *ibid.*, 18–26.

ESAIAS TEGNÉR

Born: Kyrkerud, Sweden
Date: November 13, 1782

Died: Östrabo, Sweden
Date: November 2, 1846

PRINCIPAL WORKS

POEMS: *Svea*, 1811 (*Sweden*); *Nattvardsbarnen*, 1820 (*The First Communion*); *Axel*, 1822; *Frithiof's Saga*, 1825.

Esaias Tegnér, born in the Värmland district of Sweden on November 13, 1782, was the son of Esaias Lucasson, a clergyman who changed his name to Tegnerus, after the town of Tegnaby in Småland. The poet subsequently changed his name to Tegnér. Left fatherless in childhood, the boy received some tutoring through the assistance of the crown bailiff and later, with the aid of his brother's em-

ployer, was able to enter the University of Lund. After receiving his degree in philosophy in 1802, Tegnér remained at the university as lecturer and professor of Greek for twenty-two years. During this period he slowly made progress toward being recognized as Sweden's leading national poet. After some early failures, he achieved overnight fame in 1808 with his "War Song of the Militia of Scania." Three years later his patriotic poem, *Sweden,* won him the grand prize of the Swedish Academy.

Together with Arvid Afzelius and Erik Geijer, Tegnér developed the Gothic League in opposition to modernist European trends in Swedish literature, and in 1819 he was appointed a life member of the Academy. Drawing principally on Icelandic sagas and Norse folk tales, Tegnér made his great contributions to Swedish literature in *The First Communion,* made famous by Longfellow's paraphrase in *The Children of the Lord's Supper;*

Frithiof's Saga, now translated into almost every European language, and his long narrative poem, *Axel.*

In 1824 Tegnér was named to the bishopric of Växjö, but his health broke under the burden of diocesan and parliamentary duties and for a time he became mad. He recovered sufficiently, however, to fulfill the duties of his church office from 1841 until his death at Östrabo on November 2, 1846. Two epic poems, *Gerda* and *Kronbruden,* remained unfinished when he died.

BIBLIOGRAPHICAL REFERENCES: An early study of the man and his work is Georg Brandes, *Esaias Tegnér,* 1876. See also F. Böök, *Esaias Tegnér,* 2 vols., 1946–1947.

ALFRED, LORD TENNYSON

Born: Somersby, England
Date: August 6, 1809

Died: Near Haslemere, England
Date: October 6, 1892

PRINCIPAL WORKS

POEMS: *Poems, Chiefly Lyrical,* 1830; *Poems,* 1832; *Poems,* 1842 (2 vols.); *The Princess,* 1847; *In Memoriam,* 1850; *Maud and Other Poems,* 1855; *Idylls of the King,* 1859–1885; *Enoch Arden and Other Poems,* 1864; *The Holy Grail and Other Poems,* 1869; *Ballads and Other Poems,* 1880; *Tiresias and Other Poems,* 1885; *Locksley Hall Sixty Years After,* 1886; *Demeter and Other Poems,* 1889; *The Death of Œnone,* 1892.

PLAYS: *Queen Mary,* 1875; *Harold,* 1876; *The Cup,* 1884; *The Falcon,* 1884; *Becket,* 1884; *The Promise of May,* 1886; *The Foresters,* 1892.

"Man comes and tills the field
and lies beneath."

Thus in one crisp, true line is life summed up by Tennyson. And between his birth on August 6, 1809, and his death on October 6, 1892, no poet in the whole range of English literature ever tilled the field of poetry with more diligence and versatility than Alfred, fourth son of the Rev. G. C. Tennyson, rector of the parish at Somersby in Lincolnshire, where the boy was born. Tennyson's output began at the age of six, with blank verse scribbled on a

slate, and culminated some seventy-five years later, with the much-quoted "Crossing the Bar." In between came poetry that is sometimes magnificent, often vapid and mawkish, but always characteristic of an age alternately self-confident and self-conscious, the age of Victoria.

Somersby was a quiet village containing less than a hundred inhabitants. Tennyson's father was talented (a dabbler in poetry, painting, architecture, and music) and his mother, whose maiden name was Elizabeth Fytche, was noted for her gentleness and sweet disposition. In this setting Tennyson's talent developed early. While he was attending Louth grammar school he broke into print with *Poems by Two Brothers*, a collection which actually contained the works of three members of a talented family—Alfred, Frederick, and Charles. This juvenile volume shows the influence of Byron, whom Alfred admired so greatly that when he heard of his death he took a lonely, sad walk and carved into the sandstone, "Byron is dead."

In 1828 Tennyson went to Trinity College, Cambridge. There he took an interest in politics and became a member of The Apostles, a club of young literary men. Among these friends was Arthur Henry Hallam, whose later death, at the age of twenty-three, so affected Tennyson that he published nothing for ten years. Hallam is elegized in *In Memoriam*, a loose collection of philosophical lyrics that seems to be groping for, but never quite reaching, the handhold of faith. At Cambridge Tennyson won the chancellor's medal for his poem, "Timbuctoo," and it was there he brought out in 1830 his first important volume, *Poems, Chiefly Lyrical*. Although some of the reviews of this book were unkind, perhaps justifiably so, and although the influence of another Romantic poet, Keats, is very evident, the volume marked the beginning of a career almost unmatched in popularity afforded a poet during his lifetime.

Two years later came another volume, which included "The Lady of Shalott" and "The Lotus Eaters," two poems in the smooth, melancholy tone of Tennyson at his best. Then came Hallam's death and the ten years of silence. Hallam was Tennyson's close friend and the fiancé of his sister Emily; when Tennyson heard the news of his unexpected death in Vienna, he was dreadfully shocked and shaken. Later he began working on *In Memoriam* a labor that lasted for seventeen years. Not until 1842 did Tennyson publish again, bringing out two volumes, one of which contained "Morte d'Arthur," the beginning of a series on the Arthurian legends which became *Idylls of the King*. Also in 1842 appeared "Locksley Hall," one of Tennyson's most popular poems.

The auspicious year for Tennyson was 1850. After unwise speculation had left him penniless and two bouts with nervous prostration had damaged his health, his affairs took a threefold upsurge: he married Emily Sellwood, he published *In Memoriam*, and he was appointed Poet Laureate to succeed Wordsworth. Outstanding among his "official" poems as laureate is his "Ode on the Death of the Duke of Wellington," a stiff but moving tribute. The laureateship became the first step toward elevation to the peerage, an honor bestowed on him by an admiring queen. Tennyson had twice refused this honor (tendered to him first through Gladstone and then through Disraeli), but he accepted it in 1883, becoming Baron of Aldworth and Farrington. Even before he became a peer, Tennyson's popularity had been great (for example, ten thousand copies of the first series of *Idylls of the King*, published in 1859, were sold within a few weeks) but now this tall, gaunt man, the idealized figure of a poet, became almost a living legend. So popular was he that after his death there set in a natural reaction against his sentimentality and "Victorianism." But poems like "The Lotus Eaters," "Tithonus," and "Ulysses" still ring strong and true.

Tennyson's life was quiet, unhurried. Most of it he spent at his home, Farringford, on the Isle of Wight and, after 1867, at Blackdown in Surrey, where he lived in a house which he named Aldworth. In this later period he tried his hand at poetic dramas, *Queen Mary, Harold,* and *Becket.* Only the latter became a success on the stage. In 1889, *Demeter and Other Poems* came out, twenty thousand copies of which were sold within a week. On his eightieth birthday, Tennyson received tributes from all over the world. And though the end was not far away, he still had the strength to write a romantic play, *The Foresters,* a drama on the Robin Hood theme, which was produced at Daly's Theatre in New York in 1892.

Tennyson died at eighty-three at his home, Aldworth House, and was buried in the Poets' Corner of Westminster Abbey. To many readers Tennyson, not Shakespeare, seems more fittingly called the Swan of English literature. The name seems too gentle for the oftentimes fierce Elizabethan, but very appropriate for Tennyson, who experimented widely in the technique of poetry and whose best poems glide with the grace and beauty of a swan moving slowly across an unruffled lake.

BIBLIOGRAPHICAL REFERENCES: The standard edition is *The Works of Lord Tennyson,* edited by Hallam Tennyson, 9 vols., 1908–1910. The most recent and informing of the many Tennyson biographies is Sir Charles Tennyson, *Alfred Tennyson,* 1949. See also Arthur Waugh, *Alfred, Lord Tennyson,* 1894; Hallam Tennyson, *Alfred, Lord Tennyson: A Memoir,* 2 vols., 1898; A. C. Benson, *Alfred Tennyson,* 1904; T. R. Lounsbury, *The Life and Times of Tennyson,* 1915; H. G. Nicolson, *Tennyson: Aspects of His Life, Character, and Poetry,* 1925; A. C. Bradley, *A Commentary on Tennyson's "In Memoriam,"* 1929; and T. S. Eliot, " 'In Memoriam,' " in *Essays Ancient and Modern,* 1936.

TERENCE

Born: Carthage (?)
Date: c. 190 B.C.

Died: Athens, Greece, or at sea
Date: 159 B.C.

PRINCIPAL WORKS

PLAYS: *Andria,* 166 B.C. (*The Girl from Andros*); *Heautontimorumenos,* 163 B.C. (*The Self-Tormentor*); *Eunuchus,* 161 B.C. (*The Eunuch*); *Phormio,* 161 B.C.; *Hecyra,* 160 B.C. (*The Mother-in-law*); *Adelphi,* 160 B.C. (*The Brothers*).

Publius Terentius Afer (Terence) was probably born in the North African city of Carthage in 190 or 185 B.C. Our sole source of knowledge about his life is the fourth century grammarian and commentator Donatus, who, in his commentary on Terence's plays, preserves a biographical extract from Suetonius' lost *De viris illustribus.* Terence was brought to Rome in childhood as a slave, but was given the education of a gentleman by his master, the senator M. Terentius Lucanus. After having been given his freedom, the young man took the name of his former master and added the cognomen Afer (African).

His intellectual brilliance and personal charm won Terence a place among the aristocratic literary coterie in Rome, a group of young men intent on Hellenizing Roman society and bringing Greek literature and its refinements to the Romans. His personal attractiveness, which secured him the patronage of Caecilius, the poet, and the backing of the literary and aristocratic party, stood Terence in good stead when he was accused of plagiarism and of receiving "help" from his noble friends. Although the elegance and purity of his style and language, surprising in one so young, and a foreigner, indicate that the accusation may have had some basis in truth, he was successful in repelling the charges, and continued to be lionized by Roman society.

Around 160 B.C. Terence spent some time in Greece, probably studying Greek life and institutions for future use in his writing. Tradition has it that he was lost at sea in 159 B.C., as he was returning to Italy bearing a translation of the plays of Menander.

Six plays of Terence have survived: *Andria, Hecyra, Heautontimorumenos, Eunuchus, Phormio,* and *Adelphi,* all produced between 166 and 160 B.C. Like the works of Plautus, they are modeled on Greek comedies, primarily those of Menander, but showing also the influence of Diphilus and Apollodorus. While Terence seems to have taken greater liberties with the plots and characterizations of the Greek originals than did Plautus, often combining scenes from several different plays, he nevertheless remains truer to the spirit and style of his sources. Unlike Plautus, his language is consistently temperate and refined, and he avoids the incongruity of introducing Roman allusions or traditions into his plays. Terence seems to have been less concerned with the applause of the masses than with achieving a fusion of the purity of cultivated Latin with the smoothness of Attic Greek, and he strove to introduce Greek culture and sophistication to a Rome that must have appeared to him vulgar, if not barbaric.

Terence's plays are characterized by complex but careful plot construction and by a sense of the probability of the incidents he portrays. Consistency and moderation in speech and characterization, quite different from the extravagance of Plautus's writing, mark his work. All six comedies deal with the love entanglements of young men, usually involving two love-relationships, one with a wellborn young woman and one with a courtesan, and complicated by the presence of a parent (or parents) and, as in *Phormio,* by a clever parasite. Although the characterization in the early plays follows closely the stock types of Greek comedy, Terence's later plays show considerable development toward a subtle and sympathetic understanding of human psychology.

BIBLIOGRAPHICAL REFERENCES: The standard scholarly text is *P. Terenti Afri comoediae,* edited by S. G. Ashmore, 1910. Among the translations in English are William Ritchie, *The Plays of Terence,* 1927; John Sargeunt, *Terence,* 1931; and G. E. Duckworth, *The Complete Roman Drama,* 2 vols., 1942. See also Gilbert Norwood, *The Art of Terence,* 1923. An excellent background study is William Beare, *The Roman Stage,* 1950.

WILLIAM MAKEPEACE THACKERAY

Born: Calcutta, India
Date: July 18, 1811

Died: London, England
Date: December 24, 1863

PRINCIPAL WORKS

NOVELS: *Catherine*, 1839–1840; *The History of Samuel Titmarsh and the Great Hoggarty Diamond*, 1841; *Barry Lyndon*, 1844; *Vanity Fair*, 1847–1848; *Pendennis*, 1848–1850; *Henry Esmond*, 1852; *The Newcomes*, 1853–1855; *The Virginians*, 1857–1859; *The Adventures of Philip*, 1861–1862; *Denis Duval*, 1864.

SKETCHES: *The Paris Sketch Book*, 1840; *Comic Tales and Sketches*, 1841; *The Irish Sketch Book*, 1843; *The Book of Snobs*, 1848; *Sketches and Travels in London*, 1856.

CHRISTMAS STORY: *The Rose and the Ring*, 1854.

LECTURES AND ESSAYS: *The English Humorists of the Eighteenth Century*, 1851; *The Four Georges*, 1855; *Roundabout Papers*, 1864.

William Makepeace Thackeray was born at Calcutta, India (where his father was in the service of the East India Company), on July 18, 1811, and died in London on December 24, 1863. At least until 1859, when George Eliot's *Adam Bede* appeared, he was Dickens' only possible rival as the leading Victorian novelist.

Thackeray's father, Richmond Thackeray, died in 1815; his mother thereafter married Captain Henry Carmichael-Smyth, who became the original of Colonel Newcome. In 1822 the boy was sent to the Charterhouse School, whence he proceeded to Trinity College, Cambridge, which he left without taking a degree. He studied law in a desultory fashion and wandered about Weimar and Paris dabbling in art. In 1833, through a combination of folly and ill luck, he lost most of his considerable fortune. His first thought was to make his living as an artist (he later illustrated his own writings), but he soon turned instead to literature.

Thackeray began his career by burlesquing popular contemporary novelists whose work he considered mawkish, absurd, or morally vicious, for *Fraser's Magazine;* the most important outcome of these labors was his *Catherine*, in which he attacked the vogue of the story of crime. A more important enterprise, *Barry Lyndon*, was an eighteenth century rogue story, importantly influenced by Thackeray's admiration for Fielding's *Jonathan Wild;* but the writer did not really catch the public fancy until he published *Vanity Fair* in 1847–1848. From then until the end, though his sales always ran far behind those of Dickens, his reputation was secure. In the 1850's he made two lecture tours in America; from 1860 to 1862 he edited *The Cornhill Magazine*. His domestic happiness was clouded by the insanity of his Irish wife, Isabella Shaw (whom he married in 1836, and who outlived him by many years); in his relations with his daughters he showed all the tenderness of which his kindly, but in some ways weak, nature was capable.

Thackeray was at once a cynic and a sentimentalist. The judgments he makes of his characters are often uncertain and conventional, but he portrays them with a vivid realism which

1071

in his time seemed shocking in English fiction. Many of his most successful characters are, in one way or another, rogues. "The Art of Novels," he declared, "*is* to represent Nature; to convey as strongly as possible the sentiment of reality. . . ." The heightening and idealism proper to "a tragedy or a poem or a lofty drama" he ruled out. Not by this alone was he differentiated from Dickens but also by his upper-class point of view, his lack of Dickens' enthusiasm, vitality, and inexhaustible sympathy, and by his more bookish, elegant style. His world, in its main aspects, comprises Mayfair and Bohemia. Though the two great writers did not fail to appreciate each other, Dickens was inclined to resent his rival's somewhat superior and aristocratic air toward "the art that he held in trust." Thus the tone of careless ease in Thackeray's writing is an important element in his charm, but it also indicates an important limitation.

His major novels are few in number and make up a comparatively small portion of the twenty-five odd volumes of his collected works. Probably the most brilliant are *Vanity Fair,* a stunning panorama of a corrupt upper- and middle-class society around the Waterloo crisis, with a heroine, Becky Sharp, who has been for a hundred years the most celebrated female rogue in English fiction, and *Henry Esmond,*

a novel in the form of a memoir, presenting Jacobitish and other intrigues in an eighteenth century London in some ways more congenial to Thackeray's mind and spirit than his own time. *Henry Esmond's* cool, autumnal elegance and perfect distinction of style place it forever in the aristocracy of the world's great novels. It has, too, in Beatrix Esmond, one of the most subtly and completely portrayed of all heroines of fiction. *Pendennis* is an attempt to use for fiction the materials of Thackeray's own life in the manner and spirit of Fielding's *Tom Jones.* The *Newcomes,* a family novel covering three generations, is a wider-scoped *Vanity Fair. The Virginians* gives us Esmond's grandsons in the American Revolution and in London. These are all major novels. But *The Adventures of Philip* is only a minor *Pendennis,* and *Denis Duval,* a brilliant adventure story, which represents for Thackeray a frank capitulation to romance, he unfortunately did not live to finish.

Thackeray's achievement, like that of his master Fielding, is central in the development of the English novel. Though he had neither Scott's imagination nor Dickens' brilliance, he had an unerring sense of the scope and direction of fiction. After a hundred years he still deserves to be called one of our very greatest realists.

Edward Wagenknecht

BIBLIOGRAPHICAL REFERENCES: An important event in Thackeray biography and criticism occurred in 1945–1946, when the Thackeray family allowed Gordon N. Ray to publish *The Letters and Private Papers of William Makepeace Thackeray,* 4 vols. A fifth volume is in preparation. Ray's *The Buried Life,* 1952, is a critical study; his *Thackeray: The Uses of Adversity,* 1955, and *Thackeray: The Age of Wisdom,* 1958, now make up the definitive biography. Lionel Stevenson, *The Showman of Vanity Fair,* 1947, was the last important book prepared without access to Ray's documents. Recent critical studies include John W. Dodds, *Thackeray: A Critical Portrait,* 1941; and Geoffrey Tillotson, *Thackeray the Novelist,* 1954.

Among the books published before the *Letters and Private Papers,* the most important are the writings of Thackeray's daughter, Lady Ritchie, especially *Chapters from Some Unwritten Memoirs*, 1894, and *Thackeray and His Daughter*, 1924. See also Lewis Melville, *The Life of William Makepeace Thackeray*, 2 vols., 1899; and Malcolm Elwin, *Thackeray: A Personality*, 1932. Miriam M. H. Thrall's *Rebellious Fraser's*, 1934, is important for Thackeray's apprenticeship.

THEOCRITUS

Born: Syracuse (?) *Died:* Syracuse (?)
Date: 305 (?), B.C. *Date:* c. 250 B.C.

PRINCIPAL WORKS

POEMS: The *Bucolics;* the *Epics.*

Theocritus is one of the ancient authors about whom all too little is known to satisfy scholars. Much of what has sometimes passed for fact about him has been inferred from his writings, particularly from the *Charites,* and in some cases doubt has been cast on works attributed to him. It would appear reasonable to assume, however, that he was born about 305 B.C. in Syracuse (though equal claims have been made for Cos) and that he studied as a youth and young man under the Greek master Philetas, in Cos. Becoming certain of his craft as a poet, Theocritus appealed to Hiero the Second, ruler of Syracuse, for Hiero's support as a patron (probably in 275 B.C.), but was refused. Shortly thereafter a similar plea to Ptolemy Philadelphus brought success, and Theocritus took up residence in Alexandria sometime between 275 and 270 B.C. How long he stayed there or where he went afterward is a problem for which we have only conjectures, rather than answers. Probably he went to Cos, perhaps back to Syracuse, where he probably died about 250 B.C.

Much of Theocritus' poetry illustrates the love the ancient Greeks had for their homeland. Apparently the poet, far away from Greece in Alexandria, wrote much of his poetry in the pastoral convention to express the love he had for Greece. His most famous poems, the *Bucolics,* are pastoral poems on mythical subjects. The *Epics,* a later work, include poems to Hiero and Ptolemy, also to their respective spouses. There is also a series of epigrams of doubtful authenticity and equally doubtful date. The poems of Theocritus are often referred to as idylls, a word bestowed upon them by ancient authors. Credit is usually given to Theocritus for being the inventor of bucolic poetry, and he probably was, although modern scholarship, by showing how Theocritus borrowed ideas and fragments from earlier authors, has somewhat diminished the reputation he once enjoyed.

BIBLIOGRAPHICAL REFERENCES: The best translation of Theocritus in prose is that by Andrew Lang, 1901. Verse translations are numerous. See also J. M. Edmonds, *The Greek Bucolic Poets*, 1912; and R. J. Cholmeley, Introduction to *The Idylls of Theocritus*, 1919.

DYLAN THOMAS

Born: Swansea, Wales   *Died:* New York, N. Y.
Date: October 27, 1914   *Date:* November 9, 1953

PRINCIPAL WORKS

POEMS: *18 Poems,* 1934; *Twenty-five Poems,* 1936; *The Map of Love,* 1939; *The World I Breathe,* 1939; *New Poems,* 1943; *Deaths and Entrances,* 1946; *In Country Sleep,* 1952; *Collected Poems, 1934–1952,* 1952.

SHORT STORIES AND SKETCHES: *Adventures in the Skin Trade and Other Stories,* 1955.

AUTOBIOGRAPHY: *Portrait of the Artist as a Young Dog,* 1940.

PLAYS: *The Doctor and the Devils,* 1953; *Under Milk Wood,* 1954.

ESSAYS AND BROADCASTS: *Quite Early One Morning,* 1954.

Dylan (Marlais) Thomas, born in Swansea, Wales, on October 27, 1914, regularly produced and published poetry and short fiction to the age of thirty-five. His last four years were wasted in public readings of earlier works as well as the works of other poets (for the ostensible purpose of earning more but as well to find reassurance in adulation), and new works were produced but occasionally and hurriedly under the pressure of professional commitments. It was during this latter period that Thomas disintegrated psychically to die of acute alcoholism in New York City on November 9, 1953. When the memory of his exuberant personality has dissipated, he will probably be judged the greatest lyric poet of his generation and a fiction writer of original humor and charm.

The total amount of Thomas' work could be contained in one volume; however, he was not so much a slow writer as a careful one, altering some of his poems over two hundred times. He insisted that his work be read at its face value, preferably aloud. (Thomas once said that he wanted to be *read,* not *read into.*) Much of the criticism of the obscurity of his work has been irrelevant for this reason: the reader is not supposed to find answers to anything; rather, he is to allow the words to work on him, which they do tremendously in spite of the many private and esoteric references. While some scholars have traced these to their sources for further enjoyment, the magic of the literature as it stands is the main reward.

Thomas was a tragic figure, a man of effusive good will who dissipated to death in agonies of guilt. While his poetry tortuously worked through to a celebration of the Christian belief, in his prose, as well as in his personal life, he revealed the mind of one who wished to believe, to find faith, but could not, and in not finding it knew life as a nightmare from which there was no escape except death. This was the reason for the number of images depicting horror in his work. If some of it was symbolic, it was because there was nothing in the familiar world that sufficiently expressed the horror that he saw. Extremely sensitive, imbued with an impossible ethical code by his schoolmaster father, he projected his own guilt onto the world at large, its hypocrisy and money-getting, its general inhumanity. Two symptoms of this

1074

were his telling the truth beyond the edge of tact and his profligate wastefulness of money, though he was miserable when the first resulted in hurt feelings and the second in poverty.

Thomas was essentially a rural poet, and much of what he had to say was concerned with that world, of its harmony with the rhythm of the earth in its emphasis on birth, marriage, death, rebirth, and a simple faith in God, or else with the lost world of childhood innocence. His readers were of the urban world, however, a world he feared and hated.

Thomas was educated in the Swansea Grammer School in which his father was an English master. The English scholar is often antithetical to works of writers not dead, and Dylan's later scorn of scholars in England and America may indicate that his father belittled his early efforts, just as his anti-social boisterousness indicated an overstrict childhood. However, his early poetry and prose were published frequently in the grammar school literary magazine; and when his first volume, *18 Poems,* appeared, it was received enthusiastically by critics such as Edith Sitwell, though not by the general public, some of whom wrote virulent abuses to the *Sunday Times.* The poetry of this first period was concerned almost entirely with personal problems and was made perhaps deliberately obscure by private imagery and a highly personalized style.

Until World War II Thomas lived in London much of the time. Short but broad, of huge energy, he had experiences that were in many ways those of any proud rural innocent; always scornful of hypocrisy and the unnatural, he found much to reject in the city. At the same time his great warmth and talent made him many friends among its literary leaders. His way of adapting to this life was to mock the conventions with droll acts. During the war he served as an anti-aircraft gunner; the sight of the courage and suffering induced his second creative phase, one which revealed poignant feelings for others. When he also read poetry over the B.B.C., he began to have a general public.

With the printing of *The Collected Poems of Dylan Thomas* in 1952 he became a public figure on the basis of his enthusiastic reception by reviewers and critics. His later poetry had begun to reveal the change in his attitude from one of doubt and fear to faith and hope, with love of God gained through love of man and the world of nature. It also was more verbose. It was at this time that he became unbearably dissatisfied with life, expressing this in such poems as "I Have Longed to Move Away." Part of this feeling may have been due to his growing fear of alienation from his Irish-born wife Caitlin and their three children; part of it may have been the effect of his fear of losing his powers and upon which the first fear would be based. In addition, he was miserable as a public figure. Like all provincials, he was anxious before the stranger; although he was deeply appreciated by the audiences he read to, most of these people were interested in the poet of public fame, not in the private man. For a man with a huge capacity and need to love and be loved, this experience may have been devastating. Whatever the causes, Thomas produced mostly fiction and verse plays the last few years of his life. Of these the unfinished *Adventures in the Skin Trade* deals with his urban experiences, *Under Milk Wood* with his village reminiscences. Both of these works were celebrations of innocence, written at a time when the poet said of himself, "I have seen the gates of hell."

BIBLIOGRAPHICAL REFERENCES: There is no authorized biography. Highly subjective and often conflicting details are given in two works combining biography and reminiscence: John Malcolm Brinnin, *Dylan Thomas in America*, 1955; and Caitlin Thomas, *Leftover Life to Kill*, 1957. The basic critical studies are Henry Treece, *Dylan Thomas*, 1949; and Elder Olson, *The Poetry of Dylan Thomas*, 1954. See also *Dylan Thomas: Letters to Vernon Watkins*, edited, with an introduction, by Vernon Watkins, 1957.

The best brief yet comprehensive study of the poetry and prose is John L. Sweeney's Introduction to *Selected Writings of Dylan Thomas*, 1946. See also Francis Scarfe, "Dylan Thomas: A Pioneer," in *Auden and After*, 1942; Babette Deutsch, "Alchemists of the Word," in *Poetry in Our Time*, 1952; M. W. Stearn, "Unsex the Skeleton: Notes on the Poetry of Dylan Thomas," *Sewanee Review*, LII (1944), 424–440; Robert Horan, "In Defense of Dylan Thomas," *Kenyon Review*, VII (1945), 304–310; Anon., "Salute to a Poet," *London Times Literary Supplement*, LI (Nov. 28, 1952), 776; David Daiches, "The Poetry of Dylan Thomas," *College English*, XVI (1954), 1–8; and Henry W. Wells, "Voice and Verse in Dylan Thomas' Play," *College English*, XV (1954), 438–444.

THOMAS À KEMPIS

Born: Kempen, Germany
Date: c. 1380

Died: St. Agnietenberg, Netherlands
Date: July 25, 1471

PRINCIPAL WORK

THEOLOGICAL TREATISE: *Imitatio Christi*, c. 1400 (*The Imitation of Christ*).

Thomas à Kempis, born Thomas Hammerken (or Hemerken) about 1380, was the son of a peasant whose wife was the keeper of an old-fashioned dame-school for small children. At the age of twelve, Thomas was sent to the chapter school at Deventer, where among his teachers was Florens Radewijns (Florentius Radewyn). Known at Deventer as Thomas from Kempen, the scholar gradually assumed the name by which posterity knows him. When it became apparent to Thomas and his teachers that he was suited for a monk's life, he went in 1399 to the monastery of St. Agnietenberg, near Zwolle, where the prior was his brother John. Thomas

entered the Augustinian order in 1406 and was ordained a priest in 1413 or 1414.

The remainder of his long life was spent in that monastery, except for a brief period of exile from 1429 to 1432, during the Utrecht schism. Thomas copied a great deal of material, earning money for his monastery by his labors. He also wrote original material, for which dates of composition are too vague to have any value. Included in his works are biographies of Gerhard Groot, Florentius Radewyn, and the Flemish St. Louise. He also wrote many tracts and a chronicle of the monastery of St. Agnietenberg. The most important of the writings with which his name is associated is *The Imitation of Christ,* written between 1380 and 1410 and first circulated in 1418, a moving religious document that next to the Bible is the most widely known of all religious books. Although Thomas à Kempis' authorship has been disputed, the arguments advanced against his authorship have only seemed to strengthen the belief that the work is really from his pen. Thomas was made subprior of St. Agnietenberg in 1425. He died there on July 25, 1471.

BIBLIOGRAPHICAL REFERENCES: The standard edition is the *Opera Omnia,* edited by M. J. Pohl, 1907–1922. The most recent translation of *Imitation of Christ* is that by L. Shirley-Price, 1953. A good brief biographyical study is F. R. Cruise, *Outline of the Life of Thomas à Kempis,* 1904. See also Samuel Kettlewell, *Thomas à Kempis and the Brothers of the Common Life,* 1882; and James Williams, *Thomas of Kempen,* 1910.

DANIEL PIERCE THOMPSON

Born: Charlestown, Massachusetts
Date: October 1, 1795

Died: Montpelier, Vermont
Date: June 6, 1868

PRINCIPAL WORKS

NOVELS: *The Green Mountain Boys,* 1839; *Locke Amsden,* 1847; *The Rangers,* 1851.

Born of an old American family that reached Massachusetts early in the seventeenth century, and claiming an ancestor killed at the Battle of Lexington, Daniel Pierce Thompson had reason to be interested in history. Shortly after his birth, at Charlestown, Massachusetts, on October 1, 1795, his family moved to Berlin, Vermont, a frontier settlement with neither school nor library. The chance discovery of a volume of poetry inspired him to get an education. After studying by himself and at a preparatory school, he entered Middlebury College with advanced standing, financing himself by the sale of his sheep and by poems and articles he contributed to magazines.

After graduation, Thompson tutored the son of a rich southern planter and met Thomas Jefferson, who turned the young man's thoughts toward the law. After some study, Thompson returned to Vermont and was admitted to the bar. He codified the laws of Vermont in 1834. His first fiction was the anti-Masonic *Adventures of Timothy Peacock, Esq.* (1835), whom he called a "Masonic Quixote." Association with survivors of the Revolutionary period inspired his novel *The Green Mountain Boys,* first printed on a small newspaper press. Immediately successful, the novel went through fifty editions in twenty years. Its sequel was *The Rangers,* published in 1851. Thompson also edited the anti-slavery *Green Mountain Freeman* (1849–1856).

As a man, Thompson was an old-fashioned Yankee with a keen sense of humor. A contemporary portrait shows him with thin features, a jutting chin, long nose, and a tangled mop of hair. He died at Montpelier, Vermont, June 6, 1868.

BIBLIOGRAPHICAL REFERENCES: Thompson has attracted very little attention; however, there is a full-length study that supplies all the necessary basic information: J. E. Flitcroft, *The Novelist of Vermont, A Biographical and Critical Study of Daniel Pierce Thompson*, 1929. See also L. D. Loshe, *The Early American Novels*, 1907 (rev. ed., 1930); and Van Wyck Brooks's comments in *The Flowering of New England*, 1936.

HENRY DAVID THOREAU

Born: Concord, Massachusetts
Date: July 12, 1817

Died: Concord
Date: May 6, 1862

PRINCIPAL WORKS

NATURE STUDIES AND ESSAYS: *A Week on the Concord and Merrimack Rivers*, 1849; *Walden, or Life in the Woods*, 1854; *Excursions*, 1863; *The Maine Woods*, 1864; *Cape Cod*, 1865; *A Yankee in Canada, with Anti-Slavery and Reform Papers*, 1866; *Early Spring in Massachusetts*, 1881; *Summer*, 1884; *Winter*, 1888; *Autumn*, 1894.

POEMS: *Poems of Nature*, 1895; *Collected Poems*, 1943.

LETTERS: *Letters to Various Persons*, edited by Ralph Waldo Emerson, 1865; *Familiar Letters of Henry David Thoreau*, edited by F. B. Sanborn, 1894.

Henry David Thoreau, defier of labels, was a man born before his time. Thirty or forty years later *Walden* might have surged to success on the tide of nature interest which benefited such writers as John Burroughs and John Muir. As it was, Thoreau was largely ignored by his own generation, which dismissed him as an impractical reformer. It has remained to a later period to recognize him as one of the most original thinkers and one of the best prose writers of his time.

Along with Emerson and Hawthorne, Thoreau is often referred to as a member of the "Concord Group"; of this trio, however, Thoreau alone could claim the town as his birthplace. He was born there July 12, 1817, the second son of John and Cynthia (Dunbar) Thoreau. He grew up in Concord village, attending the local school— apparently an excellent one—in preparation for Harvard College, which he entered at the age of sixteen. Despite financial difficulties during the next four years, he was graduated in 1837,

well versed in languages and skillful in the use of his pen. Already a non-conformist, during his Harvard days he disregarded honors, neglected unattractive studies, and deplored the necessity of spending five dollars for a diploma.

Unlike his literary contemporaries, Thoreau never prepared for a profession. After graduation from college he taught school in Concord for a time, together with his brother John. With the latter he made a trip on the Concord and Merrimack Rivers in 1839. John, to whom his brother was devoted, died of lockjaw in 1842. He was ill with tuberculosis at the time, a disease which took the father of the boys and, finally, Thoreau himself.

It was about 1840 that Thoreau decided to become a writer. The decision made no change in his simple manner of life: throughout his career, he preferred to support himself by the labor of his hands. Intermittently he worked at lead pencil making (his father's business), did surveying, or made gardens. It was in the capacity of gardener that he became a member of Emerson's household in 1841, though his services came to include helping Emerson to edit the Transcendentalist journal, *The Dial*. Despite Lowell's contention that Thoreau was the imitator of his employer, it seems equally likely that Emerson's interest in nature and nature lore was gained, at least in part, from Thoreau.

The independence and fearlessness of Thoreau's nature led him to speak out actively against whatever he found reason to regard as wrong. He strongly championed John Brown and the Abolitionists, for example, at a time when such a stand was highly unpopular. In 1845, following the example of Bronson Alcott, he went to jail rather than pay poll tax to a government which, as Thoreau saw it, countenanced war and slavery. He provided a living embodiment of Emerson's doctrines of self-reliance and non-conformity; but it is notable that he did so without forfeiting the love and respect of those who knew him best.

Perhaps the most important activity of Thoreau's life began in 1845, when he retired to a little hut at Walden Pond near Concord. Here, he lived for over two years, cultivating a small plot of ground and attempting to prove that a man need not go beyond his own resources for sustenance and enjoyment. The literary result of this experiment was *Walden*, his best-known work. Published in 1854, this book provided the first and best example of that literary product especially identified with America, the "nature book."

Aside from *Walden*, the only other of Thoreau's books published during his lifetime was *A Week on the Concord and Merrimack Rivers*, of which the public took little notice, only two hundred or so copies being sold. It was not until after his death that the bulk of Thoreau's writing was published, although some articles and addresses had made their appearance in contemporary periodicals, chiefly in *The Dial* and *Putnam's Magazine*. Since his death in Concord on May 6, 1862, the complete journal of Thoreau has been published; and, even though his total writing output is slim in comparison with that of some of his fellow New Englanders, it is sufficient to give him belated recognition as one of the really original and vigorous writers of the century.

The nineteenth century neglect of Thoreau, which continued for a decade or two after his death, was partly the result of the inaccurate estimates of his worth made by such respected critics as Lowell. The nature school, arising at the end of the century, has played a part in his literary revival; nevertheless, Thoreau's essential value as a writer depends only partly on the nature of his subject matter. Clarity of expression, shrewdness, and occasional humor combine to form an individual prose style of compelling charm. The integrity of the man shines through his work, and his positive views on nature and government constitute a continuing challenge to a civilization bowed down by frustrations and complexities.

BIBLIOGRAPHICAL REFERENCES: The complete works of Henry David Thoreau have been posthumously published in the Manuscript Edition, 20 vols., 1906, and in the standard Walden Edition printed from the same plates. Odell Shepherd edited *The Heart of Thoreau's Journals*, 1927. See also Bartholow V. Crawford, ed., *Henry David*

Theoreau: Representative Selections, 1934; Henry Seidel Canby, ed., *The Works of Thoreau*, 1947; and Carl Bode, ed., *The Portable Thoreau*, 1947.

The most extensive biographical study is Henry S. Canby, *Thoreau*, 1939. Other biographical studies include Henry S. Salt, *The Life of Henry David Thoreau*, 1890; Mark Van Doren, *Henry David Thoreau: A Critical Study*, 1916; Leon Bazalgette, *Henry Thoreau: Bachelor of Nature*, 1924; and Brooks Atkinson, *Henry D. Thoreau: The Cosmic Yankee*, 1927.

For briefer studies see F. O. Matthiessen, *American Renaissance*, 1941; Carl Bode, Introduction to *The Portable Thoreau*, 1947; Norman Foerster, "Thoreau as Artist," *Sewanee Review*, XXIX (1921), 2–13; Raymond Adams, "A Bibliographical Note on *Walden*," *American Literature*, II (1930), 166–168; *idem*, "Thoreau's Literary Apprenticeship," *Studies in Philology*, XXIX (1932), 617–629; Henry W. Wells, "An Evaluation of Thoreau's Poetry," *American Literature*, XVI (1944), 99–109; Randall Stewart, "The Growth of Thoreau's Reputation," *College English*, VII (1946), 208–214; Madeleine B. Stern, "Approaches to Biography," *South Atlantic Quarterly*, XIX (1946), 362–371; and S. T. Hyman, "Henry Thoreau in Our Time," *Atlantic Monthly*, CLXXVIII (1946), 137–146.

THUCYDIDES

Born: Athens, Greece
Date: 455 (?), B.C.

Died: Thrace (?)
Date: c. 400 B.C.

Principal Work

HISTORY: *History of the Peloponnesian War* (written c. 431–400 B.C.).

Thucydides was the son of Olorus, an Athenian citizen. The date of his birth is uncertain; it has been put as early as 471 B.C. and as late as 455 B.C., the latter date being the more probable. He may have spent part of his youth in Thrace, where his family owned gold-mining rights. He says that he began his history of the Peloponnesian war at the moment when the war broke out, so that he was presumably living at Athens in 431. He was certainly there the following year during the plague, of which he fell ill. In 424 he was appointed, jointly with Eucles, to defend the coastal region bordering on Thrace, and was entrusted with a naval squadron. His failure to prevent the capture of Amphipolis when it was invested by the Spartans provoked the Athenians to send him into exile. He passed the twenty years of his banishment in visit-ing the cities of the enemy and the principal battlefields of the war, and in collecting from veterans of the war the historical materials needed for his work. He returned to Athens about 403. He did not live to complete his great work, the *History* ending in 411, seven years before the peace was finally made. His death is supposed to have occurred in Thrace at the hands of an assassin about 400 B.C.

Thucydides' *History* is both highly objective and highly dramatic. In the numerous orations which he reports or constructs, he shows his precise understanding of ideological issues. His narratives are marvelously vivid; among the most memorable are his accounts of the plague at Athens and of the Syracusan campaign, which ended with the imprisonment of the expeditionary force in the rock quarries.

JAMES THURBER

Born: Columbus, Ohio
Date: December 8, 1894

Died: New York, N. Y.
Date: November 2, 1961

PRINCIPAL WORKS

ESSAYS, STORIES, SKETCHES, AND DRAWINGS: *Is Sex Necessary?*, 1929 (with E. B. White); *The Owl in the Attic and Other Perplexities*, 1931; *The Seal in the Bedroom and Other Predicaments*, 1932; *My Life and Hard Times*, 1933; *The Middle-Aged Man on the Flying Trapeze*, 1935; *Let Your Mind Alone*, 1937; *The Last Flower*, 1939; *My World—And Welcome to It!*, 1942; *Men, Women and Dogs*, 1943; *The Thurber Carnival*, 1945; *The Beast in Me and Other Animals*, 1948; *The Thurber Album*, 1952; *Thurber Country*, 1953; *Thurber's Dogs*, 1955.

FABLES AND FANTASIES: *Fables for Our Time*, 1940; *Many Moons*, 1943; *The Great Quillow*, 1944; *The White Deer*, 1945; *The Thirteen Clocks*, 1950; *Further Fables for Our Time*, 1956; *The Wonderful O*, 1957.

PLAY: *The Male Animal*, 1940 (with Elliott Nugent).

James (Grover) Thurber, born in Columbus, Ohio, on December 8, 1894, came to the East Coast by way of the Chicago *Tribune* and Paris, France, and settled down, finally, with E. B. White to make *The New Yorker* what it is today.

These journalistic meanderings started at Ohio State where Thurber began his writing career as a reporter for the university newspaper. They were interrupted by a year of war duty (unable to get into the Army because of one sightless eye, Thurber served as a code clerk in Washington and Paris) and by a second year which he took off just to read. But they were resumed in 1919, and were continued, after his graduation, on a professional basis with the Columbus *Dispatch*. Next came the *Tribune* and Paris. Thurber served as editor of the *Tribune's* Paris edition until 1929, when he returned to the

United States and began his historic relationship with White on the staff of *The New Yorker*.

The story of his beginning with the magazine has become a legend. Reputedly, Thurber was brought by White into the magazine's offices. His object was simply a job. He emerged as managing editor and remained in that capacity for six months. Eventually he joined White in the composition of the "Talk of the Town" and continued in that department until his resignation in 1933.

The resignation did not end his relations with *The New Yorker*, however. His work continued to appear in its pages in the form of frequent essays, fables, tales, and drawings, and almost all the material collected in his books first appeared in the columns of that magazine.

Is Sex Necessary? was written in

collaboration with White, its content a blend of Thurber's delightful whimsy, White's spoofing erudition, and, certainly not the least important, illustrations by Thurber himself.

The success of this first collection meant a demand for more. *The Owl in the Attic*, with an introduction by White, appeared in 1931, followed logically enough by *The Seal in the Bedroom*, and by the comically autobiographical *My Life and Hard Times*. Some fifteen additional volumes have appeared since, and with each one Thurber's reputation as the leading humorist of our age has become more firmly established. There have been numerous efforts to explain and evaluate his very particular brand of humor; no less a figure than T. S. Eliot has analyzed his genius, a quality easier to recognize than to define. Whether narrating the eternal war between the sexes, describing the homicidal effects of a baseball announcer's clichés, reviewing the frustrations brought on by recalcitrant machinery, or capturing with a few sketchy lines the canine quintessence of befuddled dogdom, Thurber is funny—sometimes quietly funny, sometimes hilariously funny, but always, it would seem, funny in a unique and inimitable way. There is whimsy in his humor, but "whimsy" is too limited a word to describe the total effect. His humor is in the American tradition of exaggeration and the tall tale (the uncle who caught the chestnut blight, the draft prospect who served four months undetected as an examiner), but there is a pathos behind it, a sort of subliminal human (or canine) tragedy that makes it something more. T. S. Eliot says that "There is a criticism of life at the bottom of it," and that "His writing and also his illustrations are capable of surviving the immediate environment and time out of which they spring." If this proves to be true, Thurber will certainly rank among the greatest of American humorists, alongside Mark Twain and Oliver Wendell Holmes.

Personally retiring to the point of shyness, Thurber heard his fame reverberate far beyond the quietly sophisticated sphere of *The New Yorker*. His introverted Walter Mitty has been brought to life on the screen by the frenetic Danny Kaye; his *Thirteen Clocks* has been performed on the stage and as a television opera; a New York bar decorated its interior with murals from his drawings. But for all this renown he lived quietly in Connecticut and, in spite of almost complete blindness, continued to write and draw. His death occurred in New York City on November 2, 1961.

BIBLIOGRAPHICAL REFERENCES: There is as yet no full-length biographical or critical study of James Thurber; however, the basic facts about his career are available in a *Time* cover article, LVIII (July 9, 1951), 88–95. There is an excellent interview by George Plimpton and Max Steele in *The Paris Review*, 11 (Fall 1955), 35–49. See also Walter Blair, *Horse Sense in American Humor*, 1942; "James Thurber: The Comic Prufrock," *Poetry*, LXII (1943), 150–159, an anonymous article; Francis Downing, "Thurber," *Commonweal*, XLI (1945), 518–519; and Gerald Weales, "The World in Thurber's Fables," *ibid.*, LXV (1957), 409–411.

COUNT LEO TOLSTOY

Born: Yásnaya Polyána, Russia
Date: August 28, 1828

Died: Astapovo, Russia
Date: November 7, 1910

PRINCIPAL WORK

NOVELS: *Kazaki*, 1863 (*The Cossacks*); *Voina i mir*, 1865–1869 (*War and Peace*); *Anna Karenina*, 1873–1877; *Smert Ivana Ilyicha*, 1884 (*The Death of Ivan Ilyich*); *Khozyain i rabotnik*, 1885 (*Master and Man*); *Kreitserova Sonata*, 1889 (*The Kreutzer Sonata*); *Voskraeseniye*, 1899 (*The Resurrection*).

AUTOBIOGRAPHY: *Destvo*, 1852 (*Childhood*); *Otrochestvo*, 1854 (*Boyhood*); *Yunost*, 1857 (*Adolescence*); *Ispoved*, 1884 (*A Confession*).

PLAY: *Vlast tmy*, 1886 (*The Power of Darkness*).

Count Leo (Lev) Nikolayevich Tolstoy, Russian author and moral philosopher, was born on August 28, 1828, at Yásnaya Polyána, near Tula, Russia, into a family of aristocratic landowners. He was educated first at home and then at the University of Kazan, which he left without taking a degree. One of his early and enduring influences was that of Rousseau. As if prompted by it he returned from Kazan to his estate with the object of improving the living conditions of his serfs. Frustrated in this task, he left in 1851 for the Caucasus where he joined the army and spent much of his time among the primitive Cossack settlers so wonderfully described in his novel *The Cossacks*, written in 1854 but not printed until 1863. In the Caucasus he finished his first important work, *Childhood*, a delightful string of autobiographic sketches which was followed up by *Boyhood* and *Adolescence*. Tolstoy took part in the Crimean campaign, and his three Sevastopol stories, with their frank realism, established his reputation. Even in these early writings he combined a profound psychological insight with an almost incredible visual and plastic power. He soon gave up the army and for a while divided his time between Moscow and his estate. In 1857 and again in 1860 he traveled extensively abroad where he became rather disappointed with the materialistic trend of Western civilization. This only fostered his sympathy with the Russian peasant masses whose simple ways of life he had admired from the outset. On his estate he actually set up, in 1859, a school for peasant children and he himself taught in it for a while on more or less Rousseau-esque lines. In 1862 he married Sophia Andreyevna Behrs. A year later he was already writing his great novel, *War and Peace*, which he finished in 1869.

In this epic of a whole people at the time of a historical crisis Tolstoy depicts, on a very broad canvas, all the strata of the Russian nation in their resistance to Napoleon's invasion in 1812. Yet the backbone of the novel is the interlacing history of two noble families—those of Tolstoy's father and mother—which in the end become united through marriage. Among the many unforgettable characters conjured up by Tolstoy's genius, that of the young Natasha Rostova is particularly wonderful. Yet Tolstoy the moralist and the seeker, quite noticeable in a number of his previous writings, comes also here to the fore. He projected his own quest into Pierre Bezukhov and Prince Andrey, but he did it objectively enough to make both of them independent of their author's views and tendencies.

Tolstoy's own "vexation of the spirit" is felt, however, much more tangibly in Levin, the hero of his next masterpiece, *Anna Karenina,* which he wrote between 1873 and 1877. The novel is a chronicle of three or four families, Tolstoy's own growing family being one of them. But this time the background is that of the 1870's when Russia, no longer in the grip of serfdom, had to cope with the problems of capitalist economy gradually encroaching upon the patriarchal countryside. Too much of a patriarchal squire at heart to welcome anything that smelled of capitalism and town civilization, Tolstoy based the very structure of this novel on the contrast between the unsophisticated countryside on the one hand and the "corrupt" city life on the other. Yet in spite of all the idyllic charms of his family life and his prosperous farming, the squire Levin was unable to escape from his inner crisis which was due to his quest for a meaning of life. Such a meaning was imparted to him at last by a simple God-fearing peasant who lived according to the teaching of the Gospel. In this way Levin anticipated Tolstoy's own conversion so pathetically described in his *A Confession,* written in 1879 and first published (abroad) in 1884.

Such a crisis and conversion had actually been latent in Tolstoy's inner make-up itself. Endowed with a spontaneous and truly pagan love of life, he was yet unable to affirm life without a meaning which he envisaged above all in terms of moral values. Far from being unexpected, his conversion was only a turning point at which the moralizing rationalist in Tolstoy took the upper hand over Tolstoy the artist. After a long quest he discovered the true meaning of life in the Sermon on the Mount which he "corrected" in such a way as to turn it against private property and all social divisions, all laws and authorities; in fact, against all civilized existence as such. The only law he acknowledged was God's commandment of brotherly love instilled in man's conscience. From the beginning of the 1880's Tolstoy wrote one eloquent pamphlet after the other in order to propagate his primitive Christian anarchism. In his brilliantly misleading book, *What is Art* (1897), he condemned all art which failed to foster the moral good among men. In another pamphlet he even made a savage onslaught on Shakespeare. His teaching soon found adherents in all parts of the world, but none of the "Tolstoyan" communities had a long lease of life. Paradoxically enough, in spite of his strange teaching of non-resistance (which was subsequently taken up by his Hindu follower, Gandhi), Tolstoy's virulent criticism of the social evils of our time helped to create in Russia that ferment which led to the revolution of 1917.

Tolstoy himself was too much of an artist to be entirely ousted by the moralist. Even with an eye on the moral "purpose" he still retained his creative power and wrote a number of masterpieces such as the haunting narrative *The Death of Ivan Ilyich, The Kreutzer Sonata, Master and Man,* and his last great novel, *The Resurrection.* Among his posthumous stories, *The Devil, The False Coupon, Father Sergius,* and *Hadji Murat* (all published in 1911) are particularly well

1084

told. As for his plays, the satirical comedy *Fruits of Enlightenment* (1891), the naturalistic peasant drama, *The Power of Darkness,* and *The Live Corpse,* unfinished, (1911), have been staged all over the world.

During the last twenty years of his life, Tolstoy became not only the most conspicuous literary figure in the world, but also one of the great moral forces of his time. Even in Russia he was allowed to say what he liked without any fear of the police or censorship. Realizing the responsibility of such a position, he did his best to live up to his own principles. He got rid of his personal property and even wanted to divide his land among the peasants, but his wife (who had to think of her large family) had responsibilities of her own which did not tally with those of her unpractical husband. Quarrels and misunderstandings between the two thus could not be avoided. In the end Tolstoy ran away from his home. During his flight he caught pneumonia and died at the small railway station, Astapovo, on November 7, 1910, at the age of eighty-two.

Janko Lavrin

BIBLIOGRAPHICAL REFERENCES: The most recent Russian edition of Tolstoy's works is *Polnoc Sobranic Sochineniy,* 1940 ff. See in English *The Centenary Edition of Tolstoy's Works,* edited by A. Maude, 1928–1937. See also D. Merezhkovsky, *Tolstoy i Dostoevsky,* St. Petersburg, 1901–1902 (2 vols.); Ivanov-Razumnik, *L. Tolstoy,* 1910; V. Veresayev, *O. Dostoevskom i Tolstom,* 1913; M. Gorky, *Vospominanya o Tolstom,* 1919; P. J. Biryukov, *L. N. Tolstoy,* 1923; N. N. Gusev, *Zhizn Tolstogo,* 1927; V. F. Bulgakov, *Tragediya Tolstogo,* 1928; N. N. Gusev, *Letopis Zhizni i Tvorchertva Tolstogo,* 1937; and I. A. Bunin *Osvobozhdenie Tolstogo,* 1937.

Studies in English include: H. Fausset, *Tolstoy,* 1927; A. Maude, *The Life of Tolstoy,* 1929–1930 (2 vols.); A. I. Nazarov, *Tolstoy, the Inconstant Genius,* 1930; Sofya A. Tolstaya, *The Diary of Tolstoy's Wife,* 1928; A. Maude, *The Final Struggle,* 1936; L. Derrick, *Tolstoy,* 1944; Janko Lavrin, *Tolstoy,* 1946; E. Simmons, *Leo Tolstoy,* 1946, 1949; Isaiah Berlin, *The Hedgehog and the Fox,* 1953; and A. L. Tolstaya, *A Life of My Father,* 1953.

H. M. TOMLINSON

Born: London, England
Date: 1873

Died: London
Date: February 5, 1958

PRINCIPAL WORKS

NOVELS: *Gallions Reach,* 1927; *All Our Yesterdays,* 1930; *The Snows of Helicon,* 1933; *Mars His Idiot,* 1935; *All Hands!* 1937 [*Pipe All Hands!*]; *The Day Before,* 1939; *Morning Light,* 1946; *The Trumpet Shall Sound,* 1957.

ESSAYS AND STUDIES: *Old Junk,* 1918; *London River,* 1921; *Waiting for Daylight,* 1922; *Gifts of Fortune,* 1926; *Under the Red Ensign,* 1926 [*The Foreshore of England*]; *Thomas Hardy,* 1929; *Between the Lines,* 1930; *Norman Douglas,* 1931; *Out of Soundings,* 1931; *The Wind Is Rising,* 1941; *The Turn of the Tide,* 1946; *The Face of the Earth,* 1950; *Malay Waters,* 1950; *The Haunted Forest,* 1951; *A Mingled Yarn,* 1953.

TRAVEL SKETCHES AND IMPRESSIONS: *The Sea and the Jungle,* 1912; *Tidemarks,* 1923; *Below London Bridge,* 1934; *South to Cadiz,* 1934.

H(enry) M(ajor) Tomlinson was born in 1873 in the East End of London and lived his youth around the docks. At the age of twelve he was employed as a shipping clerk. Hating the drudgery of the work, he loved the ships with which his labors brought him in contact. Even while working, however, he found time to read extensively, some of his favorite authors being Whitman, Melville, Emerson, and Thoreau. He also studied geology, entomology, and music.

H. M. Tomlinson started writing early in his life and began submitting his work to editors in hopes of escaping from the shipping office, but he was thirty-one before he was able to leave the job as a clerk. He became a member of the editorial staff of the London *Morning Leader* in 1904, and remained in this position until 1912, when he went on a long tour up the Amazon River on a tramp steamer. This trip and his experiences on it are the source for *The Sea and the Jungle*, his best-known travel book. In 1912 he joined the staff of the London *Daily News*, where he remained until 1917, when he became literary editor of *The Nation and Athenaeum* until 1923. From 1914 until 1917, Tomlinson was a foreign correspondent in France and Belgium. After 1923 he free-lanced as a journalist and novelist.

With the publication of *Gallions Reach* in 1927, Tomlinson achieved success as a novelist, and subsequently he devoted much of his attention to fiction. His first novel, a romance set in the Far East, won the Femina-Vie Heureuse Prize and caused Tomlinson to be associated, as an author, with Joseph Conrad. Perhaps the primary resemblance between them is their devotion to the sea, although Tomlinson seemed to share Conrad's conviction that the human state of mind, the thought process, is more important than action as such.

In his next novel, *All Our Yesterdays*, Tomlinson created a more severe tone, attacking the weaknesses of civilization. He felt that changing people's attitudes is the only hope for society. In these books, as in his later ones, he preferred settings which were unusual and exotic, places far from the main centers of life. His style is also individualistic, having a calmness and a vigor that have won him considerable praise. The books of essays which brought him a large following of readers are *Old Junk, London River*, and *Waiting for Daylight*. In these, as in his novels, a style of impressive imagery and verbal beauty accompanies the writer's gift of poetic introspection. His novels are often autobiographical, and his views of areas of the world such as the tropics border on impressionism. Although he has written much travel literature about far-off places, he was essentially a Londoner. Even so, his ability to create the mood and atmosphere of a distant place for his readers will probably continue to make him a widely read and appreciated writer whose best work has in it something of the force and yet the serenity of the sea. Tomlinson died in London on February 5, 1958.

BIBLIOGRAPHICAL REFERENCES: There is no extended body of criticism on Tomlinson. See Robert Lynd, *Books and Authors*, 1923; S. K. Ratcliffe, Introduction to *Old Junk*, 1920; John Freeman, "Mr. H. M. Tomlinson," *London Mercury*, XVI (1927), 400–408; F. P. Mayer, "H. M. Tomlinson: The Eternal Youth," *Virginia Quarterly*

Review, IV (1928), 78–82; and Helen and Richard Altick, "Square Rigger on a Modern Mission," *College English*, V (1943), 75–80.

CYRIL TOURNEUR

Born: Unknown   *Died:* Kinsdale, Ireland
Date: c. 1575   *Date:* February 28, 1626

PRINCIPAL WORKS

PLAYS: *The Revenger's Tragedy*, c. 1607; *The Atheist's Tragedy*, c. 1611.
POEMS: *A Funeral Poem upon the Death of the Most Worthy and True Soldier, Sir Francis Vere*, 1609; *A Grief on the Death of Prince Henry*, 1613.
MISCELLANEOUS: *The Transformed Metamorphosis*, 1600; *Character of Sir Robert Cecil, Earl of Salisbury*, 1612.

Cyril Tourneur, about whom little is known, was perhaps the son of Captain Richard Turnor, a follower of Sir Thomas Cecil. The young Tourneur, probably born about 1575, was a follower of the Cecils also, and served the Veres and the Earl of Essex at different times during his career. Much of that career was spent in military or diplomatic service. He probably served with the English forces in The Netherlands in the early years of the seventeenth century.

A verse satire, *The Transformed Metamorphosis*, was published in 1600, and *The Revenger's Tragedy*, which has been ascribed to Tourneur, was published in 1607. Tourneur's literary reputation rests chiefly on this play, although it was not ascribed to him until 1656, some fifty years after its performance, and its authorship has been contested. However, it is generally accepted as his work. His second surviving play, *The Atheist's Tragedy*, was published in 1611. *The Stationers' Register* contains an entry in 1612 of *The Nobleman*, a tragi-comedy by Cyril Tourneur; but this play and *The Arraignment of London*, for which he wrote one of the acts for Henslowe's company, are both lost.

He was a government courier in 1613 and a campaign soldier again in 1614. Imprisoned in 1617, he was released on Sir Edward Cecil's bond. In 1625 he accompanied Sir Edward on a naval expedition against Spain. As Lord Marshall of the Fleet, Sir Edward appointed Tourneur Secretary to the Council of War and Secretary to the Marshall's Court; but the first appointment was not approved. The expedition failed; Sir Edward's flagship, *The Royal Anna*, was badly damaged, with many of the crew killed or wounded, among them Tourneur. The ship reached port in Kinsdale, Ireland, where Tourneur was put ashore. He died there of his wounds on February 28, 1626.

Unlike many of the Elizabethan and Jacobean dramatists, Tourneur devoted most of his life to his active military career and relatively little of it to writing for the stage. T. M. Parrott considers him "a poet expressing himself in dramatic form rather than a professional playwright." The morbid splendor of his two surviving plays has attracted much critical interest.

BIBLIOGRAPHICAL REFERENCES: There are various editions of the complete and selected works: *The Plays and Poems of Cyril Tourneur*, edited by J. Churton Collins, 1878; *The Works of Cyril Tourneur*, edited by Allardyce Nicoll, 1930; *The Best Plays of Webster and Tourneur*, edited by John Addington Symonds, 1888; and *Masterpieces of the English Drama: Webster and Tourneur*, with an introduction by Ashley H. Thorndike, 1912. See also Henry W. Wells, *Elizabethan and Jacobean Playwrights*, 1939; T. M. Parrott and R. H. Ball, *A Short View of Elizabethan Drama*, 1943; and *Dictionary of National Biography*, Vol. 19.

ARNOLD TOYNBEE

Born: London, England
Date: April 14, 1889

PRINCIPAL WORKS

MISCELLANEOUS: *Nationality and the War*, 1915; *The New Europe*, 1915; *The Western Question in Greece and Turkey*, 1922; *Greek Historical Thought*, 1924; *Greek Civilization and Character*, 1924; *The World After the Peace Conference*, 1925; *Turkey*, 1926 (with K. P. Kirkwood); *A Journey to China*, 1931; *A Study of History*, 1934–1954; *Christianity and Civilization*, 1940; *Civilization on Trial*, 1948; *Prospects of Western Civilization*, 1949; *The World and the West*, 1953; *An Historian's Approach to Religion*, 1956; *Christianity Among the Religions of the World*, 1957.

Among philosophers of history Arnold (Joseph) Toynbee is unique in having made a profound appeal to scholars and general readers alike. His most impressive work to date has been his nine-volume *Study of History,* which has received careful attention from historians and philosophers of history and has afforded exciting reading to thousands who know the work through abridgements.

Toynbee, born in London on April 14, 1889, was educated at Winchester and then at Balliol College, Oxford. His academic record enabled him to be a Scholar at both schools. From 1912 to 1915 he was a fellow and tutor at Balliol. Later in his life, when his scholarly activities had given him distinguished status among commentators on history, he was awarded various honorary degrees: an Hon. D.Litt. from Oxford, Birmingham, and Co-

lumbia; a Litt.D. from Cambridge, and a D.C.L. from Princeton.

During World War I Toynbee worked at various governmental jobs, including a period with the British Foreign Office in 1918 as a member of the staff in the political intelligence department. He was a member of the Middle Eastern Section of the British Delegation to the Peace Conference in Paris in 1919.

Having engaged in the practical application of his knowledge of Middle Eastern affairs, Toynbee returned to academic life in his position as Koraes Professor of Byzantine and Modern Greek Language, Literature, and History at London University from 1919 to 1924. Recognition of his increasing competence in his fields brought him the distinction of becoming Director of Studies at the Royal Institute of International Affairs and Research Professor of International History at the University of London. He held these posts on a Sir Daniel Stevenson Foundation grant from 1925 until his retirement in 1955.

In the meantime Toynbee had initiated what developed into an impressive series of publications. In addition to writing such books as *The New Europe, The Western Question in Greece and Turkey*, and *Greek Historical Thought*, Toynbee, as both editor and writer, dealt with current international history in a series of yearbooks entitled *Survey of International Affairs* (1920–1946).

During World War II he was a director of foreign research and press services at the Royal Institute of International Affairs, and from 1943 to 1946 was director of the research department of the British Foreign Office. He was once again a member of the British delegation at the Peace Conference in 1946. Since 1934 he has been an editor of the *British Commonwealth Relations*.

Toynbee's monumental work in *A Study of History* had its beginnings in 1922; engaged in other tasks, he worked on the project intermittently until its completion in 1954, a period of study and writing at the Institute for Advanced Study in Princeton, N.J., having enabled him to complete the final volumes. A frequent visitor to the United States, he makes his permanent home in London.

The distinctive feature of Toynbee's study of history has been his claim that civilizations, not nations, are the determining factors in history; and that the life of a civilization is the story of its challenges and responses to environmental conditions. He has provoked considerable critical attack with his contention that history shows how God's influence works.

BIBLIOGRAPHICAL REFERENCES: There is no authorized biography or full-length critical study. For studies in books and periodicals see Pitirim Sorokin, *Social Philosophies of an Age of Crisis*, 1950; P. W. Martin, *Experiment in Depth: A Study of the Work of Jung, Eliot and Toynbee*, 1955; Ashley Montagu, ed., *Toynbee and History: Critical Essays and Reviews*, 1956; Richard Chase, "Toynbee: The Historian as Artist," *American Scholar*, XVI (1947), 268–282; Granville Hicks, "Arnold Toynbee: The Boldest Historian," *Harper's* CXCIV (1947), 116–124; Owen Lattimore, "Spengler and Toynbee," *Atlantic Monthly*, CLXXXI (1948), 104–105; Kenneth Kirkwood, *Arnold J. Toynbee, Philosopher of History*, 1953 (pamphlet), an address given at Karachi; R. P. Blackmur, "Reflections of Toynbee," *Kenyon Review*, XVII (1955), 357–370; K. W. Thompson, "Toynbee's Approach to History Reviewed," *Ethics*, LXV (1955), 287–303, and "Toynbee and the Theory of International Politics," *Political Science Quarterly*, LXXI (1956), 365–386; Crane Brinton, "Toynbee's City of God," *Virginia Quarterly Review*, XXXII (1956), 361–375; R. Coulborn, "Fact and Fiction in Toynbee's Study of History," *Ethics*, LXVI (1956), 235–249; F. Borkenau, "Toynbee and the Culture Cycle," *Commentary*, XXI (1956), 239–249; G. Barraclough, "Misuses of History," *Nation* CLXXXIII (1956), 392–394; and M. A. Fitzsimmons, "Toynbee: Criticism and Judgment," *Commonweal*, LXVI (1957), 43–45.

ANTHONY TROLLOPE

Born: London, England
Date: April 24, 1815

Died: Harting, England
Date: December 6, 1882

PRINCIPAL WORKS

THE CHRONICLES OF BARSETSHIRE: *The Warden*, 1855; *Barchester Towers*, 1857; *Doctor Thorne*, 1858; *Framley Parsonage*, 1861; *The Small House at Allington*, 1864; *The Last Chronicle of Barset*, 1867.

POLITICAL NOVELS: *Can You Forgive Her?*, 1864; *Phineas Finn, the Irish Member*, 1869; *The Eustace Diamonds*, 1873; *Phineas Redux*, 1874; *The Prime Minister*, 1876; *The Duke's Children*, 1880.

IRISH NOVELS: *The Macdermots of Ballycloran*, 1847; *The Kellys and the O'Kellys*, 1848; *Castle Richmond*, 1860; *The Landleaguers*, 1883.

NOVELS OF SOCIETY: *The Bertrams*, 1859; *Orley Farm*, 1862; *Rachel Ray*, 1863; *The Belton Estate*, 1866; *He Knew He Was Right*, 1869; *The Vicar of Bullhampton*, 1870; *The Way We Live Now*, 1875; *Is He Popenjoy?*, 1878; *Dr. Wortle's School*, 1881.

SHORT STORIES: *Tales of All Countries*, 1861, 1863; *Lotta Schmidt and Other Stories*, 1867; *An Editor's Tales*, 1870; *Why Frau Frohmann Raised Her Prices and Other Stories*, 1882.

MEMOIRS: *Autobiography*, 1883.

Anthony Trollope's father, Thomas Anthony Trollope, was an eccentric barrister who lost his wealth in wild speculations; his mother, Frances Trollope, kept the family together by fleeing to Belgium to escape creditors and by writing a total of 114 volumes, mostly novels. Her best-known work today is *Domestic Manners of the Americans* (1832), a caustic and grossly exaggerated account of the America she observed on an unsuccessful trip to Cincinnati in 1823 to set up a great bazaar. Since his older brother, Thomas Adolphus, was also a writer, Anthony was following a well-established family tradition.

According to his posthumous *Autobiography*, Trollope was born in London on April 24, 1815; he grew into an ungainly, oafish, and unpopular boy who spent miserable and friendless years at Harrow and Winchester, where he learned nothing. When he was nineteen, he sought work in London, first as a clerk and then as a civil servant with the Post Office. He hated his work and his lonely life in the city, and seven years later accepted with relief an appointment as traveling postal inspector in Ireland (1841–1859). Later his duties carried him on brief trips to all the continents of the world. In Ireland, Trollope's pleasant experiences with genial country people and an exhilarating landscape developed his confidence and optimism.

He married Rose Haseltine and at the age of thirty began to write, his first novels being inspired by the ruins of an Irish mansion. His early works were failures, but he persevered under difficult conditions until his fourth book, *The Warden*, found a responsive audience in 1855. This "scene from clerical life," its setting the episcopal establishment of Barchester, presents a detailed account of the day to day events of provincial life in Victorian England. Its sequel, *Barchester Towers*, with its incorrigible comic character, Bertie, was so successful that it was followed by four other novels on the same theme, the whole group constituting the perennially popular "Chronicles of Barsetshire." During this same period, Trollope also wrote other novels, the best of which are *The Three Clerks* (1858), an autobiographical account of the English civil service, and *Orley Farm*, a work which combines a plot involving a forged will with genre pictures of family life in the country.

In 1867, now confident of his powers, Trollope resigned from the Post Office and became interested in politics. He stood as Liberal candidate for Parliament in 1868 but was defeated. Nevertheless, he cut an impressive bearded figure, chatting in the London literary clubs and riding to the hounds in Southern England. All these interests are faithfully embodied in a series sometimes called the "Parliamentary Novels," among them *Phineas Finn, Phineas Redux, The Prime Minister,* and *The Duke's Children*. But Trollope could not compete with Disraeli in this field (just as he was unable to compete with Dickens in depicting city life among the lower and middle classes), and despite their appealing portraits of political life and character, his Parliamentary series was not widely read.

Trollope continued to turn out novel after novel—social manners, mild satires, histories, romances, travelogues,

and even, in *The Fixed Period* (1882), a futuristic work about life in 1980. A curiously interesting work is the story of an erring woman, in *Can You Forgive Her?*—a novel as close as he ever came to modern realism. Despite the fact that he wrote some sixty novels in all, it cannot be said of Trollope that he made the world his stage. He surveys generally a rather narrow scene, usually rural and provincial, peopled by mild villains and tame heroes. No powerful philosophical or social conviction charges his writing, and no keen analysis of human psychology opens the inner beings of his characters. "A novel," he said, "should give a picture of common life enlivened by humor and sweetened by pathos." In this endeavor Trollope succeeded so completely that Henry James said of him, "His great, his inestimable merit was a complete appreciation of the usual." He died of paralysis at Harting, Sussex, on December 6, 1882.

Trollope's posthumously published *Autobiography* disappointed his admirers and dampened his reputation, for he candidly confessed (as Arnold Bennett was to do a half-century later) that he wrote 250 words per minute, completing eight to sixteen pages a day. He is said to have earned some £70,000 from his writings. Despite the fact that he was not an inspired writer, he amused a whole generation with pleasant tales, the best of which have considerable value as sociological insights into a mellow and tranquil age now forever past.

BIBLIOGRAPHICAL REFERENCES: Although there is no complete edition of Trollope, several publishing houses have issued sets of selected groups of novels such as the Barsetshire Chronicles and the political series and his most representative titles are now available in Everyman's Library and the World's Classics. Also in progress is "The Oxford Trollope," edited by Michael Sadleir and Frederick Page. Useful one-volume editions of selections are *The Trollope Reader,* edited by Esther C. Dunn and Marion E. Dodd, 1947; and *The Bedside Barsetshire,* edited by L. O. Tingay, 1951. Also available are a new edition of the *Autobiography* and *The Letters of Anthony Trollope,* 1951, both edited by Bradford A. Booth.

The standard critical biography is Michael Sadleir, *Anthony Trollope, A Commentary,* 1927 (rev. ed., 1945). Of considerable importance also is Lucy P. Stebbins and Richard P. Stebbins, *The Trollopes: The Chronicle of a Writing Family,* 1945. For additional biography and criticism see T. H. S. Escott, *Anthony Trollope: His Works, Associates, and Literary Originals,* 1913; Hugh Walpole, *Anthony Trollope,* English Men of Letters Series, 1928; Beatrice C. Brown, *Anthony Trollope,* 1950; and A. O. J. Cockshut, *Anthony Trollope: A Critical Study,* 1955. More specialized studies include John T. Wildman, *Anthony Trollope's England,* 1940; W. G. and J. T. Gerould, *A Guide to Trollope,* 1948; and Marcie Muir, *Anthony Trollope in Australia,* 1949.

For briefer studies see also Henry James, *Partial Portraits,* 1888; James Bryce, *Studies in Contemporary Biography,* 1903; Morris E. Speare, *The Political Novel,* 1923; Lord David Cecil, *Early Victorian Novelists,* 1935; T. A. Sherman, "The Financial Motive in the Barchester Novels," *College English,* IX (1948), 413–418; F. E. Robins, "Chronology and History in Trollope's Barset and Parliamentary Novels," *Nineteenth Century Fiction,* V (1951), 303–316; Robert M. Adams, "*Orley Farm* and Real Fiction," *ibid.,* VII (1953), 27–41; Edd W. Parks, "Trollope and the Defense of Exegesis," *ibid.,* VII (1953), 265–271; and William Coyle, "Trollope as Social Anthropologist," *College English,* XVII (1956), 392–397. Michael Sadleir has compiled *Trollope, A Bibliography,* 1928.

JOHN TOWNSEND TROWBRIDGE

Born: Ogden Township, New York   *Died:* Arlington, Massachusetts
Date: September 18, 1827   *Date:* February 12, 1916

PRINCIPAL WORKS

NOVELS: *Neighbor Jackwood,* 1856; *Cudjo's Cave,* 1864; *Coupon Bonds,* 1871.
POEMS: *The Vagabonds and Other Poems,* 1869.

John Townsend Trowbridge was an American novelist who wrote for and found his greatest popularity with teen-age boys, and he himself considered his forty-odd novels as little more than hack work. He believed his only serious and great literary efforts were the series of volumes of didactic narrative poetry which later generations have forgotten, as they have almost forgotten his novels.

Trowbridge was born on a farm in Ogden Township, New York, September 18, 1827, and spent his childhood there. As he grew up, bad eyesight caused him difficulty in school. Because of his handicap, he was largely self-taught, although he acquired a great deal of learning, including a knowledge of French, Latin, and Greek. After completing a year at the academy in Lockport, New York, Trowbridge traveled to the Middle West. He taught school in Illinois in 1845, then moved back to Lockport to teach school there for a year. In 1847 he went to New York City and began to make a reputation for himself as a writer, contributing his work principally to the *Dollar Magazine.*

During the period from 1849 to 1860, Trowbridge edited periodicals and wrote for the *Atlantic Monthly,* the *Youth's Companion,* and *Our Young Folks.* His interest in writing for boys and his success in pleasing their tastes won for Trowbridge the editorship of *Our Young Folks,* a position he held from 1860 to 1873. He made his own a type of adventure fiction popular with adolescent boys and of interest to some adults. *Cudjo's Cave* is an excellent example of the type.

In 1860 Trowbridge married Cornelia Warren, who died four years later, leaving two children. The following year Trowbridge moved his family to Arlington, Massachusetts, near Boston. His second marriage was to Sarah Newton, of Arlington, in 1873. Among Trowbridge's friends were such diverse literary personalities as Oliver Wendell Holmes, Henry Wadsworth Longfellow, and Walt Whitman. He died at Arlington on February 12, 1916.

BIBLIOGRAPHICAL REFERENCES: The chief source of biographical data is Trowbridge's *My Own Story,* 1903. See also Caroline Ticknor, *Glimpses of Authors,* 1922. The brief sketch in the *Dictionary of National Biography* is by George H. Genzer.

IVAN TURGENEV

Born: Orel, Russia
Date: October 28, 1818

Died: Paris, France
Date: September 8, 1883

PRINCIPAL WORKS

NOVELS: *Rudin,* 1856; *Dvoryanskoe gnezdo,* 1858 (*A House of Gentlefolk*); *Nakanune,* 1860 (*On the Eve*); *Ottsy i deti,* 1862 (*Fathers and Sons*); *Dym,* 1867 (*Smoke*); *Veshniye vody,* 1871 (*Spring Torrents*); *Nov',* 1877 (*Virgin Soil*).

SHORT STORIES: *Zapiski okhotnika,* 1852 (*A Sportsman's Sketches*).

PLAYS: *Gde tonko tam i rviotsya,* 1847 (*The Weakest Link*); *Nakhlebnik,* 1848 (*The Parasite*); *Kholostyak,* 1849 (*The Bachelor*); *Provintzialka,* 1850 (*The Provincial Lady*); *Mesyats v derevne,* 1850 (*A Month in the Country*).

Ivan Sergeyevich Turgenev, the first of the great Russian novelists to be read widely in Europe, was born at Orel, Russia, on October 28, 1818. He was the second of three sons born to his unhappily married parents: ugly, harsh, and tyrannical Varvara Petrovna Lutovinov, who had inherited large estates at twenty-six after an unhappy childhood, and cold, handsome, philandering Sergey Nikolayeyvich Turgenev, an impecunious young cavalry officer who had married this woman six years his senior only for her money.

The child, who was to be known as the most European of the great Russian masters, first saw Europe at the age of four with his family and its entourage. Turgenev spent his earliest years in the elegance of the family mansion on the Spasskoye estate. When the family moved to their Moscow house in 1827, Turgenev began to prepare for the entrance examinations to Moscow University. By the time he entered, in 1834, he had fallen under the influence of Hegel and Schiller. In the same year, however, Colonel Turgenev transferred his son to St. Petersburg University. Then, with his wife away in Italy, the aloof, handsome colonel died.

Turgenev had written since childhood, and at St. Petersburg he continued his attempts, seeing two of his poems published a year after his graduation in 1837. In 1838 he went to Berlin to study intensively for a career as a teacher of literature, returning to St. Petersburg in 1841 to prepare for his M.A. examinations. Under the impact of an unhappy love affair, however, he failed to take his degree. The poem *Parasha* in 1843 signaled Turgenev's escape from romanticism and was praised by critics for its sensitive simplicity. When he resigned shortly thereafter from the civil service job he had taken in 1842, his tyrannical mother sharply reduced his allowance, and from that time on their relationship steadily became more acrimonious. Just then he met Madame Pauline Viardot, the ugly, magnetic opera singer to whom he was to be devoted for the rest of his life, alternately her enchanted and despairing admirer. A successful realistic sketch in *The Contemporary Review* led to others in a similar vein. Then, in February, 1847, he left Russia with Pauline Viardot and her husband despite Madame Turgenev's frantic efforts to prevent him. He left the Viardots at Berlin, and in Paris, Brussels, and Lyons he continued to work on what were to be *A Sportsman's Sketches*. Taking up residence at Courtavenel, the Viardots' summer home, in the summer of 1848, he stayed into 1849. By the summer of 1850, when he returned home because of his mother's deteriorating health, he had also composed many poems and more than half a dozen plays. For the

most part these were comedies conspicuous for their dialogue. Although some were successfully staged, Turgenev was always extremely critical of them.

His mother's death in November, 1850, made him a rich man. In March, 1852, however, he found himself under arrest. A laudatory article upon Gogol shortly after his death, combined with the suspicion created by his sketches as they appeared, caused Turgenev's arrest by the Tsar's political police. He was confined in jail for a month and then placed under house arrest at Spasskoye for a year and a half. *A Sportsman's Sketches*, collected in book form in August, 1852, was an immediate and resounding success. The realistic treatment of Russian life, particularly the plight of the peasants, was so influential that it helped bring about the emancipation of the serfs nine years later. Regaining his freedom, Turgenev worked on his first novel during 1855. Published in *The Contemporary Review* in January and February of 1856, *Rudin* was the story of a Utopian who had eloquence, honesty, faith, and enthusiasm, but who was not strong enough to achieve real love or political usefulness.

He dropped his literary work for a time in 1856 to return to Pauline Viardot in France, but her departure with another man left him desolate, and illness completed his misery. His return to Russia in 1858 was the beginning of three years of fruitful work. In January *The Contemporary Review* published *A House of Gentlefolk*, into which Turgenev had written many of his emotions arising out of his relationships with Pauline Viardot and his own family. This melancholy novel of infidelity, worldliness, and wasted lives was a resounding success. Now the most celebrated of Russian writers, he immediately set to work, this time in Vichy, on a novel based on a manuscript given him by a young soldier rightly convinced that he would not survive the Crimean War to complete it. It became *On the Eve,* appearing in *The Russian Herald* in January and February, 1860. A depiction on one level merely of a love affair, on another level it was a foreshadowing of the Russia to come, when in the 1860's so many of the nation's youth were to band together against Tsarist autocracy. Acrimonious political controversies, quarrels with Goncharov and Tolstoy, and estrangement from Madame Viardot saddened Turgenev, but he completed *Fathers and Sons,* which was published in March, 1862, in *The Russian Monthly.* This classic novel presented the age-old conflict between generations, but it was also localized in provincial Russia and set in a critical period. And in Bazaroff (often Bazarov), Turgenev created one of the first of the nihilists, men who wanted to sweep away the old and apply the tenets and methods of science to politics and other human affairs. The novel incensed both young and old, extremists and reactionaries. Turgenev, surprised and hurt, was attacked from all sides.

Except for brief visits home, the years between 1863 and 1871 were spent in Baden-Baden, some of them with the Viardot family. During this period he joined the admiring group which included Flaubert and Goncourt. In March, 1867, he published another novel, *Smoke,* in *The Russian Herald.* This love story with its portrayal of aristocrats and young revolutionaries, like *Fathers and Sons,* pleased no one. Sympathizing with

neither, castigating political persons and follies, he became in his turn a target for criticism from all quarters. During these years he continued his prolific output of short stories. The best of them, such as "A Lear of the Steppes" and "First Love," bore the same hallmarks of his art as did his novels: the psychological insight, the melancholy realism, the delicate nuances, the subtle creation of mood, and the sensitive pastel landscapes. After spending part of 1870 and 1871 in England and Scotland, he published the short, non-political novel, *Spring Torrents,* in January, 1871, in *The European Herald.* It was a great success and very soon reprinted. In 1874 he moved into a suite of rooms in the house of the Viardots, where Henry James visited him in 1875.

Turgenev spent six years planning and writing his last novel, *Virgin Soil,* published in the January and February issues of *The European Herald* in 1877. This novel, presenting to the reader a wide variety of the types who were to become revolutionaries, portrayed the aristocratic class which did not perceive itself in the process of dissolution; it also predicted with a high degree of accuracy the course that future events were to take in the writer's unhappy country. Although the novel was a best seller in France, England, and the United States, it was a failure in Russia, and Turgenev resolved to renounce fiction. In 1878, however, he began composing his *Poems in Prose,* reflections upon politics, philosophy, and his own intimate concerns. Though he was still a pessimistic agnostic, some of these works showed a lightening and a heartening at examples in man and nature of courage and defiance of death.

Turgenev's brief return to Russia in 1879 was a triumph in which honors and acclaim greeted him, and he was hailed as a pioneer and master. His academic honors conferred in Russia were soon matched by great universities in France and England. By 1882, however, when he had returned to the Viardot household, his health had begun to decline rapidly. Although he was told that he was suffering from angina pectoris, it was actually cancer of the spinal cord which confined him to his bed. In September he had virtually abandoned hope, but he lived on through a year of torment, dying quietly in Paris on September 8, 1883. His funeral in St. Petersburg, attended by delegations from 180 different organizations, was an occasion of national mourning, an acknowledgment of the passing of one of the great masters of Russian literature.

BIBLIOGRAPHICAL REFERENCES: The standard edition of Turgenev's fiction in English is *The Novels of Ivan Turgenev*, translated by Constance Garnett, 17 vols., 1919–1923. Another edition of the *Works* was translated by Isabel F. Hapgood, 7 vols., 1916. M. S. Mandell translated *The Plays of Ivan Turgenev*, 1924. Constance Garnett also translated *Three Plays*, 1934. There are also recent editions of the novels in translations by various hands. A good selected edition is *The Borzoi Turgenev*, translated by Harry Stevens, with a foreword by Serge Koussevitsky and an introduction by Avrahm Yarmolinsky, 1950. *Fathers and Sons* has been published in a Modern Library edition, translated by Constance Garnett and with an introduction by Herbert J. Muller. The best edition of *A Sportsman's Notebook* is that by Charles and Natasha Hepburn, 1950.

There are two standard biographies in English: Avrahm Yarmolinsky, *Turgenev, the Man, His Art, and His Age*, 1926; and David Magarshack, *Turgenev: A Life*, 1954. Critical studies include Edward Garnett, *Turgenev*, with an introduction by Joseph Conrad, 1924; Harry Hershkowitz, *Democratic Ideas in Turgenev's Works*, 1932; and R. A. Gettmann, *Turgenev in England and America*, 1941, with a bibliography. Studies in Russian include those by V. I. Pokrovsky, 1905; E. A. Solovyev, 1922; E. K. Semenov, 1930; and N. O. Antsiferov, 1947; in French, by E. Haumont, 1906; and André Maurois, 1931. Brief critical essays include Janko Lavrin, in *Russian Writers—Their Lives and Literature*, 1954; Irving Howe, "Turgenev: The Politics of Hesitation," in *The Political Novel*, 1957; Henry James, "Ivan Turgenev," *Atlantic Monthly*, LIII (1884), 42–55; Charles Morgan, "Turgenev's Treatment of a Love Story," *Royal Society of London: Essays by Divers Hands*, XXV (1950), 102–119; and Edmund Wilson, "Turgenev and the Life-Giving Drop," *New Yorker*, XXXIII (Oct. 19, 1957), 150–200.

MARK TWAIN
(Samuel Langhorne Clemens)

Born: Florida, Missouri
Date: November 30, 1835

Died: Redding, Connecticut
Date: April 21, 1910

PRINCIPAL WORKS

NOVELS: *The Gilded Age*, 1873 (with Charles Dudley Warner); *The Adventures of Tom Sawyer*, 1876; *The Prince and the Pauper*, 1882; *The Adventures of Huckleberry Finn*, 1884; *A Connecticut Yankee at King Arthur's Court*, 1889; *The American*

Claimant, 1892; *Tom Sawyer Abroad,* 1894; *The Tragedy of Pudd'nhead Wilson,* 1894; *Personal Recollections of Joan of Arc,* 1896.

SHORT STORIES: *The Celebrated Jumping Frog of Calaveras County and Other Sketches,* 1867; *Mark Twain's Sketches: New and Old,* 1875; *The Stolen White Elephant,* 1882; *The £1,000,000 Bank-Note,* 1893; *The Man That Corrupted Hadleyburg,* 1900; *A Double Barrelled Detective Story,* 1902; *The $30,000 Bequest,* 1906; *A Horse's Tale,* 1907; *The Mysterious Stranger,* 1916.

REMINISCENCES AND AUTOBIOGRAPHY: *Roughing It,* 1872; *Life on the Mississippi,* 1883; *Mark Twain's Autobiography,* 1924 (2 vols.).

TRAVEL SKETCHES AND IMPRESSIONS: *The Innocents Abroad,* 1869; *A Tramp Abroad,* 1880; *Following the Equator,* 1897.

ESSAYS AND HUMOROUS MISCELLANIES: *How to Tell a Story and Other Essays,* 1897; *My Debut as a Literary Person,* 1903; *Extracts from Adam's Diary,* 1904; *King Leopold's Soliloquy,* 1905; *What is Man?* 1906; *Eve's Diary,* 1906; *Christian Science,* 1907; *Is Shakespeare Dead?* 1909; *Extract from Captain Stormfield's Visit to Heaven,* 1909.

"Mark Twain" was the pen name of Samuel L(anghorne) Clemens, who was born in Florida, Missouri, on November 30, 1835. His father was a dreamy Virginia lawyer and experimenter who, in drifting westward in search of wealth through land speculation, married in Kentucky and settled finally in 1839 in Hannibal, Missouri. In this community, on the Mississippi River between Quincy and St. Louis, the boy grew up amid the scenery and in the atmosphere portrayed in *Tom Sawyer* and *Huckleberry Finn.* At twelve, following his father's death, Sam left school to become a printer; for ten years he set type as a roving journeyman as far east as New York City. In 1857 his plans to visit South America ended when Horace Bixby undertook to teach him to be a steamboat pilot. When the Civil War closed down navigation, Sam soldiered a few months with a Confederate volunteer company. With his brother Orion he went to Nevada as a clerk and then drifted into silver mining and journalism. In 1862 he adopted his pen name, a river term meaning "two fathoms deep." Fame came in 1865 with "The

Jumping Frog of Calaveras County," a tall tale. Printed lectures about a journey to the Sandwich—now Hawaiian —Islands increased his popularity, and *Innocents Abroad,* a hilarious book of fun-making at the expense of gawking American travelers in the Holy Land and in Italian art centers, solidified his position as America's leading humorist. Following his marriage in 1870 to Olivia Langdon, he settled in Hartford, Connecticut. Thereafter he alternated between periods of writing and lecturing in America and Europe. Ill-advised investments in a publishing firm and in the development of a mechanical typesetting machine—evidence of a lifelong dream of becoming a millionaire by a lucky turn of the wheel of chance— reduced him to bankruptcy in 1894, but in four years these debts were paid. A native vein of bitterness and pessimism deepened when his wife and two of their three daughters died; some of his last writings, at his wish, were issued several years after his death at his home in Redding, Connecticut, on April 21, 1910.

A humorist pokes fun at human shortcomings: Twain does so by exaggerating instances of gullibility, meanness, inexpertness, and unwise romanticism. His chief characters speak for him; the frontier humor tradition, which he inherited and which he carried to its greatest artistic successes, abetted his alternating moods of boylike playfulness and redheaded anger. His materials, though originating in anecdotes, wisecracks, and personal experience, entered like mosaics into large contexts and pictured—rather than explained in traditional essay form as did Hawthorne and Melville—the problems of his generation. Hidden behind the account of his "slothful, valueless, heedless career" in Nevada in *Roughing It* is a narrative of pioneers' "buffeting and hard striving" to establish civilization in an outpost. *The Gilded Age,* whose love story was written by Charles Dudley Warner, gave its name to, even as it half praised and half scowled on, an era of political and business dishonesty. *Tom Sawyer,* seemingly about a boy's high spirits, is a study of personal conscience set against a milieu characterized by "glaring insincerity." *Huckleberry Finn,* a first-person narrative in Missouri dialect, recounts a nature-loving boy's rebellion against an institution-ridden "sivilization" containing slavery, feuds, and fraud. *A Connecticut Yankee* flays the concept of the divine right of kings who enslave the common people and withhold from them the technological advances by which their lot might be improved; the masses of men, Twain said, can always produce "the material in abundance whereby to govern itself." A priest-led political league which betrayed "Patriotism embodied, concreted, made flesh" in the Maid of Orleans is excoriated in Twain's one biographical-historical novel, *Joan of Arc.* The posthumously published *The Mysterious Stranger* brings Satan in human form among Austrian villagers to ridicule religious and social concepts based upon an alleged "moral sense."

Twain's books reflect his view of man as an almost helpless and therefore comic free agent in a still incompletely formed society uncertain of its direction. Civilization seemed a vulgar parade of hypocrisy, scheming pretense, incompetence, bungling, pork-barrel politics, and boodlery. Yet Twain was not a thinker, not a philosopher as ordinarily fiction writers strove to be or to represent themselves. He solved no problems in his stories, as Howells tried to do; rather, Twain was, like Henry James and Stephen Crane, a pictorial artist with insight into human psychological responses during climactic moments of decision. The ordinary boy-girl or man-woman romantic relationships seldom occur in Twain's books.

A man of feeling, Twain was a sensitive barometer. As with Tom Sawyer, Huck Finn, and Pudd'nhead Wilson, Twain's mental weather fluctuated with every cloud in the social sky. He yielded to self-pity, bragged about and scolded himself, roared defiance and whimpered despondently at fate's blows, curried favors of the great and snarled at co-workers like Bret Harte and G. W. Cable, minced like a spaniel and strutted in his white suit like a king beside the dons at Oxford and Yale, who conferred honorary doctor's degrees upon him. Yet it is exactly this mercurial quality—this unexpected flash of temperament, this alternation of favorable and negative response— which enlivens his writings.

A masterly control over the English language, in its standard and Western dialect forms, made many scenes memorable, like the uproarious visit of Scotty Briggs to the fledgling parson in *Roughing It* and Sherburn's successful defiance of the lynch-hungry mob in *Huckleberry Finn.* His stories move by scenes or episodes rather than by a tightly knit plot structure woven around a clearly stated theme; yet each picture plays its role in the painter's impressionistic manner to give a single effect. In artistic manner, as in language, Twain was wholly American, wholly a product of native forces. If he was, as Dixon Wecter has suggested, "a kind of pocket miner, stumbling like fortune's darling upon native ore of incredible richness and exploiting it with effortless skill—but often gleefully mistaking fool's gold for the genuine article," the gold he found and wrought into great art remains an imperishable possession for the world's enjoyment and enrichment.

Harry R. Warfel

BIBLIOGRAPHICAL REFERENCES: The definitive edition, *The Writings of Mark Twain,* edited by Albert Bigelow Paine, 37 vols., 1922–1925, is now out of print. The best one-volume selections are *The Family Mark Twain,* with an Introduction by Albert Bigelow Paine, 1935, and *The Portable Mark Twain,* edited by Bernard DeVoto, 1946.

Mark Twain's Autobiography, edited by Albert Bigelow Paine, 2 vols., 1924, and *Mark Twain's Notebooks,* published by the same editor in 1935, provide valuable source material, though they are not always reliable. Bernard DeVoto, *Mark Twain in Eruption,* 1940, is an important addition to the autobiography. Two useful collections of correspondence are *Mark Twain's Letters,* edited by Albert Bigelow Paine, 2 vols., 1917, and *The Love Letters of Mark Twain,* edited by Dixon Wecter, 1949. The authorized biography is Albert Bigelow Paine, *Mark Twain: A Biography,* 3 vols., 1912 (reissued 1935). The best of the general Mark Twain studies are Bernard DeVoto, *Mark Twain's America,* 1932; Edward Wagenknecht, *Mark Twain: The Man and His Work,* 1935; and Dixon Wecter, *Sam Clemens of Hannibal,* 1952. See also William Dean Howells, *My Mark Twain: Reminiscences and Criticisms,* 1910; Van Wyck Brooks, *The Ordeal of Mark Twain,* 1920; Clara Clemens, *My Father, Mark Twain,* 1931; Edgar Lee Masters, *Mark Twain: A Portrait,* 1938; Bernard DeVoto, *Mark Twain at Work,* 1940; DeLancey Ferguson, *Mark Twain: Man and Legend,* 1943; Samuel C. Webster, *Mark Twain, Business Man,* 1946; Dixon Wecter, "Mark Twain," in *The Literary History of the United States,* edited by Robert E. Spiller, Willard Thorp, Thomas H. Johnson, and Henry S. Canby, Vol. II, 1948; and Kenneth R. Andrews, *Nook Farm: Mark Twain's Hartford Circle,* 1950.

For criticism and more specialized studies see the extensive bibliography in *The Literary History of the United States,* Vol. III, 1948, 442–450.

NICHOLAS UDALL (WOODALL)

Born: Hampshire, England
Date: 1505

Died: Place unknown
Date: 1556

PRINCIPAL WORKS

PLAYS: *Placidas,* c. 1534; *Ralph Roister Doister,* c. 1552–1554.

TRANSLATIONS: *Apothegms* of Erasmus, 1542.

Born in Hampshire in 1505, Nicholas Udall was educated at Winchester and Corpus Christi College, Oxford, where he served as lecturer from 1526 to 1528. When he was twenty-seven, he assisted in the preparation of verses for Anne Boleyn's coronation. From 1533 to 1547 he was Vicar of Braintree, Essex. According to E. K. Chambers, he was probably the author of a play, *Placidas*, recorded in 1534. From 1534 to 1541 he was headmaster of Eton. In 1538 he was paid for "playing before my Lord." His career at Eton ended in disgrace, for he was accused of theft and other misconduct and dismissed.

For the next fourteen years, before becoming headmaster of Westminster School, he was writer, tutor, and churchman under patronage of members of the royal household. His principles as churchman were flexible enough to permit his serving Edward VI as a Protestant and Mary Tudor as a Catholic. Before the latter he performed or produced various dialogues and interludes. The date of his only surviving play, *Ralph Roister Doister*, is uncertain, probably between 1552 and 1554—possibly in Edward's, possibly in Mary's reign. Written for performance by and before schoolboys, it may have been done when Udall was master at Eton or Westminster. (Sir Edmund Chambers favors 1553–1554 and Westminster.) The printed Epilogue praises "our most noble Queen"; but this might have been an addition for a later performance before Elizabeth I.

Udall died in 1556. After his death, Bishop John Bale in *Scriptores* credited him with several comedies and a translated tragedy. In 1564 (the memorable year of the death of Michelangelo and the birth of William Shakespeare) Queen Elizabeth saw at Cambridge an *Ezekias* by Udall. However, the author's literary reputation rests solely on *Ralph Roister Doister*. Its Prologue defends "mirth with modesty," and the play lives up to the precept quite well. With the elimination of a few words common to the vocabulary of small boys at recess, it could be produced in any modern grammer school without shocking the most staid teacher; and it has a wholesome supply of mirth. Its companion piece in the period anthologies, *Gammer Gurton's Needle,* has copious mirth, but hardly a thimbleful of modesty. *Ralph Roister Doister* is modeled on Plautus's *Miles Gloriosus*; but it shows the influence of English mystery plays and interludes. Its characters are English rather than Roman; and it shows a healthy delight in sheer slapstick. The topsy-turvy reading of Ralph's letter proposing to the Widow Custance foreshadows the mispunctuated prologue delivered by Peter Quince in the interlude of "Pyramus and Thisbe" from *A Midsummer Night's Dream*.

BIBLIOGRAPHICAL REFERENCES: Brief biographical and critical studies are presented in E. K. Chambers, *The Medieval Stage*, Vol. II (1903); and C. R. Baskervill, V. B. Heltzel, and A. H. Nethercot, *Elizabethan and Stuart Plays* (1934).

SIGRID UNDSET

Born: Kalundborg, Denmark   *Died:* Lillehammer, Norway
Date: May 20, 1882   *Date:* June 10, 1949

PRINCIPAL WORKS

NOVELS: *Fru Martha Oulie,* 1907; *Viga-Ljot og Vigdis,* 1909 (*Gunnar's Daughter*); *Jenny,* 1911; *Vaaren,* 1914 (*Springtime*); *Kristin Lavransdatter: Kransen, Husfrue,* and *Korset,* 1920, 1921, 1922 (*Kristin Lavransdatter: The Bridal Wreath, The Mistress of Husaby,* and *The Cross*); *Olav Audunssøn i Hestviken,* 1925 (*The Master of Hestviken: The Axe* and *The Snake Pit*); *Olav Audunssøn og hans børn,* 1927 (*The Master of Hestviken: In the Wilderness* and *The Son Avenger*); *Gymnedenia,* 1929 (*The Wild Orchid*); *Den brændende busk,* 1930 (*The Burning Bush*); *Ida Elisabeth,* 1932; *Den trofaste husfru,* 1936 (*The Faithful Wife*); *Madame Dorthea,* 1939.

SHORT STORIES: *Den lykkelige alder,* 1908 (*The Happy Age*); *Splinten av troldspeilet,* 1917 (*Images in a Mirror*); *De Kloge jongfruer,* 1918 (*The Wise Virgins*).

AUTOBIOGRAPHY: *Elleve år,* 1934 (*The Longest Year*).

ESSAYS IN TRANSLATION: *Men, Women, and Places,* 1939.

Sigrid Undset, born at Kalundborg, Denmark, May 20, 1882, was the daughter of Ingvald Martin Undset, a distinguished Norwegian archaeologist. As a small child, she and her mother lived with her mother's family while the father was doing archaeological work in Italy. Later her father became a university lecturer and took his family to live in Christiania (now Oslo), Norway. Two other daughters were born to the family. As a child Sigrid Undset took an interest in her father's work, and that fact influenced her own work and interests throughout life, for she had a passionate concern for the past, especially medieval Norway. As a girl she was educated at the private academy of Fru Ragna Nielsen, in Oslo. After her father's death, Sigrid Undset and her sisters continued at the academy, even though they were unable to pay the fees, thanks to the goodheartedness of Fru Nielsen. But at the age of fifteen Sigrid decided that she did not wish to prepare for the university and a scientific career, as her teachers and family had expected her to do. Having been interested in painting since she was a small child, she wished to become an artist, but the family's poverty precluded an artistic career, and she enrolled in a business school.

Finishing business school, Sigrid, still a girl, began doing clerical work, which she found distasteful. As an escape from her distasteful work, she began writing after finishing her day's work, sometimes putting in as many as eighteen hours a day at her office and home. She remained in clerical work for ten years, until her two sisters were self-supporting, but before the time she left office work she had published two novels. Neither of those first two books made any stir in literary circles, and it was not until the appearance of *Jenny,* published in 1911, that Sigrid Undset had any fame or popularity. The following year, 1912, she married A. C. Svarstad, a Norwegian artist. Three children were born to them before she and her husband separated in 1925. The oldest child, a son, was killed while fighting against the Germans at the time of the German invasion of Norway during World War II. Although reared a Lutheran, Sigrid Undset early became interested in Roman Catholicism, coming to believe that the only real heroes of history were the Christian saints and that the future of civilization lay with the Roman Church. She became a convert to the Roman Catholic Church in November, 1924.

During the following decade Sigrid Undset's greatest books were published. *The Bridal Wreath*, translated in 1923, *The Mistress of Husaby* (1925), and *The Cross* (1927) became her famous trilogy, *Kristin Lavransdatter*, issued as a single volume in 1929. This trilogy about life in medieval Norway became amazingly popular and was translated into many languages. Sigrid Undset was expected to receive the Nobel Prize for literature in 1925, but no award was made that year. She did receive the Nobel Prize in 1928. Second only to *Kristin Lavransdatter* is Sigrid Undset's tetralogy, *The Master of Hestviken*, composed of *The Axe*, translated in 1928, *The Snake Pit*, (1929), *In the Wilderness*, (1929), and *The Son Avenger*, (1930). Like *Kristin Lavransdatter*, *The Master of Hestviken* is about life in medieval Norway.

In the late 1930's Sigrid Undset turned to writing fiction about later periods, including her own. She also published a collection of essays, *Men, Women, and Places*, which illustrate her enthusiasm for Roman Catholicism. Her writings, which expressed concern for religious and racial tolerance, made her unpopular with the Nazi German government, but when World War II broke out she remained in her homeland, serving as a censor until the German invasion forced her to flee to Sweden with little more than her life. She came to the United States in 1940 and remained until her homeland was freed in 1945. During her years in America she lectured and continued writing. Upon her return to Norway she was awarded the Grand Cross of St. Olaf by her king, making her the first woman commoner ever to receive the award. During her last years Sigrid Undset lived quietly at Lillehammer, Norway, in a house dating back to Viking times. She collected old lace and other Norse antiques, and spent much of her time studying Norwegian history. She died at Lillehammer after suffering a paralytic stroke, June 10, 1949.

BIBLIOGRAPHICAL REFERENCES: There is very little criticism of Sigrid Undset in English. See Hanna Lastrop Larsen, *Sigrid Undset*, 1929; Joseph Warren Beach, *The Twentieth-Century Novel*, 1932; and Alrik Gustafson, *Six Scandinavian Novelists*, 1940.

JUAN VALERA Y ALCALÁ GALIANO

Born: Cabrá, Córdoba, Spain
Date: October 18, 1824

Died: Madrid, Spain
Date: April 18, 1905

PRINCIPAL WORKS

NOVELS: *Pepita Jiménez*, 1874; *El comendador Mendoza*, 1877 (*Commander Mendoza*); *Doña Luz*, 1879; *Juanita la larga*, 1895 (*Big Jane*).

CRITICISM: *Sobre los cuentos de Leopardi e del romanticismo en España*, 1854.

In contrast to many Spanish authors who came from humble or middle class families, Juan Valera y Alcalá Galiano, born in the town of Cabrá on October 18, 1824, was an aristocrat, his father being a naval officer and his mother a marquise of Córdoba. His education was thorough, with a degree

1102

in philosophy from Málaga (1840) and one in law from Madrid (1846). He was also a linguist who read in many languages and a poet whose first volume *Ensayos poéticos* (*Poetic Attempts*) appeared before he finished the university. For it and other critical and poetic volumes, he was elected to the Spanish Academy in 1861.

Not until he was fifty, and then by accident, did he become a novelist. While studying Spanish mysticism, he was moved to put onto paper his thinking on the differences between human and divine love. Inventing a young theological student to make his thoughts more concrete, he ended with a lengthy bit of fiction, the best psychological novel of Spain, *Pepita Jiménez*. Letters from the vacationing student to his uncle at the seminary make up the first part of the novel, a fortunate inspiration for the beginning novelist whose greatest flaw is making the conversation of his characters resemble his own. The conclusion reached in the novel, that priests are born, not made, may be somewhat biographical, since the author's early education was received in religious schools; but it does not represent Valera's own convictions, since five years later he reversed the theme in *Doña Luz*, where religion conquers carnal love and the young heroine is satisfied with platonic friendship for the priest. The two novels really treat religion as a psychological matter, rather than a social, political, or even moral problem.

Between these two novels, in 1875, came *Las ilusiones del doctor Faustino* (*The Illusions of Dr. Faust*), whose skeptical hero has to get along without magical assistance. It deals with the theme later voiced by the Generation of '98: the failure of intellectuals in modern society, through lack of will power.

More complicated in plot was *Commander Mendoza*, whose skeptical man-of-the-world hero seems to some critics an embodiment of the author. Though still analyzing sentiment and passion, Valera tells the story of the efforts of a man back from Peru to get the daughter of his former mistress married to the man of her choice instead of to the richer but older suitor favored by the fanatical mother. As a novelist, Valera shows weakness in letting the death of the mother contrive the happy ending.

In 1895, old and nearly blind, this Spaniard called "the last Humanist" dictated his final novel, *Big Jane*, which provided a photographic reproduction of the region where he was born. In this work, however, the local color is less important than the character development, and the realism is second to the happy memories of the writer's childhood.

The aristocratic Valera was never a popular author. His "elusive and mystical idealism" did not suit the tastes of the masses, nor did they understand the cosmopolitan outlook of this cultured aristocrat. But Azorín calls him "The best Spanish prose writer of us all"; and he is one of two authors (Hartzenbusch is the other) of whom the Royal Academy declared: "Anything he writes is correct Spanish." Valera died in Madrid, April 18, 1905.

BIBLIOGRAPHICAL REFERENCES: For criticism see J. D. M. Ford, *Main Currents of Spanish Literature*, 1919; S. Fishtine, *Don Juan Valera the Critic*, 1933; César Barja, *Libros y autores modernos*, 1933; P. Romero Mendoza, *Don Juan Valera*, 1940; and José A. Balseiro, *Novelistas españoles contemporáneos*, 1947.

VALMIKI

Born: Ayodhya (?), India
Date: c. 350 B.C.

Died: India
Date: Unknown

PRINCIPAL WORK

POEM: *Ramayana,* c. 350 B.C. (*The Fortunes of Rama*).

Valmiki is one of those ancient authors who tantalize scholars because so little is known or can be known about them. Valmiki may be a legend that people long ago created to account for a great work of literature, for the traditional story is that Valmiki was a wise and holy man who lived in a forest in the north of India. To Valmiki came Narada, the messenger of the gods, who recited to the holy man the virtues and adventures of Rama, the ideal hero and an incarnation of Vishnu. When he had heard the tale, Valmiki mourned that he had no poetic power to pass on the tale to other men, until one day he saw a hunter kill a heron. Moved by his pity for the bird and his anger at the man, Valmiki began to express himself in Sanskrit poetry. While he was reciting *slokas,* the god Brahma appeared and ordered Valmiki to use his new-found poetic power to sing of Rama, his love for Sita, and Rama's victory over the demons. The story of Rama is famous and has been retold many times, regardless of whoever may have composed it first. Later renditions of the *Ramayana* are Kshmendra's *Ramayana-kathasara-manjari,* Bhoja's *Ramayana-champu,* and Tulsi Das's *Ram-charit-manas.* While Valmiki may or may not have ever lived, the poem attributed to him exists and still holds meaning for its readers. Untold millions of people in India have found inspiration and pleasure in the *Ramayana.*

BIBLIOGRAPHICAL REFERENCES: The standard modern translation is *The Ramayana of Valmiki,* by Hari Prasad Shastri, 1952. Aubrey Menen, *The Ramayana,* 1956, is a satirical adaptation of the original.

SIR JOHN VANBRUGH

Born: London, England
Date: January, 1664

Died: London
Date: March 26, 1726

PRINCIPAL WORKS

PLAYS: *The Relapse,* 1697; *The Provoked Wife,* 1697; *Aesop,* 1697 (adapted from the French); *Confederacy,* 1705 (adapted from Dancourt's *Bourgeoises à la mode*); *A Journey to London* (completed by Colley Cibber as *The Provoked Husband,* 1728).

John Vanbrugh, architect and playwright, was the son of a London merchant and a daughter of Sir Dudley Carleton. His paternal grandfather had fled to England from the Low Countries to avoid persecution by the Duke of Alva. Vanbrugh was born in London in January, 1664, but very little is known of the events of his early life before he became associated with the theater, except that he seems to have studied architecture in France from 1683 to 1685. He was commissioned as an officer in the British army in 1686 and served for several years. While in France in 1690 he was imprisoned for several months in the Bastille as a suspected English spy. His best play, *The Relapse,* was an original work produced in 1697, as was *The Provoked Wife,* presented in the same year but written about 1691. Other plays which he wrote or collaborated on were adaptations from earlier English or Continental dramatists.

The Relapse was a sequel to Colley Cibber's *Love's Last Shift* (1696). Like other dramatists of the 1690's, Vanbrugh depended on comedy of manners, sex, and lively action to carry along his plays. Social problems are introduced into the plays at times, but usually only for the purpose of making some cynical humor out of them. Notable in *The Relapse* is the sudden conversion of a debauched and faithless husband to marital constancy; such a

reformation at the end of an immoral play was the dramatist's reply to charges hurled at the stage at the time that it was presenting immorality. Vanbrugh's plays, popular during his lifetime, were published in a collected edition in 1730, just four years after his death. On the side of notoriety rather than fame, Vanbrugh was one of the dramatists attacked for immorality by Jeremy Collier in his *Short View of the Immorality and Profaneness of the English Stage* (1698).

As an architect, Vanbrugh designed Castle Howard, the Haymarket Theater, Blenheim Palace, and (collaborating with Nicholas Hawksmoor) the Clarendon Building at Oxford. Vanbrugh was knighted in 1723. He was married in 1719 to Henrietta Yarborough, who bore him several children of whom a boy and a girl survived. Vanbrugh's personality and well-constructed, good-humored plays continue to hold interest for many readers in modern times. He died in London on March 26, 1726.

BIBLIOGRAPHICAL REFERENCES: The chief edition is Bonamy Dobrée and Geoffrey Webb, *Complete Works,* 4 vols., 1927–1928; this includes the letters. There are two reliable biographies: G. H. Lovegrove, *The Life, Work, and Influence of Sir John Vanbrugh,* 1902; and Laurence Whistler, *Sir John Vanbrugh,* 1938. An interesting section on Vanbrugh appears in Henry T. E. Perry, *The Comic Spirit in Restoration Drama,* 1925. Of basic importance are the evaluations in Allardyce Nicoll, *History of Restoration Comedy, 1660–1700,* 1923; and Bonamy Dobrée, *Restoration Comedy,* 1924. See also, Paul Mueschke and Jeannette Fleisher, "A Re-evaluation of Vanbrugh," *Publications of the Modern Language Association,* XL (1934), 848–889.

CARL VAN VECHTEN

Born: Cedar Rapids, Iowa
Date: June 17, 1880

PRINCIPAL WORKS

NOVELS: *Peter Whiffle,* 1922; *The Blind Bow-Boy,* 1923; *The Tattooed Countess,* 1924; *Firecrackers,* 1925; *Spider Boy,* 1928; *Parties,* 1930.

ESSAYS: *Music after the Great War,* 1915; *Music and Bad Manners,* 1916; *Interpreters and Interpretations,* 1917; *The Merry-Go-Round,* 1918; *The Music of Spain,*

1918; *In the Garret*, 1920; *The Tiger in the House*, 1920; *Red: Papers on Musical Subjects*, 1925; *Excavations: A Book of Advocacies*, 1926; *Sacred and Profane Memories*, 1932.

Carl Van Vechten was born in Cedar Rapids, Iowa, June 17, 1880. Graduated from the University of Chicago in 1903, he became assistant music critic on the *New York Times* in 1906. Although he continued to associate with music criticisms and notes for much of his career, he later became a dramatic critic and finally a novelist.

His career as a novelist began with the signal success of his first novel, *Peter Whiffle*, a satirical work which enjoyed great vogue and popularity during the 1920's. His best-known novels include *The Blind Bow-Boy* and *Firecrackers*, both stories of artistic and society sets in New York; *The Tattooed Countess*, which deals with the return to her Midwestern home of

an American woman of the world; *Nigger Heaven* (1926), about life in Harlem; *Spider Boy*, a satire on Hollywood and movie people; and *Parties*, a New York novel of the period. In his books Mr. Van Vechten uses his knowledge of and enthusiasm for many phases of the arts—music, dancing, painting, literature—as topics of commentary. As a cat-lover, Mr. Van Vechten has written some excellent essays in *The Tiger in the House* and as editor has collected other writings on cats in *Lords of the Housetops* (1921). He has established a well-deserved reputation for himself as an "unprofessional" photographer of many figures of the arts in the 1930's and 1940's.

BIBLIOGRAPHICAL REFERENCES: See Carl Van Vechten, "Notes for an Autobiography," *Colophon*, Part III (1930); also Scott Cunningham, *A Bibliography of the Writings of Carl Van Vechten*, 1924.

IVAN VAZOV

Born: Sopot, Bulgaria
Date: June 27, 1850

Died: Sofia, Bulgaria
Died: September 22, 1921

PRINCIPAL WORKS

NOVELS: *Pod igoto*, 1893 (*Under the Yoke*); *Nova zemya*, 1894 (*New Country*); *Kazalarskata tsaritsa*, 1903 (*The Empress of Kazalar*).

PLAYS: *Sluzhbogontsi*, 1903 (*The Service-Chasers*); *Borislav*, 1909; *Ivaylo*, 1911.

POEMS: *Izbavlenie*, 1878 (*Liberation*); *Epopeya na zabravenite*, 1879 (*Epic of the Heroes*); *Pod nashete nebe*, 1900 (*Under Our Heaven*); *Pesni za Makedoniya*, 1914 (*Songs for Macedonia*); *Ne shte zagine*, 1920 (*It Will Not Perish*).

Ivan (Minchov) Vazov, for thirty years the outstanding writer in Bulgaria, was Bulgaria's first great writer in the various creative fields of the novel, poetry, and the drama. During his most influential years, from 1890

to 1920, his name was used to characterize the period as "the Vazov period."

Vazov, born on June 27, 1850, received his elementary education in his native town of Sopot and at Plovdiv.

1106

Son of a conservative merchant who was financially well-to-do, the boy enjoyed a comfortable childhood. He left Bulgaria when he was nineteen, and his first creative work, which appeared in the 1870's, was poems on patriotic and revolutionary themes, published in Bucharest. During that time he made a business trip to Rumania and met the revolutionary writers Karavelov and Botev. Inspired by them and by Petko Rachev Slaveukov, the pre-revolutionary poet, he decided to give up his schooling at the University of Zagreb and devote his work to the cause of the people.

After the liberation of Bulgaria from Turkish rule in 1878 he returned to his country and served as judge of the circuit court in Berkovitsa and Vidin. From 1886 to 1889 he was a political exile in Odessa, having opposed Stambolov's Bulgarian government. When he returned to Sofia he settled down to a life of prolific writing, achieving his most notable success in 1893 with the novel *Under the Yoke,* a story of the beginnings of the Bulgarian revolt against the Turks.

His novels, plays, and poems were praised for sympathy for the common people apparent in all of his work. On October 2, 1920, he was honored by a national jubilee celebrating his completion of fifty years of creative work. He died of a heart attack in Sofia, on September 22, 1921.

BIBLIOGRAPHICAL REFERENCES: For criticism and comment see T. Minkhov, "Ivan Vazov," in *Bulgarski pisateli,* IV (1929), 3–72; E. Damiani, "Ivan Vazov, poeta della rinascita nazionale," *Nuova Antologia,* CCCLIX (1932), 286–288; and A. Werner, "Ivan Vazov," *Books Abroad,* XXIV (1950), 242–244.

LOPE DE VEGA

Born: Madrid, Spain
Date: November 25, 1562

Died: Madrid
Date: August 27, 1635

PRINCIPAL WORKS

HISTORICAL PLAYS: *Peribáñez y el comendador de Ocana,* c. 1605 (*Peribáñez and the Commander of Ocana*); *Fuente ovejuna,* c. 1619 (*The Sheep Well*); *El mejor alcalde el rey,* c. 1623 (*The King, the Greatest Alcalde*).

COMEDIES: *El acero de Madrid,* c. 1613 (*Madrid Steel*); *La dama boba,* 1613 (*The Stupid Lady*); *El perro del hortelano,* c. 1615 (*The Gardener's Dog*); *Amar sin saber a quien,* c. 1620 (*Love for Love's Sake*); *La Moza de cántaro,* c. 1627 (*The Water Seller*).

Architect of the Golden Age of the theater in Spain was Lope Félix de Vega Carpio, who could justly boast that when he started writing plays only two companies of actors were performing, while at the end of his career forty companies employing at least a thousand people were providing the Spanish capital with plays. Modern scholarship sets at about eight hundred his total dramatic output instead of the 1,800 claimed by his exuberant friend, Montalbán. At least 507 are unquestionably his, many in his own handwriting. One of the greatest, *La estrella de Sevilla* (c. 1617, *The Star of Se-*

ville) may possibly be by him, though modern scholarship discredits his authorship. The total body of his work is more than any other dramatist can claim, and though many were written in less than a day, none is wholly bad, none untouched by his genius. Publishers sent shorthand experts to the theater to copy his plays and pirate them. In the provinces managers advertised their offerings as by Lope de Vega to be sure of an audience. So great was his popularity that anything excellent, from food to jewels, was referred to as "of Lope."

This "prodigy of nature" (*monstruo de la naturaleza*), as his contemporaries called him, was the son of a worker in gold and was born in Madrid on November 25, 1562. An ecclesiastical patron entered him in the University of Alcalá, but a love affair with the wife of an actor kept him from taking orders as he had planned. This was the first of many love affairs, all of which he transmuted into important literary works. Friends had only to suggest a form of literature he had not attempted to have him compose for them a good example of it.

The theater was his great love, however. Able to write a play in verse almost faster than a scribe could copy it, he seized on anything as a plot idea. The medical fad of taking iron for the blood inspired *Madrid Steel*. A proverb was the seed of *The Gardener's Dog*. Reports of piratical activity in the Mediterranean inspired The Arabian Nights theme of *La doncella Teodora* (*The Damsel Theodora*).

In his rhymed *Arte nueva de hacer comedias* (1609, *New Art of Writing Plays*), Lope de Vega laid down the rules under which he wrote: "In the first act, state your case; in the second,

your events, so that not till the middle of the third does anybody begin to suspect what is going to come of it all. . . . Do not permit the solution till you come to the last scene."

His dramas, therefore, were full of suspense. Action, not philosophy, was what his audiences wanted, and he confessed that the audience dictated his plots, chose his characters, and wrote his plays. Though he knew the rules of the classical theater, he admitted that with a half dozen exceptions, he broke them to please the people and to be true to life. Prose and poetry, he hoped, would gain him fame, and he made no secret of the fact that he wrote plays for money. From his plays he earned $400,000, most of which he generously gave to friends in need.

While his genius touched all types of drama, his popularity rested chiefly on the type called *comedias de capa y espada*, or cape-and-sword plays which were full of intrigue and complications, with masked nobles and women disguised as men. The plots commanded the characters and stock impulses motivated the action (love easily transferred, jealousy easily aroused, honor easily offended); and an entertaining and involved plot kept the spectators guessing until matrimony at the final curtain washed away all stains on family honor. The outcome of these plays is not always logical. In his treatise on playwriting Lope de Vega declared: "At times, that which is contrary to logic for that very reason is pleasing." Good examples of this practice are *Madrid Steel*, and the gay *The Stupid Lady*.

He was also successful in religious plays with saints as heroes, in comedies of manners with lower class characters, and in heroic plays with historical or

1108

legendary characters, such as *The Sheep Well* and *The King, the Greatest Alcalde*. In addition, he composed several hundred *autos sacramentales*, short plays for the Corpus Christi season and other Church holy days.

Lope de Vega was also fertile in nondramatic works. Some one has calculated his entire output at 22,300,000 lines; it takes twenty-one quarto volumes to contain writings already published. *The Beauty of Angelica* (1602), an epic poem, runs to 11,000 lines, while he penned 10,000 lines in poetic tribute to Madrid's patron Saint Isidor. The epic, *Jerusalem Conquered* (1609), is twice that long. In 1598 he composed *La Dragontea*, an epic in ten cantos about the misdeeds of Francis Drake, and wrote 2,000 lines about the loves and adventures of a cat in his mock epic *La Gatomaquia* (1634). Fifteen hundred sonnets resulted from his poetic musing. In prose he wrote *La Arcadia* (1598), a pastoral novel. His favorite novel, *La Dorotea*, was inspired by his first love; frequently revised, it was finally published in 1632.

As a man, Lope was less admirable. He was a product of the most corrupt age of Spanish history and moved in the most corrupt circles of that age. As a boy, he showed precocity: "dedicated to the Muses from his birth," composing poetry when he was only five, and writing a play at the age of twelve. No wonder he ran away from school with a companion and toured Spain until a pawnbroker grew suspicious at the wealth they displayed and turned them over to the police.

At the university, he perfected himself chiefly in fencing, singing, and dancing. Studies over, he surrendered to his love for the theater and by fifteen was seeing his plays professionally per-

formed. His love for adventure led him in 1583 to join a naval expedition to the Azores; he returned to an intensive life of writing. Five years later he was banished from Madrid on penalty of death for a criminal libel against his mistress, Elena Osorio, daughter of a theatrical manager for whom he provided plays. From exile in Valencia he wooed Isabel de Urbina and returned boldly to the capital to elope with her. Nineteen days after their marriage, he deserted her to join the Invincible Armada; he used his leisure from military duties to write an epic poem.

Rough seas and the death of his brother made war unattractive, and following the death of his beloved Isabel he spent the next forty years in a succession of love intrigues and scandals. His two favorite children were illegitimate. Friend and associate of the nobility, serving the Duke of Alba, the Marques of Malpica, and the Count of Lemos, he reached the depths as panderer for the dissipated Duke of Sessa.

But he had his moments of repentance. In 1609 he became a *familiar* of the Inquisition. He joined three religious confraternities in two years. When his second wife, Juana, and their son Carlos died almost simultaneously, Lope entered Holy Orders. In 1614 he was ordained priest in Toledo, at a time when he was carrying on a love affair of his own and was providing mistresses for Sessa.

Truly, Lope was a strange compound of sensuality, pettiness, conceit, servility, and genius. Fortunately the last quality outweighs all the rest, and it was that quality which all Madrid recognized on Tuesday, August 28, 1635, in according him funereal honors such as have seldom been equaled for a man of letters. Ironically, when his resting place, San Estéban, was remodeled in the eighteenth century, no distinguishing mark was put on his coffin, so that Lope's present grave is uncertain. But he left his own monument in the Spanish theater.

He established the play of three acts, set down rules of versification for the expression of various emotions and situations, and brought to the stage a richness of poetic inspiration unequaled in Spanish literature. He reflected the life, customs, and ideas of the sixteenth and seventeenth centuries with realistic naturalness and poetic freedom. Inferior to Tirso de Molina in handling comedy, incapable of the poetic heights of Calderón, less careful than Alarcón in character portrayal and analysis, Lope de Vega nevertheless surpassed all his Golden Age contemporaries in skill at blending poetry and life, which he painted in vivid colors, although he did not interpret it deeply. He gave freedom and importance to women and dignity to the lower classes, and produced an enormous number of masterpieces at the time when variety was necessary to encourage a theater-going public and bring to greatness the theater of the Golden Age in Spain.

Willis Knapp Jones

BIBLIOGRAPHICAL REFERENCES: Biographical and critical studies of Lope de Vega in English include H. A. Rennert, *The Life of Lope de Vega,* 1904 (rev. ed., 1937); R. Schevill, *The Dramatic Art of Lope de Vega,* 1918; Angel Flores, *Lope de Vega: Monster of Nature,* 1930; and James Fitzmaurice Kelly, *Chapters on Spanish Literature,* 1908. See also F. A. de Icaza, *Lope de Vega, sus amores y sus odios,* 1925; Astraña Marín, *La vida azarosa de Lope de Vega,* 1935; and J. de Entrambasaguas, *La vida de Lope,* 1936, and *Estudios sobre Lope,* 1946. The Lope de Vega Number of *The Hispanic Review,* III, 3 (1935) contains articles by contemporary scholars and critics.

GIOVANNI VERGA

Born: Catania, Sicily
Date: August 31, 1840

Died: Catania
Date: January 27, 1922

PRINCIPAL WORKS

NOVELS: *I Malavoglia,* 1881 (*The House by the Medlar Tree*); *Mastro-don Gesualdo,* 1889.

SHORT STORIES: *Vita dei campi,* 1880 (*Life of the Fields*); *Novelle rusticane,* 1883 (*Country Tales*).

The greatest Italian novelist since Manzoni was born in Catania, Sicily, on August 31, 1840, of a family supposed to have come from Aragon in the thirteenth century. The Vergas were a family of patriots. The grandfather was an underground fighter for independence and a deputy to the first Sicilian parliament in 1812. During Giovanni's boyhood his mother encouraged him to read. Although he gave her credit for his decision at the age of fifteen to become a novelist, biographers point out that his teacher Pietro Abato wrote poems and novels and assigned class work that caused the young student to write a 600-page novel, *Love and Country*, about George Washington and the American Revolution. Fortunately Verga knew more about the subjects of his later fiction.

Instead of entering the university in 1860, he persuaded his father to let him use the money to publish another manuscript he had completed in four volumes. *Carbonari della montagna* concerned the adventures of his grandfather. During the next fifteen years Verga lived in Florence and Milan. In these cities, under the influence of the French writers, he wrote passable novels of middle-class life, among them the sentimental *Storia di una capinera* (1869, *Story of a Wren*). In Milan he described adultery in high society, in *Eva* (1873) and *Tigre reale* (1873).

From this distance Verga could look back on his childhood home and draw upon his impressions of Sicilian life. *Nedda*, published in 1874, was a story of a wronged girl of Sicily, a work realistic in treatment in which the writer, in spite of his attitude of scientific observation, revealed warm sympathy for his characters. He scorned being classified. When some found in him the masked pity and underlying pessimism of a Hardy and others called him a supporter of Verism, with its anti-Romanticist reaction, he retorted that "works of art may be born of any -ism. The main thing is for it to be born."

The years 1878 to 1880, after returning to Milan following the death of his favorite sister in Sicily, marked the turning point in his career. His renewed interest in the Sicilian peasants and fishermen as subjects of art was shown in the collection of short stories, *Life of the Fields*, which contained "Cavalleria Rusticana," a tale of primitive passion and violence that he was to dramatize for the great Duse in 1884, and then use as libretto for the Mascagni opera. But his greatest fame came from *The House by the Medlar Tree*, a novel dealing with Sicilian fishermen defeated in their struggle for existence, but with the town as the real protagonist. Verga's home town, under the disguise of Trezza, also figured in his last great novel *Mastro-don Gesualdo*, which tells of the downfall of a proud, ambitious peasant.

The foreword to *The House by the Medlar Tree* had announced Verga's purpose to write a Sicilian *Comédie Humaine* which he titled *I Vinti* (*The Defeated*), to show "the slow, inevitable flow of the rivers of social life." But writing was hard for him, and during the last twenty years of his life spent in his native town in southern Sicily he wrote and published little. A third novel of the series, *La Duchessa di Leyra*, was planned as a study of the Sicilian aristocracy but was never completed. He died at Catania on January 27, 1922.

The style of Verga's writing, mentioned by all critics, grew from his admiration for a moving story by a sea captain that he read when young, and which appealed to him in spite of its colloquial and illiterate style. Although an aristocrat, Verga tried to make his own writing echo the speech of the simple peasants. For most readers the wealth of detail and the keen observation of the life and customs of the lower class give his novels of Southern Italy their greatest appeal, so that D. H. Lawrence was moved to translate *Mastro-don Gesualdo* and two volumes of short stories in order to give pleasure to readers ignorant of Italian. Verga's own life was uneventful; he lived vicariously in the experiences of the impoverished people whose stories he told so well.

BIBLIOGRAPHICAL REFERENCES: The most authoritative study of Verga in English is T. G. Bergin, *Giovanni Verga*, 1931. For biographical and critical studies in Italian see A. Momigliano, *Giovanni Verga, narratore,* 1923; Luigi Russo, *Giovanni Verga,* 1934; Rosario Verde, *Giovanni Verga, drammaturgo,* 1950; Eurialo de Michelis, *Dostojevskij minore, con un saggio sul Verga europeo,* 1954; and Giorgio Santagelo, *Storia della critica Verghiana,* 1954. *Studi Verghiani,* edited by L. Perroni, 1929, is a collection of brief critical studies.

PUBLIUS VERGILIUS MARO

Born: Andes, Italy
Date: October 15, 70 B.C.

Died: Brundisium, Italy
Date: September 21, 19 B.C.

PRINCIPAL WORKS

POEMS: *Eclogues,* c. 40–37 B.C.; *Georgics,* c. 37–29 B.C.; *Aeneid,* c. 29–19 B.C.

Publius Vergilius Maro, author of one of the most familiar epics in all literature, was born in the village of Andes, in northern Italy, October 15, 70 B.C., only a few decades before the end of the Golden Age of the Roman Republic. It is claimed that his father was a potter who by hard work and an advantageous marriage had become a landowner prosperous enough to give his son a superior education. The youth studied under eminent teachers at Cremona and Milan, and under the Greek poet and grammarian Parthenius at Naples. At the age of twenty-three Vergil went to Rome to study not only poetry and philosophy but also mathematics and physics under Siro the Epicurean, whose philosophy affected Vergil's thought and writings throughout his life.

Although he was a shy, rustic, and slow-spoken youth, his personal charm and the literary ability evident in his early poems won Vergil the friendship of some of the most cultivated and powerful men in Rome, among them Octavian, Maecenas, Pollio, Horace, and Cornelius Gallus. His popularity was such that in 41 B.C., when his farm was threatened with seizure, along with surrounding territories to be divided among the victorious soldiers of the triumvirs returning from the battle of Philippi, his friends were able to intercede at Rome to have it saved. Despite his popularity in the capital, however, Vergil spent much time in retirement on his beloved farm, studying Greek and Roman history and literature.

In 42 B.C., at the request of his friend Asinius Pollio, Vergil began work on the *Eclogues,* which were finally completed about 37 B.C. These idyllic pastoral poems were based on the *Idylls* of the third century B.C. Sicilian poet, Theocritus. The setting, structure, and language of the *Eclogues* are highly imitative, but their greater complexity and artificiality reflect a wider range of observation and the background of a more highly developed civilization. They are also original in their extensive use of allegory and their many laudatory references to the author's friends.

After the publication of the *Eclogues,* Vergil took up residence at a country estate near Naples, where he spent most of the rest of his life. It was here that he wrote the *Georgics,* a didactic poem in four books on the subject of husbandry. Written at the request of Maecenas, who wished to revive an interest in the old Roman virtues of industry and a fondness for rustic life, the poems are considered to be the most technically polished and elaborate of all Vergil's work. Unlike the rather dry, strictly didactic *Works and Days* of the Greek poet Hesiod, on which they were based, the *Georgics* were obviously never intended to teach the specific techniques of successful agriculture to anyone who did not know them already. What they aimed to do, and did most successfully, was to interest the reader in the lost art of agriculture by making it attractive and interesting to him. This the author did by means of graceful language, imaginative imagery, concrete illustrations, and digressions on various subjects which added much to the charm, if not to the unity, of the work.

Vergil was forty-one years old before he embarked on his lifelong ambition, the composition of a Homeric epic which would commemorate the glory of Rome and his friend, the Emperor Augustus, and would win back the Roman people, unsettled and corrupted by long civil strife, to their primitive religion and ancient virtues. He worked on the *Aeneid* for ten years. When he died of a fever at Brundisium, Italy, on September 21, 19 B.C., after a trip to Greece, final revisions were not yet completed, but Augustus ordered that the work be preserved.

Vergil chose as his topic the voyage of the Trojan hero Aeneas to Italy after the fall of Troy, because Aeneas was the only character in the Homeric tale whom poets had connected with the legendary founding of Rome. Although Vergil borrowed heavily, not only from Homer, but also from Apollonius, Greek tragedy, and the Latin epic poet Ennius, the total conception and expression were all his own. The skillful handling of the hexameters, the imagery, the characterizations of the central figures were all original, as was the interweaving of numerous old tales and legends into one comprehensive whole. In the character of Queen Dido, particularly, we have a "modern" treatment of romantic love and its effects on the human character largely foreign to Greek classical literature. The *Aeneid* is a literary rather than a "true" epic in that it is the result of conscious artistic effort rather than of natural, gradual evolution. But there is nothing artificial in Vergil's deeply rooted patriotic sentiment nor in his unquestioning belief in the divine origin and destiny of the Roman state. His *Aeneid* remains today one of the most stirring productions of a great civilization.

BIBLIOGRAPHICAL REFERENCES: The most complete modern edition is *P. Vergili Maronis opera,* edited by Frederic A. Hirtzel, 1953. There are many translations of Vergil in English; among the most recent are *Virgil,* translated by H. Rushton Fairclough, 1946; *Virgil's Works,* translated by J. W. Mackail, 1950; and *The Aeneid of Virgil,* translated by C. Day Lewis, 1952. See also John W. Mackail, *Virgil,* 1931; and William F. J. Knight, *Roman Vergil,* 1944.

PAUL VERLAINE

Born: Metz, France
Date: March 30, 1844

Died: Paris, France
Date: January 8, 1896

PRINCIPAL WORKS

POEMS: *Poèmes saturniens,* 1866; *Fêtes galantes,* 1869; *La bonne chanson,* 1870; *Romances sans paroles,* 1874; *Sagesse,* 1881; *Jadis et naguère,* 1884; *Amour,* 1888; *Parallèlement,* 1889; *Bonheur,* 1891.

POEMS IN TRANSLATION: *Complete Works,* 1909; *Selected Poems,* 1948.

AUTOBIOGRAPHY: *Confessions,* 1895 (*Confessions of a Poet*).

The son of a former captain of engineers of Napoleon's army, Paul (Marie) Verlaine was born in Metz, March 30, 1844. He was educated in Paris, and then secured a minor position with an insurance company, thus following the tradition of many French artists and writers who have so often attached themselves to humdrum jobs that would provide a small salary and yet leave some spare time for creative work. In 1870 he married a Mlle. Mautet; and in the following year he formed the fatal friendship with Arthur Rimbaud that was to affect his life so adversely and was to be a curious forerunner of the Oscar Wilde-Lord Alfred Douglas affair that rocked England twenty years later. With Rimbaud, a much younger man of savage, indeed almost insane temperament, Verlaine wandered through England, France, and Belgium. He had long been drinking heavily, and the journey ended disastrously when he tried to shoot Rimbaud. This act cost Verlaine two years in prison at Mons, during which time he was converted to Catholicism. When he returned to France in 1875, his wife divorced him; he went to England again to earn his living as a teacher of French.

Verlaine had begun his poetic career as a member of the "Parnassian" school, led by Leconte de Lisle, whose members aimed at a detached severity in poetry; but as early as his second volume he was obviously slipping away from them by means of the eighteenth century fantasies of the *Fêtes galantes.* This phase, charming though it may have been, was not, however, Verlaine's important work. His greatest significance, beginning with *Romances sans paroles,* lies in his contribution to the Symbolist Movement.

The poets included in this general movement were at first known as the "decadents," a term that Verlaine was willing to accept. The name "Symbolists" was suggested by Moréas, and the school derived primarily from Baudelaire's poem "Correspondences," in which nature is described as a "forest of symbols." It was a reaction against the austere impersonality of the Parnassians, and can perhaps best be described by quoting Mallarmé's comment: "To name an object is to suppress three-fourths of the enjoyment of the poem. . . . to suggest it, there is the dream." Thus Symbolist poetry consists largely of vague suggestions, of half-hints, by which the poet tries to express "the secret affinities of things with his soul." "No color," Verlaine said in his poem, "The Art of Poetry," "no color, only the nuance." And again: "Take eloquence and wring its neck"—a protest against the sonorous declamations of poetry such as Hugo's. Symbolist practice led inevitably to poetry that became more and more "private" as each poet developed his own set of symbols, the ultimate, perhaps, being Rimbaud's insistence that for him each vowel had a different color—A, black; E, white; and so on. Poetry, then, finally came to resemble music; its purpose was the evocation of a mood, and the "subject" was unimportant. Behind the Symbolists clearly stood the figure of Poe, whom Baudelaire had introduced to France in the 1860's.

In France, the Symbolist Movement led to Mallarmé and finall to Paul Valéry; in England, it influenced the young William Butler Yeats as well as a number of almost-forgotten poets of the 1890's. Much of the difficulty that many readers experience in dealing with contemporary poetry stems from the Symbolists' practice of developing a "private language."

Although Verlaine regained sufficient respectability to be invited to lecture in England in 1894, his later life was that of the perfect bohemian as the term is popularly understood. He alternated between cafés and hospitals, and finally died in Paris, January 8, 1896.

BIBLIOGRAPHICAL REFERENCES: The standard study of Verlaine is E. Lepelletier, *Paul Verlaine: sa vie et son œuvre*, 1907 (Eng. trans., 1909). See also Anatole France, *La Vie littéraire* (Third Series, 1891); E. Delille, "The Poet Verlaine," *Fortnightly Review*, XLIX (March, 1891); Arthur Symons, *The Symbolist Movement in Literature*, 1908; Frank Harris, *Contemporary Portraits: First Series*, 1920; and Lawrence and Elizabeth Hanson, *Verlaine: Fool of God*, 1957.

JULES VERNE

Born: Nantes, France
Date: February 8, 1828

Died: Amiens, France
Date: March 24, 1905

Principal Works

NOVELS: *Cinq semaines en ballon,* 1863 (*Five Weeks in a Balloon*); *Voyage au centre de la terre,* 1864 (*A Journey to the Center of the Earth*); *De la terre à la lune,* 1865 (*A Trip to the Moon*); *Vingt mille lieues sous les mers,* 1870 (*Twenty Thousand Leagues under the Sea*); *L'Île mystérieuse,* 1870 (*The Mysterious Island*); *Le Tour du monde en quatre-vingts jours,* 1872 (*Around the World in Eighty Days*); *Michel Strogoff,* 1876; *Le Rayon vert,* 1882.

With the possible exception of Dumas, Jules Verne is probably the best known of all French novelists among English-speaking peoples. Born on February 8, 1828, he lived a quiet childhood in Nantes, where he attended the local lycée before going to Paris to study law. Soon after arriving in Paris, he discovered that he preferred literary work and began to write for the stage; in addition to writing several librettos for operas he also collaborated with the younger Dumas on some ephemeral plays. His first real success came with the publication of a novelette, *Five Weeks in a Balloon*, in 1863. The popularity of that short narrative encouraged Verne to continue writing what seemed at the time extravagant tales of technocracy and technology to which he added carefully prepared scientific and geographical data to provide a background of realism, in much the same way that Daniel Defoe had done in providing realistic background for his novels a century and a half before. The subject matter and lively action of Verne's tales soon gained for him an immense following in France and abroad, for his books coincided with the popular interest in science and invention beginning to sweep people's imagination during the second half of the nineteenth century. His novels, intended at the time for adult readers, still have a wide following in America, at least among youngsters, and the wide popularity of his tales is attested to by the great number of translations and foreign editions. Each novel foretells some scientific or technological development, many of which have now been reached or passed, with the result that some of Verne's devices seem crude to twentieth century readers.

The most famous of Verne's novels is Twenty Thousand Leagues Under the Sea, rewritten many times for children. In its own day the novel was a pioneer work introducing the submarine to literature decades before such craft were successfully built and used by any of the world's navies. In this case, as in others, Verne came startlingly close to later technological developments; his fictional Nautilus is propelled by electricity and functions on principles very similar to those of modern undersea craft.

Although literary scholars and even modern writers of science fiction have neglected his voluminous works, generations of readers have turned to Verne while forgetting other French authors with more serious intentions. In his own time Verne did not go unhonored. He was made a Chevalier of the Legion of Honor by the French government, and he was acclaimed by the French Academy. He died at Amiens on March 24, 1905, too early to see many of his fictional dreams of technology come true in real life.

BIBLIOGRAPHICAL REFERENCES: Verne's principal works are available in translation. For biography and criticism see Charles Lemire, *Jules Verne*, 1908; F. C. Herne, *Jules Verne: An Appreciation*, 1914; Kenneth Allott, *Jules Verne*, 1940; and G. H. Waltz, *Jules Verne*, 1943. An interesting biography intended for young people is Catherine Owens Peare, *Jules Verne: His Life*, 1956.

ALFRED DE VIGNY

Born: Loches, France
Date: March 27, 1799

Died: Paris, France
Date: September 17, 1863

PRINCIPAL WORKS

NOVEL: *Cinq-Mars*, 1826.

TALES AND SKETCHES: *Servitude et grandeur militaires*, 1835 (*Military Service and Greatness*).

POEMS: *Poèmes antiques et modernes*, 1822; *Éloa, ou la sœur des anges*, 1824; *Poèmes philosophiques*, 1843.

PLAYS: *La Maréchale d'Ancre*, 1831; *Chatterton*, 1835.

ESSAYS AND STUDIES: *Stello, ou les diables bleus*, 1832.

In French literature Alfred (Victor), Comte de Vigny is important as a great pioneer of the romantic movement in the nineteenth century, but to speakers of English he is best known as the author of a single novel, *Cinq-Mars*, a historical romance. Born at Loches on March 27, 1799, he followed a family tradition of generations and began his career as an officer in the French army in 1813, at the age of sixteen. He retired from military life in 1825, after twelve years of peacetime service. Before retiring he had already begun to write, and a volume of his verse, *Poèmes antiques et modernes*, had been published in 1822. This volume was followed by a series of narrative poems, including *Éloa* in 1824. The early poetry of Vigny, collected in 1837, was, according to his own preface to the collected edition, philosophic thought clothed in the form of poetic art. Alfred de Musset, Victor Hugo, and Lamartine, all later and important French romantic poets, were influenced by Vigny's work. In his later poetry he tried to analyze human problems and present them through Biblical symbols, as in *La Colère de Samson* (1839, *Samson's Anger*) and *Le Mont des Oliviers* (1843–1844, *The Mount of Olives*).

In addition to his poetry and his very popular novel, *Cinq-Mars*, Vigny translated Shakespeare into French, wrote studies of the poet in modern society in *Stello*, wrote plays (including one about the English poet Chatterton), and published a volume of sketches and essays on military life, *Military Service and Greatness*.

In private life Vigny was unfortunate. He was married to an Englishwoman, Lydia Bunbury, in 1828, but she shortly afterward became a permanent invalid. From 1831 to 1837 Vigny was the lover of Marie Dorval, a celebrated actress, but the affair ended unhappily. He was elected to the French Academy in 1845. Twice he ran unsuccessfully for the French Assembly, in 1848 and 1849. He died in Paris on September 17, 1863.

BIBLIOGRAPHICAL REFERENCES: This author has received little attention from English and American critics. The best study is Arnold Whitridge, *Alfred de Vigny*, 1933, which includes a bibliography. See also Anatole France, *Alfred de Vigny*, 1923. For readers of French there is Emile Lauvrière, *Alfred de Vigny*, 2 vols., 1946. S Harvey Clarke, *The Works of Vigny Judged by His Contemporaries*, 1932, is a collection of critical passages with a slight commentary. Charles W. Bird, *Alfred de Vigny's "Chatterton,"* 1941, is a source study for advanced students.

FRANÇOIS VILLON

Born: Paris, France
Date: 1431

Died: Unknown
Date: Unknown

PRINCIPAL WORKS

POEMS: *Le Petit Testament*, 1456 (*Little Testament*); *Le Grand Testament*, 1461 (*Great Testament*).

Nothing is known of the background and youth of Villon except that he was "almost certainly" born in Paris in 1431, of poor parents. His father apparently

1117

died early; his mother was still living in 1461. His name was actually Montcorbier, but he took the name of his patron (and probable relative) Guillaume de Villon, a priest and professor of canon law in Paris. The patron sent young Villon to the University of Paris, at that time one of the greatest in Europe, where he received the degree of bachelor of arts (1449) and master of arts (1452).

Shortly after Villon received his master's degree, there began the long series of embroilments with the law, incidents which scholars have dug out of the Paris archives and which make Villon's life so colorful. On June 5, 1455, he was involved in a street brawl with one Jehan le Mardi and a priest named Phillippe Chermoye, as a result of which Chermoye died of his wounds. Villon fled the city and was banished, but the sentence was remitted. Back in Paris the next year, he was so badly beaten in another brawl that he planned to go to Angers. But before his departure, near the Christmas of 1456, he and some equally disreputable friends robbed the chapel of the College of Navarre. The robbery was discovered in the spring; one of the gang turned king's evidence, and Villon was again banished from Paris. For four years he wandered about France, touching the heights and depths of the medieval world. In 1457 he was a visitor at the court of Charles, Duc d'Orléans, himself one of the great French medieval poets, and was likewise sheltered by Jean II of Bourbon. But he could not keep out of trouble; in 1460 he was sentenced to death in Orléans and was freed only as a result of the general amnesty proclaimed on the state entry of the duke's infant daughter. The summer of 1461 found

him in prison at Meung, and again he owed his release to the royal house, for Louis XI passed through the city and prisoners were consequently pardoned.

The autumn of 1462 found him back in Paris and again involved in a complicated web of trouble in which the old robbery figured. He was thrown into the Châtelet prison, tortured, and sentenced to be hanged; but the Parlement de Paris commuted his sentence to ten years' banishment from the city. After this date he vanished completely, and the most diligent research has not solved the mystery of his last years. From what is known of his life, it is likely that his death was neither edifying nor pleasant. Rabelais stated that he found refuge in London, but there is no evidence for this unlikely report.

Villon's *Testaments* are long, rambling poems in eight-line stanzas interspersed with *ballades* and *lais*. It is highly personal poetry, in which the author makes no attempt to hide the details of his sordid career—"in the thirtieth year of my age, when I have drunk so deep of shame." By ironically using the form of a "testament," he was able to include a long list of people with whom he had had dealings, bequeathing to each some appropriate memento, thus paying off old scores and expressing gratitude. The charm of the poems to modern readers lies in the unrivaled picture that is given of France at the close of the Middle Ages, a picture that cannot be gained from the romances of chivalry or the poems of courtly love. We can visualize the swarming city of Paris, the church where his mother went to pray, the taverns, the brothel where he lived with Fat Margot—for Villon had seen all aspects of contemporary life, from the court of Charles d'Orléans to the prison of Le Châtelet. There is also the frank revelation of the fascinating personality of a man who could jest about the gallows he had, more than once, narrowly escaped and the next moment write the *ballade* of his mother praying to the Virgin. Though Villon made the conventional gesture of blaming his ill-luck on Fortune, he clearly knew that his troubles were of his own making, that he was hopelessly enmeshed in vice, that the gibbet was perilously close. The only consolation he could draw was from the favorite theme of the fifteenth century—"the Dance of Death," Death the Leveller, who brings high and low alike to the same end.

Ignored during the neo-classic seventeenth and eighteenth centuries, Villon's poetry was revived by the Romanticists as part of the renewed interest in medieval literature. It appealed particularly to writers of the latter part of the nineteenth century, who, from the safety of Victorian England, enjoyed peering into the turbulent fifteenth century that had produced such contrasts as Jeanne d'Arc and François Villon.

BIBLIOGRAPHICAL REFERENCES: The *Œuvres Complètes* were edited by M. Auguste Longnon, 1892. There are two translations of Villon's poetry, that by John Heron Lepper, including the sundry translations by John Payne and others, 1926, and that of Lewis Wharton, 1935. The best study of Villon in English is D. B. Wyndham Lewis, *François Villon: A Documented Survey*, 1928. See also Gaston Paris, *François Villon*, 1901; and P. Champion, *François Villon: sa vie et son temps*, 1913.

FRANÇOIS MARIE AROUET DE VOLTAIRE

Born: Paris, France
Date: November 21, 1694

Died: Paris
Date: May 30, 1778

PRINCIPAL WORKS

NOVELS: *Zadig*, 1747; *Candide*, 1759; *L'Ingénu*, 1767; *La Princesse de Babilone*, 1768; *L'Homme aux quarante écus*, 1768.

PHILOSOPHICAL AND CRITICAL ESSAYS: *Lettres philosophiques sur les Anglais*, 1733; *Temple du goût*, 1733; *Traité sur la tolérance*, 1763; *Théâtre de Pierre Corneille*, 1764; *Dictionnaire philosophique*, 1764; *Droits des hommes*, 1768.

PLAYS: *Œdipe*, 1718; *Brutus*, 1730; *Zaïre*, 1732; *Tancrède*, 1760; *Irène*, 1778.

POEMS: *La Henriade*, 1724; *Discours en vers sur l'homme*, 1738; *La Pucelle*, 1755.

HISTORY: *Histoire de Charles XII*, 1731; *Essai sur les mœurs et l'esprit des nations*, 1754; *Le Siècle de Louis XIV*, 1756.

The man who, under the name of Voltaire, was to be remembered as the foremost spokesman of the Age of Enlightenment, was born François Marie Arouet in Paris on November 21, 1694. The son of a prosperous lawyer who numbered among his friends members of the nobility and the literary aristocracy, young François grew up in an atmosphere of wit and culture. At the age of eleven, already known in Paris as an unusually clever rhymer of verses, he was invited to the salon of the celebrated Ninon de l'Enclos, thus gaining an early entree into a dazzling world of free morals and free thought.

Although from a Jansenist family, François received his formal education at the Jesuit Collège Louis-le-Grand, where he acquired a solid classical background, familiarity with poetry and drama, and a number of noble and influential friends who were to serve him well throughout his lifetime.

While still in his school days, he became a member of the cultivated, freethinking, epicurean, and rather debauched "Society of the Temple." Resisting his father's efforts to make him a lawyer, he insisted that he would be a poet, and soon his biting verses mocking those in high places had earned him several brief exiles from Paris and, in 1717, an eleven-month sojourn in the Bastille. He emerged from prison with a finished draft of *Œdipe*, the first of the more than fifty plays he was to write during his lifetime. Some of these plays were failures, others were spectacular successes on the contemporary stage, but none has survived the test of time. Although they are interesting in their frequently exotic settings, their use of characters from French history, and their introduction of some of the elements of the less formal English drama upon the rigorously defined classical stage of France, it is for their historic interest rather than their literary or dramatic merit that they are read today.

A few years later, following another brief term in prison, a three-year exile in England brought François, who by this time had changed his name to Arouet de Voltaire, into the society of such men as Pope, Swift, and Gay, and into contact with the ideas of Bacon, Locke, and Newton. As a result of this sojourn, much of the intellectual activity of Voltaire's most productive period was devoted to synthesizing the two streams of rationalistic, freethinking ideas, French and English. Voltaire returned to France with his Deism and skepticism strengthened, and with a strong desire to cultivate liberal thought in his homeland. One of his first weapons in this cause was the *Lettres philosophiques sur les Anglais* which, in characteristically brief, epigrammatic sentences, described the political liberty, religious tolerance, and commercial enterprise of the British, contrasting them with conditions in France. When this volume was published its implied criticism of French law, religion, and institutions incurred royal wrath which forced Voltaire to flee Paris and take up residence with various wealthy sponsors in the provinces.

At the home of one of these sponsors Voltaire met the Marquise du Châtelet, the brilliant and learned woman who was to be his mistress and intellectual companion for fifteen years. The years he spent with her at Cirey were fruitful ones of intellectual development and consolidation. During that time he was appointed royal historiographer, was elected to the French Academy, wrote numerous plays, worked on several volumes of historical criticism, including the rationalistic, freethinking *Essai sur les mœurs* (1754, *Essay on Manners*), which was not published until 1754, and published the tale *Zadig* in 1747. After the Marquise du Châtelet's death in 1749 Voltaire spent three years at the court of his great admirer and patron, Frederick the Great of Prussia, years which had been intended for the creation in reality of the Platonic ideal of a philosopher-king, but which were marked by increasingly bitter quarrels and disillusionment. Upon his return to France,

Voltaire, grown rich from writings, pensions, and shrewed business ventures, purchased and settled on a great estate at Ferney, conveniently close to the Swiss border. It was during his life there that his *Traité sur la tolérance* was written and the first volume of the *Dictionnaire philosophique,* a work which epitomized Voltaire's rationalism and his universal interests, was published. At Ferney he wrote articles for Diderot's *Encyclopédie* and dedicated himself to the extirpation of "L'Infâme," the intolerance and superstition which he believed to be the inevitable accompaniment of any form of organized religion. In the midst of numerous sustained interests and activities, he spent three days writing *Candide,* the work for which he is best remembered.

In *Candide, ou l'Optimisme,* the fantastically improbable travels, adventures, and misfortunes of the young Candide, his fiancée Cunegonde, and his tutor Pangloss are recounted in a terse, dry, understated style. Voltaire, never an unqualified optimist, and progressively disillusioned by his mistress's death, the failure of his schemes for Frederick the Great, the gratuitous horror and suffering of the great Lisbon earthquake of 1755, and his acquaintance with the universal folly and wickedness of mankind derived from his wide reading, makes his exaggerated adventure tale an ironic attack on the optimistic philosophy of Leibniz and Pope, who contended that this was "the best of all possible worlds." By endowing his characters initially with a good fortune and every prospect for happiness, and then leading them through every conceivable misfortune into resigned old age, Voltaire makes the point that only by taking life as it comes and avoiding theoretical speculation about its meaning can man ward off despair. Richly spiced with a wit and humor which are as fresh today as when they were created, *Candide* is nevertheless the thoughtful and embittered product of a mind more concerned with communicating an idea than with skillful characterization or pure entertainment.

Early in 1778 Voltaire entered Paris in triumph to oversee the production of his latest play, *Irène.* There, in his hour of greatest glory, he died on May 30. Characteristically, the man whose clear, direct style made him the greatest spokesman for the anti-clerical and rationalistic ideas of the Age of Enlightenment, had died "in a state of sin," and his body had to be smuggled out of Paris at night to prevent its ignominious burial in a common ditch.

BIBLIOGRAPHICAL REFERENCES: The literature on Voltaire is tremendous. See G. Bengesco, *Bibliographie des Œuvres de Voltaire,* 4 vols., 1882–1890, for a listing of the items credited to him; and for Voltaire criticism Mary H. Barr, *Bibliography of Writings on Voltaire, 1825–1925,* 1926, and *Bibliographical Data on Voltaire from 1926 to 1930,* 1933. An edition of the *Complete Works* was published in Paris, 1877–1885. A useful one-volume edition is *The Portable Voltaire,* edited by Ben Ray Redman, 1949.

For biography and criticism see S. G. Tallentyre, *Life of Voltaire,* 2 vols., 1903, the best of the biographical studies in English; also John Morley, *Voltaire,* 1874; J. C. Collins, *Voltaire in England,* 1886; J. M. Robertson, *Voltaire,* 1922; Richard Aldington, *Voltaire,* 1925; Cleveland B. Chase, *The Young Voltaire,* 1926; and H. N. Brailsford, *Voltaire,* 1935. A good introductory study is Georges Pellissier, *Vol-*

taire philosophe, 1908. An interesting anthology is *Voltaire's England,* edited by Desmond Flower, 1951.

LEWIS WALLACE

Born: Brookville, Indiana
Date: April 10, 1827

Died: Crawfordsville, Indiana
Date: February 15, 1905

PRINCIPAL WORKS

NOVELS: *The Fair God,* 1873; *Ben Hur: A Tale of the Christ,* 1880; *The Prince of India,* 1893.

General Lewis (Lew) Wallace, though a successful realist as a soldier and politician, was a successful romantic as a novelist at the time in American literary history when the best novelists were realists. The general American reading public, however, preferred romance and sentiment, and his novel *Ben Hur,* published in 1880, became an outsanding best seller.

Wallace, born at Brookville, Indiana, April 10, 1827, studied for the bar and practiced law until the outbreak of the Mexican War, in which he served. He remained in government service, rose to the rank of major-general during the Civil War, served as president of court in the Andersonville prison

trials, acted as governor of the New Mexico Territory from 1878–1881 (during which time he wrote *Ben Hur*), and represented the United States as minister to Turkey (1881–1885). After his retirement from public life he wrote biographies, a tragedy in blank verse, and *The Prince of India.* His first novel, *The Fair God,* a tale of the conquest of Mexico by Cortez, is often considered his best. *Ben Hur* is a dramatization of the story of Christ, sentimentalized in action and language but vivid and memorable in its authentic detail. *The Prince of India* presents the legendary character of the Wandering Jew. Wallace died at Crawfordsville, Indiana, on February 15, 1905.

BIBLIOGRAPHICAL REFERENCES: For the author's own account of his life see *Lew Wallace: An Autobiography,* 1906. A brief sketch is that by Anna Lane Lingelbach in the *Dictionary of National Biography.* See also Caroline Ticknor, *Glimpses of Authors,* 1922.

HORACE WALPOLE

Born: London, England
Date: September 24, 1717

Died: London
Date: March 2, 1797

PRINCIPAL WORKS

NOVEL: *The Castle of Otranto,* 1765.

LETTERS: *Letters,* edited by Peter Cunningham, 1857–1859 (9 vols.); *Letters,* edited by Mrs. Paget Toynbee, 1903–1905 (16 vols.); *The Yale Edition of Horace Walpole's Correspondence,* edited by W. S. Lewis, 1937 ff.

MEMOIRS: *Reminiscences,* 1805; *Memoirs of the Last Ten Years of the Reign of*

George II, 1822; *Memoirs of the Reign of George III,* 1845; *Journal of the Reign of George III from 1771 to 1783,* 1859.

PLAY: *The Mysterious Mother,* 1768.

MISCELLANEOUS: *Aedes Walpolianae,* 1747; *A Catalogue of the Royal and Noble Authors of England,* 1758; *Anecdotes of Painting in England,* 1763–1771; *Historic Doubts on the Life and Reign of Richard III,* 1768.

Born in London, September 24, 1717, Horace (christened Horatio) Walpole was the son of Sir Robert Walpole, notorious British prime minister of the eighteenth century. At the age of ten Walpole was sent to Eton, where he formed friendships with boys like Thomas Ashton, Richard West, and Thomas Gray, who all became famous men. Following Eton came an academic career at King's College, Cambridge, from 1735 to 1739. Although he was supposed to enter upon a study of law after leaving the university, Walpole, in the company of Thomas Gray, made a lengthy tour of the Continent, visiting and finding delightful Paris, the Alps, Florence, and Rome. In Florence they met Horace Mann, the famous American who was destined to receive the largest number of Walpole's letters after the English dilettante became the most inveterate and voluminous writer of letters in English literary history.

Following his return to England, Walpole became a member of Parliament, serving from 1741 to 1768. In 1747 he acquired a small house in Twickenham, a residence to become famous as Strawberry Hill; famous as Walpole's home, as the center of the owner's enthusiasm for Gothic architecture and "ruins," as the home of the Strawberry Hill Press, and as a kind of park-museum-showplace. By his work on Strawberry Hill, Walpole—who was something of an expert in society, politics, literature, and painting—was to make a name for himself as a

gardener and an architect. For twenty years the house was enlarged and given additional architectural features. The Strawberry Hill Press, which published Gray's great odes, also stimulated Walpole to publication. His *Fugitive Pieces in Verse and Prose* (1758) and his tragic drama, *The Mysterious Mother,* were printed there, although his famous *The Castle of Otranto,* which was published anonymously, was not.

In his second preface to *The Castle of Otranto,* Walpole said that his novel was written to revive the supernatural elements of the earlier French romances, adding some of the aspects of the sentimental novel of the eighteenth century in England. The supernatural elements were designed to provide terror for the readers; if they did at the time, they do so no longer, being regarded often by contemporary readers as merely slightly humorous. Perhaps the chief contribution Walpole made to fiction was a reliance on stage-set backgrounds. Later Gothic writers adopted them in an effort to provide a background against which the reader would accept anything that the novelist wished to include in the action, regardless of how absurd it might be.

Outside the realm of fiction, other facets of Walpole's life loom as much more important. His memoirs, covering the last half of the eighteenth century, were written in a conscious effort to be the historian of his own times. One set covers the reign of George III, and another set covers the last years of the reign of George II. Of even greater importance to the modern student of history is Walpole's tremendous correspondence. In his letters Walpole specialized. To Horace Mann, for example, went letters on politics, while to other selected recipients, he sent letters on other topics. A vast amount of information on the culture and affairs of England and the Continent is contained in the letters; they are a source of historical knowledge which is still far from measured, and they have been compared in value to a thousand of the "documentary" films of the twentieth century.

Walpole became the fourth Earl of Orford in 1791. He never married; perhaps too busy for domestic affairs. Mme. du Deffand, the famous French wit and bluestocking, was in love with him, and Mary Berry, a neighbor whose family was intimate with Walpole, seems to have been in love with him as well. Walpole's most famous aphorism is his statement, "Life is a comedy to those who think, a tragedy to those who feel." He died in London, March 2, 1797. The auction of his Strawberry Hill collection in 1842 was one of the most celebrated sales of the nineteenth century.

BIBLIOGRAPHICAL REFERENCES: The standard modern biography is Robert W. Ketton-Cremer's *Horace Walpole: A Biography*, 1940. For biography and criticism see also Austin Dobson, *Horace Walpole*, 1890; Dorothy M. Stuart, *Horace Walpole*, 1927; K. K. Mehrota, *Horace Walpole and the English Novel*, 1934; Montague Summers, *The Gothic Quest*, 1938; Hugh Honour, *Horace Walpole*, 1957; and W. S. Lewis, "Horace Walpole Reread," *Atlantic Monthly*, CLXXVI (1945), 48–51.

SIR HUGH WALPOLE

Born: Auckland, New Zealand
Date: March 13, 1884

Died: Keswick, Cumberland, England
Date: June 1, 1941

PRINCIPAL WORKS

NOVELS: *The Wooden Horse*, 1909; *Maradick at Forty*, 1910; *Mr. Perrin and Mr. Traill*, 1911 [*The Gods and Mr. Perrin*]; *The Prelude to Adventure*, 1912; *Fortitude*, 1913; *The Duchess of Wrexe*, 1914; *The Golden Scarecrow*, 1915; *The Dark Forest*, 1916; *The Green Mirror*, 1917; *Jeremy*, 1919; *The Secret City*, 1919; *The Captives*, 1920; *The Young Enchanted*, 1921; *The Cathedral*, 1922; *Jeremy and Hamlet*, 1923; *The Old Ladies*, 1924; *Portrait of a Man with Red Hair*, 1925; *Harmer John*, 1926; *Jeremy at Crale*, 1927; *Wintersmoon*, 1928; *Hans Frost*, 1929; *Rogue Herries*, 1930; *Above the Dark Circus*, 1931 [*Above the Dark Tumult*]; *Judith Paris*, 1931; *The Fortress*, 1932; *Vanessa*, 1933; *Captain Nicholas*, 1934; *The Inquisitor*, 1935; *A Prayer for my Son*, 1936; *John Cornelius*, 1937; *The Joyful Delaneys*, 1938; *The Sea Tower*, 1939; *The Bright Pavilions*, 1940; *The Blindman's House*, 1941; *The Killer and the Slain*, 1942; *Katherine Christian*, 1943.

SHORT STORIES: *The Thirteen Travellers*, 1921; *The Silver Thorn*, 1928; *All Souls' Night*, 1933; *Head in Green Bronze*, 1938.

MISCELLANEOUS: *Joseph Conrad*, 1916; *The English Novel*, 1925; *Anthony Trollope*, 1928; *A Letter to a Modern Novelist*, 1932; *The Apple Trees*, 1932.

Hugh (Seymour) Walpole was born in Auckland, New Zealand, March 13, 1884, the son of an English minister sent in 1882 as incumbent of St. Mary's Pro-Cathedral in Auckland. As a boy, Walpole was sent to school in Cornwall, England. His family returned to England and lived in Durham, a Cathedral city; Dr. Walpole was Bishop of Edinburgh from 1910 until his death in 1929.

Walpole was educated at King's College, Canterbury, and Emanuel College, Cambridge. He began writing novels while still an undergraduate, but without success in his early literary ventures. His first journalism took the form of reviews; his first successful novel was *Fortitude,* published in 1913, and his popularity as a writer of fiction on both sides of the Atlantic stems from that year. During World War I Walpole was working in Russia with the Red Cross, and two novels grew out of his experiences there: *The Dark Forest* and *The Secret City,* awarded the James Tait Black Memorial Prize. Most of Walpole's books have a roman-tic tinge, and many of them have enjoyed very large sales. His most successful ones are parts of a tetralogy covering two hundred years of English social history: *Rogue Herries, Judith Paris, The Fortress,* and *Vanessa.* Other novels include *Mr. Perrin and Mr. Traill, The Duchess of Wrexe, The Captives, The Cathedral, The Old Ladies, Portrait of a Man with Red Hair, Hans Frost, The Inquisitor, John Cornelius, The Sea Tower,* and *The Bright Pavilions.*

At the time of King George VI's coronation, Walpole was knighted and proudly bore his title of Sir Hugh Walpole. Prolific in his fiction, Walpole also wrote short stories, critical studies, plays; did scenarios for films in both Hollywood and Britain; enjoyed great success as public lecturer on numerous lecture tours to the United States and also in Britain. W. Somerset Maugham caricatured him as Alroy Kear in *Cakes and Ale.* Walpole died at his home, Brackenburn, in the Lake District on June 1, 1941.

BIBLIOGRAPHICAL REFERENCES: The authorized biography is Rupert Hart-Davis, *Hugh Walpole,* 1952. See also Clemence Dane, *Tradition and Hugh Walpole,* 1929; Marguerite Steen, *Hugh Walpole: A Study,* 1933; Joseph Hergesheimer, *Hugh Walpole: An Appreciation,* 1919 (pamphlet); and J. B. Priestley, "Hugh Walpole," *English Journal,* XVII (1928), 529–536.

IZAAK WALTON

Born: Near Stafford, England
Date: August 9, 1593

Died: Winchester, England
Date: December 15, 1683

PRINCIPAL WORKS

ESSAYS: *The Compleat Angler, or the Contemplative Man's Recreation,* 1653.
BIOGRAPHY: *The Life of John Donne,* 1640; *The Life of Sir Henry Wotton,* 1651; *The Life of Mr. Richard Hooker,* 1665; *The Life of Mr. George Herbert,* 1670.

Izaak Walton, often called the first professional English biographer, was born of yeoman stock at St. Mary, near Stafford on August 9, 1593. In his youth he was apprenticed to an iron-monger in London and, becoming a freeman in the company in 1618, he prospered as a dealer in ironware until his retirement during the civil war. Although he was a royalist in his sympathies and his interests were literary, he never became involved in the political or literary contention of the times. In retirement, he devoted himself to his favorite pastime, fishing, out of which developed the charming yet authoritative discourse in *The Compleat Angler*.

Largely self-educated, Walton began his literary career in his late forties when he was commissioned by Sir Henry Wotton to collect material for a projected life of John Donne. Walton, who called himself "the poorest, the meanest, of all his friends," had been a member of Donne's parish of St. Dunstan's; therefore, when Wotton died before the biography had been written, Walton undertook the task of writing a brief life of the poet and divine. The result, published as an introduction to the 1640 edition of Donne's *Sermons*, has become an integral part of the great editions of Donne's poetry and prose. A life of Wotton appeared eleven years later, followed by biographies of such worthies as Bishop Sanderson, Richard Hooker, and George Herbert.

In everything he wrote, Walton presented his material from a Christian point of view, and *The Compleat Angler*, more than a study of a man's recreational pursuits, also champions the Christian virtues of peace, friendship, and goodness as opposed to the money-getting scrambling of the city. One of the writer's aims was to show how one may find peace of mind, so that the book typifies a pervading seventeenth century spirit to seek relief from the world's woes in nature and works of God. The effortless charm and clarity of the style and the freshness of the anecdotage make the work especially attractive, just as the personality of Walton himself made for the many friendships which allowed him to gather material for his less well-known biographies. The bucolic appeal of *The Compleat Angler* is universal; the more than three hundred editions printed since 1653 testify to its enduring popularity. Walton died at Winchester on December 15, 1683.

BIBLIOGRAPHICAL REFERENCES: The best modern edition is *The Compleat Walton*, edited by G. L. Keynes, 1929. Of the many editions of *The Compleat Angler*, those by R. B. Marston, 1888, and by Richard Le Gallienne, 1896, may be mentioned in particular. *The Lives*, edited by George Saintsbury, 1927, contain an important introduction by the editor. See also Stapleton Martin, *Izaak Walton and His Friends*, 1904; D. A. Stauffer, *English Biography Before 1700*, 1930; Edgar Johnson, *One Mighty Torrent*, 1937; and John Butt, "Izaak Walton's Methods in Biography," *English Association Essays*, XIX (1933), 67–84.

ROBERT PENN WARREN

Born: Guthrie, Kentucky
Date: April 24, 1905

PRINCIPAL WORKS

NOVELS: *Night Rider*, 1939; *At Heaven's Gate*, 1943; *All the King's Men*, 1946; *World Enough and Time*, 1950; *Band of Angels*, 1955.

SHORT STORIES: *Blackberry Winter,* 1946; *The Circus in the Attic,* 1947.

POEMS: *Pondy Woods and Other Poems,* 1930; *Thirty-Six Poems,* 1935; *Eleven Poems on the Same Theme,* 1942; *Selected Poems, 1923–1943,* 1944; *Brother to Dragons: A Tale in Verse and Voices,* 1953; *Promises: Poems 1954–1956,* 1957.

BIOGRAPHY: *John Brown: The Making of a Martyr,* 1929.

Robert Penn Warren, born at Guthrie, Kentucky, on April 24, 1905, has employed his Southern background in nearly all his writing. Warren's subjects are usually taken from Southern history; and although his plots abound in violent action, his chief concern is with characters engaged in a philosophical quest in which they seek to discover the meaning of their lives and the meaning of their positions in history.

Warren is probably the best educated major American novelist. After graduating from Vanderbilt University, where he was a contributor to *The Fugitive,* he took his M.A. at the University of California and received a B.Litt. from Oxford as a Rhodes Scholar. He has been notably successful at combining writing with an academic career, and was one of the founders of *The Southern Review* while teaching at Louisiana State University.

Warren's first novel, *Night Rider,* published in 1939, draws upon the Kentucky tobacco wars of the early 1900's. *At Heaven's Gate* is a novel about the daughter of a Southern financier who rebels against her father. *All the King's Men,* his best and most successful novel, won a Pulitzer Prize in 1947. It deals with the rise and assassination of a Deep South politician styled after Huey Long. The novel was also made into a play. *The Circus in the Attic* is a collection of novelettes and short stories. *World Enough and Time,* is a novel based on the famous Kentucky Tragedy, a sensational murder case of 1825. His latest novel, *Band of Angels,* relates the story of a girl who is reared as white and then discovers she is a Negro slave.

Warren has published considerable poetry, and he appears to regard himself as much a poet as a novelist. His poems have been collected in several volumes: *Pondy Woods and Other Poems, Thirty-Six Poems, Eleven Poems on the Same Theme,* and *Selected Poems. Brother to Dragons* is a book-length narrative poem on the murder of a slave by his master.

In the field of non-fiction Warren has written *John Brown: The Making of a Martyr* and *Segregation* (1956), and he has contributed to *I'll Take My Stand* (1930) and *Who Owns America?* (1936), two regional symposiums. With Cleanth Brooks he has been a leader of the New Critics, a school of criticism opposed to the historical or biographical approach to literature. Brooks and Warren have edited a number of anthologies and college textbooks.

If he had written just his thoughtful and energetic novels, Robert Penn Warren would have been a central figure in contemporary American literature. But his remarkable success at combining several literary and scholarly careers makes him a figure of still greater influence and prestige. It seems probable that his reputation will continue to mount.

BIBLIOGRAPHICAL REFERENCES: There is no full-length biographical or critical study. For briefer articles see Frederick Brantley, "The Achievement of Robert Penn

Warren," in *Modern American Poetry*, edited by B. Rajan, 1950; Charles R. Anderson, "Violence and Order in the Novels of Warren," in *Southern Renascence*, edited by Louis D. Rubin, Jr., and Robert Jacobs, 1953; Babette Deutsch, *Poetry in Our Time*, 1956; also Irene Hendry, "The Regional Novel: The Example of Robert Penn Warren," *Sewanee Review*, LIII (1945), 84–102; Robert Heilman, "Melpomene as Wallflower; or the Reading of Tragedy," *ibid.*, LV (1947), 154–166; Oscar Cargill, "Anatomist of Monsters," *College English*, IX (1947), 1–8; J. E. Baker, "Irony in Fiction: *All the King's Men*," *ibid.*, IX (1947), 122–130; Eric Bentley, "The Meaning of Robert Penn Warren's Novels," *Kenyon Review*, X (1948), 407–424; Arthur Mizener, "Amphibium in Old Kentucky," *ibid.*, XII (1950), 697–701; W. M. Frohock, "Mr. Warren's Albatross," *Southwest Review*, XXXVI (1951), 48–59; Sam Hynes, "R. P. Warren: The Symbolic Journey," *University of Kansas City Review*, XVII (1951), 279–285; and John M. Bradbury, "Robert Penn Warren's Novels: The Symbolic and Textual Patterns," *Accent*, XIII (1953), 77–89. Warren's activity as a New Critic is covered by F. P. McDowell, "Robert Penn Warren's Criticism," *Accent*, XV (1955), 173–196. For an unfriendly opinion see Norman Kelvin, "The Failure of Robert Penn Warren," *College English*, XVIII (1957), 355–364.

JAKOB WASSERMANN

Born: Fürth, Germany
Date: March 10, 1873

Died: Alt-Aussee, Austria
Date: January 1, 1934

Principal Works

NOVELS: *Die Juden von Zirndorf*, 1897 (*Dark Pilgrimage*); *Die Geschichte der jungen Renate Fuchs*, 1900 (*The Story of Young Renate Fuchs*); *Caspar Hauser oder die Trägheit des Herzens*, 1908 (*Caspar Hauser*); *Das Gänsemännchen*, 1915 (*The Goose Man*); *Christian Wahnschaffe*, 1918 (*The World's Illusion*); *Der Wendekreis I: Der unbekannte Gast*, 1920 (*World's Ends*); *Der Wendekreis II: Oberlins drei Stufen, Sturreganz*, 1922 (*Oberlin's Three Stages: Sturreganz*); *Der Wendekreis III: Ulrike Woytich*, 1923 (*Gold*); *Der Wendekreis IV: Faber oder die verlorenen Jahre*, 1924 (*Faber, or the Lost Years*); *Der Aufruhr um den Junker Ernst*, 1926 (*The Triumph of Youth*); *Der Fall Maurizius*, 1928 (*The Maurizius Case*); *Etzel Andergast*, 1931 (*Doctor Kerkhoven*).

PLAYS: *Die ungleichen Schalen*, 1912 (*Unbalanced Scales*); *Lukardis*, 1932.

BIOGRAPHY: *Deutsche Charaktere und Begebenheiten*, 1915 (*German Characters and Events*); *Hofmannsthal der Freund*, 1929 (*Hofmannsthal: A Friend*); *Christoph Columbus, Der Don Quichote des Ozeans*, 1929 (*Christopher Columbus, Don Quixote of the Seas*); *Bula Matari, Das Leben Stanleys*, 1932 (*Bula Matari: Stanley, Conqueror of a Continent*).

AUTOBIOGRAPHY: *Mein Weg als Deutscher und Jude*, 1921 (*My Life as German and Jew*); *Lebensdienst*, 1928 (*In the Service of Life*); *Selbstbetrachtungen*, 1933 (*Self-Contemplation*).

LETTERS: *Briefe an seine Braut und Gattin Julie, 1900–1929*, 1940 (first published in English as *The Letters of Jakob Wassermann to Frau Julie Wassermann*, 1935).

Perhaps no writer of modern times, unless possibly Francis Thompson, has suffered greater indignities than Jakob Wassermann in the struggle to vindicate himself as an artist. He was born of Jewish parentage at Fürth, near Nuremberg, on March 10, 1873. His father was a merchant with a narrow, conservative outlook who allowed his second wife, the boy's unsympathetic stepmother, to regulate the life of the household. In his childhood, Wassermann's literary talents were ruthlessly curbed, on the principle that if he should become a writer he would be poor and therefore worthless. In 1889 he was packed off to Vienna, where his uncle was the proprietor of a factory; but, unable to bear the routine of business, he made a temporary escape to Munich with the plan of studying to enter the university. Lacking money, he had to retreat home. He was then sent to Vienna again, this time to learn the export trade. Less than a year later, he left his new job, disgraced by a gross practical joke played on him by a fellow employee. Being of an age to perform the enforced military duty, he was thrust into the army, where anti-Semitic comrades made him the butt of pranks and insults.

After completing his year of service he held a government job in Nuremberg until, inheriting a small sum of money, he ventured to Munich again and remained as long as his resources allowed. He then obtained employment briefly at Freiburg. Destitute, he roamed as a beggar in the Black Forest. Finding his way to Zurich and then once more to Munich, he kept himself alive through working at odd jobs. A turn in his fortunes occurred, just in time to avert the collapse of his health, when he was engaged as secretary to a writer, Ernst von Wolzogen, in 1895. Shortly thereafter, he was hired as an editorial assistant by the manager of *Simplicissimus,* a periodical then in its first year of publication. Some of his poems and tales appeared in that journal in 1896, and one story gained him a prize of three hundred marks. In 1898 he returned to Austria, to live there the rest of his life. He finally succeeded in supporting himself by writing. *Dark Pilgrimage* and *The Story of Young Renate Fuchs,* both well received, inaugurated the succession of major novels that established his literary reputation. In 1901 he married Julie Speyer, of Vienna, but separated from her in 1919 and obtained a divorce several years later; he afterwards married Marta Karlweis. On New Year's Day, 1934, he died at Alt-Aussee, where he had resided for ten years.

Wassermann was strongly admired by Schnitzler, Hofmannsthal, and Thomas Mann. His work, though sometimes too diffuse, is impressive for the scope of its themes. He was especially exercised by the problems of ethical conduct and was devoted to the ideals of democratic liberalism.

BIBLIOGRAPHICAL REFERENCES: A primary source for biographical material is Jakob Wassermann, *My Life as A German Jew,* translated 1933. Studies in English include J. C. Blankenagel, *The Writings of Jakob Wassermann,* 1942, and "Jakob Wassermann's Views on America," *German Quarterly,* XXVII (1954), 51–57. For studies in German see Julie Wassermann-Speyer, *Jakob Wassermann und sein Werk,* 1923; S. Bing, *Jakob Wassermann,* 1933; and Marta Karlweis, *Jakob Wassermann,* 1935.

HUGO WAST
(Gustavo Martínez Zuviría)

Born: Córdoba, Argentina
Date: October 23, 1883

PRINCIPAL WORKS

NOVELS: *Alegre,* 1905; *Flor de durazno,* 1911 (*Peach Blossom*); *Casa de los cuevos,* 1916 (*The House of the Ravens*); *Valle negro,* 1918 (*Black Valley*); *La corbata celeste,* 1920 (*The Blue Necktie*); *Desierto de piedra,* 1925 (*Stone Desert*); *Myriam la conspiradora,* 1926 (*Myriam the Conspirator*); *Lucía Miranda,* 1929.

Gustavo Martínez Zuviría, known in literature as Hugo Wast, was born in Córdoba, Argentina, October 23, 1883. While still a university student he wrote his first novel, *Alegre,* published in 1905. Then he went on to become a Doctor of Laws (1907) and joined the University of Santa Fe as Professor of Economics and Sociology. Politics also attracted him, and he served several terms in Congress. For a long time he was Director of Argentina's National Library; more recently, Minister of Education.

After two juvenile attempts at novel writing, he published a serious novel about unmarried love, *Peach Blossom,* in 1911. Afraid that the critics of Buenos Aires would scorn any work of a provincial author, he signed it with an anagram of his first name, Gustavo, from which he made "Hugo Wast." The novel finally proved a success. During the next forty years, Wast published thirty-three books, many of them through a company that he organized. They have also appeared with Spanish and Chilean imprints to the number of 290 editions, and nearly a million and a half copies have been sold. In addition, seventy translations have appeared in eleven different languages.

Wast's best seller, *The House of the Ravens,* won for him a prize of the Ateneo in 1915. For his *Black Valley* he won the gold medal of the Spanish Academy, which later made him a corresponding member and enlarged its dictionary by the inclusion of words from his writing. *Stone Desert* was awarded the Grand National Prize of Argentine Literature for the year of its appearance.

Wast's novels can be divided into several groups. One series covers the history of his country from the earliest days of exploration and conquest, as told in *Lucía Miranda,* through the struggle for independence shown in *Myriam the Conspirator,* the period of the dictatorship dramatized in *The Blue Necktie,* and into the future in novels like *Juana Tabor* and *666* (1942).

Wast's training in economics and sociology is apparent in his problem novels set in the rural regions—*Black Valley* and *Stone Desert*—and in his fictional treatment of the urban problem in novels like *Fuente Sellada* (1914) and *Ciudad turbulenta, Ciudad alegre* (*Turbulent City, Happy City*), published in 1919. He also had young readers in mind for several novels, especially the amusing *Pata de zorra* (1924), named from the fortune teller who tried to help a university student pass his examination in Roman law.

It is for the number of readers whom

Wast's writings have attracted, rather than for any special influence he has exerted on his contemporaries, that he merits a place in Argentine literature. His ideas about writing are included in his *Vocación de escritor* (*A Writer's Calling*) published in 1946. His most recent volumes of gaucho life are *Estrella de la tarde* (*Evening Star*), published in 1954, and its sequel, *¿Le tiraría la primera piedra?* (*Would You Throw the First Stone?*).

BIBLIOGRAPHICAL REFERENCES: Wast's own account of his career is told in *Vocación de escritor*, printed as Vol. XXXI of his *Obras completas*. See also E. H. Hespelt, "Hugo Wast, Argentine Novelist," *Hispania*, VII (1924); Ruth Sedgwick, "Hugo Wast, Argentina's Most Popular Novelist," *Hispanic American Historical Review*, IX (1929), 116–26; and prefaces to his novels translated into English.

EVELYN WAUGH

Born: Hampstead, London, England
Date: October 28, 1903

PRINCIPAL WORKS

NOVELS: *Decline and Fall*, 1928; *Vile Bodies*, 1930; *Black Mischief*, 1932; *A Handful of Dust*, 1934; *Scoop*, 1938; *Put Out More Flags*, 1942; *Work Suspended*, 1942; *Brideshead Revisited*, 1945; *Scott-King's Modern Europe*, 1947; *The Loved One*, 1948; *Helena*, 1950; *Men at Arms*, 1952; *Officers and Gentlemen*, 1955; *The Ordeal of Gilbert Pinfold*, 1957.

SHORT STORIES: *Mr. Loveday's Little Outing and Other Sad Stories*, 1936; *Love Among the Ruins*, 1953; *Tactical Exercise*, 1954.

TRAVEL SKETCHES AND IMPRESSIONS: *Labels*, 1930 [*A Bachelor Abroad*]; *Remote People*, 1931 [*They Were Still Dancing*]; *Ninety-Two Days*, 1934; *Waugh in Abyssinia*, 1936; *When the Going Was Good*, 1946.

BIOGRAPHY: *Rossetti: His Life and Works*, 1928; *Edmund Campion*, 1935.

Evelyn Waugh, English satirist and Catholic apologist, was born in London, October 28, 1903, the second son of Arthur Waugh, English critic and publisher, managing director of Chapman & Hall, Limited. He was christened Evelyn Arthur St. John Waugh. An older brother is the novelist Alec Waugh.

His first writing effort, as far as his biographers know, was a 500-word novel in nine chapters entitled *The Curse of the Horse Race*, which was written when he was seven. His first published book appeared in 1928: *Rossetti: His Life and Works*.

Between those two efforts Waugh acquired an education and some experience in earning a living. He prepared for the university at Lancing School, where he won a prize for his verses. He then attended Hertford College, Oxford, for several years, but left the university without a degree. After Oxford he studied painting at Heatherley's Art School. Later he was both a schoolmaster and a journalist, working for a time on the London *Daily Express*.

Although he began his writing career with the biography of Rossetti, he found his forte in the witty, satirical style he set in *Decline and Fall,* published in 1928. He had been brought up in the intellectual circles of English middle-class society, but his independent, critical mind enabled him to see the false fronts in the most impressive performances about him. His indignation was fundamentally moral, presaging the disciplined devotion he was later to find in the Roman Catholic Church, but his manner was modern: bitter, humorous, and cutting in the distinctive fashion that Aldous Huxley in his earlier works also exemplified.

In 1928 he married Evelyn Gardner, daughter of Lord Burghclere, but the marriage was short-lived, ending in divorce two years later. He became a Roman Catholic convert in 1930. That same year saw the publication of his second satirical novel, *Vile Bodies,* a work that hinted at but did not quite reveal the growing seriousness with which he faced contemporary society. After one more novel, *A Handful of Dust,* Waugh made his first impressive mark as a distinctively Catholic writer with his biography of *Edmund Campion,* the sixteenth century English Jesuit martyr. The book proved to be a carefully written, impressive portrait, and it won for its author the Hawthornden Prize in 1936. He was married in 1937 to Laura Herbert, the youngest daughter of Aubrey Herbert, M.P.

By this time Waugh had written, in addition to his novels and biographies, several travel or near-travel books. Among them were *Labels: A Mediterranean Journal,* published in the United States under the title *A Bachelor Abroad; Remote People,* published in the United States as *They Were Still Dancing;* and *Waugh in Abyssinia.*

Although the books are entertaining and well written, they have not achieved the popularity of his novels.

Waugh received a temporary commission as a second lieutenant in the Royal Marines in the latter part of 1939. During the war he became a major in the commandos, participated in a raid on Bardia, and was one of a military team parachuted into Yugoslavia to observe Tito's campaign against the Germans. In 1942 he was transferred to the Royal Horse Guards. *Put Out More Flags* marked the transition between his satires on decadent modern society with its Bright Young People and his war novels. Other books reflecting the author's war experiences are *Men at Arms,* which won the James Tait Black Memorial Prize, and *Officers and Gentlemen.*

In 1945 Waugh won mixed critical reception but an extensive reading public with his novel *Brideshead Revisited,* a study of the changing fortunes and souls of the members of a Catholic family. The book was a book club selection in the United States. The public response to the novel made a visit to the United States and a lecture tour possible. The book was responsible for Waugh's receiving the 1945 Catholic Literary Award given by the Gallery of Living Catholic Authors.

Waugh returned briefly to his urbane cutting style with the amusing satirical novel, *The Loved One,* a work criticizing American funeral tastes, particularly as revealed by certain immense Hollywood cemeteries, and the vulgarities of love. In this work a confusion of notices from a funeral home for human beings with a similar institution for dogs puts the final ridiculous stamp on Waugh's sophisticated comment.

BIBLIOGRAPHICAL REFERENCES: The most comprehensive study is Christopher Hollis, *Evelyn Waugh*, 1954. For additional criticism see Edmund Wilson, *Classics and Commercials*, 1950; Rose Macaulay, "Evelyn Waugh," *Horizon*, XIV (1946), 360–377; Donat O'Donnell, "The Pieties of Evelyn Waugh," *Kenyon Review*, IX (1947), 400–411; Richard J. Voorhees, "Evelyn Waugh Revisited," *South Atlantic Quarterly*, XLVIII (1949), 270–280; Charles Rolo, "Evelyn Waugh: The Best and the Worst," *Atlantic Monthly*, CXCIV (1954), 80–86; and Steven Marcus, "Evelyn Waugh and the Act of Entertainment," *Partisan Review*, XXIII (1956), 348–357.

MARY WEBB

Born: Leighton, Shropshire, England   *Died:* St. Leonard's, England
Date: March 25, 1881   *Date:* October 8, 1927

PRINCIPAL WORKS

NOVELS: *The Golden Arrow*, 1916; *Gone to Earth*, 1917; *The House in Dormer Forest*, 1920; *Seven for a Secret*, 1922; *Precious Bane*, 1924; *Armour Wherein He Trusted*, 1929.

POEMS AND ESSAYS: *The Spring of Joy*, 1917; *Poems and The Spring of Joy*, 1928.

Mary (Gladys Meredith) Webb, born in Leighton, England, March 25, 1881, was the daughter of an English-Welsh schoolmaster portrayed as a charming, sympathetic man in his daughter's first novel, *The Golden Arrow*. Mary Webb must have known her father well, for she was educated largely at home, although she spent two years at a private school in Southport, England. She began to write when she was a child, trying her hand at stories and poetry, none of which has ever been published. In 1912 she married Henry Bertram Law Webb, also a schoolmaster.

Mrs. Webb's five novels appeared from 1916 to 1924, with almost no recognition at the time of their publication from either readers or critics. Her only award was the Femina-Vie Heureuse Prize for 1924–1925, which she received for *Precious Bane*. An unfinished novel, *Armour Wherein He Trusted*, was published posthumously, following her death at St. Leonard's, Sussex, October 8, 1927. When Mrs.

Webb died she was practically unknown, but in 1928 Prime Minister Stanley Baldwin praised her novels at a Royal Literary Fund dinner. After that recognition, her fame began to grow; her five novels were reprinted shortly thereafter, with introductions by Baldwin, G. K. Chesterton, and others. Whether or not that recognition is permanent, it is still too early to say. Critics are of varying opinion about her work.

Mrs. Webb's novels seem to derive from a good many earlier writers, especially George Eliot and Mrs. Gaskell, and they tend to concentrate on inner meanings which sometimes cause her books to stray away from the reality of most contemporary fiction. Her frequent didacticism, too, is contrary to the tastes of many modern readers. In *The Golden Arrow*, Mrs. Webb placed two pairs of lovers, one pair exemplary and one pair foolish. The contrasts are always obvious, and the author frequently invades the narrative with intrusive commentary and unnecessary moralizing. In *The House in Dormer Forest* there is a contrast again, this time between one family that is close to nature and another that is grasping and materialistic. Once more Mrs. Webb is obvious in preferring the former to the latter and asking the reader to do the same. In this novel, as in other of her books, there are stock characters, such as the plain, despised woman of hidden sweetness who is saved from wasting a life by the timely arrival of a husband who is the epitome of masculinity and carries about with him in obvious fashion a set of high, idealistic values. Other novels are *Gone to Earth, Seven for a Secret,* and *Precious Bane,* which is Mrs. Webb's best-known novel. Her unfinished novel, *Armour Wherein He Trusted,* took the author out of the setting she had habitually used—contemporary Shropshire—into medieval times, for the work was to be a historical romance set against the background of the First Crusade. After her death in 1927 there appeared a volume of essays and poetry written during her adult years. This collection, *The Spring of Joy,* had a preface by Walter de la Mare, in which he pointed out that her poetry and prose both contained certain poetic elements and that her prose rhythms derive from such specific seventeenth century authors as Sir Thomas Browne, author of *Religio Medici* and *Urn Burial.*

BIBLIOGRAPHICAL REFERENCES: The most comprehensive study is Thomas Moult, *Mary Webb: Her Life and Work,* 1932. See also Hilda Addison, *Mary Webb,* 1931, and the prefaces to her novels.

JOHN WEBSTER

Born: London (?), England
Date: Unknown

Died: Unknown
Date: Before 1635

PRINCIPAL WORKS

PLAYS: *Westward Ho!* 1604 (with Dekker); *Northward Ho!* 1605 (with Dekker); *The White Devil,* c. 1612; *The Duchess of Malfi,* c. 1613; *The Devil's Law Case,* 1623.
PAGEANT: *Monuments of Honour,* 1624.

The important fact in the life of John Webster is that he wrote *The White Devil* and *The Duchess of Malfi.* The scanty biographical information about this remarkable writer is an indication of the slight esteem Renaissance England granted to its great drama; it also reminds the twentieth century of how exceptional is the relatively large amount of information surviving about William Shakespeare.

Since Webster stated in the Epistle to his *Monuments of Honour* that he was born free of the Guild of Merchant Tailors, it is a reasonable assumption that the John Webster who appears in the Guild records in 1571 and 1576 was his father. A John Webster was a member of an Anglo-German acting company in 1596; a John Webster was admitted to the Middle Temple in 1598. Possibly these references are to the dramatist. Thomas Heywood referred to the dramatist as dead in 1635;

1134

but he may have died as much as ten years earlier.

The early part of Webster's dramatic career was spent as a collaborator (read "hack"?) in Philip Henslowe's prolific stable of playwrights; Webster's chief collaborators were John Marston and Thomas Dekker. Between 1610 and 1615 he reached his prime with the two celebrated tragedies which make his reputation. In these masterpieces he is a powerful and moving poet and an excellent man of the theater. Nothing in the plays before the masterpieces or in the plays after them indicates a comparable power.

BIBLIOGRAPHICAL REFERENCES: The standard edition is F. L. Lucas, ed., *The Complete Works of John Webster* (1927). Other studies include E. E. Stoll, *John Webster* (1905); Rupert Brooke, *John Webster and Elizabethan Drama* (1916); and E. K. Chambers, *The Elizabethan Stage*, Vol. III (1923).

FRANK WEDEKIND

Born: Hanover, Germany   *Died:* Munich, Germany
Date: July 24, 1864   *Date:* March 9, 1918

PRINCIPAL WORKS

PLAYS: *Frühlings erwachen*, 1891 (*The Awakening of Spring*); *Erdgeist*, 1895 (*Earth Spirit*); *Die Kammersänger*, 1899 (*The Tenor*); *Der Marquis von Keith*, 1901; *Die Büchse der Pandora*, 1903 (*Pandora's Box*); *Franziska*, 1912.

POEMS: *Die vier Jahreszeiten*, 1905.

NOVEL: *Mine-haha*, 1901.

Frank (Benjamin Franklin) Wedekind, one of the most controversial of fin-de-siècle German writers, was the son of a world-traveler doctor who at sixty-four had married an actress less than half his age. Born in Hanover, Germany, on July 24, 1864, Wedekind was graduated from Lenzburg in Switzerland in 1883. Later he worked as a journalist and as traveling secretary for Herzog's Circus. While he was with the circus he became convinced that man is essentially an animal who is healthiest when he lives entirely by his instincts, uncorrupted by bourgeois education.

After a brief period as secretary to a Parisian art dealer, Wedekind went to Munich and wrote his first play, *The World of Youth* (1890), the story of a girls' boarding school. It was followed by *The Awakening of Spring*, which presents an adolescent youth tormented by sexual drives and ruthlessly curbed by the iron discipline of society—an attempt on Wedekind's part to out-Nietzsche Nietzsche. He also attacked Ibsen and the realists of the preceding generation for being too genteel and middle class. As writer, actor, and director of the Munich Theater, he felt that the stage needed "beasts of prey," and he proceeded to supply them.

Lulu, the heroine of *Earth Spirit* and *Pandora's Box*, is a Dionysiac character who becomes sex incarnate and is finally cut down by Jack the Ripper. The hero of *The Marquis of Keith* conceives of love as sexual orgy, drives his wife to suicide, tries to build a bawdy house with stolen money but fails, and is abandoned by his mistress. These plays are not simply acted; they are mimed, danced, and screamed, as if Wedekind had Caliban within every character. Toward the end of his career, however, Wedekind reformed, thanked the judges who condemned *Pandora's Box,* and expressed a reverence for the Church. His works, like those of Strindberg, were condemned by Hitler and are now being revived as curiosities of morbid emotional and imaginative excess in the modern German theater. Wedekind died in Munich on March 9, 1918.

BIBLIOGRAPHICAL REFERENCES: Wedekind's principal plays are available in translation. For biography and criticism see Paul Fechter, *Frank Wedekind,* 1920; Arthur Kutscher, *Frank Wedekind, sein Leben und seine Werke,* 1922–1924; Fritz Dehnow, *Frank Wedekind,* 1922; and Samuel Eliot, *Tragedies of Sex,* 1923. For briefer studies see also Raimund Pissin, *Frank Wedekind,* in *Modern Essais,* 53, c. 1905; Anita Block, *The Changing World in Plays and Theatre,* 1939; and Eric Bentley, *The Playwright as Thinker,* 1946.

H. G. WELLS

Born: Bromley, England
Date: September 21, 1866

Died: London, England
Date: August 13, 1946

PRINCIPAL WORKS

PSEUDO-SCIENTIFIC NOVELS AND FANTASIES: *The Time Machine,* 1895; *The Wonderful Visit,* 1895; *The Island of Dr. Moreau,* 1896; *The Invisible Man,* 1897; *The War of the Worlds,* 1898; *The Sleeper Awakes,* 1899; *The First Men in the Moon,* 1901; *The Sea Lady,* 1902; *The Food of the Gods,* 1904; *In the Days of the Comet,* 1906; *The War in the Air,* 1908; *The World Set Free,* 1914; *Men Like Gods,* 1923; *Mr. Blettsworthy on Rampole Island,* 1928; *The King Who Was a King,* 1929; *The Autocracy of Mr. Parham,* 1930; *The Shape of Things to Come,* 1933; *The Croquet Player,* 1937; *Star-Begotten,* 1937; *The Camford Visitation,* 1937.

NOVELS OF CHARACTER: *The Wheels of Chance,* 1896; *Kipps,* 1905; *The History of Mr. Polly,* 1910; *Bealby,* 1915; *The Dream,* 1924; *Christina Alberta's Father,* 1925; *The Bulpington of Blup,* 1933; *Brynhild,* 1937; *Apropos of Dolores,* 1938.

NOVELS OF SOCIAL CRITICISM AND THEME: *Love and Mr. Lewisham,* 1900; *Tono-Bungay,* 1909; *Ann Veronica,* 1909; *The New Machiavelli,* 1911; *Marriage,* 1912; *The Passionate Friends,* 1913; *The Wife of Sir Isaac Harman,* 1914; *The Research Magnificent,* 1915; *Mr. Britling Sees It Through,* 1916; *The Soul of a Bishop,* 1917; *Joan and Peter,* 1918; *The Undying Fire,* 1919; *The Secret Places of the Heart,* 1922; *The World of William Clissold,* 1926; *Meanwhile,* 1927; *The Brothers,* 1938; *The Holy Terror,* 1939; *Babes in the Darkling Wood,* 1940; *All Aboard for Ararat,* 1941; *You Can't Be Too Careful,* 1942.

SHORT STORIES: *The Stolen Bacillus and Other Incidents,* 1895; *The Plattner Story and Others,* 1897; *The Vacant Country,* 1899; *The Country of the Blind,* 1911; *The Short Stories of H. G. Wells,* 1927.

ESSAYS AND STUDIES: *The Discovery of the Future,* 1902; *Mankind in the Making,* 1903; *This Misery of Boots,* 1907; *Socialism and Marriage,* 1908; *New Worlds for Old,* 1908; *First and Last Things,* 1908; *The Great State,* 1912 [*Socialism and the Great State*]; *God, the Invisible King,* 1917; *The Salvaging of Civilization,* 1921; *Socialism and the Scientific Motive,* 1923; *After Democracy,* 1929; *The Way to*

World Peace, 1930; *The Work, Wealth and Happiness of Mankind,* 1931; *The Science of Life,* 1931 (with Julian Huxley and G. P. Wells); *The Anatomy of Frustration,* 1936; *World Brain,* 1938; *The New World Order,* 1940; *The Common Sense of War and Peace,* 1940; *The Conquest of Time,* 1942; *'42 to '44,* 1944; *Mind at the End of Its Tether,* 1946.

HISTORY: *The Outline of History,* 1920; *A Short History of the World,* 1922.

BIOGRAPHY AND AUTOBIOGRAPHY: *Certain Personal Matters,* 1897; *The Book of Catherine Wells,* 1928; *An Experiment in Autobiography,* 1934.

H(erbert) G(eorge) Wells, one of modern England's most prolific and best-known writers, was born at Bromley, Kent, on September 21, 1866. His background was obscure; his father was an improvident shopkeeper and professional cricket player, his mother a maidservant and housekeeper. Although he had to work for a living very early in life, Wells was determined to get an education and rise in the world. After a period in which he was a draper's apprentice and a chemist's assistant, he managed to go to school at Midhurst Grammar School, where he made an exceptional academic record. He then worked for a time in a dry-goods firm in London. In 1884 he won a scholarship at the Royal College of Science, where he studied biology under Thomas Henry Huxley. He was graduated with the bachelor of science degree from London University in 1888. Following graduation, he began tutoring and working on a biology textbook until tuberculosis forced him to give up teaching. While convalescing he began to write essays and stories, and by 1891 he was in sufficiently good health to return to London. Publication of one of his essays in the *Fortnightly Review* in 1891 marked the beginning of his long and active career as a writer. For the next several years he divided his time between instruction in a correspondence school and journalism.

In 1891 Wells married a cousin, Isabel Mary Wells. The two were incompatible, however, and they were divorced in 1895, after a two-year separation. Wells later married Amy Catherine Robbins, by whom he had two sons. After the death of his second wife in 1927, Wells lived mostly in London or France.

Wells's first book of a literary rather than an academic nature was *Select Conversations with an Uncle* (1895), which was overshadowed in the same year by the first of his pseudo-scientific romances, *The Time Machine.* This novel was frequently compared to the work of Jules Verne, but Wells protested that his book was written for political ends, while Verne's was not. Although he was classified nominally as a Socialist, having joined the Fabian Society in 1903, Wells's political Utopia came to be more like Plato's republic than a Socialist or Communist state. Most readers saw only the scientific speculation in such books as *The Wonderful Visit, The Stolen Bacillus and Other Incidents, The Island of Dr. Moreau, The Invisible Man,* and *The War of the Worlds.* The power and excitement still inherent in his fiction were amply demonstrated in 1938, when a radio adaptation of *The War of the Worlds* created a few hours of panic throughout the United States.

In *The Wheels of Chance,* published in 1896, Wells wrote the first of his novels dealing with the attempts of the lower middle class to rise in the world; of this series, *Kipps* and *The History of Mr. Polly* are generally considered the best. Like Dickens, Wells was capable of treating less privileged people generously and sympathetically. From about 1905 to the period of World War I, he was a realistic novelist, using social rather than political ideas in his work and developing real, yet often highly individualized, characters. Other examples of his work from this period are *Ann Veronica* and *Mr. Britling Sees It Through*. During the same period he wrote *This Misery of Boots* and *Socialism and Marriage*, important as Fabian tracts. *New Worlds for Old* was an explanation of Wells's own version of socialism. In *Tono-Bungay*, published in 1909, he began a group of novels using themes from contemporary history, a series including *The New Machiavelli*, *The Passionate Friends*, and *The Research Magnificent*.

Following World War I, Wells turned to the writing of history, achieving a much-debated but world-wide reputation with his *Outline of History* in 1920. In this work he attempted a chronological survey of the world from its origins to the present era. Immensely popular, the book sold more than two million copies. Such a work was doomed to have shortcomings, as critics pointed out, but it did put into readable form, within two volumes, a history of the world which general readers could, and did, read with considerable profit. It was followed by a briefer account, *A Short History of the World* in 1922.

In his writings and other activities after World War I, Wells made a bid for political recognition. To this period belong *Russia in the Shadows* (1920) and *Washington and the Riddle of Peace* (1922). He himself entered politics in 1922 as a candidate for Parliament on the Labour Party ticket. Defeated, he made a second unsuccessful attempt in 1923. He continued to write during the 1920's, but none of his books attracted the attention that earlier volumes had. *The Science of Life*, published in 1929, is an erudite and monumental work which was written in collaboration with Julian Huxley and George Philip Wells, his son. During the 1930's Wells showed much interest in the New Deal experiments in the United States; his writing during the decade reflected current economic and political problems.

Three years before his death Wells completed a thesis on personality and was awarded the doctor of science degree from London University. One of his last books was *'42 to '44*, an intolerant castigation of the period discussed. He died in London on August 13, 1946.

Although he wrote a great deal, too much to be effective throughout his long career, Wells deserves an important place in contemporary literary history. His ideas, not always worked out in detail, were presented effectively and with sincerity. Although he sacrificed art to propaganda in much of his work, he spoke with eloquence and conviction to a world in crisis. Only at the end of his life did he feel that he had failed in his efforts to improve human society by thought and word.

BIBLIOGRAPHICAL REFERENCES: The standard edition, though not definitive, is *The Works of H. G. Wells*, 28 vols., 1924–1927. For an account of Wells's life, the best source is still his own *Experiment in Autobiography*, 1934. This work should be supplemented by two works by Geoffrey H. Wells, his son, *The Works of H. G.*

Wells: A Bibliography, Dictionary, and Subject Index, 1926, and H. G. Wells: A Sketch for a Portrait, 1930. Also valuable is Georges A. Connes, A Dictionary of Characters and Scenes in the Novels, Romances and Short Stories of H. G. Wells, 1926.

Recent biographical studies include Antonina Valentin, H. G. Wells: Prophet of Our Day, 1950; Norman Nicholson, H. G. Wells, 1950; and Vincent Brome, H. G. Wells, 1951. See also Van Wyck Brooks, The World of H. G. Wells, 1915; R. T. Hopkins, H. G. Wells, 1922; Sidney Dark, The Outline of H. G. Wells, 1922; Ivor Brown, H. G. Wells, 1925; Patrick Braybrooke, Some Aspects of H. G. Wells, 1928; and Montgomery Belgion, H. G. Wells, 1953.

Briefer articles in books and periodicals include E. E. Slosson, Six Major Prophets, 1917; Stuart P. Sherman, Contemporary Woodcuts, 1926; Wilbur T. Cross, Four Contemporary Novelists, 1930; André Maurois, Prophets and Poets, 1935; Ford Madox Ford, Portraits from Life, 1937; George Orwell, Dickens, Dali, and Others, 1946; Stanley Kauffman, "Wells and the New Generation," College English, I (1940), 573–582; E. K. Brown, "Two Formulas for Fiction: Henry James and H. G. Wells," ibid., VIII (1946), 7–17; Richard H. Costa, "H. G. Wells: Literary Journalist," Journalism Quarterly, XXVIII (1951), 63–68; and William J Hyde, "The Socialism of H. G. Wells," Journal of the History of Ideas, XVII (1956), 217–234.

EUDORA WELTY

Born: Jackson, Mississippi
Date: April 13, 1909

PRINCIPAL WORKS

SHORT STORIES: A Curtain of Green, 1941; The Wide Net, 1943; The Golden Apples, 1949; The Bride of the Innisfallen, 1955.

NOVELS: The Robber Bridegroom, 1942; Delta Wedding, 1946; The Ponder Heart, 1954.

ESSAYS: Short Stories, 1950; Place in Fiction, 1957.

Eudora Welty, born in Jackson, Mississippi, on April 13, 1909, writes her short stories and novels principally about the Mississippi area where she was born and has lived during most of her life. She has described with imaginative power a wide range of Southern backgrounds, never limiting herself to mere documentation: the span of history along the Natchez Trace in The Wide Net, the plantation setting of Delta Wedding, the provincial atmosphere of The Golden Apples, and the mysterious forest as re-created in her historical fable, The Robber Bride-

groom. Her art of fiction combines William Faulkner's and Katherine Anne Porter's ability to project regional sentiment into a kind of cultural symbolism, with that subtle shifting between the inner and outer worlds of character which is found also in the novels of Virginia Woolf.

Miss Welty was educated at the Mississippi State College for Women and later studied advertising copywriting. She has had shows as painter and photographer and has worked as a government publicist. Her first volume was A Curtain of Green, a collection of short stories. "The Death of a Traveling Salesman" from this book, previously printed in the magazine *Manuscript* as her first published story, established her talent for synthesizing acute observations of character, that of the dying salesman, with an evocative background, the wayside home of a poor farming couple. The other stories unite to develop a view of Southern life continued by her later work, often criticized as eccentric and grotesque. She can also be humorous, as in "Why I Live at the P.O.," "The Petrified Man," and the beautifully sustained mood of *The Ponder Heart*. But whatever her effects, she remains interested in emotions not easily expressed, in fundamental states of mind.

In *The Robber Bridegroom* she reveals an interest in outright fantasy, having based her story on a Psyche-like fable, the love of Jamie Lockhart, the outlaw, for Rosamund. *The Wide Net* is a collection of short fiction containing historical scenes of the great forest; the title story was included in the *O. Henry Prize Stories of 1942*. The stories show a blending of fantasy with reality and a further development of two of her major themes: the mysteries of personality and the essential bonds between people who affect each other's lives. In *The Golden Apples* these themes are again stressed in the story of King MacLain, who periodically vanishes and reappears unaccountably. In almost all the stories the fabulous element in her work is suggested by her titles, "Shower of Gold," "Moon Lake," "Music from Spain."

Delta Wedding is probably her most widely known book. In this novel she handles people with growing assurance as the characters come slowly into focus, viewed through the eyes of a nine-year-old girl describing late summer wedding preparations on a Mississippi plantation where a large and widely scattered family has gathered for the event. In *The Ponder Heart*, a short novel and later a Broadway play about an aging spinster and her uncle, married to a weak-minded young country girl, there is a scene which epitomizes Miss Welty's use of symbolic violence. During a thunderstorm the wife, called Bonnie Dee Peacock in keeping with the author's characteristic preference for suggestive names, is being tickled by Uncle Daniel. She dies of mingled terror and laughter, her head buried under a cushion. The ingenuity, like the writing itself, may be called precious, but Miss Welty's tone and use of idiom to enforce her themes are everywhere authoritative.

A volume of *Selected Stories* was published in 1954. It was followed by a collection of seven new stories, *The Bride of the Innisfallen* in 1955. In these, as in her earlier work, she continues to draw a sophisticated picture of eccentric variety based upon a timeless or at least changeless past. Her sensitivity to language and dialogue, her comic inventions, are entertaining, but rely on a serious conception of the symbolic or the mythic for their fullest effect.

BIBLIOGRAPHICAL REFERENCES: There is no extended biographical or critical study. For brief studies in books or magazines see Katherine Anne Porter, Introduction to *A Curtain of Green,* 1941 (reprinted in *The Days Before,* 1952); Robert Van Gelder, ed., *Writers and Writing,* 1946; Eunice Glenn, "Fantasy in the Fiction of Eudora Welty," in *A Southern Vanguard,* edited by Allen Tate, 1947; Robert Penn

Warren, "The Love and Separateness in Miss Welty," *Kenyon Review*, VI (1944), 246–259; John Edward Hardy, "Delta Wedding as Region and Symbol," *Sewanee Review*, LX (1952), 397–418; Granville Hicks, "Eudora Welty," *College English*, XIV (1952), 69–76; Harry C. Morris, "Zeus and the Golden Apples: Eudora Welty," *Perspective*, V (1952), 190–199; Robert Daniel, "The World of Eudora Welty," *Hopkins Review*, VI (1953), 461–468; and Audrey Hodgins, "The Narrator as Ironic Device in a Short Story of Eudora Welty," *Twentieth Century Literature*, I (1956), 215–219. For bibliography see Katherine H. Smythe, "Eudora Welty: A Checklist," *Bulletin of Bibliography*, XXI (1956), 207–208.

FRANZ WERFEL

Born: Prague, Czechoslovakia   *Died:* Hollywood, California
Date: September 10, 1890   *Date:* August 26, 1945

PRINCIPAL WORKS

NOVELS: *Verdi*, 1924; *Barbara oder Die Frömmigkeit*, 1929 (*The Pure in Heart*); *Die Geschwister von Neapel*, 1931 (*The Pascarella Family*); *Die vierzig Tage des Musa Dagh*, 1934 (*The Forty Days of Musa Dagh*); *Der veruntreute Himmel*, 1939 (*Embezzled Heaven*); *Das Lied von Bernadette*, 1941 (*The Song of Bernadette*); *Stern der Ungeborenen*, 1946 (*The Star of the Unborn*).

NOVELLAS AND TALES IN TRANSLATION: *Twilight of a World*, 1937.

PLAYS: *Der Spiegelmensch*, 1920; *Bocksgesang*, 1921 (*Goat Song*); *Juarez und Maximilian*, 1924; *Paulus unter den Juden*, 1926 (*Paul Among the Jews*); *Das Reich Gottes in Böhmen*, 1930 (*The Kingdom of God in Bohemia*); *Jakobowski und der Oberst*, 1944 (*Jacobowski and the Colonel*).

POEMS: *Gedichte aus den Jahren*, 1908–1945.

Franz Werfel was born into a Jewish family of Prague on September 10, 1890. His father, the owner of a glove factory, was intensely interested in art and music, but he saw in his son only a future partner and an heir to the business; consequently, he opposed the boy's early inclinations toward literature. Young Werfel was educated at the local gymnasium and spent two years, 1909–1910, at the University of Prague. Having tasted the pleasure of seeing some of his work in print, Werfel had little interest in an academic career, preferring to spend his time writing and discussing literature with literary friends who included such recognized writers as Gustav Meyrink, Max Brod, and Otokar Březina.

After leaving the university in 1910,

Werfel went to Hamburg, Germany. There he took a job in a business firm but at the same time he continued to write. Following a year of compulsory military service, from 1911 to 1912, he settled for a time in Leipzig, where he became a publisher's reader. With the opening of World War I, he took a pacifist stand, publishing pacifist poems like "Der Krieg," "Wortmacher des Krieges," and "Der Ulan," all of which appeared in *Einander* (1915). Despite his attitude toward the war, Werfel was called into the service as an officer in an artillery regiment and served during 1916–1917. In 1916 his adaptation of Euripides' *Trojan Women* had a successful season on the Berlin stage and in other cities. By the time he was thirty, Werfel had made himself a reputation in both poetry and drama; in addition, he already had written and published a short novel, *Not the Murderer* (1919). This and other of his early works have never been translated into English.

During the early 1920's Werfel's work was primarily in drama. *Der Spiegelmensch* opened simultaneously on stages in Düsseldorf, Leipzig, and Stuttgart. Werfel's first play to appear on the American stage was *Goat Song,* produced in New York in 1926. One of his most popular plays was *Juarez and Maximilian,* which after a successful run in Europe was translated into English and produced in New York before being made also into a motion picture. Three religious plays were written somwhat later in Werfel's career: *Paul Among the Jews, The Kingdom of God in Bohemia,* and *The Eternal Road* (1936). The last-named, a presentation of early Jewish history, was translated into English and produced in New York in 1937.

From 1925 on, Werfel was interested primarily in fiction, and a series of stories and short novels preceded his more important novels. In the United States his popularity came with the publication of *The Forty Days of Musa Dagh,* a novel based on the Armenian resistance to the Turks. *Hearken unto the Voice* (1937) showed the author's continued interest in the Jews and their history. *Embezzled Heaven,* also popular in America, illustrates how Werfel's religiosity caused him to become highly sympathetic to Roman Catholicism.

After World War I Werfel lived in Vienna. At the time of the *Anschluss* he fled to Paris, only to become a fugitive once more when the Germans invaded France. Eventually he reached the United States and safety. While escaping from the Germans, he had found a temporary refuge at Lourdes. While there he vowed to write a book about the young woman who had seen a vision of the Virgin Mary at that shrine. *The Song of Bernadette,* an exceptionally popular book in America, fulfilled that vow. A play, *Jacobowski and the Colonel,* was successfully produced in New York in 1944, and a collection of his verse, *Poems,* translated by E. A. Snow, was published in 1945.

Werfel and his wife Anna, who was the widow of Gustav Mahler, the composer, moved to Hollywood, California, where Werfel continued to write despite failing health. His last novel, *The Star of the Unborn,* was completed just a few days before he succumbed to a heart attack on August 26, 1945.

BIBLIOGRAPHICAL REFERENCES: Werfel's *Gesammelte Werke,* 8 vols., were published 1927–1935. The best study of the man and his work is Richard Specht, *Franz Werfel,* 1926. Studies of Werfel as one of Germany's writers-in-exile appear in Harry Slochower, *No Voice Is Wholly Lost,* 1945, and Vernon L. Parrington, *American Dreams,* 1947. See also Elisabeth Hunna, *Die Dramen von Franz Werfel,* 1947; Marysia Turrian, *Dostojewskij und Franz Werfel,* 1950; and Annemarie von Puttkamer, *Franz Werfel, Wort und Antwort,* 1952.

GLENWAY WESCOTT

Born: Kewaskum, Wisconsin
Date: April 11, 1901

NOVELS: *The Apple of the Eye*, 1924; *The Grandmothers*, 1927; *The Pilgrim Hawk*, 1940; *Apartment in Athens*, 1945.

SHORT STORIES: *Goodbye Wisconsin*, 1928; *The Babe's Bed*, 1930.

POEMS: *The Bitterns*, 1920; *Natives of Rock*, 1925.

BELLES-LETTRES: *Fear and Trembling*, 1932; *A Calendar of Saints for Unbelievers*, 1932.

Glenway Wescott, born in Kewaskum, Wisconsin, April 11, 1901, is a Middle Westerner by birth and education. He attended public schools in various Wisconsin towns and spent two years (1917–1919) at the University of Chicago. His family had hoped he would enter the ministry, while he himself entertained some hope of becoming a professional musician. After World War I he spent a year in Germany, then returned to live for a short time in New Mexico. His first book was a volume of poetry, *The Bitterns*, published in 1920; this was followed by a second book of verse, *Natives of Rock*, in 1925. His first novel, *The Apple of the Eye*, was completed during a period of several months that Wescott spent in New York City. Set against a background of rural Wisconsin, the novel relates the conflicts and forces involved in a boy's search for an understanding of the world and sex, a series of problems similiar to those probed by many contemporary novelists, who seem to be fascinated by the problems of the adolescent in the modern world. After the publication of his novel Wescott went again to Europe and during the next eight years was one of a large colony of American writers who lived abroad in the 1920's.

While in Europe he wrote *The Grandmothers*, which has received more acclaim from readers and critics than any of his other novels. It earned for Wescott the Harper Prize Novel Award for the year of publication. The novel, a saga of pioneer life in early Wisconsin, unfolds as it appears to Alwyn Tower, a young man who is very much like the author and who has his curiosity aroused by an old family photograph album. His awakened curiosity leads him to piece together the story of his family and relate the story as he finds it. This novel, like most of Wescott's fiction, interprets humanity through the desires and motives of typical human beings. The novel is illustrative, too, of the flowing, cadenced prose which is one of Wescott's strong points as a writer. The prose approaches the cadences of folk literature, and it was particularly well chosen for a novel about American pioneer life. Other works which appeared during the author's years of expatriation were *Goodbye Wisconsin*, a volume of short stories; *The Babe's Bed*, a long short story; *Fear and Trembling* a volume of essays; and *A Calendar of Saints for Unbelievers*. The most interesting of these works is *The Babe's Bed*, which is a meditation in which a young man dreams about the possible future of a baby nephew.

Returning to America in 1934, Wescott settled on a farm in Hunterdon County, New Jersey. *The Pilgrim Hawk*, published in 1940, is a novel which indicated that the author had managed to weather successfully a period of inactivity such as is some-

1143

times fatal to a writer's reputation. Ineligible for military service during World War II, Wescott sought to aid his country in other ways. An attempt to write a novel which would help Americans understand what had produced Nazism proved unsuccessful, however. An encounter with a Greek underground leader led Wescott to write another novel, *Apartment in Athens*, which describes the effect of the German occupation on one family in Athens, Greece, during World War II. The book was chosen by one of the national book clubs for its list and achieved a rather wide body of readers. Part of its value was, of course, its topicality at the time of publication.

Early in the 1950's Wescott turned to critical writing. He edited *The Maugham Reader* (1950) and *Short Novels of Colette* (1951).

BIBLIOGRAPHICAL REFERENCES: There is no full-length biographical or critical study. For brief criticism see Edmund Wilson, *Classics and Commercials*, 1950; Dayton Kohler, "Glenway Wescott: Legend-Maker," *American Bookman*, LXXIII (1931), 142–146; and C. E. Schorer, "The Maturing of Glenway Wescott," *College English*, XVIII (1957), 320–326.

NATHANAEL WEST

Born: New York, N. Y.
Date: October 17, 1903 (?)

Died: El Centro, California
Date: December 22, 1940

PRINCIPAL WORKS

NOVELS: *The Dream Life of Balso Snell*, 1931; *Miss Lonelyhearts*, 1933; *A Cool Million*, 1934; *The Day of the Locust*, 1939.

Nathanael West's literary life has an irony which almost parodies his own novels. Completely original and a deadly serious craftsman, he achieved in his short life little fame, except among a discerning few, and no popular success. Now, seventeen years after his death, two paperback editions have sold in the hundred thousands, and his *Complete Works* (1957) won critical acclaim and a place on best-seller lists.

Born Nathan Weinstein, in New York City, October 17, 1903 (?), he used the name Nathaniel von Wallenstein-Weinstein in Brown University (Ph.B., 1924), where he was labeled eccentric and a genius, and nicknamed "Pep" for the opposite characteristics the word suggests. Literary friends included I. J. Kapstein, Quentin Reynolds, and S. J. Perelman, who later married his sister Laura; but he wrote few pieces for undergraduate publications. In Paris during 1925–1926 he came under surrealist influences and wrote his first novel, *The Dream Life of Balso Snell*, a fantasy on his hero's wanderings inside the Trojan Horse, where he meets a naked man in a derby writing about Saint Puce (a flea who lived in Christ's armpit), and a twelve-year-old boy wooing his schoolmistress with Russian journals. This work was ignored following its publication in 1931.

Back in New York, West worked as a hotel manager, as associate editor of *Contact* with William Carlos Williams in 1932, and also as associate on *Americana* with George Grosz in 1933. Contact and a third little magazine, *Contempo*, contained early drafts of *Miss Lonelyhearts*, the story of an agony columnist who is destroyed when he takes too seriously the problems and miseries of his correspondents. This minor classic was issued in 1933 by a publisher who shortly afterward went bankrupt. By the time copies and plates were rescued from the unpaid printer by another publishing house, demand for the book had ceased.

West's third and weakest novel, *A Cool Million*, is a broad satire on the Horatio Alger myth, in which Lemuel Pitkin loses his teeth, eye, scalp, money, and eventually his life after being victimized by capitalists, communists, and neo-fascists. It was quickly remaindered.

Unsuccessful as a short story writer and playwright, West made a living in Hollywood writing B-grade movies. Here he took five years to finish his most mature work, *The Day of the Locust*, and in 1940 he married Eileen McKenney, of *My Sister Eileen* fame. Seven months later, on December 22, they were killed together in an auto crash at El Centro, California.

Although *The Day of the Locust* has Hollywood as its locale and minor actors and hangers-on from the periphery of the studios as its characters, the novel is no more about motion pictures than *Miss Lonelyhearts* is about newspapers. Fantastic and exaggerated in theme and treatment, West's two chief novels convey, more clearly than most twentieth century fiction, a sense of horror and revulsion from the universe man lives in and the world he makes for his fellows and himself.

BIBLIOGRAPHICAL REFERENCES: No book-length study of West has been published, but one is in preparation by James F. Light. Printed biographical information is scanty and inaccurate; for example, West's birth is given variously as 1902, 1903, 1904, and 1906.

Useful critical material is found in Robert M. Coates, Introduction to the New Directions edition of *Miss Lonelyhearts* (1946); Edmund Wilson, "Postscript," *The Boys in the Back Room*, 1941, reprinted in *Classics and Commercials*, 1950; Daniel Aaron, "The Truly Monstrous: A Note on Nathanael West," *Partisan Review*, XIV (1947), 98–106; Alan Ross, "The Dead Centre: An Introduction to Nathanael West," *Horizon*, XVIII (1948), 284–296, reprinted, with changes, in the Grey Walls Press edition of *Miss Lonelyhearts*, 1949, and the *Complete Works*, 1957; Richard B. Gehman, "Nathanael West: A Novelist Apart," *Atlantic*, CLXXXVI (1950), 69–72, reprinted in the New Directions edition of *The Day of the Locust*, 1950; Cyril M. Schneider, "The Individuality of Nathanael West," *Western Review*, XX (1955), 7–28, 254–256; Arthur Cohen, "Nathanael West's Holy Fool," *Commonweal*, LXIV (June 15, 1956), 276–278; and James F. Light, "*Miss Lonelyhearts*: The Imagery of Nightmare," *American Quartely*, VIII (1956), 316–327. See also William White, "Nathanael West: A Bibliography," *Studies in Bibliography*, XI (1958), 207–224.

REBECCA WEST
(Cicily Isabel Fairfield)

Born: County Kerry, Ireland
Date: December 25, 1892

NOVELS: *The Return of the Soldier,* 1918; *The Judge,* 1922; *Harriet Hume,* 1929; *The Thinking Reed,* 1936; *The Fountain Overflows,* 1956.
CRITICAL ESSAYS AND STUDIES: *Henry James,* 1916; *The Strange Necessity,* 1928; *D. H. Lawrence, An Elegy,* 1930; *Arnold Bennett Himself,* 1931; *Ending in Earnest: A Literary Log,* 1931; *The Court and the Castle,* 1957.
POLITICAL STUDIES: *The Meaning of Treason,* 1947; *A Train of Powder,* 1955.
TRAVEL SKETCHES AND IMPRESSIONS: *Black Lamb and Grey Falcon,* 1941.

Few writers in modern times have taken as much interest in the world about them as Rebecca West, and even fewer have done so much to illuminate that world by their writing. Miss West's interest in the condition of man began at an early age. She was born Cicily Isabel Fairfield in County Kerry, Ireland, on December 25, 1892, but spent her childhood in Edinburgh, where she attended George Watson's Ladies' College. By the time she was eighteen she was contributing to radical periodicals. One of her primary interests was female suffrage, a cause she defended in much of her early writing. It is significant that she took her pen name from the "emancipated" heroine of Ibsen's *Rosmersholm.* After a brief period on the London stage, she turned to journalism in 1911 and became a reviewer for *The Freewoman.* Becoming also an advocate of Socialism, she was for a time active in the Fabian Society.

Her first separate publication was *Henry James,* a closely reasoned and detailed analysis of that author's work. As a writer she has always admired James's powers of insight; he, along with Proust, is thought of as being one of her models. Her literary criticism is characterized by uncompromising attacks on the reputations of accepted writers. Rebecca West has always been willing to sacrifice convention for what she considers the truth.

The Return of the Soldier, her first novel, reflects the postwar emphasis on psychology. It is the story of a veteran, a victim of amnesia who is led, by a woman with whom he had had an early love affair, back to health and his wife and family. *The Judge* also displays Miss West's interest in applied psychology, although the subject here is the obsessive love of a mother for her son. Miss West's next novel, *Harriet Hume,* is subtitled *A London Fantasy;* it is just that, the end being capable of several interpretations. In this novel the writer shows her ability to draw full and carefully observed descriptions of the London scene, a power of description which was to enrich greatly her later travel writing. In the previous year she had published another volume of literary criticism, *The Strange Necessity;* with its appearance Miss West's reputation as a penetrating critic was secure.

She married Henry Maxwell Andrews, a British banker, in 1930, and she has often declared her debt to him for his help and encouragement in her literary efforts. Another book of criticism, *Ending in Earnest,* added further to her reputation as a fearless and skillful critic. The subject of her next novel, *The Thinking Reed,* is the excessive demands made by wealth upon the people who have it. The story concerns a rich American widow who marries a wealthy Frenchman.

The Meaning of Treason is a collection of essays about the Nuremberg war crimes trials, particularly that of William Joyce, "Lord Haw-Haw." In this book Miss West tries to arrive at a decision about the true significance of treasonous acts. One of the six essays in A Train of Powder deals with the same subject, but the other essays are concerned with topics as divergent as German economical growth and a lynching trial in South Carolina.

Her last novel, The Fountain Overflows, has won Miss West renewed fame in America. It tells of the dawning of awareness of an artistic gift in a member of a talented family in London. In this novel, as in her others, Miss West displays a richness of style and clarity of insight. The most impressive literary product of her career, however, is the massive Black Lamb and Grey Falcon. This book, which Miss West calls a journal of a trip through Yugoslavia, is really a fully detailed exposition of her views on history, society, and art.

In this book, as in all her others, Rebecca West brings to the reader what is perhaps her most important quality, her ability and willingness to undertake any literary, historical, or social problem that interests her and to treat it with care, detail, and courage.

BIBLIOGRAPHICAL REFERENCES: There is no comprehensive biographical study and surprisingly little criticism, although several critical studies are reported in preparation. See Patrick Braybrooke, Novelists, We Are Seven, 1926, and Philosophies in Modern Fiction, 1929; Arthur St. John Adcock, The Glory That Was Grubb Street, 1928; Frank Swinnerton, The Georgian Literary Scene, 1935; and Richard Church, British Authors, 1948 (rev. ed.).

EDWARD NOYES WESTCOTT

Born: Syracuse, New York
Date: September 27, 1846

Died: Syracuse
Date: March 31, 1898

PRINCIPAL WORKS

NOVEL: *David Harum*, 1898.
SHORT STORIES: *The Teller*, 1901.

Edward Noyes Westcott, author of the popular *David Harum*, is something of an anomaly in the history of American literature, being a banker turned author. The son of a dentist, he was born in Syracuse, New York, on September 27, 1846. He attended the public schools in Syracuse until he was sixteen and then left school to take a job as a junior clerk in a local bank. At the age of twenty he left Syracuse to work for an insurance company in New York City. He returned to Syracuse, however, to become a teller and cashier in banks in that city. In 1874 he married Jane Dows, of Buffalo, New York, and the couple had three children, two sons and a daughter.

Anxious to get ahead in life and to provide for his children's education, Westcott formed the company of Westcott and Abbott, a banking and brokerage house, in 1880. For several years the firm was successful, but the bankruptcy of an allied company caused its failure in the late 1880's, at which time Wescott took a job with the Syracuse water commission. Having to retire because of tuberculosis in 1895, Westcott went to the Adirondack Mountains to recuperate. While there he began to write for his own amusement. In 1895–1896 he went to Naples, still searching for good health, and while there he wrote *David Harum*, his famous novel about a shrewd, but good-hearted Yankee with a penchant for horse trading. The novel, rejected by six publishing houses before it was finally accepted, appeared in 1898, just a few months after the death of the author at Syracuse on March 31 of that year. Its suc-cess was immediate, with six printings within three months. Within two years over 400,000 copies were sold, and the eventual sales ran over a million copies. In 1901 *The Teller,* a group of stories, with some letters by Westcott, was published.

The popularity of *David Harum* has continued into the media of the stage and a motion picture. The novel, among the first of a type which portrayed the Yankee character as hard on the outside but gentle and kind within, is competently written; but its literary value is slight, and scholars, unlike the public, have passed it by with but slight attention.

BIBLIOGRAPHICAL REFERENCES: *The Teller,* 1901, contains a selection of letters by Edward Noyes Westcott and an account of his life. See also the sketch by Brice Harris in the *Dictionary of National Biography.*

EDITH WHARTON

Born: New York, N. Y.
Date: January 24, 1862

Died: St. Brice sous Foret, France
Date: August 11, 1937

PRINCIPAL WORKS

NOVELS: *The Touchstone,* 1900; *The Valley of Decision,* 1902 (2 vols.); *Sanctuary,* 1903; *The House of Mirth,* 1905; *The Fruit of the Tree,* 1907; *Madame de Treymes,* 1907; *Ethan Frome,* 1911; *The Reef,* 1912; *The Custom of the Country,* 1913; *Summer,* 1917; *The Marne,* 1918; *The Age of Innocence,* 1920; *The Glimpses of the Moon,* 1922; *A Son at the Front,* 1923; *Old New York,* 1924 (*False Dawn: The Forties, The Old Maid: The Fifties, The Spark: The Sixties,* and *New Year's Day: The Seventies*); *The Mother's Recompense,* 1925; *Twilight Sleep,* 1927; *The Children,* 1928; *Hudson River Bracketed,* 1929; *The Gods Arrive,* 1932; *The Buccaneers,* 1938.

SHORT STORIES: *The Greater Inclination,* 1899; *Crucial Instances,* 1901; *The Descent of Man,* 1904; *The Hermit and the Wild Woman,* 1908; *Tales of Men and Ghosts,* 1910; *Xingu,* 1916; *Here and Beyond,* 1926; *Certain People,* 1930; *Human Nature,* 1933; *The World Over,* 1936; *Ghosts,* 1937.

POEMS: *Artemis to Actaeon,* 1909; *Twelve Poems,* 1926.

CRITICISM: *The Writing of Fiction,* 1925.

AUTOBIOGRAPHY: *A Backward Glance,* 1934.

Edith Newbold Jones was born in New York City on January 24, 1862, into a wealthy, upper middle-class family of distinguished ancestry. She learned as a girl, according to her own account, to love good literature, good English, and good manners. Traveling extensively with her socially active parents, and reading under the encouragement of tutors, she acquired a perspective of people and an enjoyment of literature which led her into writing stories on her own. With the publication of poetry and stories in magazines her literary career began. But her own social circle disapproved of her work, and she in turn discovered that their good manners were motivated by status rather than love. In 1885 she married Edward Wharton, a Boston banker, but their marriage was clouded by the husband's mental breakdown. In 1907, following the example of her literary mentor and personal friend, Henry James, Mrs. Wharton went abroad to live and settled permanently in France. However, she did not forget her society; she contemplated it from a distance and re-created it in art with irony and nostalgia.

Though Edith Wharton must be considered a major writer because of her artistry, her themes are somewhat less important today than they were during the first quarter of the twentieth century. One theme she treated was that the very conventions of conduct in America tend to stifle creative activity; the second, that the rising *nouveaux riches* were adulterating the purity of upper-class standards. Essentially a writer of manners, she never attained the dispassionate view of her material that Jane Austen did, and her works are tragedies rather than comedies. Most of her novels tell the same story: the plight of an innocent victimized by the stultifying conventions of the group or the difficulties of the noble in heart in an ignoble society,

a society whose lip service to the conventions makes its successful members hypocrites and its few honest ones victims. The antagonists are essentially evil, and their inevitable triumph is the real tragedy. However, the very defeat of the protagonists gives them a spiritual victory, for their defeat, as in *The House of Mirth,* is the result of their moral integrity.

All of her works are colored by the business of maneuvering for position, usually social. The first work to achieve critical recognition was the novel *The House of Mirth,* published in 1905. The protagonist, Lily Bart, a sensitive, ethical girl, is punished by society for following the direction of her sympathies rather than the demands of the "respectable"; she makes attractive friendships rather than socially acceptable ones, is snubbed by family and old acquaintances, and commits suicide in an agony of bewildered despair. In line with the literature of revolt of the period, this novel was unique in the restraint of its style, and perhaps all the more effective for its keyed-down qualities.

Edith Wharton rejected the "middle" class with prejudiced scorn. *The Custom of the Country* is cutting in its delineation of the character of the barbarian climber, Undine Spragg. However, she felt for the lower class, especially the rural, the same sympathy and identification with its victims of convention. *Ethan Frome* is a classic story of tragic frustration. Ethan, a farmer, marries out of loneliness. When his wife's cousin comes to live with them in poverty, and they fall in love —the first love in both their lives— they cannot see any way out to consummate their love; so they attempt suicide. Mrs. Wharton, as she does in many of her short stories, adds an ironic denouement to this plot: the suicide attempt fails, both are crippled, and the wife-in-name who refused to allow them their freedom is chained to them forever as their nurse. The novel *Summer* is similar in subject, milieu, and theme.

The Age of Innocence presents a starkly classic quality in its picture of the inevitabliity of spiritual destruction suffered by two noble people because of their moral flaw, which allows their social status to take precedence over love. The protagonists, Newland Archer and Ellen Olenska, are defeated by a code of their group, a group that willingly breaks the codes only when there is an assurance of not getting caught. "It was a dull association of material and social interests held together by ignorance on the one side and hypocrisy on the other." This novel comes closest to the polished perfection of the manners genre in that there is a comic tone that restrains the pathos of the dilemma of Newland and married Ellen who, afraid to face ostracism, must either destroy their love for each other or destroy themselves. The very restraint allows the perceptive reader to live the tragedy of their thwarted emotional lives, and the impression is deep and lasting.

After 1920 only the short stories continued as art; the novels were mechanical repetitions of the earlier works or quickly contrived propaganda pieces, like *A Son at the Front*. The world that Edith Wharton had known was gone and there was little more to say.

The success of Mrs. Wharton's work was achieved by "disengaging crucial moments from the welter of existence," keeping the plot true to the characters' motivations, and using a language that was dispassionate yet moving in its clarity and restraint. Before she died, at St. Brice sous Foret, France, on August 11, 1937, she had received more honors for her work than any other woman writer in American history.

BIBLIOGRAPHICAL REFERENCES: There is no definitive biography of Edith Wharton. The most recent biographical study is Percy Lubbock, *Portrait of Edith Wharton*, 1947; the most recent critical study, Nevius Blake, *Edith Wharton: A Study of Her Ficton*, 1953. For earlier biographical and critical works see Katherine F. Gerould, *Edith Wharton: A Critical Study*, 1922; Robert M. Lovett, *Edith Wharton*, 1925; and E. K. Brown, *Edith Wharton: Étude Critique*, 1935.

See also Percy H. Boynton, *Some Contemporary Americans*, 1924; Régis Michaud, *The American Novel To-day*, 1928; N. Elizabeth Monroe, *The Novel and Society*, 1941; Alfred Kazin, *On Native Grounds*, 1942; Maxwell Geismar, *Rebels and Ancestors*, 1953; also Percy Lubbock, "The Novels of Edith Wharton," *Quarterly Review*, CCXXIII (1915), 182–201; Charles K. Trueblood, "Edith Wharton," *Dial*, LXVIII (1920), 80–91; Frances T. Russell, "Melodramatic Mrs. Wharton," *Sewanee Review*, XL (1932), 425–437; E. K. Brown, "Edith Wharton," *Études Anglaises*, II (1938), 12–26; Edmund Wilson, "Justice to Edith Wharton," *New Republic*, XCV (1938), 209–213; and Larry Rubin, "Aspects of Naturalism in Four Novels by Edith Wharton," *Twentieth Century Literature*, II (1957), 182–192.

WALT WHITMAN

Born: West Hills, Long Island
Date: May 31, 1819

Died: Camden, New Jersey
Date: March 26, 1892

POEMS: *Leaves of Grass*, 1855, 1856, 1860, 1867, 1871, 1876, 1881–1882, 1888, 1891–1892; *Drum-Taps*, 1865; *Passage to India*, 1871; *After All, Not to Create Only*, 1871; *As a Strong Bird on Pinions Free*, 1872; *Two Rivulets*, 1876; *November Boughs*, 1888; *Good-bye My Fancy*, 1891.

ESSAYS, NOTES, AND STUDIES: *Democratic Vistas*, 1871; *Memoranda During the War*, 1875–1876; *Specimen Days and Collect*, 1882–1883; *Complete Prose Works*, 1892; *An American Primer*, 1904.

LETTERS AND JOURNALS: *Calamus*, edited by Richard M. Bucke, 1897; *The Wound Dresser*, edited by Richard M. Bucke, 1898; *Letters Written by Walt Whitman to His Mother, 1866–1872*, edited by Thomas B. Harned, 1902; *Walt Whitman's Diary in Canada*, edited by William S. Kennedy, 1904; *The Letters of Anne Gilchrist and Walt Whitman*, edited by Thomas B. Harned, 1918.

NOVEL: *Franklin Evans*, 1842.

SHORT STORIES: *The Half-Breed and Other Stories*, 1927.

Walt (christened Walter) Whitman was born at West Hills, near Huntington, Long Island, May 31, 1819, the second child of Walter Whitman and Louisa Van Velsor, of English and Dutch descent. The father, a farmer and carpenter by turns, had difficulty in supporting his large family, which grew to nine children, though one died in infancy. In 1823 he moved to Brooklyn, where Walt, his only son ever to show marked ability, received a meager public school education, learned the printing trade, became a journalist, and finally a poet.

After teaching school on Long Island and starting and abandoning a newspaper, the *Long Islander*, Walt Whitman worked as a printer in New York City, and at twenty-three edited a daily paper, the New York *Aurora*. Returning to Brooklyn in 1845, he worked on the Long Island *Star* and for two years edited the Brooklyn *Eagle*, from which he was dismissed because of his editorial defense of the "free soil" faction of the Democratic Party. For three months in 1848 he was employed on the New Orleans *Crescent*, but again returned to Brooklyn and for a few months edited a "free soil" paper called the *Freeman*. Thereafter for five years he built and sold houses and dabbled in real estate. He did not edit another paper until 1857, when he took charge of the Brooklyn *Times* for approximately two years.

While employed as printer, journalist, and editor Whitman published sentimental poems and stories in newspapers and magazines, but he first became a serious poet when he printed at his own expense the first edition of *Leaves of Grass*. This book was acclaimed by Emerson and a few others, but was mostly ignored or denounced as unpoetic because the lines did not rhyme or scan, or as indecent because of the frank language. Undaunted, the poet brought out a second edition in 1856, and a third in 1860, the latter published by Thayer and Eldridge in Boston; but the outbreak of the Civil War bankrupted this firm, and Whitman did not have another commercial publisher until 1881. He himself participated in the war by ministering to the wounded, writing accounts for the New York and Brooklyn newspapers, and composing his *Drum-*

Taps poems, which he printed in 1865. After the assassination of President Lincoln he wrote what were to become his two best-known poems, "O Captain! My Captain!" and "When Lilacs Last in the Dooryard Bloom'd," which he included in an annex to the second issue of *Drum-Taps*. From 1865 until 1873, when he suffered a paralytic stroke, he was employed as a government clerk in Washington. His mother having died in 1873, for several years he lived with his brother George in Camden, N. J., a "battered, wrecked old man." Although a semi-invalid for the remainder of his life, he recovered sufficiently to make some trips, several to New York, one as far west as Denver in 1879, and another to Canada the following year.

In 1881 James Osgood, a respected Boston publisher, issued another edition of *Leaves of Grass,* but stopped distribution after the poet refused to withdraw several lines (for a new printing) which had provoked the threat of criminal prosecution. Whitman secured a new publisher in Philadelphia, first Rees Welsh and Company, followed by David McKay, who thereafter remained his publisher during his lifetime. In 1882 McKay published *Specimen Days and Collect,* a volume of prose containing sketches of the poet's early life, experiences in the hospitals, and old-age diary notes. *November Boughs,* 1888, also contained some prose, and an important literary apologia, "A Backward Glance O'er Travel'd Roads." With the income from the 1881 edition Whitman was able to buy a small house for himself in Camden, on Mickle Street, which soon began to be visited by many prominent writers and artists from England, where Whitman's reputation was greater than in his own country. At the time of his death in Camden, March 26, 1892, he was one of the best known poets in the United States, partly because of the publicity resulting from the accusations made against the Boston edition of 1881 and partly because he had relentlessly publicized himself. Consequently, the metropolitan newspapers gave many columns of space to his death, and it was even mentioned in many European papers. But he was not generally accepted by the literary critics and historians of his own country for another quarter century. By mid-twentieth century, however, he was almost universally regarded as the greatest poet America had produced. *Leaves of Grass* has now been translated in whole or in part into nearly every language of the world. Successful complete translations have been published in France, Germany, Spain, Italy, and Japan. *Leaves of Grass* is today an acknowledged masterpiece in world literature.

In its growth and structure *Leaves of Grass* is very nearly unique in literary history. Between 1855 and 1892 Whitman used the same title for nine editions of his collected poems, no two alike, and several dramatically different in size, content, and arrangement. Not only did the poet constantly revise and augment his poems, but he also altered titles, divided or combined poems, dropped some, and constantly shifted their relative positions in the book until 1881, when he solidified the order, thereafter merely annexing new poems. A posthumous tenth edition, published in 1897 contains the final annex, "Old Age Echoes," made up of poems first collected by the literary executors. On his deathbed the poet declared the 1892 edition to be definitive, but critics and biographers have often found earlier editions to be more interesting, more revealing, and even of higher literary merit—especially the first (1855) and third (1860).

Great controversy has arisen over the sexual imagery of two groups of poems first assembled in 1860 and titled "Enfans d'Adam" (later "Children of Adam") and "Calamus." Theoretically, the former group treats procreative or sexual love, the latter friendship or "manly love." Earlier critics objected to the realism of "Children of Adam"; later critics have been more concerned with the eroticism of "Calamus," but there is no universal agreement. Another critical problem is ideology vs. aesthetics. Whitman openly espoused didacticism and preferred to be known as the spokesman of democracy—and in many foreign lands he has become a symbol of American democracy—but his poems have survived as poems and not as the repository of ideas. Whitman's most characteristic poem is "Song of Myself," which celebrates *the self*, not himself primarily. Though uneven, it contains some of the finest lyrical passages in the whole range of American poetry.

Gay Wilson Allen

BIBLIOGRAPHICAL REFERENCES: The most extensive edition of Whitman's poetry and prose is the Camden Edition, *The Complete Writings of Walt Whitman*, edited by Richard M. Bucke, Horace L. Traubel, and Thomas B. Harned, 10 vols., 1902. In addition to titles already noted, supplementary material may be found in *Notes and Fragments*, edited by Richard M. Bucke, 1899; *The Gathering of the Forces*, edited by Cleveland Rodgers and John Black, 2 vols., 1920; *The Uncollected Poetry and Prose of Walt Whitman*, edited by Emory Holloway, 2 vols., 1921; *Walt Whitman's Workshop*, edited by Clifton J. Furness, 1928; *Rivulets of Prose*, edited by Carolyn Wells and Alfred F. Goldsmith, 1928; *A Child's Reminiscence*, edited by Thomas O. Mabbott and Rollo G. Silver, 1930; *I Sit and Look Out*, edited by Emory Holloway and Vernolian Schwarz, 1932; and *Walt Whitman and the Civil War*, edited by Charles I. Glicksberg, 1933.

Available one-volume editions of selections include *Walt Whitman's Complete Poetry and Selected Prose and Letters*, edited by Emory Holloway, 1938; *The Portable Walt Whitman*, edited by Mark Van Doren, 1945; *Leaves of Grass and Selected Prose*, edited by Sculley Bradley, Rinehart Editions, 1949; and *The Complete Poetry and Prose of Walt Whitman*, edited by Malcolm Cowley, 1954. Emory Holloway also edited the inclusive *Leaves of Grass*, 1924, and *Leaves of Grass: The Collected Poems*, 1942. Other editions have been prepared by Stuart P. Sherman, 1922; John Valente, 1928; Sherwood Anderson, 1933; and Carl Sandburg, 1944.

The fullest biography is by Gay Wilson Allen, *The Solitary Singer: A Critical Biography of Walt Whitman*, 1955. A companion volume is this author's *Walt Whitman Handbook*, 1946 (reissued 1957), a work useful in all Whitman studies. Allen has also edited *Walt Whitman Abroad: Critical Essays from Germany, France, Scandinavia, Russia, Italy, Spain, Latin America, Israel, Japan, and India* [in translation], 1955, and, with Charles T. Davis, *Walt Whitman's Poems*, 1955, an anthology containing extensive critical commentary. For additional biographical and critical studies see also Bliss Perry, *Walt Whitman: His Life and Works*, 1906; Basil de Sélincourt, *Walt Whitman: A Critical Study*, 1914; Emory Holloway, *Whitman: An Interpretation in Narrative*, 1926; Frederik Schyberg, *Walt Whitman*, 1933, translated by Evie Allison Allen, 1951; Henry S. Canby, *Walt Whitman, An American*, 1943; Joseph Beaver, *Walt Whitman: Poet of Science*, 1951; Roger Asselineau,

L'Évolution de Walt Whitman après la première édition des Feuilles d'Herbe, 1954; and Richard Chase, *Walt Whitman Reconsidered,* 1955.

For briefer studies see also Norman Foerster, *Nature in American Literature,* 1923; *idem, American Criticism,* 1928; Henry S. Canby, *Classic Americans,* 1931; Gay Wilson Allen, *American Prosody,* 1935; F. O. Matthiessen, *American Renaissance,* 1941; and *Literary History of the United States,* edited by Robert E. Spiller, Willard Thorp, Thomas H. Johnson, and Henry S. Canby, Vol. II, 1948.

JOHN GREENLEAF WHITTIER

Born: Haverhill, Massachusetts   *Died:* Hampton Falls, New Hampshire
Date: December 17, 1807   *Date:* September 7, 1892

Principal Works

POEMS: *Legends of New England,* 1931; *Moll Pitcher,* 1832; *Mogg Megone,* 1836; *Lays of My Home,* 1843; *Ballads and Other Poems,* 1844; *Voices of Freedom,* 1846; *Songs of Labor,* 1850; *The Chapel of the Hermits,* 1853; *The Panorama,* 1856; *The Sycamores,* 1857; *Home Ballads,* 1860; *In War-Time,* 1864; *Snow-Bound,* 1866; *The Tent on the Beach,* 1867; *Among the Hills,* 1869; *Miriam,* 1871; *The Pennsylvania Pilgrim,* 1872; *Hazel-Blossoms,* 1875; *The Bay of Seven Islands,* 1883; *St. Gregory's Guest,* 1886; *At Sundown,* 1890.

PROSE NARRATIVES: *Narrative of James Williams,* 1838; *Leaves from Margaret Smith's Journal,* 1849.

ESSAYS: *Old Portraits and Modern Sketches,* 1850; *Literary Recreations and Miscellanies,* 1854.

Time and geography link John Greenleaf Whittier with such American literary figures as Emerson, Longfellow, Lowell, and Holmes—the so-called New England Group. Whittier's New England, however, was never the same as theirs; and he stands apart from them in background, schooling, and the general direction of his writing talents. To begin with, he did not share their Puritan heritage—Whittier was a Quaker, derived from Quaker stock. Nor did he inherit a ticket of admission to the cultural benefits which nineteenth century Cambridge, Concord, and Boston were able to provide. Instead, "the American Burns" was born to the rugged labors and simple pleasures of rural life, and to such limited educational opportunities as were open to a Massachusetts farm lad.

Whittier was born near Haverhill, Massachusetts, on December 17, 1807. His birthplace was the plain colonial homestead that he later made famous in "Snow-Bound" and his boyhood environment, though not poverty-stricken, provided no luxury or special incentives to a literary career. His formal education was confined to winter sessions of a district school and two terms at Haverhill Academy. It was the village schoolmaster, Joshua Coffin, who introduced him to Burns's poems, a powerful source of inspiration to the imaginative boy.

Whittier's early poems appeared chiefly in local newspapers, one of which was published by William Lloyd Garrison. When he was about twenty-one, Whittier left home to embark on a career of itinerant journalism which led him to Boston, back to Haverhill, then to Hartford and Philadelphia. In

1833 he attended an anti-slavery convention in Philadelphia, thus launching abolitionist efforts so zealous as to engage his best strength for the next thirty years. The end of the Civil War, however, freed him to endeavors less didactic; and in 1866 "Snow-Bound" gave him not only important literary recognition but the beginnings of financial security. As the poet of rural New England and as a voice of calm and sincere religious faith, he became increasingly popular; and his seventieth and eightieth birthdays were widely celebrated. Whittier died at Hampton Falls, New Hampshire, on September 7, 1892, at the age of eighty-five.

Whittier's reputation today rests on poems which, at their best, express the very heart of rural New England. It cannot be disputed, however, that his literary reputation has suffered a marked decline during the twentieth century, nor are the reasons far to seek. For one thing, most of Whittier's anti-slavery poems have not survived the cause in which they were written. For another, the author's work, despite its sincerity and intensity, often suffers from limitations of range and craftsmanship. Finally, his poetry is direct, simple, and emotional, qualities to which modern criticism tends to turn its deaf ear. Interesting also is the now almost-forgotten *Leaves from Margaret Smith's Journal*, a fictitious but accurate account of Colonial life.

Nevertheless, "Snow-Bound" alone is enough to place posterity in debt to Whittier. The simplicity and dignity of family affection, the sharply-etched view of a winter-bound farmhouse, and the recaptured charm of a lost way of life: in these features no other American poem can display a greater, or perhaps even equal, degree of felicity.

BIBLIOGRAPHICAL REFERENCES: The standard biography is still Samuel T. Pickard, *The Life and Letters of John Greenleaf Whittier*, 2 vols., 1907 (rev. ed.). Less extensive biographical studies are Albert Mordell: *Quaker Militant: John Greenleaf Whittier*, 1933; Whitman Bennett, *Whittier: Bard of Freedom*, 1941; and John A. Pollard, *John Greenleaf Whittier: Friend of Man*, 1949.

For criticism see George E. Woodberry, *Makers of Literature*, 1901; George R. Carpenter, *John Greenleaf Whittier*, in the American Men of Letters Series, 1903; Iola K. Eastburn, *Whittier's Relation to German Life and Thought*, 1904; Norman Foerster, *Nature in American Literature*, 1923; Gay Wilson Allen, *American Prosody*, 1935; R. Brenner, *Twelve American Poets before 1900*, 1933; Arthur E. Christy, "Orientalism in New England: Whittier," *American Literature*, I (1930), 372–392; Winfield T. Scott, "Poetry in America: A New Consideration of Whittier's Verse," *New England Quarterly*, VII (1934), 258–275; and Desmond Powell, "Whittier," *American Literature*, IX (1937), 335–342.

GEORGE J. WHYTE-MELVILLE

Born: Near St. Andrews, Scotland   *Died:* Berkshire, England
Date: June 19, 1821   *Date:* December 5, 1878

PRINCIPAL WORKS

NOVELS: *Digby Grand*, 1853; *Tilbury Nogo*, 1854; *Kate Coventry*, 1856; *The Interpreter*, 1858; *Holmby House*, 1860; *Market Harborough*, 1861; *The Queen's*

Maries, 1862; *The Gladiators,* 1863; *Cerise,* 1866; *The White Rose,* 1868; *Sarchedon,* 1871; *Satanella,* 1873; *Uncle John,* 1874; *Katerfelto,* 1875.

George John Whyte-Melville was born near St. Andrews, Scotland, June 19, 1821, into society, his father being a landowner in Scotland and his mother a daughter of the Duke of Leeds. As a boy Whyte-Melville attended Eton, the famous English public school, and at the age of seventeen became a commissioned officer in the Ninety-third Highlanders Regiment. After seven years with that regiment he transferred to the Coldstream Guards and retired from the British army at the age of twenty-seven with the rank of captain. When the Crimean War broke out in 1853, Whyte-Melville volunteered his services to the government and went on active duty with the rank of major. He served with units of Turkish irregular cavalry. During his service in the Crimean War he wrote some poetry and a portion of it was published. After the war he returned to civilian life to continue writing, along with hunting, his favorite sport.

The novels of Whyte-Melville fall easily into two categories: sporting novels, for which he is best known, and historical romances. As a wealthy man of property, and a retired officer, Whyte-Melville was completely familiar with the society he depicted in his sporting novels. He wrote from first-hand knowledge of fashionable, military, and sporting people, and all of those groups furnished him with the characters, actions, and background for his fiction. His novels about fox hunting had an especial appeal for British sportsmen, for they were authentically written, with a great deal of attention to realistic detail. In addition to the realistic detail, they are also filled with

action. The best-known of the sporting novels is *Market Harborough,* a picaresque account of a series of fox-hunting episodes, with plenty of realistic detail about life among people in rural England and London society who follow the hounds. Other novels in this category are *Digby Grand, Tilbury Nogo,* and *Kate Coventry.* One interesting sidelight to these novels is that horses are often important characters.

Whyte-Melville's later fiction is largely in the field of historical romance. In 1858 he published *The Interpreter,* a novel based on the Crimean War and relating the activities of a beautiful female spy. *Holmby House* is a novel about the English Civil War of the seventeenth century, with an interesting depiction of Oliver Cromwell. In *Cerise* the author moved from backgrounds he knew well to write a novel about France and the court of Louis XIV. In *The Gladiators* and *Sarchedon* appear the times and deeds of exotic countries, the former being laid in Rome and Palestine and the latter depicting Egypt and Assyria under the rule of Semiramis. Perhaps the best of Whyte-Melville's historical novels, from one standpoint, is *Katerfelto,* the story of a famous horse of eighteenth century England.

Whyte-Melville did not write to earn money, and most of his income from his books was spent in charitable activity, especially among the poor people who were hangers-on about stables. In non-fiction, as in his novels and his charity, Whyte-Melville illustrated his love of horses with *Riding Recollections* (1875). Of his personal life little is known except that it was not happy with respect to marriage. Whyte-Melville met his death in the hunting field in White Horse Vale, Berkshire, on December 5, 1878, when one of his favorite horses stumbled and fell while at a gallop, throwing his rider and killing him instantly.

BIBLIOGRAPHICAL REFERENCES: There are interesting essays on Whyte-Melville in Lewis Melville's *Victorian Novelists*, 1906, and in *The Eighteen-sixties*, edited by John Drinkwater, 1932. See also Ernest A. Baker, *History of the English Novel*, Vol. VII, 1936.

OSCAR WILDE

Born: Dublin, Ireland
Date: October 15, 1856

Died: Paris, France
Date: November 30, 1900

PRINCIPAL WORKS

PLAYS: *Vera, or the Nihilists*, 1882; *The Duchess of Padua*, 1884; *A Florentine Tragedy*, 1885; *Lady Windermere's Fan*, 1892; *Salome*, 1893; *A Woman of No Importance*, 1893; *An Ideal Husband*, 1895; *The Importance of Being Earnest*, 1895.

NOVEL: *The Picture of Dorian Gray*, 1891.

TALES AND SKETCHES: *The Happy Prince and Other Tales*, 1888; *Lord Arthur Savile's Crime*, 1891; *A House of Pomegranates*, 1891.

POEMS: *Poems*, 1881; *The Sphinx*, 1894; *The Ballad of Reading Gaol*, 1898.

ESSAYS AND STUDIES: *Intentions*, 1891; *The Soul of Man Under Socialism*, 1891; *De Profundis*, 1905.

One of the most famous of Irish expatriates, Oscar (Fingal O'Flahertie Wills) Wilde, second son of Sir William Robert Wills Wilde and Jane Francisca Elgee Wilde, best known as "Speranza" of political fame, was born in Dublin, October 15, 1856. Early noted for his brilliance and sloth, characteristics he carried with him throughout life, he won prizes at the Portora Royal School in Ennis Killen, and later in Trinity College, Dublin. But it was in London that he first distinguished himself, although he had acquired fame at Magdalen College, Oxford, for his prize-winning poem "Ravenna" (1878) and as the most famous student of a famous master, John Ruskin.

As the leader of the Art-for-Art's-Sake school of aesthetics, Wilde was associated with his famous symbols: a peacock feather, sunflowers, dados, blue china, long hair, and velveteen breeches. A slight stigma was attached to his name even before his graduation from Oxford in 1878, but Wilde preached the doctrine that he did not care what was said as long as he was talked about. He was lampooned in cartoons, in novels, and even in comic opera; but he remained for years the center of attention, the lion of the hour, the most sought after of many famous talkers. His talents were conceded to be great by Shaw, Harris, Whistler, and, of course, Wilde himself. Even his early effusions in such magazines as *Month*, *The Catholic Mirror*, and the *Irish Monthly* were considered witty, artistic, and accomplished.

In a sense, his fortune was made in America where he lectured in the early 1880's and where his first play, *Vera*, was produced with fair success. His outrageous affectations and witty sayings and paradoxes were eagerly followed by everyone. Certainly this triumphant tour prepared England better to accept his later and best works. In 1884 his marriage to Constance Lloyd allayed somewhat the scabrous gossip of his deprecators. In fact, there seems little evidence for his homosexuality at this time. Only through hearsay and the later Wilde apologia, *De Profundis,* published posthumously in 1905, is there evidence of the depths of degradation to which he later sank. In direct contrast was his delicate language; no one ever heard him utter an oath or make an off-color remark.

Wilde's picture of the successive stages of degradation in man was openly presented in the character of Dorian Gray, who remained young outwardly while his pact with evil allowed his portrait to take on his many sins. Later Wilde's drama *Salome* aroused Philistines everywhere. Some of his poems, read at his famous trials, also caused much tongue-wagging which finally culminated in the Marquis of Queensberry's attack and Wilde's ill-advised slander suit against Lord Alfred Douglas' father. The reversal of this libel case caused Oscar Wilde to spend two years (1895–1897) in the Old Bailey and Reading Gaol, an experience which he immortalized in his famous poem. Much comment has been made on this work, regarded by many as a notable statement against man's inhumanity to man.

Many of the unsavory aspects of Wilde's personal life have been forgotten, but his witty paradoxes remain alive, especially in the plays, for his real reputation rests on his witty comedies of manners. *Lady Windermere's Fan* is a kind of moral tract with the fan used to turn public feeling from a compromising situation; in this case the mother takes on the sins of the daughter in order to prevent the daughter from making a mistake in decorum. As in all the plays, the epigrams are more noteworthy than the plot, especially in *The Importance of Being Earnest,* his last, best, and most popular drama. A *Woman of No Importance* protests the double standard, while *An Ideal Husband* suggests the old ways are best: the way to have an ideal husband is to be an ideal, old-fashioned wife. None of these plays can stand beside the work of Congreve or even Sheridan, but they keep the stream of comedy flowing from the eighteenth century into the twentieth century of Maugham and Coward.

After his release from prison, Wilde lived out a miserable few years on the Continent, estranged from his wife, cut off from his friends, always short of funds. During this time he wrote (and rewrote previously published works) under the assumed name of Sebastian Melmoth. He died at the Hôtel d'Alcace in Paris on November 30, 1900, his death still shrouding the mystery, revulsion, and untruth which colored most of his life and a great deal of his legend.

BIBLIOGRAPHICAL REFERENCES: Wilde's *Works* were published in 14 vols. in 1908. Richard Aldington edited the *Selected Works,* 1946. The standard bibliography is R. E. Cowan and William Andrews Clark, Jr., *The Library of William Andrews Clark: Wilde and Wildeiana,* 5 vols., 1922–1931. For years the standard biography was Frank Harris, *Oscar Wilde; His Life and Confessions,* 2 vols., 1916, which also contains *Memories of Oscar Wilde* by G. B. Shaw; but this work is now superseded by Hesketh Pearson, *Oscar Wilde: His Life and Wit*, 1946. V. B. Holland has made a unique contribution to biographical data in *Son of Oscar Wilde*, 1954. Critical works include Vincent O'Sullivan, *Aspects of Wilde*, 1936; Frances Winwar, *Oscar Wilde and the Yellow 'Nineties*, 1942; Edouard Roditi, *Oscar Wilde*, 1947; George Woodcock, *The Paradox of Oscar Wilde*, 1949; and St. John Ervine, *Oscar Wilde: A Present Time Appraisal*, 1951. An important brief study is Eric Bentley's essay in *The Playwright as Thinker*, 1946. Other critical articles are the chapter on Wilde in Archibald Henderson, *Interpreters of Life and the Modern Spirit*, 1911; Hugh Kingsmill, "The Intelligent Man's Guide to Wilde," *Fortnightly Review*, CL (1938), 296–303; A. H. Nethercot, "Oscar Wilde and the Devil's Advocate," *Publications of the Modern Language Association*, LIX (1944), 833–850; and Edouard Roditi, "Oscar Wilde's Poetry as Art History," *Poetry*, LXVII (1945), 322–337.

THORNTON WILDER

Born: Madison, Wisconsin
Date: April 17, 1897

PRINCIPAL WORKS

NOVELS: *The Cabala*, 1926; *The Bridge of San Luis Rey*, 1927; *The Woman of Andros*, 1930; *Heaven's My Destination*, 1934; *The Ides of March*, 1948.

PLAYS: *The Angel That Troubled the Waters and Other Plays*, 1928; *The Long Christmas Dinner and Other Plays*, 1931; *Our Town*, 1938; *The Merchant of Yonkers*, 1939; *The Skin of Our Teeth*, 1942; *The Matchmaker*, 1955 (revised from *The Merchant of Yonkers*).

Thornton (Niven) Wilder is a writer whose work displays individual qualities of wit, imaginaton, and careful workmanship, all combined with beauty and precision of style. As a novelist and playwright he has always followed his own course, even in decades when the literary current was flowing in quite different channels, such as naturalism, reportage, social documentation. Among the veering trends by which his contemporaries have reacted to the special concerns of our time, his work takes root in the humaneness and restraint of a classical tradition. A literary figure of some distinction in his own right, he has also been a teacher of students on both sides of the Atlantic, and in this role he has helped to create a cultural link between the Old World and the New.

Wilder was born in Madison, Wisconsin, on April 17, 1897, the son of Amos P. Wilder, who was at that time editor of the *Wisconsin State Journal*. When he was nine, he accompanied his family to China, where his father was consul general at Hong Kong and Shanghai. This was the first of a series of wanderings and international contacts which have in part shaped the outward pattern of his life and the inward habit of detached observation characteristic of his novels and plays. He finished high school in California and in 1915 entered Oberlin College, only to leave that school two years later for service in the Coast Artillery Corps during World War I. After the war he transferred to Yale, received his B.A. degree in 1920, studied for a year at the American Academy in Rome, and in 1921 became an instructor in a preparatory school at

Lawrenceville, New Jersey. In 1926 he received his M.A. degree from Princeton.

In the same year he published his first novel, *The Cabala,* the gracefully written story of a young American in postwar Rome and his contacts with a group of talented and wealthy aristocrats who exert a mysterious influence on affairs of state and Church. Drawn into their secret confidences and councils, he sees them at last for what they are: the pagan gods of Europe grown old and unable, in spite of their ancient wisdom, to save themselves from the sufferings and follies of ordinary humanity. With a great leap in time and space, Wilder's imagination moved to Colonial Peru for his second novel, *The Bridge of San Luis Rey,* a brief but evocative retelling of events in five lives snuffed out in the collapse of a bridge on the road between Lima and Cuzco. The stories are beautifully told; not without irony, Wilder seeks to discover the working of a providential plan in the disaster, and only at the end does the reader perceive that his characters represent in their different persons the bitterness, innocence, sorrow, and humility of love. Some critics, noting his use of the celebrated French letter writer, Madame de Sévigné, as the model for one of his characters, suggested that there was a strong element of pastiche in Wilder's writing. It is, in fact, an open secret that Wilder's mind often finds imaginative stimulus in a forgotten nineteenth century play, in Roman histories, in work as modern as James Joyce's *Finnegan's Wake.* What his critics minimize, however, is Wilder's own note, his detached but not unkind gaze to which he subjects the materials toward which his mind and im-

agination have turned. Thus his third novel, *The Woman of Andros,* is more than a story based on the *Andria* of Terence; it is another probing into hidden meanings in human experience, presented through man's blundering impulses toward truth in a twilight age that waited for the birth of a great faith.

Although Wilder's sources are usually "literary," his manipulation of them is not pedantic; he displays in whatever he touches the same sure craftsmanship and the working of a mind enlivened by considerable imagination and wit. In *Heaven's My Destination* he took the pattern of the picaresque novel and imposed on it a new subject matter, evangelistic activity in the Middle West, so that the story of George Brush becomes the amusing yet touching saga of a cornfed Faithful and his travels through a modern Vanity Fair. *The Ides of March,* epistolary in form, takes for its subject events in the closing years of Julius Caesar's life; unlike the usual popular historical novel, however, this book represents full knowledge of a past period and full imaginative and artistic domination over it.

The same note of controlled experimentation sounds in Wilder's plays. His two most noteworthy, *Our Town* and *The Skin of Our Teeth,* are at once experimental and derivative in form; we can trace his progress toward these efforts in the one-act plays and dramatic character sketches written during his Lawrenceville years and collected in *The Angel That Troubled the Waters* and *The Long Christmas Dinner. Our Town* is the account of life in a New England village, but it is acted out on a bare stage, much in the manner of

1160

Oriental drama, and the lack of furnishings such as those which clutter the modern stage becomes an effective device in centering attention upon events which make this play a morality drama revealing the religious feeling that underlies Wilder's best work. *The Skin of Our Teeth* takes elements from Joyce and European expressionism and tells, in terms of the trials and temptations of one household, of the full course of human history on the planet. But beneath this surface diversity Wilder's own note persists, the point of view of the wise observer who is not involved in what he sees but who does not, for that reason, despise what he is observing in the failures and triumphs of mankind. The play became a subject of literary controversy

when critics pointed out his debt to Joyce, but much of this curious critical flurry was negated by the fact that Joyce had in turn borrowed from the theories of Giovanni Battista Vico, eighteenth century Italian philosopher, in the writing of *Finnegan's Wake*.

Wilder's intellectual history lies open to view in his novels and plays. During World War II he served as a combat-intelligence officer with the Air Force in Italy. He has taught at the University of Chicago and at Harvard and has given special courses of lectures before various universities and learned societies throughout Europe. His most recent work is *The Matchmaker*, a revised version of *The Merchant of Yonkers*, first presented in 1939.

BIBLIOGRAPHICAL REFERENCES: There is no biography or bibliography of Wilder as yet. Three of his novels were reprinted in the *Thornton Wilder Trio*, 1956, for which Malcolm Cowley wrote a discerning and helpful preface. For criticism see Edmund Wilson, *Classics and Commercials*, 1950, and *Shores of Light*, 1952; Pierre Loving. "The Bridge of Casuistry," *This Quarter*, II (1929), 150–161; E. G. Twitchett, "Thornton Wilder," *London Mercury*, XXII (1930), 32–39; Robert McNamara, "Phases of American Religion in Thornton Wilder and Willa Cather," *Catholic World*, CXXXV (1932), 641–649; E. K. Brown, "A Christian Humanist, Thornton Wilder," *University of Toronto Quarterly*, IV (1935), 356–370; Dayton Kohler, "Thornton Wilder," *English Journal*, XXVIII (1939), 1–11; Martin Gardner, "Thornton Wilder and the Problem of Providence," *University of Kansas City Review*, VII (1940), 83–91; J. J. Firebaugh, "The Humanism of Thornton Wilder," *Pacific Spectator*, IV (1950), 426–438; and Arthur H. Ballet, " 'In Our Living and in Our Dying,' " *English Journal*, XLV (1956), 243–249. For a Marxian view of Wilder see also Michael Gold, "Wilder: Prophet of the Genteel Christ," *New Republic*, LXIV (1930), 266, and "The Economic Interpretation of Wilder," *ibid.*, LXV (1930), 31–32.

TENNESSEE WILLIAMS

Born: Columbus, Mississippi
Date: March 26, 1914

PRINCIPAL WORKS

PLAYS: *American Blues*, 1939, 1948; *Battle of Angels*, 1940; *The Glass Menagerie*, 1945; *You Touched Me!*, 1945 (with Donald Windham); *27 Wagons Full of Cotton*, 1946, 1953; *A Streetcar Named Desire*, 1947; *Summer and Smoke*, 1948; *The*

Rose Tattoo, 1951; *I Rise in Flame, Cried the Phoenix,* 1951; *Camino Real,* 1953; *Cat on a Hot Tin Roof,* 1955; *Orpheus Descending,* 1957.
NOVEL: *The Roman Spring of Mrs. Stone,* 1950.
SHORT STORIES: *One Arm and Other Stories,* 1948; *Hard Candy, a Book of Stories,* 1954.
POEMS: *Five Young American Poets,* 1939; *In the Winter of Cities,* 1956.

When *The Glass Menagerie* became the hit of the 1945 Broadway season, it was evident that America had in Tennessee Williams a playwright of new sensibility. For here he suffused the naturalism of his St. Louis upbringing with a rare theater poetry. It was also evident, and has become increasingly so, that he was a writer of the South, largely symbolized in the fading beauty and neuroses of its womanhood.

Born Thomas Lanier Williams in his grandfather's rectory in Columbus, Mississippi, on March 26, 1914, Williams has led a peripatetic life after the fashion of his shoe-salesman father. His youth consisted of aborted academic stands at the universities of Iowa and Washington and odd jobs from Florida to California; today, in well-heeled security, he still moves restlessly from Key West to Rome to New Orleans, his favorite city.

Williams' first recognition came in 1939 when his collection of one-act plays, *American Blues,* received a Group Theatre award. In 1940 the Theatre Guild backed an ill-starred production of *Battle of Angels.* Although the play never got past third-act trouble and censorship in Boston, its early demise failed to check Williams' certain but uneven career as a playwright.

The success of *The Glass Menagerie* was followed immediately by a tepid merger of Shaw and D. H. Lawrence, otherwise a vital influence upon Williams, in *You Touched Me!,* done in collaboration with Donald Windham. Two years later *A Streetcar Named Desire* brought to the stage that great portrayal of female psychosis Blanche Dubois, somewhat after the image of Strindberg's *Miss Julie,* and carried Williams' name around the world. An earlier play, *Summer and Smoke,* finally found its proper medium in the arena style and revealed Williams' fine ear for the Southern idiom.

Having examined Italianate love in *The Roman Spring of Mrs. Stone,* his only novel, Williams juxtaposed the fiery Sicilian temperament against a Gulf of Mexico sterility in *The Rose Tattoo,* a lurid, uncertain play compounded of sex and ashes. In *Camino Real,* Williams created a canvas of desiccation and despair, brilliantly theatrical but immature in its symbolism. In *Cat on a Hot Tin Roof* Williams returned to the Mississippi Delta to deal in sexual ambiguity and the decay of plantation power. Here, as so often before, the conjunctive talents of Williams as writer and Elia Kazan as director resulted in a swift, brilliant production, the "achievement of continual flow," as they called it. Their collaboration on the film *Baby Doll* (1956) accomplished a fine fusion of social protest and lingering affection for the South.

By revising *Battle of Angels* into the *Orpheus Descending* of 1957, Williams again displayed what is perhaps his greatest theatrical talent, the capacity for incessant revision, a revision which always advances into a new poetry of the theater.

BIBLIOGRAPHICAL REFERENCES: There is no full-length biographical or critical study. For discussion of Williams' work in books and periodicals are John Gassner, "Tennessee Williams: Dramatist of Frustration," *College English*, X (October 1948), 1–7; and *passim., The Theatre in Our Times*, 1954; Joseph Wood Krutch, *"Modernism" in Modern Drama*, 1953; Paul Moor, "A Mississippian Named Tennessee," *Harper's*, CXCVIII (1948), 63–71; David Sievers, *Freud on Broadway*, 1955; C. N. Stavrou, "The Neurotic Heroine in Tennessee Williams," *Literature and Psychology*, V (1955), 26–34; Kenneth Tynan, "American Blues: The Plays of Arthur Miller and Tennessee Williams," *Encounter* (London), II (1954), 13–19; Richard B. Vowles, "Tennessee Williams och Strindberg," *Svenska Dagbladet* (Stockholm), April 11, 1956, 8–9; and A. B. Waters, "Tennessee Williams: Ten Years Later," *Theatre Arts Monthly*, XXXIX (1955), 72–73, 96.

WILLIAM CARLOS WILLIAMS

Born: Rutherford, New Jersey   *Died*: Rutherford, New Jersey
Date: September 17, 1883   *Date*: March 4, 1963

PRINCIPAL WORKS

POEMS: *Poems*, 1909; *The Tempers*, 1913; *Al Que Quiere!*, 1917; *Kora in Hell: Improvisations*, 1920; *Sour Grapes*, 1921; *Spring and All*, 1922; *Collected Poems, 1921–1931*, 1934; *An Early Martyr and Other Poems*, 1935; *Adam and Eve & the City*, 1936; *The Complete Collected Poems of William Carlos Williams, 1906–1938*, 1938; *The Broken Span*, 1941; *The Wedge*, 1944; *Paterson*, Book I, 1946; *The Clouds*, 1948; *Paterson*, Book II, 1948; *Paterson*, Book III, 1949; *Collected Later Poems*, 1950; *Paterson*, Book IV, 1951; *Collected Earlier Poems*, 1951; *The Desert Music and Other Poems*, 1954; *Journey to Love*, 1956.

NOVELS: *A Voyage to Pagany*, 1928; *White Mule*, 1937; *In the Money*, 1940; *The Build-Up*, 1952.

SHORT STORIES: *The Knife of the Times*, 1932; *Life Along the Passaic River*, 1938; *Make Light of It: Collected Stories*, 1950.

ESSAYS AND BELLES-LETTRES: *The Great American Novel*, 1923; *In the American Grain*, 1925; *A Novelette and Other Prose*, 1932; *Selected Essays of William Carlos Williams*, 1954.

AUTOBIOGRAPHY: *The Autobiography of William Carlos Williams*, 1951.

LETTERS: *The Selected Letters of William Carlos Williams*, 1957.

William Carlos Williams, the New Jersey doctor who has become one of America's leading contemporary poets, was born on September 17, 1883, in Rutherford, New Jersey, where he practiced medicine from 1910 until his retirement in 1951. He received his preparatory education in Geneva and his M.D. from the University of Penn-sylvania. He did graduate work in pediatrics at the University of Leipzig. He has been writing all his adult life, and his first volume, *Poems*, was published in 1909. His long career as doctor and poet has been crowned by the receipt of many honors and awards. He received the Russell Loines Memorial Award of the National Insti-

1163

tute of Arts and Letters in 1948 and the National Book Award for Poetry in 1950. He was named a fellow of the Library of Congress in 1949 and in 1952 was appointed consultant in poetry to the Library, although objections to his politics prevented him from ever occupying the post. In 1953 he shared the Yale University Library's Bollingen Prize for 1952 with Archibald MacLeish. He holds honorary degrees from the University of Buffalo, Rutgers University, Bard College, and the University of Pennsylvania.

Williams' early poems gave litle indication of the kind of work which would make him famous later. The poems in *The Tempers,* an early volume, are heavily influenced by Yeats, Joyce, and the Imagists. Conventional in rhyme and verse pattern, they are filled with mythological and classical allusions. In the *Transitional* (1915) poems, however, Williams' characteristic free-verse form began to develop, with its short, sharp lines, colloquial speech, and rhythms arbitrarily molded to the accents of contemporary speech. Equally important was Williams' change in choice of subject matter; from a concentration on mythology and the past he turned to an intense concentration on the world he knew and lived in, and began his lifelong poetic search for the universals of human existence among the minutiae of everyday urban life. In *Al Que Quiere!* and in his "Pastorals" of city streets and back yards these changes became increasingly evident.

During the 1920's and 1930's Williams continued to write the numerous short poems which formed the *Complete Collected Poems,* and which show an ever-increasing concern with structural movement and with the inseparability of image and thought. Although sometimes marred by the opacity which his friend Ezra Pound encouraged, Williams' poems of this period are enhanced by their vivid and dynamic imagery, sometimes even going to extremes of onomatopoeia and visual patterns on the page.

Between 1928 and 1952 Williams wrote four novels: *A Voyage to Pagany, White Mule, In the Money,* and *The Build-Up.* He has also written short stories and essays. Perhaps his most important book of prose is *In the American Grain,* a minor masterpiece in which he re-creates a living American tradition from the historical figures of the national past. His prose, while casual and colloquial and sometimes even slangy, is warm and vital in the love of humanity it expresses. But it is in the realm of poetry that Williams excels as an artist, and his long poem *Paterson,* published in four books between 1946 and 1951, is the culmination of his artistic skill and sensitivity. In this poem, which has been called Williams' personal epic, he writes about what he knows best, seeking "in the particular to discover the universal." Writing about a city and a world he has been observing all his life, he seems to share Walt Whitman's ability to weave descriptions of ordinary people and commonplace incidents into a saga of American life itself. It is an older and sadder America than Whitman saw, but still worthy of the love which Williams, despite his occasional precise and biting social criticism, offers it in the creation of his masterpiece.

BIBLIOGRAPHICAL REFERENCES: There is no definitive edition of the poems. In addition to the volumes of collected verse listed under Williams' principal works, he has also published *Collected Later Poetry of William Carlos Williams,* 1950, and *Collected Earlier Poems,* 1951. The four books of *Paterson* were printed in a single volume in 1951.

For biographical information see his *Autobiography,* 1951. The most authoritative critical study is Vivienne Koch, *William Carlos Williams,* 1950. For criticism in books and periodicals see, further, Paul Rosenfeld, *Port of New York,* 1924; Yvor Winters, *Primitivism and Decadence,* 1937; Carl Rakosi, "William Carlos Williams," *Symposium,* IV (1933), 439–447; Ruth Lechlitner, "The Poetry of William Carlos Williams," *Poetry,* LIV (1939), 326–335; Vivienne Koch, "William Carlos Williams: The Man and the Poet," *Kenyon Review,* XIV (1952), 502–510; Sister M. Bernetta Quinn, "William Carlos Williams: A Testament of Perpetual Change," *Publications of the Modern Language Association,* LXX (1955), 292–322—the most comprehensive discussion of *Paterson* to date; and Frank Thompson, "The Symbolic Structure of *Paterson,*" *Western Review,* XIX (1955), 285–293.

OWEN WISTER

Born: Philadelphia, Pennsylvania *Died:* North Kingstown, Rhode Island
Date: July 14, 1860 *Date:* July 21, 1938

Principal Works

NOVELS: *The Dragon of Wantley,* 1892; *The Virginian,* 1902; *Lady Baltimore,* 1906.

SHORT STORIES: *Red Men and White,* 1896; *Lin McLean,* 1898; *The Jimmyjohn Boss and Other Stories,* 1900; *Philosophy 4,* 1903; *Padre Ignacio,* 1911; *When West Was West,* 1928.

BIOGRAPHY: *Ulysses S. Grant,* 1900; *The Seven Ages of Washington,* 1907; *Roosevelt: The Story of a Friendship, 1880–1919,* 1930.

Owen Wister, born in Philadelphia, Pennsylvania, on July 14, 1860, began his career with a serious interest in music and only later became interested in writing. After being educated in private schools in the United States and abroad, he attended Harvard University, where he was graduated with highest honors in music in 1882. He then spent two years abroad, studying composition in Paris before ill health forced his return to the United States. Following a period as the employee of a bank in New York City, he suffered a nervous breakdown and traveled to Wyoming to recuperate in the healthful atmosphere of a Western cattle ranch. From 1885 to 1888 he attended the Harvard Law School. After gradu-

ation he was admitted to the bar and practiced law in Philadelphia.

Having grown extremely fond of the West while recuperating from his illness, Wister made frequent trips back to his favorite country. Two short stories based on western life, "Hank's Woman" (1891) and "How Lin McLean Went West" (1891), published in *Harper's Magazine,* were his first published literary works to gain recognition. Such volumes as *Red Men and White* and *The Jimmyjohn Boss* followed. In the meantime, Wister was married to Mary Channing, of Philadelphia, in 1898.

Wister's only well-known novel, *The Virginian,* was enough to make him famous. The book was a best seller for

1165

years, and succeeding generations have discovered this pioneer "Western" to their delight. The volume was dedicated to another outdoorsman and lover of the West, Theodore Roosevelt, who was a close friend of Owen Wister. One of the men who illustrated an edition of *The Virginian* was Frederic Remington, the famous painter of life in the West. Owen Wister continued to write, and he explored other themes than the West, but his other works were never widely accepted, largely because of their subject matter. *Philosophy 4*, for example, was a story about life at Harvard University, with limited appeal to general readers. *Lady Baltimore* is his one venture into the field of historical romance.

In the years after World War I, Wister wrote little. His last book was *Roosevelt: The Story of a Friendship*. He died of a cerebral hemorrhage at North Kingstown, Rhode Island, July 21, 1938.

BIBLIOGRAPHICAL REFERENCES: The collected edition is *The Writings of Owen Wister*, 11 vols., 1928, which includes writings previously unpublished in book form. There is no full-scale study of Wister, but a fair and economical estimate is Jay B. Hubbell, "Owen Wister's Work," *South Atlantic Quarterly*, XXIX (1930), 440–443. Two opposing views of Wister's career are E. C. Marsh, "Representative American Story Tellers: Owen Wister," *Bookman*, XXVII (1908), 456–548; and H. W. Boynton, "A Word on the Genteel Critic: Owen Wister's Quack Novels and Democracy," *Dial*, LIX (1915), 303–306.

THOMAS WOLFE

Born: Asheville, North Carolina
Date: October 3, 1900

Died: Baltimore, Maryland
Date: September 15, 1938

PRINCIPAL WORKS

NOVELS: *Look Homeward, Angel*, 1929; *Of Time and the River*, 1935; *The Web and the Rock*, 1939; *You Can't Go Home Again*, 1940.

SHORT STORIES: *From Death to Morning*, 1935; *The Hills Beyond*, 1941.

PLAYS: *The Return of Buck Gavin*, 1924 (in *Carolina Folk-Plays: Second Series*, edited by Frederick H. Koch); *Mannerhouse*, 1948.

BELLES-LETTRES: *The Story of a Novel*, 1936.

LETTERS: *Thomas Wolfe's Letters to His Mother*, edited by J. S. Terry, 1943; *The Letters of Thomas Wolfe*, edited by Elizabeth Nowell, 1956.

MISCELLANEOUS: *A Note on Experts*, 1939; *Gentlemen of the Press*, 1942; *A Western Journal*, 1951.

Thomas (Clayton) Wolfe was born October 3, 1900, in Asheville, North Carolina. He was the youngest child in the family, with older brothers and sisters. His father, W. O. Wolfe, was a stonecutter who had been born in central Pennsylvania and who went south to live soon after the Civil War. His mother was Julia Westall, of Asheville. Wolfe was educated in public schools until he was twelve, when he was entered at the North State School under the direction of Mr. and Mrs. J. M. Roberts. Attending school here until graduation (1912–1916), he entered the University of North Carolina (1916–1920). His stay at Chapel Hill was maturing and exciting; he stood well in his classes, became interested in the Carolina Playmakers and wrote plays of his own in which he acted, and became one of the most popular and outstanding figures on the campus of his time. Encouraged by Professor Frederick H. Koch of the Playmakers, Wolfe decided to do graduate work at Harvard in George Pierce Baker's 47 Dramatic Workshop, and to make playwriting his career.

He remained three years at Harvard, two of them as student, taking his A.M. degree in 1922, and hoping to place at least one of his plays for Broadway production. During his years at Harvard, his father died, and Wolfe accepted a teaching appointment as instructor in English at New York University. He began teaching in February, 1924.

Soon afterward he was diverted from playwriting to fiction. *Look Homeward, Angel* was started in England in 1924, when Wolfe made his first visit abroad; it was finished in 1928, placed by Madeleine Boyd with Maxwell Perkins, managing editor of Scribner's, and published in October, 1929. The book was generally well received; only at home in North Carolina were the reactions antagonistic. The turmoil occasioned by *Look Homeward, Angel* in his home town hurt Wolfe; he was naïvely surprised that his novel should be so patently recognized for what it was, a very thinly disguised autobiography, and he avoided a return to Asheville until the year before his death.

Recognition came slowly for Wolfe, but surely. In 1930, in his address of acceptance of the Nobel Prize for literature, Sinclair Lewis paid Wolfe tribute on the basis of his only book, *Look Homeward, Angel,* and prophesied a great future for the younger novelist. In the meantime Wolfe was working on a second novel, a continuation of the story of Eugene Gant, which was published in 1935 as *Of Time and the River*. Although equally autobiographical, *Of Time and the River* stirred no local animosities in Asheville, perhaps because the scenes of the book were removed to Boston, New York, and Europe. In the summer of 1935 Wolfe was invited to speak at a writers' conference at Boulder, Colorado, where he delivered a series of lectures which became an account of the writer's craft and which was published the following year as *The Story of a Novel*. Also published in 1935 were the sketches and short stories called *From Death to Morning*.

By 1937 Wolfe had come to a momentous decision with himself: he had smarted from criticism and gossip which suggested too much dependence upon the guiding editorship of Maxwell Perkins, and so Wolfe decided to change publishers and become "far more objective in his approach to fiction." He signed a new contract with Harper and Brothers, and delivered to his new editor the continuing development of "the book," a work in progress incorporating some changes which Wolfe mistakenly believed to be much greater than they actually were. "The book"—Wolfe's name for the constantly accumulating manuscript of his writings—was still the story of Eugene Gant-Thomas Wolfe. Now, however, the chief protagonist was renamed George Webber, and he varied somewhat in physical appearance and family background from Eugene Gant, but the other circumstances were much the same. In 1937 Wolfe returned to Asheville to find himself recognized as famous and forgiven for the shock of *Look Homeward, Angel;* but other things had also changed, and Wolfe, the man, like Gant-Webber, the character, discovered that "You can't go home again."

In the Spring of 1938 Wolfe was invited to lecture at Purdue University. From there he started on a trip to the Far West, stopping at Denver and making a great sweep through the National Park country. In Seattle he was ill with a cold, locally diagnosed as pneumonia; he was removed to a hospital and his brother Fred was called West to attend him. When his condition grew worse, Fred Wolfe was joined by his sister, Mrs. Mabel Wheaton. Consulting physicians suspected a brain tumor; certainly an operation was indicated. The family conference determined that any operation should be done at Johns Hopkins, in Baltimore, and there Wolfe was brought in August. The operation revealed multiple tuberculosis of the brain. Wolfe never came out of the coma which followed the operation, and he died in Baltimore on September 15, 1938, less than a month before his thirty-eighth birthday. His body was taken to Asheville for burial; only in death could the wanderer "go home again."

Wolfe's third and fourth novels, *The Web and the Rock* and *You Can't Go Home Again,* were readied for posthumous publication by Edward C. Aswell, Wolfe's editor and personal friend at Harper. The novels added stature to Wolfe's increasing position as a major writer, and brought his fictional work to a reasonable conclusion. In 1941 appeared *The Hills Beyond,* another series of short stories and sketches, and "The Hills Beyond," a fragmentary and incomplete novel introducing some of the Gant-Webber family members of an earlier time in the Carolina mountains. *Mannerhouse,* a play first written by Wolfe during his stay at Harvard, appeared in published form in 1948. His *Letters to His Mother* came out in 1943. *The Letters of Thomas Wolfe,* collected and edited by his literary agent, Elizabeth Nowell, appeared in 1956; these letters constitute what amounts to an autobiography.

Before his death Thomas Wolfe was already becoming a legend. Everything about him was greater than life-size. He was six feet five inches tall; his capacities for vividly rendering sense impressions and physical appetites and energies were widely known and praised; his books confirmed the statement of the American Dream better than it had been expressed since Walt Whitman, and characters of his fiction had already entered general allusive consciousness. He is still a controversial figure, but his popularity seems to continue growing and to encourage new studies and new converts.

BIBLIOGRAPHICAL REFERENCES: There is no authorized biography. Herbert J. Muller, *Thomas Wolfe,* 1947, is the pioneer critical study. Other biographical and critical studies include Pamela Hansford Johnson, *Thomas Wolfe: A Critical Study,* 1947 [*Hungry Gulliver: An English Critical Appraisal*]; Agatha B. Adams, *Thomas Wolfe: Carolina Student,* 1950; Daniel L. Delakas, *Thomas Wolfe: La France et les romanciers français,* 1950; T. C. Pollock and Oscar Cargill, *Thomas Wolfe at Washington*

Square, 1954; and Louis D. Rubin, Jr., *Thomas Wolfe: The Weather of His Youth*, 1955. Related materials are found in Hayden Norwood, *The Marble Man's Wife*, 1947; and Maxwell Perkins, *Editor to Author: The Letters of Maxwell E. Perkins*, edited by John Hall Wheelock, 1950; and T. C. Pollock and Oscar Cargill, eds., *The Correspondence of Thomas Wolfe and Homer Andrew Watts*, 1954.

For articles on Wolfe in books see Herbert J. Muller, *Modern Fiction: A Study of Values*, 1937; Joseph Warren Beach, *American Fiction, 1920–1940*, 1941; Maxwell Geismar, *Writers in Crisis*, 1942; Alfred Kazin, *On Native Grounds*, 1942; George Snell, *Shapers of American Fiction, 1798–1947*, 1947; E. B. Burgum, *The Novel and the World's Dilemma*, 1947; F. J. Hoffman, *The Modern Novel in America, 1900–1950*, 1951; Gerald S. Sloyan, "Thomas Wolfe: A Legend of a Man's Youth in His Hunger," in *Fifty Years of the American Novel*, edited by Harold C. Gardiner, 1952; and Louis D. Rubin, Jr., "Thomas Wolfe in Time and Place," in *Southern Renascence*, edited by Rubin and Robert D. Jacobs, 1953.

See also Hamilton Basso, "Thomas Wolfe: A Portrait," *New Republic*, LXXXVII (1936), 199–202; Dayton Kohler, "Thomas Wolfe: Prodigal and Lost," *College English*, I (1939), 1–10; William Braswell, "Thomas Wolfe Lectures and Takes a Holiday," *ibid.*, 11–22; John Peale Bishop, "The Sorrows of Thomas Wolfe," *Kenyon Review*, I (1939), 7–17; Henry T. Volkening, "Thomas Wolfe: Penance No More," *Virginia Quarterly Review*, XV (1939), 196–215; E. K. Brown: "Thomas Wolfe: Realist and Symbolist," *University of Toronto Quarterly*, X (1941), 153–166; John M. Maclachan, "Folk Concepts in the Novels of Thomas Wolfe," *Southern Folklore Quarterly*, IX (1945), 28–36; Margaret Church, "Thomas Wolfe: Dark Time," *Publications of the Modern Language Association*, LXIV (1949), 629–638; and Betty Thompson, "Thomas Wolfe: Two Decades of Criticism," *South Atlantic Quarterly*, LXIX (1950), 378–392.

The Portable Thomas Wolfe, 1946, contains an excellent introduction by Maxwell Geismar.

WOLFRAM VON ESCHENBACH

Born: Eschenbach, Germany
Date: c. 1170

Died: Eschenbach
Date: c. 1220

PRINCIPAL WORKS

CHIVALRIC ROMANCES: *Parzival*, c. 1200; *Willehalm*, c. 1212.

Few facts are known about Wolfram von Eschenbach, the strongest personality of the thirteenth century epic poets writing in Middle High German. Born in Eschenbach, Germany, about 1170, he was a member of a noble Bavarian family, apparently impoverished, as he says jestingly in his poetry. Many scholars claim that he was a younger son. He served powerful overlords, like the counts of Wertheim and the Landgrave Hermann of Thüringia.

His feats of sword and spear are subjects for his boasting, rather than his poetry. He mentions being unlettered, yet the French *chanson de geste La Bataille d'Aliscans* was his source for *Willehalm* and French originals inspired much of his other poetry. His own contributions were the acute observation, deep psychology, broad toleration, and sense of humor found in his work.

Greatest of his poems is *Parzival*, a

romance of 25,000 lines believed to have been composed between 1200 and 1212. Its popularity is proved by the fifteen complete manuscripts of the work still in existence. Wolfram accredited it to the troubadour Kyot le Provençal, who has never been identified. Its praise of noble marriage and its high moral tone may derive from the personality of the author. Wolfram was admired by all as a deeply religious man; in fact, one contemporary wrote a poem selecting him as the champion of Christianity against an evil enchanter. *Willehalm* deals also with a noble knight remarkable for his chivalrous treatment of the Saracens. This work, unfinished at Wolfram's death, was continued by Ulrich von Türkheim (fl. 1235–1250) and Ulrich von dem Türlin (fl. 1261–1270). *Titurel,* a third romance left only in fragments, was completed by one Albrecht about 1260.

When the landgrave died in 1216, Wolfram apparently left Wartburg Castle and returned to his native town, where he died about 1220. He was reported buried in the Church of Our Lady in Eschenbach, but the location of his grave has never been determined.

BIBLIOGRAPHICAL REFERENCES: For commentary and criticism in English see Margaret F. Richey, *Gahmuret Anschevin: A Contribution to the Study of Wolfram von Eschenbach,* 1923; *The Story of Parzifal,* 1935; and *Essays on the Mediaeval Love Lyric,* 1943. See also A. Schulz, *Parzifal Studien,* 3 vols, 1861–1862; Ernst E. Martin, *Zur Gralsage,* 1880; Samuel Singer, *Wolframs Willehalm,* 1918, and *Wolfram und der Graal,* 1939; and Kate Laserstein, *Wolfram von Eschenbach, germanische Sendung,* 1928.

VIRGINIA WOOLF

Born: London, England
Date: January 25, 1882

Died: Lewes, Sussex, England
Date: March 28, 1941

PRINCIPAL WORKS

NOVELS: *The Voyage Out,* 1915; *Night and Day,* 1919; *Jacob's Room,* 1922; *Mrs. Dalloway,* 1925; *To the Lighthouse,* 1927; *Orlando: A Biography,* 1928; *The Waves,* 1931; *The Years,* 1937; *Between the Acts,* 1941.

SHORT STORIES: *Kew Gardens,* 1919; *The Mark on the Wall,* 1919; *Monday or Tuesday,* 1921; *The Haunted House,* 1943.

LITERARY CRITICISM: *Mr. Bennett and Mrs. Brown,* 1924; *The Common Reader,* 1925; *The Common Reader: Second Series,* 1932 [*The Second Common Reader*].

ESSAYS AND STUDIES: *A Room of One's Own,* 1929; *Three Guineas,* 1938; *The Death of the Moth,* 1942; *The Moment and Other Essays,* 1947; *The Captain's Deathbed and Other Essays,* 1950.

BIOGRAPHY: *Flush: A Biography,* 1933; *Roger Fry: A Biography,* 1940.

JOURNALS: *A Writer's Diary,* 1953.

The greatest woman novelist of this century was born Adeline Virginia Stephen in London on January 25, 1882, the daughter of Sir Leslie Stephen, eminent editor, biographer, and critic. The youngest of eight children (four were half-brothers and sisters), Virginia was frail and found her education at home in her father's superb library. Reflections of these early years were to appear in her fiction: the close-knit family group, the brilliant and domineering father, the lovely and conciliating mother, all seen in London or at seasides resembling that of their Cornish summer home. Her mother's death in 1895 was a traumatic shock, but Virginia Stephen continued reading voluminously, studying Greek, and imitating the Elizabethan prose masters. Then, following Sir Leslie's death in 1904, Vanessa, Thoby, Virginia, and Adrian Stephen took a house in the Bloomsbury district. In 1905, however, Virginia suffered the first onslaught of the mental illness which was to recur during World War I. Two years later, after Vanessa's marriage and Thoby's tragic death, Virginia and Adrian took another house among a congenial set which included economist John Maynard Keynes, artist Roger Fry, biographer Lytton Strachey, and others who became associated with the Bloomsbury Group. Reviewing books and publishing essays and criticism, Virginia Stephen worked at her art. In 1912 she married Leonard Woolf, a journalist and political essayist. Sympathetic and protective, he encouraged her in her work.

Three years later, *The Voyage Out* appeared. This story of young Rachel Vinrace's South American voyage was conventional in technique and desultory in plot, but its sensitive treatment of Rachel's maturation, abruptly stopped by death, foreshadowed a rejection of conventional plot and realistic description. *Night and Day,* longer, more sure and solid, dealt specifically with Katherine Hilbery's find-

ing of the right fiancé and generally with a young woman's intellectual and emotional growth in an environment such as Virginia Woolf's own as a girl. Her new goals and experimental methods were indicated in *Monday or Tuesday* in 1921. Its eight sketches ranged from impressionistic creation of moods in short pieces to the use of symbolic imagery in longer ones. Still others attempted to convey through highly suggestive lyrical prose the sound of music and the quality of color. (This arresting book was published by the Hogarth Press. Founded by the Woolfs in 1917, it was to publish all her books as well as work by T. S. Eliot, E. M. Forster, and Sigmund Freud.) *Jacob's Room* used some of the devices of *Monday or Tuesday* in a novel built around the magnetic Jacob Flanders, modeled on Thoby Stephen. Here the author's interest in her characters lies principally in their relationship with Jacob as he grows into manhood and even after his death in World War I. Despite uncertain health, Virginia Woolf continued to produce literary criticism and essays. A number were collected in *The Common Reader: First Series* which appeared in 1925. She ranged from the Greeks to her contemporaries, writing as a sensitive critic who was also a creative artist.

In *Mrs. Dalloway* she explored her characters' streams-of-consciousness as she depicted twelve hours in the inner and outer life of a sensitive woman. Unlike Dorothy Richardson, she revealed the interior monologues of other characters besides the central one; unlike James Joyce, she presented these thoughts so as to avoid any seemingly chaotic effect. In 1927 came her finest achievement, *To The Lighthouse.* Plotless in the ordinary sense, like

Mrs. Dalloway, this story of the Ramsays was based on her childhood. Rich in image and symbol, it treated her favorite themes of love, marriage, time, and death. She combined experiment and lyricism in "Time Passes," an interlude describing the decay of the summer home in the seven years following Mrs. Ramsay's death. In *Orlando,* a dashing Elizabethan nobleman unaccountably changes into a woman during the Restoration and continues thus into the present. This pleasant fantasy, based on Vita Sackville-West's family, re-emphasized Mrs. Woolf's interest in the merging flow of time and experience. *A Room of One's Own* discussed fiction and women, protesting against the widespread discrimination women faced. Two years later Virginia Woolf published a novel that some said signalized the end of that form. *The Waves* comprised the impressionistic interior monologues of six characters from early childhood to old age. Separated by italicized lyrical descriptions of a seaside from dawn to dark, the book's sections traced the characters' developing natures, interaction, and relationship to a dominating character named Percival who resembled Jacob Flanders. Here again Virginia Woolf intended recurrent, interrelated images and symbols to impose the unity and coherence which Bennett and Galsworthy sought through conventional plotting, narration, and description.

The Common Reader: Second Series

was followed a year later by *Flush,* a pleasant little biography of a spaniel whose mistress, Elizabeth Barrett Browning, dominates the story. *The Years* was not stylized like *The Waves.* This overlong novel emphasized the flow of time by tracing the Pargiters' fortunes from 1880 to the present. *Three Guineas* returned sharply to Virginia Woolf's feminist concerns. *Roger Fry: A Biography,* although a sympathetic memoir, lacked the characteristic incandescence of her prose. Fry's death had deepened the shadows which, cast by ill health and the specter of war, were gathering around her. On March 28, 1941, she left her work table and walked across the fields of her Sussex home into the river Ouse to her death. A note revealed her fear of oncoming incurable madness. *Between the Acts,* a poetically evocative and symbolic book built around a country pageant spanning Britain's history, showed both her weariness and continued intent to expand, here through symbol, the novel's scope. *The Death of the Moth, The Moment and Other Essays,* and *The Captain's Deathbed and Other Essays* included new and old essays displaying her characteristic perception. *A Writer's Diary,* published in 1953, is an invaluable record of the inner feelings and creative processes of this modern master. *Virginia Woolf and Lytton Strachey: Letters* (1956) reveals personal aspects of these two gifted Bloomsburyites.

Joseph L. Blotner

BIBLIOGRAPHICAL REFERENCES: The most complete biographical study is Aileen Pippett, *The Moth and the Star: A Biography of Virginia Woolf,* 1955. The following contain authoritative critical commentary: Winifred Holtby, *Virginia Woolf,* 1932; Ruth Gruber, *Virginia Woolf: A Study,* 1935; David Daiches, *Virginia Woolf,* 1942; E. M. Forster, *Virginia Woolf,* 1942; Joan Bennett, *Virginia Woolf: Her Art as a Novelist,* 1945; R. L. Chambers, *The Novels of Virginia Woolf,* 1947; Bernard Blackstone, *Virginia Woolf: A Commentary,* 1949; and James Hafley, *The Glass*

Rcof: *Virginia Woolf as Novelist,* University of California English Studies, No. 9, 1954.

See also Elizabeth N. Monroe, *The Novel and Society,* 1941; Edward Wagenknecht, *Cavalcade of the English Novel,* 1943; E. B. Burgum, *The Novel and the World's Dilemma,* 1947; Lord David Cecil, *Poets and Story-Tellers,* 1949; Elizabeth Bowen, *Collected Impressions,* 1950; D. S. Savage, *The Withered Branch,* 1950; Robert Humphrey, *The Stream of Consciousness in the Modern Novel,* 1954; and J. K. Johnstone, *The Bloomsbury Group,* 1954.

For criticism in magazines see Edwin Muir, "Virginia Woolf," *Bookman,* LXXIV (1931), 362–367; William Troy, "Virginia Woolf: The Poetic Method," *Symposium,* III (1932), 53–63, and "Virginia Woolf: The Poetic Style," *ibid.,* 153–166; J. H. Roberts, "Towards Virginia Woolf," *Virginia Quarterly Review,* X (1934), 587–612; Joseph Warren Beach, "Virginia Woolf," *English Journal,* XXVI (1937), 603–612; T. S. Eliot, "Virginia Woolf," *Horizon,* III (1941), 313–316; W. H. Mellers, "Virginia Woolf: The Last Phase," *Kenyon Review,* IV (1942), 381–387; Martin Turnell, "Virginia Woolf," *Horizon,* IV (1942), 44–56; James Southall Wilson, "Time and Virginia Woolf," *Virginia Quarterly Review,* XVIII (1942), 267–276; J. H. Roberts, " 'Vision and Design' in Virginia Woolf," *Publications of the Modern Language Association,* LXI (1946), 835–847; Dayton Kohler, "Time in the Modern Novel," *College English,* X (1948), 15–24; W. Y. Tindall, "Many Leveled Fiction: Virginia Woolf to Ross Lockridge," *College English,* X (1948), 65–71; John Graham, "Time in the Novels of Virginia Woolf," *University of Toronto Quarterly,* XVIII (1949), 186–201; Margaret Church, "Concepts of Time in the Novels of Virginia Woolf and Aldous Huxley," *Modern Fiction Studies,* I (May, 1955), 19–24; and Dean Doner, "Virginia Woolf: The Service of Style," *Modern Fiction Studies,* II (February, 1956), 1–12.

The Virginia Woolf Number of *Modern Fiction Studies,* II (February, 1956) contains a selected checklist of criticisms of Virginia Woolf with an index to studies of her separate works, 36–45.

WILLIAM WORDSWORTH

Born: Cockermouth, England
Date: April 7, 1770

Died: Rydal Mount, England
Date: April 23, 1850

PRINCIPAL WORKS

POEMS: *Lyrical Ballads,* 1798 (with Coleridge); *Lyrical Ballads,* enlarged, with Preface, 1800; *Poems in Two Volumes,* 1807; *The Excursion,* 1814; *The White Doe of Rylstone,* 1815; *Peter Bell and the Waggoner,* 1819; *The River Duddon,* 1820; *Ecclesiastical Sketches,* 1822; *Memorials of a Tour on the Continent,* 1822; *Yarrow Revisited and Other Poems,* 1835; *Sonnets,* 1838; *Poems, Chiefly of Early and Late Years,* 1842; *Collected Poems,* 1849–1850; *The Prelude,* 1850.

To compare Wordsworth with other great English poets has long been a parlor game for critics. Matthew Arnold places him below only Shakespeare and Milton; others, ranging less widely, are content to call him the greatest of the Romantics. Incontestably, however, he stands supreme among English nature poets; and the stamp of his influence so strongly marks the short, glorious period of nineteenth century Romanticism that perhaps those can be forgiven who have gone so far as to call it the Age of Wordsworth.

The second son of a lower middle-class family, William Wordsworth was born April 7, 1770, at Cockermouth in the Lake District of Cumberland. When he was eight, his mother died; the loss of his father, five years later, made him dependent upon his uncles for an education. School at Hawkshead was followed by matriculation at Cambridge, where he entered St. John's College in 1787. His career there was interrupted in 1790 by a summer tour of Switzerland, France, and Italy; and in 1791, after receiving his degree, he returned to France, ostensibly to learn the language.

Much besides language, however, quickly absorbed Wordsworth's attention. The years 1791–1792 found Wordsworth developing two passions, one for Annette Vallon and the other for the French Revolution. Both were probably sincere, while they lasted; but both were soon to suffer from a change of heart. His daughter Anne Caroline was born to Annette Vallon while Wordsworth was still in France; for reasons which have never become clear, he acknowledged the child without marrying the mother. Wordsworth's other passion, the Revolution, stirred him deeply and left an indelible impression. His enthusiasm waned chiefly because of its growing excesses and because of the accession of Napoleon. Even so, the philosophy he acquired from Michel Beaupuy and his fellow revolutionists was an important factor in making Wordsworth the great poetic spokesman for that element as yet relatively voiceless—the common man.

Back in England, Wordsworth briefly found congeniality in the circle of young freethinkers surrounding William Godwin. Godwin, future father-in-law of Percy Shelley, was a radical philosopher and the author of *Political Justice*. Like Wordsworth himself, he was an ardent disciple of Rousseau, a fact which helps to explain his temporary hold on the young man's attention. In 1795, however, a fortunate legacy enabled Wordsworth to settle at Racedown with his devoted and talented sister Dorothy. Here occurred a brush with fate which was to change the lives of two men. In meeting Samuel Taylor Coleridge, Wordsworth formed the most significant connection of his career. Mutual intellectual stimulation and constant companionship were its immediate dividends; and when, in 1797, Coleridge moved into Somersetshire, the Wordsworths followed. The next year the two men published jointly that little volume which would eventually come into its own as one of the most magnificent milestones of English literature.

Nevertheless, the initial reception of the 1798 edition of *Lyrical Ballads* gave no clue to the status it would achieve in the future. Most of its contents came from the industrious Wordsworth, including the sublime nature poem, "Tintern Abbey," and a group of shorter, ballad-like compositions in which the author undertook to preach the kindness of Nature and exalt familiar reality. Coleridge, on the other hand, attempted the project of making supernatural subjects seem real, a project carried to superb completion in his single contribution, *The Ancient Mariner*.

Laughed at by some critics and ignored by others, *Lyrical Ballads* survived its reception sufficiently well to justify a second printing in 1800. Though this edition contained some interesting new poems, its most significant feature was Wordsworth's long Preface, which amounted to a literary declaration of independence and broke completely with neo-classical theory. The main points of this credo reflected strongly the continuing influence of Rousseau and stated formally the ideals of sincerity, democracy, nature worship, and simple, natural diction to which Wordsworth and Coleridge had vowed allegiance.

With *Lyrical Ballads* as its starting point, most of Wordsworth's great poetry was compressed into the quarter century between 1798 and 1823. Many of his celebrated short poems, such as "I Wandered Lonely as a Cloud" and "The Solitary Reaper," illustrate beautiful effects and essential truths achieved through the Wordsworthian simplicity of vocabulary advocated in his famous Preface. Still, he could successfully depart from his principles when he felt the need. That he could employ more elevated diction with telling effect finds ample illustration in his excellent sonnets, as well as in such longer poems as "Tintern Abbey" and "The Prelude." The content of his work conveys feelings of humanitarianism, liberalism, and—finally and most distinctively—a thoroughly pantheistic worship of nature. Biographical interest combined with distinguished poetry are found in "The Prelude" and, to a lesser extent, in "The Excursion"; both of these were written as parts of a longer autobiographical work, *The Recluse*, which was never completed.

If Wordsworth's work could scale the heights, it could also make inexplicable plunges into utter sterility; hardly another major poet can be named who is capable of such extremes in his published poetry. Completely devoid of a sense of humor, his tendency to complacency led him into such demonstrations of bathos and infelicity as "Andrew Jones" and "The Idiot Boy." His detractors, Byron notable among them, seized on these lapses with unholy glee; and the failure of Wordsworth's critical faculty in such instances is difficult to explain.

His failures in human relationships were sometimes equally conspicuous. The friendship with Coleridge, which had had such an auspicious beginning, tapered off during the years which followed *Lyrical Ballads*. In 1803, a misunderstanding arose during a tour of Scotland, leading to a breach between the two men which was never fully mended.

In 1802 Wordsworth married his childhood friend, Mary Hutchinson, the inspiration for "She Was a Phantom of Delight." As he grew older, Wordsworth became more and more conservative in matters of religion and politics. From the government which had once been the object of his youthful censure he now received employment, being appointed, in 1813, Distributor of Stamps in Westmorland County. In 1843, long after the passing of his really creative period, he was appointed Poet Laureate, succeeding Robert Southey. He died at Rydal Mount on April 23, 1850, and was buried in Grasmere churchyard. A monument to him was erected in Westminster Abbey.

BIBLIOGRAPHICAL REFERENCES: The definitive edition, excluding *The Prelude*, is *The Poetical Works of William Wordsworth*, edited by Ernest de Selincourt and Helen Darbishire, 5 vols., 1940–1949. The variorum edition of *The Prelude* was edited by Ernest de Selincourt, 1926, 1932. Editions of the letters include *Letters of the Wordsworth Family*, edited by William Knight, 3 vols., 1907; H. C. Robinson, *Correspondence with the Wordsworth Circle, 1808–1866*, 1927; and Ernest de Selincourt, *The Early Letters of William and Dorothy Wordsworth, 1780–1805*, 1937, and *Letters of William and Dorothy Wordsworth: The Middle Years*, 2 vols., 1937. This editor also prepared the *Journals of Dorothy Wordsworth*, 2 vols., 1941.

The standard biography is George McLean Harper, *William Wordsworth, His Life, Works, and Influence*, 2 vols., 1916. See also Émile Legouis, *The Early Years of William Wordsworth, 1770–1798*, 1897; Edith Batho, *The Later Wordsworth*, 1933; and G. W. Meyer, *Wordsworth's Formative Years*, University Publications in Language and Literature, XX (1943). For criticism see Samuel Taylor Coleridge, *Biographia Literaria*, 1817; Matthew Arnold, *Essays in Criticism: Second Series*, 1888; Alfred North Whitehead, *Science and the Modern World*, 1925; Earl Leslie Griggs, ed., *Wordsworth and Coleridge: Studies in Honor of George McLean Harper*, 1939; R. D. Havens, *The Mind of a Poet*, 1941; Helen Darbishire, *The Poet Wordsworth*, 1950; and Gilbert T. Dunklin, ed., *Wordsworth: Centenary Studies Presented at Cornell and Princeton Universities*, 1951.

RICHARD WRIGHT

Born: Near Natchez, Mississippi   **Died:** Paris, France
Date: September 4, 1908   **Date:** November 28, 1960

PRINCIPAL WORKS

NOVELS: *Native Son*, 1940; *Black Boy*, 1945; *The Outsider*, 1953.
SOCIAL STUDIES: *Twelve Million Black Voices*, 1941; *Black Power*, 1954.

Richard Wright's childhood was an unpleasant one. Born near Natchez, Mississippi, on September 4, 1908, he grew up, according to his own account, as an unruly and unwanted Negro child in the American South. His father, a laborer, deserted the family when Wright was five years old, and Wright's mother became totally paralyzed when the boy was ten. Leaving the home of relatives at the age of fifteen, Wright went to Memphis, Tennessee, where he worked at various unskilled jobs. During the depression years of the 1930's he traveled north, arriving in Chicago in 1934. There, becoming interested in the labor movement and communism, he joined the Communist Party in 1936. He worked on WPA Writers' Projects in Chicago

and New York, later became a contributing editor of the *New Masses*.

Wright's "Uncle Tom's Children" won the prize offered by *Story* in 1938. Awarded a Guggenheim Fellowship the following year, he wrote *Native Son*, a fictional study of a Negro murderer. In 1940 he received the Spingarn Medal for achievement in the field of Negro interests. *Twelve Million Black Voices* is a history of the American Negro and his problems. In 1944 Wright broke with the Communists; an essay describing his career as a Party member was published in *The God That Failed* (1950). *Black Boy* is an autobiographical novel based on Wright's childhood. *The Outsider* is a novel about a Negro's experience as a Communist. *Black Power* is a nonfictional personal study of conditions in Africa, on the Gold Coast, as Wright saw them on a visit to the region in 1953. *Native Son* has been Wright's most popular novel. As a stage play produced in the United States and as a motion picture filmed in Argentina, *Native Son* was fairly successful. The author played the lead role in the motion picture version.

BIBLIOGRAPHICAL REFERENCES: For biographical and critical discussion see H. M. Gloster, *Negro Voices in American Fiction*, 1948; William A. Owens, Introduction to *Native Son*, Harper Modern Classics edition, 1957; and Nathan A. Scott, "Search for Beliefs: Fiction of Richard Wright," *University of Kansas City Review*, XXIII (1956), 19–24.

WILLIAM WYCHERLEY

Born: Clive, Shropshire, England
Date: 1640

Died: London, England
Date: January 1, 1716

PRINCIPAL WORKS

PLAYS: *Love in a Wood,* 1671; *The Gentleman Dancing Master,* 1672; *The Country Wife,* 1673; *The Plain Dealer,* 1677.

William Wycherley was born of an old family at Clive, near Shrewsbury, Shropshire, in 1640. When he was about fifteen years of age, he was sent to France, where he frequented refined circles, notably the salon of the Duchess de Montausier, the atmosphere of which was impregnated with the spirit of the Hôtel de Rambouillet. Also, while in France, Wycherley became a Catholic. In 1660 he spent a short time at Oxford, from where he went to the Inner Temple in London. In London he soon found a place in the pleasure-loving society of the town, rejoicing after eighteen years of enforced Puritan virtue; and he gravitated toward the theater, the most notable social entertainment of the day.

In 1671 his first play, *Love in a Wood,* gained him the intimacy of a royal mistress, the Duchess of Cleveland, through whose influence he secured in 1672 a commission in a foot regiment. This acquaintance with the duchess also brought him into favor with the king, which favor, however, he lost when about 1680 he married the Countess of Drogheda. This rich marriage, which led to his temporary retirement from the theater, proved disappointing, and Wycherley shortly found himself in debt and, consequently, in Fleet Prison. He was released in 1685 by the proceeds of a benefit performance of his last play, *The Plain Dealer.*

After 1704 he formed a friendship with young Alexander Pope, who "somewhat too zealously" revised many of his later verses. On his deathbed Wycherley put into posterity's quiver many barbed shafts against himself by his second marriage, ostensibly contracted to prevent the passing of his property to his nephew. He died in London on January 1, 1716.

Wycherley, with four plays, stands next after Etherege, with three plays, as the innovator of modern English comedy. Wycherley probably learned little from Etherege's cynical avoidance of genuine emotion, or from his flexible empty dialogue. Etherege transcribed life, but he lacked philosophy; life was to him a frivolous game, and to become emotionally engrossed in it was perhaps slightly vulgar. Wycherley, on the other hand, while he partook of Etherege's cynicism, felt not aloof amusement, but more than a little resentment. There is bitterness, even malice, in Wycherley's satire; he himself is not immune to his own poison.

In typical Restoration fashion, to Wycherley the greatest sin is foolishness. For instance, in *Love in a Wood,* his first play, Alderman Gripe, a hypocritical Puritan, ultimately marries a wench; Dapperwit, a fop, gets Gripe's daughter for his wife, but does not get her fortune, which he was really after. Wycherley's third play, *The Country Wife,* is an extremely realistic picture of cuckold-gulling, the great aristocratic pastime of the day. Horner, recently returned from France, pretends impotence in order better to practice his formidable art of despoiling chastity. His chief success is to win the favor of Margery, the country wife of the superannuated sensualist, Pinchwife. Without subtlety, but certainly with power, Wycherley makes his spectators partisans in condemning selfishness, pretentiousness, and hypocrisy.

The Country Wife is nowadays considered Wycherley's best play, but in his own day *The Plain Dealer* was considered his finest achievement; it is still more commonly included in anthologies. The same theme of exposing pretension and hypocrisy is present in this play as in *The Country Wife.* Manly, the Plain Dealer, has been robbed and wronged by his mistress Olivia, and his closest friend, Vernish. Wycherley's attack on selfishness and treachery in the persons of Vernish and Olivia is open and savage. Indeed, the play is not at all typical of the Restoration. It is hardly funny, hardly even amusing. Since it has more than a little of the near-repellent naturalistic abandon so noticeable in today's most esteemed playwrights, it is certain to make a strong impression on the modern reader.

BIBLIOGRAPHICAL REFERENCES: The standard edition is *The Complete Works of William Wycherley,* edited by Montague Summers, 4 vols., 1924. An early biographical study, but an interesting one, is Lord Lansdowne's *Memoirs of the Life of William Wycherley,* 1718. See also A. W. Ward, *The History of English Dramatic Literature,* 1899; Bonamy Debrée, *Restoration Comedy, 1600–1720,* 1924; Allardyce Nicoll, *A History of English Drama, 1660–1900,* Vol. I, 1952 (rev. ed.); and *Dictionary of National Biography,* Vol. XXI.

ELINOR WYLIE

Born: Somerville, New Jersey   *Died:* New York, N. Y.
Date: September 7, 1885   *Date:* December 16, 1928

PRINCIPAL WORKS

POEMS: *Nets to Catch the Wind,* 1921; *Black Armour,* 1923; *Trivial Breath,* 1928; *Angels and Earthly Creatures,* 1928; *Last Poems,* 1943.

NOVELS: *Jennifer Lorn: A Sedate Extravaganza,* 1923; *The Venetian Glass Nephew,* 1925; *The Orphan Angel,* 1926; *Mr. Hodge and Mr. Hazard,* 1928.

A woman of mercurial temperament and a dedicated artist in both poetry and prose, Elinor Wylie had one of the briefest and most integrated careers in the history of American literature. In a space of eight years she wrote four books of poems and four novels in which her tragic vision of life is grained with fantasy and satire. Within these her message is complete. Dying at forty-three, she had already made her demand on posterity for recognition of her brilliant craftsmanship and the revelation of the stoic in woman contained in her work.

Her life was a turbulent seedbed for the development of her singular talent. She was born Elinor Morton Hoyt in Somerville, New Jersey, on September 7, 1885, the oldest child of Henry Martyn and Anne (McMichael) Hoyt, both descended from old Pennsylvania families distinguished in society and public affairs. Her education was as fashionably correct as her family background. She attended private schools in Bryn Mawr and Washington, where her father, appointed to the post of assistant attorney-general of the United States in 1897, became Solicitor-General in 1903. During her schooldays her interests were divided between art and poetry, the latter chiefly through her discovery of Shelley. Following her debut and a brief, unhappy love affair, she married Philip Hichborn in 1905. For the next five years she lived the life of a fashionable young matron according to the standards of Philadelphia society and official Washington. In 1910, to the surprise of family and friends, she abandoned her husband and small son and eloped with Horace Wylie, a cultivated scholarly man fifteen years her senior. Two years later her husband committed suicide.

Because of the prominent names involved, this elopement created a scandal kept alive by gossip and the press for more than a decade.

When Horace Wylie found it impossible to obtain a divorce, the couple went to England and lived there under an assumed name. *Incidental Numbers,* her first book of poems, was privately printed in London in 1912. Published anonymously, for presentation only, it holds only occasional promise of her mature powers as a poet. Unable to remain in England under wartime conditions, she and Wylie returned to Boston in 1916. His divorce having been granted, they were married the next year. After several years of restless travel from Maine to Georgia, Horace Wylie secured a minor government post and they returned to Washington in 1919. Cut off from most of her former friends, Elinor Wylie became one of a literary group that included William Rose Benét and Sinclair Lewis, and with their encouragement she continued to write poetry. In 1921 she left Washington to make her home in New York.

She came late upon the literary scene, but with the manner of one whom no disastrous circumstance could subdue. When one possesses charm and talent, as Elinor Wylie did, and to these adds a deep knowledge of life and the craftsmanship of crystal-cool words, the result is likely to be poetry which rises phoenix-like from the ashes of disillusionment. *Nets to Catch the Wind,* published in 1921, was awarded the Julia Ellsworth Ford Prize by the Poetry Society of America. To those who knew her best she remained a person of contradictions. She could be high-handed and remote and proud (the iced chalk to which one critic compared her), but she was also comradely and mirthful and gracious, and her speech, like her writing, crackled with the wit and vigor of her mind. She had become a figure of literary legend when, having divorced Horace Wylie, she married William Rose Benét in 1923, and in the same year published her second book of poems and a successful first novel.

Although Shelley was her lifelong passion, to the extent that she often identified herself with him, he was not the only influence on her work. Her loans of power, as reflected in *Nets to Catch the Wind* and *Black Armour*, were also in the tradition of Donne and Blake, poets who found an approach to spiritual truth in a disembodied ecstasy of thought and emotion. Her erudition and wit are plain in her use of the sharpened epithet, the aristocratic scorn, the language framing stark abstractions, a delight in subtleties of thought, an imagery of symbolic birds and beasts. On the whole, the poems in these books are songs of experience, with much bitterness in the singing. *Trivial Breath* is a more uneven collection, divided as it is between lyrics of personal experience and payment of her literary debts. But there is little of the "overfine" in the elegiac moods which pervade *Angels and Earthly Creatures*. Most of these poems were written in England during the summer of 1928, when some presentiment of death seemed to have given Elinor Wylie a final certainty of vision and language. The desire for escape is less persistent, the note of resignation less profound. Instead, there is exultant affirmation of love and faith transcending all fears of death in the magnificent sonnet sequence, "One Person." These poems,

her most passionate revelation of the woman and the poet, are in the great tradition.

Her novels are like much of her poetry, exquisite and erudite. *Jennifer Lorn,* set against a droll background blending sophisticated elegance with simple manners, is a satire on the twin themes of magnificence and folly, reflected in the ambitions of an eighteenth century empire builder and the attitude of a heroine unmoved by the bustle of all practical affairs until death frees her at last from a husband who bores her and a world that intrudes upon her romantic dreaming. The artifice of *The Venetian Glass Nephew* seems on the suface as brittle as its spun-glass hero, but under its bright surface are deeper meanings in the story of a heroine willing to be transformed into a porcelain figure to decorate the sharp angles and cold corners of the world. *The Orphan Angel* is apocryphal legend, a picaresque romance in which Shelley is miraculously rescued off Viareggio and brought to America aboard a Yankee ship. *Mr. Hodge and Mr. Hazard* is a more personal fable, in many ways her best. The disillusioned poet who returns to England in the twilight of the Romantic Period is not Shelley, as many readers have supposed, but any artist who survives into a later period than his own. The summer idyl of the old poet ends in a fiasco of stale cream buns and an epigram; his fate is the crack of doom in a teacup, and the whole is an ironic allegory of the poet's tragedy and the world's indifference.

Elinor Wylie was not to share her hero's fate. In England, where she spent the summer of 1928, she fell while visiting a country house and suffered a painful but temporary back injury. In October a light stroke left one side of her face partly paralyzed. She returned to New York early in December of that year. On December 16 she had arranged the poems in *Angels and Earthly Creatures* for the printer and was sitting reading in the Benét apartment when she had a second stroke and died before her husband could summon assistance.

BIBLIOGRAPHICAL REFERENCES: *Collected Poems of Elinor Wylie* was edited by her husband, William Rose Benét, 1932. *Collected Prose of Elinor Wylie,* 1933, contains biographical and critical prefaces by Stephen Vincent Benét, William Rose Benét, Isabel Patterson, Carl Van Doren, and Carl Van Vechten. There is no authorized biography. *Elinor Wylie: The Portrait of an Unknown Lady,* 1935, is an informal biographical study by her sister, Nancy Hoyt. For brief studies in books and periodicals see Elizabeth S. Sergeant, *Fire Under the Andes,* 1927; James Branch Cabell, *Some of Us,* 1930; Emily Clark, *Innocence Abroad,* 1931; Rebecca West, *Ending in Earnest,* 1931; William Rose Benét, *The Prose and Poetry of Elinor Wylie,* 1934; Carl Van Doren, *Three Worlds,* 1936; Henry S. Canby, *American Memoir,* 1947; Mary M. Colum, *Life and the Dream,* 1947; Mary M. McClain, "Elinor Wylie's Poetry and Prose: Her Artistic Evolution," in *Writers and Their Critics,* 1956; Archibald MacLeish, "Black Armour," *New Republic,* XXXVII (December 5, 1923), Suppl., 16–18; Herbert S. Gorman, "Daughter of Donne," *North American Review,* CCXIX (1924), 679–686; Harriet Monroe, "Elinor Wylie," *Poetry,* XXXIII (1929), 266–272; Morton Dauwen Zabel, "The Pattern of the Atmosphere," *Poetry,* XL (1932), 273–282; Osbert Burdett, "The Novels of Elinor Wylie," *English Review,* LIX (1934), 488–490, 492; Dayton Kohler, "Elinor Wylie: Heroic Mask," *South Atlantic Quarterly,* XXXVI (1937), 218–228; Henry Lüdeke, "Venetian Glass: The Poetry and Prose of Elinor Wylie," *English Studies,* XX (1938), 241–250; and Julia Cluck, "Elinor Wylie's Shelley Obsession," *Publications of the Modern Language Association,* LVI (1941), 841–860.

JOHANN RUDOLF WYSS

Born: Bern, Switzerland
Date: March 13, 1781

Died: Bern
Date: March 31, 1830

PRINCIPAL WORK

NOVEL: *Der Schweizerische Robinson,* 1812–1813 (*The Swiss Family Robinson*).

Johann Rudolf Wyss, who is usually credited with being the author of *The Swiss Family Robinson,* was born in Bern, Switzerland, on March 13, 1781. He studied at several German universities and in 1806 became a professor of philosophy at the University of Bern, where he also served as the chief librarian. In his native land of Switzerland he became known as a collector and editor of Swiss folklore, publishing such volumes as *Idyllen und Erzählungen aus der Schweiz* (*Idyls and Tales from the Swiss,* 1815–1822), *Reise im Berner Oberland* (*Travels in the Bernese Uplands,* 1808), and the fifteen-volume *Die Alpenrose* (1811–1830). He was also the author of the Swiss national anthem.

Johann Rudolf Wyss, although

given credit often as the author, apparently did not compose *The Swiss Family Robinson*, but only wrote it down in revised form and had it published. The story, obviously in partial imitation of Daniel Defoe's *Robinson Crusoe* (1719), was concocted by Wyss's father, named Rudolf David, for the enjoyment of his sons. Of the father, who was a chaplain in the Swiss army, little is known, except that he was born in 1749, became a chaplain, served in Italy, and died in 1818.

The history of *The Swiss Family Robinson* is an interesting one. Apparently Pastor Wyss committed his story to writing before his son revised the manuscript and had it published at Zurich, Switzerland, under the title *Der Schweizerische Robinson, Oder der Schiffbruchige Schweizerpredige und Seine Familie. Ein Lehrreiches Buch für Kinder und Kinderfreunde zu Stadt und Land.* All that long German title can be translated as *The Swiss Family Robinson, or the Ship-*wrecked *Swiss Preacher and His Family: An Instructional Book for Children and Their Friends in City or Country.* The first known English translation was by William Godwin, British philosopher, reformer, and novelist, a short time after the Zurich edition appeared. But a Frenchwoman, Baroness de Montolieu, with Johann Rudolf Wyss's approval, enlarged the story, translated it into French, and published it in 1824. Two years later the original publisher in Zurich brought out a new German edition which incorporated the baroness's additions. The first English translation of the enlarged story was made in 1868, by Mrs. H. B. Paull, who also translated Grimm's fairy tales. Most later editions have followed Baroness Montolieu's edition. The book has been immensely popular in America and Europe with generations of children.

Wyss died in Bern on March 31, 1830.

BIBLIOGRAPHICAL REFERENCES: For brief studies of Wyss in English see William Dean Howells, Introduction to *The Swiss Family Robinson*, 1909; and R. B. Glaenzer, "The Swiss Family Robinson," *Bookman*, XXXIV (1911), 139–142. See also P. Dottin "Le Robinson suisse," *Mercure de France*, CLXIX (January 1, 1924), 114–126.

XENOPHON

Born: Athens, Greece
Date: c. 430 B.C.

Died: Corinth, Greece
Date: c. 354 B.C.

PRINCIPAL WORKS
(Dates uncertain)

HISTORY AND BIOGRAPHY: The *Hellenica*, the *Anabasis*, *Agesilaus*.

ROMANCE: The *Cyropaedia, or Education of Cyrus.*

SOCRATIC DIALOGUES: The *Memorabilia of Socrates*, the *Oeconomicus* (*Household Management*), the *Apology of Socrates*, the *Symposium*.

TREATISES: *Hippike* (*On Horsemanship*), *Hipparchicus* (*On the Cavalry General*), *Cynegeticus* (*On Hunting*), *De Vectigalibus* (*On Ways and Means*), *Polity of the Lacedaemonians, Hiero.*

Born at Athens about 430 B.C., Xenophon, son of Gryllus of the Attic deme Erchia, belonged to a well-to-do family and was a disciple of Socrates, though not a member of his intimate circle. After an adventurous participation in an expedition to overthrow the King of Persia in 401 B.C., he then spent a few years in Asia Minor with mercenary troops under Spartan command. Exiled from Athens around 394, he settled in the Peloponnese, where he lived as a country gentleman on an estate granted him by the Spartans at Scillus near Olympia. He lost this estate around 371 when the Eleans recovered Scillus from the Spartans. In 369 the decree of exile was rescinded, after Athens entered into an alliance with Sparta. Thereafter he occasionally visited Athens and sent his sons to serve in the Athenian cavalry. He died at Corinth about 354 B.C.

It is as a writer that Xenophon is best known. He wrote history, romance, and essays of practical and moral import. His most famous work is the *Anabasis,* an account of the expedition of ten thousand mercenaries hired by Cyrus, the younger brother of King Artaxerxes, to win for himself the throne of Persia. Though Cyrus' army defeated the king's, Cyrus was killed. The Greek generals having been treacherously captured and slain, Xenophon found himself in command of the hazardous retreat of the mercenaries to Trebizond on the Black Sea. After making contact with the Spartan general Thibron, Xenophon turned the mercenaries over to him; Xenophon himself remained in Asia with the Spartans for some years. The *Anabasis* is a thrilling adventure story, written in good, if somewhat uninspired, Greek.

In the *Hellenica* Xenophon completed the unfinished *History of the Peloponnesian War* of Thucydides and continued the history of Greek war and politics down to the battle of Mantinea in 362 B.C. The work is inferior to that of Thucydides both in style and in historical understanding, but it is a primary source for the history of the period it covers.

Association with Socrates supplied the material and motive for several works: The *Memorabilia of Socrates* is a defense of Socrates, with illustrative anecdotes and many short dialogues between Socrates and his friends, usually on moral questions. Xenophon lacked Plato's interest in speculative philosophy. The *Apology of Socrates* purports to explain why Socrates did not defend himself any better than he did. The *Symposium* consists of an imagined dinner party conversation at the house of Callias, with some serious philosophizing by Socrates. In general these works portray a more matter-of-fact Socrates than the protagonist of Plato's dialogues, but one probably no nearer the historical truth. Another dialogue, the *Oeconomicus,* between Socrates and Critoboulos sets forth Xenophon's views on the management of an estate. It reflects the life at Scillus and is a valuable document for the economy of the period.

A work of a different sort, the *Cyropaedia* is a romantic account of the youth and education of Cyrus the Great of Persia. It is intended to lay down the ideals of education for political leadership. It is unfavorably remarked on by Plato in the *Republic.*

Xenophon's political interests were also expressed in the laudatory *Polity of the Lacedaemonians* and in the *Hiero.* The latter is a dialogue between the King of Syracuse and the poet Simonides, dealing with the relative happiness of the despot and the private citizen and with the question of how a despot should rule in order to win the affection of his people.

Four technical treatises were also written by Xenophon: The *Hipparchicus,* on the duties of a cavalry commander; *On Horsemanship,* an author-itative manual, the first of its kind to come down to us from antiquity; *Ways and Means,* suggestions for improving the finances of Athens; and the *Cynegeticus,* a treatise on hunting, including, oddly enough, an attack on the Sophists.

Xenophon was a man of affairs, with intelligence and wide interests, who wrote plainly and with a taste for platitude. He reflects the attitudes of a Greek gentleman and for this reason alone is worth much to us for the insights his writings provide.

BIBLIOGRAPHICAL REFERENCES: E. C. Marchant edited the *Opera Omnia,* 5 vols., 1900–1919. Among available translations are the following: H. A. Holden, *Cyropaedia,* 4 vols., 1887–1890; C. L. Brownson and O. J. Todd, *Hellenica, Anabasis, Apology,* and *Symposium,* 3 vols., 1914–1923; and E. C. Marchant, *Memorabilia* and *Oeconomicus,* 1923, and *Scripta Minora,* 1925. For criticism and comment see H. Richards, *Xenophon and Others,* 1907; J. B. Bury, *Ancient Greek Historians,* 1909; Edith Hamilton, *The Greek Way,* 1930; and Kathleen Atkinson, *The Republica Lacedaemoniorum Ascribed to Xenophon: Its Manuscript Tradition and General Significance,* 1948; also A. Croiset, *Xenophon, son caractère et son talent,* 1873; and Jean Luccioni, *Xenophon et le socratisme,* 1953.

AGUSTÍN YÁÑEZ

Born: Guadalajara, Mexico
Date: May 4, 1904

PRINCIPAL WORKS

NOVELS: *Pasión y convalecencia,* 1943; *Al filo del agua,* 1947.

NOVELLAS: *Archipiélago de mujeres,* 1943.

SHORT STORIES AND SKETCHES: *Espejismo de Juchitán,* 1940; *Flor de juegos antiguos,* 1942; *Esta es mala suerte,* 1945.

BIOGRAPHY: *Fray Bartolome de las Casas, el conquistador conquistado,* 1942; *Alfonso Gutiérrez Hermosillo y algunos amigos,* 1945; *Don Justo Sierra, su vida, sus ideas y su obra,* 1950.

MISCELLANEOUS: *Genio y figuras de Guadalajara,* 1940; *El contenido social de la literatura iberoamericana,* 1944; *Yahualica,* 1946.

Agustín Yáñez, under the pseudonym of Mónico Delgadillo, has given us, in two of his books, some glimpses into his autobiography. He was born in Guadalajara, capital of the State of Jalisco, Mexico, on May 4, 1904. "Very early," he writes of himself in the third person, "there awoke in him a rigorous critical sense that inhibited the expansiveness of the child and the

1184

adolescent; but his sentimental temperament was so intense and overflowing that it could not but manifest itself, even exaggeratedly, and ended in coloring his life absolutely. Intelligence imposed on him an essential severity; . . . art was his star, his great ambition, the window through which he looked at existence." These characteristics of seriousness, austerity, and preoccupation with artistic form continued to shape his literary work.

After enrolling as a student in architecture, engineering, medicine, and philosophy, none of which he carried out, he associated himself with other young writers of Guadalajara and founded the literary journal, *Bandera de Provincias,* the establishment of which was a national event. He later moved to Mexico City, where he received the professional title of lawyer, devoted himself to university teaching and literary production, and held several public offices.

According to the aesthetic creed of Yáñez, the ideal of art is form: "Not art dehumanized, nor purely aesthetical as mere pleasure in form, nor, even less, verbalism." For him, the idea of literary form is inward, a theory of composition initiated by means of living the reality, and then reliving it in the literary work until one completes it in the appropriate verbal form. "I never write—least of all when writing novels—with the intention of sustaining a premeditated thesis, committed to predetermined conclusions." After intuiting a form, he develops it until it takes on consistency; it is then necessary to follow it, striving not to falsify characters, situations, and atmosphere.

Yáñez as a writer is very conscious and cognizant of his function. His style is elaborate, reflective, grave, and refined. "Here extend the supreme ambition and limit of my style: When I succeed in making the words sparkle like the colors in crystal and in combining them magnificently and solemnly." His knowledge of contemporary philosophy, of the Spanish classics, and of the resources of the modern novel has given to his work robustness, rigor, and an abundant vocabulary.

Almost all of Yáñez' works have reminiscence as a common ingredient. On the occasion of the commemoration of the Fourth Centennial of the founding of Guadalajara, he wrote two books: *Flor de juegos antiguos,* lyrical memories of his childhood and of the games of his province, and *Genio y figuras de Guadalajara,* in which he presents a brief description of this city in 1930 and character studies of its principal citizens throughout its history. In 1943 he published, *Archipiélago de mujeres,* a collection of seven stories, each one called by the name of a woman who represents a step on the author's "ladder of adolescence": music, revelation, desire, beauty, folly, death, and love.

In *Al filo del agua,* published in 1947, Yáñez produced his best novel and, according to many critics, the finest Mexican novel of the last twenty-five years. In a prose that is dense, unhackneyed, and subtle, he presents the life of a typical pueblo of Jalisco. In the routine and monotony of everyday life, passion and religion are the two stimuli of these townspeople. The dramas of conscience brought about by the conflicts of flesh and spirit are here analyzed with subtle introspection.

Yáñez' studies on Mexican literature have attained a high eminence. Particularly outstanding are those devoted to the chronicles of the Conquest, the novel of Lizardi, and the native myths of Mexico. At the present time Agustín Yáñez is the constitutional governor of his native state, Jalisco.

BIBLIOGRAPHICAL REFERENCES: There is no helpful criticism of Yáñez in English. For biographical and critical studies in Spanish see Manuel de Ezcurdia, *Trayectoria novelística de Agustín Yáñez*, 1954 (Mexico); F. Morton Rand, *Los Novelistas de la Revolución mexicana*, 1949 (Mexico); José Luis Martínez, *Literatura mexicana, siglo XX*, I, 1949 (Mexico); Manuel Pedro González, *Trayectoria de la novela en Mexico*, 1951 (Mexico); and Raúl Cardiel Reyes, "El ser de America en Agustín Yáñez," *Filosofía y Letras*, No. 38 (April–June, 1950), 301–321. Two collections of critical and appreciative essays by various hands have been printed in Mexican periodicals: "Homenaje a Agustín Yáñez," in *Tiras de Colores*, II, No. 27 (July, 1944), and "Homenaje a Agustín Yáñez," in *Novedades*, 1952. For studies of individual works see also the following journals printed in Mexico City: Julio Jiménez Rueda on *Archipiélago de mujeres*, *Filosofía y Letras*, No. 16 (Oct.–Dec., 1944), 232–233; Francisco Monterde on *Al filo del agua*, *ibid.*, No. 25 (Jan.–Mar., 1947), 136–140; Gabriel Méndez Plancarte on *Fray Bartolome de las Casas* in "Yáñez, el silencioso," *Abside*, VI, No. 2, 212–217; and Elena Orozco on *Don Justo Sierra* in *Filosofía y Letras*, No. 40 (Oct.–Dec., 1950). A good introduction to Yáñez is Antonio Castro Leal, Introduction to *Al filo del agua*, 1955 (2nd ed., Mexico).

WILLIAM BUTLER YEATS

Born: Sandymount, Ireland
Date: June 13, 1865

Died: Roquebrune, France
Date: January 28, 1939

PRINCIPAL WORKS

POEMS: *Mosada: A Dramatic Poem*, 1886; *The Wanderings of Oisin*, 1889; *Poems*, 1895; *The Wind Among the Reeds*, 1899; *In the Seven Woods*, 1903; *The Green Helmet and Other Poems*, 1910; *Responsibilities*, 1914; *The Wild Swans at Coole*, 1917; *Michael Robartes and the Dancer*, 1920; *Later Poems*, 1922; *The Cat and the Moon and Certain Poems*, 1924; *The Tower*, 1928; *The Winding Stair*, 1933; *Collected Poems*, 1933; *The King of the Great Clock Tower*, 1934; *A Full Moon in March*, 1935; *New Poems*, 1938; *Last Poems and Plays*, 1940; *Collected Poems*, 1949.

PLAYS: *The Countess Kathleen*, 1892; *The Land of Heart's Desire*, 1894; *The Shadowy Waters*, 1900; *Cathleen ni Houlihan*, 1902; *Where There Is Nothing*, 1902; *The Hour Glass*, 1903; *The Pot of Broth*, 1904; *The King's Threshold*, 1904; *Deirdre*, 1907; *The Unicorn from the Stars and Other Plays*, 1908 (with Lady Gregory); *Plays for an Irish Theatre*, 1911; *Four Plays for Dancers*, 1921; *Wheels and Butterflies*, 1934; *Collected Plays*, 1934; *The Herne's Egg*, 1938; *Collected Plays*, 1952.

SHORT STORIES AND TALES: *The Celtic Twilight*, 1893; *Stories of Red Hanrahan*, 1904.

MEMOIRS: *Reveries Over Childhood and Youth*, 1915; *Four Years*, 1921; *The Trembling of the Veil*, 1922; *Autobiographies*, 1926; *Estrangement*, 1926; *Reflections from a Diary Kept in 1909*, 1926; *The Death of Synge and Other Passages from an Old Diary*, 1928; *Dramatis Personae*, 1936.

ESSAYS: *Ideas of Good and Evil,* 1903; *Discoveries,* 1907; *Poetry and Ireland,* 1908 (with Lionel Johnson); *Synge and the Ireland of His Time,* 1911; *The Cutting of an Agate,* 1912; *Essays,* 1924; *A Vision,* 1925.

LETTERS: *Letters on Poetry to Dorothy Wellesley,* 1940; *Letters to Katharine Tynan,* 1953.

TRANSLATIONS: Sophocles' *King Oedipus,* 1928; *Oedipus at Colonus,* 1934.

William Butler Yeats was born at Sandymount, near Dublin, on June 13, 1865. His father, John Butler Yeats, was an artist of considerable merit who had given up a moderately lucrative law practice in order to devote himself to painting; his mother was a frail, beautiful woman who nurtured in her son a deep love for the "west country" of Ireland that was to last all his life. His early childhood and later vacations were spent there, among the green hills and lakes of Sligo which were to become, in such poems as "The Lake Isle of Innisfree," a symbol of his imaginative escape from the disappointments and unpleasant realities of life.

Much of Yeats's early life was spent in London, but between 1880 and 1887 the family was in Dublin, years which had a lasting effect on the impressionable young poet. Stimulated by his father, who loved to read aloud, Yeats discovered Shakespeare, the Romantic poets, and the Pre-Raphaelites, explored popular works on Eastern mysticism, became interested in Irish myths and folklore, and, perhaps most important, met the poets and intellectuals of the Irish Literary Revival, many of whom were to remain lifelong friends. During the period he made several attempts at poetic drama, but the plays were highly imitative and hopelessly cluttered with magic islands and timid shepherds. Back in London, Yeats embarked on a serious study of Irish folk tales in the British Museum and published his first major poem, *The Wanderings of Oisin,* in 1889.

Although the poem is superficially reminiscent of Spenser, Shelley, and his friend William Morris, the Gaelic theme and unorthodox rhythms are characteristic of Yeats's quest for a fresh tradition and an individual style.

There is, however, little that is imitative in poetic plays such as *The Countess Kathleen* and *The Land of Heart's Desire,* or in the lyrics that accompanied the former. The continued use of Irish themes evident in these volumes is indicative of an important and complex aspect of Yeats's early development. In common with the other writers of the nationalistic Irish Literary Revival, he wished to create a literature that was purely Irish in tone and subject matter. As part of the same general movement, he strove to reawaken in his people a sense of the glory and significance of Ireland's historical and legendary past. Furthermore, the remoteness of these Celtic themes was consistent with Yeats's aesthetic theory, later repudiated in part, of the separation of art from life. Finally, Irish folklore offered an answer to his search for a personal and individual mythology, for he found there a treasury of symbols hitherto unused in English poetry. Yeats's tendency to make mythical figures into private symbols was encouraged by his contacts with such Symbolist poets as Arthur Symons and Mallarmé, and by his undisciplined but enthusiastic dabbling in such esoteric subjects as "hermetic" philosophy, astrology, and spiritualism. *The Secret Rose* (1897) and

The Wind Among the Reeds are representative of Yeats's work at this time, and while the clues to the meaning of the poems in these volumes is not always readily accessible to the uninitiated reader, they reveal a major step forward in terms of artistic skill and emotional maturity.

In spite of Yeats's theoretic dissociation from contemporary Irish life and politics, he could not escape his environment, the less so because he was in love, and was to be for two decades, with the beautiful and fiery actress and nationalist, Maud Gonne. In 1899 he and Isabella Augusta, Lady Gregory, founded the Irish National Theatre Society, which presently became the famous Abbey Theatre of Dublin. During the first decade of the twentieth century, working alongside Lady Gregory and J. M. Synge, Yeats wrote several plays for the Abbey, the best of which is a patriotic propaganda piece, *Cathleen ni Houlihan*, and the tragedy *Deirdre*. In the poetry of this period, too, Yeats reacted against what he considered the sentimentality and divorce from reality of his earlier work. As the legendary past became less important, in order to rescue his imagination from abstractions and bring it closer to actuality, he pressed everything into his poetry: the theater, patriotism, contemporary controversies.

The Green Helmet characteristically shows a tremendous advance in precision of imagery and syntax, as well as an increased use of personal and contemporary themes. Yet along with the substitution of a hard, dry manner and lively, homely detail for the dreamy vagueness of the early poetry, the symbolism which he was evolving becomes more and more esoteric and obscure. In 1917, having had proposals of marriage rejected by both Maud Gonne and her daughter Iseult, Yeats precipitously married Miss Georgie Hyde-Lees. The marriage was on the whole a success; one of its curious by-products was their joint experiment in spiritualism and "automatic writing," begun by his wife as a game to distract Yeats from personal worries. From the renewed interest in the occult and the mystical which arose out of these investigations Yeats developed a system of symbols by means of which he hoped to express his philosophy of life and art. This symbolism, which Yeats discusses in detail in *A Vision*, privately printed in 1925, is extremely complex, but while it provided the poet with a device which gave unity to his ideas on history, art, and human experience, its difficulties need not be a barrier to an understanding of his poems. It is probably enough for the average reader to recognize in the gyre, or ascending spiral, and the phases of the moon, Yeats's theories regarding the cyclical natures of both human nature and history.

For the aging Yeats this concept of the cyclical character of history was in a sense his defense against time. The poems of his later years are dominated by the figure of the poet, withdrawn from the "blood and mire" of life into the eternal realm of art, smiling with "tragic joy" at the cycles of life and death, creation and destruction, which mark human existence. But Yeats could not, either in his life or in his art, consistently maintain this withdrawal. In 1923 he was made a senator of the new Irish Free State, a post he entered into with enthusiasm, if not always tact. Some of Yeats's last poems, such as

1188

the "Crazy Jane" group, are a harsh, almost bitter glorification of the physical and even the sensual. As he says in "The Circus Animal's Desertion" from *Last Poems*, he "must lie down where all the ladders start, / In the foul rag-and-bone shop of the heart." The period after 1923, when Yeats was awarded the Nobel Prize in Literature, saw the production of some of his best and most exciting poetry. On January 28, 1939, his mind still alert and active, Yeats died at Roquebrune, on the French Riviera.

No sparse biographical outline can adequately characterize the complex personality of William Butler Yeats. He was fascinated by strange and supernatural phenomena but scorned the wonders of modern science; he was by nature inclined towards mysticism, but found little that attracted him in Christianity; he was an ardent patriot who dissociated himself as far as possible from the revolutionary course his country was following; he was a disciple of the doctrine of the separation of life from art. He was all these, yet his poetry had its basis in his own quick response to life, and was indeed a criticism *of* life. Yeats himself was aware of the contradictions in his nature and in life, and throughout his career he sought for a philosophical and artistic system that would resolve the conflict between his vision of what art should be and the recognition of what life is. Perhaps he found it, but it was in many ways too private, too personal a vision to be communicated. Yeats is not always an easy poet to read, but his compact, intellectually intense, but supremely lyrical poetry deserves the careful attention it demands.

BIBLIOGRAPHICAL REFERENCES: There is no collected edition of Yeats. The definitive edition of the poems is *The Collected Poems of William Butler Yeats*, 2 vols., 1949, incorporating revisions made by the poet before his death. For those interested in a reading of the texts an indispensable work is *The Variorum Edition of the Poems of William Butler Yeats*, edited by George Daniel Peter Allt and Russell K. Alspach, 1957. A revised edition of the *Collected Plays* was published in 1952. There are two bibliographies: A. J. H. Symons, *A Bibliography of William Butler Yeats*, 1924, and Allan Wade, *A Bibliography of the Writings of William Butler Yeats*, 1953.

The standard biography is Joseph Hone, *The Life of William Butler Yeats*, 1942. For biography and criticism see also Forrest Reid, *W. B. Yeats: A Critical Study*, 1915; C. L. Wrenn, *William Butler Yeats: A Literary Study*, 1920; J. H. Pollock, *William Butler Yeats*, 1935; J. P. O'Donnell, *Sailing to Byzantium: A Study of the Later Style and Symbolism of William Butler Yeats*, 1939; Lennox Robinson, *William Butler Yeats: A Study*, 1939; Louis MacNeice, *The Poetry of William Butler Yeats*, 1941; V. K. N. Menon, *The Development of W. B. Yeats*, 1942; Peter Ure, *Towards a New Mythology*, 1946; Richard Ellman, *Yeats: The Man and the Masks*, 1948, and *The Identity of Yeats*, 1950; A. N. Jeffares, *W. B. Yeats: Man and Poet*, 1949; Donald Stauffer, *Golden Nightingale*, 1949; T. R. Henn, *Lonely Tower*, 1950; Vivienne Koch: *William Butler Yeats: The Tragic Phase*, 1951; and Virginia Moore, *The Unicorn: William Butler Yeats' Search for Reality*, 1954.

For briefer studies in books and periodicals see, further, Cornelius Weygandt, *The Time of Yeats*, 1937; Arland Ussher, *Three Great Irishmen*, 1952; R. P. Blackmur, "The Later Poetry of W. B. Yeats," *Southern Review*, II (1936), 339–362; Morton Dauwen Zabel, "Yeats at Thirty and Seventy," *Poetry*, XLVII (1936), 268–277; Cleanth Brooks, "The Vision of W. B. Yeats," *Southern Review*, IV (1938), 116–

142; W. K. Tindall, "The Symbolism of W. B. Yeats," *Accent*, V (1945), 203–212; D. S. Savage, "The Aestheticism of W. B. Yeats," *Kenyon Review*, VII (1945), 118–134; Harold H. Watts, "Yeats and Lapsed Mythology," *Renascence*, III (1951), 107–112; Peter Allt, "Yeats, Religion, and History," *Sewanee Review*, LX (1952), 624–658; Robert M. Adams, "Now That My Ladder's Gone—Yeats Without Myth," *Accent*, XIII (1953), 140–152; Richard Ellman, "The Art of Yeats: Affirmative Capability," *Kenyon Review*, XV (1953), 357–385; T. R. Henn, "W. B. Yeats and the Irish Background," *Yale Review*, XLII (1953), 351–364; Hugh Kenner, "The Sacred Book of the Arts," *Sewanee Review*, LXIV (1956), 574–590; and Peter Ure, "Yeats' Supernatural Songs," *Review of English Studies*, VII (1956), 38–51.

The Permanence of Yeats, edited by James Hall and Martin Steinmann, 1950, is a collection of essays by various hands. The special Yeats Issue of the *Southern Review*, VII (Winter, 1942), was devoted entirely to studies of Yeats as poet and mystic.

STARK YOUNG

Born: Como, Mississippi
Date: October 11, 1881

Died: New York, N. Y.
Date: January 6, 1963

PRINCIPAL WORKS

NOVELS: *Heaven Trees*, 1926; *The Torches Flare*, 1928; *River House*, 1929; *So Red the Rose*, 1934.

SHORT STORIES: *The Street of the Islands*, 1930; *Feliciana*, 1935.

PLAYS: *Guenevere*, 1906; *Addio, Madretta, and Other Plays*, 1912; *The Queen of Sheba*, 1922; *The Colonnade*, 1924; *The Saint*, 1925.

POEMS: *The Blind Man at the Window*, 1906.

ESSAYS AND SKETCHES: *Encaustics*, 1926.

THEATRICAL CRITICISM: *The Flower in Drama*, 1923; *Glamour*, 1925; *Theatre Practice*, 1926; *The Theatre*, 1927; *Immortal Shadows*, 1948.

TRAVEL SKETCHES AND IMPRESSIONS: *The Three Fountains*, 1924.

REMINISCENCES: *The Pavilion*, 1951.

Stark Young, known chiefly as the author of *So Red the Rose* and often ranked as a minor figure among the Southern Agrarians, was born in Como, Mississippi, on October 11, 1881. When a typhoid epidemic closed the preparatory school he was attending, he was allowed to enter the University of Mississippi at the age of fourteen. Graduated in 1901, he continued his studies at Columbia University, from which he received his master's degree in English in 1902.

His first career was in the classroom.

After a short period of teaching in a military school for boys he became an instructor in English at the University of Mississippi in 1904. Three years later he joined the faculty of the University of Texas, where he taught until 1915, when he became professor of English at Amherst College. In 1921 he resigned to become a member of the editorial staff of the *New Republic*, a position he held until 1947, except for one year (1924–1925) when he served as drama critic of the *New York Times*. Concurrently he was an associate editor of *Theatre Arts Monthly* from 1921 to 1940. His close association with the theater has resulted in five books of drama criticism, the plays he himself has written in both prose and verse, translations, and the direction of several plays, including Lenormand's *The Failures* and Eugene O'Neill's *Welded,* on Broadway.

Stark Young's most sustained work has been in the novel. *So Red the Rose,* one of the earliest and most popular of the Civil War novels, achieves scope and depth because the writer has dramatized against a factual historical background the symbolic conflict between opposing forces of tradition and disintegration implicit in Southern life and character. This novel and its predecessors—*Heaven Trees,* a nostalgic re-creation of plantation life in ante-bellum days, and *The Torches Flare* and *River House,* which deal with later periods of the regional experience—make up, in effect, four panels of a dramatic and somberly realized social and moral history of the South. Young has also declared his local loyalties in the essay written for *I'll Take My Stand: The South and the Agrarian Tradition,* a symposium by "Twelve Southerners" published in 1930.

BIBLIOGRAPHICAL REFERENCES: There is no full-length biographical or critical study of Stark Young, but an excellent picture of his background and personality may be gathered from his book of reminiscences, *The Pavilion,* 1951. For brief critical sketches see Donald Davidson, Introduction to *So Red the Rose,* Modern Standard Authors Series, 1953; Abbott Martin, "Stark Young and the Ransomists," Sewanee Review, XXXVIII (1930), 114–115; John Donald Wade, "Two Souths," *Virginia Quarterly Review,* X (1934), 616–619; and Emily Clark, "Stark Young's South," *ibid.,* XI (1935), 626–628.

ISRAEL ZANGWILL

Born: London, England
Date: February 14, 1864

Died: Midhurst, Sussex, England
Date: August 1, 1926

PRINCIPAL WORKS

NOVELS: *Children of the Ghetto,* 1892; *Merely Mary Ann,* 1893; *The King of the Schnorrers,* 1894; *The Master,* 1895; *The Mantle of Elijah,* 1900.

SHORT STORIES: *Ghetto Tragedies,* 1893.

PLAYS: *Children of the Ghetto,* 1899; *Merely Mary Ann,* 1903; *The Melting Pot,* 1908.

ESSAYS: *Dreamers of the Ghetto,* 1898.

Israel Zangwill, born in London on February 14, 1864, was one of the outstanding Jewish authors and leaders of his time. His family, Russian Jews, had fled Russia and settled in England before his birth. A graduate of the Jews' Free School in London, he remained at the school as a teacher in order to finance his studies at London University, which he attended at the same time he was teaching. Despite the disadvantage of this dual program, Zangwill was graduated from the university with highest honors. After graduation he left teaching for a career in journalism. He founded and edited

1191

Ariel, The London Puck, and also wrote for various other London periodicals. His critical fame began with the publication of *Children of the Ghetto: A Study of a Peculiar People,* the first of his novels of Jewish life. At the time the novel attracted considerable attention largely because of its subject matter, and Zangwill has been credited with the prevention of anti-Jewish legislation by Parliament through its publication. Other novels about Jewish people followed, including *The Last of the Schnorrers, The Master,* and *The Mantle.* Another work, *Dreamers of the Ghetto,* was a series of essays on such notable Jewish thinkers and leaders as Spinoza, Heine, and Disraeli.

Although he won fame and will probably be remembered as a novelist interpreting Jews and Jewish life, Zangwill wished to excel as a dramatist rather than as a writer of fiction; some of his most popular plays were dramatizations of novels which had been published earlier, such as *Merely Mary Ann,* his most popular comedy, and *Children of the Ghetto.* Zangwill's plays were produced in Jewish communities everywhere, in both Yiddish and English, and he tried for more than a decade to be the great dramatist of the Yiddish theater. Later critics have not been kind to his plays, and even the dramatist admitted that they were less successful artistically than they were popular.

In addition to being a writer, Zangwill was an influential Jewish leader and a popular lecturer whose work in the cause of modern Zionism was of considerable historical importance. He died in Sussex on August 1, 1926.

BIBLIOGRAPHICAL REFERENCES: The pioneer critical biography is Joseph Leftwich, *Israel Zangwill,* 1957. A briefer study appeared in Arthur St. John Adcock, *Gods of Modern Grub Street,* 1928.

STEFAN ŻEROMSKI

Born: Near Kielce, Poland
Date: November 14, 1864

Died: Warsaw, Poland
Date: November 20, 1925

PRINCIPAL WORKS

NOVELS: *Ludzie Bezdomni,* 1900 (*The Homeless*); *Popioly,* 1904 (*Ashes*); *Wierna rzeka,* 1912 (*The Faithful River*); *Wiatr od morza,* 1922 (*The Wind from the Sea*); *Puszcza jodlowa,* 1925 (*The Fir Forest*).
PLAYS: *Róża,* 1909; *Uciekla mi przepióreczka,* 1924 (*My Little Quail Has Fled*).

Stefan Żeromski was born near Kielce in Russian Poland, November 14, 1864, of an impoverished noble family. Throughout his life he chafed under this Tsarist domination, and frequently his short stories take as their subject the resistance of Polish secret organizations. Żeromski himself was even more directly involved. In 1905, during the revolt against Russia, he was imprisoned; later he went into semi-voluntary exile in France and Austrian Galicia, where he remained until the end of World War I.

Żeromski wrote plays and poetry, but his claim to greatness comes out of his novels. Most famous of these is *Ashes,* which has been called the *War and*

Peace of Poland. Although his great lyrical descriptive vein is not so evident in this work as it is in *The Wind from the Sea*, the novel possesses scope and richness of characterization to make it an authentic masterpiece.

There is a dark pessimism to Żeromski's writing which is characteristic of the Polish positivist school. Perhaps it was this quality as well as his extreme nationalism that kept him from winning the Nobel Prize. During his career he contributed many characters to the Polish national consciousness, and for that he was honored by his countrymen. He died in Warsaw on November 20, 1925.

BIBLIOGRAPHICAL REFERENCES: A good introduction to the work of Żeromski is W. Borowy, "Żeromski," *Slavonic Review*, XIV (1936), 403–416. See also Z. L. Zaleski, "Etienne Żeromski," in *Attitudes et destinées*, 1932; and Jan Lechoń, "Stefan Żeromski," *Harvard Slavic Studies*, II (1954), 323–342.

ÉMILE ZOLA

Born: Paris, France
Date: April 2, 1840

Died: Paris
Date: September 29, 1902

PRINCIPAL WORKS

NOVELS: *Thérèse Raquin*, 1867; *Madeleine Férat*, 1868; *La Fortune des Rougons*, 1871 (*The Rougon Family*); *La Curée*, 1872; *La Ventre de Paris*, 1873; *La Conquête de Plassans*, 1874; *La Faute de l'abbé Mouret*, 1875 (*The Abbe Mouret's Transgression*); *Son excellence Eugène Rougon*, 1876; *L'Assommoir*, 1877 (*Drink*); *Une Page d'amour*, 1878; *Nana*, 1880; *Pot-Bouille*, 1882; *Au bonheur des dames*, 1883; *La Joie de vivre*, 1884; *Germinal*, 1885; *L'Œuvre*, 1886 (*Labor*); *La Terre*, 1887 (*Earth*); *Le Rêve*, 1888; *La Bête humaine*, 1890; *L'Argent*, 1891; *La Débâcle*, 1892; *Le Docteur Pascal*, 1893; *Lourdes*, 1894; *Rome*, 1896; *Paris*, 1898.

CRITICAL STUDIES: *Le Roman expérimental*, 1880 (*The Experimental Novel*); *Les Romanciers naturalistes*, 1881.

TRACT: *J'accuse*, 1898 (*I Accuse*).

Probably the most important and certainly the most controversial of the French novelists of the second half of the nineteenth century was Émile Zola. Born in Paris, April 2, 1840, the son of an engineer of mixed Greek and Italian ancestry who died when his son was only seven, Zola was educated at Aix and returned to Paris in 1858 to start his career as a writer. He began as a critic, then changed, in 1867, to the writing of novels. In 1871 he published *The Rougon Family*, the first volume of twenty in a series, called the "Rougon-Macquart Novels," which was to deal with the history of a family under the Second Empire. The first of these novels attracted little attention; it was *Drink*, a merciless study of the effects of drink that placed Zola among the foremost French writers of a brilliant literary period.

In the Rougon-Macquart series it was Zola's intention to study, with scientific precision and detachment, the fortunes of the various branches of a typical French family of his time, showing, in the vast and complicated web of relationships thus created, how the members of the family were affected by their combined heredity and environment. This approach was a reaction against the romanticism of the generation of Hugo and the elder Dumas and meant an advance beyond anything that realism had as yet accomplished in fiction. The explanation of his method was set forth in his essay *The Experimental Novel*. To the literary school he thus established has been given the name of naturalism.

The naturalists claimed that they descended from Stendhal, through Balzac and Flaubert, all of whom minutely dissected the personality of the individual and the society in which he found himself, thus giving a realistic picture of the contemporary world as it actually is. The naturalists, however, went considerably further. Literature, according to them, must be scientific in its approach, not imaginative; and in this attitude they were echoing the mechanistic statements of mid-nineteenth century science. Man, according to this point of view, is merely an animal among other animals, the product of his heredity and environment which can be studied almost as in a laboratory and his behavior then predicted. When transferred to literature, this theory means, as the naturalists contended, that the novelist should invent nothing; he should observe facts and collect data as the scientist does. If the observations have been complete, if the facts are all gathered, then the behavior and even the final end of the individual can be predicted with scientific accuracy. The plot of the novel will be as inevitable as the solution to a problem in mathematics.

The scientific spirit in which Zola approached his gigantic task is shown by his submitting to his publisher a detailed outline of ten of the projected novels. Further, the sub-title of the series, "The natural and social history of a family under the Second Empire," gives the impression that he was studying his characters as an entomologist might study a colony of ants. He was astonishingly painstaking in preparing his material; if he wished to introduce some minor characters engaged in a particular trade, he was capable of spending weeks at the task of mastering the technical jargon peculiar to that trade. He was endlessly taking notes so that his details might be correct. It is not surprising that it took him twenty-five years to complete the series.

Although Zola tried to include all strata of society, the volumes by which he is best known deal with the lower—at times the lowest—classes. It is in this picture of the brutalized, almost animalistic existence of the poor that his uncompromising realism was strongest. The details aroused protest even in France; in England there was a cry of outrage from the few readers who became familiar with his work. Tennyson's lines will be remembered: "Feed the budding rose of boyhood with the drainage of your sewer." The dose was too strong for the general Anglo-Saxon reader of that day.

In the course of studying, under the microscope, the fortunes of a particular family, Zola also gave an analysis of the whole world of the Second Empire, a glittering, ornate façade with very little back of it. The hollowness of this society is best shown in *Nana*, where we are given a picture of the corruption of Paris even among the rich.

Nana, risen from the position of a simple prostitute to that of a *grande cocotte*, literally devours men; there is no amount of money too great to be spent on her. She is the epitome of the vast luxury and vice of Paris where men ruin themselves for a worthless harlot. The novel ends with the terrible irony of the dead Nana, a loathsome mass of disease, abandoned by everyone, while outside in the streets the crowds are shouting "To Berlin!"; the scene is a prelude to the downfall that is to follow.

Near the end of his life Zola became involved in a cause which brought him an international recognition far beyond his fame as an author: the Dreyfus case that split France at that time. In 1898, having become convinced that Dreyfus was the innocent victim of a plot, Zola published his famous article

I Accuse, in which he attacked the General Staff and French officialdom for seeking to persecute Dreyfus. He was tried twice for libel and had to flee to England, returning to Paris only after a general amnesty had been proclaimed.

Although Zola's scientific conception of literature is outmoded, his influence on the modern novel cannot be overemphasized. It was his work, along with that of his French imitators, that helped to shatter Victorian reticence in English literature; and, while some lamentable lapses of taste resulted, novelists were free to deal truthfully with their subjects. Dreiser's *An American Tragedy* is an example of Zola's influence on American fiction.

He died of accidental asphyxiation at his home in Paris on September 29, 1902.

BIBLIOGRAPHICAL REFERENCES: The fullest study of Zola in English is E. A. Vizetelly's rather eulogistic *Émile Zola, Novelist and Reformer*, 1904. More balanced estimates are given in R. H. Sherard, *Émile Zola: A Biographical and Critical Study*, 1903; and Matthew Josephson, *Zola and His Time*, 1929. See also F. Brunetière, *Le Roman Naturaliste*, 1883; and Henri Barbusse, *Zola*, 1932 (English translation, 1933). An account of Zola's activities in connection with the Dreyfus case is given in *Le Procès Zola*, 2 vols., 1898.

JOSÉ ZORRILLA Y MORAL

Born: Valladolid, Spain
Date: February 21, 1817

Died: Madrid, Spain
Date: January 23, 1893

PRINCIPAL WORK

PLAY: *Don Juan Tenorio,* 1844.

José Zorrilla y Moral, called the "spoiled darling of Spanish Romanticism," is its representative not only in his writing, but in his life. Born in Valladolid, February 21, 1817, he was lured, in spite of parental opposition, from the study of law by his love for

poetry. Marriage to a woman somewhat older than he, against the wishes of his stern father, widened the breach, and as a bohemian, he lived in frequent poverty. Yet he was able to visit France in 1846 to meet the leading poets of Paris and later to travel to Mexico at the request of Emperor Maximilian to direct the National Theater. He lived in Mexico from 1855 until 1866.

He sprang into fame in 1837, when as a gaunt youth he leaped into the grave of the suicide Larra and read his emotional verses about the loneliness of a poet and the sacredness of his mission. This act initiated fifteen years of literary production. He became a member of the Royal Academy in 1848. Lyrical and dramatic poetry with themes of mystery, melancholy, and religion, against a background of wild nature, characterized him. Old legends provided him with themes, and he wrapped himself in the splendor of his country's past.

As a playwright, Zorrilla was author of about twenty original dramas, all written with speed and facility and many patterned on the cape-and-sword

dramas of the Golden Age. His mastery of many verse forms established him as one of Spain's leading poets. *Don Juan Tenorio* brought him his highest fame, though he called it "the greatest nonsense ever written." In spite of its exaggerations, melodramatic improbability, and technical flaws, the drama expresses the spirit of Spain's Golden Age and is usually performed throughout the Spanish-speaking world on November 1. A good performance of it is an artistic delight. Audiences like to believe that the play, outwardly a melodramatic representation of amorous intrigues, dramatizes fundamental eternal truths, with the characters personifying the inner duality of earthy and spiritual elements inherent in human nature. Zorrilla died in Madrid, January 23, 1893.

BIBLIOGRAPHICAL REFERENCES: For criticism of Zorrilla in English see F. C. Tarr, *Romanticism in Spain*, 1939; E. A. Peers, *History of the Romantic Movement in Spain*, 1940; in Spanish, José Zorrilla's *Recuerdos del tiempo viejo*, 1880–1882, an interesting but unreliable account; N. Alonso Cortes, *Zorrilla, su vida y sus obras*, 3 vols., 1916–1920; and G. Díaz Plaja, *Introducción al estudio del romanticism español*, 1942 (2nd ed.).

ARNOLD ZWEIG

Born: Gross-Glogau, Prussia
Date: November 10, 1887

PRINCIPAL WORKS

NOVELS: *Novellen um Claudia*, 1912 (*Claudia*); *Der Streit um den Sergeanten Grischa*, 1927 (*The Case of Sergeant Grischa*); *Junge Frau von 1914*, 1931; (*Young Woman of 1914*); *De Vriendt kehrt heim*, 1932 (*De Vriendt Goes Home*); *Erziehung vor Verdun*, 1935 (*Education before Verdun*); *Einsetzung eines Königs*, 1937 (*The Crowning of a King*); *Das Beil von Wandsbek*, 1946 (*The Axe of Wandsbek*).

SHORT STORIES: *Geschichtenbuch*, 1916; *Spielzeug der Zeit*, 1933 (*Playthings of Time*); *Stufen*, 1949.

PLAYS: *Abigail und Nebel*, 1913; *Ritualmord in Ungarn*, 1914; *Die Lucilla*, 1919; *Papiergeld Brennt*, 1920; *Das Spiel vom Segeanten Grischa*, 1921; *Die Umkehr*, 1927.

ESSAYS: *Juden auf der deutschen Bühne*, 1928; *Bilanz der deutschen Judenheit*, 1934 (*Insulted and Exiled*).

The author of *The Case of Sergeant Grischa*, one of the greatest war novels ever written, was born into a Jewish middle-class family at Gross-Glogau, Prussia, on November 10, 1887. His father was Adolf Zweig, a saddler and remover, and his mother was Bianca von Spandow. He was educated at the technical school in Kattowitz, Upper Silesia, and then at several German universities, including schools at Breslau, Munich, Berlin, Göttingen, Rostock, and Tubingen, where he studied philosophy and languages and developed an interest in psychology, history, and the arts.

Arnold Zweig had planned to be a teacher, but during the course of his education he began to devote a considerable amount of time to writing; his earliest short stories date from 1909. His first novel, actually a series of episodes unified by a central character, *Claudia*, appeared in 1912. Traces of his careful, ironic style showed in that early work, an experimental book in which he portrayed the sufferings and growth of a sensitive, upper-class girl as she strives, while married to a shy professor, to free herself from her inhibitions and release her natural forces. Zweig's interest in the psychology of the individual continued to govern most of his work in the novel and drama.

During World War I he served as a private in a labor battalion in France and Serbia, and from 1917 to the armistice worked in the press section of Ober-Ost. He had already attracted some attention with his short stories and plays. *Abigail and Nebel* was presented in 1913, and *Ritualmord in Ungarn*, written in 1914, was produced seven years later as *Die Sendung Semaels* by Max Reinhardt in Berlin.

After a successful tour in Germany and Austria, the play received the Kleist Prize in 1915.

After the war Zweig lived in Bavaria to recover his strength. A play, *Das Spiel vom Sergeanten Grischa*, prepared the way for his war novel, *The Case of Sergeant Grischa*, which appeared after the Hitler *Putsch* of 1923 compelled him to leave his home in Starnberg. The novel is a powerful story about a Russian sergeant who fell victim to the power of the Prussian war machine. As a study of war and the individual, the book ranks as Zweig's best and has won a place as one of the outstanding war novels in modern literature. It demonstrated Zweig's progress from a concern with the problems of young intellectuals to an absorption in the inner lives of persons confronting situations in which their entire systems of values are upset.

Zweig lived in Berlin until he was forced to leave by the Nazis in 1933. He traveled across Europe and settled in Palestine, where he became closely identified with the Zionist movement. At the time he was suffering from a serious eye disease which forced him to dictate his books, including *Education before Verdun*, the manuscript of which was destroyed when he left Berlin. Many of Zweig's essays and some of his novels and plays show his concern for the Zionist cause; *De Vriendt Goes Home* has its setting in Palestine and centers about the Jewish problem.

Since 1948, Zweig has lived in Eastern Berlin, where he has won prizes and other honors from the Communist government. He has served as president of the East German Academy of Letters.

BIBLIOGRAPHICAL REFERENCES: The work of Arnold Zweig is discussed in W. K. Pfeiler, *War and the German Mind*, 1941. See also Werner Mahrholz, *Deutsche Literatur der Gergenwart*, 1930. A brief, specialized study is Solomon Fishman, "The War Novels of Arnold Zweig," *Sewanee Review*, XLIX (1941), 433–451.

CROSS-REFERENCE INDEX

I